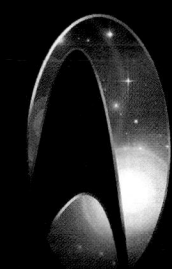

IN OUR TYPICALLY MODEST STYLE, WE'VE MADE A FEW CHANGES.

INTRODUCING THE NEWLY EXPANDED CAESARS PALACE.

Yeah, we've made a couple of improvements around here. For starters, we added a few new rooms. 1200 to be exact. All with private whirlpool spa tubs. We built three new pools. A luxurious health spa and fitness center.

New restaurants. And we also added more shopping and more things to do in our newly enlarged Forum Shops. Changes? Yeah, we've made some. Are they impressive? We think so. But remember, we're being modest.

CAESARS PALACE
LAS VEGAS

1-800-634-6661 ITT www.caesars.com

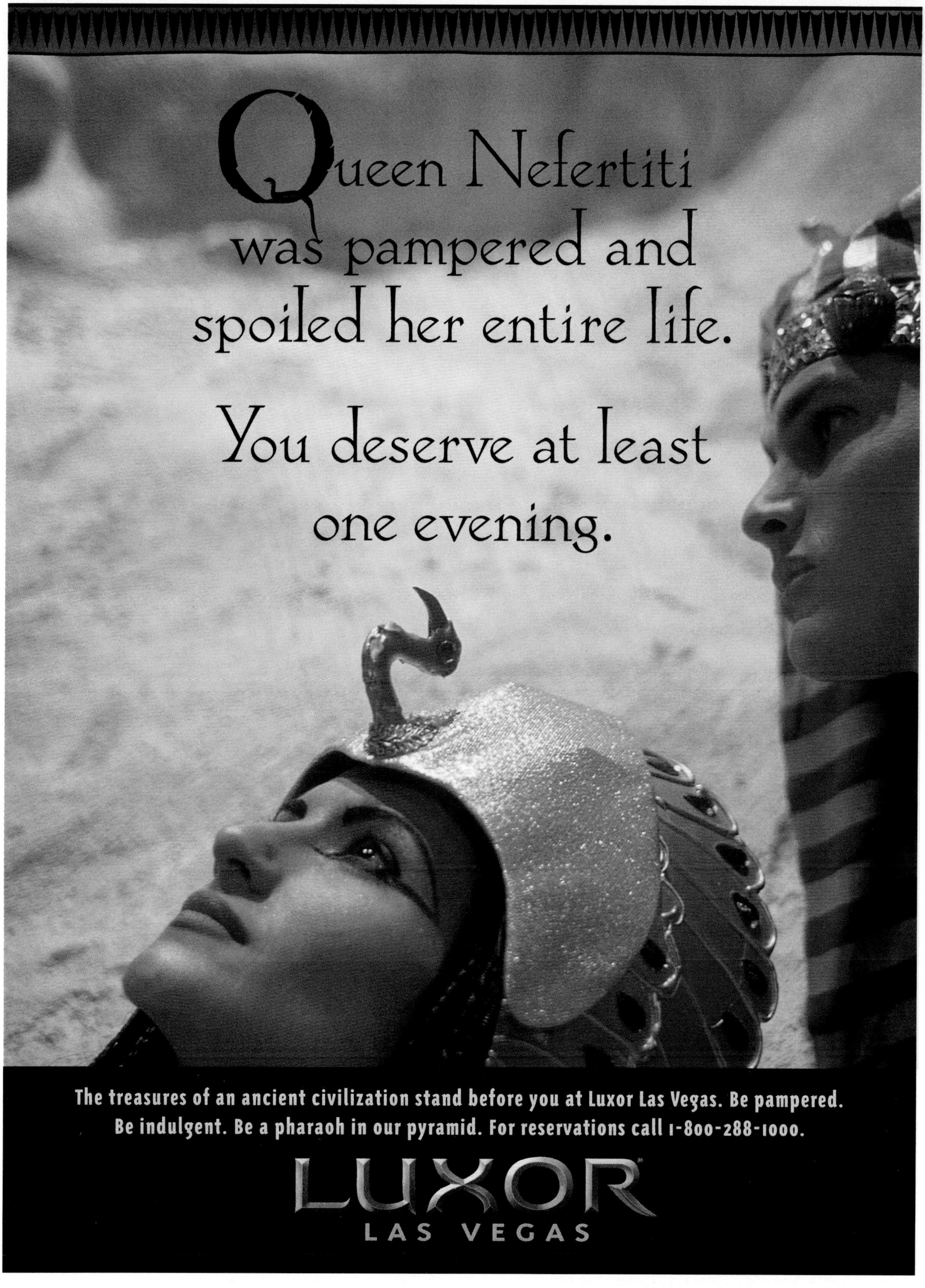
Queen Nefertiti was pampered and spoiled her entire life.
You deserve at least one evening.
The treasures of an ancient civilization stand before you at Luxor Las Vegas. Be pampered. Be indulgent. Be a pharaoh in our pyramid. For reservations call 1-800-288-1000.
LUXOR
LAS VEGAS

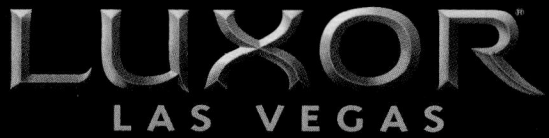

MYSTÈRE

From Cirque du Soleil

It's magical. It's mysterious. And it's performed nightly at 7:30 p.m. and 10:30 p.m. Dark Mondays and Tuesdays. Show tickets may be purchased by phone with a major credit card or at the Cirque du Soleil box offices. Box office hours: Daily 8:00 a.m. through 11:00 p.m. Watch it once. See it forever. Only at Treasure Island.

For reservations and information, call 894-7722.

Treasure Island
The Adventure Resort.

Kenneth Feld presents

SIEGFRIED & ROY
AT THE MIRAGE

TWO SHOWS NIGHTLY - 7:30 p.m. and 11:00 p.m. Dark Wednesdays and Thursdays. Tickets available at the Siegfried & Roy Theatre Ticket Office only. TICKET OFFICE HOURS: 8:30 a.m. to 11:00 p.m. daily. For more information please call 792-7777

P.O. Box 35050
Las Vegas, NV 89133-5050

(702) 868-6310 • 800-ELV-2940
Fax: (702) 838-4971

DEDICATION

This book is dedicated to Phyllis Cohen. Her thousands of phone calls, letters, and faxes, and countless hours of reading, verifying and writing have made this publication truly a labor of love. No task was ever too difficult for her to tackle.

The staff and management wish to thank her for all she has done to make us all proud of this great book.

FROM THE PUBLISHER

Dear Residents, Visitors and Newcomers:

Welcome to *Experience Las Vegas*. We hope our efforts to give you the the ultimate, all-in-one directory/guidebook will help and guide you through our great cities including Las Vegas, North Las Vegas, Henderson, and Boulder City. Las Vegas has more excitement and energy than any other city in the world. It is not only a great place to visit and enjoy the entertainment and sights, it is also a wonderful place to live. As you read through this book, you will see the many cultural offerings available, fabulous recreational areas to enjoy, schools to be proud of, strong economy, and planned communities to live in.

This book continues the efforts started by Bruce Brown, the original publisher and editor, to offer up-to-date information on Hotels, Casinos, Shows, Dining and Gaming. It answers many of the questions asked by those wanting to relocate: local government, taxes, employment information and housing.

Because of vast growth - new hotels, casinos, restaurants and businesses - *Experience Las Vegas* will be updated on a continual basis. To help you keep abreast of all the new and exciting changes, we suggest you send in the business reply card in the back of this book, so we can keep you informed when updates are available.

We hope you'll *Experience Las Vegas* with us again and again, and enjoy our book. Your comments and ideas to make our publication better for you to enjoy are greatly appreciated. Please drop us a line, we would like to hear from you.

Sincerely,

Robert Collins
Publisher,
Experience Las Vegas

HOW TO USE THIS GUIDE

Everyone experiences Las Vegas differently, and individual needs vary. Still, everyone needs reliable information. If you live in Las Vegas, visit regularly, or are planning to relocate here, *Experience Las Vegas* will make your life a lot easier and much more enjoyable. You can use *Experience Las Vegas* as a resource, a reference guide, or as your own personal concierge. Complete listings of organizations and businesses, activities, events, transportation, restaurants, entertainment, gaming, shopping, sports and recreation, children-related activities, education, parks, services, and all things relating to Las Vegas are right here at your fingertips.

The thousands of businesses listed in this directory come complete with names, addresses, zip codes, phone numbers, hours, owner's or manager's names (when available) and other pertinent information. Many businesses are listed in more than one category, providing information where and when it is needed rather than referring you to different pages. The categories themselves make selections easier to locate. For your convenience, sections are identified at the top of every page as well as page tabs.

Readers looking for a specific type of establishment or a business by name should consult the index at the end of the directory. Every entry in this book is listed in the index by name.

Experience Las Vegas gets right down to business - your business - twenty-four hours a day, seven days a week. Whether you're using it as a professional reference, helpful directory at home, or taking it with you as trusted traveling companion, we feel confident that *Experience Las Vegas* will be the only resource you'll need to answer all your Las Vegas-related questions. Find it fast. Find it first. Find it foremost in *Experience Las Vegas* - the resource that reads like a book.

Publisher
NEVADACOM MEDIA GROUP, INC.
A NEVADA CORPORATION
Robert Collins, President

Chief Operating Officer
Todd A. Molinari, Vice President

Editor in Chief
Phyllis Cohen

Managing Editor
Donna R. Fremgen

Editorial Assistance
Michelle Lupoli
Michele Powers
Audrey Fremgen

Copy Editor
Robert Weisser

Art Director
Christopher Fremgen

Publishing Consultant
Jack Godler

Business Consultant
Joel A. Goldman, *CPA*

Fulfillment Director
Fay Mancini

Photography
Covers courtesy of Tiffany Design
Inside photos courtesy of Brian Janis
at Phototechnik International
and the staff of Experience Las Vegas

Printing
Danner Press

Color Separations,
Typesetting and Graphic Design
CompuPrint Graphics & Marketing Corp.
(Parent Company of NevadaCom Media Group)

DISCLAIMER: Although the publisher has exercised the greatest care to ensure accuracy, publisher is not responsible for the accuracy of times, dates, prices, locations, etc., in this publication. It is always best to call ahead to verify any information. *Experience Las Vegas* is produced as a public service for the convenience of the user, and neither the publisher nor the advertisers shall be held liable for the accuracy, or for any errors or omissions therein. Send any corrections to *Experience Las Vegas*, P.O. Box 35050, Las Vegas, NV 89133-5050. Please do not call with corrections as we require this information in writing.

TABLE OF CONTENTS

TABLE OF CONTENTS

Welcome to Las Vegas

At the turn of the century there were only about 25 people living in the Las Vegas area. The railroad had the biggest influence on the development and growth of Las Vegas and its origins as a city on May 15, 1905. By the time Clark County was formed in 1909 there were 3,321 people living in the county.

Until 1930, growth was anything but spectacular. Tents were gradually replaced by permanent structures. Las Vegas got its first economic boost in 1931 when construction on Hoover Dam began. While the rest of the nation was experiencing the depression, the Hoover Dam project employed 5,128 workers. This along with the passage of a law legalizing gambling and six weeks' residency requirement for divorce helped Las Vegas fare much better than the rest of the nation during these years. Hoover Dam was completed in 1936 and by 1940 Clark County had a population of over 16,000.

The establishment of World War II defense industries including what is now Nellis Air Force Base helped boost the economy in the '40s. The 1940s also marked the start of the famous Las Vegas Strip and the opening of the first of the luxury hotel/casinos. The El Rancho was the first to open in 1941 followed by the Last Frontier and Bugsy Siegel's luxurious Flamingo. Resort building accelerated in the postwar years with eight more luxury hotels opening in the '50s. By 1960 the population of Clark County was 127,016, almost tripling in 10 years.

Howard Hughes came to town in 1966 and proceeded to purchase half a dozen major Strip hotels and various other properties in and around Las Vegas through his Summa Corporation. Many people see this as the end of organized crime's hold on Las Vegas and the beginning of the corporation town. Soon large corporations such as MGM and Hilton were casino operators and Las Vegas was gaining respectability. The decade saw the population more than double to 273,288 in 1970.

According to the 1990 census, Clark County had 741,459 residents, a 60.1 percent increase for the decade. Today, it is estimated that the Clark County population is 1,192,200.

Nevada's labor force has increased by 346,000 people in the last decade. Nevada gained 54,000 jobs for the year ending July 1997, a gain of 6.5 percent. Total Clark County labor force is 604,800 with about 29,800 unemployed. The median Las Vegas household income in 1997 was $41,816.

LAS VEGAS GROWTH & ECONOMY

The famous Las Vegas Sign welcomes you to the Entertainment Capital of the World.

Clark County population according to the Clark County Demographers Office is 1,170,113.

Starting in 1994, the Census Bureau included Mohave and Nye counties with Clark County. Clark County hit the 1 million population mark in January 1995, according to the Clark County Comprehensive Planning Department. The State Demographer projects that Clark County's population could be 2 million by the year 2015.

CLARK COUNTY POPULATION GROWTH

1900	About 25
1909	3,321
1920	4,859
1930	8,532
1940	16,416
1950	48,289
1960	127,016
1970	273,288
1980	463,087
1985	568,194
1990	741,459
1992	854,780
1993	898,020
1994	931,000
1995	972,460
1996	1,076,267
1997	1,119,705

U.S. Census Bureau figures

LAS VEGAS TOURISM

Las Vegas was host to 30,464,635 visitors in 1997, up 2.8 percent, and they contributed $30.5 billion to the economy, which is a small increase over the previous year, including $4,904,383,000 in gaming revenue, up 6.2 percent. The Las Vegas Convention and Visitors Authority projects 31.1 million people will visit Las Vegas this year.

Last year there were 3,749 conventions that brought 3.5 million conventioneers to the city. Conventions in 1997 had a $4.4 billion non-gaming impact on Las Vegas.

McCarran Airport had 30,305,822 people traveling through with over 15 million remaining for business or pleasure. Average automobile traffic through S. California Yermo Inspection Station reported 4,948,355. Average daily traffic on all major highways is 63,261, up 5.8 percent.

With the opening of the Stratosphere Tower, Monte Carlo, New York New York, Orleans and Reserve in addition to several expansions, Las Vegas exceeded 105,000 hotel rooms in 1997. In the mid 1980s there were only 45,815 rooms.

The busiest month is March and the slowest month is December, with the exception of Christmas and New Year's. The average length of stay is 3.1 nights and 4 days, with people most frequently staying 2 nights.

Las Vegas is no longer a place just for adults, but is rapidly becoming a vacation destination for the entire family; 8 percent of the visitors are under 21. In addition to Grand Slam Canyon, MGM Theme Park and Wet 'n Wild, Las Vegas hotels are including more family attractions in future plans.

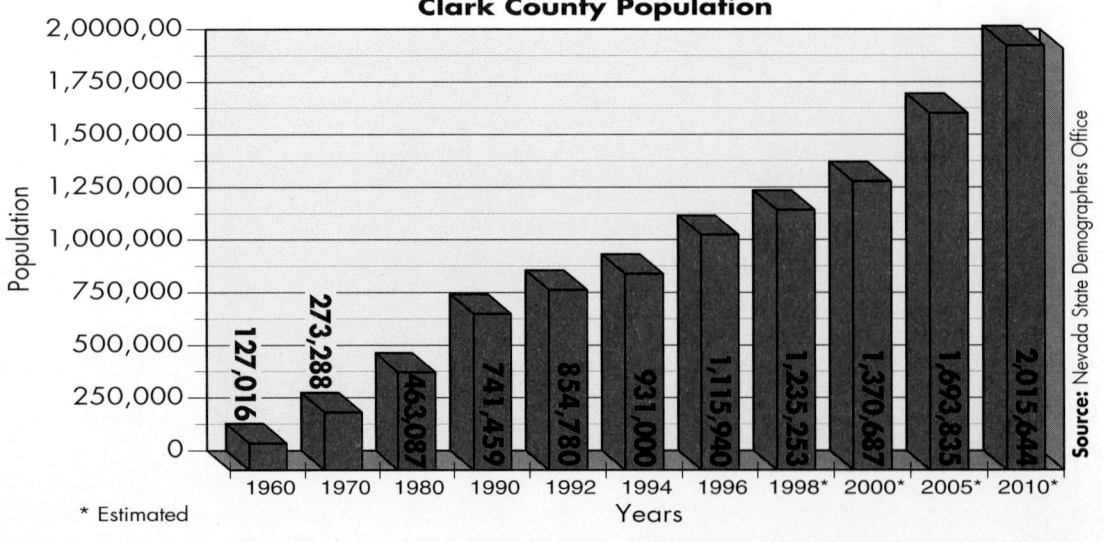

Clark County Population

* Estimated

Source: Nevada State Demographers Office

LAS VEGAS HISTORY

Sands Hotel 1952

Sands Hotel 1996

The new Venetian currently under construction, will replace the Sands Hotel

As far back as the 16th century, when the Old Spanish Trail was carved out of the wilderness to establish a route between Santa Fe and the mission of California, the Las Vegas area was a popular stop because of the natural springs and meadows. *Las Vegas* is Spanish for "the meadows."

Captain John C. Fremont led a group of pioneers into the valley in 1844 and wrote of a camping ground called Las Vegas.

In 1855 Brigham Young dispatched a 30 man group from Salt Lake with instructions to build a fort for the protection of immigrants and the mail from Indian raids and smelt the lead found in the area to produce bullets and also to teach the Indians to farm. The men, under the leadership of William Bringhurst, built an adobe fort and planted crops. Many Indians were converted and baptized but the Paiutes were not, and after a number of raids the fort was abandoned. It was also discovered that the metal they were casting into bullets was not lead but rich silver ore.

Permanent settlement was achieved in 1865, when Octavius D. Gass moved into the old Mormon mission and began developing the Las Vegas Ranch. Gass was an Arizona rancher and miner who came to Las Vegas from Eldorado Canyon. Within 10 years, Gass had acquired most of the land and water rights in the area.

In 1881, Gass was unable to repay a loan and lost the ranch to miner Archibald Stewart. Although Stewart was killed in 1884, his wife Helen managed the 1,800 acre Stewart Ranch until 1902, when she sold it to Montana Senator William Clark for $55,000. Clark needed the land as a watering stop for his Los Angeles, San Pedro, Salt Lake Railroad, later to become the Union Pacific.

Las Vegas became a town after the railroad sold 1,220 residential lots in a two day sale on May 15-16, 1905, that attracted 3,000 people. The total revenues from the lots was $265,000. Las Vegas officially became a city on March 16, 1911, by an act of the Nevada Legislature.

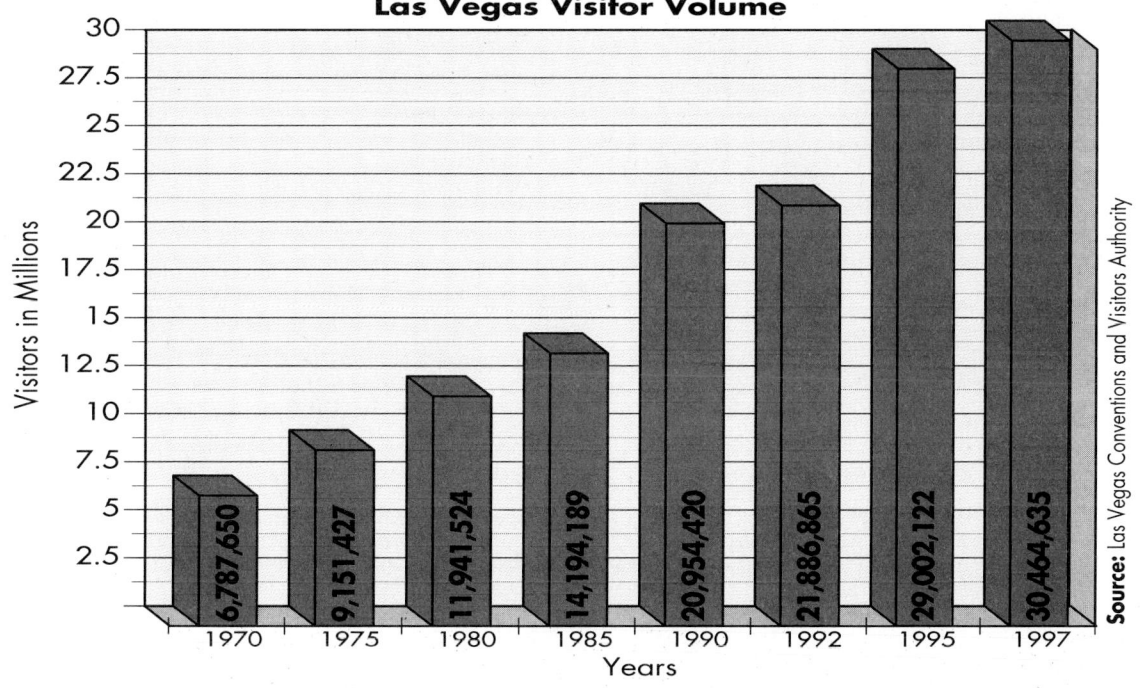

Las Vegas Visitor Volume

Visitors in Millions

Year	Visitors
1970	6,787,650
1975	9,151,427
1980	11,941,524
1985	14,194,189
1990	20,954,420
1992	21,886,865
1995	29,002,122
1997	30,464,635

Years

Source: Las Vegas Conventions and Visitors Authority

IMPORTANT DATES

1829 - Rafael Rivera is the first white man to set foot in what will one day be Las Vegas.

1855 - Thirty Mormon missionaries establish a mission.

1857 - Mission is abandoned.

1864 - Nevada becomes the 36th state in the Union. However, Las Vegas is still part of Arizona.

1865 - Octavius D. Gass builds a ranch on the site of the mission ruins. It later becomes known as the Las Vegas Ranch.

1867 - The Las Vegas area becomes part of Nevada.

1881 - Financial problems force Gass to default on loan and lose ranch to Archibald Stewart.

1902 - Stewart's widow sells the Las Vegas Ranch to Montana Senator William Clark for $55,000.

1905 - Clark's San Pedro, Los Angeles and Salt Lake Railroad auctions off parcels of land for $265,000.

1909 - Las Vegas becomes the county seat of Clark County.

1911 - Las Vegas officially becomes a city.

1931 - Gambling is legalized in Nevada.

1931 - Governor signs a six-week divorce law.

1931 - Construction starts on Boulder Dam.

1941 - The El Rancho becomes the first resort to open on the soon to be world famous Las Vegas Strip.

1946 - On New Year's Eve, the third resort on the Strip opens, Bugsy Siegel's Flamingo.

1951 - The atom bomb testing starts at the new Nevada Test Site.

1957 - Nevada Southern University (now UNLV) erects its first permanent structure.

1958 - The Las Vegas Convention Center is completed.

1963 - The new McCarran Airport opens.

1966 - Howard Hughes comes to Las Vegas and spends $300 million to purchase property, including six hotel resorts.

1969 - The International Hotel (now the Las Vegas Hilton) opens with Barbra Streisand headlining in the showroom.

1969 - Elvis Presley opens at the International.

1973 - The MGM (now Bally's) opens and with 2,100 rooms is the largest hotel in the world.

1980s - Clark County's population grows 56.9 percent.

1988 - Pepcon explosion rocks the Las Vegas Valley in May.

1989 - The Mirage Hotel opens at a cost of $610 million.

1990 - The Landmark Hotel closes. It is demolished in 1995 after attracting no bidders in Bankruptcy Court.

1990 - The Rio All Suites Hotel and Casino opens on Flamingo Rd., just off the Strip.

1990 - The Excalibur Hotel opens with 4,032 rooms, making it the largest hotel in the world.

1990 - The UNLV Runnin' Rebel Basketball team beats Duke to win its first NCAA title.

1991 - Las Vegas Events brings the Miss Universe Pageant to Las Vegas.

1992 - Main Street Station and the El Rancho close.

1993 - Three new theme hotels open; the Luxor, Treasure Island and the MGM. The MGM becomes the largest hotel in the world with 5,005 rooms.

1993 - The Dunes closes and is demolished in October.

1994 - Buffalo Bill's, Boulder Station, Boomtown and the Fiesta open.

1995 - Fremont Street Experience opens.

1996 - Stratosphere Tower, the tallest tower west of the Mississippi opens. Main Street Station reopens.

1996 - New York New York, Monte Carlo and Orleans open.

1997 - Sunset Station & Reserve open.

FACTS AND TRIVIA

Population

Clark County - 741,459 (1990 Census)
More than 90 percent of Clark County's population lives in metropolitan Las Vegas and Clark County has 63.6 percent of Nevada's total population. Clark County population is estimated now at 1,235,253 and Nevada population is 1,655,573 according to the state demographer's office. Average annual growth increase is 41,039, or 5.7 percent.

Nevada - 1,201,833 (1990 census)
Nevada - 1,655,573 (1997)

Race:
White	602,658 = 81.3%		Black	70,738 = 9.5%
Asian	26,043 = 3.5%		Am. Indian	6,416 = 0.9%
Hispanic	82,904 = 11.2%		Other	35,604 = 4.8%

Persons of Hispanic origin may be of any race and are included in figures above.

Figures below are for 1997 unless indicated. * from 1990 census.

Retirees: 167,688
*Persons over 65 years old: 117,685 (50% male & 50% female)
Persons under 18 years: 274,809
Births: 18,618
Deaths: 9,370
Population rank in U.S.: 30th
Clark County area: 5,173,760 acres (over 87% owned by the federal government)
Growth 1980 - 1990: 56.9%
Marriage Licenses: 110,696
Divorce Decrees: 9,631
Households: 637,301
Persons per household: 2.6
Median annual family income: $48,329
*Median age of population: 36.2
Percentage of persons over 24 years old with a college degree: 19.1%
Students in Clark County School District: 190,822 (6.7% increase over previous year) in 219 schools; 10th largest school district in U.S.
Median home price: $130,000
Average apartment rent: $631.22 (62% of residents own; 38% rent)
Number of physicians: 1,800
Number of dentists: 419
Number of lawyers: 2,300
Highest paid Las Vegan: Steve Wynn, $2.5 million in total compensation
Employed: 647,900
Unemployed: 25,500 (3.7%)
Labor force: 660,600 (includes Nye and Mohave counties, Feb. 1996)
Gaming industry employees: 155,338 (June 1997); 28.3% of labor force
Tourists visiting Las Vegas in 1997: 30.5 million
Visitor spending including gaming: $22,533,257,000
Gaming revenues for Clark County: $6.1 billion
There were 1,473 gaming licenses issued in Clark County, 139,218 slot machines and 3,916 live table games
Hotel/motel rooms: 105,347
Rooms added for the year: 6,275
    (Jan.-June) Occupancy rate: 86.4% (4% decrease)
        Hotels only: 90.3%   Motels only: 68.8%
Taxi cabs: 1,181
Churches: More than 500 churches & synagogues and more than 40 faiths
Golf courses: 35
Parks: 74 Clark County and 38 city
Schools: 219 primary and secondary schools.
Eating and drinking establishments in Las Vegas: More than 8,000
Office space: 14 million sq. ft. with a 9.61% vacancy rate
Industrial space: 43.7 million sq. ft., vacancy rate decreased to 5.21%. Two million sq. ft. are under construction and another 4 million sq. ft. in the planning stage
Largest hotel in the world: MGM Grand with 5,005 rooms
Largest Tree: Goodding Willow at Lorenzi Park; 68' high; 169" circumference
Largest city formed this century: Las Vegas
Largest manmade lake in the Western Hemisphere: Lake Mead with 28.5 million acre-ft. of water
Tallest building in Las Vegas: Stratosphere Tower 1,149 ft. (135 stories)
Lowest point in Nevada and Clark County: 490 ft. above sea level located at a point on the Colorado River near Laughlin
Highest point in Clark County: Charleston Peak located at Mt. Charleston, 11,918 ft.
Highest point in Las Vegas developed area: 2,921 ft. at Sahara Ave. and Hualapai Way
Clark County land area: 7,910 sq. mi., 173,760 acres
Sister City: An San, Korea

1998 LAS VEGAS SPECIAL EVENTS

JUNE
TBA - Community Foundation Golf Tournament, N. Las Vegas
6 - 7 - KidzMania '98, Cashman Field - 233-8388
12 - Nevada Broadcasters Association 3rd Annual Golf Tournament, Desert Inn Country Club - 891-0177
12 - Nevada Broadcasters Association 3rd Annual Dinner & Dance, Desert Inn Ballroom - 891-0177
13 - Home Buyers Expo, Cashman Field - (209) 221-8200
26 - Scott Walters Celebrity Golf Tournament, Stallion Mountain Country Club - 259-3741
6 - 29 - NEC Group Home Show, Cashman Field - 434-4444

JULY
3 - Campbell's Soups-Champions on Ice, Thomas & Mack
4 - Annual Fireworks Display, Sam Boyd Stadium - 895-8900
4 - July 4th Festival, Pahrump - 727-5658
4 - Water Festival & Fireworks, Mesquite
4 - Damboree, Boulder City - 293-9256
18-19 - Piccadilly Antique Fair, Cashman Field (813) 345-4431
25 - 26 - Bridal Spectacular, Cashman Field - 368-0088

AUGUST
TBA - Golf Tournament, Henderson
TBA - Miss Mesquite Pageant, Mesquite
28 - 30 - Southex Harvest Festival, Cashman Field

SEPTEMBER
TBA - Business Expo, N. Las Vegas
TBA - Virgin Valley Car Show, Mesquite
11 - 12 - Chautauqua, Boulder City - 294-6224
18 - 20 - Plus Communications Boat Show, Cashman Field - 736-5958
19 - Mariachi Festival, Thomas & Mack
22 - 25 - World Gaming Congress & Expo T/SF of Nevada, Inc., Las Vegas Hilton Convention Center - 892-0711
25 - 27 - Harvest Festival & Fair, Pahrump - 727-1555
26 - Bishop Gorman High School 5th Annual Wine Tasting & Silent Auction, Rio Hotel - 732-1945 Ext. 308
26 - 27 - Rattlin' Rails Handcar Races, Boulder City - 293-4857
26 - Wurstfest, Boulder City

OCTOBER
TBA - Harvest Carnival, Pahrump - 727-4514
TBA - Kiwanis Turkey Shoot, Pahrump - 727-1038
TBA - RiverFlight, Laughlin
3 - Knights of Columbus Golf Tournament, Pahrump - 751-3248
3 - 4 - Art in the Park, Boulder City - 294-1611
14 - 18 - Las Vegas Invitational - PGA Tour at Summerlin, Las Vegas Country Club, Desert Inn Golf Club - 382-6616
TBA - City Bus Tour, Henderson
16 - 18 - Expo, Henderson
17 - Tootsie Roll Drive, Pahrump - 751-3248
25 - St. Jude's Open House & Barbecue, Boulder City - 293-3131

NOVEMBER
10 - Veterans Day Program, Boulder City - 486-5920
21 - 22 - 1st Annual Pahrump Pow Wow, Pahrump - 727-0554
28 - Christmas Tree Lighting, Boulder City - 293-2034
28 - "Children's Christmas Party," Pahrump - 727-5107
TBA - Santa Shop/Craft Show, Pahrump - 727-7081
TBA - 7th Annual Golf Tournament, Pahrump - 727-5216
28 - 29 - Christmas Tree Festival, Mesquite

DECEMBER
1 - Festival of Lights, Mesquite
4 - 13 - National Finals Rodeo, Thomas and Mack.
TBA - Christmas Bazaar, Pahrump
TBA - Festival of Trees, Pahrump - 727-5489
TBA - Community Christmas Tree, Pahrump - 727-5800
TBA - Little Britches Rodeo, Pahrump - 727-5800
5 - Parade of Lights, Lake Mead Marina - 457-2797
5 - Christmas Parade, Boulder City - 293-2034
5 - Doodlebug Bazaar, Boulder City - 293-3992
6 - Children's Parade, Mesquite
11 - Open House, Henderson
11 - Luminaria, Boulder City - 293-2034
12 - Christmas Celebration, Henderson
12 - 13 - Christmas Bazaar, Mesquite - Live Nativity
16 - 20 - US Table Tennis Assn., LVCC - (719) 578-4583
20 - Community Caroling, Mesquite

CITIES SURROUNDING LAS VEGAS

Almost 75 percent of the country's population lives in incorporated cities. Clark County spans 7,910 sq. mi. The county has five incorporated cities: Las Vegas, North Las Vegas, Henderson, Boulder City and Mesquite.

ARDEN/ENTERPRISE
Pop. 60
7 mi. south on I-15 to Arden exit. 3 mi. west on US 160.

BLUE DIAMOND
Pop. approx. 315
20 mi. west of Las Vegas on State Route 159.
Originally called Cottonwood after Cottonwood Springs, a stop on the Old Spanish Trail, this small community was later named Blue Diamond after a division of the Flintkote Corporation which operates the nearby gypsum mine.

BOULDER CITY
Pop. 15,130
25 mi. southeast of Las Vegas on US 93, Boulder City was the nation's first planned community. The city began as a housing area for the 4,000 workers on Boulder Dam in the early 1930s. The only town in Nevada now without gambling, the selling of alcohol was illegal until 1960 when the government-owned town was established as an independent municipality. Boulder City has many lush green parks including the city center's greenbelt.

Annual Events:
April 11 - Handcar Races Long Course, 5 man teams race against the clock on a 900 ft. railroad track
April 25 - 26 - Clark County Art Show
May 2 - 3 - Spring Jamboree & Craft Fair
May 25 - Memorial Day Program
July 4 - Damboree, parade, games & fireworks
September 11 - 12 - Chautauqua, historical figures are portrayed with audience interaction
September 26 - 27 - Rattlin' Rails Handcar Races
September 26 - Wurstfest
October 3 - 4 - Art in the Park
October 25 - St. Jude's Day Celebration
November 10 - Veteran's Day Program
November 28 - Christmas Tree Lighting
December 5 - Christmas Parade, Parade of Lights and Doodlebug Bazaar
December 11 - Luminaria, traditional holiday music and program
Major Attractions:
5 mi. from Lake Mead and 8 mi. from Hoover Dam.
Bicentennial Park - Colorado St.
Boulder City Historic District - Arizona St.
Bureau of Reclamation Historical Homes - Colorado St.
Hemenway Park - 93 Bypass on Ville Dr.
Boulder City Chamber of Commerce
1305 Arizona St.
Boulder City, NV 89005
293-2034

BUNKERVILLE
Pop. 825
Located off I-15 about 80 mi. northeast of Las Vegas to Mesquite then to Riverside Rd.
This farming community in southeastern Nevada began in 1877, when settlers first attempted to tame the raging Virgin River for irrigation purposes. Oldest permanent community in Clark County.

CAL NEV ARI
Pop. 216
65 mi. south of Las Vegas, this tiny community was founded by Slim Kidwell and his wife Nancy. It began with the purchase of 640 acres, which included an abandoned airstrip, and turned into a pleasant little town near the juncture of California, Nevada and Arizona.

HENDERSON
Pop. 147,870
13 mi. southeast of Las Vegas on US 93/95.
With 74 sq. mi., Henderson is the largest city in total land area in Nevada. Once known primarily as a factory town, it was created during World War II as a federal company town for the Basic Magnesium defense plants. On January 10, 1944 the city of Henderson was officially born, named after Senator Charles B. Henderson. With the establishment of Green Valley in 1978, Henderson is now Nevada's third largest city. The Census Bureau in November 1997 confirmed that Henderson is the fastest growing city among those with a population over 100,000 people, compared to Las Vegas which finished sixth among the nation's 10 fastest growing cities.

Events:
January - City of Henderson Street Map, an annual fund-raising event
February 4 - Boss for a Day, brings students & businesses together
April 17 - 25 - Heritage Days, beauty pageant, car show, talent show, chili cookoff, parade, softball tournament, Mayor's dance and BBQ
July - Installation Dinner to honor newly elected Board of Directors for Chamber of Commerce
August - Golf tournament
October - City Bus Tour to view up-coming projects and future growth of Henderson
October 16 - 18 - Expo Days, fun, food, entertainment and carnival
December 11 - Chamber of Commerce Open House
December 12 - Christmas Celebration
Attractions:
Ethel M Chocolate Factory, Favorite Brands International
Henderson Chamber of Commerce
590 S. Boulder Hwy.
Henderson, NV 89015-7512
565-8951

CLARK COUNTY

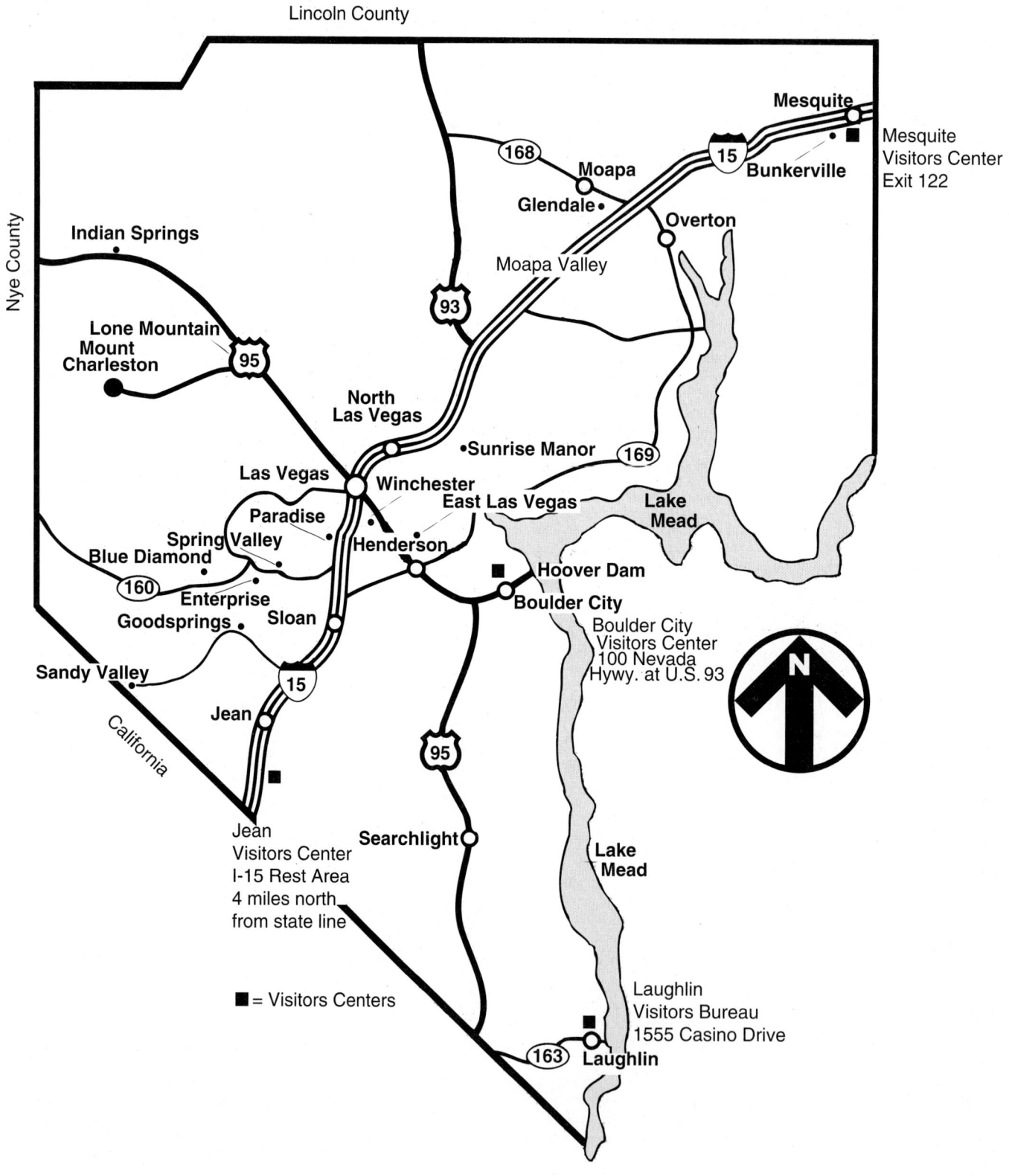

Lincoln County

Nye County

California

Indian Springs

Lone Mountain
Mount
Charleston

95

168

Moapa

Glendale

Moapa Valley

Mesquite

15

Bunkerville

Mesquite
Visitors Center
Exit 122

Overton

93

North
Las Vegas

•Sunrise Manor

169

Lake
Mead

Las Vegas   Winchester

Paradise

Spring Valley

Blue Diamond

160   Enterprise

Goodsprings   Sloan

Sandy Valley

Jean

East Las Vegas

Henderson

Hoover Dam

Boulder City

Boulder City
Visitors Center
100 Nevada
Hywy. at U.S. 93

N

15

Jean
Visitors Center
I-15 Rest Area
4 miles north
from state line

95

Searchlight

Lake
Mead

■ = Visitors Centers

Laughlin
Visitors Bureau
1555 Casino Drive

163   Laughlin

CITIES SURROUNDING LAS VEGAS

INDIAN SPRINGS
Pop. 1,422
50 mi. north of Las Vegas on US 95
Indian Springs was once a station along the Las Vegas and Tonopah Railroad's line to the mining camps of Beatty, Tonopah and Goldfield. When the mines began to play out, the rails were soon pulled up. As it has long been an important stop in the desert (beginning with the Indians), Indian Springs still provides some amenities to the passing motorist.

JEAN
30 miles south of Las Vegas, on I-15. Jean grew from a small bar and casino owned by Peter A. "Pop" Simon called Pop's Oasis. It now boasts two large hotels and casinos and a plastics plant.
Visitors Center - 1-702-874-1360

LAUGHLIN
Pop. 6,988
90 mi. south of Las Vegas on US 95 and Hwy 163. 1-1/2 hours from Las Vegas. South Pointe, as it was called in 1966, was little more than a restaurant, bar and 8 room motel located on the banks of the Colorado River on a dead-end dirt road when Don Laughlin, owner of the now Riverside Hotel, purchased the six acre site in 1966 for $235,000.

In 1983 Laughlin had only 100 residents with most of the casino workers living across the river in Bullhead City. Today over 11,035 hotel rooms in 10 resorts line the scenic Colorado River and Laughlin is Nevada's third ranked gaming area, recently passing Lake Tahoe. The gaming resort town employs over 13,000 workers and had 5 million visitors in 1997

Events:
January - Turquoise Finals Rodeo, Laughlin & Bullhead City
January - February - SCORE Laughlin desert challenge off road race
April - Rodeo Days
April - Harley Days and Laughlin River Run
May - River Days (Celebrity Water Challenge)
October - RiverFlight Hot Air Balloon Rally
Information:
Laughlin Chamber of Commerce
1725 S. Casino Dr.
P.O. Box 77777
Laughlin, NV 89028
1-702-298-2214
Laughlin Visitors Bureau
1555 S. Casino Drive
P.O. Box 502
Laughlin, NV 89029
1-702-298-3321
Bullhead Area Chamber of Commerce
1251 Hwy. 95
Bullhead City, AZ 86429
1-520-754-4121
Bullhead City was created in the early 1940s as a construction camp for the Davis Dam. The city now has a population of over 29,000 residents, primarily because of Laughlin gaming.

State Route 157 en route to Mt. Charleston

MESQUITE
Pop. 7,920
79 mi. northeast of Las Vegas on I-15. Nevada's newest city, Mesquite was originally settled by Mormon farmers attracted by the fertile soil along the Virgin River. This once quiet farming community received an economic boost with the arrival of 3 resorts. The excitement of the resorts does not detract from its tranquil surroundings.
Events:
February - Chili & Art Festival
March - Parade of Homes/Hot Air Balloon Races
April - Mesquite Heat 10K race
May - Mesquite Days Festival & Cinco de Mayo
May - Memorial Day Celebration
June - Silver State 300 Car Race
July - Fourth of July Water Festival & Fireworks
August - Miss Mesquite Pageant
September - Virgin Valley Car Show
November - Christmas Tree Festival
December - Festival of Lights
December - Children's Parade
December - Christmas Bazaar
December - Live Nativity & Candle Procession
December - Community Caroling
Attractions: Mesquite Museum, Oasis Resort, Virgin River Resort & Players Island
Mesquite Chamber of Commerce
P.O. Box 8
Mesquite, NV 89024
1-702-346-2902

MOAPA VALLEY
Pop. 5,327
50 mi. northeast of Las Vegas off I-15. This farming community consists of several towns including Moapa, Glendale, Overton, Logandale, Meadow Valley, Moapa Indian Reservation and Warm Springs along the 50-mi. long valley. The Lost City Museum located at the south end of Overton contains artifacts and displays of the ancient Pueblo Indians who inhabited the area.

Archeological finds indicate that the region was occupied by Indian civiliza-tions from as early as 1,000 B.C. Pueblo occupations of the area began around the time of Christ and spread throughout the Moapa Valley. They left the area around A.D. 1150 and sometime later the area was occupied by the Paiutes. The first permanent white settlers were sent to the area by Brigham Young in January 1865. These settlers organized three towns in the lower valley; St. Thomas, Overton and St. Joseph. St. Thomas was covered by water from Lake Mead in 1938.
Events:
April - Clark County Fair, Logandale
Attractions:
Moapa Valley is the gateway to the Valley of Fire State Park and here you will find the Overton Arm of Lake Mead National Recreation Area, Lost City Museum in Overton.
Moapa Valley Chamber of Commerce
P.O. Box 361
Overton, NV 89040
1-702-397-2160

NORTH LAS VEGAS
Pop. 93,010
North Las Vegas was incorporated in 1946 with its own mayor and city council, fire and police departments, library and recreation department.
Events:
May - Economic Development Tour
June - N. Las Vegas Community Foundation Golf Tournament
September - Business Expo
Attractions:
Nellis Air Force Base, Community College of Southern Nevada Planetarium
North Las Vegas Chamber of Commerce
1023 E. Lake Mead Blvd.
N. Las Vegas, NV 89030
642-9595

PAHRUMP
Pop. approx. 28,000 (Nye County)
63 mi. west of Las Vegas on State Route 160 in Nye County.
The Pahrump Valley is a fertile agricultural area. Fed by abundant water, the land has produced a variety of crops including cotton, alfalfa and grapes.

Pahrump is Nevada's fastest-growing unincorporated town according to state Demographer Dean Judson. The town has two-thirds of the population of Nye County, which is the fastest-growing county. There was an increase of 15 percent from July 1, 1996 - July 1, 1997
Events:
February - November - Dirt Track Auto Racing - 727-7172
February - Festival of Hearts - 727-0724
February - "Quarters," High School sports program - 751-3248
February - Fiber Craft Show - 727-8747
February - Knights of Columbus Fish Fry - 751-3248
February - March 1 - High School Rodeo - 727-5076
March - Culpepper Circus - 727-0554
April - Children's Easter Egg Hunt - 727-5800
April - Challenge Cup Relay Race - 727-5800
April - Walk-a-Thon - 727-0724
May - Valley Cruisers Car Club
May - Memorial Day Weekend Snow Mountain Powwow - 386-3916
May - Square Dance "Hoedown" - 727-5658
July - 4th of July Celebration - 727-5658
September - Pahrump Harvest Festival Parade - 727-1555
September - Harvest Festival, PRCA Rodeo & Parade - 727-5800
October - Harvest Carnival - 727-4514
October - Kiwanis Turkey Shoot Golf Tournament - 727-1038
Knights of Columbus Golf Tournament - 751-3248
October - Knights of Columbus Tootsie Roll - 751-3248
November - 1st Annual Pahrump Pow Wow - 727-0554
November - "Children's Christmas Party" - 727-5107
November - Santa Shop/Craft Show - 727-7081
November - American Heart Association's 7th Annual Golf Tournament - 727-5216
December - Festival of Trees - 727-5489
December - Little Britches Rodeo - 727-5800
Attractions:
Pahrump Valley Vineyards
Pahrump Valley Chamber of Commerce
State Route 160, Box 42
Pahrump, NV 89041 - 1-702-727-5800
1-800-633-WEST

SEARCHLIGHT
Pop. 767
57 mi. south of Las Vegas on US 95. Searchlight is a former mining camp and was once the largest community in southern Nevada. Named for the popular brand of wooden matches, Searchlight had over 10,000 residents at the turn of the century.

In recent years, Searchlight has evolved into a quiet, friendly community home to many retirees. Historical buildings, mining equipment and headframes dot the hillsides.
(also see Ghost Towns)
Attractions: Searchlight Historic Museum

LAS VEGAS CLIMATE

The sun shines almost 85 percent of the year (310 days) in Las Vegas, making it one of the sunniest cities in the United States. Hot summers and moderate winters along with low humidity combine with ideal spring and fall temperatures (average 80 degrees) to make Las Vegas an excellent year round place to live or vacation.

Las Vegas gets very little rain, averaging 4.19 inches per year. Southern Nevada is subject to flash floods. In August 1997, torrential thunderstorms and high winds left thousands of homes without power and stranded motorists in flooded roadways. Probably hit the hardest were Henderson and Boulder City, with Henderson receiving 2.28 inches and Boulder City 3.03 inches, while other parts of the valley received up to an inch and a half of rain. Las Vegas gets lots of wind, over 300 days per year. Because Las Vegas is located in the high desert, elevation 2,162 ft., the temperature ranges can be extreme. The summer months can reach a high of 115 degrees and the winter months as low as 20 degrees with only about 33 days getting below freezing.

Area weather has been recorded since 1937

Weather records:
Hottest day: 117 degrees: July 24, 1942
Coldest day: 8 degrees: Jan. 25, 1937 and Jan. 13, 1963
Longest stretch without freezing: 367 days - Dec. 17, 1994 - Dec. 19, 1995
Rainiest day (24 hours): 2.59 inches Aug. 20 - 21, 1957
Highest wind: 90 mph Aug. 8, 1989
Most snow: 9.7 inches Jan. 10 - 12, 1949
Longest without rain: 101 days, July 2 - Sept. 11, 1944
    and Sept. 2 - Dec. 11, 1995
Feb. 1997 broke all records with a rainfall of 2.8 inches.
Latest day in the year ever to hit 100 degrees June 30, 1965.
Town with the second most record high temperatures in the U.S.:
    Laughlin, Nevada
Hottest recorded temperature in Nevada:
    125 degrees June 29, 1994 in Laughlin

Annual Averages:
Annual rainfall: 4.13 inches
Wettest month: August .49 inch
Driest month: June .12 inch
Average number of days below freezing: 30.6 days
Normal number of days with rain: 27 days
Annual average humidity: 30 percent

Average wind speed: 9.3 mph
Elevation: 2,162 ft.

Telephone Numbers for Time & Temperature:
  Dial 118
  Southwest Gas Weatherline from the studios of KFM102 - 734-2010
  Las Vegas Weather - 736-6404
  National Weather Service - (recording) 736-3854
  Nevada Highway Patrol - Road Conditions - (recording) 486-3116
  Mt. Charleston/Lee Canyon snow and road condition - (recording) 658-1927
  Air Quality Index and Pollen Report - 385-4613
  NOAA Weather Radio 162.55 MhZ (special receivers)

National Weather Service
7851 S. Industrial Rd.
Las Vegas, NV 89139
Office 263-9744
Larry Jensen, *Chief Meteorologist*

Regional Flood Control District
301 E. Clark Avenue
Las Vegas, NV 89101
455-3139
Flood Safety (recording) - 455-5195
Flood Zone Information, City of Las Vegas (recording) - 229-6569
Flood Zone Info., Unincorporated Clark County (recording) - 455-5860

Clark County Air Pollution Control Division
625 Shadow Ln.
Las Vegas, NV 89106
383-1276
Michael Naylor, *Director*
After 4:30 pm, weekends and holidays - 385-1276
EPA has classified the Las Vegas area as in serious nonattainment for carbon monoxide & inhalable particulates. As of Aug. 1, 1997 there have been 110 exceedance days for carbon monoxide compared to 3 days in 1996. On particulate matter there have been 13 events, down from 35 in 1996.

TIME
Las Vegas is on Pacific Standard Time and Daylight Savings Time.
Time and temperature: Dial 118

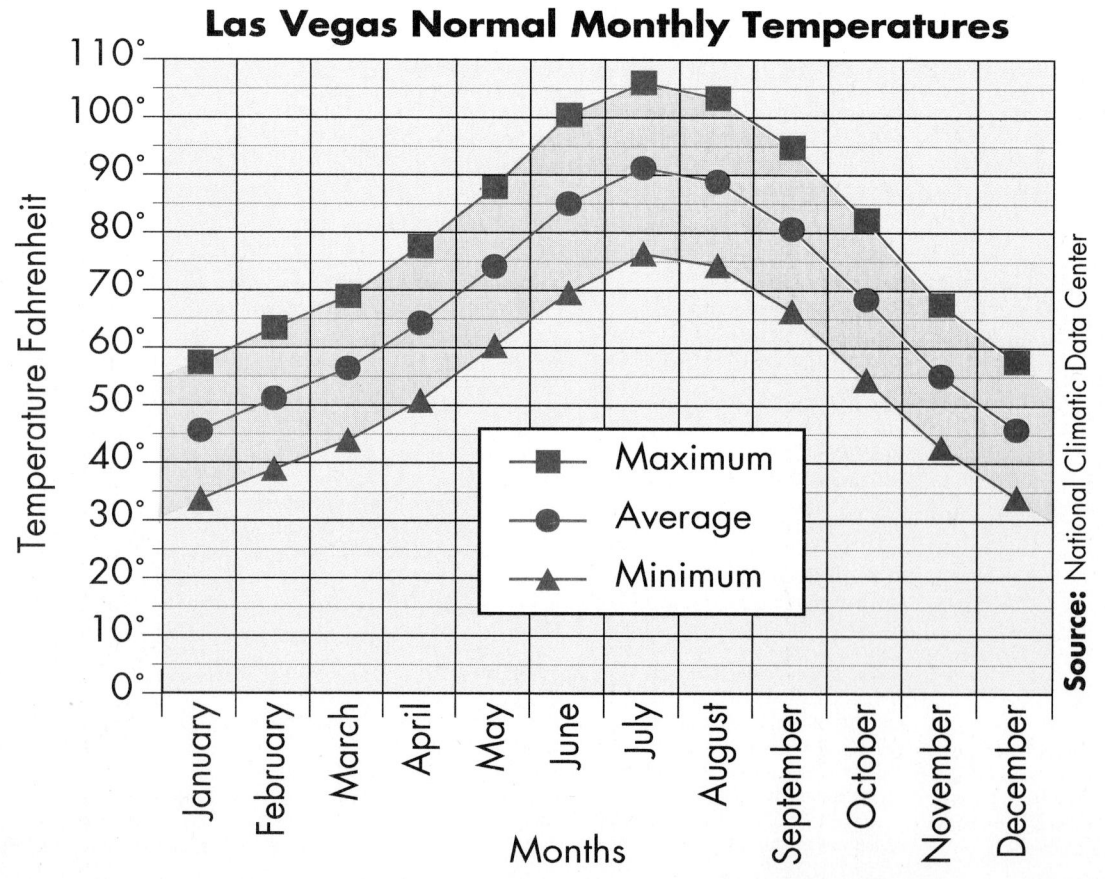

Las Vegas Normal Monthly Temperatures

NEVADA'S STATE SYMBOLS

STATE FLAG

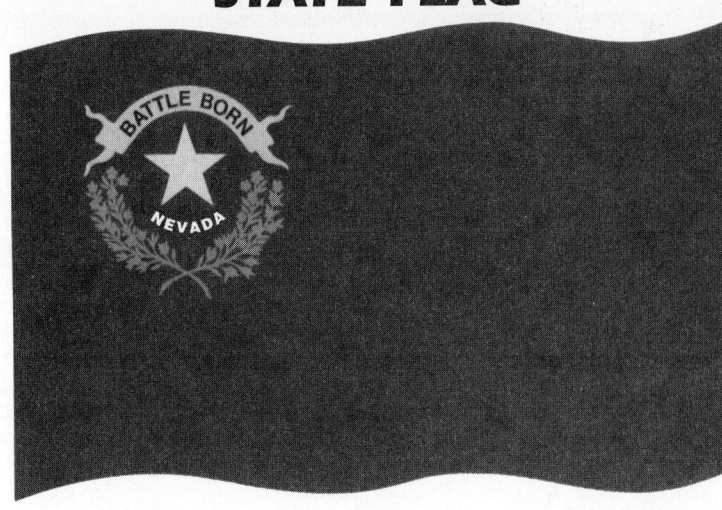

State Capital: Carson City (also territorial capital).

State Nicknames: Battle Born State, adopted March 26, 1937, also Sagebrush State, Silver State.

Origin of state name: Spanish meaning "snowcapped."

State Seal: Adopted by the state legislature in 1866, the Great Seal of the State of Nevada shows a railroad and telegraph line which depict Nevada's importance as a corridor between the Midwest and the West Coast. The tunnel, ore cart and ore-crushing mill portray mining in the Silver State, while the less prominent plow, sheaf and sickle represent agriculture.

State Flag: The current state flag was revised by the legislature in 1991, the first time in more than 60 years. The body is blue and in the upper left hand corner two sprays of sagebrush frame a large silver star with *Nevada* spelled out under the star and topped by a golden scroll that reads "Battle Born," because the state was admitted to the Union in 1864 during the Civil War. The revised flag spells out *Nevada* under the star instead of spread out around the points of the star, which was too hard to read.

State Bird: Mountain Bluebird

State Animal: Bighorn Sheep

State Tree: In 1959, the legislature designated the single-leaf pinon pine as the state tree. In 1987, the legislature also designated the bristlecone pine, notable for being the oldest plant, as the state tree.

State Flower: Shrub Sagebrush

State Motto: "All for Our Country"

State Song: "Home Means Nevada" by Mrs. Bertha Raffetto of Reno; adopted February 6, 1933.

State Grass: Indian Rice Grass

State Fossil: Ichthyosaur

State Metal: Silver

State Fish: Lahonton Cutthrout Trout

State Reptile: Desert Tortoise

State Rock: Sandstone

NEVADA COUNTIES MAP

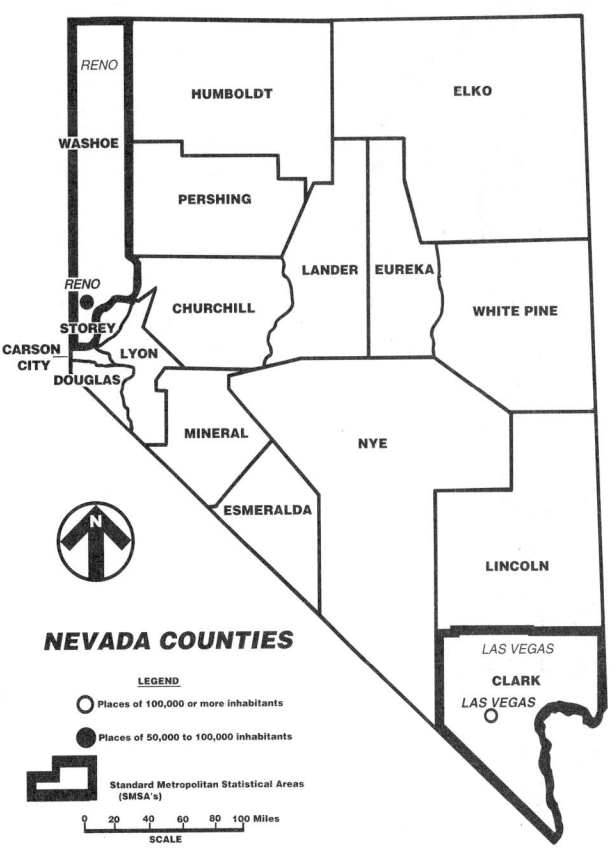

NEVADA COUNTIES

LEGEND
○ Places of 100,000 or more inhabitants
● Places of 50,000 to 100,000 inhabitants
Standard Metropolitan Statistical Areas (SMSA's)
0 20 40 60 80 100 Miles
SCALE

STATE SEAL

NEVADA STATE MAP

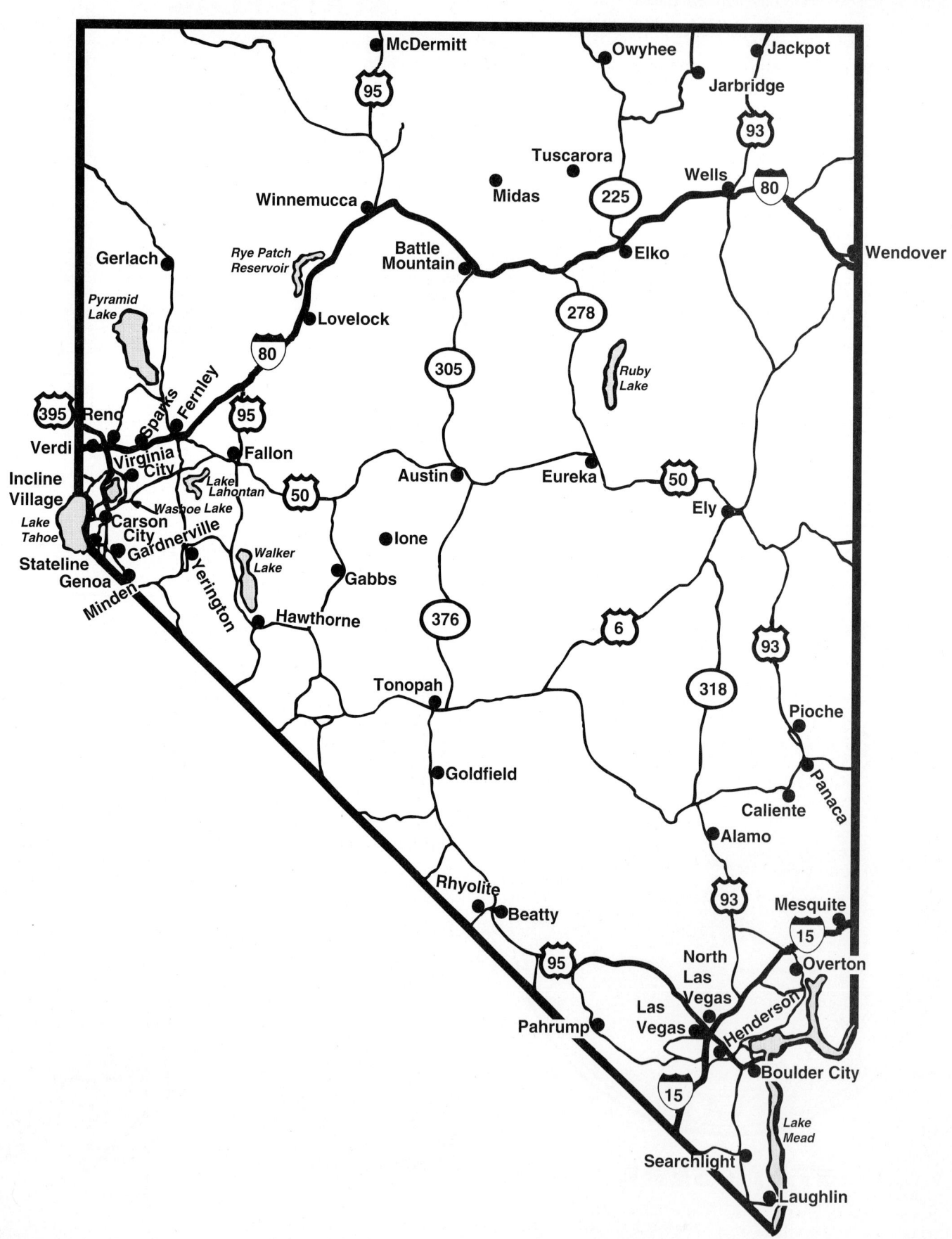

NEVADA CITIES

For information on tourism in Nevada, call the 24-hour hotline at:
1-800-NEVADA-8
or write:
Nevada Commission on Tourism
P.O. Box 30032
Reno, NV 89520

AUSTIN
Pop. 350 - Lander County - 7,030
324 mi. northwest of Las Vegas on US 50
Austin got its start as one of Nevada's mining boom towns in 1862 when a retired Pony Express rider discovered silver ore in nearby Pony Canyon.

BATTLE MOUNTAIN
Pop. 6,000 - Lander County - 6,710
413 mi. northwest of Las Vegas on I-80
Named for Indian battles fought in the area, Battle Mountain was at one time the hub of activity for the surrounding mining sites. Today it is noted for barite and turquoise mines and ranching.

CALIENTE
Pop. 1,070 - Lincoln County - 4,100
150 mi. northeast of Las Vegas. Take I-15 to the turnoff at US 93, turn north for 85 mi. to Ash Springs, continue on US 93 east to Caliente.
Caliente or Celverwell Ranch, as it was known then, played an integral part in the early days of the Union Pacific Railroad's Salt Lake to Los Angeles line. A railroad war broke out in 1900 between the Oregon Short Line and Union Pacific when both claimed the same territory. In 1902 they agreed to joint ownership which led to the line completion and the establishment of Caliente as a division point.

CARSON CITY
Pop. 50,410
State Capital of Nevada
435 mi. northwest of Las Vegas on US 95 and US 50
Originally Carson City was a supply and shipping center for the rich mines of the Comstock Lode. It became the state capital in 1864 when Nevada achieved statehood.

ELKO
Pop. 19,670 - Elko County - 47,710
469 mi. north of Las Vegas via US 95 North and I-80
Elko was an important stop for the Central Pacific and later the Western Pacific Railroads making it a central point of activity in northeastern Nevada. It was also the original site of the University of Nevada from 1874 to 1885, when it was moved to Reno. Elko is located in the high desert, elevation 5,060 ft. Elko was ranked the nations #1 small town in America by "The 100 Best Small Towns in America" in 1995.

ELY
Pop. 5,190 - White Pine County - 10,640
284 mi. north of Las Vegas at the junction of US 50, US 6 and US 93.
Established in the 1870s as a trading post and way station, Ely served local ranchers and nearby gold and silver mines until the early 1900s when copper mining became the mainstay of the town.

EUREKA
Pop. 900 - Eureka County - 1,680
361 mi. northwest of Las Vegas on US 50
Founded in 1869, Eureka was known as the "Pittsburgh of the West" because of the smelting of lead-silver ores from nearby mines. Poisonous lead fumes and flooding mines were some of the problems which eventually left Eureka a "living ghost town" by the later part of the nineteenth century.

FALLON
Pop. 8,200 - Churchill County - 23,860
383 mi. northwest of Las Vegas on US 95
With its beginnings as a ranch turned crossroads store, Fallon prospered as a result of the country's first federal reclamation and irrigation projects. Today it is still one of Nevada's largest farming areas.

FERNLEY
Pop. 9,500 - Lyon County - 29,850
410 mi. northwest of Las Vegas at the junction of Alt. US 95, Alt US 50 and I-80
Developed in 1905 as an important stop on the Southern Pacific Railroad and as an agricultural center in northwestern Nevada, Fernley is still a major farming and ranching area.It is the largest town in northern Nevada.

GOLDFIELD
Pop. 550 - Esmeralda County - 1,460
182 mi. northwest of Las Vegas on US 95
Goldfield sprang up in 1902 with the discovery of gold and silver in the nearby hills and by 1907 boasted the largest population in the state; over 20,000 people. Although the mines have long since played out, the town now profits from its own history.

HAWTHORNE
Pop. 3,630 - Mineral County - 6,860
311 mi. northwest of Las Vegas on US 95
With its beginnings as a supply and shipping center for the nearby mines, Hawthorne achieved notoriety when it became the nations largest ammunitions depot for the U.S. government in the 1930s.

INCLINE VILLAGE/CRYSTAL BAY
Pop. 9,070 - Washoe County - 311,340
With summer residents the population is about 14,000, not including visitors.
470 mi. northwest of Las Vegas
Incline Village and Crystal Bay are adjacent communities of the northeast section of Lake Tahoe.

LAKE TAHOE
(see Incline Village and South Lake Tahoe)
Captain John C. Fremont, guided by Kit Carson, is credited with being the first white man to discover this spectacular region in 1844. Its name, Tahoe, was officially adopted by the California State Legislature in 1945, and comes from the Washoe Indian dialect meaning "big water."
Lake Tahoe is the largest alpine lake on the North American continent. The lake is 22 mi. by 12 mi. and has a maximum depth of 1,645 ft. The surface area covers 191.6 sq. mi. Lake Tahoe is located 6,226 ft. above sea level. The water in Lake Tahoe is 99.9% pure, about the same as distilled water. Two-thirds of the lake is in California, the rest in Nevada.

LOVELOCK
Pop. 2,770 - Pershing County - 6,530
439 mi. northwest of Las Vegas on I-80
Originally called "Big Meadows," Lovelock was the last important stop for travelers on the Immigrant Trail. Abundant water and grass could be found here before the perilous trip across the 40 mile desert. Today farms and ranches flourish.

McDERMITT
Pop. 250 - Humbolt County - 17,520
539 mi. northwest of Las Vegas on US 95
Location of one of the world's largest mercury mines.

MINDEN
Pop. 2,400 - Douglas County - 39,590
422 mi. northwest of Las Vegas on US 395
Minden began as a railroad town in 1905 and by 1916 had grown with such impetus that it took the honors of county seat away from the fading Genoa.

PIOCHE
Pop. 770 - Lincoln County - 4,110
175 mi. northeast of Las Vegas. Take I-15 to the turnoff at US 93, turn north for 85 mi. to Ash Springs, continue on US 93 east through Caliente. Pioche is about 25 mi. from Caliente.
One of the most dangerous and lawless mining towns, Pioche boasts a legend that 75 men died violently before the town's first death by natural causes. It gained further notoriety through the scandal surrounding its "Million Dollar Courthouse."

RENO
Pop. 164,840 - Washoe County - 311,340
443 mi. northwest of Las Vegas on US 95 and I-80.
An early trading post and railroad station, Reno became a major business and transportation center during the Comstock Lode. Famous as the "Biggest Little City in the World."

SOUTH LAKE TAHOE
Pop. 35,000
Located on Hwy. 50 approx. 450 mi. north of Las Vegas.
In 1997, 3 million tourists visited Lake Tahoe, making it Nevada's fourth most popular resort area. The south shore of Lake Tahoe has over 11,500 rooms and four major hotel/casinos.

SPARKS
Pop. 61,590 - Washoe County - 311,340
440 mi. northwest of Las Vegas on US 95 and I-80.
Created in 1904 by the Southern Pacific Railroad as a switching station and maintenance facility, this community just east of Reno was named for Nevada's fourth governor, John D. Sparks.

TONOPAH
Pop. 2,760 - Nye County - 27,460
207 mi. northwest of Las Vegas on US 95
In 1900, a miner named Jim Butler was responsible for the discovery of the abundant silver deposits that would result in the creation of Tonopah. This became the first mining boomtown of the 20th century.

VIRGINIA CITY
Pop. 930 - Storey County - 3,520
435 mi. northwest of Las Vegas on State Hwy. 341
At one time the richest mining town in the world, Virginia City was established in 1859. A thriving product of the Comstock Lode, it remains much as it was during its heyday.

WELLS
Pop. 1,540 - Elko County - 47,710
419 mi. northeast of Las Vegas on US 93 and I 80.
History: Once a stop for wagon trains on the Humbolt Trail, the town of Wells was established in 1869 by the Union Pacific Railroad.

WENDOVER
Pop. 3,430 - Elko County - 47,710
400 mi. northeast of Las Vegas on US 93 and I-80.
This fast growing town on the Utah border began as a water stop for the Western Pacific Railroad. Wendover was the training site for the crew of the Enola Gay who dropped the first atomic bomb ending World War II.

WINNEMUCCA
Pop. 8,140 - Humboldt County - 17,520
466 mi. northwest of Las Vegas on US 95 and I-80.
A fur trappers trading post, a replenishing stop on the Humbolt Trail, and a stop for the Central Pacific Railroad were the beginnings of the crossroads community named for the famous Paiute Indian Chief.

YERINGTON
Pop. 2,820 - Lyon County - 29,850
368 mi. northwest of Las Vegas on US 95 and Alt. US 95.
Founded in the 1860s as a rest stop for passing miners, this agricultural community was named for H. M. Yerington, Superintendent of the Virginia & Truckee Railroad, in an attempt to lure the railroad to the town. Yerington is the county seat of Lyon County.

STATE BIRD OF NEVADA

Mountain Bluebird

NEVADA HISTORY / FACTS

NEVADA HISTORY

John C. Fremont's 1848 expedition with the legendary Kit Carson as principal scout opened the land that is now Nevada.

The region was then considered a part of the Republic of Mexico. It was ceded to the United States by the Treaty of Guadalupe Hidalgo in 1848 and the first permanent settlement was established three years later. Mormons established a community in the Carson Valley at the eastern base of the Sierra Nevada mountains and the area was administered as part of the Utah Territory.

During the 1850s, immigrants and prospectors moved into the region. In 1857 relations between the federal government and the Mormon Church became tense and Brigham Young called his followers back to Salt Lake City.

Two years later, gold was discovered on the south flank of Sun Mountain and the "Rush to Washoe" began. By then, California had been a state for nearly 10 years, yet there were scarcely 300 non-Indian people living in what is now Nevada. But the wealth of the fabulous Comstock Lode built Virginia City into a gaudy young metropolis in the wilderness and financed banks, businesses and hotels in San Francisco, railroads in several western states, and the Atlantic Cable.

The Territory of Nevada was created by an Act of Congress on March 2, 1861, and although Nevada was short of the required population for statehood, it was admitted to the Union on October 31, 1864. President Lincoln proclaimed Nevada's admission to the Union as the 36th state.

The wealth of the Comstock mines began to decline in the 1880s, causing a general decline in population. But in 1900 Tonopah boomed, and in 1903 Goldfield sprang into life 30 mi. away, bringing a new era of mining with the discovery and development of dozens of new deposits of silver and gold. These new mining cities stimulated the development of railroads, and by 1915 there were 2,000 mi. of railroad track in Nevada.

While mining camps went through their unpredictable swings from boom to bust, agriculture grew in importance as cattle and sheep outfits and hay ranches were established. Accessibility to markets got easier with the improvement of the highway system. Las Vegas, established as a railroad depot in 1905, began its growth as a great resort city 40 years later.

Through it all Nevada never lost the excitement of the frontier. Saloon gambling had gone into the back room, but it had never really stopped. In the Depression year of 1931 casino gambling was legalized as a means of raising tax revenues and Nevada's #1 industry began.

Built in 1906 at One Fremont Street, The Golden Gate is Las Vegas' oldest and most historic hotel. The first hotel in Nevada to be built out of concrete, it has survived the test of time, with the original structure still standing among the glitter and neon that is Fremont Street. Originally named Hotel Nevada when it opened, the property which it stands on was sold at auction in 1905 along with two other corner lots for a total of $1,750. The name was changed to the Sal Sagev (Las Vegas spelled backwards) in 1931 and finally named the Golden Gate in 1955.

Being the first hotel in Southern Nevada, it was also the site of the first telephone service in the area; installed in 1907, the number issued for the phone was simply "1". With only 106 rooms, making it the area's smallest hotel, the Golden Gate has the best of both worlds.

Guests of the hotel can enjoy the intimate atmosphere of a "Bed and Breakfast" and then step out the front door into the fabulous Fremont Street Experience. Las Vegas' oldest casino.

NEVADA FACTS

Population:
1,201,833 *(1990 census)* Nevada has been the fastest growing state per capita in the union for the past two decades; 1970 population was 488,738; 1997 figures estimate Nevada's population at 1,655,573, which made it the fastest growing state in the nation once again. Nevada has the 13th smallest state population.

Ten Largest Cities: *(estimates according to State Demographer)*
Las Vegas 401,703 (city) Clark County
Reno 164,840 Washoe County
Henderson 146,200 Clark County
North Las Vegas 93,010 Clark County
Sparks 61,590 Washoe County
Carson City 50,410 Independent City
Elko 19,670 Elko County
Boulder City 15,130 Clark County
Fallon 8,200 Churchill County

Nevada Counties: *16 plus one independent city, Carson City*
(population according to the 1990 census and 1997 estimates)
Carson City 40,443 - 50,410
Churchill County 17,938 - 23,860
Clark County 741,459 - 1,235,253
Douglas 27,637 - 39,590
Elko County 33,530 - 47,710
Esmeralda County 1,344 - 1,460
Eureka County 1,547 - 1,660
Humboldt County 12,844 - 17,520
Lander County 6,266 - 7,030
Lincoln County 3,775 - 4,110
Lyon County 20,001 - 29,850
Mineral County 6,475 - 6,860
Nye County 17,781 - 27,460
Pershing County 4,336 - 6,530
Story County 2,526 - 3,520
Washoe County 254,667 - 311,340
White Pine County 9,264 - 10,640
Nevada area: 110,540 sq. mi.
State dimensions: 485 mi. long by 315 mi. wide
Rank in size: 7th
Public land: 48 million acres
Federally owned land: 87%
Rank in population: 38th
Most harvested crop: Alfalfa, with almost 100,000 tons harvested annually
Total jobs - 1997: 910,800
Unemployment Rate: 3.9% (1997 seasonally adjusted)
Unemployed: 34,000
Employed: 865,900
Highest point: Boundary Peak in Esmeralda County - 13,143 feet
Lowest point: Colorado River (Laughlin) - 490 feet
Average Elevation: 5,000 ft.
Median age: 36.2
Per Capita Income: $20,209
Growth Rate from 1980 to 1990: 50.38%
Major hotel/casinos: 146 (with at least $1 million in gaming revenue)
Hotel rooms: 110,462
Gaming industry employees: (12/97) 188,572
Slot machines: 180,680 (nonrestricted)
with an average win of $27,600 per machine for a total win of $4.9 billion.
Gaming Revenue: $7.8 billion, up 5.1% from 1996.
Live table games: 5,758 for total win of $2.8 billion
430 nonrestricted gaming licenses were issued in 1997
Admitted to the union: October 31, 1864, 36th state
Natural Resources & Minerals: gold, silver, copper, lead, zinc, tungsten, uranium, manganese, titanium, iron, mercury, opal, molydenum, barite, diatomite, magnesite, talc, gypsum, dolomite, lime, turquoise, brucite, fluorspar, antimony, perlite, pumice, salt, sulfur oilshale
Agriculture: cattle, horses, sheep, hogs, poultry, hay, wheat, corn, potatoes, rye, oats, alfalfa, barley, vegetables, fruits

Transportation

Transportation to and from the Las Vegas area is both limitless and convenient. Ten of the western states are within 500 mi. of Las Vegas. Due to the large amount of tourism to the area, there are a multitude of choices available for people to meet their destination needs.

Las Vegas is often used as a jumping-off point by people wanting to get to other areas such as the Grand Canyon, Hoover Dam, the Colorado River, Reno and Disneyland. Citizens Area Transit, or CAT, is the area's largest bus system, providing transportation throughout the greater Las Vegas area. Local stops are just $1.00 and your first transfer is free. Buses also run to and from McCarran International Airport approximately every half hour. Passengers can use the system at the airport 5:30 am - 1:30 am.

The need for taxi companies is also far greater in Las Vegas than in most other cities its size. Several companies offer quality service at reasonable rates and operate 24 hours. It is always best to call as far in advance as possible. The area also has a trolley system that runs downtown, transporting people to local casino/resorts as well as providing a route on the Strip.

McCarran International Airport, key contributor in transforming a small desert community into the top tourist destination in the world, is the 12th busiest airport in the United States. With 21 airlines providing service at the airport, 30 million passengers passed through McCarran in 1997, including approximately 2 million people traveling internationally. Conveniently located only 1 mi. from the strip, McCarran averages over 800 scheduled flights and 84,000 passengers daily. A $500 million expansion, scheduled for completion by the fall of 1998, will allow the airport to keep up with the growth in flights, which has increased 200 percent since 1985. The expansion will be complete with a new "D" concourse, consisting of 26 additional gates and a tram system which will transport passengers from Terminal 1 to any of the new gates. The new concourse is consistent with McCarran's motto of giving tourists the best first and last impression of Las Vegas. It is estimated that by the year 2010, McCarran International Airport will be home to approximately 135 gates, more than double its current number.

Car rental agencies in the Las Vegas area are abundant, ranging from "Rent - A - Wreck" to "Rent - A - Vette." The options are virtually limitless. While the airport houses a number of car rental booths and limousine service to and from the destination of choice, many other agencies also offer a full line of convenient services and options. Most rentals require a major credit card and a minimum age of 25; however, it is always best to call ahead for information regarding your specific circumstances.

NEVADA MILEAGE DIAGRAM

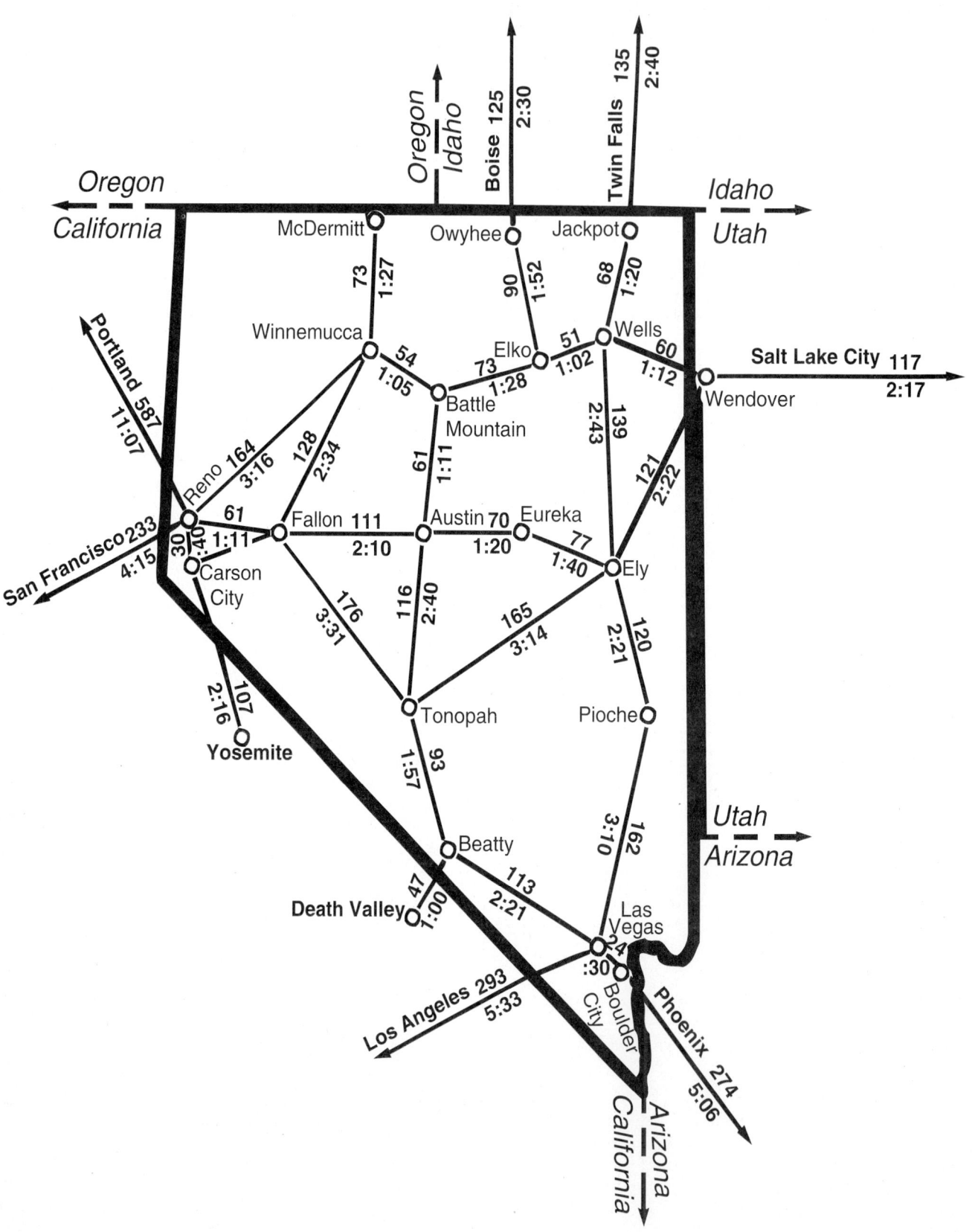

Oregon
California

Oregon
Idaho

Boise 125 2:30

Twin Falls 135 2:40

Idaho
Utah

McDermitt

Owyhee

Jackpot

73 1:27

90 1:52

89 1:20

Portland 587 11:07

Winnemucca

Elko

Wells

Salt Lake City 117 2:17

54 1:05

73 1:28

51 1:02

60 1:12

Reno 164 3:16

Battle Mountain

Wendover

128 2:34

139 2:43

61 1:11

121 2:22

San Francisco 233 4:15

61 1:11

Fallon 111 2:10

Austin 70 1:20

Eureka

30 :41

77 1:40

Carson City

Ely

176 3:31

116 2:40

165 3:14

120 2:21

107 2:16

Tonopah

Pioche

Utah
Arizona

Yosemite

93 1:57

162 3:10

Beatty

113 2:21

Las Vegas

Death Valley 47 1:00

24 :30

Boulder City

Phoenix 274 5:06

Los Angeles 293 5:33

Arizona
California

AUTO

Approximately 41 percent of Las Vegas visitors arrive by automobile, 44 percent by air, 8 percent by bus, 6 percent by RV and less than 0.4 percent by train.

The Southern California Yermo Inspection Station reported 4,948,355 vehicles passed through in 1997, up 8.7 percent from the previous year.

San Diego, Los Angeles and Salt Lake City are reached via I-15, Reno via US 95 and Phoenix via US 93. I-15 is a direct 720 mi. highway from Salt Lake to Los Angeles. The interstate also provides East Coast/West Coast access via I-80, I-70 and I-40 as well as north-south access from Mexico to Canada via I-5.

MILEAGE FROM LAS VEGAS TO STATE CAPITALS

Montgomery, AL	1,873	Lincoln, NE	1,319
Phoenix, AZ	287	Carson City, NV	438
Little Rock, AR	1,474	Concord, NH	2,772
Sacramento, CA	560	Trenton, NJ	2,515
Denver, CO	840	Santa Fe, NM	651
Hartford, CT	2,679	Albany, NY	2,619
Dover, DE	2,508	Raleigh, NC	2,335
Washington, DC	2,423	Bismarck, ND	1,340
Tallahassee, FL	2,057	Columbus, OH	2,027
Atlanta, GA	1,969	Oklahoma City, OK	1,132
Boise, ID	683	Salem, OR	944
Springfield, IL	1,688	Harrisburg, PA	2,393
Indianapolis, IN	1,856	Providence, RI	2,740
Des Moines, IA	1,499	Columbia, SC	2,219
Topeka, KS	1,319	Pierre, SD	1,246
Frankfort, KY	1,937	Nashville, TN	1,809
Baton Rouge, LA	1,644	Austin, TX	1,271
Augusta, ME	2,915	Salt Lake City, UT	431
Annapolis, MD	2,446	Montpelier, VT	2,753
Boston, MA	2,773	Richmond, VA	2,419
Lansing, MI	2,022	Olympia, WA	1,094
St. Paul, MN	1,636	Charleston, WV	2,087
Jackson, MS	1,620	Madison, WI	1,778
Jefferson City, MO	1,505	Cheyenne, WY	865
Helena, MT	906		

MILEAGE TO NEVADA CITIES & BORDER TOWNS

Baker, CA	92
Boulder City	24
Caliente	150
Carson City	435
Elko	469
Ely	284
Henderson	13
Indian Springs	41
Kingman, AZ	103
Lake Tahoe	448
Laughlin	104
Mesquite	76
Moapa	51
Pahrump	80
Reno	443
St. George, UT	127
Tonopah	207
Virginia City	435
Winnemucca	466

OTHER CITIES

Los Angeles	290
Palm Springs	280
San Diego	364
San Francisco	589

NEVADA'S ROADS

The State of Nevada maintains 5,429 mi. of paved roads; 13,448 mi. of roads are maintained by cities and counties. There are also 33,010 mi. of unimproved, dirt and gravel roads in the state.

MILEAGE TO AREA ATTRACTIONS

Death Valley Junction	110
Furnace Creek Inn	140
Scotty's Castle	170
Grand Canyon	
South Rim	290
North Rim	307
Hoover Dam	30
Lake Mead/Lake Mohave	
Overton	50
Callville Bay	36
Willow Beach	56
Lake Mead Marina	38
Cottonwood Cove	99
Mt. Charleston	34
Red Rock Canyon	16
Spring Mountain Ranch	17
Valley of Fire	50
Zion National Park	180

ROAD CONDITIONS

Arizona: (602) 241-3100 ext. 7623	California (northern): (916) 445-1534
California (southern): (916) 445-1534	Utah: (801) 964-6000
Nevada (Reno): (702) 793-1333	Nevada (Elko): (702) 738-8888

Las Vegas Area Emergency Road Conditions: 486-3116
Nevada Highway Patrol: 486-4100

BUS LINES - LONG DISTANCE

Greyhound
200 S. Main St.
Las Vegas, NV 89101
Open 24 hours
(Next to the Plaza Hotel downtown)
Fare & Schedule Information:
1-800-231-2222
Fax: 702-384-2806
Las Vegas Agent/Package Express: 702-382-2292
Package Pick-up & Delivery: 702-382-7342
Spanish: 1-800-531-5332
Group Charter: 1-800-454-2487
Charlie Tibbs, Customer Service Mgr.
Over 2,000 locations nationwide. No advance reservations are accepted and tickets can be purchased just prior to departure. Discounts are available for advance purchase, senior citizens and military.

SCHEDULE:

DEPARTURES:

Los Angeles - 9:40 am, 9:45 am, 10:30 am, 11:40 am, 12:30 pm, 2:05 pm, 2:30 pm, 4:30 pm, 5:25 pm, 5:55 pm, 10:55 pm, 11:00 pm
San Bernardino - 10:30 am, 11:40 am, 2:05 pm, 2:30 pm, 5:25 pm, 5:55 pm
Fresno - 9:45 am, 12:30 pm, 2:05 pm, 2:30 pm, 5:55 pm, 10:55 pm
Phoenix - 11:30 am, 2:45 pm, 5:35 pm
Salt Lake City - 5:45 am, 9:20 am
Kingman - 12:10 am, 6:15 am, 7:00 am, 2:45 pm, 5:35 pm
Denver - 12:30 am, 5:15 am, 5:45 am, 5:20 pm
Laughlin - 12:10 am, 6:15 am, 7:00 am, 11:30 am, 2:45 pm, 5:35 pm
Lake Havasu - 11:30 am
Reno - 8 am
San Diego - 12:40 am, 5:30 am, 6:50 am, 8:10 am, 11:40 am, 12:30 pm, 2:10 pm, 2:45 pm, 4:30 pm, 5:25 pm, 10:55 pm

ARRIVALS

Los Angeles - 1:05 pm, 1:35 pm, 2:45 pm, 3:40 pm, 4:05 pm, 4:15 pm, 5:15 pm, 8:05 pm, 8:15 pm, 11:00 pm, 11:20 pm, 12:10 am, 1:45 am
San Bernardino - 1:05 pm, 2:45 pm, 3:40 pm, 4:05 pm, 5:15 pm, 5:40 pm, 7:30 pm, 8:05 pm, 11:00 pm, 11:25 pm, 12:10 am, 1:45 am
Fresno - 7:30 pm, 11:00 pm, 12:05 am, 4:15 am, 6:10 am
Phoenix - 9:45 am, 1:20 pm, 5:00 pm, 10:45 pm
Salt Lake City - 4:35 pm, 5:20 am
Kingman - 12:10 am, 4:35 pm, 10:30 pm, 11:25 pm

Denver - 11:10 pm, 9:15 am, 1:35 pm
Laughlin - 5:10 am, 12:10 pm, 3:20 pm, 4:35 pm, 10:30 pm, 11:25 pm
Lake Havasu - 3:20 pm
Reno - 4:00 pm
San Diego - 1:05 pm, 5:15 pm, 7:30 pm, 11:00 pm, 1:45 am, 4:15 am

EXAMPLE OF FARES:
Weekend rates:
Denver: $80 *one way* - $125 *round trip*
Los Angeles: $37 - $72
Phoenix: $32 - $63
Salt Lake City: $45 - $83
San Diego: $45 - $84
Weekday rates:
Denver: $76 - $119
Los Angeles: $35 - $68
Phoenix: $30 - $60
Salt Lake City: $42 - $79
San Diego: $42 - $80
Discounts are offered if you purchase your tickets from 3 - 21 days in advance.
Some buses stop at the Lady Luck Hotel and Sunset Station after leaving the downtown station or stop at the hotel before arriving downtown. Package express service is available.

Valen Transportation & Tours
Riviera Hotel
2901 Las Vegas Blvd. S.
Las Vegas, NV 89109
702-734-5110 1-800-487-2252
Michael Valen, Pres.
Pick-ups in Las Vegas are as follows:
Golden Nugget 6:30 am Grand Canyon and Bryce Canyon, 7 am Anaheim/Disneyland
Sahara Hotel 6:45 am Grand Canyon and Bryce Canyon, 7:15 am Anaheim/Disneyland
Riviera 7:15 am Grand Canyon, 7:30 am Bryce Canyon, 8 am Anaheim/Disneyland
Included in fare are on-board meal and beverage, feature movies and no scheduled stops. Service is daily, departing Las Vegas On Mon., Wed. and Fri. at 8 am. Evening departures are 6 pm Mon., Wed., Thu., Fri. and Sat., 3:30 pm Tue. and Sun. Pick-ups and drop offs at Primm 40 minutes after departure from Riviera.
Fare: One way adult - $49; children 3 - 11 - $44; Round trip - $89; children - $79; for Grand Canyon $149 adults and $129 children 3-11 round trip.
Bryce Canyon $129 adults and children $109 round trip.

TRAIN
FREIGHT ONLY

Union Pacific Railroad
1001 Iron Horse Ct.
Las Vegas, NV 89106
702-388-9215 1-800-272-8777
Gil Escalante, Mgr. of Train Operation

Union Pacific Railroad serves the Las Vegas area with direct, single-system service to 20 states and connective service to more than 30 states. The switching and marshalling yard are located downtown west of Main St.

WESTERN U.S. TRANSPORTATION MAP

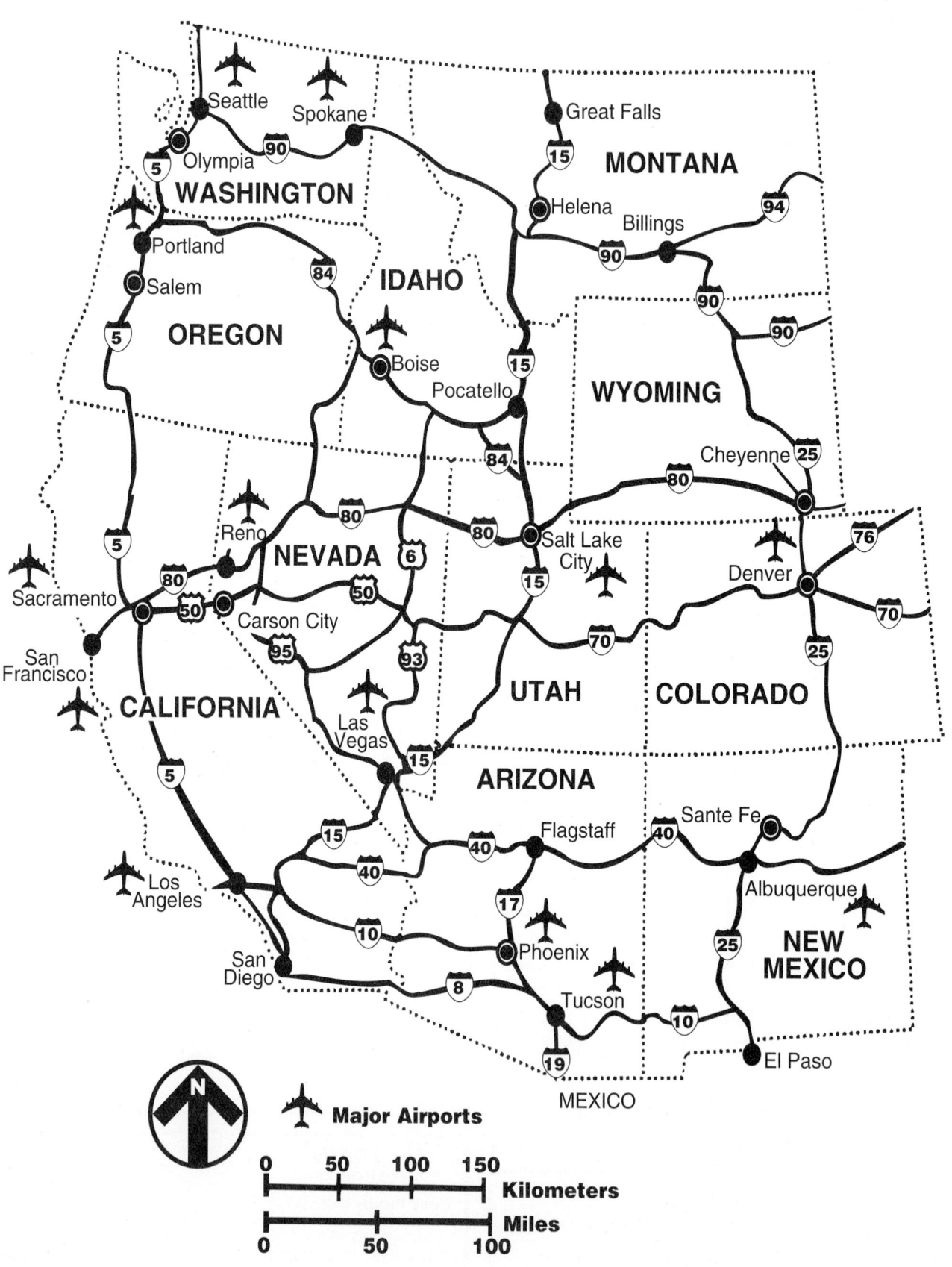

Major Airports

Kilometers
0 50 100 150

Miles
0 50 100

McCARRAN INTERNATIONAL AIRPORT

Photo: Cynthia Andersen, Clark County Dept. of Aviation

Las Vegas McCarran International Airport "The Gateway to the Great American Southwest"

McCarran International Airport

5795 Paradise Rd.
5757 Wayne Newton Blvd.-Terminal
Las Vegas, NV 89119
261-5211
Randall Walker, Clark County Dir. Aviation
General Information: 261-5743
Terminal Paging: 261-5733
Airport Emergency: 261-5911
Web site: http://McCarran.com
McCarran Construction Hotline: 261-5555
Customs Office: 388-6480
Federal Aviation Adm.: 388-6482
Traveler's Aid: 261-5234; 8 am - 5 pm
Parking Information: 261-5121
Valet: 261-4999
Parking rates: $6 for 24 hours uncovered; Garage - less than 15 min. free; Each 16 - 30 min. $2, 30 min. - 1 hr. $3. Cars may park up to 30 days without special arrangements. Valet $3.00 minimum, $10.

General Information

Approximately 30 million passengers traveled by air to Las Vegas with 15 million deplaning for business or pleasure during 1997. McCarran is the 12th busiest airport in the nation. The extraordinary increase in passenger volume was complemented by an increase in the number of takeoffs and landings, which boosted McCarran's standing to the 15th busiest airport in the world based on total aircraft operations.

On December 19, 1998 McCarran will celebrate its 50th anniversary. The airport continues to mirror the changing face of Las Vegas and enjoys the benefits of operating in the fastest growing city in the United States. The soaring popularity of Las Vegas as a vacation and business destination, the tremendous growth of the local population, and new air service to Las Vegas contributed to the double-digit growth at McCarran. Each new hotel room generates an estimated 320 passengers a year through McCarran. The next phase of mega-resort development scheduled for completion around 1999 will add an additional 12,000 rooms to Las Vegas' existing inventory, attracting even more visitors.

McCarran's facilities continue to expand in order to realize Las Vegas' potential as an international gateway and to meet the needs of the growing travel and tourism industry, local population, and thriving business economy.

On Dec. 31, 1995, McCarran celebrated the grand opening of the McCarran International Airport Connector and Roadway System which offers McCarran travelers convenient nonstop access from the Interstate system to the airport, bypassing the congested Las Vegas Strip.

A 1,400-ft. extension was added to Runway 7L-25R, making it the longest civilian runway in the United States. The runway extension enhanced airfield capacity and made possible nonstop international service to McCarran.

The 7th most popular international destination among overseas visitors, about 30 million passengers came through McCarran in 1997 of which 15,140,410 deplaned. The addition of nonstop international air service to the McCarran line-up confirmed Las Vegas' popularity.

In Nov. 1995, Condor, a Lufthansa German Airlines subsidiary, made Las Vegas aviation history by offering the first overseas nonstop scheduled service, between Cologne, Germany and Las Vegas. Airtours, a United Kingdom-based charter tour company and airline also announced direct service to Las Vegas from Manchester beginning in 1995. Demonstrating the feasibility of Las Vegas as an alternative American gateway, these flights moved McCarran toward a new level of customer service and highlighted the advantages of direct Las Vegas service to foreign visitors and international travelers.

To meet the increasing demand for parking, plans for a 6,000-space covered parking garage were set in motion. The new parking garage, together with improved passenger pick-up and roadways, was completed in November 1996. A permanent 4,200-space, fully improved parking lot opened on Russell Rd. near Kelly Ln.

Airport Parking Plaza

There are nine levels and 6,000 parking spaces in the new parking plaza which is called the "Gold Garage." Enough concrete was poured to build a sidewalk from Las Vegas to San Francisco. There are 329 mi. of post tensioning cable and 6,397 tons of reinforcing steel. Color coded lanes provide easy directions to parking locations.

McCARRAN INTERNATIONAL AIRPORT

Construction started February 23, 1995 and was completed November 4, 1996 at a cost of $83.8 million. (The original 1,500 space garage which opened in 1985 is routinely filled to capacity today. This garage is known as the "Silver Garage.") Two pedestrian bridges equipped with moving sidewalks link Gold Garage to Terminal I. Valet parking is provided, as well as parking for frequent travelers known as "Park-a-Lot." For further information, or to receive a map of the McCarran Roadway System and access to the Parking Plaza, contact the Public Information Hotline at 261-5555.

D Gates

The ultimate development of the D Gates will consist of 4 concourse wings connected to a central hub in the design of an X. The D Gates will add 26 gates, boosting passenger capacity to 45 million. The original 30 million capacity was first exceeded in 1996. Ultimately D gate will house 48 gates, nearly doubling passenger capacity of today. The first phase will cost an estimated $200 million, not including the ATS System (fixed guideway & people mover) which is an underground tram. Parking, baggage handling and ticketing will continue to occur at Terminal 1 however, the automated trasit system will move people between terminals in about 90 seconds. This Phase 1, will open June 1998 and feature new gift shops, concessions, and eateries in an environment that captures the beauty of the desert and the mystery of flight. Total approximate area of Phase 1 is 450,000 sq. ft.

The Clark County Airport System consists of six airports:

McCarran International Airport
North Las Vegas Airport
Henderson Executive Airport
Jean Airport
Overton Municipal Airport
Searchlight Airport

Owning Property

The Clark County Board of Commissioners authorized McCarran to buy property surrounding the airport to eliminate noise concerns, provide for future development and meet federal aviation requirements. When possible these properties were turned into revenue sources. McCarran now owns 350 homes, 3 apartment complexes, several commercial parks and leases land to a first class golf driving range. Occupancy for the residential properties is running at 94 percent and commercial at 92 percent. Property management generates $8 million a year and the position to expand. Because of these sources of revenue, the Department of Aviation has been able to reduce rates charged to airlines affiliated with McCarran. Since 1988, the following increases in revenue have been reported: 248 percent increase in overall growth, 286 percent increase in concessions, 29 percent increase in airline revenue. Last year, the airport generated $5.5 million in advertising revenue, $12 million in sales concessions and $24 million in gaming revenue. The Department of Aviation operates as an enterprise fund, without the use of general fund tax dollars.

McCarran International Airport is part of the Clark County Airport System, publicly owned by Clark County, and operated under the direction of the Board of County Commissioners, the authority of Dale Askew, County Manager, and the management of Randall Walker, Director of Aviation.

Other plans for McCarran include baggage claim enlargement which will increase baggage carousels from 12 to 16. Expansion will be complete in Aug.

AIRLINES SERVING McCARRAN

Air Canada:	1-800-776-3000
Am. Trans Air ATA:	1-800-225-2995
Alaska Airlines AS:	1-800-426-0333
America West HP:	1-800-235-9292
American AA:	1-800-433-7300
Canadian Airlines:	1-800-426-7000
Continental: CO:	1-800-231-0856
Condor Airlines:	1-800-524-6975
Delta DL:	1-800-221-1212
Hawaiian HA:	1-800-367-5320
KIWI International:	1-800-538-5494
Northwest NW:	1-800-225-2525
Midwest Express:	1-800-452-2022
Reno Air QQ:	1-800-736-6247
Shuttle By United:	1-800-SHUTTLE
Skywest:	1-800-453-9417
Southwest WN:	1-800-435-9792
Trans World TW:	1-800-221-2000
United UA:	1-800-241-6522
US Air US:	1-800-428-4322
Western Pacific:	1-800-930-3030

AIRPORT TRANSPORTATION

TRANSPORTATION:
Companies with counters in baggage claim area:

Allstate Car Rental:	736-6147
Avis Car Rental:	261-5595
Bell Limousine:	385-5466
Bell Limousine Shuttle:	739-7990
Dollar Rent-A-Car:	739-8408
Gray Line	
Mini Bus Service:	739-5700
Golden Year Shuttle:	360-6160
Hertz Car Rental:	736-4900
National	
Car Rental:	1-800-227-7368
Sav-Mor Car Rental:	736-1234
Airport Rent a Car:	795-0800

Photo: Photechnik International

TRANSPORTATION TO/FROM AIRPORT

Bell Trans: 739-7990
Limousines and mini-buses $3.50 per person to Strip hotels; $4.75 per person to downtown hotels one way.
Gray Line: 739-5700
Mini-buses $3.75 per person to Strip hotels one way $6.50 round trip; $4.75 per person to downtown hotels one way; $9 round trip.
Ray & Ross Airport Express: 261-3230
Strip - one way $3.50, round trip $6.00
Downtown - one way $4.50 round trip $8.00
Taxi Cab:
Examples of cab fares:
Airport to Strip hotels - $8.00 - $13.00
Airport to downtown hotels - $13.00 to $17.00
Taxis and walk-up limo and mini-bus services are available out the west doors near baggage claim.
Limo and courtesy transportation pickup for hotels is located out the east doors. This is also where group charter buses pick-up.

RADIO INFORMATION

Tune to WNRM at 530 on the AM dial for directions to McCarran's ticketing and baggage claim traffic lanes and up-to-the-minute parking availability as well as weather conditions. This station has only a 2.5 mile listening radius at the airport.

PLANE WATCHING

If you like to watch planes take off and land, McCarran has installed a parking lot along Sunset Rd. between the post office and Eastern Ave.

McCarran Airport Deplaned Passengers

Passengers in Millions

Years	Passengers
1980	5,141,664
1985	5,463,498
1986	6,220,134
1987	7,816,477
1988	8,112,238
1989	8,733,899
1990	9,505,823
1991	10,055,401
1992	10,468,062
1993	11,254,211
1994	13,399,332
1995	13,991,835
1996	15,190,526
1997	15,140,410

Source: McCarran Airport - Department of Aviation

SHOPS AND SERVICES AT McCARRAN

Auto Teller Plus System: Day & Night Teller - Between Esplanade E & W
First Aid: 261-5620 - South Mezzanine above ticketing - 8:30 am -5 pm
Information Booths: C Gate, Esplanade East, Rotunda, and Bag Claim - open 6 am - 1 am
Lockers: Near A, B and C Gates
Lost & Found: 261-5134 - South Mezzanine above ticketing
Nursery: Changing Station - Esplanade West
Police: 261-5377 - South Mezzanine above ticketing
Post Office: 361-9356 - Esplanade East/Machine - Esplanade West
Travelers Aid: 261-5234 - Bag claim area - open daily 8 am - 5 pm
Gift shops, snack bars and cocktail lounges are located at all gates and in the main lobby, as are slot machines *(571 machines throughout airport).* The main dining area is located on the north side of Esplanade West. Cocktail lounge and deli with two large screen televisions located at the west end of the rotunda. Host, a division of Marriott Corp., operates 31 food and beverage outlets at McCarran.
Stores: Most shops are open 7 am to 12:30 am.
A-1 Catering - Truck in Taxi/ Limousine Area
Alejandro's Texan Grill - Restaurant
Allstate Tours - Show Ticket Sales
Ayala's, Inc., dba Creative Candy & Gifts - Fresh Fudge/Candy
BTU Gifts And News - Gift/News
Burger King - Fast Food
Caesars World Merchandising, Inc. - Sportswear
Caesars World Merchandising, Inc. - Caesars Logo Products
Chamblis & Dougan Int'l - Gift/News
Cheers - Bar
Cigars Express, Inc. - Cigars
Cinnabon
Dan Ayala - Gift/News
Distribution Corp. of America dba Puppets, Puppets, Puppets
El Portal of Nevada - Luggage
Ethel M. Chocolates - Candy
Forget Me Not, Inc. - Cactus/Flowers
G. C. Hill - Shoeshine Concession
Hospitality Culinaire, Inc. TCBY - Yogurt in Rotunda
International Shoeshine Service - Shoeshine Concession

IPM, Inc. - Gambling/Gifts
J & D Inc. dba Trails West - Western Apparel & Gifts
L. V. Gourmet Coffee Co., Inc.
Las Vegas Fruit & Nut - Candy, Fruit
MGM Grand Merchandising, Inc. - MGM Logo Products
M & R Jewelry Corporation - Jewelry
M. R. & Whitsett Co. - TCBY & Mrs. Fields Cookies
Magna Cart-A, Inc. dba The Copper Cart - Copper Gifts & Jewelry
Marshall Rousso - Women's Apparel
Mirage Resorts - Retail Store
Mutual of Omaha and Passenger Service Center - Located under escalators between ticket counters. Services include foreign currency exchange, travel insurance, Western Union, bag storage, notary, photocopies - 261-5650
New Ventures dba Secure Seal - Baggage Wrap
The Paradise Shops dba PGA Tour Shops - PGA Tour Golf Shop
Pizza Hut
R & R Gallery c/o Serendipity-Collectibles, Gifts - Indian Jewelry
RLW, Inc. - Food Cart
RLW - Gifts/News
Rotts, Inc. dba Kids Corner KST - Toys & Children
Rotts, Inc. dba The Tie Rack and Sunglass Cache - Sunglasses and Ties
Simply Unique - Gifts, Decorative Items
Smarte Carte, Inc. - Luggage, Car Rental
Smarte Carte, Inc. - Lockers
Sparkle Plenty - Jewelry
Taco Bell & Arriba Margarita - 4 outlets - one at each concourse rotunda
Teletrip Company dba Travelex - Business Services & Flight Insurance
The Writer's Edge - Fisher Space Pens - Pens
Unibex Global Corporation dba Airport Travel Service - Travel Services
University of Gambling - Logo West
Up & Away, Inc. - Nevada Products
Vegas Memories, Inc., dba T-Shirts, LTD. - T-Shirts
WH Smith of Nevada, Inc. dba New York New York - New York New York Logo Products
Waterstone Books - Bookstore

AIR CARGO

Las Vegas International Air Cargo Center - $5 million, 78,000 sq. ft. of warehouse space - is included in Phase I improvements situated on 80 acres. It includes a 10-acre foreign trade zone with the first phase completed in January of 1996. Phase II, a 40,800 sq. ft. facility and Phase III, a 50,000 sq. ft. facility were completed in 1996. McCarran handled 157,248,238 pounds of cargo in 1997.

Air Cargo is located 1 mi. from McCarran International Airport's main terminal building, from railway service

and from the interstate. The area has 240 acres available for development .

Facilities in Phase I and II include nine primary parking positions, nine push-back aircraft parking positions, 275,000 sq. ft. of ramp area, two warehouses totaling 119,300 sq. ft. and group 5 taxiway and ramp. Phase III has a 100,000 sq. ft. warehouse and 225,000 sq. ft. of additional ramp area.

The Foreign Trade Zone utilizes 160 acres. The fifth annual Las Vegas International Air Cargo Symposium was held at the Rio Suite Hotel & Casino on May 28, 1997. The main topic was air cargo security.

TERMINALS/AIRPORTS
Charter -
International Terminal: 261-5743
International terminal is located on Kitty Hawk Way, off Paradise Rd., north of the main terminal. The 2 story, 8 gate, 183,000 sq. ft. facility opened on December 18, 1991 at a cost of $33 million. In 1997, over 30 million passengers from around the world passed through McCarran Charter/International Terminal. The facility is used by charter and commuter airlines. The facility includes US Customs and Immigration facilities.

Las Vegas Executive Terminal
(Koval Ln. & Tropicana Ave.)
275 E. Tropicana Ave.
Las Vegas, NV 89109
736-1830
Fixed base operator (FBO).

Quail Air Center
(north side of runways)
155 E. Reno Ave.
Las Vegas, NV 89119
798-0898
Private Airport.

Signature Flight Support
(West Terminal)
6005 Las Vegas Blvd. S.
Las Vegas, NV 89119
739-1100
A $2.6 million state-of-the-art terminal built in 1995.

GENERAL AVIATION AIRPORTS

North Las Vegas Air Terminal
2730 Airport Dr., Ste.101
N. Las Vegas, NV 89030
261-3800
Gus Sabo, Gen. Mgr.
Customer Service: 261-3806
North Las Vegas Air Terminal was purchased by Clark County in 1987 for $16 million to divert small planes from McCarran. The $15 million facelift, which including resurfacing the runways and a 15,600-sq. ft. terminal, was completed.

Henderson Executive Airport
1400 Executive Airport Dr.
Henderson, NV 89104
261-4800
Clark County, owner
Tom Donaldson A.A.E., Mgr., General Aviation Airports
The County will move slower, smaller general aviation aircraft to Henderson Airport to make room for the growing number of commercial airlines at McCarran Airport. The 402-acre airport was purchased by Clark County for $23.75 million.

Searchlight Airport
261-3800
Gus Sabo, Gen. Mgr.
Air strip only.

Overton Municipal Airport
1110 Airport Rd.
Overton, NV 89040
397-9617
Gus Sabo, Gen. Mgr.
The airport caters to small general avia-

tion aircraft for personal, recreational and business uses with one 4,800 ft. paved and lighted runway, in addition to a general services building, pilot lounge complete with snack bar, telephone, maps and restrooms.

Jean Airport
23600 Las Vegas Blvd. S.
Jean, NV 89019
261-4800
Tom Donaldson A.A.E., Mgr., General Aviation Airports
Only public sports airport in the country dedicated to gliding, ultralight and sky diving. Special events center for aviation related activities, contains two runways.

Bullhead - Laughlin Airport
600 Hwy. 95
Bullhead City, AZ 86430
1-520-754-3922
Airport served by:
America West: 1-800-235-9292
Sun Country: 1-800-359-5786

Boulder City Airport
1850 Buchanan Blvd.
Boulder City, NV 89005
293-5595
Tom McWhirter, Dir. of Operations
Consists of 530 acres, 2 runways and small glider/ultralight strip. Terminal building used for flights to Lake Mead and Grand Canyon. Contains flight school and skydiving club.

Civil Air Patrol USAF Auxiliary
647-2256
Search and Rescue Air Operations Center
Las Vegas Airlines: 647-3056
Flight training, charter, tours, sales
Don Alejandro's Texan Grill: 261-3844
Offers a view of planes taking off and landing, 7 am - 8 pm.
Aerleon: 647-6100
Flight training, tours, rentals, motor glider rides.

AIRLINES

In 1997, 30 million passengers passed through McCarran Airport.

Airline abbreviations:

LW: Air Nevada
AS: Alaska Airlines
AA: American
TZ: American Trans Air
HP: America West
DE: Condor
CO: Continental
DL: Delta
HA: Hawaiian Airlines
YX: Midwest Express
6G: Las Vegas Airlines
NW: Northwest
QQ: Reno Air
YR: Scenic Airlines
WN: Southwest Airlines
SY: Sun Country
TW: TWA
UA: United
US: US Air

McCARRAN INTERNATIONAL AIRPORT

ATA/American Transair
5757 Wayne Newton Blvd.
Las Vegas, NV 89119
1-800-225-2995
John Tague, Pres.
Serves 22 cities.
Hub: Chicago, Indianapolis
In 1997, there were 1,087,715 passengers.

Air Canada
1-800-776-3000
Cargo - 1-800-722-6232
Lamar Durrett, CEO
One flight daily on Thursday & Sunday to Toronto. Began service Nov. 1995.
Hub: Montreal
In 1997, there were 39,675 passengers.

Alaska Airlines
1-800-426-0333
Cargo - 261-5482
John Kelly, CEO/Pres.
Offers 5 direct flights from Las Vegas to Seattle daily. Operates routes from the Arctic to Mexico.
Hub: Seattle
In 1997, there were 606,430 passengers

America West Airlines
1-800-235-9292
Cargo -798-0644
Richard Goodmanson, Pres/CEO
William A. Franke, Chairman
Operates from B Gates.
Serves 75 cities; Operates over 80 flights daily to/from McCarran. America West also flies British Airways - 1-800-247-9297. City ticket offices located at the Riviera, MGM and New Frontier. Started service to Las Vegas Oct. 1983.
Hubs: Las Vegas, NV; Phoenix; AZ; Columbus, Ohio
In 1997, there were 5,700,041 passengers

American Airlines
1-800-433-7300
Reservations 1-800-433-7300
Automated information 1-800-223-5436
Cargo - 1-800-227-4622
Robert Crandall, CEO
Don Carty, Pres.
Mike Lincoln, Gen. Mgr.
Operates from C gates, reached by monorail. No city ticket office in Las Vegas.
Serves over 356 cities in the U.S., Canada, Mexico, Latin America, the Caribbean, Europe and Asia.
Operates approximately 100 flights daily to/from McCarran.
Hubs: Dallas/Ft. Worth, Chicago, Miami and JFK
In 1997, there were 1,268,697 passengers.

Canadian Airlines International
1-800-426-7000
Cargo - 1-800-667-7000
Kevin Jenkins, Pres.
Direct flight to Vancouver, then change flights for Calgary, Edmonton and Winnipeg. Flights to Toronto via Chicago. Service began Nov. 1995.
Hubs: Vancouver, Toronto
In 1997, there were 118,238 charter passengers.

Photo: Phototechnik International

Condor Airlines
1-800-524-6975
Cargo 261-5060
Dr. Franz Schoiber, Pres.
Operates from International Terminal. Serves 91 cities in Mexico, the Caribbean, United States, Europe, Africa & Asia.
Hub: Cologne and Frankfurt
In 1997, there were 28,559 passengers.

Continental Airlines
383-8291   1-800-525-0280
Cargo - 261-5499
Gordon Bethune, Pres./CEO
Joe Barker, Gen. Mgr.
261-5577
Operates from A & B Gates.
Serves 350 foreign and U.S. destinations. Operates 12 flights daily to/from McCarran.
Hubs: Houston, Cleveland and Newark
In 1997, there were 1,061,421 passengers.

Delta Airlines
1-800-221-1212
Cargo - 1-800-352-2746
Leo Mullin, Pres./CEO
Mike Barfield, Mgr.
Station Manager: 261-5359
City ticket office located at New Frontier Hotel - 1-800--221-1212.
Operates from A Gates. In June 1998 moves to the new D concourse.
Serves cities in the U.S., Canada, Mexico, Europe and the Orient. Delta, Delta Express, Delta Shuttle, the Delta connection carriers and Delta's worldwide partners operates 4,902 flights each day to 323 cities in 45 countries. Operates 24 flights daily to/from McCarran Crown Room Club location.
Hubs: Atlanta, Dallas/Ft. Worth, Salt Lake City, Orlando and Cincinnati
In 1997, there were 2,600,582 passengers. Western Airlines, which merged into Delta in 1987, started service to Las Vegas in 1926. Delta started service to McCarran in 1961. Skywest Airlines, which is Delta's commuter airline, no longer operates out of Las Vegas.

Hawaiian Airlines
261-3530   1-800-367-5320
5757 Wayne Newton Blvd.
Las Vegas, NV 89119
Paul Casey, Pres./Ceo

Hawaiian Airlines flies one scheduled and one charter direct from Las Vegas to Honolulu once a day. From Honolulu to Las Vegas one scherduled flight daily and one charter flight daily except Wed.
Hub: Honolulu
In 1997, there were 166,982 scheduled passengers and 209,485 charter passengers.

Midwest Express
1-800-452-2022
Timothy E. Hosksema, Pres./CEO
Operates one direct flight daily from Las Vegas to Milwaukee.
Hub: Milwaukee, Kansas City and Omaha
In 1997, there were 37,750 passengers.

Northwest Airlines
1-800-225-2525
Cargo - 261-5788
John Dasburg, Pres.
Brian McMahon, Mgr.
Station Manager: 261-5401
Operates from A Gates.
Serves over 220 cities in 20 countries on 3 continents.
Operates 20 flights daily to/from McCarran
Hubs: Detroit, Memphis and Minneapolis/St. Paul.
In 1997, there 1,088,082 passengers.

Reno Air
1-800-736-6247
Joseph O'Gorman, CEO
Serves Reno, Tucson, San Jose, Seattle, Portland, Colorado Springs, San Diego, Los Angeles, Santa Ana, Atlanta, Oklahoma City, Chicago, Anchorage, Vancouver, BC. Began service to Las Vegas in July 1992.
Hub: Reno, San Jose and Las Vegas
In 1997, there were 1,194,828 passengers.

Southwest Airlines
1-800-435-9792
Cargo - 261-3395
Baggage - 261-3301
Station Manager: 261-5910
Herb Kelleher, Pres.
Frank Stockton, Mgr.
Operates from C Gates.
Serves 45 cities in West, Midwest and South.
Leading airline serving McCarran with 140 daily nonstop departures.

Hub: Dallas' Love Field
In 1997, there were 8,224,314 scheduled passengers and 68,663 charter passengers.

TWA Airlines
1-800-221-2000
Cargo - 261-5335
Gerald Gitner, CEO
City ticket office located at New Frontier Hotel.
Operates from C Gates.
Serves more than 70 cities.
Operates flights across the U.S. the Caribbean, Europe and the Middle East.
Operates 5 flights daily to/from McCarran.
Hubs: JFK International, New York and Lambert International, St. Louis
In 1997, there were 576,343 passengers.

US Airways
1-800-428-4322
Cargo - 261-5757
Station Manager: 261-5344
Stephen W. Wolf, Pres./CEO
Bob Talbot, Mgr.
Operates from A Gates.
Serves 231 cities in the U.S., Canada, the Bahamas, Puerto Rico, Bermuda, London Frankfurt, Rome and Madrid.
Operates 10 flights daily to/from McCarran.
Hubs: Charlotte, Pittsburgh, Philadelphia and Baltimore
In 1997, there were 526,976 passengers.

United Airlines
1-800-241-6522
Shuttle by United: 1-800-SHUTTLE
Cargo - 261-5253   1-800-631-1500
Station Manager: 261-5999
Gerald Greenwald, Chairman
Victor Cornejo, Mgr.
City ticket office located at New Frontier Hotel.
Operates from C Gates.
Serves over 300 cities in the U.S., the Pacific and Europe.
Operates 39 flights daily to/from McCarran. Started serving Las Vegas in 1947.
Hubs: Chicago, San Francisco, Los Angeles, Denver, Chicago and Dulles Airport
In 1997, there were 3,159,373 passengers.

McCARRAN AIRPORT GATE MAP

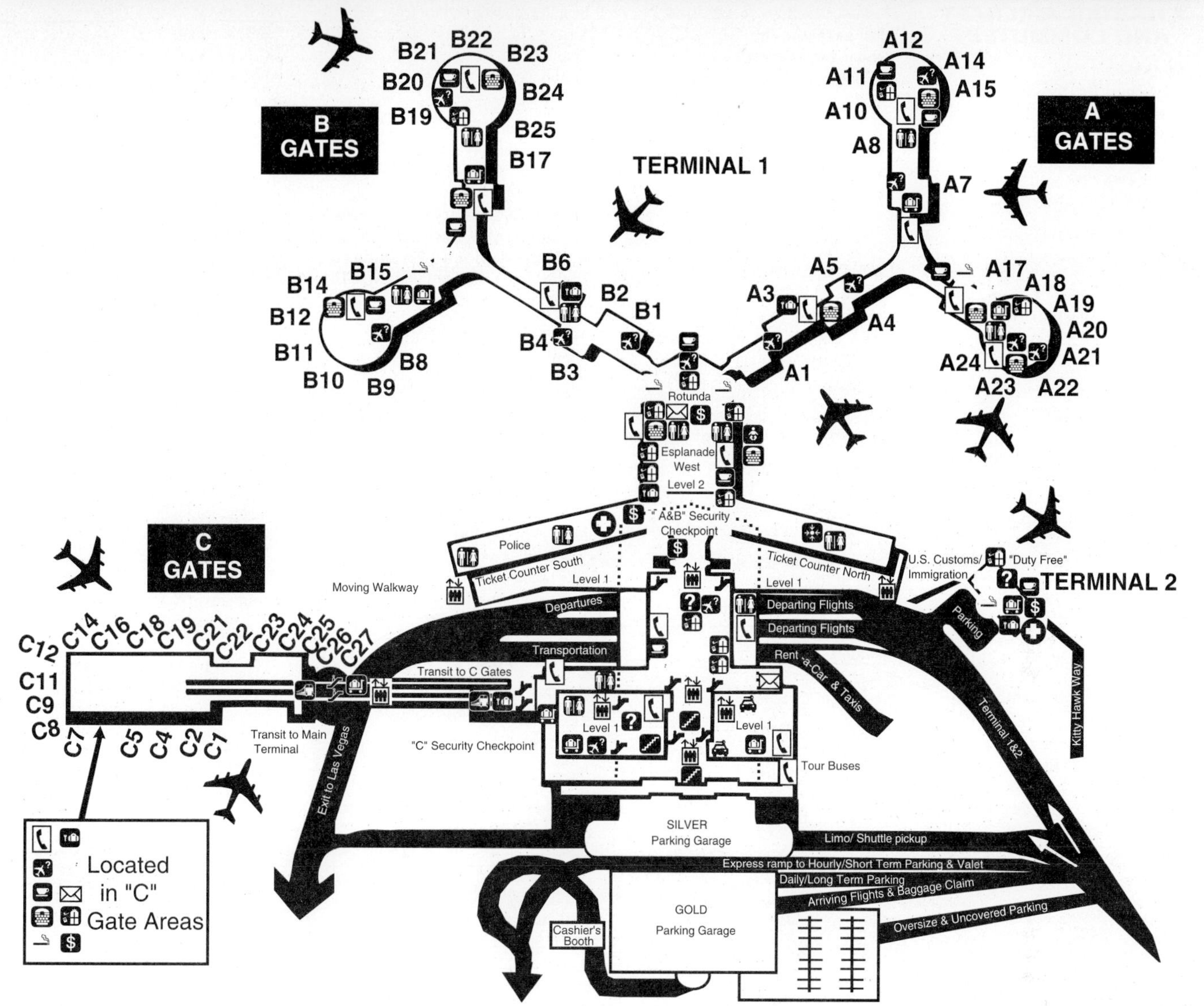

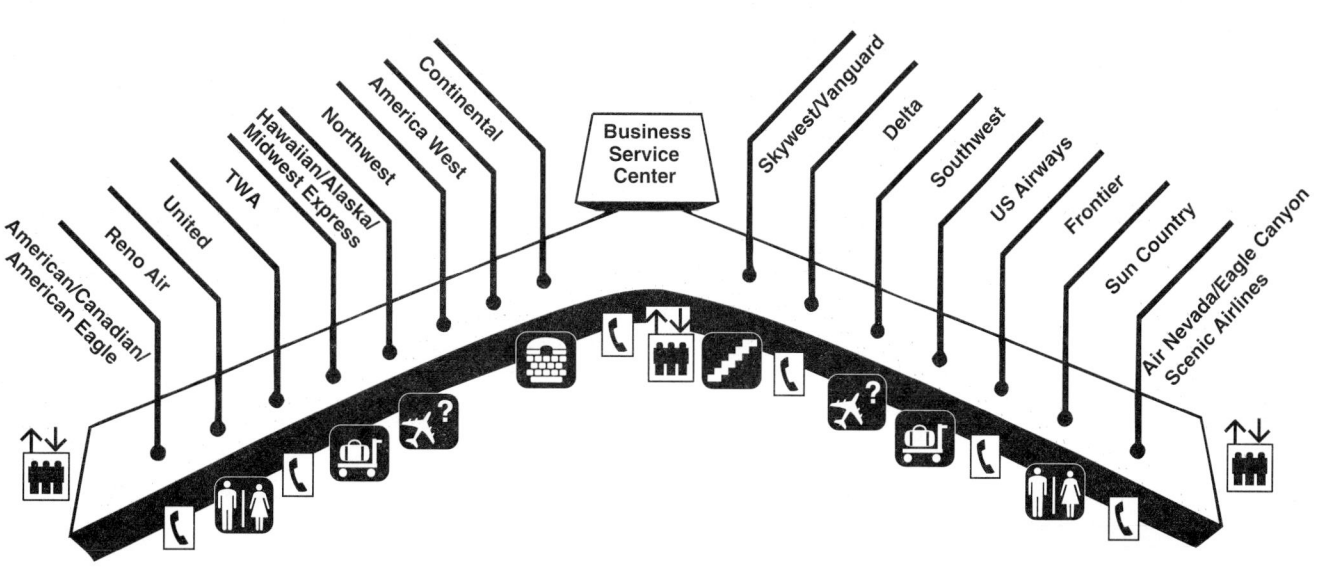

TERMINAL 1

B GATES
B21 B22 B23
B20 B24
B19 B25
B17

A GATES
A12 A14
A11 A15
A10
A8
A7

B GATES
B14 B15 B6
B12 B2
B11 B1
B10 B9 B8 B4 B3

A5 A3 A4 A1
A17 A18 A19 A20 A21 A22 A23 A24

Rotunda
Esplanade West Level 2

Police
A&B Security Checkpoint
Ticket Counter South Level 1
Ticket Counter North Level 1
U.S. Customs/ Immigration
"Duty Free"
TERMINAL 2

C GATES
C12 C14 C16 C18 C19 C21 C22 C23 C24 C25 C26 C27
C11
C9
C8 C7 C5 C4 C2 C1

Moving Walkway
Departures
Transportation
Transit to C Gates
Transit to Main Terminal
"C" Security Checkpoint
Departing Flights
Departing Flights
Rent-a-Car & Taxis
Level 1
Level 1
Tour Buses
Parking
Terminal 1&2
Kitty Hawk Way

Exit to Las Vegas

Located in "C" Gate Areas

SILVER Parking Garage
GOLD Parking Garage
Cashier's Booth

Limo/ Shuttle pickup
Express ramp to Hourly/Short Term Parking & Valet
Daily/Long Term Parking
Arriving Flights & Baggage Claim
Oversize & Uncovered Parking

AIRPORT MAIN TICKET COUNTER

American/Canadian/ American Eagle — Reno Air — United — TWA — Hawaiian/Alaska/ Midwest Express — Northwest — America West — Continental — **Business Service Center** — Skywest/Vanguard — Delta — Southwest — US Airways — Frontier — Sun Country — Air Nevada/Eagle Canyon Scenic Airlines

McCARRAN INTERNATIONAL AIRPORT

CHARTER AIRCRAFT AND COMMUTERS

Aerleon
2634 Airport Dr., Ste. 101
N. Las Vegas, NV 89030
647-6100   1-800-647-6711
fax: 647-6104
Don Flaherty, Pres.
Flight training, charter, tours.

American Eagle
1-800-433-7300
(commuter)
Dave Kennedy, Pres.
Flights to Los Angeles
(see American Airlines)

American Trans Air
1-800-225-2995
Operations - 261-3615
John Tague, Pres.
Indianapolis based charter airline with limited scheduled commercial service. American Trans Air is the largest charter airline based in the United States.

CFI Inc.
135 E. Reno Ave.
Las Vegas, NV 89119
736-0077
Ira Eichenfield, Pres.
Beechcraft Star Ships.

Charter Airlines · Jimmy Walker Jets
145 E. Reno Ave., Ste. E5
Las Vegas, NV 89119
878-2264
Jim Walker, Pres.
9 passenger Lear Jets.

Desert Southwest Airlines
1400 Executive Dr.
Henderson, NV 89012
263-9520
Chuck Herrmann, Dir. of Operations
Bob Perry, Pres.
Aircraft rentals, flight training, air taxis and charters.
Henderson Sky Harbor.

Eagle Canyon Airlines
275 E. Tropicana Ave., Ste. 220
Las Vegas, NV 89109
736-3333 1-800-446-4584
Grant Murray, Pres.
Grand Canyon and Monument Valley. Six flights daily at 8 am, 9 am, 10 am and 11 am. Air tours only 7 am and 3 pm.

Lake Mead Air
1301 Airport Rd.
Boulder City, NV 89005
293-1848
Mark Leseberg, Pres.
Air Taxi operates from Boulder City Airport.

Las Vegas Airlines
2732 Perimeter Rd.
N. Las Vegas, NV 89030
735-8007 1-800-634-6851
Donald Donohue, Pres.
9 seat Pipers.
Grand Canyon sightseeing.

Pacific Air Aviation
6900 Westcliff Dr.
Las Vegas, NV 89128
256-4320
Art Turner, Dir. of Operations

Lear Jet charter service from McCarran Airport to Canada, Mexico, Central America, South America, Caribbean, Hawaii and domestic.

Scenic Airlines
2705 Airport Dr.
N. Las Vegas, NV 89030
739-1900 1-800-634-6801
David Young, Pres.
Operates Grand Canyon tours between Las Vegas and the Canyon's South Rim airport with a fleet of nineteen 19-passenger DeHavilland Twin Otter turboprop planes.

Sun Country Airlines
1-800-359-5786
Operations - 261-3451
John Skiba, Pres.
Serves 17 cities in the U.S. and the Caribbean only in the winter. Based in Minneapolis.

Sundance Helicopter Inc.
265 E. Tropicana Ave., Ste. 130
Las Vegas, NV 89119
736-0606
Jim Granquist, Pres.
Custom charter and flight training and tour division. 6 aircraft.

CHARTER OPERATIONS

Aeroejecutivo:
Patricia Hovey, Station Mgr. - 261-3214
Aero Mexico:
*AMR Services
Air Canada:
*AMR Services
Albert Hories, Station Mgr.

Air TranAT:
*AMR Services
Ed Strickler, Station Mgr.
Alaska Airlines:
Ray Brown 261-4026
American Trans Air:
Elaine Zaniel, Station Mgr. - 261-3615
AV Atlantic:
*AMR Services
Canada 3000:
*AMR Services
Alida Offenbach,Station Mgr.- 256-0309
Canadian Airlines Int'l:
Larry Hamilton, Station Mgr. - 261-5010
Eagle Airways:
*AMR Services
Grand Airways:
Baldvin Berndsen, Station Mgr. - 261-5887
Hawaiian Airlines:
**Signature Flight Support
Miami Air Int'l:
**Signature Flight Support
Northamerica:
**Signature Flight Support
Royal Airlines:
**Signature Flight Support
Sun Country:
*AMR Services
Jack Wilson, General Mgr. of AMR Services - 261-5801
**Signature Flight Support:
Tom Kandt, Mgr. - 261-3583
(Station Managers listed with a telephone number but no address have an office in the Charter/International Terminal (CIT). AMR Services and Signature Flight Support also have offices in the CIT.)

TAXI SERVICE

TAXIS

Taxi Cab Authority
1785 E. Sahara Ave.
Las Vegas, NV 89104
486-6532
Bob Anselmo, Adm.
Controls and regulates the industry. There are 13 cab companies operating 1,181 cabs in the Las Vegas area and 2 companies serving Laughlin. Rates below are set by the meter and are the same with any area company.
Taxi rate: $2.20
Plus each 1/5 mile: $ .30
Waiting time per minute: $ .35
Each trip from McCarran Airport an additional: $1.20

Example of fares:
Downtown to airport: $13 - $17
Airport to mid-Strip: $10 - $11
Mid-Strip to Downtown: $12
Downtown to Convention Center:
                                        $10 - $12
Taxis are available 24 hours a day in front of each major hotel

ABC Union Cab Co.
736-8444

Ace Cab Co.
736-8383

Vegas Western Cab Co.
736-6121

North Las Vegas Cab Co.
5010 S. Valley View Blvd.
Las Vegas, NV 89118
643-1041
George Rodriguez, Gen. Mgr.

Desert Cab Co.
376-2688

Lucky Las Vegas Cab Co.
90 W. Oakey Blvd.
Las Vegas, NV 89102
376-2688
George Balaban, Gen. Mgr.

Nellis Cab Co.
3215 Cinder Ln.
Las Vegas, NV 89103
252-0201
Michelle Langille, Gen. Mgr.

Whittlesea Cab Co.
384-6111

Henderson Cab Co.
2030 Industrial Rd.
Las Vegas, NV 89102
384-2322
Cheryl Knapp, Gen. Mgr.

Yellow Cab Co.
873-2227

Checker Cab Co.
873-2227

Star Cab Co.
3950 W. Tompkins Ave.
Las Vegas, NV 89103
873-2227
Jack Owens, Gen. Mgr.

Fleet Delivery
3860 W. Tompkins Ave.
Las Vegas, NV 89103
876-9666
Al Foos, Gen. Mgr.
Milton Schwartz, Owner

Western Cab Co.
801 S. Main St.
Las Vegas, NV 89101
736-8000
Herb Tobman, Gen. Mgr.

CREDIT CARDS:
Yellow, Checker and Star Cabs are the only companies that currently accept credit cards. They only take American Express.

HANDICAPPED EQUIPPED:
Companies that have vans with wheel chair lifts are ABC Union, Ace and Western.

CITIZENS AREA TRANSIT - CAT BUS SERVICE

Regional Transportation Commission
301 E. Clark Ave., Ste. 300
Las Vegas, NV 89101
455-4481
Kurt Weinrich, Dir.
Information on routes and fares: 228-7433
TDD: 455-5997
Paratransit Services: 228-7433

Citizens Area Transit
Service of Regional Transportation Commission of Clark County, NV
Operated by ATC/Vancom
3210 Citizen Ave.
N. Las Vegas, NV 89030
636-0623
David A. Boggs, Gen. Mgr.
Manages local city bus system. The bus system serves 11 million mi. annually. There are 234 buses. It serves the greater Las Vegas Valley, Laughlin and Mesquite.

The Downtown Transportation Center is the starting and stopping point and transfer point for some buses. CAT® coin tokens and passes are available at 80 locations. You can purchase monthly passes and tokens at the information booth. There is also a McDonald's restaurant and newsstand.

The Regional Transportation Commission selected a new government subsidized bus system contractor, ATC/Vancom Inc. to operate and maintain a countywide bus system. The Citizens Area Transit (CAT®) began operation Dec. 5, 1992. The service has 41 routes and 225 buses operating 20 hours per day, 5:30 am - 1:30 am in residential routes and 24 hours a day along the Strip (7 routes). For specific routes and times contact the customer service at 228-7433. Buses run every 7 minutes, depending on traffic, in resort quarters; in high traffic and major arterials every 30 minutes; in residential areas every 60 minutes. Serves 3.7 million riders every month. Buses operate weekdays, weekends and holidays.

As of Jan. 1997, 36 routes are 20 hours, 6 routes 24 hours, and 2 routes *(1 government buildings and crosstown connector)* are 16 hours.

Fares:
Adult Cash Fare *(18 - 62 years)*
.... $ 1.00
Route #301 & #302 *(Strip Route)*
....$1.50
Monthly Pass...........................$20.00
CAT® Coins - 40 tokens..........$15.00
Youth *(5 - 17 years)*, Seniors *(65 and up)* & Persons with disabilities
....$.50
Monthly Pass..........................$10.00
Children *(under 5)*..........Free
Children under 5 years of age are free when accompanied by an adult paying passenger.

Transfers.....................................Free
Ask driver for a transfer when you pay your fare. Transfers are good for one hour past time of arrival.
Certified personal care attendants when traveling with customers with disabilities...............................Free
CAT® buses are accessible to customers in wheelchairs, or for those persons who need help reaching the first step.
Monthly passes can be purchased at the Downtown Transportation Center and 70 other outlets in Las Vegas. Call - CAT®-RIDE (228-7433)
Trolley transfer..........................Free
Available to persons who have a valid discount commuter card, i.e. Senior Citizens, Handicapped.
Bus routes are shown on the following pages. The route number is listed with the route name and a map route.

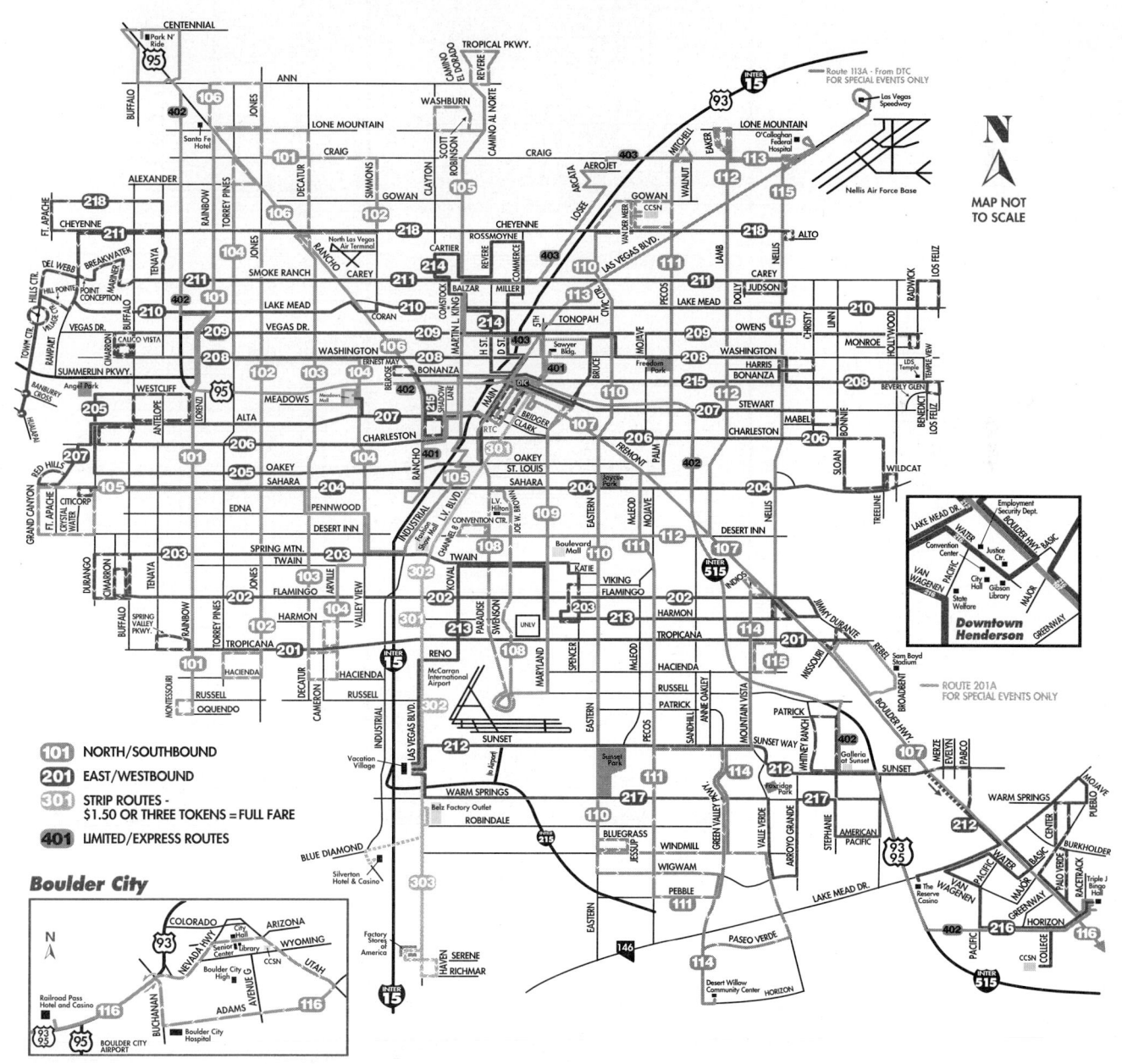

101 NORTH/SOUTHBOUND
201 EAST/WESTBOUND
301 STRIP ROUTES -
$1.50 OR THREE TOKENS = FULL FARE
401 LIMITED/EXPRESS ROUTES

Boulder City

C A T ROUTES AND SCHEDULES

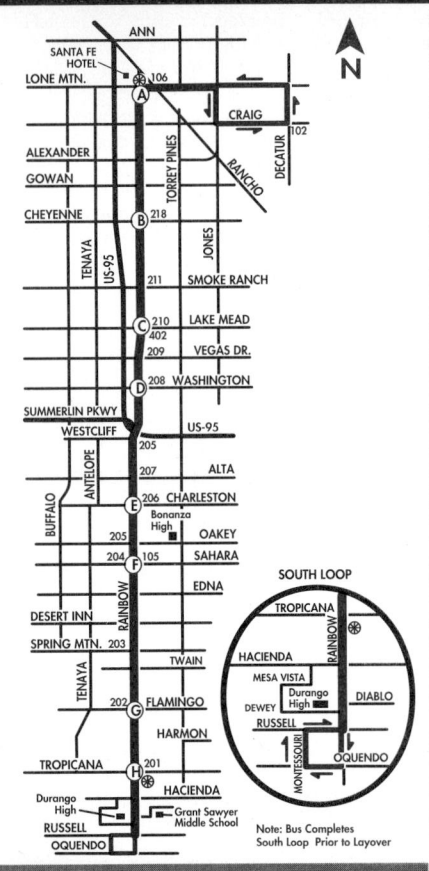

101 - Rainbow

Note: Bus Completes South Loop Prior to Layover

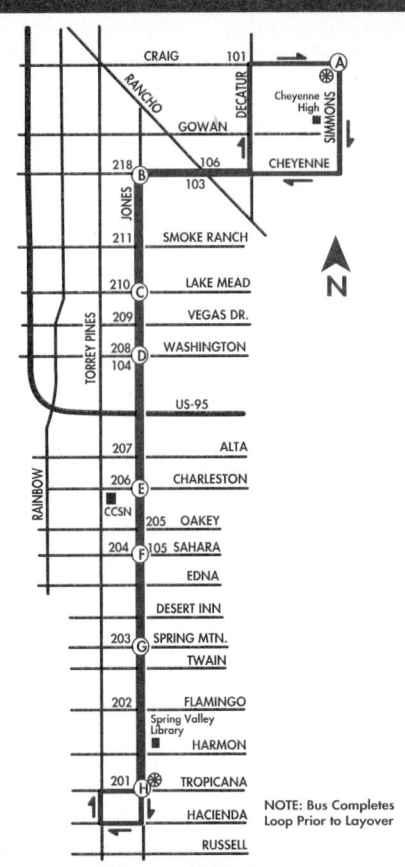

102 - Jones

NOTE: Bus Completes Loop Prior to Layover

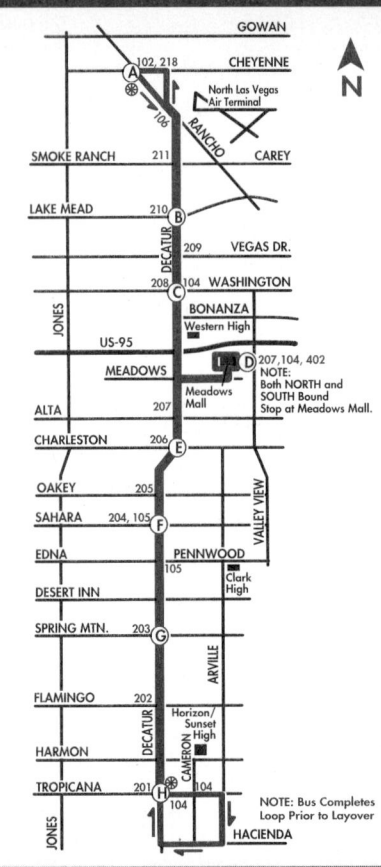

103 - Decatur

NOTE: Bus Completes Loop Prior to Layover

NOTE: 207,104, 402 Both NORTH and SOUTH Bound Stop at Meadows Mall.

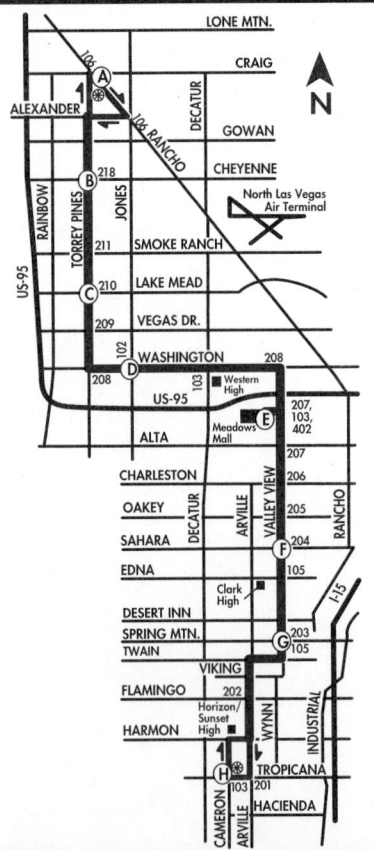

104 - Valley View/Torrey Pines

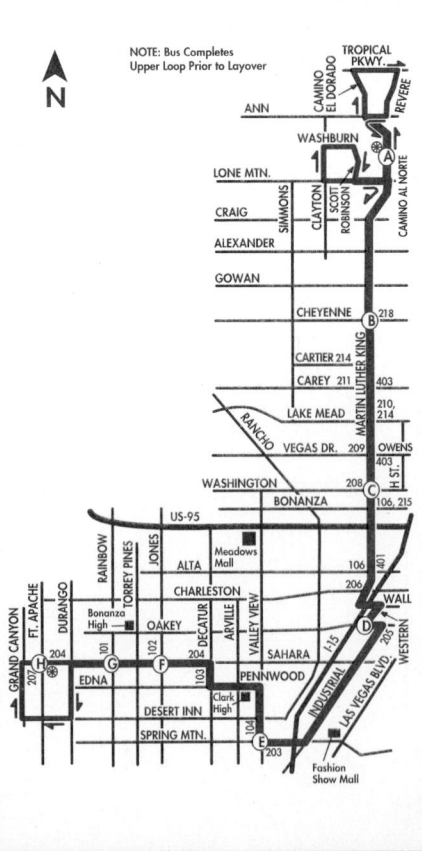

NOTE: Bus Completes Upper Loop Prior to Layover

105 - Martin L. King/W. Sahara

106 - Rancho

Experience Las Vegas

C A T ROUTES AND SCHEDULES

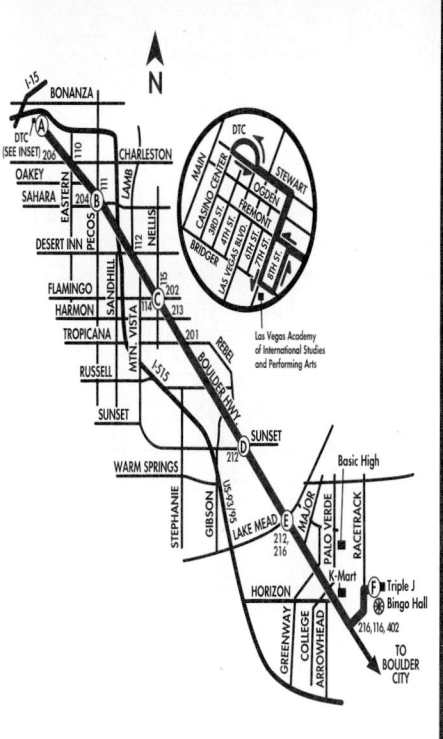

107 - Boulder Highway

108 - Paradise/Swenson

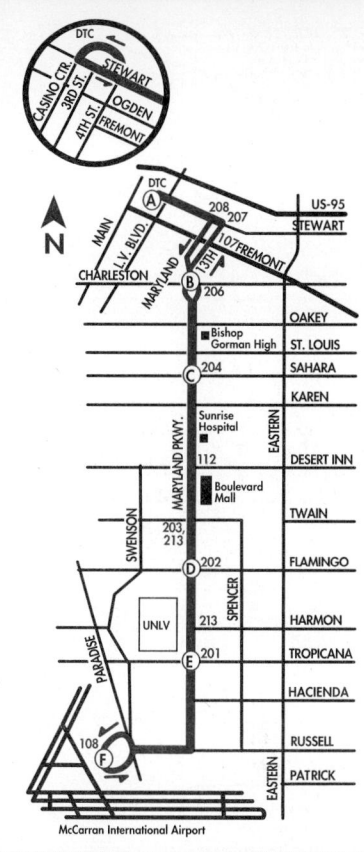

109 - Maryland Pkwy.

110 - Eastern Avenue

111 - Green Valley/Pecos

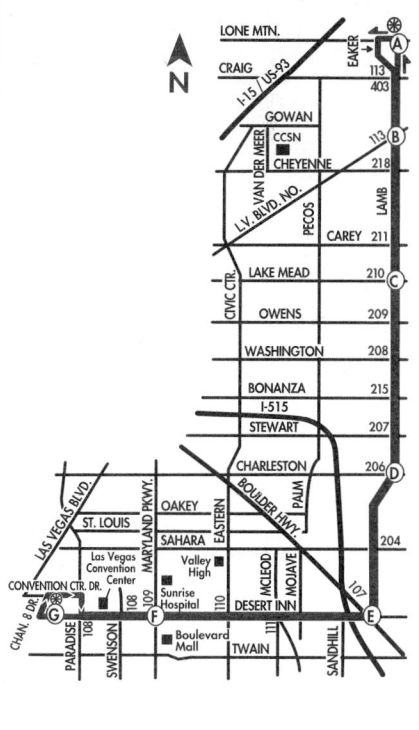

112 - Desert Inn/Lamb

C A T ROUTES AND SCHEDULES

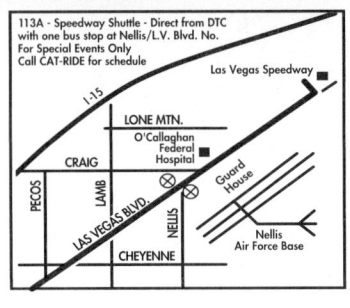

113A - Speedway Shuttle - Direct from DTC with one bus stop at Nellis/LV. Blvd. No. For Special Events Only Call CAT-RIDE for schedule

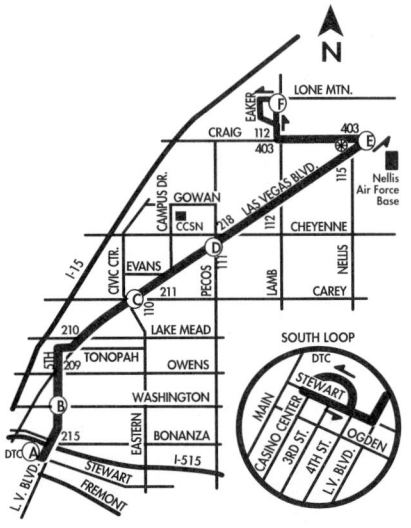

113 - Las Vegas Blvd. N.

114 - Green Valley/Mtn. Vista

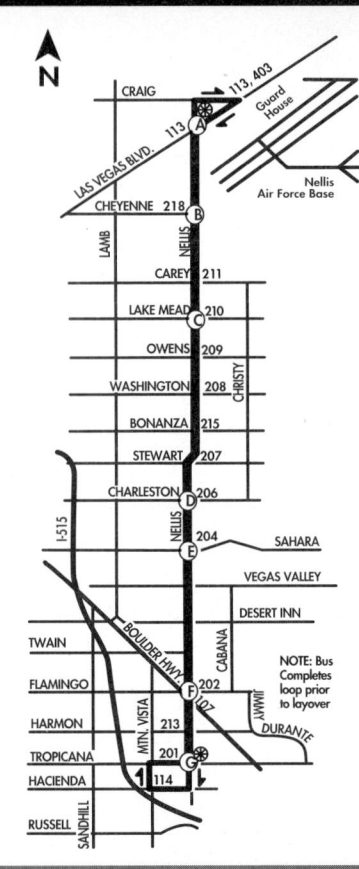

115 - Nellis

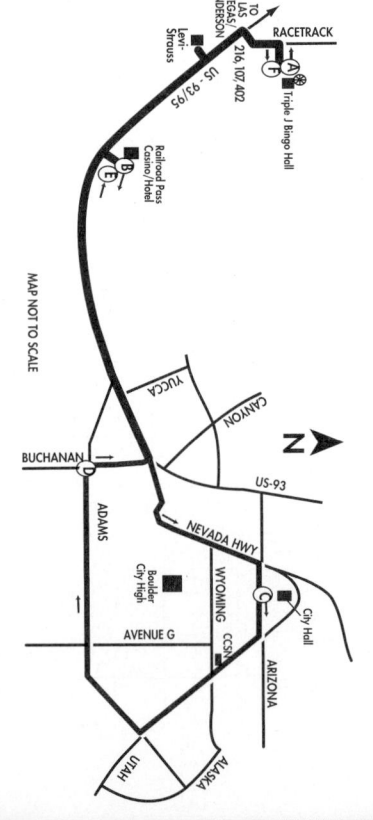

116 - Boulder City

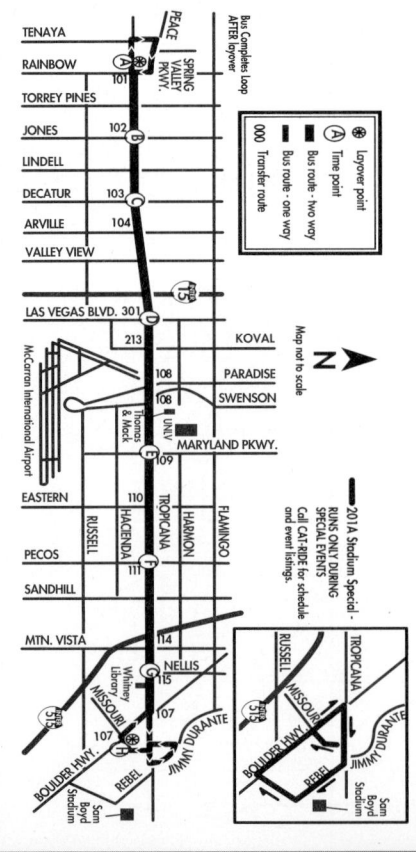

201 - Tropicana

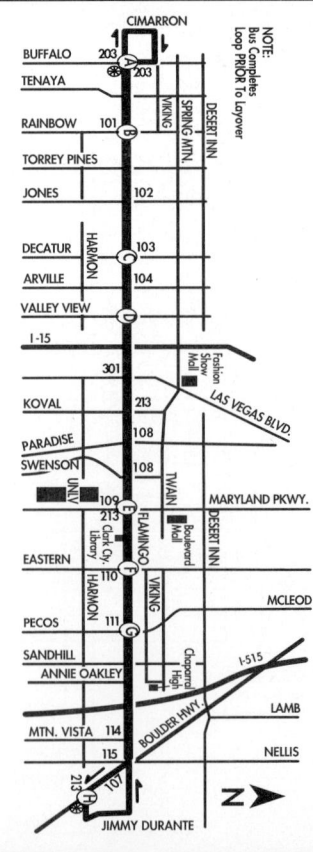

202 - Flamingo

Experience Las Vegas

Visit our website at www.experiencelasvegas.com

C A T ROUTES AND SCHEDULES

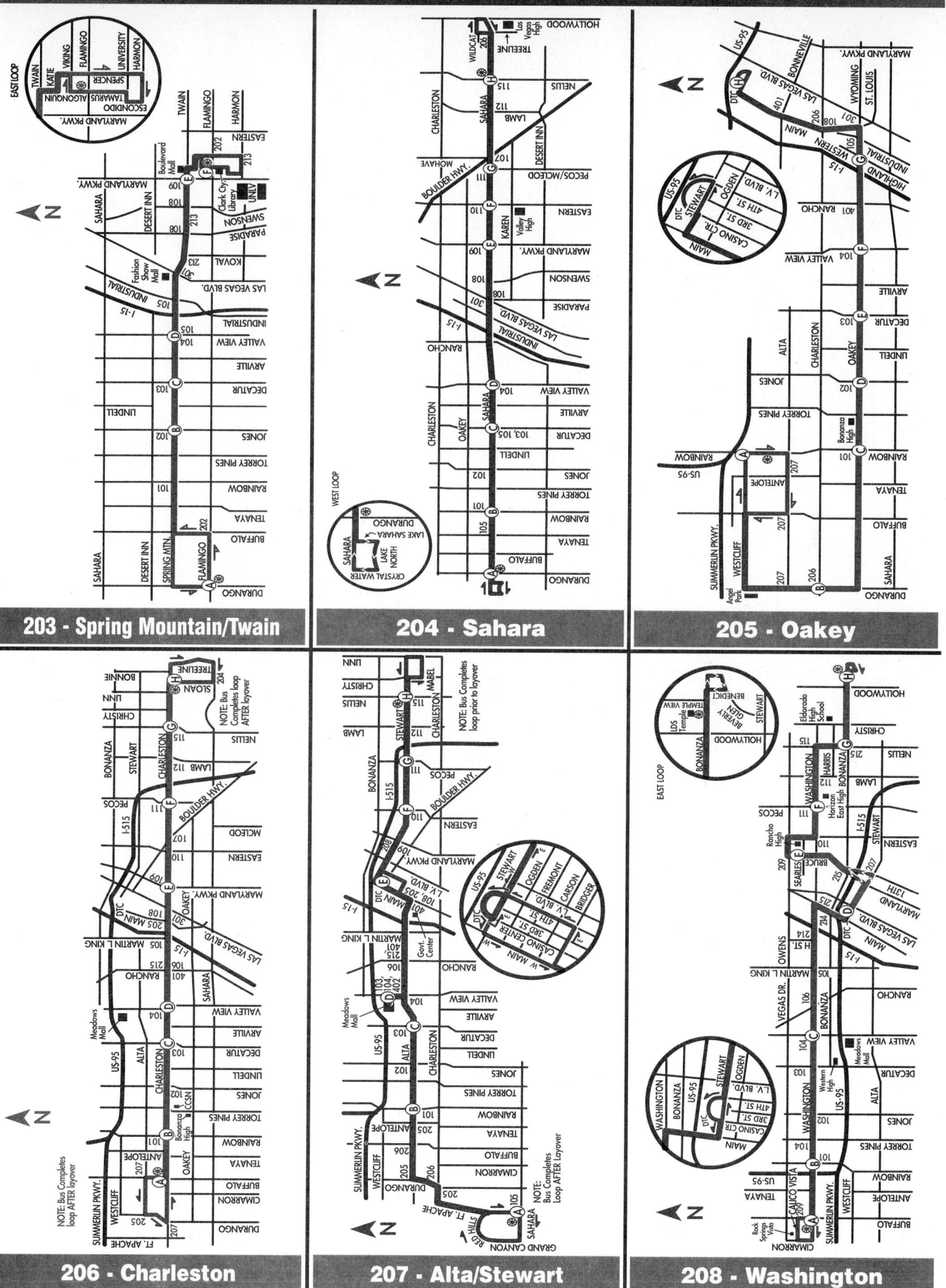

203 - Spring Mountain/Twain

204 - Sahara

205 - Oakey

206 - Charleston

207 - Alta/Stewart

208 - Washington

C A T ROUTES AND SCHEDULES

209 - Vegas/Owens

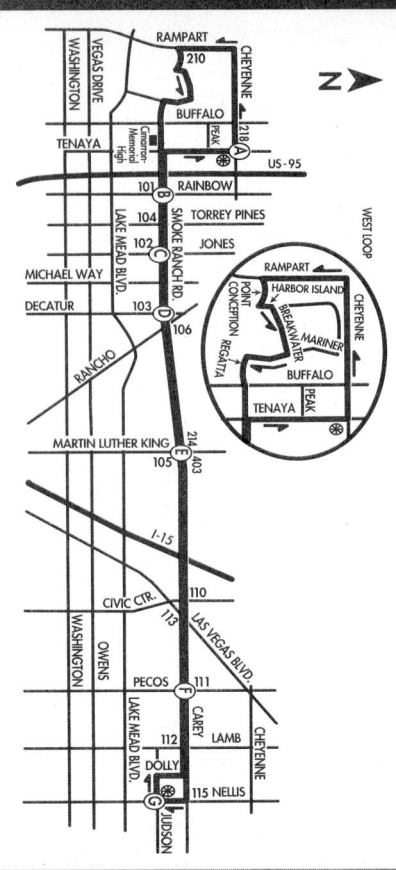

Z >

210 - Lake Mead Blvd.

211 - Smoke Ranch/Carey

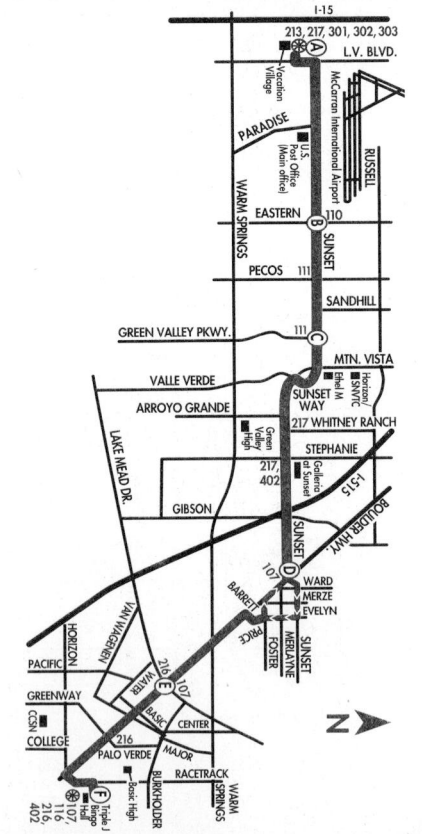

212 - Sunset/Boulder Hwy.

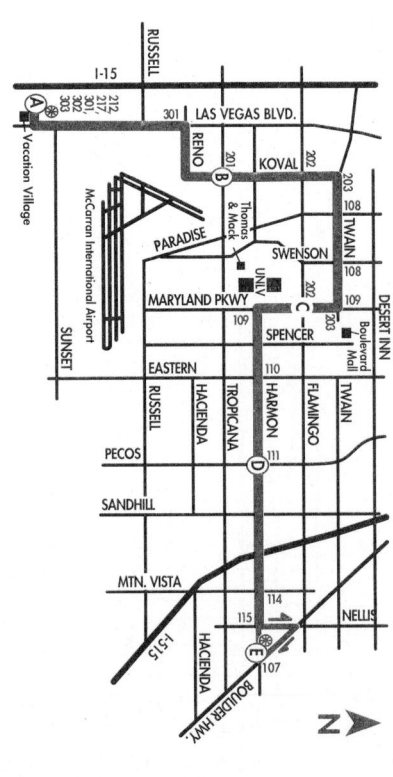

213 - Harmon/Koval

214 - H Street/D Street

C A T ROUTES AND SCHEDULES

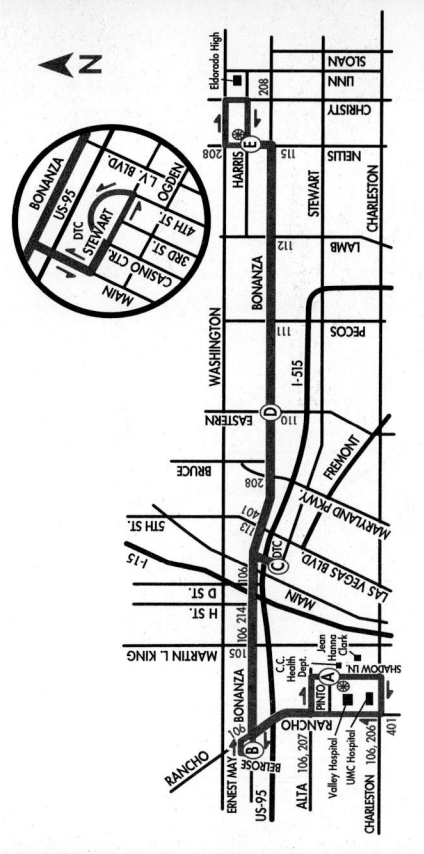

215 - Bonanza

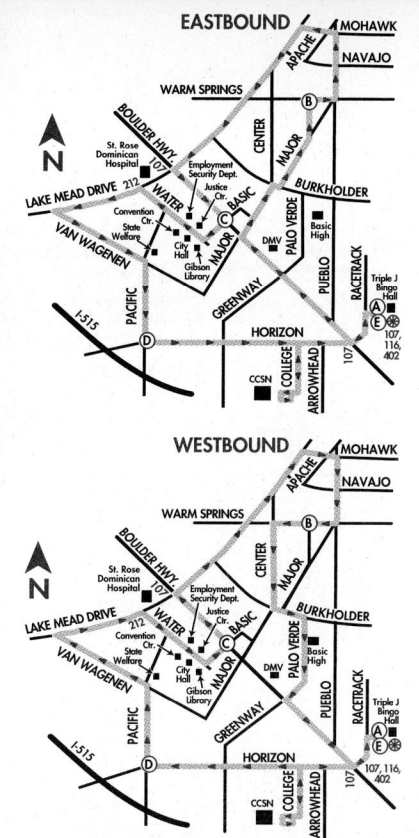

EASTBOUND

WESTBOUND

216 - Henderson

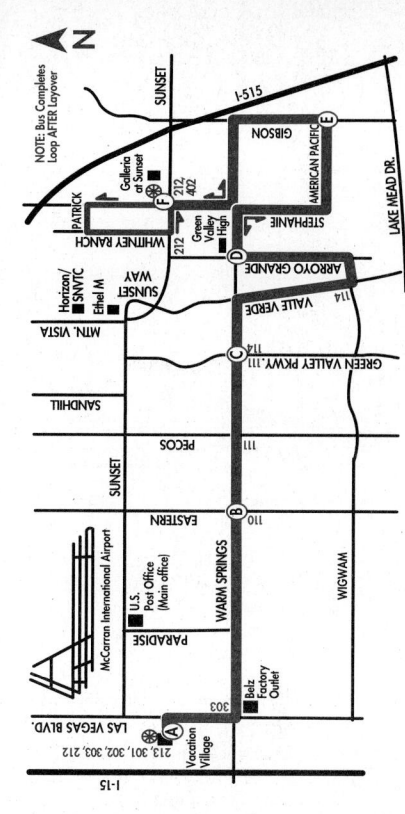

217 - Warm Springs

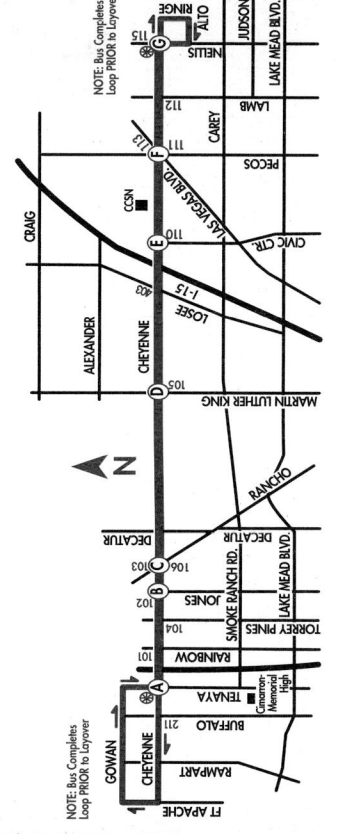
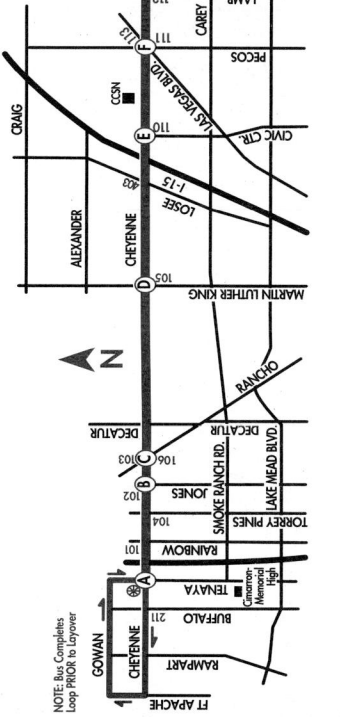

218 - Cheyenne

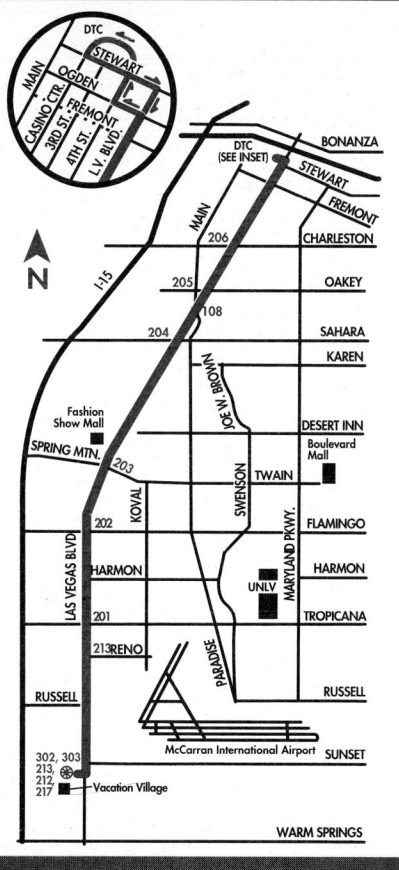

301 - Las Vegas Blvd.

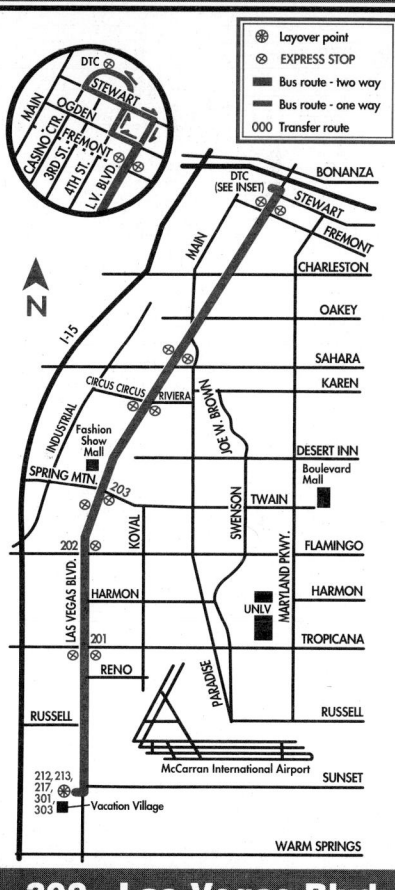

✳	Layover point
⊗	EXPRESS STOP
▬	Bus route - two way
▬	Bus route - one way
000	Transfer route

302 - Las Vegas Blvd.

TRANSPORTATION

C A T ROUTES AND SCHEDULES

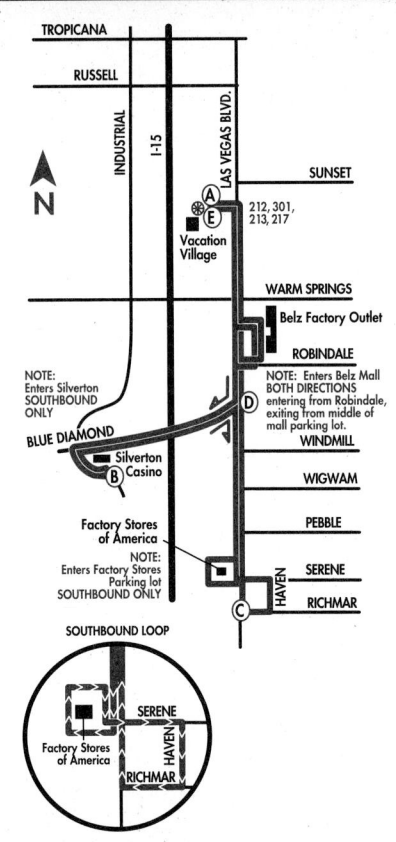

303 - Las Vegas Blvd. S.

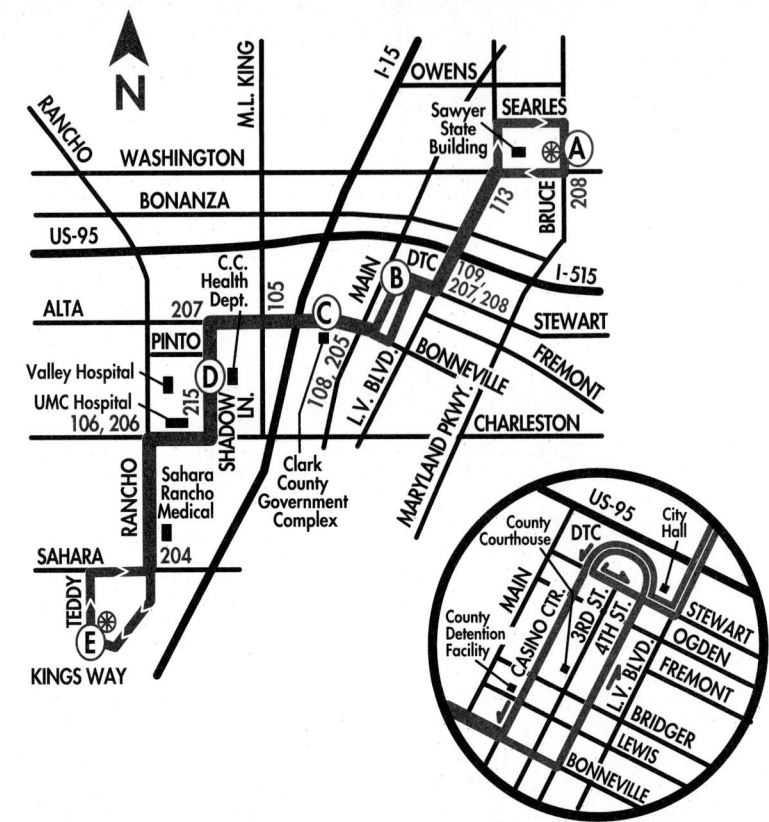

401 - Downtown Circulator

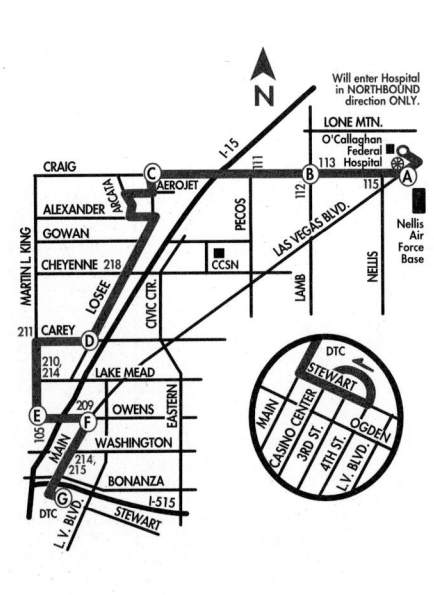

403 - Losee/Craig

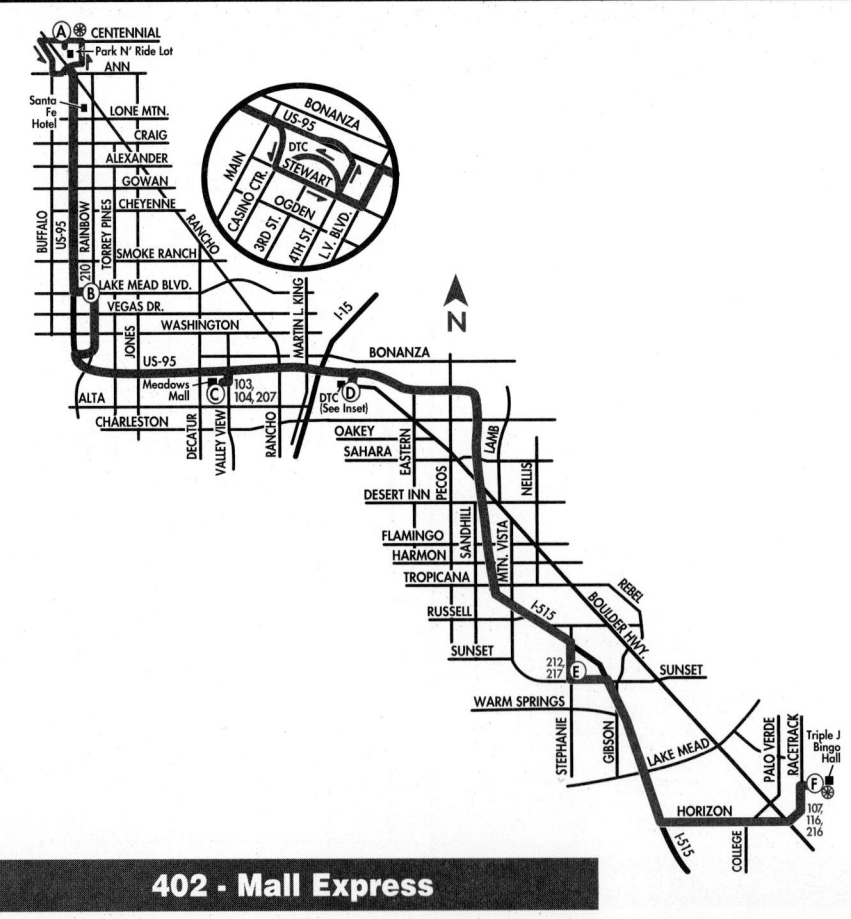

402 - Mall Express

Experience Las Vegas

TROLLEY ROUTES

TRANSPORTATION

TROLLEY

Las Vegas Strip Trolley
2030 Industrial Rd.
Las Vegas, NV 89114
382-1404
Brent Bell, Gen. Mgr.
Operates 8 trolleys on the Strip.
Strip Trolley Fare: $1.30 *(exact change)*
Schedule: 9:30 am - 2 am daily
Trolleys run approximately every 20 minutes.
Route: From the Stratosphere Tower to the Luxor including the Las Vegas Hilton with stops at the front door of each major hotel. Stratosphere Tower to 4th St. to Fremont. Fremont to Main St. then back to the Stratosphere Tower.

Downtown Trolley
Downtown Transportation Center
300 N. Casino Center Blvd.
Las Vegas, NV 89101
229-6024
Robert Hasegawa, Adm. Officer
Fare: $.50 for everyone over 5 years old, seniors and handicapped $.25. Trolley departs every 30 minutes from the South Plaza of the Downtown Transportation Center 7 am - 11:00 pm daily. Routes include downtown, Lucky Supermarket in Charleston Plaza shopping center (8 am - 9:30 pm at 20 minute intervals).

Meadows Mall Shopping Express Trolley
229-6024
Fare: $1.10 Adults; $.55 under 17 and seniors
Leaves Downtown Transportation Center 10:30 am - 5 pm Mon. through Sat.

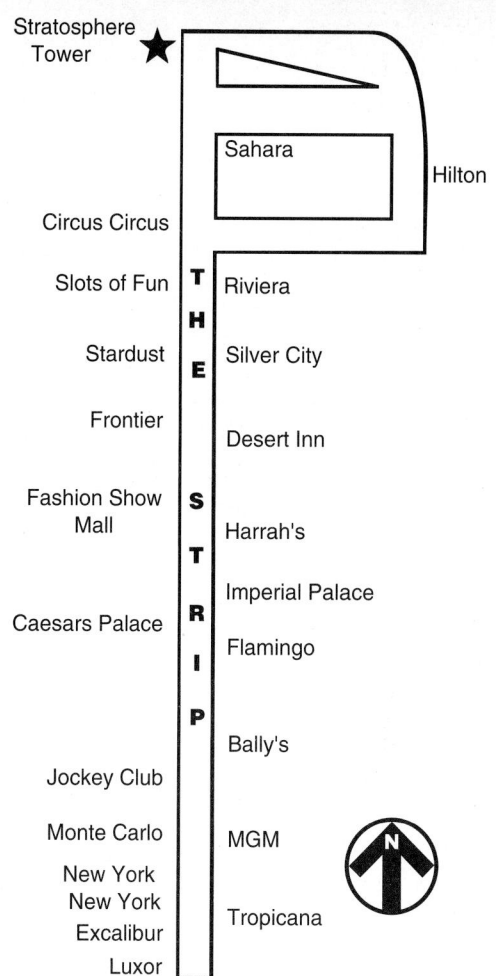

Stratosphere Tower ★

Sahara — Hilton

Circus Circus

Slots of Fun — Riviera

Stardust — Silver City

Frontier — Desert Inn

Fashion Show Mall — Harrah's

— Imperial Palace

Caesars Palace — Flamingo

— Bally's

Jockey Club

Monte Carlo — MGM

New York New York

Excalibur — Tropicana

Luxor

T H E S T R I P

THE STRIP TROLLEY STOPS

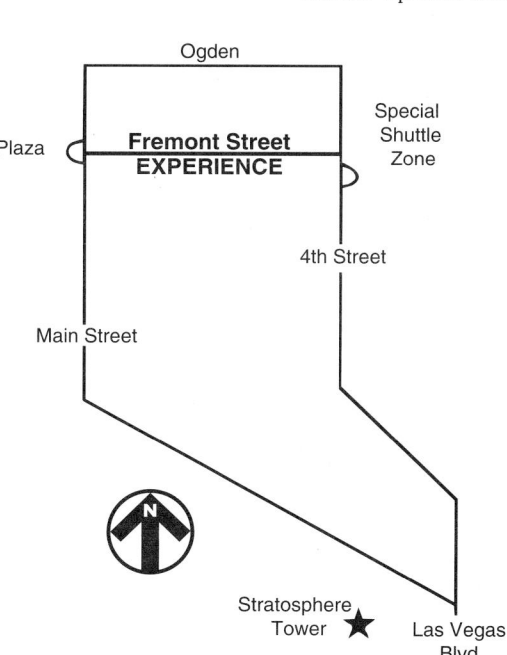

Ogden

Special Shuttle Zone

Plaza

Fremont Street EXPERIENCE

4th Street

Main Street

Stratosphere Tower ★ — Las Vegas Blvd.

DOWN TOWN TROLLEY STOPS

Photo: Phototechnik International

LIMOUSINES AND VEHICLE RENTAL

LIMOUSINES

Ambassador Limousines
3215 Cinder Ln.
Las Vegas, NV 89102
362-6200
Ray Chenoweth, Pres.
Rates: $55 per hour; 100 inch & 120
inch - $75 per hour.

Bell Transportation
1900 Industrial Rd.
Las Vegas, NV 89102
382-7060 739-7990
Jim Bell, Pres.
Rates: $27 per hour for standard chauf-
feured sedan; $33 per hour for stretch;
20 passenger minibus $38 per hr.
Bar, stereo, color TV *(Customer must
stock bar, in limo only).*
One hour minimum.

CLS of Las Vegas
4744 Paradise Rd.
Las Vegas, NV 89109
740-4545
Charlie Horky, Pres.
Rates: $52 per hour, superstretch $75
per hour. Cellular phone upon request
and personal security.

Presidential Limousine
1900 Industrial Rd.
Las Vegas, NV 89102
731-5577
Jim Bell, Pres.
Credit Cards: MC, Visa, AMX
23 Limos - 16 stretch, 6 super stretch
and 1 convertible; Lincoln and Cadillac
stretch limousines.
Chauffeur in formal tuxedo & cap.
Rates: Stretch - $45 per hour (6 ppl.);
Super Stretch - $70 per hour (8 ppl.).
Cellular phones available for $2 per
minute.
One hour minimum.

FREE HOTEL/CASINO SHUTTLES
Bally's: Monorail to MGM 9 am - 1 am
Barbary Coast: Shuttle to the Gold
Coast 10:30 am - 1 am
Boulder Station: Shuttle to and from
the Palace Station with stops at Fashion
Show Mall and the MGM on certain
shuttles.
Boyd Group Hotels: The Boyd Group of
Casinos offers a free shuttle from the
Stardust on the Strip, and from the
California and Fremont Hotels down-
town to Sam's Town on Boulder Hwy.
Fiesta: Shuttle to the Fashion Show
Mall.
Hard Rock: Shuttle to Fashion Show
Mall and the MGM 11 am - 7 pm
Mirage: Monorail to Treasure Island
New Frontier: Airport pick-up for hotel
guests.
Palace Station: Shuttle to Texas
Station, call for times
Rio: Shuttle to MGM, Fashion Show
Mall and Stardust.
Silverton: Shuttle to Fashion Show Mall.
Westward Ho: Airport pick-up.

VEHICLE RENTAL CAR RENTALS

There are many automobile rental agencies in Las Vegas with more than one
location. Rates vary but the average
price starts in the mid $20s per day for
an economy car. If you want the colli-
sion damage waiver (CDW), it averages
an extra $8 - $10.
Most agencies have free airport pick-up.
There is a 10% airport surcharge, 7%
sales tax and a 6% license tag fee added
to rental rates.
Seven agencies maintain rental desks in
the airport terminal next to the baggage
claim.
Certain requirements must be met to
rent a car. Most companies require a
major credit card and some require that
you be at least 25 years old. The agencies
that accept cash deposits require
customers to provide a round trip ticket,
a cash deposit of $100 - $250 depending
on how long you want the car, and proof
of employment.

Cut-Rate-AA Auto Rental
1613 E. Sahara Ave.
Las Vegas, NV 89104
898-1333
Richard Jacobs, Pres.
Hours: Mon. - Fri. 8 am - 5 pm, Sat. 8
am - noon
4 door American - $48 daily; $159 weekly
Used cars $8 - $12 - $0.25 per mi. extra
Accepts $150 cash w/employment
verification or MC and Visa.

Airport Rent-A-Car
4990 Paradise Rd.
Las Vegas, NV 89109
795-7380 1-800-785-8578
Hours: 6 am - 1 am
Airport Terminal: 1-800-785-8578
Barbara Kaufman, Pres.
Deluxe cars, full line of domestic and
imported; $24.99 - $89.99 daily; $129.99 -
$449.99 weekly; unlimited mileage.
Special discounts for AARP Seniors or
AAA and CAA. Preferred Customer
Program.

Alamo
6855 Bermuda Dr.
Las Vegas, NV 89119
263-8411
4263 Boulder Hwy.
Las Vegas, NV 89121
435-1449
301 Fremont St.
Las Vegas, NV 89101
388-2142
3025 Las Vegas Blvd. S.
Las Vegas, NV 89109
735-3758 1-800-327-9633
Michael Egan, Pres.
Geo - GM - $29.99 - $79 daily; $149 - $395
weekly. No mileage charge. Free pick-up
and delivery, luxury minivans and convertibles at a slightly higher rate.

Allstate
(Desk in airport terminal)
5175 Rent-A-Car Rd.
Las Vegas, NV 89119
736-6147
Open 24 hours
Union Plaza Hotel
382-2918
Nellis Air Force Base
644-5567
Riviera Hotel
794-9457
Stardust Hotel
732-6288
824 S. Decatur Blvd.
Las Vegas, NV 89107
259-3200
1835 E. Sahara Ave.
Las Vegas, NV 89104
792-9200
Nick Willden, Gen. Mgr.
Dave Willden, Pres.
Dodge, Ford, Olds $28.95 - $75.95 daily;
$145 - $350 weekly; 4 WD - $79.95. 150
free mi. daily; 1,050 free mi. weekly.

Avis
(Desk in airport terminal)
5164 Rent-A-Car Rd.
Las Vegas, NV 89119
261-5595 1-800-331-1212
East Las Vegas
641-7220

West Las Vegas
258-3400
Summerlin/Sun City
242-5111
Bally's Grand Hotel
736-1935
Caesars Palace
731-7790
Las Vegas Hilton Hotel
734-8011
C. O. Saunders, Dist. Mgr.
Craig Hoenschell, CEO
GM cars $32 - $73 daily; $129 - $269 weekly. Cash w/qualifications. Unlimited
mileage.

Brooks
3041 Las Vegas Blvd. S.
Las Vegas, NV 89109
735-3344 1-800-634-6721
S. Wicks Stephens, Pres.
Hours: 6 am - 11:30 pm
Ford, Mercury, Lincoln Towncars, GM - call
for rates.

Budget Car & Truck Rental
4744 Paradise Rd. (Airport)
Las Vegas, NV 89109
**For local reservations and locations
call 736-1212 or 1-800-527-0770 for out
of town.**
John W. Mallo, Pres.
Chrysler, Lincoln, convertibles, vans $30 - $60
daily; $99.99 - $299.99 weekly. Convertibles,
15 passenger vans; frequent renters earn
points for free golf clubs. Credit card
required. Free mileage

Dollar
(Desk in airport terminal)
5301 Rent-A-Car Rd.
Las Vegas, NV 89119
739-8408 for reservations and information
on locations, worldwide 1-800-800-4000
Gary Paxton, Pres.
Rental booths located inside Circus Circus,
Excalibur, New York New York, Monte Carlo,
MGM, Treasure Island, Mirage, Luxor and
Golden Nugget.
Chrysler - $31.99 - $69.99 daily; $149.99 -
$299.00 weekly. Credit card required. Free
mileage.

Enterprise · Las Vegas area
Administration Office
597-1600
Call for locations.
Scott Kendrick, Gen. Mgr.
3421 Boulder Hwy.
Las Vegas, NV 89121
457-0066 1-800-325-8007
Out-of-town 1-800-736-8222
Andrew Taylor, Pres.
GM - $28.99 - $49.99 daily; $129.99 -
$479.99 weekly. Daily rentals for Blazers
$69.99; Yukon & Suburban $89.99;
Camaro convertibles $59.99 daily &
$339.99 weekly.
Cash local w/qualifications only. 150 free
mi. daily; 1,050 free mi. weekly.
Will pick-up at home, office or repair shop.

Fairway
2915 Industrial Rd.
Las Vegas, NV 89109
369-8533 1-800-634-3476
Late model cars $19.95 $49.95 daily;
$139 - $249 weekly
Cash accepted, 18 year olds okay. 100
free mi. daily; $59, $69 and $79 a day for
unlimited mileage.

Hertz
McCarran Airport
(Desk in airport terminal)
736-4900 1-800-654-3131
Website WWW.Hertz.com
The Desert Inn
735-4597
Craig Koch, Pres.
$25.99 - $89.95 daily; $129.99 - $479.99 weekly
Cash accepted w/qualifications including
18 year olds. Free mileage

Ladki International Rent-A-Car
795 E. Tropicana Ave.
Las Vegas, NV 89119
1-800-245-2354
Call for locations
David Adams, Branch Mgr.
Daily $29-$69; weekly $109-$289
Economy to luxury, passenger vans,
4X4s.

Lloyd's International
3951 Las Vegas Blvd. S.
Las Vegas, NV 89119
736-2663 1-800-654-7037
Jean Pierre Raad, Fleet Mgr.
Dodge, Plymouth $24.95 - $189.95 daily;
$125.00 - $950.00 weekly. Also Corvette,
Mustangs and vans.
Cash accepted w/qualifications. 150
free mi. daily, $0.20 per mi. extra;
Cadillac 100 free mi. daily, $0.30 per mi.
extra.

National
(Desk in airport terminal)
5233 Rent-A-Car Rd.
Las Vegas, NV 89119
261-5391 1-800-227-7368
William Lobeck, Pres.
GM $36.95 - $46.95 daily; $219.99 -
$349.99 weekly
Cash accepted w/qualification. 100 free
mi. daily; unlimited mileage weekly.

Practical Rent-A-Car
3765 Las Vegas Blvd. S.
Las Vegas, NV 89109
798-5253 1-800-722-7029
Don Saari, Pres.
Hours: 8 am - 11 pm
Fords $25 - $60 daily, convertibles $65 daily,
van or convertible; $314 - $384 weekly.

Preferred Car Rental
700 Naples Dr., Ste. 101
Las Vegas, NV 89119
894-9936
Hail Fallaha, Pres.
Mitsubishi, Nissan, Ford, Dodge,
Chevrolet $21.99 - $39.95 daily; $139 -
$189 weekly; Chevy Astro vans. 150 free
mi. daily.

Rent A Vette
5021 Swenson St.
Las Vegas, NV 89119
736-2592 1-800-372-1981
Robert Wolfe, Gen. Mgr.
Corvette, Mercedes, BMW, Lexus,
Jaguar, Viper, Ferrari.

Rent-A-Wreck
2310 Las Vegas Blvd. S.
Las Vegas, NV 89104
474-0037
Charlie Fries, Pres.
New and used cars '92 - '97 - $19.95 -
$49.95 daily; $119.95 - $275 weekly.
Credit Cards only - Visa, MC, AMX,
Discover.
100 free mi. daily.

Resort Rent A Car
5080 Paradise Rd.
Las Vegas, NV 89119
795-3800 1-800-289-5343
Andy Scott, Gen. Mgr.
Daily $27 - $119; weekly $137 - $543;
unlimited Mileage.
4X4 vehicles, luxury cars, minivans, 15
passenger vans and economy to full size
sedans.

Sav-Mor
(Desk in airport terminal)
5101 Rent-A-Car Rd.
Las Vegas, NV 89119
736-1234 1-800-634-6779
Norm Jenkins, Pres.
Ford, GM Economy - full size, Toyota
$29.95 - $39.95 daily; $139 - $219 weekly. 4X4 trucks, utility, 7 and 15 passenger vans. Unlimited local mileage.

Sears Rent-A-Car
736-1212 1-800-527-0770
(for locations see Budget)

Snappy
6135 W. Sahara Ave.
Las Vegas, NV 89102
367-4999
Tom Cooper, Area Mgr.
Chrysler economy to full size $26.95 -
$42.95 daily; $159.00 - $199.00 weekly.
150 free mi. daily; 1,050 free mi. weekly.

Sunbelt
3317 Las Vegas Blvd. S.
Las Vegas, NV 89119
731-3600
Warren Spots, Pres.
Compact to luxury $39.95 - $350.00
daily; $196.00 - $450.00 weekly.
Cash requires $300.00 deposit plus
return flight tickets; credit card only on
sports cars.
Corvettes, Suzukis, Mercedes & Vipers.
100 free mi. daily; 1,000 free mi. weekly.

Thrifty
376 E. Warm Springs Rd.
Las Vegas, NV 89119
896-7600 1-800-367-2277
JHTC, Inc., Owner
Chrysler economy to full size $27.99 -
$59.99 daily; $149.00 - $299.00 weekly.
Aerostar, minivans. 150 free mi. daily;
1,050 free mi. weekly.

Thrifty
Tom Coward Lincoln-Mercury
5750 W. Sahara Ave.
Las Vegas, NV 89102
362-0315 1-800-367-2277
Tom Coward, Owner
Chrysler economy to full size $27.99 -
$59.99 daily; $149.00 - $299.00 weekly
minivans & Windstar. 150 free mi. daily;
1,050 free mi. weekly.

U. S. Rent A Car
4700 Paradise Rd.
Las Vegas, NV 89119
798-6100 1-800-777-9377
Maria Romano, Pres.
Hours: 5 am - 2 am
Geo, Olds, Chevrolet, GM $29.95 - $49.95
daily; $139.00 - $289.00 weekly.
Cars, trucks, trailers, moving equipment & U-hauls. Cash accepted w/qual-
ification.
150 free mi. daily; 1,000 free mi. duration
of rental. Short and long-term off-site
airport parking.

X-Press Rent-A-Car
3767 Las Vegas Blvd. S.
Las Vegas, NV 89109
795-4008
Sam Summa, Pres.
Compacts $29 - $39 daily, $169-$199
weekly; mini-vans $319, 21 - 25 years of
age requires an additional $10 daily.
Cash deposits or credit cards.

MOTOR HOME RENTALS

Bates Rent-a-Motor Home
3690 S. Eastern Ave., Ste. 220
Las Vegas, NV 89109
736-2070
Sandra Bates, Pres.
Hours: Mon. - Fri. 8:30 am - 5 pm; Sat.

10 am - 2 pm; Closed Sun.
Sizes: 21'-23' *(sleeps 4-6)*; 24'-27'
(sleeps 6-8); 28'-32'; 33'-36'
Rates: Mid-size - $575 - $690 weekly;
larger size $715 - $875
Mileage: 1,000 free miles weekly in
winter; 700 in summer. Daily free miles
142 in winter & 100 in summer, $.18-
$.22 per mile each additional mile.
Insurance & Deposits: reservation
deposit $500.00

Cruise America Motorhome Rental & Sales
6070 Boulder Hwy.
Las Vegas, NV 89122
456-6666
1-800-327-7799
Local and one-way rentals. Weekend,
week and longer rentals. Also camper
and motorcycle rentals.

Sahara RV Center
1518 W. Scotland Ln.
Las Vegas, NV 89102
384-8818
Hours: Mon. - Sat. 8 am - 6 pm; Sun.
10 am - 4 pm
Sizes: 18 ft. - 34+ ft.
Rates: $450 - $1,500 weekly; $275 - $485
for 3 days; $60 - $155 extra day; rates
lower Dec.1 - Feb. 28
1,000 free miles for weekly rates; 500
free miles for 3 day rate; 125 free miles
for extra day; from $.17 - $.21 each additional mile.
All units equipped with power steering,
automatic transmission, radio, dash air
conditioning, roof air conditioning,
fresh water tanks, waste holding tanks,
forced air furnace, refrigerator, stove,
oven, sink, shower, toilet, 110 volt
generator, power unit.

MOTORCYCLE/MOPED RENTALS

Cruise America Motorhome Rental & Sales
6070 Boulder Hwy.
Las Vegas, NV 89122
456-6666 1-800-327-7799
Touring, cruising and sports bikes.

Funway Rentals
5021 Swenson St.
Las Vegas, NV 89119
798-7774 1-800-372-1981
50 cc-1500 cc, Harley, Honda, Yamaha.

Iron Eagle
3867 S. Valley View Blvd.
Las Vegas, NV 89103
Harley-Davidson.

Motorcycles/Moped Rentals
Adventure Motorcycle Tours
2580 N. Nellis Blvd.
Las Vegas, NV 89115
Kawasaki & Harley-Davidson $85 daily
to $535 weekly, $150 for 8 hours & $175
for 24 hours.

Moturis Inc.
4175 W. Dewey Dr.
Las Vegas, NV 89118
597-5978
BMW, Suzuki, Honda, Gold Wing &
Harley-Davidson.

VEHICLE RENTAL

North American Motorcycle Tours Inc.
4625 E. Tropicana Ave.
Las Vegas, NV 89121
434-0200
Rentals start as low as $125 which includes bike, insurance and helmets.

TRUCK RENTAL

Ace Truck Rentals
2135 Western Ave.
Las Vegas, NV 89102
384-4565
Hours: Daily 7 am - 5 pm; Sun. 8 am - 1 pm
Rates: Pickup - $45 day; 15' moving truck - $55 day; stake truck - $55 day; 20'-24' - $60 daily
Mileage: $.25 per mile
Deposit: $200 cash w/NV drivers license, check w/guarantee card or major credit card. No rental with cash deposit on pickups & vans.
Credit Cards: Visa, MC, AMX, Discover

Ahern Rentals
1785 W. Bonanza Rd.
Las Vegas, NV 89106
648-6212
Main office
4241 S. Arville St.
Las Vegas, NV 89103
Don Ahern, Pres.
Hours: Daily 8 am - 5 pm

Rates: 22' stake truck - $64 per day
Mileage: $.20 per mile & gas
Deposit: Minimum $200 with Nevada drivers license.
Credit Cards: Visa, MC, Discover, AMX

Allstate Truck Rental
5175 Rent-A-Car Rd.
Las Vegas, NV 89119
736-6147
Nick Willden, Pres.
Hours: 24 hours
Rates: Pickups & cargo vans - $60.95 day upon availability
Mileage: pickups & cargo vans 150 miles free
Deposit: Major credit card
Credit Cards: All major

Budget Truck Rental
(local & one way)
4475 W. Tropicana Ave.
Las Vegas, NV 89103
362-8668
John Mallo, Pres.
Hours: 7 am - 5:30 pm
Rates: *(Local rates)* Pickup & cargo vans - $42.95 day; 15' moving truck - $39-$52 day
Mileage: $.10 per mile on Pickups; $.20 cargo vans; $.20 per mile on 24' moving truck
Deposit: Major credit card
Credit Cards: Visa, MC, Amx, Discover, Diners, CB, Sears

Hertz Penske Truck Rental (3)
(Local & one way)
1132 W. Bonanza Rd.
Las Vegas, NV 89106
388-9626
Las Vegas - East: 456-9905
Las Vegas - West: 645-3203
Roger S. Penske, Pres.
One way rental reservations: 1-800-222-0277 10' - 24' vans.
Rates: Daily 10' - $29.95; 14' - $39.95; 18' - $49.95; 24' - $59.95
Mileage: $.29 per mile
Deposit: $200
Credit Cards: Visa, MC, AMX, Discover

Rent A Wreck/Ryder
One way and local
2310 Las Vegas Blvd. S
Las Vegas, NV 89104
384-0401
Customer service: 1-800-327-7777
Charlie Fries, Pres.
Hours: 8 am - 5 pm
Rates: 15'-$29.95, 20'-$39.95 & 24' $49.95
Mileage: Daily $.39 a mile
Deposit: $200 credit card/cash or check
Credit Cards: MC, Visa, AMEX, Discover

Ryder Truck Rental
(local & one way)
2750 S. Maryland Pkwy.
Las Vegas, NV 89109
732-4360 1-800-GO-Ryder
Call for locations.
Local & long distance.

U-Haul Co.
1900 S. Decatur Blvd.
Las Vegas, NV 89102
251-9250
Nationwide: 1-800-460-4285
Pat Maddi, Pres. of Mktg.
There are 55 locations throughout Las Vegas area Call for locations.
Self-storage room available.
Hours: Mon. - Thu. & Sat. 7 am - 7 pm; Fri. 7 am - 8 pm; Sun. 9 am - 5 pm
U-Haul centers offer complete moving services. See Yellow Pages for additional U-Haul locations that rent trucks in the Las Vegas area.
Nationwide reservations: 1-800-528-6042.
Rates: 10'-14' vans $19.95 day; 14' plus vans $29.95 day; 24' & 26' vans $39.95 day
Mileage: $.39 per mile for 10' & 14'. $.49 per mile for 17', 24' & 26'
Deposit: $120; Protection optional $14
Credit Cards: Visa, MC, AMX, Discover

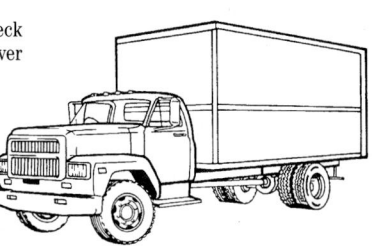

Accommodations

Las Vegas is home to 12 out of the 13 largest hotels in the world. The $1 billion MGM, the largest, encompassing a total of 114 acres, opened Dec. 18, 1993. Of the 5,005 rooms MGM offers, the largest by far is a two-story suite stretching more than 6,040 sq. ft. The MGM is also home to a 16-acre amusement park (the city's first theme park) featuring The screamer; the world's largest skycoaster, a 16,325-seat special events arena, a 17,000-seat grand theater, 171,500 sq. ft. of casino space (an area larger than Yankee stadium and the equivalent of four football fields, in four themed casino areas), a 13,500 sq. ft. spa and Grand Oasis Pool resort facility and eight restaurants.

Five years ago there was a total of 76,523 rooms in the city. Las Vegas now has 105,347 hotel and motel rooms that provide accommodations to some 30 million visitors annually. Room occupancy for 1997 was estimated at 89.5 percent based on first quarter observations.

During 1996, Las Vegas added 9,026 rooms. Projections early in the decade were that Las Vegas would not break the 100,000 mark until just before the turn of the century. Las Vegas is now way ahead of second place Orlando, which has 83,000 rooms.

Room rates in Las Vegas fluctuate greatly with conventions and major events sometimes doubling and even tripling standard rates. The average room rate for Las Vegas in 1996 was $58. If you are planning a trip to the Las Vegas area, please keep in mind that rooms are much cheaper and easier to find Sunday through Thursday, with the slowest month being December and the busiest being March. It is always best to make a reservation as far in advance as possible and to send in a deposit or leave your credit card information to guarantee your room. Prices quoted are based on normal availability and are subject to change. All rates are based on single/double person occupancy in standard rooms. Most hotels also have suites available at an additional cost; please call ahead for these quotes.

ROOM REFERRAL

Las Vegas Convention and Visitors Authority
Visitor Information Center
3150 Paradise Rd.
Las Vegas, NV 89109
892-7575
Hotel/Motel Room
Reservations Center:
383-9100   1-800-332-5333
Hours: Mon. - Fri. 7 am - 6 pm; Sat. - Sun. 8 am - 5 pm

Las Vegas Welcome Center
3333 S. Maryland Pkwy., Ste. 11
Las Vegas, NV 89109
451-7648 1-800-821-6624
Specializing in room reservations, auto and wedding arrangements.

Nevada Welcome Centers:

Boulder City Visitors Center
100 Nevada Hwy.
Boulder City, NV 89005
294-1220
Hours: 8 am - 4:30 pm

Jean Visitors Center
Interstate 15, Exit 12
P.O. Box 19470
Jean, NV 89019
1-702-874-1360
Hours: 8:30 am - 5 pm

Mesquite Visitors Center
Interstate 15, Exit 122
P.O. Box 1560
Mesquite, NV 89024
1-702-346-2902
Hours: 8 am - 5 pm

Laughlin Visitors Center
1555 Casino Dr.
Laughlin, NV 89029
1-702-298-3321
Hours: 8 am - 5 pm
Operated by The Las Vegas Convention and Visitors Authority, the center provides directions and information to visitors of the area.

PROPER TIPPING PROCEDURE

Las Vegas, known world-wide as "The Entertainment Capital of The World", and a city where anyone can find entertainment round the clock is also known for its prompt service from courteous attendants. When going out on the town in Las Vegas please remember these valuable people and follow these customary tipping procedures:

Bartenders:
Between $1.00 - $2.00 per round

Bellmen:
$1.00 - $2.00 per piece of baggage

Change Persons:
Usually 10% of winnings when hints on a particular machine pay off for you

Cocktail Waitresses:
$1.00 - $2.00 per round while drinking for free in the casino gaming area

Dealers:
A chip if you're winning or a bet made for them while you're playing is appropriate

Housekeeper:
$1.00 - $2.00 per day

Keno Runner:
15% if you're winning and a few dollars while you're actually playing

Limo Driver:
15% of your total fare

Room Service:
15 - 20% if not already included in the total bill

Showroom Maitre d' and Ushers:
$3.00 - $5.00 per person in your party, more if better seating is acquired

Taxicab Driver:
15% of the total fare

Valet Parking Attendant:
$1.00 - $2.00

Waiters and Waitresses:
15 - 20% of the total check

FREMONT STREET EXPERIENCE

Fremont Street is named after John Charles Fremont, the 19th-century explorer who established a camp May 3, 1844 near Las Vegas.

Fremont Street was first established in 1905 and has been the site of many Las Vegas firsts. It was the sight of the first paved street in Las Vegas in 1925 and where the first gaming license in Nevada was issued (the *Northern Club at 15 E. Fremont Street*). It was also the location of the first high-rise in Las Vegas, the Fremont Hotel in 1956. The Horseshoe was the first casino to install carpeting, while the Golden Nugget was the first structure designed solely as a casino.

The milestones of Fremont Street continue with the one-of-a-kind Fremont Street Experience. Construction of the project started in Sept. 1994 and was completed in Dec. 1995. Nightly on Fremont Street, on a massive space frame that towers 90 ft. above four blocks, stretching nearly 1,400 ft. and supported by 16 columns, each weighing 26,000 pounds and able to support 400,000 pounds, the Fremont Street Experience takes place. Set in the frame are nearly 2.1 million lights, and 208 speakers capable of producing 540,000 watts of sound and concert-quality music. 121 computers produce 300 colors and 65,536 combinations. Shows run on the hour beginning at 8 pm and continue until midnight. Admission is free.

While several different shows are currently running, the Fremont Street Experience will eventually have a full library of shows, that can be tailored to an unlimited number of themes, special events and holidays.

The Fremont Street Experience is a joint effort of the City of Las Vegas and the Fremont Street Experience Company, a group of 10 downtown hotels: Binion's Horseshoe, California, Fitzgeralds, Four Queens, Fremont, Golden Gate, Golden Nugget, Jackie Gaughan's Plaza, Las Vegas Club and Main Street Station.

LAS VEGAS ROOM INVENTORY

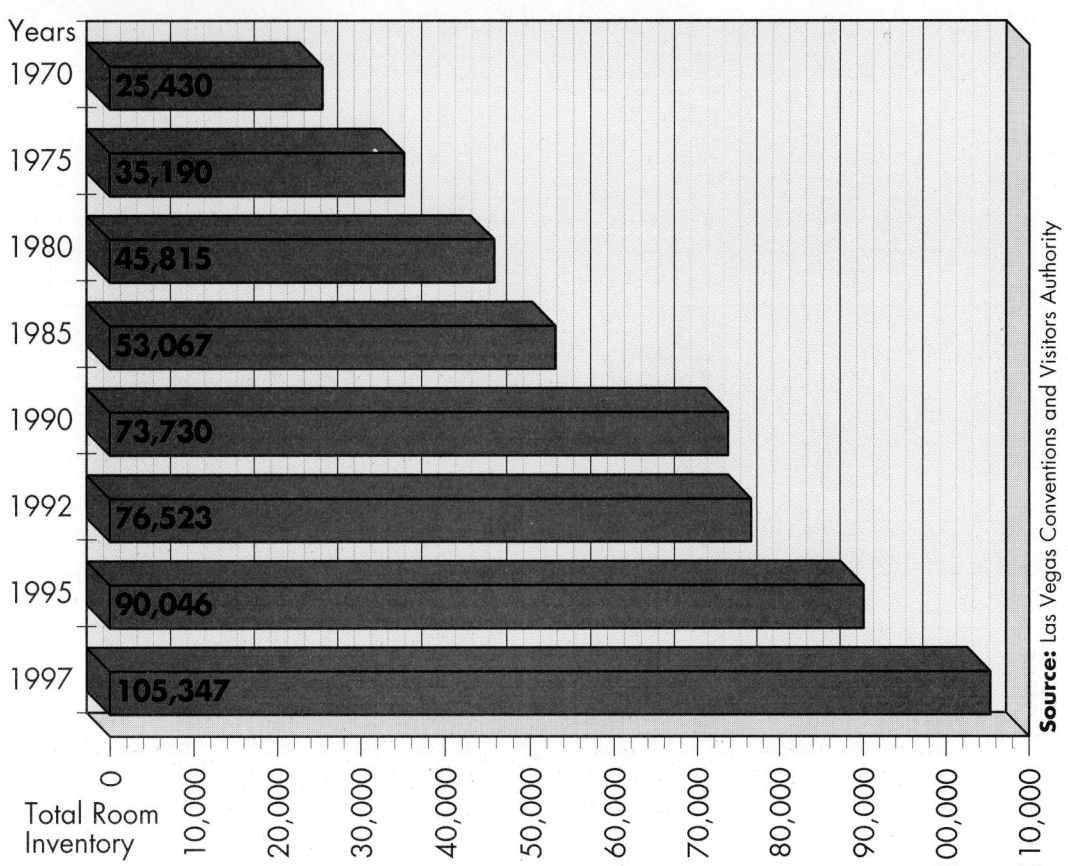

Source: Las Vegas Conventions and Visitors Authority

Years
- 1970: 25,430
- 1975: 35,190
- 1980: 45,815
- 1985: 53,067
- 1990: 73,730
- 1992: 76,523
- 1995: 90,046
- 1997: 105,347

Total Room Inventory: 0, 10,000, 20,000, 30,000, 40,000, 50,000, 60,000, 70,000, 80,000, 90,000, 100,000, 110,000

LAS VEGAS TOTAL ROOM OCCUPANCY

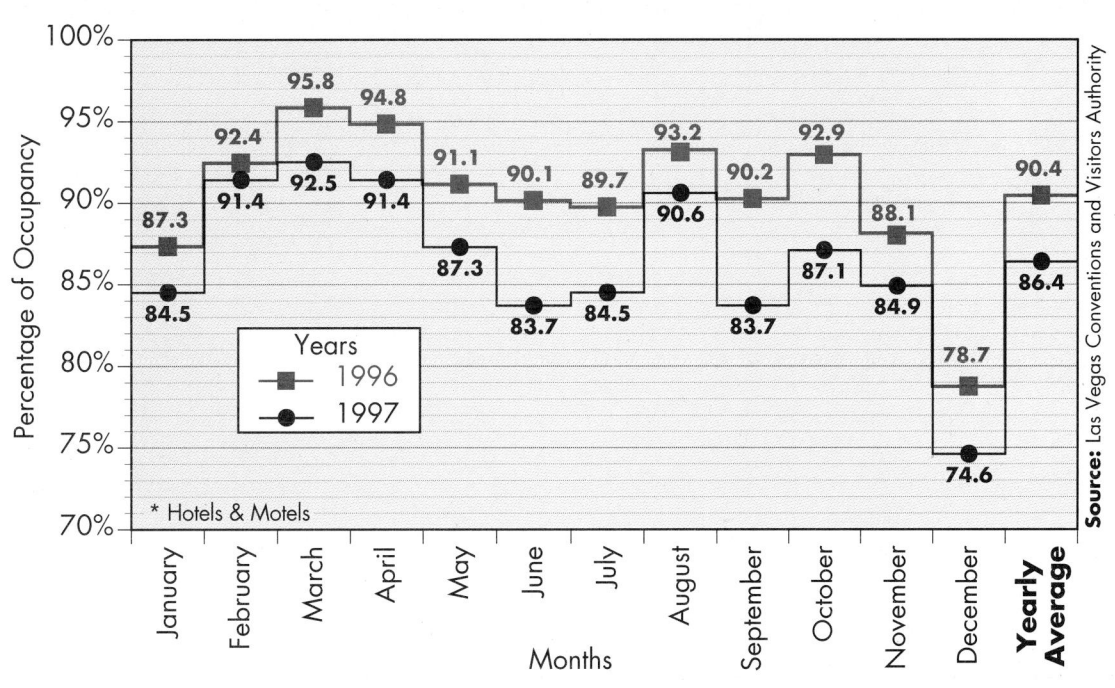

Source: Las Vegas Conventions and Visitors Authority

Month	1996	1997
January	87.3	84.5
February	92.4	91.4
March	95.8	92.5
April	94.8	91.4
May	91.1	87.3
June	90.1	83.7
July	89.7	84.5
August	93.2	90.6
September	90.2	83.7
October	92.9	87.1
November	88.1	84.9
December	78.7	74.6
Yearly Average	90.4	86.4

* Hotels & Motels

HOTELS

HOTEL/CASINO	PHONE	Rooms & Suites	Restaurants	Buffets	Weekend Brunch	Bars & Lounges	Wedding Chapels	Nightly Entertainment	Pool	Beauty Salon	Oversize Vehicle Parking	Tennis Courts	Handicap Eq. Rooms	Airline Desk	Car Rental Desk	Child Care	Meeting & Banq. Rms.	Shuttle Service	Fitness Rm.
Arizona Charlie's 740 S. Decatur Blvd.	(702) 258-5200 (800) 342-2695	255	5	•		•	•		•			•	•				•	•	
Barbary Coast 3595 Las Vegas Blvd. S.	(702) 737-7111 (800) 634-6755	200	3			•						•					•		
Bally's 3645 Las Vegas Blvd. S.	(702) 739-4111 (800) 722-5597	2814	6	•	•	•		•	•	•	•	•	•	•	•		•		•
Boulder Station 4111 Boulder Hwy.	(702) 432-7777 (800) 683-7777	300	4	•	•	•	•		•	•		•			•	•	•		
Caesars Palace 3570 Las Vegas Blvd. S.	(702) 731-7222 (800) 634-6661	2471	9	•	•	•		•	•	•		•	•	•			•		•
California Hotel 12 E. Ogden Ave.	(702) 385-1222 (800) 634-6255	781	4			•			•		•	•					•	•	
Circus Circus Hotel 2880 Las Vegas Blvd. S.	(702) 734-0410 (800) 634-3450	3746	6	•	•	•	•	•	•		•	•				•	•		
Continental 4100 Paradise Rd.	(702) 737-5555 (800) 634-6641	400	1			•		•	•		•						•	•	
Debbie Reynolds Hotel 305 Convention Center Dr.	(702) 734-0711 (800) 633-1777	192	2			•			•		•						•		
Desert Inn Resort 3145 Las Vegas Blvd. S.	(702) 733-4444 (800) 634-6906	715	4	•		•		•	•	•	•	•					•		•
Excalibur Hotel 3850 Las Vegas Blvd. S.	(702) 597-7777 (800) 937-7777	4008	6	•		•	•	•	•		•	•	•	•		•	•		
El Cortez 600 E. Fremont St.	(702) 385-5200 (800) 634-6703	308	2			•			•		•						•		
Fiesta Casino Hotel 2400 N. Rancho Dr.	(702) 631-7000 (800) 731-7333	100	5	•	•	•			•		•			•		•	•		
Fitzgeralds/Holiday Inn 301 Fremont St.	(702) 388-2400 (800) 274-5825	652	2	•	•	•			•		•			•			•		
Flamingo Hilton Hotel 3555 Las Vegas Blvd. S.	(702) 733-3111 (800) 732-2111	3642	7	•		•		•	•	•	•	•	•				•		•
Four Queens 202 E. Fremont St.	(702) 385-4011 (800) 634-6045	690	2			•		•					•	•			•		
Fremont Hotel 200 Fremont St.	(702) 385-3232 (800) 634-6460	452	4	•	•	•	•			•		•					•		
New Frontier Hotel 3120 Las Vegas Blvd. S.	(702) 794-8200 (800) 634-6966	986	2	•	•	•		•	•	•	•	•						•	
Gold Coast 4000 W. Flamingo Rd.	(702) 367-7111 (800) 331-5334	750	4	•	•	•		•	•		•	•	•		•	•	•		
Gold Spike Hotel 400 E. Ogden Ave.	(702) 384-8444 (800) 634-6703	110	1			•					•								
Golden Gate Hotel 1 Fremont St.	(702) 385-1906 (800) 426-1906	106	2			•		•			•								
Golden Nugget Hotel 129 Fremont St.	(702) 385-7111 (800) 634-3454	1907	5	•	•	•		•	•	•	•			•		•		•	•
Hard Rock Hotel / Casino 4455 Paradise Rd.	(702) 693-5000 (800) 473-7625	340	2			•			•		•								•
Harrah's 3475 Las Vegas Blvd. S.	(702) 369-5000 (800) 634-6765	2699	6	•		•		•	•	•	•					•			•
Holiday Inn - Boardwalk 3750 Las Vegas Blvd. S.	(702) 735-2400 (800) 465-4329	675	3	•		•		•	•		•					•			
Binion's Horseshoe 128 Fremont St.	(702) 382-1600 (800) 937-6537	363	6	•		•			•		•						•		
Imperial Palace Hotel 3535 Las Vegas Blvd. S.	(702) 731-3311 (800) 634-6441	2700	9	•	•	•	•	•	•	•	•	•		•		•			•
Lady Luck Casino & Hotel 206 N. Third St.	(702) 477-3000 (800) 523-9582	791	4	•	•	•			•		•			•	•	•			
Las Vegas Club 18 Fremont St.	(702) 385-1664 (800) 634-6532	410	3			•				•		•		•	•		•		
Las Vegas Hilton 3000 Paradise Rd.	(702) 732-5111 (800) 732-7117	3174	12	•	•	•	•	•	•	•	•	•	•	•	•		•	•	•
Luxor Hotel/Casino 3900 Las Vegas Blvd. S.	(702) 262-4000 (800) 288-1000	4407	7	•	•	•		•	•	•	•			•	•	•		•	•

Visit our website at www.experiencelasvegas.com

HOTELS

HOTEL/CASINO	PHONE	Rooms & Suites	Restaurants	Buffets	Weekend Brunch	Bars & Lounges	Wedding Chapels	Nightly Entertainment	Pool	Beauty Salon	Oversize Vehicle Parking	Tennis Courts	Handicap Eq. Rooms	Airline Desk	Car Rental Desk	Child Care	Meeting & Banq. Rms.	Shuttle Service	Fitness Rm.
Main Street Station 200 N. Main Street.	(702) 387-1896 (800) 713-8933	406	4	●	●	●				●				●				●		
Maxim Hotel & Casino 160 E. Flamingo Rd.	(702) 731-4300 (800) 634-6987	795	4	●	●	●		●	●	●				●		●				
MGM Grand Hotel/Casino 3799 Las Vegas Blvd. S.	(702) 891-1111 (800) 929-1111	5005	10	●	●	●		●	●	●			●	●	●	●	●	●		
The Mirage 3400 Las Vegas Blvd. S.	(702) 791-7111 (800) 627-6667	3062	10	●	●	●		●	●	●			●	●	●	●	●	●		●
Monte Carlo 3770 Las Vegas Blvd. S.	(702) 730-7000 (800) 311-8999	3002	6	●	●	●		●	●	●			●	●			●	●		●
Nevada Palace 5255 Boulder Hwy.	(702) 458-8810 (800) 634-6283	210	3	●	●	●			●		●		●				●	●	
New York New York 3790 Las Vegas Blvd. S.	(702) 740-6969 (800) 693-6763	2033	4		●	●	●	●	●	●			●	●	●		●	●		●
The Orleans 4500 W. Tropicana Ave.	(702) 365-7111 (800) 675-3267	840	4	●	●	●		●	●				●	●			●	●		
Palace Station 2411 W. Sahara Ave.	(702) 367-2411 (800) 634-3101	1028	5	●		●		●	●	●	●		●			●	●	●	
Jackie Gaughan's Plaza 1 Main St.	(702) 386-2110 (800) 634-6575	1034	2		●	●	●	●	●	●	●	●	●		●			●	
Quality Inn - Key Largo 377 E. Flamingo Rd.	(702) 733-7777 (800) 634-6617	316	1		●		●	●		●			●				●		
The Reserve Hotel 777 W. Lake Mead Dr.	(702) 558-7000 (888) 899-7770	224	3	●	●	●		●	●		●		●				●		
Rio Suite Hotel 3700 W. Flamingo Rd.	(702) 252-7777 (800) 752-9746	2563	12	●	●	●		●	●	●			●				●	●	●
Riviera Hotel 2901 Las Vegas Blvd. S.	(702) 734-5110 (800) 634-6753	2075	5	●	●	●		●	●	●			●				●		●
Royal Hotel 99 Convention Center Dr.	(702) 735-6117 (800) 634-6118	236	1			●		●					●				●		
Sahara Hotel 2535 Las Vegas Blvd. S.	(702) 737-2111 (800) 634-6666	2033	4	●		●		●	●	●	●		●	●	●		●		
Sam's Town 5111 Boulder Hwy.	(702) 456-7777 (800) 634-6371	650	8	●	●	●		●	●		●		●			●	●	●	
San Remo 115 E. Tropicana Ave.	(702) 739-9000 (800) 522-7366	751	6	●	●	●		●	●		●		●		●		●		
Santa Fe Hotel 4949 N. Rancho Dr.	(702) 658-4900 (800) 872-6823	200	7	●	●	●		●	●		●		●			●	●	●	
Showboat Hotel 2800 E. Fremont St.	(702) 385-9123 (800) 826-2800	453	4	●	●	●		●	●		●		●			●	●	●	
Silverton 3333 Blue Diamond Rd.	(702) 263-7777 (800) 588-7711	304	2	●		●			●		●		●		●				
Stardust 3000 Las Vegas Blvd. S.	(702) 732-6111 (800) 634-6757	2400	5	●	●	●		●	●	●	●		●				●		
Stratosphere 2000 Las Vegas Blvd. S.	(702) 380-7777 (800) 998-6937	2699	5	●	●	●		●	●	●	●		●				●		
Sunset Station 1301 W. Sunset Rd.	(702) 547-7777 (888) 786-7389	448	8	●	●	●		●	●		●		●			●	●	●	●
Texas Station 2101 Texas Star Ln.	(702) 631-1000 (800) 654-8888	200	7	●	●	●		●	●		●		●				●		
Treasure Island 3300 Las Vegas Blvd. S.	(702) 894-7111 (800) 944-7444	2900	8	●	●	●		●	●	●	●		●	●			●		●
Tropicana 3801 Las Vegas Blvd. S.	(702) 739-2222 (800) 634-4000	1874	7	●	●	●		●	●	●	●	●	●				●		
Vacation Village 6711 Las Vegas Blvd. S.	(702) 897-1700 (800) 338-0608	315	2			●		●	●		●		●				●	●	
Westward Ho 2900 Las Vegas Blvd. S.	(702) 731-2900 (800) 634-6651	800	2	●		●		●	●		●		●						
Western Hotel/Casino 899 Fremont St.	(702) 384-4620 (800) 634-6703	116	1		●				●										

Photo: Tiffany Design

BALLY'S

Bally's
3645 Las Vegas Blvd. S.
Las Vegas, NV 89109
739-4111   1-800-634-3434
1-800-7-Ballys FAX: 739-4405
Paul Pusateri, Pres./COO
Fritz Hubler, Vice-Pres.
Jimmy Wike, Casino Mgr.
Opened in 1973 as the MGM Grand, it is still considered one of the city's most elegant resorts. Bally's offers "a touch of class" in every aspect of service. When fire forced the closing of the hotel in November 1980, it reopened again, nine months later, with the latest in fire safety equipment. The hotel was purchased in 1986 by the Bally Corporation for $550 million. Together with MGM a monorail was opened in June 1995 offering guests free nonstop transportation between the two resorts. The monorail system was the first joint venture of its kind between two independent properties in Las Vegas at a cost of $25 million. Throughout the 1990s, Bally's Las Vegas has undergone extensive remodeling making improvements to nearly every aspect of the resort.

Rooms:
2,814 rooms including 265 suites; 2 towers (26 stories)
Rates: $99 - $129

Special Features:
Big Time Amusement video arcade, Children's Place - care for children ages 2 - 13, Health Spas: 739-4366 - The Spa at Bally's is an 11,000 sq. ft. full service health club with a wide selection of state-of-the-art fitness equipment and various other activities, Tennis Pro Shop and 8 outdoor tennis courts, Olympic size pool & Jacuzzi, Bally's 22nd Club, located on the 22nd floor of the main tower, offers premium hotel guests special amenities including

a concierge lounge in a comfortable picturesque setting overlooking Las Vegas; monorail to MGM.

Casino:
56,200 sq. ft.
Games: 1,882 slots and video machines, 49 blackjack tables, 9 crap tables, 8 roulette wheels, 1 keno lounge, 1 wheel of fortune, 4 mini-baccarat, 2 baccarat, 4 Caribbean stud, race and sports book, 3 Pai Gow poker, 4 Let It Ride, 1 War table

Entertainment:
Show Reservations: 739-4567
Jubilee Theater: *"Jubilee!"* - $49.50 - $66, continues to rate as one of Las Vegas' finest production shows with incredible sets, costumes, and special effects. *(see Pg. 165)*
Celebrity Room - Top name performers *(see Pg. 169)*
Indigo Lounge - Entertainment nightly

Dining:
Al Dente - Italiann *(see Pg. 119)*
Chang's - Asian
Seasons - Continental *(see Pg. 136)*
Bally's - steak house *(see Pg. 143)*
The Sidewalk Cafe *(see Pg. 119)*
Snack Bar
Stage Deli *(see Pg. 157)*
Terrace Cafe - seasonal *(in the pool area)*
Big Kitchen Buffet: *(see Pg. 144)*
Breakfast - 7 am - 11 am - $8.95
Brunch - 11 am - 2:30 pm - $9.95
Dinner - 4:30 pm - 10 pm - $13.95
Sunday Sterling Brunch - 9:30 am -2:30 pm - $49.95 per person *(see Pg. 144)*

Meeting & Banquet Facilities:
Bally's offers more than 180,000 sq. ft. of convention and meeting space, including side-by-side 50,000 sq. ft. ballrooms, 43 convention and meeting rooms and additional meeting rooms on the 26th floor.

Shopping & Services:
Bally's Avenue Shoppes - The stores offer items ranging from men's, women's and children's clothing; specialty items, such as gifts, artwork, collectibles and T-shirts; Bally's logo and sports logo clothing, and snacks.
Bally's Spa
The Celebration Wedding Chapel
2 Beauty salons
Allstate Tours/Universal Travel
Avis Car Rental

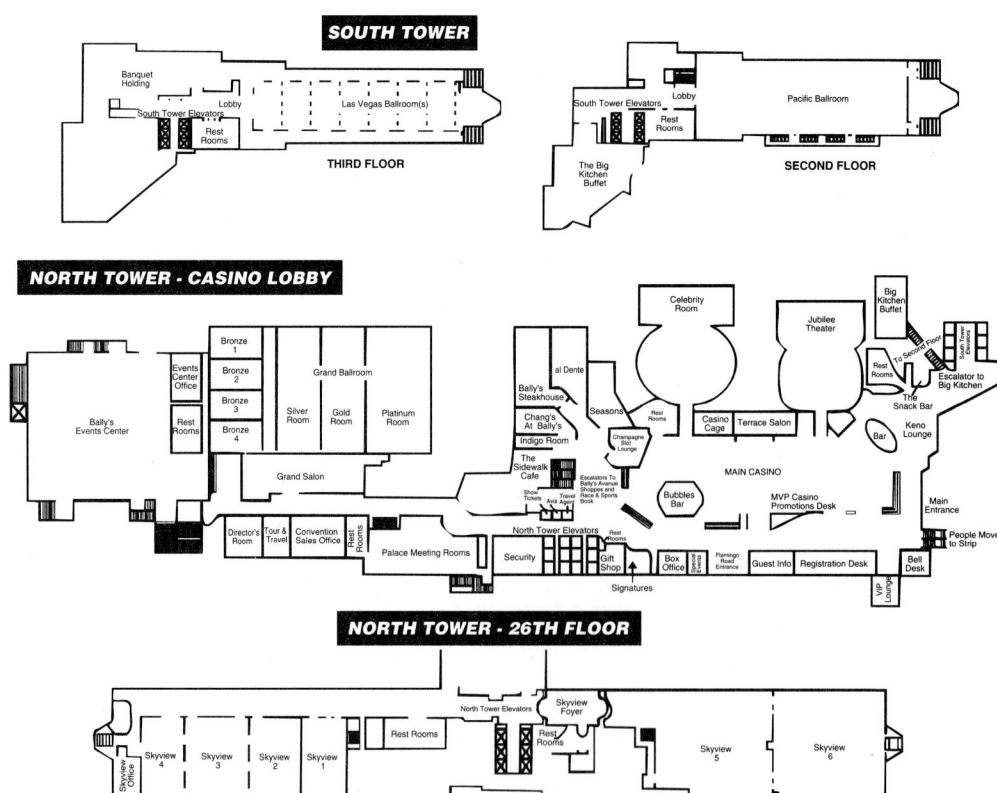

CAESARS PALACE

Caesars Palace
3570 Las Vegas Blvd. S.
Las Vegas, NV 89109
731-7110   800-634-6001
Fax: 731-7172
731-7222   800-634-6661
(room reservations)
Fax: 731-6636 *(Guest faxes)*
Paul O'Neil, Pres.
Rich Waters, Sr. VP of Casino Operations

Glittering at the heart of the Las Vegas Strip, Caesars Palace recaptures the glory that was Greece and the grandeur that was Rome in a resort/casino that has become synonymous with luxury and excitement. Graced by spectacular fountains, majestic cypress trees, beautiful landscaping and gleaming marble reproductions of classic statuary, Caesars Palace sits as an architectural marvel among world resorts known for their originality and beauty.

Rooms:
2,471 rooms including 194 suites
Rates: $109 - $199

Special Features:
Omnimax® Theatre: 731-7900, features a 70-foot high dome-shaped screen and engulfs audiences with a "sensaround" sound system, video arcade, The Forum Shops mall and Caesars mall, Brahma Shrine - Hindu God of Good Fortune, 4 swimming pools, 2 outdoor whirlpool health spa tubs.

Casino:
118,000 sq. ft.
Games: 2,050 slot and video poker machines, 65 blackjack tables, 13 crap tables, 13 roulette wheels, 1 keno lounge, 3 wheels of fortune, 3 mini-baccarat, 11 baccarat tables, 6 Pai Gow poker, 6 Pai Gow, race and sports book, 2 Caribbean stud, multiple action blackjack, 2 Let It Ride

Entertainment:
Show Reservations: 731-7333 800-445-4544
Circus Maximus - Features top name entertainment *(see Pg. 169)*
Special Sports Event Tickets: 731-7865 800- 634-6698
Cleopatra's Barge Nightclub - dancing *(see Pg. 170)*
Olympic Lounge - entertainment nightly *(see Pg. 170)*
Caesars Magical Empire - includes 2 theaters and 2 lounges *(see Pg. 169)*

Dining:
Hyakumi - Japanese *(see Pg. 125)*
Bacchanal - Continental 6-course Roman feast *(ancient Roman) (see Pg. 136)*
Caesars Magical Empire - 10 dining chambers - all continental *(see Pg. 169)*
Cafe Roma - 24 hour coffee shop *(see Pg. 144)*
Buffet:
Breakfast - Mon. - Fri. 7 am - 11 am - $11.95
Lunch - Mon. - Fri. noon - 2:30 pm - $12.45
Dinner - Sun. - Thu. 6 pm - 10 pm; Fri. - Sat. 6 pm - 11 pm - $17.95
Brunch - Sat. - Sun. 7 am - 2:30 pm- $13.95
Empress Court - Chinese *(see Pg. 114)*
LaPiazza Food Court - International cuisines
Neros - Seafood & steak house *(see Pg. 139)*
Palace Court - Gourmet French *(see Pg. 118)*
Palatium Buffet: *(see Pg. 144)*
Breakfast - Mon. - Fri. 7:30 am - 11:30 am - $7.95
Lunch - Mon. - Fri. 11:30 a.m. - 3:30 pm - $9.95
Dinner - 4:30 pm - 10 pm - $13.95
Seafood - Fri. 4 pm - 10 pm $18.95
Sat. Brunch - 8:30 am - 3:30 pm - $14.95
Sun. Champagne Brunch - 8:30 am - 3:30 pm - $14.95; children 3 - 12 $7.50; children up to 3 years free.
Terrazza - Italian *(see Pg. 124)*
PosTime Deli *(see Pg. 157)*
Snack Bar

Meeting & Banquet Facilities:
731-7200
Total Space: 170,000 sq. ft.

Shopping & Services:
The Forum Shops at Caesars - Over 100 shops in a half-million-sq.-ft.-mall.
American Express Services
Appian Way Shops
Caesars Exclusively! stores and boutiques
Laundry and dry cleaning services
Health spa and fitness center

Map labels

Covered Parking Garage
Palace Tower
Promenade Level (3rd Floor)
Spa & Fitness Center
Palace Tower Shops
Garden Of The Gods Pool Area
IMAX Race for Atlantis
La Piazza Food Court
La Piazza Lounge
The Forum Shops at Caesars
Terrazza
Empress Court
Palace Court
Emperors Club Booth
Bacchanal
Caesars Exclusively!
Caesars Adventure Arcade
Forum Casino
Cafe' Roma
Roman Tower
Appian Way Shops
Forum Tower
Forum Lounge
Omnimax Theatre
Colosseum Ballroom
Circus Maximus Showroom
Cleopatra's Barge
Hyakumi
Centurion Tower
Nero's
Cashier
Galleria Lounge
Discus Bar
Race & Sports Book Bar
The Palatium
Posttime
Planet Hollywood Entrance
Guest Registration
Palace Casino
Race Book
Sports Book
Entrance
People Mover
Caesars Magical Empire
South Front Wing
North Front Wing
The Brahma Shrine
People Mover
Caesars Ballroom
People Mover
The World of Caesar
The Temple of Caesar

CIRCUS CIRCUS

**Circus Circus
Hotel/Casino
2880 Las Vegas Blvd. S.
Las Vegas, NV 89109
734-0410   1-800-634-3450**
*Michael Ensign, Chairman/Ceo
Steve Greathouse, Gen. Mgr.
Penny Solomon, Dir. of Casino
Operations*
Circus Circus opened October 18, 1968
by Jay Sarno after he sold Caesars
Palace. The property had no rooms until
1972. In 1974, Sarno sold the casino to
William Bennett and Bill Pennington.
In 1983 Circus Circus went public and is

now one of the most successful gaming
corporations in Nevada. The first of 18
gaming properties owned and operated
nationwide by Circus Circus Enterprises,
Circus Circus led the way for family
entertainment and catering to the middle class players instead of just the high
rollers. Circus Circus completed a $75
million, five-acre indoor theme park in
August of 1993, bringing the fun of the
circus to guests, featuring the world's
largest permanent circus, a carnival
midway, Grand Slam Canyon, an arcade,
clowns and the world's most honored
circus acts all under a comfortable,
fully enclosed climate controlled 72

degree facility, the United State's
largest space-frame dome, blocking
ultra-violet rays and allowing natural light into the park area.

Rooms:
3,746 including 2 two-story suites, 14
parlor suites, 11 Jacuzzi suites and 2
Jacuzzi parlor suites and 101 regular
suites, 2,149 non-smoking rooms, 45
hearing impaired rooms, and 122 wheelchair accessible rooms.
Rates: $39 - $129
Circus Land R.V. Park: 384 spaces consists of a 24-hour convenience store,
game arcade, laundromat, pool, tot's
wading pool, Jacuzzi, saunas, playground, pet runs and disposal stations

Special Features:
Circus Midway: Free circus acts daily
11 am - midnight, 3 outdoor swimming
pools, and 2 indoor swimming pools
with whirlpools

Casino:
110,979 sq. ft.
Games: 2,700 slot and video machines,
64 blackjack tables, 3 crap tables, 7
roulette wheels, 1 keno lounge, 1 Big
Six, 5 Pai Gow poker, 10 poker tables,
race and sports book, 3 Caribbean stud,
2 Let It Ride, 1 War game

Entertainment:
Skyrise Lounge

Dining:
Plate of Plenty Buffet: - *(see Pg. 144)*
Breakfast - 6 am - 11:30 am - $2.99
Lunch - noon - 4 pm - $3.99
Dinner - 4:30 pm - 11 pm - $4.99
Sun. Champagne Brunch - 10 am - 2 pm
- $17.95 served in The Steakhouse
Circus Pizzeria - Pizza
McDonald's - fast food
Pink Pony - 24 hour coffee shop
Skyrise Deli
Westside Deli
Grand Slam Canyon Snack Bar
The Steak House - Steak *(see Pg. 143)*
Promenade Cafe *(see Pg. 149)*
Stivali - Italian *(see Pg. 124)*

Shopping & Services:
Sweet Tooth-Ice Cream
Circus Kids-Children Clothes
Vegas Only-Wearable Vegas Gifts
Headliners-Gift Shop/News Stand
Marshall Rousso-Clothing Store
Very Vegas-Souvenirs/Jewelry
Magnetized-A Magnet Shop
Market Express-Vacation Needs
Photo Stop
Personalized-Gifts
Under $10 Store
Chapel of the Fountain Wedding
Chapel: 794-3777

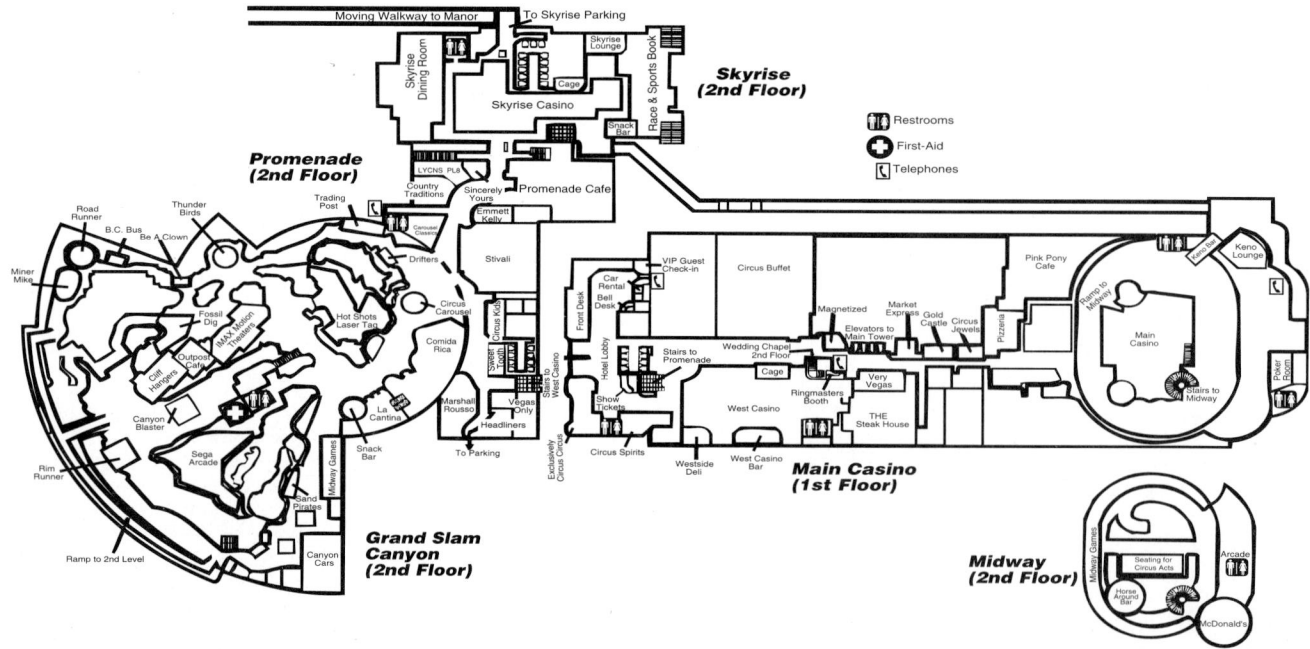

ACCOMMODATIONS

DESERT INN

**Desert Inn
Resort/Casino**
**3145 Las Vegas Blvd. S.
Las Vegas, NV 89109**
733-4444   1-800-634-6906
John Koster, Pres.
John So, Vice Pres. Hotel Operations
Arnie Shehadi, Casino Mgr.
The Desert Inn Resort/Casino recently
completed over $200 million in new ren-
ovations and expansions. Reminiscent
of the luxury resort first inspired in
1950 by the original creator, Wilbur
Clark, the newly renovated property
features lavish accommodations and
amenities in an elegant environment. A
variety of leisure and sports-oriented
activities are offered at the 150 acre
resort.

Fashioned in Mizner Palm Beach
architecture, gold leafed domed ceilings, crystal chandeliers and stately
columns adorn the 715-room resort.

Renovation and expansions in 1997
included the construction of "Villas Del
Lago," a three-story structure featuring
nine lanai suites and two opulent poolside casas. The "Palms Tower" offers 76
mini suites, three bi-level garden suites
and one 8,300 sq. ft. penthouse.
Adjacent to this tower and the existing
hotel tower, a new five-story hotel,
Grand Lobby, features a Mediterranean-
inspired mural with panoramic views of

the golf course and Las Vegas Blvd. via
expansive glass walls.

Rooms:
715 (including 99 suites, 76 mini-suites,
and 16 penthouses
Rates: $85 - $125

Special Features:
Lagoon-style swimming pool with
cabanas, bridges and waterfalls,
Jacuzzi, Health Club & Spa featuring a
salon, steam room, sauna, weight training, private whirlpools and more, 4
lighted outdoor tennis courts & Pro
Shop, 18 hole PGA Championship Golf
Course & Pro Shop.

Casino:
18,900 sq. ft.
Games: 406 slot and video machines, 31
blackjack tables, 7 crap tables, 4
roulette wheels, 9 baccarat, 2 Pai Gow,
race and sports book, keno lounge, 2
mini-baccarat, Pai Gow poker, 1 Let It
Ride, 1 Caribbean stud

Entertainment:
Crystal Room - 530 seats *(see Pg. 169)*
Show reservations: 733-4566
Starlight Lounge - Entertainment
nightly *(see Pg. 170)*

Dining:
Ho Wan - Far East *(see Pg. 115)*
Terrace Pointe Coffee Shop - 24 hours
Monte Carlo - French *(Mobil 4 star &*

DiRoNA awards) (see Pg. 118)
Portofino - Northern Italian *(see Pg.
123)*

Meeting & Banquet Facilities:
Total Meeting Capacity: 1000
Total Banquet Capacity: 800
Total Space: 30,000 sq. ft.
Total Exhibit Space: 40 8X10 booths
On property catering and special event
staff

Shopping & Services:
Regional tour information
Computer Laser printing
Gift Shop - Gifts, snacks & beverages
Hertz Rent-a-Car
Golf and Tennis Pro Shop
Desert Inn Spa & Fitness Center
The Jewelers
Beauty Shop
Barber Shop

Photo: Phototechnik International

EXCALIBUR

Excalibur Hotel & Casino
3850 Las Vegas Blvd. S.
Las Vegas, NV 89109
597-7777   1-800-937-7777
Fax: 798-3389
Don Givens, VP/Gen. Mgr.
Jim Lewis, Casino Mgr.
Opened June 19, 1990 at a cost of $290 million, as the world's largest hotel/casino at that time, with its two 28-story towers and offering 4,032 rooms, Excalibur is one of the world's most exciting resorts. It is a magical castle, complete with a moat and a fire-breathing dragon, a place that transports its guests to a medieval time when knights fought dragons for damsels in distress and King Arthur ruled the land. One might even catch a glimpse of Merlin the magician as he battles a fierce dragon, shown nightly 7 pm to midnight at the castle moat, summer show will have longer hours. Though Excalibur lost its title as the world's largest hotel/casino to MGM Grand in 1993, it has remained one of the most exciting, being the first to carry its theme throughout the entire resort.

Rooms:
4,008 - two 28 story towers
Rates: $39 - $150

Special Features:
Fantasy Faire - 2 motion simulator theaters, Arcade and midway games for all ages
Medieval Village - Daily 10 am - 10 pm-strolling entertainers, the Court Jester's stage, dozens of retail shops
The Glockenspiel Fairy Tale - Played out over the giant clock at the rear entrance top and bottom of the hour 10 am - 10 pm

Casino:
123,944 sq. ft.
Jim Lewis, Casino Mgr.
Games: 2,484 slot and video machines, 57 blackjack tables, 4 crap tables, 7 roulette wheels, 2 keno lounges, 1 big

wheel, race and sports book, 14 poker tables, 3 Pai Gow poker, 2 mini baccarat, 2 Let It Ride, 2 Caribbean stud, 1 casino War. Non-smoking areas

Entertainment:
King Arthur's Arena: 900 seats
Show Reservations: 597-7600
King Arthur's Tournament - dinner and show. *(see Pg. 169)*
Minstrel's Theatre Lounge - live entertainment *(see Pg. 170)*
Wild Bill's Saloon and Steak House - Two country bands nightly *(see Pg. 171)*
Court Jester's Stage - Free live variety acts beginning 10 am; Entertainment varies from singers to jugglers to magicians; shown every half hour.

Magic Motion Machine - Two 48 seat motion simulator theaters feature a variety of shows. An exciting three minute ride.
Hours: 10 am - midnight; $3.

Dining:
Camelot - Gourmet *(see Pg. 136)*
3 Snack Bars
Lance-A-Lotta Pasta - Italian *(see Pg. 121)*
Round Table Buffet: *(see Pg. 144)*
Breakfast - 6:30 am - 11 am - $4.49
Lunch - Mon. - Fri. 11 am - 4 pm - $5.49
Dinner - Mon. - Fri. 4 pm - 10 pm; Sat. - Sun. 11 am - 11 pm - $6.99
Sherwood Forest Cafe - 24 hour coffee shop

Sir Galahad's - Prime Rib House *(see Pg. 117)*
Wild Bills - Steak, ribs and chicken *(see Pg. 143)*

Meeting & Banquet Facilities:
1-800-811-4316
Total Space: 12,576 sq. ft.

Shopping & Services:
Medieval Village specialty shops
Canterbury Wedding Chapels
Canterbury Gardens
Full-service beauty salon

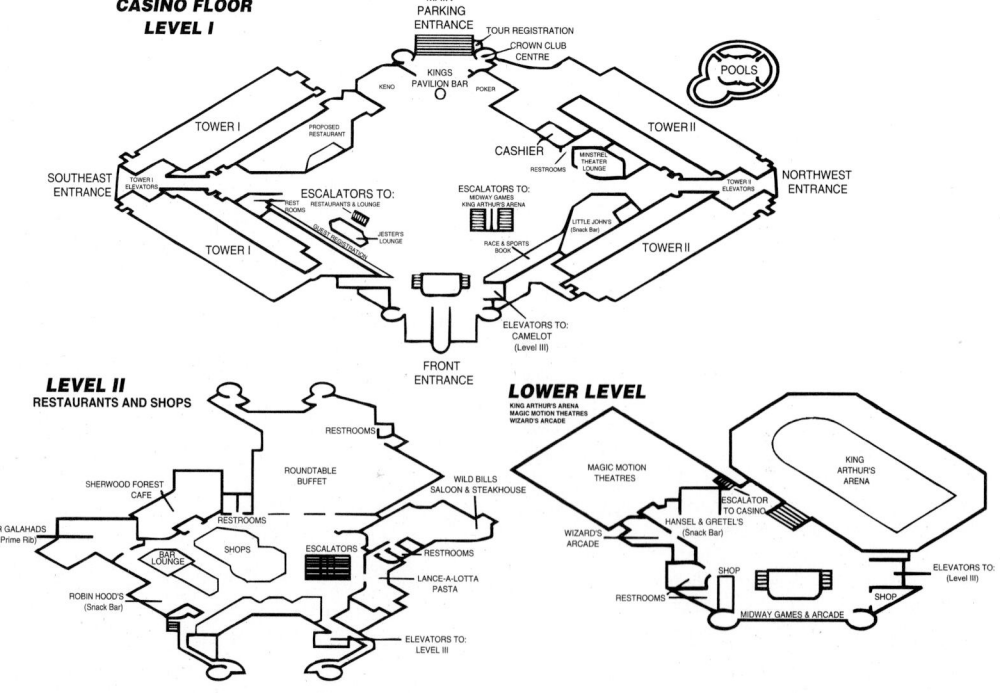

FLAMINGO HILTON

Flamingo Hilton Hotel
3555 Las Vegas Blvd. S.
Las Vegas, NV 89109
733-3111 1-800-732-2111
1-800-HILTONS
Horst Dziura, Pres.
Christopher Crider, VP/Gen. Mgr.
Joe Valella, Hotel Mgr.
Mike Boyle, Sr. VP Casino Operations
The Flamingo was opened by Benjamin "Bugsy" Siegel the day after Christmas, 1946 and was financed by "family" money. The unfinished hotel's opening was attended by movie stars and the wealthy. The first glamorous hotel on the strip, the property is located 6 mi. from downtown. The hotel suffered heavy losses and closed in January of 1947 to finish construction and reopened in March of that year at a cost of $6 million *($5 million over budget)*. Siegel operated the Flamingo until his death by assassins in June. The Flamingo had several different groups of investors until 1967 when Kirk Kerkorian purchased it. Hilton, the present owner, bought it from Kerkorian in 1970 and became the first major hotel chain to enter the gaming market. The hotel completed a $130 million-plus expansion in 1996 that included a sixth tower with 612 rooms. The new Flamingo Hilton offers guests thousands of newly restyled rooms looking out onto a 15 acre Garden of Eden. Meandering pools are secluded by tall palms and jungle-like vegetation in an exclusive tropical paradise. A wildlife habitat features live flamingos and African penguins, the wedding chapel is surrounded by lush foliage and waterfalls, the 550-seat Paradise Garden Buffet with a wide view of the grounds, offers a wide range of dishes to satisfy any palate and meeting and retail space is abundant. Also, on the property is Hilton Grand Vacations, the first timeshare complex to share space at a major Las Vegas hotel. Guests in the 201 luxury units have full access to all Flamingo Hilton facilities.

Rooms:
3,642 including 36 parlor suites and 150 mini-suites
Rates: $69 - $129

Special Features:
Separate check-in and key distribution, a state-of-the-art baggage handling system and a spacious area that seats 600. The tour lobby of the main level of the North Tower is designed to expedite check-in and registration procedures for group arrivals; interpreters available for over 35 languages, video arcade, 5 swimming pools, health club, shopping arcade, 4 tennis courts, babysitting, wheel chairs and Fax machine services.

Casino:
Gaming: 77,000 sq. ft.
Games: 1,950 slot and video machines, 7 crap tables, 8 roulette tables, 46 blackjack tables, 1 keno lounge, 1 big wheel, 2 mini-baccarat, race and sports book, 6 poker tables, Pai Gow poker, 3 Caribbean stud, 2 Let It Ride

Entertainment:
Flamingo Showroom
Reservations: 733-3333
"The Great Radio City Spectacular," starring the Radio City Rockettes - $56 - $71 dinner show including tax and tip, $49 cocktail show includes tax. *(see Pg. 169)*
"Hypno-Odyssey" - Robert Kennzington recreates classic movie scenes and "projecting subjects" thoughts onto large screens. *(see Pg. 168)*
Bugsy's Celebrity Theatre - *"Forever Plaid"* - $21.95 *(see Pg. 167/170)*

Dining:
Alta Villa - Italian *(see Pg. 119)*
Bugsy's Deli - sandwiches and snacks *(see Pg. 156)*
Conrads - Steak & Seafood *(see Pg. 140)*
Flamingo Room - American/Continental *(see Pg. 136)*
Hamada of Japan - Japanese *(see Pg. 125)*
Lindy's Deli - 24 hours *(see Pg. 150)*
Paradise Garden Buffet: *(see Pg. 144)*
Breakfast - 6 am - noon - $6.75
Lunch - noon - 2:30 pm - $7.75
Dinner - 4:30 pm -10 pm - $9.95
Seafood Buffet - Fri. 4:30 pm - 10 pm $9.95
Peking Market - Chinese *(see Pg. 116)*
Pool Grill - light snack and beverage bar - seasonal

Meeting & Banquet Facilities:
733-3211
Total Meeting Capacity: 5,400
Total Banquet Capacity: 2,000
Total Space: 55,000 sq. ft.

Shopping & Services:
Flamingo Gift Shop
Alta Villa Gift Shop
Cafe Flamingo - Exotic coffees and cookies
Flamingo Apparel - Clothing and accessories for women
D'Fitness - Men's Apparel
Alexander's Hair Salon - Full-Service Salon
Kidz Club House - Toys and clothing
Mesa Southwest - Southwest-Flavored gift wear
Ethel M Chocolates
The Jewelers
Dollar Car Rental
Flamingo Tour & Ticket
Flamingo Health Spa
Video Arcade

ACCOMMODATIONS

NEW FRONTIER HOTEL & GAMING HALL

NEW FRONTIER
3120 Las Vegas Blvd. S.
Las Vegas, NV 89109
794-8200 1-800-634-6966
Phil Ruffin, CEO
Darrell Luery, Pres.
Michael Murray, Gen. Mgr.
Paul Lovaas, Casino Mgr.
Opened in 1942 by R. E. Griffith, the Last Frontier was the second hotel to open on the Strip. The hotel was sold in 1951 to the owners of the El Rancho, the first strip hotel. After numerous expansions and a name change to the Frontier in 1955, it eventually closed in 1957 and was leased to "Doc" Bayley, who ran it until his death in 1964. In 1966, the Frontier was demolished to make way for another Frontier. Before opening in 1967, Howard Hughes purchased the property. It was sold once again in 1988 to the Elardi family who in 1997 sold it to Phil Ruffin who changed the name to The New Frontier.

Rooms:
986 including suites *(15 story tower, 7 story bldg. 3 story wing)*
Rates: $39 - $59

Special Features:
Video arcade, two outdoor tennis courts, swimming pool

Casino:
Gaming: 41,325 sq. ft.
Games: 1,105 slot and video machines, 15 blackjack tables, 4 crap tables, 2 roulette wheels, keno lounge, big wheel, race and sports book, 1 Pai Gow poker, 1 Caribbean stud, 1 Let It Ride, bingo, 3 Spanish 21, 100 times odds on craps

Dining:
Margarita's Mexican Cantina
(see Pg. 130)

Michelle's Village Cafe & Buffet:
(see Pg. 145)
Lunch - 11 am - 2 pm - $4.95
Dinner - Mon. - Thu. - 4 pm - 10 pm - $7.95; Sat. - 3 pm - 10 pm - $8.95
Sun. Brunch - 11 am - 10 pm $8.95
Friday Seafood Buffet - 4 pm -10 pm - $10.95
St. Thomas Seafood Grotto - *(see Pg. 139)*

Shopping & Services:
Hair Salon
Airline Ticket Center
Gift Shop
Flower Shop

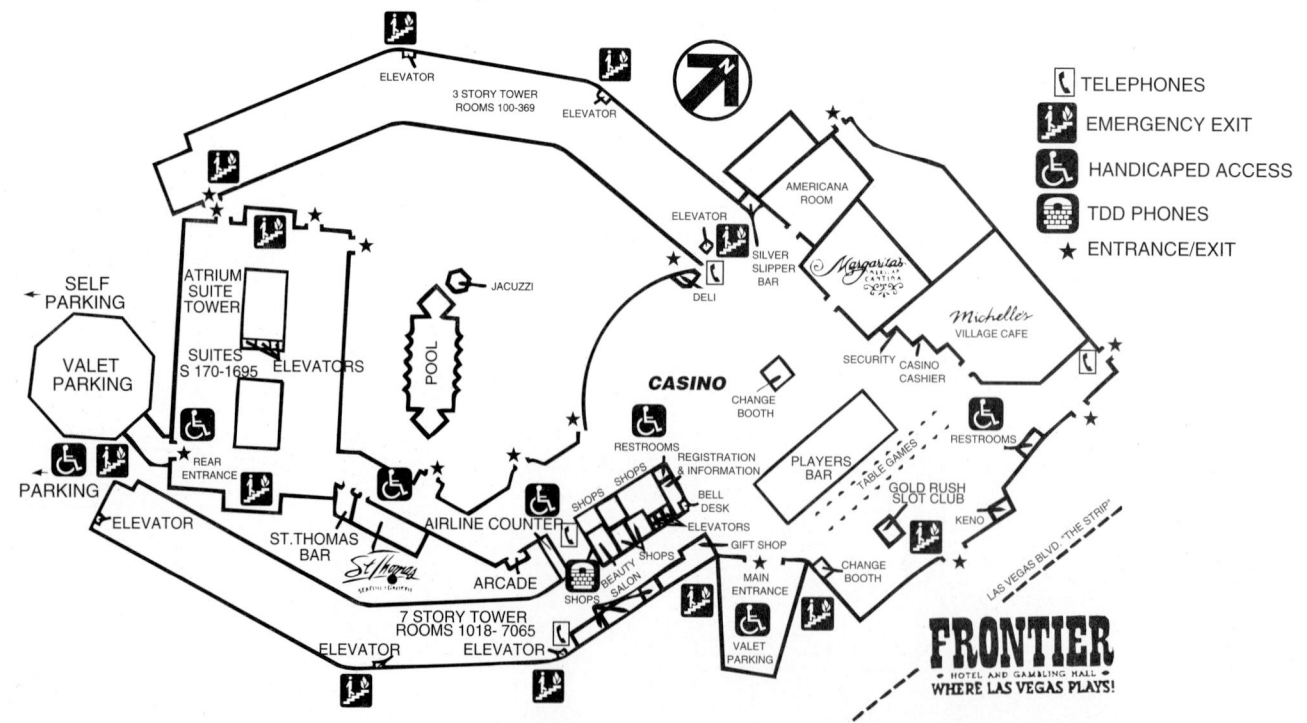

Photo: Photolechnik International

GOLD COAST

Gold Coast
4000 W. Flamingo Rd.
Las Vegas, NV 89103
367-7111 1-800-331-5334
Michael Gaughan, Chairman of the Board/CEO
Mike Growney, VP/Gen. Mgr.
Steve Carpenter, Hotel Mgr.
Alan Scano, Casino Mgr.

The Gold Coast opened in 1986 featuring Spanish architecture with intricate tile work and unusual stained glass windows and was an immediate success. The complex underwent major renovations in 1988, at which time the facility doubled its original size, adding to it a second full service casino, shops, restaurants and a 72-lane bowling center. Further additions in 1990 included a 450 room tower.

Rooms:
750 including 34 suites (10 story tower)
Rates: $40 - $55

Special Features:
Two lounges, 72-lane bowling center and pro shop, twin theaters, dance-hall/showroom, free-style swimming pool and spa.

Casino:
Gaming: 71,000 sq. ft.
Games: 2,087 slot and video machines, 6 crap tables, 3 roulette wheels, 31 blackjack tables, keno lounge, 700 seat bingo parlor - sessions 8 am - 2 am on even hours, 3 mini-baccarat, race and sports book, 5 Pai Gow poker, 1 Let It Ride

Entertainment:
East Lounge - Entertainment Mon. - Fri. - noon - 3 pm - Tue. - Sun. 9 pm -

3 am *(see Pg. 170)*
West Lounge - Karaoke nightly 8 pm - 1 am *(see Pg. 170)*
Dance Hall & Saloon - Dancing to big band sound on Sun. 1 pm - 5 pm and Tue. 7:30 pm - 11:30 pm, Latin music on Fri. and Sat. 11:30 pm - 3 am. Special shows are presented throughout the year in the ballroom. *(see Pg. 171/172)*
Twin Movie Theaters - featuring first run movies in THX Dolby digital sound.

Dining:
The Buffet: *(see Pg. 144)*
Breakfast - Mon. - Sat. 7 am - 10:30 pm - $3.45
Lunch - Mon. - Sat. 11 am - 3 pm - $4.95
Dinner - 4 pm - 10 pm - $6.95
Seafood - Wed. 4 pm - 10 pm $9.95
Sunday Brunch - 8 am - 3 pm - $6.95
Cortez Room - Steak and seafood *(see Pg. 140)*

Kate's Korner - Ice cream parlor
Mediterranean Room - Seafood and Italian *(see Pg. 121)*
Monterey Room - American and Chinese - 24 hours *(see Pg. 150)*
Terrible Mike's - Hamburgers
Bowling Center Snack Bar

Meeting & Banquet Facilities:
Total Meeting Capacity: 1,000
Total Banquet Capacity: 650
Total Space: 10,000 sq. ft.

Shopping & Services:
Barber Shop - 367-0048
Beauty Shop - 367-7073
Cole Travel Service
American Express Office
Gift Shop
Video Arcade
Terrible's Wine & Spirits

GOLDEN NUGGET

**Golden Nugget
Hotel & Casino**
129 Fremont St.
Las Vegas, NV 89101
385-7111 1-800-634-3454
Steve Wynn, Chairman

Robert Sheldon, Pres.
Richard Amalfitano, VP Casino Operations
The Golden Nugget Casino opened in 1946 and houses the largest single gold nugget in the world, *"The Hand of Faith,"* weighing a massive 61 pounds 11 ounces along with another nugget weighing in at 13 pounds and some 26 other smaller gold pieces. Rooms were not added to the casino until 1977. Present majority owner Steve Wynn purchased stock in the casino and eventually took controlling interest in 1972. Although the Golden Nugget recently underwent a $22 million renovation and expansion, the original Victorian design of the casino has remained intact for more than half a century. The lobby features beveled glass, mirrors, brass and imported marble floors. Tall palm trees, exotic sculptures and a computerized misting system now surround the entire pool and spa area, creating a cool, tropical atmosphere.

Rooms:
1,907 including one and two-bedroom suites, 27 luxury apartments and six penthouse suites
Rates: $59 - $169

Special Features:
Olympic-size heated pool/Jacuzzi, foreign language assistance, transfer arrangements, fitness center, travel arrangements, men's and women's spas with whirlpools, beauty salon, golf and tennis arrangements

Casino:
Gaming: 39,040 sq. ft.
Games: 1,323 slot and video machines, 35 blackjack tables, 7 crap tables, 3 roulette wheels, 2 keno lounges, 1 wheel of fortune, baccarat, mini-baccarat, race and sports book, 3 Pai Gow poker, 2 Caribbean stud, 2 Let It Ride, 1 Pai Gow, 2 Spanish 21

Entertainment:
The Lounge - Live music nightly *(see Pg. 170)*

Dining:
The Buffet: *(see Pg. 144)*
Breakfast - Mon. - Sat. 7:30 am - 10:30 am - $5.75
Lunch - Mon. - Sat. 10:30 am - 3 pm - $7.50
Dinner - Mon. - Sat. - 4 pm - 10 pm - $10.25
Sunday Champagne Brunch - 8 am - 10 pm - $10.95
California Pizza Kitchen *(see Pg. 120)*
Carson Street Cafe - 24 hr. coffee shop *(see Pg. 150)*
Lillie Langtry - Chinese *(see Pg. 116)*
Stefano's - Northern Italian *(see Pg. 124)*
Snack Bar

Meeting & Banquet Facilities:
Total Meeting Capacity: 1,966
Total Banquet Capacity: 1,390
Total Space: 25,900 sq. ft.

Shopping & Services:
Spa and Fitness Center
Beauty Salon
Gift Shop - Ready-to-wear merchandise, souvenirs, sundries
Gift Boutique - Jewelry and clothing

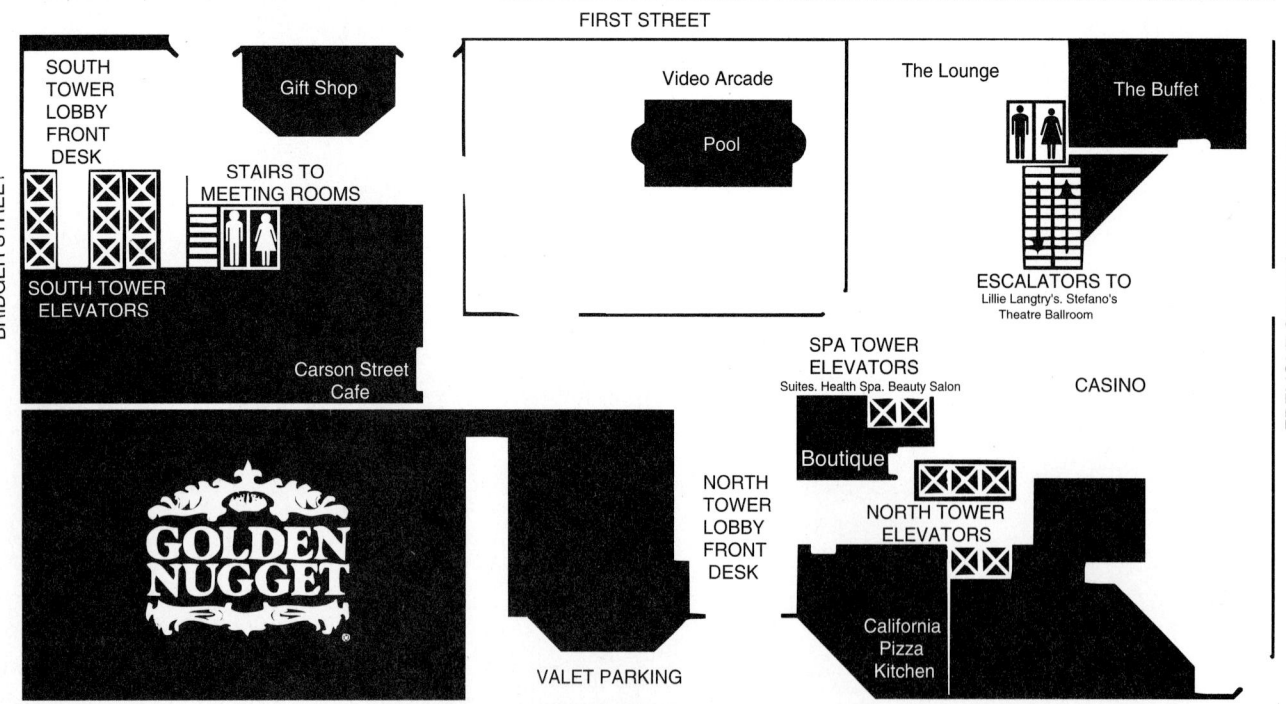

HARD ROCK HOTEL/CASINO

Hard Rock Hotel/Casino
4455 Paradise Rd.
Las Vegas, NV 89109
693-5000 1-800-HRD-ROCK
(1-800-473-7625)
Fax: 693-5010
Web site: www.hardrock.com
Gary R. Selesner, VP/Gen. Mgr.
Diane Boles, Hotel Mgr.
Willie Stephens, Dir. Casino Operations
The Hard Rock Hotel opened in March, 1995 creating the world's first rock 'n roll hotel to offer Las Vegas facilities to a new generation of people. In true Hard Rock tradition, the casino displays the greatest rock 'n roll memorabilia, a $2 million rare collection. The hotel collection features Elvis' jumpsuit, Harley Davidsons from Guns and Roses and Motley Crue, guitars from ZZ Top, Van Halen, Aerosmith and others, leather jackets from Tommy Lee Jones, the Scorpions, Iggy Pop, concert outfits and video costumes from artists like Madonna, Prince and Courtney Love, a vast collection of gold and platinum records from recording artists like David Bowie, The Beatles, Ziggy Marley, Billy Joel and Stone Temple Pilots and Elton John's piano. Nonstop rock music from Led Zeppelin to James Brown to REM is played throughout the entire property. The pool area has a sandy beach with music piped underwater, the slot machines have guitar necks for handles and the gaming chips have Jimi Hendrix on them.

Each guest to the hotel takes part in the casino's "Save The Planet" campaign in various ways. The hotel recycles glass and aluminum, steel, paper and cardboard. The housekeeping staff uses only non-toxic, biodegradable cleaning products and in order to conserve water, all rooms are equipped with low-flow toilets and all public facilities are installed with automatic shut off valves.

In addition to its other many features the Hotel also has an Electronic tote board that ticks away in seconds, the acres of remaining rainforests while displaying the earth's population as it grows. These signs are meant to make people aware of our decreasing natural resources.

The hotel is also completely wheelchair accessible and disabled rooms are available upon request.

Rooms:
340 including 28 suites *(11 story tower)*
Rates: Sun. - Thu. $75 - $250; Fri. - Sat. $135-$300; suites from $250; rooms are available for occupancy after 3 pm

Special Features:
Hard Rock Athletic Club, Hard Rock Beach Club with Tropical sand-bottom pool, two beaches, water slide, piped-in underwater music system, two whirlpools, and the only swirling Coriolis *(a tide pool that whisks swimmers around the pool's perimeter)* in Las Vegas, Baby Rock - Hard Rock Arcade featuring the latest games and a big-screen TV for viewing pleasure; complimentary Strip shuttle service and baby sitting service.

Casino:
Gaming: 28,000 sq. ft.
Games: 741 slot and video machines, *(250 feature Fender guitar handles as arms while others direct their returns to saving the rainforests and benefit various environmental organizations, making the casino the first ever to allow guests and gamblers the oppor-* *tunity to help "Save the Planet")*, 4 crap tables, 3 roulette wheels, 38 blackjack tables, 1 mini-baccarat, race and sports book, 1 Caribbean stud, 1 Pai Gow poker, 1 Let It Ride, big six wheel

Entertainment:
Show Reservations: 693-5066
The Joint - Attracts big-name performers, ticket prices are more in line with rock concerts than with headliner showroom fees. *(see Pg. 169)*
Viva Las Vegas Lounge

Dining:
Mr. Lucky's 24/7 - 24 hour coffee shop *(see Pg. 150)*
Mortoni's - Italian *(see Pg. 121)*

Shopping & Services:
Hard Rock Box Office
Sundry Shop
Hard Rock Retail Store

HARRAH'S

Harrah's
3475 Las Vegas Blvd. S.
Las Vegas, NV 89109
369-5000   1-800-634-6765
Fax: 369-5500
Website - http://harrahs.lv.com
Philip Satre, CEO
Hector Mon, Pres. Harrah's Nevada
Thom Hall, Sr. Vice Pres./Gen. Mgr.
Pat Kearns, VP of Casino Operations.
In 1972 the Holiday Inn Center Strip opened. The property, known then as the Holiday Casino, opened in 1973 by Claudine and Shelby Williams, with a Riverboat theme. Holiday Inn bought 40 percent of the casino in 1979 and the remaining 60 percent in 1983. Holiday Inn purchased the Harrah's Corporation in 1980. Holiday Corp. sold off Holiday Inns but It wasn't until April 1, 1992, that they changed the name to Harrah's. Now, just over five years and $200 million in renovations and expansions later, the new Harrah's boasts the "Great Carnivals of the World" theme, reminiscent of the Carnivale in Venice, Carnaval in Brazil, Mardi Gras in New Orleans and America's traveling carnival heritage, the new design also pays tribute to the fabulous Las Vegas entertainment legacy.

The focal point of the property's exterior features baroque-styled architecture with whimsical accents and a dramatic facade adorned with dark glass, while the carnival court, Harrah's entertainment oriented plaza, features a maypole structure complete with streamers, lights and a diaphanous tent-like cover as its center point on the Las Vegas Strip entrance of the property. Music and strolling entertainers add to the festive atmosphere.

Harrah's also features a 30 X 90 ft. mural paying tribute to the greatest Las Vegas entertainers of all time and with no exception, includes the Harrah's showgirl. The mural is the largest of its kind in all of the United States.

Rooms:
2,699 including 108 suites *(35 story towers)*
Rates: $89 - $169

Special Features:
Swimming pool/Jacuzzi, health club, arcade

Casino:
Gaming: 103,325 sq. ft.
Games: 2,200 slot and video machines, 51 blackjack tables, 8 crap tables, 8 roulette wheels, 2 keno lounges, 4 mini-baccarat, race and sports book, red dog, 8 poker tables, 4 Pai Gow poker, 3 Caribbean stud, 4 Let It Ride, 2 casino War games

Entertainment:
Show Reservations:
369-5222

Commander's Theatre - *"Spellbound"* - $34.95 per person, includes one drink *(see Pg. 168)*
The Improv - Comedy - $14.95 *(see Pg. 168)*
La Playa Lounge - Las Vegas' only indoor/outdoor lounge has the appearance of being straight from Rio de Janeiro and offers live entertainment and a nine-screen wall of video nightly

Dining:
Garden Cafe - 24 hour coffee shop *(see Pg. 158)*
Club Cappucchino - coffee and donuts
Asia - Chinese/Asian *(see Pg. 113)*
Andreotti's - Italian *(see Pg. 120)*
The Range - Steak House *(see Pg. 141)*
Fresh Market Square Buffet: *(see Pg. 144)*
Breakfast - 7 am -11 am - $6.99
Lunch - 11:30 am - 3:30 pm - $8.99
Dinner - 4 pm -10 pm - $11.99

Meeting & Banquet Facilities:
369-5138
Total Meeting Capacity: 1,905
Total Banquet Capacity: 1,411

Shopping & Services:
Carnaval Corner - Unique variety of "to go" food items, pastries, sandwiches, cigar humidor, liquors and microbrews and cappuccino counter
On Stage - Music and video store
Jackpot - Logo and star merchandise store
The Art of Gaming - Variety of eclectic art pieces
Ghirardelli's Old Fashioned Chocolate Shop
Tower of Jewels

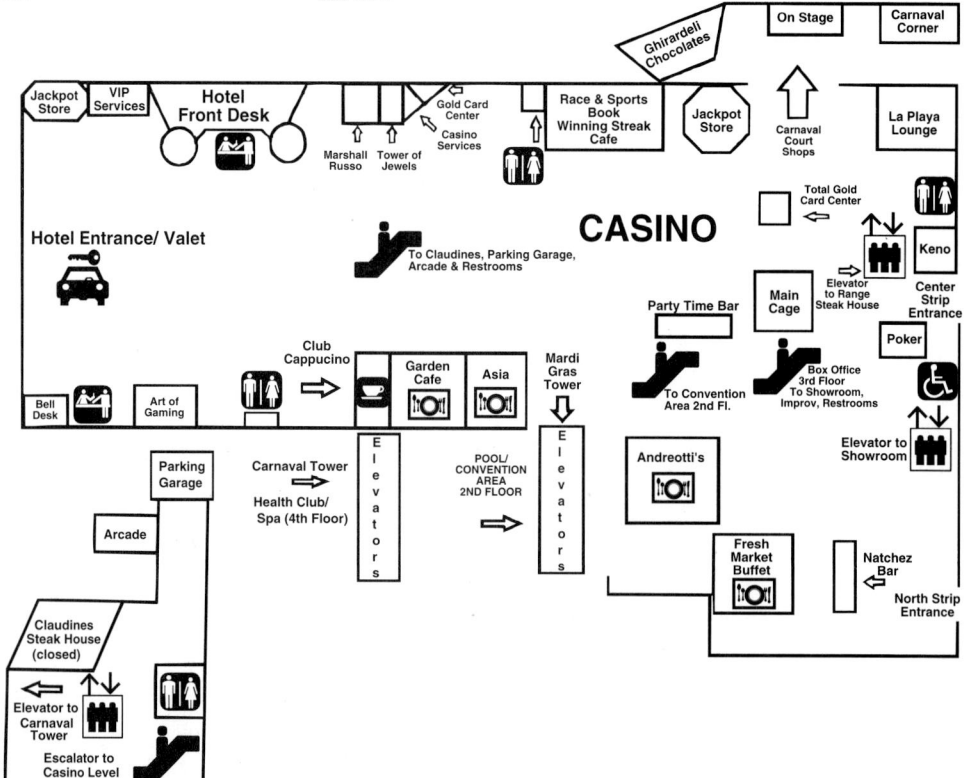

PROMENADE 2ND LEVEL

IMPERIAL PALACE

Imperial Palace
Hotel & Casino
3535 Las Vegas Blvd. S.
Las Vegas, NV 89109
731-3311 1-800-634-6441
FAX: 735-8328
Ralph Engelstad, Pres.
Ed Crispell, Gen. Mgr.
John Zabrosky, Casino Mgr.

The eleventh largest hotel in the world, the Imperial Palace is the largest privately owned hotel. Influenced by Japanese temple architecture, the beautiful Imperial Palace opened its doors on November 1, 1979. The Oriental theme is carried throughout the hotel with the food service, decor and employee uniforms. In the casino area, carved dragons and wind-chime chandeliers offer a traditional Asian atmosphere.

The Imperial Palace staff includes approximately 13% handicapped individuals which has sparked numerous awards and recognition, the highest of which was in 1991 when they were named Employer of the Year by the Pres.'s Committee on Employment of People with Disabilities. In March of 1993, the Imperial Palace also achieved another first with the opening of the Resort Medical Center, an independent 24-hour medical facility serving hotel employees, their families, Imperial Palace and other Las Vegas strip hotel guests. The Imperial Palace also hosts an annual Christmas party for Senior Citizens which provides low-income seniors and non-ambulatory convalescent center residents with a complimentary holiday dinner and show.

Rooms:
2,700 with 225 suites *(19 story tower)* including handicapped and non-smoking rooms

Rates: $49 - $250 with packages available

Special Features:
Auto Collection, Men's and Women's health clubs, Olympic-size pool with waterfall and heated spa, tour booth

Casino:
Gaming: 75,000 sq. ft.
Games: 1,844 slot and video machines, 26 blackjack tables, 4 crap tables, 1 mini-crap, 3 roulette tables, keno lounge, big wheel, mini-baccarat, race and sports book, 2 Pai Gow poker, 3 Let It Ride, 2 Caribbean stud

Entertainment:
Show Reservations - 794-3261
Imperial Theater Showroom - *"Legends in Concert"*- $29.50; children under 12 half price *(see Pg. 165)*
"Hawaiian Hot Luau Imperial Style" seasonal, Tue. and Thu.; seating beginning at 6:30 pm - $24.95; Polynesian

Buffet & Review *(Las Vegas' only poolside luau)* located at the Shangri-La Pool Area - *(May-Oct.) (see Pg. 169)*
Auto Collection - Over 200 antique, classic and special interest vehicles are on display 9:30 am - 11:30 pm
Duesenberg Lounge
Nomiya Lounge

Dining:
Show/Dinner Reservations: 794-3261
Betty's Diner
Burger Palace - Fast food
Embers - Steak & seafood *(see Pg. 141)*
Emperor's Buffet: *(see Pg. 144)*
Breakfast - 7 am - 11:30 am - $4.99
Lunch - 11:30 am - 4 pm - $5.99
Dinner - 5 pm - 10 pm - $6.99
Imperial Buffet (in Teahouse):
(see Pg. 144)
Brunch - 7 am - 2 pm - $5.95
Dinner - 5 pm - 10 pm $7.95
Champagne Brunch - Sat., Sun., and holidays - 8 am - 3:00 pm - $6.95
Ming Terrace - Cantonese/Mandarin *(see Pg. 116)*
Pizza Palace - Italian *(see Pg. 123)*
Rib House *(see Pg. 134)*
The Seahouse - Seafood *(see Pg. 139)*
Teahouse - 24 hour coffee shop *(see Pg. 150)*

Meeting & Banquet Facilities:
Total Space: 9,600 sq. ft.
Total Meeting Capacity: 960
Total Banquet capacity: 650

Shopping & Services
"We've Only Just Begun" Wedding Chapel
Resort Medical Center
Unisex Hair Salon
Health and Fitness Center
Laundry Service
Foreign Currency Exchange
Travel Agency
Video Arcade
Gift Shops
Shopping Promenade

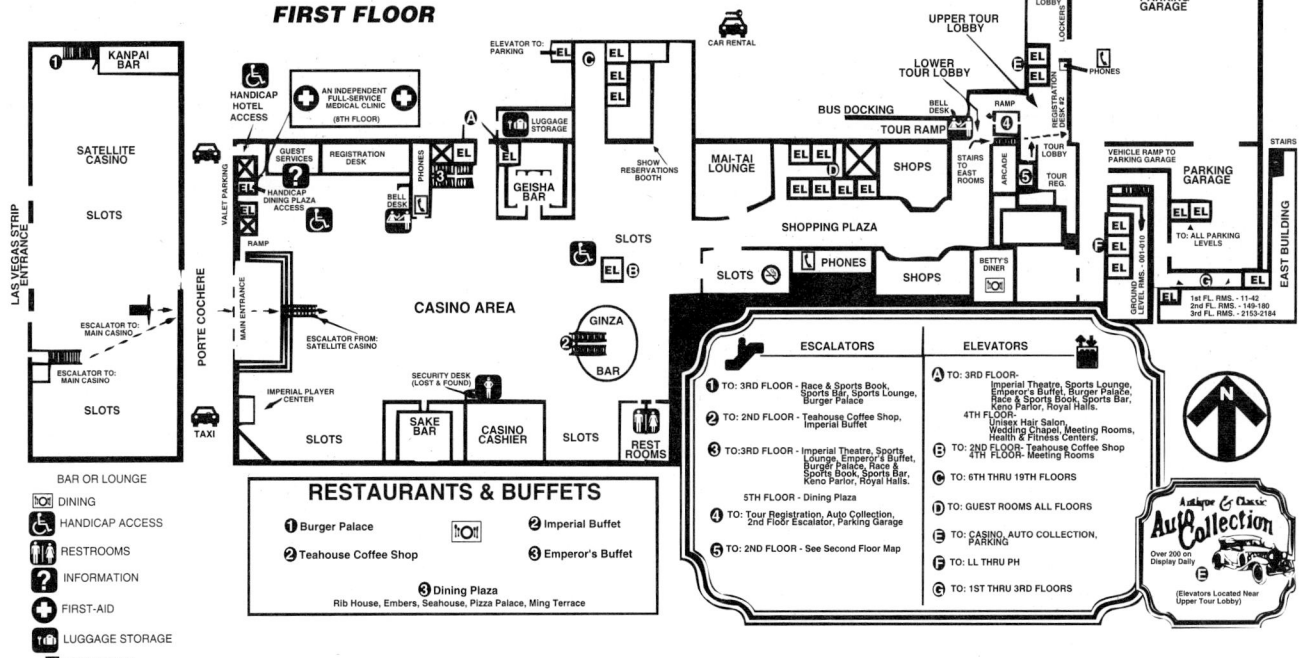

Photo: Photechnik International

LAS VEGAS HILTON

Las Vegas Hilton
3000 Paradise Rd.
Las Vegas, NV 89109
732-5111 1-800-732-7117
Fax: 732-5834
Dean Harrold, Pres.
Mark Rittorno, VP/Gen. Mgr.
Jon Jaggers, Sr. VP of Casino Operations

Billionaire Kirk Kerkorian built the resort through the International Leisure Corporation at a cost of $60 million. Opening as the International on July 2, 1969 with 1,519 rooms, Barbra Streisand appeared in the showroom. Also appearing during opening month was Elvis Presley who would go on to perform there for more than seven years and 800 engagements. The original hotel featured a total of three theaters, including Las Vegas' first legitimate theater, now the home of the resorts Benihana Village, six restaurants and 75,000 sq. ft. of convention space. In 1971 Kerkorian sold his interest in the International, which was then renamed the Las Vegas Hilton. While the history of entertainment has always been notable at the Las Vegas Hilton, the resort continues to make history today with the opening of Star Trek: The Experience™. This new venture between Paramount Parks and the Las Vegas Hilton opened January 1998 and includes everything from the Enterprise Bridge to the Quark Bar and promises to "Boldly go" where no entertainment experience has gone before.

Rooms:
3,174 including 278 suites
(30 story towers)
Rates: $89 - $259

Special Features:
Third floor, 8-acre outdoor roof-top Recreation Deck - swimming pool, 24-seat Jacuzzi spa, 6 lighted championship outdoor tennis courts with pro on call, 9-hole putting green, table tennis and the 17,000 sq. ft. Las Vegas Hilton Health Spa, complete with a full-range of exercise equipment, saunas, massage rooms and tanning beds and

Garden Snack Bar - Open 7 am - 8 pm - 732-5648
Las Vegas Hilton Country Club - provides preferred tee times to guests at its five lake, par 71, 6,815 yard golf course; Video Arcade

Casino:
Gaming: 105,500 sq. ft.
Games: 1,200 slot and poker machines, 37 blackjack tables, 7 crap tables, 6 roulette wheels, keno lounge, wheel of fortune, 6 baccarat, 1 Pai Gow poker, 2 Caribbean stud, 2 Let It Ride, 2 Pai Gow and race and sports Superbook®.

Entertainment:
Show Reservations: 732-5755
Hilton Theatre - top name performers *(see Pg. 170)*
The Nightclub - High-tech theatre and dance club *(see Pg. 171)*
Star Trek: The Experience™ - Takes guests on a warp-speed voyage through space. Includes themed shopping and dining plus a chance to become part of the Star Trek adventure. Guests entering the "SpaceQuest Casino" *(gateway to "The Experience")*, step aboard a simulated space station with three space windows creating the illusion of a passage around the globe, from sunrise to sunset. Unique offerings at the 24th century casino include SpaceQuest bonus poker and Galactic Quarters, introducing unusual twists to old favorites. The actual "Experience" is a 22 minute production which starts as a 24th century kidnapping of 27 guests by a group of hostile Klingons who then beam them aboard the bridge of the Starship Enterprise. The kidnapping ends with a 4 minute motion simulator ride. The cost is $9.95 and you must be at least 42 inches tall.

Dining:
Andiamo - Italian & Mediterranean *(see Pg. 119)*
Barronshire - Prime Rib *(see Pg. 117)*

Benihana Village - Hibachi & Benihana Seafood Grille *(see Pg. 125)*
Bistro Le Montrachet - gourmet French *(see Pg. 118)*
Buffet of Champions: *(see Pg. 144)*
Breakfast - Mon. - Fri. 7 am - 10 am - $7.99
Lunch - Mon. - Fri. 11 am - 2:30 pm - $8.99
Dinner - 5 pm - 10 pm - $12.99
Champagne Brunch - Sat. - Sun. - 8 am - 2:30 pm - $11.99
The Coffee Shop - 24 hour *(see Pg. 151)*
Garden of the Dragon - Chinese *(see Pg. 115)*
The Hilton Steak House *(see Pg. 141)*
Margarita Grille - Mexican *(see Pg. 130)*
Paddock Snack Bar - sandwiches
Quark's Bar & Restaurant - Intergalactic delicacies inside Star Trek: The Experience™
Perk Place - Gourmet Coffee and more

Meeting & Banquet Facilities:
732-5631
Total Meeting Capacity: 19,945
Total Banquet Capacity: 14,515
Total Space: 218,520 sq. ft.

Shopping & Services:
2 Shopping Promenades
Avis Rent-a-Car
Barber Shop & Beauty Salon
Convention Business Service
Empire Travel Agency
2 Gift Shops
Gourmet Shop
Arcade
Hilton Grand Vacations

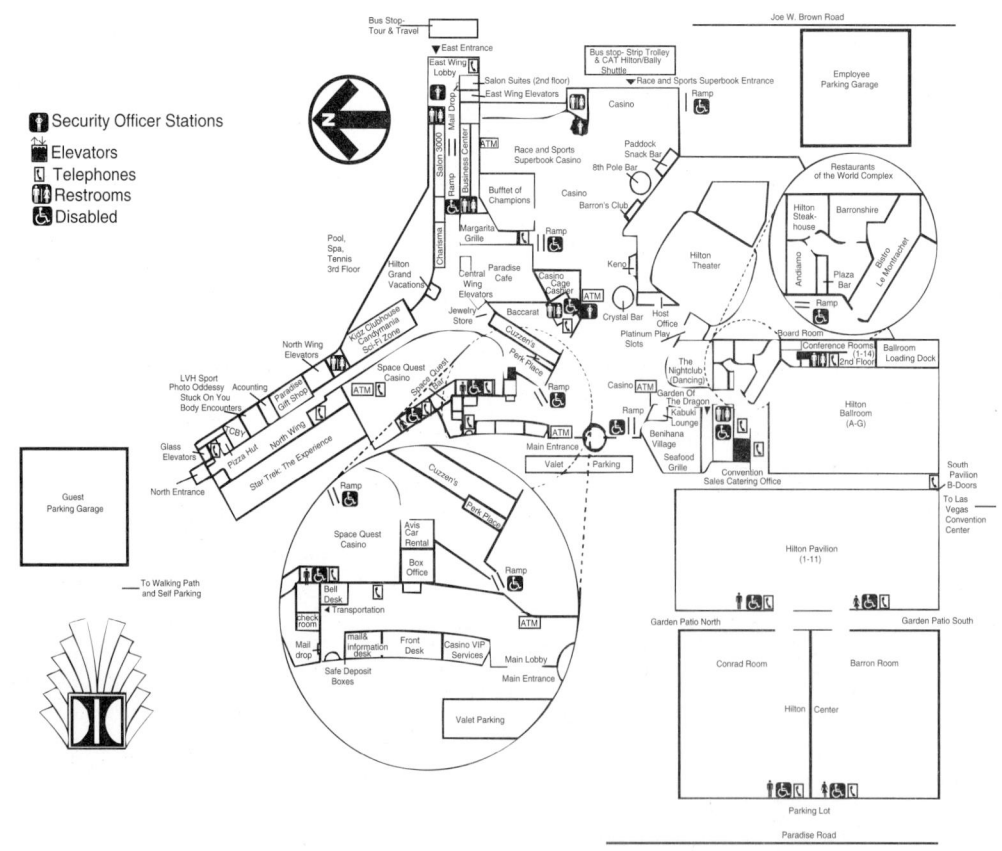

Photo: Photochnik International

LUXOR HOTEL/CASINO

Ra - Nightclub *(see Pg. 171)*
IMAX® 3D theater - Guests experience amazing state of the art film technology in a series of participatory high impact adventures. Two shows play continuously throughout the day and currently include "Super Speedway" and "Into the Deep."

Dining:
Isis - Continental *(see Pg. 136)*
Pharaoh's Pheast: *(see Pg. 144)*
Breakfast - 7 am -11:30 am - $5.99
Lunch - 11:30 am - 4 pm - $6.99
Dinner - 4 pm - 11 pm - $7.99
Millennium's - Cafe *(see Pg. 151)*
Papyrus - Polynesian-themed *(see Pg. 116)*
Pyramid Cafe - 24 hour coffee shop *(see Pg. 151)*
The Sacred Sea Room - Seafood *(see Pg. 139)*
Luxor Steak House
Nile Deli *(see Pg. 156)*

Meeting & Banquet Facilities:
Total Meeting Capacity: 1,168
Total Banquet Capacity: 2,000
Total Space: 19,933 sq. ft.

Shopping & Services:
Dollar Rent A Car
The Logo Shop
The Scarab Shop
Park Avenue Shop
Sobek's Sundries
Innerspace
Pharaoh's Photos
Spirits of the Nile
Giza Galleria - an additional nine outlets including: Treasure Chamber, Dandera's, Jewel of The Nile, Exclusivo, Tie and Sock Shop, Tiny Tut's, Ice Cream and Candy and The Vegas Store.

Luxor Hotel/Casino
3900 Las Vegas Blvd. S.
Las Vegas, NV 89119
262-4000   1-800-288-1000
Vince Matthews, VP/Gen. Mgr.
Michael Starr, Dir. of Hotel Operations
Tom Robinson, Casino Mgr.
Luxor is named after Upper Egypt's most exotic tourist destination. Ground breaking started on the Luxor in April, 1992 and the hotel opened October 15, 1993. Luxor was completed at a cost of $375 million. Another property of the highly successful Circus Circus Enterprises, the Luxor is a 30 story, bronze reflective pyramid housing the world's largest atrium, capable of housing 9 Boeing 747 airplanes comfortably. A $240 million expansion project in 1996 added 1,970 rooms in two towers. The expansion also included two new restaurants, a wedding chapel, spa, convention space and a 1,500-seat showroom.

Rooms:
4407 including 440 suites.
Rates: $49 - $249

Special Features:
"Beam of Light" shines straight from the top of the pyramid, at 40 billion times the candle power of a strong searchlight, elevators to the rooms travel at a 39-degree angle at each corner of the pyramid, worlds largest atrium soars to the apex of the pyramid 30 stories high, 10-story sphinx at front entrance, Oasis Pool and Spa with hot whirlpool, steam bath, Dry Sauna and complete fitness center, Sega VirtuaLand Arcade

Casino:
Gaming: 100,000 sq. ft. casino
Games: 2,150 slot and video machines, 69 blackjack tables, 8 crap tables, 10 roulette wheels, 3 keno lounges, 1 big wheel, 3 mini-baccarat, 3 Pai Gow poker, 8 poker tables, state-of-the-art race and sports book, baccarat, 1 Pai Gow, 2 Caribbean stud

Entertainment:
Show Reservations: 262-4400
"Imagine, A Theatrical Odyssey" - $39.95 *(see Pg. 165)*
Nefertiti's Lounge - Live music nightly *(see Pg. 170)*
Nile Bar

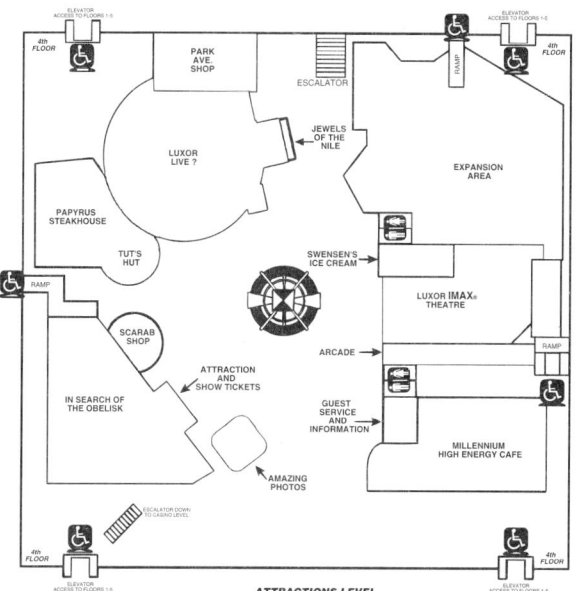

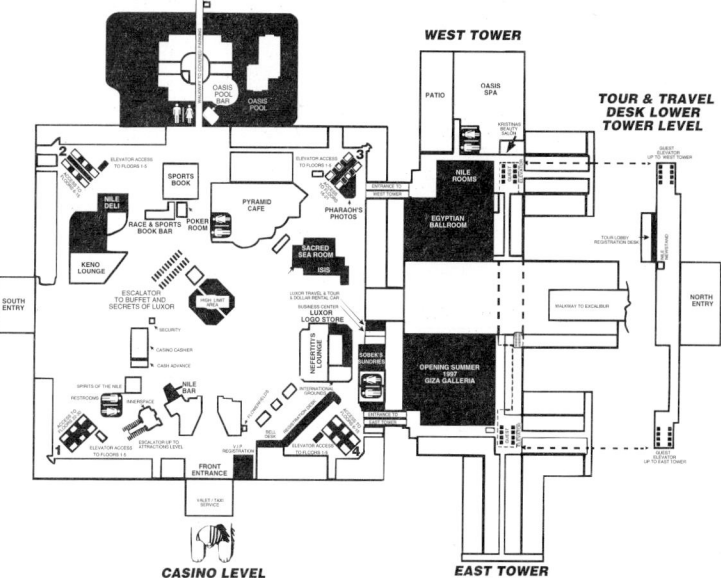

MGM GRAND

Dining:
Mark Miller's Coyote Cafe - Mexican *(see Pg. 130)*
Dragon Court - Chinese *(see Pg. 114)*
Emeril Lagasse's New Orleans Fish House - Seafood *(see Pg. 118)*
Gatsby's - French Gourmet *(see Pg. 118)*
Oz Buffet: *(see Pg. 145)*
Brunch - 7:30 am - 2:30 pm - $7.25; children under 10 $2.99
Dinner - 4:30 pm - 10 pm - $9.95; children under 10 $4.99
Grand Champagne Brunch - Sun. 9 am - 10 am - $19.95; 10 am - 2 pm - $28.95; children 12 and under 9 am - 10 am - $8.95; 10 am - 2 pm $9.95 under 5 free
The Brown Derby - Steakhouse *(see Pg. 140)*
Tre Visi Cafe *(see Pg. 124)*
La Scala *(see Pg. 136)*
Stage Deli Express *(see Pg. 157)*
Studio Cafe - 24 hour coffee shop *(see Pg. 151)*
Wolfgang Puck Cafe *(see Pg. 124)*
Food Court: McDonald's, Hamada Express, Nathan's, Mamma Ilardo's and Haagan Dazs.

Meeting & Banquet Facilities:
Total Meeting Capacity: 2,935
Total Banquet Capacity: 2,110
Total Space: 122,500 sq. ft.

Shopping & Services:
Star Lane Shops
Wedding Chapel
MGM Grand & Co.
Front Page
MGM Grand Adventures Store
Emerald City Gift Shop
Grand Spa Shop
Marshall Rousso Men's & Ladies Shop
Kenneth J. Lane Jewelry
Grand Spirits
EFX
Sport Shop

MGM Grand Hotel/Casino
3799 Las Vegas Blvd. S.
Las Vegas, NV 89109
891-1111   1-800-929-1111
Website: http://mgmgrand.com
Terrance Lanni, CEO
Daniel Wade, Pres.
Lyn Baxter, Sr. VP Casino Operations
The MGM Grand opened December 18, 1993, about 3 1/2 months ahead of schedule at a total cost of $1 billion. The brainchild of Kirk Kerkorian, majority shareholder of MGM Grand Inc., the first MGM, now Bally's, was built in 1973. Four 30-story emerald green towers soar 280 feet into the sky creating the largest hotel/casino in the world.

Rooms:
5,005 rooms including 751 suites.
Rates: $69 - $329

Special Features:
Grand Spa Resort and beach front pool, seven acres, Youth Center with professionally trained youth counselors for children ages 3 - 12, MGM Grand Adventures Theme Park - outdoor entertainment complex featuring rides, shows, themed streets, entertainment, restaurants and retail shops. *(See Children's section for additional information)*, 11,400 sq. ft. Oz midway and arcade, Four lighted tennis courts (closed until Sept.), monorail to Bally's

Casino:
171,500 sq. ft. in four theme casinos, each with unique decor - City of Entertainment, Hollywood, Grand and Sports.
Gaming: 171,500 sq. ft.
Games: 3,700 slot and video machines, 76 blackjack tables, 15 crap tables, 17 roulette wheels, 1 keno lounge, 2 big wheel, 9 mini-baccarat, 9 baccarat, state-of-the-art race and sports book, 20 poker tables, 4 Caribbean stud, 2 Pai Gow, 6 Pai Gow poker, 3 Let It Ride, 2 casino War, 1 Spanish 21

Entertainment:
Show Reservations: 891-7777
Grand Theatre:
"EFX" - starring David Cassidy - $45 - $63.64; children ages 5 - 12 $35; includes tax, gratuity and drink. *(see Pg. 165)*
Hollywood Theatre: Headline entertainers *(see Pg. 170)*
MGM Grand Garden Arena: 15,200 seats - concerts and sporting events. The Grand Garden Arena is also used for conventions and trade shows.
Center Stage Cabaret - *"Catch a Rising Star"* - $14 per person *(see Pg. 168)*
Turf Club Lounge - Live entertainment
Flying Monkey Bar - Live entertainment *(see Pg. 170)*
Betty Boop Bar - Live entertainment
Studio 54 - Night club *(see Pg. 171)*

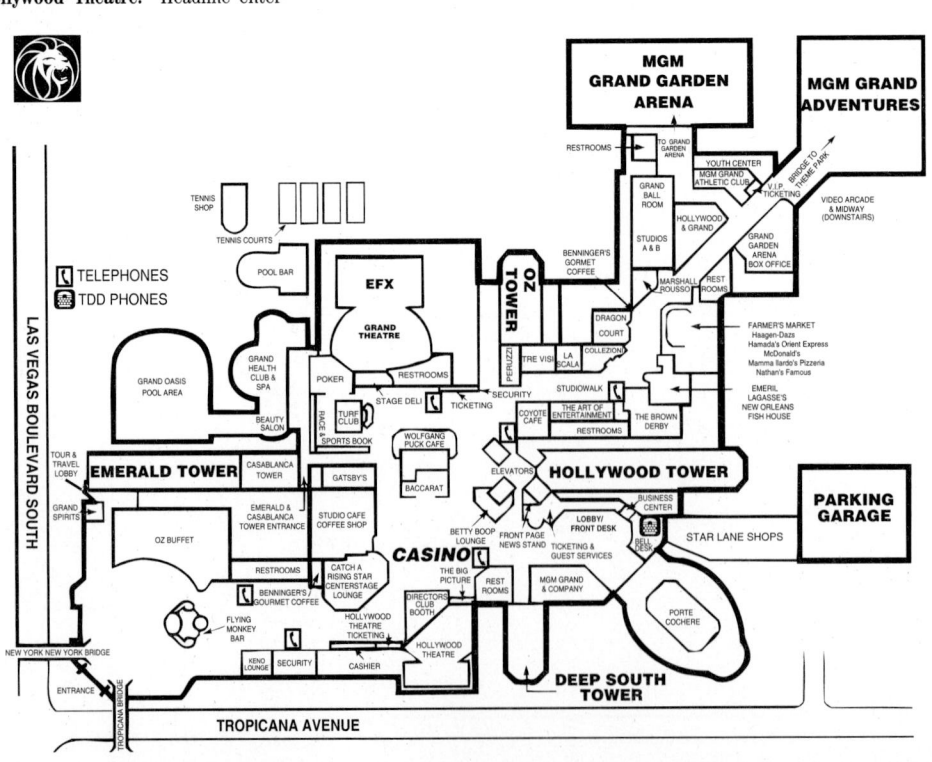

THE MIRAGE

Dining:
Restaurant reservations: 791-7111
The Melange - French *(see Pg. 118)*
The Mirage Buffet: *(see Pg. 145)*
Breakfast - 7 am - 10:45 am - $7.50
Lunch - 11 am - 2:45 pm - $8.95
Dinner - 3 pm - 9:30 pm - $12.95
Champagne Brunch - Sun. 8 am - 10 pm - $13.95
California Pizza Kitchen - gourmet pizza & pasta *(see Pg. 120)*
Caribe Cafe - 24 hour coffee shop *(see Pg. 151)*
Coconuts Ice Cream Shop
Kokomo's - Seafood and Steaks *(see Pg. 138)*
Mikado - Japanese and Sushi Bar *(see Pg. 126)*
Moongate - Cantonese and Szechuan *(see Pg. 116)*
Noodle Kitchen - BBQ's, noodle and rice dishes
Paradise Cafe - poolside cafe open during warmer months
Ristorante Riva - Northern Italian *(see Pg. 123)*

Meeting & Banquet Facilities:
Total meeting Capacity: 5,504
Total Banquet Capacity: 4,260
Total Space: 72,663 sq. ft.

Shopping & Services:
D. Fine - men's clothing
Impulse - gift and sundries, open 24 hours
The Mirage Shop - Mirage wear and gifts
The Mirage Collection
The Spa and Salon at The Mirage - includes sauna, massage and exercise room

ACCOMMODATIONS

The Mirage
3400 Las Vegas Blvd. S.
Las Vegas, NV 89109
791-7111   1-800-627-6667
Fax: 791-7446
Steve Wynn, Chairman Mirage Resorts
Mark Schorr, Pres.
Al Pulitini, Casino Mgr.
The Mirage is a Polynesian themed property which features a five-acre front entrance complete with a lagoon, waterfalls and grottos, as well as a volcano that erupts every 15 minutes. The casino is designed to resemble a Polynesian village and a tropical rain forest with waterfalls and lagoons. The registration area of the hotel has a 20,000 gallon aquarium which is home to sharks, tigerfish and other various sea life. Steve Wynn opened this $730 million resort November 1989.

Rooms:
3,062 including 260 suites & 6 bungalows w/kitchens and private pools and 8 villa apartments *(three 30 story towers)*
Rates: $79 - $399

Special Features:
Volcano, 20,000 gallon saltwater aquarium behind front desk, Royal White tiger habitat, Secret Garden, dolphin habitat, Olympic size heated pool, Jacuzzi, tropical atrium and a children's arcade.

Casino:
Gaming: 95,300 sq. ft.
Games: 2,192 slots and video machines, 73 blackjack tables, 10 crap tables, 12 roulette wheels, 2 Caribbean stud, 2 Pai Gow, 4 Pai Gow poker, 2 keno lounges, 2 wheels of fortune, 3 mini-baccarat, 8 baccarat, race and sports book, 31 poker tables, 2 Let It Ride

Entertainment:
Show Reservations: 792-7777
Siegfried & Roy Theatre - *"Siegfried & Roy"* - $89.35 per person, includes tax, two drinks, gratuity, souvenir program. *(see Pg. 166)*

The Lagoon Saloon - Live music and dancing 5 pm - 2 am *(see Pg. 170)*
Baccarat Piano Bar - Live music *(see Pg. 170)*
The Sports Bar
The Dolphin Bar - open during the warmer months

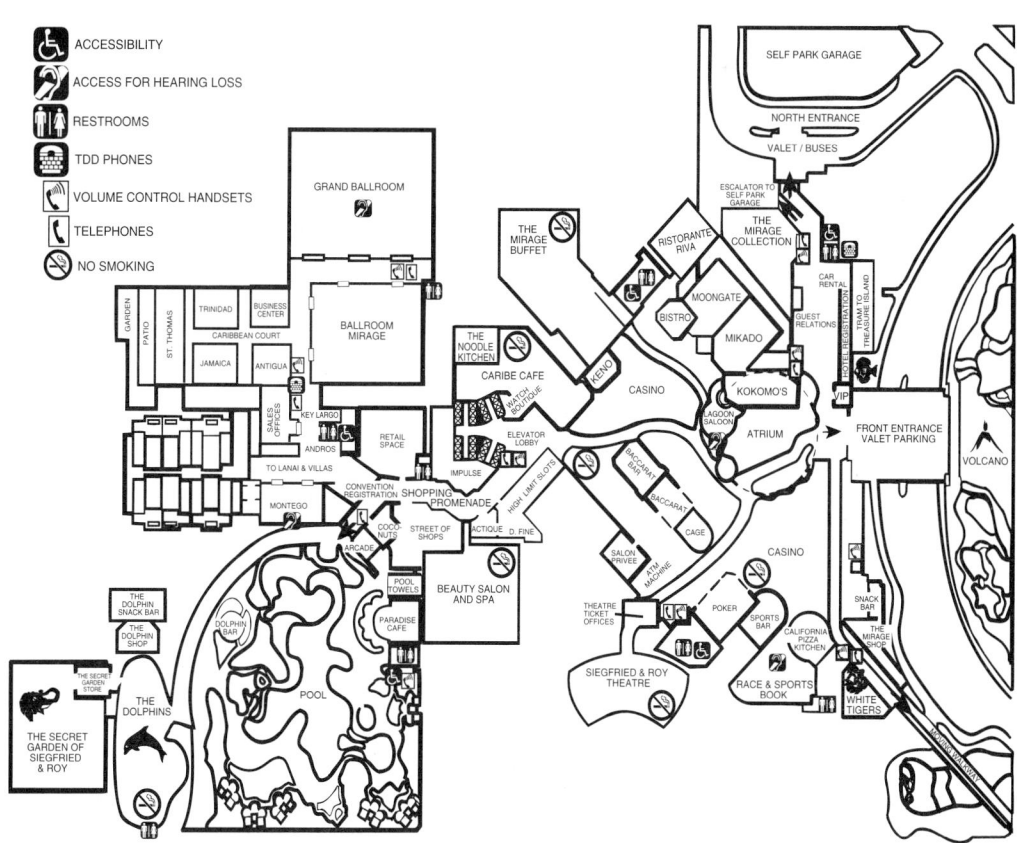

MONTE CARLO

machines, 60 blackjack tables, 8 crap tables, 3 Pai Gow poker, 1 Pai Gow, 1 Let it Ride, 4 Caribbean stud, 2 War games, 10 roulette wheels, 3 mini baccarat, 2 baccarat, 1 big six, race and sports book, 8 poker tables, 1 keno lounge

Entertainment:
Show Reservations: 730-7000
Lance Burton Theater - *"Lance Burton, Master Magician"* - $34.95 - $39.95; includes tax *(see Pg. 165)*
Microbrewery - Entertainment nightly

Dining:
Andre's - French *(see Pg. 118)*
Blackstone's - Steakhouse *(see Pg. 140)*
Buffet: *(see Pg. 145)*
Breakfast - Mon. - Sat. 7 am - 11 am - $6.49
Lunch - Mon. - Sat. 11 am - 4 pm - $8.99
Dinner - 4 pm - 10 pm - $9.49
Champagne Brunch - Sun. 7 am - 3 pm - $9.49; children 5 free
Cafe - 24 hour coffee shop *(see Pg. 151)*
Dragon Noodle Co. *(see Pg. 114)*
Market City Caffe - Italian
Monte Carlo Pub and Brewery - Pizza and Salads
Monte Carlo Food Court - McDonald's, Haagen Dazs, Nathan's, Sbarro's, Golden Bagel and Coffee

Meeting & Banquet Facilities:
1-800-311-5999
Total Meeting Capacity: 775
Total Banquet Capacity: 850
Total Space: 15,000 sq. ft.

Shopping and Services:
Bon Vivant - Apparel
Bouquet De Fleur - Florist
Club Casino Royale - Gaming merchandise
Crown Jewels
Desserts
Hypermarket - Gourmet, convenience and 1-hour photo
Lance Burton Magic Shop
Beach Club Shoppe - rent-a-raft, bathing suits
Boutique - Logo merchandise
Nouveau News
Barber and Hair Stylist Salon
Health Spa
Wedding Chapel

Monte Carlo
3770 Las Vegas Blvd. S.
Las Vegas, NV 89109
730-7000 1-800-311-8999
Website: www.monte-carlo.com
Glen Schaeffer, Pres./CFO
Tony Alamo, Sr. VP of Operations
Jim Thomason, VP/Gen. Mgr., Monte Carlo Resort/Casino
Bill Ensign, VP Casino Operations
The Monte Carlo Resort/Casino is a $344 million unique joint venture between Circus Circus Enterprises, Inc. and Mirage Resorts, Inc. The groundbreaking took place in April of 1995 and after meeting a 14 month deadline and staying within budget, the Monte Carlo opened as scheduled on June 21, 1996. During the first few months of operation, the 3,002 room resort was completely booked. Modeled after the famed Palace Du Casino in Monte Carlo, Monaco, the Monte Carlo promises to offer the experience of royalty at reasonable cost. The atmosphere includes touches such as fanciful arches, chandeliered domes, marble floors, ornate fountains and a Gothic glass and marble registration area overlooking the pool area.

Lance Burton, master magician, is currently under a 13 year contract with the resort, the longest headliner contract to date in Las Vegas. The Monte Carlo is also home to its own brewery where, from selecting and grinding their own grain to purifying their own water through reverse osmosis, the finest creations are brought to you in a unique setting complete with a catwalk so that guests can experience a birds-eye view of the entire process. The brewery also has an outdoor patio and live entertainment nightly.

Rooms:
3,002 including 259 suites
Rates: $60 - $129

Special Features:
21,000 sq. ft. pool area with Lagoon pool, kiddie pool, private heated spa, and a wave pool which produces waves up to 30 inches high. An Easy River Ride moves along at 4 miles per hour and passes under 2 rock waterfalls and a surf pond built to look and sound like an ocean boardwalk with 12 cannons forcing air currents into the water create waves 10 feet high. A fog machine gives the illusion of clouds and fog in the evening. Microbrewery - offers six varieties of beer made on premises
Lighted tennis courts

Casino:
Gaming: 90,000 sq. ft.
Games: 2,200 slot and video poker

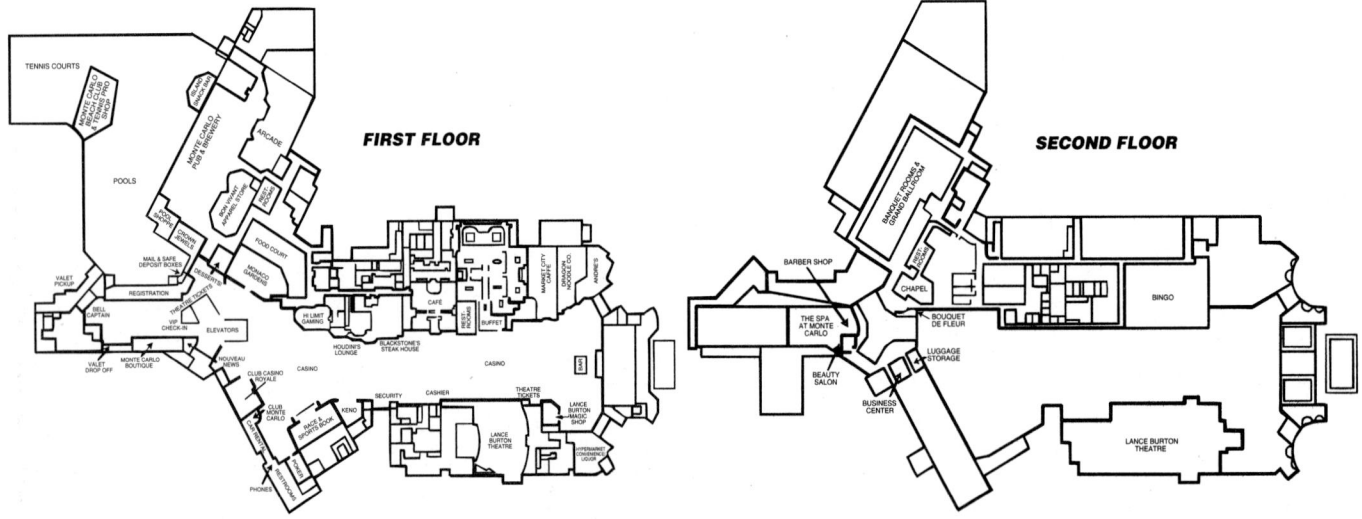

NEW YORK NEW YORK

New York New York
3790 Las Vegas Blvd. S.
Las Vegas, NV 89109
740-6969   1-800-693-6763
Scott Shou, Vice Pres. Finance/Treasurer
Thomas McCartney, Sr. VP Hotel
Operations
Jim Barrett, Mgr. Casino Operations
New York New York, *(the greatest little city in Las Vegas)*, offers guests the majesty of the Statue of Liberty, the excitement of Times Square, the ethnic flavor of Chinatown and Little Italy, and the nostalgia of Coney Island. The Big Apple is known throughout the world and its landmarks are cherished by millions. Now, Las Vegas patrons have the opportunity to enjoy the best of the New York experience by visiting a unique new property that combines the sights and sounds of America's most famous metropolis with the fun and excitement of gaming. The $460 million property recreates the classic Manhattan skyline, complete with 12 skyscrapers, at approximately a third the size of New York City architecture. The tallest building replicates the Empire State Building at 529 feet, 47 stories. Other replicas include the Statue of Liberty, a Coney Island-style roller coaster, a 300 foot version of the Brooklyn Bridge and

the Soldiers and Sailors Monument. Design elements throughout the property reflect the history, color and diversity of Manhattan's Park Avenue, Central Park, Broadway, Times Square Financial District and Greenwich Village.

Rooms:
2,033
Rates: $89 - $169

Special Features:
Coney Island Emporium with carnival rides, shooting galleries, laser tag, coin-operated games and a fiber-optic fireworks show; Manhattan Express roller-coaster *(the second of its kind to feature a 180-degree "heartline" roll maneuver that provides riders with heart-stopping action and thrills)*; Central Park with reflecting pond, Bow bridge and mosaic floor sign themed to look like "Strawberry Fields" memorial to John Lennon; Health spa and fitness center; massage facility and pool

Casino:
Gaming: 84,000 sq. ft.
Games: More than 2,400 state of the art video and slot machines, 41 blackjack tables, 8 crap tables, 7 roulette wheels, 3 mini-baccarat, 3 Caribbean stud, 1 casino War, 1 big 6, 3 Pai Gow, 1 Pai Gow Tile, 1 keno lounge, race and sports book

Entertainment:
Show Reservations: 740-6815
MADhattan Theater - *"MADhattan"* - $44 includes tax. *(see Pg. 165)*
The Empire Bar - Live entertainment nightly
The Bar at Times Square - musical entertainment nightly in a "sing-a-long" with the piano man setting
Hamiltons - Cigar Shop and Lounge

Dining:
Il Fornaio - Italian *(see Pg. 121)*
America - 24 hour coffee shop *(see Pg. 151)*
Chin Chin - Chinese *(see Pg. 113)*
Gallagher's Steak House *(see Pg. 141)*
Gonzalez Y. Gonzalez - Mexican *(see Pg. 128)*
Greenbergs - Deli *(see Pg. 156)*
Motown Cafe - Soul Food *(see Pg. 134)*
Nathan's
The Village Eateries - A variety of foods including deli, kosher, BBQ, pizza, burgers and Mexican

Shopping and Services:
Hamiltons - Cigar Shop
I Love New York-New York - Logo Shop
Houdini's Magic Shop
Vegas Express - Souvenirs
Cashman Photo Magic - Film & Film Processing
Wedding Chapel

THE ORLEANS

The Orleans
4500 W. Tropicana Ave.
Las Vegas, NV 89103
365-7111   1-800-675-3267
Website: www.orleans.com
Michael Gaughan, Pres.
Frank Toti, Casino Mgr.
The Orleans opened in December 1996 and is the newest project of Coast Hotels and Casinos, Inc., developers of the Gold Coast and the Barbary Coast properties. A combination of the city of New Orleans' most notable attractions;

the French Quarter, the Garden District and Mardi Gras, The Orleans Hotel and Casino is complete with all that is New Orleans.

The architecture of the Orleans combines a French Quarter facade with French, Spanish and Plantation Colonial influences, along with the sparkle and imagination that visitors to Las Vegas have come to expect.

Rooms:
840 including 30 suites
Rates: $69 - $89

Special Features:
Pool complex with pool, lounging pool, spa, beach and cabana area; bowling center; child care center; 12 plex movie theater; 40 foot high New Orleans-style atrium; fitness center; shuttle service to and from the Barbary Coast and the Gold Coast; arcade

Casino:
Gaming: 92,000 sq. ft.

Games: More than 2,100 slots, 65 table games which include blackjack, craps, roulette, Let It Ride, baccarat, Pai Gow poker, 16 poker tables, keno lounge, race and sports book

Entertainment:
Show Reservations: 365-7075
The Orleans Showroom - Headliner entertainment *(see Pg. 170)*
Bourbon Street Cafe - Live New Orleans-style entertainment nightly

Dining:
Canal Street Grille - Steak House *(see Pg. 140)*
Don Miguel's - Mexican *(see Pg. 130)*
Courtyard Cafe - 24 hour coffee shop *(see Pg. 151)*
French Market Buffet: *(see Pg. 145)*
Breakfast - 7 am - 10 am - $3.45
Lunch - 11 am - 3 pm - $4.45
Dinner - 4 pm - 10 pm - $7.95
Seafood Buffet - Mon. 4 pm - 10 pm - $10.95
Brunch - Sun. - 8 am - 3 pm - $7.95
Vito's Italian Restaurant - Italian *(see Pg. 124)*
Terrible Mike's - fast food
Kate's Korner - ice cream and confections

Meeting & Banquet Facilities:
Total Banquet Capacity: 2,370
Total Meeting Capacity: 3,420
Total Space: 40,000 sq. ft.

Shopping and Services:
Gift Shop - open 24 hours; sundries, logo merchandise
Beauty Salon
Barber Shop
Shuttle Service
Bowling Center Pro Shop
Child Care Center

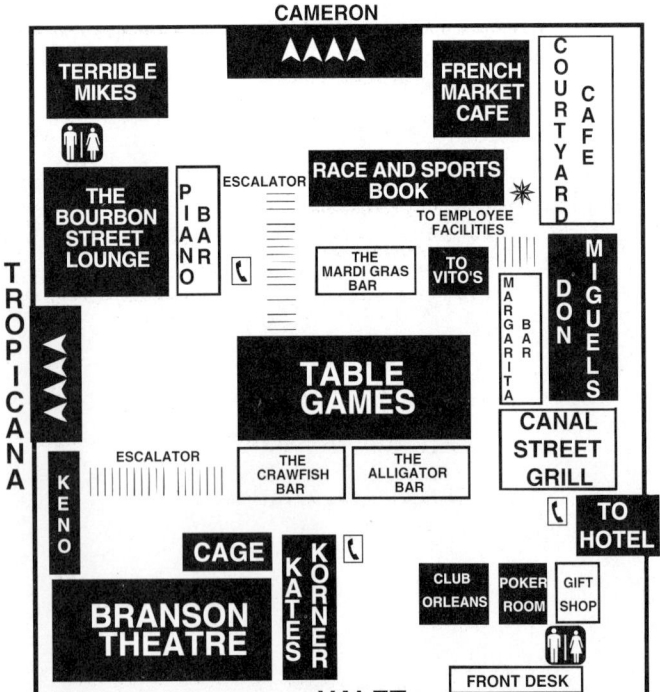

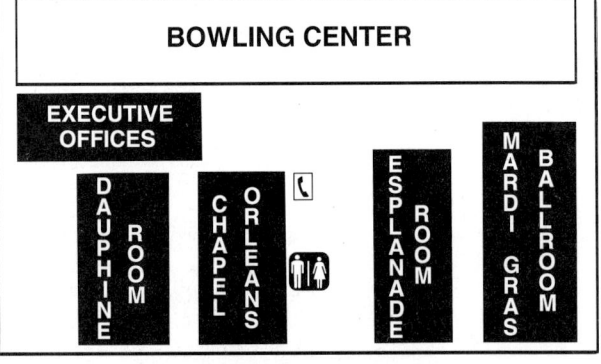

SECOND LEVEL

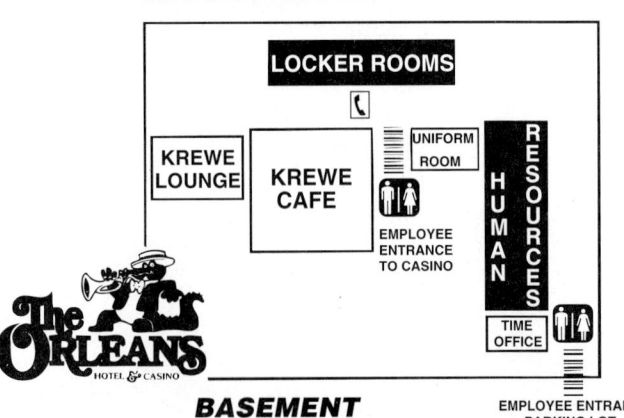

BASEMENT

PALACE STATION

Palace Station Hotel & Casino
2411 W. Sahara Ave.
Las Vegas, NV 89102
367-2411 1-800-634-3101
Blake Sartini, Pres. of Nevada Operation
Jim Hughes, VP/Gen. Mgr.
Richard St. Jean, Hotel Dir.
Tony Carolo, Casino Mgr.
Palace Station originally opened on July 1, 1976 in a one-story, 5,000 sq. ft. building known simply as The Casino, with four blackjack tables and 100 slot machines, a small bar and a buffet. Renamed Palace Station November 1983, today its hotel tower and 287,000 sq. ft. of space is a landmark on the Las Vegas skyline. Now, as part of a national, public company, more growth and expansion is master-planned for Palace Station. The display model at McCarran Airport already includes a second hotel tower, which will double the number of rooms available for an ever-growing tourist market.

Rooms:
1,028 including 74 suites
Rates: $49 - $109

Special Features:
Airport pick-up, bingo bus; shuttle bus to other casino station properties, Fashion Show Mall and MGM Grand; 2 swimming pools; arcade

Casino:
Gaming: 76,490 sq. ft.
Games: 2,250 slot and video machines, 32 blackjack tables, 5 crap tables, 3 roulette wheels, 1 Caribbean stud, 2 keno lounges, mini-baccarat, 2 Pai Gow poker, 9 poker tables, 1 Let It Ride, race and sports book, bingo parlor

Entertainment:
Loading Dock Lounge - Live entertainment nightly *(see Pg. 170)*
Palace Saloon - Live music nightly

Dining:
The Feast Buffet: *(see Pg. 145)*
Breakfast - Mon. - Fri. 7 am - 11 pm - $3.99
Lunch - Mon. - Sat. 11 am - 3:30 pm - $5.99
Dinner - 4 pm - 10 pm - $8.99
Brunch - Sun. 7 am - 3:30 pm - $7.99
The Broiler - Steaks and Seafood *(see Pg. 138)*
Oyster Bar
Guadalajara Bar & Grille - Mexican *(see Pg. 129)*
Guadalajara Lunch Buffet:
Mon. - Fri. 11 am - 2:30 pm; Sat. - Sun. noon - 3 pm - $5.95
Iron Horse Cafe - 24 hour coffee shop *(see Pg. 151)*
Pasta Palace - Italian *(see Pg. 122)*
Whistle Stop Snack Bar

Meeting & Banquet Facilities:
Total Meeting Capacity: 1,000
Total Banquet Capacity: 800
Total space: 18,500 sq. ft.

Shopping & Services:
Gift Shop
Beauty Salon
Barber Shop

THE RESERVE HOTEL & CASINO

**The Reserve
Hotel Casino**
777 W. Lake Mead Dr.
Henderson, NV 89015
558-7000 1-888-899-7770
Fax: 558-7008
Craig Neilsen, Pres.
*John R. Spina, Exec. VP of operations
and Dir.*

The Reserve opened February 10, 1998 amid fanfare with fireworks and a Congo drum procession. Ameristar developed the Reserve Hotel Casino with a corporate philosophy of building a high-quality, off-the-Strip hotel and casino with an integrated and extensively themed design. Partnering with award-winning casino theme designer Henry Conversano, whose previous projects include The Mirage Hotel Casino in Las Vegas and The Lost City at Sun City Resort Hotel and Casino in Sun City, South Africa, Ameristar's goal was to transform 37,000 sq. ft. of gaming space, four signature restaurants and three bars/lounges into an exciting and intimate safari environment.

Rooms:
224 including 8 suites
Rates: $49 - $69

Special Features:
The $125 million African Safari Animal Reserve decor has Serengeti grasslands and Congo rainforests, with a sound system that replicates the roar of lions, birds in flight, the screeching of monkeys and thunder of moving rainstorms throughout the casino and dining area. The swimming pool is in a tropical setting.

Casino:
Gaming: 37,000 sq. ft.
Games: 1,450 slot machines, 18 blackjack tables, 2 crap tables, 2 roulette

wheels, 1 mini baccarat, 1 Let-It-Ride, 1 Caribbean stud, 1 Pai Gow poker, keno, poker room, 300 seat bingo area and sports book.

Entertainment:
Wasimbas - Live entertainment and a multimedia wall showing life size videos

**Monsoon Mary's
Funky Monkey Bar**

Dining:
Pasta Mombasa - Italian *(see Pg. 122)*
Congo Jack's Cafe - Coffee Shop
Wildfire - Steaks and Seafood
Grand Safari Buffet:
Lunch - Mon. - Fri. 11 am - 4 pm $5.99

Dinner - Mon. - Fri. 4 pm - 10 pm $7.99
Weekend Brunch - Sat. - Sun. 9 am - 4 pm $6.99

Meeting & Banquet Facilities:
None

Shopping:
Gift Shop

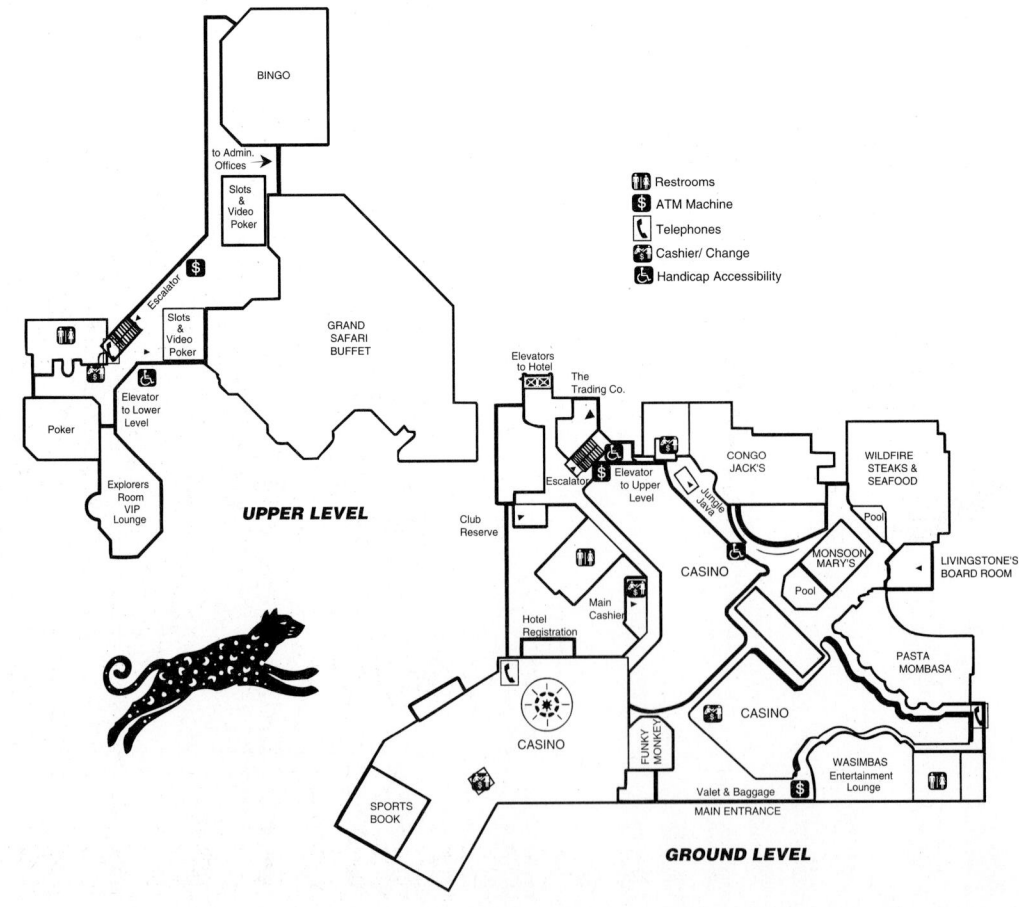

RIO SUITE HOTEL & CASINO

Rio Suite Hotel & Casino
3700 W. Flamingo Rd.
Las Vegas, NV 89103
252-7777 1-800-PLAYRIO
Fax: 252-0080

Anthony Marnell II, Chairman of the Board/CEO
James Barrett Jr., Pres.
John Lipkowitz, Sr. VP/Gen. Mgr.
Jimmy Angelo, Casino Mgr.

The Rio opened on January 15, 1990 as the only all-suite hotel/casino in the area. Expansions to the property which were completed in February 1997 at a cost of $200 million added 1,037 new suites in a new 41 story tower, one of the tallest inhabitable towers in the United States. The top of the Rio tower provides a one-of-a-kind vantage point for viewing the entire Las Vegas Strip and the surrounding valley.

Inspired by European architecture, the Rio's Masquerade Village is a combination of entertainment, food shopping and gaming, woven together in an ongoing carnival atmosphere.

Rooms:

2,563 suites - each featuring at least 600 sq. ft.
Rates: $59 - $269

Special Features:

All rooms are suites complete with in room safe; multi-level poolside recreation complex with three swimming pools, Jacuzzi, sandy beach, 2 sand volleyball courts, waterfalls, health club and spa; 18-hole championship golf course video arcade, antique slot collection.

Masquerade Show in the Sky - The first indoor entertainment experience of its kind in Las Vegas, Rio visitors are invited to take a magical journey aboard fantasy floats as they glide above the crowd to an orchestration of music, dance and Mardi Gras celebration. The Wine Cellar Tasting Room & Retail Shop - The world's largest public collection of fine and rare wines along with a complete line of tasting accessories and gifts

Casino:

Gaming: 120,000 sq. ft.
Games: 2,460 slots and video machines, 60 blackjack tables, 13 crap tables, 11 roulette wheels, 2 keno lounges, mini-baccarat, 3 Caribbean stud, 2 Pai Gow poker, 8 poker tables, race and sports book, baccarat, 3 Let It Ride

Entertainment:

Show Reservations: 252-7776
Copacabana Showroom:
"Impressionist/Comedian Danny Gans"- $60 includes tax, tip and 2 drinks *(see Pg. 167)*
Club Rio - Music videos and dancing nightly 10 pm - 4 am *(see Pg. 171)*

Jazz Lounge
VooDoo Cafe & Lounge - Live themed entertainment *(see Pg. 170)*
Outdoor poolside entertainment complex

Dining:

All American Bar & Grille - Steak and Seafood *(see Pg. 140)*
Antonio's - Northern Italian *(see Pg. 119)*
Bombolia - Mexican *(see Pg. 127)*
Buzios - Seafood/Oyster Bar *(see Pg. 138)*
Fiore Rotisserie - Continental *(see Pg. 136)*
VooDoo Cafe - Creole/Cajun
Mama Maria's Cucina - Italian and Pasta *(see Pg. 121)*
Mask - Far Eastern *(see Pg. 116)*

Napa - French Gourmet *(see Pg. 118)*
Rio Village Seafood Buffet: *(see Pg. 145)*
Breakfast - 7 am - 10 am $6.95
Lunch - Mon. - Fri. 11 am - 2:30 pm - $15.95
Dinner - Mon. - Thu. 4 pm - 10 pm; Fri. - 4 pm - 11 pm, $20.95
Brunch - Sat. - Sun. 9:30 am - 2:30 pm - $20.95
Rio Beach Cafe - 24 hour coffee shop *(see Pg. 152)*
Carnival World Buffet: *(see Pg. 145)*
Breakfast - Mon. - Fri. 8 am - 10:30 am - $6.95
Lunch - Mon. - Fri. 11 am - 3:30 pm - $8.95
Dinner - 3:30 pm - 11 pm - $10.95
Brunch - Sat. - Sun. 8:30 am - 3:30 pm - $10.95
Toscano's - Deli and Bakery *(see Pg. 157)*
Ben & Jerry's Ice Cream

Meeting & Banquet Facilities:
Total Meeting Capacity: 1,350
Total Banquet Capacity: 1,750
Total Space: 13,250 sq. ft.

Shopping & Services:
More than 600,000 sq. ft. of retail space: Alegre, Bernard K. Passman Gallery, Davante, Cashman Photo Magic, Mardi Gras Cigars, Elegant Pretenders, Gary's Island/Dick's Last Resort, Guess? Footwear, Houdini's Magic Shop, Kid Vegas, Money Magnetz, Garys Cole Haan, Napa Valley Gourmet, Nichole Miller, Nawlins, Reel Outfitter, Rio Logo Shop, Rio Sundries, Roland's Boutique, Speedo Authentic Fitness, Watch Zone and more.
All State Ticket Booth
Spa & Salon
2 Wedding Chapels and 2 1,200 sq. ft. honeymoon suites and reception facilities

ACCOMMODATIONS

FIRST LEVEL

SECOND LEVEL MASQUERADE VILLAGE

$ ATM MACHINES
C TELEPHONE
SHOE SHINE BOOTH

RIVIERA

Riviera Hotel
2901 Las Vegas Blvd. S.
Las Vegas, NV 89109
734-5110 1-800-634-6753
Fax: 794-9451
William Westerman, Chairman/CEO
Brian Benschneider, Hotel Mgr.
Mickey Falba, Casino Mgr.
The Riviera opened April 30, 1955 at a cost of $10 million. Liberace headlined in the showroom opening day and was paid a phenomenal $50,000 weekly, during a time when Las Vegas homes could be bought for less then $10,000, making entertainment history. Joan Crawford was the official hostess opening night. The nine-story hotel was the first modern high-rise in Las Vegas. Now one of the largest casinos in the world with over 100,000 sq. ft., the Riviera only had 18 table games and 116 slot machines when it opened.

Rooms:
2,075 including 156 suites and 37 rooms specially equipped to accommodate wheelchair patrons
Rates: $69 - $500

Special Features:
2 outdoor tennis courts, swimming pool with pool deck lounge and courtyard, Jacuzzi; health spa and exercise room, video arcade

Casino:
Gaming: 102,300 sq. ft.
Games: 1,576 slots and video machines, 21 blackjack tables, 4 crap tables, 2 roulette wheels, keno lounge, 1 wheel of fortune, 1 baccarat, 2 Pai Gow poker, Sic-Bo, 2 Caribbean stud, 5 poker tables, 3 Let It Ride, race and sports book

Entertainment:
Show Reservations: 794-9433
Versailles Theatre - *"Splash"* - $39.50 - $49.50 *(see Pg. 166)*

Mardi Gras Pavilion - *"An Evening at La Cage"* - $21.95 *(see Pg. 167)*
"Crazy Girls" - $18.95 plus tax includes two drinks *(see Pg. 167)*
Riviera Comedy Club - $14.95 + tax includes two drinks *(see Pg. 168)*
Le Bistro Lounge - Entertainment nightly *(see Pg. 170)*

Dining:
Kady's - 24 hour coffee shop *(see Pg. 152)*
Kristofer's - Steak and Seafood *(see Pg. 141)*
Rik'Shaw - Cantonese *(see Pg. 117)*
Ristorante Italiano - Italian *(see Pg. 123)*
World's Fare Buffet: *(see Pg. 145)*
Breakfast - 7 am - 10 am - $5.55
Brunch - 10 am - 3 pm - $6.45
Dinner - 4 pm - 10:30 pm - $8.45
Champagne Brunch - Sat. - Sun. 10 am - 3 pm $6.45
Mardi Gras Food Court - Burger King, Kabalen, Taco Riko, Panda Express, Pizza Hut, TCBY, Riksson Cafe Express and Dragon Sushi

Meeting & Banquet Facilities:
Special Services - Ice carvings, flowers, musicians and more
Total Meeting Capacity: 8,655
Total Banquet Capacity: 6,585
Total space: 125,000 sq. ft.

Shopping & Services:
Specialty Shops - Addi Gallery, Amazing Pictures, Camouflage, Chocolate Heaven, Crystal Rose, Doren Gifts, D&D, Florea Letter Art, Harris Collectibles, Kid's Inc., Las Vegas Glitz, Las Vegas Leisure Magnet Shop, Marshall Rousso, The Magic Shop, Nevada Wine Co., Norm Kaplan Shoes, Pearl Factory, Splash Co. Store, Sunglass Hut, Thunderbird Jewels and Toni's Cats
Hotel Gift Shop
Allstate Car Rental
America West Airlines ticket counter
Goodfellas Shoe Shine
Wedding Chapel
Barber Shop

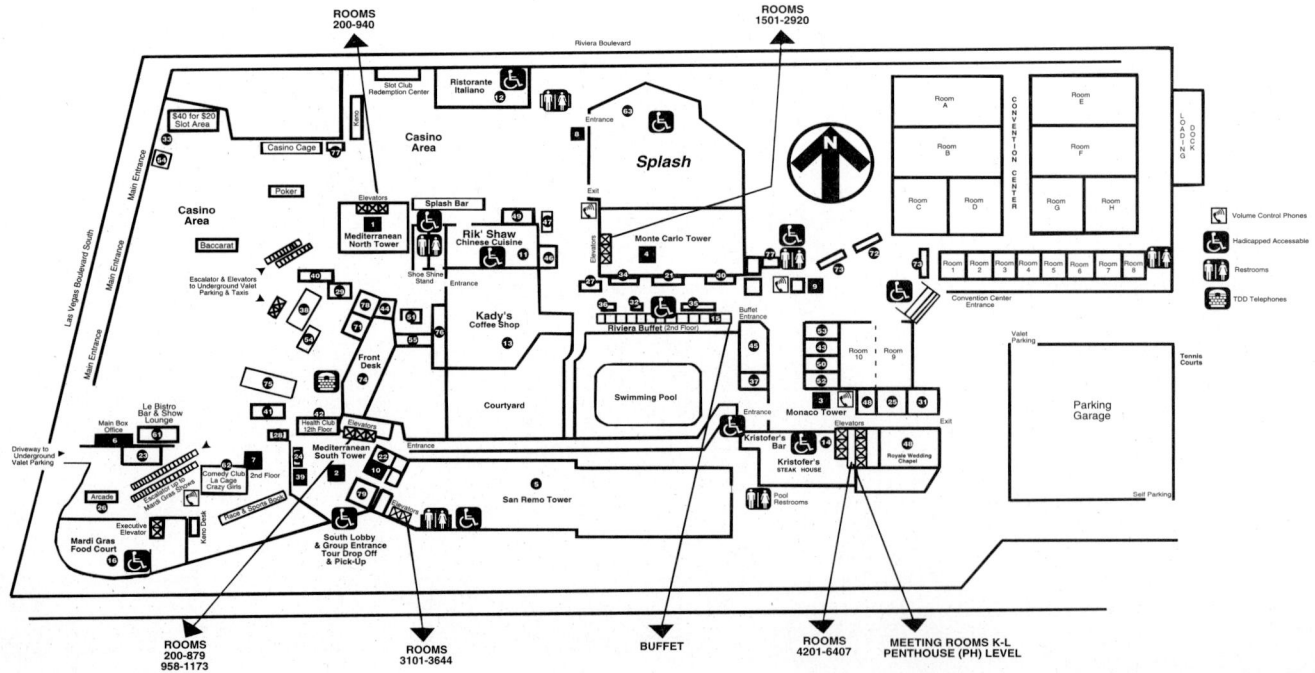

SAHARA

Sahara Hotel
2535 Las Vegas Blvd. S.
Las Vegas, NV 89109
737-2111 1-800-634-6666
Fax: 735-5921

Craig Hodgkins, Pres./Gen. Mgr.
Paul Gatlin, Casino Mgr.

The Sahara opened in December 1952, by Milton Prell with the help of a group of investors including Del Webb, whose construction company built the hotel and eventually purchased the controlling interest in 1961. Paul Lowden purchased the hotel from Del Webb in 1982 for $50 million. William Bennett purchased the hotel in October 1995 for $193 million.

A $100 million plus renovation project was completed in October 1997. Crowned "Jewel of the Desert" when it first opened, the casual atmosphere, friendly service and convenient location on the northern end of the Las Vegas Strip have continually contributed to the long-standing reputation of the Sahara.

Rooms:
2,033 including 92 suites
Rates: $29 - $89

Special Features:
"Sahara Speedway" - virtual reality Indy car racing, 2 3-D theaters, & other events; 170 ft. molded "onion" dome atop a new 80 ft. high porte cochere leading to the main entry; New pool area featuring 5,000 sq. ft. pool, 13 cabanas, circular fountains, a gazebo covered spa & snack bar.

Casino:
Gaming: 95,000 sq. ft.
Games: 1,371 slot and video machines,
25 blackjack tables, 4 crap tables, 4 roulette wheels, keno lounge, wheel of fortune, 2 Pai Gow poker, 5 poker tables, 5 Pan, race and sports book, 1 Caribbean stud, mini-baccarat, 1 Let It Ride, 1 Spanish 21, 1 casino War

Entertainment:
Show Reservations: 737-2111
Congo Showroom - Headline performers
Casbar Lounge - Nightly entertainment
(see Pg. 170)

Dining:
Caravan Room - Coffee Shop *(see Pg. 152)*
The Sahara Buffet: *(see Pg. 145)*
Breakfast - 6 am - 11 am - $2.99
Lunch - 11:30 am - 3:30 pm - $3.99
Dinner - 4 pm - 10 pm - $5.99
Sahara Steak House - Gourmet Steak *(see Pg. 143)*
Paco's Hideaway - bar & grill *(see Pg. 130)*

Meeting & Banquet Facilities:
Sales: 737-2735
Total space: 60,000 sq. ft. convention Ccenter

Shopping & Services:
Beauty Shop, Candy Shop
Luggage Shop, Flower Shop
Marshall Rousso, Jewelry Shop
Gift Shop, Logo Shop
Allstate Car Rental

SAM'S TOWN

Sam's Town Hotel & Gambling Hall
5111 Boulder Highway
Las Vegas, NV 89122
456-7777 1-800-634-6371
Bill Boyd, Pres.
Gil Peart, Casino Mgr.
The Western theme hotel opened in 1979 by Bill Boyd. Over the years the hotel/casino has continued to grow and this year Sam's Town opened a new 9-story tower with 650 rooms in July. The $90 million expansion included a 25,000 sq. ft. hotel atrium, 10,000 sq. ft. of meeting space, a food court, a parking garage, sports bar and increased sports book. Sam's Town is popular with the locals.

Rooms:
650 rooms including 33 suites; 9-story tower
Rates: $35 - $300
Sam's Town RV Park - 498 spaces phone 454-8056; 4040 S. Nellis Blvd. and 5225 Boulder Hwy.

Special Features:
56-lane bowling center - 454-8022, Coca Cola Museum, video arcade, supervised playroom for children 2-8, outdoor recreation area with pool, whirlpool and sand volleyball court.

Live music and dancing in two lounges, Roxy's Saloon and Sam's Town Western Dance Hall; daily water and laser show, Sunset Stampede at 2 pm, 6 pm, 8 pm, and 10 pm; Free Shuttle to the Stardust on the Strip and the Fremont and California Hotels downtown.

Casino:
Gaming: 81,305 sq. ft.
Games: 2,850 slots and video machines, 29 blackjack tables, 5 crap tables, 4 roulette wheels, keno lounge, bingo, 1

Pai Gow poker, 9 poker tables, race and sports book, 2 Caribbean stud, single deck blackjack, 100X odds on craps, 1 Let It Ride, 1 Spanish 21

Entertainment:
Roxy's Saloon - Live entertainment noon - 5 am *(see Pg. 170)*
Western Dance Hall - Live music 9 pm - 3 am *(see Pg. 172)*
The Final Score - Sports Bar with basketball key court, pinball, video golf, darts, pool, shuffleboard, over 30 TVs and outdoor volleyball court.
Sunset Stampede - Free water laser/light show offered four times daily in the indoor park - 2 pm, 6 pm, 8 pm & 10 pm

Dining:
Billy Bob's Western Steakhouse and Saloon *(see Pg. 140)*
Calamity Jane's Ice Cream Parlour
Chuckwagon Food Court
Diamond Lil's - Steak and Seafood *(see Pg. 140)*
Final Score Sports Bar - American
Mary's Diner - '50s Diner *(see Pg. 152)*
Papamios Italian Kitchen - Italian *(see Pg. 122)*
Smokey Joe's - 24 hour Coffee Shop *(see Pg. 152)*
Snack Bar
Great Buffet: *(see Pg. 145)*
Breakfast - Mon. - Sat. 8 am - 11 am - $4.99
Lunch - Mon. - Sat. 11 am - 3 pm - $6.99
Dinner - Sat. - Tue., Thu. 4 pm - 9 pm - $8.99, Wed. 4 pm - 9 pm $11.99, Fri. 4 pm -10 pm - $12.99
Champagne Brunch - Sun. 8 am - 3 pm - $7.99
Sunday Breakfast in the Park - 8 am - 2 pm $13.95
Willy & Jose's - Mexican *(see Pg. 131)*

Meeting & Banquet Facilities:
454-8020
Seating Capacity: 1,400
Total Space: 10,000 sq. ft.

Shopping & Services:
Western Emporium - Western Wear:
454-8017
Gift Shop

Photo: Photofechnik International

SAN REMO

Hotel San Remo
Casino & Resort
115 E. Tropicana Ave.
Las Vegas, NV 89109
739-9000 1-800-522-7366
Fax: 736-1120
Sukeaki Izumi, Pres.
Michael Hessling, Exec. VP
Harry Byrge, Casino Mgr.

In contrast to the colossal, towering hotels, the Hotel San Remo Casino & Resort exudes a European, classic old-world charm, combining a touch of elegance with a dedication to hospitality and fine service. European architecture sets the tone of this property with the unique roofline shaped by black and gold-trimmed mansards. The casino is graced by magnificent crystal chandeliers and hand-painted floral murals on its majestic high arches, lending continuity to the European theme.

Owner and President Sukeaki Izumi is a true entrepreneur. Having travelled the world over, Izumi was impressed with Las Vegas' uniqueness. He liked the friendly hospitality of the people and felt that Las Vegas was incomparable to any other city. In the late 1980s, he purchased an existing property and started a complete renovation. To complement the European theme, the hotel was named after the city of San Remo on the Italian Riviera.

Occupying 11 acres, the hotel opened in July 1989, with 322 rooms. Izumi was granted a permanent gaming license by the Nevada State Gaming Commission, and he opened the casino in February 1990. The new 18-story tower was added in June 1991. With an eye toward the future, Izumi currently has some preliminary plans to add another 1,200 room tower.

Rooms:
751 including 35 suites
Rates: Sun. - Thu. $39 - $89; Fri. - Sat. $89 - $179

Special Features:
24 hour, year-round, heated swimming pool; arcade

Casino:
Gaming: 7,889 sq. ft.
Games: 602 slot and video machines, 13 blackjack tables, 2 crap tables, roulette wheel, keno lounge, wheel of fortune, 1 Caribbean stud, 1 Let It Ride, 1 Pai Gow poker, sports book

Entertainment:
Show Reservations: 597-6028
Parisian Cabaret: *"Showgirls of Magic"* - magic/music/dance variety; *(see Pg. 168)*

Showtimes: 8 pm & 10:30 pm - $24.20 includes drink; dark Monday
Bonne Chance Lounge: Musical *(singles and duos)* - 4 pm - 5 am; dancing *(see Pg. 171)*

Dining:
Ristorante dei Fiori - 24 hour coffee shop *(see Pg. 145)*
Buffet:
Breakfast - Mon. - Fri. 6:30 am - 10:30 am - $6.95
Lunch - Mon. - Fri. 11 am - 2 pm - $6.95
Dinner - Mon. - Fri. 5 pm - 9 pm - $7.95
Champagne Brunch - Sat. - Sun. 7 am - 2 pm - $6.95
Pasta Remo - Italian *(see Pg. 123)*
Paparazzi Grille - Beef Steaks, Seafood and Chicken *(see Pg. 137)*
San Remo Sushi Bar - Sushi *(see Pg. 126)*
Luigi's Deli - Sandwiches *(see Pg. 156)*

Meeting & Banquet Facilities:
1-800-522-7366, ext. 4200
Total Meeting Capacity: 460
Total Banquet Capacity: 250
Total space: 5,600 sq. ft.

Shopping & Services:
Cucchi's Gift Shop & Player's Emporium
Miyabiya - Fine Leather Goods

Photo: Phototecknik International

SHOWBOAT

Showboat Hotel, Casino & Bowling Center
2800 E. Fremont St.
Las Vegas, NV 89104
385-9123 1-800-826-2800
Carlton Geer, Pres./CEO
Leann Schneider, VP of Finance/CFO
Marcel Baumann, VP of Hotel
   Operations
Jon Zimmerman, VP of Casino
   Operations

The Showboat Hotel, Casino and Bowling Center opened September 1954 and was the first gaming property in Las Vegas to offer the "three B's": Bingo, Bowling and Buffets. The Showboat has since become one of the most reputable names in the gaming industry. Known as "The Flagship of the Boulder Strip," the property recently underwent a $25 million renovation giving it a New Orleans atmosphere complete with southern mansions, carnival and Mardi Gras decor, and including large stained-glass windows and hand-painted murals in many areas.

Rooms:
453 including 5 suites
Rates: $29 - $89
RV Park: 84 fully equipped spaces - 383-9333
Rates: $14

Special Features:
Supervised children's playroom for ages 2-7 with up to 3 hours free; 106 lane bowling center - 385-9153; video arcade; airport shuttle; fully equipped RV Park with laundry/drycleaning facility, private showers, vending and RV amenities shop, cable TV and sewer hookups. Telephone service available.

Casino:
Gaming: 80,300 sq. ft.
Games: 1,548 slot and video machines, 14 blackjack tables, 2 crap tables, 2 roulette wheels, keno lounge, bingo, Pai Gow poker, race and sports book, 1 Caribbean stud, 2 Let It Ride, poker room, computer bingo

Entertainment:
Mardi Gras Room - Live entertainment *(see Pg. 171)*

Dining:
Captain's Buffet: *(see Pg. 146)*
Lunch - Mon. - Fri. 10 am - 3:30 pm - $4.95
Dinner - Sun., Mon., Tue. 4:30 pm - 10 pm - $6.95; Wed. - NY Steak and Shrimp Scampi Buffet - 4:30 pm - 10 pm - $7.95 Thu. - Fri. - Seafood - 4:30 pm - 10 pm - $7.95; Sat. - Prime Rib & Pasta - 4:30 pm -10 pm - $7.95
Brunch - Sat. - 8 am - 3:30 pm, Sun. 8 am - 3 pm - $6.45
Coffee Shop - 24 hours
DiNapoli - Italian *(see Pg. 120)*
Plantation Room - Steak/Seafood *(see Pg. 135)*

Meeting & Banquet Facilities:
385-9104
Total Meeting Capacity: 1,250
Total Banquet Capacity: 850
Total space: 10,000 sq. ft.

Shopping & Services:
Beauty Salon/Barber Shop
Gift Shop
Pro Bowling Shop
Shoe Shine

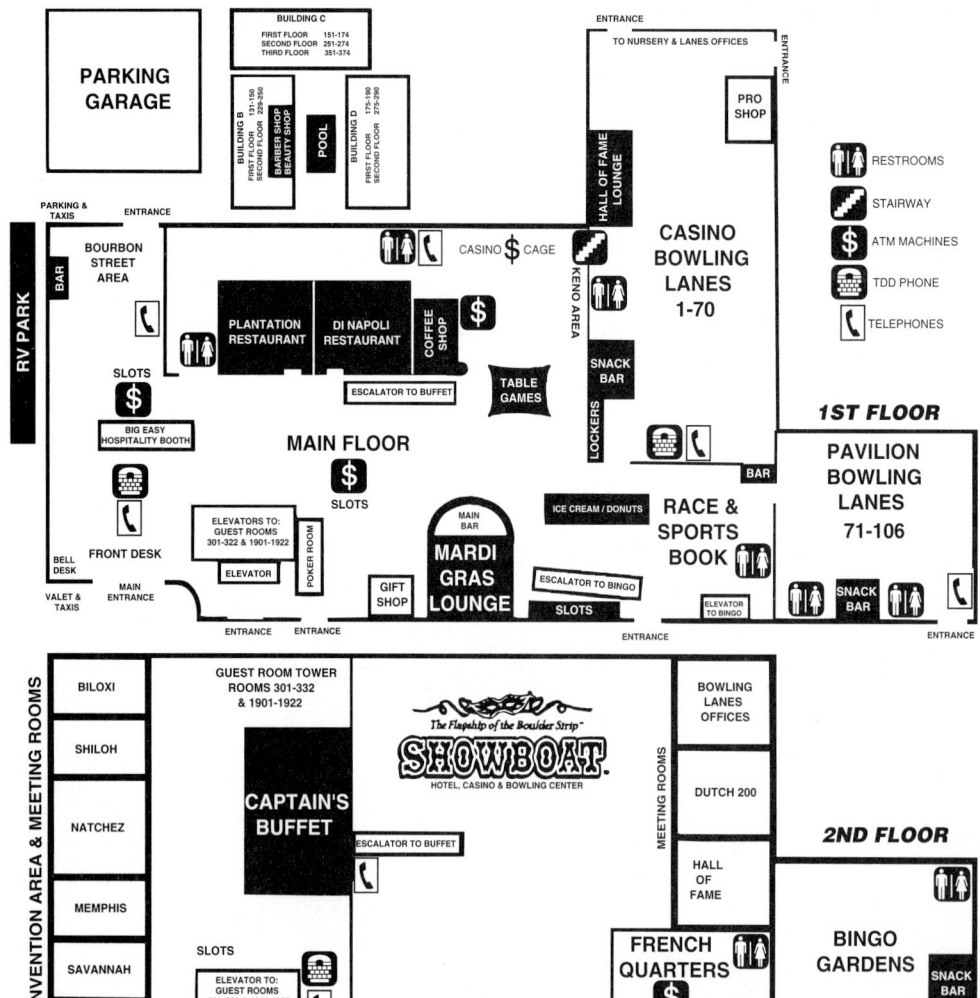

Photo: Phototechnik International

STARDUST

Entertainment:
Show Reservations: 732-6111
Stardust Showroom - "Enter The Night" - $26.90 plus tax; includes two drinks and tip (see Pg. 165)
Starlite Lounge - Entertainment nightly (see Pg. 171)
The Terrace Bar - Karaoke weekends
William B's Lounge (see Pg. 143)

Dining:
Short Stop - snack bar
Tony Roma's - ribs (see Pg. 134)
Ralph's '50s diner
Toucan Harry's - 24 hour coffee shop (see Pg. 152)
Tres Lobos - Mexican (see Pg. 131)
Warehouse Buffet: (see Pg. 146)
Breakfast - Mon. - Sat. 7 am -11 am - $4.95
Lunch - Mon. - Sat. - 11 am - 3 pm - $5.95
Dinner - 4 pm - 10 pm - $7.95
Champagne Brunch - Sun. 7 am - 3 pm - $6.95
William B's - gourmet steak

Meeting & Banquet Facilities:
Total Meeting Capacity: 2,325
Total Banquet Capacity: 1,860
Total Space: 35,464 sq. ft.

Shopping & Services:
Annee of Paris Beauty Salon
Ethel M Chocolates
Marshall Rousso's - Clothing & Accessories
Special Tee's
Stardust Barber Shop
Stardust Kids
Stardust Liquor
T-Bird Jewels
Video Arcade
Gift Shop
Stardust Logo Shop

ACCOMMODATIONS

Stardust Hotel & Casino
3000 Las Vegas Blvd. S.
Las Vegas, NV 89109
732-6111 1-800-634-6757
Fax: 732-6296
http://www.vegas.com/hotels/stardust

John Miner, VP/Gen. Mgr.
Jerry Chambers, VP Hotel Operations
Alan Abrams, Casino Mgr.

John Factor purchased and opened the hotel in 1958, after the original owner went broke and died before construction of the property was ever completed. The Stardust originally had 1,000 rooms, making it the largest hotel in the world at that time. The opening night show was the "Lido De Paris" which continued a 33-year run until 1992. The Boyd Group purchased the Stardust in 1985 and after a $300 million expansion and renovation project was completed, the "Star of the Strip" shines brighter than ever.

Although the Stardust sign has also undergone some cosmetic changes, including state-of-the-art fountain and water displays, it still remains one of the ten most recognized signs in the world today rising 182 feet into the desert sky.

Rooms:
2,400 including 200 suites
Rates: $38 - $349

Special Features:
2 swimming pools, 3 whirlpool baths, 3 championship golf courses within a five minute drive, day passes to the Las Vegas Sports Club, sightseeing tours, video arcade, shopping plaza

Casino:
Gaming: 65,538 sq. ft.
Games: 1,950 slot and video machines, 44 blackjack tables, 6 crap tables, 5 roulette wheels, 2 keno lounges, wheel of fortune, 2 baccarat, 3 Pai Gow poker, 10 poker tables, race and sports book, mini-baccarat, 2 Let It Ride, 3 Caribbean stud, multiple action blackjack book

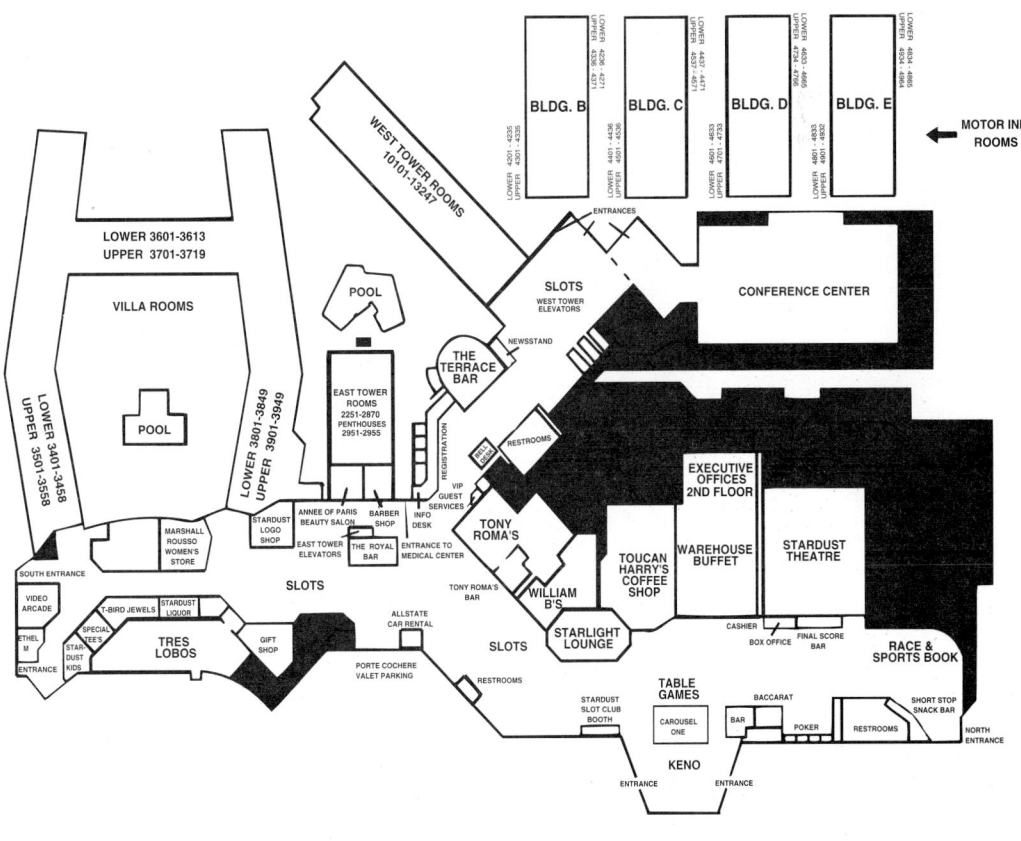

STRATOSPHERE

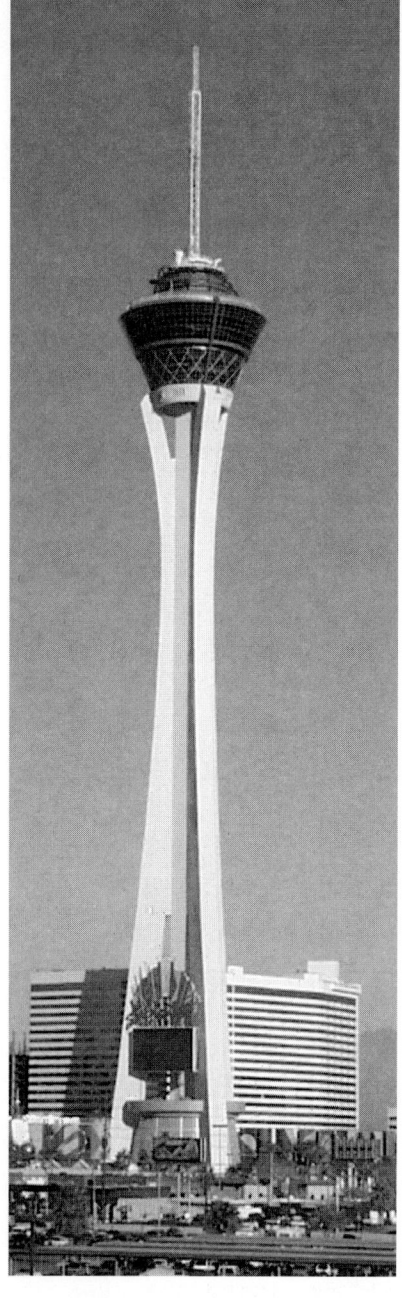

Stratosphere
2000 Las Vegas Blvd. S.
Las Vegas, NV 89104
380-7777 1-800-998-6937

Thomas Lettero, Sr. Pres
Andrew Blumen, Exec. VP/Gen. Mgr.
Mike Turngren, Dir. Casino Operations

A must-see attraction for everyone, the $550 million Stratosphere Hotel, Casino and Entertainment Complex broke ground November 5, 1991 and opened April 29, 1996. The hotel tower's top spire was lowered into place by helicopter on November 4, 1995 to signify the tower's structural completion. The 12-story tower begins at the 775-foot level and features the Pepsi Cola Observation Deck, the High Roller *(the highest rollercoaster in the world)*, the Big Shot *(the highest thrill ride in the world)*, a 220 seat cocktail lounge and a revolving restaurant which allows a unique 360 degree view of all of Las Vegas. Four high-speed double deck elevators, traveling as fast as 1,800 feet per minute, make the trip up the tower to the observation decks in only 30 seconds. The largest free-standing observation tower in the United States, soaring 1,149 feet in the air, the Stratosphere is the tallest building west of the Mississippi.

Rooms:
2,699 including 108 suites
Rates: $39 - $269

Special Features:
World's highest roller coaster, the High Roller, starting at 909 ft. above the ground; The Big Shot thrill ride shoots you 160 ft. to the 1,081 foot level; Kid's Quest child care center; four high-speed double-decker elevators travel at 1,800 ft. per minute, whisking visitors to the top of the tower in 30 seconds, where they can view Las Vegas from either the indoor or the outdoor observation deck; Dancing light show nightly, visible throughout the Las Vegas Valley.

Casino:
Gaming: 100,000 sq. ft.
Games: 2,040 slot and video games, 29 blackjack tables, 6 crap tables, 5 roulette wheels, 3 mini-baccarat, 2 Caribbean stud, 3 Pai Gow poker, 2 Let It Ride, 1 casino War, 2 three card poker, keno and sports book.

Entertainment:
Show Reservations: 380-7711
Broadway Showroom - *"American Superstars"* - Celebrity tribute - $25.25; kids 5 - 12 $18.95 *(see Pg. 167)*
Images Cabaret - *"Marshall Sylver"* - Master Hypnotist - $29.95 *(see Pg. 168)*
Broadway Showroom - *"Viva Las Vegas"* - Las Vegas revue - $11 includes tax *(see Pg. 167)*

L'Isles Bar - Caribbean/Reggae music

Dining:
Stratosphere Buffet: *(see Pg. 146)*
Breakfast - 8 am - 11 am $5.49
Lunch - 11 am - 4 pm $6.49
Dinner - Sun. - Fri. 4 pm - 9 pm; Sat. 4 pm - 10 pm $8.99
Big Sky Steak House - steaks and seafood - 24 hours *(see Pg. 140)*
Ferraro's - Italian *(see Pg. 121)*
McDonald's
Nathan's
Roxy's Diner *(see Pg. 152)*
Sister's Coffee Shop *(see Pg. 152)*
Top of the World Restaurant & Lounge - gourmet, revolves 360 degrees every hour *(see Pg. 137)*

Meeting & Banquet Facilities:
Total Space: The Stratosphere offers three separate meeting rooms each an average of 1,000 sq. ft. Call for further information.

Shopping & Services:
The same firm that built The Forum Shops at Caesars developed and operates The Tower Shops, which feature 35 stores and 11 retail kiosks including such names as Victoria's Secret, Bernini Sport, Bath & Body Works, Norman Kaplan Footwear, Sweet Factory, Swatch and Stratosphere Gifts.

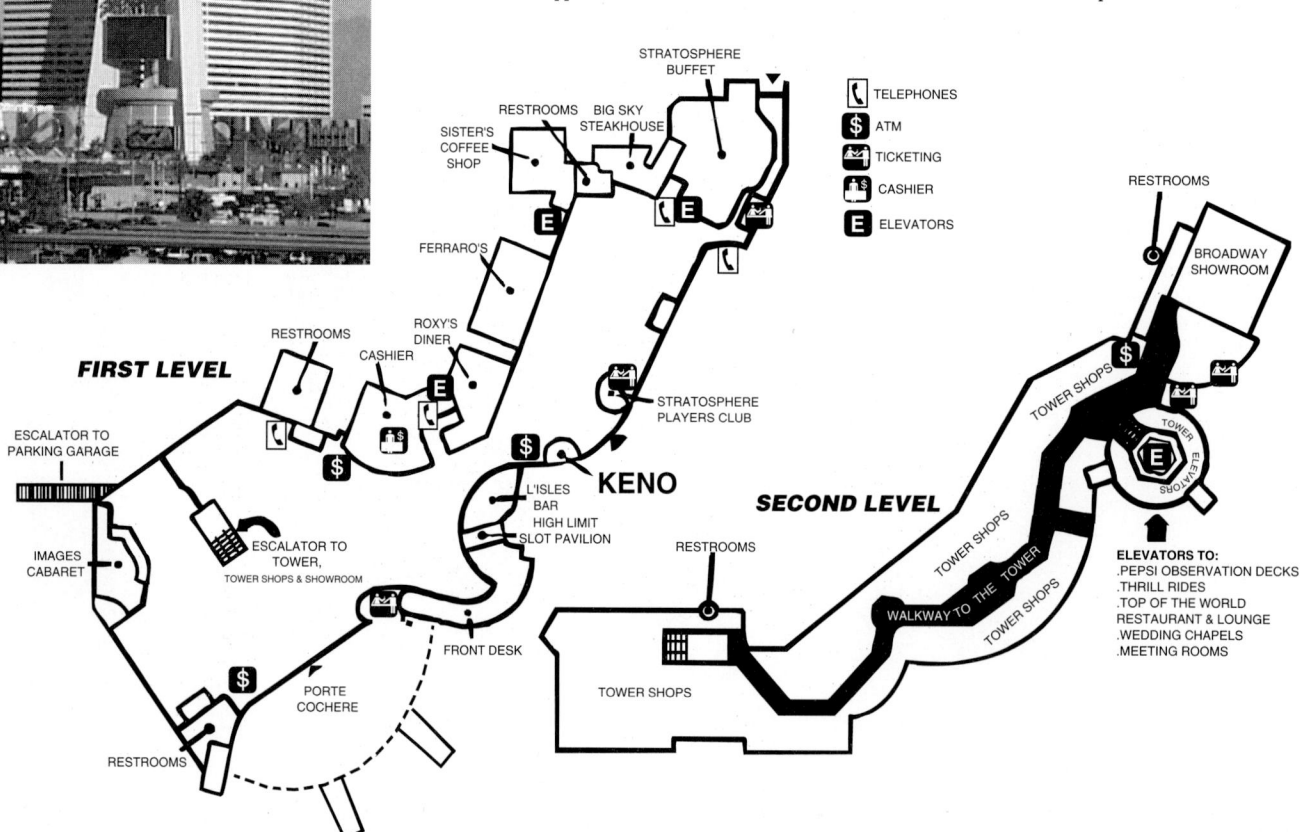

SUNSET STATION

Sunset Station
1301 W. Sunset Rd.
Henderson, NV 89014
547-7777 1-888-SUNSET9
www.sunsetstation.com
Frank Fertitta lll, Chairman/Pres./CEO
Don Marrandino, VP/Gen. Mgr.
Bart Pestrichello, Dir. Casino Operations

Sunset Station opened in June 1997 at a projected cost of $198 million, excluding pre-opening costs and capitalized interest. With intricate Spanish/Mediterranean architecture, furnishings and facades, visitors to the property feel as though they've somehow exited Las Vegas and wound up in an entirely different country. Sunset is filled with glazed tiles, fountains, ceramic-tiled columns and lots of brilliant color along with iron balconies, windows, rustic and weathered brick fronts that look and feel like a small Spanish town or a Barcelona neighborhood. The turrets of the casino structure run the gamut from mildly gothic to Ottoman Empire-inspired obelisks.

Rooms:
448 including 18 luxury king and 52 petite suites
Rates: $49 - $149

Special Features:
13-screen movie theater complex, Microbrewery, Kids Quest child-care facility, outdoor recreation facility and unique swimming pool with zero-edge entry with sofa edge for literally lounging on the water, conversation pits, circular area of swirling water, sandy volleyball play area, amphitheater and a grassy knoll area that can seat up to 4,000 for outdoor shows; Sega GameWorks video arcade

Casino:
Gaming: 80,000 sq. ft.
Games: 2,700 video poker & slot machines, 31 blackjack tables, 5 crap tables, 3 roulette wheels, 1 mini-baccarat, 2 Let It Ride, 1 Caribbean stud, 1 Spanish 21, 3 Pai Gow poker, race and sports book arena with 36-70 inch TVs, 1 keno lounge, 9 poker tables, bingo, 1 Vegas aces

Entertainment:
Show Reservations: 547-7777
Amphitheater - Headliner performances
Club Madrid - Entertainment nightly
Sunset Brewing Co. - Live entertainment

Dining:
Costa Del Sol - seafood & oyster Bar *(see Pg. 138)*
Capri - Italian
Capri Pizza Kitchen
Rosalita's - Mexican *(see Pg. 130)*

Sunset Brewing Co. Restaurant
Kenya's "Cakes of the Stars" - bakery
Fatburger - fast food
Manhattan Bagel *(see Pg. 156)*
Ben & Jerry's Scoop Shop
Sunset Cafe - 24-hour coffee shop
Feast Around the World Buffet: *(see Pg. 146)*
Breakfast - 7 am - 10:30 am - $3.99
Lunch - 11 am - 3 pm - $5.99
Dinner - 4 pm - 10 pm - $8.99
Steak and shrimp - Fri. 4 pm - 10 pm $10.99
Prime Rib - Sat. 4 pm - 10 pm $10.99
Sat. - Sun. Brunch - 7 am - 3:30 pm $7.99

Shopping and Services:
Sunset Gift Shop

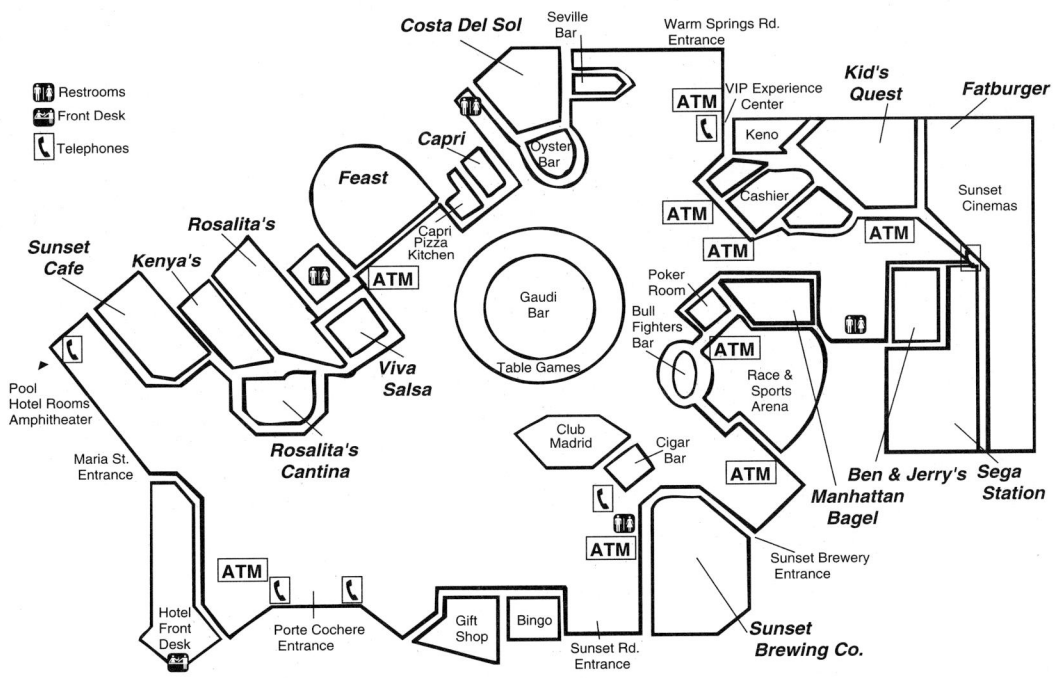

Photo: Photechnik International

TREASURE ISLAND

Treasure Island
3300 Las Vegas Blvd. S.
Las Vegas, NV 89109
894-7111 1-800-944-7444
John Strzemp, Pres.
Joe Wilcox, VP of Table Games

Treasure Island officially lowered its gangplank to the public in October 1993 at a cost of $430 million. It is a subsidiary of Mirage Resorts Incorporated, which also owns and operates the Golden Nugget Las Vegas, the Golden Nugget Laughlin and The Mirage. The company was acquired by Chairman Steve Wynn in August 1973. Wynn has guided the company from one small casino with no rooms downtown to one of the leading casino corporations in the world and is currently overseeing the development of the new Bellagio resort. Treasure Island is an idyllic getaway, based upon the village created by Robert Louis Stevenson in his novel, Treasure Island. Guests are transported to the Caribbean, to a time of pirates and dramatic sea battles at a resort that focuses on full-scale entertainment rather than standard showrooms and casinos. The lure of the pirate theme is apparent throughout the entire resort, in every nook and cranny, in a place that replicates a rich pirate capital.

Rooms:
2,900 including 212 suites
Rates: $39 - $249

Special Features:
Upon approaching Treasure Island, guests are welcomed with an exciting $32 million pirate battle presented daily. Buccaneer Bay is a unique attrac-

tion providing the sights and sounds of a bustling pirate village as waves crash against the shore, seagulls chatter and pirates call to one another as they work together on their ship, the *Hispaniola*, unloading the booty they have stolen from around the world. The British ship the *Royal Brittania* confronts the pirate ship and full-scale battle ensues as stunt men exchange fire and are thrown from their ships. The pirates, appearing to be losing the battle, make one last effort to fire their cannon at the British. The cannon hits and the *Royal Brittania* goes down. Tram leaves every 4 minutes to the Mirage from the third floor, Mutiny Bay is an 18,000 sq. ft. entertainment center offering video games, pinball and electronically simulated rides, swimming pool with a 200 ft. slide, spa and beauty salon, health club.

Casino:
Gaming: 51,152 sq. ft.
Games: 2,200 slot and video poker machines, Pai Gow, 1 mini-baccarat, 7 crap tables, 4 Caribbean stud, 52 blackjack tables, 13 poker tables, race and sports book, 8 roulette wheels, 2 keno lounges, 1 big wheels, 3 Pai Gow poker, 2 Let It Ride, race and sports book

Entertainment:
Show Reservations: 894-7722
The Showroom - *"Mystere"* - Cirque du Soleil - the world famous French-Canadian performing troupe - $69.85; children under 12 - $34.85 (see Pg. 166)

Dining:
Black Spot Grille - Mesquite Grille (see Pg. 153)
Buccaneer Bay Club - Continental (see Pg. 137)
Treasure Island Buffet: (see Pg. 146)
Breakfast - 6:45 am - 10:45 am - $5.99
Lunch - 10:45 am - 3:45 pm - $6.99
Dinner - 4 pm - 10 pm - $8.99
Sun. Brunch - 7:30 am - 3:30 pm $8.99
Lookout Cafe - 24 hour coffee shop (see Pg. 153)
Francesco's - Italian (see Pg. 121)
The Plank - steaks and seafood (see Pg. 139)
Madame Ching's - Chinese (see Pg. 116)
The Delicatessen - soups and sandwiches (see Pg. 156)
Sweet Revenge - ice cream

Meeting & Banquet Facilities:
Meeting Capacity: 1,428
Banquet Capacity: 856
Total space: 18,000 sq. ft.

Shopping & Services:
The Buccaneer Bay Shoppe - Treasure Island logo merchandise
Captain Kids - Children's logo merchandise, plush animals and toys
Crow's Nest - Treasure Island and Cirque du Soleil logo items
Damsels in Dis'Dress - Women's contemporary sportswear and accessories
Loot n' Booty - Themed logo merchandise, sundries and exotic Moroccan treasures
Treasure Chest - Watches, fine and fashion jewelry
Mystere Store - Show merchandise
Treasure Island at the Mirage Wedding Chapels
Health Club Spa and Beauty Salon

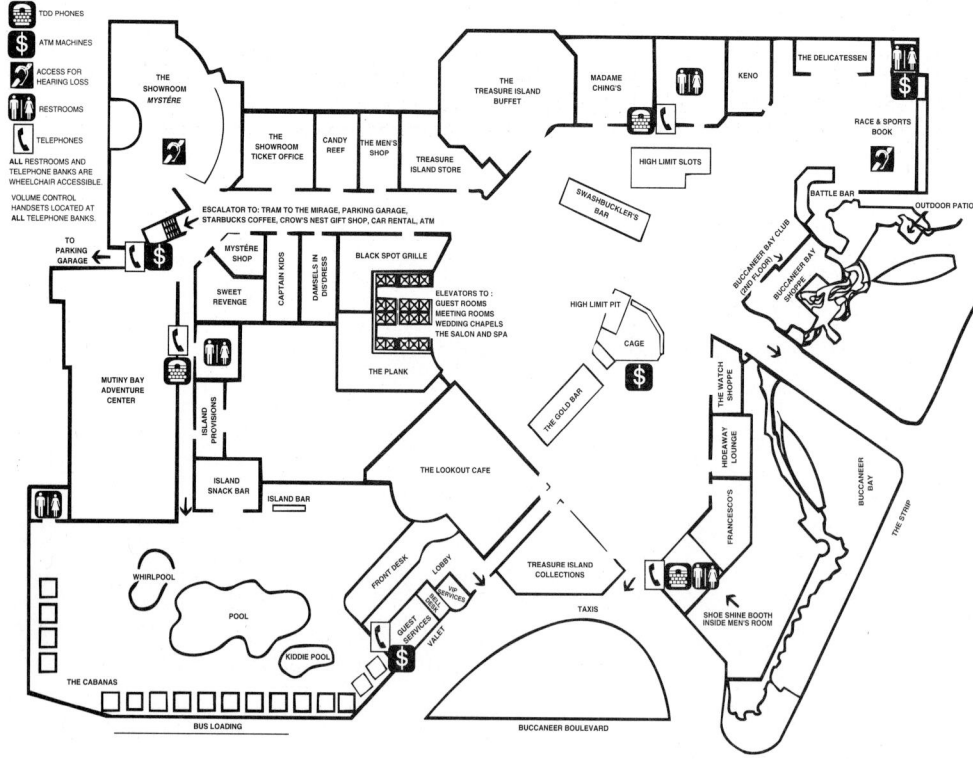

Photo: Phototechnik International

TROPICANA

**Tropicana Resort
& Casino**
3801 Las Vegas Blvd. S.
Las Vegas, NV 89109
739-2222 1-800-634-4000
Fax: 739-2469
Website http://tropicana.lv.com/
Jonathan Swain , Sr. VP of Operations
Rita Martin, Hotel Mgr.
Lee White, Casino Mgr.
Upon opening April 4, 1957, by Ben Jaffe and a group of investors, the Tropicana Resort became the unchallenged "Tiffany of the Strip," a metaphor first used by the *Saturday Evening Post* to describe the atmosphere of serene elegance conspicuously present throughout the hotel.

World famous from the day it opened, the palatial $15 million, 300-room complex sat on more than 17 acres. Unlike many other strip properties of that time, the Tropicana was designed and built as a luxury resort hotel, not as a casino and nightclub with incidental rooms. Eddie Fisher headlined in the showroom on opening night.

The Tropicana was purchased by the Ramada Corporation in 1979, the present owner. In 1989, Aztar Corporation, a publicly held company, was formed to operate the gaming division of Ramada. In 1997, the Tropicana celebrated its 40th anniversary with a new look including a brand new entrance way, a $1.4 million Baccarat room, premium slot area and an Atrium Lounge. A new edition of the Folies Bergere and an afternoon magic show, "The Illusionary Magic of Rick Thomas," debuted and a new Asian gaming room called the Jade Palace with noodle bar and a Chinese restaurant were opened.

Rooms:
1,874 including 120 suites and 80 mini-suites
Rates: $39 - $109

Special Features:
Health Club - Golden Spa Mizuno, 4,000-sq. ft. leaded stained glass dome above the main pit area, 5 acres of landscaped grounds complement lagoons, spas, waterfalls and the world's largest indoor-outdoor swimming pool, Wildlife walk, Game Arcade, Outside Elevator - Island Tower elevators to the 18th floor.

Casino:
Gaming: 45,200 sq. ft.
Games: 1,600 slot and video poker machines, 37 blackjack tables, 6 crap tables, 4 roulette wheels, 1 keno lounge, wheel of fortune, 2 Let It Ride, 4 baccarat, sports book, 3 Caribbean stud, multiple action blackjack. New Asian room opened called The Jade Palace. It contains 2 Sic-Bo, 2 Pai Gow poker, 2 Pai Gow and 2 mini-baccarat; Swim-up blackjack in pool; Pool side video poker and slots; Special instructional blackjack $1 bets only. Dealer will instruct you in rules and etiquette of the game. Roulette for a penny from - 8 pm.

Entertainment:
Show Reservations: 739-2411
Tiffany Theater - *"Folies Bergere"* - $45 - $55 *(see Pg. 165)*
"Comedy Stop" - 739-2714
Three comedians featured nightly $14.30 includes tax and 2 drinks. *(see Pg. 168)*
"The Illusionary Magic of Rick Thomas" - $8.95 *(see Pg. 168)*
Atrium Lounge - Entertainment nightly *(see Pg. 171)*

Dining:
Calypsos - 24 hour American restaurant *(see Pg. 153)*
El Gaucho Steak House *(see Pg. 141)*
Mizuno's - Japanese Steak House *(see Pg. 126)*
Pietro's Gourmet Diner - Continental Gourmet *(see Pg. 123)*
Player's Deli - soups and sandwiches
Island Buffet: *(see Pg. 146)*
Brunch - Mon. - Fri. 7:30 am - 1:30 pm - $7.95
Dinner - 5 pm - 10 pm - $9.95
Island Weekend Buffet - Sat. - Sun. 7:30 am - 2:30 pm - $9.95
Savanna - Unique dining includes buffalo & venison, chicken and seafood
Golden Dynasty - Chinese

Meeting & Banquet Facilities:
Total Meeting Capacity: 10,792
Total Banquet Capacity: 5,882
Total space: 89,830 sq. ft.

Shopping & Services:
Tropicana Box Office
Island Logo Shop
Island Wedding Chapel
The Jewelers of Las Vegas
Barber Shop
Beauty Salon
Gift Shop
Tropicana Fashions
Sports Emporium
Savmor Rent-a-Car

ACCOMMODATIONS

LAS VEGAS HOTEL MAP

WASHINGTON AVE.

WASHINGTON

95

BONANZA

95

ALTA DR.

STEWART

SEE DOWNTOWN
HOTEL MAP FOR
THIS AREA

★ARIZONA CHARLIE'S

CHARLESTON BLVD.

MAIN ST.

CASINO CTR. BLVD.

BONNEVILLE ST.

FREMONT ST.

15

LAS VEGAS BLVD

BOULDER HWY.

SHOWBOAT ★

OAKEY BLVD.

STRATOSPHERE ★

SAHARA AVE.

PALACE STATION ★

★ SAHARA

SAHARA AVE.

KAREN AVE.

DECATUR BLVD.

VALLEY VIEW BLVD.

CIRCUS CIRCUS ★

RIVIERA BLVD.
★RIVIERA

★ LAS VEGAS
HILTON

MARYLAND PKWY.

PECOS ROAD

STARDUST ★

CONVENTION CEN. DR.
★ROYAL   ★DEBBIE
         REYNOLDS

DESSERT INN RD.

FRONTIER ★
★ DESERT INN

SPRING MOUNTAIN RD.

SANDS
★ VENETIAN

TWAIN

EASTERN AVE.

TREASURE ISLAND ★

MIRAGE ★

★ HARRAH'S

PARADISE ROAD

CAESARS ★

★ IMPERIAL PALACE
★ FLAMINGO   BOURBON STREET
★ BARBARY COAST   ★ MAXIM

GOLD COAST
★   ★ RIO

FLAMINGO RD.

BELLAGIO ★   ★ BALLY'S
              ★ PARIS

FLAMINGO RD.

KOVAL LN.

W. HARMON

HARMON AVE.

★
ALEXIS   ST. TROPEZ ★
PARK

THE ORLEANS ★

HOLIDAY
BOARDWALK ★
MONTE CARLO ★   ★ POLO TOWERS
NEW YORK NY ★   ★ MGM GRAND

TROPICANA

EXCALIBUR ★   ★ TROPICANA
LUXOR ★   ★ SAN REMO

TROPICANA

RUSSELL ROAD

RUSSELL

15

LAS VEGAS BLVD.

**McCarran
International
Airport**

N

SUNSET ROAD

SUNSET ROAD

VACATION VILLAGE ★

WARM SPRINGS ROAD

LOCATIONS ARE APPROXIMATE

LAS VEGAS DOWNTOWN

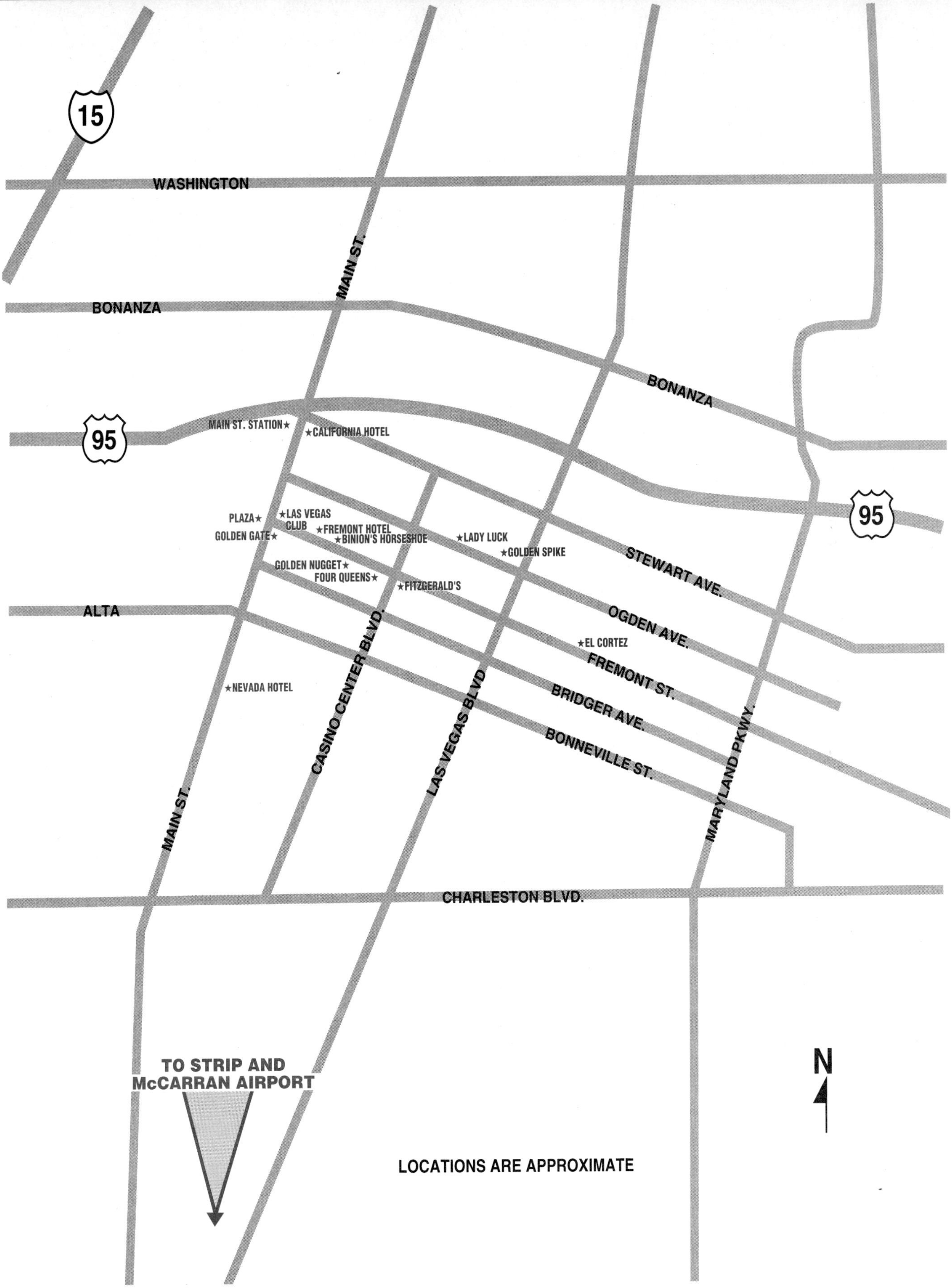

15

WASHINGTON

MAIN ST.

BONANZA

BONANZA

95

MAIN ST. STATION ★   ★ CALIFORNIA HOTEL

PLAZA ★   ★ LAS VEGAS
CLUB
GOLDEN GATE ★   ★ FREMONT HOTEL
★ BINION'S HORSESHOE   ★ LADY LUCK
★ GOLDEN SPIKE

GOLDEN NUGGET ★
FOUR QUEENS ★   ★ FITZGERALD'S

95

STEWART AVE.

OGDEN AVE.

★ EL CORTEZ

FREMONT ST.

ALTA

CASINO CENTER BLVD.

LAS VEGAS BLVD

BRIDGER AVE.

BONNEVILLE ST.

MARYLAND PKWY.

★ NEVADA HOTEL

MAIN ST.

CHARLESTON BLVD.

**TO STRIP AND
McCARRAN AIRPORT**

N

LOCATIONS ARE APPROXIMATE

ARIZONA CHARLIES

Arizona Charlie's
740 S. Decatur Blvd.
Las Vegas, NV 89107
258-5200 1-800-342-2695
TDD 258-5222
Bruce Becker, Pres.
Bucky Howard, Gen. Mgr.
Ron Lurie, Dir. of Mktg.
"Yes, there really was an Arizona Charlie. Born in 1860, his life was filled with truly amazing adventures. Arizona Charlie traveled the world with Buffalo Bill's Wild West Show and became a world champion steer roper. He tried to create a cattle empire on an island off the coast of Mexico and made a fortune during the Klondike Gold Rush. Charlie died on April 3, 1932, in Yuma, Arizona, the only date on record that it snowed in Yuma."
Rooms:
255 including 9 luxurious suites *(in a 7 story tower)*
Rates: $38 - $48 Sun. - Thu., $59 - $69 Fri., Sat. and holidays

Special Features: Pool and Jacuzzi, children's video arcade
Casino:
56,316 sq. ft.
Games: 1,400 slot and video poker machines, 16 blackjack tables, 2 crap tables, 1 roulette wheel, race and sports book, bingo parlor, Caribbean stud, 1 Let It Ride, 4 poker tables
Entertainment:
The Naughty Lady Saloon - entertainment nightly *(see Pg. 170)*
Dining:
Yukon Grille - steak house *(see Pg. 143)*
Charlie Chin's - Chinese *(see Pg. 113)*
Sourdough Cafe - 24 hours *(see Pg. 149)*
Food Court Deli
Wild West Buffet: *(see Pg. 144)*
Breakfast - 7 am - 10:30 am - $3.50
Lunch - 11 am - 3:30 pm - $4.50
Dinner - 4 pm - 10 pm - $6.50
Featuring all-you-can-eat prime rib nightly.
Meeting & Banquet Facilities:
Over 9,000 sq. ft. of banquet and meeting area with complete catering services.
Shopping & Services:
Gift Shop

BARBARY COAST

Barbary Coast
3595 Las Vegas Blvd. S.
Las Vegas, NV 89109
737-7111   1-800-634-6755
FAX: 737-6304
Michael Gaughan, Chairman
David Ross, Hotel & Gen. Mgr.
The Barbary Coast opened its doors in March 1979 with 150 beautifully decorated rooms and suites. A lavish display of stained-glass, magnificent chandeliers and plush decor, it successfully shared the Strip's famous "four corners" with its more towering neighbors. In the past 16 years the Barbary Coast has undergone three expansion programs which have added 50 rooms, increased the size of the casino and expanded the service facilities.
Rooms:
200 including 12 suites in an 8 story tower
Rates: $49 - $109

Special Features:
World's largest stained-glass mural, "Garden of Earthly Delights". Measuring 30 feet long and 5 feet high, it depicts a Victorian era fantasy and took more than 10,000 hours to complete, created by the Wallach Stained Glass Studio in Berkeley, California, it is the largest mural of its kind in the world; shuttle to Gold Coast
Casino:
32,000 sq. ft.
Games: 520 slots and video machines, 32 blackjack tables, 4 crap tables, 2 roulette wheels, 1 mini-baccarat, 4 Pai Gow poker, 1 keno lounge, race and sports book, 1 Let It Ride
Dining:
McDonald's - fast food
Michaels - gourmet steak & seafood
Victorian Room - 24 hour coffee shop
Drai's - French cuisine
Shopping & Services:
Western Union
Gift Shop

BOULDER STATION

Boulder Station
4111 Boulder Hwy.
Las Vegas, NV 89121
432-7777 1-800-683-7777
Felix Rappaport, VP & Gen. Mgr.
Rick Fields, Casino Mgr.
The $103 million project built by Station Casinos opened its doors August 23, 1994. The hotel/casino features a wide variety of gaming, dining and entertainment opportunities including Boulder Station cinemas and Kids Quest. The casino features a hand-painted sky ceiling and is based on a continuous design, with all entertainment and dining offerings radiating from a central 75,000 sq. ft. casino area creating an atmosphere of openness and easy mobility. Outside the casino stands a 160 ft. high, free standing sign featuring the world's largest color message center. Made up of 66,000 light bulbs and 2 1/2 mi. of neon, the message center transmits words and graphics over its 8,000 sq. ft. sign face.

Rooms: 300 rooms, including 6 suites
Rates: $49 - $110
Special Features:
Swimming pool, children's video arcade and redemption center, state-of-the-art 11-plex ACT III movie theaters, Kids Quest child care facility, cigar bar.
Casino: 90,000 sq. ft.
Games: Over 3,000 slots and video poker machines, 30 blackjack tables, 4 crap tables, 2 Caribbean stud, 1 Let It Ride, 2 Pai Gow poker, 3 roulette wheels, mini baccarat, 10 table poker room, 240 seat race and sports book.
70-seat keno lounge.
Entertainment:
The Railhead - live music nightly
Dining:
The Feast Action Buffet *(see Pg. 144)*
The Broiler - steak and seafood
Guadalajara Bar & Grille - Mexican
Iron Horse Cafe - Coffee Shop
Pasta Palace - Italian *(see Pg. 122)*
Food Court - featuring 8 quick-service food outlets

CALIFORNIA HOTEL

CONTINENTAL HOTEL

DEBBIE REYNOLDS

California Hotel/Casino & RV Park
12 E. Ogden Ave.
Las Vegas, NV 89101
385-1222 1-800-634-6255
Fax: 388-2660

John Repetti, Exec. Vice-Pres. and Gen. Mgr.
Pam Martin, Dir. of Hotel Operations
David Lebby, Casino Mgr.

Originally built in 1975, the California Hotel, Casino and RV Park is the cornerstone of the Boyd Gaming Corporation. The original tower of the California consisted of 300 guest rooms but in 1984 it underwent a $34 million expansion adding an additional tower with 335 new guest rooms, an enlarged casino area, restaurant and sports book. The first and only RV park in downtown Las Vegas was put into operation at the California Hotel in 1985.

Rooms: 781 including 74 suites - 11 story tower and 9 story tower
Rates: $50 - $70
RV Park: 100 Stewart Ave. - 388-2602
Rates: $12
222 spaces: 88 pull through, 192 full hookup, 30 with water and electric only; restroom, shower, laundry, dog run, swimming pool and Jacuzzi *(open year round)*, convenience store, dump sta-

tion. 20, 30 and 50 amp hook-ups. Only RV park downtown.
Special Features:
Swimming pool and Jacuzzi, video arcade, climate-controlled bridge to Main Street Station
Casino: 35,848 sq. ft.
Games: 1,100 slot and video machines, 24 blackjack tables, 6 crap tables, 2 roulette wheels, 1 keno lounge, 1 Pai Gow poker, race and sports book, 1 Caribbean stud, 1 Let It Ride, 1 mini-baccarat
Entertainment: Three cocktail lounges
Dining:
Cal Club Snack Bar
Market Street Cafe - Continental - 24 hour coffee shop *(see Pg. 149)*
Pasta Pirate - Italian/Seafood *(see Pg. 122)*
Redwood Bar & Grill - Steak & Seafood *(see Pg. 142)*
Meeting & Banquet Facilities:
Total Meeting Capacity: 500
Total Banquet Capacity: 300
Total Space: 5,435 sq. ft.
Shopping & Services:
Gift Shop
Logo Shop
Lappert's Ice Cream
Ethel M Chocolates
Aloha Specialties - Hawaiian Gifts
Video game room

Continental Hotel & Casino
4100 Paradise Rd.
Las Vegas, NV 89109
737-5555 1-800-634-6641

Ira Levy, Pres./Gen. Mgr.
Barbara Spehar, Hotel Mgr.

Rooms:
400 including 2 suites
Rates: $35 - $55

Special Features:
Airport shuttle, swimming pool, free door-to-door transportation

Casino: 33,848 sq. ft.
Games: 539 slot and video machines, 7 blackjack tables, crap table, roulette wheel, sports book

Entertainment:
Juke Box Theater - *A Tribute to the Ed Sullivan Show* - two drink minimum *(see Pg. 167)*
Juke Box Theater - *Heatwave* - $19.95
Casino Lounge - Entertainment nightly

Dining:
Big Daddy's Diner - 24 hour coffee shop
Continental Hotel Cafe *(see Pg. 150)*

Shopping & Services:
Gift Shop

Debbie Reynolds Hotel/Casino & Hollywood Movie Museum
305 Convention Center Dr.
Las Vegas, NV 89109
734-0711 1-800-633-1777

Todd Fisher, Pres.
Henry Cutrona, Hotel Mgr
Roy Warren, Casino Mgr.

Originally known as the Paddlewheel the hotel was purchased in 1984 by Horn and Hardart, the New York City automat coffee shop owners. The hotel closed October 13, 1991. In 1992, actress Debbie Reynolds purchased the hotel and refurbished the entire property. Opened in July 1993 and renamed the Debbie Reynolds Hotel, its Hollywood motif is carried out through decorations and displays of rare artifacts from Debbie's $30 million collection of Hollywood memorabilia.

Rooms: 192 rooms with 43 time-share rooms and two-room suites with parlor, wet bar, spa-size tub and king-size bed

Rates: $75 - $95
Special Features:
Movie props and costumes from famous movies are displayed throughout the hotel; Hollywood Movie Museum - memorabilia from Reynolds' vast collection dating from the silent era up to the 1960s; admission $7.95
Casino: 6,500 sq. ft.
Games: 25 slot and video machines
Entertainment:
Showroom: *Debbie Reynolds Show* - $39.95; with dinner - $55; reservations required. *(see Pg. 169)*
The Kenny Kerr Show - featuring one of Las Vegas' top female impersonators - $21.95 *(see Pg. 167)*
Broadway...Off B'Way - A tribute to major musicals - $35 *(see Pg. 167)*
Dining:
The Celebrity Cafe - 24 hours - seafood, pasta and chicken *(see Pg. 150)*
Meeting & Banquet Facilities:
Total Space: 11,300 sq. ft.
Shopping & Services:
Tinseltown Gift Shop

EL CORTEZ

FIESTA

FITZGERALDS HOTEL

El Cortez
600 E. Fremont St.
Las Vegas, NV 89101
385-5200 1-800-634-6703
Jackie Gaughan, Pres.
Frank Giannosa, Casino Shift Mgr.
The El Cortez opened in November 1941 at a cost of $325,000. Although it was completely renovated in 1983 a portion of the original building still stands. Present owner Jackie Gaughan acquired the hotel in 1963.

Rooms:
308
Rates: $23 - $40

Special Features:
Video Arcade

Casino:
Gaming: 41,300 sq. ft.
Games: 2,122 slot and video machines, 3 crap tables, 2 roulette tables, 11 blackjack tables, keno, mini-baccarat, race and sports book, 3 poker tables

Dining:
Roberta's Cafe - Steak & Seafood *P.142*
Emerald Room - 24 hour. coffee shop
Snack Bar

Meeting & Banquet Facilities:
Total Meeting Capacity: 175
Total Banquet Capacity: 150
Total Space: 2,000 sq. ft.

Shopping & Services:
El Cortez Barber Shop
Crown Beauty Shop
Gift Shop

Fiesta Casino Hotel
2400 N. Rancho Dr.
Las Vegas, NV 89130
631-7000 1-800-731-7333
George J. Maloof, Pres.
Ed Fasulo, Gen. Mgr.
John James, Casino Mgr.
Opened in December 1995, the Fiesta Hotel/Casino is a favorite among Las Vegas locals. Known as the "Royal Flush Capital of the World," Fiesta continues to solidify its reputation with the Slot House: 1,200 of the loosest and most frequently hit video poker machines on the planet.
Rooms:
100 including 4 suites
Rates: $49 - $99
Special Features:
Video poker lessons given in the Cabo Lounge at 11 am and again at 2 pm
Casino:
Gaming: 50,000 sq. ft.
Games: 1,320 slot and video machines, 2 crap tables, 2 roulette wheel, 13 blackjack tables, keno, bingo, 1 Let It Ride, 2 Pai Gow poker, race and sports

book featuring 100 individual TVs, 12 - 60" mega TVs; Sports on the Run - drive thru sports book - place sports bets from your car.
Entertainment:
Cabo Wabo Lounge - featuring nightly entertainment and cocktail parties
Dining:
Festival Buffet: *(see Pg. 144)*
Breakfast - 7 am - 11 am - $3.99
Lunch - 11 am - 3:30 pm - $5.99
Dinner - 4 pm - 10 pm - $8.99
Champagne Brunch - Sat. - Sun. 7 am - 3 pm - $7.99
Hawaiian Luau - Mon. - 3:30 pm - 10 pm - $10.99
Seafood Extravaganza - Wed. - 3:30 pm - 10 pm - $12.99
Margarita Brunch - Sun. 10 am - 3 pm - $9.99 served in Garduno's Restaurant
Garduno's - Mexican *(see Pg. 128)*
Mr. G's Diner - 24 hour coffee shop
Old San Fran. Steak House *(see Pg. 142)*
The Deli Bakery and Ice Cream Parlor *(see Pg. 156)*
Panda Express - Chinese *(see Pg. 116)*
Shopping & Services:
Fiesta Gift Shop

FITZGERALDS CASINO HOLIDAY INN
301 Fremont St.
Las Vegas, NV 89101
388-2400 1-800-274-5825
Fax: 388-2181
Bill Noonan, Gen. Mgr.
Mary Crane, Sr. Hotel Dir.
Pam Moretti-Blanner, Hotel Mgr.
Doug DuCharme, Casino Dir.
Fitzgeralds opened in 1980 as the Sundance Hotel and when purchased in 1987 was renamed Fitzgeralds. Standing 360' tall with a 10 story parking garage offering 340 spaces, it is one of the largest Holiday Inns in the world. Guests are greeted at the entrance by Nevada's largest neon rainbow and Mr. O'Lucky, a 35 ft. leprechaun.
Rooms:
652 hotel rooms; 34 stories
Rates: $40 - $100
Special Features:
One of Nevada's tallest hotels, Fitzgerald's features the largest neon rainbow in the state along with a 35 foot leprechaun.
Casino:
Gaming: 42,000 sq. ft.

Games: 1,108 slot and video machines, 20 blackjack tables, 3 crap tables, 2 roulette tables, keno, big wheel, 1 Caribbean stud, 2 Let It Ride, "21 Superbucks", race and sports book
Entertainment:
Fitzgeralds Lounge Live entertainment on the first floor of the casino with Las Vegas' "hottest" lounge acts. *(see Pg. 170)*
Dining:
Molly's Country Kitchen and Buffet:
Breakfast - 7 am - 11 am - $4.99
Lunch - 11:30 am - 4 pm - $5.49
Dinner - 5 pm - 9 pm - $7.99
Sat. & Sun. Champagne Brunch - 8 am - 4 pm - $7.99
Limerick Steak House - Steak & Seafood; Italian Specialties - Thu. - Mon. 4 pm - 10 pm *(see Pg. 141)*
Molly's - 24 hour coffee shop
McDonald's - fast food
Vincenzo's - Italian
Meeting and Banquet Facilities:
Total Meeting Capacity: 325
Total Banquet Capacity: 175
Total Space: 3,500 sq. ft.
Shopping & Services:
Gift Shop
Tour Desk
Rental Car Desk

Photo: Tiffany Design

FOUR QUEENS

Four Queens
202 Fremont St.
Las Vegas, NV 89101
385-4011 1-800-634-6045
Fax: 383-0631
Martin Gross, Gen. Mgr.
Phil Madou, Dir. of Hotel Operations
Joe Stahl, Casino Operations
The Four Queens opened in 1966 by Ben Goffstein who named the casino Four Queens because of his four daughters. Later it was acquired by the Hyatt Corporation and today is operated by the Elsinore Corporation. The Four Queens is tastefully decorated in turn-of-the-century New Orleans motif.

Rooms:
690 including 14 suites and 30 deluxe mini-suites
Rates: $49 - $150

Casino:
Gaming: 32,296 sq. ft.

Games: 1,040 slot and video machines, 28 blackjack tables, 4 crap tables, 2 roulette tables, keno lounge, 1 Pai Gow poker, 3 Caribbean stud, multiple action blackjack, 3 Let it Ride, race and sports book

Entertainment:
Royal Pavilion - *"Comedy Fun House"* Admission is free with one drink minimum
Kings' Bar - Center of casino
Hugo's Bar - In Hugo's Cellar Restaurant

Dining:
Hugo's Cellar - Gourmet *(see Pg. 141)*
Magnolia's Veranda - 24 hr. coffee shop *(see Pg. 150)*

Meeting and Banquet Facilities:
Total Meeting Capacity: 700
Total Space: 12,180 sq. ft.

Shopping & Services:
Four Queens Gift Shop
Same Day Laundry and Dry-Cleaning

Photo: Phototechnik International

FREMONT HOTEL

FREMONT HOTEL & CASINO
200 E. Fremont St.
Las Vegas, NV 89101
385-3232 1-800-634-6460
Fax: 385-6229
John Buchanan, VP/Gen. Mgr.
Connie Turner, Hotel Mgr.
Mike McCabe, Casino Mgr.
Sam Boyd's Fremont Hotel/Casino opened in 1956. Originally owed by Sam Levinson, the famous resort was the first high-rise in downtown Las Vegas. Purchased by Boyd Gaming Corp. in 1985, it has undergone over $40 million in renovations including a complete Italian marble exterior facelift. In the heart of the illustrious Glitter Gulch, the Fremont Hotel is located in the heart of the Fremont Street Experience.

Rooms:
452 including 24 suites
Rates: $29 - $79

Casino:
Gaming: 32,000 sq. ft.
Games: 1,100 slot and video machines,

16 blackjack tables, 4 crap tables, 3 roulette tables, keno lounge, race and sports book, Pai Gow poker, 1 Caribbean stud, 2 Let It Ride, 1 Spanish 21, non-smoking tables are available

Dining:
Lanai Express - Snack Bar
Lanai Cafe - American/Chinese - 24 hours *(see Pg. 150)*
Paradise Buffet: *(see Pg. 144)*
Breakfast - Mon. - Fri. 7 am - 10:30 am - $4.95
Lunch - Mon. - Fri. 11 am - 3 pm - $5.95
Dinner - Mon., Wed., Thu. and Sat. 4 pm - 11 pm - $8.95
Seafood Fantasy: Tue. and Sun. 4 pm - 10 pm , Fri. - 4 pm - 11 pm - $12.95
Sunday Champagne Brunch - 7 am - 3 pm - $7.95
Second Street Grill - American Contemporary *(see Pg. 136)*
Tony Roma's - ribs and chicken *(see Pg. 134)*

Meeting & Banquet Facilities:
385-6256
Total space: 7,400

Shopping & Services:
Gift Shop - 385-6249

GOLD SPIKE

Gold Spike Hotel & Casino
400 E. Ogden Ave.
Las Vegas, NV 89101
384-8444 1-800-634-6703
Jackie Gaughan, Owner
Mike Nolan, Gen. Mgr.

Rooms:
110 including 7 suites
Rates: $20 - $30

Special Features:
Video arcade

Casino:
Gaming: 5,820 sq. ft.
Games: 436 slot and video machines, 3 blackjack tables, keno lounge, poker table

Dining:
Diner

GOLDEN GATE

Golden Gate Hotel & Casino
1 Fremont St.
Las Vegas, NV 89101
385-1906 1-800-426-1906
Fax: 382-5349
Craig Ghelfi & Mark Brandenburg, Owners
Mike Young, Casino Mgr.
"Where Las Vegas started and the Fremont Street Experience begins"
Built in 1906 at One Fremont St., The Golden Gate is Las Vegas' oldest and most historic hotel. The first hotel in Nevada to be built out of concrete, it has survived the test of time, with the original structure still standing among the glitter and neon that is Fremont St. Originally named Hotel Nevada when it opened, the property which it stands on was sold at auction in 1905 along with two other corner lots for a total of $1,750. The name was changed to the Sal Sagev *(Las Vegas spelled backwards)* in 1931 and finally named the Golden Gate in 1955. Being the first hotel in southern Nevada, it was also the site of the first telephone service in the area; installed in 1907, the number issued for the phone was simply "1." With only 106 rooms, making it the area's smallest hotel, the Golden Gate has the best of both worlds. Guests of the hotel can enjoy the intimate atmosphere of a "bed and breakfast" and then step out the front door into the fabulous Fremont Street Experience. Las Vegas' oldest casino.
Rooms: 106 **Rates:** $35 - $49 + tax
Casino:
Gaming: 9,090 sq. ft.
Games: 445 slot and video machines, 12 blackjack tables, 2 crap tables, roulette wheel, keno lounge, Caribbean stud, 1 Let It Ride, 1 Casino War
Entertainment:
Live piano music from noon until midnight daily
Dining:
Bay City Diner *(see Pg. 150)*
San Francisco Shrimp Bar & Deli
Another first, the Golden Gate introduced the shrimp cocktail to the Las Vegas area in 1959 at a cost of 50¢. The price did not change for 32 years. Golden Gate is now known for its "famous" 99 cent shrimp cocktail.

HOLIDAY INN BOARDWALK

Holiday Inn · Casino Boardwalk
3750 Las Vegas Blvd. S.
Las Vegas, NV 89109
735-2400 1-800-HOLIDAY
Forrest J. Woodward II, Pres.
Amy Thomason, Gen. & Hotel Mgr.
Bobby Preston, Casino Mgr.
Holiday Inn Casino Boardwalk completed its casino expansion and renovation in 1996. The newest tower brought the total rooms to 675, making this the largest Holiday Inn in America. Its Coney Island theme is carried throughout the casino with its exterior including everything from the famous Coney Island rollercoaster to a full scale ferris wheel, complete with life like figures dressed in nineteenth century attire. Sold to Mirage Resorts in 1997.
Rooms: 675 deluxe rooms and suites
Rates: $39 - $169
Special Features: 2 swimming pools
Casino:
Gaming: 33,000 sq. ft.
Games: 661 slot and video poker machines, 2 roulette wheels, 13 blackjack tables, 2 crap tables, 1 wheel of fortune, race and sports book, 1 Let It Ride, 2 Spanish 21, 1 Caribbean stud
Entertainment:
Show Reservations: 730-3194
"The Dream King" - Featuring Trent Carlini as the King of Rock 'N Roll - $19.95 *(see Pg. 167)*
Mr. Dixie Dooley's Unreal Magic Show - A magic show for all ages - $8.95; children $5 *(see Pg. 168)*
Dining:
Cyclone Coffee Shop - 24 hour *(see Pg. 150)*
Deli - 24 hour
The Surf Buffet:
Breakfast - 7 am - 11 am - $3.29
Lunch - 11 am - 4:30 pm - $4.69
Dinner - 4:30 pm - 10 pm - $5.99
Shopping & Services:
Gift Shop
Enterprise Car Rental
Tour Desk

Photo: Phototechnik International

BINION'S HORSESHOE

Binion's Horseshoe
128 Fremont St.
Las Vegas, NV 89101
382-1600 1-800-937-6537
Jack Binion, Pres.
Mike Cericola, Casino Mgr.
Binion's Horseshoe was instrumental in helping to shape the Las Vegas gambling scene in the 1950s. Founded by Benny Binion, the Horseshoe has since become legendary as the home of gambling, great service and great food. Home of the best odds and the highest limits, serious players are drawn to the Horseshoe and its first bet house limit which can go as high as $1 million or more with the approval of Mr. Binion; jackpots are high as well. For instance, the Horseshoe's progressive Caribbean Stud jackpot begins at $25,000. Much of the Horseshoe's success, of course, can be attributed to the World Series of Poker which has grown in popularity each year since it began in 1970. The largest tournament of its kind in the world today, gambling's most highly publicized event attracts more than 3,000 entries and pays out millions in prize money, including a $1 million first place prize to the "world champion." This year, more than $8.5 million was paid out in total prize money.
Rooms: 363 including 13 suites
Rates: $30 - $89
Casino: Gaming: 56,929 sq. ft.
Games: 1,385 slot and video machines, 39 blackjack tables (single deck), 12 crap tables, 3 roulette wheels, 1 keno lounge, bingo, big wheel, 2 baccarat, race and sports book, red dog, 14 poker tables, 1 Caribbean stud, Pai Gow poker, 5 mini baccarat, 1 Let It Ride, 1 Spanish 21
Dining:
Binion's Ranch Steak House - Steak *(see Pg. 140)*
Buffet: *(see Pg. 144)*
Dinner - 4:30 pm - 10:30 pm - $9.95
Seafood Buffet - Fri. - $14.95
Gee Joon Chinese Restaurant - Chinese
Binion's Coffee Shop *(see Pg. 150)*
Sports Book Deli
2 Snack Bars
Shopping & Services: 2 Gift Shops

LADY LUCK

Photo: Phototechnik International

LAS VEGAS CLUB

MAIN STREET STATION

Lady Luck Hotel & Casino
206 N. Third St.
Las Vegas, NV 89101
477-3000 1-800-LADYLUCK
Fax: 477-0721
Craig Ghelfi, Gen. Mgr.
Mike Sage, Hotel Mgr.
Jim Dickstein, Casino Mgr.
The Lady Luck started in 1964 as a snack bar and newsstand with just 17 slot machines.

Rooms:
791 including 141 suites *(25 story tower and 17 story tower)*
Rates: Sun. - Thu. $49 - $109

Special Features:
Swimming pool

Casino:
Gaming: 18,350 sq. ft.
Games: 870 slot and video machines, 16 blackjack tables, 3 crap tables, 2 roulette wheels, Caribbean stud, keno lounge, 1 mini-baccarat, 2 Let It Ride, Pai Gow poker, 1 double disclosure, 1 Spanish 21, 3 card poker

Entertainment:
Show Reservations: 385-4386
Steve Wyrick World Class Magician - $27.95 plus tax & gratuities *(see Pg. 168)*
The Lady Luck Luau - Monday nights - dinner at 6 pm , show at 7:30 pm; $14.95 per person + tax.

Dining:
Burgundy Room - Gourmet *(see Pg. 136)*
The Winners' Cafe - 24 hour coffee shop
Marco Polo - Italian *(see Pg. 121)*
The Taste of the World Buffet:
(see Pg. 144)
Breakfast - 6 am - 10:30 am - $4.49
Lunch - Mon. - Fri. - 9 am - 3 pm - $4.49
Dinner - 4 pm - 10 pm - $9.95
Sat. - Sun. Brunch - 10:30 am - 6 pm - $6.49

Shopping & Services:
Gift Shop

Las Vegas Club
18 Fremont St.
Las Vegas, NV 89101
385-1664 1-800-634-6532
Mel Exber, Pres.
Brady Exber, VP/Hotel Mgr.
Frank Cornett, Gen. Mgr.
Scott Walker, Casino Mgr.
Built as the Overland Hotel in 1905. The Las Vegas Club added a 16-story tower with 185 more rooms, 18,000 sq. ft. of casino space and two new restaurants in Sept. 1996.

Rooms:
410 including 8 suites
Rates: $40 - $125

Special Features:
Sports Hall of Fame - large collection of baseball memorabilia

Casino:
Gaming: 40,000 sq. ft.
Games: 943 slot and video machines, 18 blackjack tables, 4 crap tables, roulette wheel, 1 Caribbean stud, keno lounge, 2 Let It Ride, race and sports book. Claims most liberal rules on blackjack

Entertainment:
None

Dining:
Dugout *(see Pg. 151)*
The Upper Deck
Coffee Shop - 24 hour
Great Moments - Gourmet (see Pg. 136)

Shopping & Services:
Gift Shop
Logo Apparel Shop

Main Street Station
200 N. Main St.
Las Vegas, NV 89101
387-1896 1-800-713-8933
William S. Boyd, Chairman/CEO, Boyd Gaming
Robert Boughner, Exec. VP/COO, Boyd Gaming
Bruce Fraser, VP/Gen. Mgr.
Jim Sullivan, Casino Mgr.
Boyd Gaming Corporation acquired Main Street Station in 1993 at a cost of $16.5 million and renovated the property at an additional cost of $45 million before opening in 1996. The hotel, which sports a turn-of-the-century Victorian atmosphere, is home to $3 million in one-of-a-kind historical art treasures and museum-quality antiques, together with four authentic antique sleeper cars. The Cascade rail car has been carefully preserved and is currently valued at $500,000 by the Smithsonian Institute. The cars are located in a well-lit, tree-lined streetscape stretching to the Union Plaza Hotel.
Responding to the growing nationwide thirst for microbrewed, or "craft style" beer, the Main Street Station is also home to Las Vegas' first microbrewery. Upon opening in 1996, the Triple 7 Brewery offered locals and tourists alike a new alternative for dining and entertainment.

Rooms:
406 rooms including 14 suites.
Rates: $30 - $50
Special Features:
Microbrewery; Antiques and museum quality reproductions throughout the entire property
Casino:
Gaming: More than 28,000 sq. ft.
Games: 900 state of the art machines and a variety of poker machines, 13 blackjack tables, 1 Pai Gow poker, 2 Let It Ride, 4 crap tables, 2 roulette wheels, keno lounge
Entertainment:
Triple 7 BrewPub - Live entertainment -weekends only
Dining:
Pullman Grille - Steakhouse
Cascade - 24 hour coffee shop
Triple 7 BrewPub - Sushi bar
Garden Court Buffet:
Breakfast - 7 am - 10:30 am - $4.99
Lunch - 11 am - 3 pm - $6.99
Dinner - 4 pm - 10 pm - $8.99
Seafood Buffet - Fri. 4 pm - 10 pm $12.99
Champagne Brunch - Sun. 7 am - 3 pm - $7.99
Shops and Services:
Gift Shop

ACCOMMODATIONS

MAXIM

NEVADA PALACE

PLAZA HOTEL

Maxim Hotel & Casino
160 E. Flamingo Rd.
Las Vegas, NV 89109
731-4300   1-800-634-6987
Fax: 735-3252
Larry Feil, CEO
Floyd Benedict, Hotel Mgr.
Ray Anzevino, Casino Mgr.
Opened in 1977, room remodeling began in 1993.
Rooms:
795 including 38 suites *(2 - 17 story towers)*
Rates: $39 - $59
Special Features:
Swimming pool, Jacuzzis in some suites
Casino:
Gaming: 17,250 sq. ft.
Games: 733 slot and video machines, 17 blackjack tables, 2 crap tables, 2 roulette wheels, 1 Caribbean stud, keno lounge, sports book, 1 Let It Ride
Entertainment:
Cloud Nine Lounge
Comedy Max Theater:

Show Reservations: 731-4300
Comedy Max - $16.25 includes tax and two drinks; with Grand Evening Buffet $19.95 includes tax and two drinks. *(see Pg. 168)*
Comedy Magic - $9.95 or $12.95 with buffet. *(see Pg. 168)*
Show Reservations: 734-8550
Dining:
Maxim Buffet: *(see Pg. 145)*
Brunch - Mon. - Fri. 9 am - 3 pm - $4.95
Grand Evening Buffet - 4 pm - 10 pm - $6.95
Champagne Brunch - Sat. - Sun. 9 am - 3 pm- $10.95
Jack's Colossal Deli & Snacks
Da Vinci's - Continental *(see Pg. 120)*
Tree House - Coffee Shop; 11 am - 2 am
Meeting & Banquet Facilities:
Total Meeting Capacity: 350
Total Meeting Space: 3,600 sq. ft.
Shopping & Services:
Beauty Shop
Gift Shop
T-Shirt Shop

Nevada Palace Hotel & Casino
5255 Boulder Hwy.
Las Vegas, NV 89122
458-8810 1-800-634-6283
Bill Wortman, Pres.
Bob Braner, Hotel Mgr.

Rooms:
210
Rates: $35 - $50

Special Features:
Nevada Palace VIP Travel Trailer Park
Boulder Hwy. - 451-0231
168 space RV park; swimming pool/Jacuzzi

Casino:
Gaming: 13,000 sq. ft.

Games: 499 slots and video machines, 9 blackjack tables, crap tables, 1 roulette wheels, keno lounge, 2 poker tables, 1 Let It Ride, sports book

Dining:
Boulder Cafe - 24 hour coffee shop *(see Pg. 151)*
Herman's Deli
La Bella Pasta - Italian *(see Pg. 121)*
Buffet - Sat. - Thu. 4 pm - 9 pm - $4.49, Fri. seafood - $6.99, Sat. - Sun. 8 am - noon $2.99

Shopping & Services:
Gift Shop

Jackie Gaughan's Plaza Hotel
1 Main St.
Las Vegas, NV 89101
386-2110 1-800-634-6575
Fax: 382-8281
John D. Gaughan, Sr., Pres.
Mike Nolan, Gen./Hotel Mgr.
Chris Nichols, Casino Mgr.
The hotel and casino originally opened in 1971 as the Union Plaza where the Union Pacific Depot once stood. In 1982 the casino and hotel expanded to the 1,034 rooms it has today. The hotel has twin towers with a recreational complex between them.

Rooms:
1,034 including 136 suites *(21 and 25 story towers)*
Rates: Sun. - Thu. $30 - $75; Fri. - Sat. $50 - $120

Special Features:
Adjacent to the Greyhound Bus Terminal, sports deck with lighted tennis courts, jogging track and swimming pool.

Casino:
Gaming: 57,120 sq. ft.
Games: 1,580 slots and video machines, 19 blackjack tables, 5 crap tables, 3 roulette wheels, 2 keno lounges, mini-baccarat, 1 Pai Gow poker, 12 poker tables, 13 pan tables, race and sports book

Entertainment:
Plaza Theatre - *"Xtreme Scene"* - **Showtimes:** Sat. - Thu. 8 pm & 10 pm - $19.95 includes one drink; dark Friday. *(see Pg. 167)*
Omaha Lounge - Live musical entertainment - 10 am - 4am

Dining:
Center Stage - Continental
Plaza Diner - 24 hour coffee shop
Plaza Snack Bar

Meeting & Banquet Facilities:
Total Meeting Capacity - 2,000
Total Banquet Capacity - 400
Total space: 26,800 sq. ft.

Shopping & Services:
Greyhound Bus Depot
2 Gift Shops
Beauty Shop
Barber Shop
Car Rental
Liquor Store
Coffee & Cravins'
Wedding Chapel
Ice Cream Parlor
Hawaiian Food Store and Snack Shop
Watch Specialty Shop

QUALITY INN
KEY LARGO

ROYAL HOTEL

SANTE FE

ACCOMMODATIONS

Quality Inn · Key Largo
377 E. Flamingo Rd.
Las Vegas, NV 89109
733-7777 1-800-634-6617
Kevin Thorstenson, Gen. Mgr.
Gene Browder, Casino Mgr.
Opened August 31, 1997.

Rooms:
316
Rates: $29 - $99

Special Features:
All year round pool, complimentary shuttle to airport and Strip. Rooms have refrigerators, coffee makers and wet bars.

Casino:
Gaming: 10,000 sq. ft.
Games: 180 slot and video poker, 4 blackjack tables, 1 roulette wheel and 1 crap table.

Entertainment:
Kickin' Back Lounge - entertainment nightly

Dining:
Coral Cafe - coffee shop

Meeting & Banquet Facilities:
Total Meeting Capacity: 75
Total Banquet Capacity: 75
Garden Room: 1,500 sq. ft.

Shopping & Services:
Gift Shop

Royal Hotel & Casino
99 Convention Center Dr.
Las Vegas, NV 89109
735-6117 1-800-634-6118
Fax: 735-2546
James Lang, Gen. Mgr.

Rooms:
236
Rates: $45 - $125

Special Features:
Swimming pool and lounge

Casino:
10,000 sq. ft.
Games: 155 slots and video poker machines; 3 blackjack tables; 1 roulette wheel

Dining:
Chung King III - Chinese *(see Pg. 114)*

Meeting & Banquet Facilities:
Total Meeting Capacity: 70
Total Banquet Capacity: 50
Total space: 1,040 sq. ft.

Shopping & Services:
Gift Shop

Santa Fe Hotel Casino
4949 N. Rancho Dr.
Las Vegas, NV 89130
658-4900 1-800-872-6823
Sue Lowden, Pres.
Chris Lowden, Exec. VP of Operations
Anita McFarlin, Hotel Mgr.
Joe Corradino, Casino Mgr.
This $53 million hotel opened in 1991 in northwest Las Vegas. It is owned by the Santa Fe Gaming Corporation. On December 19, 1994 a two story addition added 65,000 sq. ft. of casino and public area.

Rooms:
200
Rates: $49 - $99
Special Features:
Professional Ice Arena - featuring skating teacher & Olympic medalist, Barbara Roley-Williams; Bowling Center - 60 lanes, pro shop & snack bar; Video Arcade Nursery - children 6 months - 8 years, $10 registration fee, $2 per hour with a 3 hour maximum

Casino:
Gaming: 55,441 sq. ft.
Games: 1,766 slot and video machines, 18 blackjack tables, 2 crap tables, 2 roulette wheels, 2 Pai Gow poker, keno lounge, bingo, 5 poker tables, sports book, 1 Let It Ride

Entertainment:
Ice Lounge - Entertainment nightly with a bar overlooking the ice arena *(see Pg. 171)*

Dining:
Ben & Jerry's Ice Cream
Lone Mountain Buffet: *(see Pg. 145)*
Breakfast - Mon. - Sat. 7:30 am - 10:30 am - $3.95
Lunch - Mon. - Sat. - 11:30 am - 2:30 pm - $4.95
Dinner - 4 pm - 9 pm - $6.95, Thu. seafood night - $8.95
Classical Sun. Champagne Brunch - 7:30 am - 2:30 pm - $6.95
Ti Amo Champagne Brunch - 11 am - 5 pm $12.95
Cantina - Snack bar in ice arena
Jen's Deli - Sandwiches, salads & bagels
Kodiak Lodge - Steaks and Seafood *(see Pg. 141)*
Pablo's Cafe - 24 hour coffee shop, American & Mexican Specialties
Santa Fe Coffee Company - Fresh roasted coffees & bakery items
Suzette's - Fine French Cuisine *(see Pg. 118)*
Ti Amo - Italian *(see Pg. 124)*
Sunday Jazz Brunch: 11 am - 5 pm - $12.95

Meeting & Banquet Facilities:
Total Meeting Capacity: 1,169
Total Space: 9,701 sq. ft.
Shopping & Services:
Gift Shop
Bowling Pro Shop
Ice Skating Pro Shop

SILVERTON

TEXAS STATION

VACATION VILLAGE

Silverton
3333 Blue Diamond Rd.
Las Vegas, NV 89139
263-7777 1-800-588-7711
Fred Anthony, Sr. Vice-Pres./Gen. Mgr.
Michael Frawley, Casino Operations and Games Dir.
This Western-themed, $75 million resort opened in May 1994 under the name of Boomtown and was designed to create an authentic western atmosphere with the distinct feeling of an old mining town and campground dating back to the late 1800s.
Rooms: 304 rooms; 460 space RV park
Room rates: $29-$55 + tax
RV Rates: $18-$21
Special Features:
460-vehicle RV park; two clubhouses, pool, cable TV and telephone hookups. Shuttle bus to and from the Beltz Factory Outlet World; 3 heated swimming pools, Jacuzzis, and arcade.
Casino: **Gaming:** 32,134 sq. ft.
Games: 1,100 slot and video machines, 20 blackjack tables, 2 crap tables, 2 roulette wheels, keno, Caribbean stud

Entertainment:
Rattlesnake Ricky's Saloon - Live entertainment Sun. - Thu. from 6 pm - midnight; Fri. and Sat. 4 pm - 2 am
Dining:
Opera House - Steaks and Chops
Comstock Cafe - 24 hours
Chuck Wagon Buffet: *(see Pg. 146)*
Breakfast - 7 am - 11 am - $3.99
Lunch - 11:30 am -3:30 pm - $4.99
Dinner - 4 pm - 11 pm - $7.99
Italian - Mon. - 4 pm - 11 pm
Filet Mignon - Tue. - Wed.
Prime Rib - Fri. - Sat.
Seafood - Sun.
Champagne Brunch - Sun. 7 am - 3 pm - $5.99
Cowboy Steakout *(see Pg. 140)*
Rib Nights at The Opera House - Thu. - Sun. 5:30 pm - 10:00 pm - features all you can eat BBQ combo platter served country table style for $5.95. Monday all the spaghetti you can eat $4.95
Shopping & Services:
Gift Shop

Texas Station
3141 N. Rancho Dr.
N. Las Vegas, NV 89030
631-1000 1-800-654-8888
Fax: 631-1010
Frank Fertitta, CEO
Kevin Kelley, VP/Gen. Mgr.
Jerry Parker, Casino Mgr.
Good ol' Texas hospitality, comfort, quality and style, the Texas Gambling Hall & Hotel opened its 47-acre, 200,000 sq. ft., low-rise building on July 12, 1995. Owned by Station Casinos, Inc., a multi-jurisdictional gaming company, it is headquartered in Las Vegas. The company owns and operates Palace Station Hotel & Casino, Boulder Station Hotel & Casino, Sunset Hotel & Casino, as well as Southwest Companies, which provides slot route management and vending services in southern Nevada and Louisiana. The company also owns and operates St. Charles Riverfront Station, Inc., a riverboat and dockside gaming and entertainment facility in St. Charles, Missouri.
Rooms:
200 with 2 suites *(six-story tower)*
Rates: Sun. - Thu. $39 - $69; Fri. - Sat. $59 -$169
Special Features:
Swimming pool; Texas 12 theaters; shuttle bus to and from Palace Station and Sun City/Summerlin Community.

Casino: **Gaming:** 60,000 sq. ft.
Games: 2,008 slot machines, 23 blackjack tables, 4 crap tables,1 Let It Ride, 2 Texas Pai Gow, 1 Spanish 21, 3 roulette tables, 175-seat race and sports book, keno, 10 poker tables, bingo
Entertainment:
Armadillo Lounge - Variety of entertainment; Hours vary with performances; dancing *(see Pg. 170)*
Concert/entertainment hotline:
631-1001
Dining:
San Lorenzo - Italian *(see Pg. 124)*
Feast Around the World: *(see Pg. 146)*
Breakfast - Mon. - Fri. 7 am - 11 am - $3.99
Lunch - Mon. - Fri. - 11 am - 3:30 pm - $5.99
Dinner - 4 pm - 10 pm - $8.99
Sat. - Sun. Champagne Brunch - 7 am - 3:30 pm - $7.99
Steak & Seafood Buffet: Fri. 4 pm - 10 pm $11.99
Prime Rib Buffet - Sat. 4 pm - 10 pm $10.99
Yellow Rose Cafe - coffee shop
Stockyard Steakhouse - steaks *(see Pg. 143)*
Laredo Cantina & Cafe - Mexican *(see Pg. 129)*
China first Express - Chinese
The Deli
Pizza Kitchen
Shopping & Services:
Texas Star Gift Shop

Vacation Village
6711 Las Vegas Blvd. S.
Las Vegas, NV 89119
897-1700 1-800-338-0608
Fax: 361-6726
Lyle Thompson, Gen. Mgr.
Lolly Knapp, Hotel Mgr.

Rooms:
315 including 8 suites
Rates: $29-$65

Special Features:
Airport shuttle, children's arcade, 2 outdoor swimming pools, spa

Casino:
Gaming: 22,760 sq. ft.

Games: 584 video and slot machines, 10 blackjack tables, roulette, race and sports book

Entertainment:
Arrowhead Bar - nightly entertainment
Kookoo's Lounge - entertainment *(see Pg. 171)*

Dining:
Denny's - 24 hours
Robertos Taco Shop - 24 hours

Meeting & Banquet Facilities:
Total Meeting Capacity: 2,050
Total Banquet Capacity: 715
Total Space: 12,900 sq. ft.

Shopping & Services:
Gift Shop

WESTWARD HO

**Westward Ho
Hotel & Casino**
**2900 Las Vegas Blvd. S.
Las Vegas, NV 89109
731-2900 1-800-634-6651**
*Hans Dorweiler, VP/Gen. Mgr.
Bob Tyndall, Casino Mgr.*

Rooms:
800
Rates: $25 - $39

Casino:
Gaming: 34,427 sq. ft.
Games: 871 slots and video machines, 8 blackjack tables, 1 Let It Ride, craps, roulette, keno lounge

Entertainment:
Show Reservations: 731-2900
Lounge - *"Hurray America"* - $12.95 plus tax . *(see Pg. 167)*
Show Lounge - live music *(dark Sun.)* *(see Pg. 171)*

Dining:
Deli
The Buffet: *(see Pg. 146)*
Breakfast - 7 am - 11 am - $4.95
Brunch - 11:30 am - 2 pm - $4.95
Dinner - 4 pm - 10 pm - $6.95
Westward Ho Cafe *(see Pg. 153)*

Shopping & Services:
Gift Shop

WESTERN HOTEL

Western Hotel/Casino
**899 E. Fremont St.
Las Vegas, NV 89101
384-4620 1-800-634-6703**
*Ray Tagliaferri, Gen. Mgr.
Tony Alessandro, Casino Mgr.*

Rooms:
116
Rates: $16 - $20

Casino:
Gaming: 13,050 sq. ft.
Games: 567 slot and video machines, 8 blackjack tables, roulette wheel, keno lounge, bingo

Dining:
Snack Bar

ACCOMMODATIONS

NON-GAMING HOTELS

NON-GAMING HOTELS	PHONE	Rooms	TV	Cable TV	Pool	Heated Pool	Jacuzzi	Laundry Room	Exercise Facility	Beauty Salon	Pets Allowed	Covered Parking	Tennis Courts	Conference Room	Telephones	Kitchen or Kitchenette	Restaurant	Lounge - Bar
Alexis Park 375 E. Harmon Ave.	(702) 796-3300 (800) 582-2228	500	•		•	•		•	•					•	•		•	•
Bourbon Street 120 E. Flamingo Rd.	(702) 737-7200 (800) 634-6956	166	•				•							•	•		•	•
Courtyard-Marriott 3275 Paradise Rd.	(702) 791-3600 (800) 321-2211	149		•	•	•	•	•						•	•		•	•
Holiday Inn-Emerald Springs 325 E. Flamingo Rd.	(702) 732-9100 (800) 732-7889	150		•	•	•		•						•	•			•
Holiday Inn-Crowne Plaza 4255 Paradise Rd.	(702) 369-4400	201				•		•			•			•	•		•	•
LaQuinta Inn 3970 Paradise Rd.	(702) 796-9000 (800) 531-5900	228	•				•					•		•	•			
Polo Towers 3745 Las Vegas Blvd. S.	(702) 261-1000	250		•		•	•	•					•		•	•		•
Residence Inn-Marriott 3225 Paradise Rd.	(702) 796-9300 (800) 331-3131	192		•		•	•				•				•			
St. Tropez 455 E. Harmon Ave.	(702) 369-5400 (800) 666-5400	149		•		•	•		•					•	•		•	•
World Trade Center 901 E. Desert Inn Rd.	(702) 369-5750 (800) 390-1777	310		•		•	•	•					•		•	•		•	•

TIMESHARE

TIMESHARE	PHONE	Rooms	TV	Cable TV	Pool	Heated Pool	Jacuzzi	Laundry Room	Exercise Facility	Beauty Salon	Pets Allowed	Covered Parking	Tennis Courts	Conference Room	Telephones	Kitchen or Kitchenette	Restaurant	Lounge - Bar
Carriage House 105 E. Harmon Ave.	(702) 798-1020	143		•		•	•	•	•				•		•	•	•	•
Debbie Reynolds Resorts Inc. 305 Convention Center Dr.	(702) 734-0711	43		•		•		•				•			•	•	•	•
Hilton Grand Vacation Club 3575 Las Vegas Blvd. S.	(702) 697-2950	275	•			•	•	•				•			•	•		
Jockey Club 3700 Las Vegas Blvd. S.	(702) 798-3500	270	•			•	•	•	•						•	•		•
Olympian Palms Resort Club 3875 Cambridge St.	(702) 732-8889	25		•		•			•						•	•		
Polo Towers 3745 Las Vegas Blvd. S.	(702) 261-1000 (800) 935-2233	250		•		•	•	•	•			•			•	•		•
Ramada Vacation Suites 100 Winnick Ave.	(702) 731-6100 (800) 634-6981	300		•		•						•			•	•		

EXTENDED STAY

EXTENDED STAY	PHONE	Rooms (#)	Rooms	Kitchen or Kitchenette	TV	Cable TV	Pool	Heated Pool	Jacuzzi	Laundry Room	Exercise Facilities	Beauty Salon	Pets Allowed	Covered Parking	Tennis Courts	Conference Room	Telephones	Club House	Restaurant	Lounge - Bar
Blair House Residence Suite 344 E. Desert Inn Rd.	(702) 792-2222 (800) 553-9111	224	●		●		●	●	●								●			
Boulder Manor Apartments 4823 Boulder Hwy.	(702) 454-8969	211	●		●	●				●							●			
Brooks Residential Motel 2112 Paradise Rd.	(702) 735-2239	22	●	●		●				●							●			
Budget Suites 1500 Stardust Dr.	(702) 732-1500 (800) 752-1501	639	●		●		●	●	●	●				●	●		●			
Budget Suites 4625 Boulder Hwy.	(702) 454-4625	280	●		●	●				●			●				●			
Budget Suites 4855 Boulder Hwy.	(702) 433-3644	539	●		●		●	●	●				●	●			●			
Budget Suites 3655 W. Tropicana Ave.	(702) 739-1000	480	●		●		●	●	●					●			●			
Budget Suites 2219 N. Rancho Dr.	(702) 638-1899	704	●		●		●	●	●					●			●			
Budget Suites 3684 Paradise Rd.	(702) 699-7000	360	●		●		●	●	●					●			●			
Budget Suites 4205 W. Tropicana Ave.	(702) 889-1700	414	●		●								●	●			●			
Desert Rose Apartments 29 N. 28th St.	(702) 384-3101	240	●	●			●		●									●		
Extended Stay America 4270 S. Valley View Blvd.	(702) 221-7600 (800) 362-4040	177	●		●		●	●	●		●						●			
Extended Stay America 4240 Boulder Hwy.	(702) 433-1788	123	●		●		●		●		●									
The Falls 3825 Cambridge St.	(702) 792-9191	228	●		●		●	●	●					●				●		
4 Kings Apartments 121 N. 4th St.	(702) 384-2204	32	●	●						●		●	●							
Harbor Island 370 E. Harmon Ave.	(702) 732-9111	996	●		●	●		●	●	●		●	●	●				●		
Holiday Royale Apt. Suites 4505 Paradise Rd.	(702) 733-7676 (800) 732-7676	298	●	●		●			●								●			
Imperial Motel 1326 S. Main St.	(702) 384-8069	16	●	●								●								
La Paloma Apt. Motel 717 Las Vegas Blvd. N.	(702) 384-7381	29	●			●						●								
Las Vegas Milestone 1919 Fremont St.	(702) 387-1650	17	●			●														
Ninth Street Hotel & Apts. 117 N. 9th St.	(702) 384-1908	81		●						●										
Oakwood Corporate Apts. 600 Oakmount Dr.	(702) 735-3143 (800) 888-0808	551	●				●	●	●	●								●		
Peter Pan Motel 110 N. 13th St.	(702) 384-8422	38				●														
Squadron Executive Suites 5230 E. Craig St.	(702) 644-3300	124	●		●	●				●							●			
St. Louis Manor 2000 Paradise Rd.	(702) 369-8050	123			●	●		●	●			●								
Shelter Island 3770 Swenson Ave.	(702) 734-6788	455	●		●	●		●	●			●								
Sportsman's Royal Manor 5660 Boulder Hwy.	(702) 458-7071	196	●		●		●	●									●		●	●
Studio Plaza Apartments 915 S. Casino Center Blvd.	(702) 385-5582	75	●		●	●				●										
Sunstate Apartments 422 S. 1st St.	(702) 384-3134	168	●							●		●	●							
Thai Royal Motel 1424 S. 4th St.	(702) 384-8264	12	●	●																
Woodbridge Inn Apartments 700 E. Flamingo Rd.	(702) 732-7678	320	●			●		●	●	●		●								

ACCOMMODATIONS

MOTELS

MOTELS	PHONE	Rooms	TV	Cable TV	Pool	Heated Pool	Jacuzzi	Laundry Room	Exercise Facilities	Beauty Salon	Pets Allowed	Covered Parking	Tennis Courts	Conference Room	Club House	Telephones	Kitchen - Kitchenette	Restaurant	Lounge - Bar
Algiers Hotel 2845 Las Vegas Blvd. S.	(702) 735-3311 (800) 732-3361	105		•	•											•		•	•
Ambassador East Motel 916 E. Fremont St.	(702) 384-8281 (800) 634-6703	163	•		•		•	•					•			•	•		•
Aztec Inn 2200 Las Vegas Blvd. S.	(702) 385-4566	200		•		•		•							•	•	•	•	•
Barcelona Hotel 5011 E. Craig Rd.	(702) 644-6300 (800) 223-6330	178		•	•		•	•							•	•		•	
Best Western-Heritage Inn 4975 S. Valley View Blvd.	(702) 798-7736 (800) 528-1234	59		•		•	•	•	•		•			•		•	•		
Best Western-Main St. Inn 1000 N. Main St.	(702) 382-3455 (800) 851-1414	91	•		•			•			•					•			
Best Western-Mardi Gras Inn 3500 Paradise Rd.	(702) 731-2020 (800) 634-6501	314		•		•		•		•		•		•		•		•	•
Best Western-McCarran Inn 4970 Paradise Rd.	(702) 798-5530 (800) 626-7575	99		•			•							•					
Best Western-Nellis Motor Inn 5330 E. Craig Rd.	(702) 643-6111 (800) 546-1119	52		•	•			•			•					•			
Best Western-Parkview Inn 905 Las Vegas Blvd. N.	(702) 385-1213 (800) 548-6122	56	•					•			•					•			•
Blue Angel Motel 2110 E. Fremont St.	(702) 386-9500	84		•	•			•			•						•		
Budget Inn 301 S. Main St.	(702) 385-5560 (800) 959-9062	81		•												•			
Carriage House 105 E. Harmon Ave.	(702) 798-1020	154		•		•	•					•	•	•		•	•	•	•
Casino Royale 3411 Las Vegas Blvd. S.	(702) 737-3500 (800) 854-7666	153		•		•										•		•	•
Center Strip Inn 3688 Las Vegas Blvd. S.	(702) 739-6066 (800) 777-7737	152		•		•	•				•					•			
City Center Motel 700 E. Fremont St.	(702) 382-4766	57		•			•			•						•			
Comfort Inn 211 E. Flamingo Rd.	(702) 733-7800 (800) 634-6774	121		•	•											•			
Comfort Inn-South 5075 Koval Ln.	(702) 736-3600 (800) 228-5160	106		•	•						•					•			
Convention Center Lodge 79 Convention Center Dr.	(702) 735-1315	56	•		•			•								•			
Crest Budget Inn 207 N. Sixth St.	(702) 382-5642 (800) 777-1817	154		•	•						•					•	•		
Daisy Motel & Apartments 415 S. Main St.	(702) 382-0707	151		•	•						•					•			
Days Inn 3227 Civic Center Dr.	(702) 399-3297	120		•	•											•			•
Days Inn Downtown 707 E. Fremont St.	(702) 388-1400 (800) 325-2344	147		•	•							•				•		•	
Days Inn Town Hall Casino 4155 Koval Ln.	(702) 731-2111 (800) 634-6541	357	•			•	•	•								•		•	•
Downtown Thriftlodge Motel 629 S. Main St.	(702) 385-7796	190		•		•		•			•				•	•			
Downtowner Motel 129 N. 8th St.	(702) 384-1441 (800) 777-2566	200		•	•			•								•	•		
E-Z 8 Motel Inc. 5201 Industrial Rd.	(702) 739-9513	127		•	•			•			•					•			
Econo Lodge 1150 Las Vegas Blvd. S.	(702) 382-6001 (800) 634-6979	124	•		•											•			
Econo Lodge Downtown 520 S. Casino Center Blvd.	(702) 384-8211 (800) 223-7706	48		•				•								•	•		
Economy Inn 2028 E. Fremont St.	(702) 384-7540	58		•	•						•					•			
El Cid Hotel 233 S. Sixth St.	(702) 384-4696 (800) 688-1212	163		•				•								•	•		

MOTELS

MOTELS	PHONE	Rooms	TV	Cable TV	Pool	Heated Pool	Jacuzzi	Laundry Room	Exercise Facilities	Beauty Salon	Pets Allowed	Covered Parking	Tennis Courts	Conference Room	Club House	Telephones	Kitchen - Kitchenette	Restaurant	Lounge - Bar
Fairfield Inn by Marriott 3850 Paradise Rd.	(702) 791-0899 (800) 228-2800	129		•	•											•			
Fergusons Motel 1028 E. Fremont St.	(702) 382-3500 (800) 933-7829	66	•													•			
Fez Motel 4213 Las Vegas Blvd. S.	(702) 736-6014	42	•		•														
Firebird Inn 8025 Industrial Rd.	(702) 896-4333	47		•								•				•			
Fun City Motel 2233 Las Vegas Blvd. S.	(702) 731-3155	85		•	•			•								•	•		
Gateway Motel 928 Las Vegas Blvd. S.	(702) 382-2146	46		•								•							
Gatewood Motel 3075 E. Fremont St.	(702) 457-3660	19	•					•	•										
Glass Pool Inn 4613 Las Vegas Blvd. S.	(702) 739-6636 (800) 527-7118	48		•		•		•				•				•	•	•	•
Golden Inn Motel 120 Las Vegas Blvd. S.	(702) 384-8204	71		•	•							•				•			
Happi Inn 3939 Las Vegas Blvd. S.	(702) 736-8031 (800) 634-6727	88	•		•											•			
Holiday House 2211 Las Vegas Blvd. S.	(702) 732-2468	75		•	•											•			
Holiday Inn Express 8669 W. Sahara Ave.	(702) 256-3766	59		•		•	•	•				•				•	•		
Holiday Motel 2205 Las Vegas Blvd. S.	(702) 735-6464	41		•	•											•			•
Hops Motel 3412 Paradise Rd.	(702) 732-2494	50	•		•			•								•	•		
Howard Johnson Plaza Hotel 3111 W. Tropicana Ave.	(702) 798-1111 (800) 300-7389	150		•	•		•								•		•	•	•
Howard Johnsons-Airport 5100 Paradise Rd.	(702) 798-2777 (800) 634-6430	340		•	•			•							•			•	•
Howard Johnsons-Las Vegas Strip 1401 Las Vegas Blvd. S.	(702) 388-0301	104	•		•			•				•			•		•		
King Albert Motel 165 Albert Ave.	(702) 732-1555 (800) 553-7753	104		•	•			•				•				•			
King 8 Hotel & Gambling Hall 3330 W. Tropicana Ave.	(702) 736-8988 (800) 634-3488	298		•		•		•							•		•	•	•
Klondike Inn 5191 Las Vegas Blvd. S.	(702) 739-9351	153	•					•								•		•	•
La Quinta Motor Inn 3782 Las Vegas Blvd. S.	(702) 739-7457 (800) 687-6667	114		•	•							•				•			
La Palm Motel 2512 E. Fremont St.	(702) 384-5874	44		•	•											•	•		
Lee Motel & Deli 200 South 8th St.	(702) 382-1297	83		•				•								•	•		
Meadows Inn 525 E. Bonanza Rd.	(702) 366-0456 (800) 932-1499	150	•		•			•		•	•		•			•			•
Motel 6 195 E. Tropicana Ave.	(702) 798-0728	606		•		•		•				•				•			
Motel 6 5085 Industrial Rd.	(702) 739-6747	139		•		•		•				•				•			
Motel 6 4125 Boulder Hwy.	(702) 457-8051	161		•		•		•				•				•			
Nellis Lodge Motel 4228 Las Vegas Blvd. S.	(702) 643-9220	190		•	•			•								•			
Ogden House 651 Ogden Ave.	(702) 385-5200	102	•													•			
Par-a-Dice Inn 2217 E. Fremont St.	(702) 382-6440	53		•				•			•								
Paradise Resort Inn 4350 Paradise Rd.	(702) 733-3900	206		•	•							•				•	•		

Visit our website at www.experiencelasvegas.com

Experience Las Vegas

MOTELS

MOTELS	PHONE	Rooms	TV	Cable TV	Pool	Heated Pool	Jacuzzi	Laundry Room	Exercise Facilities	Beauty Salon	Pets Allowed	Covered Parking	Tennis Courts	Conference Room	Club House	Telephones	Kitchen - Kitchenette	Restaurant	Lounge - Bar
Queen of Hearts Hotel 19 E. Lewis St.	(702) 382-8878 (800) 835-6005	96		•	•		•									•			
Ramada, Ltd. 1501 W. Sahara Ave.	(702) 733-0001 (800) 554-4092	223		•	•		•							•		•			
Royal Motel 615 Las Vegas Blvd. S.	(702) 386-2767	13	•																
Safari Motel 2001 E. Fremont St.	(702) 384-4021	22		•	•		•									•			
Silver Queen Motel 1401 Carson Ave.	(702) 384-8157	14	•				•										•		
Somerset House 294 Convention Center Dr.	(702) 735-5097	104		•		•	•							•		•	•		
Star Motel 1418 S. 4th St.	(702) 383-9770	23	•				•										•		
Star View Motel 1217 E. Fremont St.	(702) 388-1533	25		•															
Starlite Motel 1873 Las Vegas Blvd. N.	(702) 642-1750	30	•		•														
Steven Motel 2112 N. Nellis Blvd.	(702) 452-8199	8		•			•									•	•	•	
Strip 91 Motel 2091 Las Vegas Blvd. N.	(702) 649-4593	17	•								•								
Sunrise Resorts & RV Park 4575 Boulder Hwy.	(702) 434-0848 (800) 362-4040	305		•	•			•						•		•	•		
Sunset Motel 6000 Boulder Hwy.	(702) 451-2445	24	•				•									•			
Super 8 Motel 5288 Boulder Hwy.	(702) 435-8888 (800) 825-0880	150		•	•		•	•								•		•	•
Super 8 Motel 4250 Koval Ln.	(702) 794-0888 (800) 800-8000	300		•		•	•	•			•					•		•	•
Tam O'Shanter Motel 3317 Las Vegas Blvd. S.	(702) 735-7331 (800) 727-3423	76		•	•						•					•			
Thunderbird Hotel 1213 Las Vegas Blvd. S.	(702) 383-3100	300		•	•		•				•	•						•	•
Tod Motor Inn 1508 Las Vegas Blvd. S.	(702) 477-0022	108		•	•											•	•		
Town Palms Motel 321 S. Casino Center Dr.	(702) 382-1611	90		•			•									•			
Towne & Country Motel 2033 E. Fremont St.	(702) 366-8576	29		•	•											•			
Travel Inn Motel 217 Las Vegas Blvd. N.	(702) 384-3040	57		•						•						•			
Traveler's Motel 1100 E. Fremont St.	(702) 384-7121	36								•									
Travelodge Las Vegas Strip 2830 Las Vegas Blvd. S.	(702) 735-4222 (800) 578-7878	100		•		•										•			
Travelodge South Strip 3735 Las Vegas Blvd. S.	(702) 736-3443 (800) 578-7878	126		•		•										•			
Tropicana Inn 5150 Duke Ellington Way	(702) 736-8964	118		•	•		•									•	•		
Uptown Motel 813 Ogden Ave.	(702) 382-5257	30		•															
U S Motel 2500 E. Fremont St.	(702) 384-2481	30																	
Vagabond Inn 3265 Las Vegas Blvd. S.	(702) 735-5102 (800) 522-1555	126		•		•		•			•	•				•			
Valley Motel 1313 E. Fremont St.	(702) 384-6890	22		•							•					•			
Vegas Chalet Motel 2401 Las Vegas Blvd. N.	(702) 642-2115	75									•						•		
Vegas Motel 2216 E. Fremont St.	(702) 388-1500	81		•				•			•						•		

MOTELS

MOTELS	PHONE	Rooms	TV	Cable TV	Pool	Heated Pool	Jacuzzi	Laundry Room	Exercise Facilities	Beauty Salon	Pets Allowed	Covered Parking	Tennis Courts	Conference Room	Club House	Telephones	Kitchen - Kitchenette	Restaurant	Lounge - Bar
Vegas Verdes Motel 1635 N. Main St.	(702) 642-8598	15	●													●			
Victory Hotel 307 S. Main St.	(702) 384-0260 (800) 387-9257	32	●				●												
Villa Roma Motel 220 Convention Center Dr.	(702) 735-4151	100		●		●									●				
Villager Lodge Inn 4350 Boulder Hwy.	(702) 434-9900	182			●	●	●	●							●	●			
Walden Motel 3085 E. Fremont St.	(702) 457-9090	10	●								●								
Warren House East 1025 Sierra Vista Dr.	(702) 734-8586	76		●															
White Sands Motel 3889 Las Vegas Blvd. S.	(702) 736-2515	33	●		●						●				●				
Yucca Motel 1727 Las Vegas Blvd. S.	(702) 735-2787	22	●																

AREA OUT-OF-TOWN ACCOMMODATIONS

	PHONE	Rooms	TV	Cable TV	Pool	Heated Pool	Jacuzzi	Laundry Room	Exercise Facilities	Beauty Salon	Pets Allowed	Covered Parking	Tennis Courts	Conference Room	Club House	Telephones	Kitchen - Kitchenette	Restaurant	Lounge - Bar
Boulder Dam Hotel 1305 Arizona St. Boulder City, NV 89005	(702) 293-3510																		
Desert Inn of Boulder City 800 Nevada Hwy. Boulder City, NV 89005	(702) 293-2827	26																	
Flamingo Inn Motel 804 Nevada Hwy. Boulder City, NV 89005	(702) 293-3565	16	●								●					●			
Gold Strike Inn & Casino U.S. Highway 93 Boulder City, NV 89005	(702) 293-5000 (800) 245-6380	378	●			●	●							●	●				
Best Western-Lighthouse Inn 110 Ville Dr. Boulder City, NV 89005	(702) 293-6444	70																	
Nevada Inn 1009 Nevada Hwy. Boulder City, NV 89005	(702) 293-2044	55		●	●						●				●	●			
Sands Motel 809 Nevada Hwy. Boulder City, NV 89005	(702) 293-2589	26	●												●	●			
Starview Motel 1017 Nevada Hwy. Boulder City, NV 89005	(702) 293-1658	22	●	●							●						●		
Super 8 Motel 704 Nevada Hwy. Boulder City, NV 89005	(702) 294-8888 (800) 825-0880	114	●			●	●	●			●		●		●	●	●	●	●
Western Inn 921 Nevada Hwy. Boulder City, NV 89005	(702) 294-0393	13	●													●			
Best Western-Lake Mead Hotel 85 E. Lake Mead Dr. Henderson, NV 89015	(702) 563-1712 (800) 446-2994	59	●			●									●				
Boby Motel 2100 S. Boulder Hwy. Henderson, NV 89015	(702) 565-9711	21		●		●	●				●				●	●			
Henderson Townhouse Lodge 43 Walter St. Henderson, NV 89015	(702) 564-3111	20	●								●				●	●			
Ingles Motel 1636 Boulder Hwy. Henderson, NV 89015	(702) 565-7929	28	●					●							●	●			
Outpost Motel 1104 N. Boulder Hwy. Henderson, NV 89015	(702) 564-2664	21						●			●				●	●			
Railroad Pass Hotel & Casino 2800 Boulder Hwy. Henderson, NV 89015	(702) 294-5000 (800) 654-0877	120	●		●									●	●				
Blue Sky Motel 2 Spirit Mountain Rd. Cal-Nev-Ari, NV 89039	(702) 297-9289	10	●		●		●				●							●	●
Mt. Charleston Hotel & Rest. 2 Kyle Canyon Rd. Mt. Charleston, NV 89124	(702) 872-5500	63	●				●						●		●			●	●
Mount Charleston Lodge HCR 38, Box 325 Mt. Charleston, NV 89124	(800) 955-1314	24					●				●							●	●
Bonnie Springs Motel Old Nevada, NV 89004	(702) 875-4400	50	●				●								●			●	●

Experience Las Vegas

NON-GAMING HOTELS

There are ten full-service non-gaming resorts in Las Vegas with 2,295 rooms. Non-gaming resorts cater to the travelers who want a quiet environment away from the hectic casino crowds.

Alexis Park

375 E. Harmon Ave.
Las Vegas, NV 89109
796-3300 1-800-582-2228
Fax: 796-3354
Stu Platt, Gen. Mgr.
Built in 1984 by developer Robert Schulman, the Alexis Park was the first of the luxury non-gaming hotels.
Rooms:
500 suites; rooms range in size from 500 to 1200 sq. ft.
Rates:
$99 - $500
Special Features:
Jacuzzis, 3 heated swimming pools, health spa, 9-hole putting green, telephones, cable TV, conference room.
Entertainment:
Pisces Lounge
Dining:
Pegasus - Continental
Meeting and Banquet Facilities:
Sales - 796-3333
Total meeting capacity: 8,760
Total banquet capacity: 5,940
Total space: Over 50,000 sq. ft
Shopping & Services:
Beauty Salon - 796-3364
Gift Shop

Bourbon Street

120 E. Flamingo Rd.
Las Vegas, NV 89109
737-7200 1-800-634-6956
Fax: 794-9155
Greg Regalado, Gen. Mgr.
Rooms:
166 including 4 suites
Rates:
$39 - $59
Special Features:
Telephones, TV, laundry room
Dining & Entertainment:
French Market - coffee shop
lounge - live entertainment
Meeting & Banquet Facilities:
Total Meeting Capacity: 140
Total Banquet Capacity: 100
Total Space: 1,754 sq. ft.
Shopping & Services:
Gift Shop

Courtyard by Marriott

3275 Paradise Rd.
Las Vegas, NV 89109
791-3600 1-800-321-2211
Fax: 796-7981
Chris Costella, Gen. Mgr.
Rooms:
149 including 12 suites
Rates:
$69 - $250; convention rates higher
Special Features:
Airport shuttle, heated swimming pool, Jacuzzi, laundry room, cable TV, exercise room, conference room, restaurant and lounge
Meeting Facilities:
Total meeting capacity: 78

Holiday Inn - Emerald Springs

325 E. Flamingo Rd.
Las Vegas, NV 89109
732-9100 1-800-732-7889
Lance Moore, Gen. Mgr.
Rooms:
150 including 20 deluxe suites; some suites have more than 600 sq. ft.
Rates:
$69 - $175
Special Features:
Complimentary limousine service, heated swimming pool, Jacuzzi, exercise room, cable TV, telephones.
Dining and Entertainment:
Veranda Cafe & Lounge
Meeting Facilities:
Total meeting capacity: 185 - 200
Total banquet capacity: 175
Total space: 6,000 sq. ft.

Holiday Inn – Crowne Plaza

4255 Paradise Rd.
Las Vegas, NV 89109
369-4400
John Culetsu, Gen. Mgr.
Rooms:
201 guest suites
Rates:
$95 - $165
Special Features:
All suites have a separate parlor with sofa bed, wet-bar with refrigerator, exercise room with sauna, heated outdoor pool, restaurant and cocktail lounge, shuttle, pets allowed, telephones, cable TV.
Meeting and Banquet Facilities:
Total meeting capacity: 967
Total banquet capacity: 670
Total space: 6,840 sq. ft.

La Quinta Inn

3970 Paradise Rd.
Las Vegas, NV 89109
796-9000 1-800-531-5900
Fax: 796-3537
Tom Landers, Gen. Mgr.
Rooms:
228 including 52 suites
Rates:
$85 - $250
Packages:
"Honeymoon Package" - Champagne Suite $85

Special Features:
Comp shuttle 24 hours airport and Strip, whirlpool tubs in each room and suite, some rooms with microwave and refrigerator, basic TV, free local and 800 access phone calls, conference room, heated outdoor pool, Jacuzzi, telephones, laundry room, covered parking, free continental breakfast, volleyball court; 75% non-smoking.
Meeting and Banquet Facilities:
Vanda Milligan, Convention Sales Dir.
796-9000
Total meeting capacity: 90
Total banquet capacity: 80
Total space: 2,000 sq. ft.

Polo Towers

3745 Las Vegas Blvd. S.
Las Vegas, NV 89109
261-1000
Troy Magdos, Resort Mgr.

Rooms:
250 suites and timeshare units. *(See Timeshare.)*
Rates:
$99 - $429
Special Features:
Outdoor heated pool, cable TV, spa, state-of-the-art fitness center, laundry room, covered parking, conference room, lounge, telephones, kitchens; the 19th floor of the Polo Towers offers a spectacular 180 degree view of the strip area including views of MGM, Monte Carlo, New York New York, Luxor, Excalibur, Tropicana, Caesars and the Mirage, as well as the Spring Mountain Range; two story Polo Plaza shopping center.
Entertainment:
Polo Lounge
Dining:
Fortune Gardens - Chinese
Hamada - Japanese
Marie Callender's
Starbuck's
Meeting and Banquet Facilities:
Total meeting capacity: 280
Total banquet capacity: 190
Total space: 3,926 sq. ft.
Shopping & Services:
Pony Express - gift shop and mini-mart *(in Plaza)*
Beauty Salon
International Gifts - gift shop
Winbell - gift shop
Wokohama Okadaya - gift shop
Village of Memories - gift shop
Western Jerky
VIP Tickets
Don's Jeweler
Japanese Tours
Budget Car Rental
Resort Medical Center

Residence Inn by Marriott

3225 Paradise Rd.
Las Vegas, NV 89109
796-9300 1-800-331-3131
Laurette Guess, Gen. Mgr.
Rooms:
192 suites
Rates:
$89 - $249

Special Features:
Located across from the Las Vegas Convention Center, one and two-bedroom suites with kitchens, satellite TV and VCR, pets accepted, heated swimming pool and Jacuzzi, complimentary continental breakfast, telephones, conference room, coin laundry, airport shuttle.

St. Tropez

455 E. Harmon Ave.
Las Vegas, NV 89109
369-5400 1-800-666-5400
Fax: 369-1150
Michael Wells, Gen. Mgr.
Rooms:
149 suites
Rates:
$95 - $350
Special Features:
Heated swimming pool, exercise room, video players in room, telephones, Jacuzzi, cable TV, conference room, strip and airport shuttle, restaurant and lounge
Meeting and Banquet Facilities:
Total meeting capacity: 350
Total banquet capacity: 220
Total space: 3,504 sq. ft.

World Trade Center

901 E. Desert Inn Rd.
Las Vegas, NV 89109
369-5750 1-800-390-1777
Ed Yap, Hotel Mgr.
Rooms:
310
Rates:
$35 - $125
Special Features:
Jacuzzi, heated pool, T.V., conference room, laundry room, telephones, covered parking.
Entertainment:
Mediterranean Room - lounge
Dining:
Country Cafe
Meeting & Banquet Facilities:
Total meeting capacity: 65 - 1,000
Total banquet capacity: 45 - 640
Total space: 26,100 sq. ft.

YOUTH HOSTELS

Hostels provide simple overnight accommodations, a place to prepare a meal and a friendly atmosphere for meeting other hostelers at a very reasonable cost to travelers of all ages.

Las Vegas International Hostel

1208 Las Vegas Blvd. S.
Las Vegas, NV 89104
385-9955
Vince Felgar, Owner.
Rooms: 55 beds
Rates: $11.95 nightly Sun. - Thu. for members, $14 for non-members, Fri. - Sat. $14 for members, $16 for non-members.
Special Features: Men's and women's dorms, family room, semi-private rooms.

TIMESHARE

Carriage House
105 E. Harmon Ave.
Las Vegas, NV 89109
798-1020
Amy Lowell, Gen. Mgr.

Rooms:
143 - studio, one and two bedroom suites

Rates:
$125 - $275

Special Features:
Kitchens, heated pool, spa, tennis court, cable TV, laundry room, covered parking, telephones, conference room, Kiefer's Restaurant & Lounge.

Debbie Reynolds Resorts Inc.
305 Convention Center Dr.
Las Vegas, NV 89109
734-0711
Debbie Reynolds, Owner
Henry Cutrona, Mgr.
192 rooms with 43 set aside for timeshare.

Special Features:
Cable TV, heated pool, Jacuzzi, covered parking, telephones, kitchens, restaurant , lounge, gift shop.

The Hilton Grand Vacation Club - Flamingo Hilton Las Vegas
3575 Las Vegas Blvd. S.
Las Vegas, NV 89109
697-2950
David DiBerandino, Gen. Mgr.
275-unit vacation ownership resort adjacent to the Flamingo.

Special Features:
One and two bedroom suites with full bath Jacuzzis and in house washers and dryers, heated pool, exercise room, kitchens, telephones, covered parking. Full-service deli on premises.

Jockey Club
3700 Las Vegas Blvd. S.
Las Vegas, NV 89109
798-3500
Lori Elie, Resort Mgr.

Rooms:
348 rooms of which 270 are timeshare.

Special Features:
TV, heated pool, Jacuzzi, telephones, laundry room, exercise room, kitchens, tennis court, lounge, restaurant - open for breakfast and brunch only.

Dining and Entertainment:
Turf Lounge

Olympian Palms Resort Club
3875 Cambridge St.
Las Vegas, NV 89119
732-8889
Fax: 737-1258
Jeannie Schubert, Gen. Mgr.

Rooms:
25 apartments

Rates:
$75 - $150 daily

Special Features:
Cable TV, heated pool, laundry room, telephones, kitchens.

Polo Towers
(also under Non-Gaming Hotels)
3745 Las Vegas Blvd. S.
Las Vegas, NV 89109
261-1000   1-800-935-2233
Ken Smith, VIP Mgr.

Rooms:
250 suites

Rates:
$99 - $224

Special Features:
Suites only - living room, kitchen, bed-

room (can accommodate 4 people), Pool, lounge, spa, beauty salon, kitchens, four gift shops, various other shops, Resort Medical Center, Budget Car Rental, Japanese Tours, VIP Tickets.

Ramada Vacation Suites
100 Winnick Ave.
Las Vegas, NV 89109
731-6100   1-800-634-6981
Fax: 733-0941
Ron Lovely, Resort Mgr.

Rooms:
300

Rates:
$68 - $108

Special Features:
Cable TV, heated pool, Jacuzzi, laundry room, exercise room, covered parking, telephones, kitchens.

EXTENDED STAY ACCOMMODATIONS

Blair House Residence Suites
344 E. Desert Inn Rd.
Las Vegas, NV 89109
792-2222   1-800-553-9111
Sandy Wright, Gen. Mgr.
Guest Rooms: 224, all rooms are one-bedroom suites with full kitchens
Rates: $55 - $125, weekly & monthly rates also available. All major credit cards accepted, cash payment requires a $500 deposit.
Special Features: Kitchens, cable TV, heated pool, Jacuzzi, laundry room, telephones.

Boulder Manor Apartments
4823 Boulder Hwy.
Las Vegas, NV 89121
454-8969
Rhonda Bliss, Gen. Mgr.
Rooms: 211
Rates: Studio - weekly $159, monthly $680, 1 bedroom - $169 weekly, $700 monthly
Special Features: Kitchens, cable TV, pool, laundry room, telephones.

Brooks Residential Motel
2112 Paradise Rd.
Las Vegas, NV 89104
735-2239
Janet Consorti, Mgr.
Rooms: 22 suites
Rates: $155 - $200 weekly, extended stay rates available.
Special Features: Kitchenettes, TV, pool, utilities included, laundry, telephones.

Budget Suites
1500 Stardust Dr.
Las Vegas, NV 89109
732-1500   1-800-752-1501
Elaine Olsen, Gen. Mgr.
Rooms: 639 one bedrooms
Rates: Daily, weekly & monthly from $169.50 - $189.50 per week, $49.50 - $69.50 daily.
Special features: Kitchens, telephone, cable TV, heated pool, Jacuzzis, 2 laundry facilities, conference room, tennis court, laundry room.

Budget Suites
4625 Boulder Hwy.
Las Vegas, NV 89121
454-4625
John Bayer, Gen. Mgr.
Rooms: 280 one bedroom suites
Rates: $39.50 - $59.50 Daily, $169.50 - $189.50 weekly
Special Features: Kitchens, cable TV, heated pool and Jacuzzi, telephones, laundry room, pets allowed.

Budget Suites
4855 Boulder Hwy.
Las Vegas, NV 89121
433-3644
Sarah Cervantes, Gen. Mgr.
Rooms: 539
Rates: $49.50 - $109.50, weekly $169.50 - $189.50
Special Features: 24-hour laundry facility, heated pool and hot tub Jacuzzi (7 am - 10 pm), cable TV, pets allowed, telephones, covered parking and courtesy patrol 7 pm- 3 am

Budget Suites
3655 W. Tropicana Ave.
Las Vegas, NV 89103
739-1000
Teresa Hatcher, Mgr.
Rooms: 480
Rates: $179.50 - $199.50 weekly
Special Features: Furnished, kitchens, cable TV, heated pool and Jacuzzi, 2 laundry rooms, free local calls, some covered parking.

Budget Suites
2219 N. Rancho Dr.
Las Vegas, NV 89130
638-1899
Dawn Riddle, Mgr.
Rooms: 704
Rates: $189.50 weekly
Special Features: 2 heated pools, 2 Jacuzzis, 3 laundry rooms, cable TV, some covered parking, free local calls.

Budget Suites
3684 Paradise Rd.
Las Vegas, NV 89109
699-7000
Shana Roberts, Mgr.
Rooms: 360
Rates: $179.50 - $199.50
Special Features: Furnished, kitchens, heated pool, Jacuzzi, laundry room, cable TV, free local calls, some covered parking, conference room.

Budget Suites
4205 W. Tropicana Ave.
Las Vegas, NV 89103
889-1700
Karen Labash, Mgr.

Rooms: 414
Rates: $189.50 - $209.50 weekly
Special Features: Kitchens, heated pool and Jacuzzi, laundry room, cable TV, some covered parking.

Desert Rose Apartments
29 N. 28th St.
Las Vegas, NV 89101
384-3101
James Luna, Mgr.
Rooms: 240
Rates: $315 monthly
Special Features: Clubhouse, 24-hour security, TV, heated pool, laundry room.

Extended Stay America
4270 S. Valley View Blvd.
Las Vegas, NV 89103
221-7600 1-800-362-4040
Mark Candeloro, Gen. Mgr.
Rooms: 177
Rates: weekly rates start at $238.70, $100 refundable deposit,
Special Features: One-bedroom deluxe suites with kitchenettes, exercise facility, heated pool/spa, laundry room, free local calls.

Extended Stay America
4240 Boulder Hwy.
Las Vegas, NV 89121
433-1788
Chuck Linn, Mgr.
Rooms: 123
Rates: $175 - $196 weekly
Special Features: One bedroom suites, recreation room, heated pool, direct dial phones with voice mail hook-up, satellite TV, laundry room.

EXTENDED STAY ACCOMMODATIONS

The Falls
3825 Cambridge St.
Las Vegas, NV 89119
792-9191
Sandra Surratt, Mgr.
Rooms: 228
Rates: Weekly $150 and up, monthly $580 and up
Special Features: I bedroom, all utilities paid, cable TV, heated pool and spa, laundry room, some covered parking, clubhouse.

4 Kings Apartments
121 N. 4th St.
Las Vegas, NV 89101
384-2204
Jean Bayne, Mgr.
Rooms: 32
Rates: One-bedroom $150, two-bedroom $175, extended rates available.
Special Features: Kitchenettes, no pool, color TV, laundromat, beauty shop on premises.

Harbor Island
370 E. Harmon Ave.
Las Vegas, NV 89109
732-9111
Sharon Peterson, Mgr.
Rooms: 996 studio & one-bedroom
Rates: Studio - $149.50 - $159.50 weekly, 1 bedroom - $159.50 - $169.50 weekly
Special Features: Full kitchenette and bathroom, all utilities paid, laundry room, cable TV, two indoor Jacuzzis, exercise room, pets allowed, some covered parking, tennis court and club house.

Holiday Royale Apt. Suites
4505 Paradise Rd.
Las Vegas, NV 89109
733-7676 1-800-732-7676
Alex Sugden, Gen. Mgr.
Rooms: 298 apartments
Rates: Daily, weekly or monthly, $145 - $160 weekly, rates include all utilities including direct dial phones.
Special Features: Pool, four laundry rooms, telephones, TV, some with kitchens.

Imperial Motel
1326 S. Main St.
Las Vegas, NV 89104
384-8069
Jan Baggett, Mgr.
Rooms: 16
Rates: $99 - $104 weekly, no daily rentals, extended stay rates available.
Special Features: Kitchenettes, studio apartments, TV.

La Paloma Apt. Motel
717 Las Vegas Blvd. N.
Las Vegas, NV 89101
384-7381
James Brady, Mgr.
Rooms: 29
Rates: One bedroom, no daily or weekly rates, $340 - $400 monthly, extended stay rates available.
Special Features: Kitchens, cable TV.

Las Vegas Milestone
1919 Fremont St.
Las Vegas, NV 89101
387-1650
Larry Snider
Rooms: 17
Rates: $125 - $145
Special Features: No reservations, pool, kitchenettes.

Ninth Street Hotel and Apartments
117 N. 9th St.
Las Vegas, NV 89101
384-1908
Molly Butler, Mgr.
Rooms: 81
Rates: $77 weekly, $338 monthly, extended stay rates available.
Special Features: TV, laundry room.

Oakwood Corporate Apartments
Village Green Apartments
600 Oakmount Dr.
Las Vegas, NV 89109
735-3143 1-800-888-0808
Lisa Linehan, Gen. Mgr.
Rooms: 551 apts. - furnished and unfurnished, 24-hr guarded, gated community on the Las Vegas Country Club.
Rates: Studio $580 - $630, 1 bedroom $625, 2 bedroom $835 - $1,600
Special Features: Five pools, 24 hour fitness center, clubhouse, two laundry rooms, only cats allowed.

Peter Pan Motel
110 N. 13th St.
Las Vegas, NV 89101
384-8422
Irvin Chappell, Mgr.
Rooms: 38
Rates: $84.50 - $94.50 weekly rates, $380 - $420 monthly, extended stay rates available.
Special Features: Cable TV, refrigerators.

Squadron Executive Suites
5230 E. Craig Rd.
Las Vegas, NV 89115
644-3300
Tom Lee, Mgr.
Rooms: 124
Rates: $149 - $169 weekly, $595 - $649 monthly, extended stay rates available.
Special Features: Pool, kitchens, laundry facilities, cable TV, telephones.

St. Louis Manor
2000 Paradise Rd.
Las Vegas, NV 89104
369-8050
Pat Nystrom, Mgr.
Rooms: 123
Rates: $149 - $179 weekly, $640 - $740 monthly
Special Features: Recently remodeled, fully furnished studio and one bedroom apartments include color TV and all utilities including phone and cable, swimming pool, Jacuzzi and guest laundry facilities. One cat allowed.

Shelter Island
3770 Swenson Ave.
Las Vegas, NV 89119
734-6788
Anne Stevenson, Mgr.
Rooms: 455 apartments
Rates: From $139 - $169.50 weekly including utilities, $70 deposit, pets welcome with $150 deposit
Special Features: Cable TV, pool, Jacuzzi, laundry room, kitchens.

Sportsman's Royal Manor
5660 Boulder Hwy.
Las Vegas, NV 89122
458-7071
Gary Brennan, Owner
Rooms: 196 studios and one bedrooms suites
Rates: $35 - $86 daily, $179.50 weekly, monthly rates available.
Special Features: All utilities paid, including phone and cable, heated pool and spa, 24-hour restaurant and lounge.

Studio Plaza Apartments
915 S. Casino Center Blvd.
Las Vegas, NV 89101
385-5582
Robert Chambers, Mgr.
Rooms: 75
Rates: $144.50 weekly or $560 monthly
Special Features: Cable, phone, pool, laundry facilities, barbecues, utilities furnished.

Sunrise Vista Executive Suites
3801 E. Charleston Blvd.
Las Vegas, NV 89104
459-7908
Frances Phillips, Gen. Mgr.
Rooms: 64
Rates: $149 - $169 weekly, $596 - $636 monthly, $75 deposit required
Special Features: Pool, TV and kitchenettes, laundry facilities.

Sunstate Apartments
422 S. 1st St.
Las Vegas, NV 89101
384-3134
Kathy Floyd, Mgr.
Rooms: 168
Rates: Studio $425, 1 bedroom $470
Special Features: Kitchenettes, laundry rooms, covered parking, pets allowed.

Thai Royal Motel
1424 S. 4th St.
Las Vegas, NV 89101
384-8264
Kip Psainiyom, Mgr.
Rooms: 12
Rates: $110 - $120 weekly
Special Features: Kitchens, color TV.

Woodbridge Inn Apartments
700 E. Flamingo Rd.
Las Vegas, NV 89119
732-7678
Kenneth Roberts, Mgr.
Rooms: 320 short-term rental

Rates: $157 weekly, $530 monthly
Special Features: Cable TV, heated pool and Jacuzzi, laundry room, kitchens, pets allowed.

Warren Motel Apartments
3965 Las Vegas Blvd. S.
Las Vegas, NV 89109
736-6235 1-800-331-7700
Mary Salazar, Mgr.
Rooms: 55
Rates: $146 - $172 weekly, monthly rates.
Special Features: Kitchenettes, pool, cable TV, laundromat, telephones.

MOTELS

Rates fluctuate like hotel rates as the motels usually depend on the overflow from the hotels when they are sold out. Motels fill a niche among visitors who prefer a small facility with convenient parking next to their room.

The heaviest concentrations of motels are along the extreme south end of the Strip before Flamingo Rd., the north end of the Strip between Sahara Ave. and downtown, Fremont St. east of downtown and along the side streets north of the downtown area, along Boulder Hwy. all the way to Henderson.

Algiers Hotel
2845 Las Vegas Blvd. S.
Las Vegas, NV 89109
735-3311 1-800-732-3361
Faun Crain-Olsen, Mgr.
Rooms: 105
Rates: $35 - $65
Special Features: Restaurant and lounge, pool, cable TV, telephones.

Ambassador East Motel
916 E. Fremont St.
Las Vegas, NV 89101
384-8281 1-800-634-6703
Ray Tagliaferri, Gen. Mgr.
Rooms: 163
Rates: $16 - $20
Special Features: Kitchenettes, pool, TV, telephones, banquet room, laundry room, lounge.

Apache Motel
407 S. Main St.
Las Vegas, NV 89101
382-7606
Paul Kish, Mgr.
Rooms: 42
Rates: $30 - $45 daily, $130 - $135 weekly
Special Features: Laundry room, cable TV.

Aztec Inn
2200 Las Vegas Blvd. S.
Las Vegas, NV 89104
385-4566
Bill Maxwell, Gen. Mgr.
Rooms: 200
Rates: $30 - $50
Special Features: 6,000 sq. ft. slot casino, bar, restaurant, kitchenettes, cable TV, heated pool, telephones, laundry room, conference room.

Barcelona Hotel
5011 E. Craig Rd.
Las Vegas, NV 89115
644-6300 1-800-223-6330
Jewel L. Dixon Jr., Gen. Mgr.
Rooms: 178
Rates: $30 - $125
Special Features: Restaurant and lounge with live entertainment, casino with three blackjack tables, one roulette table and over 200 slots, kitchenettes, swimming pool and spa, Laundry room, conference room, telephones, cable TV and bed and breakfast. Weekly rates available.

Barker Motel
2600 Las Vegas Blvd. N.
N. Las Vegas, NV 89030
642-1138
Danny Taylor, Mgr.
Rooms: 26
Rates: $26 - $80
Special Features: Kitchenettes, pets allowed, pool, TV.

Best Western · Heritage Inn
4975 S. Valley View Blvd.
Las Vegas, NV 89118
798-7736 1-800-528-1234
Alan Campbell, Mgr.
Rooms: 59
Rates: $59 - $235
Special Features: Continental breakfast, fresh baked cookies in the evenings, heated indoor pool and spa open 24 hours, in-room coffee makers, pets allowed, cable TV, gift shop, work-out room, telephones, laundry room, some kitchenettes, conference room, free fax and copy service for all guests.

Best Western· Main Street Inn
1000 N. Main St.
Las Vegas, NV 89101
382-3455 1-800-851-1414
Joe Signore, Mgr.
Rooms: 91
Rates: $45 - $125
Special Features: Pets allowed, pool, color TV, laundry room, telephones.

Best Western Mardi Gras Inn
3500 Paradise Rd.
Las Vegas, NV 89109
731-2020 1-800-634-6501
Philip Jaramillo, Mgr.
Rooms: 314
Rates: $49 - $129
Special Features: Airport pickup, casino with slot and video poker machines, heated swimming pool, gift shop, video arcade, beauty salon, restaurant, bar, telephones and covered parking.
Meeting and banquet facilities:
Total meeting capacity - 562
Total banquet capacity - 410

Best Western McCarran Inn
4970 Paradise Rd.
Las Vegas, NV 89119
798-5530 1-800-626-7575
Frederick Walter, Mgr.
Rooms: 99
Rates: $49 - $90
Special Features: Airport shuttle, continental breakfast, cable TV, telephones, heated pool, laundry room.

Best Western·Nellis Motor Inn
5330 E. Craig Rd.
Las Vegas, NV 89115
643-6111 1-800-546-1119
Robert Calderon, Mgr.
Rooms: 52
Rates: $40 - $100
Special Features: Satellite TV, pool, pets allowed, laundry room, telephones.

Best Western Parkview Inn
905 Las Vegas Blvd. N.
Las Vegas, NV 89101
385-1213 1-800-548-6122
Steve Pilkington, Gen. Mgr.
Rooms: 56
Rates: $44 - $98
Special Features: Pool, pets allowed, all queen beds, telephones, TV, bar, laundry room.

Black Jack Motel
2909 E. Fremont St.
Las Vegas, NV 89104
382-8093
Vipin Ghandi, Mgr.
Rooms: 23
Rates: $30
Special Features: Kitchenettes, TV, pool, small pets allowed, laundry room, telephones.

Blue Angel Motel
2110 E. Fremont St.
Las Vegas, NV 89101
386-9500
Gregg Porter, Mgr.
Rooms: 84
Rates: $27 - $49 daily, $102 weekly rates
Special Features: Kitchenettes, pool, satellite TV, laundry room, telephones, small pets allowed.

Bonanza Lodge
1808 E. Fremont St.
Las Vegas, NV 89101
382-3990
Jack Lisbyo, Mgr.
Rooms: 32
Rates: $30 - $75
Special Features: Kitchenettes, pool, satellite TV, telephones.

Budget Inn
301 S. Main St.
Las Vegas, NV 89101
385-5560 1-800-959-9062
Fax 382-9273
Herbert Moeller, Mgr.
Rooms: 81
Rates: $25 - $55
Special Features: Satellite TV, phones.

Capri Motel
3245 E. Fremont St.
Las Vegas, NV 89104
457-1429
Dilip Chohan, Mgr.
Rooms: 19
Rates: $25 - $65
Special Features: Pool, cable TV, Jacuzzi in room, kitchenettes, local calls free.

Carriage House
105 E. Harmon Ave.
Las Vegas, NV 89109
798-1020
Amy Lowell, Mgr.
Rooms: 154
Rates: $62.50 - $275
Special Features: Restaurant, lounge with entertainment, kitchenettes, airport shuttle, laundry room, heated pool, Jacuzzi, covered parking, tennis court.

Casa Malaga Motel
4615 Las Vegas Blvd. S.
Las Vegas, NV 89119
739-8362 1-800-634-6727
Randi Youngberg, Mgr.
Rooms: 44
Rates: $25 - $68.50
Special Features: Pool, TV, pets allowed, telephones.

Casablanca Inn
1801 Las Vegas Blvd. S.
Las Vegas, NV 89104
735-5300
Frank Graves, Mgr.
Rooms: 20
Rates: $35 - $65
Special Features: Cable TV, free local calls.

Casino Royale
3411 Las Vegas Blvd. S.
Las Vegas NV 89109
737-3500 1-800-854-7666
Chuck Wood, Hotel Mgr.
Rooms: 153
Rates: $35 - $125
Special Features: In-room movies, casino, heated pool, cable TV, telephones, restaurant and lounge.

Center Strip Inn
3688 Las Vegas Blvd. S.
Las Vegas, NV 89109
739-6066 1-800-777-7737
Fax: 736-2521
Angela Willis, Mgr.
Rooms: 152 including 46 suites
Rates: $29.95 - $169
Special Features: In-room fresh water spas, pool, cable TV, telephones, pets allowed, free dinner, free continental breakfast.

Cheyenne Hotel
3227 Civic Center Dr.
N. Las Vegas, NV 89030
399-3297
Tom Inda, Mgr.
Rooms: 120
Rates: $39 - $79
Special Features: Lounge, pool, cable TV, telephones.

Cimmaron Motel
3680 Boulder Hwy.
Las Vegas, NV 89121
451-4131
Bill Steele, Mgr.
Rooms: 25
Rates: $30 - $48.60
Special Features: Office open on Fri. and Sat. only, pets allowed, pool, TV.

City Center Motel
700 E. Fremont St.
Las Vegas, NV 89101
382-4766
Dora Ali, Mgr.
Rooms: 57
Rates: $30 - $42
Special Features: Small pets allowed, pool, cable TV, laundry room, free local calling.

MOTELS

Comfort Inn
211 E. Flamingo Rd.
Las Vegas, NV 89109
733-7800 1-800-634-6774
Fax: 733-7800
Jo Davidian, Gen. Mgr.
Rooms: 121
Rates: $55 - $75
Special Features: Pool, telephones, free continental breakfast, TV with pay-per-view movies.

Comfort Inn-South
5075 Koval Ln.
Las Vegas, NV 89109
736-3600 1-800-228-5160
Fax: 736-0726
Paul Sanchez, Gen. Mgr.
Rooms: 106
Rates: $47 - $80
Special Features: Pool, free continental breakfast, cable TV, telephones, pets allowed.

Convention Center Lodge
79 Convention Center Dr.
Las Vegas, NV 89109
735-1315
Joan Kilburn, Mgr.
Rooms: 56
Rates: $25 - $55, $145 - $165 weekly
Special Features: TV, pool, local calls free, refrigerators, microwaves, laundry room.

Crest Budget Inn
207 N. Sixth St.
Las Vegas, NV 89101
382-5642 1-800-777-1817
Larry Snyder, Mgr.
Rooms: 154
Rates: $29.95 - $59.95
Special Features: Kitchenettes, free breakfast, pool, cable TV, VCR, laundry room, pets allowed.

Daisy Motel & Apartments
415 S. Main St.
Las Vegas, NV 89101
382-0707
Forrest Wilkins, Mgr.
Rooms: 151
Rates: $25 - $35
Special Features: Kitchenettes, pets allowed, telephones, weekly rates, pool and laundry room, cable TV.

Days Inn Downtown
707 E. Fremont St.
Las Vegas, NV 89101
388-1400 1-800-325-2344
Fax: 388-9622
John Frank, Gen. Mgr.
Rooms: 147
Rates: $35 - $80
Special Features: Restaurant, cable TV, pool, telephones, covered parking.

Days Inn Town Hall Casino
4155 Koval Ln.
Las Vegas, NV 89109
731-2111 1-800-634-6541
Fax: 731-1113
R. G. Madsen, Mgr.
Rooms: 357 rooms including 3 suites

Rates: $29 - $80
Special Features: Casino, restaurant, lounge, gift shop, heated swimming pool and spa, telephones, TV, laundry rooms.

Del Mar Motel
1411 Las Vegas Blvd. S.
Las Vegas, NV 89104
384-5775
Alex MacFalda
Rooms: 35
Rates: $49 - $66, special 3 hour rate: $30
Special Features: Pool, two people per room only, adult movies, TV, telephones.

Desert Hills Motel
2121 Fremont St.
Las Vegas, NV 89101
384-8060
Tony Eubanks, Mgr.
Rooms: 31
Rates: $25 - $30 daily, $140 weekly
Special Features: Pool, kitchenettes, pets welcome, cable TV, free local calls, laundry room.

Desert Moon Motel
1701 E. Fremont St.
Las Vegas, NV 89101
382-5535
Mike Milo, Mgr.
Rooms: 24
Rates: $30 - $45
Special Features: Cable TV, kitchenettes, laundry room, adult movies.

Diamond Inn Motel
4605 Las Vegas Blvd. S.
Las Vegas, NV 89109
736-2565
Sam Aldabagh, Mgr.
Rooms: 44
Rates: $26 - $74
Special Features: Kitchenettes, heated pool, Jacuzzi rooms, cable TV, telephones, adult movies, weekly rates available.

Downtown Thriftlodge Motel
629 S. Main St.
Las Vegas, NV 89101
385-7796
June & Darryl Smeby, Mgrs.
Rooms: 190
Rates: $50 daily, $123.80 weekly, $437 monthly
Special Features: Heated pool, kitchenettes, cable TV, laundry room, telephones, covered parking.

Downtowner Motel
129 N. 8th St.
Las Vegas, NV 89101
384-1441 1-800-777-2566
Ada Cohen, Mgr.
Rooms: 200
Rates: $24.95 - $69.95, weekly kitchenettes starting at $135 per week
Special Features: Kitchenettes, room includes free breakfast at El Cortez, slots, pool, VCRs, refrigerators, cable TV, laundry room, telephones.

E-Z 8 Motels Inc.
5201 Industrial Rd.
Las Vegas, NV 89118
739-9513
Arthur Johnson, Mgr.
Rooms: 127
Rates: $28 - $48
Special Features: Pool, laundry facility, game room, truck parking, allows pets, telephones, cable TV.

Econo Lodge
1150 Las Vegas Blvd. S
Las Vegas, NV 89104
382-6001 1-800-634-6979
Fax: 382-9180
James Magar, Gen. Mgr.
Rooms: 124
Rates: $35 - $70
Special Features: Free coffee, direct dial phones, pool, TV.

Econo Lodge Downtown
520 S. Casino Center Blvd.
Las Vegas, NV 89101
384-8211 1-800-223-7706
Fax: 702-384-8580
Juanita Wilson, Mgr.
Rooms: 48
Rates: $35 - $60, suites $65 - $85
Special Features: Refrigerator, coffee maker, satellite TV, some kitchens, laundry room, telephones.

Economy Inn
2028 E. Fremont St.
Las Vegas, NV 89101
384-7540
Hasu Desai, Mgr.
Rooms: 58
Rates: $35 - $85
Special Features: Pets allowed, in room coffee, cable TV, pool, free local calls.

El Cid Hotel
233 S. Sixth St.
Las Vegas, NV 89101
384-4696 1-800-688-1212
Sofia Lau, Gen. Mgr.
Rooms: 163
Rates: $50 - $100
Special Features: Kitchenettes, cable TV, refrigerators in rooms, telephones, laundry room.

El Mirador Motel
2310 Las Vegas Blvd. S.
Las Vegas, NV 89104
384-6570
Paul Alspaugh, Mgr.
Rooms: 25
Rates: $35 - $59
Special Features: Pool, cable TV, telephones, pets allowed, weekly rates.

Fairfield Inn By Marriott
3850 Paradise Rd.
Las Vegas, NV 89109
791-0899 1-800-228-2800
Jodi Wanant, Gen. Mgr.
Rooms: 129
Rates: $62 - $72
Special Features: Airport shuttle, cable TV, heated pool, free local calls, meeting rooms.

Fergusons Motel
1028 E. Fremont St.
Las Vegas, NV 89101
382-3500 1-800-933-7829
Larry Ferguson, Mgr.
Rooms: 66
Rates: $29 - $100
Special Features: Kitchenettes, pets allowed, TV, pool, telephones, weekly rates available.

Fez Motel
4213 Las Vegas Blvd. S.
Las Vegas, NV 89119
736-6014
Bud Parker, Mgr.
Rooms: 42
Rates: $20 - $50
Special Features: Pool, TV.

Firebird Inn
8025 Industrial Rd.
Las Vegas, NV 89139
896-4333
Anthony Giralo, Mgr.
Rooms: 47
Rates: $35 - $49
Special Features: Cable TV, free local calls, small pets allowed, trucker rates.

A Fisher's Inn
3565 Boulder Hwy.
Las Vegas, NV 89121
457-3900
Gary Tipton, Mgr.
Rooms: 20
Rates: $32 - $52
Special Features: Continental breakfast 7 am - 11 am, free cable TV, telephones, laundry room.

Fisher Motel
1208 E. Fremont St.
Las Vegas, NV 89101
382-8131
John Ostrander, Mgr.
Rooms: 24
Rates: $25 - $35
Special Features: Cable TV, telephones.

49er Motel
3045 E. Fremont St.
Las Vegas, NV 89104
457-5754
Wayne Stokes, Mgr.
Rooms: 31
Rates: $25 - $40, weekly with kitchenette $129.50
Special Features: Studios, kitchenettes, TV.

Fun City Motel
2233 Las Vegas Blvd. S.
Las Vegas, NV 89104
731-3155
Jim Wheeler, Mgr.
Rooms: 85
Rates: $29 - $100
Special Features: Kitchenettes, local calls free, basic cable, pool, laundry facilities.

Gables Motel
1301 E. Fremont St.
Las Vegas, NV 89101
384-1637
Seng Ny, Mgr.
Rooms: 20
Rates: $35 - $45
Special Features: Cable TV, free local calls, refrigerators and microwaves in some rooms, pets allowed, donuts and coffee served in the morning.

Gateway Motel
928 Las Vegas Blvd. S.
Las Vegas, NV 89101
382-2146
Arvind Patel, Mgr.
Rooms: 46
Rates: $32.50 - $50
Special Features: Satellite TV, pets allowed.

Gatewood Motel
3075 E. Fremont St.
Las Vegas, NV 89104
457-3660
Joe Temple, Mgr.
Rooms: 19
Rates: $35 - $75
Special Features: Adult movies, small pets allowed, TV, laundry room.

Glass Pool Inn
4613 Las Vegas Blvd. S.
Las Vegas, NV 89119
739-6636 1-800-527-7118
Allen Rosoff
Rooms: 48
Rates: $29 - 69
Special Features: Restaurant and lounge, kitchenettes, only dogs allowed, satellite TV, laundry room, local calls free, fax machine. Heated pool has a glass front with a view of the Strip from under water, glass elevators.

Golden Inn Motel
120 Las Vegas Blvd. N.
Las Vegas, NV 89101
384-8204
Polly Claiborne, Mgr.
Rooms: 71
Rates: $22 - $78
Special Features: Pets allowed, pool, cable TV, telephones, refrigerators and microwaves for weekly rentals, fax machine.

Happi Inn
3939 Las Vegas Blvd. S.
Las Vegas, NV 89119
736-8031 1-800-634-6727
Donna Harris, Mgr.
Rooms: 88
Rates: $25 - $150
Special Features: King beds, refrigerators, pool, TV, telephones.

High Hat Regency Motel
1300 Las Vegas Blvd. S.
Las Vegas, NV 89104
382-8080
Rooms: 31
Rates: $25 - $85
Special Features: Kitchenettes, TV, pool, telephones.

Hitchin' Post Motel, R.V. Park
3640 Las Vegas Blvd. N.
Las Vegas, NV 89115
644-1043
Brent Childress
Rooms: 10
Rates: $30 - $50
Special Features: Cable TV, pool, laundromat.

Holiday House
2211 Las Vegas Blvd. S.
Las Vegas, NV 89104
732-2468
Yvonne Duplain, Mgr.
Rooms: 75
Rates: $54 and up
Special Features: Pool, cable TV, free local calls.

Holiday Inn Express
8669 W. Sahara Ave.
Las Vegas, NV 89117
256-3766
Mary Macy, Mgr.
Rooms: 59
Rates: $79 - $99
Special Features: Indoor pool, spa, cable TV, kitchenettes, laundry room, and spa suites, pets allowed, telephones, conference room.

Holiday Motel
2205 Las Vegas Blvd. S.
Las Vegas, NV 89104
735-6464
Yvonne Duplain, Mgr.
Rooms: 41
Rates: $30 - $60
Special Features: Pool, cable TV, phone, free coffee, local calls free.

Hops Motel
3412 Paradise Rd.
Las Vegas, NV 89109
732-2494
Warren Hopkins
Rooms: 50
Rates: $25 - $45
Special Features: Kitchenettes, pool, TV, laundry room, telephones.

Howard Johnson Plaza Hotel and Casino
3111 W. Tropicana Ave.
Las Vegas, NV 89103
798-1111 1-800-300-7389
Kevin McMullen
Rooms: 150
Rates: $49 - $110
Special Features: Airport shuttle van, restaurant, casino, pool, spa, cable TV, conference room.

Howard Johnsons - Airport
5100 Paradise Rd.
Las Vegas, NV 89119
798-2777 1-800-634-6430
Fax: 736-8295
Jim Shields, Gen. Mgr.
Rooms: 340
Rates: $35 - $95 - 1 and 2 bedroom
Special Features: Mini-Mart, restaurant and lounge, four slot machines, airport shuttle, pool, cable TV, laundry room, conference room.

Howard Johnson - Las Vegas Strip
1401 Las Vegas Blvd. S.
Las Vegas, NV 89104
388-0301
Ali Faeghi, Mgr.
Rooms: 104
Rates: $29.90 - $59
Special Features: Restaurant and coffee shop, wedding chapel, pool, 2 honeymoon suites, pay-per-view movies, TV, laundry room, pets allowed, conference room.

Jackpot Motel
1600 Casino Center Blvd.
Las Vegas, NV 89104
384-7211
Tony Swamy, Mgr.
Rooms: 22
Rates: $40 daily, short time - $20 for 1 hour.
Special Features: Cable TV, telephones.

King Albert Motel
165 Albert Ave.
Las Vegas, NV 89109
732-1555 1-800-553-7753
Pat Thorson, Mgr.
Rooms: 104
Rates: $39 - $59
Special Features: Pool, allows pets, telephones, laundry room, cable TV.

King 8 Hotel & Gambling Hall
3330 W. Tropicana Ave.
Las Vegas, NV 89103
736-8988 1-800-634-3488
Rick Ross, Gen. Mgr.
Rooms: 298 including 8 suites (2 story)
Rates: $30 - $75
Special Features: Heated swimming pool and spa, 6,000 sq. ft. casino, airport pickup and drop off, MGM drop off, restaurant and lounge, cable TV, laundry room, conference room, telephones.

Klondike Inn
5191 Las Vegas Blvd. S.
Las Vegas, NV 89119
739-9351
Jim McClean, Mgr.
Rooms: 153
Rates: $29 - $49
Special Features: Casino, restaurant, lounge, laundry room, pool, TV, telephones.

Knotty Pine
1900 Las Vegas Blvd. N.
N. Las Vegas, NV 89030
642-8300
Nancy Sadler, Mgr.
Rooms: 20
Rates: $35 - $40
Special Features: Color TV, kitchenettes.

La Quinta Motor Inn
3782 Las Vegas Blvd. S.
Las Vegas, NV 89109
739-7457 1-800-NU-ROOMS
Alex Oh, Mgr.
Rooms: 114
Rates: $59 - $89
Special Features: Pets allowed, airport shuttle, pool cable, TV, telephones.

Lamplighter Motel
2805 E. Fremont St.
Las Vegas, NV 89104
382-8791
Bill Gunn, Mgr.
Rooms: 34
Rates: $30 - $50
Special Features: Refrigerators in rooms, cable TV, telephones, only small dogs allowed.

La Palm Motel
2512 E. Fremont St.
Las Vegas, NV 89104
384-5874
Shashi Champaneri, Mgr.
Rooms: 44
Rates: $30 - $50
Special Features: Kitchenettes, color cable TV, Olympic size swimming pool, weekly rates available, telephones, laundry room.

Las Vegas Motel
1200 E. Fremont St.
Las Vegas, NV 89101
384-5670
John Ostrander, Mgr.
Rooms: 25
Rates: $25 - $35
Special Features: Cable TV, continental breakfast, telephones, laundry room.

Laughing Jackalope Motel
3969 Las Vegas Blvd. S.
Las Vegas, NV 89104
739-1915
Jim Beasley, Mgr.
Rooms: 34
Rates: $35 - $85
Special Features: Lounge, video slots, restaurant, pool, cable TV, telephones.

Lee Motel & Deli
200 South 8th St.
Las Vegas, NV 89101
382-1297
David Schaeffer, Mgr.
Rooms: 83
Rates: $21 - $38
Special Features: Kitchenettes, cable TV, laundry room, telephones, deli.

Lucky Lady Motel
1308 E. Fremont St.
Las Vegas, NV 89101
385-1093
Seng Ng
Rooms: 19
Rates: $25 - $85
Special Features: Small pets, kitchenettes, free breakfast in the El Cortez, free coffee and donuts in office, satellite TV, free local calls, microwaves.

Meadows Inn
525 E. Bonanza Rd.
Las Vegas, NV 89101
366-0456 1-800-932-1499
Paul Webberson, Mgr.
Rooms: 150
Rates: $35 - $55
Special Features: Lounge, meeting room, small pets allowed, kitchenettes, pool, TV, laundry room, covered parking, telephones.

MOTELS

Motel 6
195 E. Tropicana Ave.
Las Vegas, NV 89109
798-0728
Gene Sheridan, Gen. Mgr.
Rooms: 606
Rates: $31.99 - $61.99

Motel 6
5085 Industrial Rd.
Las Vegas, NV 89118
739-6747
John Schoofs, Mgr.
Rooms: 139
Rates: $28.99 - $39.99
Special Features: Pets allowed, cable TV, pay-per-view, telephones, laundry room, heated pool.

Motel 6
4125 Boulder Hwy.
Las Vegas, NV 89121
457-8051
Russell Whisler, Mgr.
Rooms: 161
Rates: $29.99 - $41.99
Special Features: Cable TV, phones, pets allowed, heated pool, laundry room.

Motel 8
3961 Las Vegas Blvd. S.
Las Vegas, NV 89119
798-7223
Choa-Te Chen, Mgr.
Rooms: 30
Rates: $25 - $100
Special Features: Heated pool, deli and gift shop, laundry room, heated pool.

Nellis Lodge Motel
4228 Las Vegas Blvd. N.
Las Vegas, NV 89115
643-9220
Ike Ilich, Gen. Mgr.
Rooms: 190
Rates: $44 - $54 daily, $150 weekly, $600 monthly
Special Features: All studio apartments, pool, laundromats, telephones, cable TV.

Normandie Motel
708 Las Vegas Blvd. S.
Las Vegas, NV 89101
382-1002
Brian Perceval, Mgr.
Rooms: 15
Rates: $30 - $42
Special Features: Small pets, kitchenettes, some cable, telephones.

Nylen Motel 80
3144 Las Vegas Blvd. N.
Las Vegas, NV 89115
644-9706
Russell Nylen
Rooms: 7
Rates: $12 - $35
Special Features: TV

Oasis Motel
1731 Las Vegas Blvd. S.
Las Vegas, NV 89104
735-6494
Pete Napoli, Mgr.
Rooms: 35
Rates: $42 - $64, 3 hours at varying rates
Special Features: Two adult movie channels, telephones, pool, Jacuzzis in some of the rooms.

Ogden House
651 Ogden Ave.
Las Vegas, NV 89101
385-5200
Sophia Rasile, Mgr.
Rooms: 102
Rates: $19.80
Special Features: TV, phones.

Par-a-Dice Inn
2217 E. Fremont St.
Las Vegas, NV 89101
382-6440
Dora Ali, Mgr.
Rooms: 53
Rates: $26.80 - $37
Special Features: Satellite TV, pets allowed, laundry room.

Paradise Resort Inn
4350 Paradise Rd.
Las Vegas, NV 89109
733-3900
Larry Carrion, Mgr.
Rooms: 206
Rates: $40 - $50
Special Features: Kitchenette, pool, basic cable, pets allowed, telephone, laundry room.

Ponderosa Motel
3325 E. Fremont St.
Las Vegas, NV 89104
457-0422
Ed Caballero
Rooms: 27
Rates: $30 - $45
Special Features: Pool, telephones, cable TV.

Queen of Hearts Hotel
19 E. Lewis St.
Las Vegas, NV 89101
382-8878 1-800-835-6005
Wes Yamada, Gen. Mgr.
Ann Meyers, Owner
Rooms: 100
Rates: $39 and up, $129.50 per week
Special Features: Lounge, pool, satellite TV, laundry room, some telephones, weekly rates available.

Ramada, Ltd.
1501 W. Sahara Ave.
Las Vegas, NV 89102
733-0001 1-800-554-4092
Louie LeMaster
Rooms: 223 rooms
Rates: $39 - $79
Special Features: 24-hour lounge, satellite TV, continental breakfast, pool, laundry room, telephones, conference room.

Regency Motel
700 N. Main St.
Las Vegas, NV 89101
382-2332
Barbara Toth, Mgr.
Rooms: 30
Rates: $30 - $49
Special Features: Restaurant, pets allowed, pool, TV.

Royal Motel
615 Las Vegas Blvd. S.
Las Vegas, NV 89101
386-2767
Tom Yeh, Mgr.
Rooms: 13
Rates: Single $30, double $35, family room $45
Special Features: TV.

Safari Motel
2001 E. Fremont St.
Las Vegas, NV 89101
384-4021
Bharat Chokshi, Mgr.
Rooms: 22
Rates: $30 - $45
Special Features: Pool, refrigerators, laundry facilities, telephones, cable TV.

Silver Queen Motel
1401 Carson Ave.
Las Vegas, NV 89101
384-8157
Sangetta Champaneri
Rooms: 14
Rates: $25 - $30
Special Features: Color TV, kitchenettes, laundry room.

Somerset House
294 Convention Center Dr.
Las Vegas, NV 89109
735-5097
Robert Vincent, Gen. Mgr.
Rooms: 104
Rates: $30 - $70
Special Features: Kitchenettes, conference room, free in-house movies, olympic size heated pool, free coffee in room, basic TV, laundry room.

Star Motel
1418 S. 4th St.
Las Vegas, NV 89101
383-9770
Dominga Versales, Mgr.
Rooms: 23
Rates: $30 - $40
Special Features: Kitchenettes, color TV, laundry room.

Star View Motel
1217 E. Fremont St.
Las Vegas, NV 89101
388-1533
John Ostrander, Mgr.
Rooms: 25
Rates: $25 - $35
Special Features: Cable TV.

Starlite Motel
1873 Las Vegas Blvd. N.
N. Las Vegas, NV 89030
642-1750
Judy Pong, Mgr.
Rooms: 30
Rates: $35 - $85
Special Features: Color TV, pool.

Steven Motel
2112 N. Nellis Blvd.
Las Vegas, NV 89115
452-8199
Robert French, Mgr.
Rooms: 8
Rates: $30 - $40
Special Features: Restaurant, kitchenettes, cable TV, telephones, laundry room.

Strip 91 Motel
2091 Las Vegas Blvd. N.
N. Las Vegas, NV 89030
649-4593
Glen Reaves, Mgr.
Rooms: 17
Rates: $34 - $65
Special Features: Pets allowed, color TV.

Sunrise Resorts and RV Park
4575 Boulder Hwy.
Las Vegas, NV 89121
434-0848 1-800-362-4040
Justene Thomas, Gen. Mgr.
Rooms: 305 suites, mini and one bedroom
Rates: $39 - $95
Special Features: Deli, kitchenettes, microwaves, refrigerators, pool, spa, barbecue area, cable TV, in-room movies, laundry room, telephones, meeting rooms.

Sunset Motel
6000 Boulder Hwy.
Las Vegas, NV 89122
451-2445
Allen Buell, Mgr.
Rooms: 24
Rates: $25 - $60 daily, $108 - $140 weekly
Special Features: Some kitchenettes, laundry room, TV.

Super 8 Motel
5288 Boulder Hwy.
Las Vegas, NV 89122
435-8888 1-800-825-0880
Kim Kern, Gen. Mgr.
Rooms: 150
Rates: $32 - $78
Special Features: Casino, restaurant and lounge, pool, Jacuzzi, telephones, laundry room, cable TV.

Super 8 Motel
4250 Koval Ln.
Las Vegas, NV 89109
794-0888 1-800-800-8000
Paul Harris, Gen. Mgr.
Rooms: 300
Rates: $32.88 - $61.88
Special Features: Casino, cable TV, restaurant and lounge, pets allowed, airport shuttle, free morning coffee, heated pool, laundry room, Jacuzzi, telephones, children 12 and under stay free, free local calls.

Tam O'Shanter Motel
3317 Las Vegas Blvd. S.
Las Vegas, NV 89109
735-7331 1-800-727-3423
Leah Zeldin, Mgr.
Rooms: 76
Rates: $38 - $64
Special Features: Small pets allowed, connecting rooms, pool, cable TV, telephones.

Thunderbird Hotel
1213 Las Vegas Blvd. S.
Las Vegas, NV 89104
383-3100
Sally Blumen, Mgr.
Rooms: 300
Rates: $32 - $85
Special Features: Restaurant, lounge, entertainment, pool, cable TV, pets allowed, kid's play arcade, laundry room, telephones, covered parking.

Tod Motor Inn
1508 Las Vegas Blvd. S.
Las Vegas, NV 89104
477-0022
Mel McKinney, Mgr.
Rooms: 108
Rates: $105 - $126 weekly
Special Features: Kitchenettes, cable TV, free phones, weekly maid service, pool.

Town Palms Motel
321 S. Casino Center Dr.
Las Vegas, NV 89101
382-1611
Stephen Brown, Mgr.
Rooms: 90
Rates: $34.88 - $43.60
Special Features: Cable TV, laundry room, telephones, daily, weekly and monthly rates.

Towne & Country Motel
2033 E. Fremont St.
Las Vegas, NV 89101
366-8576
Helen Hsu, Mgr.
Rooms: 29
Rates: $27 - $45
Special Features: Pool, cable TV, telephones, large rooms.

Travel Inn Motel
217 Las Vegas Blvd. N.
Las Vegas, NV 89101
384-3040
Polly Claiborne, Mgr.
Rooms: 57
Rates: $30 - $47
Special Features: Pets allowed, pool, color satellite TV, telephones, microwaves and refrigerators for weekly rentals.

Traveler's Motel
1100 E. Fremont St.
Las Vegas, NV 89101
384-7121
Rooms: 36
Rates: $25 - $60
Special Features: Pets allowed, color TV, laundry room.

Travelodge Las Vegas Strip
2830 Las Vegas Blvd. S.
Las Vegas, NV 89109
735-4222 1-800-578-7878
Patricia Ravatt, Mgr.
Rooms: 100
Rates: $39 - $69
Special Features: In room coffee, cable TV, heated pool, telephones, safes in rooms, refrigerators for rent.

Travelodge South Strip
3735 Las Vegas Blvd. S.
Las Vegas, NV 89109
736-3443 1-800-578-7878
Linda Rose, Mgr.
Rooms: 126
Rates: $49 - $99
Special Features: Heated pool, cable TV, telephones, coffee in rooms.

Tropicana Inn
5150 Duke Ellington Way
Las Vegas, NV 89119
736-8964
Marilyn Lim, Mgr.
Rooms: 118
Rates: $40 - $55

Special Features: Weekly rates available, kitchenettes, cable TV, pool, telephones, laundry room.

Uptown Motel
813 Ogden Ave.
Las Vegas, NV 89101
382-5257
Richard Raiston, Mgr.
Rooms: 30
Rates: $100 - $110 weekly, $375 - $390 monthly, extended stay rates available.
Special Features: TV.

U S Motel
2500 E. Fremont St.
Las Vegas, NV 89104
384-2481
Gene Koo, Mgr.
Rooms: 30
Rates: $30 - $45
Special Features: Some refrigerators, telephones, cable TV.

Vagabond Inn
3265 Las Vegas Blvd. S.
Las Vegas, NV 89109
735-5102 1-800-522-1555
Fax: 735-0168
Latresh Jolliff, Gen. Mgr.
Rooms: 126
Rates: $44 - $59
Special Features: Cable TV, heated pool, pets allowed, airport shuttle, complimentary continental breakfast, free local calls, laundry room, covered parking.

Valley Motel
1313 E. Fremont St.
Las Vegas, NV 89101
384-6890
Max Naik, Mgr.
Rooms: 22
Rates: $28 - $30
Special Features: Pets allowed, color cable TV, free local calling.

Vegas Chalet Motel
2401 Las Vegas Blvd. N.
N. Las Vegas, NV 89030
642-2115
Rick Desai, Mgr.
Rooms: 75
Rates: $29 - $35, weekly rates available
Special Features: Kitchenettes, pets allowed, cable TV, telephones, laundry room.

Vegas Motel
2216 E. Fremont St.
Las Vegas, NV 89101
388-1500
Dora Ali, Mgr.
Rooms: 81
Rates: $21.80 - $42 daily, weekly and monthly rates also available
Special Features: Refrigerator, satellite TV, pets allowed, some rooms with kitchenettes, laundry room.

Vegas Verdes Motel
1635 N. Main St.
N. Las Vegas, NV 89030
642-8598
Rooms: 15
Rates: $25 - $55 for regular room
Special Features: Kitchenettes, refrigerators in efficiencies, TV.

Victory Hotel
307 S. Main St.
Las Vegas, NV 89101
384-0260 387-9257
Steve Wheeler, Mgr.
Rooms: 32
Rates: $20 - $45
Special Features: TV, laundry room. The mission-style Victory Hotel was built in 1910 and was known as the Lincoln Hotel. What is now Las Vegas' oldest hotel was built to house railroad passengers and employees. The hotel is eligible for the National Register of Historic Places.

Villa Roma Motel
220 Convention Center Dr.
Las Vegas, NV 89109
735-4151 1-800-634-6535
Theodore Buban, Gen. Mgr.
Rooms: 100
Rates: $25 - $75
Special Features: Heated pool, telephones, cable TV, refrigerators.

Villager Lodge Inn
4350 Boulder Hwy.
Las Vegas, NV 89121
434-9900
Susan Black, Mgr.
Rooms: 182 suites
Rates: $59 - $99
Special Features: Full kitchen with microwave, free satellite TV, exercise facilities, 24-hour courtesy patrol, heated pool and spa, telephones, laundry room.

Walden Motel
3085 E. Fremont St.
Las Vegas, NV 89104
457-9090
Jit Mody, Mgr.
Rooms: 10
Rates: $27 - $45
Special Features: Pets allowed, color TV, newly remodeled.

Warren House East
1025 Sierra Vista Dr.
Las Vegas, NV 89109
734-8586
Mary Lou Knox, Mgr.
Rooms: 76
Rates: No daily rental, $134 - $173 weekly, $433 - $559 monthly, extended stay rates available.
Special Features: Utilities, pool, cable TV, laundry room, kitchens.

White Sands Motel
3889 Las Vegas Blvd. S.
Las Vegas, NV 89119
736-2515
Spartaco Cilleli, Mgr.
Rooms: 33
Rates: $30 - $60
Special Features: Pool, TV, free coffee, telephone, pets allowed.

Yucca Motel
1727 Las Vegas Blvd. S.
Las Vegas, NV 89104
735-2787
Bob Patel, Mgr.
Rooms: 22
Rates: $35 - $45
Special Features: TV.

AREA OUT-OF-TOWN ACCOMMODATIONS

BOULDER CITY

Boulder Dam Hotel
1305 Arizona St.
Boulder City, NV 89005
293-3510
Darlene Burk, Mgr.
The Boulder Dam Hotel is currently closed as a hotel but should reopen soon. It currently houses the Boulder City Chamber of Commerce, art gallery, shops, restaurant, gift shop. Hoover Dam Museum is relocating there late in 1998. Boulder Dam Hotel was built in 1933 to house dignitaries who came to visit Hoover Dam. The hotel has been enlarged and is currently undergoing major renovations, however, since it was built, Boulder Dam Hotel has continually maintained its original charm and hospitality. Among the guests who have stayed at the hotel are Presidents Hoover and Roosevelt, Bette Davis, Shirley Temple and Howard Hughes. Guests would mingle upstairs in the lobby and drink and gamble downstairs in the basement, both of which were illegal in the federally managed town.

Desert Inn of Boulder City
800 Nevada Hwy.
Boulder City, NV 89005
293-2827
Edith Armstrong, Mgr.
Rooms: 26
Rates: $30 - $95
Special Features: Kitchenettes, pets allowed, cable TV, telephones, heated pool, some covered parking.

Flamingo Inn Motel
804 Nevada Hwy.
Boulder City, NV 89005
293-3565
Jack Posner, Mgr.
Rooms: 16
Rates: $28.50 - $60
Special Features: Pets allowed, kitchenettes, color cable TV, refrigerators in all rooms.

Gold Strike Inn/Casino
U.S. Highway 93
Boulder City, NV 89005
293-5000 1-800-245-6380
Fax: 293-5608
David Ensign, Gen. Mgr.
Rooms:
378 *(some with lake view)*
Rates: $29 - $49

Casino:
27,440 sq. ft.
Games:
776 slot and video machines, 11 blackjack tables, 1 crap table, 1 roulette wheel, 3 poker tables, keno lounge, 1 Caribbean stud, Race and Sports Book.
Special Features:
Antique slot machine and cash register museum, gift shop, arcade, heated pool, Jacuzzi, basic cable TV, telephones, conference room.
Entertainment:
Rosebud Saloon
Tower Bar
Dining:
Buffet - Lunch 11 am - 3:30 pm $3.95, Dinner 4 pm - 10 pm $4.49, seniors (55 and older) $2.99 Tue. - Thu. $2.99 Wed. 4 pm - 10 pm $2.99
Champagne Brunch - Sat. - Sun. 7 am - 11:20 am - $4.55
Coffee Shop - 24 hour
Gold Strike Steak House
Snack Bar

Best Western-Lighthouse Inn & Resort
110 Ville Dr.
Boulder City, NV 89005
293-6444
Carl Davis, Mgr.
Rooms: 70
Rates: $60 - $70, no weekly
Special Features: Pool, Jacuzzi, laundry room, cable TV, pets allowed, telephones, continental breakfast.

Nevada Inn
1009 Nevada Hwy.
Boulder City, NV 89005
293-2044
Barbara Skinner, Mgr.
Rooms: 55
Rates: $35 - $125
Special Features: Non-smoking rooms, kitchenettes, heated pool, whirlpool, telephones, satellite TV, pets allowed.

Sands Motel
809 Nevada Hwy.
Boulder City, NV 89005
293-2589
Pat Johnson, Mgr.
Rooms: 26
Rates: $32 - $47
Special Features: Kitchenettes, cable TV, telephones, refrigerators.

Starview Motel
1017 Nevada Hwy.
Boulder City, NV 89005
293-1658
Don Schaupeter, Mgr.
Rooms: 22
Rates: $28 - $55
Special Features: Restaurant, pets allowed, satellite TV, pool.

Super 8 Motel
704 Nevada Hwy.
Boulder City, NV 89005
294-8888 1-800-825-0880
Lisa Caruso, Mgr.
Rooms: 114
Rates: $43 - $175
Special Features: Most with kitchenettes, restaurant and lounge, indoor heated pool, small pets allowed, laundry room, telephones, conference room, cable TV, spa.

Western Inn
921 Nevada Hwy.
Boulder City, NV 89005
294-0393
Maria Heaton, Mgr.
Rooms: 13
Rates: $35 - $40 daily, weekly rates available.
Special Features: Kitchenettes, satellite TV, HBO 1.

HENDERSON

Best Western-Lake Mead Hotel
85 E. Lake Mead Dr.
Henderson, NV 89015
564-1712 1-800-446-2994
James Hanily, Mgr.
Rooms: 59
Rates: $51 - $99
Special Features: Refrigerators, continental breakfast 6 am - 9 am, heated pool, satellite TV, telephones.

Boby Motel
2100 S. Boulder Hwy.
Henderson, NV 89015
565-9711
Kanji Patel
Rooms: 21
Rates: $33 - $48
Special Features: Kitchenettes, pets allowed, free phone, pool, Jacuzzi, laundry room.

Henderson Townhouse Motor Lodge
43 Water St.
Henderson, NV 89015
564-3111
Luke Benson, Mgr.
Rooms: 20
Rates: $36 - $44
Special Features: Kitchenettes, pets allowed, RV and boat parking, cable TV, telephones.

Ingles Motel
1636 Boulder Hwy.
Henderson, NV 89015
565-7929
Carol Greer, Mgr.
Rooms: 28
Rates: $35 - $45
Special Features: Kitchenettes, laundry room, WAN TV, telephones, most rooms have refrigerators and microwaves.

Outpost Motel
1104 N. Boulder Hwy.
Henderson, NV 89015
564-2664
Tom Copeland, Mgr.
Rooms: 21
Rates: $38 - $60 daily, $150 weekly
Special Features: Kitchenettes, next to Jokers Wild Casino, refrigerators in the weekly accommodations, telephones, laundry room, satellite TV, pets allowed.

Railroad Pass Hotel & Casino
2800 Boulder Hwy.
Henderson, NV 89015
294-5000 1-800-654-0877
Fax: 294-0129
Curtis Jacks, Gen. Mgr.
Rooms:
120
Rates:
$29 - $58
Special Features:
Arcade, gift shop, swimming pool, telephones, TV, conference room.
Casino:
21,480 sq. ft.
Games: Over 400 slot and video machines, 9 blackjack tables, crap table, roulette wheel, keno, race and sports book, 1 Let It Ride table.
Entertainment:
Weekends only, easy listening Fri. - Sun., 6 pm - 1 am
Dining:
Buffet: Lunch - 11 am - 3 pm, dinner - 3 pm - 9 pm - $3.99
Champagne Brunch - Sat. 8 am - 2 pm - $4.75 - Sun. 6 am - 2 pm - $4.75
Iron Rail Cafe - 24 hour
Conductor's Room - Continental

CAL-NEV-ARI

Blue Sky Motel
2 Spirit Mountain Rd.
Box 430
Cal-Nev-Ari, NV 89039
297-9289
Nancy Kidwell, Mgr.
Rooms: 10
Rates: $31 - $41, 2nd day $25
Special Features: Casino, restaurant, lounge, heated pool, cable TV, laundry room, small pets allowed.

MT. CHARLESTON

Mt. Charleston Hotel & Restaurant
2 Kyle Canyon Rd.
Mt. Charleston, NV 89124
872-5500
Sharon Hano, Gen. Mgr.
Rooms:
63 including 3 suites & 2 mini suites *(many rooms include balconies)*
Rates: $49 to $155, 48-hour cancellation required, $5 charge per person above 2nd person in room.
Special Features:
The Mt. Charleston Hotel & Restaurant was built in July 1985 in the traditional style of National Park Lodges using log and stone, with many fireplaces throughout the property.

Gold Strike Inn/Casino, U.S. Highway 93, Boulder City, NV 89005

Wraparound windows provide a sweeping view of the garden and surrounding canyon and mountains while open rafters and mounted trophies add to the Mountain Lodge atmosphere.

At the end of your busy day, come sit and relax in our spa or sauna room. The Canyon Dining room offers international cuisine in an intimate atmosphere that suggests romance to the young at heart. Enjoy your evening next to the fireplace and experience a view that is unsurpassed. The glass enclosed Cliff Hanger lounge offers a relaxing atmosphere, after which you can retire to your room and enjoy a breathtaking view and one of the best rests in Clark County. The gift shop has 13 video poker and 2 keno machines and a video arcade for children of all ages is just a few feet away. Meeting and banquet facilities can accommodate up to 200 people, and beautiful outdoor weddings. The hotel has fireplaces in many areas including the suites., satellite TV, sauna and Jacuzzi, telephones, conference room.

What is there to do on Mt. Charleston?
• Rest, relax and enjoy!!!
• Las Vegas Ski Resort is just 12 mi. from the hotel for those who want to ski and play in the snow. Mt. Charleston Hotel and Lee Canyon Ski Area offer many ski & lodging packages. To get to the Ski Area just turn left out of the hotel parking lot and turn right onto Hwy. 158. There will be signs to direct you to the ski area. For further information on ski & lodging packages call us at 1-800-794-3456.
• Rediscover our natural environment by strolling along nature's paths or hiking the various trails. There are many picnic areas for group or family fun.
• Call Mt. Charleston Hotel for information regarding ATV Tours, helicopter dinner tours, down hill and mountain bike tours and horseback riding.

Entertainment:
Cliffhanger Lounge - Offers a beautiful view of the canyon and surrounding mountains. The outdoors and the changing seasons seem to be a part of the decor in this glass enclosed room with its panoramic windows and a large fireplace. Live music nightly and a large screen TV make this the perfect place to enjoy an evening with close friends.
Dining:
Canyon Dining Room - Continental, menu choices include salads, pasta dishes, meat and fish entrees and yummy desserts. Prices are moderate and service is friendly, fireplaces throughout the room along with rich wood tones and spectacular views of the area offer a comfortable, romantic atmosphere.

Mount Charleston Lodge
HCR 38, Box 325
Mount Charleston, NV 89124
1-800-955-1314
Barbara & Collie Orcutt, Owners
Barbara Orcutt, Gen. Mgr.
Mount Charleston Resort opened in 1970 as the Mount Charleston Restaurant and Lounge at the top of Kyle Canyon in the Toiyabe National Forest, 40 minutes from the Las Vegas Strip.
In 1995, the resort opened 14 overnight lodging cabins, with another 10 cabins opened in Nov. 1997. Future plans include a wedding chapel, conference center, banquet facilities and remodeled restaurant/lounge.
Rooms:
24 standard and family size cabins, including two for handicapped guests
Rates: From $100 to $220 for a family cabin. Seasonal and weekend rates apply. Call for current rates.
Special Features:
Fireplaces, double whirlpool tubs, balconies with unobstructed mountain and canyon views from the 7,700-ft. level, outdoor barbecues, hay rides, sleigh rides, day and trail rides, pets allowed.
Restaurant: Continental cuisine with wild game menu featured.
Entertainment:
Lounge: Live entertainment Fri. - Sat. 7 pm - 11 pm, Sun. noon - 5 pm and 7 pm - 11 pm, video poker at the bar, open 24 hours.
Shops, Services:
The Christmas Shoppe; weddings and parties among spectacular mountain backdrops, Amish handmade white wedding carriage, complete wedding packages are also available.

OLD NEVADA

Bonnie Springs Motel
Old Nevada, NV 89004
875-4400
Lynn Cox, Mgr.
Rooms:
50
Rates: $55 - $125
Special Features:
Heated pool, pets allowed, kitchenettes, telephones, TV, laundry room, horseback riding, sunrise breakfast ride
Entertainment:
Lounge - Fri. - Sat. - 5 pm - 1 am, Piano Bar
Dining:
Bonnie Springs Ranch Restaurant offers a variety of steaks and daily specials.

RECREATIONAL VEHICLE PARKS

With Las Vegas fast becoming a family vacation destination, many families are traveling to the area via recreational vehicles. Many hotel/casino resort properties now have RV park facilities and over the past few years, many parks have sprung up in the Las Vegas area. Most allow pets and have shower, pool, and laundry facilities as well as cable TV hook-ups. While some offer electrical hook-ups at no additional cost, others require an additional fee. Please call ahead for details.

The following are RV parks located in the Las Vegas area. All have full hook-ups and accept pets unless otherwise indicated. Some also have stay limitations and charge extra for more than two people.

American Campgrounds
3440 Las Vegas Blvd. N.
Las Vegas, NV 89115
643-1222
Craig and Sheryl Jordan, Mgrs.

Spaces: 34
Rates: Tent area $7.50; extra tent area $10.00
Special Features: Full hook-ups, showers; grass area for tents; daily and weekly rates

Bond Trailer Lodge
284 E. Tropicana Ave.
Las Vegas, NV 89109
736-1550
Dorris Rambo, Mgr.
Spaces: 76
Rates: monthly $250.00 plus power
Special Features: Long term site, laundry, cable, telephone, storage

Boulder Lakes RV Resort & Country Club
6201 Boulder Hwy.
Las Vegas, NV 89122
435-1157
Bill Madra, Mgr.
Spaces: 417 full hook-ups
Rates: $18.90 daily; $124.20 weekly; $316.60 monthly plus power
Special Features: Showers, pool, jacuzzi, store, laundry, four tennis courts, cable and telephone service to all sites

California Hotel Casino & RV Park
200 N. Main St.
Las Vegas, NV 89101
385-1222 1-800-634-6505
Donna Timmons, Mgr.
Spaces: 94
Rates: $12.00 daily
Special Features: Showers, laundry, security, drive-thru

Canyon Trail RV Park
1200 Industrial Rd.
Boulder City, NV 89005
293-1200
Curtis and Karla Wells, Mgrs.
Spaces: 156 full hook-ups
Rates: $15.00 daily for Good Sam members, others $17.00 daily; $90.00/$100.00 weekly; $270.00/$280.00 monthly
Special Features: Showers, store, recreation hall, laundry

Circusland RV Park
500 Circus Circus Dr.
Las Vegas, NV 89109
794-3757 1-800-634-3450
Gert Pina, Mgr.
Spaces: 369 full hook-ups

Rates: $16.96-$30.74 daily
(2 week limit)
Special Features: Showers, pool and jacuzzi, store, laundry, monorail to main casino, fenced pet runs; reservations well in advance are advised

Desert Sands RV Park
1940 N. Boulder Hwy
Henderson, NV 89015
565-1945
Judith and Rodger Fleek, Mgrs.
Spaces: 300 full hook-ups
Rates: $15 daily; $95 weekly; $240 monthly
Special Features: Showers, store, pool and sauna, laundry

Showboat RV Park, 2800 Fremont Street, Las Vegas, NV 89104

RECREATIONAL VEHICLE PARKS

Circusland RV Park, 500 Circus Circus Drive, Las Vegas, NV 89109

Destiny's Oasis Las Vegas RV Resort
2711 West Windmill Ln.
Las Vegas, NV 89139
260-2020 1-800-566-4707
Fax: 263-5160
Roy Ingram, Mgr.
Spaces: 700
Rates: Vary from season to season
Special Features: Over 700 fully landscaped sites with private patios and picnic tables; phone service, cable programming, 24 hour security. Waterfalls, white sand beaches, lagoon, swimming areas, poolside cabanas, and 18 hole professional putting course on natural greens. Clubhouse Oasis bar and lounge, breakfast and lunch restaurant, media room, fitness center, showers, store, laundry, video arcade, playground, picnic tables and barbecues, tennis, horseshoes and volleyball. Shuttle service to Las Vegas Strip.

Golden Mobile Manor
252 E. Tropicana Ave.
Las Vegas, NV 89109
736-4200
Sammi and Don Kiser, Mgrs.
Spaces: 20 full hook-ups
Rates: $265.00 monthly
Special Features: Long term site; showers, laundry, pool

Hitchin' Post RV Park
3640 Las Vegas Blvd. N.
Las Vegas, NV 89115
644-1043
Jim Childress, Owner
Spaces: 195 full hook-ups
Rates: $18.00 daily; $108.00 weekly; $295.00 monthly plus power
Special Features: Good Sam; security gates, laundry, showers, pool, drive-thru spaces, phone hook-ups; motel

Holiday Travel Trailer Park
3890 S. Nellis Blvd.
Las Vegas, NV 89121
451-8005
Joy and Glen Gibson, Mgrs.
Spaces: 403 full hook-ups
Rates: $14.00 + tax daily
Special Features: Showers, pool and spa, recreation room, laundry

KOA Campgrounds- Las Vegas Resort
4315 Boulder Hwy.
Las Vegas, NV 89121
451-5527
Dave Wagner, Mgr.
Spaces: 240 hook-ups
Rates: Call for rates; major credit cards accepted
Special Features: Free shuttle to casinos, showers, pool and jacuzzi, store, daily and monthly rates

Lake Mead/Mohave
RV campgrounds with full hook-ups, groceries, showers and toilets, swimming and boating, phones and fishing.
Callville Bay Resort - 565-8958
Cottonwood Cove - 297-1464
Echo Bay Resort - 394-4000
Lakeshore Trailer Village - 293-2540
Overton Beach - 394-4040
Temple Bar - 520-767-3211
Lake Mead Marina - 293-3484

Lakeshore Trailer Village
268 Lakeshore Rd.
Boulder City, NV 89005
293-2540
Paul Montoya, Mgr.
Spaces: 84 full hook-ups
Rates: $15.00 + tax daily; $85.00 + tax weekly; $290.00 + tax monthly.
Special Features: Showers, laundry

Maycliff RV
4001 E. Sahara Ave.
Las Vegas, NV 89104
457-3553
Velma Dunlap, Mgr.
Spaces: 134 hook-ups
Rates: $245.00/$255.00 monthly plus electricity
Special Features: Showers, laundry

Mount Charleston Kyle Canyon RV Site
State Rd. 157
Las Vegas, NV 89124
1-800-280-2267
Spaces: 15 self-contained units
Rates: $55.00 daily
No water or toilets.

Nevada Palace VIP Travel Trailer Park
5325 Boulder Hwy.
Las Vegas, NV 89122
451-0232
Renee Dugan. Mgr.
Spaces: 168 full hook-ups
Rates: $15.12 daily; $105.84 weekly
Special Features: Showers, pool, laundry; pets under 20 pounds

Riviera Travel Trailer Park
2200 Palm St.
Las Vegas, NV 89104
457-8700
Carol and Wally Strom, Mgrs.
Spaces: 136 full hook-ups
Rates: $16.98 daily; $101.74 weekly; $260 monthly + tax and power
Special Features: Pool and spa, showers, store; small pets welcome; daily, weekly and monthly rates

Road Runner RV Park
4711 Boulder Hwy.
Las Vegas, NV 89121
456-4711
Stan Baldwin, Owner
Spaces: 200 full hook-ups (no reservations)
Rates: $14.00 daily; $95.00 weekly; $315 .00 monthly + power
Special Features: Showers, pool and jacuzzi, laundry, recreation room

Sam's Town RV Park
5225 Boulder Hwy.
Las Vegas, NV 89122
454-8055 1-800-634-6371
Sheila Van Horn, Mgr.
Spaces: 291 full hook-ups
Rates: $16.00 + tax daily
Special Features: Pool, showers, store, laundry

Sam's Town Nellis RV Park
4040 S. Nellis Blvd.
Las Vegas, NV 89121
454-8056
Sheila Van Horn, Mgr.

Spaces: 208 full hook-ups
Rates: $16.00 + tax daily; all major credit cards (only open in winter)
Special Features: Pool, showers, store, laundry, recreation room

Showboat RV Park
2800 Freemont St.
Las Vegas, NV 89104
1-800-826-2800
Roger Smith, Mgr.
Spaces: 84 full hook-ups
Rates: $18.00 daily
Special Features: 30 and 50 amp power services, private showers, free cable TV service for each space, laundry facilities, sewer hookup, fully staffed welcome center, food and beverage vending machines, and dog run.

Silver Nugget RV Center
2140 Las Vegas Blvd. N.
N. Las Vegas, NV 89030
649-7439
Sylvia Nicholson, Mgr.
Spaces: 152 full hook-ups
Rates: $13.75 - $15.25; $305.00 - $320.00 monthly
Special Features: Pool, jacuzzi

Silverton
3333 Blue Diamond Rd.
Las Vegas, NV 89139
263-7777 1-800-588-7711
Sharon Hathaway, Mgr.
Spaces: 460
Rates: Sun.-Thurs. $17.00; Fri.-Sat. $21.00
Special Features: 60' x 12' spaces; water park for children

Thousand Trails
4295 Boulder Hwy.
Las Vegas, NV 89121
451-7632
David Robertson, Mgr.
Spaces: 217 full hook-ups
Rates: Membership only
Special Features: Showers, pool, store

Western RV Park
1023 E. Fremont St.
Las Vegas, NV 89101
384-1033 1-800-634-6703
Ray Tagliaferri, Mgr.
Spaces: 69 full hook-ups
Rates: $10.00 daily
Special Features: Shower, laundry, small pets, arcade and casino

Dining

There are over 710 restaurants in Las Vegas offering over 30 different types of cuisine. These figures don't include 1,345 fast food and take-out restaurants, 49 ice cream and candy shops, 57 bakeries and 70 buffets.

Las Vegas has always had outstanding gourmet restaurants in the hotels, but in the past few years a number of extraordinary restaurants have opened locations in Las Vegas, including Spago's, Morton's of Chicago, and The Palm as well as some independents.

All table service establishments in the Las Vegas area (including Boulder City and Henderson) are listed in this directory. Restaurants are listed by type of food served. Many of the over 500 bars and cocktail lounges have separate dining areas and offer full dinners in addition to traditional bar menus of burgers, sandwiches, wings and fingers. (*See Entertainment.*)

Dress codes: "casual" means come as you are; "informal" or "casual elegant" indicates the restaurant's atmosphere is elegant and proper attire should be worn but you may also come as you are; "semi-formal" indicates men should wear a jacket; "formal" indicates the restaurant requires that men wear a jacket. The specialties of the house are listed along with descriptions of many of the restaurants basic decor.

Credit cards: "All major" indicates the restaurant takes MasterCard, Visa, American Express, Discover Card and usually Diners Club and Carte Blanche.

Nonsmoking areas: By law, restaurants are required to maintain a nonsmoking area if total seating capacity exceeds 50.

Prices listed are for dinner entrees only. Breakfast, lunch and salads, sandwiches, etc. may be considerably less. Because of increased competition from hotel/casinos, gourmet meals in Las Vegas are priced much less than in other cities.

RESTAURANTS - Ethnic

AMERICAN

Applebee's Neighborhood Grill & Bar
(Multiple locations listed below)
Hours: Mon. - Thu. 11 am - 11 pm; Fri. - Sat. 11 am - midnight; Sun. 10 am - 11 pm
Reservations: Accepted
Dress: Casual
Price of Entrees: $6.49 - $9.49
Credit Cards: MC, Visa, AMX
Specialties: Gourmet burgers, salads, ribs; bar area serves a variety of specialty drinks.
Atmosphere: Family atmosphere, yet comfortable for an after work drink and appetizer.

4760 W. Sahara Ave.
Las Vegas, NV 89102
878-3399

500 N. Nellis Blvd.
Las Vegas, NV 89110
452-7155

3340 S. Maryland Pkwy.
Las Vegas, NV 89109
737-4990

699 Stephanie St.
Henderson, NV 89014
433-6339

The Beach
365 Convention Center Dr.
Las Vegas, NV 89109
731-1925
Hours: 24 hours
Reservations: None
Dress: Casual
Price of Entrees: $5.95 - $15.00
Credit Cards: All major
Specialties: Philly steak, pork tenderloin, killer cheeseburgers.
Atmosphere: Big screen TVs, banquet facilities for 2,000. Comedy entertainment and piano show, DJ booth, sports book. Knowledgeable staff.

Big Dog's Bar & Grill
1511 N. Nellis Blvd.
Las Vegas, NV 89110
459-1099
Hours: 24 hours
Reservations: None
Dress: Casual

Price of Entrees: $7.95 - $12.95
Credit Cards: Visa, MC, AMX, Discover
Specialties: Prime rib, New York steak, ribs, walleye and midwestern pan fried fish.

Big Dog's Cafe
6390 W. Sahara Ave.
Las Vegas, NV 89102
876-3647
Hours: 24 hours
Reservations: None
Dress: Casual
Price of Entrees: $7.95 - $12.95
Credit Cards: Visa, MC, AMX, Discover
Specialties: Baby back ribs, chicken stir fry, chicken pasta Alfredo and specialty pizzas.

Blue Ox East Restaurant & Lounge
4130 S. Sandhill Rd.
Las Vegas, NV 89121
435-1344
Hours: 24 hours
Reservations: None
Dress: Casual
Price of Entrees: $6.00 - $13.00
Credit Cards: None
Specialties: Rack of ribs, prime rib, T-bone, rib-eye, shrimp.
Atmosphere: Casual neighborhood restaurant.

Blueberry Hill Family Restaurants
(Multiple locations & hours listed below)
Reservations: None
Dress: Casual
Price of Entrees: under $10.00
Credit Cards: Visa, MC, Diners, AMX, Discover
Specialties: Extensive breakfast menu; old fashioned buttermilk pancakes, butter cream waffles and thick cut homestyle baked bread French toast. Lunch and dinner menu includes burgers, salads, sandwiches, pasta and chicken; children's menu.

1280 S. Decatur Blvd.
Las Vegas, NV 89102
877-8867
Hours: 24 hours

1723 E. Charleston Blvd.
Las Vegas, NV 89104
382-3330
Hours: 6 am - 9 pm

3790 E. Flamingo Rd.
Las Vegas, NV 89121
433-9999
Hours: 24 hours

5000 E. Bonanza Rd.
Las Vegas, NV 89110
453-5555
Hours: 6 am - 10 pm

1505 E. Flamingo Rd.
Las Vegas, NV 89119
696-9666
Hours: 24 hours

Bob's All Family Restaurant
761 Nevada Hwy.
Boulder City, NV 89005
293-1668
Hours: 6:30 am - 2 pm
Reservations: None
Dress: Casual
Price of Entrees: $5.95 - $12.95
Credit Cards: None
Specialties: Breakfast and lunch specials.
Atmosphere: White and green garden atmosphere. Slogan - "Best Food by a Dam Site."

Bonnie Springs Ranch Restaurant
Old Nevada, NV 89004
875-4300
Hours: 8 am - 11 pm
Reservations: Accepted
Dress: Casual
Price of Entrees: $11.95 - $14.95
Credit Cards: MC, Visa, AMX
Specialties: New York steak, barbecue ribs and chicken.
Atmosphere: Barn-like setting with redwood plank tables, stone floors and white timber walls.

Boston Market
(Multiple locations listed below)
Hours: 10:30 am - 9:00 pm
Reservations: None
Dress: Casual
Price of Entrees: $4.49 - $6.99
Credit Cards: Visa, MC
Specialties: Homestyle cooking. Ham with cinnamon glaze, rotisserie roasted chicken, turkey and meat loaf.

2555 E. Tropicana Ave.
Las Vegas, NV 89121
456-3355

2650 W. Sahara Ave.
Las Vegas, NV 89102
221-4114

2081 Sunset Rd.
Henderson, NV 89014
435-4022

7291 W. Lake Mead Blvd.
Las Vegas, NV 89128
233-1111

Brick House
2850 E. Tropicana Ave.
Las Vegas, NV 89121
451-1123
Hours: 24 hours
Reservations: Suggested
Dress: Casual
Price of Entrees: $3.95 - $13.95

Credit Cards: All major
Specialties: Rigatoni with sweet red pepper sauce, baby back ribs, chicken, pasta, fresh fish.
Atmosphere: Casual, hardwood floors, fireplace, etched glass.

Brittany's Restaurant & Lounge
7770 W. Ann Rd.
Las Vegas, NV 89129
658-8998
Hours: Vary, please call ahead
Reservations: Suggested
Dress: Casual
Price of Entrees: Reasonable
Credit Cards: MC, Visa, Discover, AMX, Diners

Bugsy's Supper Club
6145 W. Sahara Ave.
Las Vegas, NV 89102
871-7194
Hours: 24 hours
Reservations: None
Dress: Casual
Price of Entrees: $9.50 - $12.95
Credit Cards: Visa, MC, AMX
Specialties: Sirloin steaks, BBQ chicken, bar menu, banquet facilities for up to 50.
Atmosphere: Golf motif.

Cantina Charlie's
2605 S. Decatur Blvd.
Las Vegas, NV 89102
258-5180
Hours: Bar 24 hours; dining room 7 am - 11 pm
Reservations: None
Dress: Casual
Price of Entrees: $6.95 - $14.95
Credit Cards: None
Specialties: Sandwiches.

Caribe Charlie's
4835 S. Rainbow Blvd.
Las Vegas, NV 89103
258-5185
Hours: 24 hours
Reservations: None
Dress: Casual
Price of Entrees: $6.95 - $14.95
Credit Cards: MC, Visa, AMX, Discover
Specialties: Appetizers, steaks, seafood, Mexican and Italian.

Carrows Restaurants

(Multiple locations listed below)
Hours: 24 hours
Reservations: None
Dress: Casual
Price of Entrees: $5.75 - $10.95
Credit Cards: All major
Specialties: Hot entrees, sandwiches, salads, soups.

169 E. Tropicana Ave.
Las Vegas, NV 89109
736-3936

2401 W. Sahara Ave.
Las Vegas, NV 89102
873-3628

3465 Boulder Hwy.
Las Vegas, NV 89121
457-4381

Big Dog's Cafe, 6390 W. Sahara Ave., Las Vegas, NV 89102

3780 Las Vegas Blvd. S.
Las Vegas, NV 89109
736-4501

4680 S. Maryland Pkwy.
Las Vegas, NV 89119
736-6908

Charlie's Bar & Grill
2089 N. Jones Blvd.
Las Vegas, NV 89108
258-5160
Hours: 24 hours
Reservations: None
Dress: Casual
Price of Entrees: Under $7.00
Credit Cards: MC, Visa, AMX
Specialties: Appetizers, sandwiches.

Charlie's Down Under
1950 Buffalo Dr.
Las Vegas, NV 89128
258-5186
Hours: 24 hours
Reservations: None
Dress: Casual
Price of Entrees: $3.25 - $7.95
Credit Cards: All but Discover
Specialties: Bar food, lunch and dinner specials.
Atmosphere: Australian motif, trees with koalas, posters, life-size surfer on wave, memorabilia.

Charlie's Lakeside
8603 W. Sahara Ave.
Las Vegas, NV 89117
258-5170
Hours: 24 hours
Reservations: None
Dress: Casual
Price of Entrees: $6.95 - $14.95
Credit Cards: MC, Visa, AMX, Diners, Discover
Specialties: Appetizers, steaks, seafood, Mexican and Italian.

Charlie's Saloon
4437 W. Charleston Blvd.
Las Vegas, NV 89102
258-5184
Hours: 24 hours
Reservations: None
Dress: Casual
Price of Entrees: $6.95 - $14.95
Credit Cards: MC, Visa, AMX
Specialties: Appetizers, steaks, seafood, Mexican and Italian.

Chili's Grill & Bar

(Multiple locations listed below)
Hours: Mon. - Thu. 11 am - 10:30 pm; Fri. - Sun. 11 am - 11 pm; happy hour Mon. - Fri. 4 pm - 6 pm
Reservations: None
Dress: Casual
Price of Entrees: $5.25 - $11.95
Credit Cards: All major
Specialties: Appetizers, fajitas, gourmet burgers, baby back ribs, Caesar salad, chili, taco salad, desserts.

2590 S. Maryland Pkwy.
Las Vegas, NV 89109
733-6462

2520 S. Decatur Blvd.
Las Vegas, NV 89102
871-0500

2751 N. Green Valley Pkwy.
Henderson, NV 89014
433-5233

Coffee Cup Cafe
558 Nevada Hwy.
Boulder City, NV 89005
294-0517
Hours: 6 am - 2 pm
Reservations: None
Dress: Casual
Price of Entrees: Inexpensive
Credit Cards: None
Specialties: Pancakes, omelets, sandwiches, soups and salads.
Atmosphere: Small breakfast and lunch cafe.

Country Cafe
3603 Las Vegas Blvd. N., Ste. 118
Las Vegas, NV 89115
644-4811
Hours: Mon. 11 am - 2 pm; Tue. - Fri. 11 am - 8 pm; Sat. 8 am - 2 pm; Closed Sun.
Reservations: None
Dress: Casual
Price of Entrees: $4.00 - $10.00
Credit Cards: None
Specialties: Steak, chicken, fried shrimp.
Atmosphere: Small and cozy.

Country Inn
(Multiple locations listed below)
Hours: Sun. - Thu. 7 am - 10 pm; Fri. - Sat. 7 am - 11 pm
Reservations: For large parties
Dress: Casual
Price of Entrees: $5.95 - $14.95
Credit Cards: All major
Specialties: Home-style breakfasts, homemade biscuits, split roasted turkey, beef and pork. Sandwiches, soups and salads. Children's menu, catering, private banquet room.
Atmosphere: Warm and friendly country setting.

2425 E. Desert Inn Rd.
Las Vegas, NV 89121
731-5035

1401 S. Rainbow Blvd.
Las Vegas, NV 89102
254-0520

1990 Sunset Rd.
Henderson, NV 89014
898-8183

Country Star American Music Grill
3724 Las Vegas Blvd. S.
Las Vegas, NV 89109
740-8400
Hours: 11 am - 9:30 pm
Reservations: None
Price of Entrees: $7 - $20
Credit Cards: All major
Specialties: American cuisine such as ribs, cornbread and chili.
Atmosphere: Memorabilia from country singers, a video wall and CD listening posts where guests can listen to the latest country hits. Second in a chain of restaurants backed by country stars Reba McIntire, Vince Gill, Tracy Lawrence and Wynona Judd.

CHARLIE'S
DOWN UNDER
Bar & Restaurant
North Buffalo & Lake Mead
Las Vegas, Nevada
702/258-5186
Featuring Charlie's famous
Danish Baby Back Ribs!
Full Rack $5.95
served 24 hours everyday
Your friendly neighborhood casino!

Crocodile Cafe
4500 E. Sunset Rd., Ste. 22
Henderson, NV 89014
456-7880
Hours: 11 am - 11 pm
Reservations: None
Dress: Casual
Price of Entrees: $6.95 - $11.95
Credit Cards: All major
Specialties: Grilled Cuban chicken, Linguine Checca, burgers, wood-fired pizza, pastas.
Atmosphere: Exhibition kitchen, very colorful, patio.

Decatur Drugs Restaurant
544 S. Decatur Blvd.
Las Vegas, NV 89107
870-2552
Hours: Mon. - Sat. 7 am - 8 pm; Sun. 9 am - 1 pm
Reservations: None
Dress: Casual
Price of Entrees: $4.50 - $5.95
Credit Cards: None
Specialties: Home-style cooking. Breakfast served anytime. Daily lunch and dinner entree specials $4.25.
Atmosphere: Coffee shop.

Denny's
(Multiple locations listed below)
Hours: 24 hours
Reservations: None
Dress: Casual
Price of Entrees: $5.00 - $7.50, Children's menu - $1.99
Credit Cards: All major
Specialties: Hot and cold sandwiches, salads, seafood, steak, shrimp.
Atmosphere: Fast friendly service.

1826 Las Vegas Blvd. S.
Las Vegas, NV 89104
384-5624

2201 W. Sahara Ave.
Las Vegas, NV 89102
873-3200

2545 Fremont St.
Las Vegas, NV 89104
384-7441

3081 S. Maryland Pkwy.
Las Vegas, NV 89109
734-1295

3771 Las Vegas Blvd. S.
Las Vegas, NV 89109
736-6265

5318 Boulder Highway
Las Vegas, NV 89122
456-1919

3397 Las Vegas Blvd.
Las Vegas, NV 89109
735-9623

Vacation Village
6711 Las Vegas Blvd.
Las Vegas, NV 89119
263-6880

RESTAURANTS - Ethnic

DIVE!
Fashion Show Mall
3200 Las Vegas Blvd. S.
Las Vegas, NV 89109
369-3483
Hours: Sun. - Thu. 11:30 am - 10 pm; Fri.
- Sat. 11:30 am - 11 pm
Reservations: None
Dress: Casual
Price of Entrees: $6.95 - $13.95
Credit Cards: All major
Specialties: 22 hot and cold gourmet
submarine sandwiches; wood oven-roast-
ed chicken, barbeque ribs, burgers, salads, fresh pasta, famous DIVE! fries,
desserts; full service bar with specialty
drinks; children's menu. DIVE! gear merchandise available at the retail counter.
Atmosphere: DIVE! blends the incredible
sights and sounds of an underwater submarine environment. Located at the Fashion
Show Mall where the nose of the life-size
submarine hangs over shoppers and a wall
of water splashes into a pool that periodically erupts with depth charges.

Draft House
4543 N. Rancho Dr.
Las Vegas, NV 89130
645-1404
Hours: 24 hours
Reservations: Accepted
Dress: Casual
Price of Entrees: $7.00 - $14.00
Credit Cards: MC, Visa, AMX, Discover
Specialties: Rotisserie chicken, brat-
wurst. Seasonal walleye pike, hand cut
fillets.
Atmosphere: Dining barn with silo.

chicago • las vegas

Drink!
200 E. Harmon Ave.
Las Vegas, NV 89109
796-5519
Hours: Tue. - Sat. 5 pm - 2 am;
Sun. 7 pm - midnight
Reservations: None
Dress: Casual
Price of Entrees: $5.95 - $9.95
Credit Cards: All major
Specialties: Seafood Belmonti, wild
mushroom pasta, mixed grill, chicken
ravioli, rigatoni liguria.

The Egg & I
4533 W. Sahara Ave.
Las Vegas, NV 89102
364-9686
Hours: 6 am - 3 pm
Reservations: None
Dress: Casual
Price of Entrees: Inexpensive
Credit Cards: MC, Visa, AMX
Specialties: Breakfasts, eggs Benedict,
Belgian waffles, sandwiches, soups, salads.
Atmosphere: Breakfast cafe with
indoor or patio dining.

Elizabeth's Little Kitchen
2112 N. Nellis Blvd.
Las Vegas, NV 89114
453-6393
Hours: Wed. - Sun. 7:30 am - 2 pm

Reservations: None
Dress: Casual
Price of Entrees: $3.50 - $5.50
Credit Cards: None
Specialties: Omelets, homemade breads
and jams.
Atmosphere: Small 24 seat diner serv-
ing home-style cooking.

Ellis Island Restaurant
4178 Koval Ln.
Las Vegas, NV 89109
733-8901
Hours: 24 hours
Reservations: Accepted
Dress: Casual
Price of Entrees: $2.95 - $12.95
Credit Cards: MC, Visa, AMX
Specialties: Steaks, steamed clams,
shrimp scampi. Sirloin steak dinner
special $2.95.
Atmosphere: Intimate.

50's Diner
3050 E. Desert Inn Rd.
Las Vegas, NV 89121
737-0377
Hours: 7 am - 2:30 pm
Reservations: None
Dress: Casual
Price of Entrees: Under $6.50
Credit Cards: MC, Visa, AMX
Specialties: Breakfast and lunch only.
Atmosphere: '50s decor, old phono jackets, pictures, and paintings. The excitement and magic of the "classic neighborhood diner" of the '50s and '60s,
where you meet your friends for home-
style good food in a relaxing friendly
"fun" atmosphere.

Furr's Cafeteria
(Multiple locations listed below)
Hours: 11 am - 8 pm
Reservations: None
Dress: Casual
Price of Entrees: $4.99 (lunch), $5.59 -
$5.99 (dinner and weekends) for cafete-
ria style all-you-can-eat buffet

Credit Cards: MC, Visa, AMX, Discover
Specialties: Homestyle cooking with all
items prepared fresh.
Atmosphere: Semi self-serve cafeteria-
style restaurant where you can pay by
the item or all-you-can-eat; senior discount.

2985 E. Sahara Ave.
Las Vegas, NV 89104
457-0166

150 S. Valley View Blvd.
Las Vegas, NV 89107
878-0901

Garden Eatery Omelet House
2160 W. Charleston Blvd.
Las Vegas, NV 89102
384-6868
Hours: 7 am - 3 pm
Reservations: None
Dress: Casual
Price of Entrees: $1.95 - $6.50
Credit Cards: MC, Visa, AMX
Specialties: Hamburgers, fried zucchini;
chicken fingers, homemade soup and chili.
Atmosphere: Casual family dining.

Golden Eagle Restaurant
2202 Paradise Rd.
Las Vegas, NV 89104
737-3888
Hours: 8 am - 11 pm
Reservations: Accepted
Dress: Casual
Price of Entrees: $10.00 - $18.00
Credit Cards: All major
Specialties: Lobster, scalone (abalone
and scallops pounded together), New
York steak.
Atmosphere: Slightly Victorian, soft, warm
rich wood and mauve colors; separate
lounge area.

The Green Shack
2504 E. Fremont St.
Las Vegas, NV 89104
383-0007
Hours: Tue. - Sun. 5 pm - varies
Closed Mon.
Reservations: None
Dress: Informal
Price of Entrees: $8.95 - $16.95
Credit Cards: MC, Visa, Discover,
Diners
Specialties: Old-fashioned batter shrimp,
New York steak, pan-fried chicken. Bar
opens at 4 pm.
Atmosphere: The oldest saloon and
supper club hosting Las Vegans since
1932. Quiet, relaxing, homestyle dining
in an authentic "Old Las Vegas" atmosphere. In business for over 60 years, the
restaurant opened as the Colorado in
1929. In 1932, the owner purchased an
old railroad barracks, painted it green
and moved it to the present location.

Happy Days Diner
512 Nevada Hwy.
Boulder City, NV 89005
294-2653
Hours: 7 am - 8 pm
Reservations: None
Dress: Casual
Price of Entrees: $3.50 - $6.99
Credit Cards: MC, Visa
Specialties: Burgers and thick shakes.
Atmosphere: Small diner and soda
fountain reminiscent of the '50s, in
business for over 60 years.

Hard Rock Cafe
4475 Paradise Rd.
Las Vegas, NV 89109
733-8400
(Also see Bars)
Hours: 11 am - midnight
Reservations: None
Dress: Casual
Price of Entrees: $5.95 - $15.95
Credit Cards: All major
Specialties: Appetizers, charbroiled
burgers, sandwiches, watermelon ribs,
lime barbecued chicken. Bar; valet
parking available.
Atmosphere: Decorated with rock
memorabilia from floor to ceiling. Hard
Rock casual wear available at entrance.

Harley Davidson
Las Vegas Cafe
3725 Las Vegas Blvd. S.
Las Vegas, NV 89019
740-4555
Hours: Sun. - Thu. 11:30 am - midnight;
Fri. - Sat. 11:30 am - 1 am
Reservations: None
Dress: Casual
Price of Entrees: $6.95 - $15.95
Credit Cards: All major
Specialties: American roadside cuisine
such as Kansas City barbecue, Harley
Hog Pork barbecue.
Atmosphere: The largest collection of
Harley Davidson memorabilia in the
world from film stars and sport stars.
Overhead conveyor belt displays the seven
newest Harley Davidson motorcycles.

Hash House
6000 Spring Mountain Rd.
Las Vegas, NV 89102
873-9479
Hours: 6 am - 2:pm
Reservations: None
Dress: Casual
Price of Entrees: $3.89 - $6.95
Credit Cards: MC, Visa
Specialties: Homemade corned-beef hash
and country fresh sausage.

Hippo & The Wild Bunch
4503 Paradise Rd.
Las Vegas, NV 89109
731-5446
Hours: 11 am - 3 am
Reservations: Suggested
Dress: Informal
Price of Entrees: $6.00 - $14.00
Credit Cards: All major
Specialties: Pastas, wood-fired gourmet pizzas, salads, burgers; exotic drinks; fresh juices and great desserts; banquet facilities available for up to 200; patio dining available.
Atmosphere: Jungle/safari motif.

The Highlander Restaurant
Highland Falls Golf Club
10201 Sun City Blvd.
Las Vegas, NV 89134
254-0767
Hours: Mon. - Fri. 6 am - 8 pm;
Sat. - Sun. 6 am - 5 pm
Reservations: None
Dress: Casual
Price of Entrees: $6.95 - $12.95
Credit Cards: MC, Visa, AMX
Specialties: Catch of the day, ribs, pork chops, steaks; birdie, eagle or wedge sandwiches.
Atmosphere: Upscale coffee shop with beautiful view.

Hilda's Restaurant
2015 Daley St.
N. Las Vegas, NV 89030
649-1094
Hours: 6 am - 4 pm
Reservations: None
Dress: Casual
Price of Entrees: $5.25 - $10.25
Credit Cards: MC, Visa, AMX, Discover
Specialties: Country-style breakfasts, chicken fried steak, meat loaf, Mexican dishes, sandwiches, homemade pies.
Atmosphere: Homey, like going to Grandma's house.

Holy Cow!
2423 Las Vegas Blvd. S.
Las Vegas, NV 89104
732-2697
Hours: 24 hours
Reservations: None
Dress: Casual
Price of Entrees: Under $12.75
Credit Cards: MC, Visa, AMX, Discover
Specialties: Baby back ribs, bratwurst, rotisserie chicken, sandwiches, burgers, appetizers. Walleye pike flown in fresh from the Midwest and served daily noon - 11 pm.
Atmosphere: Microbrewery.

Hooters
5675 W. Sahara Ave.
Las Vegas, NV 89102
248-4668
Hours: Mon. - Thu. 11 am - midnight;

Fri. & Sat. 11 am - 1 am; Sun. 11 am - 11 pm
Reservations: None
Dress: Casual
Price of Entrees: $4.50 - $11.50
Credit Cards: MC, Visa, AMX, Discover
Specialties: Wings, sandwiches, seafood and salads.
Atmosphere: Served by the "World Famous Hooter Girls."

Huntridge Drug Restaurant
1122 E. Charleston Blvd.
Las Vegas, NV 89104
384-3737
Hours: Mon. - Sat. 8 am - 7 pm;
Sun. 9 am - 4 pm
Reservations: None
Dress: Casual
Price of Entrees: $3.00 - $5.00
Credit Cards: None
Specialties: Chinese combo, top sirloin steak, daily specials.
Atmosphere: Family oriented, old fashioned diner.

The Hush Puppy
(Multiple locations & hours listed below)
Reservations: Suggested
Dress: Casual
Price of Entrees: $6.95 - $19.95
Credit Cards: MC, Visa, AMX, Discover
Specialties: Catfish and other seafood, chicken, fried oysters, frogs legs.
Atmosphere: Comfortable, casual family atmosphere.

1820 N. Nellis Blvd.
Las Vegas, NV 89115
438-0005
Hours: 5 pm - 10:30 pm

7185 W. Charleston Blvd.
Las Vegas, NV 89117
363-5988
Hours: Sun. - Thu. 5 pm - 10 pm;
Fri. - Sat. 5 pm - 11 pm

Inner Circle Restaurant
704 Nevada Hwy.
Boulder City, NV 89005
294-4482
Hours: 3 pm - 1 am
Reservations: None
Dress: Casual
Price of Entrees: $4.95 - $12.95
Credit Cards: All major
Specialties: Steaks, burgers, specialty chicken dishes, catering, lounge, banquet facilities for 300.
Atmosphere: Family oriented, bright, large picture windows.

International House of Pancakes
(Multiple locations & hours listed below)
Reservations: None
Dress: Casual
Price of Entrees: Inexpensive
Credit Cards: MC, Visa, AMX, Diners, Discover
Specialties: Popular for pancakes, waffles and other breakfast dishes. Burgers, sandwiches, salads and traditional American entrees served for lunch and dinner.
Atmosphere: Casual coffee shop.

3111 W. Tropicana Ave.
Las Vegas, NV 89103
736-3488
Hours: 24 hours

2210 Las Vegas Blvd. S
Las Vegas, NV 89104
384-6412
Hours: 6 am - 3 pm

2490 Fremont St.
Las Vegas, NV 89104
384-7881
Hours: Mon. - Fri. 7 am - 2 pm;
Sat. - Sun. 7 am - 3 pm

3260 E. Tropicana Ave.
Las Vegas, NV 89121
433-8430
Hours: Sun. - Thu. 6 am - 10 pm; Fri. - Sat. 6 am - midnight

3595 S. Rainbow Blvd.
Las Vegas, NV 89103
365-1004
Hours: 6 am - 10 pm

6870 W. Cheyenne Ave.
Las Vegas, NV 89108
656-3220
Hours: Sun. - Thu. 6 am - 11 pm;
Fri. - Sat. 24 hours

4860 Boulder Hwy.
Las Vegas, NV 89121
454-1126
Hours: Sun. - Thu. 6 am - 10 pm;
Fri. - Sat. 24 hours

3780 S. Maryland Pkwy.
Las Vegas, NV 89119
737-0375
Hours: 24 hours

1401 S. Decatur Blvd.
Las Vegas, NV 89102
877-1316
Hours: Sun. - Thu. 6 am - 10 pm;
Fri. - Sat. 24 hours

Jamms
(Multiple locations listed below)
Hours: Mon. - Sat. 7 am - 9 pm, Sun. until 8 pm
Reservations: None
Dress: Casual
Price of Entrees: $5.95 - $8.95
Credit Cards: MC, Visa
Specialties: Veal cordon bleu, chicken Florentine, meat loaf, broiled or fried seafood.
Atmosphere: Coffee shop.

2227 N. Rampart Blvd.
Las Vegas, NV 89128
228-4151

1029 S. Rainbow Blvd.
Las Vegas, NV 89128
877-0749

Jo-Ell's Restaurant
415 S. Decatur Blvd.
Las Vegas, NV 89121
870-1876
Hours: Mon. - Sat. 5:30 am - 3 pm;
Sun. 7 am - 3 pm
Reservations: None
Dress: Casual
Price of Entrees: $4.00 - $11.95
Credit Cards: MC, Discover
Specialties: American classics such as chicken-fried steaks, liver & onions, fried chicken, steaks
Atmosphere: Coffee shop.

Keuken Dutch
6180 W. Tropicana Ave.
Las Vegas, NV 89103
368-1077
Hours: 24 hours
Reservations: None
Dress: Casual

Price of Entrees: $5.99 - $11.99
Credit Cards: All major
Specialties: American and Dutch specialties; omelets, waffles, oven-baked keukens, chicken, soups, salads.
Atmosphere: Dutch motif.

L' Bombardier
4213 W. Sahara Ave.
Las Vegas, NV 89102
365-8988
Hours: 24 hours; happy hour with appetizers 5 pm - 7 pm
Reservations: Suggested
Dress: Casual
Price of Entrees: $8.95 - $18.95
Credit Cards: All major
Specialties: 16 oz. filet mignon, 16 oz. New York strip, 2 double cut lamb chops, broiled 1/2 chicken; all entrees made on mesquite grill.
Atmosphere: Aviation theme; fiber optics; waitresses and bartenders wear aviation suits; Karaoke Tue. and Wed. 9 pm - 2 am; Live entertainment Thu. - Sat. from 9 pm

Lake Mead Resort & Marina
322 Lakeshore Rd.
Boulder City, NV 89005
293-3484
Hours: Sun. - Thu. 7 am - 9 pm;
Fri. - Sat. 7 am - 10 pm
Reservations: Accepted
Dress: Casual
Price of Entrees: $5.00 - $15.00
Credit Cards: MC, Visa, Discover
Specialties: Steak, seafood, special entrees.
Atmosphere: Lounge; nautical-theme floating restaurant overlooks marina.

Legends Restaurant & Lounge
865 N. Lamb Blvd.
Las Vegas, NV 89110
437-9674
Hours: 24 hours
Reservations: None
Dress: Casual
Price of Entrees: Inexpensive
Credit Cards: MC, Visa
Specialties: Pizza, chicken sandwiches and salads.
Atmosphere: Live alternative music from Extreme Radio Fri. evenings, Grateful Dead tapes Sat. 8:30 pm - 2 am

Liberty Cafe
1700 Las Vegas Blvd. S.
Las Vegas, NV 89104
383-0101
Hours: 24 hours
Reservations: None
Dress: Casual
Price of Entrees: $5.00 - $7.00
Credit Cards: None
Specialties: Pork chops, liver and onions, trout, halibut.
Atmosphere: Located inside White Cross Drugs.

Lily's Pantry
3335 Meade Ave.
Las Vegas, NV 89102
876-6140
Hours: Mon. - Fri. 7 am - 3 pm;
Sat. 9:30 am - 1:30 pm; Closed Sun.
Reservations: None
Dress: Casual
Price of Entrees: Inexpensive
Credit Cards: None
Specialties: Salisbury steak, sky high triple decker, burgers, Philly cheese steak.

DINING

RESTAURANTS - Ethnic

The Restaurant at Los Prados
5150 Los Prados Cir.
Las Vegas, NV 89130
645-4549
Hours: Sat. - Thu. 7 am - 5 pm;
Fri. 7 am - 10 pm; closed Sun.
Reservations: None
Dress: Casual
Price of Entrees: $6.00 - $8.00
Credit Cards: MC, Visa
Specialties: Lunch, Philly steak sandwiches and pasta; dinner (Fri. only) prime rib, pasta, fish, New York steak.
Atmosphere: On Los Prados golf course; very pleasant.

Lucky Dogs
2396 S. Lamb Blvd.
Las Vegas, NV 89104
431-3991
Hours: 24 hours
Reservations: None
Dress: Casual
Price of Entrees: Inexpensive
Credit Cards: MC, Visa, AMX
Specialties: bratwurst, wood-fired pizza, ribs, chicken, smoked meats, calzones and strombolis.
Atmosphere: Doggie.

Marie Callender's

Marie Callender's
(Multiple locations & hours listed below)
Reservations: None
Dress: Casual
Price of Entrees: $6.95 - $12.00
Credit Cards: MC, Visa, Discover
Specialties: Pasta, pot pies, burgers, pot roast, meat loaf.

4800 S. Eastern Ave.
Las Vegas, NV 89119
458-2127
Hours: Mon. - Thu. 7 am - 11 pm;
Sat. 8 am - 11:30 pm; Sun. 9 am - 11 pm

600 E. Sahara Ave.
Las Vegas, NV 89104
734-6572
Hours: Sun. - Thu. 7 am - 11 pm;
Fri. - Sat. 7 am - midnight

4875 W. Flamingo Rd.
Las Vegas, NV 89103
365-6226
Hours: Sun. - Thu. 7 am - 10 pm;
Fri. 7 am - 11 pm; Sat. 8 am - 11 pm

3743 Las Vegas Blvd. S.
Las Vegas, NV 89109
798-7808
Hours: Sun. - Thu. 8 am - 11 pm;
Fri. - Sat. 8 am - 11 pm

Mollie's Kountry Kafe
3200 N. Jones Blvd.
Las Vegas, NV 89108
656-0464
Hours: 6 am - 3 pm
Reservations: None
Dress: Casual
Price of Entrees: Inexpensive
Credit Cards: None
Specialties: Country breakfasts, sandwiches, Cobb salad, chicken fried steak, halibut and pork chops.
Atmosphere: Coffee shop.

Moose McGillycuddy's
4770 S. Maryland Pkwy.
Las Vegas, NV 89119
798-8337
Hours: 11:30 am - 3:30 am
Reservations: None
Dress: Casual
Price of Entrees: $4.00 - $8.00
Credit Cards: All major
Specialties: Burgers, salads, sandwiches and appetizers.
Atmosphere: College crowd; upbeat; dancing Wed. - Sat. 9 pm - 3:30 am.

Mt. Charleston Resort
Kyle Canyon Rd. (Hwy. 157)
Mt. Charleston, NV 89124
872-5408 386-6899 1-800-955-1314
Hours: Sun. - Thu. 8 am - 9:30 pm;
Fri. - Sat. 8 am - 10:30 pm
Reservations: Accepted
Dress: Casual
Price of Entrees: $13.50 - $40
Credit Cards: All major
Specialties: Duckling with honey sauce, sauteed loin of rabbit, stuffed roast quail, chicken Kiev, venison, buffalo, pheasant, sandwiches, burgers; bar; banquet facilities for 200.
Atmosphere: Rustic-style lodge. Warm yourself at the crackling fireplace and enjoy the mountain view from 8,000 feet; deck dining available; live music on weekends featuring a German oompah band, evenings top pop and country music.

The Muleteer Restaurant
1000 E. Cheyenne Ave.
N. Las Vegas, NV 89030
649-1719
Hours: 24 hours
Reservations: None
Dress: Casual
Price of Entrees: $5.00 - $11.99
Specialties: Skillet breakfast and Mexican dinners, gourmet hamburgers.
Atmosphere: Southwest design; truck stop, separate restaurant.

Mustang Sally's Diner
280 N. Gibson Rd.
Henderson, NV 89014
566-1965
Hours: 8 am - 9 pm, closed Sun.
Atmosphere: '90s style diner with a '50s theme located in the Valley Auto Mall at Ford Country.

O'Rosie's
5795 W. Tropicana Ave.
Las Vegas, NV 89118
253-1899
Hours: Lunch Tue. - Fri. 11 am - 2 pm;
Dinner Tue. - Sat. 5 pm - 10 pm, Sun. brunch 10 am - 3 pm
Reservations: Accepted
Dress: Casual
Price of Entrees: $8.95 - $14.95
Credit Cards: All major
Specialties: Imported pastas, creative chicken, seafood, veal, steaks and salads. Children's menu.
Atmosphere: Wine country casual.

Oklahoma Kitchen
23 N. Mojave Rd.
Las Vegas, NV 89101
382-2651
Hours: Mon. - Sat. 6 am - 3 pm;
Sun. 6 am - 2 pm

Moose McGillycuddy's, 4770 S. Maryland Pkwy., Las Vegas, NV 89119

Reservations: None
Dress: Casual
Price of Entrees: Inexpensive
Credit Cards: None
Specialties: Homestyle breakfast and lunch.

Olde Philadelphia Restaurant
3430 E. Tropicana Ave.
Las Vegas, NV 89121
456-0864
Hours: 11 am - 9:30 pm
Reservations: None
Dress: Casual
Price of Entrees: $5.35 - $5.95
Credit Cards: None
Specialties: Spaghetti, ravioli and meatballs, corned beef.
Atmosphere: Sandwich shop.

Omelet House
(Multiple locations & hours listed below)
Reservations: None
Dress: Casual
Price of Entrees: Inexpensive
Credit Cards: MC, Visa
Specialties: Omelets, pancakes, homemade soups, salads and sandwiches.
Atmosphere: Coffee shop.

2160 W. Charleston Blvd..
Las Vegas, NV 89102
384-6868
Hours: 7 am - 3 pm

316 N. Boulder Hwy.
Henderson, NV 89015
566-7896
Hours: Mon. - Fri. 7 am - 2 pm; Sat. - Sun. 7 am - 3pm

3050 E. Desert Inn Rd.
Las Vegas, NV 89121
737-0377
Hours: 7 am - 2:30 pm

The Original Pancake House
4833 W. Charleston Blvd.
Las Vegas, NV 8910
259-7755
Hours: 7 am - 3 pm
Reservations: None
Dress: Casual
Price of Entrees: $4.75 - $7.25
Credit Cards: MC, Visa, Discover
Specialties: Apple pancakes with cinnamon-sugar glaze, Dutch baby.

The Park Grill
6400 S. Eastern Ave.
Las Vegas, NV 89119
597-9957
Hours: Mon. - Fri. 8 am - 3 pm
Reservations: None
Dress: Casual
Price of Entrees: Inexpensive
Credit Cards: None
Specialties: Old fashioned burgers and sourdough sandwiches.

Peppermill Restaurant & Lounge
2985 Las Vegas Blvd. S.
Las Vegas, NV 89109
735-4177
Hours: 24 hours
Reservations: None
Dress: Casual
Price of Entrees: $8.50 - $17.50
Credit Cards: MC, Visa, Discover, AMX
Specialties: Beef tip burgundy, fettuccine Del Mar, New York steak and shrimp scampi, Western beef stew, breast of chicken Oscar, sandwiches, soups and salads; huge desserts; dinner entrees are very generous portions and are served with fresh fruit.
Atmosphere: Large, comfortable booths with lots of mirrors and trees decorating the dining room. The bar and lounge features tall exotic drinks, a large circular fireplace and intimate sofa seating.

Planet Hollywood
3500 Las Vegas Blvd. S.
Las Vegas, NV 89109
791-STAR 791-7827
Hours: Sun. - Thu. 11 am - midnight;
Fri. and Sat. 11 am - 1 am
Reservations: None
Dress: Casual
Price of Entrees: $6.95 - $17.95
Credit Cards: All major
Specialties: Unusual pastas, exotic salads, vegetable burgers, gourmet pizzas, smoked and grilled meats and fish.
Atmosphere: Seats approximately 550; exciting and colorful, Hollywood memorabilia.

It's Back to the Boat for Crab Legs

$12.95

Locals know...
It's back to the Boat where all the best food values started. The 43 year tradition continues in the Plantation Room with Our 1 lb. of Alaskan King Crab Legs, and much more!

SHOWBOAT.
HOTEL, CASINO & BOWLING CENTER
2800 Fremont Street on Boulder Strip, Las Vegas, NV 89104
(702) 385-9123

We're just your size for Friendly Fun and Food and we're just your style. Locals know…It's still better at the Boat!

Served 5 p.m. - 10 p.m.
(Closed Sun. & Mon.)
Reservations Suggested
385-9156

Polaris Street Cafe
3635 Polaris Ave.
Las Vegas, NV 89103
253-9405
Hours: Mon. - Fri. 6 am - 2 pm; Closed Sat. & Sun.
Reservations: None
Dress: Casual
Price of Entrees: Inexpensive
Credit Cards: All major
Specialties: Sandwiches, salads, burgers.
Atmosphere: Small and cozy.

Poppa Gars
1624 W. Oakey Blvd.
Las Vegas, NV 89102
384-4513
Hours: Mon. - Fri. 5 am - 9 pm; Sat. 5 am - 2 pm
Reservations: None
Dress: Casual
Price of Entrees: $5.00 - $11.00
Credit Cards: None
Specialties: Breakfast, homemade soups, stuffed hamburgers, rib-eye steak, real country sausage. Homestyle cooking with all food made fresh daily. Also serves buffalo, quail and other exotic meats; restaurant can order and prepare any kind of meat.
Atmosphere: Walls are decorated with photos and trophy heads.

R U Hungry?
2120 Western Ave.
Las Vegas, NV 89102
477-0716
Hours: Mon. - Fri. 7 am - 5 pm; Closed Sat. & Sun.
Reservations: None

Dress: Casual
Price of Entrees: $4.00 - $8.00
Credit Cards: None
Specialties: Corned beef hash, sandwiches, soups; daily specials.
Atmosphere: Dining room seats 45.

Rae's of Green Valley
2531 Wigwam Pkwy.
(at Pecos Rd.)
Henderson, NV 89014
897-2000
Hours: Food served 24 hours in lounge; Dining room 7 am - 10 pm
Reservations: Suggested for parties of 6 or more.
Dress: Informal
Price of Entrees: $9.95 - $18.95
Credit Cards: MC, Visa, AMX, Diners, CB
Specialties: Steaks au poivre, blackened prime rib, Danish baby back ribs. Small banquet facilities to accommodate up to 75; lounge.
Atmosphere: Fine dining in casual elegant surroundings; rich oak in the bar and dining areas, custom stained glass designs, intimate booths, warm, friendly atmosphere. Lounge with video poker.

Red Robin Grill & Spirits
151 N. Nellis Blvd.
Las Vegas, NV 89110
453-8611
Hours: Sun. - Thu. 11 am - 10 pm; Fri. and Sat. 11 am - 11 pm
Reservations: None
Dress: Casual
Price of Entrees: $7.00 - $9.95
Credit Cards: MC, Visa, Discover, AMX
Specialties: Seafood pasta, peppercorn

sirloin steak, rib tickler platter, chicken fajita tostada, gourmet burgers. Happy hour in bar from open to close.
Atmosphere: Separate dining room.

Sammy O'Brien's
4435 Las Vegas Blvd. N.
Las Vegas, NV 89115
644-3254
Hours: 6 am - 11 pm
Reservations: None
Dress: Casual
Price of Entrees: $4.95 - $7.95
Credit Cards: MC, Visa, AMX
Specialties: Mexican food, fabulous huevos rancheros, T-bone steaks, spaghetti and meatballs.
Atmosphere: Separate level dining room; aviation memorabilia.

Shoney's
310 N. Nellis Blvd.
Las Vegas, NV 89110
437-1211
Hours: Sun. - Thu. 6 am - 11 pm; Fri. - Sat. 6 am - midnight
Reservations: None
Dress: Casual
Price of Entrees: $5.00 - $9.00; all-you-can-eat breakfast bar $4.49 - $5.39; soup, salad and fruit bar $5.29; seafood buffet $8.99 Fri. 5 pm - 9 pm.
Credit Cards: MC, Visa, AMX
Specialties: Meat loaf, pot roast, country fried steak, sandwiches, burgers.
Atmosphere: Family restaurant.

The Skillet Cafe
3923 W. Charleston Blvd.
Las Vegas, NV 89102
877-9083

Hours: Mon. - Fri. 7 am - 3:30 pm; Sat. 7 am - 1 pm; Sun. 8 am - 1:30 pm Closed Mon.
Reservations: None
Dress: Casual
Price of Entrees: Inexpensive
Credit Cards: None
Specialties: Home style breakfast and lunch.
Atmosphere: Lovely old fashioned diner.

Skyriders
2772 N. Rancho Dr.
N. Las Vegas Air Terminal
N. Las Vegas, NV 89030
646-6744
Hours: 6 am - 7 pm
Reservations: None
Dress: Casual
Price of Entrees: $6.95 - $11.95
Credit Cards: MC, Visa, Discover
Specialties: Rib-eye steaks, fresh seafood, calf's liver and onions.
Atmosphere: Located inside the new North Las Vegas Airport terminal. Patio overlooks the mountains and runways.

Smoke Ranch Junction
2425 N. Rainbow Blvd.
Las Vegas, NV 89108
656-1888
Hours: 24 hours
Reservations: None
Dress: Casual
Price of Entrees: $5.00 - $10.00
Credit cards: MC, Visa
Specialties: Steaks, fish fry Fri., burgers, sandwiches.
Atmosphere: Pleasant dining area.

RESTAURANTS - Ethnic

Sonia's Cafe & Rotisserie
3900 W. Charleston Blvd.
Las Vegas, NV 89102
870-5090
Hours: Mon. - Fri. 11 am - 7:30 pm;
Sat. 11 am - 4 pm
Reservations: None
Dress: Casual
Price of Entrees: Under $6.95
Credit Cards: None
Specialties: Rotisserie chicken, Mexican specialties, salads, California pita rolls, special red potatoes; food to go.
Atmosphere: Full service seating for 70.

SOUPER!SALAD!
You've never had it so fresh!

Souper Salad
2051 N. Rainbow Blvd.
Las Vegas, NV 89108
Hours: Mon. - Sat. 11 am - 9 pm; Sun.
11:30 am - 8 pm

4020 S. Maryland Pkwy.
Las Vegas, NV 89119
792-8555

4712 W. Sahara Ave.
Las Vegas, NV 89102
870-1444
Hours: Mon. - Sat. 11 am - 9 pm; Sun.
11:30 am - 8:30 pm
Reservations: None
Dress: Casual
Price of Entrees: $3 - $6
Credit Cards: All major
Specialties: Extensive salad bar, baked potatoes with the works, fresh soup, bread and sandwiches.

South Philly West
3123 N. Rainbow Blvd.
Las Vegas, NV 89108
645-7800
Hours: Mon. - Thu. 11 am - 9 pm;
Fri. 11 am - 10 pm; Sat. 11 am - 8 pm;
Sun. noon - 5 pm
Reservations: None
Dress: Casual
Price of Entrees: Inexpensive
Credit Cards: None
Specialties: Heros, Philly steak, Philly french fries with cheddar cheese sauce.
Atmosphere: Coffee shop.

Straight From Philly Steakout
Reservations: None
Dress: Casual
Price of Entrees: Inexpensive
Credit Cards: None
Specialties: Philly cheese steaks, chicken cheese steaks, meatballs and Italian sausage.

425 S. Decatur Blvd.
Las Vegas, NV 89107
878-6444
Hours: 24 hours

4518 E. Charleston Blvd.
Las Vegas, NV 89104
438-4737
Hours: 11 am - 11 pm

Strawberry Patch Family Restaurant
4711 Spring Mountain Rd.
Las Vegas, NV 89102
367-7775
Hours: 6 am - 10 pm
Reservations: None
Dress: Casual
Price of Entrees: $2.99 - $7.49
Credit Cards: All major
Specialties: Steak, chicken fried steak, spaghetti.
Atmosphere: Coffee shop.

Sundance Kid Cafe
4325 W. Craig Rd.
N. Las Vegas, NV 89030
655-4501
Hours: 24 hours
Reservations: None
Dress: Casual
Price of Entrees: $5.95 - $9.95
Credit Cards: Visa, MC, AMX
Specialties: Shrimp scampi, Jamaican BBQ chicken, pork chops.

Sunrise Cafe
3513 E. Charleston Blvd.
Las Vegas, NV 89104
457-6050
Hours: Mon. - Sat. 5:30 am - 2:15 pm;
Closed Sun.
Reservations: None
Dress: Casual
Price of Entrees: Inexpensive
Credit Cards: None
Specialties: Steak and eggs, ham and cheese omelettes, tenderloin, sandwiches
Atmosphere: Blue collar crowd.

T.G.I. Friday's
1800 E. Flamingo Rd.
Las Vegas, NV 89119
732-9905
(Also see Bars)
Hours: Sun. - Thu. 11 am - midnight;
Fri. - Sat. 11 am - 2 am;
Sun. 11 am - 3 pm - Brunch
Reservations: None
Dress: Casual
Price of Entrees: $7.00 - $14.00
Credit Cards: All major
Specialties: Beef fajitas, baked manicotti, baby back ribs, Fri.'s London broil, grilled halibut, salads, soups, burgers, sandwiches, extensive list of appetizers, exotic alcoholic drinks and desserts, children's menu.
Atmosphere: American bar and restaurant decorated with junk and memorabilia from floor to ceiling.

Tommy Rockers Pub & Cafe
4275 Industrial Rd.
Las Vegas, NV 89103
261-6688
Hours: 24 hours full menu
Reservations: None

Dress: Casual
Price of Entrees: $4.95 - $11.95
Credit Cards: MC, Visa, AMX
Specialties: Ribs, wide variety of burgers.
Atmosphere: Very open, colorful, live entertainment Fri. and Sat. 10 pm - 2 am

Two Dogs Tavern
3740 S. Nellis Blvd.
Las Vegas, NV 89121
433-3383
Hours: 24 hours
Reservations: None
Dress: Casual
Price of Entrees: $7.25 - $12.95
Credit cards: All major
Specialties: Baby-back ribs, steaks, burgers, bratwurst.

Two Gals
1632 Nevada Hwy.
Boulder City, NV 89005
293-1793
Hours: Sun. - Thu. 7 am - 3 pm,
Fri. - Sat. 5 pm - 8:30 pm
Reservations: None
Dress: Casual
Price of Entrees: Inexpensive
Credit Cards: MC, Visa, Discover
Specialties: Three-egg omelets, fresh muffins, Belgian waffles, vegetarian sandwiches, salads. Dinner Specials on Fri.
Atmosphere: Cozy 43 seat restaurant serving homemade food in a country setting.

USA Cafe
2855 N. Green Valley Pkwy.
Henderson, NV 89014
436-4386
Hours: 10 am - 11 pm
Reservations: None
Dress: Casual
Price of Entrees: $4.75 - $15.00
Credit Cards: MC, Visa, AMX
Specialties: Pizza, burgers, Hawg Heaven steak, USA Caesar classic salad, tequila lime chicken, Chicago-style thick crust pizza.
Atmosphere: Classic rock and roll; sawdust floors with peanut shells; very relaxed, Sun. - Tue. & Thu. live alternative music 9:30 pm - midnight for ages 17 - 21.

Wooly Bully's Restaurant & Saloon
6020 W. Flamingo Rd.
Las Vegas, NV 89103
362-2116
Hours: 24 hours
Reservations: None
Dress: Casual
Price of Entrees: $7.95 - $13.95
Credit Cards: All major
Specialties: Prime rib, Wooly burgers, ribs and chicken.
Atmosphere: Country-western; large bar; extra bunkhouse for private parties.

BRAZILIAN

Yolie's Brazilian Steak House
3900 Paradise Rd.
Las Vegas, NV 89119
794-0700

Hours: Lunch Mon. - Fri. 11 am - 3 pm;
Dinner – 5:00 pm - 11 pm
Reservations: Suggested
Dress: Informal
Price of Entrees: Fixed-price dinners $22.95
Credit Cards: All major
Specialties: Marinated mesquite-broiled meats and fish served Brazilian style. Menu items such as scampi, orange roughy, roasted half chicken, fresh catch of the day. Daily lunch specials from $4.95 - $12.95. Banquet facilities.
Atmosphere: A variety of meats cooked on a continuously revolving skewer over mesquite coals and then sliced and offered off the skewer at the table by your waiter. You are offered as much as you care to eat of all the meats. Located on the second floor of the shopping center, it offers a view of the city lights; separate piano bar; patio dining available.

CENTRAL AMERICAN

Salvadoreno Restaurant
720 N. Main St.
Las Vegas, NV 89101
385-3600
Hours: Tue. - Sun. 10 am - 9 pm
Reservations: None
Dress: Casual
Price of Entrees: Inexpensive
Credit Cards: None
Specialties: Pupusa, fried bananas, chicken pie, shrimp soup; South American cuisine.

CHINESE

168 Shanghai Restaurant
4215 Spring Mountain Rd.
Las Vegas, NV 89103
365-9168
Hours: 11 am - 9:30 pm
Reservations: None
Dress: Casual
Price of Entrees: $4.75 - $10.95
Credit Cards: MC, Visa
Specialties: Authentic Shanghai cuisine; sauteed shrimp, orange chicken, dim sum all day.
Atmosphere: Simple and casual.

Amlee Gourmet
3827 E. Sunset Rd.
Las Vegas, NV 89120
898-3358
Hours: Daily 11 am - 3 pm & 4 pm - 10 pm; Sat. and Sun. 4:30 pm - 10 pm
Reservations: On weekends
Dress: Casual
Price of Entrees: $6.95 - $24.95
Credit Cards: All major
Specialties: Sesame chicken, tangerine beef, strawberry chicken, Amlee beef, black peppercorn chicken, prawns with lobster sauce.

Asia Restaurant at Harrah's

Asia
Harrah's
3475 Las Vegas Blvd. S.
Las Vegas, NV 89109
369-5000
Hours: 5 pm - 10:30 pm
Reservations: Not required
Dress: Casual
Price of Entrees: $7.00 - $48.00
Credit Cards: All major
Specialties: Live seafood, shrimp and lobster Cantonese

Asian Garden Chinese Restaurant
701 N. Nellis Blvd.
Las Vegas, NV 89110
453-1900
Hours: Mon. - Sat. 11 am - 9:30 pm; Sun. noon - 9:30 pm
Reservations: None
Dress: Casual
Price of Entrees: $6.50 - $14.95; family style $6.50 - $8.95
Credit Cards: MC, Visa
Specialties: Roast duck, chicken green bean, lobster Cantonese; lunch buffet Mon. - Fri. 11 am - 2:30 pm $3.95.

BBQ Town
552 N. Eastern Ave.
Las Vegas, NV 89101
380-8045
Hours: 10 am - 8 pm
Reservations: None
Dress: Casual
Price of Entrees: Inexpensive
Credit Cards: None
Specialties: Oriental and Hawaiian style.

Bamboo Garden Chinese Cuisine
4850 W. Flamingo Rd.
(at Decatur Blvd.)
Las Vegas, NV 89103
871-3262
Hours: Mon. - Sat. 11 am - 10:30 pm; Sun. 5 pm - 10 pm
Reservations: Suggested
Dress: Casual
Price of Entrees: $15.00 - $20.00 per person
Credit Cards: MC, Visa, AMX, Discover
Specialties: Firecracker beef, emerald shrimp, grandfather chicken, Mongolian lamb, chicken teriyaki; banquet facilities to accommodate 60.
Atmosphere: Simple elegance in a relaxing atmosphere.

Bangkok Boom
3111 S. Valley View Blvd.
Las Vegas, NV 89102
Hours: Mon. - Sat. 11 am - 10 pm
Reservations: None
Dress: Casual
Price of Entrees: $6.00 - $22.00
Credit Cards: MC, Visa
Specialties: Kung pao chicken, sweet and sour pork, Peking duck.

Beijing Restaurant
3900 Paradise Rd.
Las Vegas, NV 89109
737-9618
Hours: 11:30 am - 11 pm
Reservations: Suggested
Dress: Informal
Price of Entrees: $7.00 - $20.00; average check $13.00 per person
Credit Cards: All major
Specialties: Vegetarian dishes, Peking duck, pine nut shrimp; banquet facilities. Lunch starting at $4.50.
Atmosphere: Collector's Oriental arts and crafts displayed, are also for sale; bar, lounge.

Canton Chinese Restaurant
3740 E. Flamingo Rd.
Las Vegas, NV 89121
458-2920
Hours: Mon. - Fri. 11 am - 10 pm; Sat. - Sun. 3 pm - 10 pm
Reservations: None
Dress: Casual
Price of Entrees: $6.00 - $11.00
Credit Cards: MC, Visa
Specialties: Moo goo gai pan, Mongolian beef, shrimp, lobster, lunch buffet 11 am - 3 pm Mon. - Sat. $3.99

Cathay House Restaurant
5300 W. Spring Mountain Rd.
Las Vegas, NV 89102
876-3838
Hours: 11 am - 10:30 pm
Reservations: Suggested
Dress: Semi-formal - Formal
Price of Entrees: $7.00 - $25.00
Credit Cards: MC, Visa, AMX, Discover, Diners
Specialties: Dim sum; duck, prawns, orange scallops. We would like to introduce you to a place of elegant dining, superb service and fine cuisine specializing in authentic Hong Kong style cuisine. The restaurant sits atop a small gradient, thus the entire dining area has a panoramic view of the glittering Las Vegas Strip. Complementing the main dining area are two banquet rooms with a capacity of 40 and 150, respectively. The larger of the two banquet rooms is equipped with a sing-along laser karaoke system and PA system. Established in 1988, our cuisine is prepared by master chefs from Hong Kong. During our lunch hour (11:00 am - 2:30 pm), dim sum, a specialty lunch is served in steaming carts. Chef Choices are created by our master chef weekly in addition to to our regular menu items.
Atmosphere: Karaoke entertainment. View of Las Vegas Strip.

Chang of Las Vegas
3055 Las Vegas Blvd. S.
Las Vegas, NV 89109
731-3388
Hours: 10 am - 2 am
Reservations: Suggested

Dress: Casual
Price of Entrees: $9.95 - $25.95
Credit Cards: Visa, MC, AMX
Specialties: Hong-Kong style Chinese cooking; shrimp-filled dumplings; dim-sum served daily.
Atmosphere: Contemporary.

Chan's Chinese Cuisine
1168 E. Twain Ave.
Las Vegas, NV 89109
796-8646
Hours: 10:30 am - 10:30 pm
Reservations: Accepted
Dress: Casual
Price of Entrees: $5.75 - $8.95
Credit Cards: None
Specialties: Beef, almond chicken; free delivery.

Charlie Chin's
Arizona Charlie's
740 S. Decatur Blvd.
Las Vegas, NV 89107
258-5200
Hours: Tue. - Sun. 5 pm - 11 pm; Closed Mon.
Reservations: Suggested
Dress: Casual
Price of Entrees: $6.50 - $8.50
Credit Cards: All major
Specialties: Pepper steak, sweet and sour pork.

Chin Chin
New York New York
3790 Las Vegas Blvd. S.
Las Vegas, NV 89109
740-NYNY
Hours: Sun. - Thu. 11 am - midnight; Fri. - Sat. 11 am - 1 am
Price of Entrees: $4.25 - $11.95
Credit Cards: All major
Specialties: Wonderful traditional Chinese food served in a bright, colorful and exciting cafe setting. Prepared in exhibition style kitchen, diners observe skilled chefs prepare a variety of sumptuous dishes from Chin Chin's signature classic shredded chicken salad to a delectable assortment of dim sum appetizers and entrees.

China Bowl Express
910 N. Rancho Dr.
Las Vegas, NV 89106
646-8646
Hours: Mon. - Thu. 11 am - 10 pm; Fri. 11 am - 11 pm; Sat. 11 am - 10 pm; Sun. 4 pm - 10 pm
Reservations: None
Dress: Casual
Price of Entrees: $5.75 - $7.50
Credit Cards: MC, Visa
Specialties: Fast food; chop suey, pork, beef, chicken.

China Doll Restaurant
2534 E. Desert Inn Rd.
Las Vegas, NV 89121
369-9511
Hours: Mon. - Fri. 11:30 am - 10 pm; Sat. - Sun. 3 pm - 10 pm
Reservations: Accepted
Dress: Casual

Price of Entrees: $6.95 - $14.95; chef's special combination dinner $24.95
Credit Cards: MC, Visa
Specialties: Spicy scallops, almond chicken, wor shu duck, minced chicken served in lettuce cups, black pepper steak kew, lunch buffet 11:30 am - 2:30 pm $4.25; delivery.

China House
4420 E. Charleston Blvd.
Las Vegas, NV 89104
438-8002
Hours: Mon. - Fri. 11:30 am - 10 pm; Sat. - Sun. 3 pm - 10 pm
Reservations: None
Dress: Casual
Price of Entrees: $4.00 - $15.95
Credit Cards: MC, Visa, AMX
Specialties: Hong Kong chow mein.

China Inn Restaurant
894 S. Boulder Hwy.
Henderson, NV 89015
566-0707
Hours: Mon. - Sat. 11 am - 10 pm; Sun. 1 pm - 10 pm
Reservations: None
Dress: Casual
Price of Entrees: $4.25 - $7.95 for combination and family dinners.
Credit Cards: MC, Visa, Discover, AMX
Specialties: Szechwan and Chinese cuisine in addition to American food.

China Joe's
(Multiple locations listed below)
Hours: Sun. - Thu. 11 am - 9:30 pm; Fri. and Sat. 11 am - 10 pm
Reservations: None
Dress: Casual
Price of Entrees: $6.95 - $8.95
Credit Cards: None
Specialties: Sesame chicken, general chicken, crab rangoon, kung pao chicken.

6126 W. Lake Mead Blvd.
Las Vegas, NV 89108
646-4848

3886 W. Sahara Ave.
Las Vegas, NV 89102
248-4848

China King
3175 N. Rainbow Blvd.
Las Vegas, NV 89108
656-2200
Hours: 11:30 am - 10 pm
Reservations: None
Dress: Casual
Price of Entrees: $5.25 - $18.95
Credit Cards: MC, Visa, Discover
Specialties: Cantonese, Szechwan and vegetarian.

China Queen
4825 S. Rainbow Blvd.
Las Vegas, NV 89103
873-3288
Hours: Mon. - Fri. 11 am - 10 pm; Sat. - Sun. noon - 10 pm
Reservations: None
Dress: Casual
Price of Entrees: $4.75 - $6.99
Specialties: Hong Kong-style; teriyaki chicken, beef, chicken or shrimp w/garlic, Mongolian beef, beef with black pepper sauce; delivery with $10 minimum; lunch special served 11 am - 3 pm $3.99.

RESTAURANTS - Ethnic

China Star
3582 S. Maryland Pkwy.
Las Vegas, NV 89109
732-1608
Hours: 11 am - 10 pm
Reservations: None
Dress: Casual
Price of Entrees: $8.50 - $11.95 for family style dinners
Credit Cards: MC, Visa, AMX, Discover
Specialties: Pine nut chicken, orange beef; private banquet rooms available.

China's Cuisine Restaurant
1945 N. Nellis Blvd.
Las Vegas, NV 89115
452-2828
Hours: Tue. - Sat. 11:30 am - 10 pm; Sun. 4 pm - 10 pm; closed Mon.
Reservations: None
Dress: Casual
Price of Entrees: $3.25 - $13.25
Credit Cards: None
Specialties: Lobster Cantonese, Mongolian beef; lunch special Tue. - Fri. 11.30 am - 2:30 pm $4.50.
Atmosphere: Small restaurant.

Chinatown Cuisine
2000 E. Charleston Blvd.
Las Vegas, NV 89104
388-0078
Hours: Mon. - Sat. 11:30 am - 10:30 pm
Reservations: None
Dress: Casual
Price of Entrees: $4.50 - $12.50
Credit Cards: MC, Visa, Discover
Specialties: Cantonese style seafood, pork, beef.

Chinatown Express
Chinatown Plaza
4255 Spring Mountain Rd., Ste. C111
Las Vegas, NV 89102
364-1122
Hours: 10 am - 10 pm
Reservations: None
Dress: Casual
Price of Entrees: $4.75 - $9.95
Credit Cards: None
Specialties: Taiwan chow mein, beef and broccoli, shrimp with snow peas, noodle dishes, sweet and sour pork.
Atmosphere: Chinese name for restaurant means "Monkey on the Mountain"; stuffed monkeys and vines hang from the ceiling; like a lovely outdoor sidewalk cafe.

Chinese Cuisine
2750 Green Valley Pkwy.
Las Vegas, NV 89014
454-6882
Hours: Mon. - Fri. 11 am - 10 pm; Sat. - Sun. noon - 10 pm
Reservations: Accepted
Dress: Casual
Price of Entrees: $4.75 - $14.95
Credit Cards: All major
Specialties: Cantonese beef, pork, chicken, seafood buffet $5.95.

Chinese New Year Restaurant
3409 S. Jones Blvd.
Las Vegas, NV 89102
873-4133
Hours: Sun. - Fri. 11 am - 11 pm;

Sat. 3 pm - 11 pm
Reservations: None
Dress: Casual
Price of Entrees: Family style $7.95 - $9.95
Credit Cards: MC, Visa, AMX
Specialties: Szechwan and Cantonese combination dinner. Nightly special. $12.95 includes appetizers, soup, main course and dessert.
Atmosphere: Cheerful and festive, friendly fast service.

Chinese Village Restaurant
(Multiple locations listed below)
Hours: 11 am - 11 pm
Reservations: None
Dress: Casual
Price of Entrees: $7.95 - $16.95
Credit Cards: MC, Visa, AMX
Specialties: Cantonese, Szechwan and Mandarin-style cooking. No MSG; free delivery.
Atmosphere: Karaoke nightly 10 pm - 2 am.

608 N. Rainbow Blvd.
Las Vegas, NV 89107
870-3888

5280 E. Craig Rd.
Las Vegas, NV 89115
643-0463

Chin's
Fashion Show Mall
3200 Las Vegas Blvd. S.
Las Vegas, NV 89109
733-8899
Hours: 11:30 am - 9:30 pm
Reservations: Preferred
Dress: Informal - casual to semi-formal
Price of Entrees: $10.00 - $28.00
Credit Cards: MC, Visa, AMX
Specialties: Gourmet Chinese; strawberry chicken, orange peel shrimp, dim sum; banquet facilities to accommodate 350.
Atmosphere: Elegant dining; local and tourist favorite. Separate lounge; piano music.

Chop Chop
5075 S. Pecos Rd.
Las Vegas, NV 89120
456-2020
Hours: 11 am - 10 pm; closed Sun.
Reservations: None
Dress: Casual
Price of Entrees: $5.95 - $10.95
Credit Cards: MC, Visa
Specialties: Chinese fast food; delivery.

Chop Chop
6812 W. Cheyenne Ave.
Las Vegas, NV 89108
658-2467
Hours: Tue. - Fri. noon - 9:30 pm; Sat. & Mon. 3:15 pm - 9:30 pm; Sun. 5 pm - 9:30 pm
Reservations: None
Dress: Casual
Price of Entrees: $6.00 - $8.95
Credit Cards: MC, Visa, Discover
Specialties: Cantonese and Szechwan; delivery.

Chung King Chinese Restaurant
3400 S. Jones Blvd.
Las Vegas, NV 89102
871-5551
Hours: 11 am - 3 pm & 5 pm - 10 pm

Reservations: Suggested
Dress: Casual
Price of Entrees: Family-style dinners for two or more $8.25 to $14.95 per person
Credit Cards: All major
Specialties: Chung King chicken, pot roast, Mongolian beef, pork a la Szechwan, fish filet in black bean sauce; buffet 11:30 am - 3 pm $5.75; Polynesian drinks.

Chung King III
Royal Hotel
99 Convention Center Dr.
Las Vegas, NV 89109
735-6117
Hours: 8 am - 11 pm
Reservations: Accepted
Dress: Casual
Price of Entrees: $9.25 - $17.95
Credit Cards: All major
Specialties: Seafood, fowl and sizzling platters; dim sum.

Cockatoo Club Chinese Restaurant
640 N. Eastern Ave.
Las Vegas, NV 89101
382-4191
Hours: Mon. - Fri. 11 am - 9:30 pm; Sat. - Sun. 3 pm - 9:30 pm
Reservations: Accepted
Dress: Casual
Price of Entrees: $4.25 - $15.00
Credit Cards: None
Specialties: Barbecue pork, beef, broccoli.

Diamond China Restaurant
3909 W. Sahara Ave.
Las Vegas, NV 89102
873-6977
Hours: 3:30 pm - 5 am; Mon. 3:30 pm - 4 am
Reservations: None
Dress: Casual
Price of Entrees: $7.00 - $9.95
Credit Cards: MC, Visa
Specialties: Seafood, chicken.

Diamond Chinese Restaurant
3449 Industrial Rd.
Las Vegas, NV 89109
796-8982
Hours: Mon. - Fri. noon - 4 am; Sat. 4 pm - 4 am; Sun. 4 pm - 2 am
Reservations: Accepted for larger parties
Dress: Casual
Price of Entrees: $5.50 - $26.95
Credit Cards: None
Specialties: Chicken chow mein, Szechwan shrimp, bird's nest soup, squid, crab and lobster dishes.

Dragon's Court
MGM Grand
3799 Las Vegas Blvd. S.
Las Vegas, NV 89109
891-7777
Hours: 6 pm - 11 pm
Reservations: Suggested
Dress: Informal
Price of Entrees: $15.00 - $30.00
Credit Cards: All major
Specialties: Mandarin and Cantonese specialties. Shark fin soup.

Dragon Noodle Co.
Monte Carlo
3770 Las Vegas Blvd. S.
Las Vegas, NV 89109
730-7777
Hours: Sun. - Thu. 11 am - 11 pm; Fri. - Sat. 11 am - midnight
Reservations: Suggested
Dress: Casual
Price of Entrees: $5.95 - $34.95
Credit Cards: All major
Specialties: Traditional Hong Kong cuisine, Peking duck, chow mein.

Dragon Palace
5006 S. Maryland Pkwy.
Las Vegas, NV 89119
795-0333
Hours: 3:30 pm - 11 pm
Reservations: None
Dress: Informal
Price of Entrees: $4.25 - $8.25
Credit Cards: MC, Visa, AMX, Discover
Specialties: Lemon chicken, sesame chicken, Mongolian beef; delivery.
Atmosphere: Warm, friendly and comfortable.

Empress Court
Caesars Palace
3570 Las Vegas Blvd. S.
Las Vegas, NV 89109
731-7731
Hours: 6 pm - 10:30 pm
Reservations: Suggested
Dress: Semiformal
Price of Entrees: $14 and up; a la carte
Credit Cards: All major
Specialties: Peking duck, orange blossom pork chops.
Atmosphere: Subtle but unmistakable Chinese look, interpreted with a contemporary flair and highlighted with Art Deco overtones.

Express Wok at Nellis
560 N. Nellis Blvd.
Las Vegas, NV 89110
459-8880
Hours: 11 am - 10 pm
Reservations: None
Dress: Casual
Price of Entrees: $2.75 - $8.95; family style $6.75
Credit Cards: None
Specialties: Moo goo gai pan, Mongolian beef, almond chicken. Delivery available to a limited area.
Atmosphere: Fast food.

Express Wok at Twain
(See Express Wok at Nellis)
860 E. Twain Ave.
Las Vegas, NV 89109
369-2128

Fair View Chinese Cuisine
1930 N. Decatur Blvd.
Las Vegas, NV 89108
647-3288
Hours: Mon. - Fri. 11:30 am - 10 pm; Sat. 3 pm - 10 pm; Sun. 4 pm - 10 pm
Reservations: None
Dress: Casual
Price of Entrees: $8.95 - $13
Credit Cards: MC, Visa, Disc.
Specialties: Peking duck; Delivery available.

Fong's Garden
2021 E. Charleston Blvd.
Las Vegas, NV 89104
382-1644
Hours: Tue. - Fri. 11:30 am - 11 pm;
Sat. - Sun. 1 pm - 11 pm
Reservations: Accepted
Dress: Casual
Price of Entrees: $6.25 to $12.50
(complete dinners)
Credit Cards: MC, Visa, AMX
Specialties: Chow mein, chop suey, lo
mein; lunch specials $3.95.

Fortune Garden
3743 Las Vegas Blvd. S.
Las Vegas, NV 89109
261-9818
Hours: 11 am - 11 pm
Reservations: Accepted
Dress: Casual
Price of Entrees: $7.50 - $28.00
Credit Cards: Visa, MC, AMX, Discover,
Diners
Specialties: Authentic Chinese Cuisine,
shark fin soup.

Fortune Inn
4408 N. Rancho Dr.
Las Vegas, NV 89130
658-8116
Hours: Mon. - Sat. 11:30 am - 10 pm;
Sun. 3:30 pm - 10 pm
Reservations: None
Dress: Casual
Price of Entrees: $6.95 - $21.95; family
dinners $10.50 to $16.50 per person.
Credit Cards: MC, Visa
Specialties: Seafood or beef in bird's
nest, Yu Hsiang scallops, cashew shrimp,
barbecue pork, General Tao's chicken;
delivery available 5 pm - 9 pm.

Full Ho Chinese Cuisine
240 N. Jones Blvd.
Las Vegas, NV 89107
878-2378
Hours: Tue. - Sat. 11 am - 10 pm;
Sun. noon - 10 pm
Reservations: None
Dress: Casual
Price of Entrees: Inexpensive
Credit Cards: MC, Visa, AMX
Specialties: Mongolian lamb, ba chen
duck, pan fried wonton.

Garden of the Dragon
Las Vegas Hilton
3000 Paradise Rd.
Las Vegas, NV 89109
732-5111
Hours: 6 pm - 11 pm
Reservations: Suggested
Dress: Informal - jacket optional
Price of Entrees: $13.50 - $38.00
Credit Cards: All major
Specialties: Gourmet Chinese dining fea-
turing an array of cuisines including spicy
Szechwan, Peking, Northern Mongolian,
Cantonese. Peking duck, lemon chicken,
sizzling lamb, abalone, shark fin soup,
Peking-style lobster.
Atmosphere: Located in the Benihana
courtyard, thunder and lightning with
rain showers appear to be taking place
just outside your dining room.

Gee Joon
Binion's Horseshoe
128 Fremont St.
Las Vegas, NV 89101
382-1600

Hours: 5 pm - 11 pm
Reservations: Suggested
Dress: Informal
Price of Entrees: $9.00 - $30.00
Credit Cards: All major
Specialties: Mongolian beef, Peking
duck, lobster, sauteed crystal prawns, stir
fried choy-sun, beef, chicken, and pork.
Gee Joon is the highest ranking hand in
Pai Gow, translated means "supreme."
Atmosphere: Elegant dining room with
white table cloths and large comfort-
able booths and romantic lighting.

Golden Dragon Chinese Cuisine
6120 W. Tropicana Ave.
Las Vegas, NV 89103
253-5148
Hours: 11 am - 10 pm
Reservations: Suggested
Dress: Informal
Price of Entrees: $5.25 - $11.95 for
combination and family dinners; $7.75 -
$24.00 for house specialties.
Credit Cards: MC, Visa, AMX
Specialties: Peking duck, Peking fla-
vored steak, Jir Jir chicken and beef;
lunch buffet 11:30 am - 2:30 pm $3.95.

Golden Flower Chinese Cuisine
3315 E. Russell Rd.
Las Vegas, NV 89120
454-1177
Hours: Mon. - Fri. 11:30 am - 10 pm;
Sat. - Sun. 4 pm - 10 pm
Reservations: None
Dress: Casual
Price of Entrees: $5.50 - $16.50; family
style dinners $8.25 - $11.75 per person
Credit Cards: MC, Visa
Specialties: Sizzling scallop, moo shu
shrimp, scallops in crispy nest,
Mongolian beef; lunch specials Mon. - Fri.
11:30 am - 3 pm $3.75 - $4.95.

**Golden Wok West
Chinese Restaurant**
504 S. Decatur Blvd.
Las Vegas, NV 89107
878-1596
Hours: 11:30 am - 10 pm
Reservations: None
Dress: Casual
Price of Entrees: $5.00 - $18.50
Credit Cards: MC, Visa, AMX
Specialties: Cantonese, Mandarin, Szechwan.

Golden Wok East
(See Golden Wok West)
4760 S. Eastern Ave.
Las Vegas, NV 89119
456-1868
Hours: Mon. - Fri. 11:30 am - 9:30 pm;
Sat. - Sun. 3 pm - 9:30 pm

Great Wall Chinese Restaurant
2202 W. Charleston Blvd.
Las Vegas, NV 89102
385-2750
Hours: Mon. - Fri. 11 am - 9:30 pm;
Sat. noon - 9:30 pm; Sun. 4 pm - 9:30 pm
Reservations: None
Dress: Casual
Price of Entrees: $3.95 - $12.95
Credit Cards: MC, Visa
Specialties: Almond duck, lobster.

Imperial Garden, 1155 E. Sahara Ave., Las Vegas, NV 89104

Green Star
101 S. Rainbow Blvd.
Las Vegas, NV 89128
877-1128
Hours: Mon. - Sat. 11:30 am - 9:30 pm;
Sun. 2:30 pm - 9:30 pm
Reservations: None
Dress: Casual
Price of Entrees: $5.00 - $10.00
Credit Cards: MC, Visa
Specialties: Cantonese, Szechwan.

Ho - Ho - Ho Restaurant
2550 S. Rainbow Blvd.
Las Vegas, NV 89102
876-5897
Hours: Mon. - Sat. 11 am - 10 pm;
Sun. 4 pm - 10 pm
Reservations: None
Dress: Casual
Price of Entrees: Moderate
Credit Cards: MC, Visa, AMX, Discover
Specialties: Traditional Mandarin &
Szechwan cuisine; delivery $1.00.

Hong Kong Chinese Restaurant
4944 E. Tropicana Ave.
Las Vegas, NV 89121
451-2828
Hours: Mon. - Sat. 11:30 am - 10 pm;
Sun. 3 pm - 10 pm
Reservations: None
Dress: Casual
Price of Entrees: $6.50 - $13.95
Credit Cards: All major
Specialties: Hong Kong, Cantonese and
Mandarin.

House of Joy
7380 S. Eastern Ave.
Las Vegas, NV 89123
896-4648
Hours: Mon. - Thu. 11 am - 10 pm;
Fri. 11 am - 10:30 pm; Sat. 11 am - 10:30 pm;
Sun. 4 pm - 10 pm
Reservations: Accepted
Dress: Casual
Price of Entrees: $6.00 - $16.00
Credit Cards: All major
Specialties: Dragon and Phoenix delight;
lounge; children's menu.

Ho Wan
Desert Inn
3145 Las Vegas Blvd. S.
Las Vegas, NV 89109
733-4547
Hours: 6 pm - 11 pm
Reservations: Required
Dress: Semi-formal
Price of Entrees: $10.00 - $36.00
Credit Cards: All major
Specialties: Whole Peking duck, chilled
black leaf lichee, prawns in black bean
sauce, minced squab.
Atmosphere: Elegant setting.

**Hunan Garden Chinese
Restaurant**
2067 N. Jones Blvd.
Las Vegas, NV 89108
646-6898
Hours: Sun. - Thu. 11 am - 9 pm;
Fri. and Sat. 11 am - 10 pm
Reservations: None
Dress: Casual
Price of Entrees: $5.00 - $15.95
Credit Cards: All major
Specialties: Triple Crown Delight
(sauteed shrimp, scallops and chicken),
orange beef, Lake Tung Ping shrimp.
Atmosphere: Cozy and clean.

**Hunan King Chinese
Restaurant**
5960 Spring Mountain Rd., Ste. 1
Las Vegas, NV 89102
221-0456   221-0489
Hours: Mon. - Fri. 11 am - 10 p.m;
Sat. - Sun. noon - 10 pm
Reservations: Accepted
Dress: Casual
Price of Entrees: $5.95 - $16.95
Credit Cards: MC, Visa, AMX
Specialties: Hunan, hot and spicy
Chinese cuisine. Hunan beef, pork in gar-
lic sauce, Kung Pao chicken, pot stickers,
lobster. Seven days lunch special combi-
nations. Full bar service. Banquet facili-
ties to accommodate up to 40.
Atmosphere: No smoking restaurant.

Imperial Garden
1155 E. Sahara Ave.
Las Vegas, NV 89104
734-6116
Hours: Mon., Wed., Thu., Sun. 11:30 am -
10 pm; Tue., Fri., Sat. 11:30 am - 10:30 pm
Reservations: Accepted
Dress: Informal
Price of Entrees: $7.00 - $14.00
Credit Cards: All major
Specialties: Cantonese, Szechwan and
Mandarin dishes; lunch buffet served daily
11:30 am - 2 pm $4.15.

Kam's Chinese Kitchen
3310 S. Nellis Blvd.
Las Vegas, NV 89121
436-0001
Hours: Mon. - Sat. 11:30 am - 9:30 pm;
Sun. 3:30 pm - 9:30 pm
Reservations: None
Dress: Casual
Price of Entrees: Inexpensive
Credit Cards: None
Specialties: Cantonese and Mandarin,
Mongolian beef, pepper steak and
vegetables.

RESTAURANTS - Ethnic

Kim Tar Restaurant
China Town Plaza
4215 W. Spring Mountain Rd.
Las Vegas, NV 89102
227-3588
Hours: 10 am - 11 pm
Reservations: None
Dress: Casual
Price of Entrees: $5.00 - $20.00
Credit Cards: All major
Specialties: Fresh seafood; live crabs, lobsters, fish, squid, clams, oysters, scallops, shrimp, beef, pork, chicken; 3 separate menus.
Atmosphere: Upscale beautiful restaurant.

King City Chinese Restaurant
4670 S. Decatur Blvd.
Las Vegas, NV 89103
Hours: 10 am - midnight
Reservations: Suggested
Dress: Informal
Price of Entrees: A la carte
Credit Cards: MC, Visa, Discover
Specialties: Hong-Kong style menu, sizzling plate and clay pot dishes, live seafood, dim sum. Lunch specials from $4.95; banquet facilities for up to 230; delivery 11 am - 10 pm; lunch specials served daily 11 am - 3 pm $4.95 - 6.95.
Atmosphere: Oriental-style building, elegant modern decor with a garden setting.

King's Garden
4570 E. Tropicana Ave.
Las Vegas, NV 89121
898-3833
Hours: Mon. - Sat. 11:30 am - 10 pm; Sun. 4 pm - 10 pm
Reservations: Accepted
Dress: Casual
Price of Entrees: $4.95 - $13.95
Credit Cards: MC, Visa, Discover
Specialties: Lemon chicken, lobster Cantonese, shrimp.

Kung Fu Plaza
3505 S. Valley View Blvd.
Las Vegas, NV 89103
247-4120
Hours: 11 am - 11 pm
Reservations: Accepted
Dress: Casual
Price of Entrees: $4.95 - $12.95
Credit Cards: All major
Specialties: Chinese and Thai crispy catfish, smoked pork salad, stuffed chicken wings, chicken satae with peanut butter sauce.

Lees Chinese Restaurant
2775 S. Nellis Blvd.
Las Vegas, NV 89121
457-1688
Hours: 11 am - 10 pm
Reservations: None
Dress: Casual
Price of Entrees: $5.25 - $8.25; combination plates $6.95 - $7.25
Credit Cards: MC, Visa, AMX, Discover
Specialties: Shrimp, scallops, chicken, pork, pepper steak. Delivery 4 pm - 10 pm to limited area with $10 minimum order; $1.50 service charge.

Lillie Langtry's
Golden Nugget
129 Fremont St.
Las Vegas, NV 89101

385-7111
Hours: 5 pm - 11 pm
Reservations: Recommended
Dress: Informal - semi-formal
Price of Entrees: $10.50 - $26.50
Credit Cards: All major
Specialties: Lobster or shrimp Cantonese, lemon chicken, stir-fried lobster with mixed vegetables, black pepper steak, Chinese-style steak with scallions; no MSG.
Atmosphere: Intimate, warmly lit, exquisite surroundings.

Lotus Garden
81 N. Nellis Blvd.
Las Vegas, NV 89110
453-3811
Hours: 11:30 am - 9:30 pm
Reservations: None
Dress: Casual
Price of Entrees: $4.00 - $13.00
Credit Cards: MC, Visa, Discover, AMX
Specialties: Traditional Chinese menu.

Madame Chings
Treasure Island
3300 Las Vegas Blvd. S.
Las Vegas, NV 89109
894-7111
Hours: Wed. - Sun. 5:30 pm - 11:30 pm
Reservations: Not required
Dress: Casual
Price of Entrees: Reasonable
Credit Cards: All major
Specialties: Built to honor Madame Ching, the most famous of female pirates, this restaurant features Szechwan and Cantonese cuisine reminiscent of old world China. Madame Ching's specialties include Grandfather chicken, steamed salmon filet and Macadamia beef.

Magic Wok
4955 E. Craig Rd.
Las Vegas, NV 89115
644-2726
Hours: Mon. - Fri. 11 am - 10 pm; Sat. noon - 9 pm
Reservations: None
Dress: Casual
Price of Entrees: $3.95 - $9.95
Specialties: Moo goo gai pan, chow mein, Szechwan.

Mandarin Court
1510 E. Flamingo Rd.
Las Vegas, NV 89119
737-1234
Hours: Mon. - Fri. 11 am - 11 pm; Sat. - Sun. noon - 11 pm
Reservations: Suggested
Dress: Informal
Price of Entrees: $8.00 - $22.00
Credit Cards: All major
Specialties: Crispy duck, orange beef; lounge specializing in Polynesian drinks; Banquet facilities for up to 150.
Atmosphere: One of the oldest and largest Chinese restaurants in Las Vegas. Romantic Forbidden City Lounge.

MB China
2100 E. Lake Mead Blvd.
Las Vegas, NV 89114
657-9007
Hours: Mon. - Fri. 10:30 am - 9 pm; Sat. and Sun. 12:30 pm - 8 pm
Reservations: None

Dress: Casual
Price of Entrees: Everything under $5.95
Credit Cards: None
Specialties: Shrimp, beef, and chicken egg foo young, moo goo gai pan; combination plates $3.20; drive thru window.

Mask
Rio
3700 W. Flamingo Rd.
Las Vegas, NV 89103
252-7777
Hours: 5 pm - 11 pm
Reservations: Required
Dress: Casual
Price of Entrees: $14.00 - $35.00
Credit Cards: All major
Specialties: Bird's nest soup, shark fin soup, and traditional favorites
Atmosphere: Chinese, Japanese Thai and Teppan delicacies entertainingly prepared and creatively served in a soothing eastern setting.

Mayflower Cuisinier
4750 W. Sahara Ave.
Las Vegas, NV 89102
870-8432
Hours: Lunch Mon. - Fri. 11 am - 3 pm; Dinner Mon. - Thu. 5 pm - 10 pm; Fri. - Sat. 5 pm - 11 pm; closed Sun.
Reservations: Suggested
Dress: Informal
Price of Entrees: $12.95 - $18.95
Credit Cards: MC, Visa, AMX, Discover, Diners
Specialties: Contemporary Chinese cuisine with Continental and French influences. Chef Ming See Woo emphasizes health and quality. No MSG is added to her preparations. Mongolian grilled lamb chops, ginger chicken ravioli with scallion-Szechwan sauce, stir fried chicken in plum wine. Semi enclosed banquet area accommodates 40; catering; 5 Star Diamond Award.
Atmosphere: Casually elegant dining room or climate controlled patio dining.

Ming Terrace
Imperial Palace
3535 Las Vegas Blvd. S.
Las Vegas, NV 89109
794-3261
Hours: 5 pm - midnight
Reservations: Suggested
Dress: Informal
Price of Entrees: $9.95 - $27.50
Credit Cards: All major
Specialties: Mandarin and Cantonese; abalone, roast duck, ginger beef, kung pao shrimp.
Atmosphere: Oriental setting with pink and black decor.

Moongate
Mirage
3400 Las Vegas Blvd. S.
Las Vegas, NV 89109
791-7111
Hours: 5:30 pm - 11 pm
Reservations: Required
Dress: Informal - semi-formal
Price of Entrees: $15.00 - $30.00
Credit Cards: All major
Specialties: Classic Szechwan and

Cantonese cuisines of China; filet of salmon, tea smoked duck, black peppered beef, strawberry chicken.
Atmosphere: Chinese courtyard setting complete with cherry blossoms.

Papyrus
Luxor
3900 Las Vegas Blvd. S.
Las Vegas, NV 89119
262-4774
Hours: 5 pm - 11 pm
Reservations: Suggested
Dress: Casual
Price of Entrees: $7.25 - $14.95
Credit Cards: All major
Specialties: Otemanu hot rock sampler; Luxor's own version of Pacific Basin hot rock grilling at your table. Served with an array of delicacies. Fine Polynesian cuisine.

Panda Express
Fiesta
2400 N. Rancho Dr.
Las Vegas, NV 89130
631-7000
Hours: Mon. - Thu. 11 am - 10 pm; Fri. - Sun. 11 am - 11 pm
Specialties: Delicious Chinese food quickly, easily, and inexpensively.

Panda Express
Boulevard Mall
3480 S. Maryland Pkwy.
Las Vegas, NV 89109
737-1616
Hours: 10 am - 9 pm
Reservations: None
Dress: Casual
Price of Entrees: Inexpensive
Credit Cards: None
Specialties: Orange chicken, spicy chicken with peanuts, vegetable chop suey, beef with broccoli.
Atmosphere: Fast food.

Peking Express Restaurant
3278 Las Vegas Blvd. N.
Las Vegas, NV 89115
644-6776
Hours: Mon. - Sat. 11:30 am - 9:15 pm
Reservations: None
Dress: Casual
Price of Entrees: Inexpensive
Credit Cards: None
Specialties: Chicken, pork, beef, seafood.

Peking Market
Flamingo Hilton
3555 Las Vegas Blvd. S.
Las Vegas, NV 89109
733-3322
Hours: Wed. - Sun. 5:30 pm - 11 pm
Reservations: Suggested
Dress: Informal
Price of Entrees: $8.00 - $20.00
Credit Cards: All major
Specialties: Mongolian beef, lemon chicken, steak kew, Peking duck; family dinners available; exotic drinks.
Atmosphere: Traditional Chinese marketplace decor. Restaurant is divided into five dining rooms with each representing a different market.

Plum Tree Inn
4215 Spring Mountain Rd.
Las Vegas, NV 89102
873-7077 / fax 873-3515
Hours: Mon. - Thu. 10 am - 10 pm;
Fri. - Sat. 10 am - 11 pm;
Sun. 11 am - 10 pm
Reservations: Recommended
Dress: Informal
Price of Entrees: $6.95 - $17.50
Credit Cards: MC, Visa, AMX
Specialties: Specializing in Mandarin
and Szechwan cuisine. Plum Tree beef,
sweet & pungent chicken, sauteed
shrimp, assorted seafoods; poultry and
duck dishes; delivery available.

Pumi Oriental Restaurant
9026 W. Sahara Ave.
Las Vegas, NV 89117
363-7466
Hours: Mon. - Sat. 11 am - 10 pm;
Sun. 4 pm - 10 pm
Reservations: Suggested
Dress: Informal
Price of Entrees: Inexpensive
Credit Cards: All major
Specialties: Walnut shrimp, chicken
soong; sushi bar.

Rainbow Chinese Cuisine
1750 S. Rainbow Blvd.
Las Vegas, NV 89102
877-2211
Hours: 11:30 am - 9:45 pm
Reservations: None
Dress: Casual
Price of Entrees: $7.50 - $15.95
Credit Cards: All major
Specialties: Chicken chow fun, lobster with
ginger. Lunch buffet served weekdays 11:30 am
- 2 pm $4.25; delivery available within a 3 mile
radius. Banquet room seats 120, full bar.

Authentic Chinese Cuisine

Rik' Shaw
Riviera
2901 Las Vegas Blvd. S.
Las Vegas, NV 89109
734-5110
Hours: Wed. - Sun. 5:30 pm - 11 pm
Reservations: Suggested
Dress: Casual
Price of Entrees: $9.95 - $24.00
Credit Cards: All major
Specialties: Two menus are featured, one
with authentic Oriental dishes, the other
with more American-style Oriental items;
Hone Sue shrimp, pineapple duck, abalone
and black mushrooms, ginger orange roughy.

Sam - Pan Chinese Restaurant
14 W. Pacific Ave.
Henderson, NV 89015
565-8985
Hours: Mon. - Sat. 11am - 10 pm;
Sun. noon - 9:30 pm
Reservations: None
Dress: Casual
Price of Entrees: $3.00 - $9.95
Credit Cards: MC, Visa, Discover
Specialties: Pepper steak, lemon chick-
en, Mongolian beef, three meats with
vegetables.

Sam Woo BBQ Restaurant
4215 Spring Mountain Rd.
Las Vegas, NV 89102
368-7628
Hours: 10 am - 5 am
Reservations: None
Dress: Casual
Credit Cards: None
Price of Entrees: To $24.95
Specialties: Roasted duck, Chinese fine
noodles, shrimp with lobster sauce,
crab and lobster.

San Francisco Bay Restaurant
900 Karen Ave.
Las Vegas, NV 89109
734-7007
Hours: 11 am - 5 am
Reservations: None
Dress: Casual
Price of Entrees: Combination dinners
$6.95 - $9.95
Credit Cards: MC, Visa
Specialties: Crab, moo shu pork, salty
steamed chicken. Karaoke after 10 pm.

Tong's Palace Restaurant
2211 Las Vegas Blvd. S.
Las Vegas, NV 89104
733-8294
Hours: 11 am - 5 am
Reservations: None
Dress: Casual
Price of Entrees: $6.25 - $29.95
Credit Cards: MC, Visa, AMX
Specialties: Roast duck - 24 hr. advance
notice, authentic Szechwan cuisine.

Wo Fat Chinese Restaurant
3700 E. Desert Inn Rd.
Las Vegas, NV 89121
451-6656
Hours: 11 am - 10 pm
Reservations: Accepted
Dress: Casual
Price of Entrees: $6.95 - $8.95
Credit Cards: MC, Visa
Specialties: Pot-roast chicken, shrimp
with tomatoes and green peppers,
clams with black bean sauce; lunch spe-
cial $3.95 - $5.95.

CUBAN

Rincon Criollo
1145 Las Vegas Blvd. S.
Las Vegas, NV 89104
388-1906
Hours: Tue. - Sun. 10 am - 10 pm
Reservations: None
Dress: Casual
Price of Entrees: $6.95 - $9.95
Credit Cards: All major
Specialties: Cuban steak, pork, seafood,
chicken and rice.

DUTCH

Keuken Dutch
6180 W. Tropicana Ave.
Las Vegas, NV 89103
368-1077
Hours: 24 hours
Reservations: None
Dress: Casual
Price of Entrees: $5.99 - $11.99
Credit Cards: MC, Visa, Discover, AMX
Specialties: Breakfast served 24 hours,
oven-baked keukens, waffles, steaks, chick-
en, sandwiches, prime rib of beef from 4 pm
Atmosphere: Dutch motif.

ENGLISH

Barronshire
Las Vegas Hilton
3000 Paradise Rd.
Las Vegas, NV 89109
732-5111
Hours: Thu. - Tue. 6 pm - 11 pm
Reservations: Suggested
Dress: Informal - Semi-formal
Price of Entrees: $18.00 - $25.00
Credit Cards: All major
Specialties: Succulent prime rib carved
tableside is the specialty, in addition to
steaks, chicken and seafood. Home of the
famed "spinning bowl" offering crisp sal-
ads with tantalizing dressings.
Atmosphere: An English-style motif is
reflected in the Barronshire.

Crown & Anchor British Pub
1350 E. Tropicana Ave.
Las Vegas, NV 89119
739-8676
Hours: 11 am - 6 am
Reservations: None
Dress: Casual
Price of Entrees: $5.95 - $8.95
Credit Cards: All major
Specialties: Fish and chips, bangers
and mash, English pies, leeks and zuc-
chini; over 30 beers on tap.
Atmosphere: Nautical decor, English
pub, darts.

Sir Galahad's Prime Rib House
Excalibur
3850 Las Vegas Blvd. S.
Las Vegas, NV 89109
597-7777
Hours: Sun. - Thu. 5 pm - 10 pm;
Fri. - Sat. 5 pm - 11 pm
Reservations: Suggested
Dress: Casual
Price of Entrees: $12.95 - $16.95
Credit Cards: All major
Specialties: Prime rib
Atmosphere: Room is decorated to look
like the interior of an old English castle.

FILIPINO

Coconut Grove
1436 E. Charleston Blvd.
Las Vegas, NV 89104
384-2925
Hours: 10 am - 7 pm
Reservations: None
Dress: Casual
Price of Entrees: $3.95 - $7.95
Credit Cards: None
Specialties: Buffet $3.99 10 am - 7 pm
Atmosphere: Island style, palm trees,
coconuts.

Epoy's New Manila Restaurant
1101 E. Charleston Blvd.
Las Vegas, NV 89104
388-8989
Hours: 11 am - 3 am
Reservations: None
Dress: Casual
Price of Entrees: $4.95 - $15.00
Credit Cards: None
Specialties: Crispy pata, lechon kawali,
inihaw sinigang, kare-kare, rellenong
talong; Karaoke.

DINING

RESTAURANTS - Ethnic

Floradel's Restaurant
900 E. Karen Ave.
Las Vegas, NV 89109
731-1003
Hours: Tue. - Sat. 10 am - 7:30 pm;
closed Sun. and Mon.
Reservations: None
Dress: Casual
Price of Entrees: Inexpensive
Credit Cards: None

Pinto's Place
2202 W. Charleston Blvd.
Las Vegas, NV 89102
474-4140
Hours: Mon. - Sat. 9 am - 5 pm
Reservations: None
Dress: Casual
Price of Entrees: $5.00 - $10.00
Credit Cards: None
Specialties: Chicken, beef or pork
adobo, pancit canton, pancitbihon, fried
fish buffet 11 am - 2 pm $4.95.
Atmosphere: Fast food on one side, buf-
fet on the other.

FRENCH

Andre's
401 S. 6th St.
Las Vegas, NV 89101
385-5016
Hours: 6 pm - 11 pm
Reservations: Suggested
Dress: Semi-formal
Price of Entrees: Dinner $19.75 -
$28.00, a la carte.
Credit Cards: Visa, MC, AMX, Diners, CB
Specialties: Maryland blue crab cakes,
marinated salmon tartare, rabbit loin
with spinach fettuccine and dijon mustard, oven roasted escolar with herb
crust, pave of veal with morel mushrooms and chive cream sauce.
Atmosphere: French country restaurant nestled in Las Vegas' oldest residential neighborhood. Remodeled home,
intimate atmosphere. Best Award of
Excellence, *Wine Spectator* magazine.
Private rooms for 8 to 60. Seasonal patio
dining; complimentary valet parking.

Andre's
Monte Carlo
3770 Las Vegas Blvd. S.
Las Vegas, NV 89109
798-7151
Hours: Sun. - Thu. 6 pm - 10 pm;
Fri. - Sat. 6 pm - 11 pm
Reservations: Suggested
Dress: Semi-formal
Price of Entrees: $22.50 - $47.00
Credit Cards: All major
Specialties: King crab and artichoke
timbale with cognac sauce, rack of lamb
with mustard herb sauce, imported sole
sauteed Veronique, abalone sauteed
almondine, thermador with lobster
essence, Maine lobster.

Bistro Le Montrachet
Las Vegas Hilton
3000 Paradise Rd.
Las Vegas, NV 89109
732-5111
Hours: Wed. - Sun. 6 pm - 10:30 pm;
closed Mon. and Tue.
Reservations: Suggested
Dress: Semi-formal - Formal
Price of Entrees: $23 - $35, a la carte
Credit Cards: All major
Specialties: Medallions of veal, roast
duck, rack of lamb, breast of pheasant,
fresh seafood, New York and filet
mignon. Best Award of Excellence from
the *Wine Spectator* magazine for wine
selection which features more than 400
hand-selected wines carefully stored in
the adjoining private wine cellar.
Atmosphere: Elegant European atmosphere with marble floors, domed ceiling
and plush booth seating. Widely recognized as one of the finest true continental
dining experiences, Bistro Le Montrachet
is a connoisseur's delight. Contemporary
French cuisine is delicately prepared and
artfully served with panache seen only in
the world's finest restaurants. Named one
of the top ten restaurants in the country
for 1995 by the American Academy of
Restaurant Sciences.

Crepes Pierrette - A French Cafe
4794 S. Eastern Ave.
Las Vegas, NV 89119
434-1234
Hours: Tue. - Sat. 8:30 am - 10 pm;
Sun. 8:30 am - 2:30 pm; closed Mon.
Reservations: Recommended
Dress: Casual
Price of Entrees: $9.95 - $18.95
Credit Cards: All major
Specialties: French crepe cuisine,
quiche, beef brochettes, filet mignon
flambeed in cognac, frogs legs, escargot,
homemade tarts, French onion soup.

Frogees on 4th
300 S. Fourth St.
Las Vegas, NV 89101
380-1122
Hours: 24
Reservations: None
Dress: Casual
Price of Entrees: $7.95 - $11.95
Credit Cards: All major
Specialties: Daily specials; 70 wines
served by the glass.
Atmosphere: French bistro; live jazz
Fri. - Sat. 10 pm - 2:30 am.

Gatsby's
MGM
3799 Las Vegas Blvd. S.
Las Vegas, NV 89109
891-7337
Hours: Mon. - Sat. seatings 5:30 - 6:30 pm,
8 - 8:30 pm, and 9 - 9:30 pm
Reservations: Required
Dress: Casual elegant
Price of Entrees: $55 - $65
Credit Cards: All major
Specialties: California French. Poached
seafood ravioli with herbed pasta and
lobster nage, ostrich with wild mush-
room risotto, seared ahi tuna.

The Melange
Mirage
3400 Las Vegas Blvd. S.
Las Vegas, NV 89109
791-7111
Hours: 5:30 pm - 11 pm
Reservations: Required
Dress: Casual elegant
Price of Entrees: $24 - $36
Credit Cards: All major
Atmosphere: French Impressionist
artist decor; no children under 5 please.

Monte Carlo Room
Desert Inn
3145 Las Vegas Blvd. S.
Las Vegas, NV 89109
733-4444
Hours: Thu. - Sun. 6 pm - 11 pm
Reservations: Suggested - required
Dress: Formal - jacket required
Price of Entrees: $26.00 - $37.00
Credit Cards: All major
Specialties: Boneless roast duckling, lamb,
veal, Cornish game hen, boneless quail, frog
legs; many dishes flamed tableside.
Atmosphere: Located on the mezzanine
level, the restaurant overlooks the
beautiful grounds of the Desert Inn.
Plush comfortable booths make your
stay comfortable, since this dining
experience will take about 3 hours.
Ladies are presented a long stem rose
at the end of the evening. 1995 Mobil
Four-Star award winner which places
The Monte Carlo in the top 2% of 20,000
establishments rated.

Napa Ristorante
Rio
3700 W. Flamingo Rd.
Las Vegas, NV 89103
252-7777
Hours: 6 pm - midnight
Reservations: Required
Dress: Semi-formal
Price of Entrees: $28 - $48
Credit Cards: All major
Specialties: Country French gourmet;
over 500 wines to choose from.

Palace Court
Caesars Palace
3570 Las Vegas Blvd. S.
Las Vegas, NV 89109
731-7547
Hours: Seatings 6 pm, 6:30 pm,
9 pm, 9:30 pm
Reservations: Required
Dress: Formal - Jacket required
Price of Entrees: $25 - $55; a la carte
Credit Cards: All major
Specialties: Chateaubriand, steak Diane,
live Maine lobster, quail, duck, fresh
salmon, lobster bisque, veal chops.
Atmosphere: Guests arrive at the
restaurant in a crystal and bronze
round elevator, framed by a bronze-
balustrade spiral staircase that is illuminated by a crystal chandelier. In the
dining area, the domed stained glass
ceiling is 16 feet in diameter. A wall of
glass overlooks the "Garden of the
Gods." Palace Court boasts a reputation
as one of the most elegant gourmet
restaurants in America.

Pamplemousse
400 E. Sahara Ave.
Las Vegas, NV 89104
733-2066
Hours: Tue. - Sun. 6 pm, 10 pm
Reservations: Required
Dress: Semi-formal - formal
Price of Entrees: $17 - $26
Credit Cards: All major
Specialties: Roast duckling, rack of
lamb, salmon, veal, fresh seafood. Your
waiter recites daily menu and tells how
the dishes are prepared.
Atmosphere: Romantic country French.

Petite Province
3715 S. Decatur Blvd.
Las Vegas, NV 89103
248-7272
Hours: 11 am - 11 pm
Reservations: Suggested
Dress: Semi-formal
Price of Entrees: $9.50 - $28
Specialties: South of France family
restaurant. Authentic Provence cuisine;
coq au vin, rack of lamb, sauteed NY
steak.
Atmosphere: Furnishings imported
from France for authenticity.

Suzette's
Santa Fe Hotel and Casino
4949 N. Rancho Dr.
Las Vegas, NV 89130
658-4900
Hours: Tue. - Sat. 5 pm - 10 pm
Reservations: Suggested
Dress: Informal
Price of Entrees: $25 - $56 and market
Credit Cards: All major
Specialties: Capon stuffed with wild
mushrooms and spinach, salmon poached
in champagne sauce with smoked scallions.

GERMAN / SWISS

Heidelberg Cafe Restaurant
610 E. Sahara Ave.
Las Vegas, NV 89104
731-5310
Hours: Mon. 11 am - 6:30 pm;
Tue. - Thu. 11 am - 8:30 pm;
Fri. - Sat. 11 am - 9:30 pm; closed Sun.
Reservations: Required
Dress: Casual
Price of Entrees: From $9.95
Credit Cards: All major
Specialties: Stuffed cabbage rolls,
schnitzel, sauerbraten, sausages, rouladen,
imported beer and wine. German
imports and gifts.
Atmosphere: Bavarian.

Swiss Cafe
3175 E. Tropicana Ave.
Las Vegas, NV 89121
454-2270
Hours: Lunch Mon. - Fri. 11 am - 3 pm;
Dinner Mon. - Sat. 5 pm - 10 pm; closed Sun.
Reservations: Suggested
Dress: Informal
Price of Entrees: $8.95 - $18.95
Credit Cards: MC, Visa, AMX
Specialties: Swiss schnitzel, veal
Monterey, tournedos "Cafe De Paris,"
duck l'orange, all entrees include med-
ley of fresh vegetables, homemade
spaetzle, soup or salad; table-side
flambe at slightly higher prices; apple
strudel.
Atmosphere: Old world charm; patio,
garden.

GREEK

Danube Cafe
(See Hungarian / Yugoslavian)

Gyro Time Restaurant
5239 W. Charleston Blvd.
Las Vegas, NV 89102
Hours: Mon. - Sat. 11 am - 8 pm
Reservations: None
Dress: Casual
Price of Entrees: $4 - $7
Credit Cards: None
Specialties: Pita sandwiches, Greek salads.

Renzio's Greek Restaurant
3200 Las Vegas Blvd. S.
Las Vegas, NV 89019
369-6112
Hours: Mon. - Fri. 10 am - 9 pm;
Sat. 10 am - 7 pm; Sun. 11 am - 6 pm
Reservations: None
Dress: Casual
Price of Entrees: Inexpensive
Specialties: Pita sandwiches, spanako-pita, baklava.

HAWAIIAN

Hawaiian Hale
3620 W. Sahara Ave.
Las Vegas, NV 89102
362-6922
Hours: Sun. - Thu. 11 am - 8:30 pm;
Fri. - 11 am - 10 pm; Sat. 11 am - 9 pm;
closed Mon.
Reservations: Accepted
Dress: Casual
Price of Entrees: $5.50 - $10.50
Credit Cards: None
Specialties: Lau lau, kahlua pig, lomi salmon poi, dry aku, poki sashimi, shrimp tempura.
Atmosphere: Hawaiian Island decor. Lounge; Banquet facilities to accommodate 60.

Island Style Restaurant
3909 W. Sahara Ave.
Las Vegas, NV 89102
871-1911
Hours: Mon. - Fri. 10 am - 7 pm;
Sat. 10 am - 5 pm
Reservations: None
Dress: Casual
Price of Entrees: Inexpensive
Credit Cards: None
Specialties: Japanese, Korean, Hawaian.
Atmosphere: Small coffee shop.

HUNGARIAN / YUGOSLAVIAN

Danube Cafe
4865 S. Pecos Rd.
Las Vegas, NV 89121
454-5535
Hours: Mon. - Fri. 10 am - 8 pm;
Sat. 10 am - 5 pm
Reservations: None
Dress: Casual
Price of Entrees: $5 - $10
Credit Cards: MC, Visa, Discover
Specialties: Moussaka, lamb chops, Hungarian goulash; also a deli with foods imported from Hungary, Yugoslavia and Greece.

INDIAN

Dosa-Den
3430 E. Tropicana Ave.
Las Vegas, NV 89121
456-4920
Hours: Wed. - Mon. 11 am - 3 pm & 5:30 pm - 9:30 pm
Reservations: Suggested
Dress: Casual
Price of Entrees: $4.50 - $7.50
Credit Cards: MC, Visa
Specialties: Masala dosa, idli, curries.
Atmosphere: Pleasant, photos of Indian culture and art, Indian music.

Gandhi India's Cuisine
4080 Paradise Rd.
Las Vegas, NV 89109
734-0094
Hours: Lunch 11 am - 2:30 pm;
Dinner 5 pm - 10:30 pm
Reservations: Accepted
Dress: Casual
Price of Entrees: $12.75 - $18.95
Credit Cards: Visa, MC, Discover, DC
Specialties: Tandoori chicken baked in clay oven, lamb and chicken curries, seafood, vegetarian dishes, fresh clay oven baked flat breads. Children's menu; banquet facilities to accommodate 189. Free delivery.
Atmosphere: Very colorful and charming giving the feel of different regions of India. Classical entertainment.

Shalimar
(Additional location listed below)
3900 Paradise Rd.
Las Vegas, NV 89109
796-0302
Hours: Lunch Mon. - Fri. 11:30 am - 2 pm;
Dinner daily 5 pm - 10:30 pm
Reservations: Accepted
Dress: Informal
Price of Entrees: $8.95 - $13.95
Credit Cards: All major
Specialties: Skinless, fat free, char-broiled chicken, meat and seafood. Naan bread, vegetable and rice dishes, chicken or seafood curries, chicken tandoori, vegetarian dishes; lamb, chicken, beef and seafood kabobs. Customer may select spice level. Banquet facilities available to accommodate 100; 11:30 am - 2 pm buffet $6.95 at Paradise location & $7.50 at Decatur location.

2605 S. Decatur Blvd.
Las Vegas, NV 89102
252-8320

ITALIAN

Al Denté
Bally's
3645 Las Vegas Blvd. S.
Las Vegas, NV 89109
739-4111
Hours: Thu. - Mon. 6 pm - 11 pm;
closed Tue. and Wed.

Reservations: Required
Dress: Semi-formal
Price of Entrees: $8.95 - $22.95, a la carte
Credit Cards: All major
Specialties: Pastas, veal Milanese, osso buco, chicken scaloppini, linguine fra diavolo, espresso and cappuccino.

Alta Villa
Flamingo Hilton
3555 Las Vegas Blvd. S.
Las Vegas, NV 89109
733-3111
Hours: Fri. - Tue. 5:30 pm - 11 pm
Reservations: Suggested
Dress: Informal
Price of Entrees: $11.50 - $19.50
Credit Cards: All major
Specialties: Pastas, osso buco, chicken Florentine. Complete six-course dinner for three or more people; $14.95 per person; music.

Andiamo
Las Vegas Hilton
3000 Paradise Rd.
Las Vegas, NV 89109
732-5111
Hours: 6 pm - 11 pm
Reservations: Suggested
Dress: Informal
Price of Entrees: $15.00 - $22.00
Credit Cards: All major
Specialties: Northern Italian specialties; fettuccine all'ara gosta e gamberi, scaloppine al marsala.
Atmosphere: The unique exhibition kitchen provides guests with a view of chefs busily creating masterpieces. In addition to the distinguished atmosphere and tempting selections, Andiamo is also known for its impressive espresso and cappuccino counter.

Anna Bella
3310 S. Sandhill Rd.
Las Vegas, NV 89121
434-2537
Hours: 4:30 pm - 10 pm
Reservations: Recommended
Dress: Casual
Price of Entrees: $8.95 - $15.95
Credit Cards: MC, Visa, AMX
Specialties: Osso buco, salmon primavera, maccheroni pasta, beef braciola.
Atmosphere: Fireplace; live accordion music.

Antonio's
Rio
3700 W. Flamingo Rd.
Las Vegas, NV 89103
252-7737
Hours: 5 pm - 11 pm
Reservations: Suggested
Dress: Informal - collared shirt/no shorts
Price of Entrees: $17.00 - $48.00
Credit Cards: All major
Specialties: Pastas, duck, osso buco, sauteed scampi, pork loin, lamb chops, veal, creamy five onion soup served in a hollowed out onion, tiramisu "the dessert of angels"; over 300 wines.
Atmosphere: Mediterranean atmosphere featuring inlaid marble floors and blue Italian sky created by an overhead dome and indirect blue lighting. The service is impeccable, surpassed only by the unique personality of the waiters from all over the world; all-exhibition cooking. Voted "most efficient service in Las Vegas." Lounge.

Bally's Sidewalk Cafe
Bally's
3645 Las Vegas Blvd. S.
Las Vegas, NV 89109
739-4111
Specialties: Steaks, seafood, pastas.

Battista's Hole in the Wall
4041 Audrie St.
Las Vegas, NV 89109
732-1424
Hours: Sun. - Thu. 4:30 pm - 11 pm;
Fri. - Sat. 4:30 pm - 10:30 pm
Reservations: Suggested
Dress: Informal
Price of Entrees: $15.95 - $29.95
Credit Cards: All major
Specialties: Finest homemade pasta, veal, steaks and seafood; Battista-style cappuccino, steak pizzaiola, steak Caruso, sausage with spaghetti. Complimentary unlimited red or white house wine is served with your dinner. Banquet facilities for 100.
Atmosphere: Old world, smoke free atmosphere; music with dinner.

RESTAURANTS - Ethnic

Bertolini's
Forum Shops
3500 Las Vegas Blvd. S.
Las Vegas, NV 89109
735-4663
Hours: Mon. - Thu. 11 am - midnight;
Fri. - Sat. 11 am - 1 am
Reservations: Accepted
Dress: Casual - Informal
Price of Entrees: $9.50 - $21
Credit Cards: MC, Visa, AMX, Diners
Specialties: Northern Italian fare, homemade pastas, veal and seafood specialties presented from open kitchen; pizza prepared in an authentic wood-burning brick oven; gelati and sorbetto are made from scratch in gelateria; bar.
Atmosphere: European-style sidewalk cafe. Dining in the indoor dining room or sidewalk dining (inside mall).

Bootlegger Ristorante
5025 S. Eastern Ave.
Las Vegas, NV 89119
736-4939
Food-to-go orders - 736-7080
Laff Line - 736-8661
Hours: Tue. - Sat. 11:30 am - 10 pm;
Sun. 4 pm - 10 pm
Reservations: Suggested
Dress: Informal
Price of Entrees: $9.95 - $18.95
Credit Cards: All major
Specialties: Over 138 items on this extensive Italian menu - lobster, seafood Diavolo, pasta with superb red and white sauces, homemade breads and soups, milkfed veal, seafood and Maria's homemade lasagna, tiramasu and other assorted Italian desserts; children's menu; private rooms - wine room 20 people; dining room 50 people; full menu delivered daily until 9 pm; early bird dinners served until 6 pm $7.95 - $9.95.
Atmosphere: Warm, romantic fireside old world atmosphere; large comfortable booths and tables; brick walls, authentic family photographs and artifacts. "Where locals and celebrities gather in Las Vegas." Cozy bar under canopy awning.

Buon Appetito Spaghetteria
6815 W. Sahara Ave.
Las Vegas, NV 89102
233-3939
Hours: 5 pm - 10 pm
Reservations: Suggested
Dress: Casual
Price of Entree: $9.95 - $14.95
Credit Cards: All major
Specialties: All pastas cooked to order, nightly specials.
Atmosphere: Very comfortable with plants and murals.

Cafe Andreatti's
Harrah's
3475 Las Vegas Blvd. S.
Las Vegas, NV 89109
369-5000
Hours: 5:30 pm - 10:30 pm
Reservations: None
Dress: Casual elegant
Price of Entrees: $9.95

Credit Cards: All major
Specialties: Seafood, cioppino, veal picatta, chicken arrosto, fettuccine, chicken parmigiana, spaghetti, salad and dessert bar. American and Italian specialties; Italian dinner menu served 5 pm - 11 pm; price begins at $5.95.
Atmosphere: Open courtyard area as well as an intimate contemporary indoor bar area where guests can enjoy a before dinner belini or a fine wine.

Gourmet Pizza

California Pizza Kitchen
Golden Nugget
129 Fremont St.
Las Vegas, NV 89101
385-7111
Hours: Lunch Mon. - Fri. 11 am - 3 pm;
Dinner Mon. - Fri. 5:30 pm - 11 pm;
Sat. - Sun. 11 am - 11 pm
Reservations: None
Dress: Casual
Price of Entrees: $6.25 - $9.25
Credit Cards: All major
Specialties: Exotic pizzas, cheeseless pizzas, two crusts, honey, whole-wheat and white, baked in wood-fired ovens; pasta dishes, salads, sandwiches.

California Pizza Kitchen
Mirage
3400 Las Vegas Blvd. S.
Las Vegas, NV 89109
791-7111
Hours: Sun. - Thu. 11 am - midnight;
Fri. - Sat. 11 am - 2 am
Reservations: None
Dress: Casual
Price of Entrees: $8.00 - $11.00
Credit Cards: All major
Specialties: Unique wood-fired gourmet pizzas, pastas, sandwiches, salads and desserts.
Atmosphere: Contemporary decor; restaurant overlooks casino.

CAPOZZOLI'S
Restaurant & Lounge

Capozzoli's
3333 S. Maryland Pkwy.
Las Vegas, NV 89109
731-5311
Hours: 9:30 pm - 4 am
Reservations: Suggested
Dress: Casual
Price of Entrees: $6.95 - $14.95
Credit Cards: All major
Specialties: Italian specialties.
Atmosphere: Entertainment Fri. - Mon.

Carluccio's Tivoli Gardens
1775 E. Tropicana Ave.
Las Vegas, NV 89119
795-3236
Hours: Tue. - Sun. 4:30 pm - 10 pm
Reservations: None
Dress: Informal
Price of Entrees: $8.99 - $12.99

Credit Cards: MC, Visa, AMX
Specialties: Seafood diablo, veal Florentine, pastas, pizza (Sicilian-style), chicken piccata.
Atmosphere: Formerly Liberace's Tivoli Gardens, the lounge area has a room done entirely in mirrors, even the piano. Banquet facilities for 25 - 55.

Che' Pasta Ristorante
4350 E. Sunset Rd.
Henderson, NV 89014
435-0036
Hours: 5 pm - 10 pm
Reservations: None
Dress: Informal
Price of Entrees: $7.95 - $15.95
Credit Cards: All major
Specialties: Angel hair pasta pomodoro, spaghetti with meatballs, ravioli and lasagna. Innovative dishes such as rigatoni with broccoli, linguini verdura, eggplant cannelloni, and tortellini pascara. Chicken, shrimp and veal.
Atmosphere: Intimate casual dining. Che Pasta offers a full service bar and lounge at which you could enjoy a pre-dinner cocktail or a relaxing after dinner liquor with an espresso or cappuccino.

Chicago Joe's Restaurant
820 S. Fourth St.
Las Vegas, NV 89101
382-JOES 382-5637
Hours: Mon. - Fri. 11 am - 10 pm;
Sat. 5 pm - 10 pm
Reservations: Suggested
Dress: Informal
Price of Entrees: $7.95 - $19.95
Credit Cards: MC, Visa, AMX
Specialties: Our famous cream garlic dressing, mushroom cap escargot, stuffed artichokes, pasta fagioli, veal Angelo, cioppino shrimp Joe, chicken Vesuvio, shrimp and mushroom Alfredo, Chicago style lobster.
Atmosphere: Converted old house, like eating at Grandma's with her own recipes.

Cipriani
2790 E. Flamingo Rd.
Las Vegas, NV 89121
369-6711
Hours: Lunch Mon. - Fri. 11:30 am - 2 pm;
Dinner Mon. - Sat. 5:30 pm - 10 pm;
Sun. - call for hours.
Reservations: Recommended

Dress: Informal
Price of Entrees: $13.00 - $35.00;
Lunch $8.00 - $15.00
Credit Cards: MC, Visa, Discover, AMX, Diners
Specialties: One of 17 best restaurants in Las Vegas per *Travel Holiday* magazine. Angel hair pasta with seafood, veal Monte Bianco, chicken abruzzese, fettuccine with salmon, lamb chops. Banquet facilities to accommodate 100.
Atmosphere: Modern decor with an open display kitchen and tableside cooking. Located under the lighthouse on Flamingo Rd.

DaVinci's
Maxim
160 E. Flamingo Rd.
Las Vegas, NV 89109
731-4300
Hours: Tue. - Sat. - 6 pm - 11 pm
Reservations: Suggested
Dress: Informal - Semi-formal
Price of Entrees: $8.95 - $36.00
Credit Cards: All major
Specialties: Dover sole carved tableside, steak Diane, veal scaloppine, orange roughy, shrimp scampi, Italian dishes.

DiNapoli
Showboat
2800 E. Fremont St.
Las Vegas, NV 89104
385-9155
Hours: Wed. - Sun. 5 pm - 11 pm
Reservations: Recommended
Dress: Informal
Price of Entrees: $5.95 - $18.95
Credit Cards: All major
Specialties: Southern Italian cuisine. Lobster fra diavolo, veal marsala, smoked salmon, ravioli, pizzas. Sun. feast featuring a variety of dishes served family style. Parties of 4 or more $8.95 per person, served 4 pm - 10 pm
Atmosphere: With recipes from the southern Italian port of Naples, Di Napoli reflects Old Rome with its statues, floral fountains, domed ceiling and marble entry, murals and Roman columns.

Capozzoli's, 3333 S. Maryland Pkwy., Las Vegas, NV 89109

Fasolini's Pizza Cafe
222 S. Decatur Blvd.
Las Vegas, NV 89107
877-0071
Hours: Mon. - Sat. 9:30 am - 10 pm;
Sun. 5 pm - 10 pm
Reservations: None
Dress: Casual
Price of Entrees: $4.95 - $10.95
Credit Cards: All major
Specialties: Gourmet pizza, pastas.
Atmosphere: '50s-style diner, neon and
glass tiles.

Ferraro's
Stratosphere
2000 Las Vegas Blvd. S.
Las Vegas, NV 89104
382-4446 Extension 4859
Hours: 4 pm - midnight
Specialties: Penne amatriciana, fettucini
alla checca, seafood and chicken dishes.
Atmosphere: Guests will enjoy their
meals surrounded by Roman columns,
vaulted ceilings, and murals that provide a tasteful and relaxing setting for
the perfect dining experience.

Ferraro's Restaurant & Lounge
5900 W. Flamingo Rd.
Las Vegas, NV 89103
364-5300
Hours: Lunch Mon. - Fri. 11:30 am - 2:30 pm;
Dinner daily 5 pm - 11 pm
Reservations: Suggested
Dress: Informal
Price of Entrees: $13.00 - $28.00
Credit Cards: MC, Visa, AMX, Diners,
CB
Specialties: Southern Italian home-style
cooking; veal osso buco, zuppa di pesce,
potato dumpling gnocchi, linguine
Portofino as well as other pasta and
seafood dishes; music 6:30 - 11 pm;
banquet facilities for 66.
Atmosphere: Art deco elegant decor; out-
door patio dining.

Fortunato's Italian Restaurant
3430 E. Tropicana Ave.
Las Vegas, NV 89121
458-3333
Hours: Mon. - Fri. 11 am - 10 pm;
Sat. 4 pm - 10 pm; closed Sun.
Reservations: Suggested
Dress: Informal - Casual
Price of Entrees: $6.95 - $14.95
Credit Cards: All major
Specialties: Tortellini, cannelloni, fet-
tuccini carbonara, veal marsala; Italian
sandwiches.

Francesco's
Treasure Island
300 Las Vegas Blvd. S.
Las Vegas, NV 89109
894-7111
Hours: 5:30 pm - 11 pm
Reservations: Recommended
Dress: Casual elegant
Price of Entrees: $8.95 - $19.95
Specialties: Swordfish carpaccio,
sauteed scallops wrapped in prosciutto,
salmon and artichokes in a vodka cream
sauce.
Atmosphere: Casually elegant contain-
ing art by Pablo Picasso, Tony Bennett,
Phyllis Diller and Tony Curtis.

Gio's Cafe Milano
3900 Paradise Rd.
Las Vegas, NV 89109
732-2777
Hours: Lunch Mon. - Fri. 11 am - 3 pm;
Dinner Mon. - Sat. 5 pm - 10 pm
Reservations: Accepted - suggested on
weekends.
Dress: Informal
Price of Entrees: $9.50 - $19.95
Credit Cards: MC, Visa, Discover, AMX,
Diners
Specialties: Giovanni's own creative
Italian recipe is a must, plus all fresh
pastas al dente, fresh pomodoro and
basil as well as daily specials, fish, veal
and chicken dishes.
Atmosphere: Real Italian trattoria atmos-
phere. Very elegant but casual, small and
charming. Winner of many awards including
"Best of the Best," Five Star Diamond Award
from the Academy of Restaurant and
Hospitality Sciences and the Academy
Awards of the Restaurant and Hospitality
Industry. This award places it in the top 25
restaurants in its category in America.

Goomba's Pasta
2603 Windmill Pkwy.
Henderson, NV 89014
263-6363
Hours: 11 am - 9 pm
Reservations: None
Dress: Casual
Price of Entrees: $1.99 - $5.49
Specialties: Beef lasagna, vegetable
toss, manicott; value meals $3.99 -
$5.29; homemade pasta.

Grotto Trattoria
4866 W. Lone Mountain Rd.
Las Vegas, NV 89130
655-3200
Hours: Tue. - Thu. 11 am - 9 pm;
Fri. - Sat. 11 am - 10 pm;
Sun. - Mon. 4 pm - 9 pm
Reservations: Suggested
Dress: Casual
Price of Entrees: Reasonable
Credit Cards: MC, Visa, Discover
Specialties: Pork marsala, Grotto chicken.

Il Fornio
New York New York
3790 Las Vegas Blvd. S.
Las Vegas, NV 89109
740-6403
Hours: Sun. - Thu. 11:30 am - 11 pm;
Fri. - Sat. 11:30 am - midnight
Reservations: Recommended
Dress: Casual
Price of Entrees: $9.00 - $16.00
Credit Cards: All major
Specialties: Pizza from wood-burning
ovens, homemade and imported pastas.
Atmosphere: Authentic Italian restaurant
and bakery where a different chef creates
new and exciting menus monthly, highlighting a single region of Italy. The bakery produces authentic Italian goodies
ranging from breads and rolls to a wide
variety of wonderful cakes, pastries, and
cookies matched only by those produced
in New York's Little Italy.
Atmosphere: Enjoy watching your meals
masterfully created in an exhibition-
style kitchen.

**Italian American Supper Club
of Southern Nevada**
2333 E. Sahara Ave.
Las Vegas, NV 89104
457-3866
Hours: Wed. - Sun. 5 pm - 10 pm
Reservations: Suggested
Dress: Casual
Price of Entrees: $6.95 - $14.95
Credit Cards: MC, Visa
Specialties: Chicken Angelo, scampi,
fettuccine carbonara. Banquet, wedding
and party accommodations for 300; bar
area.

Kitchen Cafe
4850 W. Flamingo Rd.
Las Vegas, NV 89103
222-0880
Hours: 11 am - 11 pm
Reservations: None
Dress: Casual
Price of Entrees: $9.95 - $15.95
Credit Cards: All major
Specialties: Fresh salmon, chicken
Angelo, blackened pork chops, halibut,
clams, pasta, pork chops, steaks and
seafood, Greek specialties.
Atmosphere: Casual cafe.

Lance-A-Lotta Pasta
Excalibur
3850 Las Vegas Blvd. S.
Las Vegas, NV 89101
597-7777
Hours: Lunch Sat. - Sun. 11 am - 2:30 pm;
Dinner Sun. - Thu. 5 pm - 11 pm;
Fri. - Sat. 5 pm - midnight
Reservations: None
Dress: Casual
Price of Entrees: Lunch $4.95 - $6.95;
dinner $7.95 - $15.95
Credit Cards: All major
Specialties: Pastas in a variety of styles
and sauces, lasagna, fettuccine Alfredo;
live music 5 pm - 11 pm, except Wed.

La Bella Pasta
Nevada Palace
5255 Boulder Hwy.
Las Vegas, NV 89122
458-8810
Hours: Sun. - Thu. 3 pm - 9 pm;
Fri. - Sat. 4 pm - 10 pm
Reservations: None
Dress: Casual
Price of Entrees: $6.95 - $13.95
includes salad bar
Credit Cards: All major
Specialties: Italian; breakfast buffet
Sat. - Sun. 8 am - noon $3.99.

La Strada Italian Restaurant
4640 Paradise Rd.
Las Vegas, NV 89109
735-0150
Hours: Daily 5:30 pm - 10 pm; closed Mon.
Reservations: Required
Dress: Informal
Price of Entrees: $16.95 - $25.95
Credit Cards: MC, Visa, AMX
Specialties: Osso buco, rack of lamb,
fresh seafood, steaks, pasta, veal, chicken,
homemade bread, stuffed artichokes.
Atmosphere: Live piano music Fri. and
Sat. 7 pm - 11 pm.

Mama Marie's
CUCINA

Mama Maria's Cucina
Rio
3700 W. Flamingo Rd.
Las Vegas, NV 89103
252-7777
Hours: 11 am - 11 pm
Reservations: None
Dress: Casual
Price of Entrees: $2.95 - $13.95
Credit Cards: All major
Specialties: Penne arrabiata, chicken
parmigiana, scampi.
Atmosphere: Authentic Italian specialties
are prepared from scratch featuring
family style service in warm
Mediterranean surroundings.

Marco Polo
Lady Luck
206 N. Third St.
Las Vegas, NV 89101
477-3000
Hours: Thu. - Mon. 4 pm - 11 pm
Reservations: Required
Dress: Casual
Credit Cards: All major
Price of Entrees: $12 - $15
Specialties: Seafood, linguini, bottom-
less spaghetti bowl and fresh pasta
cooked to order.
Atmosphere: Very intimate and cozy.
Seats 46; fine table-side service.

Mediterranean Room
Gold Coast
4000 W. Flamingo Rd.
Las Vegas, NV 89103
367-7111
Hours: 5 pm - 11 pm
Reservations: None
Dress: Casual
Price of Entrees: $4.95 - $25.95
Specialties: Fresh seafood and Italian
specialty dishes.
Atmosphere: Delightful Mediterranean
dining.

Milano's
3111 S. Valley View Blvd.
Las Vegas, NV 89102
876-0857
Hours: Mon. - Sat. 9 am - 9 pm; closed Sun.
Reservations: None
Dress: Casual
Price of Entrees: Inexpensive
Credit Cards: None
Specialties: Pizza, lasagna, spaghetti, ravioli.

Mortoni's
Hard Rock Hotel
4455 Paradise Rd.
Las Vegas, NV 89109
693-5000
Hours: 6 pm - 11 pm
Reservations: Preferred
Dress: Informal
Price of Entrees: $6.50 - $24.95
Credit Cards: All major
Atmosphere: Intimate, elegant dining.

DINING

RESTAURANTS - Ethnic

New York Pasta Co.
8427 W. Lake Mead Blvd.
Las Vegas, NV 89128
228-1338
Victor Williams
Hours: 5 pm - 10 pm
Reservations: None
Dress: Casual
Price of Entrees: $7.95 - $13.95
Credit Cards: All major
Specialties: Sausage and peppers, egg-plant cannelloni, veal parmigiana, scampi.
Atmosphere: Casual, intimate dining in a family oriented restaurant with lovely warehouse decor.

Nicky Blair's
3925 Paradise Rd.
Las Vegas, NV 89109
792-9900
Hours: 5 pm - 11 pm
Reservations: Suggested
Dress: Casual elegant
Price of Entrees: $13.50 - $28
Specialties: Northern and Continental cuisine. Petti di pollo, osso buco, piccata al Limone, salmone Grigliato.
Atmosphere: Beautiful decor with fireplace, piano, cigar room and banquet room.

Nora's Cuisine
6020 W. Flamingo Ave.
Las Vegas, NV 89103
873-8990
Hours: Mon. - Sat. 11 am - 2:30 pm & 4:30 pm - 10 pm
Reservations: Suggested
Dress: Casual
Price of Entrees: Reasonable
Credit Cards: None
Specialties: Chicken with artichokes, pizza

North Beach Cafe
2605 S. Decatur Blvd.
Las Vegas, NV 89102
247-9530
Hours: Mon. - Sat. 11:30 am - 10 pm; Sun. 5 pm - 10 pm
Reservations: Accepted
Dress: Casual
Price of Entrees: $9.75 - $17.50
Credit Cards: MC, Visa, AMX, Discover, Diners, CB
Specialties: Linguine pescatore, penne alla vodka, agnolotti alla crema, spaghettini al pesto. Fresh fish daily – ahi tuna, swordfish, salmon, scampi. Filet mignon, veal and chicken.
Atmosphere: Casual, quaint, cozy. Patio dining also available. Banquet room; live music Wed. - Sun.

Olive Garden Italian Restaurant
(Multiple locations listed below)
Hours: Sun. - Thu. 11 am - 10 pm; Fri. - Sat. 11 am - 11 pm
Reservations: None, except for parties of 6 or more persons
Dress: Casual - Informal
Price of Entrees: $7.75 - $13.25
Credit Cards: All major
Specialties: Lasagna, eggplant parmigiana, steak Tuscany, Venetian grilled chicken, linguine with clam sauce, shrimp primavera; children's plates $2.95

for spaghetti and $3.50 for lasagna; unlimited breadsticks and salad or soup are served with all entrees; lunch served daily starting at $4.95.
Atmosphere: Italian dinner house with a festive atmosphere serving freshly prepared Italian specialties.

1545 E. Flamingo Rd.
Las Vegas, NV 89119
735-0082

1361 S. Decatur Blvd.
Las Vegas, NV 89102
258-3453

6850 W. Cheyenne Ave.
Las Vegas, NV 89108
658-2144

80 N. Nellis Blvd.
Las Vegas, NV 89110
438-0082

4400 E. Sunset Rd.
Henderson, NV 89014
451-5133

P J Russo Inc.
2300 S. Maryland Pkwy.
Las Vegas, NV 89104
735-1264 735-5454
Hours: Mon. - Fri. 10 am - 3 am; Sat. and Sun. 5 pm - 3 am
Reservations: None
Dress: Casual
Price of Entrees: $5.00 - $7.00
Credit Cards: MC, Visa, AMX
Specialties: Homemade lasagna, New York steak and shrimp, homemade eggplant dinner.
Atmosphere: Casual

Panini
4811 S. Rainbow Blvd.
Las Vegas, NV 89103
365-8300
Hours: Mon. - Fri. 11 am - 10:30 pm; Sat. and Sun. 5 pm - 10:30 pm
Reservations: None
Dress: Casual
Price of Entrees: $8.50 - $21.95
Specialties: Salads, pastas, pizza made in a wood-burning oven.

Papamios Italian Kitchen
Sam's Town
5111 Boulder Hwy.
Las Vegas, NV 89122
454-8041
Hours: Sun. - Thu. 5 pm - 10 pm; Fri. - Sat. 5 pm - 11 pm; Sun. brunch 9 am - 2 pm
Reservations: Recommended
Dress: Casual
Price of Entrees: $5.95 - $14.00
Credit Cards: All major
Specialties: Old World and contemporary cuisine, exhibition cooking.
Atmosphere: Casual courtyard setting offers tables with a view of the spectacular waterfalls of the indoor park. Buy one entree on your birthday and get a Pasta al Dente entree of equal or lesser value absolutely free along with a Papamios T-shirt.

Pasta Mombasa at Reserve Hotel
777 W. Lake Mead Blvd., Henderson, NV

Paradise Italian Bistro
3900 Paradise Rd.
Las Vegas, NV 89109
791-5161
Hours: Mon. - Fri. 11:30 am - 2:30 pm & 5 pm - 11 pm; Sat. 5 pm - 11 pm
Reservations: Suggested
Dress: Casual
Price of Entrees: $10.00 - $25.00
Credit Cards: All major
Specialties: Osso buco, tuna ala Livornese, rack of lamb with chianti sauce.
Atmosphere: Relaxed and intimate; open view with lots of greenery.

Parma Ristorante
1750 S. Rainbow Blvd.
Las Vegas, NV 89108
258-0680
Hours: 5 pm - 10 pm
Reservations: Accepted
Dress: Informal
Price of Entrees: $9.95 - $18.95
Credit Cards: MC, Visa, AMX, Diners
Specialties: Chicken Romano, chicken Vesuvio, linguine fruta di mare, veal champagna, veal Florentine salta in boca, spaghetti a la parma, linguine with white clam sauce.
Atmosphere: Old Italy decor; very relaxed atmosphere; booths, paintings, fountains and soft lighting; small lounge.

Pasta Mia
2585 E. Flamingo Rd.
Las Vegas, NV 89121
733-0091
Hours: Mon. - Fri. 11:30 am - 9:30 pm; Sat. - Sun. 4 pm - 9:30 pm
Reservations: None
Dress: Casual
Price of Entrees: $8.50 - $13.95
Credit Cards: MC, Visa, Discover
Specialties: Linguine with fresh clams or mussels, chicken Vesuvio, calamari, angel hair with plum tomatoes, stuffed artichokes; fresh antipasto displayed in case; wine and beer.

Pasta Mia West
4455 W. Flamingo Rd.
Las Vegas, NV 89103
251-8871
Hours: 11 am - 10 pm
Reservations: None
Dress: Casual
Price of Entrees: $8.50 - $13.95
Credit Cards: MC, Visa, AMX

Specialties: Pasta with broccoli DiRabe, linguine with fresh clams or mussels, chicken Vesuvio, calamari, angel hair with plum tomatoes; fresh antipasto displayed in case; wine and beer; banquet facilities for 65.
Atmosphere: Black and white decor; patio dining.

Pasta Mombasa
Reserve Hotel
777 W. Lake Mead Blvd.
Henderson, NV 89015
558-7000
Hours: 5 pm - 10 pm
Reservations: Recommended
Dress: informal
Price of Entrees: $6.75 - $18.95
Credit Cards: All major
Specialties: Homemade pastas, steak pizzaiola, chicken piccata, grilled lamb chops, salmon Tuscano and pizza.
Atmosphere: Indoors with an outdoor cafe setting.

Pasta Palace
Boulder Station
4111 Boulder Hwy.
Las Vegas, NV 89121
432-7777
Hours: 5 pm - 10 pm
Reservations: Suggested
Dress: Casual
Price of Entrees: $6.50 - $18
Credit Cards: All major
Specialties: Complete dinners with free carafe of wine $8.95.

Pasta Palace
Palace Station
2411 W. Sahara Ave.
Las Vegas, NV 89102
367-2411
Hours: 5 pm - 11 pm
Reservations: Suggested
Dress: Casual
Price of Entrees: $5.95 - $10.95
Credit Cards: All major
Specialties: Pastas, seafood, veal, poultry. Pizza cooked in wood-burning oven.
Specials: "Mangiamo Insieme" - Shared dining, created just for you, in order to give guests a chance to enjoy a variety of delicious foods created by the chefs at Pasta Palace.
When you order your entree, it is served in two to three portions on a platter, allowing your dining partner to share the dish with you and for you to add variety to your meal by doing the same. Of course, please enjoy all that you wish of their famous Pasta Palace salad along with house specialty pasta made with homemade marinara sauce.
Atmosphere: Old Italian railroad artifacts.

Pasta Pirate
California Hotel
1212 Ogden Ave.
Las Vegas, NV 89101
385-1222
Hours: Sun. - Thu. 5:30 pm - 11 pm
Reservations: Suggested
Dress: Informal
Price of Entrees: $16 - $24
Credit Cards: All major
Specialties: Pastas, fresh fish, Alaskan king crab, steamed clams, mahi mahi, filet mignon, surf and turf.
Atmosphere: Chefs prepare your entree on a glass-enclosed mesquite grill.

Pasta Remo
San Remo
115 E. Tropicana Ave.
Las Vegas, NV 89109
739-9000
Hours: 5 pm - midnight
Reservations: Suggested on weekends
Dress: Informal
Price of Entrees: $8.95 - $16.95
Credit Cards: All major
Specialties: Calamari marinati, veal scaloppine, cannelloni, steamed clams.
Atmosphere: Casual and intimate; Authentic Italian artwork.

The Pasta Shop Restaurant
2495 E. Tropicana Ave.
Las Vegas, NV 89121
451-1893
Hours: 5 pm - 9 pm
Reservations: Suggested
Dress: Casual
Price of Entrees: $9.50 - $17.95
Credit Cards: MC, Visa, AMX
Specialties: Gourmet pastas; black pasta - tiger shrimp in saffron creme sauce, basil pasta, fettuccini teatro, linguine in clam sauce, fresh seafood and chicken specialties; watch pasta being made fresh daily; pasta by the pound to take home.
Atmosphere: Cozy and romantic.

Piero's Italian Cuisine & New England Fish Mkt.
355 Convention Center Dr.
Las Vegas, NV 89109
369-2305
Hours: 5:30 pm - 9:30 pm
Reservations: Suggested
Dress: Informal - Semi-formal
Price of Entrees: $17 - $55
Credit Cards: All major
Specialties: Famous for their osso buco; Maine lobster, pastas, fresh fish, provimi veal, calamari; extensive wine list; lounge; banquet room seats up to 250; valet parking.

Pizza Palace
Imperial Palace
3535 Las Vegas Blvd. S.
Las Vegas, NV 89109
731-3311
Hours: 11 am - midnight
Reservations: None
Dress: Casual
Price of Entrees: Inexpensive
Credit Cards: All major

Pizzeria Uno Restaurant & Bar
2540 S. Decatur Blvd.
Las Vegas, NV 89102
876-8667
Hours: 11 am - midnight
Reservations: None
Dress: Casual
Price of Entrees: $5.95 - $8.95
Credit Cards: All major
Specialties: 200-seat contemporary

restaurant features original Chicago-style deep dish pizza, pizza available by the slice, appetizers, salads, pastas, sandwiches, chicken entrees, steak fajitas and desserts. Weekday lunch special served 11 am - 3 pm for $4.95 includes an individual-sized pizza and soup or salad, served in five minutes. Delivery available.
Atmosphere: Outdoor patio.

Portofino
Desert Inn
3145 Las Vegas Blvd. S.
Las Vegas, NV 89109
733-4495
Hours: 6 pm - 11 pm
Reservations: Suggested
Dress: Semi-formal
Price of Entrees: $12 - $33
Credit Cards: All major
Specialties: Lobster, osso buco, rack of lamb, channel catfish, chateaubriand, veal marsala
Atmosphere: Located on the second floor of the hotel, the restaurant offers a view from the glass-enclosed room to the action in the casino below. The elegant setting features large velvet booths and a subtle old-world charm.

Restaurant Pietro
Tropicana Hotel
3801 Las Vegas Blvd. S.
Las Vegas, NV 89109
739-2341
Hours: 5 pm - 11 pm
Reservations: Suggested
Dress: Casual
Price of Entrees: $20 - $32
Credit Cards: All major
Specialties: Veal Pietro
Atmosphere: Small and quaint, taped instrumental music.

Ristorante Italiano
Riviera
2901 Las Vegas Blvd. S.
Las Vegas, NV 89109
794-9363
Hours: Fri. - Tue. 5:30 pm - 11 pm
Reservations: Suggested
Dress: Informal - Semi-formal
Price of Entrees: $8.95 - $32
Credit Cards: All major
Specialties: Northern and Southern Italian cuisines. Veal piccata or scaloppine, steak ala pizzaiola, osso buco. Pastas made fresh daily.
Atmosphere: A quiet and elegant restaurant capturing the charm of Italy in both ambience and cuisine.

Ristorante Riva
The Mirage
3400 Las Vegas Blvd. S.
Las Vegas, NV 89109
791-7111
Hours: 5:30 pm - 11 pm
Reservations: Required
Dress: Semi-formal
Price of Entrees: $14 - $50
Credit Cards: All major
Specialties: Pastas, cioppino, broiled salmon, veal scallopini.

RESTAURANTS - Ethnic

Romano's Macaroni Grill
2400 W. Sahara Ave.
Las Vegas, NV 89102
248-9500
Hours: Sun. - Thu. 11 am - 10 pm;
Sat. 11 am - 11 pm
Reservations: Suggested
Dress: Casual
Price of Entrees: $10 - $20
Credit Cards: All major
Specialties: Pasta of the day, fish and pizza.

San Genero Cafe
6870 Spring Mountain Rd., Ste. 9
Las Vegas, NV 89102
222-3602
Hours: Mon. - Thu. 11:30 am - 10 pm;
Fri. 11:30 am - 11 pm; Sat. 4 pm - 11 pm;
Sun. 4 pm - 10 pm
Reservations: Suggested
Dress: Casual
Price of Entrees: $8.95 - $24.95
Credit Cards: MC, Visa, AMX
Specialties: Osso buco, pasta Norma, veal chops.
Atmosphere: Comfortable; live music nightly.

San Lorenzo
Texas
3141 N. Rancho Dr.
Las Vegas, NV 89130
631-1000
Hours: Sun. - Thu. 5 pm - 10:30 pm
Fri. - Sat. 5 pm - 11 pm
Reservations: Suggested
Dress: Casual
Price of Entrees: $7.95 and up
Credit Cards: All major
Specialties: Cannelloni Florentine, scampi, al forno di giorno, Francese, spaghetti, chicken marsala, orange roughy meuniere, tiramisu.
Atmosphere: Restaurant or sidewalk cafe.

Sergio's Italian Gardens of Las Vegas
1955 E. Tropicana Ave.
Las Vegas, NV 89119
739-1544
Hours: 5:30 pm - 11 pm
Reservations: Suggested
Dress: Informal
Price of Entrees: $9.95 - $24.50
Credit Cards: All major
Specialties: Osso buco, swordfish, linguine with live Maine lobster, Dover sole, Alaskan king crab legs; full service bar with large selection of wines; banquet facilities to accommodate 70.
Atmosphere: A unique, beautiful indoor garden atmosphere with waterfalls, murals, textured concrete floors, french doors and patio seating; piano lounge.

Sfuzzi
Fashion Show Mall
3200 Las Vegas Blvd. S.
Las Vegas, NV 89109
699-5777
Hours: 11 am - 10 pm
Reservations: Suggested
Dress: Informal

Price of Entrees: $14.95 and up, a la carte
Credit Cards: Visa, MC, AMX, Diners
Specialties: Tuscan Italian cuisine, Romano crusted chicken breast.
Atmosphere: Romantic; patio dining; Mediterranean decor.

Stefano's

Stefano's
Golden Nugget
129 Fremont St.
Las Vegas, NV 89101
385-7111
Hours: 6 pm - 11 pm
Reservations: Required
Dress: Semi-formal
Price of Entrees: $10 - $25, a la carte
Credit Cards: All major
Specialties: Chicken Sorrentino, veal piccata, scampi fra diavolo, fresh fish, linguine.
Atmosphere: Friendly, romantic hospitality of the Italian countryside. The staff breaks into song every hour.

Stivali Ristorante
Circus Circus
2880 Las Vegas Blvd. S.
Las Vegas, NV 89109
734-0410
Hours: 5 pm - 11 pm
Reservations: Not required
Dress: Informal
Price of Entree: $7.95 - $20.95
Credit Cards: All major
Specialties: All pasta dishes, seafood Stivali, osso buco, single or double lobster tail and pizza.

Strings Italian Cafe
2222 E. Tropicana Ave.
Las Vegas, NV 89119
739-6400
Hours: Mon. - Thu. 11 am - 10 pm;
Fri. 10 am - 10 pm; Sat. - Sun. noon - 10 pm
Reservations: Suggested
Dress: Casual
Price of Entrees: $3.95 - $10.95
Credit Cards: All major
Specialties: Award winning dishes, lasagna pastry, tortelli alla panna.
Atmosphere: Semi-exhibition kitchen, elegant wooded winecases; bright and homey.

Terrazza
Caesars Palace
3570 Las Vegas Blvd. S.
Las Vegas, NV 89109
731-7568
Hours: Wed. - Sun. 11:30 - 2:30 pm; Dinner 5:30 pm - 11 pm every day
Reservations: Recommended
Dress: Dressy casual
Price of Entrees: $14.50 - $36
Credit Cards: All major
Specialties: Risotto, veal chop, pizzas and focaccias from wood burning oven, pasta and seafood.
Atmosphere: Rustic country Italian sectioned into four areas near the pool with terrace seating. Beautiful and elegant.

Ti Amo
Santa Fe
4949 N. Rancho Dr.
Las Vegas, NV 89130
658-4900
Hours: Wed. - Sat. 5 pm - 11 pm
Reservations: None
Price of Entrees: $5.95 - $28.95
Credit Cards: All major
Specialties: Homemade pizza from wood fired stoves, cioppino; Sun. Italian champagne brunch 11 am - 7 pm $12.95 with live jazz music.
Atmosphere: Courtyard setting.

Tiffany's
Boulder Dam Hotel
1305 Arizona St.
Boulder City, NV 89005
294-1666
Hours: Lunch Mon. - Fri. 11 am - 2 pm; dinner daily 4 pm - 10 pm
Reservations: Suggested
Dress: Casual
Price of Entrees: $9.50 - $22.95
Credit Cards: All major
Specialties: Pasta, chicken, veal, steak and seafood dishes. Veal osso buco, Mediterranean-style salmon, foccia. All of the 24 entrees are served with warm garlic bread with olive oil for dipping.
Atmosphere: Intimate 68-seat restaurant.

Tomatoes Cafe
4250 S. Rainbow Blvd.
Las Vegas, NV 89117
871-1081
Hours: Mon. - Thu. 11 am - 9 pm;
Fri. - Sat. 11 am - 10 pm; Sun. 5 pm - 9 pm
Reservations: None
Dress: Casual
Price of Entrees: Everything under $15
Credit Cards: All major
Specialties: Pasta, chicken marsala, salmon, wood-fired pizza and salads.

Tre Visi Cafe
MGM Grand
3799 Las Vegas Blvd. S.
Las Vegas, NV 89109
891-7777
Hours: 11 am - 1 am
Reservations: Suggested
Dress: Informal
Price of Entrees: $12.95 - $45
Credit Cards: All major
Specialties: Ravioli stuffed with crab meat, grilled veal with roasted potatoes and shallots, lamb shanks with wine sauce.
Atmosphere: Though indoors, it gives the feeling of being on a Mediterranean patio.

Venetian Ristorante
3713 W. Sahara Ave.
Las Vegas, NV 89117
876-4190
Hours: 24
Reservations: Suggested
Dress: Informal
Price of Entrees: $7.95 - $34.95
Credit Cards: All major

Specialties: Sauteed Venetian greens, white lemon pizza, pork neck bones, grilled halibut, chicken Angelo, all served with a side of pasta. Entrees can be ordered a la carte or as complete dinner; extensive wine list; catering and banquet facilities; take-out and delivery, phone 735-FOOD.
Atmosphere: Venice scenes and paintings both inside and outside. Although at the present location since 1966, the restaurant has been in operation in Las Vegas since 1955.

Vesuvio
1020 E. Desert Inn Rd.
Las Vegas, NV 89109
735-1170
Hours: 5 pm - 10 pm
Reservations: Suggested
Dress: Informal
Price of Entrees: $9.50 - $19.95
Credit Cards: All major
Specialties: Italian and Continental specialties; fresh Florida stone crabs, osso buco, cioppino, swordfish with capers, veal scaloppine and homemade pastas, chicken Vesuvio, fresh seafood.

Vincenzo's
Fitzgeralds
301 Fremont St.
Las Vegas, NV 89101
388-2400
Hours: Lunch Tue. - Fri. 11 am - 3 pm; Dinner Mon. - Sat. 4 pm - 10 pm
Reservations: Recommended
Dress: Informal
Price: $7.95 - $18.95
Credit Cards: All major
Specialties: Shrimp scampi, grilled salmon, fettuccine
Atmosphere: Candle-lit cafe.

Vito's Italian Restaurant
The Orleans
4500 W. Tropicana Ave.
Las Vegas, NV 89103
365-7111
Hours: 5 pm - 10:30 pm
Reservations: None
Dress: Casual
Price of Entrees: $6.95 - $24.95
Credit Cards: All major
Specialties: Pizza, daily specials, scampi, osso buco.
Atmosphere: Mediterranean, complete with pillars and Italian paintings.

Wolfgang Puck Cafe
MGM Grand
3799 Las Vegas Blvd. S.
Las Vegas, NV 89109
891-3019
Hours: Sun. - Thu. 8 am - 11 pm;
Fri. - Sat. 8 am - midnight
Reservations: None
Dress: Casual
Price of Entrees: $10 - $20
Credit Cards: All major
Specialties: Pizza, pasta, rotisserie chicken, salads, desserts.
Atmosphere: Circular restaurant decorated with brightly colored signature mosaic tiled booths which surround the open kitchen area.

JAPANESE

BENIHANA
THE JAPANESE STEAKHOUSE

Benihana Village
Las Vegas Hilton
3000 Paradise Rd.
Las Vegas, NV 89109
732-5801
Hours: 5 pm - 11 pm
Reservations: Suggested
Dress: Informal
Price of Entrees: $14.95 - $35.50
Credit Cards: All major
Specialties: In the Hibachi room, chefs prepare shrimp, chicken, steak and vegetables in front of guests on hot tables. In the new Benihana Seafood Grille a variety of sashimi and sushi appetizers are offered in addition to the tempura dinners and specialties from the deep including halibut, salmon, prawns, lobster calamari, crab and more.
Atmosphere: The facade to Benihana Village features special effects that include storms with thunder, lightning and rain as well as the relaxing sounds of crickets and frogs.

Dragon Sushi
4115 Spring Mountain Rd.
Las Vegas, NV 89102
368-4328
Hours: Sun. - Thu. 11:30 am - 10:30 pm;
Fri. - Sat. 11:30 am - 12 am
Credit Cards: MC, Visa, AMX, Discover
Price of Entrees: Inexpensive
Specialties: Sushi

Fuji Japanese Restaurant
3430 E. Tropicana Ave.
Las Vegas, NV 89121
435-8838
Ken Tsuti, Owner, Mgr.
Hours: Tue. - Sat. 4:30 pm - 10:30 pm;
Sun. 4:30 pm - 10 pm; closed Mon.
Reservations: Accepted
Dress: Casual - Informal
Price of Entrees: $6.95 - $15.95
Credit Cards: All major
Specialties: Sushi, shrimp tempura, sukiyaki and teriyaki; Combination dinners.

GINZA
JAPANESE CUISINE
SUSHI BAR

Ginza Restaurant
1000 E. Sahara Ave.
Las Vegas, NV 89104
732-3080
Hours: noon - 10 pm
Reservations: Accepted
Dress: Informal
Price of Entrees: $8 - $14
Credit Cards: All major
Specialties: Sushi bar and dining room; shrimp tempura, beef teriyaki, sukiyaki, yosenabe.

Kabuki Japanese Restaurant, 1150 E. Twain Ave., Las Vegas, NV 89109

Geisha Steak House
3751 E. Desert Inn Rd.
Las Vegas, NV 89121
451-9814
Hours: Tue. - Sun. 5 pm - 11 pm;
Reservations: Accepted
Dress: Informal
Price of Entrees: $10.95 - $22.95
Credit Cards: MC, Visa, AMX, Discover
Specialties: Lobster, scallops, shrimp, tempura, complete hibachi dinners.

Hakase Japanese Cuisine
3900 Paradise Rd.
Las Vegas, NV 89109
796-1234
Hours: Lunch Tue. - Fri. noon - 2:30 pm;
Dinner Sun., Tue. - Fri. 5 pm - 10:30 pm;
Sat. 5 pm - 10 pm; Closed Mon.
Reservations: Suggested-required weekends
Dress: Informal
Price of Entrees: $10.00 - $25.00
Credit Cards: MC, Visa, AMX, Diners, Discover
Specialties: Sushi bar, tatami room, teppan grill, sukiyaki, tempura; kimono-clad servers.
Atmosphere: Tatami Room, sit on mats.

Hamada of Japan
598 E. Flamingo Rd.
Las Vegas, NV 89119
733-3005
Hours: 5 pm - midnight;
sushi bar 5 pm - 2 am
Reservations: Suggested
Dress: Informal
Price of Entrees: $10 - $35
Credit Cards: All major
Specialties: Sushi bar, teppan grill, sukiyaki dining room, tenzaru, tonkatsu, beef sukiyaki, donburi.

Hamada of Japan
3743 Las Vegas Blvd. S.
Las Vegas, NV 89109
736-1984
Hours: 11 am - midnight
Reservations: Suggested
Dress: Informal
Price of Entrees: $11.00 - $30.00
Credit Cards: All major
Specialties: sushi bar only; also Japanese cuisine.

Hamada of Japan
Flamingo Hilton
3555 Las Vegas Blvd. S.

Las Vegas, NV 89109
733-3333
Hours: 5 pm - 12:30 am
Reservations: None
Dress: Informal
Price of Entrees: $11.50 - $42
Credit Cards: All major
Specialties: Fresh fish; Japanese beers, steak house and sushi bar.
Atmosphere: An intimate setting with elegant decorations. The quiet atmosphere has the feel of an authentic Japanese home.

Hibachi San
3480 S. Maryland Pkwy.
Las Vegas, NV 89109
731-2271
Hours: Mon. - Fri. 10 am - 9 pm;
Sat. 10 am - 8 pm; Sun. 11 am - 6 pm
Price of Entrees: Everything under $6
Credit Cards: None
Specialties: Combination platters, traditional Japanese menu.

Hyakumi Restaurant
Caesar's Palace
3570 Las Vegas Blvd. S.
Las Vegas, NV 89109
731-7731
Hours: 5 pm - 11 pm
Reservations: Required
Dress: Informal
Price: $54 - $64
Specialties: Sushi bar, seating at teppan table or order from menu a la carte or combination plate. Seafood specialties. Chef Hiroji Obayashi is one of the premiere ambassadors of Japanese cuisine and has won many awards.
Atmosphere: Dimly lit, resembling old Japanese village.

Kabocha Restaurant
4503 Paradise Rd.
Las Vegas, NV 89109
733-6616
Hours: Lunch Mon. - Sat. 11 am - 2:30 pm;
Dinner 6 pm - 2 am; Sun. 11 am - 3 pm
Reservations: None
Dress: Casual
Price of Entrees: $7.50 - $30
Credit Cards: MC, Visa, Diners, CB
Specialties: Curried dishes, gyoza, ramen and authentic Japanese appetizers; sushi to go.

Atmosphere: Japanese style coffee shop with jigsaw puzzle pictures. Laser karaoke (English & Japanese songs) 9 pm - 2 am.

Kabuki Japanese Restaurant
1150 E. Twain Ave.
Las Vegas, NV 89109
733-0066
Hours: Mon. - Sat. Lunch 11:30 am - 2 pm;
Dinner 5 pm - 10 pm
Reservations: Accepted
Dress: Casual
Price of Entrees: $9.75 - $17.95
Credit Cards: MC, Visa, AMX, Discover
Specialties: Sushi bar, tempura, teriyaki.

Kifune Restaurant
2202 W. Charleston Blvd.
Las Vegas, NV 89102
366-9119
Hours: Lunch Mon. - Fri. 11:30 am - 2:30 pm; Dinner Mon. - Sat. 5 pm - 10 pm; closed Sun.
Reservations: None
Dress: Casual
Price of Entrees: $8.75 - $12.95
Credit Cards: MC, Visa, AMX, Discover
Specialties: Teriyaki chicken, sushi bar, tempura, sake.
Atmosphere: Kimono-clad waitresses and Japanese music in a traditional setting.

Kimchee Hut
2537 S. Fort Apache Rd.
Las Vegas, NV 89117
228-2001
Hours: Mon. - Sat. 10 am - 10 pm;
Sun. 3:30 pm - 9 pm
Reservations: None
Dress: Casual
Price of Entrees: $4.49 - $5.99
Credit Cards: None
Specialties: Teriyaki BBQ, stir fry, kimchee; charbroiled and marinated foods; Korean food; value meal $7.49 includes drink and salad or soup.

Mask
Rio
3700 W. Flamingo Rd.
Las Vegas, NV 89013
252-7777
Hours: 5 pm - 11 pm
Reservations: Suggested
Dress: Casual - elegant
Price of Entrees: $8.95 - $55
Credit Cards: All major
Specialties: Japanese, Thai, and teppan delicacies expertly prepared and creatively served in a soothing traditional Eastern setting.

Mijori Japanese & Korean Restaurant
953 E. Sahara Ave.
Las Vegas, NV 89104
369-6250
Hours: Thu. - Tue. 11 am - 11 pm;
Wed. 5 pm - 11 pm
Reservations: Suggested
Dress: Casual
Price of Entrees: $7.95 - $13.95
Credit Cards: MC, Visa, AMX, Discover
Specialties: Chicken teriyaki, Korean BBQ fried shrimp, tempura.
Atmosphere: Sushi bar.

DINING

RESTAURANTS - Ethnic

Mikado
Mirage
3400 Las Vegas Blvd. S.
Las Vegas, NV 89109
791-7111
Hours: 6 pm - 11 pm
Reservations: Required
Dress: Semi-formal
Price of Entrees: $16 - $40
Credit Cards: All major
Specialties: Hibachi tables, sushi, "teppan-yaki" style lobster, steak, chicken and shrimp. A complete selection of specially prepared entrees is also available from an a la carte menu as well as a sushi bar in the garden area which offers an appetizing prelude to dinner.
Atmosphere: The experience of Mikado suggests the quiet elegance of a private Japanese home. With its placid streams, delicate gardens and exquisite murals, Mikado offers the pleasant balance of formality and informality that characterizes Japanese style.

Mikado Express
(Multiple locations & hours listed below)
Reservations: None
Dress: Casual
Price of Entrees: $2.95 - $6.00
Credit Cards: None
Specialties: Teriyaki bowls, sushi, chicken and beef lo mein; Thai style spicy chicken and beef satay; delivery available at Flamingo location.

845 S. Rainbow Blvd.
Las Vegas, NV 89128
878-3450
Hours: Mon. - Fri. 11 am - 9 pm;
Sat. noon - 9 pm

1350 E. Flamingo Rd.
Las Vegas, NV 89119
733-1930
Hours: 11 am - 8 pm

Mizuno's Teppan Dining
Tropicana
3801 Las Vegas Blvd. S.
Las Vegas, NV 89109
739-2713
Hours: 5 pm - 10:45 pm
Reservations: Suggested
Dress: Informal
Price of Entrees: $10.95 - $35
Credit Cards: All major
Specialties: Hibachi table; tempura, shrimp, lobster, steak and chicken.
Atmosphere: Enjoy watching the chef cook right at your table.

Monorail Sushi
3645 Las Vegas Blvd. S.
Las Vegas, NV 89109
891-8626
Hours: 11 am - midnight
Price of Entrees: Inexpensive
Credit Cards: MC, Visa, AMX
Specialties: Tempura, sushi

Nippon
101 Convention Center Dr.
Las Vegas, NV 89109
735-5565
Hours: 11:30 am - 2:30 pm & 5:30 pm - 10:30 pm; Sat. 6 pm - 10 pm
Reservations: Suggested
Dress: Informal

Price of Entrees: Combination dinners $16.95
Credit Cards: All major
Specialties: Shrimp tempura, Shabu-Shabu Bar; 15-seat sushi bar. Tatami room available for small parties. Karaoke Sat. 10 pm - 2 am

Shiba of Tokyo
4130 S. Decatur Blvd.
Las Vegas, NV 89103
227-0342
Hours: Mon. - Fri. 11:30 am - 11 pm;
Sat. - Sun. 5 pm - 7 pm
Reservations: Suggested
Dress: Casual
Price of Entrees: $10.95 - $35.00
Credit Cards: All major
Specialties: Lava boat, beef teriyaki and tempura, sushi, hibachi tables, don buri mono.
Atmosphere: Sushi bar, hibachi.

Shilla Restaurant
2721 W. Sahara Ave.
Las Vegas, NV 89102
362-5050
Hours: 11 am - 11 pm
Reservations: Suggested
Dress: Casual
Price of Entrees: $10.00 - $15.00
Credit Cards: All major
Specialties: Sushi, Japanese and Korean food, table BBQ, sashimi, tatami room.

Shogun Japanese Restaurant
4941 W. Craig Rd.
Las Vegas, NV 89130
396-3381
Hours: 11 am - 11 pm
Price of Entrees: $6.50 - $14.50
Credit Cards: MC, Visa
Specialties: Sushi, tempura, teriyaki.

Sushi Bar
San Remo
115 E. Tropicana Ave.
Las Vegas, NV 89109
739-9000
Hours: 6 pm - midnight
Reservations: None
Dress: Casual
Price of Entrees: $2.50 and up; combinations $16 - $22
Credit Cards: All major
Specialties: Sushi available a la carte and served on a getas or in dinner combinations; Japanese beers and wine.
Atmosphere: 20 seat sushi bar located at the rear of the casino.

Sushi House Manda
230 W. Sahara Ave.
Las Vegas, NV 89102
382-6006
Hours: Lunch Mon. - Fri. 11:30 am - 1 pm; Dinner Sun. - Thu. 5 pm - 9:30 pm; Fri. - Sat. 5 pm - 11 pm
Reservations: None
Dress: Casual
Price of Entrees: $16.95 - $19.95
Credit Cards: MC, Visa
Specialties: Sushi bar with a selection of 20 different types of rolls.

Teriyaki
6710 W. Cheyenne Ave.
Las Vegas, NV 89108
658-2866
Hours: Mon. - Sat. 11 am - 9:30 pm;
Sun. noon - 9 pm
Reservations: None
Dress: Casual
Price of Entrees: $2.77 - $5.66
Credit Cards: None
Specialties: Beef, shrimp, chicken teriyaki.

Teriyaki II
(see Teriyaki above)
4060 S. Jones Blvd.
Las Vegas, NV 89103
221-8181
Hours: Mon. - Sat. noon - 9:30 pm;
Sun. 11 am - 9 pm

Teriyaki III
(see Teriyaki above)
4161 S. Eastern Ave.
Las Vegas, NV 89119
735-5730
Hours: Mon. - Sat. 11 am - 9:30 pm;
Sun. 11 am - 9 pm

Teriyaki Bowl
4604 W. Sahara Ave.
Las Vegas, NV 89102
870-3656
Hours: Mon. - Sat. 10:30 am - 9:30 pm;
Sun. 11:30 - 9 pm
Reservations: None
Dress: Casual
Price of Entrees: Inexpensive $2.89 - $6.09
Credit Cards: None
Specialties: Curry and teriyaki sauces, beef, chicken and shrimp, soft noodles; no MSG.

Teriyaki Cafe
2520 S. Eastern Ave.
Las Vegas, NV 89109
641-5648
Hours: Mon. - Sat. 11 am - 9:30 pm;
Sun. 11 am - 9 pm
Reservations: None
Dress: Casual
Price of Entrees: $6 - $8
Credit Cards: None
Specialties: Curry and teriyaki sauces, beef, chicken and shrimp, soft noodles; no MSG.

Teriyaki King
4019 S. Maryland Pkwy.
Las Vegas, NV 89119
735-1565
Hours: Mon. - Sat. 11 am - 9 pm
Reservations: None
Dress: Casual
Price of Entrees: $3.95 - $7.95
Credit Cards: None
Specialties: Teriyaki, curried beef, vegetable or shrimp tempura.

Teru Sushi
700 E. Sahara Ave.
Las Vegas, NV 89104

734-6655
Hours: Mon. - Sat. 5 pm - 11 pm;
Closed Sun.
Reservations: Accepted
Dress: Informal
Price of Entrees: $15.00 - $25.00
Credit Cards: MC, Visa, AMX
Specialties: Sushi bar, tempura, yakitori.

Togoshi Ramen
855 E. Twain Ave.
Las Vegas, NV 89109
737-7003
Hours: 11:30 am - 11 pm
Reservations: None
Dress: Casual
Price of Entrees: $5 - $10.25
Credit Cards: None
Specialties: Japanese noodle soup, ramen noodles with a variety of toppings, shumai, eel.

Tokyo Restaurant
953 E. Sahara Ave.
Las Vegas, NV 89104
735-7070
Hours: 5 pm - 10 pm
Reservations: Accepted
Dress: Casual
Price of Entrees: $9.95 - $18.50
Credit Cards: All major
Specialties: Yosenabe, steamed clams, tempura.
Atmosphere: Japanese style decoration; sushi bar; banquet facilities accommodate 50; catering.

Western Garden
3943 Spring Mountain Rd.
Las Vegas, NV 89102
876-0243
Hours: Noon - 11 pm
Reservations: Accepted
Dress: Casual
Price of Entrees: Under $13.50
Credit Cards: None
Specialties: Barbecue beef, teriyaki chicken, tempura.

KOREAN

B-Won
953 E. Sahara Ave.
Las Vegas, NV 89104
791-3992
Hours: 3 pm - 2 am
Reservations: None
Dress: Casual
Price of Entrees: $6.99 - $12.99
Credit Cards: MC, Visa, AMX
Specialties: Carbi-marinated short ribs, hot fish soup; Karaoke bar.

Ging-Seng Bar-B-Que
2975 Las Vegas Blvd. S.
Las Vegas, NV 89109
735-2050
Hours: 24 hours
Reservations: Accepted
Dress: Casual
Price of Entrees: $9.95 - $15.95
Credit Cards: MC, Visa, AMX

Specialties: Beef, chicken and pork dishes, fish soup, fried fish; sushi bar.
Atmosphere: Two separate dining rooms - Korean and Japanese.

Ho Ban
953 E. Sahara Ave.
Las Vegas, NV 89104
737-5044
Hours: 11 am - 11 pm
Reservations: None
Dress: Casual
Price of Entrees: $8.00 - $9.50
Credit Cards: MC, Visa
Specialties: Chopped chae noodles with vegetables, pan fried squid.

King Se-Jong Hong Restaurant
1500 Las Vegas Blvd. S.
Las Vegas, NV 89104
384-5264
Hours: 9 am - 10 pm
Reservations: None
Dress: Casual
Price of Entrees: $7.50 - $11.50
Credit Cards: Visa
Specialties: Barbecue beef, yellow corbina and mackerel.

OK Korean Restaurant & Market
17 E. Oakey Blvd.
Las Vegas, NV 89104
382-4989
Hours: 24 hours
Reservations: None
Dress: Casual
Price of Entrees: $6.99 - $12.99
Credit Cards: MC, Visa, AMX, Discover
Specialties: Squid, fried rice, beef and pork.

Sahara Korean Restaurant
953 E. Sahara Ave.
Las Vegas, NV 89104
893-3423
Hours: 10 am - 11 pm
Reservations: None
Dress: Casual
Price of Entrees: $6.99 - $13.99
Credit Cards: MC, Visa
Specialties: Barbecued beef, short ribs, chicken.

Seoul Korean Bar-B-Q Restaurant
953 E. Sahara Ave.
Las Vegas, NV 89104
369-4123
Hours: 11 am - 11 pm
Reservations: Suggested
Dress: Casual
Price of Entrees: $5.25 - $15.95
Credit Cards: MC, Visa
Specialties: Crab casserole, broiled adka fish, short ribs, hot and spicy pork. Lunch special served 11 am - 3 pm $5.99.
Atmosphere: Food is served from the kitchen or you can cook it yourself at your table on the gas-fired brazier.

So Kong Tong Restaurant
953 E. Sahara Ave.
Las Vegas, NV 89104
369-9909
Hours: 10 am - 10 pm
Reservations: None
Dress: Casual
Price of Entrees: $6.99 - $15.99
Credit Cards: MC, Visa
Specialties: Crab soup, barbecue fish, barbecue leaves, pan-fried squid with vegetables, short ribs.
Atmosphere: Korean fare.

MEXICAN / SOUTHWEST

Alberto's Mexican Food
(Multiple locations & hours listed below)
Reservations: Accepted
Dress: Casual
Price of Entrees: $3.95 - $7.95
Credit Cards: All major
Specialties: Home of the sizzling fajitas, chicken, beef, pork, seafood.

3025 Las Vegas, Blvd. S.
Las Vegas, NV 89109
732-8226
Hours: 11 am - 2 am

5550 W. Charleston Blvd.
Las Vegas, NV 89102
878-8669
Hours: Mon. - Sat. 11 am - 10 pm; Sun. 11 am - 9 pm

3466 S. Decatur Blvd.
Las Vegas, NV 89102
362-8226
Hours: 11 am - 8:40 pm

Amigo's
1725 E. Warm Springs Rd.
Las Vegas, NV 89102
361-8929
Hours: Mon. - Thu. 10 am - 8 pm; Fri. - Sat. 10 am - 9 pm

Arriba Restaurant
89 E. Lake Mead Dr.
Henderson, NV 89015
566-1690
Hours: Sun. - Thu. 11 am - 9 pm; Fri & Sat. 11 am - 10 pm
Reservations: None
Dress: Casual
Price of Entrees: $3.95 - $5.95
Credit Cards: None
Specialties: Chile rellenos, carne asada, tamales.
Atmosphere: Small, cozy place.

Bombolia
Rio
3700 W. Flamingo Rd.
Las Vegas, NV 89103
252-7777
Hours: 11 am - 11 pm
Reservations: Accepted
Dress: Casual
Price of Entrees: $4.50 - $10.95
Credit Cards: All major
Specialties: Seafood fajitas, quesadillas, enchiladas, specialty drinks.

Carlos'
1300 Arizona St.
Boulder City, NV 89005
293-5828
Hours: Tue. - Fri. 4 pm - 9 pm; Sat. - Sun. 4 pm - 9 pm
Reservations: None
Dress: Informal - Casual
Price of Entrees: $4.95 - $12.95
Credit Cards: MC, Visa, Discover
Specialties: Seafood, quesadillas, sizzling fajitas, crab tostadas, steaks, combination platters; bar.

Casa Flores Restaurant
930 Nevada Hwy.
Boulder City, NV 89005
294-1937
Hours: Sun., Mon., Wed., Thu. 4 pm - 10 pm;

Chevy's Mexican Restaurant, 4090 S. Eastern Ave., Las Vegas, NV 89119

Fri. - Sat. 4 pm - 11 pm; closed Tue.
Reservations: Accepted
Dress: Informal
Price of Entrees: $5.25 - $10.25
Credit Cards: MC, Visa, AMX
Specialties: Mexican shrimp, steak picado, fajitas, chimichangas, fajita dinners, roast pork (carnitas). Everything homemade. Food to go and catering. Children's menu; banquet facilities accommodate 40-50. Cantina lounge.
Atmosphere: Typical south of the border in fiesta season.

Casa Vera Cruz
1002 N. Rancho Dr.
Las Vegas, NV 89106
631-5944
Hours: Sun. - Thu. 10 am - 8 pm; Sat. 9 am - 10 pm
Reservations: None
Dress: Casual
Price of Entrees: Inexpensive
Credit Cards: None
Specialties: Shrimp with onions, Vera Cruz style fresh fried fish, enchiladas.

Chapala Mexican Restaurant
(Multiple location & hours listed below)
Reservations: Accepted
Dress: Casual
Price of Entrees: $4.50 - $10
Credit Cards: MC, Visa
Specialties: Fajitas, tostada salad, Mazatlan red snapper; bar.

3335 E. Tropicana Ave.
Las Vegas, NV 89121
451-8141
Hours: 11 am - midnight

2101 S. Decatur Blvd.
Las Vegas, NV 89102
871-1915
Hours: Sun. - Thu. 11 am - 11 pm; Fri. - Sat. 11 am - midnight

Chevy's Mexican Restaurant
4090 S. Eastern Ave.
Las Vegas, NV 89119
731-6969
Hours: Sun. - Thu. 11 am - 10 pm; Fri. - Sat. 11 am - 11 pm
Reservations: Accepted for parties of 8 or more.
Dress: Casual
Price of Entrees: $5.95 - $13.95
Credit Cards: MC, Visa, AMX
Specialties: "The freshest food in town." All items are made from fresh ingredients daily. Quail and jumbo shrimp fajitas, com-

bination platters, endless tortillas made before your very eyes, handmade tamales, fresh chips and salsa, Margaritas. Lounge. Children's menu. Banquet facilities to accommodate 60 - 100.
Atmosphere: South of the Border, cantina style. Fun and festive. A great place to bring the kids!

Chili's Grill & Bar
(See American)

Cordobe's Restaurant Mexicano
(Multiple locations listed below)
Hours: Mon. - Fri. 10:30 am - 9 pm; Sat. 10 am - 5 am; Sun. 10:30 am - midnight
Reservations: None
Dress: Casual
Price of Entrees: $5.75 - $10.95
Credit Cards: None
Specialties: Enchiladas, tacos and green chile burritos.
Atmosphere: Fri. - Sun. live entertainment 9 pm - 3 am.

235 N. Eastern Ave.
Las Vegas, NV 89101
382-3803

4255 E. Charleston Blvd.
Las Vegas, NV 89104
431-2122

2560 S. Maryland Pkwy.
Las Vegas, NV 89109
369-2286

Coyote's Cantina
4350 E. Sunset Rd.
Henderson, NV 89014
458-3739
Hours: 11 am - 11 pm
Reservations: Accepted
Dress: Informal
Price of Entrees: $7.95 - $12.95
Credit Cards: All major
Specialties: Shrimp chile rellenos, chile Colorado, chile verde burritos, fajitas, grilled chicken breasts with sweet red pepper sauce, shrimp fajitas, costillas de puerco, enchiladas de puerco adovado, chicken or beef tamales, Mexican pizza, fried ice cream; cantina with six different flavors of margaritas. Children's menu. Banquet facilities accommodate 30.
Atmosphere: Very Southwestern. Traditional Old Mexico atmosphere; cantina area with video poker.

RESTAURANTS - Ethnic

Cozymel's, 355 Howard Hughes Center, Las Vegas, NV 89109

Cozymel's
355 Howard Hughes Center
Las Vegas, NV 89109
732-4833
Hours: Sun. - Thu. 11 am - 10 pm;
Fri. - Sat. 11 am - midnight
Reservations: Recommended
Dress: Casual
Price of Entrees: Reasonable
Credit Cards: All major
Specialties: Salmon, tropical sea bass
Vera Cruzana, shrimp and lamb fajitas.
Truly authentic Mexican dishes from
family recipes.

Don Alejandro's Texan Grill
McCarran Airport
Las Vegas, NV 89119
261-3113
Hours: 6 am - 10 pm
Reservations: None
Dress: Casual
Price of Entrees: $8.00 - $12.00
Credit Cards: All major
Specialties: Mexican fare.

Dona Maria's Mexican Restaurant
910 Las Vegas Blvd. S.
Las Vegas, NV 89101
382-6538
Hours: 8 am - 10 pm
Reservations: Accepted
Dress: Informal
Price of Entrees: $8.00 - $10.95
Credit Cards: MC, Visa, Discover, AMX
Specialties: Red, green, cheese and
sweet homemade tamales, snapper Vera
Cruzana, chicken enchiladas. Tamales
sold for take-home singly or by the half-
dozen; guitar music.

Dona Maria's Restaurant
4889 E. Craig Rd.
Las Vegas, NV 89115
644-5209
Hours: Mon. - Sat. 8 am - 9 pm;
Closed Sun.
Reservations: Accepted
Dress: Casual
Price of Entrees: $6.25 - $9.00
Credit Cards: MC, Visa
Specialties: Steak Rio Grande, enchi-
ladas, fajitas.

El Azteca
226 W. Sahara Ave.
Las Vegas, NV 89102
382-8448
Hours: Tue. - Sun. 11 am - 9:30 pm;
Closed Mon.
Reservations: None
Dress: Informal
Price of Entrees: Inexpensive
Credit Cards: MC, Visa, AMX
Specialties: Steaks, enchiladas, tamales.

El Burrito West
633 N. Decatur Blvd.
Las Vegas, NV 89107
870-1969
Hours: Sun. - Thu. 11 am - 9:30 pm;
Fri. - Sat. 11 am - 10:30 pm

El Burrito
8508 Del Webb Blvd.
Las Vegas, NV 89134
255-1069
Hours: Mon. - Thu. 11 am - 9 pm;
Fri. - Sat. 10 am - 11 pm; Sun. noon - 9 pm
Reservations: None
Dress: Casual
Price of Entrees: Inexpensive
Credit Cards: MC, Visa, Discover
Specialties: Burritos, tamales, tacos,
chile rellenos, fried ice cream.

El Cordobes
5020 E. Tropicana Ave.
Las Vegas, NV 89122
433-8226
Hours: 10 am - 9 pm
Reservations: None
Dress: Casual
Price of Entrees: $5.75 - $10.95
Credit Cards: None
Specialties: Steak picado, chimichangas,
seafood, chile verde, chile Colorado,
machaca, menudo, chile rellenos and
huevos rancheros. Banquet facilities to
accommodate 45.
Atmosphere: Homey atmosphere.

El Jalisco Mexican Restaurant
3400 S. Jones Blvd.
Las Vegas, NV 89102
251-4742
Hours: Mon. - Fri. 9 am - 9 pm;
Sat. & Sun. 8 am - 11 pm
Reservations: None
Dress: Casual
Price of Entrees: $6.95 - $11.95
Credit Cards: All major
Specialties: Lunch specials - $4.95; fish,

shrimp, chicken breast, rib eye, fajitas
chicken a la Vera Cruzana, pollo a la casa.
Atmosphere: Soft, clean, light and airy.

El Matador
(Inside Cattleman's)
2645 S. Maryland Pkwy.
Las Vegas, NV 89109
732-1691
Hours: 5 pm - 11 pm
Reservations: None
Dress: Casual
Price of Entrees: $5.95 - $11.95
Credit Cards: Visa, MC, AMX, Discover
Specialties: Flautas de pollo, caldo de
pescado, carne de puero; seafood, combina-
tion plates. Live music; bar open 24 hours.

El Sinaloense
953 E. Sahara Ave.
Las Vegas, NV 89104
796-3811
Hours: 7 pm - 4 am
Reservations: None
Dress: Casual
Price of Entrees: $10.00 - $15.00
Credit Cards: None
Specialties: Carne asada, enchiladas,
chicken.
Atmosphere: Night club; live entertain-
ment Fri. - Tue. 8 pm - 4 am.

El Sombrero Cafe
807 S. Main St.
Las Vegas, NV 89101
382-9234
Hours: Mon. - Sat. 11 am - 10 pm;
closed Sun.
Reservations: None for small parties.
Dress: Informal
Price of Entrees: $6.00 - $9.00
Credit Cards: MC, Visa, AMX
Specialties: Enchiladas, green chile,
red chile, chile rellenos, tamales, com-
bination platters, sopaipillas.
Atmosphere: Small 48 seat restaurant
in business at the same location for over
45 years.

El Taco Fresco
4825 W. Flamingo Rd.
Las Vegas, NV 89103
247-6633
Hours: 24 hours
Reservations: None
Dress: Casual
Price of Entrees: Inexpensive
Credit Cards: None
Specialties: Carne asada, steak fajitas,
tortas, taco salad.

El Taquito
2350 Bonanza Rd.
Las Vegas, NV 89101
387-5588
Hours: 7 am - 11 pm
Reservations: None
Dress: Casual
Price of Entrees: $5.00 - $14.00
Credit Cards: None
Specialties: Chile rellenos, tamales,
enchiladas, tacos and seafood.
Atmosphere: Live entertainment Fri., -
Sun. 4 pm - 11 pm.

El Tenampa
556 N. Eastern Ave.
Las Vegas, NV 89101
598-1716
Hours: Call for hours

Reservations: None
Dress: Casual
Price of Entrees: Inexpensive
Specialties: Burritos, homemade flour
and corn tortillas, tacos and seafood. All
food homemade.

El Torito Cafe
2126 S. Boulder Hwy.
Henderson, NV 89015
564-2309
Hours: Vary; please call
Reservations: None
Dress: Casual
Price of Entrees: Inexpensive
Credit Cards: None
Specialties: Mexican food and chicken
fried steak, hamburgers.

Esmeraldas Cafe
1000 E. Charleston Blvd.
Las Vegas, NV 89104
388-1404
Hours: 11 am - 9 pm
Reservations: None
Dress: Casual
Price of Entrees: $1.50 - $7.50
Credit Cards: None
Specialties: Salvadoran, Mexican.

Garduno's Restaurant & Cantina
Fiesta
2400 N. Rancho Dr.
Las Vegas, NV 89130
631-5111
Hours: Sun. - Thu. 10 am - 10 pm;
Fri. - Sat. 10 am - 11 pm
Reservations: None
Dress: Casual
Price of Entrees: $3.95 - $15.95
Specialties: Variety of chiles, Mexican
seafood, special Mexican desserts, nine
different types of fajitas, homemade tor-
tillas, sopaipilla and sweet corn cake;
margarita brunch Sun. 10 am - 3 pm $9.99.

Gonzalez Y. Gonzalez
New York New York
3790 Las Vegas Blvd. S.
Las Vegas, NV 89109
650-6500
Hours: 11 am - noon
Reservations: None
Price of Entrees: $4.00 - $17.00
Credit Cards: All major
Specialties: Fajitas, arroz con pollo,
carne asada.
Atmosphere: Mexican courtyard.

Granpa Flores Mexican Restaurant
3149 N. Rancho Dr.
Las Vegas, NV 89130
645-1196
Hours: 8 am - 10 pm
Reservations: Accepted
Dress: Casual
Price of Entrees: $4.50 - $9.50
Credit Cards: MC, Visa
Specialties: Carne asada, chicken pica-
do, green chile and pork with nopalitos
(green cactus). Children's menu.
Atmosphere: Authentic Mexican.

Macayo Vegas, 3 locations in Las Vegas (see listings)

Gringos
2081 N. Decatur Blvd.
Las Vegas, NV 89108
636-0688
Hours: Sun. - Thu. 9 am - 11 pm;
Fri. - Sat. 9 am - midnight
Reservations: None
Dress: Casual
Price of Entrees: $2.99 - $5.29
Credit Cards: MC, Visa
Specialties: Enchiladas, chile verde, burritos, chimichangas and chalupa.

Guadalajara
Palace Station
2411 W. Sahara Ave.
Las Vegas, NV 89102
367-2411
Hours: 11 am - 11 pm
Reservations: None
Dress: Informal
Price of Entrees: $5.95 - $10.95
Credit Cards: All major
Specialties: Crab meat enchiladas, steak especiale, tacos al carbon, steak Guadalajara, margarita, or chips and salsa $.99.
Atmosphere: Authentic Guadalajara ambience.

Guadalajara Bar & Grille
Boulder Station
4111 Boulder Hwy.
Las Vegas, NV 89121
432-7777
Hours: 11 am - 4 pm;
Dinner Sun. - Thu.. 4 pm - 10 pm;
Fri. - Sat. 4 pm - 11 pm
Reservations: None
Dress: Casual
Price of Entrees: $7.95 - $17.00
Credit Cards: All major
Specialities: Daily specials; fajita lunch special $5.95.

La Bombilla
537 E. Twain Ave.
Las Vegas, NV 89109
733-9166
Hours: 11 am - 11 pm
Price of Entrees: $2.75 - $8.00
Credit Cards: All major
Specialties: Menudo, fajitas, burritos, tacos and enchiladas.

La Cabana
526 S. Martin Luther King Blvd.
Las Vegas, NV 89106
366-0039
Hours: 9 am - 9 pm
Reservations: None
Dress: Casual
Price of Entrees: $3.25-$10.95
Credit Cards: MC, Visa
Specialties: Traditional Mexican menu.

La Fiesta
2550 S. Rainbow Blvd.
Las Vegas, NV 89102
871-5172
Hours: Mon. - Sat. 7 am - 10 pm;
Sun. 7 am - 9 pm
Reservations: Accepted
Dress: Informal
Price of Entrees: $5.95 - $9.95
Credit Cards: All major
Specialties: Specializing in original and authentic Mexican food; homemade tamales, fajitas, chile Colorado, carne asada carnitas, higado encevollado. Children's menu.
Atmosphere: Simple and yet very upbeat. Relaxed and comfortable. Harp player on weekends.

La Playita
2238 N. Pecos Rd.
Las Vegas, NV 89115
459-4169
Hours: Mon. - Thu. 10 am - 10 pm;
Fri. - Sun. 10 am - midnight
Reservations: None
Dress: Casual
Price of Entrees: $5 - $12
Credit Cards: None
Specialties: Green chile, seafood.

La Salsa
Forum Shops
3500 Las Vegas Blvd. S.
Las Vegas, NV 89109
735-8226
Hours: Sun. - Thu. 11 am - 11 pm;
Fri. - Sat. 11 am - midnight
Reservations: None
Atmosphere: Mexican courtyard setting with a view of the Forum Shop's "talking fountain" which presents a show every hour.

La Salsa Taqueria
Boulevard Mall
3480 S. Maryland Pkwy.
Las Vegas, NV 89109
369-1234
Hours: Mon. - Fri. 10 am - 7 pm;
Sat. 10 am - 8 pm; Sun. 10 am - 6 pm
(Not a full service restaurant)

Laredo Cantina & Cafe
Texas
3141 N. Rancho Dr.
Las Vegas, NV 89130
631-1044
Hours: 5 pm - 11 pm
Reservations: Suggested
Dress: Casual
Price of Entrees: $11.95 and up
Credit Cards: All major
Specialties: Parrillado, enchilada suizas, tacos al carbon and burrito de Laredo. Self-serve salsa bar.

Lindo Michoacan Mexican Restaurant
2655 E. Desert Inn Rd.
Las Vegas, NV 89121
735-6828
Hours: Mon. - Wed. 11 am - 10 pm;
Thu. - Fri. 11 am - 11 pm;
Sat. - Sun. 9:30 am - 11 pm
Reservations: Accepted
Dress: Casual
Price of Entrees: $8.95 - $16.25
Credit Cards: All major
Specialties: Steak Tampiquena, Steak Cilantro, Cabrito, Camarones Rancheros, burritos, tacos, chicken with cactus, fresh seafood and 20 combination platters. Daily specials $4.95 includes beverage. Live music.

Los Antojos
2520 S. Eastern Ave.
Las Vegas, NV 89121
457-3505
Hours: 9 am - 10:30 pm; Closed Thu.
Reservations: None
Dress: Casual
Price of Entrees: Inexpensive
Credit Cards: None
Specialties: Mexico City style tortas, flautas, quesadillas, marinated pork, $5.99.
Atmosphere: Small coffee shop.

Macayo Vegas
(Multiple locations listed below)
Hours: 11 am - 11 pm
Reservations: Not accepted on Fri. & Sat.
Dress: Informal
Price of Entrees: $3.95 - $11.95
Credit Cards: All major
Specialties: Chili rellenos, chimichangas, tamales.

1741 E. Charleston Blvd.
Las Vegas, NV 89104
382-5605

4457 W. Charleston Blvd.
Las Vegas, NV 89102
878-7347

1375 E. Tropicana Ave.
Las Vegas, NV 89109
736-1898

DINING

La Fiesta, 2550 S. Rainbow Blvd., Las Vegas, NV 89102

RESTAURANTS - Ethnic

Mamacita's Mexican Food
1322 Fremont St.
Las Vegas, NV 89101
474-7033
Hours: Mon. - Sat. 7 am - 9 pm;
Sun. 7 am - 7 pm
Reservations: None
Dress: Casual
Price of Entrees: $4.95 - $10.95
Credit Cards: MC, Visa, AMX
Specialties: Steak picado, chimichangas, chile verde, fajitas; free delivery.
Atmosphere: Quiet, large windows, small waterfall, trees, flowers and ceiling fans; catering.

Manuel's Mexican Food
6055 E. Lake Mead Blvd.
Las Vegas, NV 89115
453-3377
Hours: Mon. - Sat. 5 pm - 9 pm
Reservations: None
Dress: Casual
Price of Entrees: $4.00 - $8.00
Credit Cards: MC, Visa
Specialties: Chile rellenos, tacos, burritos.

Margarita Grille
Las Vegas Hilton
3000 Paradise Rd.
Las Vegas, NV 89109
732-5111
Hours: 4 pm - 11 pm; closed Wed.
Reservations: Suggested
Dress: Informal
Price of Entrees: $7.95 - $14.50
Credit Cards: All major
Specialties: Carne asada, chimichangas, sizzling beef, chicken or shrimp fajitas, spicy burritos, combination dinners. Fresh fruit margaritas and daiquiris. Chocolate tacos.

Margarita's Mexican Cantina
New Frontier
3120 Las Vegas Blvd. S.
Las Vegas, NV 89109
794-8200
Hours: 11 am - 10:30 pm
Reservations: None
Dress: Informal
Price of Entrees: $5.95 - $12.50
Credit Cards: All major
Specialties: Fresh tortillas (watch them being made at entrance), pollo pepita, flambe ole, sizzling fajitas - chicken, pork, beef or shrimp, quesadillas; giant 45-ounce margaritas for $8.50 and you keep the glass.
Atmosphere: Old Mexican courtyard.

Maria Conchita
4375 W. Desert Inn Rd.
Las Vegas, NV 89102
227-0410
Hours: Mon. - Fri. 10 am - 7 pm;
Sat. 10 am - 3 pm
Reservations: None
Dress: Casual
Price of Entrees: $4.75 - $5.85
Credit Cards: None
Specialties: Chile Colorado, pancho plate, chile verde; pick-up window.
Atmosphere: Coffee shop.

Maria's Mexican Restaurant
3762 E. Flamingo Rd.
Las Vegas, NV 89121
898-7299
Hours: 11 am - 10 pm
Reservations: Suggested
Dress: Casual
Price of Entrees: $4.50 - $8.50
Credit Cards: None
Specialties: Emilio's Special Salad, Caesar salad with chicken relleno, taquitos, steak picado.
Atmosphere: 15 tables, hacienda style.

Mariana's Cantina
Eldorado Club
140 S. Water St.
Henderson, NV 89015
564-1811
Hours: 4 pm - 10 pm
Reservations: Suggested
Dress: Informal
Price of Entrees: $5.95 - $11.95
Credit Cards: All major
Specialties: Jumbo shrimp, sincronizada, fajitas.

Marisca's Las Islitas
2437 N. Las Vegas Blvd.
Las Vegas, NV 89104
649-9198
Hours: 10 am - 9 pm
Reservations: None
Dress: Casual
Price of Entrees: $2.00 - $7.00
Credit Cards: None
Specialties: Seafood, fajitas, enchiladas, chile.

Marisca's Las Islitas II
911 Pecos Rd.
Las Vegas, NV 89101
642-3123
Hours: 9 am - 8 pm
Price of Entrees: $2.00 - $7.00
Credit Cards: None
Specialties: Raw shrimp, sopaipillas, quesadillas.

Mark Miller's
Coyote Cafe
& Grill Room
MGM Grand
3799 Las Vegas Blvd. S.
Las Vegas, NV 89109
891-7777
Hours: 9 am - 11 pm in Coyote Cafe; 5:30 pm - 9:45 pm in Coyote Grill Room.
Reservations: None for cafe; reservations required for dinner in the dining room.
Dress: Casual
Price of Entrees: $18 - $32
Credit Cards: MC, Visa, Discover, Diners
Specialties: Hot and spicy modern Southwestern cuisine such as Texas Hill Country venison, grilled rack of Colorado lamb, black beans, enchiladas, jerk chicken tacos and cajun creole.
Atmosphere: Hand painted coyotes, lizards and other desert art throughout terra cotta stone cafe.

Mi Tierra
3205 N. Tenaya Way
Las Vegas, NV 89129
656-1600
Hours: Mon. - Thu. 11 am - 10 pm; Fri. - Sat. 11 am - 10:30 pm; Sun. 11 am - 9 pm
Reservations: None
Dress: Casual

Rosalita's Cantina at Sunset Station, 1301 W. Sunset Rd., Henderson, NV

Price of Entrees: Reasonable
Credit Cards: All major
Specialties: Tex-Mex menu.
Atmosphere: Old mission style restaurant with open kitchen. Watch tortillas being made at entrance. Live mariachis Fri. and Sat. 6 pm - 9 pm.

Don Miguel's
The Orleans
4500 W. Tropicana Ave.
Las Vegas, NV 89103
365-7550
Hours: 11 am - 11 pm
Reservations: None
Dress: Casual
Price of Entrees: $6.00 - $14.00
Credit Cards: All major
Specialties: Shrimp rancheros, enchiladas, fajitas, seafood, combination platters; complimentary chips with salsa and guacamole and margaritas served with all dinners.
Atmosphere: Mirror and brass ceiling treatments, large wall mural, margarita bar and display tortilla cooking makes for a wonderful dining experience.

Pablo's Cafe
Santa Fe
4949 N. Rancho Dr.
Las Vegas, NV 89130
658-4900
Hours: 24 hours
Reservations: None
Dress: Casual
Price of Entrees: $3.00 - $9.00
Credit Cards: All major
Specialties: Prime rib, fajitas, ribs.

Paco's Hideaway
Sahara Hotel
2535 Las Vegas Blvd. S.
Las Vegas, NV 89109
737-2111
Hours: 5 pm - 10:30 pm
Reservations: Suggested
Dress: Casual
Price of Entrees: $4.95 - $12.95
Specialties: Enchiladas, tacos, fajitas, tamales, New York steak sauteed with peppers, onions, mild chiles and tomatoes.

Pancho's Mexican Restaurant
3720 E. Sunset Rd.
Henderson, NV 89015
898-8488
Hours: 7 am - 9 pm
Reservations: None
Dress: Casual
Price of Entrees: $3 - $8.50
Credit Cards: None
Specialties: 3 lb burrito, super nachos, Mexican pizza.

Ricardo's
(Multiple locations listed below)
Reservations: Accepted
Dress: Informal
Price of Entrees: $5.95 - $15.95
Credit Cards: All major
Specialties: Sizzling fajitas, carne asada, chile rellenos, combination platters; children's menu; separate bar and lounge area. Luncheon buffet 11 am - 2:30 pm, $7.25 for adults, $4.25 for children, includes soft drink (not available at Meadows Mall); food and drink specials Mon. - Fri. 4 pm - 6 pm.
Atmosphere: Strolling guitar player entertains diners during the evening (varies with location, please call ahead).

Meadows Mall
4300 Meadows Ln.
Las Vegas, NV 89107
870-1088
Hours: Mon. - Sat. 11 am - 10 pm;
Sun. 11 am - 9 pm

2380 E. Tropicana Ave.
Las Vegas, NV 89119
798-4515
Hours: Sun. - Thu. 11 am - 10 pm;
Fri. - Sat. 11 am - 11 pm

4930 W. Flamingo Rd.
Las Vegas, NV 89103
871-7119
Hours: Sun. - Thu. 11 am - 10 pm;
Fri. - Sat. 11 am - 11 pm

Rosalita's Cantina
Sunset Station
1301 W. Sunset Rd.
Henderson, NV 89014
547-7777
Hours: Sun. - Thu. 5 pm - 10 pm;
Fri. - Sat. 5 pm - 11 pm

VIVA MERCADO'S

"Home of the Best Chile Rellenos"
We prepare with your health in mind.

WINNER of the Zagat Survey's,
"Best Mexican Restaurant in Las Vegas."

WINNER of the American Academy of Restaurant and Hospitality Sciences's
"5 Star Award and in the Top 10 Mexican Restaurants in the Nation."

WINNER of the Review Journal's,
"Best of Las Vegas from '94 to '98.

Lunch from $5.⁷⁵

Dinner from $7.⁹⁵

Family Owned & Operated

6182 West Flamingo Road
871-8826

OPEN DAILY
11 A.M. TO 10 P.M.

4500 East Sunset Road
435-6200

DINING

Reservations: None
Dress: Casual
Price of Entrees: $8.99 - $26.99
Credit Cards: All major
Specialties: Paella de Mariscos, burrito del mar with shrimp, crab scallops and fish, traditional fajitas, large assortment of tacos, enchiladas, quesadillas, fresh fish and poultry wrapped in banana leaves, green chile lamb empanadas, and Mexican desserts such as chocolate tacos and tropical fruit tacos; Sun. brunch features fresh suckling pig coated with Yucatan spices, posole and delicious South-of-the-Border breakfast items; tortilla making station and the Cerreza Bar, where Rosalita's offers Sol beer, exclusive to the Las Vegas area. All meals are made from scratch from traditional family recipes.

Santa Rosa Taco Shop
23 E. Basic Rd.
Henderson, NV 89015
558-7540
Hours: 8 am - 11 pm
Reservations: None
Dress: Casual
Price of Entrees: $2.00 - $7.00
Credit Cards: None
Specialties: Chimichanga, burritos, fish tacos, fajitas.

Tacos El Popeye
3216 Civic Center Dr.
Las Vegas, NV 89109
649-1218
Hours: 8 am - 8 pm
Reservations: None
Dress: Casual
Price of Entrees: $2.00 - $10.00
Credit Cards: None
Specialties: Seafood, chile rellenos, octopus, enchiladas.

Tacos Latinos
1558 N. Eastern Ave.
Las Vegas, NV 89101
399-3966
Hours: 8 am - 11 pm
Reservations: None
Dress: Casual
Price of Entrees: $2.00 - $6.00
Credit Cards: None
Specialties: Tacos, burritos.

Tacos Mexico
(Multiple locations listed below)
Hours: 24 hours
Reservations: None
Dress: Casual
Price of Entrees: Inexpensive
Credit Cards: None
Specialties: Combination plate, tacos, burritos.

1205 E. Charleston Blvd.
Las Vegas, NV 89104
385-6806

3820 W. Sahara Ave.
Las Vegas, NV 89102
365-7673

1612 Civic Center Dr.
N. Las Vegas, NV 89030
399-7953

Toto's Mexican Restaurant
2055 E. Tropicana Ave.
Las Vegas, NV 89119
895-7923
Hours: 11 am - 11 pm
Reservations: Suggested
Dress: Casual
Price of Entrees: $5.95 - $11.95
Credit Cards: All major
Specialties: Camarones envueltos, enchiladas de espinacas and taquitos del mar.

Toto's Mexican Restaurant
806 Buchanan Blvd.
Boulder City, NV 89005
293-1744
Hours: Sun. - Thu. 11 am - 9:30 pm;
Fri. - Sat. 11 am - 10:30 pm
Reservations: Accepted
Dress: Casual
Price of Entrees: $5.95 - $11.95
Credit Cards: MC, Visa, AMX, Discover
Specialties: Chile verde, camarones, combination New York steak and jumbo shrimp wrapped in bacon.
Atmosphere: 2 separate dining rooms, one non-smoking.

Tres Lobos
Stardust
3000 Las Vegas Blvd. S.
Las Vegas, NV 89109
732-6111
Hours: Tue. - Thu. 5 pm - 11 pm;
Fri. - Sat. 5 pm - midnight
Reservations: None
Dress: Informal
Price of Entrees: $6.95 - $11.95
Credit Cards: All major
Specialties: Chimichangas, flautas, jumbo Mexican shrimp, enchiladas and steaks; deep-fried ice cream, mud pie, sopaipillas; some American dishes such as Gulf shrimp and T-bone steak. Tres Lobos features authentic Mexican dishes, margaritas and Mexican beers.
Atmosphere: Courtyard-style dining room designed to suggest the courtyard of a stately mansion, complete with fountains, trees, statuary and other interesting artifacts; music.

Viva Mercado's Mexican Restaurant
(Additional location listed below)
Barley's Casino & Brewing Co.
4500 E. Sunset Rd.
Henderson, NV 89014
435-6200
Hours: Sun. - Thu. 11 am - 10 pm;
Fri. - Sat. 11 am - 11 pm
Reservations: For parties of 6 or more.
Dress: Informal
Price of Entrees: $7.95 - $16.95
Credit Cards: Visa, MC, AMX, Discover
Specialties: Traditional homemade Mexican and Southwest cooking. Fresh salsa, chile rellenos, quesadillas, steak asada, enchiladas poblanos, pork tenderloin. No animal fats used. Children's menu. Mon. - Fri. Fiesta menu - build your own combination or chicken fajita 2 pm - 5 pm $6.95. Five Star Diamond Award by the National Hospitality Association.
Atmosphere: Soft garden open-market style.

6182 W. Flamingo Rd.
Las Vegas, NV 89103
871-8826

Willy and Jose's
Sam's Town
5111 Boulder Hwy.
Las Vegas, NV 89122
454-8044
Hours: Sun. - Thu. 4 pm - 10 pm;
Fri. - Sat. 4 pm - 11 pm
Reservations: Suggested
Dress: Informal
Price of Entrees: $6.00 - $14.00
Credit Cards: All major
Specialties: Authentic Mexican food. Flautas, fajitas, enchiladas, tostadas grandes, no name burritos, combination plates and steaks, chicken and seafood prepared Mexican-style.
Atmosphere: South-of-the-Border Mexican cantina decor.

RESTAURANTS - Ethnic

Z'Tejas Grill
3824 S. Paradise Rd.
Las Vegas, NV 89109
732-1660
Hours: 11 am - 11 pm
Reservations: Accepted
Dress: Casual - Informal
Price of Entrees: $7.00 - $17.00
Credit Cards: All major
Specialties: Southwestern, Cajun and Tex-Mex. Stuffed pork tenderloin, cotija chicken pasta, aliso-glazed salmon, Sonoran crab, stuffed shrimp; entrees are served with a choice of two side dishes, hot corn custard, black beans and rice; banquet facilities are available for parties of 150 or more; valet parking.
Atmosphere: Southwest decor; misted patio.

MIDDLE EASTERN

House of Kabob
4110 S. Maryland Pkwy.
Las Vegas, NV 89119
732-2285
Hours: Mon. - Sat. 11 am - 9 pm; Sun. noon - 8 pm
Reservations: None
Dress: Casual
Price of Entrees: $3.00 - $13.95
Credit Cards: MC, Visa, AMX, Diners
Specialties: Shawirma beef or chicken shishkabob, moussaka.
Atmosphere: Floral scapes, wall mural; traditional music.

Mediterranean Cafe & Market
4147 S. Maryland Pkwy.
Las Vegas, NV 89119
731-6030
Hours: Mon. - Fri. 9:30 am - 11:30 pm; Sat. noon - 11 pm
Reservations: Required on Wed. and Sat.
Dress: Casual
Price of Entrees: $4.99 - $8.25
Credit Cards: All major
Specialties: Combination Middle Eastern vegetarian plates; hummus, spinach pie, stuffed grape leaves, shishkabob, kibbe; market has imported cheeses, spices, oils and candies.
Atmosphere: Outside patio, water fountain, arts and crafts from Mediterranean countries; taped music.

MOROCCAN

Mamounia Moroccan Restaurant
4632 S. Maryland Pkwy.
Las Vegas, NV 89119
597-0092
Hours: 5 pm - 11 pm
Reservations: Suggested
Dress: Informal
Price of Entrees: $12.95 - $20.95
(6 course dinner)
Credit Cards: MC, Visa
Specialties: Authentic Moroccan cuisine; shishkabobs made with marinated beef, chicken or lamb; lamb shank, couscous, braised lamb, Cornish hen, seafood and chicken pastillas, baklava, pastilla. Catering available.
Atmosphere: Authentic Moroccan decor. Belly dancers entertain while you dine; large imported rugs cover the walls and floor. Diners sit around a low table seated on large floor pillows or banquette, which has a back support.

Mamounia Moroccan Restaurant, 4632 S. Maryland Pkwy., Las Vegas, NV 89119

Marrakesh Restaurant
3900 Paradise Rd.
Las Vegas, NV 89109
736-7655
Hours: 5:30 pm - 10:30 pm
Reservations: Recommended
Dress: Informal
Price of Entrees: $23.95 for 7-course fixed price dinner.
Credit Cards: MC, Visa, AMX
Specialties: French Moroccan cuisine; scampi, shish kebab, lemon chicken, Cornish hen, pastilla.
Atmosphere: Diners sit on large floor pillows and are entertained by belly dancers while they dine. The dinner starts and ends with traditional hand washing in rose water, since most of the food is eaten with the hands.

PERSIAN

Habib's Persian Restaurant
4750 W. Sahara Ave.
Las Vegas, NV 89102
870-0860
Hours: 11:30 am - 3 pm & 5:30 pm - 10 pm
Reservations: Suggested
Dress: Semi-formal
Price of Entrees: $8.50 - $14.95
Credit Cards: All major
Specialties: Middle Eastern and Persian, banquet facilities for 80, catering.
Atmosphere: Romantic and contemporary, patio dining.

THAI

Bangkok 9
663 Stephanie St.
Henderson, NV 89014
898-6881
Hours: Mon. - Sat. 11 am - 10 pm; Sun. noon - 9 pm
Reservations: None
Dress: Casual
Price of Entrees: $5.95 - $7.95

Credit Cards: MC, Visa, Discover
Specialties: Thai-Chinese food; spinach salad with chicken, garlic pepper, sweet & sour. Banquet facilities to accommodate 45. Catering available; delivery after 6 pm.
Atmosphere: Exotic cuisine in a contemporary setting.

Bangkok Orchid
4662 E. Sunset Rd.
Henderson, NV 89014
458-4945
Hours: 11 am - 10 pm
Reservations: None
Dress: Casual
Price of Entrees: $6.95 - $12.95
Credit Cards: MC, Visa, AMX
Specialties: Spicy beef salad, Thai noodles, Thai red curry, spicy catfish, combination seafood, garlic shrimp.
Atmosphere: Beautiful silk flowers and plants.

Chiang Mai Restaurant
2560 Las Vegas Blvd. N.
N. Las Vegas, NV 89030
642-9111
Hours: 10:30 am - 10 pm
Reservations: None
Dress: Casual
Price of Entrees: $4.95 - $12.95
Credit Cards: None
Specialties: Spicy squid, shrimp with pepper sauce, garlic pork and chicken, Tom yum poe tak soup.

Friendship Restaurant
556 N. Eastern Ave.
Las Vegas, NV 89101
384-2444
Hours: Mon. - Sat. 11 am - 9 pm; Sun. noon - 8 pm
Reservations: None
Dress: Casual
Price of Entrees: $4.95 - $11.95
Credit Cards: MC, Visa
Specialties: Spicy, sweet and sour pork; deep fried pompano.

King & I
1107 E. Tropicana Ave.
Las Vegas, NV 89119
739-8819
Hours: Mon. - Sat. 11 am - 10 pm; Sun. 1 pm - 9 pm
Reservations: None
Dress: Casual
Price of Entrees: $5.95 - $11.95
Credit Cards: MC, Visa
Specialties: Pad Thai, crispy duck, rice and noodles; delivery available.

King & I
2904 Lake East Dr.
Las Vegas, NV 89117
256-1568
Hours: Mon. - Thu. 11 am - 9:30 pm; Fri. - Sat. 11 am - 10 pm; Sun. 3 pm - 9 pm
Reservations: None
Dress: Casual
Price of Entrees: $6.95 - $12.95
Credit Cards: All major
Specialties: Pud Thai, King and I stir fry chicken wings, Royal Grand Palace spicy seafood combination, beef, chicken or pork stir fry and Singapore noodles; delivery available.
Atmosphere: Warm and friendly Thai atmosphere.

Komol Restaurant
Commercial Center
953 E. Sahara Ave.
Las Vegas, NV 89104
731-6542
Hours: Mon. - Sat. 11 am - 10 pm; Sun. noon. - 10 pm
Reservations: Accepted
Dress: Very casual
Price of Entrees: $5.95 - $14.95 family style
Credit Cards: MC, Visa, AMX, Discover
Specialties: Authentic Thai cuisine plus Thai vegetarian and Chinese food. Pud Thai, Thai beef salad, tom yum goong, chicken chili mint, beef panang, chicken curry, tom yum mushroom, Mongolian beef, sesame beef.
Atmosphere: A homestyle atmosphere with lovely hand painting on the walls, flower decoration. Banquet facilities to accommodate 60.

Ocha
1201 Las Vegas Blvd. N.
Las Vegas, NV 89101
386-8631
Hours: 10 am - 6 am
Reservations: None
Dress: Casual
Price of Entrees: $5.95 - $14.95
Credit Cards: MC, Visa
Specialties: Chicken, noodles, Pad Thai, deep fried pompano.

Pad Thai Restaurant
850 S. Rancho Dr.
Las Vegas, NV 89106
870-2899
Hours: Mon. - Sat. 11 am - 10 pm; Closed Sun.
Reservations: None
Dress: Casual
Price of Entrees: $5.95 - $11.95
Credit Cards: All major
Specialties: Pad Thai noodles, chicken curry, Gulf of Siam seafood.

Ocha, 1201 Las Vegas Blvd. N., Las Vegas, NV 89101

Plawan Thai Chinese Cuisine
2536 Fremont St.
Las Vegas, NV 89104
384-0484
Hours: Mon. - Sat. 11 am - 10 pm
Reservations: None
Dress: Casual
Price of Entrees: $5.95 - $14.95
Credit Cards: MC, Visa, AMX
Specialties: Super lunch special $4.95; beef broccoli, curry, hot & spicy soup, coconut soup; delivery.

Prommare's Thai Food
6362 W. Sahara Ave.
Las Vegas, NV 89102
221-9644
Hours: Wed. - Mon. 11 am - 10 pm; Sun. 5 pm - 10 pm, Closed Tue.
Reservations: None
Dress: Casual
Price of Entrees: From $9.95
Credit Cards: None
Specialties: Seafood soup, Pad Thai noodles, curries, catfish, crab, squid, chicken, beef, pork.

Siam Garden
3297 Las Vegas Blvd. N.
Las Vegas, NV 89115
644-7770
Hours: noon - 9 pm
Reservations: None
Dress: Casual
Price of Entrees: $5.95 - $12.95
Credit Cards: None
Specialties: Catfish, beef broccoli, chicken chow mein, sun beef, papaya salad.

Tai Pei Restaurant
500 Las Vegas Blvd. S.
Las Vegas, NV 89101
384-7555
Hours: Mon. - Sat. 11 am - 9 pm
Reservations: None
Dress: Casual
Price of Entrees: Inexpensive
Credit Cards: None
Specialties: Mongolian beef, duck, seafood, beef with chile pepper.

Tanya Restaurant
210 W. Sahara Ave.
Las Vegas, NV 89102
388-9923
Hours: Mon. - Sat. 11:30 am - 4:30 am; Sun. 5 pm - 4:30 am
Reservations: None
Dress: Casual
Price of Entrees: $5.95 - $18.95
Credit Cards: MC, Visa, Discover
Specialties: Maine lobster, roast duck

Thai BBQ Restaurant
1424 S. Fourth St.
Las Vegas, NV 89104
383-1128
Hours: 11 am - 9 pm
Reservations: None
Dress: Casual
Price of Entrees: $5.50 - $7.25
Credit Cards: All major
Specialties: Chicken, duck, pork, spareribs, salad.

Thai Classic
AUTHENTIC THAI CUISINE

Thai Classic Restaurant
5980 Spring Mountain Rd.
Las Vegas, NV 89102
227-8424
Hours: Mon. - Sat. 10 am - 10 pm; Sun. 4 pm - 10 pm
Reservations: None
Dress: Casual
Price of Entrees: $5.95 - $9.95
Credit Cards: MC, Visa, AMX
Specialties: Bangkok shrimp, Thai basil and chile, seafood basket.

Thai Cuisine
601 N. Nellis Blvd.
Las Vegas, NV 89110
459-6009
Hours: 11 am - 11 pm
Reservations: None
Dress: Casual
Price of Entrees: $5.95 - $15.95
Credit Cards: Visa
Specialties: Pad Thai, combination fried rice, chicken or pork satay, seafood combination platter.
Atmosphere: Trees, authentic Thai decorations.

Thai & Chinese Food — THAI GARDEN

Thai Garden
5600 Spring Mountain Rd.
Las Vegas, NV 89102
873-9798
Hours: Mon. - Sat. 11 am - 11 pm
Reservations: None
Dress: Casual
Price of Entrees: $5.95 - $12.95
Credit Cards: All major
Specialties: Shrimp with lobster, seafood shrimp curry, spicy squid.

Thai Room
3355 E. Tropicana Ave.
Las Vegas, NV 89121
458-8481
Hours: Mon. - Fri. 11 am - 10 pm; Sat. noon - 10 pm; closed Sun.
Reservations: Suggested
Dress: Casual
Price of Entrees: $6.95 - $13.95; family dinners $10.95 - $13.95 per person
Credit Cards: MC, Visa, Discover
Specialties: Mongolian beef, lobster in curry, Pad Thai noodles, almond chicken, Thai spicy curries; spicy dishes may be ordered mild, medium, hot or very hot. Buffet Mon. - Fri. 10 am - 2 pm $4.95
Atmosphere: Warm and delightful with soft music.

Thai Spice
4433 W. Flamingo Rd.
Las Vegas, NV 89103
362-5308
Hours: 11 am - 10 pm; Fri. - Sat. 11 am - 11 pm
Reservations: Suggested
Dress: Informal
Price of Entrees: $6.95 - $13.95
Credit Cards: All major
Specialties: Siamese duckling, Pad Thai, mee krob; Specialties can be ordered on a heat scale from 1 to 10.

Tycoon Restaurant
4425 E. Tropicana Ave.
Las Vegas, NV 89121
898-6003
Hours: 11 am - 9 pm
Reservations: Accepted
Dress: Semi-formal
Price of Entrees: $6.50 - $20.00
Credit Cards: None
Specialties: Chinese and Thai, spicy; Free delivery $10 min.; Banquet facilities to accommodate 30 people.

Vegas Chinese & Thai Restaurant
115 N. 4th St.
Las Vegas, NV 89101
382-1928
Hours: 10 am - 10 pm

Reservations: None
Dress: Casual
Price of Entrees: Inexpensive
Credit Cards: MC, Visa
Specialties: Mongolian beef, shrimp, chicken.

Xinh Xinh Restaurant
220 W. Sahara Ave,
Las Vegas, NV 89102
Hours: 10 am - 10 pm
Reservations: None
Dress: Casual
Price of Entrees: $4.95 - $8.95
Credit Cards: MC, Visa
Specialties: Traditional Thai cuisine.

VIETNAMESE

A touch of **Ginger**

A Touch of Ginger
4110 S. Maryland Pkwy.
Las Vegas, NV 89119
796-1779
Hours: 11 am - 9 pm
Reservations: Accepted
Dress: Casual
Price of Entrees: $2.95 - $9.50
Credit Cards: None
Specialties: House special - curry chicken, imperial rolls, spring rolls, Mandarin ginger chicken, Mongolian beef, spicy shrimp; buffet 11:30 am - 3 pm $3.95; banquet facilities available.

Pho Chien
3839 W. Sahara Ave.
Las Vegas, NV 89102
873-8749
Hours: 10 am - 9 pm
Reservations: None
Dress: Casual
Price of Entrees: $4.95 - $16.95
Credit Cards: None
Specialties: Beef noodle soup, noodles, shrimp, chicken, pork, stir-fry vegetables, stuffed steamed rice cakes.

Cafe Nicolle, 4760 W. Sahara Ave., Las Vegas, NV 89102 *(see page 135)*

DINING

RESTAURANTS - Ethnic

Pho So 1
4745 Spring Mountain Rd.
Las Vegas, NV 89102
252-3934
Hours: 10 am - 10 pm
Reservations: None
Dress: Casual

Price of Entrees: $5.00 - $7.50
Credit Cards: None
Specialties: Beef and broccoli, chicken with lemon grass, grilled shrimp and pork, shrimp with lemon grass (cooked at your table).
Atmosphere: Oriental decor.

Saigon Restaurant
4251 W. Sahara Ave.
Las Vegas, NV 89102
362-9978
Hours: 10 am - 10 pm
Reservations: Accepted
Dress: Casual

Price of Entrees: Up to $8.75
Credit Cards: All major
Specialties: Shrimp stir fry, squid, chicken in coconut curry, beef and vegetarian dishes.

RESTAURANTS - SPECIALTY

BARBECUE

Big Sky Feast Ranch House Cookin'
Stratosphere
2000 Las Vegas Blvd. S.
Las Vegas, NV 89104
382-4446
Hours: 24
Reservations: None
Dress: Casual
Credit Cards: All major
Specialties: All you can eat BBQ feast $12.95; 1 lb prime rib 13.95.

D & W Open Pit BBQ
3603 Las Vegas Blvd. N.
Las Vegas, NV 89115
643-7616
Hours: Mon. - Fri. 11 am - 10 pm; Sat. noon - 11 pm; closed Sun.
Reservations: None
Dress: Casual
Price of Entrees: Inexpensive
Credit Cards: None
Specialties: Barbecue beef, ribs, chicken, pork.

Memphis Championship Barbecue
4379 Las Vegas Blvd. N.
Las Vegas, NV 89115
644-0000
Hours: Mon. - Fri. 11 am - 10 pm; Sat. 11 am - 10 pm; Sun. noon - 9 pm
Reservations: None
Dress: Casual
Price of Entrees: $5 - $14
Credit Cards: All major
Specialties: Ribs, beef, chicken and pork, Southern style; peanuts are served, throw shells on the floor.
Atmosphere: Free-standing building, comfortable southern funky.

Mountain Springs Saloon
HCR 33 Box 3325
Mountain Springs, NV 89124
875-4266
Highway 160 at Mile Marker 21; Located about 16 miles west of I-15 on Blue Diamond Rd.
Hours: 9 am - 11 pm, later on weekends
Dress: Very casual
Price of Entrees: $5 - $14
Credit Cards: None
Specialties: Smoked barbecue pork or beef ribs, breast of chicken, porterhouse steak, burgers, barbecued beef or pork sandwiches; Fri. and Sat. - Live entertainment from 7 pm; Sun. 3 pm - 8 pm.
Atmosphere: Country setting, horseshoe pit, picnic tables, indoor fireplace; banquet facilities.

Rib House
Imperial Palace
3535 Las Vegas Blvd. S.
Las Vegas, NV 89109
731-3311
Hours: Tue. - Sat. 5 pm - 11 pm
Reservations: Suggested

Tony Roma's A Place for Ribs, 2040 N. Rainbow Blvd., Las Vegas, NV 89108

Dress: Casual
Price of Entrees: $9.95 - $16.95
Credit Cards: All major
Specialties: Barbecued ribs and chicken, original sauces and down-home flavors.

T-Bone's Texas Bar-B-Que
4734 E. Flamingo Rd.
Las Vegas, NV 89121
456-9898
Hours: Mon. - Sat. 10 am - 10 pm
Reservations: None
Dress: Casual
Price of Entrees: $4.25 - $12.95
Credit Cards: MC, Visa
Specialties: Beef brisket, slow-cooked with a hickory-smoked Southwestern sauce, burgers, baby back ribs, peach cobbler. Buckets to go also available.
Atmosphere: Hometown cafe.

TONY ROMA'S
•FAMOUS FOR RIBS•

Tony Roma's A Place for Ribs
Fremont
200 Fremont St.
Las Vegas, NV 89101
385-3232
Hours: Sun. - Thu. 5 pm - 11 pm; Fri. - Sat. 5 pm - midnight
Reservations: None
Dress: Informal
Price of Entrees: $5.95 - $13.95
Credit Cards: All major
Specialties: Barbecued baby back ribs, broiled chicken breast, steaks, barbecued shrimp, onion ring loaf, potato skins. Ribs served Cajun-style, Carolina honey-style or Tony Roma's award-winning style.

Tony Roma's A Place for Ribs
Stardust
3000 Las Vegas, Blvd. S.
Las Vegas, NV 89109
732-6111

Hours: Sun. - Thu. 5 pm - 11 pm; Fri. - Sat. 5 pm - midnight
Reservations: None
Dress: Informal
Price of Entrees: $6.95 - $26.95
Credit Cards: All major
Specialties: Barbecued baby back ribs, broiled chicken breast, steaks, onion ring loaf.

Tony Roma's A Place for Ribs
(Multiple locations listed below)
Hours: Sun. - Thu. 11 am - 10 pm; Fri. - Sat. 11 am - 11 pm
Reservations: None
Dress: Informal
Price of Entrees: $8.49 - $15.99
Credit Cards: All major
Specialties: Barbecued baby back ribs, broiled chicken breast, steaks, famous onion ring loaf.
Atmosphere: Casual

620 E. Sahara Ave.
Las Vegas, NV 89104
733-9914

2040 N. Rainbow Blvd.
Las Vegas, NV 89108
638-2100

Uncle Ben's Bar-B-Que
616 N. H St.
Las Vegas, NV 89106
648-6779
Hours: Mon. - Sat. 11 am - 8:30 pm
Reservations: None
Dress: Casual
Price of Entrees: Inexpensive
Credit Cards: None
Specialties: Beef or pork ribs, barbecued chicken, pork chops.
Atmosphere: Coffee shop.

CAJUN / CREOLE SOUTHERN / SOUL

Big Mama's Cookin'
3765 Las Vegas Blvd. S.
Las Vegas, NV 89109
597-1616
Hours: Sun. - Thu. 11 am - midnight; Fri. - Sat. 11 am - 2 am
Reservations: None
Dress: Casual
Price of Entrees: $5.95 - $11.95
Credit Cards: None
Specialties: BBQ ribs, gumbo and jambalaya, New Orleans seafood, fried chicken, fried catfish, barbecue, blackened red fish, oysters, sandwiches, salads, candied yams, black-eyed peas, red beans.

Chez Place
910 N. Martin Luther King Blvd.
Las Vegas NV 89106
648-8411
Hours: 24 hours
Reservations: Suggested
Dress: Casual
Price of Entrees: Inexpensive
Credit Cards: All major
Specialties: Creole-style dishes; Southern style breakfast; bar.
Atmosphere: Live music occasionally, call ahead.

Kathy's Southern Cooking
6407 Mountain Vista St.
Henderson, NV 89014
433-1005
Hours: Mon. - Thu. 11 am - 9 pm; Fri. - Sat. 11 am - 10 pm; Sun. 1 pm - 8 pm
Reservations: None
Dress: Casual
Price of Entrees: $6.99 - $17.99
Credit Cards: MC, Visa
Specialties: Catfish, fried chicken, chicken fried steak, gumbo, chitlins, barbecued ribs, pork chops, sweet potato pie.

Motown Cafe
New York New York
3790 Las Vegas Blvd. S.
Las Vegas, NV 89109
740-6440
Hours: Mon. - Thu. 7:30 - midnight; Fri. - Sun. 7:30 pm - 2 am
Reservations: None
Dress: Casual
Price of Entrees: $10.95 - $17.95
Credit Cards: All major
Specialties: Chicken waffles, heatwave chicken, pork chops, Smokey's ribs and Southern fried chicken.
Atmosphere: Marvin Gaye and Diana Ross rooms. Largest record (32 ft.) on the ceiling. Staircase decorated with gold CDs from Motown records. Daily live entertainment noon - 11:30 pm. Karaoke Wed.-Thu. 9 pm - 11 pm.

Plantation Room
Showboat
2800 E. Fremont St.
Las Vegas, NV 89104
385-9123
Hours: 5 pm - 11 pm
Reservations: Suggested
Dress: Informal
Price of Entrees: $12.95 - $19.50
Credit Cards: All major
Specialties: Mesquite broiled fresh fish or steaks, jambalaya, ribs, duck.
Atmosphere: Elegant Southern mansion.

Sadie's
505 E. Twain Ave.
Las Vegas, NV 89101
796-4177
Hours: Tue. - Sat. 11 am - 9:45 pm; Sun. 1 pm - 7:45 pm; closed Mon.
Reservations: None
Dress: Casual
Price of Entrees: $6.95 - $14.95
Credit Cards: MC, Visa
Specialties: Southern-style cooking, smothered pork chops, ham hocks and lima beans, fried catfish, gumbo, fried chicken ribs, collard greens, yams, black-eyed peas, sweet potato pie, corn muffins.
Atmosphere: Lounge; Louisiana atmosphere.

Tallulah Too Catering Service
600 W. Jackson St.
Las Vegas, NV 89106
646-8404
Hours: Mon. - Thu. 6 am - 10 pm; Fri. - Sat. 6 am - midnight; Sun. 10 am - 6 pm
Reservations: None
Dress: Casual
Price of Entrees: $1.99 - $7.95
Credit Cards: MC, Visa
Specialties: Louisiana style cooking, seafood gumbo, oxtails, deep-fried catfish, Texas style ribs, liver and onions all served with cornbread; banquet facilities.
Atmosphere: Lounge; Louisiana atmosphere.

CONTINENTAL CUISINE

Anthony's
1550 E. Tropicana Ave.
Las Vegas, NV 89119
454-0000
Hours: Lunch Mon. - Fri. 11 am - 3 pm; Dinner Mon. - Sat. 5 pm - 11 pm, Fri. - Sat. until midnight ; closed Sun.
Reservations: Suggested
Dress: Informal
Price of Entrees: $9.25 - $24.50
Credit Cards: All major
Specialties: Veal, pastas, chicken, chateaubriand; extensive wine list.

The Aristocrat Restaurant
850 S. Rancho Dr.
Las Vegas, NV 89106
870-1977
Hours: Lunch - Daily 11 am - 2 pm; Dinner - Daily 5 pm - 10 pm
Reservations: Suggested
Dress: Informal
Price of Entrees: $25.50 - $32.50
Credit Cards: All major
Specialties: Fresh seafood, osso buco, chicken Oscar, duck, scampi.
Atmosphere: Live music - accordion from 6:30 pm.

Boison's
4503 Paradise Rd.
Las Vegas, NV 89109
732-9993
Hours: Dinner 6 pm - 11 pm
Reservations: Suggested
Dress: Informal
Entrees: $11.00 - $54.00
Credit Cards: All major
Specialties: Rack of lamb, beef Wellington, fresh seafood, roast duck, oysters Rockefeller, flaming desserts, over 70 varieties of wine; banquet facilities for 150.
Atmosphere: Winner of the International Hospitality Award of Excellence, grand piano, waiters in tuxedos, romantic with winery theme.

The Boston Grill & Bar
3417 S. Jones Blvd.
Las Vegas, NV 89102
368-0750
Hours: 24 hours with dinner menu served 4 pm - 11 pm
Reservations: Suggested for dinner.
Dress: Casual - Informal
Price of Entrees: $8.00 - $15.00
Credit Cards: MC, Visa, Discover
Specialties: New England fried clams, Boston baby back ribs, filet mignon; Full bar; banquet facilities to accommodate 150; delivery.
Atmosphere: Contemporary - Boston memorabilia; video poker machines.

Cafe Nicolle
4760 W. Sahara Ave.
Las Vegas, NV 89102
870-7675
Hours: Mon. 11 am - midnight; Tue. - Sat. 11 am - 2 am
Reservations: Suggested
Dress: Informal
Price of Entrees: $8.95 - $18.95
Credit Cards: All major
Specialties: Chicken, veal, lamb chops, seafood, Caesars salad, quiche, crepes.
Atmosphere: Mist-cooled patio dining during warmer months and heaters in the winter; live entertainment Thu. - Sat.

Greens Supper Club
2241 N. Green Valley Pkwy.
Henderson, NV 89014
454-4211
Hours: 8 am - 10:30 pm
Reservations: No
Dress: Informal
Price of Entrees: $9.95 - $17.95
Credit Cards: All major
Specialties: Chateaubriand, roast rack of lamb, prime rib, veal, pastas, orange roughy. Adjacent lounge serves breakfast and traditional bar food 24 hours and breakfast served midnight to 11 am.

Kiefer's Atop the Carriage House
105 E. Harmon Ave.
Las Vegas, NV 89109
739-8000
Hours: Sun. - Thu. 5 pm - 11 pm; Fri. - Sat. 5 pm - midnight; Breakfast - Mon. - Sat. 7 am - 11 am; Sun. 7 am - noon.
Reservations: Suggested
Dress: Informal - Semi-formal
Price of Entrees: $16.95 - $25.95
Credit Cards: All major
Specialties: Chicken cordon bleu, orange roughy Oscar, steaks au poivre, fresh seafood and shellfish.
Atmosphere: Spectacular view of Las Vegas, the Strip and the sunset. Banquet facilities to accommodate 50; full service catering. Piano bar Thu. - Sat. 7 pm - 11 pm, until 1 am Fri. and Sat.

Kiefer's
15 Lake Mead Dr.
Henderson, NV 89115
565-0122
Hours: Lunch daily 11 am - 2 pm; Dinner Mon. - Sat. 5 pm - 11 pm; Sun. 5 pm - 10 pm
Reservations: Suggested
Dress: Informal
Price of Entrees: $9.95 - $24.95
Credit Cards: All major
Specialties: Steaks, fresh seafood, lobster, veal, crab, pastas, oyster bar; Banquet facilities to accommodate up to 100; bar and lounge; food specials served in lounge, burgers $1.50, steak sandwich $4.95.

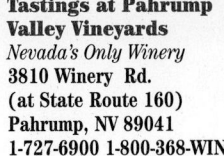

Tastings at Pahrump Valley Vineyards
Nevada's Only Winery
3810 Winery Rd.
(at State Route 160)
Pahrump, NV 89041
1-727-6900 1-800-368-WINE
Hours: Wed. - Sun. Lunch noon - 3 pm; Dinner 5 pm - 9 pm; Sun. 5 pm - 8 pm
Reservations: Strongly suggested.
Dress: Informal
Price of Entrees: Lunch $5.95 - $8.50; Dinner $10.95 - $18.95
Credit Cards: All major
Specialties: Chicken-scampi thermidor, tournedos Rossini, Cajun prime rib, duck l'orange and assorted ice creams made on premises. Complimentary wine tasting at your table. Because we produce and serve Pahrump Valley Vineyards' own wine, bottle prices are very reasonable. Private labeling for special events makes the dining experience unique and fun.
Atmosphere: Intimate and romantic dining with a great view of Charleston Peak; superb cuisine in an atmosphere of quiet elegance. Two viewing towers and a wrap-around veranda for dining "al fresco." Patio dining and outdoor BBQ. Restaurant seats up to 45 and can be reserved for large groups.

Philips Supper House
4545 W. Sahara Ave.
Las Vegas, NV 89102
873-5222
Hours: 4:30 pm - 11 pm
Reservations: Suggested
Dress: Informal
Price of Entrees: $14.95 - $28.95
Credit Cards: All major
Specialties: Wide selection of seafood, prime beef, and Italian specialties. Excellent banquet facilities for parties, meetings, receptions or special occasions; seats 80; separate lounge area.
Atmosphere: Edwardian New England home in the desert. The dining areas range from open rooms decorated in soft wood tones to intimate alcove seating which gives one a feeling of privacy. Piano bar with robot player.

Play It Again Sam
4120 Spring Mountain Rd.
Las Vegas, NV 89102
876-1550
Hours: 11:30 am - 4 am
Reservations: Accepted
Dress: Informal
Price of Entrees: $10.95 - $18.95
Credit Cards: All major
Specialties: Chicken, pastas, seafood, beef; fresh seafood specials nightly. Alaskan crab legs by the pound, appetizers, burgers, sandwiches and salads; banquet facilities accommodate up to 70.
Atmosphere: Casa Blanca atmosphere; live jazz music in lounge. Happy Hour 3 pm - 7 pm with 1/2 price well drinks and domestic beer; complimentary buffet.

Philips Supper House, 4545 W. Sahara Ave., Las Vegas, NV 89102

RESTAURANTS - SPECIALTY

Renata's
4451 E. Sunset Rd.
Henderson, NV 89014
435-4000
Hours: Tue. - Sat. 5 pm - 11 pm; 24-hour bar menu served in adjacent lounge.
Reservations: Suggested
Dress: Informal - Semi-formal
Price of Entrees: $9.25 - $18.00
Credit Cards: All major
Specialties: Fresh seafood, duck, swordfish, rack of lamb, appetizers and an extensive wine list; Chinese specialties; breakfast specials in lounge, 24 hour bar; early bird 2 for 1, Chinese menu from 5 pm - 6:30 pm nightly.
Atmosphere: Elegant dining. Private dining room, LeBistro Du Vin, seats up to 26 people.

ECLECTIC/ CALIFORNIA

Spago
Forum Shops
3500 Las Vegas Blvd. S.
Las Vegas, NV 89109
369-6300
Hours: Cafe daily 11 am - 11 pm; Fri. - Sat. until 1 am; Restaurant Sun. - Thu. 5:30 pm - 10 pm; Fri. - Sat. until midnight
Reservations: Suggested for dining room
Dress: Informal
Price of Entrees: $21 - $27, a la carte
Credit Cards: All major
Specialties: California-style cuisine; smoked salmon and sturgeon, grilled swordfish, sauteed crab cakes, black pepper linguine, grilled free-range chicken, Sonoma lamb, roasted Chinese duck, seared venison; menu changes daily. The cafe, which seats 125, serves appetizers, salads, pizza, sandwiches and complete entrees.
Atmosphere: The main dining room seats 175 with it's exhibition kitchen decorated in copper and tile with colorful art covering the walls. The "outdoor" cafe is available for lunch and more casual dining. Private room to accommodate up to 20 persons and banquet room upstairs to accommodate up to 100; separate bar; gift shop with Spago logo souvenirs available.

Winchester Tap
2327 S. Eastern Ave.
Las Vegas, NV 89104
641-7673
Hours: 24
Reservations: Suggested
Dress: Casual
Price of Entrees: $8 - $14
Credit Cards: All major
Atmosphere: Casual black and white; pool tables and dart boards.

GOURMET DINING

Seasons
Bally's
3645 Las Vegas Blvd. S.
Las Vegas, NV 89109
795-3990
Hours: Tue. - Sat. 6 pm - 11 pm
Reservations: Recommended
Dress: Semi-formal
Price of Entrees: $30 - $50

Credit Cards: All major
Specialties: Filet mignon, fresh Maine lobster, pheasant, chateaubrian, broiled veal chops.
Atmosphere: Decor and menu changes with the seasons. Seating in private alcoves makes for a romantic evening.

Michael's
Barbary Coast
3595 Las Vegas Blvd. S.
Las Vegas, NV 89109
737-7111
Hours: 6 pm - 11 pm with seatings at 6 pm and 6:30 pm, 9 pm and 9:30 pm
Reservations: Required
Dress: Semi-formal
Price of Entrees: $30 - $70; a la carte
Credit Cards: All major
Specialties: Baked escargot, Dover sole, rack of lamb, veal fricassee or piccata. Distinguished Restaurants of North America award.
Atmosphere: Small, intimate room with great service and attention to every detail.

Bacchanal Room
Caesars Palace
3570 Las Vegas Blvd. S.
Las Vegas, NV 89109
731-7525
Hours: Tue. - Sat. with seatings at 6 pm and 6:30 pm, 9 pm and 9:30 pm
Reservations: Required
Dress: Semi-formal
Price of Entrees: $69.50 fixed price menu
Credit Cards: All major
Specialties: Seven-course "Roman Feast" with rack of lamb, filet mignon, Cornish game hen, veal chops, daily fresh fish. Wine, with a selection of three, is included with meal and your glass is kept full by wine goddesses. Caesars chocolates and cappuccino and espresso are included with the meal.
Atmosphere: Belly dancers entertain and occasionally stop to massage gentlemen diners' shoulders and offer grapes. One of the finest restaurants in Las Vegas for over 26 years; music.

Camelot
Excalibur
3850 Las Vegas Blvd. S.
Las Vegas, NV 89109
597-7449
Hours: Wed., Thu., Sun. 6 pm - 10 pm; Fri. 6 pm - 11 pm; Sat. 5 pm - 11 pm
Reservations: Required
Dress: Casual
Price of Entrees: $18.95 - $32.95
Credit Cards: All major
Specialties: Ostrich, buffalo, antelope, festive duck and various fish dishes.
Atmosphere: Beautiful room, food cooked in plain view behind glass.

Flamingo Room
Flamingo Hilton
3555 Las Vegas Blvd. S.
Las Vegas, NV 89109
733-3111
Hours: Breakfast 7 am - noon; Dinner 5 pm - 11 pm
Reservations: Suggested
Dress: Informal
Price of Entrees: $14.95 - $19.95
Credit Cards: All major

Specialties: Broiled swordfish, steaks and chicken.
Atmosphere: The multi level dining room has a view of the pool area.

Second Street Grill
Fremont
200 Fremont St.
Las Vegas, NV 89101
385-6277
Hours: Sun. - Mon. and Thu. 5 pm - 10 pm; Fri. - Sat. 5 pm - 11 pm
Reservations: Suggested
Dress: Semi-formal
Price of Entrees: $13.95 - $34.95
Credit Cards: All major
Specialties: Wok charred salmon, bamboo-steamed Hawaiian snapper, veal chops, French pressed coffee, traditional and contemporary American with a Pacific Rim influence, fresh seafood, beef dry aged 31 days, veal and chicken.
Atmosphere: Upscale room, intimate yet with a casual elegance.

Burgundy Room
Lady Luck
206 N. Third St.
Las Vegas, NV 89101
477-3000
Hours: 5 pm - 11 pm
Reservations: Suggested
Dress: Semi-formal - Informal
Price of Entrees: $12.95 - $39.95
Credit Cards: All major
Specialties: Live Maine lobster, lobster thermidor, rack of lamb, chateaubriand, veal Oscar, beef Wellington.

Great Moments Room
Las Vegas Club & Hotel
18 E. Fremont St.
Las Vegas, NV 89101
385-1664
Hours: 5:30 pm - 10:30 pm
Reservations: Recommended
Dress: Informal
Price of Entrees: $11.00 - $25.00
Credit Cards: All major
Specialties: Flamed pepper steak, prime Angus beef, bouillabaisse.
Atmosphere: English hunting club decor.

Isis
Luxor
3900 Las Vegas Blvd. S.
Las Vegas, NV 89119
262-4773
Hours: 6 pm - 11 pm
Reservations: Suggested
Dress: Semi-formal
Price of Entrees: $24 and up a la carte
Credit Cards: All major
Specialties: Continental dining; beef, seafood and chicken specialties.
Atmosphere: Guests enter the restaurant through an intimate colonnade walk of caryatid statues. Inside the housing, authenticated reproductions of Egyptian artifacts modeled after the Egyptian Museum in Cairo. The ceiling is vaulted with hundreds of gold Egyptian stars.

La Scala
MGM Grand
3799 Las Vegas Blvd.
Las Vegas, NV 89109
891-1111
Hours: 5:30 pm - 11 pm

Reservations: Required
Dress: Casual elegant
Price of Entrees: $25 - $60
Menu changes daily. Lobster linguine, fish of the day and rack of lamb.
Atmosphere: Casual elegant decor modeled after the famous opera house in Milan, Italy. Dining booths replicate a theater balcony. Waterfall in center of room and two on the back walls. Musical instruments and opera posters adorn the walls. The full service bar features a wine rack that holds 2,000 of the finest wines.

Canyon Dining Room
Mt. Charleston Hotel & Restaurant
2 Kyle Canyon Rd.
Mt. Charleston, NV 89124
1-872-5500
Hours: Sun. - Thu. 7 am - 9:30 pm; Fri. - Sat. 7 am - 10:30 pm
Reservations: Suggested
Dress: Casual - Informal
Price of Entrees: $9.95 - $25.00
Credit Cards: All major
Specialties: Steaks, seafood, veal, Italian dishes. For $179 per person, Sundance Helicopter will deliver you to the Mt. Charleston Hotel for dinner. The meal is included in the price. The evening starts at Signature Flight Services at 5:30 pm where you will be whisked over Red Rock Canyon to the hotel, where you have dinner and return over downtown Las Vegas and the Strip at 7:30 pm.
Atmosphere: Very calm and peaceful; large windows with a beautiful view of Kyle Canyon.

Center Stage
Jackie Gaughan's Plaza Hotel
1 S. Main St.
Las Vegas, NV 89101
386-2464
Hours: 5 pm - midnight
Reservations: Required
Dress: Informal
Price of Entrees: $5.95 - $12.95
Credit Cards: All major
Specialties: Steaks, roast prime rib of beef, broiled pork chops, chicken, Alaskan crab legs.
Atmosphere: Spectacular glass-domed room is located at the end of Fremont St. on the second floor of the hotel, the Center Stage offers the best view of the Fremont Street Experience downtown.

Fiore
Rio Suite Hotel
3700 W. Flamingo Rd.
Las Vegas, NV 89103
252-7777
Hours: 5 pm - 11 pm
Reservations: Recommended
Dress: Semi-formal
Price of Entrees: $26 - $48
Credit Cards: All major
Specialties: Country cuisine from around the world presented in a new American style. Menu selections change daily. Chefs create any request.
Atmosphere: World class dining in an estate setting. Serene cigar terrace featuring vintage cigars. The Fiore herb terrace provides the freshest herbs available.

Paparazzi Grille
San Remo
115 E. Tropicana Ave.
Las Vegas, NV 89109
739-9000
Hours: 6 pm - midnight
Reservations: Suggested
Dress: Semi-formal
Price of Entrees: $16.95 - $29.95
Credit Cards: All major
Specialties: Beef Wellington, veal, duck, seafood, chateaubriand; exquisite cuisine and gourmet continental delicacies; music.
Atmosphere: Rich dark wood interior.

Top of the World Restaurant
Stratosphere
2000 Las Vegas Blvd. S.
Las Vegas, NV 89104
380-7711
Hours: 5 pm - 11 pm, until midnight on Fri. and Sat.
Reservations: Suggested
Dress: Casual - Elegant
Credit Cards: All major
Specialties: Steaks, fresh fish, lobster.
Atmosphere: Restaurant revolves once an hour; spectacular 360-degree view of Las Vegas.

Buccaneer Bay Club

Buccaneer Bay Club
Treasure Island
3300 Las Vegas Blvd. S.
Las Vegas, NV 89109
894-7111
Hours: 5 pm - 10:30 pm

Reservations: Required
Dress: Casual- Elegant
Price of Entrees: $14.95 - $28
Credit Cards: All major
Specialties: Salmon, spit roasted duckling, lobster, center prime rib.
Atmosphere: Enjoy a panoramic view of Buccaneer Bay and the hourly sea battle while dining on gourmet fare.

HEALTH FOOD

Carrot Patch Nutrition Center/Mr. Greengenes
3661 S. Maryland Pkwy.
Las Vegas, NV 89109
735-2800
Hours: Lunch counter Mon. - Fri. 10 am - 4 pm; Sat. 11 am - 4 pm; Store hours: Mon. - Sat. 9 am - 6 pm; Sun. 11 am - 5 pm
Reservations: None
Dress: Casual
Credit Cards: MC, Visa, AMX, Discover
Specialties: Veggie burger, homemade soups, salads, taco salad, sandwiches; fresh juices.

Erby's Sunshine Foods
4596 Spring Mountain Rd.
Las Vegas, NV 89102
222-1022
Hours: Mon. - Fri. 10 am - 7 pm; Sat. 10 am - 4 pm
Reservations: None
Dress: Casual
Price of Entrees: $4.00 - $7.00
Credit Cards: All major
Specialties: Veggie burgers, Greek wonder salad, smoothies, tabouli wrap, bible sandwich.

Fresh Blend Smoothie and Juice Bar
(Multiple locations listed below)
Hours: Mon. - Thu. 7 am - 10 pm; Sat. 8 am - 10 pm; Sun. 9 am - 10 pm
Reservations: None
Dress: Casual
Credit Cards: None
Specialties: Fresh juice, smoothies, cinnamon rolls, soups and healthy snacks.

4500 E. Sunset Rd., Ste. 117
Henderson, NV 89014
436-5582

2600 W. Sahara Ave.
Las Vegas, NV 89102
257-7113

Juice Blenders
4632 S. Maryland Pkwy.
Las Vegas, NV 89119
795-2676
Hours: Mon. - Sat. 8:30 am - 8 pm
Reservations: None
Dress: Casual
Credit Cards: None
Specialties: Fresh juices and fruit smoothies, sandwiches and salads.

Power Smoothie
7762 W. Sahara Ave.
Las Vegas, NV 89117
228-1125
Hours: Mon. - Fri. 7 am - 10 pm; Sat. 10 am - 8 pm; Sun. 11 am - 6 pm
Reservations: None
Dress: Casual
Price of Entrees: $3 - $6
Credit Cards: MC, Visa

Specialties: Subs and pitas, smoothies, salads.
Atmosphere: Coffee shop.

Rainbow's End
1100 E. Sahara Ave.
Las Vegas, NV 89104
737-7282
Hours: Mon. - Sat. 9 am - 9 pm; Sun. 11 am - 6 pm
Reservations: None
Dress: Casual
Credit Cards: MC, Visa, AMX
Specialties: Sandwiches and fresh juices. All vegetarian food. Complete selection of natural herbs and vitamins.

Wild Oats Community Market & Cafe
(Multiple locations & hours listed below)
Reservations: None
Dress: Casual
Credit Cards: None
Specialties: Salads, homemade soups, "super natural" sandwiches, steamed vegetables and organic brown rice, natural burritos, vegetarian chili.

3455 E. Flamingo Rd.
Las Vegas, NV 89121
434-8115
Hours: Cafe hours: 10 am - 8 pm; Store hours: 8 am - 9 pm

6720 W. Sahara Ave.
Las Vegas, NV 89102
253-7050
Hours: Cafe: daily 10 am - 8 pm; Store: 8 am - 9 pm

DINING

RESTAURANTS - SPECIALTY

SEAFOOD

Benihana Seafood Grille
Las Vegas Hilton
(See Japanese)

The Broiler
Boulder Station
4111 Boulder Hwy.
Las Vegas, NV 89121
432-7777
Hours: Sun. - Thu. 5 pm - 10 pm;
Fri. - Sat. 5 pm - 11 pm
Reservations: Suggested
Dress: Casual
Price of Entrees: $11.00 - $23.00
Credit Cards: All major
Specialties: 1 lb crab leg dinner and all-you-can-eat soup and salad bar, $16.95; Sun. brunch 10 am - 3 pm $13.95.

The Broiler
Palace Station
2411 W. Sahara Ave.
Las Vegas, NV 89102
367-2411
Hours: 11 am - 11 pm;
Fri. - Sat. noon - 11 pm
Reservations: Suggested
Dress: Informal
Price of Entrees: $7.95 - $35.00
Credit Cards: All major
Specialties: Mesquite-grilled salmon, halibut, shark, sea bass, catfish; fish and meats are cooked on glass-enclosed broiler. One pound crab leg dinner served Mon. - Fri. 11 am to 11 pm; Sat. - Sun. noon - 11 pm $16.95; complete lobster tail dinner served 4 pm - 11 pm $28.95; oyster bar located at entrance.

Buzios Seafood Restaurant
Rio Suite Hotel
3700 W. Flamingo Rd.
Las Vegas, NV 89103
252-7777
Hours: 11 am - 11 pm
Reservations: None
Dress: Informal
Price of Entrees: $13.50 - $45.95
Credit Cards: All major
Specialties: Featuring the finest North and South Pacific seafood flown in fresh daily. Chowders, cioppino, bouillabaisse, steamed mussels, clams, king crab legs, lobster capellini, fresh oysters flown in daily. Buzios serves 16 wines by the glass.
Atmosphere: All exhibition cooking area offers diners the unique opportunity to see their food prepared before them.

Captain's Galley
455 S. Decatur Blvd.
Las Vegas, NV 89107
870-7682
Hours: Mon. - Sat. 11 am - 9:30 pm
Reservations: None
Dress: Casual
Price of Entrees: $8.50 - $12.50
Credit Cards: All major
Specialties: Fresh clams, oysters, lobster, crab legs, pasta, steaks, chicken.
Atmosphere: Nautical theme.

Buzios Seafood Restaurant at Rio, 3700 W. Flamingo Rd., Las Vegas, NV

Costa Del Sol
Sunset Station
1301 W. Sunset Rd.
Henderson, NV 89014
547-7801
Hours: Sun. - Thu. 5 pm - 10 pm
Reservations: Suggested
Dress: Casual - Elegant
Price of Entrees: $9.99-$21.99
Credit Cards: All major
Specialties: Choose your own topping to complement your entree such as "The Mirabella" chunks of gulf shrimp in asiago cream sauce served over your favorite fish or seafood entree, or try one of the other specialties like filet mignon with wild mushroom ragout, rack of lamb with brandy mint jus or spicy corn-meal encrusted oysters, fried crispy and served with cajun tartar sauce.
Atmosphere: Mediterranean fishing village with boats and fishing wharf motif.

Emeril Lagasse's New Orleans Fish House
MGM Grand
3799 Las Vegas Blvd. S.
Las Vegas, NV 89109
891-7374
Hours: 11 am - 10:30 pm
Reservations: Suggested
Dress: Informal
Price of Entrees: $20 - $38
Credit Cards: All major
Specialties: Chef Emeril Lagasse's blend of modern Creole/Cajun cooking features his delectable signature dish, Emeril's BBQ shrimp. Also on the menu-fresh fish flown in daily and many other delicious entrees. All dishes are homemade from the bread to the tantalizing desserts featuring banana cream pie with banana crust and caramel. Grilled duck, Louisiana lump crabmeat cakes, tuna steak, grilled creole spiced ribeye steak.

Joe's Crab Shack
1991 N. Rainbow Blvd.
Las Vegas, NV 89108
646-3996
Hours: Sun. - Thu. 11 am - 10 pm;
Fri. - Sat. 11 am - 11 pm
Reservations: Recommended
Dress: Casual
Price of Entrees: Inexpensive
Credit Cards: All major
Specialties: Seafood combo, fried oysters, coconut shrimp, Blue and Alaskan snow crabs, King crab legs.
Atmosphere: Fishing shack with indoor and outdoor seating available; servers entertain you while you dine on the freshest seafood available.

Kim Tar Seafood Restaurant
Chinatown Plaza
4215 Spring Mountain Rd.
Las Vegas, NV 89102
227-3588
Hours: 10 am - 11 pm
Reservations: Suggested
Dress: Casual-Elegant
Price of Entrees: $4.75 - $12.95
Credit Cards: All major
Specialties: Lobster, crab, shrimp, scallops, clams, chicken and pork.
Atmosphere: Oriental theme with mirrored windows and a Buddha greeting you at the door.

Kokomo's
Mirage
3400 Las Vegas Blvd. S.
Las Vegas, NV 89109
791-7111
Hours: Lunch 11 am - 2:30 pm;
Dinner 5:30 pm - 11:00 pm
Reservations: Suggested
Dress: Informal
Price of Entrees: $19.50 - $30.00
Credit Cards: All major
Specialties: Steaks and fresh seafood, roast prime rib, Dungeness crab cakes, lamb chops, loin of pork, swordfish.
Atmosphere: Exotic "outdoor" restaurant situated within the tropical rain forest of the atrium. Guests dine in the controlled open-air environment surrounded by waterfalls and a sparkling interior lagoon.

Landry's Seafood House
2610 W. Sahara Ave.
Las Vegas, NV 891
251-0101
Hours: 11 am - 10 pm; Fri. and Sat. til 11 pm
Reservations: Accepted for large parties.
Price of Entrees: $10.95 - $17.95
Credit Cards: All major
Specialties: Crawfish, blackened Ahi tuna, oysters on the half-shell, certified Angus beef, pastas.

La Barca Mexican Seafood Restaurant
2517 E. Lake Mead Blvd.
Las Vegas, NV 89115
657-9700
Hours: Fri. - Sun. 10 am - 10 pm
Reservations: Accepted
Dress: Casual
Price of Entrees: Inexpensive
Credit Cards: None
Specialties: Site of restaurant scene in movie *Leaving Las Vegas*; specialties include fish and shrimp taco, ocean perch, 45-ounce shrimp cocktail, seven-seas soup.
Atmosphere: Relaxed; mariachi music.

Joe's Crab Shack, 1991 N. Rainbow Blvd., Las Vegas, NV 89108

The Plank at Treasure Island, 3300 Las Vegas Blvd. S., Las Vegas, NV 89109

The Lobster House
3763 Las Vegas Blvd. S.
Las Vegas, NV 89109
740-4430
Hours: 5 pm - 11:30 pm
Reservations: Suggested
Dress: Casual - Elegant
Price of Entrees: $17.50 - $49.50
Credit Cards: All major
Specialties: Live Maine lobster, Alaskan king crab legs, prime rib.

Mediterranean Room
Gold Coast
4000 W. Flamingo Rd.
Las Vegas, NV 89103
367-7111
Hours: 5 pm - 11 pm
Reservations: Suggested
Dress: Informal
Price of Entrees: $4.95 - $24.95
Credit Cards: All major
Specialties: Swordfish, cioppino, veal picante.

Nero's
Caesars Palace
3570 Las Vegas Blvd. S.
Las Vegas, NV 89109
731-7731
Hours: Sun. - Fri. 5:30 pm - 10 pm;
Sat. 5:30 pm - 10:30 pm
Reservations: Suggested
Dress: Semi-formal
Price of Entrees: $18.50 - $50, a la carte
Credit Cards: All major
Specialties: Fresh seafood and prime aged beef, chicken, veal.
Atmosphere: Art deco, contemporary with excellent service.

Palm Restaurant
Forum Shops
3500 Las Vegas Blvd. S.
Las Vegas, NV 89109
732-7256
Hours: 11:30 am - 11 pm
Reservations: Suggested
Dress: Informal
Price of Entrees: $15.95 - $140 for 7 lb lobster
Credit Cards: MC, Visa, AMX, CB, Diners
Specialties: Live Maine lobster, prime steaks.

The Plank
Treasure Island
3300 Las Vegas Blvd. S.
Las Vegas, NV 89109
894-7111
Hours: 5:30 pm - 10:30 pm
Reservations: Suggested
Dress: Casual
Price of Entrees: $14.95 - $40
Credit Cards: All major
Specialties: Island stuffed lobster, swordfish, Alaskan king crab.
Atmosphere: Relaxing, nautical and library decor.

Red Lobster Restaurant
200 S. Decatur Blvd.
Las Vegas, NV 89107
877-0212
Hours: Sun. - Thu. 11 am - 10 pm;
Fri. - Sat. 11 am - 11 pm
Reservations: Accepted , call ahead seating.
Dress: Informal
Price of Entrees: $7.99 - $34.99
Credit Cards: All major
Specialties: Part of a nationwide chain specializing in seafood flown in fresh daily; bar; children's menu.
Atmosphere: Comfortable, homey.

2325 E. Flamingo Rd.
Las Vegas, NV 89119
731-0119

Rosewood Grille & Lobster House
3339 Las Vegas Blvd. S.
Las Vegas, NV 89109
792-9099
Hours: 4:30 pm - 11 pm
Reservations: Suggested
Dress: Semi-formal
Price of Entrees: Starting at $19.50
Credit Cards: All major
Specialties: Fresh seafood and steaks; live jumbo Maine lobster (3 - 9 lbs) steamed whole and served with drawn butter, roast rack of lamb, poached salmon, scampi Portofino; fresh strawberries and Dom Perignon; Award of Excellence from the *Wine Spectator* magazine for wine selection. Formerly Ye Olde Lobster House.
Atmosphere: Elegant dining room features spacious booths and impeccable service.

The Sacred Sea
Luxor
3900 Las Vegas Blvd. S.
Las Vegas, NV 89119
262-4772
Hours: 5 pm - 11 pm
Reservations: Suggested
Dress: Informal
Price of Entrees: $10.95 - $25.95
Credit Cards: All major
Specialties: Fresh and saltwater seafood shipped daily from the East and West coasts, cioppino, shellfish, veal chops, New York steaks and poultry.
Atmosphere: Egyptian theme restaurant boasts murals and hieroglyphic reproductions of fishing on the Nile, as well as intricate tile mosaics. The room's centerpiece is a fishing boat mast and sail centered in a dramatic angled window.

St. Thomas Seafood Grotto
New Frontier
3120 Las Vegas Blvd. S.
Las Vegas, NV 89109
794-8240
Hours: Sun. - Thu. 11 am - 2:30 pm and 5 pm - 10 pm; Sat. 8 am - 2:30 pm and 5 pm - 11 pm
Reservations: Suggested
Dress: Informal
Price of Entrees: $12.95 - $18.95
Credit Cards: MC, Visa, AMX
Specialties: Salmon fettucini, halibut St. Thomas, thresher shark, mahi-mahi island style. Oriental specialties.
Atmosphere: Waterfalls and a babbling brook highlight this open air restaurant that overlooks the pool area.

Seahouse
Imperial Palace
3535 Las Vegas Blvd. S.
Las Vegas, NV 89109
731-3311
Hours: Fri. - Tue. 5 pm - 11 pm
Reservations: Suggested
Dress: Informal
Price of Entrees: $9.95 - $29.95
Credit Cards: All major
Specialties: Fresh seafood, Alaskan king crab legs, shrimp fettuccine, live Maine lobster, New York steak, San Francisco cioppino, filet mignon and Australian lobster tail combination.
Atmosphere: Quaint New England decor.

Señor Frogs
3190 W. Sahara Ave.
Las Vegas, NV 89102
873-3345
Hours: 11 am - 5 am
Reservations: Only for parties of 6 or more.
Dress: Casual
Price of Entrees: Reasonable
Credit Cards: All major
Specialties: Swordfish, halibut, lobster tails, Alaskan king crab legs, fried shrimp, prime steaks, prime rib, baby back ribs; banquet facilities for up to 150. Valet parking.

Starboard Tack
2601 Atlantic Ave.
Las Vegas, NV 89121
457-8794
Hours: Mon. - Thu. 11 am - 10 pm;
Fri. 11 am - 11 pm; Sat. 3 pm - 1 am;
Sun. 3 pm - 11 am
Reservations: Suggested
Dress: Informal
Price of Entrees: $14 - $20
Credit Cards: All major
Specialties: Fresh catch of the day, prime Eastern beef, jumbo prawns, steamed clams, mahi-mahi.
Atmosphere: Quiet nautical theme with three fireplaces. Banquet facilities; lounge.

The Tillerman
2245 E. Flamingo Rd.
Las Vegas, NV 89119
731-4036
Hours: 5 pm - 11 pm
Reservations: Suggested
Dress: Informal
Price of Entrees: $15.95 - $36.95
Credit Cards: All major
Specialties: Voted "Best Seafood House" in Las Vegas. Award of Excellence from the *Wine Spectator* magazine for wine selection. Farm raised salmon from Norway, Australian whole lobster, rainbow trout, thresher shark, Florida red snapper, Alaskan crab, tuna, swordfish, orange roughy, chicken and pasta dishes; salad brought to table in a lazy Susan. Small intimate lounge. Banquet facilities available to accommodate 25 - 85.
Atmosphere: High ceilings with retractable skylights and large ficus trees create a unique dining setting.

The Tillerman, 2245 E. Flamingo Rd., Las Vegas, NV 89119

DINING

RESTAURANTS - SPECIALTY

STEAKHOUSES

Alan Albert's
3763 Las Vegas Blvd. S.
Las Vegas, NV 89109
795-4006
Hours: 5 pm - 11:30 pm
Reservations: Suggested
Dress: Informal
Price of Entrees: $14.50 and up
Credit Cards: Visa, MC
Specialties: Steaks, veal steak, lamb chops, lobster

All American Bar & Grille
Rio Suite Hotel
3700 W. Flamingo Rd.
Las Vegas, NV 89103
252-7767
Hours: 11 am - 11 pm
Reservations: Suggested
Dress: Informal
Price of Entrees: $11.95 - $25.95
Credit Cards: All major
Specialties: Steaks and seafood, pork ribs cooked on a mesquite grill located at the entrance of the dining room. All meals include salad, sourdough bread, potato and vegetable. Burgers and sandwiches served in the All American Bar and Grill at the entrance to the restaurant. Lunch menu served 11 am - 5 pm, $4.50 - $7.25.

Big Sky Steakhouse
Stratosphere
2000 Las Vegas Blvd. S.
Las Vegas, Nv 89104
380-7777
Hours: 4 pm - 11 pm
Reservations: Suggested
Dress: Casual - Elegant
Price of Entrees: $9.95 - $14.95
Credit Cards: All major
Specialties: Prime rib and thick steaks.
Atmosphere: Reminiscent of how the West once was with chuckwagons, spectacular 3-d scenery and hardwood flooring.

Billy Bob's Steakhouse & Saloon
Sam's Town
5111 Boulder Hwy.
Las Vegas, NV 89121
454-8031
Hours: 4:30 pm - 10 pm
Reservations: Recommended
Dress: Casual
Price of Entrees: $13 - $22
Credit Cards: All major
Specialties: 28-ounce ribeye steak.

Atmosphere: Casual dining in a western setting with a large rotating water wheel in the dining room.

Binion's Horseshoe Steakhouse
Binion's Horseshoe
128 Fremont St.
Las Vegas, NV 89101
382-1600
Hours: 5 pm - 10:45 pm
Reservations: Recommended
Dress: Casual - Informal
Price of Entrees: $16.00 - $34.00
Credit Cards: All major
Specialties: Steaks, prime rib, seafood.
Atmosphere: Outside glass elevator to the 24th floor of the Horseshoe and a great view of Las Vegas.

Blackstone's
Monte Carlo
3770 Las Vegas Blvd. S.
Las Vegas, NV 89109
730-7777
Hours: 5:30 pm - 11 pm
Reservations: Suggested
Dress: Informal
Price of Entrees: $17 - $37
Credit Cards: All major
Specialties: Top sirloin, filet mignon, veal chops, halibut, roast duck, lamb chops.
Atmosphere: European elegance.

Bob Taylor's Original Ranch House Supper Club
6250 Rio Vista St.
Las Vegas, NV 89130
645-1399
Hours: Sun. - Thu. 5 pm - 10 pm;
Fri. - Sat. 5 pm - 11 pm
Reservations: Suggested
Dress: Casual - Informal
Price of Entrees: $11.95 - $35.95
Credit Cards: All major
Specialties: Thick steaks cooked over a crackling mesquite grill, seafood, chicken; 28-ounce Diamond Jim Brady cut.
Atmosphere: Old West style stone and wood ranch house frequented in the past by such celebrities as Frank Sinatra and Sammy Davis, Jr; location of the skeet-shooting scene from *Viva Las Vegas*. Recently reopened with only a few cosmetic changes the new owners will maintain the atmosphere and the very best quality food and finest service available in Las Vegas.

The Broiler
Palace Station
2411 W. Sahara Ave.
Las Vegas, NV 89102
367-2408
Hours: Mon. - Fri. 11 am - 11 pm;
Sat. - Sun. noon - 11 pm
Reservations: Suggested
Dress: Casual
Credit Cards: All major
Specialties: Australian lobster, steaks, 1 lb Alaskan king crab $16.95.

Brown Derby
MGM Grand
3799 Las Vegas Blvd. S.
Las Vegas, NV 89109
891-7318
Hours: 5:30 pm - 11 pm
Reservations: Suggested
Dress: Informal
Price of Entrees: $16 - $45, a la carte
Credit Cards: All major
Specialties: Mesquite-broiled corn-fed beef, dover sole, rack of lamb.

Canal Street Grille
The Orleans
4500 W. Tropicana Ave.
Las Vegas, NV 89103
365-7111
Hours: 5 pm - 11 pm
Reservations: Suggested
Dress: Casual - Elegant
Price of Entrees: $12.95 - $24.95
Credit Cards: All major
Specialties: prime rib, steaks, fresh seafood.
Atmosphere: Enter through a door of intricately carved glass and dine in elegance New Orleans-style.

Carvers
2061 West Sunset Rd.
Henderson, NV 89014
433-5801
Hours: Mon. - Thu. 5 pm - 9:30 pm;
Fri. - Sat. 5 pm - 10 pm; Sun. 5 pm - 9 pm
Reservations: Suggested
Dress: Informal
Price of Entrees: $16 - $23
Credit Cards: MC, Visa, AMX, Diners
Specialties: prime rib, veal chops, roasted salmon, duck
Atmosphere: Rustic, elegant with rich wood tones and high vaulted ceilings; cigar friendly.

Cavalier Restaurant
3850 E. Desert Inn Rd.
Las Vegas, NV 89121
451-6221
Hours: 24 hours; Lunch 11 am - 4 pm;
Dinner 4 pm - 11 pm; Breakfast 11 pm - 11 am
Reservations: Only for parties of 5 or more.
Dress: Casual
Price of Entrees: $8.95 - $19
Credit Cards: MC, Visa, AMX
Specialties: Prime rib, NY steak, prawns; all dinners include salad bar; bar and lounge.

The Coachman's Inn
3240 S. Eastern Ave.
Las Vegas, NV 89109
731-4202
Hours: 24 hrs
Reservations: Suggested
Dress: Casual
Price of Entrees: $10.00 - $40.00
Credit Cards: MC, Visa, AMX, Discover
Specialties: Famous prime rib (three cuts), chicken Angelo, seafood, Australian lobster; bar; patio.
Atmosphere: Intimate and comfortable. Fireplace, dark wood, open beamed ceiling. No windows. Reminiscent of a mountain chalet. Bar area. Banquet facilities available to accommodate 35 people.

Conductor's Room
Railroad Pass
2800 Boulder Hwy.
Henderson, NV 89015
294-5000
Hours: 5 pm - 10 pm
Reservations: None
Dress: Casual
Price of Entrees: $5 - $25
Specialties: Steaks and seafood.

Conrads
Flamingo Hilton
3555 Las Vegas Blvd. S.
Las Vegas, NV 89109
733-3502
Hours: Thu. - Mon. 5:30 pm - 11:30 pm
Reservations: Suggested
Dress: Informal
Price of Entrees: $25.00 - $60.00
Credit Cards: All major
Specialties: Steaks, lobster, prime rib, Beluga caviar, dover sole, swordfish, lobster bisque.
Atmosphere: Uniquely decorated to accentuate the glamour of Old England.

Cortez Room
Gold Coast
4000 W. Flamingo Rd.
Las Vegas, NV 89103
367-7111
Hours: 5 pm - 11 pm
Reservations: Suggested - Required
Dress: Informal
Price of Entrees: $7 - $15
Credit Cards: All major
Specialties: Prime rib, 1 1/4 pound porterhouse, broiled half chicken, baby back ribs; fresh bread along with the potato of your choice are served with entrees.
Atmosphere: Dining room has a Spanish decor with large comfortable booths.

Cowboy Steakout
Silverton Hotel & Casino
3333 Blue Diamond Rd.
Las Vegas, NV 89139
263-7777
Specialties: Cowboy Steakout served poolside every Tue. during the spring and summer 5 pm - 9 pm. 14-ounce T-bone steak includes spuds and corn in the husk from the "hot" wagon. $7.77 per person.

Diamond Lil's
Sam's Town
5111 Boulder Hwy.
Las Vegas, NV 89122
454-8009
Hours: Fri. - Sat. 5:30 pm - 10:30 pm;
Sun. 5:30 pm - 11 pm
Reservations: Accepted
Dress: Semi-formal
Price of Entrees: $15 - $20
Credit Cards: All major
Specialties: USDA choice beef broiled over mesquite; 18 ounce porterhouse steak, veal, lamb, baby back ribs, prime rib, lobster tail, variety of fresh fish, blackened, baked or broiled.
Atmosphere: Sparkling Old West elegance.

El Gaucho Steak House
Tropicana
3801 Las Vegas Blvd. S.
Las Vegas, NV 89109
739-2222
Hours: 5 pm - 11 pm
Reservations: Suggested
Dress: Informal
Price of Entrees: $16.95 - $29.95
Credit Cards: All major
Specialties: Center cut New York steak, prime rib of beef, filet mignon, top sirloin, T-bone, porterhouse, and seafood specialties such as the El Gaucho duet, an 8-ounce filet mignon and lobster tail, swordfish Mazatlan, halibut steak, black bean soup, beer-battered onion rings; dinners are served with a relish tray, salad, loaf of hot bread, and entrees served with baked potato or rice and vegetable. Diners can select the cut of meat from the glass case.

The Embers
Imperial Palace
3535 Las Vegas Blvd. S.
Las Vegas, NV 89109
731-3311
Hours: Wed. - Sun. 5 pm - 11 pm
Reservations: Suggested
Dress: Informal
Price of Entrees: $9.95 - $39.95
Credit Cards: All major
Specialties: Roast prime rib, steaks, fresh seafood, veal, Caesar salad, flaming desserts.

Gallaghers
New York New York
3790 Las Vegas Blvd. S.
Las Vegas, NV 89109
740-6450
Hours: 4 pm - 11:30 pm
Reservations: Suggested
Dress: Casual - Elegant
Price of Entrees: $17.95 - $75
Credit Cards: All major
Specialties: Offering prime New York porterhouse and filet mignon steaks as well as the freshest seafood available.
Atmosphere: New York City's original steakhouse since 1927 now available at New York New York for your dining pleasure.

Gentleman Jack's Supperclub
3620 E. Flamingo Ave.
Las Vegas, NV 89121
435-1299
Hours: 11 am - midnight
Reservations: Suggested
Dress: Informal
Price of Entrees: From $19.95
Credit Cards: All major
Specialties: Seafood, steaks, penne amatriciana, rack of lamb, roast duck, filet mignon.
Atmosphere: Quiet, elegant.

Golden Steer
308 W. Sahara Ave.
Las Vegas, NV 89102
384-4470
Hours: 4:30 pm - 11:30 pm
Reservations: Suggested
Dress: Informal
Price of Entrees: $20.00 - $30.00
Credit Cards: All major

Hungry Hunter, 2380 S. Rainbow Blvd., Las Vegas, NV 89102

Specialties: Steaks, prime rib, quail, seafood, Italian cuisine. The portions are large and the quality superior; lounge; banquet facilities; valet parking.
Atmosphere: Old West motif with seating in several dining areas; local and tourist favorite since 1959.

Gold Strike Inn Steakhouse
Gold Strike Inn
Highway 93
Boulder City, NV 89005
293-5000
Hours: 5 pm - 10 pm
Reservations: Recommended
Dress: Casual
Price of Entrees: $7 - $22
Credit Cards: All major
Specialties: Lemon-lime roughy, shrimp, prime rib, chicken, stuffed turkey.

Hilltop House Supper Club
3500 N. Rancho Dr.
Las Vegas, NV 89130
645-9904
Hours: Sun. - Mon. 5 pm - 9 pm; Wed. - Sat. 5 pm - 9 pm; closed Tue.
Reservations: None
Dress: Informal
Price of Entrees: $7.50 - $38.95
Credit Cards: All major
Specialties: Pan fried lobster tails, steaks, frog legs, chicken. Fresh salad bar, homemade desserts, small bar; children's menu.
Atmosphere: Home-like atmosphere.

Hilton Steakhouse
Las Vegas Hilton
3000 Paradise Rd.
Las Vegas, NV 89109
732-5111
Hours: 5:30 pm - 10:30 pm
Reservations: Required
Dress: Semi-formal
Price of Entrees: $19 - $37
Credit Cards: All major
Specialties: New York, rib eye and T-bone steaks, fresh seafood, chicken, lamb chops. Steaks are prepared over aromatic mesquite wood.
Atmosphere: Texas-sized meals in an atmosphere reminiscent of the American Southwest. Casual, yet elegant, Western

ambience lends to this unique dining experience. Rich mahogany booths and chairs, etched glass and distinct pieces of modern art.

Hugo's Cellar
Four Queens
202 Fremont St.
Las Vegas, NV 89101
385-4011
Hours: 5:30 pm - 10:30 pm
Reservations: Suggested - Required
Dress: Semi-formal
Price of Entrees: $24.00 - $49.00
Credit Cards: All major
Specialties: Steaks, prime rib, tournedos Hugo, roast rack of lamb, broiled swordfish, veal; salad cart brought to your table, included with entree; chocolate dipped fruits served with whipped cream for dessert. Award of Excellence from the *Wine Spectator* magazine for wine selection.
Atmosphere: Wine cellar atmosphere in an intimate setting. Ladies receive a long-stemmed rose as they are seated.

Hungry Hunter
2380 S. Rainbow Blvd.
Las Vegas, NV 89102
873-0433
Hours: Mon. - Thu. 11 am - 2:30 pm; limited cafe menu 3 pm - 5 pm; Mon. - Thu. 5 pm - 9:30 pm; Fri. - Sat. 5 pm - 10 pm; Sun. 4:30 pm - 10 pm
Reservations: Suggested
Dress: Casual - Informal
Price of Entrees: $12.95 - $32.95
Credit Cards: All major
Specialties: Prime rib and steaks such as Signature Whiskey Peppercorn Filet, rack of lamb, grilled swordfish and shrimp scampi, linguine. All dinners are complete with soup and our personal lazy Susan salad bar prepared at your table; children's menu; banquet facilities to accommodate up to 50. Twilight Dining $9.95 (call for hours).

Jeremiah's Steakhouse
171 E. Tropicana Ave.
Las Vegas, NV 89109
736-3044
Hours: Sun. - Thu. 4:30 pm - 10 pm; Fri. - Sat. 4:30 pm - 11 pm
Reservations: Accepted
Dress: Casual - Informal
Price of Entrees: $7.95 - $18.95; early

bird menu 4:30 pm - 6:30 pm $7.95 - $10.95
Credit Cards: All major
Specialties: USDA choice steaks, prime rib, fresh seafood, chicken dishes, 40-item salad bar.
Atmosphere: Bar; lounge; subdued lighting.

Kodiak Lodge
Santa Fe
4949 N. Rancho Dr.
Las Vegas, NV 89130
658-4900
Hours: 5 pm - 10 pm
Reservations: None
Dress: Casual
Price of Entrees: $11.95 - $32
Credit Cards: All major
Specialties: Alaskan king crab, prime rib, rotisserie pork and chicken.
Atmosphere: Hunting lodge complete with large stuffed bear.

Kristofer's
Riviera
2901 Las Vegas Blvd. S.
Las Vegas, NV 89109
734-5110 or 794-9233
Hours: 5:30 pm - 11 pm
Reservations: Recommended
Dress: Casual elegant
Price of Entrees: Fixed-price dinners from $21.95
Credit Cards: All major
Specialties: Complete dinners include Caesar salad, wine, a crock of cheese and crackers, freshly baked sourdough rye, entree and desserts. Swordfish, cajun-style blackened redfish, broiled salmon filets, lamb chops, steaks, prime rib, chicken.
Atmosphere: Main dining room features a copper-and-glass-enclosed exhibition kitchen and comfortable rattan furnishings and brass ceiling fans. The bar and lounge feature a spectacular view of the hotel's swimming pool and beautiful surroundings.

Lawry's, The Prime Rib
4043 E. Howard Hughes Pkwy.
Las Vegas, NV 89109
893-2223
Hours: Sun. - Thu. 5 pm - 10 pm; Fri. - Sat. 5 pm - 11 pm
Reservations: Suggested
Dress: Casual - Eegant
Price of Entrees: $19.95 - $29.95
Credit Cards: All major
Specialties: Prime rib, lobster and fresh fish of the day.

Limericks Steak House
Fitzgeralds
301 Fremont St.
Las Vegas, NV 89101
388-2460
Hours: Mon. - Fri. 5 pm - 11 pm; Sat. - Sun. 5 pm - 1 am
Reservations: Suggested
Dress: Informal
Price of Entrees: $6.95 - $16.95
Credit Cards: All major
Specialties: Beef Wellington, orange roughy.
Atmosphere: Irish castle setting.

DINING

Lone Star Steakhouse and Saloon
(Multiple locations listed below)
Hours: Sun. - Thu. 11 am - 10 pm; Fri. and Sat. 11 am - 11 pm
Reservations: Only for 8 or more.
Dress: Casual
Price of Entrees: $9.45 - $19.95
Credit Cards: All major
Specialties: Mesquite grilled steaks, baby back ribs, grilled chicken breast, Lone Star chile; mesquite grilled burgers, grilled chicken, soups, salads, homemade cobbler; steaks are hand-cut each day; bar.
Atmosphere: Fun and friendly up beat atmosphere, servers gather to do country line dancing when certain songs are played; large buckets of peanuts at each table and you are encouraged to throw the shells on the floor. True Texas atmosphere with bull heads and cattle drive murals on the walls; patio.

1290 E. Flamingo Rd.
Las Vegas, NV 89119
893-0348

1611 S. Decatur Blvd.
Las Vegas, NV 89102
259-0105

3131 N. Rainbow Rd.
Las Vegas, NV 89108
656-7125

210 N. Nellis Blvd.
Las Vegas, NV 89110
453-7827

Morton's of Chicago
Fashion Show Mall
3200 Las Vegas Blvd. S.
Las Vegas, NV 89109
893-0703
Hours: Mon. - Sat. 5 pm - 11 pm; Sun. 5 pm - 10 pm; lounge opens at 5 pm
Reservations: Recommended
Dress: Semi-formal
Price of Entrees: $18.95 - $30.95, a la carte
Credit Cards: MC, Visa, AMX, Diners
Specialties: Double filet mignon, rib-eye, 24-ounce porterhouse steak, swordfish steak, domestic rib lamb chops, Sicilian veal chops, whole baked Maine lobsters, lemon chicken; sharing is permitted. Morton's doesn't have a menu; items are presented on a cart for your selection before cooking. Prime grain-fed beef from the Midwest is cooked on an open grill in their exhibition kitchen. Private dining room, The Board Room, available for parties up to 60; complimentary valet parking available.
Atmosphere: White tablecloths, dark wood paneling and lots of mahogany. The service is impeccable. Large separate comfortable bar/lounge area.

Old San Francisco Steak House & Dance Hall
Fiesta
2400 N. Rancho Dr.

Las Vegas, NV 89130
631-7000
Hours: 5 pm - 10 pm
Price of Entrees: $8.95 - $26.95
Specialties: Steak and seafood. "The Girl on the Red Velvet Swing" maneuvers a suspended 20 foot swing over the restaurant stage area hourly 6:30 pm - 8:30 pm.

Outback Steakhouse
(Multiple locations & hours listed below)
Reservations: None
Dress: Casual
Price of Entrees: $9.95 - $16.99
Credit Cards: All major
Specialties: Specially seasoned steaks, Blooming onion, chicken, fish, ribs, prime rib, and pasta.
Atmosphere: Australian theme decor. Aussie memorabilia decorates each restaurant along with large booths and tables, blond woods in a warm and comfortable environment. Happy hour daily 4 pm - 7 pm, 2 for 1 drinks.

3685 W. Flamingo Rd.
Las Vegas, NV 89118
253-1020
Hours: Sun. - Thu. 4 pm - 10:30 pm; Fri. - Sat. 4 pm - 11:30 pm

4141 S. Pecos Rd.
Las Vegas, NV 89121
898-3801
Hours: Mon. - Thu. 4 pm - 10:30 pm; Fri. - Sat. 3 pm - 11 pm; Sun. 1 pm - 10 pm

4423 E. Sunset Rd.
Henderson, NV 89014
451-7808
Hours: Mon. - Thu. 4 pm - 10 pm; Fri. - Sat. 3:30 pm - 11:30 pm; Sun. noon - 9:30 pm

1950 N. Rainbow Blvd.
Las Vegas, NV 89108
647-1035
Hours: Mon. - Thu. 4 pm - 10 pm; Fri. - Sat. 4 pm - 11:30 pm; Sun. 4 pm - 10:30 pm

8671 W. Sahara Ave.
Las Vegas, NV 89117
228-1088
Hours: Mon. - Thu. 4 pm - 10 pm; Fri. - Sat. 4 pm - 11 pm; Sun. 4 pm - 10 pm

Palm Restaurant
Forum Shops
3500 Las Vegas Blvd. S.
Las Vegas, NV 89109
732-7256
Hours: 11:30 am - 11 pm
Reservations: Suggested
Dress: Informal
Price of Entrees: $15 - $140, a la carte
Credit Cards: All major
Specialties: Prime aged steaks, jumbo lobsters 3-7 lb, fresh seafood, fresh crab cakes, pasta, veal and chops. Private rooms available. $12 fixed price lunch or a la carte. Banquet facilities available to accommodate 50. Comfortable bar with New York tradition.

Atmosphere: The first Palm Restaurant opened in 1926 in New York City and there are 12 locations in major cities throughout the United States.

Paparazzi Grille
Hotel San Remo
115 E. Tropicana Ave.
Las Vegas, NV 89109
739-9000
Hours: Wed. - Sun. 5 pm - 11 pm
Reservations: Suggested
Dress: Informal
Price of Entrees: $13 - $38
Specialties: Prime rib, fresh seafood and poultry.

Plantation
Showboat
2800 E. Fremont St.
Las Vegas, NV 89104
385-9156
Hours: Tue. - Sat. 5 pm - 10 pm
Reservations: Suggested
Dress: Informal
Price of Entrees: $8.95 - $10.95
Credit Cards: All major
Specialties: Prime steaks, seafood crabs legs.
Atmosphere: Southern mansion setting.

GREAT BEGINNINGS

Pullman Grill
Main Street Station
200 N. Main St.
Las Vegas, NV 89101
387-1896
Hours: Thu. - Mon. 5 pm - 10 pm
Reservations: Suggested
Dress: Casual
Price of Entrees: $12.95 - $25.95
Credit Cards: All major
Specialties: Black angus prime rib, veal marsala, filet mignon.
Atmosphere: Richly appointed parlor setting with authentic antique rail car set the mood for a truly unique dining experience.

The Range Steak House
Harrah's
3475 Las Vegas Blvd. S.
Las Vegas, NV 89109
369-5000
Hours: Sun. - Thu. 5:30 pm - 11 pm; Fri. - Sat. 5:30 pm - 11:30 pm
Reservations: Recommended
Dress: Casual - Elegant
Price of Entrees: $15.95 - $39.95
Credit Cards: All major
Specialties: Bone in filet, halibut T-bone, calostoga chicken; lounge seats 60; live music from 6 pm weekends featuring jazz and blues.
Atmosphere: Elegant dining; high vaulted ceilings, warm wood tones; glass elevators allow a fantastic view of Strip overlooking Caesars Palace, the Mirage, and the new Bellagio hotel and casino.

Redwood Bar & Grill
California Hotel
12 Ogden Ave.
Las Vegas, NV 89101
385-1222
Hours: 5:30 pm - 11 pm
Reservations: Suggested
Dress: Informal
Price of Entrees: $13 - $40
Credit Cards: All major
Specialties: Porterhouse steak, steak Diane, lobster thermidor, prime rib.
Atmosphere: Dark wood paneling and country English decor; piano music.

Roberta's Cafe
El Cortez
600 Fremont St.
Las Vegas, NV 89101
386-0692
Hours: 4 pm - 11 pm
Reservations: Suggested
Dress: Informal
Price of Entrees: $6.95 - $26
Credit Cards: All major
Specialties: Prime rib, crab legs, New York steak $11.95, whole broiled Maine lobster.

Rosewood Grille
3339 Las Vegas Blvd. S.
Las Vegas, NV 89109
735-0151
Hours: 4:30 pm - 11:30 pm
Reservations: Required
Dress: Informal
Price of Entrees: $18.50 - $29.95
Credit Cards: All major
Specialties: Live Maine lobster, thick steaks and fresh seafood.
Atmosphere: Quiet and intimate.

Ruth's Chris Steak House
(Multiple locations & hours listed below)
Reservations: Suggested
Dress: Semi-formal
Price of Entrees: $18.95 - $34 a la carte
Credit Cards: All major
Specialties: Ruth's Chris steaks come only from selected Midwestern beef, corn fed, aged and never frozen, then served to you sizzling. To complement an already perfect meal, choose from an award winning wine list. The Flamingo Rd. location offers a special late night menu from 11 pm with a selection of lighter choices including pasta. Award of Excellence from the *Wine Spectator* magazine for wine selection. Proprietor's reserve dining room available for private parties. Separate cocktail lounge.
Atmosphere: Elegant brass, leather and etched glass decor.

3900 Paradise Rd.
Las Vegas, NV 89109
791-7011

Wildfire at Reserve Hotel, 777 W. Lake Mead Blvd., Henderson, NV 89015

Hours: Mon. - Fri. 11 am - 10:30 pm;
Sat. - Sun. 4:30 pm - 10:30 pm

4561 W. Flamingo Rd.
Las Vegas, NV 89103
248-7011
Hours: 4:30 pm - 3 am

Sahara Steak House
Sahara
2535 Las Vegas Blvd. S.
Las Vegas, NV 89109
737-2111
Hours: 6 pm - midnight
Reservations: Suggested
Dress: Semi-formal
Price of Entrees: $16.95 - $38
Credit Cards: All major
Specialties: Steak Diane, veal chops, fresh broiled fish, rack of lamb; bananas Foster, cafe diablo.
Atmosphere: Many entrees are flamed tableside in what is one of the first gourmet rooms on the Strip.

Sizzler Buffet Court & Grill
(Multiple locations listed below)
Reservations: None
Dress: Casual
Price of Entrees: $6.99 - $13.99
Credit Cards: All major
Specialties: Charbroiled steaks, seafood and chicken served semi-self service. Large salad, soup, dessert and Mexican bar.

4901 S. Eastern Ave.
Las Vegas, NV 89119
736-3120
Hours: Sun. - Thu. 11 am - 9 pm;
Fri. - Sat. 11 am - 9:30 pm

307 S. Decatur Blvd.
Las Vegas, NV 89107
878-1223
Hours: Sun. - Thu. 11 am - 9:30 pm;
Fri. - Sat. 11 am - 10 pm

3553 S. Rainbow Blvd.
Las Vegas, NV 89103
227-0131
Hours: Mon. - Thu. 11 am - 9 pm;
Fri. - Sat. 11 am - 9:30 pm

Steakhouse
Bally's
3645 Las Vegas Blvd. S.
Las Vegas, NV 89109
739-4661
Hours: Thu. - Mon. 6 pm - 11 pm
Reservations: Suggested
Dress: Casual - Elegant
Price of Entrees: $19.50 - $55
Credit Cards: All major
Specialties: Steaks, chops, fresh seafood, whole Maine lobster.
Atmosphere: Exclusive New York club setting.

The Steak House
Circus Circus
2880 Las Vegas Blvd. S.
Las Vegas, NV 89109
734-0410
Hours: 5 pm - midnight
Reservations: Suggested
Dress: Relaxed
Price of Entrees: $14.95 - $27.95
Credit Cards: All major
Specialties: Finest 21 day aged beef cooked over an open-hearth exhibition mesquite grill. Porterhouse, New York, top sirloin, filet mignon cooked to your specification in full view in their display kitchen; intimate bar and lounge.
Atmosphere: Excellent service with a comfortable oak and brass decor have made The Steak House the number one steak house in the *Review-Journal* readers poll for nearly a decade.

Stockyard Steak House
Texas
3141 N. Rancho Dr.
Las Vegas, NV 89130
631-1000
Hours: Sun. - Thu. 5 pm - 10 pm;
Fri. - Sat. 5.pm - 11 pm
Reservations: Suggested
Dress: Informal
Price of Entrees: $13.99 - $40
Credit Cards: All major
Specialties: Finest aged, corn-fed beef cooked on a sizzling open-flame grill.

The result is a thick, juicy, flavor-packed steak. A wide variety of fresh seafood including King crab legs, shrimp and lobster tails, and fresh oysters.
Atmosphere: Relaxed.

Wild Bill's Saloon & Steakhouse
Excalibur
3850 Las Vegas Blvd. S.
Las Vegas, NV 89109
597-7777
Hours: Sun. - Thu. 5 pm - 10 pm;
Fri. - Sat. 5 pm - 11 pm
Reservations: None
Dress: Casual
Price of Entrees: $7.95 - $19.95
Credit Cards: All major
Specialties: 24-ounce T-bone, sirloin, filet mignon, St. Louis-style barbecued ribs and country-fried chicken, spare ribs. Sun. express breakfast buffet $6.99.
Atmosphere: "Real food cooked by real cowboys" served in a western-theme atmosphere divided into three different motifs. Big screens showing early cowboy movies. Live country music and dancing nightly 7 pm - 11 pm.

Wildfire
Reserve Hotel
777 W. Lake Mead Blvd.
Henderson, NV 89015
558-7000
Hours: Mon. - Fri. 5 pm - 10 pm; Sat. - Sun. 5 pm - 11 pm
Reservations: Recommended
Dress: Informal
Price: $9.95 - $22.95
Credit Cards: All major
Specialties: Rosemary chicken and fettuccine, veal Oscar, roast pork loin, steak and lobster and Bourbon Street fireside steak.
Atmosphere: Secluded, circular dining area with casino noises excluded. A romantic cave-like setting.

William B's
Stardust
3000 Las Vegas Blvd. S.
Las Vegas, NV 89109
732-6111
Hours: Sun. - Thu. 5 pm - 11 pm;
Fri. - Sat. 5 pm - midnight
Reservations: Suggested

Dress: Informal
Price of Entrees: $14.95 - $42
Credit Cards: All major
Specialties: Prime rib, steaks, chops and seafood.
Atmosphere: Turn-of-the-century elegance.

Yolie's Brazilian Steak House
3900 Paradise Rd.
Las Vegas, NV 89119
794-0700
Hours: Lunch Mon. - Fri. 11 am - 3 pm;
Dinner 5:00 pm - 11 pm
Reservations: Suggested
Dress: Informal
Price of Entrees: Fixed price dinners at $22.95
Credit Cards: All major
Specialties: Marinated mesquite-broiled meats and fish served Brazilian style. Menu items such as scampi, orange roughy, roasted half chicken, fresh catch of the day. Daily lunch specials from $4.95 - $12.95. Banquet facilities.
Atmosphere: A variety of meats cooked on a continuously revolving skewer over mesquite coals and then sliced and offered off the skewer at the table by your waiter. You are offered as much as you care to eat of all the meats. Located on the second floor of the shopping center, it offers a view of the city lights; separate piano bar; patio dining available.

Yukon Grille
Arizona Charlie's
740 S. Decatur Blvd.
Las Vegas, NV 89107
258-5200
Hours: 5 pm - 11 pm
Dress: Casual
Reservations: Recommended
Price of Entrees: $9.95 - $19.95
Credit Cards: All major
Specialties: 20-ounce porterhouse, veal center cut rib chop, lamb rib chop, salmon filet, prime rib.
Atmosphere: 1890s Gold Rush atmosphere with a large stone fireplace.

Yolie's Brazilian Steak House, 3900 Paradise Rd., Las Vegas, NV 89119

BUFFETS & BRUNCHES

BUFFETS
(Alphabetical by Hotel)

Wild West Buffet
Arizona Charlie's
740 S. Decatur Blvd.
Las Vegas, NV 89107
258-5200
Breakfast - 7 am - 10:30 am - $3.50
Lunch - 11 am - 3:30 pm - $4.50
Dinner - 4 pm - 10 pm - $6.50

Big Kitchen Buffet
Bally's
3645 Las Vegas Blvd. S.
Las Vegas, NV 89109
739-4111
Breakfast - 7 am - 11 am - $8.95
Brunch - 7:30 am - 2:30 pm - $9.95
Dinner - 4:30 pm - 10 pm - $13.95
Diners have their food cooked fresh to order. View of the Las Vegas Strip.

Sunday Sterling Brunch
Bally's
(Served in the Steak House)
Hours: 9:30 am - 2:30 pm, last seating at 1:00 pm
Reservations: Required
Price: $49.95

Binion's Buffet
Binion's Horseshoe
128 Fremont St.
Las Vegas, NV 89101
382-1600
Dinner - 4:30 pm - 10:30 pm - $9.95
Friday's buffet includes shrimp and crab bar in addition to the regular buffet $14.95.

The Feast
Boulder Station
4111 Boulder Hwy.
Las Vegas, NV 89121
432-7777
Breakfast - 7 am - 11 am - $9
Lunch - 11 am - 2 pm - $5.99
Dinner - 4 pm - 10 pm - $8.99, T-bone steak Thu. $9.99, Seafood Fri. $11.49
Sun. Brunch - 7 am - 3:30 pm - $7.99
Diners can watch meals being prepared.
Sunday Signature Brunch - 10 am - 3 pm $13.95 *served in The Broiler*

Surf Buffet
Holiday Inn Boardwalk
3750 Las Vegas Blvd. S.
Las Vegas, NV 89109
735-2400
Hours: Daily 7 am - 10 pm
Breakfast - $3.29
Brunch - $4.69
Dinner - $5.99

Miss Ashley's Boarding House Buffet
Buffalo Bill's
Jean, NV 89019
382-1111
Breakfast - Sun. - Thu. 8 am - 8 pm;
Fri. - Sat. 8 am - 9 pm - $4.95
Lunch - Sun. - Thu. 8 am - 8 pm;
Fri. - Sat. 8 am - 9 pm - $4.95
Dinner - Sun. - Thu. 8 am - 8 pm;
Fri. - Sat. 8 am - 9 pm - $5.95

Palatium Buffet
Caesars Palace
3570 Las Vegas Blvd. S.
Las Vegas, NV 89109
731-7110
Breakfast - Mon. - Fri. - 7:30 am - 11:30 am - $7.95
Lunch - Mon. - Fri. - 11:30 am - 3:30 pm - $9.95
Dinner - 4:30 pm - 10 pm - $13.95
Friday seafood buffet - 4 pm - 10 pm $18.95 and $3.00 extra for lobster
Brunch - Sat. - 8:30 am - 3:30 pm - $14.95
Champagne Brunch - Sun. - 8:30 am - 3:30 pm - $14.95
Children 4 - 12 - $7; children under 4 - free.

Cafe Roma
Caesars Palace
3570 Las Vegas Blvd. S.
Las Vegas, NV 89109
731-7110
Breakfast - Mon. - Fri. - 7 am - 11 am - $11.95
Lunch - Mon. - Fri. - noon - 2:30 pm - $12.45
Dinner - Sun. - Thu. - 6 pm - 10 pm; Fri. - Sat. 6 pm - 11 pm - $17.95
Brunch - Sat. - Sun. - 7 am - 2:30 pm - $13.95

Plate of Plenty
Circus Circus
2880 Las Vegas Blvd. S.
Las Vegas, NV 89109
734-0410
Breakfast - 6 am - 11:30 am - $2.99
Brunch - noon - 4 pm - $3.99
Dinner - 4:30 pm - 11 pm - $4.99
Sunday Champagne Brunch *served in The Steak House*, 10 am - 2 pm, $17.95, children 6-12 $8.95

Round Table Buffet
Excalibur
3850 Las Vegas Blvd. S.
Las Vegas, NV 89109
597-7777
Breakfast - 6:30 am - 11 am - $4.49
Lunch - 11 am - 4 pm - $5.49
Dinner - Sun. - Fri. 4 pm - 10 pm; Sat. 4 pm - 11 pm - $6.99

Festival Buffet
Fiesta
2400 N. Rancho Dr.
Las Vegas, NV 89130
631-7000
Breakfast - 7 am - 11 am - $3.99
Lunch - 11 am - 3 pm - $5.99
Dinner - 4 pm - 10 pm - Tue., Thu. - Sun. $8.99
Hawaiian Luau - Mon. $10.99
Seafood and filet mignon Wed. $12.99

Champagne Brunch - Sat. - Sun. 7 am - 3 pm - $7.99
Margarita Brunch - Sun. 10 am - 3 pm - $9.99 *served in Garduno's*

Molly's Country Kitchen and Buffet
Fitzgeralds
301 E. Fremont St.
Las Vegas, NV 89101
388-2400
Breakfast - Mon. - Fri. 7 am - 11 am - $4.99
Lunch - Mon. - Fri. 11:30 am - 4 pm - $5.49
Dinner - Nightly 5 pm - 10 pm - $7.99
Champagne Brunch - Sat. - Sun. 8 am - 4 pm - $7.99

Paradise Garden
Flamingo Hilton
3555 Las Vegas Blvd. S.
Las Vegas, NV 89109
733-3111
Breakfast - 6 am - noon - $6.75
Lunch - noon - 2:30 pm - $7.75
Dinner - Sat. - Thu. 4:30 pm - 10 pm - $9.95
Seafood Buffet - Fri. $9.95

Paradise Buffet
Fremont
200 Fremont St.
Las Vegas, NV 89101
385-3232
Breakfast - Mon. - Sat. 7 am - 10:30 am - $4.95
Lunch - Mon. - Sat. 11 am - 3 pm - $5.95
Dinner - Mon., Wed., Thu., & Sat. 4 pm - 11 pm - $8.95; Tue., Fri. & Sun. - 4 pm - 10 pm; (Seafood Fantasy) - $12.95
Champagne Brunch - Sun. 7 am - 3 pm $7.95
Atmosphere: Tropical rain forest setting.

The Buffet
Gold Coast
4000 W. Flamingo Rd.
Las Vegas, NV 89103
367-7111
Breakfast - Mon. - Sat. 7 am - 10:30 am - $3.45
Lunch - 11 am - 3 pm - $4.95
Dinner - 4 pm - 10 pm - $6.95
Seafood buffet - Wed. 4 pm - 10 pm - $9.95
Brunch - Sun. 8 am - 3 pm - $6.95

The Buffet
Golden Nugget
129 E. Fremont St.
Las Vegas, NV 89101
385-7111
Breakfast - Mon. - Sat. 7 am - 10:30 am - $5.75
Lunch - Mon. - Sat. 10:30 am - 3 pm - $7.50
Dinner - Mon. - Sat. 4 pm - 10 pm - $10.25
Sunday Champagne Brunch - 8 am - 10 pm - $10.95

Gold Strike Buffet
Gold Strike Inn
U.S. Highway 93
Boulder City, NV 89005
293-5000
Lunch - Mon - Fri. 11 am - 3:45 pm - $3.95; Sat. - Sun. noon - 3:30 pm - $4.23
Dinner - 4 pm - 10 pm - $4.49; Wed. $2.99
Seniors - Tue. - Thu. - $2.99
Brunch - Sat. - Sun. - 7 am - 11:30 am - $4.25

Fresh Market Square Buffet
Harrah's
3475 Las Vegas Blvd. S.
Las Vegas, NV 89109
369-5000
Breakfast - 7 am - 11 am - $6.99
Lunch - 11:30 am - 3:30 pm - $8.99
Dinner - 4 pm - 10 pm - $11.99

Emperor's Buffet
Imperial Palace
3535 Las Vegas Blvd. S.
Las Vegas, NV 89109
731-3311
Breakfast - 7 am - 11:30 am - $4.99
Lunch - 11:30 am - 4 pm - $5.99
Dinner - 5 pm - 10 pm - $6.99

The Imperial Buffet at Teahouse
Imperial Palace
Weekday Brunch - 7 am - 2:30 pm - $5.95
Champagne Prime Rib Dinner - 5 pm - 10 pm - $7.95
Champagne Brunch - Sat. - Sun. - 8 am - 3 pm - $6.95

Jesters Court
Jokers Wild
920 N. Boulder Hwy.
Henderson, NV 89015
564-8100
Buffet Lunch - Mon. - Fri. 10 am - 3 pm - $3.75
Dinner - Sat. - Thu. 4 pm - 9 pm $4.95; Fri. - $6.95 *seafood buffet*
Saturday Brunch - 9 am - 3 pm - $4.25;
Sunday Champagne brunch - $6.95; Children age 5 - 8 - $2.99

Taste of the World Buffet
Lady Luck
206 N. Third St.
Las Vegas, NV 89101
477-3000
Breakfast - 6 am - 10:30 am - $4.49
Lunch - Mon. - Fri. 10:30 am - 2 pm - $4.49
Dinner - Mon. - Fri. 4 pm - 10 pm - $9.95
Weekend Brunch - Sat. - Sun. 10:30 am - 6 pm - $6.49

Buffet of Champions
Las Vegas Hilton
3000 Paradise Rd.
Las Vegas, NV 89109
732-5111
Breakfast - Mon. - Fri. 7 am - 10 am - $7.99
Lunch - Mon. - Fri. 11 am - 2:30 pm - $8.99
Dinner - 5 pm - 10 pm - $12.99 (Children under 12 half price)
Champagne Brunch - Sat. - Sun. - 8 am - 2:30 pm - $11.99

Pharaoh's Pheast
Luxor
3900 Las Vegas Blvd. S.
Las Vegas, NV 89119
262-4740
Breakfast - 6:30 am - 11:30 am - $5.99
Lunch - 11:30 am - 4 pm - $7.49
Dinner - 4 pm - 11 pm - $9.99
Children under 10 half price. Children under 4 free.

Oz Buffet
MGM Grand
3799 Las Vegas Blvd. S.
Las Vegas, NV 89109
891-1111
Brunch - 7:30 am - 2:30 pm - $7.25; children under 10 - $2.99
Dinner - 4:30 pm - 10 pm - $9.95; children under 10 - $4.99
Brown Derby Grand Champagne Brunch - Sun. 9 am - 10 am $19.95 - 10 am - 2 pm $28.95, children under 12, 9 am - 10 am $8.95; 10 am - 2 pm $9.95; children under 5 free

The Maxim Buffet
The Maxim
160 E. Flamingo Rd.
Las Vegas, NV 89109
731-4300
Brunch - Mon. - Fri. 9 am - 3 pm- $4.95
Grand Evening Buffet - 4 pm - 10 pm - $6.95
Weekend Champagne Brunch - 9 am - 3 pm - $10.95

Mirage Buffet
The Mirage
3400 Las Vegas Blvd. S.
Las Vegas, NV 89109
791-7111
Breakfast - 7 am - 10:45 am - $7.50; children - $5.75
Lunch - 11 am - 2:45 pm - $8.95; children - $6.50
Dinner - 3 pm - 10 pm; until 11 pm on Fri. and Sat. - $12.95; children - $8.50
Sunday Champagne Brunch - 8 am - 10 pm - $13.95 (breakfast entrees until 3 pm); children under 10 - $10.00

The Buffet
Monte Carlo
3770 Las Vegas Blvd. S.
Las Vegas, NV 89109
730-7777
Breakfast - Mon. Sat. 7 am - 11 am - $6.49
Lunch - Mon. Sat. 11 am - 4 pm - $6.99
Dinner - 4 pm - 10 pm $9.49
Champagne Brunch - Sun. 7 am - 3 pm - $9.49; children under 5 free

La Bella Pasta Buffet
Nevada Palace
5255 Boulder Hwy.
Las Vegas, NV 458-8810
458-8810
Dinner - Sat. - Thu. 4 pm - 9 pm - $4.49
Fri. Seafood - 4 pm - 9 pm $6.99
Sat. - Sun. Brunch - 8 am - noon $2.99

Michelle's Village Cafe
New Frontier
3120 Las Vegas Blvd. S.
Las Vegas, NV 89109
794-8200
Lunch - 11 am - 2 pm - $4.95
Dinner - Mon. - Thu. 4 pm - 10 pm - $7.95
Friday Seafood Buffet - 4 pm - 10 pm - $10.95
Saturday Seafood Buffet - 3 pm - 10 pm - $8.95
Sun. - 11 am - 10 pm - $8.95

French Market Buffet
The Orleans
4500 W. Tropicana Ave.
Las Vegas, NV 89103
365-7111
Breakfast - 7 am - 10 am - $3.45
Lunch - 11 am - 3 pm - $4.45
Dinner - 4 pm - 10 pm - $7.95
Seafood buffet - Mon. - 4 pm - 10 pm- $10.95
Brunch - Sun. 8 am - 3 pm - $7.95

The Feast at Palace Station, 2411 W. Sahara Ave., Las Vegas, NV 89102

The Feast
Palace Station
2411 W. Sahara Ave.
Las Vegas, NV 89102
367-2411
Breakfast - Mon. - Sat. 7 am - 11 am - $3.99
Lunch - Mon. - Fri. 11 am - 3 pm - $5.99
Dinner - 4 pm - 10 pm - $8.99
Sun. Champagne Brunch - 7 am - 3:30 pm - $7.99
The Palace Station Buffet is an action buffet where diners watch their meals prepared for them.

Railroad Pass Buffet
Railroad Pass
2800 Boulder Hwy.
Henderson, NV 89015
294-5000
Lunch - Mon. - Fri. 11 am - 2:30 pm - $4.29
Dinner - 3 pm - 10 pm - $4.29
Champagne Brunch - Sat. & Sun. 8 am - 2 pm - $4.55

Grand Safari Buffet
The Reserve Hotel
777 West Lake Mead Dr.
Henderson, NV 89015
558-7000
Lunch - 11 am - 4 pm - $5.99
Dinner - 4 pm - 10 pm - $7.99
Brunch - Sat. - Sun. 9 am - 4 pm - $6.99

Carnival World Buffet
Rio
3700 W. Flamingo Rd.
Las Vegas, NV 89103
252-7777
Breakfast - Mon. - Fri. 8 am - 10:30 am - $6.95
Lunch - Mon. - Fri. 11 am - 3:30 pm - $8.95
Dinner - 3:30 pm - 11 pm - $10.95
Brunch - Sat. - Sun. 8:30 am - 3:30 pm - $10.95
Five different food stations including Brazilian, Mexican, American, Italian and Chinese and a dessert pavilion; live entertainment. Private dining room for large parties up to 20.

Rio Village Seafood Buffet
Rio
3700 W. Flamingo Rd.
Las Vegas, NV 89103
252-7777
Fresh seafood flown in daily
Breakfast - 7 am - 10 am - $6.95
Lunch - Mon. - Fri. 11 am - 2:30 pm - $15.95
Dinner - Mon. - Thu. 4 pm - 10 pm; Fri. - 4 pm - 11 pm - $20.95
Sat. - Sun. Brunch - 11 am - 3 pm - $20.95

World's Fare Buffet
Riviera
2901 Las Vegas Blvd. S.
Las Vegas, NV 89109
734-5110
Breakfast - Mon. - Fri. 6 am - 10 am $5.45
Brunch - Mon. - Fri. 10 am - 2 pm - $6.45
Dinner - 4 pm - 10:30 pm - $8.45
Champagne Brunch - Sat. & Sun. 10 am - 3 pm - $6.45

Sahara Buffet
Sahara
2535 Las Vegas Blvd. S.
Las Vegas, NV 89109
737-2111
Breakfast - Mon. - Fri. 6 am - 11 am - $2.99
Lunch - Mon. - Fri. 11:30 am - 3:30 pm - $3.99
Dinner - 4 pm - 10 pm - $5.99

The Great Buffet
Sam's Town
5111 Boulder Hwy.
Las Vegas, NV 89122
456-7777
Breakfast - Mon. - Sat. 8 am - 11 am - $4.99
Lunch - Mon. - Sat. 11 am - 3 pm - $6.99
Dinner - Sat. - Tue. & Thu. - 4 pm - 9 pm - $8.99; Wed. 4 pm - 9 pm - $11.99; Fri. 4 pm - 10 pm - $12.99
Champagne Brunch - Sun. 8 am - 3 pm - $7.99
Children 6 & under half price.
Breakfast in the Park - Sun. 9 am - 2 pm - $13.95

Ristorante dei Fiori Buffet
San Remo
115 E. Tropicana Ave.
Las Vegas, NV 89109
739-9000
Breakfast - 6:30 am - 10:30 am - $6.95
Lunch - 11 am - 2 pm - $6.95
Dinner - 5 pm - 9 pm - $7.95
Champagne Brunch - Sat. - Sun. 7 am - 2 pm - $6.95

Lone Mountain Buffet
Santa Fe
4949 N. Rancho Dr.
Las Vegas, NV 89130
658-4900
Breakfast - 7:30 am - 10:30 am - $3.95
Lunch - 11:30 am - 2:30 pm - $4.95
Dinner - 4 pm - 9 pm - $6.95
Seafood Buffet - Thu. 4 pm - 9 pm $8.95
Champagne Brunch - Sun. 7:30 am - 2:30 pm - $6.95
Children under 8 - $3.50
Italian Champagne Brunch - Sun. 11 am - 5 pm - $12.95 *served in Ti Amo Italian Restaurant*

DINING

BUFFETS & BRUNCHES

CAPTAIN'S BUFFET

Captain's Buffet
Showboat
2800 E. Fremont St.
Las Vegas, NV 89104
385-9123
Lunch - Mon. - Fri. 10 am - 3:30 pm - $4.95
Dinner - Sun. - Tue. 4:30 - 10 pm - $6.95;
Wed. - 4:30 - 10 pm - $7.95 *(New York strip steak)*; Thu. & Fri. 4:30 - 10 pm - $7.95 *(Seafood Extravaganza)*; Sat. 4:30 pm - 10 pm - $7.95 *(prime rib and pasta)*
Weekend Brunch - Sat. 8 am - 3:30 pm; Sun. 8 am - 3 pm $6.45

Chuckwagon Buffet
Silverton
3333 Blue Diamond Rd.
Las Vegas, NV 89139
263-7777
Breakfast - 7 am - 11 am - $3.99
Lunch - 11:30 am - 3:30 pm - $4.99
Dinner - 4 pm - 10 pm - $7.99
Italian - Mon. - $7.99
Filet mignon buffet Tue. & Wed. $7.99,
Prime rib buffet Thu. & Sat. $7.99,
Seafood buffet Fri. & Sun. - $7.99

Warehouse Buffet
Stardust
3000 Las Vegas Blvd. S.
Las Vegas, NV 89109
732-6111
Breakfast - 7 am - 11 am - $4.95
Lunch - Mon. Sat. 11 am - 3 pm $5.95
Dinner - 4 pm - 10 pm $7.95
Champagne Brunch - Sun. 7 am - 3 pm - $6.95

Buffet
Stratosphere
2000 S. Las Vegas Blvd.
Las Vegas, NV 89104
380-7777
Breakfast - Daily 8 am - 11 am - $5.49
Lunch - Daily 11 am - 4 pm - $6.49
Dinner - Sun. - Fri. 4 pm - 9 pm; Sat. 4 pm -10 pm - $8.99

Feast Around the World
Sunset Station
1301 W. Sunset Rd.
Henderson , NV 89014
547-7777
Breakfast - 7 am - 10:30 am - $3.99
Lunch - 11 am - 3 pm - $5.99
Dinner - 4 pm - 10 pm - $8.99
Late Night Feast - Fri. & Sat. 11 pm - 4 am $4.49
Weekend Brunch - Sat. - Sun. 7 am - 3:30 pm $7.99

Feast Around the World
Texas
2101 Texas Star Ln.
Las Vegas, NV 89130
631-1000
Breakfast - 7 am - 10:30 am - $3.99 children under 9 $2
Lunch - 11 am - 3:30 pm - $5.99 children $3
Dinner - 4 pm - 10 pm - $8.99 children $4.50
Fri. Steak & Shrimp - 4 pm - 10 pm - $10.99 children $5.50
Prime rib - Sat. 4 pm - 10 pm - $10.99 children $5.50
Champagne Brunch - Sat. - Sun. 7 am - 3:30 pm - $7.99 children $4.00
Children under 3 eat free.

THE TREASURE ISLAND BUFFET

Treasure Island Buffet
Treasure Island
3300 Las Vegas Blvd. S.
Las Vegas, NV 89109
894-7111
Breakfast - 6:45 am - 10:45 am - $5.99
Lunch - 10:45 am - 3:45 pm - $6.99
Dinner - 4 pm - 10:30 pm - $8.99
Brunch - Sun. 7:30 am - 3:30 pm - $8.99

Island Buffet
Tropicana
3801 Las Vegas Blvd. S.
Las Vegas, NV 89109
739-2222
Brunch - Mon. - Fri. 7:30 am - 1:30 pm - $7.95
Dinner - 5 pm - 10 pm - $9.95
Weekend Champagne Brunch - Sat. - Sun. 7:30 am - 2:30 pm - $9.95

The Buffet
Westward Ho
2900 Las Vegas Blvd. S.
Las Vegas, NV 89109
731-2900
Breakfast & Brunch - 7 am - 2 pm - $4.95
Dinner - 4 pm - 10 pm - $6.95

OUTSTANDING HOTEL SUNDAY CHAMPAGNE BRUNCHES

Bally's Sterling Buffet
Served in The Steakhouse. Omelets cooked to order, sushi bar, eggs Benedict made with crabmeat and real champagne; $49.95 per person served 9:30 am - 2:30 pm.

Boulder Station Signature Champagne Brunch
Served in the Broiler. Sun. 10 am - 3 pm $13.95 consists of seafood bar, clams on the half shell, Washington oysters, crab and shrimp cocktail, carving station and omelet station.

Circus Circus Champagne Sunday Brunch
Served in The Steak House, Sun. 10 am - 2 pm $17.95 per person; children 6 - 12 $8.95. Reservations suggested 734-0410.
A combination of self- and full-service, buffet-style and ordering at the table provides the quality atmosphere The Steak house is known for. Carving stations, eggs made to order, and the option to order succulently prepared filet mignon, New York strip, salmon filet, chicken breast and more.

Sam's Town - Breakfast in The Park
Champagne brunch served Sun. 9 am - 2 pm $13.95. Guests eat in a park setting indoors among the trees, greenery and waterfalls. 456-7777 for information.

DINING AT A GLANCE

LATE NIGHT DINING

Big Dogs
Blue Ox East
Coachman's Inn
Ellis Island
Fratelli's Ristorante
L'Bombardier
The Peppermill Restaurant & Lounge
Wooly Bully's
All major hotel/casinos have 24 hour coffee shops.

FINER RESTAURANTS OPEN FOR LUNCH

Bertolini's - *Italian*
Caesars Palace - Terrazza- *Italian*
Cafe Michelle - *Continental*
Cathay House - *Chinese*
Chevy's - *Mexican*
Chin's - *Chinese*
Cipriani - *Italian*
Coyote's - *Mexican*
Ferraro's - *Italian*
Gentleman Jack's - *Steakhouse*
Gold Coast - Cortez Room - *Steak*
Greens Supper Club - *Continental*
Hard Rock Cafe - *American*
Lone Star - *Steak*
Macayo Vegas - *Mexican*
MGM Grand - Emeril Lagasse's- *Seafood*
Mirage - Kokomo's - *Seafood*
Mi Tierra - *Mexican*
New Frontier - St Thomas - *Seafood*
New York New York-Motown Cafe - *American*
Nippon - *Japanese*
Olive Garden - *Italian*
Orleans-Don Miguels-*Mexican /Seafood*
Palm - *Steak*
Peppermill Restaurant - *American*
Play It Again Sam - *Continental*
Renata's - *Continental*
Ricardo's - *Mexican*
Rio - All American *Steakhouse*
Rio - Buzios Oyster Bar - *Seafood*
Ruth's Chris - *Steakhouse*
Shalimar - *Middle Eastern*
Showboat - Di Napoli - *Italian*
Spago - *Italian*
Swiss Cafe - *Swiss*
TGI Fridays - *American*
Tony Roma's - Barbecue - *Sahara Ave.*
The Venetian - *Italian*
Viva Mercado's - *Mexican*
Yolie's - *Steak*
Z' Tejas - *Southwestern*

PATIO DINING

Barley's Casino and Brew Pub
Buccaneer Bay Club - Treasure Island
Cadillac Grille
Cafe Michelle - *Continental*
Cafe Nicolle - *Continental*
Charlie's Lakeside Bar & Grill
Chevy's - *Mexican*
Coffee Pub - *Sandwich/Salad*
Crocodile Cafe - *American*
Culturati An American Bistro
The Egg and I - *Breakfast*
Ferraro's - *Italian*
Hippo & The Wild Bunch - *American*
Lone Star Steak House - *Steak*
Macayo Vegas (Tropicana Ave.) - *Mexican*
North Beach Cafe - *Italian*
Pasta Mia - *Italian* (N. Flamingo location)
Pizzeria Uno Restaurant & Bar
Samueli's - *Deli*
Sergio's Italian Gardens

Sfuzzi - *Italian*
Strings - *Italian*
Terrazza - Caesars Palace - *Italian*
TGI Fridays - *American*
Tommy Rocker's - *American*
Yolie's - *Brazilian steak house*
Z'Tejas Grill - *Mexican*

RESTAURANTS WITH A VIEW

Buccaneer Bay Club - Treasure Island view of hourly sea battle in Buccaneer Bay
Cathay House - Strip
Center Stage - Plaza - "Glitter Gulch"
Flamingo Room - pool area
Harrah's - The Range - Strip
Binion's Horseshoe - Steakhouse - city
Kiefer's - Strip and west
Lake Mead - lake and surrounding mountains
Las Vegas Hilton - "Garden of The Dragon" - Benihana gardens
La Terrazza - Sahara - pool area and grounds
The Mirage - Kokomo's - tropical rain forest, atrium, waterfalls, lagoon
Monte Carlo Room - Desert Inn
Mt. Charleston Lodge - Kyle Canyon
New Frontier - St. Thomas Seafood Grotto - waterfalls, brook and pool
Palace Court - Caesars Palace - pool
Riviera - Kristofer's - pool and its breathtaking surroundings
Stratosphere - Top of The World -Gourmet- 360-degree view of Las Vegas
Tastings of Pahrump - two viewing towers and wrap-around veranda for views of the entire area
Terrazza - Caesars Palace - poolside terrace
Treasure Island - Lookout Cafe - casino and pool area
Tropicana - Tropics - view of pool area
Yolie's Brazilian Steakhouse - city lights

FOUR-STAR RESTAURANTS

(MOBIL DINING GUIDE)

Monte Carlo Room - Desert Inn - *French*
Palace Court - Caesars Palace - *French*

DINING WITH MUSIC

Aristocrat - *Violin*
Bacchanal Room - Caesars Palace - *Belly dancers and traditional Middle-Eastern music*
Battista's Hole in the Wall - *Italian songs*
The Beach - *Piano and DJ*
Cafe Nicole - *Piano and vocals*
Chez Place - *Live music weekends only*
Country Star Cafe - *C.D. listening posts*
Coyote's - *Strolling mariachis*
El Sinalaense - *from 8 pm Fri. - Tue. Club music*
El Taquito - *Mariachi music*
Gandhi India's Cuisine - *Classical Indian music*
Kiefer's - *Piano bar*
Kifune - *Traditional Japanese music*
La Barca - *Mariachi music*
Lance-A-Lotta Pasta - Excalibur - *Strings*

La Strada - *Piano on weekends*
L'Bombardier - *Live entertainment starting 9 pm*
Mi Tierra - *Mariachi performers Fri. & Sat.*
Motown Cafe -NY NY - *Motown favorites*
Mount Charleston Resort - *Live German band, top pops and country music on alternating weekends only*
North Beach Cafe - *piano and vocals*
Palace Court - Caesars Palace - *Piano*
Paparazzi Grill - Hotel San Remo - *Easy listening*
Play It Again Sam - *Piano*
Primavera - Caesars Palace - *Italian guitars*
The Range - Harrah's - *Jazz & Blues from 6 pm*
Ricardo's - *Strolling guitarist*
Roxy's Diner - The Stratosphere - *Music of the '50s and '60s*
Sergio's - *Piano bar*
Sushi House Manda - *Jazz*
USA Cafe - *Alternative music from 9:30 pm*
Wild Bills - Excalibur - *Country bands*
Yolie's Brazilian Steakhouse - *Separate piano bar*

ANNUAL DINING EVENTS AND FOOD EVENTS

Community College of Southern Nevada - Culinary students at the college prepare dinners throughout the school year which are served to the public at a moderate price in Russell's dining room. Call 651-4020 for more information.

Sunset Park - Craft Fair & Rib Burn Off - Held in May.

Greek Food Festival - Held annually during October; next year's event will be the 24th year that St. John Greek Orthodox Church has sponsored this event. Call 221-8245 or the info line at 248-3896.

Italian Festival & Cook-off - Held annually in October at the Rio Hotel. Free admission to event with samples of food for sale at various booths, grape stomping, pizza tasting, spaghetti eating contest.

Meet The Winemaker Dinners - Presented by the culinary students at UNLV. Dinner held in November, hosted by various restaurants such as Renata's, Andre's French Restaurant and Kiefer's. For information call the hotel college at 895-4467.

October Fest - Held annually at the Nevada Palace during the first week in October, featuring authentic German foods, music and domestic and imported beers; call 458-8810 for further information.

San Gennaro Feast - Sponsored by the Italian American Club and Budweiser, the outdoor Italian food fair is held annually at the end of August. The festival features a variety of food and craft booths, continuous entertainment, games, a beauty pageant, talent contest, and more.

Taste of Las Vegas - Selections from fine Las Vegas restaurants set up in street fair style with live bands. Benefits the Children's Miracle Network. Held each year in May.

Taste of the Nation - Annual events featuring a variety of foods from participating Las Vegas restaurants. Event is held annually in April to benefit the Share Our Strength (SOS) fight against hunger. Call 895-4710 for information.

UNLV College of Hotel Administration - Culinary students at the university prepare lunches and dinners throughout the school year which are served to the public at a moderate price in the dining hall at the William F. Harrah College of Hotel Administration. Call 895-4467 for information.

UNLVino - Annual wine-tasting to benefit UNLV's hotel school's scholarship fund. Held annually during April at Bally's Hotel and Casino.

DINNER SHOWS

"Caesars Magical Empire"
Caesars Palace
731-7333
Price: Dinner, 3 shows, tax and gratuity - $75; Children ages 5-12 are half price; individual party bookings for parties of 4-12 persons featuring an additional "Seance" experience offered at slightly higher prices.
Hours: Daily from 4:30 pm Seating at 4:30 pm and continuing until 11 pm
Menu: "Spirited" gourmet menu featuring three courses and including your choice of salmon, chicken or veal.

"King Arthur's Tournament"
Excalibur
597-7600
Price: Dinner, show, tax and gratuity - $29.95
Hours: 6 pm and 8:30 pm
Seating at 5:30 pm and 8 pm
Menu: Three-course medieval feast eaten with the fingers in traditional manner.

"The Great Radio City Music Hall Spectacular"
Flamingo Hilton
733-3333
Featuring the world famous Radio City Rockettes.
Price: Dinner, show, tax and gratuity - $45.00 - $55.00
Hours: Seating at 5:45 pm Sat. - Thu. for 7:45 pm show.

"Hawaiian Hot Luau"
Imperial Palace
794-3261
Price: Dinner, show, tax and gratuity - $25.95
Hours: Tue. and Thu. starting at 7 pm; presented throughout warmer months poolside starting in April.
Menu: Polynesian-style seafood dinner buffet presented poolside. Price includes tax, admission, all-you-can-eat island and seafood buffet and unlimited mai tais, pina coladas and fruit punch. Entertainment is a music and dance review, "Drums of the Island."

DINING

CATERING & BANQUET ROOMS

CATERING

Affairs Catering
4850 W. Flamingo Rd.
Las Vegas, NV 89103
368-4106
Party planning - all special events.

Bon Appetit Catering
953 E. Sahara Ave.
Las Vegas, NV 89104
Credit Cards: All major
Full service party planning and catering
for all your party needs.

The Educated Palate
871-4593
All items cooked from scratch; quality
service at very affordable prices for 20
to 240 people.

Gourmet Cafe Catering Company
330 S. 3rd St.
Las Vegas, NV 89101
388-8222
Credit Cards: MC, Visa, AMX
Full service coordinating and catering
for all your needs. Specializing in ethnic
and theme parties for 30 to 4,000 people.

Kiefer's
15 E. Lake Mead Rd.
Henderson, NV 89015
565-0122
Credit Cards: All major
Full service catering for every occasion;
from small groups to elaborate celebrations accommodating 20 - 1000 people.

Plump Turkey Country Inn
(Multiple locations listed below)
Credit Cards: All major
Complete party planning and full ser-
vice catering.

2425 E. Desert Inn Rd.
Las Vegas, NV 89121
731-5035

1401 S. Rainbow Blvd.
Las Vegas, NV 89102
254-0520

1990 W. Sunset Rd.
Henderson, NV 89014
898-8183

Rainbow Catering
2013 S. Highland Dr.
Las Vegas, NV 89102
384-9153
Catering for all occasions, specializing
in cakes and pastries.

Renaissance Catering
3999 Renate Dr.
Las Vegas, NV 89103
367-2277
Full service catering and party planning.

Tropical Gardens
3808 E. Tropicana Ave.
Las Vegas, NV 89121
434-4333 1-800-668-7080

Able to create and prepare any menu
imaginable to fit the needs of any occasion, for as few as 20 or as many as 500!
Just ask, and our more than two
decades of experience is yours for making business meetings, conventions,
promotional events, cocktail parties,
wedding receptions, showers, and bach-
elor/bachelorette parties effective, professional, worry-free occasions.

**UNLV College of Hotel
Administration**
UNLV Catering
4505 S. Maryland Pkwy.
Las Vegas, NV 89154
895-3980
Caters parties of 80 or more; available
evenings Mon. - Fri. and anytime on
weekends.

Waiters on Wheels
735-6325
Credit Cards: All major
Buffet style food delivery service for
your catering needs.

BANQUET ROOMS

Andre's
401 S. Sixth St.
Las Vegas, NV 89101
385-5016
Seats 8-85 in several separate eating
areas; reserve ASAP. Deposit of 50% of
estimated total per person upon booking.

Beijing Restaurant
3900 Paradise Rd.
Las Vegas, NV 89109
737-9618
Seats up to 100; separate room for
smaller groups. Menu varies. $10 and up
per person. Deposit of 25% of total.

Big Dog's Catering Division
6390 W. Sahara Ave.
Las Vegas, NV 89102
876-1106
Two private banquet rooms. The
Pedigree Room accommodates up to
175 and Bailey's accommodates up to
25. Private bar and dance floor.

Boison's
4503 S. Paradise Rd.
Las Vegas, NV 89109
732-9993
Up to 60 in separate dining room. $14 -
$24 per person.

Brittany's
7770 W. Ann Rd.
Las Vegas, NV 89129
658-8998
Accommodates 20 to 240 guests. Menus
starting at $10.95, tax and gratuity
included. Outside catering available.

Calico Jack's Banquet Hall
8200 W. Charleston Ave.
Las Vegas, NV 89117233-5574
Able to accommodate 25 to 125 people
at a cost of between $10 and $18.50;
$125 deposit required.

Carrows Restaurant
169 E. Tropicana Ave.
Las Vegas, NV 89109
736-3936
Up to 40 in separate room, except Fri. and
Sat., $7 - $10 per person plus tax and tip.
$75 room rent.

Cathay House Restaurant
5300 Spring Mountain Rd.
Las Vegas, NV 89102
876-3838
Up to 130 in separate room; separate
menus. $13 - $100 per person plus tax
and tip.

Country Inn
1990 W. Sunset Rd.
Henderson, NV 89014
898-8183
Consultation, planning, decorating, food,
beverage and entertainment. Banquet
room seating up to 75. Outside catering.

Country Inn
1401 S. Rainbow Blvd.
Las Vegas, NV 89102
254-0520
Consultation, planning, decorating,
food, beverage and entertainment.
Banquet room seating up to 75.

Emerald Gardens
891 S. Rampart Blvd.
Las Vegas, NV 89128
242-5700
Credit Cards: All major
Comfortably accommodates up to 350
people; indoor and outdoor banquet
facilities; $1,000 deposit required.

Golden Steer
308 W. Sahara Ave.
Las Vegas, NV 89102
384-4470
Up to 50 in separate room. Menu is negotiable. Approximately $20 - $30 plus tax
and tip per person. $400 - $500 deposit. No
outside catering.

Jeremiah's Restaurant
171 E. Tropicana Ave.
Las Vegas, NV 89109
736-3044
James Winso, Gen. Mgr.
Up to 35 in main dining room, no separate rooms. Menu negotiable; no deposit;
no outside catering.

Kiefers
15 E. Lake Mead Dr.
Henderson, NV 89015
565-0122
Credit Cards: All major
Up to 175 in separate rooms. Four separate banquet menus; $100 deposit
required.

Kiefer's Atop the Carriage House
105 E. Harmon Ave.
Las Vegas, NV 89109
739-8000
Restaurant can accommodate 40 people. Outside catering available.

**King City Chinese
Seafood Restaurant**
4670 S. Decatur Blvd.
Las Vegas, NV 89103
876-9588
Credit Cards: MC, Visa
Seating up to 100 people, also outside
catering; 25% deposit required.

Macayo West
4457 W. Charleston Blvd.
Las Vegas, NV 89107
878-7347
Up to 180 persons Sun. - Thu. in separate room. Deposit required.

Macayo Vegas
1741 E. Charleston Blvd.
Las Vegas, NV 89104
382-5605
Up to 50 people.

Mandarin Court
1510 E. Flamingo Rd.
Las Vegas, NV 89119
737-1234
Credit Cards: All major
Up to 120 in separate room; starting at
$12 per person plus tax, tip and bever-
age; $50 - $200 deposit.

**Mt. Charleston
Hotel & Restaurant**
2 Kyle Canyon Rd.
Mt. Charleston, NV 89124
456-1606 872-5500 1-800-794-3456
Credit Cards: All major
Two separate banquet rooms. First can
accommodate about 200 people, while a
second smaller room can accommodate
up to 35 people. No outside catering;
deposit required.

Paradise Food Service
9457 Las Vegas Blvd.
Las Vegas, NV 89123
897-2287
Indoor seating for up to 275; outdoor
seating for up to 1,200. Wedding receptions, banquets, meetings, BBQs, corporate functions.

Philips Supper House
4545 W. Sahara Ave.
Las Vegas, NV 89102
873-5222
Credit Cards: All major
Up to 80 in separate room. Different
banquet menus range from $27 to $52
per person plus tax, tip and beverage.
Deposit $200.

**Piero's Italian Cuisine & New
England Fish Market**
355 Convention Center Dr.
Las Vegas, NV 89109
369-2305
Credit Cards: All major
Private parties from 10 to 70 people in five
separate dining areas; separate banquet
menu. $50 per person plus tax and tip,
pianist available. Deposit is 50% of total
estimated bill. No outside catering.

Play It Again Sam
4120 Spring Mountain Rd.
Las Vegas, NV 89102
876-1550
Credit Cards: All major
Up to 150 persons. Menu negotiable;
price ranges from $10.95 to $17.95 per
person plus tax and tip. $100 deposit.
No outside catering.

Red Lobster
(Multiple locations listed below)
200 S. Decatur Blvd.
Las Vegas, NV 89107
877-0212

Not available on Fri. or Sat. evenings. Seating for 60 with varied menu; $14.50 - $17.00 plus tax and tip, or order off menu, no deposit for groups under 25.

2325 E. Flamingo Rd.
Las Vegas, NV 89121
731-0119
Not available on Fri. or Sat. evenings. Seating for 100 with separate banquet menu; $15 plus tax and tip.

Señor Frogs
3190 W. Sahara Ave.
Las Vegas, NV 89102
873-3345
Hours: 11 am - 5 am. 50 to 150 in separate room. Separate banquet menu; deposit required. No outside catering.

Starboard Tack
2601 Atlantic St.
Las Vegas, NV 89104
457-8794
Up to 45 in separate area of main dining room. Separate banquet menus priced from $8.95 to $15.95 per person plus tax and tip; $100 deposit. Outside catering available.

Sunset Gardens
3931 E. Sunset Rd.
Las Vegas, NV 89120
456-9986
Credit Cards: All major

Three separate rooms accommodate 50, 125 and 350 people comfortably; in house catering and entertainment available. Menu prices start at $14.95 plus $10 per head for open bar; $1,500 deposit required.

The Tillerman
2245 E. Flamingo Rd.
Las Vegas, NV 89119
731-4036
Credit Cards: All major
Up to 80 in separate areas. Separate banquet menus $29 - $34 includes tax; $100 deposit; add 17% gratuity.

Tricia's Teas
Red Rooster Antique Mall
1109 Western Ave.
Las Vegas, NV 89102
876-0682
Private tea parties can be scheduled in this unique vintage tea room. All teas are by reservation only. Teas, scones, with jam and Devonshire creme, cucumber sandwiches, fresh fruits, croissants, tea cakes. No outside catering. Proper tea attire, please; vintage clothing available. Gentlemen welcome and children 5 and older.
Atmosphere: Victorian private room. Unusual and wonderful experience.

The Victorian Room
2800 W. Sahara Ave.
Las Vegas, NV 89102
252-8379
Credit Cards: MC, Visa
Accommodating up to 85 persons; room rental $150 per hour plus price per person for food; adjacent patio allows for indoor/outdoor atmosphere; entertainment available upon request; $500 deposit required.

Wet 'n Wild - Las Vegas
2601 Las Vegas Blvd. S.
Mailing address:
2310 Paseo Del Prado, Ste. A-220
Las Vegas, NV 89102
737-3819
Recorded Information: 734-0088
Offices/Group Info: 871-7811
Birthday parties for 20 to convention gatherings for 5,000, Wet'n Wild can service the smallest to largest parties. Wet'n Wild offers over 16 acres of thrilling chutes, slides, flumes, floats and plunges and creatively caters for a spectacular display of cuisine. The experienced staff at the park can customize any function ranging from a Polynesian luau with a steel drum band

to an old fashioned western barbecue to an elegant sit-down dinner.

Wet'n Wild can accommodate up to 5,000 guests in the park. It also offers a 2-acre outdoor picnic facility known as the Picnic Plaza. The Picnic Plaza, which can be reserved for up to 2,000 guests, includes more than 100 picnic tables, two volleyball courts, horseshoe pits, the Trampoline Thing, and many more fun games. There are several other entertainment options including disc jockeys and live bands.

Discounted group rates available. Half off the price of all day admission for senior citizens and children under 3 are free. For more information on group or convention rates, children and spouse programs and coupons programs, please call 871-7811.

Yolies Brazilian Steak House
3900 Paradise Rd.
Las Vegas, NV 89109
794-0700
Credit Cards: All major
Up to 200 in main dining area. Regular seven course fare $22.95 per person plus tax and tip; 30 percent deposit. Outside catering available.

DINING - MISCELLANEOUS

DINING SERVICE HOME DELIVERY

Waiters on Wheels
(WOW) 735-MEAL (6325)
Delivery throughout Las Vegas from over 75 fine restaurants. Order from any of the menus in their menu guide, add $6 for delivery and in about an hour you have got your lunch or dinner. Waiters on Wheels takes the order, places it with the restaurant, picks it up and delivers it to your home or office.
Hours: Mon. - Fri. 10 am - 10 pm; Sat. 11 am - 10 pm; Sun. 3 pm - 10 pm
Credit Cards: MC, Visa, AMX, Diners

The Custom Cook
5432 Rose Hills St.
Las Vegas, NV 89129
658-9921
David Lessnick
Specializes in preparing low-fat, healthy meals in client's home. They do shopping and prepare two weeks' (10) dinners on their own equipment. Each dinner is an entree, with enough for three to four people and side dishes.

AMERICAN/HOTEL COFFEE SHOPS

HOTEL RESTAURANTS - All hotels have 24 hour coffee shops. Many have daily specials in addition to late night specials served after 11 pm or midnight until about 7 am. Breakfast is usually served 24 hours.

Specials listed below are subject to change without notice.

Grillhouse
Alystra Casino
333 W. Sunset Rd.
Henderson, NV 89015
564-8555
Hours: 24 hours
Reservations: None
Dress: Casual
Price of Entrees: $5.95 - $15.95
Credit Cards: MC, Visa, Discover
Specialties: Pasta, whole chicken, baby back ribs, steaks and daily dinner specials.
Atmosphere: Charming and colorful.

Sourdough Cafe
Arizona Charlie's
740 S. Decatur Blvd.
Las Vegas, NV 89107
258-5200
Hours: 24 hours
Reservations: None
Dress: Casual
Price of Entrees: $4.55 - $10.95
Credit Cards: All major
Specials: Breakfast specials: bacon and eggs, pancakes and bacon or biscuits and gravy served Mon. - Fri.; $1.59 midnight - 7 am

Sidewalk Cafe
Bally's
3645 Las Vegas Blvd. S.
Las Vegas, NV 89109
739-4111
Hours: 24 hours
Reservations: None
Dress: Casual
Price of Entrees: $8.50 - $13.50
Credit Cards: All major
Specials: Prime rib dinner $7.77, served 5 pm - 5 am. Voted #1 coffee shop by *Lifestyle* magazine.

Victorian Room
Barbary Coast
3595 Las Vegas Blvd. S.
Las Vegas, NV 89109
737-7111
Hours: 24 hours
Reservations: Not required
Dress: Casual
Price of Entrees: $10 - $35
Credit Cards: All major
Specials: Breakfast special served for $1.94 from 11 pm - 7 am
Specialties: Chinese and American.

Barcelona Restaurant
Barcelona Hotel & Casino
5011 E. Craig Rd.
Las Vegas, NV 89115
644-6300
Hours: 24 hours
Reservations: None
Dress: Casual
Specialties: Soup and sandwich $2.99; ham steak and eggs $1 (24 hours); Home cooking from scratch.
Atmosphere: Country cafe.

Brewer's Cafe
Barley's Casino & Brewing Co.
4500 E. Sunset Rd.
Henderson, NV 89014
458-BREW(2739)
Hours: Mon. - Fri. 11 am - 11 pm, Sat. - Sun. 7 am - 11 pm
Reservations: None
Dress: Casual
Specialties: Pasta, wood-fired pizza, salads; children's menu.
Atmosphere: Micro-brewery and restaurant; patio dining.

Iron Horse Cafe
Boulder Station
4111 Boulder Hwy.
Las Vegas, NV 89121
432-7777
Hours: 24 hours

Reservations: Suggested
Dress: Casual
Price of Entrees: $2.50 - $14
Credit Cards: All major
Specialties: 16-oz T-bone steak, $7.95. Chinese specialties served 11 am - 5 pm

Cafe Roma
Caesars Palace
3570 Las Vegas Blvd. S.
Las Vegas, NV 89109
731-7110
Hours: 24 hours
Reservations: None
Dress: Casual
Price of Entrees: $8.75 - $21.95
Credit Cards: All major

Market Street Cafe
California Hotel
12 Ogden Ave.
Las Vegas, NV 89101
385-1222
Hours: 24 hours
Reservations: None
Dress: Casual
Price of Entrees: Inexpensive
Credit Cards: All major
Specials: NY strip served 11 pm - 9 am $2.99.
Specialties: American and Oriental.

Promenade
Circus Circus
2280 Las Vegas Blvd. S.
Las Vegas, NV 89109
734-0410
Hours: 24 hours
Reservations: None
Dress: Casual
Price of Entrees: Inexpensive
Credit Cards: All major
Specials: Daily chef's selection served weekdays 11 am - 11 pm.
Specialties: Breakfast, lunch and dinner favorites. 1 lb prime rib - $7.99, 1 lb burger - $3.99.

DINING - MISCELLANEOUS

Continental Hotel Cafe
Continental Hotel
4100 Paradise Rd.
Las Vegas, NV 89109
737-5555
Hours: 24 hours
Reservations: None
Dress: Casual
Credit Cards: All major
Specials: 6 oz. filet w/ jumbo shrimp $5.95

The Celebrity Cafe
Debbie Reynold's Hotel
305 Convention Center Dr.
Las Vegas, NV 89109
734-0711
Hours: 24 hours
Reservations: None
Dress: Informal
Price of Entrees: $8.95 - $15.95
Credit Cards: All major
Specials: Daily luncheon specials $3.95
Specialties: Trout almondine, broiled salmon, roast pork loin.
Atmosphere: Large portraits of legendary film stars adorn the walls.

Terrace Pointe
Desert Inn
3145 Las Vegas Blvd. S.
Las Vegas, NV 89109
733-4580
Hours: 24 hours
Reservations: None
Dress: Informal
Price of Entrees: Moderate
Credit Cards: All major
Specials: Daily dinner specials are served 5 pm - 11 pm.

The Emerald Room
El Cortez
600 Fremont St.
Las Vegas, NV 89101
385-5200
Hours: 24 hours
Reservations: None
Dress: Casual
Price of Entrees: Inexpensive
Credit Cards: All major
Specials: Varies daily.
Specialties: Prime rib, steaks, sandwiches.

Cactus Joe's Cafe
Eldorado Club
140 S. Water St.
Henderson, NV 89015
564-1811
Hours: 24 hours
Reservations: None
Dress: Casual
Price of Entrees: Inexpensive
Credit Cards: MC, Visa, AMX
Specials: Changes daily.

Sherwood Forest Cafe
Excalibur
3850 Las Vegas Blvd. S.
Las Vegas, NV 89109
597-7777
Hours: 24 hours
Reservations: None
Dress: Casual

Price of Entrees: Under $10.25
Credit Cards: All major
Specials: Changes daily.

Mr. G's
Fiesta
2400 N. Rancho Dr.
Las Vegas, NV 89130
631-7000
Hours: 24 hours
Reservations: None
Dress: Casual
Credit Cards: All major
Specials: Late night specials: $2.95 choice of barbecue ribs, steak and eggs, served 11 pm - 7 am; T-bone steak dinner $9.95, served 24 hours. Prime-rib special served 4 pm - midnight $6.95

Lindy's
Flamingo Hilton
3555 Las Vegas Blvd. S.
Las Vegas, NV 89109
733-3111
Hours: 24 hours
Price of Entrees: Inexpensive
Credit Cards: All major
Specialties: Sandwiches, salads; patio dining.

Magnolia's Veranda
Four Queens
202 Fremont St.
Las Vegas, NV 89101
385-4011
Hours: 24 hours
Reservations: None
Dress: Casual
Price of Entrees: $6 - $15
Credit Cards: All major
Specials: Prime rib served daily 4 pm - 2 am $5.95; two breakfast specials served midnight - 8 am; pancakes, or biscuits and gravy $2.49.

The Lanai
Fremont
200 Fremont St.
Las Vegas, NV 89101
385-3232
Hours: 24 hours
Reservations: None
Dress: Casual
Price of Entrees: Inexpensive
Credit Cards: All major
Specials: Prime rib $5.95, served 5 pm - 11 pm; sirloin steak and two lobster tails $8.88, served 4 pm - 2 am.
Specialties: American food in addition to a Chinese menu served 11 am - 1 am.

Monterey Room
Gold Coast
4000 W. Flamingo Rd.
Las Vegas, NV 89103
367-7111
Hours: 24 hours
Reservations: None
Dress: Casual
Price of Entrees: Inexpensive
Credit Cards: All major
Specials: Bacon and eggs - $1.95, served 11 pm - 6 am; ham and eggs - $2.95, served 11 pm - 6 am; 16-ounce T-bone $7.95, served 24 hours.
Specialties: Chinese and American.

Bay City Diner
Golden Gate
1 E. Fremont St.
Las Vegas, NV 89101
382-6300
Hours: 24 hours
Reservations: None
Dress: Casual
Price of Entrees: $3.75 - $9.95
Credit Card: All major
Specials: Porterhouse steak $7.77 served 24 hours.

Carson Street Cafe
Golden Nugget
129 Fremont St.
Las Vegas, NV 89101
385-7111
Hours: 24 hours
Reservations: None
Dress: Casual
Price of Entrees: $6.95 - $18.50
Credit Cards: All major
Specials: 8 ounce ham steak, 2 eggs served from 11 pm - 6 am - $3.95.
Atmosphere: Light and cheery atmosphere of a European sidewalk cafe.

Mr. Lucky's 24/7
Hard Rock Hotel
4405 Paradise Rd.
Las Vegas, NV 89109
693-5000
Hours: 24 hours
Reservations: None
Dress: Casual
Price of Entrees: $6.95 - $13.95
Credit Cards: All major
Specialties: Pizza, fresh fish, homemade chicken pie.
Atmosphere: Casual, upbeat, coffee shop-style dining.
Specials: Steak and shrimp $6.95. Served 24 hours.

Garden Cafe
Harrah's
3475 Las Vegas Blvd. S.
Las Vegas, NV 89109
369-5000
Hours: 24 hours
Reservations: None
Dress: Casual
Price of Entrees: Inexpensive
Credit Cards: All major
Specials: Steak and lobster $9.95 with salad bar $11.95 served daily 5 pm - 11 pm; Steak & crab legs or steak and scampi, both $7.95 and served 3 pm - 11 pm; Daily double breakfast $2.99 or steak and eggs $3.99, both served 11 pm - 5 am.

Cyclone Coffee Shop
Holiday Inn/Casino Boardwalk
3750 Las Vegas Blvd. S.
Las Vegas, NV 89109
735-2400
Hours: 24 hours
Price of Entrees: $2.00 - $9.95
Credit Cards: All major

Binion's Horseshoe Coffee Shop
Binion's Horseshoe
128 Fremont St.
Las Vegas, NV 89101
382-1600
Hours: 24 hours
Reservations: None
Dress: Casual
Price of Entrees: $6.25 - $23
Credit Cards: On $10 or more
Specials: 16 ounce T-bone $6.75, served 5 pm - 11:45 pm; prime rib $5.75, served 24 hours; breakfast special served 2 am until 2 pm - $2.95. The smoked-ham available with the breakfast special covers the entire plate.

Teahouse Coffee Shop
Imperial Palace
3535 Las Vegas Blvd. S.
Las Vegas, NV 89109
731-3311
Hours: 24 hours
Reservations: None
Dress: Casual
Price of Entrees: $6.95 - $13.95
Credit Cards: All major
Specials: Bacon rolled filet mignon - $7.95; prime rib - $6.95; Steak sandwich $5.95 all served from 11 am - 11 pm.

Canal Street
Jerry's Nugget
1821 Las Vegas Blvd. N.
N. Las Vegas, NV 89030
399-3000
Hours: 24 hours
Reservations: None
Dress: Casual
Price of Entrees: Inexpensive
Credit Cards: All major
Specials: Prime rib $7.95, $10.50 and $21, served 24 hours.
Specialties: Great desserts.

Jesters Court
Jokers Wild
920 N. Boulder Hwy.
Henderson, NV 89015
564-8100
Hours: 24 hours
Reservations: None
Dress: Casual
Price of Entrees: $3.95 - $5.95
Credit Cards: All major
Specials: $.99 big breakfast served 11 pm - 11 am; $4.95 prime rib served 24 hours. Buffet - lunch served Mon. - Fri. 10 am - 3 pm $3.75; dinner nightly 4 pm - 9 pm $5.45. Sat. brunch served 9 am - 3 pm - $3.95; Sun. champagne brunch - $5.45. Children age 5 - 8 $3.99.

King 8 Coffee Shop
King 8 Hotel & Gambling Hall
3330 W. Tropicana Ave.
Las Vegas, NV 89103
736-8988
Hours: 24 hours
Reservations: None
Dress: Casual
Price of Entrees: Inexpensive
Credit Cards: All major
Specialties: Changes daily.
Atmosphere: Coffee shop.

Winners Cafe
Lady Luck
206 N. 3rd St.
Las Vegas, NV 89101
477-3000
Hours: 24 hours
Reservations: None
Dress: Casual
Price of Entrees: $4.95 - $9.00
Credit Cards: All major
Specials: Prime rib - 4 pm - 11 pm - $5.45
Specialties: Hawaiian and American dishes.

Dugout
Las Vegas Club
18 Fremont St.
Las Vegas, NV 89101
385-1664
Hours: 24 hours
Reservations: None
Dress: Casual
Price of Entrees: $7.00 - $8.95
Credit Cards: All major
Specials: Prime rib $5.95; trout $6.95.

The Coffee Shop
Las Vegas Hilton
3000 Paradise Rd.
Las Vegas, NV 89109
732-5111
Hours: 24 hours
Reservations: None
Dress: Casual
Price of Entrees: $7.25 - $13.50
Credit Cards: All major

Ligouri's
Ligouri's Casino
1133 Boulder Hwy.
Henderson, NV 89015
565-1688
Hours: 24 hours
Reservations: None
Dress: Casual
Price of Entrees: Daily specials from $3.75
Credit Cards: None
Specials: Changes daily.
Specialties: Homemade ham & bean soup and homemade chile, prime rib, liver & onions, chicken & dumplings.

Pyramid Cafe
Luxor
3900 Las Vegas Blvd. S.
Las Vegas, NV 89119
262-4770
Hours: 24 hours
Reservations: None
Dress: Casual
Price of Entrees: Inexpensive
Credit Cards: All major
Specials: None
Atmosphere: Three dimensional busts of Egyptian gods and goddesses decorate the cafe.

Millennium
Luxor
3900 Las Vegas Blvd. S.
Las Vegas, NV 89119
262-4765
Hours: 11 am - 11 pm; Fri. - Sat. 11 am - midnight
Reservations: None
Dress: Casual
Price of Entrees: Inexpensive
Credit Cards: All major
Specials: Steak & eggs $2.99, served 11 pm - 6 am except Wed.

America Cafe, New York New York, 3790 Las Vegas Blvd. S., Las Vegas, NV

Garden Cafe
Mahoney's Silver Nugget Casino
2140 Las Vegas Blvd. N.
N. Las Vegas, NV 89030
399-1111
Hours: 24 hours
Reservations: None
Dress: Casual
Price of Entrees: $3.99 - $6.99
Credit Cards: MC, Visa
Specials: 24-hour breakfast specials for $1.25; daily lunch specials.

Studio Cafe
MGM Grand
3799 Las Vegas Blvd. S.
Las Vegas, NV 89109
891-1111
Hours: 24 hours.
Reservations: none
Dress: Casual
Credit Cards: All major
Specials: Changes daily.

Tree House
Maxim
160 E. Flamingo Rd.
Las Vegas, NV 89109
731-4300
Hours: 24 hours
Reservations: None
Dress: Casual
Price of Entrees: $3.95 - $13.95
Credit Cards: All major
Specials: Half-baked chicken $3.95; served noon-11 pm $3.95; graveyard specials from $2.49.
Atmosphere: Open air restaurant overlooks the casino action.

Coyote Cafe
MGM Grand
3799 Las Vegas Blvd. S.
Las Vegas, NV 89109
891-1111
Hours: 9 am - 10:30 pm
Reservations: none
Dress: Casual
Price of Entrees: $7.00 - $16.00
Specials: Daily specials.

Caribe Cafe
Mirage
3400 Las Vegas Blvd. S.
Las Vegas, NV 89109
791-7111
Hours: 24 hours
Reservations: None
Dress: Casual
Price of Entrees: $8.95 - $16.00
Credit Cards: All major
Specials: Prime rib dinner served noon-midnight - $14.
Specialties: Create your own burger. Member of Las Vegas Lean, menu item made to contain less fat.

Monte Carlo Cafe
Monte Carlo
3770 Las Vegas Blvd. S.
Las Vegas, NV 89109
730-7777
Hours: 24
Reservations: None
Dress: Casual
Credit Cards: All major

Boulder Cafe
Nevada Palace
5255 Boulder Hwy.
Las Vegas, NV 89122
458-8810
Hours: 24 hours
Reservations: None
Dress: Casual
Price of Entrees: Inexpensive
Credit Cards: All major

Michelle's Village Cafe
New Frontier
3120 Las Vegas Blvd. S.
Las Vegas, NV 89109
794-8200
Hours: 24 hours
Reservations: None
Dress: Casual
Price of Entrees: $7.95 - $12.95
Credit Cards: All major
Specials: 12-ounce prime rib served noon - midnight for $5.95; 20-ounce for $8.95; $4.95 all you can eat buffet 11 am - 2 pm; seafood buffet Mon. - Thu. 4 pm - 10 pm - $7.95, Fri. 3 pm - 10 pm - $10.95, Sat. 4 pm - 10 pm - $8.95 & Sun. 11 am - 10 pm - $8.95.

America Cafe
New York New York
3790 Las Vegas Blvd. S.
Las Vegas, NV 89109
740-6969
Hours: 24 hours

Reservations: None
Dress: Casual
Price of Entrees: $3.00 - $17.00
Credit Cards: All major
Specials: Changes daily
Atmosphere: Features a 90' x 20' map of the U.S. complete with mountains, rivers and amber waves of grain so that you can find your home town and eat there too.

Courtyard Cafe
The Orleans
4500 W. Tropicana Ave.
Las Vegas, NV 89103
365-7111
Hours: 24 hours
Reservations: None
Price of Entrees: $4.95 - $12.95
Credit Cards: All major
Specialties: Steak and eggs served 11 pm - 6 am, 10-ounce prime rib or 16 ounce porter-house steak for $7.95.
Atmosphere: Warm and friendly.

Iron Horse Cafe
Palace Station
2411 W. Sahara Ave.
Las Vegas, NV 89102
367-2411
Hours: 24 hours
Reservations: None
Dress: Casual
Price of Entrees: $5.95 - $10.95
Credit Cards: All major
Specials: New York steak or prime rib served 24 hours, $6.95; 16 ounce T-bone served 24 hours, $7.95; baby back ribs served 24 hours $7.95. Complete Chinese dinner specials served 11 pm - 5 am, $6.45; $1.99 breakfast special served 10 pm - 7 am.
Specialties: Chinese and American menu.

Plaza Diner
Jackie Gaughan's Plaza Hotel
1 Main St.
Las Vegas, NV 89101
386-2110
Hours: 24 hours
Reservations: None
Dress: Casual
Price of Entrees: $1.98 - $8.95
Credit Cards: All major
Specials: Eggs with bacon or sausage $2.25 - 24 hours.
Atmosphere: '50s outdoor diner.

Poker Palace Restaurant
Poker Palace Casino
2757 Las Vegas Blvd. N.
N. Las Vegas, NV 89030
649-9280
Hours: 24 hours
Reservations: None
Dress: Casual
Price of Entrees: Inexpensive
Credit Cards: None
Specials: Complete prime rib dinner $5.99, served 24 hours.

Railroad Pass Coffee Shop
Railroad Pass Hotel & Casino
2800 Boulder Hwy.
Henderson, NV 89015
294-5000
Hours: 24 hours
Reservations: None
Dress: Casual
Price of Entrees: $4.00 - $8.00
Credit Cards: All major

DINING

DINING - MISCELLANEOUS

Congo Jack's Cafe
Reserve Hotel
777 W. Lake Mead Blvd.
Henderson, NV 89015
558-7000
Hours: 24 hours
Reservations: None
Dress: Casual
Price of Entrees: $6.50 - $13.95
Credit Cards: All major
Specialties: Blackened shrimp Alfredo, Boudin, stuffed and smothered pork chops, Burmese curry, whole fish and Chinese and Italian dishes.
Atmosphere: You are greeted at the entrance by a life size wrecked airplane, Congo Jack hangs from the ceiling on a parachute and stuffed monkeys are snooping around the plane.

Beach Cafe
Rio
3700 W. Flamingo Rd.
Las Vegas, NV 89103
252-7777
Hours: 24 hours
Reservations: None
Dress: Casual
Credit Cards: All major
Specialties: Steak and lobster served 4 pm - 10 pm - $7.95; 10-ounce prime rib $12.95; 10-ounce T-Bone steak - $12.95.
Atmosphere: Restaurant overlooks the beach and pool area.

Kady's Brasserie
Riviera
2901 Las Vegas Blvd. S.
Las Vegas, NV 89109
734-5110
Hours: 24 hours
Reservations: None
Dress: Casual
Price of Entrees: $7.95 - $14.95
Credit Cards: All major
Specialties: Breakfast special featuring ham and eggs - $2.99, served midnight-6:30 am; all you can eat pancakes served midnight - 6 am - $1.99; 1 lb crab legs $9.95 served 5 pm - midnight.

'50s Diner
Roadhouse Casino
2100 Boulder Hwy.
Henderson, NV 89015
564-1150
Hours: 24 hours
Reservations: None
Dress: Casual
Price of Entrees: $2.95 and up
Credit Cards: major
Specialties: Blue plate specials from $2.95.
Atmosphere: Authentic '50s diner.

Caravan Dining Room
Sahara
2535 Las Vegas Blvd. S.
Las Vegas, NV 89109
737-2111
Hours: 24 hours
Reservations: None
Dress: Casual
Price of Entrees: $1.99 - $16.99
Credit Cards: All major

Congo Jack's Cafe at **Reserve Hotel,** 777 W. Lake Mead Blvd., Henderson, NV

Specialties: 1-lb NY steak served 5 pm to 11 pm - $7.95; graveyard specials midnight - 6 am - 7 oz. NY steak and eggs - $1.99; 1 lb King crab - $7.95.

Mary's Diner
Sam's Town
5111 Boulder Hwy.
Las Vegas, NV 89122
454-8073
Hours: 7 am - 11 pm
Reservations: None
Dress: Casual
Price of Entrees: $4.95 - $9.50
Credit Cards: All major
Specialties: Daily blue plate specials $4.95; soup and sandwich served 11 am - 4 pm - $2.95 at the counter.
Specialties: Burgers, sandwiches, real malts and shakes and blue plate specials daily.
Atmosphere: Authentic '50s diner.

Smokey Joe's
Sam's Town
5111 Boulder Hwy.
Las Vegas, NV 89122
454-8073
Hours: 24 hours
Reservations: None
Dress: Casual
Price of Entrees: $6.95 - $11.00
Credit Cards: All major
Specialties: Steak and eggs $4.95; 3/4 lb ham steak and 3 eggs $3.95, 11 pm - 11 am; both include hash browns & coffee; prime rib with salad bar $8.95; soup and salad bar lunch $2.99, dinner $4.99.
Specialties: Chinese menu also served 11 am - 11 pm, Fri. & Sat. 11 am - 2 am

Ristorante dei Fiori
San Remo
115 E. Tropicana Ave.
Las Vegas, NV 89109
739-9000
Hours: 24 hours
Reservations: None
Dress: Casual
Price of Entrees: $6.95 - $18.95
Credit Cards: All major
Specialties: $4.49 steak and eggs served 24 hours; $3.95 prime rib dinner served 24 hours.

Pablo's Cafe
Santa Fe
4949 N. Rancho Dr.

Las Vegas, NV 89130
658-4900
Hours: 24 hours
Reservations: None
Dress: Casual
Price of Entrees: Inexpensive
Credit Cards: All major
Specialties: 10 oz. chef cut prime rib $5.95, $2.49 breakfast specials served 11 pm - 11 am.
Specialties: American and Southwestern dining.

Santa Fe Coffee Company
Santa Fe
4949 N. Rancho Dr.
Las Vegas, NV 89130
658-4900
Hours: 7 am - 10 pm
Specialties: A variety of coffee and pastries, rolls, cookies, muffins and cakes.

Showboat Coffee Shop
Showboat
2800 E. Fremont St.
Las Vegas, NV 89104
385-9123
Hours: 24 hours
Reservations: None
Dress: Casual
Price of Entrees: $5 - $10.95
Credit Cards: All major
Specialties: Changes daily; Dinner specials 4:30 pm - 10:30 pm; 16 ounce T-bone steak $7.95 served 24 hours.

The Country Cupboard
Silver City Casino
3001 Las Vegas Blvd. S.
Las Vegas, NV 89109
732-4152
Hours: 24 hours
Reservations: None
Dress: Casual
Price of Entrees: Inexpensive
Specialties: 12-ounce T-bone steak $4.99, served 24 hours.

Comstock Coffee Shop
Silverton
3333 Blue Diamond Rd.
Las Vegas, NV 89139
263-7777
Hours: 24 hours
Reservations: None
Dress: Casual
Specialties: Prime rib $6.95 3 pm - 6 pm, huge $1 strawberry shortcake.

Skyline Casino Coffee Shop
Skyline Casino
1741 N. Boulder Hwy.
Henderson, NV 89015
565-9116
1-800-621-0187
Hours: 24 hours
Reservations: None
Dress: Casual
Price of Entrees: Inexpensive
Credit Cards: All major
Specials: $1.99 breakfast specials, three to choose from, served 24 hours; prime rib $5.95, served 4 pm - 10 pm; Lunch buffet $4.99; dinner buffet $7.99; steak & eggs $3.95 served 11 pm - 11 am

Toucan Harry's
Stardust
3000 Las Vegas Blvd. S.
Las Vegas, NV 89109
732-6111
Hours: 24 hours
Reservations: None
Dress: Casual
Price of Entrees: Inexpensive
Credit Cards: All major
Specials: Prime rib $5.95 served 24 hours; steak and lobster $7.95 served 3 pm - 2 am and Tue. until 9 pm; late night breakfast 11 pm - 7 am - $2.89.
Specialties: American menu as well as Chinese specialties served 11 am - 2 am.

Sister's Coffee Shop
Stratosphere
2000 Las Vegas Blvd. S.
Las Vegas, NV 89109
380-7777
Hours: 24 hours
Reservations: None
Credit Cards: All major
Price of Entrees: $4.95 - $14.95
Atmosphere: Country western.

Roxy's Diner
Stratosphere
2000 Las Vegas Blvd. S.
Las Vegas, NV 89109
380-7777
Hours: Noon - 10 pm
Reservations: None
Dress: Casual
Price of Entrees: $5.00 - $9.00
Specials: Great burgers, blue plate specials served daily.
Atmosphere: Reminiscent of a '50s diner complete with singing and dancing waiters who entertain while they serve you. Hula hoops and poodle skirts optional.

Sunset Cafe
Sunset Station
130 W. Sunset Rd.
Henderson, NV 89015
547-7777
Hours: 24 hours
Reservations: None
Dress: Casual
Price of Entrees: $2.99 - $14.99
Credit Cards: All major

The Yellow Rose Cafe
Texas Station
3141 N. Rancho Dr.
Las Vegas, NV 89130
631-1000
Hours: 24 hours
Reservations: None
Dress: Casual
Price of Entrees: $6.50 - $8.95
Credit Cards: All major
Specials: 6 ounce NY steak and 3 eggs
served 11 pm - 11 am $3.49; 16-ounce sir-
loin $5.95; $1.99 breakfast specials served
Sun. - Thu. 11 pm - 11 am.

Tom's Cafe
Tom's Sunset Casino
444 W. Sunset Rd.
Henderson, NV 89015
564-5551
Hours: 6 am - 11 pm
Reservations: None
Dress: Casual
Price of Entrees: $.99 - $10.95
Specialties: Omelets, ribs, pork chops,
chicken.
Atmosphere: Southwest.

Lookout Cafe
Treasure Island
3300 Las Vegas Blvd. S.
Las Vegas, NV 89109
894-7111
Hours: 24 hours
Reservations: None
Dress: Casual
Price of Entrees: $7.50 - $14.50
Credit Cards: All major
Specials: Daily specials.
Atmosphere: Overlooking the casino and
the lushly landscaped swimming pool.

Black Spot Grille
Treasure Island
3300 Las Vegas Blvd. S.
Las Vegas, NV 89109
894-7111
Hours: Sun. - Thu. 11 am - 11 pm;
Fri. - Sat. 11 am - 12:30 am
Reservations: None
Dress: Casual
Price of Entrees: $6.95 - $12.95
Credit Cards: All major
Specialties: Calzones, strombolis, burg-
ers, pastas and salads.

Calypsos
Tropicana
3801 Las Vegas Blvd. S.
Las Vegas, NV 89109
739-2222
Hours: 24 hours
Reservations: None
Dress: Casual
Price of Entrees: $6.95 - $14.95
Credit Cards: All major
Specials: Prime rib sandwich - $5.95 served
on club roll with fries, NY steak $13.95.

Chuckwagon
Virgin River
Interstate 15, Exit 122
Mesquite, NV 89024
1-800-346-7721
Hours: 24 hours
Reservations: None
Dress: Casual
Price of Entrees: $5.95 - $11.95
Credit Cards: All major
Specialties: Prime rib, crab legs, surf &
turf, shrimp.

Westward Ho Cafe
Westward Ho
2900 Las Vegas Blvd. S.
Las Vegas, NV 89109
731-2900
Hours: 24 hours
Reservations: None
Dress: Casual
Price of Entrees: $5.95 - $10.95
Credit Cards: All major

CAFES/COFFEE HOUSE

Art from the Heart
4020 N. Tenaya Way
Las Vegas, NV 89129
656-8250
Hours: Sun. - Fri. 6 am - 9 pm; Sat. 7 am - 7 pm
Atmosphere: For the art enthusiast,
works of art are on display in an otherwise traditional coffee house setting.

The BeanTree
2620 Regatta Dr., Ste. 112
Las Vegas, NV 89128
242-2233
Hours: Mon. - Sat. 7 am - 6 pm;
Sun. 8 am - 3 pm
Reservations: None
Dress: Casual
Price of Entrees: $3.00 - $5.00
Credit Cards: MC, Visa, AMX
Specialties: Daily sandwich specials,
salads and desserts.
Atmosphere: Casually elegant with
rough tiled floor; lakeside patio seating.

Blue Angel Coffee and Market
252 Convention Center Dr.
Las Vegas, NV 89109
732-4250
Hours: Mon. - Sat. 8 am - 10 pm;
Sun. 11 am - 10 pm

Bonjour French & European Bakery
4012 S. Rainbow Blvd.
Las Vegas, NV 89103
221-4320
Hours: Mon. - Fri. 8 am - 6 pm;
Sat. 8 am - 3 pm
Reservations: None
Dress: Casual
Specialties: An authentic French bakery
specializing in cakes, pastries, breads, soups,
salads, sandwiches, quiche; coffee bar.

Borders Book Shop & Cafe
2323 S. Decatur Blvd.
Las Vegas, NV 89102
258-0999
Hours: Mon. - Sat. 9 am - 10 pm;
Sun. 9 am - 8:45 pm
Specialties: Gourmet coffee, espresso,
cappuccino, cheesecakes, pies and
decadent desserts.
Atmosphere: Located inside Borders
Book Shop; "The coffee bar for the book
lover;" live entertainment and speakers.

Brewed Awakening
2305 E. Sahara Ave., Ste. F
Las Vegas, NV 89104
457-7050
Hours: Mon. - Fri. 6 am - 8 pm;
Sat. 7 am - 5 pm; Sun. 9 am - 4 pm
Reservations: None
Dress: Casual
Credit Cards: All major
Specialties: Coffee roasting, gourmet
gifts, sandwiches, soups, salads.

Cafe Ah Go-Go, 6985 W. Sahara Ave.,
Las Vegas, NV 89117

Buzzy's Espresso
4755 S. Maryland Pkwy.
Las Vegas, NV 89119
261-9779
Hours: Mon. - Fri. 7 am - 6 pm;
Sat. 9 am - 5 pm
Reservations: None
Dress: Casual
Credit Cards: None
Specialties: Light lunch, sandwiches
and desserts.

Cafe Ah Go-Go
6985 W. Sahara Ave.
Las Vegas, NV 89117
Hours: Mon. - Fri. 5:30- am - 6 pm;
Sat. 7 am - 6 pm; Sun. 7 am - 3 pm
Specialties: Strictly drive thru; espres-
so, hot and iced coffee drinks, flavored
specialty coffees, muffins and croissants.

Cafe Copioh
4550 S. Maryland Pkwy.
Las Vegas, NV 89119

739-0305
Hours: Tue. - Thu. 11 am - 3 am;
Fri. 3 pm - 3 am; Sat. 6pm - 3 am;
Sun. 6 pm - midnight
Reservations: None
Dress: Casual
Price of Entrees: Inexpensive
Credit Cards: None
Specialties: Gourmet coffee, herbal tea,
sandwiches, homemade pastries, cheese
cake, cappuccino and espresso.

Cafe Espresso Roma
4440 S. Maryland Pkwy.
Las Vegas, NV 89119
369-1540
Hours: 8 am - 10 pm
Reservations: None
Dress: Casual
Credit Cards: None
Specialties: Espresso, cappuccino, cafe
au lait, Italian sodas, quiche, salads and
pastries.
Atmosphere: Semi-self service; clientele
of students and artists; Mon. night poet-
ry readings at 7:30 pm.

Cafe Neon
(Inside The Attic Vintage Clothing Store)
1018 S. Main St.
Las Vegas, NV 89101
388-4088
Hours: Mon. - Sat. 10 am - 6 pm; Closed Sun.
Reservations: None
Dress: Casual
Credit Cards: None
Specialties: Coffee, pastries, sandwiches.

DINING

DINING - MISCELLANEOUS

Bonfiglio's Corner Store & Deli
8524 W. Sahara Ave.
Las Vegas, NV 89117
363-8018
Hours: 8 am - 1 am
Credit Cards: All major
Specialties: Italian deli sandwiches.

Bugsy's Deli
Flamingo Hilton
3555 Las Vegas Blvd. S.
Las Vegas, NV 89109
733-3111
Hours: Sun. - Thu.. 11 am - 11 pm;
Fri. - Sat. 11 am - 2 am
Specialties: Sandwiches, hot dogs, danish and donuts.

Casba
855 E. Twain Ave.
Las Vegas, NV 89109
791-3344
Hours: Mon. - Thu. 9 am - 10 pm;
Fri. 9 am - 3 pm; Sun. 10 am - 9:30 pm;
closed Sat.
Reservations: Suggested
Dress: Casual
Price of Entrees: $8.99 - $22.99
Credit Cards: MC, Visa, AMX
Specialties: Glatt Kosher cuisine. Hungarian goulash, shislik, seasoned ground beef meatball kabob, veal chops, deli sandwiches.
Atmosphere: Elegant Kosher atmosphere.

Celebrity Deli
4055 S. Maryland Pkwy.
Las Vegas, NV 89119
733-7827
Hours: Mon. - Sat. 9 am - 8 pm;
Sun. 9 am - 4 pm
Reservations: Accepted
Dress: Casual
Price of Entrees: $6.95 - $13.95
Credit Cards: All major
Specialties: Romaine steak, brisket and potato pancakes; children's menu; catering and delivery.
Atmosphere: Very pretty and airy; patio dining.

Danube Cafe and Market
4865 S. Pecos Rd.
Las Vegas, NV 89121
454-5535
Hours: Mon. - Fri. 10 am - 8 pm;
Sat. 10 am - 5 pm
Credit Cards: MC, Visa, Discover
Specialties: Greek-Mediterranean deli

Deli - Bakery & Ice Cream Parlor
Fiesta Casino Hotel
2400 N. Rancho Dr.
N. Las Vegas, NV 89130
631-7000
Hours: 10 am - midnight
Specials: Emack and Bolio's ice cream.
Specialties: Sandwiches, jumbo Kosher hot dogs and a variety of cheeses; fresh baked hams.

Deli Delite
6261 Industrial Rd.
Las Vegas, NV 89118
896-2282
Hours: Mon. - Fri. 7 am - 3 pm
Credit Cards: None
Specialties: Deli sandwiches, bagels.

Deli 300
3430 E. Tropicana Ave.
Las Vegas, NV 89112
458-1028
Hours: Mon. - Sat. 11 am - 5 pm
Credit Cards: None
Serving Las Vegas for over 25 years; previously of Maryland Square.
Specialties: Corned beef, pastrami, bagels, cream cheeses, homemade soups and salads, and 330 different sandwiches made to order.

The Delicatessen
Treasure Island
3300 Las Vegas Blvd. S.
Las Vegas, NV 89109
894-7111
Hours: Mon. - Fri. 11 am - midnight;
Sat. - Sun. 9 am - midnight
Credit Cards: All major
Specialties: Corned beef, pastrami, sandwiches, matzo ball soup, New England clam chowder, in-house bakery fresh breads.

Delicious Italian Deli
6110 Spring Mountain Rd.
Las Vegas, NV 89102
873-9250
Hours: Mon. - Sat. 9 am - 6 pm
Credit Cards: None
Specialties: pasta fagoli soup, hot pastrami.

Einstein Brothers Bagels
(Multiple locations & hours listed below)
9041 W. Sahara Ave.
Las Vegas, NV 89117
254-0919
Hours: Mon. - Sat. 6 am - 7 pm;
Sun. 7 am - 5 pm
Credit Cards: MC, Visa
Specialties: 17 varieties of bagels, 10 assorted cream cheeses, low-fat menu available.

2560 S. Decatur Blvd.
Las Vegas, NV 89102
227-8776

1405 W. Sunset Rd.
Henderson, NV 89014
547-6300

4624 Maryland Pkwy.
Las Vegas, NV 89119
795-7800

8300 W. Cheyenne Ave.
Las Vegas, NV 89129
645-3771

Fritter's Cafe and Deli
316 Bridger Ave.
Las Vegas, NV 89101
384-3115
Hours: Mon. - Fri. 7:30 am - 4:45 pm
Credit Cards: None
Specialties: 15 assorted sandwiches made to order.

Gina Marie Deli
1725 E. Warm Springs Rd.
Las Vegas, NV 89119
Credit Cards: None
Specialties: Italian deli.

Greenbergs
New York New York
3790 Las Vegas Blvd. S.
Las Vegas, NV 89109
740-6969
Hours: Sun. - Thu. 10 am - 11 pm;
Fri. - Sat. 10 am - midnight
Specialties: Serving up Dr. Brown's soda and egg creams in traditional deli setting.

Harrie's Bagelmania
855 E. Twain Ave.
Las Vegas, NV 89109
369-3322
Hours: Mon. - Sat. 6:30 am - 5 pm;
Sun. 6:30 am - 3 pm
Reservations: None
Dress: Casual
Credit Cards: None
Specialties: Fresh baked New York-style bagels and delicatessen; soups, potato pancakes, meat knishes, egg dishes.

Jen's Deli
Santa Fe Hotel & Casino
4949 N. Rancho Rd.
Las Vegas,NV 89130
658-4900
Hours: 11 am - 10 pm
Specialties: Soups, salads and New York-style sandwiches.

Kathee's Deli
228 Las Vegas Blvd. N.
Las Vegas, NV 89101
386-8002
Hours: Mon. - Fri. 9 am - 4 pm;
Sat. 10:30 am - 1:30 pm
Reservations: None
Dress: Casual
Credit Cards: None
Specialties: Hot and cold sandwiches; delivery available.

Landmark Deli
252 Convention Center Dr.
Las Vegas, NV 89109
731-0041
Hours: Mon. - Sat. 9 am - 4 pm
Credit Cards: None

Luigi's Place
San Remo
115 E. Tropicana Ave.
Las Vegas, NV 89109
739-9000
Hours: 11 am - 10 pm
Specialties: Italian meatball and sausage sandwiches, deli sandwiches, potato salad & hot dogs.

Manhattan Bagel
Palace Station
2411 W. Sahara Ave.
Las Vegas, NV 89102
221-6842
Hours: Sun. - Thu. 7 am - 10 pm;
Fri. - Sat. 7 am - midnight
Specialties: 11 varieties of bagels and a large assortment of cream cheeses.

Manhattan Bagel
Sunset Station Hotel & Casino
1301 W. Sunset Rd.
Henderson, NV 89014
434-8883
Hours: Sun. - Thu. 7 am - 10 pm; Fri. - Sat. 6 pm - midnight
Credit Cards: All major
Specialties: 19 varieties of bagels, danish and muffins.

Max C's Deli
605 Las Vegas Blvd. S.
Las Vegas, NV 89101
382-6292
Hours: Mon. - Fri. 8 am - 4:30 pm;
Sat. 9 am - 2 pm
Reservations: None
Dress: Casual
Credit Cards: None
Specialties: Twenty varieties of overstuffed sandwiches, many named after prominent Las Vegans. Free office delivery to limited area.

Minuto's Italian Deli
6160 W. Tropicana Ave., Ste. 8
Las Vegas, NV 89103
Hours: Tue. - Sun. 9 am - 7 pm
Credit Cards: None
Specialties: Fresh mozzarella and homemade sausage, Italian imported and domestic products.

Montesano's Italian Deli
(Multiple locations listed below)
Hours: Mon. - Sat. 10 am - 10 pm
Credit Cards: MC, Visa, AMX
Specialties: Boar's Head meats, imported cheeses, meats and groceries; catering; old-school NY style Italian deli.

4835 W. Craig Rd.
Las Vegas, NV 89130
656-3708

4105 W. Sahara Ave.
Las Vegas, NV 89102

Mountain Hams and Country Deli, Inc.
4613 Faircenter Pkwy.
Las Vegas, NV 89102
385-4267
Hours: Mon. - Sat. 9 am - 6 pm
Credit Cards: All major
Specialties: Spiral-sliced honey-glazed hams, sandwiches, baked fresh, stoneground wheat and white breads, homemade soups.

Mrs. Bagel Deli Mart
8504 Del Webb Blvd.
Las Vegas, NV 89134
242-5754
Hours: Mon. - Sat. 7 am - 9 pm
Credit Cards: All major

New York Sabrett
3525 S. Valley View Blvd.
Las Vegas, NV 89103
222-0889
Hours: Mon. - Fri. 10 am - 5 pm;
Sat. 10 am - 3 pm
Reservations: None
Dress: Casual
Price of Entrees: Inexpensive
Credit Cards: None
Specialties: Salads, hot dogs, deli sandwiches.

Nile Deli
Luxor
3900 Las Vegas Blvd. S.
Las Vegas, NV 89119
262-4790
Hours: 6 am - 1 am
Specialties: Kosher style delicatessen; hot pastrami sandwiches, reubens, fresh baked breads and pastries.

Park Deli
3900 Paradise Rd.
Las Vegas, NV 89109
369-3354
Hours: Mon. - Fri. 7:30 am - 6 pm;
Sat. 9 am - 3 pm; closed Sun.
Reservations: None
Dress: Casual
Price of Entrees: Inexpensive
Credit Cards: None
Specialties: Sandwiches, soups, salads; patio.

Parthenon Greek Market and Deli Cafe
3655 S. Durango Dr.
Las Vegas, NV 89117
255-1088
Hours: Mon. - Sat. 11 am - 7 pm
Credit Cards: All major
Specialties: Greek deli items.

PosTime Deli
Caesars Palace
3570 Las Vegas Blvd. S.
Las Vegas, NV 89109
Hours: 9:30 am - 6 pm
Specialties: Assortment of salads, onion rings, grilled and cold sandwiches, french fries and fresh fruit.

Plaza Deli
3301 Spring Mountain Rd.
Las Vegas, NV 89102
871-1047
Hours: Mon. - Fri. 8 am - 4 pm
Credit Cards: None
Specialties: Sandwiches, soups and salads.

Prima Deli
3423 S. Rainbow Blvd.
Las Vegas, NV 89102
Hours: Mon. - Sat. 9 am - 6 pm
Credit Cards: MC, Visa, Discover
Specialties: Subs and pizzas.

Rafi's Place
6135 W. Sahara Ave.
Las Vegas, NV 89102
253-0033
Hours: Mon. - Thu. 11 am - 8 pm;
Fri. 10 am - 2 pm; closed Sat.;
Sun. 4 pm - 8 pm
Reservations: None
Dress: Casual
Credit Cards: None
Specialties: Glatt Kosher deli. Sandwiches, salads, roasted chicken, BBQ beef ribs.

Rainbow Deli
2550 S. Rainbow Blvd., Ste. E-16
Las Vegas, NV 89102
227-3663
Hours: Mon. - Fri. 8 am - 4 pm;
Sat. 8 am - 3 pm
Credit Cards: None
Specialties: Sandwiches, bagels and home of Barbara's Cookies.

Ritz Deli
35 E. Basic Rd.
Henderson, NV 89015
558-6486
Hours: Mon. - Fri. 8:30 am - 9 pm;
Sat. 9 am - 8 pm; Sun. 10 am - 8 pm
Credit Cards: None
Specialties: Sandwich shop and convenience store.

Sal's New York Deli
5333 Arville St
Las Vegas, NV 89118
222-0966
Hours: Mon. - Fri. 7:30 am - 4 pm;
Closed Sat. and Sun.
Reservations: None
Dress: Casual
Credit Cards: None
Specialties: Sandwiches, salad and soup.

Samueli's
2744 N. Green Valley Pkwy.
Henderson, NV 89014
454-0565
Hours: Mon. - Thu. 7 am - 9 pm;
Fri. and Sat. 7 pm - 10 pm; Sun. 7 am - 8 pm
Reservations: None
Dress: Casual
Price of Entrees: Dinner entrees $8.95 - $12.95
Credit Cards: MC, Visa, Discover
Specialties: Kosher delicatessen and bakery; grilled calves liver and onions, sauteed chicken livers, corned beef and cabbage, stuffed cabbage, broiled salmon; over 50 different sandwiches; seven pound New York-style cheesecakes, breads, cakes, danish; catering.
Atmosphere: Contemporary style dining room or outdoor patio dining.

Stage Deli
Bally's
3645 Las Vegas Blvd, S.
Las Vegas, NV 89109
739-4111
Hours: Sun. - Thu. 7:30 am - 8 pm;
Fri. - Sat. 7:30 am - 9 pm
Specialties: Pastrami, corned beef, and brisket straight from New York.

Stage Deli
MGM Grand
3799 Las Vegas Blvd. S.
Las Vegas, NV 89109
891-1111
Hours: 8 am - 10 pm

Stage Deli of Las Vegas
Forum Shops
3500 Las Vegas Blvd. S.
Las Vegas, NV 89109
893-4045
Hours: Sun. - Thu. 7:30 am - 11 pm;
Fri. - Sat. 7:30 am - midnight
Reservations: None
Dress: Casual
Price of Entrees: $5.95 - $13.95
Credit Cards: All major
Specialties: Over 300 items on the menu. "Skyscraper" sandwiches named after celebrities. Specialty meats and desserts flown in from NYC. Royal Flush dinners. Hot and cold platters. Oven roast prime brisket of beef, stuffed cabbage, roast half chicken, corned beef and cabbage, large overstuffed sandwiches such as roasted turkey breast or pastrami, potato pancakes, homemade salads and soups, egg creams, desserts; catering; banquet facilities for 200 people.
Atmosphere: Following in the tradition of the famous New York Stage Deli. New York deli atmosphere, New York show posters, art, deli display cases. Located near the "talking fountain" in the Forum Shops at Caesars.

Teresa's Italian Deli
318 W. Sahara Ave.
Las Vegas, NV 89102
385-0006
Hours: Mon. - Fri. 10 am - 4 pm
Credit Cards: None
Specialties: Italian homemade breads, sausage and pasta fagiola.

Toscano's
Rio Suite Hotel
3700 W. Flamingo Rd.
Las Vegas, NV 89103
252-7698
Hours: Sun. - Thu. 7 am - 1 am; Fri. - Sat. 7 am - 2 am
Specialties: Authentic New York deli; fresh baked breads, pastries and danish; fresh cured and smoked meats done on the premises.

Valley View Deli, Inc.
5190 S. Valley View Blvd.
Las Vegas, NV 89118
597-9618
Hours: Mon. - Fri. 6 am - 4 pm
Credit Cards: None
Specialties: Italian deli.

Victoria's Deli
2797 S. Maryland Pkwy.
Las Vegas, NV 89109
792-2227
Hours: Mon. - Sat. 10 am - 5 pm
Credit Cards: All major
Specialties: Build your own sandwiches, specials available for parties and weekly functions.

PIZZA
(Also see Italian Restaurants)
Not all area pizza restaurants are listed.

Americana Pizza
2162 N. Lamb Blvd.
Las Vegas, NV 89115
459-6686
Hours: 11 am - 11 pm
Price of Entrees: $3.99 - $12.99
Credit Cards: None
Specialties: Sicilian, thin crust, thick crust and New York-style pizza, chicken wings.

Ann's Pizza
6119 Clarice Ave.
Las Vegas, NV 89107
877-6444
Hours: 10 am - 10 pm
Price of Entrees: $3.25 - $18.99
Credit Cards: None
Specialties: Pizza, calzone, chicken wings.

Antonio's Pizza
6651 Smoke Ranch Rd.
Las Vegas, NV 89128
647-0227
Hours: 10 am - 11 pm
Price of Entrees: $5.99 - $21.99
Credit Cards: MC, Visa
Specialties: Antonio's supreme pizzas, foot long Philly sandwich, chicken fingers.

Artie's Pizza and Wings of Green Valley
4401 E. Sunset Rd.
Henderson, NV 89014
451-9464
Hours: Sat. - Thu. 11:30 am - 10 pm;
Fri. 11:30 am - 11 pm
Price of Entrees: $3.95 - $12.95
Credit Cards: None

B.J.'s Pizza
6847 W. Flamingo Rd.
Las Vegas, NV 89103
362-1121
Hours: Sun. - Thu. 10 am - 10 pm;
Fri. - Sat. 10 am - midnight
Credit Cards: None
Specialties: Baked ziti, pizza, linguini and clam sauce.

Back East Pizza & Video Delivery
529 E. Twain Ave.
Las Vegas, NV 89109
733-1575
Hours: Sun. - Thu. 10 am - 11 pm;
Fri. - Sat. 10 am - 2 am
Price of Entrees: $3.99 - $20.00
Credit Cards: None
Specialties: Chicken wings, Philly cheese steak, pizza; for $1.00 service charge we will deliver your food and the latest video rentals right to your door.

Beach Pizza
8512 W. Lake Mead Blvd.
Las Vegas, NV 89128
255-8646
Hours: Mon. - Thu. 11 am - 10 pm;
Fri. - Sat. 11 am - 11 pm; Sun. noon - 10 pm
Price of Entrees: $2.25 - $18.95
Credit Cards: None
Specialties: DelRay pizza, eggplant parmigiana, Hang-10 pizza combo.

Bella Roma Pizza
4120 S. Maryland Pkwy.
Las Vegas, NV 89109
451-4644
Hours: 24 hours
Price of Entrees: $1.75 - $22.00
Credit Cards: All major
Specialties: Chicken fingers, half rack of ribs, pizza.

Boston Pizza
1507 Las Vegas Blvd. S.
Las Vegas, NV 89101
385-2595
Hours: 10 am - 4 am
Price of Entrees: $1.95 - $15.95
Credit Cards: None
Specialties: Cheese steaks, chicken wings, heros, medium crust pizza.

Capri Pizza
4080 Paradise Rd.
Las Vegas, NV 89109
796-0019
Hours: 24 hours
Price of Entrees: $2.95 - $21.95
Credit Cards: MC, Visa
Specialties: Chicken wings, chicken parmigiana, pizza.

Chicago Pizza Works
3660 W. Craig Rd.
Las Vegas, NV 89130
647-7722
Hours: 9 am - 10 pm
Price of Entrees: $3 - $15
Specialties: Chicago-style pizza.

Circle K. Piccadilly Pizza
(Additional location listed below)
(2885 S. Decatur Blvd.
Las Vegas, NV 89102
873-3606
Hours: 10 am - 10 pm
Price of Entrees: $2.25 - $22.50
Specialties: Pizza

3200 Fremont St.
Las Vegas, NV 89104
457-7001

Fat Boys Pizza
1401 E. Charleston Rd.
Las Vegas, NV 89104
471-7411
Hours: 11 am - 1 am
Price of Entrees: $4.50 - $13.50
Specialties: Meatball parmigiana, Fat Boy combo pizza, chicken wings.

DINING

DINING - MISCELLANEOUS

Flight Line Pizza
4955 E. Craig Rd.
Las Vegas, NV 89115
644-0557
Hours: 11 am - midnight
Price of Entrees: $4 - $16
Specialties: Chicken wings, pizza.

Giuseppe's Pizza
5645 S. Eastern Ave.
Las Vegas, NV 89119
739-0304
Hours: Mon. - Fri. 11 am - 9 pm;
Sat. 11 am - 7 pm; closed Sun.
Credit Cards: None
Specialties: 6-item pizza and 2 for 1
pizza special daily.

Good Fella's Pizza
6680 W. Flamingo Rd.
Las Vegas, NV 89103
362-1955
Credit Cards: None

The Great Pizza Pie Experience
545 E. Sahara Ave.
Las Vegas, NV 89104
731-0460
Hours: 24 hours
Price of Entrees: $5 - $17
Credit Cards: None
Specialties: Pizza, chicken fingers,
wings, burgers, calzones.

Godfather's Pizza
(Multiple locations listed below)
2269 N. Green Valley Pkwy.
Henderson, NV 89014
456-3900
Hours: Mon. - Thu. 11 am - 11 pm;
Fri. - Sat. 11 am - midnight
Reservations: None
Dress: Casual
Price of Entrees: $7.99 - $18.99
Credit Cards: MC, Visa, Discover
Specialties: Pizza; dine in and take out;
lunch buffet: Mon. - Fri. 11 am - 2 pm
$4.99, $3.50 for seniors, 10 and under
$.25 x age.

3265 E. Tropicana Ave.
Las Vegas, NV 89121
458-8211

2555 S. Rainbow Blvd.
Las Vegas, NV 89102
252-0511

3051 N. Rainbow Blvd.
Las Vegas, NV 89108
645-1150

Hungry Howie's Pizza & Subs
2775 S. Nellis Blvd.
Las Vegas, NV 89121
431-1515
Hours: Sun. - Thu. 10 am - 11 pm;
Fri. - Sat. 10 am - midnight
Price of Entrees: $5.99 - $13.99
Specialties: Delivery available.

Justino's Pizza, Subs & Wings
2208 S. Nellis Blvd.
Las Vegas, NV 89122
431-9464
Hours: Mon. - Thu. 11 am - 9:30 pm;
Fri. - Sat. 10 am - 9:30 pm
Price of Entrees: $3.95 - $14
Credit Cards: MC, Visa

Little Caesars Pizza
There are 21 Little Caesars in Las Vegas,
N. Las Vegas, Boulder City and
Henderson. Call corporate office for
location nearest you 870-5909.
Hours: Open daily 11 am, various clos-
ing times

Mama Illardo's Pizza
26 Fremont St.
Las Vegas, NV 89101
474-6788
Hours: 10:30 am - 1 am
Price of Entrees: $1.99 - $17.99
Specialties: Pizza with the works.

Marco's Pizza
860 E. Twain Ave.
Las Vegas, NV 89109
737-5161
Hours: Tue. - Thu. 11 am - 11 pm; Fri. 11
am - midnight; Sat. noon - midnight;
Sun. noon - 11 pm; Mon. 4 pm - 11 pm
Price of Entrees: $3 - $20
Credit Cards: MC, Visa, Discover
Specialties: Chicken fingers, wings,
submarine sandwiches, pizza and pasta.

Metro Pizza
(Multiple locations listed below)
2250 E. Tropicana Ave.
Las Vegas, NV 89119
736-1955
Hours: Mon. - Thu. 11 am - 10 pm; Fri. -
Sat. 11 am - 11 pm; Sun. noon - 10 pm
Reservations: None
Dress: Casual
Price of Entrees: Pizzas $5.50 - $21.35
Specialties: Appetizers, pastas, subs
and pizzas.

4001 S. Decatur Blvd.
Las Vegas, NV 89103
362-7896

3870 E. Flamingo Rd.
Las Vegas, NV 89119
458-4769

Milano's Pizza
(Multiple locations listed below)
4640 S. Paradise Rd.
Las Vegas, NV 89109
794-0630
Hours: Sun. - Thu. 9 am - 11 pm;
Fri. - Sat. 24 hours
Price of Entrees: $3.50 - $27.50
Credit Cards: None
Specialties: Cheese steak, calzone.

3111 S. Valley View Blvd.
Las Vegas, NV 89102
876-0857
Hours: Mon. - Sat. 9 am - 9 pm

2916 Lake East Dr.
Las Vegas, NV 89117
255-2600
Hours: Mon. - Thu. 10 am - 10 pm;
Fri. - Sat. 10 am - 11 pm

Montesano's
4105 W. Sahara Ave.
Las Vegas, NV 89102
876-0348
Hours:
Dress: Casual
Specialties: Pizzas, calzones, frittatas,
pastas. Delivery available to limited area.

Most Valuable Pizza
3437 N. Rancho Dr.
Las Vegas, NV 89130
645-4087
Hours: Tue. - Sun. 5 pm - 11 pm
Price of Entrees: Inexpensive
Credit Cards: None
Specialties: Pizza, submarine sandwiches,
chicken.

New York City Pizza
1553 N. Eastern Ave.
Las Vegas, NV 89101
399-2288
Hours: Noon - 11 pm
Reservations: None
Dress: Casual
Price of Entrees: $8.51 - $22.96 (King Kong)
Credit Cards: MC, Visa, AMX
Specialties: Limited citywide delivery.

New York Pizza and Pasta
(Additional location listed below)
Hours: Sun. - Thu. 11 am - 10 pm;
Fri. - Sat. 11 am - 11 pm
Price of Entrees: $4.50 - $25.00
Credit Cards: All major
Specialties: Pasta, stuffed pizza, calzone.

3131 N. Rancho Dr.
Las Vegas, NV 89130
645-3337

2400 S. Jones Blvd.
Las Vegas, NV 89102
871-1159

Odyssey Pizza
1930 Fremont St.
Las Vegas, NV 89104
386-9484
Hours: 10 am - midnight
Price of Entrees: $4.00 - $21.00
Credit Cards: None
Specialties: 16" 2 item pizza and a
bucket of wings for $21; delivery.

Payless Pizza and Ribs
469 S. Decatur Blvd.
Las Vegas, NV 89107
877-1900
Hours: Mon. - Sat. 10 am - 10 pm
Price of Entrees: $3.25 - $21.95
Credit Cards: None
Specialties: Ribs, pizza, stromboli, calzone.

Papa John's Pizza
(Multiple locations listed below)
Hours: Sun. - Thu. 11 am - 11 pm;
Fri. - Sat. 11 am - midnight
Price of Entrees: $5 - $15
Credit Cards: All major

3460 E. Sunset Rd.
Henderson, NV 89114
433-6262

4860 Eastern Ave.
Las Vegas, NV 89121
450-7272

4444 W. Craig Rd.
N. Las Vegas, NV 89031
639-6262

242 N. Nellis Blvd.
Las Vegas, NV 89110
434-5252

1411 N. Jones Blvd., Ste. 100
Las Vegas, NV 89108
638-7272

Peter Piper Pizza
(formerly Pistol Petes)
(See also Children)
(Multiple locations listed below)
Price of Entrees: $4.39 - $10.99
Credit Cards: All major
Specialties: Birthday party packages;
rides and arcade.

560 S. Decatur Blvd.
Las Vegas, NV 89107
877-8873
Hours: Mon. - Thu. 11 am - 10 pm;
Fri. 11 am - 11 pm; Sat. 10 am - 11 pm;
Sun. 10 am - 10 pm

3430 E. Tropicana Ave.
Las Vegas, NV 89121
454-6366
Hours: 11 am - 10 pm

350 N. Nellis Blvd.
Las Vegas, NV 89110
459-1200
Hours: 11 am - 10 pm

2401 E. Lake Mead Blvd.
Las Vegas, NV 89101
399-1115
Hours: 11 am - 10 pm

Pizza Hut
There are 58 Pizza Huts in Las Vegas, N.
Las Vegas, Henderson and Boulder City.
Call corporate office for location near-
est you 1-800-948-8488.

Pizzeria Uno Restaurant & Bar
2540 S. Decatur Blvd.
Las Vegas, NV 89102
876-8667
Hours: Sun. - Thu. 11 am - midnight;
Fri. - Sat. 11 am - 1 am
Reservations: None
Dress: Casual
Price of Entrees: $5.99 - $9.99
Credit Cards: All major
Specialties: 200-seat contemporary
restaurant features original Chicago-
style deep dish pizza, pizza available by
the slice, appetizers, salads, pastas,
sandwiches, chicken entrees, steak fajitas and desserts. Weekday lunch special
served 11 am - 3 pm for $4.99 includes
an individual-sized pizza and soup or
salad. Delivery available.
Atmosphere: Outdoor patio.

Scaturro's Pizza
900 E. Karen Ave.
Las Vegas, NV 89109
734-2929
Hours: Mon. - Sun. 11 am - 11 pm; Fri.
and Sat. 11 am - 1 am; Sat. noon - 11 pm
Reservations: None
Dress: Casual
Price of Entrees: Pasta entrees from $5.25
Credit Cards: None
Specialties: Lasagna, eggplant - full menu.

Sunset Pizza
6400 S. Eastern Ave.
Las Vegas, NV 89119
798-8272
Hours: 11 am - 11 pm
Reservations: None
Dress: Casual
Price of Entrees: $5.95 - $9.95
Credit Cards: None
Specialties: Pasta, strombolis, pastries.

Tropicana Pizza
Delivery citywide
1105 E. Tropicana Ave.
Las Vegas, NV 89119
798-6707

4310 E. Tropicana Ave.
Las Vegas, NV 89121
434-2212

4825 W. Flamingo Rd.
Las Vegas, NV 89103
251-4770

765 N. Nellis Blvd.
Las Vegas, NV 89110
452-6363

Villa Pizza
(Multiple locations listed below)
2211 S. Maryland Pkwy.
Las Vegas, NV 89104
734-2188
Hours: Mon. - Thu. 11 am - 1 am;
Fri. - Sat. 11 am - 2 am
Reservations: None
Dress: Casual
Price of Entrees: $4.00 - $10.00
Credit Cards: MC, Visa, Discover, Diners
Specialties: Wings, pizza, stuffed pizza, calzones, pasta.
Atmosphere: Upbeat.

7777 W. Sahara Ave.
Las Vegas, NV 89117
255-4488

639 Stephanie St.
Henderson, NV 89014
458-7344

869 S. Boulder Hwy.
Henderson, NV 89015
565-8844

3620 W. Sahara Ave.
Las Vegas, NV 89102
368-0368

HOTEL PIZZA RESTAURANTS
The following hotels have pizza restaurants. Information on some can be found under *Italian Restaurants*: Caesars Palace, Circus Circus, Golden Nugget, Imperial Palace, MGM, Mirage, New York New York, Sam's Town, Stardust, Stratosphere, Tropicana.

FAST FOOD RESTAURANTS
Bono's
4902 S. Eastern Ave.
Las Vegas, NV 89119
456-6248
Hours: Mon. - Fri. 10:30 am - 10:30 pm;
Sat. - Sun. 10:30 am - 7:30 pm
Vienna hot dogs, polish sausage and Italian beef and sausage sandwiches.

Bono's II
310 E. Warmsprings Rd.
Las Vegas, NV 89119
438-3939

Bono's III
737 S. Rainbow Blvd.
Las Vegas, NV 89128
258-6339

Burger Express
3200 S. Las Vegas Blvd.
Las Vegas, NV 89109
733-9963
Hours: 9 am - 9 pm
Credit Cards: None
Specialties: Vegetarian hamburgers.

Capriotti's Delaware Subs
(Multiple locations listed below)
Hours: Mon. - Sat. 10 am - 7 pm
Eastern-style cheese steak sandwiches. Fresh roasted roast beef and turkey.

322 W. Sahara Ave.
Las Vegas, NV 89102
474-0229

3981 E. Sunset Rd.
Las Vegas, NV 89120
898-4906

Chicago Hot Dogs
1078 N. Rancho Dr.
Las Vegas, NV 89106
647-DOGS (3647)
Hours: 11 am - 8 pm; Drive thru 11 am - 9 pm
Direct from Chicago, all Vienna brand hot dogs; hamburgers and Italian beef sandwiches.
Atmosphere: Kick back and relax, Chicago memorabilia.

In-N-Out Burger
(Multiple locations listed below)
Hours: Sun. - Thu. 10:30 am - 1 am;
Fri. and Sat. 10:30 am - 1:30 am
First locations outside of California for this popular burger place founded in 1948.

2900 W. Sahara Ave.
Las Vegas, NV 89102
1-800-786-1000

4888 S. Industrial Rd.
Las Vegas, NV 89103
1-800-786-1000

51 N. Nellis Blvd.
Las Vegas, NV 89110
1-800-786-1000

4705 S. Maryland Pkwy.
Las Vegas, NV 89109
1-800-786-1000

1960 Rock Springs Dr.
Las Vegas, NV 89106
1-800-786-1000

Tommy's Burgers
2635 E. Tropicana Ave.
Las Vegas, NV 89121
458-2533
Hours: Mon. - Sat. 10 am - 9 pm

FRANCHISES
CHICKEN
Church's
4480 Spring Mountain Rd.
Las Vegas, NV 89102
362-8999

El Pollo Loco
4011 E. Charleston Blvd.
Las Vegas, NV 89104
459-0987

Farm Basket
2554 E. Tropicana Ave.
Las Vegas, NV 89121
451-6922

Kentucky Fried Chicken
District Office
4122 N. Eastern Ave.
Las Vegas, NV 89101
435-7551

Kenny Rogers Roasters
Corporate Office
4340 S. Valley View Blvd.
Las Vegas, NV 89103
248-1559

Popeye's
2421 W. Bonanza Rd.
Las Vegas, NV 89106
646-2883

HAMBURGERS
A & W Root Beer
1410 Nevada Hwy.
Boulder City, NV 89105
293-2340

Burger King
Executive Office
3421 E. Tropicana Ave., Ste. J
Las Vegas, NV 89121
454-6900

Carl's Jr.
Headquarters
2950 E. Flamingo Rd.
Las Vegas, NV 89121
734-2276

Dairy Queen
3880 W. Sahara Ave.
Las Vegas, NV 89102
876-9255

Fatburger
2700 E. Sunset Rd.
Suite C29
Las Vegas, NV 89120

Great American Burgers
6775 W. Flamingo Rd.
Las Vegas, NV 89103
365-1250

Jack-In-The-Box
Business Office
10650 Treena St., Ste. 301
San Diego, CA 92131
619-693-5225

McDonald's
Regional Office
2030 E. Flamingo Rd.
Las Vegas, NV 89119
796-3200

Skooters
6150 W. Charleston Blvd.
Las Vegas, NV 89102
258-6179

Sonic Drive-In
4825 Las Vegas Blvd. N.
Las Vegas, NV 89115
643-1470

Wendy's
General Offices
1614 E. Lake Mead Blvd.
N. Las Vegas, NV 89030
642-9011

FISH
Long John Silver's
4466 E. Charleston Blvd.
Las Vegas, NV 89104
459-1963

HOT DOGS
Nathan's
3799 Las Vegas Blvd. S.
Las Vegas, NV 89109
597-0131
MGM Grand - food court and theme park.

Wienerschnitzel
4001 W. Sahara Ave.
Las Vegas, NV 89102
362-0418

MEXICAN
Del Taco
3715 W. Flamingo Rd.
Las Vegas, NV 89103
364-9520

Roberto's Taco Shops
Business Office
4660 S. Eastern Ave., Ste. 102
Las Vegas, NV 89119
434-1216

Taco Bell
1210 S. Valley View Blvd.
Las Vegas, NV 89102
880-5818

SANDWICH
Arby's Roast Beef
Main Office
3901 S. Maryland Pkwy., Ste. A
Las Vegas, NV 89119
734-7091

Blimpie Subs & Salads
1146 W. Sunset Rd.
Las Vegas, NV 89119
898-7850

Port of Subs
3961 Maryland Pkwy.
Las Vegas, NV 89119
737-9211

Schlotzsky's Deli
3200 Las Vegas Blvd. S.
Las Vegas, NV 89109
735-1906

Subway
3991 Industrial Rd.
Las Vegas, NV 89103
734-6222

MISCELLANEOUS
Baskin Robbins 31 Flavors
3620 W. Sahara Ave.
Las Vegas, NV 89102
873-5383

Haagen Dazs Ice Cream Shoppe
4300 Meadows Ln.
Las Vegas, NV 89107
878-7551

Mrs. Fields Cookies
3200 Las Vegas Blvd. S.
Las Vegas, NV 89109
369-2778

TCBY Yogurt
2191 E. Tropicana Ave.
Las Vegas, NV 89119
739-0025

Winchell's Donut House
4469 W. Flamingo Rd.
Las Vegas, NV 89103
873-0000

GOURMET & SPECIALTY FOODS - RETAIL

GOURMET FOODS

Gilcrease Orchard
7800 N. Tenaya Way
Las Vegas, NV 89131
645-1126
Hours: 7 am - noon, June - Oct.
65-acre orchard where you can pick your own apples, pears, apricots, peaches, plums and figs right from the tree. Bring your own containers; fruit is priced at 15¢ - 50¢ per pound.
Directions: Northwest on US 95, turn right on Ann Rd., left on the first street, right on the next street, to 7800 N. Tenaya Way.

Honeybaked Hams
(Multiple locations listed below)
Hours: Mon. - Fri. 10 am - 7 pm;
Sat. 10 am - 5 pm
Credit Cards: MC, Visa, AMX, Discover
Original spiral-sliced ham; hams, sandwiches and party platters.
To ship anywhere in the U.S. - 1-800-367-2426.

3585 S. Maryland Pkwy.
Las Vegas, NV 89109
369-8100

1110 S. Rainbow Blvd.
Las Vegas, NV 89129
258-9200

Mountain Hams & Country Deli
4613 W. Charleston Blvd.
Las Vegas, NV 89102
385-4267
Hours: Mon. - Sat. 9 am - 6 pm
Credit Cards: Visa, MC, AMX, Discover
Spiral-sliced hams, party platters, sandwiches.

Trader Joe's
(Multiple locations listed below)
Hours: 9 am - 9 pm
Gourmet foods at low value prices, wines, beer and liquor.

2716 Green Valley Pkwy.
Henderson, NV 89014
433-6773

2101 S. Decatur Blvd.
Las Vegas, NV 89102
367-0227

Village Meats and Wines
5025 S. Eastern Ave.
Las Vegas, NV 89119
Hours: Tue. - Fri. 10 am - 6 pm;
Sat. 10 am - 5 pm
Credit Cards: MC, Visa
Fresh meats caviar, imported wines and cheeses.

SPECIALTY FOODS

BAKERIES

Albina's Italiano American Bakery
3035 E. Tropicana Ave.
Las Vegas, NV 89121
433-5400
Hours: Mon. - Sat. 8 am - 6 pm;
Sun. 8 am - 5 pm
Credit Cards: None
Specialties: Italian pastries, pies, all occasion cakes, cannolis.

Bay Area Biscotti Co.
3125 Ali Baba Ln.
Las Vegas, NV 89118
795-8700 1-800-497-9556
Italian cookies, 6 flavors; wholesale, retail.

Bonjour French & European Bakery
4012 S. Rainbow Blvd.
Las Vegas, NV 89103
221-4320
Hours: Mon. - Sat. 8 am - 6 pm
Credit Cards: None
Specialties: Cakes, pastries, strudel, danish and coffee cakes.

CHESAPEAKE BAGEL BAKERY®

Chesapeake Bagel Bakery
850 S. Rancho Dr.
Las Vegas, NV 89106
258-9595
Hours: 6:30 am - 6 pm
Reservations: None
Dress: Casual
Specialties: Sandwiches, salads and pastries.

Cinnabon
(Multiple locations listed below)
Hours: Mon. - Fri. 9 am - 9 pm;
Sat. 9 am - 8 pm; Sun. 10 am - 6 pm
Credit Cards: None
Specialties: Cinnamon buns, jarred cinnamon, recipe book and specialty coffees.

Boulevard Mall
3480 S. Maryland Pkwy.
Las Vegas, NV 89109
731-0522

Meadows Mall
4300 Meadows Ln.
Las Vegas, NV 89107
870-8160

Galleria Mall
1300 W. Sunset Rd.
Henderson, NV 89014
436-4005

Cookies By Design
4760 W. Sahara Ave.
Las Vegas, NV 89102
259-0020
Hours: Mon. - Thu. 8 am - 6 pm;
Fri. 8 am - 5 pm; Sat. 11 am - 3 pm
Credit Cards: MC, Visa, AMX, Discover
Personal message delivered with a cookie bouquet. Cookie arrangements with a holiday theme, company logo or club insignia. Local delivery or shipped anywhere.

Diamond Bakery Inc.
4255 Spring Mountain Rd.
Las Vegas , NV 89102
368-1886
Hours: 9 am - 9 pm
Credit Cards: MC, Visa, AMX
Specialties: Cakes, pies and pastries.

DiGruccio's
1725 E. Warm Springs Rd.
Las Vegas, NV 89119
897-1015
Hours: 3 am - 6 pm
Credit Cards: None
Specialties: Breads, challah bread, cakes, pastries.

Eclair
Fashion Show Mall
3200 S. Las Vegas Blvd.
Las Vegas, NV 89109
369-6117
Hours: 8 am - 9 pm
Credit Cards: None
Specialties: Eclairs and fruit tarts.

Freed's Bakery
4780 S. Eastern Ave.
Las Vegas, NV 89119
456-7762
Hours: Tue. - Sat. 7 am - 8 pm;
Sun. and Mon. 7 am - 6 pm
Credit Cards: None
Same day wedding and birthday cakes.

Frogees on 4th
300 N. 4th. St.
Las Vegas, NV 89015
Hours: 24
Credit Cards: All major
Specialties: Breads, pastries, danish, pies and tarts.

Great Buns Bakery
3270 E. Tropicana Ave.
Las Vegas, NV 89121
898-0311
Hours: Mon. - Sat. 7 am - 5 pm
Credit Cards: None
Full line of bread, coffee cake and 30 different types of pastries; also a full line of fat-free and sugar-free breads.

Jelly Belly Bakery
1951 N. Decatur Blvd.
Las Vegas, NV 89107
646-0068
Hours: Mon. - Sat. 7 am - 3 pm
Credit Cards: None
Specialties: Cakes, cookies and pastries.

Jerry's Nugget Bakery
1821 Las Vegas Blvd. N.
N. Las Vegas, NV 89030
399-3000
Hours: Mon. - Tue. noon - 8 pm;
Wed., Thu. & Sun. 10 am - 10 pm;
Fri. - Sat. 10 am - midnight
Credit Cards: All major
Specialties: Largest selection of the freshest and finest baked goods in Las Vegas, including wedding cakes.

John's Bakery
5006 S. Maryland Pkwy.
Las Vegas, NV 89107
Hours: 8 am - 1 pm
Credit Cards: None
Specialties: Wedding cakes, all occasion cakes, pastries and pies.

Kenya's Cakes of The Stars
Sunset Station
1301 W. Sunset Rd.
Henderson, NV 89014
450-7661
Hours: 8 am - 11 pm
Credit Cards: All major
Specialties: Star, wedding and all occasion cakes, cookies pastries and pies.

Kenya's Gourmet Bakery
3945 E. Patrick Ln., Ste. F
Las Vegas, NV 89120
261-0900
Hours: Mon. - Fri. 8:30 am - 5 pm;
Sat. 8:30 am - 4:30 pm
Credit Cards: MC, Visa, AMX, Discover

Krispy Kreme
7015 W. Spring Mountain Rd.
Las Vegas, NV 89103
222-2320
Hours: Mon. - Thu. 5:30 - midnight; Fri. - Sat. 5:30 am - 1 am; Sun. 5:30 am - 11 pm 24 hour drive thru
Credit Cards: None
Price: $4.25 per dozen for glazed, $4.89 per dozen assorted, $.55 per donut glazed, $.60 assorted
Atmosphere: See 270 dozen donuts an hour float down the conveyor belt before your eyes.

Las Vegas Cheese Cakes
4343 N. Ranch Dr.
Las Vegas, NV 89130
655-0101
Hours: Mon. - Sat. 11 am - 6 pm
Credit Cards: None
Specialties: Assorted New York - style cheese cakes.

Mrs. Fields Cookies
(Multiple locations & hours listed below)
Fashion Show Mall
3200 Las Vegas Blvd. S.
Las Vegas, NV 89109
369-2778
Hours: 8:30 am - 9 pm
Credit Cards: MC, Visa, AMX, Disc.

Boulevard Mall
3680 S. Maryland Pkwy.
Las Vegas, NV 89109
369-8030
Hours: 9 am - 9 pm
Credit Cards: MC, Visa, AMX

Mrs. Williams Diabetic Delights
3466 S. Decatur Blvd.
Las Vegas, NV 89102
362-1243
Hours: Mon. - Sat. 10 am - 5:30 pm
Credit Cards: MC, Visa, Discover
Sugar free pies, muffins, cheesecake, candy.

Nana's Cookies and Gifts
4343 N. Rancho Dr., Ste. 136
Las Vegas, NV 89130
656-3710 1-800-656-2627
Credit Cards: All major
Cookie bouquet baskets, cookie tins, gift baskets. Local and nationwide delivery.

Pastry Chef Bakery
608 S. Decatur Blvd.
Las Vegas, NV 89107
870-1418
Hours: 7 am - 3 pm
Credit Cards: None
Specialties: Wedding and all occasion cakes, pastries, cookies, pies and doughnuts.

Rancho Bakery
850 S. Rancho Dr.
Las Vegas, NV 89106
870-6449
Hours: Mon. - Fri. 6 am - 6 pm;
Sat. 6 am - 4 pm
Credit Cards: None
Handcrafted, quality baked pastries and breads.

Toscano's Baking Co.
Rio
3700 W. Flamingo Rd.
Las Vegas, NV 89103
252-7777
Hours: 24 hours
Credit Cards: All major
Located in the Beach Cafe.
Fresh baked breads, cakes and pies.

Sam's Cheesecake Factory
1350 E. Flamingo Rd.
Las Vegas, NV 89119
791-0988
Hours: Mon. - Fri. 8 am - 6 pm;
Sat. 9 am - 5 pm
Credit Cards: None
Sandwiches, quiche, soups and salads;
over 24 flavors of cheesecakes, mousse,
layer cakes pies, baklava. Delivery.

Selma's Cookies
3315 E. Russell Rd., Ste. 4-G
Las Vegas, NV 89120
434-9660
Hours: Mon. - Fri. 8:30 am - 5:30 pm;
Sat. 11 am - 5 pm
Credit Cards: MC, Visa, AMX

Slice of Heaven Cheese Cake
3330 E. Tropicana Ave.
Las Vegas, NV 89121
450-6254
Hours: Please call ahead
Credit Cards: MC, Visa
Specialties: Over 50 varieties of cheese
cakes, including fat free; also a large
assortment of sweet specialty desserts,
pastries and cookies. Let us design a
special custom creation for you.

Universal Bakery
2340 Bonanza Rd.
Las Vegas, NV 89109
385-7721
Hours: Mon. - Sat. 9 am - 8 pm;
Sun. 10 am - 6 pm
Credit Cards: None
Specialties: Mexican, French and Italian
pastries by special order, breads, all
occasion cakes and cookies.

ICE CREAM

Ben & Jerrys
Santa Fe
4949 N. Rancho Dr.
Las Vegas, NV 89130
655-3450
Hours: 11 am - 11 pm; Fri. - Sat. 11 am -
1 am

**Danielle's Chocolates
and Ice Cream**
4760 W. Sahara Ave.
Las Vegas, NV 89102
259-7616
Hours: Mon. - Thu. 10 am - 9 pm;
Fri. - Sat. 10 am - 11 pm
Credit Cards: MC, Visa, AMX

Haagen Dazs Ice Cream Shoppe
Meadows Mall
4300 Meadows Ln.
Las Vegas, NV 89107
878-7551
Hours: Mon. - Fri. 9 am - 9 pm;
Sat. - Sun. 9 am - 6 pm
Credit Cards: None

Italcream
3871 S. Valley View Blvd.
Las Vegas, NV 89103
873-2214
Hours: Mon. - Fri. 8 am - 4 pm
Credit Cards: None
Italian sorbetto, gelato, ices and other
desserts.

Jerome's Frozen Custard
9402 Del Webb Blvd.
Las Vegas, NV 89134
243-9226
Hours: 11 am - 9 pm
Specialties: Custard made fresh daily.

Leatherby's Family Creamery
577 E. Sahara Ave.
Las Vegas, NV 89104
641-6088
Hours: Sun. - Thu. 11 am - 11 pm;
Fri. and Sat. 11 am - midnight
Credit Cards: None
Specialties: Sandwiches and old-fash-
ioned ice cream; table service.

Luv It Frozen Custard
505 E. Oakey Blvd.
Las Vegas, NV 89104
384-6452
Hours: Mon. - Thu. 11 am - 10 pm;
Fri. 11 am - 11 pm; Sat. noon - 11 pm;
Sun. 1 pm - 10 pm
Credit Cards: None

Swenson's
(Multiple locations & hours listed below)
Credit Cards: None
Specialties: Ice cream specialties,
sandwiches, salads, soup.

4500 E. Sunset Rd.
Henderson, NV 89014
454-1900
Hours: Sun. - Thu. 11 am - 10 pm;
Fri. - Sat. 11 am - midnight

Forum Shops
3500 Las Vegas Blvd. S.
Las Vegas, NV 89109
737-3113
Hours: Mon. - Thu. 10 am - 11 pm;
Fri. - Sun. 10 am - midnight

Luxor
3900 Las Vegas Blvd. S.
Las Vegas, NV 89119
597-5330
Hours: Sun. - Thu. 10 am - midnight;
Fri. - Sat. 10 am - 1 am

CANDY

American Candy Gram
1-800-824-7363
24 hour candy delivery service to anywhere in the country.

Ayala's Inc.
(Multiple locations & hours listed below)
Credit Cards: None
Specialties: Homemade assorted fudge
as well as a large assortment of other
candies.

228 Las Vegas Blvd. N.
Las Vegas, NV 89101
383-3180

5757 Wayne Newton Blvd.
Las Vegas, NV 89119
739-8838
Hours: 7 am - 11 am

Chocolate Chariot
Forum Shops
3500 Las Vegas Blvd. S.
Las Vegas, NV 89109
735-2639
Hours: Sun. - Thu. 10 am - 11 pm;
Fri. - Sat. 10 am - midnight
Credit Cards: All major
Fancy candies.

Chocolate Heaven
(Multiple locations listed below)
Hours: 9 am - midnight
Credit Cards: All major
Specialties: Brittle, fudge, choco-
lates, assorted candies; complete line
of sugarfree varieties.

Riviera
2901 Las Vegas Blvd. S.
Las Vegas, NV 89109
792-2639

Bally's
3645 Las Vegas Blvd. S.
Las Vegas, NV 89109

Chocolate Puppy
2099 N. Jones Blvd.
Las Vegas, NV 89108
648-0399
Hours: Mon. - Thu. 10 am - 9 pm;
Fri. and Sat. 10 am - 10 pm
Credit Cards: MC, Visa, Discover
Fudge, chocolate dipped items, diabetic
candies, flavored popcorn; canisters, bas-
kets, gifts shipped and homemade crafts.

**Danielle's Chocolates
& Ice Cream**
4760 W. Sahara Ave., Ste. 11
Las Vegas, NV 89102
259-7616
Hours: Mon. - Thu. 10 am - 9 pm;
Fri. - Sat. 10 am - 11 pm
Credit Cards: MC, Visa, AMX
Gourmet candy and ice cream; pocket
sandwiches; watch candy being made.

Erotic Edibles
2375 E. Tropicana Ave.
Las Vegas, NV 89119
739-9688
Hours: 9 am - 5 pm
Credit Cards: All major
Specialties: Adult milk chocolate creations.

Ethel M Chocolates
1-800-438-4356
Hours: Vary by location
Credit Cards: MC, Visa, AMX
15 locations throughout Las Vegas including
all shopping malls, the airport, the factory
store in Green Valley, and the California,
Circus Circus, Flamingo, Frontier, Harrah's,
Plaza, Stardust, Tropicana Hotels and
O'Shea's Casino. For a shop near you or for
mail orders, call 1-800-4-ETHEL-M.

Executive Sweets
3147 Industrial Rd.
Las Vegas, NV 89109

Hours: Mon. - Fri. 10 am - 4 pm
Credit Cards: MC, Visa
Specialties: Hand dipped assorted choco-
late creations.

**Rocky Mountain
Chocolate Factory**
(Multiple locations & hours listed below)
Credit Cards: All major
Retail chocolatier, manufactures own
candy and caramel and candy apples,
fudge and miscellaneous confections.

9155 Las Vegas Blvd. S.
Las Vegas NV 89123
361-7740
Hours: Mon. - Sat. 10 am - 8 pm;
Sun. 10 am - 6 pm

Beltz Factory Mall
7400 Las Vegas Blvd. S., Unit 24-25
Las Vegas, NV 89123
361-7553
Hours: Mon. - Sat. 10 am - 9 pm;
Sun. 10 am - 6 pm

See's Candy
(Multiple locations & hours listed below)
Credit Cards: None
For shop locations and mail order,
1-800-347-7337.

Fashion Show Mall
3200 Las Vegas Blvd. S.
Las Vegas, NV 89109
737-8880
Hours: Mon. - Fri. 10 am - 9 pm;
Sat. 10 am - 7 pm; Sun. noon - 6 pm

Meadows Mall
4300 Meadows Ln.
Las Vegas, NV 89107
878-5267
Hours: Mon. - Fri. 10 am - 9 pm;
Sat. - Sun. 10 am - 6 pm

Boulevard Mall
3534 S. Maryland Pkwy.
Las Vegas, NV 89109
732-1826
Hours: Mon. - Fri. 10 am - 9 pm;
Sat. 10 am - 7 pm; Sun. 11 pm - 6 pm

Sweet Factory
(Multiple locations & hours listed below)
Credit Cards: MC, Visa,
Fill a bag yourself with a variety of old-
fashioned candies from barrels.

3680 S. Maryland Pkwy.
Las Vegas, NV 89109
731-4619
Hours: Mon. - Fri. 10 am - 9 pm;
Sat. 10 am - 7 pm; Sun. 11 am - 6 pm

Forum Shops
3500 Las Vegas Blvd. S.
Las Vegas, NV 89109
732-3877
Hours: Sun. - Wed. 10 am - 11 pm;
Thu. - Sat. 10 am - midnight

Meadows Mall
4300 Meadows Ln.
Las Vegas, NV 89107
258-7995
Hours: Mon. - Fri. 10 am - 9 pm;
Sat. - Sun. 10 am - 6 pm

Sweet Zone
(Beltz Factory Mall)
7400 Las Vegas Blvd. S.
Las Vegas, NV 89123
260-4561
Hours: Mon. - Sat. 10 am - 9 pm;
Sun. 10 am - 6 pm
Credit Cards: None
Specialties: Assorted dipped choco-
lates, candies and nuts.

DINING

GOURMET & SPECIALTY FOODS - RETAIL

COFFEE

Gloria Jeans Coffee Beans
Boulevard Mall
3680 S. Maryland Pkwy.
Las Vegas, NV 89109
791-0144
Hours: Mon. - Fri. 9:30 am - 9 pm;
Sat. 9:30 am - 7 pm; Sun. 10:30 am - 6 pm
Credit Cards: MC, Visa, AMX
Over 65 varieties of whole bean coffee, bulk teas, coffee and espresso makers, grinders, mugs and unique gift items for the coffee lover. Serving espresso, cappuccino, coffee, tea and cold coffee drinks.

Jitter's Gourmet Coffee
(Multiple locations & hours listed below)
Credit Cards: MC, Visa, AMX, Discover
Coffee bar and gourmet coffee and gift items; cappuccino, espresso, pastries, sandwiches, salads; coffee beans roasted on premises; indoor and patio seating; trendy little cafe catering to the yuppie crowd.

2457 E. Tropicana Ave.
Las Vegas, NV 89121
898-0056
Hours: Mon. - Sat. 6 am - 11 pm;
Sun. 7 am - 9 pm

8441 W. Lake Mead Blvd.
Las Vegas, NV 89128
256-1902
Hours: Mon. - Sat. 6 am - 11 pm;
Sun. 7 am - 9 pm

Galleria Mall
671 Mall Ring Circle
Henderson, NV 89130
898-6626
Hours: Mon. - Fri. 6 am - 5:30 pm;
Sat. and Sun. 7 am - 5:30 pm

Sip of Seattle
136 S. Rainbow Blvd.
Las Vegas, NV 89123-5330
363-8144
Hours: Mon. - Fri. 6:30 am - 5 pm; Sat.
7:30 am - 4 pm; Sun. 8:30 am - noon
Credit Cards: None
Bulk coffee beans, Seattle's best coffee, sandwiches, quiche and muffins.

Spill the Beans Coffee House
4825 W. Flamingo Rd.
Las Vegas, NV 89103
876-8797
Hours: Mon. - Thu. 7 am - 7 pm;
Fri. - Sat. 7 am - 10 pm; Sun. 9 am - 2 pm
Credit Cards: MC, Visa, Discover
Coffee bar, gourmet coffee, whole coffee beans and related items; live music Fri. and Sat.

Starbucks Coffee
(Multiple locations & hours listed below)
Fashion Show Mall
3200 Las Vegas Blvd. S.
Las Vegas, NV 89109
794-4010
Hours: Mon. - Fri. 8 am - 9 pm; Sat. 9 am
- 7 pm; Sun. 9 am - 6 pm

Mission Center
1340 E. Flamingo Rd.
Las Vegas, NV 89119
737-9099
Hours: Sun. - Thu. 5:30 am - 10 pm; Fri.
5:30 am - 11 pm; Sat. 5:30 am - 11 pm

Polo Towers
3743 Las Vegas Blvd. S.
Las Vegas, NV 89109
739-9780
Hours: Sun. - Thu. 5:30 am - 10:30 pm;
Fri. - Sat. 5:30 am - midnight
Credit Cards: All major
Specialties: Espresso, cappuccino, coffee beans and related products, pastries.

Boulder Station
4111 Boulder Hwy.
Las Vegas, NV 89121
457-3313
Hours: Mon. - Thu. 6 am - 11 pm; Fri. -
Sat. 6 am - midnight; Sun. 7 am - 11 pm

Barnes & Noble Bookstore
567 Stephanie St.
Henderson, NV 89014
436-5104
Hours: Mon. - Thu. 6 am - 10 pm; Fri.
6 am - midnight; Sat. 7 am - midnight;
Sun. 7 am - 10:30 pm

4732 Fair Center Pkwy.
Las Vegas, NV 89102
258-1223
Hours: Sun. - Thu. 6 am - 10 pm; Fri. -
Sat. 6 am - 11 pm; Sun. 7 am - 10 pm

850 S. Rancho Dr.
Las Vegas, NV 89106
870-6993
Hours: Sun. - Thu. 6 am - 11 pm;
Fri. - Sat. 6 am - midnight

4500 E. Sunset Rd.
Henderson, NV 89014
433-6015
Hours: Mon. - Thu. 5:30 am - 11 pm; Fri.
5:30 am - midnight; Sat. 6:30 am - midnight; Sun. 6:30 am - 11 pm

2530 S. Decatur Blvd.
Las Vegas, NV 89103
248-9166
Hours: Mon. - Thu. 5:30 am - 10 pm; Fri.
5:30 am - 11 pm; Sat. 6 am - 11 pm; Sun.
6 am - 10 pm

9151 W. Sahara Ave.
Las Vegas, NV 89117
233-5797
Hours: Mon. - Thu. 5:30 am - 10 pm; Fri. -
Sat. 5:30 am - 11 pm; Sun. 6 am - 10 pm

**Sweeney's Gourmet
Coffee Roasters**
671 Middlegate Rd.
Henderson, NV 89015
558-3779
Hours: Mon. - Fri. 9 am - 4 pm
Credit Cards: MC, Visa,
Coffee bar, gourmet coffee and teas, spices and sweets.

Whole Bean
3441 W. Sahara Ave.
Las Vegas, NV 89102
368-2633
Hours: Mon. - Fri. 7 am - 6 pm;
Sat. 9 am - 1 pm; Sun. 10 am - 2 pm
Credit Cards: MC, Visa, Discover
Gourmet coffee beans freshly roasted on premises and related gift items.

The Treasure Island Buffet

Experience Las Vegas
Visit our website at www.experiencelasvegas.com

Entertainment

Where else but in Las Vegas can you visit a Castle, a Pyramid, a Desert Oasis, New York, New Orleans, the Roman Empire, dragons, pirates and a 35-foot leprechaun, all within a 15-minute drive of each other? From the bright lights and neon signs to beautiful showgirls and spectacular displays of magic and music, the "Entertainment Capital of the World" has something for everyone!

The young and the youthful at heart can enjoy theme parks like MGM Grand Adventures at the MGM Grand "City of Entertainment," ice skating at the Santa Fe, virtual reality and arcades in just about all of the major hotels, as well as quality afternoon showroom extravaganzas ranging from "Viva Las Vegas" at the Stratosphere to the hilarious humor of "Comedy Magic" at the Maxim. The 21 and older crowd can engage in nonstop nightclubs such as Club Rio, Drink!, Studio 54, Ra and Club Utopia. Spectacular shows including "EFX" at MGM, "Splash" at the Riviera, "Legends in Concert" at the Imperial Palace, "Imagine" at Luxor and "Enter the Night" at the Stardust are among many available 7 days a week, and on nights when shows are dark, many of the hotels offer headliner performances from some of today's hottest stars.

From the amazing magic of master magicians such as Lance Burton or Siegfried and Roy to the hypnotic performances of Marshall Sylver and the colorful acrobatic and aerial feats of Cirque du Soleil's "Mystere," to the high energy and wonderful choreography of Las Vegas showgirls, including the fabulous Radio City Music Hall's Rockettes at the Flamingo Hilton, Las Vegas offers quality performances by top notch entertainers 365 days a year!

Many of the hotels and casinos offer free entertainment, such as Merlin fighting off a fierce dragon at Excalibur, the circus acts at Circus Circus, an erupting volcano at the Mirage and a full-fledged battle between the British and pirates at Treasure Island. Motion simulator rides are available at several of the hotels, including "In Search of the Obelisk" at the Luxor, "Race for Atlantis" at Caesars Forum Mall and the new "Star Trek Experience" at the Las Vegas Hilton.

Many lounges offer top entertainers, like "Kristine W" at the Las Vegas Hilton, for a small minimum or cover charge. Still other hotels offer "Fun Books" which provide discounts to many of their attractions. Modern multiplex theaters can be found at several hotels featuring the latest in theater technology as well as fully serviced concession areas.

The downtown Fremont section also offers entertainment, including the magnificent 2-million-light, 65,536-color-combination "Fremont Street Experience" which, with a variety of shows displayed nightly, provide an unmatched entertainment experience! Along with the sights of this illuminating display, 208 speakers produce 540,000 watts of concert-quality sound and music. Not to be missed!

TICKETS

TicketMaster
Administration Office (*no sales*)
2030 E. Flamingo Rd.
Las Vegas, NV 89119
893-3000
Ticket & Show Information
893-3033 - 24 hours
Charge by phone - 474-4000
Credit Cards: MC, Visa
Ticketmaster charges you a handling
charge of approx. $3.00 per ticket.
Tickets can also be purchased (walk-
ins only, no phone orders) at
Ticketmaster outlets at:
Blockbuster Music
4555 W. Charleston Blvd.
Las Vegas, NV 89102

Robinson May
Fashion Show Mall
3200 Las Vegas Blvd. S.
Las Vegas, NV 89109

Robinson May
1304 W. Sunset Rd.
Henderson, NV 89014

Smith's
(*see Shopping for locations*)

Tower Records
4110 S. Maryland Pkwy.
Las Vegas, NV 89119

Tower Records
4580 W. Sahara Ave.
Las Vegas, NV 89102

Thomas & Mack Center
Ticket Office
Tropicana / Swenson
4505 S. Maryland Pkwy.
Las Vegas, NV 89154
895-3900
To charge tickets by phone, call
TicketMaster.
Hours: Mon. - Fri. 10 am - 6 pm;
Sat. 10 am - 4 pm
Ticket window sales: Cash, check, MC,
Visa
Mail: Money order or cashier's checks
are preferred. A flat convenience fee
per order will be added.

Fax: You can fax your Visa or MC num-
ber, expiration date, and your address
and they will mail your tickets to you.
Fax - 895-1099.
Group sales - 895-1002
Thomas and Mack Center charges
$4.00 per car for parking at all events.

V.I.P. Tickets
3743 Las Vegas Blvd. S.
Las Vegas, NV 89109
1-800-442-3311 895-7555
Concert, sports and theater ticket
sales, specializing in Las Vegas Best
events. Corporate accounts accepted.
Charge by phone, delivery available, all
major credit cards accepted.

All State Ticketing
Corporate Office
999 E. Tropicana Ave.
Las Vegas, NV 89119
798-5606 1-800-634-6787
19 locations; show tickets and tours
and guest-related services; Bally's,
Lady Luck, Maxim, Palace Station, Rio,

Sahara, Westward Ho, McCarran
Airport and Tourist Centers.

All State Ticketing
5030 Paradise Rd.
Las Vegas, NV 89119
597-5970 1-800-634-6787
Credit Cards: MC, Visa, Discover, AMX
Ticket booths are located at 19 hotels;
$2.50 service fee on each ticket sold.

Ticket outlets at most hotels sell tickets to various hotel shows, but not to
all shows. Some show tickets can be
purchased only at that hotel's own box
office, others just by picking up the
phone and making a reservation
directly with the hotel. The policies
and where to pick up tickets as well as
how far in advance tickets can be purchased for all shows are listed below.

ENTERTAINMENT AT A GLANCE

SPECTACULAR STAGE
PRODUCTIONS
Bally's, Jubilee!
Flamingo Hilton, Radio City Spectacular
Imperial Palace, Legends in Concert
Luxor, Imagine
MGM Grand, EFX
Mirage, Siegfried & Roy
Monte Carlo, Lance Burton's Magic
New York New York, Madhattan
Riviera, Splash II
Stardust, Enter the Night
Treasure Island, Mystere
Tropicana, Les Folies Bergere

MEDIUM-SCALE
PRODUCTIONS / VARIETIES
Debbie Reynolds, Broadway...Off B'way
Flamingo, Forever Plaid
Plaza, Xtreme Scene
Riviera, Crazy Girls
Stratosphere, Viva Las Vegas (daytime)
Westward Ho, Hurray America

IMPERSONATORS
Continental Hotel, Tribute to Ed Sullivan
Holiday Inn/Boardwalk, The Dream King
Debbie Reynolds, Kenny Kerr Show
Imperial Palace, Legends in Concert
Rio, Danny Gans
Riviera, La Cage
Stratosphere, American Superstars

MAGIC / HYPNOTISM
Caesars Palace, Caesars Magical Empire
Flamingo Hilton, Hypno-Odyssey
Harrah's, Spellbound
Holiday Inn/Boardwalk, Unreal Magic Show
Lady Luck, Steve Wyrick Magic
Mirage, Siegfried & Roy
Monte Carlo, Lance Burton
San Remo, Showgirls of Magic
Stratosphere, Marshall Sylver-Hypnotist
Tropicana, Rick Thomas

COMEDY
Harrah's, An Evening at the Improv
Holiday Inn/Boardwalk, Comedy Club
MGM Grand, Catch Rising Star
Maxim, Comedy Max
Rio, Danny Gans
Riviera, Riviera Comedy Club
Tropicana, Comedy Stop

NUDITY
(*The following shows have some
topless numbers*)
Bally's, Jubilee!
Lady Luck, Sexy Magic
Continental, Heatwave
Plaza, Xtreme Scene
Riviera, Splash II (Late Show)
Riviera, Crazy Girls
San Remo, Showgirls of Magic
Stardust, Enter the Night
Tropicana, Les Folies Bergere

DAYTIME SHOWS
Circus Circus, Circus Acts under Big Top
Holiday Inn/Boardwalk, Unreal Magic Show
Maxim, Comedy Magic
Stratosphere, Viva Las Vegas
Tropicana, Rick Thomas

FREE OUTDOOR
ENTERTAINMENT
Golden Nugget, Carillo Brothers
Harrah's, Carnival Fantastique
Treasure Island, Pirate Battle
Mirage, Volcano

DINNER SHOWS
Caesars Palace, Caesars Magical Empire
Debbie Reynolds, Debbie Reynolds Show
Excalibur, King Arthur's Tournament
Flamingo Hilton, Radio City Spectacular
Imperial Palace, Hawaiian Hot Luau

HOTEL SHOWROOM
ENTERTAINMENT
Arizona Charlie's, Grand Palace
Bally's, Celebrity Room
Boulder Station, The Railhead
Caesars Palace, Circus Maximus
Desert Inn, Crystal Room
Hard Rock Hotel, The Joint
Las Vegas Hilton, Hilton Theatre
MGM, Hollywood Theatre
Orleans, Orleans Showroom
Riviera, Grand Ballroom
Sahara, Congo Theatre
Silverton, Opera House Theatre
Sunset Station, Club Madrid
Texas Station, Armadillo Lounge

CASINO LOUNGE
ENTERTAINMENT
Arizona Charlie's, Naughty Lady Saloon
Boulder Station, Railhead Saloon
Caesars Palace, Olympic Lounge
California Hotel, Redwood Bar & Grill
Desert Inn, Starlight Lounge
Excalibur, Minstrel's Theatre Lounge
Fiesta, Cabo Lounge
Fitzgerald's, Fitzgerald's Lounge
Flamingo Hilton, Bugsy's Lounge
Gold Coast, West or East Lounge
Golden Nugget, The Lounge
Harrah's, Court of Two Gators
Imperial Palace, Imperial Lounge
Las Vegas Hilton, The Nightclub
Luxor, Nefertiti's Show Lounge
MGM Grand, Flying Monkey Bar
Mirage, Lagoon Saloon
Palace Station, Loading Dock Lounge
Plaza, Omaha Lounge
Rio, Club Rio
Riviera, Le Bistro Lounge
Sahara, Casbar Lounge
Sam's Town, Roxy's Saloon
San Remo, Bonne Chance Bar
Santa Fe, Ice Lounge
Showboat, Mardi Gras Lounge
Silverton, Rattlesnake Rick's Lounge

Skyline Casino, Skyline Lounge
Stardust, Skylite Lounge
Texas Station, Armadillo Lounge
Treasure Island, Battle Bar
Tropicana, Atrium Lounge
Vacation Village, Kookoo's Lounge
Westward Ho, Show Lounge

DANCE CLUBS
The Beach
Cleopatra's Barge, *Caesars Palace*
Drink!
Dylan's Dance Hall & Saloon
Wild Bill's, *Excalibur*
Gold Coast Dance Hall, *Gold Coast*
The Nightclub, *Las Vegas Hilton*
Ra, *Luxor*
Studio 54, *MGM Grand*
Pink E's
Club Rio, *Rio*
Rockabilly's
Western Dance Hall & Saloon, *Sam's Town*
Silver Saddle Saloon
The Tap House
Armadillo Lounge, *Texas Station*
Tommy Rockers
Utopia
Village Pub
The Wet Spot

TOPLESS BARS
Can-Can Room
Centerfold Lounge
Cheetah's Topless Lounge
Club Paradise
Crazy Horse Saloon
Gentlemen's Club
Girls of Glitter Gulch
Little Darlings
Olympic Garden
Palomino Club
Satin Saddle Club
Tally - Ho
Tender Trap
What's Up
Wild J's Gentlemen's Club

SPECTACULAR STAGE PRODUCTIONS

PLEASE NOTE: Productions are listed alphabetically not necessarily by artistic merits. Prices subject to change without notice, please check with Box Office or Ticket Service. It is also suggested to reserve tickets well in advance of your requested date as many shows sell out fast.

EFX
MGM Grand
Theatre: Grand Theatre
Seats: 1,700
891-7777
Type of Show: David Cassidy stars as "The Effects Master." EFX features a cast of 70 in a $45 million surrealistic, high-tech journey through space and time in an original moving adventure highlighted by music and dance. Over 250 spectacular visual effects and pyrotechnics in a state-of-the-art theater that is designed to take the audience to a world far beyond imagination.
Showtimes: Tuesday - Saturday 7:30 pm & 10:30 pm
Price: $49.50 & $70; $35.00 for children ages 5 - 12 includes tax, gratuity and souvenir program.

Enter the Night
Stardust
Theatre: Stardust Theatre
Seats: 900
732-6325
Ticket Policy: Reserved ticket seating; tickets go on sale at 9 am and can be purchased one day in advance at the Stardust Box Office. Reservations by phone can be made up to 2 weeks in advance.
Type of Show: Contemporary, high-tech musical extravaganza. Cast of 40 performers and live musicians; 82 minutes; Features a full-color, three-dimensional laser system and internationally known specialty performers: Aki (billed as the Showgirl for the 21st Century), The Scott Brothers (an amazing dance duo performing high-energy routines that showcase their unique dance talents and robot-like maneuvers) and lead vocalist Jennifer Page (one of the finest female vocalists on the strip).
Showtimes: 7:30 pm & 10:30 pm Tuesday - Thursday & Saturday; one show on Sunday & Monday at 8 pm; dark on Friday; show runs indefinitely. Adults only, no one under 21.
Price: $29.85 - $55 includes tax, tip & two drinks.

Imagine
Luxor
Theatre: Imagine Theatre
Seats: 1,200
262-4400
1-800-228-1000 1-800-557-7428
Ticket Policy: Reservations can be made up to 6 days in advance and can be secured with a major credit card; changes can be made up to 72 hours before the show.
Type of Show: A Theatrical Odyssey; transports guests to a mysterious lost world, an undersea garden and a cyberworld. Amazing aerial acts, unique choreography and astounding illusions allow the imagination to run wild.
Showtimes: Wednesday - Monday at 7:30 pm & 10:30 pm; dark Tuesday.
Price: $39.95 includes tax and gratuity Separate self-service bar located in the theater lobby.

Jubilee!
Bally's
Theatre: Jubilee Theatre
Seats: 1,035
739-4441 1-800-237-SHOW
Ticket Policy: Reserved seat ticket policy. Tickets available only at Bally's; Tickets can be purchased six weeks in advance. Tickets on sale at Bally's box office, open 10 am - 10 pm daily or charge by phone.
Type of Show: $14 million extravaganza featuring a cast of over 100 opened in 1981. Show includes "The Sinking of the Titanic" and "The Destruction of the Temple of Samson." Bally's added a new $5 million opening number to the 17-year-old show. The opening features a 16 minute performance based on Jerry Herman's Hundreds of Girls, featuring 74 performers in extravagant costumes. Remodeling of the show's finale in 1995 brought about an additional $1 million extravaganza incorporating scenes and dance numbers from classic Fred Astaire and Ginger Rogers movies.
Showtimes: Thursday - Saturday at 8 pm & 11 pm; Sunday & Wednesday at 8 pm; dark Friday; show runs indefinitely; (no one under 18).
Price: $46.50 - $66 per person including tax.

Lance Burton
"Master Magician"
Monte Carlo
Theatre: Lance Burton Theatre
Seats: 1,260
730-7777
Lance Burton dazzles his audiences with mind-boggling magic and 10 new illusions including "The Flying Car" considered the grandest illusion in the show.
Type of Show: Magic
Showtimes: Tuesday - Saturday 7:30 - 10:30
Price: $34.95 and $39.95 includes tax; drinks extra and available at lobby bar.

> The Dunes Hotel & Casino was the first to introduce topless showgirls in 1957 with its presentation of Minsky Goes to Paris. The Folies Bergere at the Tropicana began in 1959 and is still there as the longest running production show.

Les Folies Bergere, Best of
Tropicana
Theatre: Tiffany Theatre
Seats: 920
739-2411
Ticket Policy: Call hotel for show reservations. Tickets can be purchased up to one month in advance. Available at two ticket booths in casino, All State Ticketing and all major hotels. Assigned seats.
Type of Show: The longest running production show in Las Vegas, the "Folies" came to the Tropicana from Paris, France. As extravagant as ever, the show combines award winning sequences from the past with stunning new numbers, dazzling sets and lines of beautiful show girls. Novelty acts and elaborately costumed topless showgirls have been entertaining audiences since 1959. Must be 16 to attend.
Showtimes: 8:00 pm & 10:30 pm; dark Thursday. Seating half hour before show.
Price: $45.00 - Table Seating, $55.00 Booth Seating. Includes tax & gratuities.

Legends in Concert at Imperial Palace

Legends in Concert
Imperial Palace
Theatre: Imperial Theater
Seats: 850
794-3261
Ticket Policy: 3 days in advance, tickets can be purchased at All State ticket counters.
Type of Show: Live impersonations and recreations of legendary superstars.
Showtimes: 7:30 pm & 10:30 pm; dark Sunday except holidays; Show started May 1983 and runs indefinitely.
Price: $29.50 per person includes two drinks, tax and gratuity included, children 12 and under half price.

Madhattan
New York New York
Theatre: Madhattan Theatre
Seats: 1,000
For reservations and additional information, ~~740-6815~~
Type of Show: Music and comedy show starring ~~SHOW CLOSED~~ the Ambassadors of the Big Apple, ~~NEW SCHEDULE~~ the heart and soul of New York's underground ~~NOT AVAILABLE~~ performers. ~~AT PRESS TIME~~ the hope and excitement from Manhattan to Madhattan, in a marriage of New York's finest song, dance and comedy.
Showtimes: Tuesday - Saturday 7:30 pm - 10 pm
Price: $39.95 plus tax.

HOTEL SHOWROOM ENTERTAINMENT
Many Las Vegas showrooms have gone to a computerized ticketing system. Gone are the Maitre d's and Captains at many showrooms and ushers seat you in your preassigned seat. Reservations or tickets can be purchased at the individual hotels or ticket counters located in most hotels or directly from the hotel.
Bally's Celebrity Theatre, Caesars Palace, MGM Grand, Orleans, Sahara and the Desert Inn have changing big-name show policies. The Tropicana, Mirage and Las Vegas Hilton also have celebrity entertainment when the main show is dark.
    Most shows last from 75 to 90 minutes. The smaller shows can last about an hour. Seating usually begins one hour before the show begins. There is a 10 percent entertainment tax on all shows and is included in the price where noted.

Imagine at Luxor

SPECTACULAR STAGE PRODUCTIONS

Mystere
Treasure Island
Theatre: The Showroom
Seats: 1,538
894-7722
Ticket Policy: Tickets can be purchased up to 90 days in advance over the phone with a major credit card or in person at the Treasure Island or Mirage box office. The box office is open daily 8 am - 11 pm Tickets may also be purchased at all TicketMaster ticket centers.
Type of Show: World-renowned French-Canadian theatrical troupe Cirque du Soleil. The show features 8 main numbers and many specialty acts such as stilt-walkers, comedians, clowns and acrobats all going at the same time. The $20 million show features a cast of 72 artists with a live 10-piece band.
Showtimes: 7:30 pm & 10:30 pm, Wednesday - Sunday, dark Monday & Tuesday.
Price: $69.85 includes tax per person; children 12 and under $34.85 includes tax.

Mystere at Treasure Island

Splash ll at Riviera

Splash II
Riviera
Theatre: Versailles Theater
Seats: 950
477-5274
Ticket Policy: Call Riviera "Splash II" reservations up to four weeks in advance, also available at All State Ticket Booths.
Type of Show: $5 million production show takes the audience on a magical journey to Atlantis, Shangri-la and the Abyss, featuring a 20,000 gallon water tank, sea creatures, high divers and synchronized swimmers. Other specialty acts include motorcycle riding, comedy and magic. Early show is covered.
Showtimes: 7:30 pm family show & 10:30 pm adult show nightly
Price: $45 and $56 includes tax.

Photo: Phototechnik International

Siegfried & Roy:
"Masters of Illusion"
Mirage
Theatre: Siegfried & Roy Theatre
Seats: 1,504
792-7777
Ticket Policy: Tickets go on sale daily at 8 am and can be purchased up to three days in advance. Tickets available only at the Mirage ticket office. Reserved seating. Phone reservations accepted from Mirage, Treasure Island and Golden Nugget hotel guests.
Type of Show: Siegfried and Roy perform mind-boggling illusions with their famous white tigers in this $30 million production show which premiered in February 1990, three months after the Mirage opened.
Showtimes: Friday - Tuesday 7:30 pm & 11 pm
Although the show is on an indefinite run the showroom is used periodically for star entertainment when Siegfried and Roy are on vacation.
Price: $89.35 per person includes tax, two drinks, gratuities and souvenir program.

Siegfried & Roy "Masters of Illusion" at the Mirage

The Great Radio City
Spectacular
Flamingo Hilton
Theatre: Showroom
Seats: 775
733-3333
Ticket Policy: Tickets may be purchased seven days in advance and are available at hotel box office and All State Ticket Booths.
Type of Show: The Rockettes with Paige O'Hara
Showtimes: 7:45 pm with seating beginning at 5:45 pm for dinner show, 10:30 pm with seating beginning at 9:30 pm for the cocktail show; show is dark on Friday; show runs indefinitely.
Price: Dinner show from $56.00 to $71.00; $49.00 for cocktail show, includes two drinks, tax and tip.

Barbra Streisand

Barbra Streisand appeared at the Riviera in 1963, her Las Vegas debut. In 1969, she appeared at the opening of Kirk Kerkorian's International Hotel (now the Las Vegas Hilton). On December 31, 1993 and January 1, 1994, she again appeared at a Kirk Kerkorian hotel, The MGM Grand. She was paid $20 million for the two performances, her first in 25 years. The hotel reported over 1 million requests for some of the 30,000 tickets sold at $500 to $1,000 each.

MEDIUM-SCALE PRODUCTION / VARIETY

Broadway...Off B'way!
Debbie Reynolds Hotel
Theater: Star Theatre
733-2243
Ticket Policy: Available at hotel box office or at All State Ticket counters.
Type of Show: A musical extravaganza saluting New York's biggest hit shows including *42nd Street, Cabaret, Grease, Evita* and more.
Showtimes: Sat. 3:00 pm & 7:00 pm, Sun. 3:00 pm, 7:00 pm & 9:30 pm, Mon. 9:30 pm
Price: $35.00 plus tax and tip. $32.00 for seniors, military & children under 16.

Crazy Girls
Riviera
Theatre: Crazy Girls Theatre
794-9433
Ticket Policy: Available at Mardi Gras Box Office or charge by phone up to three weeks in advance
Type of Show: Topless variety show featuring the best comedy, music, dance and song in addition to some of the sexiest showgirls on the strip.

Showtimes: 8:30 pm & 10:30 pm nightly except Monday, with an additional midnight show on Saturday.
Price: $23 and $28 includes two drinks, plus tax and tip. VIP seating and dinner optional at an additional cost.

Forever Plaid
Flamingo Hilton
Theatre: Bugsy's Lounge
Seats: 230
733-3333
Ticket Policy: Tickets can be purchased at the Flamingo ticket booth, All State and T-Tours one month in advance.
Type of Show: Musical spoof of the four-part harmony groups of the '50s and '60s, such as The Four Freshmen and The Four Lads. The fictitious Plaids are killed on February 9, 1964, when a school bus filled with teenagers smashes into their car and stops them in mid-note, but God brings the four back to earth's stage for one more chance. The ghostly quartet brings back memories of every "Four" of that era, with style,

panache and easy good humor.
Showtimes: Tuesday - Sunday at 7:30 pm & 10 pm
Price: $21.95; drinks not included

Heatwave
Continental Hotel
Theatre: Jukebox Theater
Seats: 200
737-5555
Ticket Policy: Up to 3 days in advance at ticket office
Type of Show: Fleshy Dance Review
Showtimes: Tues. - Wed. at 8 pm, Thurs. 10 pm, Fri. - Sat. 10 pm & midnight
Price: $19.95 + tax and gratuity, two drinks included.

Hurray America
Westward Ho
Theater: Crown Room
731-2900
Ticket Policy: Available at All State ticket counters.
Type of Show: Small-scale production show with music, comedy and lots of audience involvement. Show features The Walkers and the Hurray America Band.

Showtimes: Daily 7 pm, Monday 9 pm, dark Wednesday & Saturday
Price: $12.95 plus tax incl. one drink

Viva Las Vegas
Stratosphere
Theatre: Broadway Theatre
Type of Show: Variety daytime show
Showtimes: Monday - Saturday 2 pm and 4 pm
Price: $11 includes tax

The Xtreme Scene
Jackie Gaughan's Plaza Hotel
Theatre: Plaza Theatre
Seats: 600
386-2444
Ticket Policy: Up to 3 days in advance at ticket office
Type of Show: Adults only performance features fabulous showgirls, comedy and one of the area's best female vocalists.
Showtimes: Saturday - Thursday 8 pm & 10 pm
Price: $19.95 + tax with one drink included.

IMPERSONATORS

A Tribute to the Ed Sullivan Show
Continental Hotel
Theater: Jukebox Theater
Seats: 200
737-5555
Ticket Policy: No reservations needed, may be picked up at front desk.
Type of Show: Variety featuring Steve Rossi and the Walkers, with impressions of Elton John, Barbra Streisand, Liberace, Dolly Parton and many more.
Showtimes: Thu. - Mon. 8 pm
Price: Two drink minimum

American Superstars
Stratosphere
Theatre: Broadway Showroom
Seats: 780
380-7700 • (800) 99-TOWER
Type of Show: Six multitalented featured acts and six equally talented beautiful dancers delivering high-energy interpretations of America's favorite entertainment superstars backed by the rock and roll sounds of an exceptional seven-piece band. Also included are a large-screen multimedia presentation, exceptional lighting and spectacular costumes. Performances included are renowned singer Delona Simon as Diana Ross, Damian Brantley as Michael Jackson and 11 year Nevada State Fiddle Champion Johnny Potashas as Charlie Daniels.
Showtimes: Fri. - Wed. 7:30 and 10 pm
Price: $25.25 for adults and $18.95 for children 4 - 12, tax and tip included.

Danny Gans
Rio
Theatre: Copacabana Showroom
Seats: 430
252-7776
Ticket Policy: Purchase tickets at show ticket booth. No reservations, tickets can be purchased up to two weeks in advance.

Type of Show: Comic, impressionist Danny Gans known as the man of many voices and an L.A. hit, now in Las Vegas, creates a multitude of impressions that are guaranteed to amuse and astound audiences; creating a large variety of voices and moods, Danny Gans is unbelievable.
Showtimes: Wed. - Sun. 8 pm. Show runs indefinitely.
Price: $60.00 includes tax, gratuity and two drinks.

The Dream King
Holiday Inn Casino Boardwalk
Theatre: The Lighthouse Showroom
Type of Show: Starring Trent Carlini in

a fantastic tribute to Elvis Presley.
Ticket Policy: For ticket information and reservations call 730-3194; reservations taken same day.
Showtimes: Tue. - Sun. 8:30 pm
Price: $19.95 per person plus tax.

The Kenny Kerr Show
Debbie Reynolds Hotel
Theatre: Star Theatre
Seats: 500
733-2243
Ticket Policy: Tickets can be purchased at All State ticket booths or phone hotel for reservations.
Type of Show: Female impersonator

revue starring Kenny Kerr and some of the best impersonators anywhere starring as some of the most famous performers of all time.
Showtimes: 7:30 pm; Sat. 10 pm
Price: $21.95 includes tax & gratuity.

An Evening at La Cage
Riviera
Theatre: La Cage Showroom
794-9433
Ticket Policy: Available at Mardi Gras box office or charge by phone up to three weeks in advance.
Type of Show: Female impersonator revue starring Frank Marino and others impersonating such show biz performers as Tina Turner, Michael Jackson, Madonna, Diana Ross, Bette Midler, Whoopi Goldberg and Whitney Houston.
Show times: 7:30 pm, 9:30 pm with an additional 11:15 pm show on Wed. - Sat. dark Tue., show runs indefinitely.
Price: $26 and $32 includes two drinks, tax and tip with VIP seating and dinner optional at an additional cost.

Legends in Concert
Imperial Palace
Theatre: Imperial Theater
Seats: 850
794-3261
Ticket Policy: 3 days in advance, tickets can be purchased at All State ticket counters.
Type of Show: Live impersonations and recreations of legendary superstars.
Showtimes: 7:30 pm & 10:30 pm; dark Sun. except holidays; show started May 1983 and runs indefinitely.
Price: $29.50 per person includes two drinks, tax and gratuity included, children 12 and under half price.

ENTERTAINMENT

MAGIC / HYPNOTISM

Caesars Magical Empire
Caesars Palace
731-7333
(See Dining for more information)
Price: Dinner, 3 magic shows, tax and gratuity - $75; children ages 5-12 are half price.
Hours: Daily from 4:30 pm and continuing until 11 pm.

Dixie Dooley's World of Unreal Magic
Holiday Inn Casino Boardwalk
Theatre: The Lighthouse Showroom
Ticket Policy: For ticket information and reservations, call 730-3194.
Type of Show: Family; magic and illusions.
Showtimes: Tue. - Sat. 4 pm and 5:30 pm
Price: Free with purchase of a drink.

Hypno-Odyssey
Flamingo Hilton
Theatre: Flamingo Showroom
Seats: 635
733-3333
Ticket Policy: Up to two weeks in advance. Tickets on sale at hotel box office and All State ticket booths. Maitre d' seating.
Type of Show: Robert Kennzington recreates classic movie scenes and "projecting subjects thoughts" onto large screen.
Showtimes: 9 pm Fri. Seating at 8 pm.
Price: $24.95 plus tax and gratuity

Lance Burton
"Master Magician"
Monte Carlo
(See Spectacular Stage Productions)

Rick Thomas, The Magic of
Tropicana
Theatre: Tiffany Theatre
Seats: 1,100
739-2411
Ticket Policy: Call hotel for show reservations. Tickets must be purchased in person at the Tropicana box office.
Type of Show: Combines exotic birds, white Bengal tigers, original illusions and exciting choreography in a fantastic production for all ages.
Showtimes: Sat. - Thu. 2 pm & 4 pm
Price: $12.95 for table seating and $17.95 for booth seating.

Showgirls of Magic
San Remo
Theatre: Parisian Cabaret
Seats: 170
597-6028
Ticket Policy: Tickets can be purchased one week in advance at the box office in the hotel, or at the "Money Club." Tickets also available at All State ticket booths.
Type of Show: Female illusionists.

Showtimes: Tue. - Fri. and Sun. 8 pm and Sat. 8 pm and 10:30 pm; dark Mon.
Price: $24.20 includes tax, gratuity and one cocktail.

Siegfried & Roy:
"Masters of Illusion"
Mirage
(See Spectacular Stage Productions)

Sammy Davis, Jr.
When Sammy Davis, Jr. died in 1990, the marquee lights on the Strip were turned off for 10 minutes in his honor, something never done before in Las Vegas. It was recently done again for George Burns.

Spellbound
Harrah's
Theatre: Commander's Theatre
Seats: 525
369-5222
Ticket Policy: Tickets available at Harrah's ticket booth or any All State ticket booth one month in advance.
Type of Show: Magical, musical extravaganza starring Joaquin Ayala, Mexico's master of illusion, in a spectacular display of illusion, dance laser sets and lights.
Showtimes: 7:30 pm & 10 pm; dark Sun.
Price: $34.95, plus tax, gratuity and one drink.

Steve Wyrick World Class Magic
Lady Luck
Theatre: Lady Luck Theater
Seats: 550
385-4386
Ticket Policy: All State ticket counters
Type of Show: Illusions; featuring the largest illusion in Las Vegas, "The Blades of Death," an illusion not even attempted by the great Houdini.
Showtimes: Tue. - Sun. 7:30 pm family performance; 10:30 pm tasteful topless show.
Price: $22.95 and $27.95.

Marshall Sylver
Stratosphere
Theatre: Images Cabaret
Seats: 300
380-7700 • (800)99-TOWER
Type of Show: Dubbed the greatest hypnotist of all time, the world's leading expert in subconscious reprogramming amazes audiences while dazzling lighting, rock music pyrotechnics and a "fly girls" type dance troupe perform in elaborate costumes. Sylver puts his audience participants in a trance, taking them through mind boggling activities, convincing them to eat fire, walk on broken glass and speak in tongues.
Showtimes: Wed. - Fri. 9 pm, Sat. 7:30 pm & 10 pm
Price: $32.95 includes tax.

COMEDY ENTERTAINMENT

An Evening at the Improv
Harrah's
369-5111
Ticket Policy: Reservations made up to 30 days in advance. Tickets may be purchased at Harrah's ticket booth or any All State ticket booth.
Type of Show: Las Vegas' longest running comedy show; stand-up comedians
Showtimes: Tue. - Sun. 8 pm & 10:30 pm
Price: $14.95 plus tax.

Catch a Rising Star
MGM Grand
Theatre: Center Stage Cabaret
891-7777
Type of Show: Award winning club starring top stand-up comedians and featuring three new acts each week.
Showtimes: Nightly at 7:30 pm & 10 pm
Price: $14.00 plus tax.

Comedy Max
Maxim
Theatre: Showroom
Seats: 121
731-4300
Ticket Policy: Tickets available at the Maxim or any All State ticket booths.
Type of Show: Three stand-up comedians are featured nightly.
Showtimes: Nightly 7 pm & 9 pm
Price: $16.25 includes tax, gratuity and two drinks. For $19.95 you are entitled to complimentary tickets to "Comedy Magic" & "Comedy Max" performances, which includes buffet.

Comedy Magic
Maxim
Theatre: Showroom
Seats: 121
731-4300
Type of Show: Comedy day-club with magic

Showtimes: Mon. - Sat. at 1 pm and 3 pm
Price: $9.95 includes tax and gratuity and two drinks; $12.95 includes tax, gratuity and brunch.

Comedy Stop
Tropicana
Theatre: Mezzanine level
Seats: 400
739-2714
Ticket Policy: Up to a month in adv. at box office, and All State ticket outlets
Type of Show: Three different stand-up comedians are featured each week.
Showtimes: 8 pm & 10:30 pm nightly
Price: $14.30 plus tax per person includes two cocktails.

Riviera Comedy Club
Riviera
Showroom: Comedy Club Show Room
794-9433

Ticket Policy: Available at Mardi Gras box office or charge by phone up to three weeks in advance
Type of Show: Stand-up comedy in an intimate setting reminiscent of a Manhattan nightclub with its neon studded walls and canopy entrance. In addition to headliner comedians, the club features performances by ventriloquists, hypnotists, and shock comedians.
Showtimes: Nightly 8 pm & 10 pm with an additional 11:45 pm show Fri. and Sat.
Price: $18 and $24 includes two drinks, tax and tip. VIP seating and dinner optional at additional cost.

DAYTIME SHOWS

Big Top Circus
Circus Circus
734-0410
Main Arena houses world famous circus acts continuously 11 am - midnight daily. Free entertainment.

Broadway...Off B'way
Debbie Reynolds Hotel
733-2243
Showtimes: Sat. & Sun. matinee 3 pm (children over 6)
Price: $35 plus tax and gratuity.

Comedy Magic
Maxim
731-4300
Showtimes: Mon. - Sat. 1 pm & 3 pm; dark Sun.
Price: $9.95 includes tax and gratuity, two drinks; $12.95 includes tax & gratuity, brunch & two drinks.

Dixie Dooley's
World of Unreal Magic
Holiday Inn Casino Boardwalk
735-2400

Showtimes: Daily 4 pm and 5:30 pm
Price: $8.95 adults, $5.00 children plus tax & gratuity.

Rick Thomas, The Magic of
Tropicana
Theatre: Tiffany Theatre
Seats: 1,100
739-2411
Ticket Policy: Call hotel for show reservations. Tickets must be purchased in person at the Tropicana box office.

Type of Show: Combines exotic birds, white Bengal tigers, original illusions and exciting choreography in a fantastic production for all ages.
Showtimes: Sat. - Thu. 2 pm & 4 pm
Price: $12.95 for table seating and $17.95 for booth seating.

Viva Las Vegas
Stratosphere
380-7777
Showtimes: Mon. - Sat. 2 pm & 4 pm
Price: $11 includes tax and gratuity.

FREE HOTEL OUTDOOR ENTERTAINMENT

Carillo Brothers High Wire Act
Golden Nugget
Act is performed outdoors on 5/8 inch rope suspended over 30 feet in the air. Witness amazing high wire acts and acrobatic feats. Mon. - Sat., four performances daily starting at 3:20 pm.

Carnival Fantastique
Harrah's
The only outdoor acrobatic show on the Strip. It contains fireworks at the beginning and end of each performance and features a bungee act performed around

an outdoor fountain. Twelve performers put on a 20 minute show five times a day, six days a week. The only time performances will be cancelled will be due to high winds.

Pirate Battle
Treasure Island
See an exciting $23 million pirate battle presented daily. This unique attraction, named Buccaneer Bay, has the British ship *Brittania* confronting the pirate ship *Hispaniola*, as the pirates unload their booty. A full-scale battle ensues as stunt men exchange fire and are thrown

from their ships. The pirates, appearing to be losing the battle, make one last ditch effort to fire their cannon at the British. The cannon hits and the *Brittania* goes down. The Buccaneer Bay Show is at 4 pm, 5:30 pm, 7 pm, 8:30 pm and 10 pm and 11:30 pm daily.

Volcano
Mirage
See and hear a realistic pina-colada scented, 54 foot high volcano, erupt every 15 minutes from 6 pm until midnight in front of the hotel.

Fremont Street Experience
(Downtown Area)
On Fremont Street, on a massive space frame that towers 90 feet above four blocks, the Fremont Street Experience takes place. The show runs on the hour beginning at 8 pm and continues until midnight.

Inside the space frame are 2 million lights capable of producing 65,536 color combinations. Accompanying the light display is a state-of-the-art sound system with 208 speakers mounted within the space frame that can produce a combined 540,000 watts of concert-quality sound and music.

DINNER SHOWS

Caesars Magical Empire
Caesars Palace
731-7333
Price: Dinner, 3 shows, tax and gratuity - $75; Children ages 5-12 are half price; Individual party bookings for parties of 4-12 persons featuring an additional "Seance" experience are offered at slightly higher prices.
Hours: Daily from 4:30 pm. Seating at 4:30 pm and continuing until 11 pm.
Menu: "Spirited" gourmet menu featuring three courses and including your choice of salmon chicken or veal.

Debbie Reynolds
Debbie Reynolds Hotel
Theatre: Star Theatre
Seats: 500
733-2243
Ticket Policy: Tickets can be purchased at All State ticket booths or phone hotel for reservations.
Type of Show: Music variety show starring Debbie Reynolds.
Showtimes: Mon. - Fri. at 7:30 pm; Dark Sat. and Sun.
Price: $39.95 includes tax and gratuity; $55.00 includes dinner.

Hawaiian Hot Luau
Imperial Palace
794-3261
Price: Dinner, show, tax and gratuity $24.95.
Hours: Tue. and Thu. starting at 7 pm; presented throughout warmer months poolside and indoor during the cooler months.
Menu: Polynesian-style seafood dinner

King Arthur's Tournament at Excalibur

buffet presented poolside. Price includes tax, admission, all-you-can-eat island and seafood buffet and unlimited mai tais, pina coladas and fruit punch. Entertainment is a music and dance review, "Drums of the Island."

King Arthur's Tournament
Excalibur
Theatre: King Arthur's Arena
Seats: 900
597-7600 1-800-933-1334
Ticket Policy: Tickets can be purchased up to six days prior to the per-

formance at the Excalibur ticket booth, by phone with a major credit card by phoning 597-7600 and area All State ticket outlets. Excalibur ticket booth open 8 am until 10 pm
Type of Show: The show features a cast of 50 performers and takes audiences back to the Middle Ages when knights held jousting tournaments and battled each other for the hands of fair maidens. The medieval theme show features magic, dancing, a jousting tournament and a festive wedding celebration, all guided by magical Merlin. The energy

from this performance radiates through the audience, who become an intricate part of this mystical journey back to the days of King Arthur. The bold special effects enhance the show while you dine on a dinner of Cornish game hen served without flatware in the authentic medieval manner.
Showtimes: Both shows are dinner shows at 6 pm & 8:30 pm; show runs indefinitely.
Price: $29.95 per person includes show, tax, dinner and gratuity.

The Great Radio City Spectacular
featuring the world famous Radio City Rockettes.
Flamingo Hilton
Theatre: Showroom
Seats: 775
733-3333
Ticket Policy: Tickets may be purchased seven days in advance and are available at hotel box office and All State Ticket Booths.
Type of Show: The Rockettes with Paige O'Hara.
Showtimes: 7:45 pm with seating beginning at 5:45 pm for dinner show, 10:30 pm with seating beginning at 9:30 pm for the cocktail show; dark on Fri.; show runs indefinitely.
Price: Dinner show from $56.00 to $71.00; $49.00 for cocktail show, includes two drinks, tax and tip.

HOTEL SHOWROOM ENTERTAINMENT

Most hotel showrooms feature headline entertainment. Tickets can usually be purchased through Ticketmaster or the individual hotel box office. Call theaters for show information.

Arizona Charlie's
Theatre: Grand Palace
258-5100
Seats:: 625
Ticket Policy: Tickets available at Arizona Charlie's ticket booth
Entertainment Hotline: 258-5188

Bally's
Theatre: Celebrity Room
739-4567 1-800-237-SHOW

Seats: 1,450
Featuring top performances by some of todays hottest entertainers.
Ticket Policy: Reserved seat ticket policy. Tickets can be purchased four weeks in advance. Tickets on sale at Bally's box office, open 10 am - 10 pm daily or charge by phone.

Bally's
Theatre: Bally's Events Center
739-4567 for information
No tickets sold by phone.
Seats: 5,200
Ticket Policy: Reserved-seat tickets on sale at Bally's box office, open 10 am-10 pm daily and through Ticketmaster.

Boulder Station
Theatre: The Railhead
432-7777
Seats: 427
Ticket Policy: Reservations up to 3 weeks in advance. Tickets may be purchased at any Station Casino or Ticketmasters.

Caesars Palace
Theatre: Circus Maximus
731-7333 1-800-445-4544
Seats: 1,126
Top celebrity performances held throughout the calendar year.
Ticket Policy: Reserved seat ticket policy; tickets can be purchased one month in advance and available only at Caesars.
Showtimes: Varies

Price: Prices vary and include tax but do not include beverage.

Desert Inn
Theatre: Crystal Room
733-4566
Seats: 530
Ticket Policy: Reservations taken ten days in advance. No tickets, payment received at table.

Hard Rock Hotel
Theatre: "The Joint"
Seats: 1,400
693-5066
Concert Hotline: 226-4650
Ticket Policy: Hard Rock box office noon - 8 pm or through Ticketmaster; 21 and over only for all concerts.

HOTEL SHOWROOM ENTERTAINMENT

Las Vegas Hilton
Theatre: Hilton Theatre
Seats: 1,650
732-5755 1-800-222-5361
Ticket Policy: Reserved seat ticket policy. Tickets can be purchased up to three days in advance at the box office or with credit card by phone.
Open for concerts by some of today's best performers.

MGM Grand
Theatre: Hollywood Theatre
Seats: 650
891-7777 • (800) 929-1111
Ticket Policy: Seats are reserved and gratuities are included. Drinks are extra.

The Grateful Dead
The Grateful Dead attracted 122,533 fans to their three day concert in May, 1995. The shows grossed $3.7 million.

MGM Grand
Theatre: Grand Garden
Seats: 16,325
891-7777
Ticket Policy: Tickets for events held at the Grand Garden are available at the hotel or through TicketMaster - 474-4000.
Type of Show: The Grand Garden Theater houses Las Vegas' finest championship boxing, concerts and sporting events. Christened by Barbra Streisand on December 31, 1993, her first performance in more than two decades; home of the annual Bud Light Cup professional Bull Riders Finals, typically held during the second week in October.

Orleans
Theatre: The Orleans Showroom
365-7075
Ticket Policy: May be purchased up to three months in advance

Riviera
Theatre: Grand Ballroom

794-9280
Headliners appear occasionally.

Sahara
Theatre: Congo Theatre
Seats: 700
737-2515
Ticket Policy: Tickets available at Sahara and through Ticketmaster. May call up to four days in advance.

Silverton
Theatre: Opera House Theatre
Seats: 600
263-7777
Headliners appear occasionally.

Sunset Station
Theatre: Club Madrid
547-7777
Headliners appear occasionally.

Texas Station
Theatre: Armadillo Lounge
631-1000
Special Events Hotline: 631-1001
Headliners appear occasionally.

PROPER TIPPING PROCEDURE
When going out on the town in Las Vegas please remember these valuable people listed below and follow the customary tipping procedures:
Bartenders: Between $1.00 - $2.00 per round
Change Persons: Usually 10% of winnings when hints on a particular machine pay off for you
Cocktail Waitresses: $1.00 - $2.00 per round while drinking for free in the casino gaming area
Keno Runner: 15% if you're winning and a few dollars while you're actually playing
Limo Driver: 15% of your total fare
Showroom Maitre d' and Ushers: $3.00 - $5.00 per person in your party, more if better seating is acquired
Taxicab Driver: 15% of the total fare
Valet Parking Attendant: $1.00 - $2.00
Waiters and Waitresses: 15 - 20% of the total check

CASINO LOUNGE ENTERTAINMENT

Casino lounges became a popular Las Vegas entertainment venue in the early '60s when many big name performers would retreat to the lounge after finishing their midnight show. The lounges would remain open with performances until the early morning hours. Today most play until 1 or 2 am. You'll find a variety of music, from country to contemporary; from jazz to rock and roll. You probably won't recognize the names, but most are very talented performers. Most places have no cover charge and no reservations are required. Usually a one or two drink minimum is required although some lounges require no minimum purchase.

Arizona Charlie's
Naughty Lady Saloon
258-5200
Hours: 4 pm - 12:30 am, no cover and no minimum

Boulder Station
Railhead Saloon
432-7575
Live music; two drink minimum
Hours: Fri. - Sat. 10 pm - 3 am
Concerts are presented often with various prices depending on entertainer.

Caesars Palace
Olympic Lounge
731-7110
Musical entertainment
Hours: 9 pm - 2 am; no cover, no minimum.

Cleopatra's Barge
Continuous entertainment and dancing on the floating barge
Hours: 9 pm - 4 am

Palace Court Restaurant
Piano
Hours: 6 pm - 11:30 pm

California Hotel
Redwood Bar and Grill
385-1222
Piano music
Hours: 6 pm - 11 pm

Desert Inn
Starlight Lounge
733-4444
200-seat intimate theatre with continuous music daily 5 pm - 3 am.

Excalibur
Minstrel's Theatre Lounge
597-7777
Hours: 8 pm - 3 am, 2 drink minimum

Wild Bills
Live country music and dancing
Hours: Wed. - Sun. 5:30 pm - 2 am; Mon., 7 pm - 2 am; Tue., 5:30 pm - 11:15 pm

Fiesta
Cabo Lounge
631-7000
Live entertainment
Hours: 8 pm - midnight

Fitzgerald's
Fitzgerald's Lounge
388-2400
Piano bar
Hours: noon - midnight

Flamingo Hilton
Bugsy's Celebrity Lounge
733-3111
Musical entertainment nightly except Thur. after the "Forever Plaid" show beginning at 10:45 pm

Gold Coast
West Lounge
367-7111
Karaoke
Hours: 8 pm - 1 am

East Lounge
Hours: Mon. - Fri. noon - 6 pm; Tue. - Sun. 9 pm - 3 am

Dance Hall
Live music / D.J.
Hours: Tue. 7:30 pm - 11:30 pm, Sun. 1 pm - 5 pm (DJ)
Fri. - Sat. 11 pm - 3 am (Latin Band)

Golden Nugget
"The Lounge"
385-7111
Hours: 9 pm - 2 am; dark Mon.

Harrah's
Court Of Two Gators
369-5000
Entertainment and dancing
Hours: 8 pm - 2 am

Imperial Palace
Imperial Lounge
731-3311
Hours: vary, call ahead

King 8
Lounge
736-8988
Hours: Tue. - Sat. 8 pm - 2 am

Las Vegas Hilton
The Nightclub
732-5422
Dance to the beat of rock, jazz, funk and motown performed by Kristine W & The Sting and Louie Louie nightly, two drink minimum.

Luxor
Nefertiti's Show Lounge
795-8118
Live music
Hours: 9 pm - 3 am

MGM Grand
Flying Monkey Bar
891-1111
Live entertainment
Hours: 3 pm - 2 am

Mirage
Lagoon Saloon
791-7111
Dancing and entertainment
Hours: 10 pm - 3 am

Baccarat Lounge
Piano
Hours: 4 pm - 4 am

Palace Station
Loading Dock Lounge
367-2411
Popular musical groups
Hours: Mon. - Tue. 5:15 pm - 1 am; Wed. - Sun. 5:15 pm - 2:30 am

Jackie Gaughan's Plaza Hotel
Omaha Lounge
386-2110
Live music
Hours: noon - 6 am

Rio
Club Rio
252-7777
Live Music
Hours: Wed. - Sat. 11 pm - 3 am

Mambo's Lounge
Live music, dancing.
Hours: 9 pm - 2:30 am

VooDoo Lounge
Hours: 11 am - 3 am

Riviera
Le Bistro Lounge
734-5110
Mon. nights "Jazz on the Strip"
Hours: 6 pm - 2 am

Roadhouse
564-1150
Live music & dancing
Hours: 2 pm - midnight

Sahara
Casbar Lounge
737-2111
Live music
Hours: Tue. - Sun. 9:30 pm - 1:30 am
Two drink minimum

Sam's Town
Roxy's Saloon
456-7777
Live country music
Hours: Begins at noon

Western Dance Hall
Live music & dancing
Hours: 9 pm - 3 am
No cover / no minimum

Las Vegas' first nightclub with legal gambling was the Meadows. Opened in 1931, it was located on the road between Las Vegas and Boulder City to attract men working on Hoover Dam and boasted the first floor show in the state

---

San Remo
Bonne Chance Bar
739-9000
Hours: Tue. - Sun. noon - 3 am

Santa Fe
Ice Lounge
658-4900
Live music
Hours: Tue. - Sat. 7 pm - 1 am

Showboat
Mardi Gras Lounge
385-9123
Hours: Tue. - Sun. 11:45 pm - 4:30 am

Silverton
Rattlesnake Ricky's Lounge
263-7777
Hours: 8 pm - 2 am, two drink minimum, no cover

Skyline Casino
565-9116
Skyline Lounge
Live music
Hours: Fri. - Sat. 8 pm - 2 am

Stardust
Starlite Lounge
732-6111
Hours: 5 pm - 2 am

Texas
Armadillo Lounge
631-1000
Live music
Hours: Vary; call ahead
Live concerts
Entertainment Hotline- 631-1001

Treasure Island
Battle Bar
894-7111
View the live pirate battle on the outdoor patio overlooking Buccaneer Bay.
Hours: 11 am - 1 am

Tropicana
Atrium Lounge
739-2222

Live entertainment
Hours: 6 pm - 4 am

Vacation Village
Kookoo's Lounge
897-1700
Live music
Hours: Various days, usually about four days a week

Westward Ho
Show Lounge
731-2900
Live music
Hours: 6 pm - midnight

DANCE CLUBS

The Beach
365 Convention Center Dr.
Las Vegas, NV 89109
731-9298
Ticket Office - 731-1925
Hours: 24 hours
Fun: Video poker, race & sports book
Atmosphere: Eight bars including a dance & party area, a sing-along piano bar, restaurant; dancing nightly occasional concerts "A Place to Party." The two-story, 25,000 sq. ft. night club is open 24 hours.
Bars: Beach Sports Bar & Piano bar
Entertainment: Live bands Wed. & Thu. 10 pm - 1 am

Cleopatra's Barge
Caesars Palace
3570 Las Vegas Blvd. S.
Las Vegas, NV 89109
731-7110
Hours: Tue. - Sun. 9 pm - 4 am
Cover: No cover, 2 drink minimum. on Friday & Saturday
Fun: Located in casino
Entertainment: Continuous; Live band & DJ, 9 pm - 4 am
Food: In hotel restaurants
Atmosphere: Replica of the majestic ships that sailed the Nile in ancient Egypt. The ornate vessel is replete with oars and furled sails.
Credit cards: All major

Drink!
200 E. Harmon Ave.
Las Vegas, NV 89109
796-5519

Studio 54 at MGM Grand

Cover: $10 Thu. - Sat.
Entertainment: Thu. disco music with The Boogie Knights; Friday the sounds of Dr. Funkenstein; Sat. DJ; closed Mon.

Dylan's Dance Hall & Saloon
4660 S. Boulder Hwy.
Las Vegas, NV 89121
451-4006
Fun: Video poker; happy hour 7 pm - 10 pm
Entertainment: Wed. - Sat. 7 pm - 3 am country music, DJ
Food: Appetizers

Wild Bills
Excalibur
3850 Las Vegas Blvd. S.
Las Vegas, NV 89109
597-7777
Bar hours: 5 pm - 11:30 pm
Cover: None
Fun: Located in hotel/casino
Entertainment hours: Sun. - Thu. 7 pm - 10:30 pm; Fri. - Sat. 7 pm - 11:15 pm
Entertainment: Two bands nightly; free line dance lessons 9:30 pm - 10 pm
Food: 5 pm - 10 pm
Atmosphere: Large open bar and dinner house. Large stage on dance floor. Two big screens showing old western movies.
Credit cards: All major

Gold Coast Dance Hall & Saloon
Gold Coast Hotel
4000 W. Flamingo Rd.
Las Vegas, NV 89103
367-7111
Bar hours: Doors open at 6:30 pm
Cover: $5
Fun: Casino
Entertainment hours: Sun., Mon., Wed. & Thu. 8 pm - 2 am; Tue. 7:30 pm - 11:30 pm; Fri. & Sat. 9 pm - 3 am
Entertainment: Latin music sound & DJ Sunday 1 pm - 5 pm
Food: In casino
Atmosphere: Free dance lessons at 6:30 pm; large dance floor
Credit cards: None

The Nightclub
Las Vegas Hilton
3000 Paradise Rd.
Las Vegas, NV 89109
732-5755
Bar hours: 24 hours

Ra at Luxor, 3900 Las Vegas Blvd. S., Las Vegas, NV 89119

Cover: No cover, no minimum
Seats: 450
Entertainment hours: 8 pm - 4 am
Food: In hotel restaurants
Atmosphere: Dance floor, great light and sound system; live contemporary music featuring Kristine & The Sting
Credit Cards: All major

Ra
Luxor
3900 Las Vegas Blvd. S.
Las Vegas, NV 89119
262-5900
Hours: Wed. - Sat. 10 pm - 6 am
Cover: Men $10, out of town ladies $5 and local ladies have free admittance.
Dress Code: Collared shirts and sports jackets
Atmosphere: Cigar lounge, karaoke lounge, 110 ft. sushi bar and VIP booth. Futuristic Egyptian theme.

Studio 54
MGM Grand
3799 Las Vegas Blvd. S.
Las Vegas, NV 89109
891-1111
Hours: Mon. - Sat. 10 pm - 5 am
Dress Code: Collared shirts and dress shoes
Cover: Men $10 weekdays and $20 Fri. and Sat., ladies admitted free.
Atmosphere: Three story high energy, trend setting nightclub which showcases state-of-the-art sound, music and lighting. Four separate dance floors and bars.

Pink E's
3695 W. Flamingo Rd.
Las Vegas, NV 89103
252-4666
Happy hour 4 pm - 7 pm; Ladies Night on Thu.
Bar hours: 24 hours
Fun: 55 pool tables, video poker, shuffleboard, ping pong, darts
Entertainment: Bands, DJ, comedians, variety
Food: 24 hours
Credit cards: All major

Club Rio
Rio
3700 W. Flamingo Rd.
Las Vegas, NV 89103
252-7777
Located in the Copacabana Entertainment Complex. Large circular dance floor.
Bar hours: Wed. - Sat. 10:30 pm - 4 am
Cover: Men $10; ladies free
Hours: Wed. - Sat., doors open at 11 pm
Dress Code: Collared shirts and dress shoes
Entertainment: Live bands Wed. midnight - 4 am. Great dance tunes and videos on 12 large video screens, each one 12 feet by 12 feet. See yourself on the video wall as the camera pans the dance floor. Live concerts.
Atmosphere: Las Vegas' premiere music video night club. Dress code strictly enforced. Huge dance floor. Wed., live music by "Boogie Knights." First drink for ladies is free.

DANCE CLUBS

Rockabilly's
3785 Boulder Hwy.
Las Vegas, NV 89121
641-5800
Bar hours: 6 pm - 4 am
Cover: None
Fun: Slots, 3 pool tables
Entertainment: 6 pm - 3 am; Disc jockey plays new country
Food: Mesquite grill
Atmosphere: Largest country western nightclub in town; large dance floor; homey atmosphere with a large living room area for intimate conversation; dance lessons at 7:30 pm; enclosed bar off dance floor for quiet socializing.

Western Dance Hall & Saloon
Sam's Town
5111 Boulder Hwy.
Las Vegas, NV 89121
456-7777
Bar hours: 7 pm - 3 am
Cover: None
Fun: Dance lessons 7:30 pm - 9 pm
Entertainment: Mon. - Sat. 9 pm - 3 am; DJ
Food: In casino
Atmosphere: Happy hour 7 pm - 9 pm; all drinks $1.00; free dance lessons start at 7:30 pm; Sun. is karaoke night 9 pm - 3 am; Western atmosphere with rail seating around the dance floor and booth seating; good atmosphere and great dancers; Mon. is ladies night, all drinks are $1.00 for ladies; located on second floor above casino.
Credit cards: None

Silver Saddle Saloon
2501 E. Charleston Blvd.
Las Vegas, NV 89104
382-6921
Bar hours: 24 hrs.
Cover: Fri. - Sat. $1.00; no cover on weekdays.
Fun: Slots and 2 blackjack tables
Entertainment: Live band; Sun. - Thu. 9 pm - 2 am; Fri. - Sat. 9 pm - 4 am
Food: 24 hours bar food
Atmosphere: Country western
Credit cards: None

The Tap House
5589 W. Charleston Blvd.
Las Vegas, NV 89102
870-2111
Bar hours: 24 hours
Fun: Progressive video poker; big screen TV, shuffleboard, 2 pool tables, foosball

Entertainment: Sat. 9 pm - 2 am; Live '50s and '60s music.
Food: Full bar menu served in the lounge; hickory smoked ribs and chicken, deep dish pizza, chicken wings (voted best in Las Vegas by the R-J Readers poll); $1.99 breakfast special; private banquet room.
Atmosphere: Cleveland Indians bar; happy hour 4 pm - 6 pm
Credit cards: MC, Visa, AMX, Discover

Armadillo Lounge
Texas
2101 Texas Star Ln.
N. Las Vegas, NV 89030
631-1000
Entertainment: Thu. 9 pm - 1 am and Fri. - Sat. 10 pm - 2 am, Loveshack Sun. 4 pm - 8 pm, Jerry Tiffe band and Monday 7 pm - 11 pm various country bands. Dark Tue. and Wed. karaoke 8 pm - 11 pm

Tommy Rockers
4275 Industrial Rd.
Las Vegas, NV 89103
368-7625
Entertainment: Fri. & Sat. 10 pm - 2 am; live music by Tommy Rocker, The One Man Band.

Utopia
3765 Las Vegas Blvd. S.
Las Vegas, NV 89109
593-5935
Three unique rooms, live music, dance and electronica; banquet facilities
Live dance: 11 pm - 5 am Sun. - Thu., Mon. and 11 pm - 8 am, Fri. 10 pm - 5 am

Village Pub
4563 E. Sunset Rd.
Henderson, NV 89104
454-1887
Video poker machines, juke box, large bar.
Food: separate dining area, pizza, burgers, subs, wings and finger food and dinners.
Credit Cards: MC, Visa

The Wet Spot
4440 S. Maryland Pkwy.
Las Vegas, NV 89119
791-0977
Fun: Video poker, 2 pool tables and happy hour 1 pm - 6 pm, two for one
Food: 24 hours bar food
Entertainment: Tue. - Sat. 10:30 pm - 2 am live band

ENTERTAINMENT AT A GLANCE

BARS AND LOUNGES WITH LIVE MUSIC

BIG BAND

Boulder Station - Mon.
Gold Coast Dance Hall and Saloon
Pepper's Lounge (occasionally)
Plaza Hotel (occasionally)
Santa Fe - Mon. 7 pm - 11 pm
Skyline Casino - Sun. 4:30 pm - 9:30 pm
Texas - Sun. 2 pm - 10 pm
Vacation Village

BLUES

Boulder Station
Mad Dogs & Englishmen
Moulin Rouge
Sand Dollar
Shifty's

COUNTRY

Cellar Lounge
Cheyenne Saloon
Dylan's Dance Hall & Saloon
Excalibur - Wild Bills
Gold Coast Dance Hall - Nite Club
High Country Bar & Grill
Idle Spurs Tavern
Palladium - Nite Club (DJ)
Rockabilly's - DJ
Saddle 'N Spurs Saloon
Sam's Town - Roxy's Saloon
Sam's Town Western Dance Hall & Saloon - Nite Club
Santa Fe - Ice Lounge
Silver Dollar Saloon
Silverton - Rattlesnake Rick's Lounge
Sit 'n Bull Lounge
Texas - Armadillo Honkey Tonk

JAZZ

Castaways
Gold Coast
Harrah's - Court of Two Gators Lounge
Hob Nob
Play It Again Sam
Pogo's

KARAOKE

Boulder Station
Continental
Ellis Island
Favorites
Gold Coast
New Manila
Tanya Restaurant

ROCK

Beach
Drink!
Joshua's Pub
Moose McGillycuddy's

ROCK 'N' ROLL

Boulder Station
Double Downs
Gold Coast Dance Hall - Nite Club
New York New York
Roadhouse
The Tap House

HOTELS WITH DANCING

Boulder Station - Railhead
Caesars Palace - Cleopatra's Barge
Excalibur - Wild Bills
Gold Coast - Dance Hall
Hard Rock Hotel - Viva Las Vegas Lounge
Harrah's - Court of Two Gators
Las Vegas Hilton - The Nightclub
Luxor - Ra
MGM Grand - Studio 54
Maxim - Cloud Nine Lounge
Nevada Palace - Silverado Saloon
Palace Station - Loading Dock Lounge
Rio - Mambo's Lounge
Rio - Club Rio
Sahara - Casbar Lounge
Sam's Town - Roxie's Lounge
Sam's Town - Western Dance Hall
Texas - Armadillo Honkey Tonk
Treasure Island - Doubloon Saloon
Tropicana - Atrium Lounge

RESTAURANTS WITH GOOD BARS

Cadillac Grille
Cafe Nicolle
Cavalier
Cousins
Ellis Island
Hard Rock Cafe
Hippo & The Wild Bunch
Kiefer's

Nicky Blairs
Peppermill
Planet Hollywood
Play It Again Sam
Renata's
TGI Friday's
Tommy Rocker's Pub & Cafe

BARS WITH GOOD RESTAURANTS

Big Dog's Bar & Grill
Big Dog's Cafe & Casino
Barley's
Beano's
The Cellar
Charlie's Lakeside
Draft House
Four Kegs
Hard Rock Cafe
Holy Cow
Keg-A-Brew
Kilroy's
Kopper Keg
L. J.'s Sports Bar
Mad Matty's
Magoo's
O'Aces
Planet Hollywood
Skip's Gold Coin Saloon
TGI Friday's
Triple Play
Village Pub

BARS & COCKTAIL LOUNGES

There are 500 bars and cocktail lounges in the Las Vegas area, and this doesn't include the hotel bars or restaurant lounges. Unless otherwise indicated, the bars and lounges listed are open 24 hours. Most have at least one pool table and bar top video poker. Most have the traditional bar food such as burgers, sandwiches, chicken wings and fingers, breakfast. Some have full menus and separate dining areas and are indicated.

Andy Capz Pub
1631 N. Decatur Blvd.
Las Vegas, NV 89108
647-1178
Video poker; pool tables; home of the Denver Broncos, British draft beer.
Food: Served 24 hours.

Atomic Liquors
917 Fremont St.
Las Vegas, NV 89101
384-7371
Video poker, juke box. Bar opened in 1945; package liquor.
Food: None

BJ's Lounge
218 E. Tropicana Ave.
Las Vegas, NV 89109
736-9439
Video poker; pool tables; package liquor.
Food: Italian deli, appetizers, pizza; wings .10¢ each, midnight - 8 am; Karaoke Fri. - Sun. 8 pm - midnight.

B.T.'s Pub
1651 Palm St.
Las Vegas, NV 89104
457-0010
Video slot machines, pool table, dart boards and horseshoes; sports bar.
Food: Sandwiches, pizzas.

Barley's Casino Brew & Pub
The Green Valley Town Center
4500 E. Sunset Rd.
Henderson, NV 89014
458-2739
Casino, 2 restaurants and a microbrewery. Able to produce 3,000 barrels of beer each year.

Back Stop Sports Pub
533 Ave. B
Boulder City, NV 89005
294-8445
Gaming is not legal in Boulder City, the only city in Nevada that doesn't have gaming; advertises a "free beer to everyone any day the sun does not shine in Boulder City."
Entertainment: Live band Fri. - Sat. 9 pm - 2 am pool tables, arcade games, and foosball. Happy hour 3 pm - 6 pm.

The Ball Park Lounge
7380 S. Eastern Ave., Ste. 101
Las Vegas, NV 89123
361-1961
Video poker, progressive machines; darts, video games; juke box; large friendly bar.
Food: Separate dining area with food served 24 hours; appetizers, sandwiches, burgers, dinner entrees.

The Bank Club
1930 E. Fremont St.
Las Vegas, NV 89101
474-9262
Neighborhood bar; video poker; 2 pool tables, dart board; free video tournaments Fri. & Sat.; Fri. & Sat. live music from 7 pm, ladies night Thu.

Barcelona Lounge
5021 E. Craig Rd.
Las Vegas, NV 89115
644-6300
Four 21 tables, slots, video poker, and video keno, sports book.
Motel with 174 rooms on premises.
Entertainment: Live band Tue. - Sun.
Hours: 4:30 pm - 2 am
Food: $1.99 breakfast special, lunch and dinner.

The Barking Frog
5150 Spring Mountain Rd.
Las Vegas, NV 89102
248-4370
15 video poker machines, 12 pool tables
Food: 24 hours
Friday - Sun. live entertainment; karaoke and DJ.

Barley's Casino & Brewing Co.
4500 E. Sunset Rd.
Henderson, NV 89014
458-BREW(2739)
Hours: Mon. - Fri. 11 am - 11 pm; Sat. - Sun. 7 pm - 11 pm

Andy Capz Pub, 1631 N. Decatur Blvd., Las Vegas, NV 89108

Micro-brewery and restaurant. 199 slot and video poker machines, 6 table games, sports book.

Barley Pops
3328 E. Charleston Blvd.
Las Vegas, NV 89104
457-3353
Video poker; 2 pool tables, 2 dart boards; neighborhood bar.
Food: 24 hours

The Beach
365 Convention Center Dr.
Las Vegas, NV 89109
731-9298
Video poker, race & sport book; eight bars including dance & party area; live music.
Hours: 24 hours
Food: 11 am - 9 pm, full menu

Beano's Casino
7200 W. Lake Mead Blvd.
Las Vegas, NV 89128
255-9150
35 video poker and keno machines; big screen; blue collar bar.
Food: 24 hours; separate dining room with a full menu; steaks a specialty; daily specials; MC, Visa.

Beers and Cheers
713 E. Ogden Ave.
Las Vegas, NV 89101
474-9060

Video poker; pool tables, darts, basketball machine; pool and dart leagues; casino workers.
Food: Pizza & snacks.

Big Dog's Bar and Grill
1511 N. Nellis Blvd.
Las Vegas, NV 89110
459-1099
35 video poker machines; slot club; entire bar decorated in doggie memorabilia, fun atmosphere.
Food: Separate dining area with food served 24 hours; appetizers, steak, ribs, chicken; all major credit cards accepted.

Big Dog's Cafe & Casino
6390 W. Sahara Ave.
Las Vegas, NV 89102
876-3647
35 video poker machines with progressive video poker; slot club; big screen TV; fun atmosphere; entire bar decorated in dog pictures and dog memorabilia.
Food: Separate dining room serving food 24 hours; breakfast served midnight to 10 am; entrees priced at $7.95 to $16.50, include pastas, fajitas, steak, ribs; cappuccino and espresso; NY steak & eggs $2.99 served daily midnight to 11 am; all major credit cards.

The Big Game Club
4747 Fair Center Pkwy.
Las Vegas, NV 89102
870-0087
35 video poker machines
Food: Mon. - Thu. 11 am - 11 pm; Fri. 11 am - 1 am; Sat. - Sun. 8:30 am - 11 pm

Bighorn Casino
3016 E. Lake Mead Blvd.
N. Las Vegas, NV 89030
642-1940
Video poker & keno, live 21 tables
Entertainment: Tue. - Sun., live music from 8 pm - 2 am
Food: Separate dining room

Big John's
3430 E. Tropicana Ave.
Las Vegas, NV 89131
458-5629
Video poker; 3 pool tables.

Bikini Cafe
4611 Las Vegas Blvd. S.
Las Vegas, NV 89119
739-6800
Bikini clad waitresses, swimming pool, bikini memorabilia on walls of celebrities in bikinis, video poker machines.
Entertainment: Happy hour 1 pm - 3 pm Sunday Bikini Jazz Invitational Midnight - 4:30 am
Food: 24 hours; breakfast, burritos, tacos, burgers, Kosher sandwiches.

Bird Off Paradise
501 E. Twain Ave.
Las Vegas, NV 89109
733-9200
Video poker; two pool tables; neighborhood bar.

Bleachers Sports Pub & Grill
3720 E. Sunset Ave.
Las Vegas, NV 89120
435-1480
Video poker; 2 pool tables, darts, pinballs & golf; big screen TV & 8 TVs
Entertainment: occasional live music; Happy hour 4 pm - 7 pm; ladies night Wed.
Food: 24 hours; separate dining area serving appetizers, burgers, dinner entrees; daily specials.

Blue Diamond Saloon
6935 Blue Diamond Rd.
Las Vegas, NV 89124
896-1455
15 video machines, dart machine, pool table, juke box. Live country music Fri. & Sat. 8 pm - 2 am; Dallas Cowboy bar; Sun. jam session 4 pm - 9 pm; Large dance floor.
Food: 6 am - 11 pm

The Blue Ox Tavern
5825 W. Sahara Ave.
Las Vegas, NV 89102
871-2536
Bar top video poker; 1 pool table, darts; big screen TV; Vikings bar.
Food: traditional bar menu, breakfast and dinner menu; baby back ribs, chicken wings .20¢; 1/3 pound burgers, $2.35

Blue Ox East
Restaurant Lounge
4130 Sandhill Rd.
Las Vegas, NV 89121
435-1344

Blue Ox West
Cocktail Lounge
3111 S. Valley View Blvd.
Las Vegas, NV 89102
873-5276
Video poker; satellite TV; sports bar; Minnesota Vikings.
Food: 24 hours; ribs, salads & sandwiches

Bob's Paradise Bar & Grill
2210 Paradise Rd.
Las Vegas, NV 89104
650-3412
Video poker, pool, shuffleboard, darts, ping pong. Happy hour 3 pm - 6 pm daily; live music Fri. - Sat. from 10 pm

Bonanza Lounge
4300 E. Bonanza Rd.
Las Vegas, NV 89107
452-7955
35 video poker and keno machines, progressive; juke box; video poker bar.
Food: Full rack of baby back ribs, $8.95; breakfast special 11 pm - 11 am, $1.49

Bond-Aire Club Bar
284 E. Tropicana Ave.
Las Vegas, NV 89109
798-7726
Video poker, pool table; neighborhood bar.
Food: Pizza

BARS & COCKTAIL LOUNGES

Boodles Lounge & Restaurant
7002 W. Charleston Blvd.
Las Vegas, NV 89128
363-3606
Progressive video poker
Food: 10 am - midnight; traditional bar food and dinner entrees

Boomer's
3200 Sirius Ave.
Las Vegas, NV 89102
368-1863
Video poker, 2 pool tables
Food: 10 am - 6 pm

Boomerang's
6650 Vegas Dr.
Las Vegas, NV 89108
631-4711
Video poker machines, 4 pool tables, pinball, foosball, darts, full beach sand volleyball court
Entertainment: Wed. & Sun. karaoke 9 pm, Fri. & Sat. DJ from 9 pm, exciting special events call for details
Food: 24 hours; pizza, finger foods & appetizers; Villa Pizza, Roberto's Taco Shop

Boston Bar & Grille
3417 S. Jones Blvd.
Las Vegas, NV 89102
368-07500
Bar top video poker, pool tables; happy hour 4 pm - 7 pm, $1.00 drinks & free appetizers
Food: Separate dining area; complete dinners served 3 pm - 11 pm; live music Fri. - Sat. from 10 pm; all major credit cards accepted.

Bottle Collector's
Liquor Shop Lounge
1328 Las Vegas Blvd. S.
Las Vegas, NV 89104
382-6645
Video poker machines; neighborhood bar & liquor store; collectibles

Brickhouse
2850 E. Tropicana Ave.
Las Vegas, NV 89121
451-1123
10 video poker machines; 5 TV sets; New York bar.
Food: 24 hours, pasta, ribs, chicken and salads, breakfast and graveyard specials; free-standing brick building, fire place, 80 seat dining room

Buck's Tavern
1204 N. Nellis Blvd.
Las Vegas, NV 89110
452-3246
Video poker; pool tables & pool leagues; juke box
Food: 24 hours
Entertainment: Special occasions; karaoke Fri. & Sun. 8 pm - 2 am

Bugsy's Supper Club
6145 W. Sahara Ave.
Las Vegas, NV 89102
871-7194
15 slot machines; sports bar with golfer's motif, all NFL games; Happy hour 5 pm - 7 pm, graveyard specials include 1/2 price drinks.
Food: 24 hours, all meals served at low prices; DMX stereo system, patio dining, totally remodeled

Bunkhouse Saloon
124 S. 11th St.
Las Vegas, NV 89101
384-4536
Video poker; pool tables, darts. This saloon, with a cowboy decor, is owned by a judge and is popular with the downtown legal community.
Food: Free snacks Mon., free barbecues occasionally
Entertainment: Occasional music; country western atmosphere with saddles, Old West art

Bushy Lou's
3246 E. Desert Inn Rd.
Las Vegas, NV 89121
735-3832
15 poker machines; large screen TV; sponsors dart teams
Food: 24 hours; spaghetti, biscuits & gravy, nachos supreme grande & potato skins with daily German specials. Beer garden with a German theme. 25 taps, imports & micro with every beer known to man available.

Butch Cassidy's
5225 E. Tropicana Ave.
Las Vegas, NV 89122
434-0678
Video poker; 2 pool tables, darts
Food: 24 hours; sandwiches & burgers $3.75 - $4.75; appetizers; daily dinner specials

CD's Sport Lounge
3025 E. Desert Inn Rd.
Las Vegas, NV 89121
737-1600
Video poker; pool, foosball, darts; big screen; Happy hour Sun. - Thu. 4 pm - 7 pm, sports bar

The Cadillac Grille
2801 N. Tenaya Way
Las Vegas, NV 89102
255-5555
Video poker
Food: Mon. - Tue. 7 am - 1 am; Wed. - Sun. 24 hours; mesquite grilled steaks, ribs, chicken and fish
Entertainment: Occasional

Calico Jack's Saloon
8200 W. Charleston Blvd.
Las Vegas, NV 89117
255-6771
Progressive video poker; pool table, video games
Food: 24 hours

Cantina Charlie's
2605 S. Decatur Blvd.
Las Vegas, NV 89102
258-5180
Progressive video poker; full menu
Food: 8 am - 8 pm

Capri Lounge
3665 N. Nellis Blvd.
Las Vegas, NV 89115
651-0564
Video machines; 2 pool tables; juke box; neighborhood bar
Food: Served in separate dining room from 11 am (closing time varies)

Captains Quarters
2610 Regatta Dr.
Las Vegas, NV 89129
256-6200
Poker machines; juke box; 2 pool tables, darts
Food: Gino's Pizza located in bar

Cariba Charlie's
4835 S. Rainbow Blvd., Ste. 303
Las Vegas, NV 89103
258-5185
Progressive video poker
Food: Dining room serving a full menu; all major credit cards accepted.

Castaways
1690 N. Decatur Blvd.
Las Vegas, NV 89108
648-1961
Video poker; Miami Dolphins sports bar; large screen TV & monitors
Food: 24 hours; shrimps, steak & grilled chicken breast; MC, Visa
Entertainment: Thu. jazz 9 pm - 1 am

Cavalier
3850 E. Desert Inn Rd.
Las Vegas, NV 89121
451-6221
Video poker
Food: 24 hours; MC, Visa & AMX

Cellar Lounge
3601 W. Sahara Ave.
Las Vegas, NV 89102
362-6268
Bar top video poker; white collar crowd
Entertainment: Blues Wed. & Thu. 3 pm - 7 am
Food: $2.95 bacon & eggs, sandwiches; daily dinner specials; full menu

Champagne Cafe
3557 S. Maryland Pkwy.
Las Vegas, NV 89109
737-1699
Video poker; juke box; neighborhood bar
Food: Sandwiches & White Castle hamburgers 3 for $1.50; great burgers & dinners 10 am - 3 am; MC, Visa

Champs
3603 Las Vegas Blvd. N.
Las Vegas, NV 89115
644-8321
Video poker; pool table, darts; sponsor of 22 pool & 4 softball teams
Food: Bar food 10 am - 10 pm

Charlie's Bar
2089 N. Jones Blvd.
Las Vegas, NV 89108
258-5160
Video poker; big screen TV, 2 pool tables
Food: Full menu; MC, Visa, AMX

Charlie's Bar Down Under
1950 N. Buffalo Dr.
Las Vegas, NV 89128
258-5186
35 video poker machines
Food: 24 hours, pizzas, ribs, salad, dinner specials Fri. & Sat. 5 pm - 10 pm

Charlie's Lakeside Bar & Grill
8603 W. Sahara Ave.
Las Vegas, NV 89117
258-5170
Bar top video poker
Food: Separate dining area & terrace dining; scampi, prime rib, filet mignon, liver and onions, entrees $6.95 - $15.95; Sun. brunch 11 am - 4 pm; all major credit cards accepted

Charlie's Saloon
4437 W. Charleston Blvd.
Las Vegas, NV 89102
258-5184
Video poker
Food: none

Cheers Bar & Grill
1220 E. Harmon Ave.
Las Vegas, NV 89119
734-2454
Video poker; 3 pool tables
Food: Daily 10 am - 10 pm

Cheyenne Saloon
3103 N. Rancho Dr.
Las Vegas, NV 89130
645-4139
Bar top progressive video poker; 4 pool tables; country bar; Happy hour daily 2 pm - 6 pm; Blues Wed. - Sat. 10 pm - 2 am
Food: 24 hours; dinner specials Fri. night from 5 pm - 11 pm

Chicago Inn
1502 N. Jones Blvd.
Las Vegas, NV 89108
646-1696
Video poker; pool table; neighborhood bar

Chris's Place
1725 E. Warm Springs Rd.
Las Vegas, NV 89119
361-2252
Video poker; big screen TVs
Food: 24 hours; separate dining area; breakfast, steaks, ribs, appetizers

Chubby's Pub & Grub
4702 E. Flamingo Rd.
Las Vegas, NV 89121
458-5774
Video poker; pool, shuffleboard; Chicago sports bar; Cubs & Bears
Food: Bar food 9 am - 1 am

Chuckster's
4632 S. Maryland Pkwy.
Las Vegas, NV 89109
736-7808
Video poker; big screen TV; pool table
Food: Served daily 10 am - 2 am; sandwiches, dinner entrees; MC, Visa. Happy hour 4 pm - 6 pm; free buffet Fri. 4 pm - 6 pm German food a specialty. Talent night every Thu. night starting 8 pm

City Limits
3297 Las Vegas Blvd. N.
N. Las Vegas, NV 89030
643-7166
Video poker; 2 pool tables; pool leagues

Clubhouse Tavern
4001 Las Vegas Blvd. N.
Las Vegas, NV 89115
643-2337
Bikers bar; video poker machines, 3 pool tables, pool leagues, dart machine; annual hog roast on Mothers Day; Swap meet twice a year; Happy hour Mon. - Fri. 4 pm - 6 pm
Entertainment: Live music Friday - Sun. rock & roll 10 pm - 2 am; 6 pm - midnight open jam session
Food: Free barbecue Sun. 6 pm

Club Monaco
1487 E. Flamingo Rd.
Las Vegas, NV 89119
737-6212
Video poker, gourmet appetizers
Entertainment: 9 pm - 2 am & piano bar; Intimate, contemporary atmosphere.

The Coachman's Inn
3240 S. Eastern Ave.
Las Vegas, NV 89109
731-4202
Video poker; restaurant; all major credit cards accepted

Cooler Lounge
1905 N. Decatur Blvd.
Las Vegas, NV 89108
646-3009
Video poker, darts, 2 pool tables; neighborhood crowd
Entertainment: live music on weekends

Country Roads Lounge
8025 Industrial Rd.
Las Vegas, NV 89139
896-4824
Video machines, darts & juke box; packaged liquor. Karaoke every other Sat. 7 pm - 11 pm

Crown & Anchor Pub
1350 E. Tropicana Ave.
Las Vegas, NV 89119
739-8676
Poker machines, foosball, pool table, darts
Food: 11 am - midnight extensive menu, limited menu after midnight; Sun. roast lamb or beef 5 pm - 10 pm
Entertainment: Sat. live music, popular music 11 pm - 3 am

DT's Lounge
530 S. Martin Luther King Blvd.
Las Vegas, NV 89106
386-6786
Video poker, 3 pool tables; neighborhood bar
Food: Traditional bar food

Danny's Bar
4213 Boulder Hwy.
Las Vegas, NV 89121
451-4171
Bar top video poker, video slots; juke box; neighborhood bar
Food: 24 hours - specials

Danny's II
1750 S. Rainbow Blvd.
Las Vegas, NV 89102
878-3392
Bar top video poker; pool table; juke box
Food: Served 24 hours, burgers, ribs, sandwiches, steaks

Davey's Locker
1149 E. Desert Inn Rd.
Las Vegas, NV 89109
735-0001
Progressive video poker
Food: Hot dogs, sandwiches, homemade chili

Dealers Choice Lounge
4552 Spring Mountain Rd.
Las Vegas, NV 89102
367-6798
Bar top video poker; big screen TV; 4 pool tables, dart board, ping pong
Food: 11 am - 3 am Mexican food

Dean's Den
4808 S. Nellis Blvd.
Las Vegas, NV 89121
458-1867
Video poker machines; Small neighborhood bar

The Debriefing Room
1250 S. Burnham Ave.
Las Vegas, NV 89104
384-9601
Free pool, video machines and juke box
Hours: Open Mon. - Thu. 10 am - midnight; Fri. - Sat. 8 pm - midnight; Sun. noon - 10 pm
Food: Hot dogs, chips; Karaoke occasionally, call ahead

Decatur Express
2650 S. Decatur Blvd.
Las Vegas, NV 89102
362-7500
Bar top video poker; 2 pool tables, 2 electronic dart machines, video games; pool tournaments; Happy hour 6 pm

Decatur Package Liquor & Cocktails
546 S. Decatur Blvd.
Las Vegas, NV 89107
870-2522
Video poker, electronic dartboard and pinball machines; neighborhood bar
Food: 6 am - 9 pm adjacent restaurant; daily specials

Deluxe Bar
2820 E. Lake Mead Blvd.
N. Las Vegas, NV 89030
649-0825
Package liquor; neighborhood bar; pool table, poker machines

Desert Market & Lounge
2343 W. Gowan Rd.
N. Las Vegas, NV 89030
646-2443
15 Video poker machines; pool tables
Food: None, market on premises

Dew Drop Inn
4200 Boulder Hwy.
Las Vegas, NV 89121
458-3184
Video poker; darts, pool table; neighborhood bar

Dino's Lounge
1516 Las Vegas Blvd. S.
Las Vegas, NV 89104
382-3894
Video poker; 2 pool tables, electronic darts; neighborhood bar

Dispensary Lounge
2451 E. Tropicana Ave.
Las Vegas, NV 89121
458-6343
Video poker; neighborhood crowd
Food: Sandwiches, Caesar salad & appetizers served 11 am - 1 am; Visa & MC for $20+; couches for lounging and make your own tacos Fri. 5 pm - 7 pm

Favorites, 4110 S. Maryland Pkwy., Las Vegas, NV 89119

Doc Holiday's
3685 S. Rainbow Blvd.
Las Vegas, NV 89103
253-0000
Bar top progressive video poker; darts; 16 TVs, big screen TV
Food: separate dining area; 24 hours; appetizers, burgers, sandwiches; daily dinner specials $5.95 - $7.95

Don Felipe's Nite Club
2560 Las Vegas Blvd. N.
N. Las Vegas, NV 89030
642-5550
Video poker; 3 pool tables; 75¢ draft beer; Hispanic bar
Entertainment: Live band Sat. 10 pm - 4 am; Sun. 8 pm - 1 am
Food: Separate dining room

Door Sports Tavern
1820 E. Lake Mead Blvd.
N. Las Vegas, NV 89030
399-0711
Video poker; 2 pool tables, shuffleboard
Entertainment: Fri. & Sat. live classic rock band 8 pm - 2 am
Food: 9 am - 6 pm; bar food

Double Down Saloon
4640 Paradise Rd.
Las Vegas, NV 89109
791-5775
Video poker; pool tables, electronic darts, pinball, juke box; live entertainment

Draft House Bar & Grill
4543 N. Rancho Dr.
Las Vegas, NV 89130
645-1404
35 video poker machines, some progressive; Lucky Dog slot club; Green Bay Packers bar; Packer & Draft House sportswear; 14 beers on draft; Wisconsin theme decor
Food: Separate dining room with food served 24 hours; full menu including steaks, pastas & salad, dinner entrees $8.95 - $15.95. All major credit cards

Drink!
200 E. Harmon Ave.
Las Vegas, NV 89109
796-5519
Food: Tue. - Sat. 8 pm - 2 am; closed Sun. & Mon, full menu
Entertainment: Dr. Funkenstein and Boogie Nights midnight - 2:30 am

Duffy's Tavern
4420 E. Charleston Blvd.
Las Vegas, NV 89104
453-3454
15 video poker machines; shuffleboard, darts; neighborhood bar
Food: Hot dogs

Duffy's Tavern II
40 N. Nellis Blvd.
Las Vegas, NV 89110
438-3050
Video poker bar; darts, shuffleboard
Food: Hot dogs

Duffy's Tavern III
3085 S. Nellis Blvd.
Las Vegas, NV 89121
451-9221
Dart lanes & dart shop; video poker
Food: Mon. - Tue. 4 pm - 11 am; Wed. - Sun. 8 pm - midnight; Mexican food

Ellis Island
4178 Koval Ln.
Las Vegas, NV 89109
733-8901
Video poker; free poker tournaments on Tue., Wed., & Thu.
Entertainment: Karaoke entertainment daily 7 pm - 3 am
Food: 24 hours; complete menu; all major credit cards

Ernie's Bar
1901 N. Rancho Dr.
Las Vegas, NV 89106
646-3447
56 machines; satellite TV; friendly neighborhood bar; sports crowd
Food: 24 hours; extensive menu

Fast Break Lounge
2245 N. Decatur Blvd.
Las Vegas, NV 89108
648-8081
Video poker; pool tables, shuffleboard; country bar

Favorites
4110 S. Maryland Pkwy.
Las Vegas, NV 89119
796-1776
Bar-top video poker; 2 pool tables, darts, shuffleboard, basketball machine, video games
Entertainment: 18 piece band Thu. 9 pm - 11 pm; Karaoke, Sun. evenings
Food: 24 hours; traditional bar menu; MC, Visa

5th Avenue Pub
906 S. 6th St.
Las Vegas, NV 89101
385-5000
Video poker machines, some with progressives; ATM machine; karaoke Sat. evenings.
Food: 7 am - 9 pm breakfast, steak, shrimp, burgers & appetizers; MC, Visa

BARS & COCKTAIL LOUNGES

Final Score Sports Bar
Sam's Town
5111 Boulder Hwy.
Las Vegas, NV 89122
456-7777
Hours: Sun. - Wed. 10 am - 3 am; 24 hours Thu.- Sat.
Watch telecast of top sporting events; burgers, sandwiches. Interactive computerized games, indoor basketball key court, virtual reality
Entertainment: Live Fri. & Sat. 9 pm - 1 am; Karaoke Mon., Wed. & Thu.

Finnegan's Pub
6000 S. Eastern Ave.
Las Vegas, NV 89119
795-8795
Video poker; pool tables, darts; juke box, big screen TV
Food: Breakfast, sandwiches, burgers, appetizers

Finnegan's Pub
3889 E. Craig Rd.
N. Las Vegas, NV 89030
644-7080
Video poker & Mega poker
Food: Breakfast, hot and cold sandwiches, appetizers

Foothills Express
714 N. Rainbow Blvd.
Las Vegas, NV 89107
878-2281
Progressive video poker & keno; big screen TV, jukebox
Food: 24 hours; breakfast, ribs, burgers, appetizers; daily specials

Foothills Lounge
6125 W. Tropicana Ave.
Las Vegas, NV 89103
871-8302
Progressive video poker, shuffleboard, darts, video games; big screen TV
Food: From Foothills Pizza; appetizers, pizza, ribs

Foothills Ranch
3377 N. Rancho Dr.
Las Vegas, NV 89130
658-6360
Video poker and video keno; big screen TV
Food: 24 hours; separate dining room

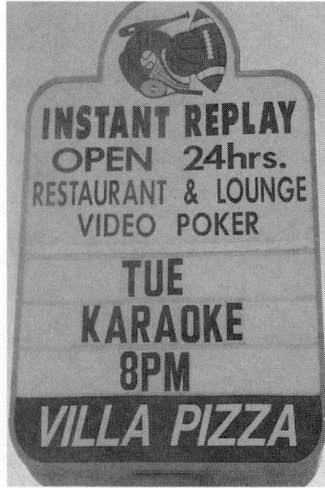

49er Saloon & Casino
1556 N. Eastern Ave.
Las Vegas, NV 89101
649-2421
Video poker; pool tables; neighborhood bar

Four Kegs East
4972 S. Maryland Pkwy.
Las Vegas, NV 89119
736-4444

Four Kegs West
276 N. Jones Blvd.
Las Vegas, NV 89107
870-0255
Video poker; video games; big screen TV
Food: 24 hours; separate dining area and banquet room; Sicilian pizza, hickory smoked baby back ribs, sandwiches, appetizers; chicken wings; $1.99 three egg omelette 24 hours

Four Mile Bar
3650 1/2 Boulder Hwy.
Las Vegas, NV 89121
431-6936
Video Poker, electronic darts; Neighborhood Bronco bar
Entertainment: Karaoke sat. 9 pm
Food: 24 hours with daily lunch specials

Foxfire Lounge
348 N. Nellis Blvd.
Las Vegas, NV 89110
452-4979
Video poker; 3 pool tables, foosball, dart machines, arcade games; neighborhood Chargers bar
Food: None

Frankie's Bar & Cocktail Lounge
1712 W. Charleston Blvd.
Las Vegas, NV 89102
387-9256
Video poker; neighborhood bar
Food: Sandwiches served

Friendly Fergies
2430 Las Vegas Blvd. S.
Las Vegas, NV 89104
598-1985
Video poker, slots; juke box; neighborhood bar

The Front Row Lounge
4180 S. Jones Blvd.
Las Vegas, NV 89103
876-7667
Video poker; 2 pool tables, darts; juke box; neighborhood bar
Entertainment: Live Fri. & Sat. evenings
Food: Appetizers

Gabby's
2303 E. Lake Mead Blvd.
N. Las Vegas, NV 89030
642-5303
Video poker, shuffleboard
Food: Hot dogs

Gabe's Bar
1622 Las Vegas Blvd. N.
N. Las Vegas, NV 89030
649-7187
Video poker; pool table; neighborhood bar opened in 1945; package liquor
Food: Cheeseburgers, burritos & snacks

Gators Lounge
4402 N. Rancho Dr.
Las Vegas, NV 89130
645-6411
Video poker; darts

Gizmo's Grub & Pub
3895 Boulder Hwy.
(Enter from Lamb Blvd.)
Las Vegas, NV 89121
641-6919
Poker machines; pool tables; neighborhood bar
Food: 10 am - noon for .99¢ wings, pasta, pizzas & appetizers
Entertainment: Karaoke Sat. 9 pm - 1 am

Glass Pool Lounge
4611 Las Vegas Blvd. S.
Las Vegas, NV 89119
739-6800
Video poker; neighborhood bar
Entertainment: Karaoke Wed. - Sat. 9 pm - 2 am contests every Sat. with cash prizes given.
Food: 24 hours; burgers & sandwiches

Gloria's Depot
3720 W. Tropicana Ave.
Las Vegas, NV 89103
798-7884
Video poker, pool table; neighborhood bar.
Food: 24 hours; lunch specials

Gloria's II
1966 N. Rainbow Blvd.
Las Vegas, NV 89108
647-0744
Video poker, 2 pool tables, juke box
Food: 24 hours; midnight - 8 am graveyard specials, full menu

Gold Mine Bar & Grill
252 Convention Center Dr.
Las Vegas, NV 89109
696-9722
Video poker, keno machines; juke box, sports ticker; gold mine theme, rock walls, beams, gold cart, trestle above bar; live entertainment
Food: 24 hours; full menu, specials & food to go

Golden Eagle
2202 Paradise Rd.
Las Vegas, NV 89104
737-3888
Video poker and juke box
Food: separate restaurant open 8 am - 10:30 pm

The Gold Mine
23 S. Water St.
Henderson, NV 89015
565-9391
Poker machines; 2 pool tables, darts; Fri. - nine ball leagues
Entertainment: Pool tournaments, raffles & T-shirts
Food: Sun. 10 am - 8 pm; Mon. - Sat. 10 am - 2 am; deli type

The Gourmet Cafe
330 S. Third St., Ste. 100
Las Vegas, NV 89101
388-8222
Video poker
Food: 7 am - 3 pm; sandwiches, salads, & homemade soup; MC, Visa, AMX; closed Sat.

Green's Lounge & Kitchen
2241 N. Green Valley Pkwy.
Henderson, NV 89014
454-4211
Video poker bar with lots of large comfortable booths
Food: 8 pm - 10:30 pm full menu.

The Guadalajara Nite Club
1600 Las Vegas Blvd. N.
N. Las Vegas, NV 89030
642-4722
Video poker; Ranch-style Latin nite club
Hours: 2 pm - 6 am
Entertainment: Traditional Mexican music

The Hard Hat Cocktail Lounge
1675 Industrial Rd.
Las Vegas, NV 89102
384-8987
Video poker; pool tables, darts; blue collar bar; payroll checks cashed
Food: Mon. - Fri.; dinner specials

Hard Rock Cafe
4475 Paradise Rd.
Las Vegas, NV 89109
733-8400
Video poker in bar; recorded rock music; one of 79 Hard Rock Cafes worldwide, the first located in London in 1971. Decorated with memorabilia from rock stars from floor to ceiling; retail sales of Hard Rock sportswear located just inside front entrance
Hours: 11 am - midnight
Food: Appetizers, burgers, sandwiches, American entrees; all credit cards

The Heights Lounge
465 S. Decatur Blvd.
Las Vegas, NV 89107
878-5433
Bar top video poker; pool table, darts, pinball, video games; package liquor
Food: Fried foods

Hogg's Breath Saloon
3100 E. Lake Mead Blvd.
N. Las Vegas, NV 89030
649-4911
Video poker; pool, darts; juke box; neighborhood bar
Entertainment: Occasional live entertainment, call ahead.

Holy Cow! Casino, Cafe & Brewery
2423 Las Vegas Blvd. S.
Las Vegas, NV 89104
732-2697
90 video poker machines including bartop & progressive; slot club; only brewpub in Las Vegas where beer is made & served on premises; three different beers on tap at all times, Asle Ale, Wheat Beer and Red Ale. On the mezzanine level you can view the beer being made. TV monitors & six big screen TVs
Food: 24 hours; separate dining area; Wisconsin Bratwurst, rotisserie chicken, ribs, steaks & American specialties; MC, Visa, AMX

Hooters
5675 W. Sahara Ave.
Las Vegas, NV 89102
248-4668
$1.00 draft beer
Food: Mon. - Thu. 11 am - 11 pm; Fri. - Sun. 11 am - midnight

The Huddle Lounge
4844 S. Eastern Ave.
Las Vegas, NV 89121
458-1056
Video poker; pool tables, electronic darts; neighborhood bar
Food: 24 hours; corn dogs, fried zucchini, mushrooms, chicken wings & fingers
Entertainment: Karaoke Fri. & Sat. 9 pm - 3 am; Sun. 4 pm - 7 pm

Kilroys, 1021 S. Buffalo Dr., Las Vegas, NV 89128

Huntridge Package Liquor & Cocktails
1122 E. Charleston Blvd.
Las Vegas, NV 89104
384-7377
Video poker and keno machines;
neighborhood Raiders bar
Food: Bar food in the evening

Ichabod's Lounge
3300 E. Flamingo Rd.
Las Vegas, NV 89121
451-2323
Bar top video poker; pool table; big
screen TV
Food: 8:30 pm - 10:30 pm; separate dining area; sandwiches, salads, burgers,
appetizers, entrees $4.00 - $14.95

Idle Spurs Tavern
1113 S. Rainbow Blvd.
Las Vegas, NV 89102
363-7718
Poker machines; shuffleboard, 3 pool
tables, free pool on graveyard & all day
Sun.; country atmosphere
Entertainment: live country music
Thu. - Sun.y 7 pm - midnight
Food: Snack bar

Inner Circle
(In Super 8 Motel)
704 Nevada Hwy.
Boulder City, NV 89005
294-4482
Hours: Sun. - Thu. 10 am - midnight,
Fri. - Sat. 10 am - 1 am
No gaming in Boulder City. Attached to
motel; clientele consists of tourists and
locals; big screen TV; darts; karaoke
Thu. 8 pm
Food: 7 am - 1 am

Inn Zone D. I.
2542 E. Desert Inn Rd.
Las Vegas, NV 89109
369-9892
Video poker
Food: Separate dining area; breakfast
special served midnight to noon., $1.59

Inn Zone Flamingo
4850 W. Flamingo Rd.
Las Vegas, NV 89103
871-4034
Bar top video poker; pool table, video games
Food: 24 hours; lunch & dinner specials;
$1.49 breakfast special 11 pm - 11 am

Inn Zone Rainbow
238 S. Rainbow Blvd.
Las Vegas, NV 89128
363-2424
Video poker; juke box; big screen TV
Food: 24 hours; separate dining area;
daily specials

Instant Replay
7777 W. Sahara Ave.
Las Vegas, NV 89117
243-7777
Video poker; Buffalo Bills sports bar;
sponsors softball teams
Food: 24 hours, Italian food

Irene's Cocktail Lounge
5480 Spring Mountain Rd.
Las Vegas, NV 89102
873-5758
Progressive video poker, .05¢ & .25¢;
2 pool tables, darts; free pool Sat.
Food: 8 am - 4 am; burgers, sandwiches
& finger food; delivery available

**Jack Potter's
Quarter Club & Cafe**
4485 S. Jones Blvd.
Las Vegas, NV 89103
248-4211
Video machines
Food: 24 hours; lunch & dinner specials; sports bar with Dallas as home
team; 3 large & 6 regular size TVs.

Jacks or Better Eatery & Pub
1645 N. Lamb Blvd.
Las Vegas, NV 89115
453-4888
Bar top video poker; dart leagues; pool
& poker tournaments shuffleboard 3
pool tables; juke box
Food: Complete menu with separate
dining room. 2½ pound Hoss burgers. If
you can eat one you get in their Hall of
Fame; if you eat two, both are free and
if you can do it in under 30 minutes, you
win $100.

Jack's Place
5067 E. Bonanza Rd.
Las Vegas, NV 89110
453-4333
Video poker, slots; pool tables, electronic
darts; free music on juke box; large
screen TV
Hours: 10 am - 2 am

Jakes
2301 S. Eastern Ave.
Las Vegas, NV 89104
457-0053
Video poker; pool, steel & soft tip darts;
juke box; neighborhood bar
Food: specials with separate dining
area 10 am - 6 pm

Jonathan's Pub
3310 S. Nellis Blvd.
Las Vegas, NV 89121
435-3282
Progressive video poker; video games
Food: 6:30 am - 10:30 pm; breakfast spe-
cial 6:30 am - 10:30 am $1.95; Great
White burger $2.90; baby back ribs
$8.95 half rack; $10.95 full rack, and on
Fri. beer battered fish special.
Entertainment: Live entertainment
Friday 9 pm 'til late.

Joshua's Pub
3650 S. Decatur Blvd.
Las Vegas, NV 89103
367-7201
Progressive video poker & video keno; 2
pool tables, darts; weekly poker tournament Mon. 1:30 am
Entertainment: Live Saturday 10 pm - 2
am
Food: Delivered from various restaurants around town via your phone order

Keg-A-Brew
5310 W. Sahara Ave.
Las Vegas, NV 89102
367-2303
Progressive video poker; 2 big screen TVs
Food: 24 hours; separate dining room

Keg Room
2365 E. Bonanza Rd.
Las Vegas, NV 89101
384-7260
Video poker; dartboard; neighborhood
bar in business 33 years

Kelly's Kasino
164 W. Oakey Blvd.
Las Vegas, NV 89102
382-8713
Video poker; pool table, electronic darts
Food: Hot dogs

Kilroys
1021 S. Buffalo Dr.
Las Vegas, NV 89128
363-4933
Bar top video poker
Food: Separate dining room; full menu;
fresh ground charbroiled burgers; MC, Visa

Kilroys Decatur
310 S. Decatur Blvd.
Las Vegas, NV 89107
2596400
Poker machines, juke box; upper class
neighborhood bar
Food: Salads, burgers, chicken sandwiches and appetizers

King of Clubs
1401 N. Decatur Blvd.
Las Vegas, NV 89108
646-1501
Video poker & keno machines; pool table
Food: Hot dogs

Kooter's Klub
1511 S. Main St.
Las Vegas, NV 89101
366-1533
Video poker; juke box; 2 pool tables;
neighborhood bar

Kopper Keg East
4550 E. Tropicana Ave.
Las Vegas, NV 89121
454-0711
Video poker; paycheck cashing; Happy
hour 3 pm - 6 pm
Food: 8 am - midnight; lunch specials

Kopper Keg West
2257 S. Rainbow Blvd.
Las Vegas, NV 89102
254-4299
Video poker; pinball and video games;
big screen; paycheck cashing; Happy
hour 3 pm - 6 pm
Food: 8 am - midnight; daily lunch specials

L. J.'s Sports Bar & Grill
4405 W. Flamingo Rd.
Las Vegas, NV 89103
871-1424
Bar top video poker; 2 pool tables, electronic dartboard, golf machine; 43 TV
monitors, juke box; sports bar decorated with sports memorabilia
Food: 24 hours; separate dining area;
appetizers, burgers, sandwiches, dinner
entrees; MC, Visa, AMX

Lake Mead Lounge
846 E. Lake Mead Dr.
Henderson, NV 89015
565-0297
Video poker; juke box; blue collar bar
Food: Separate dining room; full menu -
Mexican & American. Specials: Prime
rib, 16 ounce porterhouse steak, filet
and shrimp; MC, Visa

The Lakes Lounge
2920 Lake East Dr.
Las Vegas, NV 89117
363-9733
Video poker; juke box
Food: 24 hours; dinner 5 pm - 10 pm pot
roast and prime rib; $2.95 New York
steak sandwich; Visa & MC accepted.

Lally's of Las Vegas
1750 N. Rancho Dr.
Las Vegas, NV 89106
648-6897
Bar top video poker; dartboard & pool
table; juke box
Entertainment: Karaoke Fri. & Sat.
9 pm - late
Food: Lunch 11 am - 2 pm;
Dinner 5 pm - 10 pm

Las Vegas Bar & Liquor
1617 E. Sahara Ave.
Las Vegas, NV 89104
735-2562
Video machines, pinball, bumper pool,
CD player
Food: 24 hours, finger foods; 3 drawings
Fri. 8 pm, 9:30 pm and 11 pm; extensive
liquor collection, in-house or out; 99
bottles of beer on the wall
Entertainment: Karaoke Sun.

Las Vegas Lounge
900 E. Karen Ave.
Las Vegas, NV 89109
737-9350
Video poker, pool table, dart room
Food: Full menu - daily specials

Legends Restaurant & Lounge
865 N. Lamb Blvd.
Las Vegas, NV 89119
437-9674
15 slots, pool table with leagues, steel
tipped and soft tipped dart leagues
Food: pizza, chicken finger & wings,
hoagies and appetizers
Entertainment: Grateful Dead tapes
Sat. 8:30 pm - 2 am

ENTERTAINMENT

BARS & COCKTAIL LOUNGES

The Lift
3045 S. Valley View Blvd.
Las Vegas, NV 89102
876-3920
35 video poker & keno machines; 3 dart boards; 12 TV monitors; juke box; package liquor
Food: 24 hours; half pound burger with fries, $2.50; steak sandwich with fries, $1.75

Liguori's Bar & Casino
1133 N. Boulder Hwy.
Henderson, NV 89015
565-1688
103 slots & videos, 2 live poker tables
Food: 24 hours; full service; separate dining room Italian cuisine; lunch & dinner specials

Loading Dock
4510 Arville St.
Las Vegas, NV 89103
221-0495
Poker machines; 2 pool tables, 2 electronic dart boards; juke box; blue collar bar
Food: 11 am - 6 pm; daily specials; separate dining room

Lone Star Steakhouse & Saloon
(Additional location listed below)
1290 E. Flamingo Rd.
Las Vegas, NV 89119
893-0348
Hours: 11 am - 11 pm
Fun and friendly upbeat atmosphere, waiters and waitresses break out in song and dance when certain country songs are played; large buckets of peanuts at each table and you are encouraged to throw the shells on the floor. True Texas atmosphere with bull heads and cattle drive murals on the walls; bar; patio.

1611 S. Decatur Blvd.
Las Vegas, NV 89102
259-0105

Loose Caboose
3175 E. Tropicana Ave.
Las Vegas, NV 89121
433-8060
Bar top video poker; 14 TVs and large screen TV - two satellites; 2 pool tables, video poker; neighborhood crowd
Food: 24 hours; MC, Visa

Loose Caboose Saloon
15 N. Nellis Blvd.
Las Vegas, NV 89110
452-4500
Bar top progressive video poker; 2 pool tables, darts; big screen TV; juke box.
Food: 24 hours; separate dining area; daily dinner specials; MC, Visa

Lucky Dogs
2396 S. Lamb Blvd.
Las Vegas, NV 89104
431-3991
Video poker
Food: 24 hours; $7.25 - $12.95

Lucky Lil's Saloon
957 E. Sahara Avenue
Las Vegas, NV 89104
696-0202
Video poker; 2 pool tables; darts
Food: 11 am - 7 pm; finger foods, hamburgers & subs, steaks, ribs & chicken.
Happy hour Mon. - Thu. 4 pm - 7 pm

Lucky Nickel Saloon
2075 Palm St.
Las Vegas, NV 89104
457-6911
Video poker; 2 pool tables, 2 steel dart bars, foosball, pinball; blue collar bar
Food: Daily specials

M. G. Backroads
4636 Wynn Rd.
Las Vegas, NV 89103
368-0416
Video poker; pool table; neighborhood bar
Food: 24 hours

Mad Matty's Bar & Grille
8100 W. Sahara Ave.
Las Vegas, NV 89117
254-9997
35 video poker machines; pool tables, dart boards; TV monitors
Food: 24 hours, view of Las Vegas from dining room

Madison Avenue
855 E. Twain Ave.
Las Vegas, NV 89109
735-4535
Video poker; pool table, darts, air hockey, pinball
Food: 24 hours; French dip, prime rib, steakburgers, Philly steak sandwiches, eggrolls & fried zucchini

Magoo's
(Additional location listed below)
7360 W. Cheyenne Ave.
Las Vegas, NV 89129
395-7360
Video poker

3234 Decatur Blvd
Las Vegas, NV 89130
631-8595
Video poker

Magoo's Hideaway
6985 W. Sahara Ave.
Las Vegas, NV 89117
873-6466
Video poker; 2 pool tables, darts; juke box
Food: 24 hours; separate dining room & patio; traditional bar food & dinner entrees

Magoo's West
5765 W. Tropicana Ave.
Las Vegas, NV 89118
368-1515
Video poker; big screen TV
Food: 24 hours; separate dining area; MC, Visa.

Magoo's East
2585 E. Flamingo Rd.
Las Vegas, NV 89121
732-1515
Bar top video poker, 2 pool tables, foosball; juke box
Food: 24 hours; separate dining room; fireplace in dining room

Mahoney's Pub
6870 Spring Mountain Rd.
Las Vegas, NV 89102
871-1220
Video poker & keno; darts, 3 pool tables; pool leagues; TV monitors; Green Bay bar
Food: Traditional bar menu

Marker Down
3939 Spring Mountain. Rd.
Las Vegas, NV 89102
876-4114

Progressive video poker; 2 pool tables foosball, electronic darts, pinball, shuffleboard; juke box; blue collar bar
Entertainment: Live music Fri. 10 pm - 2 am
Food: 24 hours, traditional bar menu

Messin Around Lounge
2740 E. Lake Mead Blvd.
N. Las Vegas, NV 89030
642-7848
Video poker; pool table, shuffleboard, darts; juke box; neighborhood bar
Food: Bar food
Entertainment: Go-Go dancers Fri.-Sun. 7:30 pm - 2:30 am

Michael's Pub
4012 S. Rainbow Blvd.
Las Vegas, NV 89103
871-1381
Progressive video poker; pool table, pinball, video games; big screen TV
Food: 24 hours; weekend champagne brunch Sat. - Sun. 9 am - 3 pm $6.95

Magoo's
7360 W. Cheyenne Ave.
Las Vegas, NV 89129

Mirabelli's Sports Bar & Grill
3990 W. Russell Rd.
Las Vegas, NV 89118
736-2454
Video poker; pool table
Food: separate dining room; served Mon. - Thu. 7 am - 2 pm; Fri. 7 am - 5 pm; Sat. free hot dogs & chili; closed Sun., '49ers bar.

Money Plays
4755 W. Flamingo Rd.
Las Vegas, NV 89117
368-1828
Video poker; shuffleboard; beer & wine bar
Food: available next door at Guido's
Entertainment: Live band Sat. from 10 pm; no cover charge
Famous for "100 yard club"; 1/2 yard beers; drink 200 and you receive a 100 yard jacket.

Moose McGillycuddy's Pub & Cafe
4770 S. Maryland Pkwy.
Las Vegas, NV 89119
798-8337
2 pool tables; foosball; Happy hour daily 4 pm - 9 pm, all drinks and appetizers half price; 12 draft beers on tap
Entertainment: Live band Sat. night
Food: 11:30 am - midnight; extensive menu

Mountain Springs Saloon
U.S. 160 Mountain Springs
Blue Diamond, NV 89004
875-4266
Video poker; gift shop open on weekends, horseshoes
Hours: 9 am - 11 pm & later on weekends
Entertainment: Live music Fri. - Sun. 7 pm - 2 am
Food: Smoked barbecue served noon - 10 pm; separate dining room

Mt. Charleston Resort
Kyle Canyon Rd.
Mt. Charleston, NV 89124
872-5408
Fireside cocktail lounge
Entertainment: live entertainment on weekends; horse-drawn sleigh rides/hay rides (seasonal)
Food: Breakfast, lunch & dinner with wild game a specialty

Mugshots Lounge West
1810 S. Rainbow Blvd.
Las Vegas, NV 89102
362-8777
Progressive video poker; pool table; big screen TV; Dallas Cowboys bar
Food: 24 hours; steamed clams in beer $6.95 per dozen, Sun. peel & eat shrimp .25¢ each.

Mugshots Lounge East
3342 S. Sandhill Rd.
Las Vegas, NV 89121
454-6100
Video poker; pool tables; darts
Food: 24 hours; daily specials, steamed clams $5.50; Fri. all you can eat tacos $3.25; MC, Visa

Mugshots Eatery & Pub
1120 N. Boulder Hwy.
Henderson, NV 89015
566-6577
Video poker; big screen TV
Food: 24 hours; separate dining room; lunch & dinner specials; steak, sea & shore, pork chops, shrimp, and Italian dinners; Fri. all the hard tacos you can eat for $2.95; steamed clams in beer $6.95 per dozen, peel & eat shrimp 25¢ each
Entertainment: Fri. & Sat. 8 pm - 2 am live music

Murphy's Pub
3985 E. Sunset Rd.
Las Vegas, NV 89120
458-5516
Video poker; 4 pool tables, darts; CD player; home of the Denver Broncos
Entertainment: Karaoke Sat. 8 pm - 2 am

The New Montana Bar & Kitchen
1736 Las Vegas Blvd. N.
N. Las Vegas, NV 89030
642-4704 • 642-4271
Bar top video poker; foosball; 2 pool tables; juke box; country atmosphere

New Town Tavern
600 Jackson Ave.
Las Vegas, NV 89106
647-3995
20 video poker machines
Entertainment: Occasional
Food: 24 hours; soul food; separate dining room. Specials such as smoked neckbones, ox tail and smothered pork chops are served 2 pm - 10 pm

New Twenty Five Club
4531 Las Vegas Blvd. N.
Las Vegas, NV 89115
643-6415
Video poker; 2 pool tables; darts; juke box
Food: 24 hour; bar food with daily specials

The Nice Place
3021 E. Charleston Blvd.
Las Vegas, NV 89104
386-2622
Video poker; 3 pool tables; juke box; neighborhood bar
Food: Bar food

Noreen's Cocktail Lounge
2799 E. Tropicana Ave.
Las Vegas, NV 89121
458-7557
Video poker & keno; pool table; juke box; neighborhood Steelers bar
Food: Snacks

North Star Bar & Grill
5150 Camino Al Norte
N. Las Vegas, NV 89030
642-4690
Video poker; 3 pool tables, dart board; juke box.
Food: 24 hours, full menu

O'Aces Bar & Grill
3003 N. Rainbow Blvd.
Las Vegas, NV 89108
645-2237
Video poker, 2 pool tables; juke box; neighborhood bar, satellite TV
Food: Up-scale dinner 5 pm - 10:30 pm at a reasonable price

Off Ramp Lounge
3935 E. Charleston Blvd.
Las Vegas, NV 89104
438-4565
Video poker; 3 pool tables, pool leagues, foosball, dart boards; Dallas Cowboys bar
Food: 24 hours; serving burgers, steaks & appetizers, soups

Office Bar 1
4608 Paradise Rd.
Las Vegas, NV 89109
737-7756
Video poker machines; 2 pool tables; darts; juke box; neighborhood bar
Food: Subs

Office Bar 2 & Lounge
953 E. Desert Inn Rd.
Las Vegas, NV 89109
735-2349
Slots; 2 TVs, juke box, neighborhood bar

Office Bar 3 & Lounge
3240 S. Arville St.
Las Vegas, NV 89102
368-4180
Video poker & keno; 2 pool tables; comfortable over 30s crowd
Food: 24 hour, bar food with specials

Office Bar 5 & Grill
3375 E. Russell Rd.
Las Vegas, NV 89120
451-1626
Video poker; juke box; neighborhood older crowd
Food: 24 hours, daily specials

Office Bar 6 & Grill
2570 E. Tropicana Ave.
Las Vegas, NV 89121
454-0770
Video poker, pool table, darts, shuffleboard, older neighborhood crowd
Food: 24 hours, bar food with specials

Office Lounge 7 & Restaurant
2660 S. Maryland Pkwy.
Las Vegas, NV 89109
737-1966
Video poker; pool tables; big screen television; juke box; New York Giants bar
Food: Served 24 hours in Eli & Wongs; Italian and Chinese food

Our Place Lounge
4000 Boulder Hwy.
Las Vegas, NV 89121
431-3106
15 video machines; 2 pool tables; darts
Food: Free food Mon. night football

O'Aces Bar & Grill, 3003 N. Rainbow Blvd., Las Vegas, NV 89108

Ozzie's
5020 Spring Mountain Rd.
Las Vegas, NV 89102
368-3870
Video poker, juke box
Food: Hot dogs

P.J. Lounge
2300 S. Maryland Pkwy.
Las Vegas, NV 89104
735-5454
24 bartop video poker, 2 keno, pool table, large screen TV
Food: 10 am - 3 am; lasagna, spaghetti & meatballs, eggplant parmigiana, jumbo fried shrimp; MC, Visa, AMX

P.T.'s Bar & Grill
(Additional locations listed below)
347 N. Nellis Blvd.
Las Vegas, NV 89110
452-9555
15 video poker; 2 pool tables, dart boards

4424 Spring Mountain Rd.
Las Vegas, NV 89102
368-3744

1631 N. Rancho Dr.
Las Vegas, NV 89106
646-6657

3435 N. Nellis Blvd.
Las Vegas, NV 89110
644-6767

2875 S. Nellis Blvd.
Las Vegas, NV 89121
641-1750

8584 W. Lake Mead Blvd.
Las Vegas, NV 89134
228-0758

4604 W. Sahara Ave.
Las Vegas, NV 89102
258-0224

4825 W. Flamingo Rd.
Las Vegas, NV 89103
367-1606

739 S. Rainbow Blvd.
Las Vegas, NV 89128
878-3083

532 E. Sahara Ave.
Las Vegas, NV 89104
792-4121

3790 Cambridge St.
Las Vegas, NV 89109
792-4475

P.T.'s Slot Casino
46 S. Water St.
Henderson, NV 89015
564-4994
15 video poker machines, 2 pool tables, dart boards

Paddy's Pub & Eatery
4160 S. Pecos Rd.
Las Vegas, NV 89104
435-1684
Bar top video poker, Guinness on tap, New Castle brown Ale, Irish pub
Food: 11 am - 10 pm

The Pat Hand Lounge
6250 Mountain Vista St.
Henderson, NV 89014
435-7414

Bar top video machines; 2 pool tables; darts; neighborhood bar
Food: 24 hours, appetizers

Patrick's Restaurant & Lounge
6142 W. Flamingo Rd.
Las Vegas, NV 89103
871-9378
Video poker, big screen TV
Food: 7 pm - 11 pm; separate dining area; filet mignon, tiger shrimp, burger & fries; MC, Visa, AMX

Pecos Saloon
3704 E. Owens Ave.
Las Vegas, NV 89110
399-4722
Video poker
Entertainment: Country western bar; Karaoke once a month
Food: 11 am - 9 pm; burgers, wings & dinner

The Original Pepe Muldoon's
4341 N. Rancho Dr.
Las Vegas, NV 89130
655-7373
Bar top video poker; electronic dart board; Happy hour Mon. - Fri. 4 pm - 6 pm with free buffet; Irish & Mexican pub

Peppermill Lounge
2985 Las Vegas Blvd. S.
Las Vegas, NV 89109
735-7635
Plush couches arranged with large trees between create an intimate atmosphere; during the cooler months relax by the large circular fireplace; soft contemporary music plays in the background; large menu of specialty and exotic drinks; video poker
Food: Appetizers; adjacent 24-hour coffee shop *(see Restaurants)*; all major credit cards

Pepper's Lounge
2929 E. Desert Inn Rd.
Las Vegas, NV 89121
731-3234
Video poker; mature white collar crowd
Food: Appetizers & dinners

Pete's Place
3095 E. Fremont St.
Las Vegas, NV 89104
457-7400
Bar top video poker; payroll checks cashed; neighborhood bar
Food: 24 hours; sirloin tips, surf & turf, New York steak, also daily specials & graveyard specials

Philly Pub
2202 W. Charleston Blvd.
Las Vegas, NV 89102
384-8836
Video poker; darts, pool table; sports bar
Food: 11 am - 10 pm, lunch specials $3.50

Pink E's Fun Food & Spirits
3695 W. Flamingo Rd.
Las Vegas, NV 89103
252-4666
55 pool tables, video poker, shuffleboard, pingpong & darts; Happy hour 4 pm - 7 pm, ladies night Thu.
Food: 24 hours
Entertainment: Live bands, DJs & comedians

BARS & COCKTAIL LOUNGES

Planet Hollywood
Forum Shops
3500 Las Vegas Blvd. S.
Las Vegas, NV 89109
791-7827
Seats approximately 550 people.
Food: Unusual pastas, exotic salads, vegetable burgers, gourmet pizzas, meats and fish

Players Lounge
3514 Cambridge St.
Las Vegas, NV 89109
735-8595
Video poker; 2 pool tables; darts; neighborhood bar
Food: 24 hours; pizza, ribs & hamburgers

Pogo's Lounge
2103 N. Decatur Blvd.
Las Vegas, NV 89108
646-9735
Video poker; pool table
Entertainment: Fri. jazz 9:30 pm - 2 am
Food: 9 pm - 1 am

The Point After Lounge
925 N. Pecos Rd.
Las Vegas, NV 89101
399-3309
Video poker; 5 pool tables, 2 foosball tables, darts; sports bar; paychecks cashed; Happy hour 3 pm - 6 pm
Food: Fri. - Sat. 8 am - 2 am; .15¢ chicken wings
Entertainment: Wed. karaoke 9 pm - 1 am

19th Floor Lounge
Polo Towers
3745 Las Vegas Blvd. S.
Las Vegas, NV 89109
261-1000
Video poker; spectacular view of Las Vegas from the 19th floor. Dance to live music nightly 9 pm - 2 or 3 am

Pooh Bear Lounge
3508 E. Lake Mead Blvd.
N. Las Vegas, NV 89030
642-5170
Video poker, 3 pool tables & juke box
Food: 24 hours; appetizers

Porky's Bar and Grill
6138 W. Charleston Blvd.
Las Vegas, NV 89102
258-6344
Video poker; 2 pool tables, electronic darts, neighborhood bar
Food: Bar food
Entertainment: Live music Wed. 5 pm - 9 pm

Popo's Saloon & Casino
2501 E. Lake Mead Blvd.
N. Las Vegas, NV 89030
649-8022
41 video poker; pool table, darts, horseshoes; very clean neighborhood bar, slogan is "A friendly and comfortable place to play"
Food: 24 hour, bar food

Pub Bar & Liquors
1000 S. Torrey Pines Dr.
Las Vegas, NV 89107
870-9915
Video poker and keno machines; darts, pool table, 2 juke boxes; older crowd in daytime & younger rock crowd at night

Pug's Pub
5006 S. Maryland Pkwy.
Las Vegas, NV 89119
795-7847
Video poker; 8 TVs, juke box; Happy hour Mon. - Fri.
Food: 4 pm - 7 pm, specials
Entertainment: Karaoke Fri. & Sat.

Quenchers Lounge
3430 E. Tropicana Ave.
Las Vegas, NV 89121
454-7770
15 video poker; 2 pool tables, darts
Food: 8 am - 10 pm, bar food

R Bar
6000 W. Charleston Blvd.
Las Vegas, NV 89102
259-0120
Video poker & keno, shuffleboard, big screen TV
Food: 24 hours; separate dining area; breakfast specials served 2 am - 10 am; full rack of baby back ribs $9.25

Ram's Head Lounge
2207 Las Vegas Blvd. S.
Las Vegas, NV 89104
734-1026
Bar top video poker; neighborhood bar

Randy Kiefer's
Play It Again Sam
4120 Spring Mountain Rd.
Las Vegas, NV 89102
876-1550
Bar top video poker; Humphrey Bogart *Casablanca* decor throughout the restaurant and piano bar. Clientele is the suit crowd; Happy hour Mon. - Fri. 3 pm - 7 pm
Entertainment: live piano & jazz music 7 days 9 pm - 3 am; small dance floor
Food: Adjacent restaurant; all major credit cards.

Rascal's Lounge
860 E. Twain Ave.
Las Vegas, NV 89121
791-0670
Bar top video poker, 3 pool tables, darts, pinball machine
Food: Traditional bar menu; daily specials

Red Dawg Saloon
3650 Las Vegas Blvd. N.
Las Vegas, NV 89115
643-7740
Video poker, pool table, country western
Food: 2 pm - 10 pm dinner special

Red Rock Inn
5350 W. Charleston Blvd.
Las Vegas, NV 89102
870-2604
Video poker, pool tables, neighborhood bar located in old house
Food: Chicken wings, fries, finger foods

Renata's Lounge
4451 E. Sunset Rd.
Henderson, NV 89014
435-4000
Video poker & keno
Food: 24 hours, appetizers, burgers, sandwiches, steamers, pastas, steak & eggs served 11 pm - 6 am for $2.95; bacon and eggs $1.95; adjacent restaurant

Rice Paddy Bar
5183 W. Charleston Blvd.
Las Vegas, NV 89102
878-4781
Video poker; pool table
Food: Free hot dogs

Roadhouse Casino
2100 Boulder Hwy.
Henderson, NV 89015
564-1150
127 slots, low prices at bar; 59¢ drinks
Food: $.99 breakfast; blue plate specials, '50s style large dinner
Entertainment: Live music 7 days 3 pm - midnight

Road Runner Saloon
4425 E. Stewart Ave.
Las Vegas, NV 89110
438-3448
Mega video poker, nickel progressive, pool table, juke box
Food: Appetizers, burgers, sandwiches, breakfast, dinners

Road Runner Saloon
6910 E. Lake Mead Blvd.
Las Vegas, NV 89115
459-1889
Video machines & juke box
Food: 24 hours; full menu
Entertainment: Bands & karaoke occasionally

Ropers Sports Lounge
1987 N. Nellis Blvd.
Las Vegas, NV 89115
459-1333
Video poker; 2 pool tables, foosball, ping pong; sports bar
Food: Located next door to Santora's Pizza and Subs restaurant pass through window 11 am - 11 pm; MC & Visa

Rum Runner Lounge
1801 E. Tropicana Ave.
Las Vegas, NV 89109
736-6366
9 pool tables, foosball, poker machines
Food: Barbecue ribs and Mexican specialties, dinner specials from $3.95.

Runway 21
4955 E. Craig Rd.
Las Vegas, NV 89115
644-0923
Video poker, 4 pool tables, video games, darts, juke box, military crowd

Runway 25
6295 S Pecos Rd.
Las Vegas, NV 89120
436-7925
Airplane motif; replica of an airplane hangar with over 200 model airplanes on display, video poker
Food: Full service menu

Saddle 'N Spurs Saloon
2329 N. Jones Blvd.
Las Vegas, NV 89108
646-6292
Video poker & keno, pool table, darts, large screen TV, juke box
Entertainment: Live country music, Thu. 8 pm - midnight, Fri. & Sat. 9 pm - 2 am
Food: 3 pm - 11 pm bar food

Sagebrush Saloon
2162 N. Lamb Blvd.
Las Vegas, NV 89110
452-7038
Video poker; pool table; neighborhood bar
Food: Noon - 10 pm; appetizers
Entertainment: Karaoke Fri. 9 pm - late

Sahara Avenue Saloon
3345 E. Sahara Ave.
Las Vegas, NV 89104
457-2020
50 progressive video poker & keno machines; video poker bar
Food: Separate restaurant with full menu

Sammy O'Brien's
4435 Las Vegas Blvd. N.
Las Vegas, NV 89115
644-3254
Video poker
Food: Served 6 am - 9 pm breakfast & Mexican specials Tue. & Thu., homemade soups, separate dining room

Sand Dollar Lounge
3355 Spring Mountain Rd.
Las Vegas, NV 89102
871-6651
Video poker, pool table, dart board, juke box, sponsors fund raisers & benefits
Food: Hot dogs
Entertainment: Blues Sun. - Thu. 10 pm - 2 am & Fri. - Sat. 9 pm - 5 am

Scoreboard Lounge
2400 S. Jones Blvd.
Las Vegas, NV 89102
368-2711
Bar top video poker; darts, video games; big screen TV; Happy hour 3 pm - 6 pm, $1.50 draft, $1.25 bottled beer
Food: Steak and ribs; separate dining room

Scotty's Lounge
2300 E. Desert Inn Rd.
Las Vegas, NV 89102
369-4225
Video poker; neighborhood bar
Food: 9 am - 12:30 am; steak & ribs; graveyard specials on finger food & drinks

Scoundrel's East Saloon
420 N. Nellis Blvd., Ste. 812
Las Vegas, NV 89110
452-9469
15 video poker machines; darts, shuffleboard; large screen TV
Food: 8 am - midnight
Entertainment: Live music Thu. - Sun. 8 pm - 1 am. "A nice place, not just a bar"

Scoundrel's Pub
4360 S. Decatur Blvd.
Las Vegas, NV 89103
871-4390
Progressive video poker; 2 pool tables; pool & dart leagues
Food: 24 hours; bar food; dinner 4 pm - midnight; Tue. 4 pm - midnight tacos special $.75; Wed. chicken wings 12 for $1.50 on graveyard, $2.00 special 24 hours 4 oz. top sirloin steak sandwich with fries; $2.25 for 2 Scoundrel Mcmuffins

Scoundrel's Pub II
4850 Camino Al Norte Dr.
N. Las Vegas, NV 89030
642-8014

Screw Balls
2460 W. Warm Springs Rd.
Las Vegas, NV 89119
361-4488
Video poker; darts, pool, pinball; Neighborhood bar, sports oriented sponsors softball teams
Food: 24 hours; Italian cuisine

Serene Room Lounge
(Additional locations listed below)
3661 S. Maryland Pkwy.
Las Vegas, NV 89109
735-6454
Progressive video poker; darts; Happy hour Mon. - Sat. 2 pm - 6 pm & all day Sun.
Food: 11 am - 2 am; traditional bar food menu along with Italian specialties

Serene II
545 E. Sahara Ave.
Las Vegas, NV 89104
892-9600

Serene 3 Lounge
3441 W. Charleston Blvd.
Las Vegas, NV 89102
876-9670

Serene 5 Lounge
2354 E. Bonanza Rd.
Las Vegas, NV 89101
386-9698

Serene West Lounge
5740 W. Charleston Blvd.
Las Vegas, NV 89102
878-7063

7-11 Bar
2520 S. Arville Street
Las Vegas, NV 89102
362-2415
Video poker; sports bar
Food: noon - 9 pm, appetizers, sandwiches, burgers, chili

Shanty Bar & Grill
1817 N. Boulder Hwy.
Henderson, NV 89015
565-1146
Video poker, 2 pool tables, neighborhood bar
Food: Fri. 10 am - 8 pm; Sat. 10 am - 9 pm; $1.00 area delivery; daily specials; chicken, fish, & ham

Shifty's Cocktail Lounge
3805 W. Sahara Ave.
Las Vegas, NV 89102
871-4952
Video poker; darts, pool table
Entertainment: Live music on Fri. & Sat. beginning at 10 pm
Food: 24 hours, bar food, best tacos in town, daily specials

Silver Saddle Saloon
2501 E. Charleston Blvd.
Las Vegas, NV 89104
382-6921
Video poker & 2 live blackjack tables; honky tonk setting
Entertainment: 7 days, Fri. 9 pm - 1 am; Sat. 9 am - 4 am; Country music with large dance floor
Food: 6 am - 2 am; lunch and dinner specials

Six & Eights Cocktail Lounge
2973 Industrial Rd.
Las Vegas, NV 89109
731-1328
Mega video poker; 2 pool tables; Friendly atmosphere
Food: Sandwiches

Skinny Dugan's Pub
4127 W. Charleston Blvd.
Las Vegas, NV 89102
877-0522
Video poker
Entertainment: DJ on Fri. & Sat., Cribbage night on Wed. 7 pm
Food: 24 hours

Sly Fox Lounge
3266 Las Vegas Blvd. N.
Las Vegas, NV 89115
643-8096
Video poker; 2 pool tables, 9 ball pool league; $1.00 draft beer and $1.25 well drinks, juke box, neighborhood bar
Food: 1/4 pound hamburgers $2.75, 1/2 pound hamburger $3.75

Smoke Ranch Junction
2425 N. Rainbow Blvd.
Las Vegas, NV 89108
656-1888
Video poker
Food: 24 hours

Smuggle Inn
1305 Vegas Valley Dr.
Las Vegas, NV 89109
731-1305
Video poker; neighborhood bar
Food: 11 am - midnight, bar food

Snafu Bar & Grill
4090 Las Vegas Blvd. N.
Las Vegas, NV 89115
644-2401
Video poker; juke box; Happy hour daily 3 pm - 6 pm, domestic beer $1.50
Food: 3 pm - 9 pm
Entertainment: Live entertainment Fri. & Sat. 8 pm - midnight

Sneakers
2250 E. Tropicana Ave.
Las Vegas, NV 89119
798-0272
Fruit margaritas; sports singles bar catering to white collar & college crowd; large screen TV, 10 TVs throughout broadcasting sporting events; MC, Visa, AMX
Food: Dining room serving gourmet burgers, sandwiches, salads, tacos, chili, appetizers, desserts

Sonny's Saloon & Casino
3449 Industrial Rd.
Las Vegas, NV 89109
731-5553
Video poker
Food: adjacent Diamond Chinese Restaurant

Spanky's Pub
6720 W. Cheyenne Ave.
Las Vegas, NV 89108
645-5524
Bar top video poker, 2 pool tables, pool league, darts, dart leagues
Food: 24 hours; dinners 5 pm - 11 pm; Prime rib, London broil; separate dining room; all major credit cards
Entertainment: Live band Fri. - Sat. 9 pm - 2 am

Sporting Chance Saloon
2808 N. Craig Rd.
N. Las Vegas, NV 89030
631-4099
Video poker, pool table, electronic darts, golf machine
Food: 24 hours

Sportsman's Lounge
5660 Boulder Hwy.
Las Vegas, NV 89122
458-7071
Video poker, 4 pool tables, CD juke box
Food: 24 hours; separate dining room, bar food

Stadium Saloon
6016 Boulder Hwy.
Las Vegas, NV 89122
433-8550
Video poker, 2 pool tables, juke box, large screen TV, well drinks & domestic beers $1.25 no drink over $2.00

Stagecoach Saloon
1200 Nevada Hwy.
Boulder City, NV 89005
293-0926
Pool table, golf machine, bowling machine, shuffleboard, juke box; Country western crowd
Food: Bar food

Stage Door Casino
4000 Audrie St.
Las Vegas, NV 89109
733-0124
Video poker; neighborhood & tourist bar that also contains a souvenir shop and liquor store
Food: hot dogs & shrimp cocktail

The Stake Out Bar & Grill
4800 S. Maryland Pkwy.
Las Vegas, NV 89119
798-8383
Video poker; 2 pool tables in the loft, happy hour 3 pm - 7 pm; free hors d'oeuvres on Fri. 4 pm - 6 pm
Food: Appetizers, burgers, chicken, subs, Philly cheese steak sandwiches, sandwiches, daily specials

Star Golf Lounge
3000 Meade Ave.
Las Vegas, NV 89102
247-4653
Target golf range; pool, darts, Washington Redskins bar
Entertainment: Wed. 5 pm - 9 pm, Karaoke Fri. - Sat. 5 pm - late

Stateside Lounge
931 Las Vegas Blvd. N.
Las Vegas, NV 89101
382-2337
2 pool tables, horseshoes & video machines
Food: 24 hours; full menu

The Still
9495 Las Vegas Blvd. S.
Las Vegas, NV 89123
361-7012
Video poker, 2 pool tables, shuffleboard, large backwoods theme bar with tin roof; separate banquet room
Food: Separate dining area. Home of the "Jiant" Jethroburger which weighs over two pounds $8.00 - $10.25; appetizers, sandwiches. Breakfast 7 am - 11 am also pinto beans and corn bread

Strike Zone
3726 E. Flamingo Rd.
Las Vegas, NV 89121
456-4800
Video poker, foosball, 1 pool table, video magic machine, darts. Happy hour 3 pm - 6 pm
Food: Snack food

Sugar Bears
4015 N. Nellis Blvd.
Las Vegas, NV 89115
644-1933
Video poker; pool table
Food: 5 am - midnight, breakfast, burgers, chicken

Sugar Daddy's
4020 Boulder Hwy.
Las Vegas, NV 89121
457-7520
Video poker, pool table, juke box, darts, older rock 'n roll crowd
Food: Sandwiches & pizza

Sum Place Else
3355 S. Procyon Ave.
Las Vegas, NV 89102
876-3399
Hours: 7 am - midnight
Video poker; pool table; blue collar bar
Food: 9 am - 3 pm; Sat. 9 am - noon; breakfast & lunch specials

Sundance Kid Cafe
4325 W. Craig Rd.
N. Las Vegas, NV 89030
655-4501
Video poker, satellite TV; train runs around the bar
Food: 11 am - 11 pm; full menu, graveyard special
Entertainment: Occasional, call ahead

Sunrise Casablanca
6320 E. Charleston Blvd.
Las Vegas, NV 89122
452-8080
Gamemaker machines; pool table, dart boards; great view of the city; Happy hour Mon. - Fri. 3 pm - 7 pm
Graveyard special: Domestic beer .75¢ with free pool, daily 2 am - 5 am
Food: Deli

Sunrise Cedar Bar
1602 N. Nellis Blvd.
Las Vegas, NV 89115
453-6496
Video poker; country western bar
Food: 24 hours

Sunrise Liquors
2601 E. Charleston Blvd.
Las Vegas, NV 89104
382-0282
Video poker; pool table, neighborhood bar. Barbecue every month and party the last Fri. or Sat. of each month 4 pm - 11 pm

ENTERTAINMENT

BARS & COCKTAIL LOUNGES

Sunrise Lounge & Restaurant
6055 E. Lake Mead Blvd.
Las Vegas, NV 89115
438-6944
Video poker, 2 pool tables, giant screen TV
Food: 6 am - 9 pm; breakfast special $2.19, separate dining room

Swizzle Stick Lounge
2740 N. Green Valley Pkwy.
Henderson, NV 89014
456-0010
Video poker
Food: 8 am - midnight; separate dining area, appetizers, breakfast, sandwiches; daily specials

T-Bird Restaurant & Lounge
3330 E. Tropicana Ave.
Las Vegas, NV 89121
458-4567
Bar top video poker; 2 pool tables. Large white collar bar with separate dining area
Food: 24 hours, Sicilian pizza, sandwiches, burgers, appetizers and dinners. Breakfast specials midnight - 11 am; 1/2 lb. burger and fries $3.25

T. G. I. Friday's
1800 E. Flamingo Rd.
Las Vegas, NV 89109
732-9905
Hours: Sun. - Thu. 11 am - midnight; Fri. - Sat. 11 am - 1 am
No gaming; QVC machines; 6 TV monitors; white collar singles bar, especially on Fri. evenings; Happy hour daily 4 pm - 7 pm & 10 pm - midnight with $1.99 hors d'oeuvres
Food: Appetizers & full menu
(Also see American Restaurants)

The Tap House
5589 W. Charleston Blvd.
Las Vegas, NV 89102
870-2111
Progressive video poker, big screen TV, shuffleboard; Cleveland Indians bar; Happy hour 4 pm - 6 pm
Entertainment: Live music Fri. & Sat. 9 pm - 2 am, oldies music
Food: Hickory smoked ribs & chicken, deep dish pizza, chicken wings, breakfast specials; private banquet room; MC, Visa, Discover, AMX.

Tequila Red's
1590 E. Flamingo Rd.
Las Vegas, NV 89119
735-4142
Bar top video poker, 3 dart boards, tournaments, 2 pool tables
Food: 11:30 am - 2 am, burgers, Mexican specialties, entrees, daily specials.
Entertainment: Thu. - Mon. Karaoke 9:30 pm - late

Terry's Villa
1203 E. Charleston Blvd.
Las Vegas, NV 89104
384-6963
Video poker; pool table
Entertainment: Sat. karaoke 8 pm
Food: Bar menu

Thirstbusters Lounge
697 N. Valle Verde Dr.
Henderson, NV 89014
454-9200
Video poker, video games, big screen TV; over 120 beers from all over the world with eight on draft
Food: 24 hours; separate dining room; breakfast, burgers, sandwiches, salads, appetizers, dinner entrees.

Thumpers
3870 E. Flamingo Rd.
Las Vegas, NV 89121
435-4557
Video poker
Food: 24 hours; dinners 5 pm - 11 pm; full menu; separate dining area; Visa, AMX

Time In Lounge
6120 W. Tropicana Ave.
Las Vegas, NV 89103
367-3644
Bar top video poker; 2 pool tables, dart boards
Food: 8 am - midnight; separate dining area; full menu; delivery service

Tom and Jerry's
Grub and Steak Pub
4550 S. Maryland Pkwy.
Las Vegas, NV 89119
736-8550
Sports bar; Tue. & Fri. $1.00 drinks, Wed. $1.50 pitchers; Thu. - Sat. Ladies night 10 pm - 2 am (ladies drink free)
Food: Window to Mexican restaurant
Entertainment: Tue. & Sat. 10 pm - 2 am live entertainment, Wed. & Fri. DJ

Tommy Rocker's Pub & Cafe
4275 S. Industrial Rd.
Las Vegas, NV 89103
261-6688
Bar top video poker
Food: Separate restaurant area, patio, full menu; Beach bar concept with open air deck; MC, Visa, AMX
Entertainment: Live entertainment 10 pm - 2 am Fri. & Sat.

Tony B's Bar & Lounge
5890 Boulder Hwy.
Las Vegas, NV 89122
451-8524
Video poker, pool table; Happy hour Mon. - Fri. 4 pm - 6 pm;
Entertainment: Live entertainment on special occasions

Torrey Pines Pub
6374 W. Lake Mead Blvd.
Las Vegas, NV 89108
648-7775
Bar top video poker, 2 pool tables, golf game, big screen TV; New York Giants; home of the 25 ounce mug
Food: 6:30 am - 1 am, until 2 am on Fri. & Sat.; breakfast, burgers, dinner entrees; 16 oz. charbroiled Porterhouse, $8.25; separate dining room

The Trap House
6131 Clarice Ave.
Las Vegas, NV 89107
878-4272

Video poker, 2 pool tables, electronic dart board, juke box, 35" TV screen; '49ers bar
Food: Free hot dogs & chili dogs, nachos on weekends

Trisha's Lounge
4900 E. Tropicana Ave.
Las Vegas, NV 89121
454-0100
Bar top video poker, 2 pool tables, darts, tournaments, CD juke box & TV monitors, neighborhood bar
Food: 8 am - 11 pm; chicken fried steak, beef tips, roast beef
Entertainment: Sat. karaoke 9 pm - 1 am

The Triple Play
1875 S. Decatur Blvd.
Las Vegas, NV 89102
364-0808
35 video poker & keno, satellite TV; sports bar
Food: 24 hours; famous Philly sandwiches beef or chicken; MC, Visa, AMX, Discover

Turf Lounge
Jockey Club
3700 Las Vegas Blvd. S.
Las Vegas, NV 89109
736-3899
Video poker
Entertainment: Live entertainment Tue. & Fri. 10 pm - 2 am
Food: Breakfast only 8 am - noon

Twin Lakes Liquor
1032 N. Rancho Dr.
Las Vegas, NV 89106
648-8121
Video poker machines, 1 pool table
Entertainment: DJ Thu. 9 pm - 2 am

Ukulele Lounge
620 Las Vegas Blvd. N.
Las Vegas, NV 89101
382-7364
25 poker machines, juke box, pool table
Food: 10 am - 8 pm; specials

USA Cafe
2855 Green Valley Pkwy
Henderson, NV 89014
436-4386
Video poker; pool table
Entertainment: Live entertainment, Thu. & Sun. 9:30 pm - 2 am
Food: 10 am - 11 pm extensive menu, daily specials; 2 for 1 lunch Mon. - Fri.

The Villager Lounge
886 S. Boulder Hwy.
Henderson, NV 89015
565-0466
Video poker, 2 pool tables, darts; juke box; neighborhood bar
Food: 10 am - 9 pm, finger food

The Waterhole
4740 S. Arville St.
Las Vegas, NV 89103
876-5520
Video poker, foosball, darts
Food: 24 hours; mooseburger $2.99; 16 drafts, complete menu

Westcliff Station
7614 Westcliff Dr.
Las Vegas, NV 89128
255-1627
Video poker, 2 pool tables, 2 dart boards, sports bar, large screen TV, 26 TV monitors, sofa area; Los Angeles Raiders bar
Food: Separate dining area, dinner specials 5 pm - 10 pm; MC, Visa

Whiskey Creek
4741 E. Charleston Blvd.
Las Vegas, NV 89104
431-8805

Whiskey Creek Saloon II
9151 Las Vegas Blvd. S.
Las Vegas, NV 89123
798-3039
Video poker; pool table; slots tournament 8 pm on varying nights
Food: Free food Wed. & Sat. 6 pm
Entertainment: Occasionally

Winchester Cap
2327 S. Eastern Ave.
Las Vegas, NV 89104
641-7673
Video poker
Food: 24 hours; pizza, steaks, sandwiches, salads, Oriental & Mexican
Entertainment: Fri. & Sat. 9 pm - 11 pm

Windy City Pub
3050 E. Desert Inn Rd., Ste. 130
Las Vegas, NV 89121
732-7373
Sports bar with video poker, pool & dart tournaments; Happy hour 3 pm - 7 pm & 3 am - 7 am
Food: Noon - midnight; full menu

Winn-Dee Bar
2440 Las Vegas Blvd. N.
N. Las Vegas, NV 89030
649-9469
Video poker, pool tables, pinball, bowling machines & trivia machine.
Entertainment: Fri. & Sat. 9 pm - 3 am; Sun. 7 pm - 11 pm; live band plays country, rock and blues
Food: 24 hours, bar food menu

Wooly Bully's Food & Spirits
6020 W. Flamingo Rd.
Las Vegas, NV 89103
362-2116
Bar top video poker; pool table
Food: 24 hours; appetizers, burgers, sandwiches, salads, tacos; children's menu; separate room for private parties

Z Sports Bar
5285 Industrial Rd.
Las Vegas, NV 89118
798-6262
Bar top video poker; Happy hour daily specials, large, bright, open bar with high ceilings and loft
Food: Bar food; MC, Visa, AMX

GAY BARS

Angles Lounge
4633 Paradise Rd.
Las Vegas, NV 89109
791-0100
24 hours, cruise bar, video poker; other fun & games; pool tables; Happy hour Mon. - Fri. 5 pm - 7 pm, dance floor
Atmosphere: Cruise bar

Back Door Lounge
1415 E. Charleston Blvd.
Las Vegas, NV 89104
385-2018
Bar hours: 24 hours; other fun & games, foosball
Atmosphere: older gay men, casual gay bar

Backstreet Bar & Grill
5012 S. Arville St.
Las Vegas, NV 89109
876-1844
24 hours, slots; other fun & games, pool table; large dance floor, Rustler hour noon - 2 pm, 5 pm - 7 pm, 3 am - 5 am
Atmosphere: Country bar

The Buffalo
4640 Paradise Rd.
Las Vegas, NV 89109
733-8355
24 hours; Happy hour noon - 2 pm, 5 pm - 7 pm; slots
Atmosphere: Standard Levis gay bar

Choices
1729 E. Charleston Blvd.
Las Vegas, NV 89104
382-4791
24 hours; Video poker; other fun & games; pool tables; Happy hour 2 pm - 6 pm drinks $2.25
Specials: Sun. all you can drink $5.00 (beer), midnight - 3 am
Atmosphere: Cruise bar

Flex
4371 W. Charleston Blvd.
Las Vegas, NV 89102
385 - FLEX (3539)
Video bar poker; pool tables
Food: Full menu 24 hours; bar & gourmet food
Entertainment: Up-scale dance club; DJ Fri., Sat., Tue. & Thu. 10 pm - 6 am; Sun. 4 pm - midnight.

The Gipsy
4605 Paradise Rd.
Las Vegas, NV 89119
731-1919
Video poker; state of the art lighting sound & video
Hours: Tue. - Sun. 10 pm - 5 am or 6 am
Entertainment: Tue. - amateur strip show; Wed. - Queens on Paradise; Thu. - Gong Show; Sat. - Dance & song show

Goodtimes Bar & Grill
1775 E. Tropicana Ave.
Las Vegas, NV 89119
736-9494
24 hours; video poker, pool tables
Happy hour daily 5 pm - 7 pm; Mon. liquor bust midnight - 3 am $5.00 for unlimited well drinks & draft
Entertainment: Big screen TV; Disco open Sat. & Mon. 10 pm - 4 am with DJ Ken

Lace for Women
4633 Paradise Rd.
Las Vegas, NV 89109
791-1947
Video poker, pinball
Hours: Sun. - Thu. 10 pm - 3 am; Fri. - Sat. 10 pm - 5 am
Entertainment: Disco open Fri. & Sat. 10 pm - 5 am; special shows; Happy hour 6 pm - 8 pm
Atmosphere: Primarily women's bar, outdoor patio.

Las Vegas Eagle
3430 E. Tropicana Ave.
Las Vegas, NV 89121
458-8662
24 hours; video poker, tournament on Wed., slots; other fun & games; pool tables;

Happy hour 10 am - 2 pm, 5 pm - 7 pm; Liquor bust Tue. & Sat. 9 pm - 1 am; Wed. & Fri. underwear party 10 pm - 3 am; Live DJ Wed., Fri. & Sat. 10 pm - 4 am; Slot tournament Thu. with free well drinks and draft beer 8 pm
Atmosphere: Leather Levi bar

Snick's Place
1402 S. Third St.
Las Vegas, NV 89104
385-9298
24 hours; video poker
Food: Pizzas, chips, snacks
Atmosphere: Friendly neighborhood bar; oldest gay bar in town.

Tropical Island
3430 E. Tropicana Ave.
Las Vegas, NV 89121
456-5525
Hours: 6 pm - late
Video poker, pool table, darts; other fun & games; call for details; free slots tournament Sat. from 9 pm; Located next to Eagle, available for private parties.

TOPLESS BARS

Can-Can Room
3155 Industrial Rd.
Las Vegas, NV 89109
737-1161
Hours: 7 pm - 5 am
Cover: $10 cover, one drink $10 minimum.
Entertainment: Continuous 3 pm - 5 am
Atmosphere: Totally nude, no alcohol served.
Credit cards: All major

Centerfold Lounge
1024 N. Boulder Hwy.
Henderson, NV 89015
564-7865
Hours: Noon - 6 am
Cover: None
Entertainment: 1 pm - 4 am continuous
Drinks: Begin at $3.25
Atmosphere: Friendly local bar

Cheetah's Topless Lounge
2112 Western Ave.
Las Vegas, NV 89102
384-0074
Hours: 24 hours
Cover: $5.00 cover buys membership card for free return visits.
Drinks: Prices start at $3.75
Atmosphere: Plush high energy club which features eight girls dancing on the main stage as well as several girls dancing on the side stages.
Credit cards: All major

Club Paradise
4416 Paradise Rd.
Las Vegas, NV 89109
734-7990
Hours: Mon. - Fri. 4 pm - 6 am, Sat. & Sun. 6 am - 6 am; Happy hour Mon. - Fri. 4 pm - 7 pm; five stages; tableside dancing
Cover: $10
Choreographed fantasy shows; house masseuse offers neck rubs at your table.

Crazy Horse Saloon No. 1
4034 Paradise Rd.
Las Vegas, NV 89109
732-1116
Hours: 24 hours

Cover: 7 pm - 3 am, $5 charge includes membership card for free return visits; no cover during day.
Entertainment: Continuous 24 hours, over 100 girls each day, private dances for customers
Drinks: Prices start at $3.75

Crazy Horse II Gentlemen's Club
2476 Industrial Rd.
Las Vegas, NV 89102
382-8003
Hours: 24 hours
Cover: 7 pm - 4 am, $10 cover includes membership card for free return visits.
Entertainment: 24 hours daily
Drinks: Prices start at $4.25
Atmosphere: Three large stages; largest number of girls in topless bars with as many as 300 on hand each day; pool tables; free hotel shuttle
Credit cards: All major

Girls of Glitter Gulch Gentlemen's Club
20-22 Fremont St.
Las Vegas, NV 89101
385-4774
Hours: Sun. - Thu. noon - 4 am; Fri. & Sat. noon - 6 am
Cover: No cover
Entertainment: Continuous noon - 4 am
Drinks: Start at $5.75
Atmosphere: Four stages, center bar, VIP area; Happy hour 4 pm - 7 pm; DJ, state of the art lighting and sound.

Larry's Villa
2401 W. Bonanza Rd.
Las Vegas, NV 89106
647-2713
Hours: 24 hours
Cover: None
Drinks: Begin at $2.00
Fun: Video poker
Entertainment: Dancers noon - 4 am
Food: Snacks
Atmosphere: Girls accept money in garter only, no table dancing.

Little Darlings
1514 Western Ave.
Las Vegas, NV 89102
366-8514
Hours: Mon. - Sat. 11 am - 6 am, Sun. 6 pm - 4 am
Cover: Nonresidents $20, Nevada residents $10
Drinks: Non-alcoholic, all are free
Entertainment: Main & VIP stage with 100 girls daily and DJ
Atmosphere: Theme rooms, fantasy booths, private dancers - all nude.

Olympic Garden
1531 Las Vegas Blvd. S.
Las Vegas, NV 89104
385-9361
Hours: 2 pm - 6 am
Cover: No cover before 6 pm; $5.00 cover from 6 pm - 6 am
Drinks: Prices begin at $4.00
Entertainment: 2 pm - 6 am; Happy hour: Tue. - Sat. 2 pm - 8 pm
Atmosphere: Seven stages in a plush setting, VIP room; over 80 dream girls; Beer & Bad Boys "The All American Dream Team Male Review!"
Credit cards: All major

Palomino Club
1848 Las Vegas Blvd. N.
N. Las Vegas, NV 89030
642-2984
Hours: 2 pm - 4 am
Cover: $10.00 cover plus a two drink minimum ($12.00)
Atmosphere: Located in North Las Vegas for over 20 years, the Palomino can offer both alcohol & total nudity; private room for bachelor parties.

Satin Saddle Club
1818 Las Vegas Blvd. N.
N. Las Vegas, NV 89030
649-3590
Hours: 5 pm - 3 am
Drinks: Prices begin at $3.00

Showgirls
3247 Industrial Rd.
Las Vegas, NV 89109
894-4167
Hours: Mon. - Sat. 11 am - 4 am
Cover: $20.00
Entertainment: Fully nude continuous shows on the main stage

Tally - Ho
2580 S. Highland Dr.
Las Vegas, NV 89109
792-9330
Hours: 24 hours
Cover: $10 with one drink minimum
Entertainment: Stylish nude entertainment in a very unique gentlemen's tavern; lunch served.

Tender Trap
311 E. Flamingo Rd.
Las Vegas, NV 89109
732-1111
Hours: 4 pm - 5 am
Cover: None
Entertainment: 3 pm - 5 am
Drinks: Prices begin at $3.25
Fun: Video poker; Happy hour 3 pm - 6 pm
Atmosphere: Small, intimate, friendly club, continuous show.
Credit cards: All major

What's Up
1101 N. Boulder Hwy.
Henderson, NV 89015
565-3346
Hours: 1 pm - 5 am
Cover: None
Entertainment: 1 pm - 5 am
Drinks: Prices begin at $2.75

Wild J's Gentlemen's Club
2923 S. Industrial Rd.
Las Vegas, NV 89109
892-0416
Hours: Mon. - Sat. noon - 4 am; Sun. 6 pm - 2 am
Cover: Before 6 pm $5 , after 6 pm $10
Drinks: Non-alcoholic, juice bar
Atmosphere: One center stage with three special shows a night. Stars are from porno industry.

ENTERTAINMENT

MOVIE THEATRES

Boulder Station Cinemas
Boulder Station
4111 Boulder Hwy.
Las Vegas, NV 89121
221-ACT3

ACT III Theatres
11-Theater complex features THX sound.
Admission: $6.50 adults; children under 12 and senior citizens $3.75; matinees $3.75 for all seats on movies starting before 6 pm; Late night shows Fri. & Sat.

Boulder Theatre
1225 Arizona St.
Boulder City, NV 89005
293-3145

Features first run movies. The Boulder Theatre is registered as a National Historical Landmark. The theater opened May 14, 1932 with the movie "It's Tough to be Famous" starring Douglas Fairbanks, Jr.

Century Desert 16
2606 S. Lamb Blvd.
Las Vegas, NV 89121
641-2500

Syufy Enterprises
First run movies, handicapped accessibility.

Cinedome 12
3200 S. Decatur Blvd.
(at Desert Inn Rd.)
Las Vegas, NV 89102
362-2550
362-2133 (Recorded Message)
Admission: $6.75 adults; children 2 - 11 and seniors 65+ $4.00, matinees $4.00 for movies starting before 6 pm

Cinedome 12
851 S. Boulder Hwy.
Henderson, NV 89015
566-1570
457-3700 (Recorded Message)
Syufy Enterprises
Admission: General admission $6.75; children 2 - 11 and seniors 65+ $4.00. Bargain matinees weekdays before 5:45 pm; video arcade

The Vitagraph Theater was the first movie theater in Nevada. It opened in Reno in 1903.

Cinema 8
3025 E. Desert Inn Rd.
(at Pecos)
Las Vegas, NV 89121
734-2124
Stewart Blair
United Artist - second-run features.
Admission: $1.00 all shows all the time.

Gold Coast Twin
Gold Coast
4000 W. Flamingo Rd.
Las Vegas, NV 89103
367-7111 Ext. 671
Syufy Enterprises
First run movies.
Admission: Adults $6.75, children & seniors 65+ $4.00; Matinees $4.00 before 6 pm on weekdays.

Green Valley Cinemas
4500 E. Sunset Rd.
Henderson, NV 89014
458-2880
United Artists
8 screens; ADA accessibility, Assistel Listening Devices, THX sound system, DTS digital sound, cup holder armrests
Admission: $6.75 adults; $5.00 students; 12 & under and seniors $4.00; matinees before 6 pm $4.00

Magic Motion Machine
Excalibur Hotel
3850 Las Vegas Blvd. S.

Las Vegas, NV 89109
597-7777
Hours: Mon. - Fri. 10 am - 11:30 pm; Sat. - Sun. 9 am - 12:30 am
Admission: $3.00
Dynamic Motion Simulator - seats are hydraulically synchronized to the action you are watching on the screen. Six different features are presented in two separate theaters with features changing throughout the day. Rides last three minutes.

Mountain View Dollar Cinema
3400 S. Jones Blvd.
Las Vegas, NV 89102
889-6500
Second run features - three screens.
Admission: $1.00 all shows all the time

Omnimax
Caesars Palace
3570 Las Vegas Blvd. S.
Las Vegas, NV 89109
731-7900
Specially made films create an awesome visual display projected via 70 mm film, which is 10 times the frame size of ordinary 35 mm film. Complementing the visual projection is a sophisticated nine-channel "sensaround" sound system emanating from 10 speaker banks. A total of 89 speakers engulf the audience which is seated in 368 luxurious seats which recline 27 degrees.
Admission: Adults $7.00, children under 12, seniors 55+, students with ID, hotel guests and military personnel $5.00; Children under 4 free.

Show hours: Every hour on the hour; Sun. - Thu. 2 pm - 10 pm; Fri. & Sat. 11:40 am - 11 pm; box office opens 10 am - 10 pm; audio headsets available for the hearing impaired.

Planetarium
Community College of Southern NV
3200 E. Cheyenne Ave.
N. Las Vegas, NV 89030
651-5059 (Recorded message)
Show times: Public presentations are Wed. & Fri. at 6 pm & 7:30 pm and 5:30 pm & 7:30 pm Sat.
Interesting and educational movies with 360 degree screen viewing. The planetarium also offers telescope viewing after last performance, weather permitting. Many astronomical objects can be viewed depending on the time of year and visibility.
Admission: General admission $3.50; children under 12, seniors 65+, CCSN & UNLV students w/ID $2.25. Shows are usually presented on Fri. & Sat. Call for times and reservations.

Rainbow Promenade Theater
2321 N. Rainbow Blvd.
Las Vegas, NV 89128
225-4828
Admission: General admission $6.75 adults; $4.00 children 12 and under & seniors; matinees $4.00 for all shows before 6 pm; listening devices for the hearing impaired.

Rancho-Santa Fe Theater
5101 N. Rancho Dr.
Las Vegas, NV 89130
645-5518
Syufy Enterprises
16 screen motion picture theater; Assistel Listening Devices
Admission: Adults $6.75; Before 5:45 pm and on weekends before 2:00 pm $4.00, seniors and children $4.00

Redrock 11 Theaters
5201 W. Charleston Blvd.
Las Vegas, NV 89102
878-9255
870-1423 (Recorded message)
Syufy Enterprises

Admission: $6.75 adults; $4.00 children under 12; $4.00 seniors 65+; $4.00 matinees Mon. - Fri. before 5:45 pm and weekends & holidays before 2 pm

Showcase Cinemas
Showcase Mall
Las Vegas Blvd. S.
Las Vegas, NV 89109
225-4828
United Artists Theater
Admission: $6.75 adults; $4.00 children 12 and under and seniors; matinees $4.00 for all shows starting before 6 pm; listening devices for the hearing impaired.

Sunrise Dollar 751 Cinema
751 N. Nellis Blvd. (at Bonanza Rd.)
Las Vegas, NV 89110
438-5321 (Recorded message)
United Artist
Second-run movies on seven screens.
Admission: $1.00 all seats all the time

Sunset Station Cinemas
1301 W. Sunset Rd.
Henderson, NV 89014
221-2283
THX, Dolby Stereo Digital and Sony Dynamic Digital Sound
Admission: $6.50 adults; $3.75 children under 12 and seniors; matinees $3.75 for all shows before 6 pm; late night shows Fri. & Sat.

Texas 12 Cinemas
Texas
2101 Texas Star Ln.
Las Vegas, NV 89130
221-ACT3
ACT III Theaters
THX, Dolby Stereo Digital and Sony Dynamic Digital Sound
Admission: $6.50 adults; $3.75 children & seniors, all shows $3.75 before 6 pm & all Mon., late night shows Fri. & Sat.

Torrey Pines Discount Cinema
6344 W. Sahara (at Torrey Pines)
Las Vegas, NV 89102
876-4334
Fountain Cinemas
First-rate movies and some foreign and specialty films shown on four screens.
Admission: 99¢

The first feature film, made in 1913, was *Moving Pictures of Tonopah* made in Tonopah.

DRIVE-IN MOVIE THEATER

Vegas 4 Drive In Theatre
4158 W. Carey Ave.
Las Vegas, NV 89030
646-3565
Syufy Enterprises
First run, current releases & double features.
Admission: $5.50 adults; children under 12 free.
Hours: Sun. - Thu. 7 pm - 10 pm; Fri. - Sat. 6:30 pm - 10:30 pm; show starts after dusk.

INTERESTING FILM FACTS

132 Motion Pictures were filmed in Las Vegas and Surrounding Areas since 1932

1932 - Airmail	1981 - History of the World Part I	1993 - The Good Son
1933 - The White Sister	1981 - Thief	1994 - 8 Seconds
1936 - Boulder Dam	1982 - Megaforce	1994 - Roadflower
1937 - Slim	1982 - Things Are Tough All Over	1994 - Star Trek: Generations
1940 - One Million B.C.	1983 - Breathless	1995 - Casino
1941 - Fremont Street History	1984 - Cannonball Run 2	1995 - Destiny Turns on the Radio
1946 - Heldorado	1984 - Deadly Impact	1995 - Get Shorty
1946 - Lady Luck	1984 - Oh God, You Devil	1995 - Leaving Las Vegas
1947 - Bells of San Angelo	1984 - Oxford Blues	1995 - Showgirls
1948 - Hazard	1984 - Romancing the Stone	1995 - Texas Payback
1949 - The Lady Gambles	1984 - Starman	1996 - Bogus
1950 - 711 Ocean Drive	1985 - Beer	1996 - Eraser
1950 - Dark City	1985 - Fever	1996 - Father Hood
1952 - The Las Vegas Story	1985 - Lost in America	1996 - Feeling Minnesota
1955 - The Girl Rush	1985 - Prizzi's Honor	1996 - Mars Attacks
1956 - Crashing Las Vegas	1985 - Rocky 4	1996 - MTV
1956 - Hollywood or Bust	1986 - Black Moon Rising	1996 - Sgt. Bilko
1957 - Jet Pilot	1986 - Iron Eagle	1996 - That Thing You Do
1957 - The Amazing Colossal Man	1986 - Over the Top	1996 - The Great White Hype
1957 - The Joker Is Wild	1986 - Salvador	1997 - Arlete
1957 - Wild Is the Wind	1986 - The Hitcher	1997 - Austin Powers, Int'l Man of Mystery
1960 - Ocean's Eleven	1987 - Heat	1997 - Beavis & Butthead Do America
1964 - Dr. Strangelove	1988 - Aria	1997 - Con Air
1964 - Kiss Me Stupid	1988 - Cherry 200	1997 - Fear and Loathing in Las Vegas
1964 - Viva Las Vegas	1988 - Midnight Run	1997 - Fools Rush In
1966 - The Professionals	1988 - Nightbreaker	1997 - My Giant
1967 - Hombre	1988 - Picasso's Trigger	1997 - Perdita Durango
1968 - In Cold Blood	1988 - Rainman	1997 - Shut Up and Dance
1968 - Name of the Game	1988 - Rambo III	1997 - Top of the World
1968 - The Stalking Moon	1989 - Eddie & the Cruisers II	1997 - Vegas Vacation
1969 - Bob & Carol & Ted & Alice	1989 - Elvira Mistress of the Dark	1998 - Lethal Weapon IV
1969 - Hell's Angels	1989 - K-9	
1969 - Where It's At	1989 - Kill Me Again	
1970 - The Ballad of Cable Hogue	1989 - Tango & Cash	
1970 - The Only Game in Town	1990 - Guns	
1971 - Diamonds Are Forever	1990 - Solar Crisis	
1972 - The Godfather	1991 - Delusion	
1974 - Harry & Tonto	1991 - Harley Davidson & The Marlboro Man	
1974 - The Gambler	1991 - Hot Shots	
1975 - Bite the Bullet	1991 - Lionheart	
1977 - Grand Theft Auto	1991 - Payoff	
1977 - The Gauntlet	1992 - Best of the Best II	
1978 - Corvette Summer	1992 - Bugsy	
1978 - Superman	1992 - Cool World	
1979 - Electric Horseman	1992 - Honey, I Blew Up the Kid	
1979 - Going in Style	1992 - Pure Country	
1979 - Players	1992 - Reckless Kelly	
1980 - Melvin & Howard	1992 - This Is My Life	
	1992 - Universal Soldier	
	1993 - Another Stakeout	
	1993 - City Slickers II	
	1993 - Honeymoon in Vegas	
	1993 - I Love Trouble	
	1993 - Indecent Proposal	

ENTERTAINMENT

Live Singing, Live Dancing, Live Orchestra ...
...*Real Entertainment!*

T·D·C Entertainment Group, LLC
proudly presents

...*off B'way!*"
Las Vegas

Music Director / Arranger
Brian W. Tidwell

Musical Supervisor
Joe DeLuca

Vocal Coach
Joni Yeater

Associate Producers
Thomas Christensen
Daryl E. Deck

Artistic Director / Choreographer
Christopher Tompkins

Associate Choreographer
Arlene DeLuca

Hair & Make-up Designs
Paul Parnell

Costume Designs
Jeff Rowen

Graphic Design
Heather C. Peko

at the

Debbie Reynolds

HOTEL / CASINO / HOLLYWOOD MOVIE MUSEUM
305 Convention Center Drive • Las Vegas, NV 89109

RESERVATIONS
702-693-6309 OR 1-800-978-6309

    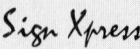   

Experience Las Vegas   *Visit our website at www.experiencelasvegas.com*

Gaming

Las Vegas, founded by Mormons, energized by the railroad and the construction of Hoover Dam, was built by gaming, which last year contributed over $7.6 billion to the state's economy. With 125,273 electronic gaming devices in operation in Clark County alone over the past year, more than $3.5 billion in revenue was generated between September 1996 and August 1997.

When admitted to the Union in 1864, gaming had already been a part of Nevada's lifestyle for years.

Gaming was illegal in Nevada for a brief period starting in 1861, and again in 1910, but in 1915 limited gaming was allowed by the legislature and in 1931 the legislature approved a bill allowing gaming much as it is today. So for approximately 120 years it has legally existed and flourished in Nevada.

During the early years of Las Vegas, gaming took place in small bars and casinos downtown. In 1941, a giant step was taken when the El Rancho Vegas opened on Las Vegas Blvd. S. at Sahara Ave. It was the first resort on the soon-to-be famous Las Vegas Strip.

Casino gaming did not become a major industry until after World War II, when it flourished in response to increasing social acceptance and population booms in California and other western states.

The Flamingo was Nevada's first major, plush resort hotel/casino, and marked a turning point in the history of Nevada's gaming.

The evolution of legalized gaming, reputable casino operators and controlled industry regulations now assures patrons of an honest game. Today the Silver State annually attracts millions of visitors who are as willing to take a chance as were the pioneers who brought their adventurous spirit to Nevada.

GAMING FACTS & INFORMATION

IMPORTANT GAMING GROWTH DATES

1861	Prohibition of all forms of gambling
1864	Nevada admitted to Union
1869	Legislature legalized gambling
1910	All forms of gambling prohibited
1915	Limited gaming permitted
1931	Legislature legalized gaming
1941	El Rancho Vegas opens
1946	Flamingo opens
1955	Legislature created Nevada Gaming Control Board
1959	Legislature created Nevada Gaming Commission
1966	Howard Hughes buys six major resorts

STATE GAMING LICENSES

Statewide there are 2,555 gaming licenses. Slot machines account for approximately 62 percent of all money won by Nevada casinos. During the 1980s, Nevada's gross gaming revenues climbed from $2.4 billion to $5.2 billion. Statewide total win for the fiscal year ending June 30, 1997 was $7.3 billion. There are 429 non-restricted gaming licenses, 148 non-restricted slots only licenses and 1,978 restricted licenses in the state. Restricted licenses allows 15 slot machines or less. In the state there are 197,144 slot machines and 5,716 table games.

Nevada collected $570 million in gross gaming taxes in 1997.

CLARK COUNTY GAMING LICENSES

Non-restricted games and slots - 143
Non-restricted slots only - 88
Restricted slots - (15 or fewer) - 1,139
Fiscal year 6/30/97 1,370 gaming licenses

There were 125,273 electronic gaming devices in operation in Clark County generating more than $3.6 billion in revenue from September 1996 to August 1997.

BLACK BOOK

The Nevada Gaming Control Board established a list in 1966 of excluded persons from casinos called the Black Book. The Gaming Control Board meets to decide if a person should be included on the list. Individuals on the list are slot cheaters, organized crime figures, and others with notorious and unsavory reputations.

CLARK COUNTY

Total gaming revenue from non-restricted locations for Clark County for the fiscal year ending June 30, 1997 was $5,844,400,005. The games visitors play most frequently are slot machines, preferred by 52 percent of the visitors who gamble. Next is blackjack, which 17 percent play. Eleven percent of the visitors to Las Vegas don't gamble at all.

1997 GROSS GAMING REVENUE FOR CLARK COUNTY

January	$538,719,083	7.2%
February	$516,727,047	5.9%
March	$488,041,938	-4.4%
April	$501,549,251	9.0%
May	$537,518,197	11.6%
June	$475,618,943	1.5%

* Percentage change from same month the previous year.

1997 GROSS GAMING REVENUE FOR NEVADA

January	$646,676,560	4.4%*
February	$634,668,621	5.0%
March	$630,399,661	-3.8%
April	$635,942,417	8.3%
May	$682,600,497	9.6%
June	$618,960,037	0.9%
July	$671,110,700	4.6%

* Percentage change from same month the previous year.

LARGEST CASINOS IN LAS VEGAS

1)	MGM Grand	171,500 sq. ft.
2)	Excalibur	123,944
3)	Rio	120,000
4)	Caesars Palace	118,000
5)	Circus Circus	110,979
6)	Las Vegas Hilton	105,500
7)	Riviera	102,300
8)	Luxor	100,000

Nevada Gaming Control Board
555 E. Washington Ave.
2nd Floor
Las Vegas, NV 89158
486-2000
William A. Bible, Chairman
Brian Harris, Member/Directs Audits & Electronic Services
Steve Ducharme, Member/Overseas Enforcement
The 1955 legislature created the Nevada Gaming Control Board within the Nevada Tax Commission. Its purpose was to inaugurate a policy to eliminate the undesirable element in Nevada and to provide regulations for the licensing and operation of gaming.

The Gaming Control Board maintains a staff of approximately 220 in Las Vegas including attorneys, investigators, accountants, electronics technicians, and law enforcement experts.

Nevada Gaming Commission
Capital Plaza
1919 E. College Pkwy.
Carson City, NV 89706
687-6530
Bill Curran, Chairman
Arthur Marshall, Member
Augie Gurrola, Member
Sue Wagner, Member
Deborah Griffin, Member
The Nevada Gaming Commission was created by the 1959 Nevada Legislature. The five member lay body, appointed by the Governor, serves in a part-time capacity. By statute, the membership of the commission limits plural representation by members of a profession or major industry. Members are appointed to four year terms.

The primary responsibilities of the commission include acting on the recommendations of the State Gaming Control Board in licensing matters and ruling over work permit appeal cases. The Commission is the final authority on licensing matters, holding the power to approve, restrict, limit, condition, deny, revoke, or suspend any gaming license.

Additionally, the Commission is charged with the responsibility for adopting, amending, or repealing regulations consistent with the policy, objective and purpose of the statutes of this state.

GAMING TAXES

Gross revenue:
3% on first $50,000
4% on $50,000 - $134,000
6-1/4% on more than $134,000
Slot fees: Casinos pay $80
Quarterly license fee of $20 per machine.
Annual slot fee of $250 per machine
Restricted gaming license pays annual tax of $250 per machine plus quarterly license fee of $1,365 for 15 machines; $61 for one, up to 5 machines.
Quarterly table game fee: $12.50 for one game to $20,300 plus $25 for each game over 35 for 36 or more games.
Annual table game fee: $100 on the first table to $16,000 for casinos with 17 or more games plus $200 for each game over 16.
Entertainment tax: 10% on anything connected with entertainment in casinos.
Casino entertainment tax: 10%

Players that hit a jackpot of $1,200 or more on slot or video poker machines or $1,500 on keno are required to file Form W-2G. The player is required to sign the form and show identification with their social security number. The player must report his winnings to the IRS as income. Gambling losses can be deducted from gambling winnings, but you must have proof of your losses, such as a diary with detailed information. You can not deduct more in losses than winnings.

Casino cash transactions in excess of $10,000 must be reported to the Nevada Gaming Control Board, as per Regulation 6-A of the National Banking Laws.

Many insiders are aware of the 30% tax on gross winnings of non-resident aliens that is imposed according to U.S. tax laws. There is some good news here, however. A close examination of the various tax treaties has revealed that a total of at least fifteen countries are exempt from the normal 30% withholding required by tax code. Tax treaties supersede tax code. This means that residents of these countries will avoid all tax burden from any form of gambling while in the United States merely by requesting treaty exemption on IRS form 1001. A passport may be requested for verification of residence.
Czech Republic, Denmark, Finland, France, Germany, Hungary, Italy, Liechtenstein, Malta, Netherlands, Russia, Slovenia, Spain, Tunisia and United Kingdom.

CASINOS

Alystra Casino
333 W. Sunset Rd.
Henderson, NV 89015
564-8555
Phil Rossi, Gen. Mgr.
Games: 271 slot machines, 2 blackjack tables, Grillhouse restaurant, bar with live evening entertainment

Arizona Charlie's
740 S. Decatur Blvd.
Las Vegas, NV 89107
258-5200
Bucky Howard, Casino Mgr.
Gaming: 56,316 sq. ft.
Games: 1,400 slot and video poker machines, 16 blackjack tables, 2 crap tables, 1 roulette wheel, race and sports book, bingo parlor, Caribbean Stud, 1 Let It Ride, 4 poker tables

Bally's
3645 Las Vegas Blvd. S.
Las Vegas, NV 89109
739-4111
Jimmy Wike, Casino Mgr.
Gaming: 56,200 sq. ft.
Games: 1,882 slots and video machines, 49 blackjack tables, 9 crap tables, 8 roulette wheels, 1 keno lounge, 1 wheels of fortune, 4 mini-baccarat, 2 baccarat, 4 Caribbean stud, race and sports book, 3 Pai Gow poker, 4 Let It Ride, 1 war table

Barbary Coast Hotel & Casino
3595 Las Vegas Blvd. S.
Las Vegas, NV 89109
737-7111
Ted Reynolds, Casino Mgr.
Gaming: 32,000 sq. ft.
Games: 520 slots and video machines, 32 blackjack tables, 4 crap tables, 2 roulette wheels, 1 mini-baccarat, 4 Pai Gow poker, 1 keno lounge, race and sports book, 1 Let It Ride

Barcelona
5011 E. Craig Rd.
Las Vegas, NV 89115
644-6300
Jewel Dixon, Casino Mgr.
Gaming: 2,220 sq. ft.
Games: 319 slots, 3 blackjack tables, race and sports book, 1 roulette, 1 poker table

Barley's Casino & Brewing Co.
4500 E. Sunset Rd.
Henderson, NV 89014
458-BREW
Scott Garawitz, Casino Mgr.
Gaming: 199 slot and video poker machines, 6 blackjack table, sports book, micro-brewery

The Beach
365 Convention Center Dr.
Las Vegas, NV 89109
731-1925
Doug Culver, Gen. Mgr.
Games: 30 slots, race and sports book

Boulder Station
4111 Boulder Hwy.
Las Vegas, NV 89121
432-7777
Rick Fields, Casino Mgr.
Casino: 90,000 sq. ft..
Games: Over 3,000 slots and video poker machines, 30 blackjack tables, 4 crap tables, 2 Caribbean stud, 1 Let It Ride, 2

Pai Gow Poker, 3 roulette wheels, mini-baccarat, 10 table poker room, 240 seat race and sports book, 70-seat keno lounge.

Buffalo Bill's
I-15 S., CA/NV Stateline
Primm, NV 89019
382-1111   800-367-7383
Mike Cray, Casino Mgr.
Gaming: 46,000 sq. ft.
Games: 1,669 slot and video machines, 4 crap tables, 4 roulette wheels, 28 blackjack tables, 1 keno, 1 wheel of fortune, race and sports book, 2 Caribbean stud, 4 Let It Ride, 1 Pai Gow

Caesars Palace
3570 Las Vegas Blvd. S.
Las Vegas, NV 89109
731-7110
Rich Waters, Sr. VP Casino Operations
Gaming: 118,000 sq. ft.
Games: 2,050 slot and video poker machines, 65 blackjack tables, 13 crap tables, 13 roulette wheels, 1 keno lounge, 3 wheels of fortune, 3 mini-baccarat, 11 baccarat tables, 6 Pai Gow poker, 6 Pai Gow, race and sports book, 2 Caribbean stud, multiple action blackjack, 2 Let It Ride

California Hotel · Casino & RV Park
12 Ogden Ave.
Las Vegas, NV 89101
385-1222
David Lebby, Casino Mgr.
Gaming: 35,848 sq. ft.
Games: 1,100 slot and video machines, 24 blackjack tables, 6 crap tables, 2 roulette wheels, 1 keno lounge, 1 Pai Gow poker, race and sports book, 1 Caribbean stud, 1 Let It Ride, 1 mini-baccarat

Casino Royale
3411 Las Vegas Blvd. S.
Las Vegas, NV 89109
737-3500
Juan Garcia, Gen. Mgr.
Gaming: 6,000 sq. ft.
Games: 502 slot and video machines, 7 blackjack tables, 2 crap tables, 1 roulette wheel, 2 Spanish 21, 1 Caribbean stud

Circus Circus Hotel/Casino
2880 Las Vegas Blvd. S.
Las Vegas, NV 89109
734-0410
Penny Solomon, Dir. Casino Operations
Gaming: 110,979 sq. ft.
Games: 2,700 slot and video machines, 64 blackjack tables, 3 crap tables, 7 roulette wheels, 1 keno lounge, 1 big six, 5 Pai Gow poker, 10 poker tables, race and sports book, 3 Caribbean stud, 2 Let It Ride, 1 war game

Continental Hotel & Casino
4100 Paradise Rd.
Las Vegas, NV 89109
737-5555
Ira Levy, Casino Mgr./CEO
Gaming: 33,848 sq. ft.
Games: 539 slot and video machines, 7 blackjack tables, crap table, roulette wheel, sports book

Desert Inn Hotel & Casino
3145 Las Vegas Blvd. S.
Las Vegas, NV 89109
733-4444
Arnie Shehadi, Casino Mgr.
Gaming: 18,900 sq. ft.
Games: 406 slot and video machines, 31 blackjack tables, 7 crap tables, 4 roulette wheels, 9 baccarat, 2 Pai Gow, race and sports book, keno lounge, 2 mini-baccarat, Pai Gow poker, 1 Let It Ride, 1 Caribbean Stud

Debbie Reynolds Hollywood Hotel
305 Convention Center Dr.
Las Vegas, NV 89109
734-0711
Roy Warren, Casino Mgr.
Gaming: 6,500 sq. ft.
Games: 25 slot and video machines

El Cortez Hotel & Casino
600 E. Fremont Street
Las Vegas, NV 89101
385-5200
Frank Giannosa, Casino Shift Mgr.
Gaming: 41,300 sq. ft.
Games: 2,122 slot and video machines, 3 crap tables, 2 roulette tables, 11 blackjack tables, keno, mini-baccarat, race and sports book, 3 poker tables

Ellis Island Casino
4178 Koval Ln.
Las Vegas, NV 89109
733-8901
Gary Ellis, Pres.
Gaming: 27,000 sq. ft.
Games: 410 video poker and slot machines, sports book, 6 blackjack tables, micro-brewery, restaurant and lounge

Excalibur Hotel & Casino
3850 Las Vegas Blvd. S.
Las Vegas, NV 89109
597-7777
Jim Lewis, Casino Mgr.
Gaming: 123,944 sq. ft.
Games: 2,484 slot and video machines, 57 blackjack tables, 4 crap tables, 7 roulette wheels, 2 keno lounges, 1 big wheel, race and sports book, 14 poker tables, 3 Pai Gow poker, 2 mini baccarat, 2 Let It Ride, 2 Caribbean stud, 1 casino war. non-smoking areas

Fiesta Casino & Hotel
2400 N. Rancho Dr.
Las Vegas, NV 89130
631-7000
John James, Casino Mgr.
Gaming: 50,000 sq. ft.
Games: 1,320 slot and video machines, 2 crap tables, 2 roulette wheel, 13 blackjack tables, keno, bingo, race and sport book, 1 Let It Ride, 2 Pai Gow poker

Fitzgeralds Hotel
301 E. Fremont St.
Las Vegas, NV 89101
388-2400
Doug DuCharme, Casino Dir.
Gaming: 42,000 sq. ft.
Games: 1,108 slot and video machines, 20 blackjack tables, 3 crap tables, 2 roulette tables, keno, big wheel, 1 Caribbean stud, 2 Let It Ride, "21 Superbucks," race and sports book

Flamingo Hilton Las Vegas
3555 Las Vegas Blvd. S.
Las Vegas, NV 89109
733-3111
Mike Boyle, Sr. VP Casino Operations
Gaming: 77,000 sq. ft.
Games: 1,950 slot and video machines, 7 crap tables, 8 roulette tables, 46 blackjack tables, 1 keno lounge, 1 big wheel, 2 mini-baccarat, race and sports book, 6 poker tables, Pai Gow poker, 3 Caribbean stud, 2 Let It Ride

---

CLARK COUNTY GAMES

1997 Non-restricted Licenses Only

Slot Machines:	197,144
Crap Tables:	463
Roulette Wheels:	408
Blackjack Tables:	3,536
Keno Games:	174
Mini-Baccarat:	92
Baccarat:	86
Race Books:	104
Sports Pools:	131
Caribbean Stud:	138
Let It Ride:	205

GAMING

CASINOS

Four Queens
202 E. Fremont St.
Las Vegas, NV 89101
385-4011
Joe Stahl, Dir. Casino Operations
Gaming: 32,296 sq. ft.
Games: 1,040 slot and video machines, 28 blackjack tables, 4 crap tables, 2 roulette tables, keno lounge, 1 Pai Gow poker, 3 Caribbean stud, multiple action blackjack, 3 Let it Ride, race and sports book

Fremont Hotel & Casino
200 Fremont St.
Las Vegas, NV 89101
385-3232
Mike McCabe, Casino Mgr.
Gaming: 32,000 sq. ft.
Games: 1,100 slot and video machines, 16 blackjack tables, 4 crap tables, 3 roulette tables, keno lounge, race and sports book, Pai Gow poker, 1 Caribbean stud, 2 Let It Ride, 1 Spanish 21, non-smoking tables available

Gold Coast
4000 W. Flamingo Rd.
Las Vegas, NV 89103
367-7111
Alan Scano, Casino Mgr.
Gaming: 71,000 sq. ft.
Games: 2,087 slot and video machines, 6 crap tables, 3 roulette wheels, 31 blackjack tables, keno lounge, 700 seat bingo parlor - sessions 8 am - 2 am on even hours, 3 mini-baccarat, race and sports book, 5 Pai Gow poker, 1 Let it Ride

Gold Spike Hotel & Casino
400 E. Ogden Ave.
Las Vegas, NV 89101
384-8444
Mike Nolan, Gen. Mgr.
Gaming: 5,820 square feet
Games: 436 slot and video machines, 3 blackjack tables, keno lounge, poker table

Gold Strike Inn/Casino
U.S. Hwy. 93
Boulder City, NV 89005
293-5000
Tony Korfman, Gen. Mgr.
Gaming: 27,440 sq. ft.
Games: 776 slot and video machines, 11 blackjack tables, 1 crap table, 1 roulette wheel, keno lounge, 3 poker tables, 1 Caribbean stud, race and sports book

Golden Gate Hotel & Casino
1 E. Fremont St.
Las Vegas, NV 89101
382-6300
111 S. Main St. *(Hotel)*
382-3510
Las Vegas, NV 89101
1-800-426-0521
Mike Young, Casino Mgr.
Gaming: 9,090 sq. ft.
Games: 445 slot and video machines, 12 blackjack tables, 2 crap tables, roulette wheel, keno lounge, Caribbean stud, 1 Let It Ride, 1 Casino War *(Las Vegas' oldest hotel and casino)*

Golden Nugget Hotel & Casino
129 E. Fremont St.
Las Vegas, NV 89101
385-7111

Richard Amalfitano, VP Casino Operations
Gaming: 39,040 sq. ft.
Games: 1,323 slot and video machines, 35 blackjack tables, 7 crap tables, 3 roulette wheels, 2 keno lounges, 1 wheel of fortune, baccarat, mini-baccarat, race and sports book, 3 Pai Gow poker, 2 Caribbean stud, 2 Let It Ride, 1 Pai Gow, Sports pool, 2 Spanish 21

Hard Rock Hotel & Casino
4455 Paradise Rd.
Las Vegas, NV 89109
693-5000   800-HRD-ROCK
Willie Stephens, Dir. Casino Operations
Gaming: 28,000 sq. ft.
Games: 741 slot and video machines, 4 crap tables, 3 roulette wheels, 38 blackjack tables, 1 mini-baccarat, race and sports book, 1 Caribbean Stud, 1 Pai Gow poker, 1 Let It Ride, big six wheel

Harrah's
3475 Las Vegas Blvd. S.
Las Vegas, NV 89109
369-5000
Pat Kearns, VP of Casino Operations
Gaming: 103,325 sq. ft.
Games: 2,200 slot and video machines, 51 blackjack tables, 8 crap tables, 8 roulette wheels, 2 keno lounges, 4 mini-baccarat, race and sports book, red dog, 8 poker tables, 4 Pai Gow poker, 3 Caribbean stud, 4 Let It Ride, 2 casino war games

Holiday Inn Boardwalk Hotel & Casino
3750 Las Vegas Blvd. S.
Las Vegas, NV 89109
735-1167
Bobby Preston, Casino Mgr.
Gaming: 33,000 sq. ft.
Games: 661 slot and video poker machines, 2 roulette wheels, 13 blackjack tables, 2 crap tables, 1 wheel of fortune, race and sports book, 1 Let It Ride, 2 Spanish 21, 1 Caribbean stud

Binion's Horseshoe
128 Fremont St.
Las Vegas, NV 89101
382-1600
Mike Cericola, Casino Mgr.
Gaming: 56,929 sq. ft.
(Features no limit action)
Games: 1,385 slot and video machines, 39 blackjack tables (single deck), 12 crap tables, 3 roulette wheels, 1 keno lounge, bingo, big wheel, 2 baccarat, race and sports book, red dog, 14 poker tables, 1 Caribbean stud, Pai Gow poker, 5 mini-baccarat, 1 Let It Ride, 1 Spanish 21

Imperial Palace Hotel & Casino
3535 Las Vegas Blvd. S.
Las Vegas, NV 89109
731-3311
John Zabrosky, Casino Mgr.
Gaming: 75,000 sq. ft.
Games: 1,844 slot and video machines, 26 blackjack tables, 4 crap tables, 1 mini-crap, 3 roulette tables, keno lounge, big wheel, mini-baccarat, race and sports book, 2 Pai Gow poker, 3 Let It Ride, 2 Caribbean stud

Jerry's Nugget
1821 Las Vegas Blvd. N.
N. Las Vegas, NV 89030
399-3000
Charles Woods, Gen./Casino Mgr.
Gaming: 25,144 sq. ft.
Games: 777 slot and video machines, 7 blackjack tables, crap table, roulette wheel, keno lounge, bingo, race and sports book, 24-hour restaurant, snack bar, lounge

Joker's Wild
920 N. Boulder Hwy.
Henderson, NV 89015
564-8100
Ron Harbison, Gen. Mgr.
Gaming: 23,698 sq. ft.
Games: 656 slot and video machines, 9 blackjack tables, roulette wheel, 1 craps table, 1 Let It Ride, sports book, keno lounge, 24-hour restaurant and buffet, lounge with live entertainment

King 8 Hotel & Gambling Hall
3330 W. Tropicana Ave.
Las Vegas, NV 89103
736-8988
Rick Ross, Gen. Mgr.
Gaming: 4,516 sq. ft.
Games: 230 slot and video, 5 blackjack, crap table, roulette, keno lounge, 1 Let It Ride, 1 poker tables, sports book, live entertainment in lounge

Klondike Inn
5191 Las Vegas Blvd. S.
Las Vegas, NV 89119
739-9351
Jim Parks, Gen. Mgr.
Gaming: 6,800 sq. ft.
Games: 415 video poker and slot machines, 4 blackjack tables, 1 roulette wheel

Lady Luck Casino & Hotel
206 N. Third St.
Las Vegas, NV 89101
477-3000
Jim Dickstein, Casino Mgr.
Gaming: 18,350 sq. ft.
Games: 870 slot and video machines, 16 blackjack tables, 3 crap tables, 2 roulette wheels, Caribbean Stud, keno lounge, 1 mini-baccarat, 2 Let It Ride, Pai Gow poker, 1 double disclosure, 1 Spanish 21, 3 card poker

Las Vegas Club
18 E. Fremont St.
Las Vegas, NV 89101
385-1664
Scott Walker, Casino Mgr.
Gaming: 40,000 sq. ft.
Games: 943 slot and video machines, 18 blackjack tables, 4 crap tables, roulette wheel, 1 Caribbean stud, keno lounge, 2 Let It Ride, race and sports book, claims most liberal rules on blackjack

Las Vegas Hilton
3000 Paradise Rd.
Las Vegas, NV 89109
732-5111
Jon Jaggers, Sr. VP of Casino Operations
Gaming: 105,500 sq. ft.
Games: 1,200 slot and poker machines, 37 blackjack tables, 7 crap tables, 6

roulette wheels, keno lounge, wheel of fortune, 6 baccarat, 1 Pai Gow poker, race and sports book, 2 Caribbean stud, 2 Let It Ride, 2 Pai Gow

Ligouri's Restaurant & Casino
1133 N. Boulder Hwy.
Henderson, NV 89015
565-1688
John Ligouri, Casino Mgr.
Games: 103 slot and video machines, 2 poker tables, restaurant

Luxor
3900 Las Vegas Blvd. S.
Las Vegas, NV 89119
262-4000
Tom Robinson, Casino Mgr.
Gaming: 100,000 sq. ft.
Games: 2,150 slot and video machines, 69 blackjack tables, 8 crap tables, 10 roulette wheels, 3 keno lounges, 1 big wheel, 3 mini-baccarat, 3 Pai Gow poker, 8 poker tables, state-of-the-art race and sports book, baccarat, 1 Pai Gow, 2 Caribbean stud

Main Street Station
200 N. Main Street
Las Vegas, NV 89101
387-1896   1-800-713-8933
Jim Sullivan, Casino Mgr.
Gaming: More than 28,000 sq. ft.
Games: 900 state of the art machines and a variety of poker tables, 13 blackjack tables, 1 Pai Gow poker, 2 Let It Ride, 4 crap tables, 2 roulette wheels, keno lounge

Maxim Hotel & Casino
160 E. Flamingo Rd.
Las Vegas, NV 89109
731-4300
Ray Anzevino, Casino Mgr.
Gaming: 17,250 sq. ft.
Games: 733 slot and video machines, 17 blackjack tables, 2 crap tables, 2 roulette wheels, 1 Caribbean stud, keno lounge, sports book, 1 Let It Ride

MGM Grand Hotel & Theme Park
3799 Las Vegas Blvd. S.
Las Vegas, NV 89109
891-1111
Lyn Baxter, Sr. V/P Casino Operations
Gaming: 171,500 sq. ft.
Games: 3,700 slot and video machines, 76 blackjack tables, 15 crap tables, 17 roulette wheels, 1 keno lounge, 2 big wheel, 9 mini-baccarat, 9 baccarat, state-of-the-art race and sports book, 20 poker tables, 4 Caribbean stud, 2 Pai Gow, 6 Pai Gow poker, 3 Let It Ride, 2 Casino War, 1 Spanish 21

The Mirage
3400 Las Vegas Blvd. S.
Las Vegas, NV 89109
791-7111
Al Pulitini, Casino Mgr.
Gaming: 95,300 sq. ft.
Games: 2,192 slots and video machines, 73 blackjack tables, 10 crap tables, 12 roulette wheels, 2 Caribbean stud, 2 Pai Gow, 4 Pai Gow poker, 2 keno lounges, 2 wheels of fortune, 3 mini-baccarat, 8 baccarat, race and sports book, 31 poker tables, 2 Let It Ride

Monte Carlo Resort & Casino
3770 Las Vegas Blvd. S.
Las Vegas, NV 89109
730-7777
Bill Ensign, VP Casino Operations
Gaming: 90,000 sq. ft.
Games: 2,200 slot and video poker machines, 60 blackjack tables, 8 crap tables, 3 Pai Gow poker, 1 Pai Gow, 1 Let it Ride, 4 Caribbean stud, 2 war games, 10 roulette wheels, 3 mini baccarat, 2 baccarat, 1 big six, race and sports book, 8 poker tables, 1 keno lounge, roulette tables, 15 blackjack tables, keno lounge, 1 Caribbean stud, sports book

Nevada Palace Hotel & Casino
5255 Boulder Hwy.
Las Vegas, NV 89122
458-8810
Peter Maksymec, Gen. Mgr.
Gaming: 13,000 sq. ft.
Games: 499 slots and video machines, 9 blackjack tables, crap tables, 1 roulette wheels, keno lounge, 2 poker tables, 1 Let It Ride, sports book

New Frontier Hotel & Gambling Hall
3120 Las Vegas Blvd. S.
Las Vegas, NV 89109
794-8200
Phil Lovaas, Casino Mgr.
Gaming: 41,325 sq. ft.
Games: 1,105 slot and video machines, 15 blackjack tables, 4 crap tables, 2 roulette wheels, keno lounge, big wheel, race and sports book, 1 Pai Gow poker, 1 Caribbean Stud, 1 Let It Ride, bingo, 3 Spanish 21, 100 times odds on craps

New York New York Hotel & Casino
3790 Las Vegas Blvd. S.
Las Vegas, NV 89109
740-6969
Joe Barrett, Mgr. Casino Operations
Gaming: 84,000 sq. ft.
Games: More than 2,400 state of the art video and slot machines, 41 blackjack tables, 8 crap tables, 7 roulette wheels, 3 mini-baccarat, 3 Caribbean stud, 1 casino war, 1 big 6, 3 Pai Gow, 1 Pai Gow Tile, 1 keno lounge, 1 race and sports book

Opera House Saloon & Casino
2542 Las Vegas Blvd. N.
N. Las Vegas, NV 89030
649-8801
Jack Broeder, Gen. Mgr.
Gaming: 4,419 sq. ft.
Games: 160 slot and video machines, 4 blackjack tables, 24-hour restaurant and bar

Orleans Hotel & Casino
4500 W. Tropicana Ave.
Las Vegas, NV 89103
365-7111
Frank Toti, Casino Mgr.
Gaming: 92,000 sq. ft.
Games: More than 2,100 slots, 65 table games which include blackjack, craps, roulette, Let It Ride, baccarat, Pai Gow poker, 16 poker tables, keno lounge, race and sports book

O'Sheas Casino
3555 Las Vegas Blvd. S.
Las Vegas, NV 89109
697-2711
Chris Crider, Gen. Mgr.
Gaming: 40,492 sq. ft.
Games: 412 slot machines, 40 blackjack tables, 7 crap tables, 8 roulette wheels, 1 Pai Gow, 3 Caribbean stud, 2 Let It Ride, 5 poker tables, race and sports book, 1 big six, Sic-Bo
Restaurant: O'Sheas Food Park - Subway Sandwiches, Burger King, Dunkin Donuts, Baskin Robbins, Jay's Pizza, Orient Express

Palace Station Hotel & Casino
2411 W. Sahara Ave.
Las Vegas, NV 89102
367-2411
Tony Carolo, Casino Mgr.
Gaming: 76,490 sq. ft.
Games: 2,250 slot and video machines, 32 blackjack tables, 5 crap tables, 3 roulette wheels, 1 Caribbean stud, 2 keno lounges, mini-baccarat, 2 Pai Gow poker, 9 poker tables, 1 Let It Ride, race and sports book, bingo parlor

Jackie Gaughan's Plaza
1 Main St.
Las Vegas, NV 89101
386-2110
Chris NIchols, Casino Mgr.
Gaming: 57,120 sq. ft.
Games: 1,580 slots and video machines, 19 blackjack tables, 5 crap tables, 3 roulette wheels, 2 keno lounges, mini-baccarat, 1 Pai Gow poker, 12 poker tables, 13 Pan tables, race and sports book

Poker Palace
2757 Las Vegas Blvd. N.
N. Las Vegas, NV 89030
649-3799
Brad Feitush, Gen. Mgr.
Gaming: 9,950 sq. ft.
Games: 407 slot and video machines, 6 blackjack tables, 2 poker tables, race and sports book, roulette, restaurant, lounge, two complete casinos, one smoking, the other nonsmoking with separate ventilation systems, 16 computerized betting terminals

Pot O' Gold
120 Market St.
Henderson, NV 89015
564-8488
Thomas Brosenne Jr.
Games: 200 slots, 4 blackjack tables, bingo

Quality Inn Key Largo Casino
377 E. Flamingo Rd.
Las Vegas, NV 89109
733-7777
Brent Vockrodt, Gen. Mgr.
Gaming: 10,000 sq. ft.
Games: 248 slots and video machines, 3 blackjack tables, 1 crap table, 1 roulette wheel

Railroad Pass Hotel & Casino
2800 Boulder Hwy.
Henderson, NV 89015
294-5000
Curtis Jacks, Gen. Mgr.
Gaming: 21,480 sq. ft.
Games: Over 400 slot and video machines, 9 blackjack tables, crap table, roulette wheel, keno lounge, race and sports book, 1 Let It Ride

Rainbow Club & Casino
122 S. Water St.
Henderson, NV 89015
565-9776
Oscar Portillo, Gen. Mgr.
Gaming: 8,100 sq. ft.
Games: 490 slot and video machines, 24-hour restaurant, bar

The Reserve Hotel Casino
777 W. Lake Mead Dr.
Henderson, NV 89015
558-7000

Joe Cottine, Dir. of Casino Mkt.
Gaming: 37,000 sq. ft.
Games: 1,450 slot machines, 18 blackjack tables, 2 crap tables, 2 roulette wheels, 1 mini-baccarat, 1 Let-It-Ride, 1 Caribbean stud, 1 Pai Gow poker, keno, poker room, 300 seat bingo area and sports book.

Rio Suite Hotel & Casino
3700 W. Flamingo Rd.
Las Vegas, NV 89103
252-7777
Jimmy Angelo, Casino Mgr.
Gaming: 120,000 sq. ft.
Games: 2,460 slots and video machines, 60 blackjack tables, 13 crap tables, 11 roulette wheels, 2 keno lounges, mini-baccarat, 3 Caribbean stud, 2 Pai Gow poker, 8 poker tables, race and sports book, baccarat, 3 Let It Ride

Riviera Hotel
2901 Las Vegas Blvd. S.
Las Vegas, NV 89109
734-5110
Mickey Falba, Casino Mgr.
Gaming: 102,300 sq. ft.
Games: 1,576 slots and video machines, 21 blackjack tables, 4 crap tables, 2 roulette wheels, keno lounge, 1 wheel of fortune, 1 baccarat, 2 Pai Gow poker, Sic-Bo, 2 Caribbean stud, 5 poker tables, 3 Let It Ride, race and sports book

Royal Hotel Casino
99 Convention Center Drive
Las Vegas, NV 89109
735-6117
James Lang, Gen. Mgr.
Gaming: 10,000 sq. ft.
Games: 121 slots and video machines, race & sports book, bar

Clark County & Nevada Gaming Revenues

Legend:
- Nevada Gaming
- Clark County Gaming

Year	Nevada Gaming	Clark County Gaming
1970	369,287,000	604,351,000
1975	770,337,000	1,174,627,000
1980	1,617,194,799	2,478,454,000
1985	2,256,763,000	3,370,619,000
1990	4,104,001,000	5,459,441,000
1992	4,381,710,000	5,867,539,000
1995	5,717,567,000	7,368,612,000
1997	6,152,415,000	7,802,221,000

Years (vertical axis) — Dollars in Billions (horizontal axis: 0, .5, 1, 1.5, 2, 2.5, 3, 3.5, 4, 4.5, 5, 5.5, 6, 6.5, 7, 7.5, $8)

Source: Las Vegas Convention & Visitor Authority; Nevada State Gaming Control Board

Experience Las Vegas

GAMING

CASINOS

Sahara Hotel
2535 Las Vegas Blvd. S.
Las Vegas, NV 89109
737-2111
Phil Gatlin, Casino Mgr.
Gaming: 95,000 sq. ft.
Games: 1,371 slot and video machines, 25 blackjack tables, 4 crap tables, 4 roulette wheels, keno lounge, wheel of fortune, 2 Pai Gow poker, 5 poker tables, 5 Pan, race and sports book, 1 Caribbean stud, mini-baccarat, 1 Let It Ride, 1 Spanish 21, 1 casino war

Sam's Town Hotel & Gambling Hall
5111 Boulder Hwy.
Las Vegas, NV 89122
456-7777
Gil Peart, Casino Mgr.
Gaming: 81,305 sq. ft.
Games: 2,850 slots and video machines, 29 blackjack tables, 5 crap tables, 4 roulette wheels, keno lounge, bingo, 1 Pai Gow poker, 9 poker tables, race and sports book, 2 Caribbean stud, single deck blackjack, 100X odds on craps, 1 Let It Ride, 1 Spanish 21

Hotel San Remo
Casino & Resort
115 E. Tropicana Ave.
Las Vegas, NV 89109
739-9000
Harry Byrge, Casino Mgr.
Gaming: 7,889 sq. ft.
Games: 602 slot and video machines, 13 blackjack tables, 2 crap tables, roulette wheel, keno lounge, wheel of fortune, 1 Caribbean Stud, 1 Let It Ride, 1 Pai Gow poker, sports book

Santa Fe Hotel Casino
4949 N. Rancho Dr.
Las Vegas, NV 89130
658-4900
Joe Corradino, Casino Mgr.
Gaming: 55,441 sq. ft.
Games: 1,766 slot and video machines, 18 blackjack tables, 2 crap tables, 2 roulette wheels, 2 Pai Gow poker, keno lounge, bingo, 5 poker tables, sports book, 1 Let It Ride

Sassy Sally's Casino
32 Fremont St.
Las Vegas, NV 89101
382-5777
Jim Gish, Gen. Mgr.
Gaming: 7,000 sq. ft.
Games: 147 slot and video machines, restaurant and bar

Showboat Resort & Casino
2800 E. Fremont St.
Las Vegas, NV 89104
385-9123
Jon Zimmerman, VP. of Casino operations
Gaming: 80,300 sq. ft.
Games: 1,548 slot and video machines, 14 blackjack tables, 2 crap tables, 2 roulette wheels, keno lounge, bingo, Pai Gow poker, race and sports book, 1 Caribbean stud, 2 Let It Ride, poker room, computer bingo

Silver City Casino
3001 Las Vegas Blvd. S.
Las Vegas, NV 89109
732-4152
Joe Amato, Casino Mgr.

Gaming: 15,258 sq. ft.
Games: 482 slot and video machines, 16 blackjack tables, 1 crap table, 1 roulette wheel, 1 Let It Ride, restaurant, bar

Silver Saddle Saloon
2501 E. Charleston Blvd.
Las Vegas, NV 89104
474-2900
Charlie Howell, Mgr.
Games: 75 slots, 2 blackjack tables

Silverton Hotel & Casino
(Formerly Boomtown Hotel/Casino)
3333 Blue Diamond Rd.
Las Vegas, NV 89139
263-7777 1-800-588-7711
Michael Frawley, Casino Operations and Games Dir.
Gaming: 32,134 sq. ft.
Games: 1,100 slot and video machines, 20 blackjack tables, 2 crap tables, 2 roulette wheels, keno, Caribbean stud

Mahoney's Silver Nugget
2140 Las Vegas Blvd. N.
N. Las Vegas, NV 89030
399-1111
Dennis Gushue, Gen. Mgr.
Gaming: 18,622 sq. ft.
Games: Over 300 slot and video machines, 5 blackjack tables, crap table, keno lounge, bingo, 2 poker tables, sports pool, 1 Spanish 21, 1 21 madness, restaurant, bar, bowling

Skyline Casino
1741 N. Boulder Hwy.
Henderson, NV 89015
565-9116
Gaming: 8,500 sq. ft.
John Kish, CEO/Owner
Dean Joyner, Gen. Mgr.
Games: 401 slot and video machines, 4 blackjack tables, 1 poker table, sports book, restaurant, lounge with live entertainment

Slots-A-Fun
2880 Las Vegas Blvd. S.
Las Vegas, NV 89109
734-0410
Joe Amato, Casino Mgr.
Gaming: 16,733 sq. ft.
Games: 598 slot and video machines, 22 blackjack tables, 1 crap table, 2 roulette wheel, red dog, 1 Let It Ride, 1 Caribbean Stud, snack bar, bar

Stardust Hotel & Casino
3000 Las Vegas Blvd. S.
Las Vegas, NV 89109
732-6111
Alan Abrams, Casino Mgr.
Gaming: 65,538 sq. ft.
Games: 1,950 slot and video machines, 44 blackjack tables, 6 crap tables, 5 roulette wheels, 2 keno lounges, wheel of fortune, 2 baccarat, 3 Pai Gow poker, 10 poker tables, race and sports book, mini-baccarat, 2 Let It Ride, 3 Caribbean stud, multiple action blackjack

Stratosphere
2000 Las Vegas Blvd. S.
Las Vegas, NV 89104
380-7777 1-800-998-6937
Mike Turngren, VP Casino Operations
Gaming: 100,000 sq. ft.
Games: 2,040 slot and video games, 29 blackjack tables, 6 crap tables, 5 roulette wheels, 3 mini-baccarat, 2 Caribbean stud, 3 Pai Gow poker, 2 Let It Ride, 1 casino war, 2 three card poker, keno and sports book.

Sunset Station
1301 W. Sunset Rd.
Henderson, NV 89014
547-7777
Bart Pestrichello, Dir. Casino Operations
Gaming: 80,000 sq. ft.
Games: 2,700 video poker & slot machines, 31 blackjack tables, 5 crap tables, 3 roulette wheels, 1 mini-baccarat, 2 Let It Ride, 1 Caribbean stud, 1 Spanish 21, 3 Pai Gow poker, race and sports book arena with 36-70 inch TVs, 1 keno lounge, 9 poker tables, bingo, 1 Vegas aces

Texas Station
2101 Texas Star Ln.
N. Las Vegas, NV 89030
631-1000 800-654-8888
Jerry Parker, Casino Mgr.
Gaming: 60,000 sq. ft.
Games: 2,008 slot machines, 23 blackjack tables, 4 crap tables, 1 Let It Ride, 2 Texas Pai Gow, 1 Spanish 21, 3 roulette tables, 175-seat race and sports book, keno, 10 poker tables, bingo

Tom's Sunset Casino
444 W. Sunset Rd.
Henderson, NV 89015
564-5551
Tom Yarbrough, Gen. Mgr.
Gaming: 7,340 sq. ft.
Games: 287 slot and video machines, 1 poker table, sports book, 24-hour restaurant, bar

Town Hall Casino
4155 Koval Ln.
Las Vegas, NV 89109
732-1499
Bill Walker, Gen. Mgr.
Gaming: 4,600 sq. ft.
Games: 155 slot and video machines, 3 blackjack tables, 24-hour restaurant, bar, motel

Travel Centers of America
Truck Plaza
8050 Industrial Rd.
Las Vegas, NV 89139
361-1176
Gladys Giralo, Mgr.
Gaming: 644 sq. ft.
Games: 96 slots, 3 blackjack tables, 1 Let It Ride, truck stop, restaurant

Treasure Island
3300 Las Vegas Blvd. S.
Las Vegas, NV 89109
894-7111
Joe Wilcox, VP of Table Games
Gaming: 51,152 sq. ft.
Games: 2,200 slot and video poker machines, Pai Gow, 1 mini-baccarat, 7 crap tables, 4 Caribbean stud, 52 blackjack tables, 13 poker tables, race and sports book, 8 roulette wheels, 2 keno lounges, 1 big wheels, 3 Pai Gow poker, 2 Let It Ride, race and sports book

Triple J Bingo Hall & Casino
725 S. Racetrack Rd.
Henderson, NV 89015
566-5555 1-800-642-7777
Donnie Clifton, Gen. Mgr.
Gaming: 22,660 sq. ft.
Games: 70 slot and video machines, 1 blackjack table, bar, restaurant

Tropicana Resort & Casino
3801 Las Vegas Blvd. S.
Las Vegas, NV 89109
739-2222
Lee White, Casino Mgr.
Gaming: 45,200 sq. ft.
Games: 1,600 slot and video poker machines, 37 blackjack tables, 6 crap tables, 4 roulette wheels, 1 keno lounge, wheel of fortune, 2 Let It Ride, 4 baccarat, sports book, 3 Caribbean stud, multiple action blackjack. New Asian room called the Jade Palace with 2 Sic-Bo, 2 Pai Gow poker, 2 Pai Gow and 2 mini-baccarat.

Swim-up blackjack in pool; Poolside video poker and slots; special instructional blackjack $1 bets only. Dealer will instruct you in rules and etiquette of the game. Roulette for a penny noon - 8 pm.

Vacation Village
6711 Las Vegas Blvd. S.
Las Vegas, NV 89119
897-1700
Lyle Thompson, Casino Mgr.
Gaming: 22,760 sq. ft.
Games: 584 video and slot machines, 10 blackjack tables, roulette, race and sports book

Western Hotel/Casino
899 Fremont St.
Las Vegas, NV 89101
384-4620
Tony Alessandro, Casino Mgr.
Gaming: 13,050 sq. ft.
Games: 567 slot and video machines, 8 blackjack tables, roulette wheel, keno lounge, bingo

Westward-Ho Hotel & Casino
2900 Las Vegas Blvd. S.
Las Vegas, NV 89109
731-2900
Bob Tyndall, Casino Mgr.
Gaming: 34,427 sq. ft.
Games: 871 slots and video machines, 8 blackjack tables, 1 Let It Ride, craps, roulette, keno lounge

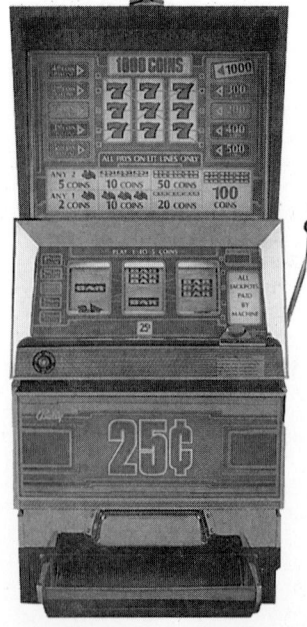

NONRESTRICTED SLOTS-ONLY CASINOS

COMPS

Comps are free meals, rooms, and other amenities given to a casino guest at no charge because of casino play. Whether you play slot machines or table games, you now qualify at most casinos. If you are a slot player, you must join the slot club. You will be issued a card which looks much like an ATM card. You insert the card in the slot on the slot machine and the amount of money you insert is tracked. You rack up points, the more you put in, the more points you earn. Points are good for meals, rooms, merchandise and more.

If you play the tables, you want to ask the pit boss to rate your play. Many casinos require you to apply for a player card, some just take your name. Each year casinos give out more than a half-billion dollars worth of comps. Unless you are playing above $5 per hand, you need to ask if you qualify for a comp. Below is a chart on how long and how much you need to play for certain comps. Of course, it depends on the casino you are playing. Twenty-five dollars a hand at a small casino will get you much more than $25 at the Mirage or Caesars Palace.

$ Per Hand	Comp
$5-$10	Coffee Shop: Breakfast, lunch
$10-$25	Coffee Shop: Anytime; Casino rate on room
$25-$100	Show tickets; Gourmet restaurants, free room.
$100-$250	Room, food, beverage.
$250+	Room, food, beverage, suite, limo, golf, airfare

Aztec Inn
2200 Las Vegas Blvd. S.
Las Vegas, NV 89104
385-4566
Bill Maxwell, Gen. Mgr.
Gaming: 3,120 sq. ft.
Games: 100 slot and video machines

Beano's Casino
7200 W. Lake Mead Blvd.
Las Vegas, NV 89128
255-9150
Barry Moore
Games: 35 video poker & keno machines

Big Dog's Bar & Grill
1511 N. Nellis Blvd.
Las Vegas, NV 89110
459-1099
Tom Weisner
Games: 35 video poker machines

Big Dog's Cafe & Casino
6390 W. Sahara Ave.
Las Vegas, NV 89102
876-3647
Tom Weisner
Games: 35 video poker machines

Big Game Club, The
4747 Fair Center Pkwy.
Las Vegas, NV 89102
870-0087
Sheldon Stunkel
Games: 35 slot machines

Bonanza Lounge
4300 E. Bonanza Rd.
Las Vegas, NV 89107
452-7955
Peter Mandas
Games: 35 poker & keno machines

Captain's Quarters
2610 Regatta Dr.
Las Vegas, NV 89129
256-6200
Steven Stein
Games: 28 slot machines

Castaways Casino
1690 N. Decatur Blvd.
Las Vegas, NV 89108
648-1961
Ronald Coury
Games: 35 video poker machines

Charlie's Down Under
1950 N. Buffalo Dr.
Las Vegas, NV 89128
258-5186
Bruce Becker
Games: 35 video poker machines

Charlie's Lakeside Bar & Grill
8603 W. Sahara Ave.
Las Vegas, NV 89117
258-5170
Ernest Becker
Gaming: 1,950 sq. ft.
Games: 35 slot machines, bar and restaurant

Coin Castle Casino
15 E. Fremont St.
Las Vegas, NV 89101
385-7474
Jim Gish, Gen. Mgr.
Gaming: 3,100 sq. ft.
Games: 114 slot and video machines

Danny's Slot Country
4213 Boulder Hwy.
Las Vegas, NV 89121
451-4974
Barbara Davidson, Gen. Mgr.
Gaming: 1,200 sq. ft.
Games: 75 slot and video machines, adjacent bar

Draft House Bar & Grill
4543 N. Rancho Dr.
Las Vegas, NV 89130
645-1404
Tom Weisner
Games: 35 video poker machines

Ernie's Bar
1901 N. Rancho Dr.
Las Vegas, NV 89106
646-3447
Melvin Wolzinger
Games: 56 slot machines

Eureka Casino
595 E. Sahara Ave.
Las Vegas, NV 89104
794-3464
Buck Burkett, Gen. Mgr.

Gaming: 4000 sq. ft.
Games: 252 slot and video machines, bar, small restaurant

Foothills Express
714 N. Rainbow Blvd.
Las Vegas, NV 89107
878-2281
Randy Miller
Games: 35 video & keno machines, restaurant

Foothills Ranch
3377 N. Rancho Dr.
Las Vegas, NV 89130
658-6360
Randy Miller
Games: 35 video poker & keno machines, restaurant

49er Saloon & Casino
1556 N. Eastern Ave.
Las Vegas, NV 89101
649-2421
Bertha Ravetti
Games: 22 slot machines

Friendly Fergie's Casino & Saloon
2430 Las Vegas Blvd. S.
Las Vegas, NV 89104
598-1985
Allen Gyger
Games: 27 video poker machines

Gloria's II
1966 N. Rainbow Blvd.
Las Vegas, NV 89108
647-0744
Gloria Peterman
Games: 20 video games

Gold Rush Casino
1195 W. Sunset Rd.
Henderson, NV 89015
454-0544
Steve McLaughlin, Gen. Mgr.
Games: 183 video poker machines

Green's Supper Club
2241 N. Green Valley Pkwy.
Henderson, NV 89104
454-4211
Pete Kypreos
Games: 40 video poker machines

Holy Cow Casino Brewery & Cafe
2423 Las Vegas Blvd. S.
Las Vegas, NV 89104
732-2697
Vicki Egan, Gen. Mgr.
Gaming: 2,500 sq. ft.
Games: 76 slot and video machines, video roulette, 1 video blackjack, restaurant, brew-pub

Howard Johnson
3111 W. Tropicana Ave.
Las Vegas, NV 89103
798-1111
Kevin McMullen
Games: 63 slot machines

Lake Mead Lounge
846 E. Lake Mead Dr.
Henderson, NV 89015
565-0297
Stephen Hampe
Games: 117 slot machines and video poker

The Lift
3045 S. Valley View Blvd.
Las Vegas, NV 89102
876-3920
Randal Markin
Games: 35 video poker & keno machines

Loose Caboose Saloon
3175 E. Tropicana Ave.
Las Vegas, NV 89121
433-8060
Katherine Garrison, Mgr.
Games: 15 slot machines

Mad Matty's Bar & Grille
8100 W. Sahara Ave.
Las Vegas, NV 89117
254-9997
Madison Graves
Games: 35 video poker machines

Mardi Gras Inn
3500 Paradise Rd.
Las Vegas, NV 89109
731-2020
Julian Perez, Gen. Mgr.
Games: 50 slot machines

Miss Lucy's Gambling Hall & Saloon
129 N. 3rd St.
Las Vegas, NV 89101
385-3131
Games: 16 slot machines

Mugshots Eatery & Pub
1120 N. Boulder Hwy.
Henderson, NV 89015
566-6577
Ross Anfuso
Games: 39 slot machines

One Eyed Jacks
2823 N. Green Valley Pkwy.
Henderson, NV 89014
434-0690
John Alderfer
Games: 25 slot machines

PJ's Lounge
2300 S. Maryland Pkwy.
Las Vegas, NV 89104
735-5454
Paul Russo
Games: 35 video poker machines

P.T.'s Pub
1631 N. Rancho Dr.
Las Vegas, NV 89106
646-6657
Thomas Boeckle
Games: 35 video machines

P.T.'s Pub
532 E. Sahara Ave.
Las Vegas, NV 89104
792-4121
Philip Boeckle
Games: 29 video poker machines

P.T.'s Slot Casino
46 S. Water St.
Henderson, NV 89015
564-4994
Philip Boeckle
Games: 45 video poker machines

Peppermill Lounge
2985 Las Vegas Blvd. S.
Las Vegas, NV 89109
735-7635
William Paganetti
Games: 15 slot machines

NONRESTRICTED SLOTS-ONLY CASINOS

Queen of Hearts Hotel & Casino
19 E. Lewis St.
Las Vegas, NV 89101
382-8878
Wes Yamada, Gen. Mgr.
Games: 18 slot machines

R Bar
6000 W. Charleston Blvd.
Las Vegas, NV 89102
259-0120
Don Hanson
Games: 20 video poker & keno machines

Rainbow Vegas Hotel & Casino
401 S. Casino Center Blvd.
Las Vegas, NV 89101
386-6166   634-6635
Roy Atuczo, Gen. Mgr.
Gaming: 20,000 sq. ft.
Games: 95 slot machines

Roadhouse Casino
2100 Boulder Hwy.
Henderson, NV 89015
564-1150
Robert McMackin
Games: 122 slot machines

Roadrunner Casino
754 S. Boulder Hwy.
Henderson, NV 89015
566-9999
Scott Skochenko, Gen. Mgr.
Games: 103 slot machines

Renata's
4451 E. Sunset Rd.
Henderson, NV 89014
435-4000
Bud Lang, Gen. Mgr.
Gaming: 10,000 sq. ft.
Games: 199 slot and video machines

Sahara Avenue Saloon
3345 E. Sahara Ave.
Las Vegas, NV 89104
457-2020
Margaret Hoover
Games: 50 video poker & keno machines

Sassy Sally's Casino
32 Fremont St.
Las Vegas, NV 89101
382-5777
James Gish
Games: 181 slot machines

Skinny Dugan's Pub
4127 W. Charleston Blvd.
Las Vegas, NV 89102
877-0522
Robert Keck
Games: 35 slot machines

Smoke Ranch Junction
2425 N. Rainbow Blvd.
Las Vegas, NV 89108
656-1888
Rick Winzen, Gen. Mgr.
Games: 20 slot machines

Stage Door Casino
4000 Audrie St.
Las Vegas, NV 89109
733-0124
Ronald Markin
Games: 50 slot machines

Terrible's Town Casino
642 Boulder Hwy.
Henderson, NV 89015
564-7118
Steve Beckman, Gen. Mgr.
Gaming: 3,800 sq. ft.
Games: 112 slots, bowling, snack bar

The Gambler's Casino
2501 E. Lake Mead Blvd.
North Las Vegas, NV 89030
649-8022
Games: 32 video poker machines

The Village Pub
4365 E. Sunset Rd.
Henderson, NV 89014
454-1887
Gary Ellis & Jaime Holcumb
Games: 40 slot machines

Thirstbuster Lounge
697 N. Valle Verde Dr.
Henderson, NV 89014
454-9200
Jackie Sofia, Gen. Mgr.
Games: 40 video poker machines

Triple Play, The
1875 S. Decatur Blvd.
Las Vegas, NV 89102
364-0808
Charles Pape
Games: 35 video poker & keno machines

Ukulele Lounge
620 Las Vegas Blvd. N.
Las Vegas, NV 89101
382-7364
Patrick Mandel
Games: 24 poker machines

GAMING LESSONS

Many different games are played in the casinos in Las Vegas, such as Red Dog, Pai Gow and Caribbean Stud. Most dealers will be happy to explain the game or give you a guide that shows how to play the game.

The following casinos offer free instruction in various casino games. The instructor will cover the rules of the game, language, etiquette and how to play the game.

Bally's Gaming University
739-4111
Receive free souvenir diploma and match play coupons. Classes are held Mon. - Fri. blackjack 10 am, craps 11 am, roulette 1 pm, baccarat 1:30 pm, Pai Gow 2 pm, craps 3 pm, blackjack 4:30 pm.

Caesars Palace:
731-7110
Instructions given at tables adjacent to the Olympic Casino box office. Lessons are offered Monday - Friday in blackjack, craps, Pai Gow, poker, roulette and mini-baccarat. Starts at 11 am.

Circus Circus
734-0410
Craps at noon and 3:30 pm on Fri., blackjack and roulette 10:30 am - 12 pm Mon. - Fri. except holidays.

Excalibur
597-7777
Lessons daily, craps 12:00 am, blackjack 11 am, roulette 11:15 am poker 10 am and 6 pm followed by a beginners low-limit game

Flamingo Hilton
733-3111
Lessons Mon. - Fri. craps at noon.

Harrah's
369-5000
Instructions given in roulette, blackjack, craps, baccarat and Pai Gow poker. Free lessons in all games are offered Mon. - Fri. 9 am - 3 pm.

Imperial Palace
731-3311
Lessons Mon. - Fri. 11 am - 7 pm and Fri. 10 am in main casino area for blackjack, and daily at 11 am and 3 pm for craps. Using mock chips, classes last an hour. Lots of practice and question time, roulette and mini-baccarat classes.

Lady Luck
477-3000
Lessons in craps and blackjack are held Mon. - Fri. 11 am. Other games upon request

MGM Grand
891-1111
Lessons given daily by gaming veterans. Mini-baccarat 9:30 am, roulette 10:15 am, blackjack 11:30 am, craps 12:15 pm, Pai Gow, Caribbean stud and Let It Ride 2 pm, live poker 10 am.

Riviera
734-5110
Free instructions in gaming Mon. - Fri.

craps 10 am, blackjack 11:15 am, roulette 12:15 pm, baccarat 1 pm, Let It Ride 2:30 pm, Caribbean stud 2 pm

Sahara
737-2111
Neil Ritchie, Instructor. Lessons offered Mon. - Fri. Blackjack noon, craps 11:30 am.

Sam's Town
456-7777
Casino lessons are conducted every weekday 11 am - 5 pm. Call for game schedule. All are held in the main casino. Participants receive a "Certified Gambler" certificate.

San Remo
739-9000
One hour live gaming lesson is held every hour in Japanese at 4:30 pm - 10:30 pm. Free deck of cards to all participants.

Slots-A-Fun
734-0410
Free gaming lessons offered Mon. - Fri. Blackjack 10:30 am, roulette 11:00 am craps 11:30 am.

Stardust:
732-6111
Classes given Mon. - Fri. 10 am - 6 pm in all phases of gaming.

Tropicana:
739-2222
Craps Mon. - Fri. at noon. Special instructional blackjack $1 bets only, dealer will instruct you in rules and etiquette of the game at 11 am. Roulette for a penny at 1 pm.

Sunset Station, 1301 W. Sunset Rd., Henderson, NV 89014

BLACKJACK

Many people are under the impression that the object in the game of Blackjack is to get as close to 21 as possible. Nothing could be further from the truth. The name of the game is to beat the dealer. Once you understand the basics of Blackjack you will see that you can win with a 12 as easily as you can 21!

At the start of the game the dealer gives everyone playing as well as himself two cards. One of the dealers cards is always face up.

King, queen, jack and ten all count as 10; aces count as 1 or 11; All other cards count at their face value.

The player always has first choice as to whether to take an additional card. After all players have made their choice the dealer then exposes his bottom card. If the dealer has 16 or less he must take a card, if he has 17 or more he stands. If the total of your cards are closer to 21 then the dealer's, you win; if the dealer goes over 21 you win; if both you and the dealer have the same total it's a push and you get to keep your bet. If you have taken a third card and have gone over 21, you lose.

For strategy sake always assume that the dealer's bottom card is a 10 value card, so add 10 to whatever the dealer has showing. For example if the dealer has a 5 face up then assume that he has 15.

After you are dealt your first two cards you have 4 options.

1. You may take any total of cards that will bring you to your stopping point or puts you over 21.

2. You may double down. You do this by matching your bet with the same

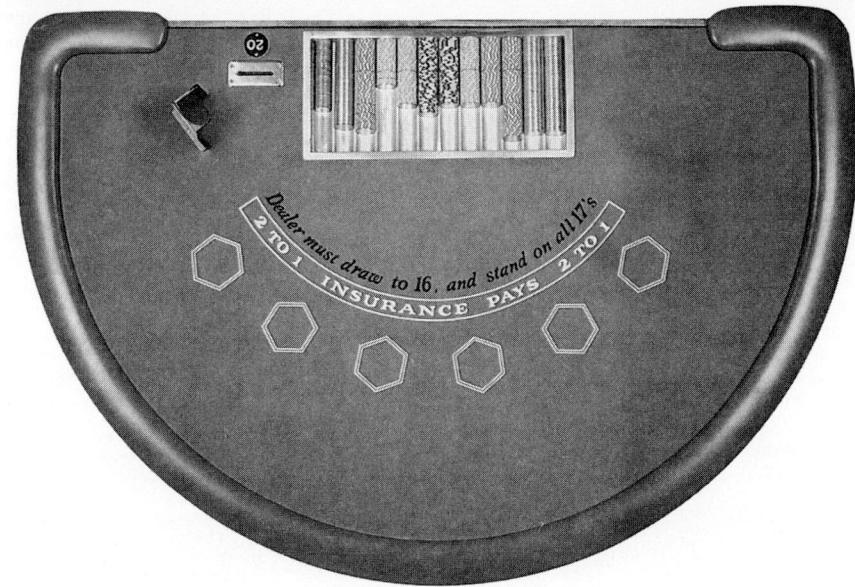

amount and you receive one card. You should always double down when your first two cards total 11. You should double down when your first two cards total 10 and the dealer's up card is 9 or less.

3. You may split any pair. To split you must match your bet and then you will play two separate hands. You receive one card on each hand if you split aces; all other cards you can take as many cards as you want. Always split aces and eights. Never split 4s, 5s or 10s.

4. You may surrender. To surrender you let the dealer know that you want to give up half of your bet. The dealer will then take half your bet and your cards and your hand will be over. In the event that the dealer has an ace showing he will ask if you want insurance. Insurance is betting that the dealer has a Blackjack. Insurance costs up to half of your bet; and is a good bet only if you have Blackjack yourself because the dealer is going to pay you no matter what he has.

Once again, assuming that the dealer's bottom card is a 10 strategy tells you that if the dealer has 12 - 16 and you have 12 - 16, you want to stay. If the dealer has 17 or more you want to hit your hand until you have at least 17.

Gaming instructions courtesy of:
DAVID WILHITE
GAMING SEMINARS & CASINO NIGHTS
for information call: 368-2096

BACCARAT

Baccarat is played with eight decks of cards dealt out of a shoe. The easy part about baccarat is that the player makes no decision what-so-ever except where to make a bet. After the bets are made the rules come into play.

All cards are worth their face value, ace is one and face cards are worth 10.

The object of the game is to get as close to nine as possible. The player and the banker each receive 2 cards to begin. The two cards are added together and all totals over ten are reduced to their single digit value. For example, if the player's two cards total 15, the 1 is dropped and the value is 5.

The bettor has the option of betting on the player or the banker, with the house taking whatever position is left. The player position wins even money, the banker position wins even money less a 5% commission.

The only difference between baccarat and mini-Baccarat is that in baccarat the player gets to handle the cards.

The rules for baccarat are as follows:

The player draws if two card total is 0 - 5.
The player stands if two card total is 6 or 7.
The player stands if two card total is 8 or 9 (Natural)
The bank draws if two card total is 0 - 2.

The bank draws if two card total is 3 and player's third card is not an 8.
The bank draws if two card total is 4 and player's third card is 2 - 7.
The bank draws if two card total is 5 and player's third card is 4 - 7.

The bank draws if two card total is 6 and player's third card is 6 or 7.
The bank stands if two card total is 8 or 9 (Natural). There are never more than three cards drawn for either the player or the banker.

GAMING

CRAPS

Although craps may appear to be one of the hardest games to play, in all reality it is the simplest. Most bets in craps consist of 1 or 2 steps. The fun part of craps is that if you want to make just one bet that's all you have to make. You do not have to bet every roll of the dice.

A The bet that most people make is the Pass Line bet, and it is a 2 step bet. Step 1: If the shooter rolls a 7 or 11 you win, if he rolls a 2, 3 or 12 you lose. If the shooter rolls a 4, 5, 6, 8, 9 or 10, that establishes his point which takes you to Step 2: If the shooter has a point of 5 he must roll the 5 again before he rolls a 7. If the 7 shows first you lose, if the 5 shows you win. Any other number will not affect your bet. Also once the point has been established you cannot pick up your Pass Line bet, it must stay until won or lost.

B The Come bet is the second most popular bet. It is almost exactly like the Pass Line bet except that you are betting on the next number rolled. The Come bet is made directly in front of you in the Come area, and it is a two step bet just like the Pass Line. The only exception is that when the shooter rolls a number the money is then put in the box of the number that was rolled.

C The Don't Pass Line is the exact opposite of the Pass Line, with the exception that if 12 is rolled on the first roll it is a push.

D The Don't Come bet is the exact opposite of the Come, once again with the exception that 12 on the first roll is a push.

E The Odds bet is the money behind your Pass bet and is put down once the point has been established. If the point is 4 or 10, for each additional $1 you put down you will win $2. If the point is 5 or 9 you put down $2 to win $3 and if the point is 6 or 8 you put down $5 dollars to win $6. The odds on Don't Pass and Don't Come are opposites.

F Place bets are made after the point has been established. You tell the dealer that you want to place a number and he will put your money on the outline of the number that you pick. This bet is a 1 step bet, that number you win or 7 you lose. The proper amount to bet on the 4 or 10 is $5 and you will win $9, for the 5 or 9 $5 will win you $7 and for the 6 or 8 $6 will win you $7. You can put these bets down anytime after the point and you can pick them up anytime.

G The Field bet is betting that you are going to win or lose on the next roll of the dice. The Field bet is betting on 2, 3, 4, 9, 10, 11 or 12. 5, 6, 7 and 8 are losers. Most places pay double on 2 or 12.

H Hardway bets are betting only on the pairs 22, 33, 44, 55. If that number shows any other way you lose or if the number 7 shows you lose.

I Proposition bets are betting on 2, 3, 11 or 12 for the next roll of the dice. 2 and 12 pay $30 for $1, 3 and 11 pay $15 for $1.

J Any Craps is betting on 2, 3 or 12; if one of them show you win $8 for $1.

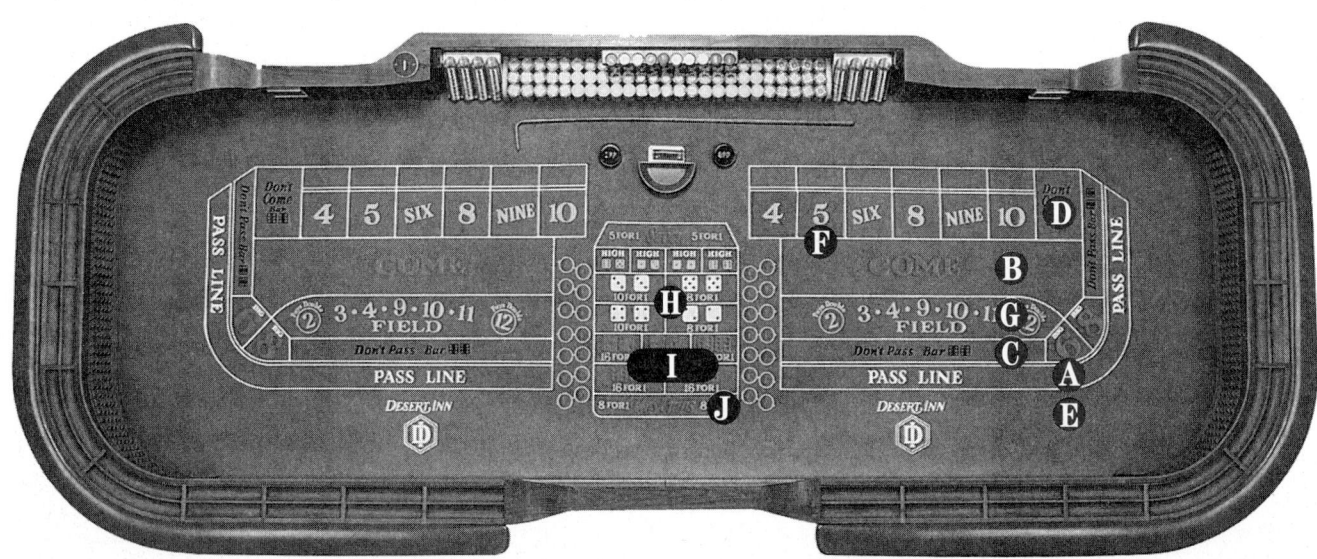

CARIBBEAN STUD

Caribbean Stud is a version of poker that everyone has played at home.

The player makes an initial bet called the ante. The player and dealer each receives five cards, with one of the dealer's cards exposed. The player then decides on whether he can beat the dealer or not. If the player thinks he can beat the dealer he must double his ante, or the ante will be forfeited.

The dealer will expose his hand and he must have an ace and king or better in his hand. If the dealer does not have an ace and king or better, the player gets paid on the ante only. If the dealer does qualify the two hands are compared and the higher hand wins. The ante always wins even money and the back bet wins based on a set payoff.

The player also has the option of making a 1 dollar bet on the progressive. This bet is made before the cards are dealt and you receive the payoff whether the dealer qualifies or not.

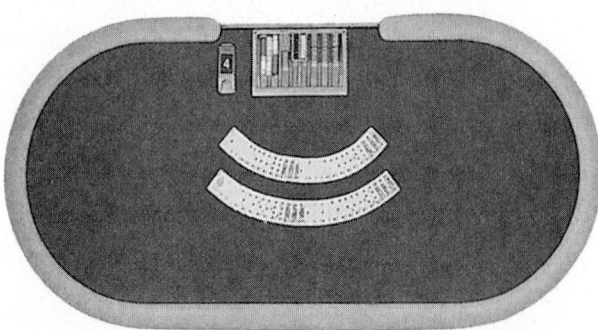

PAI GOW POKER

Pai Gow poker is played with a standard 52 card deck plus one joker. The joker can be used as an ace or to fill in any straight or flush.

Each player and the dealer receives seven cards, which are put into two hands: a high hand and a low hand. The only rule that the player has to follow is that the five card hand must be higher then the two card hand.

The game begins when the dealer pushes a button on the shuffler that generates a number from 1 to 7. This tells the dealer who gets the first hand. To win, both of your hands must beat both of the dealer's hands. If you win one hand and lose one hand, it's a push. Because your odds of winning are the same as the dealer's, if you win the house charges a 5 percent commission.

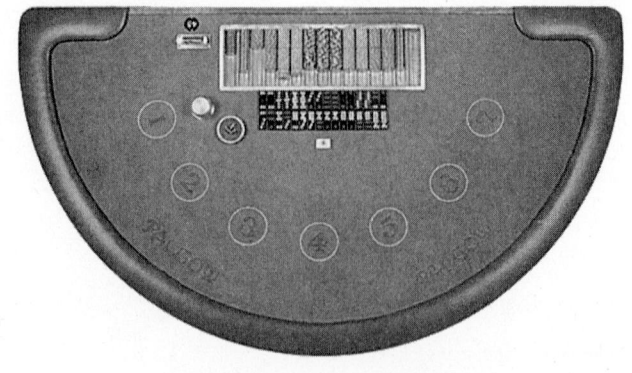

WHEEL OF FORTUNE

The Wheel of Fortune is played by making a bet on one or more of the spaces marked on the wheel.

The payoffs on the wheel are exactly what they say, 1 pays $1, 2 pays $2, 5 pays $5, 10 pays $10, 20 pays $20 and 40 pays $40 for each dollar bet.

The wheel is spun after the bets are made and when it stops all bets are paid.

LET IT RIDE

Let It Ride is similar to the game of five card stud, with the exception that the player can take back up to two-thirds of their bet.

Players make three equal bets in the circles in front of them. The players each receive three cards and the dealer deals two cards face down in front of him. The player looks at his cards and decides if he wants to let his bets ride or pull back the first bet. The dealer then exposes one of his cards and the player then decides if he wants to let the second bet ride or pull it back. The player's third bet must always stay. The dealer then turns over his second card and then each player's hand in turn and either pays or takes the bets. The player wins if he has a pair of 10s or better.

Let It Ride also has a bonus payout that can be played for one dollar. The payout ranges from $4 for two pair up to $20,000 for the Royal Flush.

ROULETTE

What makes roulette so popular is that you bet a number, if it comes up you win, if it doesn't you lose.

When you buy your chips from the dealer you tell him what value you would like to play with. The value of the chips range from 25¢ up to $500, depending on what casino you play at.

Everyone receives their own color of chip, so if more than one person wants to bet on the same number there is no confusion. Remember that the chips are only good on that table and must be cashed out before you leave.

All of the payoffs in roulette are based on a 36 to 1 payoff.

Straight-up: any one individual number pays 35 to 1. **F**
Split: Any two connecting numbers pay 17 to 1. **G**
Street: Any three numbers across pays 11 to 1. **H**
Corner: Any four numbers making a square pays 8 to 1. **I**

Five Numbers: The only place you can bet 5 numbers is 0, 00, 1, 2 and 3. This bet pays 6 to 1. **J**
Six Numbers: Any two rows of three numbers across pay 5 to 1. **K**
Outside bets: Odd, even, red, black, 1-18 and 19-36 pays even money. **A B C**
Outside bets: 1-12, 13-24 and 25-36 pays 2 to 1. **D**
Column: Pays 2 to 1. **E**

KENO

Keno is a form of bingo with the exception that you get to pick what numbers and how many numbers you want. You may pick anywhere from 1 to 20 numbers, and then depending on how much you bet determines your payoff. After marking the numbers that you want with an X you give the ticket to the Keno person who will give you a copy. Make sure that the copy is the same as the one you gave because the copy is the one that all winners are paid on.

The game consists of 80 numbered balls from which 20 are drawn for each game.

You may play as many tickets that you wish on each game, or you may play as many as 100. If you play one game at a time, the ticket must be redeemed at the end of each game if you have a winner.

Keno has some very high returns for the money invested. For example, you can win up to $1,000,000 for a $3 bet.

Gaming instructions courtesy of:

DAVID WILHITE

GAMING SEMINARS & CASINO NIGHTS

for information call: (702) 368-2096

BIG TIPPER

Australian media mogul Kerry Packer won $6 million at a Strip hotel. Mr. Packer tipped the dealers $2 million over the two day period. As with all Strip casinos, the dealers split their tips equally. Dealers made $800 and $1,500. It is said he tipped a waitress $250,000 over the New Year's Holiday.

LOCALS CASINOS

The off-Strip casinos where the locals prefer to play:

1) Gold Coast
2) Palace Station
3) Sam's Town
4) Showboat
5) Santa Fe Hotel
6) Rio Suite Hotel
7) Arizona Charlie's
8) Boulder Station
9) Texas
10) Fiesta
11) Orleans
12) Sunset Station

GAMING

FACTS / SLOT CLUBS

DICE AND CARDS

The Paul-son Dice & Card Company produces over 1,000,000 pairs of dice each month. The dice are manufactured to a tolerance of 0.0002 inch so that no numbers will come up more than others. Paul-son manufactures 3.5 million decks of playing cards. World's largest gaming supply manufacturer.

PHONE BETTING

Excalibur and Circus Circus in Las Vegas have sports betting by phone with a $350 minimum deposit. Play teams, totals, props, parlays, and futures on all major sporting events. Bet as little as $50 or as big as $10,000. All you have to do is dial their toll free number. To set up your account, go to the sports book at any of the three properties, call 1-800-879-1379, ext. 6700.

SLOT CLUB INFORMATION

The Las Vegas Advisor Guide to Slot Clubs

Jeffery Compton
Huntington Press (1995)
1-800-244-2224
ISBN - 0-929712-75-7
118-page book that takes you on a tour of southern Nevada slot clubs - separating the good from the bad and revealing strategies and insider tips that show you how to get more from the casinos than you ever imagined possible.

Price: $6

MEGABUCKS

Suzanne Henley, a Las Vegas resident, broke the world's record for the largest slot jackpot at New York - New York Hotel and Casino, winning $12,510,559 on the Megabucks progressive slot system in 1997. She had played $100 before the four double diamonds lined up on the pay line hit. The win broke the previous record set in Jan. 1996 by John Tippen of Hawaii at the Las Vegas Hilton with a payout of $11.9 million. This is the 45th Nevada Megabucks jackpot since the system began in Mar. 1986. To date, IGT's Nevada Megabucks has paid out more than $211 million in primary jackpots. Henley, who is 46 years old, will receive a check for $500,422 annually for the next 24 years.

THREE-REEL SLOT MACHINE

A 22-symbol, three-reel slot machine has 10,648 possible combinations of symbols.

SLOT MACHINES

These *"one-armed bandits"* can be found in every casino and many stores, restaurants and bars, with a variety of models and coin denominations to please every player. There are three to nine reelers, crisscrosses, multiples, progressive, and specialty machines such as 21, keno, video poker, and video horse racing and dog racing.

MGM GRAND

When the MGM Grand opened, it took $3.5 million to fill the machines and provide change. It took 39 armored cars two days to bring in the money.

SLOT CLUBS

Slot club players receive a card, similar to an ATM card, that is inserted into a machine before you begin play. You are awarded points by how much you put into the machine, which are redeemable for cash, merchandise and comps. Membership is free. You must be 21 and have a photo ID.

Bally's: MVP - shows, dinners, merchandise discounts, more

Barbary Coast: The Fun Club - gifts, hotel redemptions

Big Dog's Hospitality Group: Lucky Dog Slot Club

Boulder Station: Boarding Pass

Caesars Palace: Emperors Club - gifts and rewards including comps, cash, special parties.

California Hotel: Slot Club - cash

Casino Royale: Club Royale - discounts for restaurant, hotel, free T-shirts

Circus Circus: Ringmaster Club - hotel comps, discounts, cash, prizes

Desert Inn: Player's Club - hotel, restaurant, theater comps, pro, logo, gift shop merchandise.

Excalibur: Crown Club - cash or merchandise

Fiesta: Amigo Club - free food and beverage, novelty items, special entertainment packages

Flamingo Hilton: Flamingo Players Club - for slot and table players. Hotel rooms, meals, shows

Four Queens: Reel Winners Club - casino scrip, merchandise, gift certificates

Fremont: Five Star Slot Club - cash and merchandise

Gold Coast: The Club - gift certificates to merchants, hotel amenities

Golden Nugget: 24 Karat Club - bonus points earned are used as cash toward purchases at the hotel's restaurants, gift shops, spa, shows, hotel rooms, slot tokens

Harrah's: Gold Card - discounts and hospitality services

Binion's Horseshoe: points for cash back, comps, gift of the month

Imperial Palace: Imperial Club - complimentary meals, show tickets, rooms, exclusive gift merchandise, cash-back privileges

Jerry's Nugget: The More Club - cash, meals, gift shop

Las Vegas Hilton: Club Magic - cash, merchandise, hotel amenities

MGM Grand: MGM Player Card - room discounts, invitations to parties, retail shop discounts, preferred room, show reservations

Mirage: Club Mirage - special room rates, comp meals, shows, cash rebates

Nevada Palace: Players Circle

The Orleans: Club Orleans Slot Club

Reserve: Club Reserve - Self comp is available through slot machines for buffet and cafe, gift certificates for gift shop

Riviera: Star Club - merchandise

Sahara: Club Sahara

Sam's Town: Sam's Town Club - cash, comps and special events

Santa Fe: Desert Fortune Club

Showboat: Slot Club - cash, gifts and discounts

Stardust: Slot Club - cash awards

Treasure Island: The Treasure Island Club - points redeemed for cash, goods and services, dollar machines or higher

Tropicana: Island Winners Club - comp points for shows, meals, cash

SPORTS BOOK

During football season many hotels have special parties for Sunday and Monday night football. Big screen televisions along with food and drinks are served usually in one of the hotel's lounges, showrooms or ballrooms. A few of the plusher, state-of-the-art race and sports books are found at Caesars Palace, Las Vegas Hilton, MGM, Rio and Bally's.

Arizona Charlie's
258-5200
Mary Sapp, Mgr.
Hours: 8 am - 11 pm

Bally's
739-4111
John Avello, Dir.
Hours: Mon. - Thu. 8 am - 11 pm, Fri. - Sat. 6 am - 2 am, Sun. 6 am - 6 pm

Barbary Coast
737-7111
Jerry Ludt, Sports Mgr.
Robert Muniz, Race Mgr.
Hours: Race 8 am until last race

The Beach
731-1925
365 Convention Center Dr.
Las Vegas, NV 89109
Sports book satellite of Barbary Coast

Boulder Station
432-7777
Roy Haskell, Sports Mgr.
Hours: Race 8 am until last race. Sports Mon. - Thu. 8:30 am - 11 pm, Fri. - Sat. 6 am - 3 am, dog races Tue. - Sat. 4:30 pm until last race. Closed Sun. & Mon.

Caesars Palace
731-7110
Vinnie Magliulo, Sports Mgr.
Hours: Sports 9 am until last major event
Race: Mon. - Wed. 8:30 am - 4:30 pm, Thu. 8:30 am - 11:30 pm, Fri. 8:30 am - 12:30 am, Sat. 8:30 am - midnight, Sun. 8:30 am -6 pm
32,000 sq. ft. book with 650 seats and 38 video screens, a three-color marquee displays bets

California Hotel
385-1222
Mario Pirastau, Mgr.
Hours: Mon. - Thu. 10 am until last event, Fri. - 10 am - 10 pm Sat. 8 am - 10 pm, Sun. 8 am until last event
Sports book only

Circus Circus
734-0410
Jeff Stonebeck, Mgr.
Hours: 8:30 am until last event

Continental
737-5555
Satellite operated by Leroy's Horse & Sports
Hours: 8 am until last event

Desert Inn
733-4444
Rob Terch, Dir.
Hours: 7:30 am until last race or sports event

El Cortez
385-5200
Jerry Subject, Mgr.
Hours: 8:30 am - 10:30 pm; during football season, open 24 hours

Excalibur
597-7777
Eric St. Clair, Mgr.
Hours: Mon. - Thu. 8 am - 9 pm, Fri. 7 am - 1 am, Sat. 7 am - 2:30 am and Sun. 7 am - 10 pm Race hours are Sat. - Thu. 8 am - 8:30 pm and Fri. 8 am - 10:30 pm

Fiesta
631-7000
Mark Nelson, Mgr.
Hours: 9 am - 8 pm
Hours: Mon. - Thu. 8:30 am - 10:30 pm, Fri. 8:30 am - 3 am, Sat. 7 am - 3 am, Sun. 7 am - 10:30 pm
Drive-thru sports book. Three drive up lanes. Drive-thru hours: Mon. - Thu. 9:30 am - 10 pm, Fri. 9:30 am - 3 am, Sat. 7:30 am - 3 am, Sun. 7:30 am - 10 pm

Fitzgeralds
388-2400
Satellite operated by Leroy's Horse and Sports Place
Sports book only
Hours: Mon. 11 am - 8 pm, Tue. 11 am - 7:30 pm, Wed. 9 am - 8 pm, Thu. 8 am - 7:30 pm, Fri. 11 am - midnight, Sat. 8 am - midnight, Sun. 8 am - 6:30 pm

Flamingo Hilton
733-3111
Mark Goldman, Mgr.
Hours: 8:30 am - start of last game
Race book offers parimutuel wagering, sports book

Four Queens
385-4011
Satellite of Leroy's
Sports Book Only
Hours: Mon. - Thu. 10 am - 7:30 pm, Fri. 10 am - midnight, Sat. 8 am - midnight, Sun. 9 am - 7 pm

Fremont
385-3232
Carol Boyd, Mgr.
Hours: Mon. - Thu. 8 am - 9 pm, Fri. 8 am - 1:45 pm, Sat. 7 am - 1:45 pm, Sun. 7 am - 9 pm

Gold Coast
367-7111
Liz Lucas, Race Mgr.
Bert Osbourne, Sports Mgr.
Hours: Race 8 am until last race 24 hours during football season, Sun. - Thu. 7 am - 11 pm, Fri. and Sat. 24 hours

Golden Nugget
385-7111
Hours: 9 am until last event

Harrah's
369-5000
Howard Greenbaum, Mgr.
Hours: Sports - 9 am until last event, Fri. - Sat. 9 am - 1:30 am, race - 8 am until last race

Las Vegas Hilton
732-5111
Art Manteris, Sports Mgr.
Lou D'Amico, Race Mgr.
Hours: Mon. - Thu. 8:30 am - 12:15 am, Fri. - Sat. 7 am - 4 am, Sun. 7 am - 9 pm
Race Hours: Sun. - Thu. 9 am - 9 pm, Fri. - Sat. 9 am - 10 pm

Holiday Inn Casino Boardwalk
735-1167
Bob Bernacchi, Mgr.
Hours: Sun. - Thu. 8 am - 10:30 pm, Fri. - Sat. 7 am - 10:30 pm

Binion's Horseshoe
382-1600
Katherine Manix, Race Mgr.
Nick Bogdonavich, Sports Mgr.
Hours: Sports - Mon. - Thu. 8 am - 10 pm, Fri. 8 am - 3 am, Sat. 7 am - 10 pm, Sun. 7 am - 10 pm Race - 8 am - 10:30 pm Tickets cashed 24 hrs.

Imperial Palace
731-3311
Jay Kornegay, Dir.
Hours: Sun. 7 am - 10 pm, Mon. - Thu. 8 am - 11 pm, Fri. 8 am - 2 am, Sat. 7 am - 2 am, Drive Up Hours: Mon. - Thu. 9 am - 9 pm, Fri. 9 am - 11 pm, Sat. 8 am - 11 pm, Sun. 8 am - 8 pm Enter off Koval Ln. between Sands and Flamingo Rd.

Las Vegas Hilton
732-5111
Art Manteris, Sports Mgr.
Rick Herron, Race Mgr.
Hours: Mon. - Fri. 9 am - 11 pm Sat. - Sun., 8 am - 11 pm
30,500 sq. ft. book with seating for over 400 patrons. Called *"The Superbook."*

Las Vegas Club
385-1664
Tom Vincenta, Mgr.
Hours: Mon. - Fri. 9 am - 11:30 pm, Sat and Sun. 24 hours, race hours 9 am - 10 pm daily

Leroy's Horse and Sports Place Office
735-0101
675 Grier Dr.
Las Vegas, NV 89119
382-1561
Vic Salerno, Owner
Hours: Mon. - Fri. 8:30 am - 5 pm
Leroy's operates 42 satellite sports books around the state.

Luxor
730-5530
Eric St. Clair, Mgr.
Mike Davis, Race Mgr.
Hours: Sun. - Thu. 8 am - 9 pm, Sat. - Sun. 8 am - 1 am
Race hours: 8 am - 9 pm

MGM Grand
891-1111
Dennis Dahl, Sports Mgr.
William Hall, Race Mgr.
Hours: Sports - Mon. - Thu. 8:30 am - 9 pm, Fri. and Sat. 8:30 am - midnight, Sun. 8:30 am - 8 pm
Race: 8:30 am until last race

Maxim
731-4300
Operated by Leroy's Sports Book
Sports book only
Hours: Mon. 10 am - 10 pm, Tue. - Wed. 10 am - 7:30 pm, Thu. 10 am - 9 pm, Fri. 10 am - 2 am

Mirage
791-7111
Robert Walker, Sports & Race Dir.
Hours: Sports - Mon. - Thu. 8 am - 11 pm, Fri. - Sat. 6 am - 3:30 am, Sun. 6:30 am - 11 pm
Race: 8:30 am until last race

Monte Carlo
730-7777
Kevin Klein, Race & Sports Mgr.
Hours: Mon. - Thu. 8 am - 10 pm, Fri. 7 am - 2 am, Sat. 7 am - 3 am, Sun. 7 am - 10 pm. Race hours are the same.

Nevada Palace
458-8810
Satellite operated by Leroy's Horse & Sports Book
Hours: 8 am - 11 pm

New Frontier
794-8200
Lenny Del Genio, Mgr.
Hours: 9 am - 9 pm
Sports book only

New York New York
740-6969
Martha Ditsworth, Race & Sports Book Mgr.
Sports hours: Mon., Tue. & Thu. 8:30 am - 10 pm, Wed. 8:30 am - 10:30 pm, Fri. 8:30 am - 11:30 pm, Sat. 8:30 am - 10 pm and Sun. 8:30 am - 9 pm Race book hours are the same.

Orleans
365-7111
Don Williams, Sports Mgr.
Robert Muniz, Race Mgr.
Sports hours: Mon. - Thu. 8 am - 11 pm, Fri. & Sat. 24 hours
Race hours: Mon. - Thu. 7 am - 9:30 pm, Fri. - Sat. 7 am - 10:30 pm, Sun. 7 am - 6:30 pm

Palace Station
367-2411
Pete Glanz, Sports Mgr.
Hours: Mon. - Thu. 8:30 am - 11 pm, Fri. 8:30 am - 3 am, Sat. 6 am - 3 am, Sun. 6 am - 11 pm
Race hours: 8:30 am until last race

Plaza
386-2110
Jerry Subject, Mgr.
Hours: 8 am until last race
Sports: 8 am - 10:30 pm

Reserve
558-7000
D. Wayne Maulder, Mgr.
Sports hours: open 24 hours

Rio
252-7777
Roger Sims, Dir.
Race hours: 8:30 am until 8:30 pm
Sports hours: Sun. - Thu. 8:30 am - 8 pm, Fri. - Sat. open 24 hours

Riviera
734-5110
Gary Jones, Mgr.
Race hours: 8 am until last event
Sports hours: Mon. - Wed. 9 am - 9:30 pm, Thu. 9 am - 8:30 pm, Fri. 9 am - 1 am, Sat. 7 am - 1 am, Sun. 7 am - 8:30 pm

Sahara
737-2111
Andy DeLuca, Dir.
Hours: Mon. - Thu. 8:30 am - 8 pm, Fri. 8:30 am - 11 pm, Sat. 7:30 am - 11 pm, Sun. 7:30 am - 8 p.m

Sam's Town
456-7777
Norm Kelly, Sports Mgr.
Tony Paonessa, Race Mgr.
Race Hours: 8 pm until the last race
Hours: Mon. - Thu. 8 am - 9 pm, Fri. - Sat. 8 am - 4 am, Sun. 8 am - 9 pm

Hotel San Remo
739-9000
Operated by Leroy's Sports Book
Hours: Mon. - Thu. 11 am - 7:30 pm, Fri. and Sat. 8 am - 4 am, Sun. 8 am - 9 pm

Santa Fe
658-4900
Steve Klein, Mgr. of Sports & Race
Hours: Mon. 9:30 am - 10 pm, Tue. - Wed. 9:30 am - 8:30 pm, Thu. 9:30 am - 9:30 pm, Fri. 9:30 am - 3:30 a.m, Sat. 7 am - 3:30 am, Sun. 7 am - 9:30 pm

Showboat
385-9123
Bruno Sciotto, Mgr.
Hours: Race Book - 8 am - 9 pm, Sports Book - 8 am to last game.

Skyline
565-9116
LeRoy's
Sports Book Only
Hours: 11 am - 8 pm

Stardust
732-6111
Joe Lupo, Dir.
Hours: Mon. - Thu. 8 am - 10 pm, Fri. - Sun. 8 am until last event - Tickets cashed 24 hours
Over 60 monitors and big screens. Telephone wagering, $1,000 deposit required to open your personal phone account.

Sunset Station
547-7777
Rob Perry, Race & Sports Dir.
Sports Hours: Mon - Thu. 8 am - 11 pm, Fri. 8 am - 3 am, Sat. 6 am - 3 am, Sun. 6 am - 11 pm. Race hours are 8 am until 1/2 hour after last race.

Texas
631-1000
Terry Downey, Mgr.
Hours: Sun. - Thu. 8:30 am - 11 pm and Fri. - Sat. 8:30 am - 3 am. Tickets can be cashed 24 hours.

Treasure Island
894-7111
Jim Croley, Mgr.
Hours: 9 am - midnight

Tropicana
739-2222
Jack Love, Mgr.
Hours: Mon. 10 am - 9 pm, Tue. - Thu. 10 am - 8 pm, Fri. 10 am - midnight, Sat. 7 am - midnight, and Sun. 7 am - 10 pm Sports book only

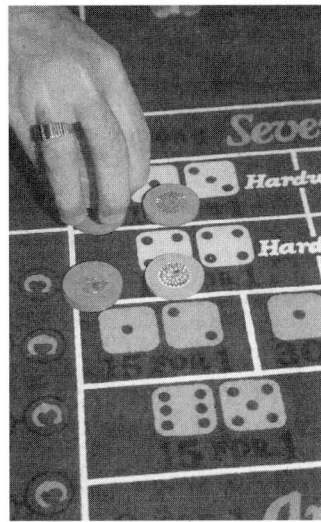

Photo: Photolechnik International

GAMING

POKER ROOMS

Arizona Charlie's
258-5200
David Nais , Mgr.
Seven Card Stud, $1-$4, Texas Hold'em, $1-$4 - last card $8; 4 tables

Boulder Station
432-7777
Rory Haskell, Mgr.
Seven Card Stud $1-$5, Texas Hold'em $1-$4-$8-$8, $3-$6-$12-$12, $3-$6-$6, Omaha $1-$4-$8-$8; 10 tables

Circus Circus
734-0410
Jerry Harwell, Mgr.
$1-$3 Seven Card Stud, $1-$4, $2-$4, Hold'em $3-$6, Omaha $3-$6; 10 tables

El Cortez
385-5200
Scott Furman, Mgr.
Seven Card Stud $1-$3, Hold'em $1-$3-$6; 3 tables

Excalibur
597-7777
Patty Sherman, Mgr.
Seven Card Stud $1-$5, Texas Hold'em $2-$6, Jackpot poker; 11 tables

Flamingo Hilton
733-3111
Steve Baker, Mgr.
Seven Card Stud $1-$5, Texas Hold'em $1-$4-$8-$8; 6 tables

Gold Spike Hotel
384-8444
Rosita White, Mgr.
Seven Card Stud, $1-$3-$6; 1 table

Gold Strike Hotel
477-5000
Seven Card Stud, Texas Hold 'em; 1 table

Gold Strike Inn
293-5000
Jerry Marshall, Mgr.
Seven Card Stud $1-$5, Texas Hold'em, $1-$3-$6-$6; 3 tables

Harrah's
369-5000
Chuck Stiles, Mgr.
$1-$5 Seven Card Stud, Texas Hold'em $1-$4-$8-$8; 8 tables

Binion's Horseshoe
382-1600
Jim Albrecht, Mgr.
$1-$5 Seven Card Stud, $1-$4-$8, $4-$8, $10-$20, $15-$30, Texas Hold'em $4-$8, Omaha, $4-$8, $10-$20, Omaha Hi-Lo; 14 tables

King 8 Hotel and Gambling Hall
736-8988
Starts at 6 pm; 2 tables

Ligouri's Bar & Casino
565-1688
Lee Ann McCormick, Mgr.
Closed Mondays; 2 tables

Luxor
262-4210
Jim Weitzel, Mgr.
Seven Card Stud $1-$4, $5-$10, $1-$4-$8-$8, Texas Hold'em, $1-$4-$8-$8 Hi-Lo; 8 tables

MGM Grand
891-1111
Mark Jacobs, Mgr.
Seven Card Stud: $15-$30 Seven Card Stud $1-$5, Texas Hold'em $1-$4, $10-$20, Omaha $1-$4, $15-$30; 20 tables

Mahoney's Silver Nugget
399-1111
James J. Sauner, Mgr.
Seven Card Stud, Hold-'em; 2 tables

Mirage
791-7111
Doug Dalton, Mgr.
Seven Card Stud $1-$5, $5-$10, $15-$30, $40-$80, $75-$150, $150-$300, $200-$400 *(varies)* Horsegame, $3-$6, $6-$12, $10-$20, $20-$40, $40-$80, $75-$150 Hold 'em, $4-$8, $10-$20 Omaha 8 or better; 31 tables

Monte Carlo
730-7777
Becky Hughes, Mgr.
Seven Card Stud $1-$5, $5-$10, Seven Card Hi/lo 8 or better $1-$5; 8 tables

Nevada Palace
458-8810
Bob Peckinpaugh, Mgr.
2 table - poker room opens at 10 am
Seven Card Stud $1-4, Hold'em $1-4-8-8,

Orleans
365-7111
David Hricsina, Mgr.
Seven Card Stud $1-$5, Hold'em $4-$8, $6-$12 Hold'em with a half kill, $4-$8-$8 Omaha hi/lo split with a half kill; 20 tables

Palace Station
367-2411
Greg Nares, Mgr.
Seven Card Stud: $1-$4, $1-$3-$6 on the end limit, Texas Hold 'em, $2-$4 with a $2 blind, $1-$4-$8-$8 with a $1-$2 blind; 9 tables.

Plaza
386-2110
Jerry Rowell, Mgr.
Seven Card Stud, $1-$4, Hold'em $1-$3-$3-$6, Omaha $3-$6, Pan $1-$2, $5-$10 and $25-$50; 12 poker & 13 pan tables

Reserve
558-7000
Larry Sanders, Mgr.
$1-$5 Seven Card Stud, Texas Hold'em $1-$4-$8-$8, 6 tables

Rio
252-7777
Carol Trimble, Mgr.
Seven Card Stud, $1-$4, Hold'em $1-$4-$8-$8; 8 tables

Riviera
794-9255
Rick Vetter, Mgr.
Seven Card Stud, $1-$4, Texas Hold'em, $1-$4-$8-$8, Hi/lo Split $1-$5, $3 & $6, Jackpot Poker; 5 tables

Sahara
737-2111
Fred Masters, Mgr.
Seven Card Stud, $1-$5, Hold'em, $1-$4-$8 and $1-$4-$8-$8, Hi/lo Split $5-$10; 5 Pan tables and 5 tables

Sam's Town
456-7777
Dick Gatewood, Mgr.
Seven Card Stud, $1-$4, Hold'em $1-$4-$8-$8, Omaha $3-$6 and $4-$8; 9 tables

Santa Fe
658-4900
Olivia Elliott, Mgr.
$1-$4 Seven Card Stud, $3-$6 Texas Hold 'em, $1-$4 Omaha Hi/low 8 or better with a half kill; 5 tables

Showboat
385-9123
Gary Dewitt, Mgr.
$1-$5 Seven Card Stud, Texas hold 'em, $1-$3-$6-$6; 3 tables

Skyline Casino
565-9116
1 table

Stardust
732-6111
Bob Rihel, Mgr.
Seven Card Stud $1-$4, Hold'em $3-$6; 10 tables

Sunset Station
547-7777
George Steedle, Mgr.
Seven Card Stud $1-$5, Seven Card Stud with deuces wild $1-$5, Hold'em $3-$6-$9, Omaha High $3-$6-$9; 9 tables

Texas
631-1000
A. J. Martin, Mgr.
Seven Card Stud $1-$5, Texas Hold'em $1-$4-$8-$8, $6-$8, $4-$8 Omaha high only and pot limit Texas Hold 'em; 10 tables

Tom's Sunset Casino
564-5551
Seven Card Stud $1-$4, Texas Hold 'em $1-$4; 1 table

FUN BOOKS

Many casinos issue fun books with a variety of coupons good for free drinks, match play at the gaming tables, free souvenirs and discounts. Most casinos require an out-of-state drivers license and/or airline ticket or room key.

Barbary Coast: Fun books available to hotel guests upon check-in.

Continental: Fun books available to hotel guests upon check-in.

El Cortez: No fun books handed out, only mailed upon request to out-of-towners.

Excalibur: Fun Books available at guest information booth.

Fitzgeralds: Guest will receive Fun Book upon check-in at hotel or with Fitzgerald's card membership.

Flamingo Hilton: Fun Books are available at Players Club.

Gold Strike Inn *(Boulder City)*: At cashier's cage, must show out of state ID, comp drink, free all day keno, free souvenir

Harrah's: Customer Center in Casino will give free membership to Slot Club.

Imperial Palace: Coupons available in front of hotel.

Lady Luck: Mad money booth in Casino. Promotions will give free Slot Card Membership to everyone

O'Sheas Casino: Casino Cage Fun Books redeemed at Slot Club Promotions Booth in Casino.

Railroad Pass *(Henderson)*: At hotel desk, free drink, free souvenir, discount in gift shop

Rio: Fun Book at Casino Cage

Riviera: Slot Club cards free at Redemption Booth in Casino with flyer given outside front door

Sahara: Fun Books available at the Sahara Welcome Center. Must show out of state ID or room key

San Remo: Fun books available to hotel guests upon check-in.

Showboat: Slot Card membership free to everyone 21 and over with photo ID

Silver City: Fun Books available at the Welcome Center

Silverton: Fun books are given to guests at hotel registration.

Skyline: available at cashier's cage. Free souvenir, cocktail, lucky buck, $.50 in nickels, food discounts, drawing entry.

Slots-A-Fun: Coupons for fun book available at Circus Circus.

Stardust: Fun Books available at Logo Shop in Hotel. Slot Club membership cards at Slot Booth in Casino.

Photo: Phototechnik International

BINGO

For information on bingo, pick up a free copy of the *Bingo Bugle* at any bingo parlor.

BINGO PARLORS

Arizona Charlie's
258-5200
Judy Jones, Mgr.
Hours: 24 hours on odd hours
Paper, double action games 11 am - 1 am, $1,000 guarantee 11 am, 7 pm and 1 am

Eldorado Casino
564-1811
Barbara Devine, Mgr.
Hours: 7 pm and 9 pm party sessions

Fiesta
631-7000
J. D. Duke, Mgr.
Hours: 9 am - 11 am on odd hours

Gold Coast
367-7111
Hours: Ten sessions daily from 8 am - 2 am on even hours
Lyn Brown, Mgr.
Bonanza Bingo, Progressive starts at $25,000 five times daily, 10 am, 2 pm, 6 pm and 10 pm & midnight sessions. Free donuts and coffee at 8 am and 10 am

Gold Spike
384-8444
Hours: 6:30 am - 9:30 am

Binion's Horseshoe
382-1600
Harvey Puller, Mgr.
Hours: 8 am - 2 am on even hours
All paper games, $4, $6, $10, $12 cards, special games. Thousand dollar guaranteed for Bonanza coverall 10 am - midnight.

New Frontier
794-8200
Jim Pappa, Mgr.
Hours: 11 am - 9 pm on odd hours
Paper: $3, $6, $9, $10

Jerry's Nugget
399-3000
Janet Arida, Mgr.
Hours: 11 am - 11 pm
Paper: $3, $6, $9 and $12
Free donuts and coffee at 11 am session. Double action sessions at 11 am, 3 pm and 9 pm

Palace Station
367-2411
Allen Karol, Mgr.
Hours: 9:30 am, 11 am, 1 pm, 3 pm, 5 pm, 7 pm, 9 pm and 11 pm

$3, $6, $9, $12 and $18 cards. Free coffee and donuts at 9:30 am session. Thousand dollar guaranteed coverall at 3 pm and 7 pm

Reserve
558-7000
Iona Alderete, Mgr.
Hours: 9 am - 11 pm, every odd hour. Paper only, $3, $6, $9 and $18

Sam's Town
454-8063
Marie Zorne, Mgr.
Hours: 9 am - 1 am
Paper: $3, $6, $9, and $15
Free continental breakfast at 9 am session. Double and triple action bingo Monday at 1 pm and Thursday at 9 pm Thousand dollar guaranteed coverall at 3 pm and 11 pm.

Santa Fe
658-4900
Jeannie Abbott, Mgr.
Hours: 8 am - midnight, Fri. and Sat. til 2 am
Paper: $3, $6, $9 and $12, computers

Showboat
385-9123
Linda Sanchez, Mgr.

Hours: 9 am - 1 am on odd hours
Boards and paper, minimum $3, card $1, $2, $3, and $5, bonus card with $5 buy-in, double bingo at 5 pm, 7 pm and 1 am.

Silver Nugget
399-1111
Gene Blyer, Mgr
Hours: 10 am - 10 pm.
$3, $6, $9, $10 and $14 rainbow
Free bonus strip on buy-in and wild bingo on Wed.

Sunset Station
547-7777
Dee Goss, Mgr.
Hours: Starts at 8 am every even hour until midnight

Texas
631-1000
Diane Reilly, Bingo Mgr.
Hours: 9 am - 11 pm on odd hour
Paper: $3, $6, $9, $12 and $9, $18 rainbow

Western
384-4620
Sherrion Breen, Mgr.
Hours: 8 am, 11 am, 2 pm, 7 pm, 9 pm
$1 bingo, boards and paper

GAMING STORES

The Bud Jones Co.
3640 S. Valley View Blvd.
Las Vegas, NV 89103
876-2782
Bernard Jones, Owner
Hours: Mon. - Fri. 8 am - 4 pm
Credit Cards: MC, Visa
Supplier of gaming equipment to casinos, personalized casino quality chips for home games.

C. J's Casino Emporium
2780 Las Vegas Blvd. S.
Las Vegas, NV 89109
893-0660

2000 Las Vegas Blvd. S.
Las Vegas, NV 89109
380-1220
Catalog sales: 257-2220
Carl Fredericksen, Owner
Casino products for home use, slots, poker, cards, dice and more

Dags Gaming Supplies
5609 Avenida Filla St.
Las Vegas, NV 89108
656-1400
Dennis Goodman
Hours: 8 am - 5 pm
Credit Cards: None
Gaming supplies, layouts, chips, furniture.

Gamblers Book Club
630 S. 11th St.
Las Vegas, NV 89101
382-7555   1-800-522-1777
Edna Luckman, Gen. Mgr.
Howard Schwartz, Marketing Dir.
Hours: Mon. - Sat. 9 am - 5 pm
Credit Cards: MC, Visa, Discover
New and used books and publications on gambling. Carries almost everything ever written on gambling, including various systems. Catalog available.

Gamblers General Store
800 S. Main St.
Las Vegas, NV 89101
382-9903   1-800-322-2447
Wendy Butler, Mgr.

Hours: 9 am - 5 pm
Credit Cards: MC, Visa
Slot and poker machine, gambling books and tapes, table layouts, chips, cards and anything else that has to do with gambling, unique gift items. Largest gambling supply store in the world. Call for catalog.

Gaming Books International
7441 Lake Mead Blvd.
Las Vegas, NV 89128
477-7771
James Richards, Gen. Mgr.
Hours: Call for appointment
Credit Cards: Visa, MC
Gaming books, video, cassettes.

Paul-son Dice & Card Inc.
2121 Industrial Rd.
Las Vegas, NV 89102
384-2425   800-546-DICE
Eric Endy, Gen. Mgr.
Hours: Mon. - Fri. 8:30 am - 5 pm
Credit Cards: MC, Visa

Dice, cards, casino chips, custom table layouts and casino furniture. Tables and party items available for rent.

Videotronics Inc.
3280 W. Hacienda Ave., Ste. 201
Las Vegas, NV 89118
795-0787   800-440-8854
Hours: Mon. - Fri. 8 am - 5 pm
Slot machines, poker machines, antiques, retail and wholesale. For Sat. and Sun. appointments, call 433-3939.

Vintage Slots
3379 Industrial Rd.
Las Vegas, NV 89109
369-2323   1-800-228-7568
Rudy Lewis, Owner
Hours: 9 am - 5 pm
Credit Cards: All major cards
Slot and poker machines, juke boxes, coke machines and game room furnishings. Buy, sell, trade.

GAMING

GAMING MISCELLANEOUS

RACE & SPORTS BOOKS

A number of resort casinos feature race and sports book wagering. Live closed-circuit race broadcasts and your favorite sports via satellite are featured on giant screen TVs. The largest books in town are at the Las Vegas Hilton, Caesars Palace and the Stardust.

Sports events include professional and college football, professional baseball, professional hockey, professional and college basketball, the Indianapolis 500, the Kentucky Derby, and major championship boxing.

Employees at the race and sports books will be able to answer any questions and will take bets on almost any horse race and sports event occurring in the United States, excluding Nevada.

FOOTBALL BETTING

To make a straight bet, you wager $11 to win $10. If you win, you get $21 back, your $11 bet plus $10 won. A minus sign on the board denotes the favorite and a plus sign denotes the underdog. To win, your team must cover the point spread which follows the plus/minus sign. Parlay bets involve two or more teams and over/under bets are the total points scored by both teams.

CALIFORNIA SUPER LOTTO TICKETS

Dry Lake Mini-Mart
I-15 S. at State Line
(on the California/Nevada border)
Hours: 6 am - 10:30 pm
The closest place to Las Vegas to buy California Super Lotto tickets. Tickets are $1 each. Customers can either pick their own five numbers or have the computer randomly select a combination.
Latest lottery results: 382-1212 ext. 5402

LARGEST LEGAL BET ON A SUPERBOWL

The largest legal bet on a Superbowl was placed in 1991, at the closed Little Caesars. Bob Stupak, partner in the Stratosphere, placed $1 million on the game and won.

1998 SUPERBOWL WAGERING

A record $77.3 million was wagered in Nevada's 115 sport books on the 1998 Superbowl between the Denver Broncos and the Greenbay Packers.

POKER

Poker is played with one deck of playing cards and dealt only by professional dealers. Games featured include Seven Card Stud, Texas Hold 'em, Seven Card Stud High-Low split, Razz and Omaha High-Low Split. The two most popular games in Las Vegas poker rooms are Texas Hold'em and Seven Card Stud.

The games, the limits and the amount of rake *(house commission)* are clearly posted in the poker area.

The eighth annual Queens Poker Classic was held in March 1998. The tournament featured 22 events and over $2.5 million in prize money.

For information on poker and poker rooms pick up a free copy of the *Card Player* at any poker room.

ANNUAL WORLD SERIES OF POKER

A southern California man turned a $220 buy-in at a satellite game into $1 million in the 26th Annual World Series of Poker at Binion's Horseshoe. The annual event is held in April and May.

CASINO PAYCHECK PROMOTIONS

Alystra: Paycheck drawing and free drink ticket

Arizona Charlie's: Maximum prize $10,000

Boulder Station: Maximum prize Camaro, GMC truck

Fiesta: Paycheck pinata

Gold Coast: win up to $250,000

Binion's Horseshoe: pull on slot, top prize $1 million

Opera House: Maximum prize $500

Palace Station: Maximum prize Camaro, GMC Truck

Rio: Poker wheel, maximum prize $25,000

Sam's Town: Scratch Pay Daze and win up to $250,000

Santa Fe: Cash, food offers,

Showboat: Progressive jackpot

Silver Nugget: Maximum prize $5,000

Silverton: Payroll Pick'em up Buck

Texas: Paycheck Round-up, cash prizes. Every paycheck is a guaranteed winner.

Sightseeing

Sightseeing in Las Vegas and surrounding areas is endless. Days are filled with visits to area museums, fantastic day shows at hotel/casino resorts, hiking in area canyons and day trips to places like the Grand Canyon, Mount Zion National Park and Hoover Dam, while nights are filled with fantastic battles between the pirates and the British, dragons vs. wizards and erupting volcanos.

Exciting tours are available through many reputable companies throughout the Las Vegas area, who offer tours of the Grand Canyon and many other points of interest at reasonable fees. Helicopter rides are the most popular, while other less conventional tours are available. Tours such as hot air balloon and RV tours of the Las Vegas Valley are becoming increasingly popular. Call ahead to reserve as many of these tours are booked well in advance.

SUGGESTED SIGHTSEEING ITINERARY

Day One:

- Start your day at the Luxor with a tour of the King Tut Museum, view the impressive replica of the ancient Egyptian tomb and artifacts.

- Go over to the Mirage to see the world-famous white tigers and take a tour of the dolphin habitat or visit Siegfried & Roy's Magic Garden of exotic animals.

- Walk next door to Caesars Palace, have lunch at the world-famous Planet Hollywood in the Forum Shops. Spend some time seeing the Forum's sensational free entertainment and browse through the many interesting stores.

- Catch a show at the amazing Omnimax Theatre or the new Imax presentation "Race for Atlantis" show.

- Have dinner at Hard Rock Hotel or Cafe, and see their impressive collection of music memorabilia.

- After dark, catch the Pirate Battle at Treasure Island and walk over to the Mirage to see the volcano erupt. Both are "must see" events.

Day Two:

- If May through Sept., spend the morning having fun in the sun at Wet'n Wild.

- Grab Holy Cow! micro brewery and head over to Circus Circus to check out the circus performances in the midway. Grand Slam Canyon, adjacent to Circus Circus, offers an excellent variety of amusement park rides and high-tech features in an air-conditioned environment.

- Just down the street, the MGM offers more of the same kind of excitement in their Grand Adventure Park.

- Back to your hotel and get ready for a dinner at the Top of the World Restaurant at the Stratosphere Tower.

- That evening, continue downtown to see the light and sound show of the Fremont Street Experience.

Day Three:

- Get an early start to Boulder City for a series of enjoyable and informative tours. On the way, visit the Ethel M Chocolate Factory and see candy being made. Then to Favorite Brands International, see how marshmallows are made, and taste-test your way through the plant. Then visit the Ocean Spray plant, and learn about cranberries and take a free tour of their bottling facilities. Continue to Hoover Dam for a tour of that historic site.

- Have lunch at one of the quaint restaurants in Boulder City amid its many art and craft shops.

- Drive back to Las Vegas via Highway 146 to I-15 South to State Line and take a ride on Desperado, one of the world's largest and fastest roller coasters.

- Head back to the hotel to get ready for dinner at the Rio Carnival World Buffet.

- That evening, relax at one of the city's semi-professional or university sporting events or take in one of the extraordinary shows offered throughout the Strip.

Day Four:

- Dress comfortably and get an early start to visit some of the most beautiful sights around Las Vegas, starting with a drive through scenic Red Rock Canyon.

- Drive on to Spring Mountain Ranch State Park and tour the house once owned by Howard Hughes and other famous people.

- A little way down the road is Old Nevada, a restoration of a frontier town, complete with gunfights and public hangings. Have lunch in the local saloon, where you can participate in a melodrama staged at various times throughout the day.

- Adjacent to the Village is Bonnie Springs Ranch. Spend some time in its petting zoo and then take a horse ride.

- If you're visiting during the summer months, plan to spend an evening at Theater Under the Stars at Spring Mountain Ranch. If you're out of season, drive back to town for dinner at Kiefer's Atop the Carriage House for a delicious meal in an elegant yet informal setting with a breathtaking view of the city lights.

Day Five:

- Take a trip over to the Liberace Museum, which is one of the most popular attractions in Las Vegas. The museum houses a tremendous amount of Liberace memorabilia, along with the world's largest rhinestone.

- One more stop for historical perspective: the Imperial Palace Auto Collection displays more than 200 vehicles previously owned by famous — and infamous — folks.

- Drive up to Mount Charleston in time so you can enjoy a drink and lunch out on the patio with a spectacular mountain view or inside the lodge, sitting in front of a roaring fire. Depending on the season, take advantage of the opportunity to see the sights on a hay ride or sleigh ride.

- For this evening, plan on a sensational three-hour sunset cruise on Lake Mead aboard the Desert Princess with dinner and dancing.

Other options for nature lovers to replace some of the city trips:

- Valley of Fire State Park is about an hour from Las Vegas, and it offers a spectacular wildlife experience, including ancient petroglyphs and Anasazi Indian artifacts.

- Just a bit farther is Mount Zion National Park, which is about three hours from Las Vegas and has some of the most diverse and majestic sandstone landscapes in the country.

- A trip to Grand Canyon would be tough to make a day trip, since it's just over 300 miles from Las Vegas. But it's a one-and-only attraction, which some people will want to fit into their Las Vegas vacation.

GUIDED TOURS

Air Nevada
2634 Airport Drive, Ste. 103
N. Las Vegas, NV 89030
736-8900 1-800-634-6377
Fax 795-8116
Myron Caplan, President
Grand Canyon -
Deluxe Air & Ground Tour: (GCU 2) Adults $189; children $139. Hotel transfers, air tour plus motor coach excursion through the park and complete meal. Tour duration 8 hours.
Grand Canyon Air Only Tour: (GCU 3) Adults $139; children $109. Hotel transfers, aerial excursion over and through the Grand Canyon. Tour duration 4-5 hours.
Grand Canyon "on your own" Air & Ground Tour: (GCU 5) Adults $149; children $119. Hotel transfers and air tour narration along with several hours of "on your own time" at the South Rim. Tour duration 7 1/2 hours.
Grand Canyon West Rim Air Tour: (GCU4) Adults $89; children $69. Hotel transfers, aerial tour of Hoover Dam, Lake Mead and the western portion of the Grand Canyon. Tour duration 2 1/2 hours.
Grand Canyon - West "Indian Country": Tour (GCW1) Adults $159; children $129. The West Rim's native people, the Hualapai Indians, will share with you their history and legends. You will enjoy an Indian barbecue in the wilderness overlooking the Colorado River and the Grand Canyon. Tour duration 5 hrs.
Grand Canyon Overnight Tour: $299 single; $199 pp double. Hotel transfers, aerial tour, one night's lodging at Grand Canyon. Overnight passengers must travel to the park on the afternoon flight and from the park on the morning flight. Extra nights available at additional cost.
"Grand" Overnight Tour: $379 single; $319 pp double. An extended version of the above tour. The extras include time for a ground tour, lunch and a screening at the IMAX Theatre.
Bryce Canyon/Grand Canyon: Tour COMBI - Adults $339; children $279. Deluxe air and ground tour with flight over the Las Vegas Strip, Valley of Fire and Zion National Park, a guided ground tour at Bryce Canyon and an air tour with views of Lake Powell and Grand Canyon. Tour duration 10 hours.
Bryce Canyon: Tour BCERON - $339 pp double occupancy; $279 children. Overnight tour includes a wonderful aerial tour and lodging at Grand Canyon.
Los Angeles/Grand Canyon: Tour (CA3) - Adult $269 Children $269. Jet service between Los Angeles and Las Vegas with optional stopover in Las Vegas. Air and ground tour of Grand Canyon National Park.
Optional West Rim All-Terrain Vehicle Tour Combination: Valley of Fire, over 2 hours guided tour, equiopment and lunch. Allow 8 hours - $269.
Independence Tour: Designed for individual free time, narrated flight to south rim of Grand Canyon. Allow 8 1/2 hours. Adults $149; children $119.

Tour the Grand Canyon

Air Vegas Airlines
500 Hwy. 146
Sky Harbor Airport
Henderson, NV 89015
736-3599 1-800-255-7474
Fax: 361-8967
Jim Petty
Operates from Sky Harbor Airport to the Grand Canyon, Monument Valley, Arizona and Bryce Canyon in Utah. Tours begin at $139.
Grand Canyon & Monument Valley Premium Crown Tour: Adults $389; children 2 - 11 $349 - A spectacular air tour over the Grand Canyon. Bus transfer to South Rim. Approx. 10 hours.
Grand Canyon Air Tour: Adults $139; children 2 -11 $119 - Spectacular flight takes you over the famous Hoover Dam, Lake Mead and finally the majestic Grand Canyon. Comfortable window seating for everyone. Approx. 3 hours from hotel back to hotel.
Deluxe Air & Ground Tour: Adults $189; children 2 - 11 $139 - Includes everything offered in the Air Tour plus: Touch down at the Grand Canyon Airport and begin a fully guided bus tour, with several stops along the South Rim. A delicious lunch. Approx. 8 1/2 hours from hotel back to hotel.
Overnight Tour: One night accommoda-

tions at the Grand Canyon - single $299; double $199; triple $179; quad $169.
Grand Canyon & Bryce Canyon National Park - Adults $389; children 2 - 11 $349. A spectacular air tour over Valley of Fire and Zion National Park, landing in Bryce Canyon; Continental breakfast, coffee, tea. 1 hour flight from Bryce Canyon to Grand Canyon. Tour time approx. 9 hours.
Grand Canyon & Monument Valley **Crown Tour:** Adults $389; children 2 - 11 $359 - Air tour over the Grand Canyon. Magnificent view of Glen Canyon Dam and Lake Powell, sightseeing Monument Valley. Tour time is approx. 12 hours.

Allstate Tours
999 E. Tropicana Ave.
Las Vegas, NV 89119
597-5970 1-800-634-6787
Motorcoach to Grand Canyon departs every Tue., Thu. & Sat. from the Riviera Terminal at 7:30 am. Adults $159; children $139 round trip.

Black Canyon Raft Tours
1297 Nevada Hwy.
Boulder City, NV 89005
293-3776 1-800-696-7238 (RAFT)
Ron Opfer, General Manager
Tour operates from Feb. 1 through Nov. 30. Eleven mile raft tour down the Colorado

River (Lake Mohave) from just below Hoover Dam to Willow Beach Resort and Marina. Trip takes about 5 hours. Departure 9:45 am daily from the Expedition Depot and includes transportation to starting point and back to Expedition Depot, narration en route and a picnic on the river. Price: $64.95 - $74.95; group rates also available.

Cactus Jack's Wild West Tour Co.
2217 Paradise Rd., Ste. A
Las Vegas, NV 89104
731-9400 1-800-367-7612
John Early, President
Tour description of Grand Canyon Flight "The Unforgettable Experience."
Land Air Tour: Includes hotel pickup, stars' homes, a visit to Hoover Dam, buffet luncheon, and a 1 1/2 hour aerial excursion through the Grand Canyon. Approx. 7 1/2 hours - $109.50 per person (includes airport fees).
Grand Canyon Deluxe South Rim: Includes hotel pickup, narrated air excursion into the Grand Canyon; land at the South Rim for a narrated bus tour through Grand Canyon National Park and a buffet lunch. Approx. 7 1/2 hours - $129 per person.
Hoover Dam Cruise: Includes all transfers. Continental breakfast at check-in. Stars' homes. A 1 1/2 hour cruise on Lake Mead. Lunch. Hoover Dam. Ethel M Chocolate Factory. Approx. 7 hours - $31.95 per person.
Hoover Dam Deluxe: Includes all transfers. Stars' homes. Hoover Dam. Lunch. Ethel M Chocolate Factory. Cranberry World. Approx. 7 hours - $29.95 per person.
Hoover Dam Express: Includes all transfers. Continental breakfast at check-in. Stars' homes. Hoover Dam. Ethel M Chocolate Factory. Two departures daily. Approx. 4 1/2 hours - $19.95 per person.
Laughlin: Includes all transfers. Continental breakfast at check-in. Travel through Searchlight, NV where gold was discovered in 1890. Free fun book. Lunch. River taxis available. Two departures daily Approx. 10 hours - $4.95 per person.
Grand Canyon Bus Tour: Includes all transfers. Stars' homes. Travel through the world's largest Joshua Tree forest. Enjoy an Indian guided ground tour and lunch on the rim. Approx. 14 hours - $109.50 per person.
Air Ground Deluxe: Includes all transfers, air tours, guided ground tour on Grand Canyon South Rim-lunch is included. Approx. 7 hours - $179.50 per person.

Desert Action Inc. · 4x4 Tours
2810 S. Highland Dr.
Las Vegas, NV 89109
796-9355
Rick Lend, President
Off-road tours using 4-wheel drive vehicles. Length of tours 4 - 7 hours; $50-$159 per person. Visit the Grand Canyon, Red Rock Canyon, El Dorado Canyon, Mount Charleston and Valley of Fire. Enjoy the great outdoors in an air-conditioned jeep.

GUIDED TOURS

Desert Eco-Tours
Southern Nevada
Zoological-Botanical Park
1775 N. Rancho Dr.
Las Vegas, NV 89106
647-4685
Half or full day jeep tours with trained naturalists to geological or gem collecting sites, ancient Native American camp sites, ghost towns and wildlife viewing. Daily year 'round.

Drive-Yourself Tours
8170 S. Eastern Avenue
Las Vegas, NV 89123
565-8761   Fax: 565-5786
Tour #1 - Las Vegas
Tour #2 - Red Rock Canyon
Tour #3 - Valley of Fire
Tour #4 - Mount Charleston
Tour #5 - Hoover Dam/Lake Mead
Tour #6 - Las Vegas to Laughlin
Tour #7 - Laughlin/Colorado River
Self-guided audiocassette tapes with maps. Ask for the tours at your hotel's concierge desk, also available at Las Vegas Chamber of Commerce office.

Eagle Canyon Airlines, Inc.
275 E. Tropicana Avenue Ste. 22
Las Vegas, NV 89109
736-3333   1-800-446-4584
Grant Murray, President
McCarran Airport
Grand Air Tour: Adults $149 - 3 1/2 hours hotel to hotel
Air tour of Hoover Dam: Includes Lake Mead, the Colorado River and the many plateaus and canyons within the Grand Canyon. Free Spirit Tour with Helicopter Option - $159 per person without helicopter and $249 with helicopter. Enjoy the Canyon at your own pace, approx. 7 hours.
The Time Saver Tour: $99 per person, designed for people with limited time - approx, 2.5 hours hotel to hotel.
Canyon Overnight Tour: $199 per person double occupancy. Narrated air tour of Lake Mead, Hoover Dam, Colorado River and the Grand Canyon. Includes one night hiotel accommodation, approx. 12 hours.
Grand Deluxe Overnight Tour: $229 double occupancy. Combines popular Air/Ground Tour with one night accommodations, approx. 24 hours.

Fantasy Adventure
P. O. Box 17298
Anaheim, CA 92817
1-800-455-6323
Al Ogrodski, President
Credit cards: MC, Visa
Grand Canyon Tour: *(Air Nevada Airlines)* Narrated tour over Hoover Dam, scenic Lake Mead and the western portion of the Grand Canyon. Approx. 7 1/2 hours, $269 plus tax per person.
Four Wheel Ride: In the Valley of Fire, picnic style meal, hotel shuttle. Approx. 2 1/2 hours - $149-year round. Morning, afternoon and sunset tours are available.
Water Sports Adventure: One price

includes a full day of unlimited water sports, beach activities, lessons, drinks and a BBQ lunch. Approx. 8 hours from 9 am ending at 5 pm between May and October. Adults $129, 12 - 17 $99, 6 - 11 $49, children 5 and under free.

Forrest Hummer Tours
4503 Paradise Rd., Ste. 1
Las Vegas, NV 89109
798-HUMM   Fax: 896-8330
Forrest B. Johnson
Tours are approx. 3 hours total time, 2 tours daily. Minimum of two people and no small children. We provide pick up and return to hotel. US Government approved. Tour Guides - US & Japanese speaking available; casual dress; private tours available. Hummer Desert (Off Road) Adventure and Red Rock Canyon Tour - now for the first time in Las Vegas, you can take a private tour to Red Rock Canyon and desert in the most powerful off road vehicle in the world...the HUMMER! More exciting than even the best Disneyland ride! Tours are every day of the week: 2 tours daily - 9 am and 2 pm; closed Christmas Day.

Tour Hoover Dam

Gray Line Tours of Southern Nevada
1550 S. Industrial Rd.
Las Vegas, NV 89102-2699
384-1234 1-800-634-6574
Fax - 387-6401
Credit cards: All major.
Laughlin Day Tour: $7.95 per person. Hotel pick-up at 8 am and noon. Departs Laughlin at 4:30 pm and 8:30 pm. Includes lunch or dinner buffet.
Hoover Dam Express: $25.95 per person. Includes admission to Visitors Center, escorted interior tour of dam, tour of Ocean Spray and complimentary 30-minute beverage stop at the Gold Strike. Departs 8 am and noon. Tour duration 5 1/2 hours.
Deluxe Hoover Dam & City Highlights Tour: $31.95. Includes admission to Visitors Center, escorted interior tour of dam, tour of Ocean Spray and the Heritage Museum and complimentary buffet lunch at the Gold Strike. Departs daily at 10 am and has you back to hotel about 6 pm.
"The Grand" Hoover Dam Tour: $47.95 per person. 1 1/2 hour paddlewheeler cruise on Lake Mead with a light lunch

and 2 hours at Hoover Dam. Tour includes a stop at the Ethel M Chocolate Factory; Hhotel pick-up daily at 10 am and return to hotel at 6 pm.
The City Tour: $28 per person. Ride through Green Valley, buffet lunch, Ethel M Chocolate Factory, Cranberry World, top of Stratosphere Tower and downtown Fremont Street Experience. Hotel pick-up at 10 am and returns at 6 pm.
Valley of Fire & Desert Tour: $34.75 per person. Tour the Valley of Fire, Lost City Museum and lunch at Echo Bay Resort and Marina. Tour operates Tue., Wed. and Thu. with hotel pick-up at 8 am and return at 4 pm.
Red Rock Canyon & Mt. Charleston Tour: $30.75 per person. Tour includes lunch at the Mt. Charleston Lodge. Tour operates Tue., Wed. and Thu. with hotel pick-up at 8 am and return at 5 pm.
Colorado River Raft Tour: $74.95 per person. Float down this famous river and enjoy a picnic box lunch and back to Las Vegas over Hoover Dam. Tour operates Feb. 1 through Nov. 30. Hotel pick-up daily at 8 am and returns at 4 pm.
Flightseeing & Rafting Grand Canyon & Colorado River Tour: $165 per person; children 9 and under $115. Float 11 miles down the Colorado River from Hoover Dam through the placid, majestic Black Canyon. Enjoy a picnic box lunch along the river on your way to Willow Beach. Then board the bus for a ride over the Hoover Dam to the Boulder City Airport for an aerial view of the Grand Canyon. Tour operates April through Oct. Hotel pick-up at 8 am and return at 6 pm.
Grand Canyon Air Tour & Hoover Dam: $110 per person; children 9 years and under $68.50. Motor coach to the Boulder City Airport where you will board a Lake Mead airplane for your 1 1/2-hour aerial tour of the Grand Canyon. Tour includes Hoover Dam and Ocean Spray Cranberry World. Hotel pick-up daily at 8 am and return at 6 pm.
Grand Canyon Morning & Afternoon Express: $99 per person. Panoramic 1 1/2 hour aerial flight over Hoover Dam, Lake Mead and the Canyon's Great Gorge. Tour operates daily with hotel pick-up at 8 am and 2 pm.
Grand Canyon West Rim Motorcoach Tour: $99 per person. Day tour of the Hualapai Indian Reservation, located 120 miles southeast of Las Vegas on the west rim of the Grand Canyon. Tour includes a barbecue lunch at Guano Peak, 3500 feet above the winding Colorado River. Hotel pick-up 7 am Tour duration 10 1/2 hours.
Grand Canyon West Rim Air/Ground Tour: $144 per person. Fight leaves from Boulder City Airport to the Hualapai Indian Reservation, located 120 miles southeast of Las Vegas on the west rim of the Grand Canyon. Tour includes a barbecue lunch at Guano Peak, 3500 feet above the winding Colorado River. Hotel pick-up 8 am and 10 am. Tour duration is 7 1/2 hours.

Grand Canyon: $158. Motorcoach to the Grand Canyon. Includes park admission, lodging and taxes. Tour operates March 1 through October 31. Operates Mon., Wed. and Fri.; Hotel pick-up at 7 am.

Deluxe South Rim Grand Canyon Day Tour: $149 per person. Tour includes two meals and light snack, admission to park and escorted tour. Tour operates Tue. - Sat.; hotel pick-up at 6:45 am and return at 9 pm.

Death Valley: $99 per person. Tour Death Valley with a 2 hour stop and buffet at the Furnace Creek Ranch. On the trip back to Las Vegas, the tour stops at the Amargosa Opera House. Tour operates Sept. through May. Hotel pick-up daily at 7 am and return at 6:30 pm. Special reduced fares for children 17 years and under and seniors 62 and over.

Guaranteed Tours
3734 Las Vegas Blvd. S.
Las Vegas, NV 89109
369-1000
Tony Mancuso, Owner

Lake Mead Boat Cruise: $39.95; seniors 62 and older and ages 2 - 12 $37.50. Hoover Dam, spend 2 hours sightseeing and picture taking. Approx. 8 hours.

Night Cruise Champagne Dinner: $48.50 and $45.50. Approx. 5 hours.

Country Star: $26.95 and $24.95. Hoover Dam mini-tour and free lunch at Country Star American Music Grill. Approx. 7 hours.

City Deluxe Tour: $27.95 and $25.95. Star's homes to Boulder City, then Hoover Dam and the Visitor's Center. Approx. 7 1/2 hours.

City Mini Tour: $18.95 and $17.50. Designed for the one with limited time but wanting to see the sights and wonders of our surrounding history. Approx. 4 hours.

City Tour of Las Vegas: $29.95 and $27.95. First visit star's homes then on to World of Clowns, Ethel Ms Chocolate Factory and Desert Botanical Gardens. Sightsee at downtown Fremont Street and enjoy a buffet. Approx. 5 hours.

Real Estate Showcase Tour: $19.95. Come see why Las Vegas is the fastest growing community in the United States. Approx. 5.5 hours.

Mesquite: - $5 and $3. Travels directly to Rancho Mesquite Casino/Resort Hotel, complimentary buffet and casino coupons. Approx. 9 hours.

Helicopter-Night Lights of Las Vegas: $69. Breathtaking flight over Las Vegas Strip and downtown's "Glitter Gulch." Approx. 1 hour.

Grand Canyon Below the Rim: $249. Birds-eye view of Lake Mead and Hoover Dam. Approx. 2 hours.

Red Rock: $32.95 and $29.95. Visit Spring Mountain State Ranch then Red Rock Visitors Center. Approx. 4 1/2 hours.

Heli USA
275 E. Tropicana Avenue
Las Vegas, NV 89109, Ste. 240
736-8787   1-800-359-8727
Nigel Turner, President

Apollo Night Flight: Fly over dazzling Las Vegas Strip. $65 per person - approx. 1 hour.

Aphrodite Dinner Flight: Most popular night tour. Dine at Planet Hollywood then a flight over the Strip. $99 per person - approx. 3 hours.

VIP Experience: For those who want privacy and their own picnic, this is the ultimate, from Las Vegas through the Grand Canyon then land at the Ramada. $2,000 (private helicopter holds 1 - 6 passengers), approx. 4 hours.

The Pegasus Flight & Indian Adventure: Grand Canyon above and below the rim, tribal BBQ. $349 per person, approx. 7 hours.

Sky Chariot: For those with limited time, this flight is the ideal way to see the Grand Canyon. $249, about 2 1/2 hours.

Pegasus Grand Canyon Flight: Includes landing for a picnic at the bottom of the Grand Canyon. $299 per person - approx. 3 1/2 hours.

Grand Canyon Voyage: Float through the Black Canyon, river rafting and picnic. $369 per person, approx. 8 hours.

Interstate Tours
1400 Wyoming St., Ste. 3
Boulder City, NV 89005
293-2268 1-800-245-1166
Judy Strand, President

Grand Canyon Wilderness: Approx. 10 hours hotel to hotel, $109.50 per person, seniors $98.50 and children 2 - 11, $76.50. Continental breakfast & hearty Indian barbecue. Travel across Hoover Dam. Ride through the magnificent Black Canyon and Mohave Desert to Indian Country. The Hualapai Indians take you on a 4 1/2 guided motor tour along the Canyon rim. Share an Indian BBQ.

Ask about our unique full and half day air and motor excursions to Zion; Bryce Canyon; Death Valley; Laughlin; Hoover Dam; Oatman.

Mini City Hoover Dam Cruise: $39.50, seniors $35.50 and 2 - 11 $27.50. Free hospitality coffee at check-in. Light Champagne lunch on the *Desert Princess*, celebrity homes, Cranberry World West, Hoover Dam, Ron Lee's World of Clowns.

Mini City Deluxe Hoover Dam: $32.50, seniors $29.50 and children $22.50. Spend 2 hours at Hoover Dam, celebrity homes, Cranberry World West, and Ron Lee's World of Clowns.

Express Hoover Dam: $23.50, seniors $21.50 and children $16.50. Drive through Boulder City to Hoover Dam, stop at Ethel Ms Chocolate Factory and Botanical Gardens.

Death Valley National Monument: $109.50, seniors $98.50 and children $76.50. Travel through Death Valley

Junction, see the Amargosa Opera House, tour historic Borax Museum and lunch at Pahrump Winery.

Zion National Park: $109.50, seniors $98.50 and children $76.50. Travel through rural Utah. See the red cliffs of St. George, and the Virgin River gorge. Enjoy a picnic lunch in the park.

Jackpot Tour Service
4740 S. Valley View Blvd., Ste. 200
Las Vegas, NV 89103
795-7878
Ray King, President

Jackpot Tour to Laughlin: Tour operates Tue., Wed., Fri. and Sat. Duration: 10 hours. This narrated motorcoach tour takes you through the once flourishing mining town of Searchlight on your way to the Gold River Hotel and Casino on the banks of the Colorado River. You will receive a casino fun book loaded with discounts and a complimentary buffet during your 6 hour stay.

Lake Mead Cruise: Tour operates Wed. and Sat. Duration: 7 1/2 hours. Tour begins with a stop at the Ethel M Chocolate Factory and Botanical Gardens. After a drive through historical Boulder City and the magnificent Hoover Dam, you will board the *Desert Princess*, a three-level Mississippi-style paddlewheeler. On the way back to Las Vegas you will stop at the Railroad Pass for a buffet lunch and a casino fun book.

Hoover Dam Mini Tour: $14.50 Tour operates Tue., Wed., Fri. and Sat. Duration: 4 hours. Tour includes the

dam ($5 entrance fee not included), Ethel M Chocolate Factory and Botanical Gardens.

"Best Dam Cruise": $36 per person. Board Mississippi style paddlewheeler on Lake Mead, buffet lunch at Railroad Pass Hotel. Tour operates Tue. & Sat.

Lake Mead Cruise & Hoover Dam, Too: $36.00 per person. Visit Lake Mead and Hoover Dam, buffet lunch and Ethel M Factory. Operates Wed. and Sat.

Key Tours
3305 W. Spring Mountain Rd., Ste.16
Las Vegas, NV 89102
362-9355
Joe Mattes, General Manager

Tour #1: Laughlin Tour - $5 per person includes lunch and fun book. Six hours of fun in Laughlin. Operates daily.

Primm Tour - $5 per person includes complimentary buffet, ferris wheel ride, train ride and carousel ride. Operates Wed. and Fri.

Tour #2: - Hoover Dam Tour - $17 per person includes Hoover Dam, Ethel M Chocolate Factory and Botanical Gardens. Tour offered Tue., Wed. and Sat. Add $8 optional tour of dam.

Lake Mead Air
1301 Airport Rd.
Boulder City, NV 89005
293-1848
Earl Leseberg, President
Grand Canyon, Hoover Dam and Lake Mead; $89 per person, minimum 2 fares.

SIGHTSEEING

GUIDED TOURS

Lake Mead Cruises
P.O. Box 62465
Boulder City, NV 89006-2465
293-6180
Meg Fair, Sales Manager
Credit cards: MC, Visa, AMX, Discover
The *Desert Princess*, a 250 passenger three-deck sternwheeler, has two fully enclosed, climate-controlled decks and an open top deck. Food and beverages are available on all cruises. Reservations are required for all meal cruises.
Sightseeing Cruises: 10 am - 4 pm April 1 - Oct. 31, 1 1/2 hour narrated cruise to Hoover Dam. Full beverage service and snack bar available. Adults $16; children 11 and under $6. From Nov. 1 - March 31 there are only three sightseeing cruises at 10 am, noon and 2 pm
Early Dinner Cruise: 6:30 pm - 8:30 pm Sun. - Thu. Apr.1 - Oct. 31; Nov. 1 - Mar. 31 on Sun. only 5:30 - 7:30 pm, 2-hour cruise to Black Canyon and Hoover Dam with dinner. Fare: Adults $29; Children $15.
Breakfast Buffet Cruise: 10 am Sun., April 1 - Oct. 31, 2-hour cruise with breakfast buffet. Adults $21; children $10. Sun. only, Nov. 1 - March 31.
Dinner/Dance Cruise: 7:30 pm Fri. and Sat. evenings, April 1 - Mar. 31. 3-hour cruise featuring live music for dancing and choice of 3 entrees including New York steak, charbroiled chicken and Alaskan halibut. $43 per person. This cruise is not recommended for children.

The *Desert Princess* is also available for wedding receptions, parties and reunions for groups from 25 to 250.

Las Vegas Airlines
P.O. Box 15105
Las Vegas, NV 89114
735-8007   647-3056   1-800-634-6851
Donald Donahue, President
Grand Canyon Air Tour Only: 3 hours hotel to hotel $149.50 adult, $124.50 children - no restrictions.
Grand Canyon Deluxe Air & Ground Tour: 7 hours $199.50, adult, $159.50 children 2 - 11.
Grand Canyon Overnight Tour: $225 single; $215 double, $186 triple, $177 quad.
Grand Canyon Special Air: 2 hours hotel to hotel, $95 adults, $75 children.
Grand Canyon Freedom Tour: 7 hours - $175 adult, $145 children.
Local Tour: 35 minute flight $65 adults, $45 children.
One Way Air Tour: Las Vegas and Grand Canyon $119 adults, $109 children.

Las Vegas Helicopters
3712 Las Vegas Blvd. S.
Las Vegas, NV 89109
736-0013
Gerald Schlesinger, President
Hours: dusk - midnight, until 1 am on Saturdays and holidays
Price: $45
Dusk to late-night views of the Las Vegas Strip from 500 feet aboard a Bell Jetranger helicopter.
Tour: Flight over the Mirage Golf Course from Tropicana to downtown; $45.
Grand Canyon Tours: Hotel to hotel air

only $249.
Deluxe Tour: $299
VIP Tour: $359 with champagne.
Flight Weddings: $229 plus $50 for the minister, champagne included.

North American Motorcycle
4625 E Tropicana Ave.
Las Vegas, NV 89121
434-0200
Kris Miller, Vice Pres.
Guided tours on Harley Davidson motorcycles to Lake Mead, Grand Canyon, Bryce, Zion and Death Valley. Four to five day tours for groups of 4 - 10 adults. Also motorcycle rentals for self-guided tours.

Scenic Airlines
2705 Airport Dr.
N. Las Vegas, NV 89030
638-3300 1-800-634-6801
David Young, President
Scenic's 19-seat deHavilland Twin Otter has large panoramic windows, high wings so visibility is not blocked and comfortable seats along with headsets that narrate tour in the language of your choice, over 20 available. All tours include hotel pick-up and drop-off, flight certificate and color souvenir book.

Scenic offers ten flights from Las Vegas to the Grand Canyon and return daily in addition to the tours listed below.
Fees: Fees include the National Park User Fee; federal excise tax and the Las Vegas Airport Passenger Facility Charge and are generally collected at check in. Fees listed are subject to change at any time.
Highlights Air Tour: Adults $99, children $79. YRLG-1 Fees: $10.50; Scenic's 1 hour 15 minute tour offers a bird's-eye view of Western Grand Canyon, Hoover Dam and Lake Mead.
Classic Air Tour: Adults $149, children $119. YRLG-2 Fees: $13.00; complete aerial sightseeing tour of Grand Canyon. Tour may land at Grand Canyon to deplane or enplane other passengers. Approx. 3 1/2 hours.
Mini-Deluxe: Adults $169, children $149. YRLG-3 Fees: $13.00; features

transfers to and from the South Rim to enjoy walking along the Rim, hiking into the Canyon or a variety of optional activities such as local helicopter or airplane flights, or the IMAX Theatre experience. Includes snack sack. Approx. 7 1/2 hours.
Premium Deluxe: Adults $239, children $189. YRLG-5 Fees: $13.00; includes limousine transfers from hotel; VIP Rainbow Club check-in with welcome refreshments; prime time flight departures; delicious buffet lunch at the Rim with breathtaking views; bus excursion of the South Rim; expanded Rim time; and admission to the IMAX Theatre experience. Approx. 7 1/2 hours.
Helicopter Combo: Adults $279, children $249. YRLG-H Fees: $13.00; includes a bus transfer to the Rim; a buffet meal; plus an exciting 25-minute helicopter flight at the Grand Canyon with Papillon Grand Canyon Helicopters. Approx. 7 1/2 hours.
Overnight Tour: $209 single, $189 double, $169 triple and $159 quad; children $149. YRLG-6 Fees: $13.00; Includes 1 night accommodations at the Grand Canyon; Rim transfers to enjoy either a sunrise or sunset. This tour is available on designated flights.
Flight and Hike Option: $289 single, $249 double, $229 triple and $219 quad; children $199. YRLG-7 Fees: $13.00; Includes two nights accommodations at Grand Canyon, hotel transfers as well as a one-day unlimited transfer pass on a local shuttle; admission to the IMAX Theatre experience, free time for hiking, a box lunch, and official Scenic Airlines backpack, water bottle and T-shirt.
Grand Deluxe: Adult $199, children $169 YRLG-4 Fees: $19. Includes a bus excursion through the National Park; a buffet meal, and complimentary transfer.
Grand Deluxe Planet Hollywood: Adult $199, children $169 YRLG-4P Fees: $19. Includes a bus excursion through the National Park; with dinner at Planet Hollywood, and complimentary transfer.
Grand Overnight Deluxe: $309 single, $269 double, $259 triple and $249 quad; children $229. YRLG-8 Fees: $19.00;

Combines the best of the Grand Deluxe YRLG-4 plus overnight accommodations at the Grand Canyon allowing passengers the most Canyon viewing time.
Monument Valley Grand Excursion: $389, children $349. YRLM-2 Fees: $18.00; includes aerial sightseeing flight to Grand Canyon; rest stop with continuing flight to Monument Valley; approximately 3 1/2-hour ground excursion with Navajo taco lunch and Indian culture experience; aerial sightseeing of Rainbow Bridge and Lake Powell; includes seldom seen northern and eastern portions of Grand Canyon; bus transfer to a popular viewpoint from the South Rim. Approx. 12 hours.
Monument Valley with Grand Canyon Overnight: $429 single, $409 double, $389 triple and $379 quad; children $369. YRLM-3 Fees: $18.00; includes everything listed in the Monument Valley Grand Excursion Tour (YRLM-2) plus one night hotel at Grand Canyon and admission to the IMAX Theatre experience.
Monument Valley with Two Nights Hotel: $479 single, $439 double, $419 triple and $409 quad; children $399. YRLM-4 Fees: $18.00; includes everything listed in the Monument Valley Grand Excursion Tour (YRLM-2) plus hotel for one night at Grand Canyon and one night in the Lake Powell area; IMAX Theatre.
Bryce Canyon Deluxe: Adults $269, children $219. YRLB-1 Fees: $16.00; includes air tour of Valley of Fire and Zion en route; meal at Bryce, ground tour at Bryce Canyon with photo stops at lookout points; air tour of the spectacular East End of Grand Canyon. Approx. 7 1/2 hours.
Bryce and Grand Canyons Deluxe: Adults $329, children $269. YRLB-2 Fees: $16.00, includes air tour of Valley of Fire and Zion en route, meal at Bryce, ground tour at Bryce Canyon with photo stops at lookout points; air tour of the spectacular East End of Grand Canyon; bus excursion in the Grand Canyon National Park with photo stops along the Rim; a buffet meal; admission to the IMAX Theatre experience. Approx. 12 hrs.
Bryce Canyon with Overnight Accommodation: $389 single, $349 double, $329 triple and $319 quad; children $289. YRLB-3 Fees: $16.00; includes air tour of Valley of Fire and Zion en route, meal at Bryce, ground tour at Bryce Canyon with photo stops at lookout points; air tour of the spectacular East End of Grand Canyon, at Grand Canyon includes hotel transfers, transfers to the Rim to enjoy a sunrise or sunset, and an additional transfer to the Village with free time for hiking or walking along the Rim; hotel accommodations for one night at the Grand Canyon; admission to the IMAX Theatre experience; colorful Scenic backpack and water bottle.
"The Best of the West" Bryce, Grand Canyon and Monument: $619 single, $579 double, $559 triple and $549 quad; children $469. YRLB-4 Fees: $20.00; Includes air tour of Valley of Fire and

Visit Lake Mead

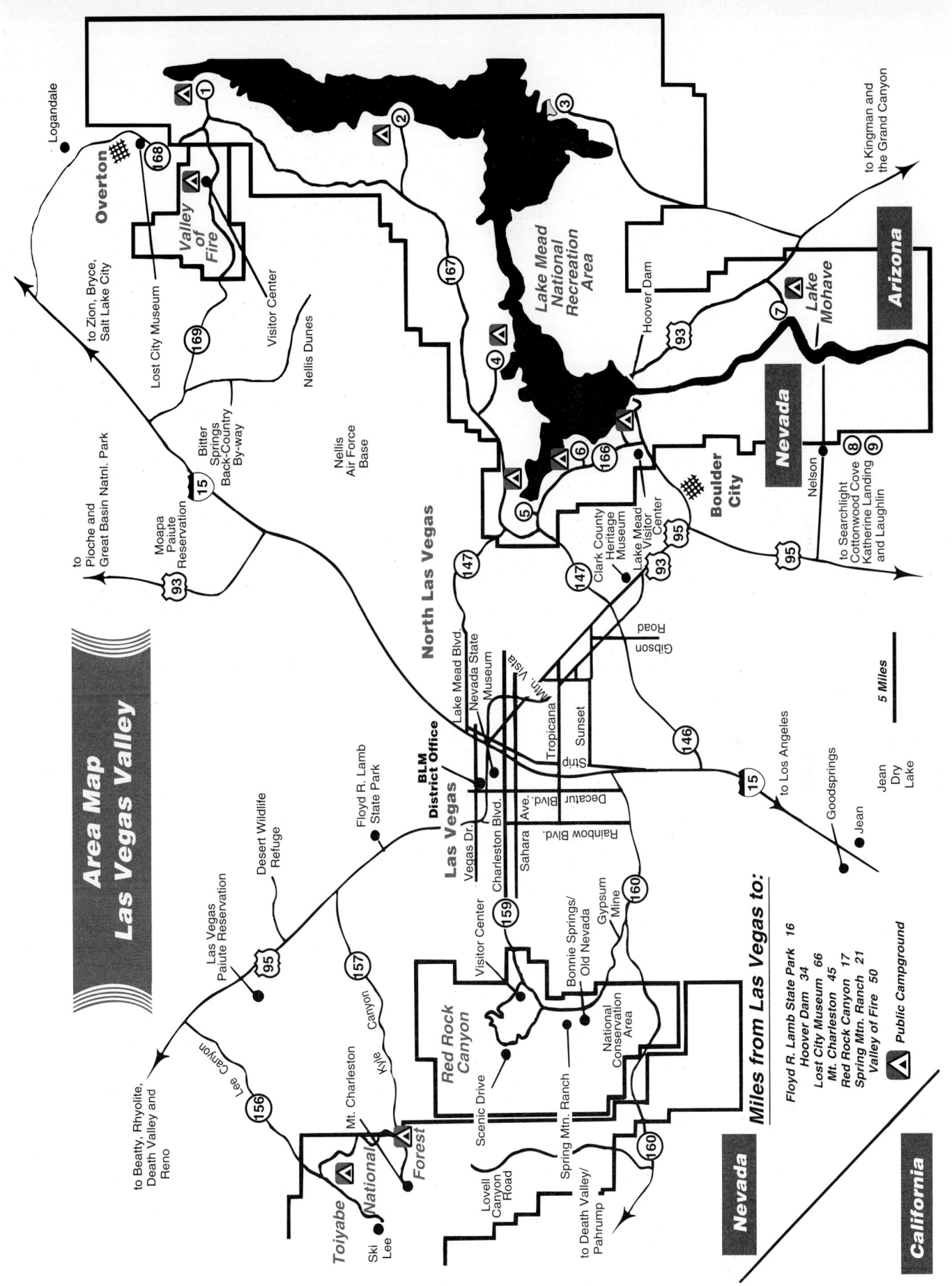

Area Map
Las Vegas Valley

Miles from Las Vegas to:

Floyd R. Lamb State Park 16
Hoover Dam 34
Lost City Museum 66
Mt. Charleston 45
Red Rock Canyon 17
Spring Mtn. Ranch 21
Valley of Fire 50

△ Public Campground

GUIDED TOURS

Zion en route; delicious meal at Bryce; ground tour at Bryce Canyon with photo stops at lookout points; air tour of the spectacular East End of Grand Canyon; transfers and hotel for one night at Grand Canyon; transfers to the Rim to enjoy a sunrise or sunset; admission to the IMAX Theatre experience; colorful Scenic backpack and water bottle; scenic flight to Monument Valley; 3 1/2 hour Monument Valley ground tour including an authentic Navajo taco lunch; aerial sightseeing of Rainbow Bridge and Lake Powell; hotel accommodations in the Lake Powell area including transfers; includes aerial sightseeing of seldom-seen northern and eastern portions of Grand Canyon.

Sierra Nevada Airways
2772 N. Rancho Dr.
Las Vegas, NV 89130
631-3119
Theresa Heisserman
Grand Canyon Deluxe Air/Ground Tour - $135 per person.
Deluxe Air Tour - $80 per person
Custom tours also available.

Sundance Helicopters
265 E. Tropicana Ave. Ste. 130
Las Vegas, NV 89119
736-0606 1-800-653-1881
Fax 736-4107
Rick Eisenreich, President
The air conditioned, jet powered helicopter allows guests to enjoy breathtaking scenery while the pilot narrates over a background of exhilarating music.
Grand Canyon Picnic: Fly into the depths of the incredible wonder that nature has created. $299 per person, approx. 3 1/2 hours.
The Escape: This exciting tour explores 40 miles of the Grand Canyon at rim level. $249 per person, approx. 2 1/2 hrs.
Expedition: The rugged desert terrain,

the crystal blue waters of Lake Mead, the mighty Hoover Dam from above and below and the spectacular Grand Canyon. $339 per person, approx. 8 hrs. Option to land and enjoy a champagne picnic in the canyon, add $50 per person.
Rock 'N Rotor: Experience dining at the world famous Hard Rock Cafe with a spectacular night flight over the Las Vegas Strip in one great package tour. $119 per person, approx. 3 hours.
Dinner Adventure Tour: Depart Las Vegas in a modern helicopter for an evening you will always remember. Land at Mount Charleston and enjoy fine dining. $179 per person, approx. 4 hrs.
City Lights: A twenty mile loop over downtown and the fabulous Strip at dusk. $59 per person.
Tours also available from the Primadonna at Primm. Tour prices range from $19 to $199 and are available on Saturdays.

Teddy Bear Express
2235 E. Flamingo Rd., Ste. 300E
Las Vegas, NV 89119
737-6062
Laughlin - Sun., Tue., Thu. 8 am. Departs from five pickup locations. Free.
Primm - Mon., Wed., Fri. 8 am. Same departure points. Free.

Thrillseekers Unlimited
3172 N. Rainbow Blvd., Ste. 321
Las Vegas, NV 89108
699-5550
Rich Hopkins, Owner
Kevin Biernacki, Director of Operations
Hours: Varies
"The Time of Your Life": Thrillseekers offers Adrenaline Sports Tours including firewalking, bungy jumping, in-line skating, rock climbing, para-gliding, snow-boarding, mountain boarding, sky-diving all in 1 week!! Includes resort accommodations, photo and video

transportation, energy snacks or create your own dream package year round. Call for details and media pack; prices range from $75 to $1745.
Credit Cards: MC, Visa

Tours of Distinction
3430 E. Flamingo Rd., Ste. 318
Las Vegas, NV 89121
454-3838 1-888-471-8687
Anne McCall, President
For motorcoach tours departing from Las Vegas, Tours of Distinction have convenient pick-ups on both sides from the Showboat Hotel and Arizona Charlie's.

UNLV
Continuing Education
4505 S. Maryland Pkwy.
Las Vegas, NV 89154
895-3394
The university sponsors a variety of trips to all parts of the world with an emphasis on education. Lectures and classes are conducted on campus before your trip begins to acquaint you with your destination.

**Valen Transportation & Tours
(Riviera)**
2901 Las Vegas Blvd. S.
Las Vegas, NV 89109
734-5110 1-800-487-2252
Mike Valen
Daily departure from Las Vegas on Tue. through Sat. to the Grand Canyon at 7:30 am and return at approximately 9 pm. Service aboard the fully equipped Valen coaches includes meals and beverages, historical lectured tour and video documentaries en route, baggage handling, all taxes, entrance fees to park, souvenir Grand Canyon book and Wild West Explorer Certificate.

Wolff Adventures
240 N. Jones Blvd., Ste. 212
Las Vegas, NV 89107
233-3061 1-800-997-2708
Bonnie Wolff, President
Your connection to tours in and around Las Vegas; specializing in group tours and special events; tours include Grand Canyon flights and motor coach, ATV adventure, Hoover Dam, Lake Mead cruises, free Laughlin day trip, Stateline, Colorado River raft, jet ski tour of Hoover Dam, house boat rentals, golf packages, horseback riding and paintball for group packages.

LAUGHLIN TOURS

Blue River Safari: 298-0910
Departs the *Colorado Belle* to Lake Havasu. 8 hour trip; $60 adults; $30 children 6 - 15 yrs; children under 6 free.

Fiesta Queen/Little Belle: departs from Edgewater: 298-1047; 150 passenger sidewheeler, 11 am - 6:30 pm; 1 1/2 hour tours. Adults $10; children 12 and under $6; under 4 free.

USS Riverside: 65-foot, 100-passenger luxury tour boat owned by the Riverside Hotel offers fully narrated tours of the casino area to Davis Dam. The tour lasts an hour and twenty minutes. Adults $10; children 3 - 12 $6; children under 3 free; 298-2535.

SIGHTSEEING IN LAS VEGAS

The following sightseeing suggestions are listed under their categories elsewhere in greater detail. Consult index.

STRIP AREA

"Welcome to Fabulous Las Vegas" sign
Located on the median of the Strip about a mile south of the Hacienda Hotel. The sign was built in the late 1950s when traffic from Southern California had to go through Las Vegas.

Las Vegas Strip
Three and a half miles of Las Vegas Blvd. South from the Sahara Hotel to the Luxor Hotel, the Strip supposedly got its name when people started referring to "that strip of land," which was the Los Angeles Highway (Old US 91) three miles south of downtown. Thomas E. Hull built the first hotel on the Strip, the old El Rancho, which opened April 3, 1941.
The Strip, from Russell Rd. to Sahara Ave. is one of eight officially designated state scenic byways. The resorts that line the Strip paid for the $13.2 million Strip Beautification Project.

The Strip Trolley
Shuttle buses that look like trolleys, the Strip Trolleys carry visitors up and down the Strip, stopping at each major hotel from the Luxor to the Sahara. The trolley also goes off the strip to the Convention Center and Las Vegas Hilton on Paradise Rd. Hours of operation are 9:30 am to 2 am approximately every 15 minutes. Fare: $1.30.

Tropicana Hotel
4,000 sq. ft. leaded stained-glass dome located over the casino just inside the front entrance.
Island - Five acre water park with the largest indoor/outdoor swimming pool in the world. The pool features a water slide, spas and even a swim-up blackjack table and video poker. The water park is home to penguins, flamingos and swans. Koi fish can be seen in the lagoons.
Wildlife Walk - A variety of exotic birds, butterflies and wildlife are on display in the walkway between the casino and the island tower.

Luxor Hotel
The pyramid-shaped hotel opened October 15, 1993.
A Beam of Light (40 billion candle power) shines straight from the top of the pyramid.
10-story sphinx at front entrance, whose eyes shoot lasers that interact with the obelisk and lagoon.
The Atrium contains over 29 million sq. ft. of space, enough room for nine Boeing 747s.

Featuring a variety of attractions including an IMAX Theatre with a seven story screen and 3-D films, a series of "participatory" high impact adventures involving cutting-edge movie technology; exotic scenery and artifacts; a full-size replica of King Tut's tomb; intriguing cast of players, guides, entertainers.
"Imagine - A Theatrical Odyssey" transports guests to a mysterious lost world, an undersea garden and a futuristic cyberworld. Amazing aerial acts, unique choreography and astounding illusions allow the imagination to run wild.

Photo: Phototechnik International

Experience Las Vegas

Excalibur Hotel

The Excalibur Hotel is the fourth largest hotel in the world with 4,032 rooms.

Magic Motion Machine - Dynamic Motion Simulator, where the seats are hydraulically synchronized to the action you are watching on the screen. Two different features are presented in two separate theaters. Ride lasts three minutes. Also located on the lower level are carnival games, video arcade games, snack bars, shops, concessions and King Arthur's Court.

Medieval Village - The Fantasy Factory's strolling Renaissance performers entertain guests daily 10 am - 10 pm on the Medieval Village level. The shows include jugglers, puppets, mimes, magicians and more performing continuously with each show lasting about 20 minutes.

MGM Grand Hotel and Theme Park

"The City of Entertainment," Worlds Largest Hotel (5,009 rooms) opened December 18, 1993.

Guests enter the hotel through a 125 ft. polished gold bronze, full bodied replica of the MGM lion. It is the largest in the world.

Theme Park - 18-acre theme park features 10 rides and shows.

Studio 54 - Three story nightclub as well as Rainforest Cafe.

Monorail - 1.6 mile rail running between the MGM and Bally's Hotel. The system, which cost $25 million to build, shuttles an average 13,000 passengers a day.

Hard Rock Hotel and Cafe
4475 Paradise Rd.
693-5000

One of 80 Hard Rock Cafes located around the world. The Hard Rock features the largest neon guitar sign in the world, a restaurant and bar with rock n' roll music and the most extensive collection of rock n' roll memorabilia in the world. At the entrance you can purchase the popular Hard Rock casual wear featuring the Hard Rock logo with the Las Vegas location.

UNLV - University of Nevada, Las Vegas
4505 S. Maryland Pkwy.
895-3011

Founded in 1957, UNLV has over 20,000 students. The 335-acre campus is located one mile from the Strip.

UNLV Aboretum: 895-3392 - Self-guided tour takes you through display of more than 40 species of trees and shrubs.

Barrick Museum of Natural History-895-3381 - Features Smithsonian traveling exhibits and permanent displays. *(See Museums for more information.)*

Donna Beam Fine Art Gallery: 895-3893 - Exhibits works from nationally prominent artists in addition to works from students and faculty. *(See Art Galleries for more information.)*

Performing Arts Centers - Artemus W. Ham Concert Hall and Judy Bayley Theatre.

Flashlight - Art piece by Claes Oldenburg; located outside the Judy Bayley Theatre.

Hard Rock Hotel and Cafe

Desert Research Institute
Southern Nevada Science Center
755 E. Flamingo Rd.
898-0400

The Desert Research Center conducts research projects in such areas as water resources, atmospheric sciences, biological sciences, energy and environmental engineering. The State of Nevada established the Desert Research Institute in 1959 specifically for conducting statewide research to help manage Nevada's most valuable environmental resources; it now conducts research all over the globe. Its 400 scientists, technicians and support staff participate in over 100 research projects a year. The non-profit research center is part of the statewide division of the University and Community College System of Nevada, with a $5.9 million, 2,000 sq. ft. center adjacent to the UNLV campus.

Bally's

(Formerly the MGM Grand) Opened in 1973, Bally's is one of the more glamorous casinos.

Shopping Arcade - Over 20 stores located on the lower level.

Bally's offers backstage tours of "Jubilee" for groups of 25 or more.

Barbary Coast

World's largest stained-glass mural, "Garden of Earthly Delights," is located just inside the main entrance to the casino.

Flamingo Hotel

Bugsy Siegel opened the Flamingo in 1946. It was what was called a "carpet joint," the first of the glamorous casinos. The new 15 acre water habitat features flamingos, swans and African penguins.

The Magic & Movie Hall of Fame
O'Sheas Casino

Over 5,000 exhibits of magic, ventriloquist and movie memorabilia. Live magic performed. Show: Wed. - Sun. 11:30 am - 1:30 pm; museum Wed. - Sun. 10 am - 6 pm.
Admission: $9.95 adults; $3 children.

Caesars Palace

Fountains, statues and shrines located in front of the hotel. Omnimax - surrounded by a huge; dome-shaped screen and a sophisticated nine-channel "Sensaround" sound system with 89 speakers, viewers are whisked into space, under the sea or high above the Rocky Mountains with realistic sight and sound. *(See Movie Theaters for additional information)*

Brahma Shrine - A place for prayer, the four-faced statue presides over carved elephants from within a structure which is a mosaic of twinkling mirrors. The four faces represent the Four Divine States of Mind: Loving Kindness, Compassion, Sympathy and Equanimity.

Forum Shops - A half million sq. ft. of some of the finest specialty shops and restaurants in the world. Fifteen-foot robotic replicas of Roman gods perform under a massive domed rotunda around the Festival Fountain. The 48 foot ceilings emulate the Mediterranean sky by changing colors with the time of day, and store fronts resemble Roman Streets. *(See Shopping for more information.)*

Caesars Magical Empire - An unprecedented dining and entertainment experience where guests descend into an underground world of mysticism, illusions, wizards and sorcerers. Nowhere in the Caesars Magical Empire will things be always as they seem. During dinner service and throughout the entire facility, mysterious happenings will amaze and delight.

After the feasting is completed in one of the 10 dining chambers, visitors will be guided through a catacomb maze of corridors along an aqueduct of cascading waters, leading to a vast, seven-story-high magical realm. There, they may wander at their leisure, discovering mysterious nooks and corridors that will offer more surprises. Within this central pavilion of wonders will be beverage lounges - relaxing, if not always pre-

dictable, adult retreats for spirited libation - and adjoining the activity will be a boutique of magical games and treasures.

Highlighting the experience will be two live-entertainment theaters that will spotlight the talents of various magicians. Shows will emphasize audience participation in an opulent, but relatively intimate setting, so that guests can join in the fun.

Festival Fountain - Seven minute special effects show presented every hour on the hour 10 am - 11 pm.

Be sure to catch the performance of Atlantis every hour. It is a brief but very intense encounter with divine denizens of the deep, Titans of myth from the murky sea bed.

Cinema Ride: 3-D motion simulator rides; galactic light Atlantis; submarine race, Coaster Crazy and Haunted Graveyard Run. Daily 10 am - 11 pm.

Don Pablo Cigar Company
3025 Las Vegas Blvd. S.
369-1818

Watch Cuban cigar masters hand-roll cigars using tobacco from five countries. Mon. - Sat. 9 am - 6 pm.

Imperial Palace

The Imperial Palace Auto Collection, with over 200 vehicles on display from a rotating collection of more than 800 antique and special-interest automobiles, is on display in a plush, gallery-like setting. *(See Museums for more information.)*

Mirage

Opened in 1989 at a cost of over $610 million; 8th largest hotel in the world with 3,049 rooms.

Volcano - See and hear a realistic pina colada scented, 54 foot high volcano, erupts every 15 minutes from 6 pm until midnight in front of the hotel.

Dolphin Exhibit - The hotel's $14 million, 1.5 million gallon lagoon is home to five bottle-nosed dolphins. View of dolphins at play from above and below water level. *(For additional information call 791-7188.)*

White Tigers - See the white tigers from the Siegfried & Roy show in their compound on display 24 hours a day near the south entrance. Free admission on Wed. 10:30 am - 3 pm

Aquarium - A 20,000 gallon saltwater aquarium runs the entire length of the front desk area.

Mirage

SIGHTSEEING IN LAS VEGAS

Treasure Island

Guests are welcomed with an exciting $23 million pirate battle presented daily. This unique attraction, named Buccaneer Bay, has the British ship *The Brittania* confronting the pirate ship *Hispaniola* as the pirates unload their booty. A full-scale battle ensues as stunt men exchange fire and are thrown from their ships. The pirates, appearing to be losing the battle, make one last ditch effort to fire their cannon at the British. The cannon hits and the *Brittania* goes down. The Buccaneer Bay Show is at 4 pm, 5:30 pm, 7 pm, 8:30 pm, 10 pm and 11:30 pm daily.

Fashion Show Mall

With close to 1 million sq. ft. of fine shops, department stores and restaurants, you can find what you are looking for at the Fashion Show Mall. Saks, Neiman's, Macy's and Robinson May are just a few of the over 160 stores within the mall. *(See Shopping for additional information.)*

Walk of Fame - Located at the Fashion Show Mall Strip entrance, the "Stars on the Strip" contains an inlaid brass star and the prints and signatures of Las Vegas entertainers in a 3 x 3 concrete square.

American Museum of Historical Documents - Located in the Fashion Show Mall, the American Museum of Historical Documents has over 200 original historical documents preserved and framed as works of art. *(See Museums for additional information.)*

Sfuzzi at the Fashion Show Mall features a 10 1/2 x 12 1/2 foot replica of the Mona Lisa.

Scandia
2900 Sirius Ave.
364-0070

• Batting range (baseball or softball) - 25 pitches $1.25; also by time - 15, 30 and 60 minutes
• Miniature golf - $5.95 per round, per person; children under 5 free with an adult
• Bumper boats - $3.95
• Lil' Indy Raceway - $3.95
• Video arcade and redemption games
• Snack bar
Unlimited use wristbands which include 10 tokens $15.95
Parties - groups: 364-0071
Hours: Sun. - Thu. 10 am - 11 pm; Fri. - Sat. 10 am - midnight; closes one hour earlier in winter.

Las Vegas Hilton

Star Trek: The Experience opened in January 1998 at a cost of $70 million is 65,000 sq. ft. Hilton Hotels and Paramount Parks brings the formidable world of Star Trek to life. Star Trek: The Experience launches the visitor into a new realm of technologically and creatively advanced entertainment experiences.

Star Trek: The Experience is uniquely designed with a totally interactive entertainment approach in which each visitor assumes the identity of a Starfleet or alien crew member and participates as

Circus Circus

this character in the extraordinary and imaginative world of Star Trek. With this identity, the visitor will see, feel, touch, and live the adventure of Star Trek like never before, becoming immersed in the futuristic environment. While maneuvering through the multi-million dollar venue, the visitor will encounter an unmatched variety of entertainment elements including the ultimate simulated ride and challenging interactive video and virtual reality stations. Star Trek: The Experience will transport guests aboard the *USS Enterprise* where they'll venture to the bridge, travel on a turbolift, speed along the grand corridor and brave an exciting shuttlecraft mission through space and time.

SpaceQuest Casino - 20,000 sq. ft., designed by renowned futurist Syd Mead. Takes guests more than 350 years into the future and on board a space station orbiting the Earth. Inside, three 10- by 24-ft. "space windows" above the casino creates the illusion of a passage around the globe as space taxis, delivery ships, even limousines race by.

Debbie Reynolds Hollywood Movie Museum
305 Convention Center Dr.

Movie costumes and props from Debbie Reynolds' vast collection on dis-

play. Film clips date back from the silent era to the 1960s serve as a backdrop to the revolving display. World's largest private collection. Multimedia Extravaganza featuring wide screen film clips and surround sound.
Tours hourly Mon. - Fri. 10 am - 10 pm; Sat. & Sun. 11 am - 4 pm; $7.95 per person.

Las Vegas Convention Center

The nation's largest single level convention facility with 1.6 million square feet of meeting and exhibit space.

In 1997, the Las Vegas Convention Center hosted 50 conventions with 1,229,424 delegates. *(See Convention Section for additional information.)*

Stardust Hotel

One of the most recognized signs in the world, The Stardust was erected in 1967 and stands 188 ft. tall, contains 26,000 bulbs and over 30 miles of wiring.

Riviera Hotel

The Riviera opened in 1955 at a cost of $10 million. Feature shows: Splash, An Evening at La Cage, Crazy Girls and The Riviera Comedy Club.

The Mardi Gras Food court - Located just inside the south Strip entrance, features eight quick serve food outlets.

Circus Circus

Free circus acts are performed on the midway continuously from 11 am until midnight daily. In addition to the circus acts, the midway features a variety of carnival games where people of all ages can win prizes.

Grand Slam Canyon - Five-acre indoor theme park with a roller coaster, a water flume ride, children's rides and laser tag.

Monorail - A monorail transports guests from the Circus Manor and RV Park to the main casino.

Guinness World of Records Museum
2780 Las Vegas Blvd. S.
792-3766

See the famous Guinness Book brought to three-dimensional life. Amazing videos, life-sized replicas, unique displays and interactive computers and data banks are imaginatively divided into six "worlds" with over 35 exhibits. Open daily 9 am - 8 pm $4.95 for adults, $3.95 for seniors, students and military, $2.95 for 12 and under; 4 and under free.

Wet'n Wild - Las Vegas
2601 Las Vegas Blvd. S.
737-3819

Wet'n Wild, located on the world famous Las Vegas Strip, offers locals and visitors a fun way to beat the hot desert sun. The 16 acre water park features over a dozen breathtaking chutes, slides, flumes, floats and plunges. Wet'n Wild's 1 1/2 million gallons of fresh water is maintained at comfortable temperatures and circulated through a state-of-the-art filtering system.

Holy Cow! Micro Brewery
2423 Las Vegas Blvd. S.
732-2697

Cow-themed restaurant, bar and microbrewery. The microbrewery features four microbrews each day brewed right on the premises. Free brewery tours are offered daily from 11 am - 5 pm Gift shop, video poker. Holy Cow has won medals; Amber Gambler, Pale Ale, Rebel Red Ale, Hefeweis Bavarian Wheat Beer, various specials.

Stratosphere

Tallest free-standing observation tower in the U.S. The tower, which is three times taller than any other building in Las Vegas, soars 1,149 ft. - or more than 135 stories, the tallest building west of the Mississippi.

A 360-seat revolving restaurant and 220-seat cocktail lounge are located on the top of the tower.

World's highest roller coaster, High Roller, starting at 909 feet above the ground; The Big Shot thrill ride shoots you 160 feet to the 1,081 ft. level.

Four high-speed double-decker elevators travel at 1,400 ft. per minute, whisking visitors to the top of the tower in 45 seconds, where they can view Las Vegas from either the indoor or the outdoor observation deck. Admission charges: observation deck $5; thrill rides $5.

Nightly "dancing" light show synchronized to music visible throughout the Las Vegas valley every 15 minutes.

Las Vegas Hilton

DOWNTOWN

Fremont Street Experience -

Nightly on Fremont St. downtown, on a massive space frame that towers 90 ft. above four blocks, the Fremont Street Experience takes place. The show runs on the hour beginning at 8 pm and continues until midnight. Admission is free.

Inside the space frame are 2 million lights capable of producing 65,536 color combinations. Accompanying the light display is a state-of-the-art sound system with 208 speakers mounted within the space frame that can produce a combined 540,000 watts of concert-quality sound and music.

The graphic display system alone contains 121 computers, including 30 within the space frame, and a single master computer located in the Fremont Street Experience offices. Combined, the graphic display system computers contain 100 gigabytes of storage - comparable to about 250 personal home computers.

Eventually, the Fremont Street Experience will have a library of several shows, which can be tailored to an unlimited number of themes, special events and holidays.

The Fremont Street Experience downtown revitalization project is a joint effort of the city of Las Vegas and the Fremont Street Experience Company, a coalition of 11 hotels within the Fremont Street Experience.

Plaza Hotel

View from the Center Stage Restaurant after dark.

Bank of 14 penny progressive slot machines with a jackpot of over $500.

Las Vegas Club

Sports Hall of Fame - Collection of baseball memorabilia that is second only to the Cooperstown Hall of Fame.

Golden Gate

Built as the Overland Hotel in 1905. The Las Vegas Club added a 16-story tower with 185 more rooms, 18,000 square feet of casino space and two new restaurants in Sept. 1996. Home of the 99 cent shrimp cocktail.

Golden Nugget

Not only the most elegant casino downtown but one of the most elegant in Las Vegas. The front of the hotel is encased in Italian marble and is the only casino downtown without neon.

World's largest gold nugget - The Hand of Faith, on display just off the hotel lobby, weighs in at 61 pounds, 11 ounces.

Binion's Horseshoe

Opened in 1951 by gambler Benny Binion, the Horseshoe has a reputation of not being afraid to take any bet no matter how large.

You can have your picture taken free of charge, 4 pm - midnight, in front of $1 million; 100 $10,000 bills arranged inside a giant horseshoe display.

A spectacular view of Las Vegas from the Binion's Ranch Restaurant on the top floor, reached via glass elevator.

Old Fort

Las Vegas Blvd. N. at Washington. Enter from Cashman Field parking lot. The oldest historical site in southern Nevada, built by the Mormon missionaries from Utah in 1855. *(See Museums for additional information.)*

Reed Whipple Cultural Arts Center
821 Las Vegas Blvd. N.
229-6211

The center hosts a variety of cultural events and classes.

Las Vegas Museum of Natural History
900 Las Vegas Blvd. N.
384-3466

One of the finest prehistoric dinosaur collections and over 300 modern-day animals. Extensive wildlife art gallery includes award winning wood sculptures. Animated dinosaurs, bat flight room, a large wildlife art collection, a children's hands-on room, a world wildlife room, and a gift shop. *(See Museums for more information.)*

Las Vegas Library - Lied Discovery Children's Museum -

Located inside the main library, this private, non-profit children's museum is designed to provide enjoyable learning experiences. This 22,000 sq. ft. $2 million hands-on museum has 130 exhibits devoted to science, humanities and the arts. The exhibits, designed for children 8 and older, include a newspaper newsroom, a radio and television studio and many others devoted to science and technology.
(See Museums for more information.)

Reed Whipple Cultural Arts Center

EAST

Antique Shops

There are over 30 antique shops located on E. Charleston Blvd. between Maryland Pkwy. and Eastern.

Nature Park

Mojave and Bonanza - An untouched 96 acre remnant of the Old Las Vegas Meadows. Mesquite, cottonwood and elm trees provide sheltered homes to birds, cottontails, snakes and the endangered desert tortoise.

Mormon Temple
827 Temple View Dr., off E. Bonanza
452-5011

Located at the base of Sunrise Mountain on a beautifully landscaped 12 acre site, this is one of only 42 temples of the Church of Jesus Christ of Latter-Day Saints and was dedicated in 1989. A 13 ft. high gold leaf statue of an ancient prophet stands atop one of six gracefully tapered spires rising above the impressive copper roof. The temple is used for baptisms and marriages and provides an atmosphere of meditation. The temple is open only to members of the Mormon Church although non-members may walk the grounds and enjoy the great view of Las Vegas.
Grounds hours: Tue. - Fri. 5:30 am - 10 pm; Sat. 5:30 am - 8 pm

View from Sunrise Mountain

Sunrise Mountain offers an excellent view of the entire Las Vegas valley, especially good vantage point to view the lights of Las Vegas at night.

WEST

Siegfried and Roy's House
4200 Vegas Dr.

The home where the stars and the animals of the Mirage show live.

Zoological Botanical Park
1775 N. Rancho Dr.
648-5955

This one acre zoo is home to over 250 birds and animals, including a Bengal Tiger and a lion; children's petting zoo. *(See Children for more information.)*

Yucca Mountain Information Office
4101 Meadows Ln.
295-1312

Exhibits and displays about the U.S. Department of Energy study of Yucca Mountain to determine whether it can safely isolate 77,000 tons of high level nuclear waste from the environment. There is also an extensive collection of printed and audiovisual materials as well as a staff member to answer your questions. Admission is free. Hours: Tue. - Sat. 10 am - 6 pm; evening hours by appointment.
Yucca Mountain tours: 794-7434

Tours of Yucca Mountain, the proposed nuclear waste repository located 100 miles northwest of Las Vegas, are occasionally conducted. The tour, with transportation provided, is open to any U.S. citizen over the age of 14 years. Reservation must be made at least 14 days in advance and positive ID provided.

Golden Nugget

SIGHTSEEING

SIGHTSEEING IN LAS VEGAS

Meadows Mall
4300 Meadows Ln.

With 140 specialty stores, an indoor oasis pool, colorful carousel animals and curious dinosaur bones. Meadows Mall holds as many surprises as the desert itself.
Hours: Mon. - Fri. 10 am - 9 pm; Sat. - Sun. 10 am - 6 pm

Lorenzi Park
3333 W. Washington

60 acre park with picnic, play, tennis facilities and pond. Originally a guest ranch that opened in the 1930s.

Nevada State Museum & Historical Society

Located at Lorenzi Park, the Nevada State Museum contains permanent exhibits highlighting the history, natural history, and Native American cultures of the region and a schedule of changing exhibits features art, history and science. The Cahlan Library is open weekdays for those interested in Nevada history research; museum gift shop. This 35,000 sq. ft. facility opened in 1982.
(See Museums for more information.)

Las Vegas Art Museum
Sahara West Library
9600 W. Sahara Ave.

Three separate galleries - Main Gallery, Mini Gallery and Southwest Gallery; exhibits change monthly; outstanding annual shows and competitions.
Hours: Tue. - Sat. 10 am - 5 pm; Sun. 1 pm - 5 pm

Desert Demonstration Gardens
3701 W. Alta Dr.
258-3205

2.4 acres with 11 different landscape areas and over 180 species of vegetation designed to show the beauty of water-efficient landscaping. Resource room and amphitheater for demonstrations and lectures.
Hours: 8 am - 5 pm

Charleston Heights Arts Center
800 S. Brush St.
229-6383

Center for cultural performances, art displays, classes and a variety of other programs.
Hours: Mon. & Thu. 1 pm - 8:30 pm, Tue. & Wed. 10 am - 8:30 pm, Fri. 10 am - 5:30 pm, Saturday 9 am - 4:30 and Sun. 1 pm - 4:30 pm

NORTHWEST

Santa Fe Hotel Ice Arena
4949 N. Rancho Dr.

17,000 sq. ft. of ice with a 2,500 seat arena.
Admission: Adults $5, children 3 - 12 $4, children 2 and under free; $1.50 figure skate rental and $2 hockey skate rental

Gilcrease Nature Sanctuary
8103 Racel St.
645-4224

Non-profit safe-haven for exotic game birds and wildlife. Aviaries and small habitats for birds and animals, all in a beautiful setting filled with trees and flower-lined pathways. The sanctu-

Liberace Museum

ary is home to The Wild Wing Project, southern Nevada's only non-profit, federally licensed wildlife rehabilitation organization. School tours available.
Hours: Wed. -Sun. 11 am - 3 pm or by appointment
Admission: $3 adults, $1 for children 6 and older, under 6 free.

Gilcrease Orchard
7800 N. Tenaya Way
645-1126

Bring your own containers and pick your fruit yourself; about 40 cents per pound, depending on the fruit.
Hours: 7 am - noon

SOUTH

Liberace Former Home
4982 Shirley St.

The former residence of Liberace is now used for special functions. House may be rented for parties.

Liberace Museum
1775 E. Tropicana Ave.

Displays of custom automobiles, rare and antique pianos, the famous Liberace wardrobe, the world's largest rhinestone and other memorabilia. Admission donations go to the Liberace Foundation for the Performing and Creative Arts; gift shop.
(See Museums for more information.)

Nevada Institute for Contemporary Art
3455 E. Flamingo Rd.
434-2666
Hours: Tue., Wed., Fri. 10 am - 6 pm; Thu. 10 am - 8 pm; Sat. - Sun. 10 am - 3 pm
Admission: Free

Pet Kingdom 2000
2431 E. Tropicana Ave.
451-9123

Pet store with unique pets, animals and reptiles

McCarran Airport

McCarran is the ninth busiest airport in the United States. Special parking lot to watch planes take off and land on Sunset Rd., across from the main post office.

McCarran Aviation History and McCarran Art Gallery - Part of the airport's public art program features rotating exhibits showcasing the talents of southern Nevada artists.

Kiosks containing artifacts and video displays. Long range plan is to develop a museum documenting the history of aircraft in Southern Nevada. The free exhibit is open to the public 24 hours a day. *(See Transportation for more information.)*

Sunset Park
Sunset at Eastern

Largest park in Las Vegas with 324 acres. *(See Parks for more information.)*

Wayne Newton's Home
Pecos at Sunset

Casa de Shenandoah is the 53-acre home of the "Midnight Idol."

BOULDER STRIP

Sam's Town
5111 Boulder Hwy.

Sunset Stampede - Free water laser/light show offered four times daily in the Mystic Falls Indoor Park - 2 pm, 6 pm, 8 pm & 10 pm

The Final Score - Sports Bar with basketball key court, pinball, video golf, darts, pool, shuffleboard, over 30 TVs and outdoor volleyball court.

Silver Bowl Sports Complex
6800 E. Russell Rd.

Concerts, UNLV football. 36.9-acre park with six lighted ballfields, archery, playground, soccer field and restrooms. Circus Circus Radio Controlled Aircraft Field located 1/4 mile north of stadium. Remote Controlled Car Track for 1/4, 1/8 and 1/10 scale cars is located in the south parking lot.

Archery range located 1/4 mile south of stadium. The Silver Bowl Sports Complex covers 420 acres.

NORTH LAS VEGAS

Nellis Air Force Base
Salt Lake Hwy.

Nellis began as the Army Air Corps Gunnery School in 1941. Located 8 miles northeast of Las Vegas, Nellis Air Force Base covers more than 11,000 acres and restricted ranges cover over 4,742 sq. mi. The base was renamed in 1950 after Lt. William Nellis, who was killed in action in 1944 on his 70th P-47 combat mission over Luxembourg. There are 9,100 military and civilian personnel at Nellis. Free guided tours lasting approximately 90 minutes are offered Tue. and Thu. at 2 pm; reservations required.

Community College of Southern Nevada
651-4000

Officially dedicated in 1971, and moving to its present 80-acre facility in 1975, the community college has an enrollment of nearly 27,000 students at three campuses and 50 academic centers.

Planetarium - Located at Community College of Southern Nevada, the Planetarium features interesting and educational movies. The planetarium also offers telescope viewing after each performance, weather permitting. Many astronomical objects can be viewed depending on the time of year and visibility. Call 651-4759 for shows.
(See Movie Theaters for more information.)

HENDERSON

Favorite Brands International
1180 Marshmallow Ln.
564-3878

See how marshmallows are made in their Henderson factory and sample fresh-off-the-line marshmallows. The factory store sells Favorite Brand international products and gift items.

Clark County Heritage Museum
1830 S. Boulder Hwy.

New exhibit center with a 12,000 year timeline of southern Nevada history. Heritage Street living history area with renovated historic structures and a Nevada ghost town (unrestored). Outdoor railroad and ranching displays, and a Southwestern gift shop on this 25 acre site. *(See Museums for more information.)*

Santa Fe Hotel Ice Arena

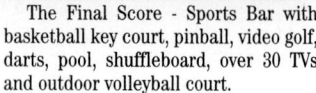

Ron Lee's World of Clowns
330 Carousel Pkwy.
434-3920

A factory where clown sculptures are made. A museum of circus memorabilia, a gift gallery full of clown related items, and an archives filled with clown and animated sculptures. *(Also listed under Children and Cultural Arts.)*

GREEN VALLEY HENDERSON

Mountasia Family Fun Center
2050 Olympic Ave.
898-7777

Two 18 hole miniature golf courses, roller skating, roller blading, arcade with over 100 video games, go carts (must be 54 inches or more to drive, 44 inches or more to be passenger), Bumper Boats (must be 44 inches to drive and 32 inches to be a passenger), large clubhouse with game rooms, McDonalds.

Hours: Mon. - Thu. 2 pm - 10 pm; Fri. 2 pm - midnight; Sat. 10 am - midnight; Sun. 10 am - 10 pm

Ethel M Chocolate Factory/Cactus Garden
2 Cactus Garden Dr.
433-2500

Self guided tour takes you through the factory to see how these gourmet chocolates are made. Video monitors provide taped explanations of the process. At the end of the tour you are treated to a free sample in the gift shop. In the 2.5 acre cactus garden, you'll discover an arid landscape with over 350 species of cactus, succulents and desert plants from the Southwest and other deserts of the world.

Hours: Daily 8:30 am - 7 pm

Cranberry World West Ocean Spray
1301 American Pacific Dr.
566-7160

Visitors Center features free plant tours, a museum with interactive exhibits, a film in the Cranberry Cinema and samples from the demonstration kitchen; gift shop.

Hours: Daily 9 am - 5 pm

Green Valley Sculpture Information Center
2501 N. Green Valley Pkwy.

Life-like bronze statues line Green Valley Pkwy. near Sunset Rd. in the Green Valley area of Henderson. Works include permanent and rotating outdoor pieces by J. Seward Johnson, Lita Albuquerque, Lloyd Hamrol, Lee Sido, Alan Osborn and Isaac Witkin. The center has a location map and information on the sculptures and the Green Valley area. *(See Cultural Arts for more information.)*

BOULDER CITY

Hemenway Park
Ville Dr. S. off Manna Dr.

4.6 acre park with an open play area, two gazebos, playground, basketball court, two lighted tennis courts, picnic facilities. Park offers a panoramic view of Lake Mead and bighorn sheep come out of the River Mountains to graze during the early summer until late fall, usually around noon - 3 pm.

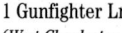

Boulder Dam Hotel

Boulder Dam Hotel
1305 Arizona St.
293-3510

Built in 1933 to house dignitaries who came to visit Hoover Dam. Surrounding buildings in the historical district were built in the 1920s and 1930s during construction of the dam. Not used as a hotel now but will be renovated in the future. *(See Accommodations for more information.)*

Hoover Dam
Located 40 miles southeast of Las Vegas on US 93.

Guided tour info.: 293-8321
Hours: 8:30 am - 5:30 pm; 8 am - 6:45 pm Memorial Day through Labor Day.
Admission: Adults $6.00, seniors $5, children 6 - 16 $2, children 5 and under free.

Lake Mead
(See Recreation Areas.)

OUT FROM LAS VEGAS

Pahrump Valley Vineyards
3810 Winery Rd.
Pahrump, NV 89048
727-6900   1-800-368-WINE

Located 60 miles west of Las Vegas, just off Highway 160. Look for the win-ery sign as you enter Pahrump on Highway 160 from Las Vegas. Turn east on Winery Road.

Hours: 10 am - 4:30 pm
Admission: Free

The Pahrump Valley Vineyards sit against the western slope of Mt. Charleston. Wine tasting and hourly tours of Nevada's only winery are offered daily. The Mediterranean-style winery uses imported California juice to make all its wines. The grapes, planted in the winter, won't be ready for three years. The winery produced 12,000 cases of wine last year and predicts 16,000 cases this year. The winery is dedicated to producing premium quality wines that showcase the unique flavors of the fruit with finesse and balance. The wines can be purchased by the bottle or the case at the winery. Cases can also be ordered with personalized labels. The winery was visited by over 100,000 people last year.

Tasting Restaurant serves lunch Wed. -Sun. noon - 3 pm and dinner 5 pm - 9 pm; reservations are required for dinner. Relax in an ambiance of quiet elegance. High-backed wing chairs offer privacy for intimate dining. The cocktail lounge with wrap-around windows, three sto-ries up, offers a spectacular view of the valley. *(Also see Restaurants.)*

Browse through the souvenir shop. The winery hosts a grape-stomping festival each year.

Old Nevada
1 Gunfighter Ln.
(West Charleston Blvd., 20 miles to the west)
Old Nevada, NV 89004
875-4191

Original 1902 Stamp Mill (crushes ore to retrieve gold) and a replica of an 1860 chapel.

Full scale recreation of an Old West town with wooden sidewalks and buildings featuring a restaurant, saloon, museum and shops. Shootouts and hangings hourly in the streets. On Saturdays and Sundays, special children's show lets kids be part of a posse to catch the bad guy. Melodrama and Cowboy Shows daily at 11:30 am, noon, 2 pm, 2:30 pm, 4:30 pm & 5 pm

Hours: 10:30 am - 5 pm
Admission: Adults $6.50, children 5 - 11 $4, under 5 free, seniors $5.50

PRIMM

Buffalo Bill's Hotel & Casino
Primadonna, NV 89019
382-1111 1-800-FUNSTOP

$90 million hotel/casino features the tallest roller coaster drop in the world, a water-flume ride, and a ghost town attraction; Buffalo Bill's is connected to Primadonna by western-style train; Carolee's Movie Theater featuring first run movies; video arcade; two state-of-the-art motion simulator theaters. Buffalo-shaped swimming pool with water slide and jacuzzi.

Primadonna Monorail to Whiskey Pete's, Ferris Wheel, Carousel, eight lane bowling alley
(Also see Recreation Areas for more sightseeing outside of Las Vegas.)

WEST OF LAS VEGAS ON CHARLESTON BLVD. (159)

Brownstone Canyon
Located off West Charleston Blvd., Brownstone Canyon is part of the Red Rock National Conservation Area. To reach Brownstone Canyon, travel west on Charleston until you see a powerline road heading westward. Travel about five miles on the powerline road or the wash to the fence closing off the upper end of the canyon. Motor vehicles are prohibited beyond the fence but mountain bikes, hikers and horseback riders are welcome.

Signs of early Indian life in the area can be seen, as well as unusual rock formations and varied plant life. The area offers an excellent view of the Las Vegas valley.

Bonnie Springs
Located 20 miles west of Las Vegas, this 115 acre desert park has a motel, three museums, train, restaurant, Old West shows, an old mining town and a petting zoo with over 100 animals.

Pahrump Valley Vineyards

SIGHTSEEING

SIGHTSEEING IN LAS VEGAS

Lovell Canyon

Travel west on Charleston Blvd. to the Sky Mountain Resort/Lovell Canyon turnoff and travel 9.3 miles. Turn left at Bluebird and travel a half mile.

A wide variety of flowers, plants and trees as well as small wildlife can be seen in the area. The higher elevation makes this a great escape from the heat of the valley. Primitive camping areas and fire pits. No facilities are available.

NORTH OF LAS VEGAS ON U.S. 95

Corn Creek

Located about 22 miles north on U.S. 95. Turnoff is about 8 miles past Kyle Canyon Rd. Corn Creek turnoff is on the right; travel about four miles on a well-graded dirt road to parking area.

Part of the vast Desert Mountain Wildlife Range supervised by the U.S. Fish and Wildlife Service. Open to visitors year-round from 5 am until 9 pm. Foot paths take visitors around the spring-fed ponds and pastures. Displays with information explain about the area. The area attracts a vast variety of birds; over 250 species have been identified. A picnic area has tables, grills, restrooms and water.

Cold Creek · Willow Creek

Located 35 miles north of Las Vegas on US Highway 95 to the turnoff to the Indian Springs Prison. It is about another 12 miles past the prison and up into the foothills. When you see some houses

steer to the road on the right, you will come first to the Cold Creek area about a mile down the road. About 2 miles further is the Willow Creek area.

Located at the northern end of the Spring Mountains, the area offers picnicking, hiking, camping and other backroad exploring. The Bonanza Trailhead is a 12-mile hike into Lee Canyon. There are no formal campgrounds. Area is maintained by the U. S. Forest Service and is part of the Desert National Wildlife Range. Permits are required for overnight use.

Desert National · Wildlife Range

Turn-off is located 18 miles past Cheyenne Boulevard on U.S. 95.

Spring Mountains

Located 30 miles northwest of Las Vegas. 316,000-acre range is supervised by the U.S. Forest Service. President Clinton designated it a recreation area in 1993. A dedication ceremony for the new Spring Mountains National Recreation Area was held in October.

The area encompasses the Las Vegas Ranger District of the Toiyabe National Forest which includes the 43,000-acre Mt. Charleston Wilderness area and lands extending from Mount Sterling in the north to Mount Potosi in the south.

NORTH OF LAS VEGAS ON I-15

VALLEY OF FIRE STATE PARK
(See Recreation Areas.)

Bitter Springs Trail Back Country Byway

45 miles north of Las Vegas on I-15, then east for 4.5 miles on the Valley of Fire State Park Rd. The 28-mile Byway journey will begin at Valley of Fire State Park, then cut through the foothills of the Muddy Mountains, through several dry washes, past abandoned mining operations and terminate on North Shore Dr. in the Lake Mead National Recreation Area. Along the way you will view lush desert streams, burnt-red butte formations, bighorn sheep and wild horses and burros and dramatic views of Lake Mead and the western reaches of the Grand Canyon.

EAST OF LAS VEGAS ON U.S. 93

Rogers Springs

Part of the Lake Mead National Recreation area, Rogers Springs is located 15 miles south of Overton on North Shore Rd., just past the Echo Bay turnoff. Large tamarisk trees shade the natural warm spring gravel-bottom shallow wading pool. The day-use area has picnic tables.

Devil's Paint Pots/Fortification Mountain

Located 40 miles from Las Vegas. Cross over Hoover Dam into Arizona and about 2 1/2 miles past the dam will be a turnoff on the left. Travel 4 miles on a graded road to the lake.

Primitive camping along the lake's shore or picnicking. Some rock fire pits are located along the shore. From this area you will have spectacular views of the lake and the surrounding mountains, with the different colors of earth. The hike to the top of Fortification Mountain will take several hours; the trail is long and steep.

SOUTH OF LAS VEGAS ON U.S. 95

Christmas Tree Pass

Just off U.S. 95 between Searchlight and Laughlin, a dirt road marked Christmas Tree Pass snakes through the Newberry Mountains for 17 miles to S.R. 163. Along this road is a collection of rock formations, cacti, sagebrush, pinon pines and junipers. During the Christmas season it has become traditional that passing visitors decorate these trees with any number of unusual "ornaments." A side trip off this road, before you reach S.R. 163, takes you into Grapevine Canyon and a profusion of ancient petroglyphs, thousands of years old.

Keyhole Canyon

Take U.S. 93/95 to the Laughlin turnoff, U.S. 95, past the turnoff to Nelson about 6 miles; follow the dirt road east, past the second powerline, turn right and watch for the spur road to the left, about 5 miles from the highway. Varied rock formation and ancient Indian art. Great place for rock climbing.

Botanical Gardens at the Mirage

Stealth F-117 - Nellis Air Force Base

Light Show at Fremont Street Experience

Lake Mead National Recreation Park

Family Interests

CHILDREN IN LAS VEGAS

According to the 1990 census, approximately 182,000 children under the age of 18 live in Clark County. Sixty-nine percent of Las Vegas households have no children, 14 percent have one child, 11 percent have two children and 6 percent have three or more.

There were 17,895 babies born in Clark County in 1997. The Clark County School District is the largest district in the state and the 10th largest school district in the nation.

FAMILIES VISITING LAS VEGAS

During 1997, 88 percent of the visitors to Las Vegas were 21 or over; however, with the addition of the MGM Theme Park, Grand Slam Canyon at Circus Circus and family attractions at many other major hotels, Las Vegas is fast becoming a family vacation destination.

Las Vegas has the same - if not more - entertainment as any other American city for people under the age of 21. In recent years the city has developed many family attractions, such as Wet 'n Wild on the Strip, Scandia Fun Center and the Las Vegas Mini Grand Prix, to name just a few. Hotels such as Circus Circus cater to families with children by offering circus acts and a carnival midway.

The legal age to drink or buy alcohol or gamble is 21 in all of Nevada. Persons under 21 are not allowed in the casino areas of the hotels, except to pass through to other areas. The laws are strictly enforced in both casinos and bars.

Curfew for unchaperoned youths under 18 is midnight on weekends, holidays and summer months. Weeknight (Sun. - Thu.) curfew is 10 pm during the school year.

AMUSEMENT CENTERS

Cinema Ride
Forum Shops
3500 Las Vegas Blvd. S.
Las Vegas, NV 89109
369-4008
Hours: 10 am - 11 pm
3-D motion simulator rides, Galactic Light Atlantis, Submarine Race, Coaster Crazy and Haunted Graveyard Run.

Circus Circus Hotel & Casino
2880 Las Vegas Blvd. S.
Las Vegas, NV 89109
734-0410
Video arcade, pool, monorail, McDonald's, Grand Slam Canyon. Located off the mezzanine is a carnival midway with games of chance, arcade games, shops and restaurants and snack bars open 10 am - 1 am; Free live circus acts in the center ring daily 11 am - midnight every half hour.

Crystal Palace Skating Centers
(Multiple locations listed below)
3901 N. Rancho Dr.
Las Vegas, NV 89130
645-4892

4680 Boulder Hwy.
Las Vegas, NV 89121
458-7107

4740 S. Decatur Blvd.
Las Vegas, NV 89103
253-9832

1110 E. Lake Mead Dr.
Henderson, NV 89015
564-2790

Cyber Station
Forum Shops
3500 Las Vegas Blvd. S.
Las Vegas, NV 89109
893-3350
Hours: Sun. - Thu. 10 am - 11 pm;
Fri. - Sat. 10 am - midnight
Large video arcade and fun center featuring the latest games.

Discovery Zone
2020 Olympic Ave.
Henderson, NV 89014
434-9950
Hours: Mon. - Thu. 10 am - 8 pm; Fri. - Sat. 10 am - 9 pm; Sun. 11 am - 7 pm
Admission: $5.99 per child, club discount rate $3.99
Time is unlimited, specially designed indoor padded playground with slides, swings, tunnels and things to climb on and through where fitness is disguised as fun for children to age 12. Socks are required for all play participants. Adults can participate free of charge but cannot drop children off; snack bar, overnight camp-ins.

Excalibur Hotel & Casino
3850 Las Vegas Blvd. S.
Las Vegas, NV 89109
597-7777
Hours: 9:30 am - midnight
Located on the lower level are carnival games, video games, a snack bar, concessions, and the Magic Motion Machine (*See Theaters*).

Grand Slam Canyon Indoor Amusement Park
Circus Circus
2880 Las Vegas Blvd. S.
Las Vegas, NV 89109
794-3745
Hotline: 794-3939
Hours: Sun. - Sat. 10 am - closing time varies
Admission: Free. All day wrist band, which entitles you to unlimited rides are $13.95 per person age 10 and over; $9.95 ages 3-9; free for under 3 years. Nevada residents receive $2 off all day wrist band.

Five-acre theme park fully enclosed within a pink glass dome, climate controlled year round. Grand Slam's attractions include Bumper Cars; the Canyon Blaster, the only indoor double-loop double-corkscrew roller coaster in the Unit-

Circus Circus Hotel & Casino, 2880 Las Vegas Blvd. S., Las Vegas, NV 89109

ed States; the Rim Runner, a three-and-a-half minute water flume ride that plummets from the peaks into a spectacular splashdown; and an interactive, nonviolent laser tag game called Hot Shots.

Cliffhangers (net climb and ball crawl area); Thunderbirds (children's airplane ride); Miner Mike (mini roller coaster); Road Runner (mini Himalayan ride); Drifters (balloon ferris wheel); and Fossil Dig (play area) will appeal to smaller children; B.C. Bus is a ride for the whole family.

Within the dome are roaring robotic dinosaurs, and replicas of a fossil wall, tar pits, and a Native American cliff dwelling. Canyon Country peaks soar 140 feet skyward and a 90-foot waterfall cascades amid caves, canyons, and lush vegetation.

Gymboree
918 S. Valley View Blvd.
Las Vegas, NV 89107
877-0074
Hours: Mon. - Sat. 9:30 am - 7:30 pm
Preschool exercise classes and play program that stresses semi-structured play and bonding between parent and child. Enrollment is required.

Las Vegas Mini Grand Prix
1401 N. Rainbow Blvd.
Las Vegas, NV 89108
259-7000 Fax: 259-7001
Hours: Sun. - Thu. 10 am - 11 pm;
Fri. - Sat. 10 am - midnight
Call for information on party or group rates. Four tracks of racing: Adult Grand Prix, Raised Oval Super Stock Cars, Go-karts (1/3 mile track) and Kiddie Karts (ages 4-7). 5,000 sq. ft. game and party room, located just 15 minutes from the Las Vegas Strip.

Luxor
3900 Las Vegas Blvd. S.
Las Vegas, NV 89119
262-4000
Hours: 9 am - midnight
18,000 sq. ft. Virtualand arcade. "Luxor Live" and "In Search of the Obelisk" each lasting 15-20 minutes in two separate theaters, dealing with the past, present and future; Sega Virtualand Arcade - Virtual Formula Race Cars, F-16 Flight Simulators; IMAX theater shows 2 special features throughout the day.

MGM Grand Adventures
Theme Park
3805 Las Vegas Blvd. S.
Las Vegas, NV 89109
891-1111
Theme park: 891-7979
Hours: Daily 10 am - 6 pm (winter); noon - 8 pm (spring); 10 am - 10 pm (summer)
Admission Winter: Adults $12; children 10 and under $10; under 42 inches free. Nevada residents receive $2 off. There are also special event and summer admission prices which vary; please call. Park is limited to 9,000 people per day. The MGM Grand Adventures theme park is an outdoor entertainment complex featuring 7 rides, 3 theater shows, 15 restaurants and shops, 6 theme streets and wandering MGM characters. Rides include Grand Canyon Rapids (rapids ride), Over the Edge (flume ride), peddlin' paddle boats, Les bumper boats, the Lightning Bolt (dark coaster ride), Parisian Taxis (bumper cars) and of course, The Screamer. The world's highest Skycoaster thrill-attrac-

tion, The Screamer puts 1 to 3 people in a flight harness and lifts the flyers to the top of a 250-foot launching tower. Flyers pull their own ripcord which sets in motion a 100-foot free-fall plunge before they swoop into a 70 mph swing.

McDonald's
3801 S. Maryland Pkwy.
Las Vegas, NV 89119
735-2266
Hours: Sun. - Thu. 6 am - 10 pm;
Fri. - Sat. 6 am - 11 pm
Large, 3-story, air conditioned, indoor playland. Of the 54 local McDonald's, 10 have indoor soft play areas.

Mountasia Family Fun Center
2050 Olympic Ave.
Henderson, NV 89014-2242
898-7777
Hours: Mon. - Thu. 2 pm - 10 pm;
Fri. 2 pm - midnight; Sat. 10 am - midnight; Sun. 10 am - 10 pm
Two 18 hole miniature golf courses, roller skating, roller blading, arcade with over 100 video games, Go Carts (must be 54 inches or more to drive, 44 inches or more to be passenger), Bumper Boats (must be 44 inches to drive and 32 inches to be a passenger), large, clubhouse with game rooms, McDonalds.

Peter Piper Pizza
(see Children's Parties)

Pocket Change
Meadows Mall
4300 Meadows Ln.
Las Vegas, NV 89107
878-8776
Hours: Mon. - Fri. 10 am - 9 pm;
Sat. - Sun. 10 am - 6 p.m
Over 70 games.

Rad Trax
3650 S. Decatur Blvd.
Las Vegas, NV 89103
253-7568
Hours: Mon. - Fri. 2 pm - 10 pm;
Sat. - Sun. noon - 11 pm
Family style slot car racing tracks. The center offers a complete line of cars, performs repairs and rents slot cars, 3 tracks and video arcade.

Slot Car City
4430 E. Charleston Blvd.
Las Vegas, NV 89104
438-1760
Hours: Daily 3 pm - 11 pm; Wed. 6 pm - 11 pm
18 lanes on 2 high speed tracks and drag strip. Scale speeds over 1,000 mph.

Stratosphere
2000 Las Vegas Blvd. S.
Las Vegas, NV 89104
382-4446
World's highest roller coaster, High Roller, starting at 909 feet above the ground; The Big Shot, a 30-second thrill ride, shoots 16 passengers 160 feet to the 1,081 foot level, reaching up to 4-1/2 G-forces and negative 1 G-force descending. Four high-speed double-decker elevators travel at 1,400 ft. per minute, whisking visitors to the top of the tower in 45 seconds, where they can view Las Vegas from either the indoor or the outdoor observation deck.
Admission: observation deck $5, Nevada residents $4; thrill rides $5

Treasure Island
3300 Las Vegas Blvd. S.
Las Vegas, NV 89109
894-7111
Hours: 9 am - 1 am, later on weekends
Mutiny Bay - an 18,000 sq. ft. entertainment center offering video games and electronically simulated rides.

Ultrazone
2555 S. Maryland Pkwy
Las Vegas, NV 89109
734-1577
Hours: Mon. - Thu. 3 pm - 4 am;
Fri. 3 pm - 1 am; Sat. 10 am - 1 am;
Sun. 10 am - 11 pm
Admission: 15 minute game $7 per player; fee for membership $10 per year
Live-action laser game. A minimum of two and a maximum of 24 players (on 3 teams) can play the game at one time. Players compete in a 5,000 sq. ft. arena with an elaborate maze. Points are scored by shooting targets on opponents' vests or by gaining access to the other team's base.

Wet 'n Wild
2601 Las Vegas Blvd. S.
734-0088
(see Water Parks, this section)

GO CARTS

Formula K Family Fun Park
2980 S. Sandhill Rd.
Las Vegas, NV 89121
431-7223
Hours: Mon. - Thu. 3 pm - 10 pm;
Fri. 3 pm - midnight; Sat. noon - midnight; Sun. noon - 10 pm
Admission: $3.50 for 5 minute ride; children under 54" ride free with an adult.
Also mini go carts for children 5 and up.

Las Vegas Mini Grand Prix
1401 N. Rainbow Blvd.
Las Vegas, NV 89108
259-7000 Fax: 259-7001
Hours: 10 am - 11 pm, please call for party and group rates.
Four tracks for racing: Adult Grand Prix, Raised Oval Super Stock Cars, Go-Carts (1/3 mile track) and Kiddie Karts (4-7 years).
5,000 sq. ft. game and party room; located just 15 minutes from the Las Vegas Strip.

Scandia Family Fun Center
2900 Sirius Ave.
Las Vegas, NV 89102
364-0070
Hours: Sun. - Thu. 10 am - 10:30 pm;
Fri. - Sat. 10 am - midnight; closes 1 hour earlier in winter.
Admission: $3.95 per race, children under 54" ride free with an adult (must be at least 3 years old)

MINIATURE GOLF

Formula K Family Fun Park
2980 S. Sandhill Rd.
Las Vegas, NV 89121
431-7223
Michael Stephanie
Hours: Mon. - Thu. 3 pm - 10 pm; Fri. 3 pm - midnight; Sat. noon - midnight; Sun. noon - 10 pm
Admission: 18 holes $3.50
Two 18 hole miniature golf courses.

Mountasia Family Fun Center
2050 Olympic Ave.
Henderson, NV 89014-2242
898-7777
Doug Eichholz, Gen. Mgr.
Hours: Mon. - Thu. 2 pm - 10 pm; Fri 2 pm - midnight; Sat. 10 am - midnight; Sun. 10 am - 10 pm
Admission: $4 children 12 or under; $5.50 for adults; $4.50 seniors; $14.00 family of four. Miniature golf.

Scandia Family Fun Center
2900 Sirius Ave.
Las Vegas, NV 89102
364-0070
Wayne Larson, Gen. Mgr.
Hours: Sun. - Thu. 10 am - 10 pm; Fri. - Sat. 10 am - midnight; closes 1 hour earlier in winter.
Admission: $5.95 per person; 1/2 price replay; children 5 & under play free with adult.
Three miniature golf courses of varying difficulty. Also Li'l Indy Raceway, bumper boats, batting range and video arcade.

SKATING - ICE

Sahara Ice Palace
800 E. Karen Ave.
Las Vegas, NV 89109
862-4262
Greg Toy, Mgr.
Hours: Daily: Noon - 2:00 pm, Tue. - Wed. 5:45 pm - 7:45 pm, Fri. - Sat. 8:00 pm - 10:00 pm
Price: General public $5, children under 12 and seniors over 55 $4, skate rentals $2
Plans include "Learn to Skate" program, group lessons, broomball and a hockey league starting in April. Tuesday night is "Gospel Skating" to Christian music. Small arcade, small restaurant opening soon, birthday party room and private ice available

Santa Fe Hotel Ice Arena
4949 N. Rancho Dr.
Las Vegas, NV 89130
658-4993
William Coblentz, Ice Arena Mgr.
Hours: Call for hours. They vary from day to day. Senior citizens most Wednesdays noon - 2 pm
Admission: adults $5; children 3 - 12 $4; children 2 and under free; $1.50 skate rental, $2 hockey skate rental.
17,000 sq. ft. of ice with a 2,500 seat arena.

SKATING - ROLLER

Crystal Palace
(Multiple locations listed below)
3901 N. Rancho Dr.
Las Vegas, NV 89130
645-4892

4680 Boulder Hwy.
Las Vegas, NV 89121
458-7107

4740 S. Decatur Blvd.
Las Vegas, NV 89103
253-9832

1110 E. Lake Mead Dr.
Henderson, NV 89015
564-2796
Please call for information on hours, fees and skate rentals.

Mountasia Family Fun Center
2050 Olympic Ave.
Henderson, NV 89014
898-7777
Hours: Mon. - Thu. 3 pm - 10 pm;
Fri. 3 p.m - midnight; Sat. noon - midnight; Sun. 11 am - 8 pm
Roller skating and roller blading, skate anytime, $2 in-line skate rental; $4 quad skate rental. Prices apply to all ages. Children's sizes as small as size 9. You can bring your own skates.

WATER PARKS

Wet 'n Wild · Las Vegas
2601 Las Vegas Blvd. S.
Las Vegas, NV 89109
Mailing address:
2310 Paseo Del Prado, Ste. A220
Las Vegas, NV 89102
737-3819   1-800-565-0786
Recorded Info: 734-0088
Offices/Group Info: 871-7811
Wet 'n Wild, located on the world famous Las Vegas Strip, offers locals and visitors a fun way to beat the hot desert sun. The 24 acre water park features over a dozen breathtaking chutes, slides, flumes, floats and plunges. Wet 'n Wild's 1.5 million gallons of fresh water are maintained at comfortable temperatures and circulated through a state-of-the-art filtering system.

There is fun and thrills for all ages at Wet 'n Wild with rides for the most courageous of daredevils to the relaxing Lazy River®. Some of the rides for the not-so-faint-at-heart are Der Stuka® and Bomb Bay®. Der Stuka® is a seven story

free fall into a refreshing catch pool and Bomb Bay® sends its passengers down a 76-foot slide like a missile projectile. Kids can enjoy the giant water playground complete with sea squirts and other aquatic contraptions.

Between June 26 and July 31, Wet 'n Wild will put on an entertainment extravaganza called Summer Nights and Las Vegas has little to compare. The park extends its hours from 10 am - 10 pm, fills the night air with music from live bands and has numerous games and contests.

For group events, Wet 'n Wild offers 2 acres of outdoor picnic facilities known as the Picnic Plaza. The Picnic Plaza, which can be reserved for up to 2,000 guests, includes more than 100 picnic tables, 2 volleyball courts, horseshoe pits, the Trampoline Thing, and many more fun games. The entire park can also be reserved for special occasions for up to 5,000 guests.

The park is staffed with certified lifeguards. Picnic facilities are available as are snack bars and locker facilities with showers and towel rentals. Wet 'n Wild's Beach Trends shop offers the latest fashions in swim apparel and all the sun care items you need to make your outing enjoyable.

The 1998 season is scheduled from early May through the end of September. **General admission prices:** $22.95 for ages 10 and up; $16.95 for ages 3 - 9 years; under 3 years free; seniors receive 1/2 off full day's general admission. **For more information or for group rates call:** 871-7811 or 800- 565-0786.

ZOOS & ANIMALS

(Also see Pets)

Pets Lost and Found: 873-3455

Dewey Animal Care Center
No-kill animal shelter.

Henderson Animal Shelter
565-2033

Nevada SPCA
897-1844

Animal Foundation
384-3333

**Las Vegas Valley Humane
Society**
434-2009

In July 1995 the Clark County Commission unanimously approved a 30 year conservation habitat for the desert tortoise, allowing developers to bulldoze other habitats in exchange for paying a $550 per acre developing fee. The County uses this to maintain 500,000 acres in the El Dorado Valley, south of Las Vegas, as a protected Desert Tortoise Habitat.

In order to prevent wild horses and burros from crossing State Route 160 near Mountain Springs, the Bureau of Land Management has built three underpasses. There are open ranges on the south side of the highway and reliable water sources on the north side so concrete culverts were built to save the Red Rock herd.

Bonnie Springs Ranch
1 Bonnie Springs Ranch Rd.
Old Nevada, NV 89004
(20 miles west on Charleston Blvd.)
875-4191
Alan Levinson, Pres.
Hours: 10:30 am - 5 pm
Admission: Free
Petting zoo, large animal zoo, duck pond and bird aviary. Many other animals roam the mountains in the Red Rock area such as wild donkeys, wild horses, coyotes, polecats, deer, elk and big horn sheep.

The Secret Gardens of Siegfried and Roy

Dolphin Habitat
The Mirage
3400 Las Vegas Blvd. S.
Las Vegas, NV 89109
791-7111
Hours: Mon. - Fri. 11 am - 7 pm;
Sat. & Sun. 9 am - 7 pm
Admission: $3; children under 10 free.
Bottlenose dolphins frolic in a 1.5 million gallon pool.

The Flamingo Hilton
3555 Las Vegas Blvd. S.
Las Vegas, NV 89109
733-3111
Hours: 24 hours
The Flamingo Hilton features a lush wildlife habitat amid cascading waterfalls, rockscapes, palm trees, water slides and linked swimming pools. There are 18-inch tall penguins, pink-plumed flamingos, wood ducks, swans, brightly colored Japanese koi, native hummingbirds and finches that live in the garden.

**Gilcrease Bird Preserve &
Wild Wing Project**
8103 Racel Rd.
Las Vegas, NV 89131
645-4224
(Also see Pets)
Hours: Sat. - Sun. 10 am - 3 pm
Admission: $3 adults; $1 children; 6 and under free.
A sanctuary and rehabilitation for orphaned and injured birds. For orphaned or injured birds of prey, call 658-0166. For hummingbirds, songbirds or any other wildlife, call 876-0387. Over 1,100 rehabilitated animals released back into the wild in 1994.

Nevada Zoological Foundation
1775 N. Rancho Dr.
Las Vegas, NV 89106
647-4685
Dedicated to conservation education and recreation.

**The Southern Nevada
Zoological-Botanical Park**
1775 N. Rancho Dr.
Las Vegas, NV 89106
648-5955
Pat Dingle
Hours: 9 am - 5 pm
Admission: $5 general, $3 for senior citizens and children ages 2 - 12, free to children under age 2.
Exhibits a variety of endangered cats as well as the last family of Barbary apes in the United States, chimpanzees,. eagles, ostriches, emus, talking parrots, wallabies, flamingos, large exotic reptiles and every species of venomous reptile native to southern Nevada. The zoo also features exhibits by the Las Vegas Gem Club and botanical displays of endangered cycads and rare bamboos.

There are educational-recreational opportunities at the park for all types of visitors, both the general public who explores the park unguided and organized groups and classes looking for more formal activities.

A snack bar and gift shop are available on grounds. The zoo also offers half day or full day Desert Eco-Tours via jeep, year round. Reservations required.

White Tiger Exhibit
The Mirage
3400 Las Vegas Blvd. S.
Las Vegas, NV 89109
791-7111
Hours: 24 hours
Exact replica of the White Tiger's original habitat; Tigers on display 24 hours.

**The Secret Gardens of
Siegfried and Roy**
The Mirage
3400 Las Vegas Blvd. S.
Las Vegas, NV 89109
791-7111
Admission: $10, children under 10 years of age are free.
Hours: Mon. - Fri. 11 am - 5:30 pm;
Sat. & Sun. 10 am - 5:30 pm

CULTURAL ARTS

Class Act
Allied Arts Council
401 S. Fourth St., Ste. 110
Las Vegas, NV 89101
386-4804
Goal is to introduce students to different forms of artistic expression such as dance, theater, music and visual arts. Targeting school children of all ages, Class Act is a three-way partnership between Allied Arts Council, the Junior League and CCSD.

Las Vegas Civic Ballet
821 Las Vegas Blvd. N.
Las Vegas, NV 89101
229-6211
Joel Mur, Pres.
For boys and girls ages 10-23. Must have 3 years of classical ballet training. Auditions are held twice a year for 2 concerts per year at Reed Whipple Center.

Nevada Dance Theatre
UNLV
3425 S. Lamb Blvd.
Las Vegas, NV 89119
547-1040

Professional ballet company offering a variety of programs each season.

**Academy of Nevada
Dance Theatre**
4850 Harrison Dr.
Las Vegas, NV 89121
898-6306
Bruce Steivel, Dir.
Official school of Nevada Dance Theatre. Offers pre-ballet, ballet, jazz and tap for ages 3 to adult.

Nevada School of the Arts
315 S. 7th St.
Las Vegas, NV 89109
386-2787
Dr. Paul Hesselink, Dean
Provides instruction in music and visual arts for ages 3 to senior citizens.

Rainbow Company
821 Las Vegas Blvd. N.
Las Vegas, NV 89101
229-6553
Karen McKenney, Artistic Dir.
Children's theater group for ages 10 - 17 years. No previous experience required.

The ensemble is a group of about 30 students who participate in classes and productions throughout the year at Reed Whipple Center.

Reed Whipple Cultural Center
821 Las Vegas Blvd. N.
Las Vegas, NV 89101
229-6211
Pat Harris, Coordinator
Offers a variety of classes for youths and adults of all ages and abilities in all the arts. Call for a class schedule.

Sign Design Theatre Company
2718 S. Highland Dr.
Las Vegas, NV 89109
731-3738
Richard Smith, Dir.
Children's company whose plays are sung and signed simultaneously. Open to deaf or hearing impaired children ages 4 - 17.

DANCE

**Preston's Class Act Dance &
Gymnastics School**
6250 Mountain Vista St.
Henderson, NV 89014
451-3939

Nancy Preston, Dir.
Ballet, tap, jazz, cheerleading and gymnastics for ages 2 1/2 to adult.

**Janet Kravenko School of
Dance · Dance Rage**
3400 S. Jones Blvd., Ste. 11
Las Vegas, NV 89102
876-2806
Janet Kravenko, Owner
Contemporary jazz for teens; ballet, tap, jazz, modern dance, acrobatics; children's musical theater workshop; pre-dance classes for children ages 3 to adults.

Rainbow Performing Arts Center
21 N. Mojave Rd.
Las Vegas, NV 89101
384-6268
Dan Garner, Dir.
Ballet, tap, jazz, and street jazz; modern acting and musical theater.

ASSISTANCE - YOUTH

Boys Town of Nevada
821 N. Mojave Rd.
Las Vegas, NV 89101
642-7393
Hotline: 1-800-448-3000
Tom Waite, Dir.
The Boy's Town 20-acre campus opened March 1991 for boys and girls ages 10 to 17. The Boy's Town program focuses on teaching children interpersonal skills in a family setting with 5 separate homes with a maximum of 6 children in each home, living with a married couple that act as counselors and surrogate parents. There is also a short term residential program which provides emergency shelter for boys and girls.

Big Brothers/Big Sisters of Southern Nevada
1785 E. Sahara Ave.
Las Vegas, NV 89104
731-2227
Donation Center: 222-9000
Elizabeth Painter, Social Work Supv.
Program for children ages 6-14, from single parent homes, to spend time on a monthly basis with a trained adult volunteer (one they have been matched with) sharing in activities and learning skills.

Catholic Charities of Nevada
Regina Hall
215 Palo Verde Dr.
Henderson, NV 89015
565-0688
Myra Davis, Adm.
Residential group home for abused and neglected female adolescents.

Children's Developmental Center
6910 Edna Ave., Ste. 110
Las Vegas, NV 89117
367-0306
Sue Germeroth, Dir.
Preschool for children under age 7 with behavioral problems. Support group also available.

Child Haven
Clark County Juvenile Court Service
701 N. Pecos Rd.
Las Vegas, NV 89101
455-5390
Peggy Leavitt, Div. Supv.
Provides temporary shelter for children under 18, who have been abandoned, neglected, abused or dependent children until placed in a protected environment. Children are placed in protective custody in Child Haven by police or by a Child Protective Services Officer. A new $1.1 million school was made possible with a donation from the Andre Agassi Foundation and the support of the Clark County School District, the County Commission and a group of business people led by interior designer Leslie Paraguirre. The 7 room, 10,000 sq. ft. Agassi Center for Education replaces a 2 room facility built in 1973.

Child Protective Services
Clark County Juvenile Court
3410 E. Bonanza Rd.
Las Vegas, NV 89101
455-5200
Neglect & Abuse Hotline: 399-0081

Carol Stillian, Div. Supv.
Investigates reports of child abuse and neglect. CPS receives nearly 3,500 calls per month.

Clark County Family & Youth Services
601 N. Pecos Rd.
Las Vegas, NV 89101
455-5200
Kirby Burgess, Dir.
The department processes youths who violate the law and supervises those on probation. The department investigates complaints of child abuse and neglect. Provides a variety of services designed to protect, care for and rehabilitate and counsel the youth of Clark County. Call for programs and details.

To work, a youth under 18 needs a work permit from Juvenile Court Services at 601 N. Pecos Rd. (455-5240). Limitations are set for 14 and 15 year olds during the school year.

Parenting Project
601 N. Pecos Rd.
Las Vegas, NV 89101
455-5295
Sarah Beers/Dianne Sivoli, Program Coordinators
The Parenting Project offers programs to help parents be more effective in raising their children. Programs support a positive learning environment using presentation, videos, experimental role play and group discussion. The following three programs are currently offered:

The Nurturing Parents and Families Program targets parents of children from birth to 5 years.

The Practical Parenting Program helps parents of 5 - 10 year olds gain an understanding of their children's behavior and assists them in devising a plan for encouraging appropriate behaviors and handling problem behaviors.

Families Back in Control is a 6 week program designed to maximize family strengths and reduce behavioral problems in children.

For information on any of these programs please call Sarah Beers or Dianne Sivoli.

Clark County School District
2832 E. Flamingo Rd.
Las Vegas, NV 89121
799-5011
Dr. Brian Cram, Supt. of Schools
Public Information: 799-5302
Programs for school aged children include those for the physically handicapped, emotionally handicapped, mentally handicapped, academically talented and learning disabled.

Special Education Services
2625 E. St. Louis Ave.
Las Vegas, NV 89104
799-7449
Dr. Brian Cram, Supt. of Schools
Tests and evaluates students beginning at age 3 to determine their needs.

Substance Abuse Services
601 N. 9th St.
Las Vegas, NV 89101
799-8444

Karla McComb, Asst. Dir.
Abuse Hotline (recording): 399-0081
Provides information and education of substance abuse to parents and students. Offers Student/Parent Drug Intervention Program geared toward students who have had problems with drugs or alcohol in school or related activities.

FHP Health Care's Fit Kids Club
700 E. Warm Springs Rd.
Las Vegas, NV 89119
269-7500
Barbara Pinjuv Peters, Program Mgr.
Your child can learn good health habits and it's fun. Club members receive a membership card, surprise gift, activity book and quarterly newsletter. Becoming a member is free.

Family Cabinet, Inc.
300 W. Boston Ave.
Las Vegas, NV 89102
385-KIDS
Carl Rowe, CEO
Non-profit agency coordinating family services. Information on child care providers, parenting and prenatal services and classes.

Family & Child Treatment Center of Southern Nevada
4800 W. Charleston Blvd., Ste. 140
Las Vegas, NV 89102
258-5855
Fran Marshall, Exec. Dir.
Family and child treatment, victim counseling, parenting classes

Head Start
Economic Opportunity Board
1818 Balzar Ave.
Las Vegas, NV 89106
647-2710
Jean S. Childs, Adm.
Provides low-income and handicapped children, ages 3 - 5, a comprehensive and meaningful pre-school experience. There are 13 Head Start sites.

Juvenile Work Permits
455-5240

Las Vegas Center For Children
6171 W. Charleston Blvd.
Las Vegas, NV 89102
258-9766

Nevada Children's Center
2929 S. Decatur Blvd.
Las Vegas, NV 89101
221-4900
Kellie Isbell, Adm. Dir.
Non-profit organization offering counseling programs for troubled southern Nevada children ages 5-13.

Las Vegas Housing Authority
420 N. 10th St.
Las Vegas, NV 89101
386-2727
Frederick Brown, Exec. Dir.
Provides a variety of youth activities and assistance for residents of Housing Authority properties.

Lorenzi Adaptive Recreation Center
3333 W. Washington Ave.
Las Vegas, NV 89107
229-6358
Cathy Watson
Adaptive/Recreation Div.: 229-6358
Adaptive Outreach Ctr.: 229-4796
Serves developmentally disabled youth up to age 22.

Nevada Association for the Handicapped
6200 W. Oakey Blvd.
Las Vegas, NV 89102
870-7050
Vince Triggs, Dir.
Helps children 6 months - 18 years with disabilities and behavioral problems.

Nevada Business Services
930 W. Owens Ave.
Las Vegas, NV 89106
647-4929
Kabili Tayari, Exec. Dir.
Occupational training and job placement for economically disadvantaged students. Eligibility for this federally funded program is based on income.

Nevada Child Seekers
25 TV 5 Dr.
Henderson, NV 89014
458-7009
Jill LeMasurier, Exec. Dir.
Provides assistance to parents and authorities in identifying and locating missing children. Also available are counseling, referral and rehabilitation programs and services, fingerprinting at no charge and photo ID for children for $6.

Nevada Department of Children and Family Services
6171 W. Charleston Blvd.
Las Vegas, NV 89102
486-6100
Christa Peterson, Deputy Adm.
Children's Behavioral Services, Early Childhood Services and Centralized Intake offers crisis respite services, treatment for pre-schoolers, children and teens, parenting classes, inpatient care and counseling. For emergency referrals call 486-3540.

Nevada Dept. of Motor Vehicles
2701 E. Sahara Ave.
Las Vegas, NV 89104
486-4368
(See Newcomers for other offices)
Residents at least 10 years of age who don't drive may apply for an identification card. Applicants must show a social security card and birth certificate. Fee: $4 under 18 years, $10 for ages 18 and older.

Nevada Homes for Youth
525 S. Thirteenth St., Ste. 208
Las Vegas, NV 89104
380-2889
Ron Moore, Exec. Dir.
Private, non-profit organization that finds immediate housing for youths 17-21 who have no one to help them. Teaches independent living to homeless young adults, provides counseling.

ASSISTANCE - YOUTH / HOTLINES

Project Youth Life Skills Center
1201 W. Miller Ave.
Las Vegas, NV 89106
647-5800
Hours: 10 am - 6 pm
Programs for children, including academic tutoring.

Rock Solid Recreation Center
800 N. Rancho Dr.
Las Vegas, NV 89106
646-4626
Pastor Richard Box, Adm.
Recorded information: 226-0188
Hours: Mon. - Fri. 3 pm - 9 pm;
Sat. 2 pm - 9 pm; Sun. 1 pm - 6 pm
Non-profit Christian community recreation center designed to meet the immediate needs of area youths by providing direction through recreation, education and vocational training; bookstore, cafe.

Ronald McDonald House
2323 Potosi St.
Las Vegas, NV 89102
252-4663
Emma Addis, Exec. Dir.
"The House That Love Built." Ronald McDonald House is a home-away-from-home for the families of seriously ill children receiving specialized treatment at area hospitals. The House provides an environment for emotional support to parents and siblings of sick children. Scheduled to open in 1998.

St. Jude's Ranch for Children
100 St. Jude St.
Boulder City, NV 89005
293-3131
Father Herbert A. Ward
Established in 1966, St. Jude's is a licensed, non-profit, non-sectarian and professionally supervised residential childcare facility dedicated to helping abused, neglected and troubled children and teens. Children ages 5 to 18 live in cottages with married couples and attend local schools. Most of the ranch's funding is from individual donations. Gift shop and tours available.

Sunrise Children's Hospital
3186 S. Maryland Pkwy.
Las Vegas, NV 89109
731-8000
Allan Stipe, Pres./CEO
Sunrise is the only medical facility with hospital and triage equipment specifically for children. The pediatric emergency treatment room is exclusively for children.

School Refusal Clinic
University of Nevada Las Vegas
4505 S. Maryland Pkwy.
Las Vegas, NV 89154
895-3305
Christopher Kearney, Clinic Dir.
For children ages 5 - 12 who have difficulties remaining in school. Assessment and potential treatment of problem.

We Can
5440 W. Sahara Ave., Ste. 202
Las Vegas, NV 89102
368-1533
Dr. Paula Ford, Exec. Dir.
Working to eliminate child abuse and neglect. Provides child abuse and neglect prevention programs. Non-profit organization is the Southern Nevada Chapter of the National Committee to Prevent Child Abuse and an affiliate of Parents Anonymous.

Westcare Inc.
401 S. Martin Luther King Blvd.
Las Vegas, NV 89106
385-2020
Youth Services: 385-3330
Runaway Hotline: 385-3335
Richard Steinberg, Pres.
WestCare is Nevada's largest non-profit social service agency providing treatment for drug and alcohol abusers, high-risk youths and troubled families. Provides a number of programs, including an adolescent detoxification program, to help the youth of southern Nevada, including Boys Treatment Program, Emergency Placement and Runaway

Youth Project, and emergency shelter for abused and neglected youths and runaways as well as a 24-hour crisis hotline.

WIC
(Multiple locations listed below)
2917 W. Washington Ave.
Las Vegas, NV 89107
646-5600   1-800-8-NEV-WIC

235 N. Eastern Ave.
Las Vegas, NV 89101
385-2100

3266 Las Vegas Blvd. N.
Las Vegas, NV 89115
643-2515
Barbara Ludwig, Dir.
Women, Infants and Children program which is administered through 30 clinics throughout the state; immunization and special supplemental food program with nutrition education, packages of nutritious foods and referrals to additional sources of aids from infancy to 5 years. Must meet income and dietary risk requirements.

HOTLINES

Abuse and Neglect Hotline
399-0081

Alcoholics Anonymous
598-1888

Drug Hotline
799-8414
60 taped messages in 12 categories related to substance abuse and other areas of help for young adults.

Homework Hotline
799-5111
Hours: Mon. - Thu. 3:30 pm - 5:30 pm
Sponsored by TV 10, Prime Cable and the Clark County School District. Callers state their questions and are provided a direct response over the phone. Some questions will be responded to live during the hotline television show on Prime Cable, Channel 48, Mon.-Thu. 5 pm - 6 pm.

Narcotics Anonymous
369-3362

National Youth Crisis Hotline
1-800-448-4663
Helps runaways and would be suicides. Referrals given.

"Focus on Recovery"
Rehab Hotlines
1-800-234-0420 / 1-800-274-2042

Runaway Hotline
1-800-621-4000
Information and referrals for would-be runaways; legal, medical, lodging and transportation help.

Teen to Teen
871-6585
Hours: Mon. - Fri. 3 pm - 6 pm
Confidential counseling service provided by teens to teens. Counselors trained by Metropolitan Police, Rape Crisis Center, Life Line Pregnancy Assistance Center, Suicide Prevention, Juvenile Court Service and sponsored by Life-Line.

Thomas & Mack Center
Parents Concert Hotline: 895-3900
Recorded preview of all concerts as well as a rating by arena management of the acts' on-stage conduct.

Youth Runaway/Emergency Shelter
385-3335
Temporary shelter and counseling offered.
(See Assistance for a complete list of hotlines)

YOUTH PROGRAMS

Las Vegas offers a number of quality programs and activities for area youths. Many are offered throughout the year while others are offered during 12 month school track breaks.

AFTER SCHOOL PROGRAMS & ACTIVITIES

Boys & Girls Club
2850 S. Lindell Rd.
Las Vegas, NV 89102
367-2582
Ginger Trueblood, Dir. of Program Activities

School Time Out Program
(See Boys & Girls Club for addresses)
Hours: Mon. - Fri. 7 am - 8:30 pm
Fees: $38 weekly with $17 membership, $32 fall membership for after school programs

Break Out! Program
500 Harris St.

Henderson, NV 89015
565-2121
Paul Widman, Coordinator
Educational recreation program for children in year-round schools during their quad and track breaks. Activities include field trips, tournaments, arts and crafts, sports and games, library special events and more. Offered at Silver Springs Recreation Center (435-3814) and Valley View Recreation Center (565-2121) for grades K-5; Mon. - Fri. 7 am - 6 pm; Fee: $45 week or $10 day per child.

Camp Lee Canyon
Clark County Parks and Recreation
Mt. Charleston, NV 89124
455-8200
John Hulme, Camp Dir.
Located on 27 acres in Toiyabe National Forest 45 minutes from Las Vegas, the camp is available for groups and organizations that want a serene setting for

retreats and seminars. Facilities include basketball court, tennis court, picnic facilities and restrooms. Camp held year round.
Camp Odyssey - Hands-on experience in the arts and sciences for ages 13-15.
Omnicamp - An Adventure in Science and Lee Canyon Arts Camp are held in July for children 8-12. Both camps are sponsored by the Clark County Parks and Recreation Department. For information call Darlene Bichel, 455-8241.
Lee Canyon Arts Camp features music, visual arts, drama, dance and creative writing, campfire activities, hiking, a talent show and more.
Physically and mentally challenged individual campers will stay in cabins supervised by trained counselors. A registered nurse is on duty.

Foxtail Camp
385-3677
Yolanda Pierce, Camp Dir.
Frontier Girl Scout Council's summer

camp for girls ages 7 to 17, held each year June through August. Girls take part in games, sports, arts, fashion, nature study, hiking and fitness.

Girl Scout Drop-In Centers
2020 McGuire St.
Las Vegas, NV 89106
647-6064
Herbert Gerson

Doolittle Center
1950 N. J St.
Las Vegas, NV 89106
229-6374

Safekey Program
2601 E. Sunset Rd.
Las Vegas, NV 89120
455-8251
Mary Wolfe, Safekey Coordinator
Clark County - 455-8251; Las Vegas - 229-6705; Henderson - 565-2124; Boulder City - 293-9256
Hours: When school is held 9 am - 3:11 pm, Safekey offers two programs:

YOUTH PROGRAMS

Program I: 7 am - 8:30 am and Program II: 3:11 pm - 6 pm. When school is held 8:30 am - 2:41 pm, please check with your school for appropriate time schedule.
Fee: 3 day minimum for all programs. Listed fees are for 3 - 5 days. School hours 9 am - 3:11 pm, Program I: 1 child $8 - $12, 2 children $12 - $21, 3 children $17 - $30, 4 children $23 - $39 and 5 children $28 - $48; Program II: 1 child $16 - $26, 2 children $28 - $43, 3 children $39 - $62, 4 children $52 - $81 and 5 children $64 - $100.
An after-school recreation/enrichment program for children, K-5 who need supervision until parents get off work. Safekey is held at the child's elementary school.

The after-school program is administered by the City of Las Vegas Department of Parks and Leisure Activities, the Clark County Department of Parks and Recreation and surrounding cities' parks departments in cooperation with the Clark County School District and area elementary schools. The program runs Monday through Friday in conjunction with the school calender. Students are provided a snack, time to do homework as well as special programs, games and activities.

In addition to Safekey, several after-school teen programs are offered through Brinley Community School, Burkholder Middle School, Greenspun Junior High School and Thurman White Middle School

Teen Trackers
Sponsored by the Clark County Parks and Recreation Dept.
455-8200
Program is offered at Paradise Community Center and Sunrise Community Center. For teens ages 13 - 15.
Hours: Mon. - Fri. 7:30 am - 3 pm and 3 pm - 7 pm
$7 per day or $30 per week.

Track Break Program
Clark County Parks & Recreation
455-8200
Hours: Mon. - Fri. 7:30 am - 3 pm with open recreation 3 pm - 7 pm

Fees: $7 per day per child; $30 per week Supervised activities such as field trips, special events, parties, games and arts and crafts. For ages 6 - 12 who attend year-round school. This program is held Mon. - Fri. at Paradise, Sunrise and Parkdale Community Centers. Call the individual community centers.

YMCA
4141 Meadows Ln.
Las Vegas, NV 89107
877-9622
Offers a variety of programs for children during breaks, weekends and the summer months.

CHILDCARE

Clark County has over 500 licensed daycare providers with just under 21,000 slots for children, according to statistics provided by city, county and state licensing officials. Twelve centers are licensed for 24 hour care. There are also 110 home-care facilities.

The following is a list of government agencies and professional associations and businesses that can help find competent infant and child care:

Clark County Child Care Assn.
734-0504

Clark County Social Services
455-3894

Family Cabinet
385-5437

Home Sweet Home
896-1132

Kids Care Connection
871-5555

Las Vegas Department of Business Activities
229-6918

North Las Vegas Business Licensing
657-2258

State of Nevada Child Care Licensing
486-5099

BABYSITTING
(Also see Day Care)

The following baby-sitting services are all licensed and bonded and provide services anywhere in the Valley. Most have a 4 hour minimum with maximum hours unlimited. Most, unless otherwise stated, go to homes, hotels, motels or RVs.

Around the Clock Child Care
3871 S. Valley View Blvd.
Las Vegas, NV 89103
365-1040
Margaret Oliveri, Dir.
24 hours - Sitters come to you with 2 hours notice preferred.
Prices are the same day or night - up to 2 children - $36 for the first 4 hours and $7 - $8 each additional hour.

Four Seasons Babysitting Service
Quail Park 2
601 Rancho Dr., Ste. B31
Las Vegas, NV 89106
384-5848
Opal Holton, Owner
24 hours. Sitters come to you with as little as l hour notice. Prices are the same day or night - up to 2 children is $24 for the first 4 hours and $5 each additional hour; 3 - 4 children $30 the first 4 hours and $7 each additional hour.

Grandma Dotti's Babysitting Agency
3838 Raymert St.
Las Vegas, NV 89121
456-1175
Dotti Brooks, Owner
24 hours. Sitters come to you with as little as 1 hour notice. Prices are the same day or night, up to 2 children, $25 for the first 4 hours and $6 each additional hour; $27 for first 4 hours and $7 each additional hour for 3 children, call for additional rate information; hotel rates vary.

Nanny's & Granny's Babysitting Service
6440 Coley Ave.
Las Vegas, NV 89102
364-4700
Carol Hale, owner
24 hours; Will go to home or hotel; Homes: 1 - 2 children $32 for 4 hours, $6 each additional hour; Hotels: $35 for 4 hours, $6 each additional hour.

Sunshine Sitters
823 Las Vegas Blvd. S.
Las Vegas, NV 89101
385-9966
Licensed and bonded in-room baby sitting. For 1 - 2 children $28 for 4 hours and $6 each additional hour.

DAY CARE

To enroll any child in a day care or preschool facility, it is required by law to provide that facility with records proving current immunizations and a doctor's certificate stating the child is in good health and not the carrier of any communicable diseases or illnesses.

If in need of a referral for child care facilities, the following agencies can be of assistance in locating the childcare

center or licensed individual closest to your home or place of employment. These agencies also provide the licensing for such facilities and individuals. Clark County has more than 500 licensed day care facilities including licensed private homes, where up to 6 children can be taken at once.

CHILD CARE REFERRAL AND LICENSING

Clark County Social Services
Child Care Licensing
1600 Pinto Ln.
Las Vegas, NV 89106
455-3894

Clark County Child Care Assoc.
734-0504
Referral service to licensed child care.

City of Las Vegas Department of Business Activity
Privilege License Division
Child Care Licensing
400 E. Stewart Ave.
Las Vegas, NV 89101
229-6281

CHILD CARE CENTERS/PRESCHOOL/ INFANT NURSERIES

A to Z Childcare and Learning Center
5653 S. Mojave Rd.
Las Vegas, NV 89120
433-1411
Laura Garcia, Center/Infant Dir.
Center for infants and children to age 6. $20 daily; for infants to 12 months $95 weekly, for children to 6 years $75 weekly.

ABC Preschool & Daycare
1730 N. Pecos Rd.
Las Vegas, NV 89115

642-5176
Nancy Schmitt, Preschool Dir.
Ages: 2 - 5 years
$78 weekly includes meals; $35 registration fee required.

Adventures in Learning
3338 Oneida Way
Las Vegas, NV 89109
893-3080

Anna Johnson, Preschool/Center/Infant Dir.
Ages: Infant to 12 years
$83 weekly plus $35 registration fee.

Babyland Infant Center
3825 Raymert Dr.
Las Vegas, NV 89121
451-1633
Pamela Amante, Owner
Hours: Mon. - Fri. 7 am - 6 pm
Ages: birth - 3 years
$95 weekly plus $35 registration fee; lunch included.

Bright Start Children's Center
2785 S. Rainbow Blvd.
Las Vegas, NV 89102
362-4453
Call for nearest location
Hours: Mon. - Fri. 6 am - 6:30 pm
Ages: Infants - 10 years
Infants $121 weekly; children $100 weekly; $40 initial registration fee. Part time rates available; snacks and lunch provided.

Building Blocks Child Care
7570 W. Peace Way
Las Vegas, NV 89117
873-7340
Nelda Blodgett, Ctr. Dir.
Diana Sickles, Infant Dir.
Ages: Infants - 11 years
$80 - $110 per child plus $50 registration fee. Infants, $30 ages 2 and up; snacks included; part time rates available.

Photo: Phototechnik International

CHILD CARE

Captain Kidd's Child Care
3883 E. Mesa Vista Way
Las Vegas, NV 89120
456-1133
Patty Walker, Dir.
Ages: 1 - 9 years
A variety of learning experiences. $35 -
$105 weekly plus $40 registration fee
part time rates available; snacks and
lunch provided.

**Central Christian
Preschool/Child Care**
3375 S. Mojave Rd.
Las Vegas, NV 89121
735-5448
Debra Bult, Center/Preschool Dir.
Ages: 2 - 10 years
$90 weekly plus $30 registration fee.

Child Kingdom
3551 E. Sunset Rd.
Las Vegas, NV 89120
451-9801
Arlene Gonzalez/Vickie Parra, Center Dirs.
Ages: 12 months - 10 years
$80 - $95 weekly plus $40 registration
fee; part time rates available.

**Children's Paradise
Day Care Center**
4220 McLeod Dr.
Las Vegas, NV 89121
454-0440
Holly Clifford, Center/Preschool Infant Dir.
Ages: 6 weeks to 10 years
$85 - $110 weekly, plus registration fee
$25 first child and $15 each additional
child. Part time rates available for ages 2
and over; night time care available.

Cinderella Careskool
4270 S. Maryland Pkwy.
Las Vegas, NV 89119
732-0230
Steve Pelican, Dir.
Hours: 24 hours
Ages: Children 2 - 12 years
$85 - $97 weekly; meals provided; part
time rates $4 hourly or $24 daily; drop-
ins accepted. Breakfast and dinner provided at additional cost.

Creative Kids Learning Center
Corporate Office
871-0078
(Call for nearest location)
Ages: 2 - 12 years
Hours: Mon. - Fri. 6:30 am - 6:30 pm
$200 biweekly plus $50 registration fee;
snacks provided; part time rates available. Transportation to and from public
schools.

Education Station
3451 Michael Way
Las Vegas, NV 89108
655-6888
Dean & Kathleen Mierau, Dirs.
Hours: 6 am - midnight, 7 days
$190 - $224 weekly plus $40 registration
fee, meals additional; part time rates
available.

Fielday School
3570 N. Buffalo Dr.
Las Vegas, NV 89108
655-6565
Carol Fink, Center/Preschool/Infant Dir.
Ages: 3 - 5 years
$95 - $120 weekly plus $35 registration
fee; part time rates available; snacks
and lunch provided.

Gold Coast Hotel
4000 W. Flamingo Rd.
Las Vegas, NV 89103
367-7111
Ruth Hall, Dir.
Child care facility - Free to hotel guests
and visitors; 2 - 8 years of age, must be
out of diapers. Open 9 am - 11:45 pm
daily and staffed by 12 licensed and
trained caretakers. The center features
movies, toys, crafts and a listening center where children can listen to music
or stories; 3 hour limit per day.

Creative Kids Learning Center

The Green Frog
4610 Monterrey Ave.
Las Vegas, NV 89121
458-2828
Aysha DeFresta, Ctr. Dir.
Ages: 2 years and up
$85 - $90 plus registration fee, $35 for
one child; $60 for 2 or more children; 5%
discount for 2 or more children; part
time rates available; lunch and snacks
provided.

Hallmark Academy
3460 S. Arville St.
Las Vegas, NV 89102
367-8337
Jean Gregory, Center/Preschool Dir.
Mary Ann Spears, Infant Dir.
$23 daily or $90 - $100 weekly plus $35
registration fee; meals and snacks
provided.

Happy Days Preschool/Child Care
(Multiple locations listed below)
2950 E. Tropicana Ave.
Las Vegas, NV 89121
451-8952
Hours: 6:30 am - 6:30 pm
$45 - $90 weekly plus $25 registration
fee; part time rates available; lunch and
snacks provided.

3710 S. Sandhill Rd.
Las Vegas, NV 89121
458-2875

Herb Kaufman Headstart Daycare
4020 Perry St.
Las Vegas, NV 89122
434-5329
Helen Simms, Preschool/Center/Infant Dir.

Ages: Infants to 5 years
$80 - $120 weekly; $40 for Headstart stu-
dents; plus $20 family registration.

**Hill & Dale Child
Development Center**
3720 E. Tropicana Ave.
Las Vegas, NV 89121
458-2243
Diane Wimberly, Preschool Dir.
Cindy Snyder, Center/Infant Dir.
Jetaun Legg, Infant Dir.
Ages: 6 weeks to 10 years

Holy Family Day Care Center
451 E. Twain Ave.
Las Vegas, NV 89109
735-4358
Connie Johnson, Center Dir.
Ages: Infants to 6 years
$55 - $80 weekly plus $30 registration fee;
breakfast, lunch and snack provided.

**Imagination Plus Child Devel-
opment Center**
3525 Sunset Rd.
Las Vegas, NV 89120
433-1044
Mary Butler, Preschool Dir.
Hours: Mon. - Fri. 6 am - 7 pm
$93 - $120 weekly plus $40 registration
per family; meals and hot lunch provided;
part time rates also available, drop ins
welcome. Focus on social, emotional,
physical and mental growth and development of child.

Kids Connection
1085 Betty Ln.
Las Vegas, NV 89110
438-0017
$95 - $110 weekly plus registration fee,
$40 first child, $30 second child; meals
and snacks provided; part time rates available.

Kid's Cove
4975 E. St. Louis Ave.
Las Vegas, NV 89104
431-2222
Astrid Volkert, Center Dir.
Ages: 2 - 8 years
$75 - $80 weekly plus $40 registration
fee; snacks provided, part time rates
also available.

Kid's Korral Inc.
5370 Lake Mead Blvd.
Las Vegas, NV 89115
459-0091
Della Keller, Center Dir.
Ages: 1 - 9 years
$35 - $105 weekly plus registration fee;
part time rates available, lunch and
snacks available at additional fee.

Kids Quest
Boulder Station
4111 Boulder Hwy.
Las Vegas, NV 89121
432-7777
Hours: Sun. - Thu. 9 am - midnight;
Fri. - Sat. 9 am - 1 am
Ages: 6 weeks to 12 years
Thousands of square feet of non-stop
fun, excitement and adventure, with
toy-filled play areas, hearty physical
challenges and the latest interactive
media. The Quest play area offers over
35 challenging activities. Other areas
include Construction Lane, Paint 'N
Puzzle, Barbieland, Mini-Arcade, Interactive CD-ROM computers, Laser
Karaoke Stage and the Movie Room. $5
per hour per child.

Kindercare Learning Center
4845 Community Ave.
Las Vegas, NV 89121
456-5772
(Call for nearest location)
Ages: 2 months - 12 years
$96 - $140 weekly plus registration fee,
$45 first child, $70 second child; meal
and snacks provided.

**Learning Blocks Preschool &
Child Care Center**
5540 Spring Mountain Rd.
Las Vegas, NV 89102
247-4767
Heather Kuenzi, Center Dir.
Ages: Infants to 10 years
$70 - $260 biweekly plus $45 to $55 registration fee; snacks provided; drop ins
welcome.

The Learning Tree
4640 E. Desert Inn Rd.
Las Vegas, NV 89121
456-4986
Leslie Chaney, Center Dir.
Ages: 18 months - 11 years
$78 - $88 weekly plus $35 registration
per child; snacks provided; part time
rates available.

Lillie's Little Players
1965 University Cir.
Las Vegas, NV 89109
731-5714
Lillie Gresham, Center Dir.
Ages: Infants to 4 years
$87.50 - $100 weekly; meals and snacks
provided; part time rates available.

Lit'l Scholar Academy
3233 E. Desert Inn Rd.
Las Vegas, NV 89121
732-4292
(Call for nearest location)
Ages: 3 - 12 years
$80 - $125 weekly plus $35 registration
fee per family; drop ins welcome; part
time rates available for ages 3 and up;
meals and snacks provided, nighttime
hours available.

MGM Grand Youth Center
3799 Las Vegas Blvd. S.
Las Vegas, NV 89109
891-3200
Mike Messner, Center Dir.
Ages: 3 - 12 years
Theme park for those 6 - 16 years of age. Supervised activities for ages 3 - 16 for MGM hotel guests. The center offers daily excursions for 6 - 16 yearolds and a fun activity center for 3 - 12 yearolds, supervised by an enthusiastic staff of educators and recreational specialists.

Montessori Academy of So. Nevada
6000 W. Oakey Blvd.
Las Vegas, NV 89102
870-5117
Connie Mormon, Ctr. Dir.
Ages: Infants - 12 years
Hours: 24 hours
$85 - $105 weekly plus $35 registration fee; snacks provided; night time hours also available.

Mother Goose College
2760 S. Jones Blvd.
Las Vegas, NV 89102
362-5801
Janice Brown, Ctr. Dir.
Hours: Open 24 hours
Ages: Newborns - 11 years
$75 - $90 weekly plus $35 family registration fee; part time rates also available; snacks provided. Night time hours available.

My Little Schoolhouse
3790 Redwood St.
Las Vegas, NV 89103
362-9255
Jacqueline Valella, Center/Preschool/Infant Dir.
Ages: Infants - 6 years
$88 - $103 weekly plus $35 family registration fee; snacks provided; part time rates available.

Nellis Baptist Day Care
4300 N. Las Vegas Blvd.
Las Vegas, NV 89115
643-8800
Beth Brosemer, Center Dir.
Barbara Sinyard, Infant Dir.
Ages: 6 weeks - 5 years
Call for information on rates and availability.

Once Upon a Time Learning Center
5055 Duneville St.
Las Vegas, NV 89118
368-7757
Gayle Gleicher, Center Dir.
Hours: 5 am - 8:30 pm
Ages: 2 years - 11 years
Call for information on rates and availability.

Paradise Park Recreation Center
4770 S. Harrison Dr.
Las Vegas, NV 89121
455-7513
Barbara Chesley, Preschool Dir.
Ages: 3 - 5 years
$7 daily or $30 weekly track break program for children in area 12-month schools.

The Pumpkin Shell
1934 S. Walnut St.
Las Vegas, NV 89104
641-8118
Darnetha Ellison, Center/Infant Dir.
Ages: Infants - 9 years
$95 - $105 weekly plus registration fee; part time rates available.

Robert Jones Gardens Headstart
1750 Marion Dr.
Las Vegas, NV 89115
438-3770
Vanita Ditto, Preschool Dir.
Ages: 3 - 5 years
Federally funded free program for income eligible families; snack and lunch served.

Romp 'N Play Nursery
3412 S. Decatur Blvd.
Las Vegas, NV 89102
873-9091
Donna Kutlesa, Center Dir.
Ages: 18 months - 8 years
$75 - $95 weekly plus $35 family registration; part time rates available; walk ins welcome.

Santa Fe Hotel
4949 N. Rancho Dr.
Las Vegas, NV 89130
658-4900
Nursery open 9 am - 11 pm for children 6 months - 8 years.
$10 enrollment fee plus $2 per child for a maximum of 3 hours; parents must remain in the hotel/casino at all times.

Seton Academy
1592 E. Hacienda Ave.
Las Vegas, NV 89119
736-4246
Mary Hayes, Preschool Dir.
Ages: 2 - 10 years
$350 - $445 monthly plus $65 registration; part time rates available.

Small World Learning Center
10 N. 28th St.
Las Vegas, NV 89101
386-1006
Ethel Howard, Center/Infant Dir.
Ages: 6 weeks - 11 years
$70 - $90 weekly plus registration fee of $25 - $55; part time and drop ins welcome; meals provided at additional cost.

Sweet Pea Day Care Center
1441 E. Hacienda Ave.
Las Vegas, NV 89119
798-2772
Loretta Christa, Center Dir.
Ages: 1 - 12 years
$65 - $85 weekly plus $20 registration per family; lunch provided at additional fee; part time rates available.

Teacher's Apple
2253 E. Desert Inn Rd.
Las Vegas, NV 89109
731-4650
Sue Patel, Center/Preschool/Infant Dir.
Hours: Mon. - Fri. 7 am - 7 pm; Sat. 8 am - 6:30 pm
Ages: Infants - 12 years
$70 - $90 weekly with no registration fee; lunch and snack provided; drop ins welcome at a rate of $3 per hour; night time hours available.

Teddy Bear Junction
1905 E. Warm Springs Rd.
Las Vegas, NV 89119
361-1795
Mary Standridge, Preschool Dir.
Ages: 6 weeks - 10 years
Call for information regarding hours, rates and availability.

Toddle Towne
2775 S. Jones Ave.
Las Vegas, NV 89102
254-6000
Suzanne Anderson, Preschool Dir.
Laura Mastrodonato, Center/Infant Dir.
Ages: Infants and up
$21 - $24 daily, $85 - $95 weekly plus $35 registration fee; drop ins welcome - please call in advance for availability; part time rates available; lunch and snacks provided.

University United Methodist Child Development
4412 S. Maryland Pkwy.
Las Vegas, NV 89109
733-7157
Amy Robinson, Center/Preschool/Infant Dir.
Ages: 3 months - 6 years
$85 - $115 weekly plus $30 family registration; snacks provided; part time rates available.

Vegas Valley Christian Day Care
5515 Mountain Vista St.
Las Vegas, NV 89120
451-9665
Veronica Siebler, Preschool/Center Dir.
Ages: 2 - 12 years
$81 - $109 weekly plus $35 registration; snacks provided; drop ins welcome and part time rates also available.

Winchester Community Center
3130 McLeod Dr.
Las Vegas, NV 89121
455-7340
Patrick Gassey, Preschool Dir.
Ages: 3 - 5 years
Six week activity learning program providing creative learning, playtime, story time and music programs.
$89 Mon., Wed. & Fri. program
$59 Tue. & Thu. program

GROUP CARE HOMES

Johnnie Beatty
Little People Group Care Home
4604 S. Sandhill Rd.
Las Vegas, NV 89121
458-8900
Katherine Hunter, Center Dir.
Ages: Infants - 4 years
$20 per day or $85 weekly plus $15 registration. Part time rates and drop ins welcome; meals and snacks provided.

Bellas Infant Nursery
1517 Raindance Way
Las Vegas, NV 89109
734-1602
Adele Bellas, Infant Dir.
Ages: Infants - 3 years
$95 weekly with no registration fee.

Children's Developmental Group Care
6910 Edna Ave.
Las Vegas, NV 89117
367-0306
Sue Germeroth, Preschool/Center Dir.
Ages: 2 years and older
$115 weekly with no registration; snacks provided. High risk individual care facility for children with special needs.

Susan's Day Care
3977 Avila St.
Las Vegas, NV 89103
873-3610
Susan Marvosh
Ages: Infants - 12 years
$3 hourly; $15 daily; $75 weekly; meals and snacks provided; drop ins welcome.

Patty Cake, Patty Cake Baker's Daycare
4788 San Rafael Ave.
Las Vegas, NV 89120
434-1799
Debra Miller-Baker
Ages: Infant and up
$3.50 hourly with a 4 hour minimum; $20 daily; $80 weekly; meals and snacks provided; drop ins welcome.

HOTEL ACTIVITIES FOR CHILDREN

Many of the Las Vegas hotel/casinos have facilities for children, such as swimming pool with lifeguards on duty in the warmer months and video arcades. Circus Circus and MGM Grand are recommended as two of the best places to stay if you have children and want them to have plenty to do. All hotels have a listing of bonded baby-sitting services. Listed are the hotels and what they have to offer children and their showroom policies.

Children are not allowed to linger in casinos but may pass through on their way to someplace else or while standing in a line that extends into the casino area. *(For more information on shows, see Entertainment)*

Arizona Charlie's
740 S. Decatur Blvd.
Las Vegas, NV 89107
258-5200
Video arcade

Bally's Grand Hotel
3645 Las Vegas Blvd. S.
Las Vegas, NV 89109
734-4029
Large video arcade, swimming pool, tennis courts.
Celebrity Room: Star entertainment. Children of all ages welcome.
Reservations: 739-4567

Boulder Station
4111 Boulder Hwy.
Las Vegas, NV 89121

432-7777 1-800-683-7777
Swimming pool, children's video arcade and redemption center, movie theaters, Kids Quest child-care center.

Caesars Palace
3570 Las Vegas Blvd. S.
Las Vegas, NV 89109
731-7110
Adventure Fun Center Video Arcade, pool, tennis courts, La Piazza Food Court, Festival Fountain in the Forum Shops
(Caesars continued on page 226)

HOTEL ACTIVITIES FOR CHILDREN

Circus Maximus Showroom: Star entertainment. Children 6 and older welcome.
Reservations: 731-7333
Omnimax Theatre: *(see Entertainment)*

Circus Circus Hotel & Casino
2880 Las Vegas Blvd. S.
Las Vegas, NV 89109
734-0410
Video arcade, pool, monorail, McDonald's, Grand Slam Canyon. Located off the mezzanine is a carnival midway with games of chance, arcade games, shops and restaurants and snack bars open 10 am - 1 am. Free live circus acts in the center ring daily from 11 am - midnight.

Desert Inn Hotel
3145 Las Vegas Blvd. S.
Las Vegas, NV 89109
733-4444
Swimming pools, tennis courts, golf course
Crystal Room: Star entertainment. Children 8 and over are welcome.
Reservations: 733-4566.

Excalibur Hotel & Casino
3850 Las Vegas Blvd. S.
Las Vegas, NV 89109
597-7777
Video arcade, swimming pool. The Fantasy Factory's strolling Renaissance performers entertain guests daily 10 am - 10 pm on the Medieval Village level. The shows include puppets, mimes, magicians, jugglers and more with each show lasting about 20 minutes. On the lower level are carnival games, video games, a snack bar, concessions.
The Magic Motion Machine and King Arthur's Court *(see Theaters):* Each evening at 6 pm and 8:30 pm "King Arthur's Tournament" appears at a cost of $29.95. Enjoy dancing and music, magic and jousting while dining. A giant fire-breathing dragon moved into the castle moat. The 51 foot robot monster battles Merlin the Magician for domain in the mystical moat every hour on the hour 8 pm - 1 am daily, weather permitting.

Flamingo Hilton
3555 Las Vegas Blvd. S.
Las Vegas, NV 89109
733-3111
Pool with water slides, shopping mall; "Rockettes" - All Ages - Dancers from Radio City Music Hall; Sat. - Thu. 5:45 pm seating for 7:45 pm Dinner Show; Sat. - Thu. 10 pm cocktail show; "Forever Plaid" over 5 years of age - 50s musical with a story line; Tue. - Sun. 7:30 pm & 10 pm; dark Monday.
Reservations: 733-3333

Gold Coast Hotel & Casino
4000 W. Flamingo Rd.
Las Vegas, NV 89103
367-7111
Video arcade, 72 lane bowling center, ice cream and soda shop, twin movie theaters. Child care facility - free to hotel guests and visitors; open 9 am - midnight daily and staffed by 12 licensed and trained caretakers. The center features movies, toys, crafts and a listening center where children can listen to music or stories.

Harrah's
3475 Las Vegas Blvd. S.
Las Vegas, NV 89109
369-5000
Swimming pool
Holiday Theatre: "Spellbound," children any age are welcome; dark Sundays. Shows are 7:30 pm and 10 pm at a cost of $34.95.

Imperial Palace
3535 Las Vegas Blvd. S.
Las Vegas, NV 89109
731-3311
Imperial Palace's auto collection contains over 800 antique and classic automobiles, with over 200 on display at one time. Open daily 9:30 am - 11:30 pm.
Admission: Adults $6.95, Children under 12 $3, under 5 free, seniors $3.
"Legends in Concert": Stars from the past and present re-created. Shows nightly at 7:30 and 10:30, except Sunday. Children 6 and older admitted to both shows.
Admission: $29.50 per person (includes two drinks); children 12 and under $14.95.

Roller Coaster at Circus Circus - Grand Slam Canyon

Las Vegas Hilton
3000 Paradise Rd.
Las Vegas, NV 89109
732-5111
Video arcade
Star Trek Experience: Must be over 42 inches tall.

Luxor
3900 Las Vegas Blvd. S.
Las Vegas, NV 89119
262-4000
Admission: $4 for "Luxor Live" film and $5 for "In Search of the Obelisk" a flight simulator. The attractions, each lasting 20-25 minutes, features two films dealing with the past, present and future.
IMAX Theater: shows 3-D movies at a cost of $8.50 or $7.50 for the regular theater show.
Sega Virtualand Arcade.

King Tut's Museum: Full-scale reproduction of the world's largest atrium with over 29 million cu. ft. of space.

MGM Grand
3805 Las Vegas Blvd. S.
Las Vegas, NV 89109
891-1111
Show: EFX; children 5 and older may attend.
The MGM Grand Adventures theme park: features acres of rides, shows, theme streets, entertainment, restaurants and shops. Rides include The Screamer, Grand Canyon Rapids (rapids ride), Over the Edge (flume ride), Lightning Bolt (dark coaster), and Parisian Taxis (bumper cars).
Hours: Daily 10 am - 6 pm (winter hours); 10 am - 10 pm (summer hours)
Admission: Purchase a wrist band for unlimited admission to all park attractions and thrill rides: 13 years & older $10; 4-12 years $8; Las Vegas residents receive a $2 discount. Park is limited to 9,000 people per day.
Swimming pool with beach, four tennis courts

King Looey Activity Center: 891-3200
Pre-school Room: 3 - 6 years Playhouse, tumbling mats, puppets and much more. 7 - 12 year olds have a special game room offering foosball, ping pong, mini pool table, board games and a variety of other fun things. Both groups can go to the Arts and Crafts Room, also a lounge area complete with large screen TV/VCR showing the latest in children's films. Available only to registered guests.

Mirage
3400 Las Vegas Blvd. S.
Las Vegas, NV 89109
791-7111
See Siegfried & Roy's white tigers on display 24 hrs. a day in their glass enclosed compound in front of the hotel, just off the south entrance. Free admission.

The Secret Gardens of Siegfried and Roy: Siegfried and Roy reveal their most cherished and well guarded secret: that the world's most exotic animals can live side by side with one another and with mankind. Through the garden, Siegfried and Roy are seeking to renew the public's sense of responsibility to preserve nature. The haven represents what is possible when humans and animals work, play and share their lives together. Here, six rare animal breeds reside; the Royal White Tigers of Nevada, the White Lions of Timbavatim, heterozygous Bengal Tigers, an Asian Elephant, a panther and a snow leopard. As with the Mirage's Dolphin Habitat, the Secret Garden offers an educational program to children enrolled in the Clark County School District.
Hours: 11 am - 5:30 pm
Located next to the swimming pool is the Dolphin Environment, where six happy Atlantic bottlenose dolphins cavort in their $14 million habitat. The dolphins may be seen from the windows on the side of the dolphin pool or from the outdoor balcony.
Hours: Mon. - Fri. 11 am - 7 pm; Sat. - Sun. 9 am - 7 pm
Admission: $3 per person; Free for children under 10 when accompanied by adult - 791-7188.
Nightly beginning at dark and continuing every 15 minutes until midnight, blasts of steam and smoke rip out of the realistic volcano in front of the hotel. Admission is free.
"Siegfried & Roy": Evenings except Wed. and when star entertainment is featured. Children 5 and older welcome.
Reservations: 792-7777

Rio
3700 W. Flamingo Rd.
Las Vegas, NV 89103
252-7777
Swimming pool with sand beach, beach volleyball, pizza parlor, ice cream shop.

Santa Fe Hotel
4949 N. Rancho Dr.
Las Vegas, NV 89130
658-4900
Bowling center, ice skating; nursery open 9:30 am - 11 pm for children ages 6 months to 6 years.

Sahara
2535 Las Vegas Blvd. S.
Las Vegas, NV 89109
737-2111
Swimming pool, video arcade.

Showboat Hotel
2800 Fremont St.
Las Vegas, NV 89104
385-9123
Video arcade, bowling center.

Stardust
3000 Las Vegas Blvd. S.
Las Vegas, NV 89109
732-6111
Swimming pool, video arcade
"Enter the Night": Must be 21 to attend. Ralph's 50s diner.

FAMILY INTEREST

Stratosphere
2000 Las Vegas Blvd. S.
Las Vegas, NV 89104
382-4446
World's highest roller coaster, High Roller, starting at 909 ft. above the ground; The Big Shot thrill ride shoots you 160 feet to the 1,081 ft. level; four high-speed double-decker elevators travel at 1,400 feet per minute, whisking visitors to the top of the tower in 45 seconds, where they can view Las Vegas from either the indoor or the outdoor observation deck.

Admission: Observation deck $5; thrill rides $5

Treasure Island
3300 Las Vegas Blvd. S.
Las Vegas, NV 89109
894-7111
Each hour the resort features a live sea battle between a pirate ship and the Royal Brittania in front of the hotel. Swimming pool.
Mutiny Bay: an 18,000 sq. ft. entertainment center offering video games and electronically simulated rides.

Mystere - Circus: Children may attend any performance. Special price for children under 12, $26.40 (including tax).

Tropicana Resort
3801 Las Vegas Blvd. S.
Las Vegas, NV 89109
739-2222
Arcade, wildlife walk, island pool area.
"Folies Bergere": Children are welcome at the 8 pm dinner show.
Reservations: 739-2411

Photo: Phototechnik International

LIBRARIES

The Las Vegas-Clark County Library District Young People's Library publishes "Kids Quarterly" which lists dates and times of weekly story times and other children's activities such as movies, classes and music. To receive "Kids Quarterly," sign up at any branch library or call 382-3493.
Young Adult Book Link: Children 12 - 18 will hear a review of young adult books available at the library. Different review each week - 594-7700.
Immunization Clinics: The Clark County Health Department conducts a free shot clinic for ages 2 months - 21 years at various branch libraries on certain days of the month. Call 383-1307 for more information.
Gene Nelson, Children's Services, 228-1940

Clark County Library
1401 E. Flamingo Rd.
Las Vegas, NV 89119
733-3616
Monteria Hightower, Adm.
Hours: Mon. - Thu. 9 am - 9 pm;
Fri. - Sat. 9 am - 5 pm; Sun. 1 pm - 5 pm

Enterprise Library
25 E. Shelbourne Ave.
Las Vegas, NV 89123
269-3000
Judith Gray, Adm.
Young People's Library: 269-8027

Green Valley Library
Young People's Library
2797 Green Valley Pkwy.
Henderson, NV 89014

435-1840
Young People's Library: 435-2078
Sally Feldman, Librarian
Hours: Mon. - Thu. 9 am - 9 pm;
Fri. - Sat. 9 am - 5 pm; Sun. 1 pm - 5 pm.

Las Vegas Library
833 Las Vegas Blvd. N.
Las Vegas, NV 89101
382-3493
Young People's Library: 382-2003
Marylou Wigley, Adm.
Hours: Mon. - Thu. 9 am - 9 pm;
Fri. - Sat. 9 am - 5 pm; Sun. 1 pm - 5 pm

Lied Discovery Children's Museum
833 Las Vegas Blvd. N.
Las Vegas, NV 89101
382-KIDS
Hours: Mon. - Thu. 9 am - 9 pm;
Fri. - Sat. 9 am - 5 pm; Sun. noon - 5 pm

Rainbow Library
3150 N. Buffalo Dr.
Las Vegas, NV 89128
243-7323
Young People's Library: 243-7307
Jane Richardson, Adm.
Hours: Mon. - Thu. 9 am - 9 pm;
Fri. - Sat. 9 am - 5 pm; Sun. 1 pm - 5 pm

Sahara West
9600 W. Sahara Ave.
Las Vegas, NV 89117
228-1940
Ann Lang Evin, Adm.
Hours: Mon. - Thu. 9 am - 9 pm;
Fri. - Sat. 9 am - 5 pm; Sun. 1 pm - 5 pm

Spring Valley Library
Young People's Library
4280 S. Jones Blvd.
Las Vegas, NV 89103
368-4940
Beryl Andrus Zundel, Adm.
Hours: Mon. - Thu. 9 am - 9 pm;
Fri. - Sat. 9 am - 5 pm; Sun. 1 pm - 5 pm

Summerlin Library
Young People's Library
1771 Inner Circle Dr.
Las Vegas, NV 89134
256-1414
Richard Lee, Adm.
Hours: Mon. - Thu. 9 am - 9 pm;
Fri. - Sat. 9 am - 5 pm; Sun. 1 pm - 5 pm

Sunrise Library
Young People's Library
5400 Harris Ave.
Las Vegas, NV 89110
453-1180
Laura Golod, Adm.
Hours: Mon. - Thu. 9 am - 9 pm;
Fri. - Sat. 9 am - 5 pm; Sun. 1 pm - 5 pm

West Charleston Library
6301 W. Charleston Blvd.
Las Vegas, NV 89102
878-3682
Young People's Library: 878-2606
Marie Cuglietta, Adm.
Hours: Mon. - Thu. 9 am - 9 pm;
Fri. - Sat. 9 am - 5 pm; Sun. noon - 5 pm

West Las Vegas Library
951 W. Lake Mead Blvd.
Las Vegas, NV 89106

647-2117
Kelly Richards, Dir.
Hours: Mon. - Thu. 9 am - 9 pm;
Fri. - Sat. 9 am - 5 pm; Sun. 1 pm - 5 pm

Whitney Library
5175 E. Tropicana Ave.
Las Vegas, NV 89122
454-4575
Young People's Library: 454-4649
Barb Carey, Adm.
Hours: Mon. - Thu. 9 am - 9 pm;
Fri. - Sat. 9 am - 5 pm; Sun. 1 pm - 5 pm

North Las Vegas City Public Library
2300 Civic Center Dr.
N. Las Vegas, NV 89030
633-1070
Anita Laruy, Dir.
Hours: Mon. 9 am - 6 pm; Tue. - Thu. 9 am - 9 pm; Fri. - Sat. 9 am - 6 pm

Henderson Library
280 S. Water St.
Henderson, NV 89015
565-8402
Zuki Landow, Dir.
Hours: Mon. - Thu. 9 am - 9 pm;
Fri. - Sat. 9 am - 5 pm; Sun. noon - 4 pm

Boulder City Library
813 Arizona St.
Boulder City, NV 89005
293-1281
Duncan McCoy, Dir.
Hours: Mon. - Thu. 9 am - 8:30 pm;
Fri. 9 am - 5 pm; Sat. 11 am - 4 pm;
Sun. 1 pm - 4 pm

MUSEUMS

(For a complete list see Cultural Arts)

Guinness World of Records Museum
2780 Las Vegas Blvd. S.
Las Vegas, NV 89109
792-3766
Oli Manlet, General Mgr.
Hours: 9 am - 6 pm
Admission: Adults $4.95; seniors, students, military $3.95; children 5 - 12 $2.95; under 5 free
See the famous Guinness Book brought to life. Amazing videos, life-sized replicas, unique displays and interactive computers and data banks are imaginatively divided into six "worlds." Over 35 exhibits including "The human world," the world's most tattooed woman, Krystyne Kolorful in **The Amazing Humans Section;** The Guinness jukebox, which plays record-breaking songs that have made music history, including Michael Jackson's

"Thriller," in **The Music Arts and Entertainment World;** the most poisonous jellyfish in **The Animal World;** and historical film footage of man's courage in space at **The Space Achievements Display.** The Razzle Dazzle **World of Las Vegas** highlights some of the unique events in Las Vegas, including the world's only swim-up craps table, the only nuclear bomb ever exploded out of a canyon, celebrity weddings and much more. Gift shop.

Imperial Palace Auto Collection
Imperial Palace Hotel & Casino
3535 Las Vegas Blvd. S.
Las Vegas, NV 89109
794-3174
Richie Clyne, Adm.
Hours: 9:30 am - 11:30 pm
Admission: Adults $6.95; children under 12 $3; under 3 free
Over 200 antique, classic and special interest automobiles on display at one

time from the 750 vehicle collection. Vehicles are constantly rotated from storage and nationwide tours to give the Auto Collection a fresh appeal for repeat visitors. The cars are displayed in a plush gallery-like setting located on the fifth floor of the hotel's parking facility. See Hitler's 1939 Mercedes-Benz, W.C. Fields' 1938 Cadillac limo, JFK's 1962 "Bubbletop" limo and a whole room devoted to Duesenbergs. The auto collection features a gift shop, which contains a wide variety of automobile memorabilia and books.

Las Vegas Natural History Museum
900 Las Vegas Blvd. N.
Las Vegas, NV 89101
384-3466
Marilyn Gillespie, Dir.
Hours: Daily 9 am - 4 pm
Admission: adults $5; children 4 - 12 $2.50

Exhibits include **The Prehistoric Room,** where children of all ages can enjoy the new 35-foot long Tyrannosaurus Rex, Triceratops, Ankylosaur (complete with three hatchlings) and the raptor, Deinonychus, fossils of a four-tusked elephant, a prehistoric crocodile and a saber-toothed cat to name a few; and **The International Wildlife Room,** where over 26 species of animals can be found. Features include dynamic mounts pf animals from around the world. Here visitors can find a zebra being attacked by two lions, a caribou fighting off two wolves, monkeys, a warthog and a grizzly bear defending his kill. Each exhibit has an information placard so viewers learn as well as look. **The Wild Nevada Room** features the scenic, harsh beauty of the Silver State's Mojave Desert. All animals on exhibit here can be found within a 100

KIDS LOVE...

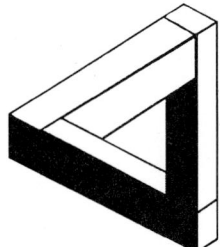

EXHIBITS

Crawl and slide through the Toddler Towers, be a star on the Performing Arts stage, pilot the Space Shuttle or Gyrochair, create color computer prints and toe tap a tune on the Musical Pathway. Stand in a giant bubble, play disc jockey at KKID radio, and use your body to generate electricity - it's all yours to enjoy at Discovery!

SCIENCE TOWER

Bend sound waves in the Echo Tubes; check out conditions around the Las Vegas Valley at the Weather Station and the Periscope; thrill to the sights and sounds you create with the neon and fiber optic display - visit the Tower and be a scientist!

PROGRAMS

Workshops, performances, and demonstrations are scheduled throughout the year for kids of all ages. We also offer a gift shop, lunch area, birthday rentals, group tours, and museum rentals.

ADMISSION

Adults, $5; Seniors, military, children 12 and older, $4; Children 3 through 11, $3 • Children 2 and under FREE. Members Free - ask about becoming a Museum member! Children 11 and under must be accompanied by an adult. Admission fees subject to change without notice.

At Lied Discovery you can **TOUCH** over 100 hands-on exhibits. **SEE** displays that demonstrate the wonders of the arts and sciences. **EXPLORE** one of the country's largest children's museums.

EXPERIENCE something new to do with your family at Lied Discovery.

HOURS

Tuesday through Saturday, 10 AM - 5 PM; Sunday, Noon - 5 PM Closed Monday, except on school holidays

Lied Discovery Children's Museum

833 Las Vegas Blvd., North • Las Vegas, NV 89101 • Call 382-3445

Share The Wonders

Las Vegas
NATURAL HISTORY MUSEUM

An Exciting Journey
Through Nature
Featuring:

- **Animated Dinosaurs**
- **Marine Life - Featuring Sharks**
- **Nevada's Wildlife** • **Hands-On Room for Kids**
- **Gift Shop** • **International Wildlife Room**

HOURS:
9 A.M. - 4 P.M.
EVERYDAY!!!

ADMISSION:
$5.00 Adults $2.50 Children
$4.00 Seniors/Military   *Under 4 Years - Free*

LAS VEGAS
NATURAL
HISTORY
MUSEUM

900 Las Vegas Blvd. N.
Las Vegas, NV 89101
(702) 384-3466

Library & Museum

Bonanza Rd.

N. Las Vegas Blvd.

Las Vegas
Natural
History
Museum

Washington Ave.

Cashman Field & Convention Center

MUSEUMS

mile radius of Las Vegas. Exhibit literature features interactive displays using audio, hands-on and olfactory sensory displays. **The Marine Life Room** offers visitors the feeling of being underwater, painted in cool blue colors to resemble the ocean floor. Here they can see recreations of sharks and fish, including Great White, Tiger and Hammerhead sharks. It is here that in a 3,000 gallon shark tank & display visitors can observe shark feedings on Saturdays at 2 pm; other tanks are occupied by various other strange creatures from the deep, such as trigger and porcupine fish. Additional information is made available through a shark video. In **The Young Scientists' Center** the budding genius or the merely curious can have a great time in this hands-on interactive room; and in **The Learning Center** a classroom, complete with teaching aids, has been developed for use during the various workshops and summer classes held at the museum. In addition to the many exhibits, various programs are offered throughout the year so that all children are given the opportunity to experience the museum.

World of Clowns, 330 Carousel Pkwy., Henderson, NV 89014

Lied Discovery Children's Museum
833 Las Vegas Blvd. N.
Las Vegas, NV 89101
382-3445
Suzanne LeBlanc, Exec. Dir.
Lied Discovery Children's museum is a non-profit children's museum designed to provide enjoyable learning experiences. This 22,000 sq. ft. $2 million hands-on museum has over 100 interactive exhibits devoted to the sciences, arts, radio station, tornado, science tower, and many other exhibits devoted to science and technology. Workshops, performances and demonstrations are scheduled throughout the year. Toddle Towers, located on the first floor, is for children under 5. There is also a gift shop, birthday room, group tours, snack bar and museum rentals available.

World of Clowns
330 Carousel Pkwy.
Henderson, NV 89014
434-1700
Ron Lee, Mgr.
Hours: Mon. - Fri. 8 am - 5 pm;
Sat. & Sun. 9 am - 5 pm
Factory tours/visitors center; clown sculptures, "Lara" a live clown, merry-go-round and Gallery.

PARKS AND RECREATION

Boulder City Parks & Recreation Dept.
900 Arizona St.
Boulder City, NV 89005
293-9256
Roger Hall, Dir.
Recreation classes and sports, municipal golf course, swimming pool and racquetball complex.

City of Las Vegas Parks & Leisure Activities
749 Veteran's Memorial Dr.
Las Vegas, NV 89101
229-6297
David Kuiper, Dir.

Clark County Parks & Recreation Dept.
2601 E. Sunset Rd.
Las Vegas, NV 89120
455-8200
Glenn Trowbridge, Dir.

Henderson Parks & Recreation Dept.
240 Water St.
Henderson, NV 89015
Information Line: 565-4264
Recreation and Leisure Activities
Sports Office: 434-4131
Black Mountain Aquatic Complex:
565-2888
Steve Rongyocsik, Dir.

North Las Vegas Recreation Dept.
1638 N. Bruce St.
N. Las Vegas, NV 89030
633-1600
Eric Dabney, Dir.

COMMUNITY CENTERS

Boulder City Recreation Center
900 Arizona St.
Boulder City, NV 89005
293-9256
Roger Hall, Dir.

Hours: Mon. - Thu. 7:30 am - 6 pm;
Fri. 9 am - noon; Sat. - Sun. 1 pm - 5 pm

Swimming Pool and Racquetball Complex
861 Ave. B.
Boulder City, NV 89005
293-9286

Charleston Heights Arts Center
800 S. Brush St.
Las Vegas, NV 89107
229-6383
Cassandra McGuire, Ctr. Coordinator
Hours: Mon. & Thu. 1 pm - 8:30 pm; Tue. - Wed. 10 am - 8:30 pm; Fri. 10 am - 5:30 pm; Sat. 9 am - 4:30 pm; Sun. 1 pm - 4:30 pm

Chuck Minker Sports Complex
275 N. Mojave Rd.
Las Vegas, NV 89101
229-6563
Danny Higgons, Ctr. Coordinator
Variety of classes and programs for all ages, recreational activities.
Hours: Mon. - Fri. 7 am - 9:30 pm; Sat. 9 am - 5 pm; Sun. 10 am - 4 pm

Doolittle Community Center
1901 N. J St.
Las Vegas, NV 89106
229-6374
Phil Thompson, Ctr. Coordinator
Supervised activities & field trips for children, outdoor pool, indoor & outdoor basketball. Classes and programs for youths and adults.
Hours: Mon. - Fri. 9 am - 9 pm, Sat. 9 am - 4 pm

Lorenzi Adaptive Recreation Center
3333 W. Washington Ave.
Las Vegas, NV 89110
229-6358
Recreation for the developmentally disabled 7 - 22 years.
Hours: Mon. - Fri. 1 pm - 6 pm

Lorna J. Kesterson Valley View Recreation Center
500 Harris St.
Henderson, NV 89015
565-2121
Paul Widman, Ctr. Coordinator
Hours: Mon. - Fri. 8 am - 9 pm;
Sat. 9 am - 5 pm; Sun. 1 pm - 5 pm
Class for dance, art, drama and exercise for adults and children. Summer camp program; full size gym, 3 racquetball courts, 6 meeting rooms, kitchen and multi-fitness room. Next to the facility are 4 lighted tennis courts, 2 sand volleyball courts and a basketball court.

Lowden Community Center
3333 Cambridge St.
Las Vegas, NV 89109
455-7169
Adam Leonard, Ctr. Coordinator
Mon., Wed. & Fri. 9:30 am - 6 pm;
Tue. & Thu. 11 am - 6 pm
Parks & recreation office, family youth providers, children's library.

Mirabelli Community Center
6200 Elton Ave.
Las Vegas, NV 89107
229-6359
Sue Bartling, Ctr. Coordinator
Programs and classes for all ages; basketball and recreational activities.
Hours: Mon. - Fri. 9 am - 7 pm;
Sat. 11 am - 3 pm

North Las Vegas Recreation Center
1638 N. Bruce St.
N. Las Vegas, NV 89030
633-1600
Jody Davis, Ctr. Coordinator
Hours: Tue. - Fri. 10 am - 9 pm;
Sat. 9 am - 5 pm
Safekey, gym classes, karate, fitness center, racquetball court, dance classes & open activity game room.

Northwest Community Center
6841 W. Lone Mountain Rd.
Las Vegas, NV 89108
Recreation: 229-4794
Senior Activities: 229-4765
Lifetime Sports: 229-6772
Adaptive Recreation: 229-4796
Hours: Mon. - Fri. 7 am - 6 pm

Orr Community Center
1520 E. Katie Ave.
Las Vegas, NV 89119
455-7196
Sharon Lopez, Ctr. Coordinator
Hours: Mon. - Fri. 10 am - 6:30 pm
Crafts, exercise, gymnastics & sports, martial arts, modeling & dance classes, intramural sports leagues.

Paradise Community Center
4770 S. Harrison Ave.
Las Vegas, NV 89121
455-7513
Jacque Alter, Program Supv.
Classes for youth and adults, recreational programs, outdoor pool.
Hours: Mon. - Fri. 7:30 am - 7 pm; Sat. 9 am - 5 pm
Break Program: Mon. - Fri. 7:30 am - 7 pm
Track Break Program: Mon. - Fri. 7:30 am - 7 pm, $7; 7:30 am - 3 pm, ages 6 - 12

Parkdale Community Center
3200 Ferndale St.
Las Vegas, NV 89121
455-7517
Marie Kirker, Recreation Leader III
Recreational programs, physical fitness classes, art & craft classes, outdoor pool and basketball.
Hours: Mon. - Fri. 7:30 am - 7 pm;
Sat. 10 am - 2 pm
After school: Mon. - Fri. 3 pm - 7 pm
Track Break: Mon. - Fri. 7:30 am - 3 pm

Photo: Phototechnik International

Rafael Rivera
2900 E. Stewart Ave.
Las Vegas, NV 89101
229-4600
Lance Mecham, Ctr. Coordinator
Hours: Mon. - Fri. 9 am - 8 pm;
Sat. 9 am - 5 pm

Reed Whipple Cultural Center
821 Las Vegas Blvd. N.
Las Vegas, NV 89101
229-6211
Patricia Harris, Cultural Field Supv.
A wide variety of classes, programs, performances and showings of performing and visual arts.
Hours: Mon. - Thu. 1 pm - 9 pm, Tue. -
Wed. 10 am - 9 pm, Fri. 10 am - 6 pm;
Sat. 9 am - 5 pm; closed Sun. except for
performances.

Silver Springs Recreation Center
1951 Silver Springs Pkwy.
Henderson, NV 89014
435-3814
Kurt Williams, Ctr. Coordinator
Supervised children's activities and Kid
Zone 7 am - 6 pm. Adult classes, weight
room, basketball, outdoor Olympic size
pool.
Hours: Mon. - Fri. 8 am - 9 pm;
Sat. 9 am - 5 pm; Sun. 1 pm - 5 pm;
$65 pre-registration required includes
all activities, field trips and T-shirt.

Stupak Community Center
300 W. Boston Ave.
Las Vegas, NV 89102
229-2488
Deb Massey, Ctr. Coordinator
Hours: Mon. - Thu. 7:30 am - 8:30 pm;
Fri. 8:30 am - 8 pm; Sat. 9 am - 5 pm

Sunrise Community Center
2240 Linn Ln.
Las Vegas, NV 89115
455-7600
Randy Reese, Ctr. Coordinator
Classes and programs for all ages,
including Seniors on the Go. Outdoor
pool and basketball.
Hours: Mon. - Fri. 7:30 am - 6 pm; Sat.
9 am - 5 pm
Break Program: Mon. - Fri. 10 am - 3 pm

Whitney Community Center
5700 Missouri Ave.
Las Vegas, NV 89122
455-7573
Robert Dwyer, Ctr. Coordinator
Adult and youth classes and recreational activities, basketball court available.
Hours: Mon. - Fri. 8 am - 9 pm; Sat.
10 am - 3 pm
Teen Drop-In Program Hours: Mon. -
Fri. 12:30 pm - 6 pm

Winchester Community Center
3130 S. McLeod Dr.
Las Vegas, NV 89121
455-7340
Dan Skea, Ctr. Coordinator
Films, concerts, classes and programs
for all ages.
Hours: Mon. - Fri. 8 am - 9 pm; Sat.
9 am - 5 pm

COMMUNITY SCHOOLS

Facilities available to provide the youth
and adults of southern Nevada with a
wide variety of classes and programs in
the arts, physical fitness, self help and
fun recreational activities. Costs vary
with each activity.

Baker Park Community School
Fremont Jr. High
1020 E. St. Louis Ave.
Las Vegas, NV 89104
733-6599
Linda Ryan, Ctr. Coordinator
Hours: Mon. - Thu. 3 pm - 9 pm;
Fri. noon - 6 pm

Becker Community School
9151 Pinewood Hills Dr.
Las Vegas, NV 89134
229-2482
Sue Ann Porter, School Coordinator
Hours: Mon. - Fri. 3:30 pm - 7 pm

Brinley Community School
6150 Smoke Ranch Rd.
Las Vegas, NV 89108
646-9046
Ken Brensinger, Ctr. Coordinator
Hours: Mon. - Fri. 2 pm - 7 pm

**Charleston Heights
Community School**
Garside Middle High
300 S. Torrey Pines Dr.
Las Vegas, NV 89107
878-8644
Mark Romeo, Ctr. Coordinator
Hours: Mon. - Fri. 3 pm - 7 pm

Clark Community School
4291 Pennwood Ave.
Las Vegas, NV 89102
365-9272
Brenda Bouie, Coordinator
Hours: Mon. - Thu. 3 pm - 7 pm;
Fri. 3 pm - 6 pm

Johnson Community School
340 Villa Monterey Dr.
Las Vegas, NV 89128
229-6175
Ray Call, Center Coordinator
Hours: Mon. - Fri. 3 pm - 7 pm

Robison Community School
4740 N. Marion Dr.
Las Vegas, NV 89110
459-0201
Marc Walters, Ctr. Coordinator
Hours: Mon. - Thu. 1 pm - 8 pm

PUBLIC POOLS

Most public swimming pools open
Memorial Day and close Labor Day.
Admission: Adults $2; children under
18 $1
(See Sports for complete list of pools)

Municipal Pool
430 E. Bonanza Rd.
Las Vegas, NV 89101
229-6309
Slated to open early 1998. Enclosed pool
will be opened year-round; call for
hours.

**Lorin L. Williams
Municipal Indoor Pool**
Basic High School
500 N. Palo Verde Dr.
Henderson, NV 89015
565-2123
Open year-round.
Admission: Adults $2; children under 18 $1
Hours: Tue. & Thu. 7:30 pm - 9 pm;
Sat. & Sun. 11 am - 5 pm
Lap Swimming: Mon. - Fri. 5:30 am - 7 am;
Mon., Wed. and Fri. 6:30 pm - 8:30 pm

Silver Springs Pool
1951 Silver Springs Pkwy.
Henderson, NV 89014
435-3819
Open Memorial Day to Labor Day.
Admission: Adults $2, children under 18 $1
Hours: Call

Boulder City Swimming Pool
861 Ave. B
Boulder City, NV 89005
293-9286
Plastic bubble enclosed during winter
months - open year-round.

YMCA
4141 Meadows Ln.
Las Vegas, NV 89107
877-9622
Membership or daily fee.
Indoor Olympic sized pool.

CHILDREN'S PARTIES

Crystal Palace, 3901 N. Rancho Dr., Las Vegas, NV 89130

Astro Jump of Las Vegas
435-5867
Karen Cruz, Mgr.
Hours: 8 am - 8 pm
15 x 15 ft. inflatable dinosaurs, castles,
elephants & dragons. Delivered and
taken down at the end of the day; birthdays, carnivals, fund raisers and company picnics.

Burger King Restaurants
Executive Office
3421 E. Tropicana Ave.
Las Vegas, NV 89121
Call for nearest location
Party at Burger King. Package includes
cake, present for birthday child, decorations, kids meals and (at locations with

playground) supervised play time for
$32 up to 10 children and $2 each additional child. Prices and provisions may
vary with each restaurant.

Crystal Palace
(Multiple locations listed)
3901 N. Rancho Dr.
Las Vegas, NV 89130
645-4892
David Morgan, Owner
Parties can be booked at $60 for up to
10 children, $6 each additional. Price
includes admission and skates, pizza or
hot dogs, ice cream, soft drinks and the
use of the party table for whole sessions. Party invitations are available.

CHILDREN'S PARTIES

Call for more information and reservations for parties.

4680 Boulder Hwy.
Las Vegas, NV 89121
458-7107

4740 S. Decatur Blvd.
Las Vegas, NV 89103
253-9832

1110 E. Lake Mead Dr.
Henderson, NV 89015
564-2790

Discovery Zone
2020 Olympic Ave.
Henderson, NV 89014
434-9575
Marsha Perry, Gen. Mgr.
Hours: Mon. - Thu. 10 am - 8 pm; Fri. - Sat. 10 am - 9 pm; Sun. 11 am - 7 pm
Private rooms for birthday parties. Party room for 45 minutes, 1 hour of play time, birthday cake; $7.99 - $12.99 per child; 10 child minimum Fri. - Sun.

Gold Coast Bowling Center
4000 W. Flamingo Rd.
Las Vegas, NV 89103
367-4700
Sheila Delaney, Group Sales Coordinator
Party package includes two games of bowling, shoe rental, hot dogs and soda, party hats and balloons; $5.00 per child; $6.00 per child includes pizza instead of hot dogs.

Lied Discovery Children's Museum
833 Las Vegas Blvd. N.
Las Vegas, NV 89101
382-3445
Doreen Bartoli, Dir.
Party includes invitations, guided museum tour, souvenir T-shirt, customized cake, party favors and refreshments. Happy Birthday Room available for children's parties.

McDonald's
McDonald's Regional Office
2030 E. Flamingo Rd.
Las Vegas, NV 89119
796-3200
Call for nearest location
For as little as $45 (for up to 10 children; $2.50 each additional child) let McDonald's take all the worries out of your child's party. Price includes Hamburger Happy Meals for each child and one adult host, cake, ice cream, games, gift for birthday child, decorations and use of party room (if restaurant has one). Prices and provisions may vary slightly with each restaurant. Reservations should be made 1 - 1 1/2 weeks in advance.

Mountasia Family Fun Center
2050 Olympic Ave.
Henderson, NV 89014-2242
898-7777
Doug Eichholz, Gen. Mgr.
Hours: Mon. - Thu. 2 pm - 10 pm; Fri. 2 pm - midnight; Sat. 10 am - midnight; Sun. 10 am - 10 pm
Two 18 hole miniature golf courses, roller skating, roller blading, arcade with over 100 video games, Go Carts (must be 54 inches or more to drive, 44 inches or more to be passenger), Bumper Boats (must be 44 inches to drive and 32 inches to be a passenger), large clubhouse with game rooms, McDonald's.

Peter Piper Pizza
(Multiple locations & hours listed below)
701 S. Decatur Blvd.
Las Vegas, NV 89107
877-8873
Hours: Sun. - Thu. 10 am - 10 pm; Fri. & Sat. 10 am - 11 pm
Minimum 6 children $6.45 per child; deluxe package $8.95. Includes invitations, cake, ice cream, pizza, drinks, balloons, party favors and game tokens.

Games include video games, skeeball, kiddie rides. Tokens can be purchased at $.25 each.

3430 E. Tropicana Ave.
Las Vegas, NV 89121
454-6366
Hours: Sun. - Thu. 11 am - 10 pm; Fri. & Sat. 11 am - 11 pm
Minimum 6 children - $5.45 per child; includes invitations, cake, ice cream, pizza, drinks, balloons, party favors and game tokens. Games include video games, skeeball, kiddie rides. Tokens can be purchased at $.25 each.

350 N. Nellis Blvd.
Las Vegas, NV 89110
459-1200
Hours: Sun. - Thu. 11 am - 10 pm; Fri. & Sat. 11 am - 11 pm
Minimum 6 children - Mon. - Thu. $5.95 per child; Fri. - Sun. $6.45 per child; includes invitations, cake, ice cream, pizza, drinks, balloons, party favors and game tokens. Games include video games, skeeball, kiddie rides. Tokens can be purchased at $.25 each.

2401 E. Lake Mead Blvd.
N. Las Vegas, NV 89030
399-1115
Hours: Sun. - Thu. 11 am - 10 pm; Fri. & Sat. 11 am - 11 pm
Minimum 6 children - birthday parties: $5.45 per child; includes invitations, cake, ice cream, pizza, drinks, balloons, party favors and game tokens. Games include video games, skeeball, kiddie rides. Tokens can be purchased at $.25 each.

Santa Fe Hotel Ice Arena
4949 N. Rancho Dr.
Las Vegas, NV 89130
658-4991
17,000 sq. ft. of ice with a 2,500 seat arena. Prices include admission and skates. $80 Ice Castle pkg. - Party room for 1 hour and skating; $100 Stanley Cup pkg. - The above plus cake, punch, party favors and decorations and 30 minute skating lesson for birthday child. Prices quoted are for 10 children. Ice Castle $5 each additional child; Stanley Cup $5 each additional child.
For further information and reservations contact William Coblentz 658-4983.

Scandia Family Fun Center
2900 Sirius Ave.
Las Vegas, NV 89102
364-0070
Wayne Larson, Gen. Mgr.
Parties-groups: 364-0071
Hours: Sun. - Thu. 10 am - 11 pm; Fri. - Sat. 10 am - midnight; closes 1 hour earlier in winter.
Batting range (baseball or softball) - 25 pitches $1.25; also by time - 15, 30 and 60 minutes.
Miniature golf - $5.95 per round per person; children under 5 free with adult.
Bumper boats - $3.95
Lil' Indy Raceway - $3.95
Unlimited use wristbands including 10 tokens - $15.95
Video arcade and redemption games; snack bar.

Spence Tumble Bus
(Multiple locations listed below)
4860A W. Lone Mountain Rd.
Las Vegas, NV 89130
658-9003
Gymnastics, dance studio features birthday parties at the gym or their Tumble Bus will come to you. Bus is equipped with rope course, climbing wall, obstacle course, cargo net, crazy barrel, rings, tumble mats and mini trampoline. $125 for up to 15 children.

1000 Stephanie Pl.
Henderson, NV 89014
436-7333

Sue-Z-Q Rides & Expo.
565-1590
Welcome to your special events and company picnics; full size children's carnival with rides and games.

Ultrazone
2555 S. Maryland Pkwy.
Las Vegas, NV 89109
734-1585
Sam Eigen, Pres.
"The Ultimate Birthday Party" Players compete in a 5,000 sq. ft. arena with an elaborate maze - safe, supervised, for all ages.

Zoological Botanical Park
1775 N. Rancho Dr.
Las Vegas, NV 89106
647-4685
Facility can be rented for parties $3 per person, minimum 15 people.

Lied Discovery Children's Museum, 833 Las Vegas Blvd. N., Las Vegas, NV 89101

YOUTH ORGANIZATIONS

SCOUTS & YOUTH ORGANIZATIONS

Big Brothers / Big Sisters Of Southern Nevada, Inc.
1660 E. Flamingo Rd.
Las Vegas, NV 89119
731-2227
Willie Baer, Exec. Dir.
Preventive program which matches young people from single parent families with appropriate role models.

Boys and Girls Club of Las Vegas
(Multiple locations & hours listed below)
P. O. Box 26689
Las Vegas, NV 89126
Administration Office: 367-2582
Debbie Verges, Exec. Dir.
Non-profit, charitable organization that conducts activities and projects for youth ages 7-18. Services such as education and guidance, athletic leagues, workshops, crafts and camping, track-break program. The clubs serve approximately 10,167 children each year in 8 permanent units.

2850 Lindel Rd.
Lied Memorial Unit
Las Vegas, NV 89102
368-0317
Hours: Mon. - Fri. 7 am - 8:30 pm

2801 E. Stewart Ave.
28th Street Unit
Las Vegas, NV 89101
388-2828
Hours: Tue. - Fri. 7 am - 8:30 pm;
Sat. 10 am - 5 pm

800 N. Martin Luther King Blvd.
Andre Agassi Unit
Las Vegas, NV 89106
646-8457
Hours: Tue. - Fri. 7 am - 8:30 pm;
Sat. 10 am - 5 pm

2530 E. Carey Ave.
North Las Vegas Unit
N. Las Vegas, NV 89030
649-2656
Hours: Mon. - Fri. 7 am - 8:30 pm

1011 Dumont St.
Cambridge Unit
Las Vegas, NV 89109
792-1388
Hours: Mon. - Fri. 2:30 pm - 8:30 pm,
Sat. 11 am - 4:30 pm

4412 S. Maryland Pkwy.
University Church Unit
Las Vegas, NV 89119
796-7880
Hours: Mon. - Fri. 7 am - 7:30 pm

3200 E. Cheyenne Ave.
Cheyenne Campus Unit
N. Las Vegas, NV 89030
651-4447
Hours: Mon. - Thu. 3:30 pm - 10:30 pm
Only for students' children.

6375 W. Charleston Blvd.
West Charleston Campus Unit
Las Vegas, NV 89102
651-5642
Hours: Mon. - Thu. 3:30 pm - 10:30 pm
Only for students' children

Boy Scouts of America
Boulder Dam Area Council
1135 University Rd.
Las Vegas, NV 89119
736-4366
Ronald Garland, Scout Exec.
Open to youth ages 6 to 20. The Boulder Dam Area Council has over 25,260 members in 982 troops in Clark and Nye counties in Nevada, LaPaz and Mojave counties in Arizona and Riverside and San Bernardino counties in California. Provides youth with an organized program in outdoor skills.
Hours: Mon., Tue., Thu. & Fri. 8:30 am - 5 pm; Wed. 8:30 am - 7 pm; Sat. 10 am - 4 pm $7 fee
1st Grade - Tiger Cub
2nd - 5th Grade - Cub Scout
6th - 12th Grade - Boy Scouts
14 - 21 years - Explorer

4-H Programs - Nevada Cooperative Extension
2345 Red Rock St.
Las Vegas, NV 89102
222-3130
Rosemary West, Youth Program Spec.
4-H is a youth program conducted by volunteers which allows boys and girls to "learn by doing," Members choose projects based on their own interests, developing life skills and forming attitudes that will enable them to become self-directing, productive and contributing members of society. Some 4-H projects are bicycling, consumer education, aerospace and animal sciences. 5 - 19-year-olds can be regular 4-H members enrolled in any number of 4-H projects. There is no membership registration fee although some projects may require materials which may involve a minimal purchase. The 4-H emblem is a green four-leaf clover with a white "H" on each leaf, symbolizing Head, Heart, Hands and Health; the green clover is symbolic of growth. The 4-H emblem was patented in 1924.

Girl Scouts
Frontier Girl Scout Council
2530 Stewart Ave.
Las Vegas, NV 89101
385-3677
Pat Miller, Exec. Dir.
8,400 members in 410 troops.
A variety of activities for girls age 5 - 17. Conducts training courses, workshops, seminars, projects, camping trips and other activities for girls.
Hours: Mon. - Fri. 9 am - 5 pm; $7 membership plus troop dues.
5 - 6 year old - Daisy
1st - 3rd grade - Brownie
3rd - 6th grade - Junior

Girl Scouts
Henderson Scout House
1210 N. Boulder Hwy
Henderson, NV 89015
558-3232

Henderson Boys & Girls Club
401 Drake St.
Henderson, NV 89015
565-6568
A non-profit organization which serves over 2,000 children 6 - 18 through 3 locations & several outreach programs; arts & crafts; after school homework program; indoor flag football; basketball; wrestling; T-ball & pitching machine league.

Young Men's Christian Association (YMCA)
4141 Meadows Ln.
Las Vegas, NV 89107
877-9622
Hours: Mon. - Fri. 6 am - 10 pm;
Sat. 8 am - 7 pm
Swim classes, gymnastics, basketball courts, camping and martial arts as well as cultural programs. Also offered are Youth Outreach and Wellness. The YMCA is a complete fitness facility.

CHILDREN'S SPORTS ORGANIZATIONS

Over 17,000 players, ages 4 - 18, participate in southern Nevada baseball and soccer leagues.
Special Events Clark County Parks & Recreation Hotline: 455-8206

BASEBALL/SOFTBALL

Little League Baseball
Little League Central
641-7703
Robert Fleming - Dist. Administrator
Green Valley
Paradise Valley (American)
Paradise Valley (National)
Red Rock
Spring Valley
Western
North Las Vegas
Henderson
Ages 6 - 14. Season ends in June; sign up in January.

ASA Junior Olympic Girls Fast Pitch
737-1960   735-4840
Dee Prince, Nevada State Deputy Junior Olympic Commissioner
Class A League
Traveling Tournament Teams (experienced)
Ages 10 - 18
Girls will travel and be exposed to college scouts for purposes of earning scholarships.

Henderson Girls Fast Pitch League
737-1960
Dee Prince
Class B League
Ages 10 - 18; strictly for recreation

Photo: Phototechnik International

T Ball
Sunrise Community Center
2240 Linn Ln.
Las Vegas, NV 89115
455-7600
Randy Reese, Recreation Leader III
For ages 5 - 7; Learn fundamentals of T-Ball (like softball); Wed. & Fri. 5:30 pm - 6:30 pm, Sept. - Oct.; resumes in the spring.
(See Parks for list of baseball and softball fields)

Batting Cages
Scandia Family Fun Center
2900 Sirius Ave.
Las Vegas, NV 89102
364-0070
Wayne Larson, Gen. Mgr.
Baseball and softball cages
(See Amusement Centers)

Baseball School
Junior Stars
850 Las Vegas Blvd. N.
Las Vegas, NV 89101
386-7200
Don Logan, Asst. Gen. Mgr.
Program formed by the Las Vegas Stars offers youngsters a chance to learn baseball from Stars players and attend games. Sunday games free, April - September.
For 5 - 15 years; each Sunday, members receive promotional gifts; clinic with players & picnics; about 10 games are free plus T-shirt; $5 per person per year.

Photo: Phototechnik International

YOUTH ORGANIZATIONS

Las Vegas Baseball Academy
(Multiple locations listed below)
2901 S. Highland Dr.
Las Vegas, NV 89109
369-5822
Mike Martin/Jerry DeSimone, Pres.
Hours: Mon. - Fri. 2 pm - 8 pm
Camps throughout the year; ages 6 - 18;
individual lessons & batting cages.

5325 W. Sahara Ave.
Las Vegas, NV 89102
876-5822

BASKETBALL

Doolittle Center Youth Basketball League
1901 J Street
Las Vegas, NV 89106
229-6374
Phil Thompson, Ctr. Coordinator
January - March

Boys & Girls Clubs Biddy Basketball
2850 S. Lindell Rd.
Las Vegas, NV 89102
367-2582
Paul Marsh
Boys and girls grades 2 - 5; take part in an organized sport at an early age; Julius Erving, Larry Bird and Darnell Valentine are all former "Biddy" Players. Division I is recreational. Division II is for the more skilled player. Sign up in November for January and February.

Clark County Youth Basketball Leagues
455-8245
Mike Krauss, Sports Supv.
For boys and girls ages 7 - 14. Team registration only - Pee Wee $160 registration fee; Midgets $180 registration fee; Junior $180 registration fee; Senior $180 registration fee. Must maintain age requirements to March 4, 1998; $14 per team per game. Call for mailing list.

BASKETBALL COURTS (GYMNASIUMS)
(Also see Community Centers and Schools)

Chuck Minker Sports Complex
275 N. Mojave Rd.
Las Vegas, NV 89101
229-6563
Danny Higgins, Ctr. Coordinator
Hours: Mon. - Fri. 7 am - 9:30 pm;
Sat. 9 am - 5 pm; Sun. 10 am - 4 pm

Las Vegas Sporting House
3025 Industrial Rd.
Las Vegas, NV 89109
733-8999
Private club; guest fees are between $12 and $20.

Sports Club Las Vegas
2100 Olympic Ave.
Henderson, NV 89014
454-6000
Private club.

YMCA
4141 Meadows Ln.
Las Vegas, NV 89107
877-9622
Bill Starmer, Pres.
Hours: Mon. - Fri. 6 am - 10 pm;
Sat. 8 am - 7 pm
2 indoor courts.

BICYCLE & MOTOCROSS

Nellis Meadows BMX
4949 E. Cheyenne Ave.
(At park on Cheyenne and Nellis)
Las Vegas, NV 89115
Peter & Gayle Price
Hours: Saturdays only
Bicycle motocross track.

BMX Program
452-6053
Bicycle motocross for all ages at the Nellis Meadows BMX Track. Each rider is required to join the league at a cost of $35 per year. All minors must have parents' written permission to participate in races; sign up for races is between noon and 1:30 pm; races start at 3 pm.
BMX Hotline: 453-1663

Las Vegas Valley Bicycle Club
254-5554
Barry Vinik, Pres.
Teenagers welcome; meetings 1st Thu. of each month at 7 pm; USCF affiliated.

National Bicycle League
3958 Brown Park Dr., Ste. D
Hilliard, OH 43026
1-800-886-2691
Bob Tedesco, CEO
National Association for BMX Program. Grand National Races held in Sept. in Louisville, Kentucky.

BOWLING
(Also see Sports & Recreation)
Call individual bowling alleys for information on youth leagues.

Sam's Town
5111 Boulder Hwy.
Las Vegas, NV 89122
454-8022
Rose Jaramillo, Jr., Program Dir.
Youth bowling program for children; parties, tournaments and special events.
Registration fee: $10 plus weekly fee of $4.50 - $6.
No youth leagues in summer.

Santa Fe
4949 N. Rancho Dr.
Las Vegas, NV 89130
658-4995
C. W. Wyatt
Offers pee wee bumper bowling league for children 3 - 6 in the summer only.

The gutters are filled with a balloon so the ball doesn't go and the alleys are adjusted to fit their size and ability.

BOXING

Golden Gloves of Nevada
1602 Gragson Ave.
Las Vegas, NV 89109
649-3535
Hal Miller, Pres.
Amateurs and professionals.

U.S.A. Amateur Boxing Federation of Nevada
734-8093
Hal Miller, Pres.

Nevada Partners - Sugar Ray Leonard Boxing Gym
710 W. Lake Mead Blvd.
N. Las Vegas, NV 89030
399-5627
Richard Steele, Gym Mgr.
Open to youths 9 and older. Training given.

FOOTBALL

Southern Nevada Pop Warner Youth Football Conference
4064 Schiff Dr.
Las Vegas, NV 89103
Pop Warner Football Office: 873-4096
For ages 7 - 14. Sign ups start mid-July.
Registration fee: $100 certification fee and $20 per player - $55 cheerleader.

GOLF
(See Sports for complete list of golf courses)

Southern Nevada Junior Golf Association
3430 E. Flamingo Rd., Ste. 244
Las Vegas, NV 89121
433-0626
Jane Schlosser, Exec. Dir.
For ages 6 - 18; Itty Bitty Golf for children 3 - 5 years. Call for registration forms.

GYMNASTICS

Desert Gymnastics
1924 Rock Springs Dr.
Las Vegas, NV 89128
341-5852
Denise Vigil, Owner

Hours: Vary
Walking & young teens.

The Las Vegas Flyers Gymnastics
1122 Vista Dr.
Las Vegas, NV 89102
877-2266
Dusty Ritter, Coach
Hours: Mon. - Fri. 3:30 pm - 8 pm;
Sat. 9 am - 3 pm
Gymnastics instruction for recreation and competition; 18 months to adult.

Green Valley Athletic Club
2100 Olympic Ave.
Henderson, NV 89014
454-6000
Tammy Miller, Gymnastics Dir.
Gymnastics classes for ages 3 - 5; members only.

Gymboree
918 S. Valley View Blvd.
Las Vegas, NV 89107
877-0074
Hours: Tue. - Thu. 9:15 am - 12:30 pm & 5:30 pm - 8 pm; Sat. 9:30 am - noon
Playing, learning, developing and growing, all in an environment of fun for infants, toddlers and pre-schoolers to age 4 in 45 minute classes. Gymboree's parent/child play program includes trained teachers, over 40 pieces of special play equipment, plus parenting information, tips and resources.

Gym-Cats West
440 Parkson Ave., Ste. B
Henderson, NV 89015
566-1414
Cassandra Rice, Dir.
Hours: Mon. - Fri. 11 am - 9 pm;
Sat. 8 am - 3 pm
Ages: 12 months - 18 years
First class free - 8 weeks $82
Competitive boys and girls teams. Trampoline and tumbling classes, introduction to a circus school.

Gym Tyme
276 S. Decatur Blvd.
Las Vegas, NV 89107
870-5766
Hours: Mon. - Fri. 10 am - 8 pm;
Sat. 9 am - 9 pm
Ages: Children 1 - 12
Trampoline fun, bars, balance beams; also fitness & piano classes.

Spence Tumble Bus Gymnastics & Dance Co.
4860A W. Lone Mountain Rd.
Las Vegas, NV 89130
436-7333
Olympic training for boys and girls ages 18 months to 18 years; cheerleading classes, dance; mentally and physically disabled students welcome.

HOCKEY

Boom Boom's Fan Club
P.O. Box 70065
Las Vegas, NV 89170-0065
798-7825   386-8884
Laurie Wanser, Special Project Coordinator
Monthly newsletter and a chance to win an autographed hockey stick.

MARTIAL ARTS

Karate for Kids
(Multiple locations listed below)
5020 E. Tropicana Ave.
Las Vegas, NV 89122
434-5566
Appointments: 876-5424
Tae Kwon Do USA Family Center; adult programs available. Free orientation class; hours vary.

6105 W. Flamingo Rd.
Las Vegas, NV 89103
876-5424

2549 Wigwam Pkwy.
Henderson, NV 89014
897-7225

5075 E. Bonanza Rd.
Las Vegas, NV 89110
438-9767

3270 N. Buffalo Dr.
Las Vegas, NV 89129
645-5425

Allen Sarac's Professional Karate Centers of Las Vegas
(Multiple locations listed below)
4451 E. Sunset Rd., Ste. 6
Henderson, NV 89014
456-6323
Allen Sarac
Hours: Sun. - Fri. 11 am - 8 pm;
Sat. 10 am - 5 pm

420 N. Nellis Blvd., Ste. A9
Las Vegas, NV 89110
438-5425

3625 S. Rainbow Blvd.
Las Vegas, NV 89103
365-1171

SOCCER

Nevada State Youth Soccer Assn.
1200 S. Jones Blvd.
Las Vegas, NV 89102
593-8508
Hot Line: 594-KICK
Skip Henderson, Pres.
Rainbow Youth Soccer League: 593-2475
Non-competitive league for boys and girls ages 4 - 14. Sign-ups are in May and Jan.
Sagebrush Youth Soccer League: 225-9929
Nevada South Youth Soccer League: 898-8845
Tournament Information: 585-1777
For more information: 363-2848
U.S. Youth Soccer Association: 1-800-4SOCCER
Ray Thompsett, Exec. Dir.
To foster the physical, mental and emotional growth and development of America's youth through the sport of soccer at all levels of age and competition. Non-profit.

SWIMMING

(See also Public Pools in Parks & Recreation - Children Section)

Boulder City Swim Team
861 Avenue B
Boulder City, NV 89005
293-9286
Mike Polk & Stana Hurlburt, Coaches

Beginner, intermediate & advanced; Groups meet Mon. - Fri. 2:30 pm - 4:30 pm; Beginning group meets 3 pm - 4 pm; All groups compete in various meets.

Fremont Swim Club
5112 Overland Ave.
Las Vegas, NV 89107
878-5447
Memorial Day weekend through Sept. 30.

Las Vegas Sandpiper Swim Team
2800 S. Eastern Ave.
Las Vegas, NV 89109
737-7799

Sports Club Las Vegas
454-6000
Members only.

TENNIS

Nevada Junior Intermountain Tennis Association
792-8384
Parent company of Nevada Tennis Association.

Nevada Tennis Association
2840 E. Flamingo Rd., Ste. E-2
Las Vegas, NV 89121
792-8384
Sandy Foley, Exec. Dir.
Coordinates all junior activities for greater Las Vegas.

Sunset Park Tennis
2180 E. Warm Springs Rd., Ste. 1013
Las Vegas, NV 89119
647-3434
Junior tennis ages 4 - 18.

TRACK & FIELD

Amateur Athletic Union (AAU)
456-7339
P.O. Box 72346
Las Vegas, NV 89170
Tony Kyriacou, Chairman
Cross country, track and field and others.

Las Vegas Lizards Track and Field
456-7339
Tony Kyriacou, Head Coach
Year round running club open to ages 6 - 18.

Las Vegas Track Club
645-9618
Deloy Martinez, Pres.
Hotline: 594-0970
Distance running club open to all ages.

USA Track & Field
(Multiple locations listed below)
3922 Scotsman Way
N. Las Vegas, NV 89030
399-0448
Carl Wallace, Local Pres.
Governing body of track & field in the United States.

3336 Turtle Vista Cir.
Las Vegas, NV 89117
Doug Garner, National Chairperson
Hotline: 226-4722

TOURS

City of Las Vegas Fire Dept.
383-2888
Children meet real firemen and paramedics. See real emergency vehicles, equipment; watch a firefighter "suit up" in firefighting gear. Also see how and where firemen live when they are on duty and see where they learn life saving and emergency information and techniques. Children are encouraged to ask questions and are given information on prevention and what to do in an emergency. Know which facility you wish to visit when calling for arrangements.

Clark County Ambassador Program
455-3530
Tours of the Government Center which includes a brief history and overview of Clark County government as well as the southwestern influences in the architecture of the building.

Cranberry World West - Ocean Spray
1301 American Pacific Dr.
Henderson, NV 89014
566-7160
Teri Laursen, Gen. Mgr.
Hours: 9 am - 5 pm, except major holidays
10,000 sq. ft. Visitors Center features free plant tours, a museum with interactive exhibits, a film in the Cranberry Cinema and sample juices & baked goods from the demonstration kitchen. Visitors watch plant activities from a special observation deck. Gift shop.

Ethel M. Chocolate Factory
2 Cactus Garden Dr.
Henderson, NV 89014
458-8864
Self-guided behind-the-scene look at what goes into making Ethel M. Chocolate. At the end of the tour you will be treated to a free sample of their work from the gift shop.
Located outside the Ethel M. Chocolate Factory is a 2 1/2 acre botanical garden with over 350 species of cactus and other desert plants.
Gift shop and self guided tours: daily 8:30 am - 7 pm

Favorite Brands
8203 Gibson Rd.
Henderson, NV 89015
564-3878   Tour Info: 564-5400
See how marshmallows are made. Free sample at end of tour. Gift shop
Self guided tour: Mon. - Sat. 9 am - 4:30 pm

Las Vegas Library
833 Las Vegas Blvd N.
Las Vegas, NV 89110
382-3493
Tour the entire library or just the children's section. Learn how to use computers to find books and learn how to use the Library of Congress system. Tour lasts 1 - 1 1/2 hours. During school hours are preferable, but not required. Contact Nancy French (Young People's Library) to arrange tour in advance.

McCarran Airport
5795 Paradise Rd.
Las Vegas, NV 89119
261-5153

A closer look at airport operations is offered to youth groups, schools and civic groups by the Clark County Department of Aviation. Tours are conducted Mon. - Fri. and must be arranged in advance.

Nellis Air Force Base
Las Vegas, NV 89191
652-4018
Guided tours of the Thunderbird planes are offered Tue. and Thu. at 2 pm. Tours last approximately 90 minutes. Three week notice is required.

Old Las Vegas Mormon Fort
908 N. Las Vegas Blvd.
Las Vegas, NV 89101
486-3511
Phares Woods, Park Supv.
Walk in tours from 8 am - 3:30 pm; oldest historic site in southern Nevada.

Ron Lee's World of Clowns
330 Carousel Pkwy.
Henderson, NV 89014
434-1700
Hours: Open Sun. - Fri. 8 am - 5 pm;
Sat. 9 am - 6 pm
Ride the carousel, electric train, museum containing clown memorabilia, statues & animated cartoon figures, cafe. Reservations a must.

Saturn of West Sahara
5325 W. Sahara Ave.
Las Vegas, NV 89102
362-0733
Buck Weaver, Tour Guide
The largest collection of space shuttle pictures in the world. Free airplanes,

pictures and pilot licenses; 5 years and older; reservations a must.

Sunrise Children's Hospital
3186 S. Maryland Pkwy.
Las Vegas, NV 89109
731-8000
Janet Delaney
Tours limited to 15 children. Children over 7 get general tour of hospital including the emergency room, kitchen, neonatal unit and nursery (just looking through windows) and pediatrics ward. Children 4 - 7 may also visit the hospital where they learn all about doctors and nurses and how they help children. Each child receives a coloring book on this tour. Tours should be scheduled in advance and are held Mon. - Fri. 10 am - 3 pm; 25 minute tour.

United States Post Office
1001 E. Sunset Rd.
Las Vegas, NV 89119
361-9242
Free tour of the main post office facility to see how the mail system works.

Yucca Mountain Science Center
4101B Meadows Ln.
Las Vegas, NV 89107
295-1312
Melinda D'Ouville, Mgr.
Hours: Open to the public Tue. - Sat. 10 am - 6 pm
Call for group arrangements. Science wonders; hands-on computer activities; science education materials & videos; information on how the government is handling high level radioactive waste.

CHILDREN'S TOY STORES

F.A.O Schwartz at the Forum Shops, 3500 Las Vegas Blvd. S., Las Vegas, NV 89109

Animal Crackers
Forum Shops
3500 Las Vegas Blvd. S.
Las Vegas, NV 89109
796-0121
Hours: 9 am - midnight

The Disney Store
(Multiple locations & hours listed below)
Fashion Show Mall
3200 Las Vegas Blvd. S.
Las Vegas, NV 89109
737-5400
Hours: Mon. - Fri. 10 am - 9 pm;
Sat. 10 am - 7 pm; Sun. noon - 6 pm

Boulevard Mall
3680 S. Maryland Pkwy.
Las Vegas, NV 89109
893-3390
Hours: Mon. - Fri. 10 am - 9 pm;
Sat. 10 am - 8 pm; Sun. 11 am - 6 pm

Forum Shops
3500 Las Vegas Blvd. S.
Las Vegas, NV 89109
732-9560
Hours: Mon. - Thu. & Sun. 10 am - 11 pm;
Fri. & Sat. 10 am - midnight

Galleria at Sunset
1300 W. Sunset Rd.
Henderson, NV 89014
433-3666
Hours: Mon. - Sat. 10 am - 9 pm;
Sun. 11 am - 6 pm

The Elf Shelf
6366 W. Sahara Ave.
Las Vegas, NV 89102
248-8888
Hours: Mon. - Sat. 10 am - 6 pm;
Sun. 11 am - 5 pm

Unusual toys, collectible dolls, educational toys, games and bears. Toy hospital and adoption center.

Imagination Unlimited
(Multiple locations listed below)
4934 E. Tropicana Ave.
Las Vegas, NV 89122
434-5696
Hours: Mon. - Sat. 10 am - 6 pm;
Sun. 11 am - 5 pm
Premier doll store, both play and collectibles; 1,500 dolls on display; large variety of specialty toys.

3262B Civic Center Dr.
N. Las Vegas, NV 89030
649-3311
Hours: Mon. - Sat. 10 am - 6 pm; Closed Sun.
Model trains, radio control aircraft and plastic models; roll-playing games.

Kay Bee Toy & Hobby Shops Inc.
(Multiple locations & hours listed)

Boulevard Mall
3452 S. Maryland Pkwy.
Las Vegas, NV 89109
737-5112
Hours: Mon. - Fri. 10 am - 9 pm;
Sat. 10 am - 8 pm; Sun. 11 am - 6 pm

Meadows Mall
4300 Meadows Ln.
Las Vegas, NV 89107
878-0904
Hours: Mon. - Fri. 10 am - 9 pm;
Sat. 10 am - 6 pm; Sun. 10 am - 6 pm

Kay Bee Toy Liquidators
Belz Outlet Mall
7400 Las Vegas Blvd. S.
Las Vegas, NV 89123
361-8683
Hours: Mon. - Sat. 10 am - 9 pm;
Sun. 10 am - 6 pm

Kids Inc.
Riviera Hotel
2901 Las Vegas Blvd. S.
Las Vegas, NV 89109
733-6690
Hours: Flexible

Replay
(Multiple locations listed below)
4425 E. Tropicana Ave.
Las Vegas, NV 89121
433-6802
Hours: Mon. - Sat. 10 am - 6 pm;
Sun. noon - 5 pm
Used toys sold at 40% - 80% below original price.

6620 W. Flamingo Rd.
Las Vegas, NV 89103
891-TOYS

Toys 'R' Us
(Multiple locations listed below)
4000 S. Maryland Pkwy.
Las Vegas, NV 89119
732-3733
Hours: Mon. - Sat. 9:30 am - 9:30 pm;
Sun. 10 am - 6 pm
The world's largest toy store.
Credit Cards: MC, Visa, AMX, Discover

4550 Meadows Ln.
Las Vegas, NV 89107
877-9070

1425 W. Sunset Rd.
Henderson, NV 89014
454-8697

Warner Bros. Studio Store
Forum Shops
3500 Las Vegas Blvd. S.
Las Vegas, NV 89109
893-7711
Loralee Neuwirth, Gen, Mgr.
Hours: Sun. - Thu. 10 am - 11 pm;
Fri. - Sat. 10 am - midnight
Credit Cards: All major
Over 8,000 sq. ft. of clothing, toys, souvenirs and collectibles with the Warner Bros. characters and name. Store features a 16 ft. video screen playing Warner Bros. cartoons, videos and clips from upcoming movies.

Whippersnapperz
2555 S. Jones Blvd., Ste. F1B
Las Vegas, NV 89102
368-6810
Hours: Mon. - Sat. 9:30 am - 6 pm;
Sun. noon - 5 pm during holidays
Fabulous gifts for infants through teenagers; craft classes.

The Great Outdoors

Lake Mead is the only lake in Nevada with an outlet to the sea. It flows into the Gulf of California. It took 3 years to fill Lake Mead after Hoover Dam was completed. Lake Mead was named for Elwood Mead, the Bureau of Reclamation chief during the construction of the dam. The water level at Lake Mead is 1,187 ft. above sea level. Lake Mead National Recreation Area is comprised of both Lake Mead, formed by Hoover Dam, and Lake Mohave, formed behind Davis Dam, the land surrounding these lakes and an isolated island of land on the Shivwits Plateau on the North Rim of the Grand Canyon.

Although the name conjures the image of water, more than 87 percent of the recreation area is land based with a wealth of natural and cultural resources. Lake Mead was created in 1935 and is the largest man-made lake in the United States. It extends 110 miles up from Hoover Dam, has 550 miles of shoreline, covers 1,501,216 acres (2,337 sq. mi.) and has 290.7 sq. mi. of water surface area. The average depth of the lake is 280 ft.; its widest point is 8 mi.; and average elevation is 1,160 ft. above sea level. There are 237 mi. of surfaced roads in the park and 800 mi. of unimproved backcountry roads. No off-road use is permitted. Wildlife such as bighorn sheep, mule deer, coyotes, bats, kit foxes, bobcats, ringtail cats, desert tortoises, lizards, snakes and birds can be seen in the area. The average water temperature during the summer is 83 degrees. During 1997, 9,447,9763 people visited Lake Mead National Recreational Area.

There are a total of nine marinas on Lakes Mead and Mohave. All marinas provide boat rentals, fuel, general store, dry storage and slip rentals and launch ramps. The most popular beach area at Lake Mead is located at Boulder Beach. *(For fishing information see Sports.)* Weather report: Lake Mead/Lake Mohave: 736-3854. 24-Hour Emergency: 293-8932 or Marine Band Channel 16. A $5 fee per week is charged per vehicle entering the Lake Mead National Recreation Area. A 36-page boating access guide for Nevada's lakes and reservoirs is available free from the Nevada Department of Wildlife at 4747 W. Vegas Dr.; call 486-5127 for further information.

In addition to the Lake Mead area, several other recreational areas are located in southern Nevada and surrounding areas. Red Rock Canyon in Las Vegas offers spectacular views of ancient rock formations on a 13 mile scenic drive, and the Valley of Fire in nearby Overton, Nevada, is the area's oldest state park. Its name was derived from the brilliant red sandstone formations created over 150 million years ago. As the sun sets on The Valley of Fire the canyon seems to come alive with a breathtaking show of color. It is here that ancient Indian petroglyphs can be seen at both the Atlotl Rock and Petroglyph Canyon areas of the park.

Mount Charleston is located 45 miles from Las Vegas, offering visitors the best of both worlds. While Las Vegas is experiencing temperatures in the mid 60s to mid 70s during the winter months and into early spring, visitors to Mount Charleston (which is only a 20 minute drive from the Valley) can enjoy snowmobiling, sledding and skiing.

Death Valley in California is 136 miles away and Grand Canyon National Park is only five and a half hours or 300 miles away.

LAKE MEAD RECREATION AREA

Photo: Photolechnik International

Lake Mead
National Recreation Area
601 Nevada Hwy.
Boulder City, NV 89005
293-8907
Alan O'Neill, Superintendent

Alan Bible Visitors Center
601 Nevada Hwy.
Boulder City, NV 89005
293-8990
Four miles northeast of Boulder City on
US 93 at Lakeshore Rd. (SR 166).
Hours: 8:30 am - 4:30 pm
Closed Christmas, Thanksgiving and
New Years Day.
Movies, exhibits, books, brochures and
topographic maps and nautical charts
as well as drinking water and restrooms
are available.
Discovery hikes on Sat., evening lectures on Fri. nights and slide programs are a few of the weekly activities
available free to the public by the park
to help visitors learn more about the
area during the Fall and Winter.
Call the center at 293-8906 for more
information. *(For information on area
of Boulder Beach, tune in to 1610 on
your AM radio.)*

Boulder City Visitors Center
100 Nevada Hwy.
Boulder City, NV 89005
294-1220
Located about 2 miles west of the Alan
Bible Visitors Center. Operated by the
Las Vegas Convention and Visitors
Authority, at the intersection of US 93
and the Nevada Highway. Tourist
information on Nevada and Las Vegas,
restrooms, water and telephones.

Lake Mead Fish Hatchery
245 Lakeshore Rd.
Boulder City, NV 89005
486-6738
Hours: 8 am - 4 pm
Produces 500,000 9-inch rainbow trout
annually. Located one mile north of
Boulder Beach.

BOULDER BEACH
Directions from Las Vegas: US 93 to SR
166; 28 mi. southeast of Las Vegas and
about a 40 minute drive. There is a half
mile stretch of swim beach and group
picnic area.

Lakeshore Trailer Village
268 Lakeshore Rd.
Boulder City, NV 89005
293-2540
RV sites, laundry and showers.

Lake Mead Marina
Seven Crown Resorts
322 Lakeshore Rd.
Boulder City, NV 89005
293-3484   1-800-752-9669
Beverly Chandler, Gen. Mgr.
Store, restaurant & lounge, motel, full
service marina.
Boat rentals: 20 foot ski boat $225 per
day or $45 per hour with $225 deposit;
Patio boats $175 per day or $35 per hour
with $175 deposit; fishing boats $100
per day or $20 per hour with $100
deposit. Price does not include gas -
two hour minimum rental. Credit cards:
MC, Visa, Discover; Hours: 7 am - 6 pm

Lake Mead Lodge
322 Lakeshore Rd.
Boulder City, NV 89005
293-2074
Rooms: 43; Rate: $50 - $65; 3 room suite
$125
Pool and cable TV; pets allowed for $5
per night; banquet room.

Lake Mead Cruises
707 Wells Rd.
Boulder City, NV 89005
293-6180
(See Sightseeing for more information)

LAS VEGAS BAY & MARINA
Directions from Las Vegas: 17 miles
south on US 93/95 to Lake Mead Dr. (SR
147) in Henderson. Located approximately 25 miles from Las Vegas, it is a
35 minute drive.

Las Vegas Bay Ranger Station
Lake Shore Rd.
Henderson, NV 89015
565-8368

Las Vegas Bay Marina
P.O. Box 91150
Henderson, NV 89009
565-9111
Robert Gripentog, Gen. Mgr.
Store, restaurant/lounge, full service
marina, boat rental.

CALLVILLE BAY
Directions from Las Vegas: 30 miles
southeast of Las Vegas on US 93/95 to
Lake Mead Dr. (SR 147), North Shore
Rd. (SR 149) and Callville Bay Rd.

Callville Bay Resort and
Marina
HCR 30, Box 100
Las Vegas, NV 89124
565-8958
Rod Taylor, Gen. Mgr.
Store, cafe/lounge, RV park, full service
marina, auto fuel, public showers,
houseboat rental. Forever Resorts 1-
800-255-5561, boat rentals 565-4813.
Credit Cards: MC, Visa, AMX.

ECHO BAY
(Seven Crown Resorts management)
Directions from Las Vegas: 54 miles
southeast on US 93/95 to Lake Mead Dr.
(SR 147), North Shore Rd. to Echo Bay.

Echo Bay Resort
Via Star Route 89010
Overton, NV 89040
394-4000   1-800-PLAYNOW
Larry Ewing, Gen. Mgr.
Store, restaurant/lounge, full service
marina, RV park, upper and lower campgrounds, motel, houseboat rental, boat
rental, airstrip. Free 2,500 sq. ft. meeting room to registered groups.

OVERTON BEACH
Directions from Las Vegas: 60 miles
northeast via I-15 to SR 169.

Overton Beach Resort
Overton, NV 89040
394-4040
Paul Chandler, Jr., Gen. Mgr.
Store, snack bar, trailer village/RV park.
MC, Visa.

TEMPLE BAR
(Seven Crown Resorts)
Directions from Las Vegas: 75 miles
southeast via US 93 over Hoover Dam to
Temple Bar Rd.

Temple Bar Resort
P.O. Box 545
1 Main St.
Temple Bar, AZ 86443
1-520-767-3211   1-800-752-9669
Dave Gabriel, Gen. Mgr.
Store, restaurant/lounge, motel, RV
park, boat rentals, full service marina.
Paved 3,500 ft. day airstrip, recreation
area, swim/beach area.

HOOVER DAM
Located 40 miles southeast of Las Vegas
and about a 45 minute drive on US 93.
It cost $16 million to build the dam in
the 1930s. To build the Dam today would
cost $4 billion and that figure doesn't
include environmental impact studies.

Bureau of Reclamation
Visitor Services
Box 299
Boulder City, NV 89005
293-8367
Robert Johnson, Regional Dir.
Congress, in 1928, passed the Boulder
Canyon Project Act; construction on the
dam was started in 1931 and completed in 1935. Hoover Dam turned the vio-
lent Colorado River into the still waters
of Lake Mead. The 17 generators provide power to Arizona, southern
California and southern Nevada. More
than 5,000 men worked day and night,

at an average pay of about 62 cents an
hour, for almost five years to erect the
giant concrete structure between the
deep, rugged walls of Black Canyon.
Ninety-six workers died during
construction. The 726.4 ft. high structure
is 660 feet thick at its base. It took 4.4
million cubic yards of concrete to build
the dam.
Hoover Dam expanded the power
plant in 1992 from 1,340 megawatts to
2,040 megawatts and built a new visitors
center, snack bar and parking garage.
Nevada gets 25 percent of the energy
that is produced by Hoover Dam.
Nevada Power gets 4.3 percent of its
power from Hoover Dam.
Guided tour information: 294-3523
Tours: Summer 8:30 am - 5:45 pm, winter 9:15 am - 4:15 pm
Admission: Adults $8, seniors $7, children under 16 $2. Hard Hat Tour $25 for
all. 1,030,000 people took the tour in
1997. Tours began in 1937, two years
after President Roosevelt dedicated the
structure.
Improvements to the Monument
area recently include a parking garage,
information center and new elevators.
Free movie, "The Hoover Dam
Experience" is available at the dam for
viewing at no charge.
Snacketeria: 293-4364
40-seat snack bar located at the edge of
the dam.

Boulder City - Hoover Dam
Museum
444 Hotel Plaza
Boulder City, NV 89005
294-1988
Pat Lappin, Curator
Hours: 10 am - 4 pm
Established for the preservation of
historical artifacts relating to the
workers and construction of Hoover
Dam. Free 28-minute movie screenings
of "The Construction of Hoover Dam."
Admission by donation; gift shop.

Hoover Dam Visitors Bureau
1228 Arizona St.
Boulder City, NV 89005
294-3515
Hours: 9 am - 5 pm
Admission: $6 for adults; children under
9 free. 28 minute movie on the construction
of Hoover Dam is shown throughout the
day. Parking $2.

DAM CONSTRUCTION
ACCIDENTS
During the construction of
Hoover Dam, 96 men lost their
lives. Although it is rumored that
some of the men were buried alive
in the cement, this is not true.
The first man to die was R. G.
Tierney, a surveyor who drowned
in the Colorado River on
December 20, 1922.
The last person died exactly 13
years later. Patrick Tierney, an electri-
cal apprentice, fell from one of the
dam's intake towers into the
Colorado River far below. The
Tierneys were father and son.

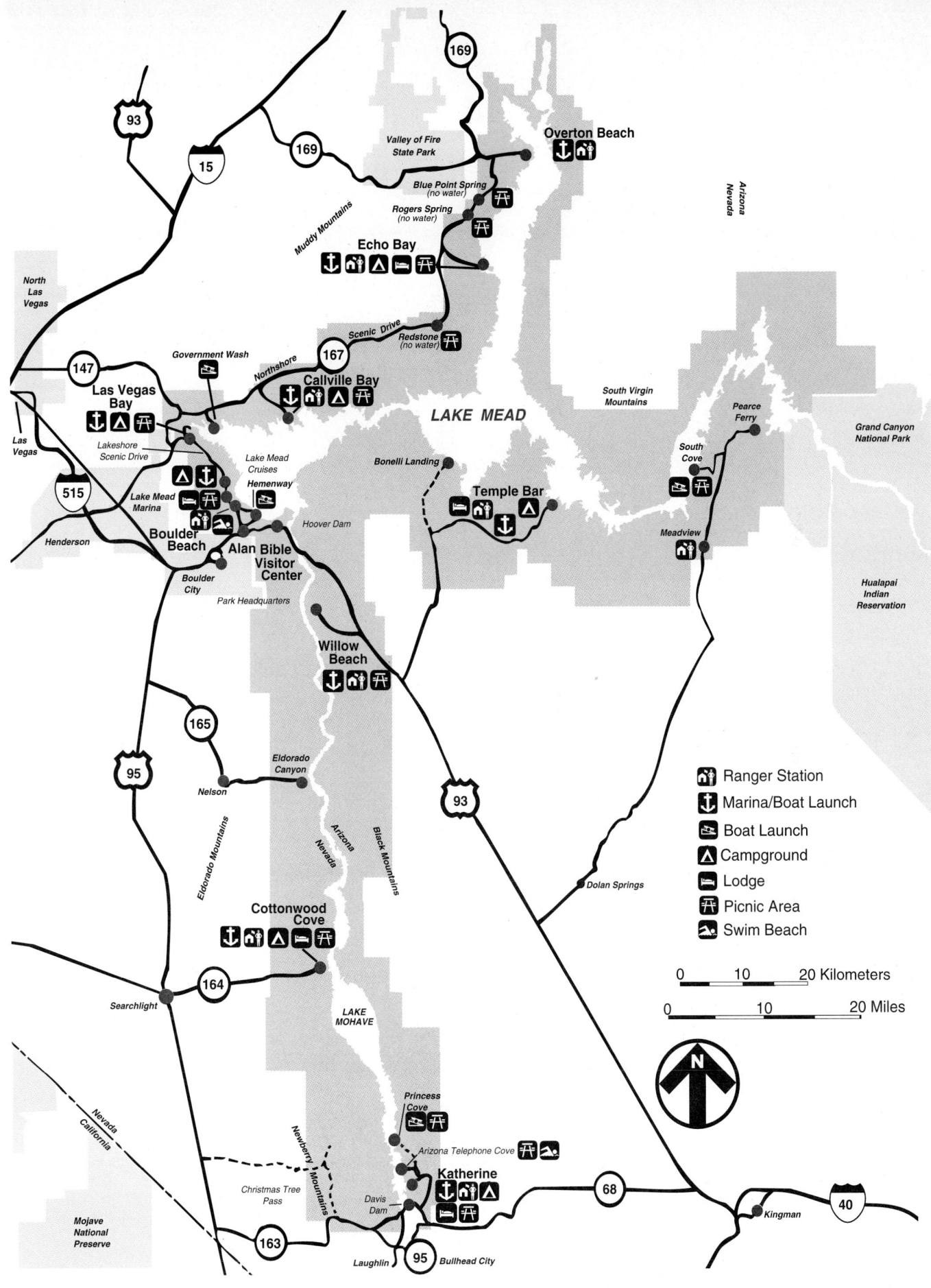

93

15

169

169

Valley of Fire
State Park

Overton Beach

Blue Point Spring
(no water)

Rogers Spring
(no water)

Echo Bay

Muddy Mountains

North
Las
Vegas

Scenic Drive

Redstone
(no water)

147

Government Wash

Northshore

167

Callville Bay

LAKE MEAD

South Virgin
Mountains

Arizona
Nevada

Grand Canyon
National Park

Pearce
Ferry

South
Cove

Las Vegas
Bay

Las
Vegas

Lakeshore
Scenic Drive

Lake Mead
Cruises

Hemenway

Bonelli Landing

Temple Bar

Meadview

515

Lake Mead
Marina

Henderson

Boulder
Beach

Alan Bible
Visitor
Center

Boulder
City

Hoover Dam

Park Headquarters

Hualapai
Indian
Reservation

Willow
Beach

165

95

Eldorado
Canyon

Nelson

Eldorado Mountains

Arizona
Nevada

Black Mountains

93

Dolan Springs

Cottonwood
Cove

164

Searchlight

LAKE
MOHAVE

Nevada
California

Newberry Mountains

Christmas Tree
Pass

Princess
Cove

Arizona Telephone Cove

Mojave
National
Preserve

Davis
Dam

Katherine

68

40

Kingman

163

95

Laughlin   Bullhead City

Legend

- 👫 Ranger Station
- ⚓ Marina/Boat Launch
- 🚤 Boat Launch
- ⛺ Campground
- 🛏 Lodge
- 🎪 Picnic Area
- 🏊 Swim Beach

0   10   20 Kilometers

0   10   20 Miles

N

Lake Mead Riverboat - *Desert Princess*

LAKE MOHAVE

Lake Mohave is a slender body of water backed up 67 miles behind Davis Dam. At its widest point in the Cottonwood Basin, it is about 4 mi. across. Lake Mohave has 150 miles of shoreline and 44 sq. mi. of water surface.

DAVIS DAM
1-520-754-3628
Hours: 7:30 am - 3:30 pm (Arizona time) for self-guided tours.
Directions from Las Vegas: US 95 south to SR 163; about 95 miles and an hour and a half drive.

Completed in 1953, Davis Dam is an earth and rock-filled embankment with a concrete spillway, gravity structure, intake structure and power plant. Davis Dam regulates the flow of water to the lower Colorado River region. Spanning the Colorado River near Laughlin, Davis Dam backs up the river's waters to form Lake Mohave, 67 miles downstream from Hoover Dam.

KATHERINE LANDING

Katherine Landing
1-520-754-3245
Open year round. For general information in vicinity of Katherine Landing, tune in to 1610 on AM radio.
National Park Service: 1-520-754-3272
Area information, maps, publications and campground information.
Hours: 8 am - 4 pm
Directions from Las Vegas: 100 miles south of Las Vegas via US 95 and SR 163 just past Davis Dam make a left turn; about 4 miles to marina.

Lake Mohave Resort
(Seven Crown Resorts)
Katherine Landing
Bullhead City, AZ 86430-4016
1-520-754-3245 1-800-752-9669
Horace Schuler, Gen. Mgr.
Free boat launch, sandy beach and swim area, picnic area, store, restaurant, lounge, full service marina, gas station, motel with 52 rooms.
Rates: $60 - $69 w/kitchenette $73 - $83; RV park - 40 sites - $18 with full hook-ups, showers, laundry.

WILLOW BEACH
Directions from Las Vegas: About a one hour drive south via US 93. Turnoff is about 14 miles south of Hoover Dam; 50 miles from Las Vegas.
Open year round. Located in a quiet cove on Lake Mohave 11 miles down from Hoover Dam.

Willow Beach Harbor
Willow Beach Rd.
Willow Beach, AZ 86445
1-520-767-4747
Gary Wirth, General Manager
Boat Rental Only: Open 8 am - 5 pm; 2 hr. min.- $70 deposit, Deck Boat - $225 for 24 hrs., fishing boat - $70 for 8 hours.

Willow Beach National Fish Hatchery
1-520-767-3456
Run by U.S. Fish & Wildlife Service
Hours: Display building open 7 am - 3:30 pm
Self-guiding tour. This hatchery raises rainbow trout for distribution in the Colorado River below Hoover Dam.

Black Canyon Raft Tours
1297 Nevada Hwy.
Boulder City, NV 89005
293-3776
1-520-767-3311
Willow Beach river raft tour leaves daily from the Expedition Depot at 9:45 am. Bus takes you to starting point just below Hoover Dam where you start your 11 mile ride down the Colorado to Willow Beach. The trip takes 5 hours.
Price: $74.95 adults, $64.95 with own transportation to Boulder City, $35 - $45 for children under 12.

COTTONWOOD COVE
Directions from Las Vegas: US 95 south to Searchlight; 14 miles east of Searchlight on SR 164; 1 1/2 hours and a 70 mile drive from Las Vegas.

Open year round. Cottonwood Cove is a secluded desert oasis located on the Nevada shoreline midway on Lake Mohave.

Cottonwood Cove Resort
1000 Cottonwood Cove Rd.
Cottonwood Cove, NV 89046
297-1464
Gary Wirth, Gen. Mgr.
Cottonwood Cove Motel - 24 rooms
Rates: Winter $35 - $60; summer $90 - $95; convenience store, restaurant; RV park with 72 sites, summer $20 per night, winter $17; full hook-ups, showers & laundry, full service marina; boat rental; Park Service campground RV park with 145 sites, $10 per night; primitive camping.

NELSON LANDING
Directions from Las Vegas: US 95 south to SR 165 then 18 miles to Lake.
In 1974 a flash flood buried this resort under a 45-foot wall of mud. The resort and marina were never rebuilt and there are no facilities. About a mile walk from parking area to water.

CAMPING

Lake Mead Recreation Area
Alan Bible Visitors Center: 293-8906
Location: 25 miles southeast of Las Vegas on US 93/95.
Fee: $10 per night.
Season: Open year round.
Eight campgrounds with about 1,000 campsites. Campgrounds offer water faucets, restrooms, picnic tables and barbecue grills.

BOAT RENTAL

Seven Crown Resorts
1-800-752-9669
Operates concessions at Echo Bay, Lake Mead Resort, Temple Bar, Katherine Landing *(Lake Mohave Resort)*

Lake Mead Resort
Fishing boat (V-hull 40 HP) - 4 hours $50, 1 day $100 and weekly $500.
Patio Boat - 4 hours $100, 1 day $175 and weekly $800.
Commander 150 ski boat - 4 hours $145, 1 day $225 and weekly $1,050.

Echo Bay Resort
Fishing boat - 4 hours $35, 1 day $50 and weekly $275.
Patio Boat - 4 hours $100, 1 day $175 and weekly $800.
Commander 150 ski boat - 4 hours $145, 1 day $225 and weekly $1,050.

Temple Bar Resort
Fishing boat - 4 hours $35, 1 day $60 and weekly $275.
Patio Boat - 4 hours $100, 1 day $175 and weekly $800.
Commander 150 ski boat - 4 hours $145, 1 day $225 and weekly $1,050

HOUSE BOATS
1-800-752-9669
Reservations for summer season should be made six months to a year in advance. A deposit of $300 is required to book the reservation.

Lake Mead/Lake Mohave
From 3 to 7 days ranges from $550-$1,550, different for summer season, value season and early board.
Houseboats may be operated during daylight hours only. Pets are welcome.

Forever Resorts
Operates concessions at:
Callville Bay: 565-8958, 565-4813
Marina: 1-800-255-5561
Cottonwood Cove: 297-1005

MT. CHARLESTON

Mt. Charleston, part of the Toiyabe National Forest and the Las Vegas Ranger District, is located 45 mi. northwest of Las Vegas via US 95 North. Make a left turn off US 95 onto Kyle Canyon Rd. (North State Hwy. 157) or a few mi. farther to Lee Canyon Rd. (North State Hwy. 156). The two are connected by Hwy. 158 on the upper portion.

The Las Vegas Ranger District encompasses 316,000 acres of forest land of the 3.5 million acre Toiyabe National Forest. On the drive to Mt. Charleston the cactus, yucca and creosote bush on the desert floor are soon replaced by junipers and pinon pine as you gain elevation. At the 6,500 ft. level you will see ponderosa pine, mountain mahogany and oakbrush. Even higher up are aspen firs. Charleston Peak is the highest in the Spring Mountain range at 11,918 feet. There are 52 mi. of hiking trails, 160 picnic spots and 150 campsites in 7 camp grounds and RV camps. At the top of Kyle Canyon Rd. is the Mt. Charleston Restaurant and Lounge, and a short distance down the mountain is the Mt. Charleston Hotel, a popular place for weddings and weekend escapes. At the end of Lee Canyon Rd. is Lee Canyon Ski Area. Here you will also find a coffee shop and cocktail lounge open the same hours as the ski area and weekends during summer months.

The mountain has a population of 1,053, along with an elementary school, community center and library.

Forest land covers 12 percent of Nevada, or 8.6 million acres.

United States Department of Agriculture Forest Service
(Las Vegas District Office)
2881 S. Valley View Blvd., Ste. 16
Las Vegas, NV 89102
873-8800
24-hour Information: 222-1597
James Tallerico, District Ranger

Kyle Canyon Ranger Station
Located on Kyle Canyon Rd. (#157) just past Deer Creek Rd. (#158)
Mt. Charleston, NV 89124
872-5486
U. S. Forest Service: 878-8800
Lee Canyon Guard Station: 872-5442
Fire, Emergency & Medical Services: 872-5306
To Report Wildfires: 647-5090
Kyle Fire Office: 872-0010

Mt. Charleston Hotel
Kyle Canyon Rd.
Mt. Charleston, NV 89124
872-5500
(see Accommodations)

Mt. Charleston Restaurant & Lounge
Kyle Canyon Rd.
Mt. Charleston, NV 89124
872-5408   386-6899

Las Vegas Ski & Snow Board Resort
Lee Canyon Rd.
Mt. Charleston, NV 89124
1-702-872-5462
Office: 646-0008
Snow Report: 593-9500

Mt. Charleston Riding Stables
Kyle Canyon Rd.
Mt. Charleston, NV 89124
872-7009
The following is a list of parks, scenic areas, picnic and camping areas in the Las Vegas Ranger District of the Toiyabe National Forest. Most picnic and camping areas are open from Memorial Day to Labor Day. Not all sites are open on weekdays.

A recreation site is divided into camp or picnic units. Each camp or picnic unit is provided with a parking spur, table, barbecue grill and/or open fire ring. Within walking distance are water hydrants and toilets.

CAMPGROUNDS
Some campgrounds are group RV camp areas as well as group picnic areas and are on a reservation system; some are on a first-come, first-served basis. Call toll free 1-800-280-2267, request a reservation for a campsite on the Toiyabe National Forest, Las Vegas Ranger District and give the name of the campground in which you wish to reserve a campsite.

Camping is limited to 5 days; $10 per day for single family sites and $20 for multi-family sites. Daily fees are for a 24 hour period running 2 pm - 1 pm. A self service pay station is located at the entrance; you must pay within 30 minutes of entering the campground.

Kyle Canyon
Kyle Canyon Rd. (157), left side just past Deer Creek Rd.
Elevation: 7,000' - 19 single-family camp units; 6 multi-family units, toilets. Open 7 days a week. $10 single and $20 double.

Fletcher View
Kyle Canyon Rd. (157) just past Kyle Canyon Campgrounds
Elevation: 7,000' - 11 single-family camp units - $10.

Hilltop
Deer Creek Rd. via Kyle Canyon Rd.
Elevation: 8,400' - 31 single-family camp units, (half of the units are reserved); 3 double family units, 1 triple. $10 single, $20 double and $30 triple. Coin operated showers.
NOTE: Trailers and motor homes are not recommended due to narrow road and short parking spaces.

McWilliams
Lee Canyon Rd. (156)
Elevation: 8,500' - 31 single family units; 9 multi-family camp units which are reserved; toilets.
$10 single and $20 double.
NOTE: Two or three families may share a multi-family unit.

Dolmite
Lee Canyon Rd. (156)
Elevation: 8,500' - 31 single-family camp sites; toilets; half of these sites are reserved. $10 single. Open 7 days a week.
NOTE: Some facilities have disabled access.

Old Mill
Clark Creek Canyon Rd. via Lee Canyon Rd. (156)
Elevation: 8,300' - 18 tent campsites, $3 per vehicle, open weekends only.

GROUP RV CAMPS
Kyle RV Camp
Kyle Canyon Rd. (157)
Elevation: 7,100' - no facilities, limit is 10 vehicles or fewer self-contained RVs.
Daily use fee: $10 family price; $20 multi-family

PICNIC AREAS
Picnic areas are first-come, first-served. Each single-family unit has a parking spur, table and barbecue grill or grate. There is no charge for picnic use at family units in these sites. Gates open at 8 am and close at 8 pm. These are day-use sites only and overnight camping is not allowed. Open 7 days a week from May to Sept. 30.

Old Mill
Clark Creek Canyon Rd. via Lee Canyon Rd. (156)
Elevation: 8,300' - 61 single-family units, 13 multi-family units, 5 flush toilets, horseshoe pits, volleyball poles; bring your own equipment.

Deer Creek
Deer Creek Rd. via Kyle Canyon Rd. (158)
Elevation: 8,200' - 11 single-family units, one vault toilet. No water available after Sept. 30.
NOTE: This is a walk-in area only. To protect this unique environment, no vehicles are allowed. Parking lot is on highway, about 1/4 mi. from picnic units.

Cathedral Rock
Kyle Canyon Rd. to end (157)
Open only on weekends. Construction still in progress.
Elevation: 7,600' - 75 single-family units, 5 flush toilets, 1 vault toilet, group picnic area. 2 units; $3 vehicle; $70 for 60 people; $85 for 75 people.

GROUP PICNIC AREAS
To reserve group picnic, call toll free 1-800-280-2267.
There is an $8.25 additional fee for booking reservations; $16.50 for group rates. Groups can select from several sites and reserve areas or group units for large picnics.
Hours: 8 am - 8 pm
Parking is limited; car pooling is recommended.

Cathedral Rock
Kyle Canyon Rd. (157)
Two group units.
Fee: 75 people, $85; 60 people $70; $3 per vehicle. Flush toilet, large tables, barbecue grills.

Mahogany Grove
Deer Creek - (158) via Kyle Canyon Rd.; 1/4 mile from parking lot
Two units - 60 people - $70 per unit.
Fee: No charge.

Foxtail
Lee Canyon Rd. (156)
Three units - Each unit can accommodate 75 people.
Fee: $85 per unit.

Foxtail Snow Play Area: The best place on the hill to sled, toboggan and inner tube. Obstacles have been cleared for safety. *(For hiking areas in Toiyabe National Forest, see Sports.)*

GRAND CANYON NATIONAL PARK

Grand Canyon National Park · South Rim
P.O. Box 129
Grand Canyon, AZ 86023
1-520-638-7888
Grand Canyon Visitor Center
South Rim: 1-520-638-7763
Grand Canyon Village: 1-520-638-7805
Open year round
Hours: 8 am - 5 pm; 7 am - 9 pm during summer months
Fees: Autos and motor homes - $10

Grand Canyon Chamber of Commerce
P.O. Box 3007
Grand Canyon, AZ 86023
1-520-638-2901
Bernie Scherr, Gen. Mgr.
Directions from Las Vegas: US 93 southeast to Kingman; from Kingman take I-40 east to Williams, and north on 64. Three hundred miles southeast of Las Vegas, about a 5 1/2 hour drive.
Altitude: 6,860 ft.
History: The first non-Native American to discover the Grand Canyon was Don Lopez de Cardenas, a captain in Coronado's expedition in 1540. The Grand Canyon became a National Monument in 1908 and a National Park in 1919. The mile deep gorge is 4 to 18 mi. wide, 217 mi. long and covers an area of over 1,900 sq. mi. (1,218,375 acres).

Over 20 licensed concessionaires conduct motorized and oar powered raft trips down the river on 3 - 12 day excursions. You can also explore the canyon by plane, helicopter, foot or burro. For more information, contact the Visitors Center or Chamber of Commerce.
Grand Canyon Airlines:
National Park Airport: 638-2463
Tours: Scenic Airlines: 638-3300
Air Nevada: 736-8900
Lake Mead Air: 293-1848
River Rafting:
For a complete list of authorized river companies, write to the park.

Grand Canyon National Park
P. O. Box 129
Grand Canyon, AZ 86023
The following company has Las Vegas departure and return:
Arizona River Runners
P. O. Box 47788
Phoenix, AZ 85068
1-800-477-7238

Grand Canyon Railway
Williams, AZ
1-800-THE-TRAIN
Leaves the historic 1908 Williams depot daily at 9:30 am and arrives at the south rim of the Grand Canyon at noon, departs at 3:15 pm; 2 1/4 hour trip each way. During winter months, train operates on the weekends only.
Fare: Roundtrip - Adults $49.50, children 2 - 16 $19.50, children under 2 free. Overnight packages also available. An authentic steam train pulls reconditioned 1920s Harriman coach cars and follows a track originally used to bring supplies to mining operations in the canyon.

Grand Canyon/IMAX Theater
1-520-638-2468
AZ Hwy. 64
World's largest motion picture system featuring "Grand Canyon - The Hidden Secrets." The screen is 82 ft. wide and six stories high with Stereo Surround Sound.

Horseback Riding and Mule Trips
Bright Angel Transportation Desk
Open 6 am - 7 pm
Reservations: 1-303-297-2757

ACCOMMODATIONS:

Grand Canyon National Park Lodges
Fred Harvey
P.O. Box 699
Grand Canyon, AZ 86023
1-520-638-2631
Bright Angel Lodge 4037 $56 - cabins $66 - $112

El Tovar Lodge	$112 - $277
Kachina Lodge	$102 - $112
Thunderbird Lodge	$102 - $112
Maswick Lodge	$72 - $107
Yavapai Lodge	$83 - $98

Moqui Lodge (located at park entrance) $93
For same day reservations:
1-602-638-2631
Rates subject to change.

CAMPING
1-800-365-2267

Desert View Campground
1-520-638-7850
No reservations required.

Trailer Village
1-602-638-2401
$18 per night.

Grand Canyon National Park · West Rim
1-520-638-7888
Directions from Las Vegas: 120 mi. from Las Vegas via US 93 across the Hoover Dam to the Dolan Springs turn off, continue about 28 mi. on Pierce Ferry Rd., then follow signs to Grand Canyon West. The final 20 miles is a dirt road with a 20 mph speed limit.
Located on the Hualapai Indian Reservation.
Entrance fee: $10 per person
A tram travels along 3.2 mi. of the Canyon Rim (included in entrance fee). Western barbecue served on a spectacular overlook, horseback riding, rafting and canoeing on the Colorado River, helicopter flights to the bottom of the canyon, flight through 40 mi. of the Grand Canyon.

Grand Canyon National Park · North Rim
North Rim: 1-520-638-7888
Directions from Las Vegas: I-15 north through St. George to Washington to Route 9 and Route 89A to Route 67 into Canyon. Follow Kaibab Plateau (North Rim Pkwy.) 43 mi. through forests and meadows to park entrance. The entrance to the North Rim is about 300 miles from Las Vegas.

Although the North and South rims are only 10 air miles apart, it is either a 15 mi. hike or a 214 mi. drive to get to the other side. Of the nearly 4 million yearly visitors to the Grand Canyon, only about 10 percent travel to the more remote North Rim.

Open Mid-May until Mid-Nov.; after summer day use only until first snowfall.
Hours: 24 hours
Fees: $10 per car, $4 for pedestrians and cyclists
Altitude: 8,200 ft.
Average summer daytime temperature low to mid 70s - nights in the 40s.
Weather info.: 1-602-638-2245
Concessions and Facilities (North Rim): Park Service Information Center, Grand Canyon Lodge Dining Room, gift shop, snack bar, camper store (groceries), gas station, pizza restaurant.

Grand Canyon North Rim Trail Rides
P.O. Box 58
Tropic, Utah 84776
1-520-638-2611
Open Mid-May - Mid-Oct.
Trail rides - horse and mule.

For North Rim Accommodations:

T W Recreational Services, Inc.
51 N. Main St.
Cedar City, Utah 84720
1-801-586-7686
Accommodations: 200 rooms in motel units and cabins at the lodge.
Rates: $76 - $115
Campground: 1-800-525-0924 *(reservations required.)* Closes October 27. 80 sites - $10 per night.

GREAT OUTDOORS

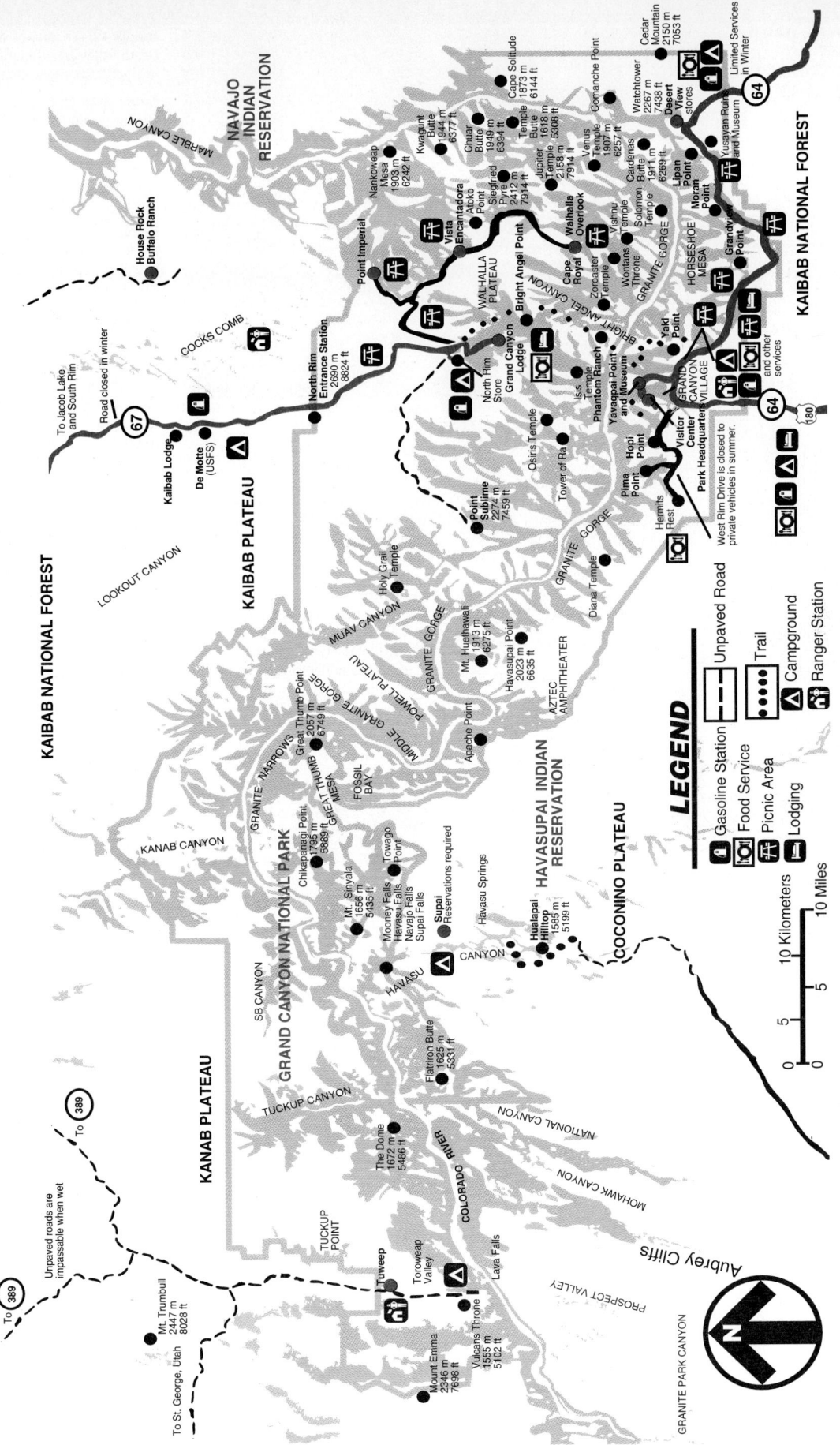

NAVAJO INDIAN RESERVATION

MARBLE CANYON

House Rock
Buffalo Ranch

COCKS COMB

To Jacob Lake
and South Rim

Road closed in winter

67

Kaibab Lodge

De Motte
(USFS)

KAIBAB PLATEAU

KAIBAB NATIONAL FOREST

LOOKOUT CANYON

Nankoweap
Mesa
1903 m
6242 ft

Kwagunt
Butte
1944 m
6377 ft

Chuar
Butte
1949 m
6394 ft

Cape Solitude
1873 m
6144 ft

Temple
Butte
1618 m
5308 ft

Siegfried
Pyre
2412 m
7914 ft

Jupiter
Temple
2158 m
7914 ft

Venus
Temple
1907 m
6257 ft

Watchtower
2267 m
7438 ft

Comanche Point

Cedar
Mountain
2150 m
7053 ft

Limited Services
in Winter

Desert
View
stores

64

Yusayan Ruins
and Museum

KAIBAB NATIONAL FOREST

Point Imperial

Vista
Encantadora

Atoko
Point

Walhalla
Overlook

Cardenas
Butte
1911 m
6299 ft

Lipan
Point

Moran
Point

Grandview
Point

Vishnu
Temple

Solomon
Temple

HORSESHOE
MESA

North Rim
Entrance Station
2690 m
8824 ft

WALHALLA
PLATEAU

Bright Angel Point

Cape
Royal

Zoroaster
Temple

Wotans
Throne

GRANITE GORGE

North Rim
Store

Grand Canyon
Lodge

BRIGHT ANGEL CANYON

Yaki
Point

GRAND
CANYON
VILLAGE

64

180

Isis
Temple

Phantom Ranch

Yavapai Point
and Museum

and other
services

Osiris Temple

Tower of Ra

Visitor
Center

Park Headquarters

Hopi
Point

Pima
Point

Hermits
Rest

West Rim Drive is closed to
private vehicles in summer.

Holy Grail
Temple

MUAV CANYON

GRANITE GORGE

Diana Temple

GRANITE GORGE

Mt. Huethawali
1913 m
6275 ft

Havasupai Point
2023 m
6635 ft

AZTEC
AMPHITHEATER

POWELL PLATEAU

GRANITE NARROWS

Great Thumb Point
2057 m
6749 ft

MIDDLE GRANITE GORGE

Apache Point

Chikapanagi Point
1795 m
5889 ft

GREAT THUMB MESA

FOSSIL BAY

Towago
Point

HAVASUPAI INDIAN
RESERVATION

COCONINO PLATEAU

KANAB CANYON

Mt. Sinyala
1656 m
5435 ft

Mooney Falls
Havasu Falls
Navajo Falls
Supai Falls

Supai
Reservations required

Havasu Springs

Hualapai
Hilltop
1585 m
5199 ft

HAVASU CANYON

HAVASU

SB CANYON

GRAND CANYON NATIONAL PARK

KANAB PLATEAU

Flatirox Butte
1625 m
5331 ft

TUCKUP CANYON

MOHAWK CANYON

NATIONAL CANYON

To 389

Unpaved roads are
impassable when wet

The Dome
1672 m
5466 ft

COLORADO RIVER

TUCKUP POINT

To 389

Tuweep

Toroweap
Valley

Lake Falls

PROSPECT VALLEY

Aubrey Cliffs

Mt. Trumbull
2447 m
8028 ft

To St. George, Utah

Mount Emma
2346 m
7698 ft

Vulcans Throne
1555 m
5102 ft

GRANITE PARK CANYON

N

LEGEND

Gasoline Station	Unpaved Road
Food Service	Trail
Picnic Area	Campground
Lodging	Ranger Station

0   5   10 Kilometers

0   5   10 Miles

Experience Las Vegas

NATIONAL PARKS

ZION NATIONAL PARK
Springdale, Utah 84767
1-435-772-3256 *(Main Visitors Center)*
1-435-586-9548 *(Kolob Canyon Visitor Center)*

Directions from Las Vegas: 159 miles northeast of Las Vegas - approximately a 3 hour drive. I-15 north through St. George; take Hurricane-Zion turnoff to Hwy. 9 east to Springdale and the south entrance of the park. For road conditions, call 1-801-772-3256 or dial 1610 on your AM radio for general park information.

The erosional features carved by the Virgin River into the Navajo sandstone of the Zion Canyon give this park one of its most outstanding features. The diversity of rock formations as well as that of the flora and fauna make Zion one of the most scenic and majestic of Utah's National Parks.

The main Visitor's Center is located at the south entrance; open 8 am - 8 pm daily except Christmas and New Years and provides information, slide programs, exhibits, book sales and a museum.

Entrance Fees: $10 per vehicle for 7-day permit; $25 for a Zion-only year pass, $50 for a Golden Eagle Passport, which allows admission to any National Park.

There are 340 campsites between two campgrounds inside the south entrance; $10 per night per site, first-come, first-served. One is open year round.

Grotto Picnic Area is the only designated picnic ground, with fire grates, picnic tables, water and restrooms. The Zion Lodge has overnight facilities, with 120 rooms and cabins available year-round, a restaurant, snack bar and gift shop. Also available through the lodge are tram tours and horseback riding in the summer season.

Bryce-Zion Trail Rides, Inc.
P.O. Box 128
Tropic, UT 84776
1-801-679-8665
1 hour $12; 3 hours $35.

For further information about the lodge, etc.:

Zion Canyon Lodge, TW Recreational Services
451 North Main St.
Cedar City, UT 84720
1-801-772-3213
Same day reservations 1-303-297-2757.

GREAT BASIN NATIONAL PARK

Baker, NV 89311
234-7331
Rebecca Mills, Park Superintendent
From Las Vegas take I-15 north to US 93, US 50 and Nevada Hwy. 487. Park headquarters are 5 mi. west of Baker and 68 mi. east of Ely.
Great Basin Park, established in 1986, is Nevada's first and only national park and the second newest of the nation's more than 50 national parks. The parks 77,100 acres features limestone caves, ancient Bristlecone Pines, camping,

Great Basin Mountains

hiking and picnicking. Lehman Caves, Wheeler Peak Scenic Area and Alpine Lakes Loop Trail are also located within the park.
Hours: Memorial Day thru Labor Day; Visitors Center 8: 30 am - 4:30 pm
Admission: Adults $4; children 6 - 15 $3, Golden Age & Golden Access $2.

DEATH VALLEY PARK

National Park Service Visitors Center

Death Valley National Park
State Route 190
Death Valley, CA 92328
1-760-786-2331
Richard H. Martin, Park Superintendent
Hours: 8 am - 6 pm; Nov. 1 - Easter 8 am - 7 pm
Information center, museum, camping facilities. Orientation film shown hourly (Auditorium 500 seats). Evening programs and interpretive programs are available in the cooler months.

Death Valley Chamber of Commerce
1-760-852-4524
Fees: $10 per vehicle to enter park, $5 per person for people on a bus, hiking, or riding a bike or motorcycle. Permit is valid for 7 days.
Directions from Las Vegas: US 95 north to Lathrop Wells; State Route 373 south to Death Valley Junction; State Route 190 to Death Valley. Drive time: About 2 1/2 hours and 136 mi. to park entrance and visitors center.
History: Herbert Hoover named Death Valley a National Monument in 1933. Death Valley National Park encompasses over 3,000 sq. mi. of desert in both California and Nevada. The lowest point in the Western Hemisphere is at Badwater, 282 ft. below sea level. Just a short distance to the south stands Telescope Peak, which rises to 11,049 ft.
Many early pioneers heading west almost lost their lives crossing the valley with its extreme temperatures, so they named it "Death Valley." Borax, a salty white mineral, was mined in Death Valley.
A total of 1.3 million people visited the park in 1997.

Furnace Creek Ranch
P.O. Box 1, Highway 190
Death Valley, CA 92328
1-760-786-2345
Cal Jepson, Gen. Mgr.
Open year round; 224 Guest rooms, fairway and pool view rooms.
Rates: $90 - $125
Special Features: 18 hole golf course; swimming pool - naturally warm spring-fed 84 degrees year round, 2 tennis courts (illuminated), horseback riding, recreation - shuffleboard, volleyball and basketball, Borax Museum, general store, gas station, landing strip for light planes.
Restaurants: Steakhouse, Coffee Shop, 19th Hole Bar & Grill.

Furnace Creek Inn
1-760-786-2345
Toni Jepson, Gen. Mgr.
Located 1 mi. on State Route 190 from Furnace Creek Ranch, it uses the same address and phone number. Open year round. Built by Borax and railroad barons in the late 1920s. 66 guest rooms.
Rates: $235 - $325; extra person $14. Special summer rates.
Restaurants: Jacket suggested for dinner which is served 6 pm - 10 pm.
Hours: Daily 7 am - 10 am, noon - 2:30 pm, 6 pm - 10 pm; Sunday Brunch served 11 am - 2 pm, $18 plus tax.
Lobby Lounge: noon - midnight, live entertainment
Special Features: 18 hole golf course, swimming pool, 4 illuminated tennis courts, massage, room service, bar and snack service at the pool.
Furnace Creek Ranch and Inn both conduct tours of Death Valley. Afternoon tea is served at the Inn 4 pm-5 pm $8.95.

Stove Pipe Wells Village
State Route 190 (24 miles NW of Visitors Center)
P.O. Box 187
Death Valley, CA 92328
1-760-786-2387
Open year round; 82 guest rooms.
Rates: $53 - $76
Special Features: Swimming pool, grocery store, service station, restaurant and bar.

Death Valley Junction
Death Valley Junction was built in 1923 by the Pacific Coast Borax Company.

Amargosa Opera House
California State Route 190
(near intersection of 127)
Death Valley Junction, CA 92328
1-760-852-4316
(30 mi. east of Death Valley)
Marta Becket
Performances: Sat. and Mon. at 8:15 pm during Nov., Feb., March and Apr.; Sat. only during May, Oct., Dec. and Jan.; Closed June through Sept.
Admission: Adults $10, children 12 and under $8.
New York dancer Marta Becket discovered this abandoned theater in 1967; refurbished it and began one-woman ballet and mime performances.

Amargosa Hotel
Death Valley Junction, CA 92328
1-760-852-4441
Marta Becket
(Next to Opera House)
Rooms: 20
Rates: 1 bed $35 plus tax; 2 beds $45 plus tax

Scotty's Castle
State Route 267
Death Valley, CA 92328
1-760-786-2392
(About 1 hour drive north of Visitors Center on State Routes 190 and 267)
From Las Vegas: US 95 north through Beatty about 35 more miles to the junction with State Route 267. Scotty's Castle is about 170 miles from Las Vegas.
Fifty minute tour admission: $8 adults; $4 children 6 - 11; under 5 free.
Tours conducted 9 am - 5 pm - Castle open 8:30 am - 6 pm.
Built in the 1930s by Chicago insurance executive Albert Johnson at a cost of close to $2 million, but was never completed. Friend and prospector Walter Scott, known as "Death Valley Scotty," took credit for the project and lived in the castle after Johnson's death. Located at 3,000 ft. in Grapevine Canyon.

Campgrounds and RV Park:
Information: 1-760-786-2331
Reservations for winter only Oct. - Apr. 30
1-800-365-2267
There are nine campgrounds located throughout the park with more than 1,500 campsites. With the exception of the Furnace Creek Campground from Oct. to Apr., all campsites are available on a first come basis. Fee $10 in summer. Backcountry camping is available in many areas and some are free.
Furnace Creek
Wildrose
Mesquite Springs
Thorndike
Mahogany Flats
*Sunset
*Texas Springs
Stovepipe Wells
*Emigrant
            *Closed in summer

RED ROCK CANYON

Directions from Las Vegas:
West on Charleston Boulevard 20 miles;
about a half hour drive to Visitors Center.

Red Rock Canyon Visitors Center

Bureau of Land Management
1000 Scenic Drive
Las Vegas, NV 89126
363-1921
Dave Wolf, Conservation Mgr.
Located off State Route 159
(Charleston Blvd.) at entrance to park.
Hours: Daily 8:30 am - 4:30 pm
(Seasonal changes)
Exhibits, hiking, climbing and picnic area
information in addition to restrooms,
telephones, drinking water.
Fees: $5 and yearly pass $20.
History: In 1967 this geologically diverse
canyon was designated a Bureau of Land
Management-owned recreation area by
the Secretary of the Interior. Red Rock
Canyon Recreation Lands encompasses
83,100 acres.
About 600 million years ago Red Rock
Canyon was beneath a sea. As the sea
receded it left dense beds of gray limestone.
  Then about 65 million years ago a thrust fault
occurred, which is a fracture in the earth's crust
 where one rock plate is thrust horizontally
over another. This thrust fault shoved the older
gray limestones up and over the younger red
sandstones creating the sharp contrast we see
today. Red Rock is visited by 1,500,000 people
annually.
Thirteen Mile Scenic Drive: This road is one
way and comes out about three miles further west
down State Route 159. The Loop Road is open for
day use only, 7 am - dusk.
For information on the 20 miles of hiking
trails at Red Rock, see Sports Section.

U. S. Department
of the Interior

Bureau of Land Management
Las Vegas District Office
4765 Vegas Drive
Las Vegas, NV 89108
647-5000

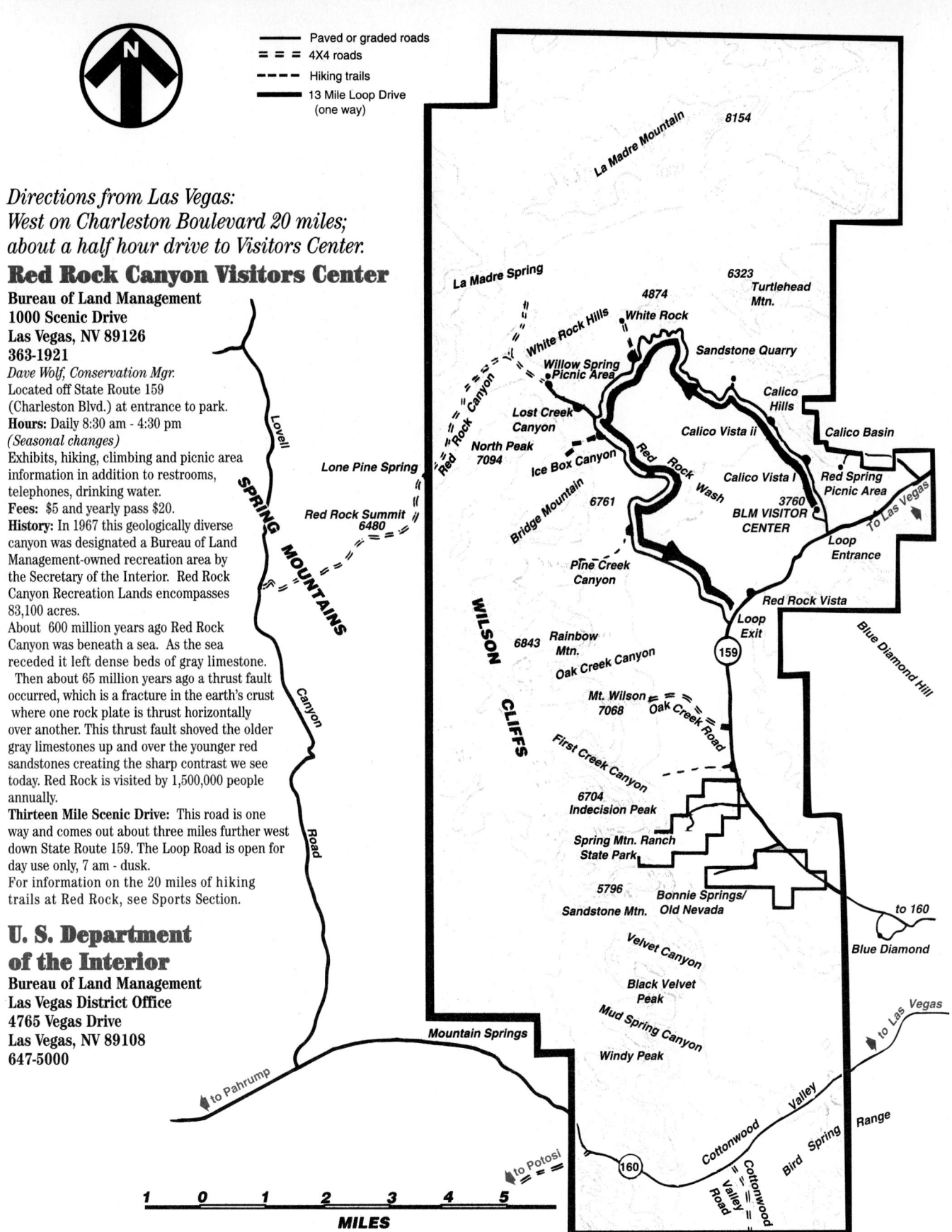

DEATH VALLEY NATIONAL MONUMENT

See page 250 for Campsite Information

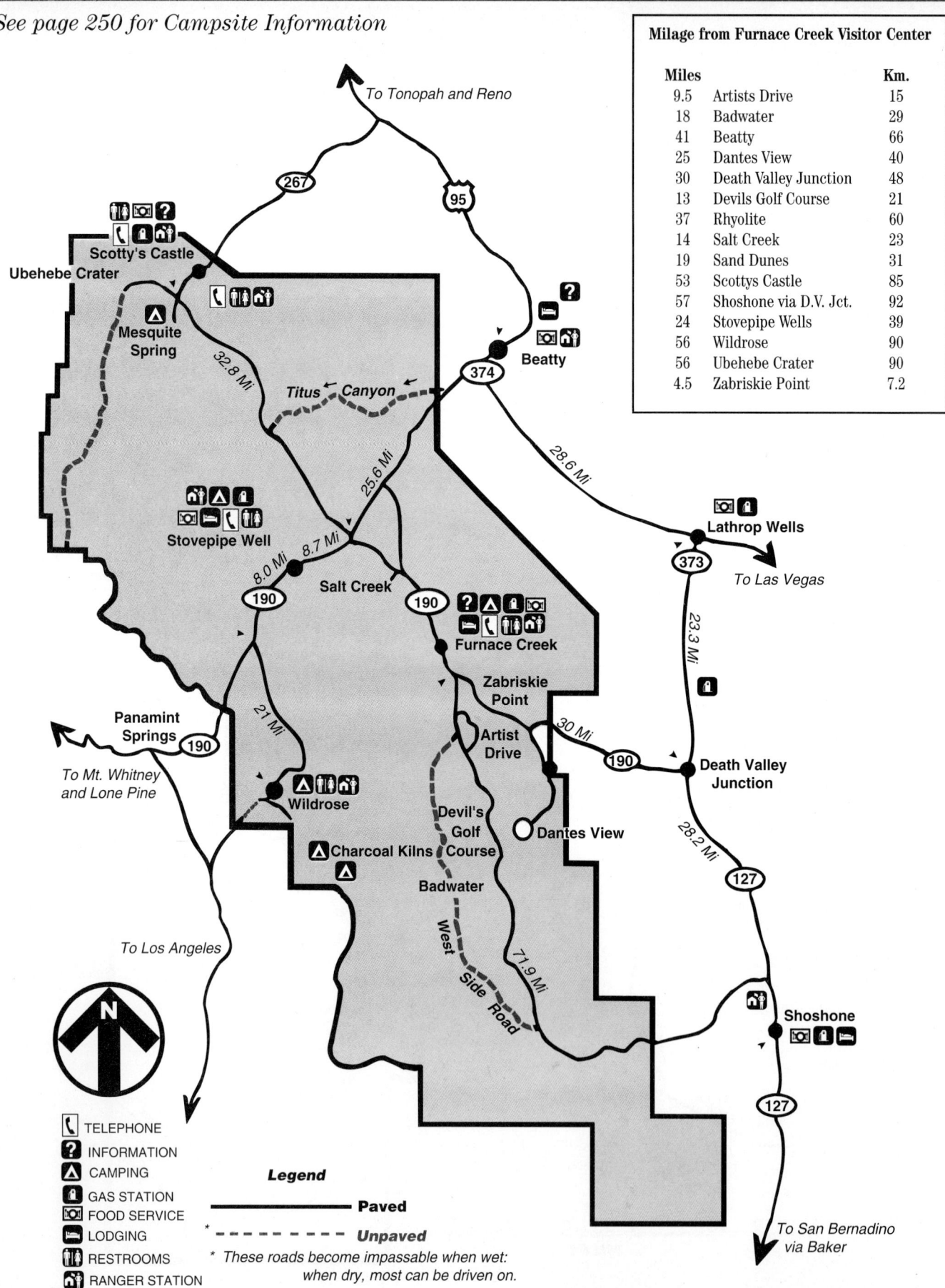

Milage from Furnace Creek Visitor Center

Miles		Km.
9.5	Artists Drive	15
18	Badwater	29
41	Beatty	66
25	Dantes View	40
30	Death Valley Junction	48
13	Devils Golf Course	21
37	Rhyolite	60
14	Salt Creek	23
19	Sand Dunes	31
53	Scottys Castle	85
57	Shoshone via D.V. Jct.	92
24	Stovepipe Wells	39
56	Wildrose	90
56	Ubehebe Crater	90
4.5	Zabriskie Point	7.2

To Tonopah and Reno

267

95

Scotty's Castle

Ubehebe Crater

Mesquite Spring

32.8 Mi.

Titus   Canyon

Beatty

374

25.6 Mi.

28.6 Mi.

Stovepipe Well

8.7 Mi.

8.0 Mi.

Lathrop Wells

190

Salt Creek

To Las Vegas

190

23.3 Mi.

Furnace Creek

Zabriskie Point

Panamint Springs

190

21 Mi.

Artist Drive

30 Mi.

190

Death Valley Junction

To Mt. Whitney and Lone Pine

Wildrose

Dantes View

127

28.2 Mi.

Devil's Golf Course

Charcoal Kilns

Badwater

To Los Angeles

West Side Road

71.9 Mi.

Shoshone

127

N

To San Bernadino via Baker

TELEPHONE

INFORMATION

CAMPING

GAS STATION

FOOD SERVICE

LODGING

RESTROOMS

RANGER STATION

Legend

——————— **Paved**

* - - - - - - - **Unpaved**

* *These roads become impassable when wet:*
   when dry, most can be driven on.

SPRING MOUNTAIN RANCH STATE PARK

GREAT OUTDOORS

Of the 13 state parks in Nevada, three are located in Southern Nevada. In addition to the state parks, the Nevada State Parks Division also manages five recreation areas and five historic sites throughout the state.
District VI office: 486-5126.

Spring Mountain Ranch State Park
P.O. Box 124
Blue Diamond, NV 89004
875-4141
Jan Prida, Park Supvr.
Hours: Day use only 8 am - 7 pm, in winter 8 am - 4:30 pm
Fee: $5 per vehicle and senior pass free for Nevada residents.
Tour of Main Ranch House and Visitors Center
Hours: Fri. and Mon. noon - 4 pm; Sat. and Sun. and State holidays 10 am - 4 pm On Tue., Wed., and Thu. there are no walking tours.
Directions from Las Vegas: West on Charleston Blvd. (State Route 159) about 18 miles from Las Vegas; about a half hour drive.
History: Situated at the base of the Wilson Cliffs, travelers along the Old Spanish Trail used the area of the ranch as a rest stop in the 1830s because of the spring fed creek running through the ranch. Chester Lauck of the comedy team "Lum & Abner" radio show built the ranch house in 1948 that stands today and is used as a visitors center for the park. German born actress Vera Krupp purchased the ranch in 1955 and raised Herefords and Brahmas. Because of health reasons she sold the ranch to Howard Hughes in 1967. The Nevada Division of State Parks bought the 528 acre ranch in 1974.
Facilities located in Park:
Picnic facilities, interpretive trails, play area, stage for theatrical programs and concerts, ranch house.

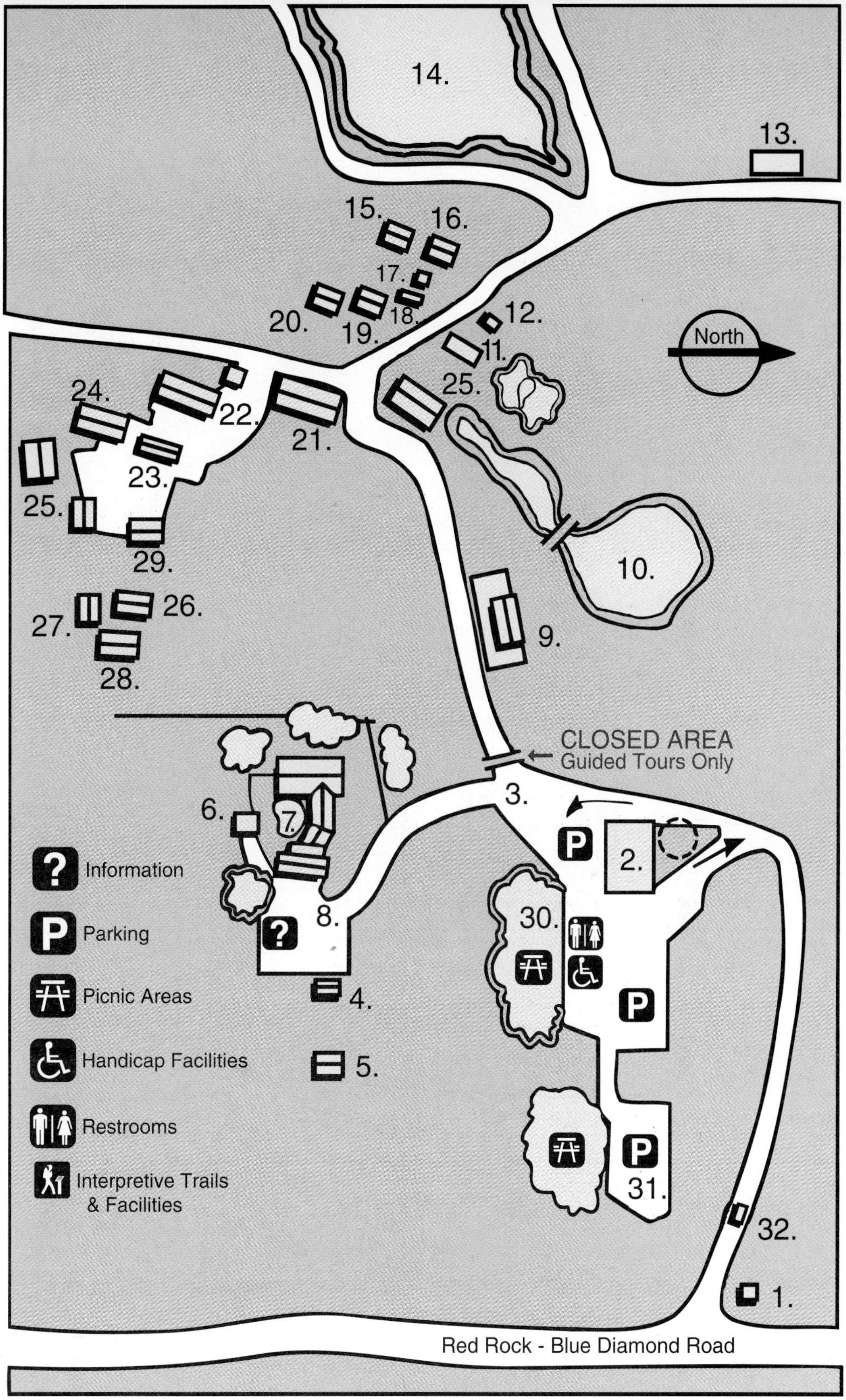

KEY:
1. Main Gate
2. Corral Complex
3. Main House Drive Gateposts
4. Kennel
5. Stable
6. Residence Hot Water System; Chiller/Boiler Air Conditioner
7. Swimming Pool
8. Main Ranch House, Visitor Center
9. Corral and Shed
10. Old Reservoir
11. Fish Pond
12. Two-Hole Outhouse
13. Wilson Family Cemetery
14. Irrigation Reservoir
15. Board and Batten Cabin
16. Stone Cabin, c. 1864
17. Spring House, Fig Spring

18. Watering Trough
19. Stone Blacksmith Shop, c 1864
20. Metal Storage Shed, c. 1910
21. Hay and Horse Barn
22. Shop
23. Chinchilla Breeding Shed
24. Bunkhouse
25. Ranger Residence
26. Poultry House
27. Milking Barn
28. Farm Implement Shed
29. Foreman's Residence, c. 1929
30. Family Picnic Area
31 Group Use Area
32. Fee Booth

Information
Parking
Picnic Areas
Handicap Facilities
Restrooms
Interpretive Trails & Facilities

Red Rock - Blue Diamond Road

FLOYD LAMB STATE PARK

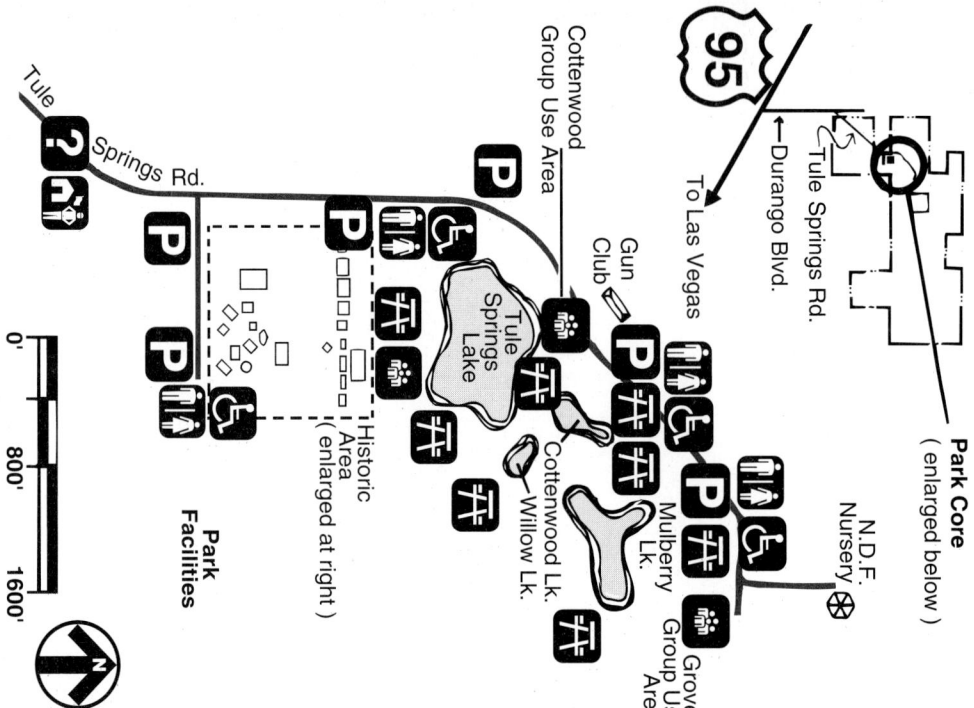

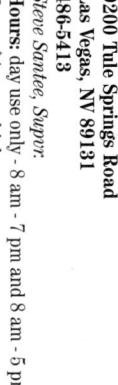

Floyd Lamb State Park
9200 Tule Springs Road
Las Vegas, NV 89131
486-5413
Steve Santee, Supvr.
Hours: day use only - 8 am - 7 pm and 8 am - 5 pm in winter.
Fees: $4 per vehicle

Directions from Las Vegas: Ten miles north on US 95 to Tule Springs Road.

History: Originally known as Tule Springs, this park was an early watering stop for Indians. It later became a privately owned working ranch, as well as a guest/dude ranch in the 1950s.

Facilities located within Park: Picnic facilities, fishing lakes, walking/bicycling path, trapshooting range, horseback riding; ducks and geese roam throughout the park. Special programs are presented throughout the year at the park.

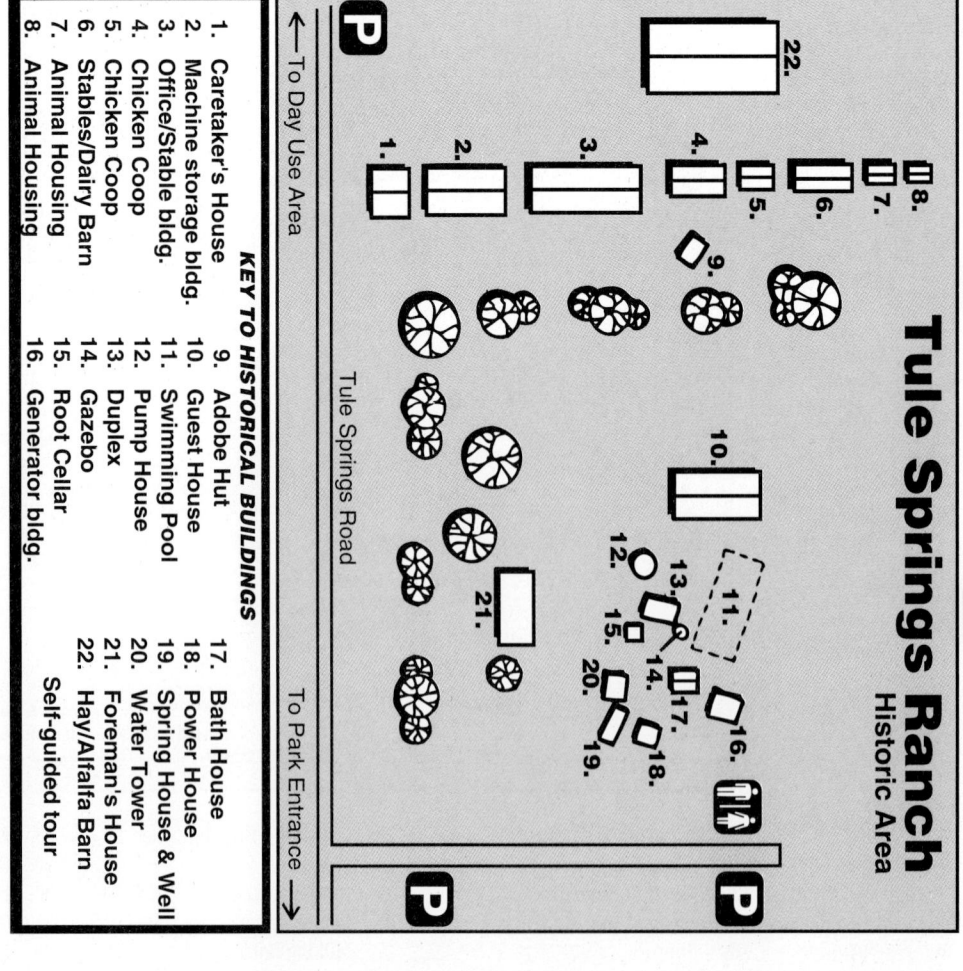

KEY TO HISTORICAL BUILDINGS

1. Caretaker's House	9. Adobe Hut	17. Bath House
2. Machine storage bldg.	10. Guest House	18. Power House
3. Office/Stable bldg.	11. Swimming Pool	19. Spring House & Well
4. Chicken Coop	12. Pump House	20. Water Tower
5. Chicken Coop	13. Duplex	21. Foreman's House
6. Stables/Dairy Barn	14. Gazebo	22. Hay/Alfalfa Barn
7. Animal Housing	15. Root Cellar	Self-guided tour
8. Animal Housing	16. Generator bldg.	

VALLEY OF FIRE STATE PARK

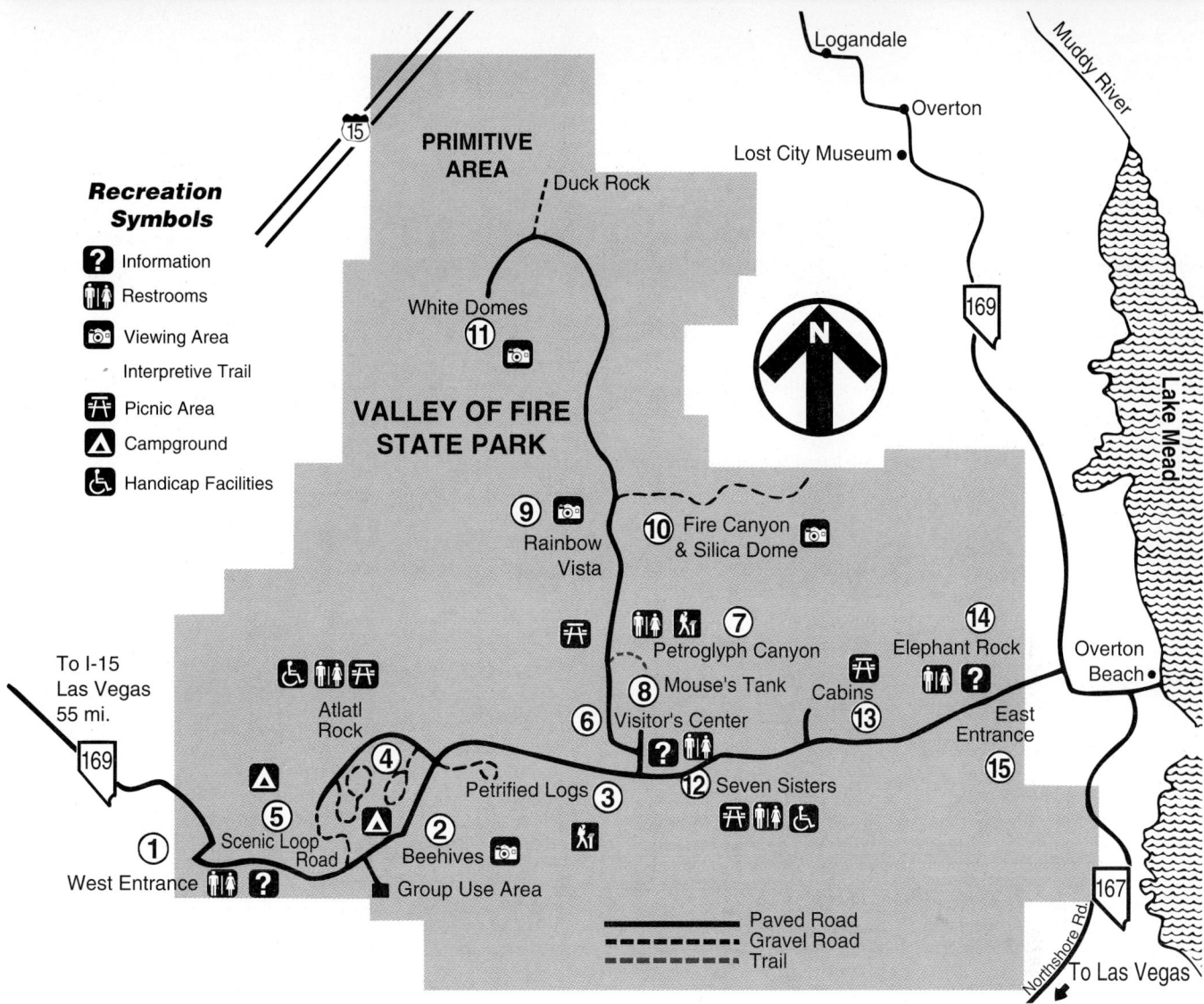

Recreation Symbols

- ? Information
- Restrooms
- Viewing Area
- Interpretive Trail
- Picnic Area
- Campground
- Handicap Facilities

PRIMITIVE AREA

Duck Rock

White Domes ⑪

VALLEY OF FIRE STATE PARK

N

Logandale

Overton

Lost City Museum

Muddy River

169

Lake Mead

⑨ Rainbow Vista

⑩ Fire Canyon & Silica Dome

⑦ Petroglyph Canyon

⑭ Elephant Rock

Overton Beach

⑧ Mouse's Tank

Cabins

East Entrance

⑥ Visitor's Center

⑬

⑮

To I-15 Las Vegas 55 mi.

169

Atlatl Rock

Petrified Logs ③

⑫ Seven Sisters

④

① West Entrance

⑤ Scenic Loop Road

② Beehives

Group Use Area

167

Northshore Rd.

To Las Vegas

——— Paved Road
- - - - Gravel Road
· · · · Trail

GREAT OUTDOORS (side tab)

Valley of Fire State Park Visitors Center
Box 515
Overton, NV 89040
397-2088
Gary Rimbey, Park Supvr.
Hours: Daily 8:30 am - 4:30 pm
Fees: $4 per vehicle; camping fee $11
Directions from Las Vegas: About 1 hour drive from Las Vegas, Valley of Fire is 55 mi. northwest on I-15 to State Route 169 to the visitors center. Also accessible via Lake Mead Blvd., North Shore Road and State Route 169. This route is about 10 miles longer but much more scenic.
History: Valley of Fire, dedicated in 1935, is Nevada's oldest state park. It encompasses over 46,000 acres and derives it's name from brilliant red sandstone formations that were formed from great shifting sand dunes over 150 million years ago. Complex uplifting and faulting of the region, followed by extensive erosion, have created the present topography. Ancient Indian petroglyphs can be seen at Atlotl Rock and Petroglyph Canyon.

MAPPING OF VALLEY OF FIRE STATE PARK

1. West Entrance Station: Maps, points of interest and information.

2. The Beehives: Unusual sandstone formations weathered by the eroding forces of wind and water. located near the group area entrance.

3. Petrified Logs: Logs and stumps washed into the area from ancient forest about 225 million years ago. There are two interpretive trails leading to the petrified logs.

4. Atlatl Rock: Site of many Indian petroglyphs, including a depiction of the atlatl ("at-lat-l"), a notched stick used to add speed and distance to a thrown spear. The atlatl was a predecessor to the bow and arrow.

5. Scenic Loop Road: A two mile trip around some of the Valley's most interesting formations such as Arch Rock and Piano Rock.

6. Visitor Center: Information, books, film and exhibits on the Valley and surrounding areas. Ranger Station located here.

7. Petroglyph Canyon Self Guiding Trail: A half mile (.8 km) round trip walk to Mouse's Tank through a sandy canyon, with trail markers to point out interesting features, including fine examples of pre-historic Indian rock writings.

8. Mouse's Tank: Named for a renegade Indian who used the area as a hideout in the 1890's. Mouse's Tank is a natural basin in the rock where water collects after a rainfall. Water occasionally remains in the tank for several months.

9. Rainbow Vista: A favorite photo point with a panoramic view of multi-colored sandstone.

10. Fire Canyon/Silica Dome: A trail offers an easy three mile (4.8 km) round trip walk from Rainbow Vista. From the vantage point, visitors have an excellent view of the deep red sandstone of Fire Canyon, and the unique geological features of Silica Dome.

11. White Domes Area: Brilliant contrast of sandstone colors with unique plants to the area such as the yucca. White Domes is a moderate, seven mile (11.2 km) round trip hike from Rainbow Vista. Please report in at the Visitor Center before going out, and be sure you have plenty of water on the hike.

12. Seven Sisters: Fascinating red rock formations, easily accessible from the road. Picnic areas provide a relaxing stop during your Valley tour.

13. The Cabins: Now a picnic area, these stone cabins were built with native sandstone by the CCC (Civilian Conservation Corps) in the 1930's as a shelter for passing travelers.

14. Elephant Rock: This well known formation accessible via a short trail from the east entrance station.

15. East Entrance Station: Mounted maps, information, restrooms and points of interest.

CAMPSITES

Death Valley National Monument
Campgrounds and RV Parks:
Information: 1-760-786-2331
Reservations for winter only Oct. - Apr. 30
1-800-365-2267
There are 9 campgrounds located throughout the park with more than 1,500 campsites. With the exception of the Furnace Creek Campground from Oct. to Apr., all campsites are available on a first come basis. Fees are $10 a night. Backcountry camping is available in many areas and some are free.

Toiyabe National Forest
Location: 35 mi. northwest of Las Vegas on US 95 and State Hwys. 156, 157, and 158.
Reservations: 1-800-280-2267 or 873-8800 for information.
Fee: $10 for single family sites; $20 for multi-family sites.
Season: 5 campgrounds are open May 1 through mid Sept. Handicapped sites available; flush or vault toilets.

Katherine Landing
602-754-3245
Open year round. For general information in vicinity of Katherine Landing, tune in to 1610 on AM radio.

Photo: Photodschnik International

National Park Service
602-754-3272
Area information, maps, publications and campground information.
Hours: 8 am - 4 pm
Directions from Las Vegas: 100 mi. south of Las Vegas via US 95 and State Route 163; just past Davis Dam make a left turn; about 4 mi. to marina.

Lake Mead Recreation Area
Alan Bible Visitors Center: 293-8906

Location: 25 mi. southeast of Las Vegas on US 93/95.
Fee: $10 per night.
Season: Campgrounds are open year round.
10 campgrounds with 810 campsites plus group camping for 125 and group camping for 90 motorhomes. Campgrounds offer water faucets, restrooms, picnic tables and barbecue grills.

Sportsmen's Park
P.O. Box 652
Laughlin, NV 89029
298-3377
26-acre park located on the Colorado River with picnic facilities, restrooms, 59 RV campsites, fishing, boat launch ramp, handicap access. No fee for day use, 6 am - 10 pm; $6 per day for camping, 11 am - 11 pm, with a 14-day limit.

Valley of Fire State Park
Visitors Center: 397-2088
Location: 35 mi. northwest of Las Vegas on I-15 and 20 mi. west on Hwy. 169.
Reservation: First-come basis
Fee: $11 per night
Season: Campgrounds are open year round.
51 campsites; water faucets, restrooms, hot showers and picnic tables.

Virgin River Canyon Recreation Area
St. George, UT
435-688-3246
Located 15 mi. southwest of St. George on I-15, east at the rest area exit. Fishing, trails, picnic tables, grills, restrooms, water available. 1st come-1st serve basis; 77 sites, $6 per day.

GHOST TOWNS

CALICO GHOST TOWN
P.O. Box 638
Yermo, CA 92398
1-619-254-2122 1-800-2-CALICO
Located 160 mi. south of Las Vegas. I-15 to Ghost Town Rd. exit 10 mi. north of Barstow.
Hours: 7 am - dusk; shops 9 am - 5 pm
Admission: $6 adults, $3 children.
Although today this is a thriving tourist attraction, Calico is actually a reproduction of its former self. A prosperous silver mining community from 1881 to 1896, when the price of silver dropped so low, mining here was abandoned. However, the discovery of boride kept the town going until 1907, after which it was completely abandoned.
In 1950, Walter Knott (of Knott's Berry Farm) purchased the town and rebuilt it with a mind toward authenticity and modern convenience.
With a 110-unit tree-lined campground, Calico is operated as part of the park system of San Bernardino County.

ELDORADO CANYON - NELSON
Pop. 50
42 mi. south of Las Vegas via US 95 to State Route 165.
In 1839 gold and silver were discovered in Eldorado Canyon and almost $5 million was removed in the 40 years of operations. This small mining town sprang up to accommodate the mines of the Eldorado Canyon. During it's heyday, it achieved a reputation as one of the most notorious towns in the West.
Today Nelson presents it's past through historic buildings and ancient mining ruins and is still inhabited by a few residents.

GOODSPRINGS
Pop. approx. 100
37 mi. south of Las Vegas via I-15 to Jean and State Route 161.
Founded in the 1860s, Goodsprings became a large silver and lead producer in the 1890s. This once thriving mining town still sports remains of its past. Clearly visible among the few occupied homes and businesses are abandoned mining buildings and equipment.
In January 1942, Goodsprings received notoriety as the base camp for film legend Clark Gable, who was awaiting word on the fate of his wife, actress Carole Lombard, whose plane crashed on nearby Potosi Mountain.
The Pioneer Saloon has been serving for over 75 years from what is said to be the oldest tin building in Nevada.

JOHNNIE
Pop. 0
Located 50 miles northwest of Las Vegas just east of State Route 160.
Johnnie produced more than $1 million in gold from 1904 until it was shut down at the beginning of World War II.

OATMAN
Pop. 100 - 200
Located on old US Route 66, 30 mi. from Laughlin.
Born as a tent camp for miners in 1906, Oatman was a gold-mining center. Shootouts are held along the many false-front buildings on Main Street which house shops, saloons and restaurants. Wild burros roam the streets.
Oatman Chamber of Commerce
Oatman, AZ 86433
1-520-768-9907

PIOCHE
Pop. 800 - Lincoln County - 4,020
175 mi. northeast of Las Vegas. Take I-15 to the turnoff at US 93, turn north for 85 mi. to Ash Springs, continue on US 93 east through Caliente. Pioche is about 25 mi. from Caliente.
One of the most dangerous and lawless mining towns, Pioche boasts a legend that 75 men died violently before the town's first death by natural causes. It gained further notoriety through the scandal surrounding it's "Million Dollar Courthouse." The Pioche cemetery's Boot Hill and many buildings in the old business district still exist. Pioche had a population of 10,000 in 1871.
Pioche Chamber of Commerce:
962-5544

POTOSI
Pop. 0
25 mi. southwest of Las Vegas via I-15 south to the Arden exit, US 160 West.
Site of Nevada's oldest lode mine, with the discovery of lead deposits by Mormons from the Las Vegas Mission in 1856, the Potosi mine was a producer of lead, zinc and silver well into the 20th century.

RHYOLITE
Pop. 0
Located 114 mi. northwest of Las Vegas via US 95 north to Beatty, State Route 374 4 miles west of Beatty.
A mining boomtown in the Bullfrog District 1905 - 1908, Rhyolite now sits a ghostly reminder of the prosperous town it once was, with over 6,000 residents in 1907. Different from most mining towns which were just tent cities, Rhyolite had a community swimming pool, ten-

nis court, hospital, two churches, a red light district, an opera house, hotel, two-story school, a railroad depot that still exists today, three banks and a newspaper.
The famous "Bottle House" was built almost entirely of bottles by saloon keeper Tommy Kelly from 31,000 Anheuser Busch beer bottles he collected from the 48 saloons in town. This and the railroad depot turned museum are major attractions here amid the ruins.

SANDY & SANDY VALLEY
Pop. 806
36 mi. southwest of Las Vegas. I-15 to Jean and State Route 161.
A small milling community that sprang up in the 1890s to service the Keystone Mine in the nearby Spring Mountains.

SEARCHLIGHT
Pop. 760
Fifty-seven mi. south of Las Vegas on US 95.
This mining town began around 1879 and in 1907 was the most important community in southern Nevada. However, by 1910 depletion of high grade ore soon reduced the population of Searchlight greatly, and those remaining made a living from ranching or catering to the highway traffic.

MOJAVE DESERT GHOST TOWNS
North of I-15 between the Nevada state line and Baker are many former mining towns all within a short drive of Las Vegas.

CITIES WITHIN A FIVE HOUR DRIVE

ARIZONA

Arizona has 204 golf courses, 2 national parks, 15 national monuments, 5 national forests, professional basketball and football teams, spring professional baseball training camps, and horse and greyhound racing.

Arizona Office of Tourism
1100 W. Washington
Phoenix, AZ 85007
1-602-230-7733
Travel center: 1-800-842-8257

BULLHEAD CITY
Located 95 mi. south of Las Vegas via US 95 to Hwy. 163; directly across the Colorado River from Laughlin.

Bullhead City was created in the early 1950s when construction crews moved to the area to build Davis Dam, which formed Lake Mohave. Bullhead City is the fastest growing city in the state, due to the Laughlin casinos.

Bullhead City Chamber of Commerce
1251 Hwy 95
P.O. Box 66
Bullhead City, AZ 86430
1-520-754-4121

FLAGSTAFF
pop. 52,000
265 mi. southeast of Las Vegas via US 93 to I-40.

Flagstaff is one of the highest cities in the nation at 7,000 ft. The area has four classic seasons with skiing at the Snow Bowl just outside of town. Flagstaff is home to Northern Arizona University with over 13,000 students. Several Indian art festivals are held each summer. The Grand Canyon is only 90 minutes from Flagstaff.

Annual Events:
February - Flagstaff Winter Festival
June - Pine Country Pro Rodeo
July - Annual Festival of Native American Arts; Indian Arts Association Pow Wow
August - Annual Festival in the Pines

Flagstaff Chamber of Commerce
100 W. Rte. 66
Flagstaff, AZ 86001
1-520-774-4505

Convention & Visitors Bureau
1-520-779-7611
Visitors Center: 1-520-774-9541
1-800-842-7293

LAKE HAVASU CITY
pop. 42,000
Directions from Las Vegas: 150 mi. south of Las Vegas on US 95 to I-40 east.

Founded in the mid-1960s by Bob "Chainsaw" McCulloch to test his outboard motors. In 1971 he bought the London Bridge, had it dismantled and shipped to Long Beach and then trucked to Lake Havasu.

Annual Events: October - London Bridge Days

Lake Havasu Area Visitors & Convention Bureau
1930 Mesquite Ave., Ste. 3
Lake Havasu City, AZ 86403
1-520-855-4115 1-800-242-8278

PHOENIX
Maricopa County
Directions from Las Vegas: US 93 south, 287 mi.

Population: 2,500,000, metro 1,200,000
The Phoenix area grew by 69 percent between 1970 and 1990; nation's ninth largest city. Twenty-three communities make up the Phoenix area with a total population of about 2 million people. Located on 430 sq. mi. in the heart of the Sonoran Desert at an elevation of 1,110 ft. Warm temperatures and low humidity, with an average temperature of 54 degrees in January and 90 degrees in July, make Phoenix a desirable place to vacation or to live.

Attractions:
Big Surf (water theme park):
947-7873
Phoenix Greyhound Park
(dog racing): 273-7181
Phoenix International Raceway
(auto racing): 252-2227
Phoenix Zoo: 273-1341
State Capitol: 542-4900
Turf Paradise (horse racing Oct. - May): 942-1101

Professional Sports:
Phoenix Cardinals NFL team, plays Aug. through Dec. at Sun Devil Stadium in Tempe. Sun Devil Stadium also hosts the annual nationally televised Fiesta Bowl on New Year's Day.
Phoenix Suns NBA team play Oct. through Mar. at America West Arena.

Five professional baseball teams have spring training facilities in the Phoenix area during Mar. and Apr.
Golf:
Phoenix has 108 golf courses from 9-hole to 18-hole championship courses. The Phoenix Open is held in Jan. and the Arizona Open is held in Nov.

Information Sources:
Phoenix & Valley of the Sun Convention & Visitor Bureau
One Arizona Center
400 E. Van Buren St., Ste. 600
Phoenix, AZ 85004-2290
1-602-254-6500
FAX: (602) 253-4415

Visitor Information Center
Northwest Corner of Adams and Second St.
Hyatt Regency Hotel Block
Hours: 8 am - 4:30 pm, Mon. - Fri.
Visitor Information and Activity Hotline: 1-602-252-5588

Phoenix Chamber of Commerce
1-602-254-5521

SEDONA
pop. 16,000
Directions from Las Vegas: US 93 south to Kingman; from Kingman take I-40 east to 179.

This area continues as a thriving mecca for art lovers and collectors who are drawn to this community by the more than 25 commercial galleries featuring paintings, sculptures and art objects. The natural beauty of the red rocks makes this resort area unique in the country, and provides a beautiful backdrop for the many boutiques found here containing unique mementos and handmade arts and crafts.

Sedona/Oak Creek Chamber of Commerce
Corner 89A/Forest Rd.
Sedona, AZ 86336
1-520-282-7722   1-800-288-7336

CALIFORNIA

LOS ANGELES
Directions from Las Vegas: I-15 south about 282 mi. southwest of Las Vegas.
Population: 3,638,100; average temperature 57 degrees in Jan. and 70 degrees in July.

Attractions:
Catalina Island
Chamber of Commerce: 310-510-1520
Crystal Cathedral
Garden Grove: 714-971-4000
Disneyland, Anaheim: 714-999-4565
Hollywood Bowl
Hollywood: 213-850-2000
Hollywood Wax Museum
Hollywood: 213-462-8860
Knott's Berry Farm
Buena Park: 714-220-5200
Los Angeles Zoo
Los Angeles: 213-666-4090
Magic Mountain
Valencia: 818-367-5965
Movieland Wax Museum
Buena Park: 714-522-1155
NBC Studios Tour
Burbank: 818-840-3537
Sunset Strip - Sunset Blvd.
Universal Studios Tour
Universal City: 818-622-3801

Sports:
California Angels: 714-634-2000
Hollywood Park (horse racing)
310-419-1500
Los Alamitos (horse racing)
714-995-1234
Los Angeles Clippers (basketball)
213-748-0500
Los Angeles Dodger (baseball)
213-224-1500
Los Angeles Kings (hockey)
310-673-1300
Los Angeles Lakers (basketball)
310-673-1300
Mighty Ducks (hockey)
714-995-1234
Santa Anita (horse racing)
818-574-7223

Information Sources:
Anaheim Chamber of Commerce
100 S. Anaheim Blvd., Ste. 300
Anaheim, CA 92805
714-758-0222

Big Bear Lake Valley Chamber of Commerce
630 Bartlett Rd.
P.O. Box 2860
Big Bear Lake, CA 92315
909-8664

Los Angeles Chamber of Commerce
350 S. Bixel St.
Los Angeles, CA 90017
213-580-7500

Los Angeles Visitors and Convention Bureau
685 S. Figueroa St.
Los Angeles, CA 90071
213-689-8822   1-800-CATCHLA

Palm Springs Convention and Visitors Bureau
69-930 Highway 111, Ste. 201
Rancho Mirage, CA 92270
619-770-9000
1-800-96 RESORTS

Santa Barbara Visitors Center
1 Santa Barbara St.
P.O. Box 299
Santa Barbara, CA 93102
805-965-3021

SAN DIEGO
Directions from Las Vegas: I-15 south 331 mi. southwest of Las Vegas.

San Diego is the southern most city in California, with Tijuana just across the border. San Diego has 70 mi. of beaches and the sun shines almost every day of the year. The average temperature is 58 degrees in Jan. and 70 degrees in July.

Attractions:
Mission Bay Visitors & Information Center
2688 E. Mission Bay Dr.
San Diego, CA 92109
619-276-8200
Balboa Park (northeast of downtown, north of Russ Blvd.): 619-239-0512
Del Mar (horse racing): 619-755-1141
Navy Base, Broadway Pier: 619-532-1430
Old Town - North of I-5
and Washington St.
San Diego Chargers (football):
619-280-2111
San Diego Gulls (hockey):
619-224-4625
San Diego Padres (baseball):
619-283-4494
San Diego Sports Arena 619-225-9813
San Diego Wild Animal Park
Escondido: 619-234-6541
San Diego Zoo: 619-234-3153
Sea World: 619-226-3901

Information Sources:
San Diego Chamber of Commerce
402 W. Broadway, Ste. 1000
San Diego, CA 92101
1-619-232-0124

San Diego Convention and Visitors Bureau
11 Horton Plaza
San Diego, CA 92101
1-619-236-1212

CITIES WITHIN A FIVE HOUR DRIVE

UTAH

CEDAR CITY
pop. over 20,000
Interstate 15 north through St. George
175 mi. from Las Vegas.
Utah Tourism: 1-800-233-8824

Attractions:
Brian Head Ski Resort
Major Events: June - Sept. - Utah
Shakespearean Festival

Information Source:
**Cedar City Chamber of
Commerce**
280 N. Main St.
Cedar City, UT 84720
1-801-586-4484

ST. GEORGE
pop. 38,000
Take I-15 north from Las Vegas about 2
hours and 125 mi. from Las Vegas.

Attractions:
St. George Mormon Temple - completed
in 1877, the St. George Temple was built
even before the Salt Lake Temple.

Walking guides to St. George are avail-
able from the Visitors Center, which
lists 22 points of interest including
Brigham Young's winter home, the old
Washington County Courthouse and the
Tabernacle.

Major Attractions:
Zion National Park

Information Sources:
**St. George Chamber of
Commerce**
100 E. St. George Blvd.
St. George, UT 84770
1-801-628-1658

**Washington County Travel and
Convention Bureau:**
1-800-869-6635

HOT SPRINGS

Out from Las Vegas are several hot spring sites, both public and private which
are enjoyed most in the cold winter months.

ARIZONA HOT SPRINGS
A 6 mile hike of approximately 5 hours. Starting at the Alan Bible Visitors
Center, travel east on US 93 about 4.2 mi. beyond Hoover Dam. There is parking in White Rock Canyon on the right. Go through the canyon down to the
river and head south for 1/4 mile. In a side canyon you will find the hot
springs. The springs can also be reached by boat.

GOLDSTRIKE HOT SPRINGS
A treacherous 6 mile hike of approximately 4 hours. Beginning at the Alan
Bible Visitor Center at Lake Mead, take US 93 east. Just past the Gold Strike
Casino (about 1/2 mile) is a paved road which takes off on the right and after
a steep descent becomes a dirt road. After parking in an open wash, hike into
the canyon parallel to the highway. Follow this rocky wash to the hot springs.
Springs can also be reached by boat.

ROGERS SPRINGS
Part of the Lake Mead National Recreation area, Rogers Springs is located 15
mi. south of Overton on North Shore Rd., just past the Echo Bay turnoff. Large
tamarisk trees shade the natural warm spring gravel-bottom shallow wading
pool. The day-use area has picnic tables.

Sports & Recreation

Sports enthusiasts world over love Las Vegas. On any given day, Las Vegas offers limitless possiblities from watersports to rock climbing to hunting for elk, bighorn sheep and wild turkey, to teeing off on any number of championship golf courses or serving it up on one of the fine tennis courts available.

For those who prefer to observe rather than to participate, Las Vegas is the undisputed boxing capital of the world, hosting such phenomenal bouts as in 1994, when George Foreman defeated Michael Moorer to win the IBF and WBA heavyweight titles at the MGM Grand Garden Arena. Las Vegas was also the site for Mike Tyson's comeback in 1995. The annual National Finals Rodeo is held at the Thomas & Mack Center the first week in December. The world's richest rodeo attracts the top 15 money winners in seven events.

Las Vegas is a leader in off-road racing with national races held in the area annually. Located on Las Vegas Blvd. S., near Nellis Air Force Base, Las Vegas Motor International Speedway holds professional stock car and drag races throughout the year. The 135,000-seat Speedway opened in 1996 and contracted with Indy Racing League, beginning September, 1996.

The mild weather in Las Vegas makes for great golfing year-round. Clark County currently has more than 30 golf courses, with many more proposed. In the Las Vegas area there are 35 eighteen hole courses and one nine hole course. Las Vegas is a stop on the PGA, with the Las Vegas Invitational held in October when players from around the world are invited to compete for over $15 million in prizes. Las Vegas is also a stop on the LPGA held in November at the Desert Inn Country Club.

Tennis anyone? There over 200 tennis courts in the area, many of which are lighted for night-time play, and local racquetball facilities have turned out a number of top contenders in the sport. Las Vegas is home to No. 1 ranked tennis star Andre Agassi and tennis great Michael Chang lives in nearby Henderson.

If it's bowling you are after, four hotel-casinos and three casinos have bowling centers. The Showboat Hotel is the oldest stop on the PBA Tour, held each January.

Through the fall and into the spring months, you can actually snow ski and water ski in the same day, with Lake Mead and Mt. Charleston both less than one hour outside of town.

The University of Nevada Las Vegas Runnin' Rebels basketball team was the 1990 NCAA National Champions and second in 1991.

Horseback riding is available at a number of places including Bonnie Springs Old Nevada, where horseback riding is available seven days a week and takes you through the spectacular Red Rock Canyon, for a totally unique sightseeing experience.

Amateur sports in Las Vegas include soccer, basketball, flag football and softball among others. Home of one of the few privately operated softball complexes in the United States, the Las Vegas Softball Center is located on Las Vegas Blvd. S., south of Blue Diamond Rd. The center has five fields and offers year-round competition.

AERIAL SPORTS

AIRPLANE RIDES

Classic Biplanes
655-3653
North Las Vegas Airport
Rides, tours and aerobatics

FLIGHT INSTRUCTION

Aerleon Inc.
North Las Vegas Airport
2634 Airport Dr., Ste. 101
N. Las Vegas, NV 89030
647-6100
Don Flaherty, Owner
Hours: 7 am - 9 pm daily
Single and multi-engine FAA approved flight training, motor glider training/rental; pilot supplies

Desert Southwest Airlines
500 E. Hwy. 146
Las Vegas, NV 89124
263-9520
Chuck Herman, Dir. of Operations
Primary and advanced training; charter, sightseeing and aerial photography; single and multi engine aircraft; aircraft rentals.

Sundance Helicopters Inc.
265 E. Tropicana Ave., Ste. 130
Las Vegas, NV 89109
736-0606
Rick Eisenreich, Pres.
Custom charter flight training and tours.

Ultralight Flying Machines Inc.
14555 Eldorado Canyon
Henderson, NV 89015
564-1922
Don "Hawk" Wyatt, Pres.
US UA instructors, sales and rentals, repairs and demo rides, 70 planes. Closed Monday.

HANG GLIDING

The U.S. Hang Gliding Association
P. O. Box 1330
Colorado Springs, CO 80901
1-719-632-8300 1-800-616-6888
Instructions all over the country, call for information.

Flyaway, 200 Convention Center Dr., Las Vegas, NV 89109
The country's only skydiving simulator

PARACHUTE JUMPING

Flyaway
200 Convention Center Dr.
Las Vegas, NV 89109
731-4768
Gary Speer, Owner
Hours: Seasonal; please call ahead
The country's only skydiving simulator. Indoor 21 foot vertical wind tunnel with air speed up to 115 mph. $24 for first fall; $19.50 for repeat flights. After about 15 minutes of instructions you get about fifteen minutes of flying time in the tunnel shared by five other flyers. Flights are videotaped and copies can be made. Flyaway has an observation gallery which the $2 admission applies to your flight if you fly.

Skydive Las Vegas Inc.
1401 Airport Rd.
Boulder City, NV 89005
293-1860
Michael Hawkes, Pres.
Boulder City Airport; free shuttle; licensed instructor; beginner, novice, expert.
Discover skydiving with the Tandem Jump. After a half hour lesson you'll jump with your instructor with you with a parachute built for two. Beginning jumps $199

Thrillseekers Unlimited
3172 N. Rainbow Blvd., Ste. 321
Las Vegas, NV 89108
699-5550
Fax: 699-5551
Rich Hopkins, Owner
Credit Cards: MC, Visa

Price: $189; $75 for photos and video
Paragliding: Thrillseekers offers paragliding from beginning to Class III rating; Towing available!! Several take off spots around Las Vegas. Learn to fly with the pros!!

The British School of Paragliding
P. O. Box 50382
Henderson, NV 89016
896-6000
Patrick Sugrue, Pres.
Paragliding $350 per day; trike instructions $1000; pagojets.

HOT AIR BALLOONING

Las Vegas, Laughlin, and Reno all have annual balloon races and events. The Las Vegas Balloon Classic is held in October at the Silver Bowl Park. The event attracts over 100 balloons and features craft and food booths, demonstrations and exhibits.

Balloon Safaris
2039 Civic Center Dr., Ste. 282
N. Las Vegas, NV 89030
259-6705
Roger Stadtmueller
Hot air balloon flights with licensed pilots. Season runs from November to the end of April. Specials available.

Nevada High Inc.
873-8393
Joe Hanna, Pres.
Balloon rides, advertising, instruction in your balloon or theirs. Balloon rides $125 per person.

The Ultimate Balloon Adventure
2013 Clover Path
Las Vegas, NV 89128
221-9199
Bob Bowers, Pres.
Fly with commercially licensed pilots in a colorful hot air balloon. Flights start before sunrise or just before sunset when the air is still. Each flight is totally unique and a different experience. Daily one to one and a half hour flight with champagne celebration $125.00 per person with a minimum of two people. Pre-dawn flights $175.00 per person.

BUNGEE JUMPING

A. J. Hackett Bungy
810 Circus Circus Dr.
Las Vegas, NV 89109
385-4321
Mike Champoux, Gen. Mgr.
Hours: Vary; call for details
Cost: One jump - $59; $25 every jump after first; every 4th jump free
Credit Cards: M/C, Visa
201 foot tower with elevator, jump into a sparkling pool. Free T-shirt and certificate with first jump. 90,000 gallon pool to touch water from 171 feet.

Thrillseekers Unlimited
3172 N. Rainbow Blvd., Ste. 321
Las Vegas, NV 89108
699-5550
Fax: 699-5551
Rich Hopkins, Owner
Credit Cards: MC, Visa
Cost: $100 for 2 jumps

The Screamer
MGM Grand Adventures Theme Park
3805 Las Vegas Blvd. S.
Las Vegas, NV 89109
891-1111
The Screamer puts 1 - 3 people in a flight harness and lifts the flyers to the top of a 250 ft. launching tower. Flyers pull their own ripcord which sets in motion a 100 ft. free-fall plunge before they swoop into a 70 mph swing.
Call for hours and prices.

AUTO RACING & ATV RIDING

AUTO RACING

Las Vegas Motor Speedway
7000 Las Vegas Blvd. N.
Las Vegas, NV 89115
644-4444
Richie Clyne, CEO
Robert Bahre, Pres.
NASCAR type auto racing track was completed September 1996 at a cost of $72 million. Host to Indy Car and Indy Racing League events, the raceway offers seats

for 135,000 on 1,500 acres. The first race was held September 15, 1996, a 200-mile Indy Racing League Event.

ATV AND MOTORCYCLE CASUAL USE AREAS

Eldorado Dry Lake Area - US 93/95 to US 95 heading for Laughlin. You'll see the dry lake bed on the right.

Nelson Hills Area - US 93/95 to US 95 toward Laughlin. Continue past the dry lake bed to Highway 165. Turn left and travel 3.6 miles to the second power line road. Turn right and proceed south to cleared area.
Jean Dry Lake Area - I-15 south to the Sloan exit. Turn right and cross under I-15. Turn right onto the old Los Angeles Highway. Travel 9 miles and turn left onto the county maintained road, where you will see the dry lake bed on your left.

Las Vegas Dunes Area - I-15 north to the Apex/Las Vegas Blvd. exit. Turn right on Las Vegas Boulevard and travel 1.7 miles. Turn left onto the pipeline road.
Dry Lake Valley Area - I-15 north to the Pioche/Ely exit. Turn left and proceed under the freeway. Use the power line road 1/2 mile from the exit or choose an existing jeep trail within the next three miles.

BOWLING

BOWLING

Most bowling centers are located in hotel/casinos where you can bowl 24 hours a day. All the bowling centers listed below have the most up-to-date equipment and pro shops. The Showboat, the largest bowling center in Nevada, is the oldest stop on the PBA tour which is held in January. The Santa Fe has Bowlervision, which tracks the speed and path the ball takes from the time it leaves your hand until it hits the head pin.

BOWLING LANES

Boulder Bowl
504 California St.
Boulder City, NV 89005
293-2368
Dick Winters, Owner
Hours: varies; open bowling Sat. - Sun. 10 am - 6 pm & 9:30 pm - midnight; League play evenings beginning at 5:30 pm

Gold Coast Hotel
4000 W. Flamingo Rd.
Las Vegas, NV 89103
367-4700
Robert Prevost, Mgr.
Hours: 24 hrs.
Fees: Mon. - Fri. $1.90 per game; Srs. (55 & up) $1.35; Jrs.(16 & under) $1.55; $1.25 shoe rental
Sat., Sun. & holidays $1.90 for all
72 lanes; closed periodically for league bowling; Pro shop & resident pro.

Terrible's Town Casino & Bowl
642 S. Boulder Hwy.
Henderson, NV 89015
564-7118
Steve Beckman, Mgr.
Hours: 24 hrs.
Fees: Mon. - Fri. $1.75, under 12 $1.24; Sat & Sun. $1.95 for all; Shoes $1.25
16 lanes, bar, slot & video poker machines & snack bar.

The Orleans Hotel
4500 W. Tropicana Ave.
Las Vegas, NV 89103
365-7111
Mike Monyak, Mgr.
Hours: 24 hrs.
Fees: adults $2.10; Srs. & Jrs. $1.60 5:30 pm - 9:30 pm - league play
70 lanes & a pro shop.

Sam's Town Hotel
5111 Boulder Hwy.
Las Vegas, NV 89122
456-7777
Mike Kaufman, Mgr.

League coordinator: 454-8022
Hours: 24 hrs.
Fees: Mon. - Fri. $1.70; Jr. & Srs. $1.30; Sat. -Sun. & holidays $1.75 for all; shoe rental $1.50
Closed for league bowling Sun - Fri 5:30 pm - 11 pm; Sat. 5:30 pm - 9 pm
56 lanes, automatic scoring, pro shop & resident pro.

Santa Fe Hotel
4949 N. Rancho Dr.
Las Vegas, NV 89130
658-4995
Bud Horn, Mgr.
Hours: 24 hrs.
Fees: based on per hour, per lane. Mon. - Fri. 9 am - 5:30 pm - adults; $8.50; Jrs. (18 and under) & Srs. (55 and over) $7.50; Mon. - Thu. 6 pm - midnight $10.50; Fri. - Sat. 6 pm - midnight $12.50; Sat. - Sun 9 am - 5:30 pm $12; Daily - midnight - 8 am $7.50; shoes $1.50
60 lanes & pro shop.

Showboat Hotel
2800 Fremont St.
Las Vegas, NV 89104
385-9153
Jack Cook, Mgr.
Hours: 24 hrs.
Closed during league bowling.
Fees: adults $2.50; Jrs. (18 & under) & Srs. (55 and over) $1.65; shoe rental - $1.75
106 championship lanes, PBA host, pro shop & resident pro.

Silver Nugget
2140 Las Vegas Blvd. N.
N. Las Vegas, NV 89030
657-2750
Donna Ibierski, Mgr.
Hours: 9 am - midnight
Fees: $1.50 before 6 pm; $2 after 6 pm; Jrs. & Srs. $1.50; Shoe rental $1
The only bowling alley in Las Vegas with Cosmic Bowling & laser lights.

Sunset Lanes
4565 E. Sunset Rd.
Henderson, NV 89014
736-2695
Jimmy Fuji, Gen. Mgr.
Hours: Sun. - Thu. 8:30 am - 1 am; Fri. - Sat. 24 hrs.
Fees: $1.50 before 6 pm; $2.10 after 6 pm; shoe rental $1.50
For league information call Kathy at above number.
40 lanes

BOWLING EQUIPMENT & APPAREL

Other than the pro shops, which are located in the bowling alleys there are three stores that specialize in selling bowling supplies.

Action Bowling Supply
5645 S. Eastern Ave.
Las Vegas, NV 89119
891-8855
Frank Harper, Owner
Hours: Mon. - Fri. noon - 7 pm; Sat. 10 am - 8 pm

Excellence Pro Shop
2101 S. Decatur Blvd., Ste. 12
Las Vegas, NV 89102
873-4493
Gary Higashi, Owner
Hours: Mon. - Sat. 10 am - 6 pm

Todd's Bowling Supply
2245 N. Decatur Blvd.
Las Vegas, NV 89108
646-7273
Jack Todd, Owner
Hours: Wed. - Sat. noon - 7 pm

BOWLING ORGANIZATIONS

For league information you can contact your local bowling alley or one of the following associations:

Las Vegas Women's Bowling Association
3111 S. Valley View Blvd., Ste. 0102
Las Vegas, NV 89102
362-0276
Linda Spaulding, Secretary
Promotes bowling in sanctioned leagues.

Southern Nevada Bowling Association
3111 S. Valley View Blvd., Ste. 0102
Las Vegas, NV 89102
362-5550
Walter Kuhn, Pres.
Men's association.

SPORTS

BASEBALL, BILLIARDS AND BOXING

BASEBALL/SOFTBALL

Amateur Softball Association
260-7803
Ralph Reuber

Boulder City Parks & Recreation
293-9256
Tay Deering

City of Las Vegas
229-2089
Bobby McRoy

Clark County
455-8200
Mike Krauss

Henderson
434-4131
Lenore Budyach

National Softball Association
896-3053
Marty Lally

North Las Vegas
633-1605
Neil Gallant

Scandia Family Fun Center
2900 Sirius Ave.
Las Vegas, NV 89102
364-0070
Wayne Larson, Gen. Mgr.
Parties-groups: 364-0071
Hours: Sun. - Thu. 10 am - 11 pm; Fri. - Sat. 10 am - midnight; closes one hour earlier in winter.
Batting range (baseball or softball) - 25 pitches $1.25; also by time - 15, 30 and 60 minutes

Sports Hall of Fame
(Las Vegas Club)
18 Fremont St.
Las Vegas, NV 89109
385-1664
Hours: 24 Hours
Admission: Free
Primarily baseball memorabilia including World Series bats from 1946 through 1958.

BILLIARDS

In addition to the listings below, most area bars have pool tables.

The Barking Frog
5150 Spring Mountain Rd.
Las Vegas, NV 89102
248-4370
John Card, Mgr.
Hours: 24 hrs.
Fees: $5 per table
Facilities: 13 9 ft. tournament tables, dance floor, video poker, big-screen TV, 24 hour restaurant serving primarily Italian food.

Crystal Palace Billiards
2411 E. Bonanza Rd.
Las Vegas, NV 89101
384-6734
Frank Torres, Mgr.
Hours: 24 hrs.
Fees: 1 person - $3 hr.; 2 people - $6 hr.; 3 people - $8.10 hr.; 4 people $10 hr.
22 tables, one snooker table, refreshments, slot and video games.

Cue Club
953 E. Sahara Ave.
Las Vegas, NV 89104
735-2884
Henry Nojiec, Owner
Hours: 24 hrs.
Fees: $3.50 per hr. per person
Facilities: 46 tables, 1 snooker table, video poker, arcade games. Tournaments. Food - burgers, fingers, beer. Monday night is ladies night.

Cue-Topia
860 E. Twain Ave.
Las Vegas, NV 89109
737-6998
Betty Miers, Mgr.
Hours: 24 hrs.
Fees: $3.60 per hr. per person
Facilities: 19 tables; cue shop and repair. Children welcome.

Family Billiards
1089 E. Tropicana Ave.
Las Vegas, NV 89119
736-1568
Jim Bunker

Hours: 24 hrs.
Fees: $2.50 per hr. per person
Facilities: 14 tables
No one under 21; 24 hour grill, video poker.

Mickey's Cue & Brews
7380 S. Eastern Ave.
Las Vegas, NV 89123
361-2060
Brian Stark, Mgr.
Hours: 24 hrs.
Fees: $4 per person per hr.
Facilities: 13 tables and 4 small bar tables; tournaments

Pink E's Fun, Food & Spirits
4170 S. Valley View Blvd.
Las Vegas, NV 89117
252-4666
Mike Smith, Gen. Mgr.
Cover Charge: After 8 pm $2 - $4
Fees: $.50 per game on pink tables and $6.00 per hour on regulation-size tables. Restaurants, daiquiri bar, dance floor, big-screen TV and monitors, video poker and video games. Playboy magazine pin-ups in the men's restroom and Playgirl magazine pin-ups in the women's restroom.

Pool Sharks
3650 S. Decatur Blvd.
Las Vegas, NV 89103
222-1011
Lou Butera, Mgr.
Hours: 24 hrs.
Fees: $3.50 per hour or $7 per hour for 2 or more people
Facilities: 21 4.5' x 9' tables; 5 bar size

Sidepocket East
2162 N. Lamb Blvd.
Las Vegas, NV 89115
459-7711
Randy Glockzin
Hours: Sun. - Thu. 11 am - midnight; Fri.-Sat. noon - 2 am
Cover charge: Before 4 pm: 1 - 3 people - $3 per hour; 4 - 6 people: $4 per hour; After 4 pm 1 - 2 people $4 per hour; 3 - 4 people $5 per hour; 5 - 6 people $6 per hour
Facilities: 12 tables

BOXING

Las Vegas plays host to many professional fight championships each year. Major cards are held at MGM Grand Garden, Caesars Palace, The Mirage and the Las Vegas Hilton in addition to the Thomas & Mack Center. Minor cards are held occasionally at the Silver Nugget, Boulder Station, Buffalo Bills, Arizona Charlie's, Sahara, Riviera, Bally's and other hotels in addition to the matches held at the Golden Gloves Gym. The first legal prize fight in the United States was held in Carson City on March 17, 1897. It was a fight between Gentleman Jim Corbett and Bob Fitzsimmons.

Nevada State Athletic Comm.
555 E. Washington Ave., Ste. 1500
Las Vegas, NV 89101
486-2575
Marc Ratner, Exec. Dir.

Barry's Boxing
3850 Vanessa Dr.
Las Vegas, NV 89103
368-2696
Pat Barry
Amateur boxing.
Dues: $35 per month

Golden Gloves Gym
1602 Gragson Ave.
Las Vegas, NV 89101
649-3535
Hal Miller
Amateurs and professional.
Dues: $25 for amateur and $35 for pros.

Nevada Partners
Sugar Ray Leonard Boxing Gym
710 W. Lake Mead Blvd.
N. Las Vegas, NV 89030
399-5627
Richard Steele, Mgr.
Hours: Mon. - Fri. 8 am - 6 pm; Sat. 10 am - 2 pm
Open to all youths of Las Vegas, 9 years and older, training and amateur boxing matches.

Top Rank Gym
3041 Business Ln.
Las Vegas, NV 89103
739-1501
Mitch Hampp, Mgr.
(not open to the public)

CYCLING AND RUNNING

CYCLING AND RUNNING

BIKE TRAILS/ROUTES

Red Rock Scenic Loop:
14.7 miles beginning and ending at the Red Rock Visitors Center. This wide, one way road goes through scenic Red Rock Canyon. The course goes uphill for the first 5 miles, the next 8 miles are either flat or downhill and then ending with a steep slope. There are also a lot of switchbacks along the loop.

Las Vegas to Red Rock:
An 11 mile course along West Charleston Blvd. from Rainbow Blvd. to the Red Rock Visitors Center. The road has bike paths and a good shoulder. You could either head back from here which

would make this a 22 mile ride or add the Red Rock Scenic Loop described above for a 37 mile ride.

Highway ride from Red Rock to Blue Diamond:
Travel from the Visitors Center uphill to the city park in Blue Diamond and back again. The ride is 7.6 miles in each direction. The road has good shoulders and offers long grades of flat recuperation stretches.

Floyd Lamb State Park:
Take U.S. 95 north to Durango, turn right, then it's about 3 miles to the park entrance. Round trip is approximately 20 miles with a good shoulder all the way.

Las Vegas to Boulder City/Lake Mead:
Starting on Boulder Highway, near

Tropicana Ave., head east on Boulder Highway to Boulder City. There is a shoulder and a gradual hill all the way to Boulder City, the trip is about 25 miles one-way. If you continue through Boulder City you can reach Lake Mead.

Old Los Angeles Highway:
Start at Hacienda Ave. and head south on Las Vegas Blvd. going toward Jean.

MOUNTAIN BIKING

Mt. Charleston:
Bikes are allowed only on the Bristlecone Pine Trail in the Mt. Charleston area of Toiyabe National Forest. This course is a six-mile loop which climbs 1,400 ft. This area can be at the top of the Lee Canyon ski area or at the end of the dirt road just before the McWilliams Campground.

Cottonwood Valley:
Take I-15 south to the Blue Diamond Rd. exit (160). Go 5.9 miles west from I-15 and turn-off to the left. Parking is located .5 mile from the highway where the pack-in, pack-out sign is. The course is a 14 mile circle.

BICYCLE RENTALS/TOURS

Bikes USA
1539 N. Eastern Ave.
Las Vegas, NV 89101
642-2453
David Lutz, Owner
Hours: Mon. - Fri. 10 am - 6 pm; Sat. 10 am - 5 pm
BMX racing, recumbent, repairs, rentals, touring & commuting

There's More Fun On Board For You!

THE ALL NEW 'BOAT FEATURES:

- 453 deluxe rooms including 4 suites & 1 hospitality room

- Beautifully renovated 80,000 square foot casino including 1500 high-paying slot and video poker machines, table games, keno, and a race & sports book

- 4 great restaurants including The Captain's Buffet, our 24 hour Coffee Shop and 2 specialty restaurants - Di Napoli featuring Southern Italian cuisine, and the Plantation Room, featuring steak and seafood

- 106-lane championship bowling center - Home of the PBA Tour

- Las Vegas' largest bingo parlor, offering the "highest payouts in town"

- Live entertainment in the Mardi Gras Lounge

- Meeting facilities for 25 to 1100 people

- Convenient valet services as well as covered and surface parking

- Free airport shuttle

- Fully-equipped RV Park with 84 spaces available

SHOWBOAT

HOTEL, CASINO & BOWLING CENTER
2800 Fremont Street • On the Boulder Strip
Las Vegas, Nevada • 89104
(800) 826-2800 • (702) 385-9123
www.showboat-lv.com

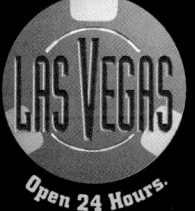

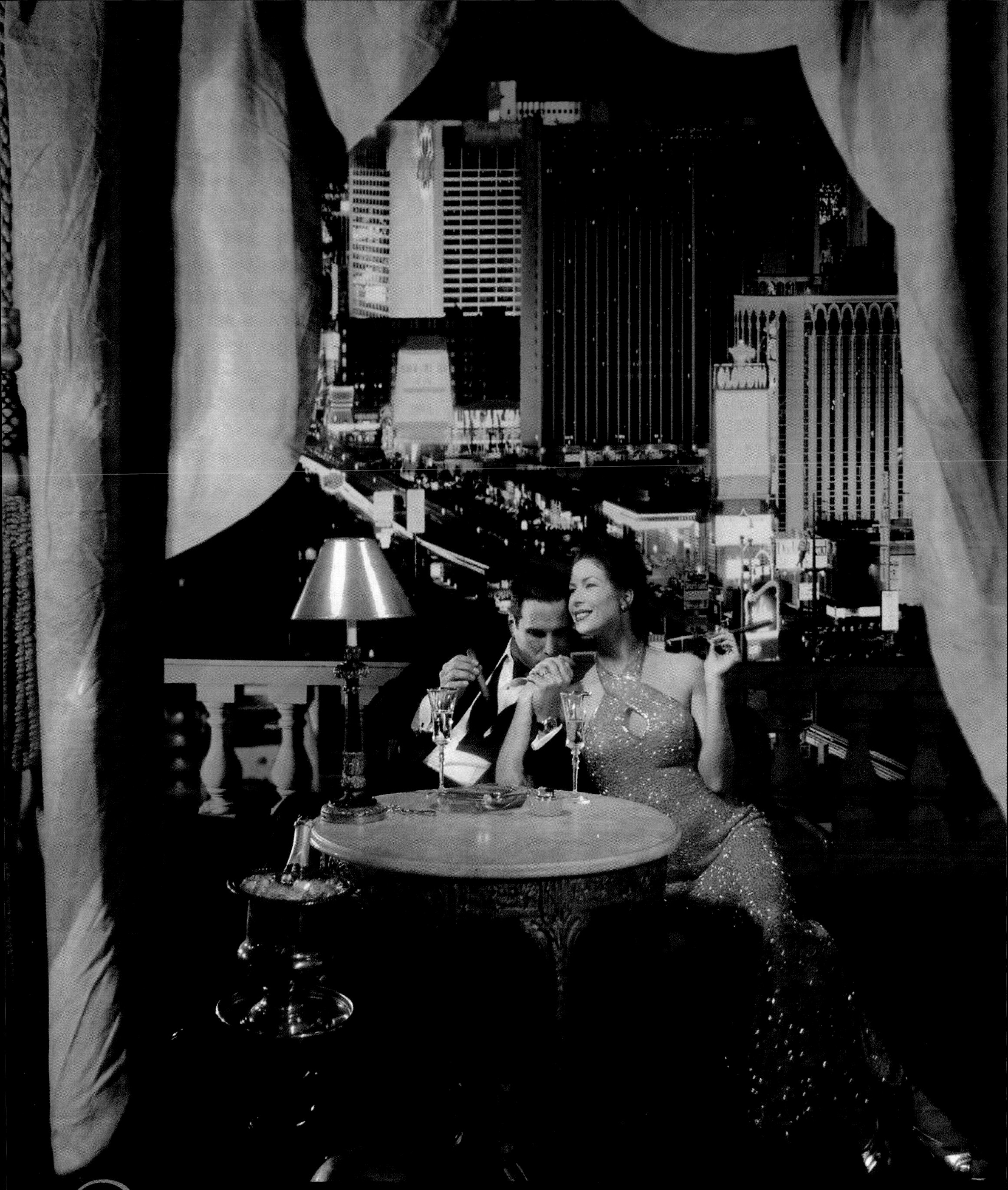
SMOOTH, WITH PLENTY OF CHARACTER.
We satisfy even the most discriminating taste. Call your travel agent today.
www.lasvegas24hours.com
LAS VEGAS
Open 24 Hours.

Award-Winning Entertainment at Unbelievable Values

Nightly
8:30 & 10:30 p.m.
Midnight Show Saturdays
Must be 21
Dark Mondays

$**18**^{95*}
plus taxes
Includes 2 Drinks

Ticket price does not include applicable fees & service charge.

Nightly
7:30 & 9:30 p.m.
11:15 p.m.
Show Saturdays
Dark Tuesdays

$**21**^{95*}
plus taxes
Includes 2 Drinks

Ticket price does not include applicable fees & service charge.

Crazy Girls SM

**Las Vegas' Sexiest Topless Revue
Voted #1 Showgirls**

NORBERT ALEMAN presents

La Cage SM

Starring
FRANK MARINO as Joan Rivers
and an All-Star cast of Female Impersonators

Nightly
8 & 10 p.m.
11:45 p.m. Show
Fridays & Saturdays

$**14**^{95*}
plus taxes
Includes 2 Drinks

Ticket price does not include applicable fees & service charge.

**EIGHT-TIME WINNER
"SHOW OF
THE YEAR"**
Must be 18
Nightly
7:30 & 10:30 p.m.

$**39**^{50*}
plus taxes
VIP Seating Available

Ticket price does not include applicable fees & service charge.

Riviera
Comedy Club
Named #1 Comedy Club

Splash SM

RIVIERA SM
Hotel & Casino
The Entertainment Center of Las Vegas

The Alternative for Grown-Ups

Re-defining the "High Roller"
Where the Mid-range player is King.

by Craig Ghelfi
General Manager

*T*here have always been two kinds of players in Las Vegas: those who watch things happen and those who make things happen. I want you to be the kind of player who makes things happen.

This may astonish you, but it is very easy to make sure you get the absolute best out of Las Vegas. And by **"absolute best,"** I mean: fully-stocked stretch limousines waiting for you at the airport, a maitre'd who picks up your dinner check, and complimentary hotel suites for you and your friends.

It doesn't matter if you like to play slots, table games or Keno. At Lady Luck Casino Hotel in Downtown Las Vegas, any player can obtain V.I.P. status or "full comps" by gambling what other casinos consider "small time." In fact, it will surprise you how little it takes to receive V.I.P. complimentary status at Lady Luck. **"All comps are not created equal"**.

How do we compare to the Las Vegas Strip? You decide. The Strip has luxury suites with whirlpools and gold fixtures. So do we. We have two elegant towers with 162 luxurious suites (792 rooms and suites). We also

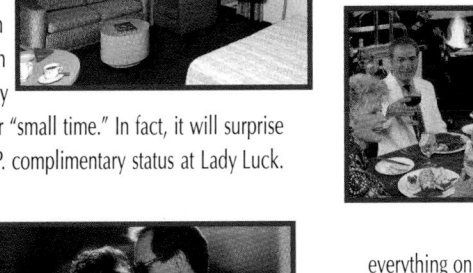

know all our V.I.P. players by their first names. So when you need personal attention, you get it.

The Strip has sprawling attractions and gigantic pools. Our heated pool sparkles just as blue and Lady Luck is less than a block away from the Fremont Street Experience. You decide if and when you want attractions. The Las Vegas Strip has huge restaurants. Ours are more intimate. *USA Today* calls our prime rib dinner "the best value" and "tops for flavor," and this is just our buffet! The Burgundy Room, our fine dining room, is a choice of Chaines des Rotisseurs, an international organization of classically trained restaurateurs. Our newest addition, the Marco Polo Room, serves guests exceptional Italian cuisine in a cozy, yet elegant atmosphere.

At Lady Luck, having V.I.P. status means more, it's where the mid-range player is king.

Once we rate your play, we will tell you exactly what you can expect... and it will be the best.

If you love to golf, we'll help you choose the right course. When big events like basketball, ice hockey, concerts and rodeos come to Las Vegas, we'll set you up in our plush Thomas and Mack Arena suite, with stocked bar and closed-circuit TV. We have another private box at the Las Vegas Motor Speedway and you can be right there for the biggest races.

We take care of other details too... like placing complimentary copies of *USA Today* outside your door and refreshments in our private Gold Club lounge. When we host extravagant gaming tournaments, casino events or V.I.P. parties, you'll be invited to

bring your friends. But perhaps the best reason to stay and play at Lady Luck is for the personalized service and attention we offer our V.I.P. guests. They're like family to us, and they don't have to play a bundle to get a bundle back.

Now I don't expect you to believe everything on pure faith, but you really can make this happen. I'll prove it. Just call one of our V.I.P. Hosts and give them your name, address, and birth date. Tell them you just read our ad in Experience Las Vegas.

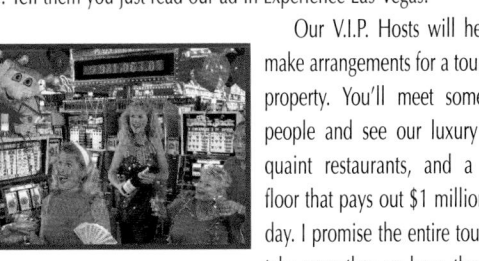

Our V.I.P. Hosts will help you make arrangements for a tour of our property. You'll meet some great people and see our luxury suites, quaint restaurants, and a casino floor that pays out $1 million every day. I promise the entire tour won't take more than an hour, there is no

obligation, and your call will be confidential. If you like what you find, I'll be delighted to give you everything I promised. And, if you decide Lady Luck is not for you, we'll part friends and you've only lost an hour.

If you would like to accept my invitation or require more details...dial **1-800-634-6580 (out-of-state) or 477-3000 (in Nevada)**, ask for a V.I.P. Host, and put me to the test. I'm sure you'll be pleasantly surprised how easy it is to make this happen. At Lady Luck, you really are this important.

Lady Luck
Casino Hotel • Downtown Las Vegas

Nevada is even more colorful after dark.

During the day, Nevada is a whirl of blue and green, a place of cool lakes and tall pines.

At night, Nevada is brighter still, its Vegas Strip a blaze of neon hues. The options for fun

are equally colorful: skiing in the Sierra Nevadas, boating in Lake Tahoe, nightlife in Vegas.

At America West Vacations, we'll show you how electrifying Nevada can be.

Our exciting vacation packages include:

- Roundtrip airfare on America West Airlines
- Hotel accommodations
- 500 bonus FlightFund® miles
- All airport passenger facility charges
- Vacation Welcome Pack
- Express document delivery
- 24-hour customer service
- Optional Avis rental car

Call your professional Travel Agent or America West Vacations and prepare for departure to any of our exciting destinations.

America West Vacations®
1-800-356-6611
www.americawest.com

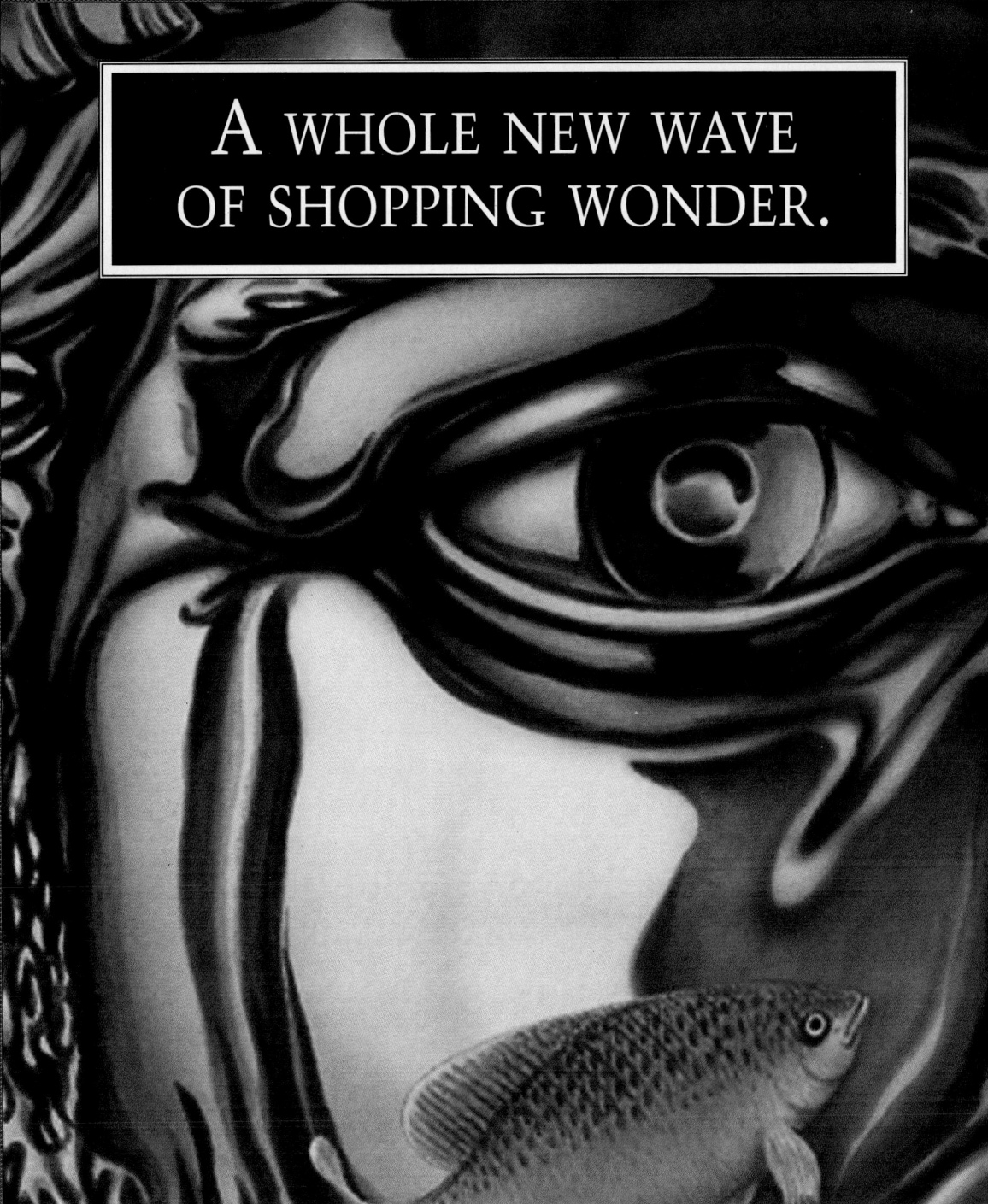

A WHOLE NEW WAVE OF SHOPPING WONDER.

Behold! It's more magnificent than ever. Twice the space. Thirty-nine new stores and restaurants. And the breathtaking spectacle of the destruction of Atlantis, an incredible animatronics tour de force in which Titans of the deep face off in a struggle for total oceanic power. The Forum Shops was a marvel to begin with. You may have already been enchanted by its dancing waters, ever-changing skies and talking statues. You may have already enjoyed its peerless shopping and dining. And, by all means, continue to do so. But prepare to be swept away by a whole new wave of shopping wonder. Visit soon.

VISA

Preferred Here

THE FORUM SHOPS AT CAESARS
THE SHOPPING WONDER OF THE WORLD

Visit The Coney Island of Las Vegas!™

Surrounded By Megaresorts

THE BEST LOCATION ON THE STRIP!

- **Lowest Minimums on The Strip!**
- **5 X Odds on Craps**
- **Over 650 Slots** (98.6% Payback On $1 Slots)
- **24-Hour Surf Buffet**
- **Nightly Entertainment**
- **"21" Madness**
- **Spanish 21**
- **Caribbean Stud**
- **Let It Ride**

RESERVATIONS:
1-800-635-4581

The Fun Place To Be!

BOARDWALK CASINO

On the Strip, Next to the Monte Carlo

www.hiboardwalk.com • 3750 Las Vegas Boulevard, South • Las Vegas, NV 89109

The World's First Rock & Roll Hotel and Casino

SHOWCASE

STARRING

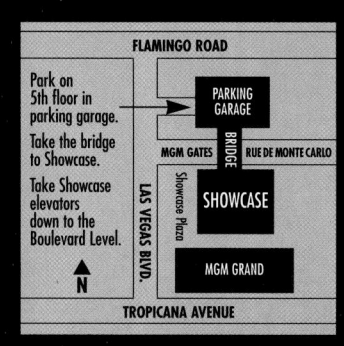

FLAMINGO ROAD

Park on 5th floor in parking garage.

Take the bridge to Showcase.

Take Showcase elevators down to the Boulevard Level.

PARKING GARAGE

MGM GATES | BRIDGE | RUE DE MONTE CARLO

Showcase Plaza

LAS VEGAS BLVD.

SHOWCASE

MGM GRAND

N

TROPICANA AVENUE

SHOWCASE is open 7 days a week • For more information call 702-597-3122
3769 South Las Vegas Boulevard • Las Vegas, NV 89109

Supercharged Excitement!

Las Vegas 500K IRL Race

October 8-11, 1998   Las Vegas Motor Speedway

WELCOME TO Fabulous LAS VEGAS NEVADA

For Ticket Information
Call 702-644-4443

Schedule of Events

Las Vegas Bike Week
Oct. 1-4
Featuring the AMA
Superbike Series

NASCAR Craftsman
Truck Series Race
Nov. 7-8

Call your travel
professional for a
Funjet Vacation Package

LAS VEGAS MOTOR Speedway

LAS VEGAS

PEP BOYS
INDY RACING LEAGUE

We Come to Race

www.lvms.com

When it comes to entertainment - We've got it all!

When it comes to live entertainment the Thomas & Mack Center and Sam Boyd Stadium deliver all the fun, action and excitement you expect! From Touchdowns to Trapeze, Slap Shots to Slam Dunks and Rodeo to Rock n' Roll, we've got exactly what you're looking for!

THOMAS & MACK
CENTER

SAM BOYD
STADIUM

For a complete schedule of events call the Thomas & Mack Center Ticket Office at (702)895-3900 or visit our web site at tmc.unlv.edu

Just for you, Nevada's newest mall, Dillard's, JCPenney, Mervyn's California, Robinsons•May, over 130 specialty shops, restaurants and natural attractions. Galleria at Sunset is at your service: 600 seat food court, valet parking, taxi call service, gift certificates, strollers, wheelchairs.

OPEN LATE ON SATURDAYS UNTIL 9:00 PM.

Hours: Mon - Sat 10am - 9pm • Sun 11am - 6pm
702-434-0202 • 1300 W. Sunset Road • www.galleriaatsunset.com

MEGASTARS @ IMPERIAL PALACE

THE ORIGINAL LEGENDS IN CONCERT
THE WORLD'S GREATEST TRIBUTE SHOW

Escape the City Streets
8221 W. Charlston Blvd.
Las Vegas, NV 89117
596-2953
Jared Fisher, Pres.
Hours: 10 am - 6 pm
Mountain bike tours & rentals, half day $20, fullday $25, a week $85. Includes bike, maps, equipment & delivery.

BICYCLE SHOPS

Bicycle Depot
2801B Green Valley Pkwy.
Henderson, NV 89014
458-0888

5665 W. Sahara Ave.
Las Vegas, NV 89102
252-4316
Leo Marquez, Gen. Mgr.
Hours: Mon. - Fri. 9:30 am - 7 pm; Sat. 9:30 am - 5 pm; Sun. 11 am - 5 pm
Credit Cards: All major

Bicycle King
2470 E. Tropicana Ave.
Las Vegas, NV 89121
451-2580
Lincoln Salisbury, Mgr.
Hours: Mon. - Fri. 9 am - 6 pm; Sat. 9 am - 5 pm
Credit Cards: MC & Visa
The largest bicycle track & Yakima dealer in southern Nevada.

Bike Stuff
1268 Wyoming Ave.
Boulder City, NV 89005
Jeff Spriggs, Owner
293-2453
Hours: Mon. - Sat. 10 am - 6 pm
Credit Cards: MC & Visa

Bike Trail
6816 W. Cheyenne Ave.
Las Vegas, NV 89108
656-2026
Tony Garza, Sales and service
Hours: Mon. - Fri. 10:30 am - 6 pm; Sat. 10:30 am - 4 pm

Bike World
2320 E. Flamingo Rd.
Las Vegas, NV 89119
735-7551

1901 S. Rainbow Blvd.
Las Vegas, NV 89102
254-1718
Jim Martinez, Gen. Mgr.
Hours: Mon. - Fri. 10 am - 6 pm; Sat 10 am -5:30 pm; Sun. 10 am - 5 pm
Credit Cards: All major

Cyclery 'N Cafe
7016 W. Charleston Blvd.
Las Vegas, NV 89117
228-9460
Richard Craig, owner
Hours: Mon. - Fri. 10 am - 7 pm; Sat. - Sun. 10 am - 5 pm
Coffee bar and bike shop; rentals, scheduled rides.

First Choice Bicycle
1000 E. Charleston Blvd.
Las Vegas, NV. 89104
382-5775
Stacey Steele, owner
Hours: Mon. - Sat. 9 am - 6 pm

House of Bikes
6162 W. Spring Mountain Rd.
Las Vegas, NV 89102
871-0871
Jerry Morgan, Mgr.
Hours: Mon. - Fri. 10 am - 6 pm; Sat. 10 am - 5 pm
Credit Cards: All major

Peloton Sports
911 N. Buffalo Dr.
Las Vegas, NV 89128
363-1991
Deya Hawk, Mgr.
Hours: Mon. - Fri. 10 am - 7 pm; Sat. 9 am - 5 pm
Credit Cards: MC, Visa, Discover
Specialty shop selling higher end equipment with an emphasis on customer service.

McGhies Ski Chalet
4503 W. Sahara Ave.
Las Vegas, NV 89102
252-8077

3310 E. Flamingo Rd.
Las Vegas, NV 89121
433-1120
Randy McGhie, Owner
Hours: Mon. - Fri. 10 am - 7 pm; Sat. 10 am - 6 pm; Sun 11 am - 5pm
Mountain bikes and bike accessories, snow skis, snowboards, wakeboards and water skis

CLUBS AND ORGANIZATIONS

Las Vegas Valley Bicycle Club
228-4076
Leanne Miller, Pres.
Jim Matthews, Membership Chairman
Hotline: 897-7800
USCF sanctioned club affiliated with N.O.R.B.A. and L.A.W. USCF Affiliated. With over 300 members, the club holds a variety of rides and events each weekend; mid-week training rides; monthly meetings

Nellis Meadows Bicycle Motocross Track (BMX)
4949 E. Cheyenne Ave.
Las Vegas, NV 89115
452-6053
Peter Price, Pres.
Hotline: 453-1663
Fees: $35 per year for membership in National Bicycle League *(required)*
Clark County Parks and Recreation, in conjunction with the National Bicycle League, offers bicycle motocross for all ages.

RUNNING

A variety of races and fun runs of all lengths are held almost every weekend. The best source of information on races is the Running Store listed below. The Friday edition of the *Review Journal* has a "Running/Fitness" column which has race results and coming events. The Annual Las Vegas International Marathon is held in February.

The Running Store
4350 E. Sunset Rd.
Henderson, NV 89014
898-7866
Larry LaHondy, Mgr.
Hours: Mon. - Sat. 10 am - 6 pm; Sun. 11 am - 5 pm
Carrying everything for the runner including footwear, clothes, accessories. Information on upcoming races and registration available at the store.

Las Vegas Track Club
594-0970
Deloy Martinez, Pres.
The 600-member Las Vegas Track Club sponsors weekly races. Annual dues: adult $16; student $8; family $24.

SPORTS

FISHING & HUNTING

FISHING LICENSES

In 1997 95,000 rainbow trout were planted in Lake Mead. 198,000 were planted in Mohave. These were considered catchable fish at least 10 inches long.

License Requirements:
To be eligible for a resident license, a person must be a citizen of the United States and physically present in the State of Nevada for at least 6 months immediately proceeding his application for a license.
Resident anglers under 12 years of age are not required to have a license to fish in Nevada.
Nevada's license year runs from March 1st through the last day in February.

RESIDENT LICENSES AND PERMITS
General Fishing License 30: $21.00 *(For persons 16 years or older)*
Junior Fishing License 31: $5.00 *(For persons 12 through 15 years)*
Senior Fishing License 32: $5.00 *(For persons 65 years or older)*
General Combination Hunting & Fishing License 24: $39.00
(For persons 16 years or older)
Junior Combination Hunting & Fishing License 26: $8.00
(For persons 12 through 15 years)
Sr. Combination Hunting & Fishing License 25: $8.00
(For persons 65 years or older)
Serviceman's Fishing License 33: $6.00
(For NV residents who are on active duty outside of Nevada)
Short Term Fishing Permit: 1 day fishing permit: $7.00
For each consecutive day added to a 1-Day Permit to fish *(must be purchased at the same time 1-day permit is purchased)*: $2.00
Indian's Hunting & Fishing 01: Free *(For resident Indians with a certificate of eligibility. The license is available only through Dept. of Wildlife)*
Disabled Veteran's Combination Hunting & Fishing License 03: Free
For veterans who reside in Nevada and have incurred a service-connected disability which is considered 50% or more.
Disabled Person Fishing License 05: $5.00
Disabled Person Combination
Hunting & Fishing License 06: $8.00

NONRESIDENT LICENSES AND PERMITS
Nonresident License - Regular Fishing License 37: $51.00
(For persons 16 years or older)
Junior Fishing License 38: $9.00 *(For persons 12 through 15 years)*
Colorado River Fishing License 39: $21.00
(for person 14 years of age or older)
The department will issue a special license to nonresidents who are 14 years of age or over to fish in the reciprocal waters of the Colorado River, Lake Mead and Lake Mohave.
Short Term Fishing Permit:
1-Day Permit: $12.00
For each consecutive day added to a 1-Day Permit to fish: $4.00
NAC 502.285 Fishing in reciprocal waters of Colorado River, Lake Mead and Lake Mohave.
When fishing in those waters, each person who is 14 years of age or over must possess:
(a) An Arizona special use stamp, in addition to a Nevada fishing license or permit or a special annual license issued pursuant to subsection 1; or
(b) A Nevada special use stamp, in addition to an Arizona fishing license, unless he is fishing from the shore of the state in which he is licensed. The fee for the special use stamp is $3 and the stamp is effective from January 1 to December 31, inclusive.
In addition to the requirements of paragraph **(a)**, a person who has a Nevada fishing license must have a Nevada trout stamp to possess trout.
Trout Stamp: $5.00
Second Rod Stamp Fee: $10.00

NEVADA STATE FISHING RECORDS FOR LOCAL WATERS:

Large-mouth Bass	11.0 lbs.	Mohave 1972
Striped Bass*	67.1	Mohave 1997
Carp	30.8	Mohave 1976
Black Crappie	3.2	Mead 1976
Silver Salmon	8.12	Mead 1974
Red-ear Sunfish*	0.14	Lamb 1988
Green Sunfish	1.6	Lamb 1992
Rainbow Trout	16.4	Mohave 1971
Channel Catfish*	26.4	Mohave 1978
	* not a state record	

FISHING & HUNTING

Nevada Department of Wildlife
4747 Vegas Dr.
Las Vegas, NV 89108 - 486-5127
William Molini, Admin.
Nevada has 215 fishable waters encompassing approximately 385,026 surface acres and 529 fishable streams with 2,750 miles of fishable length.

In 1997, 95,000 rainbow trout were planted in Lake Mead; 198,000 were planted in Lake Mohave. Lake Mead harvested 1.4 million fish and Lake Mohave harvested 256,000 fish in 1996. Lake Mead is known primarily for large-mouth and striped bass and Lake Mohave for its rainbow trout, large-mouth bass and striped bass. Channel catfish and bluegill are found in both lakes. The largest striped bass taken from Lake Mohave was 67 pounds, 1 ounce in 1997.

Within Las Vegas, Lorenzi Park and Sunset Park have ponds stocked with rainbow trout in the cooler months and channel catfish during the summer. Floyd Lamb State Park just north of Las Vegas also has fishing.

Region III Regulations
Seasons/Hours: Open year round, any hour of the day or night.
Limits: 10 trout and 15 warm-water game fish of which not more than 10 may be black bass.
Colorado River: Season is open year round any hour of the day or night (except closed as posted immediately below dam). Rainbow trout, large-mouth bass, striped bass and channel catfish are the most prevalent species found in the river. Limits are 10 trout, 10 black bass, 10 striped bass and 25 catfish. Minimum size for black bass is 13 inches. No limit on other game fish.

Lake Mead: Season is open year round any hour of the day or night except for posted areas. The Lake Mead Hatchery outflow stream to Lake Mead is closed to fishing. Large-mouth bass, striped bass, channel catfish, crappie and sunfish are the most prevalent species found in the lake. Limits are 5 trout, 6 large mouth black bass, 25 catfish, 15 crappie and 20 striped bass. No limit on other game fish.

Lake Mohave: Season is open year round, any hour of the day or night except for posted areas. Limits are 10 trout, 6 black bass, 20 striped bass, 25 catfish and 15 crappie. No limit on other game fish.
Lorenzi Park Pond: Urban pond - Season is open year round and hours are when park is open to public use. The pond is stocked with rainbow trout in the winter and channel catfish during the spring and summer. Limit is 3 game fish, singly or in the aggregate. License required for age 12 and over.
Sunset Park Pond: 12 acre urban pond - Season is open year round, hours are

when park is open to public use. The pond is stocked every other week with 300 pounds of rainbow trout in the winter and channel catfish during the spring and summer. Limit is 3 game fish, singly or in the aggregate. License required for age 12 and over.
Trail Canyon Reservoir: Stocked by Nevada Division of Wildlife with Rainbow and Brook Trout. The lake elevation is 8,000 feet. It is located via a dirt road 11 miles north of Dyer on Nevada Hwy. 264. Also, nearby Chiatovich Creek has good fishing. No established campgrounds or motels but primitive camping sites are available.
Tule Lake at Floyd Lamb State Park: Urban pond - Season is open year round and hours are when park is open for public use. Limit is 3 game fish, singly or in the aggregate. License required for age 12 and over.
Virgin River System: Season is open year round, any hour of the day or night. Limits are 5 trout, 6 black bass, 25 catfish, 15 crappie and 10 striped bass. No limit on other game fish.

Lake Mead Hatchery
245 Lake Shore Road
Boulder City, NV 89005
486-6738
John Mckay, Supervisor
Hours: 8 am - 4 pm
Nevada Trout Hatchery System
Visitors are welcome at all Nevada Fish Hatcheries between the hours of 8:00 am to 4:00 pm weekdays except holidays. Tours can be arranged by contacting the hatchery supervisor prior to a planned visit. Station staff will gladly answer questions about the facility and its operation.

FISHING BAIT & TACKLE

Blue Lake Bait & Tackle
5485 E. Lake Mead Blvd.
Las Vegas, NV 89115
452-8299
Marvin Walker, Owner
Hours: Daily 5 am - 7 pm

Rainbows End Bass & Gas
1330 E. Lake Mead Dr.
Henderson, NV 89015
564-5660
Mark Johnson, Owner
Hours: 5 am - 10 pm

Sandy Cove Bait Store
5225 E. Lake Mead Blvd.
Las Vegas, NV 89115
459-2080
Jack Evans, Owner
Hours: 6 am - 9 pm

Sportsman's Bait & Tackle Shop
5660 Boulder Hwy.
Las Vegas, NV 89122
458-7071
Hours: 24 hrs.

Sunset Bait & Tackle
1000 E. Lake Mead Dr.
Henderson, NV 89015
565-0696
William Scott, Owner
Hours: 5 am - 6 pm

FISHING SUPPLIES

(also see Sporting Goods Stores)

Active Sports
348 N. Nellis Blvd.
Las Vegas, NV 89110
452-6555
John Goodman
Hours: 7:30 pm - midnight

Clearwater Flyfishing
3031 E. Charleston Blvd.
Las Vegas, NV 89104
388-1022
Tom Guisewhite, Owner
Hours: Mon. - Fri. 10 am - 6 pm; Sat.
10 am - 5 pm
Complete line of flyfishing materials
and full line of custom rods and reels.

FISHING GUIDES

Anglers Guide Service
161 E. Rancho Dr.
Henderson, NV 89114
564-1558
Bill Spellman
30 years experience on Lake Mead and
Mohave; striper specialist.

Donoho's Guide Service
451-4004
Pat Donoho
Professional equipment and free drinks
furnished; striped or black bass; satisfaction guaranteed or your money
refunded.

Fish, Inc.
1500 Palamino Dr.
Henderson, NV 89015
565-8396
Jim Goff
No fish - no pay! Bass and stripers.

Jr's Guide Service
361-7039
Jim Robinson, Capt. U.S.C.G.
Black bass and stripers; 30 years experience on Lakes Mead and Mohave.

Karen Jones Fishing Guide
1018 Cutter St.
Las Vegas, NV 89105
871-1399
$100 per person, $200 for two people,
$250 for three people and $300 for four
people *(maximum)*. All prices include
bait and equipment.

HUNTING

Department of Wildlife
Region III Headquarters
4747 Vegas Dr.
Las Vegas, NV 89108
486-5127
Mike Wickersham, Regional Mgr.

Operation Game Thief: This is a
program similar to Secret Witness
where concerned citizens can report
wildlife violations to Nevada's Game
Wardens. Rewards are offered upon
conviction of the violators and the
caller can remain anonymous. Toll free
number is 1-800-992-3030.

BIG GAME

Nevada Department of Wildlife
P.O. Box 30040
Reno, NV 89520-3040
688-1500
William Molini, Admin.
Hunting informational brochures and
tag applications are distributed in early
March.

Tags for deer, antelope, elk, mountain goat and any subspecies of bighorn
sheep may be obtained only through the
application process. Hunters pay a
nonrefundable $5 application fee for
each big game species applied for.
Applications must be mailed to the
Nevada Department of Wildlife through
the postal service. Last year 17,473 buck
tags and 1,840 doe tags were issued for
the general resident and non-resident
hunt. The 1998 season begins August 8
and lasts through January 3, 1999.

"*Resident*" means a person who is a
citizen of the United States who has actually been physically present in the State
of Nevada for at least 6 months immediately preceding his application for a
license, tag, or permit, and who intends
to make Nevada his permanent home.

1997 Big Game Quotas
Antelope: 1,153
Elk: 740
Bighorn Sheep: 147
Rocky Mountain Goat: 6
Mule Deer: 21,191

SMALL GAME

Upland game hunting for chukar, quail,
rabbits and sage grouse as well as
waterfowl hunts starts in mid to late
November; pheasant hunting is early
November. Shooting hours are from
sunrise to sunset.

Small game seasons and regulations
brochures are available at the
Department of Wildlife or at any fishing
and hunting license agent.

LICENSES, TAGS AND FEES

(License year - March 1, 1998 through March 1, 1999)
Upland Game Bird, Migratory Game Bird and Rabbit
Resident Hunting Licenses:
General Hunting License 20 $24.00
(For persons 16 years or older)
Junior Hunting License 21 $5.00
(For persons 12 - 15 years)
Senior Hunting License 22 $5.00
(For a person 65 years or older with 6 mos. of NV residence)
Serviceman's Hunting License 23 $6.00
(For a NV resident who is a serviceman on active duty outside NV)
Severe Handicap Hunting License 04 $5.00
(This license is available only through the Dept. of Wildlife)
Indian's Hunting and Fishing License 01 Free
(This license is available only through the Dept. of Wildlife)
Disabled Veteran's Hunting and Fishing License 03 Free
(This license is available only through the Dept. of Wildlife)
Combination License 24 $39.00
(For persons 16 years or older)
Junior Combination License 26 $8.00
(For persons 12 - 15 years)
Senior Combination Hunting and Fishing License 25 $8.00
(For a person 65 years or older with 6 or more mos. of NV residence)
Severe Handicap Combination Hunting and Fishing License 06 $8.00
(This license is available only through the Dept. of Wildlife)

Nonresident and Alien Licenses;
1-day Upland Game and Waterfowl Permit $16.00; $5.00 each consecutive day
Regular Hunting License Class 28 $111.00
(For persons of any age)

STAMPS
(Required regardless of residency)
State Duck Stamp $5.00
*(For a person 12 - 65 years who hunts any migratory game bird, except
common snipe, coot, gallinule, white-winged dove, mourning dove and
band-tailed pigeon)*
Federal Migratory Bird Hunting Stamp $12.50
(For a person 16 years or older who hunts migratory waterfowl)

SPECIAL TAGS OR SEALS
Tundra Swan Tag $5.00
Turkey Tag $20.00

SPORTS

GOLF

Las Vegas averages 320 days of sunshine a year and has over 30 golf courses in the area. These two elements along with year round access make Las Vegas one of the best places in the world to enjoy golf.

Las Vegas is a stop for both the PGA and the LPGA.

Reservations for tee time should be made three days in advance at most courses. Starting times for same day play are taken but for first available time. During the summer months, the biggest demand for tee times is the early morning hours. When making a tee time, it is best to call early and have a credit card ready.

Las Vegas has two municipal courses, the Las Vegas Golf Club and the Desert Rose Golf Course. The $52 million Shadow Creek, a private club, is owned by the Mirage and is by invitation only. Las Vegas' five private clubs have initiation fees that range from $20,000 to $30,000, with monthly dues ranging from $270 to $360.

All courses have excellent teaching professionals, club rentals and practice facilities. Most also have pro shops and restaurants.

Many new courses have opened within the last 12 months and still more are opening in the area within the next 12, included in these are Mount Charleston Golf Resort, which opened August 1997, Rio Secco, set among the Black Mountain Range in Las Vegas and the Callaway Golf Center which was completed October 1997 at the south end of the Las Vegas Strip.

Hours for most courses are 6 am until sundown.

Photo: Photoechnik International

GOLF COURSES

Angel Park Golf Club
est. 1989
100 S. Rampart Blvd.
Las Vegas, NV 89128
254-4653
Pro shop: 254-0565
Tee times: 7 1/2 days in advance for card holders and 60 days in advance for resort guests.
36-hole Arnold Palmer designed municipal course, open to the public.
Orrin Vincent, Director of Golf
Andy Deiro, Tom Vold, Head Pros
Palm Course: Well bunkered course with many elevation changes; surrounded by desert canyon; fast bent-grass greens.
Tees:
Professional: 6,530 yds. par 70 USGA rating 70.9, slope rating 129
Championship: 5,857 yds. par 70 USGA rating 67.6, slope rating 114
Resort: 5,438 yds. par 70 USGA rating 65.4, slope rating 110
Forward: 4,570 yds. par 70 USGA rating 66.2, slope rating 111
Green fees: Twilight fees are $60.
Mountain Course Tees:
Professional: 6,722 yds. par 71 USGA rating 72.4, slope rating 128
Championship 6,235 yds. par 71 USGA rating 70.3, slope rating 117
Resort: 5,751 yds. par 71 USGA rating 67.1, slope rating 116
Forward: 5,164 yds. par 71 USGA rating 69.9, slope rating 119
Green fees: $110 includes cart. Club rentals $25. No 9-hole rates available.
Cloud Nine Course: The course features replicas of 12 of the most famous and challenging par-3 holes in the world. Nine holes are lighted for night play.
Hours: 6 am - 10 pm
Green fees: $22 for 18 holes *(walking)*. 18-hole Championship Putting Course: Night lighted putting course, complete water hazards and sand traps.
Green fees: $8
Facilities: Pro-shop, night lighted driving range, putting green, restaurant and snack bar; banquet facilities.

Badlands Golf Club
est. 1996
(Peccole Ranch)
9119 Alta Dr.
Las Vegas, NV 89117
242-4653
Joel Villanos, Dir. of Golf
Tee Times: 30 days in advance
Johnny Miller Signature Design Course has a unique desert terrain with spectacular view of Red Rock Canyon, Par 72.
Tate Stull, Head Pro
Tees: Black 7,100 yards; Blue 6,800 yards; White 6,500 yards; Red 5,300 yards
Green Fees: Mon. - Thu. $98; Fri. - Sun. $115
Club Rentals: $35
Designed by U. S. Open Champion Johnny Miller
Facilities: Driving range, clubhouse, bar, restaurant and putting green

Black Mountain Golf and Country Club
est. 1959
500 Greenway Rd.
Henderson, NV 89015
565-7933
Tee times: Four days in advance.
Semi-private club for 18 holes; desert landscaped course with lots of sand bunkers and two large lakes, but still a good course for beginners.
Brett Mulligan, Head Pro
Tees: Championship: 6,541 yds. par 72, USGA 72.4, slope 130
Men's: 6,223 yds. par 72, USGA 71.2, slope 123
Ladies': 5,476 yds. par 73, USGA 71.6, slope 125
Green Fees: Mon. - Fri. $52; Sat. - Sun. $57, includes cart.
Seniors over 63 years $40 *(walking)* Tues. and Thu. except holidays, cart $12
Carts mandatory on weekends $12 per person
Club rentals: $13.
Facilities: Pro shop, driving range, putting green, restaurant, snack bar and bar

Boulder City Municipal Golf Course
est. 1972
1 Clubhouse Dr.
Boulder City, NV 89005
293-9236
Tee times: seven days in advance; weekends - nine days in advance
Public course for 18 holes; flat desert course.
Tony Fiorentini, Head Pro
Tees: Championship: 6,561 yds. par 72, USGA 70.2, slope 110
Men's: 6,132 yds. par 72, USGA 68.3, slope 103
Ladies': 5,566 yds. par 72, USGA 70.7, slope 114
Green Fees: $27 walk; $36 ride anytime
Carts: *(optional)* $9 per person for 18 holes; $5 per person for 9 holes
Club rentals: $15
Facilities: Pro shop, driving range, putting green, four chipping greens, snack bar.

The Calloway Golf Center
est. 1997
6730 Las Vegas Blvd. S.
Las Vegas, NV 89119
896-4100
John Boreta, Dir. of Golf
A 42 acre golf training facility offering the best in golf instruction, evaluation and practice to players of all skill levels. The driving range includes 110 lighted practice stations and natural grass hitting areas. The landing area provides a country club setting with rolling hills, ten elevated greens and trees overhanging the sand traps and greens. Specially designed challenges, including island greens which are positioned adjacent to three waterfall features encourage precise shot making. The Divine nine is a par 3, nine hole lighted golf course featuring lakes, water rapids and waterfalls. The challenging golf holes range from 125 to 200 yards in length and feature PGA quality 6,000 ft. greens.
Tees: Championship: 1,152 yds.
Men's: 1,033 yds.
Ladies': 988 yds.
Green Fees: $35 walking or $45 with cart
Club Rental: $25
Facilities: St. Andrews Golf Shop, Calloway Performance, David Leadbettor Golf Academy, driving range, chipping and putting greens, restaurant and full bar

Canyon Gate Country Club
est. 1989
2001 Canyon Gate Dr.
Las Vegas, NV 89117
363-0481 363-0303
Andy Anderson, Dir. of Golf
Tee times: call after 7:30 am for tee times up to 14 days in advance; dress code.
Lush, narrow fairway with many bunkers and mounds and lots of water.
Private course *(members only)*, 18 holes
Membership fee: $30,000 and $362 monthly dues.
Tees: Championship: 6,742 yds. Par 72, USGA 73.0, slope 125
Men's: 6,259 yds. par 72 USGA 70.9, slope 121
Ladies': 5,141 yds. par 72, USGA 69.7, slope 121
Green Fees: Monthly membership dues $362; Guest of members pay $75 *(includes cart)* to play 18-holes and club rentals $25. Not open to the public
Facilities: Pro shop, driving range, putting green, restaurant, snack bar, bar, 2 tennis courts, spa, steam room, weight room, and 2 swimming pools.

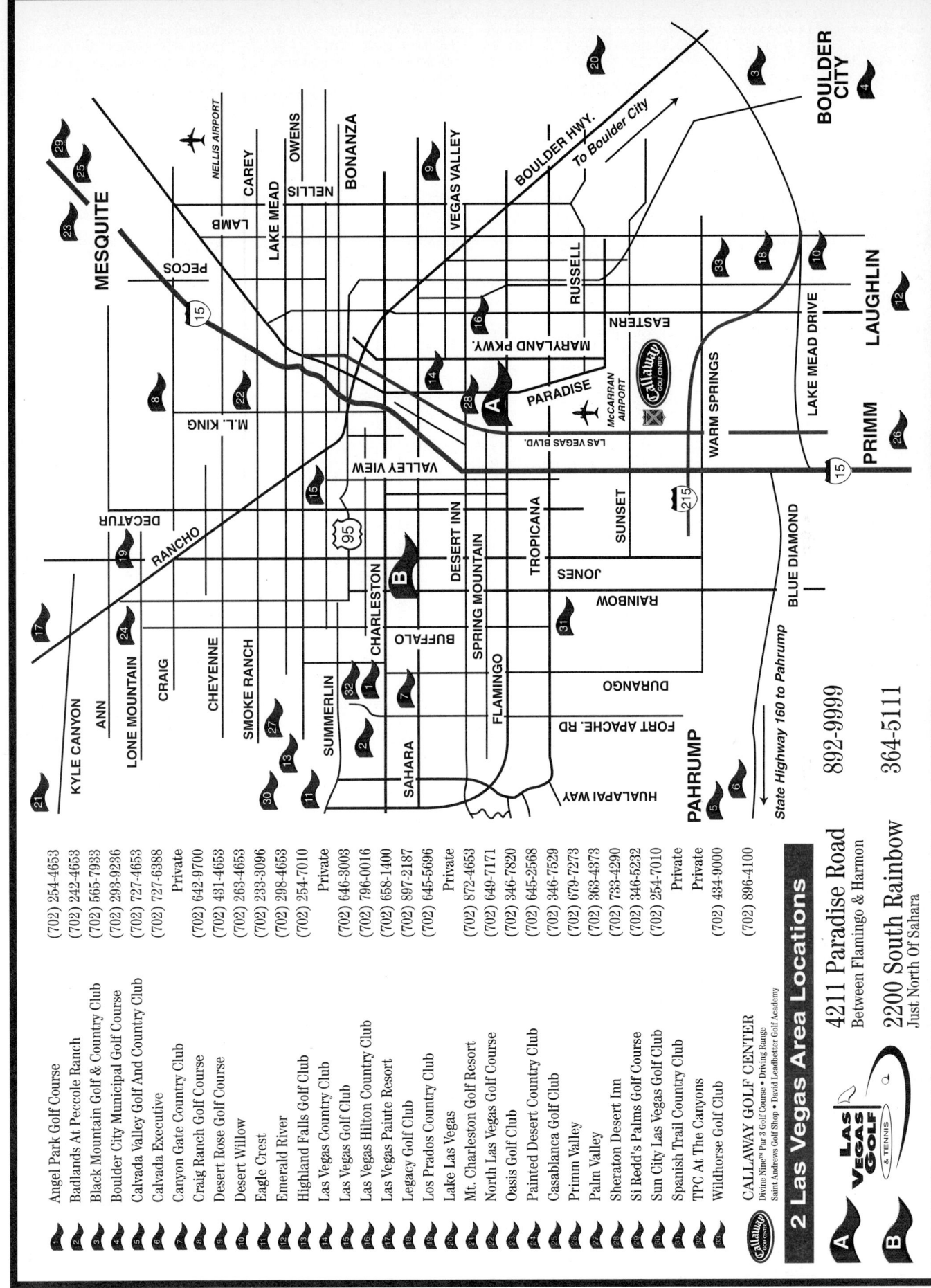

2 Las Vegas Area Locations

1	Angel Park Golf Course	(702) 254-4653
2	Badlands At Peccole Ranch	(702) 242-4653
3	Black Mountain Golf & Country Club	(702) 565-7933
4	Boulder City Municipal Golf Course	(702) 293-9236
5	Calvada Valley Golf And Country Club	(702) 727-4653
6	Calvada Executive	(702) 727-6388
7	Canyon Gate Country Club	Private
8	Craig Ranch Golf Course	(702) 642-9700
9	Desert Rose Golf Course	(702) 431-4653
10	Desert Willow	(702) 263-4653
11	Eagle Crest	(702) 233-3096
12	Emerald River	(702) 298-4653
13	Highland Falls Golf Club	(702) 254-7010
14	Las Vegas Country Club	Private
15	Las Vegas Golf Club	(702) 646-3003
16	Las Vegas Hilton Country Club	(702) 796-0016
17	Las Vegas Paiute Resort	(702) 658-1400
18	Legacy Golf Club	(702) 897-2187
19	Los Prados Country Club	(702) 645-5696
20	Lake Las Vegas	Private
21	Mt. Charleston Golf Resort	(702) 872-4653
22	North Las Vegas Golf Course	(702) 649-7171
23	Oasis Golf Club	(702) 346-7820
24	Painted Desert Country Club	(702) 645-2568
25	Casablanca Golf Club	(702) 346-7529
26	Primm Valley	(702) 679-7273
27	Palm Valley	(702) 363-4373
28	Sheraton Desert Inn	(702) 733-4290
29	Si Redd's Palms Golf Course	(702) 346-5232
30	Sun City Las Vegas Golf Club	(702) 254-7010
31	Spanish Trail Country Club	Private
32	TPC At The Canyons	Private
33	Wildhorse Golf Club	(702) 434-9000
	CALLAWAY GOLF CENTER	(702) 896-4100

CALLAWAY GOLF CENTER
Divine Nine™ Par 3 Golf Course • Driving Range
Saint Andrews Golf Shop • David Leadbetter Golf Academy

A **4211 Paradise Road**
Between Flamingo & Harmon
892-9999

B **2200 South Rainbow**
Just North Of Sahara
364-5111

State Highway 160 to Pahrump

LAS VEGAS GOLF & TENNIS

GOLF

Craig Ranch Golf Course
est. 1953
628 W. Craig Rd.
N. Las Vegas, NV 89030
642-9700
Henry Sandler, Head Pro
Tee times: seven days in advance.
Public course *(privately owned)*; Short, narrow, tight course.
Tees: Men's: 6,000 yds. par 70, USGA 66.8, slope 101
Ladies': 5,221 yds. par 70, USGA 69, slope 103
Green Fees: $15 for 18 holes, walking; $21 with cart; $9 for 9 holes, walking; $13.50 with cart
Cart Rentals: *(optional)* $8 per person for 18 holes; $4.50 per person for 9 holes;
Club rentals: $8 for 18 holes; $5 for 9 holes
Facilities: Pro shop, driving range, putting green, chipping green, snack bar.

Desert Inn Golf Club
est. 1951
3145 Las Vegas Blvd. S.
Las Vegas, NV 89109
733-4290 733-4288
Dave Johnson, Dir. of Golf
Kevin Paulson, Head Pro
Tee times: Hotel guests up to a year in advance with room reservation.
Resort course for 18 holes, hosting all three major pro golf tours; the PGA, LPGA and Senior PGA. Tight and long undulating greens. Of the four holes over 500 yards, the 578-yard, par-5 fifth hole is the longest. The shortest hole is the par-3 173-yard 16th with a tee shot across water to a bunkered green.
Tees: Championship: 7,193 yds. par 72, USGA 73.9, slope 124
Men's: 6,732 yds. par 72, USGA 72.1 slope 121
Blue: 6,319 yds. par 72, USGA 69.8, slope 118
Ladies': 5,884 yds. par 72, USGA 72.7, slope 121
Green Fees: Desert Inn guests - $150; carts included
Non-hotel guests $215; $6 golf shoes;
Club Rentals: $40
Facilities: Pro shop, driving range, putting green, deli-style restaurant, snack bar on course, bar, tennis courts, spa.

Desert Rose Golf Course
est. 1960
formerly Winterwood Golf Course
5483 Clubhouse Dr.
Las Vegas, NV 89122
431-4653
Eric Eubanks, Head Pro
Tee times: weekends three days in advance; weekdays seven days.
Open to the public; moderate length, wide fairways and fast greens.
Tees: Championship: 6,600 yds. par 71, USGA 70.7, slope 117
Men's: 6,135 yds. par 71, USGA 68.7, slope 108
Ladies': 5,458 yds. par 71, USGA 69.6, slope 115
Green Fees: Residents: $37 weekdays;

$39 weekends; twilight rate $29 weekdays; $31 weekends; Non-residents: $65; $51 twilight rate Mon. - Thu.; $73 Fri. - Sun.
Carts optional, no individual fees
Club rentals: $15 for 18 holes; $7.50 for 9 holes
Facilities: Pro shop, driving range, two putting greens, restaurant, banquet room, snack bar, and bar.

Desert Pines Golf Club
est. 1997
3401 E. Bonanza Rd.
Las Vegas, NV 89101
366-1616
Dale Williams, Dir. of Golf/Head Pro
Tee Times: Nonresidents 30 days, residents 3 days in advance
Play on water; undulated greens and pot bunkers
Tees: Championship: 6,800 yds. par 71, USGA 70.4, slope 122
Mens: 6,450 yds. par 71, USGA 66.8, slope 112
Ladies': 5,873 yds. par 71, USGA 66.8, slope 112
Green Fees: $115 Mon. - Thu.; $130 Fri. - Sun. includes cart
Club Rental: $50
Facilities: Pro shop, restaurant and snack bar, country club atmosphere, state-of-the-art driving range *(fully automatic)*, banquet facilities.

Desert Willow Golf Course
est.1996
Sun City MacDonald Ranch Green Valley Parkway
2020 W. Horizon Ridge Pkwy.
Henderson, NV 89012
263-4653
Joe Spatz, Dir. of Golf/Head Pro
Tee Times: 3 days in advance
Open to the public; 18-hole executive length course.
Tees: Championship: 3,811 yds. par 60, USGA 59.1, slope 91
Mens: 3,454 yds. par 60, USGA 58.1, slope 89
Ladies': 3,108 yds. par 60, USGA 56.9, slope 88
Green Fees: $35 walking for 18 holes, $45 with carts; $20 walking for 9 holes, $26 with carts; Seniors 55 and older - $25 walking or $35 with cart for 18 holes; $15 walking or $21 with cart for 9 holes; Non-residents: $50 walking or $60 with cart for 18 holes; $30 walking or $36 with cart for 9 holes
Cart Rentals: $10 for 18 holes or $6 for 9 holes
Club Rentals: $25
Facilities: Putting green, driving range, pro shop, bar, restaurant and banquet facilities.

Eagle Crest Golf Club
Jon Spatz, Head Professional
This Casper/Nash-designed par 60 executive course opened recently in Summerlin. A private course, it is only open to residents of Sun City.

Highland Falls Golf Club
est. 1993
10201 Sun City Blvd.
Las Vegas, NV 89134
254-7010

Scott Greer, Dir. of Golf
Sean Connett, Head Pro
Tee times: seven days in advance
18 holes
Designed by golf course architect Greg Nash and golfer Billy Casper. Course is shorter than Palm Valley course and plays a little tighter and has more bunkers; hilly course with numerous elevation changes. Course offers a great view of Las Vegas with a peak elevation of 3,053 feet.
Tees: Men's: 6,017 yds. Par 72, USGA 68.6, slope 116
Championship: 6,512 yds. par 72, USGA blue 71.2, slope 126
White tees: 6,017 yds. par 72, USGA 68.6, slope rating 116
Gold tees: 5,579 yds. par 72, USGA 67.1, slope 112
Ladies': 5,099 yds. par 72, USGA 68.8, slope 110
Green Fees: Resident 18 holes $43; 9 holes $25; guest of resident 18 holes $53; 9 holes $30; resident rates apply to Sun City residents only
Nonresident before noon 9 holes $50; before noon 18 holes $95; Summer rates $50 before noon and $40 after noon includes cart
Club rentals: $30
Facilities: Pro shop, driving range, chipping and putting greens, club house, restaurant, bar

Las Vegas Country Club
est. 1967
3000 Joe W. Brown Dr.
Las Vegas, NV 89109
734-1122
Bill Farkas, Jr., Brett Bidwell and John Creaney, Golf Pros
Private course *(members only)*
Memberships: $20,000 to $35,000 and $1,165 per quarter.
Course features bent grass greens and hybrid Bermuda fairways.
Tees: Championship: 7,164 yds. par 72, USGA 72.8, slope 128
Men's: 6,718 yds. par 72, USGA 70.8, slope 123
Ladies': 5,581 yds. par 72, USGA 71.7, slope 121
Green Fees: Private course, members and their guests only
Facilities: 42,000 sq. ft. clubhouse with pro shop, three restaurants and bar; locker rooms and spa; driving range, putting green; 2 indoor and 4 outdoor tennis courts

Las Vegas Golf Club
est. 1949
4300 W. Washington Dr.
Las Vegas, NV 89107
646-3003
Jeff Curran, Dir. of Golf
Tom Carlson, Head Pro
Tee times: seven days in advance
Municipal course for 18 holes; mature course, lots of trees; little water.
Tees: Championship: 6,631 yds. par 72, USGA 71.8, slope 117
Men's: 6,337 yds. par 72, USGA 70.3, slope 114
Ladies': 5,715 yds. par 72, USGA 71.2, slope 113

Green Fees: Residents - $10.50 for 18 holes; $9 with shared cart; Nonresidents $16.75 walking or $25.75 with cart; Seniors with Nevada Drivers License $5 walking for 9 or 18 holes; $9 with cart
Cart Rentals: 18 holes $9; 9 holes - $6.75;
Club rentals: $15 for 9 holes; 18 holes $25
Facilities: Pro shop, night lighted driving range, putting green, restaurant, snack bar, bar and beverage cart staff who patrol the course.

Las Vegas Hilton Country Club
est. 1961
Formerly Sahara Country Club
1911 E. Desert Inn Rd.
Las Vegas, NV 89109
796-0013
Sammy Eshragh, Gen. Mgr.
Rick Fite, Head Pro
Tee times: ten days in advance: 1-800-468-7918
Public course *(privately owned)*, 18 holes; mature course with lots of trees.
Tees: Championship: 6,815 yds. par 71, USGA 72.1, slope 130
Men's: 6,418 yds. par 71 USGA 70.2, slope 121
Ladies': 5,741 yds. par 71, USGA 69.5, slope 103
Green Fees: Mon. - Thu. before 1 pm - $120; $80 after 1 pm; $45 after 3 pm; $150 weekends until 1 pm; $90 after 1 pm; $45 after 3 pm; platinum plus rates: $45 9-hole rate in the am only
Discount to American Golf Club Members
Carts: Mandatory
Club Rentals: $40 Callaways or Big Bertha's; $25 for American Golf Classics
Facilities: Pro shop, night lighted driving range, putting green, snack bar and bar; banquet facilities.

Las Vegas Paiute Resort
est.1995
(near Mount Charleston)
10325 Nuvakai Dr.
Las Vegas, NV 89133
658-1400 1-800-711-2833
Scott McDade, Golf Pro
Tee Times: sixty days in advance.
The 51 members of the Las Vegas Paiute Tribe *(located 18 miles northwest of downtown Las Vegas on US 95, Snow Mountain Exit, turn right)* dedicated the two $11.4 million golf courses on the nation's first multi-course resort developed on Indian Land. Nu-Wav Kaiv is Paiute for Snow Mountain and Tav-Ai Kaiv is Paiute for Sun Mountain. Pete Dye designed courses integrated into the native desert. With an emphasis on resort play, the courses have wide fairways, easy entry to greens and a wide variety of tee length and angles.
Nu-wav Kaiv Tees:
Tournament: 7,158 yds., par 72, USGA 73.9, slope 125
Championship: 6,665 yds. par 72, USGA 71.2, slope 120
Men's: 6,035 yds. par 72, USGA 68.6, slope 112
Ladies': 5,341 yds. par 72, USGA 70, slope 117

Tav-Ai Kaiv Tees: Tournament: 7,112 yds. par 72, USGA 73.3, slope 130
Championship: 6,631 yds. par 72, USGA 70.9, slope 121
Mens: 6,074 yds. par 72, USGA 68.8, slope 116
Ladies: 5,465 yds., par 72, USGA 71.0, slope 123
Green fees: $85 off season and $110 in season *(Mar. 1 - May 31 and Sept. 10 - Nov. 16)* includes cart and range facilities.
Club Rentals: $35 for steel or $45 for graphite
Facilities: Pro shop and clubhouse.

Legacy Golf Club
est. 1989
130 Par Excellence Dr.
Henderson, NV 89014
897-2200
Pro shop: 897-2187
David Barnhart, Head Pro
Craig Smith, Dir. of Golf
Tee times: up to two months in advance. Public course *(privately owned)*. Rated among the top 100 golf courses in the country. Wall to wall turf, two lakes, rolling terrain and lots of trees; number 10 signature tee is designed in the shape of diamonds, hearts, clubs and spades; features US open qualifiers and AJGA.
Tees: Championship: 7,233 yds. par 72, USGA 74.9, slope 136
Men's: 6,744 yds. par 72, USGA 72.1, slope 128
Ladies': 5,340 yds. par 71, USGA 71.0, slope 120
Green Fees: $120 weekdays & $125 weekends including cart (mandatory); $65 twilight rate after 11:30 pm; nongolfing passengers $10; no 9 hole rates;
Club rentals: $25
Facilities: Clubhouse, pro shop, driving range, putting green, restaurant, snack bar and bar; beverage cart and banquet facilities.

Los Prados Country Club
est. 1985
5150 Los Prados Circle Dr.
Las Vegas, NV 89130
645-5696
Keith Flatt, Head Pro
Tee times: ten days in advance.
Semi-private course for 18 holes; short and tight, well bunkered, fast greens. Course borders desert.
Tees: Championship: 5,358 yds. par 70, USGA 65.0 slope 107
Men's: 4,937 yds. par 70, USGA 62.2, slope 101
Ladies': 4,474 yds. par 70, USGA 64.4, slope 104
Green Fees: Residents: $30; after 1 pm Mon. - Thu. $40 for 18 hole with cart; Sat.-Sun. & holidays $45, no 9 hole rates.
Club rentals: $20
Facilities: Pro shop, putting green, restaurant, snack bar and bar, dress code enforced, no personal coolers.

Mount Charleston Golf Resort
est. 1997
1 Kyle Canyon Rd.
Mount Charleston, NV 89124
872-4653
Jeff Bruckner, Dir. of Golf
Joe Lescenski, Head Pro

Tee Time: seven day advance notice; nonresidents: sixty days notice
Golf at 7,000 feet, fresh mountain air-scented by aspens, pinions and pines; crystal creeks and waterfalls, comfortable temperatures to inspire year-round play
Tees:
Oak: 3,200
Pine: 2,747
Rose: 2,498
Green Fees: Clark County Residents: Mon. - Fri. -$35, Sat. - Sun. - $49 includes cart; $5 extra for cart prolink which allows for viewing of upcoming greens; Nonresidents: $75 includes cart
Club Rental: $25
Facilities: 9-hole golf course including a par 5 over lake area and a par 6 to the canyon allowing for various changes in green area. Miniature golf, full pro shop, free picnic area, snack bar, club house, chipping and putting greens. Future projects include negotiations with the forestry dept. for additional prime land to increase the size of the course allowing for additional tee off locations; 16,000 - 17,000 sq. ft. alpine village family fun center to open in mid-spring of 1998 including a video arcade, convenience store, gift shops and restaurant area; iceskating rink with surrounding ampitheater for viewing of winter staged performances. Plans for Asian and western villages are also being proposed.

North Las Vegas Golf Course
est. 1971
324 E. Brooks Ave.
N. Las Vegas, NV 89030
633-1833
Tee times: seven days in advance
Municipal course for 9 holes *(night lighted)*
Small, 18-acre par 3 course. First night lit course in Nevada. From April 1 to November 10 Last tee time is 10 pm, course closes at midnight
Hilly par-3 course. Longest hole is 212 yards.
Tees: Men's: 1,158 yds. par 27, USGA 52.6 *(based on 18 holes)*; slope n/a
Green Fees: weekdays: $5, seniors $4, students $4.50; weekends: $6.50, $7.50 after 5 pm
Hand Carts: $2
Club rentals: $10 including pull cart
Facilities: Pro shop, putting green and snack bar.

Painted Desert Golf Course
est. 1987
5555 Painted Mirage Rd.
Las Vegas, NV 89129
645-2568
Office: 645-2570
Rebecca Allen, Head Pro & Dir. of Golf
Tee times: seven days in advance.
Public course *(privately owned)* of 18 holes; desert target design course consisting of lush fairway landing pads amidst natural desert landscape.
Tees: Championship: 6,840 yds. par 72, USGA 73.7, slope 136
Men's: 6,323 yds. par 72, USGA 71, slope 128
Ladies': 5,711 yds. par 72, USGA 73, slope 127
Green Fees: Residents and Members of American Golf $50, twilight rates after 2 pm $35; non-residents Mon. - Thu. $100 and Fri.-Sun. $120
Club Rentals: $25 - $40, $35 after 2 pm
Facilities: Pro shop, driving range, putting green, snack bar & bar.

Palm Valley Golf Club
est. 1991
(Sun City)
9201 Del Webb Blvd.
Las Vegas, NV 89134
363-4373
Scott Greer, Dir. of Golf
Tee times: Nonhomeowners tee times taken 7 days in advance at 6 am for weekends and 3 days in advance for weekdays.
18-hole semi-private course. Bent grass greens. Tough layout on rolling & wide-open terrain.
Tees: Championship: Blue 6,849 yds,, par 72, USGA 72.3. slope 127
Men's: White 6,341 yds.. par 72, USGA 69.8, slope 124
Ladies: Red 5,502 yds., par 72, USGA 71.5, slope 124
Ladies: Gold 5,757 yds., par 72, USGA 67.5, slope 119
Cart Rentals: $13
Club Rentals: $15 - $30
Facilities: Pro shop, driving range, two putting greens, snack bar & bar. Additional facilities for members.

Rio Secco Golf Club
est. 1997
2851 Grand Hills Dr.
Las Vegas, NV. 89012
361-7044
Frank Campagna, Dir. of Golf
Clif Vanetti, Head Pro
Tee times: 30 days in advance. 18 holes - 72 par course that is not yet rated set in the rolling foothills of the Black Mountain Range.
Tees: Range Tournament: 6,375 yds.
Championship: 7,332 yds.
Men's: 6,951 yds.
Ladies': 5,778 yds.
Green Fees: $190 includes cart rental.
Club Rentals: $40
Facilities: Pro shop, putting & chipping green, driving range, & Harmon School of Golf with Tiger Woods' coach, Butch Harmon. This is an open school, where the teacher - student ratio is 1:3. The cost of this school is $2,000 - one day & $4,000 - three days.

Shadow Creek
(Private Golf Course)
N. Las Vegas, NV 89030
Mirage Resorts
By invitation only, not open to the public

SouthShore Golf Club
29 Grand Mediterra Blvd.
Henderson, NV. 89011
558-0022
John Herndon, Dir. of Golf & Head Pro
Southern Nevada's only Jack Nicklaus Signature Golf Course. Only open to members of the SouthShore Golf Club. The Jack Nicklaus designed layout is a 71 par course with an elevation ranging from 1,400 - 1,750 ft. A challenging course, forcing drives over canyons and water, with strategic bunkering.
Tees: Championship: 6,917 yds. par 71, USGA 72.8, slope 133
Blue: 6,524 yds. par 71, USGA 70.7, slope 130
White: 6,204 yds. par 71, USGA 69.2, slope 123
Ladies: 4,830 yds. par 71, USGA 66.5, slope 110
Green Fees: For members only
Facilities: Clubhouse, restaurant, bar and new course opens in April named the Links at Monte Lago.

Spanish Trail Country Club
est. 1984
5050 Spanish Trail Ln.
Las Vegas, NV 89113
364-0357   364-5050
Jesse Thorp, Gen. Mgr.
Robert Trent Jones, Jr. Golf Course Designer
Jerry Roberts, Head Pro
Private course *(Members only)* - 27 holes; consisting of bent grass greens, undulating fairways and lakes. Not open to the public.
Tees: Championship: 7,107 yds. par 72, USGA 73.8, slope 139
Men's: 6,516 yds. par 72 USGA 71.1, slope 131
Ladies': 5,761 yds. par 72, USGA 74.4, slope 138
Green Fees: Private membership only
Facilities: 45,000 sq. ft. club house, pro shop, driving range, putting green, restaurant, banquet room, lounge, snack bar & grill.

SPORTS

GOLF

Stallion Mountain Country Club
est. 1990
5500 E. Flamingo Rd.
Las Vegas, NV 89122
456-3160
For information call Carol Goree, Dir. of Mktg.
456-2440
Mike Hawkins, VP/Gen. Mgr.
Joe Kelly, Dir. of Golf
Neil Pierce, Head Pro
Membership fees: Initiation fee of $9,500 and $200 in monthly dues.
Tee times: 7 days in advance
Private course - 54 holes; rolling terrain, lots of bunkers, mature trees and wall-to-wall grass.
3 courses
South Course:
Tees: Championship: 6,914 yds. par 72, USGA 71.7, slope 119
Men's: 6,493 yds. par 72, USGA 70.0, slope 115
Ladies': 5,473 yds par 72, USGA 71.3, slope 121
Ladies: Championship 6,849 yds., par 72, USGA 71.7, slope 119
North Course: opened 1991.
Tees: Championship 6,661 yds. par 72.
Men's: 6,052 yds. par 72.
Women's: 5,210 yds par 72, USGA 68.9, slope 115
West Course:
Tees: Championship 7,212 yds, par 72, USHGA 73.6, slope 127
Mens: 6,519 yds, par 72, USGA 70.2, slope 121

Ladies: 5,465 yds., par 72, USGA 70.3, slope 118
Green Fees: Members and guests only
Facilities: 3 golf courses, pro shop, John Jacobs Golf School, 16-acre practice facility with driving range and putting green and unlimited practice balls; restaurant, snack bars and bar.
West Course: opened 1995 Championship on water on 10 holes 7,200 yards, bent grass greens, pennlinks greens 18 hole, par 72- 7,212 yards.
Course Highlights - Phase III
Championship: 7,212 yds. par 72, USGA 73.5, slope 127
Men's: 6,519 yds. par 72, USGA 70.2, slope 121
Ladies: 5,465 yds. par 72, USGA 70.2, slope 118

Sunrise Vista Golf Course
est. 1972
formerly Nellis Golf Course
Building T 1619
2841 Kinley Dr.
Nellis AFB, NV 89191
652-2602
John Elkins, Dir. of Golf
John Little, Head Pro
Tee time: three days in advance; active duty have priority.
Flat course for use by active duty and retired military personnel and Department of Defense civilian employees
Tees: Championship: 6,813 yds. par 72, USGA 71.8, slope 114

Men's: 6,429 yds. par 72, USGA 70.1, slope 110
Ladies': 5,506 yds. par 72, USGA 69.5, slope 107
Green Fees: Sliding scale for military by rank.
Facilities: Pro shop, lighted driving range, two putting greens, chipping greens, restaurant, snack bar & bar.

Tournament Players Club at Summerlin
est. 1991
1700 Village Center Dr.
Las Vegas, NV 89134
256-0111 256-0222
Private course
Mike Davis, Gen. Mgr. & Dir. of Golf
Brain Hawthorne, Head Pro
Course includes large greens with subtle breaks, four water hazards and five natural washes.
Stadium course serves as headquarters for the Las Vegas Invitational. Built, designed and managed by the PGA; rated 12th in the TPC network.
Tees: Championship: 6,866 yds., par 72, USGA 72.1, slope 129.
Men's: White: 6,292 yds. par 72, USGA 69, slope 118; Blue: 6,866 yds. par 72, USGA 72.4, slope 127; Gold: 7,243 yds. par 72, USGA 74.3, slope 139
Ladies': 5,395 yds. par 72, USGA 70.4, slope 122.
Green Fees: Private, members and guests only.

Facilities: Pro shop, driving range, putting green, tennis courts, pool, bar, restaurant & banquet room.

Wildhorse Golf Club
est. 1961
2100 W. Warm Springs Rd.
Henderson, NV 89014
434-9009
Tee times: Seven days in advance.
18 hole semi-private course
Charles Packard, Head Pro
Tees: Championship: 7,041 yds. USGA 75.5, slope 135
Men's: Gold - 6,465 yds. par 72, USGA 72.2, slope 129; Blue - 6,513 yds. par 72, USGA 72.2, slope 129; White - 5,954 yds. par 72, USGA 9.7, slope 124; Black - 5,911 yds par 72, USGA 69.7, slope 124
Ladies': Gold - 6,513 yds. par 72, USGA 78.0, slope 137; Silver - 5,331 yds. par 72, USGA 71.3, slope 125; White - 5,954 yds. par 72, USGA 74.5, slope 130; Red - 5,372 yds. par 72, USGA 71.3, slope 125
Green Fees: Clark County Residents with American Golf Card: Weekdays $50 for 18 holes; Non-residents: $95 for 18 holes Mon. - Thurs; $110 weekends
Club Rental: $20 - $40
Mandatory carts included in fees
Facilities: Pro shop, driving range, putting green, restaurant, snack bar, bar & tennis courts.

GOLF ORGANIZATIONS

Las Vegas Invitational & Sr. Invitational
1680 Village Center Circle, Ste. C-3
Las Vegas, NV 89134
382-6616 242-3000
Charlie Baron, Tournament Mgr.
The Las Vegas Invitational is a pro-am held each October at the Tournament Players Club in Summerlin. The 15th Annual Las Vegas Invitational featured a $1.8 million purse, one of the richest on the PGA tour.

Las Vegas Women's Golf Association
870-9959
Deon Johnson, Pres.
Amateur tournaments throughout the year consisting of several local club teams.

Southern Nevada Junior Golf Association
3430 E. Flamingo Rd., Ste. 224
Las Vegas, NV 89121
433-0626
Jane Schlosser, Exec. Dir.
Non-profit organization dedicated to the development of youth through supervised golf, social activities and tournaments.

Southern Nevada Golf Association
5205 Consul Ave.
Las Vegas, NV 89122
641-4080
Stuart Reid, Pres.
Regional golf association for the USGA. Meeting held at the Las Vegas Golf Course on the first Thursday of each month.

Southern Nevada Inner-City Youth Golf Association
Sponsored by the City of Las Vegas

Parks and Leisure Activities, Southern Nevada Inner-City Youth Golf Association is an educational and athletic scholarship and teaching program to provide the youth of Las Vegas the opportunity to learn the life skills acquired through playing the game of golf.

GOLF RANGES

Green Valley Golf Range
1351 W. Warm Springs Rd.
Henderson, NV 89014
434-4300
Clinton Weaver
Hours: 24 hrs.
Price: $5 small; $7 medium; $9 large
Lighted, free-standing golf range with 95 hitting stations. Forty stations are shaded and have mist sprayers for summer and heaters for winter. Pitching and putting green, and a practice sand trap. Professional instruction, snack bar, clubs available.

Star Golf Lounge
3000 Meade Ave.
Las Vegas, NV 89102
247-4653
Bill Kenneman, Owner
Hours: Mon. - Fri. 9 am - 2 am; 24 hrs. weekends
Lighted target golf range with a tavern.

GOLF TOURS

Las Vegas Golf Tours
2245 N. Green Valley Pkwy. Ste. 204
Henderson, NV 89014
434-8187
Mon. - Fri. 8 am - 3 pm

World Class Golf
1631 E. Sunset Rd., Ste. C105
Las Vegas, NV 89119
361-8778 1-800-332-8776

GOLF EQUIPMENT & SUPPLIES

Besides the golf stores listed below, every course has a pro shop

Akropolis Sports Center
3890 Swenson St.
Las Vegas, NV 89109
735-2000
Buddy McDonald
115,000 sq. ft. sports center with two ice rinks, roller rink, an Olympic-size pool, full court basketball gym, athletic club, and quarter-mile running track. The facility will also house a bar and restaurant.

Golf War
1918 N Decatur Blvd.
Las Vegas, NV 89108
647-6584
Dennis Morrell
Hours: 9:00 am - 7:00 pm Mon. - Sat.; Sun. 10:00 am - 6:00 pm
Custom golf clubs, golf equipment and supplies.

Las Vegas Golf & Tennis
4211 Paradise Rd.
Las Vegas, NV 89109
892-9999
12,000 sq. ft. store with golf and tennis equipment and clothing, multi-station driving area, putting green, golf repair center and tennis stringing and service.
Hours: Mon. - Fri. 8 am - 9 pm; Sun. 9 am - 8 pm
Credit cards: All major credit cards

2200 S. Rainbow Blvd.
Las Vegas, NV 89102
364-5111
Voss Boreta, Pres.
Hours: Mon. - Fri. 8 am - 7 pm; Sat. 8 am - 6 pm; Sun. 9 am - 5 pm
Credit cards: All major credit cards

Nevada Bob's
4043 S. Eastern Ave.
Las Vegas, NV 89119
451-3333
Robert Lucia, Owner

2303 N. Rainbow Blvd.
Las Vegas, NV 89108
646-0007
Hours: Mon. - Fri. 9 am - 7 pm; Sat. 9 am - 6 pm; Sun. 10 am - 5 pm
Credit cards: all major credit cards

R. C.'s Golf Shop
3310 S. Nellis Blvd., Ste. 28
Las Vegas, NV 89121
434-8880
Chuck Lellos, Owner
Hours: Mon. - Sat. 8 am - 5 pm; Sun. 10 am -2 pm
Credit cards: MC, Visa

5120 W. Charleston Blvd.
Las Vegas, NV 89130
877-0999
Hours: Mon. - Sat. 8 am - 5 pm

Roger Dunn Golf Shop
2261 N. Green Valley Pkwy.
Henderson, NV 89014
456-4653
Joe Davis, Mgr.
Hours: Mon. - Fri. 9 am - 7 pm; Sat. 9 am - 6 pm; Sun. 10 am - 5 pm
Credit cards: MC, Visa, Discover, AMX.

World Class Sports
1631 E. Sunset Rd., Ste. C105
Las Vegas, NV 89119
361-8778
John Tassone, Owner
Hours: 6 am - 8 pm .
Reservations for golf tee times, provide shuttle service to and from golf courses and golf club rentals.

HEALTH & FITNESS CENTERS

Chuck Minker Sports Complex
275 N. Mojave Rd.
Las Vegas, NV 89101
229-6563
Danny Higgins, Mgr.
Hours: Mon. - Fri. 7 am - 9:30 pm; Sat. 9
am - 5 pm; Sun. 10 am - 4 pm
Membership fees: $15 mo., $105 yr.;
Seniors $10 per month or $80 per year
Co-ed fitness center. Fully equipped
weight rooms, sauna, jacuzzi, aerobic
classes; fat & fitness testing; blood
pressure testing & circuit training; gym
w/volleyball, basketball and badminton
courts; racquetball courts; gymnastics
for youngsters, martial arts and court
leagues. Showers and lockers. The
gymnasium is available for rent to
organizations and groups of 10 people
or more for $20 per hour. First aid
and CPR training.

24 Hour Fitness Center
3055 S. Valley View Pkwy.
Las Vegas, NV 89102
368-1111

2605 S. Eastern Ave.
Las Vegas, NV 89109
641-2222

3141 N. Rainbow Blvd.
Las Vegas, NV 89128
656-7777

2893 N. Green Valley Pkwy.
Henderson, NV 89014
458-3122
Steve Clinefelter, Area Dir.
Hours: 24 hrs.
Membership fee: Initiation varies; $12-
$30 month
Co-ed. Free weights and machines, life-
cycles, stairmasters, rower, sprint,
Eagle & Nautilus equipment, aerobic
classes, child care.

Gold's Gym
2720 W. Sahara Ave.
Las Vegas, NV 89102
877-6966
Steve Madrid, Mgr.

3750 E. Flamingo Rd.
Las Vegas, NV 89121
451-4222
Sean Paxton, Mgr

7501 W. Lake Mead Rd.
Las Vegas, NV 89128
360-8205
Hours: 24 hrs.
Membership fee: $10 - $30 mo.
Specializing in weight training, aero-
bics; child care provided

Jazzercise · 647-TRIM
Sara Griffith, Franchised Instructor
Over 45 classes taught throughout the
Las Vegas area at various times of the
day. Baby-sitting available at some
classes.
Fee: $3.99 per week

**Judy Gillette's For Women Only
Fitness Center**
1142 S. Rainbow Blvd.
Las Vegas, NV 89102
258-1226

4451 E. Sunset Rd.
Henderson, NV 89014
898-3909

Judy Gillette, Owner
Hours: Mon., Wed., Fri. 6 am - 9 pm,
Tues., Thu. 7 am - 9 pm, Sat. 7 am - 4 pm
Membership fees: Personalized
For women only. Offers a variety of body
testing to find the perfect program for
your personal training and fitness plan.
Clients are assigned a personal trainer
to teach, coach and guide them through
workout to achieve their goal.

Las Vegas Athletic Club
3315 Spring Mountain Rd.
Las Vegas, NV 89102
362-3720

5090 S. Maryland Pkwy.
Las Vegas, NV 89119
795-2582

3830 E. Flamingo Rd.
Las Vegas, NV 89121
898-5822

5200 W. Sahara Ave.
Las Vegas, NV 89102
364-5822

2655 S. Maryland Pkwy.
Las Vegas, NV 89109
734-5822
Hours: Vary, please call
Membership fee: Initiation fee, $20 -
$30 mo. and specials
Guest fee: $10; week $25
Indoor & outdoor pools, racquetball,
handball & volleyball, Nautilus, Kaiser &
Bodymaster Equipment, free weights, aerobic & aqua aerobic, whirlpools, sauna,
steam room, tanning & massage, lounge,
snack bar and child care provided. Not all
services available at all locations.

Las Vegas Sporting House
3025 Industrial Rd.
Las Vegas, NV 89109
733-8999
Norm & Jennifer Jenkins
Hours: 24 hrs.
Membership fees: $50 week, $125
month; $15.00 daily.
65,000 sq. ft. club; 10 racquetball courts,
2 squash courts, 2 tennis courts, basketball and volleyball courts; indoor & outdoor running track; indoor & outdoor

pools, hydro-tone, sauna, steam rooms &
jacuzzi, aerobic classes, state-of-the-art
exercise equipment & weights; cardio
and strength training, boxing, yoga, tai
chi, shiatsu, massage. Full service
restaurant and bar, beauty salon, travel
agency, car detailing, child care.

Polo Towers Fitness Center
3743 Las Vegas Blvd. S.
Las Vegas, NV 89109
261-1030
Rick Nelson
Hours: Mon. - Sat. 6 am - 9 pm; Sun.
9 am - 5 pm
State of the art equipment includes
Cybex, Vesa Climber, ClimbMax,
Concept II Rower and Butt Blaster.
Refreshment bar and steam room.
Membership Fee: $35 month, rates $25
weekly, $8 daily.

Q The Sports Club
601 S. Rainbow Blvd.
Las Vegas, NV 89128
258-7080
Dan Gorski, Mgr.
Steam room, sauna, jacuzzi, lap pool,
massage and physical therapy; personal
training; aerobic schedule, lectures and
special events; Tanning Center; The Q
Cafe; Q-4 Kids Fitness & Children's
Center.
47,000 sq. ft.
Membership fee: $249 initiation, $35-
$57 monthly; corporate rates available.

Sunrise Fitness Center
765 N. Nellis Blvd.
Las Vegas, NV 89110
459-4241
Cindy Green, Mgr.
Hours: Mon. - Fri. 6 am - 10 pm; Sat. -
Sun. 8 am - 8 pm
Membership fees: $245 year
(no initiation); call for rates
Co-ed. Nautilus Equipment; cardiovascular equipment *(Lifecycles, Stairmaster,
etc.)* free weights, aerobic & water aerobic; pool, jacuzzi, sauna, steam room,
child care.

UNLV
McDermott Physical Educ. Complex
*It is best to enter the university from
the back; take Swenson to Harmon.*
4505 S. Maryland Pkwy.
Las Vegas, NV 89154
895-3150
Mac Hayes, Mgr.
Use of the university all-weather track
and shower facilities.
Fee: $2

Work 4 It
Personalized fitness
6376 W. Spring Mountain Rd.
Las Vegas, NV 89102
222-0803
Cindy Braden, Mgr.
Work 4 It provides personalized
conditioning and rehabilitation programs as well as nutritional and diet
supplement evaluation and information designed for the individual.

Bennett Family YMCA
(co-ed fitness facility)
4141 Meadows Ln.
Las Vegas, NV 89107
877-9622
Bill Starmer, Pres.
Hours: Mon. - Fri. 6 am - 10 pm; Sat. 8
am - 7 pm
Please call for membership rates. No
one is denied YMCA services due to
inability to pay.
Credit cards: MC, Visa.
72,000 sq. ft. facility with Nautilus &
Universal equipment; stairmasters &
rowing machines; aerobic & water aerobic, 25-meter indoor lap pool, track, two
full basketball gyms, outdoor walking
track, tennis and racquetball courts and
whirlpool and sauna. Health and fitness
classes and summer day camp.

HOTEL SPAS AND FITNESS CENTERS

Alexis Park
375 E. Harmon Ave.
Las Vegas, NV 89109
796-3300
Brian Hannig, Mgr.
Masseuse, two jacuzzis, beauty salon,
weight room, locker rooms, showers,
aquatic exercise and Jazzercise.
Hours: 6 am - 8 pm

HEALTH & FITNESS CENTERS

Bally's
(separate facilities for men & women)
3645 Las Vegas Blvd. S.
Las Vegas, NV 89109
739-4366
Kevin Land, Spa Dir.
Work out room, spa, sauna, massage.
Fees: $18 usage
Hours: 6 am - 7:30 pm

Caesars Palace
(separate facilities for men & women)
3570 Las Vegas Blvd. S.
Las Vegas, NV 89109
731-7110
Ken Henderson, Spa Dir.
Universal gym equipment; steam & whirlpool, for guests of the hotel only.
Fees: $16 use fee
Hours: 7 am - 7 pm

Desert Inn
(separate facilities for men & women)
3145 Las Vegas Blvd. S.
Las Vegas, NV 89109
733-4571
Mark Burgett, Spa Mgr.
Workout room, free weights, Kaiser equipment, stairmaster, treadmills, sauna, whirlpools, massages. Complete health club and spa facility.
Fees: $25
Hours: Mon. - Fri. 6:30 am - 7 pm; Sat. - Sun. 7 am - 7 pm

Flamingo Hilton
(separate facilities for men & women)
3555 Las Vegas Blvd. S.
Las Vegas, NV 89109
733-3535
Mosha Rosenblum, Spa Mgr.
Whirlpools, saunas, steam room, Universal equipment, treadmills, stairmasters, video aerobic, exercise room

with complete spa facilities, tanning beds (*$10 per session*), massage (*$45 for 1/2 hour*), television lounge, snooze room. Towels, safe deposit box, toiletries and sandals provided.
Fees: $15 usage
Hours: 7 am - 8 pm

Harrah's
(separate facilities for men & women)
3475 Las Vegas Blvd. S.
Las Vegas, NV 89109
369-5007
Kerry Printy, Spa Dir.
Complete health club & spa facilities. Lifecycles, treadmills, rowing machines, universal weights; heated pool, jacuzzi & saunas. Massage by appointment.
Fees: $12 for use of facilities; $18 for nonguests
Hours: Mon. - Fri. 6 am - 7 pm; Sat. 6 am - 6 pm; Sun. 8 am - 6 pm

Imperial Palace
(separate facilities for men & women)
3535 Las Vegas Blvd. S.
Las Vegas, NV 89109
731-3311
Winona Sylvia, Mgr.
Paramount stairmaster, Universal & Nautilus equipment, massages, tanning beds, steam room, sauna.
Fees: $10 use fee
Hours: 7 am - 7 pm

Las Vegas Hilton
3000 Paradise Rd.
Las Vegas, NV 89109
732-5111
Craig Bjokne, Spa Dir.
24 seat jacuzzi and state-of-the-art health spa.
Fees: $17 for day pass
Hours: 6 am - 8 pm

Luxor Oasis Spa
3900 Las Vegas Blvd. South
Las Vegas, NV 89119
Scott Hamann, Spa & Pool Mgr.
Steam rooms, saunas, indoor whirlpools, lockers, robes and complimentary juices and fruit, weight room and cardiovascular equipment including lifecycles and treadmills; outdoor pool; Trainer always on duty.
Fees: $20 a day; Swedish massage $40 for 1/2 hour or $70 for 55 min.
Hours: 6:30 am - 7:30 pm

MGM Grand
3799 Las Vegas Blvd. So.
Las Vegas, NV 89109
891-3077
Charlotte Bowdle, Spa Mgr.
Steam, sauna, hot and cool whirlpools and fitness equipment. A cardiovascular /weight training area.
Fees: $20; massages, facials, manicures and body treatments available.
Hours: 6:30 am - 7:30 pm

Monte Carlo
3770 Las Vegas Blvd. S.
Las Vegas, NV 89109
252-7777
Alan Espina, Spa Dir.
Sauna, steam, hot and cold whirlpool, fully equipped gym, showers, lockers, lounge area, Swedish massage.
Fees: $20
Hours: 6:30 am - 7:30 pm

New York New York
3790 Las Vegas Blvd. S.
Las Vegas, NV 89109
740-6955

Keskie Young, Spa Dir.
Fitness center, cardio-vascular equipment, free weights, circuit training, body massage - $60 - $65 for 55 minutes; hydro therapy woman's spa only - $20 for 20 minute soak.
Fees: $15
Hours: 7 am - 7 pm

Rio Spa
3700 W. Flamingo Rd.
Las Vegas, NV 89103
252-7777
Deanna Fortuneato, Spa Dir.
Fees: $16
Hours: 6:30 am - 7 pm

Riviera Executive Fitness
(separate facilities for men & women)
2901 Las Vegas Blvd. S.
Las Vegas, NV 89109
794-9441
Jeff Ross, Spa Dir.
Complete health & spa facilities. Exercise room, weights, sauna, whirlpools, massages.
Fees: from $10 per day
Hours: 7 am - 7 pm

Tropicana Spa
3801 Las Vegas Blvd. S.
Las Vegas, NV 89109
739-2680
Carol Peterson, Spa Dir.
Co-ed gym with separate men's and women's spa facilities. Universal equipment, whirlpool, sauna, steam and massage.
Fees: $15 pass
Hours: 7 am - 7 pm

HIKING & ROCK CLIMBING

MT. CHARLESTON
Toiyabe National Forest
Located 34 miles north of Las Vegas via US 95. For information on hiking in the Toiyabe National Forest contact the U.S. Forest Service at 2881 S. Valley View, Ste. 16, 873-8800 or stop by the Lee Canyon or Kyle Canyon ranger stations, 872-5486.

Toiyabe Forest offers 52 miles of marked and maintained hiking trails for all abilities.
SOUTH LOOP:
8.3 miles one way; very strenuous; 6 hours one way. The hike to Charleston Peak is very difficult and not recommended for one day. Trail begins at 7,600 feet at Cathedral Rock Camp Ground and continues to 11,918 feet. The gate to Cathedral Rock Picnic Area is open 8 am to 8 pm. At the top of Mount Charleston Peak you can see nearly 300 miles in each direction on clear days.
NORTH LOOP:
10.3 miles; very strenuous; 8 hours one way. Trail begins at 8,400 ft. and ends at 11,918 ft. Charleston Peak. The trailhead is a short distance from the Hilltop Campground on State Route 158; park at the second turnout on the left.

After reaching Charleston Peak you can continue another 9 miles to the Cathedral Rock Picnic Area. There are many spots along these trails for campsites. Trail offers excellent views of the Las Vegas valley.
CATHEDRAL ROCK:
1.4 miles one way; moderately strenuous; 1 hour each way. Begins at the end of Hwy. 157, across from the Cathedral Rock picnic area. The trailhead is located near the first parking lot as you enter the picnic area. The hike takes you from 7,600 feet to 8,600 feet. One of the most colorful areas in the summer when the wildflowers are blooming. In the early part of the summer a waterfall can be seen about half way up the trail. At the top of the trail is a spectacular view of Kyle Canyon.
MARY JANE FALLS:
1.2 miles one way; strenuous; 1 hour each way. Take Highway 157 toward Cathedral Rock; travel 2.1 miles west of the ranger station to Echo Road. After traveling .35 miles, take the left fork off Echo Road and continue up until the road ends. Good views of the opposite side of the canyon. Caves and two springs cascade down steep-terraced cliff walls at Mary Jane Falls.

GRIFFITH PEAK:
Take Hwy. 157 to marker 12 to Harris Springs. Hike begins at 8,400 feet and climbs to 10,500 feet, after 5 miles the trail meets the South Loop trail. This hike offers great views of the Las Vegas valley and Lake Mead.
TRAIL CANYON:
2 miles one way; moderately strenuous; 1 3/4 hours each way. Take Hwy. 157 toward Cathedral Rock; travel 2.1 miles west of the ranger station. When the road makes a sharp left toward Cathedral Rock keep going straight on Echo Rd. After traveling .35 miles to the fork in the road veer to the right. Continue a short distance further until it makes a right U-turn, becoming Crestview Dr. The trailhead and parking are located on the left side of the curve. This 2-mile hike connects to the North Loop. The first part of the hike follows an old road and then a foot trail. A number of trails dot the limestone walls along the way.
FLETCHER CANYON:
1 mile one way; moderate; 30 minutes one way. Trail starts about a half-mile from the intersection of Hwys. 157 and 158. There is a small turnout on the left for parking. The trail follows the closed-

off road to the right. The hike gently meanders through pinon and ponderosa pines and mountain mahogany and comes to a small spring at the end of the trail.
BRISTLECONE LOOP TRAIL:
6.1 miles round trip; moderate; 4 1/2 hours. Take State Route 156 south to where it ends in the upper parking lot of the Lee Canyon Ski area. The trail is located to the left, at the end of the parking lot. The Bristlecone Loop Trail is the only trail located outside the wilderness area, making it accessible to mountain bikes.
EASY WALKING TRAILS:
Robbers Roost
850 yards round trip; moderate; 20 minutes. Travel 3.2 miles north on State Route 158 from State Route 157. Parking is on the right, the trailhead is on the left. This trail leads to a couple of limestone caves. Legend has it that the caves were used as a hideout for bandits during the days of the old Mormon Trail.
Desert View
Along Deer Creek Rd. where you have a panoramic view of the entire valley. The walkway is paved and accessible by wheelchairs. It is about 150 yards from road.

MT. CHARLESTON HIKING AREA MAP

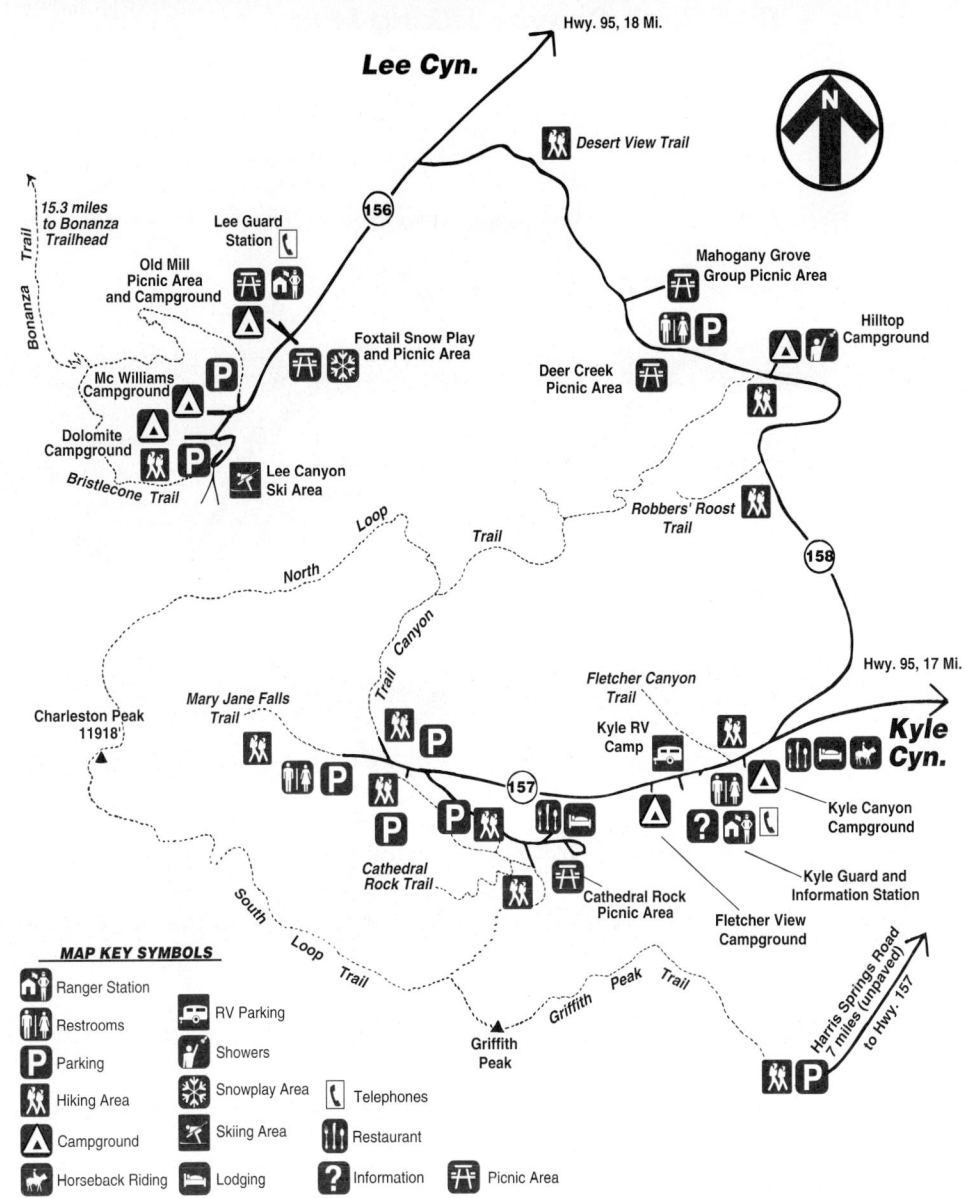

Hwy. 95, 18 Mi.

Lee Cyn.

Desert View Trail

156

15.3 miles to Bonanza Trailhead

Bonanza Trail

Lee Guard Station

Old Mill Picnic Area and Campground

Foxtail Snow Play and Picnic Area

Mahogany Grove Group Picnic Area

Hilltop Campground

Deer Creek Picnic Area

Mc Williams Campground

Dolomite Campground

Bristlecone Trail

Lee Canyon Ski Area

North *Loop* *Trail*

Canyon *Trail*

Robbers' Roost Trail

158

Hwy. 95, 17 Mi.

Kyle Cyn.

Fletcher Canyon Trail

Kyle RV Camp

Charleston Peak 11918'

Mary Jane Falls Trail

157

Kyle Canyon Campground

Kyle Guard and Information Station

Cathedral Rock Trail

Cathedral Rock Picnic Area

Fletcher View Campground

South *Loop* *Trail*

Griffith *Peak* *Trail*

Griffith Peak

Harris Springs Road 7 miles (unpaved) to Hwy. 157

MAP KEY SYMBOLS

Ranger Station	RV Parking
Restrooms	Showers
Parking	Snowplay Area
Hiking Area	Skiing Area
Campground	Lodging
Horseback Riding	Information

Telephones

Restaurant

Picnic Area

Bristlecone Loop

1/4 mile; easy. Take State Route 156 south to where it ends in the upper parking lot of the Lee Canyon Ski area. The trail is located to the left, at the end of the parking lot. On this short quarter mile trail you have a view of the cliffs of Mummy Mountain and of the ski slopes. This trail continues to a 5 mile hike.

LAKE MEAD NATIONAL RECREATION AREA

Located 30 miles southeast of Las Vegas via US 93/95 through Boulder City.

For information on hiking trails in the Lake Mead Recreation Area stop by the Alan Bible Visitors Center.

Guided hikes and lectures conducted by volunteers are held at the Alan Bible Visitors Center during the cooler months on weekends. Group size is limited so call Lake Mead National Recreation Area for information and reservations at 293-8900.

Boulder City - River Mountain Hiking Trail

5.5 mile moderate hike. This 55-year-old trail was built by the Civilian Conservation Corps. Trailhead located on truck bypass (US 93) just beyond the traffic light on the left. Spectacular view of Lake Mead, Boulder City, and the Las Vegas valley. Desert bighorn sheep may also be seen from this trail.

Bowl of Fire

Mile marker #18 - North Shore Rd. - moderately strenuous 8-mile hike through a scenic area of sculptured, multi-colored sandstone to an overlook with a dramatic view of the area.

Boy Scout Canyon

From Boulder City take Utah St. past the recycling center - strenuous 8-mile hike down a steep canyon through volcanic rock formations to an overlook with a view of the Colorado River.

Fortification Hill

3 miles east of Hoover Dam on Arizona side. Take US 93 to improved road 70. Strenuous 5-mile hike to the top of an extinct volcano with a view of the Boulder Basin. Not an approved hike unless accompanied by a professional group such as the Sierra Club.

Natural Arch

East of Hoover Dam about 6 miles. No marker, turn off before White Rocks Canyon. Moderately strenuous 6 1/2-mile hike traversing a narrow wash through ancient river beds to the natural arch in Black Canyon.

U.S. Government Construction Railroad Trail

Hike begins on Lake Shore Dr. opposite Alan Bible Visitor Center, 4 miles north of Boulder City. The trail follows an abandoned railroad grade through four tunnels on a level 2.6 mile, one-way route.

RED ROCK

Located 20 miles west of Las Vegas on West Charleston Blvd. For information on the 25 miles of hiking trails in the Red Rock area stop by the visitors center, open 8 am to 6 pm. Call 363-1921.

Bridge Mountain

Five miles one way, difficult. Natural bridge and views of Red Rock Canyon Area.

Calico Hills

1 mile one way, easy. Slick rock sandstone hills.

From Sandstone Quarry:

Turtlehead Peak

5 miles, very strenuous. 1700' climb with spectacular views.

Calico Tanks

2.5 miles, moderately strenuous. Many natural water tanks.

From White Rock Spring parking area:
Hermit's Cabin - 3 miles, moderate. A small cabin can be seen in the canyon to the east.

From the Lost Creek parking area:

Lost Creek

0.7 miles, easy. Leads to a seasonal waterfall.

From the Willow Spring Picnic Area:

Willow Spring / Lost Creek Loop

1.5 miles, moderate. This trail follows the northeast side of the canyon past Paiute roasting pits to the Lost Creek parking lot. From there, take the right-hand trail back to Willow Spring.

La Madre Spring - 6 miles, moderate. Trail follows the Rocky Gap Rd. across La Madre Wash and takes the right-hand fork to the northeast. At the dam, a path continues up the creek to the spring.

Top of the Escarpment

14 miles, strenuous. Follow the Rocky Gap Rd. and take the left-hand fork after crossing La Madre Wash. From Red Rock Summit follow the ridge easterly to the top of the escarpment. Then walk along the escarpment south for about 1/4 mile and then east and down toward the head of the North Fork of Pine Creek. From here non-experienced hikers should not continue and there is no obvious route. Experienced hikers can continue across the sandstone towards the rounded dome of Bridge Mountain to a pool of water with large Ponderosa pine trees.

From Ice Box Canyon overlook:

Ice Box Canyon

2.5 miles, moderately strenuous. The trail crosses the wash and stays to the north side of the canyon until the canyon narrows. The trail then drops into the wash and follows it to a seasonal waterfall.

SPORTS

HIKING & ROCK CLIMBING

From Pine Creek Canyon overlook:

Pine Creek Canyon

4 - 5 miles, moderate to moderately strenuous. The trail follows an old road past the Horace Wilson homestead to where the canyon divides. From there either of the washes can be followed to seasonal waterfalls.

Oak Creek Canyon

5 - 6 miles, moderately strenuous. From the Scenic Loop exit follow State Route 159 south for 1.6 miles to the dirt road leading to Oak Creek Canyon. From the road closure at the end of the dirt road follow the trail around Potato Knoll to the left. Sandy beaches and seasonal waterfalls can be found in the canyon.

First Creek Canyon

5 miles, moderately strenuous. From the scenic loop exit follow State Route 159 south for 2.6 miles to a large dirt parking lot at the trailhead. Follow the closed dirt road to the mouth of the canyon. A trail follows the canyon on the left side for a distance with some rock scrambling required.

VALLEY OF FIRE

Mouse's Tank

Length: 0.3 mile one way. Drive northeast on I-15 approximately 55 miles then turn right on Nevada Highway 169 to Valley of Fire Park. The trail follows Petroglyph Canyon west from the parking area. After a relatively straight section the road veers sharply left and then drops into the first of several natural water tanks.

Fire Canyon - Silica Dome

Length: 1 mile one way

Center about 18 miles from I-15. After 0.2 miles turn left and continue about 1.5 miles to end of paved road. Trail follows an old road now closed to motorized vehicles; superb view.

White Domes

Length: 3.5 miles one way. Follow directions for Fire Canyon - Silica Dome. The unsigned trailhead is at the north end of parking lot. Several hundred yards from trailhead, the signed White Dome trail branches left. View to north and northeast is spectacular. For information 1-702-397-2088.

GUIDED HIKES

Community College of Southern Nevada
3200 E. Cheyenne Ave.
N. Las Vegas, NV 89030
651-4000
Mike Metty, Dean for Rural & Urban Centers
Ext. 4622
Hiking and adventure classes are offered through community education, non-credit classes and leisure activities.

Friends of Nevada Wilderness
P.O. Box 19777
Las Vegas, NV 89132
363-4805
Lois Sagel, Treas.
Non-profit coalition of organizations and individuals providing public education and information on Nevada's public lands. Conducts bi-monthly meetings and wilderness hikes. Publishes newsletter.

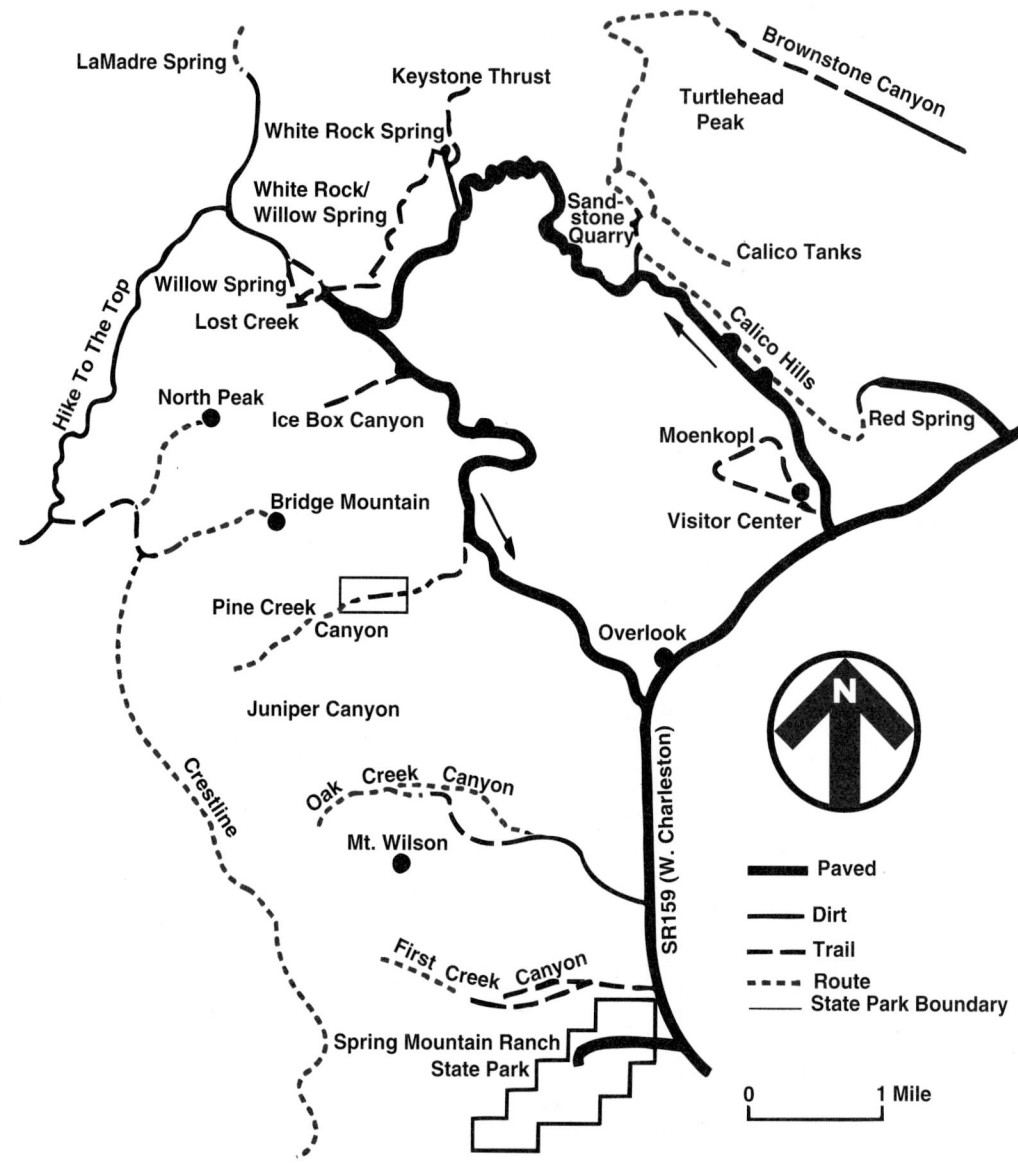

Red Rock Canyon Hiking Map

LaMadre Spring
Keystone Thrust
White Rock Spring
Brownstone Canyon
Turtlehead Peak
White Rock/ Willow Spring
Sand- stone Quarry
Calico Tanks
Hike To The Top
Willow Spring
Lost Creek
Calico Hills
North Peak
Ice Box Canyon
Red Spring
Moenkopi
Visitor Center
Bridge Mountain
Pine Creek Canyon
Overlook
Juniper Canyon
Crestline
Oak Creek Canyon
SR159 (W. Charleston)
Mt. Wilson
N
First Creek Canyon
Spring Mountain Ranch State Park

Paved
Dirt
Trail
Route
State Park Boundary

0   1 Mile

Lake Mead National Recreation Area
Alan Bible Visitors Center
Lakeshore Rd.\US 93
Boulder City, NV 89005
293-8906
Ellie Richardson, Supvr.
Guided hikes and lectures led by National Park Service volunteers.

Las Vegas Mountaineers Club
434-4323
Richard Baugh, VP
Purpose is to promote interest and enjoyment of non-motorized outdoor activities in the mountains and

back-country. Organized day and overnight trips include rafting, kayaking, bicycling, bird watching, rock hounding and photography.

Las Vegas Wash Ranger Station
293-8943
Thomas Valenta, Supvr.

Nevada Division of State Parks
875-4141
Jan Prida, Supvr.

Red Rock
Bureau of Land Management
HCR 33 Box 5500
Las Vegas, NV 89124
363-1921

Chris Miller, Mgr.
Planned hikes and walks in the Red Rock area. Promotes multiple use of trails throughout the valley.

Red Rock Audubon Society
P.O. Box 96691
Las Vegas, NV 89193
293-2716
Connie Lyons, Pres.
John Bialecki - 363-6615
Conducts weekly field trips and events, open to the public. Meetings are held at the Centel Building, 300 S. Valley View, Rooms 4 & 5 at 7:30 pm on the 3rd Wed. of every month except summer months and Dec.

SPORTS STORES

Desert Outfitters
2101 S. Decatur Blvd.
Las Vegas, NV 89102
362-7177
Hours: Mon. - Sat. 10 am - 6 pm
Specializing in recreational prospecting and mining equipment and supplies for the outdoors.

Desert Rock Sports
8201 W. Charleston Blvd.
Las Vegas, NV 89117
254-1143
Mike Ward, Owner
Hours: Mon. - Fri. 9 am - 7 pm; Sat. 9 am - 6 pm; Sun. 10 am - 6 pm
Credit Cards: MC, Visa, Discover, AMX
Climbing, hiking and mountaineering equipment; hiking trail information.

Peak Sports
3065 E. Patrick Ln.
Las Vegas, NV 89120
458-8870
Hours: Mon. - Fri. 2 pm - 9 pm; Sat. 10 am - 10 pm; Sun. noon - 8 pm
Located inside Rocks & Ropes.
Climbing, backpacking, telemark skiing; rentals available.

Sierra Club
641-9362
Dave Brickey, Pres.
647-5459
Call 363-3267 for recorded listing of outings. Sponsors a variety of hikes and activities.
Meets 2nd Wed. of each month at the Clark County Library on Flamingo Rd. at 7 pm.

University of Nevada Las Vegas
4505 S. Maryland Pkwy.
Las Vegas, NV 89154
895-3394
Offers a variety of programs through non-credit continuing education classes. Catalog is published in Jan., Apr. and Aug.

ROCK CLIMBING

The best place to climb in the area is Calico Hills area of Red Rock Canyon. Information on climbing in the area is available at the places listed below.
(See Hiking and Rock Climbing)

Jackson Hole Mountain Guide & Climbing School
P.O. Box 248
Blue Diamond, NV 89004
223-2176
Mark Limage and Andrew Fulton, Guides
Hours: Rock climbing classes 8 am - 5 pm
Rates: Basic beginning rock climbing course $65.00 per person - about 5 1/2 hours mostly done at Red Rock Canyon. A day of technical rock climbing - private guiding: $230.00 per person, $100.00 for second person. Half day $120.00, hike $45.00 per person, group rates available on request.
Based out of Jackson Hole, Wyoming next to Grand Teton and Yellowstone Park. Operates throughout the west at various locations such as Sierra Nevada, Joshua Tree National Monument, Devils Tower in Wyoming and various other states.

Rocks and Ropes
3065 E. Patrick Ln., Ste. 4
Las Vegas, NV 89119
434-3388
Trent Billingsley and Patrick Putnam, Co-Owners
Hours: Mon. - Fri. 11 am - 10 pm; Sat. 10 am - 10 pm; Sun. noon - 8 pm
Rates: $10 a day plus $6 for all the equipment you'll need. 10,000 feet of sculpted textured walls for simulated rock climbing with more than 80 routes. Rock climbing tours and 5 day camps available. Monthly rates available. Tuesday nights are ladies nights; women of all ages climb free.

Sky's the Limit
HCR 33, Box 1
Las Vegas, NV 89124
363-4533
Laura Sanders, Pres.
Randall Grandstaff, CEO
Climbing school and guides service by accredited climbers. Introductory course "Discover Climbing" at $169 for 1/2 day and $250 for full day for private guiding. Course includes 6 1/2 hours of instruction and transportation.
"Basic Rock Craft Course" offers classes at Red Rock, two days of climbing and transportation for $220; All equipment is provided; accredited by the AMGA.

Thrillseekers Unlimited
3172 N. Rainbow Blvd., Ste. 321
Las Vegas, NV 89108
699-5550
Fax: 699-5551
Rich Hopkins, Owner
Credit Cards: MC, Visa
Price: $150 a day
Rock climbing, guide, outdoor climbing gym. Safe and supervised instruction

and gear provided. Private and birthday parties. Do something unique for your next get together!

Photo: Phototechnik International

HORSE / EQUESTRIAN

The National Finals Rodeo moved from Oklahoma City in 1985 and is now held annually at Thomas & Mack Center the first week of Dec. The world's richest rodeo, with over $3.3 million in prize money, attracts the top 15 money winners in seven events. The 1998 NFR will be held December 4 - 13. The Helldorado Rodeo is held in May at the Thomas & Mack Center.

HORSEBACK RIDING STABLES

Cowboy Trail Rides
387-2457
Red Rock Canyon Riding Stables Located on the Red Rock scenic road at marker 10, Cowboy Trail Rides offers a variety of horseback rides at Lovall Canyon, Mt. Charleston, Valley of Fire and Red Rock Canyon. Choose hour-long rides to overnight trips, cattle drives, fishing trips, barbeques and more.
Rates: $25 an hour; overnight $225, which includes meals.

Mountain-T Ranch
140 Kyle Canyon Rd.
HCR 38 Box 140
Las Vegas, NV 89124
656-8025
Chuck Traynor, Supvr.
Guided Trail rides by appointment into the Mount Charleston foothills.
Hours: Call for reservation
Rates: Rides from 1 to 6 hours. The 6 hour ride includes lunch on the trail and a barbecue upon your return to the ranch. 1 - 1 1/2 hour $20; 2 hours and 20 minutes $30; 3 1/2 hours $50; 4 1/2 hours $65; 6 hours $100.

Silver State "Old West" Tours
798-6565
Hourly rides and group events in the Red Rock Canyon area beginning at Spring Mountain Ranch State Park. Rides range from an hour-long horseback tour of the ranch for $25 to all day ride which includes lunch for $97.50.

STABLES/ARENAS

Horseman's Park
5800 E. Flamingo Rd.
Las Vegas, NV 89122
455-8281
Bob Powers, Supvr. of Park
Horseman's Maintenance: 455-7548
Reservations: 455-8281
620 acre park with 320 permanent stalls, two arenas including a lighted rodeo and show arena, cutting area for day use, shower facilities.

Silk Purse Ranch
8101 Racel St.
Las Vegas, NV 89131
645-3223
Cathy Armiger, Mgr.
English riding and training, horse boarding - no horse rentals.

TACK STORES

Horse 'n Around Tack and Saddlery
1859 N. Decatur Blvd.
Las Vegas, NV 89108
646-1859
Chuck Punelli, Owner

Horse N Around Too
2540 W. Warm Springs Rd.
Las Vegas, NV 89119
361-4350
Chuck Punelli, Owner
Hours: Mon. - Fri. 9 am - 6 pm; Sat. 9 am - 5 pm
Credit cards: Visa, MC, AMX
English saddles, boots and tack; complete western tack.

Jones Feed & Tack
6515 W. Lone Mountain Rd.
Las Vegas, NV 89130
645-1992
Lee Croaro, Owner
Hours: Mon. - Fri. 6 am - 9 pm; Sat. 8 am - 6 pm; Sun. 8 am - 5 pm
Horse supplies, western tack, saddle repair, Purina animal feed.

Silk Purse Tack Shop
8101 Racel St.
Las Vegas, NV 89131
645-3224
Margaret McManee, Owner
Hours: Call for hours

Snowy River Feed & Tack
3084 N. Nellis Blvd.
Las Vegas, NV 89115
644-1935
Kimberly Story, Owner
Hours: Mon. - Sat. 8 am - 5:30 pm; Sun. 9 am - 1 pm
Feed, horse tack supplies, dog and cat supplies, rabbits, ducks, poultry, rats and mice.

V & K Wakimoto Farm Store
11925 Las Vegas Blvd. S.
Las Vegas, NV 89123
361-3441
Karen Wakimoto, Owner
Hours: Mon. - Sat. 8 am - 5:30 pm; Sun. 11 am - 3 pm
Feed, tack, pet supplies and alfalfa hay.

PROFESSIONAL SPORTS

Photo: Phototechnik International

SPORTS

1998 LAS VEGAS STARS SCHEDULE

APR. 7 - 10	EDMONTON	JUNE 22 - 25	OMAHA
APR. 11 - 14	CALGARY	JUNE 30 - JULY 3	NASHVILLE
APR. 25 - 28	MEMPHIS	JULY 13 - 16	FRESNO
APR. 30 - MAY 3	OKLAHOMA	JULY 21 - 24	IOWA
MAY 13 - 16	TUCSON	JULY 25 - 28	ALBUQUERQUE
MAY 17 - 20	VANCOUVER	AUG. 6 - 9	NEW ORLEANS
MAY 26 - 29	COLORADO SPRINGS	AUG. 11 - 14	SALT LAKE
MAY 30 - JUNE 2	SALT LAKE	AUG. 27 - 30	TACOMA
JUNE 4 - 7	FRESNO	AUG. 31 - SEPT. 3	TUCSON

Las Vegas has been home to over a dozen professional sports franchises since 1977. These include four soccer teams, Seagulls, Quicksilvers, Americans and the Dustdevils; three basketball teams, Dealers of the Western Basketball Association, Silvers from the Continental Basketball Assn. and the Silver Streaks; two football teams that folded before the season began, the Las Vegas Aces of the World Football League and the Nevada Aces Professional Spring Football League, Las Vegas Posse of Canadian Football Team and the Las Vegas Sting Arena Football; The Las Vegas Gamblers semi-pro hockey team; Las Vegas Flash roller hockey; all now defunct. The Las Vegas Stars baseball team, which will begin their 16th season, is the area's most successful professional sports franchise.

Many professional events are also held in Las Vegas. Two major golf tournaments, the PGA Las Vegas Invitational and the Las Vegas Senior Classic, which draws top players from the Senior Tour, are held annually.

The National Finals Rodeo moved from Oklahoma in 1985 and is now held annually at Thomas & Mack Center in early December. The world's richest rodeo, with $3.3 million in prize money, attracts the top 15 money winners in seven events.

Las Vegas is also the undisputed boxing capital of the world. Many championship fights are held at the Mirage, Caesars Palace and the MGM Grand Garden.

PROFESSIONAL TEAMS

In 1994, Las Vegas had two pro football teams, two pro soccer teams, a pro volleyball team, a pro roller hockey team, a pro baseball team and a pro ice hockey team. Only the Las Vegas Stars baseball team and the Las Vegas Thunder pro hockey teams remain. Both teams have been highly successful and are owned by the same family. The Los Angeles Kings, led by Wayne Gretzky beat the New York Rangers at Caesars Palace in 1991, in the first outdoor NHL game since 1925.

HOCKEY

Las Vegas Thunder Hockey
P. O. Box 70065
Las Vegas, NV 89170-0065
798-7825
Bob Strumm, Gen. Mgr.
Chris McSorley, Head Coach
Tickets: individual tickets - $10, $13 and $16; Season tickets - $300, $475, $600, $850 and $1,100. Ticket available through TicketMasters, the Thomas & Mack Box Office or Stars and Thunder Store at the Meadows Mall.

Henry Stickney, owner of the Las Vegas Stars baseball team, has brought a professional hockey team to Las Vegas to play at the Thomas & Mack Center. The International Hockey League team plays 41 regular season home games

and 41 road games, plus playoffs. The season runs from October through April. Games are broadcast on KENO 1460 AM. During the 96/97 season, 316,561 fans attended the 42 home games held at the Thomas & Mack Center.

BASEBALL

Las Vegas Stars
850 Las Vegas Blvd. N.
Cashman Field
Las Vegas, NV 89101
386-7200
Mandalay Sports Enterprises, Owner
Don Logan, Gen. Mgr.
Jerry Royster, Mgr.
Individual tickets: Club level $8, Field level $7, Plaza level $6, Reserved level $5, General Admission $4, Junior, Senior and Military $3.
Season Tickets: $200, $275, $300, $400 and $500.
Tickets available at all TicketMaster outlets or at the Cashman Field ticket office which opens at noon.

The Las Vegas Stars, Class AAA baseball team in the Pacific Coast league and affiliate of the San Diego Padres, moved to Las Vegas for the 1983 season from Spokane, Washington. The Stars play a 70 game home schedule, with all home games at 9,370-seat Cashman Field. The season is from early April through Labor Day. The Stars have been the most successful professional sports franchise Las Vegas has had, winning the league championship in 1986 and

1988 and attracting 313,128 fans in 1997. Stars games are broadcast on KBAD 920 AM.
The Stars have averaged 4,437 fans per game for home games at Cashman Field.

SPORTS MEDIA

LAS VEGAS SPORTS SHOWS
RADIO:
KDWN - AM 720 - 6 pm - 7 pm Tues. & Wed. Sports topics; Thu. 8 pm Sunset Station with Ron Futrell ; 9 pm Pigskin Power Preview; Midnight Sat. - Sun. Stardust line; UNLV football; Los Angeles Dodgers
KNUU - AM 970 - 9 pm - 11 pm Thu. - Mon. Between the Lines
KRLV - AM 1340- Weekends NASCAR, official broadcaster, live at race time; 5 - 6 pm sports corner
KENO - AM 1460 - San Francisco 49er Football, Chicago Bears, Dallas Cowboys, USC Football, Las Vegas Stars Baseball, Chicago Cubs, LA Lakers, NBA Game of the Week, LA Kings, Championship Boxing
KVBC - FM 105.1 - Sports in the evening
KXNO - AM 1140 - All sports station
KBAD - AM 920 - Sports, play by play and sports talk

TELEVISION:
K17TV - Cable channel 17
ESPN - Cable channel 19
KUPN - Cable channel 21
ESPN 2 -Cable channel 31

1998 LAS VEGAS THUNDER SCHEDULE

JAN 2	at MANITOBA 5:30 pm	FEB. 22	AT LONG BEACH 4:00 pm
JAN. 3	at CHICAGO 5:00 pm	FEB. 24	MANITOBA 7:05 pm
JAN. 6	MILWAUKEE 7:05 pm	FEB. 27	SAN ANTONIO 7:05 pm
JAN. 9	UTAH 7:05 pm	MAR. 1	at MANITOBA 4:30 pm
JAN. 12	at UTAH 6:00 pm	MAR. 3	at MILWAUKEE 5:00 pm
JAN. 14	GRAND RAPIDS 7:05 pm	MAR.. 7	at HOUSTON 5:00 pm
JAN. 16	HOUSTON 7:05 pm	MAR. 8	at ORLANDO 3:00 pm
JAN. 17	HOUSTON 8:05 pm	MAR. 10	SAN ANTONIO 7:05 pm
JAN. 20	CINCINNATI 7:05 pm	MAR. 13/14	at KANSAS CITY 5:30 pm
JAN. 23	LONG BEACH 7:05 pm	MAR. 15	at HOUSTON 4:00 pm
JAN. 24	at LONG BEACH 7:05 pm	MAR. 20 21	LONG BEACH 7:05 pm
JAN. 27	FORT WAYNE 7:05 pm	MAR. 22	at SAN ANTONIO 4:00 pm
JAN. 30/31	SAN ANTONIO 7:05 pm	MAR. 24	MICHIGAN 7:05 pm
FEB. 3	MANITOBA 7:05 pm	MAR. 27/28	DETROIT 7:05 pm
FEB. 4	at UTAH 6:00 pm	MAR. 31	ORLANDO 7:05 pm
FEB. 6	SAN ANTONIO 7:05 pm	APR. 3	at SAN ANTONIO 5:30 pm
FEB. 8	MANITOBA 2:05 pm	APR. 4	at HOUSTON 5:00 pm
FEB. 9/11	ALL STAR-ORLANDO, FL	APR. 7	LONG BEACH 7:05 pm
FEB. 13	LONG BEACH 7:05 pm	APR. 10	UTAH 7:05 pm
FEB. 15	HOUSTON 2:05 pm	APR. 11	SAN ANTONIO 7:05 pm
FEB. 20/21	UTAH 7:05 pm	APR. 12	at LONG BEACH 3:00 pm

SHOOTING & ARCHERY

ARCHERY

Pacific Archery Sales
4084 Schiff Dr.
Las Vegas, NV 89103
367-1505
Dan Bozarth, Owner
Hours: Mon. - Fri. 9 am - 9 pm; Sat. 9 am - 5 pm
Equipment sales and shooting lanes

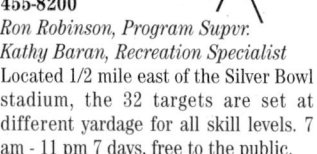

Silver Bowl Sports Complex Archery Range
6800 E. Russell Rd.
Las Vegas, NV 89122
455-8200
Ron Robinson, Program Supvr.
Kathy Baran, Recreation Specialist
Located 1/2 mile east of the Silver Bowl stadium, the 32 targets are set at different yardage for all skill levels. 7 am - 11 pm 7 days, free to the public.

SHOOTING

It is prohibited by law to discharge firearms in metropolitan areas, National Parks, Wildlife Preserves, Conservation Areas or Military Installation.

Active Sports
348 N. Nellis Blvd.
Las Vegas, NV 89110
452-6555
John Goodman, Owner
Indoor range, pistols and .22 rimfire rifles. Gunsmith on site.
Hours: 7:30 am - midnight

The American Shooters Supply and Gun Club
3440 S. Arville St.
Las Vegas, NV 89102
362-4321
Ron Montoya, Owner
Hours: Mon. - Sat. 9 am - 9 pm; Sun. 10 am - 6 pm
50 yard indoor rifle/pistol range; instruction; leagues.

The Gun Store
2900 E. Tropicana Ave.
Las Vegas, NV 89121
454-1110
Rick Crawford, Mgr.
Hours: 9 am - 7 pm
Pistols, revolvers, submachine guns.

Nevada Pistol Academy
4610 Blue Diamond Rd.
Las Vegas, NV 89139
897-1100
Dave Floyd, Mgr.
Hours: 10 am - 7 pm
Handguns and .22-caliber rimfire rifles.

The Pawn & Gun Shop
1212 N. Boulder Hwy.
Henderson, NV 89015
564-4266
Linda & Jim Reid, Owners
Hours: Mon. - Sat. 9 am - 5:45 pm
Handgun calibers only *(rifles of handgun calibers and rimfire rifles are allowed)*. NRA-certified instructors on duty. Gun cleaning and boresighting.

Shooters Emporium
3160 W. Sahara Ave.
Las Vegas, NV 89102
367-0025
Edwin M. Elliott, Owner
Hours: Mon. - Fri. 8 am - 5 pm
All shooting supplies.

GUN CLUBS

Boulder Rifle & Pistol Club
Boulder City, NV 89005
293-1885
Turn south off Utah St. on dirt road before dump, follow signs. Open to the public without charge within designated areas; many organized matches also open to the public. No glass targets allowed. Dawn to dusk. Outdoor range.

Desert Sportsman's Rifle & Pistol Club
P.O. Box 517
Las Vegas, NV 89125
642-9928
Lee Avant, Pres.
Range located at 12201 W. Charleston Blvd. near Red Rock Canyon, the private club features six ranges located on 480 acres. $75 annual membership fee and membership in the NRA required.

Las Vegas Gun Club
9400 Tule Springs Rd.
(Floyd Lamb State Park)
Las Vegas, NV 89131
645-5606
Steve Carmichael, Pres.
Hours: Open to the public Fri. - Sun. 9 am - 5 pm; Wed. 5 pm - 10 pm trapshooting; Thu. noon - dark skeet shooting
$5.50 a round of 25 targets.
Trap and skeet; Shells, rental guns and instruction are available; league shooting on Wednesday.

PAINTBALL

Paintballs Adventure Quest
1401 N. Decatur Blvd., Ste. 33A
Las Vegas, NV 89108
647-0000
Las Vegas' only indoor paintball field with 10,000 sq. ft. indoor area as well as 7 tournament grade quality fields for outdoor play.
Hours: Mon., Tue., Thu., Fri. & Sat. 6 pm - 11 pm
Gun Rental: F - 4 Illustrator $15, Tippman Prolite $20, Mini Mag W/ VL 3000 hopper $40 *(includes 300 paintballs)*; Included with rental packages is a 2-piece camo uniform, gloves, goggles, co-2 and 100 paintballs.
Complete pro shop and repair station

SNOW SKIING

Photo: Phototechnik International

SNOW SKIING

Just a 47 mile drive northwest of Las Vegas, 11,912 foot Mount Charleston located in the Toiyabe National Forest, offers Las Vegas a place to ski and play in the snow. There are lodges, a hotel, ski area, a snow play area, a winter use

campground, a golf course, snowmobile and cross country ski area in addition to downhill skiing Nov. - Apr. with the aid of snowmaking equipment.
Southern Utah's Brian Head, about a 3 1/2 hour drive and 180 miles via I-15 north, is the closest major ski area. Northern Nevada has the greatest con-

centration of ski areas in America with a total of 16 different resorts within the Tahoe area. Tahoe averages about 40 feet of snow a year and the season usually last from Nov. to May.

Las Vegas Ski & Snowboard Resort at Lee Canyon
State Hwy. 156
Mt. Charleston, NV 89124
385-2754
Russell Highfield, Mgr./Owner
Local Snow Report : 593-9500
Dept. of Transportation Report *(local):* 486-3116
US 95 North to State Hwy. 156 (Lee Canyon) and about 16 miles to the mountain. Ski area is located 45 miles north of Las Vegas.
Lift Tickets: Adult full day $28; children 12 and under and seniors $21; Half-day afternoon *(1 pm - 4 pm)* adults $22, children $15; night skiing 4 pm-10 pm adults $28, children $21
Season Pass: $560, seniors $410 students 13-17 $470, children 12 and under $410.
Hours: lifts operate 9 am - 4 pm ; night skiing 4:30 pm - 10 pm on Saturday.

Season *(depending on snow)* Dec. to Mar.
8,500 ft. elevation
Three double chairlifts carry skiers to over 40 acres of maintained ski slopes surrounded by over 600 acres of forested terrain. Snowmaking equipment and an average snowfall of 80 inches.
Chair 1: (3,000 ft.) four runs intermediate to advanced
Chair 2: (3,000 ft.) five runs beginning intermediate to advanced
Chair 3: novice
Summit Elevation: 9,320 ft.
Vertical drop: 1,030 ft.
Runs: 13 Beginning: 15%; intermediate: 80%; advanced: 5%; longest run: 3,000 feet. Forty acres of groomed slopes.
Facilities: Ski school, Ski shop, rentals, snowmaking, day lodge, coffee shop and lounge.

Las Vegas Ski & Snowboard Resort at Lee Canyon Rentals
3119 N. Rancho Rd.
Las Vegas, NV 89130
646-0008
Russell Highfield, Pres.
Hours: 7:30 am - 6 pm

LEE CANYON SKIERS MAP

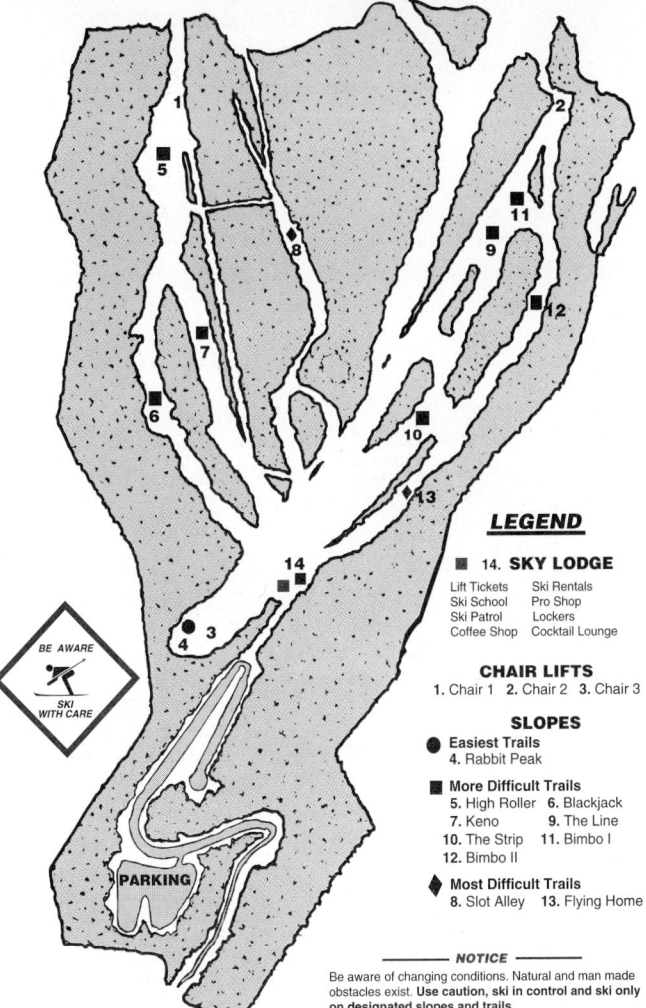

LEGEND

■ 14. **SKY LODGE**

Lift Tickets	Ski Rentals
Ski School	Pro Shop
Ski Patrol	Lockers
Coffee Shop	Cocktail Lounge

CHAIR LIFTS
1. Chair 1 2. Chair 2 3. Chair 3

SLOPES
● **Easiest Trails**
    4. Rabbit Peak

■ **More Difficult Trails**
    5. High Roller 6. Blackjack
    7. Keno 9. The Line
    10. The Strip 11. Bimbo I
    12. Bimbo II

◆ **Most Difficult Trails**
    8. Slot Alley 13. Flying Home

—— **NOTICE** ——
Be aware of changing conditions. Natural and man made obstacles exist. **Use caution, ski in control and ski only on designated slopes and trails.**

BE AWARE / SKI WITH CARE

PARKING

Lee Canyon Bus, tours & special programs
Free Lee Canyon bus leaves at 7:30 am
Call for information.

Thrillseekers Unlimited
3172 N. Rainbow Blvd., Ste. 321
Las Vegas, NV 89108
699-5550
Fax: 699-5551
Rich Hopkins, Owner
Credit Cards: MC, Visa
Thrillseekers offer snowboarding at Lee Canyon or Brian Head. Groups or individuals. Beginner to advanced tricks.

SKI RESORTS

Brian Head Resort
P.O. Box 190008
Brian Head, Utah 84719
1-801-677-2035
(8 am-4 pm Office)
Henry Hornberger, Gen. Mgr.
I-15 to Parowan, Utah, then 12 miles southwest of Parowan on Utah 143. Located 200 miles north of Las Vegas, Brian Head is about a 3 1/2 hour drive.
Hours: 9 am - 4:30 pm *(Utah is one hour ahead of Las Vegas)*
Runs: 10 novice, 20 intermediate, 10 advanced
Lifts: 5 triple chairs, 2 double chairs

Vertical Drop: 1,300 ft.
Longest Run: 4,934 ft.
Lift Tickets: Adult $35; Children 6 - 12 and seniors 60 & over $20;
Half day adult $28; children and seniors $17
Children under 6 free with adult
Season Passes: Valid Nov. 7 - Apr. 15; Adult $599, second adult $499; age 13 - 18 $299; age 6 - 12 $249
Rentals: Adults skis, boots, poles - $17 one day; $15 additional days; Children skis, boots, poles - $11 one day; $9 additional days
Lessons: Beginner's Special - $39 includes rental, lift, ticket and lesson
Private Lessons: $69 per hour and $21 additional person
Child Care Center at Brian Head Station: reservations recommended. Infants up to age 2 $50/full day. Children over age 2 $35/full day.
Hours: 8:30 am - 4:30 pm
Facilities: Ski school, ski shops, rentals, base lodges, restaurants, lounge, grocery store, accommodations nearby, NASTAR ski course.
Cross Country Center: 1-801-677-3012
Brian Head Ski Shuttle
Bates Travel: 736-2070
Bus leaves area ski shops on Wednesdays and Saturdays and returns the same day

after the lifts close. The shuttle price is $52 per person which includes lift ticket and a ski party.

Elk Meadows
150 S. W. Village Lodge Cir.
Beaver, Utah 84713
1-801-438-5433 1-888-881-7669
Snow report: 1-801-438-5433
I-15 north to Beaver, Utah, then 18 miles east of Beaver on Utah 153. Located 244 miles north of Las Vegas, Elk Meadows is about a 4 hour drive.
Hours: 9 am - 4 pm (Utah is one hour ahead of Las Vegas)
Runs: 30 runs plus off-trail skiing; 14% beginner, 62% intermediate, 24% advanced.
Lifts: one triple chair, two double chair, one poma and one t-bar.
Vertical Drop: 1,200 ft.
Longest Run: 4,000 ft.
Lift Tickets: Adults $30; Children 12 - 17 $25; Seniors 60 - 70 $15; Seniors 71 and over and children under 6 are free; weekdays adults $15, children $15
Season Passes: Adult $260; student $150; College students $210; seniors $150; family of four or less $599; each additional member add $100
Ski Rental: Keep all year Nov. - Apr., boots poles and skis: Adult $80; children 7 - 12 $60
Facilities: Ski school, rentals, restaurants, lounge, general store, gift shops, accommodations, lodges. Elk Meadows also caters to snowboarders.

CROSS COUNTRY SKIING

Mt. Charleston
Scout Canyon - State Route 156 north of the Lee Forest Service Station. Watch for a gravel road on the right. Drive up road about 100 yards to a plowed parking area.
Bristlecone Trail - Trail head is located at the top of Lee Canyon Rd., at the Alpine Ski area.
Macks Canyon - About 14 miles up Lee Canyon. Park in cleared area where you see the "Chains" sign.
Information on cross country trails can be obtained at any of the local ski shops or maps of cross country ski areas can be obtained at the USFS, 2881 S. Valley View Blvd., Ste. H, Las Vegas, NV 89102.

SKIING EQUIPMENT

It's All Downhill
5636 W. Charleston Blvd.
Las Vegas, NV 89102
258-SNOW
Snowboards, skateboards, wakeboards and clothing; rentals and repairs.

McGhies Ski Chalet
4503 W. Sahara Ave.
Las Vegas, NV 89102
252-8077
Hours: Mon. - Fri. 10 am - 7 pm; Sat. 10 am - 6 pm; Sun. 11 am - 5 pm
Credit Cards: MC, Visa, AMX, Discover
Mountain bikes, roller blades, skis, backpacking, water skis.

3310 E. Flamingo Rd.
Las Vegas, NV 89121
433-1120
Hours: Mon. - Fri. 10 am - 7 pm; Sat. 10 am - 6 pm; Sun. 11 am - 5 pm

Credit Cards: MC, Visa, AMX, Discover
Mountain bikes, roller blades, skis, backpacking, water skis.

Nu Style
4534 E. Tropicana Ave.
Las Vegas, NV 89121
456-6390
Hours: Mon. - Fri. 10 am - 7 pm; Sat. 10 am - 6 pm; Sun. noon - 5 pm
Snowboards

Play It Again Sports
2001 S. Rainbow Blvd.
Las Vegas, NV 89102
228-1713

8380 W. Cheyenne Ave.
Las Vegas, NV 89129
645-5548
Hours: Mon. - Sat. 9 am - 8 pm; Sun. 11 am - 6 pm
Skis and snowboards and accessories

Sports 1 & Ski Slope
1062 N. Rancho Dr.
Las Vegas, NV 89106
647-6000
Hours: Mon. - Sat. 11 am - 6 pm
Team uniforms, sports accessories and ski equipment.

Sub Skates Etc.
840 N. Rainbow Blvd.
Las Vegas, NV 89107
258-3635

3736 E. Flamingo Rd.
Las Vegas, NV 89021
Hours: Mon. - Fri. 11 am - 7 pm; Sat. 10 am - 7 pm; Sun. 11 am - 5 pm
Snowboards, sub skates, roller blades, wake boards, clothing, shoes and accessories.

SKI CLUBS

Las Vegas Ski Club
458-0469
Cindy Hanrahan
Formed in 1962, the Las Vegas Ski club has over 500 members. The club sponsors activities and trips for skiers of all abilities. The meetings are held at Oasis Las Vegas Resort the 1st and 3rd Thu. of each month at 8 pm.

Alpine Ski Club
362-7669
Raul Wood, Vice Pres.
Meets at Tommy Rockers every Thu. 7 pm - 9 pm for business and social; one trip monthly
Membership: $25 per season includes T-shirt and discount card

SNOWMOBILE

Mt. Charleston - at Mack Canyon, Scout Canyon Rd.

SNOWMOBILE DEALERS

Red Carpet Kawasaki/Polaris/Honda
4260 Boulder Highway
Las Vegas, NV 89121
451-1121
Hours: Mon. - Sat. 9 am - 6 pm

Rip Cove High Performance
575 W. Lake Mead Dr.
Henderson, NV 89015
564-8895
Hours: Mon. - Fri. 10 am - 6 pm; Sat. 9 am - 5 pm

SPORTS

SKATING

Santa Fe Hotel Ice Arena, 4949 N. Rancho Dr., Las Vegas, NV 89130

SKATING

ICE SKATING

Sahara Ice Palace
800 E. Karen Ave.
Las Vegas, NV 89109
862-4262
Greg Toy, Mgr.
Hours: Daily: Noon - 2:00 pm, Tue. - Wed. 5:45 pm - 7:45 pm, Fri. - Sat. 8:00 pm - 10:00 pm
Price: General public $5, children under 12 and seniors over 55 $4, skate rentals $2
Plans include "Learn to Skate" program, group lessons, broomball and a hockey league starting in Apr. Tuesday night is "Gospel Skating" to Christian music. Small arcade, a small restaurant opening soon, a birthday party room and private ice available

Santa Fe Hotel Ice Arena
4949 N. Rancho Dr.
Las Vegas, NV 89130
658-4993
William Coblentz, Ice Arena Mgr.

17,000 sq. ft. of ice with a 2,500 seat arena.
Hours: Call for hours. They vary from day to day. Senior citizens most Wednesdays noon - 2 pm
Admission: adults $5; children 3 - 12 $4; children 2 and under free; $1.50 skate rental, $2 hockey skate rental.

ROLLER SKATING

Crystal Palace
3901 N. Rancho Dr.
Las Vegas, NV 89130
645-4892

4680 Boulder Hwy.
Las Vegas, NV 89121
458-7107

9295 W. Flamingo Rd.
Las Vegas, NV 89117
253-9832

1110 E. Lake Mead Dr.
Henderson, NV 89015
564-2790
Hours: Tue.- Thu. 7 pm - 9:30 pm; Fri.- Sat. 7 pm - 11 pm; Sun. all closed except Boulder Hwy. 7 pm - 10 pm
Admission: Tue.- Thu. $5 plus $1 skate rental; Fri. - Sat. $6 plus $1 skate rental *(you may bring your own skates)*; speed skates $2, roller blades $3; Call for specials
Snack bar and arcade at each location. Roller Hockey Youth Clinic at all locations. Call for dates and times. $60 for 6 week clinic. Meets twice a week, ages 14 and under are required to go to clinic.

Mountasia Family Fun Center
2050 Olympic Ave.
Henderson, NV 89014
898-7777

Mike Nichol, Gen. Mgr.
Hours: Mon. - Thu. 3 pm - 10 pm Fri. 3 pm - midnight, Sat. 10 am - midnight, Sun. 10 pm - 10 pm
Admission: Skate anytime $4; $2 roller blade rental fee Prices apply to all ages. Can bring own skates.

Thrillseekers Unlimited
3172 N. Rainbow Blvd., Ste. 321
Las Vegas, NV 89108
699-5550
Fax: 699-5551
Rich Hopkins, Owner
Credit Cards: MC, Visa
Thrillseekers offers in-line skating tour of the Strip. Also lessons for beginners to advanced stunt skating, complete skating teams for performances, parties and grand openings.

SKATING EQUIPMENT

Las Vegas Skates
3421 E. Tropicana Ave.
Las Vegas, NV 89121
898-0080
Hours: 11 am - 7 pm
Skateboards, roller blades, etc.

Nevada Blade & Wheel
6160 W. Tropicana Ave.
Las Vegas, NV 89103
220-5008
Michael Ourada
Hours: Mon. - Fri. 9 am - 6 pm; Sat. 9 am - 8 pm; Sun. 11 am - 6 pm
Roller blades, ice skates, hockey, skating equipment and team equipment.

Sub Skates, etc.
840 N. Rainbow Blvd.
Las Vegas, NV 89107
258-3635

3736 E. Flamingo Rd.
Las Vegas, NV 89121
435-1978
Hours: Mon. - Fri. 11 am - 7 pm; Sat. 10 am - 7 pm; Sun. 11 am - 5 pm
Credit Cards: Visa, MC, Discover, AMX
Rollerblades, snowboards, skateboards; accessories, shoes and clothing. Snowboard and rollerblade sales and rentals.

TENNIS & RACQUETBALL

Many parks in Las Vegas and surrounding areas have tennis courts which are open to the public. All Clark County high schools, most junior high schools and even a few of the area elementary schools have courts that are open for public play when school is not in session. Many apartment complexes have tennis facilities as a part of their amenities. Las Vegas was host of the 1995 Davis Cup Semifinals in September at Caesars Palace.

Courts are also available at many hotels for public play. Priority is given to guests of the hotel, so it is best to call for information and reservations.

Las Vegas is the home of top ranked Andre Agassi and Michael Chang.

Tennis information and tournaments can be found in Paul Bauman's tennis column appearing every Thursday in the Review-Journal.

COUNTY PARKS WITH TENNIS COURTS

Guinn Middle School
6480 Fairbanks Rd.
Las Vegas, NV 89103
455-8200
4 lighted courts

Hidden Palms
8855 Hidden Palms Pkwy.
Las Vegas, NV 89123
455-8200
2 lighted courts

Laurelwood Park
4300 Newcastle Rd.
Las Vegas, NV 89103
455-7573
2 lighted courts

Orr Middle School
1562 E. Katie Ave.
Las Vegas, NV 89119
799-5573
4 courts

**Paradise Park
Community Center & Park**
4770 S. Harrison Dr.
Las Vegas, NV 89121
455-7513
2 lighted courts

Paul Meyer Park
4525 New Forest Dr.
Las Vegas, NV 89117
455-7513
2 lighted courts

Sunset Park
2575 E. Sunset Rd.
Las Vegas, NV 89120
455-8243
8 lighted courts

**Sunrise Community
Center & Park**
2240 Linn Ln.
Las Vegas, NV 89115
455-7600
2 courts

**Whitney Community
Center & Park**
5700 Missouri Ave.
Las Vegas, NV 89122
455-7573
3 lighted courts

**Winchester Community
Center & Park**
3130 S. McLeod Dr.
Las Vegas, NV 89121
455-7340
2 lighted courts

Winterwood Park
5310 Consul Ave.
Las Vegas, NV 89122
455-8200
2 lighted courts

RURAL PARK TENNIS COURTS

Bowler Park - 2 lighted courts
Lee Canyon Youth Camp - 1 court
Leavitt Memorial Park - 1 lighted court
Overton Town Park - 2 lighted courts

CITY PARK TENNIS COURTS

Angel Park - 2 lighted courts
Baker Park - 4 courts
Bob Baskin Park - 4 lighted courts
Bruce Trent Park - 2 lighted courts
Bunker Family Park - 2 lighted courts
Gary Dexter Park - 2 courts
James A. Gay III Park - 2 lighted courts
Hills Park - 2 lighted courts
Lorenzi Park - 8 lighted courts, fee and reservations
Ethel Pearson Park - 2 lighted courts
Von Tobel Park - 3 courts

NORTH LAS VEGAS PARK TENNIS COURTS

**Hartke Park/Pool
Neighborhood Center**
1638 N. Bruce St.
N. Las Vegas, NV 89030
3 lighted courts

Joe Kneip Park
2127 McCarran St.
N. Las Vegas, NV 89030
2 lighted courts

Cheyenne Sports Complex
3500 E. Cheyenne Ave.
N. Las Vegas, NV 89030
5 lighted courts

Petitti Park
2505 N. Bruce St.
N. Las Vegas, NV 89030
4 lighted courts

HENDERSON PARK TENNIS COURTS

Black Mountain - 2 lighted courts
Discovery Park - 2 lighted courts
Morrell Park - 2 lighted courts
Mountain View Park - 2 lighted courts
O'Callaghan Park - 4 lighted courts
Paseo Verde Park - 2 lighted courts
Pecos Legacy Park - 2 lighted courts
Silver Springs Park - 2 lighted courts
River Mountain - 2 lighted courts
Thurman White School Park - 4 courts
Wells Park - 2 lighted courts

BOULDER CITY PARK TENNIS COURTS

Boulder City High School - 4 courts
Central Park - 4 lighted courts
Hemenway Park - 4 lighted courts
Garrett Junior High - 4 courts
(For park locations see Parks and Event Centers)

OTHER PUBLIC TENNIS COURTS

UNLV
4505 S. Maryland Pkwy.
Las Vegas, NV 89154
895-3207
Harmon Ave., enter campus from Swenson
Larry Easley, Facilities Coordinator
Hours: 8 am - 10 pm
12 lighted outdoor courts
Fee: $5 per person, per day - reservations advised
$1 million Frank and Vicki Fertitta Tennis Complex. The complex includes seating for 2,000 spectators, tennis courts, a stadium club, offices and meeting rooms and locker rooms.

YMCA
4141 Meadows Ln.
Las Vegas, NV 89107
877-9622
Jay Johnson, Pro
5 lighted outdoor courts
Hours: Mon. - Fri. 6 am - 10 pm; Sat. 8 am - 7 p.m
Fee: $3 per person, members free; no reservations necessary

HOTEL TENNIS COURTS

Bally's
739-4111
Adolph Huddleston, Jeff Foley and Rita Agassi, Pros
David Pate, Tennis Dir.
8 lighted outdoor courts
$10 court charge per hour for hotel guests; $15 for nonguests; reservations
Pro shop: 739-4598

Desert Inn
733-4577
Marty Hennessey, Pro
4 lighted outdoor courts
No charge for hotel guests; $10 per day for non-guests.
Reservations; lessons/rentals available; ball machines at $20 a hour; open to the public
Hours: 6 am - 10 pm
Pro shop
Tennis clinic
Hours: Mon. - Sat. 8:30 am - 10 am
Fee: $18

Flamingo Hilton
733-3444
John McCauley, Pro
4 lighted outdoor courts
Hours: Mon. - Thu. 7 am - 8 pm; Fri. - Sun. 7 am - 7 pm
Fee: $12 per hour for hotel guests, $16 for nonguests

Frontier
794-8200
2 lighted outdoor courts
no fee for guests; reservations
Hours: 8 am - 11 pm

Las Vegas Hilton
732-5111
Sam Aparicio, Pro
6 lighted outdoor courts
Hilton guests only, no reservations taken
Hours: 6:30 am - 10 pm

MGM Grand
891-3085
Lornie Kuitle, Pro
4 lighted courts. Private and group lessons, kids tennis camps and guest partner matchup.
Hours: 24 hrs.
Fees: $20
Pro shop, rentals.

Plaza
386-2110
4 rooftop, lighted courts; Not open to public; rentals available
Hours: 8 am - 6 pm

Riviera
734-5110
3 lighted outdoor courts
priority to guests, no fee; public welcome, $10
Hours: 7 am - 7 pm

TENNIS CLUBS

Canyon Gate Country Club
2001 Canyon Gate Dr.
Las Vegas, NV 89117
363-0303
Tom Sullivan, Dir. of Tennis
Four lighted tennis courts. Private club.

SPORTS

TENNIS & RACQUETBALL

Las Vegas Country Club · Pro Tennis Inc.
3000 Joe W. Brown Dr.
Las Vegas, NV 89109
732-1861
Johnny Lane & Susan Campbell, Pros
Hours: 8:30 am - 9 pm
2 indoor courts & 4 lighted outdoor courts
Private club.

Las Vegas Racquet Club
3333 Raven Ave.
Las Vegas, NV 89139
361-2202
Christi McKee, Dir.
Hours: Mon. - Thur. 10 am - 5 pm
3 lighted outdoor courts.
Fee: $5 per day

Las Vegas Sporting House
3025 Industrial Rd.
Las Vegas, NV 89109
733-8999
2 lighted outdoor courts open 24 hrs.
Private club - reservations required.
Fee: $20 per person for use of all facilities for nonmembers.

Spanish Oaks Tennis Club
2201 Spanish Oaks Dr.
Las Vegas, NV 89102
876-5836
Bob Stewart, Admin.
Sammy Aparicio, Pro
Hours: 24 hrs.
For members only, 6 lighted outdoor courts.

Spanish Trail
7450 Mission Hills Dr.
Las Vegas, NV 89113
367-2711
Dan Knight, Pro
Hours: Mon. - Thu. 8 am - 8 pm; Fri. - Sun. 8 am - 4. pm
$1 million sunken stadium court, 12 outdoor courts; 9 lighted.
Private club.
Open only to residents of Spanish Trail. Nonresidents can apply for *"Social Membership"* which is the purchasing of membership of current holders. Contact the country club to inquire about availability - 364-5050.

Sports Club Las Vegas
2100 Olympic Ave.
Henderson, NV 89014
454-6000
Six pros on premises.
Open to members and guests only.
Hours: Mon. - Fri. 5 am - 11 pm; Sat. - Sun. 7 am - 9 pm
6 indoor courts & 7 outdoor courts, including 4 lighted courts.

Sunset Tennis Club
Lorenzi Park
2601 E. Sunset Rd.
Las Vegas, NV 89107
260-9803
Gerry Springer
8 lighted outdoor courts
Open to public; reservation required.
Fee: $3 per hour before 7 pm; $5 per hour after 7 pm
Club operates under a lease agreement with Clark County.
Matt Springer, tennis instruction: 647-2157
Lessons are available at $30 per hour for individual lessons to anyone 6 years and older. Groups are $8 for a one hour lesson.

Photo: Phototechnik International

Wild Horse Country Club
1 Showboat Country Club Dr.
Henderson, NV 89014
434-9000
Ann Rockwell, Tennis Dir.
Marcus Wittington, Tennis Pro
2 lighted tennis courts; open to the public.

TENNIS EQUIPMENT

Las Vegas Discount Golf & Tennis
4211 Paradise Rd.
Las Vegas, NV 89109
892-9999
Hours: Mon. - Fri. 8 am - 9 pm; Sat. - Sun. 8 am - 8 pm

2200 S. Rainbow Blvd.
Las Vegas, NV 89102
364-5111
Voss Boreta, Owner
Hours: Mon. - Fri. 8 am - 7 pm; Sat. 8 am - 6 pm; Sun. 9 am - 5 pm
Credit Cards: All major
Pro-Line equipment; repair & stringing.

Nevada Bob's
4043 S. Eastern Ave.
Las Vegas, NV 89119
451-3333

3480 S. Jones Blvd.
Las Vegas, NV 89102
362-9904
Hours: Mon. - Fri. 9 am - 7 pm, Sat. 9 am - 6 pm, Sun. 10 am - 5 pm
Credit Cards: All major
Complete Pro-Line

TENNIS ORGANIZATIONS

Nevada Tennis Association
2840 E. Flamingo Rd., Ste. E-2
Las Vegas, NV 89121
792-8384
Sandy Foley, Exec. Dir.
Members receive current information on upcoming tennis events. Tennis leagues & team competition for men & women of all abilities. Free tennis programs for youths & minorities. NTA can give referrals for tennis instructions.

Nevada Youth Tennis Foundation
792-8384
Sandy Foley, Exec. Dir.
Implements grass roots tennis. Free summer camps in 5 locations; one & a half hours of lessons twice weekly for three weeks. The top 20 children who show potential receive free lessons.

RACQUETBALL

Caesars Palace Hotel
3570 Las Vegas Blvd. S.
Las Vegas, NV 89109
731-7110
Ken Henderson, Dir. of Leisure Services
One court in Caesars Spa, open to public, reservations required.
Fee: $10 - up to 4 players per court hour.
Racquet rental: $2
Hours: 6 a.m - 8 pm

Chuck Minker Sports Complex
275 N. Mojave Rd.
Las Vegas, NV 89101
229-6563
Danny Higgins, Center Coordinator
Fee: $7 per hour for two people; $35 monthly membership of two people
Hours: Mon. - Fri. 7 am - 9:30 pm; Sat. 9 am - 5 pm; Sun. 10 am - 4 pm
8 public courts.

Las Vegas Athletic Club
2655 S. Maryland Pkwy.
Las Vegas, NV 89104
733-1919
Fee: $10 per person/per court hr. includes use of full spa facilities.
Hours: 24 hrs.
9 public courts.

3315 Spring Mountain Rd.
Las Vegas, NV 89102
362-3720
Fee: $10 per person/per court hr. includes use of full spa facilities.
Hours: Mon - Fri. 5 am - 11 pm; Sat. - Sun. 8 am - 8 pm
7 public courts.

Las Vegas Sporting House
3025 Industrial Rd.
Las Vegas, NV 89109
733-8999
Mike Coulter, Mgr.
Fee: $20 per person; $15 for hotel guests, includes full use of facilities
Hours: 24 hrs.
10 courts - 2 squash courts

University of Nevada Las Vegas
4505 S. Maryland Pkwy.
Las Vegas, NV 89154
895-3150
Mac Hayes, Dir.
Fee: $2 guest fee, students free with valid ID.
Hours: Mon. - Fri. 6 am - 9 pm; Sat. 8 am - 4 pm; Sun. 10 am - 4:30 pm
8 courts

YMCA
4141 Meadows Ln.
Las Vegas, NV 89107
877-9622
Fee: $10 per visit plus $3 per hour on court
Hours: Mon. - Fri. 6 am - 10 pm; Sat. 8 am - 7 pm
4 courts.

UNLV SPORTS

University of Nevada Las Vegas
4505 S Maryland Pkwy
Las Vegas, NV 89154
Charles Cavagnaro, Athletic Dir.
Department of Athletics: 895-3614

MEN'S SPORTS

Baseball
Basketball
Golf
Football
Soccer
Swimming and Diving
Tennis

WOMEN'S SPORTS

Basketball
Cross Country
Indoor Track
Outdoor Track
Softball
Swimming and Diving
Tennis

UNLV moved to the Western Athletic Conference for the 1996 - 97 school year. Some top pro athletes that graduated from UNLV are quarterback Randall Cunningham, shortstop Matt Williams, and forward Larry Johnson.

WAC expanded from 10 members to its current 16 universities and became the country's first true "Super Conference" in 1996. It is the third largest major conference in undergraduate enrollment with over 270,000 students. The WAC also has 1.5 million alumni and boasts a combined seating capacity of over 935,000 in its stadiums and arenas. Las Vegas has been selected to host the 1997 and 1998 WAC Men's and Women's Basketball Tournaments.

UNLV has outstanding athletic facilities, such as the Thomas & Mack Center for basketball and the Sam Boyd Silver Bowl for football. Also available are tennis facilities, pool, all-weather track, baseball stadium and a soccer field. Classes are offered in a variety of sports. UNLV is a member of the National Collegiate Athletic Association (NCAA) and is affiliated with the Big West Conference. Intercollegiate Division I competition for both men and women is offered in 14 sports.

UNLV BASEBALL

Rod Soesbe, Head Coach
895-3499
24-41, 1st season

UNLV FOOTBALL

Jeff Horton, Head Coach
Now in his 4th year.
13-32
For season ticket information and highlights: 895-3900
Football Department: 894-3400
All home games played Saturdays at Sam Boyd Silver Bowl.
UNLV ended the 1997 season with a 55-48 over-time loss to San Jose. They ended the season 3-8. The first opponent for the 1998 season will be Northwestern on Sept. 5th.

UNLV Football

UNLV BASKETBALL

Bill Bayno, Head Coach
All home games played at Thomas & Mack on the UNLV campus, Tropicana Ave. at Swenson. At UNLV for the 1996/97 season coach Bayno was the fourth head coach at UNLV in the last three years.
Tickets:
Thomas & Mack box office: 895-3900 or available at TicketMaster locations.
UNLV is committed to paying former coach Rollie Massimino nearly $1,000.00 per day into 1999 under the terms of his $1.88 million contract buyout.

UNLV Basketball

UNLV BASKETBALL STATISTICS AND FACTS

UNLV will open its 41st season in November. UNLV played its first game in 1958.
UNLV won the NCAA National Championship in 1990 and almost repeated the following year but were beaten in the final minutes by Duke.

UNLV had the longest home winning streak going in 1992 at 59 games until being stopped by Indiana on Feb. 14, 1993.
UNLV has won 10 of 11 Big West Conference championships since joining in 1983.
UNLV's overall record is 815 wins against 294 losses since 1958.

1998 UNLV FOOTBALL SCHEDULE

Sept. 9 at Northwestern	Oct. 24 at Southern Methodist
Sept. 12 Air Force	Oct. 31 Tulsa
Sept. 19 at Wisconsin	Nov. 14 at Rice
Sept. 26 at Colorado State	Nov. 21 Texas Christian
Oct. 3 Nevada Reno	
Oct. 10 at Brigham Young	Home games played at the Sam Boyd
Oct. 17 Wyoming (homecoming)	Silver Bowl

1998 UNLV BASKETBALL HOME SCHEDULE

Nov. 10 USDBL 7:35 pm	Jan. 22 BYU* 7:35 pm
Nov. 9 Melbourne 7:35 pm	Jan. 24 Utah* 7:35 pm
Nov. 15 LMU 7:35 pm	Jan. 26 Chaminade 7:35 pm
Dec. 17 Chicago State 7:35 pm	Feb. 7 Wofford 7:35 pm
Dec. 20 Syracuse 9:00 pm	Feb. 14 UTEP* 7:35 pm
Dec. 23 UC Irvine 7:35 pm	Feb. 16 New Mexico* 9:00 pm
Dec. 27 UCLA 9:30 pm	Feb. 26 Wyoming* 7:35 pm
Dec. 30 UNR 7:35 pm	Feb. 28 Colorado State* 7:35 pm
Jan. 10 Air Force* 7:35 pm	*WAC Game

1998 UNLV BASEBALL SCHEDULE

Jan. 30 at UCSB 2:00 pm	Mar. 25 Portland State 3:05 pm
Jan. 31 - Feb. 1 at UCSB 1:00 pm	Mar. 27 at TCU 2:30 pm
Feb. 3 - 4 S. Utah 3:05 pm	Mar. 28 - 29 at TCU 1:00 pm
Feb. 6 Utah 3:05 pm	Apr. 3 New Mexico 7:05 pm
Feb. 7 - 8 Utah 1:05 pm	Apr. 4 - 5 New Mexico 1:05 pm
Feb. 10 -11 Pepperdine 3:05 pm	Apr. 10 Air Force 7:05 pm
Feb. 13 UNR 3:05 pm	Apr. 11 - 12 Air Force 1:05 pm
Feb. 14 - 15 - 16 UNR 1:05 pm	Apr. 17 SJSU 7:00 pm
Feb. 20 at CS Full. 7:05 pm	Apr. 18 - 19 SJSU 1:00 pm
Feb. 21 - 22 at CS Full. 1:05 pm	Apr. 24 at Rice 7:00 pm
Feb. 27 Fresno State 3:05 pm	Apr. 25 at Rice (DH) 2:00 pm
Feb. 28 - Mar. 1 Fresno State 1:05 pm	May 1 TCU 7:05 pm
Mar. 5 - 8 UNLV Coors/Classic	May 2 TCU 1:05 pm
Mar. 13 at Grand C 3:00 pm	May 3 TCU 5:05 pm
Mar. 14 - 15 at Grand C 1:00 pm	May 5 Arizona State 5:05 pm
Mar. 17 Arizone 7:05 pm	May 8 at New Mexico 2:00 pm
Mar. 18 Arizona 5:05 pm	May 9 - 10 at New Mexico 1:00 pm
Mar. 20 Rice 3:05 pm	May 13 - 16 WAC Tournament
Mar. 21 - 22 Rice 1:05 pm	May 21 - 24 NCAA Regionals

UNLV Hocky

SAM BOYD STADIUM

TOTAL SEATING 45,287

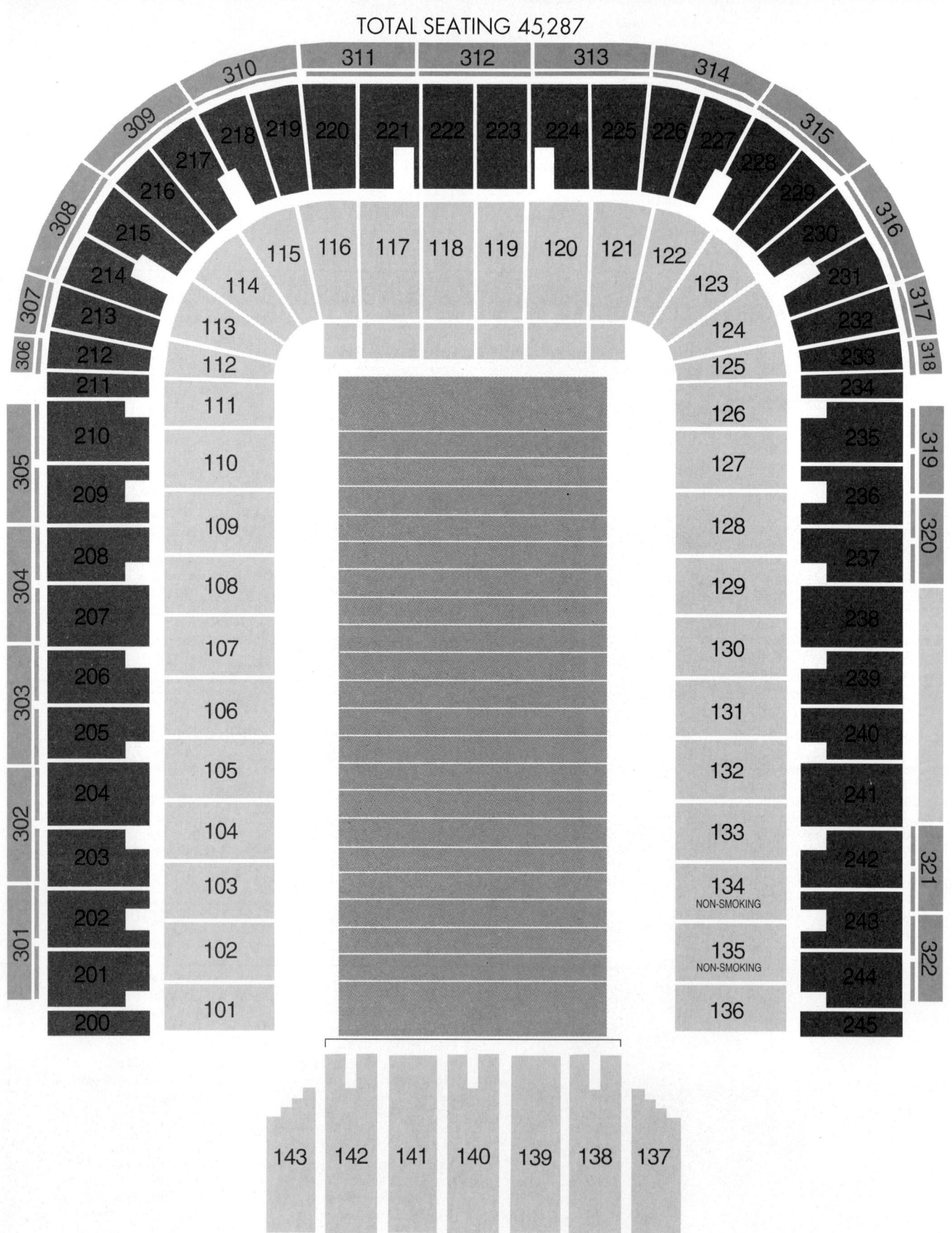

THOMAS & MACK STADIUM

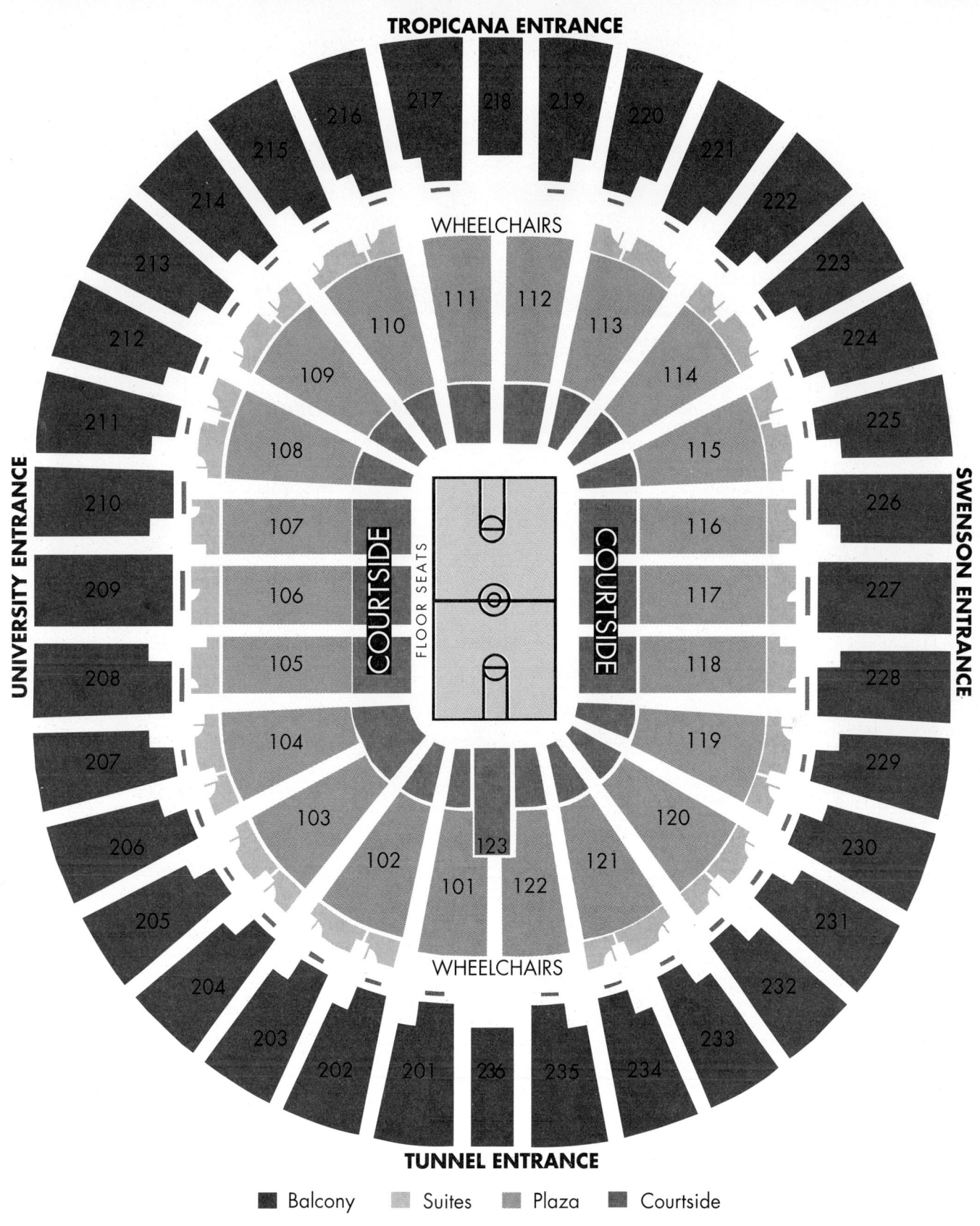

TROPICANA ENTRANCE

WHEELCHAIRS

217 218 219

216 220

215 221

214 222

213 223

212 224

211 225

UNIVERSITY ENTRANCE

210 226

209 227

208 228

207 229

206 230

205 231

204 232

203 233

202 201 236 235 234

SWENSON ENTRANCE

SPORTS

111 112

110 113

109 114

108 115

107 116

COURTSIDE   FLOOR SEATS   COURTSIDE

106 117

105 118

104 119

103 120

102 123 121

101 122

WHEELCHAIRS

TUNNEL ENTRANCE

◼ Balcony   ◼ Suites   ◼ Plaza   ◼ Courtside

WATER SPORTS

DIVING

The National Park Service has buoyed off a designated underwater trail at Boulder Beach, near the Pyramid Island Causeway. Call the National Park Service 293-8906 for more information.

A A I Neptune Divers
5831 E. Lake Mead Blvd.
Las Vegas, NV 89115
452-5723
Stephen Castle, Pres.
Hours: Thu. - Tue. 10 am - 5:30 pm; Basic open water instruction $150 plus books
Instruction, scuba equipment, rentals & repairs.

American Cactus Divers
3985 E. Sunset Blvd.
Las Vegas, NV 89120
433-3483
Jerry Yost, Owner
Hours: Mon. - Fri. 9 am - 6 pm; Sat. - Sun. 8 am - 4 pm
Instruction, scuba equipment sales & service, rentals.

Blue Seas Scuba Center
4661-A Spring Mountain Rd.
Las Vegas, NV 89102
367-2822
Hours: Mon. - Fri. 11 am - 7 pm; Sat. 9 am - 5 pm; Sun. noon - 5 pm
Equipment, instruction & in-store training pool.

Boulder City Divers
1637 Nevada Hwy.
Boulder City, NV 89005
294-5060
Rick Stevens, owner
Hours: Mon. - Fri. 9 am - 6 pm; Sat. - Sun. 8 am - 6 pm
Complete scuba instruction & full service dive center.

Desert Divers Supply
5720 E. Charleston Blvd.
Las Vegas, NV 89122
438-1000
Arthur Haugen, Owner
Hours: Mon. - Fri. 10 am - 7 pm; Sat. - Sun. 8 am - 6 pm
Masks, fins, tanks, boots, regulators & wet suits; open-water diver instructor training

Photo: Phototechnik International

Colorado River Diver
1321 Nevada Hwy.
Boulder City, NV 89005
293-6648
Ron & Vicki Ruiz, owners
Hours: Mon. - Fri. 10 am - 6 pm; Sat. 8:30 - 6 pm; Sun. 8:30 am - 3 pm
Full retail dive center; including sales, rental, service & instruction.

Neptune Divers
600 W. Sunset Rd.
Henderson, NV 89015
564-5253
Dwight Carter, Owner
Hours: Mon. - Fri. 10 am - 5 pm; Sat. 9 am - 5 pm; Sun. 11 am - 5 pm
Complete line of scuba equipment & flexible classes.

PERSONAL WATER CRAFT

Jet Away
5535 E. Lake Mead Blvd.
Las Vegas, NV 89115
565-4994
Joe Frohlich, Owner
Hours: 8 am - 6 pm
3 seater ski doos & sit down jet skis
Rental: $100 8 am - 6 pm

Wolff Adventures
240 N. Jones Blvd., Ste. 212
Las Vegas, NV 89107
233-3061 1-800-997-2708
Bonnie Wolff, Pres.

Photo: Phototechnik International

Personal watercraft rentals, jet ski tours of Hoover Dam; Grand Canyon tours and ATV tours and rentals also available.

RAFTING & CANOEING

The Black Canyon of the Colorado River can be run throughout the year.
The best place to launch is just below Hoover Dam. The 11 mile trip to Willow Beach is exciting and the steep canyon walls offer beautiful scenery with wild burros and Big Horn Sheep roaming the bluffs. The river is calm, flowing about 5 mph. A permit is required for both rafting and canoeing from the U.S. Dept. of Interior, Bureau of Reclamation, Lower Colorado Region. For a permit application, apply at least two weeks in advance of your launch date. You can write to them at: P.O. Box 60400, Boulder City, NV 89006 or call at: 293-8204 Mon. - Thu.

Black Canyon Raft Tours
1297 Nevada Highway
Boulder City, NV 89005
293-3776
One day guided raft trip down the Colorado River. Leaves at 9:30 am from Boulder City and returns at 3 pm.

Down River Outfitters
P.O. Box 61235
Boulder City, NV 89006
293-1190
Patty Beloud, owner
Rentals; self guided.
Launched just below Hoover Dam to Willow Beach or beyond.
Shuttle service is provided at additional cost. 1st departure at 8:30 am returns at 4 pm & the 2nd departure at 10 am is an overnight trip.
14 day notice is required along with a trip permit from the U. S. Dept. of Interior, Bureau of Reclamation, Lower Colorado Region.

CANOEING

Boulder City Water Sports
1108 Nevada Highway
Boulder City, NV 89005
293-7526
Bobbie Werly, Owner
Hours: 8 am - 6 pm
Canoe, kayak & waverunner rentals.

SWIMMING

Most public pools are open from Memorial Day to Labor Day. A variety of aquatics programs including learn-to-swim, lifeguard training and aquacise are offered through both the city and county.
Admission: adults $ 1.50, seniors *(over 55)* $1, children 3 - 17 $.50, Season passes: Seniors (over 55) $20; individual $25, each additional family members $5.
County: 455-8200
City: 229-6310

Baker Pool
(city)
1100 E. St. Louis Ave.
Las Vegas, NV 89104
229-6395
Hours: Mon. - Sat. 1 pm - 5:45 pm

BMI Pool
107 W. Basic
Henderson, NV 89015
565-2168
Hours: Open Memorial Day through Labor Day
Mon., Wed., Fri. 12:30 pm - 5 pm; Tue.& Thu. 12:30 pm - 5 pm & 6 pm - 8 pm; Sat. - Sun. 11 am - 6 pm

Boulder City Swimming Pool
861 Avenue B
Boulder City, NV 89005
293-9286
Steve Corry, superintendent
Hours: Adults - Mon. - Fri. 5:30 am - 9 am; noon - 1 pm; Sat. 7 am - 9 am
Open swim: Mon. - Fri. 4:30 pm - 7:30 pm; Sun. 1 pm - 5 pm
Fee: Adults $1.50; children & seniors $1
Open year-round with plastic bubble enclosure during winter months.

Brinley Pool
(city)
2480 Maverick St.
Las Vegas, NV 89108
229-6784
Hours: Mon. - Fri. 1 pm - 5 pm; Sat. 1 pm - 4:45 pm

Cragin Pool
(city)
900 Hinson St.
Las Vegas, NV 89107
229-6394
Hours: Mon. - Fri. 1 pm - 5 pm

Desert Inn
(county)
3750 Vista Del Monte Dr.
Las Vegas, NV 89121
455-7531
Hours: 1 pm - 5 pm

Doolittle
(city)
W. Lake Mead & J St.
Las Vegas, NV 89106
229-6398
Hours: Mon. - Sat. 1 pm - 5:45 pm

Garside
(city)
300 S. Torrey Pines Dr.
Las Vegas, NV 89107
229-6393
Hours: Mon. - Sat. 1 pm - 5 pm

Hadland
(city)
2800 Stewart Ave.
Las Vegas, NV 89101
229-6397
Hours: Mon. - Sat. 1 pm - 6 pm

Hartke
1301 E. Tonopah Ave.
N. Las Vegas, NV 89030
649-5811
Hours: Tue.- Sat. noon - 6 pm

Las Vegas Athletic Club
3315 Spring Mountain Rd.
Las Vegas, NV 89102
362-3720
Outdoor pool - closed in winter.

5090 S. Maryland Pkwy.
Las Vegas, NV 89119
795-2582

3830 E. Flamingo Rd.
Las Vegas, NV 89121
451-2526

5200 W. Sahara Ave.
Las Vegas, NV 89102
364-5822

2655 S. Maryland Pkwy.
Las Vegas, NV 89109
Rudolph Smith, owner
Hours: vary
Fee: $10 per day; $25 per wk.; includes
full use of facilities.
Child care provided.

Las Vegas Sporting House
3025 Industrial Rd.
Las Vegas, NV 89109
733-8999
Indoor/outdoor pools
Hours: 24 hrs.
Fee: $12 per visit for guest of member;
$15 per visit if staying at a hotel;
$20 for locals
Child care provided.

**Lorin L. Williams Municipal
Indoor Pool**
Basic High School
500 N. Palo Verde Dr.
Henderson, NV 89015
565-2123
Hours: Sat. - Sun. 11 am - 5 pm;Tue.-
Thu. 7:30 am - 9 pm; Open year-round
Fee: Adults over 16 - $1, children - $.50;
under 4 free

Maslow
(city)
3920 Lana Ave.
Las Vegas, NV 89109
458-9809
Hours: Mon. - Sat. 1 pm - 5 pm

Paradise
(county)
4770 S. Harrison Ave.
Las Vegas, NV 89106
455-8200
Hours: 1 pm - 5 pm

Parkdale
(county)
3200 Ferndale St.
Las Vegas, NV 89121
455-7523
Hours: 1 pm - 5 pm

Photo: Phototechnik International

Petitti
2505 N. Bruce St.
N. Las Vegas, NV 89030
649-5811
Hours: Tue.- Sat. noon - 6 pm

Sierra Nevada Arms Pool
(city)
1971 Carrera Dr.
Las Vegas, NV 89106
229-2472
Hours: Mon. - Sat. 1 pm - 5 pm

Silver Springs Pool
1951 Silver Springs Pkwy.
Henderson, NV 89014
435-3819
Hours: Mon. - Fri. 1 pm - 5 pm, Sat. -
Sun. 11 am - 5 pm
Open Memorial Day - Labor Day.

Sports Club Las Vegas
2100 Olympic Ave.
Henderson, NV 89014
454-6000
Indoor & outdoor Olympic sized pools.
Open only to members & guests of
members.

Sunrise
(county)
2240 Linn Ln.
Las Vegas, NV 89115
455-7610
Hours: 1 pm - 5 pm

Sunset
(county)
2575 E. Sunset Rd.
Las Vegas, NV 89120
361-9930
Hours: 1 pm - 5 pm

Trails Community Pool
(city)
1920 Spring Gate Ln.
Las Vegas, NV 89134
229-4629
Hours: Mon. - Fri. 1 pm - 5 pm; Sat. 1 pm
- 5:45 pm

**UNLV - McDermott Physical
Education Complex**
4505 S. Maryland Pkwy.
Las Vegas, NV 89154
895-3150
Hours: Mon. - Fri. 1 pm - 3 pm; Sat. 1 pm
- 5 pm; Sun. 10 am - 5 pm
Fee: Community ID $15 - 2 month
minimum; $5 charge for ID; $2 for each
facility for passes.
Weight room, basketball court, racquetball
court, swimming pool, track.

Von Tobel
(county)
2436 N. Pecos Rd.
Las Vegas, NV 89115
455-7625
Hours: 1 pm - 5 pm

Walker
1509 June Ave.
N. Las Vegas, NV 89030
649-5811
Hours: Tue.- Sat. 12 pm - 6 pm

Whitney Pool
(county)
5700 Missouri Ave.
Las Vegas, NV 89122
455-7573
Hours: 1 pm - 5 pm

Bennett Family YMCA
4141 Meadow Ln.
Las Vegas, NV 89107
877-9622
Hours: Mon. - Fri. 6 am - 10 pm; Sat. 8
am - 7 pm
Rates: Adults $10; Young adults ages 13
- 17 $5; Children ages 3 - 12 $4; Seniors
$5
Membership Fee: $29 - $48 depending
on age and family structure; various
enrollment plans; MC, Visa
3 indoor heated pools, full basketball
court, tennis, racquetball, track, boxing
area, saunas, whirlpool, private sun
decks, all facilities are co-ed.

SPORTS

VOLLEYBALL

Las Vegas Volleyball Club
5277 Cameron St., Ste. 110
Las Vegas, NV 89118
252-4244
Heather Iannoni, Mgr.
17,000 sq. ft. indoor volleyball facility.
Leagues, tournaments, clinics, private
instruction, equipment, court rental,
youth programs and open play. Retail
Outlet.
Fees: League play is $180 - $270 per
team for a six-week session; court rental
$25 per hour; open play $5 per person
Hours: Open play 3 pm - 5:30 pm;
leagues 7 pm - 10 pm

Clark County Parks & Recreation
2601 E. Sunset Rd.
Las Vegas, NV 89120
455-8241   455-8245
Sunset park has six lighted sand volleyball
pits; leagues.

Nevada Outdoor Volleyball Association
878-1775
Presents amateur volleyball association.
Hosts tournaments, special events.

SPORTING GOODS STORES

Big 5 Sporting Goods
4295 E. Charleston Blvd.
Las Vegas, NV 89104
641-2224
Andrew Jakus, Mgr.

2797 Maryland Pkwy.
Las Vegas, NV 89109
734-6664
Bruce Butler, Mgr.

1140 S. Decatur Blvd.
Las Vegas, NV 89102
878-6100
Steve Kain, Mgr.
Hours: Mon. - Fri. 10 am - 9 pm, Sat.
9 am - 9 pm, Sun. 10 am - 6pm
Credit Cards: MC, Visa, AMX
Sports clothing, shoes, fishing, guns and
ammo.

Copeland's Sports
3860 S. Maryland Pkwy.
Las Vegas, NV 89119
794-0119

2060 N. Rainbow Blvd.
Las Vegas, NV 89108
636-2866

S79 N. Stephanie St.
Henderson, NV 89014
436-3089
Hours: Mon. - Sat. 10 am - 7 pm; Sun.
11 am - 7 pm
Complete line of sporting equipment.

Desert Outfitters
2101 S. Decatur Blvd., Ste. 5 & 6
Las Vegas, NV 89102
362-7177
Rick Kasky, Owner
Hours: Mon. - Sat. 10 am - 6 pm
Emergency supplies, camping equipment, prospecting supplies and metal
detectors *(sell & rent)*

Holiday Hockey & Sport
4611 N. Rancho Dr.
Las Vegas, NV 89130
645-4301
Randy Huartson
Hours: Mon. - Fri. 11 am - 8 pm; Sat.
11 am -6 pm; Sun. noon - 7 pm
Hockey equipment, roller skates and in-
line gear.

The Jock Shop
5785 W. Sahara Ave.
Las Vegas, NV 89102
871-4910
Dean Weible, Owner
Hours: Mon. - Fri. 9 am - 6 pm; Sat. 9 am
- 5 pm
Credit Cards: All major
Sports clothing and footwear; silk
screening and embroidering of shirts
and jackets

Jumbo Sports
3071 N. Rainbow Blvd.
Las Vegas, NV 89108
645-0410
Steve Davis
Hours: Mon. - Sat. 10 am - 9 pm; Sun. 10
am - 6 pm
Credit Cards: MC, Visa, Discover, AMX
72,000 sq. ft. sporting goods store featuring a variety of name-brand sports
equipment, and athletic apparel and
footwear.

Just 4 Feet
Forum Shops
3500 Las Vegas Blvd. S.
Las Vegas, NV 89109
791-3482
Hours: 9 am - 1 am
Credit Cards: MC, Visa, AMX
18,000 sq. ft. store with 7,000 athletic
shoe styles, 90 percent of the styles
worldwide, as well as other athletic
apparel. Store also has an indoor basketball court, and a 9 screen video viewing wall tuned to sporting events.

Las Vegas Golf & Tennis
4211 Paradise Rd.
Las Vegas, NV 89109
892-9999 1-800-933-7777
Bill Stauffer, Mgr.
Hours: 8 am - 9 pm

2200 S. Rainbow Blvd.
Las Vegas, NV 89102
364-5111
Richard Gale, Mgr.
Hours: Mon. - Fri. 8 am - 7 pm; Sat. 8 am
- 6 pm; Sun. 9 am - 5 pm
Credit Cards: MC, Visa, AMX, Discover, CB

M & G Sporting Goods
3111 S. Valley View Blvd., Ste. 0105
Las Vegas, NV 89102
362-3111
Deborah Straub, Mgr.
Hours: Mon. - Fri. 8 am - 6 pm; Sat. 9
am - 1 pm
Credit Cards: MC, Visa
Team and institutional uniforms and
equipment. Umpire apparel.

Nevada Bob's
3311 E. Flamingo Rd.
Las Vegas, NV 89121
451-3333

3480 S. Jones Blvd.
Las Vegas, NV 89102
362-9904

2303 N. Rainbow Blvd.
Las Vegas, NV 89105
646-0007
Hours: Mon. - Fri. 9 am - 7 pm; Sat. 9 am
- 6 pm; Sun. 10 am - 5 pm
Credit Cards: all major
Complete line of golf, tennis, running,
and racquetball clothing and equipment.

Peloton Sports
911 N. Buffalo Dr.
Las Vegas, NV 89128
363-1991
Deya Hawk, Mgr.
Hours: Mon. - Fri. 10 am - 7 pm Sat.
9 am - 5 pm
Bicycles and bicycle equipment.

The Penalty Box
6380 W. Flamingo Rd.
Las Vegas, NV 89103
362-4884
Kimberly Nolan
Hours: Mon. - Fri. 11 am - 7 pm; Sat.
9 am - 7 pm; Sun. noon - 5 pm
Ice hockey, roller hockey and figure
skating equipment and accessories.

Play It Again Sports
2001 S. Rainbow Blvd.
Las Vegas, NV 89102
228-1713
John Eberle, Mgr.

8380 W. Cheyenne Ave.
Las Vegas, NV 89119
645-5548
Hours: Mon. - Sat. 9 am - 8 pm; Sun. 11
am - 6 pm
Credit Cards: MC, Visa
New and used sports equipment, con-
signment

Rebel Store
At Thomas & Mack Center
4505 S. Maryland Pkwy
Las Vegas, NV 89154-0022
895-4207
Sally Olson, Mgr.
Hours: Mon. - Fri. 10 am - 6 pm; Sat. 10
am - 4 pm
Credit Cards: MC, Visa
One of a kind merchandise at great low
prices. Runnin' Rebels, Las Vegas Thunder
and Las Vegas Posse merchandise

Sub - Skates Etc.
840 N. Rainbow Blvd.
Las Vegas, NV 89107
258-3635

3736 E. Flamingo Rd.
Las Vegas, NV 89121
435-1978
Barry Lidecker, Owner
Hours: Mon. - Fri. 10 am - 7 pm; Sat. 10
am - 7 pm; Sun. 11 am - 5 pm
Skateboards, supplies, snowboards,
roller blades and clothing.

Sportco Sporting Goods
2803 N. Green Valley Pkwy.
Henderson, NV 89014
454-9878
Rob Campbell, Owner
Hours: Mon. - Fri. 10 am - 7 pm; Sat. 9
am - 5 pm; Sun 11 am - 5 pm
Credit Cards: MC, Visa, AMX
Equipment, apparel, team outfitters,
letter jackets.

The Sports Authority
2620 S. Decatur Blvd.
Las Vegas, NV 89102
368-3335
Ron Reda, Mgr.

3651 S. Maryland Pkwy.
Las Vegas, NV 89109
796-5557
John Robinson, Mgr.

1431 E Sunset Rd.
Henderson, NV 89014
433-2071
Donna Testimer
Hours: Sat. 10 am - 9 pm Sun. 11 am - 6 pm
Credit Cards: MC, Visa, Discover, AMX
Sporting goods store, apparel, and
equipment.

Turf Sporting Goods
3558 S. Procyon Ave.
Las Vegas, NV 89103
873-2478
John Waroe, Owner
Hours: Mon. - Fri. 9 am - 6 pm; Sat.
10 am - 4 pm
Credit Cards: MC, Visa, AMX, Discover
Sporting goods, team outfitters.

*(Also see specialized areas for
additional store listings)*

Shopping and Services

The metropolitan Las Vegas area has more than 25 million sq. ft. of retail space with a vacancy rate of approximately 9.5 percent. There are four regional shopping malls, The Boulevard, The Meadows, The Galleria and The Fashion Show Mall with an average occupancy rate of 98 percent.

The Boulevard Mall completed a $60 million expansion in August 1992 and is currently the largest shopping mall in Nevada. The Forum Shops at Caesars Palace, a 250,000 sq. ft. upscale mall with over 70 shops and restaurants, opened in May 1992. Ribbon cutting ceremonies, held August 29, 1997, marked the opening of the Forum Shops' newest section, adding approximately 283,000 sq. ft. with 35 new stores and two new restaurants.

Two factory outlet malls, The Belz Factory Outlet World Mall and Vegas Pointe Stores, are located two miles south of the Strip (Hacienda) on Las Vegas Blvd.

The Galleria at Sunset, the newest regional mall, opened February 28, 1996. The mall has 900,000 sq. ft. and features Robinsons-May, Dillard's, Mervyn's, and JC Penney. The Showcase Mall, located on the Strip next to MGM Grand, contains 300,000 sq. ft. and includes a Coca Cola retail store, GameWorks, United Artists Theaters, Official All Star Cafe, Ethel M Chocolates and M&M's World.

COST OF LIVING - RETAIL SALES

ADDITIONAL ON PAGE 310

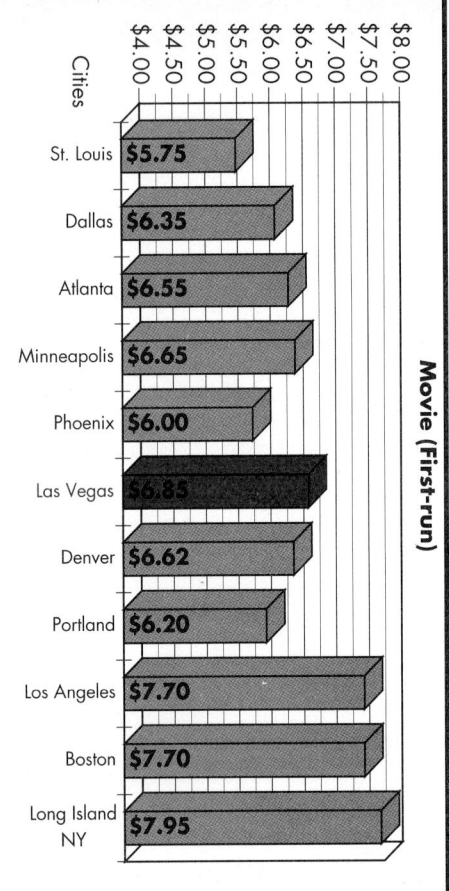

Movie (First-run)

Cities	
St. Louis	$5.75
Dallas	$6.35
Atlanta	$6.55
Minneapolis	$6.65
Phoenix	$6.00
Las Vegas	$6.85
Denver	$6.62
Portland	$6.20
Los Angeles	$7.70
Boston	$7.70
Long Island NY	$7.95

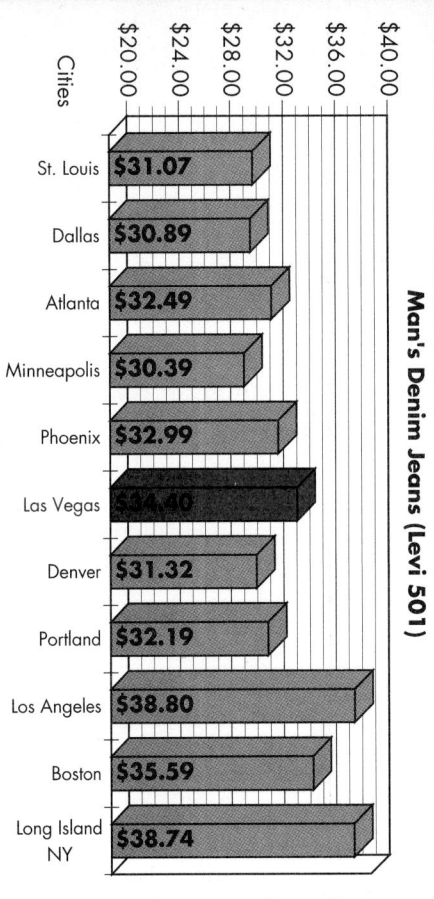

Man's Denim Jeans (Levi 501)

Cities	
St. Louis	$31.07
Dallas	$30.89
Atlanta	$32.49
Minneapolis	$30.39
Phoenix	$32.99
Las Vegas	$34.40
Denver	$31.32
Portland	$32.19
Los Angeles	$38.80
Boston	$35.59
Long Island NY	$38.74

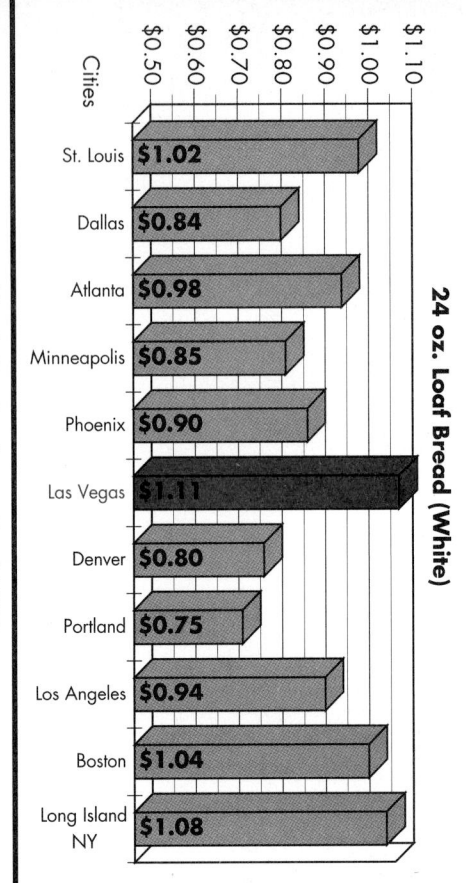

24 oz. Loaf Bread (White)

Cities	
St. Louis	$1.02
Dallas	$0.84
Atlanta	$0.98
Minneapolis	$0.85
Phoenix	$0.90
Las Vegas	$1.11
Denver	$0.80
Portland	$0.75
Los Angeles	$0.94
Boston	$1.04
Long Island NY	$1.08

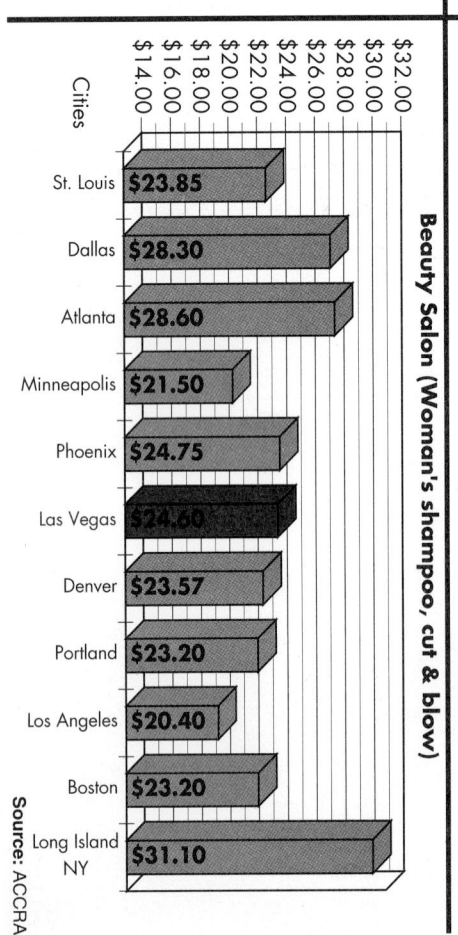

Beauty Salon (Woman's shampoo, cut & blow)

Cities	
St. Louis	$23.85
Dallas	$28.30
Atlanta	$28.60
Minneapolis	$21.50
Phoenix	$24.75
Las Vegas	$24.60
Denver	$23.57
Portland	$23.20
Los Angeles	$20.40
Boston	$23.20
Long Island NY	$31.10

Source: ACCRA

Source: Nevada State Department of Taxation

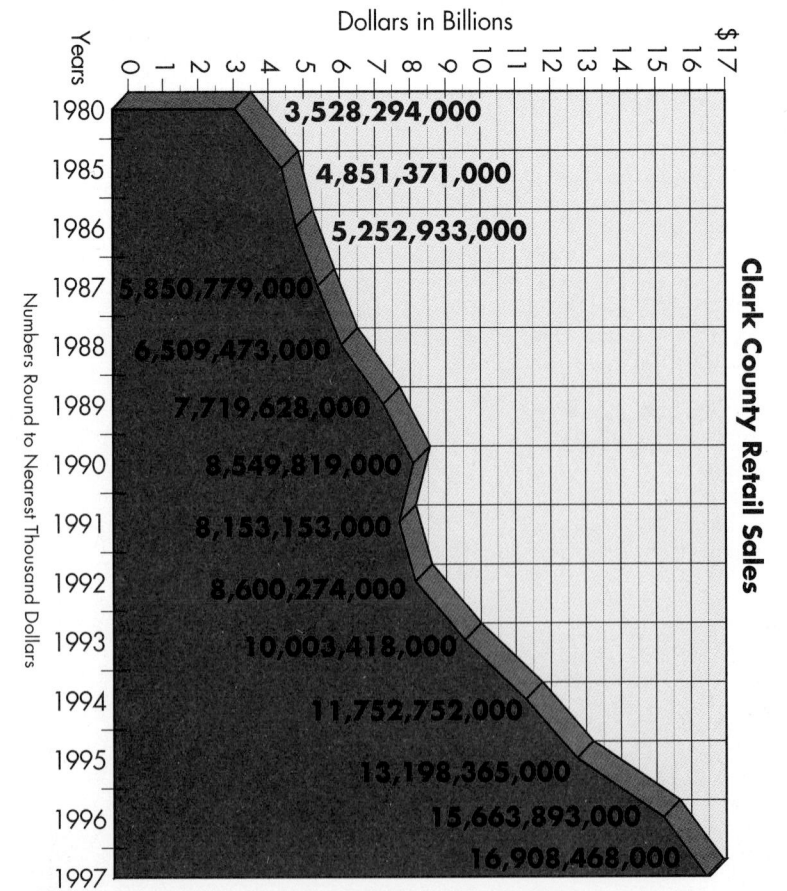

Clark County Retail Sales

Dollars in Billions

Numbers Round to Nearest Thousand Dollars

Years	
1980	3,528,294,000
1985	4,851,371,000
1986	5,252,933,000
1987	5,850,779,000
1988	6,509,473,000
1989	7,719,628,000
1990	8,549,819,000
1991	8,153,153,000
1992	8,600,274,000
1993	10,003,418,000
1994	11,752,752,000
1995	13,198,365,000
1996	15,663,893,000
1997	16,908,468,000

Experience Las Vegas

Visit our website at www.experiencelasvegas.com

BOULEVARD MALL

Photo: Phototechnik International

**3528 S. Maryland Pkwy.
Las Vegas, NV 89109
732-8949**

*MEPC American Properties
Robert Touma, General Mgr.
Sue Brandt, Marketing Dir.*
734-1562
over 150 tenants - opened 1968
Area: 1,250,000 sq. ft. *(largest mall in Nevada)*

Hours: Mon. - Fri. 10 am - 9 pm; Sat. 10 am - 8 pm; Sun. 11 am - 6 pm
Valet parking: located at main entrance on Maryland Pkwy (complimentary).

Customer Service Desk: wheelchairs available free of charge, strollers available for rent, mall gift certificates good at any Boulevard store or restaurant, postage stamps, automatic teller machines located throughout the mall.

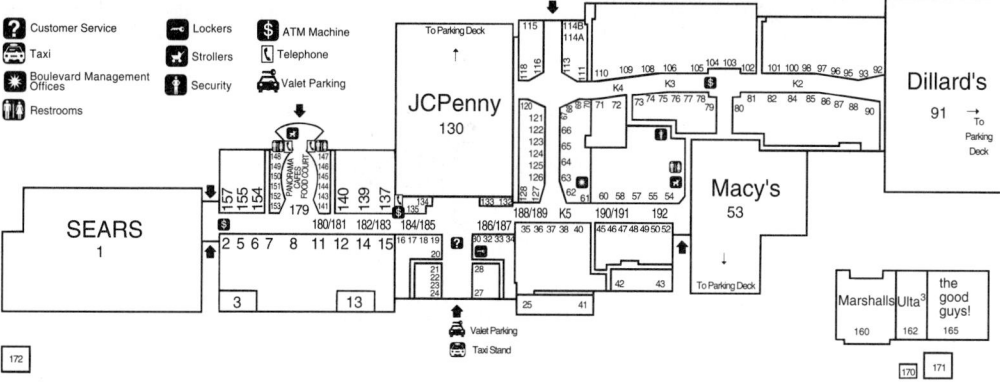

SHOPPING

PANORAMA CAFES FOOD COURT
150 Baskin Robbins: 732-9998
151 Big Easy Cajun: 734-7759
141 Cinnabon: 731-0522
153 Everything Yogurt & Salad Cafe: 734-3688
144 Flamers Charbroiled Hamburgers: 734-5939
145 Great Steak & Potato Company: 791-5453
146 Hibachi San: 731-2271
143 La Salsa: 369-1234
152 Orange Julius/Dairy Queen: 734-8283
148 Panda Express: 737-1616
147 Sbarro: 369-1314
149 The Soup & Sandwich Company: 733-1222
179 Tropical Sno: 892-8240

RESTAURANTS
172 Applebee's Neighborhood Grill & Bar: 737-4990
171 IHOP: 737-0375
155 McDonald's: 369-2039

SERVICES
114A Americana Realty: 734-5555
193 Foreign Currency Exchange
74 Glamour Shots: 731-3777
42 Great Expectations Hair Salon: 733-9096*
70 Natural Beauty Salon & Cosmetics: 796-0712
115 Kiddie Kandids: 792-2766
50 LensCrafters Optique: 737-0741
193 Phone Cards
13 Prestige Travel: 794-2811*
114B Stark Express Shoe Repair: 369-1102
6 Styles Hair Salon: 733-6623
92 Trade Secret Beauty Salon: 731-4669
170 Ted Weins Firestone: 732-9626
162 Ulta 3 Cosmetics & Salon: 735-4714

SHOES
18 Bostonian: 791-0111
104 Famous Footwear: 735-8030
87 Foot Action: 794-4492
12 Footlocker: 737-8646
121 Kids Footlocker: 737-7312
140 Kinney Shoes: 735-3930
77 Lady Footlocker: 369-3662
101 Leed's: 369-9409
76 Naturalizer: 791-0722
80 Nine West: 796-5530
73 Sam & Libby: 734-8455
128 Wild Pair: 369-9356

OTHER AREAS
ATM Machine
Boulevard Management Office
Restrooms
Public Telephones
Valet Parking
Taxi
Strollers
Lockers
Security Office
  *(Dial *16 free from any mall pay phone)*
Customer Service Center
  *(Dail *19 free from any mall pay phone)*

* *Indicates exterior entrance*

ACCESSORIES, MEN'S & WOMEN'S
311 Afterthoughts: 369-4048
75 Afterthoughts: 369-0600
48 Best of Times: 792-2708
63 Claire's Boutique: 791-3320
67 Sporting Eyes: 791-0775
20 Sunglass Designs: 732-7933
K3 Sunglass Designs Too: 796-7655

APPAREL, MEN'S, WOMEN'S & CHILDRENS
16 Colorado: 792-8678
95 County Seat: 737-0228
40 The Gap: 734-6620
60 GapKids: 734-7077
82 Going to the Game: 893-4699
111 Gymboree: 369-4055
85 Hot Cats: 796-1870
55 Howard & Phil's: 732-0070
122 Jagged Edge: 733-0077
182 Lineback's: 737-3434
189 Moa 4 Kids: 794-0064
88 Mr. Rags: 791-5600
49 Sports Logo: 734-4770
191 Stringers: 732-3129
96 Wilson's, The Leather Experts: 796-0083

APPAREL, MEN'S
54 B'Koz: 893-3078
14 Coda: 737-8626
35 Harris & Frank: 735-1102
36 J. Riggings: 733-8025
33 JW: 737-8464
38 Oak Tree: 369-3171
46 Pacific Wave: 735-2332
108 Structure: 735-8144

APPAREL, WOMEN'S
47 5-7-9: 796-8068
78 August Max Woman: 893-2686
110 Cacique: 369-4338
17 Calla Bay Swimwear: 737-3116
100 Casual Corner/Petite Sophisticate: 792-0808
137 Charlotte Russe: 792-2110

82 Contempo Casuals: 369-5877
72 Dress Barn: 369-8510
106 Express: 733-7977
57 Lane Bryant: 791-5021
15 Lerner, New York: 734-8291
109 The Limited: 369-0221
180 Mario's of Palm Springs: 893-9322
90 Modern Women: 733-0053
154 Roland's of Las Vegas: 369-8443
84 Victoria's Secret: 732-1767
102 Wet Seal: 796-8859

CARDS, GIFTS & SPECIALTY
125 African & World Imports: 734-1900
183 Allstate Keychains: 735-5305
188 Animal World: 791-0335
105 Bath & Body Works: 735-0290
135 The Body Shop: 737-0005
116 Brookstone: 794-0880
187 Chop Chop: 735-7867
113 The Disney Store: 893-3390
3 Franklin Covey: 733-7701*
1 Hallmark: 734-6617
123 Hot Topic: 731-3011
185 Linda Ray's Gifts: 893-9926
81 The Mole Hole: 699-5536
184 Name Express: 732-8077
69 The Nature Company: 792-0877
120 The San Francisco Music Box Company: 369-2888
124 Sanrio Surprises: 737-7637
86 Spencer Gifts: 737-8380
58 Things Remembered: 735-7745
23 The Tinderbox: 737-1807
98 Yorkville Gifts: 836-9380

DEPARTMENT STORES
91 Dillard's: 734-2111
130 J.C. Penney: 735-5131
53 Macy's: 791-2100
160 Marshalls: 737-1117
1 Sears: 894-4200

FOOD
68 Ethel M. Chocolates: 369-8438
24 General Nutrition Center: 733-7742
126 Gloria Jean's Gourmet Coffees: 791-0144
21 Hot Dog on a Stick
127 Mrs. Fields Cookies: 369-8030
66 Pretzel Time: 735-6136
22 See's Candies: 732-1826
62 Sweet Factory: 731-4619
K4 Tropik Sun Fruit & Nut: 791-5233

HOBBY, LEISURE & ELECTRONICS
K2 360 Communications: 733-2007
97 B. Dalton Bookseller: 735-0008
157 Champs Sports: 369-0903
37 El Portal Luggage: 735-6433
27 Frisky Pet Center: 737-5118
165 Good Guys: 892-9200
2 Kay Bee Toy & Hobby: 737-5112
K5 Nordic Trak: 893-6684
45 Radio Shack: 369-5933
32 Ritz Camera: 735-5705
103 Sam Goody: 734-1424
71 Software Etc.: 794-2700
64 Suncoast Motion Picture Company: 369-1418
139 Wherehouse Records: 733-1724

HOME FURNISHINGS
30 The Bombay Company: 893-4633

JEWELRY
52 Bailey, Banks & Biddle: 734-2577
133 The Chainery: 731-5151
79 Crescent Jewelers: 737-1988
61 Gordon's: 791-6939
118 The Jewelers: 796-6000
19 Lundstrom Jewelers: 733-7565
132 Marks Bros. Jewelers: 796-6540
190 Silver City: 737-7373
28 Tiffin's Jewelers: 369-3113
134 Whitehall Co. Jewelers: 731-5211
34 Zales: 735-3482

FASHION SHOW MALL

3200 Las Vegas Blvd. S.
Las Vegas, NV 89109
369-0704   369-8382
Fashion Show Management, Inc.
The Hahn Co.
Wendy Garrison Crawford, V/P & Gen. Mgr.
136 tenants - opened 1981
Area: 827,000 sq. ft.
Hours: Mon. - Fri. 10 am - 9 pm; Sat. 10 am - 7 pm; Sun. noon - 6 pm
Valet Parking: located at the south entrance to Neiman Marcus; the north entrance to Saks Fifth Avenue, the east entrance to the mall next to Chin's and in the underground parking lot in the Blue Lot. Car wash available Wed. - Sat. 10 am - 2 pm

Concierge Desk: strollers and wheelchairs, general information, bus schedules. The Concierge Desk provides a variety of business and hospitality services including copying, fax transmissions, show and tour bookings, car rentals and gift certificates.

Macy's, Dillard's, Saks Fifth Avenue, Robinsons-May, Nieman Marcus, 15 different cafes in the food court & 4 restaurants.

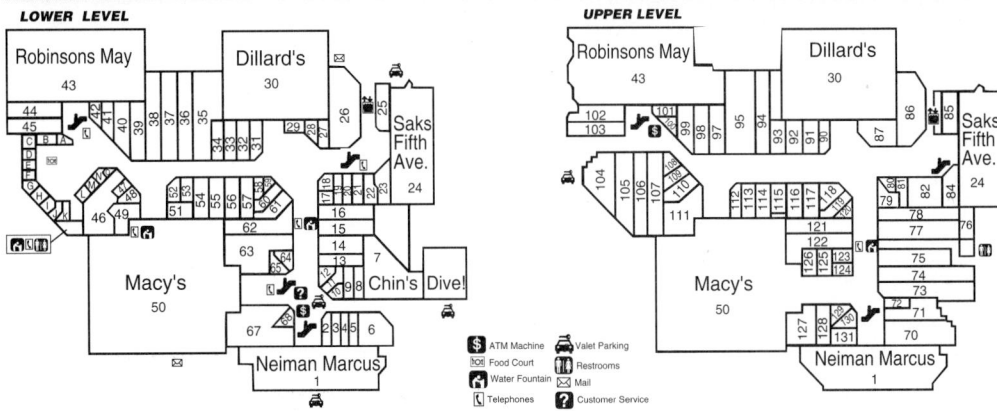

CHILDREN'S APPAREL
84 Brats: 735-2728
37 The Disney Store: 737-5400
27 Gymboree: 369-8909
FAMILY APPAREL
75 Abercrombie & Fitch: 737-5018
94 Banana Republic: 794-0747
26 GAP: 796-0010
86 Millers Outpost: 796-5021
MEN'S APPAREL
75 Abercrombie & Fitch: 737-5018
73 Amici: 369-9133
87 Bally: 737-1968
94 Banana Republic: 794-0747
17 Custom Shop Shirtmakers: 731-6882
11 Detour: 894-5030
26 GAP: 796-0010
15 Harris & Frank: 737-7545
21 Melwanis: 733-6676
86 Millers Outpost: 796-5021
127 Schwartz Big & Tall: 733-9111
126 Shirt Shoppe: 731-5157
22 St. Croix Knit: 794-4333
70 Structure: 732-2825
14 Uomo: 733-8230
WOMEN'S APPAREL
75 Abercrombie & Fitch: 737-5018
78 Ann Taylor: 734-8614
87 Bally: 737-1968
94 Banana Republic: 794-0747
91 B.C.B.G.: 737-0681
34 bebe: 892-8083
80 Betsey Johnson: 735-3338
16 Cache: 731-5548
107 Casual Corner: 737-1134
56 Chico's: 791-3661
38 Contempo Casuals: 369-1789
95 Express, Inc.: 737-8999
26 GAP: 796-0010
116 Jessica McClintock: 733-4003
121 Lillie Rubin: 735-2131
122 The Limited: 737-4880
93 Liz Claiborne: 796-8772
49 Macy Woman: 733-6220

13 Marshall-Rousso: 737-5011
115 Mondi: 735-3411
79 Nicole Miller: 734-7767
97 Petite Sophisticate: 733-6563
23 Private Collections: 731-6689
62 Talbots/Talbots Petites: 893-1706
125 United Colors of Benetton: 737-3811
85 Wet Seal: 796-0344
SPECIALTY APPAREL
124 Accento: 369-2324
20 A Pea in the Pod: 893-8484
87 Bally: 737-1968
52 Destination Las Vegas: 734-5080
11 Detour: 894-5030
44 Diane's Swimwear: 792-9904
92 The Icing: 650-9006
39 Miller Stockman: 737-7236
79 Nicole Miller: 734-7767
60 North Beach Leather: 731-0630
127 Schwartz Big & Tall: 733-9111
7 Tennis Lady/Tennis Man: 731-5001
67 Victoria's Secret: 737-1313
SHOES
53 Aerosole: 796-4144
73 Amici: 369-9133
78 Ann Taylor: 734-8614
87 Bally: 737-1968
119 Bianca: 369-0048
108 Brass Boot: 731-6502
105 Footlocker: 737-5623
26 GAP: 796-0010
12 Johnston & Murphy: 737-0114
48 Jones New York: 735-5496
54 Lady Foot Locker: 735-7030
40 Leeds Shoes: 737-1198
13 Marshall-Rousso: 737-5011
65 Michael Rossi Shoes: 792-8088
129 Norman Kaplan Footwear: 733-6303
68 Rococo: 792-2221
130 Scarpe: 369-3500
113 Selby Las Vegas: 733-1740
JEWELRY
31 Bailey, Banks & Biddle: 731-3355
90 Ben Bridge: 733-0003

42 The Chainery: 731-0670
18 Berger & Son Fine Jewelers: 737-7118
131 The Gold Factory: 737-5151
100 Kay Jewelers: 369-0013
51 Lundstrom: 734-6612
29 Whitehall Co. Jewelers: 737-1174
112 Zales Jewelers: 731-0103
DEPARTMENT STORES
30 Dillard's: 733-2008
50 Macy's: 731-5111
1 Neiman Marcus: 731-3636
43 Robinsons-May: 737-8708
24 Saks Fifth Avenue: 733-8300
ART GALLERIES
99 Centaur Sculpture Galleries: 737-0004
110 The Rock & Hollywood Gallery: 731-1292
45 Southwest Spirit Gallery: 737-5595
46 Walt Disney Gallery: 650-2201
35 Williams-Sonoma: 734-5699
36 Wyland Galleries: 699-9970
CARDS, GIFTS, BOOKS, TOYS
114 Carlan's Gifts: 734-6003
57 Discovery Channel Store: 792-2121
37 The Disney Store: 737-5400
71 El Portal Luggage: 369-0606
98 Expanding Wall-Cards: 792-2333
109 Game Keeper: 735-5360
128 Papyrus: 733-0073
25 Serendipity Gallery of Collectibles: 733-2080
111 Waldenbooks: 733-1049
46 Walt Disney Gallery: 650-2201
SPECIALTY SHOPS
87 Bally: 737-1968
117 Bath & Body Works: 693-5944
32 The Body Shop: 737-1198
52 Destination Las Vegas: 734-5080
57 Discovery Channel Store: 792-2121
37 The Disney Store: 737-5400
71 El Portal Luggage: 369-0606
9 Electronics Boutique: 731-1146
2 Future Tronics: 734-6464
109 Game Keeper: 735-5360
3 Gloria Jean's Coffee Bean: 943-1344
10 H2O Plus: 893-1332

118 Louis Vuitton: 731-9860
8 Omni Pharmacy & Drug Store: 731-1162
82 Optique by Lenscrafters: 732-8233
58 Optica: 735-8557
110 The Rock & Hollywood Gallery: 731-1292
103 Sam Goody's Musicland: 794-0079
81 San Francisco Music Box Co.: 735-7700
62 Sharper Image: 731-3113
120 Solstar Sunglasses: 737-1464
102 Suncoast Motion Picture Co.: 893-0100
72 Sun Shade Optique: 733-9331
64 Swatch: 796-8344
101 Universal Flags: 737-3524
67 Victoria's Secret: 737-1313
46 Walt Disney Gallery: 650-2201
35 Williams-Sonoma: 734-5699
FOOD SPECIALTY
123 Ethel M. Chocolates: 796-6662
3 Gloria Jean's Coffee Bean: 732-2326
4 Mrs. Field's Cookies: 369-2778
5 See's Candies: 893-3338
28 Starbucks: 794-4010
41 Sweet Factory: 369-6100
35 Williams-Sonoma Grand Cuisine: 734-5699
FOOD COURT
A Dairy Queen: 732-7019
B Orange Julius: 732-7019
C 1 Potato 2: 369-1656
D Hot Dog On-A-Stick: 737-3182
E Sbarro: 796-2998
F Burger Express: 733-9963
G Aloha Teriyaki: 737-7375
H Yang's Wok: 732-9606
I Schlotzsky's Deli: 735-1906
J Renzio's Greek Food: 369-6112
K Chicken Plus: 733-3910
L Wetzel's Pretzels: 369-2544
M Dagwood's: 731-1600
N French Express: 796-9445
O E'Claire: 369-6117
RESTAURANTS
104 Morton's of Chicago, The Steak House: 893-0703
Entry Dive!: 369-3483
7 Chin's: 733-8899
Entry Sfuzzi: 699-5777
SERVICES & GENERAL INFORMATION
1 Beauty Terrace: 369-3636
43 Elizabeth Arden Salon: 737-8708
82 Optometrist/Dr. Chen K. Young, O.D.: 737-0506
24 Saks Fifth Avenue Hair Salon: 733-8300
Concierge Desk:
  Show Tickets, Tours, Strollers, Postage
76 Management Offices: 369-0704
ATM Machines located near Customer Assistance lower level, Food Court lower level, and Kay Jewelers upper level.

FORUM SHOPS AT CAESARS PALACE

3500 Las Vegas Blvd. S.
Las Vegas, NV 89109
893-4800
Simon DeBartolo Group, Inc.
Jeff Silbert, Gen. Mgr.
Maureen Taylor Crampton, Mktg. Dir.
70 stores - opened May 11, 1992 with 250,000 square feet. The new phase, added 283,000 sq. ft. for a total of 533,000 sq. ft. and opened August 29, 1997 with 35 additional stores doubling the original size
Gross Leasable Area (GLA): 533,000 sq. ft. *(The Forum Shops at Caesars is the most successful shopping center in the nation, with average annual sales of over $1,200 per square foot. The industry average is $300 per square foot.)*
Hours: Sun. - Thu. 10 am - 11 pm; Fri. - Sat. 10 am - midnight *(Some establishments open earlier and stay open later.)*
Valet parking: located at south entrance, between Caesars and the Forum Shops, via the underground traffic tunnel
Customer Service Center: Located at the people mover entrance. Offers a variety of services including gift certificates, postal service and free wheelchair and stroller rental.

Security
ATM Machine
Telephones
Valet Parking
Restrooms

SHOPPING

The Forum Shops has two distinct entertainment features:

1. Festival Fountain: fifteen foot robotic replicas of Roman gods perform under a massive domed rotunda. Bacchus and his entourage present the magnificent sound, light and water show every hour on the hour beginning at 10 am.

2. The Atlantis Fountain Show: features a recreation of the mythical sinking of Atlantis. Life-like characters of Atlas, Gadrius and Alia and special fire, water, steam and sound effects bring the fall of Atlantis to life on the hour beginning at 11 am.

Providing the backdrop for the Lost City of Atlantis show, the 50,000 gallon marine aquarium is one of the newest attractions at the Forum Shops.

Barrel-vaulted ceilings emulate a Mediterranean sky by changing from dusk to dawn every hour. Store front facades resemble Roman streets with columns and arches, piazzas, fountains and statuary. Tenants are upscale specialty retail shops and restaurants.

The multimillion dollar Forum Shops attract an average of 40,000 people daily. A 283,000 sq. ft. expansion opened on August 29, 1997 and includes 35 new stores and two restaurants.

WOMEN'S APPAREL
116 Ann Taylor: 794-0494
188 bebe: 735-8885
179 Cache': 796-3532
130 DKNY*
121 Escada: 791-2300
200 Express: 892-0424
158 Max Mara*
190 St. John: 893-0044
148 Shauna Stein: 893-9786

MEN'S APPAREL
126 Bernini: 893-7786
151 Bernini Collections: 893-1786
168 Cuzzens: 732-1329

157 Hugo Ross: 696-9444
176 Kerkorian: 892-0430
117 The Knot Shop: 369-4144
201 Structure: 892-0421
166 Vasari: 792-2476

CHILDREN'S APPAREL & TOYS
102 Animal Crackers: 796-0121
149 Baby Guess*
132 FAO Schwartz: 796-6500
150 Gap Kids: 737-1550
177 Kids Kastle: 369-5437

SPECIALTY APPAREL
130 Abercrombie & Fitch Co.: 731-0712
131 A/X Armani Exchange: 733-1666
194 Banana Republic: 650-5623
103 Beyond the Beach: 791-5989
147 Diesel: 791-5927
152 Emporio Armani: 650-5200
174 French Room: 796-1067
150 Gap: 737-1550
124 Gianni Versace: 796-7222
120 Guess: 737-1816
203 Images by Crazy Shirts: 893-7780
138 Lacoste: 791-7617
133 The Polo Store/Ralph Lauren: 650-5656
173 Rose of Sharon: Size 14 & up: 791-0151
162 Sloanes: 737-0900
169 Versus: 796-7332
114 Victoria's Secret: 893-0903

SPECIALTY SHOPS
155 Alfred Dunhill: 650-2992
145 Bath & Body at Home: 796-4902
207 Christian Dior: 737-9777
186 Davante: 737-8585
115 Disney Store: 732-9560
165 Estee Lauder: 737-9011
195 Field of Dreams: 792-8233

149 Guess Home Collection*
105 Magic Masters: 735-1800
142 NIKETOWN: 650-8888
185 Porsche Design: 369-0410
202 Sports Logo: 792-2338
110 Sunglass Hut International: 369-8383
128 Swatch: 796-1522
136 Victoria's Secret Bath & Fragrance: 765-5435
144 Virgin Megastore: 696-7100
178 Warner Brothers Studio Store: 893-7711

LEATHER
164 El Portel Luggage: 765-6044
156 Fendi: 893-2616
122 Gucci: 369-7333
125 Louis Vuitton: 732-1227

ENTERTAINMENT
204 Cinema Ride: 369-4008
205 Cyber Station: 893-3350
140 IMAX

JEWELRY
184 Bulgari: 734-2001
160 Fred Joaillier: 650-0090
153 Hyde Park: 794-3541
111 M.J. Christensen Jewelers: 734-2300
182 N. Landau Hyman: 737-7117
161 Opals & Gems of Australia: 696-1882
113 Roman Times: 733-8687
198 Zero Gravity: 731-3565

SHOES
172 Avventura: 731-1300
134 Footworks -792-8400
197 Just for Feet: 791-3482
137 Salvatore: 696-9786
127 Salvatore Ferragamo*
170 Shoooz at the Forum: 734-7600
181 Stuart Weitzman: 369-9222

119 Via Veneto: 369-7414

GIFTS
112 Brookstone: 734-8400
175 Caesars Exclusively: 731-7851
193 Crystal Galleria: 369-2622
101 The Endangered Species Store: 794-4545
159 Ice Accessories Las Vegas: 696-9700
129 Lalique: 731-2155
100 Magnet Maximus: 791-5227
167 The Museum Company: 792-9220
192 Planet Hollywood Superstore: 369-6001
189 West of Santa Fe: 737-1993

ART GALLERIES
108 Antiquities: 792-2274
118 Galerie Lassen: 731-6900
163 Galleria di Sorrento: 369-8000

RESTAURANTS
183 Bertolini's: 735-4663
146 Caviarteria: 792-8560
143 The Cheesecake Factory: 792-6888
154 Chinois*
107 La Salsa: 735-8226
171 Palm Restaurant: 732-7256
191 Planet Hollywood: 791-7827
180 Spago: 369-6300
104 Stage Deli: 893-4045

SPECIALTY FOOD
104 Cafe Express
106 Chocolate Chariot: 735-2639
109 David's Cookies
109 Heidi's Yogurt
198 Sweet Factory: 732-3877
109 Swensen's Ice Cream: 737-3113

SERVICES
ATM Bank of America ATM/Cash
PC Phone Card Machine
206 Allstate Ticketing & Tours: 732-9579
206 Business/Postal Service
206 Customer Service Center
199 Foto Forum: 893-3686

GENERAL INFORMATION
123 Management Office/Security

*Coming soon

THE GALLERIA AT SUNSET

1300 W. Sunset Rd.
Henderson, NV 89014
434-2409
Alan Schmiedicker, Gen. Mgr.
Area: 900,000 sq. ft.
Mall opened February 28, 1996.
Over 130 stores and restaurants and four department stores.

Major tenants: Dillard's (208,000 sq. ft.) JC Penney (126,000 sq. ft.) Robinsons-May (180,000sq. ft.) Mervyn's (83,000 sq. ft.)

Hours: Mon. - Sat. 10 am - 9 pm, Sun. 11 am - 6 pm

The Galleria Mall is the first new regional mall in the Las Vegas valley in 14 years and the first for Henderson. The mall contributes about 1,000 new jobs.

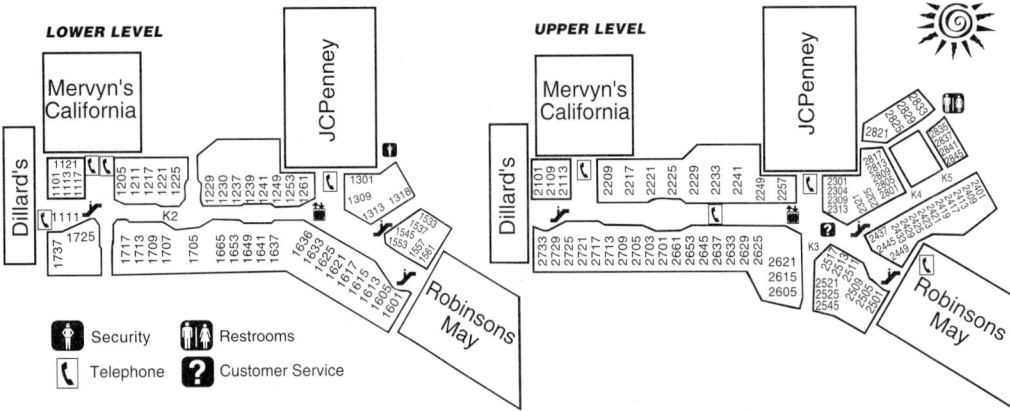

LOWER LEVEL — **UPPER LEVEL**

Security | Restrooms
Telephone | Customer Service

2225 Bath & Body Works: 454-8831
2525 The Body Shop: 434-4434
1217 Carlton Cards: 898-8333
2645 The Disney Store: 433-3666
1717 El Portal Luggage: 456-1314
2509 The Game Keeper: 898-8952
2313 Garden Botanika: 436-1300
2725 Kay Bee Toys: 436-1778
2709 The Mole Hole: 451-0814
2233 Natural Wonders: 898-2286
2513 Nava Hopi Gallery: 458-2254
2701 Off The Wall: 434-4364
2637 Papyrus: 898-4889
1725 Sam Goody: 436-6002
2109 Spencer Gifts: 436-5514
2413 Suncoast Motion Picture Company: 454-8865
2217 Things Remembered: 458-4088
2629 Thomas Kinkade Gallery: 898-4080
2505 Uniquely Crystal: 547-3577
2445 Wicks n' Sticks: 898-3582
HOME FURNISHINGS
2729 Bath Elegante: 435-2294
2449 The Kitchen Sink: 898-3005
1621 Lechter's Housewares: 435-5207
2709 The Mole Hole: 451-0814
2513 Nava Hopi Gallery: 458-2254
2701 Off The Wall: 434-4364
2417 Select Comfort: 433-5335
2629 Thomas Kinkade Gallery: 898-4080
JEWELRY
1261 Ben Bridge Jeweler 456-8807
2437 Crescent Jewelers: 454-1550
1117 Gordon's Jewelers: 436-1558
K2 Intrigue Jewelry: 433-7313
1205 Kay Jewelers: 434-1530
2621 M.J. Christensen Jewelers: 433-0100
1545 The Whitehall Co. Jewelers: 451-2667
2257 Zales Jewelers: 436-0766
LUGGAGE/HANDBAGS
1717 El Portal Luggage: 456-1314
PERSONAL & PROFESSIONAL SERVICES
Bank America ATM 111/2835
1121 Expressly Portraits: 433-5851
1537 Fast-Fix Jewelry Repair: 547-6223
2501 Kiddie Kandids: 436-7121
2511 1 Hour Photo Kits Cameras: 435-8840
1617 Lenscrafters: 436-0040
2101 Master Cuts: 433-5444
1561 Prudential Southwest Realty: 456-7400
1113 Regis Hairstylists: 898-6600
1533 1 Hour Photo Ritz Camera: 433-6524
1301 Trade Secret: 898-1878
2241 Venusto: 898-7171
K3 360 Communications: 454-7558
SPECIALTY
2429 Electronics Boutique: 435-2217
1717 El Portal Luggage: 456-1314
1229 Friskey Pet Center: 434-6100
2637 Papyrus: 898-4889
1133 Sunglass Hut International: 436-4042
2629 Thomas Kinkade Gallery: 898-4080
SPORTING GOODS & APPAREL
1641 Champs Sports: 456-0903
1705 Foot Action: 458-8388
2309 Foot Locker: 456-0587
1253 Lady Foot Locker: 456-0616
2425 Pro Image: 458-1202

DEPARTMENT STORES
Dillard's: 435-6300
JC Penney: 451-4545
Mervyn's California: 454-8881
Robinsons-May: 458-7300
ACCESSORIES
2419 Claire's Boutique: 484-4377
1717 El Portal Luggage: 456-1314
2325 Hot Topic: 456-6605
K2 Intrigue Jewely: 433-7313
2653 Pacific Sunwear: 433-0003
K4 Sunglass Hut: 436-4042
1636 Sunglass Hut II: 436-4045
APPAREL-CHILDREN'S
2645 The Disney Store: 433-3666
1625 Gap Kids/Baby Gap: 434-3110
1249 Gymboree: 898-8010
1665 The Limited Too: 451-8007
APPAREL-MEN'S
2703 Beyond The Beach: 433-6544
1239 Eddie Bauer: 898-0035
1633 The Gap: 434-3011
1241 Harris & Frank: 433-5746
2325 Hot Topic: 456-6605
2705 J. Riggings: 456-2461
2209 Miller's Outpost: 435-0390
2721 Miller Stockman: 456-5140
2721 Western Wear: 456-5140
2653 Pacific Sunwear: 433-0003
2221 Structure: 898-3706
APPAREL-WOMEN'S
1221 Ann Taylor: 454-2518
1230 bebe: 458-0518
2703 Beyond The Beach: 433-6544
1713 Cache': 454-0026
1649 Cacique: 451-2730
1309 Charlotte Russe: 898-8677
2225 Express: 433-5529
1239 Eddie Bauer: 898-0035
1637 5-7-9: 456-1922
1633 The Gap: 434-3011
2325 Hot Topic: 456-6605

1653 Lane Bryant: 898-1211
1237 Lerner New York: 898-9880
2229 The Limited: 451-2629
2209 Miller's Outpost: 435-0390
2721 Miller Stockman: 456-5140
2721 Western Wear: 456-5140
2717 Motherhood Maternity: 898-8302
2653 Pacific Sunwear: 433-0003
2661 Victoria's Secret: 456-3002
1211 Windsor Fashions: 456-1120
MEN & WOMEN'S SPECIALTY APPAREL
2703 Beyond The Beach: 433-6544
1239 Eddie Bauer: 898-0035
1633 The Gap: 434-3011
2325 Hot Topic: 456-6605
2209 Miller's Outpost: 434-0390
2721 Miller Stockman: 456-5140
2721 Western Wear: 456-5140
2653 Pacific Sunwear: 433-0003
2425 Pro Image: 458-1202
BEAUTY/HEALTH
2225 Bath & Body Works: 454-8831
2525 The Body Shop: 434-4434
2313 Garden Botanika: 436-1300
2409 General Nutrition Center: 434-1641
2101 Master Cuts: 433-5444
1113 Regis Hairstylists: 898-6602
1301 Trade Secret: 898-1878
2241 Venusto: 898-7171
SHOES - MEN'S, WOMEN'S & CHILDREN'S
2633 Aerosoles: 456-8956
1221 Ann Taylor: 454-2518
1641 Champs Sports: 456-0903
1615 Famous Footwear: 451-8368
1705 Foot Action: 458-8388
2309 Foot Locker: 456-0587
2625 J. Stephens Florsheim: 456-4858
1253 Lady Foot Locker: 456-0616
1707 Leeds: 456-5844
2517 Naturalizer: 434-3237
1225 Easy Spirit: 454-8474
2653 Pacific Sunwear: 433-0003

1557 Payless Shoesource/Payless Kids: 454-6569
2249 Wild Pair: 454-5655
ELECTRONICS, MUSIC, & HOME ENTERTAINMENT
2429 Electronics Boutique: 435-2217
2509 The Game Keeper: 898-8852
2511 1 Hour Photo Kits Cameras: 435-8840
2105 Radio Shack: 435-5021
1533 1 Hour Photo Ritz Camera: 433-6524
1725 Sam Goody: 436-6002
2413 Sun Coast Motion Picture Company: 454-8865
ENTERTAINMENT
2401 Tilt: 451-3688
EYEWEAR
1617 Lenscrafters: 436-0040
2653 Pacific Sunwear: 433-0003
1636 Sunglass Hut: 436-4045
FOOD
Food Court
2809 Bourbon Street Grill: 436-1335
2801 Cinnabon: 436-4005
2813 Dairy Queen: 433-1273
2817 Edo Japan: 898-9696
2829 Flamers Grill: 451-0760
2841 Garden Botanika: 898-6482
2805 Hot Dog On A Stick
2837 McDonald's: 456-0968
2825 Olympia Greek Cafe: 898-4936
2833 Panda Express: 898-8947
2845 Sbarro: 434-6162
RESTAURANTS
2605 Chevy's: 434-8323
1721 Java Centrale 898-8060
2545 Trilussa: 456-3306
SPECIALTY FOODS
2423 Auntie Anne's Soft Pretzels: 435-5660
2801 Cinnabons: 436-4005
2433 Gloria Jeans Gourmet Coffee: 451-2345
1553 Great American Cookie Company: 433-5588
1721 Java Centrale: 898-8060
2521 Sweet Factory: 436-6466
GIFTS, BOOKS, STATIONERS & RECORDS
2713 B. Dalton Bookseller: 434-1331

THE MEADOWS MALL

4300 Meadows Ln.
Las Vegas, NV 89107
878-4849
Yarmouth Group Property Management
Frank Wheat, Jr., Gen. Mgr.
Heather McCombs, Mrktg. Dir.
140 Tenants - opened 1978
Area: 950,000 sq. ft.
Hours: Mon. - Fri. 10 am - 9 pm; Sat. - Sun. 10 am - 6 pm
Anyone who has ever seen a cactus flower bloom or the colors of a dazzling desert valley sunset knows the desert is a special place. Meadows Mall reflects this image. With 140 specialty stores, an indoor oasis pool, colorful carousel animals and curious dinosaur bones, Meadows Mall holds as many surprises as the desert itself. Without the heat, of course.
Valet parking: At Blue Entrance - north side of mall
Customer Convenience Center: located on the lower level. Gift certificates, stroller rental and wheelchairs are available as well as information.

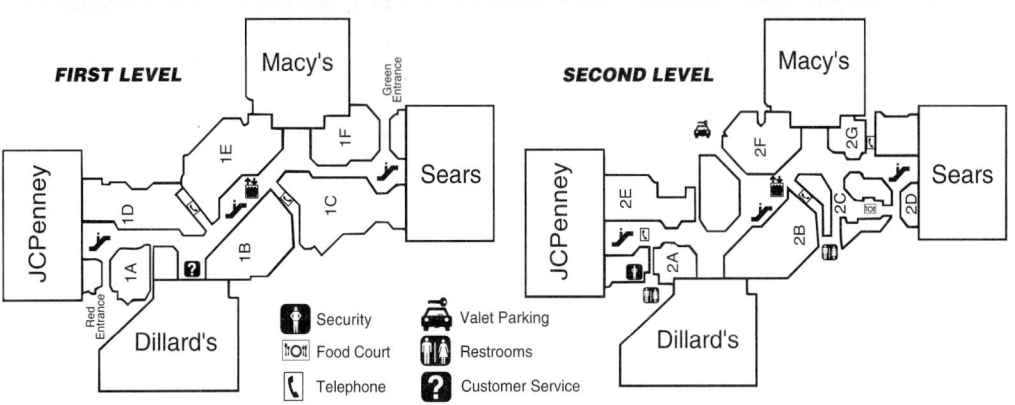

SHOPPING

DEPARTMENT STORES
Dillard's: 870-2039
JC Penney: 870-9182
Macy's: 258-2100
Sears: 259-4200

MEN'S AND WOMEN'S ACCESSORIES
1F Sunglass Hut: 877-2828
2A Sunglass Hut: 259-9030

MEN'S APPAREL
1F Coda: 870-4156
2D Gingiss Formalwear: 878-6885
2F Jay Jacobs-Men: 877-1084
1F JW: 870-0806
1A Pacific Sunwear of California: 878-3250

WOMEN'S APPAREL
2B Casual Corner: 870-1141
1E Charlotte Russe: 878-0002
2B Contempo Casuals: 870-1510
1E Express: 870-2028
2A Fredrick's of Hollywood: 870-8129
1B Jay Jacobs-Women: 877-0232
1E Lane Bryant: 877-4989
1C Lerner New York: 878-9517
1E The Limited: 877-1949
1A Motherhood Maternity: 878-0229
2B Petite Sophisticate: 877-1970
1D Size 5-7-9: 870-4811
1B Victoria's Secret: 878-9270
2B Windsor Fashions: 878-4849

FAMILY APPAREL
1B The Disney Store: 258-2692
1D The Gap: 878-2446
2G Graphic Shirts: 878-8779
1C Gymboree: 880-4228
1A Hot Cats: 877-9918
20 Hot Topic: 870-0081
2A Life Uniforms: 870-9752
2F Miller Stockman: 870-2951
2G Miller's Outpost: 878-0130
2F Mr. Rags: 822-5800
2B Wilson's Suede & Leather: 870-1320

FOOD
2F The Coffee Beanery: 258-1674
1F The Cookie Chef: 878-1985
2A Ethel M Chocolates: 877-2777
1D General Nutrition Company (GNC): 878-8785
1A Haagen Dazs Ice Cream: 878-7551
1C Hickory Farms: 878-7746
1A Pretzel Time: 259-0309
2F See's Candies: 878-5267
1D Sweet Factory: 258-7995

FOOD COURT/RESTAURANTS
2C Best Burger: 878-6383
2C China Inn: 878-4849
2C Cinnabon: 870-8160
2C Dairy Queen: 878-4849
2F DiMartino's Italian Eatery: 822-6767
2C Edo Japan: 878-5333
2C The Great American Cookie Company: 870-5588
2C Great Steak & Fry: 258-8181
2C Hot Dog on a Stick: 878-6510
2C McDonald's: 878-5342
2C Nach-O Fast: 870-2775
2C 1 Potato 2: 877-1718
2C Renzio's Greek Food: 877-2885
2F Ricardo's Mexican Restaurant: 870-1088
2C Schlotzsky's Deli: 259-4775
2C Villa Pizza: 870-1400

SHOES
1D Athletic X-Press: 878-4353
2F Florsheim Shoes: 870-5597
2G Foot Action: 870-1899
1B Foot Locker: 878-8226
2E Footquarters: 258-4109
1B Kinney Shoes: 870-4014
1D Lady Foot Locker: 870-8260
1F Leed's: 878-8945
2G Payless ShoeSource: 877-9768
2G Perfect Fit Shoes: 877-1301
1A Stride Rite: 878-4317
2B The Wild Pair: 877-2218

HOBBY & LEISURE
1C B. Dalton Booksellers: 878-4405
1C Champs Sports: 258-5943
1A Electronics Boutique: 258-9177
2F The Game Keeper: 878-1188
2A K-B Toys: 878-0904
1D Kits Camera One Hour Photo: 259-6779
2A Lemstone Books: 870-9996
1F Meadows Pets: 870-0939
1F Pocket Change: 878-8776
2C The Pro Image: 878-2468
1D Sam Goody: 877-0505
2A Stars 'N Thunder: 259-6880
2E Suncoast Motion Picture Co.: 878-9260
2F Waldenbooks: 870-4914
2G The Wherehouse: 870-8253

HOME FURNISHINGS
2C The Bombay Company: 258-1978
2G Cellular USA: 877-2402
2B The Kitchen Sink: 870-4485
2E La-Z-Boy Gallery: 870-1617
2E Lechters Housewares: 259-0006
1C Off The Wall: 870-7525
2A Radio Shack: 878-4233
1C Wicks n' Sticks: 878-3580

JEWELRY & GIFTS
1B Afterthoughts: 258-0272
1C Amy's Hallmark: 878-1423
1C Bath & Body Works: 878-2595
1F Ben Bridge Jewelers: 878-4849
2F Carlton Cards: 878-1113
2A The Chainery: 870-8444
2C Claire's Boutique: 877-6119
1B Crescent Jewelers: 258-8866
1B The Disney Store: 258-2692
2D El Portal Luggage: 870-3121
2C Gordon's Jewelers: 878-1936
2A Hiland's Gifts & Tobacco: 878-7720
2F The Icing: 878-4849
1E Intrigue Jewelry: 870-5179
1A Kay's Jewelers: 878-4133
2F Lundstrom Jewelers: 870-3020
2F M. J. Christensen Jewelers: 878-7832
2E Spencer Gifts: 870-8770
1D Things Remembered: 877-1966
1F Zale's Jewelers: 878-8001

SERVICES
1F Bank of America: ATM: 654-1110
2F Fast 1-Hour Foto: 878-2025
2C Glamour Shots: 870-6880
1A Great Expectations: 870-1710
1B Lenscrafters: 877-6779
2F Lisa's Beauty Supply House: 878-4849
2A Mastercuts: 878-4849
1F New Home Concepts: 877-4397
1B Norwest Bank: ATM: 365-3310
1F Regis Hairstylists: 870-8022

BELZ FACTORY OUTLET WORLD MALL

**7400 Las Vegas Blvd. S.
at Warm Springs Rd.
Las Vegas, NV 89123
896-5599**

Belz Enterprises
Maria Fleming, Gen. Mgr.
Tenants: 140 - Opened November 19, 1993
Area: 575,000 sq. ft.
Hours: Mon. - Sat. 10 am - 9 pm,
Sun. 10 am - 6 pm
Factory stores feature name brand merchandise at up to 75 percent off department store prices. 275,000 sq. ft. expansion was completed in 1996.

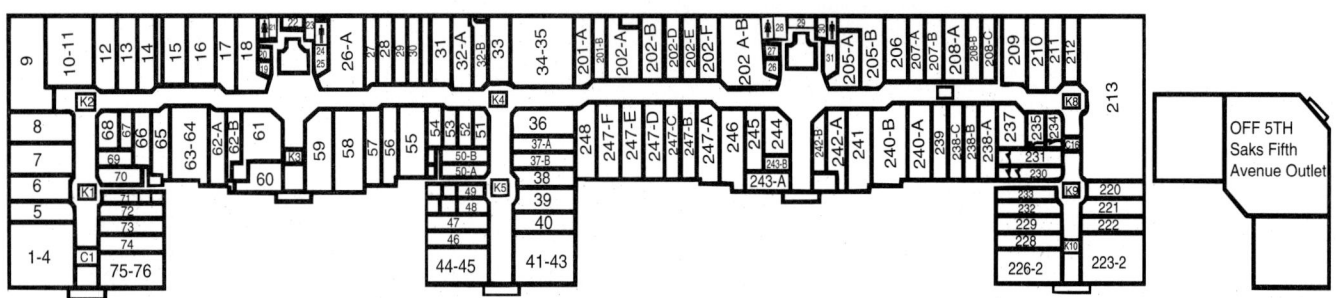

ACCESSORIES
211 American Tourister: 260-3014
72 Afterthoughts: 897-3525
67 Amity Leather/Wallet Works: 897-1108
C1 Black Hills Gold: 361-8401
60 Bruce Alan Bags: 361-5355
5 California Luggage I: 361-8113
232 California Luggage II: 897-1556
51 Claire's Accessories: 260-4363
39 Designer Brands Accessories: 896-2018
71 El Mundo: 896-3991
240B Esprit: 269-4450
243A Fossil: 897-4770
K1 Frenchy's: 896-2216
50B The Hat Co.: 897-1666
48 The Jewelers I: 263-0990
212 The Jewelers II: 361-5444
K2 Jewelry Factory Outlet I: 896-7460
C8 Jewelry Factory Outlet II: 896-5320
208B Leathermode: 269-7227
18 Leggs/Hanes/Bali: 897-8449
K9 Madhatter: 897-5058
242C Momento: 270-2018
52 90 Park: 896-1940
56 Ross Simon: 897-1790
70 Stone Mountain Bags: 897-0613
K4 Sunglass Hut I: 897-8584
K8 Sunglass Hut II: 263-4296
49 Tie One On: 897-8225
231 Ultra Jewelers: 260-8699

BOOKS, RECORDS & TAPES
62B Music 4 Less: 896-0272
38 Publishers Warehouse: 897-2240

CAMERAS & ELECTRONICS
210 Black & Decker: 270-7750
226/7 Bose: 896-5567
228 Casio: 269-9591
73 Wolf Camera & Video: 896-4271

FOOTWEAR
247B Bostonian/Clark: 269-6730
245 Etienne Aigner: 897-5181
59 Famous Footwear: 896-1287
206 Fila: 896-3452
208C Florsheim: 260-4926
17 Hush Puppies: 263-0013
27 Naturalizer: 896-1087
1-4 Nike: 896-7444
223/5 Reebok: 260-7910
222 Rockport: 260-7912

46 Stride Rite: 361-4471
37A Unisa: 361-2954
233 Vans Shoes: 897-6768

HEALTH & BEAUTY AIDS
242B Designer Fragrance: 260-8185
66 Fragrance Outlet: 896-3901
54 Perfumania: 361-1899
50A Prestige Fragrance: 896-1343
69 Vitamin World: 896-1053
234 Wizard of Eyes: 361-1104

HOUSEWARES & LINENS
36 Corning-Revere: 361-241
32A Famous Brands Housewares: 896-3221
14 Kitchen Collection: 896-2882
203A/B Lenox: 263-4889
246 Noritake: 897-7199
65 Oneida: 897-7589
58 Pfaltzgraff: 896-5977
244 Royal Doulton: 260-4192
10-11 Springmaid: 361-0288
242A Waterford/Wedgwood: 896-1606
207B Welcome Home: 896-3623

JEWELRY
C1 Black Hills Gold: 361-4801
48 The Jewelers I: 263-0990
212 The Jewelers II: 361-5444
K2 Jewelry Factory Outlet I: 896-7460
C8 Jewelry Factory Outlet II: 896-5320
231 Ultra Jewelers: 260-8699
56 Diamond Exchange: 837-8555

LINGERIE
202F Jockey: 896-6602
18 Leggs/Haines/Bali/Playtex: 897-8449
47 Maidenform: 270-9691
238B Olga/Warner: 269-6541

MEN'S, WOMEN'S & CHILDREN'S APPAREL
28 Adolfo II: 361-0171
241 American Outpost: 263-5054
230 Ashworth: 260-4230
74 Baby B'Gosh: 263-0033
33 Bass Apparel: 897-0934
202D Big Dogs: 269-7170
16 Blue Wave: 896-0481
29 Bon Worth: 361-3457
209 Bramptons: 260-8850
61 Bugle Boy: 896-4667
9 Burlington Brands: 263-0030

32B Buster Brown: 269-1473
44-45 Carter's: 896-4532
248 Casual Corner: 269-6304
201A Casual Corner Woman: 269-6311
37B Chez Magnifique: 896-1767
235 Coastal Cotton: 270-8772
41-43 Danskin: 361-2900
55 Designer Labels for Less: 896-0755
63-64 Dress Barn: 361-3634
63-64 Dress Barn Woman: 361-3634
71 El Mundo: 896-3991
15 Ellen Ashley: 897-3566
240B Esprit: 269-4450
247F Fitting Image: 260-4161
243A Fossil: 897-4770
53 Fresh Produce: 896-6336
26A Geoffrey Beene: 897-4575
240A Grand & Company: 897-8430
247A Group U.S.A.: 269-6710
6 Harris & Frank: 361-4643
247C HE-RO Group: 269-6575
26B Izod: 896-2636
202F Jockey: 896-6602
247D Jones NY Country: 263-1151
220 Koret: 269-9692
208B Leathermode: 269-7227
34-35 Levi Outlet: 361-4622
202E Little Big Dogs: 269-7170
13 London Fog: 270-9644
57 Lucia: 361-1368
205A Nautica: 270-4041
221 Ocean Pacific: 897-8266
75-76 Oshkosh B'Gosh: 897-1727
201B Petite Sophisticate: 269-6309
238A Primary Years: 269-8610
68 Rafael: 897-7603
22/5 Reebok: 260-7910
247E Reel Studio Store: 269-9790
208A Rue 21: 260-8815
40 SBX: 361-8078
237 So Fun! Kids!: 260-8809
213 Spiegel: 263-1173
202B Starter: 361-1355
205B Umbro: 270-3101
12 Van Heusen: 897-5417
202A We're Entertainment: 260-4450

GREEN FOOD COURT
FC22 Burger King: 263-0023
FC23 Chao Praya I: 896-2523
FC19 Great American Cookie Co.: 897-7229
FC24/25 Rocky Mountain Chocolates: 361-7553

FC21 Sbarro's Pizza: 896-5105
FC20 Steak & Spud: 361-1948

BLUE FOOD COURT
FC31 Baskin Robbins: 260-8900
FC27 Bean Stalk: 260-8898
FC31 Blimpies: 260-8900
FC 28 Chao Praya II: 896-2606
FC26 Pretzel Zone: 897-5635
FC29 Rockey's Philly Cheesesteaks:
FC29 California Salads
FC30 Umbertos: 269-6591

SNACKS
C9 Sweet Zone (Central) 260-4561
C2 Sweet Zone (North): 897-9458
C16 Sweet Zone (South): 361-3663
C12 Great American Cookie Company: 897-7229

SPORTSWEAR & EQUIPMENT
230 Ashworth: 269-8228
61 Bugle Boy: 896-4667
41-43 Danskin: 361-2900
53 Fresh Produce: 896-6336
205 Nautica: 270-4041
1-4 Nike Factory Store: 896-7444
238C Major T's: 260-1420
223/5 Reebok: 260-7910
202B Starter Outlet: 361-1355

TOYS, GIFTS & SOUVENIRS
236 Baldwin Brass: 260-4700
229 Flashback: 269-9661
240A Grand & Company: 897-8430
30 Greetings 'N' More: 897-4261
239 Harry & David: 269-8228
C17 Linda Ray's Gifts: 269-6755
C18 Name Express: 269-8077
207A Natives: 270-9119
K10 Orient Express: 269-0640
C2 Preferred Equities: 896-9705
K38 Preferred Equities: 896-5710
31 Toy Liquidators: 361-8683

ANNEX ONE
A1 Calvin Klein Outlet: 270-4366
A6 OFF 5TH-Saks Fifth Avenue: 263-7692

INFORMATION CENER
Mall Office: 896-5599

DISCOUNT MALL & SWAP MEETS

DISCOUNT MALL

VEGAS POINTE PLAZA
(Formerly Las Vegas Factory Stores of America)
9155 Las Vegas Blvd. S., Las Vegas, NV 89123, 897-9090

Ginny Perkins, Gen. Mgr.
Hours: Mon. - Sat. 10 am - 8 pm, Sun.
10 am - 6 pm
Opened in 1992
255,115 sq. ft.
Open air strip mall
Features bargains up to 70% by major
name manufacturers.

APPAREL
Activewear: 260-8037
Farah/Savane: 361-0477
Izod: 896-4003
Kasper A.S.I.: 361-1778
Nothing over $20: 260-8030
Ocean Pacific: 361-4454
VF Factory Outlet: 896-7565
Van Heusen: 897-0016
Westport Ltd.: 361-4543
Westport Woman: 361-0841

LINGERIE/HOSIERY
Barbizon: 361-8488

FOOTWEAR
Banister Shoe: 361-0061
Converse: 896-5226
Dexter: 896-0713
Factory Brand Shoes: 361-5080
Florsheim: 361-1254
Nine West: 897-7044

SAS Shoes: 896-0728
Shoe Pavilion: 897-4655

FOOD
Rocky Mountain Chocolate Factory: 361-7740

JEWELRY/COSMETICS
Black Hills Gold: 897-2248
Perfumania: 361-3302
Prestige Fragrance & Cosmetics: 896-4090

HOME ACCESSORIES
Famous Brands Housewares: 896-7333
Farberware: 263-1129
Libbey Glass: 897-2710
Mikasa: 897-0737
WestPoint Stevens Bed & Bath: 361-5542

BOOKS/NOTIONS/PAPER
Book Warehouse: 896-5344
Paper Factory: 897-2290
Souvenir Shop: 260-8691

LEATHER GOODS/LUGGAGE
American Tourister: 897-2327
Leather Loft: 361-0904

MISCELLANEOUS
Management Office: 897-9090
Sunglass Hut: 897-7730
Whiskey Creek Saloon: 896-8908

SWAP MEETS

The Fantastic Indoor Swap Meet, 1717 S. Decatur Blvd., Las Vegas, NV 89102

Broadacres Swap Meet
2930 Las Vegas Blvd. N.
N. Las Vegas, NV 89030
642-3777
Jake Bowman, Mgr.
Hours: Fri. - Sun. from 6:30 am
Admission: Friday $.50; Sat. - Sun. $1
26 acres open-air swap meet with
1,000 vendor spaces, new and used
merchandise.

Eastern Indoor Swap Meet
1560 N. Eastern Ave.
Las Vegas, NV 89101
399-3433
Eugene Pak, Mgr.
Hours: Wed. - Mon. 9:30 am - 7:30 pm

Rancho Swap Meet
2909 W. Washington Ave.
Las Vegas, NV 89107
631-1717
Hours: Wed. - Mon. 10 am - 7 pm

**The Fantastic Indoor Swap
Meet**
1717 S. Decatur Blvd.
Las Vegas, NV 89102
877-0087
Bernie Krebs, Mgr.
Hours: Fri. - Sun. 10 am - 6 pm
Admission: $1 adults; children 12 &
under free
Indoor swap meet - 650 merchants

J & R Swap Meet
3901 Las Vegas Blvd. N.
Las Vegas, NV 89115
644-7927
Rick Jewell, Mgr.
Hours: Wed., Fri., Sat. & Sun. 7 am - 4
pm; open to vendors 6:30 am
Admission: Sat. and Sun. $ .50

SHOPPING CENTERS

Listed below are all the major centers in Las Vegas; small neighborhood strip centers are not listed.

Alamosa Plaza
2929-2949 E. Desert Inn Rd.
Las Vegas, NV 89121
Major tenants: Peppers Lounge, Hurst Dental Clinic

Albertson's
1421 N. Jones Blvd.
Las Vegas, NV 89107
Opened 1992
Major tenants: Albertson's, 100,000 sq. ft.

Albertson's Payless Shopping Center
4821 W. Craig Rd.
Las Vegas, NV 89130
Opened 1993
Major tenants: Albertson's, Payless

Albertson's Shopping Center
1955 N. Nellis Blvd.
Las Vegas, NV 89115
85,270 sq. ft.
Major tenants: Albertson's, Blockbuster, Radio Shack, Chief Auto Parts

Albertson's
Boulder Hwy. & Lake Mead
100,000 sq. ft.
Opened 1994
Major tenants: Albertson's & Sav-On

Albertson's Shopping Center
8140-8170 Windmill Pkwy.
Henderson, NV 89014
Major tenants: Albertson's

A Mall
Sahara Ave. & Maryland Pkwy.
Las Vegas, NV 89104
Major tenants: Oshman's Sporting Goods, The Jester

Auto Giant Center
Eastern Ave. & Karen Ave.
Las Vegas, NV 89109
103,000 sq. ft.
Opened 1973
798-6767
Major tenants: Family Fitness Center, Jack-in-the Box

Avenue Shoppes at Bally's
3645 Las Vegas Blvd. S.
Las Vegas, NV 89109
739-4111
Specialty shops and services

Bargain Bazaar
1401 N. Decatur Blvd.
Las Vegas, NV 89108
Major tenants: Thrifty, Lucky's, Payless

Best in the West
Lake Mead & Rainbow Blvd.
Las Vegas, NV 89108
384-4488
415,000 sq. ft.
Realty Holdings Group
Opened 1996
Major tenants: Best Buy, Home Place, PetsMart, Borders, Old Navy and Lil' Things

Best on the Boulevard
Maryland Pkwy. & Katie Ave.
Las Vegas, NV 89119
206,000 sq. ft.
Opened 1995

Major Tenants: Best Buy, Cost Plus, Best Products, Bookstar, Home Place, Hallmark and Blockbuster

Bonanza Square
2300-2448 E. Bonanza Rd.
at Eastern Ave.
Las Vegas, NV 89101
120,000 sq. ft.
Opened 1976
Major tenants: Lucky's, Hancock Fabrics, Sun Drug, Al Phillips, FIB, Sizzler

Boulder Marketplace
Boulder Hwy. & Major Ave.
Henderson, NV 89015
180,000 sq. ft.
Opened 1989
Major tenants: Lucky's, Payless, Miller's Outpost

The Cannery
3455 E. Flamingo Rd.
Las Vegas, NV 89121
Major tenants: Red Carpet Car Wash, Wild Oats Market

Canyon Lakes
9002-9232 W. Sahara Ave.
Las Vegas, NV 89117
118,00 sq. ft.
Opened 1990
Major tenants: Albertson's, Sav-On Drugs, Al Phillips

Central Valley
Boulder Highway & Flamingo Rd.
Las Vegas, NV 89121
108,000 sq. ft.
Opened 1977

Major tenants: Albertson's, Sav-On Drugs, Big O Tires, JB's Restaurant

Charleston Commons
15-201 N. Nellis Blvd.
Las Vegas, NV 89110
350,506 sq. ft.
Opened 1990
Major tenants: Wal-Mart, Ross, Red Robin Restaurant, Petsmart

Charleston Heights Center
Decatur Blvd. & Alta Dr.
Las Vegas, NV 89107
133,000 sq. ft.
Opened 1963
Major tenants: Ross, Pep Boys, Decatur Drug, Peter Piper Pizza, Arizona Charlie's

Charleston-Lamb
1255 S. Lamb Blvd.
Las Vegas, NV 89110
150,000 sq. ft.
Opened 1982
Major tenants: Albertson's, Big 5 Sporting Goods, Major Video

Charleston Plaza
1700-1900 E. Charleston Blvd.
Las Vegas, NV 89104
283,900 sq. ft.
Opened 1959
Major tenants: Home Club, Lucky's, Sav-On Drugs, Computer City and Service Merchandise

Charleston Square
4400-4600 E. Charleston Blvd.
at Lamb Blvd.
Las Vegas, NV 89104
262,393 sq. ft.
Opened 1979
Major tenants: Von's, Payless Drugs

SHOPPING

SHOPPING CENTERS cont.

Cheyenne Commons
3041-3075 N. Rainbow Blvd.
at Cheyenne Ave.
Las Vegas, NV 89108
363,688 sq. ft.
Opened 1992
Major tenants: Wal-Mart, Ross, Family Fitness, Las Vegas Sports and Pier One

Cheyenne Crossing
3210 Tenaya Way
at Cheyenne Ave.
Las Vegas, NV 89129
140,403 sq. ft.
Opened 1992
Major tenants: Target

Cheyenne Plaza
3250-3278 Las Vegas Blvd. N.
at Cheyenne Ave.
Las Vegas, NV 89115
Major tenants: Thrifty, Von's, Macayo's, Dollar Mania

Cheyenne Village
Cheyenne Ave. & Rainbow Blvd.
Las Vegas, NV 89108
Major tenants: Olive Garden

Chinatown Plaza
4205 Spring Mountain Rd.
Las Vegas, NV 89102
221-8448
Terry Chen, Mgr.
90,000 sq. ft.
25 tenants including 7 restuarants
Free shuttle: 497-0188
A majestic "Gate of the Heaven" invites visitors into the complex. In front of the stores is a 28-ft. tall gilded sculpture of Priest Xuanzang & His Three Disciples. The center contains many fine shops, including the town's largest Asian supermarket, and a wedding chapel where civil or true Chinese weddings are performed.
Tenants: 99 Ranch Market, America Asia Travel Center, Beauty Point Hair Salon, Chinatown Florist, Chong Hing Jewelers, Great Wall Book Store, Double Happiness Wedding Chapel, Marco Polo Furniture, Ginseng & Tea House, Zen Entertainment Zone, Diamond Bakery, Snack House, Chinatown Express Restaurant, Kim Tar Seafood Restaurant, Pho Vietnam Restaurant, Sam Woo BBQ Restaurant, 168 Shanghai Restaurant, Plum Tree Inn, Dragon Sushi Japanese Restaurant, DD's Cafe, Rainbow Medical Center, United Pacific Real Estate, Valley Oriental Artworks, Dr. Diep *(Optometrist)*, Far East Trade & Expo Center and Images of the East

Cinema 8 Center
3025 E. Desert Inn Rd.
Las Vegas, NV 89121
Major tenants: Cinema 8 Theaters, Nevada Career Institute

Civic Center Plaza
2100 Civic Center Dr.
N. Las Vegas, NV 89030
186,311 sq. ft.
Opened 1966
Major tenants: Sprint Central, Fashion Discount Mall, Southwest Gas

College Park
2031 E. Lake Mead Blvd.
N. Las Vegas, NV 89030
163,936 sq. ft.
Opened 1959
Major tenants: Lucky's, Newberry, Miller's Outpost, Sav-On Drugs and Blockbuster Video

Commercial Center
Sahara Ave. & Maryland Pkwy.
Las Vegas, NV 89104
300,000 sq. ft.
Opened 1959
Commercial Arts Building: 732-7794
Holland Realty: 385-3226 *(New Orleans Square)*
Americana Commercial Group: 732-8888
Westmark Commercial Group: 458-2911
Major tenants: Aaron Brothers and White Cross Drugs

The Crossroads at Sunset
Sunset Rd. & Stephanie St.
Henderson, NV 89014
130,000 Sq. Ft.
Major tenants: Toys 'R' Us, Sports Authority, Pier 1

Decatur Crossing
202 S. Decatur Blvd.
at Meadows Ln.
Las Vegas, NV 89107
200,000 sq. ft.
Opened 1987
Major tenants: Target, Marshall's, Learning is Fun, Strouds

Decatur Lake Mead Shopping Village
1901-1971 N. Decatur Blvd.
at Lake Mead Blvd.
Las Vegas, NV 89108
Major tenants: Pioneer Market, Radio Shack, Hancock Fabrics, Price Rite, Big O Tires

Decatur Meadows
310-398 S. Decatur Blvd.
Las Vegas, NV 89107
111,258 sq. ft.
Opened 1979
Major tenants: Vons, Aaron Brothers, Leewards, The Wherehouse

Decatur Twain
3650 S. Decatur Blvd.
Las Vegas, NV 89103
49,500 sq. ft.
Major tenants: Green Valley Grocery, Joshua's Pub, Rentronics, Postal Express Plus, Garlic Cafe

Desert Shores Village
2620 Regatta Dr.
Las Vegas, NV 89128
Opened 1991
Major tenants: For Women Only, Captain's Quarters, Beach Cafe, Myers Bakery

Eastgate Plaza
2295 E. Sahara Ave.
Las Vegas, NV 89104
Major tenants: Albertson's, Music World

Epicenter
(formerly Metz Plaza)
3765 Las Vegas Blvd. S.
Las Vegas, NV 89109
Major tenants: Utopia Night Club

The Family Center
1100 S. Decatur Blvd.
at Charleston Blvd.
Las Vegas, NV 89102
Major tenants: Lucky's, Big 5, Blockbuster Video, Bank of America

Flamingo Arville Plaza
4405-4467 W. Flamingo Rd.
at Arville St.
Las Vegas, NV 89103
Minor tenants: LJ's Sports Bar, Pasta Mia, Fremont Medical, Nevada Federal Credit Union, State Farm Insurance

Flamingo-Jones
6110-6190 W. Flamingo Rd.
Las Vegas, NV 89103
Major tenants: Albertson's, Susie's Deals, Al Phillips

Foothills Center
6125 W. Tropicana Ave.
Las Vegas, NV 89103
Major tenants: Samplers Shoppes, Foothills Lounge, Petco

Francisco Center
2470 E. Desert Inn Rd.
Las Vegas, NV 89121
118,400 sq. ft.
Opened 1971
Major tenants: Vons, Ross Dress for Less, Inn Zone D.I.

Franklin Center
5200 Boulder Hwy.
at Nellis Blvd.
Las Vegas, NV 89122

Fremont Plaza
Jones Blvd. & Expressway
Las Vegas, NV 89108
105,000 sq. ft.
Opened 1980
Major tenants: Smith's Food King, Sav-On Drugs

Fremont Street Experience Retail Complex
Fremont St. at 4th & Las Vegas Blvd.
Las Vegas, NV 89101
50,000 sq. ft.
Opened 1996
Located at the base of the new 1,500 car garage.

Galleria Commons
Warm Springs Rd. & Stephanie St.
Henderson, NV 89015
369-4800
CB Commercial
284,000 sq. ft.
Major tenants: Home Base, Stein Mart, Arby's, Boxer's World

Gemco East
Boulder Hwy. & Sahara Ave.
Las Vegas, NV 89121
149,700 sq. ft.
Opened 1979
Major tenants: Elite Indoor Swap Meet

Gemco West
W. Sahara Ave./Duneville St.
Las Vegas, NV 89102
146,000 sq. ft.
Opened 1980
Major tenants: American Federal, The Tavern

Gold's Plaza
3726-3790 E. Flamingo Rd.
Las Vegas, NV 89121
90,743 sq. ft.
Opened 1978
Major tenants: Norwest Bank, Gold's Gym, Hancock Fabrics, Blueberry Hill

Green Valley Town Center
(70 acre entertainment and retail complex)
Sunset Rd. & Green Valley Pkwy.
Henderson, NV 89014
350,000 sq. ft.
Opened 1995
Major tenants: United Artist Theatre, Wherehouse, Green Valley Athletic Club, Olive Garden, Discovery Zone, Mountasia, Starbucks Coffee, Petco

Green Valley Towne & Country
Sunset Rd. & Green Valley Pkwy.
Henderson, NV 89014
129,000 sq. ft.
opened 1989
Major tenants: Lucky's, One Eyed Jacks, Movies to Go, United Artists Theatre, Discovery Zone, Barley's Casino & Brewery

Henderson Shopping Village
830-884 S. Boulder Hwy.
Henderson, NV 89015
112,000 sq. ft.
Opened 1984
Major tenants: Smith's Food King, Checker Auto Parts

K-Las Vegas
Rancho Dr. & Washington Ave.
Las Vegas, NV 89108
109,000 sq. ft.
Opened 1970
Major tenants: K-Mart, Mac Frugals

K Mart Center
Sahara Ave./McLeod Dr.
Las Vegas, NV 89121
140,000 sq. ft.
Opened 1970
Major tenants: K-Mart, Mac Frugals, Pier I Imports, Leatherby's, Furr's Cafeteria

K-Mart Center
Race Track & Sausalito
115,000 sq. ft.
Opened 1992
Major tenants: K-Mart

Kinko's Plaza
4440 S. Maryland Pkwy.
Las Vegas, NV 89119
Opened 1977
Major tenants: Kinko's Copy Center, Sports Pub, Cafe Espresso Roma

Lake Mead Plaza
Lake Mead Blvd. & Jones Blvd.
Las Vegas, NV 89108
106,000 sq. ft.
Opened 1994
Major Tenants: Lucky's, Sav-On

Lake Mead Station Factory Stores
Nevada Hwy. & McKinley St.
176,500 sq. ft.
Opened 1993

Lakes Plaza
W. Sahara Ave. & Ft. Apache Rd.
100,000 sq. ft.
Opened 1995
Major tenants: Lucky's, Baskin-Robbins

Las Vegas Plaza Shopping Center
3025 Las Vegas Blvd. S.
Las Vegas, NV 89109
Major tenants: Silver City Casino, Tower of Jewels

Loma Vista Shopping Center
4530-4560 Meadows Ln.
at Decatur Blvd.
Las Vegas, NV 89107
646-5711
Wing Fong & Associates
275,000 sq. ft.
Opened 1979
Major tenants: Mervyn's, Toys 'R' Us, Home Express, Sav-On Drugs

Lone Mountain Plaza
4854 W. Lone Mountain Rd.
at N. Decatur Blvd.
Las Vegas, NV 89130
369-4800
CB Commercial
124,475 sq. ft.
Opened June, 1992

Major tenants: Vons, Little Caesars Pizza, Prestige Travel

Los Prado Mall
Buchanan & US 93
100,000 sq. ft.
Opened 1982
Major tenants: Vons & Sav-On

Lucky's
Nellis Blvd. & Bonanza Rd.
Las Vegas, NV 89110
Major tenants: Lucky's, Thrifty, American Federal

Lucky's/Sav-On
Warm Springs Rd. & Eastern Ave.
185,000 sq. ft.
Opened 1995

Maryland Crossing
4001-4055 S. Maryland Pkwy.
at Flamingo Rd.
Las Vegas, NV 89119
163,050 sq. ft.
Opened 1987
Major tenants: Target, Payless Shoe Source, Suzie's Deals, Quicksilver

Maryland Square
3661 S. Maryland Pkwy
Las Vegas, NV 89109
220,688 sq. ft.
Opened 1965
Major tenants: Payless Drugs, Sports Authority, Al Phillip's, US Bank

Mercado Del Sol
1110 - 1150 S. Rainbow Blvd.
Las Vegas, NV 89102
Major tenants: Blue Haven Pools

Mission Center
4020 S. Maryland Pkwy.
Las Vegas, NV 89109
302,000 Sq. Ft.
Opened 1978
Major tenants: TJ Max, Toy's 'R' Us, Lucky's, Sav-On, Cafe Michelle

Mission Paseo
8885 W. Sahara Ave.
Las Vegas, NV 89117
Major tenants: Design Center, Beano's Bar & Grill, Blockbuster Video, FIB

Mountain View Plaza
3420 S. Jones Blvd.
Las Vegas, NV 89102
Major tenants: Chung King, Cafe Cappuccino, Calvary Chapel, Mountain View Cinema 3, Just Wood

Nellis Crossing
1200-1300 S. Nellis Blvd.
at Charleston Blvd.
Las Vegas, NV 89104
220,730 sq. ft.
Opened 1987
Major tenants: Target, Mervyn's, Miller's Outpost

North Mesa Plaza
Craig Rd. & Martin Luther King Blvd.
Las Vegas, NV 89030
Major tenants: Vons

North Ranch Plaza
Craig Rd. & Decatur Blvd.
Las Vegas, NV 89108
113,000 sq. ft.
Opened 1992
Major tenants: Albertson's, Payless

Nucleus Shopping Plaza
900-1058 W. Owens Ave.
at H St.
Las Vegas, NV 89106
130,000 sq, ft.
Rebuilt 1993
Major tenants: Nevada Business Service, Community Health Center, Wells Fargo Bank

Ocotillo Plaza
Eastern Ave. & Tropicana Ave.
Las Vegas, NV 89121
118,000 sq. ft.
Opened 1987
Major tenants: Albertson's, Petsmart, Jitters

Owens / Eastern Center
Eastern Ave. & Owens Ave.
Las Vegas, NV 89101
108,000 sq. ft.
Opened 1969
Major tenants: Albertson's, Eastern Indoor Swap Meet

Paradise Cinema Shopping Center
3330 E. Tropicana Ave.
Las Vegas, NV 89121
Major tenants: Paradise Cinema

Paradise Marketplace
3830-3870 E. Flamingo Rd.
Las Vegas, NV 89121
148,714 sq. ft.
Opened 1988
Major tenants: Smith's Food King, Las Vegas Athletic Club, Petco, Just-a-Buck

Park Place
1095 E. Twain Ave.
Las Vegas, NV 89109
224,407 sq. ft.
Opened 1979
Major tenants: Mervyn's, Service Merchandise, Vons, Strouds

Parkway Springs Plaza
2241-2295 N. Green Valley Pkwy.
at Warm Springs Rd.
Henderson, NV 89014
128,585 sq. ft.
Opened 1990
Major tenants: Albertson's, Payless, Roger Dunn Golf Shop

Paseo Plaza
2600 W. Sahara Ave.
Las Vegas, NV 89102
55,000 sq. ft.
Opened 1995
Major tenants: Java Centrale, Boston Market, Bonjour Bagel, Landry's Seafood House, Put 'n on the Ritz

Pebble Marketplace
1000 N. Green Valley Pkwy.
Henderson, NV 89014
160,000 sq. ft.
Opened 1997
Major tenants: Smith's Food & Drug, Bank of America

Pecos Legacy Center
2556-2584 Wigwam Pkwy.
Henderson, NV 89014
Opened 1994
Major tenants: Mega Foods, Blockbuster, State Farm Insurance

Pecos-McLeod Plaza
3050 E. Desert Inn Rd.

Las Vegas, NV 89121
Opened 1988
Major tenants: Learning Is Fun, Pizza Hut, Break Room Pub

Pecos Plaza
Pecos Rd./Russell Rd.
Las Vegas, NV 89120
136,000 sq. ft.
Opened 1987
Major tenants: Vons, Michael's, Blockbuster Video

Pecos-Tropicana Center
3265 E. Tropicana Ave., Ste. 1E
Las Vegas, NV 89121
451-1911
KSK Property
604,629 sq. ft.
Opened 1990
Major tenants: Wal-Mart, Sams Club, Sheplers, Home Express

Pecos Windmill Plaza
2667 Windmill Pkwy
at Pecos Rd.
Henderson, NV 89014
120,000 sq. ft.
Opened 1994
Major tenants: Vons

Pioneer Plaza Shopping Center
4110 S. Maryland Pkwy.
Las Vegas, NV 89119
Opened 1978
Major tenants: Tower Records, Favorites Lounge, Citibank, Pioneer Citizens Bank

The Plazas
2800 W. Sahara Ave.
Las Vegas, NV 89102
Office and retail
Major tenants: American Bank of Commerce, Coffee Pub

SHOPPING

SHOPPING CENTERS cont.

Plaza Desert Inn
3700-3788 E. Desert Inn Rd.
at Sandhill Rd.
Las Vegas, NV 89121
Major tenants: Lucky's, Baskin Robbins

Polo Plaza
3743 Las Vegas Blvd. S.
Las Vegas, NV 89109
60,000 sq. ft.
Opened 1993
Major tenants: Chevy's, Marie
Callender's, Fortune Garden

Premier Plaza
2101 S. Decatur Blvd.
Las Vegas, NV 89102

PriceRite
498 S. Boulder Hwy.
Henderson, NV 89015
117,000 sq. ft.
Opened 1994
Major tenants: PriceRite Warehouse

The Pueblo at Summerlin
Lake Mead Blvd. & Scholar Ln.
Las Vegas, NV 89134
39,841 sq. ft.
Opened 1994
Major tenants: Jitters, Di Martino's
Italian Restaurant, Farmers Insurance

Rainbow Center
6820 Spring Mountain Rd.
at Rainbow Blvd.
Las Vegas, NV 89102
Major tenants: Lucky's, Chief Auto
Parts, Mahoney's

Rainbow Design Mart
1200-1242 S. Rainbow Blvd.
Las Vegas, NV 89102
65,000 sq. ft.
Opened 1991
Major tenants: La-Z Boy Furniture,
Country Interiors, Nevada Tile Center

Rainbow-Dunes Center
Rainbow Blvd. & Spring Mountain Rd.
Las Vegas, NV 89102
101,000 sq. ft.
Opened 1983
Major tenants: K-Mart, Payless Shoes,
Burger King

Rainbow Express Village
1750 S. Rainbow Blvd.
Las Vegas, NV 89102
Major tenants: Danny's II Bar, Parma
Ristorante, Old Santa Fe Furniture

Rainbow-Expressway
110-240 S. Rainbow Blvd.
Las Vegas, NV 89128
104,000 sq. ft.
Opened 1983
Major tenants: Albertson's, Thrifty,
Wells Fargo Bank, Carl's Jr.

Rainbow Plaza
900-1100 S. Rainbow Blvd.
Las Vegas, NV 89128
311,089 sq. ft. *(combined with Rainbow
Plaza II)*
Opened 1989
Major tenants: Lucky's, Payless,
Hallmark

Rainbow Plaza II
800 S. Rainbow Blvd.
Las Vegas, NV 89128
311,089 sq. ft. *(combined with Rainbow
Plaza)*
Opened 1992
Major tenants: Home Depot, Furniture
Depot

Rainbow Ridge Plaza
3104-3174 N. Rainbow Blvd.
Las Vegas, NV 89129
Opened 1990
Major tenants: Albertson's, Payless

Rainbow Shopping Center
101 S. Rainbow Blvd.
Las Vegas, NV 89128
Major tenants: Video Tyme & Norwest
Bank

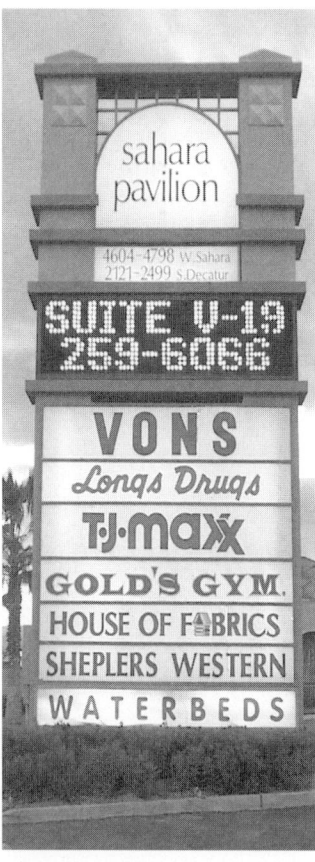

Rainbow Springs West
Rainbow Blvd. & Spring Mountain Rd.
Las Vegas, NV 89117
873-7440
Rainbow Springs, Inc.
335,838 sq. ft
opened 1990
Major tenants: Wal-Mart, Sam's Club,
Sizzler, Loose Caboose, Club Funtime,
Payless Shoe Source

Rampart Plaza
8524-8532 Del Webb Blvd.
at Rampart Blvd.
Las Vegas, NV 89134
Opened 1992
Major tenants: Nevada Bob's &
Domino's

Rancho Sierra
4402-4500 N. Rancho Dr.
Las Vegas, NV 89130
300,000 sq. ft.
Opened 1990
Major tenants: Miller's Outpost, K-
Mart, Smith's, Mac Frugal's

Rancho Town & Country
850 S. Rancho Dr.
at Charleston Blvd.
Las Vegas, NV 89102
79,467 sq. ft.
Major tenants: Smith's Food King,
Blockbuster Video

Renaissance Center East
2250 E. Tropicana Ave.
Las Vegas, NV 89119
192,000 sq. ft.
Opened 1981
Major tenants: Lucky's, Ricardo's
Restaurant, Sprint Central, PriceRite,
Sneaker's

Renaissance Center West
4001 S. Decatur Blvd.
Las Vegas, NV 89103
168,036 sq. ft
Opened 1986
Major tenants: PriceRite, First
Security Bank, Video Park, Ricardo's,
Pier 1

Renaissance III
3230 E. Flamingo Rd.
Las Vegas, NV 89121
220,752 sq. ft.
Opened 1988
Major tenants: PriceRite, Video Park,
Payless Drugs, TruValue, Phillips Jr.
College, Carousel Commons Food Court

Runnin' Rebel Plaza
4550 S. Maryland Pkwy.
Las Vegas, NV 89119
Major tenants: Arthur Murray,
Alphagraphics, Tom & Jerrys

Sahara Decatur Plaza
5001-5099 W. Sahara Ave.
Las Vegas, NV 89102
190,000 sq. ft.
Opened 1988
Major tenants: Circuit City, Charlie's
Cantina

Sahara Paradise Plaza
2200 Paradise Rd.
Las Vegas, NV 89104
Major tenants: Rose of Sharon, Golden
Eagle

Sahara Pavilion North
4604-4798 W. Sahara Ave.
Las Vegas, NV 89102
329,000 sq. ft.
Opened 1989
Major tenants: Drug Emporium, TJ
Maxx, Silo, House of Fabrics, Vons,
Shepler's Western Wear, Formal Affair

Sahara Pavilion South
2500 S. Decatur Blvd.
Las Vegas, NV 89102
258-4330
Pan Pacific Development Co.
132,000 sq. ft.
Opened 1990
Major tenants: Sports Authority, Gold's
Gym, Michaels, Pizzeria Uno, Chili's

Sahara Rainbow Center
2550 S. Rainbow Blvd.
Las Vegas, NV 89102
Major tenants: Sahara Jewelers, La
Fiesta Mexican Restaurant

Sahara Square
1155 E. Sahara Ave.
Las Vegas, NV 89104
Major tenants: Imperial Garden,
Country Store, American Red Cross

Sahara Towne Square
2510-2660 S. Maryland Pkwy.
Las Vegas, NV 89109
162,000 sq. ft.
Opened 1988
Major tenants: Smith's Food King,
Blockbuster Video, Chili's

Sahara West Center
3441 W. Sahara Ave.
Las Vegas, NV 89102
105,000 sq. ft.
Opened 1989
Major tenants: Blockbuster Video,
Golden House

Sahara West Center
2200-2260 S. Rainbow Blvd.
Las Vegas, NV 89102
Opened 1989
Major tenants: Home Base, Las Vegas
Discount Golf & Tennis, McDonald's

Sandhill Square
Sandhill Rd. & Flamingo Rd.
Las Vegas, NV 89121
Major tenants: Blue Ox East

Showcase Mall
3769 Las Vegas Blvd. S
Las Vegas, NV 89109
597-3122
192,000 sq. ft.
Opened 1996
Major tenants: United Artist Theater,
World of Coca-Cola, Official All-Star
Cafe, GameWorks, M&M's World &
Ethel M. Chocolates

Smith's
8555 W. Sahara Ave.
Las Vegas, NV 89117
Major tenants: Smith's Food & Drug

Smith's Center
2211 N. Rampart Blvd.
at Lake Mead Blvd.
Las Vegas, NV 89128
796-5500
The Equity Group
114,000 sq. ft.
Opened 1992
Major tenants: Smith's Food and Drug

Somerset Shopping Center
294 Convention Center Dr.
Las Vegas, NV 89109
735-6244

South Shores Center
8510-8584 W. Lake Mead Blvd.
at Rampart Blvd.
Las Vegas, NV 89134
133,000 sq. ft.
Opened 1991
Major tenants: Albertson's, Payless
Drugs, Video Tyme, Al Phillips

Spanish Oaks
3500-3698 W. Sahara Ave.
Las Vegas, NV 89102
150,000 sq. ft.
Opened 1977
Major tenants: Sav-On Drugs, Al Phillips

Spring Mountain Center
3301-3499 S. Jones Blvd.
Las Vegas, NV 89102
144,000 sq. ft.
Opened 1976
Major tenants: Miller's Outpost, Thrifty Drugs, The Boston Grill & Bar, Nevada State Bank

Spring Oaks Plaza
Decatur Blvd. & Spring Mountain Rd.
Las Vegas, NV 89103
114,000 sq. ft.
Opened 1979
Major tenants: Lucky's, Mac Frugal's, Carl's Jr.

Spring Valley Marketplace
4825-4845 S. Rainbow Blvd.
Las Vegas, NV 89103
Major tenants: Cariba Charlie's, Century Pharmacy, 7 Eleven, Al Phillips

Spring Valley Town Center
6831 W. Flamingo Rd.
at Rainbow Blvd.
Las Vegas, NV 89103
149,621 sq. ft.
Opened 1989
Major tenants: Lucky's, Payless, Movies to Go

Star Lane at the MGM Grand
3799 Las Vegas Blvd. S.
Las Vegas, NV 89109
MGM Grand Merchandising
Bob Bowman, Pres.
22 tenants
Opened 1995
A 40,000 sq. ft. underground shopping mall at the entrance to the MGM Grand Hotel & Theme Park Monorail. There are 11 retail shops and four "Outpost" booths. The shop area features a 1940s and 1950s Hollywood motif.
Major tenants: Haagen Dazs Ice Cream, Yummy's Coffee & Deserts, Photo Magic, Star Magnet, the Pearl Factory, El Portal, Biker Road, Kenneth Jay Lane, Houdini Magic, America West Airlines Ticket Office, Grand Candy Co., Emerald City Gift Shop.
Hours: 9 am - midnight; times subject to change.

Stephanie Street
Stephanie St., south of Sunset Rd.
Henderson, NV 89014
420,000 sq. ft. center.
Opened 1995
Major tenants: Circuit City, Home Place, Best Products, Barnes & Noble

Sunrise
Boulder Hwy./Charleston Blvd.
Las Vegas, NV 89104
135,000 sq. ft.
Opened 1965
Major tenants: Montgomery Ward

Sunrise City
2797 S. Maryland Pkwy.
Las Vegas, NV 89109
101,000 sq. ft.
Opened 1973
Major tenants: Lucky's, Big 5 Sporting Goods, Office Depot

Sunrise Marketplace
420-560 N. Nellis Blvd.
Las Vegas, NV 89110
181,256 sq. ft.
Opened 1988
Major tenants: Smith's, Video Park, House of Fabrics, Applebee's

Sunrise Mountain Plaza
5000 E. Bonanza Rd.
Las Vegas, NV 89110
132,500 sq. ft.
opened 1983
Major tenants: K-Mart, Video Tyme, Blueberry Hill

Sunset Mountain Vista Plaza
4600 E. Sunset Rd.
Henderson, NV 89014
110,00 sq. ft.
Opened 1992
Major tenants: Smith's, Video Tyme, Chief Auto Parts

Sunset Place
Sunset Rd. & Sandhill Rd.
Las Vegas, NV 89124
118,000 sq. ft.
Opened 1988
Major tenants: K-Mart, Bleacher's Pub, Payless Shoe Source

Sunset Plaza
1080 W. Sunset Rd.
Henderson, NV 89014
272,286 sq. ft.
Opened 1992
Major tenants: Costco, Home Depot

Target
Spring Mountain Rd. & Rainbow Blvd.
125,000 sq. ft.
Opened 1993
Major tenants: Target

Times Square
4000 S. Rainbow Blvd.
Las Vegas, NV 89013
130,000 sq. ft.
Opened 1978
Major tenants: Vons, Sav-On, Michael's Pub

Tonopah Plaza
Rancho Dr. & Cheyenne Ave.
Las Vegas, NV 89108
100,000 sq. ft.
Opened 1982
Leasing: 795-7900
Major tenants: Lucky's

Town & Country Plaza
Rancho Dr. and Charleston Blvd.
87,300 sq. ft.
Opened 1978
Major tenants: Smith's

Tropicana East Centre
4750-4900 S. Eastern Ave.
Las Vegas, NV 89119
200,000 sq. ft.
Opened 1981
Major tenants: Circuit City, Cloth World, Marie Callender's, World Gym, Burlington Coat Factory

Tropicana Marketplace
6120-6160 W. Tropicana Ave.
Las Vegas, NV 89103
142,853 sq. ft.
Opened 1988
Major tenants: Smith's Food King, Spring Valley Travel, Mammoth Video, Little Professor Books

Tropicana Nellis Shopping Village
4900 E. Tropicana Ave.
Las Vegas, NV 89121
Major tenants: Nevada State Bank, Radio Shack, Pykettes

Tropicana Plaza
3430 E. Tropicana Ave.
at Pecos Rd.
Las Vegas, NV 89121
115,400 sq. ft.
Opened 1974
Major tenants: Miller's Outpost, Peter Piper Pizza

Twin Lakes Plaza Shopping Center
910 N. Rancho Dr.
Las Vegas, NV 89106

University Gardens
4632-4634 S. Maryland Pkwy.
Las Vegas, NV 89119
Major tenants: Wherehouse Records, Nevada Copy Systems

University Plaza
Tropicana Ave. & Maryland Pkwy.
Las Vegas, NV 89119
100,000 sq. ft.
Opened 1970
Major tenants: Vons, University Drugs, Checker Auto Parts

Valley Oaks Plaza
3846-3888 W. Sahara Ave.
at Valley View Blvd.
Las Vegas, NV 89102
121,000 sq. ft.
Opened 1993
Major tenants: Payless, Albertsons

Vegas Valley Plaza
2755-2875 S. Nellis Blvd.
at Vegas Valley Blvd.
Las Vegas, NV 89121
135,000 sq. ft.
Opened 1992
Major tenants: Lucky's, Sav-On, PT's Pub, Video Tyme

Victory Village
300 E. Lake Mead Dr.
Henderson, NV 89015
Major tenants: Wal-mart

Village East
5025 S. Eastern Ave.
Las Vegas, NV 89119
Major tenants: Bootlegger Ristorante, Village East Cleaners, Village East Drugs

Vista Plaza
Tropicana Ave. & Mountain Vista St.
Las Vegas, NV 89121
Major tenants: Lucky's, Kopper Keg

Vons
6010 W. Cheyenne at Jones Blvd.
Las Vegas, NV 89108
Major tenants: Vons & Video Tyme

Von's Food Center
Pecos & Russell
136,000 sq. ft.
Opened 1987
Major tenants: Vons & Michaels

Wal-Mart
300 E. Lake Mead Dr.
Henderson, NV 89015
110,00 sq. ft.
Opened 1994
Major Tenants: Wal-Mart

Warm Springs Marketplace
7271 S. Eastern Ave.
Las Vegas, NV 89123
185,000 sq. ft.
Opened 1995
Major tenants: Lucky's, Sav-On

Warm Springs Plaza
7380 S. Eastern Ave.
at Warm Springs Rd.
Las Vegas, NV 89123
Opened 1990
Major tenants: BallPark Lounge, Park Animal Hospital, Flower Fair

WestLake
4505 W. Sahara Ave.
Las Vegas, NV 89102
Opened 1987
Major tenants: Spartan Health Foods, McGhies Ski Chalet, The Egg & I Restaurant

West Sahara Town Plaza
6322-6398 W. Sahara Ave.
Las Vegas, NV 89102
Opened 1988
Major tenants: Big Dog's, Torrey Pines Cinema, Green Valley Grocery

Westland Fair South
4601 W. Charleston Blvd.
Las Vegas, NV 89102
411,630 sq. ft.
opened 1969; renovated 1990
Major tenants: Service Merchandise, Builders Square, Smart & Final, Petsmart, Computer City

Magic's Westland Plaza
1601 W. Owens Ave.
Las Vegas, NV 89106
235,170 sq. ft.
Opened October 1994
Major tenants: Vons

Whitney Ranch Center
605-649 Stephanie St.
at Sunset Rd.
Henderson, NV 89014
256,167 sq. ft.
Opened October 1991
Major tenants: Target, Vons, Ross, Learning Is Fun

Winchester Plaza
1700 E. Desert Inn Rd.
Las Vegas, NV 89109

Windmill Pecos Plaza
Windmill/Pecos
130,000 sq. ft.
Opened 1994
Major tenants: Vons

Winterwood Pavilion
2200-2350 S. Nellis Blvd.
Las Vegas, NV 89104
163,000 sq. ft.
Opened 1990
Major tenants: Anna's Linens, Vons, Carl's Jr., Heilig-Meyers, Blockbuster Video

SHOPPING

DEPARTMENT STORES

Dillard's
Fashion Show Mall
3200 Las Vegas Blvd. S.
Las Vegas, NV 89109
733-2008
Maria Rokovitz, Store Mgr.

Meadows Mall
4300 Meadows Ln.
Las Vegas, NV 89107
870-2039
Karen Linquist, Store Mgr.

Boulevard Mall
3700 S. Maryland Pkwy.
Las Vegas, NV 89109
734-2111
Steve Dohm, Store Mgr.

Galleria
1320 W. Sunset Rd.
Henderson, NV 89014
435-6300
Mark Stevens, Store Mgr.
Hours: Mon. - Sat. 10 am - 9 pm; Sun. noon - 6 pm
Credit Cards: MC, Visa, AMX, Discover, Dillard's Charge, Diner's Club, CB
Quality fashions for the whole family, housewares, linens and gifts. Services include a beauty salon, travel service, gift wrapping and gift certificates.

J. C. Penney Co.
Boulevard Mall
3542 S. Maryland Pkwy.
Las Vegas, NV 89109
735-5131
Michael Merchant, Store Mgr.
Hours: Mon. - Fri. 10 am - 9 pm; Sat. 10 am - 7 pm; Sun. 11 am - 6 pm

Meadows Mall
4400 Meadows Ln.
Las Vegas, NV 89107
870-9182
Howard Couch, Store Mgr.
Hours: Mon. - Fri. 10 am - 9 pm; Sat. - Sun. 10 am - 6 pm

Galleria
1300 W. Sunset Rd.
Henderson, NV 89014
451-4545
King Watts, Store Mgr.
Hours: Mon. - Sat. 10 am - 9 pm; Sun. 11 am - 6 pm
Credit Cards: MC, Visa, AMX, Penney's Charge
Catalog phone: 1-800-222-6161

K-Mart Discount Stores
2671 Las Vegas Blvd. N.
N. Las Vegas, NV 89030
642-2183

3760 E. Sunset Rd.
Las Vegas, NV 89120
458-8008

5050 E. Bonanza Rd.
Las Vegas, NV 89110
459-2000

4500 N. Rancho Dr.
Las Vegas, NV 89130
658-5977

2975 E. Sahara Ave.
Las Vegas, NV 89104
457-1037
(Auto service center at this location)

3455 S. Rainbow Blvd.
Las Vegas, NV 89103
367-8300

732 S. Racetrack Rd.
Henderson, NV 89015
564-8860
Steve Pratt, Dist. Mgr.
(Auto service center at this location)
Hours: 8 am - 10 pm
Credit Cards: MC, Visa, Discover, AMX

Macy's
Boulevard Mall
3634 S. Maryland Pkwy.
Las Vegas, NV 89109
791-2100
Michael Ellis, Store Mgr.
Hours: Mon. - Fri. 10 am - 9 pm; Sat. 10 am - 8 pm, Sun. 11 am - 7 pm

Meadows Mall
4100 Meadows Ln.
Las Vegas, NV 89107
258-2100
Linda King, Store Mgr.

Hours: Mon. - Fri. 10 am - 9 pm; Sat. 10 am - 8 pm; Sun. 11 am - 8 pm
Shop by phone: 1-800-626-4800
Credit Cards: Broadway Charge, MC, Visa, AMX

Fashion Show Mall
3200 Las Vegas Blvd. S.
Las Vegas, NV 89109
731-5111
Charles Anderson, Store Mgr.
Hours: Mon. - Fri. 10 am - 9 pm; Sat. 9 am - 8 pm; Sun. 11 am - 7 pm
Personal Shopper: 731-5111 ext. 4444
Credit Cards: Macy's Charge, MC, Visa, AMX
Contemporary and designer fashions for men and women, children's clothing, jewelry, cosmetics, crystal and silver, everything for the kitchen, linens, electronics, gifts.

Mervyn's California
1300 S. Nellis Blvd.
Las Vegas, NV 89110
453-8800
Blondell Jones, Store Mgr.

1155 E. Twain Ave.
Las Vegas, NV 89109
737-1500
Lisa Davise, Store Mgr.

4700 Meadows Ln.
Las Vegas, NV 89107
870-9000
Michele Jacobson, Store Mgr.

Galleria
1300 W. Sunset Rd.
Henderson, NV 89014
454-8881
Linda Ethridge, Store Mgr.
Hours: Mon. - Sat. 10 am - 9 pm; Sun. 9 am - 9 pm
Credit Cards: MC, Visa, Discover, AMX, Mervyn's Charge
Clothing for the whole family, jewelry, shoes, linens, gift items.

Montgomery Ward & Co.
2875 E. Charleston Blvd.
Las Vegas, NV 89104
385-6600
Gary Martin, Store Mgr.

2120 S. Decatur Blvd.
Las Vegas, NV 89107
251-7300
Brian Waltman, Store Mgr.
Hours: Mon. - Fri. 10 am - 9 pm; Sat. 10 am - 8 pm; Sun. 11 am - 6 pm
Credit Cards: MC, Visa, AMX, Ward's
Complete department store with everything for the home, family and the automobile.

Neiman Marcus
Fashion Show Mall
3200 Las Vegas Blvd.
Las Vegas, NV 89109
731-3636
Terri Monsour, Store Mgr.
Hours: Mon. - Fri. 10 am - 8 pm; Sat. 10 am - 7 pm; Sun. noon - 6 pm
Credit Cards: Neiman Marcus, all major credit cards
Contemporary and designer fashions for men and women, jewelry, cosmetics, gifts.

Robinsons-May
Fashion Show Mall
3200 Las Vegas Blvd. S.
Las Vegas, NV 89109
737-8708
Vicki Raynolds, Store Mgr.
Hours: Mon. - Fri. 10 am - 9 pm; Sat. 9 am - 8 pm; Sun. 10 am - 7 pm

Galleria
1304 W. Sunset Rd.
Henderson, NV 89014
458-7300
Bob Steinforth, Store Mgr.
Hours: Mon. - Sat. 10 am - 9 pm; Sun. 10 am - 7 pm
Credit Cards: Robinsons-May Charge, MC, Visa, Discover

Saks Fifth Avenue
Fashion Show Mall
3200 Las Vegas Blvd. S.
Las Vegas, NV 89109
733-8300
Mari Landers, Store Mgr.

Hours: Mon. - Wed. 10 am - 8 pm; Thu. - Fri. 10 am - 9 pm; Sat. 10 am - 7 pm; Sun. noon - 6 pm
Credit Cards: Saks Charge and all major credit cards
Contemporary and designer fashions for men and women, jewelry, cosmetics, gifts.

Sears Roebuck & Co.
Boulevard Mall
3450 S. Maryland Pkwy.
Las Vegas, NV 89109
894-4200
Chris Adams, Store Mgr.
Hours: Mon. - Fri. 10 am - 9 pm; Sat. 10 am - 8 pm; Sun. 10 am - 6 pm

Meadows Mall
4000 Meadows Ln.
Las Vegas, NV 89107
259-4200
Ron Rude, Store Mgr.
Hours: Mon. - Fri. 10 am - 9 pm; Sat. 10 am - 7 pm; Sun. 10 am - 6 pm
Credit Cards: Sears Charge, Discover
Complete department store with everything for the home, family and the automobile.

Target
278 S. Decatur Blvd.
Las Vegas, NV 89107
870-1981

4001 S. Maryland Pkwy.
Las Vegas, NV 89119
732-2218

1200 S. Nellis Blvd.
Las Vegas, NV 89110
438-8866

3210 N. Teneya Wy.
Las Vegas, NV 89129
645-5440

605 Stephanie St.
Henderson, NV 89014
451-5959

3550 S. Rainbow Blvd.
Las Vegas, NV 89103
253-5151
Ray Sconiers, Dist. Team Leader
Hours: 8 am - 10 pm
Credit Cards: MC, Visa, Discover, AMX, Dayton's, Hudson's, Marshall Field's

Wal-Mart
201 N. Nellis Blvd.
Las Vegas, NV 89110
452-9998

3075 E. Tropicana Ave.
Las Vegas, NV 89121
451-8900

3625 S. Rainbow Blvd.
Las Vegas, NV 89103
367-9999

3041 N. Rainbow Blvd.
Las Vegas, NV 89108
656-0199
Hours: 24 hours

300 E. Lake Mead Dr.
Henderson, NV 89015
564-3665
Jim Bennett, District Mgr.
Hours: 7 am - 11 pm
Credit Cards: Visa, MC, Discover
Two new stores are opening in 1998 in North Las Vegas and Henderson.

ANTIQUE SHOPS

Most of the antique dealers in Las Vegas are located along East Charleston, between Maryland Pkwy. and Eastern. Antique Square Shopping Center, at the corner of Charleston and Eastern, is home to about 21 antique shops.

A Antique & Collector's Gallery
6125 W. Tropicana Ave., Ste. A
Las Vegas, NV 89103
889-1444
Hours: Mon. - Sat. 10 am - 5 pm; Sun. noon - 5 pm

Ack's Attic
530 Nevada Hwy.
Boulder City, NV 89005
293-4035
Robert Ackerson, Owner
Hours: By appointment only
Dolls, paintings, coins, baseball cards, comic books.

Albion Book Company
2466 E. Desert Inn Rd.
Las Vegas, NV 89121
792-9554
Lisa Horine, Owner
Hours: 10 am - 8 pm
Antique, used, and out of print books.

Anello's Collectibles of All Kinds
1115 Western Ave.
Las Vegas, NV 89102
366-1664
Tony Anello, Owner
Hours: Mon. - Sat. 10 am - 5 pm; Sun. noon - 5 pm
Marbles, cigarette lighters, casino memorabilia, old toys, die cast vehicles, buttons, Coca Cola items.

Antique Palace
6125 W. Tropicana Ave.
Las Vegas, NV 89103
873-3749
Sharon Melton, Owner
Hours: By appointment only
Furniture, kitchenware, jewelry, Louis XIV reproductions, crystal, china and sterling.

Antique Warehouse
4175 S. Cameron St., Ste. 1
Las Vegas, NV 89103
251-3447
Kurt Howe, Owner
Hours: Mon. - Sat. 10 am - 5 pm; Sun. 11 am - 4 pm
Toys, dolls, autographs, jewelry, ceramics and furnishings.

Antiquities International
Forum Shops
3500 Las Vegas Blvd. S.
Las Vegas, NV 89109
792-2274
Toby Stoffa, Owner
Hours: Mon. - Thu. 10 am - 11 pm, Fri. - Sat. 10 am - midnight
Credit cards: All major
Antiques from the 40s and 50s, autographs, rock and roll guitars, photos and Hollywood props.

Buzz & Co. Fine Antiques
2034 E. Charleston Blvd.
Las Vegas, NV 89104
384-2034
Buzz Parsons
Hours: Mon. - Sat. 10 am - 4 pm
Fine European and American antique furniture, silver, music boxes, paintings, lamps, bronzes, china and crystal.

Estate Antiques
2032 E. Charleston Blvd.
Las Vegas, NV 89104
388-4289
David Arenaz, Owner
Hours: 10 am - 4 pm
Fine glass, pottery, jewelry (costume and fine), highest price paid for antiques - buy and sell.

Fields of Dreams
1647 E. Charleston Blvd.
Las Vegas, NV 89104
385-2770
Lillian Potter, Owner
Hours: Mon. - Sat. 10 am - 4 pm; Sun. 11 am - 2 pm
Furniture, Coca-Cola memorabilia, pottery, art glass, jewelry, primitives and Victorian items.

Gallery of History
3601 W. Sahara Ave.
Las Vegas, NV 89102
731-2300
Todd Axelrod, Owner
Hours: Mon. - Fri. 8 am - 5 pm
Historical documents, letters, manuscripts, photographs and signatures of famous people who shaped the world.

Grace Cottage of Lordsly
2616 E. Charleston Blvd.
Las Vegas, NV 89104
386-0518
James Hardy, Owner
Hours: Mon. 10 am - 4 pm; Tue. - Fri. 10 am - 6 pm; Sat. 10 am - 4 pm
Old world elegance in the Victorian era. Specializing in furniture and fine china.

Granny's Nook and Cranny
2032 E. Charleston Blvd.
Las Vegas, NV 89104
598-1983
Kathryn Rayls, Owner
Hours: Tue. - Sat. 10 am - 4 pm
Antiques and collectibles. China, linens, jewelry, pottery, furniture.

J.B. New & Used Furniture Co.
5920 Boulder Hwy.
Las Vegas, NV 89122
451-1310
Hazel Flippin, Owner
Hours: Mon. - Sat. 9 am - 6 pm
Furniture, wagons, wagonwheels, claw-foot bathtubs, cream separators and wind-up record players.

Janean's Antiques
538 Nevada Hwy.
Boulder City, NV 89005
293-5747
Janean Gegen, Owner
Hours: Mon. - Sat. 10 am - 4 pm
Furniture, jewelry, frames, linens.

Las Vegas Antique Slot Machine Co.
4820 W. Montara Cir.
Las Vegas, NV 89121
456-8801
Mike Andrews, Owner
Hours: 9 am - 5 pm
Slots going back as far as 1898; restoration.

Maudie's Antique Cottage
3310 E. Charleston Blvd.
Las Vegas, NV 89104
457-4379
Ariana Saint Jennings, Owner
Hours: Mon. - Sat. 10 am - 5 pm ; closed Wed. and Sun.

Victorian antiques. Antique glassware, furniture, linens, new and antique dolls and Teddy bears.

Nicholas Antonio Antiques
2016 E. Charleston Blvd., Ste. 6
Las Vegas, NV 89104
385-7772
Nick Gaudino, Owner
Hours: Mon. - Sat. 10 am - 3 pm
Swords, knives and other antiques.

Nicolas & Osvaldo Antiques
2020 E. Charleston Blvd.
Las Vegas, NV 89104
386-0238
Robert Nichols
Hours: Mon. - Sat. 10 am - 5 pm; closed Sun.
An exquisite collection of fine European and American antiques and collectibles. Antique statues, china, crystal, furniture and more.

Ratcliff's Antiques
2532 E. Desert Inn Rd.
Las Vegas, NV 89121
796-9686
Ronald Ratcliff, Owner
Hours: Mon. - Sat. 10 am - 5 pm; Sun. 10 am - 4 pm
Silver, artwork, furniture, crystal, china, lamps, brass, marble and bronze.

Las Vegas Antiques
6115 W. Tropicana Ave.
Las Vegas, NV 89103
248-1956
Tom Phillips, Owner
Hours: Mon. - Sat. 10 am - 6 pm; Sun. noon - 5 pm
Sterling, art, glass, unusual items, jewelry and china. Will buy antiques; house calls made.

Roaring 20's Player Pianos
618 Mt. Elbert Way
Boulder City, NV 89005
294-1484
Joanne Biger, Owner
Hours: By appointment
Antique player pianos.

Romantic Notions/Antiques
6125 W. Tropicana Ave., Ste. F
Las Vegas, NV 89103
248-1957
Carol & Peter Sidlow
Hours: Mon. - Sat. 10 am - 5 pm
Vintage laces, ribbons, linens, buttons, paintings, advertisements and road maps

The Sampler Shops
6115 W. Tropicana Ave.
Las Vegas, NV 89103
368-1170
Susan Boaz, Gen. Mgr.
Hours: Mon. - Sat. 10 am - 6 pm, Sun. noon - 5 pm
Antique and interior design mall. Over 40,000 sq. ft. of antiques, collectibles, jewelry and fine home interiors. Over 200 merchants.

Silver Horse Antiques
1651 E. Charleston Blvd.
Las Vegas, NV 89104
385-2700
Leslie Bell, Mamie Lewis
Hours: Tue. - Fri. 10 am - 5 pm; Sat. 10 am - 4 pm
Victorian antiques and collectibles from furniture to old bottles and china.

Sugarplums Etc.
2022 E. Charleston Blvd.
Las Vegas, NV 89104
385-6059
Jeane Parris
Hours: Tue. - Sat. 10 am - 4 pm
Antique glassware, porcelain figurines, silver and jewelry. Large collection of antique perfume bottles.

Sunshine Clocks Antiques
1651 E. Charleston Blvd.
Las Vegas, NV 89104
363-1312
Raymond Emery, Owner
Hours: Tue. - Fri. 10 am - 5 pm; Sat. 10 am - 4 pm
Antique clocks including grandfather clocks and mantle clocks. Antique clocks restored and repaired. Located inside Silver Horse Antiques.

Vintage Slot Machine
3379 Industrial Rd.
Las Vegas, NV 89109
369-2323
Rudy Lewis, Owner
Largest selection of antique slots.

The Yesteryear Mart
1626 E. Charleston Blvd.
Las Vegas, NV 89104
384-6946
Vince Betke, Owner
Hours: Mon. - Sat. 10 am - 4 p.m
Antique furniture, jewelry, ceramics, lamps and crystal.

Because of the many of car dealerships in the area, below is just a sampling of what is available for most of today's cars.

SHOPPING

AUTO RETAIL DEALERS

ACURA
Falconi's Acura of Las Vegas
5550 W. Sahara Ave.
Las Vegas, NV 89102
367-6400
Sales Hours: Mon. - Sat. 8 am - 10 pm
Service Hours: Mon. - Fri. 7:30 am -
5:30 pm

AUDI
Chaisson Motor Cars
2333 S. Decatur Blvd.
Las Vegas, NV 89102
871-1010
Sales Hours: Mon. - Sat. 8:30 am - 8 pm
Service Hours: Mon. - Fri. 7:30 am -
5:30 pm; Sat. 8 am - 2 pm

BMW
Chaisson Motor Cars
2333 S. Decatur Blvd.
Las Vegas, NV 89102
871-1010
Sales Hours: Mon. - Sat. 8:30 am - 8 pm
Service Hours: Mon. - Fri. 7:30 am -
5:30 pm; Sat. 8 am - 2 pm

BUICK
Desert Buick GMC Trucks, Inc.
6400 W. Sahara Ave.
Las Vegas, NV 89102
253-6400
Sales Hours: Mon. - Sat. 9 am - 9 pm
Service Hours: Mon. - Fri. 7 am - 6 pm;
Sat. 8 am - 2 pm

CADILLAC
Cashman Cadillac
2711 E. Sahara Ave.
Las Vegas, NV 89104
457-0300
Sales Hours: Mon. - Fri. 8 am - 7 pm;
Sat. 8 am - 5 pm
Service Hours: Mon. - Fri. 7:30 am -
5:30 pm; Sat. 8 am - 1 pm

CHEVROLET / GEO
Fletcher Jones Chevrolet - Geo
444 S. Decatur Blvd.
Las Vegas, NV 89107
870-9444
Sales Hours: Mon. - Sat. 8:30 am - 9 pm
Service Hours: Mon. - Fri. 7 am - 6 pm;
Sat. 7 am - 1 pm

CHRYSLER-PLYMOUTH
Las Vegas Chrysler Plymouth
2100 S. Decatur Blvd.
Las Vegas, NV 89102
870-9793
Sales Hours: Mon. - Sat. 8 am - 9 pm
Service Hours: Mon. - Fri. 7 am - 9 pm;
Sat. 8 am - 4 pm

DODGE
Chapman's Las Vegas Dodge, Inc.
3470 Boulder Hwy.

Las Vegas, NV 89121
457-1061
Sales Hours: Mon. - Fri. 8 am - 9 pm;
Sat. 8 am - 7 pm
Service Hours: Mon. - Fri. 7 am - 6 pm;
Sat. 8 am - 2 pm

FORD
Friendly Ford
660 N. Decatur Blvd.
Las Vegas, NV 89107
870-7221
Sales Hours: Mon. - Fri. 8:30 am -
10 pm; Sat. 8:30 am - 9:30 pm
Service Hours: Mon. - Fri. 7:30 am -
11 pm; Sat. 8 am - 4 pm

GMC
Desert Valley GMC
330 N. Gibson Rd.
Henderson, NV 89014
558-3300
Sales Hours: Mon. - Sat. 9 am - 9 pm
Service Hours: Mon. - Fri. 7 am - 6 pm;
Sat. 8 am - 2 pm

HONDA
Las Vegas Honda Automobiles
1700 E. Sahara Ave.
Las Vegas, NV 89104
369-3099
Sales Hours: Mon. - Sat. 8 am - 10 pm
Service Hours: Mon. - Fri. 7:30 am -
5:30 pm; Sat. 8 am - 2 pm

HUMMER
Towbin Super Stores
5555 W. Sahara Ave.
Las Vegas, NV 89102
253-7000
Sales Hours: Mon. - Fri. 9 am - 9 pm;
Sat. 9 am - 8 pm
Service Hours: Mon. - Fri. 7 am - midnight;
Sat. 8 am - 2 pm

HYUNDAI
Fletcher Jones Hyundai
4900 Alta Dr.
Las Vegas, NV 89107
870-9444
Sales Hours: Mon. - Sat. 8 am - 10 pm
Service Hours: Mon. - Fri. 7 am - 6 pm;
Sat. 8 am - 1 pm

INFINITI
Towbin Super Stores
5555 W. Sahara Ave.
Las Vegas, NV 89102
253-7000
Sales Hours: Mon. - Fri. 9 am - 9 pm;
Sat. 9 am - 8 pm
Service Hours: Mon. - Fri. 7 am - 6 pm;
Sat. 8 am - 2 pm

ISUZU
Courtesy Oldsmobile-Isuzu-Kia
5800 W. Sahara Ave.
Las Vegas, NV 89102
221-8000
Sales Hours: Mon. - Sat. 9 am - 10 pm
Service Hours: Mon. - Fri. 7 am - 6 pm;
Sat. 7 am - 1 pm

JAGUAR
Chaisson Motor Cars
2333 S. Decatur Blvd.
Las Vegas, NV 89102
871-1010
Sales Hours: Mon. - Sat. 8:30 am - 8 pm
Service Hours: Mon. - Fri. 7:30 am -
5:30 pm; Sat. 8 am - 2 pm

JEEP-EAGLE
Jim Marsh Jeep-Eagle-Mazda-Volvo
2570 S. Eastern Ave.
Las Vegas, NV 89109
457-8033
Sales Hours: Mon. - Fri. 8 am - 9 pm;
Sat. 8 am - 6 pm
Service Hours: Mon. - Fri. 7 am - 5:30
pm; Sat. 8 am - 12 pm

KIA
Courtesy Oldsmobile-Isuzu-Kia
5800 W. Sahara Ave.
Las Vegas, NV 89102
221-8000
Sales Hours: Mon. - Sat. 9 am - 10 pm
Service Hours: Mon. - Fri. 7 am - 6 pm;
Sat. 7 am - 1 pm

LAMBORGHINI
Towbin Super Stores
5555 W. Sahara Ave.
Las Vegas, NV 89102
253-7000
Sales Hours: Mon. - Fri. 9 am - 9 pm;
Sat. 9 am - 8 pm
Service Hours: Mon. - Fri. 7 am - 6 pm;
Sat. 8 am - 2 pm

LAND ROVER
Chaisson Motor Cars
2333 S. Decatur Blvd.
Las Vegas, NV 89102
871-1010
Sales Hours: Mon. - Sat. 8:30 am - 8 pm
Service Hours: Mon. - Fri. 7:30 am -
5:30 pm; Sat. 8 am - 2 pm

LEXUS
Fletcher Jones Lexus
3130 S. Rancho Dr.
Las Vegas, NV 89102
364-2727
Sales Hours: Mon. - Fri. 8 am - 8 pm;
Sat. 8 am - 7 pm
Service Hours: Mon. - Fri. 7 am - 6 pm

LINCOLN-MERCURY
Signature Lincoln Mercury
3030 E. Sahara Ave.
Las Vegas, NV 89104
457-0321
Sales Hours: Mon. - Fri. 9 am - 9 pm;
Sat. 9 am - 7 pm
Service Hours: Mon. - Fri. 7 am - 7 pm;
Sat. 8 am - 2 pm

MAZDA
Jim Marsh Jeep-Eagle-Mazda-Volvo
2570 S. Eastern Ave.
Las Vegas, NV 89109
457-8033

Sales Hours: Mon. - Fri. 8 am - 9 pm;
Sat. 8 am - 6 pm
Service Hours: Mon. - Fri. 7 am - 5:30 pm;
Sat. 8 am - 12 pm

MERCEDES-BENZ
Fletcher Jones Import Center
3100 S. Rancho Dr.
Las Vegas, NV 89102
364-2700
Sales Hours: Mon. - Fri. 8:30 am - 8 pm;
Sat. 9 am - 5 pm
Service Hours: Mon. - Fri. 7 am - 6 pm

MITSUBISHI
Fletcher Jones Mitsubishi
444 S. Decatur Blvd.
Las Vegas, NV 89107
870-9444
Sales Hours: Mon. - Sat. 8 am - 9 pm
Service Hours: Mon. - Fri. 7 am - 6 pm;
Sat. 8 am - 1 pm

NISSAN
Nissan West
5050 W. Sahara Ave.
Las Vegas, NV 89102
871-7000
Sales Hours: Mon. - Sat. 8 am - 10 pm
Service Hours: Mon. - Fri. 7 am - 7 pm;
Sat. 8 am - 4 pm

OLDSMOBILE
Courtesy Oldsmobile-Isuzu-Kia
5800 W. Sahara Ave.
Las Vegas, NV 89102
221-8000
Sales Hours: Mon. - Sat. 9 am - 10 pm
Service Hours: Mon. - Fri. 7 am - 6 pm;
Sat. 7 am - 1 pm

PONTIAC
Pat Clark Pontiac Sales & Service
2575 E. Sahara Ave.
Las Vegas, NV 89104
457-2111
Sales Hours: Mon. - Sat. 8 am - 9 pm
Service Hours: Mon. - Fri. 7 am - 6 pm;
Sat. 8 am - 2 pm

PORSCHE
Gaudin Motor Co.
2121 E. Sahara Ave.
Las Vegas, NV 89104
731-2121
Sales Hours: Mon. - Sat. 8:30 am - 10 pm
Service Hours: Mon. - Fri. 7 am - 7 pm;
Sat. 8 am - 5 pm

AUTO DEALERS & SERVICES

ROLLS ROYCE
Chaisson Motor Cars
2333 S. Decatur Blvd.
Las Vegas, NV 89102
871-1010
Sales Hours: Mon. - Sat. 8:30 am - 8 pm
Service Hours: Mon. - Fri. 7:30 am -
5:30 pm; Sat. 8 am - 2 pm

SATURN
Saturn of Henderson
310 Gibson Rd.
Henderson, NV 89014
558-8888
Sales Hours: Mon. - Fri. 7 am - 10 pm;
Sat. 8 am - 10 pm
Service Hours: Mon. - Fri. 7 am - 7 pm;
Sat. 8 am - 5 pm

SUBARU
Findlay Subaru
3024 Fremont St.
Las Vegas, NV 89104
457-1021
Sales Hours: Mon. - Sat. 8 am - 9 pm
Service Hours: Mon. - Sat. 7 am - 6 pm

SUZUKI
Courtesy Pontiac Suzuki
6900 W. Sahara Ave.
Las Vegas, NV 89102
242-6000
Sales Hours: Mon. - Sat. 9 am - 10 pm
Service Hours: Mon. - Fri. 7 am - 6 pm;
Sat. 7 am - 1 pm

TOYOTA
Toyota West Sales & Service, Inc.
2025 S. Decatur Blvd.
Las Vegas, NV 89102
871-4111
Sales Hours: Mon. - Fri. 8 am - 10 pm;
Sat. 9 am - 10 pm
Service Hours: Mon. - Fri. 7 am - 10 pm;
Sat. 7 am - 4 pm

VOLKSWAGON
Chaisson Motor Cars
2333 S. Decatur Blvd.
Las Vegas, NV 89102
871-1010
Sales Hours: Mon. - Sat. 8:30 am - 9 pm
Service Hours: Mon. - Fri. 7:30 am -
5:30 pm; Sat. 8 am - 2 pm

VOLVO
Jim Marsh Jeep-Eagle-Mazda-Volvo
2570 S. Eastern Ave.
Las Vegas, NV 89109
457-8033
Sales Hours: Mon. - Fri. 8 am - 9 pm;
Sat. 8 am - 6 pm
Service Hours: Mon. - Fri. 7 am - 5:30
pm; Sat. 8 am - 12 pm

VALLEY AUTO MALL
Gibson Rd., 1-1/2 miles south of Sunset
Henderson, NV 89015
566-1888
Ford Country, Henderson Chevrolet,
Saturn of Henderson, Desert Valley GMC,
Towbin Nissan, Chaisson BMW, Courtesy
Imports, Chapman Chrysler-Plymouth-
Jeep, Findlay Oldsmobile, Findlay Toyota
and Tobin Dodge - $75 million auto mall
housing 11 dealerships.

AUTO DETAILING

Charleston West Car Wash
4820 W. Charleston Blvd.
Las Vegas, NV 89102
878-4825
Hours: Mon. - Sat. 8 am - 2 pm; Sun. 9
am - 1 pm
Complete auto detailing

Mr. Magic Mobile Car Wash
592-9229
Hours: Mon. - Fri. 9 am - 4 pm
Mobile service to home or office. Cars,
boats, motor homes; wash, wax, detail.

Oasis Car Wash
3425 E. Flamingo Rd.
Las Vegas, NV 89121
433-3680
Hours: 8 am - 1:30 pm
We feature 100% hand car wash and
detailing.

Terrible's Detail Plus
4310 W. Flamingo Rd.
Las Vegas, NV 89103
876-9105
Hours: Mon. - Sat. 8 am - 10 pm; Sun. 9
am - 11 pm
Credit Cards: Visa, MC, AMX, Terrible
Herbst

AUTOMOBILE CLUB

California State Automobile Association
Nevada Division - AAA
3312 W. Charleston Blvd.
Las Vegas, NV 89102
870-9171
From Las Vegas, Henderson, Boulder
City: 1-800-222-4357
Richard Purvis, Mgr.
Hours: Mon. - Fri. 8:30 am - 5 pm
Emergency Road Service for members
only - 24 hours

TOWING

City Wide Towing
2306 Crestline Loop
N. Las Vegas, NV 89030
649-2305   649-5030
AAA

South Strip Towing
3975 W. Hacienda Ave.
Las Vegas, NV 89118
736-0515
Mark Keller, Gen. Mgr.
Hours: 24 hours

24-HOUR SERVICE AND REPAIR

The Car Doctor
3705 S. Industrial Rd.
Las Vegas, NV 89109
732-0112
Credit Cards: Visa, MC, AMX, Discover
Sixteen radio-dispatched mobile units,
stocked with hundreds of parts. Service
comes to you or large jobs done at shop.

SERVICE AND REPAIR

Auto Service Systems
980 N. Nellis Blvd.
Las Vegas, NV 89110
438-0802

3540 S. Jones Blvd.
Las Vegas, NV 89103
367-0810

1754 E. Charleston Blvd.
Las Vegas, NV 89104
384-7636

4022 W. Charleston Blvd.
Las Vegas, NV 89102
878-1050

Boulder Highway Texaco
4172 Boulder Hwy.
Las Vegas, NV 89121
458-7900
Hours: 6 am - 11 pm
Mechanic on duty: 8 am - 5 pm

Boyd's West Sahara 76
4401 W. Sahara Ave.
Las Vegas, NV 89102
876-3743
Hours: 24 hours
Mechanic on duty: Mon. - Sat. 8 am - 5 pm

Flamingo & Jones Texaco
6055 W. Flamingo Rd.
Las Vegas, NV 89103
876-3020
Credit Cards: Visa, MC, AMX, Discover
Mechanic on duty: 8 am - 5 pm; Sat. 9
am - 5 pm; Sun. 10 am - 3 pm

Flamingo Pecos Texaco
3380 E. Flamingo Rd.
Las Vegas, NV 89121
456-0096
Hours: 24 hours
Mechanic on duty: 7 am - 7 pm

Fleming's Spring Mountain Chevron
6075 Spring Mountain Rd.
Las Vegas, NV 89102
871-5870
Hours: 6 am - 10 pm
Mechanic on duty: 8 am - 5 pm

Jim's Texaco
2051 E. Sahara Ave.
Las Vegas, NV 89104
457-2675
Hours: 6 am - 10 pm
Mechanic on duty: Mon. - Fri. 7 am - 5 pm;
Sat. 7 am - 2 pm

Mr. E's Texaco
2233 Paradise Rd.
Las Vegas, NV 89104
735-9447
Hours: 24 hours
Mechanic on duty: Mon. - Sat. 8:30 am - 6 pm

Pep Boys
4155 S. Jones Blvd.
Las Vegas, NV 89103
362-3833
Hours: Mon. - Sat. 7 am - 10 pm, Sun. 8
am - 6 pm
Credit Cards: All major
Complete automotive parts and repair
and maintenance.

Russell Road Texaco
2424 E. Russell Rd.
Las Vegas, NV 89120
736-2139
Hours: 6 am - midnight
Mechanic on duty: Mon. - Fri. 8 am - 5
pm; Sat. - Sun. 8 am - 3 pm

Sahara-Decatur Texaco
2500 S. Decatur Blvd.
Las Vegas, NV 89102
873-7846
Hours: Mon. - Fri. 6 am - 11 pm; Sat. 7
am - 10 pm; Sun. 7 am - 9 pm
Mechanic on duty: Mon. - Fri. 8 am - 5
pm; Sat. 8 am - 2 pm

Triangle Service
901 W. Sunset Rd.
Henderson, NV 89015
458-3037
Hours: 6 am - 10 pm
Mechanic on duty: Mon. - Fri. 8 am - 5 pm;
Sat. 8 am - 2 pm

1197 E. Tropicana Ave.
Las Vegas, NV 89119
736-7371
Hours: 6 am - 10 pm
Mechanic on duty: Mon. - Sat. 9 am - 5 pm

University Texaco
1175 E. Flamingo Rd.
Las Vegas, NV 89119
732-0999
Hours: 6 am - 11 pm
Mechanic on duty: Mon. - Fri. 8 am - 6 pm;
Sat. 8 am - 3 pm

SHOPPING

BALLOONS, BASKETS, FLOWERS & GIFTS

Awesome Blossoms
3140 S. Valley View Blvd., Ste. 10
Las Vegas, NV 89102
362-5002
Carolyn, Mgr.
Hours: Mon. - Fri. 8 am - 5 pm; Sat.
8 am - 1 pm
Full service florist
Credit Cards: All major
Flowers, plants, balloons, candies, and
gift baskets. Phone orders taken to 5
pm, will deliver 24 hours a day.

Baskets & Gifts
2800 W. Sahara Ave.
Las Vegas, NV 89102
368-0001
Bobbi Tsatsa, Mgr.
Hours: Mon. - Sat. 9 am - 5 pm
Credit Cards: Visa, MC, AMX
Custom gift baskets for all occasions.

Basket Case
2450 Losee Rd.
N. Las Vegas, NV 89030
399-8585
Marie Hanlon, Owner
Hours: Mon. - Fri. 10 am - 5 pm
Credit Cards: Visa, MC
Total gift packages, gourmet food baskets.

Cookie Bouquets
5643 W. Charleston Blvd.
Las Vegas, NV 89102
877-2674
Dianne Shorkey, Owner
Hours: Mon. - Fri. 8 am - 5 pm; Sat. 10
am - 1 pm
Credit Cards: MC, Visa, Discover
Cookies baked fresh daily as an "edible
alternative to flowers or balloons" and
made into attractive bouquets to be
delivered locally or nationwide.

Flowerama of America
3685 S. Decatur Blvd.
Las Vegas, NV 89103
222-0084
Ronda Thompson, Owner
Hours: Mon. - Fri. 7:30 am - 8 pm, Sat.
8:30 am - 8 pm, Sun. 10 am - 5 pm
Fresh arrangements, green and blooming plants, balloons.

**A French Bouquet Flower
Shoppe**
2121 E. Tropicana Ave.
Las Vegas, NV 89119
739-8484
Robert Werner, Owner
Hours: Mon. - Sat. 8 am - 6 pm; Sun.
10 am - 5 pm

4001 S. Decatur Blvd.
Las Vegas, NV 89103
365-6464
Hours: Mon. - Sat. 8 am - 6 pm
Credit Cards: all major
FTD and Teleflorist wire service.
Telephone orders accepted with major
credit cards.

Gift Baskets & Beyond
248-0242
Dyana Ashman
Unique custom personalized baskets in
Las Vegas.

International Orchid Florist
5015 W. Sahara Ave., Ste. 127
Las Vegas, NV 89102
252-7433
Ingorn Sirintr, Owner
Tropical and exotic arrangements (floral
and balloons), free delivery is available.

**Mrs. Williams Diabetic
Delights**
3466 S. Decatur Blvd.
Las Vegas, NV 89102
362-1243
Janet Dietz, Owner
Hours: Mon. - Sat. 10 am - 5:30 pm
Credit Cards: MC, Discover (over $15)
Sugarless pies, cakes and chocolates.
Gift baskets.

Teddy Bearing Gifts
3512 Wynn Rd.
Las Vegas, NV 89103
362-6013
Pat, Owner
Hours: Mon. - Fri. 10 am - 6 pm
Credit Cards: All major
Balloon shop and assorted Teddy Bears.

A Touch of Glass
3650 S. Decatur Blvd.
Las Vegas, NV 89103
873-0220
Eric Peppers, Owner
Hours: Mon. - Fri. 10 am - 6 pm; Sat. 2
pm - 7 pm; Sun. noon - 5 pm
Credit Cards: All major
Personalized gifts, flowers and balloons,
custom engraved items.

The Whole Bean
3441 W. Sahara Ave.
Las Vegas, NV 89102
368-2633
Lance George, Owner
Hours: Mon. - Fri. 7 am - 6 pm; Sat. 9 am
- 1 pm
Credit Cards: Visa, MC, Discover
Gift baskets for the caffeine set.

GIFTS

Bonanza Gift Shop
2460 Las Vegas Blvd. S.
Las Vegas, NV 89104
385-7359
Lynn Morris, Mgr.
Hours: 8 am - midnight
Credit Cards: All major

"World's largest gift store," with a wide
variety of gift items and Las Vegas souvenirs including toys, magic and gag
items, jewelry and clothing.

Carlan's
Fashion Show
3200 Las Vegas Blvd. S.
Las Vegas, NV 89109
734-6003   1-800-733-6003
Susan Polda, Mgr.
Hours: Mon. - Fri. 10 am - 9 pm; Sat. 10
am - 7 pm; Sun. noon - 6 pm
Credit Cards: All major
Fine gifts and collectibles. Waterford,
pewter, plates, dolls, Hummel and
Disney.

The Christmas Goose
4750 W. Sahara Ave., Ste.12
Las Vegas, NV 89102
877-1158
Jeanette Sherrick
Hours: Mon. - Sat. 10 am - 6 pm; Sun.
noon - 4 pm
Credit Cards: All major
Collectibles, country, hand-painted and
one-of-a-kind items.

The Collectors Gallery
5025 S. Eastern Ave.
Las Vegas, NV 89119
736-7353
Leona Bravin, Mgr.
Hours: Mon. - Sat. 10 am - 6 pm
Credit Cards: Master, Visa AMX,
Discover
Hummel figurines, Precious Moments,
Swarovski crystal and Department 56.

Cost Plus World Market
3840 S. Maryland Pkwy.
Las Vegas, NV 89109
794-2070
Jim Strand, Gen. Mgr.
Hours: Mon. - Sat. 9 am - 9 pm; Sun.
10 am - 7 pm
Ever-changing mix of more than 20,000
products from over 40 countries.
Collectibles, rugs, textiles, furniture,
housewares, gourmet food and specialty
cookware. Over 100 types of beer from
about 25 countries.

Country Hutch
6360 W. Sahara Ave.
Las Vegas, NV 89102
871-6664
Hours: Mon. - Sat. 10 am - 6 pm

193 N. Pecos Rd.
Henderson, NV 89014
263-4777
Hours: Mon. - Sat. 10 am - 6 pm; Sun.
Noon - 5 pm
Credit Cards: Visa, MC
Handcrafted gifts, furniture, specialty
items and collectibles.

Diamond's Treasure
9012 W. Sahara Ave.
Las Vegas, NV 89117
254-1161
Diamond Foss, Owner
Hours: Tue. - Sat. noon - 6 pm
Credit Cards: None
Dolls, plates and collectibles.

LeMelange-Gifts
4161 S. Eastern Ave.
Las Vegas, NV 89119
731-5730
Georgia Ritter, Mgr.
Hours: Tue. - Sat. 10 am - 5 pm or by
appointment
Credit Cards: MC, Visa, AMX, Discover
Unique imported and domestic collectibles.

The Nature Company
3680 S. Maryland Pkwy.
Las Vegas, NV 89109
792-0877
Ann Montgomery, Mgr.
Hours: Mon. - Fri. 10 am - 9 pm; Sat.
10 am - 8 pm; Sun. 11 am - 6 pm
Credit Cards: All major
Located at the Boulevard Mall. Nature
inspired products. The Nature
Company's goal is to encourage the
observation, understanding and appreciation of the natural world.

Tuesday Morning
4750 W. Sahara Ave.
Las Vegas, NV 89102
878-0455
Alesha Pyzer, Mgr.

8520 Del Webb Blvd.
Las Vegas, NV 89134
363-7073
Vaughn Donnelly , Mgr.

7380 S. Eastern Ave.
Las Vegas, NV 89123
897-5077
Sheila Stewart, Mgr.
Hours: Mon. - Sat. 10 am - 6 pm; Thu. 10
am - 8 pm; Sun. noon - 6 pm
Credit Cards: MC, Visa, Discover
Specializes in famous maker, first quality gift items at up to 80 percent off. Uses
"event selling" concept - open for differ-
ing lengths of time. Open Feb. 12 - Mar.
31, Apr. 23 - June 30, Aug. 6 - Sept. 20,
Oct. 1 - Dec. 31.

CLOTHING & WESTERN APPAREL

Ample Boutique
3846 W. Sahara Ave.
Las Vegas, NV 89102
362-0212
Susan Locklin, Mgr.
Hours: Mon. - Sat. 10 am - 6 pm, Sun.
noon - 5 pm

Bricktop & Boris
900 E. Karen Ave.
Las Vegas, NV 89109
735-3007
Gayle Ravese, Mgr.
Hours: Mon. - Fri. 10 am - 7 pm, Sat. 10
am - 6:30 pm
Original in-house designs and exciting
shoes and accessories.

Buffalo Exchange
4110 S. Maryland Pkwy.
Las Vegas, NV 89119
791-3960
Jonathan Hesser, Mgr.
Hours: Mon. - Sat. 11 am - 7 pm
Buy, sell and trade. Designer, vintage
and denim fashions for men and women.

Burlington Coat Factory
5959 W. Sahara Ave.
Las Vegas, NV 89102
247-1268
Joe Garcia, Store Mgr.

4750 S. Eastern Ave.
Las Vegas, NV 89119
451-5581
Hours: Mon. - Sat. 10 am - 9 pm; Sun. 11
am - 6 pm
Men's, women's and children's clothing,
baby furniture and accessories; gifts
and home furnishings. Discounts as
high as 60 percent.

Cache
3500 Las Vegas Blvd. S.
Las Vegas, NV 89109
796-3532
Kris Tecza, Mgr.

3200 Las Vegas Blvd. S.
Las Vegas, NV 89109
731-5548
Anne Yesin, Mgr.
Hours: Mon. - Thu. 10 am - 11 pm, Fri. -
Sun. 10 am - midnight
Designer clothes for women.

Country Comforts
854 E. Sahara Ave.
Las Vegas, NV 89104
697-7000
Joy Chambers, Mgr.
Hours: Mon. - Sat. 9:30 am - 5:30 pm
Shoes, hats and custom orders.

Designing Women
600 S. 6th St.
Las Vegas, NV 89101
385-0888
Johnny Heintz, Store Mgr.
Hours: Mon. - Fri. 10 am - 5:30 pm; Sat.
11 am - 5 pm
Credit Cards: Visa, MC
Designer resale and consignment boutique.

Rebel Store
(Located at Thomas & Mack Center)
Swenson St. and Tropicana Ave.
Las Vegas, NV 89154
895-4207
Sally Olson, Mgr.
Hours: Mon. - Fri. 10 am - 6 pm; Sat. 10
am - 4 pm

Credit Cards: Visa, MC
T-shirts, shorts, novelty items, jackets,
hats, sweats. Official team shop of the
Runnin' Rebels; owned and operated by
UNLV.

Rose of Sharon
2244 Paradise Rd.
Las Vegas, NV 89109
791-5655
Pam Cain, Mgr.
Hours: Mon. - Fri. 10 am - 8 pm; Sat. -
Sun. 10 am - 6 pm

3500 Las Vegas Blvd. S.
Las Vegas, NV 89109
791-0151
Lori Holoway, Mgr.
Hours: Sun. - Thu. 10 am - 11 pm; Fri. -
Sat. 10 am - midnight
Credit Cards: All major
Women's apparel sizes 14 and up.

Star Costume & Theatrical Supplies
4601 W. Sahara Ave.
Las Vegas, NV 89102
871-3395
Debra Salls, Owner
Hours: Mon. - Fri. 10 am - 6:30 pm; Sat.
10 am - 3 pm
Costume rental, dancewear, theatrical
make-up, feather boas.

William's Costume Company
1226 S. 3rd St.
Las Vegas, NV 89104
384-1384
Nancy Baker
Hours: Mon. - Sat. 10 am - 5:30 pm and
for rentals 10 am - 5 pm
Credit Cards: Visa, MC, Discover
Costume sales and rentals.

WESTERN APPAREL

Adams Western Store
1415 Western Ave.
Las Vegas, NV 89102
384-6077   1-800-345-5581
Vicki Paulbick, Owner
Hours: Mon. - Sat. 9 am - 5:30 pm
Credit Cards: Visa, MC, Discover, AMX
Western and English style riding appar-
el for men, women and children. Also
Western and English tack. Complete
line of accessories including boots,
belts and hats.

Boot Barn
7265 Las Vegas Blvd. S.
Las Vegas, NV 89119
260-1888
Jim Parrish, Mgr.
Hours: Mon. - Fri. 10 am - 9 pm; Sat.
9:30 am - 7 pm; Sun. 10 am - 6 pm
Giant selection and lowest prices.

Cowtown Boots
2989 S. Paradise Rd.
Las Vegas, NV 89109
737-8469
Mark Akers, Mgr.
Hours: Mon. - Sat. 10 am - 9 pm; Sun.
noon - 6 pm
Credit Cards: Visa, MC, Discover, AMX
Cowtown Boots in addition to other
prominent boot brands; factory direct
outlet featuring 7,000 - 10,000 pairs of
handcrafted, first quality, all leather
boots; western apparel.

D Bar J Hat Co.
3873 Spring Mountain Rd.
Las Vegas, NV 89102
362-HATS 1-800-654-1137
1-800-DBARJ4U
David Johnson, Pres.
Hours: Mon. - Fri. 8:30 am - 5 pm; Sat.
9:30 am - 3 pm
Credit Cards: Visa, MC
Western, Panama, straw, felt hats, custom made; repair and renovation. The
only manufacturer of authentic Mexican
style sombreros in North America.

Gary Tucker Custom Boots
4648 W. Sahara Ave.
Las Vegas, NV 89102
877-9777
Hours: Mon. - Sat. 10 am - 5 pm
Wooden pegs, hand lasted leather boots.
Texas boots made in Las Vegas.

Howard & Phils Western Wear
Boulevard Mall
3528 S. Maryland Pkwy.
Las Vegas, NV 89109
732-0070
Gary Kramer, Mgr.
Hours: Mon. - Fri. 10 am - 9 pm; Sat.
10 am - 8 pm; Sun. 11 am - 6 pm
Credit Cards: All major
Western wear, boots, hats, belt buckles,
jewelry, leather, suede jackets and coats.

Intermountain Farmers
4295 W. Tropicana Ave.
Las Vegas, NV 89103
362-7515
Robert Hughes, Mgr.
Hours: Mon. - Sat. 8 am - 5:30 pm
Credit Cards: MC, Visa, Discover
Feed, farm supplies, fertilizers, fencing,
livestock equipment, clothing and tack.

Miller Stockman Fine Western Apparel
Fashion Show Mall
3200 Las Vegas Blvd. S.
Las Vegas, NV 89109
737-7236
Janel Miller, Mgr.
Hours: Mon. - Fri. 10 am - 9 pm; Sat. 10
am - 7 pm; Sun. noon - 6 pm

Meadows Mall
4300 Meadows Ln.
Las Vegas, NV 89107
870-2951
Jason Glasgow, Mgr.
Hours: Mon. - Fri. 10 am - 9 pm; Sat. 10
am - 7 pm; Sun. noon - 6 pm

1300 W. Sunset Rd.
Henderson, NV 89014
456-5140
Kelly Squire, Mgr.

Hours: Mon. - Sat. 10 am - 9 pm, Sun. 11
am - 6 pm
Credit Cards: Visa, MC, AMX, Discover
Famous name brand clothing, boots and
hats for the whole family.

Shepler's Western Store
4700 W. Sahara Ave.
Las Vegas, NV 89102
258-2000
Glenn Woolbright, Mgr.
Hours: Mon. - Sat. 10 am - 9 pm; Sun.
11 am - 6 pm

3025 E. Tropicana Ave.
Las Vegas, NV 89121
898-3000
Rob Eichelberger, Mgr.
Hours: Mon. - Sat. 10 am - 9 pm; Sun. 11
am - 6 pm
Credit Cards: Visa, MC, Discover, AMX
A complete selection of famous name
brand western wear and accessories
from "The World's Largest Western
Stores"; boots, jeans, shirts, hats, outer-
wear and accessories.

Tumbleweed Western Wear
4213 Las Vegas Blvd. S.
Las Vegas, NV 89119
736-2182
Hours: Mon. - Sat. 10 am - 6 pm
Credit Cards: Visa, MC, Discover
Pants, shirts, suits, exotic boots and
hats. Square dance apparel. Also available in big and tall sizes.

West of Santa Fe
Forum Shops
3500 Las Vegas Blvd. S.
Las Vegas, NV 89109
737-1993
Alvin Degna, Owner
Hours: 10 am - midnight
Credit Cards: Visa, MC, AMX
Western apparel, boots, belts, hats,
Indian and Southwest jewelry,
Southwestern gifts.

Western Emporium
Sam's Town
5111 Boulder Hwy.
Las Vegas, NV 89122
454-8017
Kathy Ross, Mgr.
Hours: Sun. - Thu. 9 am - 10 pm; Fri. -
Sat. 9 am - midnight
Credit Cards: Visa, MC
Large selection (25,000 sq. ft.) of
famous name brand, western clothing,
boots and hats. Also available are a
variety of gift items, jewelry, western
art, freshly roasted coffee beans, penny
candies by the pound and T-shirts.

DRY CLEANING - TAILORS

Al Phillips The Cleaners Inc.
(Also see 24 Hour Businesses)
Corporate Office
3250 W. Ali Baba Ln.
Las Vegas, NV 89118
798-7333
Al Phillips has 13 locations in the Las Vegas area.

Fast 'N Fresh Cleaners, Inc.
2488 E. Desert Inn Rd.
Las Vegas, NV 89121
735-6860
Hours: Mon. - Fri. 7 am - 8 pm, Sat. 8 am - 5 pm
Same day service. Alterations, shoe repair, office uniforms pick-up and delivery.

Galloping Valet
5965 W. Sahara Ave., Ste. C
Las Vegas, NV 89102
362-1046
Hours: Mon. - Fri. 7 am - 7 pm; Sat. 8 am - 5 pm
Laundry and dry cleaning pick-up and delivery. No minimum. Alterations and shoe shines also available.

Tiffany Cleaners
953 E. Sahara Ave.
Las Vegas, NV 89104
735-0186
Hours: Mon. - Fri. 7 am - 6 pm; Sat. 9 am - 5 pm
Pickup and delivery. Alterations, suede and leather, fur storage, wedding gowns cleaned and preserved.

Vogue Cleaners
550 S. Decatur Blvd.
Las Vegas, NV 89107
878-1955
Hours: Mon. - Fri. 7 am - 7 pm; Sat. 8 am - 6 pm
Alterations and laundry.

Ballan's Custom Tailors
3977 Maryland Pkwy.
Las Vegas, NV 89119
369-0099
David Ballans, Owner
Hours: Mon. - Sat. 10 am - 6 pm
Perfect fitting pants and shirts.

Boston's Custom Tailor & Alteration
2105 E. Lake Mead Blvd.
N. Las Vegas, NV 89030
642-8605
Johnny Boston, Owner
Hours: Mon. - Sat. 10 am - 6 pm
Men's and women's alterations. One day service.

George Yaghi Tailors
3333 S. Maryland Pkwy.
Las Vegas, NV 89109
731-4717
George Yaghi, Owner
Hours: Mon. - Fri. 10 am - 7 pm; Sat. 10 am - 6 pm
Credit Cards: All major
Men's & ladies custom tailoring and alterations. Free estimates; same day service. Also serves in your home or business.

Kathy's Tailor
4264 E. Charleston Blvd.
Las Vegas, NV 89104
438-2027
Kathy Vaughn, Owner
Hours: Mon. - Fri. 9:30 am - 7 pm; Sat. 10 am - 6 pm
Custom tailoring and alterations for men and women. Tuxedo rentals and dry cleaning.

Magic Thimbles
3300 S. Jones Blvd.
Las Vegas, NV 89102
871-5490
Hours: Mon. - Fri. 9 am - 4 pm; Sat. 10 am - 2 pm
Tailoring and alterations for men and women.

FURNITURE - JEWELERS

A Mexican/Tile Imports
5320 Cameron St., Ste. 4
Las Vegas, NV 89117
221-1617
Hours: Mon. - Fri. - 9 am - 5 pm; Sat. 9 am - 3 pm
Factory direct prices. Authentic furniture, leather, wood, Old World & rustic. Tile, rugs and artifacts.

Ethan Allen Home Interiors
1540 S. Rainbow Blvd.
Las Vegas, NV 89102
878-4444
Hours: Mon. - Sat. 10 am - 6 pm; Sun. noon - 5 pm
Fine home furnishings & complimentary interior design.

Leather King Furniture
3507 S. Maryland Pkwy.
Las Vegas, NV 89109
734-7212

2021 N. Rainbow Blvd.
Las Vegas, NV 89108
636-1195
Hours: Mon. - Fri. 10 am - 6 pm; Sat. 9 am - 6 pm; Sun. noon - 5 pm
Major name brands for less

Levitz Furniture Corporation
90 S. Martin Luther King Blvd.
Las Vegas, NV 89106
366-9097
Hours: Mon. - Sat. 10 am - 9 pm; Sun. 11 am - 6 pm
Discount furniture.

Marco Polo Furniture
4215 Spring Mountain Rd., Ste. 107
Las Vegas, NV 89103
227-8988   1-800-866-3690

4300 Meadows Ln., Ste. 201
Las Vegas, NV 89107
870-1818

Galleria
1300 E. Sunset Rd., Ste. 1615
Henderson, NV 89014
898-1169
Hours: Mon. - Fri. 11 am - 8 pm; Sat. - Sun. 10 am - 9 pm
Nevada's only Oriental furniture store.

McMillan's
1760 S. Rainbow Blvd.
Las Vegas, NV 89102
258-9933
Hours: Mon. - Sat. 10 am - 6 pm; Sun. noon - 5 pm

Walker Furniture
301 S. Marin Luther King Blvd.
Las Vegas, NV 89106
384-9300
Hours: Mon. - Fri. 9 am - 9 pm; Sun. 11 am - 6 pm
100,000 foot showroom featuring famous name brands.

Aloha Tropical Leis & Hawaiian Heritage Gold Jewelry
2867 Bamboo Ct.
Henderson, NV 89014
263-3222
Norma O'Nan, Owner
Hours: Call for appointment
Hand made bangles, pendants, earrings and rings. All jewelry has flowers of Hawaii and names are engraved in Hawaiian.

Bailey Banks and Biddle
Boulevard Mall
3622 S. Maryland Pkwy.
Las Vegas, NV 89109
734-2577
Lance Yates, Mgr.
Hours: Mon. - Fri. 10 am - 9 pm; Sat. 10 am - 8 pm, Sun. noon - 7 pm

Fashion Show Mall
3200 Las Vegas Blvd. S.
Las Vegas, NV 89109
731-3355

Ginger Urbanski, Mgr.
Hours: Mon. - Fri. 10 am - 9 pm; Sat. 10 am - 7 pm; Sun. noon - 6 pm
Credit Cards: All major
Custom jewelry designers and manufacturers. Fine watches. Jewelry and watch repairs.

Ben Bridge Jewelers
3200 Las Vegas Blvd. S.
Las Vegas, NV 89109
733-0003
Patick Stout, Mgr. - 3 locations
Hours: Mon. - Fri. 10 am - 9 pm; Sat. 10 am - 7 pm; Sun. noon - 6 pm

Bernard K. Passman
Rio Hotel
3700 W. Flamingo Rd.
Las Vegas, Nv 89103
791-3376
Peter Englehart, Mgr.
Hours: Sun. - Thu. 10 am - 11 pm; Fri. - Sat. 10 am - midnight
Bernard K. Passman is a pioneer in Black Coral as a fine art medium. He is one of the foremost experts in the world in black coral.

Cartier
Caesars Palace
3570 Las Vegas Blvd. S.
Las Vegas, NV 89109
733-6652
Mariam Afshai, Mgr.
Hours: 10 am - 11 pm
Credit Cards: all major
Famous Cartier jewelry, watches, clocks, perfumes, leather goods and fine gift items. Repairs to any Cartier jewelry and watches.

J. Christensen Jewelers. Inc.
4300 Meadows Ln., Ste. 2072
Las Vegas, NV 89107
878-7832
Carl Christensen, Mgr.
Hours: Mon. - Fri. 10 am - 9 pm; Sat. - Sun. 10 am - 6 pm
Oldest full service jeweler in town, since 1939. Repairs, custom orders and more.

JEWELERS - LIQUOR STORES

Corbeille's Jewelers
3882 W. Sahara Ave.
Las Vegas, NV 89102
221-0929
Dean Corbeille, Owner
Hours: Mon. - Sat. 10 am - 6 pm
Custom made jewelry and design. Remounting and remodeling.

Don's Jewelers
Polo Plaza
3743 Las Vegas Blvd. S., Ste. 114
Las Vegas, NV 89109
262-6950
Don Chaplin, Owner
Hours: Mon. - Sat. 9:30 am - 5:30 pm
Expert watch and jewelry repair. Custom designing and name brand watches.

J. Edwards Jewelry Distributing Co.
6235 S. Pecos Dr.
Las Vegas, NV 89120
547-4852
Jodi Zeller, Mgr.
Hours: Mon. - Sat. 10 am - 6 pm
Guaranteed lowest prices in town.

Gabriel Jewelers
900 E. Karen Ave., Ste. B105
Las Vegas, NV 89109
898-2282
Gabriel DeLeon, Jr.
Hours: Mon. - Fri. 10 am - 6 pm; Sat. 10 am - 5 pm
Fine 14K and 18K jewelry. Custom manufacturing, family owned and operated.

Gemonte Jewelers
1350 E. Flamingo Rd.
Las Vegas, NV 89119
731-1139
Hours: Mon. - Sat. 10:30 am - 6 pm
Diamonds, custom jewelry and repairs done on premises.

Gold Castle
3850 Las Vegas Blvd. S.
Las Vegas, NV 89109
739-0033
Gail Miller, Mgr.
Hours: 9 am - 11 pm
Fine jewelry at outlet prices.

Huntington Jewelers
3661 S. Maryland Pkwy.
Las Vegas, NV 89109
732-1977
Richard Huntington, Owner
Hours: Mon. - Fri. 9 am - 5:30 pm
"A trusted name in Las Vegas for over 40 years." Engraving, manufacturing and repairs.

Jeffrey H. White, Inc.
6767 W. Tropicana Ave., Ste. 212
Las Vegas, NV 89103
248-1087
Jeff White, Owner
Hours: Mon. - Fri. 8 am - 5 pm
Credit Cards: MC, Visa
Diamond broker, jewelry appraisals, jewelry sales and custom jewelry. One-of-a kind custom designs, jewelry design and redesign, upgrading diamonds. Local design jeweler since 1985. Graduate gemologist, secure and personalized location.

John Fish Jewelers
Commercial Center
953 E. Sahara Ave.
Las Vegas, NV 89104
731-1323
John Fish, Pres.
Hours: Mon. - Sat. 9:30 am - 5:30 pm
Credit Cards: all major
Watches, jewelry, custom designing and manufacturing, gemologist and appraiser.

Las Vegas Manufacturing Jewelers
4624 W. Sahara Ave.
Las Vegas, NV 89102
259-8011
Dan Gold, Owner
Hours: Mon. - Sat. 9:30 am - 6 pm
Large selection of fine jewelry.

The Jeweler's
2400 Western Ave.
Las Vegas, NV 89102
382-7411
Hours: Vary by store

Tower of Jewels
953 E. Sahara Ave.
Las Vegas, NV 89104
735-4145
Jack Weinstein, Pres.
Hours: Vary by store
Credit cards: All major
Manufacturers of fine custom jewelry. Appraising, jewelry and watch repair.

Whitehall Company Jewelers
3530 S. Maryland Pkwy.
Las Vegas, NV 89109
731-5211
Raul Nelson, Mgr.
Hours: Mon. - Fri. 10 am - 9 pm; Sat. 10 am - 8 pm; Sun. 10 am - 6 pm
200 stores nationwide. Huge selection of large diamonds.

Zale's Jewelers
3568 S. Maryland Pkwy.
Las Vegas, NV 89109
735-3482
Jim Carrillo, Regional Mgr.
Hours: Mon. - Fri. 10 am - 9 pm; Sat. 10 am - 8 pm; Sun. 11 am - 6 pm
Largest retail diamond chain in the United States. Over 1,200 stores nationwide including Hawaii and Puerto Rico.

Badger Beverage Mart
5600 W. Spring Mtn. Rd.
Las Vegas, NV 89102
362-1433
Hours: Tue. - Sat. 8 am - midnight; Sun. 8:30 am - 6:30 pm; Mon. 8 am - 9:30 pm
Credit Cards: Visa, MC, AMX, Discover
Huge selection of foreign and domestic liquor, wine and beer.

Drive-In Liquor
185 W. Lake Mead Blvd.
Henderson, NV 89015
565-6800
Elizabeth Garcia, Owner
Hours: 10 am - 10 pm
The only drive-in liquor store, large selection.

Keg World
3675 S. Decatur Blvd.
Las Vegas, NV 89103
876-5347
Duncan Harvey, Vice Pres.
Hours: Mon. - Fri. 10 am - 6 pm; Sat. 10 am - 4 pm; Sun. 11 am - 2 pm
Keg beer, home beer dispensing equipment.

Las Vegas Wine Co.
3050 E. Desert Inn Rd.
Las Vegas, NV 89121
893-8466
Dominic Borra, Owner
Hours: Mon. - Sat. 10 am - 7 pm; Sun. 11 am - 3 pm
Credit Cards: Visa, MC, Discover, AMX
Over 650 wines in stock, gift baskets, factory fresh cigars.

Lee's Discount Liquor
3480 E. Flamingo Rd.
Las Vegas, NV 89121
458-5700
20,000 sq. ft. store with over 400,000 bottles.

1780 S. Rainbow Blvd.
Las Vegas, NV 89102
870-6300

789 N. Nellis Blvd.
Las Vegas, NV 89110
459-2200
Hae Un Lee
Hours: Mon. - Thu. 9 am - 10 pm; Fri. - Sat. 9 am - 11 pm, Sun. 9 am - 9 pm
Credit Cards: All Major
Spirits and wines at discount prices; beer-keg rentals available; wine storage lockers for rent at Flamingo store; prices as low as $8 a month.

Mr. Radz Homebrew
4972 S. Maryland Pkwy.
Las Vegas, NV 89119
736-8504
Greg Radziewicz
Hours: Mon. - Sat. 11 am - 6 pm; Sun. 1 pm - 5 pm

R. G. Liquors
4080 Paradise Rd.
Las Vegas, NV 89109
734-2600
Sal Garcia, Owner
Hours: Mon. - Sat. 9 am - 9 pm; Sun. 9 am - 5 pm
Credit Cards: Visa, MC, AMX
Friendly service with best prices.

Speakeasy Liquor & Market
1006 E. Charleston Blvd.
Las Vegas, NV 89104
382-3542
Roger Kosa, Owner
Hours: Mon. - Sat. 8 am - 11 pm; Sun. 9 am - 9 pm
Micro-brew, keg beer and gift boxes.

Spirits Plus
4880 W. Flamingo Rd.
Las Vegas, NV 89103
873-6000
Hours: Mon. - Thu. 8 am - 11 pm; Fri. - Sat. 8 am - midnight; Sun. 8 am - 10 pm

4401 E. Sunset Rd.
Henderson, NV 89014
451-4146
Mark Anderson
Hours: Sun. - Thu. 10 am - 10 pm; Fri. & Sat. 9 am - 11 pm
Credit Cards: Visa, MC, Discover
Fine wines, liquor, liquor catering.

Terrible's Discount Liquor
Gold Coast Hotel
4000 W. Flamingo Rd.
Las Vegas, NV 89103
367-7111
Ruth Hall, Mgr.
Hours: 24 hours
Credit Cards: All major

Town Pump Liquors
6040 W. Sahara Ave.
Las Vegas, NV 89102
876-6615
Hours: 8 am - midnight

953 E. Sahara Ave.
Las Vegas, NV 89104
735-8515

1725 E. Warm Springs Rd.
Las Vegas, NV 89119
897-9463

4410 W. Craig Rd.
N. Las Vegas, NV 89030
645-9700
Bob Darrell, Owner
Hours: 8 am - 10 pm
Credit Cards: Visa, MC

Western Emporium Liquor Depot (Sam's Town)
5111 Boulder Hwy.
Las Vegas, NV 89122
454-8017
Kathy Ross, Mgr.
Hours: Sun. - Thu. 9 am - 10 pm; Fri. - Sat. 9 am - midnight

SHOPPING

LUGGAGE & LUGGAGE REPAIR

California Luggage Outlet
Belz Factory Outlet
7400 Las Vegas Blvd. S.
Las Vegas, NV 89123
361-8113
Tim Lavelle, Mgr.
Hours: Mon. - Sat. 10 am - 9 pm; Sun.
10 am - 6 pm
Credit Cards: All major
Skyway, Samsonite, Dakota and many
more.

El Portal Luggage
Fashion Show Mall
3200 Las Vegas Blvd. S.
Las Vegas, NV 89109
369-0606
Hours: Mon. - Fri. 10 am - 9 pm; Sat.
10 am - 7 pm; Sun. noon - 6 pm

Forum Shops
3500 Las Vegas Blvd. S.
Las Vegas, NV 89109
892-0029
Hours: Sun. - Thu. 10 am - 11 pm; Fri. -
Sat. 10 am - midnight

Boulevard Mall
3574 S. Maryland Pkwy.
Las Vegas, NV 89109
735-6433
Hours: Mon. - Fri. 10 am - 9 pm; Sat.
10 am - 6 pm; Sun. 11 pm - 6 pm

Meadows Mall
4300 Meadows Ln.
Las Vegas, NV 89107
870-3121
Hours: Mon. - Fri. 10 am - 9 pm; Sat. &
Sun. 10 am - 6 pm

1300 W. Sunset Rd., Ste. 1717
Henderson, NV 89014
456-1314
Hours: Mon. - Sat. 10 am - 9 pm, Sun.
11 am - 6:30 pm

McCarran Airport
5757 Wayne Newton Blvd.
Las Vegas, NV 89119
736-0076
Hours: 7 am - 7 pm

MGM Grand
3799 Las Vegas Blvd. S.
Las Vegas, NV 89109
798-4455
Donny Borsack, Gen. Mgr.
Hours: 9 am - midnight
Credit cards: All major
Fine quality leather luggage, handbags,
business cases and unique gifts.
Featuring the work of internationally
famous designers. For mail orders and
information, call 1-800-723-7568.

Louis Vuitton
Fashion Show Mall
3200 Las Vegas Blvd. S.
Las Vegas, NV 89109
731-9860

Mary Olson, Store Mgr.
Hours: Mon. - Fri. 10 am - 9 pm; Sat. 10
am - 7 pm; Sun. noon - 6 pm

Forum Shops
3500 Las Vegas Blvd. S.
Las Vegas, NV 89109
732-1227
Diane Kalchbrenner, Store Mgr.
Hours: Mon. - Wed. 10 am - 11 pm; Thu.
- Sun. 10 am - midnight

Neiman Marcus
3200 Las Vegas Blvd. S.
Las Vegas, NV 89109
731-3636
David Ferguson, Store Mgr.
Hours: Mon. - Fri. 10 am - 8 pm; Sat. 10
am - 7 pm; Sun. noon - 6 pm

Saks Fifth Avenue
3200 Las Vegas Blvd. S.
Las Vegas, NV 89109
733-8300
Della Gonyea, Store Mgr.
Hours: Mon. - Wed. 10 am - 8 pm, Thu. -
Fri. 10 am - 9 pm, Sat. 10 am - 7 pm, Sun.
noon - 6 pm
Credit Cards: All major
Luggage, handbags, business cases and
accessories exclusively by Louis
Vuitton.

Samsonite Company Store
9175 Las Vegas Blvd. S.
Las Vegas, NV 89123
897-2327

Elvie Hoffman, Mgr.
Hours: Mon. - Sat. 10 am - 8 pm; Sun. 10
am - 6 pm

7400 Las Vegas Blvd. S., Ste. 146
Las Vegas, NV 89123
260-3014
Darlene Rivera, Mgr.
Hours: Mon. - Sat. 10 am - 9 pm, Sun. 10
am - 6 pm
Credit Cards: All major

LUGGAGE REPAIR

**Commercial Shoe Repair &
Luggage**
850 S. Rancho Dr.
Las Vegas, NV 89106
880-7455
Mary Watson, Owner
Hours: Mon. - Fri. 8:30 am - 5:30 pm,
Sat. 9 am - 3 pm
Credit Cards: Visa, MC
Service while you wait.

Nevada Leather & Luggage
953 E. Sahara Ave.
Las Vegas, NV 89104
731-4900
Steve Matulich, Owner
Hours: Mon. - Fri. 9:30 am - 5 pm, Sat
10 am - 1 pm (closed 2nd Sat. of month)
Credit Cards: All major
Everything for the traveler.

MUSIC

Best Buy
3820 S. Maryland Pkwy.
Las Vegas, NV 89119
732-8283
Hours: Mon. - Sat. 10 am - 9 pm; Sun.
10 am - 6 pm
CDs & cassettes.

Blockbuster Music
4555 W. Charleston Blvd.
Las Vegas, NV 89102
259-6606
Hours: Sun. - Thu. 10 am - 10 pm; Fri. -
Sat. 10 am - 11 pm
Books, magazines, cassettes and CDs.

Disc Go Round
3967 S. Maryland Pkwy.
Las Vegas, NV 89119
731-1445

2570 S. Decatur Blvd.
Las Vegas, NV 89102
221-1759
Hours: Mon. - Sat. 10 am - 9 pm
CDs, stickers, posters and T-shirts.

Famous Video & Music
2555 E. Tropicana Ave.
Las Vegas, NV 89121
433-4003
Hours: 10 am - 11 pm
Buy and sell new and used tapes and
compact discs.

J-Mar's Records
2620 S. Maryland Pkwy.
Las Vegas, NV 89109
796-6366
Hours: Mon. - Fri. 11 am - 6 pm; Sat.
11 am - 5 pm
Collectible CDs, records and tapes.

Music 4 Less
7400 Las Vegas Blvd. S.
Las Vegas, NV 89123
896-0272
Hours: Mon. - Sat. 10 am - 9 pm; Sun.
10 am - 6 pm
CDs and cassettes.

Odyssey Records
1600 Las Vegas Blvd. S.
Las Vegas, NV 89104
384-4040
Julie Mernin, Store Dir.
Hours: 24 hours
12" single records and CDs.

Record City
300 E. Sahara Ave.
Las Vegas, NV 89104
735-1126

Hours: Mon. - Sat. 10 am - 6 pm; Sun.
noon - 5 pm

101 S. Rainbow Blvd.
Las Vegas, NV 89128
258-1229
Hours: Mon. - Sat. 10 am - 6 pm; Sun.
noon - 5 pm

3300 S. Decatur Blvd.
Las Vegas, NV 89102
364-1070
Hours: Mon. - Sat. 10 am - 6 pm

4157 S. Maryland Pkwy.
Las Vegas, NV 89119
731-1191
Hours: Mon. - Sat. 10 am - 6 pm

4555 E. Charleston Blvd.
Las Vegas, NV 89104
457-8626
Hours: Mon. - Sat. 10 am - 6 pm; Sun.
noon - 5 pm

553 E. Sahara Ave.
Las Vegas, NV 89104
369-6466
Leonard Leavitt, Pres.
Hours: Mon. - Sat. 10 am - 6 pm
Credit Cards: Visa, MC
Collectibles, books and videos. Las
Vegas' most complete selection of used
compact discs, tapes, LPs, 45s and
videos.

Sam Goody's Musicland
Fashion Show Mall
3200 Las Vegas Blvd. S.
Las Vegas, NV 89109
794-0079
Hours: Mon. - Fri. 10 am - 9 pm; Sat. 10
am - 8 pm; Sun. 11 am - 6 pm

Meadows Mall
4300 Meadow Ln.
Las Vegas, NV 89109
877-0505
Hours: Mon. - Fri. 10 am - 9 pm; Sat. -
Sun. 10 am - 6 pm
CDs, tapes and movies.

Tower Records & Video
4110 S. Maryland Pkwy.
Las Vegas, NV 89119
731-0800 731-2022

4580 W. Sahara Ave.
Las Vegas, NV 89102
364-2500
Shop by phone: 1-800-ASK-TOWER
Russ Solomon, Pres.
Hours: 10 am - midnight
Records, CDs, audio and videotapes,
magazines and out-of-town newspapers.

The Wherehouse
Meadows Mall
4300 Meadow Ln.
Las Vegas, NV 89107
870-8255
Hours: Mon. - Fri. 10 am - 9 pm; Sat. -
Sun. 10 am - 6 pm

3482 S. Maryland Pkwy.
Las Vegas, NV 89119
733-1724

4500 E. Sunset Rd.
Henderson, NV 89014
434-8005
Hours: Sun. - Thu. 10 am - 10 pm; Fri.
Sat. 10 am - 11 pm
For the location nearest you call
1-800-WHEREHOUSE

PERSONAL CARE - HEALTH & BEAUTY

TANNING SALONS

All Tanning Salons of Nevada
2249 N. Green Valley Pkwy.
Henderson, NV 89014
433-9800
Jay & Priscilla Strommen, Owners
Hours: Mon. - Fri. 9 am - 10 pm; Sat.
9 am - 8 pm; Sun. 10 am - 8 pm

A Tropical Tan
3111 S. Valley View Blvd.
Las Vegas, NV 89102
876-2826
Hours: Mon. - Fri. 9 am - 8:30 pm; Sat.
11 am - 6:30 pm
"We spoil you." VIP Rooms.

Body Heat Tanning Salon
3870 E. Flamingo Rd.
Las Vegas, NV 89121
547-6500
Hours: Mon. - Fri. 8 am - midnight; Sat.
8 am - 9 pm; Sun. 10 am - 7 pm
We make tanning fun and affordable all
year round.

Bronze 'N' Beauty
4443 W. Flamingo Rd.
Las Vegas, NV 89103
365-9090
Hours: Mon. - Thu. 7 am - 10 pm; Fri.
7 am - 8 pm; Sat. - Sun. 11 am - 7 pm
The only ultrasun in town.

Neon Sun Tanning (4)
6128 W. Lake Mead Blvd.
Las Vegas, NV 89108
647-0273
Tonia Ryan, Mgr.
Hours: 8 am - 10 pm
Ultrabronz beds.

Rio Tan (5)
2570 S. Decatur Ave.
Las Vegas, NV 89102
362-8410
Hours: 9 am - 10 pm
Ultrabronz or Wolff beds.

The Tanning Place
2563 Wigwam Pkwy.
Henderson, NV 89014
263-8060
Hours: Mon. - Sat. 9:30 am - 9:30 pm
Unique tanning in elegant surroundings.

Totally Tan
1033 S. Rainbow Blvd.
Las Vegas, NV 89117
878-8267
Hours: Mon. - Thu. 9 am - 11 pm; Sat.
9 am - 10 pm; Sun. 9 am - 8 pm
State of the art high pressure tanning.

BEAUTY SALONS

A Hairitage
319B Water St.
Henderson, NV 89015
565-7503 565-7368
Phyllis Thompson, Owner
Hours: Mon. - Fri. 8 am - 9 pm; Sat. 8 am
- 6 pm; Sun. 10 am - 4 pm
Full family service salon.

A Little Off the Top
3209 W. Sahara Ave.
Las Vegas, NV 89104
258-5411
Dave Thompson, Owner
Hours: Mon. - Fri. 10 am - 6 pm, Sat.
10 am - 5 pm
Features ladies in lingerie to cut your
hair. *"A Gentleman's Salon."*

Amour Beauty Center
2663 Windmill Pkwy.
Henderson, NV 89014
896-0097
Cheryl Santorelli, Owner
Hours: 8 am - 8 pm
Nails, facials and waxing.

Anastasia Salon
1700 E. Desert Inn Rd., Ste. 207
Las Vegas, NV 89109
732-2703
Mary Gibbons, Owner
Hours: Tue. - Sat. 10 am - 6 pm, Mon.
noon - 6 pm
Hair, nails and massage.

Beauty Center Ultra Salon (4)
6160 W. Tropicana Ave.
Las Vegas, NV 89103
367-1333
Kathy Smith
Hours: Mon. - Fri. 9 am - 8 pm; Sat. 9 am
- 6 pm; Sun. 11 am - 5 pm
Full service salon; hair, nails, skin, massage, retail.

Brand New Look Hair Salon
1811 S. Jones Blvd.
Las Vegas, NV 89102
362-2979
Bob Brand
Hours: Tue. - Fri. 9 am - 7:30 pm; Sat.
9 am - 6 pm
Nails, hair and facial services.

Cache'
4850 W. Flamingo Rd.
Las Vegas, NV 89103
876-7445
Andrea Jones
Hours: Mon. - Sat. 9 am - 9 pm
Full service salon. Creative cuts, highlighting, custom coloring and corrections, cellophane, hair extensions,
men's hair replacement, braiding, spiral
and body perms, relaxers, curls, flat
iron work, make-up specialists, chair
massage, pedicures and full service nail
care, beauty and wedding packages.

Celebrity Beauty Salon
4455 E. Tropicana Ave.
Las Vegas, NV 89121
435-9490
Diane Romero, Owner
Hours: Fri. - Tue. 9 am - 5 pm; Wed. -
Thu. 9 am - 6 pm
Full service salon.

Deja Vu Hairstyling
690 N. Valle Verde Dr.
Henderson, NV 89014
458-0898
Kari Lee, Owner
Hours: Mon. - Fri. 8 am - 8 pm; Sat. 8 am
- 6 pm
Hair, sculptures, pedicures, makeovers
and facial waxing

Diva Studio
3159 W. Tompkins Ave.
Las Vegas, NV 89103
736-2011
Lisa Brooks
Hours: Mon. - Sat. 9 am - 7 pm
Full skin, manicuring, hair services and
massage.

Foxy Lady
2400 S. Jones Blvd., Ste. 11
Las Vegas, NV 89102
871-6500
Alice Arredondo
Hours: Mon. - Fri. 9 am - 6 pm; Sat. -
Sun. 9 am - 4 pm
Hair, nails and wedding packages.

Hair Forum
1909 N. Decatur Blvd.
Las Vegas, NV 89108
648-9000
Bette Raymond, Owner
Hours: Tue. - Sat. 9 am - 5 pm; Mon
10 am - 5 pm
Hair and nails. Facials by Linda.

A Pampered You
706 N. Rainbow Blvd.
Las Vegas, NV 89107
878-9090
Kathy Flood, Owner
Hours: Tue. - Sat. 8 am - 7 pm; Mon.
8 am - 5 pm
Hair, facials, manicures, pedicures and
waxing.

Park Avenue
4660 E. Sunset Rd.
Henderson, NV 89014
433-0030
Hours: Mon. - Sat. 8 am - 7 pm
Latest techniques in permanent make-
up, hair and nails.

Profiles
900 E. Karen Ave., Ste. C-116
Las Vegas, NV 89109
737-5888
Araceli Wayne, Owner
Hours: Flexible
Hair styling, facials and manicures.

Salon Sahara
2535 Las Vegas Blvd. S.
Las Vegas, NV 89109
792-2340
Gary Waysack, Owner
Hours: 9 am - 7 pm
Full service salon.

Scandals
4001 S. Decatur Blvd.
Las Vegas, NV 89103
367-3930
Jack Coskey, Mgr.
Hours: Mon. - Sat. 9 am - 6:30 pm
Salon and day spa; Vichy shower, massage rooms, facial rooms, body treatment rooms, cafe, car wash service;
employs over 65 professionals.

Somerset Hair Creations
252 Convention Center Dr.
Las Vegas, NV 89109
735-6008
Marjorie Nelson, Owner
Hours: 9 am - 5 pm
Male and female perms, facials, waxing
and massage

**Special Effects Hair & Nail
Studio**
3310 S. Jones Blvd., Ste. C
Las Vegas, NV 89102
871-9277
Barbara Deanin, Owner
Perms, color, cut, manicures, pedicures
and artificial nails.

Studio 302
2235 E. Flamingo Rd.
Las Vegas, NV 89119
796-8004
Elizabeth Mullin, Owner
Hours: Mon. - Sat. 9 am - 7 pm
Tanning, skincare, hair and nails.

Topps Hair Salon
1600 N. Nellis Blvd.
Las Vegas, NV 89115
438-4127
Cary Shannon, Owner
Hours: Tue. - Fri. 9 am - 7 pm; Sat. 9 am
- 5 pm; Sun. 10 am - 4 pm
Full service salon.

Scandals, 4001 S. Decatur Blvd., Las Vegas, NV 89103

SHOPPING

PERSONAL CARE - HEALTH & BEAUTY

SKIN CARE

Advanced Skin Care
Facial Salons
2200 S. Rancho Dr.
Las Vegas, NV 89102
382-7546
Carolyn Vanzlow, Owner
Hours: Mon. - Sat. 10 am - 6 pm
Facials, make-up and waxing.

Ambiance Massage & Facials
923 S. Rainbow Blvd.
Las Vegas, NV 89128
877-1144
Ellen Green
Hours: Tue. - Fri. 9 am - 7 pm; Sat. - Mon. 9 am - 5 pm
Licensed and certified massage therapists.

Armando's Make-up Studio
4161 S. Eastern Ave.
Las Vegas, NV 89119
733-9223
Armand S. Martine, Owner
Hours: Tue. - Sat. 10 am - 6 pm
Make-up lessons, facials, massages and waxing.

Biogime Skin Care
6600 W. Charleston Blvd., Ste. 101
Las Vegas, NV 89102
878-1855
Olene Alvarez, Owner
Hours: Mon. - Fri. 10 am - 6 pm; Sat. 10 am - 2 pm
All natural skin products and nutritional products.

Cosmetique Skin and Nails
5000 E. Bonanza Rd., Ste. E
Las Vegas, NV 89110
438-9951
Janice Jones, Mgr.
Hours: Mon. - Sat. 9 am - 5 pm
European skin care, deep cleansing, treatment for acne skin, eyebrow arching, lash and brow tinting, body waxing.

Strictly Skin
3742 E. Tropicana Ave.
Las Vegas, NV 89121
434-1716
Karen Douglas, Owner
Hours: Tue. - Sat. 10 am - 6 pm
Scientific skin care, facials, waxing, acne care.

MASSAGE

Angel's Touch
2550 S. Rainbow Blvd.
Las Vegas, NV 89102
873-7795
Mary Green, Owner
Hours: Sun. 10 am - 6 pm; Mon. 10 am - 8 pm; Tue. - Fri. 10 am - 10 pm; Sat. 10 am - 8 pm
Stress relieving therapeutic massage. Deep tissue manipulation, sports massage, mud packs, salt scrubs, herbal wrap. One hour therapeutic massage $50. Will also travel to you.

Body Benefits Massage
497-1987
We pamper you at your location, 24 hours 7 days. Licensed certified therapists. Swedish, deep tissue and body scrubs.

Hands On
4750 S. Eastern Ave.
Las Vegas, NV 89119
451-4550

Ari Stein, Owner
We treat pain, soft tissue therapy, stress relief at home, office or hotel.

Heavenly Hands
2605 S. Decatur Blvd.
Las Vegas, NV 89102
493-5222
Massage, steam and aromatherapy. 24 hour outcall service also available.

Oasis of Hands
Green Valley Athletic Club
2100 Olympic Ave.
Henderson, NV 89014
454-6000
Misty Chadwick, Mgr.
Hours: Mon. - Fri. 9 am - 9 pm; Sat. 8 am - 8 pm; Sun. 10 am - 8 pm reservations recommended.
A variety of therapeutic and relaxing massage techniques. Skin care services, waxing and body treatments.

The Rubb
3025 Industrial Rd.
Las Vegas, NV 89109
497-Rubb
Mark Brooks, Owner
Hours: Open 24 hours
Specializing in Swedish oil, accupressure, sports massage and Shiatsu.

TATTOOS & BODY PIERCING

Doc's Las Vegas Tattoo Company
731 Las Vegas Blvd. S.
Las Vegas, NV 89101
384-6911
Hours: 11 am - 1 am

Over 100 years' experience; Nevada's oldest tattoo parlor; featured in *Tattoo Magazine* seven times; piercing now available.

Imagination Station
4310 E. Tropicana Ave., Ste. 2
Las Vegas, NV 89121
451-8050
Hours: noon - midnight; nail salon 10 am - 10 pm
Quality work at reasonable prices; full service tattoo parlour, nail salon and tanning; permanent makeup; body piercing available.

Tattoo Revolution
3143 Industrial Rd.
Las Vegas, NV 89109
791-3488
Hours: Mon. - Sat. noon - midnight; Sun. noon - 8 pm
All styles, all free hand, all guaranteed! Specializing in portraits and tribal tattoos; all work done by award winning artists; body piercing available.

Tattoos R Us
101 E. Charleston Blvd.
Las Vegas, NV 89104
387-6969

616 Las Vegas Blvd. S.
Las Vegas, NV 89101
678-6162
Hours: Sun. - Thu. 10 am - 10 pm; Fri. - Sat. 10 am - midnight
Over 50,000 designs; specializing in freehand, fine line, tribal, new school and coverups; body piercing available.

SPECIALTY FOODS & SUPERMARKETS

SPECIALTY FOOD

Cost Plus World Market
3840 S. Maryland Pkwy.
Las Vegas, NV 89109
794-2070
Jim Straub, Gen. Mgr

2151 N. Rainbow Blvd.
Las Vegas, NV 89108
638-8844
Debbie Hayden, Gen. Mgr.
Hours: Mon. - Sat. 9 am - 9 pm; Sun. 10 am - 7 pm
Ever-changing mix of more than 20,000 products from over 40 countries. Collectibles, rugs, textiles, furniture, housewares, gourmet food and specialty cookware. Over 100 types of beer from about 25 countries.

Fun City Popcorn, Inc.
3395 Pinks Pl.
Las Vegas, NV 89102
367-2676
Hours: Mon. - Fri. 8 am - 4 pm
Popcorn, pretzels and churros.

Gilcrease Orchard
7800 N. Tenaya Way
Las Vegas, NV 89131
645-1126
Hours: 7 am - noon
Bring your own containers and pick your fruit yourself; about 40 cents per pound, depending on the fruit.

99 Ranch Market
4155 W. Spring Mountain Rd.
Las Vegas, NV 89102
364-8899
George Wang, Mgr.
Hours: 9 am - 10 pm
Largest Asian supermarket in town. Located in the Chinatown Plaza.

Trader Joe's
2716 Green Valley Pkwy.
Henderson, NV 89014
433-6773
John Persichitte, Mgr.

2101 S. Decatur Blvd.
Las Vegas, NV 89102
367-0227
Michael Shields, Gen. Mgr.
Hours: 9 am - 9 pm
Credit Cards: VISA, MC, Discover
Gourmet foods at low value prices, wines, beer and liquor. Coffee beans, meatless entrees, fresh salads, nuts, dried fruits, fat-free foods, bread, and candy.

Wild Oats Community Market
3455 E. Flamingo Rd.
Las Vegas, NV 89121
434-8115
Steve Miller, Mgr.

6720 W. Sahara Ave.
Las Vegas, NV 89102
253-7050
Mike Circuit, Mgr.
Hours: 8 am - 9 pm
Credit Cards: MC, Visa, Discover
Natural food grocery store; sponsors free nutrition and health seminars.

SUPERMARKETS

Smith's Food and Drug Centers
6130 W. Tropicana Ave.
Las Vegas, NV 89103
871-0904

3850 E. Flamingo Rd.
Las Vegas, NV 89121
451-2246

8555 W. Sahara Ave.
Las Vegas, NV 89117
341-7474

450 N. Nellis Blvd.
Las Vegas, NV 89110
452-4718

2540 S. Maryland Pkwy.
Las Vegas, NV 89109
735-8928

232 N. Jones Blvd.
Las Vegas, NV 89107
870-5175

850 S. Rancho Dr.
Las Vegas, NV 89106
870-8494

4440 N. Rancho Dr.
Las Vegas, NV 89130
645-6100

2211 N. Rampart Blvd.
Las Vegas, NV 89128
256-5200

2255 Las Vegas Blvd. N.
N. Las Vegas, NV 89030
642-1000

1000 N. Green Valley Pkwy.
Henderson, NV 89014
260-0060
Groceries, florist dept., one-hour photo, Chinese Kitchen, pharmacy, dry cleaners *(some locations)*, video rentals, service desk, stamps, money orders and Ticketmasters.

MAJOR CHAINS
Albertson's: 17
PriceRite Warehouse & Foods: . . 4
Lucky's: 25
Smith's: 13
Vons: 17

PHOTO FINISHING & PHOTOGRAPHERS

PHOTO FINISHING

Allen Photo/Digital Imaging
3223 Industrial Rd.
Las Vegas, NV 89109
735-2222
Hours: Mon. - Fri. 8 am - 5:30 pm, Sat.
9 am - 3 pm
Reprographic services, photographic processing, in-plant processing and printing. Pick-up and delivery.

Express Photo
3041 Las Vegas Blvd. S., Ste. 7
Las Vegas, NV 89109
369-8822
Hours: 8 am - midnight
Color prints, camera and video equipment.

Fast 1-Hour Foto
Meadows Mall
4300 Meadows Ln.
Las Vegas, NV 89107
878-2025
Hours: Mon. - Fri. 10 am - 9 pm; Sat. - Sun. 10 am - 6 pm
Passports, photo restoration and one-hour enlargements.

Films Developed in 30 Minutes
3041 Las Vegas Blvd. S.
Las Vegas, NV 89109
369-8822
Kobi Deri, Mgr.
Hours: 8 am - midnight
Credit Cards: Visa, MC, AMX, Diners Club
Multi-service.

Film Developed While You Wait
3049 Las Vegas Blvd. S., Ste. 25
Las Vegas, NV 89109
369-4040
Hours: 8 am - 7:30 pm
Rated one of the three best photo labs in North America

Kinko's
4440 S. Maryland Pkwy.
Las Vegas, NV 89109
735-4402
Hours: Mon. - Fri. 8:30 am - 9:30 pm; Sat. 8:30 am - 4:30 pm
Fast reprints and photo greeting cards.

Michael's One Hour Photo Lab
3547 S. Maryland Pkwy.
Las Vegas, NV 89109
737-1404
Hours: Mon. - Fri. 9 am - 6 pm; Sat. 10 am - 5 pm
One hour film and slide developing, video transfers and old photos copied.

1 Hour Photo Shack
4632 S. Maryland Pkwy.
Las Vegas, NV 89119
798-7373
Hours: Mon. - Fri. 8:30 am - 7 pm; Sat. 10 am - 4 pm
Quick and quality prints.

Cashman Enterprises, 3660 Cinder Ln., Las Vegas, NV 89103

Photo Finish
3121 S. Industrial Rd.
Las Vegas, NV 89109
732-1878   1-800-945-0056
Hours: Mon. - Fri. 8:30 am - 6 pm; Sat. 10 am - 2 pm
Film processing, custom print services, digital imaging, lab services. Pick-up and delivery.

Smiths
One-hour location
6130 W. Tropicana Ave.
Las Vegas, NV 89103
871-0904
Hours: Mon. - Sat. 8 am - 9 pm; Sun. 10 am - 7 pm
1 hour photos.

Walgreen One-Hour Photo Labs
2995 E. Flamingo Rd.
Las Vegas, NV 89121
737-6545
Hours: 9 am - 9 pm

Wal-Mart
1 hour photo lab
3075 E. Tropicana Ave.
Las Vegas, NV 89121
451-6663
Hours: Mon. - Sat.   9 am - 9 pm, Sun. 10 am - 8 pm
Credit Cards: MC, Visa

PHOTOGRAPHERS

Brian Janis Phototechnik
8401 Campana Dr.
Las Vegas, NV 89117
252-8311   1-800-362-3624
Fax: 252-4566
Brian Janis, Owner

Create a special setting for your photos or pose with a fabulous showgirl, celebrity lookalikes...the possibilities are endless.

Glamour Shots
Boulevard Mall
3680 S. Maryland Pkwy.
Las Vegas, NV 89109
731-3777
Hours: Mon. - Fri. 10 am - 9 pm; Sat. 10 am - 8 pm; Sun. 10 am - 6 pm

Meadows Mall
4300 Meadows Ln.
Las Vegas, NV 89107
870-6880
Kenny Villegas, Owner
Hours: Mon. - Fri. 10 am - 9 pm; Sat. - Sun. 9 am - 7 pm
Credit Cards: MC, Visa, AMX, Discover
Makeover, hairstyling and high fashion photo sessions. Instant viewing of video proofs; portrait packages starting at $35.

Photos & Flowers
5785 W. Sahara Ave., Ste. 100
Las Vegas, NV 89102
873-3686
Hours: Mon. - Fri. 8:30 am - 5 pm

3830 Meadows Ln.
Las Vegas, NV 89107
258-1554
Mike & Judy Maguire, Owners

Hours: Mon. - Fri. 8:30 am - 5 pm; Sat. - Sun. 8:30 am - 3 pm
Credit Cards: MC, Visa, Discover, AMEX, Diners Club
Floral arrangements, gift items, photo processing and cafe.

Cashman Enterprises
3660 Cinder Ln.
Las Vegas, NV 89103
871-8300

Photo Magic
MGM Grand Hotel & Casino
Star Lane Mall
891-FOTO (891-3686)

Cashman's Photo Magic
Stratosphere Hotel & Casino
The Tower Shops
438-FOTO (438-3686)

Cashman's Photo Magic
Rio Suite Hotel & Casino
Masquerade Village
876-FOTO (876-3686)

New York New York Hotel & Casino
Mezzanine Shops
643-FOTO (643-3686)

Cashman's Photo Magic Fuji Kiosk
Fremont Street Experience
647-FOTO (647-3686)

Foto Forum
The Forum Shops at Caesars
893-FOTO (893-3686)
Six conveniently located retail stores to provide for all photographic needs; showroom and restaurant photography and photography taken on thrill rides.

Vogue Photography Studios & Portraits While You Wait
3049 Las Vegas Blvd. S., Ste. 25
Las Vegas, NV 89109
Specializing in glamour & boudoir shots & family reunions. Complete makeover. First in Las Vegas with high tech state of the art.

SHOPPING

PSYCHIC

The Psychic
4110 S. Maryland Pkwy.
Las Vegas, NV 89119
732-8552
Hours: Mon. - Sat. 10:30 am - 6 pm
Character and coffee cup readings, understanding your dreams. Reading $15.

Psychic Eye Book Shops
953 E. Sahara Ave.
Las Vegas, NV 89104
369-6622

4810 Spring Mountain Rd.
Las Vegas, NV 89102
368-7785

3315 E. Russell Rd.
Las Vegas, NV 89120
451-5777
Hours: Mon. - Fri. 10 am - 9 pm; Sat. 10 am - 8:30 pm; Sun. noon - 6 pm

6848 W. Charleston Blvd.
Las Vegas, NV 89117
255-4477
Robert Leysen, Owner

Hours: Mon. - Fri. 10 am - 9 pm; Sat. 10 am - 8:30 pm; Sun. 11 am - 6 pm
Specialize in new age book supplies, self help, philosophy, occult books.

The Psychic Institute
4800 S. Maryland Pkwy.
Las Vegas, NV 89119
798-8448
Dawn Miller, Owner
Hours: 10 am - 9 pm
Personal consultations, classes, hypnosis and yoga as well as a variety of metaphysical books.

Experience Las Vegas

TOBACCO

Churchill Tobacco Emporiom
3144 N. Rainbow Blvd.
Las Vegas, Nv 89108
645-1047
George Arnold, Owner
Hours: Mon. - Sat. 10:30 am - 7 pm; Sun.
11 am - 4 pm
The best selection of hard-to-get rare cigars. Humidors, cigar accessories, imported cigarettes and great prices.

Don Pablo Cigar Co.
3025 Las Vegas Blvd. S., Ste. 117
Las Vegas, NV 89109
369-1818 1-800-537-4957
Bob Schear, Pres.
Hours: Mon. - Sat. 9 am - 6 pm; Sun.
10 am - 4 pm
Credit Cards: MC, Visa, AMEX, Discover
Cigars handmade on premises, using fine tobacco leaves from five different countries; watch them being made.

Ed's Pipes Tobacco & Gifts
Maryland Square
3661 S. Maryland Pkwy.
Las Vegas, NV 89109
734-1931 1-800-688-6222
Helen Dobbs, Owner
Hours: Mon. - Fri. 9 am - 6 pm; Sat. 9 am - 5 pm; Sun. noon - 4 pm
Credit Cards: MC, Visa
Tobacco in every form plus related paraphernalia. Figurines, mugs and other fine gift items.

Hiland's Tobacco & Gifts
Meadows Mall
4300 Meadows Ln.
Las Vegas, NV 89107
878-7720
Phil Lyons, Mgr.
Hours: Mon. - Fri. 10 am - 9 pm; Sat. -
Sun. 10 am - 6 pm
Credit Cards: All major
Various fine cigars, pipes and tobacco collections.

Las Vegas Cigar Company
3755 Las Vegas Blvd. S.
Las Vegas, NV 89109
262-6100
Richard V. Galdieri, Pres.
Hours: 8 am - 9 pm
Credit Cards: MC, Visa
Watch as cigars are made by hand. Everything sold is made on premises.

Las Vegas Tribal Smoke Shop
1225 N. Main St.
Las Vegas, NV 89101
387-6433
Hours: Mon. - Sat. 7 am - 8 pm; Sun.
8 am - 7 pm

1 Nuvakai UD 95 North
Snow Mountain Exit
645-2957
Hours: 7 am - 6 pm
Credit Cards: MC, Visa
Cigarettes sold by the carton, all brands at lowest prices.

Mr. Bill's Pipe & Tobacco Shop
4510 E. Charleston Blvd.
Las Vegas, NV 89104
459-3400   1-800-688-0302

4632 S. Maryland Pkwy.
Las Vegas, NV 89119
739-8840

1014 S. Sunset Rd.
Henderson, NV 89014
434-4423

2559 S. Rainbow Blvd.
Las Vegas, NV 89102
362-4427

4441 W. Flamingo Rd.
Las Vegas, NV 89103
221-9771

3220 N. Jones Blvd.
Las Vegas, NV 89108
395-7264
James Russell, Pres.
Hours: Mon. - Sat. 9 am - 9 pm Sun.
10 am - 9 pm
Credit Cards: MC, Visa, Discover, AMX
All forms of tobacco, related paraphernalia. Crystals, mugs, shaving sets and other fine gift items.

Royal Cigar Society
3900 Paradise Rd.
Las Vegas, NV 89109
732-4411
Corbett Crumpley, Mgr.
Las Vegas' largest selection of cigars. Cigarettes, tobacco, novelties, espresso and cappuccino bar and private smoking lounge. Sign up for membership.

Smokers Paradise
3310 S. Nellis Blvd.
Las Vegas, NV 89121
435-4096
Sheila Lively, Mgr.
Hours: Mon. - Fri. 8 am - 8 pm; Sat 9 am - 8 pm; Sun. 10 am - 7 pm
Cigar humidors, Clove cigarettes, major brands and generics and supplies.

Tinder Box
3536 S. Maryland Pkwy.
Las Vegas, NV 89109
737-1807
Jeff Kappuls, Mgr.
Hours: Mon. - Fri. 10 am - 9 pm; Sat.
10 am - 8 pm; Sun. 11 am - 6 pm
Credit Cards: All major
Pipes, tobacco, cigars, foreign cigarettes and related gift items.

Tobacco Road
3650 E. Flamingo Rd.
Las Vegas, NV 89121
435-8511

1129 S. Rainbow Blvd.
Las Vegas, NV 89102
254-8511
Ed Kotoch, Pres.
Hours: 9 am - 10 pm
Credit Cards: MC, Visa, AMX
All forms of tobacco and related paraphernalia; jewelry, crystals, T-shirts and other fine gift items.

TRAVEL AGENCIES

Admiral Cruise Center
3050 E. Desert Inn Rd., Ste. 138
Las Vegas, NV 89121
Hours: Mon. - Fri. 9 am - 5:30 pm
"Our only business is cruising."

Around the World Travel, Inc.
2003 Las Vegas Blvd. S.
Las Vegas, NV 89104
731-1006
Hours: Mon. - Fri. 9 am - 5 pm, Sat. 9 am - 3 pm

California State Automobile Assoc.
NV Division Travel Agency
3312 W. Charleston Blvd.
Las Vegas, NV 89102
870-9171
Hours: Mon. - Fri. 8:30 am - 5 pm

Carefree Travel
4545 E. Tropicana Ave.
Las Vegas, NV 89121
456-6717
Hours: Mon. - Fri. 9 am - 5:30 pm; Sat.
10 am - 2 pm
"Never a service charge."

Cheyenne Travel & Cruise
3161 N. Rainbow Blvd.
Las Vegas, NV 89108
645-1104
Hours: Mon. - Fri. 8:30 am - 6 pm, Sat.
10 am - 2 pm
All airlines.

Cole Travel Service
520 S. Sixth St.
Las Vegas, NV 89101
382-5133
Bob Cole, Mgr.
Hours: Mon. - Fri. 9 am - 5:30 pm

Dillard's Travel
4200 Meadows Ln.
Las Vegas, NV 89107
258-1584
Hours: Mon. - Sat. 10 am - 9 pm; Sun. 10 am - 3 pm
International and domestic vacation planning.

Prestige Travel, 6175 Spring Mountain Rd., Las Vegas, NV 89102

Discount Travel
3305 Spring Mountain Rd., Ste. 7
Las Vegas, NV 89102
251-1101
Hours: Mon. - Fri. 8 am - 7:30 pm
Airlines, cars, hotels and cruises

Escape Travel
544 E. Sahara Ave.
Las Vegas, NV 89104
734-8987
Hours: Mon. - Fri. 8:30 am - 5 pm
Vacation packages, airline tickets, cruises and business travel.

Good Times Travel, Inc.
624 N. Rainbow Blvd.
Las Vegas, NV 89107
878-8900
Hours: Mon. - Fri. 9 am - 6 pm; Sat.
10 am - 2 pm
Your passport to good times.

Happy Tours Travel
2330 E. Bonanza Rd.
Las Vegas, NV 89101
380-3000
Hours: 10 am - 6 pm
Complete travel packages.

Horizon Travel
3315 E. Russell Rd.
Las Vegas, NV 89120
451-0406
Hours: Mon. - Fri. 8:30 am - 6 pm, Sat.
10 am - 3 pm
A full service travel agency.

Mickey Cole Travel Service
Gold Coast
4000 W. Flamingo Rd.
Las Vegas, NV 89103
876-1410
Mickey Cole, Pres.
Hours: Mon. - Sat. 9 am - 6:30 pm, Sun.
9 am - 5 pm

Prestige American Express Travel
Corporate Office
6175 Spring Mountain Rd.
Las Vegas, NV 89102
251-5552
Hours: Mon. - Fri. 7:30 am - 6 pm, Sat.
10 am - 5 pm

Uniglobe Benchmark Travel
4511 W. Sahara Ave.
Las Vegas, NV 89102
228-3700 1-800-655-1173
Carl & Marty Quillin, Owners
Hours: Mon. - Fri. 8:30 am - 5:30 pm;
Sat. 10 am - 2 pm
24 hour Rescue Line
Uniglobe Benchmark Travel will provide you with all the information you need to come to our dazzling city.

24 HOUR BUSINESSES

AUTO PARTS

Chief Auto Parts
525 E. Sahara Ave.
Las Vegas, NV 89104
734-0724

3455 S. Decatur Blvd.
Las Vegas, NV 89102
362-1540

DRY CLEANERS

Al Phillips The Cleaners
2700 Green Valley Pkwy.
Henderson, NV 89014
456-248

2201 E. Tropicana Ave.
Las Vegas, NV 89119
736-6029

4130 Koval Ln.
Las Vegas, NV 89109
733-1043

6190 W. Flamingo Rd.
Las Vegas, NV 89103
367-8383

8578 W. Lake Mead Blvd.
Las Vegas, NV 89134
228-5843

GENERAL MERCHANDISE

Wal-Mart Discount Cities
201 N. Nellis Blvd.
Las Vegas, NV 89110
452-9998

3075 E. Tropicana Ave.
Las Vegas, NV 89121
451-8900

3625 S. Rainbow Blvd.
Las Vegas, NV 89103
367-9999

3041 N. Rainbow Blvd.
Las Vegas, NV 89108
656-0199

GROCERY STORES

All grocery stores throughout Las Vegas are open 24 hours with the exception of some major holidays.

PHARMACIES

Sav-On Drugs
1360 E. Flamingo Rd.
Las Vegas, NV 89119
731-5373

3550 W. Sahara Ave.
Las Vegas, NV 89102
873-7171

2011 E. Lake Mead Blvd.
N. Las Vegas, NV 89030
642-9780

4410 E. Bonanza Rd.
Las Vegas, NV 89110
452-5652

4014 S. Rainbow Blvd.
Las Vegas, NV 89103
873-5917

8320 W. Cheyenne Ave.
Las Vegas, NV 89129
658-3834

PRINTING/COPYING

Kinko's
4440 S. Maryland Pkwy.
Las Vegas, NV 89119
735-4402

4750 W. Sahara Ave.
Las Vegas, NV 89102
870-7011

608 S. 4th St.
Las Vegas, NV 89101
383-7022

671 Mall Ring Cir.
Henderson, NV 89014
436-7370

RECORDS / TAPES

Odyssey Records
1600 Las Vegas Blvd. S.
Las Vegas, NV 89104
384-4040
Julie Mernin, Store Dir.

UNIQUE SHOPPING

Back to the 50's
6870 S. Paradise Rd.
Las Vegas, NV 89119
361-1950 1-800-224-1950
Hank Cartwright, Owner
Hours: Mon. - Sat. 9 am - 6 pm
Take a trip down memory lane and visit our showroom. We'll ship your purchase anywhere in the world. Elvis Presley memorabilia and limited edition merchandise. John Wayne, Beatles, James Dean and Marilyn Monroe nostalgia are available. Over 300 items for $30 or less. Call for free catalog.

Houdini's Magic Shop
Locations: MGM Grand, New York New York & The Rio in the Masquerade Village
24 hour order line: 633-9110
Magic, pranks and gags.

Las Vegas Harley Davidson
2495 E. Sahara Ave.
Las Vegas, NV 89104
431-8500
Don Andress, Owner
Hours: Mon. - Sat. 9 am - 6 pm, Sun. 10 am - 5 pm
Harley Owners Group: 454-1544
Motorcycles, T-shirts, motor clothing, accessories, boots, helmets, motorcycle parts and supplies.

Ray's Beaver Bag
727 Las Vegas Blvd. S.
Las Vegas, NV 89101
386-8746
Ray Potter, Owner
Hours: Mon. - Fri. 9 am - 6 pm; Sat. 10 am - 4 pm
Pelts of fox, beaver and wolverine; cookbooks with recipes from the Revolutionary War, earrings made from rattlesnake fangs, even a "jackalope." Basically a black powder gun store.

Revenge, Inc.
3700 S. Highland Ave., Ste. 6
Las Vegas, NV 89103
365-1010
Lynn McClain, Owner

Hours: Call for hours
Retail sales of the unusual; headless teddy bears, horse manure bouquets, voodoo dolls, hair kits for vain men, coal in stocking, candy box with half-eaten chocolates.

Sexy Dress
2600 S. Maryland Pkwy.
Las Vegas, NV 89109
382-SEXY
Bruce Dyer, Owner
Hours: Sun. - Fri. 11 am - 7 pm; Sat. 10 am - 6 pm
Nevada's largest sexy clothing store featuring Club, Party, Casino, Dance, Tramp, and Swimwear.

Smokey's Sportcards, Inc.
3734 Las Vegas Blvd. S.
Las Vegas, NV 89109
739-0003 1-800-766-5397
Smokey Scheinman
Hours: Mon. - Sat. 9 am - 6:30 pm; Sun. 10 am - 5 pm
Credit Cards: Visa, MC
Largest distributor of sports cards in the world. In addition to the retail shops, Smokey's operates a warehouse which is one of the largest mail-order businesses in the country.

Stamp Oasis
4750 W. Sahara Ave.
Las Vegas, NV 89102
878-6474
Jim Freedman, Owner
Hours: Mon. - Sat. 10 am - 6 pm; Sun. noon - 5 pm
Credit Cards: All major
Over 35,000 fun rubber stamps and related items.

The Jungle Zone
Meadows Mall
4300 Meadows Ln.
Las Vegas, NV 89107
877-5600
Jason Buchanan, Owner
Hours: Mon. - Fri. 10 am - 9 pm; Sat. - Sun. 10 am - 6 pm
Fine jewelry, eclectic art and hand

beaded crafts. Music from reggae to new age to nature. Professional body piercing, including navels and nipples.

Warner Bros. Studio Store
Forum Shops
3500 Las Vegas Blvd. S.
Las Vegas, NV 89109
893-7711
Loralee Neuwirth, Gen. Mgr.

Hours: Sun. - Thu. 10 am - 11 pm; Fri. - Sat. 10 am - midnight
Credit Cards: All major
Over 8,000 sq. ft. of clothing, toys, souvenirs and collectibles with the Warner Bros. characters and name. Store features a 16 ft. video screen playing Warner Bros. cartoons, videos and clips from upcoming movies.

SHOPPING

WORLD'S LARGEST GIFT SHOP

Bonanza Gift Shop, 2460 Las Vegas Blvd. S., Las Vegas, NV 89104
"World's largest gift store," with a wide variety of gift items and Las Vegas souvenirs including toys, magic and gag items, jewelry and clothing. (*See page 300 for information*)

COST OF LIVING - RETAIL SALES

ADDITIONAL ON PAGE 284

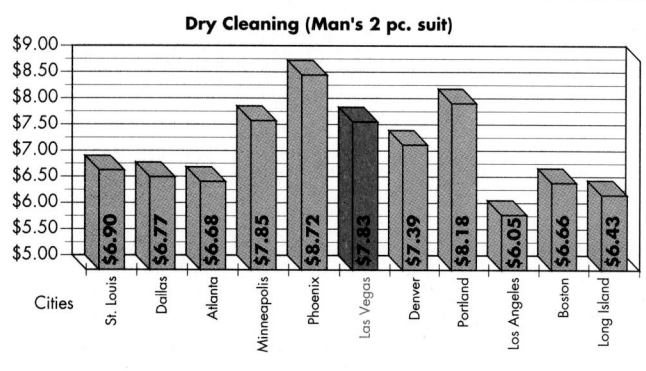

Dry Cleaning (Man's 2 pc. suit)

City	Price
St. Louis	$6.90
Dallas	$6.77
Atlanta	$6.68
Minneapolis	$7.85
Phoenix	$8.72
Las Vegas	$7.83
Denver	$7.39
Portland	$8.18
Los Angeles	$6.05
Boston	$6.66
Long Island	$6.43

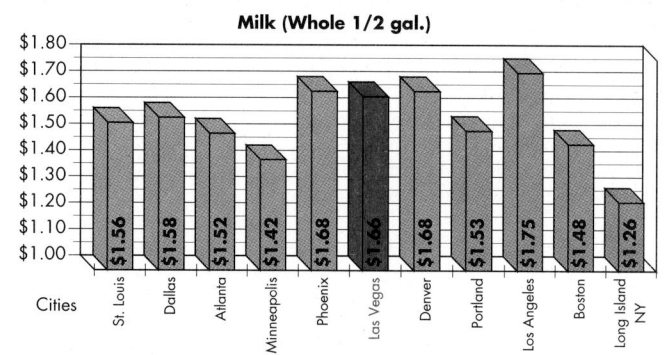

Milk (Whole 1/2 gal.)

City	Price
St. Louis	$1.56
Dallas	$1.58
Atlanta	$1.52
Minneapolis	$1.42
Phoenix	$1.68
Las Vegas	$1.66
Denver	$1.68
Portland	$1.53
Los Angeles	$1.75
Boston	$1.48
Long Island NY	$1.26

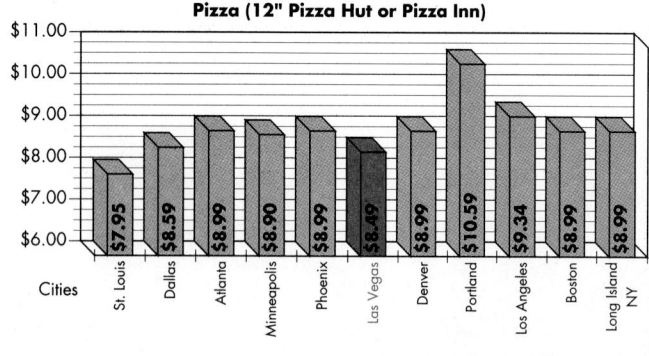

Pizza (12" Pizza Hut or Pizza Inn)

City	Price
St. Louis	$7.95
Dallas	$8.59
Atlanta	$8.99
Minneapolis	$8.90
Phoenix	$8.99
Las Vegas	$8.49
Denver	$8.99
Portland	$10.59
Los Angeles	$9.34
Boston	$8.99
Long Island NY	$8.99

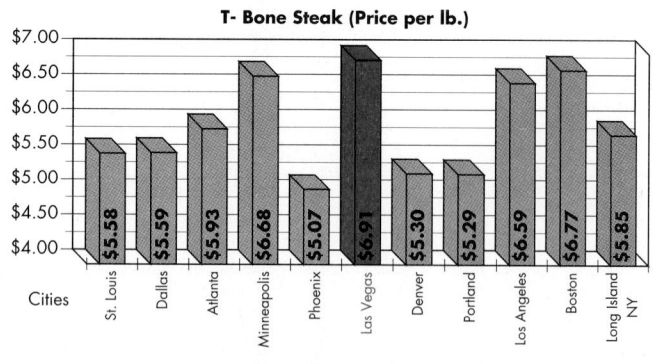

T- Bone Steak (Price per lb.)

City	Price
St. Louis	$5.58
Dallas	$5.59
Atlanta	$5.93
Minneapolis	$6.68
Phoenix	$5.07
Las Vegas	$6.91
Denver	$5.30
Portland	$5.29
Los Angeles	$6.59
Boston	$6.77
Long Island NY	$5.85

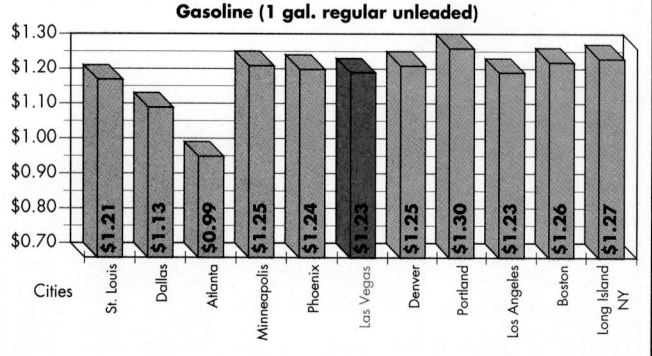

Gasoline (1 gal. regular unleaded)

City	Price
St. Louis	$1.21
Dallas	$1.13
Atlanta	$0.99
Minneapolis	$1.25
Phoenix	$1.24
Las Vegas	$1.23
Denver	$1.25
Portland	$1.30
Los Angeles	$1.23
Boston	$1.26
Long Island NY	$1.27

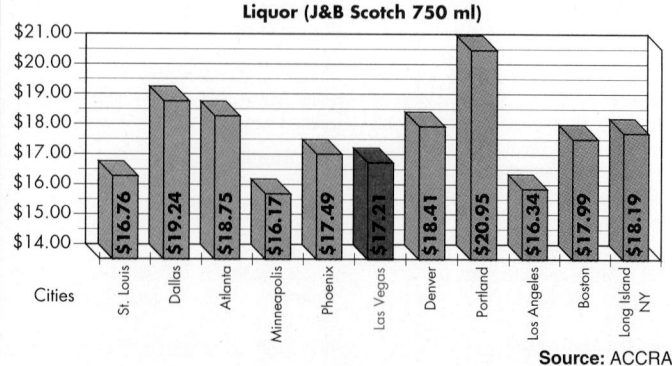

Liquor (J&B Scotch 750 ml)

City	Price
St. Louis	$16.76
Dallas	$19.24
Atlanta	$18.75
Minneapolis	$16.17
Phoenix	$17.49
Las Vegas	$17.21
Denver	$18.41
Portland	$20.95
Los Angeles	$16.34
Boston	$17.99
Long Island NY	$18.19

Source: ACCRA

Convention

Las Vegas has more exhibition space - 761,522 sq. ft. - than any other U.S. city, and it is third in the country, behind New York and Chicago, in number of trade shows. The Las Vegas Convention Center, with a total of 1.3 million sq. ft., is the largest single-level convention complex in the United States.

The Convention Center opened in 1959 to boost midweek visitor volume. Initially it included the recently demolished rotunda, 18 meeting rooms and a 90,000 sq. ft. North Hall. In its first year of operation it hosted 8 conventions attended by 22,519 delegates.

In 1997 Las Vegas hosted 3,749 conventions attended by 3.5 million delegates, or 11.6 percent of all visitors, resulting in an economic impact of $4.4 billion. Conventions in Las Vegas have increased over 400 percent in the last ten years.

Las Vegas can accommodate conventions of any size. Along with the Convention Center, there is more than 100,000 sq. ft. of meeting space at Cashman Field Center not to mention the many hotel convention facilities, such as the 1,006,396 sq. ft. Sands Expo and Convention Center.

The Consumer Electronics Show in January and the COMDEX Show in November are the largest annual conventions. Each one is attended by over 100,000 delegates. The 1997 COMDEX was the largest convention ever held in Las Vegas with over 225,000 delegates, providing a $341 million lift for the local economy. The busiest convention months are September through November and January through April.

The Las Vegas Convention Center and the Cashman Field Center are operated by the Las Vegas Convention and Visitors Authority, a governmental agency which promotes Southern Nevada as a convention and vacation destination. The LVCVA receives the majority of its funds from the Clark County and Las Vegas hotel and motel room tax.

Las Vegas Convention and Visitors Authority

Las Vegas Convention Center
3150 Paradise Rd.
Las Vegas, NV 89109
892-0711 Fax: 892-2824
Manny Cortez, Pres.: 733-2300
Rossi Ralenkotter,
  VP of Marketing: 733-2244
Thomas A. Smith, VP of Operations
The Las Vegas Convention Center has 1.3 million sq. ft. of total space. Ten exhibit halls, divisible by movable walls, provide 761,522 sq. ft. and the South Hall has 120,000 sq. ft. Lobby and concourse areas total 85,200 sq. ft.; there are 91 meeting rooms with seating capacities ranging from 50 to 7,500. Total meeting space is 150,630 sq. ft. with a total Grand Lobby Registration area of 85,200 sq. ft. Parking for 4,472 cars. Banquet services for 12,000. LVCC exhibit and meeting space averages 15 cents per net sq. ft.

Cashman Field Center

850 Las Vegas Blvd. N.
Las Vegas, NV 89101
386-7100
Events: 386-7184
Larry Griffith, Mgr. of Facilities
Seating Capacity (Theater): 1,940
Stage Area: 3,015 sq. ft. permanent stage
Use: Fine arts events, concerts and meetings.
Seating Capacity (Stadium): 9,370; field is 148,500 sq. ft.
Use: Las Vegas Stars AAA baseball
Built in 1983 at a cost of $27 million, Cashman encompasses 534,000 sq. ft. of improvements on a 50-acre site. It has 98,100 sq. ft. of exhibit space; 16 meeting rooms on two levels comprising 17,500 sq. ft.; parking for 2,608 vehicles, at $2 per space utilized; food and beverage services available through ARA Services. By the end of 1998, the meeting rooms and exhibit hall will be doubled in size to over 200,000 sq. ft.

Henderson Convention Center

200 Water St.
Henderson, NV 89015
565-2171
Lisa Jolly, Convention Center Services Supv.
The Henderson Convention Center consists of a 10,000 sq. ft. ballroom that can accommodate up to 800 people for meetings and 600 for banquets. It can be divided into four separate rooms and six break-out conference rooms accommodating up to 20 people. Rooms open to an outdoor garden area. Parking for 200 vehicles.

Sands Expo & Convention Center

201 E. Sands Ave.
Las Vegas, NV 89109
733-5556 Fax: 733-5353
Jeff Beckelman, VP Sales
Total exhibit space: 105,000 sq. ft.
Total Space: 1,006,396 sq. ft.
The Sands Expo is the largest privately owned convention center in the United States.
Meeting capacity: 108 meeting and conference rooms with over 100,000 sq. ft.
Theater seats: 2,300
Lobby: 50,000+ sq. ft.
Banquet capacity: 29,870
Parking: 1,000+ cars
Upper Level
Ceiling height: 32 1/2 ft.; Lobby: 50,000+ sq. ft.
Exhibit Hall A: 178,000 sq. ft.
Exhibit Hall B: 189,000 sq. ft.
Exhibit Hall C: 188,000 sq. ft.
Exhibit Hall D: 105,500 sq. ft.
Street Level
Ceiling Height: 14 ft.
Exhibit Hall G: 380,000 sq. ft.; Lobby: 20,000+ sq. ft.;
Public telephones: 100; Food service: 4 snack bars and on-site 6,000 sq. ft. kitchen.

LAS VEGAS HOTEL CONVENTION FACILITIES

In addition to the Las Vegas Convention Center, the following hotels have meeting and convention space. The major convention hotels are the Las Vegas Hilton, Sahara, Bally's, Caesars Palace, MGM, the Mirage, Riviera, and Tropicana.

Hotel	Total Square Feet
Arizona Charlie's	9,348
Alexis Park	37,766
Bally's	175,909
Best Western Mardi Gras Inn	8,260
Bourbon Street	1,753
Buffalo Bills	31,000
Caesars Palace	109,606
California Hotel	5,300
Circus Circus	15,000
Courtyard by Marriott	1,250
Debbie Reynolds	3,200
Desert Inn	30,060
El Cortez	2,000
Fiesta	840
Fitzgeralds	7,000
Flamingo Hilton	53,830
Four Queens	8,406
Fremont	6,838
Gold Coast	10,675
Golden Nugget	25,550
Hard Rock Hotel	12,000
Harrah's	18,996
Holiday Inn	2,392
Imperial Palace	34,595
King 8	1,000
LaQuinta	1,820
Las Vegas Club	3,600
Las Vegas Hilton	220,000
Luxor	20,000
Maxim	3,603
MGM	122,451
Mirage	86,069
Monte Carlo	15,000
Nevada Palace	5,000
New York New York	12,300
Orleans	40,000
Palace Station	18,500
Plaza	21,100
Quality Inn	1,400
Residence Inn	580
Rio	18,408
Riviera	91,216
Royal Hotel	27,314
Sahara	52,514
Sam's Town	10,000
Sands Expo	1,000,000
San Remo	6,134
Santa Fe	9,701
Showboat	13,900
Stardust	34,845
St. Tropez	4,096
Stratosphere Tower	6,600
Treasure Island	15,526
Tropicana	89,830
Vacation Village	10,200
Whiskey Pete's	8,000

LAS VEGAS CONVENTION FACTS

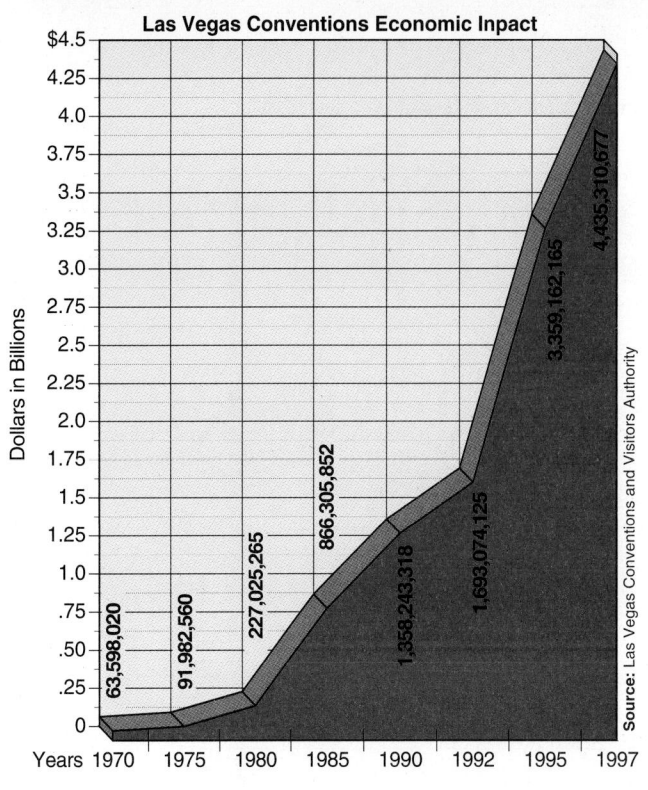

Las Vegas Conventions Economic Inpact

Dollars in Billions

Years: 1970, 1975, 1980, 1985, 1990, 1992, 1995, 1997

- 63,598,020
- 91,982,560
- 227,025,265
- 866,305,852
- 1,358,243,318
- 1,693,074,125
- 3,359,162,165
- 4,435,310,677

Source: Las Vegas Conventions and Visitors Authority

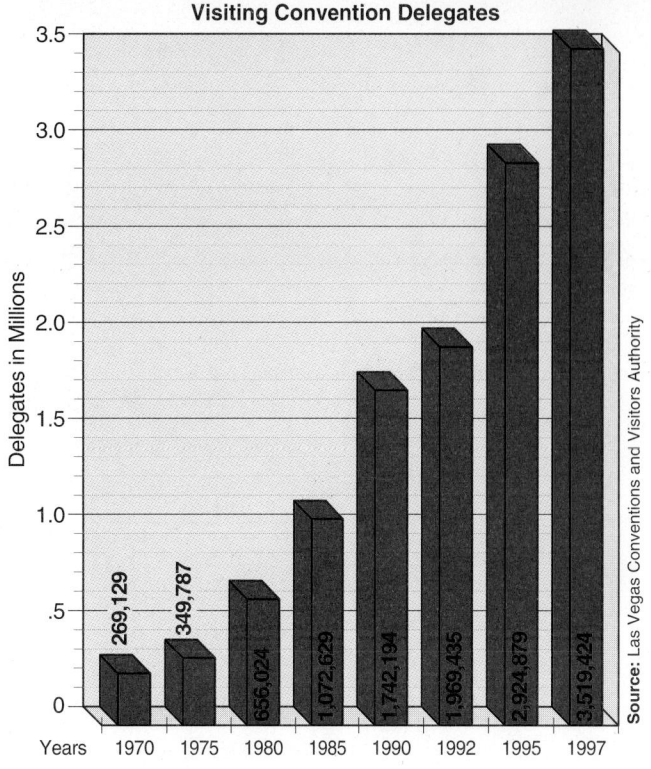

Visiting Convention Delegates

Delegates in Millions

Years: 1970, 1975, 1980, 1985, 1990, 1992, 1995, 1997

- 269,129
- 349,787
- 656,024
- 1,072,629
- 1,742,194
- 1,969,435
- 2,924,879
- 3,519,424

Source: Las Vegas Conventions and Visitors Authority

Conventions Held In Las Vegas

Year

- 1970: 296
- 1975: 393
- 1980: 449
- 1985: 480
- 1990: 1,011
- 1992: 2,199
- 1995: 2,826
- 1997: 3,749

Conventions Held

Source: Las Vegas Conventions and Visitors Authority

CONVENTION

LAS VEGAS CONVENTION CENTER

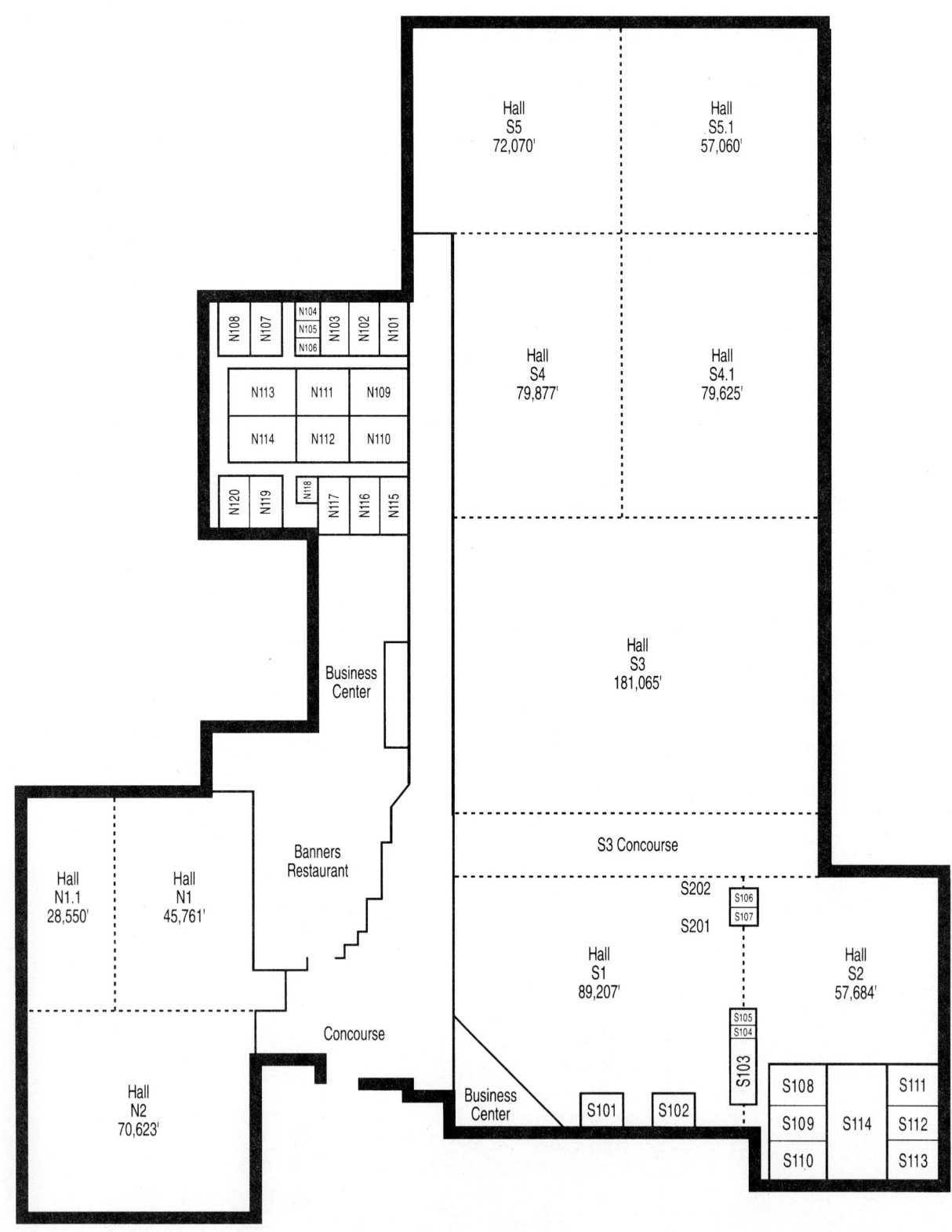

Hall
S5
72,070'

Hall
S5.1
57,060'

N108 N107 N104 N105 N106 N103 N102 N101

N113 N111 N109

N114 N112 N110

N120 N119 N118 N117 N116 N115

Hall
S4
79,877'

Hall
S4.1
79,625'

Business
Center

Hall
S3
181,065'

S3 Concourse

Hall
N1.1
28,550'

Hall
N1
45,761'

Banners
Restaurant

S202

S201

S106
S107

Hall
S1
89,207'

Hall
S2
57,684'

Concourse

S105
S104

Hall
N2
70,623'

Business
Center

S103

S101 S102

S108 S111

S109 S114 S112

S110 S113

LEVEL ONE

LAS VEGAS CONVENTION CENTER

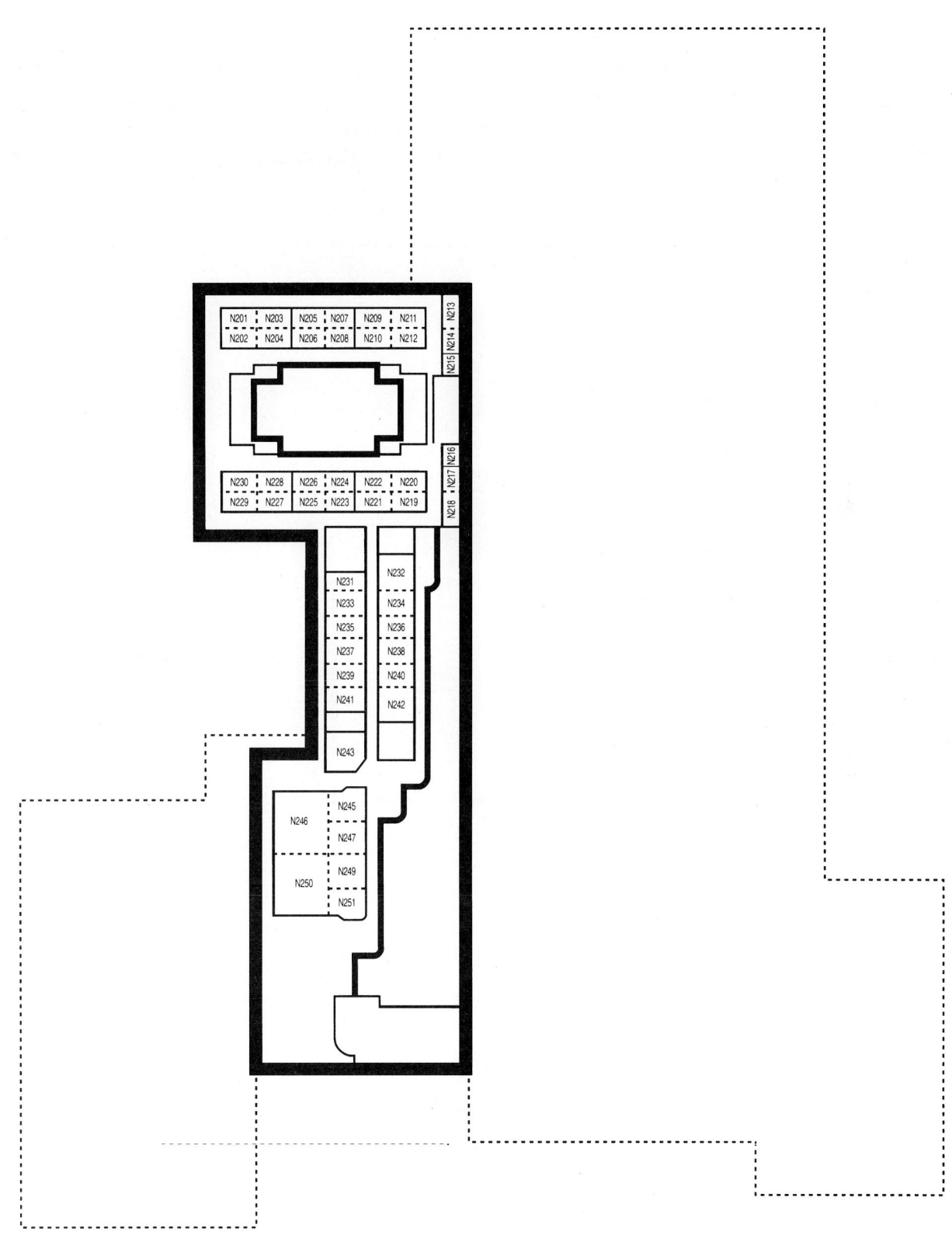

LEVEL TWO

LAS VEGAS CONVENTION CENTER

ADA ACCESS

LEVEL TWO

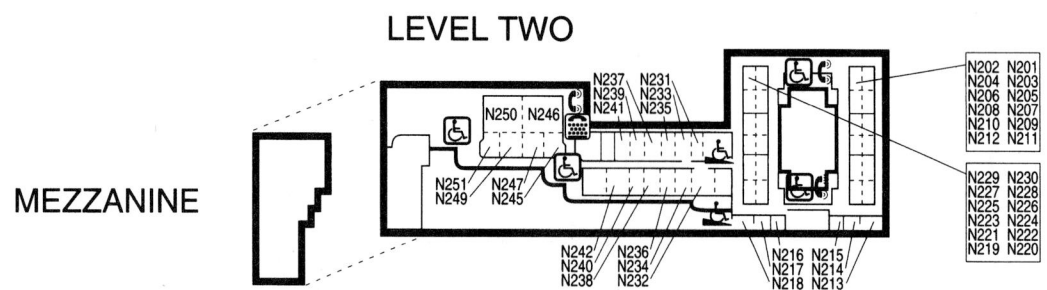

MEZZANINE

LEVEL ONE

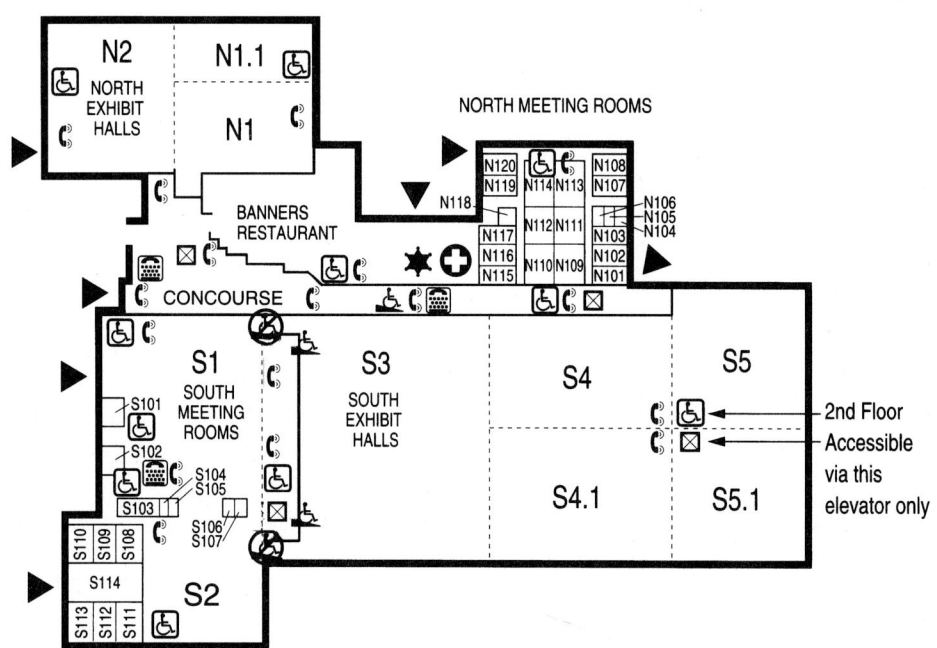

Legend

Ⓚ Ramp (Non-Accessible)		▶ Automatic Doors	
♿ Ramp		⊠ Elevator (Accessible)	
★ LVCVA Security		☐ Lower Level to Restrooms, Phones, Food Stand	
ℂ Telephones (Volume Control)		✚ First Aid Station	
⌨ TDDs Available Here		♿ Restrooms (Accessible)	

CASHMAN FIELD CENTER

ADA ACCESS

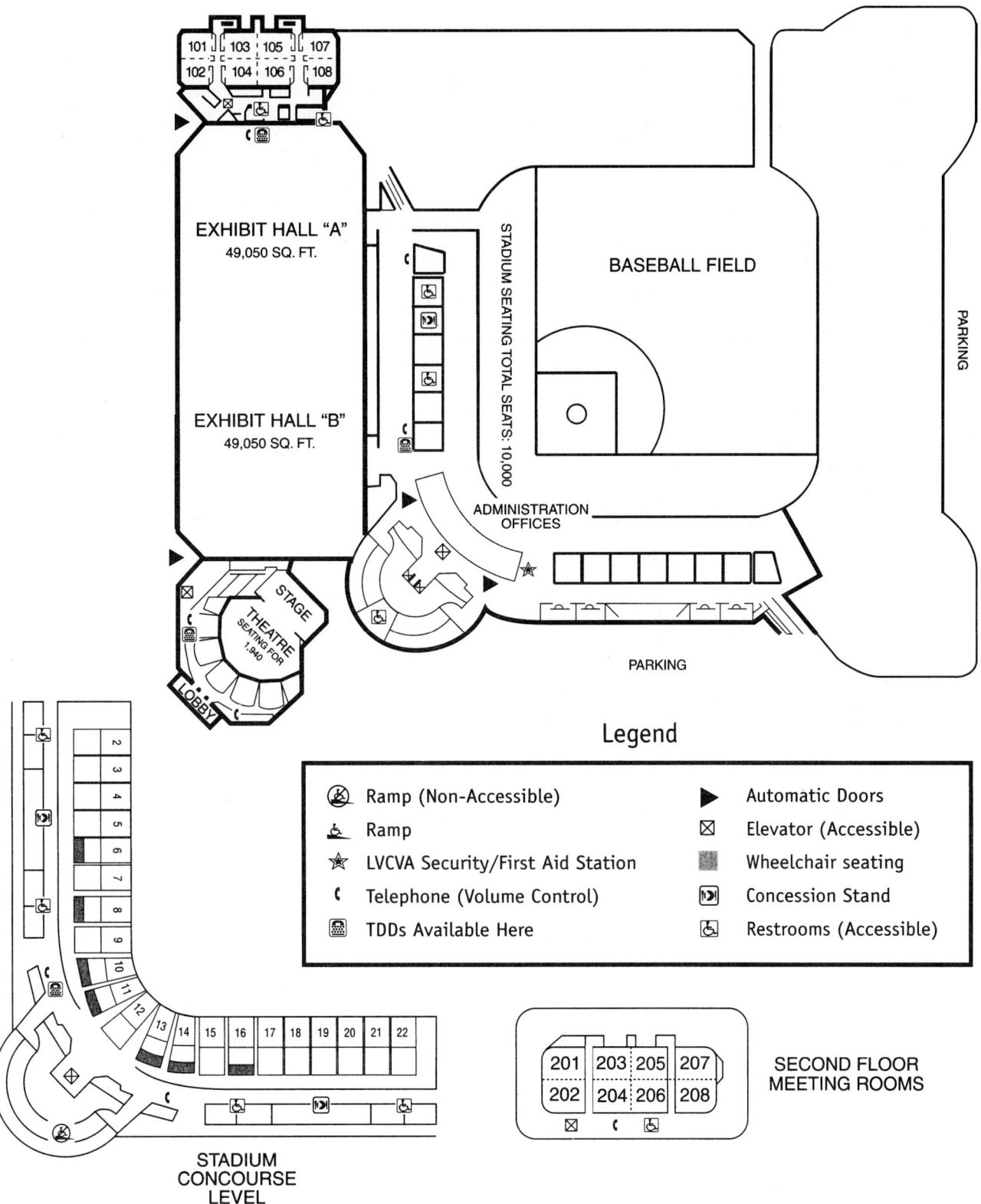

Legend

- ⊘ Ramp (Non-Accessible)
- ♿ Ramp
- ★ LVCVA Security/First Aid Station
- ℂ Telephone (Volume Control)
- ⌨ TDDs Available Here

- ▶ Automatic Doors
- ⊠ Elevator (Accessible)
- ▓ Wheelchair seating
- ▷ Concession Stand
- ♿ Restrooms (Accessible)

SECOND FLOOR MEETING ROOMS

STADIUM CONCOURSE LEVEL

CASHMAN FIELD CENTER

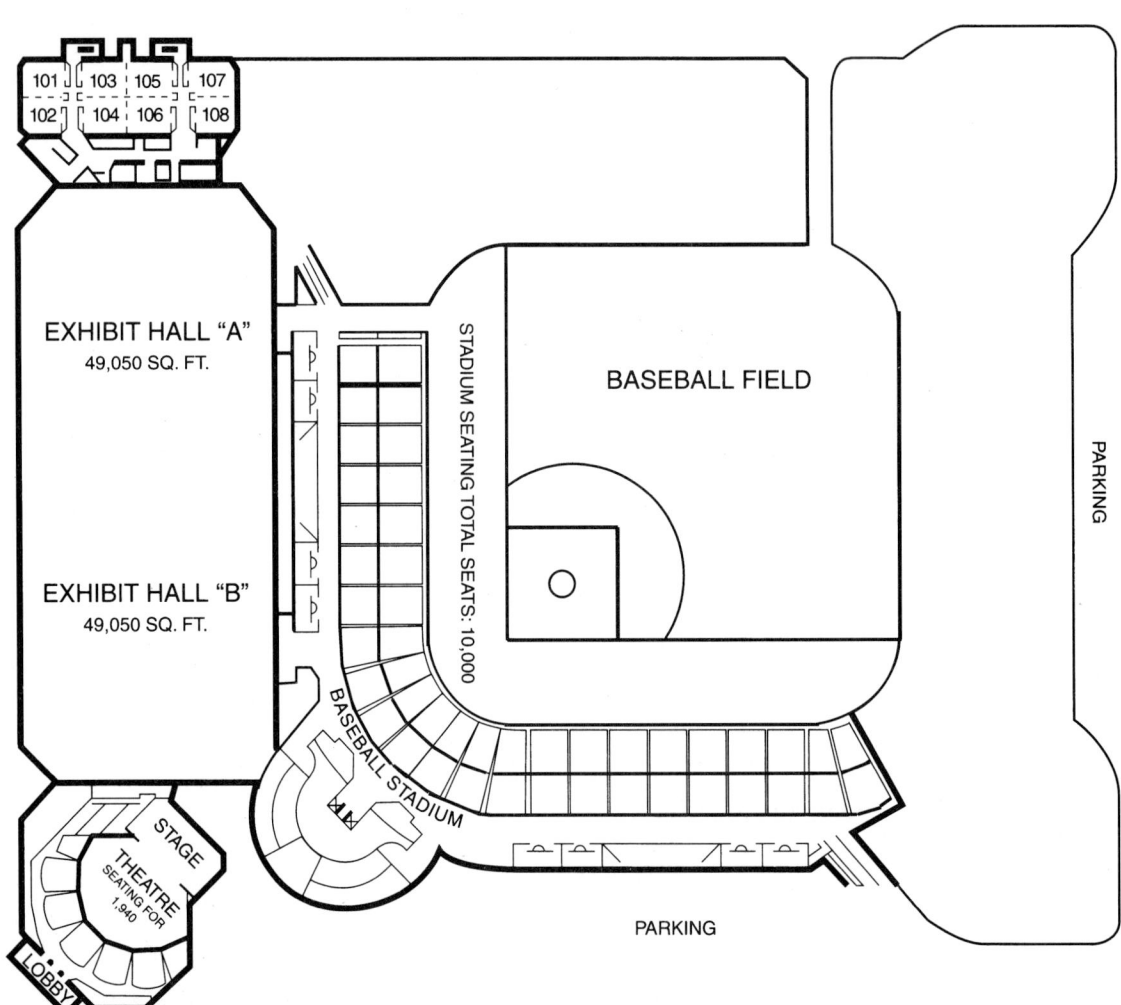

CASHMAN EXHIBIT HALLS A & B

SQUARE FEET	MINIMUM CEILING HEIGHT	ELECTRIC ROLL-UP DOOR	HANGAR DOOR
98,100	2/3 @ 35' 1/3 @ 25'	2 - 7' 9" x 30'	2 - 24' x 28' 1 - 24' x 24'

CASHMAN MEETING ROOMS

ROOM FEET	SQUARE CEILING HEIGHT	MINIMUM THEATER STYLE	SEATING
101-2	1,083 each	12'	100 each
103-4-5-6	1,113 each	12'	100 each
107-8	1,083 each	12'	100 each
201-2	1,083 each	12' 6"	100 each
203-4-5-6	1,113 each	12' 6"	100 each
207-8	1,083 each	12' 6"	100 each

UTILITIES

Air conditioning, water, natural gas, steam electric (120V single-phase, 208V single and three-phase, 480V single and three-phase with unlimited capacity), modern telephone system, overhead lighting throughout.

MEETING ROOMS

8 Meeting Rooms – First Floor
8 Meeting Rooms – Second Floor
Single Meeting Rooms – 16 at 1,083 square feet each
Double Meeting Rooms – 8 at 2,166 square feet each
Quadruple Meeting Rooms – 2 at 4,453 square feet each

SANDS EXPO CENTER

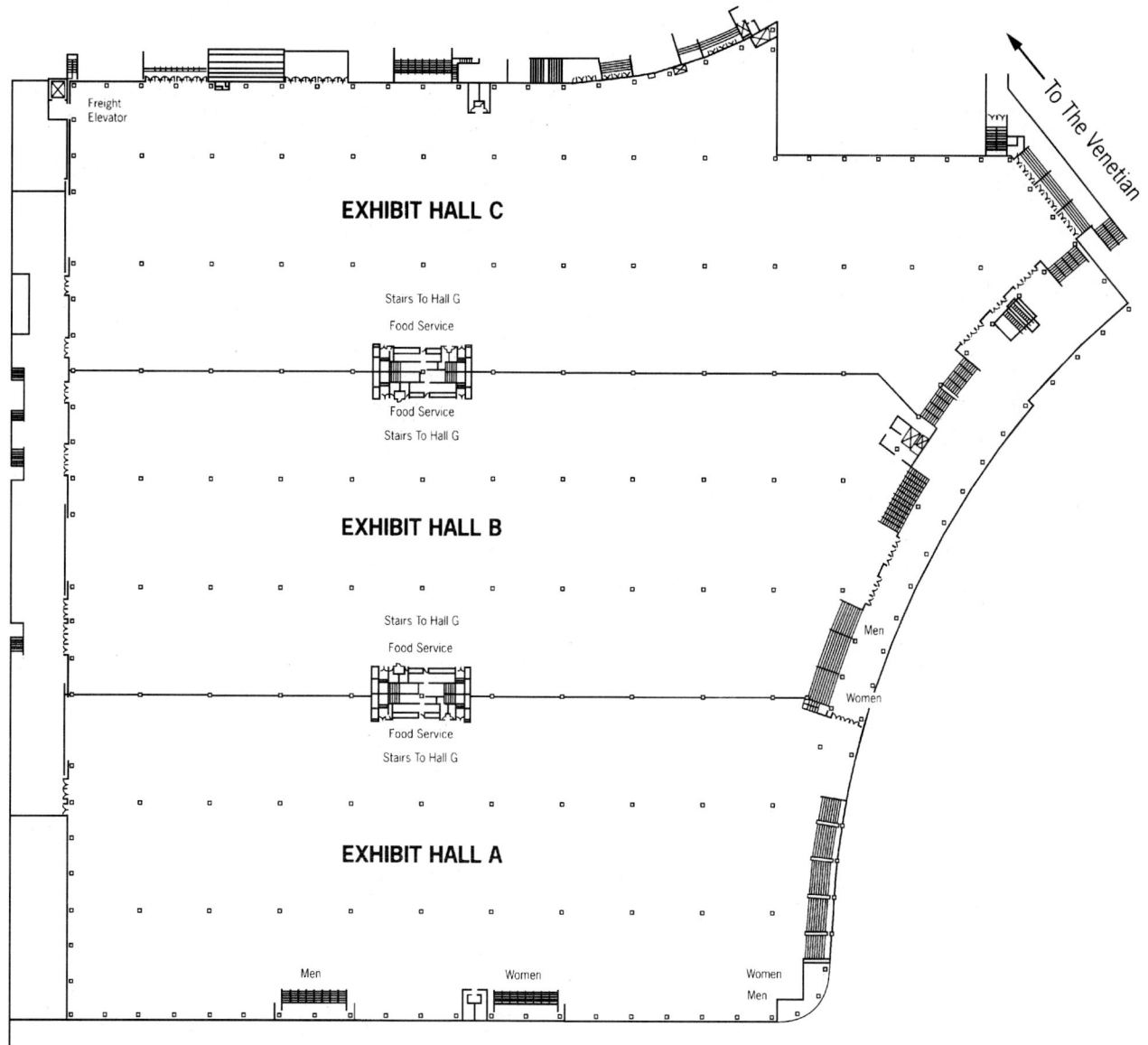

EXHIBIT HALL C

Stairs To Hall G

Food Service

Food Service

Stairs To Hall G

EXHIBIT HALL B

Stairs To Hall G

Food Service

Food Service

Stairs To Hall G

EXHIBIT HALL A

Freight
Elevator

To The Venetian

Men

Women

Men

Women

Women

Men

UPPER LEVEL

Experience Las Vegas

SANDS EXPO CENTER

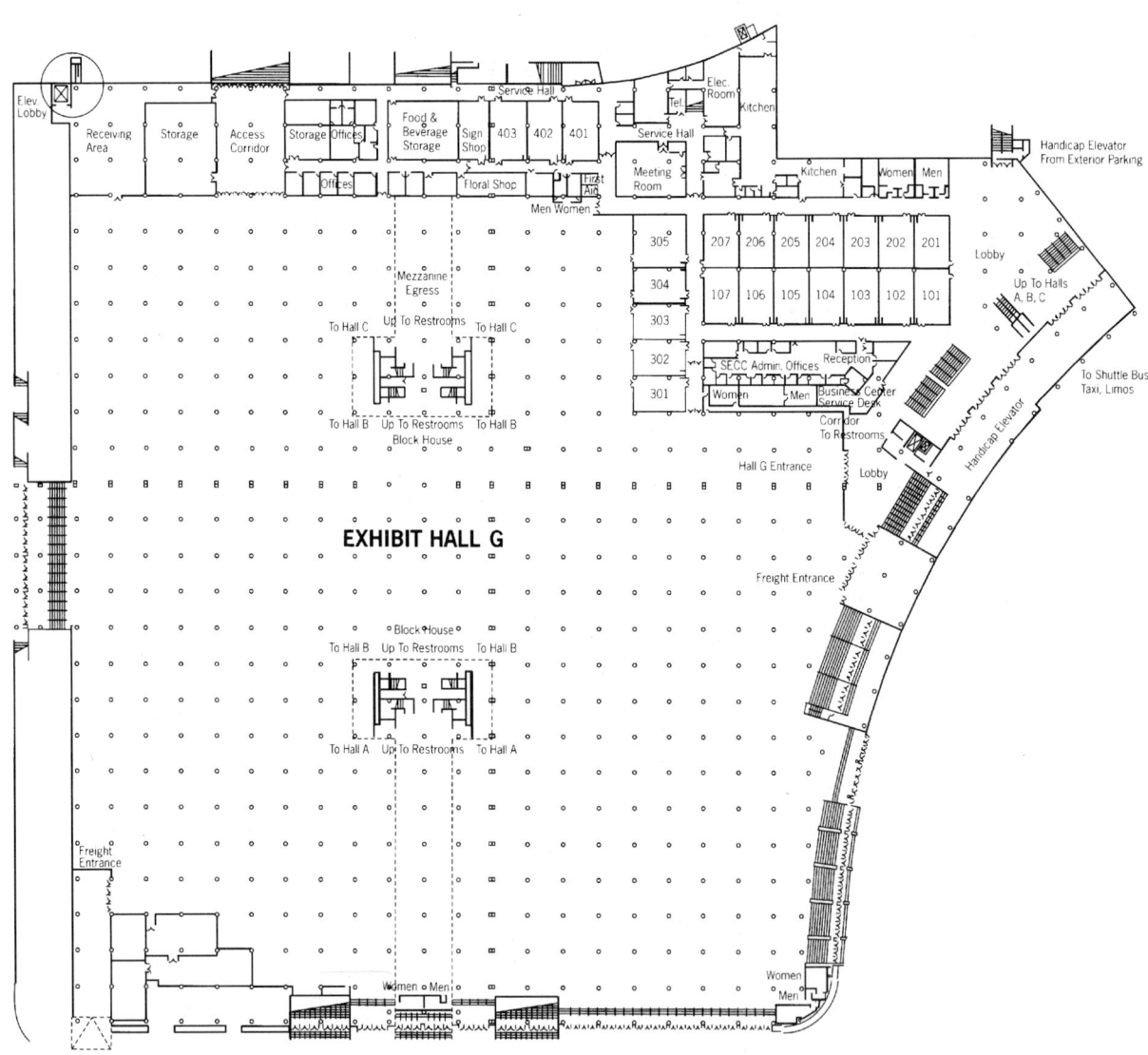

STREET LEVEL

SANDS EXPO CENTER

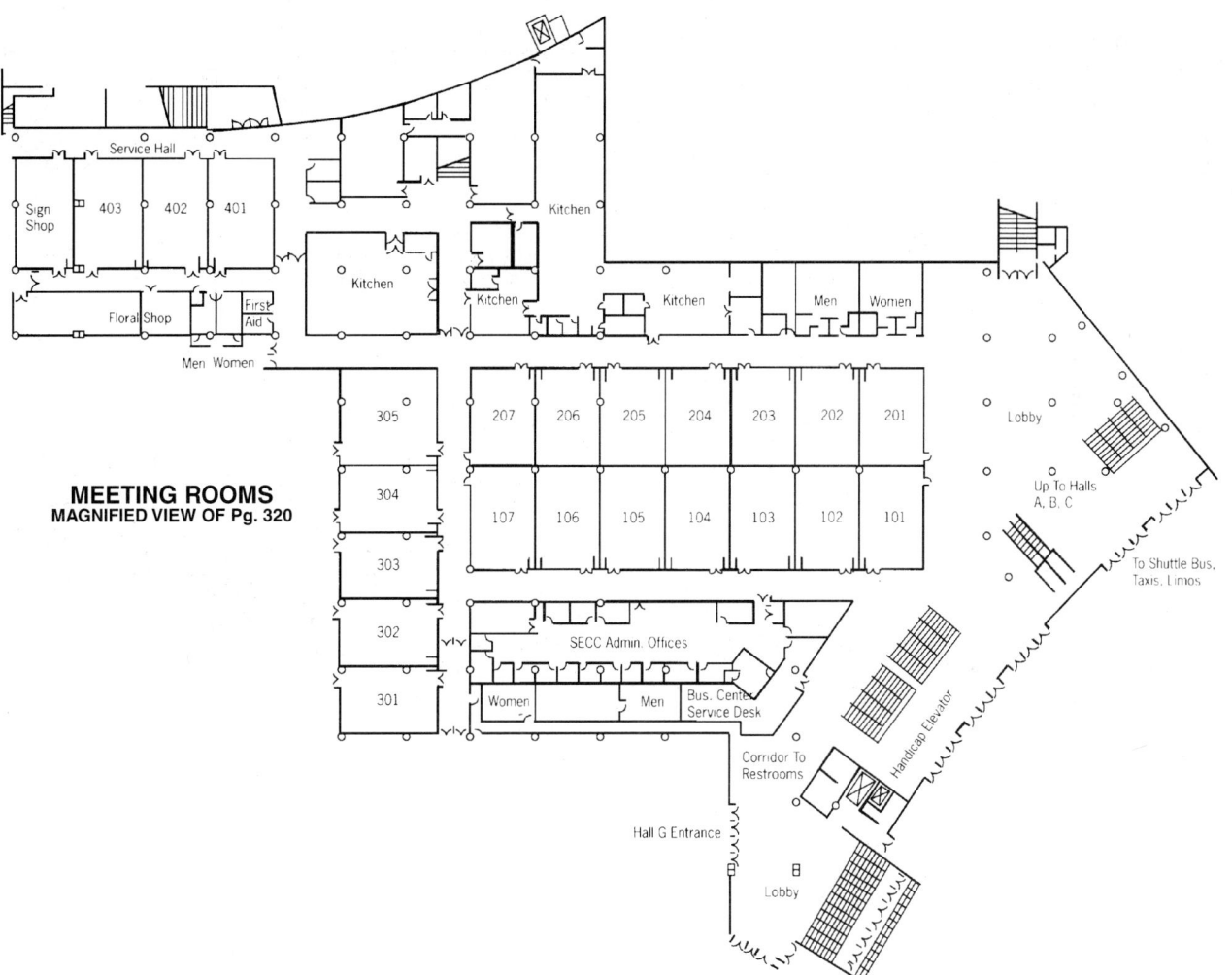

MEETING ROOMS
MAGNIFIED VIEW OF Pg. 320

STREET LEVEL

CONVENTION

SANDS EXPO CENTER

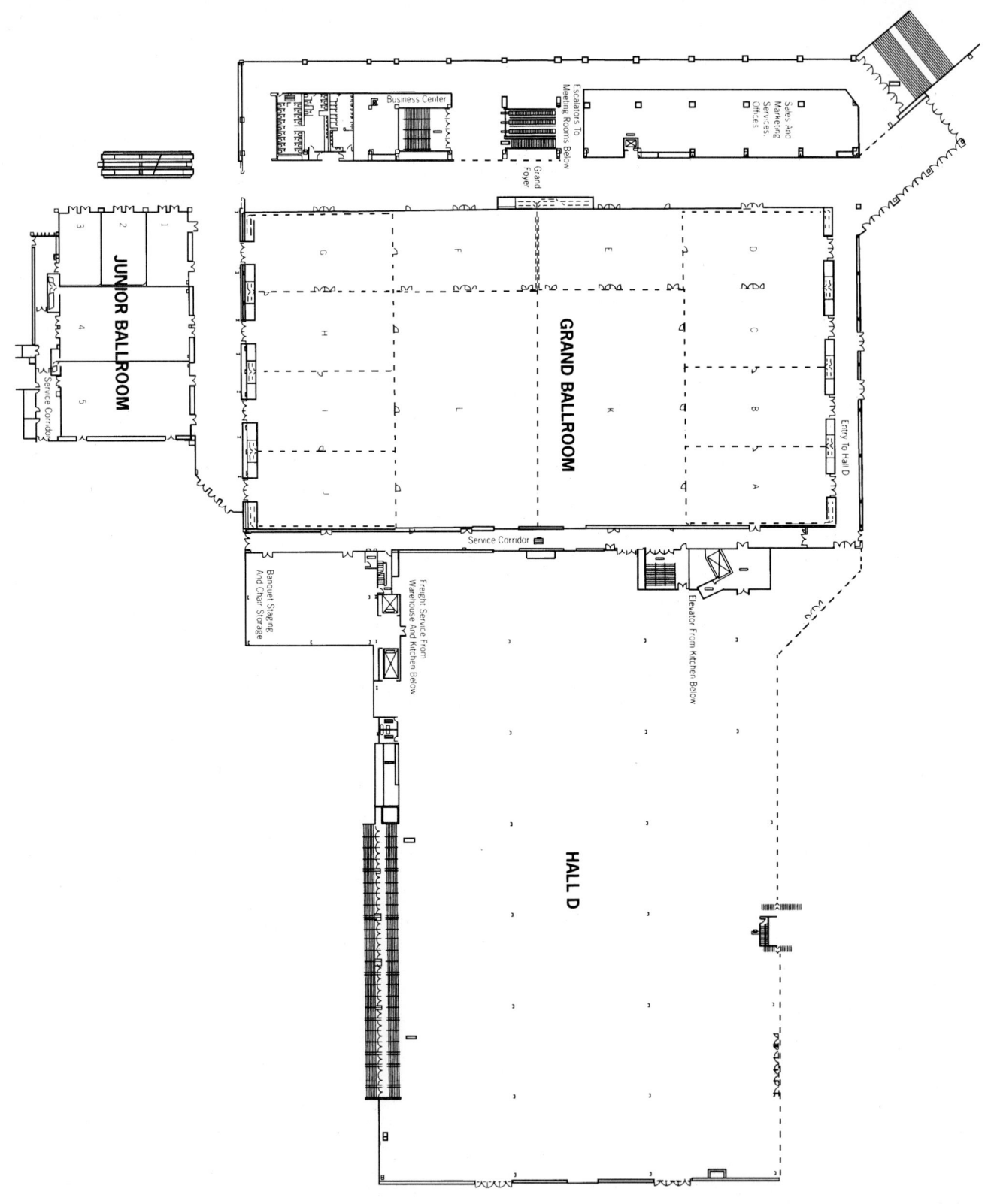

UPPER LEVEL

SANDS EXPO CENTER

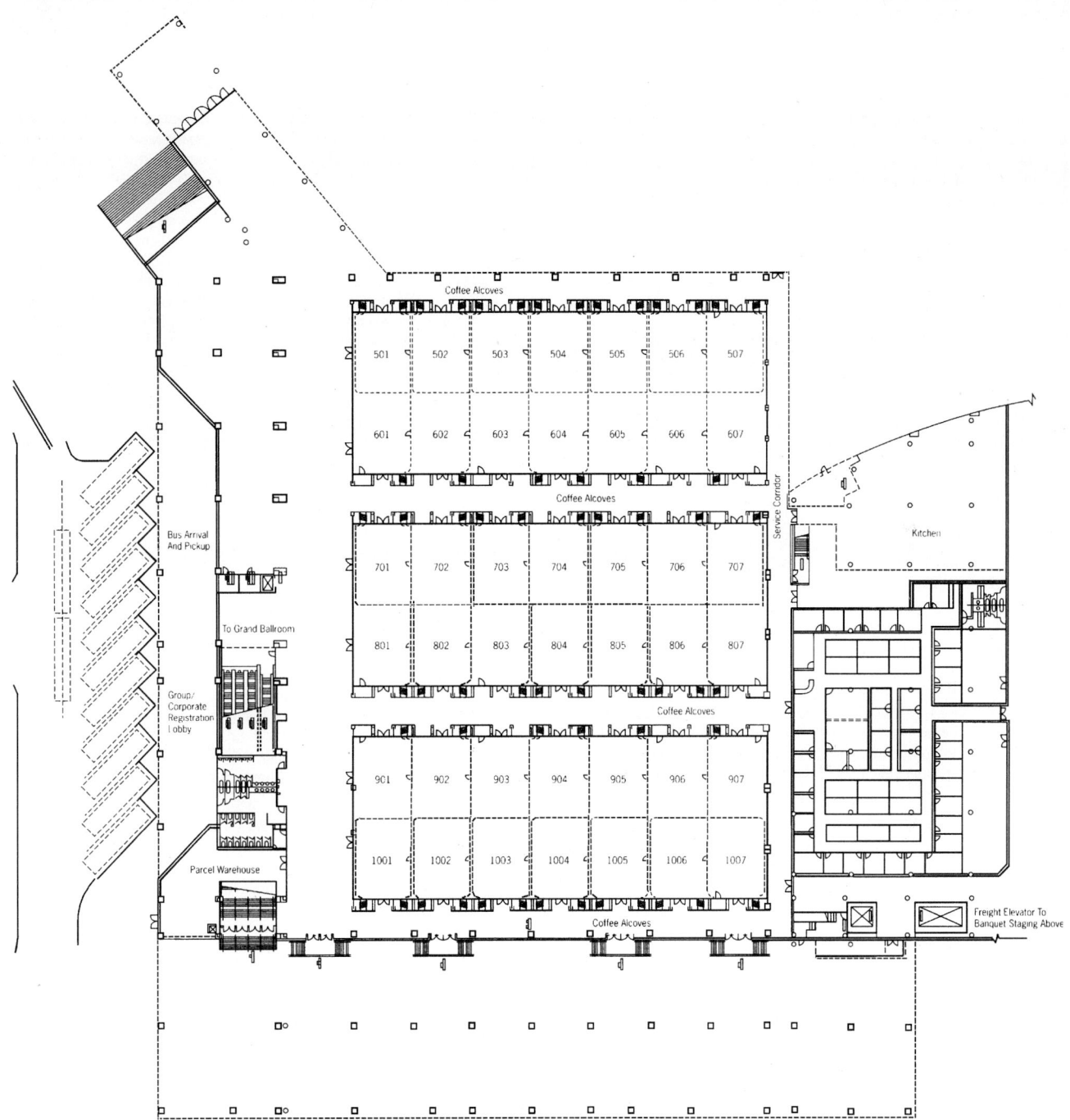

STREET LEVEL

1998 CONVENTION CALENDAR

JANUARY

2 - 7	*Western Beauty Rep. Assn., Tropicana *National:* 800
8 - 11	Consumer Electronic Show, Conv. Ctr., various *National:* 100,000
16 - 18	*Model-T Ford Club, Imperial Palace *National:* 200
16 - 22	*Cotter & Co., Bally's *National:* 1,100
18 - 20	Limousine & Chauffeur Trade Show, MGM Grand *National:* 3,000
18 - 21	Giftsource West Las Vegas, Sands Expo *National:* 10,000
18 - 21	Souvenir Super Show, Sands Expo, various *National:* 50,000
18 - 22	*Minnesota Credit Union League, Stardust *National:* 360
19 - 21	Nightclub & Bar Convention & Trade Show, Bally's *National:* 10,000
19 - 21	Cottage Industry Miniature Trade Assn., Riviera *National:* 1,000
19 - 22	Club Managers Assn. of America, Conv. Ctr., LV Hilton *National:* 3,400
23 - 26	*Hall Kinion Inc., Bellagio *National:* 1,000
27 - 30	Shooting Hunting Outdoor Trade Show & Convention, Conv. Ctr.-LV Hilton *National:* 35,000
28 - 2/2	*Contact Lens Assn. of Ophthalmologists, MGM Grand *National:* 1,500

FEBRUARY

1 - 5	*Exhibitor Show, Bally's *National:* 4,800
2 - 3	*New Vision Endodontics
2 - 4	*Inside Self-Storage Expo, Tropicana *National:* 2,800
2 - 5	*Western Veterinary Conf., Riviera *International:* 14,000
2 - 6	*Affiliated Manufactures Home Dealers, Harrah's *International:* 60
6 - 8	Non-Commissioned Officers Assn. of the USA, Bally's *National:* 50
7 - 10	*SuperValu Stores, Inc., MGM Grand *National:* 300
8 - 11	Natl. Roofing Contractors Assn., Conv. Ctr.-LV Hilton *National:* 8,000
8 - 11	Western Shoe Associates, Sands Expo *National:* 25,000
9 - 1	*Electric West, Conv. Ctr., LV Hilton *National:* 5,000
9 - 12	Comptel/Conferon, Bally's *National:* 1,500
10 - 12	Natl. Grocers Assn., Conv. Ctr., Bally's *National:* 5,000
13 - 16	Southern California Volleyball Assn., Cashman Field *Regional:* 3,000
15 - 18	*Western Sizzlin' Inc., Mirage *National:* 500
15 - 20	World Aquaculture Society, Bally's *National:* 2,500
17 - 20	Men's Apparel Guild in California, Conv. Ctr., LV Hilton *National:* 10,000
17 - 20	*Women's Apparel Vegas, Riviera, various *International:* 5,000
17 - 20	*Western Petroleum Marketers Assn., MGM Grand *Regional:* 3,000
18 - 20	*Broadcast Cable Financial Mgmt. Assn., Tropicana *National:* 300
22 - 25	Intl. Festivals & Events, Luxor *International:* 300
22 - 26	Associated Surplus Dealers, Sands Expo, LV Hilton *National:* 50,000
22 - 27	*Creative Painting Show, Tropicana, various *National:* 8,000
23 - 25	*Stan A. Huber Consultants Inc., Monte Carlo *National:* 40
26 - 28	*Pipeliner's Reunion Group, Riviera *National:* 300

MARCH

1 - 5	Osteopathic Physicians & Surgeons of Ca., Bally's *National:* 6,000
1 - 5	*Re/max Intl. Inc., Bally's *National:* 6,000
2 - 5	*Electronic Realty Associates Inc., Mirage *International:* 4,000
2 - 6	Snowsports Industries of America, Conv. Ctr., various *National:* 28,000
2 - 9	Natl. Child Care Assn., Riviera *National:* 1,300
5 - 8	Natl Assn. of Dental Labs, Bally's *National:* 300
5 - 9	*Truly Nolen, Bally's *National:* 100
7 - 12	Intl. Franchise Assn., MGM Grand *National:* 800
9 - 12	National Postal Forum, LV Hilton *National:* 6,300
9 - 12	*Telecard World, Caesars Palace, Riviera *National:* 8,000
11 - 14	*American Feed Industry Assn., Riviera *National:* 500
12 - 14	Natl. Truck Equipment Assn., Conv. Ctr., HDQ TBA *National:* 4,000
12 - 15	Assn. of Chiropractic Colleges, Alexis Park *National:* 500
12 - 15	*Allstate Insurance Co./Incentive, Treasure Island *International:* 300
15 - 19	*Global Sports Vacation Inc./ Lady Luck Cup, Santa Fe, various *National:* 400
16 - 19	Sun Refining & Marketing Co., Bally's *National:* 2,600
16 - 22	American College of Legal Medicine, Tropicana *National:* 360
17 - 19	Natl. Assn. of Pizza Operators Inc., Conv. Ctr., MGM Grand *National:* 12,000
17 - 20	*Assn. for Financial Technology, MGM Grand *National:* 150
19 - 25	Automotive Oil Change Assn., MGM Grand *National:* 1,100
20 - 25	Soc. of Permanent Cosmetic Professionals, Harrah's *National:* 250
23 - 25	Assn. for Computer Operations Management, Conv. Ctr., Bally's *National:* 3,500
23 - 25	American Home Sewing & Craft Assn., Bally's *National:* 3,000
24 - 26	Pacific Equipment & Technology Expo, Conv. Ctr., LV Hilton *National:* 5,000
27 - 31	Miller Brewing Co., LV Hilton *National:* 500
27 - 4/2	*Parts Plus AAAD, MGM Grand *National:* 2,000

APRIL

1 - 3	*Intl. Data Base Mgmt. Assn., Riviera *International:* 3,000
2 - 5	Calif. Society of Pediatric Dentists, Tropicana *National:* 300
4 - 12	*Global Sports Vacation Inc./Lady Luck Cup, Santa Fe Various *National:* 400
5 - 10	*Natl. Assn. of Campus Card Users, Tropicana *National:* 1,000
5 - 10	*Natl. Independent Automobile Dealers Assn., MGM Grand *National:* 700
6 - 9	*Natl. Assn. of Broadcasters, Con. Ctr., LV Hilton *National:* 90,000
10 - 12	*Intl. Principals Conversations, Caesars Palace *National:* 300
14 - 16	*Natl. Manufactured Housing Congress, Caesars Palace *National:* 1,300
14 - 20	American Salvage Pool Assn., Tropicana *International:* 200
16 - 19	Natl. Science Teachers Assn., Conv. Ctr., LV Hilton *National:* 15,000
19 - 21	*American Resort Development Assn., Bally's *National:* 2,100
19 - 23	*Webber Supply, Monte Carlo *National:* 200
22 - 24	Intl. Wireless Communications Expo, Conv. Ctr., LV Hilton *National:* 8,000
22 - 26	Altrusa Intl., Harrah's *International:* 100
23 - 26	*Mountain West Council of Optometrists, Bally's *National:* 1,800
24 - 25	Nevada State Education Assn., Desert Inn *Regional:* 220
24 - 26	*Omega Psi Phi Fraternity Inc., Riviera *National:* 500
25 - 29	Natl. Systems Contractors Assn., Conv. Ctr., LV Hilton *National:* 6,000
26 - 29	*YMCA of the USA, Bally's *National:* 550
27 - 29	Natl. Art Materials Trade Assn., Conv. Ctr., LV Hilton *International:* 4,000
27 - 30	Thorn Emi Rental Americas (Rent-A-Center), Bally's *National:* 1,800
29 - 5/1	*Parcel Shippers Assn., Alexis Park *National:* 200
30 - 5/3	*Greater Beneficial Union of Pittsburgh, Harrah's *National:* 150

MAY

4 - 6	*Professional Insurance Agents of CA/NV, Tropicana *Regional:* 350
4 - 8	Instrument Society of America, Sahara *National:* 500
4 - 8	Networld+Interop, Conv. Ctr., *National:* 60,000
6 - 8	Futureshow, Bally's *National:* 3,000
14 - 16	*Academy of General Dentistry, Alexis Park *National:* 40
17 - 21	Newspaper Purchasing Management Assn. Inc., Harrah's *National:* 125
19 - 21	*Intl. Council of Shopping Centers, Conv. Ctr., *International:* 30,000
25 - 28	Ice Skating Institute of America, Mirage *National:* 600
27 - 29	*Intl. Lighting & Expo Conference, Conv. Ctr., Mirage *International:* 10,000
29 - 6/4	Soc. for In Vitro Biology, Bally's
31 - 6/3	Writing Instrument Manufacturers Assn., Inc., Bally's *National:* 350

JUNE

7 - 10	Daughters of the Nile, Bally's *National:* 5,000
10 - 13	Intl. Silk Flower Show, Conv. Ctr., LV Hilton *National:* 10,000
10 - 14	*Office Network, Alexis Park *National:* 800
16 - 19	*Nevada School Food Service Assn., Harrah's *Regional:* 300
18 - 20	Natl. Apartment Assn., Conv. Ctr., LV Hilton *National:* 5,000
19 - 21	*U.S. Junior Chamber of Congress, Imperial Palace *National:* 400
19 - 26	Controlled Release Society, Mirage *National:* 1,400
20 - 23	Giftsource West Las Vegas, Sands Expo, TBA *National:* 10,000
22 - 25	U.S. Junior Chamber of Commerce, Conv. Ctr., MGM Grand, Bally's *National:* 5,500
26 - 7/4	Western Dredging Assn., Mirage *National:* 1,200
27 - 29	Karel Exposition Management, Sands Expo *National:* 5,000
27 - 7/4	*Institute of Internal Auditors, Stardust *National:* 280
28 - 7/1	Natl. Environmental Health Assn., Riviera *National:* 850

JULY

1 - 4	Intl. Bowling Pro Shop Assn., Riviera *International:* 500
6 - 9	*Mine Safety & Health Administration, Stardust *National:* 700
11 - 14	Natl. Assn. of College & University Business Officers, Bally's *National:* 2,500
13 - 21	*Amerisource Tradeshow, Conv. Ctr., LV Hilton *National:* 1,900
14 - 16	Intermountain Farmers Assn., Tropicana *Regional:* 400
19 - 23	Bakery, Confectionery & Tobacco Workers, Riviera *National:* 800
20 - 23	Natl. Conference of State Legislators, Conv. Ctr., LV Hilton *National:* 7,000
26 - 31	Sigma Gamma Rho Sorority Inc, *National:* 800
27 - 31	Natl. Assn. of Letter Carriers, Conv. Ctr., LV Hilton *National:* 16,000
31 - 8/7	Improved Benevolent Protective Order of Elks of the World, Cashman Field *International:* 16,000

AUGUST

5 - 9   The Drifters Inc., Flamingo Hilton *National:* 500
6 - 9   Beauty & Barber Supply Institute, Conv. Ctr., LV Hilton
      National: 16,000
9 - 12   *School Transportation News, Riviera *National:* 900
10 - 13   *United Steel Workers of America, Conv. Ctr., MGM Grand
      National: 5,000
12 - 23   American Accounting Assn., Bally's *National:* 5,000
16 - 20   Associated Surplus Dealers, Sands Expo, Various *National:* 32,000
22 - 27   *Disabled American Veterans, LV Hilton *National:* 5,000
23 - 28   *Women Marines Assn., Stardust *National:* 500
27 - 30   Western Shoe Associates, Sands Expo, Various *National:* 25,000
31 - 9/3   *Men's Apparel Guild in California, Conv. Ctr, LV Hilton
      National: 90,000

SEPTEMBER

8 - 12   Natl. Assn. of Dental Laboratories, Bally's *National:* 800
10 - 16   *Defense Credit Union Council Cone, Riviera *National:* 1,000
14 - 15   Tortilla Industry Assn., Bally's *International:* 700
14 - 16   American Public Works Assn., Conv. Ctr., TBA *National:* 11,000
22 - 25   World Gaming Congress & Expo, Conv. Ctr., LV Hilton
      National: 22,000
27 - 10/3   Intl. Assn. of Hydrologists, Riviera *National:* 600

OCTOBER

4 - 7   Intl. Foundation of Employee Benefit Plans, HDQ TBA
      International: 10,000
6 - 8   Intl. Sanitary Supply Assn., Conv. Ctr., LV Hilton *National:* 10,000
11 - 15   *Assn. of State Dam Safety Officials, Riviera *National:* 650
17 - 20   Advertising Media Credit Executives Assn., Tropicana
      International: 150
18 - 23   United Union of Roofers Waterproofers & Allied Workers,
      Riviera *National:* 600

19 - 21   Natl. Electrical Contractors Assn., Conv. Ctr., LV Hilton
      National: 8,000
19 - 21   Natl. Business Aircraft Assn., Conv. Ctr., LV Hilton *National:* 20,000
22 - 24   Diocesan Conference, Cashman Field, Boulder Station
      Regional: 1,500
22 - 25   Natl. Assn. of Retail Collection Attorneys, Bally's *National:* 350
25 - 27   Assn. for Services Management Intl., Conv. Ctr., LV Hilton
      National: 1,000
26 - 29   Nursing Education Institute, Tropicana *National:* 1,000

NOVEMBER

3 - 6   Specialty Equipment Market Assn., Conv. Ctr, *National:* 60,000
3 - 6   *APAA/ASIA/MEMA/APAA, MGM Grand/Sands, Bally's/Sands
      Mirage/Sands *National:* 65,000
3 - 6   Automotive Warehouse Distributors Assn. Inc., Mirage
      National: 3,000
16 - 19   Softbank Comdex, Conv. Ctr., various *International:* 210,000
19 - 23   Natl. Chrysanthemum Society *National:* 200
29 - 12/2   *Soc. of California Accountants, Bally's *National:* 600

DECEMBER

2 - 6   U. S. Custom Harvesters Inc., Alexis Park *National:* 700
6 - 8   *Pacific Lodging Congress, Mirage *National:* 400
6 - 9   Entomological Society of America/American Phytopathological,
      LV Hilton *National:* 5,150
6 - 9   *American Academy of Otolaryngic Allergy, Mirage *National:* 250
13 - 17   Natl. Federation of State H.S. Assn., LV Hilton *National:* 2,800
14 - 16   National Ground Water Assn., Conv. Ctr, LV Hilton *National:* 5,000
16 - 20   U.S. Table Tennis Assn., Conv. Ctr, various *National:* 2,800

* New Booking

CONVENTION SUPPORT SERVICES

ADVERTISING

Collegiate Graphics
2901 S. Highland Dr., Ste. 12A
Las Vegas, NV 89109
737-0771
Jim Simonson
Screen printed T-shirts, sweatshirts, caps and visors

Desert Specialties, Inc.
3900 Schiff Dr.
Las Vegas, NV 89103
253-0450
Mike Pearlmutter, Pres.
Novelties and custom imprinted sportswear

Logo-Motion
8812 Silver Mountain Ct.
Las Vegas, NV 89134
256-8836
Robin Bernazzani, Pres.
Advertising specialty items

Ocean Desert Sales
2901 S. Highland Dr., Bldg. 4
Las Vegas, NV 89109
384-0606
John LaFronz, Dir. of Operations
Custom screen printing done on premises, T-shirts, caps, visors, etc.

AUDIO VISUAL / LIGHTING

A-1 Audio
3780 Scripps Way
Las Vegas, NV 89103
364-0203
Tony Caporale, Mgr.
Audio, video, film equipment and P.A. systems; specialized entertainment and production equipment and fabrication

American Audio Access Recording Services
804 Vincent Way
Las Vegas, NV 89128
363-6150
La Nae MacBan, Pres.
Record conventions, high speed cassette duplicating

AVW Audio Visual Inc.
7000 Placid St., Ste. 102
Las Vegas, NV 89119
263-1484
Hoagie Herman, Gen. Mgr.
Professional audiovisual rental company

Broadcast Productions, Inc.
6020 W. Flamingo Rd., Ste. 14
Las Vegas, NV 89103
227-5252
Tony Sacca, Mgr.
Full service video/television company from concept to completion

Cinema Services of Las Vegas
4445 S. Valley View Blvd.
Las Vegas, NV 89103
876-4667
Barbara Brennan Deibert, Pres.
Sell and rent lighting equipment for theaters, films and movies

Encore Productions
3285 W. Tompkins Ave.
Las Vegas, NV 89103
739-8803
Phil Cooper, Pres.
Full service production company
Audiovisual rentals, staging, lighting

Goodwyn Production Group
2626 S. Rainbow Blvd., Ste. 104
Las Vegas, NV 89102
363-2260

MaryAnn Ferguson, Pres.
Norm Nusbaum, Dir./Cameraman
Beta Cam SP video for broadcast and business

GES Audio Visual
3300 Bircher Dr.
Las Vegas, NV 89118
263-3711
Jeff Abodeely, Gen. Mgr.
Sound and lighting effects

Infovision
3111 S. Valley View Blvd., Ste. A217
Las Vegas, NV 89102
227-8439
Michael Otero, Pres.
State-of-the-art video film and television production services specializing in 16mm-35mm productions

J R Lighting
236 S. Rainbow Blvd., Ste. 480
Las Vegas, NV 89128-5329
363-2220
Jim Reid, Pres.
Booth lighting

Kilby's Video Productions
3871 S. Valley View Blvd., Ste. 23
Las Vegas, NV 89103
736-6461
Darryl Kilby, Pres.
Television production

Laguna Productions
2708 S. Highland Dr.
Las Vegas, NV 89109
731-5600
Douglas Momary, Pres.
Television production

Las Vegas Video & Sound Rentals, Inc.
4221 Thiriot St.
Las Vegas, NV 89103
362-4660
Larry Hamm, Pres.
Rent and sell audiovisual equipment; provide material for conventions, rental

Masterpiece Productions
2340 Paseo Del Prado, Ste. D202
Las Vegas, NV 89102
438-7005
Sharon Marie Houlihan
Concept to completion, film/tape productions

Media Solutions
4301 S. Valley View Blvd., Ste. 20
Las Vegas, NV 89103
871-0570
Billy Graham, Pres.
Audiovisual rentals

Multivision Video & Film
4291 Polaris Ave.
Las Vegas, NV 89103
798-8802
Bob Berkowitz, Pres.
Video walls

COMDEX

Comdex is the largest trade show in the United States. Over 2,200 exhibitors and 200,000 delegates attend each November. The COMDEX founder, Sheldon Adelson, sold COMDEX to Tokyo-based Softbank Corporation for $800 million cash.

CONVENTION

CONVENTION SUPPORT SERVICES

NTV Productions
5665 S. Valley View Blvd., Ste. 4
Las Vegas, NV 89118
795-2688
Nancy Turney, Pres.
Video tape duplication

Post Digital
1771 E. Flamingo Rd., Ste. 206A
Las Vegas, NV 89119
734-0001
Jerry Wayne, Pres.
Digital audio and video editing

SGA Production Staging
4601 E. Cheyenne Ave., Ste. 101
Las Vegas, NV 89115
643-8141
Mark Reed, Pres.
Audience risers and full scale audio and lighting

TVM Studios
3230 W. Hacienda Ave.
Las Vegas, NV 89118
261-0051
Ted V. Mikels, Pres.
Complete film and video productions and post facilities

Transfer West Duplication
6000 S. Eastern Ave., Ste. 10-I
Las Vegas, NV 89119
895-9900
Rob Retting, General Mgr.
Las Vegas's premier video and audio duplicating facility

Vegas Post Group
721 E. Charleston Blvd., Ste. 2
Las Vegas, NV 89104
388-0277
Raul Romero, Pres.
Professional video editing and duplication

Video Transfers
6224 Brittany Way
Las Vegas, NV 89107
870-9110
Edward Malkiewicz, Pres.
Tape to tape transfers 8mm-16mm film to BHS; European conversions

Vincent Video Resources
500 N. Rainbow Blvd., Ste. 300
Las Vegas, NV 89107
221-1956   Fax - 221-1901
Fabian Vincent, Pres.
Complete video and film production; duplicating and packing services available

Vision Control
4535 W. Russell Rd., Unit 1
Las Vegas, NV 89118
222-0877
Randy Premetz, Pres.
Advanced display systems; video walls, projection cubes, data display

Visual Concepts Displays
4682 Via Torino St.
Las Vegas, NV 89103
871-8191
Peter Schmitt, Pres.
Display work, props and theme parties

Z A V Services
4275 W. Bell Dr., Ste. 7
Las Vegas, NV 89118-1753
248-6770   1-800-370-6770
Sharon Dow, Mgr.
Video and audio display systems

BANQUET ROOMS
(See Restaurant Section)

BUSINESS SERVICES

USA Hosts Business Services
3150 Paradise Rd., Ste. 100
Las Vegas, NV 89109
(located inside the Las Vegas Convention Center)
735-1963   Fax: 735-2145
Liz Halamka, Gen. Mgr.
Hours: Mon. - Fri. 9 am - 5 pm, as well as show hours.
Equipment rental:
Cellular phones $5 per day plus $1.50 per minute airtime including long distance 486 and 586.
Thermal fax machine $140 for show plus phone line.
IBM computer and printer pricing on request.
Standard desktop copier $275 for show.
Support personnel: Four hour minimum and advance notice required.
Receptionist $10/hour and up
Data entry $12/hour and up
Secretary $15/hour and up
Desktop publisher $20/hour and up
Interpreter $30/hour and up
Other services:
Office supplies, copies, color transparencies, conference room rental, office equipment rental, self-service fax machine, computer time, business card printing machine

Business Centers of Las Vegas Convention Center-USA Hosts
1055 E. Tropicana Ave., Ste. 625
Las Vegas, NV 89119
798-0000
Kathleen Spurney, Gen. Mgr.
Equipment rentals and temporary labor for conventions.

CATERING
(See Restaurant Section)

Connecting Point
2905 W. Charleston Blvd.
Las Vegas, NV 89102

COMMUNICATIONS

A-AAA Radio Rentals
4640 S. Arville St., Ste. E
Las Vegas, NV 89103
253-5390
Jean McIntosh, Pres.
Cellular and radio rental

Action Page
3610 S. Highland Dr., Ste. C1
Las Vegas, NV 89103
873-7243
Barbara Volk, General Mgr.
Digital and voice pagers, short or long term leasing and rental, pick-up and delivery

AT&T Wireless Services
3763 Howard Hughes Pkwy.
Las Vegas, NV 89109
734-1010
Las Vegas Convention Center Business Center
Hand-held cellular phone rentals

Cellular City
4700 Paradise Rd., Ste. 2050
Las Vegas, NV 89109
873-2489   1-800-535-2489
Al Fasano, Pres.
Cellular phone rental, $3.00 per day with free pick-up and delivery

Crescent Communications
3430 Polaris Ave.
Las Vegas, NV 89102
361-1867
David Vargas, Rental Mgr.
Motorola 2 way radio rental

Las Vegas 2-Way Communications
4132 S. Rainbow Blvd., Ste. 322
Las Vegas, NV 89103
736-2186   1-800-397-1293
Ned Carey
Motorola radio rentals, cellular phones

Nextel Communications
3610 S. Highland Dr.
Las Vegas, NV 89103
873-5000   491-0103
Bob Mearns, General Mgr.
Radio paging, 2-way portable radio and radio repeating service, daily or weekly rental

COMPUTER

Best Computer Rentals
3867 Valley View Blvd., Ste. 6
Las Vegas, NV 89103
368-7784
John Swinford, Pres.
Computer rentals

Business Computer Rentals
3560 Polaris Ave., Ste. 23
Las Vegas, NV 89103
871-8009   1-888-222-1655
Charles Growden, Pres.
Computer renting and leasing

Connecting Point
2905 W. Charleston Blvd.
Las Vegas, NV 89102
870-6411
Brenda Cook, Pres.
Computer equipment and service department

Michada Computers
4080 Lake Mead Blvd., Ste. 100
Las Vegas, NV 89115
642-4444
Harold Ross, Pres.
Computers and computer parts

Personal Computer Rentals
1631 E. Desert Inn Rd.
Las Vegas, NV 89109
731-1880
Larry Laidlow, Pres.
Systems, monitors, peripherals, printers, local delivery and installation; technical assistance and support; daily, weekly, monthly

Strickland Business Systems
3145 W. Post Rd.
Las Vegas, NV 89118
896-1442
Rich Strickland, Pres.
Copier and fax rentals by the day or week

CONVENTION SERVICES

All American Convention Services
4050 W. Harmon Ave., Ste. 6
Las Vegas, NV 89103
227-0970
Scott Svinning, Pres.
Set-up, storage and rental

American Decorators
553 E. Twain Ave.
Las Vegas, NV 89109
737-0688
Marty Shadin, Pres.
Props, backdrops and theme parties

BMK Corporation
2232 S. Nellis Blvd.
Las Vegas, NV 89104-6213
431-9119
Betty Kostiner, Pres.
Packing and shipping, copy and fax service

Bradstreet Productions
4170 S. Decatur Blvd., Ste. D1
Las Vegas, NV 89103
876-1520   1-800-854-1555
Joe Jarred, Pres.
Video production and entertainment

Clear Span Tents
4275 Arcata Way
N. Las Vegas, NV 89030
642-0887
Jack Freestone, Gen. Mgr.
Tents and canopies for conventions and special events

Epic Enterprises of Nevada
2275A Renaissance Dr.
Las Vegas, NV 89119
795-3999
Robert Colvin, V/P
Convention program planners

GES Exposition Services
1624 Mojave Rd.
Las Vegas, NV 89104
457-5075
Daryl Clove, Gen. Mgr.
GES Exposition Services serves the trade show, special event and exposition industry with planning and design, freight handling, signage, installation and dismantling, custom and rental exhibits, carpet and furnishings and electrical, plumbing and audiovisual service. Headquartered in Las Vegas, GES is North America's leading trade show contractor, with 35 offices serving major markets in the U.S. and Canada.

Las Vegas Expo
3764 Scripps Dr.
Las Vegas, NV 89103
248-6200
Bob Cordaro, Pres.
Labor services

Nevada Association for the Handicapped
6200 W. Oakey Blvd.
Las Vegas, NV 89102
870-7050
Annie Baca
Packaging, light assembly and all mail services

Nevada Exhibitors Service
3305 Spring Mountain Rd., Ste. 60
Las Vegas, NV 89102
362-2273
Lee Robson, Jr., Pres.
Exhibit installation specialists

Patrick Signs
4420 Arville St., Ste. 27
Las Vegas, NV 89103
873-4463
Patrick Dean, Pres.

Plus Communications, Inc.
1455 E. Tropicana Ave., Ste. 175
Las Vegas, NV 89119-6507
736-5958
Harry Sleight, Pres.
Convention services, special events and meeting planning

Positive Show Solutions Technology
4065 S. Procyon Ave., Ste. D
Las Vegas, NV 89103
895-7778
Judith L. Pulizzano, Pres.
Labor to set up and dismantle, rental furniture, floral service, storage, transportation, full-service facility

Sho-Aids, Inc.
4050 W. Harmon Ave.
Las Vegas, NV 89103
735-5811
Andy Codamo, Pres.
Nationwide company specializing in shipping, installing, dismantling, tracing and storing exhibits

STS Display & Exhibit Group
3650 Ali Baba Ln., Ste. 103
Las Vegas, NV 89118
891-8777
Meg Merritt, Pres.
Set up and dismantling, graphics, booth staffing and training

Thorndike & Associates
3238 Oquendo Rd.
Las Vegas, NV 89120
454-9334
Teri Thorndike
Receptionists, models, demonstrators and dancers

Universal Event Services, Inc.
3220 Pepper Ln.
Las Vegas, NV 89120
458-0121   FAX 458-1228
Gerry Grouberi, Pres.
Exhibit labor and support services, carpet and furniture rental

USA Hosts
1055 E. Tropicana Ave., Ste. 625
Las Vegas, NV 89119

798-0000   1-800-634-6133
Fax: 702 597-0264
Gail Knowles, Vice Pres.
Arrangement of all necessary group services; hotel accommodations, airport transfers, specialized sightseeing tours, theme parties, entertainment and convention shuttles

Vegas Events
240 N. Jones Blvd., Ste. 212
Las Vegas, NV. 89107
233-3061   1-800-997-2708
Convention services and special events planning

Victoria's Destination Services
2929 E. Desert Inn Rd., Ste. 20
Las Vegas, NV 89121-3607
794-2492
Vicki Marshall, Pres.
Convention services, special events and meeting planning models, production department, theme parties, entertainers and speakers

COORDINATORS

Accent Las Vegas Inc.
P.O. Box 26115
Las Vegas, NV 89126-0115
870-0184
Caryl Mahaffey, Pres.
Full service DMC where service is perfection

Activity Planners Inc.
3110 Polaris Ave., Ste. 4
Las Vegas, NV 89102
362-8002
Karen Gordon, Pres.
Custom tours, spouse programs, theme parties, destination management

ASAP
3430 E. Flamingo Rd., Ste. 318
Las Vegas, NV 89121
458-0090
Sunny Barkley, Pres.

Full custom planning and arrangement services, group travel, airport greeting, shuttle, group tours, spouse and special interest programs, step-on guides, activities galore, special events

Baskow & Assoc.
2948 E. Russell Rd.
Las Vegas, NV 89120
733-7818
Jaki Baskow, Pres.
Spouse programs, party planners, celebrity lookalikes, models, actors, entertainers

Bass Creative Bookings
6188 S. Sandhill Rd.
Las Vegas, NV 89120
898-2277
Wendy Bass
Models, demonstrators and dance fashion shows

C A T S Inc.
1350 E. Flamingo Rd., Ste. 133
Las Vegas, NV 89119
739-8272
Nancy Goodwin, Pres.
Airport transfers, spouse programs, show reservations

Clayton Nicholas Design
3230 Polaris Ave., Ste. 6
Las Vegas, NV 89102
365-1233
Clay Nicholas, Pres.
Trimmers, display personnel, props and sets

Convention Services, Inc.
6235 Stevenson Way
Las Vegas, NV 89120
434-4124 Fax: 735-6942
Steve Cahill, Pres.
Install and dismantle booths

Convention Ease
3720 W. Desert Inn Rd., Ste. A
Las Vegas, NV 89102
365-1057
Gaya Trombley, Pres.
Models, interpreters, hostesses, show and restaurant reservations

Creative Concepts
3135 Industrial Rd., Ste. 212
Las Vegas, NV 89109
792-4111
Renee Hale-Pursel, Pres.
Party planning, models, entertainment

Creative Endeavors
2408 Chapman Dr.
Las Vegas, NV 89104-3455
731-2449
Thomas Licata, Pres.
Corporate meeting, special event planning, "Flair with care"

Dan Nelson Productions
6165 Harrison Dr., Ste. 10
Las Vegas, NV 89120
798-8909
Dan Nelson, Pres.
Custom theatrical productions, costumes, spouse programs, complete coordinating services and special events

Destinations by Design
145 E. Reno Ave., Ste. E8
Las Vegas, NV 89119
798-9555 Fax: 798-7641
Joyce Sherman, Pres.
Theme parties, props, casino nights, unique venues, entertainment, production, unique decor, models, spouse programs, show reservations, transportation, tours, special events

Exquisite Impressions
P.O. Box 72246
Las Vegas, NV 89170
898-9968
Gerald Robinson, Pres.
Special events coordinator

Farrington Productions
4350 Arville St., Ste. 27
Las Vegas, NV 89103
362-3000
Blair Farrington, Pres.
Full-service production company; corporate events, industrial shows, theme parties, special events, models, costumes, dancers and variety acts

GES Convention Service
1624 Mojave Rd.
Las Vegas, NV 89104
457-5075
Daryl Clove, Mgr.
Spouse programs, seminars, entertainment, hostesses, special events

Inventive Incentives
2210 E. Flamingo Rd., Ste. 300
Las Vegas, NV 89108
893-6444 Fax: 893-6413
Robyn Johnson, Pres.
Meeting planning, promotions, special events

Judy Venn & Associates, Inc.
3401 W. Charleston Blvd.
Las Vegas, NV 89102
259-4494
Lawanda Baldwin, Dir.
Temporary booth personnel broker, providing hostesses/hosts

Key Tours
3305 W. Spring Mountain Rd., Ste. 16
Las Vegas, NV 89102
732-4055 1-800-326-4053
Steve Lurenz, Pres.
Meet & greet service, transportation, baggage coordination, tours, party planning, also ground handlers

CONVENTION

CONVENTION SUPPORT SERVICES

Las Vegas Entertainment Productions
4990 Paradise Rd., Ste. 103
Las Vegas, NV 89119
871-9007
Lou Marek, Pres.
Complete convention service. Decorations, theme parties, entertainers and dancers

Las Vegas Expo Inc.
3764 Scripps Dr.
Las Vegas, NV 89103
248-6200
Bob Cordero, Pres.
Set-up for conventions

Lenz Agency
1591 E. Desert Inn Rd.
Las Vegas, NV 89109
733-6888
Richard Weber, Pres.
Models, narrators, celebrity lookalikes, entertainers, dancers, hostesses

Marilyn Mayblum Productions
2411 Mason Ave.
Las Vegas, NV 89102
896-6619
Marilyn Mayblum, Pres.
"Murder Mystery Vegas Style" is a special event with different themes and costumes

Meeting & Incentive Management Inc.
5030 Paradise Rd., Ste. D-103
Las Vegas, NV 89119
798-3031
Sharon Geraci, Pres.
Meeting and party planning, theme parties and hotel reservations

NYF Inc.
4790 Polaris Ave.
Las Vegas, NV 89103
258-0876
Glenn Ya, Pres.
Retail home and Christmas shows

Park's People
50 S. Jones Blvd., Ste. 200
Las Vegas, NV 89107
870-0555
Pat Park, Pres.
Theme parties, tours and sporting events

The Party Company
260 Mayflower Ave.
N. Las Vegas, NV 89030
642-8131 Fax: 642-5805
Sam Spalding, Pres.
Convention service consultants, professional designers, theme parties, entertainment, props, plant rental, musical entertainment

Rising Inc.
3135 Industrial Rd., Ste. 233
Las Vegas, NV 89109
796-0559 Fax: 796-5233
Grant Philipo, Pres.
Stage shows, photos, film, costume, sets and theme parties

Safaris
1771 E. Flamingo Rd., Ste. 213A
Las Vegas, NV 89119
733-6778
Keith Davies, General Mgr.

Nation's largest DMC, specializing in unique theme and sporting events, entertainment, custom tours, creative spouse programs, complete air and ground services

Supreme Agency Inc., Int'l
2245 N. Green Valley Pkwy., Ste. 288
Henderson, NV 89014
433-3393
Socorro Keenan
Entertainers, models, lookalikes, actors, magicians, theme parties

Thrillseekers Unlimited
3172 N. Rainbow Blvd., Ste. 321
Las Vegas, NV 89108
699-5550 Fax: 699-5551
Rich Hopkins, Owner
Credit Cards: MC, Visa
Price: Varies
Thrillseekers and extreme athletes perform various events including skydiving, paragliding, bungee jumping, fire-walking, stunt in-line skating and rock climbing; All Adrenaline Sports

Vegas Events
240 N. Jones Blvd., Ste. 212
Las Vegas, NV 89107
233-3061 1-800-997-2708
Specializing in group events and parties including team building activities and spouse programs. Custom planning services

DELIVERY SERVICES

Airborne Express
3245 E. Patrick Ln.
Las Vegas, NV 89119
1-800-247-2676
Hours: Mon. - Fri. 8 am - 5 pm

Airgroup Express Inc.
5030 Paradise Rd.
Las Vegas, NV 89119
798-6909
Hours: 24 hours

DHL Worldwide Express
1-800-225-5345
Hours: Mon. - Fri. 8 am - 5 pm

**Express Mail
(U.S. Postal Service)**
1-800-222-1811
Hours: Mon. - Fri. 8 am - 4 pm

Federal Express
5870 S. Eastern Ave.
Las Vegas, NV 89119
1-800-238-5355
Hours: Mon. - Fri. 8 am - 5:30 pm

Fleet Delivery Service
3860 W. Tompkins Ave.
Las Vegas, NV 89103
367-4555
Hours: 24 hours

Southern Nevada Courier Service
5282 Holbrook Dr.
Las Vegas, NV 89103
871-0565
Hours: Mon. - Fri. 8 am - 5 pm
Service Area: Local, domestic

United Parcel Service
1-800-742-5877
Hours: Mon. - Fri. 8:30 am - 5:30 pm

DESIGN AND CONSTRUCTION

A & D Scenery, Inc.
3200 Sirius Ave., Ste. F
Las Vegas, NV 89102
362-9404
Alan DeLeon, Pres.
Rental and fabrication and storing, erecting and dismantling of displays, exhibits and payroll service

Apple Convention Services Inc.
3200 Sirius Ave., Ste. F
Las Vegas, NV 89102
362-9401
Alan DeLeon, Pres.
Exhibit fabrication and storage, transportation, rentals and payroll service

C B Display Services Inc.
5141 S. Procyon Ave.
Las Vegas, NV 89118
739-9301
Dennis Birsa, Pres.
Trade show contractor

Coastal International
4855 W. Harmon Ave., Ste. A
Las Vegas, NV 89103
645-4300
Lou Genzano, Vice Pres.
Installation and dismantling of exhibits

Convention Service, Inc.
6235 Stevenson Way
Las Vegas, NV 89120
434-4124
Lisa Raiano, City Mgr.
Exhibit installation and dismantling service

Display & Exhibit House of Las Vegas
5880 Bunch St.
Las Vegas, NV 89122
456-8200
Donald Harmer, Pres.
Licensed union contractor; all sizes of custom rental booths, installation, dismantling, storage, transportation

Display & Exhibit Rental
5050 Steptoe St.
Las Vegas, NV 89122
456-8200
Stephanie Harmer, Pres.
Custom rental booths, furniture, carpet, construction of exhibits

Exhibit Installation Specialists Inc.
3580 W. Reno Ave.
Las Vegas, NV 89118
736-8950
Joseph Nuzzi, Pres.
Warehouse, set-up and dismantle

Freeman Companies
7000 Placid St., Ste. 101
Las Vegas, NV 89119
263-1404
Garry Rappaport, Pres.
300,000 sq. ft. facility; support to conventions, trade shows and meetings as well as a depot for distribution of equipment and personnel

Fritkin-Jones Design Group, Inc.
4030 Industrial Center Dr., Ste. 502
N. Las Vegas, NV 89030
643-0079
Design and construction

GES Exhibit Services
1624 Mojave Rd.
Las Vegas, NV 89104
457-5075
Daryl Clove, Mgr.
Rentals, design and custom fabrication

Giltspur Exposervices
4545 Cameron St., Ste. C
Las Vegas, NV 89103
367-1650
Bernie Massett, City Mgr.
Installation, dismantling and warehousing

Heritage Communications of Nevada
874 American Pacific Dr.
Henderson, NV 89015
558-1600
Shawn Garrity, Pres.
Custom exhibit and refurbishing, portable and rental systems, installation, dismantle and storage, graphics and design, lighting and audiovisual

Kenmark Scenic Studio, Inc.
4440 Arville St., Ste. 28
Las Vegas, NV 89103
873-2003
Mark Short, Pres.
Scenic backdrops

National Moving & Storage
6065 S. Polaris Ave.
Las Vegas, NV 89118
362-4186
Dick Morony, Pres.
Storage, erecting and dismantling

Nevada Exhibitors Service
3305 Spring Mountain Rd., Ste. 60
Las Vegas, NV 89102
362-2273
Lee Robson, Jr., Pres.
Exhibitor service

Sho-Link Inc.
4675 S. Valley View Blvd.
Las Vegas, NV 89103
798-1186
Dan Stock, City Mgr.
Provide installation and labor for conventions

Skyline Display & Designing
6255 Industrial Rd.
Las Vegas, NV 89118
361-3440
Robert Stone, Pres.
Communications company that sells custom lightweight exhibits and high impact graphics

United Production Services
3081 Business Ln.
Las Vegas, NV 89103
597-9798
Mike Brown, Pres.
Staging and grandstand specialists

VIP Coast to Coast Exhibitor Service
658-7779
Lou Zachea, City Mgr.
Set-up trade show exhibits

Federal Express Building, 1121 W. Cheyenne, Las Vegas

DISPLAYS AND PROPS

Abstracta/Exposure/Expose Displays
3242 E.Desert Inn Rd., Ste. 6
Las Vegas, NV 89121
731-3070
Cendy Converse, Pres.
Trade show displays and graphics, sales and rentals

Apple Foam & Plastics
1151 Grier Dr., Ste. 1
Las Vegas, NV 89119
361-7999
Lloyd Hill, Pres.
Distributor of graphic arts material

Events Designs
4881 W. Hacienda Ave., Ste. 3
Las Vegas, NV 89118
365-8980
Ken Hurdle, Pres.
Corporate events

Hollywood Props
2716 S. Highland Dr.
Las Vegas, NV 89109
732-7767
Duane Smith, Pres.
25,000 sq. ft. of unusual props and scenery to design theme parties, parades, grand openings and special events; specializing in Western themes

JR & Sons, Inc.
2017 W. Gowan Rd.
N. Las Vegas, NV 89030
646-0403
Joseph Pokorny, Pres.
Portable stage risers

Las Vegas Party Tents
7120 W. Azure Dr.
Las Vegas, NV 89130
251-1997
Al Strand, Pres.
Canopies for all occasions

Ralph Jones Display
2576 E. Charleston Blvd.
Las Vegas, NV 89104
382-4398
Ralph Jones, Pres.
Major credit cards
Creative services; scenic painting and banners

ENTERTAINMENT
(Also see Party Planning)

AAA-Guarnieri Music
6324 Stonegate Way
Las Vegas, NV 89102
871-3506

Ann C. George, Pres.
Musicians, singers, dancers, magicians, jugglers, circus acts

A All Star Norm Prentice Variety Music & Entertainment
806 Pioneer St.
Las Vegas, NV 89107
878-0100
Norm Prentice, Pres.
All types, sizes and styles of entertainment

Always Entertaining
3690 S. Eastern Ave., Ste. 163
Las Vegas, NV 89109
737-3232
Maria Battaglia, Pres.
Specialized themed entertainment packages for trade shows and corporate events, stage productions and fashion shows, lookalikes, models, bands, dancers and fabulous showgirls

A One Man Band
3941 Cutting Horse Ave.
N. Las Vegas, NV 89030
531-1855
Gabriel Magno
All music from the '40s to the '90s including Italian and Spanish, vocal, keyboard and guitar

Bobby Morris Agency
1629 E. Sahara Ave.
Las Vegas, NV 89104
733-7575   459-3315
Specializing in complete spectrum of convention entertainment since 1966

Brass-on-the Grass Band
225-3054
Walter J. Blanton
Blues, Latin, bop standards, jazz and New Orleans

Caribbean Delights
3838 Raymert Dr.
Las Vegas, NV 89121
898-2243
Diana Aird, Pres.
Full service event and scene party planning. Authentic Caribbean, Latin American and African cuisine, authentic entertainment in each area

Creative Casting & Acting
900 E. Karen Ave., Ste. D116
Las Vegas, NV 89109
737-0611
Margee Butto
Live entertainment, singers, actors and karaoke equipment rentals

Crosswynd
4616 W. Sahara Ave., Ste. 102
Las Vegas, NV 89102
228-9017
Kate Mucci
Classic, medieval and Celtic music, folk harpist and guitarist

Dave Coady's Irish Express
6206 Meadowbrook Ln.
Las Vegas, NV 89103
873-6486
Dave Coady
Specializes in Irish and American music

Dan Nelson Productions
6165 Harrison Dr.
Las Vegas, NV 89120
798-8909
Theatrical productions, spouse programs and costumes

David London Productions
3369 Berwyck St.
Las Vegas, NV 89121
458-6423
David London, Pres.
Music, entertainment and shows of all kinds

Dick Ryan Magic
1715 Delores Ave.
Henderson, NV 89014
458-3217
Dick Ryan, Pres.
Magician/product presenter for exhibits; close-up magic for hospitality suites and receptions

Don Burke
2925 Linkview Dr.
Las Vegas, NV 89134
255-1468
Don Burke
Big band, Dixieland, anytime and anywhere, from 4 to 17 piece orchestra

The Festival Trumpeters
225-3054
Walter J. Blanton
Best trumpeters in Las Vegas

Fireworks America
6300 Bannock Way
Las Vegas, NV 89107
Indoor fireworks for entertainment events, laser displays, full range of outdoor fireworks

Hal Belfer & Associates
3111 S. Valley View Blvd., Ste. 218
Las Vegas, NV 89102
364-4959
Hal Belfer, Pres.
Producing, writing, directing and staging, major stars

Hot Wax Music Productions
618 E. Carson Ave., Ste. 288
Las Vegas, NV 89101
437-4595
Steve Melanson, Pres.
Music and video productions, professional disc jockeys, dance floor and lighting

Jay Cameron
3105 Palora Ave.
Las Vegas, NV 89121
457-1362
Jay Cameron
Jazz sax man and tape backing, distinguishes your booth or party

Jim Maffett Band
9117 Dolente Ave.
Las Vegas, NV 89129
254-6250
Jim Maffett
Eight piece band with vocalist; theme parties, German, Dixieland and dances

Lantis Fireworks
384-2595
Ken Lantis, Pres.
Aerial and ground displays anywhere, laser productions

Las Vegas Karaoke Productions
2350 E. Patrick Ln., Ste. 2
Las Vegas, NV 89120
898-1567
Gene Dawley
Dancers, models, actresses and variety acts

Limelight Productions & Entertainment
3448 Clandara Ave.
Las Vegas, NV 89120
794-0486
Tom Nelli
Strolling musicians, string quartet and all types of music

Million Dollar Entertainment
653 N. Benedict Dr.
Las Vegas, NV 89110
452-3211   452-7964
Paul Bowman, Pres.
Six piece country western band and country comedy

Musicians Union of Las Vegas Local #369
3701 Vegas Dr.
Las Vegas, NV 89108
647-3690
Dan Trinter, Pres.
Live music groups for all occasions

One Eyed Jacks Steel Drum Band
P.O. Box 80846
Las Vegas, NV 89180
647-8221
Jack Cenna
Caribbean music, salsa, reggae and calypso

CONVENTION SUPPORT SERVICES

Polynesian Entertainment Productions
2983 Pinehurst Dr.
Las Vegas, NV 89109
739-9311
Rozita Lee, Pres.
Unique Polynesian and international show

Rattlesnake Whiskey! Productions, Inc.
6655 W. Sahara Ave., Ste. B200
Las Vegas, NV 89115
438-4660
Only Old West entertainment specialist in Las Vegas, can-cans, gunfights and quick draw competitions

Rosario Music
208 N. Torrey Pines Dr.
Las Vegas, NV 89107
870-0594
Russ Martino
Bands and mariachi for all occasions

Sandy Hackett Entertainment
269 Hickory Hollow Dr.
Las Vegas, NV 89123
368-6611
Richard Sacks, Dir. of Operations
Name entertainment, stars, props and theme parties

Sasha Semenoff Music
2125 Michael Way
Las Vegas, NV 89108
648-6471
Strolling musicians, single musicians to big band

Soc. Preserv. & Encourgement· Barber Shop Quartet Sing. Am.
2245 Green Valley Pkwy., Ste. 290
Henderson, NV 89014
221-9895   362-8680
Bob Lindstrom, Chorus Mgr.
Las Vegas Gamble-Aires

Sun Cats Band
3049 Wonderview Dr.
Las Vegas, NV 89134
255-6714
Ann Holland
Lively music including boogie, Dixieland, Latin, rock and standard, small band with big sound

Sweet Adelines International
Home: 896-1805
Work: 458-2123
Angie Yokay
Award-winning Valley of Fire 35 member chorus

The Classics According to John Henry
654 Radwick Dr.
Las Vegas, NV 89110
438-1687
John Henry
Pianist performing classics; single or four man ensemble, tapes and brochures available

The Gaming Steward
733-4080   1-800-732-8007
Janet Steward, Pres.
Gaming seminars with literature included

You Name It Entertainment
4535 W. Sahara Ave., Ste. 105
Las Vegas, NV 89102
871-3300
Richard Ballen, Pres.
Magicians, mimes, clowns

GROUND HANDLERS / RECEPTIVE OPERATORS

Airgroup Express Inc.
5030 Paradise Rd., Ste. B208
Las Vegas, NV 89119
798-6909
Rich Scaglione
24 hour - 7 days - heavy cargo, domestic and international

BMA, Inc.
5538 S. Eastern Ave.
Las Vegas, NV 89119
798-8000
Rex Jarrett, Jr., Pres.
Destination management

Cactus Jack's Wild West Tour Company
2217 Paradise Rd., Ste. A
Las Vegas, NV 89104
731-9400
John Early, Mgr.

Destination Services
3900 Paradise Rd., Ste. 117
Las Vegas, NV 89109
732-4055
Gayle Spratt

Estrada Tours
5030 S. Paradise Rd., Ste. 206B
Las Vegas, NV 89119
451-5583
Aurora Gomez, Mgr.

FunQuest Inc. · Trans Global Vacation
3900 Paradise Rd., Ste. 281
Las Vegas, NV 89109
737-5556   Fax: 737-5251
Bill Thurman, Operations Mgr.

Funway Holidays Funjet
6330 S. Eastern Ave.
Las Vegas, NV 89119
736-8902   Fax: 736-2066
Pauline Appleby, VP Nevada Operations

Garth Tours
P.O. Box 26837
Las Vegas, NV 89126
228-3707   Fax: 228-9361
Vincent Garth, Pres.

National Tour Co.
1801 E. Tropicana Ave., Ste. 28
Las Vegas, NV 89119
798-1244   Fax: 798-3576
Ken Partridge, Pres.

Ra·Mar Tours
P.O. Box 11048 Airport
Las Vegas, NV 89111
739-7506
Maria Grinspanas, Mgr.

Reservation Fax, Inc.
P.O. Box 19750
Las Vegas, NV 89132
878-4141   Fax: 1-800-848-8845
Darin Gangwish, Pres./CEO

Safaris Events
1771 E. Flamingo Rd., Ste. 213A
Las Vegas, NV 89119
733-6778   Telex: 283-0991
Fax: 733-7960
Keith Davies, Mgr.

Silver State Tour & Travel
5030 Paradise Rd., Ste. D101
Las Vegas, NV 89119
736-0034
Bill & Jean Howard

USA Hosts
5030 Paradise Rd., Ste. 101
Las Vegas, NV 89119
798-0034
Raja Hand, General Mgr.
Travel arrangements

World of Vacations
3900 Paradise Rd., Ste. 117
Las Vegas, NV 89109
732-2838
Steve Lurenz, Destination Supv.

OFFICE SUPPLIES

Copy Shoppe
1900 Civic Center Dr.
N. Las Vegas, NV 89030
649-6031
Hours: Mon. - Fri. 8 am - 6 pm; Sat. 9 am - 5 pm

Ideal Office Equipment
1200 S. 3rd St.
Las Vegas, NV 89104
384-3814
Hours: Mon. - Fri. 7:30 am - 5 pm

Office Depot
(Multiple locations listed below)
Maureen Ryan, General Mgr.
Hours: Mon. - Fri. 7 am - 9 pm; Sat. 9 am - 9 pm; Sun. 10 am - 6 pm
Credit Cards: Mastercard, Visa, Discover, AMEX, Office Depot
Office supplies, computers, office furniture, copy center

3630 W. Sahara Ave.
Las Vegas, NV 89102
222-1890

270 S. Martin Luther King Blvd.
Las Vegas, NV 89106
387-2582

3265 E. Tropicana Ave.
Las Vegas, NV 89121
434-3555

3247 Maryland Pkwy.
Las Vegas, NV 89109
892-9897

Office Max
(Multiple locations listed below)
Hours: Mon. - Fri. 7 am - 9 pm; Sat. 9 am - 9 pm; Sun. 10 am - 6 pm
Credit Cards: All major
Print shop, computers and office furniture and supplies

4995 S. Eastern Ave.
Las Vegas, NV 89119
736-4411

2837 S. Maryland Pkwy.
Las Vegas, NV 89109
732-4244

2640 S. Decatur Blvd.
Las Vegas, NV 89102
221-0471

Office Max, 2201 N. Rainbow Blvd., Las Vegas, NV

549 Stephanie St.
Henderson, NV 89014
451-7774
1-800-788-8080

41 N. Nellis Blvd.
Las Vegas, NV 89110
437-8962

2201 N. Rainbow Blvd.
Las Vegas, NV
647-4878

OFFICE FURNITURE RENTAL

Aaron Rents & Sells
4345 S. Industrial Rd.
Las Vegas, NV 89103
798-7644
Hours: Mon. - Fri. 9 am - 7 pm; Sat. 9 am - 5 pm

Brook Furniture Rental
4850 W. Flamingo Rd., Ste. 45
Las Vegas, NV 89103
871-3351
Convention services

Custom Office Furniture
301 Martin Luther King Blvd.
Las Vegas, NV 89106
384-6996
Hours: Mon. - Fri. 9 am - 6 pm; Sat. 9 am - 5 pm

Ideal Office Equipment
1200 S. 3rd St.
Las Vegas, NV 89104
384-3814
Hours: Mon. - Fri. 7:30 am - 4 pm

Sarret Office Equipment
555 S. Casino Center Blvd.
Las Vegas, NV 89101
384-8105
Hours: Mon. - Fri. 8 am - 5 pm
Office supplies and office furniture

Somers Convention Furniture Rental, Inc.
3926 W. Ponderosa Way
Las Vegas, NV 89118
739-0229
Debbi Somers, Pres.
Convention furniture

PARTY PLANNING AND SUPPLIES

Partyland
3129 N. Rainbow Blvd.
Las Vegas, NV 89108
645-9601
Lori Naipo, Gen. Mgr.
Large discount party chain

Party Supply House
6060 Laredo St.
Las Vegas, NV 89102
876-1100
Tom Straub, Pres.
Hours: Mon. - Fri. 9 am - 7:30 pm;
Sat. 9 am - 6 pm; Sun. 10 am - 4 pm
Over 8,000 square feet of party supplies

The Party Line
4834 Jadero Dr.
Las Vegas, NV 89117
259-9766   Fax: 259-6694
Marlena Pier
No cost referral agency. Need a caterer,
DJ, location, flowers or photographs?
"Doing the best parties for the best people"

Pretty Party Place
(Multiple locations listed below)
Hours: Mon. - Fri. 9:30 am - 9 pm;
Sat. 9 am - 6:30 pm
Credit Cards: MC, Visa
Party and wedding supplies, baking and
candy making supplies, helium rentals

2718 N. Green Valley Pkwy.
Henderson, NV 89014
433-0676

2630 S. Decatur Blvd.
Las Vegas, NV 89102
362-3631

Thrillseekers Unlimited
3172 N. Rainbow Blvd., Ste. 321
Las Vegas, NV 89108
699-5550   Fax: 699-5551
Rich Hopkins, Owner
Credit Cards: MC, Visa
Price: Varies
Thrillseekers will plan your event or par-
ties from concept to performance and
transportation

PHOTOGRAPHY

Advanced Photographics
2318 Howard Dr.
Las Vegas, NV 89104
431-9206
Barbara Oddo, Owner
Over a decade of fine art photography

Allen Photographics
3223 Industrial Rd.
Las Vegas, NV 89109
735-2222   Fax: 734-2222
Photo processing laboratories

Brian Janis Phototechnik
8401 Campana Dr.
Las Vegas, NV 89117
252-8311   1-800-362-3624
Fax: 252-4566
Brian Janis, Owner

Cashman Photo Enterprises Inc.
3660 Cinder Ln.
Las Vegas, NV 89103
871-8300
Morgan Cashman, Pres.
Photos taken in showrooms and restaurants

Elite Photo Graphics
3230 W. Hacienda Ave., Ste. 302
Las Vegas, NV 89118
597-2822
Randy Becker, Pres.
Exhibit photos, signs, lithographs.

Films Developed in 30 Minutes
3041 Las Vegas Blvd. S.
Las Vegas, NV 89109
369-8822
Film 30 minute, slides 1 hour development

Photo Finish
3121 Industrial Rd.
Las Vegas, NV 89109-1136
732-1878
Photo processing

Rainbow Multi-media Productions
3620 E. Flamingo Rd., Ste. 6
Las Vegas, NV 89121
456-4050
Arnie Altman, Pres.
Photography, video, slide presentations,
music, disc jockey, emcee

A French Bouquet, 2121 E. Tropicana Ave., Las Vegas, NV 89119

PLANTS, FLOWERS and BALLOONS
(Also see Flowers in Marriage Section)

Balloon Sculptures
4251 W. Sahara Ave., Ste. A
Las Vegas, NV 89102
220-8000   Fax: 220-8008
Helen Hsueh
Sculptures and arches

Exhibit Plant and Floral Co.
1818 S. Industrial Rd.
Las Vegas, NV 89102
384-4490
Special event plant rental

A French Bouquet
(Multiple locations listed below)
2121 E. Tropicana Ave.
Las Vegas, NV 89119
739-8484 Shop
739-9977 Office
For all your floral and plant needs

4009 S. Decatur Blvd., Ste. 9
Las Vegas, NV 89103
365-6464

Outside-In Design
6000 S. Eastern Ave., Ste. 10J
Las Vegas, NV 89119
597-0300
Linda Freeman, Pres.
Plant rental and floral designs

Paradise Florists & Gifts
3661 S. Maryland Pkwy., Ste. 17
Las Vegas, NV 89109
735-0173
Jan Hughes, Owner
Orders taken 7 days, no plant rental

The Plantworks
3930 Graphic Center Dr.
Las Vegas, NV 89118
795-3600
Silk plants, silk trees, flowers and
containers

Rain Forest
4171 S. Maryland Pkwy.
Las Vegas, NV 89119
732-9555
David Weingarten, Owner
Balloons, fruit and gourmet baskets

Showtime Florists
2532 W. Pebble Dr.
Las Vegas, NV 89123
361-1444
Nelson Werner, Pres.
Plants and landscaping

The Big Balloon
850 E. Sahara Ave.
Las Vegas, NV 89104
362-4808
George McLean, Pres.
In business for 18 years, extensive trade
show and convention experience and
references

PRINTING

Creel Printing Co.
2701 Westwood Dr.
Las Vegas, NV 89109
735-8161
Hours: Mon. - Fri. 8 am - 5 pm
Full service printer

Kinko's Copies
(Multiple locations listed below)
Open 24 hours

4440 S. Maryland Pkwy.
Las Vegas, NV 89119
735-4402

4750 W. Sahara Ave.
Las Vegas, NV 89102
870-7011

830 S. 4th St.
Las Vegas, NV 89101
383-7022

Kwik Kopy Number 275
923 E. Charleston Blvd.
Las Vegas, NV 89104
382-1838
Hours: Mon. - Fri. 8 am - 6 pm;
Sat. 9 am - noon

PDQ Printing
(Multiple locations & hrs. listed below)
3820 S. Valley View Blvd.
Las Vegas, NV 89103
876-3235
Hours: Mon. - Fri. 8:30 am - 5:30 pm

3901 W. Charleston Blvd.
Las Vegas, NV 89103
878-1701
Hours: Mon. - Fri. 8 am - 6 pm;
Sat. 8 am - 4 pm
Shipping at Charleston location

3520 W. Reno Ave.
Las Vegas, NV 89138
739-7446
Hours: Mon. - Fri. 8 am - 4:30 pm

300 S. 4th St.
Las Vegas, NV 89101
598-4455
Hours: Mon. - Fri. 8:30 am - 5 pm
Printing, packaging, shipping

PIP Printing
4912 S. Eastern Ave.
Las Vegas, NV 89119
435-8400
Carla Perkins, Owner
Hours: Mon. - Fri. 8 am - 5 pm
Quick copies and printing

Southwest Printers
3721 Meade Ave.
Las Vegas, NV 89102
367-2544   Fax: 367-2821
Hours: Mon. - Fri. 8 am - 5 pm

RECORDERS

Associated Reporters of Nevada
720 S. 4th St., Ste. 202
Las Vegas, NV 89101
382-8778
Barbara Seaton, Owner

Ready Reporting Services
P.O. Box 80804
Las Vegas, NV 89180
363-3274
Daxelle Reddy

CONVENTION SUPPORT SERVICES

RENTAL

Ahern Party Rental
(Multiple locations listed below)
Don Ahern, Pres.
Tables, chairs, slide projectors, PA systems, event booths, helium tanks, complete rental, tents and catering. Hi-Reach equipment, forklifts, boomlifts. Tractors, trailers, saws, pumps, trucks and a complete line of equipment.

4631 S. Industrial Rd.
Las Vegas, NV 89103
891-8533

4241 Arville St.
Las Vegas, NV 89103
362-1800

5915 S. Industrial Rd.
Las Vegas, NV 89118
736-4922

Artistic Garden Arts
5617 S. Valley View Blvd.
Las Vegas, NV 89118
736-1556
Statuary, fountains and waterfalls; sales and rentals

Bash Lighting Services
5277 Cameron Ave., Ste. 160
Las Vegas, NV 89118
367-2274
Michael Cannon, VP Operations
Consultations, rentals, service, sales, and theatrical lighting equipment

Bill Rents It Custom Exhibit Rentals
1880 Pasadena Blvd.
Las Vegas, NV 89115
452-8966
Bill Lewin, Pres.
Rent custom exhibits

Characters Unlimited
709 Foot Hill Court
Boulder City, NV 89005
294-0563
Talking and animated character mannequins

Clear Span Tents
4275 Arcata Way
N. Las Vegas, NV 89038
642-0887
Jack Freestone, Mgr.
Creative designs in tents and canopies; sales, rentals and service

Desert Cash Register
6010 Boulder Hwy.
Las Vegas, NV 89122
437-8722
Bob Lackey, Pres.
Rent and sell cash registers 24 hours a day, 7 days a week

Eagle Scaffolding & Equipment Company
3629 W. Hacienda Ave.
Las Vegas, NV 89118
740-4041
Ken McNabb, Pres.
Rent scaffolding and equipment

Herda's Discount Appliance Warehouse
3025 S. Highland Dr.
Las Vegas, NV 89109
737-1047
Nick Herda, Pres.
16 years in business, rent big screen, video equipment and other appliances

Mountain Business Products
6266 S. Sandhill Rd.
Las Vegas, NV 89120
798-4998
Bob Tatalovich, Pres.
Rentals for copiers, fax and typewriters

PJ's Display
3111 S. Valley View Blvd., Ste. E117
Las Vegas, NV 89102
253-9865
Pamela Jackson, Pres.
Store fixture, display case rentals and mannequins

Rebel Rents (Party Division)
4231 Bertsos Dr.
Las Vegas, NV 89103
252-0152
Sam Emerson, Owner
Hours: Mon. 8 am - 6 pm;
Tue. - Sat. 8 am - 5 pm
Party goods, party tent, delivery

Fastsigns, 4604 W. Sahara Ave.
Las Vegas, NV 89102

Spectrum Office System
1727 N. Rancho Dr.
Las Vegas, NV 89106
438-5990
Gary Gattermeyer, Owner
Delivery, sales and service

Strickland Business Systems
3145 W. Post Rd.
Las Vegas, NV 89118
896-1442
Rich Strickland, Owner
Panasonic copier and fax rentals, daily and weekly

United Rent-All
1020 E. Twain Ave.
Las Vegas, NV 89109
733-8847
Ray Suhadolnik, Owner
Party equipment, home owner repair equipment and banquet tables and chairs

SECRETARIAL SERVICES

Abacus & Quill
4161 S. Eastern Ave., Ste. E-8
Las Vegas, NV 89119
732-0889
Wendy Cole, Owner
Business consultant, typing, writing, ghost writing. Rents small meeting room, capacity 16 people

Confidential Plus Secretarial
2275-D Renaissance Dr.
Las Vegas, NV 89109
740-8067
Judie Sallee, Owner
Word processing, typing, resumes, notary, copies and all secretarial services

Labor Force
1155 E. Sahara Ave.
Las Vegas, NV 89104
894-4117   Fax: 894-4129

Office Team
1771 E. Flamingo Rd., Ste. 211A
Las Vegas, NV 89119
732-1180   Fax: 732-1016

SHIPPING and MAILING

(Also see Post Offices in Government Section)

Federal Express
1-800-238-5355
5870 S. Eastern Ave.
Las Vegas, NV 89119

316 Bridger Ave.
Las Vegas, NV 89101

3840 W. Sahara Ave.
Las Vegas, NV 89102

6075 S. Spencer St.
Las Vegas, NV 89109
Over-night shipping

SIGNS

Classic Graphics
3111 Joe W. Brown Dr.
Las Vegas, NV 89109
791-5190
Cathy Gordon, Mgr.
Custom signs

Corky's Signs & Displays
1536 Western Ave.
Las Vegas, NV 89102
382-0012
Corky Rux, Pres.
All phases of signs except electrical

Creative Signs
2200 Patrick Ln., Ste. 2
Las Vegas, NV 89119
798-7760
John Davis
Paper signs, banners and showcards

Fastsigns
3973 S. Maryland Pkwy.
Las Vegas, NV 89119
792-9225
Richard Hood
1 day signs and lettering

Fastsigns
4604 W. Sahara Ave.
Las Vegas, NV 89102
878-3838
Ken Anderson
Signs and lettering; 24 hour turnaround

Hiett Dezigns
4350 S. Arville St., Ste. 16
Las Vegas, NV 89103
367-3949
James Hiett, Pres.
Full stage equipment; neon, strobes, fiberoptics, fog machines

Las Vegas Signs & Designs
1400 Industrial Rd.
Las Vegas, NV 89102
388-1044
Dennis Gomez, Pres.
Interior and exterior, fiberoptics, neon and vinyl

Mikohn Interior Signs
4181 W. Oquendo Rd.
Las Vegas, NV 89118
798-2015
Signs and graphics, sales and rentals

Patrick's Signs
4420 S. Arville St., Ste. 27
Las Vegas, NV 89103
873-4463   Fax: 873-5657
Michael Thompson, VP
Custom signs, storefronts, vinyl lettering, show cards, vehicle lettering, job site signs, screenprinting, real estate signs, ADA signs, custom banners, convention

Signage
4330 W. Desert Inn Rd., Ste. I
Las Vegas, NV 89102
871-2503
Mike Wall, Pres.
Priority graphics and lettering

U Need a Sign
3400 Sirius Ave., Ste. H
Las Vegas, NV 89102
362-3838
Barbara Naughton, Sec.-Treas.
Logos, route lettering, banners, vinyl lettering and graphics and more

SPEAKERS

Denise Tighe & Associates
Northshore Office Building
3320 N. Buffalo Dr., Ste. 106
Las Vegas, NV 89129
656-9036
Denise M. Tighe
Speaker, entrepreneur, business education instructor

Desert Research Institute
755 E. Flamingo Rd.
Las Vegas, NV 89119
895-0408   Fax: 895-0496
Dr. James V. Taranik, Pres.
Conducts environmental research for government and industry to help manage natural resources. Video and speaker presentations available for groups

Las Vegas Chamber of Commerce
3720 Howard Hughes Pkwy.
Las Vegas, NV 89109
735-1616
Provides community experts free on many topics including gaming, education, marketing, tourism and business

Mavis Benson
309 Yardarm Way
Las Vegas, NV 89128
254-8030
Workshops, lectures and consultation

Stop All Stalkers
5025 S. Eastern Ave., Ste. 16
Las Vegas, NV 89119
226-5142
Joyce Brown
Non-profit, all-volunteer group presents 45 minute speech regarding stalker crimes

The Learning Center
2972 Meade Ave.
Las Vegas, NV 89102
365-8885
Linda Montgomery
Taking the fear out of the byte, earning with computers

Thrillseekers Unlimited
3172 N. Rainbow Blvd., Ste. 321
Las Vegas, NV 89108
699-5550   Fax: 699-5551
Rich Hopkins, Owner
Credit Cards: MC, Visa
Price: Varies
Thrillseekers Unlimited offers extreme sports athletes for speaking engagements. Subjects include extreme sports, management, extreme sports in advertising-sky diving, bungee jumping, in-line skating, paragliding, rock climbing, firewalking and all other sports. Clients include Brut, ESPN2 and Power Bar.

UNLV Speakers Bureau
4505 S. Maryland Pkwy.
Las Vegas, NV 89154
895-3101
Diane Russell
Staff and faculty in various areas of expertise for conventions and assorted clubs

Victoria's Destination Services, Inc.
2690 Chandler Ave., Ste. 1
Las Vegas, NV 89120
794-2492 1-800-317-7724
Fax: 794-3451
Extensive list of nationally recognized speakers

Wiener Communications Group
1500 Foremaster Ln., Ste. 2
Las Vegas, NV 89101-1103
221-0068
Valerie Wiener
Corporate communications, media relations, speeches and writing

WJM Management Co.
6847 W. Tree Haven Ct.
Las Vegas, NV 89102
873-2760
Woodrow Smith, Jr.
Lectures, seminars, finance and business consulting

Dr. Adele Zorn, FAACS
3104 Calle De El Cortez
Las Vegas, NV 89102
876-5398
Diplomat/board certified sexologist

TECHNICAL

Effects Network Inc.
5277 S. Cameron St., Ste. 130
Las Vegas, NV 89108
736-8458
Scott Christensen, Pres.
Custom sets, EFX - displays

Protech Theatrical Service Inc.
3431 N. Bruce St.
N. Las Vegas, NV 89030
639-0290
Richard Tarbell, Pres.
Stage rigging, equipment and curtains

Scenic Technologies
4170 W. Harmon Ave., Ste. 6
Las Vegas, NV 89103
876-1451
Kevin Baxley, Pres.
Mechanized effects and show control systems

Source Corporation
3620 W. Reno Ave., Ste. K
Las Vegas, NV 89118
739-9110
Ginny McCord, Pres.
Production systems, desktop video, GVG110 component production switcher, Sony BVW 65-70, broadcast equipment maintenance and parts

Trade Show Electrical
3073 S. Highland Dr.
Las Vegas, NV 89109
731-6007
Bill Suszko, Vice Pres.
Temporary electrical and plumbing service for trade shows

TEMPORARY PERSONNEL
(Also see Employment in Newcomer section)

Acutemps Temporary Service
2909 W. Charleston Blvd.
Las Vegas, NV 89102
877-6775
Lynn Murray, Owner
Blue and white collar personnel

Adecco Personnel Services
1050 E. Flamingo Rd., Ste. E225
Las Vegas, NV 89119
731-2267
Claire Watson, Pres.
Attendants, clerical and laborers

American Protective Services
51 N. Pecos Rd.
Las Vegas, NV 89101
459-3131
Xavier D. Peterson
Full service

Anne O'Briant Agency
2213 Paradise Rd.
Las Vegas, NV 89104
870-4499
Anne O'Briant, Mgr.
Specializing in conventions and trade shows exclusively; spokespersons, hostesses and models

ATS Temporary Staffing
1700 E. Desert Inn Rd., Ste. 118
Las Vegas, NV 89109
731-2066
Marla Allen, Treasurer
All facets of convention help

B'More Security
1928 Western Ave., Ste. 5
Las Vegas, NV 89102
598-1941   1-800-598-0184
Roscoe Baltimore, Pres.
Convention patrol service

Acutemps Temporary Service, 2909 W. Charleston Blvd., Las Vegas, NV 89102

Burns International Security Services
2770 S. Maryland Pkwy., Ste. 318
Las Vegas, NV 89109
737-5316
Daniel D. Crate, General Mgr.
Trained and uniformed security for conventions and special events

Classic Models, Ltd.
3305 Spring Mtn. Rd., Ste. 12
Las Vegas, NV 89102
367-1444   Fax: 367-6457
Wendy Wenzel, Pres.
Nationwide trade show specialist, hostesses, models, narrators, celebrity look-a-likes, interpreters, famous speakers

Convention Support Service
2909 W. Charleston Blvd.
Las Vegas, NV 89102
877-6775
*Deborah Boccio,
Director of Business Development*
All convention needs

Eastridge Temps Services
4220 S. Maryland Pkwy., Ste. 205
Las Vegas, NV 89119
732-8861
Diane Ray
Convention personnel; hostesses, laborers, booth attendants and secretarial

Green Valley Security
6135 Harrison Ave., Ste. 3
Las Vegas, NV 89120
261-0440
Jeff Sellers, Owner

Holiday Models Corporation
900 E. Desert Inn Rd., Ste. 101
Las Vegas, NV 89109
735-7353   Fax: 796-5676
Scott Griffith, Pres.
Trade show receptionists, spokespersons, VIP show and gourmet restaurant reservations, hospitality suite and theme party production, musical talent

Kelly Temporary Services
3770 Howard Hughes Pkwy., Ste. 145
Las Vegas, NV 89109
796-0203

1160 Town Center Dr., Ste. 190
Las Vegas, NV 89134
255-4708

Loomis Fargo & Company
1427 Gragson Ave.
Las Vegas, NV 89101
642-9686
Kris Waugh, Sales Mgr.

Manpower Temporary Service
3625 Pecos-McLeod
Las Vegas, NV 89121
893-2626

Manpower-Industrial
314 Las Vegas Blvd. N.
N. Las Vegas, NV 89101
386-2626

8170 W. Sahara Ave.
Las Vegas, NV 89117
363-8170

Mercy Medical Services
1130 S. Martin Luther King Blvd.
Las Vegas, NV 89102
386-9985
Robert Forbuss, CEO
Special event medical standby

Official Security
2404 Santa Paula Dr.
Las Vegas, NV 89104
369-4366
Darryl Cronfeld

Olsten Staffing Service
5440 W. Sahara Ave., Ste. 101
Las Vegas, NV 89102
794-0069

601 Whitney Ranch Dr.
Henderson, NV 89014
454-2335
Jill Elliot, Branch Mgr.
Exclusive provider of casual labor for the Las Vegas Convention and Visitors Authority; secretaries, booth aids, models, general laborers

CONVENTION SUPPORT SERVICES

Lawrence-Mayflower Moving & Storage, 4725 S. Valley View Blvd., Las Vegas, NV

Pinkerton Security
4045 S. Spencer St., Ste. A47
Las Vegas, NV 89119
876-9299
Steve Heaney

Pro-Tect Security
3111 Joe W. Brown Dr., Ste. B
Las Vegas, NV 89109
735-0110
Pat Hamilton

Quest Intelligence Bureau, Ltd.
2770 Maryland Pkwy., Ste. 417
Las Vegas, NV 89109
892-0061   Fax: 892-0552
Robert Doty, Pres.
"When the challenge is preparedness, the solution is Quest"

Remedy · The Intelligent Temporary Service
1900 E. Flamingo Rd., Ste.161
Las Vegas, NV 89119
369-0292
Ted Hirsch, Pres.
Set-up, registration and labor provided

Security Unlimited
2231 E. Desert Inn Rd.
Las Vegas, NV 89109
733-0022
Annette Lexis

S.O.A. Security
1611 E. Charleston Blvd., Ste. 3
Las Vegas, NV 89104
386-8065
Lynn Strocchia

Todays Temporary
2300 W. Sahara Ave., Ste. 55
Las Vegas, NV 89102
382-4888
Mike Johnson, Operations Mgr.
Temporary bookkeepers; accounting and legal

Universal Security Service, Inc.
2303 E. Sahara Ave., Ste. 204
Las Vegas, NV 89104
457-3066
George Rahas, Owner

We Serve, Inc.
1515 E. Tropicana Ave., Ste. 340
Las Vegas, NV 89119
798-6556
Bill Overly
Security for conventions and special events

Wells Fargo Guard Service, Inc.
3305 W. Spring Mountain Rd., Ste. 66
Las Vegas, NV 89102
365-1585
Jerry Ashenfelter, Branch Mgr.

Western Temporary Services Inc.
2650 S. Maryland Pkwy., Ste. A3B
Las Vegas, NV 89109
735-4334
Joan Ehlen, Mgr.

TRANSFER AND STORAGE

Capitol North American
1780 S. Mojave Rd.
Las Vegas, NV 89104
457-5353
Mitch Rittenhouse, General Mgr.
Moving company

Las Vegas Transfer and Storage
6065 S. Polaris Ave.
Las Vegas, NV 89118
362-4186
Richard Morony, Pres.
Storing, erecting and dismantling

Lawrence-Mayflower Moving & Storage
4725 S. Valley View Blvd.
Las Vegas, NV 89103
736-2920
Bill Hibbitt, General Mgr.
Moving and storage

Puliz Moving & Storage
3840 E. Craig Rd.
N. Las Vegas, NV 89030
644-6160
Allen Puliz, Pres.
Moving and warehousing

TRANSLATORS

Castillo & Associates
4535 W. Sahara Ave., Ste. 105
Las Vegas, NV 89102
1-800-683-3898
Enrique F. Castillo, Pres.
Translating, interpreting and moderating

Communication Accessing Network
2657 Windmill Pkwy., Box 295
Henderson, NV 89014
896-5457
Catherine Black, Dir.
TTD/voice qualified interpreters for the deaf; coordination of interpreter needs

Communications Consulting Service
900 Alan Shepard St.
Las Vegas, NV 89128
363-2000
Richard Smith, Owner
Translation from and into nearly every language; multilingual typesetting, word processing

Latin Chamber of Commerce
829 S. 6th St., Ste. 3
Las Vegas, NV 89101
385-7367
Otto Merida, Executive Director
Provides recommendations

Pro-File Translation
376 W. Viewmont Dr.
Henderson, NV 89015
565-6674
Bruce Gonyea, Pres.
Translations, tours and shopping services

Trans-Inter Communications Co.
300 E. Fremont St., Ste. 100
Las Vegas, NV 89101
477-0134   Fax: 477-0882
Mary Kozlowski, Pres.
Large pool of interpreters and translators available through the U.S. Dept. of State's Language Services Division. Translation services in any language from Armenian to Zulu. Wide array of simultaneous interpretation equipment, which can be rented or bought.

TRANSPORTATION

Adventure Charters & Tours
1305 N. Main St.
Las Vegas, NV 89101
383-0500
Robert Worthen, Pres.
Buses - charter rental

Bell Trans
1900 Industrial Rd.
Las Vegas, NV 89102
Charter Limousine: 385-5466
Charter Bus: 736-4428

Exposition Transportation Inc.
6230 Greyhound Ln., Ste. G
Las Vegas, NV 89122
433-0530
Kristin Vlahof, Business Coordinator
Freight, storage and local transportation

Garth Tours
P.O. Box 26837
Las Vegas, NV 89126
228-3707
Vincent H. Garth, Sr., Tour Operator

Gray Line Tours of Southern Nevada
1550 S. Industrial Rd.
Las Vegas, NV 89102
384-1234
Richard Myler, VP Sales and Marketing
Group and individual ground transportation and sightseeing

K-T Services Coach USA
4020 E. Lone Mountain Rd.
N. Las Vegas, NV 89031
644-2233
Ray Ross
Chartered buses

Protrav Motor Coach Services
1515 E. Tropicana Ave.
Las Vegas, NV 89119
739-7714
Valerie Smith
Consistently reliable service

Superior Tours
4740 S. Valley View Blvd., Ste. 200
Las Vegas, NV 89103
798-7311
Jeff Whitker, Pres.
Charters and sightseeing

Bell Trans
1900 Industrial Rd.
Las Vegas, NV 89102

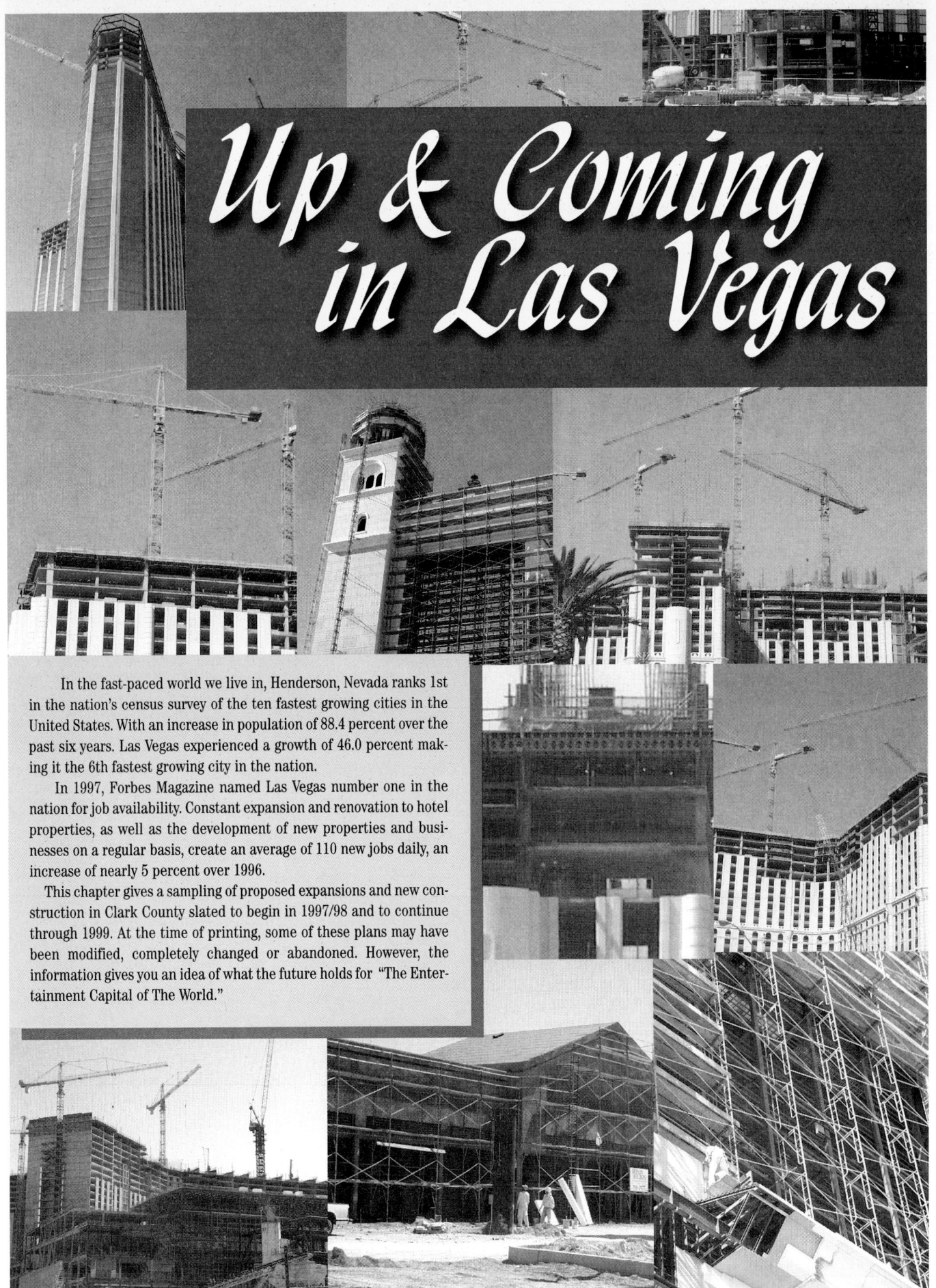

Up & Coming in Las Vegas

In the fast-paced world we live in, Henderson, Nevada ranks 1st in the nation's census survey of the ten fastest growing cities in the United States. With an increase in population of 88.4 percent over the past six years. Las Vegas experienced a growth of 46.0 percent making it the 6th fastest growing city in the nation.

In 1997, Forbes Magazine named Las Vegas number one in the nation for job availability. Constant expansion and renovation to hotel properties, as well as the development of new properties and businesses on a regular basis, create an average of 110 new jobs daily, an increase of nearly 5 percent over 1996.

This chapter gives a sampling of proposed expansions and new construction in Clark County slated to begin in 1997/98 and to continue through 1999. At the time of printing, some of these plans may have been modified, completely changed or abandoned. However, the information gives you an idea of what the future holds for "The Entertainment Capital of The World."

BELLAGIO

Bellagio
3650 Las Vegas Blvd. S.
Las Vegas, NV 89109

Groundbreaking took place November 1, 1995 for Bellagio, billed as the most extravagant and expensive hotel ever built. The $1.25 billion project is being built by Mirage Resorts chairman Steve Wynn.

Located on the 122-acre site of the legendary Dunes Hotel and Golf Course at the corner of Flamingo Rd. and Las Vegas Blvd. the resort is inspired by the idyllic village of Bellagio overlooking Italy's magnificent Lake Como. The complex will overlook a 9 acre lake with an array of lights and water jets providing a $30 million water ballet.

Bellagio's 36-story tower will feature 3,000 guest rooms and 400 suites that achieve an unmatched level of luxury and lavishness, decorated with European antiquities and artwork. Average room rates at the resort are projected to start at $168 a night. Shopping will include the most exclusive of international retailers, such as Chanel, Tiffany & Co., Giorgio Armani, and Gucci among others. A gallery housing $150 million in fine art will feature works by Picasso, Renoir and Rembrandt. Bellagio will also encompass a 15,000 square foot conservatory with massive floral displays that will change periodically, and extensive ballroom and meeting facilities including halls of 45,000 and 25,000 sq. ft. as well as smaller rooms. Each hall will have outdoor balconies overlooking the pool and garden. Entertainment at the Bellagio will be provided by a $70 million production created by Cirque du Soleil. The company has been the innovator of some of the most critically acclaimed performances in the world, including the very successful "Mystere" production at Treasure Island. A monorail will transport guests traveling between the Bellagio and the Monte Carlo, and a second monorail connecting the Bellagio to the Mirage is also proposed.

MANDALAY BAY

Mandalay Bay
3950 Las Vegas Blvd. S.
Las Vegas, NV 89109

Construction on Mandalay Bay, formerly known as Project Paradise, began in February 1997 on the former site of the Hacienda Hotel and Casino, which was imploded on New Year's Eve before a national television audience. Plans for the property include a 3,700-room, 43-story resort destination presenting a highly lush and adventuresome experience, surrounding a 10-acre tropical lagoon at the back of the property.

This "created environment" will contain, among other things, a sand and surf beach with Hawaii-style waves, a three-quarter mile lazy river ride and a swim-up shark tank. A self-contained 417-room Four Seasons Hotel will be part of the Mandalay, aiming to become the first five-star luxury resort on the Las Vegas Strip, the Four Seasons will have its own entrance, lobby and express elevators.

The architectural concept of Mandalay Bay reflects an ancient South Seas culture, as if a Forbidden City were discovered in an exotic island jungle. Inside the resort, visitors will enjoy spectacular waterfalls, terraced gardens, and mystical statuary. Also included will be a 12,000-seat arena, a nightclub, and a showroom

The $950 million resort is expected to open in Spring of 1999.

UP & COMING

PARIS LAS VEGAS

Paris Las Vegas
3665 Las Vegas Blvd. S.
Las Vegas, NV 89109

Paris Las Vegas was proposed by Bally Entertainment's Arthur Goldberg in 1995. The resort is being built on a 24 acre site on the southwest corner of Las Vegas Blvd. and Flamingo Rd., the last prime location left on the "Golden Mile" of the Las Vegas Strip. Hilton Hotels took over as developer when they acquired Bally's in 1996, adding to its position as the largest casino corp. in the world.

Ground was broken for Paris Las Vegas on April 18, 1997. The $750 million project is scheduled for completion in early 1999. The resort incorporates turn-of-the-century as well as modern motifs from the renowned "City of Lights."

The 34-story resort will consist of 2,914 rooms, including 300 suites; 85,000 sq. ft. of casino space including 100 table games, 2,500 slot and video machines and a race and sports book; 119,030 sq. ft. of convention and banquet facilities, 13 restaurants and bars, and a 25,000 sq. ft. health spa. Its signature attraction will be a 50-story replica of the Eiffel Tower, which will include a gourmet restaurant-bar on the mezzanine and an elevator to the top for spectacular views of the Las Vegas Valley. The design plan also includes many other replicas of Parisian landmarks, including the Arc de Triomphe, the Opera House, Parc Monceau, and the Rue de la Paix.

The 31,523 sq. ft. shopping area will resemble a Parisian street scene. Via a recreation of a Paris Metro station, the resort will be connected to the monorail that travels between Bally's and the MGM Grand.

Also incorporated into the new resort are art nouveau sculptures and paintings done by French Impressionists for an absolutely authentic atmosphere. The opening of Paris Las Vegas will give visitors all the excitement and magic of Paris, bringing the spirit, images, and savoir faire of the "City of Lights" to the "City of Neon Lights."

THE VENETIAN

The Venetian
3355 Las Vegas Blvd. S.
Las Vegas, NV 89109
733-5000 1-800-446-4678

Like the fabled city to which it owes its name, the Venetian promises to be a shimmering center of beauty, romance, power, and passion. The first phase of a $2 billion luxury resort, the Venetian is inspired by the splendor of Italy's most romantic city.

From the gondola-filled lagoon that beckons visitors along the Strip to reproductions of well-known architectural landmarks, the property depicts Renaissance Venice.

The first phase, scheduled to open in spring 1999, will house 3,000 luxury suites, a 100,000 sq. ft. casino with over 50 table games and 1,250 slot machines, 1.6 million sq. ft. of meeting space in the soon-to-be-expanded Sands Expo, an elegant 80,000 sq. ft. grand ballroom, the Grand Canal Shops featuring 750,000 sq. ft. of exclusive retail shops and boutiques, a four-level theater entertainment venue, as well as a second world-class theater and a luxury spa with spectacular pools in an Italian rooftop garden setting.

A sister tower, the Lido, is slated as the second phase of the project. The two towers, with a total of 6,000 suites, will make the resort the largest hotel property in the world.

ALADDIN

ALADDIN
3667 Las Vegas Blvd. S.
Las Vegas, NV 89109

Aladdin Gaming LLC President and chief executive officer Richard Goeglein recently unveiled the casino, retail and entertainment complex that will lead Las Vegas into the 21st Century – the $1.3 billion Aladdin Project – which will be completed in the spring of 2000.

The Aladdin Project is the first mixed-use development to offer two distinctly different hotels and casinos targeting different demographic groups, nearly one-half million square-feet of high-end retail, entertainment and dining facilities, a 7,000-seat premier concert venue and Las Vegas' first European-style luxury gaming salon. All of these attractions are seamlessly connected for secure and comfortable access from either Las Vegas Boulevard or Harmon Avenue.

Goeglein said the 34-acre redeveloped Aladdin site, owned by Aladdin Holdings LLC, will include the $826 million Aladdin Hotel & Casino with 2,600 new rooms; the 462,000-square-foot Desert Passage retail and mixed-use development; more than 150,000 square-feet of casino space, including a luxurious European-style gaming salon; and the 1,000-room music-themed hotel and casino developed by Planet Hollywood. The existing Aladdin Theater of the Performing Arts will undergo an $8-10 million renovation.

"The unique offerings of the new Aladdin will successfully draw incremental numbers of tourists to Las Vegas each year," said Goeglein.

The Aladdin will be strategically located at the mid-point of the Las Vegas Strip, at the center of all significant development currently underway in Las Vegas.

"When it is completed, this exciting destination will provide more than 7,000 jobs for Nevadans," Goeglein said.

Planet Hollywood Hotel & Casino on the Aladdin site

ACCOMMODATIONS - FUTURE PROJECTS

The Bellagio, Mandalay Bay, Paris Las Vegas, and Venetian are the four new hotel/casino projects breaking ground along the famed Las Vegas Strip.

At a projected combined cost of $4.5 billion, the four mega-resorts will create approximately 20,000 new jobs while visitors to the area are expected to increase by about 13% to more than 33 million people annually. There are also other projects on the drawing board.

EXISTING HOTEL/CASINO PROPERTY EXPANSIONS AND FUTURE PROJECTS

Site of the Aladdin Hotel
After the implosion, the Aladdin site will have two hotels and two casinos. The new Aladdin will have 2,500 rooms and a second, operated by Planet Hollywood will have 1,000 rooms. The new Aladdin project is scheduled to open in the spring of the year 2000.

The New Frontier Hotel & Gambling Hall
3120 Las Vegas Blvd. S.
Las Vegas, NV 89109
794-8200   1-800-634-6966
The Frontier Hotel & Gambling Hall was recently purchased by Kansas businessman Phil Ruffin from Margaret Elardi and her sons for $165 million. Shortly after receiving his gaming license and taking control of the property in early 1998, Ruffin's plans include $20 million in renovations to the Hotel.

Marriott
MGM Grand and Marriott have signed a joint venture agreement to build a 1,500 room nongaming Marriott Hotel adjacent to the MGM Hotel and Casino on the Strip. Construction of the property is scheduled to start in mid-1998 with completion expected by the end of 1999. The hotel will also house 40,000 sq. ft. of meeting space. While the hotel is to be a nongaming property, the MGM also has plans to build an additional 30,000 square feet of casino space near the Marriott location, bringing the total MGM casino space to over 200,000 sq. ft.

Rio Suite Hotel & Casino
3700 W. Flamingo Rd.
Las Vegas, NV 89103
252-7777   1-800-PLAYRIO
Fax: 252-0080
The Rio Suite Hotel & Casino has begun the first phase of its newest master plan, which includes a new 3,000 room hotel and casino resort property on the 43-acre property directly adjacent to the resort's current site depending on on-going evaluations about the market. A new road will allow additional access to the strip area. Other plans include expansions to the existing Rio Suite property. Although details regarding a theme or cost of the venture have not yet been disclosed, the new road and additions as well as further construction are estimated at $200 million. Improvements slated for the existing property include a 100,000 sq. ft. convention center, 10,000 additional square feet of retail space, 9 "Palazzo" suites and a concierge suite level in both Rio towers. The new road and additions are scheduled to open in several stages throughout 1998 and 1999.

Riviera Hotel
2901 Las Vegas Blvd. S.
Las Vegas, NV 89109
734-5110
A second convention and entertainment center is being built, bringing the total to 181,000 sq. ft. The $20 million project will also refurbish rooms and suites.

Silverton
3333 Blue Diamond Rd.
Las Vegas, NV 89130
263-7777
Silverton will add 600 rooms to its existing 304.

FUTURE HOTEL PROPOSALS

Neonopolis
Proposed for the east end of the Fremont Street Experience at Fremont St., Fourth St., Ogden Ave. and Las Vegas Blvd., plans for this project were initiated by World Entertainment Centers of Atlanta, Georgia. Estimated cost of this project is $84 million, and include a nongaming hotel, restaurants, retail shops, and a 24-screen movie theater.

Winter Wonderland Hotel/Casino Resort
Currently under consideration is Winter Wonderland, the nation's first indoor ski slope. Architect for the project is the Minneapolis-based Cunningham Group. The project, proposed by Richard Tam Investments for an 11-acre site at Koval Ln. and Harmon Ave. would include a 1,200 room hotel with 85,000 sq. ft. of casino space, several restaurants and retail shops, as well as an indoor ski slope with a 125-ft. drop and a 350-ft. mountain exterior with a cable car running down its side.

Santa Fe Galleria Hotel & Casino
This is expected to be completed in the summer of 1999. It will be located on Sunset Rd. adjacent to the Galleria Mall. The plans are for a 300 room hotel, 75,000 sq. ft. casino, 2,500 seat ice arena, 1,000 seat performing arts center, six restaurants, pool, spa, banquet and meeting rooms, and a children's activity center. The developer is Santa Fe Gaming Corporation.

TIME SHARE PROPERTIES

Las Vegas Lodge
Situated on 2.2 acres, costing $2.6 million, and with a value of $90 million, the Las Vegas Lodge, a 5-story, 66-unit time share complex proposed by Silverleaf Resorts, a Dallas-based company, will feature 1 and 2 bedroom units and a top-floor lounge and restaurant. Lodge construction is anticipated to begin in early 1998. Units will cost approximately $11,000 weekly and sales are slated to commence in mid-1998. Additional plans call for a second 9-story tower housing an additional 96 units, to begin construction in mid-1999.

RECREATION

PROPOSED PROJECTS

Adventure Kingdom
Emerald Isle Productions and Entertainment, Inc. announced plans for a 125-acre theme park, non-gaming hotel, convention center, and RV park to be built west of the Stratosphere Hotel and Casino in an area now occupied by Stupak Park. Information from city documents indicates that Emerald Isle will pay $4.5 million for the park.

Plans for Adventure Kingdom include a 2,700 room nongaming hotel complete with six grand ballrooms, 14 meeting rooms and business facilities, as well as a 2-acre swimming lagoon complete with waterfalls and water slides.

The theme park will be divided into seven sections, including Land of Little People, Old West Adventure, Nether World, Adventure Land, 2525 Future Adventure Land, Adventure Kingdom U.S.A. and Prehistoric Land, complete with prehistoric Robotic dinosaurs roaming through the area. No starting date for the project has been announced.
Developer: American Nevada Corporation

MEDIA

TELEVISION

1998 has brought changes to Las Vegas Television viewing. Currently the 61st largest television market in the United States, local television has added its first 10 o'clock evening news show. Prime Cable, the *Las Vegas Sun* and KLAS-TV Channel 8 have created a 24-hour all-news network that began on April 1, 1998. The channel includes a live 30-minute news show at 10 pm with reports from the *Sun* and KLAS "Eyewitness News." Estimated cost of the new department is $3 million, with approximately 20 new jobs being created.

MOVIE PRODUCTION

Movie Studio
Close to $97 million was spent in Nevada on movie production in 1997. In 1998 a $10 million studio-production plant will be built in Henderson. Black Mountain Studios will have multiple sound stages, production and post-production equipment, and Old West back lots.

ASSISTANCE

MEDICAL CENTERS

Hartwell Medical Center
Located at 1776 Warm Springs Rd. phase 1 of a 26,000 sq. ft. medical office building will offer primary care and medical services. Expected to open in the winter of 1998, the cost is $3.5 million.
Developer: Dasco Company

Parkway Medical Plaza
Developed by St. Rose Dominican Hospital and American Nevada Corp. is a 94,000 sq. ft., $15 million medical office building consisting of a surgical center, full diagnostics, lab & radiology, rehab services and physician practices.
Developer: Marshall Erdman & Associates

St. Rose Dominican Hospital · West Center
Phase 2 $100 million expansion consisting of 132 bed, full service, acute care hospital expected to be completed in December 1999.
Developer: HKS Architects

NEWCOMERS

Versailles
In October 1997, plans for a luxury condominium complex called The Versailles were approved by the Las Vegas City Council. Slated for construction in 1998, with floor plans from 3,000 to 13,500 sq. ft. and prices from $1.1 million to $5.5 million, the three 135-foot towers will provide breathtaking views of the Las Vegas Valley. Early plans call for two 2-story penthouse suites as well as a number of other smaller condominiums on the lower levels.

While plans call for three 12-story towers, Taurus Development, which expects to break ground on the project early in 1998, speculates between 20 and 40 condominiums per tower rather than the 56 units allowed for by the city council, providing for more spacious condos.

With a toll-free phone number of 888-LOUIS XV, the complex will boast a strictly French palace motif. The 14.5-acre property will also include full concierge service, spa and salon facilities, as well as elaborate gates and gardens at the property borders.

GOVERNMENT - BUSINESS

GOVERNMENT

New Courthouse

A $90 million Federal Courthouse is being built across from the old one at 300 Las Vegas Blvd. S. at the site of the "Minami Hole," started by a Japanese developer who went broke before starting a hotel there.

BUSINESS PARKS

Galleria Corporate Center

At a $20 million cost, a 160,000 sq. ft. master-planned center will feature small medical and office buildings. Date of completion to be announced.
Developer: Griffin Realty Company

Green Valley Corporate Center

Due to open late in 1999, a 90 acre master-planned office park, at a cost of $194.6 million. It will be located at Green Valley Pkwy. and Lake Mead Dr. with adjacent restaurant, retail shops, and child care facilities.
Developer: American Nevada Corporation

Horizon Ridge

A two story office project containing 30,000 sq. ft. will open in mid-1998 at Horizon Ridge and Green Valley Pkwy. at a cost of $3 million.
Developer: Scott Fulwider

The Plaza at Corporate Center

At a cost of $23.4 million, phase one will feature 56,862 sq. ft. of office space in a two story building expected to be completed in the summer of 1998.
Developer: American Nevada Corporation

Rainbow Corporate Center

Opening late in 1998 at a cost of $17 million, 2 three story buildings containing 155,000 sq. ft. will be located at the corner of Washington Ave. and Rainbow Blvd.
Developer: Rainbow Corporate Center LLC

Silverado Business Park

Costing $8 million it is expected to be completed in mid-1998. It will consist of three buildings, 165,000 sq. ft. of industrial space at Pecos Rd. between Alexander and Craig Rds.
Developer: Transwestern Property Company

Summergate Corporate Center - Phase II

Situated at the corner of Buffalo Dr. and Lake Mead Blvd. will be a two story building with about 50,000 sq. ft. of office space. At a cost of $5 million it is expected to open late in 1998.
Developer: TLC Enterprises

Sun Plaza

To be built at Fourth St. and Lewis Ave. and completed in mid-1999, it will consist of a 14 story building with 280,000 sq. ft. of office space.
Developers: Nevada State Bank and American Nevada Corporation

TechPark at Corporate Center

A $25.1 million, 200,000 sq. ft. office space divided among six buildings.

Phase 2 is expected to be completed in early 1998 and phase 3 in late 1998.
Developer: American Nevada Corporation

Trident Business Park

Expected to be completed late in 1998, a total of nine buildings are planned at the corner of Sahara Ave. and Miller Ln. totaling 6,500 - 19,500 sq. ft. at a cost of $10.2 million.
Developer: Trident Homes of Nevada

Warm Springs Crossing

It contains four concrete buildings for office, showroom and warehouse space, located at Warm Springs Rd. southwest of I-15. Phase 2 is expected to be completed in the spring of 1998 at a cost of $22.5 million.
Developer: Jackson-Shaw Company

TRANSPORTATION

PROPOSED PROJECTS

Clark County Regional Transportation Commission

301 E. Clark Ave., Ste. 300
Las Vegas, NV 89101
455-4481

Currently on the drawing board, The Clark County Regional Transportation Commission is planning nearly 20 miles of monorail servicing both sides of the Las Vegas Blvd. strip area. Tourists would be able to board a train at McCarran International Airport and be dropped off at their hotel destination. All of this is several years down the road at a projected cost of hundreds of millions of dollars.

The first phase of the monorail master plan proposed by the Commission includes a fixed system running from Cashman Field to the general area of the Stardust Hotel & Casino on the Las Vegas Strip. RTC figures indicate that this route would be the easiest and quickest for resort employees and tourists alike who are traveling between the Strip and downtown. Phase one cost estimates are around $380 million.

On a much smaller scale, development of a monorail system may progress as soon as the summer of 1998 with the expansion of an already operating system between the MGM Grand and Bally's. The expansion would extend the current system to include the Las Vegas Hilton and the Las Vegas Convention Center.

Mirage Resorts is already building a monorail between the Bellagio and the Monte Carlo. Talks with Caesars Palace would extend this system to Treasure Island.

While the monorail connecting the Bellagio and the Monte Carlo will run on private property and require no special permits, a project connecting the properties to Treasure Island may require county approval depending on the route taken.

McCarran Airport

Airport Information Systems Integration

Computer technology that will better efficiency of passenger check-in, baggage claim, boarding procedures and flight information.
Developer: EDS and ARING

Automatic Transit System / People Mover

A monorail that will transport passengers from Terminal 1 to "D" gates is expected to be completed by summer, 1998 at a cost of $79.2 million.
Developer: Max Riggs, AEG Westinghouse, Benedict

Baggage Claim Expansion

In the summer of 1998 there will be 16 new baggage carousels and new curbside roadway at a cost of $18.6 million.
Developer: Sletten Construction

"D" Gates

At a cost of $190 million, there will be an additional 26 gates opening. Completion is expected in the summer of 1998.
Developer: Perini/Henderson

ENTERTAINMENT - SPORTS

ENTERTAINMENT

Fremont Street Experience

Fremont Street Experience will be spending $1.2 million for improvements. The light show will be extended north on First and Third Sts. and there will be more landscaping and wider sidewalks. This project will take about two years.

SPORTS

Future Projects:

Mountain Spa
2810 W. Charleston Blvd.

Las Vegas, NV 89102
870-1234

A 637-acre master-planned destination resort and golf course community with 27 holes of championship golf, a 526-room resort hotel and spa, plus custom home sites is currently planned. Starting construction and completion dates are currently unavailable while the property is still undergoing financial negotiations. At present time estimates from Mountain Spa Development put a completion date at mid-1999.
Developer: Jack Sommer

Mount Charleston Golf Resort
1 Kyle Canyon Rd.
Mount Charleston, NV 89124
872-4653

Future projects for the resort include negotiations with the Forestry Department for additional prime land to increase the size of the course, allowing for additional tees. Also scheduled for completion in mid-1998 are a 16,000-17,000 sq. ft. Alpine Family Fun Center, including a video arcade, convenience store, gift shops and restaurant area, as well as an ice skating rink with a surrounding outdoor amphitheater for viewing of planned winter performances.

Plans for Asian and Western villages are also being considered.

Silver Canyon

A new 18-hole golf course is being proposed for the south end of Eastern Ave.

Rhodes Ranch

Nine thousand homes are being built on 1,700 acres at Durango and Warm Springs Rd.

SHOPPING & SERVICES

PLANNED PROJECTS

Car Country Factory Stores

Boulder Hwy.
Henderson, NV 89015
This will be a 225,000 sq. ft. factory mall with 65 stores located on 23 acres.

At the California-Nevada stateline, a new, 1 million square foot factory outlet mall and entertainment complex is planned adjacent to the Primadonna Hotel-Casino. One hundred well-known retailers, manufacturers, and designers are slated to set up shop at the center. The Gordon Company is the developer.

Paseo Verde Plaza

Situated at the corner of Lake Mead Dr. and Valle Verde, a 110,000 sq. ft. shopping center should open late spring of 1998 at a cost of $8.7 million.
Developer: American Nevada Corporation

Pebble Market Place

A 160,000 sq. ft. shopping center located at Pebble Rd. and Green Valley Pkwy. is expected to be completed at a cost of $13.2 million in the summer of 1998.
Developer: American Nevada Corporation

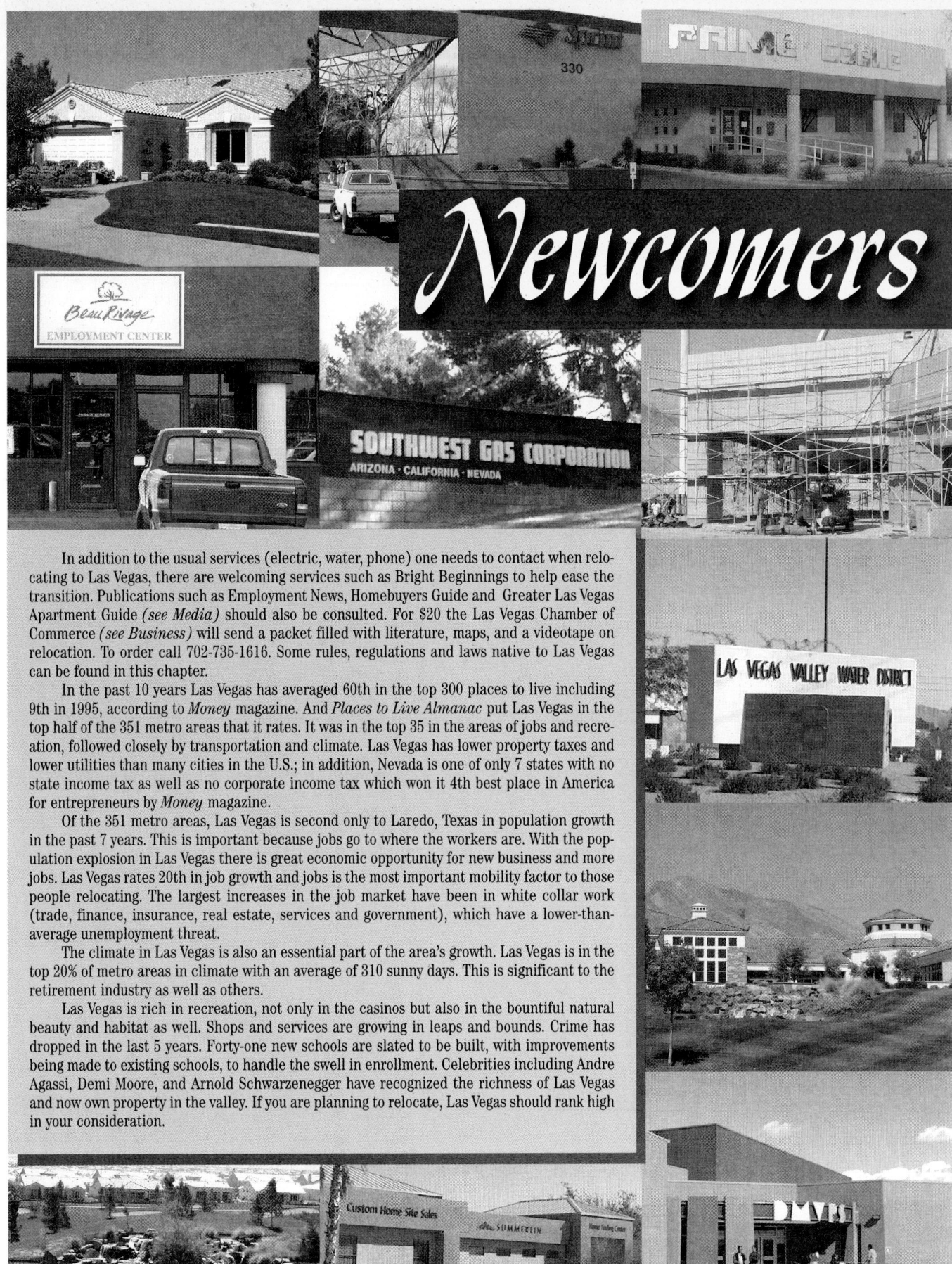

Newcomers

In addition to the usual services (electric, water, phone) one needs to contact when relocating to Las Vegas, there are welcoming services such as Bright Beginnings to help ease the transition. Publications such as Employment News, Homebuyers Guide and Greater Las Vegas Apartment Guide *(see Media)* should also be consulted. For $20 the Las Vegas Chamber of Commerce *(see Business)* will send a packet filled with literature, maps, and a videotape on relocation. To order call 702-735-1616. Some rules, regulations and laws native to Las Vegas can be found in this chapter.

In the past 10 years Las Vegas has averaged 60th in the top 300 places to live including 9th in 1995, according to *Money* magazine. And *Places to Live Almanac* put Las Vegas in the top half of the 351 metro areas that it rates. It was in the top 35 in the areas of jobs and recreation, followed closely by transportation and climate. Las Vegas has lower property taxes and lower utilities than many cities in the U.S.; in addition, Nevada is one of only 7 states with no state income tax as well as no corporate income tax which won it 4th best place in America for entrepreneurs by *Money* magazine.

Of the 351 metro areas, Las Vegas is second only to Laredo, Texas in population growth in the past 7 years. This is important because jobs go to where the workers are. With the population explosion in Las Vegas there is great economic opportunity for new business and more jobs. Las Vegas rates 20th in job growth and jobs is the most important mobility factor to those people relocating. The largest increases in the job market have been in white collar work (trade, finance, insurance, real estate, services and government), which have a lower-than-average unemployment threat.

The climate in Las Vegas is also an essential part of the area's growth. Las Vegas is in the top 20% of metro areas in climate with an average of 310 sunny days. This is significant to the retirement industry as well as others.

Las Vegas is rich in recreation, not only in the casinos but also in the bountiful natural beauty and habitat as well. Shops and services are growing in leaps and bounds. Crime has dropped in the last 5 years. Forty-one new schools are slated to be built, with improvements being made to existing schools, to handle the swell in enrollment. Celebrities including Andre Agassi, Demi Moore, and Arnold Schwarzenegger have recognized the richness of Las Vegas and now own property in the valley. If you are planning to relocate, Las Vegas should rank high in your consideration.

COST OF LIVING INDEX

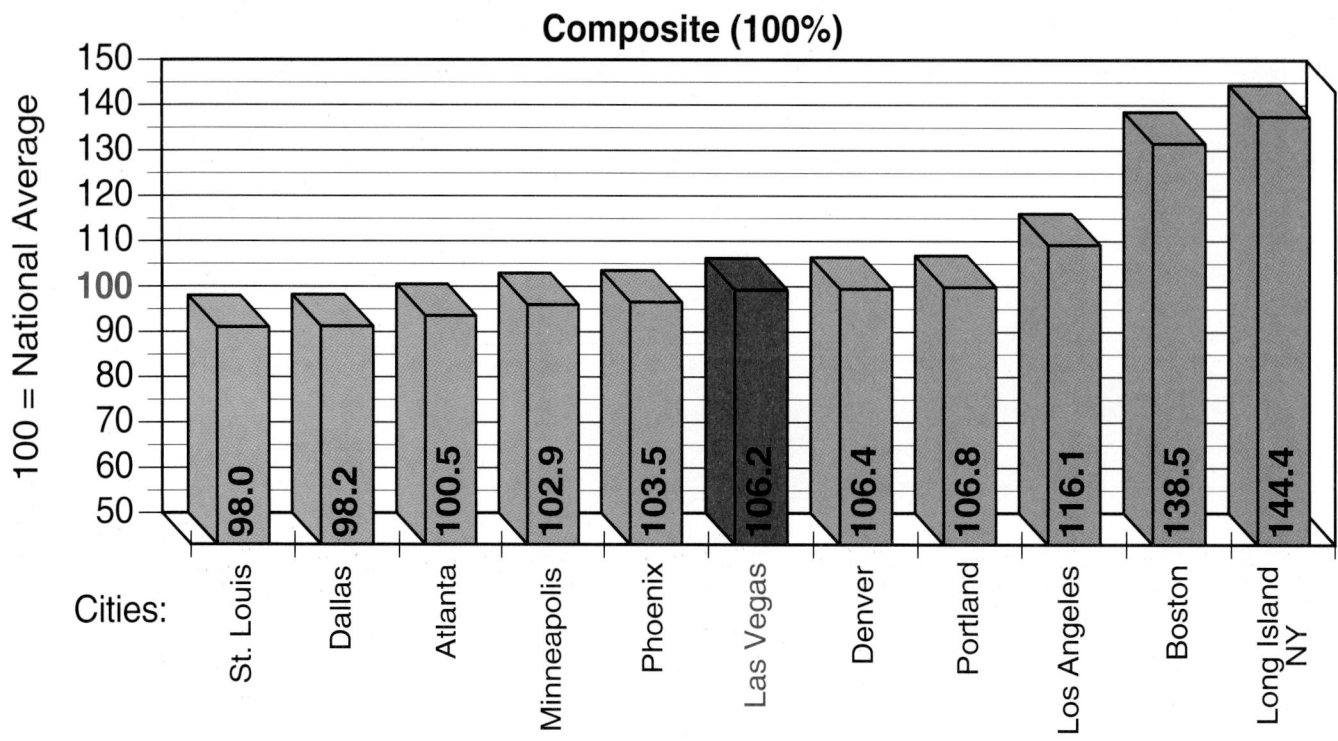

Composite (100%)

100 = National Average

City	Value
St. Louis	98.0
Dallas	98.2
Atlanta	100.5
Minneapolis	102.9
Phoenix	103.5
Las Vegas	106.2
Denver	106.4
Portland	106.8
Los Angeles	116.1
Boston	138.5
Long Island NY	144.4

Cities:

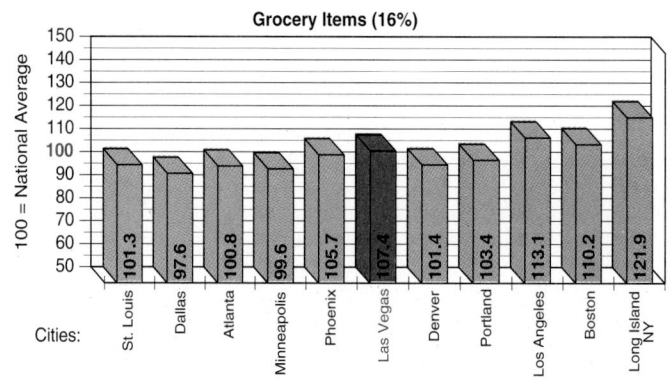

Grocery Items (16%)

100 = National Average

City	Value
St. Louis	101.3
Dallas	97.6
Atlanta	100.8
Minneapolis	99.6
Phoenix	105.7
Las Vegas	107.4
Denver	101.4
Portland	103.4
Los Angeles	113.1
Boston	110.2
Long Island NY	121.9

Cities:

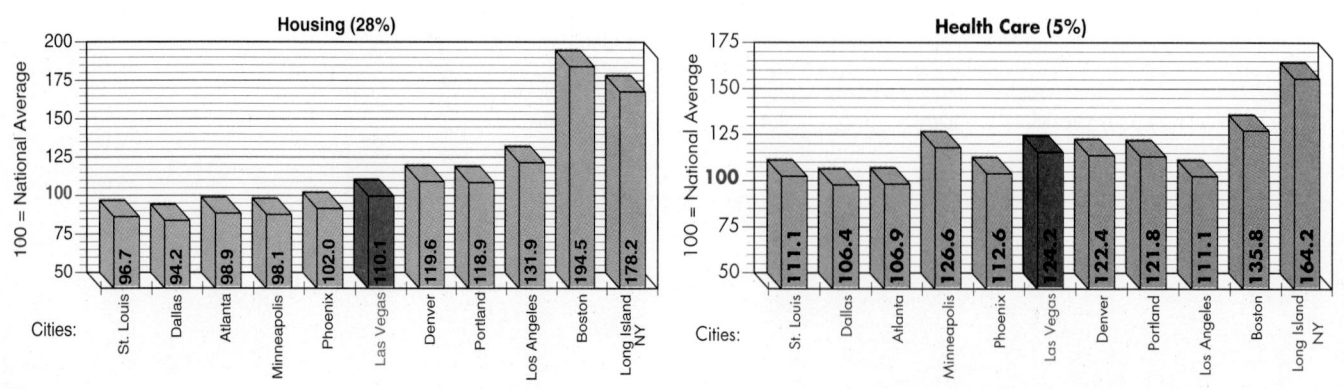

Housing (28%)

100 = National Average

City	Value
St. Louis	96.7
Dallas	94.2
Atlanta	98.9
Minneapolis	98.1
Phoenix	102.0
Las Vegas	110.1
Denver	119.6
Portland	118.9
Los Angeles	131.9
Boston	194.5
Long Island NY	178.2

Cities:

Health Care (5%)

100 = National Average

City	Value
St. Louis	111.1
Dallas	106.4
Atlanta	106.9
Minneapolis	126.6
Phoenix	112.6
Las Vegas	124.2
Denver	122.4
Portland	121.8
Los Angeles	111.1
Boston	135.8
Long Island NY	164.2

Cities:

Source: ACCRA

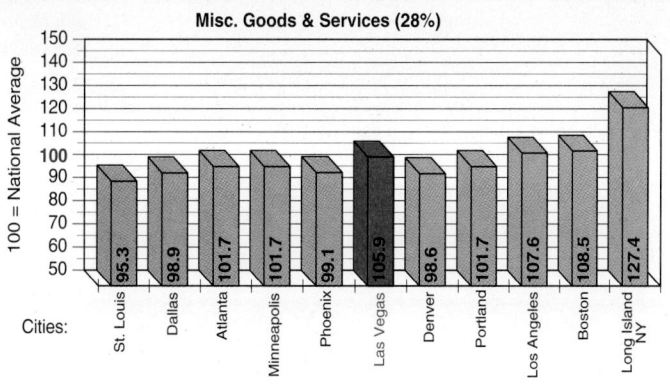

Misc. Goods & Services (28%)

100 = National Average

St. Louis 95.3, Dallas 98.9, Atlanta 101.7, Minneapolis 101.7, Phoenix 99.1, Las Vegas 105.9, Denver 98.6, Portland 101.7, Los Angeles 107.6, Boston 108.5, Long Island NY 127.4

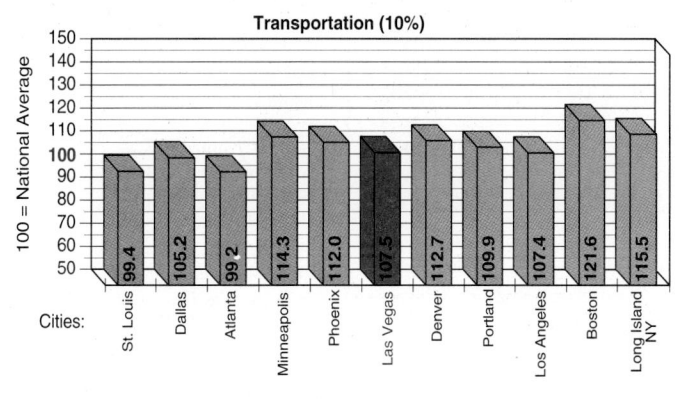

Transportation (10%)

100 = National Average

St. Louis 99.4, Dallas 105.2, Atlanta 99.2, Minneapolis 114.3, Phoenix 112.0, Las Vegas 107.5, Denver 112.7, Portland 109.9, Los Angeles 107.4, Boston 121.6, Long Island NY 115.5

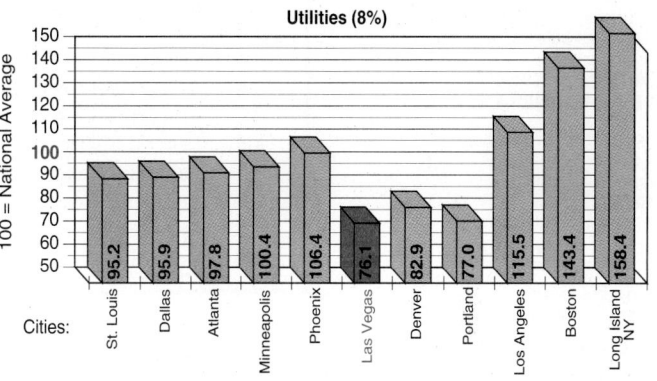

Utilities (8%)

100 = National Average

St. Louis 95.2, Dallas 95.9, Atlanta 97.8, Minneapolis 100.4, Phoenix 106.4, Las Vegas 76.1, Denver 82.9, Portland 77.0, Los Angeles 115.5, Boston 143.4, Long Island NY 158.4

Source: ACCRA

LAS VEGAS HOUSING MARKET

LAS VEGAS HOUSING MARKET

Median price house: $126,650
Average rent: $631.22

Housing Costs - 1996
Median price of new home:

2 bedroom:	$95,500
3 bedroom:	$111,500
4 bedroom:	$146,900

Average home sold:

2 bedroom:	$107,580
3 bedroom:	$119,574
4 bedroom:	$186,670

Median price of condominium:

2 bedroom:	$72,250
3 bedroom:	$97,500
4 bedroom:	$143,000

Average price of condominium:

2 bedroom:	$85,288
3 bedroom:	$104,794
4 bedroom:	$146,614

WHO LIVES IN LAS VEGAS

Population: July 1996: 1,119,705
July 1997: 1,170,113

Total Households: 416,051

Male/Female: 49% / 51%

Married: 51%

Adults with College Degrees:
(1990 census) 19.6%

Births:	17,895
Deaths:	9,255
Marriages:	103,871
Divorces:	8,700

Median Household Income:
$38,389
Average number of persons
per household (1990): 2.6

EMERGENCY NUMBERS

Nevada Power Company	367-5555
Southwest Gas Corp.	365-1111
Sprint Telephone	611 or 385-2211
AT&T	1-800-222-3000
Prime Cable	383-4000
Metro Police or Fire Dept.	911
Secret Witness	385-5555
F.B.I.	385-1281
Forest & Range Fires	647-5090
Bureau of Alcohol, Tobacco and Firearms	388-6584
U.S. Secret Service	388-6571
U.S. Marshals Service	388-6355
Drug Enforcement Administration	388-6635
Emergency Road Conditions	486-3116
American Red Cross	384-1225
Oil & Toxic Chemical Spill	1-800-424-8802
Suicide Prevention Center - Clark County	731-2990
Rape Crisis Center	366-1640
Poison Center	732-4989
Domestic Violence	646-4981
Child Abuse & Neglect	399-0081
Time & Temperature	118
Clark County Health District	385-1291
Runaway Youth Hotline	385-3335
Better Business Bureau	735-6900
Consumer Affairs	486-7355

WELCOME SERVICES

Bright Beginnings
889 S. Rainbow Blvd., Ste. 580
Las Vegas, NV 89128
256-7782
Cheri Petroni
A personalized session acquainting newcomers with
community resources.

Desert Newcomer Club
564-3216
Nanct Zangl, Pres.
Meets last Thu. of each month at Green Valley
library.

Newcomers Club of Las Vegas
458-5744
Josephine Bergman, Reservation Chairman
Nancy Hasselman, Pres.
Meets every 3rd Thu. at 11:30 am at the Showboat.
Their charity is Safe Nest which is a home for abused
women and children.

Welcome Wagon International
507 Sutters Mill Ct.
Henderson, NV 89014
898-0567   1-800-779-3526   474-1313

Jan Nygard, Field Mgr.
Welcoming service for newcomers.

Westside Newcomers Club
341-8690
Pearl DePietro, Pres.
Social club for women who have lived in Las Vegas for
less than 3 years. Meets 2nd Wed. of each month at various casinos and third Wed. at Sahara library.

RESIDENTIAL REAL ESTATE FIRMS

Listed are some of the top real estate
companies in terms of realtors or offices.
There are many more fine companies in
Las Vegas but due to space limitations,
we cannot list them all.

AMERICANA GROUP
BETTER HOMES AND GARDENS

Americana Group Realtors ·
Better Homes & Gardens
Interstate relocation:
796-7777
1-800-456-4885
5420 W. Sahara Ave., Ste. 101
Las Vegas, NV 89102
362-1111
Gene Freedman

3790 Paradise Rd., Ste. 100
Las Vegas, NV 89109
796-7777
Mark Misceivic

9408 Del Webb Blvd.
Las Vegas, NV 89134
256-3333
Myron Nalder

620 N. Rainbow Blvd.
Las Vegas, NV 89107
870-7777
Jan O'Brien

2625 N. Green Valley Pkwy.
Henderson, NV 89014
458-8888
Mark Stark

3240 E. Tropicana Ave.
Las Vegas, NV 89121
796-7777
Lesley Barr

8241 Bermuda Beach Dr.
Las Vegas, NV 89128
276-8680
Jan Bravin

Americor Realty
4509 W. Sahara Ave.
Las Vegas, NV 89102
365-1033
John La Duke

Award Realty
3015 S. Jones Blvd.
Las Vegas, NV 89102
873-7400   1-800-945-0222
Michael Fowler

Century 21 Real Estate
Each office is independently owned and
operated.

Aaimheigh
6010 W. Cheyenne Ave., Ste. 11
Las Vegas, NV 89108
655-7000
Rod Johnson

TOP TEN LARGEST REAL ESTATE FIRMS		
# 1	Americana Group Realtors	582 Agents
# 2	Liberty Realty	328 Agents
# 3	Century 21 - Moneyworld	233 Agents
# 4	Realty Executives	224 Agents
# 5	Properties Plus	220 Agents
# 6	General Realty Group	169 Agents
# 7	Coldwell Banker	160 Agents
# 8	Prudential Southwest Realty	134 Agents
# 9	Americor Realty	92 Agents
#10	Rossum Realty Unlimited	72 Agents

Act 1
3430 E. Flamingo Rd.
Las Vegas, NV 89121
451-2605
Jerry Abel

Action Network Realty
2551 N. Green Valley Pkwy.
Henderson, NV 89014
458-7653
Breese Rusk

Affordable Realty
3626 Pecos-McLeod, Ste. 1
Las Vegas, NV 89121
791-0709
Susan M. Reed

Barrett & Co.
2885 S. Jones Blvd.
Las Vegas, NV 89102
252-7100
Bob Barrett

Consolidated Realty
2820 E. Flamingo Rd., Ste. D
Las Vegas, NV 89121
732-7282
Bette Leal

Gordon Realty
3501 W. Charleston Blvd.
Las Vegas, NV 89102
878-2121
Mike Gordon

Henderson Realty
18 S. Water St.
Henderson, NV 89015
564-2515
Duane Laubach

JR Realty
101 E. Horizon Dr., Ste. A
Henderson, NV 89015
564-5142
Jackie Wooldridge

Moneyworld Realtors
4310 E. Tropicana Ave.
Las Vegas, NV 89121
435-8300
Michael Donovan

Moneyworld Realtors
6431 W. Sahara Ave.
Las Vegas, NV 89102
876-2700
Mike West

Realty Associates
3100 S. Valley View Blvd.
Las Vegas, NV 89102
871-1441   1-800-844-7356
Jack Matthews

Sell-Abration Realty
1555 E. Flamingo Rd., Ste. 200
Las Vegas, NV 89119
731-2100
Lois Mazgaj

Summerlin
8455 W. Lake Mead Blvd.
Las Vegas, NV 89128
242-4228
Sue Gray

Boulder Dam
1664 Nevada Hwy.
Boulder City, NV 89005
293-4664
Ellen Lamb

Coldwell Banker
Anchor Realty
1497 Nevada Hwy.
Boulder City, NV 89005
293-5757
Katie Cartlidge

Meadows
Premier Inc.
3844 Meadows Ln., Ste. A
Las Vegas, NV 89107
877-6200
Robert Penton

Rainbow
Premier Inc.
2975 S. Rainbow Blvd., Ste. C
Las Vegas, NV 89102
871-9500
Bob Hamrick

Tropicana
Premier Inc.
3690 E. Tropicana Ave.
Las Vegas, NV 89121
458-7070
Steve Baird

ERA Realty
ERA Professional Realty
2620 Regatta Dr., Ste. 116
Las Vegas, NV 89128
363-7573
Joan Berry

ERA Sunbelt Realty
3101 Spring Mountain Rd., Ste. 1
Las Vegas, NV 89102
364-1699
Raymond Smith

ERA Western Properties
6655 W. Sahara Ave., Ste. A116
Las Vegas, NV 89102
873-4372
Harlene Bailey

ERA Palma
2570 E. Tropicana Ave.
Las Vegas, NV 89121
456-5003
Joe Gioeli

General Realty Group, Inc.
6330 S. Eastern Ave., Ste. 2
Las Vegas, NV 89119
736-4664
Jay Dana

101 S. Rainbow Blvd.
Las Vegas, NV 89128
870-4664
Jay Dana

1211 E. Charleston Blvd.
Las Vegas, NV 89104
312-3272

721 E. Charleston Blvd., Ste. 4
Las Vegas, NV 89104
499-2272
Ricardo Monterroso

Liberty Realty
4055 S. Spencer St., Ste. 108
Las Vegas, NV 89119
735-5052

2685 S. Rainbow Blvd.
Las Vegas, NV 89102
248-8899
Richard Bell

Properties Plus
Properties Plus
2001 E. Flamingo Rd., Ste. 115
Las Vegas, NV 89119
732-7587
Shoni Hetland

8064 W. Sahara Ave.
Las Vegas, NV 89117
256-7587
Joseph Sherry

434 N. Rancho Rd., Ste. 222
Las Vegas, NV 89130
658-7587
Joseph Sherry

Prudential Southwest Realty
Prudential Southwest Realty
2950 S. Rancho Dr.
Las Vegas, NV 89102
251-1010
David Boyer
Executive Office - 871-8600

3663 E. Sunset Rd., Ste. 102
Las Vegas, NV 89120
454-7400
Sandy Ford

2001 S. Rainbow Blvd.
Las Vegas, NV 89102
243-3500
Red Mattson

Realty Executives
Realty Executives
1-800-533-6166
1903 S. Jones Blvd.
Las Vegas, NV 89102
873-4500
Jeff Moore

1231 Town Center Dr., Ste. 100
Las Vegas, NV 89134
648-4500
Jeff Moore

2920 N. Green Valley Pkwy.
Henderson, NV 89014
795-4500
Fafie Moore

1803 S. Jones Blvd., Ste. 100
Las Vegas, NV 89102
566-4500
Fafie Moore

Rossum Realty Unlimited
3875 S. Jones Blvd., Ste. 101
Las Vegas, NV 89103

368-1850
Elizabeth Rossum

Venture Realty Group
3560 S. Jones Blvd.
Las Vegas, NV 89103
368-3300
Deborah Musso

REAL ESTATE GUIDES & INFORMATION

Coldwell Banker Buyers Guide
Available at grocery and convenience stores.

Greater Las Vegas Association of Realtors
1750 E. Sahara Ave.
Las Vegas, NV 89104
732-8177
Paddy Ryan, Interim Exec. V.P.
Local real estate association whose members follow a code of ethics established by the National Association of Realtors. Promotes real estate sales through board members.

Homebuyers Guide
1456 E. Tropicana Ave.
Las Vegas, NV 89119
891-8420
Irene Boyle, Nevada Division Mgr./Ass. Publisher
Monthly guide to new home communities.

Homes & Living
Mountain House, Inc.
2500 Chandler Ave., Ste. 1
Las Vegas, NV 89120
891-0095 1-800-247-6996
Terry Tebbs, Publisher
Monthly new homes magazine.

Homes of Las Vegas Century 21
Real estate guide of properties offered for sale through Century 21 offices. Available free throughout Las Vegas.

Home Scene
900 S. Main St.
Las Vegas, NV 89101
224-5555
Pete Bodnar, Mgr.
A Nifty Nickel Publication
News and guide to homes and real estate published the 4th Fri. of every month.

Las Vegas Homes Illustrated
5825 W. Sahara Ave., Ste. G
Las Vegas, NV 89102
367-3439
T. C. Turpin, Publisher
Biweekly magazine listing homes and property for sale through brokers.

Metropolitan Real Estate Guide
1201 Arville St.
Las Vegas, NV 89102
870-3435
Paul Brauner, Pres.
Full color guide featuring pictures of homes for sale through licensed realtors. Available free at stores throughout Las Vegas.

Las Vegas Review-Journal & Sun
Sunday combined edition. Real estate section each Sun.; classified ads daily. Classified ads are the same in both newspapers.

The Real Estate Book
4330 S. Valley View Blvd., Ste. 102
Las Vegas, NV 89103
367-7200
Beverly Croft, Pres.
Pictures and information on homes.

Today's Homes of Las Vegas
3139 S. Eastern Ave.
Las Vegas, NV 89109
731-4000
Alain Romeriez, Gen. Mgr.
Free monthly homes for sale by realtors guide.

House Detective
Televised Sun. mornings at 9 am on KTNV-TV Channel 13. Information and pictures of homes for sale in Las Vegas through licensed realtors.

New Homes Las Vegas TV
Sun. mornings 7 am on Fox Channel 5.

HOME BUILDERS

American West Development
2700 E. Sunset Rd.
Las Vegas, NV 89120
736-6434
Larry Canarelli, Pres.

Avanti Homes
2325 Renaissance Dr.
Las Vegas, NV 89119
798-6800
Rex Lewis, Pres.

Beazer Homes
770 E. Warm Springs Rd.
Las Vegas, NV 89119
837-2100
Warren Kiggins

Coleman Homes
1635 Village Center Dr., Ste. 100
Las Vegas, NV 89134
243-9800
Ron Ray, Pres.

Capital Pacific Homes
3200 Soaring Gulls Dr., Ste. 7
Las Vegas, NV 89129
362-2000
Scott Coler, Pres.

Del Webb Corporation
9555 Del Webb Blvd.
Las Vegas, NV 89134
363-2111
Frank Pankratz, Gen. Mgr.

Falcon Development
2290 S. Jones Blvd., Ste. 110
Las Vegas, NV 89102
871-6677
Fred Ahlstrom, Pres.

Gem Homes
777 W. Lake Mead Blvd.
Las Vegas, NV 89106
221-1177
Steve Rebeil

Kaufman & Broad
4755 Industrial Rd.
Las Vegas, NV 89103
261-1300
Jay L. Moss, Pres.

Lewis Homes of Nevada
3325 W. Ali Baba Ln., Ste. 603
Las Vegas NV 89118
736-8960
Robert Lewis, Pres., NV Div.

Pacific Homes
1095 E. Twain Ave.
Las Vegas, NV 89109
369-8119
Steve Molasky, CEO

Pardee Construction of Nevada
4835 S. Rainbow Blvd., Ste. 301
Las Vegas, NV 89103
876-2634
Ray Landry, Asst. V/P of Sales

Perma-Bilt Homes
7150 Pollock Dr., Ste. 104
Las Vegas, NV 89119
896-9100
Daniel Schwartz, Pres.

Plaster Development
(Signature Homes & Monogram Homes Inc.)
801 S. Rancho Dr., Ste. E4
Las Vegas, NV 89106
385-5031
Richard Plaster, Pres.

Pulte Homes
1635 Village Center Dr., Ste. 250
Las Vegas, NV 89134
256-7900
Steven Petruska, Div. Pres.

Rhodes Homes
4630 S. Arville St., Ste. B
Las Vegas, NV 89103
433-4663
James M. Rhodes, Pres.

Richmond American Homes
6400 S. Eastern Ave., Ste. 18
Las Vegas, NV 89119
736-1770
Kent Lay, Div. Pres.

Robert V. Jones Corporation
3275 S. Jones Blvd., Ste. 105
Las Vegas, NV 89102
227-6600
Gary Lake, Pres.

Stanpark Construction
8080 W. Sahara Ave., Ste. A
Las Vegas, NV 89117
255-7753
Dave Carver, Pres.

Sterling S. Development
5365 Cameron St.
Las Vegas, NV 89118
871-0555
Michael Stratton, Pres.

Torino Construction Corporation
4820 Alpine Pl., Ste. E202
Las Vegas, NV 89107
258-4474
Brett Torino, CEO

U. S. Home
3075 E. Flamingo Rd., Ste. 100
Las Vegas, NV 89121
451-6222
Steve Hackney, Pres.

Woodside Homes
3855 S. Jones Blvd., Ste. 102
Las Vegas, NV 89103
889-7800
Chip Nelson, Pres.

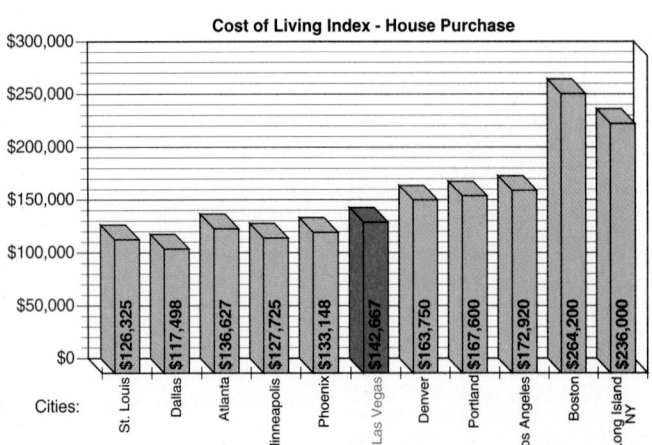

Cost of Living Index - House Purchase

City	Amount
St. Louis	$126,325
Dallas	$117,498
Atlanta	$136,627
Minneapolis	$127,725
Phoenix	$133,148
Las Vegas	$142,667
Denver	$163,750
Portland	$167,600
Los Angeles	$172,920
Boston	$264,200
Long Island NY	$236,000

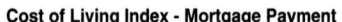
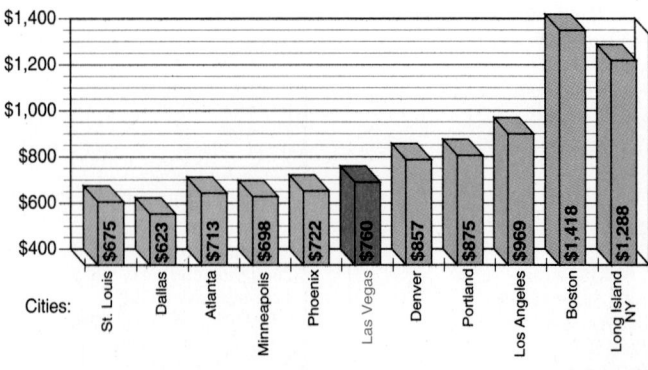

Cost of Living Index - Mortgage Payment

City	Amount
St. Louis	$675
Dallas	$623
Atlanta	$713
Minneapolis	$698
Phoenix	$722
Las Vegas	$760
Denver	$857
Portland	$875
Los Angeles	$969
Boston	$1,418
Long Island NY	$1,288

Source: ACCRA

HOUSING DEVELOPMENT
MASTER PLANNED COMMUNITIES

Model Home Center 10351

Summerlin is named after Howard Hughes' grandmother. Hughes began acquiring the 39 sq. mi. parcel of land west of Las Vegas in the 1950s in a land swap with the federal government.

Canyon Gate
8700 W. Sahara Ave.
Las Vegas, NV 89117
352 acres
Developer: Torino Industries

Desert Shores Community Association
2500 Regatta Dr.
Las Vegas, NV 89128
254-1020
Judy Farrah, Gen. Mgr.
986 acres, 4 lakes and 3,100 homes when completed.
Developer: RA Homes

Eldorado
Craig Rd./Camino El Norte
1,080 acres, 1,583 homes
Developer: Pardee Construction Company

Green Valley Ranch
American Nevada Corp.
2501 N. Green Valley Pkwy., Ste. 200
Henderson, NV 89014
263-4963
Tony Traub
South of Lake Mead Dr./Between Pecos and Valley Verde Dr.
1,311 acres
Developer: American Nevada Corp.
Prices begin in the low $100s in 17 neighborhoods.

Lake Las Vegas Resort
1605 Lake Las Vegas Pkwy.
Henderson, NV 89011
735-1919 1-800-564-1603
Sherri O'Boyle, V/P Marketing
Sales Office: 564-1600
Located in Henderson east on Lake Mead Dr. for 7 mi. Turn left on Lake Las Vegas Pkwy. Located 17 mi. east of Las Vegas.
The $4 billion development is a 2,243 acre resort and master plan residential development. It consists of a 320 acre manmade lake, 250,000 sq. ft. village center with up to 6 hotels and 5 golf courses planned. Homesites planned from $255,000 to $2.5 million.
Southshore - Private residential development within Lake Las Vegas Resort. First private Jack Nicklaus Gold Course in Nevada. Approximately 361 residences and approximately 500 sin-

gle family homes. For information call 702-564-1600 or 800-564-1603.
Developer: Transcontinental Corp. of Santa Barbara and The Bass Family Interests of Fort Worth, TX.

The Lakes
W. Sahara Ave./Durango Rd.
1,302 acres
Developer: Collins Brothers & Buck Graves
Semi-custom homes for the homebuyer with discriminating taste and an eye for design, open spacious floor plans, oversize lots *(1/3 to 3/4 acres)*, mountain views and superior construction. Homes priced from $299,000.

Las Palmas
50 S. Jones Blvd., Ste. 101
Las Vegas, NV 89107
870-0212
Jim Zeiter
Developer: Las Palmas L.L.C.
Clayton / Lone Mountain
140 acres - 714 homes

Los Prados
Lone Mountain Rd./Jones Blvd.
5020 Burr Oak St.
Las Vegas, NV 89130
645-1562
Sylvia Leby
372 acres, 1,300 homes
Developer: U. S. Homes

MacDonald Ranch
2920 N. Green Valley Pkwy., Ste. 212
Henderson, NV 89014
458-0001
Richard C. MacDonald
Lake Mead Dr./US 93/95 in Henderson
Project will consist of 2,500 homes, one hotel, two golf courses, office and retail space. There are 557 homes at present. This community consists of four villages. The first to be completed is Sunridge which is family oriented; 60 acres of parks, public and private schools. Del Webb's Sun City (*MacDonald Ranch*) is not complete. Foothills is an upscale community consisting of an 18 hole golf course and country club. Fourth village is unnamed.
Developer: Richard MacDonald

Mountain Spa Resort
Far Northwest Las Vegas near Floyd Lamb State Park
It's a $1 billion, 636 acre golf course, hotel, casino and residential development. When completed, it will feature about 1,120 residential units including custom

homes, estate homes and condominiums, 363 room hotel, 40,000 sq. ft. retail center and 90,000 sq. ft. of office space.
Developer: Jack Sommer

The Orchards
3325 W. Ali Baba Ln., Ste. 603
Las Vegas, NV 89118
736-8960
Ron Rulof
East Charleston/Hollywood Blvd.
380 acres - 1,200 homes

Painted Desert
Painted Mirage Rd.-Ann Rd./Rancho
Las Vegas, NV 89129
462 acres
Developer: Painted Desert Development
375 homes and condominiums

Peccole Ranch
W. Charleston and Sahara near Fort Apache
632 acres, 17 neighborhoods with 1,822 homes, not all completed
Developer: Bill Peccole

Rancho Del Norte
Craig Rd./Camino Del Norte
N. Las Vegas, NV 89031
642-4420
Developer: C.R.I.B., Ltd.
320 acres; priced from $99,990

Rancho Las Palmas
4835 S. Rainbow Blvd., Ste. 301
Las Vegas, NV 89103
876-2634
Ray Landry
Developer: Pardee Construction
610 Palmwood
540 acres

Seven Hills
Lake Mead Dr./Eastern Ave. in Henderson
Seven Hills will include 23 neighborhoods totaling 3,000 homes and more than 150 acres of planned community parks, picnic sites and ball parks.
Developer: Terry Johnson and Forest City Enterprises

Southfork
404 Presque Isle
Henderson, NV 89014
896-3600
Developer: The Developer of Nevada
378 acre master plan priced from $90s to $200s; 3 neighborhoods.

Spanish Trail
West Tropicana at Rainbow Blvd.
Sales and Information
6767 W. Tropicana Ave., Ste. 100
Las Vegas, NV 89103
362-9797 1-800-331-6274
Michael Fahey
640 acres - 26 models - gated community
Developer: Spanish Trail

Spring Valley
W. Flamingo Rd./Rainbow Blvd.
1,160 acres
Developer: Pardee

Summerlin
Summerlin Information Center
1500 N. Town Center Dr.
Las Vegas, NV 89134
791-4500
Karen Wofford
US 95 North to Summerlin Pkwy.
22,500 acres with more than 150 model homes open. Sold 2,060 homes in 1997; 44,000 residents.
Subdivisions: Villages - The Hills - The Hills South - The Pueblo - The Trails - The Crossing - Sun City - the Canyons - The Arbors and The Willows
Developer: The Howard Hughes Corporation

Sun City Summerlin
US 95 North to Summerlin Pkwy.
Sales Office
10351 Sun City Blvd.
Las Vegas, NV 89134
363-5454 1-800-843-4848
Frank Pankratz, Gen. Mgr.
14 floor plans prices from 120,000's to more than $200,000.
Occupancy high restricted to at least one person 55 or older and no one in permanent residence under 19. Since 1988, the 2,530-acre master-planned community has reported sales of 6,818 homes and is home to over 11,000 residents.

Whitney Ranch
Whitney Ranch Pkwy. between Sunset and Russell Rds.
510 acres
Developer: American West
There are six communities at Whitney Ranch. Cimarron was the first built, followed by Candle Creek, Candle Creek II, Sandstone, Indian Creek and The Canyons. There are professional offices, a park and three schools.

APARTMENT COMPLEXES

APARTMENTS

There are 115,866 multi-family units in Clark County. The average apartment rent is $631.22 with a vacancy rate of 3.6 percent.

The average rent is:
Studio:	$450.00
One Bedroom	$550.00
Two Bedroom	$725.00
Three Bedroom	$850.00

Nevada Apartment Association
5030 Paradise Rd., Ste. C101
Las Vegas, NV 89119
547-3550
Sherry Byrns, Pres.
John Terranova, Exec. Dir.
Hours: Mon. - Fri. 9 am - 4 pm
Protects rights of both tenants and property owners.

Listed below are apartment communities with approximately 500 units or more. Most apartments provide trash and water unless otherwise indicated. Also see extended stay accommodations.

Canyon Lake
2200 S. Fort Apache Rd.
Las Vegas, NV 89117
363-4415
504 apartments
Water & sanitation furnished; 7 months lease; 1 bedroom $660 - $675; 2 bedrooms $780-$795; 3 bedrooms $870-$880.

Crystal Creek Apartments
3001 W. Warm Springs Rd.
Henderson, NV 89014
451-8144
528 units
3 swimming pools, 2 whirlpool spas, 2 lighted tennis courts, 2 clubhouses with 24 hour fitness centers, men's and women's saunas and reserved covered parking; 1 bedroom $630-$640; small 2 bedrooms $735-$745 with fireplace $760, large two bedrooms $770-$780; 3 bedrooms $875-$885.

Crystal Cove
3309 Sky Country Ln.
Las Vegas, NV 89117
254-1133
444 apartments
Clubhouse and weight room, pools and spas, lighted tennis court, attached garage with opener, washer & dryer, children's playground. Month to month; $640-$950, 1 bedroom $640-$655; 2 bedrooms $750-$850; 3 bedrooms $865-$950.

Desert Club
3950 Koval Ln.
Las Vegas, NV 89109
732-1244
658 apartments
Gated entry; five pools, jacuzzis, clubhouse, racquetball courts, 5 fitness rooms, roman tubs. Water and sanitation furnished; 6 month and 12 month lease, 1 bedroom $620-$680; 2 bedrooms $775-$840.

Eagle Trace Apartments
5370 E. Craig Rd.
Las Vegas, NV 89115
643-3833
984 apartments. 5 swimming pools, 6 hot tubs, 2 racquetball courts, 1 basketball court, sand volleyball, 2 tennis courts, Kiddy Rec Center *(activities planned)* and 2 playgrounds, 3 fitness centers; 1 bedroom $540-$635; 2 bedrooms 2 baths $695-$750; 3 bedrooms $795-$835.

Grand Plaza Apartments
4308 Koval Ln.
Las Vegas, NV 89109
733-8888
660 apartments
15 pool areas and laundry facilities; 1 bedroom $525, 2 bedrooms, 1 bath $545; 2 bedrooms, 2 bath $585; 3 bedrooms $650.

Harbor Island
370 E. Harmon Ave.
Las Vegas, NV 89109
732-9111
998 apartments
Furnished studio and one bedroom; all utilities paid except telephone.
No lease required; studio $149.70 per week, $598 per month; one bedroom $159.50 per week, $638 per month.

La Tierra Apartments
8600 Starboard Dr.
Las Vegas, NV 89117
363-8033
896 apartments
Washer & dryer, 5 pools, spas, play areas, weight room. 6 month/1 year lease; 1 bedroom $585, 2 bedrooms $639, 3 bedrooms $790.

The Meridian at Hughes Center
250 E. Flamingo Rd.
Las Vegas, NV 89109
796-6666
Ken Scroggs
680 furnished and unfurnished apartments. Maid service available; eight floor plans; complete health club, lighted tennis courts, lagoon-sized swimming pool and one smaller one, spas, meeting rooms, full-time concierge, movie theater. Studio $685-$850; 1 bedroom $710-$1,100; 2 bedrooms $835-$1,485.

Nellis Oasis Executive Suites
5025 Nellis Oasis Ln.
Las Vegas, NV 89115
643-7340
408 apartments - furnished
Studio $530 monthly; 3 month lease $500/month; 6/month lease $435 month.

Oakwood Apartments
600 Oakmount Dr.
Las Vegas, NV 89109
735-3143
551 apartments
Located on the Las Vegas Country Club, just behind the Las Vegas Hilton. Five pools, spas, fitness center. Water, sanitation, and gas; furnished and unfurnished; 6 month or 1 year leases.
Furnished studio 6 month lease $630-$730, 12 month lease $580-$680; 1 bedroom furnished 6 month lease $880-$955, 12 month lease, $830-$905; 1 bedroom unfurnished 6 month lease $675-$885, 12 month lease, $625-$845; 2 bedrooms furnished 6 month lease $1,325-$1,440, 12 month lease, $1,275-$1,390; 2 bedrooms unfurnished 6 month lease $885-$1,100, 12 month lease $835-$1,100.

APARTMENT GUIDES

Copies can be obtained at convenience stores and supermarkets or call to have a guide sent to you.

For Rent Magazine
7330 Smoke Ranch Rd., Ste. A
Las Vegas, NV 89128
255-3700
Craig Holmes, Sales Mgr.
United Advertising Publications

Greater Las Vegas Apartment Guide
4425 Spring Mountain Rd., Ste. 300
Las Vegas, NV 89102
736-3943
Craig Simmons, Publisher
Haas Publishing Companies, Inc. Monthly pocket-size apartment guide distributed free throughout Las Vegas.

Las Vegas Review-Journal and Las Vegas Sun
Classified ads are the same in both newspapers.

Oasis Heritage
4870 E. Nellis Oasis Ln.
Las Vegas, NV 89115
644-1880
720 apartments
1 bedroom $530, 2 bedroom, 2 bath $635, 3 bedroom $775 with 6 month lease.

Oasis Paradise
3295 Casey Ave.
Las Vegas, NV 89120
458-8838
624 units
1 bedroom $630 - $655, 2 bedroom, 2 bath $730 - $790, 3 bedroom $925 - $950.

Oasis Ridge
3040 E. Charleston Blvd.
Las Vegas, NV 89104
457-4004
477 units
6 month lease - 1 bedroom $520, 2 bedrooms $625, 3 bedrooms $750.

Paradise Bay Club
4185 S. Paradise Rd.
Las Vegas, NV 89109
796-3500
544 apartments
Clubhouse with fitness center, 4 pools, 4 spas, alarm system, ceiling fans. Water & sanitation furnished; 6 month, 9 month or 12 month leases available; 1 bedroom $570-$635; 2 bedrooms $760-$820.

Pueblo Verde
2362 Green Valley Pkwy.
Henderson, NV 89014
456-0029
609 apartments
Located on the Wild Horse Country Club, Pueblo Verde's features include swimming pools and spas, lighted tennis court, basketball court, weight room, clubhouse, washer & dryer. Small pets welcome. Water and sanitation furnished, studios $535-$555;

Cost of Living Index - Rent Payment

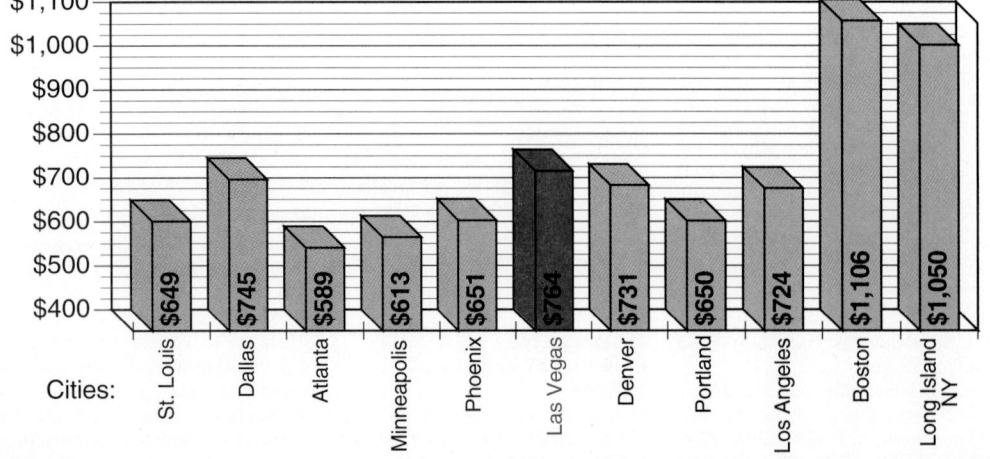

Cities:	St. Louis	Dallas	Atlanta	Minneapolis	Phoenix	Las Vegas	Denver	Portland	Los Angeles	Boston	Long Island NY
	$649	$745	$589	$613	$651	$764	$731	$650	$724	$1,106	$1,050

Source: ACCRA

1 bedroom $580-$600; 2 bedrooms, 1 bath $670-$690; 2 bedrooms, 2 bath $700-$710; 3 bedrooms, 2 bath $840-$850; 3 bedroom townhouses $930.

Renaissance Villas
(2 complexes with 844 apartments)
5419 W. Tropicana Ave.
Las Vegas, NV 89103
367-1001
1 bedroom $599 - $649, 2 bedroom $729 - $869 with 6 month lease

5445 W. Reno Ave.
Las Vegas, NV 89118
367-6710
Eight floor plans; full size washer & dryer, microwave, alarm system, fireplace available, pools and spas, tennis court and recreation center; water and sanitation furnished; 6 month leases available, $599-$839, 1 bedroom $599-$689, 2 bedrooms $698-$859.

Shelter Island
3770 S. Swenson St.
Las Vegas, NV 89119
734-6788
454 apartments
No lease required. Studio $149.50 per week; 1 bedroom $159.50 per week.

Summerhill Pointe
9501 W. Sahara Ave.
Las Vegas, NV 89117
254-7777
576 apartments
Three pools and spas, weight room, children's playground. Water & sanitation furnished. 3 month lease, then month to month; 1 bedroom $585, 2 bedrooms $695-$725; 3 bedrooms $695- $795.

Sundance Village
6500 W. Charleston Blvd.
Las Vegas, NV 89102
870-1982

532 apartments
Water & sanitation furnished; 6 months lease; 1 bedroom $495, 2 bedrooms, 1 bath $555; 2 bedrooms, 2 bath $605, 3 bedrooms $760-$825.

Sunterra Apartments
1901 N. Jones Blvd.
Las Vegas, NV 89108
646-3000
444 apartments
Activity center, pools and spas. 6 month or 12 month leases available, $500-$730; 1 bedroom $525, 2 bedrooms $595, 3 bedrooms $750.

Wildflower Apartments
6666 W. Washington Ave.
Las Vegas, NV 89107
877-0111
540 apartments

Three pools and spas, lighted tennis courts, basketball court, children's playground. Water & sanitation furnished. Studio $494, Jr. 1 bedroom $509, 1 bedroom $529, 2 bedrooms, 1 bath $594, 2 bedrooms, 2 baths $634, 3 bedrooms $764.

Westwood Pointe
5070 River Glen Dr.
Las Vegas, NV 89103
871-6552
468 apartments
24-hour monitored gate, pools and whirlpools, lighted tennis courts. 3 month lease, $580-$900 and 6 and 12 month leases, $555-$875, 1 bedroom $555, 2 bedrooms, 1 bath $625; 2 bedrooms, 2 baths $665; 3 bedrooms $775-$875.

PUBLIC UTILITIES

ELECTRIC

Nevada Power Company
Administrative Offices
6226 W. Sahara Ave.
Las Vegas, NV 89102
367-5000
Hours: Mon. - Fri. 8 am - 6 pm; drive-thru 24 hours
Charles A. Lenzie, Chairman
Turn on or turn off: 367-5555
Emergency: 367-5555
24 Hour Phone Service: 367-5555
Spanish: 367-5554
Hearing and Speech Impaired: 367-5080
Energy-saving programs info: 367-5111
Call Before You Dig: 1-800-227-2600

Henderson
227 Water St.
Henderson, NV 89015
367-5555
Hours: Mon. - Fri. 8 am - 5 pm

North Las Vegas
1820 E. Lake Mead Blvd.
N. Las Vegas, NV 89030
367-5555
Hours: Mon. - Fri. 7 am - 7 pm
Nevada Power began supplying service to the area in 1906. The company used a 90-horsepower single-cylinder gasoline engine.

Nevada Power gets only 4 percent of its power from Hoover Dam. Most of the utility's energy is generated by coal-fired and natural gas plants in the West. Nevada Power utilizes purchased power for 45 percent of southern Nevada's power. Residential air conditioning accounts for almost 50 percent of the yearly energy use in Las Vegas. Thirteen thousand miles of power lines deliver 14 million megawatt hours of electricity to Nevada Power's over 500,000 customers.

Monthly bills can also be paid at Nevada Power Ready Pay locations at most Albertson's, some Lucky's with 65 locations in all; contact Nevada Power, 367-5555. Customers must bring their monthly billing statement with them. Customer can pay by electronic fund transfer or use ATM debit card at the Sahara office.
Serves over 500,000 customers in Southern Nevada.
Rate: $68.86 excluding franchise tax per 1,100 kilowatt hours. There is a $5 customer service charge on all bills. The average residential bill is $73 per month. Energy charge is $.06034, deferred energy adjustment ($.00229); franchise tax rates change on a quarterly basis.
Residential Deposit: Customers with good credit from Nevada Power or another power company are not required to post a deposit. If a deposit is required it is 1 1/2 times the average monthly bill. The average deposit is about $100.
Connection: Connection charge of $15 will appear on your first bill.

Boulder City Utilities
City Council
401 California St.
Boulder City, NV 89005
293-9244
Hours: Mon. - Thu. 7 am - 6 pm

WATER

Southern Nevada receives 85 percent of the water it uses from the Colorado River, which supplies Lake Mead, and 15 percent from ground water. Las Vegans use, on the average, 178 gallons of water per day per person, an inflated figure because of the large amount of tourists visiting the city. The Las Vegas Valley is expected to use its entire water supply by the year 2010.
Las Vegas water has 79 milligrams per liter of hardness. The median for public water is 128 milligrams per liter in the West.

Las Vegas Valley Water District
1001 S. Valley View Blvd.
Las Vegas, NV 89153
870-2011
Patricia Mulroy, Gen. Mgr.
258-3104
Water Conservation Hotline: 258-3102
Customer Service: 870-4194
Water quality: 258-3215
Emergency: 258-3150 after 5 pm
Call Before You Dig: 1-800-227-2600
Hours: Mon. - Fri. 8 am - 5 pm

Las Vegas Valley Water District

Serves 196,444 customers in the Las Vegas and the Clark County area. The cities of North Las Vegas, Henderson and Boulder City supply water for residents within their city. The monthly water bill consists of a service charge, based on the size of the meter that serves you, and a water usage charge. Monthly bills can be paid at Albertson's and Lucky grocery stores.
Rate: The monthly *(30 days)* service charge is $3.67 for a 5/8" meter to $208.17 for a 12" meter. Consumption rate is 98 cents per thousand gallons up to the threshold and $1.42, $1.92 and $2.27 after the threshold is exceeded. The average single family residential customer uses 27,000 gallons monthly and has a 5/8" meter. The typical homeowner pays an average bill of $30-$35 in summer and $15-$20 in winter.
Residential Deposit: $100 deposit can be waived if you are buying the home or provide a letter of credit from another utility showing one year of good credit. If deposit is required, it is returned at the end of one year of good credit.

City of North Las Vegas · Sewer, Water & Garbage
2200 Civic Center Dr.
N. Las Vegas, NV 89030
633-1484
Linda Hinson, City Mgr.
Hours: Tue. - Fri. 7 am - 5:45 pm

City of Henderson · Sewer & Water
240 S. Water St.   2600 N. Green Valley Pkwy.
Henderson, NV 89015   Henderson, NV 89014
565-2110   454-9607 - *Kurt Segler, Utility Services Mgr.*
Hours: Mon. - Fri. 7:30 am - 5:30 pm   **Hours:** Mon. - Fri. 7:30 am - 5:30 pm

Desert Demonstration Gardens
3701 W. Alta Dr.
Las Vegas, NV 89107
258-3205
Hours: 8 am - 5 pm
Eleven different landscape areas with over one thousand species of vegetation designed to show the beauty of water-efficient landscaping. Operated by the Las Vegas Valley Water District. The Water District has put together a 42-page plant and gardening guide focusing on plants best suited to a desert climate. Call 258-3102.

PUBLIC UTILITIES

GARBAGE

Nevadans recycle 17 percent of their waste.

Silver State Disposal
770 E. Sahara Ave.
Las Vegas, NV 89104
735-5151 1-800-752-8719
Tom Isola, Pres.
Service: Residential service twice weekly
Rate: $29.10 quarterly
Container rentals: three sizes $12.50 - $17.50 per month; mobile cans for residences are $3 per month.
Drop boxes: 20 and 28 cu. yd. boxes available. Phone 399-1900.

City Dump
Apex Waste Management Center
735-5151
I-15 north to Exit 64
The Sunrise Mountain Landfill closed October 5, 1993. The dump is located 30 mi. north of Las Vegas on I-15 at Apex, Exit 64; turn right to gate.
Hours: 7 am - 5 pm
Fee: There is no charge to dump residential trash if you show your Nevada drivers license and your current Silver State Disposal bill; otherwise the charge is $4.50 per cu. yd.

Cheyenne Transfer Station
315 W. Cheyenne Ave.
at Commerce St.
N. Las Vegas, NV 89030
399-1900
Hours: 7 am - 5 pm
Hazardous materials accepted.
Fee: $6 per cu. yd.

Black Mountain Transfer Station
1214 McCormick Rd.
Henderson, NV 89015
565-8568
Hours: 7 am - 5 pm
Fee: $6 per cu. yd.

Shelbourne Road Transfer Station
Las Vegas Blvd. S./Shelbourne Rd.
Las Vegas, NV 89123
Hours: 7 am - 4:45 pm
Fee: $6 per cu. yd.

Recycling Facility
Recycle Nevada
333 W. Gowan Rd.
N. Las Vegas, NV 89030
399-1112
Accepts recyclable items. Call 734-5400 Mon.-Fri. 8 am - 5 pm for more information.

Boulder Disposal, Inc.
2500 Utah St.
Boulder City, NV 89005
293-2276
Hours: Landfill - 7 days, 8 am - 5 pm; Recycling - 7 days 8:30 am 4:30 pm

Illegal Dumping
County and City: 383-1027
Keep deserts clean and report illegal dumper and receive one-half of their fine as a reward.

GAS

Southwest Gas Corporation
Corporate Office
5241 Spring Mountain Rd.
Las Vegas, NV 89102
876-7011
Michael Maffie, Pres./CEO

Customer Service & Operation Center
4300 W. Tropicana Ave.
Las Vegas, NV 89103
365-1100
Turn-on or turn-off: 365-1555
Gas appliance adjustment or repair: 365-1555
Bill inquiries: 365-1555
Emergency: 365-1111
Hours: Mon. - Fri. 8 am - 5 pm

North Las Vegas Office
2115 Civic Center Dr.
N. Las Vegas, NV 89030
365-1555
Hours: Mon. - Fri. 8 am - 5 pm

Henderson Office
108 Market St.
Henderson, NV 89015
565-8941
Hours: Mon. - Fri. 8 am - 5 pm
Southwest Gas technicians will do minor repairs and adjustments to gas appliances, adjustments on appliances and relight pilots free in the fall. Serves 285,000 customers in southern Nevada.
Rate: $.47 per therm; average monthly bill in summer is $17.54 and in winter is $40.50.
Residential Deposit: $50 or letter of credit from another gas or electric company, or through a guarantor.
Connection: $25 connection charge. Water and power must be on to begin service. Someone must be home on the day your connection is scheduled between the hours of 8 am and 6 pm and usually next day service. If you want same-day turn-on the connection charge is $40. Basic service charge is $6.

SEWER

Clark County Sanitation District
5857 E. Flamingo Rd.
Las Vegas, NV 89122
434-6600
E. James Gans, Dir.
Billing inquiries and connection: 458-1180
Toll free: 1-800-782-4324
Emergency after hours: 795-3111
Hours: Mon. - Fri. 8 am - 4:30 pm
Serves 92,378 customers in the unincorporated portion of the Las Vegas Valley and the communities of Laughlin, Overton, Searchlight and Blue Diamond.

Charge: condominiums $136.20; single family residence $187.72; single family residence with pool $204.89; commercial rates based on plumbing fixtures.
Deposit: None
Payment: Quarterly, semi-annually or annually.

CABLE TV

(For cable listing see Media)

Prime Cable
121 S. Martin Luther King Blvd.
Las Vegas, NV 89106
383-4000

Henderson Office
11 S. Water St.
Henderson, NV 89015
383-4000

Boulder City Office
508 Nevada Hwy., Ste. 5
Boulder City, NV 89005
383-4000
Harris Bass, VP/Gen. Mgr.
Serves more than 280,390 households in southern Nevada. Prime offers 59 channels, including 6 premium stations and 8 pay-per-view services. Installation varies, although Prime often runs installation specials.
Rate: Basic cable, 49-channel standard service is $26.15 per month Additional fee of $10.95 each per month for premium channels. MasterCard, Visa accepted. "Broadcast Basic" package with 14 channels for $8.38 a month with a $19.80 installation charge.
Deposit: $25 with good credit. If you have a credit problem, the deposit is $50.

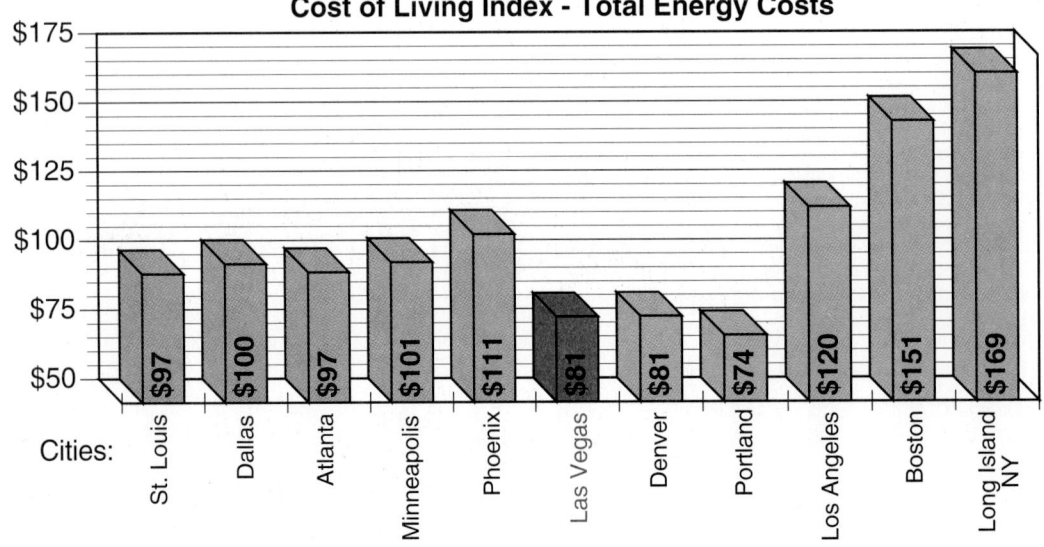

Cost of Living Index - Total Energy Costs

Cities:	St. Louis	Dallas	Atlanta	Minneapolis	Phoenix	Las Vegas	Denver	Portland	Los Angeles	Boston	Long Island NY
	$97	$100	$97	$101	$111	$81	$81	$74	$120	$151	$169

Source: ACCRA

TELEPHONE

Sprint/Central Telephone Nevada
Administrative Offices
330 S. Valley View Blvd.
Las Vegas, NV 89152
244-7400
New residential service: 244-7400
1-800-877-7077
Repair service: 385-2211 Ext. 611
Payment inquiries: 244-7700
Business service: 244-7711
Emergency: 385-2211
Local information & directory assistance:
411 - 555-1212
Long distance information & directory
assistance: 1-area code-555-1212
New charges or custom features: 811
Hours: Mon. - Fri. 7:30 am - 6:30 pm,
Sat. 9 am - 5:30 pm
Steve McMann, President

Renaissance Office
2340 E. Tropicana Ave.
Las Vegas, NV 89119

North Las Vegas Office
2121 Civic Center Dr.
N. Las Vegas, NV 89030

Henderson Office
104 Water St.
Henderson, NV 89015
Hours: Mon. - Fri. 8 am - 6 pm

Boulder City Office
503 Ash St.
Boulder City, NV 89005
Hours: Mon. - Fri. 8 am - 5 pm
Serves over 1.4 million customers in
Southern Nevada.
Charge: $7.18 per month for basic service
and $3.49 federal subscriber line
charge. Business service is $16.38 per
line plus federal line charge.
Deposit: Minimum $50 deposit for resi-
dential and $50 per line for business.
Deposit is returned with interest once
Sprint credit is established.
Connect Charge: The connect charge for
new homes and new businesses varies.
Payment: Payments can be made in
person at any of the Sprint offices,
through the mail or through any of the
20 Western Union "Easy Pay" locations
throughout Las Vegas.
    For bills of $50 or more, payment
can be made using Visa or MasterCard
at any Sprint office or over the phone.
Payment is past due 15 days after
monthly bills are mailed.
Custom Features: Available custom
features include Speed Calling, Call
Waiting, Cancel Call Waiting, Call
Within, Call Forward, Three-way
Calling, Long Distance Restriction,
Caller ID, Caller ID Block, Call Trace,
Return Call, Selective Call Acceptance,
Selective Call Rejection, Selective Call
Forward, Selective Call Ring, Total
Voice and Redial Call along with Sprint
Voice Mail Service, Sprint Paging, and
Lifeline Assistance, Speed-Call 8,
Speed-Call 30 and Three-Way calling
and Total Number.

LONG DISTANCE COMPANIES

When you connect phone service with
Sprint Central, you will be asked to
select a long distance company within
30 days. If you change after the initial
period, you will be charged $12.

AT&T
Business: 1-800-222-0400

Access Long Distance
3753 Howard Hughes Pkwy., Ste. 131
Las Vegas, NV 89109
385-3311
Ronda Mayfield, Office Mgr.

C R C Corporation
4275 E. Sahara Ave., Ste. 6
Las Vegas, NV 89104
641-5177
Richelle Shaw, Operations Mgr.

Express Tel
2225 E. Flamingo Rd., Ste. 305
Las Vegas, NV 89119
731-2776   1-800-748-6777
Mike Jasper, Sales Mgr.

WORLDCOM
4315 S. Industrial Rd., Ste. 225
Las Vegas, NV 89103
262-9200   1-800-859-5369
Mark Jensen, Branch Mgr.

MCI Telecommunications Inc.
1771 E. Flamingo Rd., Suite 209A
Las Vegas, NV 89119
733-6001   1-800-876-4624
John McInerney, Sales Mgr.

Sprint
Residential: 1-800-767-7759

FIRST TELEPHONE IN NEVADA
The first telephone in Las Vegas was
installed in 1907 in a cigar store at the
Nevada Hotel. The phone number was 1.

CELLULAR TELEPHONE SERVICE

In 1993, the cellular phone industry was
virtually nonexistent. Today more than
25 million cellular phones are in use in
the United States, and Las Vegas has the
highest use per capita, over 15 percent.
Southern Nevada coverage extends
from Laughlin to Indian Springs and
State Line to Mesquite.

A T & T Wireless
734-1010
Sales & Administration
3763 Howard Hughes Pkwy.,
Ste. 100 & 200
Las Vegas, NV 89109
892-1100
Customer Centers:
3280 E. Flamingo Rd.
Las Vegas, NV 89121
433-5100

3010 S. Rancho Dr.
Las Vegas, NV 89102
873-1000

1934 Rock Springs Blvd.
Las Vegas, NV 89128
256-2440
Paul Taylor, VP/ Gen. Mgr.
Deposit: Depending on credit history,
deposit can range from zero to $1,000.
Activation charge: $25
Monthly service: Monthly rates range
from $9.95 and $.65 per minute to
$149.99 with 500 free minutes and 26
cents per minute. Unlimited weekends
and evenings 45 minutes included
at peak time.

360 Communications
Corporate Office
840 Grier Ave.
Las Vegas, NV 89119
360-2000

3520 S. Maryland Pkwy.
Las Vegas, NV 89109
733-2007

1300 W. Sunset Rd., Ste. K3
Henderson, NV 89014
454-7558

4022 S. Industrial Rd.
Las Vegas, NV 89103
894-5051

929 S. Rainbow Blvd.
Las Vegas, NV 89117
258-8899

5101 S. Pecos Rd.
Las Vegas, NV 89120
456-4991

7175 W. Spring Mountain Rd.
Las Vegas, NV 89117
364-1116

Administration Sales
4022 Industrial Rd.
Las Vegas, NV 89103
893-8100

4001 S. Decatur Blvd., Ste. 2
Las Vegas, NV 89103
873-1663

2249 N. Rampart Blvd.
Las Vegas, NV 89134
256-8873

2340 E. Tropicana Ave., Ste. A
Las Vegas, NV 89119
739-7019

2121 Civic Center Dr.
N. Las Vegas, NV 89030
642-4439
Kevin Halpin, Gen. Mgr.
Convenience Centers also located at the
Boulevard Mall and both Sam's Clubs.
Deposit: None up to $750 depending
on credit.
Activation charge: $10
Monthly service:
Basic Plus Plan: $28.95 plus $.40 per
minute or $.29 per minute with 35 free
minutes; free Sun. local usage.
Bronze Plan: $79.95 per month, with
200 minutes and $.32 per minute after 200.
Silver Plan: $129.95 per month, after
380 minutes outgoing calls $.26 per
minute and incoming calls $.13 per
minute; 50% off incoming calls.
Gold Plan: $179.95 per month, after 650
minutes outgoing calls $.25 per minute
and incoming calls $.125 per minute;
free Sun. usage and 50% off incoming calls.
Platinum Plan: $229.95 per month,
after 950 minutes outgoing calls $.25
per minute and incoming calls $1.25 per
minute; free Sun. usage and 50% off
incoming calls.
Valley Plan: No roam $11.95 Sun., free
local calls.
Security Plan: $17.95 120 minutes per
month off peak.
*Peak time is Mon. - Sat. 7 am - 7 pm.
Off peak are all other times including
holidays.

The first long distance call made
from Las Vegas was in January 1929.

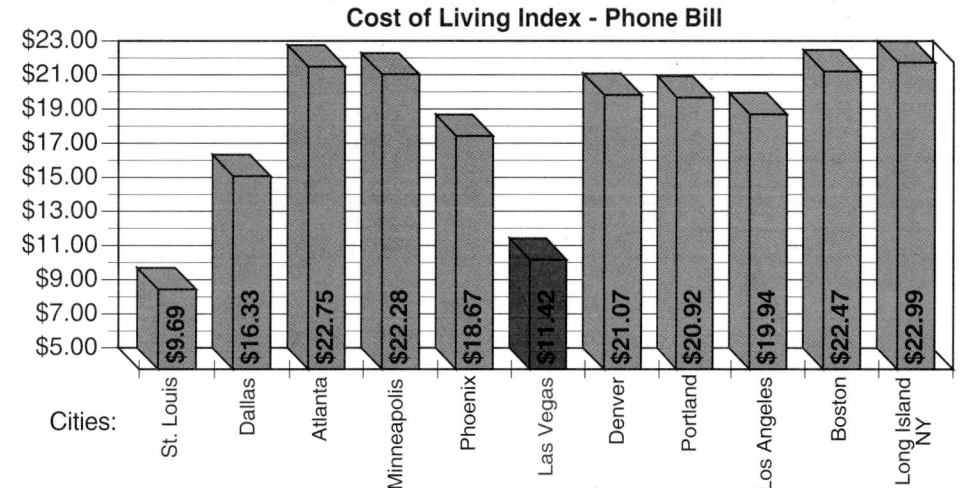

Cost of Living Index - Phone Bill

Cities:		
St. Louis	$9.69	
Dallas	$16.33	
Atlanta	$22.75	
Minneapolis	$22.28	
Phoenix	$18.67	
Las Vegas	$11.42	
Denver	$21.07	
Portland	$20.92	
Los Angeles	$19.94	
Boston	$22.47	
Long Island NY	$22.99	

Source: ACCRA

DRIVERS LICENSE / REGISTRATION

Nevada Dept. of Motor Vehicles & Public Safety
2701 E. Sahara Ave.
Las Vegas, NV 89104
486-4368
Douglas Kraemer, Deputy Dir.
Full service office
Hours: Mon. - Fri. 6 am - 6 pm, Sat. 6 am - 2 pm
Information: 486-4368
Drive Test Appointments: 486-4368
Renewal Appointments: 486-4368
Recorded Information: 486-4368

North Las Vegas Office
4021 W. Carey Ave.
N. Las Vegas, NV 89030
486-4368
Full service office
Hours: Mon. - Fri. 7:30 am - 5:30 pm, Sat. 7:30 am - 3:30 pm
Drive Test Appointments: 486-4368
Renewal Appointments: 486-4368

Flamingo Office
8250 W. Flamingo Rd.
Las Vegas, NV 89117
486-4368
Full service office
Hours: Mon. - Fri. 8 am - 8 pm; Sat. 8 am - 4 pm
Drive Test Appointments: 486-4368
Renewal Appointments: 486-4368

North Las Vegas Office
4110 Donovan Way
N. Las Vegas, NV 89030
486-5655
Express office
CDL Drive Test Appt: 486-5655
Hours: Mon. - Fri. 8 am - 5 pm
Express drivers license and vehicle registration renewal services. Full service for commercial vehicles.

Henderson Office
875 S. Boulder Hwy.
Henderson, NV 89015
486-4368
Express Office
Hours: Mon. - Fri. 8 am - 5 pm
Full service office except vehicle inspections. Express offices provide renewal services for drivers licenses and vehicle registration.

DRIVERS LICENSE

DMV drivers license travel team goes to rural areas of Clark County certain days of each month. Call for information and date and times in area.

New residents have 30 days to register their vehicles and obtain a Nevada drivers license.

You can pick up a Nevada driver's handbook at any Dept. of Motor Vehicles Office or call 486-4368 and one can be mailed to you.

Drivers License is valid for four years. Minimum age for drivers is 16 years of age.
New Residents: Apply at any one of the full service offices.

Documents required: Proof of name and age, current drivers license, birth certificate, passport or immigration papers. Proof of social security number,

Nevada Dept. of Motor Vehicles & Public Safety

social security card or payroll documents. Must pass a vision test and, if not in possession of a valid out-of-state drivers license, must take a written test also. The passing score for the written test is 80 percent. If your license has expired, you also must pass a driving test.
Fee: $20.50; age 65 or older $15.50.
To Renew: DMV offers a renewal by mail service. You may renew your drivers license at any full service or express office. If you have had three or more traffic tickets in four years, you will need to go to a full service office for testing.
Fee: $20.50; age 65 or older $15.50.
Change of address: You must change your address within ten days of moving. You can change your address by mail or in person. There is no fee.
Change of Name: You must visit any full service or express office and bring proof of name change *(marriage certificate or court order)*, age and social security number.
Fee: $6.00
Instruction permit: Applicant must be at least 15 1/2 years of age, successfully pass the written and vision examinations, and be accompanied by a licensed driver who is at least 21 when driving. Permit is good for 8 months.
Fee: $20.50
Identification card: Residents age 10 and above can apply for an identification card. Applicants must show birth certificate and social security card.
Fee: $10.00; age 65 and over $5.00.

VEHICLE REGISTRATION

New Residents: New residents have 30 days to register their vehicles in Nevada. There is no grace period for vehicle plates, and Nevada does not recognize grace periods from other states.
Documents needed to register a vehicle:
1) Current registration certificate
2) Out-of-state license plates
3) Title - unless it is held by a lien holder
4) Nevada evidence of insurance card - you must have a liability insurance policy in the amount to cover $15,000 for the death or injury of one person; $30,000

for the death or injury of two or more persons; and $10,000 for property damage. Proof must be carried in vehicle.
5) Emission Control Inspection Certificate obtained from authorized service stations and inspection stations, for 1968 and newer year autos.
Fee: about $18.50 *(cost varies)* plus certificate fee of $6.00.
There are 325 licensed emission control stations in the metro Las Vegas area. Most gas stations and dealers are licensed stations.
Exempt from smog test:
Diesel-powered trucks with GVW of 8,500 pounds and more, 1967 and older year model vehicles, and motorcycles.
6) Vehicle inspection certificate verifying the identification number of the vehicle. These certificates can be obtained at the Sahara, Carey or W. Flamingo office.
Renewal: Current registration or renewal notice, and emission control inspection certificate, if required. Drop boxes have now been installed in DMV lobbies *(except the W. Flamingo office)* which will enable them to process and return your registration in one week. *(The West Flamingo office has express renewal service.)*
Vehicle purchased in state from dealer:
1) Green copy of dealers report of sale
2) Nevada evidence of insurance card
3) If used vehicle, you need an emission control inspection.
If transferring plates from another vehicle, you will need registration certificate or license plate number.
Vehicle purchased from dealership out of state:
All applicable bills of sale, contracts, manufacturer's certificates of origin, lease agreements required. Use/sales tax is 7% of full purchase price, 5% of trade, if appropriate, is credited. Reciprocity of taxes paid to another state credited upon verification.
Vehicle purchased from private party:
Five percent sales tax is collected at time of registration based on the manufacturer's suggested retail price. If an authorized appraisal is presented, the 5% sales tax can be calculated from that figure.

Basic registration fFee: Registration fee is determined by
1) Manufacturer's suggested retail price 2) Age of vehicle
3) Weight of vehicle. For passenger cars and light trucks under 8,500 pounds $27.00 + $6.00 fee for the support of the Nevada Highway Patrol + a road privilege tax assessed on the value of the vehicle. Trucks 6,000 - 8,499 pounds $38.00 and trucks 8,500 -10,000 pounds $48.00 in addition to above additional fees. Heavy duty vehicles, such as trucks over 8,500 GVW, motor homes and buses, fees are $21 plus certificate fee of $6. Motorcycles $33 plus a $6 fee for motorcycle safety.
Personalized plates: $36.00 and $20.00 annual renewal fee in addition to all other applicable fees. Maximum of seven spaces.
Certificate of title fee: $20.00, vehicle registered outside Nevada $35.00.

SOME IMPORTANT MOTOR VEHICLE LAWS

Nevada license plates issued to you are not transferable to any individual or company other than your spouse. When selling a vehicle, you must remove your license plates by law.

If you cancel or allow to expire your vehicle liability insurance because the vehicle is inoperable, you must turn in your license plates to the Department of Motor Vehicles if these plates are not yet expired.

Seat belts must be worn when operating vehicle.

Children under the age of 5 or less than 40 pounds must be secured in a child safety seat.

The speed limit in school zones is 15 mph and 25 mph around school crossings.

You are required to stop coming from both directions for school buses loading or unloading students.

The speed limit is 25 mph in business and residential areas, 65 mph on highways and freeways.

Open containers of alcohol are prohibited in the passenger compartment of a motor vehicle.

Vehicle owner must carry liability insurance and provide proof, if asked. Drivers must carry a minimum of $15,000 bodily injury, $30,000 per-person per-accident, and $10,000 property damage insurance written by a licensed Nevada insurance company.

It is legal to make right turns on red lights after coming to a stop. It's all right to make a U-turn at intersections unless otherwise specified.

AUTO REGISTRATION
As of August, 1997, 832,648 vehicles were registered in Clark County.

AUTO INSURANCE
In Nevada, vehicle owners must carry liability insurance. There are 1.4 million vehicles registered in Nevada. There are 318 insurance companies that write coverage in Nevada.

EMPLOYMENT

Las Vegas has consistently had the highest new job growth rate in the nation. Clark County had a total work force of 604,800 and an unemployment rate of 29,800 in June 1997. Job growth in Las Vegas was nearly three times the national average. Nevada is a right-to-work state. The state's right-to-work laws prevent labor organizations from establishing "closed shop" policies that preclude hiring of non-union personnel. Nevada's right-to-work law states that no person shall be denied the opportunity to obtain or retain employment because of nonmembership in a labor union.

The Nevada labor force has increased by 346,000 people in the last decade. Nevada gained 54,000 jobs for the 12 month period ending June 1997, a gain of 6.5 percent. Employment was 847,900 and unemployment was 36,100 as of May 1997.

The service industry dominates the Las Vegas and Nevada job market with almost 50 percent of the state's total work force employed in this sector. In Las Vegas, 52 percent of the work force are employed in the service industry. Nevada ranks 49th nationally in jobs generated by agriculture, ahead of only Rhode Island.

If you are hired in a food and beverage or child care position, you must obtain a health card from the Clark County Health District. If you are hired in hotel or gaming, you are required to have a Sheriff's Work Card. If you handle or work directly around liquor, you will be required to have an Alcohol Awareness Card.

SPECIAL EMPLOYMENT CARDS/CERTIFICATION

Sheriff's Card

Las Vegas Metropolitan Police Department
601 Fremont St.
Las Vegas, NV 89101
229-3465
Hours: Mon. - Fri. 8 am - 4 pm

To work at any Las Vegas hotel/casino, employees will need to obtain a Sheriff's Card. The employer will give you a signed referral to get the card. The Police Department charges $35 for the card and $5 for fingerprinting you and running a background check. Renewals are $20 and the card is good for 5 years. For renewal appointments call 229-0312; cash only. Two forms of ID are required.

Health Card

Clark County Health Department
625 Shadow Ln.
Las Vegas, NV 89106
383-1226

To work as a food handler or in child care, you must obtain a health card. The health district will give you a TB test and a two hour class. Cost is $10 for the certificate which you can obtain prior to being hired.

Techniques of Alcohol Management (TAM)
557 E. Sahara Ave., Ste. 223
Las Vegas, NV 89104
647-1954

If you serve alcohol, you must obtain a TAM card. You will be required to attend a four-hour course to get certification. Bartenders, cocktail waitresses, security officers, casino management and anyone who sells alcohol is required to have a card. Refresher classes are two hours and cost $10, cash only.

MEDIAN CLARK COUNTY

Manufacturing:

Administrative Services	$25.63
Executive	$63.13
Sales	$27.83
Accountants	$18.40
General Office	$11.34
Secretaries *(except legal & medical)*	$11.86
Supervisors	$16.67
Janitors	$9.73
Electricians	$18.21
Laborers	$9.16
Mechanics	$20.26
Wholesale & Retail Trade Managers	$22.02

Administration:

Fast Food Services	$11.20
Food & Beverage	$15.84
Executives	$39.37
Marketing/PR	$24.42
Personnel	$21.46
Sales	$27.54
Warehouse	$17.29

Professionals:

Accountants	$16.18
Buyers	$17.85
Pharmacists	$29.80

Sales:

Cashiers *(non-gaming)*	$7.88
Clerks	$8.42

Clerical:

Bookkeepers	$13.23
Accounting Clerk	$9.68
General Office	$8.90
Receptionists	$8.03
Payroll	$11.22
Switchboard Operators	$8.21

Service:

Bartenders	$6.31
Chefs	$14.07
Security Guards	$7.21
Waiters & Waitresses	$4.58

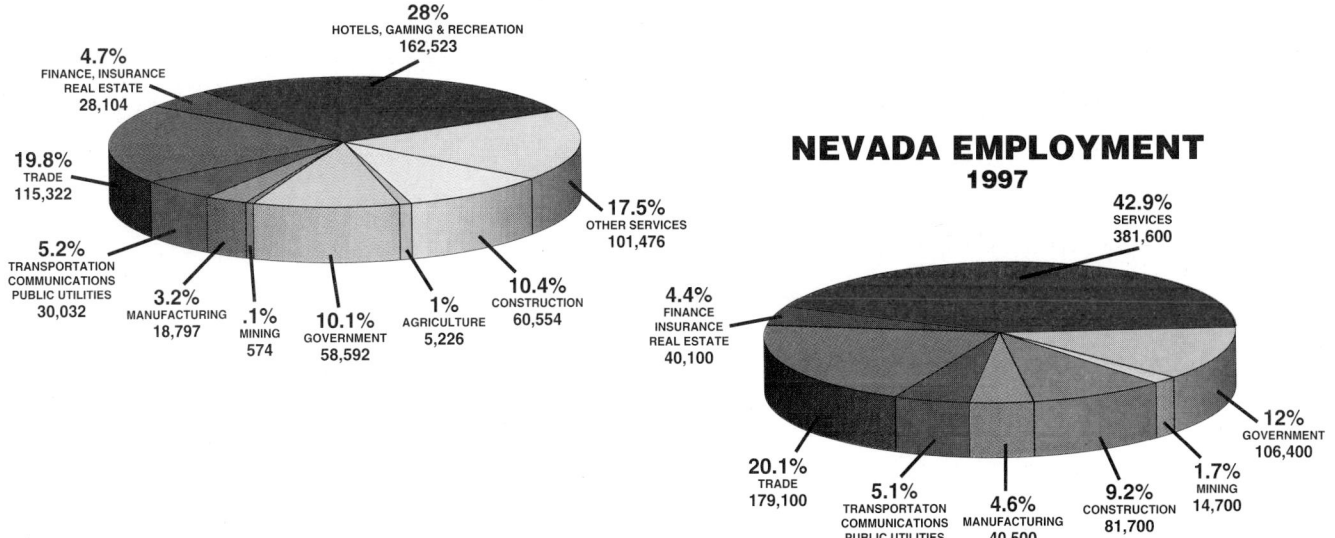

CLARK COUNTY EMPLOYMENT
JUNE 1997

28% HOTELS, GAMING & RECREATION 162,523
4.7% FINANCE, INSURANCE REAL ESTATE 28,104
19.8% TRADE 115,322
5.2% TRANSPORTATION COMMUNICATIONS PUBLIC UTILITIES 30,032
3.2% MANUFACTURING 18,797
.1% MINING 574
10.1% GOVERNMENT 58,592
1% AGRICULTURE 5,226
10.4% CONSTRUCTION 60,554
17.5% OTHER SERVICES 101,476

NEVADA EMPLOYMENT
1997

42.9% SERVICES 381,600
4.4% FINANCE INSURANCE REAL ESTATE 40,100
20.1% TRADE 179,100
5.1% TRANSPORTATON COMMUNICATIONS PUBLIC UTILITIES 45,400
4.6% MANUFACTURING 40,500
9.2% CONSTRUCTION 81,700
1.7% MINING 14,700
12% GOVERNMENT 106,400

Source: Dept. of Employment, Training & Rehabilitation

EMPLOYMENT

Clark County Work Force

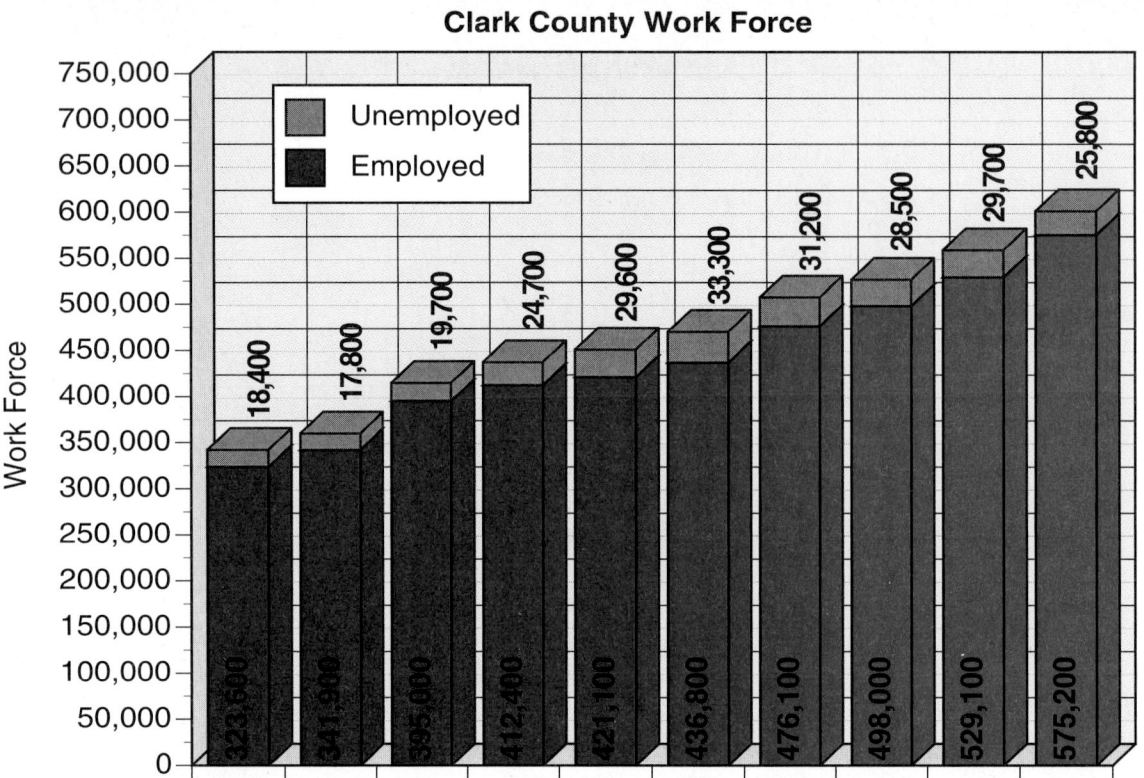

Hourly Wages

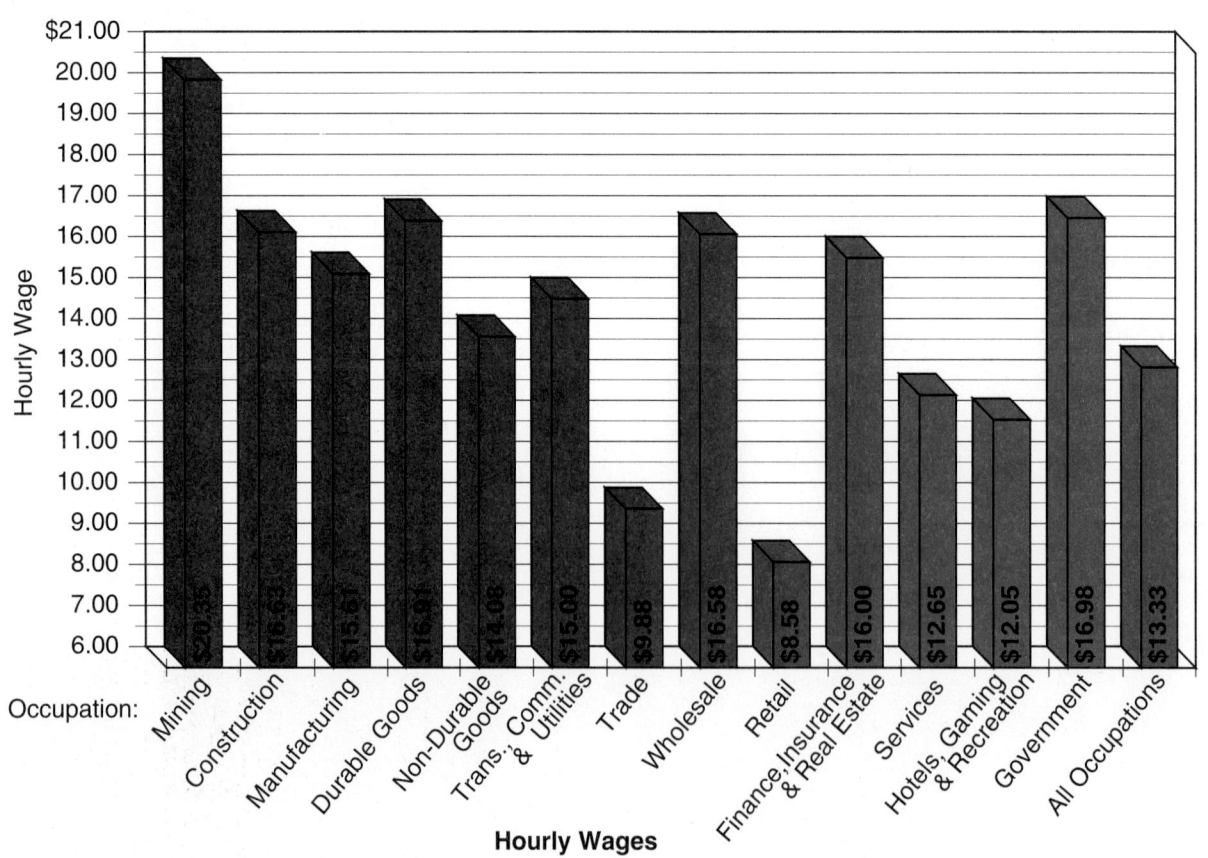

Source: Dept. of Employment, Training & Rehabilitation

GOVERNMENT OFFICIALS YEARLY SALARIES

Nevada Governor	$90,000
Las Vegas Mayor	$47,830
Las Vegas City Manager	$120,509
Clark County Commissioners	$54,000
Las Vegas City Councilmen	$36,407
Sheriff	$84,000
Clark County School District Superintendent	$138,753
Clark County District Attorney	$100,800
County Clerk	$72,000
County Assessor	$72,000
County Treasurer	$72,000
Public Administrator	$72,000

LABOR INFORMATION AND ASSISTANCE

American Civil Liberties Union of Nevada
325 S. 3rd St., Ste. 25
Las Vegas, NV 89101
366-1226
Gary Peck, Exec. Dir.

National Labor Relations Board
600 Las Vegas Blvd. S., Ste. 400
Las Vegas, NV 89101
388-6416
*Stephen E. Wamser, Resident Officer
Cornele A. Overstreet, Regional Dir.*
Investigates complaints of unfair labor practices and assists in finding a settlement. If either side declines to settle, the board issues a formal complaint and an administrative judge hears the case.

Nevada Equal Rights Commission
1515 E. Tropicana Ave., Ste. 590
Las Vegas, NV 89119
486-7161
William H. Stewart, Adm.
Handles employer discrimination complaints and sexual harassment as well as housing and public accommodation complaints and employment.

Nevada State Labor Commission
555 E. Washington Ave.
Las Vegas, NV 89101
486-2650
David J. Dahn, Labor Commissioner
Settles disputes between employees and employers over wages. Makes sure workers are treated fairly. Enforces the state's labor laws. Ensures that minimum wage and overtime is being paid.

State of Nevada Department of Industrial Relations
2500 W. Washington Ave.
Las Vegas, NV 89106
486-5150
Lisa Wyman, Asst. Adm.
Occupational safety & health.

U.S. Department of Labor
Wage and Hour Division
1050 E. Flamingo Rd., Suite 321
Las Vegas, NV 89119
699-5581
Enforces minimum wage and overtime laws.

EMPLOYMENT SERVICES

Nevada Employment Security Department
North Las Vegas Office
2827 Las Vegas Blvd. N.
N. Las Vegas, NV 89030
486-5600
Ronald Fletcher, Mgr.

Henderson Office
119 Water St.
Henderson, NV 89015
486-6710
Charles Smith, Mgr.

902 W. Owens St.
Las Vegas, NV 89106
486-5300
Brenda Harris, Mgr.
Provides basic employment and unemployment services for residents of Henderson, Boulder City and neighboring zip code areas.

The Nevada Employment Service provides a well-trained staff and a computerized job bank system free of charge to employers and job seekers.

MINIMUM WAGE

Federal: $5.15 hour
State of Nevada *(Firms that are exempt from Federal law)*:
Persons age 18 and up: $5.15 hour
Persons less than age 18: $4.38 hour
State law prohibits an employer from applying tips against the minimum wage.

Hotel/Casinos Job Lines

Bally's	739-4299
Binions Horsehoe	385-5225
Caesars Palace	731-7386
California Hotel	388-2669
Circus Circus	794-3732 Option 1
Silver City	794-3732 Option 1
Slots of Fun	794-3732 Option 1
Desert Inn	733-4784
Excalibur	597-7200
Fiesta	631-7003
Flamingo Hilton	733-3179 Option 1
Four Queens	385-4011 Ask for Hot Line
Fremont	385-6250
Golden Nugget	386-8181
Hard Rock Casino	594-5022
Harrahs	369-5050
Imperial Palace	794-3191
Las Vegas Hilton	732-5717
Luxor	262-4600
MGM Grand	891-2121
Mirage/Treasure Island	792-5267
Nevada Palace	458-8810 Ext. 7200
New York New York	740-6660
Orleans	365-7099
Reserve	567-7700
Rio	252-7634
Riviera	794-9651
Sahara	737-2700
Sam's Town	454-8015
Santa Fe	658-4967
Showboat	385-9101
Silverton	263-7777 Ask for Hot Line
Stardust	732-6364
Station Casinos Palace/Boulder/Sunset/Texas	456-5627
Tropicana	739-2473
Westward Ho	731-6374

Job Lines

Clark County Personnel	455-4565
Current Jobs - County	455-3174
Governor's Committee on Employment of People with Disabilities	486-4318
TDD	486-5244
New Employment Security	486-3300
Senior Citizens Employment Service	382-0721
Nevada Business Service	638-8750

Utility Companies

Las Vegas Water District	258-3220
Nevada Power Company	367-5200
Southwest Gas Corporation	365-2085
Sprint/Centel Phone Company	244-7566
Prime Cable	384-9260

Financial Institutions

Bank of America	654-1241
Household Credit Services	243-1400
Nevada Federal Credit Union	457-1000 Option 8
Norwest Financial	765-3824
US Bank	1-800-780-1436
Wells Fargo	791-6251

Federal Agencies

Bureau of Reclamation	293-8000
Environmental Protection Agency	798-2418
Federal Information Center	1-800-688-9889
Housing and Urban Development	388-6500 Option 7
Internal Revenue Service	455-1016 Option 1
National Park Service	293-8906
Nellis Air Force Base	652-3464
United States Postal Service	361-9385
U.S. Forestry Service	778-0233
Veterans Administration	636-3020

Government Agencies

Boulder City, City of	293-9430
Clark County Library District	382-7919 Option 7
Clark County School District	799-1000
Henderson, City of	565-2318
Las Vegas, City of	229-6346
Las Vegas Convention and Visitors Authority	226-5030
Metropolitan Police Department	226-7506
Nevada, State of	486-2920
North Las Vegas, City of	633-1000 Option 3
University Medical Center	383-2490
University of Nevada, Las Vegas	895-1666

EMPLOYMENT / UNEMPLOYMENT

Nevada Employment Service helps job seekers find work; provides counseling, testing, job development and referral to training programs as needed; helps employers find qualified workers; provides screening, testing, job analysis and other personnel services; furnishes vital labor market information, aids in cutting training and turnover costs and identifying employees with training potential, all without charge. Provides special services for veterans, minorities, younger, older, handicapped and rural workers and others with specific needs.

Industrial Labor Office
1001 N. "A" St.
Las Vegas, NV 89106
486-3441
Bart Bartholomew, Supvr.
Serves employers and job seekers in the short-term labor market. Also place domestics and provides rural manpower services.

Processes claims of those out of work and pays unemployment benefits to the eligible unemployed. These benefits are financed by contributions to unemployment insurance trust funds by employers of the state in which the worker was previously employed. Claims for certain other federally authorized benefits are also processed.

Nevada Business Services
930 W. Owens Ave.
Las Vegas, NV 89106
647-1682
Richard Blue, Exec. Dir.

920 W. Owens Ave.
Las Vegas, NV 89106
638-8750

940 W. Owens Ave.
Las Vegas, NV 89106
646-7675
Non-profit job training and human resource firm that provides employment and training opportunities to economically disadvantaged residents, dislocated workers and residents with special barriers to employment.

EMPLOYMENT AGENCIES

Adecco Personnel Services
1050 E. Flamingo Rd., Ste. E225
Las Vegas, NV 89109
731-2267
Light industrial, secretarial, marketing.

All Jobs Employment Agency
3870 E. Flamingo Rd.
Las Vegas, NV 89121
454-2000
All types of positions.

Allen & Associates
1700 E. Desert Inn Rd., Ste. 118
Las Vegas, NV 89109
731-2066
Profession job placement. National executive search.

Appleone Employment
1019 S. Decatur Blvd.
Las Vegas, NV 89107
258-3010

3900 Paradise Rd., Ste. G
Las Vegas, NV 89109
734-8110

UNEMPLOYMENT

Las Vegas Unemployment Rate:

Year	Rate
1990:	4.7%
1991:	5.6%
1992:	6.6%
1993:	7.1%
1994:	6.1%
1995:	5.4%
1996:	5.3%
1997:	4.3%

The average unemployed worker receiving unemployment insurance receives $183.85 per week, with the maximum being $258. There is a 26 week limit on collecting unemployment.

In Las Vegas the unemployment rate was 5.3 percent in January 1997. There were 558,800 people in the labor force, 529,100 persons employed, 29,700 unemployed. In Nevada, employment was 896,100 and unemployment was 43,600. Approximately $144.4 million in benefits were paid out in 1996.

Nevada's Unemployment Insurance Program (UI) is administered by the Unemployment Insurance Division.

3510 E. Tropicana Ave.
Las Vegas, NV 89121
898-1856
All positions

ATC Health Care Services
4055 S. Spencer St., Ste. 102
Las Vegas, NV 89119
732-9800
Nursing, technical, office and administrative.

Career Connectors Employment Service
4015 W. Charleston Blvd.
Las Vegas, NV 89102
877-2008
Administrative, bookkeeping, clerical, general labor, light industrial, medical and dental. Permanent or temporary.

Eastridge Personnel Services
(Also listed under Temporary Employment)
4220 S. Maryland Pkwy., Ste. 205A
Las Vegas, NV 89119
732-8855
732-8861 temporary

2685 S. Rainbow Blvd., Ste. 109
Las Vegas, NV
257-3827 full time
257-2200 temporary
Temporary and permanent positions in clerical, labor, light industrial.

Robert Half International
1771 E. Flamingo Rd., Ste. 211A
Las Vegas, NV 89119
739-9797
Lynn Gerard, Branch Mgr.
All types of permanent and temporary from entry level to top level management.

Heritage Employment
2975 S. Rainbow Blvd., Ste. F1
Las Vegas, NV 89102
221-6222
All types and levels of permanent positions.

Labor World of Las Vegas
1551 S. Commerce St.
Las Vegas, NV 89101
382-2100

The Matrix Group Personnel Services
501 S. Rancho Dr., Ste. H-53
Las Vegas, NV 89106
598-0070
Darlene Karn, Pres.
Permanent and temporary positions in all positions and levels.

St. Vincent Job Development
1501 Las Vegas Blvd. N.
Las Vegas, NV 89101
384-3837

Snelling Personnel Services
1050 E. Flamingo Rd., Ste. 142
Las Vegas, NV 89119
369-0087
Permanent and temporary positions in all levels.

SOS Staffing
3160 W. Sahara Ave., Ste. A14
Las Vegas, NV 89102
367-2113

3505 E. Flamingo Rd., Ste. 3
Las Vegas, NV 89121
451-2331
Permanent and temporary positions in all levels.

Talent Tree Staffing Services
2920 S. Jones Blvd.
Las Vegas, NV 89102
362-8600

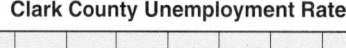

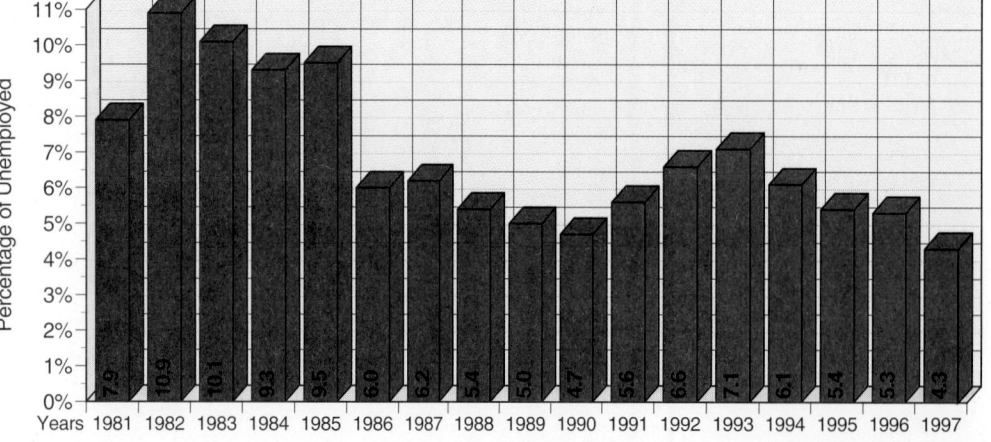

Clark County Unemployment Rate

Years	1981	1982	1983	1984	1985	1986	1987	1988	1989	1990	1991	1992	1993	1994	1995	1996	1997
%	7.9	10.9	10.1	9.3	9.5	6.0	6.2	5.4	5.0	4.7	5.6	6.6	7.1	6.1	5.4	5.3	4.3

Source: Dept. of Employment, Training & Rehabilitation

TEMPORARY EMPLOYMENT AGENCIES

Accountants By Acumen
1771 W. Charleston Blvd.
Las Vegas, NV 89102
877-6775
All levels, white collar and executive search.

Acutemps Personnel
1771 E. Flamingo Rd.
Las Vegas, NV 89119
739-9797
Clerical, accounting, executive, both blue and white collar positions.

ATS Temporary Services
1700 E. Desert Inn Rd., Ste. 118
Las Vegas, NV 89109
731-2066
Accounting, finance, administrative, secretarial and engineering.

Axis Temps
320 E. Charleston Blvd., Ste. B
Las Vegas, NV 89104
384-2947
Unskilled, skilled and technical.

Eastridge Temps
4220 S. Maryland Pkwy., Ste. 205A
Las Vegas, NV 89119
732-8861

320 S. Boulder Hwy., Ste. 102
Henderson, NV 89015
566-9662

2685 S. Rainbow Blvd., Ste. 109
Las Vegas, NV 89102
257-3827 full time
257-2200 temporary
Positions in clerical, industrial and labor.

Interim Personnel
2245A Renaissance Dr.
Las Vegas, NV 89119
736-1585

Kelly Temporary Services
3770 Howard Hughes Pkwy., Ste. 145
Las Vegas, NV 89109
796-0203

1100 Town Center Dr.
Las Vegas, NV 89134
255-4708

Labor Express
1235 E. Charleston Blvd.
Las Vegas, NV 89104
474-9494
Construction and industrial.

Labor Force Temporary Personnel Service
1155 E. Sahara Ave., Ste. 18
Las Vegas, NV 89104
894-4117
Temporary industrial and clerical positions.

Labor Express
35 E. Lake Mead Dr.
Henderson, NV 89015
558-4231

Manpower Inc. of Southern Nevada
314 Las Vegas Blvd. N.
Las Vegas, NV 89101
893-2626

Industrial
8170 W. Sahara Ave., Ste. 207
Las Vegas, NV 89117
363-8170

Technical
3626 Pecos McLeod
Las Vegas, NV 89121
893-2626

Nevada Industrial Labor Office
Nevada Employment Security
1001 N. A St.
Las Vegas, NV 89106
486-3441
Hours: 6 am - 3 pm
Short-term labor placement.

Remedy Intelligent Staffing
1900 E. Flamingo Rd., Ste. 161
Las Vegas, NV 89119
369-0292

Clerical, marketing, light industrial, conventions and technical.

Staffing Resources
4620 S. Valley View Blvd.
Las Vegas, NV 89103
795-7767
Sue Peck
Temporary employment agency.

Talent Tree Personnel Services
2920 S. Jones Blvd., Ste. 220
Las Vegas, NV 89102
362-8600
Temporary clerical positions.

Todays Temporary
2300 W. Sahara Ave., Ste. 550
Las Vegas, NV 89102
382-8677
Temporary clerical positions.

Volt Service Group
1050 E. Flamingo Rd.
Las Vegas, NV 89119
732-8658
No fee to applicant. General labor, clerical, light industrial, warehousing, customer service, assembly.

LABOR UNIONS

American Federation of Government Employees #1978
P. O. Box 60966
Boulder City, NV 89006-0966
293-8379
Criag Calderwood, Pres.
Federal workers at Hoover Dam.

American Postal Workers Union
1641 E. Sunset Rd.
Las Vegas, NV 89119
361-2798
Billy Harrell, Pres.

Bartenders and Beverage #165
1630 S. Commerce St.
Las Vegas, NV 89102
384-7774
Pat Benzenbower, Sec./Treas.
Bartender and beverage dispensers.

Bricklayers and Tilesetters #3
4720 Wynn Rd.
Las Vegas, NV 89103
873-0332
Tim Egan, Business Mgr.

Carpenter's Local Union #1780
501 N. Lamb Blvd.
Las Vegas, NV 89110
453-2206
Dan O'Shea, Pres.

City Employees Association
857 N. Eastern Ave.
Las Vegas, NV 89101
649-6606
Mikey Gluskin, Pres.

Clark County Classroom Teachers Assn.
2950 E. Rochelle Ave.
Las Vegas, NV 89121
733-3063
Sue Strand, Pres.

Culinary Workers Local #226
1630 S. Commerce St.
Las Vegas, NV 89102
385-2131
Hatty Canty, Pres.
$22 month to be listed on job referral list. 40,000-45,000 members.

Glaziers #2001
3432 N. Bruce St.
N. Las Vegas, NV 89030
399-4555
Bill Smirk, Business Rep.

Insurance Workers Professional Division Local #2201
400 S. Jones Blvd.
Las Vegas, NV 89107
Tom Cotter, Pres.
259-0946

I.A.T.S.E. Local #720
3000 S. Valley View Blvd.
Las Vegas, NV 89102
873-3450
Enrico Grippo, Pres.
Stagehands, wardrobe, movie location.

I.B.E.W. #396
3520 Boulder Hwy.
Las Vegas, NV 89121
457-3011
Michelle Bonelli, Pres.
Electricians.

I.B.E.W. Local #357
4321 East Bonanza Rd.
Las Vegas, NV 89110
452-9357
Carl Johnson, Pres.
Electricians.

I.H.B.C.L. Local #872
4200 E. Bonanza Rd.
Las Vegas, NV 89110
452-4440
Dalton Hooks, Sec./Treas.
International hodcarriers, building and common laborers.

International Assn. of Firefighters #1908
5650 W. Charleston Blvd.
Las Vegas, NV 89102
870-1908
Robert Trenkle, Pres.

International Assn. Of Machinists #845
1033 N. Nellis Blvd.
Las Vegas, NV 89110
452-4699
Mike Aupperle, Pres.

International Operating Engineers #12
360 Shadow Ln.
Las Vegas, NV 89106
598-1212
John Haslam, Nevada District Rep.

International Union Operating Engineers #501
301 Deauville St.
Las Vegas, NV 89106
382-8452
Michael Russell, Business Rep.
Brian Reive, Business Rep.

Ironworkers Local #433
100 Shiloh Dr.
Las Vegas, NV 89110
452-8445
Max Price, Business Rep.

I.T.P.E. · N.M.U/M.E.B.A., AFL-CIO
720 E. Charleston Blvd., Ste. 202
Las Vegas, NV 89104
384-7171
Theatla Jones, VP
Cab workers (*Yellow, Checker, Star, and Henderson*); Food servers at Nellis Air Force Base.

Las Vegas Police Protective Association
1250 Burnham Ave., Ste. 200
Las Vegas, NV 89104
384-8692
Andy Anderson, Pres.

Millwrights and Machinery Erectors #1827
501 N. Lamb Blvd.
Las Vegas, NV 89110
452-8998
Charles Kessler, Financial Sec./Treas.

Musicians Union of Las Vegas Local #369
3701 W. Vegas Dr.
Las Vegas, NV 89108
647-3690
Dan Trinter, Pres.

Nevada Service Employees Union
1250 Burnham Ave.
Las Vegas, NV 89104
386-8849
Barbara Aupperle, Pres.

Nevada State AFL-CIO
4200 E. Bonanza Rd.
Las Vegas, NV 89110
531-6532
Claude (Blackie) Evans, Exec. Sec./Treas.

LABOR UNIONS

Painters Local #159
5130 E. Charleston Blvd., Ste. 3
Las Vegas, NV 89122
452-2140
Gerald Kmetz, Business Rep.

Plasterers & Cement Masons Union #797
4201 E. Bonanza Rd., Ste. 103
Las Vegas, NV 89110
452-9199
Shell Sherman, Bus. Mgr.

Plumbers and Pipefitters Local #525
760 N. Lamb Blvd.
Las Vegas, NV 89110
452-1520
Billy Anderson, Business Mgr.

Road Sprinkler Fitters Local #669
P.O. Box 92207
Henderson, 89009
568-6331
Gerald Singleton, Business Mgr.

Roofers Local #162
4200 E. Bonanza Rd., Ste. 102
Las Vegas, NV 89110
453-5801
William Penrose, Business Mgr.

Screen Actors Guild of Nevada
3900 Paradise Rd., Ste. 206
Las Vegas, NV 89109
367-8217
Michael Justin, Pres.

Service Employees International Union AFLCIO-CLC Local #1864
1250 S. Burnham Ave., Ste. 216
Las Vegas, NV 89104
383-1022
Kathy Nauman, Exec. Dir.

Sheet Metal Local #88
4321 E. Bonanza Rd.
Las Vegas, NV 89110
452-4799
Jim Long, Business Mgr.

Teamsters Local #14
305 Wall St.
Las Vegas, NV 89102
384-7841
Gary D. Mauger, Sec./Treas.

Teamsters Local #995
300 Shadow Ln.
Las Vegas, NV. 89106
385-0995
Mike Magnani, Sec./Treas.
Convention help, warehousing, construction, freight, hotel front desk, valet parking; $20 month to be listed on the referral list.

Teamsters Local #631
307 Wall St.
Las Vegas, NV 89102
385-1455
Robert McClone, Sec./Treas.

Textile Processors Service Trades Health Care Professional & Technical

Employees Int'l Union Local #311
1311 S. Casino Center Blvd.
Las Vegas, NV 89104
382-4919
Mary Caldwell, VP

United Food & Commercial Workers Union #711
1201 N. Decatur Blvd., Ste. 116
Las Vegas, NV 89108
648-7112
Roberta West, Pres.
Grocery industry.

United Steel Workers Of America Local #711A
1754 Industrial Rd.
Las Vegas, NV 89102
477-7620
Duane Skiver, Pres.

United Steel Workers of America #4856
47 Water St.
Henderson, NV 89015
565-8207
Billy Hand, Pres.

COMPANIES WITH OVER 1,000 EMPLOYEES

Aladdin Hotel and Casino
Arizona Charlie's Hotel and Casino
ATC/Vancom of Nev Ltd Ptrshp
Bally's Casino/Hotel - Las Vegas
Boulder Station Hotel & Casino
Caesars Palace
California Hotel and Casino
First & Ogden
Central Telephone - Nevada
Circus Circus Casinos, Inc .- Las Vegas
Citibank (Nevada), NA
City of Henderson
City of Las Vegas
City of North Las Vegas
Clark County
Clark County School District
Colorado Belle Hotel & Casino
Desert Inn

Desert Springs Hospital
Edgewater Hotel & Casino
El Cortez
Excalibur Hotel & Casino
Fiesta Hotel & Casino
Flamingo Hilton Corporation
Flamingo Hilton - Laughlin Inc.
Four Queens Hotel & Casino
Frontier Hotel & Gambling Hall
Gold Coast Hotel & Casino
Gold River Gambling Hall & Res
Gold Strike Hotel & Gambling
Golden Nugget, #2
Grand Resorts, Inc.
Greyhound Exposition Services
Hard Rock Hotel & Casino
Harrah's Del Rio
Holiday Casino

Horseshoe Club, The
Household Credit Services, Inc.
Imperial Palace Inc.
Las Vegas Hilton Corporation
Las Vegas Metropolitan Police
Luxor Hotel
MGM Grand Hotel, Inc.
Mirage Casino-Hotel
Mission Industries
Monte Carlo Resort & Casino
Nevada Power Company
New York New York Hotel & Casino
Orleans Hotel and Casino
Palace Station Hotel & Casino
Post Office Las Vegas 89114
Ramada Express Inc.
Rio Suite Hotel & Casino
Riverside Resort & Casino

Riviera Hotel and Casino
Sahara Hotel and Casino
Sam's Town
Santa Fe Hotel & Casino
Showboat Hotel and Casino
Silver State Disposal Service, Inc.
Southern Nevada Memorial Hospital
Stardust Hotel & Casino
State of Nevada
Stratosphere Tower, Casino & Hotel
Sunrise Hospital
Sunset Station Hotel & Casino
Texas Gambling Hall & Hotel
Treasure Island at the Mirage
Tropicana Hotel & Country Club
Union Plaza Hotel & Casino
University of Nevada, Las Vegas
Valley Hospital Medical Center
Whiskey Pete's & Kactus Kate's

LAS VEGAS CELEBRITY RESIDENTS

Andre Agassi
Marty Allen
Paul Anka
Susan Anton
Desi Arnez, Jr.
Lance Burton
Sam Butera
Johnny Carson
David Cassidy
Jim Colbert
Natalie Cole
David Copperfield
Randall Cunningham

Robert Gamez
Danny Gans
Robert Goulet
Kenny Kerr
Gladys Knight
Jerry Lewis
Rich Little
Greg Maddux
Phyllis McGuire
Vince Neil
Sandy Nelson
Wayne Newton
Louie Prima & Keely Smith

Debbie Reynolds
Kenny Rogers
Siegfried & Roy
Steve Rossi
Arnold Schwarzenegger
Brook Shields
Marshall Sylver
Mark Slaughter
Rip Taylor
Mike Tyson
Dionne Warwick
Barry White
Bruce Willis & Demi Moore

Education

The Clark County School District covers 7,910 sq. mi. with an estimated 1997 population of 1,170,113. Cities and rural areas served by the district reach as far north as Indian Springs and Mesquite and as far south as Laughlin and Searchlight.

Bond issues totaling $1.25 billion were approved in 1994 and 1996, and are building 41 new schools, providing improvements to existing schools and new technology.

In 1997-1998, 6 new elementary schools, 3 middle schools and 2 high schools opened, bringing the total to 219 schools. There are 142 elementary schools, 31 middle schools, 28 high schools, 14 alternative schools and 4 special schools. The district predicts 110 new schools will be needed in the next 10 years.

Official student enrollment for the 1997-1998 school year is 190,822, an increase of 6.7 percent over the previous year. Clark County is the largest school district in the state and the 10th largest in the nation. More than 60 percent of Nevada's total public school enrollment is in Clark County. In June 1997 the number of graduates, including Adult Education Graduates, was 7,452.

The 1998-1999 estimated figure for enrollment is 202,388. In 1998-1999, 3 middle schools and 5 elementary schools will be built. Paradise school will be relocating to a new free-standing building at UNLV. This will give UNLV students the opportunity to work directly with children.

As of September 1997, approximately 20,927 full time, part time, substitute and temporary staff were employed by the school district. Of those, 12,517 are licensed, 701 are administrative personnel, 105 are school police and 7,604 are support staff, which includes cafeteria workers, teacher aides and student workers. In elementary school, the student-teacher ratio is 21.78.

The final General Operating Fund Budget for the 1997-1998 school year is $855,877,005. The State provides 31.1 percent of the budget, federal aid and other sources provide 4.5 percent. Local sales tax (41 percent), property tax (20.2 percent), and motor vehicle and franchise taxes (3.2 percent) contribute 64.4 percent of the budget. Per pupil expenditure for the 1996-1997 school year was $4,486.24. The operating dollar was spent as follows: employee compensation 46.1 percent, support staff/school police 16.2 percent, administration 5.5 percent, fixed charges - retirement and insurance 18.9 percent, utilities/postage/property insurance 3.3 percent, textbooks/instructional materials/field trips 3.9 percent, other 6.1 percent includes $8.7 million for the execution of capital leases [buses] and transfers of $12.2 million and 2.2 million for the capital replacement program and budget stabilization, respectively; or 3.0 percent.

Nevada law requires that students be five years old on or before September 30th to enter kindergarten and six years old on or before September 30th to enter first grade. Kindergarten is part of the regular school program but is not compulsory. State law requires all children ages 7 to 17 to attend school. Students attend 180 days of school for the year.

Parents must have a certified birth certificate, up-to-date immunization records from a doctor or health department administering them, two proofs of address (utility bill and rent receipt), and the name and address of the previous school attended, if there is one. At the time of student's enrollment, additional information will be asked of the parents, such as the parents' social security numbers.

Immunization shots are mandatory if a child is to attend Clark County schools. Immunizations are available at any public health center in addition to area immunization clinics. Further information is available by calling the Clark County Health District at 383-1351.

Specific information regarding assigned school attendance areas can be obtained by calling the school district zoning office at 799-7573. Students must attend their assigned school unless a zone variance is obtained under special circumstances. Questions regarding a zone variance can be answered by the principal.

The school district provides bus transportation for students living 2 or more miles from the assigned school. Students attending a school on a zone variance, and who live less than 2 miles from school, are not bused. About 50,000 students ride the district's 740 buses. Specific information can be obtained from the school office, from the Clark County School District Transportation Department at 799-8100 or from your school.

Source: Clark County School District 1997 Annual Report

PUBLIC EDUCATION

Clark County School District
2832 E. Flamingo Rd.
Las Vegas, NV 89121
799-5011
Brian Cram, Supt. of Schools
799-5310

**Clark County School District
Community Relations**
4212 Eucalyptus Ave.
Las Vegas, NV 89121
799-5301
Robert McCord, Dir.

**Clark County Department of
Administrative Services**
Desert Conservation Plan
500 S. Grand Central Pkwy.
Las Vegas, NV 89155-8270
455-3530

Public information and education materials are available upon request. The Desert Conservation Plan is responsible for the implementation of the provisions of Section 10(a)1(B) Incidental Take Permit, issued by the United States Fish & Wildlife Service, pursuant to the Endangered Species Act. Through an interlocal agreement with the cities of Las Vegas , North Las Vegas, Henderson, Boulder City and Mesquite, Clark County serves as the plan administrator, responsible for the collection of mitigation fees, implementation of the plan and adhering to all compliance measures associated with the permit. The Desert Conservation Plan and its accompanying

30-year permit is intended to promote a balance between economic stability and environmental integrity in Clark County.

Nevada Dept. of Education
Southern Nevada Office
1820 E. Sahara Ave., Ste. 207
Las Vegas, NV 89104
486-6455
Mary Peterson,Supt. of Public Instruction
Establishes courses of study, textbooks and graduation requirements and sets the standards for content and administration of student testing.

CLARK COUNTY
SCHOOL DISTRICT

**Clark County School
Board of Trustees**
2832 E. Flamingo Rd.
Las Vegas, NV 89121
799-1072
Mary Beth Scow (District A)
Ruth Johnson (District B)
Shirley Barber (District C)
Larry Mason (District D) Vice President
Lois Tarkanian (District E) Clerk
Susan Brager (District F) President
Judy Witt (District G)
The publicly elected board has seven members. They serve overlapping four-year terms and set policy. The board meets every second and fourth Thursday at 5:30 pm at the Education Center in the Board Room. The seven members are elected by the citizens of Clark

County to make and adopt school district policy. Individuals who wish to address the board may do so by calling the Superintendent's Office at 799-5310 by 2 pm the day of the board meeting.

**Clark County School District
Assessment Center**
601 N. 9th St.
Las Vegas, NV 89101
799-8550
Dr. Stella Helvie, Dir.
Hours: Mon. - Fri. 7:30 am - 4:30 pm
Places non-English speaking students.

Home Schooling
Connie Geldbach
Oversees district's Home-School Program; in 1996-97 there were 1,665 home-schooled students.

Educare
850 S. Durango Dr.
Las Vegas, NV 89128
341-8058
Connie Carter, Licensed Consultant
Service for home-schooling. Administers diagnostic tests, writes curriculum and tutors students.

Indian Education Program
601 N. 9th St.
Las Vegas, NV 89101
799-8515
Jack Spicer, Coordinating Teacher
Tutorial program for grades K-8.

Adult Education
2701 E. St. Louis Ave.
Las Vegas, NV 89104
799-8650
Claudette Whitson, Adm.
Career development center that is staffed by counselors and support personnel who provide counseling services and placement in educational programs to adult residents who do not have a diploma.

**Clark County Public Education
Foundation**
2832 E. Flamingo Rd., Box 7
Las Vegas, NV 89121
799-1042
Judi K. Steele, Exec. Dir.
The Clark County Public Education Foundation is an independent, non-profit corporation created by business and community leaders to work in collaboration with the school district as a catalyst for educational change through innovation.

Nevada State PTA
(LV Area Council)
1620 W. Charleston Blvd.
Las Vegas, NV 89102
258-7885
Stuart Reid, Treas.
Provides a forum for parents to share ideas and concerns as well as to get a better idea of what is going on in school.

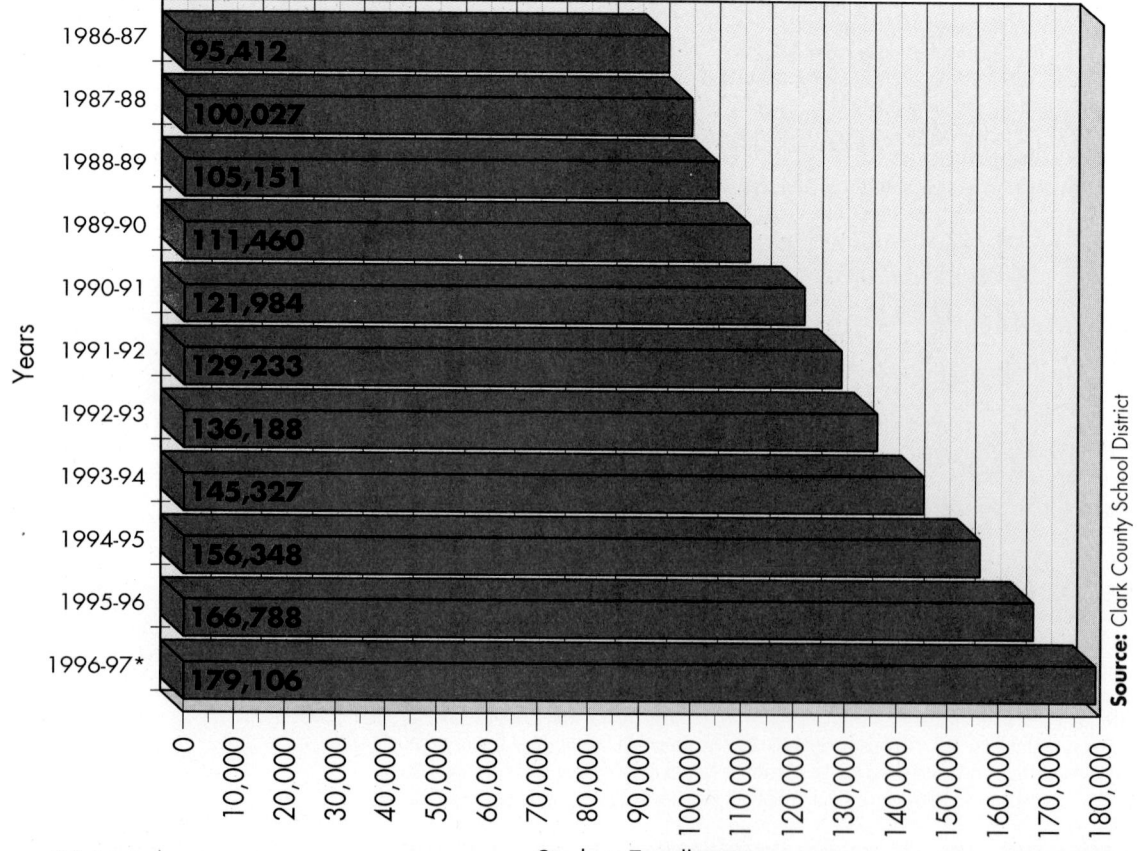

Clark County Public School Enrollment

Years	Student Enrollment
1986-87	95,412
1987-88	100,027
1988-89	105,151
1989-90	111,460
1990-91	121,984
1991-92	129,233
1992-93	136,188
1993-94	145,327
1994-95	156,348
1995-96	166,788
1996-97*	179,106

Source: Clark County School District

* Estimated

1998-99 Clark County School District Calendar
9-Month Schools

July 1	Twelve-month administrators begin work year
July 3	Independence Day observed *(twelve-month employees only)*
August 3	Eleven-month administrators return
August 11	Ten-month secondary deans return
August 12	New teachers report
August 17	Ten-month administrative specialists and coordinators return
August 19	Teachers on leave of absence return along with all other licensed employees
August 20 - 21	School registration
August 24	Classes begin
September 7	Labor Day *(no school)*
October 23	End of first nine weeks *(44 days)*
October 30	Nevada Day observed *(no school)*
November 11	Veteran's Day *(no school)*
November 26 - 27	Thanksgiving Day & Family Day *(no school)*
December 18	Winter break begins at end of day *(no school December 21 - January 1)*
January 4	Classes resume
January 15	End of second nine weeks *(46 days)*
January 18	Martin Luther King, Jr. Day *(no school)*
January 19	Second semester begins
February 15	Presidents' Day *(no school)*
March 19	End of the third nine weeks *(43 days)*
March 26	Spring break begins at end of day *(no school March 29 - April 2)*
April 5	Classes resume
May 31	Memorial Day observed *(no school)*
June 2	End of fourth nine weeks *(47 days)*, end of second semester *(90 days)* and end of school year *(180 days)*
June 3	End of teachers' work year
June 4, 7 & 8	Emergency days if needed
June 10	End of ten-month secondary dean's work year
June 14	End of ten-month administrator's work year
June 30	End of twelve & eleven-month Administrator's work year

1998 Clark County School District Calendar
11 & 12 - Month Schools

January 5	9-month, 11-month, and 12-month tracks 2, 3, 4, 5 classes resume
January 16	9-month end of second report period
January 19	Observe Martin Luther King's Birthday *(no school)*
January 26	12-month track 1, classes resume
February 16	Observe Presidents' Day *(no school)*
March 6	11-month end of second report period
March 13	12-month track 5 end of second report period
March 20	9-month end of third report period
April 3	12-month tracks, 1, 2, 3, 4 end of second report period
April 3	Spring Break Begins (April 6-10, incl.)
April 13	9-month, 11-month, 12-month tracks 1, 2, 3, 4 classes resume
April 20	12-month track 5 classes resume
May 25	Memorial Day *(no school)*
June 4	9-month end of fourth report period
June 25	11-month
July 3	Independence Day Observed *(no school)*
July 17	12-month track 5 end of third report period
August 7	12-month tracks 1, 2, 3, 4 end of third report period End of school year

EDUCATION COST

It cost Clark County $4,195 to educate each child in the Clark County School District for 1996-97.

COST OF BUILDING SCHOOLS

The approximate cost of building schools in the Clark County School District is as follows:

Elementary school	$5 million
Middle school	$17 million
High school	$32 - $34 million

PUBLIC ELEMENTARY SCHOOLS

Elementary Schools: 142

School lunch: $1.30

School Hours: 9 am - 3:11 pm; some 8:30 am - 2:41 pm

Area Superintendents:

Marjorie Connor, Northeast - 799-7943

Dr. Michael Robinson, Northwest - 799-4254

Dr. Maurice Flores, Southeast - 799-8077

Dr. Carla Steinforth, East - 799-8497

Dr. Marsha Irvin, East Central - 799-2142

Eva Simmons, Southwest - 799-4270

Dr. Kay P. Carl, Asst. Superintendent of Elementary Div. - 799-5475

Kirk L. Adams
580 Fogg St.
Las Vegas, NV 89110
799-8800
Cardon Allred, Princ.

O.K. Adcock
100 Newcomer St.
Las Vegas, NV 89107
799-4185
Laura Fesenmeyer, Princ.

Lee Antonello
1101 Tropical Pkwy.
N. Las Vegas, NV 89031
799-8380
Andrea Klafter-Phillips, Princ.

Selma F. Bartlett
1961 Wigwam Pkwy.
Henderson, NV 89014
799-5750
Bradley Reitz, Princ.

John R. Beatty
8685 Hidden Palms Pkwy.
Las Vegas, NV 89123
799-5700
Jimmy Chapman, Princ.

Will Beckley
3223 S. Glenhurst Dr.
Las Vegas, NV 89121
799-7700
Sandra E. Carmody, Princ.

Rex Bell
2900 Wilmington Way
Las Vegas, NV 89102
799-5910
Manuel Madrid, Princ.

Patricia Bendorf
3550 W. Kevin St.
Las Vegas, NV 89117
799-4440
Elizabeth Duncombe, Princ.

William G. Bennett
2750 S. Needles Hwy.
Laughlin, NV 89029
298-3378
Gladys Laughlin, Princ.

Blue Diamond
912 Village Ln.
Blue Diamond, NV 89004
875-4226
Anecia Nelson, Princ.

John W. Bonner
765 Crestdale Ln.
Las Vegas, NV 89134
799-6050
Debrah Franklin, Princ.

PUBLIC ELEMENTARY SCHOOLS

Grant Bowler
1425 Whipple Rd.
Logandale, NV 89021
398-3233
John (Ken) Ligon, Princ.

Joseph L. Bowler
851 Vincent Leavitt Ave.
Bunkerhill, NV 89007
346-1900
Richard Davis, Princ.

Walter Bracken
1200 N. 27th St.
Las Vegas, NV 89101
799-7095
Wendy Roselinsky, Princ.

Lucille Bruner
4289 Allen Ln.
N. Las Vegas, NV 89030
799-0620
Carol Threats, Princ.

Richard H. Bryan
8050 Cielo Vista Ave.
Las Vegas, NV 89128
799-1460
Bart Mangino, Princ.

Roger M. Bryan
8255 W. Katie Ave.
Las Vegas, NV 89117
799-1270
Carol Bumgamer, Princ.

Marion Cahlan
2801 Ft. Sumter Dr.
N. Las Vegas, NV 89030
799-7103
Jean Jackson, Princ.

Arturo Cambeiro
2851 Harris Ave.
Las Vegas, NV 89101
799-1700
Cenie Nelson, Princ.

Roberta Cartwright
1050 Gary St.
Las Vegas, NV 89123
799-1350
Emily Aguero, Princ.

M. J. Christensen
9001 Mariner Cove Cir.
Las Vegas, NV 89117
799-4390
Joan Gray, Princ.

Clyde C. Cox
3855 Timberlake Dr.
Las Vegas, NV 89115
799-4990
Jan Bennington, Princ.

David M. Cox
(Year-round)
280 Clark Dr.
Henderson, NV 89014
799-5730
John Ward, Princ.

Lois Craig
2637 E. Gowan Rd.
N. Las Vegas, NV 89030
799-4910
Gloria Brooks, Princ.

Crestwood
1300 Pauline Way
Las Vegas, NV 89104
799-7890
Sue Bernheisel, Princ.

Paul E. Culley
1200 N. Mallard St.
Las Vegas, NV 89108
799-4800
Dennis Cobia, Princ.

Cynthia Cunningham
(Year-round)
4145 Jimmy Durante Blvd.
Las Vegas, NV 89122
799-8780
James Fincher, Princ.

Jack Dailey
2001 E. Reno Ave.
Las Vegas, NV 89119
799-5690
Dora Herman, Princ.

Laura Dearing
3046 S. Ferndale St.
Las Vegas, NV 89121
799-7710
Judith Mutnick, Princ.

C. H. Decker
(Year-round)
3850 S. Redwood St.
Las Vegas, NV 89103
799-5920
David Smith, Princ.

Herbert A. Derfelt
1900 S. Lisa Ln.
Las Vegas, NV 89117
799-4370
Susan Steaffens, Princ.

Ruthe Deskin
4550 N. Pioneer Way
Las Vegas, NV 89129
799-4600
James Perkins, Princ.

P. A. Diskin
(Year-round)
4220 S. Ravenwood Dr.
Las Vegas, NV 89103
799-5930
Charles Santelman, Princ.

Harvey N. Dondero
(Year-round)
4450 S. Ridgeville St.
Las Vegas, NV 89103
799-5940
Robert Wondrash, Princ.

John Dooley
1940 Chickasaw Dr.
Henderson, NV 89015
799-8060
Clint Phillips, Princ.

Ira J. Earl
(Year-round)
1463 Marion Dr.
Las Vegas, NV 89110
799-7310
Earnestine Nix, Princ.

Marion B. Earl
6650 W. Reno Ave.
Las Vegas, NV 89110
799-8181
Ronald Fagen, Princ.

Elbert Edwards
(Year-round)
4551 Diamond Head Dr.
Las Vegas, NV 89110
799-7320
John S. Lindley, Princ.

Dorothy Eisenberg
(Year-round)
7770 Ruby Valley Ave.
Las Vegas, NV 89129
799-4680
Curtis Jones, Princ.

Ruth Fyfe
4101 W. Bonanza Rd.
Las Vegas, NV 89107
799-4191
Dale (Rick) Slater, Princ.

Fay Galloway
(Year-round)
701 Tamarak Dr.
Henderson, NV 89015
799-8920
Susan Leibowitz, Princ.

James Gibson
271 Leisure Cr.
Henderson, NV 89014
799-8730
Margaret Moore, Princ.

Dan Goldfarb
1651 Orchard Valley Dr.
Las Vegas, NV 89122
799-1550
Bridget Bilbray, Princ.

Goodsprings
385 San Pedro St.
Goodsprings, NV 89019
874-1378
Anecia Nelson, Princ.

Oran Gragson
(Year-round)
555 N. Honolulu St.
Las Vegas, NV 89110
799-7330
Theresa Lee Douglass, Princ.

R. Guild Gray
2825 S. Torrey Pines Dr.
Las Vegas, NV 89102
799-5950
Beatrice Soares, Princ.

Dorothy Eisenberg, 7770 Ruby Valley Ave., Las Vegas, NV 89129

William E. Ferron
4200 Mountain Vista St.
Las Vegas, NV 89121
799-7720
Jean Serum, Princ.

Lilly & Wing Fong
2200 James Bilbray Dr.
Las Vegas, NV 89108
799-4890
Jeffrey H. Dwyer, Princ.

Doris French
3235 E. Hacienda Ave.
Las Vegas, NV 89120
799-7730
Jerry Boles, Princ.

E. W. Griffith
324 Essex Dr.
Las Vegas, NV 89107
799-4200
Phoebe Spohn, Princ.

Addeliar Guy
4028 La Madre Way
N. Las Vegas, NV 89031
799-3150
Kathy Kulas, Princ.

Doris Hancock
1661 Lindell Rd.
Las Vegas, NV 89102
799-4205
Roy Shupe, Princ.

Harley Harmon
5351 S. Hillsboro Ln.
Las Vegas, NV 89120
799-7740
Anthony Ulintz, Princ.

George E. Harris
3620 S. Sandhill Rd.
Las Vegas, NV 89121
799-7750
Aileen Pequeen, Princ.

Lomie G. Heard
Nellis Air Force Base
42 Baer Dr.
Las Vegas, NV 89115
799-4920
Danny Kilgore, Princ.

Helen Herr
6475 Eagle Creek Ln.
Las Vegas, NV 89115
799-8860
Karen McVeigh, Princ.

Fay Herron
(Year-round)
2421 N. Kenneth
N. Las Vegas, NV 89030
799-7123
Tom Hutton, Princ.
Fay Herron was the first school to start year-round classes in 1973.

Halle Hewetson
(Year-round)
701 N. 20th St.
Las Vegas, NV 89101
799-7896
Thomas Maveal, Princ.

Charlotte Hill
7440 Bates St.
Las Vegas, NV 89123
799-5720
Frances Spicer, Princ.

Edna F. Hinman
450 Merlayne Dr.
Henderson, NV 89015
799-8990
Alan Bowman, Princ.

Indian Springs
400 Sky Rd.
Indian Springs, NV 89018
382-8011
Mark Coleman, Princ.

Walter Jacobson
8400 Bosack Dr.
Las Vegas, NV 89128
799-4320
Francie Summers, Princ.

Helen Jydstrup
(Year-round)
5150 Duneville St.
Las Vegas, NV 89128
799-8140
Nadine Nielsen, Princ.

Edythe & Lloyd Katz
(Year-round)
1800 Rock Springs Dr.
Las Vegas, NV 89128
799-4330
Mary Ann Ward, Princ.

Marc Kahre
(Year-round)
7887 W. Gowan Rd.
Las Vegas, NV 89129
799-4660
Carol Lark, Princ.

Frank Kim
7600 Peace Way
Las Vegas, NV 89117
799-5990
Mark Christensen, Princ.

Martha P. King
888 Adams Blvd.
Boulder City, NV 89005
799-8260
James La Buda, Princ.

Martin Luther King, Jr.
2260 Betty Ln.
Las Vegas, NV 89115
799-7390
Sue Jonas, Princ.

Robert E. Lake
2904 Meteoro St.
Las Vegas, NV 89109
799-5530
Alma Vining, Princ.

Allen Dean LaMar
8680 W. Hammer Ln.
Las Vegas, NV 89129
799-4580
Thomas O'Roarke, Princ.

Lincoln
3010 Berg St.
N. Las Vegas, NV 89030
799-7133
James Shipp, Princ.

Walter V. Long
2000 S. Walnut Rd.
Las Vegas, NV 89104
799-7456
DeLloyd Hammond, Princ.

Mary and Zel Lowman
4225 N. Lamont St.
Las Vegas, NV 89115
799-4930
Ruby Epps, Princ.

William Lummis
(Year-round)
9000 Hillpointe Rd.
Las Vegas, NV 89128
799-4380
Rick Watson, Princ.

Robert Lunt
(Year-round)
2701 Harris St.
Las Vegas, NV 89101
799-8360
Elena Villa, Princ.

Ann Lynch
4850 Kell Ln.
Las Vegas, NV 89115
799-8820
Andrew Martinez, Princ.

Nate Mack
(Year-round)
3170 Laurel Ave.
Henderson, NV 89014
799-7760
Teddie Brewer, Princ.

Ernest May
(Year-round)
6350 W. Washburn Rd.
Las Vegas, NV 89130
799-4690
James Phil Barra, Princ.

Gordon McCaw
57 Lynn Ln.
Henderson, NV 89015
799-8930
Janet Dobry, Princ.
Detailed re-creation of a 19th-century silver mine in a mountain. The $200,000 McCaw School of Mines Project consists of five mining display rooms and simulations of an open pit mine, a mine elevator and a tunnel.

Estes M. McDoniel
1831 Fox Ridge Dr.
Henderson, NV 89014
799-7788
Eva White, Princ.

James B. McMillan
(Year-round)
7000 Walt Lott Dr.
Las Vegas, NV 89108
799-4350
Doretta B. Worsham, Princ.

J. T. McWilliams
1315 Hiawatha Rd.
Las Vegas, NV 89108
799-4770
Cecil Jackson, Princ.

J. E. Manch
4351 Lamont St.
Las Vegas, NV 89115
799-4900
Donna Barber, Princ.

John F. Mendoza
(Year-round)
2000 N. Sloan Ln.
Las Vegas, NV 89122
799-8680
Deborah Powell Willis, Princ.

Andrew Mitchell
900 Ave. B
Boulder City, NV 89005
799-8280
Marilyn Miks, Princ.

Sue H. Morrow
1070 Featherwood Ave.
Henderson, NV 89015
799-3550
Gary Namba, Princ.

Mt. Charleston
HCR 38 Box 275
End of Yellow Pine Rd.
Mt. Charleston, NV 89124
872-5438
Anecia Nelson, Princ.

Mountain View
(Year-round)
5436 E. Kell Ln.
Las Vegas, NV 89115
799-7350
David Harcourt, Princ.

Ulis Newton
571 Greenway Rd.
Henderson, NV 89015
799-0500
David Mendelson, Princ.

Paradise
851 E. Tropicana Ave.
Las Vegas, NV 89109
799-5660
Trudi Abbel, Princ.

John S. Park
931 Franklin Ave.
Las Vegas, NV 89104
799-7904
Linda Ragan Agreda, Princ.

Claude & Stella Parson
4100 Thom Blvd.
Las Vegas, NV 89130
799-4530
Herbert Freeman, Princ.

Ute Perkins
1255 Patriots Way
Moapa, NV 89025
1-702-864-2444
Frank Cooper, Princ.

Clarence A. Piggott
9601 Red Hills Dr.
Las Vegas, NV 89117
799-4450
Linda Kemp, Princ.

Vail Pittman
6333 Fargo Ave.
Las Vegas, NV 89107
799-4213
Linda Gross, Princ.

Red Rock
408 Upland Blvd.
Las Vegas, NV 89107
799-4223
Lynn Meyer, Princ.

Doris M. Reed
2501 Winwood St.
Las Vegas, NV 89108
799-4777
Shelly Channel, Princ.

Harry Reid
300 Michael Wendell Way
Searchlight, NV 89046
297-1224
Anecia Nelson, Princ.

Betsy Rhodes
7350 Tealwood St.
Las Vegas, NV 89131
799-3450
Ken Fowler, Princ.

Aggie Roberts
227 Charter Oak Dr.
Henderson, NV 89014
799-1320
Janice Stromberg, Princ.

C. C. Ronnow
(Year-round)
1100 Lena St.
Las Vegas, NV 89101
799-7159
Billy Chapman, Princ.

Bertha Ronzone
5701 Stacey Ave.
Las Vegas, NV 89108
799-4780
Catherine Conger, Princ.

Lewis E. Rowe
4338 S. Bruce St.
Las Vegas, NV 89109
799-5540
Marianne Long, Princ.

Richard J. Rundle
(Year-round)
425 N. Christy Ln.
Las Vegas, NV 89110
799-7380
David Price, Princ.

Sandy Valley
Hopi & Pearl
Sandy Valley, NV 89019
723-5344
Anecia Nelson, Princ.

PUBLIC ELEMENTARY SCHOOLS

C. T. Sewell
(Year-round)
700 E. Lake Mead Dr.
Henderson, NV 89015
799-8940
Carolyn Edwards, Princ.

Helen M. Smith
7101 Pinedale Ave.
Las Vegas, NV 89128
799-4300
David Spitler, Princ.

C. P. Squires
1312 E. Tonopah Ave.
N. Las Vegas, NV 89030
799-7169
Betty Roqueni, Princ.

Stanford
5350 Harris Ave.
Las Vegas, NV 89110
799-7272
Celia Isbell, Princ.

Sunrise Acres
2501 Sunrise Ave.
Las Vegas, NV 89101
799-7912
Art Ochoa, Princ.

Myrtle Tate
2450 N. Lincoln Rd.
Las Vegas, NV 89115
799-7360
Marie Wakefield, Princ.

Robert L. Taylor
400 McNeil Dr.
Henderson, NV 89015
799-8950
Lisa Babcock, Princ.

Ruby S. Thomas
(Year-round)
1560 E. Cherokee Ave.
Las Vegas, NV 89109
799-5550
Elsie Harris, Princ.

Jim Thorpe
1650 Patrick Ln.
Henderson, NV 89014
799-0740
Sylvia Springer, Princ.

R. E. Tobler
6510 W. Buckskin Ave.
Las Vegas, NV 89108
799-4500
Alice Wisdom, Princ.

Bill Y. Tomiyasu
(Year-round)
5445 S. Annie Oakley Dr.
Las Vegas, NV 89120
799-7770
Patricia Daley-Blomstrom, Princ.

Harriet Treem
1698 Patrick Ln.
Henderson, NV 89014
799-8760
Sharon Garhardt, Princ.

Twin Lakes
3300 Riverside Dr.
Las Vegas, NV 89108
799-4790
Barbara Fox, Princ.

J. M. Ullom
4869 E. Sun Valley Dr.
Las Vegas, NV 89121
799-7780
Anthony Vicari, Princ.

John Vanderburg
2040 Desert Shadow Trail
Henderson, NV 89012
799-0540
Carolyn Reedom, Princ.

Vegas Verdes
4000 El Parque Ave.
Las Vegas, NV 89102
799-5960
William Partier, Princ.

Virgin Valley
150 North Yucca St.
Mesquite, NV 89027
346-5761
Phyllis Leavitt, Princ.

Gene Ward
1555 E. Hacienda Ave.
Las Vegas, NV 89119
799-5650
Patricia Hodges, Princ.

Rose Warren
6451 Brandywine Way
Las Vegas, NV 89107
799-4233
Steve Rudish, Princ.

Kermit R. Booker, Sr., 2277 Martin Luther King Blvd., Las Vegas, NV 89106

Howard Wasden
2831 Palomino Ln.
Las Vegas, NV 89107
799-4239
Diane Reitz, Princ.

Cyril Wengert
(Year-round)
2001 Winterwood Blvd.
Las Vegas, NV 89122
799-8600
Scott Ober, Princ.

Whitney
5005 Keenan Ave.
Las Vegas, NV 89122
799-7790
Francine Mayfield, Princ.
Replaces old school which first opened
in 1927.

Louis Wiener Jr.
450 E. Eldorado Ln.
Las Vegas, NV 89123
799-5760
Margaret Appuglise, Princ.

Elizabeth Wilhelm
609 W. Alexander Rd.
N. Las Vegas, NV 89030
799-1750
Vee Wilson, Princ.

Tom Williams
3000 E. Tonopah Ave.
N. Las Vegas, NV 89030
799-7179
Linda Griffith, Princ.

Eva Wolfe
4027 W. Washburn Rd.
N. Las Vegas, NV 89031
799-1860
Ryleen Hinkle, Princ.

Gwendolyn Woolley
3955 Timberlake Dr.
Las Vegas, NV 89115
799-4970
Holly Jaacks, Princ.

Elaine Wynn
5655 Edna Ave.
Las Vegas, NV 89102
799-8160
Jacqueline Locks, Princ.

ELEMENTARY SPECIAL EDUCATION

Special Student Asst. Supervisor: 799-5471
Special Education Services: 799-7446
Special Education Programs: 799-7468
Judi Miller, Coordinator

Child Find Project
2625 E. St. Louis Ave.
Las Vegas, NV 89104
799-7463
Fulfills needs of unserved handicapped
children ages 3 to 21. Eligible children
are provided with free diagnostic
evaluation, development of an appropriate
educational program and placement
recommendations.

Miley Achievement Center
5850 Euclid Ave.
Las Vegas, NV 89120
799-5631
Karyn Durbin, Coordinator

John F. Miller
1905 Atlantic St.
Las Vegas, NV 89104
799-7401
Diana Dowling, Princ.

Seigle Diagnostic Center
2625 E. St. Louis Ave.
Las Vegas, NV 89104
799-7446
Tippy Reid, Dir.

Helen J. Stewart
2375 E. Viking Rd.
Las Vegas, NV 89109
799-5588
Leni Proctor, Princ.

Variety
2601 Sunrise Ave.
Las Vegas, NV 89101
799-7938
Beverly J. Minnear, Princ.

PRIME 6 SCHOOLS

Prime 6 schools, which used to be sixth
grade centers, now accept kindergarten
through sixth grade. Sixth graders now
attend middle schools. For more information about Prime 6 schools, call 799-0670.
School Hours: 8:15 am - 2:45 pm
Lunch: $1.30

Kermit R. Booker, Sr.
2277 Martin Luther King Blvd.
Las Vegas, NV 89106
799-4720
Beverly Mathis, Princ.

Kit Carson
1735 N. D St.
Las Vegas, NV 89106
799-7113
Linda Gipson, Princ.

H. P. Fitzgerald
2651 N. Revere St.
N. Las Vegas, NV 89030
799-0600
Leary Adams, Princ.
Fitzgerald is the first new school built
in the predominantly black northwest
neighborhood in 27 years.

Matt Kelly
1900 N. J St.
Las Vegas, NV 89106
799-4750
Jeremy Hauser, Princ.

Madison
1030 J St.
Las Vegas, NV 89106
799-4760
Garrett Kerkstra, Princ.

Quannah McCall
800 Carey Ave.
N. Las Vegas, NV 89030
799-7149
Mary Manchego, Princ.

PUBLIC MIDDLE SCHOOLS

Asst. Superintendent: 799-5481
School Hours:
Grades 6 thru 8: 8:15 am - 2:26 pm
Grades Year-round: 8 am - 2:33 pm
Lunch: $2.35

Ernest A. Becker
9151 Pinewood Hills Dr.
Las Vegas, NV 89128
799-4460
Cathy Andrews, Princ.

Jim Bridger
2505 N. Bruce St.
N. Las Vegas, NV 89030
799-7185
Douglas R. Gougar, Princ.

Harold J. Brinley
(Year-round)
2480 Maverick St.
Las Vegas, NV 89108
799-4550
Alan McNulty, Princ.

B. Mahlon Brown
307 N. Cannes St.
Henderson, NV 89015
799-8900
Emilo Fernandez, Jr., Princ.

Lyal Burkholder
355 W. Van Wagenen St.
Henderson, NV 89015
799-8080
Diana Chalpant, Princ.

Helen C. Cannon
5850 Euclid Ave.
Las Vegas, NV 89120
799-5600
Chris Erbe, Princ.

James E. Cashman
4622 W. Desert Inn Rd.
Las Vegas, NV 89102
799-5880
Evans Rutledge, Princ.

John C. Fremont
1100 E. St. Louis Ave.
Las Vegas, NV 89104
799-5558
Russell Ramirez, Princ.

Elton M. Garrett
1200 Ave. G
Boulder City, NV 89005
799-8290
Shauna Zobel, Princ.

Frank F. Garside
300 S. Torrey Pines Dr.
Las Vegas, NV 89107
799-4245
Sandra Metcalf, Princ.

Robert O. Gibson
3900 W. Washington Ave.
Las Vegas, NV 89107
799-4700
Denise Williams-Robinson, Princ.

Barbara and Hank Greenspun
140 N. Valle Verde Dr.
Henderson, NV 89014
799-0920
Leroy Hurd, Princ.

Kenny C. Guinn
4150 S. Torrey Pines Dr.
Las Vegas, NV 89103
799-5900
Jan Boyer, Princ.

Hyde Park
900 Hinson St.
Las Vegas, NV 89107
799-4260
Patricia LaMonica, Princ.

Walter Johnson
(Year-round)
7701 Ducharme Ave.
Las Vegas, NV 89128
799-4480
James Cavin, Princ.

Duane Keller
301 N. Fogg St.
Las Vegas, NV 89110
799-3220
Lauren Kohut-Rost, Princ.

K. O. Knudson
2400 Atlantic St.
Las Vegas, NV 89104
799-7470
Mary Ramirez, Princ.
K. O. Knudson will offer a magnet program emphasizing performing and creative arts.

Lied
5350 W. Tropical Pkwy.
Las Vegas, NV 89130
799-4620
Paul Osboid, Princ.

Mack Lyon
179 S. Anderson St.
Overton, NV 89040
397-8610
Katherine Christensen, Princ.

Roy W. Martin
2800 E. Stewart Ave.
Las Vegas, NV 89101
799-7922
John Kelley, Princ.

Mike O'Callagan
(Year-round)
1450 Radwick Dr.
Las Vegas, NV 89110
799-7340
Roberta Holton, Princ.

William E. Orr
1562 E. Katie Ave.
Las Vegas, NV 89119
799-5573
Barbara Rosenburg, Princ.

Dell H. Robison
(Year-round)
825 Marion Dr.
Las Vegas, NV 89110
799-7300
John Hummel, Princ.

Grant Sawyer
(Year-round)
5450 Redwood St.
Las Vegas, NV 89118
799-5980
Ronnie Smith, Princ.

J. D. Smith
1301 Tonopah Ave.
N. Las Vegas, NV 89030
799-7080
Theresa Nicholson, Princ.

Theron L. Swainston
(Year-round)
3500 W. Gilmore Ave.
N. Las Vegas, NV 89030
799-4860
Susan Overmoen, Princ.

Ed Von Tobel
(Year-round)
2436 N. Pecos Rd.
Las Vegas, NV 89115
799-7280
Ron Montoya, Princ.

Charles I. West
2050 Sapphire Stone Ave.
Las Vegas, NV 89106
799-3121
Lois Venger, Princ.

Thurman White
1661 Galleria Dr.
Henderson, NV 89014
799-0777
Emil Wozniak, Princ.

C. W. Woodbury
3875 E. Harmon Ave.
Las Vegas, NV 89121
799-7660
Joe Murphy, Princ.

SCHOOL FACTS OF INTEREST

TEST SCORES

ACT - The average composite score for Clark County students taking the test was 21.2 out of a possible 35. For Nevada the average was 21.3 while the national average was 21.8.

SAT - 2,264 Clark County students took the 1996-1997 test and averaged 502 on the verbal and 509 on the math. *(National averages are 505 and 511 respectively.)* The maximum for each section is 800.

DROPOUTS

Clark County dropout rate was 10.8 percent for the 1995-96 school year, down from 11.7 percent the previous year. According to the 1990 Census, Nevada has the highest percentage of dropouts in the nation.

EXPULSION

Total expulsions during the 1996-97 period were 167. Reasons for expulsion were:

Arson 7
Assault/Battery 26
Substance Possession 5
Extortion/Robbery 4
Fighting 3
Immoral conduct 1
Sexual Harassment 1
Major Campus Disruption 1
Theft 9
Threats 4
Weapons 92

Trial re-enrollments were approved in 1996-97 for 65 students expelled that year and in prior years, and 20 students had expulsions rescinded.
Source: Clark County School District

COLLEGE BOUND

Nevada ranks last among states in sending its high school graduates to college. Nationwide, 53.5 percent of high school graduates in the nation go on to college. In Nevada, the rate is only 32.8 percent. Nevada is just slightly below the national average in percentage of ninth-graders that go on to graduate from high school. The national average is 71.2 percent; Nevada's is 70.9 percent.

COLLEGE EDUCATION

According to the 1990 census, 13.8 percent of the Clark County adults over age 25 have Bachelor's degrees or higher.

FOREIGN EXCHANGE STUDENTS

EF Foundation for Foreign Study
1-800-44-SHARE
Chris or Mike Cutler

Founded in 1979, the foundation puts together host families and students. Both must complete an application and screening process. Students age 15-18 study in Las Vegas for a semester or an academic year. The Foreign Exchange Program offers opportunities for more than 50,000 students from 25 countries.

SENIOR HIGH SCHOOLS

Asst. Superintendent
Leonard Paul - 799-5466

Area Superintendent
Stephen Augspurger - 799-5398

Area Superintendent
Pamela Hicks - 799-8492

Area Superintendent
Steve McCoy - 799-2137

Director of Curriculum
Alice Dallimore - 651-5065

Director of School-to-Work Programs
Kathleen Frosini - 799-8462

School Hours: 7:20 am - 1:31 pm

Clark County students are required to obtain a minimum of 22.5 high school course credits to receive a diploma.

In 1996-97, 18,671 students in grades 9-12 were enrolled in occupational programs, or 46 percent of all high school students in the district.

Area Technical Trade Center (ATTC)
444 W. Brooks Ave.
N. Las Vegas, NV 89030
799-8300
Estella Hodgkin, Princ.
Student attends the home school for comprehensive classes for half day and A.T.T.C. for selected vocational programs. Program is for students in their junior and senior years.

Basic
400 Palo Verde Dr.
Henderson, NV 89015
799-8000
Horace Smith, Princ.

Bonanza
6665 W. Del Rey Ave.
Las Vegas, NV 89102
799-4000
Sue DeFrancesco, Princ.

Boulder City
1101 Fifth Ave.
Boulder City, NV 89005
799-8200
Bill Garis, Princ.

Chaparral
3850 Annie Oakley Dr.
Las Vegas, NV 89121
799-7580
Bob Chesto, Princ.

Cheyenne
3200 W. Alexander Rd.
N. Las Vegas, NV 89030
799-4830
Richard Brown, Princ.

Cimarron-Memorial, 2301 N. Tenaya Way, Las Vegas, NV 89128

Cimarron-Memorial
2301 N. Tenaya Way
Las Vegas, NV 89128
799-4400
Ken Bedrosian, Princ.

Ed W. Clark
4291 W. Pennwood Ave.
Las Vegas, NV 89102
799-5800
Wayne Tanaka, Princ.

Durango High School
7100 W. Dewey Dr.
Las Vegas, NV 89113
799-5850
Allen Coles, Princ.

Eldorado
1139 N. Linn Ln.
Las Vegas, NV 89110
799-7200
Tom Barberini, Princ.

Green Valley
460 Arroyo Grande Ave.
Henderson, NV 89014
799-0950
Betty Sabo, Princ.

Indian Springs Jr. & Sr.
400 Sky Rd.
Indian Springs, NV 89018
382-8011
Mark Coleman, Princ.

Las Vegas High School
6500 E. Sahara Ave.
Las Vegas, NV 89122
799-0180
Barry Gunderson, Princ.

Laughlin Jr./Sr. High School
1900 Cougar Dr.
Laughlin, NV 89029
298-1996
Dick Edwards, Princ.

Moapa Valley High School
2400 St. Joseph Dr.
Overton, NV 89040
397-2611
Dean Allen, Princ.

Mojave
5302 Goldfield St.
N. Las Vegas, NV 89031
799-0432
Gail Dixon, Princ.

Palo Verde
333 S. Pavilion Center Dr.
Las Vegas, NV 89134
799-1450
Theresa Smith, Princ.

Rancho
1900 E. Owens Ave.
N. Las Vegas, NV 89030
799-7000
Ernie Jauregui, Princ.

Silverado
1650 Silver Hawk Ave.
Las Vegas, NV 89123
799-5790
Aldeane Ries, Princ.

South Nevada Vocational Technical Center
5710 Mountain Vista St.
Las Vegas, NV 89120
799-7500
Daniel A. Berg, Princ.
Comprehensive high school that offers courses needed for graduation as well as elective vocational programs.

Valley
2839 S. Burnham Ave.
Las Vegas, NV 89109
799-5450
Carol Leavitt, Princ.

Virgin Valley Jr. & Sr.
820 Valley View Dr.
Mesquite, NV 89027
346-2780
Ray DePalma, Princ.

Western
4601 W. Bonanza Rd.
Las Vegas, NV 89107
799-4080
Ronan Matthew, Princ.

MAGNET SCHOOLS

Starting in the early 1970s, magnet schools and programs were created as vehicles for voluntary desegregation in public schools across the nation. By providing unique educational programs absent in neighborhood schools, the establishment of magnet schools and programs is a way to offer students opportunities to choose educational experiences based on their special interests and abilities.

Types of magnets: A magnet program serves a specific number of students from more than one attendance area in a school that also provides a regular program to students in a specific attendance area. A magnet school is a school which serves more than one attendance area, with the total school population participating in the identified magnet program. Magnet schools offer unique

instructional programs related to the magnet theme to all students attending the school.

Admission requirements: Students and parents may choose from the magnet schools and magnet programs offered by the school district based on interest, talent, and abilities. Application forms are available at each of the magnet sites. The period for submitting an application for enrollment in a magnet school/program for the following school year is: Elementary School - January thru 3rd Fri. in February; High School - November thru 3rd Fri. in February; Middle School - Last Fri. in January thru 1st Fri. in March.

The district currently operates 14 magnet schools & programs.

Magnet School District Office: 799-5479

Academic Fast Track
Charles I. West
2050 Sapphire Stone Ave.
Las Vegas, NV 89106
799-3121
Lois Venger, Princ.
Grades 6 - 8

Academy of Aerospace & Aviation
Rancho High School
1900 E. Owens Ave.
N. Las Vegas, NV 89030
799-7000
Ernie Jauregui, Princ.

Academy of Creative Arts & Language
Knudson Middle School
2400 Atlantic St.
Las Vegas, NV 89104
799-7470
Information: 799-8621
Mary Ramirez, Princ.
Grades 6 - 8

Academy for Mathematics, Science, Engineering & Applied Tech.
Clark High School
4291 W. Pennwood Ave.
Las Vegas, NV 89102
799-5800
Wayne Tanaka, Princ.
Grades 9-12
The math and science component will prepare students to succeed in the nation's most competitive colleges, while the engineering and applied technology component will provide hands-on technical experience along with developing students' problem-solving and critical-thinking skills. Operates as a school within a school.

Academy of Medical & Allied Health Professionals
Rancho High School
1900 E. Owens Ave.
N. Las Vegas, NV 89030
Ernie Jauregui, Princ.
Grades 9-12

MAGNET SCHOOLS

Academy of Science and Mathematics
Hyde Park Middle School
900 Hinson St.
Las Vegas, NV 89107
799-4263
Patricia LaMonica, Princ.
Grades 6-8

Academy of Travel & Tourism
Valley High School
2839 S. Burnham Ave.
Las Vegas, NV 89109
799-5450
Carol Leavitt, Princ.
Grades 9-11
Operates as a school within a school for students who wish to enter the tourism industry.

Business, Law, Computers and
Technology Careers
Advanced Technologies
Academy
2501 Vegas Dr.
Las Vegas, NV 89106
799-7870

Michael Kinnaird, Princ.
Grades 9-12
Limited comprehensive high school offering state-of-the-art computers and technologies to prepare students for occupational and professional career courses.

Communication and Creative Arts
C.V.T. Gilbert Magnet School for
Communication & Creative Arts
2101 W. Cartier
N. Las Vegas, NV 89030
799-4730
June Eshelman, Princ.
Grades 1-5

Academic Enrichment and Global
Studies
Jo Mackey Magnet School
2726 Engelstad St.
N. Las Vegas, NV 89030
799-7139
Annie Barnes, Princ.
Grades 1-5

Math/Science Magnet School
Mabel Hoggard
950 N. Tonopah Dr.
Las Vegas, NV 89106
799-4740
Bill Evans, Princ.
Grades 1-5
The Hoggard Math/Science Magnet School is the first elementary magnet school in Clark County. Part of the school district's new Prime 6 desegregation plan, children selected by lottery only.

Performing Arts School
Las Vegas Academy of Int'l
Studies & Performing and
Visual Arts
315 S. 7th St.
Las Vegas, NV 89101
799-7800
Robert Gerye, Princ.
Grades 9-12
Courses offered include five foreign languages; world's governments and related cultural courses. The Performing Arts school will offer courses in theater, dance, vocal/instrumental music and orchestra.

Pre-International Baccalaureate
Program
Valley High School
2839 S. Burnham Ave.
Las Vegas, NV 89109
799-5450
Carol Leavitt, Princ.
Grades 9-12
Academic excellence. Rigorous four-year college preparatory program.

Vocational High School
Vo-Tech
5710 Mountain Vista St.
Las Vegas, NV 89120
799-7500
Daniel Berg, Princ.
Four-year comprehensive vocational high school. VoTech's 1,500 students are served by over 75 academic and vocational teachers.

ALTERNATIVE PROGRAMS / SCHOOLS

Biltmore
801 Veterans Memorial Dr.
Las Vegas, NV 89101
799-7880
William Troeger, Princ.

Classroom on Wheels
439 S. Decatur Blvd.
Las Vegas, NV 89107
870-7201
Angela M. Pernatozzi, Exe. Director
Free bi-lingual pre-school 3-5 years; accredited drug prevention program.

Jefferson
1941 Jefferson St.
No. Las Vegas, NV 89030
799-8330
Thurban Warrick, Princ.

East Horizon High School
3801 E. Washington Ave.
Las Vegas, NV 89110
799-8850
Gina White, Site Administrator

North Horizon High School
444 Brooks Ave.
N. Las Vegas, NV 89030
799-8375
Patricia Green, Site Administrator

South Horizon High School
5710 Mountain Vista St.
Las Vegas, NV 89120
799-8770
Dr. Frank Roqueni, Site Administrator

West Horizon High School
4560 W. Harmon Ave.
Las Vegas, NV 89103
799-8150
Carolyn Chatman, Princ.
Maria Chairez, Dir. of Horizon Project
Hours: 7 am - 12:30 pm
High school with flexible hours to fit around working students or young parents with credit deficiencies to prevent them from dropping out.

Sunset
4560 W. Harmon Ave.
Las Vegas, NV 89103
799-8150
Bob Tobias, Princ.
Hours: 1 pm - 8:25 pm
High school with hours to fit around working students or young parents with credit deficiencies to prevent them from dropping out.

Sunset East
(Evening High School)
900 Hinson St.
Las Vegas, NV 89107
799-8880
Dr. Frank Roqueni, Princ.

Washington
1901 N. White St.
N. Las Vegas, NV 89030
799-8320
Matt Lusk, Princ.

Adult Education Programs
2701 E. St. Louis Ave.
Las Vegas, NV 89104
799-8655
Claudette Whitson, Director
Adults 17 and over who have not received their diplomas.

Clark County Dept. of Parks &
Recreation - Active Learning
Program
455-8200
Joanne Lorrey,
Program Recreation Supervisor
Activities and preparation to formal instruction for children at least age 3 by September 30 to age 5. The program is held at East Las Vegas Community Center, Parkdale Community Center, Sunrise Community Center, Winchester Community Center and Paradise Park Community Center. *(See Parks Section for locations.)* Classes last 7 weeks and run from 9 am - 11:30 am and noon to 2:30 pm, 2 or 3 days per week depending on child's age.

COMMUNITY COLLEGE OF SOUTHERN NEVADA

Adult Basic Skills Center
Community College of
Southern Nevada
6375 W. Charleston Ave.
Las Vegas, NV 89102
651-5033
Terri Kaulentis, Coordinator
Literacy program for adults.

Clark County Library District's
Literacy Program
1401 E. Flamingo Rd.
Las Vegas, NV 89119
733-1127
Monteria Hightower, Literacy Coor.
Talking Books: 733-1925
Computer assisted literacy in libraries is offered at 11 different libraries for English speaking adults who read at or below 5th grade level.

Economic Opportunity Board
Head Start
708 S. 6th St.
Las Vegas, NV 89101
647-2906
Jean S. Childs, Adm.
Provides low-income and handicapped children ages 3 to 5 a comprehensive and meaningful pre-school experience.

East Horizon High School, 3801 E. Washington Ave., Las Vegas, NV 89110

Experience Las Vegas

CLASSES AND TRAINING

CLASSES

Clark County Department of Parks and Recreation
2601 E. Sunset Rd.
Las Vegas, NV 89120
455-8200
Glenn Trowbridge, Dir.
Recreation classes and activities, special interest workshops, cultural and educational offerings and senior citizens' programs. Over 175 classes and programs in all areas are offered to children, teens and adults at the following community centers:

Kenny Guinn Junior High School Satellite Center:
455-8393

Whitney Community Center:
455-7573

Paradise Park Community Center:
455-7513

Parkdale Community Center:
455-7517

Sunrise Community Center:
455-7600

Winchester Community Center:
455-7340

Orr Community Center:
455-7196

Von Tobel Community Center:
455-7699

(See Parks Section for addresses of centers)
Class costs vary and begin at $18-$23; some classes are free; active learning classes $50-$80.

Community Centers and Community Schools
City of Las Vegas
749 Veteran's Memorial Dr.
Las Vegas, NV 89101
229-6297
Stephen Mead, Recreation Mgr.
Classes and workshops in such areas as arts and crafts, computers, dance, drama, gymnastics, martial arts, modeling, physical fitness, music, languages, tutoring and sports. Classes begin in the spring and fall with the school year. Classes range in price from $20 to $37 with workshops $7 to $15. Computer classes $60 for 8 weeks.

Community College of Southern Nevada Continuing & Community Education
6375 W. Charleston Blvd.
Building B, Room 104
Las Vegas, NV 89102
651-5786
Terri Kaulentis, Program Coordinator
The community college offers more than 300 non-credit classes, activities, seminars and workshops for Southern Nevadans to sharpen professional skills, develop new interests and lifelong learning programs.

Reed Whipple Cultural Center
821 Las Vegas Blvd. N.
Las Vegas, NV 89101
229-6211
Bettye Keeton, Class Coordinator
Offers classes and workshops for adults, teens and children in theater, dance, fine arts, music and other areas. Regular class session lasts 10 weeks.

Nevada Cooperative Extension Service
2345 Red Rock St., Ste. 100
Las Vegas, NV 89102-3160
731-3130
Elwood Miller, Dir.
Cooperative Extension brings research information from the University of Nevada, Reno to the residents of the state's rural and urban communities. Extension helps people improve their lives through an educational process which uses scientific knowledge focused on issues and needs. In addition to the 4-H program, numerous other youth programs are available.

UNLV
Cont. Educ. - Frazier Hall, Rm. 109
4505 S. Maryland Pkwy.
Las Vegas, NV 89154
895-3394
Dr. Paul Aizley, Dean
Each year Continuing Education offers over 1,150 credit and non-credit courses aimed at encouraging lifelong education. Community interest courses on a variety of topics, such as business, real estate, computers, exploring trips, etc. Catalogs are mailed to all households in Las Vegas before the spring and fall semester or call and one will be mailed to you. Register by phone using Visa, MasterCard and Discover.

Las Vegas · Clark County Library District CALL PROGRAM
(Computer Assisted Literacy in Libraries)
Clark County Library
1401 E. Flamingo Rd.
Las Vegas, NV 89119
733-1127
Hours: Mon. - Thu. 9 am - 1 pm & 4 pm - 8 pm

Las Vegas Library
833 Las Vegas Blvd. N.
Las Vegas, NV 89101
382-3493
Hours: Mon. - Thu. 9 am - 9 pm; Fri. - Sat. 9 am - 5 pm; Sun. 1 pm - 5 pm

West Las Vegas Library
951 W. Lake Mead Blvd.
Las Vegas, NV 89106
647-1668
Hours: Mon. - Thu. 9 am - 9 pm; Fri. - Sat. 9 am - 5 pm; Sun. 1 pm - 5 pm

TRAINING

Department of Employment Claimant Employment Program
123 Water St.
Henderson, NV 89015
486-6790

2827 Las Vegas Blvd. N.
N. Las Vegas, NV 89030
486-5600
Designed to implement programs to provide jobs and related job training for the unemployed and underemployed residents of Southern Nevada.

The Community Employment and Training Center
902 W. Owens Ave.
Las Vegas, NV 89106
486-5300
Carol Jackson, Dir.
Janice Mace, Supervisor
Unemployment information, job service, veterans assistance, Job Corps program.

Life Line Pregnancy Vocational Education Center
1800 S. Industrial Rd., Ste. A
Las Vegas, NV 89102
871-6585
Lynn Richmond-Scales, Exec. Dir.
Vocational program referral, computer training; assistance and counseling.

Nevada Business Services
930 W. Owens Ave.
Nucleus Plaza
Las Vegas, NV 89106
647-1329
Richard Blue, Exec. Dir.
Occupational training and job placement for economically disadvantaged. Eligibility for this federally funded program is based on income. Call 647-4929 for more information.

Nevada Homes for Youth
525 S. 13th St.
Las Vegas, NV 89101
380-2889
Ron Moore, Exec. Dir.
Teaches teens, 16 to 21, life skills and independent living. Classes are taught at UNLV and various other locations. Students can earn one-half credit toward graduation.

Nevada Partners
710 W. Lake Mead Blvd.
N. Las Vegas, NV 89030
399-5627
Mujahid Ramadan, Dir.
Nevada Partners offers life skill courses and works with business and government to find full-time employment for low-income, unemployed people in Southern Nevada.
Nevada Partners helps at-risk and disadvantaged and chronically unemployed citizens 16 and up with job referrals and training. Job seekers are trained on-site or referred to outside agencies. Its new Training Facility and Sugar Ray Leonard Gym at Revere St. and W. Lake Mead Blvd. in North Las Vegas opened in December, 1994. The 20,000 sq. ft. job-training facility also houses a boxing gym.

The Vocational Assessment Center Dept. of Employment Training & Rehabilitation
628 Belrose Ave.
Las Vegas, NV 89107
486-7895
Terry Sokey, Supervisor
Evaluates people with medical problems. Provides employment subcontract activities to industry such as packaging, assembling and mailing services.

TUTORING

Computertots
2455 Marlene Ct.
Henderson, NV 89014
898-8687
Beth DeLuca, Dir.
Program: Computer classes for children; Computertots (3-5) and Computer Explorers (6 & up)

Futurekids
2555 S. Jones Blvd., Ste. F-1B
Las Vegas, NV 89102
256-9880
Sue Bolton, Owner
Computer literacy plus; ages 3-12; (over 1,200 locations around the globe); keyboarding, animation, robotics & desktop publishing

Kaplan Educational Centers
4632 S. Maryland Pkwy., Ste. 23
Las Vegas, NV 89119
798-5005   1-800-527-8378
Deborah Herman, Dir.
Test preparation for LSAT, MCAT, GMAT, GRE.

Learning to Learn
2075 E. Tropicana Ave.
Las Vegas, NV 89121
435-4323
Jeanine Rodgers, Dir.
Tutoring for adults and children with learning problems. Help for reading and behavior problems.

Miss Dee's Tutoring
228-8363
Specializing in LD, ASL, ADHD and other special needs; completely mobile service.

Sylvan Learning Center
5280 S. Eastern Ave., Ste. A-3
Las Vegas, NV 89119
795-7323

3885 S. Decatur Blvd., Ste. 1040
Las Vegas, NV 89103
876-4090
Tutoring in reading, math, study skills; college prep exam.

EDUCATIONAL STORES

Imagination Unlimited
4934 E. Tropicana Ave.
Las Vegas, NV 89121
434-5696
Hours: Mon. - Thu. & Sat. 10 am - 6 pm; Fri. 10 am - 7 pm; Sun. 11 am - 5 pm
Credit Cards: MC, Visa, Discover, AMX
Specialty toy store; toys, hobbies, games, puzzles, dolls, educational.

Learning Is Fun
Corporate Office
Charles Ivy, Owner
Hours: Mon. - Fri. 10 am - 7 pm; Sat. 10 am - 6 pm; Sun. noon - 5 pm
Books, educational toys and teaching aids, CD-ROM, software, videos and cassettes; located in Target Center.

3062 Sheridan St.
Las Vegas, NV 89102
876-5437

4047 S. Maryland Pkwy.
Las Vegas, NV 89119
791-KIDS
Closed Sundays

290 S. Decatur Blvd.
Las Vegas, NV 89107
258-5437

673 Stephanie St.
Henderson, NV 89014
456-5437

Whippersnapperz
2555 S. Jones Blvd.
Las Vegas, NV 89102
368-6810
Fern Greenwald, Mgr.
Models, challenging puzzles, magic kits, electronic and chemistry sets, computer software, newborn and toddler learning toys; creative and educational toy store.

COLLEGE EDUCATION - UNLV

University of Nevada - Las Vegas
4505 S. Maryland Pkwy.
Las Vegas, NV 89154
895-3011 1-800-334-UNLV
Web site: http://www.unlv.edu
President *Carol Harter* 895-3201
Admissions Office 895-3443
Bookstore 895-3290
Campus Tours 895-3443
James Dickinson Library ... 895-3285
      Circulation ... 895-3531
      Reference 895-3280

University and Community College - System of Nevada Board of Regents
  James Eardley
  Shelley Berkley
  Jill Derby
  David Phillips
  Dorothy Gallagher
  Mark Alden
  Madison Graves
  Nancy Price
  Thalia Dondero
  Howard Rosenberg
  Tom Weisner
The university is a state coeducational institution governed by the publicly elected Board of Regents.

History
The first college-level class in Southern Nevada was held in 1951 in a room at Las Vegas High School, with one full-time faculty member, James Dickinson, and 12 students.
In 1957, the University was founded officially as a Southern Regional Division of the University of Nevada (Reno) and opened its first classroom and administration building on 80 acres of land. Twenty-nine students received degrees at the first commencement ceremonies in 1964. The following year the university was named Nevada Southern University. In January 1969 the university was given its present name, when it was granted autonomy under the state's higher education system, giving it status equal to that of the University of Nevada, Reno.
The 335 acre campus has a student body of 20,000 with 9,855 being full-time for the fall '97 semester. More than 1,100 full-time and part-time faculty are involved in teaching, research and community service. All UNLV programs are accredited by the Northwest Association of Schools and Colleges. Classes run from 7 am to 10 pm weekdays, with some classes held on Saturday.
Graduate Students: 4,020
New Freshman and Undergraduate Transfers: 2,561
UNLV offers more than 148 undergraduate, master's and doctoral degree programs. The university is organized into the following colleges:
  College of Business
  College of Education
  Howard R. Hughes
      College of Engineering
  College of Fine Arts
  College of Health Sciences
  William F. Harrah College
      of Hotel Administration
  College of Liberal Arts
  College of Science

Graduate College: 895-3320
Continuing Education: 895-3394

Over 200 classes are offered each semester in a variety of areas including business, real estate, computers, arts, recreation, architecture and construction management. Call for a catalogue.
The 1997 legislature allocated $5.4 million over the next 2 years toward the creation of a law school for the Nevada University System. The first class will begin in the fall of 1998.

Admission Requirements:
Students must have graduated from an accredited high school (or have GED); have a minimum cumulative high school G.P.A. of 2.50 on a 4.0 scale or 2.0 for Nevada residents; submit scores on either the ACT or SAT. Each student applying for admission is charged a non-refundable $40 application fee and a mandatory health fee of $20.

Tuition:
The undergraduate fee is $66.50 per credit hour. Graduate student tuition is $90 per credit. Tuition for out-of-state residents is $5,435 per year. Residents of Mojave County in Arizona, San Bernardino and Inyo Counties in California qualify for a special $106 per credit "Good Neighbor Out-of-State" tuition; 752 undergraduate and graduate foreign students were among the 3,763 non-resident students who attended UNLV last fall.

UNLV's Runnin' Rebels were the national NCAA basketball champions in 1990. They play all their home games at Thomas & Mack Center on the campus. The center is also used for other events such as concerts, wrestling, hockey and skating. Thomas & Mack Center Box Office - 895-3900; Rebels Box Office - 895-3267.
(See Sports Section for UNLV sports information)

UNLV could be considered the cultural center of Las Vegas. Over 400 events per year are held at one of the four performing arts centers located on campus.
KUNV 91.5FM: 895-3877
Request Line: 895-3976
Art Gallery: 895-3893
Marjorie Barrick Museum
  of Natural History: 895-3381
Arboretum: 895-3392
Judy Bayley Theatre
  Box Office: 895-3801
Black Box
  Theatre Box Office: 895-3801
Artemus Ham Concert Hall
  Box Office: 895-3801
Charles Vanda
  Master Series: 895-3535
National Association
  of Jazz Education: 895-3738
Nevada Dance Theatre: 732-3838
Nevada School of the Arts: .. 895-3502
  895-3801
Concerts, special classes, lectures, etc.
  (24 hour recorded message)
Student Activities: 895-3667

1998 UNLV CALENDAR

SPRING SEMESTER 1998:

December 15:	Applications for undergraduate admission due for Spring 1998.
January 2:	Final date to apply for undergraduate admission for Spring semester 1998. All supporting documents must be submitted by this date.
January 5:	Initiation of application for May graduation due.
January 12:	"Dead Day."
January 19:	Martin Luther King holiday.
January 20:	Instruction and late registration begin.
January 26:	Final date for late registration, course additions, changes or fee payment. None of these will be accepted after this date.
January 26:	Applications for May graduation due in advisor's office.
February 2:	Final date to submit an application for May graduation without a late penalty fee.
February 16:	Washington's Birthday recess.
February 23:	Final date to submit an application for May graduation with a late penalty fee.
March 13:	Mid-semester.
March 22:	Final date to drop a course or withdraw from classes, except for short courses (see class schedule).
April 6:	Spring recess begins.
April 12:	Spring recess ends.
April 16:	Honors Convocation.
May 4 - 8:	Study week.
May 8:	Instruction ends.
May 11 - 16:	Final examinations.
May 16:	Semester ends.
May 16:	Commencement.
May 19:	Final grade sheets due in deans' office 9:00 am.

SUMMER SEMESTER 1998:

May 18:	Summer I begins.
June 5:	Summer I ends.
June 8:	Summer II begins.
July 3:	Independence Day recess.
July 10:	Summer II ends.
July 13:	Summer III begins.
August 14:	Summer III ends.

FALL SEMESTER 1998:

August 31:	Instruction begins.
September 4:	Last date to register, add or change.
September 7:	Labor Day recess.
October 23:	Mid-semester.
October 30:	Nevada Day recess.
November 11:	Veterans Day recess.
Nov. 26/29:	Thanksgiving recess.
Dec. 7-11:	Study week.
December 11:	Instruction ends.
Dec. 14-19:	Final examinations.

EDUCATION

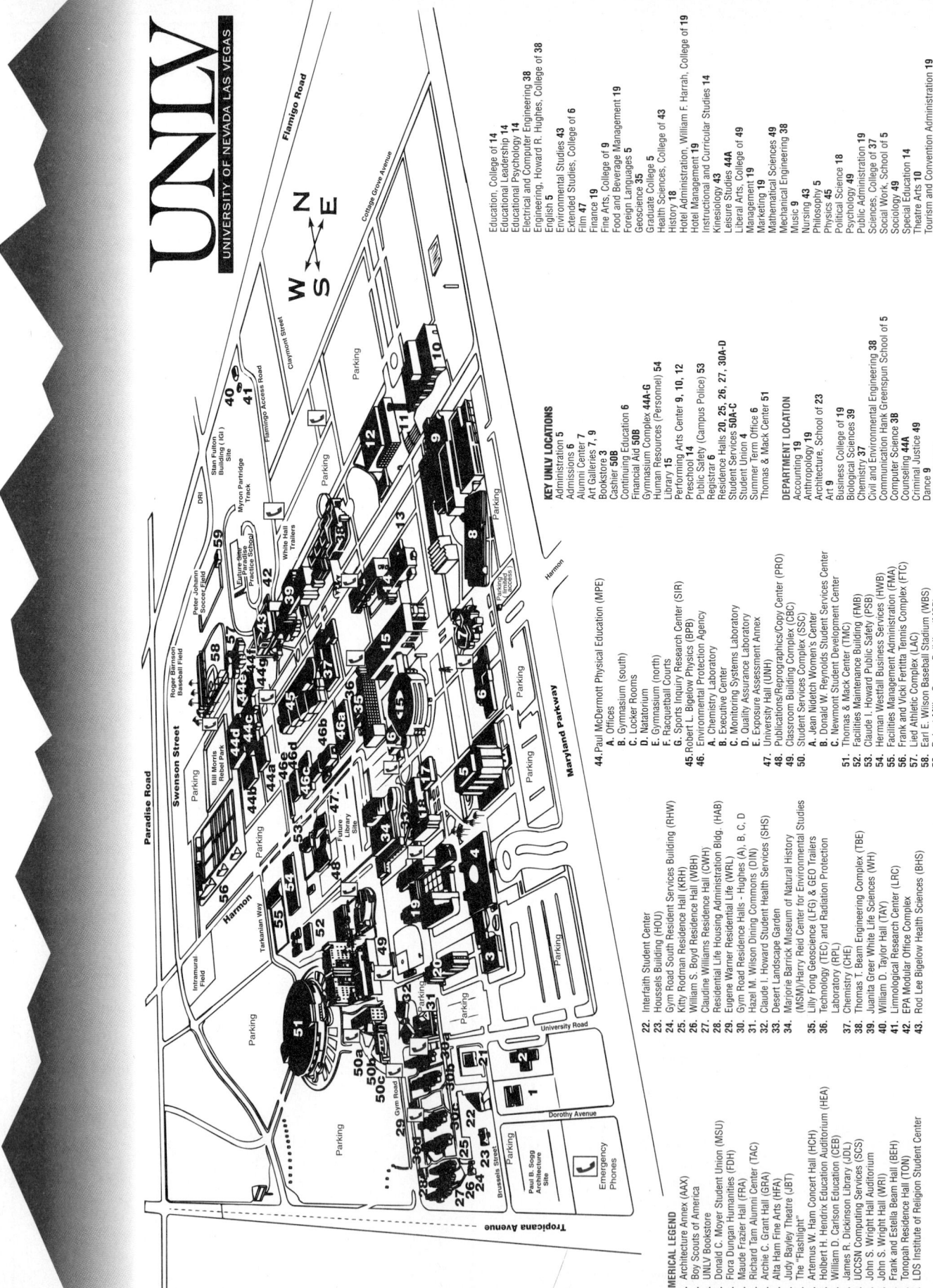

UNLV
UNIVERSITY OF NEVADA LAS VEGAS

NUMERICAL LEGEND

1. Architecture Annex (AAX)
2. Boy Scouts of America
3. UNLV Bookstore
4. Donald C. Moyer Student Union (MSU)
5. Flora Dungan Humanities (FDH)
6. Maude Frazier Hall (FRA)
7. Richard Tam Alumni Center (TAC)
8. Archie C. Grant Hall (GRA)
9. Alta Ham Fine Arts (HFA)
10. Judy Bayley Theatre (JBT)
11. The "Flashlight"
12. Artemus W. Ham Concert Hall (HCH)
13. Holbert H. Hendrix Education Auditorium (HEA)
14. William D. Carlson Education (CEB)
15. James R. Dickinson Library (JDL)
16. UCCSN Computing Services (SCS)
17. John S. Wright Hall Auditorium
18. John S. Wright Hall (WRI)
19. William D. Taylor Hall (TAY)
20. Tonopah Residence Hall (TON)
21. LDS Institute of Religion Student Center
22. Interfaith Student Center
23. Houssels Building (HOU)
24. Gym Road South Resident Services Building (RHW)
25. Kitty Rodman Residence Hall (KRH)
26. William S. Boyd Residence Hall (WBH)
27. Claudine Williams Residence Hall (CWH)
28. Residential Life Housing Administration Bldg. (HAB)
29. Eugene Warner Residential Life (WRL)
30. Gym Road Residence Halls - Hughes (A), B, C, D
31. Hazel M. Wilson Dining Commons (DIN)
32. Claude I. Howard Student Health Services (SHS)
33. Desert Landscape Garden
34. Marjorie Barrick Museum of Natural History (MSM)/Harry Reid Center for Environmental Studies
35. Lilly Fong Geoscience (LFG) & GEO Trailers
36. Technology (TEC) and Radiation Protection Laboratory (RPL)
37. Chemistry (CHE)
38. Thomas T. Beam Engineering Complex (TBE)
39. Juanita Greer White Life Sciences (WH)
40. William D. Taylor Hall (TAY)
41. Limnological Research Center (LRC)
42. EPA Modular Office Complex
43. Rod Lee Bigelow Health Sciences (BHS)

44. Paul McDermott Physical Education (MPE)
   A. Offices
   B. Gymnasium (south)
   C. Locker Rooms
   D. Natatorium
   E. Gymnasium (north)
   F. Racquetball Courts
   G. Sports Inquiry Research Center (SIR)
45. Robert L. Bigelow Physics (BPB)
46. Environmental Protection Agency
   A. Chemistry Laboratory
   B. Executive Center
   C. Monitoring Systems Laboratory
   D. Quality Assurance Laboratory
   E. Exposure Assessment Annex
47. University Hall (UNH)
48. Publications/Reprographics/Copy Center (PRO)
49. Classroom Building Complex (CBC)
50. Student Services Complex (SSC)
   A. Jean Nidetch Women's Center
   B. Donald W. Reynolds Student Services Center
   C. Newmont Student Development Center
51. Thomas & Mack Center (TMC)
52. Facilities Maintenance Building (FMB)
53. Claude I. Howard Public Safety (PSB)
54. Herman Westfall Business Services (HWB)
55. Facilities Management Administration (FMA)
56. Frank and Vicki Fertitta Tennis Complex (FTC)
57. Lied Athletic Complex (LAC)
58. Earl E. Wilson Baseball Stadium (WBS)
59. Robert Miller Soccer Building (MSB)

KEY UNLV LOCATIONS

Administration 5
Admissions 6
Alumni Center 7
Art Galleries 7, 9
Bookstore 3
Cashier 50B
Continuing Education 6
Financial Aid 50B
Gymnasium Complex 44A-G
Human Resources (Personnel) 54
Library 15
Performing Arts Center 9, 10, 12
Preschool 14
Public Safety (Campus Police) 53
Registrar 6
Residence Halls 20, 25, 26, 27, 30A-D
Student Services 50A-C
Student Union 4
Summer Term Office 6
Thomas & Mack Center 51

DEPARTMENT LOCATION

Accounting 19
Anthropology 19
Architecture, School of 23
Art 9
Business College of 19
Biological Sciences 39
Chemistry 37
Civil and Environmental Engineering 38
Communication Hank Greenspun School of 5
Computer Science 38
Counseling 44A
Criminal Justice 49
Dance 9
Economics 19

Education, College of 14
Educational Leadership 14
Educational Psychology 14
Electrical and Computer Engineering 38
Engineering, Howard R. Hughes, College of 38
English 5
Environmental Studies 43
Extended Studies, College of 6
Film 47
Finance 19
Fine Arts, College of 9
Food and Beverage Management 19
Foreign Languages 5
Geoscience 35
Graduate College 5
Health Sciences, College of 43
History 18
Hotel Administration, William F. Harrah, College of 19
Hotel Management 19
Instructional and Curricular Studies 14
Kinesiology 43
Leisure Studies 44A
Liberal Arts, College of 49
Management 19
Marketing 19
Mathematical Sciences 49
Mechanical Engineering 38
Music 9
Nursing 43
Philosophy 5
Physics 45
Political Science 18
Psychology 49
Public Administration 19
Sciences, College of 37
Social Work, School of 5
Sociology 49
Special Education 14
Theatre Arts 10
Tourism and Convention Administration 19
Urban Affairs, Greenspun College of 44A

EDUCATION

**FOR UNLV
TEAM SCHEDUALS
SEE
SPORTS & RECREATION**

University of Nevada Las Vegas Enrollment

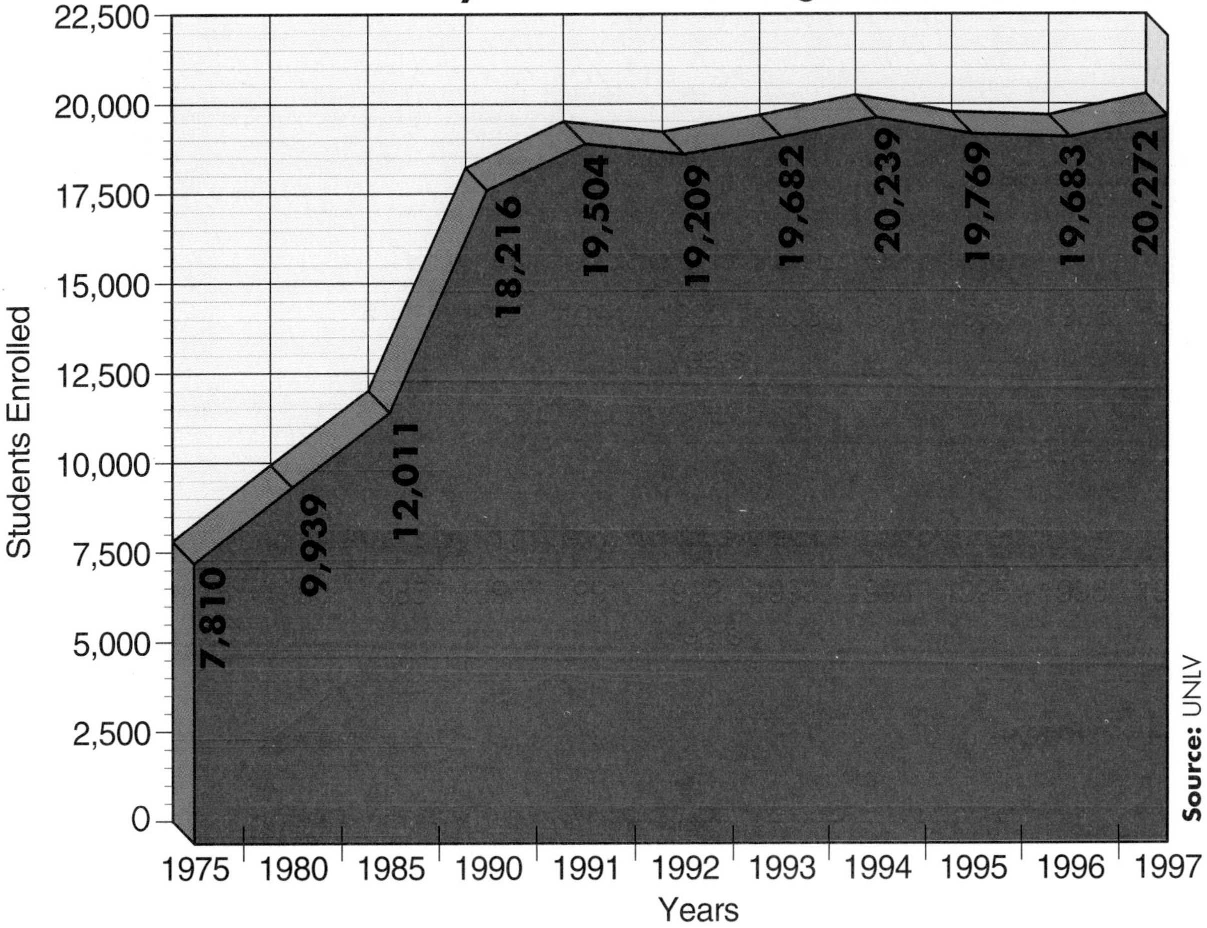

Students Enrolled

22,500
20,000
17,500
15,000
12,500
10,000
7,500
5,000
2,500
0

7,810 9,939 12,011 18,216 19,504 19,209 19,682 20,239 19,769 19,683 20,272

1975 1980 1985 1990 1991 1992 1993 1994 1995 1996 1997

Years

Source: UNLV

COLLEGE EDUCATION - COMMUNITY

COMMUNITY COLLEGE OF SOUTHERN NEVADA

Community College of Southern Nevada
3200 E. Cheyenne Ave.
N. Las Vegas, NV 89030
651-4000
Richard Moore, President
http://www.ccsn.nevada.edu
Admissions: 651-4060
Registration & Records: 643-7026
Bookstore: 651-4645
Executive Offices:
820 Shadow Ln.
Las Vegas, NV 89106
383-6648

Spring 1997 enrollment at the Community College of Southern Nevada's three campuses was just over 26,000 students.

By educating and training the region's workforce since 1971—more than a quarter million people—CCSN is strongly linked to Southern Nevada's economic development and diversity, helping to support business attraction, retention and expansion.

More than 35,000 students enroll annually in college general education courses, university transfer coursework and job skill training. CCSN serves the 1 million people and 42,000 sq. mi. of Clark, Esmeralda, Lincoln and Nye counties with three campuses in the Las Vegas Valley and 50 extension centers.

At CCSN, students are serious about education and demonstrate a strong work ethic—90 percent are already employed. They are dedicated part-time scholars with full-time jobs. Through the Boys & Girls Clubs of Las Vegas, CCSN also provides free evening youth services for students' children. In the record 1995 graduating class, 83 percent achieved honors or high honors in 70 career fields. These graduates changed their lives and futures by improving their productivity and the profitability of employers.

Building on a quarter-century foundation of excellence, CCSN's taken special steps to help craft one of the finest community colleges in America, cutting edge in 17 different fields. Our goal: creating world-class programs to match a world-class city.

The record: CCSN's dental hygiene program is rated number two in America, while our award-winning culinary program ranks third! Both of these leading national programs are earmarked for state of the art expansion.

Next in line for expansion: our computing and information technologies program; resorts and gaming; nursing and other health professions; automotive technology; air conditioning and criminal justice.

The formula for success: faculty-driven and student-centered education. Our expert faculty is hand-selected against a two-fold criteria—excellence in their field and a demonstrated passion to help others learn. Seven-days-a-week classes and support centers are available from early morning to late evening to match the round-the-clock work and lifestyle of Southern Nevadans. The concept is simple: adaptable classes to meet the needs of busy working adults and employers.

Crafting partnerships with the Clark County School District, CCSN combines resources to help high school students begin to take college courses and transition to college level training and education. Special efforts help youngsters, who are behind in their requirements graduate from high school, thereby reducing Nevada's dropout rates and creating more successful lives. The key: public schools and public colleges combine talents and energy to gain students job training and academic success while still in high school.

CCSN will build out its current main 80-acre campuses—Cheyenne in the north, West Charleston in the west valley and Henderson in the southeast—over the next 10 years. To complete Cheyenne Campus, a 100,000 sq. ft. building with 2 floors each the size of football fields became operational in fall 1995. The ground floor houses the finest community college resort industry training center with 5 kitchens, restaurant, bakery, and hotel/casino operations and management training areas.

A computer interactive learning center on the second floor, and a related center operational in early 1996 in a 75,000 sq. ft. building at West Charleston Campus, provide more than 800 computer work stations, featuring a mixture of Power Macs, Pentium class computers and AS400 mainframes, the mainstay of our unique resort industry and other business sectors.

The centers have network access to laser printers, library resources, the Internet and University System mainframes. Software will allow students to access complete learning experiences covering virtually all the college's course material. Currently half-developed, buildout of the West Charleston Campus should occur within 7 or 8 years. Remodeling of existing structures expanded award-winning medical programs, such as dental hygiene. The Nevada Legislature approved design planning funds for a $25 million academic facility with construction starting in late 1997. An Army ROTC program started in fall 1995, along with a horticulture program spun off from the Henderson campus. A broadcasting program will commence when KNPR Public Radio builds it station on this campus by 1998.

Funds were also recently allocated to design-plan a $17 million building and related facilities to support more classrooms, labs and faculty offices and to expand learning resource centers at the Henderson Campus. Expect to see these advancements operating within the next few years. Henderson will also be strengthening its academic college and industrial technology programs and develop general aviation industry programs.

With projections for a regional population of 2 million in the next 15-20 years, the UCCSN Board of Regents has given CCSN the conceptual go-ahead to identify and obtain several 40-acre and 20-acre sites around the Las Vegas Valley for new campuses.

The 1995 Legislature also allocated funds to design-plan a $5 million special college unit in Summerlin which could start construction soon. It will house an "Honors College" program for students majoring in advanced science and technology fields with a guaranteed transfer to selected top western universities for its graduates.

Other programs include a Weekend College, "First Course Free" financial aid to Nevada high school graduates who have never taken a college course, and special college credit programs for high school students to help them graduate or prepare for college.

Business partnership and apprenticeship programs are expected to expand and result in customized training programs, internships and job placements. These have been extremely successful given the generosity of many companies in contributing funds, equipment, technical expertise and ingenuity to the process. Customized training to contracted businesses comes with an ironclad guarantee. CCSN guarantees employers that workers will succeed in specific job training or upgrade programs, or there's no charge for those who fail the final performance test.

These, as well as CCSN's community and continuing education programs, are part of the Rural and Urban Centers Campus. The latest additions are campus extensions in Boulder City and Sun City which offer the new Silver Sage College programs, an initiative to provide lifelong learning for active senior adults.

General Admission Requirements:
a) high school graduate or GED holder;
b) at least 18 years old;
c) or qualify under open door policy;
d) or an international student;
e) or a high school student with recommendation by high school principal.

For additional information regarding admission, call 651-4060.

Tuition & Fees: $38 per credit hour for the 1996 spring and summer semesters; $36.50 per credit hour for the 1997 fall and 1998 spring semesters. Non-resident fee of $15.50 per credit hour in addition to tuition for up to six credits; $1,600 per semester in addition to tuition for seven or more credits.

The Planetarium presents public performances featuring Cinema 360 hemispheric motion pictures and programs which reproduce the motions of the sun, moon and planets against the background of the stars on a 30 foot dome. 644-5059
(See Theaters for more information)

1998 COMMUNITY COLLEGE CALENDAR

SPRING SEMESTER 1998

Dec. 1 - 10: Early telephone registration for Spring 1998 semester - currently enrolled only.

Dec. 11 - Jan. 9: Continued telephone registration - open to all admitted students

Dec. 11 - Jan. 9: In-person registration - new students and senior citizens only.

Jan. 9: Payment due for early registrants

Jan. 12 - 16: Telephone registration continues for all students, after the purge (payments due the same day). In-person registration - new students and senior citizens only.

Jan. 16: Final date for 100% refund for Spring 1998 semester.

Jan. 19: Martin Luther King, Jr. holiday.

Jan. 20: First day of instruction for Spring 1998 semester.

Jan. 20 - 26: Late registration period for Spring 1998 Semester.

Jan. 26: Final date for 75% refund.

Jan. 30: Final date to drop a course without a grade of *W*.

Feb. 16: Presidents' Day Holiday.

Mar. 6: Last day to apply for Spring 1998 graduation.

Mar. 16: Last day to officially change from audit to credit or credit to audit.

Apr. 6 - 12: Spring recess (Monday - Sunday).

Apr. 23: Final date to officially withdraw from Spring 1998 semester.

Apr. 28 - May 7: Early telephone registration Fall 1998 semester - currently enrolled students only.

May 8 - Aug. 21: Early telephone registration Fall 1998 semester - open to all admitted students.

May 8 - Aug. 21: In-person registration Fall 1998 semester - new students and senior citizens only.

May 8 - 14: Final examination period for Spring 1998 semester.

May 14: Last day of semester.

May 17: Commencement.

COLLEGE EDUCATION - COMMUNITY

1998 COMMUNITY COLLEGE CALENDAR (Cont.)

SUMMER SEMESTER 1998

Apr. 21 - May 29: Early telephone registration for Summer 1998 sessions. Open to all admitted students. In-person registration for Summer sessions - new students and senior citizens only.

May 25: Memorial Day observed.

May 29: Payment due for early registrants.

June 2 - 5: Telephone registration continues for all students, after the purge (payments due same day). In-person registration - new students and senior citizens only.

June 5: Final date for 100% refund for Summer 1998 semester.

June 8: 1st four week session begins, six week session begins, eight week session begins, ten week session begins.

June 8 - 9: Late registration period for 1st four and six week sessions.

June 8 - 12: Late registration period for eight and ten week sessions.

June 9: Final date for 75% refund - 1st four and six week sessions.

June 12: Final date for 75% refund - six, eight and ten week sessions.

June 15: Final date to drop a course without a grade of *W* - all sessions.

June 19: Final date to officially withdraw from 1st four week session.

June 19: Final date to officially change from audit to credit or credit to audit for the 1st four week session.

June 25: Last day to apply for Summer 1998 graduation.

June 25: Final date to officially withdraw from six week session.

June 25: Final date to officially change from audit to credit or credit to audit for the six, eight and ten week sessions.

July 2: 1st four week session ends.

July 2: Final date for 100% refund for 2nd four week session.

July 3: Independence Day observed.

July 6: 2nd four week session begins.

July 6 - 7: Late registration period for 2nd four week session.

July 7: Last date for 75% refund - 2nd four week session.

July 10: Final date to drop a course without a grade of *W* - 2nd four week session.

July 17: Six week session ends.

July 17: Final date to officially withdraw from eight week session.

July 20: Final date to officially withdraw from 2nd four week session.

July 24: Final date to officially withdraw from ten week session.

July 31: 2nd four week and eight week sessions end.

Aug. 14: Ten week sessions end.

FALL SEMESTER 1998

Apr. 21 - May 5: Early telephone registration for Fall 1998 semester - currently enrolled students only.

May 6 - Aug. 21: Continued telephone registration - open to all admitted students.

May 6 - Aug. 21: In-person registration - new students and senior citizens only.

Aug. 21: Payment due for early registrants.

Aug. 25 - Sept. 4: Telephone registration continues for all students, after the purge (payments due same day). In-person registration - new students and senior citizens only.

Sept. 4: Final date for 100% refund for Fall 1998 semester.

Sept. 7: Labor Day holiday.

Sept. 8: First day of instruction for Fall 1998 semester.

Sept. 8 - 14: Late registration period for Fall 1998 semester.

Sept. 14: Final date for 75% refund.

Sept. 21: Final date to drop a course without a grade of *W*.

Oct. 26: Last date to officially change from audit to credit or credit to audit.

Oct. 29: Last date to apply for Fall 1998 graduation.

Oct. 30: Nevada Day holiday observed.

Nov. 11: Veterans Day holiday observed.

Nov. 25: Final date to officially withdraw from Fall 1998 semester.

Nov. 26 - 29: Thanksgiving Day recess (Thursday - Sunday).

Dec. 14 - 18: Final examination period for Fall 1998 semester.

Dec. 18: Final day of semester.

Henderson Campus Community College of Southern Nevada
700 College Dr.
Henderson, NV 89015
564-7484
The Henderson campus opened in 1981 and consists of a 23,500 sq. ft. building situated on 75 acres.

Health Sciences Center
6375 W. Charleston Blvd.
Las Vegas, NV 89102
651-5000
Opened in 1988, the 22,000 sq. ft. facility houses four of the college's Health Occupations departments along with the Family Practice Medical Clinic and Family Medicine Residency Program of the University of Nevada School of Medicine and serves over 5,000 patients per month. Dental Hygiene & Dental Assisting Program (651-5685).
The college also operates a dental clinic with low-cost patient care services available to the general public. Call 877-3999 for dental clinic appointments.

Center for Business and Industry Training
3200 E. Cheyenne Ave.
N. Las Vegas, NV 89030
651-4000
Computer training and housekeeping.

LICENSED PRIVATE SCHOOLS

Nevada Dept. of Education Southern Nevada Office
1820 E. Sahara Ave., Ste. 205
Las Vegas, NV 89104
486-6455
Establishes courses of study, textbooks and graduation requirements and sets the standards for content and administration of student testing. Schools listed are licensed by the Nevada State Department of Education.

SCHOOLS

All Saints Episcopal School
4201 W. Washington Ave.
Las Vegas, NV 89107
878-1205
Gloria Durling, Dir.
Grades: K, 3 & 4; 124 students

Bright Start Learning Center
8451 Bosech Dr.
Las Vegas, NV 89128
255-9252
Tammy Joslin, Dir.
Grades: K; 12 students

Children's Oasis School
720 Rancho Del Norte Dr.
Las Vegas, NV 89031
649-5425
Michelle Wood, Dir.
Hours: Mon. - Fri. 6:30 am - 6:30 pm
Grades: 12 weeks to 12 years; 230 students
Private, non-profit; social, intellectual, music, movement, arts and crafts; social and language development.

Christian Center Schools
571 Adams Blvd.
Boulder City, NV 89005
293-7773
Debbie Behre, Adm.
Grades: K - 8; 90 students

Church of Scientology Mission of the Children
1018 E. Sahara Ave., Ste. D
Las Vegas, NV 89104
737-8668
Tracy Yeich, Dir.
Grades: K - 12; 22 students

Citibank Child Care Center
2720 Crystal Water Way
Las Vegas, NV 89163
256-0394
Helen Unangst, Dir.
Grades: K; 24 students

Calvary Church Christian School
3005 E. Cedar Ave.
Las Vegas, NV 89101
382-5998
Don Dunagan, Adm.
Grades: K - 12; 217 students

Community College of Southern Nevada
3200 E. Cheyenne Ave.
N. Las Vegas, NV 89030
651-4000
Two-year associate degree and certificate of achievement programs.

Echoes Christian Academy
1608 Gragson Ave.
Las Vegas, NV 89101
649-8744
Cynthia Watson, Princ.
Grades: K - 12; 39 students

Faith Lutheran Jr - Sr High School
1251 Robin St.
Las Vegas, NV 89106
648-7047
John Haynal, Princ.
Grades: 6 - 12; 490 students

First Christian Child Development Center
101 S. Rancho Rd.
Las Vegas, NV 89106
384-4839
Natalie Madden, Dir.
Grades: K; 28 students

First Good Shepherd Lutheran
301 S. Maryland Pkwy
Las Vegas, NV 89101
382-8610
James E. Krafft, Princ.
Grades: K - 6; 218 students

First Presbyterian Academy
1515 W. Charleston Blvd.
Las Vegas, NV 89102
382-3611
Jean Witmer, Dir.
Grades: K - 8; 186 students

LICENSED PRIVATE SCHOOLS

Gateway Christian Academy
1900 Gateway Rd.
Las Vegas, NV 89115
452-7111
Brent Fleshman, Princ.
Grades: K - 8; 50 students

Bishop Gorman High School
1801 S. Maryland Pkwy.
Las Vegas, NV 89104
732-1945
David W. Erbach, Princ.
Grades: 9 - 12; 1,140 students

Green Valley Christian School
711 Valle Verde Ct.
Henderson, NV 89014
454-4056
Kelly Marchello, Dir.
Grades: K - 3; 270 students

Griffith United Methodist Day School
1701 E. Oakey Blvd.
Las Vegas, NV 89104
382-7836
Karen Bigelow, Dir.
Grades: K; 35 students

The Hebrew Academy
9700 W. Hillpointe Rd.
Las Vegas, NV 89134
255-4500
Dr. Roberta Sabbath, Dir.
Grades: Pre-K - 8; 275 students
Annual tuition: $6,200
Private, non-profit and
non-denominational school.

Jewish Community Day School of Las Vegas
2761 Emerson Ave.
Las Vegas, NV 89121
650-2800
Dr. Jerome Kutliroff, Dir.
Grades: K - 6; 40 students

Lake Mead Christian Academy
540 E. Lake Mead Dr.
Henderson, NV 89015
565-5831
Gayle Sue Blakeley, Adm.
Grades: K - 12; 250 students

Las Vegas Day School
3198 S. Jones Blvd.
Las Vegas, NV 89102
362-1180
Neil H. Daseler, Dir.
Grades: Pre-K - 8; 520 students
Founded in 1961, Las Vegas Day School
offers a disciplined environment that
stresses work and study habits to prepare students for college.

Las Vegas Jr. Academy
6059 W. Oakey Blvd.
Las Vegas, NV 89102
871-7208
Jim Hawkins, Princ.
Grades: K - 10; 156 students

Maranatha Academy
2727 Civic Center Dr.
N. Las Vegas, NV 89030-5148
399-4315
Roy Manibusan, Dir.
Grades: Pre-K & 3 - 8; 80 students

The Meadows School
8601 Scholar Ln.
Las Vegas, NV 89128
254-1610
William Richardson, Headmaster
Grades: K - 12

Independent, non-sectarian college
preparatory school located on a new 40-
acre campus in Summerlin. The school,
which opened in 1984, has 752 students
with a maximum of 20 students per class.
Tuition is $8,000 - $10,000 per year.

Montessori Academy
6000 W. Oakey Blvd.
Las Vegas, NV 89102
878-3744
Main office: 870-5117
Connie Mormon, Dir.
Grades: 1 - 6; 250 students
24-hour child care.

Mother Goose College
2760 S. Jones Blvd.
Las Vegas, NV 89102
362-5801
Janice Brown, Dir.
Grades: K; 18 students

Bishop Gorman High School, 1801 S. Maryland Pkwy., Las Vegas, NV 89104

Mountain View Christian School
3900 E. Bonanza Rd.
Las Vegas, NV 89110
452-1300
Crystal VanKempen-McClanahan, Princ.
Grades: Pre-K - 12; 650 students

New Horizons Academy
2393 Potosi St.
Las Vegas, NV 89102
876-1181
Roger Gehring, Dir.
Grades: K - 12; 62 students
Non-profit learning institution for children
with learning disabilities.

New Life Christian Academy
1229 E. Carson Ave.
Las Vegas, NV 89101
387-1255
Zandra Oshinski, Princ.
Grades: K - 12; 65 students
A.C.E. curriculum instilling Biblical
character traits.

Our Lady of Las Vegas
3036 Alta Dr.
Las Vegas, NV 89107
878-6841
Gerald Streit, Princ.
Grades: Pre-K - 8; 350 students

Paradise Christian Academy
2525 Emerson Ave.
Las Vegas, NV 89121
732-8256
Mike Elliott, Adm.
Grades: K, 4 - 8; 220 students

Primetime Preschool & Child Care Center
4514 Meadows Ln.
Las Vegas, NV 89107
258-8858
Sherry Overby, Dir.
Grades: Pre-K; 11 students

Redeemer Lutheran School
1730 N. Pecos Rd.
Las Vegas, NV 89115
642-6144
Joyce Miskey, Dir.
Grades: K - 6; 165 students

St. Anne's School
1813 S. Maryland Pkwy.
Las Vegas, NV 89104
735-2586
Phyllis Joyce, Princ.
Grades: Pre-K - 8; 350 students

St. Christopher's School
1840 N. Bruce St.
N. Las Vegas, NV 89030
657-8008
Carol Haeberlin, Princ.
Grades: K - 8; 300 students

St. Francis de Sales School
1111 Michael Way
Las Vegas, NV 89108
647-2828
Gloria Hagstrom, Princ.
Grades: K - 8; 301 students

St. Joseph's Elementary
1300 Bridger Ave.
Las Vegas, NV 89101
384-6909
Lynda Ballard, Princ.
Grades: 1 - 8; 280 students

St. Viator's Elementary
4246 S. Eastern Ave.
Las Vegas, NV 89119
732-4477
William C. Langley, Princ.
Grades: Pre-K - 8; 695 students

Shiloh Christian School
6701 W. Charleston Blvd.
Las Vegas, NV 89102
878-6418
Lois Cadwallader, Princ.
Grades: K - 10; 415 students

Spring Valley Christian Academy
7570 W. Peace Way
Las Vegas, NV 89117
873-1200
Mark Blodgett, Princ.
Grades: K - 12; 25 students

Trinity Christian School
950 E. St. Louis Ave.
Las Vegas, NV 89104
734-0562
Harry Hendrickson, Princ.
Grades: K - 6; 246 students

Junior/Senior High (7-12)
950 E. Sahara Ave.
Las Vegas, NV 89104
735-5778
Harry Hendrickson, Princ.
Grades: 7 - 12; 185 students

Pre-School
928 E. Sahara Ave.
Las Vegas, NV 89104
732-2787
Derald Grauberger, Princ.
Grades: 18 mo. - 5 yr.; 70 students

Trinity United Methodist Kindergarten
6151 W. Charleston Blvd.
Las Vegas, NV 89102
870-4749
Pamela Troll, Adm.
Grades: Pre-K; 115 students

University Baptist Academy
1490 E. University Ave.
Las Vegas, NV 89119
732-3385
Dr. Juan Sclafani, Dir.
Grades: K - 12; 62 students

University of Nevada Las Vegas
4505 S. Maryland Pkwy
Las Vegas, NV 89119
895-3011
Carol Harter, Pres.

Variety Day Home
990 D St.
Las Vegas, NV 89106
647-4907
Sister Diane Maguire, SHF Dir.
Grades: 6 mo. - 5 yr.; 218 students

Warren Walker Pre School
2150 Windmill Pkwy., Ste. A
Henderson, NV 89014
896-0780
Carolyn Kessler, Dir.
Tuition: $3,000 - $5,000
Provides unique experience for children
ages 2-6; emphasis on social development, cooperation, increasing attention
span and creating lifelong love of learning; 9,000 sq. ft.

Warren Walker West
9001 Hillpointe Rd.
Las Vegas, NV 89134
242-3230
Carolyn Kessler, Dir.
Tuition: $3,000 - $5,000
Licensed private facility is available for 2
1/2 years through Kindergarten; 5,000 sq. ft.

Warren Walker School
2150 Windmill Pkwy.
Henderson, NV 89014
896-0780
Janet Smith, Dir.
Grades: K - 8
Tuition: $7,100 per year.
Non-parochial private school; nurturing
environment, small class size; extended
day program.

OCCUPATIONAL SCHOOLS

There are 112 non-degree and degree occupational schools in Southern Nevada. The following schools are licensed by the Commission on Post-secondary Education. Many of these schools offer VA benefits, government loans and grants as well as pay-as-you-go plans.

Commission on Post-secondary Education
1820 E. Sahara Ave., Ste. 111
Las Vegas, NV 89104
486-7330
David Perlman, Adm.
Regulates and licenses private schools.

A-1 Truck Driver Training
1105 Industrial Rd.
Boulder City, NV 89005
293-7335
Gene Breeden, Owner
Program: Truck Driving

Academy of Dog Grooming
7530 Westcliff Dr.
Las Vegas, NV 89128
386-5302
Cathi Boyle, Dir.
Program: Dog Grooming

Academy of Hair Design
4445 W. Charleston Blvd.
Las Vegas, NV 89102
878-1185
Sandy Durham, Owner
Program: Hair, Nails & Aesthetician Course (skin care & make-up)

Academy of Medical Careers
5243 W. Charleston Blvd., Ste. 2
Las Vegas, NV 89102
259-6263
William Paul, Pres.
Program: Medical Assistant, Medical Insurance Biller, Health Claims Examiner

Academy of Professional Cocktail Servers & Bartenders
5734 W. Charleston Blvd.
Las Vegas, NV 89102
878-1664
Patty Gustin, Owner
Program: Bartender/Cocktail

Academy of Travel & Tourism
1651 E. Sunset Rd., Ste. A107
Las Vegas, NV 89119
361-0149
Michael Williams, Dir.
Program: Travel Agent

Aerleon
2634 Airport Dr., Ste. 101
Las Vegas, NV 89030
647-6100
Don Flaherty, Owner
Program: Flight Training

All-Rite Trade School
93 W. Lake Mead Dr.
Henderson, NV 89015
564-3124
Leonard Dejoria, Owner
Program: Locksmith, Small Engine Repair, Truck Driving, Bartending, Cocktail Waitress

American Locksmith Institute of Nevada
875 S. Boulder Hwy.
Henderson, NV 89015
565-8811
Eugene Altobella, Owner
Program: Basic Locksmith

American Real Estate School
2320 Paseo Del Prado, Ste. B-301
Las Vegas, NV 89102
368-3161
Tom Matejko
Program: Pre-Licensing and Sales

Americana School of Real Estate
3790 Paradise Rd., Ste. 100
Las Vegas, NV 89109
796-8888
Gayle Brown, Dir.
Program: Real Estate

B.A.D.G.E. Corporation
953 E. Sahara Ave., Ste. 224
Las Vegas, NV 89104
893-9750
Connie Heinen, VP
Post Secondary Education Institution; Emergency Medical Technicians, Security Officer, Women's Defense, First Aid, CPR

Barbizon School of Modeling & Talent Agency
1515 E. Tropicana Ave., Ste. 785
Las Vegas, NV 89119
798-4120
Jed Snyder, Pres.
Program: Modeling - Male, Female, Pre-teen

CDF Gaming Machine Repair School
1111 Grier Dr., Ste. B
Las Vegas, NV 89119
361-8994
Randall Melton, Dir.
Program: Slot Repair

Casino Gaming School
900 E. Karen Ave., Ste. 218
Las Vegas, NV 89109
388-7477
Nick Kallos, Owner
Program: Casino Dealing

Claims Administration Training Group
1700 E. Desert Inn Rd., Ste. 304
Las Vegas, NV 89109
796-1913
Darlien Breeze, Dir.
Program: Workers Compensation Specialist, Hotel Front Desk Training

CompUSA Training Center
3535 W. Sahara Ave.
Las Vegas, NV 89102
227-4250
Winn Than, Dir.
Program: Computer Software

Computer City
4731 Faircenter Pkwy.
Las Vegas, NV 89102
258-7410
Leonard Kirkley, Dir.
Program: Software Application

Computer Skills Institute
1820 E. Sahara Ave., Ste. 201
Las Vegas, NV 89104
732-4900
Bob Anderson, Dir.
Program: Word Processing

Contractor's License Center
4440 S. Maryland Pkwy., Ste. 205
Las Vegas, NV 89119
733-9598
Patty Norberg, Dir.
Program: Contractor Pre-License, insurance Pre-License

CPR Plus
3355 W. Spring Mountain Rd., Ste. 12
Las Vegas, NV 89102
252-8969
Julie Schultz, Dir.
Program: First Responder, EMT Basic, EMT Intermediate

Creative Casting
900 E. Karen Ave., Ste. D116
Las Vegas, NV 89109
737-0611
Margie Butto, Owner
Program: Acting

Dahan Institute of Massage Studies
3430 E. Tropicana Ave., Ste. 62
Las Vegas, NV 89121
434-1338
Serge Dahan, Owner
Program: Massage

Electronic Technology Institute
3330 E. Tropicana Ave., Ste. G
Las Vegas, NV 89121
435-5610
Shirley Valenzuela, Dir.
Program: Electronics & Computer Repair

Embry-Riddle Aeronautical University
99 MSS/DPE
4475 England Ave., Ste. 217
Nellis AFB, NV 89191
643-0762
Maryanne Willquer, Dir.
Program: Professional Aero, Aviation Business Mgt., Aviation Admin., Aviation Mgt., Aeronautical Science, Aircraft Maint. - AS
VA & SACS approved.

H & R Block
1416 S. Decatur Blvd.
Las Vegas, NV 89102
877-0900
Dave Livingston, Dist. Mgr.
Program: Tax

Hearts & Flowers
4810 S. Nellis Blvd.
Las Vegas, NV 89122
451-7030
Sharon Cowlishaw, Dir.
Program: Advanced Floral Design and Basic Floral Design

Heritage College
3305 W. Spring Mountain Rd., Ste. 7
Las Vegas, NV 89102
368-2338
Matthew Klabacka, Owner
Program: Medical Front Office, Medical Assistant and Travel and Tourism, Paralegal, Computerized Business

Interior Design Institute
4225 S. Eastern Ave., Ste. 4
Las Vegas, NV 89119
369-9944
Nancy Wolf, Dir.
Program: Interior Design, Decor Fundamentals, Commercial Design

International School of Dog Grooming
2929 E. Desert Inn Rd., Ste. 25
Las Vegas, NV 89121
734-1033
Maryanne Harker, Owner
Program: Beginning and Advanced Dog grooming

John Casablancas Modeling & Career Center
2080 E. Flamingo Rd., Ste. 219
Las Vegas, NV 89119
733-8080
Paula Kelly, Dir.
Program: Basic Acting/TV, Professional Development, Fashion Modeling

Kaplan Educational Centers
4632 S. Maryland Pkwy., Ste. 23
Las Vegas, NV 89119
798-5005   1-800-527-8378
Fred Stow, Dir.
Program: Test Preparation, Tutoring, LSAT, MCAT, GMAT, GRE

Key Real Estate School
3620 E. Flamingo Rd., Ste. 4
Las Vegas, NV 89121
313-7000
Ted Federwitz, Dir.
Program: Real Estate

Las Vegas College
3320 E. Flamingo Rd.
Las Vegas, NV 89121
434-0486
Bob McCart, Dir.
Program: Business Mgt., Admin. Asst., Court Reporting, Word Processing, Paralegal

Las Vegas School of Dealing
3850 Valley View Blvd.
Las Vegas, NV 89103
368-1717
Anthony Toti, Pres.
Program: Casino Dealing

The Learning Center
2972 Meade Ave.
Las Vegas, NV 89102
878-8885
Linda Montgomery, Owner
Program: Computerized Office Specialist, Computerized Accounting, Certified Network Engineer (CNE), Certified Network Administrator (CNA), Microsoft (CSE)

License Information Service
4110 S. Maryland Pkwy., Ste. 17
Las Vegas, NV 89119
388-1615
Blair Edwards, Owner
Program: Contractor Pre-License

Marinello School of Beauty
5000 E. Bonanza Rd.
Las Vegas, NV 89110
431-6200
Gail Moore, Dir.
Program: Cosmetology & Manicuring

Mercy Medical Services Training Center
1130 S. Martin Luther King Blvd.
Las Vegas, NV 89102
386-9985
Mark Dascalos, Dir.
Program: EMT Intermediate, EMT Basic, First Responder

OCCUPATIONAL SCHOOLS

National Academy for Casino Dealers
557 E. Sahara Ave., Ste. 110
Las Vegas, NV 89104
735-4884
Joe Rizzi, Dir.
Program: Casino Dealing

National Bartenders School
3333 S. Maryland Pkwy.
Las Vegas, NV 89109
731-6499
Carol Logan, Dir.
Program: Bartending

National Schools
4480 W. Spring Mountain Rd., Ste. 700B
Las Vegas, NV 89102
364-0495
Len Nelson, Pres.
Program: Real Estate Pre-License, Real Estate Broker

Nevada Career Institute
3025 E. Desert Inn Rd.
Las Vegas, NV 89121
893-3300
Karen Eisner, Dir.
Program: Medical Assistant, Bilingual Medical Assistant, Surgical Assisting & Surgical Technology and Medical and Dental Management and Billing

Nevada Dog Grooming School
1233 E. Sahara Ave.
Las Vegas, NV 89104
734-0774
Roy Mule', Owner
Program: Basic Dog Grooming, Adv. Dog Grooming

Nevada Jewelry Manufacturing School
953 E. Sahara Ave., Ste. B27
Las Vegas, NV 89104
735-4191
Edgardo Mazzola, Owner
Program: Watch Repair, Stone Setting, Jewelry Manufacturing & Repair

Nevada School of the Arts
315 S. 7th St.
Las Vegas, NV 89101
386-2787
Dr. Paul Hesselink, Dean
Program: Musical instruments and voice for ages 3 - adult, visual arts for ages 6 - 14 years

Nevada School of Insurance
3305 Spring Mountain Rd., Ste. 50
Las Vegas, NV 89102
362-2069
Gary Rutherford, Owner
Program: Insurance Pre-License, Securities

Nevada Training Corp.
2215 Renaissance Dr., Ste. C
Las Vegas, NV 89119
798-6929
Connie Spaan, Dir.
Program: Bartending & Cocktails, Phlebotomy Technicians

Nova Southeastern University
2320 Paseo Del Prado, Ste. 307
Las Vegas, NV 89102
365-6682
Steven Rudish, Dir.
Program: Education Spec.-ME, Education Spec.; 15 Masters Programs

On-Track Computer Training Corp.
3800 Howard Hughes Pkwy.
Las Vegas, NV 89109
699-9332
Danette Adams, Dir.
Program: Computer Software

Personalized Casino Instruction
920 S. Valley View Blvd.
Las Vegas, NV 89107
877-4724
Joel Lauer, Owner
Program: Table Games - contact school for details

Physicians Institute of Therapeutic Massage
1140 Almond Tree Ln., Ste. 312
Las Vegas, NV 89104
369-5472
Carol Barrett, Dir.
Program: Therapeutic massage

Las Vegas School of Dealing, 3850 Valley View Blvd., Las Vegas, NV 89103

Prestige Travel School
6175 W. Spring Mountain Rd.
Las Vegas, NV 89102
251-5552
Edie Gupton, Dir.
Program: Travel Aagent, Travel Agent Computer

Productivity Point International
2580 Sorrel St.
Las Vegas, NV 89102
365-1900
Keith Rowins, Gen. Mgr.
Program: Software Training

Quality Air Service Training
3141 Westwood Dr.
Las Vegas, NV 89109
731-1617
Leroy Brown, Adm.
Program: Heating and Air Conditioning

Queen Bee Floral Design School
3342 S. Sandhill Rd.
Las Vegas, NV 89121
451-4022
Nancy Broesel, Dir.
Program: Advanced Floral, Basic Floral

Real Estate Academy
6655 W. Sahara Ave., Ste. A116
Las Vegas, NV 89102
221-2222
Harlene Bailey, Owner
Program: Real Estate

Real Estate School of Nevada, Inc.
4180 S. Sandhill Rd., Ste. B10
Las Vegas, NV 89121
454-1936
Teresa Keyes, Dir.
Program: Real Estate

Red Rock Floral Design School
5409 W. Charleston Blvd.
Las Vegas, NV 89102
870-2530
Peggy Jakobiak, Owner
Program: Floral Design

Rollers Institute of Cosmetology
953 E. Sahara Ave., Ste. 11B
Las Vegas, NV 89104
732-1986
Jeanette Labbe, Dir.
Program: Cosmetology, Manicuring and Aesthetician

San Joaquin Valley College
862-4488
Scheduled to re-open late 1998
Program: Admin. Medical Assistant, Veterinary Technology, Clinical Medical Assistant, Dental Assisting, Pharmacy Technology

Silver State Schools
4480 W. Spring Mountain Rd., Ste. 700
Las Vegas, NV 89102
364-5005
Lender Alexander, Dir.
Program: Real Estate Pre-License, Real Estate Broker, Hotel Management, Computer Operations

Southern Nevada School of Real Estate
3441 W. Sahara Ave., Ste. C5
Las Vegas, NV 89102
364-2525
Randall Van Reken, Owner
Program: Real Estate Pre-License

Southern Nevada University of Cosmetology
3430 E. Tropicana Ave.
Las Vegas, NV 89121
458-6333
Judith Hloros, Dir.
Program: Cosmetology, Manicuring and Hair Design

University of Phoenix - Nellis
4475 England Ave.
Nellis AFB, NV 89191
652-5527
Steve Soukup, Dir.
Program: Org. Management - MA, MBA

University of Phoenix - Las Vegas
2975 S. Rainbow Blvd., Ste. D
Las Vegas, NV 89102
876- 5004   876-1687

333 N. Rancho Dr.
Las Vegas, NV 89106
638-7279

4 Sunset Way
Henderson, NV 89014
433-7008
Steve Soukup, Dir.
Program: Business Admin. - MBA, Management - BSB, Administration - BSB, Org. Management - MA

Vegas Career School
3333 S. Maryland Pkwy.
Las Vegas, NV 89109
792-6299
John Rosich, Pres.
Program: Salesmanship, Insurance, Real Estate, Timeshare Sales, Front Desk Operation, Casino Dealing

Webster University - Las Vegas Graduate Center
3430 E. Flamingo Rd., Ste. 350
Las Vegas, NV 89121
435-6660
Joseph Estrada, Dir.
Program: Human Resource Devl. - MA, Management - MBA, Computer Resources - MA, Computer Resource - MBA, Management - MA, Human Resource Dev. - MBA
Part of a worldwide network of campuses, with the main campus in St. Louis, Webster offers graduate-level curriculums at their Las Vegas campus and is accredited by the North Central Association of Colleges and Schools.

Western Business Academy
1055 E. Tropicana Ave., Ste. 575
Las Vegas, NV 89119
736-6789
Tija Muntean, Dir.
Program: Secretary Sciences, Typing, Word Processing, Accounting, Computer Appl., Bookkeeping, Medical Billing, Windows and Excel

World Travel Institute
150 S. Decatur Blvd.
Las Vegas, NV 89107
870-7394
Sharon Holmes-Reed, Owner
Program: Travel Agent

Las Vegas has become a haven for new businesses and an ideal location for corporate headquarters, especially as a West Coast distribution center. The favorable tax climate, availability of land, low utility costs, duty-free foreign trade zones, mostly-skilled labor force and weather and quality of life along with the location are strong assets in attracting economic development.

A national study by the Corporation for Enterprise Development gave Nevada high marks in economic performance because of "stellar employment conditions and equity." The study gave the state low marks in business vitality because of "drastically sparse diversification in the industrial base." The study rated Nevada's annual pay and health coverage as only moderate.

The Census Bureau reported 29,932 private business establishments in Nevada with 536,506 employees with an average salary of $20,892 (March 1990). As of August 1997 there were 33,632 business licenses issued in Clark County and 5,004 in the city of Las Vegas. Seventy-three percent of the businesses in Las Vegas employ less than 10 people, accounting for only 9.2 percent of the jobs. The major employers with more than 1,000 employees make up 0.4 percent of the businesses but account for 35.5 percent of the jobs.

During 1997, according to the Nevada Commission on Economic Development, 75 companies relocated to Nevada and 73 companies expanded, creating 6,886 new jobs during 1997, continuing the steady rise in jobs since the 1983 inception of Economic Development.

Nevada is a fee-based state, not a corporate tax-based state. Although it is not a cheap place to do business it does have a good business climate as well as a good location.

(See Government Section for more tax information)

BUSINESS ASSOCIATIONS

Better Business Bureau
1022 E. Sahara Ave.
Las Vegas, NV 89104-1515
735-6900
Sylvia Campbell, Exec. Dir.
Maintains records on how companies have conducted business with their customers and how long they have been in business. Handles and investigates truth in advertising complaints and manufacturer warranty problems.

Asian Chamber of Commerce
900 E. Karen Ave., Ste. C215
Las Vegas, NV 89109
737-4300
Robert Young, Pres.

Boulder City Chamber of Commerce
1305 Arizona St.
Boulder City, NV 89005
293-2034
Cheryl Ferrence, Exec. Dir.

Urban Chamber of Commerce
1048 W. Owens Ave.
Las Vegas, NV 89106
648-6222
Nick Nixon, Exec. Dir.
The voice of the urban community with over 150 members.

Clark County Comprehensive Planning
500 S. Grand Central Pkwy., Ste. 3012
Las Vegas, NV 89155-1741
455-4181
Richard B. Holmes, Dir.
Population data projections and maps for growth in geographical areas.

Community Resources Mgt.
500 S. Grand Central Pkwy.
Las Vegas, NV 89155-1212
455-5025
Douglas Bell, Mgr.
Helps fund nonprofit organizations.

Fremont Street Experience
425 Fremont St., Ste. 808
Las Vegas, NV 89101
382-6397
Mark Paris, Pres.
Promotes, develops, and improves downtown Las Vegas.

Henderson Chamber of Commerce
590 S. Boulder Hwy.
Henderson, NV 89015
565-8951
Alice Martz, Exec. Dir.
754 members

Henderson Economic Development
240 Water St.
Henderson, NV 89015
565-2409
Ann Barron, Dir.
Attracts businesses to area, assists clients in obtaining permits.

Las Vegas Chamber of Commerce
3720 Howard Hughes Pkwy.
Las Vegas, NV 89109
735-1616
Pat Shalmy, Pres.
Tourist and Show Information:
735-1616

Member Sales: 735-2718
Member Services: 641-LVCC (5822)
Organization founded in 1911 whose purpose is to represent, promote, and protect its more than 5,000 members by creating a more powerful network and information center and to observe legislation where business has an interest.

Las Vegas Convention and Visitors Authority
3150 Paradise Rd.
Las Vegas, NV 89109
892-0711
Manny Cortez, Pres.
Tourist and Brochure Information:
892-7575
Hotel-Motel Room Reservation Center:
892-0777
Boulder City Visitors Bureau:
294-1220
Jean Visitors Bureau:
874-1360   874-1574
Visitor Information Center:
892-7575
Markets Southern Nevada as a tourist destination and convention site. A government entity, the LVCVA is funded through the 10 percent room tax.

Las Vegas Chamber of Commerce, 3720 Howard Hughes Pkwy., Las Vegas, NV 89109

Las Vegas Events, Inc.
770 E. Warm Springs Rd., Ste. 140
Las Vegas, NV 89119
260-8605 • Fax: 260-8622
Kirk Hendrix, Pres.
Organization started in 1985 to bring special events to Las Vegas. Las Vegas Events was responsible for bringing the 1991 Miss Universe Pageant, the National Rodeo Finals, the Budweiser Las Vegas Silver Cup Unlimited Hydroplane Races, the Bud Light Las Vegas Championship & World Cup and the Las Vegas Marathon.

Las Vegas News Bureau
3150 Paradise Rd.
Las Vegas, NV 89109
735-3611
Myram Borders, Bureau Chief
Las Vegas media liaison and publicity organization operated by the Las Vegas Convention and Visitors Authority. The bureau provides news release features on new developments at Las Vegas hotels and helps visiting travel editors with stories on Las Vegas. The bureau maintains over 1 million photographs of Las Vegas.

Latin Chamber of Commerce
829 S. 6th St., Ste. 3
Las Vegas, NV 89101
385-7367
Otto Merida, Exec. Dir.
Rose Dominguez, Pres.
There are 567 members.

Nevada Association of Independent Businesses
3131 Meade Ave., Ste. 1B
Las Vegas, NV 89102
251-8166
Phil Stout, Exec. Dir.
This organization of over 800 businesses monitors business interests and legislation that affects businesses.

Nevada Commission on Economic Development
555 E. Washington Ave.
Las Vegas, NV 89101
486-2700

Capitol Complex
Carson City, NV 89710
1-702-687-4325   1-800-336-1600

Bob Shriver, Exec. Dir.
Created in 1983 to diversify the state's economy and attract new businesses to Nevada. The commission attracted 75 businesses to Nevada in 1997, creating 6,886 jobs.

Nevada Development Authority
3773 Howard Hughes Pkwy., Ste. 140
S. Las Vegas, NV 89109
791-0000   1-800-634-6858
Fax: 796-6483
Somer Hollingsworth, Pres.
The Nevada Development Authority is a nonprofit organization dedicated to the expansion and diversification of business and industry in Southern Nevada and to help established companies. In 1997, the Development Authority helped bring 37 new companies to Las Vegas and 3,048 jobs.

Nevada Office of Small Business
(Nevada Commission on Economic Development)
555 E. Washington Ave.

Las Vegas, NV 89101
486-2700
Bob Shriver, Dir.
Information and business start-up packages.

Nevada Resort Association
3773 Howard Hughes Pkwy., Ste. 1
Las Vegas, NV 89109
735-4888
Richard Bunker, Pres.
Lobbying organization for the Southern Nevada gaming industry.

Nevada Small Business Development Center
3720 Howard Hughes Pkwy., Ste. 130
Las Vegas, NV 89109
734-7575
Sharolyn Craft, Center Dir.

19 W. Brooks Ave., Ste. B
N. Las Vegas, NV 89030
399-6300
Janis Stevens, Center Dir.
Co-sponsored by the U.S. Small Business Administration, the Small Business Development Center assists small business owners in all aspects of business at no charge.

North Las Vegas Chamber of Commerce
2290 McDaniel St.
N. Las Vegas, NV 89030
642-9595
Richard Conner, Exec. Dir.
450 members.

North Las Vegas Economic Development
2266 Civic Center Dr.
N. Las Vegas, NV 89030
633-1529
Phyllis Martin, Exec. Dir.
Aids new businesses.

Office of Business Development
400 Las Vegas Blvd. S.
Las Vegas, NV 89101
229-6551
Jeff Maresh, Acting Dir.
Promotes and assists new businesses in Las Vegas.

Philippine Chamber of Commerce
2700 State St., Ste. 16
Las Vegas, NV 89109
796-5502
Charlie Lee, Pres.
165 members.

UNLV Center for Business & Economic Research
3720 Howard Hughes Pkwy., Ste. 130
Las Vegas, NV 89109
734-7575
R. Keith Schwer, Dir.
The Center is a university based organization founded in 1975, providing research and analysis services to clients in business and government. It combines the expertise of trained professionals with state-of-the-art technology to get results that help businesses keep a competitive edge and government agencies produce a quality product.

U. S. Small Business Administration
301 E. Stewart Ave.
Las Vegas, NV 89101
388-6611
John E. Scott II, District Dir.
Offers business publications, workshops, counseling and financial assistance to qualified applicants. The Las Vegas District SBA has a business loan portfolio of 1,400 loans worth more than $240 million.

Score
(Service Corps of Retired Executives)
301 E. Stewart Ave.
Las Vegas, NV 89101
388-6104
Sherman Kerner, Local Chapter Chairman

Sponsored by the U.S. Small Business Administration. Operates a counseling center made up of retired men and women from all types of business to help individuals who are presently in business and need help with problems, all free of charge. Conducts workshops on how to start and maintain businesses.

U. S. Commercial Service International Trade Administration
1755 E. Plumb Ln., Ste. 152
Reno, NV 89502
1-702-784-5203
Jere Dabbs, Dir.
Will research a product's export potential and provides information on overseas markets and contacts.

PRECIOUS METALS
Nevada ranks first in the nation in gold production (1996) and is the second largest gold producing region in the world, second only to South Africa.

Nevada produces 68 percent of the nation's gold and over 40 percent of the nation's silver. In 1996 7 million troy ounces of gold and 20.7 million ounces of silver were produced. Nevada's gold production accounts for 11.1 percent of the world supply. In 1996, Nevada was the nation's leading producer of barite, lithium carbonate and mined magnesite, and was second in the production of diatomite.

In 1996, there were more than 14,400 Nevadans directly employed in the mineral industry at an average annual salary of $47,540, the highest of any sector in the state. It is estimated that another 48,000 jobs are involved with supplying goods and services to the industry. In 1996, approximately $3.3 billion in mineral commodities were produced in Nevada. There were over 1.1 million barrels of oil produced from oil fields located in Nye and Eureka counties.

Las Vegas Exports

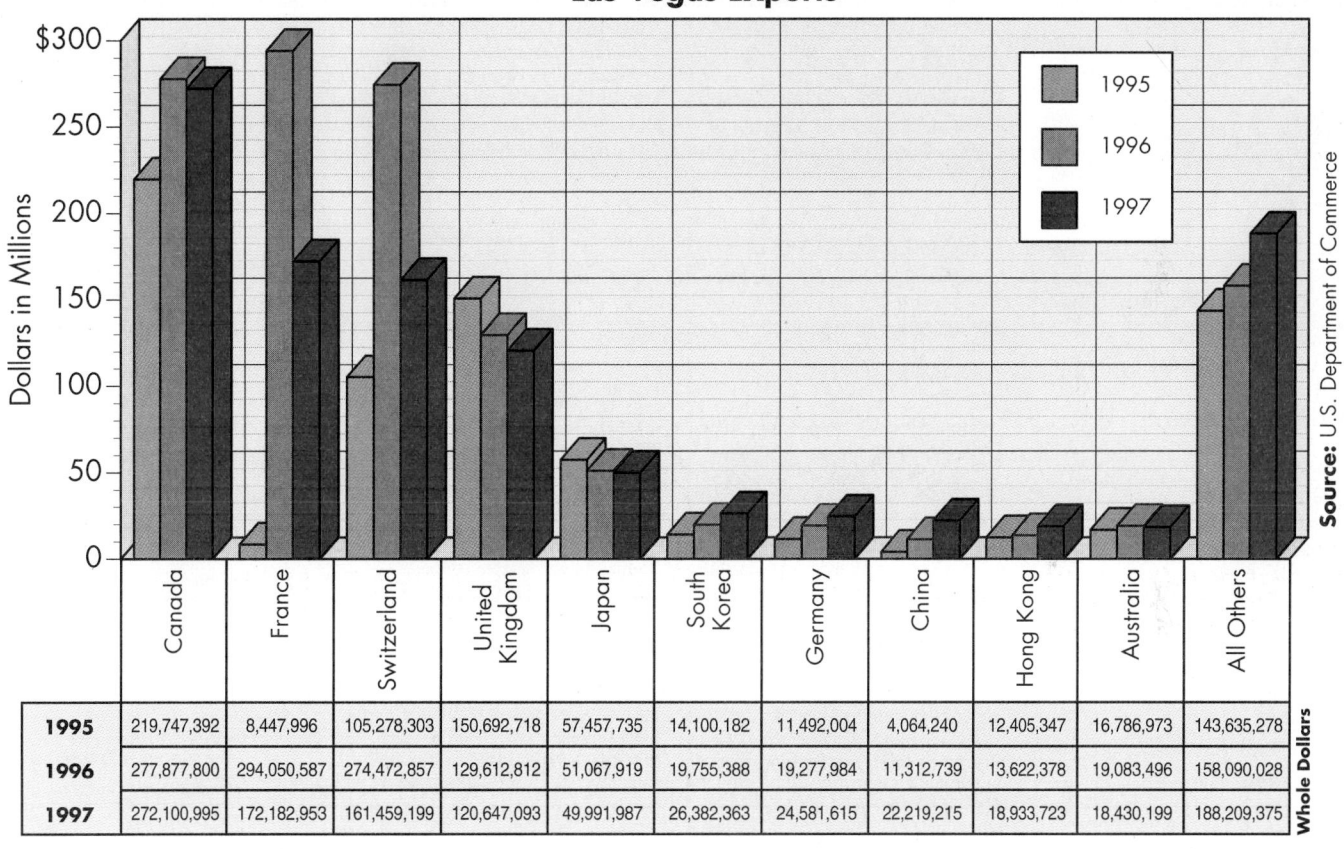

	Canada	France	Switzerland	United Kingdom	Japan	South Korea	Germany	China	Hong Kong	Australia	All Others
1995	219,747,392	8,447,996	105,278,303	150,692,718	57,457,735	14,100,182	11,492,004	4,064,240	12,405,347	16,786,973	143,635,278
1996	277,877,800	294,050,587	274,472,857	129,612,812	51,067,919	19,755,388	19,277,984	11,312,739	13,622,378	19,083,496	158,090,028
1997	272,100,995	172,182,953	161,459,199	120,647,093	49,991,987	26,382,363	24,581,615	22,219,215	18,933,723	18,430,199	188,209,375

Source: U.S. Department of Commerce

EXPORTS
According to Nevada's Department of Economic Development, in 1996 we exported $1.2 billion worth of products, a 70.4 percent increase over 1995.

MAIN EXPORT NATIONS:
1. France .... $294 million
2. Canada .... $277 million
3. Switzerland .... $274 million
4. United Kingdom .... $129 million
5. Japan .... $51 million

FIVE TOP PRODUCTS EXPORTED:
1. Primary metal products .... $392 million
2. Waste and scrap products .... $280 million
3. Miscellaneous Products (mostly gaming supplies) .... $125 million
4. Electric products (mostly gaming machines) .... $86 million
5. Medical instruments .... $39 million

FOREIGN TRADE ZONE #89
Grantee: Nevada Development Authority
3773 Howard Hughes Pkwy., Ste. 140 South
Las Vegas, NV 89109
791-0000   1-800-634-6858   Fax: 796-6483
Jerry Sandsrom, VP of Client Services
The U.S. Secretary of Commerce created Foreign Trade #89 in 1986 and is helping Las Vegas to become an international business destination. From the initial 5,000 sq. ft. the Foreign Trade Zone has grown to over 200,000 sq. ft. with 100 international companies and 56 domestic companies utilizing the facility. A complete customs facility opened in December 1992 at the McCarran Charter International Air Cargo Center. A Foreign Trade Zone is an area where foreign products can be stored and assembled without payment of duties until they are shipped to U.S. markets.

BUSINESS - GOVERNMENT AGENCIES

Below is a list of government agencies you need to go through before opening a new business. Depending on the type of business license you are applying for, you will need an inspection from the building department and fire department. *(See Government Section)*

Assessor - Clark County
500 S. Grand Central Pkwy.
Las Vegas, NV 89101
455-3882
Mark Schofield
Personal property tax

BUSINESS LICENSES

**Clark County Business
License Department**
500 S. Grand Central Pkwy.
Las Vegas, NV 89155
455-4252   1-800-328-4813
Ardel Jorgensen, Dir.
Mon. - Fri. 9 am - 4:30 pm

**City of Las Vegas Business
Activities Department**
400 E. Stewart Ave., Room 107
Las Vegas, NV 89101
229-6281
George Stevens, Dir.
Mon. - Fri. 8 am - 5 pm

**City of North Las Vegas City
Hall, Licensing Division**
2266 Civic Center Dr.
N. Las Vegas, NV 89030
633-1519
Don Schmeiser, Dir.
Tue. - Fri. 7 am - 6 pm

Henderson City Hall
240 Water St.
Henderson, NV 89015
565-2045
Dave Lee, Adm.
Mon. - Thu. 7:30 am - 5:30 pm

Boulder City
401 California St.
Boulder City, NV 89005
293-9219
Robert Boyer, Dir.
Mon. - Thu. 7 am - 6 pm

County Clerk
200 S. 3rd St.
Las Vegas, NV 89101
455-3156
Loretta Bowman
To register a fictitious name. Forms can be obtained at any commercial bank. Your signature must be notarized, and you will need the original and two copies and $15 filing fee.

Clark County Health District
625 Shadow Ln.
Las Vegas, NV 89106
385-1291
Dr. Otto Ravenholt
Chief Health Officer
Food and beverage establishments as well as many other businesses must be inspected and follow Health Department guidelines.

**Gaming Control Board
State of Nevada**
555 E. Washington Ave., Ste. 2600
Las Vegas, NV 89101
486-2000
Bill Bible, Chairman
Gaming licenses

**Immigration & Naturalization
Services**
Employer Relations Office
3373 Pepper Ln.
Las Vegas, NV 89120
451-3597
Forms: 1-800-870-3676
Employers are required to obtain a signed I-9 form from the employee within 72 hours of hire. The employer must document proof of employee's right to work in the United States by social security card, driver's license, birth certificate, passport, etc.

Internal Revenue Service
4750 W. Oakey Blvd.
Las Vegas, NV 89102
455-1016
Brian McMahon, Dir.
Information: 1-800-829-1040
Forms: 1-800-829-3676
Request an application for an employer identification number (form SS-4); Form 941 for Social Security and income tax withholding. Required if you pay wages, or are a partnership or corporation.

**Nevada Employment Security
Department**
Unemployment Insurance
1830 E. Sahara Ave., Ste. 313
Las Vegas, NV 89104
486-8222
Susanne Cooper, Manager
Mon. - Fri. 8 am - 5 pm
Unemployment compensation insurance taxes are paid by employers to make unemployment payments to laid-off workers. Any business that employs one or more persons and pays wages totaling $225 or more per calendar quarter must pay unemployment. Contributions for a new employer fall between 0.25 percent to 5.40 percent with the standard rate being 3.0 percent of the taxable wage. There are 18 categories, based on employee turnover in the past with new employers paying the mandatory 2.95 percent until they get an experienced rating to qualify them for lower rates. The average Nevada employer will pay 1.5 percent on the first $16,400 a year in wages. Refundable deposit based on 2.95 percent of estimated payroll is required to get started.

**Nevada Occupational Safety
& Health**
2500 W. Washington Ave., Ste. 113
Las Vegas, NV 89106
486-5020
Jimmy Garrett, Safety Manager
Enforcement agency inspecting restaurants on complaint

Privileged Permits
Department of Business Activity
400 E. Stewart Ave.
Las Vegas, NV 89101
229-2291
George Stevens, Dir.
Issues privileged permits in 25 categories for liquor, gaming, child care, fire arms, astrology, hypnosis, psychic arts, burglar alarms, locksmiths, pawn shops, massage, second hand dealers, escort services, martial arts, rock concerts, and teen dances. Police Department conducts a background investigation and the request goes before the city council.

Public Utilities Commission
555 E. Washington Ave., Room 4500
Las Vegas, NV 89101
486-2600
Judy Sheldrew, Chairman
Licenses utility services and motor carriers operating in Nevada. Regulates electricity, telephones, gas, water and railroads.

Secretary of State
Capitol Complex
Carson City, NV 89710
1-702-687-5203   1-800-274-2754
Dean Heller, Secretary of State
There are no financial reporting requirements for a corporation in Nevada, and the only action necessary to keep the corporation in good standing is to maintain a resident agent in the state and to file a list of current officers annually. The fee to incorporate is $125 for shares of $25,000 or less. It cost $85 a year to keep a corporation alive in Nevada. At the end of fiscal year 1997 there were approximately 116,000 companies in good standing in Nevada. In 1996-1997 32,000 companies incorporated with the Secretary of State's office, a 20 percent increase over the previous year.

**State Industrial Insurance
System** (SIIS)
Workers Compensation Insurance
1700 W. Charleston Blvd.
Las Vegas, NV 89126-0929
388-3225
Douglas Dirks, Gen. Mgr.
Policy Holder Service Office
1210 S. Valley View Blvd.
Las Vegas, NV 89102
259-5989
Douglas Dirks, General Mgr.
Workman's compensation insurance for employee accidents is required if you pay wages. Premiums are paid by employers into the system to take care of medical expenses and rehabilitation costs for injured workers. Premiums are collected on each $100 of payroll based on loss experience of the industry classification, to a cap of $36,000. Premium rates vary by occupation, with riskier job classifications, such as mining, having higher rates than safer classifications such as clerical positions. To apply for SIIS the employer fills out an application and pays a deposit based on the industry classification and projected payroll. Deposit formula: monthly payees must deposit 2 months of estimated premiums; quarterly payees must deposit 4 months of estimated premiums. There are presently approximately 60,000 employers in the system. Beginning January 1994, employers must choose a managed health-care system for injured workers. If you need more information contact:
Department of Industrial Relations
Division of Industrial Insurance Regulation
2500 W. Washington Ave., Ste. 102

Las Vegas, NV 89106
486-5001
Ron Swirczek, Administrator

**Taxation, Department of
State of Nevada**
555 E. Washington Ave., Ste. 1300
Las Vegas, NV 89104
486-2300
Robert Palmer, Tax Adm.
Assesses the amount of sales tax your business will pay. They will either require a bond of cash (check) security deposit based on your projected sales paid quarterly or monthly. You also obtain your State Business License here.

ZONING

Clark County Zoning Division
500 S. Grand Central Pkwy.
Las Vegas, NV 89155
455-4314
Richard Holmes, Dir.

**City of Las Vegas Community
Planning and Development Dept.**
731 S. 4th St.
Las Vegas, NV 89101
229-6301
Theresa O'Donnell, Dir.

**City of North Las Vegas Dept. of
Comm. Planning & Development**
2266 Civic Center Dr.
N. Las Vegas, NV 89030
633-1537
Don Schmeiser, Dir.

**City of Henderson Planning
Division**
240 Water St.
Henderson, NV 89015
565-2088
Mary Kay Peck, Dir.

**City of Boulder City
Department of Community
Development**
401 California St.
Boulder City, NV 89005-0367
293-9292
John Fullard, Dir.

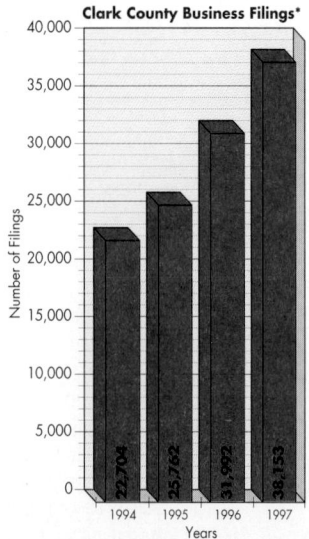

Clark County Business Filings*

Years	Number of Filings
1994	22,704
1995	25,762
1996	31,992
1997	38,153

Source: Secretary of State

* Includes corporations, limited liability companies, limited partnerships and limited liability partnerships

COMMERICAL REAL ESTATE BROKERS

Americana Commercial Group
3790 Paradise Rd.
Las Vegas, NV 89109
796-8888
Mark Stark, CEO

Bill Hammons & Assoc.
4409 S. Pecos Rd.
Las Vegas, NV 89121
435-7011
Bill Hammons, Pres.

CB Commercial
1900 E. Flamingo Rd., Ste. 180
Las Vegas, NV 89119
369-4800
John Records, Senior VP

Century 21 Realty Associates
3100 S. Valley View Blvd.
Las Vegas, NV 89102
362-5150
Jim Whitworth, Broker/Mgr.

The Commercial Group
700 S. 8th St.
Las Vegas, NV 89101
471-6767
Dave Nevenkirch, Pres.

Cornerstone Company
820 Rancho Ln., Ste. 85
Las Vegas, NV 89106
383-3033
Richard Truesdell, Pres.

Diversified Realty
911 N. Buffalo Dr., Ste. 201
Las Vegas, NV 89128
222-2222
Randy Black, Pres.

ETN Real Estate
2920 S. Jones Blvd., Ste. 200
Las Vegas, NV 89102
737-8000
E. Thomas Naseef, Pres.
Management, leasing, sales, analysis and development. Office, retail and industrial.

Encore Realty & Commercial Inc.
8100 W. Sahara Ave.
Las Vegas, NV 89117
242-4000
Randel Aleman, Pres.

The Equity Group
2300 W. Sahara Ave., Ste. 1130, Box 2
Las Vegas, NV 89102
796-5500
Scott Godino, Pres.

First Commercial Real Estate Services
4427 S. Polaris Ave.
Las Vegas, NV 89103
798-9988
Kevin Buckley, Pres.

Jan Bernard Realty
1514 S. Eastern Ave.
Las Vegas, NV 89104
383-3333
Jan Bernard, Owner/Broker

Lee & Assoc.
1771A E. Flamingo Rd., Ste. 108
Las Vegas, NV 89119
739-6222
Greg Morrell, Pres.

Prudential Southwest Realty Jack Matthews & Co. Commercial
2950 S. Rancho Dr., Ste. 100
Las Vegas, NV 89102
251-1010
Jim Wade, Pres.

Real Properties Ltd.
2764 Lake Sahara Dr., Ste. 115
Las Vegas, NV 89117
794-4000
Ted Stoever, Pres.

Realty Executives of Nevada
1903 S. Jones Blvd., Ste. 100
Las Vegas, NV 89102
873-4500
Jeff Moore, Corporate Broker

Realty Holdings Group
340 Lewis Ave., Ste. 1104
Las Vegas, NV 89101
384-4488
Keith Bassett, Pres.

Rossum Realty LTD
3875 S. Jones Blvd.
Las Vegas, NV 89103
368-1850
Beth Rossum, Broker

SBO Corporation
6787 W. Tropicana Ave., Ste. 235
Las Vegas, NV 89103
892-7777
Healey Mendicino, Pres.
Business specialist; commercial, land, industrial and income property

Stuart Mixer & Associates, Inc.
3800 Howard Hughes Pkwy. Ste. 1220
Las Vegas, NV 89109
735-5700
Michael Mixer, CEO

Vista Management
2295-A Renaissance Dr.
Las Vegas, NV 89119
798-7970
Michael Saltman, Pres.

Westmark Commercial Group
3737 Pecos McLeod, Ste. 101
Las Vegas, NV 89121
458-2911
Joseph Abdenour, Pres.

COMMERICAL PROPERTY MANAGERS

The Commercial Group
700 S. 8th St.
Las Vegas, NV 89101
798-6767
Dave Nevenkirch, Pres.
Manages almost 1/2 million square feet of retail space.

HOWARD HUGHES

Howard Hughes came to Las Vegas in 1966. Within four years he had purchased the Desert Inn, Sands, Castaways, Frontier, Silver Slipper, and the Landmark. He also purchased an air charter service, Channel 8, the North Las Vegas Airport, Harolds Club in Reno, and acres of land at the Strip and Sahara, all for less than $300 million. This was the beginning of the end of the "Mafia"-run Las Vegas and the beginning of corporate-run Las Vegas.

Commercial Specialists
2320 Paseo Del Prado
Las Vegas, NV 89102
364-0909
Kevin Donahoe, Pres.
Currently 678,000 sq. ft. under management

Dermody Properties
1900 E. Flamingo Rd.
Las Vegas, NV 89119
794-0000
Michael Dermody, Pres.
Largest industrial developer in Nevada with warehousing, retail and distribution outlets.

The Equity Group
2300 W. Sahara Ave., Ste. 1130, Box 2
Las Vegas, NV 89102
796-5500
Scott Godino, Pres.
Manages 2 million square feet of retail and office space; primarily retail.

E. Thomas Naseef & Co.
2920 S. Jones Blvd., Ste. 200
Las Vegas, NV 89102
737-8000
E. Thomas Naseef, Pres.
Management, leasing, sales, analysis, and development; office, retail, and industrial.

The Howard Hughes Corporation
3800 Howard Hughes Pkwy.
Las Vegas, NV 89109
791-4000
John Goolsby, Pres.
Hughes Center, Hughes Cheyenne Center, Hughes Airport Center, Summerlin Business Park.

MDL Group
400 S. Maryland Pkwy.
Las Vegas, NV 89101
388-1800
Carol Cline & Curt Anderson, Co-Owners

Palms Business Centers B. H. Miller Contractors
3137 W. Tompkins Ave.
Las Vegas, NV 89103
367-3000
Lee W. Phelps, Gen. Mgr.

The Ribeiro Corp.
195 E. Reno Ave.
Las Vegas, NV 89119
798-1133
Johnny A. Ribeiro, Pres.
Manages over 3 million square feet of office and industrial space.

Transwestern Property Co.
1050 E. Flamingo Rd.
Las Vegas, NV 89119
731-0954
Faye Murphy, Property Manager
Leasing, building and construction management; accounting and reporting systems. Manages 583,000 square feet of industrial and retail space.

The Howard Hughes Corporation, 3800 Howard Hughes Pkwy.
Las Vegas, NV 89109

OCEAN SPRAY

Ocean Spray opened a $50 million plant in Henderson in 1994. The 200,000 sq. ft. plant has a capacity of 30 million cases of juice annually and employs 150 people. The average salary is $30,000.

OFFICE SPACE

Las Vegas has 10.2 million sq. ft. of office space with a vacancy rate of 13.24 percent. Lease rates range from $1.95 to $2.25 per sq. ft. There is approximately 1,848,960 sq. ft. currently planned or under construction, which will push the total office inventory close to 12 million sq. ft.

Airport Center
5030 Paradise Rd.
Las Vegas, NV 89119
57,994 sq. ft. - 2 floors
Leasing - 739-9411

Airport East
6075 S. Eastern Ave.
Las Vegas, NV 89119
124,000 sq. ft.
Lee & Assoc. - 739-6222

Alexander Dawson Building I & II
4045 - 4055 Spencer St.
Las Vegas, NV 89119
175,000 Sq. Ft. - 2 & 6 floors
CB Commercial - 369-4800

Alpine Court
4820 Alpine St.
Las Vegas, NV 89114
48,000 sq. ft. - 2 floors
Americana Commercial - 796-8888

Alta Quail
1640 Alta Dr.
Las Vegas, NV 89106
56,000 sq. ft.
Ribeiro Corp. - 798-6050

AmBank Business Center
4435 Spring Mountain Rd.
Las Vegas, NV 89102
45,000 sq. ft. - 3 floors
E. Thomas Naseef - 737-8000

Atrium Business Tower
333 N. Rancho Dr.
Las Vegas, NV 89106
138,440 sq. ft. - 9 floors
CB Commercial - 369-4800

Bank of America Center
101 Convention Center Dr.
Las Vegas, NV 89109
318,000 sq. ft. - 8 floors
CB Commercial - 369-4800
$1.35 - $1.60 sq. ft./mo.

Bank of America Plaza
300 S. Fourth St.
Las Vegas, NV 89101
255,000 sq. ft. - 16 floors
Realty Holdings Group - 384-4488
$1.95 - $2.15 per sq. ft.

Bank of America West
6900 Westcliff Dr.
Las Vegas, NV 89128
88,000 sq. ft. - 8 floors
Realty Holdings Group - 384-4488
$1.95 - $2.15 per sq. ft.

Bird Building
5325 S. Rainbow Blvd.
Las Vegas, NV 89118
47,600 sq. ft. - 2 floors

Bonneville Square I
Bonneville Square II
530 Las Vegas Blvd. S.
Las Vegas, NV 89101
75,200 sq. ft. for both buildings - 8 floors

Bridger Law Building
701 E. Bridger
Las Vegas, NV 89101
50,000 sq. ft. - 10 floors

Cambridge Quail Park
1601-1681 E. Flamingo Rd.
Las Vegas, NV 89119
50,000 sq. ft. - 1 floor
Ribeiro Corp. - 798-6050

Cameron Commerce Center
4685 Cameron Rd.
Las Vegas, NV 89107
162,000 sq. ft.

Century Park
1771 E. Flamingo Rd.
Las Vegas, NV 89119
113,500 sq. ft. - 2 floors
$1.40 per sq. ft.

Lakes Business Park, W. Sahara Ave./Crystal Water Way, Las Vegas, NV 89128

Charleston Tower
1701 W. Charleston Blvd.
Las Vegas, NV 89102
88,000 sq. ft. - 6 floors

Charleston/Valley View
3811-3841 W. Charleston Blvd.
Las Vegas, NV 89102
88,000 sq. ft.
CB Commercial - 369-4800

Citibank Park
3900 Paradise Rd.
Las Vegas, NV 89109
85,000 sq. ft. - 2 floors
The Schulman Group - 737-6822

Clark Place
301 E. Clark Ave.
Las Vegas, NV 89101
108,000 sq. ft. - 10 floors
CB Commercial - 369-4800

Coldwell Banker Plaza
Rainbow Blvd./Edna Ave.
Las Vegas, NV 89102
36,000 sq. ft. - 1 floor

Consolidated Business Center
2235 E. Flamingo Rd.
Las Vegas, NV 89119
43,000 sq. ft. - 2 floors

Copper Pointe
4510, 4530, 4570 S. Eastern Ave.
Las Vegas, NV 89119
35,000 sq. ft. - 1 floor

Credit Union Plaza
3100 W. Sahara Ave.
Las Vegas, NV 89102
44,000 sq. ft. - 2 floors
The Equity Group - 796-5500

The Crossings Business Center
Summerlin Pkwy./Town Center Dr.
Las Vegas, NV 89134
Howard Hughes Corp. - 791-4400
128-acre business park

Desert Inn Office Park
2725-2785 E. Desert Inn Rd.
Las Vegas, NV 89121
101,000 sq. ft. - 2 floors

Desert Professional Building
2225 E. Flamingo Rd.
Las Vegas, NV 89119
45,000 sq. ft. - 2 floors
Nova Commercial - 735-3300

Eastern Business Park
6000 S. Eastern Ave.
Las Vegas, NV 89119
CB Commercial - 369-4800

Executive Center East
1515 E. Tropicana Ave.
Las Vegas, NV 89119
82,236 sq. ft. - 1 floor
Lee & Associates - 739-6222

Executive Center West
4555 W. Tropicana Ave.
Las Vegas, NV 89103
35,000 sq. ft. - 1 floor
E. Thomas Naseef - 737-8000

Executive Park & Executive Park West
6773 & 6833 W. Charleston Blvd.
Las Vegas NV 89102
102,000 sq. ft. - 1 floor

Executive Towers
401 S. Third St.
Las Vegas, NV 89101
38,000 sq. ft. - 5 floors

FIB Building
302 E. Carson Ave.
Las Vegas, NV 89101
140,000 sq. ft. - 11 floors
Americana Commercial - 796-8888

The Financial Center
3300 W. Sahara Ave.
Las Vegas, NV 89102
207,000 sq. ft. - 6 floors
Cornerstone Co. - 383-3033

Flamingo Executive Park
1050 E. Flamingo Rd.
Las Vegas, NV 89119
137,000 sq. ft. - 3 floors
Wilshire Pacific Realty - 646-6636

Flamingo Lakes
2820 - 2880 E. Flamingo Rd.
Las Vegas, NV 89121
54,000 sq. ft. - 1 floor
Terra West - 362-8776

Flamingo-Pecos Plaza
3400 E. Flamingo Rd.
Las Vegas, NV 89121
34,300 sq. ft. - 3 floors

Fountain Park
3670 S. Eastern Ave.
Las Vegas, NV 89109
80,000 sq. ft. - 7 floors

Goodman Building
520 S. Fourth St.
Las Vegas, NV 89101
30,000 sq. ft. - 3 floors

Green Valley Civic Center
2625 Green Valley Pkwy.
Henderson, NV 89014
10-acre professional office complex
60,000 sq. ft. - 2 floors
Americana Realtors - 796-8888

Green Valley Corporate Center
Green Valley Pkwy./Lake Mead Dr.
Henderson, NV 89014
250,000 sq. ft.
American Nevada Corp. - 458-8855

Green Valley Professional
2501 Green Valley Pkwy.
Henderson, NV 89014
53,000 sq. ft. - 2 floors
American Nevada Corp. - 458-8855

Greystone & Greystone II
1850 - 2030 E. Flamingo Rd.
Las Vegas, NV 89119
191,000 sq. ft. - 2 floors
CB Commercial - 369-4800

Hilton Corporate Plaza
3930 Howard Hughes Pkwy.
Las Vegas, NV 89109
85,915 sq. ft. - 5 floors
Howard Hughes Corp. - 699-5000

Hughes Center
3720 - 3800 Howard Hughes Pkwy.
Las Vegas, NV 89109
735,000 sq. ft.
Howard Hughes Corp. - 791-4439
Upon completion of the 120 acres, Hughes Center will have over 2 million square feet of office space.

Karen Executive Center
1050 E. Sahara Ave.
Las Vegas, NV 89104
40,000 sq. ft. - 4 floors
CB Commercial - 369-4800

Lakes Business Park
W. Sahara Ave./Crystal Water Way
Las Vegas, NV 89128
Priority One Commercial - 228-7464

La Mirada Office Park
Jones Blvd./Edna Ave.
Las Vegas, NV 89102
60,000 sq. ft.
E. Thomas Naseef - 737-8000

La Plaza Business Center
4220 S. Maryland Pkwy.
Las Vegas, NV 89119
104,230 sq. ft. - 2 floors

Legacy Business Park
Wigwam Pkwy./Green Valley Pkwy.
Henderson, NV 89014
89,000 sq. ft. - 11 acres
Priority One Commercial - 228-7464

Magna Executive Center
2001 E. Flamingo Rd.
Las Vegas, NV 89119
55,200 sq. ft. - 1 floor
Bruttomesso Realty - 369-9999

Marabeya Business Park
6655 W. Sahara Ave.
Las Vegas, NV 89102
98,000 sq. ft. - 2 floors
CB Commercial - 369-4800

Maryland Parkway Building
2770 S. Maryland Pkwy.
Las Vegas, NV 89119
50,000 sq. ft. - 1 floor

Mid Towne Plaza
1111 Las Vegas Blvd. S.
Las Vegas, NV 89104
54,000 sq. ft. - 3 floors
H & L Realty - 385-3226

Nevada Financial Center
2300 W. Sahara Ave.
Las Vegas, NV 89102
158,000 sq. ft. - 12 floors
CB Commercial - 369-4800

Newport Center
3790 Paradise Rd.
Las Vegas, NV 89109
31,500 sq. ft. - 3 floors

Norwest Plaza
201 Las Vegas Blvd. S.
Las Vegas, NV 89101
24,000 sq. ft. - 3 floors
Cornerstone Co. - 383-3033

Park 2000
6075 S. Eastern Ave.
Las Vegas, NV 89119
138,000 sq. ft.
Office, retail and warehouse space
Ribeiro Corp. - 798-6050

Park Flamingo East
2110 E. Flamingo Rd.
Las Vegas, NV 89119
102,275 sq. ft. - 3 floors
Nova Commercial - 735-3300

Park Flamingo West
2080 E. Flamingo Rd.
Las Vegas, NV 89119
118,000 sq. ft. - 2 floors
Nova Commercial - 735-3300

Park Sahara I, II, III
1810-1860 E. Sahara Ave.
Las Vegas, NV 89104
117,000 sq. ft. - 3 floors

Parkway Center
3101 S. Maryland Pkwy.
Las Vegas, NV 89109
31,500 sq. ft. - 3 floors

Phoenix Building
330 S. 3rd St.
Las Vegas, NV 89101
66,000 sq. ft. - 11 floors
CB Commercial - 369-4800

Philadelphia Square
4160 - 4180 S. Pecos Rd.
Las Vegas, NV 89121
32,500 sq. ft. - 2 floors

The Plazas
2800 W. Sahara Ave.
Las Vegas, NV 89102
2 story office/retail

The Plazas
2975 S. Rainbow Blvd.
Las Vegas, NV 89102
38,000 sq. ft. - 2 floors

Quail Park I & II, 801 & 601 S. Rancho Dr., Las Vegas, NV 89106

The Plazas Office Park
2330 Paseo Del Prado
Las Vegas, NV 89102
123,000 sq. ft. - 3 floors
Fidelity Realty - 362-2111

The Plaza at Summerlin
Summerlin Pkwy. &
Hills Village Center Circle
Las Vegas, NV 89134
88,000 sq. ft. - 3 floors
Howard Hughes Corp. - 791-4439

Plaza Vegas I & II
3305-3355 Spring Mountain. Rd.
Las Vegas, NV 89102
80,000 sq. ft. - 1 floor
Ribeiro Corp. - 798-6050

Pointe Flamingo Office Park
Flamingo Rd./Eastern Ave.
Las Vegas, NV 89119
135,000 sq. ft. - Class A office park
Major Tenant: Chevy's Mexican Restaurant

Pueblo Medical Center
8551 W. Lake Mead Blvd.
Las Vegas, NV 89128
Howard Hughes Corp. - 791-4000

Quail Bonita I & II
600-601 Whitney Ranch Dr.
Henderson, NV 89014
77,000 sq. ft. - 1 floor
Ribeiro Corp. - 798-6050

Quail Park I & II
801 & 601 S. Rancho Dr.
Las Vegas, NV 89106
124,000 sq. ft.
Ribeiro Corp. - 798-6050

Quail Park III & IV
2810 & 2820 W. Charleston Blvd.
Las Vegas, NV 89102
51,000 sq. ft. - 1 floor
Ribeiro Corp. - 798-6050

Quail VI
2810 W. Charleston Blvd.
Las Vegas, NV 89102
100,000 sq. ft. - 4 floors
Ribeiro Corp. - 798-6050

Quail Orient
501 S. Rancho Dr.
Las Vegas, NV 89106
71,000 sq. ft. - 1 floor
Ribeiro Corp. - 798-6050

Quail Park West
2881 S. Valley View Blvd.
Las Vegas, NV 89102
Space starting at 1,320 sq. ft.
Ribeiro Corp. - 798-6050

R & R Plaza
8068 - 8084 W. Sahara Ave.
Las Vegas, NV 89117
Space from 1,200 sq. ft.
Jack Matthews & Co. - 368-4114

Rancho Sahara Medical I & III
Rancho Dr. & Sahara Ave.
Las Vegas, NV 89102
97,100 sq. ft. - 2 floors

Renaissance Office Park
2255 Renaissance Dr.
Las Vegas, NV 89119
140,000 sq. ft. - 1 floors
CB Commercial - 369-4800

Sahara Executive Building
1785 E. Sahara Ave.
Las Vegas NV 89104
67,200 sq. ft. - 2 floors
CB Commercial - 369-4800

Sahara/Rancho Medical Center
2200, 2300, 2320 S. Rancho Dr.
Las Vegas, NV 89102
121,000 sq. ft. - 2 floors
Prudential Hallmark Realty - 251-1010

Sahara Vista I
5440 W. Sahara Ave.
Las Vegas, NV 89102
40,000 sq. ft. 3 floors
Realnet Commercial Brokerage - 221-1111

Silver State Building
770 E. Sahara Ave.
Las Vegas, NV 89104
32,000 sq. ft. - 4 floors

Spanish Oaks Plaza
3150-3180 W. Sahara Ave.
Las Vegas, NV 89102
41,700 sq. ft. - 2 floors
E. Thomas Naseef - 737-8000

Tropicana Plaza
1055 E. Tropicana Ave.
Las Vegas, NV 89119
50,000 sq. ft. - 1 floor

Valley View Office Park
Charleston Blvd./Valley View Blvd.
Las Vegas, NV 89102
84,000 sq. ft. - 7 floors
CB Commercial - 369-4800

Valley View Pointe
Valley View Blvd./Flamingo Rd.
Las Vegas, NV 89103
64,000 sq. ft. - 2 floors
CB Commercial - 369-4800

Vantage Point
4100 W. Flamingo Rd.
Las Vegas, NV 89103
42,000 sq. ft. - 2 floors

Wells Fargo Tower
3800 Howard Hughes Dr.
Las Vegas, NV 89109
259,000 sq. ft. - 17 floors
Howard Hughes Corp. - 791-4440

Weston Park
6600 W. Charleston Blvd.
Las Vegas, NV 89102
43,000 sq. ft.

Winchester Plaza
1700 E. Desert Inn Rd.
Las Vegas, NV 89109
44,000 sq. ft. - 2 floors

901 Building
901 S. Rancho Dr.
Las Vegas, NV 89102
73,000 sq. ft. - 2 floors

1555 Business Center
1555 E. Flamingo Rd.
Las Vegas, NV 89119
44,000 sq. ft. - 1 floor
GFS of Nevada Inc. - 362-6444

3770 Building
3770 Spring Mountain Rd.
Las Vegas, NV 89102
66,000 sq. ft. - 3 floors

4310 Building
4310 S. Paradise Rd.
Las Vegas, NV 89109
32,000 sq. ft. - 2 floors

BUSINESS

INDUSTRIAL PARKS

(For retail space see Shopping Section)

Aerojet Facilities
1 Aerojet Way
N. Las Vegas, MNV 89030
435-7011
121,075 sq. ft.
Bill Hammond & Associates

Airport East
6075 Eastern Ave.
Las Vegas, NV 89119
Ribeiro Corp. - 736-6901

Airport Industrial Park
Ensworth St. & I-15
Las Vegas, NV 89119
30 acres
Major Tenants: Merillat Industries, Bonanza Beverage and Kalco

Allen Aerojet
1840-1900 Aerojet Way
N. Las Vegas, NV 89030
209,665 sq. ft.
Major Tenants: Val Pac and Wal-Mart
CB Commercial - 369-4800

Angeles Warehouse
3600 Oquendo Rd.
Las Vegas, NV 89120
160,000 sq. ft.
Burke Commercial - 739-6222

APEX
11401 US 93 North
Las Vegas, NV 89115
21,000 acres
Major Tenants: Georgia-Pacific and Chemstar

Arville Commerce Center
4610 - 4650 Arville St.
Las Vegas, NV 89103
Major Tenants: GE Appliances, NEC Business Communications, Closets by Design
America Property Enterprises - 367-4900

Basic Management Inc.
W. Lake Mead Dr.
Henderson, NV 89015
1,000 acres
Major Tenants: Pioneer Chlor/Alkali, Kerr McGee, Chemstar & Titanium Metals

Birtcher Palms Business Center
3300 Birtcher Dr.
Las Vegas, NV 89118
20 acres, 111,945 sq. ft.
Major Tenants: American Casino Enterprise, FHP, PRN Home Health Care, Honeywell & Interactive Flight Technologies
CB Commercial - 369-4800

Black Mountain Business Park
Cassia Way/Gibson Rd.
Henderson, NV 89015
200 acres
Major Tenants: Serrot Corp., Big O Tires
Victory Valley Land Co. - 565-6485

Black Mountain Distribution Center
882 American Pacific Dr.
Henderson, NV 89014
104,420 sq. ft.
Opened 1996
CB Commercial - 369-4800

Boulder City Business Center
Wells Rd.
Boulder City, NV 89005
678 acres
Major Tenant: L. A. Dept. of Power & Water

Brookspark
19 W. Brooks Ave., Ste. A
N. Las Vegas, NV 89030
60 acres, 218,000 sq. ft.
Major Tenants: Able Distributing, Angelic Linen, Casino Tokens & Dolphin Machine
Sterling Realty - 642-1177

Brookhallow Business Park
LV Technology Center
7310 Smoke Ranch Rd.
Las Vegas, NV 89128
100,000 sq. ft. opened 1990
Major Tenants: Perma Built Homes, Del Webb
Brookhallow Properties - 254-1000

Brookhallow Business Park, LV Technology Center
7310 Smoke Ranch Rd., Las Vegas, NV 89128

Cameron Business Park
4545 Cameron St.
Las Vegas, NV 89103
103,312 sq. ft. opened 1987
Major Tenants: Gilspur Exposition
CB Commercial - 369-4800

Cameron Commerce Center
4701 Cameron St.
Las Vegas, NV 89103
163,300 sq. ft. opened 1995
Major Tenants: Walker Zanger and Western Title
CB Commercial - 369-4800

Capital Business Park
3645 Losee Rd.
N. Las Vegas, NV 89030
150,000 sq. ft.
Burke Commercial - 739-6222

Centerpointe Business Park
4040 S. Industrial Rd.
Las Vegas, NV 89103
130,000 sq. ft. office-warehouse
Major Tenants: Sprint Cellular
The Tiberti Co. - 382-7070

Cheyenne Business Park
Cheyenne East of Lamb
Las Vegas, NV 89115
150,000 sq. ft.
Lee & Associates - 739-6222

Collins Business Park
Mirror Ct.
Henderson, NV 89015
20 acres
Major Tenants: Greyhound Exposition, Excalibur, Graybar Electric, Arneson Marine

Craig Commerce Center
2625-2711 Craig Rd.
Las Vegas, NV 89115
218,360 sq. ft. opened 1996
Major Tenants: Norsat, Inc.
369-4800

Cypress Center Business Park
Industrial Rd./Post Rd.
Las Vegas, NV 89118
118,960 Sq. ft.
Major Tenants: DHL Airways, Bell Atlantic
Pascoe Investment - 942-8846

Desert Inn Industrial Park
3300 E. Desert Inn Rd.
Las Vegas, NV 89121
Major Tenants: Dupont/MSA, Norwest Bank
SF Nevada LLC - 368-0046

Eastern Business Park
6000 S. Eastern Ave.
Las Vegas, NV 89119
157,200 sq. ft. opened 1986
Major Tenants: Opportunity Village and Gaming Systems, Inc.
SF Nevada - 368-0046

Fisher Industrial Park
1500 Industrial Rd.
Boulder City, NV 89005
30 acres
Major Tenants: Fisher Pen, Ennis Business Forms, Fradella Industries, Dennet Brothers, Park Plaza

Foremost Airport East
Patrick Ln./Eastern Ave.
Las Vegas, NV 89119
Major Tenants: Good Body Fitness, ARC materials
Leasing - 893-3366

Gateway to Las Vegas
Russell Rd./I-15
Las Vegas, NV 89118

Gibson Business Park
8201 Gibson Rd.
Henderson, NV 89015
200 acres, opened 1989
Major Tenants: Favorite Brands, Intl., Ocean Spray, Super Brands, Hydro-Craft, Pacific Industrial, Play Pal, Ocean Spray.
Am Pac Development Co. - 735-2200

Golden Triangle Industrial Park
I-15/Craig Rd.
N. Las Vegas, NV 89030
320 acres
Major Tenants: A. C. Houston Lumber
Stewart Mixer - 735-5700

Green Valley Commerce Center
7-15 Sunset Way 250 and 391
Henderson, NV 89014
112 acres opened 1980
Major Tenants: Ethel M. Chocolates, Service Merchandise, Clintas, International Seal, TV-5, Hospitality Network YCM
American Nevada Corp. - 458-8855

Hacienda Business Centre
5270 S. Cameron St.
Las Vegas, NV 89118
20 acres
Major Tenants: Bash Lighting, Las Vegas Volleyball Club
SBO Commercial - 892-7777

Hacienda Distribution Center
5277 Cameron St.
Las Vegas, NV 89118
107,500 sq. ft. opened 1990
CB Commercial - 369-4800
Major Tenants: The Effects Network, Warren's Homework, Las Vegas Volleyball

Hacienda Polaris Business Park
Hacienda Ave./Polaris Ave.
Las Vegas, NV 89118
163,156 sq. ft.
Lewis Homes - 736-8690

Harmon Distribution Center
Cameron St./Harmon Ave.
Las Vegas, NV 89103
245,000 sq. ft.
RFG Management Inc. - 771-0321

Harmon Industrial Park
4170 W. Harmon Ave.
Las Vegas, NV 89103
380,000 sq. ft.
CB Commercial - 369-4800
Major Tenants: GE Supply, WMS Gaming, Fastenal

Henderson Industrial Park
Industrial Park Rd.
Henderson, NV 89015
100 acres
Major Tenants: K.W. Pipeline, Henderson Trophies, Pacific Mechanical Supply

Highland Industrial Center
1001 S. Highland Dr.
Las Vegas, NV 89109
Major Tenants: Circus Circus, United Refrigeration
Transwestern Property - 731-1551

Highland Industrial Park
2901 S. Highland Dr.
Las Vegas, NV 89109
306,000 sq. ft.
Major Tenants: Quality Wood Products,
Collegiate Graphics
American Management - 362-4042

Hughes Airport Center
6700 S. Paradise Rd./Sunset Rd.
Las Vegas, NV 89119
390 acres, 750,000 sq. ft. eventually 4.5
million sq. ft.; foreign trade zone with
rail service.
Major Tenants: U. S. Postal Service
Regional Service Hub, EG&G-Special
Projects, Hughes Aircraft, Bally's
Manufacturing, GES, Lockheed
Engineering, Mikohn, Venada Aviation
The Howard Hughes Corp. - 791-4440

Hughes Cheyenne Center
Cheyenne Ave./Martin Luther King Blvd.
N. Las Vegas, NV 89030
321,800 sq. ft. opened 1995
209 acres - total build-out to be 4.3 mil-
lion sq. ft.
Tenants: Lechters Inc., Federal Express,
Rykoff-Sexton
Howard Hughes Corp. - 791-4400

Industrial Business Park
8000 E. Lake Mead Dr.
Henderson, NV 89015
Major Tenants: Savage Brothers,
Thatcher Chemical

Kiel Ranch Business Park
Carey Ave.
N. Las Vegas, NV 89030
20 acres
Major Tenants: Westco Food Service,
Vega Enterprises, Unitog, Allegis Pipe

**L & B Harmon Industrial
Center**
4170 W. Harmon Ave.
Las Vegas, NV 89103
140,000 sq. ft. opened 1988
Major Tenants: GE Supply, WMS Gaming
CB Commercial - 369-4800

Lake Mead Industrial Park
East Lake Mead Dr. at Olsen Dr.
Henderson, NV 89015
59 acres
Major Tenants: Good Humor-Breyers
Ice Cream, Hilt's Molds

Las Vegas Corporate Center
4301 N. Pecos Rd.
Las Vegas, NV 89115
112 acres - $60 million project
Major Tenants: ETA, La-Z-Boy, Lockheed
Martin, Loral Corp., Milgray

Las Vegas Enterprise Park
Martin Luther King Blvd., between
Lake Mead Blvd. and Vegas Dr.
Las Vegas, NV 89106
74-acres
Major Tenants: US Veterans Administration
The City of Las Vegas - 229-6551

Las Vegas Technology Center
Prairie Falcon Rd./Tenaya Wy.
Las Vegas, NV 89108
400-acres
Major Tenants: Columbia Sunrise
Mountainview, Multi Pure Corporate

Headquarters, Sierra Health Services,
University of Nevada School of
Medicine, Westwood Studios
The City of Las Vegas - 229-6551

Letica Industrial Park
Jean, NV 89019
57 acres
Major Tenants: Letica Corporation

Lewex Business Center
3245 Polaris Ave.
Las Vegas, NV 89102
170,604 sq. ft. opened 1990
Major tenants: Tacki-Mac
Lewis Properties - 737-9000

Lone Mountain Mesa
2700 Lone Mountain Rd.
N. Las Vegas, NV 89030
80 acres, 122,700 sq. ft.
Major Tenants: Western Casework,
Anderson Lumber
CB Commercial - 369-4800

Las Vegas Technology Center , Tenaya Wy., Las Vegas, NV 89108

Majestic Post Industrial Center
3480-3550 Bircher Dr.
Las Vegas, NV 89118
115,000 sq. ft. opened 1995
Major Tenants: Casino Data Systems,
Discount Package Supply
Majestic Realty Company - 896-5564

McCarran Airport Center
Bermuda Rd./Warm Springs Rd.
Las Vegas, NV 89123
100 acres-400,000 sq. ft.
Major Tenants: United Parcel Service,
Len Gordon Company, Freeman
Thomas & Mack Co. - 368-4200

McCarran Beltway
Bermuda Rd./Beltway
Las Vegas, NV 89119
292,000 sq. ft.
Major Tenants: Freeman Decorating,
Sullivan Transfer
CB Commercial - 369-4800

McCarran Center
444 E. Warm Springs Rd.
Las Vegas, NV 89119
600,000 sq. ft.
Major Tenants: Sigma Game, Pacific

Healthcare, Southland Corp. Reno Air,
Beazer Homes
Thomas & Mack Co. - 360-1008

McKellar Business Park
6000 S. Eastern Ave.
Las Vegas, NV 89119
157,204 sq. ft.
Major Tenants: Fisk Electric, United
Payphone, ATI Medical
CB Commercial - 369-4800

McKellar Industrial Park
3696 Scripps Way
Las Vegas, NV 89103
Jack Matthews - 386-4114
Americana Commercial Group - 796-8888

Mesa Vista Business Center
Wynn Rd./Mesa Vista Ave.
Las Vegas, NV 89118
160,000 sq. ft. opened 1995
Major Tenants: Boise Cascade, Frazee
Paint
CB Commercial - 369-4800

Mojave Industrial Park
1675 S. Mojave Ave.
Las Vegas, NV 89104
Lee & Assoc. - 739-6222

Monarch Business Center
4375 S. Valley View Blvd. &
Flamingo Rd.
Las Vegas, NV 89103
123,780 sq. ft. opened 1990
Major Tenants: Kirk Paper, Monarch
Title
CB Commercial - 369-4800

Nellis Industrial Park
Craig Rd./I-15
N. Las Vegas, NV 89030
206 acres
Major Tenants: Basic Food Flavors,
Intermec, J. B. Chemical, Kool Seal,
MACtac, McGrann Paper, Nikkiso,
Rotocast, Plastics, Sweetheart, T. J.
Maxx, Universal Urethane, WAVE
Dermody Properties - 794-0000

**New Horizon Campus
Industrial Park**
501 Conestoga Way
Henderson, NV 89015
217 acres

Major Tenants: Levi Strauss, Leggs,
future home of Car Country

North Park One Business Center
2191 W. Mendenhall Dr.
N. Las Vegas, NV 89031
107,500 sq. ft. opened 1995
Major Tenants: Bekins Moving &
Storage, Treadco
CB Commercial - 369-4800

Pacific Industrial
American Pacific/Gibson
Henderson, NV 89015
Major Tenants: Applied Hardcoating
Technologies
Lee & Associates - 369-9012

Palms Airport Center
Palms Airport Dr./Paradise Rd.
Las Vegas, NV 89119
23 acres, 371,000 sq. ft.; build to suit up
to 150,000 sq. ft.
Major Tenants: Kleindfelder, International
Gaming Technology, AC Coin, Coca-Cola,
General Services Administration, Jackpot,
SRI Instruments
The Palms Business Centres - 367-3000

The Palms Business Centres
Palms North - Rancho Dr./Mead Ave.
Palms South - Industrial Rd./Tompkins
Palms III - Industrial Rd./Palms Center
Palms IV - Rigel Ave./Meade Ave.
Palms Airport - Paradise Rd./Palms Airport
Post Palms - Industrial Rd./Post Rd.
Six locations with space ranging from 400
sq. ft. to over 25,000 sq. ft. Build-to-suit
up to 600,000 sq. ft.
The Palms Business Centres - 367-3000

Park 2000
Eastern Ave. at Sunset Rd.
Las Vegas, NV 89119
120 acres, 416,778 sq. ft. opened in 1986
Major Tenants: AT&T Information
Systems, Namark Cap & Emblem Company
Ribeiro Corp. - 736-6901

Patrick Airport Park
3035-3095 Patrick Ln.
Las Vegas, NV 89120
223,000 sq. ft.
Major Tenants: Associated Business
Products, Annie the Maid, Sun Country
Airlines, Westcor
Stuart Mixer Commercial - 735-5700

Peachtree Distribution Center
Craig Rd./Losee Rd.
Las Vegas, NV
206,000 sq. ft.
Major Tenants: Val Pak
CB Commercial - 369-4800

Pecos Industrial Complex
4300 N. Pecos Rd.
Las Vegas, NV 89115
86,400 sq. ft. opened 1985
Major Tenants: Eagle Telecom, Swann
Trucking
H&L Realty & Management - 385-3226

Plaza Vegas
3301 Spring Mountain Rd.
Las Vegas, NV 89102
354,941 sq. ft. opened 1978
Major Tenants: Tango Pools, Interstate,
Blynco Valley
Ribeiro Corp. - 876-7868

BUSINESS

INDUSTRIAL PARKS

Tropicana Industrial Park, 5115 Industrial Rd., Las Vegas, NV 89118

Polaris Business Park
6065 S. Polaris Ave.
Las Vegas, NV 89118
166,400 sq. ft.
Major Tenants: National Procurement, Supreme Lobster
CB Commercial - 369-4800

Post Palms Business Center
6285 S. Industrial Rd.
Las Vegas, NV 89118
20 acres
Major Tenants: PRN Extended Group, Key Products
Palms Business Centers - 361-2444

Presidio Industrial Plaza
2716 S. Highland Dr.
Las Vegas, NV 89109
American Management Co. - 382-8339

Quail Air Control
135-195 E. Reno Ave.
Las Vegas, NV 89119
91,331 sq. ft. opened 1986
Major Tenants: Fletcher Jones, Ribeiro Corp.
Ribeiro Corp. - 798-6050

Quail Industrial Park
3550 W. Quail Ave.
Las Vegas, NV 89118
Lee & Assoc. - 739-6222

Raco
1841 E. Craig Rd.
N. Las Vegas, NV 89030
203,000 sq. ft.
CB Commercial - 369-4800

Russell Road Distribution Center
4155 Russell Rd. & 5845 Wynn Rd.
Las Vegas, NV 89118
410,000 sq. ft. opened 1996
Major Tenants: Marriot Host Services, Cable Design Technologies
Majestic Realty Co. - 896-5564

SDC Building
4170 W. Harmon Ave.
Las Vegas, NV 89103
CB Commercial - 369-4800

Sandhill Airport Park
6320 S. Sandhill Rd.
Las Vegas, NV 89120
107,400 sq. ft. opened 1996
547-1110

Sahara Commerce Center
Sahara & Lamb
Las Vegas, NV 89104
95,676 sq. ft.
Stuart Mixer Commercial - 735-5700

Sky Harbor Industrial Park
Lake Mead Dr.
Henderson, NV 89015
947 acres
Major Tenant: Levi Strauss

South Arville Center
5560-5570 S. Arville St.
Las Vegas, NV 89118
CB Commercial - 369-4800

South Pointe
6355 Windy St.
Las Vegas, NV 89119
130,000 sq. ft.
CB Commercial - 369-4800

South Tech
4305 S. Industrial Rd.
Las Vegas, NV 89103
Office, showroom, warehouse
12 acres
Major Tenants: Pitney Bowes, NCR, USA Today
USA Commercial Real Estate Group - 734-1737

Southern Nevada Industrial Center
Losee/Craig Rd.
N. Las Vegas, NV 89030
213 acres
Major Tenants: Hackney & Sons, Arcata, Clear Pack West, Matrix Electromedical, Moen, Inc. Powerlogistic, Val-Pak
Americana Commercial - 796-8888

The Spectrum of Las Vegas
71 N. Pecos Rd.
Las Vegas, NV 89101
116 acres, 487,000 sq. ft.
Major Tenants: Bank of America, Coca-Cola, Milgard, Owens Precision Fabricators
Lewis Properties - 737-9000

Spring Mountain Business Park
3949 W. Spring Mountain. Rd.
Las Vegas, NV 89102
386,000 sq. ft.
Major Tenants: H & H Enterprise, Nevada Bindery
SF Nevada LLC - 368-0046

Suncrest Commerce Center
Mary Crest Rd./Gibson
Henderson, NV 89015
157,000 sq. ft. opened 1996
CB Commercial - 369-4800

Sunset Industrial Park
740 W. Sunset Rd.
Las Vegas, NV 89119
564-2747

Tiberti Industrial Complex
4675 S. Valley View Blvd.
Las Vegas, NV 89103
Major Tenants: Lockheed, 48 Hour Mini-Blind, G & B Optics
Tiberti Co. - 382-7070

Tropicana Industrial Park
5115 Industrial Rd.
Las Vegas, NV 89118
739-7434

Valley Business Center
200 Gibson Rd.
Henderson, NV 89014
160,000 sq. ft. opened 1996
Lee & Associates - 739-6222

Valley View Commerce Center
5130 - 5230 S. Valley View Blvd.
Las Vegas, NV 89118
Major Tenants: Sanborn Sourdough Bakery
SBO Commercial - 892-7777

Valley View Industrial Center
4045 W. Harmon Ave.
Las Vegas, NV 89103
300,000 sq. ft. opened 1979
Major Tenants: Con Marle, Watkins-Sheppard, AM Reprographics
CB Commercial - 369-4800

Warm Springs Crossing
Warm Springs & Industrial Rd.
Las Vegas, NV 89118
160,000 sq. ft. opened 1997
Lee & Associates - 739-6222

WestOne Business Center
3455 & 3555 W. Reno Ave.
Las Vegas, NV 89118
174,200 sq. ft. opened 1990
Major Tenants: Al Phillips, Equinox International
CB Commercial - 369-4800

Westone Business Center
3250 & 3350 W. Ali Baba Ln.
Las Vegas, NV 89118
124,260 sq. ft. opened 1993
Major Tenants: Spicers Paper, Al Phillips
CB Commercial - 369-4816

Wind River Industrial Park
4301 S. Valley View Blvd.
Las Vegas, NV 89103
137,000 sq. ft.
CB Commercial - 369-4800

Wynn Road Business Center
5475 Wynn Rd.
Las Vegas, NV 89119
128,226 sq. ft. opened 1996
Major Tenants: Universal Brass, Unicor
CB Commercial - 369-4816

6065 Polaris
6065 Polaris Ave.
Las Vegas, NV 89118
160,000 sq. ft.
CB Commercial - 369-4800

South Tech, 4305 S. Industrial Rd., Las Vegas, NV 89103

Financial

Wells Fargo Bank was the first bank to open it's doors in Nevada, in 1860. Along the way, Wells Fargo acquired First Interstate Bank, and currently has over 50 locations in the state. Aside from its many full service facilities, Wells Fargo also has many in-store locations at Lucky's supermarkets.

State chartered banks in Nevada showed combined net earnings of $19.1 million as of June 1, 1997. These banks had assets of $3.4 billion at the end of June 1997. This drastic reduction from the year before is due to the Bank of Nevada becoming a nationally chartered bank.

Four community banks in the Las Vegas area - BankWest, Community Bank of Nevada, Commercial Bank and Las Vegas Business Bank - cater to small to mid-size businesses and professionals and provide personal service.

Obtaining cash in Las Vegas is quick and easy. Most of the major hotels and casinos have full-service ATMs in the Cirrus, Instant Teller or Plus networks as well as provide quick foreign currency exchange. Check-cashing businesses are scattered throughout the Las Vegas area, handling in and out-of-state checks and savings account access in exchange for a small fee. Personal identification is required when obtaining these services and verification is required.

Low on funds? Throughout southern Nevada and Las Vegas, pawn brokers will exchange cash for your valuable items, including but not limited to jewelry, electronics, tools and cameras. While these exchanges can be made quickly and easily, it is wise to keep in mind that pawnbrokers usually pay only 10% to 15% of the actual value of any given item. Items can be retrieved within a given time specified at the time of exchange.

BANKS & FINANCIAL INSTITUTIONS

**Department of Business
& Industry**
*State of Nevada, Financial
Institutions Division*
2501 E. Sahara Ave., Ste. 300
Las Vegas, NV 89104
486-4120
Lyndon Evans, Deputy Commissioner
Licenses and regulates state chartered
financial institutions.

BANKS

Bank of America Nevada
Headquarters
300 S. Fourth St.
Las Vegas, NV 89101
654-1000
75 branches in Nevada
George Smith, Chairman/CEO
Assets: $4,393,603,000
Deposits: $3,749,437,000
Loans: $2,538,773,000
Hours: Mon. - Thu. 9 am - 5 pm; Fri.
9 am - 6 pm
Drive-thru hours: same
Call 654-1000 (Las Vegas) to locate a
branch with Saturday hours
ATM: Versatel and Plus
Valley Bank was the successor to the
Bank of Las Vegas, which was founded in
1964 under the direction of E. Perry
Thomas and Jerome Mack. The same year
they also started Valley Bank of Reno,
merging the two in 1969 to form Valley
Bank of Nevada. Bank of America merged
with Security Pacific and acquired Valley
Capital Corporation on April 22, 1992, in
a $5 billion deal that was the largest
merger in banking history. They all now
operate as Bank of America Nevada.
Information: 654-1000
Outside Las Vegas metro area: 1-800-
388-2265

Branches
4801 W. Charleston Blvd.
Las Vegas, NV 89102

3155 N. Rancho Dr.
Las Vegas, NV 89130

4361 N. Rancho Dr.
Las Vegas, NV 89129

1140 E. Desert Inn Rd.
Las Vegas, NV 89109

4111 E. Charleston Blvd.
Las Vegas, NV 89104

4850 W. Flamingo Rd.
Las Vegas, NV 89103

3680 E. Flamingo Rd.
Las Vegas, NV 89121

4080 Spring Mountain Rd.
Las Vegas, NV 89102

3580 S. Jones Blvd.
Las Vegas, NV 89103

300 S. Decatur Blvd.
Las Vegas, NV 89107

1380 E. Flamingo Rd.
Las Vegas, NV 89119

801 N. Nellis Blvd.
Las Vegas, NV 89110

1077 E. Sahara Ave.
Las Vegas, NV 89104

3430 E. Tropicana Ave.
Las Vegas, NV 89121

1801 S. Rainbow Blvd.
Las Vegas, NV 89102

3150 N. Rainbow Blvd.
Las Vegas, NV 89130

901 S. Rancho Ln.
Las Vegas, NV 89106

5950 W. Sahara Ave.
Las Vegas, NV 89102

3828 E. Desert Inn Rd.
Las Vegas, NV 89121

835 N. Martin Luther King Blvd.
Las Vegas, NV 89106

2060 N. Las Vegas Blvd.
N. Las Vegas, NV 89030

2798 N. Green Valley Pkwy.
Henderson, NV 89014

107 Water St.
Henderson, NV 89015

8667 E. Windmill Pkwy.
Henderson, NV 89014

900 Nevada Hwy.
Boulder City, NV 89005

Bank of America, 2595 Fremont St., Las Vegas, NV 89104

4290 S. Rainbow Blvd.
Las Vegas, NV 89103

8581 W. Lake Mead Blvd.
Las Vegas, NV 89128

2595 Fremont St.
Las Vegas, NV 89104

4800 W. Tropicana Ave.
Las Vegas, NV 89103

4795 S. Maryland Pkwy.
Las Vegas, NV 89119

101 Convention Center Dr.
Las Vegas, NV 89109

6900 Westcliff Dr.
Las Vegas, NV 89128

2200 E. Warm Springs Rd.
Las Vegas, NV 89119

2254 S. Nellis Blvd.
Las Vegas, NV 89122

Vons Supermarket Branches
Hours: Mon. - Fri. 9 am - 7 pm; Sat.
9 am - 6 pm; Sun. noon - 5 pm
ATM: Versatel and Plus

2254 S. Nellis Blvd.
Las Vegas, NV 89104

2500 E. Desert Inn Rd.
Las Vegas, NV 89121

3325 E. Russell Rd.
Las Vegas, NV 89120

4610 W. Sahara Ave.
Las Vegas, NV 89102

4854 Lone Mountain Rd.
Las Vegas, NV 89031

1061 W. Owens Ave.
Las Vegas, NV 89102

605 Stephanie St.
Henderson, NV 89014

6000 W. Cheyenne Blvd.
Las Vegas, NV 89108

2667 E. Windmill Pkwy.
Henderson, NV 89014

BankWest of Nevada
3500 W. Sahara Ave.
Las Vegas, NV 89102
248-4200
Larry Woodrum, Pres.
Assets: $138,209,000
Deposits: $126,921,000
Loans: $97,243,000
Hours: Mon. - Fri. 9 am - 5 pm
BankWest provides personalized service
to small businesses and professionals.

California Federal Bank
398 S. Decatur Blvd.
Las Vegas, NV 89107
1-800-843-2265
Carl Webb, Pres.
Hours: Mon. - Thu. 9 am - 4 pm; Friday
9 am - 5:30 pm
ATM: Cirrus and Star

Branches
2891 N. Green Valley Pkwy.
Henderson, NV 89014

3990 S. Maryland Pkwy.
Las Vegas, NV 89119

Citibank*
Wilfried Jackson, Pres.
Assets: $11,986,179,000
Deposits: $879,009,000
Loans: $103,092,000
Hours: Mon. - Thu. 9 am - 5 pm; Fri.
9 am - 6 pm; Sat. 9 am - 1 pm
ATM: Star and Plus
Regional credit card center is located in
Nevada at Summerlin.
Visa & MC assistance: 1-800-950-5114
Savings and Checking: 1-800-756-7047
Customer Service: 1-800-756-7047
*Nevada retail activities only, except
total assets.

Consumer Banking Branches
8701 W. Sahara Ave.
Las Vegas, NV 89117
228-2500

3900 Paradise Rd.
Las Vegas, NV 89109
796-3030

4065 S. Jones Blvd.
Las Vegas, NV 89103
364-5664

4110 S. Maryland Pkwy.
Las Vegas, NV 89119
734-3106

2215 N. Rampart Blvd.
Las Vegas, NV 89128
363-8488

Commercial Bank
2820 W. Charleston Blvd.
Las Vegas, NV 89102
258-9990
John S. Gaynor, President
Assets: $69,322,000
Deposits: $59,696,000
Loans: $37,097,000
Hours: Mon. - Thu. 9 am - 4 pm; Fri.
9 am - 5 pm
Drive-thru: Mon. - Fri. 7:30 am - 5:30 pm

Community Bank of Nevada
1400 S. Rainbow Blvd.
Las Vegas, NV 89102
878-0700
Edward Jamison, Pres.
Assets: $90,768,000
Deposits: $131,303,000
Loans: $57,753,000
Hours: Mon. - Thu. 9 am - 5 pm; Fri.
9 am - 6 pm; Sat. 9 am - 1 pm
Serves small and mid-sized businesses.

Continental National Bank
(See First Security Bank of Nevada)

First Republic Savings Bank
2510 S. Maryland Pkwy.
Las Vegas, NV 89109
792-2200
James Baumberger, Pres./CEO
Assets: $2,140,506,000
Deposits: $1,353,355,000
Loans: $1,919,804,000
Hours: Mon. - Fri. 9 am - 5 pm; Sat.
10 am - 1 pm

Branch
6700 W. Charleston Blvd.
Las Vegas, NV 89102
880-3700
Hours: Mon. - Fri. 9 am - 5 pm

First Security Bank of Nevada
Headquarters
530 Las Vegas Blvd. S.
Las Vegas, NV 89101
David J. Smith, Pres./CEO
Assets: $467,304,000
Deposits: $431,669,000
Loans: $243,521,000
Hours: Mon. - Thu. 9 am - 4 pm; Fri.
9 am - 9 pm
Drive-thru: Mon. - Thu. 8 am - 4:30 pm;
Fri. 9 am - 6 pm
ATM: None
Information: 251-1100
Locally owned bank serving professionals and small and medium-sized businesses. First Security acquired Nevada Community Bank in 1993 and Continental National Bank and American Bank of Commerce in 1997.

Branches
4813 S. Eastern Ave.
Las Vegas, NV 89119

4950 W. Flamingo Rd.
Las Vegas, NV 89103

3340 W. Sahara Ave.
Las Vegas, NV 89112
(no drive-thru)

2925 S. Rainbow Blvd.
Las Vegas, NV 89102

701 N. Valle Verde Dr.
Henderson, NV 89014

770 E. Warm Springs Rd.
Las Vegas, NV 89119

1234 W. Sahara Ave.
Las Vegas, NV 89102

4050 Losee Rd.
N. Las Vegas, NV 89030

1690 E. Flamingo Rd.
Las Vegas, NV 89119

4425 Spring Mountain Rd.
Las Vegas, NV 89102

2980 W. Sahara Ave.
Las Vegas, NV 89102

727 S. 9th St.
Las Vegas, NV 89101

Las Vegas Business Bank
Al Alvarez, Pres.
Total Assets: $33,712,000
Deposits: $28,209,000
Loans: $19,256,000
Hours: Monday - Friday 9 am - 5 pm
Branch Hours: Mon. - Thu. 9 am - 4:30 pm;
Fri. 9 am - 6 pm
Drive-thru: Mon. - Thu. 9 am - 5 pm; Fri.
9 am - 6 pm
Serves small and mid-sized businesses.

Branches
3885 S. Maryland Pkwy.
Las Vegas, NV 89119
794-0070

6085 W. Twain Ave.
Las Vegas, NV 89103
220-3302

Nevada State Bank
Headquarters & Main Office
201 S. 4th St.
Las Vegas, NV 89101
383-4193
33 branches statewide
Roy Simmons, Chairman
George B. Hoffman, Pres.
Subsidiary of Zions Bancorporation
Assets: $567,745,000
Deposits: $500,498,000
Loans: $276,185,000
ATM: Star, Plus, Reddi-Access
Information: 383-0009
Reddi-Response: 1-800-462-3555
Acquired Sun State Bank in October 1997

Branches
3345 S. Maryland Pkwy.
Las Vegas, NV 89109
737-7006

3480 W. Sahara Ave.
Las Vegas, NV 89102
248-6417

6100 Spring Mountain Rd.
Las Vegas, NV 89102
367-8390

4970 E. Tropicana Ave.
Las Vegas, NV 89121
898-8730

2017 N. Nellis Blvd.
Las Vegas, NV 89115
438-2231

4240 W. Flamingo Rd.
Las Vegas, NV 89103
364-2440

9454 Del Webb Blvd.
Las Vegas, NV 89134
254-5959

4343 E. Sunset Rd.
Henderson, NV 89014
383-0009

1027 Nevada Hwy.
Boulder City, NV 89005
293-7682

Smith's Food Locations
Hours: Mon. - Sat. 10 am - 8 pm; Sun.
noon - 5 pm

3850 E. Flamingo Rd.
Las Vegas, NV 89121
458-4715

2540 S. Maryland Pkwy.
Las Vegas, NV 89109
369-5609

6130 W. Tropicana Ave.
Las Vegas, NV 89103
873-2834

232 N. Jones Blvd.
Las Vegas, NV 89107
258-2902

450 N. Nellis Blvd.
Las Vegas, NV 89110
453-2067

4440 N. Rancho Dr.
Las Vegas, NV 89130
658-8441

2211 N. Rampart Blvd.
Las Vegas, NV 89134
256-5003

8555 W. Sahara Ave.
Las Vegas, NV 89117
228-1597

2255 Las Vegas Blvd. N.
N. Las Vegas, NV 89030
649-4496

4602 E. Sunset Rd.
Henderson, NV 89014
456-3776

830 S. Boulder Hwy.
Henderson, NV 89015
566-8862

Norwest Banks
John Campbell, Pres.
Customer Service: 1-800-331-1816
Information: 765-3310
Outside Las Vegas: 1-800-792-0110
Acquired Primerit Bank for $175 million in July 1996. Norwest has adopted interstate banking rules; unable to break down figures by state.

Branches
1775 N. Decatur Blvd.
Las Vegas, NV 89108
765-2800

2625 E. Desert Inn Rd.
Las Vegas, NV 89121
765-2700

4016 S. Rainbow Blvd.
Las Vegas, NV 89103
765-2375

3104 N. Rainbow Blvd.
Las Vegas, NV 89108
765-2250

2283 Rampart Blvd.
Las Vegas, NV 89128
765-2100

910 W. Owens Ave.
Las Vegas, NV 89106
765-2850

9325 W. Sahara Ave.
Las Vegas, NV 89117
765-2000

6120 W. Tropicana Ave.
Las Vegas, NV 89103
765-2300

21 Marion Dr.
Las Vegas, NV 89110
765-1600

3333 E. Tropicana Ave.
Las Vegas, NV 89121
765-2550

1000 Nevada Hwy.
Boulder City, NV 89005
765-2900

546 S. Boulder Hwy.
Henderson, NV 89015
765-2600

1411 W. Sunset Rd.
Las Vegas, NV 89119
765-2500

2331 N. Green Valley Pkwy.
Henderson, NV 89014
765-2525

3300 W. Sahara Ave.
Las Vegas, NV 89102
765-3009
Hours: Mon. - Thu. 9 am - 5 pm; Fri.
9 am - 6 pm; Sat. 10 am - 1 pm
Drive-thru: Mon. - Thu. 8 am - 4:30 pm;
Fri. 8 am - 6 pm

1700 E. Charleston Blvd.
Las Vegas, NV 89104
765-1950
Hours: Mon. - Fri. 9 am - 6 pm
Drive-thru: same

4800 W. Charleston Blvd.
Las Vegas, NV 89102
765-1850
Hours: Mon. - Fri. 9 am - 6 pm; Sat.
9 am - 1 pm
Drive-thru: same

201 Las Vegas Blvd. S.
Las Vegas, NV 89101
765-1900
Hours: Mon. - Fri. 9 am - 6 pm
No drive-thru

8190 W. Sahara Ave.
Las Vegas, NV 89117
765-1800
Hours: Mon. - Fri. 9 am - 6 pm; Sat.
9 am - 1 pm
Drive-thru: same

BANKS & FINANCIAL INSTITUTIONS

3900 Meadows Ln.
Las Vegas, NV 89107
765-2200
Hours: Mon. - Fri. 9 am - 7 pm; Sat.
9 am - 1 pm
Drive-thru: same

3726 E. Flamingo Rd.
Las Vegas, NV 89121
765-2575
Hours: Mon. - Fri. 9 am - 6 pm
No drive-thru

103 S. Rainbow Blvd.
Las Vegas, NV 89128
765-1875
Hours: Mon.y - Fri. 9 am - 7 pm; Sat.
9 am - 1 pm
Drive-thru: same

6145 Spring Mountain Rd.
Las Vegas, NV 89102
765-2350
Hours: Mon. - Fri. 9 am - 7 pm; Sat.
9 am - 1 pm
Drive-thru: same

9350 W. Lake Mead Blvd.
Las Vegas, NV 89134
765-2150
Hours: Mon. - Fri. 9 am - 6 pm; Sat.
9 am - 1 pm

2690 E. Sunset Rd.
Las Vegas, NV 89120
765-1500
Hours: Mon. - Fri. 9 am - 7 pm; Sat.
9 am - 1 pm
Drive-thru: same

3745 S. Maryland Pkwy.
Las Vegas, NV 89119
765-2750
Hours: Mon. - Fri. 9 am - 7 pm; Sat.
9 am - 1 pm
No drive-thru

5140 E. Bonanza Rd.
Las Vegas, NV 89110
765-1975
Hours: Mon. - Fri. 9 am - 7 pm; Sat. 9
am - 1 pm
Drive-thru: same

2025 Civic Center Dr.
N. Las Vegas, NV 89030
765-1700
Hours: Mon. - Fri. 9 am - 6 pm; Sat.
9 am - 1 pm.
No drive-thru

Pioneer Citizens Bank of Nevada
Main Office
230 Las Vegas Blvd. S.
Las Vegas, NV 89101
382-3440
Louis Capurro, Chairman
William E. Martin, Pres.
Assets: $630,086,000
Deposits: $562,209,000
Loans: $357,204,000
Hours: Mon. - Thu. 9 am - 4 pm; Fri.
9 am - 5:30 pm
Drive-thru: Mon. - Thu. 8:30 am - 5 pm;
Friday 8:30 am - 5:30 pm
ATM: Plus and Starr
Information: 731-2222 1-888-605-7475

Branches
4170 S. Maryland Pkwy.
Las Vegas, NV 89119
734-5710

4949 Spring Mountain Rd.
Las Vegas, NV 89102
873-4837

8400 W. Lake Mead Blvd.
Las Vegas, NV 89128
363-1999

4001 E. Sunset Rd.
Henderson, NV 89014
454-1121

U. S. Bank
Southern Nevada Headquarters
2300 W. Sahara Ave.
Las Vegas, NV 89102
386-3611
13 Southern Nevada branches
Peter Landis, Pres./CEO
Assets: $1,144,657,000
Deposits: $1,042,671,000
Loans: $726,590,000
Hours: Mon. - Thu. 9 am - 5 pm; Fri.
9 am - 6 pm; Sat. 9 am - 1 pm
ATM: UBANK
The Portland, Oregon-based bank expanded into Nevada in 1992 by buying 30 branches from Bank of America Nevada/Valley and Security Pacific, twelve of which are in the Las Vegas area. This created the third largest bank system in Nevada. U. S. Bank's Nevada headquarters are in Reno.

The June 1995 issue of Money magazine rated U. S. Bank the best in Nevada in a survey of 428 banks in the United States with assets over $300 million. The ranking cited U. S. Bank's soundness, safety, free checking, home banking features and the banks willingness to lend money to its customers.

Branches
3681 S. Maryland Pkwy.
Las Vegas, NV 89119
737-7127

9004 W. Sahara Ave.
Las Vegas, NV 89117
254-8090
Hours: Mon. - Thu. 9 am - 4:30 pm; Fri.
9 am - 5:30 pm; Sat. 9 am - 1 pm
ATM location

801 E. Charleston Blvd.
Las Vegas, NV 89104
387-1919

2135 Decatur Blvd.
Las Vegas, NV 89102
364-4888

4320 E. Tropicana Ave.
Las Vegas, NV 89121
434-2225

5940 W. Flamingo Rd.
Las Vegas, NV 89103
386-3780
Hours: Sat. 9 am - 4 pm
ATM location

4550 E. Sunset Rd.
Henderson, NV 89014
451-1020
Hours: Sat. 9 am - 1 pm
ATM location

65 W. Lake Mead Dr.
Henderson, NV 89015
565-8987

948 N. Nellis Blvd.
Las Vegas, NV 89110
438-4690
Hours: Sat. 9 am - 1 pm
ATM location

2300 W. Sahara Ave.
Las Vegas, NV 89102
386-3658

2200 E. Lake Mead Blvd.
N. Las Vegas, NV 89030
657-8224

6175 W. Sahara Ave.
Las Vegas, NV 89102
362-3990
Hours: Mon. - Thu. 9 am - 5 pm; Fri.
9 am - 6 pm
ATM location

Albertson's Supermarket branches
Hours: Mon. - Fri. 10 am - 7 pm; Sat.
10 am - 4 pm; Sun. noon - 4 pm

8570 W. Lake Mead Blvd.
Las Vegas, NV 89129
254-7450

1955 N. Nellis Blvd.
Las Vegas, NV 89115
459-8660

3864 W. Sahara Ave.
Las Vegas, NV 89102
227-3355

2475 E. Tropicana Ave.
Las Vegas, NV 89121
454-5577

3160 N. Rainbow Blvd.
Las Vegas, NV 89108
658-3601

4821 W. Craig Rd.
Las Vegas, NV 89130
645-7203

1421 N. Jones Blvd.
Las Vegas, NV 89108
647-2077

Wells Fargo Bank
Headquarters
3800 Howard Hughes Pkwy.
Las Vegas, NV 89109
1-800-777-3000
Paul Haven, CEO
Wells Fargo acquired First Interstate. 53 full service locations in Nevada - 24 in southern Nevada. Wells Fargo has adopted interstate banking rules; unable to break down figures by state
Branch hours: Mon. - Thu. 9 am - 4 pm;
Fri. 9 am - 5:30 pm or 6 pm
Drive-thru: 9 am - 5 pm; except
Sahara/Rainbow, Spring Mountain/Valley

View, Sunset/Eastern, Pecos/Wigwam, and Civic Center/Lake Mead branch in North Las Vegas 7 am - 7 pm
ATM: 381 in Nevada; Cirrus, The Exchange, Star, Plus, Armed Forces Financial Network
Day & Night Bank by Phone: 1-800-869-2554

Las Vegas Main Office
300 Carson Ave.
Las Vegas, NV 89101

Branches
5757 Wayne Newton Blvd.
Las Vegas, NV 89119

4578 Boulder Hwy.
Las Vegas, NV 89121

1501 E. Charleston Blvd.
Las Vegas, NV 89104

791 N. Nellis Blvd.
Las Vegas, NV 89110

1700 S. Main St.
Las Vegas, NV 89104

3433 S. Maryland Pkwy.
Las Vegas, NV 89109

Nellis AFB
4325 N. Washington Blvd.
Las Vegas, NV 89191

2501 S. Rainbow Blvd.
Las Vegas, NV 89102

3255 E. Sahara Ave.
Las Vegas, NV 89104

3755 Spring Mountain Rd.
Las Vegas, NV 89102

3555 S. Jones Blvd.
Las Vegas, NV 89103

9410 W. Lake Mead Blvd.
Las Vegas, NV 89108

2420 E. Sunset Rd.
Las Vegas, NV 89120
Saturday hours: 9 am - 1 pm

4720 S. Eastern Ave.
Las Vegas, NV 89119

801 N. Rancho Dr.
Las Vegas, NV 89106

6110 W Cheyenne Ave.
Las Vegas, NV 89108

4595 W. Charleston Blvd.
Las Vegas, NV 89102
Saturday hours: 9 am - 1 pm

2103 Civic Center Dr.
N. Las Vegas, NV 89030
385-8011
Saturday hours: 9 am - 1 pm

112 S. Water St.
Henderson, NV 89015
564-2552

101 Pecos Rd.
Henderson, NV 89014

2196 Olympic Ave.
Henderson, NV 89014
Hours: Mon. - Fri. 9 am - 7 pm; Sat.
9 am - 6 pm; Sun. noon - 4 pm

412 Nevada Hwy.
Boulder City, NV 89005
293-1232

924 W. Owens Ave.
Las Vegas, NV 89106
Handles no cash; only loans, credit
cards, IRAs and CDs

Lucky In-Store Branches
Hours: Mon. - Fri. 9 am - 7 pm; Sat.
9 am - 6 pm; Sun. noon - 4 pm

4120 S. Rainbow Blvd.
Las Vegas, NV 89103

2835 S. Nellis Blvd.
Las Vegas, NV 89121

1300 E. Flamingo Rd.
Las Vegas, NV 89119

2021 E. Lake Mead Blvd.
Las Vegas, NV 89115

2400 E. Bonanza Rd.
Las Vegas, NV 89101

2747 S. Maryland Pkwy.
Las Vegas, NV 89109

4500 E. Tropicana Ave.
Las Vegas, NV 89121

4801 W. Spring Mountain Rd.
Las Vegas, NV 89102

1001 S. Rainbow Blvd.
Las Vegas, NV 89128

1200 S. Decatur Blvd.
Las Vegas, NV 89102

1324 W. Craig Rd.
Las Vegas, NV 89130

1760 E. Charleston Blvd.
Las Vegas, NV 89104

2300 E. Tropicana Ave.
Las Vegas, NV 89119

2550 S. Fort Apache Rd.
Las Vegas, NV 89117

3736 E. Desert Inn Rd.
Las Vegas, NV 89121

4420 E. Bonanza Rd.
Las Vegas, NV 89110

5975 W. Tropicana Ave.
Las Vegas, NV 89103

610 N. Nellis Blvd.
Las Vegas, NV 89110

6140 W. Lake Mead Blvd.
Las Vegas, NV 89108

6850 W. Spring Mountain Rd.
Las Vegas, NV 89102

7271 S. Eastern Ave.
Las Vegas, NV 89119

8350 W. Cheyenne Ave.
Las Vegas, NV 89129

2851 Green Valley Pkwy.
Henderson, NV 89014

724 Boulder Hwy.
Henderson, NV 89015

Drive-ups
990 Sierra Vista Dr.
Las Vegas, NV 89117

2460 E. Tompkins Ave.
Las Vegas, NV 89101

Wells Fargo Bank

In 1860, Wells Fargo Express &
Banking Compnay opened the
state's first bank in Virginia City.

CREDIT UNIONS

Credit unions are member-owned, not-
for-profit financial cooperatives.

Aerospace Credit Union
2915 W. Charleston Blvd.
Las Vegas, NV 89102
877-4660
Mike Johnson, Pres.
Hours: Mon. - Fri. 8 am - 5 pm
Members: 2,500
Mostly engineers and electrical workers.

Bally's Federal Credit Union
(See WestStar Federal)

**Boulder Dam Federal
Credit Union**
530 Ave. G
Boulder City, NV 89005
293-7777
Bill Ferrence, Pres.
Hours: Mon. - Thu. 9:30 am - 5 pm; Fri.
9:30 am - 6 pm
Members: 21,500
Full service; open to people who live or
work in Boulder City.

Clark County Credit Union
5 branches in Nevada
Main Office
2625 N. Tenaya Way
Las Vegas, NV 89128
228-2228
Wayne Tew, Pres.
Hours: Mon. & Fri. 9 am - 6 pm; Tue. -
Thu. 9 am - 5:00 pm
ATM: Star and Plus
Information: 228-2228
Outside Las Vegas: 1-800-748-6885
Phone Center: Sat. 8 am - 6 pm
Members: 22,655
Full service; open to county and med-
ical employees.

Branches
401 S. Third St.
Las Vegas, NV 89101
367-4339

3780 E. Flamingo Rd.
Las Vegas, NV 89121
367-4339

202 W. Pacific Ave.
Henderson, NV 89015
367-4339

3100 W. Sahara Ave., Ste. 208
Las Vegas, NV 89102
367-4339

Clark County Credit Union

Cumorah Credit Union
3 branches in Nevada
Anthony Mook, Pres.
ATM: Plus
Members: over 8,000
Full service; open to LDS only.

Branches
3990 S. Eastern Ave.
Las Vegas, NV 89119
735-2181
Hours: Mon. - Thu. 9 am - 5 pm; Fri.
9 am - 5:30

1725 S. Rainbow Blvd., Ste. 12
Las Vegas, NV 89102
242-6598
Hours: Tue. - Thu. 9 am - 5 pm; Fri. 9
am - 5:30 pm; Sat. 8:30 am - 2:30 pm
No drive thru

1905 Green Valley Pkwy.
Henderson, NV 89014
263-8753
Hours: Tue. - Fri. 9 am - 5 pm; Sat.
8:30 am - 2:30 pm
Drive-thru: Mon. - Thu. 8:30 am - 5:30 pm;
Fri. 8:30 am - 6 pm; Sat. 8:30 am - 3 pm

Ensign Federal Credit Union
218 N. 15th St.
Las Vegas, NV 89101
382-5010
Norman Gates, Pres.

Hours: Mon. & Fri. 7 am - 6 pm; Tue. -
Thu. 8:30 am - 5 pm
Drive-thru: same
ATM: None
Members: 7,000
Full service; open to LDS only.

IBEW Plus Credit Union
4315 E. Bonanza Rd.
Las Vegas, NV 89110
452-4445
Rita Allyene, Mgr.
Hours: Mon. - Thu. 9 am - 5:30 pm; Fri.
9 am - 6:30 pm; Sat. 9 am - 4 pm
Members: Approximately 6,000
Electrical workers and other local unions.

Branch
6378 W. Sahara Ave.
Las Vegas, NV 89102
871-4746

Kolob Credit Union
810 S. Boulder Hwy.
Henderson, NV 89015
564-2646
Kent Rhees, Mgr.
Hours: Mon. - Thu. 9 am - 5:30 pm; Fri.
9 am - 6 pm
ATM: Co-op, Star, Explore, Plus, Amex,
Cirrus, Visa, MC & Discover

Members: 4,100
Full service; open to LDS or Kerr
McGee employees or relatives, Basic
Management, Chamber of Commerce
members, Basic High School students
or if you live or work in Henderson.

Las Vegas Federal Credit Union
3100 W. Sahara Ave., Ste. 206
Las Vegas, NV 89102
251-8011
Ron Helvie, Pres./ Mgr.
Hours: Mon. - Fri. 9:30 - 5 pm
No ATM
Members: 900
Open to Musician's Union & various
small businesses.

**Las Vegas U.P. Employees
Federal Credit Union**
320 N. 10th St.
Las Vegas, NV 89101
382-9688
Sam Villafana, Pres.
Hours: Tue. - Fri. 9 am - 5 pm
Members: 1,700
Open to Union Pacific Railroad and
Plaza Hotel employees and families.

Network Federal Credit Union
Main Office
3100 W. Sahara Ave., Ste. 115
Las Vegas, NV 89102
873-7300
Roger Ballard, Pres.
Hours: Mon. - Fri. 9:30 am - 5:30 pm
ATM: Star, Pulse, Plus, Instanteller,
Cirrus, INN
Information: 873-7300
Members: 18,000
Full service; open to employees and
families of various employers.

Branches
2699 N. Tenaya Way
Las Vegas, NV 89128
873-7300

3230 E. Flamingo Rd., Ste. 6
Las Vegas, NV 89121
873-7300

FINANCIAL

CREDIT UNIONS

Nevada Federal Credit Union
Corporate Office
2645 S. Mojave Rd.
Las Vegas, NV 89121
457-1000 1-800-388-3000
(10 branches in southern Nevada)
Brad Beal, Pres.
Hours: Mon. - Thu. 9 am - 5 pm; Fri.
9 am - 6 pm
ATM: Star, Cirrus, Armed Forces
Financial Network
Information: 457-1000
Members: 75,000
Full service; open to active or retired
military, UNLV students or graduates
thereof, 55 or older, various casinos,
businesses and churches.

Branches
Express Office
5000 E. Bonanza Rd., Ste. M
Las Vegas, NV 89110

3630 E. Tropicana Ave.
Las Vegas, NV 89121

555 N. Maryland Pkwy.
Las Vegas, NV 89101

4251 Griffiss Ave.
Nellis AFB
Las Vegas, NV 89191

3100 W. Sahara Ave., Ste. 102
Las Vegas, NV 89102

Express Office
6010 W. Cheyenne Ave.
Las Vegas, NV 89108

2645 S. Mojave Rd.
Las Vegas, NV 89121

853 S. Rainbow Blvd., Ste. 5-10
Las Vegas, NV 89128

1090 W. Sunset Rd.
Henderson. NV 89014

Silver State Schools
Federal Credit Union
Main Office
4221 S. McLeod Dr.
Las Vegas, NV 89121
6 branches in Nevada
J. Alan Pughes, Pres.
Hours: 11 am - 2 pm
ATM: Plus, Star
Information: 733-8820
Members: 35,000
Full service; open to Clark County
School District, UNLV & CCSN employ-
ees & families and some stakes of the
Mormon Church.

Branches
6830 W. Sahara Ave.
Las Vegas, NV 89102

5910 W. Lake Mead Blvd.
Las Vegas, NV 89108

169 N. Nellis Blvd.
Las Vegas, NV 89110

657 N. Stephanie Ave., Ste. C7
Henderson, NV 89014
Hours: Mon. - Fri. 9:30 am - 6 pm

Green Valley High School
460 Arroyo Grande Blvd.
Henderson, NV 89014

Sonepco
3100 W. Sahara Ave.
Las Vegas, NV 89102
871-0977
Sue Longson, Pres.
Hours: Mon. 10 am - 5:30 pm; Tue. - Fri.
9 am - 5:30 pm
Members: 3,500
Open to employees and families of
Nevada Power Co.

SWG Federal Credit Union
5241 Spring Mountain Rd.
Las Vegas, NV 89102
876-7229
Shirley Shutt, Mgr.
Hours: Mon. - Fri. 10 am - 5 pm
Members: 2,500
Open to employees and families of
Southwest Gas.

Stage Employees
Local 720
3000 S. Valley View Blvd.
Las Vegas, NV 89102
873-3450
Enrico Grippo, Pres.
Hours: Mon. - Fri. 10 am - 4:30 pm
Members: 1,229
Open to members and family of union.

USA Federal Credit Union
2790 E. Flamingo Rd.
Las Vegas, NV 89121
732-1552
Ed Effey, Pres.
Hours: Mon. - Fri. 9 am - 5 pm
Members: 600
Mostly military & retired military

US Lime Employees Federal
Credit Union
138 Magnesium St.
Henderson, NV 89015
564-1360
Hours: Mon. - Fri. 4:30 pm - 8:30 pm
Members: 150
Savings & loan only; open to Chemstar
employees and families.

Westside Federal Credit Union
418 Madison Ave.
Las Vegas, NV 89106
648-4626
David Yancy, Pres.

Hours: Mon. - Fri. 10 am - 6 pm; Sat. 9
am - noon
ATM: none
Members: 3,400
Savings & loan; open to everyone.

Weststar Federal Credit Union
3 branches in Nevada
Don Paulson, Pres.
ATM: Exchange, Interlink, Plus
Information: 791-4777
Members: 23,704
Full service; employees and families of
Arizona Charlie's, Fletcher Jones,
Howard Hughes Prop., State of Nevada,
UNLV, MGM, Bally's and others.

Branches
4639 Faircenter Pkwy., Ste. F
Las Vegas, NV 89102
Hours: Mon. - Thu. 9 am - 5 pm; Fri.
9 am - 6 pm

110 E. Harmon Ave.
Las Vegas, NV 89109
Hours: Mon. - Thu. 9 am - 5 pm; Fri.
9 am - 6 pm
Drive-Thru: Mon. & Fri. 7:30 am - 6 pm;
Tue. - Thu. 8 am - 6 pm

3760 Pecos-Mcleod
Las Vegas, NV 89121
Hours: Mon. and Fri. 9 am - 5:30 pm;
Tue. - Thu. 9 am - 5 pm

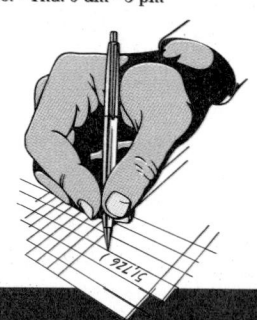

INVESTMENT

The State Securities Division of
Commerce is responsible for the regulation and licensing of all investment
houses, stockbrokers and investment
counselors in Nevada. Before investing
with a firm or individual, you may
inquire with this department to check
for previous complaints and the legiti-
macy and length of time in business.

Secretary of
State Securities Division
555 E. Washington Ave.
Las Vegas, NV 89101
486-2440
Investor Hotline: 1-800-758-6440
Donald Reis, Deputy Secretary of State
Set up by the Secretary of State, the
hotline is designed to give investors a
chance to report misconduct involving
securities and to check out new investment offerings and advisers.

Dean Witter Reynolds
3800 Howard Hughes Pkwy.
Ste. 800
Las Vegas, NV 89109
737-7275
Gary Abraham, Branch Mgr.
Full service brokerage.

1645 Village Center Dr.
Las Vegas, NV 89134
228-4083
Allan Duff, Branch Mgr.

701 N. Green Valley Pkwy.
Henderson, NV 89014
270-8880
Alan Mann, Branch Mgr.

Edward Jones & Co.
3505 E. Flamingo Rd., Ste. 6
Las Vegas, NV 89121-5033
436-7777
Robert K. Peddicord, Investment Rep.

2660 S. Rainbow Blvd. Ste. J-107
Las Vegas, NV 89102-5147
221-9222
Linda Schultz, Investment Rep.

404 Nevada Hwy.
Boulder City, NV 89005
294-3050
Wendell W. Whitman, Investment Rep.

LPL Financial Services
1601 E. Flamingo Rd., Ste. 18
Las Vegas, NV 89119-5278
791-5622
Ken & Linda Parker, Branch & Office Mgrs.

Merrill Lynch
Pierce Fenner & Smith
Jan Krug, Resident VP
Full service, investment and insurance.

2300 W. Sahara Ave., Ste. 1200
Las Vegas, NV 89102
227-7000

1645 Village Center Dr., Ste. 271
Las Vegas, NV 89134
228-2272

PaineWebber
3800 Howard Hughes Pkwy., Ste. 1200
Las Vegas, NV 89109
731-1121
Randy Stewart, Branch Mgr.
Full service brokerage.

Prudential Securities Inc.
3763 Howard Hughes Pkwy., Ste. 330
Las Vegas, NV 89109
796-0135
Kevin Kitchin, Branch Mgr.
Full service brokerage.

Shearson Lehman Brothers
3800 Howard Hughes Pkwy., Ste. 1100
Las Vegas, NV 89109
792-2000
Theodore Schlazer, Investment Executive

Smith Barney
3800 Howard Hughes Pkwy., Ste. 1100
Las Vegas, NV 89109
792-2000
Joe Polanski, VP, Resident Mgr.
Full service brokerage.

Stratton Investors
Financial Services
3690 S. Eastern Ave., Ste. 200
Las Vegas, NV 89109
732-1448
Gary W. Stratton, Pres.

Signal / USA
3900 Paradise Rd.
Las Vegas, NV 89109
734-8721
David Berkowitz, Pres.
Full service brokerage.

OBTAINING CASH

WIRE SERVICE

Western Union
Credit card money transfer MC, Visa:
1-800-225-5227
Telegram and Mailgram services:
1-800-325-6000
For the nearest agent: 1-800-325-6000

Barbary Coast Hotel · Strip
3595 Las Vegas Blvd. S.
Las Vegas, NV 89109
731-1876

The Telegraph Office · Downtown
517 Fremont St.
Las Vegas, NV 89101
385-3593
Send or receive funds; open 24 hours.

There are many other locations throughout the Las Vegas area where you can send or receive telegrams or Money Transfers; not all locations do all services. Money can be sent to most casino cages, but money can't be sent out from the casino.
Smith's Food and Drug Centers and Mail Boxes Etc., both with locations throughout Las Vegas, are Western Union agents. Consult the white pages of the phone book or call the toll free number listed for the location nearest you.

American Express Moneygram
1-800-926-9400

Excalibur
3850 Las Vegas Blvd. S.
Las Vegas, NV 89109
798-7020
Can receive money, but cannot wire out. Transactions at casino cage.

Greyhound · Trailways · Downtown
200 S. Main St.
Las Vegas, NV 89101
384-9561

Mutual of Omaha Travelers
McCarran Airport ticket counter
5757 Wayne Newton Blvd.
Las Vegas, NV 89119
261-5650
Other locations throughout Las Vegas including all Smith's Food and Drug Centers. Check the Yellow Pages or call the toll free number above for the nearest location.

CHECK CASHING

Local Checks
When opening a new checking account with other than cash, a hold may be put on your account before the funds are available for withdrawal.
Most businesses will only accept local personal checks with a guarantee check card. Some casinos will cash a check if you have filled out a check cashing application and have received approval.
All casinos and many bars will cash local payroll checks.

Out of State Checks
Most hotels will cash a check at the casino cashier if you are staying in the hotel and have a drivers license and major credit card. The hotels/casinos are linked to a central credit system and $500 is about the most you can cash for any single trip unless you have filled out a check cashing application in advance and they approve the limit you set for your stay in the city.

American Express Cardholders
American Express cardholders can cash personal checks for travelers checks at the American Express Offices. You can cash a check for up to $1,000 for any 7 day period with a green American Express card, $5,000 with a gold card and $10,000 with a platinum card. If you don't have a check, you can use a counter check; all you need to know is the name of your bank. The funds are charged to your checking account, not your card.

TRAVELERS CHECKS

Travelers checks can be cashed at any hotel/casino and are accepted by all businesses. If you intend to gamble, you must cash the checks at the casino cashier first, as they are not accepted at the tables. You will probably need a photo ID.

AMERICAN EXPRESS CARDMEMBER & TRAVELERS CHEQUES SERVICES

MGM Grand
3799 Las Vegas Blvd. S.
Las Vegas, NV 89109
739-8474
Foreign currency bought and sold, American Express travelers cheques, American Express Gift Cheques. Cardmembers can cash personal checks, receive replacement cards and make card payments.

Gold Coast · Cole Travel
4000 W. Flamingo Rd.
Las Vegas, NV 89103
876-1410
American Express travel service.

CHECK CASHING SERVICES

Check cashing services will cash a variety of checks, money orders and cashiers checks, and even savings account with passbook. They charge a high percentage of the face value. Check cashing services do not have cash on hand but issue you a check guaranteed by their firm which you can easily cash at a bank or casino. *(For a complete list, consult the Yellow Pages)*

AAA Check Cashing Inc.
3317 Las Vegas Blvd. S.
Las Vegas, NV 89109
732-3326
Hours: 6 am - 10 pm

American Check Exchange
4015 N. Nellis Blvd.
Las Vegas, NV 89115
644-7400
Hours: Mon. & Fri. 10am - 6pm; Tue. & Thu. 10 am - 5 pm; Sat. 10 am - 4 pm

Cash Plus
4914 Boulder Hwy.
Las Vegas, NV 89121
434-3718
Hours: Mon. - Fri. 9 am - 6 pm; Sat. 9 am - 4 pm

Courtesy Check Cashing
3265 Las Vegas Blvd. S.
Las Vegas, NV 89109
792-1370
Hours: 9 am - 10 pm

Fremont Check Cashing Service
517 Fremont St.
Las Vegas, NV 89101
382-4600
Hours: Mon. - Thu. 9 am - 10 pm; Fri.- Sat. 9 am - midnight; Sun. 9 am - 5 pm

Interstate Check Cashing
112 N. 3rd St.
Las Vegas, NV 89101
384-9880
Hours: Sun. - Thu. 9 am - 9 pm; Fri. - Sat. 9 am - 11 pm

Mail & More
2039 Civic Center Dr.
N. Las Vegas, NV 89030
649-1017
Hours: Mon. - Fri. 8:30 am - 5 pm

Nationwide Check Cashing Service
515 E. Fremont St.
Las Vegas, NV 89101
382-7227
Hours: 24 hours

Sahara Check Cashing Service
1939 Las Vegas Blvd. S.
Las Vegas, NV 89104
733-1770
Hours: Mon. - Sat. 8 am - 11:30 pm; Sun. 9 am - 9 pm

Strip Check Cashing Service
3735 Las Vegas Blvd. S.
Las Vegas, NV 89109
734-6900
Hours: 8 am - 10 pm

3041 Las Vegas Blvd. S.
Las Vegas, NV 89109
732-2541
Hours: 10 am - 6 pm

Twain Check Cashing
855 E. Twain Ave.
Las Vegas, NV 89109
734-2425
Hours: Mon. - Fri. 9 am - 7 pm; Sat. 9 am - 4 pm
Check cashing, money orders, mail boxes, Western Union.

CREDIT CARDS

Cash advances on your MasterCard or Visa are available at all casinos, but the fee is high: about $50 for each $1,000.
Local banks will give a cash advance on certain major credit cards and the fee isn't as high.

AUTOMATIC TELLER MACHINES

All hotel/casinos, 7-11s and bank branches in Las Vegas have ATM machines. When using automatic teller machines at locations other than your bank, a $1 - $2 service charge will be charged to your account.

Plus System
1-800-THE PLUS
MasterCard, Visa, American Express - Express Cash, Discover, Plus System, INN, Instant Teller, Star Exchange, JCB Cards.

Cirrus
200 Plus System ATMs statewide

Day & Night Teller
1-800-424-7787 for locations nationwide Cirrus Day & Night teller machines statewide.

FOREIGN CURRENCY

Most hotel casinos will exchange foreign currency from major countries. They will charge a fee in addition to the actual exchange rate.

Advantage Check Cashing
4914 Boulder Hwy.
Las Vegas, NV 89121
434-3718
Hours: Mon. - Fri. 8 am - 6 pm; Sat. 9 am - 4 pm
Foreign currencies purchased.

American Express
MGM Grand
3799 Las Vegas Blvd.
Las Vegas, NV 89109
739-8474
Hours: 8 am - 6 pm
Foreign currency bought and sold, foreign traveler's checks and drafts.

Bank of America
101 Convention Center Dr.
Las Vegas, NV 89109
654-3848
Hours: Mon. - Thu. 9 am - 5 pm; Fri. 9 am - 6 pm
Foreign currencies bought and sold, foreign, travelers cheques, foreign drafts and wire service.

Foreign Money Exchange
3025 Las Vegas Blvd. S.
Suite 224
Las Vegas, NV 89109
791-3301
Hours: Mon. - Fri. 8:30 am - 5 pm
Offers free information on more than 43 countries, including daily exchange rates and currency regulations.

Mutual of Omaha/Travelex
McCarran Airport between ticket counter
5757 Wayne Newton Blvd.
Las Vegas, NV 89119
261-5650
Hours: 6 am - 9:30 pm
Exchange foreign currency; flight and travel insurance; money wiring.

Twain Check Cashing
855 E. Twain Ave.
Las Vegas, NV 89109
734-2425
Hours: Mon. - Fri. 9 am - 7 pm; Sat. 9 am - 4 pm
Foreign currency purchased.

CASINO CREDIT

Establishing a line of credit is usually done in advance of your trip and a limit is set for each visit. Contact the casino cashier's cage for more information. Upon approval, markers are issued at the gaming tables and you are given chips.

FINANCIAL

PAWNBROKERS

State law allows pawnbrokers to charge no more than 10 percent monthly interest on items in hock. There is a $5 service charge which is paid at the time of redemption. Most will hold merchandise for 120 days, longer if interest is paid. Ten to 15 percent of value of item hocked is usually given. Pawnbrokers handle jewelry, guns, cameras, coins, televisions, VCRs and anything of value.

Ace Loan Co.
215 N. 3rd St.
Las Vegas, NV 89101
384-5771
Hours: Mon. - Sat. 8:30 am - 6 pm

American Jewelry & Coin
616 Las Vegas Blvd. S.
Las Vegas, NV 89101
385-2274
Hours: Mon. - Thu. 11 am - 8 pm; Fri. & Sat. 11 am - midnight

Arrow Buy & Sell
1901 Las Vegas Blvd. N.
Las Vegas, NV 89104
399-9950
Hours: Mon. - Sat. 9 am - 6 pm

ASAP Auto Pawn
1241 N. Boulder Hwy.
Henderson, NV 89015
565-5626
Hours: Mon. - Sat. 9 am - 7 pm; Sun. 10 am - 4 pm

Auto Pawn
6250 Mountain Vista St., Ste. H
Henderson, NV 89014
454-7300
Hours: Mon. - Sat. 9 am - 6 pm

Bargain Pawn
1901 Las Vegas Blvd. N.
N. Las Vegas, NV 89030
642-5958
Hours: Mon. - Sat. 9 am - 6 pm

Bobby's Jewelry & Loan
626 Las Vegas Blvd. S.
Las Vegas, NV 89101
382-2486
Hours: Mon. - Sat. 9 am - 6 pm

Boulder City Pawn Shop
1644 Nevada Hwy.
Boulder City, NV 89005
293-7296
Hours: Mon. - Fri. 9 am - 6 pm; Sat.9 am - 5 pm

Cash 4 U Pawn Shop
2216 E. Charleston Blvd.
Las Vegas, NV 89104
383-0988
Hours: 9 am - 7 pm

City Loan & Jewelry
1832 Las Vegas Blvd. N.
N. Las Vegas, NV 89030
649-8533
Hours: Mon. - Sat. 9 am - 6 pm

Desert Inn Pawn
3050 E. Desert Inn Rd.
Las Vegas, NV 89121
737-3385
Hours: Mon. - Fri. 8 am - 6 pm; Sat. 8 am - 2 pm

First Class Pawn & Jewelry
821 N. Rancho Dr.
Las Vegas, NV 89106
631-7296
Hours: 9 am - 8 pm
Drive-thru: Wed. - Sat. 4 pm - midnight; Sun. 9 am - 6 pm
Pawn, jewelry repair, TV and VCR repair.

Gold & Silver Pawn Shop
715 Las Vegas Blvd. S.
Las Vegas, NV 89101
385-7912
Hours: 24 hours

The Hock Shop Ltd.
808 Las Vegas Blvd. S.
Las Vegas, NV 89101
384-3042
Kit Jory
Hours: Mon. - Fri. 8:30 am - 2 am; Sat. - Sun. 8:30 am - 5:30 pm
Service since 1953.

John's Loan & Jewelry
128 S. 1st St.
Las Vegas, NV 89101
382-3489 383-0744
Hours: Mon. - Sat. 8:30 am - 7 pm; Sun. 8:30 am - 3:30 pm
Loans on Doulton, Lladro and Hummel figurines.

Las Vegas Auto Title Loan Store
1613 E. Sahara Ave.
Las Vegas, NV 89104
893-9800
Hours: 9 am - 5 pm; Sat. 8 am - 2 pm

Las Vegas Loan & Jewelry
114 N. 3rd St.
Las Vegas, NV 89101
385-5317
Hours: 9:30 am - 8 pm

Nevada Loan & Jewelry
1720 Las Vegas Blvd. N.
N. Las Vegas, NV 89130
649-5626
Hours: Mon. - Sat. 9 am - 6 pm

Pawn & Gun Shop
1212 N. Boulder Hwy.
Henderson, NV 89015
564-2676
Hours: Mon. - Sat.9 am - 5:45 pm
Pawn shop and 8-lane pistol range.

The Pawn Place
119 N. 4th St.
Las Vegas, NV 89101
385-7296
Hours: 9 am - 10 pm, 24 hour window

Pioneer Jewelry & Loan Co. Inc.
111 N. 1st St.
Las Vegas, NV 89101
384-2970
Hours: 24 hours
Gemologist on premise.

Poor Richards
1700 Las Vegas Blvd. N.
Las Vegas, NV 89101
649-5626
Hours: Mon. - Sat. 9 am - 6 pm

Quick Bill's
508 S. Boulder Hwy.
Henderson, NV 89015
566-5626
Hours: Mon. - Sat. 9 am - 6 pm

Sahara Pawn
2400 S. Jones Blvd., Ste. 15
Las Vegas, NV 89102
253-7296
Hours: 9 am - 7 pm

Slim's Ready Cash
114 N. 3rd St.
Las Vegas, NV 89101
382-1971
Hours: Mon. - Sat. 9 am - 6 pm

Stoney's Loan & Jewelry Co.
126 S. 1st St.
Las Vegas, NV 89101
384-2686
Hours: Mon. - Sat. 8:30 am - 5:15 pm; Sun. 8:30 am - 3:45 pm
Oldest pawn shop in Nevada

Super Pawn
11 branches in Nevada
Corporate Office
3021 Business Ln.
Las Vegas, NV 89103
735-4444
Steven A. Mack, Pres.
For information or to find the store nearest you, call 225-1000.
Hours: 9:30 am - 7 pm
Credit Cards: All major
Largest pawn shop in the world.

The Pawn Place
6250 Mountain Vista St.
Henderson, NV 89014
451-3800
Hours: 9 am - 7 pm

US Auto Pawn
1633 N. Boulder Hwy.
Henderson, NV 89015
564-6465
Hours: Mon. - Sat. 10 am - 6 pm

Government

CLARK COUNTY
HEALTH DISTRICT

CLARK COUNTY
GOVERNMENT
CENTER
500

COUNTY GOVERNMENT

Clark County government has three-fold responsibilities as a regional, city, and town entity. Clark County provides regional services to the entire county and provides city services to the residents of the unincorporated areas of the county including residents within the county limits in Las Vegas, generally the area located south of Sahara Ave. The five incorporated cities within the county are Las Vegas, North Las Vegas, Henderson, Boulder City and Mesquite. There is talk of consolidating the Las Vegas and Clark County government offices and some services in the Las Vegas area.

The City of Las Vegas encompasses 80 sq. miles and has a population of 401,703. The boundaries are north of Clark County at Sahara Ave. and south of North Las Vegas; to the east of East Las Vegas at Nellis Blvd. and west past Rancho Dr. The city stretches to the base of Mount Charleston, south to Desert Inn Rd. and north just past Kyle Canyon Rd. There are areas of land in the northwest section of the city that have not been annexed to the city.

CITY GOVERNMENT

The City of Las Vegas has operated under what is commonly known as a "council-manager" form of government since January 1, 1944. Under this form of government, by a charter adopted by the state legislature, the citizens elect four City Councilmen and a Mayor who comprise the City Council. The mayor is elected at large by all the voters of the city. Each Councilman is elected from one of four wards in the city. The Mayor and City Councilmen serve four-year terms.

The City Manager, hired by the Council, is responsible for the day-to-day operation of the city government. Below the City Manager is the City Attorney's office and two Deputy City Managers, responsible for 14 major departments within the organization. Departments are further divided into logical divisions to perform their respective functions.

Las Vegas' budget for fiscal year 1997-1998 is $483.8 million total. The general fund is $240.6 million and the non-general fund is $243.2 million.

UNITED STATES
POSTAL SERVICE
POST OFFICE
Las Vegas, NV

James C. Brown Jr.
Facility

700
FEDERAL BUREAU OF INVESTIGATION

DEPARTMENT OF MOTOR VEHICLES AND PUBLIC

LAS VEGAS
METROPOLITAN POLICE DEPARTMENT
SOUTHWEST AREA COMMAND
JERRY KELLER, SHERIFF

CITY OF LAS VEGAS
NORTHWEST NEIGHBORHOOD
SERVICES CENTER

CITY OF LAS VEGAS

City Hall
400 E. Stewart Ave.
Las Vegas, NV 89101
229-6011
Hours: Mon. - Fri. 8 am - 5 pm
Citizens Complaint Hotline - 229-6615
Web site - http://www.vegas.com/CLV

Neighborhood Services
914 W. Owens Ave.
Las Vegas, NV 89106
229-2540
Neighborhood Services Manager:
Kathy Somers
Mayor: *Jan Laverty Jones* - 229-6241
Council: *Michael McDonald*
Ward 1 - 229-6405
Council: *Arnie Adamsen*
Ward 2 - 229-6405
Council: *Gary Reese*
Ward 3 - 229-6405
Council: *Larry Brown*
Ward 4 - 229-6405

Ward 1 is generally comprised of the oldest, centralized part of the city, including the urban downtown area and the special impact area of West Las Vegas.

Ward 2 extends west of Decatur Blvd. to the base of the western mountain range. Its southern border runs along Sahara then dips to Desert Inn to include The Lakes. Its northern border runs along Vegas Dr. then extends north to Cheyenne Ave., west of U.S. 95.

Ward 3 includes the land west of Nellis Blvd., east of Boulder Highway, north of Charleston Blvd. and south of Owens Ave.

Ward 4 is comprised mostly of rural residential housing located north of Vegas Dr. and for the most part, west of Decatur Blvd.

North West Planning Center
7551 Sauer Dr.
Las Vegas, NV 89128
Scott Albright, Neighborhood Planner
Plans for zoning.

MUNICIPAL JUDGES
City of Las Vegas Municipal Court
400 E. Stewart Ave.
Las Vegas, NV 89101
229-4783

General Information (recording)
229-6421
Court sessions run Monday - Friday 7 am - 5 pm with five sessions each day. Traffic Court check-in times are 7 am, 9 am, noon, 2 pm, 5 pm.

Department 1:
Judge Toy R. Gregory - 229-6584
Department 2:
*Judge Seymore H. Brown,
Chief Judge* - 229-6584
Department 3:
Judge Nancy Saitta - 229-6061
Department 4:
Judge Valerie J. Vega - 229-6509
Department 5:
Judge Cedric Kerns - 229-6061
Department 6:
Judge Ron Parraguirre - 229-2059

Michael Havemann, Administrator
Judges Chambers - 229-6584

LAS VEGAS AGENCIES

City Attorney
Brad Jerbic
400 E. Stewart Ave.
Las Vegas, NV 89101
229-6201
Criminal Div. - 229-6201

City Council
Jan Laverty Jones, Mayor
400 E. Stewart Ave.
Las Vegas, NV 89101
229-6241

City Engineer
Dennis Anderson, City Engineer
420 N. 4th St.
Las Vegas, NV 89101
229-6272

City Lobbyist
Myron Leavitt
400 E. Stewart Ave.
Las Vegas, NV 89101
229-6958

City Manager
400 E. Stewart Ave.
Las Vegas, NV 89101
229-6501

Clerk
Roni Ronemus
400 E. Stewart Ave.
Las Vegas, NV 89101
229-6311

Detention & Enforcement
Mike Sheldon, Dir.
3300 E. Stewart Ave.
Las Vegas, NV 89101
229-6617

Finance & Business Licensing
George W. Stevens, Dir.
400 E. Stewart Ave.
Las Vegas, NV 89101
229-6321

General Services
Ralph Shackleford, Dir.
400 E. Stewart Ave.
Las Vegas, NV 89101
229-6234

Human Resources
Richard Anderson, Dir.
416 N. 7th St.
Las Vegas, NV 89101
229-6315

Intergovernment & Community Relations
Lynn Macy, Deputy City Mgr.
400 E. Stewart Ave.
Las Vegas, NV 89101
229-6958

Judicial Services
Michael Havemann, Court Adm.
400 E. Stewart Ave.
Las Vegas, NV 89101
229-6421

Parks & Leisure Activities
Dave Kuiper, Dir.
749 Veterans Memorial Dr.
Las Vegas, NV 89101
229-6297

Planning & Development Dept.
Theresa O'Donnell, Dir.
731 S. 4th St.
Las Vegas, NV 89101
229-6301

Public Works Dept.
Dick Geocke, Dir.
400 E. Stewart Ave.
Las Vegas, NV 89101
229-6276

Other Departments and General Information
400 E. Stewart Ave.
Las Vegas, NV 89101
229-6011

COUNCIL, BOARDS AND COMMISSIONS

City of Las Vegas boards meet on the following days and times and are open to the public.

City Council
City Council Chambers, 2nd & 4th Mon., 9 am

Child Welfare Board
City Council Chambers, 2nd Wed., 3 pm

Civil Service Board
City Council Chambers, 2nd Wed., 4:45 pm at 416 N. 7th St.

Parks & Recreation Advisory Board
2nd Wed., 5:30 pm at Veterans Memorial Dr.

Planning Commission
City Council Chambers, 2nd & 4th Thu. 7 pm

Senior Citizens Law Project Quarterly
Howard Cannon Senior Citizens Center, 4th Mon., 4:00 pm

Senior Citizens Project Advisory Board
450 East Bonanza Rd., meets 2nd Thurs. each month excluding August

Traffic & Parking Commission
City Council Chambers, 4th Thu., 2 pm

Board of Zoning Adjustment
City Council Chambers, 1st Tue., 6 pm

Recommending Committee
City Mgr. Conference Rm. 10th floor, City Hall, every other Monday, 4:00 pm

City Council Chambers are located at City Hall, 400 East Stewart Ave.

Las Vegas City Council meetings are re-broadcast on TV Cable Channel 4

NORTH LAS VEGAS

North Las Vegas encompasses 53.7 sq. mi. The population in 1990 was 47,707; it had increased to 83,830 in 1996. The City of North Las Vegas offices are open four days a week with most offices closed on Mondays. Most offices are open 7 am - 6 pm
The North Las Vegas City Council meets at 7 pm on the 1st and 3rd Wed. of each month at City Hall.

**City of North Las Vegas -
City Hall**
2200 Civic Center Dr.
North Las Vegas, NV 89030
633-1007
Michael Montandon, Mayor
Information - 633-1000

Building & Safety Dept.
Roger Condie, Dir.
2266 Civic Center Dr.
N. Las Vegas, NV 89030
633-1577

City Attorney
Richard Mauer
2200 Civic Center Dr.
N. Las Vegas, NV 89030
633-1045

City Council
Michael Montandon, Mayor
2200 Civic Center Dr.
N. Las Vegas, NV 89030
633-1010

City Council
Michael Montandon - 633-1011
John Rhodes - 633-1011
Paula Brown - 633-1011
William E. Robinson - 633-1010
Stephanie Smith - 633-1010

City Engineer
Jim Bell
2266 Civic Center Dr.
N. Las Vegas, NV 89030
633-1233

City Manager
Linda Hinson
2200 Civic Center Dr.
N. Las Vegas, NV 89030
633-1002

Clerk
Eileen Sevigny, City Clerk
2200 Civic Center Dr.
N. Las Vegas, NV 89030
633-1031

Deputy City Manager
Patrick Importuna, Dir.
2200 Civic Center Cr.
N. Las Vegas, NV 89030
633-1005

Economic Development
Phyllis Martin, Dir.
2200 Civic Center Dr.
N. Las Vegas, NV 89030
633-1527

Finance
Vytas Vaitkus, Dir.
2200 Civic Center Dr.
N. Las Vegas, NV 89030
633-1462

Fire Dept.
Michael Massey, Fire Chief
2626 E. Carey Ave.
N. Las Vegas, NV 89030
633-1117

Licensing Division
Don Schmeiser
2200 Civic Center Dr.
N. Las Vegas, NV 89030
633-1519

Maintenance & Operations
Larry K. McCutchen, Supt.
3120 Losee Rd.
N. Las Vegas, NV 89030
633-1279

Municipal Court
Warren VanLandschoot,
Municipal Court Judge
2240 Civic Center Dr.
N. Las Vegas, NV 89030
633-1131

Parks & Recreation
Eric Dabney, Dir.
324 E. Brooks St.
N. Las Vegas, NV 89030
633-1171

Public Works Dept.
Gary W. Holler, Dir.
2266 Civic Center Dr.
N. Las Vegas, NV 89030
633-1200

Other Departments and General Information
2200 Civic Center Dr.
N. Las Vegas, NV 89030
633-1000

HENDERSON

Henderson encompasses 74 sq. mi. with a population now estimated at 130,380. For fiscal year 1997-1998, the budget is $163,856,133. The City of Henderson offices are open 4 days a week with most offices closed on Fridays. Office hours are 7:30 am - 5:30 pm

The Henderson City Council meets the 1st Tue. of each month at 7 pm in the City Hall chambers.

The City of Henderson opened a $13.8 million courthouse and jail complex in 1995. The 113,000 sq. ft. Robert A. Swadell Justice Facility houses two Henderson Municipal Court and two Clark County Justice Court Hearing Rooms and a 144-cell jail.

City of Henderson
City Hall
240 Water St.
Henderson, NV 89015
565-2085
Information - 565-2323

Building & Safety Division
Joe Titus, Dir.
240 Water St.
Henderson, NV 89015
565-2099

Business License
Dave Lee, Dir.
240 Water St.
Henderson, NV 89015
565-2050

City Attorney
Shauna Hughes
240 Water St.
Henderson, NV 89015
565-2083

City Council
Jim Gibson, Mayor
240 Water St.
Henderson, NV 89015
565-2085

Councilmen
Jim Gibson - 565-2085
Ward 1 - *Amanda Cyphers* - 565-2403
Ward 2 - *Andy Hafen* - 565-2404
Ward 3 - *Jack Clark* - 565-2405
Ward 4 - *David Wood* - 565-2402

City Manager
Philip Speight
240 Water St.
Henderson, NV 89015
565-2080

Clerk
Susan Robinson
240 Water St.
Henderson, NV 89015
565-2057

Economic Development
Ann Barron, Dir.
240 Water St.
Henderson, NV 89015
565-2315

Engineering/Public Works Dept.
Mark Calhoun, Dir.
240 Water St.
Henderson, NV 89015
565-2140

Finance Dept.
Steve Hanson, Dir.
240 Water St.
Henderson, NV 89015
565-2056

Fire Chief
Joe Hill
223 Lead St.
Henderson, NV 89015
565-2022   565-2016

Human Resources
240 Water St.
Henderson, NV 89015
565-2069

Justice of the Peace
Rodney Burr & Kent Dawson
243 Water St.
Henderson, NV 89015
455-7962

Municipal Court
Ken Proctor, Municipal Court Judge
243 Water St.
Henderson, NV 89015
565-2075

Parks & Recreation
Steve Rongyocsik, Dir.
240 Water St.
Henderson, NV 89015
565-2120

Planning Division
Mary Kay Peck, Dir.
240 Water St.
Henderson, NV 89015
565-2088

Police Chief
Tommy Burns
223 Lead St.
Henderson, NV 89015
565-2003

Other Departments and General Information
240 Water St.
Henderson, NV 89015
565-2323

BOULDER CITY

Boulder City encompasses 34.3 sq. mi. with a population of approximately 14,460. The city of Boulder City offices are open 4 days a week with most offices closed on Fridays. Hours are 7 am - 6 pm.

The Boulder City Council meets at 7 pm every 2nd and 4th Tue. at City Hall.

City Hall
401 California Ave.
Boulder City, NV 89005
293-9202

Building Dept.
Paul Donahue, Building Official
401 California Ave.
Boulder City, NV 89005
293-9282

Business License
Robert E. Boyer
401 California Ave.
Boulder City, NV 89005
293-9219

City Attorney
B. G. Andrews
401 California Ave.
Boulder City, NV 89005
293-9238

City Council
Robert Ferraro, Mayor
401 California Ave.
Boulder City, NV 89005
293-9208
Information - 293-9208

Boulder City's Mayor is appointed among its Councilmen.

Robert Ferraro, Mayor - 293-3114
Bill Smith - 294-2240
Bryan Nix - 293-2626
Mike Pacini - 293-5615
Robert Kenneston - 293-3327

City Manager
John Sullard
401 California Ave.
Boulder City, NV 89005
293-9202

Clerk
Vicki Mayes
401 California Ave.
Boulder City, NV 89005
293-9208

Community Development
401 California Ave.
Boulder City, NV 89005
293-9292
Planning and zoning department.

Engineer
Phillip Henry, City Eng.
401 California Ave.
Boulder City, NV 89005
293-9233

Finance
Robert E. Boyer
401 California Ave.
Boulder City, NV 89005
293-9246

Fire Dept.
Dean Molburg, Fire Chief
1101 Elm St.
Boulder City, NV 89005
293-9228

Municipal Court
501 Ave. G
Boulder City, NV 89005
293-9278
Judge Victor Miller
Judge Mark Denton

Parks & Recreation
Roger Hall, Dir.
900 Arizona St.
Boulder City, NV 89005
293-9256

Planning/Zoning
401 California Ave.
Boulder City, NV 89005
293-9282
John Sullard,
Acting Community Dev. Dir.

Police Dept.
David Mullin, Police Chief
1005 Arizona St.
Boulder City, NV 89005
293-9224

Public Works Dept.
Alan Gove, Dir.
401 California Ave.
Boulder City, NV 89005
293-9200

GOVERNMENT

CLARK COUNTY

Clark County Government Center, 500 S. Grand Central Pkwy., Las Vegas, NV 89155

Clark County is a regional "city" and town government, spanning 7,910 sq. mi., about the size of Connecticut and Rhode Island combined. The County provides numerous regional services to the county's incorporated cities, urban unincorporated areas, or a rural "towns." The population for Clark County is now estimated at 1,119,705 according to the State Demographer (includes Mojave and Nye counties). The county has five incorporated cities: Las Vegas, North Las Vegas, Henderson, Boulder City and Mesquite. Clark County's budget for fiscal year 1997-1998 is $2,243,268,587.

Clark County consolidated its offices in June 1995 to a new 385,000 sq. ft., $48.5 million government center.

NEVADA LEGISLATURE
The formation of Clark County was approved by the Nevada legislature on July 1, 1909.

CLARK COUNTY AGENCIES

County of Clark
200 S. Third St.
Las Vegas, NV 89101
455-4011
County emergency - 455-5710

Administrative Services
Thom Reilly, Dir.
500 S. Grand Central Pkwy.
Las Vegas, NV 89155
455-3530

Air Pollution Control District
Mike Naylor, Dir.
625 Shadow Ln.
Las Vegas, NV 89106
383-1276
Night recording - 383-1420
To report excessive dust from construction or uncommon odors, call 383-1276 and an enforcement officer will respond to your complaint.

Assessor
Mark Schofield
500 S. Grand Central Pkwy.
Las Vegas, NV 89155
455-3882
The assessed gross value of property in 1997-1998 is $20 billion. There are 401,557 parcels of land on the tax roll.

Assessor · Satellite Office
Las Vegas
1949 N. Decatur Blvd.
Las Vegas, NV 89108
Hours: Mon. - Fri. 8 am - 5 pm

Assessor · Satellite Office
Henderson
872 S. Boulder Hwy.
Henderson, NV 89015
Hours: Mon. - Fri. 8 am - 5 pm

Aviation
Randall Walker, Dir.
McCarran Int'l Airport
P.O. Box 11005
Las Vegas, NV 89111
261-5211

Building
Robert Weber, Dir.
500 S. Grand Central Pkwy.
Las Vegas, NV 89155
455-3000

Business License
Ardel Jorgensen, Dir.
500 S. Grand Central Pkwy.
Las Vegas, NV 89155
455-4252

Clerk
Loretta Bowman
200 S. Third St.
Las Vegas, NV 89101
455-3156

Constables
Elected to four year terms by township.
Las Vegas . . . . *Bob Nolan*
Boulder City . . . . . *Larry Markotay*
Bunkerville . . . . . . *Erik L. Laub*
Goodsprings . . . . . *Walter Martin*
Henderson . . . . . . *Earl Mitchell*
Laughlin . . . . *Pat Ketterer*
Mesquite . . . . *Duane Thurston*
Moapa . . . . *Gary Leavitt*
Moapa Valley . . . . *Harry Perkins*
North Las Vegas . . *Lou Tabat*
Searchlight . . . . . *Chuck Golden*

Comprehensive Planning
Richard Holmes, Dir.
500 S. Grand Central Pkwy., Ste. 3012
Las Vegas, NV 89155-1741
455-4181

Comptroller
Therral Jackson
500 S. Grand Central Pkwy.
Las Vegas, NV 89155
455-3895

Information on the five major town advisory boards in the county:

Paradise:
Meets the 1st & 3rd Tue. preceding County Commission meetings.
 Paradise Park Community Center
 4770 Harrison Dr.
Mary Jane Harvey, Chairman - 451-9775
Maria Newell, Secretary - 451-6034

Spring Valley:
Meets second Tue. of month
 Spring Valley Library
 4280 S. Jones Blvd.
Dorothy Kidd, Chairwoman - 361-1688
Pam Reno, Secretary - 363-8204

Sunrise Manor:
Meets Thu. preceding County Commission meetings.
 Sunrise Manor Town Hall
 1106 N. Nellis Blvd.
Michael Dias, Chairman - 384-0124
Aggie Roberts, Secretary - 641-9210

Whitney:
Meets 3rd Tue. of the month.
 Whitney Library
 5175 E. Tropicana Ave.
Jack Hurley, Chairman - 433-0744
Vickie Blackwell, Secretary - 435-5057

Winchester:
Meets second Thu. of the month.
 Winchester Community Center
 3130 S. McLeod Dr.
Christine Makowsky, Chairman - 641-8798
Maria Newell, Secretary - 451-6034

Clark County Government Center
500 S. Grand Central Pkwy.
Las Vegas, NV 89155
Switchboard: 455-4011

Offices located at Clark County Government Center:

Commission Chambers	455-3500
Permit Application Center Building	455-3000
Current Planning	455-4314
Community Development	455-5025
Elections	455-2780
Public Response Office	455-4191
Quality Resource Center	455-3179
Treasurer	455-4323
Community Room/Cafeteria	
Assessor	455-3882
Public Works	455-6000
Administration	455-6002
Design Engineering	455-6050
Construction Mgmt.	455-6050
Community Information	455-2762
Traffic Management	455-6100
Recorder	455-4336
Business License	455-4252
Comprehensive Planning	455-4181
Human Resources	455-4565
Risk Management	455-4544
General Services	455-4425
Geographic Info. Systems	455-3855
Information Systems	455-3282
Equal Opportunity Division	455-5760
Community Resources	455-5025
Comptroller	455-3895
District Attorney-Civil Div.	455-4761
Internal Audit	455-3269
Parks & Recreation	455-8200
Commissioners	455-3500
Administrative Services	455-3530
County Manager	455-3530
County Clerk-Commission Div.	455-4431
Finance	455-3542

County Clerk · Commission Division
Pat Harrison, Asst. Clerk to the Board of County Commissioners
500 S. Grand Central Pkwy.
Las Vegas, NV 89155
455-4431

County Commissioner
500 S. Grand Central Pkwy.
Las Vegas, NV 89155
455-3500
Dist A. - *Bruce Woodbury* (R)
Dist B. - *Mary Kincaid* (D)
Dist C. - *Lance Malone* (R)
Dist D. - *Yvonne Atkinson Gates* (D)
Dist E. - *Myrna Williams* (D)
Dist F. - *Erin Kenny* (D)
Dist G. - *Lorraine Hunt* (R), Vice Chairperson

County Manager
Dale Askew
500 S. Grand Central Pkwy.
Las Vegas, NV 89155
455-3530

District Attorney
Stewart Bell
200 S. Third St.
Las Vegas, NV 89155
455-4711

District Attorney · Civil Division
Mary Miller, County Counsel
500 S. Grand Central Pkwy.
Las Vegas, NV 89155
455-4761

District Attorney · Family Support Division
C. A. Watts, Acting Dir.
301 E. Clark Ave., Ste. 400
Las Vegas, NV 89101
455-4755

DISTRICT JUDGES
Eighth Judicial District Court

Clark County Courthouse
200 S. Third St.
Las Vegas, NV 89155
455-4641
Dept. 1 - *Gene Porter* - 455-4641
Dept. 2 - *Nancy A. Becker* - 455-4645
Dept. 3 - *Joseph Pavlikowski* - 455-4648
Dept. 4 - *Kathy Hardcastle* - 455-4652
Dept. 5 - *Jeffery D. Sobel* - 455-4655
Dept. 6 - *Joseph Bonaventure* - 455-4658
Dept. 7 - *Mark Gibbons* - 455-4662
Dept. 8 - *Lee Gates* - 455-4681
Dept. 9 - *Stephen Huffaker* - 455-4666
Dept. 10 - *Jack Lehman* - 455-4668
Dept. 11 - *Michael L. Douglas* - 455-4527

Dept. 12 - *Myron Leavitt* - 455-4793
Dept. 13 - *Don Chairez* - 455-4313
Dept. 14 - *Donald Mosley* - 455-4304
Dept. 15 - *Sally Loehrer* - 455-4305
Dept. 16 - *John McGroarty* - 455-3306
Administrator -
  Charles Short - 455-4277
Discovery Commissioner -
  Thomas W. Biggar - 455-4390

In 1996, 55,893 cases were filed in Clark County District Court with about half of the cases being family-related. The Family Court began hearing all family-related cases on January 11, 1995.

Family Court
Clark County Courthouse
601 N. Pecos Rd.
Las Vegas, NV 89101
Dept. A - *Terrance Marren* - 455-5990
Dept. B - *Gloria Sanchez* - 455-5991
Dept. C - *Steve Jones* - 455-5992
Dept. D - *Gerald Hardcastle* - 455-5993
Dept. E - *Frances Ann Fine* - 455-5994
Dept. F - *Bob Gaston* - 455-5995
Dept. G - *Cynthia Steel* - 455-6940
Dept. H - *Gary Redmon* - 455-6944
Administrator -
  Christina Chandler - 455-2383

Family Court handles divorces, adoptions, guardianship, abuse and neglect cases, parental rights arguments and anything else involving juveniles and families.

Community Resources
Douglas Bell, Mgr.
500 S. Grand Central Pkwy.
Las Vegas, NV 89155
455-5025

Elections
Kathryn Ferguson, Registrar of Voters
500 S. Grand Central Pkwy.
Las Vegas, NV 89155
455-2780

Equal Opportunity Division
George L. Cotton, Mgr.
500 S. Grand Central Pkwy.
Las Vegas, NV 89155
455-5760

Finance
Rosemary Vissiliadis, Dir.
500 S. Grand Central Pkwy.
Las Vegas, NV 89155
455-3530

Fire Dept.
Earl Greene, Fire Chief
575 E. Flamingo Rd.
Las Vegas, NV 89119
455-7311

General Services
Earl Hawkes, Dir.
500 S. Grand Central Pkwy.
Las Vegas, NV 89155
455-4425

Geographic Information Systems
David Edwards, Mgr.
500 S. Grand Central Pkwy.
Las Vegas, NV 89155
455-3855

Health District
Dr. Otto Ravenholt, Chief Health Officer
625 Shadow Ln.
Las Vegas, NV 89106
385-1291

Child Support/Paternity Hearing Masters
Clark County Courthouse
Las Vegas, NV 89101
Special Hearing Masters:
Thomas Leeds, Child Support/Paternity
Jennifer Henry, Guardianship

Special Juvenile Hearing Masters:
Dept. 1 - *Sylvia G. Beller* - 455-5301
Dept. 2 - *Fernando Guzman* - 455-5302
Dept. 3 - *Fred Fischer* - 455-5303
Dept. 4 - *Jack Fields* - 455-2435
Violence Hearing Master

JUSTICE COURT
JUSTICE OF THE PEACE
Las Vegas Township
200 S. Third St.
Las Vegas, NV 89155
455-4436
Justice Court civil evictions and small claims - 455-4478
Traffic citation info. - 455-5944
Dept. 1 - *Deborah Lippis* -
  455-4380 - Chief Judge
Dept. 2 - *Doug Smith* - 455-4122
Dept. 3 - *Daniel Ahlstrom* - 455-4124
Dept. 4 - *James Bixler* - 455-3469
Dept. 5 - *William Jansen* - 455-4381
Dept. 6 - *Nancy Oesterle* - 455-5510

Boulder Township
Kerry Passey, Administrator
401 California Ave.
Boulder City, NV 89005
455-8000
Victor Miller - 455-8000

Bunkerville Township
Cecil Leavitt - 346-5711

Goodsprings Township (Jean, NV)
Janet Smith - 874-1405

Henderson Township
200 S. Water St.
Henderson, NV 89015
455-7951
Rodney Burr - 455-7962
Kent J. Dawson - 455-7980

Laughlin Township
Billy Moma - 298-4622

Mesquite Township
Brent Walker - 346-5298

Moapa Township
Marley Robinson - 864-2333

Moapa Valley Township (Overton, NV)
Lanny Waite - 398-3213

North Las Vegas Township
1916 N. Bruce St.
North Las Vegas, NV 89030
455-7801
Stephen Dahl - 455-7804

Searchlight Township
Wendell Turner - 297-1252

Current Planning
Rick Holmes, Mgr.
500 S. Grand Central Pkwy.
Las Vegas, NV 89155
455-4314

Human Resources
Cheryl Miller, Dir.
500 S. Grand Central Pkwy.
Las Vegas, NV 89155
455-4565

GOVERNMENT

Information Systems
Steve Chapin, Dir.
500 S. Grand Central Pkwy.
Las Vegas, NV 89155
455-3282

Internal Audit
Jeremiah P. Carroll II, Dir.
500 S. Grand Central Pkwy.
Las Vegas, NV 89155
455-3269

Las Vegas Valley Water Dist.
Patricia Mulroy, Gen. Mgr.
1001 S. Valley View Blvd.
Las Vegas, NV 89153
870-2011
Water Conservation Hotline - 258-3102

Organizational Development Center
Ron Cameron, Dir.
500 S. Grand Central Pkwy.
Las Vegas, NV 89155
455-3179

Parks and Recreation
Glenn Trowbridge, Dir.
500 S. Grand Central Pkwy.
Las Vegas, NV 89155
455-2452

Public Response Office
Jim Foreman, Mgr.
500 S. Grand Central Pkwy., Ste. 2017
Las Vegas, NV 89155
455-4191

Public Works/Engineer
Martin J. Manning, Dir.
500 S. Grand Central Pkwy.
Las Vegas, NV 89155
455-6000
Community Development
General Info. - 455-4600

Public Administrator
Jared Shafer

1700 Pinto Ln.
Las Vegas, NV 89106
455-4332

Recorder
Judy Vandever
500 S. Grand Central Pkwy.
Las Vegas, NV 89155
455-4336

Regional Transportation
Kurt Weinrich, Dir.
301 E. Clark Ave., Ste. 300
Las Vegas, NV 89101
455-4481

Risk Management
Robert Mulroy, Mgr.
500 S. Grand Central Pkwy.
Las Vegas, NV 89155
455-4544

Sheriff
Jerry Keller
400 E. Stewart St.
Las Vegas, NV 89101
795-3111

Treasurer
500 S. Grand Central Pkwy.
Las Vegas, NV 89155
455-4323

BOARD OF COUNTY COMMISSIONERS

Schedule of Board Meetings:
Administrative agenda -
    Meets at 9 am 1st and 3rd Tue. of each month.
Zoning agenda -
    Meets 9 am 1st and 3rd Wed. each month.
Clark Co. Liquor & Gaming Licensing Board -
    Meets 9 am the last working day of each month.
Board of Trustees -
    Meets 1:30 pm Wed. following the 1st and 3rd Tue. of each month.
Board of Directors, Las Vegas Valley Water District -
    Meets 1:30 pm 1st and 3rd Tue. of each month.
Metropolitan Police Department Fiscal Affairs -
    Meets 3rd Mon. of each month at 8 am.
Parks & Recreation Advisory Committee -
    Meets 3rd Thu. of each month at 2:30 pm.
Planning Commission -
    Meets 1st and 3rd Tue. and the following Thu. at 7 pm.
Regional Transportation Commission -
    Meets 2nd Thu. of the month at 9:15 am.
Board of Trustees, Sanitation -
    Meets 1st and 3rd Tue. of the month at 1:45 pm.
Board of Trustees, University Medical Center -
    Meets 1st and 3rd Tue. of the month at 2 pm.

All meetings are held in the
Clark County Commission Chambers at 500 S. Grand Central Pkwy.

Clark County Commission meetings are re-broadcast on
TV Cable Channel 4-UNLV. For agenda and meeting times, call 455-4431.

CLARK COUNTY - WHERE TO COMPLAIN

Airport Noise Complaint Hotline: 261-3694	To Report a Fire Hazard: 455-7316
Airport Parking Hotline: 261-5121	Gang Hotline Recorder: 229-4264
Arson Hotline:..........................455-7322	Graffiti Hotline: 385-3473
Child Abuse/Neglect Hotline: 399-0081	Metro Narcotics: 229-4141
Clark County Animal Control: 455-7710	Nevada Equal Rights Commission-
Complaints/Nuisances:...................455-4191	Discrimination or Harassment on the Job: ..486-7161
Construction Control - Excess Dust: 383-1276	City of Las Vegas Animal Control: 229-6348
Dirty Restaurant: 383-1251	School District:........................799-5005
Dumping (illegal): 383-1027	Secret Witness: 385-5555

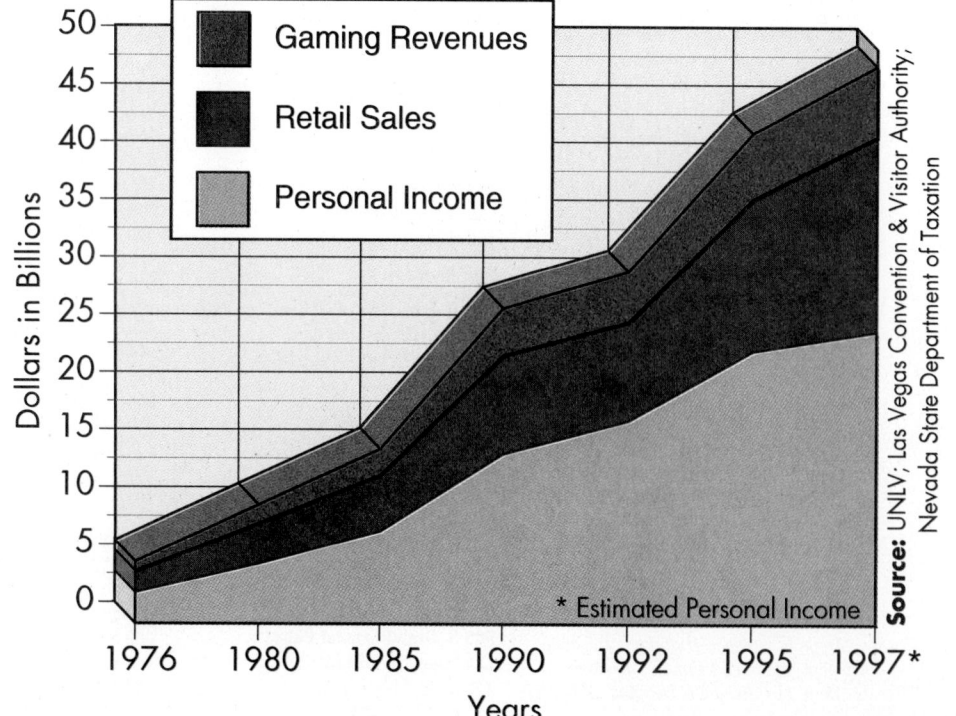

Clark County Combined Circulating Money

Legend:
- Gaming Revenues
- Retail Sales
- Personal Income

Y-axis: Dollars in Billions (0, 5, 10, 15, 20, 25, 30, 35, 40, 45, 50)

X-axis: Years (1976, 1980, 1985, 1990, 1992, 1995, 1997*)

* Estimated Personal Income

Source: UNLV; Las Vegas Convention & Visitor Authority; Nevada State Department of Taxation

STATE GOVERNMENT

The Grant Sawyer State Office Building, a 223,000 sq. ft. complex, opened in January 1995 at Washington Ave. and Las Vegas Blvd. across from Cashman Field.

Executive Branch
State Capitol Complex
Carson City, NV 89710
687-5670
To call any State of Nevada office from Las Vegas, dial 486-3000 and give the operator the extension desired (last four digits of number). To call any state office toll free, dial 1-800-992-0900 and give the operator the extension desired.

Attorney General
Frankie Sue Del Papa (D)
555 E. Washington Ave.
Las Vegas, NV 89101
486-3420   687-4170

Chief Deputy A.G.
Don Haight
555 E. Washington Ave.
Las Vegas, NV 89101
486-3420

Colorado River Commission
555 E. Washington Ave., Ste. 3100
Las Vegas, NV 89101
486-2670
George M. Caan, Dir.

DEPARTMENT OF BUSINESS & INDUSTRY

Department of Business & Industry
Consumer Affairs Div.
Claudia Cormier, Dir.
1850 E. Sahara Ave., Ste. 101
Las Vegas, NV 89104
486-7355

Financial Institutions
Lyndon Evans, Deputy Commissioner
2501 E. Sahara Ave., Ste. 300
Las Vegas, NV 89104
486-4120

Insurance Division
Pam Mackay, Chief Deputy Commissioner
2501 E. Sahara Ave., Ste. 302
Las Vegas, NV 89104
486-4009

Real Estate Division
Joan Buchanan, Adm.

2501 E. Sahara Ave., Ste. 202
Las Vegas, NV 89104
486-4033

Telemarketing Division
Patricia Morris German, Commissioner
1850 E. Sahara Ave., Ste. 101
Las Vegas, NV 89104
486-7325

CONSERVATION AND NATURAL RESOURCE

Conservation and Natural Resource
Pete Morros, Dir.
123 W. Nye Ln.
Carson City, NV 89710
687-4360

Division of Forestry
Robert Ruffridge, So. Regional Forester
4747 W. Vegas Dr.
Las Vegas, NV 89108
486-5123

Division of State Parks
Roy E. Orr, Regional Mgr.
4747 W. Vegas Dr.
Las Vegas, NV 89108
486-5126

Division of Wildlife
Mike Wickersham, Regional Supv.
4747 W. Vegas Dr.
Las Vegas, NV 89108
486-5127

Environmental Protection Division
L. H. Dodgion, Adm.
333 W. Nye Ln.
Carson City, NV 89710
687-4670

Water Resources Division
Mike Turnipseed, State Eng.
123 W. Nye Ln.
Carson City, NV 89710
687-4380

NEVADA STATE GENERAL FUND
Revenue Forecast for Fiscal Year 1998-1999

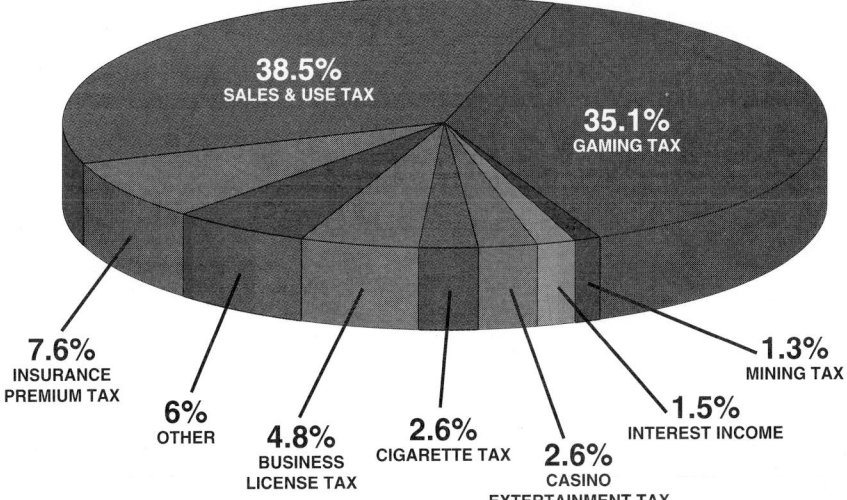

38.5% SALES & USE TAX
35.1% GAMING TAX
7.6% INSURANCE PREMIUM TAX
6% OTHER
4.8% BUSINESS LICENSE TAX
2.6% CIGARETTE TAX
2.6% CASINO EXTERTAINMENT TAX
1.5% INTEREST INCOME
1.3% MINING TAX

PROJECTED REVENUE	(000)
MINING TAX	19,428
INTEREST INCOME	23,370
CASINO ENTERTAINMENT TAX	40,138
CIGARETTE TAX	39,981
BUSINESS LICENSE TAX	74,175
OTHER	93,249
INSURANCE PREMIUM TAX	116,682
GAMING TAX	541,720
SALES & USE TAX	593,686

Source: Nevada State Dept. of Administration

STATE GOVERNMENT

Grant Sawyer State Building
555 E. Washington Ave.
Las Vegas, NV 89101

Offices located at Grant Sawyer Building:

ROOM	OFFICE	TELEPHONE	FAX LINE
1500	Athletic Commission	486-2575	486-2577
3900	Attorney General	486-3420	486-3768
4800	Atty. for Injured Workers	486-2830	486-2844
4900	Business & Industry	486-2750	486-2758
	Cafeteria	486-3407	
1003	Capitol Police	486-2935	486-2012
3100	Colorado River Comm.	486-2670	486-2695
5400	Economic Development	486-2700	486-2701
1700	Employee Assistance Prog.	486-2929	
1700	Equal Employment Oppr.	486-2905	
4300	Environmental Protection	486-2850	486-2863
2600	Gaming Administration	486-2000	486-2045
2500	Gaming Audit	486-2060	
2100	Gaming Enforcement	486-2020	
	After Office Hours	486-2156	
1800	Gaming Electronic Serv.	486-2043	
2200	Gaming Investigations	486-2260	
2300	Gaming Tax and License	486-2008	
5100	Governor	486-2500	486-2505
3300	Hearing Division	486-2525	486-2555
4100	Labor Commission	486-2650	486-2660
4400	Legislative Bureau	486-2800	486-2810
5500	Lieutenant Governor	486-2400	486-2404
1200	Mail Room	486-2485	
5400	Motion Pictures	486-2711	486-2712
5600	*Nevada Magazine* Editorial	486-2433	486-2789
5600	*Nevada Magazine* Sales	486-2434	
1400	Personnel	486-2900	486-2925
4600	Public Service Comm.	486-2600	486-2590
2900	Sec. of State Corporate	486-2880	486-2888
5200	Sec. of State Securities	486-2440	486-2452
1300	Taxation	486-2300	486-2373
5600	Tourism	486-2424	486-2789
3200	Victims of Crime Program	486-2740	486-2825
4200	Water Resources	486-2770	486-2781

Clark County Desert Conservation Plan
500 S. Grand Central Pkwy.
Las Vegas, NV 889155-8370
455-3530
Public Information and Educational materials available upon request. The Desert Conservation Program is responsible for the implementation of the provisions of the Section 10(a)1(B) Incidental Take permit, issued by the United States Fish & Wildlife Service, pursuant to the Endangered Species Act. Through an interlocal agreement with the cities of Las Vegas, North Las Vegas, Henderson, Boulder City and Mesquite, Clark County serves as the plan administrator, responsible for the collection of mitigation fees, implementation of the Plan, and adhering to all compliance measures associated with the permit. The Desert Conservation Plan and its accompanying 30-year permit is intended to promote a balance between economic stability and environmental integrity in Clark County.

Controller
Darrel R. Daine
Capitol Complex
Carson City, NV 89710
687-4330

Dairy Commission
Leon Webster, Area Supv.
1840 E. Sahara Ave., Ste. 111
Las Vegas, NV 89104
486-8212

Economic Development
Robert E. Shriver, Exec. Dir.
Capitol Complex
Carson City, NV 89710
687-4325

Department of Education
Frank South, Team Leader
1820 E. Sahara Ave., Ste. 205
Las Vegas, NV 89104
486-6455

EMPLOYMENT SECURITY

Employment Security
Stan Jones, Dir.
500 E. Third St.
Carson City, NV 89713
687-4635

Field Auditor
Susanne Cooper,
Compliance Audit Investigator
1830 E. Sahara Ave., Ste. 202
Las Vegas, NV 89104
486-8222

Henderson Office
119 Water St.
Henderson, NV 89015
486-6710
Charles Smith, Mgr.

Las Vegas Office
902 W. Owens St.
Las Vegas, NV 89106
486-5300
Brenda Harris, Mgr.

North Las Vegas
2827 Las Vegas Blvd. N.
N. Las Vegas, NV 89030
486-5600
Ron Fletcher, Mgr.

Fire Marshal Division
Bryon Slobe, Acting State Fire Marshal
Capitol Complex #207
Carson City, NV 89710
687-4290

Gaming Commission
Bill Curran, Chairman
Marilyn Epling, Exec. Sec.
1150 E. Williams St.
Carson City, NV 89710
687-6530

Gaming Control Board
(Also listed under Taxes)
Bill Bible, Chairman
555 E. Washington Ave., Ste. 2600
Las Vegas, NV 89101
486-2000

Governor
Bob Miller (D)
Capitol Complex
Carson City, NV 89710
687-5670

Governor · Las Vegas Office
Catherine Cortez, Exec. Asst.
555 E. Washington Ave.
Las Vegas, NV 89101
486-2500

Lt. Governor
Lonnie Hammargren (R)
555 E. Washington Ave.
Las Vegas, NV 89101
486-2400

DEPARTMENT OF HUMAN RESOURCES

Training and Rehabilitation
Charlotte Crawford, Acting Dir.
505 King St., Ste.600
Carson City, NV 89710
687-4730

Bureau of Services to the Blind
Al Roybal, District Mgr.
628 Belrose St.
Las Vegas, NV 89107
486-5333

Welfare Division
Gail Matthews, Social Worker Mgr.
700 Belrose St.
Las Vegas, NV 89107-2235
486-5000

Job Training Partnership Act (JTPA)
Barbara Weinberg, Dir.
400 W. King St., Ste.108
Carson City, NV 89710
687-4310

Labor Commission
David J. Dahn,
Deputy Labor Commissioner
555 E. Washington Ave.
Las Vegas, NV 89101
486-2650

Local Government · Employee Management Relations Board
Shari Thomas, Commissioner
2501 E. Sahara Ave., Ste. 203
Las Vegas, NV 89104
486-4504

Department of Minerals
Russ Fields, Executive Dir.
400 W. King St., Ste. 106
Carson City, NV 89710
687-5050

Nevada Commmission on Economic Development · Motion Picture Div.
Bob Hirsch, Dir.
555 E. Washington Ave.
Las Vegas, NV 89101
486-2711
Nevada's Motion Picture Division of the State Commission on Economic Development attracted over $90 million in revenue to Nevada during the 1996-97 fiscal year. Nevada is in the top 10 in location filming nationwide with 279 projects.

Motor Vehicle and Public Safety Dept. of
Donald Denison, Deputy Dir.
8250 W. Flamingo Rd.
Las Vegas, NV 89117
486-4200

North Las Vegas Driver's License Div.
4021 W. Carey Ave.
N. Las Vegas, NV 89030
486-4368

Registration Div.
8250 W. Flamingo Rd.
Las Vegas, NV 89117
641-0090

Registration and Drivers License Division
2701 E. Sahara Ave.
Las Vegas, NV 89104
486-4368

Commercial Drivers License
4110 Donovan Way
N. Las Vegas, NV 89030
486-5655

874 S. Boulder Hwy.
Henderson, NV 89015
486-4368
Donna West, Asst. Chief

Public Service Commission
555 E. Washington Ave.
Las Vegas, NV 89101
486-2600
John Mendoza, Chairman

Secretary of State
Dean Heller (R)
Capitol Complex
Carson City, NV 89710
687-5203   1-800-274-2754

Secretary of State ·
Las Vegas Office
555 E. Washington Ave.
Las Vegas, NV 89101
486-2880
Marlene McFall, Supv.
Securities Division - 486-2440

State Industrial Insurance
System
Douglas Dirks, Gen. Mgr.
515 E. Musser St.
Carson City, NV 89714
687-5284

1700 W. Charleston Blvd.
Las Vegas, NV 89102
388-3225

(See Business Section for further information)

STATE LICENSE EXAMINATION BOARDS

Architecture
2080 E. Flamingo Rd., Ste. 225
Las Vegas, NV 89119
486-7300

Barber Examiners
3250 Civic Center Dr.
N. Las Vegas, NV 89030
399-9041

Contractors
4220 S. Maryland Pkwy.,
Building D, Ste. 800
Las Vegas, NV 89119
486-3500

Cosmetology
1785 E. Sahara Ave., Ste. 255
Las Vegas, NV 89104
486-6542

Landscape Architecture
1395 Haskell, Ste. C
Reno, NV 89502
359-8110

Marriage & Family Counselor
Examiners
1555 E. Flamingo Rd., Ste. 303
Las Vegas, NV 89119
486-7388

Nursing
4335 S. Industrial Rd., Ste. 420
Las Vegas, NV 89103
739-1575

Pharmacy
1201 Terminal Way, Ste. 212
Reno, NV 89502
322-0691

Pharmacy
4220 S. Maryland Pkwy., Ste. 314
Las Vegas, NV 89119
486-7380

Taxation Dept. of
Robert Palmer, Tax Adm.
555 E. Washington Ave.
Las Vegas, NV 89101
486-2300

Taxicab Authority
Robert Anselmo, Adm.
1785 E. Sahara Ave., Ste. 200
Las Vegas, NV 89104
486-6532

Treasurer
Bob Seale (D)
Capitol Complex
Carson City, NV 89710
687-5200

UNIVERSITY OF NEVADA SYSTEM

University of Nevada
Dr. Carol Harter, Pres.
4505 Maryland Pkwy
Las Vegas, NV 89154
895-3201

University Regents
District 1
Sub-District A   Howard Rosenberg
Sub-District B   Jim Eardley
District 2
Sub-District A   David Phillips
Sub-District B   Tom Weisner
Sub-District C   Shelley L. Berkley
Sub-District D   Mark Alden
Sub-District E   Thalia Dondero
Sub-District F   Nancy Price
Sub-District G   Maddy Graves
District 3
Sub-District A   Dorothy Gallagher
Sub-District B   Jill Derby

Community College of
Southern Nevada
3200 E. Cheyenne Ave.
N. Las Vegas, NV 89030
651-4000
Richard Moore, Pres.

Weights and Measures,
Bureau of
Kevin Coyne, Senior Inspector
2300 McLeod Dr.
Las Vegas, NV 89104
486-4690

LEGISLATIVE BRANCH

The Nevada legislature meets every 2 years on the odd-numbered years, beginning the 3rd Mon. in January and lasting through at least June. The 1997 legislature met from January 20th to July 7th at a cost of $15.3 million. Of the 21 State Senators, 13 represent Clark County; of the 42 State Assemblymen, 26 represent Clark County. To call the legislature the toll free number is 1-800-367-5057. There is a full time legislative staff located in Las Vegas, 486-2800.

SOUTHERN NEVADA ASSEMBLYMEN

Dist. 1
Clarence W. (Tom) Collins (D) - 645-2817
Dist. 2
Merle Berman (R) - 228-0020
Dist. 3
John J. Lee (D) - 258-5447
Dist. 4
Deanna Braunlin (R) - 256-1935

Dist. 5
Barbara K. Cegavske (R) - 873-0711
Dist. 6
Wendell P. Williams (D) - 646-1018
Dist. 7
Morse Arberry Jr. (D) - 229-2330
Dist. 8
Barbara Buckley (D) - 222-9901
Dist. 9
Chris Giunchigliani (D) - 366-1663
Dist. 10
David Goldwater (D) - 796-5644
Dist. 11
Douglas A. Bache (D) - 642-8099
Dist. 12
Genie Ohrenschall (D) - 384-5922
Dist. 13
Dennis Nolan (R) - 262-1000
Dist. 14
Ellen M. Koivisto (D) - 438-5723
Dist. 15
Jack D. Close, Sr. (R) - 731-6873
Dist. 16
Dario Herrera (D) - 651-4047
Dist. 17
Bob Price (D) - 642-5669
Dist. 18
Mark Manendo (D) - 451-8654
Dist. 19
Saundra Krenzer (D) - 437-9209
Dist. 20
Kathleen A. Von Tobel (R) - 496-6559
Dist. 21
Sandra Tiffany (R) - 451-7301
Dist. 22
Genevieve Segerblom (D) - 293-2626
Dist. 23
Richard Perkins (D) - 566-6542
Dist. 28
Vonne Chowning (D) - 642-8683
Dist. 41
David R. Parks (D) - 736-6929
Dist. 42
Harry Mortenson (D) - 876-6944

SENATORS

Dist. 1
Jon Porter (R) - 294-1004
Dist. 2
Ray Shaffer (D) - 647-8683
Jack Regan (D) - 452-3988
Dist. 3
Valerie Wiener (D) - 871-6536
Bob Coffin (D) - 384-9501

Dist. 4
Joe Neal (D) - 399-2114
Dist. 5
Ann O'Connell (R) - 434-4020
Bill O'Donnell (R) - 873-2724
Dist. 6
Ray Rawson (R) - 651-5591
Dist. 7
Dina Titus (D) (4 yr) - 895-3756
Kathy Augustine (R) (2 yr) - 387-5922
Dist. 8
Michael A. Schneider (D) - 876-5121
Mark James (R) - 791-0308

JUDICIAL BRANCH

Nevada State Supreme Court
225 Bridger Ave.
Las Vegas, NV 89101
486-3200

Supreme Court Building
Carson City, NV 89710
687-5180   1-800-992-0900, ext. 5180
Miriam Shearing, Chief Justice
Cliff Young
Charles E. Springer
A. William Maupin
Robert E. Rose
Janette Bloom, Clerk of the Court
Jeanne C. Richards, Chief Deputy Clerk

1998 NEVADA LEGAL HOLIDAYS

New Years Day	January 1	Thursday
Martin Luther King Jr.	January 19	Monday
Presidents Day	February 16	Monday
Easter	April 12	Sunday
Memorial Day (observed)	May 25	Monday
Independence Day	July 4	Saturday
Labor Day	September 7	Monday
Columbus Day (observed)	October 12	Monday
Nevada Day	October 30	Friday
Veterans Day	November 11	Wednesday
Thanksgiving	November 26	Thursday
Christmas	December 25	Friday

NEVADA GOVERNOR

The youngest Governor in Nevada was 35 year old Emmett Boyle, who served from 1915 to 1922. The oldest was 66 year old Lewis Bradley, who served from 1871 to 1878.

FEDERAL GOVERNMENT

Foley Federal Building, 300 Las Vegas Blvd. S., Las Vegas, NV 89101

FEDERAL AGENCIES

Foley Federal Building
300 Las Vegas Blvd. S.
Las Vegas, NV 89101
388-6351
Information - 1-800-688-9889

Agriculture, Div. of
Thomas Smigel, Regional Mgr.
2300 McLeod St.
Las Vegas, NV 89104
486-4690

U. S. Forest Service
Las Vegas Ranger District
Jim Tallarico, District Ranger
2881 S. Valley View Blvd., Ste. 16
Las Vegas, NV 89102
873-8800

ARMED FORCES

Nellis Air Force Base
Salt Lake Hwy.
Las Vegas, NV 89191
652-1110
 Nellis began as the Army Air Corps Gunnery School in 1941. Located 8 mi. northeast of Las Vegas, Nellis Air Force Base covers more than 11,000 acres and restricted ranges cover over 4,742 sq. mi. The base was renamed in 1950 after Lt. William Nellis who was killed in action in 1944 on his 70th P-47 combat mission over Luxembourg. There are 9,100 military and civilian personnel at Nellis.
 Nellis Air Force Base is the largest and busiest base in the Air Combat command and is home to the famed Thunderbirds air demonstration squadron. Free guided tours lasting approximately 90 minutes are offered Tuesdays and Thursdays at 2 pm. It concludes with a walk through the Thunderbird Museum. To take tour, visitors must check in at the Nellis Visitor's Center. Reservations are required, call 652-4018 or 652-7200.

ARMED FORCES RECRUITING STATIONS

Air Force
242 S. Decatur Blvd.
Las Vegas, NV 89107
877-4478

Army
1995 N. Nellis Blvd., Ste. D
Las Vegas, NV 89115
459-2123

557 E. Sahara Ave.
Las Vegas, NV 89104
733-6770

732 S. Boulder Hwy.
Henderson, NV 89015
566-6766

242 S. Decatur Blvd., Ste. B109
Las Vegas, NV 89107
258-4702

Army National Guard
4130 S. Sandhill Rd.
Las Vegas, NV 89121
435-2861

Marine Corps
557 E. Sahara Ave.
Las Vegas, NV 89104
796-1881

242 S. Decatur Blvd.
Las Vegas, NV 89107
258-3391

732 S. Boulder Hwy.
Henderson, NV 89015
565-5560

3603 Las Vegas Blvd. N.
Las Vegas, NV 89115
644-1958

Navy
732 Boulder Hwy.
Henderson, NV 89015
564-5606

242 S. Decatur Blvd.
Las Vegas, NV 89107
258-4707

557 E. Sahara Ave.
Las Vegas, NV 89104
735-7099

1937 N. Nellis Blvd.
Las Vegas, NV 89115
459-6655

Bankruptcy Court
Robert Clive Jones, Judge - 388-6505
Linda B. Riegle, Judge - 388-6120
300 Las Vegas Blvd. S.
Las Vegas, NV 89101
388-6257 (clerk)

Bureau of Land Management
General Information
4765 W. Vegas Dr.
Las Vegas, NV 89108
647-5000
Michael Dwyer, District Mgr.
Eighty-three percent of the land in Nevada is controlled by federal agencies.

Congress of the United States
Richard Bryan, Senator (D)
300 Las Vegas Blvd. S., Ste. 1110
Las Vegas, NV 89101
388-6605
 269 S. R. O. B.
 Washington, D.C. 20510-2804
 1-202-224-6244

Harry Reid, Senator (D)
528 E. Charleston Blvd.
Las Vegas, NV 89101
474-0041
 Hart Senate Office Bldg.
 Washington D.C. 20510-2803
 1-202-224-3542

Jim Gibbons, Congressman (R)
850 S. Durango Dr., Ste. 107
Las Vegas, NV 89128
255-1651
 100 Cannon Office Bldg.
 Washington, D.C. 20515-2802
 1-202-225-6155

John Ensign, Congressman (R)
1000 E. Sahara Ave., Ste. 108
Las Vegas, NV 89104
731-1801

Sonia Joya, District Dir.
414 Cannon, House Office Bldg.
Washington, D.C. 20515-2801
1-202-225-5965

Customs
 (Also listed under
 Protective/Emergency Services)

Jack Pansky, Port Dir.
McCarran Int'l Airport
P.O. Box 11049
Las Vegas, NV 89111
388-6480

DISTRICT COURT

District Court
300 Las Vegas Blvd. S.
Las Vegas, NV 89101
388-6351 (clerk)

District Court Judges:
David Hagen - 388-6447
Lloyd D. George, Chief Judge - 686-5888
Howard D. McKibben - 388-5880
Philip M. Pro - 388-6942
Edward C. Reed, Jr. - 686-5919

District Court Magistrates
(Presides over petty offenses, bail hearings and pretrial motions)
Lawrence R. Leavitt - 388-6516
Robert J. Johnston - 388-6222
Roger Hunt - 388-6996
Phyllis Halsey Atkins - 686-5855
Robert A. McQuaid, Jr. - 686-5858

Pretrial Service Agency
330 S. 3rd St., Ste. 820
Las Vegas, NV 89101
388-6780

Probation and Parole Office
411 Bonneville Ave., Ste. 400
Las Vegas, NV 89101
388-6428

Energy, Dept. of
Terry Johnson, Mgr.
232 Energy Way
N. Las Vegas, NV 89030
295-1000

Environmental Protection Agency
Jay Messer, Dir.
944 E. Harmon Ave.
Las Vegas, NV 89119
798-2100

U.S. Dept. of Housing & Urban Development
Paul A. Pradia, State Coordinator
333 N. Rancho Dr., Ste. 700
Las Vegas, NV 89119
388-6500 388-6776

Food and Drug Administration
Luis Chavarria, Resident in Charge
300 Las Vegas Blvd. S.
Las Vegas, NV 89101
388-6361

Immigration and Naturalization
3373 Pepper Ln.
Las Vegas, NV 89120
451-3597

Internal Revenue Service
4750 W. Oakey Blvd.
Las Vegas, NV 89102
455-1016

Internal Revenue Service · Tax Forms
Brian P. Mahon, Dir.
4750 W. Oakey Blvd.
Las Vegas, NV 89102
455-1030
1-800-829-3676 (tax forms)
1-800-829-1040 (tax info.)

Reporting tax fraud 1-800-859-8519

For assistance call Problem Resolution - 1-800-829-1040, or write to the:

Taxpayer Advocate
Internal Revenue Service
1111 Constitution Ave., N.W.
Washington, D.C. 20224

> ### NEVADA PROVING GROUND
> Established by the U.S. Atomic Energy Commission in southern Nevada in December 1950, above-ground atomic testing began in 1951. In 1962, it was shifted underground. The test site is 1,350 sq. mi. - slightly larger than Rhode Island. Testing ended in 1992, at which time 925 nuclear tests had been conducted.

Internal Revenue Service Building, 4750 W. Oakey Blvd., Las Vegas, NV 89102

LABOR, DEPT. OF

Apprenticeship and Training
George E. Ramsey, State Dir. - Nevada
301 E. Stewart Ave., Rm 311
Las Vegas, NV 89101
388-6771

Wage & Hour Division
General Information
1050 E. Flamingo Rd.
Las Vegas, NV 89119
699-5581

National Labor Relations Board
Stephen Wamser, Resident Officer

600 Las Vegas Blvd. S.
Las Vegas, NV 89101
388-6416

Post Office
Main Office
1001 E. Sunset Rd.
Las Vegas, NV 89199
1-800-275-8777
Answer Line - 361-9200
Cliff Rucker, Postmaster

Small Business Administration
John Scott, District Dir.
301 E. Stewart Ave.
Las Vegas, NV 89101
388-6611

Social Security Administration
Barbara Salzman, District Mgr.
5460 W. Sahara Ave.
Las Vegas, NV 89102
248-8717
800-772-1213 *(information)*

1820 E. Lake Mead Blvd.
N. Las Vegas, NV 89030
649-1982
Barbara Salzman, District Mgr.
800-772-1213 *(information)*

Veterans Administration
Information & Assistance
1-800-827-1000

FRANKLIN DELANO ROOSEVELT

In 1935 Franklin Delano Roosevelt was the first President to visit Las Vegas. John F. Kennedy was the second, when he delivered a speech at the Convention Center in September 1963.

POSTAL SERVICE

There are 39 full service post offices and contract stations in the Las Vegas metropolitan area.

Main Post Office
General Mail Facility
1001 E. Sunset Rd.
Las Vegas, NV 89199
1-800-275-8777
Serves Zips: 89119, 89193
Hours: Mon. - Fri. 6:30 am - 10 pm;
Sat. 8 am - 4 pm
Cliff Rucker, Postmaster - 361-9200
Postal answer line - 361-3444
(recorded info. using touch tone phone)
Zip Code information - 1-800-275-8777
Express Mail pick-up - 1-800-222-1811
General Delivery:
Downtown Post Office Mon. - Fri. 9 am-2 pm; Sat. 9 am - 1 pm
Same-day postmark:
Any post office before 5 pm or the Main Post Office outside collection box before 10 pm.
Express Mail:
Accepted until 10 pm at Main Post Office and Industrial Road Post Office until 7:45 pm for next day delivery to 11 western states.
Post Office Boxes: Five sizes
Small $ 20.00 - $29.00 - $52.00
for 6 mos.
Large $86.00 - $144.00 - $157.50
for 6 mos.
Money Orders: up to $700 - 85¢ each
Passport Applications:
Main Post Office - 1-800-275-8777
   Passport Office U.S. Dept. of State
1) Previous U.S. passport or certified birth certificate
2) Two identical photos (2" X 2")
3) Proper ID (such as drivers license)

4) Personal appearance
   (over 13 years of age)
5) $65 fee; under 18 years $40
Hours: Mon. - Fri. 8:30 am - 4:30 pm

POST OFFICES

General Mail Facility ·
Zip 89193
1001 E. Sunset Rd.
Las Vegas, NV 89199
1-800-275-8777 or 228-7231
Hours: Mon. - Fri. 6:30 am - 10 pm;
Sat. 8 am - 4 pm

McCarran Airport · Zip 89111
5757 Wayne Newton Blvd.
Las Vegas, NV 89111
361-9356
Hours: Mon. - Fri. 9 am - 5 pm
Closed 1 pm - 2 pm

Blue Diamond · Zip 89004
2 Diamond St.
Blue Diamond, NV 89004
Hours: Mon. - Fri. 8 am - 4:30 pm, closed
noon- 12:30 pm; Sat. 8 am - 11:30 am

Bonanza Station · Zip 89106 & 27
901 W. Bonanza Rd.
Las Vegas, NV 89127
Hours: Mon. - Fri. 9 am - 5 pm

Boulder City · Zip 89005 & 06
1101 Colorado St.
Boulder City, NV 89005
Hours: 8:30 am - 5:30 pm; Sat. 10 am - 1 pm

Downtown Station · Zip 89101 & 25
301 Stewart Ave.
Las Vegas, NV 89125
Hours: Mon. - Fri. 9 am - 5 pm;
Sat. 9 am - 1 pm

East Las Vegas ·
Zip 89112, 21, 22 & 60
4948 Mountain Vista St.
Las Vegas, NV 89112
Hours: Mon. - Fri. 9 am - 5 pm;
Sat. 9 am - 2 pm

Federal Station · Zip 89 101
300 Las Vegas Blvd. S.
Las Vegas, NV 89101
Hours: Mon. - Fri. 9 am - 4 pm,
closed 1 pm - 2 pm

Garside · Zip 89102, 07 & 26
1801 S. Decatur Blvd.
Las Vegas, NV 89126
Hours: Mon. - Fri. 9 am - 5 pm;
Sat. 9 am - 3 pm

Henderson ·
Zip 89009, 89011 & 89015
404 S. Boulder Hwy.
Henderson, NV 89015
565-8388
Hours: Mon. - Fri. 8:30 am - 5 pm

Henderson / Green Valley
Zip 89012, 14 & 16
2722 N. Green Valley Pkwy.
Henderson, NV 89016
Hours: Mon. - Fri. 7:30 am - 5 pm;
Sat. 10 am - 3 pm

Huntridge Station · Zip 89104,
10, 16 & 85
3115 E. Olive St.
Las Vegas, NV 89116
Hours: Mon. - Fri. 9 am - 5 pm;
Sat. 10 am - 2 pm

Nellis AFB Branch · Zip 89191
4250 Griffiss St.
Las Vegas, NV 89191

Nellis AFB - 652-4679
Hours: Mon. & Thu. 8:30 am - 5 pm;
Tue. & Wed. 8:30 am - 4 pm

North Las Vegas ·
Zip 89030, 31, 33, 36 & 115
1414 E. Lake Mead Blvd.
N. Las Vegas, NV 89030
Hours: Mon. - Fri. 8:30 am - 5 pm

Paradise Valley ·
Zip 89109, 19 & 32
4975 S. Swenson St.
Las Vegas, NV 89119
Hours: Mon. - Fri. 8:30 am - 5 pm

Red Rock Vista Station ·
Zip 89108, 29, 30, 31, and 33
2449 N. Tenaya Way
Las Vegas, NV 89128
Hours: Mon. - Fri. 9 am - 5 pm;
Sat. 8 am - 2 pm

Spring Valley ·
Zip 89103, 13, 17 & 80
3375 S. Rainbow Blvd.
Las Vegas, NV 89103
Hours: Mon. - Fri. 9 am - 5 pm;
Sat. 9 am - 2 pm

Strip Station ·
Zip 89114
3100 S. Industrial Rd.
Las Vegas, NV 89114
Hours: Mon. - Fri. 8:30 am - 5 pm

Summerlin ·
Zip 89128, 34, 37
1611 Spring Gate La.
Las Vegas, NV 89134
Hours: Mon. - Fri. 9 am - 5 pm;
Sat. 9 am - 2 pm

GOVERNMENT

Sunrise Carrier Unit ·
ZIP 89110 & 15
4885 E. Carey Ave.
Las Vegas, NV 8911 15
Hours: Mon. - Fri. 9 am – 4 pm;
Sat. 9 am – noon

Sunset Station ·
Zip 89118, 20, 23, & 39
950 S. Pilot Rd., Ste. M
Las Vegas, NV 89119
No window

University Branch D POBU ·
Zip 89170
4632 S. Maryland Pkwy.
Las Vegas, NV 89170
Hours: Mon. - Fri. 9 am - 4:30 pm

CONTRACT STATIONS

Sun Drugs · Zip 89101
2410 E. Bonanza Rd.
Las Vegas, NV 89101
382-1166
Hours: Mon. - Fri. 9 am - 4:20 pm;
Sat. 9 am - 1:30 pm

The Galleria · Zip 89102
2160 W. Charleston Blvd.
Las Vegas, NV 89102
385-9563
Hours: Mon. - Fri. 9 am - 5 pm;
Sat. - Sun. 8:30 am – noon

Mail Center USA · Zip 89102
4375 W. Desert Inn Rd.
Las Vegas, NV 89102
367-0665
Hours: Mon. - Sat. 8:30 am - 5:30 pm;
Sat. 9 am - 2 pm

Rainbow Drug · Zip 89102
1725 S. Rainbow Blvd.
Las Vegas, NV 89102
363-3043
Hours: Mon. - Fri. 9 am - 5 pm;
Sat. 9 am - 1 pm

Forum Shops · Caesars Palace
Zip 89109
3500 Las Vegas Blvd. S.
Las Vegas, NV 89109
893-4800
Hours: Sun. - Thu. 10 am - 11 pm;
Fri. - Sat. 10 am - Midnight

Landmark Pharmacy · Zip 89109
252 Convention Center Dr.
Las Vegas, NV 89109
731-0041
Hours: Mon. - Fri. 8:30 am - 4:30 pm;
Sat. 10 am - 2 pm

Package Plus II · Zip 89110
5000 E. Bonanza Rd.
Las Vegas, NV 89110
437-1459
Hours: Mon. - Fri. 9 am - 6 pm;
Sat. 8 am - 3:30 pm

Bonfiglio's Corner · Zip 89117
8524 W. Sahara Ave.
Las Vegas, NV 89117
363-8018
Hours: Mon. - Fri. 9 am - 5 pm, closed
2:20 - 3:30 pm; Sat. 9 am - 12 pm

Village East Drugs · Zip 89119
5025 S. Eastern Ave.
Las Vegas, NV 89119
736-7018
Hours: Mon. - Fri. 8 am - 4 pm

Village East Drugs · Zip 89119
2301 E. Sunset Rd.
Las Vegas, NV 89119
361-8800
Hours: Mon. - Fri. 9 am - 5 pm

NEVADA ZIP CODES

Carson City	897**	Carson City
Churchill	89406	Fallon
Clark	89004	Blue Diamond
	89005	Boulder City
	89007	Bunkerville
	89039	Cal-Nev-Ari
	89046	Cottonwood Cove
	89019	Goodsprings
	89012, 89014	Henderson-Green Valley
	89009, 89011, 89015	Henderson
	89018	Indian Springs
	89019	Jean
	891**	Las Vegas
	89029	Laughlin
	89021	Logandale
	89024	Mesquite
	89025	Moapa
	89124	Mtt. Charleston
	89191	Nellis AFB
	89046	Nelson
	89030, 89031, 89033, 89036	North Las Vegas
	89040	Overton
	89046	Searchlight
	89019	Stateline
Exclusive	89152	Sprint/Central Telephone
Clark County	89163	Citibank
Zip Codes	89155	Clark County Courthouse
	89125	General Delivery
	89153	LV Valley Water District
	89191	Nellis Air Force Base
	89151	Nevada Power Company
	89199	Postmaster
	89150	Southwest Gas Company
	89158	State of Nevada Mail Room
	89154	UNLV
Douglas	89705	Carson City
	89410	Gardnerville
	89411	Genoa
	89413	Glenbrook
	89423	Minden
	89449	Stateline
	89448	Zephyr Cove
Elko	89822	Carlin
	89823	Deeth
	89801	Elko
	89824	Halleck
	89825	Jackpot
	89826	Jarbidge
	89801	Jiggs
	89801	Lamoille
	89801	Lee
	89830	Montello
	89831	Mountain City
	89833	Ruby Valley
	89834	Tuscarora
	89835	Wells
	89883	Wendover
Esmeralda	89010	Dyer
	89013	Goldfield
	89047	Silverpeak

Eureka	89821	Beowawe
	89822	Carlin
	89823	Crescent Valley
	89316	Eureka
Humboldt	89404	Denio
	89414	Golconda
	89421	McDermitt
	89425	Orovada
	89426	Paradise Valley
	89438	Valmy
	89445	Winnemucca
Lander	89310	Austin
	89820	Battle Mountain
Lincoln	89001	Alamo
	89008	Caliente
	89017	Hiko
	89042	Panaca
	89043	Pioche
Lyon	89403	Dayton
	89408	Fernley
	89428	Silver City
	89429	Silver Springs
	89439	Smith
	89444	Wellington
	89447	Yerington
Mineral	89415	Hawthorne
	89420	Luning
	89422	Mina
	89427	Schurz
Nye	89020	Amargosa Valley
	89003	Beatty
	89409	Gabbs
	89022	Manhattan
	89023	Mercury
	89041	Pahrump
	89045	Round Mountain
	89049	Tonopah
Pershing	89418	Imlay
	89419	Lovelock
Storey	89440	Virginia City
Washoe	89704	Carson City
	89402	Crystal Bay
	89405	Empire
	89412	Gerlach
	89451	Incline Village
	89424	Nixon
	895**	Reno
	894**	Sparks
	89439	Verdi
	89442	Wadsworth
White Pine	89311	Baker
	89304	Duckwater
	89315	East Ely
	89301	Ely
	89317	Lund
	89318	McGill
	89319	Ruth

** This city has more than one five-digit Zip code.

Package Plus of LV · Zip 89121
4754 E. Flamingo Rd.
Las Vegas, NV 89121
435-1521
Hours: Mon. - Fri. 9 am - 5:30 pm;
Sat. 10 am - 3 pm

Copy Plus · Zip 89129
4016 N. Tenaya Way
Las Vegas, NV 89129
656-4537
Hours: Mon. - Fri. 8:30 am - 6 pm;
Sat. 9 am - 1 pm

Rainbow Drug · Zip 89134
9430 Del Webb Blvd.
Las Vegas, NV 89134
255-2234
Hours: Mon. - Fri. 9 am - 5 pm;
Sat. 9 am - 1 pm

Hallmark Gold Crown ·
Zip 89005
806 Buchanan Blvd.
Boulder City, NV 89005
293-1799
Hours: Mon. - Fri. 9 am - 5 pm,
closed 1 pm - 2 pm; Sat. 9 am - 1 pm

Green Valley Drug · Zip 89014
2712 N. Green Valley Pkwy.
Henderson, NV 89014
456-5000
Hours: Mon. - Fri. 9 am - 5 pm;
Sat. 9 am-3 pm

AKA Thunderbird · Zip 89115
3603 Las Vegas Blvd. N.
Las Vegas, NV 89115
643-2198
Hours: Mon. - Fri. 9 am-6 pm

LAS VEGAS AREA ZIP CODE MAP

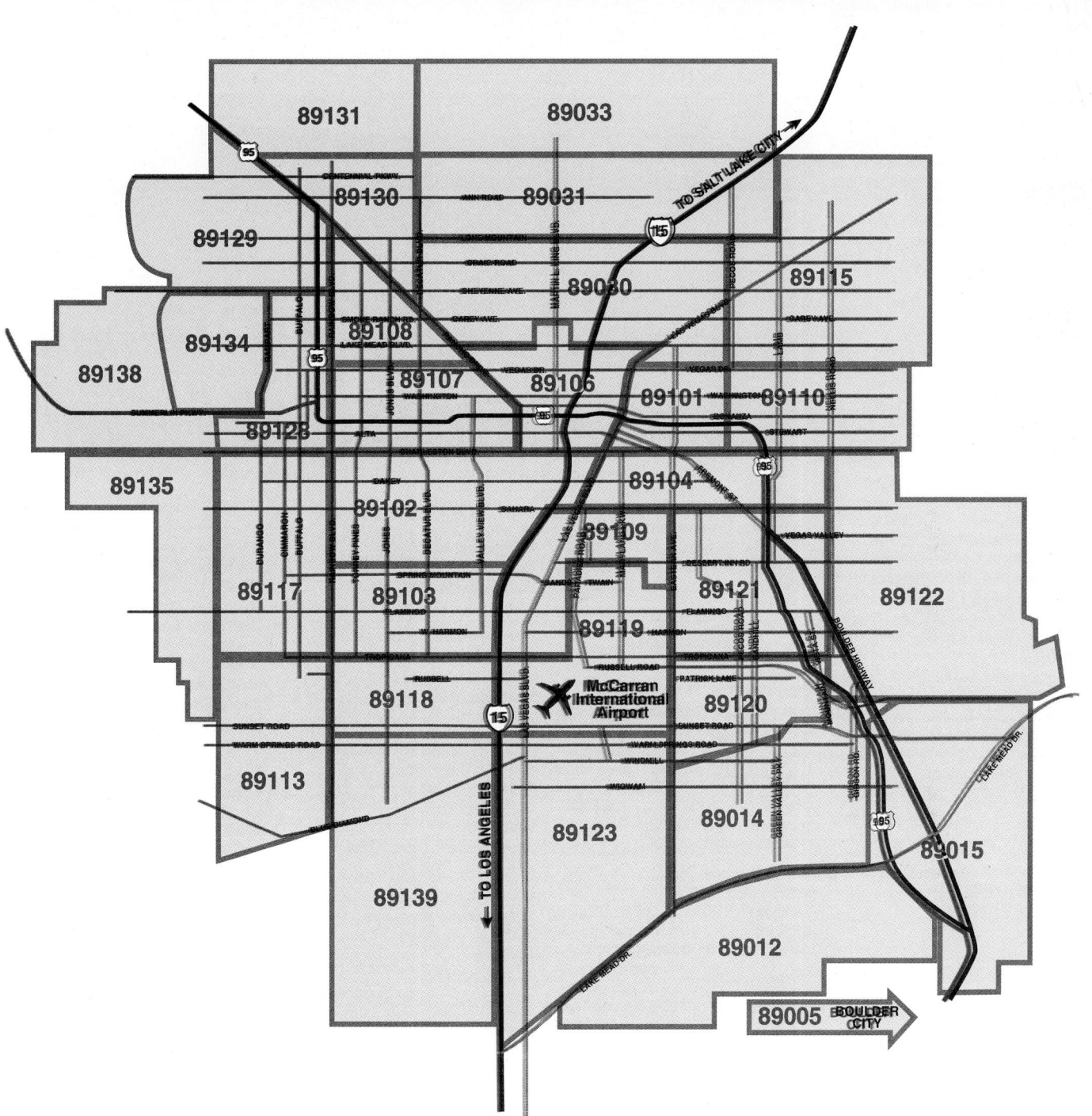

POST OFFICE EXPRESS LOCATIONS

Listed below are Express offices located inside Lucky Grocery Stores and the post offices that they report to.
Hours: Mon. - Sat. 10:30 - 7:30 pm; Sun. 11 am - 7 pm

Lucky Post Office Express
Redrock Vista Station
8350 W. Cheyenne Ave.
Las Vegas, NV 89129
655-4641   631-4843

Garside Station
6850 Spring Mountain Rd.
Las Vegas, NV 89102
248-7027

Garside Station
4801 Spring Mountain Rd.
Las Vegas, NV 89102
362-3951

Paradise Station
2300 E. Tropicana Ave.
Las Vegas, NV 89119
736-5189

Paradise Station
7271 S. Eastern Ave.
Las Vegas, NV 89119
263-7109

Huntridge Station
4420 E. Bonanza Rd.
Las Vegas, NV 89110
453-2219

Henderson
7245 S. Boulder Hwy.
Henderson, NV 89015
558-4072

PROTECTIVE / EMERGENCY SERVICES

911 EMERGENCY

for police-fire-ambulance serving Clark County (Las Vegas, North Las Vegas, Henderson, Boulder City, Blue Diamond and Laughlin).

Emergency means a situation in which property or human life is in jeopardy. The 911 hotline does not require a coin from pay phones and displays caller address if caller is unable to speak. If caller cannot speak English the 911 operator plugs the call into a language bank and the call is interpreted in English for emergency operator.

Las Vegas Metropolitan Police Department
Jerry Keller, Sheriff
400 E. Stewart Ave.
Las Vegas, NV 89101
Emergency 911

Non-emergency	229-3111
Secret Witness	385-5555
Information	795-3111
Sexual Assault	229-3421
Juvenile Detail	229-3561/2
Gang Hotline	229-4264
Prevention Detail	229-3597
SWAT Hot Line	229-7922
Missing Persons	229-2907
Abuse Line	229-3364
Domestic Violence	229-4451

Serves Las Vegas, Blue Diamond, Cal-Nev-Ari, Cottonwood Cove, Primm, Jean, Nelson, Searchlight, Moapa and Overton.

1,362 commissioned, 942 civilian personnel and 347 commissioned detention. Las Vegas has a ratio of 1.67 commissioned officers for every 1,000 residents.

Las Vegas Police Patrol
McCarran Airport
229-3328

Las Vegas Police Patrol
Northeast Area Command
831 N. Mojave Rd.
Las Vegas, NV 89101
229-3403

Las Vegas Police Patrol
Northwest Area Command
6208 Hargrove Ave.
Las Vegas, NV 89107
229-3426

Las Vegas Police Patrol
Southeast Area Command
2390 E. St. Louis Ave.
Las Vegas, NV 89104
229-3206

Las Vegas Police Patrol
Southwest Area Command
5925 Spring Mountain Rd.
Las Vegas, NV 89102
229-2848

Metropolitan Police Department (Southwest Area Command), 5925 Spring Mountain Rd., Las Vegas, NV 89102

Las Vegas Police Patrol
Downtown Area Command
400 S. 4th St.
Las Vegas, NV 89101
229-4848

Police Bureau Substations

Laughlin:
Emergency 911
Non-emergency: 298-2223

Mt. Charleston:
Emergency: 1-800-492-6505
Non-emergency: 872-5797

Lee Canyon:
Emergency: 1-800-492-6505
Non-emergency: 872-5797

UNLV Campus Police
4505 S. Maryland Pkwy
Las Vegas, NV 89154
895-3668
David Hollenbeck, Police Chief

North Las Vegas Police Department
1301 E. Lake Mead Blvd.
N. Las Vegas, NV 89030
J. E. Tillmon, Police Chief
Emergency 911
Non-emergency 649-9111

Henderson Police Department
223 Lead St.
Henderson, NV 89015
Tommy Burns, Police Chief
Emergency 911
Non-emergency 565-8933

Boulder City Police Department
1005 Arizona St.
Boulder City, NV 89005
David Mullin, Police Chief
Emergency 911
Non-emergency 293-9224

Las Vegas City Jail at City Hall
400 Stewart Ave.
Las Vegas, NV 89101
Michael Sheldon, Dir.
Information 229-6429

Las Vegas Department of Detention and Enforcement
3300 E. Stewart Ave.
Las Vegas, NV 89101
229-6617
Michael Sheldon, Dir.

Clark County Jail
330 S. Casino Center
Las Vegas, NV 89101
455-3950
David Sweikert, Deputy Chief
Information - 455-3900

Clark County Animal Control
4800 W. Dewey Dr.
Las Vegas, NV 89118
455-7710
Joe Boteilho, Chief

U. S. Customs Service
(Also listed under Federal Agencies)
McCarran International Airport
P. O. Box 11049
Las Vegas, NV 89111
388-6480
Office of Enforcement - 388-6042
Jack Pansky, Port Dir.

District Attorney · Clark County
200 S. 3rd St.
Las Vegas, NV 89101
455-4711
Stuart Bell, District Attorney
Responsible for prosecuting all felony, gross misdemeanor and juvenile offender cases within the county as well as all misdemeanor outside the county's four incorporated areas and enforces, through the courts, payments of child support.

Las Vegas Constable
200 S. Third St.
Las Vegas, NV 89101
455-4099
Bob Nolan, Constable

Nevada Attorney General
Las Vegas Central
555 E. Washington Ave.
Las Vegas, NV 89101
486-3420
Frankie Sue Del Papa
Consumer Fraud - 486-7353
Worker Comp Fraud - 687-4076
Gaming Unit - 486-6400

Nevada Gaming Control Board
555 E. Washington Ave., Ste. 2600
Las Vegas, NV 89101
486-2000
Bill Bible, Chairman

1997 LAS VEGAS CRIME INDEX

	1997	1996	1995
Murder	148	163	122
Rape	574	475	571
Robbery	3,809	3,650	3,782
Aggravated Assault	4,527	4,123	5,102
Burglaries	13,162	11,656	12,230
Larcenies	28,072	28,952	30,445
Auto Theft	8,703	7,925	7,991

Metro police responded to 854,796 calls during 1997.

PRISON POPULATION

Nevada is ninth in the nation in incarcerating prisoners. According to state Prisons Department Director Robert Bayer, there are 8,262 in-house prisoners in Nevada as of September 1997. It costs about $15,164 per year to keep an inmate in Nevada prisons. Figures do not include local jails. In 10 years (July 1985 - July 1995) Nevada's prison population increased 100.4 percent.

Nevada Highway Patrol
2601 E. Sahara Ave.
Las Vegas, NV 89104
486-4100
Michael Hood, Chief
Emergency Dial Operator and ask for Zenith 1-2000
Road Conditions - 486-3116
Cellular Emergency - *NHP

Postal Inspector
1001 E. Sunset Rd.
Las Vegas, NV 89199
796-6839
Robert Hernandez

U.S. Department of Justice
Drug Enforcement Administration
600 Las Vegas Blvd. S., Ste. 640
Las Vegas, NV 89101
388-6635
Keith Baudoin, Asst. Special Agent in Charge

Federal Bureau of Investigation
700 E. Charleston Blvd.
Las Vegas, NV 89104
385-1281
Bobby Siller, Special Agent in Charge

Immigration & Naturalization Service
3373 Pepper Ln.
Las Vegas, NV 89120
451-3597
Christine Davis, Officer in Charge

U.S. Attorney
701 E. Bridger Ave.
Las Vegas, NV 89101
388-6336
Kathryn Landreth

U.S. Marshal
300 Las Vegas Blvd. S., Ste. 424
Las Vegas, NV 89101
388-6355
Herbert L. Brown, U.S. Marshal

U.S. Dept. of Treasury
Secret Service
600 Las Vegas Blvd. S.
Las Vegas, NV 89101
388-6571
Joseph Saitta, Special Agent

Bureau of Alcohol, Tobacco & Firearms
600 Las Vegas Blvd. S., Ste. 540
Las Vegas, NV 89101
388-6584
Ed Verkin, Resident Agent in Charge

U.S. National Park Service
601 Nevada Hwy
Boulder City, NV 89005
293-8908
Emergency - 293-8932
Law enforcement agency for Lake Mead National Recreation Area
Alan O'Neill, Supt.

CORONER / MEDICAL EXAMINER

Clark County Coroner
1704 Pinto Ln.
Las Vegas, NV 89106
455-3210
Ron Flud, Chief Coroner
Death Certificate copy - 383-1223

FIRE / PARAMEDIC

Clark County Fire Department

There are 505 combat firefighters and 61 support personnel in Clark County. There are five separate City and County fire departments.

Las Vegas Fire Dept. #1
500 N. Casino Center Blvd.
Las Vegas, NV 89101
383-2888
Emergency - 911
Cellular Emergency - *NHP
Mario Trevino, Chief of Dept.

Clark County Fire Dept. #18
575 E. Flamingo Rd.
Las Vegas, NV 89119
455-7311
Earl Greene, Fire Chief

Las Vegas Fire Dept. #2
900 S. Durango Dr.
Las Vegas, NV 89117

Las Vegas Fire Dept. #3
2645 W. Washington Ave.
Las Vegas, NV 89106

Las Vegas Fire Dept. #4
4215 S. 15th St.
Las Vegas, NV 89104

Las Vegas Fire Dept. #5
1020 Hinson St.
Las Vegas, NV 89107

Las Vegas Fire Dept. #6
190 Upland Blvd.
Las Vegas, NV 89107

Las Vegas Fire Dept. #8
633 N. Mojave Rd.
Las Vegas, NV 89101

Las Vegas Fire Dept. #9
6841 W. Lone Mountain Rd.
Las Vegas, NV 89108

Las Vegas Fire Dept. #42
7331 W. Cheyenne Ave.
Las Vegas, NV 89129

Clark County Fire Station #11
5150 Las Vegas Blvd. S.
Las Vegas, NV 89119

Clark County Fire Station #12
3001 Industrial Rd.
Las Vegas, NV 89109

Clark County Fire Station #13
McCarran Airport
Las Vegas, NV 89119

Clark County Fire Station #14
3260 Topaz St.
Las Vegas, NV 89121

Clark County Fire Station #15
3480 S. Valley View Blvd.
Las Vegas, NV 89102

Clark County Fire Station #16
150 N. Nellis Blvd.
Las Vegas, NV 89110

Clark County Fire Station #17
5110 Andover Dr.
Las Vegas, NV 89122

Clark County Fire Station #19
5710 Spencer St.
Las Vegas, NV 89119

Clark County Fire Station #20
5710 Judson Ave.
Las Vegas, NV 89115

Clark County Fire Station #21
4950 S. Valley View Blvd.
Las Vegas, NV 89118

Clark County Fire Station #22
6685 W. Flamingo Rd.
Las Vegas, NV 89103

Clark County Fire Station #23
4520 E. Alexander Rd.
Las Vegas, NV 89115

Clark County Fire Station #24
7525 Industrial Rd.
Las Vegas, NV 89139

Clark County Fire Station #25
5210 S. Pecos Rd.
Las Vegas, NV 89120

N. Las Vegas Fire Station #51
2626 E. Carey Ave.
N. Las Vegas, NV 89030
633-1117

N. Las Vegas Fire Station #52
2001 E. Cheyenne Ave.
Las Vegas, NV 89115

N. Las Vegas Fire Station #53
3001 N. Martin Luther King Blvd.
Las Vegas, NV 89106

N. Las Vegas Fire Station #54
5438 Camino Al Norte St.
N. Las Vegas, NV 89030
Michael Massey, Chief of Department
Emergency 911

Henderson Fire Department
Administration
223 Lead St.
Henderson, NV 89015
565-2016

Henderson Fire Dept. #91
600 College Dr.
Henderson, NV 89015
565-2131

Henderson Fire Dept. #92
486 Gibson Rd.
Henderson, NV 89015
565-2132

Henderson Fire Dept. #93
100 Burkholder Blvd.
Henderson, NV 89015
565-2133

Henderson Fire Dept. #94
400 Valley Verde Dr.
Henderson, NV 89015
565-2041

Henderson Fire Dept. #95
2300 Pebble Pl.
Henderson, NV 89015
565-2819
Joe Hill, Chief of Dept.
Emergency 911

Boulder City Fire Department
1101 Elm St.
Boulder City, NV 89005
293-9228
Emergency - 911
Dean Molburg, Chief of Dept.

AMBULANCE & PARAMEDICS

Mercy Ambulance
1130 S. Martin Luther King Blvd.
Las Vegas, NV 89102
John Wilson, CEO
Non-emergency dispatch - 384-3400
Emergency 911

Serving Las Vegas since 1954, Mercy Ambulance operates through a performance-based contract with Clark County. Mercy operates 48 ambulances that respond to an average of 370 calls a day.

TAXATION INFORMATION

(Also see Business Section for business taxes)

The State Department of Taxation publishes a 16-page pamphlet called the "taxpayers' bill of rights" which details the responsibilities of the agency and the taxpayer and identifies the rights for business owner taxpayers.

Department of Taxation Office - Main Office
1550 E. College Pkwy., Ste. 115
Carson City, NV 89706
Larry Scott, Revenue Dir.
687-4820 (Revenue)
Paul Ferrin, Acting Audit Dir.
687-4830 (Audit)

Department of Taxation Office - Reno District Office
Kietzke Plaza
4600 Kietzke Ln.
Building O, Ste. 263
Reno, NV 89502
688-1295
Thelma De Voss, Dir.

Department of Taxation Office - Las Vegas District Office
Grant Sawyer Office Building
555 E. Washington Ave.
Las Vegas, NV 89101
486-2300
Bob Palmer, District Mgr.

Nevada Taxpayers Association
2303 E. Sahara Ave.
Las Vegas, NV 89104
457-8442
Carole Vilardo, Pres.
Private advocacy and research group.

TAXES

Alcoholic Beverage Tax
Beer: .09 per gallon
Liquor: 1/2 of 1% to 14% alcohol (dry wine) - $.40 per gallon
14% to 22% alcohol (sweet wine) $.75 per gallon
Over 22% alcohol (liquor) $2.05 per gallon
Cigarette & Tobacco Excise Tax:
1.75 cents per cigarette, but no less than 35 cents per package. Other tobacco products at 30 percent of wholesaler's cost. Almost $50 million a year is raised from this tax.
Estate Tax: Imposed on the transfer of the taxable estate of a deceased person who is a resident of Nevada in the amount of the maximum credit allowable against the federal estate tax for the payment of state death taxes.
Gasoline Tax: State gasoline tax is 23 cents a gallon. Nevadans pay 18.4 cents a gallon federal tax, up to 10 cents a gallon local tax and 73/410th of a cent a gallon into a fund to clean up leaking gasoline tanks.
Inheritance Tax: None
Personal Income Tax: None
Personal Property Tax: None on household goods owned by a single family.

Property Tax - County Assessor
500 S. Grand Central Pkwy.
Las Vegas, NV 89155
455-3891
Mark Schofield, Clark County Assessor
Hours: Mon. - Fri. 8 am-5 pm

The Nevada constitutional limit and statutory limit is $5 and $3.64 respectively per $100 assessed valuation. A typical tax bill on a $100,000 home for 1996-97 was $819 per year for the County and $1,059 for the City. Las Vegas residents pay about $3.03 per $100 of assessed value.

Assessment is 35% of full cash value. Taxable value for land is full cash value; for improved land cash value based on actual use; for improvements value is replacement cost less depreciation at 1 1/2% per year to 50 years.

The assessed value of taxable Clark County property is $20 billion for 1997-98. This is a 10% increase over the 1996-97 value.

Real Property Transfer Tax - 55 cents for each $500 of value or fraction thereof, when value exceeds $100.

Sales Tax - Department of Taxation
555 E. Washington Ave.
Las Vegas, NV 89101
486-2300
Bob Palmer, District Supv.

The aggregate rate of sales and use tax is 7% in Southern Nevada. The components making up the 7% tax rate are: State Sales and Use Tax 2%; Local School Support Tax 1 1/2%; Basic and supplemental City and County Relief Tax 2 1/4%; Control of Floods 1/4%.
Food for home consumption or prescription drugs are exempt from tax.

Taxable sales for fiscal year 1997 were $16,476,941,732 in Clark County, an increase of 12.1% from 1996; $24,408,113,890 in Nevada, an increase of 9.3% from 1996.
Sales Tax on Services: Almost none.

BUSINESS TAXES

Admissions Tax: None.
Business Licenses: *See Business Section.*
Business License Tax: Approved in 1991 by the legislature, the law went into effect July 1, 1991 with the first quarterly payment due Sept. 30, 1991. All Nevada businesses must pay a one-time fee of $25 and a fee of $100 ($25 per quarter) per year for each employee. Sole proprietorships are exempt.
Capital Stock Tax: None.
Chain Store Tax: None.
Corporate Income Tax (taxes measured by net income): None.
Franchise Tax: None.
Inventory Tax: None.
Room Tax: 10 percent in Clark County for resort hotels. Non-resort hotels where an occupant stays over 30 days, 4 percent. Downtown room tax is 10 percent if the hotel is part of the Fremont Street Experience, and 9 percent for hotel adjacent to the project.
Unitary Tax: None.

State Business License Tax: one time $25 filing fee for all businesses. Any business that has employees must pay a quarterly tax based on the number of employees. Many different formulas are used to calculate the rate, which if you had just one employee would be $25 per quarter. The number does not include a sole proprietor.

State Dept. of Taxation - Las Vegas District Office
Grant Sawyer Office Bldg.
555 E. Washington Ave., Ste. 1300
Las Vegas, NV 89101
486-2300
Bob Palmer, District Mgr.

Unemployment Insurance Tax
Employment Security Div.
1830 E. Sahara Ave., Ste. 202
Las Vegas, NV 89104
486-8222
Stan Jones, Dir.
Unemployment Compensation Insurance taxes are paid by employers to make unemployment payments to laid-off workers. Any business that employs one or more persons and pays wages totaling $225 or more per calendar quarter must pay unemployment. Contributions for a new employer fall between 0.25 percent to 5.40 percent with the standard rate being 2.95 percent of the taxable wage. There are 18 categories, based on employee turnover in the past with new employers paying the mandatory 2.95 percent until they get an experienced

rating to qualify them for lower rates. The average Nevada employer will pay 1.4 percent on the first $18,000 a year in wages. The department paid out approximately $159.6 million in benefits during 1997 compared to $145.2 million in 1996. Each employer pays out $570 per year for each employee.

Workers Compensation Insurance
State Industrial Insurance System
1700 W. Charleston Blvd.
Las Vegas, NV 89126
388-3114
Douglas Dirks, Dir.
Premiums are collected on each $100 of payroll based on loss experience of the industry classification, to a maximum of $36,000 in 1997. Premium rates vary by occupation, with riskier job classifications, such as mining, having higher rates than safer classifications, such as clerical positions.

GAMING AND ENTERTAINMENT TAXES

Nevada Gaming Control Board
555 E. Washington Ave.
Las Vegas, NV 89101
486-2000
Bill Bible, Chairman
There are many different gaming taxes imposed. Contact the Tax and License Division of the Gaming Control Board for information. Gaming revenue tax is 6.25 percent on revenues above $134,000 a month; 4 percent on revenues between $50,000 and $134,000 a month; 3 percent on revenues up to $50,000 a month; additional fee of $100 to $1,000 per table game and $250 on each slot machine per year. Total state gaming tax contribution for FY 1997 was $570 million. Taxes from gaming revenue make up about 42 percent of the state's general fund budget. Since 1955, the tax rate on large casinos has only risen from 5.5 percent of gross winnings to 6.25 percent.

FEDERAL INCOME TAX

Internal Revenue Service
(Also listed under State Government)
4750 W. Oakey Blvd.
Las Vegas, NV 89102
455-1016
1-800-829-1040 1-800-829-0433
Web site - http:www.ustreas.gov
Information, tax forms and pamphlets
Hours: Mon. - Fri. 7:30 am - 3:30 pm

VOTER REGISTRATION

VOTER REGISTRATION

Clark County Election Department
500 Grand Central Pkwy.
Las Vegas, NV 89155
455-2780
Voter Hotline - 455-VOTE

Nevada is a closed primary state, which means you cannot vote for partisan offices in a primary election unless you are registered with the political party.

Kathryn Ferguson, Registrar of Voters, conducts all federal, state, county and municipal elections and supervises voter registration.

Municipal elections were held in May and June 1996.

Primary Election - Sept. 1, 1998
General Election - Nov. 3, 1998

Qualifications for voter registration are:

1. You must be a United States citizen
2. You must be 18 years of age by election day.
3. You must have continuously resided within the State and Clark County at least 30 days, and your precinct for 10 days before the next ensuing election.
4. Persons convicted of a felony or dishonorably discharged from the military must have had their civil rights restored.

Registration can be done in person or through the mail. Applications are available at over 132 sites including post offices, schools, DMV and libraries, a few banks, United Blood Service, Chamber of Commerce, City Clerk's office and utility companies. If you register by mail, you must provide a social security number, Nevada driver's license number or state identification number on the application.

Absentee Voting - 455-2780; absentee ballots must be received by the election department no later than 7 pm on election day.

REGISTRATION

You may register to vote at the Clark County Election Department or at any City Clerk's office located in Boulder City, Henderson, Las Vegas, North Las Vegas and Mesquite, or with any Field Deputy Registrar (455-2780).

1. Registration closes for the September 1st primary election on August 1st at 9:00 pm
2. Registration closes for the November 3rd general election on October 3rd at 9:00 pm
3. Registration closes 3 weeks prior to any special election.

During the last five (5) days prior to the close of registration for any election, the Clark County Election Department is open 8:00 am - 9:00 pm, including Saturday, which is always the last day to register.

For information about party affiliation, absentee ballot or special voting instructions, call 455-2780.

Voter registration is permanent unless you fail to vote in the State's General Election held in November of the even-numbered years.

You may change your address by calling the Election Department at 455-2780 up to one week prior to the close of registration and in person the last week of registration.

Approximately fifteen days before any election, you will be mailed a sample ballot. On the front of each sample ballot will be a label stating the name and address of your polling location. Polls are open on election day from 7 am - 7 pm

Registered voters in Nevada are 817,657 as of July 1997. During last November's election, 56.3 percent of the registered voters cast their ballots. During the Municipal election held June 6, 1995, 61,862 people cast their ballot. There are 39,233 inactive and 464,530 active registered voters in Clark County as of September 1997.

POLITICAL ORGANIZATIONS

League of Women Voters of Las Vegas Valley
4413 Mark Ave.
Las Vegas, NV 89108
631-4998
Ruth Mills, Pres.
Meets 3rd Sat. 8:30 am at Mardi Gras Hotel.

DEMOCRATIC

Clark County Democratic Party
1785 E. Sahara Ave., Ste. 496
Las Vegas, NV 89104
735-1600
Charlie Waterman, Pres.
Meets about four times a year. Call for information.

Democratic Party of Nevada State Chairman
Paul Henry, Chairman

North Las Vegas Democratic Club
2201 W. Evans Ave.
N. Las Vegas, NV 89030
648-5328
Annie Walker, Pres.
Meets 3rd Tue. 7:30 pm at N. Las Vegas Lions Club.

Paradise Democratic Club
405 Antelope Way
Las Vegas, NV 89128
363-2456
John Ponticello, Pres.
Meets 3rd Wed. of each month at the Police Protective Assn.

Women's Democratic Club
2680 Copper Cove Dr.
Henderson, NV 89014
897-0775
Caren Levenson, Pres.
Meets 3rd Thu. 11:30 am.

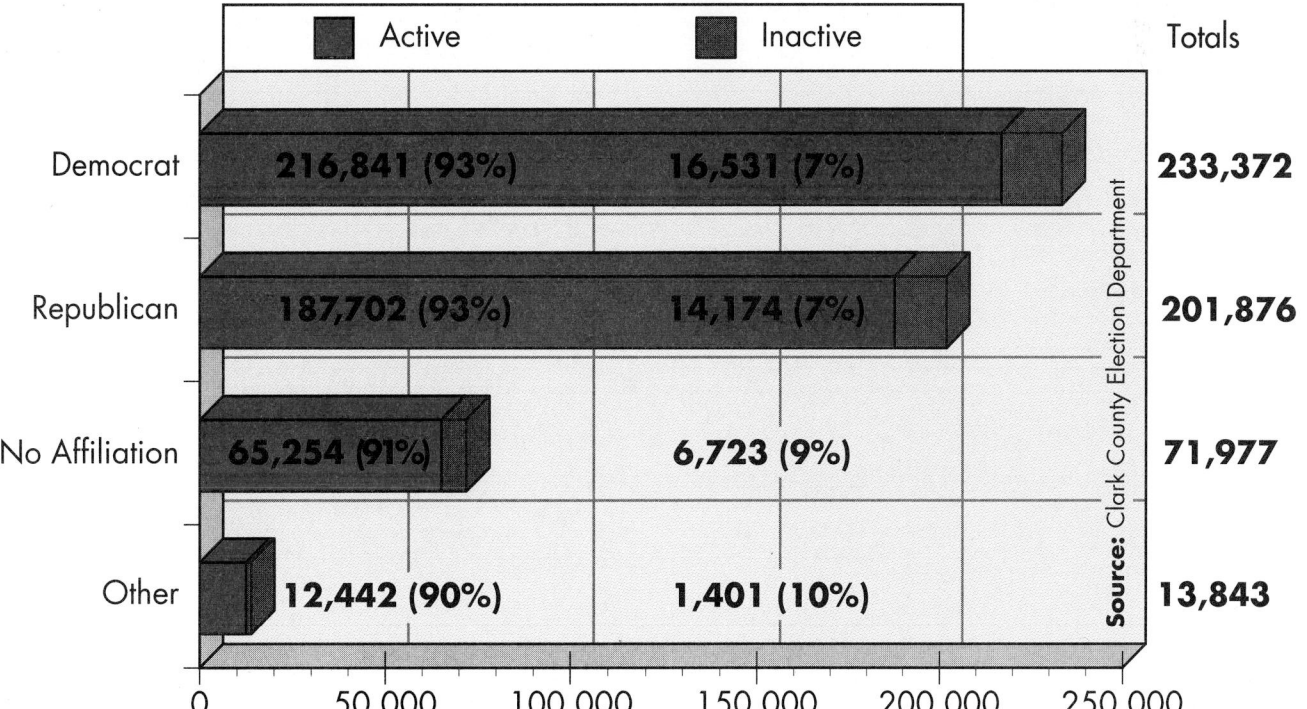

Clark County Registered Voters

	Active	Inactive	Totals
Democrat	216,841 (93%)	16,531 (7%)	233,372
Republican	187,702 (93%)	14,174 (7%)	201,876
No Affiliation	65,254 (91%)	6,723 (9%)	71,977
Other	12,442 (90%)	1,401 (10%)	13,843

Source: Clark County Election Department

Total Registered Voters = 521,068

VOTER REGISTRATION

REPUBLICAN

Active Republicans Women's Club
711 Rancho Cir.
Las Vegas, NV 89109
878-5534
Liz Roberts, Pres.
Meets 2d Thu. 5:30 pm.

Boulder City Republican Women's Club
1611 Bermuda Dunes Dr.
Boulder City, NV 89005
293-6676
Jo Marshall, Pres.
Meets 3rd Thu. 11:30 am.

Republican Women of Henderson
3113 Trueno Rd.
Henderson, NV 89014
451-8080
Mary Ann Hantout, Pres.
Meets 2nd Thu. 11:30 am.

Nevada Republican Men's Club
1824 Goldring Ave.
Las Vegas, NV 89106
383-6767
Susan Turner, Treas.
Meets 1st Mon. 11:30 am. Everyone of voting age is welcome, including women and other political parties.

Republican Party of Nevada
6114 W. Charleston Blvd.
Las Vegas, NV 89102
258-9182
John Mason, State Chairman

Clark County Central Committee
6116 W. Charleston Blvd.
Las Vegas, NV 89102
258-9184
Milton I. Schwartz, County Chairman
Meets 3rd Tue. bi monthly 7 pm at Showboat Hotel.

Republican Women of Las Vegas
356 Humboldt Dr. N.
Henderson, NV 89014
897-1345
Carol LaCosta, Pres.
Helen Klatt, State Pres.
Meets 2nd Wed. of each month (except July and August) at Debbie Reynolds Hotel - 11:30 am, guest speakers.

Spring Mountain Republican Women
2328 Brighton Shore St.
Las Vegas, NV 89128
242-9012
Joan Dimmitt, Pres.
Meets 3rd Sat. 10 am.

Green Valley Republican Women
2012 Aspen Brook Dr.
Henderson, NV 89014
897-4682
Nickie Diersen, Pres.
Meets 2nd Sat. 10 am.

LIBERTARIAN

Libertarian Party of America
Watergate Hotel
2600 Virginia Ave. N.W., Ste. 100
Washington, D.C.20037
1-800-682-1776
Jim Burns, Party Chairman

Independent American Party
415 S. 6th St.
Las Vegas, NV 89101
893-9332
Brian Lusk, County Chairman
Teresia Avila, State Chairperson
Meets 1st Tue. of each month at the Oxford Court.

Facts of Interest

Only one woman was ever legally hanged in Nevada. Elizabeth Potts was sent to the gallows in June 1890 for the murder of Miles Faucett.

The world's first execution by lethal gas took place in Nevada State Prison in Carson City in 1924.

The first Nevada State Prison was established in 1862 in the Warm Springs Hotel, located east of Carson City.

In 1892, the U.S. Postal Service opened an office in the then-tiny hamlet of Las Vegas.

The first courthouse was built in Genoa County, seat of Carson County in the Utah Territory, in 1860.

Lovelock has the only round courthouse in Nevada. There are only two in the country.

The only wooden courthouse still in use in Nevada is in Fallon, built in 1903.

Dorothy Porter, a former Ziegfeld dancer, was the first woman elected to a major city council. In 1953, she was elected Mayor of North Las Vegas. The first African-American to be elected to the Nevada legislature was Woodrow Wilson of Las Vegas, who served in the State Assembly as a Republican in 1966.

Registered voters in Clark County
(through March 1998)

Democratic 233,372
Republican 201,876
Nonpartisan 71,977
Libertarian 2,462
Independent American 9,727
Green Party 122
Nat. Law 330
Reform Party 122
Other 1,080

Total Clark County eligible voters: 521,068

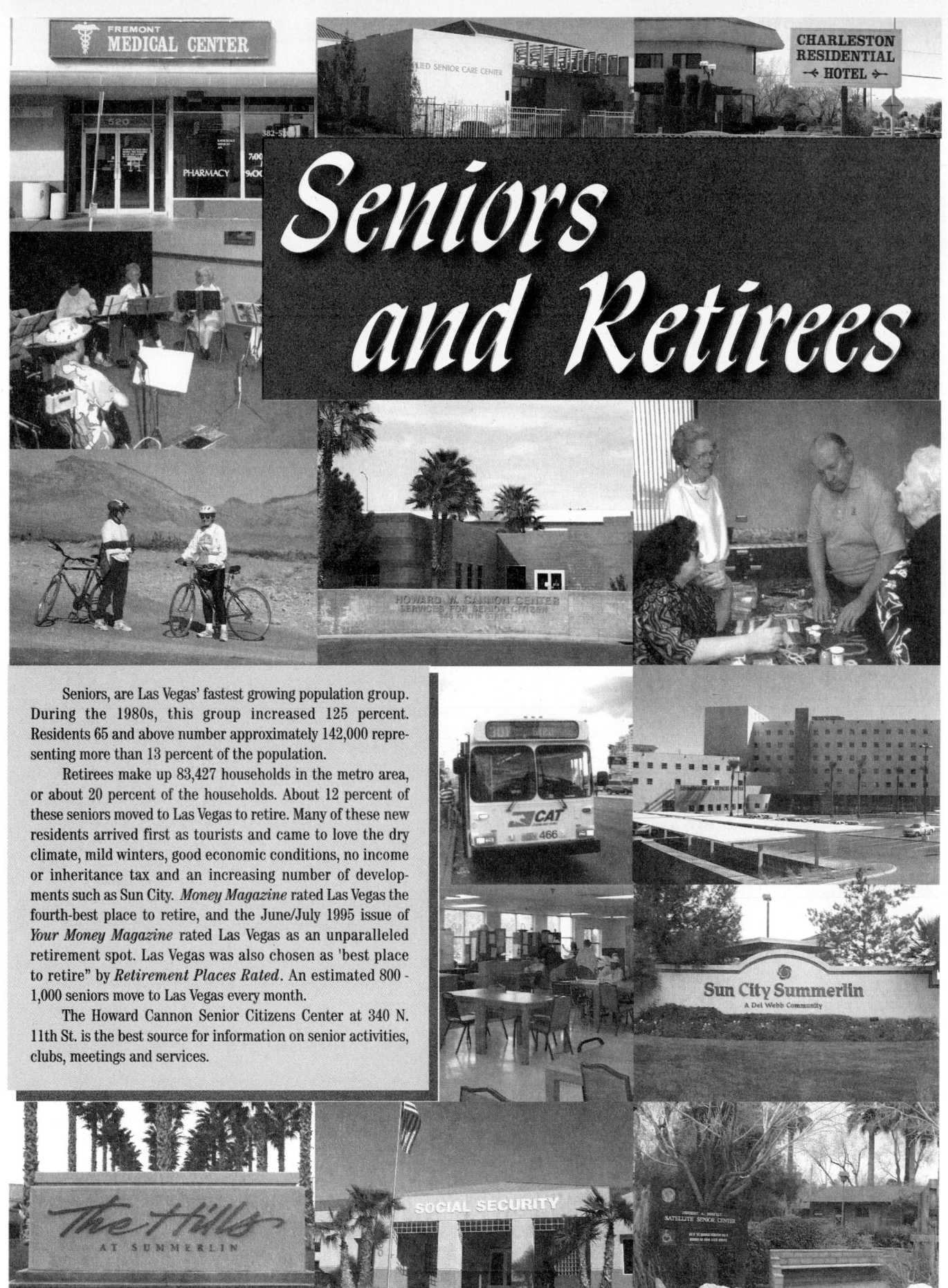

Seniors and Retirees

Seniors, are Las Vegas' fastest growing population group. During the 1980s, this group increased 125 percent. Residents 65 and above number approximately 142,000 representing more than 13 percent of the population.

Retirees make up 83,427 households in the metro area, or about 20 percent of the households. About 12 percent of these seniors moved to Las Vegas to retire. Many of these new residents arrived first as tourists and came to love the dry climate, mild winters, good economic conditions, no income or inheritance tax and an increasing number of developments such as Sun City. *Money Magazine* rated Las Vegas the fourth-best place to retire, and the June/July 1995 issue of *Your Money Magazine* rated Las Vegas as an unparalleled retirement spot. Las Vegas was also chosen as 'best place to retire" by *Retirement Places Rated*. An estimated 800 - 1,000 seniors move to Las Vegas every month.

The Howard Cannon Senior Citizens Center at 340 N. 11th St. is the best source for information on senior activities, clubs, meetings and services.

SENIOR HELP & REFERRAL

American Association for Retired Persons (AARP)
340 N. 11th St.
Las Vegas, NV 89101
386-8661
Mildred Willard,
State Office Coordinator
National organization of people age 50 and over that serves their needs and interests through legislative advocacy, research, informative programs and community services. An $8 annual fee includes subscription to *Modern Maturity* magazine as well as discounts on travel, discount prescriptions by mail, supplemental health insurance at group rates, auto and homemaker's insurance and volunteer services.

Clark County Neighborhood Justice Center
1600 Pinto Ln.
Las Vegas, NV 89106
455-3898
Ruth Urbin, Div. Mgr.
The NJC helps residents of Clark County resolve conflicts at no cost through a comprehensive information and referral program and through mediation services.

Clark County Public Guardian/Administrator
(Also listed under Family)
1700 Pinto Ln.
Las Vegas, NV 89106
455-4332
Jared E. Shafer, Public Guardian/Adm.
The public guardian handles cases involving people with diminished physical and mental capacity who are unable to manage their own affairs. The office's goal is to prevent exploitation of the elderly and mentally or physically impaired.

Economic Opportunity Board of Clark County
2228 Comstock Dr.
Las Vegas, NV 89030
647-2010
Information & Referral - 647-1510
James Tyree, Exec. Dir.
Federally funded social services agency. Senior day care centers and foster grandparents.

Eldercare Helpline
1-800-677-1116
Toll-free telephone number responds to the needs of seniors, families and professional caregivers to know more about the wide range of senior services offered in Nevada.

HELP of Southern Nevada
953 E. Sahara Ave., Bldg. #35B, Ste. 208
Las Vegas, NV 89104
369-4357
Denice Conrad, Exec. Dir.
Information and referral to senior agencies in Clark County.

Howard Cannon Senior Service Center
(Also listed under Senior Centers)
340 N. 11th St.
Las Vegas, NV 89101
366-1522
Carol Hunter, Dir.
The Howard W. Cannon Center opened in 1987 and provides a variety of services to seniors under one roof. Persons age 60 and older can access the following services Mon. - Fri. 9 am - 4 pm: center social work, assistance provided for seniors with problems, information and referral, loan of medical equipment.
   The following organizations have representatives at Cannon Senior Center:

Nevada State Welfare Office
486-3600
Medical Assistance for the Aged (MAABD) (seniors 65 and up).

Senior Citizens Law Project
229-6596
Legal advice, information and referral

American Association of Retired Persons
386-8661
Volunteer tax service.

Catholic Charities of Southern Nevada
382-0721
Senior Companion, Senior Community Service Employment Program and Retired Senior Volunteer Program (RSVP).

Patient Billing Services
384-1987
Processing insurance claims, problem solving and insurance counseling.

Cannon Senior Medical Center
384-2273
General practice by Dr. James Laird and vision screening by Opticare 2000.

Clark County Social Services
455-4342
Senior citizen protective services, Clark County medical cards.

Other agencies that provide services but are not housed at the center:

DMV - 1st Mon. of the month
Sheppard Eye Clinic - every other Thu.
C.A.T. tickets - available every day.
Public Guardian - training two times a month on Wed. - 455-4332
Clark County Assessor Office - once a year to assist with application on rent rebate.
More information on the services listed can be found in other sections.

Las Vegas Metropolitan Police Dept.
400 Stewart Ave.
Las Vegas, NV 89101
229-3364
Abuse and neglect detail

Las Vegas Senior Citizens Center
451 E. Bonanza Rd.
Las Vegas, NV 89101
229-6454
Lettie Peters, Programs Coordinator
Hours: Mon. - Sat. 9 am - 10 pm
Facilities: Gymnasium, swimming pool, billiard room, restaurant, library, banquet room and meeting rooms.

Lend-a-Hand Program, Inc.
400 Utah St.
Boulder City, NV 89005
294-2363
Margaret Lotspeich, Program Dir.
Home care, light meals, friendly visits, errands, exercising.

Direct Dental Services

This program was started by Donna Rose, a member of the state's Long-Term Care Facilities Administrators Board of Examiners. It has been described as a "M.A.S.H." dental unit, formed in 1996 after a pilot study proved such a service was needed. A portable dentist's office is housed in a van which visits 23 facilities, 13 of which are in Clark County. Patients in adult care facilities were not receiving adequate dental care because of the difficulty in finding dentists who were willing to accept Medicaid patients. (Medicaid pays only 20 - 30 percent of the cost of a dental visit.) There can be nothing but admiration for Dr. Eric Homze and Dr. Joseph Eberly of Reno for undertaking this work and accepting whatever Medicaid will pay. Thanks to this program, the state legislature has increased the amount that Medicaid will pay.

Nevada Division of Aging Services
340 N. 11th St., Ste. 203
Las Vegas, NV 89101
486-3545
Carla Sloan, Adm.
Nursing home ombudsman administers federal grants for nutrition and social service programs, office of elder rights. Serves as advocate for Nevada's senior population. Major function is to develop programs to help seniors maintain their independence and improve their quality of life. Community Home-Based Initiatives Program (CHIPS) for seniors eligible to receive home and personal care assistance (no medical services).

Nevada State Welfare
340 N. 11th St.
Las Vegas, NV 89101
486-3600
Homemaker Services - 486-5000
Food stamps and medical assistance for the aged.

Senior Citizens Protective Services Program
Clark County Social Services
340 N. 11th St.
Las Vegas, NV 89101
455-4291
Deanna Taha, Supv.
Investigates allegations of senior abuse, neglect and exploitation.

Social Security Administration
5460 W. Sahara Ave.
Las Vegas, NV 89102
248-8717

1820 E. Lake Mead Blvd.
N. Las Vegas, NV 89030
649-1982   1-800-772-1213

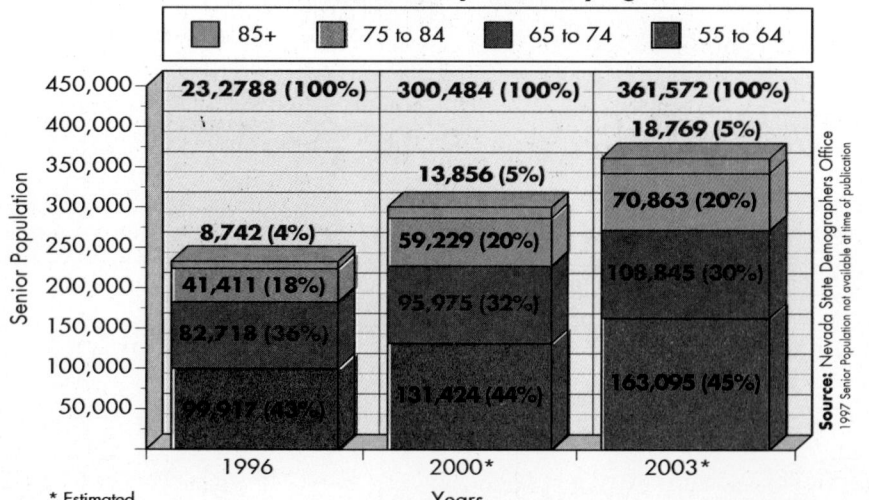

Clark County Seniors By Age

| | 85+ | 75 to 84 | 65 to 74 | 55 to 64 |

Senior Population

	1996	2000*	2003*
Total	23,2788 (100%)	300,484 (100%)	361,572 (100%)
85+	8,742 (4%)	13,856 (5%)	18,769 (5%)
75 to 84	41,411 (18%)	59,229 (20%)	70,863 (20%)
65 to 74	82,718 (36%)	95,975 (32%)	108,845 (30%)
55 to 64	99,917 (43%)	131,424 (44%)	163,095 (45%)

Source: Nevada State Demographers Office
1997 Senior Population not available at time of publication

* Estimated

Years

SENIOR ASSOCIATIONS

American Association for Retired Persons (AARP)
340 N. 11th St.
Las Vegas, NV 89101
386-8661
Mildred Willard,
State Office Coordinator
(See Senior Help & Referral)

National Association of Senior Friends
3101 S. Maryland Pkwy., Ste. 314
Las Vegas, NV 89109
735-5510
Pamela Carnevale, Dir.
One year membership: $15
Provides seniors, 50 and over, with many benefit programs including social events and educational programs on medical and other issues. Regularly scheduled free health care screenings and wellness programs. Hours: Mon. - Fri. 9 am - 4 pm.

Mountain View Chapter
8524 Del Webb Blvd.
Las Vegas, NV 89134
255-5404
Mimi Saft, Supv.
One year membership: $15

Nevada Council of Senior Citizens
P.O. Box 12112

Las Vegas, NV 89112-0112
645-1048
Don Fuller, Pres.
Civic minded seniors sharing ideas and encouraging activity and free thinking. Meets once a month on Wed. 10 am - noon at Clark County Library.

RTC Paratransit System
301 E. Clark Ave., Ste. 300
Las Vegas, NV 89101
228-4800

Sue Joseph, Mgr.
Operated by CAT. Door to door service. Provides alternative service to people who, because of physical or mental disabilities, can't use the regular bus system. Reservations a must; 30 trips for $30.

Retired Public Employees of Nevada
5171 N. Pioneer Way
Las Vegas, NV 89129
645-1048

Kathryn Howell, Legislative Chairman
Meets every 2nd Mon. at 2 pm at American Legion Hall, Memorial Dr.

Retired Senior Volunteer Program (RSVP)
(Multiple locations listed below)
340 N. 11th St.
Las Vegas, NV 89101
382-0721
Valerie Kalmerton, Dir.
Provides retired persons the opportunity to participate in the community through volunteer work and helping other seniors.
RSVP Programs include telephone reassurance - volunteers daily call seniors who live alone and have nobody to watch after their welfare.

27 E. Texas Ave.
Henderson, NV 89015
565-6690
Juliette Parlow, Dir.

Senior Tripster, Inc.
450 E. Bonanza Rd.
Las Vegas, NV 89101
387-0007
Geri Wulf, Dir.
Meets second Thu. of each month at 1 pm. Open to seniors who are interested in traveling.

SENIOR CENTERS

There are 13 senior centers in the Las Vegas area. A variety of activities can be found at the centers such as bingo, cards, classes, dancing, socializing and dining. Special senior services can be found or are scheduled at many centers. The communities of Searchlight, Overton, Mesquite, Pahrump, Indian Springs, Amagosa Valley and Beatty also have senior centers.
(See also Community Centers)

Arturo Cambeiro Center
Nevada Assn. of Latin Americans
330 N. 13th St.
Las Vegas, NV 89101
382-6252
Ruth Magana, Dir.
Hours: Mon. - Fri. 8 am - 4 pm
Nutrition program, special events, scheduled activities; Spanish/English library; Spanish and Englishspeaking staff.

Boulder City Senior Center
1001 Arizona St.
Boulder City, NV 89005
293-5510   293-3320
Marilyn Moore, Adm.
Regularly scheduled activities, workshops and classes; lunches daily.
Hours: Mon. - Fri. 8 am - 3 pm

Derfelt Senior Center
3333 W. Washington Ave.
Las Vegas, NV 89107
229-6601
Lana Reich, Center Supv.
Hours: Mon. - Fri. 8 am - 4 pm
Located in Lorenzi Park. Regularly scheduled activities, workshops and classes.
Facilities: Activity room, classroom and passive garden.

Doolittle Satellite Senior Center
1940 N. J St.

Las Vegas, NV 89106
229-6125
Jerlys Baker, Program Specialist
Hours: Mon. - Fri. 9 am - 2 pm
The center provides leisure activities for people 55 and over.

Dula Gymnasium
441 E. Bonanza Rd.
Las Vegas, NV 89101
229-6307
Marilyn Louden, Program Specialist
Hours: Mon. - Fri. 8 am - 5:30 pm
Table tennis, basketball and weight room.

EOB Senior Center
330 W. Washington Ave., Ste. 1
Las Vegas, NV 89106
647-2536
Hazel Geran, Project Dir.
Hours: Mon. - Fri. 8 am - 4:30 pm
Programs and services in health, education and social activities.

Henderson Senior Center
27 E. Texas St.
Henderson, NV 89015
565-6990
Edie Barker, Dir.
Hours: Mon. - Fri. 8 am - 4 pm; Mon. - Thu. 6 pm - 10 pm; Sat. 9 am - 11:30 am
Regularly scheduled activities, workshops and classes; senior information and assistance. Black Mountain Nutrition Program provides meals for seniors Mon. - Fri. 11:30 am - 12:30 pm; Sat. brunch 9 am - 11:30 am. Suggested donation for persons 60 and over $1.25 per meal, under 60 $3 per meal. Seniors who are homebound are eligible to have their noon meals delivered.

Howard W. Cannon Senior Service Center
(Also listed under Senior Help)
340 N. 11th St.
Las Vegas, NV 89101
366-1522
Carol Hunter, Dir.
Hours: Mon. - Fri. 9 am - 4 pm
Provides a single point of access for the major public services available to senior citizens.

Hollyhock Adult Day Care Center
(also listed under Physically Handicapped and Handicapped-Mentally)
380 N. Maryland Pkwy.
Las Vegas, NV 89101
382-0588
Mary Jo Greenlee, Adm.
Hours: Mon. - Sat. 7:30 am - 5:30 pm
Operated by the EOB, designed to meet the specific needs of elderly and impaired individuals. $35 per day; $18.50 if below federal poverty level guidelines.

Lied Senior Center, 901 N. Jones Blvd., Las Vegas, NV 89108

SENIORS

Katherine Center · Reformation Lutheran Church
580 E. St. Louis Ave.
Las Vegas, NV 89104
732-2054
Aldina Mang, Coordinator
Hours: Mon. - Fri. 9 am - 12:30 pm
Non-profit church organization. Regularly scheduled activities, workshops and classes. Senior meal site and drop-in center.

Las Vegas Senior Citizens Center
451 E. Bonanza Rd.
Las Vegas, NV 89101
229-6454
Activities: 229-6307
Lettie Peters, Center Coordinator
Hours: Mon. - Sat. 9 am - 10 pm
Facilities: Gymnasium, billiard room, library, snack bar and meeting rooms.

Lied Senior Care Center
901 N. Jones Blvd.
Las Vegas, NV 89108
648-3425
Mary Jo Greenlee, Adm.
Hours: Mon.-Thu. 7 am - 8 pm; Fri. 7 am - 10 pm, closed Saturday, Sunday 7 am - 5:30 pm
Provides day supervision to functionally impaired adults.

Lowden Center
333 Cambridge St.
Las Vegas, NV 89109
455-7169
Dorothy Schwartz, Coordinator
Hours: Mon. & Fri. 8 am - 6 pm
Ceramics, health programs, games, field trips, speakers and fitness activities.

Northwest Community Center
6841 W. Lone Mountain Rd.
Las Vegas, NV 89108
229-4794
Michael Habighorst, Coordinator
Hours: Mon. - Fri. 7 am - 6 pm
Senior Activities - 229-4765

Parkdale Center
3200 Ferndale St.
Las Vegas, NV 89121
455-7517
Marie Kirker, Coodinator
Hours: Mon. - Fri. 7:30 am - 7 pm
Social activities and monthly trips.

Salvation Army Friendship Circle Adult Day-Time Center
830 E. Lake Mead Dr.
Henderson, NV 89015
565-9578
Lieutenant Colonel James Sullivan, Adm.
Hours: Mon. - Fri. 7 am - 5 pm
Provides preventive nursing service, counseling, recreation, snacks and hot lunches.

Sunrise Community Center
2240 Linn Ln.
Las Vegas, NV 89115
455-7600
Randy Reese, Coordinator
The Sunrise Center Seniors meet for luncheons, workshops and field trips each month.

Whitney Senior Center
5700 Missouri Ave.
Las Vegas, NV 89122
455-7576
Bob Dwyer, Center Coordinator
Hours: Mon. - Fri. 9 am - 4 pm
Senior meal site and drop-in center; regular activities.

Derfelt Senior Center, 3333 W. Washington Ave., Las Vegas, NV 89107

EMPLOYMENT - EDUCATION - VOLUNTEER

SENIOR EMPLOYMENT

AARP Community Service Employment Program
330 W. Washington Ave.
Las Vegas, NV 89106
648-3356
Jacqueline Phillips, Dir.
Seniors 55 and over of lower income are provided with part time employment with non-profit host agencies.

Catholic Charities of Southern Nevada
Senior Community Employment Service
340 N. 11th St.
Las Vegas, NV 89101
382-0721
Maffy Forester, Dir.
Finds employment for seniors (55 and over) and provides counseling with employment problems.

HELP of Southern Nevada
953 E. Sahara Ave., Ste. 208
Las Vegas, NV 89104
369-4357
Desiree Kelly, Dir.
Displaced homemaker program. Provides job seeking skills training, job placement and access to needed social services to any client who has lost main source of income through a death, divorce or disability of a spouse.

Nevada Business Service
55-Plus Program
930 W. Owens Ave.
Las Vegas, NV 89106
647-1329
Richard Blue, Jr., Exec. Dir.
Hours: Mon. - Fri. 8 am - 5 pm
Federal funded training program for low income adults.

Nevada Employment Security
2827 Las Vegas Blvd. N.
N. Las Vegas, NV 89030
486-5600
Stan Jones, Adm.
Hours: Mon. - Fri. 8 am - 5 pm

119 S. Water St.
Henderson, NV 89015
486-6710
Nevada Employment Service helps job seekers find work. Provides counseling, testing, job development and referral to training programs as needed free of charge. Provides special services for veterans, minorities, younger, older, handicapped, rural workers and others with specific needs.

SENIOR EDUCATION

55 Alive
2413 Desert Glen Dr.
Las Vegas, NV 89134-8874
256-5459
Walter Wilgus, State Coordinator
Tup Tupper, Coordinator
Mature driving program that provides classroom instruction by trained volunteers. Program for older students. UNLV offers most of the spring and fall semester classes to seniors age 62 and over free of charge with the exception of lab fees on a first-come, first-serve basis depending on space availability. Senior citizens also qualify to attend summer classes at 50 percent of the regular cost. For further information, call the programs for older students at 895-4469. UNLV also offers a special senior program called EXCELL (Extended Education Center for Lifelong Learning). Study program geared toward the intellectual stimulation and the interests of the participants. The $45 per semester fee covers as many study groups participants desire, but does not cover necessary learning materials. Currently, there are over 250 students participating in 22 study groups per week. For information call 895-3394.

VOLUNTEER

Foster Grandparent Program
Economic Opportunity Board
330 W. Washington Ave.
Las Vegas, NV 89106
647-1515
Frederick Morgan, Project Dir.
Seniors are placed in community sites

where they offer guidance, understanding, affection and love to children with special needs and problems. Receive a stipend of $2.45 an hour.

Lend A Hand
400 Utah St.
Boulder City, NV 89005
294-2363
Margaret Lotspeich, Program Dir.
Volunteers provide a variety of services to Boulder City seniors such as transportation, meals, shopping, running errands and support.

Park Ambassador Program
229-4924
Stephanie Geary, Dir.
Senior volunteers circulate, greet and assist visitors at Paradise Park, Sunset Park, and Paul Meyer Park.

Retired Senior Volunteer Program (RSVP)
340 N. 11th St.
Las Vegas, NV 89101
382-0721
Valerie Kalmerton, Dir.

27 E. Texas Ave.
Henderson, NV 89015
565-0669
Juliette Parlow, Dir.
Provides recruitment, screening and placement in volunteer positions in the community for seniors 60 and over. RSVP sends volunteers to hospitals, senior centers and wherever there is a need. Currently volunteers are serving public and private non-profit agencies in Southern Nevada.

(See also Volunteer & Assistance for complete list of programs)

MEDIA - RECREATION - SOCIAL CLUBS

PUBLICATIONS and MEDIA

Las Vegas Golden Age
2528 E. Fremont St.
Las Vegas, NV 89104
795-2446
Ann Wilson Enterprises, Inc.
Bimonthly senior's newspaper.
Subscription: $20 annually.

Nevada Senior World
2340 Paseo Del Prado, Ste. 304
Las Vegas, NV 89102
367-6709
Steve Fish, Publisher
Monthly newspaper dedicated to informing, serving and entertaining mature adults in Las Vegas. Available free throughout Las Vegas or by subscription at $14.95 per year.

Senior Press
3335 Wynn Rd.
Las Vegas, NV 89102
871-6780
Bruce Spotleson, Publisher
Monthly seniors magazine.
Subscription: $12 per year.

KORK · AM 920
Targets senior market with big bands, ballads and Broadway format.

RECREATION

Clark County School District
2832 E. Flamingo Rd.
Las Vegas, NV 89121
799-5304
Ray Willis, Dir.
Offers free gold cards to seniors 62 and over, which allows them to attend school sporting events, plays and concerts free of charge.

Four Queens Club 55
202 Fremont St.
Las Vegas, NV 89101
385-4011
Joe Cottone, Club Mgr.
Entitles seniors age 55 and over to social activities and discounts at the hotel along with other merchants.

Nevada Senior Games Inc. (Olympics)
P.O. Box 27947
Las Vegas, NV 89126-1946
294-2954 Fax 242-3919

Biking on a beautiful day in Las Vegas

Roger Owen, Exec. Dir.
Seniors 50 and over compete in any of 34 events, grouped in five-year intervals. The 1998 Senior Olympics are scheduled Oct. 1 - 11.
Sports training sessions meet at Dula Gym, Senior Center, 441 E. Bonanza Rd. several days a week. For information call 229-2208.

Senior Citizen Programs Division of the City of Las Vegas
Dept. of Parks & Leisure Activities
749 Veterans Memorial Dr.
Las Vegas, NV 89101
229-6724
Amy Carver, Mgr. of Senior Citizens programs

Senior Tripsters
(Also listed under Social Clubs)
387-0007
Geraldine Wulf, Dir.
Out-of-town organized group excursions for seniors.

SOCIAL CLUBS

Clark County Seniors Chapter of National Council of Senior Citizens

645-4487
Don Fuller, Pres.
Affiliated with national organization in Washington, D.C. Started in 1961 to promote establishment of monthly Medicare meetings. Dues $12 per year. National magazine lobbyists for senior issues. Seniors are invited to attend to express views and to keep active in community, state and national affairs. No age barrier; dues are $5 for locals.

Retired Eagles Activities
384-1596
Elizabeth Hixenbaugh, Pres.
Affiliated with Eagles Fraternal Organization in Las Vegas. Open to all. Retired persons are welcome. Fund raising for charities, pot luck and bingo. Meets 3rd Wed. of each month, except June, July and August.

Senior Tripsters Inc.
(Also listed under Recreation)
387-0007
Geraldine Wulf, Dir.
Travel club - $7 yearly dues. Discounts for seniors; newsletter distributed monthly.

Senior Activities (Band Practice)

Photo: Phototechnik International

SENIOR LEGAL AND TRANSPORTATION

SENIOR LEGAL

Senior Citizens Law Project
Howard Cannon Senior Services Ctr.
340 N. 11th St.
Las Vegas, NV 89101
229-6596
Sheri Vogel, Dir.
Hours: Mon. - Fri. 9 am - 4 pm
Help for seniors 60 and above with wills, living wills, homesteading and terminating joint holdings. Legal advice on many matters including bankruptcy. Complex problems are referred to lawyers referral or an estate planner who offers free advice to seniors as well as prepares living trusts. Clients are responsible for filing fees and other court costs.
(See also Lawyer Referral)

TRANSPORTATION

C.A.T.® Paratransit Services
301 Clark Ave.
Las Vegas, NV 89101
228-4800   TTD 455-2199
Curb-to-curb bus service for disabled. You must fill out an application to qualify. Rides are scheduled 24 hours to 14 days in advance and each ride is $1. Over 14,000 people are signed up for this service.

EOB Senior Citizens Transportation Project
800 W. Bonanza Rd.
Las Vegas, NV 89106
646-2063
John Gerena, Transportation Adm.
Provides door-to-door transportation and route service for seniors 55 and over. Reservations can be made up to two weeks in advance. Service only on Fri. 7 am - 4 pm, $10 round trip.

Senior Ride Program
Division for Aging Services
340 N. 11th St., Ste. 203
Las Vegas, NV 89101
486-6535
Bruce McAnnany,
Chief Compliance Investigator
State of Nevada Division for Aging Services sells and distributes subsidized taxicab transportation coupon books usable with any cab company in Clark County for seniors 60 years of age and older and permanently disabled persons. Register Mon. - Fri. 9 am - 4 pm. Price of 20 $1.00 coupons is $10. After registration, maximum order per person is two books per distribution. Distribution is quarterly.

BINGO BUS
Many casinos have courtesy buses that pickup seniors at various retirement communities, mobile home estates and

senior centers. The following hotels have regular scheduled bus service to their casinos for senior citizens.
Arizona Charlies - 2 buses, 2 vans; 8 am - 11:30 pm
Binion's Horseshoe - 5 buses, 3 vans; 7 am - 11 pm
Gold Coast - 7 buses; 9:30 am - 12:15 am
Palace Station - 7 buses; 8:30 am -6:30 pm
Santa Fe - 3 buses; 7 am - 10 pm

Photo: Phototechnik International
C.A.T.® Paratransit Services

SENIORS

SENIOR MEDICAL & SPECIAL NEEDS

MEDICAL & HEALTH

Alzheimer's Disease and Related Disorders
(Also listed under Health Care)
3441 W. Sahara Ave., Ste. A8
Las Vegas, NV 89102
248-2770
Judy Hetherington, Pres.
366-0899
Provides information about Alzheimer's Disease as well as group support meetings and referrals.

Arthritis Foundation
2660 S. Rainbow Blvd., Ste. 102
Las Vegas, NV 89102
367-1626
Nikki Sobrowski, Exec. Dir.
Offers referrals to doctors, information, a water exercise program and educational programs for arthritis sufferers and interested persons.

Cannon Senior Medical Center
340 N. 11th St.
Las Vegas, NV 89101
384-2273
Dr. James Laird, Dir.
Medical Equipment Loan Program
366-1522
Provides medical and podiatry services to persons 55 and older. Primary care services include routine screening, management of chronic illness and immunizations. Sliding fee scale based on income.

Clark County Health District
625 Shadow Ln.
Las Vegas, NV 89106
385-1291
Senior Health Program: 383-1355

3262 Civic Center Dr.
N. Las Vegas, NV 89030
642-3525

129 W. Lake Mead Dr.
Henderson, NV 89015
564-3232

1001 Arizona St.
Boulder City, NV 89005
293-3320
Fran Courtney, Dir.
Clinics for seniors age 60 and over. Immunizations and blood pressure checks.

Lifeline · St. Rose Dominican
102 E. Lake Mead Dr.
Henderson, NV 89015
564-4543
Sharon Moxley, Dir.
Personal medical emergency support.

Opticare
8467 W. Lake Mead Blvd.
Las Vegas, NV 89128
369-1555

3575 Pecos McLeod
Las Vegas, NV 89121
369-1555
Norma Jean Perry, Coordinator
Free evaluations for vision, cataracts, glaucoma. Also eyeglass adjustments.

Senior Advantage Resource Center
9310 Sun City Blvd., Ste. 101
Las Vegas, NV 89134
363-1150
Kristyne Blake, Senior Coordinator
Free benefits offered through Valley Health System, Valley and Summerlin Medical Center for age 50 and older.

Sunrise Senior Friends
(Multiple locations listed below)
8524 Del Webb Blvd.
Las Vegas, NV 89134
255-5405
Pamela Carnevale, Mgr.
One-year membership $15. Provides seniors 50 and over, with many benefit programs including social events and educational programs on medical and other issues. Regularly scheduled free health care screenings and wellness programs.

3101 S. Maryland Pkwy., Ste. 314
Las Vegas, NV 89109
735-5510

2809 N. Green Valley Pkwy.
Henderson, NV 89014
434-6500

Senior Dimensions Service Center
Div. of Health Plan of NV
900 S. Rancho Dr.
Las Vegas, NV 89106
646-8304
Dave Allazetta, Adm.
Marti Stefanowiczi, Senior Coordinator
Services are provided at no cost to the 28,011 seniors in Southern Nevada and 3,126 in Northern Nevada who are members. Services include health education and literature, volunteer placement, social services, and educational, recreational and cultural activities.

Silver Advantage Program
University Medical Center
1800 W. Charleston Blvd.
Las Vegas, NV 89102
383-2095
Charmaine Endres, Coordinator
Silver Advantage is a free health education program for adults over 50 years of age. In addition to social and educational activities, Silver Advantage works in conjunction with insurance to provide savings on health care.

Valley Hospital Medical Center
Offers seniors the Seniors Advantage Program, which offers health education, counseling and physician referrals amongst its many services. For further information, call 388-4665.

SENIOR MEALS

Senior Nutrition Program
531 N. 30th St.
Las Vegas, NV 89101
385-5284
Dawn Baker, Dir.
Meals on Wheels program for homebound seniors age 60 and over delivers over 550 hot lunches to homes, senior housing and senior sites Mon. - Fri., site lunch on Saturday.

320 meals are also served at 11 sites throughout the area. Donation of $1.75 per meal is requested but not required; under age 60 pay $3 per meal. Program is administered by Catholic Charities of Southern Nevada.

Dolittle Senior Center - 11:30 am
1901 J. St.
Las Vegas, NV 89106
229-6125

Hollyhock Day Care - noon
380 N. Maryland Pkwy.
Las Vegas, NV 89101
382-0588

Jaycee Adult Park - 11:30 am
5805 W. Harmon Ave.
Las Vegas, NV 89103
364-4931

Katherine Senior Center - 11:30 am
580 E. St. Louis Ave.
Las Vegas, NV 89104
732-2054

Lied Center - noon
901 N. Jones Blvd.
Las Vegas, NV 89107
648-3425
Adult day care clients.

Lowden Center - 11:30 am Mon., Wed., Fri.
3333 Cambridge St.
Las Vegas, NV 89109
455-7169

Sartini Plaza - 11:15 am
900 S. Brush St.
Las Vegas, NV 89107
878-8581

Sister Mercita Weis Center - 11:30 am
531 N. 30th St.
Las Vegas, NV 89101
385-5284

Sunrise Gardens - noon
3601 El Conlon Ave.
Las Vegas, NV 89102
873-3335

Arturo Cambeiro Senior Center - 11:30 am
330 N. 13th St.
Las Vegas, NV 89101
382-6252

Whitney Senior Center - 11:30 am Mon. - Fri.
5700 Missouri Ave.
Las Vegas, NV 89122
455-7576

Black Mountain Nutrition Program
27 E. Texas Ave.
Henderson, NV 89015
565-7980
Black Mountain Nutrition Program provides meals for seniors Mon. - Fri. 11:30 am - 12:30 pm; Sat. noon - 12:30; Sun. 10:30 am - 1:30 pm. Suggested donation for persons 60 and over is $1.25 per meal, under 60 $3 per meal. Seniors who are homebound are eligible to have their noon meals delivered.

SENIOR SPECIAL NEEDS

AARP #1189
340 N. 11th St.
Las Vegas, NV 89101
386-8661
Mildred Williard, State Office Coordinator
Automobile, home owner's, and health insurance, towing service, investment program, optical and pharmacy service, tax programs. Membership is $8 annually.

Clark County Social Services
1600 Pinto Ln.
Las Vegas, NV 89106
455-4270
Verla Davis, Dir.
Alternative Health Program: (short term): 455-3651
Homemaker Home Health Aid Service: (long term): 455-4431
Nursing Home Placement: 455-3565

Clark County Social Services · Cannon Center
340 N. 11th St.
Las Vegas, NV 89101
455-4342
Deanna Taha, Supv.
Senior citizens protective services, Clark county medical cards.

Hollyhock Adult Day Care Center
380 N. Maryland Pkwy.
Las Vegas, NV 89101
382-0588
Mary Jo Greenlee. Dir.
Hours: Mon. - Sat. 7 am - 5:30 pm
Day care for the physically handicapped adult. Medical supervision, social activities and daily nutrition are provided for persons who or frail or who suffer from memory disorders.

Family Home Hospice
1701 W. Charleston Blvd.
Las Vegas, NV 89102
383-0887
Renee Meldrum, VP
Home health care nurses come to patient's home.

Friendship Circle Adult Daytime Center
Salvation Army
830 E. Lake Mead Dr.
Henderson, NV 89015
565-8836
Holly Forbush, Dir.
Day care center for frail and elderly persons who require some daily attention. Facility is open Mon. - Fri. 7 am - 5 pm. The fee is $35 per day or $8 per hour. Hot lunches are served and snacks are provided as well as activities, classes, social counseling and music therapy.

Independent Living Program
6200 W. Oakey Blvd.
Las Vegas, NV 89102
870-7050
Mary Evilsizer, Dir.
Provides training in living skills to handicapped.

SENIOR HOUSING & ASSISTANCE

SENIOR SPECIAL NEEDS (CONTINUED)

Interim Health Care
4055 S. Spencer Dr., Ste. 116
Las Vegas, NV 89119
369-5533
Lilly Gonzales, Adm.
Providers of health care specialists for home care or staffing.

Las Vegas Home Care Inc.
2375 S. Jones Blvd., Ste. 17
Las Vegas, NV 89102
221-9848
Pat Reznak, Adm.
Private in-home care management and coordination.

Lied Senior Care Center
901 N. Jones Blvd.
Las Vegas, NV 89108
648-3425
Mary Jo Greenlee, Dir.
Provides adult supervision of handicapped or frail adults. Nutritious meals, classes and therapy are available.

PRN Extended Care
3022 W. Post Road
Las Vegas, NV 89118
896-5759
Marti Norris, Adm.
Provides nursing at home, health aides, homemaker services available, physical therapy, occupational therapy and speech therapy, medical social workers. Accepts Medicare, Medicaid and private insurance.

6233 Industrial Rd.
Las Vegas, NV 89118
367-1885
Gaynor Gardner, Adm.
Nurses attend to homebound patients to administer medication and baths. Only for Medicare patients and only under doctor's orders.

Senior Companion Program
340 N. 11th St.
Las Vegas, NV 89101
382-0721
Dawn Baker, Project Dir.
Seniors 60 and older giving companionship to elderly and frail Las Vegas and Henderson residents. Volunteers receive stipends ($2.45 hour) and mileage from Catholic Charities of Southern Nevada. To qualify, you must have a car and a monthly income of less than $700.

SENIOR HOUSING

NURSING HOMES & LONG TERM CARE FACILITIES

A 'Legant Elder Care (3)
9708 Enniskeen Ave.
Las Vegas, NV 89129
242-9440
Celeste Post, Adm./Owner
6 beds - upscale retirement home with a bed and breakfast atmosphere.

9712 Enniskeen Ave.
Las Vegas, NV. 89129
242-9440
Assisted living.

3517 Kilbarry Ct.
Las Vegas, NV 89129
242-9440
Dementia/Alzheimer's.

Boulder City Care Center
601 Adams Blvd.
Boulder City, NV 89005
293-5151
Tammy McDermott, Adm.
87 beds.

Charleston Residential Care Hotel
2121 W. Charleston Blvd.
Las Vegas, NV 89102
382-7746
Margaret McConnell, Adm.
125 beds.

Cheyenne Care Center Inc.
2856 E. Cheyenne Ave.
N. Las Vegas, NV 89030
644-1888
Darrin Cook, Adm.
98 bed skilled nursing home.

Cheyenne Residential
2860 E. Cheyenne Ave.
N. Las Vegas, NV 89030
644-7777
Walter Hanson, Adm.
240 bed care facility.

Delmar Gardens of Green Valley
100 Delmar Gardens Dr.
Henderson, NV 89014
361-6111
Chad Stenslie, Adm.
184 bed nursing and rehabilitation center with home-like atmosphere; outstanding health care and rehabilitative services and social and recreational programs.

Desert Lane Care Center
660 Desert Ln.
Las Vegas, NV 89106
382-5580
Paul Boyar, Adm.
172 beds.

The Elderly Aristocrat
2380 Mohigan Way
Las Vegas, NV 89109
796-9952
Doug St. Clair, Adm.
5 beds
Assisted living in a home-like setting. Private and semi-private rooms.

El Jen Convalescent Hospital
5538 W. Duncan Dr.
Las Vegas, NV 89130
645-2606
James Toomey, Adm.
104 beds.

Emmanuel Health Care Center
2035 W. Charleston Blvd.
Las Vegas, NV 89102
386-7980
Bobbye Greet, Adm.
100 beds.

Henderson Convalescent Hospital
1180 E. Lake Mead Dr.
Henderson, NV 89015
565-8555
Carol Barnicoat, Adm.
264 beds.
Pro-active programs, therapy and

rehabilitation. Medicare, Medicaid, VA, county and private insurance accepted.

Integrated Health Services of Las Vegas
2170 E. Harmon Ave.
Las Vegas, NV 89119
794-0100
Rick Denning, Adm.
120 beds.

Las Vegas Health Care & Rehabilitation Center
2832 S. Maryland Pkwy.
Las Vegas, NV 89109
735-5848
Julie Mason, Adm.
77 beds.
24 hour skilled care nursing.

Life Care Center of Las Vegas
6151 Vegas Dr.
Las Vegas, NV 89108
648-4900
Joyce Dahlen, Exec. Dir.
229-bed long term care facility. Licensed nurses 24 hours, chapel, ice cream parlor, gift shop, library, transportation, beauty shop.

North Las Vegas Care Center
3215 E. Cheyenne Ave.
N. Las Vegas, NV 89030
649-7800
Brent Hoffman, Adm.
Alzheimer's living center, physical, occupational and speech therapy; Medicare/Medicaid certified.

Shadow Mountain
5659 W. Duncan Dr.
Las Vegas, NV 89130
645-1900
Kelli Toomey, Adm.
116 beds.

Torrey Pines Care Center
1701 S. Torrey Pines Dr.
Las Vegas, NV 89102
871-0005
Linda Gelinger, Adm.
116 licensed beds.
24 hour skilled nursing, rehabilitation, recreation, transportation.

Vegas Valley Convalescent Hospital
2945 Casa Vegas St.
Las Vegas, NV 89109
735-7179
Philip Hibnick, Adm.
102 licensed beds.

Willow Creek Memory Care Residence
4025 S. Pearl St.
Las Vegas, NV 89121
433-1994
Dianna Higgs, Dir.
Resident care facility for Alzheimer's and dementia.

SENIOR HOUSING ASSISTANCE

Clark County Nursing Home Placement
1600 Pinto Ln.
Las Vegas, NV 89102
455-3565
Sue Robinson, Supv.

Adult Care Association of Nevada
458-7733 645-2291
Gerri Killough, Pres.
Information on member care homes and vacancies.

State of Nevada Dept. of Human Resources
Health Division
4220 S. Maryland Pkwy.,
Bldg. D, Ste. 810
Las Vegas, NV 89119
486-6515
Lisa Jones, Supv.
Provides list of bed and board homes. Group homes are privately owned and run, licensed homes where seniors can live and receive care in a homelike atmosphere. There are approximately 200 of these homes in the Las Vegas area.

Clark County Health District
625 Shadow Ln.
Las Vegas, NV 89106
385-1291
Marge Mouer, Supv.
Home care.

Housing Authority of the City of Las Vegas
420 N. 10th St.
Las Vegas, NV 89101
386-2727
Frederick Brown, Exec. Dir.

Housing Authority of North Las Vegas
1632 Yale St.
N. Las Vegas, NV 89030
649-2451
Bob Sullivan, Dir.

Housing Authority of the County of Clark
5390 E. Flamingo Rd.
Las Vegas, NV 89122
451-8041
William Cottrell, Exec. Dir.

Housing Options for Seniors
Jewish Family Serv. Agency
3909 S. Maryland Pkwy., Ste. 205
Las Vegas, NV 89119
732-0304
Holly Mercy, Clinical Dir.
Non-profit, non-sectarian agency that provides seniors with an impartial, objective list of housing options and a person to help evaluate each. JFS family therapy services has affordable rates.

State of Nevada, Division for Aging Services
Ombudsman Program
340 N. 11th St., Ste. 203
Las, Vegas, NV 89101
486-3545
Bruce McAnnany, Compliance Officer
Investigates complaints about area nursing homes. Provides information on nursing home placement and/or alternatives available; community home-based initiatives program (65+).

SENIORS

SENIOR HOUSING & DEVELOPMENTS

MOBILE HOMES

Las Vegas Jaycees Senior Community
5805 W. Harmon Ave.
Las Vegas, NV 89103
364-4931
80-acre low-income mobile home park for seniors. The lots rent for $180 a month to qualified seniors. Applications are available at the manager's office.

RETIREMENT APARTMENTS

Camlu Retirement Apartments
4255 Spencer St.
Las Vegas, NV 89119
732-0652
Janet and Richard West, Adms.
124 full-service apartments from $935. Three meals, transportation, maid service and utilities included and weekly linens.

Carefree Senior Living Apartments
1600 S. Valley View Blvd.
Las Vegas, NV 89102
259-6687
Ken Templeton, Pres.
Rents start at $535 from three different floor plans, landscaped, pool with waterfalls.

3210 S. Sandhill Road
Las Vegas, NV 89121
641-4700
Rents start at $570. Gated community, shuttle service, luxury club house, pool, spa, elevators and garages available.

Country Club at the Meadows
300 Promenade Blvd.
Las Vegas, NV 89107
258-1121
June Kremer, Mgr.
304 unit apartment development for adults 55 and over. Priced from $540 per month for a junior one bedroom, $605 - $625 for a one bedroom, $725 - $745 for a two bedroom/two bath unit. Full-time concierge, 24 hour guarded gate and alarm systems. Shuttle bus

Country Club at Valley View
1400 S. Valley View Blvd.
Las Vegas, NV 89102
878-6266
Judy Bale, Mgr.
312 units starting at $510 - $745 per month.

Gramercy Park
2001 E. Tropicana Ave.
Las Vegas, NV 89119
736-8666
JoAnn Palcynsky, Mgr.
240 apartments $555 - $755 per month. Pool, indoor spa, fitness center, nine hole putting green and deck shuffleboard court.

Heritage Park Apartments
3555 Stober Blvd.
Las Vegas, NV 89103
873-9977
Barbara Steinman, Mgr.
189 one and two bedroom apartments $485 - $620 month. Electronic gates, swimming pool and jacuzzi.

Ida's Senior Housing
213 N. 6th St.
Las Vegas, NV 89101
366-1600
Lee Black, Mgr.
30 apartments for Social Security recipients. Single independents only. Studios $360 per month furnished; unit includes utilities, housekeepers, free use of laundromat, and security gates and garden area; non-smoking units.

Montara Meadows
3150 E. Tropicana Ave.
Las Vegas, NV 89121
435-3150
Judy and Paul Lauff, Owners
174 apartments from $1,150 per month. Three full meals a day, swimming pool, transportation, maid service, security and utilities included.

Paradise Cove Retirement Community
4330 S. Eastern Ave.
Las Vegas, NV 89119
369-1552
Judy Davidson, Mgr.
120 apartments from $945 month. Security, maid service, one meal per day and continental breakfast, swimming pool and transportation.

Del Webb Corp. - Sun City, 10351 Sun City Blvd., Las Vegas, NV 89134

Saratoga Palms East
3850 Mountain Vista St.
Las Vegas, NV 89121
458-8041
Bonnie Wenneberg
152 units $490 - $695. 2 pools, 2 spas and large patios.

The Grand Court of Las Vegas
6650 W. Flamingo Rd.
Las Vegas, NV 89103
732-2800
Ruth Barraza, Dir.
152 apartments - Independent $1,500 - $2,400; assisted care $2,100 - $2,300 per month; security, maid service, transportation, recreation room and utilities included; meal plan also available.

Villa Monterey

1270 Burnham Ave.
Las Vegas, NV 89104
474-7700
Emily Hill, Mgr.
320 apartments from $505 - $610. One and two bedroom apartments; 24 hour gated community, pool, clubhouse, social activities.

SENIOR HOUSING DEVELOPMENTS

Los Prados
5150 Los Prados Circle
Las Vegas, NV 89130
645-1562
100 homes completed with a total of 1,400 planned. Priced at $134,500 - $220,000. Golf course, tennis courts, library, restaurant.

Promenade at the Meadows
401 Promenade Blvd.
Las Vegas, NV 89107
877-9520
186 homes priced $125,000 - $150,000. 24 hour security, clubhouse, swimming pool and shuffleboard.

Quail Estates West
2851 S. Valley View Blvd.
Las Vegas, NV 89102
367-1537
200 homes priced from $106,500, swimming pool/spa, guarded gate, activities Director.

Del Webb Corp. - Sun City Las Vegas
10351 Sun City Blvd.
Las Vegas, NV 89134
363-5454   1-800-843-4848
Housing community with over 6,000 homes completed for adults 55 and over. Community includes social hall, swimming pools, golf courses, tennis courts and exercise room. Community opened in 1988, median price $209,000, population over 12,000.

Del Webb Corporation - McDonald Ranch
2000 W. Horizon Ridge
Henderson, NV 89012
269-4300
Housing community with over 550 homes completed (2,500 projected) for

adults 55 and older. Community includes social hall, swimming pools, golf course, tennis courts and exercise room. Groundbreaking began May 1995. Median price $150,000. Population 1,200, projected 4,700.

HOSPICE

Clark County Health District
Home Care Hospice
625 Shadow Ln.
Las Vegas, NV 89106
383-1341
Sue Kolrey, Care Coordinator
Under direction of patient's private physician, this program offers home care to the terminally ill.

Family Home Hospice
Sierra Health Services, Inc.
1701 W. Charleston Blvd.
Las Vegas, NV 89102
383-0887
Rene Meldrum, Adm.

Horizen Hospice Care
2920 S. Rainbow Blvd., Ste. 140
Las Vegas, NV 89102
361-6801
Karin Maxfield, Dir.
Medicare certified, providing supportive care to terminally ill clients. Primarily in the home; in-patient is available.

Nathan Adelson Hospice
4141 Swenson St.
Las Vegas, NV 89119
733-0320
Betsy Gornet, Adm.
20 units
An accredited acute care facility serving the terminally ill and their families. There are five clusters with four suites in each cluster. Each suite is tastefully decorated and opens on to a private patio. The hospice is built around an enclosed aviary and a large open atrium with trees, fountain and waterfall. All patients are accepted due to the support of community foundations. It is named for the founder of Sunrise Hospital, Nathan Adelson.

Option Care Hospice
3900 W. Charleston Blvd.
Las Vegas, NV 89102
258-0011
Ron Memo, Pres.
Professional care, guidance and support.

Safe Harbor Hospice
3910 Pecos-McLeod
Las Vegas, NV 89121
435-7660
In-patient hospice.

4011 McCleod Dr.
Las Vegas, NV 89121
Fred Schultz, Exec. Dir.
Provides hospice services to patients in their own homes.

More than 1 million people live in the Las Vegas area, and more than 31 million people visit annually. Many of these people require assistance at some point. Clark County has some of the finest hospitals and care centers in the country, offering 24 hour assistance for everything from a simple cold to drug addiction and depression, from support groups to hospitalization. Support groups ranging from Aid for AIDS of Nevada to the Suicide Prevention Center have groups that meet on a regular basis as well as 24 hour hotlines for those with immediate needs. For medical referrals, call the Nevada State Medical Association at 798-6711.

There are 9 hospitals in the area, all of which offer 24 hour care. Sunrise Hospital has 688 beds and is the largest health care facility in the state. Las Vegas also has a number of fine clinics and assistive services available to help with the problems facing people today. Most offer bilingual assistance and some, such as the Resort Medical Services of Las Vegas, will even make room calls to your hotel during your visit. Several local pharmacies offer 24 hour prescription pick-up services.

Rehabilitation centers abound in the area, offering quality care for people requiring special assistance to meet the needs of everyday living. The New Covenant House on Buffalo Rd., in Las Vegas is due to be completed by the end of 1998. While some offer inpatient facilities for extensive therapy, others are outpatient providers and have flexible hours.

For those in need of financial assistance, many organizations and programs can provide the necessary resources to get them on the path to becoming self-supporting. One such group, Catholic Charities of Southern Nevada, ensures the basic needs of families. Eighteen programs are currently available to serve everyone in need, reguardless of race, color or age. For every dollar raised by Catholic Charities, 86 cents goes to the poor, homeless and less fortunate, while only 14 cents goes toward overhead.

Assistance can mean anything from quick medical care to consumer help to equal rights. Southern Nevada and the Las Vegas area offer programs and facilities to meet all of these needs.

ASSISTANCE HOTLINES
all are 24 hours

Addiction Treatment Center 383-1347	Gang Hot Line 229-4264
Aid for AIDS of Nevada Hotline 382-2326	Help of Southern Nevada 369-4357
AIDS Hotline .1-800-342-AIDS	Lupus Foundation 645-6736
AIDS Information 383-1393	Mental Health Crisis Unit-Emerg. 486-8020
Al-anon Family Groups .642-7438	Narcotics Anonymous 369-3362
Alcoholics Anonymous .598-1888	National Domestic Violence Hot Line 1-800-SAFE
American Red Cross 384-1225	Nevada Child Seekers 458-7009
Bridge Counseling Center 474-6450	Nevada Network Against Domestic Violence .1-800-5001556
Child Abuse and Neglect Hotline 399-0081	Planned Parenthood Answer Line 1-800-322-1020
Child & Adult Sexual Assault Center 366-1640	Poison Center - Sunrise Hospital 732-4989
Childhelp USA 1-800-4-A-CHILD	Runaway Hotline . . . . .385-3335 or 1-800-231-6946
City of Las Vegas Animal Control 229-6348	Secret Witness 385-5555
Crisis Evaluation Team .876-4357	Senior Citizens Protective Services 455-4291
Community Action Against Rape 385-2153	Suicide Prevention Center 731-2990
Domestic Crisis Shelter 646-4981	Toughlove 386-5632
Domestic Crisis Temp. Assistance 877-0133	Veterans Benefit Info. 1-800-827-1000
Family Resource Center 385-3335	We Can 399-0081
Gamblers Anonymous .385-7732	Youth Crisis Hotline 1-800-448-4663

HOSPITALS

There are eight medical/surgical hospitals in the metropolitan area with over 2,000 beds. Clark County has 1,480 licensed physicians. University Medical Center is a nonprofit hospital owned by Clark County and is associated with the University of Nevada School of Medicine and by law must treat everyone.

The "Personal Health Choices" report on what 24 surveyed medical treatments cost at various Nevada hospitals can be obtained for $6.00 from:

Health Division, Bureau of Health Planning
505 E. King St., Room 102
Carson City, NV 89701-4749
1-702-687-4720

Problems with hospital bills: call the Commission for Hospital Patients - 486-4009.

Nevada State Division of Health
1-702-687-4740

HOSPITALS

Boulder City Hospital
901 Adams Blvd.
Boulder City, NV 89005
293-4111
Kim Candell, Dir.
24 hour emergency services, 73 beds. Nonprofit.

Desert Springs Hospital
2075 E. Flamingo Rd.
Las Vegas, NV 89119
733-8800
Health Referral: 733-6875
Tom Koenig, CEO
24 hour emergency services, 225 beds with 16-bed maternity ward. Medical/surgical hospital.

Desert Springs Hospital Nutrition Clinic
4225 S. Eastern Ave., Ste. 8
Las Vegas, NV 89119
369-7961
Virginia Train, Registered Dietician
Nutrition counseling.

Lake Mead Hospital Medical Center
1409 E. Lake Mead Blvd.
N. Las Vegas, NV 89030
649-7711
Physician referral: 649-3627
Ernest Libman, CEO
24 hour emergency services, 199 beds. Private medical/surgical hospital with more than 700 physicians on call.

MountainView Hospital & Medical Center
3100 N. Tenaya Way
Las Vegas, NV 89128
255-5000
Mark Howard, CEO
Owned by Columbia Sunrise Hospital, this 200,000-sq. ft. facility with 120 beds opened in January 1996. When completed, it will have 400 rooms.

Nellis Federal Hospital
4700 Las Vegas Blvd. N.
Las Vegas, NV 89191
653-2222
Military and VA hospital opened in 1994. The hospital has 118 beds, 66 of which are for Air Force personnel and 52 for local veterans.

St. Rose Dominican Hospital
Adrian Dominican Order of Sisters
102 E. Lake Mead Blvd.
Henderson, NV 89015
564-2622
Rod Davis, Pres.
24 hour emergency services, 147 beds, medical/surgical hospital. This nonprofit hospital opened in 1942 as the Basic Magnesium Hospital and was purchased for $1 by the Adrian Dominican Sisters in 1947.

Summerlin Medical Center
1635 Village Center Circle
Las Vegas, NV 89134
233-7000
K. D. Justyn, CEO
State-of-the-art $70 million, 265,000 square foot facility recently opened with 149 beds. It is part of Universal Health Services.

Sunrise Hospital & Medical Center
3186 S. Maryland Pkwy.
Las Vegas, NV 89109
731-8000
Physicians Info: 731-8211
Children's Hospital: 731-8000
Poison Control Center: 732-4989
Physicians Referral: 1-800-COLUMBIA
A. Jerald F. Mitchell, CEO
24 hour emergency services, 688 beds, medical/surgical hospital (largest hospital in Nevada).

Sunrise Mountain View Hospital & Medical Center
3100 N. Tenaya Way
Las Vegas, NV 89128
731-8000
Mark Howard, CEO
215,000 square foot, $50 million facility with 110 beds opened January 1996.

Photo: Phototechnik International

St. Rose Dominican Hospital, 102 E. Lake Mead Blvd., Henderson, NV 89015

HOSPITALS

THC Las Vegas
Transitional Hospital
5100 W. Sahara Ave.
Las Vegas, NV 89102
871-1418
Dale Kirby, CEO
52 bed facility for critically ill and medically complex patients.

University Medical Center of
Southern Nevada
1800 W. Charleston Blvd.
Las Vegas, NV 89102
383-2000
William Hale, CEO
24 hour emergency services, 545 bed medical-surgical hospital. Clark County-

owned nonprofit hospital with nearly 1,000 physicians on staff. Hospital opened in 1931 with 20 beds and one doctor and one nurse. Affiliated with the University of Nevada School of Medicine. Nevada's only Burn Care Center; Nevada's major Trauma Center.

Valley Hospital Medical Center
620 Shadow Ln.
Las Vegas, NV 89106
388-4000
Roger Collins, Managing Dir.
24 hour emergency services, 416 bed medical-surgical hospital. Home of "Flight for Life" helicopter transport of patients within 160 mile radius.

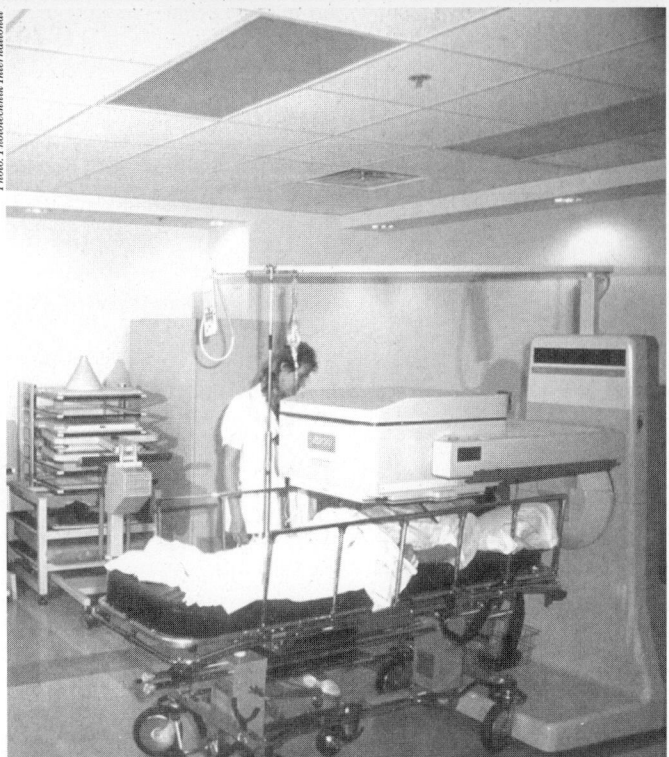
Photo: Photoechnik International

AMBULANCE

911 for Emergency

AAA Advanced Air Ambulance
145 E. Reno Ave., Ste. E7
Las Vegas, NV 89119
798-4600   1-800-222-9993
Complete bedside to bedside transport; ICC-CCU registered nurses and MDs; certified and licensed aircraft and equipment. 24-hour, 7-day service.

Mercy Ambulance
1130 S. Martin Luther King Blvd.
Las Vegas, NV 89102
386-9985
Emergency - 911
Non-emergency - 384-3400
Paramedic ambulance, local and long distance. Medicare; MC, Visa, AMX

MEDICAL CLINICS

Clark County Health District
(Multiple locations listed below)
625 Shadow Ln.
Las Vegas, NV 89106
385-1291
Otto Ravenholt, Dir.
Hours: Mon. - Fri. 8 am - 4 pm
Nonprofit public health agency providing a vast variety of health care, health education, and health related services including childhood and adult immunizations, home health care, hospice care, free health screening for seniors, family planning, sexually transmitted disease testing and treatment (including AIDS), child health programs and issuing health cards for food handlers. Anyone is eligible for clinic services. Many services are free or offered at a nominal charge. AIDS tests are conducted Monday - Friday, 8 am - 4 pm at a cost of $10; fee can be waived if patient cannot afford it.

129 W. Lake Mead Dr., Ste. 10
Henderson, NV 89015
564-3232

Community Health Centers
of Southern Nevada
916 W. Owens Ave.
Las Vegas, NV 89106
Appointments: 631-8800
Administration: 631-8818
Ed Martinez, Exec. Dir.

Community Health Centers
of Southern Nevada
Senior Medical Center
340 N. 11th
Las Vegas, NV 89101
384-2273

Community Health Centers
of Southern Nevada
Homeless Program
916 W. Owens Ave.
Las Vegas, NV 89106
631-8815

Doyne Medical Clinic Inc.
1706 W. Bonanza Rd.
Las Vegas, NV 89106-4704
631-6860
Dr. Martin Doyne, Pres.

Family Medical Group
4550 E. Charleston Blvd.
Las Vegas, NV 89122
459-5500
Hours: Mon. - Fri. 8 am - 8 pm; Sat. 8 am - 3 pm; Sun. 10 am - 3 pm

Flamingo Medical Center
2860 E. Flamingo Rd.
Las Vegas, NV 89121
733-7600
Arthur Gresen, M.D.
Hours: Mon. - Fri. 8 am - 5 pm

Fremont Medical Center
(Multiple locations & hours listed below)
520 Fremont St.
Las Vegas, NV 89101
382-5200
24 hrs., no appointment necessary.

4415 W. Flamingo Rd.
Las Vegas, NV 89103
382-5200
Dr. J. Corey Brown
Hours: Mon. - Fri. 7 am - 10 pm; Sat. - Sun. 9 am - 7 pm

595 W. Lake Mead Dr.
Henderson, NV 89015
566-5500
Dr. V. Corey Brown
Full service health care facility
Hours: Mon. - Fri. 7 am - 9 pm; Sat. - Sun. 8 am - 6 pm

331 N. Buffalo Dr.
Las Vegas, NV 89128
228-5477
Steve Goldstein, CEO
Hours: Mon. - Fri. 8 am - 5 pm

Galleria Urgent Care
600 Whitney Rd., Ste. A1
Henderson, NV 89014
454-8898
Dr. Michael Schlaack, Owner
Hours: Mon. - Fri. 7 am - 10 pm; Sat. & Sun. 8 am - 6 pm

Green Valley Urgent Care
Sponsored by
St. Rose Dominican Hospital
6301 Mountain Vista St., Ste. 100
Henderson, NV 89014
451-3636
Dr. Michael Schlaack, Owner
Hours: Mon. - Fri. 8 am - 7 pm; Sat. - Sun. 8:30 am - 5 pm

Hogan Clinic
(Multiple locations & hours listed below)
4241 S. Nellis Blvd.
Las Vegas, NV 89121
898-1405
Dr. James Hogan
Hours: Mon. - Thurs. & Sun. 6 am - 11 pm; Fri. & Sat. 24 hours

2975 Industrial Rd.
Las Vegas, NV 89109

735-0010
Hours: 24 hours daily

Hogan Clinic of Green Valley
4 Sunset Way, Ste. B2
Henderson, NV 89014
434-1111
Hours: Mon. - Fri. 7 am - 9 pm; Sat. 9 am - 2 pm

Industrial Medical Group
of Las Vegas
3673 Polaris Ave.
Las Vegas, NV 89103
871-1721
Janet Brown, Mgr.
Hours: 24 hours daily
Specializing in industrial medicine.

Industrial Medical Group
of Henderson
222 Lead St.
Henderson, NV 89015
564-2433
Janet Brown, Mgr.
Hours: Mon. - Fri. 8 am - 6 pm
Specializing in industrial medicine.

Industrial Medical Group
of North Las Vegas
151 W. Brooks Ave.
N. Las Vegas, NV 89030
399-6545
Janet Brown, Mgr.
Hours: Mon. - Fri. 8 am - 5 pm
Specializing in industrial medicine.

Inn-House Doctor
300 Fremont St.
Las Vegas, NV 89101
382-9100
Walter Krause, Owner
Physicians on-call for in-room treatment.

ASSISTANCE

MEDICAL CLINICS

Las Vegas Medical Center
(Multiple locations & hours listed below)
495 E. Sahara Ave.
Las Vegas, NV 89104
731-6060
Carol Eupdike, Adm.
Hours: 8 am - 5 pm

150 E. Harmon Ave.
Las Vegas, NV 89109
796-1116
Hours: 24 hours

Lone Mountain Medical Centre
4830 Lone Mountain Rd.
Las Vegas, NV 89130
645-8555
Hours: Mon. - Fri. 8 am - 6 pm; Sat. 8 am - noon

Nevada Medical Center
(Multiple locations & hours listed below)
3880 S. Jones Blvd.
Las Vegas, NV 89103
362-1051
Steven Fales, Pres.
Hours: Mon. - Fri. 8 am - 6:30 pm

601 S. Rancho Dr.
Las Vegas, NV 89106
384-9374
Steven Fales, Pres.
Hours: Mon. - Fri. 8 am - 3:45 pm

3150 N. Tenaya Way
Las Vegas, NV 89128
385-5972
Steven Fales, Pres.
Hours: Mon. - Fri. 9 am - 4 pm

Premier Family Medical Center
111 E. Harmon Ave.

Las Vegas, NV 89109
891-8606
Lane H. Friedman, M.D., Medical Dir.
Hours: 24 hours daily
Appointments available, walk-ins welcome. Lab tests, x-rays, urgent care. Located next to the MGM.

Pueblo Medical Center
8551 W. Lake Mead Blvd.
Las Vegas, NV 89128
256-8474
Hours: Mon. - Fri. 8 am - 8 pm; Sat. - Sun. 8 am - 4 pm
Family practice, urgent care.

Rainbow Medical Center
(Multiple locations listed below)
4920 W. Lone Mountain Rd.
Las Vegas, NV 89130
655-0550
Denise Brewer, Supvr.
Hours: Mon. - Fri. 9 am - 7 pm; Sat. 9 am - 3 pm

731 N. Nellis Blvd.
Las Vegas, NV 89110
438-4003
Anthony Pollard, Clinic Adm.

1341 S. Rainbow Blvd.
Las Vegas, NV 89117
255-4200
Eddie Kachnik, Clinic Adm.

Resort Medical Centers
3743 Las Vegas Blvd. S.
(Polo Plaza)
Las Vegas, NV 89109
735-3600
Gerald Malone

Smoke Ranch Medical Centre
6663 Smoke Ranch Rd.
Las Vegas, NV 89128
646-1661
Mona Goldsmith, Adm.
Hours: Mon. - Fri. 8 am - 8 pm; Sat. 8 am - noon

Southwest Medical Associates
888 S. Rancho Dr.
Las Vegas, NV 89106
877-8600
Dr. A. Marlon, CEO

Summit Medical Group
(Multiple locations & hours listed below)
600 Whitney Ranch Dr.
Bldg. B, Ste. 9
Henderson, NV 89014
434-3616
Sherif Abdou, M.D., Adm.
Hours: Mon. - Fri. 9 am - 5 pm

2600 S. Rainbow Blvd., Ste. 106
Las Vegas, NV 89102
252-0009
Sherif Abdou, M.D.
Hours: Mon. - Fri. 9 am - 5 pm

University Medical Center Quick Care Center
(Multiple locations & hours listed below)
University Medical Center
1000 S. Valley View Blvd.
Las Vegas, NV 89107
383-2074
Linda DeSapio, Regional Dir.
Hours: 7 am - 11 pm daily

2760 Lake Sahara Dr.
Las Vegas, NV 89117
254-4900

Kay Clayton, Regional Dir.
Hours: 8 am - 8 pm daily

4331 N. Rancho Dr.
Las Vegas, NV 89130
658-4507
Kay Clayton, Regional Dir.
Hours: 8 am - 8 pm daily

61 N. Nellis Blvd.
Las Vegas, NV 89110
644-8701
Linda DeSapio, Regional Dir.
Hours: 7 am - 11 pm daily

1769 Russell Rd.
Las Vegas, NV 89119
261-3600
Linda DeSapio, Regional Dir.
Hours: 24 hours daily

UNLV Student Health Services
4505 S. Maryland Pkwy.
Las Vegas, NV 89154
895-3370
Lori Winshell, Dir.
Hours: Mon. - Thurs. 8 am - 8 pm
24-hour health issue hotline: 895-4679
Over 70 recorded messages. For a copy of the brochure listing the topics and the code numbers, call Student Psychological Services at 895-3627.

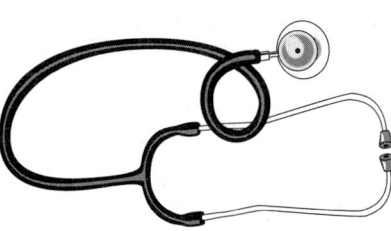

LICENSING BOARDS

Bureau of Licensure and Certification
(Multiple locations listed below)
1550 E. College Pkwy., Ste. 158
Carson City, NV 89710
687-4475
Richard Panelli, Acting Bureau Chief

Health Facilities and Consumer Health Protection
4220 S. Maryland Pkwy., Ste. 810
Las Vegas, NV 89119
486-6515
Lisa Jones, Supvr.
Licenses and regulates hospitals, hospices, and nursing facilities.

Nevada Association of Hospitals & Health Systems
4600 Kietzke Ln., Ste. A108
Reno, NV 89502
827-0184
Jeanette Belz, Pres.
Lobbyists for hospitals, educational seminars.

Nevada Donor Network
4580 S. Eastern Ave.
Las Vegas, NV 89119
796-9600
Ken Richardson, Dir.
Marti Stefanowicz

Non-profit organization that specializes in finding organ donors. About 300 people in Southern Nevada are waiting for organ transplants.

Nevada State Medical Association
2590 E. Russell Rd.
Las Vegas, NV 89120
798-6711
Frank V. Nemac, Pres.
Lobbyists for doctors, the medical society has over 600 members. The society answers medical inquiries and requests for physician information.

MEDICAL SCHOOL

University of Nevada School of Medicine
2040 W. Charleston Blvd.
Las Vegas, NV 89102
486-3578
Robert Daugherty, Jr., M.D., Ph.D.
Family Center - 877-3999
Genetics - 385-5011
Internal Medicine - 486-3578
Nutrition - 383-2520
Obstetrics/Gynecology - 383-2271
Pediatrics - 383-2741
Surgery - 385-1980
Established in 1969, the school is a four

year degree granting institution with 184 full time faculty members and 602 volunteer faculty members and operates on an annual budget of $50 million. It was started in 1969 with the help of $4 million from Howard Hughes after he read an ad supporting a medical school in Nevada.

For the past three years, the American Academy of Family Practice has placed in the top ten medical schools in the United States in percentage of graduates entering family practice. More than 1,000 students have been admitted to the school in it's 25 years of existence.

Sunrise Mountain View Hospital & Medical Center, 3100 N. Tenaya Way, Las Vegas, NV 89128

ADDICTION CLINICS & COUNSELING

Bridge Counseling Associates
1701 W. Charleston Blvd., Ste. 320
Las Vegas, NV 89102
474-6450
Mark Disselkoen, Exec. Dir.
Chemical dependency.

Economic Opportunity Board
522 W. Washington Ave.
Las Vegas, NV 89106
648-0663
Vilius Paskevicius, Dir.
Alcohol and substance abuse treatment; inpatient and outpatient counseling at minimal cost.

Lied Residence for Women
Salvation Army
39 W. Owens Ave.
N. Las Vegas, NV 89030
649-1469
Dr. Mel Adkins, Clinical Dir.
32-bed chemical dependency program for women with drug and alcohol problems. 72-unit transitional housing complex; 2 year program.

UNLV Client Services Center
4505 S. Maryland Pkwy.
Room 226 - Carlson Education Bldg.
Las Vegas, NV 89154
895-3106
Tom Sexton, Dir.
Counseling services. Support for persons facing marital difficulties, family communication problems, individual crisis, parenting problems and career decisions. Groups include adult children of alcoholics, incest, survivors, and divorce. Sliding scale fee of $5 to $25.

Veterans Administration
1703 W. Charleston Blvd.
Las Vegas, NV 89102
636-3000
Ramon J. Reevey, Dir.
Alcohol treatment program for honorably discharged veterans and dependents.

We-Care Foundation
2216 S. Sixth St.
Las Vegas, NV 89104
369-0613
Gerry Fletcher, Dir.
Provides rehabilitation for women with a drinking problem.

WestCare
(Also listed under Mental Health and Subsistence and Low Income)
401 S. Martin Luther King Blvd.
Las Vegas, NV 89106
385-2020
Detoxification: 383-4044
Richard E. Steinberg, Pres.
Private nonprofit social service agency providing treatment for drug and alcohol abusers.

ADDICTION SUPPORT GROUPS

Adult Children of Alcoholics
(Also listed under Support Groups)
P.O. Box 29332
Las Vegas, NV 89126
369-2262
No fee. Provides support groups using 12 step program for alcoholism, women's issues, relationships, and incest.

Alcoholics Anonymous
1431 E. Charleston, Ste. 7
Las Vegas, NV 89104
598-1888
Jack Fisher, Mgr.
Offers a 12 step program for alcoholics.

Al-Anon Family Groups
2314 E. Cheyenne Ave.
Las Vegas, NV 89115
642-7438
Support group for family members of alcoholics.

Alateen
2314 E. Cheyenne Ave.
Las Vegas, NV 89115
642-7438
Young people whose lives are affected by someone else's drinking.

Cocaine Abuse
5900 Brockton Ave.
Riverside, Ca. 92506
1-800-888-9383
National referral line for drug and alcohol abuse.

Debtors Anonymous
737-7047
Bonnie
Meets every Thursday at 7 pm at Central Christian Church, 3375 S. Mojave Road.

Gamblers Anonymous
P.O. Box 12936
Las Vegas, NV 89112
385-7732
Group support for compulsive gamblers. There are 41 groups in Las Vegas with over 45 meetings each week.

Narcotics Anonymous
P.O. Box 26636
Las Vegas, NV 89126
369-3362
Support group meetings held daily.

National Council on Problem Gambling Inc.
3006 S. Maryland Pkwy., Ste. 405
Las Vegas, NV 89109
369-9740
1-800-522-4700 24 hr. help line
For persons throughout the United States seeking assistance and information on problem and compulsive gambling.

Nevada Council on Problem Gambling
3006 S. Maryland Pkwy., Ste. 405
Las Vegas, NV 89109

369-9740
Carol O'Hare, Exec. Dir.
Education and treatment referral for problem gambling.

Nicotine Anonymous
456-8138
Meet Thursday and Saturday at 5 pm, Wednesday at 5:15 pm, and Sunday at 2 pm at Triangle Club, 4600 S. Nellis Blvd., and Mon. 6 pm at Montevista Hospital Conference Room 2. Helps you to stop smoking.

Overeaters Anonymous
Hot Line: 593-2945
12 step program for compulsive eaters. Meetings daily in homes, support groups.

Samaritan House
1001 N. Fourth St.
Las Vegas, NV 89101
386-6999
Care and shelter for male alcoholics.

Sex Addicts Anonymous
732-7811
Support meetings held throughout the week in various locations. For men and women suffering from sexual addiction or dependency.

Sex & Love Addicts Anonymous
737-7047
12 step program for those with compulsive patterns of sex and those preoccupied with relationships. Call for times and locations.

Treatment for Compulsive Gamblers
876-4357
Ongoing outpatient treatment program 4 times a week for 4 to 6 weeks at Charter Hospital; $5 fee is donated to the Nevada Council on Problem Gaming and Consumer Credit Counseling.

MENTAL HEALTH & CHEMICAL DEPENDENCY

Charter Hospital of Las Vegas
7000 W. Spring Mountain Rd.
Las Vegas, NV 89117
876-4357
Lynn Rosenbach, Adm.
Bill Parks, Deputy Adm.
Mental health - inpatient hospital. 84-bed chemical dependency hospital for treatment of drug and alcohol abuse and compulsive gambling; 24 hours.

Montevista Hospital
5900 W. Rochelle Ave.
Las Vegas, NV 89103
364-1111
Dale Reynolds, Adm.
80 beds - 24 hour drug, alcohol abuse, depression, stress, phobias, eating disorders.

Rainbow Charter Hospital of Las Vegas
Patient Counseling Center
2972 Rainbow Blvd., Ste. B
Las Vegas, NV 89117
254-8348

Southern Nev. Adult Mental Health Services
Las Vegas Mental Health Center
6161 W. Charleston Blvd.

Las Vegas, NV 89102
486-6000
106 bed facility operated by the State of Nevada.

The Southeast Mental Health Center
1820 E. Sahara Ave., Ste. 109
Las Vegas, NV 89104
486-8280

Sunset Charter Hospital of Las Vegas
Counseling Ctr., Ste. 307
3663 E. Sunset Rd., Ste. 105
Las Vegas, NV 89120
794-0004

WestCare
(Also listed under Addiction Clinics & Counseling and Subsistence & Low Income.)
401 S. Martin Luther King Blvd.
Las Vegas, NV 89106
385-2020
Richard E. Steinberg, Pres.
Detoxification: 383-4044
Provides beds and counseling services to people suffering from alcoholism.

PHARMACIES

Landmark Pharmacy
252 Convention Center Dr.
Las Vegas, NV 89109
731-0041
Hours: Mon. - Fri. 8 am - 7 pm;
Sat. 8 am - 6 pm
Delivery service; wheelchair and crutch rental.
Credit Cards: MC, Visa, Disc., AMX

Rite Aid
Formerly Payless Drugs
(11 locations in the Las Vegas area)
For nearest location call 1-800-685-5355.

Village East Drugs
5025 S. Eastern Ave.
Las Vegas, NV 89119
736-7018
Hours: Mon. - Sat. 9 am - 9 pm;
Sun. 9 am - 7 pm
Home health care equipment - rental and sales.

24-HR. PHARMACIES

Smith's Food & Drug Center
2540 S. Maryland Pkwy. (at Sahara)
Las Vegas, NV 89109
791-0517

Sav-on Drugs
(Locations with 24 hr. pharmacies)
(Multiple locations listed below)
3550 W. Sahara Ave.
Las Vegas, NV 89102
873-7171

2011 E. Lake Mead Blvd.
N. Las Vegas, NV 89030
642-9780

1360 E. Flamingo Rd.
Las Vegas, NV 89119
731-5373

4410 E. Bonanza Rd.
Las Vegas, NV 89110
452-5652

Walgreens
(6 locations in the Las Vegas area)
6787 W. Tropicana Ave.
Las Vegas, NV 89103
Drive-thru prescription service
1-800-925-4733 for the pharmacy nearest you.

Walmart Pharmacy
3075 E. Tropicana Ave.
Las Vegas, NV 89121
451-0774

ASSISTANCE

HEALTH CARE AIDS

Clark County Health District: 385-1291
Offers free AIDS tests.
National Aids Hotline: 1-800-342-AIDS
Answers questions about AIDS - 24 hours.

Aid for AIDS of Nevada (AFAN)
(Multiple locations listed below)
2300 S. Rancho Dr., Ste. 211
Las Vegas, NV 89102
382-2326
Hotline: 474-2437

West Side Center
908 W. Owens Ave., Bldg. 5
Las Vegas, NV 89106
648-0177
Hotline: 474-2437
Jeff Smith, Executive Dir.
Non-profit agency that strives to reduce the occurrence of AIDS by providing education to the public, health care providers and those in high-risk groups. Provides assistance to people with AIDS. There are 2,846 cases in Clark County as of January 31, 1998.

Alzheimer's Disease Association
(Also listed in Seniors and Retirees)
3441 W. Sahara Ave.
Las Vegas, NV 89102
248-2770
Judy Hetherington, Exec. Dir.
Provides information and referrals about Alzheimer's Disease as well as group support meetings. There are 21,600 Alzheimer's patients in Clark County.

American Cancer Society
1325 E. Harmon Ave.
Las Vegas, NV 89119
798-6877
1-800-ACS-2345
Willette Balard, Regional Exec. Dir.
Extends a variety of rehabilitation and recovery programs, including support groups, to cancer patients. Also offers public and professional education on the prevention and detection of cancer. Other educational topics and services also offered.

American Diabetes Association
2785 E. Desert Inn Rd., Ste. 140
Las Vegas, NV 89121
369-9995
Debbie Devald, Exec. Dir.
Health fairs, awareness programs, youth programs, money for research and information.

American Heart Association
6370 W. Flamingo Rd., Ste. 1
Las Vegas, NV 89103
367-1366
John McNeil, Exec. Dir.
The nation's largest voluntary health organization dedicated to reducing early death and disability from cardiovascular diseases. Provides various heart health education services including CPR training.

American Lung Association
3375 Glen Ave., Ste. 7
Las Vegas, NV 89121
431-6333
John Holck, Exec. Dir.
Offers a variety of services to patients with lung diseases and their families.

American Red Cross
1155 E. Sahara Ave., Ste. 27
Las Vegas, NV 89104
791-3311
Rick Diebold, Exec. Dir.
Provides various health and educational programs to the public. Provides emergency relief to victims of floods, fires, and other disasters, as well as services for military personnel.

The Angel Planes
2700 Chandler Ave., Ste. A8
Las Vegas, NV 89120
261-0494
Ann McGee, Pres.
Provides free air transportation to treatment centers outside Las Vegas for families living in Southern Nevada. Sponsors annual Angel Plane Airfest at Boulder City Airport each March.

Arthritis Foundation
2660 S. Rainbow Blvd., Ste. B102
Las Vegas, NV 89102
367-1626
Nikki Sobkowski, Exec. Dir.
Offers doctors referrals, information, a water exercise program, and educational programs for arthritis sufferers and interested persons. Over 155,000 children and adults are afflicted with arthritis in Las Vegas.

Association of Anorexia Nervosa and Associated Disorders (ANAD)
368-0828
Non-profit group for people with anorexia and bulimia. ANAD offers free counseling, referrals, advocacy, and information.

City of Hope
Power of Life Chapter
3792 Decade St.
Las Vegas, NV 89121
Rose Levine, Pres.
451-2424
Cinthia Savage, Dir.
1-800-544-3541

City of Hope
Summerlin Chapter
2612 Saltbush Dr.
Las Vegas, NV 89134
255-4584

Garvin Haist, Pres.
Fundraisers for research to find cures for all forms of life-threatening diseases. City of Hope is supported by thousands of volunteers, organized in chapters and industry groups throughout the country, and by a nationwide network of donors. The City of Hope philosophy is to heal the whole person, not only physically but also emotionally and spiritually, and provide support and counseling for families.

Clark County Dental Society
(Also listed under Doctor Referral and Dental)
1785 E. Sahara Ave.
Las Vegas, NV 89117
733-8700
Connie Ballard - Exec. Dir.
Organization of dentists belonging to American Dental Association.

Clark County Medical Society
2590 E. Russell Rd.
Las Vegas, NV 89120
739-9989
Lisa Puled, Exec. Dir.
Nonprofit affiliate of American Medical Association. Physician referrals.

Cystic Fibrosis Foundation
1516 E. Tropicana Ave., Ste. A1
Las Vegas, NV 89119
597-0435
Regale Komzak, Dir.
Fundraising arm of the foundation to support patient care and research program. Dedicated to finding a cure for this country's leading genetic killer of children and young adults.

Down Syndrome Organization of Southern Nevada
5300 Vegas Dr.
Las Vegas, NV 89108-2347
648-1990
Kathy Treants, Pres./CEO
Helps people with Down syndrome achieve their potential in the community. Referrals to community services are provided to families, professionals, and concerned individuals.

Easter Seal Society of Nevada
(Also listed under Handicapped)
5785 W. Tropicana Ave., Ste. 2
Las Vegas, NV 89103
873-4000
Donald Stromquist, Pres.
Speech and physical therapy.

Family Planning Institute
501 S. Rancho Dr.
Las Vegas, NV 89106
382-0303
Takes care of women's needs. Pap smears, birth control, GYN exams and pregnancy terminations.

Healthinsight
901 Rancho Ln., Ste. 200
Las Vegas, NV 89106
385-9933
Sheri Steelman, Dir.
Health care quality improvement.

Help Them Walk Again Foundation for Spinal Research
(Also listed under Handicapped)
5300 W. Charleston Blvd.
Las Vegas, NV 89102
878-8360
Joanne Toadvine, Dir.
Non-profit organization specializing in spinal injury rehabilitation.

Hemophilia Foundation of Nevada
67 E. Lake Mead Dr.
Henderson, NV 89015
564-4368
Renee Paper, R.N., Program Dir.
Sponsors seminars, information/literature on bleeding disorders and complications, including hepatitis and HIV.

Juvenile Diabetes Foundation
4220 S. Maryland Pkwy., Ste. 214
Las Vegas, NV 89119
732-4795
Colleen Ashworth, Exec. Dir.
The Juvenile Diabetes Foundation is dedicated to financing research that will improve treatment, develop prevention, and find a cure for diabetes and its complications. Offers referral service as well as education and support programs.

Lupus Foundation of Las Vegas
1555 E. Flamingo Rd., Ste. 439
Las Vegas, NV 89119
645-6736
Cathy Osborn, Pres.
Lupus is a genetic, chronic, inflammatory illness that affects over 1 million people nationwide. The goal of the local chapter is to provide funds for medication for low-income patients and to establish a clinic in Las Vegas to serve lupus patients.

March of Dimes Birth Defects Foundation
2755 E. Desert Inn Rd., Ste. 260
Las Vegas, NV 89121
732-9255
Denise Chamberland, Division Dir.
Prevention of birth defects and advocacy of awareness and public education.

Multiple Sclerosis National Society
(Also listed under Handicapped)
6000 S. Eastern Ave., Ste. 5C
Las Vegas, NV 89119
736-7272
Program services: 736-9369
Rick Smith, Chapter Pres.
Equipment and support groups.

Muscular Dystrophy Association
(Also listed under Handicapped)
2245-D Renaissance Dr.
Las Vegas, NV 89119
739-7833
Patient services: 739-7669
Jo Ann Malone, District Dir.
Extends a variety of medical and community services to patients of any neuromuscular disease covered by the MDA.

National Kidney Foundation of Nevada
3050 E. Desert Inn Rd., Ste. 121
Las Vegas, NV 89121
735-9222
Gary Davis, Exec. Dir.
Raises and provides money for kidney patients in the state of Nevada.

Planned Parenthood of Southern Nevada
3220 W. Charleston Blvd.
Las Vegas, NV 89102
878-7776

Suzanne Gurstner, Adm. Dir.
Hours: Mon. - Thu. 9 am - 6 pm; Fri. 9 am - 4 pm; Sat. 9 am - 2 pm
Provides a variety of birth control and family planning, counseling, educational, and medical services for women; HIV-AIDS testing ($25) and counseling. 24 hour Planned Parenthood Answer Line - 1-800-322-1020. Confidential answers on sex, pregnancy, birth control, and sexually transmitted diseases.

Ronald McDonald House of Greater Las Vegas
2323 Potasi St.
Las Vegas, NV 89102
252-HOME(4663)
Emma L. Addis, Exec. Dir.
"The House That Love Built"
A 12,500 sq. ft., 12-bedroom home away from home for families of seriously ill children.

Senior Friends
(Multiple locations listed below)
3101 S. Maryland Pkwy., Ste. 314
Las Vegas, NV 89109
735-5510
Pam Carnivale, Exec. Dir.
Non-profit organization. Health screening, educational classes, discounts on optical and hearing aids.

8524 Del Webb Blvd.
Las Vegas, NV 89134
255-5404
Mimi Saft-Combs, Dir

Susan G. Komen Breast Cancer Foundation
Las Vegas Chapter
3223 W. Charleston Blvd., Ste. 207
Las Vegas, NV 89102
822-2324
Joan C. Heffner, Pres.
Helps to fight breast cancer and to support people affected.

United Blood Services
(Multiple locations listed below)
Main Center
6930 W. Charleston Blvd.
Las Vegas, NV 89117
228-4483
David Denney, Dir.
Non-profit organization collects blood for all hospitals.

600 Whitney Ranch Dr., Ste. C12
Henderson, NV 89014
434-1838

3935 E. Charleston Blvd.
Las Vegas, NV 89104
438-9850

4343 N. Rancho Dr., Ste. 244
Las Vegas, NV 89130

United Way Services, Inc.
1660 E. Flamingo Rd.
Las Vegas, NV 89119
734-2273
(See Clubs and Organizations Section)

REFERRALS

DOCTOR REFERRAL

Referral Nevada State Chiropractic Assn.
434 Washington St., Ste. C
Reno, NV 89503
702-324-2299

Clark County Dental Society
(Also listed under Dental & Healthcare.)
1785 E. Sahara Ave.
Las Vegas, NV 89117
733-8700
Connie Ballard, Exec. Dir.
Emergency Service 24 hours daily.

Board of Medical Examiners
1105 Terminal Way, Ste. 301
Reno, NV 89502
702-688-2559

Boulder City Hospital
293-4111
Physician-on-call.

Clark County Medical Society
2590 Russell Rd.
Las Vegas, NV 89120
739-9989

Call for Health
733-6875
Staffed by registered nurses to provide referral and information - Desert Springs Hospital.

Direct Doctor Referral Service
Valley Hospital
388-4852 1-800-322-8322

Columbia
1-800-COLUMBIA
Physician referral.

Lake Mead Hospital
649-3627
Physician referral.
St. Rose Dominican Physician Referral Program
564-4508

UMC Physicians Referral
383-2060

HEALTH PROFESSIONAL LICENSING & REFERRALS

If you have been mistreated or grossly overcharged, you can file a complaint with the appropriate board.

Audiologist and Speech Pathologists, Board of (Reno)
1-702-784-4887

American Society of Plastic & Reconstructive Surgeons Inc.
1-800-635-0635

Dental Examiners, State Board of
486-7044

Dispensing Opticians
735-0223

Hospitals, Office of Hospital Patients
486-8255

Marriage and Family Counselors, Board of
486-7388

Nurses and Nurse Practitioners, Board of Nursing
1-702-786-2778

Optometry, Board of (Carson City)
1-702-883-8367

Osteopaths
732-2147

Physicians, Board of Medical Examiners
486-6244

Physicians' Assistants, Board of Medical Examiners
1-702-688-2559

Nevada State Medical Assoc.
1-702-825-6788

Physical Therapists
1-702-876-5535

Podiatrists
1-733-7617
1-702-688-2555

HANDICAPPED

PHYSICALLY HANDICAPPED

The 1990 Census indicated there are more than 55,000 physically disabled people in the Las Vegas metropolitan area. There are 49 million disabled nationwide with higher than average in the Las Vegas area. There are 123,995 disabled people in Clark County, 13.5 percent of the population. The Americans with Disabilities Act is a federal law passed in 1990 that ensures the disabled access to employment, public buildings, and services such as restaurants, businesses, and hotels.

Adaptive Outreach Center
3333 W. Washington Ave.
Las Vegas, NV 89107
Adaptive Recreation Div.: 229-4900
Adaptive Outreach: 229-4796
Lorenzi Adaptive Center: 229-6358
Project D.I.R.T.: 648-2370
Adult Recreation: 648-4398
John Chambers, Chief of Adaptive Rec.
Serves physically challenged youth and adults with a wide variety of programs for all abilities. The cost varies with each activity. Programs are scheduled Monday through Saturday and the hours vary. The main goal is to provide leisure opportunities to citizens with disabilities to enhance their quality of life.

Assistive Technology Center
2820 W. Charleston Blvd., Ste. B19
Las Vegas, NV 89102
259-0789
Linn Thome, Mgr.
Teaches how to operate a wheelchair, navigate a handicap ramp, or finance the purchase of equipment.

Bureau of Vocational Rehabilitation
State of Nevada
628 Belrose St.
Las Vegas, NV 89158
486-5230
Carol Jackson, Dir./Mgr.
Occupational guidance and counseling for the rehabilitation of the physically handicapped.

CAT® Paratransit Services
301 Clark Ave.
Las Vegas, NV 89101
228-4800   TTD 455-2199
Door-to-door bus service for disabled sponsored by the Regional Transportation Commission. You must fill out an application to qualify. Rides are scheduled 24 hours to 14 days in advance and each ride is $1. Over 14,000 people are signed up for this service.

Clark County School District
Child Find Project
2625 E. St. Louis Ave.
Las Vegas, NV 89104
799-7463
Judy Miller, Coordinator
Diagnostic evaluation and placement recommendations of handicapped individuals to age 21 who are not enrolled in the school district. Services are available to all individuals.

Children's Special Health Care Services
1161 S. Valley View Blvd.
Las Vegas, NV 89102
486-7680
Yvonne Silva, Adm.
State agency providing, to qualified families, financial assistance in paying for medical care for children with birth defects or acquired medical disabilities.

Department of Justice
ADA Information Line: 1-800-514-0301
Teletypewriter: 1-800-514-0383
Technical assistance on ADA standards for accessible design. Instructions on how to file an official ADA complaint.

Easter Seal Society of Nevada
5785 W. Tropicana Ave., Ste. 2
Las Vegas, NV 89103
873-4000
Physical and occupational therapy for young children.

ASSISTANCE

HANDICAPPED

**Equal Employment
Opportunity Commission**
1-800-669-4000
Teletypewriter: 1-800-669-6820
Technical assistance on the ADA's provisions regarding employment and information on filing complaints.

Goodwill Industries
(Also listed under Handicapped-Mentally and Low Income)
6171 McLeod St.
Las Vegas, NV 89120
597-1107
Steve Chartrand, Pres./CEO
Vocational and occupational rehabilitation for the physically handicapped.

**Governor's Committee on
Employment of People with
Disabilities**
2601 E. Sahara Ave.
Las Vegas, NV 89104
Teletypewriter: 486-4318/486-4320
Suzanne Thomas, Community Program Consultant
Employment opportunities for the disabled; equipment and aid.

**E.O.B. Mentally Handicapped
Transportation**
800 W. Bonanza Rd.
Las Vegas, NV 89106
646-4203
John Del Mar, Dir.
Transportation assistance for mentally disabled from home to the Hollyhock Adult Day Care Center.

**Help Them Walk Again
Foundation**
5300 W. Charleston Blvd.
Las Vegas, NV 89102
878-8360
Joanne Toadvine, Dir.
Physical therapy services to disabled persons.

**Henderson Convalescent
Hospital**
1180 E. Lake Mead Dr.
Henderson, NV 89015
565-8555
Carol Barnicoat, Adm.
266-bed facility providing therapy and rehabilitation - physical and speech. Short and long term.

Hollyhock Adult Day Care
380 N. Maryland Pkwy.
Las Vegas, NV 89101
382-0588
Mary Jo Greenlee, Dir.
Day care for the physically handicapped adult. Medical supervision, social activities and daily nutrition are provided.

Las Vegas Blind Center
1001 N. Bruce St.
Las Vegas, NV 89101
642-6000
Katherine Law, Dir.
Non-profit organization and training center for the blind.

Lorenzi Adaptive Rec Center
3333 W. Washington Ave.
Las Vegas, NV 89107
229-6358   229-4905
Serves developmentally disabled youth up to age 22; the A. G. E. Program serves those age 23 and over.

Multiple Sclerosis National Soc.
6000 S. Eastern Ave., Ste. 5C
Las Vegas, NV 89119
736-7272
Program services: 736-9369
Rick Smith, Chapter Pres.
Equipment, physical therapy, and support groups.

**Muscular Dystrophy
Association**
2245-D Renaissance Dr.
Las Vegas, NV 89119
739-7833
Patient services: 739-7669
Jo Ann Malone, District Dir.
Diagnostic and medical treatment, referrals, orthopedic equipment and physical therapy.

**Nevada Association for the
Handicapped**
6200 W. Oakey Blvd.
Las Vegas, NV 89102
870-7050
Vince Triggs, Dir.
Services for the physically handicapped, sensory impaired, and their families.

Nadine Ford Development Center
870-7050
Provides outreach programs, training and the state's first full-time day-care and preschool for disabled children.

**Nev. Bureau of Services to the
Blind and Visually Impaired**
628 Belrose St.
Las Vegas, NV 89158
486-5333
Al Roybal, District Mgr.
Services to the visually impaired, blind and deaf-blind.

**Nevada Disability Advocacy and
Law Center**
401 S. 3rd St.
Las Vegas, NV 89101
383-8150
Travis Wall, Exec. Dir.
Non-profit organization protects the rights of people with disabilities. Receives and investigates complaints.

Nevada Rehabilitation Division
505 E. King St., Room 502
Carson City, NV 89710
687-4440

New Vista Ranch
7875 N. Rainbow Blvd.
Las Vegas, NV 89131
645-7432
Dick & June Herman, Pres.
Private, non-profit residential facility for disabled adults. Operates Thrift Store at 4000 Boulder Hwy.

**Spina Bifida and
Hydrocephalus Association**
3196 S. Maryland Pkwy., Ste. 104
Las Vegas, NV 89109
796-7242
Variety of services to those afflicted and their families.

Sunset Park
2601 E. Sunset Rd.
Las Vegas, NV 89120
455-8200
Playground designed for disabled children.

HANDICAPPED
MENTALLY

**Bureau of Vocational
Rehabilitation**
628 Belrose St.
Las Vegas, NV 89158
486-5230
Daryl Teegarden, Dir./Mgr.
Vocational rehabilitation for handicapped individuals.

Danville Service Corp.
2626 S. Rainbow Blvd., Ste. 203
Las Vegas, NV 89102
227-8558
Mark Inouye, Dir.
Operates six intermediate care residential facilities in the Las Vegas area under contract with the State of Nevada for people with disabilities. Danville matches people with mental retardation with jobs and provides the necessary support so the person will succeed in the workplace.

Goodwill Industries
6171 McLeod St.
Las Vegas, NV 89120
597-1107
Steve Chartrand, Pres./CEO
Vocational and occupational rehabilitation.

Haven of Hope (St. Vincent)
1501 Las Vegas Blvd. N.
Las Vegas, NV 89101
382-9781
Jesse Kent, Program Dir.
Mentally ill people are counseled by caseworkers and helped with survival basics.

Hollyhock Adult Day Care
(Also listed under Handicapped and Senior Centers)
380 N. Maryland Pkwy.
Las Vegas, NV 89101
382-0588
Mary Jo Greenlee, Dir.
Day care; medical supervision, social activities, and daily nutrition.

**Nevada Association
for the Handicapped**
6200 W. Oakey Blvd.
Las Vegas, NV 89102
870-7050
Vince Triggs, Dir.
Variety of services for handicapped and families.

**Nevada State Desert
Developmental Center**
Desert Regional Center
1300 S. Jones Blvd.
Las Vegas, NV 89158
486-6200
Stanlee Dodd, Ed.D., Regional Dir.
Variety of services for handicapped and families; residential facility.

**Opportunity Village Association
of Retarded Citizens**
6300 W. Oakey Blvd.
Las Vegas, NV 89102
259-3700
Ed Guthrie, Exec. Dir.
Vocational and occupational services and opportunities for retarded adults (18 and over). In its 44 years, this private, non-profit agency has helped thousands of mentally handicapped adults lead more productive lives with training and employment. Opportunity Village completed an $8 million construction project in 1994 that includes new recreational facilities and headquarters. Currently, more than 300 adults receive training at the facility. Opportunity Village maintains thrift stores at 921 S. Main St. and on Boulder Hwy. in Henderson.

Special Children's Clinic
1161 S. Valley View Blvd.
Las Vegas, NV 89102
486-7670
Karen Cummings, Clinic Dir.
Diagnosis and treatment or referral services to developmentally delayed children from birth to three years.

**Southern Nevada Alliance
for the Mentally Ill**
(Also listed under Counseling)
P.O. Box 85373
Las Vegas, NV 89185
486-6000
Janyce Benson, Pres.
No cost. Provides referrals for mental health care. Provides social services information and sponsorship of support groups and mental health care education.

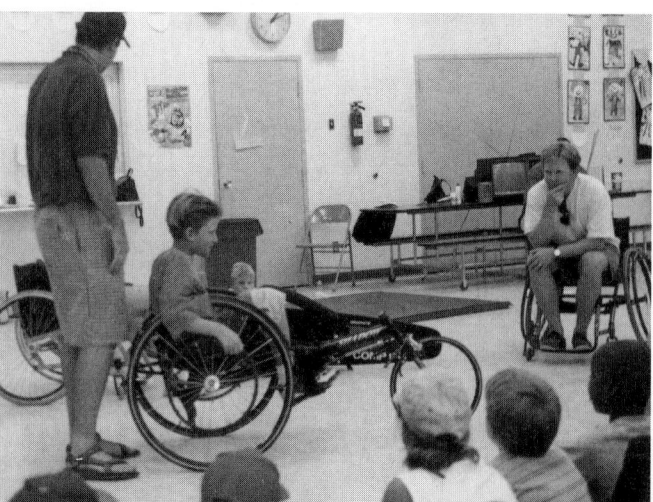

COUNSELING

Baby Pearls Program
3105 Merritt Ave.
Las Vegas, NV
876-3848
Dolly Earl, Dir.
Prenatal education and case management.

Bridge Counseling Associates
(Also listed under Addiction)
1701 W. Charleston Blvd., Ste. 320
Las Vegas, NV 89102
474-6450
Mark Disselkoen, Exec. Dir.
Deals with chemical dependency, family and marital problems, stress, depression and other mental health needs.

Community Counseling Center
1120 Almond Tree Ln., Ste. 207
Las Vegas, NV 89104
369-8700
Ronald Lawrence, Exec. Dir.
Non-profit group. One-on-one counseling for drug abuse or alcohol.

Family and Child Treatment Center of Southern Nevada
4800 W. Charleston Blvd., Ste. 140
Las Vegas, NV 89102
258-5855
Fran Marshall, Exec. Dir.
Deals with sexually abused children, adults sexually abused as children, rape, physical and psychological abuse and neglect, relationships, stress adjustment problems and depression.

LDS Social Services
513 S. 9th St.
Las Vegas, NV 89101
385-1072
Christian Anderson, Dir.
Provides pregnancy counseling for all residents.

Nevada State Desert Developmental Center
(Also listed under Handicapped-Mentally)
Desert Regional Center
1300 S. Jones Blvd.
Las Vegas, NV 89158
486-6200
Stanlee Dodd, Ed.D., Regional Dir.

Planned Parenthood
3220 W. Charleston Blvd.
Las Vegas, NV 89102
878-7776
Kimula Schoffner, Clinical Mgr.
Pregnancy testing, counseling, and referrals. Testing and treatment for sexually transmitted diseases.

Southern Nevada Adult Mental Health Services
West Charleston Counseling Center
6161 W. Charleston Blvd.
Las Vegas, NV 89102
486-6000
Crisis line: 486-8020
Provides a variety of inpatient and outpatient services and programs for diagnosis, treatment and rehabilitation. This facility also houses a psychiatric hospital. With the exception of the psychiatric hospital, services and programs available here are also available at 1820 E. Sahara Avenue.

Counseling Center
1820 E. Sahara Ave., Ste. 109
Las Vegas, NV 89104
486-8280

Southern Nevada Child and Adolescent Mental Health Center
6171 W. Charleston Blvd.
Las Vegas, NV 89158
486-6100
Christa Peterson, Adm.
Provides numerous services and programs to children and adolescents suffering from behavioral and emotional problems, and their families.

N. Las Vegas Counseling Center
2308 E. Cheyenne Ave.
N. Las Vegas, NV 89030
486-5610
Dr. N. Parson, Site Mgr.
Provides numerous services and programs to children and adolescents suffering from behavioral and emotional problems, and their families.

Southern Nevada Alliance for the Mentally Ill
(Also listed under Handicapped.)
P.O. Box 85373
Las Vegas, NV 89185
898-9790
Janyce Benson, Pres.
Self-help organization of mentally ill persons, their friends and families whose goals are mutual support, education and advocacy for the victims of severe mental illness.

Southern Nevada Sightless
1001 N. Bruce St.
Las Vegas, NV 89101
642-6000
Katherine Law, Dir.
Provides counseling, referral, advocacy, adjustment training, recreation, work activities.

UNLV Client Services Center
4505 S. Maryland Pkwy.
Las Vegas, NV 89154
895-3106
Tom Sexton, Dir.
Professional counseling for adults, children and couples in parenting, marriage, communication problems, career decisions and other crises. The center is part of the Greenspun School of Urban Affairs and charges a sliding scale fee ranging from $5 to $25; $15 for initial intake interviews.

SUPPORT GROUPS

(Also see Addiction Support Groups)

Active Blind and Visually Impaired of Nevada
4537 Brighton Dr.
Las Vegas, NV 89121
454-9958
Kurt Boucher, Pres.
Meetings held at Denny's Restaurant, Maryland Pkwy. 2nd Monday of each month. Hospitality hour 6 pm. Peer counseling to the newly blinded at 7 pm. Assist in jobs for blind and recreational activities.

Adult Children of Alcoholics
P. O. Box 29332
Las Vegas, NV 89126
369-2262
Help for children of alcoholics: 12-step program. Call for meeting times and locations.

Aid for AIDS of Nevada (AFAN)
(Also listed under Health Care)
1111 Desert Ln.
Central Community Center
Las Vegas, NV 89102
382-2326
Hotline: 474-2437
National Hotline: 1-800-342-2437
David Parks, Pres.
Non-profit agency that strives to reduce the occurrence of AIDS by providing education to the public, health care providers and those in high risk groups. Provides assistance to people with AIDS. AFAN's large community center provides a variety of social events and a daily lunch program.

Aid for AIDS of Nevada (AFAN)
West Community Service Center
(Also listed under Health Care)
908 W. Owens Ave., Bldg. 5
Las Vegas, NV 89106
648-0177
David Parks, Pres.
Provides support group, food pantry, financial assistance, buddy program, and educational outreach.

Alzheimer's Support Group
648-3425
Kate Mead
Meets the 2nd Wednesday of each month at E.O.B., Lied Senior Center, 901 N. Jones Blvd.

Bereaved Parents Program
3141 Nottingham Dr.
Las Vegas, NV 89121
393-1810
Loss of child support group. Monthly meetings. Bereaved Parents is a non-denominational organization.

Better Breathers Club
American Lung Association
3375 Glen Ave., Ste. 7
Las Vegas, NV 89121
431-6333
Bunny Grangaard, Dir.
Support group for people with lung problems. Meetings held on 3rd Wednesday of each month at Parish Hall, Christ Church Episcopal, 2000 S. Maryland Pkwy. Rap sessions 1 pm; guest speaker 2 pm.

Bridge Counseling Associates
(Also listed under Addiction Clinics)
1701 W. Charleston Blvd., Ste. 320
Las Vegas, NV 89102
474-6450
Mark Disselkoen, Exec. Dir.
Chemical dependency, marital and family problems, mental health issues. Understand how drugs affect your life and how to adapt to a drug-free life-style.

Candlelighters for Childhood Cancer
3201 S. Maryland Pkwy., Ste. 512

Las Vegas, NV 89109
737-1919
Eleyna Olivas, Exec. Dir.
Support groups for families with children diagnosed with cancer.

Clark County SIDS
455-3894
Meets 3rd Tuesday of each month at 7 pm at Clark County Social Services office, 1600 Pinto Lane.

Children of Older Parents
6161 W. Charleston Blvd.
Las Vegas, NV 89102
486-6263
Laurie Moore
Call for meeting times and days. Support group for adults concerned about aging parents.

Co-Dependency Help Line
1-800-888-9383
Non-profit support group for people having problems facing life or who come from dysfunctional families.

Community Action Against Rape (CAAR)
(Also known as Rape Crisis Center.)
749 Veterans Memorial Dr.
Las Vegas, NV 89101
385-2153
Hotline: 366-1640
Renata Cirri, Exec. Dir.
Independent, non-profit sexual abuse prevention and intervention service. Emergency shelter, food and clothing. Assistance in obtaining no-cost counseling and/or additional medical care. CAAR is the only agency providing crisis intervention to sexual assault victims in Southern Nevada. In 1997, the agency assisted 869 primary victims and 1,779 secondary victims. United Way Agency.

Depression Support Group
876-4357
Group for people suffering from depression and manic depressive illness. Free group meetings 7 pm - 8:30 pm Mondays at Charter Hospital.

Divorced, Separated and Widowed Adjustment, Support Groups, Inc.
P.O. Box 26504
Las Vegas, NV 89126
735-5544 225-1785
Park Baker
Non-profit corporation. Small and caring support groups that meet each week for men and women 7:30 pm - 9:30 pm at no cost.

Emotions Anonymous
221-0744
A 12 step program to help individuals cope with emotional problems.

Equal Rights for Divorced Fathers
387-6266
Ernest Del Casal, Exec. Dir.
Weekly support meetings. Works with fathers to continue contact with their children.

ASSISTANCE

COUNSELING

Family & Child Treatment Center of Southern Nevada (FACT)
4800 W. Charleston Blvd., Ste. 140
Las Vegas, NV 89102
258-5855
Fran Marshall, Exec. Dir.
Counseling for childhood sexual abuse, adults molested as children, physical and emotional abuse and neglect, elderly abuse, and rape.

Families of Murder Victims
564-5919
Eva Collenberger
Meets twice monthly on the 2nd Thursday at 7 pm and 4th Saturday at 11 am at the Stop DUI offices at 3321 Sunrise Ave., Ste. 107.

Grief/Loss Support Class
First United Methodist Church
231 S. 3rd St.
Las Vegas, NV 89101
382-9939
Support for persons seeking to cope with grief duo to death, divorce, or other significant loss.

Junior League of Las Vegas
461 S. Decatur Blvd.
Las Vegas, NV 89107
732-3257
LuAnn Kutch, Pres.
Programs provided include the Repeat Boutique Thrift Shop, 1040 E. Twain Ave., Las Vegas, 89109; Done in a Day; education grants.

Las Vegas Fibro Myalgia Chronic Fatigue Syndrome
647-4791
Sheryl Brewer, Support Group Leader
Lois Davidson, Co-Support Group Leader
Educate patients and the community regarding the illness. Meets 2nd Sunday at Sunrise Hospital, 3 pm in Rendezvous Room.

Las Vegas Stroke Club
438-7911   369-3249 (evenings)
Bette Lou Schaum, Pres.
Survivors of strokes and their families meet 2nd Wednesday at 7 pm at 2040 W. Charleston Blvd.

Lupus Foundation of Las Vegas
(Also listed under Health Care)
1555 E. Flamingo Rd., Ste. 439
Las Vegas, NV 89119
645-6736
Cathy Osborn, Pres.
Lupus is a genetic, chronic, inflammatory illness that affects over 1 million people nationwide. The goal of the local chapter is to provide funds for medication for low-income patients and to establish a clinic in Las Vegas to serve lupus patients.

Nathan Adelson Hospice Support Group
4141 S. Swenson St.
Las Vegas, NV 89119
733-0320
Adult Bereavement Support Group meets 1st and 3rd Thursday at 10 am.

Parents and Friends of Lesbians and Gays
438-7838
Support group for gays and their parents.

Parents Anonymous
368-1533
Sandy Sultz, Facilitator
Meeting Tuesday 6:30 - 8 pm at St. Viator Community Center, 4320 Channel 10 Dr.; Thursday 7 pm - 8:30 pm at Community Counseling Center, 1120 Almond Tree Ln.

Recovery Inc.
362-7368
Anxieties, fears, and temperamental behavior. Four meetings each week.

Resolve Through Sharing
731-8222
Infant or pregnancy loss support group; Meets the 2nd Tuesday at Sunrise Hospital.

Sex and Love Addicts Anonymous
737-7047
Free 12-step program for those with compulsive patterns of sex and relationships; call for times and locations.

Southern Nevada Adult Mental Health Services
6161 W. Charleston Blvd.
Las Vegas, NV 89102
486-6000
Support group for mentally ill.

Southern Nevada Amputee Support Group
P.O. Box 29255
Las Vegas, NV 89126
458-8230
Butch Plotner, Pres.
Provides and promotes resources and information to assist amputees in independent living.

Stop DUI
3321 Sunrise Pkwy., Ste. 107
Las Vegas, NV 89101
456-7867
Sandy Heverly, Pres.
As-needed group support meetings

Stroke of Luck Support Group
242-9653
Meets 3rd Wednesday 2 pm at the Summerlin Library.

Suicide Prevention Center
3838 Raymert St.
Las Vegas, NV 89121
731-2990
24 hour hotline.

Survivors of Suicide
731-2990
Support group for those who have lost a family member through suicide; meetings held twice monthly in the evening; ask for Dorothy or the SOS coordinator.

Widowed Person Service of Southern Nevada
385-6922
Volunteers help newly widowed persons through tough times one-on-one.

MILITARY / VETERAN

ASSISTANCE

American Red Cross
(Also listed under Health Care)
1155 E. Sahara Ave., Ste. 27
Las Vegas, NV 89104
791-3311
Rick Diebold, Exec. Dir.
Provides information, counseling and referrals as well as financial assistance to military personnel and their families.

Deputy Commission for Veterans' Affairs
1700 Vegas Dr., Room 1719
Las Vegas, NV 89106
636-3070
Steve Clark
Offers a variety of services regarding rehabilitation, benefits, education, and employment, including filing for claims, appeals, compensation, and pensions.

Disabled American Veterans Dept. of Nevada
702-883-8937
Nick Condos, Commander

Nellis AFB Family Services Center
Nellis Air Force Base, NV 89191
652-6070
Col. Gerald Muehlberger
Provides a number of services to active and retired military personnel and their families as well as Department of Defense civilians and their families.

Nellis AFB Family Support Center
Nellis Air Force Base, NV 89191
652-3327
Provides relocation services, employment guidance, and financial guidance support groups for single parents, young mothers, and foreign-born spouses. Also provides information and referral services and enrichment in parent and family development. For active and retired military personnel and their families, and Department of Defense civilians and their families.

Nellis AFB Social Actions Office
Nellis Air Force Base, NV 89191
652-9420
Chief Capt. McGriff
Offers services on substance abuse problems, information about community organizations, and management of human resources programs to active and retired military personnel and their families and Department of Defense civilians and their families.

Michael O'Callaghan Federal Hospital
Nellis Air Force Base
4700 Las Vegas Blvd. N.
Las Vegas, NV 89191-6601
653-2222
Col. David Young, Hospital Commander
118-bed facility is shared by the Air Force and the Veterans Administration. The hospital has an emergency room, a dental clinic, an obstetrical nursing unit, an intensive care unit, and psychiatric nursing unit for the Veterans Administration and outpatient clinic for Air Force personnel.

Southern Nevada Veterans Memorial Cemetery
1900 Buchanan Blvd.
P.O. Box 878
Boulder City, NV 89005
486-5920

Veterans Administration Clinic
1700 Vegas Dr.
Las Vegas, NV 89106
636-3000
Hours: Mon. - Fri. 8 am - 4 pm

Alcohol Treatment Center and Outpatient Clinic
Regional Veterans Administration Benefit Office
4800 Alpine Pl., Ste. 11
Las Vegas, NV 89102
1-800-827-1000
Hours: Mon. - Fri. 8 am - 3:45 pm

Veteran Housing Center
5000 E. Bonanza Rd., Ste. X2
Las Vegas, NV 89110
459-8387

Veterans Outreach Center
1040 E. Sahara Ave., Ste. 1
Las Vegas, NV 89104
388-6368
Matt Watson, Team Leader
Offers a variety of therapy, counseling, and support group programs.

Veterans in Politics
P.O. Box 43776
Las Vegas, NV 89116
459-0842
David Mofchum, Pres.

DEPARTMENT OF VETERANS AFFAIRS
ADDELIAR D. GUY, III
AMBULATORY CARE CENTER

REHABILITATION

SUBSISTENCE & LOW INCOME

Horizon Specialty Hospital
640 Desert Ln.
Las Vegas, NV 89106
382-3155
Scott Weiss, Adm.
Specialize in rehabilitation.

**Dept. of Human Resources
Bureau of Vocational
Rehabilitation**
(Also listed under Handicapped)
628 Belrose St.
Las Vegas, NV 89158
486-5230
Daryl Teegarden, District Mgr.

J H C Health Center
1001 Shadow Ln.
Las Vegas, NV 89106
388-3500
Vera Smith, Manager
Physical therapy and vocational evaluation for the industrially injured with referral from physician and/or insurance company.

**Nevada Community Enrichment
Program**
2820 W. Charleston Blvd., Ste. D37
Las Vegas, NV 89102
259-1903
Bob Hogan, Dir.
Non-profit full-day speech and physical rehabilitation service.

Nevada Rehabilitation Division
505 E. King St., Room 502
Carson City, NV 89710
687-4440

**Nova Care Outpatient
Rehabilitation**
(Multiple locations listed below)
6848 W. Charleston Blvd.
Las Vegas, NV 89117
870-8564
Larry Urban, Gen. Mgr.
Rehabilitation for sports injuries, pool facilities, extended hours until 9 pm on Mon., Wed. and Fri. and 8 am - noon on Sat. Bilingual Therapist.

2055 East Sahara Ave.
Las Vegas, NV 89104
796-0945
Alison Ames-Orci, P.T., Clinic Mgr.
Central Las Vegas location. Pool facilities, sports medicine, shoulder and knee injuries, TMJ treatment.

3870 East Flamingo Rd., Ste. A12
Las Vegas, NV 89121
434-0100
Alex Delgado, P.T., Clinic Mgr.
Spine therapy, swimming pool, bilingual therapist, use of Las Vegas Athletic Club facilities.

2628 W. Charleston Blvd.
Las Vegas, NV 89102
259-1990
Miriam Franta, P.T., Clinic Mgr.
Neurological injuries, spine therapy.

501 S. Rancho Dr., Ste. D21
Las Vegas, NV 89106
388-1100
Randy Allen, P.T., Clinic Mgr.
Hand and upper extremity therapy, BTE equipment for testing, pediatric therapist (NDT trained), bilingual services.

4 Sunset Way, Ste. A1
Henderson, NV 89014
898-8186
Jeff Diedrich, P.T., Clinic Mgr.
Combined upper extremity and cervical spine evaluation and treatment programs; spine therapy; hand, foot, and ankle therapy; bilingual therapist.

8420 W. Lake Mead Blvd., Ste. 100
Las Vegas, NV 89128
243-7744
Scott Pensivy, P.T., Clinic Mgr.
Located at Lake Mead and Rampart Blvd. Sports medicine, neurological injuries, spine therapy.

Rancho Rehabilitation Center
University Medical Center
4333 N. Rancho Dr.
Las Vegas, NV 89130
656-0470
Dr. Firooz Mashhood, Medical Dir.
University Medical Center rehabilitation center for adults and children 7 years and older.

**Rehabilitation Hospital of
Nevada · Las Vegas**
1250 S. Valley View Blvd.
Las Vegas, NV 89102
877-8898
Dennis Falk, CEO
60-bed comprehensive acute rehabilitation hospital. This 56,500 square foot, $13.9 million facility opened in January 1993 and offers special programs for head trauma, orthopedic, and general rehabilitation. Outpatient services for aftercare and followup.

Sunrise Hospital
Rehab West 300
3186 S. Maryland Pkwy.
Las Vegas, NV 89109
731-8629
Samuel Wise, Medical Dir.
The 30-bed unit opened in 1989 and recently was accredited by the Commission of Accreditation of Rehabilitation Facilities, the only accredited inpatient facility in Southern Nevada. Specially trained physical therapists, occupational therapists, speech and language pathologists, social workers, recreation therapists, dietitians, doctors, and nurses operate the unit.

**Univ. Medical Center
Rehabilitation Centers**
Transitional Care Center
1800 W. Charleston Blvd.
Las Vegas, NV 89102
383-2250
Byron Brown, Dir.

Work 4 It
6376 W. Spring Mountain Rd.
Las Vegas, NV 89102
222-0803
Cindy Braden, Pres.
Work 4 It provides personalized conditioning and rehabilitation programs as well as nutritional and diet supplement evaluation and information designed for the individual.

American Red Cross
(Also listed under Health Care)
1155 E. Sahara Ave., Ste. 27
Las Vegas, NV 89104
384-1225
Rick Diebold, Exec. Dir.
Provides various health and educational programs to the public. Provides emergency relief to victims of disasters and services for military personnel.

**Catholic Charities
of Southern Nevada**
808 S. Main St.
Las Vegas, NV 89101
385-2662
Michael Husted, Exec. Dir.
The purpose of CCSN is to establish programs and service centers ensuring the basic needs of the poor, homeless, and disadvantaged people in Southern Nevada will be met, as far as resources allow, and in cooperation with other local agencies. The 25 current programs serve people of all races and ages. For every dollar donated 86 cents goes to the needy and 14 cents goes for overhead and expenses.

Clark County Pro Bono Project
382-3113
Lana Perry, Supvr.
You may also call: 386-1070 ext. 136.
Low-cost legal assistance for low income residents of Clark County.

**Clark County Social Services
Direct Assistance Service**
(Multiple locations listed below)
1600 Pinto Ln.
Las Vegas, NV 89106
455-4270
Denell Hahn, Dir.
Hours: Mon. - Fri. 7 am - 5 pm
Rural Clark County: 1-800-492-3177
Financial or medical assistance by County eligibility standards: 455-3108
If zip codes are 89030, 89031, 89106, 89115, 89130, or if homeless and in 89101: 455-7208
If 60 years or older: 455-4342
Provides medical cards and monthly financial assistance for qualified applicants; provides indigents with food and shelter; provides out of area transportation back to place of residence.

Satellite Office
3333 S. Cambridge St.
Las Vegas, NV 89109
455-8656
Hours: Mon. - Fri. 7:30 am - 4:30 pm

Satellite Office
940 W. Owens Ave.
Las Vegas, NV 89106
455-7208
Hours: Mon. - Fri. 7 am - 4 pm

Clean and Sober Living House
1419 Harmony Hill Dr.
Henderson, NV 89014
898-0054
Paul Benton, Dir.
A transitional living environment for working males recovering from alcoholism.

Community Food Bank
4601 E. Cheyenne Blvd., Ste. 111
Las Vegas, NV 89115
643-0074
Bessie Bragg, Dir.
Programs to feed the hungry in Las Vegas.

**Deseret Industries
Welfare Services Center**
1300 Las Vegas Blvd. N.
Las Vegas, NV 89101
649-8191
Darrel Smith, Unit Mgr.
Deseret Industries is an arm of the Church of Jesus Christ of Latter-day Saints. The center houses a thrift shop, employment and referral center and food distribution center for the needy through the Bishop's Storehouse. Food distributions are done through referral slips from LDS Bishops.

Economic Opportunity Board
2228 Comstock Dr.
N. Las Vegas, NV 89030
647-2010
Information and referral: 647-1510
James Tyree, Executive Dir.

**Economic Opportunity Board
Project Home Program**
330 W. Washington Ave., Ste. 7
Las Vegas, NV 89106
647-3307
Beverly Johnson, Dir.
Provides housing assistance, through several programs that promote self-sufficiency, to homeless families with minor children or those threatened with homelessness.

Golden Rule, Inc.
624 E. Stewart Ave.
Las Vegas, NV 89110
383-0847
Bonnie Polley, Coordinator
Offers affordable rent for men and women (no children) coming out of jail, treatment, emergency shelter, or off the street who desire to get back into the mainstream. Also for the unemployed and the working poor.

Goodwill Industries of Nevada
(Also listed under Handicapped-Mentally and Handicapped)
6171 McLeod St.
Las Vegas, NV 89120
597-1107
Steve Chartrand, Pres./CEO
Provides jobs and training to the disadvantaged. Goodwill depends on public donations and income from its three stores. Provides food baskets for the needy on holidays.

Goodwill Industries Thrift Store
(Multiple locations listed below)
3461 Boulder Hwy.
Las Vegas, NV 89121
641-7523

2560 S. Duneville St.
Las Vegas, NV 89102
251-1929
9 am - 6 pm

31 N. Nellis Blvd.
Las Vegas, NV 89110
437-7194
9 am - 6 pm

Habitat for Humanity
4375 E. Stewart Ave.
Las Vegas, NV 89110
638-6477
Jim Evans, Exec. Dir.
Constructs homes for low income residents.

SUBSISTENCE & LOW INCOME

HELP of Southern Nevada
953 E. Sahara Ave.
Bldg. 35B, Ste. 208
Las Vegas, NV 89104
369-4357
Denice Conrad, Exec. Dir.
HELP was founded 24 years ago by the Junior League of Las Vegas. Since opening it has turned into a social services agency that provides a variety of services including alternative sentencing program for nonviolent convicts, home weatherizing for low income families, helps displaced homemakers support themselves, and provides travelers aid information and assistance to stranded clients. HELP is funded by state and local governments and private donations.

Homeless Advocacy Project
2756 N. Green Valley Pkwy.
Henderson, NV 89014
256-5077 (job hotline)
Helping the homeless help themselves.

**Housing Authority of
the City of Las Vegas**
420 N. 10th St.
Las Vegas, NV 89101
386-2727
Frederick Brown, Exec. Dir.
Directs housing programs for low income families and the elderly of Las Vegas. Agency administers aid to 3,768 families of which 1,670 are elderly and 2,098 are non-elderly families.

**Housing Authority
of Clark County**
5390 E. Flamingo Rd.
Las Vegas, NV 89122
451-8041
Bill Cottrell, Exec. Dir.
Offers a variety of low rent housing and assistance programs.

**Housing Authority of the City
of North Las Vegas**
1632 Yale St.
N. Las Vegas, NV 89030
649-2451
Bob Sullivan, Dir.

**Howard W. Cannon Center
*Services for Senior Citizens***
340 N. 11th St.
Las Vegas, NV 89101
366-1522
Carol Hunter, Acting Dir.
Services include Nevada State Welfare; CHIP-NV Aging Service - Age 65; Cannon Center Administration; Clark County Social Services; Representative Payee; Senior Companion; Senior Law Project - Age 60; AARP; Cannon Senior Medical Center; RSVP; Senior Employment; Opticare 2000 - 2nd and 4th Thu. 9 am - 10 am; Vision Screening (369-1555) - prior sign up required.

Jewish Family Service Agency
3909 S. Maryland Pkwy., Ste. 205
Las Vegas, NV 89119
732-0304
Adrienne Rosenberg, Exec. Dir.
Services include marriage counseling; individual, group, and family counseling; food and shelter; information and referrals. Housing options for seniors, homesharing.

Las Vegas Rescue Mission
480 W. Bonanza Rd.
Las Vegas, NV 89106
382-1766
Rev. Edward Compton, Dir.
Christian-based non-profit organization. Provides emergency shelter (must call first), clothing and food for needy men, women and children. Meals served 5 pm daily.

Lutheran Social Ministry
1501 N. Main St.
Las Vegas, NV 89101
383-4054
Provides weekend emergency food, shelter and clothing. Sat. 9 am - 1 pm; Sun. noon - 2 pm.

M*A*S*H Village
1559 Main St.
Las Vegas, NV 89101
229-4806
Ken Robinson, Dir.
40,000 square foot facility. The city and county built the Mobilized Assistance and Shelter for the Homeless (MASH) at the corner of Owens and North Main St. The center provides medical, rehabilitation, child care, training and job placement and 300 beds. Construction was completed late 1995.

Nevada Legal Services, Inc.
Clark Co. Legal Serv. Prg.
701 E. Bridger Ave., Ste. 101
Las Vegas, NV 89101
386-1070
Terry Bratton, Program Dir.
Provides free legal assistance in civil matters to low income citizens of Clark County.

Nevada Partners Inc.
710 W. Lake Mead Blvd
N. Las Vegas, NV 89030
399-5627
Mujaid Ramadam, Executive Dir.
Nevada Partners offers life skills courses and works with businesses and government to find full-time employment for low-income, unemployed citizens of Clark County. Programs offered include Summer Youth Employment, Women in Transition, Life Skills, and Job Readiness Training.

Nevada State Welfare Division
(Multiple locations listed below)
700 Belrose St.
Las Vegas, NV 89107
486-5000
Hours: Mon. - Fri. 7 am - 5 pm
Gail Mathews, Social Welfare Mgr.
Food stamps, Aid to Dependent Children, medical services, employment and training for those in need. Clients are assisted by the office nearest their zip code. During 1997 there were 703,124 food stamp recipients, 269,656 people receiving temporary assistance for needy families, and 710,515 people receiving Medicaid in Clark County.

Owens Office
1040 W. Owens Ave.
Las Vegas NV 89106
486-5040
Dave Wallace, Social Welfare Mgr.

Charleston Office
3700 E. Charleston Blvd.
Las Vegas, NV 89104
486-4535
Barbara Clark, Social Welfare Mgr.

***Howard Cannon
Senior Center Office***
340 N. 11th St.
Las Vegas, NV 89101
486-3600
Barbara Clark, Social Welfare Mgr.
Information and assistance for food stamps and medical coverage; issues Medicaid cards.

Henderson Office
538A S. Boulder Hwy.
Henderson, NV 89015
486-6748
Paula Petruso, Social Welfare Mgr.
All services available.

St. Vincent's
150l Las Vegas Blvd. N.
Las Vegas, NV 89101
383-1163
Frank Richo, Residential Svcs Dir.
383-0700
Dining Room: 385-7801
Shelter: 384-0409
Thrift Store: 385-2662
Haven of Hope: 382-4900
Family Assistance: 383-0766
Provides temporary shelter for the homeless. Provides emergency clothing, meals (daily at noon) and showers (7:30 am - 9:30 am for men and 1:30 pm - 2:30 pm for women and children).
Catholic Charities of Southern Nevada Child Programs - adoption, Holy Family Day Care in Las Vegas, Marian Residence and Regina Hall - 735-4358
Crisis Intervention Programs - emergency assistance, Haven of Hope, immigration services, refugee assistance, St. Vincent Dining Room, St. Vincent Shelter.
Senior Programs - Black Mountain, Las Vegas Senior Nutrition Programs, Meals on Wheels Program - 385-5284, Retired Senior Volunteer Program, Senior Community Service Employment, Senior Companion Program and Crossroads Transitional Housing for Senior Men.

St. Vincent's Thrift Stores
(Multiple locations listed below)
808 S. Main St.
Las Vegas, NV 89101
382-4604
Call 382-9781 - 24-hour pick-up line for tax deductible donations.

4921 Vegas Dr.
Las Vegas, NV 89108
647-6729

1519 Las Vegas Blvd. N.
Las Vegas, NV 89101
383-2846

1767 N. Rancho Dr.
Las Vegas, NV 89106
646-2150

4137 S. Sandhill Rd.
Las Vegas, NV 89104
547-4429

Salvation Army
35 W. Owens Ave.
Las Vegas, NV 89106
870-4430   649-8240
Lt. Col. Jim Sullivan, Coordinator
Provides counseling for individuals and families, also in emergency situations, food, clothing and financial assistance,

when available. The day center provides child care, laundry facilities, storage lockers, phones, showers and assistance in finding a job. Emergency Lodge provides temporary housing and meals to the stranded and homeless. *Salvation Army Thrift Stores are located at the following addresses:*
429 N. Main St.
4001 W. Charleston Blvd.
471 N. Boulder Hwy., Henderson
2035 Yale St., North Las Vegas
5200 Boulder Hwy.
801 N. Lamb Blvd.

**Salvation Army Command
Offices and Worship**
2900 Palomino Ln.
Las Vegas, NV 89107 - 870-4430
Adult Rehabilitation Center
2035 Yale St.
Lied Transitional Housing Complex
45 W Owens Ave.
**Henderson Corp and Family
Services and Adult Day Care
Center "Friendship Circle"**
830 E. Lake Mead Dr., Henderson

Variety Day Home
990 D St.
Las Vegas, NV 89106
647-4907
Sister Diane Maguire, Dir.
Child care for children 6 months to 6 years for low-income working parents; sliding scale fee.

HOMELESS
It is estimated that there are nearly 11,000 homeless people in Las Vegas. The five emergency shelters have 400 beds.

FAMILY

**Catholic Charities
of Southern Nevada**
808 S. Main St.
Las Vegas, NV 89101
385-2662
Michael Husted, Exec. Dir.

Clark County District Attorney
200 S. 3rd St.
Las Vegas, NV 89155
455-4711

**Clark County
Family Support Division**
301 E. Clark Ave., Ste. 400
Las Vegas, NV 89155
455-4755
Hours: 7 am - 6 pm

Clark County · Civil Division
500 Grand Central Pkwy., Ste. 5075
Las Vegas, NV 89106
455-4761

Clark County Public Guardian
(Also listed under Senior Help)
1700 Pinto Ln.
Las Vegas, NV 89106
455-4332
Jared Shafer, Public Guardian
Takes care of Clark County residents who are not able to take care of themselves or their affairs, such as seniors, disabled and children.

Crossroads Family Shelter
1526 N. Main St.
Las Vegas, NV 89101
385-2777
Adult Men's Residence: 39 W. Owens Ave.
Adult Women's Residence: Pathways,
37 W. Owens Ave.
639-0277
Crossroads is a division of Catholic
Community Services. Provides shelter,
social services, medical services, education and job-finding assistance.

DOMESTIC VIOLENCE
If you are a victim of domestic violence, you can get a Temporary
Protective Order (TPO) that will
make it illegal for that person to
come within a certain number of feet
of you. This distance is set by the
judge. To obtain the order, go to the
TPO office in the Family Court
Building, Eighth Judicial District
Court, 3464 E. Bonanza Rd., Las
Vegas. The phone number is 455-3400.
The order has to be signed by a judge,
then put into Metro's computer and
served upon the person.

Domestic Crisis Shelter
646-4981
Estelle Fuller, Dir.
Shelter for abused women and children
for up to 5 weeks.

Displaced Homemakers Center
*(Also listed under Subsistence and
Low Income-Family as HELP of
Southern Nevada)*
953 E. Sahara Ave.
Bldg, 35B, Ste. 208
Las Vegas, NV 89104
369-4357
Denice Conrad, Exec. Dir.
The center emphasizes job placement
and offers career counseling and testing
for job skills. It serves as a network to
link employers with women seeking to
enter the work force.

Economic Opportunity Board
*(Also listed under Subsistence and
Low Income)*
Project Home Program
330 W. Washington Ave.
Las Vegas, NV 89106
647-3307
James Tyree, Exec. Dir.
Provides emergency assistance, including
food, shelter, employment, transportation, health and services that promote
self-sufficiency to homeless families or
those threatened with being homeless.

Economic Opportunity Board
Women, Infants and Children
2224 N. Comstock Dr.
N. Las Vegas, NV 89030
647-2171
Cheryl Sonnenberg, Administrator
Supplemental food, physical examinations,
immunizations, nutritional counseling.
Other locations are 5A and 5B Tonopah
Ave., N. Las Vegas, NV 89030. The phone
numbers are 647-3319 and 649-4272.

Economic Opportunity Board
Child and Family Services
708 S 6th St.
Las Vegas, NV 89101
387-0179
Child Care Assistance: 387-0985
**WISH (Wellness Incentive for Self
Help) Counselor:** 387-0321
Head Start Information: 387-5579
Social Services Supervisor: 387-1714

Epicenter on the Parkway
2100 S. Maryland Pkwy.
Las Vegas, NV 89104
732-8776
Bonnie Polley, Coordinator
Supports the needs of families and individuals who are ineligible for or unaware of
assistance available through Clark County.

**Family and Child Treatment
Center of Southern Nevada**
4800 W. Charleston Blvd.
Las Vegas, NV 89102
258-5855
Fran Marshall, Exec. Dir.
Deals with sexually abused children,
adults sexually abused as children,
rape, physical and psychological abuse
and neglect, relationships, stress
adjustment problems and depression.

**Family Cabinet Inc.
of Clark County**
300 W. Boston Ave.
Las Vegas, NV 89102
385-5437
Carl Rowe, Exec. Dir.
Non-profit organization that coordinates family services. The agency operates as a centralized clearinghouse for
prenatal care, child-care resource and
referral, and parenting education.

HELP of Southern Nevada
*(Also listed under Subsistence and Low
Income as Displaced Homemakers Center.)*
953 E. Sahara Ave.
Bldg. 35B, Ste. 208
Las Vegas, NV 89104
369-4357
Denice Conrad, Exec. Dir.
Referral to services. Helped over 35,000
families and individuals last year.

Holy Family Day Care Center
451 E. Twain Ave.
Las Vegas, NV 89109
735-4358
Connie Johnson, Dir.
Provides day care for low-income families
with assistance from Catholic Charities of
Southern Nevada and United Way.

Jean Nidetch Women's Center
4505 S. Maryland Pkwy
Las Vegas, NV 89154-2025
895-4475
Fax: 895-0601
Conee Spano, Dir.
Educational, directional, and career
guidance. The center helps women who
want to return to school after prolonged
absence, or are just entering college as
mature adults. The center also offers
information and referrals, scholarships,
workshops, seminars, support groups,
child care, and a resource center.

Jewish Family Service Agency
*(Also listed under Subsistence and
Low Income)*
3909 S. Maryland Pkwy., Ste. 205
Las Vegas, NV 89119
732-0304
Adrienne Rosenberg, Exec. Dir.
Services include marriage counseling; individual, group, and family counseling; food
and shelter; information and referrals.

Las Vegas Rescue Mission
*(Also listed under Subsistence and
Low Income)*
608 N. E St.
Las Vegas, NV 89106
382-5924
Rev. Edward Compton, Dir.

**Lied Transitional Housing
Apartments**
45 W. Owens Ave.
N. Las Vegas, NV 89030
642-7252
John Evans, Adm.

M*A*S*H Village
*(Also listed under Subsistence and
Low Income)*
1559 Main St.
Las Vegas, NV 89101
229-4806
Ken Robinson, Dir.
The Las Vegas/Clark County M*A*S*H
(Mobilized Assistance and Shelter for
the Homeless) is a comprehensive, one-
stop regional crisis and intervention center for homeless and at-risk individuals
and families with children. M*A*S*H will
help the homeless of southern Nevada
break the cycle of poverty and transition
to permanent economic and social self-
sufficiency. Basic services such as showers, clothing, food, or other immediate
needs are provided.

Nevada Homes for Youth
525 S. 13th St.
Las Vegas, NV 89101
380-2889
Ronald C. Moore, Exec. Dir.
Will find immediate housing for youths
17-21 who have no one to help them.
Transitional housing for up to 1 year.
Counseling and employment assistance.

**Nevada Network Against
Domestic Violence**
Hotline: 1-800-500-1556
Information and referral: 1-800-230-1955

St. Vincent's
150l Las Vegas Blvd. N.
Las Vegas, NV 89101
Family Assistance: 383-0766
United Social Ministries: 453-9455

**The Salvation Army Family
Welfare Services**
35 W. Owens Ave.
Las Vegas, NV 89106
649-8240

The Shade Tree
1560 N. Main St.
Las Vegas, NV 89101
385-0072
Shelter: 385-4596

Brenda Divon, Exec. Dir.
Shelter and assistance for homeless
women and women with children.
Shade Tree is a domestic violence support group and Southern Nevada's only
24 hour emergency shelter for women
and their children, providing them with
telephone access and a mailing address.

**Southern Nevada Domestic
Violence Task Force**
225-4113

**TADC (Temporary Assistance
for Domestic Crisis)**
Estelle Murphy, Exec. Dir.
Counseling: 877-0133
Hotline 646-4981: Domestic
Non-profit agency offering temporary
emergency shelter available to victims
of domestic violence; 24 hour crisis telephone line; crisis intervention program
concerning physical abuse in the home.

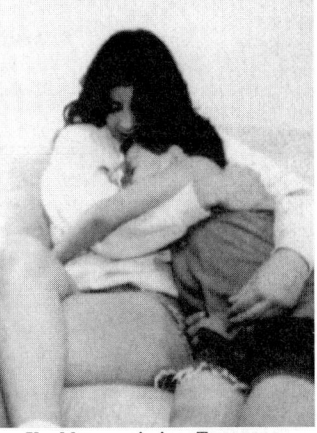
Used by permission, Temporary
Assistance for Domestic Crisis

We Can
5440 W. Sahara Ave., Ste. 202
Las Vegas, NV 89102
368-1533
Dr. Paula Ford, Exec. Dir.
Child abuse prevention, parenting support and education.

WestCare Inc.
401 S. Martin Luther King Blvd.
Las Vegas, NV 89106
385-2020
Richard E. Steinberg, Pres.
Runaway Hotline: 385-3330
Youth Services: 385-3330
Family Services: 385-3330
Family Resource Project: 385-3330
Private non-profit social service agency
providing treatment for drug and alcohol abusers, high risk youth and troubled families.

The Women's Development Center
953 E. Sahara Ave., Ste. 201
Las Vegas, NV 89104
796-7770
Candace Ruisi, Exec. Dir.
Food, housing, counseling, child care
and educational workshops for homeless women and children.

ASSISTANCE

1997 Welfare Recipients & Grants Paid

MEDICAID	Elegibles	Grants Paid
January	95,327	$35,281,130
February	94,951	$29,891,674
March	96,207	$29,706,674
April	94,820	$33,519,029
May	94,299	$36,059,889
June	94,742	$27,605,497
July	92,594	$31,477,584
August	94,442	$36,928,530
September	94,097	$35,451,638
October	94,535	$36,237,109
November	94,769	$30,469,618
December	96,741	$29,859,082

FOOD STAMPS	Recipients	Grants Paid
January	87,777	$6,945,400
February	85,592	$6,763,021
March	82,479	$6,401,121
April	80,215	$6,121,281
May	78,580	$5,898,192
June	76,956	$5,754,116
July	76,685	$5,768,036
August	75,412	$5,683,529
September	75,304	$5,683,598
October	75,541	$5,792,284
November	74,466	$5,629,793
December	75,800	$5,769,218

TANF*	Recipients	Grants Paid
January	28,973	$3,049,490
February	29,038	$3,140,992
March	30,008	$3,200,690
April	29,137	$3,116,708
May	28,720	$3,020,681
June	28,934	$2,989,743
July	27,896	$2,900,072
August	28,854	$2,942,126
September	28,157	$2,892,285
October	28,348	$2,877,672
November	28,333	$2,927,710
December	29,465	$2,984,225

Source: State of Nevada Department of Human Resources, Welfare Division

* Temporary Assistance for Needy Families

EQUAL RIGHTS

American Civil Liberties Union of Nevada
366-1226
Chad Kendrick, Exec. Dir.
Organization dedicated to defending the Bill of Rights. ACLU's commitment is to protect individual liberty against abuse of power or infringement by government at any level.

Anti-Defamation League
1-800-446-ANTI (2684)
David Lehrer, Regional Dir.
Represents victims of discrimination.

Immigration and Naturalization Service
3373 Pepper Ln.
Las Vegas, NV 89120
451-3597

National Conference of Christians and Jews
913 E. Charleston Blvd., Ste. B
Las Vegas, NV 89104
387-6225
Susan Boswell, Regional Dir.
A nonsectarian civic organization that promotes religious, racial, and ethnic inclusiveness in American society.

Nevada Equal Rights Commission
1515 E. Tropicana Ave., Ste. 590
Las Vegas, NV 89119
486-7161
William H. Stewart, Adm.
State Agency handles employment, housing and public accommodations complaints.

ATTORNEYS

State Bar of Nevada Lawyer Referral Service
382-0504
Hours: Mon. - Fri. 9 am - 4 pm
Confirmed initial 30 minute appointment with an attorney who specializes in the type of legal problem client is experiencing.

Nevada State Bar Association
201 Las Vegas Blvd. S., Ste. 200
Las Vegas, NV 89101
382-2200
Attorney complaints; intervenes between lawyer and client.

Clark County Bar Association
P.O. Box 657
Las Vegas, NV 89125
387-6011
Tom Sheets, Pres.
Voluntary organization dedicated to professional education and community service.

Nevada Law Foundation
1833 W. Charleston Blvd.
Las Vegas, NV 89102
384-1204
Suzan Baucum, Exec. Dir.
Non-profit organization provides funding to legally disadvantaged and law related educational programs. Funds are provided through the interest on Lawyers Trust Accounts or IOLTA.

Nevada Legal Services
Clark County Legal Services Program
701 E. Bridger Ave., Ste. 101
Las Vegas, NV 89101
386-1070
Wayne Presseo, Exec. Dir.
Provides free legal assistance and civil matters to low income citizens of Clark County.

Pro Bono Project
P.O. Box 867
Las Vegas, NV 89125-0867
382-4090

Dennis M. Hetherington, Exec. Dir.
Provides free legal assistance to low income residents of Clark County. Sponsored by the Nevada Law Foundation, the project covers family matters, bankruptcy, probate, real estate law, consumer product complaints, debt collection, accident and property damage. They do not handle criminal cases, traffic citations or fee-generating cases.

Senior Citizens Law Project
340 N. 11th St.,
Las Vegas, NV 89101
229-6596
Sheri Vogel, Exec. Dir.

UNLV Legal Help
4505 S. Maryland Pkwy.
Las Vegas, NV 89154
895-3645   474-7262
Peter Bellon, Attorney
This service is offered for students only and is available on Tuesday from 6 pm - 8 pm and on Wednesday from 11 am - 1 pm and 6 pm - 8 pm

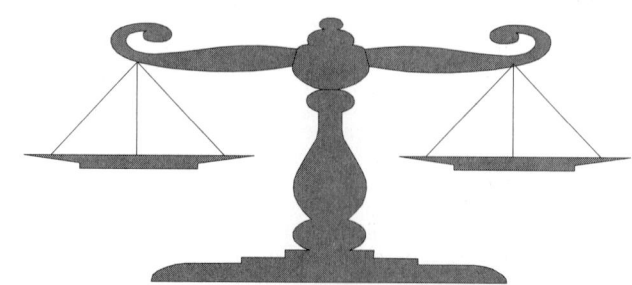

CONSUMER HELP

If you have a problem with a business or an agency, the first step is to deal with the highest level within the company, such as the owner or manager. If you cannot get satisfaction, then call one of the following agencies. Also see particular area in this directory for regulating agency which may help you resolve a problem.

To check if a business is licensed, to verify the owner of a business, or to register a complaint:
Clark County: 455-4125
City of Las Vegas: 229-6281
Henderson: 565-2045
Boulder City: 293-9219

Attorney General
Consumer Affairs Division
555 E. Washington Ave., Ste. 3900
(second floor)
Las Vegas, NV 89101
486-3777

Better Business Bureau
1022 E. Sahara Ave.
Las Vegas, NV 89104-1515
735-6900
Sylvia Campbell, Exec. Dir.
Information on charities: 735-6001
Hours: Mon. - Fri. 8 am - 5 pm
Private non-regulatory agency. Consumers can obtain a telephone report at no cost on a company that will reveal the company's date of license and how they have conducted business with their customers, including the number of customer complaints and how the customer responded to those complaints. Handles and investigates complaints, truth in advertising and mediation and arbitration on auto manufacturer warranty problems.

Bureau of Consumer Protection
1-202-326-3650

Clark County Health District
383-1251
Claire A. Schmutz, Dir.
Complaints about food establishments for unhealthy food handling conditions or unclean environments.

Clark County Social Service
Neighborhood Justice Center
1600 Pinto Ln.
Las Vegas, NV 89106
455-3898
Ruth Urban, Mgr.

Created by the 1991 Nevada Legislature, the Neighborhood Justice Center offers free mediation services to anyone with a dispute with a neighbor or business as an alternative to small-claims court. The center provides trained mediators who meet with both parties.

Consumer Affairs Division
State of Nevada
Dept. of Business and Industry
1850 E. Sahara Ave., Ste. 101
Las Vegas, NV 89104
486-7355
Patricia Morse-Jarman, Commissioner
Hours: Mon. - Fri. 7 am - 6 pm
Enforcement of Nevada Revised Statutes for Deceptive Trade Practices.

Consumer Credit
Counseling Service
3650 S. Decatur Blvd., Ste. 30
Las Vegas, NV 89103
364-0344
Michele Johnson, Executive Dir.
Non-profit community agency offering free financial counseling and money management education. Debt management program allows CCCS to serve as a third party mediator between debtor and creditors. United Way agency.

Contact 13 KTNV-ABC
3355 S. Valley View Blvd.
Las Vegas, NV 89102
876-4301
Call about consumer related problems.

District Attorney
Clark County
200 S. Third St.
Las Vegas, NV 89101
455-4711

Las Vegas Metropolitan Police Department
Fraud Detail
400 E. Stewart Ave.
Las Vegas, NV 89101
229-3285

Nevada State Barber Board
1539 S. Virginia St.
Reno, NV 89509
1-702-786-9889

Board of Architecture
2080 E. Flamingo Rd., Ste. 225
Las Vegas, NV 89119
486-7300

Dept. of Business and Industry
2501 E. Sahara Ave., Ste. 302
Las Vegas, NV 89104
486-4009

Federal Trade Commission
Regional Office
San Francisco, CA
1-415-356-5270

Financial Institution Division
2501 E. Sahara Ave., Ste. 300
Las Vegas, NV 89104
486-4120

Insurance Division
2501 E. Sahara Ave., Ste. 302
Las Vegas, NV 89104
486-4009
Call for a copy of the "Comparison Guide to Buying Automobile Insurance."

Manufactured Housing Div.
486-4135

Real Estate Division
2501 E. Sahara Ave.
Las Vegas, NV 89104
486-4033

Board of Contractors
4220 S. Maryland Pkwy.
Bldg. D, Ste. 800
Las Vegas, NV 89119
486-3500
Information on complaint and bond proceedings; to find out if a contractor is licensed.

Board of Cosmetology
1785 E. Sahara Ave., Ste. 255
Las Vegas, NV 89104
486-6542

Board of Veterinary
Medical Examiners
4600 Kietzke Ln., Ste. 265
Reno, NV 89502
702-688-1788
(Also see Health Care Licensing Boards)

Mediators of Southern Nevada
631-2790
Charlotte Kiefer
MSN is a nonprofit organization that promotes mediation as a way of resolving disputes.

National Fraud
Information Center
1-800-876-7060

Nevada Apartment Association
5030 Paradise Rd., Ste. C101
Las Vegas, NV 89119
547-3550
Acts as mediator in tenant-landlord disputes.

Nevada Arbitration Association
3271 S. Highland Dr., Ste. 705A
Las Vegas, NV 89109
737-7334
Julius Conigliaro, Exec. Dir.
Arbitration service as an alternative to court. Alternate dispute resolution. Settles commercial and construction contracts.

Nevada Legal Service
Landlord/Tenant Hotline: 386-8753

Nevada State Bar Association
Las Vegas
201 Las Vegas Blvd. S., Ste. 200
Las Vegas, NV 89101
Wayne Brevins, Acting Dir.
Attorney complaints: 382-2200
Intervenes in lawyer and client disputes; an arbitrator makes decision.

Public Utility Commission
555 E. Washington Ave., Ste. 4600
Las Vegas, NV 89101
486-2600
John Mendoza, Chairman
Hours: Mon. - Fri. 8 am - 5 pm
No charge to public.
Handles consumer complaints regarding local utility services.

Taxicab Authority
1785 E. Sahara Ave., Ste. 200
Las Vegas, NV 89104
486-6532
Robert Anselmo, Adm.
Hours: 24
Handles complaints against taxi companies and drivers.

Transportation Service
Authority
687-6016

U. S. Attorney's Office
388-6336

RIGHTS - EMPLOYER DISPUTES

American Civil Liberties Union of Nevada
366-1226

Equal Employment Opportunity Commission
3300 N. Central Ave., Ste. 690
Phoenix, AZ 85012
1-602-640-5000
Help against discrimination because of race, sex, religion, national origin and age.

National Labor Relations Board
600 Las Vegas Blvd. S., Ste. 400
Las Vegas, NV 89101

388-6416
Cornele A. Overstreet, Regional Dir.
Negotiates settlements between employers and employees in complaints of unfair labor practices. If no settlement is reached, a formal complaint is filed and an administrative judge hears the case.

Nevada Equal Rights Commission
1515 E. Tropicana Ave., Ste. 590
Las Vegas, NV 89119
486-7161
William H. Stewart, Adm.

The commission hears employer discrimination and sexual harassment complaints, as well as housing and public accommodations complaints.

Nevada State Labor Commissioner
Southern Nevada Division
555 E. Washington Ave., Ste. 4100
Las Vegas, NV 89101
486-2650
Settles disputes between employers and employees; makes sure employees are treated fairly. Enforces the state's labor laws.

U. S. Department of Labor
Federal Wage & Hour Div.
1050 E. Flamingo Rd., Ste. 321
Las Vegas, NV 89119
699-5581
Dan Ford, Compliance Officer
Enforces minimum wage and overtime.

MULTI-CULTURAL ORGANIZATIONS / ASSISTANCE

AFRICAN-AMERICAN ASSOCIATIONS

African-American Museum & Research Center
The Walker Foundation
705 W. Van Buren Ave.
Las Vegas, NV 89106
647-2242
Gwen Walker, Pres.
African-American Museum & Research Center. Promotes and preserves history of people of African descent.

Urban Chamber of Commerce
1048 W. Owens Ave.
Las Vegas, NV 89106
648-6222
Fax: 648-6223
Dorothie T. Clark, Pres.
Aid and information for businesses in the Las Vegas Valley.

Black Business Directory
1048 W. Owens Ave.
Las Vegas, NV 89106
646-4223
Warren Maxey, Pres.
Community service hotline to inform consumers about products, services, and upcoming special events. Single copies free locally or $4.95 for out of state mailing.

KCEP - FM 88
330 W. Washington Ave.
Las Vegas, NV 89106
648-0104
Request line: 647-3688
Sherman Rutledge, Gen. Mgr.
Nonprofit soul/urban contemporary radio station operated by the Equal Opportunity Board.

Las Vegas Sentinel Voice
900 E. Charleston Blvd.
Las Vegas, NV 89104
380-8100
Ramon Savoy, Publisher
African-American community newspaper.

Dr. Martin Luther King Jr. Center
1316 Morgan Ave.
Las Vegas, NV 89106
631-1913
Operated by the Dr. Martin Luther King Jr. Committee, the center offers youth recreational activities, tutorial programs, legal services, health screenings, youth committee meetings, and information hotline.

NAACP Community Development Resource Center
1785 E. Sahara Ave., Ste. 440
Las Vegas, NV 89104
796-4090
Frank Hawkins, Dir. of Center Operations
Designed to provide education to low and moderate income consumers about general banking practices, procedures, specific loan products, and services offered by U.S. banks for consumers and small businesses.

AMERICAN INDIAN ASSOCIATIONS

Las Vegas Indian Center
2300 W. Bonanza Rd.
Las Vegas, NV 89106
647-5842
Richard Arnold, Exec. Dir.
Provides a variety of services to American Indians.

Las Vegas Paiute Tribe
1 Paiute Dr.
Las Vegas, NV 89106
386-3926
Alfreda Mitri, Chairperson
Provides wide range of social services.

Moapa Tribe
1 Lincoln Dr.
P.O. Box 340
Moapa, NV 89025
702-865-2787

HISPANIC ASSOCIATIONS

According to the 1990 census, the Hispanic population in Las Vegas is 82,904, which represents 11.2 percent of the population.

Hispanic Media:
KAFT - Cable channel 27
KBLR - Cable channel 9
KDOL 1280-AM - Spanish language radio
KLAV 970-AM
El Mundo - local Spanish newspaper
Vida En Las Vegas - Spanish life-style tabloid
Imagenes of Las Vegas - free monthly magazine
Ahora - Free semimonthly newspaper

El Mundo
845 N. Eastern Ave.
Las Vegas, NV 89101
649-8553
Eddie Escobedo, Sr., Publisher
Weekly independent Spanish language newspaper. Circulation: 25,000.

Image of Southern Nevada
391-7127
Volunteer organization concerned with the needs and advancement of Hispanic Americans.

Latin Chamber of Commerce
829 S. 6th St.
Las Vegas, NV 89125
385-7367
Otto Merida, Exec. Dir.

Nevada Association of Latin Americans
323 N. Maryland Pkwy.
Las Vegas, NV 89101
382-6252
Dr. Ali Almeida, Exec. Dir.

Helps undocumented or aliens whose immigration papers have expired or have other legal problems, housing, etc.

Nevada Treatment Center
(Hispanic Services)
1721 E. Charleston Blvd.
Las Vegas, NV 89104
382-4226
Margaret Piasecki, Exec. Dir.
Provides assistance in AIDS-related services, drunken driving, methadone detoxification and maintenance.

ASIAN ASSOCIATIONS

Asian Chamber of Commerce
900 E. Karen Ave., Ste. C215
Las Vegas, NV 89109
737-4300
Monthly luncheons.

Japanese American Club of Las Vegas
1316 S. 8th St.
Las Vegas, NV 89104
382-4443
Meets 4th Monday 7 pm at the Nevada Power Co.

MEDICAL TRANSLATION

Resort Medical Centers
Imperial Palace Hotel
3743 Las Vegas Blvd. S., Ste. 106
Las Vegas, NV 89109
735-3600
Dr. Gerald Malone
24-hour medical care. No appointment necessary. House calls available. Free shuttle service. Lab/x-ray/medications. Multi-lingual staff - Japanese, Filipino, Spanish, German, French, English, Italian, Arabic, Tagalog.

DENTAL

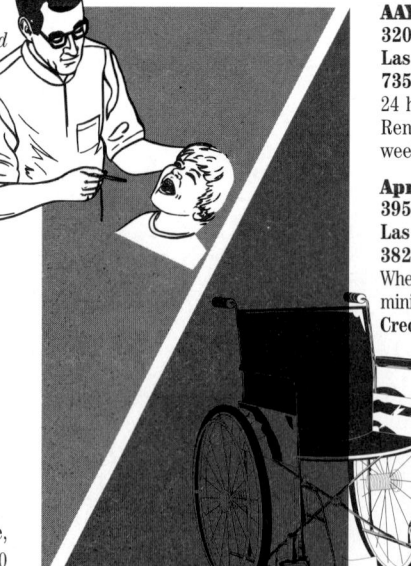

Clark County Dental Society
(Also listed under Doctor Referral and Health Care)
1785 E. Sahara Ave.
Las Vegas, NV 89117
255-7873
Connie Ballard, Exec. Dir.
Referral and emergency referral, 24 hours 7 days; provides arbitration services.

Community College of Southern Nevada
Health Sciences Center
6375 W. Charleston Blvd.
Las Vegas, NV 89102
651-5000
Theresa Raglin, Dir.
Dental clinic appts.: 651-5510
For dental hygiene $8 registration fee, clean teeth $26 - $56, x-rays $10 - $70 for full mouth, bitewings $30.

HOSPITAL EQUIPMENT

AAY'S Medical Supply
3200 S. Eastern Ave.
Las Vegas, NV 89109
735-1992
24 hr service - free delivery for oxygen. Rental-sales-service. Scooters $100 per week. Complete home care center.

Apria Health Care
3955 W. Mesa Vista Ave., Ste. 11
Las Vegas, NV 89118
382-0773
Wheelchair rentals; will deliver; One month minimum.
Credit Cards: MC, Visa, or $100 deposit.

Medical Mart
2797 S. Maryland Pkwy.
Las Vegas, NV 89109
369-9107
Hours: Mon. - Fri. 8:30 am - 5:30 pm; Sat. 9:30 am - 2 pm
Home health care equipment and supplies; some rentals available. Repair service - personalized instruction.

Total Home Care
3261 S. Highland Dr.
Las Vegas, NV 89109
796-1016
Hours: Mon. - Fri. 9 am - 5 pm; Sat. 9 am - noon
Purchases and rentals available; will deliver.

United Rent All
1020 E. Twain Ave.
Las Vegas, NV 89109
733-8847
Hours: Mon. - Sat. 8 am - 5:30 pm
Hospital equipment and wheelchairs; delivery available.
Credit Cards: MC, Visa, AMX, Disc.

Cultural Arts

While Las Vegas is best known for it's high-energy, extravagant stage productions complete with showgirls in glitzy costumes, it also has a softer side that provides a multitude of cultural diversions. Southern Nevada offers its audiences some of the finest opera, theater, classical music and ballet, as well as a variety of museums and fine arts galleries to stimulate the senses.

Las Vegas is the proud home of the Nevada Symphony Orchestra, offering performances by area artisans; the Nevada Opera Theater, currently in its 12th season; the Las Vegas Civic Ballet, now in its 16th year of combining captivating choreography with ballet, hip hop, jazz and modern dance techniques.

The annual Las Vegas Children's Summer Concert Series, a southern Nevada favorite for 13 years, allows children ages 3 and older the unique opportunity to experience many of the performing arts programs available in the area. There are more than 90 not-for-profit cultural arts organizations in the area, with the Allied Arts Council as the umbrella organization.

The Judy Bailey Theater, Artemus Ham Concert Hall, Black Box Theater and Paul Harris Theaters all make their home at the University of Nevada, Las Vegas - the "Cultural Arts Center of Southern Nevada."

The Cultural and Community Affairs Division of the City of Las Vegas Department of Parks and Leisure Activities presents performances throughout the year at the Charleston Heights Arts Center, the Hills Amphitheater at Summerlin, the Reed Whipple Cultural Center and the Sammy Davis, Jr. Festival Plaza at Lorenzi Park.

The Las Vegas Cultural Corridor, near Cashman Field on Las Vegas Blvd. N., is home to the Las Vegas Library, Lied Discovery Children's Museum, Reed Whipple Cultural Arts Center, the National History Museum and the Mormon Fort.

ART ORGANIZATIONS

Allied Arts Council
401 S. 4th St., Ste. 110
Las Vegas, NV 89101
731-5419
Constance DeVereaux, Dir.
Hours: Mon. & Fri. 9 am - 1 pm
Membership: Individual $25; Family $30; Senior/Student $20
Corporate Rates: Business Patron $250; Silver Patron $500; Gold Patron $1,000; Arts Round Table $2,500 and up. Non-profit organization founded in 1962, the Allied Arts Council is the coordinating body and communicating network for the areas many arts organizations. The council's purpose is to further the development and appreciation of the visual and performing arts, stimulate the enrichment and expansion of the arts in communities served. The Allied Arts Council publishes the "Datebook," the monthly calender of the arts, which is distributed to its members.

Arts Advisory Council of Henderson-Green Valley
901 N. Green Valley Pkwy., Ste. 200
Henderson, NV 89014
458-8855
Sherri Smith, Dir. Pub. Relations
Provides cultural experiences that foster awareness and appreciation of the arts and the humanities thereby enhancing the quality of life in our community. Sponsors annual "Nevada Shakespeare in the Park" at Foxridge Park in September as well as other theatrical performances, concerts and art exhibits. All "Shakespeare in the Park" events are open to the public and are free of charge.

African-American Cultural Arts Foundation
P.O. Box 4997
Las Vegas, NV 89127
459-7159
Katherine James, Pres.
AACAF is a non-profit tax exempt charitable foundation supporting the arts. "Enrich your child's life with culture and he/she will mentally reach higher and expand outside his/her environment".

Boulder City Arts Council
130 S. Arizona St.
Boulder City, NV 89005
294-1499
Alice Isenberg, Pres.
A presenting organization for visual and performing arts.

Boulder City Art Guild
1495 Nevada Hwy.
Boulder City, NV 89005
293-2138
Mary Alice Mooney, Pres.
Gallery hours: noon - 5 pm
Presents Clark County Artists Show at Bicentennial Park. The show features fine arts, no crafts.

Business and the Arts
7555 Spanish Bay Dr.
Las Vegas, NV 89113
362-8885
Angie Wallin, Exec. Dir.
Cultural tours and local art events.

City of Las Vegas-Division of Cultural & Community Affairs
Dept. of Parks & Leisure Activities
749 Veterans Memorial Dr.
Las Vegas, NV 89101
229-6511
Joanne Nivison, Div. Mgr.
The Charleston Heights Arts Center and Reed Whipple Cultural Center host a variety of performances and art exhibits.

Clark County Parks and Recreation Dept.
Cultural Affairs Division
2601 E. Sunset Rd.
Las Vegas, NV 89120
455-8247
Joan Lolmaugh, Mgr.

Clark County School District Fine Arts Division
2832 E. Flamingo Rd.
Las Vegas, NV 89121
799-5478
Marcia Neel, Coordinator
Statewide advocacy organization for arts education in school districts. Offers low-cost professional cultural performances and demonstrations in all mediums to local schools.

Henderson Parks and Recreation Dept.
240 Water St.
Henderson, NV 89015
565-4264
Steve Rongyocsik, Adm.
Sponsors the civic orchestra and various other events in Henderson and Green Valley.

KLVX-TV Channel 10
4210 Channel 10 Dr.
Las Vegas, NV 89119
799-1010
Tom Axtell, Dir.
Public television. Publishes "Antenna," a monthly program information guide available to members who contribute $35 or more annually ($20 for senior citizens).

KNPR Public Radio
5151 Boulder Hwy.
Las Vegas, NV 89122
456-6695
Lamar Marchese, Gen. Mgr.
89.5 FM; public radio with information on cultural happenings in addition to cultural programming. Sponsors six summer concerts at Hills Park in Summerlin.

KUNV-FM Radio
University of Nevada, Las Vegas
4505 S. Maryland Pkwy.
Las Vegas, NV 89154
895-3877
Don Fuller, Gen. Mgr.
91.5 FM; non-commercial community radio station at UNLV provides cultural information and entertainment, such as jazz and classical music.

Las Vegas Arts Commission
749 Veterans Memorial Dr.
Las Vegas, NV 89101
229-6844
Lisa Stamanis, Sr. Vis. Arts Specalist
Advisory body to the Las Vegas City Council on the acquisition and placement of art in public places.

Las Vegas/Clark County Library District
833 Las Vegas Blvd. N.
Las Vegas, NV 89101
382-3493
Kristy Price, Sched. & Prod. Serv. Mgr.
Art galleries at each branch library; theaters at the Summerlin, Clark County and West Las Vegas libraries; Lied Children's Museum at the Las Vegas Library; and children's activities.

Liberace Foundation for the Performing and Creative Arts
(Also under Museums)
1775 E. Tropicana Ave.
Las Vegas, NV 89119
798-5595
Myron Martin, Dir.
Since its incorporation by the late entertainer in 1976, the foundation has funded more than 1,300 individual scholarships in the arts and is currently awarding grants to 59 schools and colleges across the nation. The foundation is funded by donations from the Liberace Museum and proceeds from special events.

National Endowment for the Arts
1100 Pennsylvania Ave., N.W.
Washington, D.C. 20506
202-682-5400
Katherine Higgins, Acting Chairman
Federal agency that provides grant funds distributed by the Nevada State Council of the Arts.

Nevada Alliance for the Arts
7555 Spanish Bay Dr.
Las Vegas, NV 89113
362-8885
Roger Peltyn, President
Angie Wallin, Exec. Dir.
Statewide arts advocacy organization.

Nevada School of the Arts
(Also under Music)
315 S. 7th St.
Las Vegas, NV 89101
386-2787
Dr. Paul Hesselink, Dean
Nevada School of the Arts offers quality

music and visual arts instruction to students of all ages at various locations throughout Las Vegas. With 400 students, NSA classes are taught in spring and fall semesters; private lessons are also available.

Nevada Screenwriters
631-0878
Joe Wheeler
Meets 1st Sat. of the month at 10 am at the Las Vegas Library, 833 Las Vegas Blvd N. The group discusses all aspects of writing for film and television.

Nevada State Council on the Arts
602 N. Curry St.
Carson City, NV 89703
687-6680
Susan Boskoff, Dir.
State agency that provides grants to artists and art organizations. In 1996, Clark County applicants received $272,450 in grants. Grants were awarded in four areas: Design Arts, Project, Development and Organizational Support.

Sociedad Cultural Hispana, Inc.
2065 Wagon Wheel Ave.
Las Vegas, NV 89119
736-3881
Fidel Torea, Pres.
Founded in 1974 to promote, perpetuate and maintain the cultural heritage of Hispanics.

UNLV Performing Arts Center
4505 S. Maryland Pkwy.
Las Vegas, NV 89154
895-3535
Box Office: 895-3801
Jeff Koep, Dean College of Fine Arts
Box Office Hours: Mon. - Fri. 10 am - 6 pm; Sat. 10 am - 4 pm

Las Vegas - Clark County Library
1401 E. Flamingo Rd.
Las Vegas, NV 89119

ART CENTERS

Cashman Field Theatre
850 Las Vegas Blvd. N.
Las Vegas, NV 89101
386-7100
Don Ahl, Dir.
Facilities: 1,940 seat theater
Use: Speakers & gospel

**Charleston Heights
Arts Center**
800 S. Brush St.
Las Vegas, NV 89107
229-6383
Box Office: 229-6382
Priscilla Romas, Field Supvr.
Operated by City of Las Vegas
Facilities: 365 seat auditorium
Use: Art gallery, film series, New West
theatre
Hours: Mon. & Thu. 1 pm - 9 pm; Tue. -
Wed. 10 am - 9 pm; Fri. 10 am - 6 pm;
Sat. - 9 am - 4 pm; Sun. 1 pm - 5 pm
Tickets to most events are available at
the box office or through TicketMasters.

**Community College of
Southern Nevada**
Nicholas Horn Auditorium
3200 E. Cheyenne Ave.
N. Las Vegas, NV 89030
651-4052   631-5483
Wendy Riggs, Dir. of Performing Arts.
Facilities: 524 seat theater
Use: Theater productions are presented
regularly, usually twice a semester.
Box Office: 651-4478
Hours: Mon. - Fri. 3 pm - 7 pm; Sat.
1 pm - 4 pm
CCSN Art Gallery: 1,500 sq. ft. of
intriguing architecture and dramatic
lighting to challenge the eye.
CCSN Little Theatre: Intimate 130-
seat environment to bring the audience
close to the action.
CCSN Recital Hall: 143-seat facility
with sparkling sound and lighting.

Fox Ridge Park Amphitheater
Valley Verde and Fox Ridge Dr.
Henderson, NV 89014
Carolyn Andersen, Coord. for Spec. Events
Use: Shakespeare in the Park, concerts.

**Government Center
Amphitheater**
500 S. Grand Central Pkwy.
Las Vegas, NV 89155
455-8242
Dorothy Wright, Adm.
Facilities: 3,000 seat capacity on
approximately 1 1/2 acres. Accommodates
almost any type of major public gathering,
theater or ceremony. The central
amphitheater represents the center of
the community and public life of
openness and accessibility to all.

Hills Park Amphitheater
Hillpointe Dr. & Rampart Blvd.
Las Vegas, NV 89134
229-4674
Joanne Nivison, Div. Mgr.
Located at Hills Park in Summerlin.

**Huntridge Performing Arts
Theatre**
1208 E. Charleston Blvd.
Las Vegas, NV 89104
477-7703
Hotline: 386-4868
Richard Lenz
(Also under Historical Sites)
Facilities: 549 seats
Use: Movie house, live theater and con-
cert hall which features alternative,
new music, and metal bands and a
dance floor. This art deco, former
movie theater opened in 1944.

**Las Vegas-Clark County Library
District**
Flamingo Branch
1401 E. Flamingo Rd.
Las Vegas, NV 89119
733-7810
Sally Ahlstedt, Theater Mgr.
Facilities: 399-seat theater auditorium
with a modified thrust stage, 110-seat
jewel box theater and conference room
Use: Community groups

Green Valley Library
2797 N. Green Valley Pkwy.
Henderson, NV 89014
435-1840
Sally Feldman, Adm.
Facilities: 2 conference rooms, seating
for 50 in Sunset Room.

Las Vegas Library
833 Las Vegas Blvd N.
Las Vegas, NV 89101
382-3493
Mary Lou Wigley, Adm.
Facilities: 2 program rooms seating 75.

Rainbow Library
3150 N. Buffalo Dr.
Las Vegas, NV 89128
243-READ
Jane Richardson, Adm.
Facilities: Amphitheater: capacity 500;
2 conference rooms: capacity 160

Spring Valley Library Auditorium
4280 S. Jones Blvd.
Las Vegas, NV 89103
368-4411
Beryl Andrus-Zundel, Adm.
Facilities: 165-seat theater
Use: Community groups

*Summerlin Library & Performing
Arts*
1771 Inner Circle Dr.
Las Vegas, NV 89134
256-5111
Richard Lee, Adm.
Facilities: theatre 291-seat
Use: Actors Repertory Theatre, Las
Vegas Gambelaires, Las Vegas Brass
Band and Signature Productions

Sunrise Library Auditorium
5400 Harris Ave.
Las Vegas, NV 89110
453-1104
Laura Golod, Librarian
Facilities: 250-seat auditorium
Use: Concerts, recitals, meetings

Reed Whipple Cultural Arts Center, 821 Las Vegas Blvd. N., Las Vegas, NV

West Charleston Library
6301 W. Charleston Blvd.
Las Vegas, NV 89102
878-3682
Marie Cuglietta, Librarian
Facilities: 280-seat auditorium

West Las Vegas Library
951 W. Lake Mead Blvd.
Las Vegas, NV 89106
647-2117
Joyce Thomas, Theater Mgr.
Facilities: 11,700 sq. ft. 299 seat
auditorium/theater
Use: Theater and other performances
Theater features opaque skylights, a
nine-piece orchestra pit, and a fly tower
to lower seats, props, and lighting onto
a 2,000 sq. ft. stage.

Whitney Concert Hall
5175 E. Tropicana Ave.
Las Vegas, NV 89122
454-4575
Barbara Carey, Adm.
Facilities: 198-seat recital hall and con-
ference room
Use: Concert hall

**Las Vegas Academy of
International Studies,
Performing and Visual Arts**
315 S. 7th St.
Las Vegas, NV 89101
(auditorium located at Clark & 9th St.)
799-7800
Robert Gerye, Prin.
(Also under Art Class)
Facilities: 1,400-seat auditorium
Use: Theater, concerts, performances

Masonic Memorial Temple
2200 W. Mesquite Ave.
Las Vegas, NV 89106
382-6055
Facilities: Auditorium

**Reed Whipple Cultural Arts
Center**
821 Las Vegas Blvd. N.
Las Vegas, NV 89101
229-6211

Patricia Harris, Ctr. Coordinator
Operated by the City of Las Vegas
Facilities: 300-seat multipurpose theater;
80-seat intimate theater; Dance studio,
meeting rooms, rehearsal rooms, pottery
studio, art gallery.
Use: Las Vegas Civic Symphony, Las
Vegas Civic Ballet, Rainbow Company,
Sunset Symphony
Office Hours: Mon. & Thu. 1 pm - 8 pm;
Tue. & Wed. 10 am - 9 pm; Fri. 10 am -
6 pm; Sat. 9 am - 5 pm
The center offers four class sessions
each year in theater, dance, music,
painting and other fine arts for adults
and children.

**Sammy Davis Jr. Festival Plaza
Amphitheater**
Lorenzi Park
720 Twin Lakes Dr.
Las Vegas, NV 89107
229-2390
Priscilla Romas, Field Supvr.
Facilities: First phase was completed
in October 1992. The $2 million, 500-
seat Southwestern-style amphitheater
with a fully equipped 28x56 ft. stage
with a basket-weave design floor, is
used for a variety of festivals and performances. The facility also includes
dressing rooms, box office, kitchen,
projection booth, restrooms and concession area.

Silver Springs Amphitheater
1950 Silver Spring Pkwy.
Henderson, NV 89014
435-3814
Kurt Williams, Rec. Coordinator
Resembles small Roman amphitheater.
Very unique, holds about 200 people
including grass area. Used for rehearsals
and plays.

UNLV Performing Arts Centers
4505 S. Maryland Pkwy.
Las Vegas, NV 89154
895-3535
Jeff Koep, Dean College of Fine Arts
Tickets through Internet:
http://pac.nevada.edu

Amphitheater
Facilities: 300-seats, 20 X 20-ft. stage
Use: Theatrical events, outdoor classes and lectures. Located on the campus green in front of the Moyer Student Union.

Artemus W. Ham Concert Hall
Facilities: 1,885-seat concert hall
Opened in 1976, this acoustically excellent facility serves as a cultural home for the broadest possible range of performances including light operas, folk and pop music, ballet, jazz and full symphonic productions. Seating 1500 patrons on the main floor and another 500 in the balcony. The halls elevated seating provides excellent sight lines from every part of the house.
Use: UNLV Symphonic and Chamber Music Society, Charles Vanda Master Series

Black Box Theatre
Facilities: 175-seat studio theater
Use: Theatrical events

Judy Bayley Theatre
Facilities: 556-seat theater. Drama theater, construction shop for scenery, costume storage and design areas, dressing and make-up facilities, and a "green room" for theatrical critiques.
Use: Nevada Dance Theatre and other performing arts. Opened in 1972.

Paul Harris Theatre
Facilities: 99-seat theater
Use: Theatrical performances

Studio One
Facilities: 140-seat theater
Use: Dance performances

Thomas and Mack Center
Tropicana & Swenson
Las Vegas, NV 89119
895-3761
Pat Christenson, Exec. Dir.
Facilities: 18,500 seats
Use: UNLV Basketball, Las Vegas Thunder Hockey, National Finals Rodeo, major concerts

Opened in 1983, this multipurpose events center is the site for basketball games, major concerts, hockey games, tennis matches and ice shows. Meeting rooms and banquet facilities. Houses the Administrative Office of the Department of Intercollegiate Athletics, the center's operating staff and upcoming events ticket sales. Home of the UNLV Runnin' Rebels.

Sam Boyd Silver Bowl
Boulder Hwy./Russell Rd.
Las Vegas, NV 89122
895-3900
Pat Christenson, Exec. Dir.
Facilities: 32,000seats
Use: UNLV football, major concerts

West Las Vegas Arts Center
947 W. Lake Mead Blvd.
Las Vegas, NV 89106
229-4800
Marcia Robinson, Ctr. Coordinator
Hours: Tue. 1 pm - 9 pm; Wed - Fri 10 am - 7 pm; Sat. 10 am - 5 pm
Facilities: 700 sq. ft. exhibit room, dance floor, recording studio
Use: Arts facility for visual arts, musical and dance arts. Saturday matinees at 1 pm and jam sessions.

Winchester Community Center
3130 S. McLeod Dr.
Las Vegas, NV 89121
455-7340
Dan Skea
Operated by the Clark County Parks & Recreation Dept.
Facilities: Classrooms, rehearsal space, gallery and 300-seat auditorium.

Zelzah Shrine Temple
2222 W. Mesquite Ave.
Las Vegas, NV 89106
382-5554
Jim Denny, Potentate
Facilities: Ballroom

Rock Concert at Thomas and Mack Center, Tropicana & Swenson, Las Vegas, NV 89119

ARTEMUS W. HAM CONCERT HALL SEATING CHART

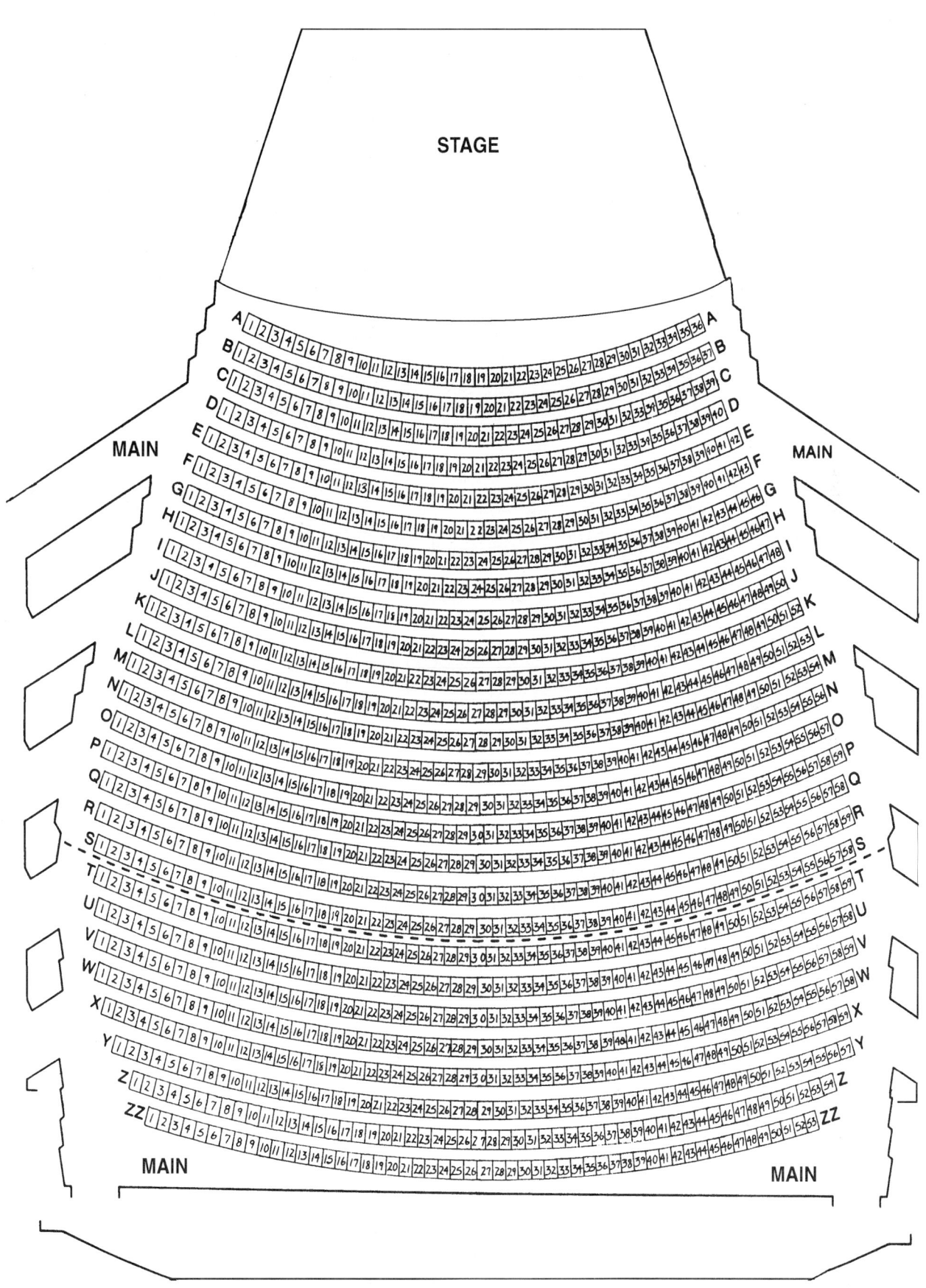

JUDY BAYLEY THEATRE SEATING CHART

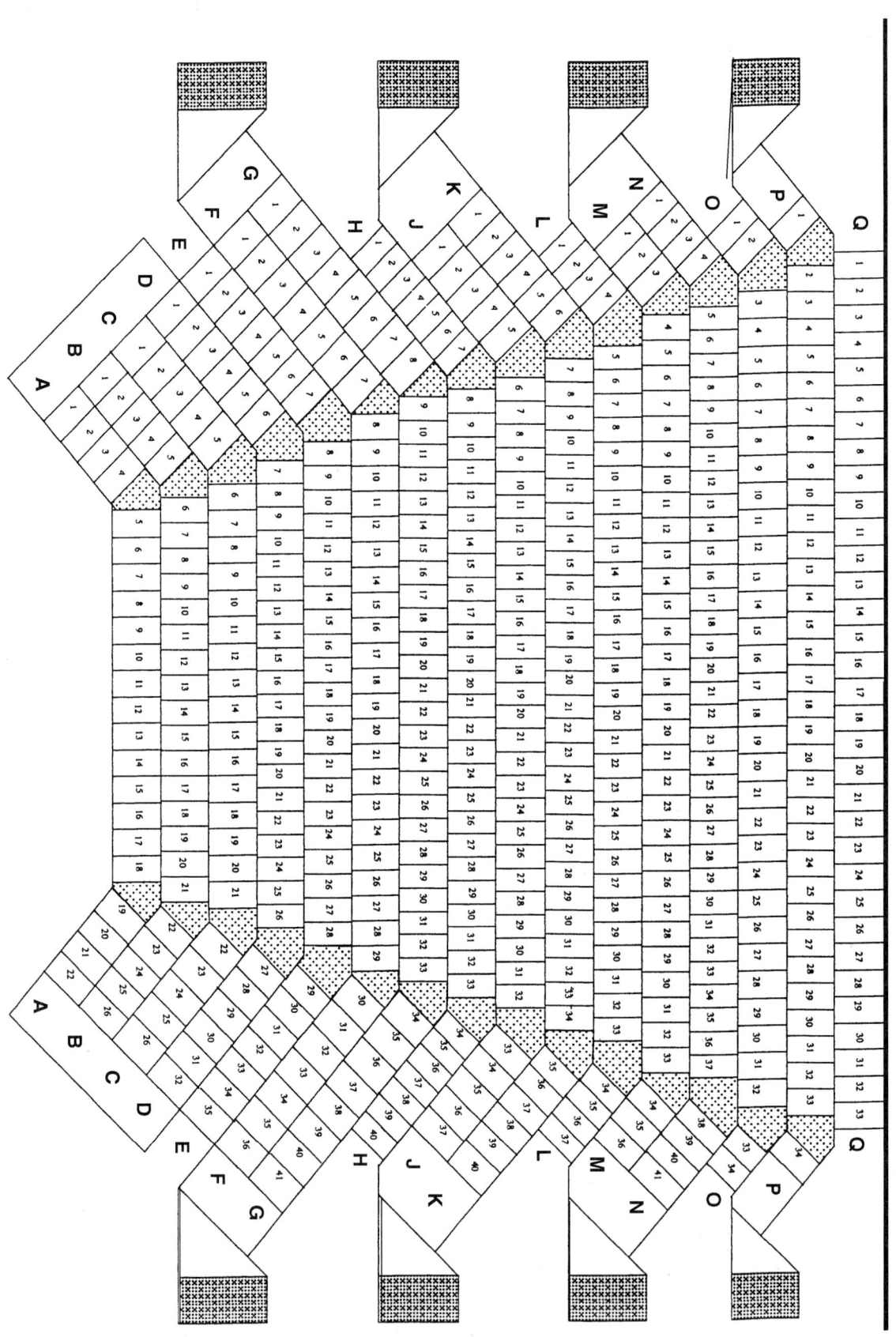

ART IN PUBLIC PLACES

**Green Valley
Outdoor Sculpture Museum**

**Green Valley Outdoor
Sculpture Museum**
Sculpture Information Center
901 N. Green Valley Pkwy., Ste. 200
Henderson, NV 89014
458-8855
The 18 life-like bronze statues line
Green Valley Pkwy. near Sunset Rd. and
throughout the Green Valley area of
Henderson. Works include permanent
and rotating pieces by J. Seward
Johnson, Lita Albuquerque, Lloyd
Hamrol, Lee Sido, Alan Osborn and
Isaac Witkin. A location map of these
sculptures can be found on page 446 of
this book.
Green Valley Sculptures:
1. "Match Point"
 by J. Seward Johnson, Jr.
2. "Companions"
 by J. Seward Johnson, Jr.
3. "Sharing Headlines"
 by J. Seward Johnson, Jr.

4. "The Right Light"
 by J. Seward Johnson, Jr.
5. "Attic Trophy"
 by J. Seward Johnson, Jr.
6. "Green Valley High Gator"
 by Don Winton
7. "Greenspun Junior High Dolphin"
 by Wyland
8. "Time To Go Fishing"
 by J. Seward Johnson, Jr.
9. "Par, What?"
 by J. Seward Johnson, Jr.
10. "Second Hand News"
 by J. Seward Johnson, Jr.
11. "Generation Bridge"
 by J. Seward Johnson, Jr.
12. "The Linden Tree"
 by Isaac Wilkin.
13. "Big Sister"
 by J. Seward Johnson, Jr.
14. "Ediface Brace"
 by Leo Sido.
15. "Things To Do"
 by J. Seward Johnson, Jr.
16. "Obelisk"
 by Lila Albuquerque.
17. "Serpent Mound"
 by Lloyd Hamrol.
18. "Waterpower"
 by J. Seward Johnson, Jr.

**Other sculptures located in and
around Las Vegas:**

"Circle of Life"
by William Limebrook
Pueblo at Summerlin, Lake Mead Blvd.
at Scholar Ln.

"Environmentally Interactive
Sculptural System"
by Patrick Zentz
UNLV - Richard Tam Alumni Center

"Flashlight"
by Claes Oldenberg
$130,000 sculpture commissioned to
symbolize the university; UNLV

"The Water Bearers"
by Glenna Goodacre
5241 Spring Mountain Rd., Southwest
Gas

"Winged Figures of the Republic"
Largest cast bronze statues in U.S.;
Nevada side of Hoover Dam.

"Double Negative"
by Michael Heizer
Earth art near Overton.

"Tribute to a Cowboy"
by Deborah Copenhaver
Monument to Benny Binion - downtown.

"Ground Zero"
by William J. Maxwell
Facade of City Hall
The 100 x 280-ft. wall was transformed
into a kaleidoscope of colors and shadows
crisscrossing and moving with the sun.
In the evening southwest images are
brought to life by lighted projections
reflected in the waters of the pool below.
The city removed the malfunctioning
fountain last year.

McCarran Airport:
"Control Tower"
by Peter Shire
Ticketing area.

"Lost Showgirl Civilization"
bronze shoe sculpture
by Rhonda Zwillinger
Shopping promenade.

"Vaquero"
by New Mexico artist Luis Jimenez
Fiberglass sculpture of Vaquero astride
a bucking horse; located outside
approach to ticketing.

"Ghost Gems"
by John Torreano
Five gem shapes made of aluminum and
glass placed to look like they spilled;
located outside approach to ticketing.

"Mast and Sails"
by Luis Jimenez
Desert Shores, Spinnaker Cove

"Lorenzi Bust"
by Mauro Possobon
Lorenzi Park

"Spirit Tower"
by Rita Deanin Abbey
20-ft.-tall, 10-ton steel sculpture.
Summerlin Library, 1771 Inner Circle Dr.

"Reflections Center"
Railroad/Colorado St. Boulder City
Sculpture garden with over half-dozen
pieces on display.

"Monument to Old Fort"
Old Las Vegas Mormon Fort 908 Las
Vegas Blvd. N.
Stone monument erected in 1939 by the
Daughters of Utah Pioneers. Knocked
over during area construction in 1970s,
it revealed a sealed time capsule of origi-
nal documents.

"Memorial to American Gold Star
Mothers"
Dedicated May 30, 1952 by a mother
whose sons died in World War I, World
War II, and the Korean War. Las Vegas
Blvd./Bonanza Rd.

"Setsuko"
by Montana artist Deborah Butterfield
Full-scale cast bronze horse - on display
in Summerlin in the courtyard of the
Plaza East Office Building, Village
Center Circle.

"Flashlight" by Claes Oldenberg at UNLV

GREEN VALLEY OUTDOOR SCULPTURE GARDEN

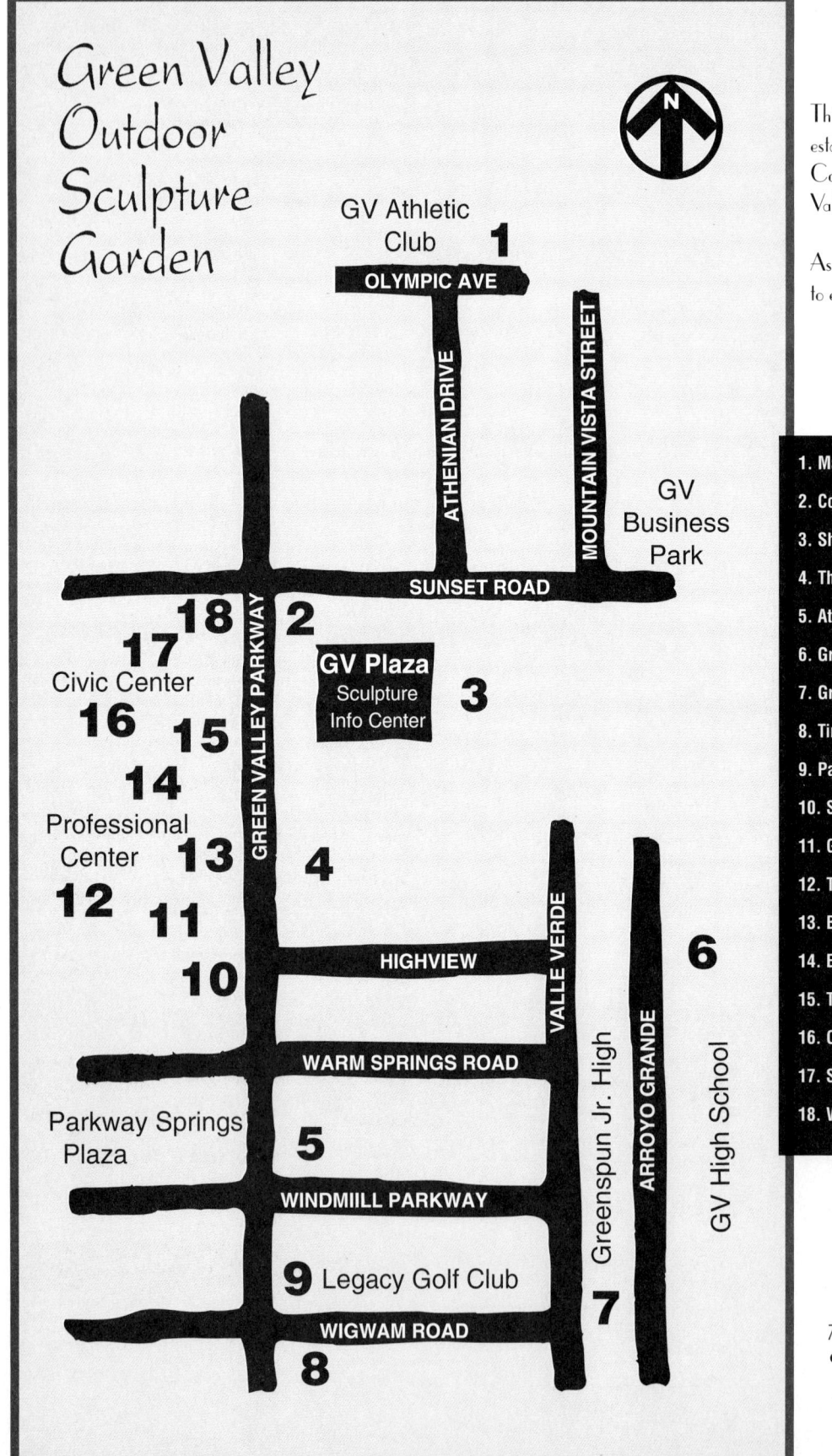

Green Valley Outdoor Sculpture Garden

GV Athletic Club

OLYMPIC AVE

1

ATHENIAN DRIVE

MOUNTAIN VISTA STREET

GV Business Park

SUNSET ROAD

18 **2**

17

Civic Center

16 **15**

14

Professional Center **13**

12 **11**

10

GREEN VALLEY PARKWAY

GV Plaza
Sculpture
Info Center

3

4

HIGHVIEW

VALLE VERDE

6

WARM SPRINGS ROAD

Parkway Springs Plaza

5

Greenspun Jr. High

ARROYO GRANDE

GV High School

WINDMIILL PARKWAY

9 Legacy Golf Club

7

WIGWAM ROAD

8

This unique collection of original art was established in 1984 by American Nevada Corporation, the developer of Green Valley.

As you tour the community, we invite you to enjoy these distinctive works of art.

1. Match Point - J. Seward Johnson, Jr.

2. Companions - J. Seward Johnson, Jr.

3. Sharing Headlines - J. Seward Johnson, Jr.

4. The Right Ligh t - J. Seward Johnson, Jr.

5. Attic Trophy - J. Seward Johnson, Jr.

6. Green Valley High Gator - Don Winton

7. Greenspun Junior High Dolphin - Wyland

8. Time To Go Fishing - J. Seward Johnson, Jr.

9. Par, What? - J. Seward Johnson, Jr.

10. Second Hand News - J. Seward Johnson, Jr.

11. Generation Bridge - J. Seward Johnson, Jr.

12. The Linden Tree - Isaac Wilkin

13. Big Sister - J. Seward Johnson, Jr.

14. Ediface Brace - Lee Sido

15. Things To Do - J. Seward Johnson, Jr.

16. Obelisk - Lila Albuquerque

17. Serpent Mound - Lloyd Hamrol

18. Waterpower - J. Seward Johnson, Jr.

American Nevada
corporation
A Greenspun Company

ART GALLERIES - NONPROFIT

Bank of America Nevada Art Collection
Bank of America Plaza
300 S. 4th St.
Las Vegas, NV 89101
654-8428
Bonnie Earl Solari, Curator
Hours: Mon. - Fri. 9 am - 5 pm
Bank of America's $6 million collection is open to the public and on display at their downtown office building. The collection contains several hundred pieces of Southwestern art. Tours by reservation once a month.

Boulder City Art Gallery
Boulder Dam Hotel
1305 Arizona St.
Boulder City, NV 89005
293-2138
Mary Alice Mooney, Pres.
Hours: Mon. - Sat. 10 am - 5 pm; Sun. noon - 5 pm
Local artists featured; original fine arts.

Charleston Heights Art Gallery
800 S. Brush St.
Las Vegas, NV 89107
229-6383
Lisa Stamanis, Gallery Dir.
Hours: Mon. & Thu. 1 pm - 9 pm; Tue. & Wed. 10 am - 9 pm; Fri. 10 am - 6 pm; Sat - Sun. 1 pm - 5 pm

Clark County Government Center
500 S. Grand Central Pkwy.
Las Vegas, NV 89106
455-7340
Changing exhibits shown in the County Room Rotunda.

Clark County Heritage Museum
(Also see Museums)
1830 S. Boulder Hwy.
Henderson, NV 89015
455-7955
Mark Ryzdynski, Head Adm.
Hours: 9 am - 4:30 pm
Admission: adults $1.50; seniors and children $1
Heritage Gallery offers a lively selection of changing exhibits.

Contemporary Arts Collective
103 E. Charleston Blvd.
Las Vegas, NV 89104
382-3886
Joy Prendergast, Curator
Hours: Fri. - Sun. noon - 4 pm; Wed. & Thu. 6 pm - 8 pm

Community College of Southern Nevada
Department of Fine Arts
3200 E. Cheyenne Ave.
N. Las Vegas, NV 89030
651-4006
Dr. Tom Ferguson, Chairman

CCSN Art Gallery
3200 E. Cheyenne Avenue
N. Las Vegas, NV 89030
651-4113   651-4473
Kim Fink, Dir.
Hours: Mon. - Fri. 8 am - 4 pm; Sat. 10 am - 2 pm

Donna Beam Fine Art Gallery
4505 S. Maryland Pkwy
Las Vegas, NV 89154
UNLV: 895-3893
Jerry Schefcik , Dir.
Hours: Mon. - Fri. 9 am - 5 pm
(Extended hours for special exhibits)
Richard Tam Alumni Center
UNLV: 895-3621
Fred Albrecht, Dir.
Hours: Mon. - Fri. 8 am - 5 pm
Changing art exhibits on display.
Jessie Metcalf Gallery
UNLV: 895-3621
UNLV - located on the second floor of the Richard Tam Alumni Center. Mon. - Fri. 8 am - 5 pm
Jerry Schefcik, Programmer
Artemus Ham Concert Hall Lobby
UNLV - changing art exhibits on display.

Fletcher Jones Cultural Gallery
(Also see Museums)
833 Las Vegas Blvd. N.
Las Vegas, NV 89101
382-3445
Inside the Lied Discover Museum

Las Vegas Art Museum
6132 W. Charleston Blvd.
Las Vegas, NV 89102
360-8000
Joe Palermo, Dir.
Hours: Tue. - Sat. 10 am - 5 pm; Sun. 1 pm - 5 pm
Gift Shop Hours: Tue. - Sat. 10 am - 5 pm; Sun. 1 pm - 5 pm
Three separate galleries -Main Gallery, Mini Gallery and Southwest Gallery; exhibits change monthly; outstanding annual shows and competitions.

Lied Museum, 833 Las Vegas Blvd. N., Las Vegas, NV. 89101

Las Vegas · Sahara West Library
9600 W. Sahara Ave.
Las Vegas, NV 89117
228-4274
Denise Shapiro, Gallery Mgr.
Currently there are twelve galleries in six branches:

Clark County Library Main Gallery & Photographic Exhibition Hall
1401 E. Flamingo Rd.
Las Vegas, NV 89119
2 galleries

Enterprise Library
25 E. Shelborne Ave.
Las Vegas, NV 89123

Green Valley Library
2797 N. Green Valley Pkwy.
Henderson, NV 89014

Rainbow Library
3150 N. Buffalo Dr.
Las Vegas, NV 89128

Sahara West Library
Fine Arts Museum
9600 W. Sahara Ave.
Las Vegas, NV 89117

Spring Valley Library
4280 S. Jones Blvd.
Las Vegas, NV 89103

Summerlin Library & Performing Arts Center
1771 Inner Circle Dr.
Las Vegas, NV 89134

Sunrise Library
5400 Harris Ave.
Las Vegas, NV 89110

West Charleston Library
6301 W. Charleston Blvd.
Las Vegas, NV 89102

West Las Vegas Library
951 W. Lake Mead Blvd.
Las Vegas, NV 89106

Whitney Library
5175 E. Tropicana Ave.
Las Vegas, NV 89122

Lost City Museum
(Also see Museums)
721 S. Moapa Valley Blvd.
Overton, NV 89040
397-2193
Kathryne Olson, Curator
Admission: $2, daily 8:30 am - 4:30 pm
Changing art exhibits

McCarran Art Gallery
261-5743
McCarran International Airport
South end of baggage claim
Hours: 24 hours
Part of the airport's public art program; features rotating exhibits showcasing the talents of southern Nevada artists.

Nevada Institute for Contemporary Art (NICA)
3455 E. Flamingo Rd. (The Cannery)
Las Vegas, NV 89121
434-2666
Mark Masuoka, Dir.
Arlene Blut, Dir. Devlpmt.
Hours: Tue., Wed. & Fri. 10 am - 6 pm; Thu. 10 am - 8 pm; Sat. - Sun. 10 am - 3 pm
5,000-sq. ft. facility features 6 exhibits per year. The facility will be used to educate Clark County elementary school students in the area of arts. Brings contemporary art to southern Nevada. Nonprofit.

Nevada State Museum and Historical Society
700 Twin Lakes Dr.
Las Vegas, NV 89107
486-5205
Changing art exhibits and displays
(Also see Museums)

Reed Whipple Cultural Center Art Gallery
821 Las Vegas Blvd. N.
Las Vegas, NV 89101
229-6211
Lisa Stamanis, Sr. Vis. Arts Spec.
Hours: Mon. & Thu. 1 pm - 9 pm; Tue. - Wed. 10 am - 9 pm; Fri. 10 am - 6 pm; Sat. 9 am - 5 pm; Sun. 1 pm - 5 pm

Winchester Community Center Gallery
3130 S. McLeod Dr.
Las Vegas, NV 89121
455-7340
Dan Skea, Cult. Progm. Super.
Hours: Mon. - Fri. 9 am - 9 pm; Sat. 9 am - 6 pm

Clark County Heritage Museum, 1830 S. Boulder Hwy., Henderson, NV 89015

PRIVATE CONTEMPORARY ART GALLERIES

Addi Galleries International
2901 Las Vegas Blvd. S. (Riviera Hotel)
Las Vegas, NV 89109
796-6552   1-800-428-2537

3645 Las Vegas Blvd. S. (Bally's)
Las Vegas, NV 89109
737-9795   1-800-428-2537
Paul Addi, Jr., Owner
Hours: 9 am - 11 pm
Leroy Neiman, Ting, Red Skelton, Wahlbuck, Lu Hong sculpture, Pam Foss bronzes, original serigraphs. Original handcast paper sculpture. 1000 sq. ft.

Antigua De Mexico
3375 S. Decatur Blvd., Ste. 18
Las Vegas, NV 89102
253-0101
Hours: Mon. - Fri. - 10 am - 6 pm; Sun. noon - 5 pm
Mexican hand crafted furniture and folk art and oil paintings.

Art Affair
3871 S. Valley View Blvd., Ste. 9
Las Vegas, NV 89103
368-7888
Dugan Elkins
Hours: Mon. - Fri. 9 am - 5:30 pm
Oils, limited-edition prints, serigraphs, etchings, watercolors, paper sculpture. Local and national artists, custom framing. Melanie Taylor Kent, Earle, Olivia, Luango, Nagel. Locals Roy Purcell, Laura Nann, Don Harper, Yanush Godeski. Brokerage service; 5,000 sq. ft.

Art Encounter
3979 Spring Mountain Rd.
Las Vegas, NV 89102
227-0220
Rod Maly
Hours: Tue. - Fri., 10 am - 6 pm; Sat. & Mon. noon - 5 pm
2,000 works of oils, watercolors, drawings, photographs, sculptures, pottery and jewelry for sale on consignment by over 100 artists; 6,000 sq. ft. Nevada's largest fine art gallery.

Art From the Heart
4020 N. Tenaya Way
Las Vegas, NV 89129
656-8250
Barbara Sindelir
Art classes: watercolors, oils, pastels, beginning drawing, children's art classes, creative play, young at art, junior high artists. One-person shows and group shows. Coffee bar with occasional entertainment.

Bernard K. Passman Gallery
3700 W. Flamingo Rd. (Rio Hotel)
Las Vegas, NV 89103
791-3376
Bernard K. Passman, Owner
Hours: 10 am - 11 pm
Bernard Passman is recognized as the artist who pioneered exotic black coral as a fine art and jewelry medium. He has been sculpting since the end of World War II in mediums ranging from stone, clay, and metal to exotic woods. There are always two Royal Guards in front of his gallery as tribute to his numerous commissions for royalty and heads of state worldwide.

Brent Thomson Gallery
1672 Nevada Hwy.
Boulder City, NV 89005
293-4652
Connie Thomson
Hours: Mon. - Fri. 9 am - 5 pm; Sat. 10 am - 3 pm
Contemporary Southwest, landscapes, pottery, custom framing. Monotype etchings, oils, acrylics. Local and national artists - Amado Pena, Jr., Brent Thomson. Art is both created and presented. Print making studio, workshop and gallery. Publisher of fine intaglio prints; 1,600 sq. ft.

Carrara Galleries, 1236 S. Rainbow Blvd., Las Vegas, NV 89102

Carrara Galleries
1236 S. Rainbow Blvd.
Las Vegas, NV 89102
877-4399
Mary K. Carrara & Richard A. Thomas
Hours: Mon. - Sat. 10 am - 6 pm; Sat. 10 am - 6 pm; Sun. 10 am - 4 pm
Alvar, Dali, Neiman, Simbari, Erte, Peter Max and Lichtenstein.

Celebrity Estates
2735 Industrial Rd.
Las Vegas, NV 89109
735-0553
Thomas Schrade
Bronze art sales, furniture, paintings, retail and wholesale and marble statues.

Centaur Sculpture Galleries, Ltd.
3200 S. Las Vegas Blvd. (Fashion Show Mall)
Las Vegas, NV 89109
737-0004
Richard Perry
Hours: Mon. - Fri. 10 am - 9 pm ; Sat. 9:30 am - 7 pm; Sun. noon - 6 pm
Special showings every 4 - 6 wks.

Acrylic, bonded bronze, bonded sand, cut glass, resins, wood, wood resins, fossilized stone - Bill Mack, Michael Wilkinson, Geoffrey Smith, Mark Hopkins, Rick Cain and Alice Riordon.

Coleman's Clay Studio & Gallery
6230 Greyhound Ln., Ste. E
Las Vegas, NV 89122
451-1981
Elaine Coleman, Sec./Treas. & Owner
Hours: Tue. - Fri. 10 am - 2 pm; Sat. 10 am - 4 pm
A unique studio workshop and gallery. The first of its kind in Las Vegas. The gallery features top national artists as well as student work.

Crockett Gallery
2800 W. Sahara Ave., Ste. 7C
Las Vegas, NV 89102
253-6336
Caty Crockett
Hours: Mon. - Sat. 10 am - 6 pm
Original fine art, glass, sculpture, metal work, watercolors, oils and pastels.

Crystal Galleria
(Forum Shops)
3500 Las Vegas Blvd. S.
Las Vegas, NV 89109
369-2622
Vincent J. Browne
Hours: Sun. - Thu. 10 am - 11 pm; Fri. & Sat. 10 am - midnight
Unique art glass, Lilique, Waterford & Baccarat Crystal, Lladro, Hummel, Disney Collectibles, Daume & Orrefors.

Debora Spanover Gallery Fine Arts
(Liberace Plaza)
1775 E. Tropicana Ave. Ste. 22
Las Vegas, NV 89119
739-0072
Debora Spanover
Hours: Mon. - Fri. 10 am - 4 pm; Sat. 10 am - 2 pm; by appointment
Special showings throughout the year. Original paintings, serigraphs, lithographs, sculptures, animation art, posters. Erte, Rockwell, Neiman, Warhol, Kent, Yamagata and more.

Demos Gallery
1775 E. Tropicana Ave., Ste. 13
Las Vegas, NV 89119
798-8900
Joan Samara, Owner
Hours: Mon. - Fri. 10 am - 6 pm; Sat. 10 am - 5 pm
Library of catalogs for ordering art decor, home and office, consultation, antique prints, original watercolors. Limited and open edition graphics, oils, poster art, custom framing. Ray McCarty, Barbara Wood, 19th century prints, etchings and engravings, botanical prints, political, contemporary and traditional art. Evalynne Lathrop-Engel. Cartoons, Civil War steel engraving. Special showing on occasion.

Duncans Framing Gallery
3220 N. Rancho Dr.
Las Vegas, NV 89130
656-3403
Will Duncan
Hours: Tue. - Sat. 9 am - 6 pm
Southwest and contemporary art, specializing in all types of custom framing. Large art selection and wood carvings.

Eternal Treasures
1725 S. Rainbow Blvd., Ste. 5
Las Vegas, NV 89102
256-9134
Fax: 256-9201
Flagship gallery in a chain of 13; featuring multi-denominational religious and inspirational fine art; custom framing available.

Fire and Water Studio of Fine Art
555 Hotel Plaza St.
Boulder City, NV 89005
294-4177
Sharon Heher
Hours: Tue. - Sat. 10 am - 3 pm
The gallery sells personalized gourmet gift & picnic baskets, custom picture framing, ceramics and pottery and two-dimensional art by local artists.

Galerie Lassen
(Forum Shops)
3500 Las Vegas Blvd. S.
Las Vegas, NV 89109
731-6900
Christian Lassen
Hours: 10 am - midnight
2,700-gallon saltwater aquarium and sign. High tech video wall. Features works of artists Doug Wylie, Christian Lassen, James Colman, William DeShazo, Michael David Ward, Dario Campanile.

Galleria Di Sorrento Gallery
(Forum Shops)
3500 Las Vegas Blvd. S.
Las Vegas, NV 89109
369-8000
John Russo
Hours: Mon. - Fri. 10 am - 11 pm; Sat. - Sun. 10 am - midnight
Original paintings, bronze and acrylic sculptures, art glass vases and bowls. Unique art forms.

Glass Artistry, Inc.
4200 W. Desert Inn Rd.
Las Vegas, NV 89102

Gallerie Michelangelo
(Caesars Palace)
3570 Las Vegas Blvd. S.
Las Vegas, NV 89109
796-5001
Larry Yaker
Hours: 10 am - midnight
Original works by contemporary artists;
LeRoy Neiman, Erte, Leonardo
Nierman, Charlene Mitchell, Miguel
Prados and Bill Mack.

Gallery of History
3601 W. Sahara Ave.
Promenade Ste.
Las Vegas, NV 89102
731-0785
Todd Axelrod
Hours: Mon. - Fri. 8 am - 5 pm
Largest dealer of original historical doc-
uments in the world. Documents are
framed as works of art.

Glass Artistry Inc.
4200 W. Desert Inn Rd.
Las Vegas, NV 89102
221-8494
Rita Malkin
Hours: Mon. - Fri. 9 am - 5 pm
Custom stained glass windows, unique
one-of-a kind fused glass art pieces.
Etched and carved glass.

Igitian Modern Art Gallery
5808 Spring Mountain Rd., Ste. 107
Las Vegas, NV 89102
365-5600
Henry Igitian, Curator
Hours: Tue. - Sat. 10 am - 6 pm
All modern Russian artists from
Armenia. Sculptures and original printings.

**Left of Center Art Gallery and
Studio**
*(in the Richardson Construction
Company building)*
2207 W. Gowan Rd.
N. Las Vegas, NV 89030
647-7378
Vicki Richardson
Hours: Thu. - Fri. 3 pm - 6 pm; Sat.
10 am - 2 pm or by appointment
Showcases minority artists.

Liguori's Gallery
1306 Nevada Hwy.
Boulder City, NV 89005
293-5450 1-800-292-3233
Steven Liguori
Hours: 9 am - 6 pm
In-house artist Steven Liguori designed
the Veterans Memorial Monument at
Boulder City Veterans Cemetery. Native
American art, southwest art and jewel-
ry. Also operates shop at Hoover Dam.

Mixed Media, Ltd.
3355 S. Highland Dr., Ste. 109
Las Vegas, NV 89109
796-8282 1-800-772-8282
Brad Whiting
Hours: Mon. - Fri. 8 am - 5 pm or by
appointment
Fine art posters and graphics, catalog
available in September; design and consulting.

Moonstruck Gallery
6322 W. Sahara Ave.
Las Vegas, NV 89102
364-0531 1-800-421-9133
Sharon Schafer and Denise Mrochek
Hours: Mon. - Sat. 10 am - 7 pm
Special showing throughout year. More
than 3,500 sq. ft. of gallery space in
Moonstruck's 5,600 sq. ft. premises is
available for special events and meetings to local groups. Moonstruck also
presents free community events, seminars, craft demonstrations and workshops
on an ongoing basis; preserving and presenting historical documents.
Hand crafted musical instruments, fine
contemporary Southwest art, prints,
limited editions, hand crafted collectibles.
Preferred gallery of Disney Art Editions.
Custom framing.

Moonstruck Gallery, 6322 W. Sahara Ave., Las Vegas, NV 89102

The Museum Company
(Forum Shops)
3500 Las Vegas Blvd. S.
Las Vegas, NV 89109
792-9220
Pat Caspary, Manager
Hours: 10 am - midnight
Museum reproductive art, jewelry, gifts.

Planet Mirth Productions
5115 S. Industrial Rd., Ste. 107
Las Vegas, NV 89118
Earl Chaney
Hours: Mon. - Sat. noon - 8 pm
Clowns, wildlife, personalities, portraits
and landscapes featuring Jim Howle,
artist of the century.

P. S. Galleries
(Bally's Hotel)
3645 Las Vegas Blvd. S.
Las Vegas, NV 89109
733-0705
Dorothy Homola & Lynne Gordon
Hours: 9 am - 11 pm
Bronze, pewter and alabaster sculp-
tures; Ron Lee clowns, sculptured wall
hangings, Tom Clark gnomes.

Regal Art Gallery
3315 E. Russell Rd.
Las Vegas, NV 89120
436-4146
William Dahmer
Hours: Mon. - Fri. 9:30 am - 5:30 pm;
Sat. 9:30 am - 5 pm
Fine art and custom framing. Thomas
Kinkade, Terry Redlin, G. Harvey and
Marty Bell.

Ron Lee's World of Clowns
330 Carousel Pkwy.
Henderson, NV 89014
434-3920
Ron Lee, Owner
Hours: Mon. - Fri. 8 am - 5 pm; Sat.
9 am - 5 pm
Admission: Factory tour of clown makers and sculptures, $200,000 carousel,
live clowns and gallery, Carousel Cafe
and 30,000 sq. ft. manufacturing facility.

Ryan Gallery
2972 S. Rainbow Blvd.
Las Vegas, NV 89102
368-0545
Gail Buy
Hours: Mon. - Sat. 9 am - 5 pm
Art, jewelry, art furniture and fine crafts.

Serendipity Gallery
(Fashion Show Mall)
3200 Las Vegas Blvd. S.
Las Vegas, NV 89109
733-2080
Adelle Cuaron, Mgr.
Hours: Mon. - Fri. 10 am - 9 pm; Sat.
10 am - 7 pm; Sun. noon - 6 pm
Lladro, Armani, Swarovski, Dept. 56 &
all major collectibles.

Studio West
8447 W. Lake Mead Blvd.
Las Vegas, NV 89128
228-1901
Jana & Gary Porter
Hours: Mon. - Fri. 10 am - 6 pm; Sat.
10 am - 5 pm
Paintings, etchings, limited-edition
prints, posters, needlepoint; custom
framing; featuring Thomas Kinkade.

Trinity Black Fine Art Gallery
2657D Las Vegas Blvd. N.
N. Las Vegas, NV 89030
399-1125
Lillian Moore, Owner
Hours: Tue. - Fri. 10 am - 6 pm; Sat.
10 am - 5 pm
Features African and multicultural art
by local, national and international
artists. Special showings by scheduled
artists. Custom framing.

Unique Art Gallery
925 S. Rainbow Blvd.
Las Vegas, NV 89128
870-2121
Ken McDonald
Hours: Mon. - Sat. 10 am - 5:30 pm
Special showings on occasion, subject
matter varies. Oils, acrylics, watercolors,
sculpture by local artists and others.
Art classes; 1,400 sq. ft.

Walt Disney Gallery
(Fashion Show Mall)
3200 Las Vegas Blvd. S.
Las Vegas, NV 89109
650-2201
David Wicburg, Mgr.
Hours: Mon. - Fri. 10 am - 9 pm, Sat.
10 am - 7 pm, Sun. noon - 6 pm
Gallery is divided into 4 themed areas:
animation gallery, collectibles gallery,
contemporary gallery, gallery shop;
4,600 sq. ft.

Winged Horse Gallerie
3750 S. Valley View Blvd., Ste. 8
Las Vegas, NV 89103
227-3445
Mary Ann Sachs & Linda Verga
Hours: Mon. - Fri. 10 am - 5 pm; Sat. by
appointment
Contemporary ceramic, wood and
bronze sculpture, paintings, assemblages,
collages.

Zero Gravity
(Forum Shops)
3500 Las Vegas Blvd. S.
Las Vegas, NV 89109
731-3565
Eddie Rosenberg
Hours: Sun. - Thu. 10 am - 11 pm; Fri. -
Sat. 10 am - midnight
Art and sculptures by Tabra, Titanium
by Spector and Kaleidoscope by
Enchanted Vision.

ART CLASSES

Community College of Southern Nevada
3200 E. Cheyenne Ave.
N. Las Vegas, NV 89030
651-4006
Kim Fink, Dir.
The college offers non-credit classes and activities in a variety of areas and subjects. Call the Division of Community Education at 651-4057.

Joe Behar's Community Drama Workshop
(Also under Theater)
457-0234
Joe Behar, Dir.
Meets Mondays at 8 pm; Sam's Town, 5111 Boulder Hwy., for drama workshop at no cost.

Las Vegas Academy of International Studies, Performing & Visual Arts
315 S. 7th St.
Las Vegas, NV 89101
799-7800
Robert Gerye, Prin.

Performing arts magnet school will offer courses in theater, dance, vocal/instrumental music and orchestra.

Las Vegas Art Centre
Art Encounter
3979 Spring Mountain Rd.
Las Vegas, NV 89102
227-0220
Rod Maly
Classes taught in drawing, oil painting, calligraphy, watercolor, acrylics, pencil and more.

Nevada School of the Arts
315 S. 7th St.
Las Vegas, NV 89101
386-2787
Dr. Paul Hesselink, Dean
Provides instruction in music, visual arts and children's musical theater to all ages and abilities. Founded in 1977, NSA is a local, non-profit organization and is supported by a grant from the Nevada State Council on the Arts. NSA will reach nearly 400 students per semester, from age 3 to adult, with a

faculty of 50 during the 1997-98 season. NSA offers both private and class instruction. The only Nevada member of the National Guild of Community Schools of the Arts.
(Also under Arts Organizations and Music)

Reed Whipple Cultural Center
821 Las Vegas Blvd. N.
Las Vegas, NV 89101
229-6211
Classes are offered for adults, teens and children in dance, theater, music, painting, photography, pottery, weaving and more. Call for a free brochure detailing all classes.

Simba Jambalaya Dance Theatre
1953 N. Decatur Blvd.
Mailbox 331
Las Vegas, NV 89108
647-8808
Laverne Ligon, Exec. Dir.
Dance classes for ages 3 through adult professionals in ballet, jazz, tap, African and hip hop.
(Also under Dance)

UNLV
Continuing Education
4505 S. Maryland Pkwy.
Las Vegas, NV 89154
895-3394
Community and general interest classes and workshops.

UNLV College of Fine and Performing Arts
4505 S. Maryland Pkwy.
Las Vegas, NV 89154
895-3237
Jeff Koep, Dean
Lee Sido, Chairman
Degrees offered: Art - B.A., B.F.A., M.F.A.; Dance - B.A., B.S.; Music - B.A., B.M., M.M.; Theater Arts - B.A., M.A., M.F.A.
The College of Fine and Performing Arts presents hundreds of performances, recitals, and art shows each year in its concert hall, theaters, galleries, and studios.
(Also see Education Section)

Art Encounter, 3979 Spring Mountain Rd., Las Vegas, NV 89102

Art Affair, 3871 S. Valley View Blvd., Ste. 9, Las Vegas, NV 89103

ART GROUPS and LECTURE

ART GROUPS

The Desert Quilters of Nevada
451-2949
Gail Smith, Pres.
Non-profit group that promotes and preserves the art of quilting, applique and related fiber arts.

Fiber Arts Guild
6317 O'Bannion Dr.
Boulder City, NV 89102
254-5743
Jan Flores, Pres.
Handweaving, spinning and related arts; group meets 2nd Sat. of each month at 9 am *(Sept. - June).*

Nevada Camera Club
P.O. Box 19451
Las Vegas, NV 89132
458-6382 or 564-3980
Frank Porter, Pres.
Group of amateur photographers. Sponsor print competitions; monthly meetings are open to the public.

Membership is $24 per year, $15 for juniors 17 and under and seniors 63 and over.

Nevada Clay Guild
P. O. Box 50004
Henderson, NV 89016
736-2484   293-5154
Julie Heileman, Pres.
Non-profit organization whose members are involved in clay crafts and arts as professionals, teachers and students.

Nevada Watercolor Society
P. O. Box 27224
Las Vegas, NV 89126
256-7002
Kathy Morton-Stanton, Pres.
Founded in 1969, this non-profit organization's goal is to develop a membership devoted to encouraging, educating and promoting transparent watercolor paintings. Monthly meetings Sept.-May 2nd Wed. 7 pm at Moonstruck Gallery. Open to the public.

LECTURE

Barbara Greenspun Lecture Series
UNLV Artemus W. Ham Concert Hall
Box Office: 895-3801
Public is invited free to this annual series. Admission is by ticket only on a first come, first served basis. Tickets are limited to 2 per person.

Barrick Lecture Series
UNLV Artemus W. Ham Concert Hall
Joann Prujan, Proj. Coordinator
Free annual series of lectures, featuring nationally and internationally known guest speakers. Tickets are available on a first come, first served basis, with a 2 ticket limit per person. Watch newspapers for ticket availability.

Borders Book Shop
2323 S. Decatur Blvd.
Las Vegas, NV 89102
258-0999
Dennis McGraw, Mgr.
Coffee bar and book store. Poetry readings, workshops, light music, book discussion and story time.

Community College of Southern Nevada
Distinguished Speaker Series
Tickets: 651-LIVE
Price: Adults $15, Seniors and Students $10
Call for schedule of speakers.

University Forum Lecture Series
Free Lecture Series: 895-3401
UNLV
Series of free public lectures sponsored by the College of Liberal Arts and underwritten by the UNLV Foundation. Pre-registration or tickets are not required, simply attend at the time and place indicated.

UNLV Information Line: 895-3131
Concerts, special classes, lectures, etc.

HISTORICAL

HISTORICAL ORGANIZATIONS

Archaeo - Nevada Society
3930 El Camino Rd.
Las Vegas, NV 89103
876-6944
Helen Mortenson, Pres.
An incorporated, non-profit organization since 1966. Local group interested in various aspects of historic and prehistoric archeology.

Boulder City Historical Assoc.
663 Ave. D
Boulder City, NV 89005
293-1716
Virginia (Teddy) Fenton, Historian
Preserving the history of Boulder City and the Hoover Dam construction era. Currently running temporary museum in Hotel Plaza downtown Boulder City. Eventually hopes to have a permanent location in the proposed railroad museum between Boulder City and Henderson. In the future wants to relocate to the Boulder Dam Hotel.

Clark County Museum Guild
565-8073
Judy Hampton, Pres.
(Also see Museums)
Fund raisers for the Clark County Heritage Museum, located in Henderson on a 25-acre site featuring regional memorabilia, historic structures and artifacts. The 8,000 sq. ft. exhibit center features regularly changing exhibits that tell the story of southern Nevada from prehistoric times through the 20th century. Heritage St. features homes relocated to the museum from area locations, which were restored to recreate the lifestyles of important periods. Railroad cars with the original Boulder City train depot are featured in a special display along with an 1880s era ghost town.

Clark County Nevada Genealogical Society
225-5838 *(voice mail)*
Group meets 3rd Thu. of each month 7 pm at the Katherine Center. Seminars in Mar. and Oct.

Friends of the Fort
P.O. Box 667
Las Vegas, NV 89125-0667
Runs the Old Las Vegas Fort and is responsible for all related operations.

Las Vegas Historic Preservation Commission
388-9602
Richard Segerblom, Chairman
Recommends neighborhoods, buildings and sites that should be protected. Commission can halt the demolition of historic buildings for up to 60 days while the commission and building owners consider other options.

The Las Vegas History Foundation, Inc.
3108 Colanthe Ave.
Las Vegas, NV 89102
259-9299
Bill Mors, Prod. Multi-Media Prod.

The Las Vegas History Foundation is a non-profit educational corporation organized to fulfill the program as outlined. Dedicated to the preservation of the past, the understanding of the present, the fulfillment of the future.

Nevada Division of Historic Preservation and Archeology
Nevada Cultural Affairs Commission
Carson City, NV 89705
687-6360
Ron James, Dir.
Established to fund restoration around the state.

Nevada Historical Society
1650 N. Virginia St.
Reno, NV 89503
688-1190
Peter Bandurraga, Dir.
The state's oldest museum with library and archives. Housing the most complete repository of materials relating to the history of Nevada. Las Vegas Historic Preservation Commission formed by the City Council.

McCarran Aviation History
McCarran Airport
(Over baggage claim, 2nd floor)
Kiosks containing artifacts and video displays. Long range plan is to develop a museum documenting the history of aircraft in southern Nevada. The free exhibit is open to the public 24 hours a day.

Preservation Association of Clark County
P. O. Box 96686
Las Vegas, NV 89193-6686
895-3894
Cathie Kelly, Pres.
Non-profit organization established in 1974 for the preservation of Clark County heritage.

Southern Nevada National Railway Historical Society
565-5742
William Brandt, Pres.
Local charter of a national organization focusing on collecting and sharing information on the history of the railroads in southern Nevada and information on railroads in general. A railroad museum in Las Vegas is a future goal.

Living History Program
Spring Mountain State Park
875-4141
Karen Rennick, Park Interpreter
Presented weekends in Sept/Oct. Re-enactment of life in southern Nevada from the early 1900s. Actors portray mountainmen, explorers, settlers, and ranchers. Historic figures are dressed in period costume and demonstrate old-time skills and crafts.

Nevada's Early Exploration Routes

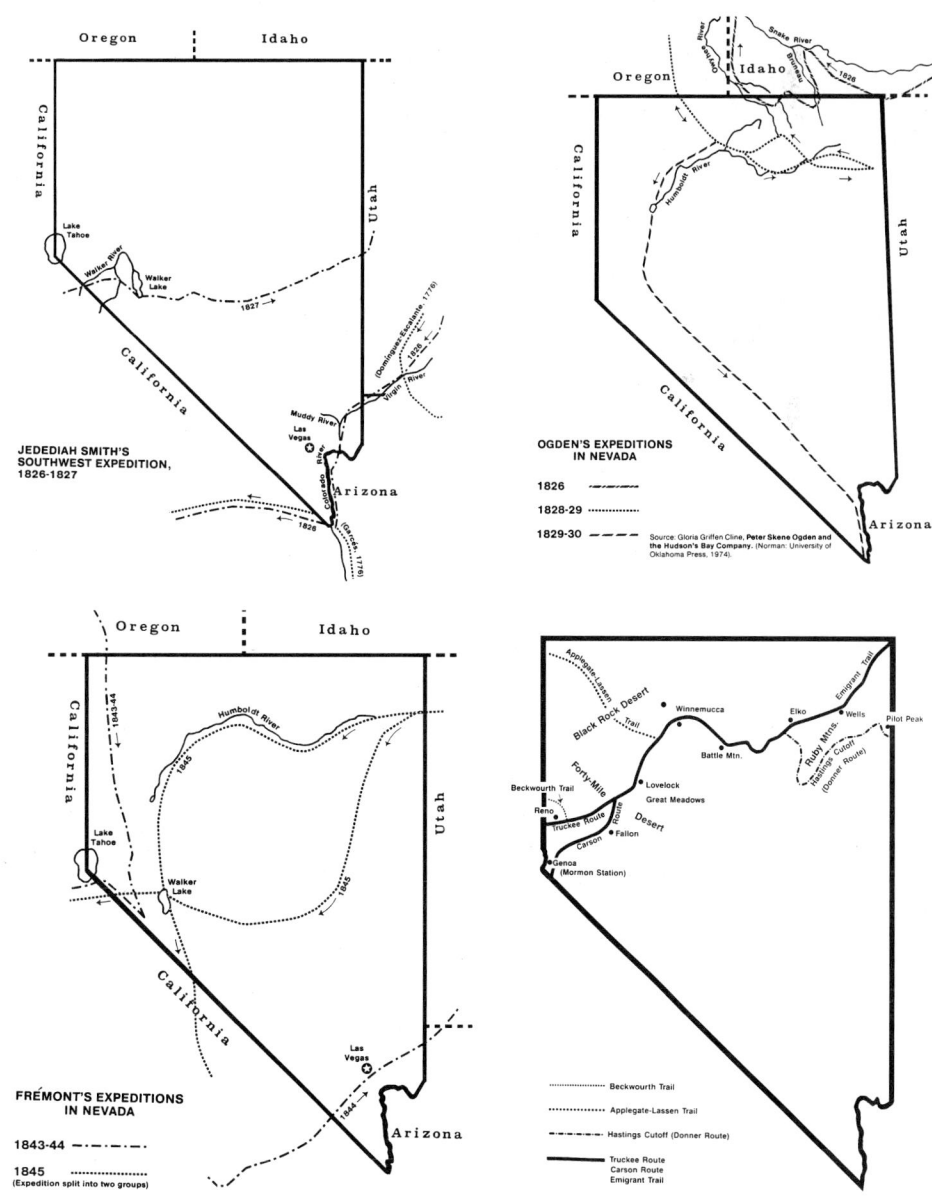

NEVADA HISTORICAL MARKERS - CLARK COUNTY

6 El Dorado Canyon
US 95 at SR 60 *(near Nelson)*
31 Old Spanish Trail
US 91 in West Mesquite
32 Old Spanish Trail (1829-1850)
Fantasy Park, 1/4 mi. E. of N. Las Vegas
Blvd. & Washington Ave.
Stretching for 130 miles across Clark
County, this historic horse trail became
Nevada's first route of commerce in
1829 when trade was initiated between
Santa Fe and Los Angeles. The trail was
later used by the '49ers and Mormon
pioneers. Concrete posts marking the
trail were erected in 1965.
33 Old Spanish Trail
Center of town, Blue Diamond
34 Old Spanish Trail
SR 16 at Mountain Springs Summit
35 Las Vegas Mormon Fort *(Nevada's
Oldest Building)*
N. Las Vegas Blvd. & Washington Ave.
At this location Las Vegas had its beginning on June 14, 1855, when 30 Mormon
missionaries arrived from Utah. They
built a 150-ft. square adobe fort enclos-
ing 8 two-story houses, cultivated small
gardens and fields, planted fruit and
shade trees and established friendly
relations with the Paiutes.
After the Mormons departed in
1858, Octavius Decatur Gass developed
Las Vegas Rancho, using the adobe
structures as headquarters. He farmed
800 acres, supplying produce to miners
and travelers.
Mrs. Helen J. Stewart, owner of
the property from 1882 to 1903, expanded the ranch to 1,800 acres, which she
sold to the San Pedro, Los Angeles &
Salt Lake Railroad Company as the Las
Vegas townsite, auctioned on May 15,
1905, starting contemporary Las Vegas.
One of the Fort houses remains as a
monument to the 1855 pioneers.
36 Moapa Valley
SR 12, 2 mi. N. of Logandale
37 Powell of Colorado
At Echo Bay on Lake Mead
40 Las Vegas *(The Meadows)*
West Charleston/Valley View Road, Las
Vegas
The famous Las Vegas Springs rose from
the desert floor here sending two
streams of water across the valley to
nurture the native grasses and create
lush meadows in the valley near Sunrise
Mountain. The water gushed forth with
such force that a man could not sink in
the Springs.
The natural oasis of meadow and
mesquite forest was the winter homeland
of Paiutes who spent the summers in
the Charleston Mountains.
An unknown Spanish-speaking
sojourner, whether padre, trapper or
trader, named Las Vegas "The
Meadows," and marked it as such on a
map of the Southwestern Desert.
Antonio Armijo stopped at the
Springs in 1829-30, traveling a route
which became known as the Old
Spanish Trail. After 1830, the route was
traveled by Spanish traders, emi-
grants and frontiersmen, who rested
beside the Springs. On one of his western

exploration trips, John C. Fremont
camped here on May 3, 1844.
Because of the artesian water
here, Mormons established the Las
Vegas Mission and Fort in 1855; the
Valley became a huge cattle ranch from
1866 to 1904; and the San Pedro, Los
Angeles & Salt Lake Railroad Company
acquired water rights and land and
created the City of Las Vegas in 1905.
41 Lost City
SR 12, 2 miles south of Overton
56 Virgin Valley
US 91 in Mesquite
86 Tule Springs
In Tule Springs Park, 15 miles NW of Las
Vegas
102 Goodsprings
Off I-15, 7 miles in Goodsprings
103 Gypsum Cave
Private road off I-15 at Apex S. 6 mi.
104 The Camel Corps
SR 77 at jct. with SR 76
115 Potosi
FAS 538, 7 miles north of Blue Diamond
Jct.
116 Searchlight
US 95
140 Old Spanish Trail
(Garces's Expedition)
US 95 at jct. with SR 77
141 Old Spanish Trail
(Armijo's Route)
SR 41, 6 miles east of Henderson
142 Old Spanish Trail
(Mt. Springs Pass)
Mt. Springs Pass of I-15 at Arden cross-
ing
150 Nevada's First State Park
Visitor Center, Valley of Fire State Park
168 Arrowhead Trail
SR 40 in Valley of Fire State Park
**188 Von Schmidt State Boundary
Monument**
5 1/2 mi. N. of Needles, CA at Colorado
River
**190 Original Homesite of Pioneer Las
Vegan "Pop" Squires**
(1865-1958)
Fremont St., Las Vegas
Squires founded the *Las Vegas Age*
newspaper and was the voice of the
community for more than a quarter century. A visionary, he helped make
Hoover Dam a reality.
195 The Last Spike
Off I-15, 4.6 miles northeast of Jean
197 Arrowhead Trail II
Jct. US Hwy. 93-95, 2.5 miles south of
Henderson
The name "Arrowhead Trail" is of doubtful
origin. This portion was regularly used
between the 1860s and 1924. Earlier it
was an alternate wagon route to the
Mormon settlement at San Bernardino,
California.
Heading south along this trail
toward Bishop Mountain, one would
turn through El Dorado Pass and continue on to Nelson, Searchlight, Nipton,
Wheaton Springs and then to San
Bernardino.
The trail was popular as an early
automobile road (1914-1924) when
communities along the route volunteered
the reconstruction of the historic trail

and local Chambers of Commerce vigorously
promoted its use between Los Angeles
and Salt Lake City.
214 Rafael Rivera
Off Mountain Vista Rd. at entrance to
Vo-Tech School
This historical marker commemorates
the valor and service of pioneer scout
Rafael Rivera, the first Caucasian of
record to view and traverse Las Vegas
Valley. Scouting for Antonio Armijo's 60-
man trading party from Abiquiu, NM in
January 1830, young Rivera ascended
Vegas Wash 20 miles east of this marker
and blazed a route to the Mojave River
in California by way of the Amargosa
River.
Rivera's pioneering route became
a vital link in the Old Spanish Trail, with
Las Vegas Springs a most essential stop
on this popular route to Southern
California. John C. Fremont mapped the
trail in 1844. Three years later, following
an extension of the course to Salt Lake
Valley, the route became known in this
area as the Mormon Trail. Today the Old
Spanish Trail closely parallels I-15.
224 Kyle (Kiel) Ranch
Kyle Ranch park, Carey and Losee Rd.,
North Las Vegas
In 1856 the farm was created by
Mormon missionaries as an Indian
farm. Conrad Kiel bought the farm from
the federal government in 1875. The

Kiel Ranch was one of only two major
ranches in Las Vegas Valley throughout
the 19th century. The Kiel tenure was
marked by violence. Neighboring rancher Archibald Stewart was killed in a
gunfight here in 1884. Edwin and
William Kiel were found murdered on
the ranch in October 1900.
The San Pedro, Los Angeles & Salt
Lake Railroad purchased the ranch in
1903 and later sold it to Las Vegas
banker John S. Park, who built the
elegant white mansion in 1911.
Subsequent owners included
Edwin Taylor (1924-39), and Edwin
Losee (1939-58), who developed the
Boulderado Dude Ranch here, a popular
residence for divorce seekers and
celebrities.
In the late 1950s, business
declined and the ranch was sold. In
1976, 27 acres of the original ranch
were purchased jointly by the City of
North Las Vegas and its Bicentennial
Committee as a historic project. A $1.1
million restoration was approved by
the North Las Vegas City Council. The
city plans to sell off 22 acres of the site.
Restoration was underway on the main
house, but the white house burned a
couple of years ago. Still standing are
the old adobe house built in 1855 and
the doll house, a small wooden building.

CLARK COUNTY HISTORICAL SITES

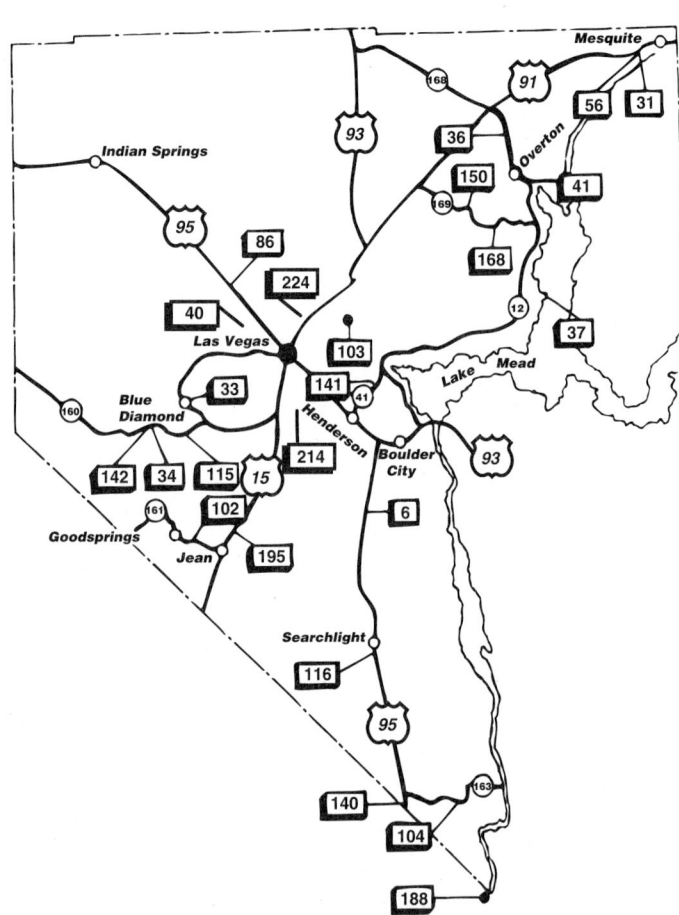

HISTORICAL BUILDINGS IN LAS VEGAS

Of the almost 66,000 properties listed on the National Register, 215 are located in Nevada with 35 being in Clark County. Properties on the National Register can be significant at the local, state or national level. One of the requirements is that the structure retains its original integrity.

A free booklet on the historical neighborhood around downtown Las Vegas is published by the Nevada State Museum and Historical Society and available at the museum.

Six historical Las Vegas homes scheduled to be demolished have been moved to the Clark County Heritage Museum during the past decade. The homes have been restored and decorated in furnishing from the era.
(Also see Museums)

Apache Hotel
128 Fremont St.
Las Vegas, NV 89101
Now the Horseshoe, the Apache was built in 1931 and still lies behind the Binion's neon sign.

Big Springs
Las Vegas Water District
3700 W. Charleston Blvd.
Las Vegas, NV 89102
The famous springs which John C. Fremont described in 1844 supplied all the water for the Las Vegas Valley until the 1950s, when Lake Mead water began to supply the town. Located on Las Vegas Valley Water District property and not accessible to the public.

Boggs Building
319 E. Fremont St.
Las Vegas, NV 89101
Built in 1932 to house the J. C. Penney Department Store.

Carl Ray Professional Building
417 E. Fremont St.
Las Vegas, NV 89101
This Spanish Colonial adobe structure was built in 1929 and was the city's first major office building.

The Church of Jesus Christ of Latter Day Saints, 1st Ward
1300 N. 8th St.
Las Vegas, NV 89101
This Tudor-style building was built in 1932.

El Portal Theater
310 Fremont St.
Las Vegas, NV 89101
Las Vegas' first modern theater was built in 1928. Now occupied by El Portal Gifts.

Fifth St. School
400 S. Fourth St.
Las Vegas, NV 89101
This mission-style building was built with money from President Franklin D. Roosevelt's New Deal in 1936 and was placed on the National Register of Historic Places in 1988.

Golden Gate Casino
1 E. Fremont St.
Las Vegas, NV 89101
Parts of this structure date back to 1906. The oldest portion was part of the Hotel Nevada until the 1930s, when it was renamed Sal Sagev (Las Vegas spelled backwards).

Green Shack Restaurant
2504 Fremont St.
Las Vegas, NV 89104
The restaurant, which opened in 1930, is one of the few remaining original buildings along what was a dirt road leading to the Hoover Dam construction site.

Hitching Post Wedding Chapel
226 Las Vegas Blvd. S.
Las Vegas, NV 89101
Originally constructed as a private residence in 1923, it has been a wedding chapel since 1934.

Huntridge Theater
1208 E. Charleston Blvd.
Las Vegas, NV 89104
Built in 1944 to entertain wartime plant workers, the Huntridge was once owned by movie star Irene Dunne. The World War II international-style building also served the movers and shakers of the era. Silver-screen stars such as Frank Sinatra, Jane Russell and Vincent Price often turned up for premiers. Attorney General Frankie Sue Del Papa once was an usherette there.

Ice Plant Site
612 S. Main St.
Las Vegas, NV 89101
Built in 1908 to supply ice for the community and the railroad. It produced ice until 1983. The building was destroyed by fire in 1988.

Las Vegas Academy
315 S. Seventh St.
Las Vegas, NV 89101
This Art Deco structure, designed in 1931 by Reno architects George A. Ferris and Son, is Las Vegas' only example of this style. The elaborate detail carvings of flora and fauna, with the heroic figures over the portals, contribute to the beauty of this edifice. The neighborhood around the high school was named a historic district by the National Register of Historic Places. Name changed in 1993 when it became a magnet high school for performing visual arts and international studies.

Las Vegas Hospital
201 N. 8th St.
Las Vegas, NV 89101
This adobe structure, built in 1931, was used as a hospital into the 1960s. It was placed on the National Register of Historical Places in 1987, and was destroyed by fire in 1988.

Old Las Vegas Mormon Fort State Historical Park
908 Las Vegas Blvd. N.
Las Vegas, NV 89101
Phares Woods, Park Supervisor
The Old Fort is a remnant of the complex of adobe structures built by Mormon colonists in 1855. The story of the fort reflects the growth of Las Vegas as its economy changed from ranching to railroading to recreation.

Little Church of the West
4617 Las Vegas Blvd. S.
Las Vegas, NV 89119
739-7971

Victory Hotel, 307 S. Main St., Las Vegas, NV 89101

The Little Church of the West opened in 1942. It is listed because it is one of the earliest chapels and has a unique type of architecture.

Moulin Rouge
900 W. Bonanza Rd.
Las Vegas, NV 89106
648-4420
Las Vegas' first interracial casino opened in 1955 with national fanfare, only to close several months later.

Post Office/Federal Building
301 E. Stewart Ave.
Las Vegas, NV 89101
This 20th century neoclassical structure was completed in 1933 as part of the Hoover administration's massive building program and was used until 1967, when the current federal building was erected. Originally housing the U.S. District Courts, the building now is occupied principally by the Post Office. Original cost of the entire building in 1931 was $220,553.

Railroad Cottages
200-400 block of Clark and Garces Ave.
The 7 bungalow-style cottages represent a remnant of Las Vegas' first subdivision built between 1909 and 1911. The original 64 cottages were built to house the railroad workers. Listed on the National Register of Historic Places.

J. D. Smith House
624 S. 6th St.
Las Vegas, NV 89101
Civic leader and dentist Dr. J. D. Smith built this showplace home in 1932. Designed by architects Nordstrom and Warner, the completion of the house was featured in full-page newspaper ads. The home has been restored by the Smith family for use as professional offices.

Twin Lakes Resort
3333 W. Washington Ave.
Las Vegas, NV 89107
Now Lorenzi Park, some of the buildings, like the ones that house the Las Vegas Art Museum, still exist. The resort was built in the 1940s.

Victory Hotel
307 S. Main St.
Las Vegas, NV 89101
384-0260
The mission-style Victory Hotel was built in 1910 and was known then as the Lincoln Hotel. Las Vegas' oldest remaining hotel was built to house railroad passengers and employees. The hotel is eligible for the National Register of Historic Places.

Frank Wait House
900 block of Ogden Ave.
Frank Wait, an early police officer, began building his stone house in 1930. He and his wife spent the next 10 years searching the surrounding desert for the petrified wood, fossils and quartz pieces that form the walls and stone chimney. The house was finished in 1940. His picture is still embedded in a piece of clear quartz on one of the outside walls. *(Private residence)*

Wengert House
600 E. Charleston Blvd.
Las Vegas, NV 89104
This Tudor-Revival residence was built in 1936 by civic leader Cyril Wengert. It has been restored and houses law offices.

Westside School
300 W. Washington Ave.
Las Vegas, NV 89106
This lovely Mission-style school was constructed in 1922 for the children of Old Town, the original townsite on the other side of the railroad tracks. The building was restored with federal funds and is now a community center of West Las Vegas.

Steven R. Whitehead House
333 N. 7th St.
Las Vegas, NV 89101
Designed by A. L. Worswick, this Mission-style residence was constructed in 1929. It has had several alterations, but they have been in keeping with the original design.

LIBRARIES

The Las Vegas-Clark County Library District serves the public with 11 urban and rural libraries. Nine new building projects and $10 million for books were approved by voters in the $80 million bond issue in 1991. The West Charleston and Summerlin Libraries opened in January and August 1993, respectively. In 1994, the Rainbow Library opened in March; Laughlin Library opened in April; Whitney Library opened in June; Clark County Library opened in November. The West Las Vegas Library Theatre opened in June 1995. Sahara West Library broke ground in April 1995. The Enterprise Library, last of the bond issue buildings, broke ground in the Spring and was completed in 1996.

Of the 14 Las Vegas area libraries, including the Henderson Library, Boulder City Library and UNLV's James Dickerson Library, most can accommodate cultural events, concerts, lectures, forums and seminars, art exhibits and displays.

The Library District has 2.2 million items in its collection with emphasis in areas such as foundation and grants, career and job, medical and health services, consumer interest, Southwest region, Nevada and Las Vegas, bilingual and Spanish language materials, an African American collection, large-print books and books on tape. Thirty-five percent of the total collection is for young people. Information is presented by the library district in various formats, including print, CDs, audio and video cassettes and CD-ROM. In fiscal year 1996-97, the district spent approximately $3,785,514 on books and information materials.

Finding what you want or need has been aided by the use of computers and on-line databases. Some libraries house special collections and most have active young people's department. Libraries provide access to computers, typewriters and copy machines. Available for check-out are books, videos, CDs and tapes. A library card is issued free of charge. Picture identification with current address is requested. Cards may be obtained and used at any library in Nevada.

The Library District publishes the quarterly *Off the Shelf* with library news and calendar of events and exhibits, upcoming concerts, talking books, art exhibits, lectures and films. Most programs are free of charge. During 1996 more than 140,878 persons attended 3,683 young people's programs. **Loan periods:** All materials, 3 weeks, major motion pictures on video, 3 days. **Overdue Charges:** There are no overdue charges for paperback books, magazines or children's books. Overdue charges are .25 cents per day with a $4 per item maximum. To replace lost or stolen library cards, $1. To reserve an item, $1. Call the library hotline for more information: 382-7919.
(Boulder City, Henderson and North Las Vegas have their own library districts.)

Las Vegas-Clark County Library District
Library Hours: Mon. - Thu. 9 am - 9 pm; Fri. - Sat. 9 am - 5 pm; Sun. 1 pm - 5 pm

Photo: Phototechnik International

Green Valley Library
2797 N. Green Valley Pkwy.
Henderson, NV 89014

Las Vegas Library
Library District Headquarters
833 Las Vegas Blvd. N.
Las Vegas, NV 89101
382-3493
Darrell Batson, Library Dist. Dir.
Mary Lou Wigley, Library Adm.
Library Hours: Mon. - Thu. 9 am - 9 pm; Fri. - Sat. 9 am - 5 pm; Sun. 1 pm - 5 pm

Microcomputer Lab
382-3493 Ext. 215
Hours: Mon. - Thu. 9 am - 9 pm, Sat. 9 am - 5 pm; Sun. 1 pm - 5 pm

Clark County Library
1401 E. Flamingo Rd.
Las Vegas, NV 89119
733-7810
Monteria Hightower, Library Adm.
Library Hours: Mon. - Thu. 9 am - 9 pm; Fri. - Sat. 9 am - 5 pm; Sun. 1 pm - 5 pm

Microcomputer Lab
733 - 1113
Hours: Mon. - Thu. 11 am - 8:45 pm; Fri. - Sat. 9 am - 4:45 pm; Sun. 1 pm - 4:45 pm

Talking Books Services
733-1925
Library Hours: Mon. - Thu. 9 am - 9 pm; Fri. - Sat. 9 am - 5 pm; Sun. 1 pm - 5 pm
Catalog with the latest acquisitions are sent periodically. Books are sent to and returned by patrons free through the mail.

Enterprise Library
25 E. Shelbourne Ave.
Las Vegas, NV 89123
269-3000
Judith Gray, Library Adm.
Library Hours: Mon. - Thu. 9 am - 9 pm; Fri. - Sat. 9 am - 5 pm; Sun. 1 pm - 5 pm
This 20,000 sq. ft. facility is known as a construction trade library with part of the ceiling left open to show pipes, ducts, etc.

Green Valley Library
2797 N. Green Valley Pkwy.
Henderson, NV 89014
435-1840
Sally Feldman, Library Adm.
Hours: Mon. - Thu. 9 am - 9 pm; Fri. - Sat. 9 am - 5 pm; Sun. 1 pm - 5 pm

Henderson Library
Lydia Malcolm Branch
80 N. Pecos Rd.
Henderson, NV 89014
263-7522
Zuki Landau, Library Dir.
Hours: Mon. - Thu. 9 am - 9 pm; Fri. - Sat. 9 am - 5 pm; Sun. noon - 4 pm
Opened September 30, 1995; 4,000 sq ft. full service library; programming room.

Rainbow Library
3150 N. Buffalo Rd.
Las Vegas, NV 89128
243-7323
Jane Lorance, Library Adm.
Hours: Mon. - Thu. 9 am - 9 pm; Fri. - Sat. 9 am - 5 pm; Sun. 1 pm - 5 pm
The 28,000 sq. ft. facility provides 100,000 items in its collection with 500 general interest magazine titles and 20 newspapers for browsing and circulation; young people's materials, including a separate section for young adults; numerous business directories and a health reference center on CD - ROM. HSA Architects designed the building featuring desert landscaping and a 500 capacity amphitheater, 160 capacity conference room and 12-seat meeting room.

Sahara West Library
9002 W. Sahara Ave.
Las Vegas, NV 89117
228-1940
Ann Langevin, Library Adm.
Hours: Mon. - Thu. 9 am - 9 pm; Fri. - Sat. 9 am - 5 pm; Sun. 1 pm - 5 pm
122,000 sq. ft. hub Sahara West Library was completed in 1997. The Nevada Museum of art operates a 30,000 sq. ft. exhibit space. There is a 220-seat multipurpose room.

Spring Valley Library
4280 S. Jones Blvd.
Las Vegas, NV 89103
368-4411
Beryl Andrus-Zundel, Library Adm.
Hours: Mon. - Thu. 9 am - 9 pm; Fri. - Sat. 9 am - 5 pm; Sun. 1 pm - 5 pm

Summerlin Library and Performing Arts Center
1771 Inner Circle Dr.
Las Vegas, NV 89134
256-5111
Richard Lee, Library Adm.
Hours: Mon. - Thu. 9 am - 9 pm; Fri. - Sat. 9 am - 5 pm; Sun. 1 pm - 5 pm
The 40,165 sq. ft. facility has a book capacity of 100,000 volumes, 150 periodical titles, a separate young people's library and story room, a gallery and a 291-seat performance theater with fly tower and proscenium stage. Designed by Robert Fielden and Associates, it is the center of a cultural hub in the community of Summerlin.

Sunrise Library
5400 Harris Ave.
Las Vegas, NV 89110
453-1104
Laura Golod, Library Adm.
Hours: Mon. - Thu. 9 am - 9 pm; Fri. - Sat. 9 am - 5 pm; Sun. 1 pm - 5 pm

West Charleston Library
6301 W. Charleston Blvd.
Las Vegas, NV 89102
878-3682
Maria Cuglietta, Library Adm.
Hours: Mon. - Thu. 9 am - 9 pm; Fri. - Sat. 9 am - 5 pm; Sun. 1 pm - 5 pm
The 38,900 sq. ft. library features a medical and health services special collection which correlates with the curriculum of the adjacent satellite branch of the Community College of Southern Nevada, donor of the library land site. The library, designed by Welles-Pugsley Architects, includes all library services, a collection capacity of 100,000 volumes; a 289-seat lecture hall, a gallery, conference room, quiet study and typewriter rooms.

> The first public library in Nevada opened in Reno in 1895.

West Las Vegas Library
951 W. Lake Mead Blvd.
Las Vegas, NV 89106
647-2117
Kelly Richards, Library Adm.
Hours: Mon. - Thu. 9 am - 9 pm; Fri. - Sat. 9 am - 5 pm; Sun. 1 pm - 5 pm
An 11,666 sq. ft. theater with 299 seats, adjacent to the 12,200 sq. ft. library, fulfills the cultural needs of the community.

Whitney Library
5175 E. Tropicana Ave.
Las Vegas, NV 89122
454-4575
Barbara Carey, Adm.
Hours: Mon. - Thu. 9 am - 9 pm; Fri. - Sat. 9 am - 5 pm; Sun. 1 pm - 5 pm
The 23,350 sq. ft. facility provides full library services, a book collection capacity of 120,000, a young people's library with computer area and story room, a 198-seat recital hall and a Southwest regional collection room.

NORTH LAS VEGAS

North Las Vegas District Library
2300 Civic Center Dr.
N. Las Vegas, NV 89030
633-1070
Anita Laruy, Library Adm.
Hours: Mon. 9 am - 6 pm; Tue. - Thu. 9 am - 9 pm; Fri. - Sat. 9 am - 6 pm

HENDERSON

Henderson District Public Library
280 Water St.
Henderson, NV 89015
565-8402
Zuki Landau, Dir.
Hours: Mon. - Thu. 9 am - 9 pm; Fri.- Sat. 9 am - 5 pm; Sun. noon - 4 pm

Pittman Branch Library
1608 Moser St.
Henderson, NV 89015
565-5816
Michelle Eagleson, Librarian
Hours: Mon. - Thu. 10 am - 6 pm

LIBRARIES

BOULDER CITY

Boulder City Library
813 Arizona St.
Boulder City, NV 89005
293-1281
Duncan R. McCoy, Library Dir.
Hours: Mon. - Thu. 9 am - 8:30 pm; Fri. 9 am - 5 pm; Sat. 11 am - 4 pm; Sun. 1 pm - 4 pm

Photo: Photetechnik International

OUTREACH LIBRARIES

Chester Stupak Community Center Library
300 W. Boston Ave.
Las Vegas, NV 89102
474-0023
Hours: Mon. - Thu. 4 pm - 8 pm; Sat. - Sun. 10 am - 3 pm
Homework center with circulating Spanish language books for both children and adults. Regularly scheduled story times for children in Spanish.

Salvation Army Day Center Library
33 W. Owens Ave.
N. Las Vegas, NV 89030
639-0277
Hours: 7:30 am - 11:30 am and 1 pm - 4:30 pm
Small reading library to serve the homeless. Non-circulating.

RURAL AREA LIBRARIES

Blue Diamond Branch Library
14 Cottonwood St.
Blue Diamond, NV 89004
875-4295
Tammy Dennison, Branch Mgr.
Hours: Tue. - Wed. 2 pm - 7 pm; Thu. 1 pm - 8 pm; Sat. 10 am - 1 pm

Bunkerville Branch Library
150 W. Virgin St.
Bunkerville, NV 89007
346-5238
Carolyn Leavitt, Library Ass.
Hours: Mon. 4 pm - 8 pm; Tue. - Thu. 1 pm - 5 pm; Sat. 9 am - 1 pm

Goodsprings Branch Library
365 W. San Pedro Ave.
Goodsprings, NV 89019
874-1366
Peggy Stephens, Branch Mgr.
Hours: Mon. - Thu. 3 pm - 7 pm; Sat. 10 a.m - 2 pm

Indian Springs Branch Library
715 Gretta Ln.
Indian Springs, NV 89018
879-3845
Dodie Patrick, Branch Mgr.
Hours: Tue. - Thu. 11 am - 7 pm; Sat. 9 am - 3 pm

Laughlin Branch Library
2840 S. Needles Hwy.
Laughlin, NV 89028
298-1081
Joyce Pipkin, Librarian
Hours: Mon., Wed. & Thu. 9 am - 6 pm; Tue. 9 am - 9 pm; Fri. & Sat. 9 am - 5 pm; Sun. 1 pm - 5 pm
30,000 sq. ft.; opened in April 1994.

Mesquite Branch Library
121 W. First North St.
Mesquite, NV 89024
346-5224
Geraldine Zarate, Branch Mgr.
Hours: Mon. & Wed. 12 noon - 8 pm; Tue. & Thu. 10 am - 6 pm; Fri. & Sat. 9 am - 5 pm

Moapa Town Branch Library
1340 E. Hwy 168
Moapa, NV 89025
864-2438
Lynn Wren, Branch Mgr.
Hours: Tue. - Wed. 1 pm - 5 pm; Thu. noon - 8 pm; Sat. 9 am - 1 pm

Moapa Valley Branch Library
350 N. Moapa Valley Blvd.
Overton, NV 89040
397-2690
Tonia Payne, Librarian
Hours: Mon. - Thu. noon - 8 pm; Fri. - Sat. 9 am - 5 pm

Mount Charleston Branch Library
1252 Aspen Ave.
Las Vegas, NV 89124
872-5585
Sandra Gibson, Branch Mgr.
Hours: Mon. - Tue. noon - 8 pm; Wed. - Thu. noon - 5 pm; Sat. 9 am - 3 pm

Sandy Valley Branch Library
650 W. Quartz Ave.
Sandy Valley, NV 89019
723-5333
Gwen Doty, Branch Mgr.
Hours: Mon. - Tue.; Sat. 1 pm - 5 pm; Wed. - Thu. 5 pm - 9 pm

Searchlight Branch Library
200 Michael Wendell Way
Searchlight, NV 89046
1-702-297-1442
Lynn Rhodes, Branch Mgr.
Hours: Tue. - Wed. 1 pm - 6 pm; Thu. 1 pm - 7 pm; Sat. 9 am - 1 pm

SPECIAL LIBRARIES

James R. Dickinson Library
University of Nevada Las Vegas
4505 S. Maryland Pkwy.
Las Vegas, NV 89154
895-3286
Kenneth E. Marks, Ph.D., Library Dean
Circulation: 895-3531
Reference: 895-3290
Government Documents: 895-3409
Special Collections: 895-3252
Hours: Hours vary with school: 895-3285, recorded hours and information
Serves the university and community with a collection of nearly 2 million items, from books to photographs. Anyone with a Las Vegas-Clark County Library District card and a Nevada drivers license with a Clark County address and a credit card can check out up to five items.

Bureau of Reclamation
Park & Boulder Hwy.
Boulder City, NV 89005
293-8000
Robert Johnson, Dir.
Hours: Mon. - Fri. 7:30 am - 4 pm
Public may use materials on premises. No charge-outs.

Clark County Law Library
304 E. Carson St.
Las Vegas, NV 89101
455-4696
Kevin Clanton, Director
Ann Jarrell, Ref. Librarian
Hours: Mon. - Fri. 8 am - 5:30 pm; Sat. 10 am - 5 pm
The Law Library serves as a depository for all legal material for southern Nevada. It maintains local ordinances, state statutes, federal laws, legal texts and encyclopedias, legal periodicals and case reports.

Lake Mead National Recreational Area Library
601 Nevada Hwy.
Boulder City, NV 89005
293-8907
Katherine Rohde, Chief of Interpretation
Hours: Mon. - Fri. 8:30 am - 4:30 pm

Las Vegas Family History Center
509 S. Ninth St.
Las Vegas, NV 89101
382-9695
Deon J Sanders, Dir.
Church of Jesus Christ Latter Day Saints
Hours: Tue. - Sat. 9 am - 6 pm

Nellis Air Force Base Library
554 SVS/SVRL Nellis Air Force Base
4311 N. Washington Blvd.
Las Vegas, NV 89191-7064
652-4484
Sharron Cooper, Dir.
Hours: Mon. - Thu. 10 am - 8 pm; Fri. - Sun. 10 am - 6 pm

Nevada State Library and Archives
Capitol Complex
401 North Carson
Carson City, NV 89710
687-5160 800-922-2880

Library District Stats:
12 urban library branches
11 rural library branches
2 outreachlibraries
2,027,685 items in the collection
5,013,074 items circulated

140,879 persons attended 3,683 young peoples library programs

877,970 library card holders
517,966 active library card holders

15 art galleries
2 museums, Lied and Las Vegas Museum in Sahara West Library

Rainbow Library, 3150 N. Buffalo Rd., Las Vegas, NV 89128

MUSEUMS

Marjorie Barrick Museum of Natural History
University of Nevada, Las Vegas
4505 S. Maryland Pkwy.
Las Vegas, NV 89154
895-3381
Donald Baepler, Dir.
Aurora Giguet, Curator
Hours: Mon. - Fri. 7:45 am - 4:45 pm;
Sat. 10 am - 2 pm
Admission: Free
Exhibits of real desert animals; archeology, anthropology and natural history of Nevada and the Southwest; Smithsonian traveling exhibits; Native American crafts. Student art exhibits also on display. Gift shop with Native American and nature items. Located next to the museum is a 2-acre garden featuring desert plants.

Boulder City - Hoover Dam Museum
444 Hotel Plaza St.
Boulder City, NV 89005
294-1988
Pat Lappin, Curator
Hours: 10 am - 4 pm
Established for the preservation of historical artifacts relating to the workers and construction of the Hoover Dam. Free 28-minute movie screenings of "The Construction of Hoover Dam." Admission by donation; gift shop.

Bruno's Indian and Turquoise Museum
1306 Nevada Hwy.
Boulder City, NV 89005
293-4865
Steven Liguori, Owner
Hours: 9 am - 6 pm
Admission: Free
A history of native American people and educating the public about mineralogy. A unique museum which offers historic detailing regarding mining and jewelry making. A trading post and gallery are also on site.

Clark County Heritage Museum
1830 S. Boulder Hwy.
Henderson, NV 89015
455-7955
Mark Ryzdynski, Head Adm.
Hours: 9 am - 4:30 pm
Admission: adults $1.50; seniors and children $1
Located in Henderson on a 25-acre site, the Clark County Heritage Museum features regional memorabilia, historic structures and artifacts. The 8,000 sq. ft. exhibit center features regularly changing exhibits that tell the story of southern Nevada from prehistoric times through the 20th century. Heritage St. features homes relocated to the museum from area locations, which were restored to recreate the lifestyles of important periods. Railroad cars with the original Boulder City train depot are featured in a special display along with an 1880s era ghost town.

Las Vegas Natural History Museum, 900 Las Vegas Blvd. N., Las Vegas, NV 89101

Debbie Reynolds' Hollywood Movie Museum
305 Convention Center Dr.
Las Vegas, NV 89109
733-2243
Michael Rennie, Curator
Tour Hours: Hourly Mon. - Fri. 10 am - 10 pm; Sat - Sun. 11 am - 4 pm
Admission: $7.95 per person
Movie costumes and props from Debbie Reynolds' vast collection on display. Film clips dating back from the silent era to the 1960s serve as a backdrop to the revolving display. World's largest private collection. Multimedia extravaganza featuring wide screen film clips and surround sound.

Desert Valley Museum
31 W. Mesquite Blvd.
Mesquite, NV 89024
346-5705
Verde Hughes, Curator
Hours: Mon. - Sat. 8 am - 5 pm
Admission: Free
Contributions by locals. Pioneer vintage quilts, wedding dresses, feather pillows, old telephones, old movie projectors, numerous handmade items.

Gallery of History
3601 W. Sahara Ave.
Las Vegas, NV 89102
731-2300
Todd M. Axelrod, Pres.
Hours: Mon. - Fri. 8 am - 5 pm
Historical documents, letters, manuscripts, photographs and signatures of famous people who shaped the world. Prices range from $200 to over $100,000.

Guinness World of Records Museum
2780 Las Vegas Blvd. S.
Las Vegas, NV 89109
792-3766
Information: 792-0640
Oli Manlet, Gen. Mgr.
Hours: 9 am - 6 pm
Admission: adults $4.95; seniors, students, military $3.95; children 12 and under $2.95; children to 4 years free
Las Vegas' greatest three-dimensional display of all that is superlative around the globe. The museum is imaginatively divided into six "worlds," bringing the Guinness Book of World Records vividly to life. The 5,200 sq. ft. museum has exhibits, displays, rare videos, artifacts and computerized data banks.

Imperial Palace Auto Collection
Imperial Palace Hotel & Casino
3535 Las Vegas Blvd. S.
Las Vegas, NV 89109
794-3174
Richie Clyne, Adm.
Hours: 9:30 am - 11:30 pm
Admission: Adults - $6.95; children under 12 - $3; under 3 years free.
Over 200 antique, classic and special interest automobiles on display from the 750 vehicle collection. Vehicles are constantly rotated from storage and nationwide tours to give the Auto Collection a fresh appeal for repeat visitors. The cars are displayed in a plush gallery-like setting located on the fifth floor of the hotel's parking facility. See Hitler's 1939 MercedesBenz, W.C. Fields' 1938 Cadillac limo, and JFK's 1962 "Bubbletop" limo and a whole room devoted to Duesenbergs. The Auto Collection features a gift shop, which contains a wide variety of automobile memorabilia and books.

Las Vegas Art Museum
4600 W. Sahara Ave.
Las Vegas, NV 89117
360-8000
Joe Palermo, Pres.
Dr. James Mann, Curator
Hours: Tue. - Sat. 10 am - 3 pm; Sun. noon - 3 pm
Admission: $3, under 12 years free, $2 for seniors and $1 for students. Docent available for 3 or more.
Exhibits in three galleries change monthly. Museum gift shops sells art at reasonable prices.

Las Vegas Natural History Museum
900 Las Vegas Blvd. N.
Las Vegas, NV 89101
384 - 3466
Marilyn Gillespie, Dir.
Hours: 9 am - 4 pm
Admission: Adults $5; seniors, military & students $4; children 4 - 12 $2.50; under 4 years free
Seven models of prehistoric dinosaurs growl from above while a robotic exhibit demonstrates how they moved their arms, legs and mouths. Extensive wildlife art gallery includes award winning wood sculptures. Over 300 modern-day animals, bat flights room, 300 gallon shark tank and shark display, a large wildlife art collection, a children's hands-on room, a world wildlife room and a gift shop.

Las Vegas Neon Museum
Howard Scholes, Dir. Collections
The Neon Museum is scheduled to open soon, showing Las Vegas history through neon. Young Electric Signs has pledged to give the city 27 signs. The city also has some that are in storage for the museum.

Liberace Museum
1775 E. Tropicana Ave.
Las Vegas, NV 89119
798-5595
Myron Martin, Adm.
Hours: Mon. - Sat. 10 am - 5 pm; Sun. 1 pm - 5 pm
Admission: Adults $6.95; seniors $4.50; students $3.50; children under 12 $2.
Displays of custom automobiles, rare and antique pianos, the famous Liberace wardrobe, the world's largest rhinestone and other memorabilia. Admission donations go to the Liberace Foundation for the Performing and Creative Arts which funds scholarships and awards grants to colleges across the nation; gift shop.

McCarran International Airport
Aviation Heritage Exhibit
Located over the baggage claim area, the exhibit features 6 kiosks containing photographs, artifacts and memorabilia donated by families of the pioneers of local aviation. Within a year the display is expected to expand to 30 kiosks.

Liberace Museum, 1775 E. Tropicana Ave., Las Vegas, NV 89119

Lied Discovery Children's Museum, 833 Las Vegas Blvd. N., Las Vegas, NV 89101

Lied Discovery Children's Museum
833 Las Vegas Blvd. N.
Las Vegas Library
Las Vegas, NV 89101
382-3445
Suzanne LeBlanc, Dir.
Workshops Hotline: 382-KIDS
Hours: Tue. - Sat. 10 am - 5 pm; Sun. noon - 5 pm; Closed Mon. except for federal holidays
Admission: Adults $5; seniors, students, military with ID $4; children 3 - 11 $3; under 3 years free. School groups of 10 or more $1. Tour groups $2.50 per person.
A private, non-profit children's museum designed to provide enjoyable learning experiences, this 22,000 sq. ft. $2 million hands on museum has 130 hands-on exhibits devoted to science, humanities and the arts. The exhibits, designed for children 8 and older, include a newspaper newsroom, a radio and television studio and many others devoted to science and technology. Workshops, performances and demonstrations are scheduled throughout the year and are designed for children of all ages. Toddler Towers located on the first floor is for children under 8 years. Gift shop, birthday room, group tours, snack bar, museum rentals, located at the library.

Lost City Museum of Archeology
721 S. Moapa Valley Blvd.
Overton, NV 89040
(60 miles NE of Las Vegas)
397-2193
Kathryne Olson, Curator
Hours: 8:30 am - 4:30 pm
Admission: 18 years and over $2.
Exhibits interpret the span of human occupation in southern Nevada beginning 12,000 years ago and continuing through the white settlers. One of the most complete collections of early Pueblo Indian artifacts in the Southwest including a full-scale reconstruction of a Pueblo village. Other exhibits relate to the Mormon farmers who first settled the Moapa Valley in 1855. Changing art exhibits.

Magic and Movie Hall of Fame
3555 Las Vegas Blvd. S.
(O'Sheas Casino)
Las Vegas, NV 89109
737-1343
Valentine Vox, Gen. Mgr.
Hours: Tue. - Sat. 10 am - 6 pm
Admission: Adults $4.95; children 12 and under $3
Over 20,000 sq. ft. and over 120 exhibits of magic, movie and ventriloquist memorabilia. Live magic and illusions are presented. "It's Magic" appears in the Houdini Theatre at 11:30 am, 1:30, 3 & 4:30 pm

Nevada State Museum & Historical Society
700 Twin Lakes Dr.
Lorenzi Park
Las Vegas, NV 89107
486-5205
Shirl Naegle, Dir.
Hours: 9 am - 5 pm
Admission: Adults $2.00; children under 18 free
Permanent exhibits highlight the history, natural history, and Native American cultures of the region and a schedule of changing exhibits features art, history and science. The Cahlan Library is open weekdays for those interested in Nevada history and for research; museum gift shop. This 35,000 sq. ft. facility opened in 1982.

Old Las Vegas Mormon Fort State Historic Park
908 Las Vegas Blvd. N.
Las Vegas Blvd. & Washington Ave.
(enter Cashman Field north entrance)
Las Vegas, NV 89101
486-3511
Phares Woods, Pk. Super.
Hours: 8:30 am - 3:30 pm
Admission: Free
The fort was built by Mormon settlers in 1855. Las Vegas' oldest building was purchased by the state from the city in 1990 for $300,000 to preserve it as a state park. Visitors to the Park will see only a remnant of the original structures.

Riverside Resort Hotel and Casino Auto Exhibition Hall
1650 Casino Dr.
Laughlin, NV 89029
298-2535
Mark Osborn, Curator
Hours: Sun. - Thu. 9 am - 10 pm; Fri. - Sat. 9 am - 11 pm
Admission: Free
34,000 sq. ft., featuring over 70 antique, classic and sports cars as well as a number of antique motorcycles. The oldest car on display is an 1886 Benz Replica.

Searchlight Museum
200 Michael Wendell Way
Searchlight, NV 89046
297-1682
Mark Ryzdynski, Head Adm.
Hours: Mon. - Fri. 9 am - 5 pm; Sat. 9 am - 1 pm
Admission: Free
The Searchlight Museum, which is a satellite of the Clark County Heritage Museum, reports the rich history of Searchlight, a prosperous mining town at the turn of the century. Housed in the Searchlight Community Center.

Nevada State Museum & Historical Society, 700 Twin Lakes Dr., Lorenzi Park, Las Vegas, NV 89107

MUSIC

Brown Bag Concerts
The Performing Arts Society of NV
6301 Machalite Bay Ave.
Las Vegas, NV 89130
658-6741
John Meren & Tom Gallagher, Co-founders
Concerts every Mon. at the Debbie Reynolds Celebrity Cafe with luncheon. Concert at Sun City once a month, residents and invited guests.
Admission: Varies
Reservations: 658-6741
Sponsors escorted tours to concerts out of the Las Vegas area with transportation, room and concert tickets all included. The Performing Arts Society of Nevada is composed of three branches: Brown Bag Concerts, Las Vegas Lyric Opera and National Globe Theatre.

Charles Vanda Master Series
UNLV Performing Arts Center
4505 S. Maryland Pkwy
Las Vegas, NV 89154
895-3535
Information: 895-3801
Jeff Koep, Dean College of Fine Arts
Founded in 1976 by the late Charles Vanda to bring classical and performing artists from all over the world to Las Vegas. All performances in the Artemus W. Ham Concert Hall at 8 pm.
Individual tickets: $4 to $62.25

Community College of Southern Nevada
3200 E. Cheyenne Ave.
N. Las Vegas, NV 89030
651-4002
Dr. Tom Ferguson
Musical concerts are presented from time to time on campus as funds and artists are available.

Henderson Civic Symphony Orchestra
Valley View Recreation Center
500 Harris St.
Henderson, NV 89015
565-2121

Brad Pfiel, Conductor
Sponsored by the Henderson Parks and Recreation Department, the Henderson Civic Symphony is a 50-member orchestra in its 11th season.

Las Vegas Civic Symphony
821 Las Vegas Blvd. N.
Las Vegas, NV 89101
229-6211
Al Lewis, Conductor
Founded in 1974 by the City of Las Vegas. Membership is from local student and adult musicians. All performances are free of charge.

Las Vegas Lyric Opera
The Performing Arts Society of NV
6301 Malachite Bay Ave.
Las Vegas, NV 89130
658-6741
John Meren & Tom Gallagher, Co-founders
Periodic Concerts and operas at the Clark County Library
Admission: Varies
Reservations: 658-6741
Sponsors escorted tours to concerts out of the Las Vegas area with transportation, room and concert tickets all included. The Performing Arts Society of Nevada is composed of three branches: Las Vegas Lyric Opera, National Globe Theatre and Brown Bag Concerts.

Las Vegas Music Teachers Association
5012 Churchill Ave.
Las Vegas, NV 89107
877-1743
Refers to teachers for piano, organ, voice, flute, violin, cello, harp and guitar.

Las Vegas Youth Orchestra
2832 E. Flamingo Rd.
Las Vegas, NV 89121
385-8948
Karl Reinarz, Dir.
85-member youth orchestra formed in 1976. Students audition in the spring for

positions. The advanced orchestra under the direction of Karl Reinarz performs four or five times a year and the intermediate orchestra is under the direction of John Sullivan. Season runs from Sept. to May.
The orchestra is sponsored by the City of Las Vegas Cultural and Community Affairs Division and the Clark County School District.
Tickets: Adults $4; students, seniors and handicapped $3

National Globe Theatre
6301 Malachite Bay Ave.
Las Vegas, NV 89130
John Meren & Tom Gallagher, Co-founders
Periodic plays and musicals. Prices vary. Shows at Clark County Library Theatre and Winchester Community Theater.

Nevada Chamber Symphony
2229 Marlboro Dr.
Henderson, NV 89014
433-9280
Peggy Trasatti, Chairman
Founded in 1985 as the Serenata Chamber Orchestra. Featuring both instrumental and vocal soloists, the symphony is led by Conductor Rodolfo Fernandez. Nevada Chamber Symphony performs an indoor season Oct. through May and an outdoor season June through Aug. Concerts are held at the Clark County Library and Henderson Civic Center sponsored by the Clark County Library and Summerlin Hills Park. Concerts are on Sun. at 3 pm and are free but tickets are required. For further information and to confirm location, call 433-9280.

Nevada Opera Theatre
4080 Paradise Rd., Ste. 15
Las Vegas, NV 89109
699-9775
Tickets: 451-6331
Eileen Hayes, Gen. Dir.

12th Anniversary Season
Performs three productions a year, in addition to approximately 30 dates a year for civic and community organizations. All main stage productions are performed at the Artemus Ham Concert Hall on the UNLV campus, Clark County library and Summerlin Hills Park.
Individual Ticket Prices: $8 - $25, available at the Performing Arts Box Office at UNLV.

Nevada School of the Arts
(Also listed under Arts Organizations and Art Classes)
315 S. 7th St.
Las Vegas, NV 89101
386-2787
Dr. Paul Hesselink, Dean
Provides instruction in fine music arts to all ages and abilities. Founded in 1977, NSA is a local, non-profit organization and is supported by a grant from the Nevada State Council on the Arts and the National Endowment for the Arts. NSA will reach nearly 400 students per semester, from age 3 to adult, with a faculty of 50 during the 1997-98 season. NSA offers both private and class instruction.

Nevada Symphony Orchestra
557 E. Sahara Ave., Ste. 211
Las Vegas, NV 89104
792-4337
Janice Tanno, Pres. & C.O.B.
Nevada Symphony Orchestra, in its 18th season, is a 65 to 100-member symphony with concerts held at Artemus W. Ham Concert Hall. Outdoor pop concerts, usually 4, are held at Hills Park, Summerlin.
Admission: Tickets to individual performances $15 for general admission and $45 for reserved cabaret seat *(includes buffet)* through TicketMasters. Special group rates.

Las Vegas Youth Orchestra, 2832 E. Flamingo Rd., Las Vegas, NV 89121

Nevada Symphony Orchestra, 557 E. Sahara Ave., Ste. 211, Las Vegas, NV 89104

Performing Arts Box Office.
The Southern Nevada Musical Arts Society is a non-profit community organization founded in 1963 encompassing the Musical Arts Orchestra *(fine local professionals),* the Musical Arts Chorus *(a group of about 80 members)* and the Musical Arts Singers *(a select group of 22 semi-professionals)* under the direction of Dr. Douglas R. Peterson. These groups perform not only at the Artemus Ham Hall at UNLV but also at CCSN, Reed Whipple and Clark County Flamingo library.

UNLV · Department of Music
4505 Maryland Pkwy.
Las Vegas, NV 89154
895-3332
Paul Kreider, Chairman
Courses in music are offered in the fields of education, performance, and composition. The Music Department's sponsored events series include the Student Recital Series, the Student Ensemble Series, the Sponsored Events Series and the Faculty Recital Series. Listed are the Jazz Ensemble, UNLV Opera Theatre schedules and the Wind Symphony.

UNLV Choral Ensembles
895-3008
University Chorus, the Chamber Chorale, the Varsity Men's Glee Club and the Women's Chorus are all part of UNLV's choral ensembles. All concerts are presented at Artemus Ham Concert Hall on the UNLV campus.

Winchester Community Center
3130 S. McLeod Dr.
Las Vegas, NV 89121
455-7340
Operated by the Clark County Parks & Recreation Department

The Performing Arts Society of Nevada
6301 Malachite Bay Ave.
Las Vegas, NV 89130
658-6741
John Meren & Tom Gallagher, Co-founders
The Performing Arts Society is comprised of the Las Vegas Lyric Opera Company, the National Globe Theatre and Brown Bag Concerts.

Reed Whipple Cultural Center
821 Las Vegas Blvd. N.
Las Vegas, NV 89101
229-6211

Sierra Winds
UNLV
4505 S. Maryland Pkwy.
Las Vegas, NV 89154
895-3332

Stephen Caplan, Dir.
Founded in 1982 and named by Jan Laverty Jones in a city proclamation as Culture Ambassador for the City of Las Vegas. The group is one of the nation's top chamber music ensembles. For two consecutive years has been chosen by the *Review-Journal* as the #1 fine arts performance group.
Admission: Adults $30; seniors, students and military $22. Tickets for individual events will be available for $10; seniors and students $8

Southern Nevada Community Concert Association
1620 Stonehaven Dr.
Las Vegas, NV 89108-2014
Information: 895-3801
Agnes Capps, Pres.
Membership: 648-8962
Admission: Adults $40; students $15

Works with Columbia Artists to bring a diversity of outstanding talent to Las Vegas, one of the most prominent being the New York Theatre Ballet. Season runs from Oct. to April. All performances take place at UNLV's Artemus Ham Hall and begin at 8 pm.

Southern Nevada Musical Arts Society
3950 Springhill Ave.
Las Vegas, NV 89121
451-6672
UNLV Box Office: 895-3801
UNLV Music Dept.: 895-3332
Dr. Douglas Peterson, Music Dir.
Membership Fee: Adults $35; seniors, students, military, handicapped $25
Individual performances: Adults $10; seniors, students, military, handicapped $7. Tickets available at UNLV

JAZZ

The Bank Club
1930 E. Fremont St.
Las Vegas, NV 89101
474-9262
Live jazz on Fri. & Sat. 7 pm - 11:30 pm

Cafe Sensations
4350 E. Sunset Rd.
Henderson, NV 89014
456-7803
Various artists 8:30 pm - 11:30 pm

Cappozolli's
3333 S. Maryland Pkwy.
Las Vegas, NV 89109
731-5311
Fri. - Sat. 11 pm - 4 am, Sun. - Mon. 10 pm - 4 am

KUNV · 91.5 FM
Jazz music
Call the KUNV concert hotline at 895-FM91 for up-to-date on all jazz, including concerts and lounges.

Gold Coast
4000 W. Flamingo Rd.
Las Vegas. NV 89103
367-7111
Sorta Dixie Jazz Band, noon - 6 pm in the East Lounge.

Las Vegas Jazz Society
P.O. Box 60396
Las Vegas, NV 89106
269-3374
Art Goldberg, Pres.
Non-profit organization dedicated to the support, encouragement and presentation of live jazz in southern Nevada. Publishes "The Jazz Note," a newsletter which is a source of information.

Le Bistro Lounge
(Riveria Hotel)
2901 Las Vegas Blvd. S.
Las Vegas, NV 89103
734-5110
Mon. at 9 pm; hosted by Don Menza

Manhattan of Las Vegas
2600 E. Flamingo Road
Las Vegas, NV 89121
737-5000
Marv Kovel All-Stars, Sun. 5:30 pm - 9:30 pm

North Beach Cafe
2605 S. Decatur Blvd.
Las Vegas, NV 89102
Bruce Westcott, piano, Wed. - Sun. 6 pm

Paradise Bistro
3900 Paradise Rd.
Las Vegas, NV 89109
Frank Leone, Tue. - Sat. 7 pm - 11pm

Play It Again Sam
4120 Spring Mountain Rd.
Las Vegas, NV 89102
876-1550
Kathy Lamar, Wed. - Sun. 9 pm - 2 am

Pogo's Lounge
2103 N. Decatur Blvd.
Las Vegas, NV 89108
646-9735
Live jazz Friday beginning at 9 pm, jam sessions. Irv Kluger & the All-Star Band

Riviera Hotel
2901 las Vegas Blvd. S.
Las Vegas, NV 89109
Jazz on the Strip with the Don Menza Quartet & Special Guests, Mon. 9 pm & 11 pm
Lon Bronson's All-Star Band, Mon. & Sat. 1:30 am

Ruth's Chris Steak House
4561 W. Flamingo Rd.
Las Vegas, NV 89103
Joe Darro Trio, Wed. - Sat., 10 pm - 2 am

Santa Fe Hotel Casino
4949 N. Rancho Dr.
Las Vegas, NV 89130
658-4900
The Jazz Brunch with the Jazz Organization in the Pavilion every Sun. noon - 3:30 pm; Fri. - Sat. 5 pm - 9 pm the Mike Breene Trio

DANCE

Academy of Nevada Dance Theatre
4850 Harrison Dr.
Las Vegas, NV 89121
898-6306
Bruce Steivel, Dir.
Official school of the Nevada Dance Theatre. Offers jazz, tap, pre-ballet and ballet for ages 3 through adult and professional. Fees begin at $36 a month depending on the number of classes taken.

American Dance Company
2188 E. Desert Inn Rd. Suite 10
Las Vegas, NV 89109
735-9181
1-888-298-2998
Linda deBecker Shoemaker, Pres.
A non-profit corporation that provides talented young artists the opportunity to perform professionally. American Dance Company is comprised of dancers age 15 years and up. The company's productions will be based on American Events, educating our audiences through dance.

Community College of Southern Nevada
3200 E. Cheyenne Ave.
N. Las Vegas, NV 89030
651-4006
Kelly Roth, Dir. Dance
Classes in jazz, ballet, ballroom and tap dancing will be taught by professional dancers and choreographers. The college also offers non-credit classes and activities in a variety of areas and subjects. Call the Division of Community Education at 651-4057.

Fern Adair Conservatory of the Arts
3265 E. Patrick Ln.
Las Vegas, NV 89120
458-7575
Fern Adair, Pres., Art. Dir.
Dance conservatory, annual concert, summer camp, karate, theater & gymnastics

Kirov Ballet

Las Vegas Civic Ballet Association
P.O. Box 159
Las Vegas, NV 89125
229-6211
Aurora Jesus, Pres.
Founded in 1981 by Jeanne Roberts and the Las Vegas City Cultural and Community Affair Division to provide young Las Vegas dancers between the ages of 10 and 23 years with a program designed to bridge the gap between dance auditions and concerts. The youth company utilizes professional dancers and choreographers as guest artists. Performances are held twice a year at the Reed Whipple Cultural Center.
Tickets: General admission $5; Students, seniors and disabled $3; children $2. Tickets are available at Reed Whipple.

The Las Vegas Dance Theatre Studio
3248 Civic Center Dr.
N. Las Vegas, NV 89030
649-3932
Dance studio; beginner to professional, children to adult; tap, ballet, and jazz.

Merluzzi Dance Theatre
1137 S. Rainbow Blvd.
Las Vegas, NV 89102
254-6712
Christine Merluzzi
Tap, ballet, jazz and gymnastics. Children mornings and afternoons; adults evenings.

Nevada Dance Theatre
1555 E. Flamingo Rd., Ste. 112
Las Vegas, NV 89119
732-3838
Bruce Steivel, Art. Dir.
Founded in 1972, Nevada Dance

Theatre is Nevada's only professional ballet company presenting both classical and contemporary ballet performances. Four programs are offered each season, September to May, including "The Nutcracker" in December, plus galas and the Black & White ball, the highlight of the social season. All performances are held at UNLV Performing Arts Center. Season subscriptions and single tickets plus children, senior, group discounts are available.
Thu. - Fri. performances 8 pm; Sat. performances 2 pm and 8 pm Sun. performances 2 pm and 7 pm
Tickets available through the UNLV Performing Arts Box Office: 895-3801.
1998 Season

Simba Jambalaya Dance Theater
1953 N. Decatur Blvd.
Mailbox 331
Las Vegas, NV 89108
647-8808
LaVerne Ligon, Exec. Dir.
Dance classes for ages 3 through adult professionals in ballet, jazz, tap, African and hip hop.

Department of Dance Arts (UNLV)
University Dance Department
4505 S. Maryland Pkwy
Las Vegas, NV 89154
895-3827
Louis Kavouras, Chairman Dance Arts Dept.
Provides theoretical and technical preparation in ballet, modern, jazz and other dance forms. Specialization may be directed toward performance and choreography or toward general dance studies and teaching. Performances held in UNLV's Alta Fine Arts Building, Studio One.
Tickets: General admission $8; seniors and students $5

FILM

Charleston Heights Arts Center
City of Las Vegas Cultural and
Community Affairs Division
800 S. Brush St.
Las Vegas, NV 89107
229-6383
Admission: $2.00
Presents a variety of films, such as
dance and musical films and documen-
taries and international films, through-
out the year. All films begin at 7:30 pm
Call for a free detailed film brochure.

**Jaycee Park Family Film
Festival**
Jaycee Park
St. Louis & Eastern Ave.
Las Vegas, NV 89104
229-6211
Free weekly festival presented Thu. at 8
pm during July and Aug. outdoors at the
park.

**Las Vegas-Clark County Library
District**
Film series shown at most branches
throughout the year. Call your local
branch. Admission is free.

The International Film Series
UNLV
Dr. Hart Wegner, Dir. Film Studies each
Thu. 7 pm, Room A106 in the classroom
building complex. Free, open to the pub-
lic. Call 895-3547 for mailing list.

Winchester Community Center
3130 S. McLeod Dr.
Las Vegas, NV 89121
455-7340
Patrick Gaffey, Cult. Specialist
Admission: $2
Films presented by the Cultural
Division of Clark County Parks and
Recreation Department.

THEATRE

Rainbow Company Theatre, 821 Las Vegas Blvd. N., Las Vegas, NV 89101

Acting Achievements Studio
1612 Metropolitan St.
Las Vegas, NV 89102
877-6654
Lorie Noble, Dir.
Acting studio - individual instruction

Actors Repertory Theatre
1824 Palo Alto Circle
Las Vegas, NV 89108
647-7469
Georgia Neu, Art. Dir.
Formed in 1987, the group will produce
plays at the new Summerlin Library and
Performing Arts Center. This season there
will be seven shows. Price for six shows $87,
for seven shows $96. For seniors and stu-
dents, six shows are $75 and seven
shows are $84. Individual tickets are
$12.50-$22.
Tickets: Regular season subscription
$42; Seniors $34. Individual performances: $15 for matinee and $20 for
Sat. performances. Children and
seniors $12.50 and $15
Show times: Fri. 8 pm; Sat. 2 pm and 8
pm; Sun. 2 pm
1998 Fall Season:
Oct.: The Compleat Works of Wllm
Shkspr (abridged)
Dec.: ART's Version of A Christmas
Carol
All presented at Summerlin

Creative Talent
900 E. Karen Ave., Ste. D 116
Las Vegas, NV 89109
737-0611
Carl & Marge Butto, Art. Dirs. & Pres.

Production company for Off-Broadway
theater. Now in its 5th season presents
five shows annually.

Charles Vanda Master Series
(see Music)

**Community College of
Southern Nevada Dept. of
Theatre**
Nicholas J. Horn Theatre
3200 E. Cheyenne Ave.
N. Las Vegas, NV 89030
651-5483
Wendy Riggs, Art. Dir.

Jade Productions
P. O. Box 94802
Las Vegas, NV 89193-4802
263-6385
Joy Demain, Pres.
Non-profit theatre company creates
high quality working experiences for
performers, musicians, directors and
technicians who love to work in live theatrical endeavors.

**Joe Behar's Community Drama
Workshop**
457-0234
Joe Behar, Dir.
Meets Mon. 8 pm, Sam's Town, 5111
Boulder Hwy., for drama workshop at no
cost.

Las Vegas Little Theatre
3844 Schiff Dr.
Las Vegas, NV 89103
362-7996
Paul & Sue Thornton

Las Vegas Little Theatre is a non-profit
theater, now in its 19th season, that
produces five comedies from Sept.
through May. Performances held at the
Spring Valley Library.
Tickets: For information call theaere.
Individual performances: General admission $10; students and seniors $9; musicals $12 and $10.

Lear Casting
1112 S. 3rd St.
Las Vegas, 89104
385-9000
Marilee Lear
Casts parts and extras in motion
pictures filmed in Las Vegas.

New West Theatre
3540 W. Sahara Ave., Ste. 235
Las Vegas, NV 89102
258-8022
Brian Strom, Art. Dir.
Co-sponsored by the City of Las Vegas
with performances held at the
Charleston Heights Arts Center, 800 S.
Brush St.. The production season
includes comedies, dramas and musicals.
Tickets: Season tickets Adults $35; stu-
dents, seniors and handicapped $25.
Individual performances: general
admission $12.50; students, seniors and
handicapped $9; children under 5 not
admitted.

The Off-Broadway Theatre
900 E. Karen Ave., Ste. D 116
Las Vegas, NV 89109
737-0611

Carl Butto, Art. Dir.
Afternoon and evening classes in drama
workshops; children's and teen classes
on Sat.; 99-seat theater for classes and
small performances; casts extras, theater group.

**The Performing Arts Society of
Nevada**
6301 Malachite Bay Ave.
Las Vegas, NV 89130
658-6741
Fax: 658-6741
*John Meren & Tom Gallagher,
Co-founders*
Parent company of Brown Bag
Concerts, Las Vegas Lyric Opera and
National Globe Theatre. Purpose is to
provide venues for talented performers
and to make performances easily accessible.

Rainbow Company Theatre
821 Las Vegas Blvd. N.
Las Vegas, NV 89101
229-6553
Karen McKenney, Art. Dir.
Formed in 1977 primarily as a children's
theater group for ages 7 - 17, sponsored
by the City of Las Vegas, Cultural and
Community Affairs Branch of the
Department of Parks and Leisure Activities.
Tickets: Season tickets: Adults $20; stu-
dents and seniors $12; Children 12 and
under $6. Individual performances:
Adults $5; seniors and handicapped $3;
children $2.

Photo: Rainbow Company Theatre

Photo: Rainbow Company Theatre

Signature Productions
3255 Mustang St.
Las Vegas, NV 89108
878-7529
Karl Larsen, Pres.
Non-profit community theater group that began in 1988. Usually a two play season with auditions held for each play, musicals.

Sign Design Theatre Company
2300 W. Sahara Ave., Ste. 300
Las Vegas, NV 89102
341-3877
Mindy Silberlicht, Dir.
A non-profit organization open to all deaf or hearing impaired children 4-17

years old. Children learn sign language as well as dance and drama. Sign Design Theatre Company uses the performing arts as a vehicle to promote awareness of the deaf and hearing-impaired community.

Super Summer Theatre
P.O. Box 89147
Las Vegas, NV 89180
594-PLAY
Mary Gafford, Publicity
Super Summer Theatre runs from June 10 through August 20, Wed. - Sat. each year at Spring Mountain State Park. Broadway musicals and Shakespeare productions are presented 12 to 13

nights each, with three different productions each summer put on by local community theatre or university groups. Tickets available at the UNLV Performing Arts box office.
Tickets: Wed. - Thu. Adults $5; seniors, students and handicapped $3; Fri. - Sat. $7 and $4; children under 6 free. Gates open at 6 pm Nobody admitted after 8 pm

Theatre in the Valley
500 Harris St.
Henderson, NV 89015
458-7529
Ed Clayton, Pres.
Community theater group formed in 1992 in the Green Valley - Henderson area. The group has planned a season of three plays presented at the Valley View Recreation Center. Plays are presented Fri. & Sat. evening 8 pm and Sun. 2 pm Tickets are $5 - $8. No summer performances

Tuacahn Amphitheater and Center for the Arts
Box 1996
St. George, Utah 84771
1-800-746-9882
Glen Goodwin, Exec. Dir.

UNLV Department of Theatre Arts
4505 S. Maryland Pkwy.
Las Vegas, NV 89154
895-3666
Joe Aldridge, Chairman, Dept. of Theatre Arts
The Department of Theatre Arts provides cultural enrichment for the university

and the community through its production programs
University Theater - all performances are held in the Judy Bayley Theatre, Artemus Ham Hall, Black Box Theatre or the Paul C. Harris Theatre on the campus. Performances are 8 pm Wed. - Sat. & 2 pm Sun.
Individual tickets may be purchased at the Performing Arts Center Box Office. Call 895-3801 for more information.

Utah Shakespearean Festival
351 W. Center St.
Cedar City, Utah 84720
1-801-586-7878   1-800-752-9849
Donna Law, Fest. Dir. Mktg.
Performances are held in Cedar City, Utah, 180 miles northeast of Las Vegas, on the campus of Southern Utah University in the summer from the end of June 25 through Sept. 5.
Six plays in daily rotation in two theatres. In addition to the plays there are other festival events, including the Green Show, The Royal Feast, tours and seminars. This summer will be the 37th season for the festival. Tickets for performances range in price from $10 to $38 depending on time of performance and theater. Plays presented this year are: Romeo and Juliet, The Taming of the Shrew, All's Well that Ends Well, King John, Relative Values, Joseph and the Amazing Technicolor Dreamcoat

Clubs & Organizations

Due to the vast and diverse population of Las Vegas, the growing need for clubs, associations and organizations, both professional and recreational, has become undeniable. In Clark County alone, there are more than 25 different ethnic interest groups meeting on a weekly basis.

Other clubs and organizations, civic and social, join people with similar interests throughout the community. They are available for people in all walks of life; providing support, assistance, reassurance and comfort, as well as a way to adjust for those who are new to the area.

Many professional organizations are also on the rise in Las Vegas. Nonprofit Foundations such as the Clark County Public Education Foundation help to raise money for the growing needs of the area. Assistive and volunteer organizations help provide rehabilitation, support and in many instances, a second chance to people who are in need in the community. Last year alone, the Las Vegas chapter of the United Way raised $7.8 million for human care services.

Military and Veterans clubs provide assistance and support to veterans, their families and friends, and ex-prisoners of war, as well as food, clothing and other donations to area homeless, seniors and other needy families. The Key Foundation has provided these needs to more than 1,500 individuals in the Las Vegas area.

Recreational clubs such as the Vegas Valley 4 Wheelers and the Swing Dancers Club join people with similar interests for fun and recreation and meet throughout the month; while the Friends of Nevada Wilderness meets every two months at various locations. Because many of these groups meet in a variety of locations, times and days of meetings often change so it is best to call ahead to obtain the most current information.

FOUNDATIONS

**Clark County Public
Education Foundation**
2832 E. Flamingo Rd.
Las Vegas, NV 89121
799-1042
Judi Steele, Exec. Dir.
Nonprofit group raises money and collects donations for the Clark County School District's over 200 schools.

**The Liberace Foundation for
the Performing & Creative Arts**
1775 E. Tropicana Ave.
Las Vegas, NV 89119
798-5595
Myron Martin, Exec. Dir.
Supports scholarship grants for the arts to 57 schools, universities and organizations.

**Make-A-Wish Foundation
of Nevada**
4625 Wynn Rd.
Las Vegas, NV 89103
367-1440
Karla Jacobson, Exec. Dir.
Wishes granted to children between the ages of 2 1/2 and 18 years that have life threatening illnesses.

**Nevada Childhood Cancer
Foundation**
2235 E. Flamingo Rd.
Las Vegas, NV 89119
735-8434
*Dave Thomas, Director of Family
Services*
Not-for-profit organization founded to address the psychological, educational, social and emotional needs of children and families of children diagnosed with cancer, AIDS or sickle cell anemia.

Nevada Donor Network
4580 S. Eastern Ave.
Las Vegas, NV 89119
796-9600
Ken Richardson, Exec. Dir.

Non-profit Medicare provider, federally designated human organ and tissue bank for the state of Nevada.

Nevada Zoological Foundation
1775 N. Rancho Dr.
Las Vegas, NV 89106
647-4685
Pat Dingle, Exec. Dir.
Call or write for additional information. Dedicated to conservation, education and recreation.

**Southern Nevada Cancer
Research Foundation**
2020 Palomino Ln., Ste. 210
Las Vegas, NV 89106
384-0013
*Kathleen Van Wagenen, Program
Coordinator*
Non-profit federal grant. Clinical and pharmaceutical trials as cancer treatment in southern Nevada.

UNLV Foundation
4505 S. Maryland Pkwy.
Las Vegas, NV 89154-1006
895-3641
Dr. John Gallagher, Exec. Dir.
Raises funds on behalf of the University of Nevada, Las Vegas and represents UNLV to the community.

**University Medical Center of
S. Nevada Foundation, Inc.**
1800 W. Charleston Blvd.
Las Vegas, NV 89102
383-2326
*Rick Pyatt, Chairman
Colleen Courtney, Dir.*
An independent non-profit organization chartered to raise funds for UMC and the Children's Miracle Network.

PROFESSIONAL

American Marketing Association
P.O. Box 72098
Las Vegas, NV 89170
593-0883
Peter Shevelin - 364-0558
Marketing professionals. Monthly luncheon meetings; quarterly newsletter. Meets 1st Thursday of the month at 11:30 am at Palace Station.

The Business Network Int'l.
3462 Sioux Way
Las Vegas, NV 89109
731-6065
Leslie Taylor, Exec. Dir.
13 meeting locations
Tue., Wed., Thu., Fri. 7 am - 8:30 am
Wed., Thu. 11:30 am - 1 pm
Business networking group. Since only one person from each type of business is in each group, call Leslie Taylor for opening.

**Credit Managers Association
of California · Las Vegas Chapter**
2810 W. Charleston Blvd., Ste. 47
Las Vegas, NV 89102
259-2622
Kitty Boozer, Chapter Mgr.
Member owned company. Credit professional group meetings, credit reporting, construction form filing, collection department. Call for times of meetings.

Educational Networking Group
2810 W. Charleston Blvd.
Las Vegas, NV 89102
259-2622
Rand Peterson, Chairman
Member owned company meets 4th Wednesday of each month at 11:30 am at Palace Station. Guest speakers. Part of Credit Managers Association of California.

Leads Club
822-2001 1-800-783-3761
Scott Rotheiser, Dir.
Founded in 1978, this is the world's oldest and largest networking organization. Has more than 300 chapters in the United States and Australia.

**Professional Secretaries
International · Oasis Chapter**
2648 Ontario Drive
Las Vegas, NV 89128
360-8400
Patti Speer, Pres.
Meets 2nd Tuesday at 5:30 pm at various locations.

**Public Relations Society of
America · Desert Sands Chapter**
P.O. Box 81742
Las Vegas, NV 89180
244-7575
Vince Alberta, Pres.
Meets last Friday of the month at Chin's Restaurant in the Fashion Show Mall at noon.

ASSOCIATIONS

**American Association
of Travel Agents**
Escape-Carson Wagonlit Travel
544 E. Sahara Ave.
Las Vegas, NV 89104-2798
734-8987
Leonard J. Yelinek, Pres.
Trade organization for travel agents. Upholds standards for integrity in travel.

**American Association of
University Women**
Hot Line: 1-800-821-4364
*Lynn Ossolinski, NV Pres.
Sandy Bernard, National Pres.*
Organization that promotes education for women. Bachelor Degree or higher required for membership.

Associated General Contractors
4052 Industrial Rd.
Las Vegas, NV 89103
796-9986
*Steve Holloway, Exec. VP
Linda Harris, Pres.*
Commercial construction association specializing in legislative lobbying, safety services, safety inspection, OSHA representation, CPR and first aid training.

**Association of Record
Managers & Administrators
Silver State Chapter**
894-7519
Jeana McLellan, Dir.
Seminars are held for dues paying members and guests. Provides information on record management, document imaging, regulations, retention/destruction of office records/files.

Citizen's Grand Jury Assn.
6185 Pecos Rd., Ste. 175
Las Vegas, NV 89120
361-7018
Larry Engel, Spokesman
A not-for-profit unincorporated association registered with the Secretary of State and dedicated to educating the public on the issues of the Grand Jury.

Clark County Bar Association
517 S. 9th St.
Las Vegas, NV 89101
387-6011
Patty Blakeman, Exec. Dir.
A voluntary fraternal association for attorneys and members of the local judiciary. Provides member services and benefits.

Clark County Child Care Assn.
P. O. Box 15372
Las Vegas, NV 89114
656-8922
Kay Fischer, Pres.
Provides a phone referral service to the community for licensed child care.

**Clark County Classroom
Teachers Association**
2950 E. Rochelle Ave., Ste. C
Las Vegas, NV 89121
733-3063
Sue Strand, Pres.
Union representing teachers on contract issues.

Clark County Genealogical Soc.
225-5838   Fax: 258-4099
Robert Kennard, Jr., Pres.
Workshop and meeting 3rd Thursday 7 pm at 580 E. St. Louis Avenue. Seminars in spring and fall; October - Family History Month.

Clark County Medical Society
2590 E. Russell Rd.
Las Vegas, NV 89120
739-9989
Mitch Keamy M.D., Pres.
Mails referral background information on member physicians, takes grievances on member physicians excluding billing disputes and malpractice claims.

**Employers Association of
Southern Nevada**
2303 E. Sahara Ave.
Las Vegas, NV 89104
457-0556
Don Forman, Exec. Dir.
Non-profit association affiliated with the Builders Association, Pool & Spa, Floor Covering and Glazers. Handles union contracts, bookkeeping, meeting, and fundraising projects, and sets up community affairs.

**Equal Rights for Divorced
Fathers**
23 N. Mojave Rd., Ste. A
Las Vegas, NV 89101
387-6266
Support and educational association for divorced and separated fathers.

Fremont Street Experience
425 Fremont St.
Las Vegas, NV 89101
382-6397
Kim Daskas, Adv. & PR Dir.
Manages operation of the Fremont Street Experience.

ASSOCIATIONS

CLUBS

Employers Association of Southern Nevada, 2303 E. Sahara Ave. Las Vegas, NV 89104

Greater Las Vegas Association of Realtors
1750 E. Sahara Ave.
Las Vegas, NV 89104
732-8177
Judie Wood, Exec. VP
Professional trade association for realtor members.

International Association of Financial Planning
1609 E. Sahara Ave.
Las Vegas, NV 89104
733-3002
John Dube, Pres.
Helps individuals, corporations and groups to reach their financial goal.

Las Vegas Ad Club
Lotus Broadcasting
4660 S. Decatur Blvd.
Las Vegas, NV 89103
876-1460
Eric Bonnici, Pres.
Industry organization for all people involved in advertising. Monthly meetings at various locations, usually membership luncheons. Various socials during the year. Addy awards presented annually.

Manufactured Home Community Owners Association
4055 S. Spencer St., Ste. 107
Las Vegas, NV 89119
731-1900
Marolyn Mann, Exec. Dir.
Trade association for manufactured home community owners, legislative well being and continuing education for management.

National Association of Retired Federal Employees
(Multiple locations listed below)
Las Vegas Chapter East 2275
Paradise Community Center
438-6715
Edward Donahue, Sec.
Meets 2nd Tuesday of each month.

Chapter West 423
Charleston Heights Arts Center
255-7082
Gloria Hill, Sec.
Meets 2nd Friday of each month.

Nevada Apartment Association
5030 S. Paradise Rd., Ste. C101
Las Vegas, NV 89119
547-3550
David Bauman, Pres.
An association for apartment owners in the Las Vegas Valley. Protects owners' rights.

Nevada Association of Independent Business
3131 Mead Ave.
Henderson, NV 89102
251-8166
Phil Stout, Pres.
Fights against over-regulation and excessive taxation of small business.

Nevada Broadcasters Assn.
1050 E. Flamingo Rd., Ste. S110
Las Vegas, NV 89119
794-4994
Robert Fisher, Exec. Dir.
Protects, promotes and enhances the broadcasting industry. Organizes programs and activities that further broadcasting.

Nevada Casino Dealers Assn.
1120 E. Fremont St.
Las Vegas, NV 89101
474-9766
Tony Badillo, Pres.
Lobbying for working conditions and job security.

Nevada Hotel & Motel Assn.
4820 Alpine Pl., Ste. F203
Las Vegas, NV 89107
878-9272
Van Heffner, Pres.
Membership organization concerned with legislative measures and various other services.

Nevada Press Association
P.O. Box 1030
Carson City, NV 89702
1-702-885-0866
Kent Lauer, Exec. Dir.
Non-profit association which represents newspapers throughout the state.

Nevada Resort Association
3773 Howard Hughes Pkwy.
Las Vegas, NV 89109
735-4888
Richard Bunker, Pres.
Hotel/casino trade association and lobbying group.
.
Nevada Taxpayers Association
2303 E. Sahara Ave., Ste. 203
Las Vegas, NV 89104
457-8442
Carole Vilardo, Pres.
Conservative government research group funded by businesses, monitors local and state government tax and spending policies.

Retail Association of Nevada
305 N. Carson St., Ste. 203
Carson City, NV 89701
1-702-882-1700
Mary Lau, Exec. Dir.
Office open Mon. - Fri. 8 am - 5 pm.
Advocate for the retail industry.

Southern Nevada Homebuilders Association
3685 S. Pecos McLeod
Las Vegas, NV 89121
794-0117
Irene Porter, Exec. Dir.
Trade association for membership and contracts. Represents all members on issues that pertain to the home building industry.

State Bar of Nevada
600 E. Charleston Blvd.
Las Vegas, NV 89104
382-2200
Wayne Blevins, Dir.
Administers bar exams, disciplines attorneys, lawyer referral. Client's security fund and fee dispute component.

GAY ASSOCIATIONS

National HIV and Aids Hotline: 474-2437

Community Counseling Center
1120 Almond Tree Ln., Ste. 207
Las Vegas, NV 89104
369-8700
Ron Lawrence, Exec. Dir.
Counsels on criminal justice, such as DUI, marriage counseling and group therapy for HIV patients.

Gay & Lesbian Community Center of Southern Nevada
912 E. Sahara Ave.
Las Vegas, NV 89104
733-9800
Holly Lee, Pres.
Non-profit organization that supports the well being of the gay and lesbian community by providing information and services through projects and programs.

Golden Rainbow
1111 Desert Ln.
Las Vegas, NV 89102
384-2899
Sue Melfi, Exec. Dir.
Provides housing and financial assistance for people with HIV/AIDS in Southern Nevada.

Lambda Business Association
1801 E. Tropicana Ave., Ste. 9
Las Vegas, NV 89119
593-2875
Paul Sanchez, Pres.
Gay and gay-friendly business owners association. Publishes the Lambda Business Directory.

Las Vegas Bugle
3131 Industrial Rd.
Las Vegas, NV 89109
369-6260   Fax 369-9325
Rob Schlegel, Publisher
Monthly gay-oriented magazine.

Metropolitan Community Church
1140 Almond Tree Ln., Ste. 304 (Office)
Las Vegas, NV 89104
369-4380
Rev. B. J. Beau McDaniels
Sunday service at 10 am at 1208 E. Charleston Blvd. Wednesday service at Almond Tree Ln. at 6 pm.

Some of the following clubs and organizations list locations formeetings, but locations change frequently, as do officers. Call ahead for information.

BOOKS

Clark County Library Great Books Discussion Group
454-1941
Jane Macia
Classics-oriented discussion held the 2nd and 4th Tuesday of each month at 7 pm at the Clark County Library on Flamingo Rd.

Fiction Discussion Group
258-6479
Held at Borders Book Shop 3rd Tuesday of each month.

Las Vegas Writer's Guild
254-0788
Mike Flashner, Dir.
Non-profit literary organization. Meeting 2nd Wednesday of each month at West Sahara Library, 7 pm. Critique meetings held throughout the month.

Nevada Screenwriters
393-2141
Joe Wheeler
Meets 1st Saturday of the month at 10 am at the Las Vegas Library, 833 Las Vegas Blvd. N.

CAR CLUBS

British Auto Club
658-8195
John Inman
Meets 1st Wednesday of each month at 7 pm in the Duesenberg Room at the Imperial Palace.

Classic Chevy Club
593-5572
Don Nisley, Pres.
Meets 3rd Thursday at 7:30 pm at various locations.

Classic Thunderbird Club
255-3322
Bob Tayler
Meetings at different times at various locations.

Corvette Association
876-4268
Jerry McCorkle
Meets 2nd Thursday of each month at 7:30 pm, at the Tap House, 5589 W. Charleston Blvd.

Electric Auto Association
736-1910
Gail Lucas
Meets 3rd Thursday of each month at 7 pm at Desert Research Institute, 755 E. Flamingo Rd. Guest speakers and videos. Demonstrations of cars at various schools.

F-100's Ltd. of Las Vegas
877-2312
Tony Costa
Meets 1st Thursday of each month at Villa Pizza, Sunset Rd. & Eastern Ave. at 7:30 pm

ORGANIZATIONS

CLUBS

Harley Owners Group
Las Vegas, NV 89104
645-7293
Fred Soukup
General meetings are held at The Still, 9495
Las Vegas Blvd. S.

Kit Car Club
645-7658
Bill McCord, Pres.
Harry Hartung, VP
Cars are built from scratch with kits.
Meets 1st Saturday of each month at 1
pm, Kelly's Custom Auto, 5151 S.
Procyon Ave., Ste. 108.

Las Vegas Cruisin' Association
739-7641
Art Kam, Pres.
Cruises 3rd Friday of each month at different locations.

Las Vegas Kart Club
5719 E. Carey Ave.
Las Vegas, NV 89115
438-3398
Don Dayton, Pres.
Meets 1st Wednesday at 7:30 pm; call for
location. Go-cart racing. Race 2nd and 4th
Saturday of the month at 6 pm in the summer and 2nd and 4th Sunday of the month
at 9 am in the winter at Las Vegas Motor
Speedway. Oldest racing club in Las Vegas.

Las Vegas Valley
Model A Ford Club
255-7858
Delroy Hering, Pres.
Vintage 1928-1931. Meets 2nd Thursday of
each month at 7 pm for dinner and 8 pm
for meeting in the R-Bar Restaurant, 6000
W. Charleston Blvd.

Las Vegas Porsche Club
876-7982
Paul Broadway, Pres.
Meets once a month at various locations.

Model T Club of Las Vegas
451-0449
Peter Proschold, Pres.
Harold Mann, Contact - 646-6063
Meets the 3rd Tuesday of each month at
7 pm in the Duesenberg Room at the
Imperial Palace.

Mustang Club
658-5800
Dean Dike, Treas.
Meets 1st Wednesday of each month at 7
pm at the Financial Center, 3300 W.
Sahara Ave.

Nevada Car Club Council
593-5572
Don Nisley, Pres.
Composed of 35 different car clubs to promote unity, develop representation for
political issues concerning autos, trucks
and motorcycle enthusiasts. Meets 4th
Wednesday of each month at 6:30 pm at
various locations; facilitates and coordinates events between member car clubs.

Nevada Car Owner's Association
458-9146
Jim Sohns, Pres.
Meets at R-Bar, 6000 W. Charleston Blvd.,
3rd. Monday of each month at 7:30 pm.

Nevada United Four Wheelers
Association
645-5458
Dick Franta, Pres. - 451-5842
P.O. Box 46521, Las Vegas, NV 89114
Representing all four wheelers in NV.

Packard Club
452-5892
Paul Baker or Jim Donaldson
Meetings vary. Picnics, tours, active in
parades.

Silver State 4 X 4 Club
658-9822
Robin Haywood, Pres.
Meets 2nd and 4th Wednesday each month
at Denny's, Boulder Hwy., at 7:30 pm.

Southern Nevada Buick Club
458-4104
Richard King, Dir.
Monthly meeting 4th Thursday of each
month at 7 pm at Desert Buick. Newcomers
are welcome.

Southern Nevada Land
Cruisers Club
293-3023
Debbie Parris, Sec.
Jim Arby, Pres. - 454-5290
Toyota 4X4's only. Meets 2nd and last
Wednesday of each month at 7:30 pm at
Denny's, Sahara Ave. and Rancho Rd.

Southern Nevada Off Road
Enthusiasts
Hot Line: 452-4522
Joe Ross, Pres.
Meetings held 2nd Tuesday of each
month at Eagles Hall, 1601 E.
Washington Ave. Off road racing cars,
clean up projects in the desert.

Southern Nevada Street Rod
Association
368-2542
Gene Blake
Family oriented social club - active in
charities, meets 1st Tuesday of each
month at 7 pm; meeting places vary.

Sports Car Club of America
368-6926
Dave Roberts
Open meeting 1st Tues. of each month at
Texas Hotel, on Rancho Rd. and Lake Mead
Blvd. at 7:30 pm. Auto crosses, road racing,
rallies. Membership open to everyone.

Studebaker Club
642-2643
Lorraine Hall, Pres.
National organization - Family oriented,
social functions, yearly international
meetings. Meet locally 2nd Wednesday
of each month at Carrow's, S. Rancho
Rd. and Sahara Ave. at 6:30 pm.

Vegas Valley 4 Wheelers
646-6046
Gene Elliot, Pres.
Meets 1st and 3rd Wednesday of each
month at 7:30 pm at The Tap House at
W. Charleston and Decatur Blvds.

Veteran's Motor Club of America
871-6478
Frank Nicholson
1st Tuesday of each month at R-Bar on
Charleston and Jones Blvds.

COMPUTER CLUBS

Association of Information
Technology Professionals
(formerly DPMA)
www.normt.com
Norman Tornek, Dir.

Clark County Commodore Group
645-2402
Al Jackson, Pres.
Meets 9 am every other Saturday at
Nevada Power, 6226 W. Sahara Ave.

Las Vegas MacIntosh
Users Group
896-1137
Brian Corr, Pres.
Monthly meetings at various locations,
1st Saturday of month. Special interest
group meetings throughout month.

Las Vegas OS/2 User Group
474-1133
Chip Shapiro, Treas.
shapiro@netcom.com

Las Vegas P. C. Users Group, Inc.
363-4785
Chuck Buchhiet, Pres.
General meeting 2nd Thursday of each
month, 6:15 pm at High Desert Training
Room at Community College - no charge.

Southern Nevada Amiga
Users Group
293-1913
Mark Richey, Pres.
mrichey@skylink.net
Ron Gratreaks, VP
captj@skylink.net
Meets every other Saturday at 9 am at
Nevada Power Company.

SNUG - Southern Nevada
Users Group
658-6462
David Gaberel, Pres.
Meets 2nd Monday of each month, 7 pm - 9
pm at Nevada Power Company, Jones and
Torrey Pines. Demonstrations of programs.

Sun City Summerlin
Computer Club
Fran Wise, Pres.
franwise@juno.com

DANCE

International Folk Dances
732-4871
Donna Killian
International Ethnic Express Folk Dancers
sponsor general dance classes 7:15 pm -
8:45 pm and beginners classes 6:30 pm -
7:15 pm Wednesday at Baker Park
Community School.

Las Vegas B-Sharp Square
Dance Club
870-1792
Doug & Eva Pushard, Chairpersons
Advanced square dancers meet every
Friday night 7:30 pm - 10:30 pm at
Knights of Columbus, 10th & Ogden. Out
of town guests welcome.

Movers & Groovers
458-1302
Marie Pelliccioni
Swing dancers meet Sunday 8 pm - midnight at Skinny Dugans, 4127 W.
Charleston Blvd.

Over 40 Dance Group
368-1155   451-9712
Jean Szafraniec
Meets 1st Saturday of the month for dinner and dancing at 6 pm at the Moose
Lodge on Bruce and Washington.

Stardusters Square Dancers
451-1288
Dance Thursday nights from 7:30 pm -
9:30 pm at Helen J. Stewart School,
Viking Rd.

Square and Round Dancers of
Southern Nevada
451-1288 or 454-2217
Thursdays from 7:30 pm - 9:30 pm at St.
Viator Community Center. Contact this
association for all square dances.

Swing Dance Club of Las Vegas
733-6393   456-0562
Christi Reagen
Meets every Friday for dancing at
Pepper's Lounge, 2929 E. Desert Inn Rd.
at 8 pm.

Swing Dancers
693-5955
For singles and couples; dance at 8 pm
Thursdays and Saturdays at Sonia's Bar,
1243 E. Sahara Ave. and Maryland Pkwy.

U.S. Amateur Ballroom
Dancers Association
876-5637
Susan Sheridan
Monthly lesson, dance and meeting 8 pm -
11 pm Saturday at 4550 S. Maryland Pkwy.

ENVIRONMENTAL, CONSERVATION and HUMANE

Air & Waste Management Assn.
500 S. Martin Luther King Blvd.
P.O. Box 167
Las Vegas, NV 89106
367-3455
Greg Sanks, Pres.
Promotes better understanding of environmental concerns; monthly luncheons.

Animal Foundation of Nevada
700 N. Mojave Rd.
Las Vegas, NV 89101-2401
384-3333
Mary Herro, Pres.
Non-profit organization - low cost spay
and neuter, adoption center.

Citizen Alert
P.O. Box 1681
Las Vegas, NV 89125
796-5662
Richard Nielsen, Exec. Dir.
Statewide environmental group.

Desert Research Institute
755 E. Flamingo Rd.
Las Vegas, NV 89154
895-0400
Dr. James V. Taranik, Pres.
Part of the University of Nevada system,
dedicated to environmental research.

Friends of Nevada Wilderness
P.O. Box 19777
Las Vegas, NV 89132
870-1350
Mark Saylor
Meeting every two months at different
locations. Organization for wilderness
study. Looks for cultural sites and caves.

The Nature Conservancy
1771 E. Flamingo Rd., Ste. 111B
Las Vegas, NV 89119
737-8744
Steve Hobbs, Dir.
Non-profit organization involved with preservation, through land acquisition, of rare and endangered animals, plants and wild lands.

Red Rock Audubon Society
P.O. Box 96691
Las Vegas, NV 89193
363-6615   293-2716
Bird alert: 649-1516
John Bialecki, Pres.
Meetings and field trips September - June; bird watching and wild flower appreciation. Trees and shrubs are planted at wildlife refuges. Membership $35 annually; $21 seniors, $20 students and $38 family. Membership includes newsletter.

Sierra Club
P.O. Box 19777
Las Vegas, NV 89132
647-5459   363-3267
Bill Marr, Chairman
Dave Brickey, Pres.
To explore, enjoy and protect wild lands. Hiking, backpacking, skiing, pot-luck and other activities.

ETHNIC / RELOCATED

Armenian American Cultural Society
269-9394
Gil Suabian
Meets 3rd Sunday of the month at The California Club. Picnics, parties and cultural events

Brooklyn Club of Las Vegas
896-8163
Gene Venezia, Pres.
Social events; bowling league.

Canadian Club of Southern Nevada
242-8311
Ray Elgaard
Call for times and locations of meetings. Social engagements for individuals of Canadian heritage and friends of Canada to come together both socially and professionally.

Danish-American Friendship Club of Las Vegas
262-6913
John Kobberoe, Pres.
Socials held at different locations.

Daughters of the British Empire
456-7228
Patricia Nell, Pres.
Meet once a month at different homes. Charitable functions throughout the year. Locations and days vary.

Desert Newcomers Club
436-4126
Pat Alberto, Pres.
Women's social organization. Meets 10 am at Green Valley Library, last Thursday of each month.

Filipino American Club of Nevada
4201 W. Rochelle Ave.
Las Vegas, NV 89103
873-0237
Nelinda McKellar, Pres.
Meets 3rd Thursday of each month. Call for times and locations.

German - American Club
1110 E. Lake Mead Blvd.
N. Las Vegas, NV 89030
649-8503
Vickie Sponseller, Pres. - 649-8503
Dinners every Saturday night, live music, $10 initially then $20 annually for membership.

German Mardi Gras of Las Vegas
362-1949
Doris Tramont, Pres.
Meets 3rd Tuesday of the month at 7 pm at Clubhouse on Blue Diamond Road.

Image of Southern Nevada
391-7127   435-5545
Volunteer organization concerned with the needs and advancement of Hispanics.

Italian American Club
2333 E. Sahara Ave.
Las Vegas, NV 89104
457-3866
Joe Tegano, Gen. Mgr.
Meets 7 pm first Tuesday of the month.

Japanese-American Club
382-4443
Dean Kajioka, Pres.
Monthly meetings at 7 pm 4th Monday at Nevada Power Company, 6226 W. Sahara Avenue. All persons interested in membership are invited.

Jewish Women's International Club
Summerlin Chapter 1827
242-0842
Lillian Goodman, VP
Meets 3rd Wednesday of each month at the Santa Fe at 9:30 am for breakfast.

Jewish Junction
(Jewish Professionals Organization)
P.O. Box 15208
Las Vegas, NV 89114
268-3026
Robert Silverberg, Pres.
Call for various times and meeting places. Happy hours and occasional Shabbat dinners.

Las Vegas Nebraskans
363-4688
Steve Kushner, Pres.
Connie Ballard
Social Club affiliated with the University of Nebraska Alumni Assn. For more information, call Connie.

Las Vegas Newcomers Club
Meets 3rd Thursday of the month at 11:30 am at the Gold Coast. You don't have to be a newcomer to join. Everyone welcome.

Las Vegas Hawaiian Civic Club
452-0507
Pauline Clark
Meets 4th Sunday of each month at various locations.

Las Vegas Indian Center
2300 W. Bonanza Rd.
Las Vegas, NV 89106
647-5842
Richard Arnold, Dir.
Social and economic aid to Native Americans.

Latin Action of Las Vegas
257-1567
Meets 2nd and 4th Sunday of the month, 7 pm at Nevada Power, 6226 W. Sahara Ave.

The Minnesota Club
878-5340
Sandra Dinsmore, Pres.
The Minnesota Club meets quarterly. All former Minnesotans are invited.

Nevada Association of Latin Americans
323 N. Maryland Parkway
Las Vegas, NV 89101
382-2252
Dr. Abie Armeida, Pres.
Child care, English and Spanish classes, assistance with teen problems, job referrals.

New York Club
456-2425
Hank Brown, Pres.
Meets 7 pm 4th Tuesday of each month at Vacation Village. Refreshments served; first visit is free, all New Yorkers welcome.

Sons of Erin
458-9445   388-1177
Tom Joyce, Pres.
Meets 2nd Tuesday of the month at the Maxim Hotel at 7:30 pm.

Sons of Italy
317 Fremont St.
Las Vegas, NV 89101
384-3964
Phil Carlino, Pres.
Provides scholarships, contributes to Coolys Anemic Research and to Italian Language and Cultural Programs.

Sons of Norway
227-9842
Siri Poehls, Pres.
Meetings 1st Thursday of each month at 6:30 pm at Spring Valley Library.

SWEA
(Swedish Women Educational Association)
896-9995
Siv Domeiv, Pres.
Meets 3rd Wednesday of the month at 7 pm; call for locations.

Towne Club
648-9333
Yolanda Moreria, Pres.
Women's Social Club meets 4th Tuesday of each month at 11:30 am at various restaurants.

VASA Order of America-Valhalla #715
6586 W. Treadway Ln.
Las Vegas, NV 89103
873-5811
Inga-Britt Barnes, District Deputy Historian
Swedish American Fraternal organization. Open to all five Nordic countries. Call for meeting times.

Vegas Viking Sons of Norway Lodge
227-9842
Meets 1st Thursday of the month 6:30 pm at Spring Valley Library, 4280 S. Jones Blvd.

Westside Newcomers Club
221-7243
Pearl DiPietro, Pres.
Meets for lunch 2nd Wednesday of each month at various restaurants and for coffee 3rd Wednesday of each month at the Sahara Library.

Windy City Vegans
642-6881
Social-business meetings held for former Chicagoans 3rd Sunday of each month at 4:30 pm at the Windy City Pub, 3050 E. Desert Inn Rd.

FRATERNITIES AND SORORITIES

Beta Sigma Phi
878-3483
Pam Austin, Pres.
Social sorority dealing with cultural and community affairs. Worldwide organization.

Zeta Master Chapter of Beta Sigma Phi
648-4486

Laurette Theta Chapter of Beta Sigma Phi
878-9523

Preceptor Mu Chapter of Beta Sigma Phi
873-3428

GAMES

Cribbage Night
877-0522
Meets Wednesday at Skinny Dugan's Pub, 4127 W. Charleston Blvd.

Fun Pinochle Group
733-6387
Non-smoking group
Meets at 6:30 pm Tuesday for double-deck pinochle at First Church of Religious Science, 1420 E. Harmon Ave.

Las Vegas Bridge Center
1111 Las Vegas Blvd. S., Ste. 309
Las Vegas, NV 89104
735-5141
Meets Mon. - Sat. 12:30 pm & 7 pm; Sun. 1 pm & 6 pm; party bridge Thursday 9:30 am

Las Vegas Chess Club
399-1552
Meets 2nd and 4th Thursday of the month 5 pm - 9 pm at the Rainbow Library.

Las Vegas Backgammon Club
458-9359
Mike Maxikul
Meets Tuesday at 7 pm in the Turf Lounge at the Jockey Club, 3700 Las Vegas Blvd. S.

Las Vegas Scrabble Club
Sunday Scrabble
878-5405
Sue
Meets 1st and 3rd Sundays 1 pm - 4:30 pm at Spring Valley Library. No charge - open to public.

Las Vegas Scrabble Club
454-0620
Garry Greenside
Meets Tuesdays at noon at 3047 Zane Circle.

Monday Night Pinochle Club
247-1435
Meets every Monday at Leatherby's, 577 E. Sahara Ave.

Nevada Backgammon Assn.
P.O. Box 230
2620 S. Maryland Pkwy.
Las Vegas, NV 89109
893-6025
Howard Markowitz, Dir.
Holds major tournaments semi-annually.

CLUBS

Oasis of Las Vegas
2214 S. Rainbow Blvd.
Las Vegas, NV 89102
362-0606
Michael Valentine, Owner
A non-gaming club featuring all board games, ping-pong and darts. The purpose of the club is to provide the games you like to play in a warm comfortable atmosphere. No alcohol is served but food can be delivered by Waiters on Wheels in just 15 minutes. The cost is $5 an hour; open from noon until midnight. Must be over 16 years old or accompanied by an adult.

Over 50 Singles Pinochle Club
645-7559
Louise
Call for meeting times and locations.

GARDEN CLUBS

Cactus and Succulent Society of Southern Nevada
258-3205
Peter Ducomb, Pres.
Meets 1st Thursday of each month at 7 pm at Lorenzi Park.

Carnation Garden Club
877-1832
Sandy Gunderson, Pres.
Meets 1st Thursday of each month at 9:30 am at Lorenzi Park Garden Club Bldg.

Flower Arrangers Guild
876-1226
Jane Koerwitz, Pres.
Meets 2nd Thursday of each month at 9:30 am in the Lorenzi Park Garden Club Bldg.

Greater Las Vegas Orchid Society
870-9639
Tony Billitere, Pres.
Meets 1st Sunday of each month at 2 pm at Lorenzi Park Garden Club Bldg.

Growers Study Guild
363-3991
Scotty Nogaim, Pres.
Meets at the Garden Club in Lorenzi Park 2nd Wednesday of each month at 11:30 am.

Hoe and Grow Garden Club
293-2365
Emily Henderson, Pres.
Meets 2nd Tuesday, 7 pm in Boulder City Library.

Las Vegas Bonsai Society
876-6728
Steve Lilly, Pres.
Meets 2nd Wednesday of each month at 7:30 pm at Lorenzi Park Garden Club Bldg.

Las Vegas Chrysanthemum Society
735-0855
Ruth Ann Waite, Pres.
Meets at Garden Club in Lorenzi Park 2nd Tuesday of each month at 7:30 pm.

Las Vegas Council of Garden Clubs
459-0583
Barbara Appel, Pres.
Meets four times a year. Closed to the public.

Las Vegas Iris Society
255-1263
Hiromi Uyeda, Pres.
Meets 1st Monday each month 7 pm at Garden Club in Lorenzi Park.

Las Vegas Valley Rose Society
646-6048
Jackie Jackson, Pres.
Meets on the 2nd Thursday at 7:30 pm at the Garden Club in Lorenzi Park.

Nevada Garden Center
3331 W. Washington Ave.
(Lorenzi Park)
Las Vegas, NV 89107
878-4846

Rose Garden Club
454-1941
Jane Macia, Pres.
Meets 3rd Thursday 11 am in Garden Club Bldg. in Lorenzi Park; lunch and speaker.

Southern Nevada Iris Society
294-5059
Howard Wald, Pres.
Meeting approximately 6 times a year, hosts the largest iris show in the U.S.

Sunset Garden Club
896-1144
Julio A. Menasco, Pres.
Meets 2nd Tuesday of each month at 9:30 am at Green Valley Library in Henderson.

HOBBY CLUBS

Antique Bottles and Collectibles
Nevada Memorabilia
452-1263
Dottie Dougherty
Meets 1st Wednesday of the month at 7 pm at Elks Lodge, 4100 W. Charleston.

Clark County Gem Collectors, Inc.
496-1153
Frank Rowley, Pres.
Meets 7 pm 1st Tuesday of the month at Dula Senior Citizens Center, Henderson. Public is invited.

Fossil Finders of Southern Nevada
254-0047
Scott Kramer, Pres.
Meets 3rd Monday of the month at 7 pm at the Las Vegas Library, 833 Las Vegas Blvd. N.

Frontier Amateur Radio
269-9551
Bill Scarborough, Pres.
Meets the 3rd Saturday of each month at 8 am at Rae's Country Inn, Henderson.

Garden Railway Society
P.O. Box 2777
Las Vegas, NV 89124
Ardel Henrichsen, Pres.
Train meetings once a month at various locations.

Geological Society of Southern Nevada
269-8336
Kurt Goebel, Pres.
For professional geologists only. Meets monthly at Desert Research Institute.

Gold Searchers of Southern Nevada
642-8972
Sam Johnson, Pres.
Meets 1st Wednesday of each month at 6:45 pm at Orr Middle School Cafeteria. Guest speakers; club has its own claims for members' use.

Las Vegas Doll Show
P.O. Box 90669
Henderson, NV 89009
564-2395
Sharon Briner, Show Chairman - 565-1600
Meets once a month. Call for information. Annual doll show in the fall.

Las Vegas Gem Club
565-5256
Jack Toogood, Pres.
Meets 7:30 pm 2nd Monday of the month at Saturn of Henderson on Gibson Rd.

Lucky 100 Prospecting Club
362-0056
Tom Jeeves, Pres.
Small prospecting club, looking for new claims. Meets 3rd Wednesday of each month at American Legion Post, Veterans Memorial Dr.

Southern Nevada Rock Art Enthusiasts
457-8690
Nancy Wier, Pres.
Meets 1st and 3rd Thursday of each month at 7 pm at the Las Vegas Library, 830 Las Vegas Blvd. N. Study Indian engravings. All ages welcome.

Southern Nevada Stamp Club
5708 W. Charleston Blvd.
Las Vegas, NV 89102
452-5427
Betty Mauck, Greeter
Meets 1st and 3rd Friday of the month at 7 pm at Winchester Community Center at 3130 S. McLeod Dr. Trades stamps, films, education programs and socializing.

INVESTMENT CLUBS

Black Chip Investment Club
873-0965
Monthly meetings held in members' homes. Follows guidelines of the National Association of Investors Corp. Analyzes growth potential of corporations listed on all stock exchanges.

MISCELLANEOUS

Clark County Nevada Genealogical Society
225-5838
Robert Kennard, Jr., Pres.
Meets 3rd Thursday of each month at 580 E. St. Louis Ave., Katherine Center, at various times.

Country Farm Retreat
361-7018
Larry Engel
Researches living together on farms. Call for details on seminars and meetings.

Darwin Magic Club
737-8927
Dr. Morton Greene
Meets socially every Wednesday after 10 pm at The Jockey Club, across from the Aladdin Hotel & Casino. Prominent magicians from all over the world drop in.

Hispanics in Politics
732-8031
Monthly breakfast meeting, 7 am Wednesday at Dona Maria Tamales Restaurant, 910 Las Vegas Blvd. S. Public is welcome.

Snafu Brewers Club
736-8504
Meets 2nd Friday of each month at 7 pm at Mr. Radz Homebrew Supply, 4972 S. Maryland Pkwy. People interested in making their own beer.

Las Vegas Brewers Guild
Meets 1st Friday of the month at 7 pm at Mr. Radz Homebrew Supply.

Las Vegas Childrens Books
256-6267
Lorraine Lange, Pres.
Meets the last Wednesday of each month. Call for information.

Las Vegas Mothers of Twins Club
223-0266
Korri Ward, Pres.
Advocates education, provides community resources and social support of mothers of twins or higher order. Meets 3rd Thursday of the month at Medical Building, 3300 W. Charleston Blvd.

Las Vegas Mutual UFO Network
242-2294
Monthly meetings, Mondays at 7 pm at The R Bar, 6000 W. Charleston Blvd. Public is invited.

Las Vegas Writers Poetry Group
878-8820
Dennis DeLong, Dir.
Meets the last Thursday of each month at the West Charleston Library in Health Science conference room.

Mensa
453-0731   366-8111
Jim Jarvis
For a free brochure call 1-800-666-3672. An organization focusing on the development of human intelligence. Qualifications require passing a standardized test.

Parents Without Partners
656-2867
Stephanie Edelman, VP
Discussion groups, dances, dinners, outings and parties on a regular basis.

Society of American Magicians
737-8927
Dr. Morton Greene, Hypnotist
About 60 members meet the 1st Wednesday of every month at 8 pm at the Jockey Club at 3700 Las Vegas Blvd. S.

Tall Club of Las Vegas
253-5552
Marcy Morgan
Open to women 5'10" and over and men 6'2" and over. Meets Thursdays at 5:30 pm at Jimmy Murphy's, 6138 W. Charleston Blvd.

TOPS
(Take Off Pounds Sensibly)
732-8215
Pat Thompson
Meets Wednesdays 7 pm, William Orr School, 1562 E. Katie St. near Blvd. Mall.

MUSIC

Barber Shop Quartet & Chorus
Las Vegas Gamble Aires - 657-2277
John Mackey, Pres.
Member of Society for the Preservation and Encouragement of Barber Shop Quartet Singing in America. 90-man organization that produces Christmas and Spring Shows. 1997 Division Champions of S.P.E.B.S.Q.S.A. far western district. Meets at 7:30 pm Thursday at Christ Lutheran Church, 111 N. Torrey Pines.

ORGANIZATIONS

Desert Chorale
3016 Carlotta Circle
Las Vegas, NV 89121
796-0668
Nancy Helm, Dir.
Community choral group meets every Wednesday at Palora Church on Palora Ave.

Guitar Society of Las Vegas
1305 E. Vegas Valley Dr.
Las Vegas, NV 89109
733-0482
Oscar Carrescia, Pres.

Las Vegas Songwriters Assn.
223-7255
Weekly workshops 7 pm every Thursday.

Las Vegas Jazz Society
Hot Line: 369-3374
Art Goldberg, Pres. - 431-4137
Concert series and picnics.

Sweet Adelines
Celebrity City Chorus: 223-7893
Rehearsals 7 pm Tuesdays at the Henderson Senior Center. Open to women of all ages.
Valley of Fire Chorus: 875-4242
Rehearsals 7:30 pm Tuesdays at Our Lady of Las Vegas Catholic Church, 3050 Alta Drive; newcomers welcome.

Sweet Adeline's Young Women in Harmony
547-6121
Free singing lessons for girls in the sixth grade through high school. Rehearsal at 6 pm Tuesdays at Community Lutheran Church, 3720 E. Tropicana Ave.

The Quiet Music Society
361-7018
Larry Engel
Group gathers to listen to live performances of classical music while enjoying dinner 3rd Tuesday of each month at Winchester Center.

PETS

Absolutely Cats
Sandra Whitley, Pres. - 658-2287
Donna Cornelius, Secretary - 395-4333
Open to cat-minded persons; not-for-profit organization assists with the placement and adoption and behavioral problems in cats.

Black Mountain Kennel Club of Nevada
565-1277
Terri Bounty
Meets 3rd Wednesday of each month at 7 pm at Henderson Chevrolet on Sunset and Stephanie. Shows held in April and October at Sam Boyd Silverbowl practice field, training and educational programs.

Southern Nevada Koi Club
876-8813
Colleen Weaver, Pres.
Meets 3rd Saturday of the month at 9 am in the Spring Valley Library, 4280 S. Jones Blvd. Membership includes subscription to Koi Magazine.

Southern Nevada Turtle and Tortoise Club
4527 E. Harmon Circle
Las Vegas, NV 89122
456-1476
Help Line: 223-3348
Fax: 566-4575
The Southern Nevada Turtle and Tortoise Club was founded in 1996 and works to disseminate information regarding proper husbandry of the exotic turtles and tortoises kept in captivity here in Southern Nevada. We hold monthly meetings, publish a quarterly newsletter and run a rescue and adoption service. In addition, we have a help line in place so turtle and tortoise keepers may call for advice, veterinary referrals or current club information.

Las Vegas Avicultural Society
631-6031
Linda Smith, Membership Chairman
Meets 2nd Sunday of each month at North Las Vegas Elks Lodge, 2939 Van Der Meer St. Speakers on birds as pets, breeding and care; Non-profit; 2 Bird Marts a year.

Las Vegas Cat Club
(Cat Fanciers Association)
6708 Old Castle Dr.
Las Vegas, NV 89109
Sandra Whitney, Show Coordinator - 658-2287
Linda Jeske - 368-6266
Shows held at Cashman Field and are open to purebred and household pets. Cat show held annually, non-profit organization for the benefit of other feline organizations.

Nevada Dog Fanciers
458-4075
Jean Sharp
Meets 8 pm 4th Monday of each month in Dog Fanciers Park, 5800 E. Flamingo Rd.

Silver State Kennel Club
878-8683
Mike Connell, Pres.
AKC licensed all-breed club. Shows held in April and October at Dog Fanciers Park.

SNFF
(S. Nevada Feline Fanciers)
565-8449
Barbara Mongan, Pres.
Member of the American Cat Association.

Silver State Miniature Horse Club
452-1985
Kathy Councilman, Secretary
Meets 2nd Monday of every month at 7:30 pm. Call for information. Breeders, showers and pet owners welcome.

RECREATION

The Adventurers
650-2629
Activities group meets for hiking, cliff dives, parties and other events.

Healthy Strides
Walking group meets at 10 am Monday, Wednesday and Friday at Doolittle Senior Satellite, 1901 N. J St.

Las Vegas Far-Out Explorers Society
733-0536
Gary Hoffman, Pres.
Monthly meetings to bring experienced adventure travelers together to share experiences of travel off the beaten path outside the United States.

Las Vegas Track Club
645-9618
Runners Hotline: 594-0970
Deloy Martinez, Pres.
Meets every Saturday (except when there's a sponsored T-shirt race). Call for times and locations.

Las Vegas Valley Bike Club
228-4076
Leanne Miller, Pres.
Meets 1st Thursday of each month at 7 pm at Nevada Power Co., 6226 W Sahara Ave., weekend rides, mountain bike rides, poker runs and special event rides. Road, mountain and tandem bikes. Open to the public.

Las Vegas Womens Bowling Assn.
362-0276
Linda Spaulding
Meets 10 times a year at various houses. Go-between for about 500 leagues.

Nevada Camera Club
477-9900
Jerome Hamilton, VP
Meets 2nd and 4th Friday at UMC Office Building, 2040 W. Charleston Blvd. at 7 pm.

Southern Nevada Bowling Assn.
362-5550
Otis Reid
Affiliated with the American Bowling Congress. Non-profit, gives league members membership cards.

Southern Nevada Horseshoe Pitchers Association
736-7348
Don Weaver, Pres.
Year-round leagues. Meets every Tuesday at 6:30 pm at Jaycee Park.

The American Volkssport Assn.
255-3770
Terry Kunz
Fun-filled, safe exercise in a stress-free environment. Walking, biking, swimming, cross-country skiing, snow shoeing, roller skating and ice skating.

Tri Club
248-7000
Supports and trains for triathlons.

SINGLES

Bachelors and Bachelorettes Toastmasters
367-0284
All singles club meets every Wednesday of the month at 6 pm at the Macayo Restaurant, 5589 Charleston Blvd.

Christian Singles Connection
393-4939
Activities for new non-denominational singles.

Dinner with Singles
226-4023
Business and professional people meet for weekly dinners at various restaurants. Non-profit.

Funtimers Singles
Hot Line: 387-3887
Irma Schultz, Pres.
Meets Wednesday 6 pm at the Silver Saddle and Friday 5 pm at The Hop, Tropicana Ave. Walks in different malls Sunday at 9 am followed by Sunday brunch.

Guys and Dolls
897-2431
Single seniors 55-plus
Meets every Tuesday for dinner at 5 pm.

JCCSN Jewish Singles 39 Again
Meets 2nd and 4th Wednesday 5:30 pm - 7:30 pm at Big Dogs, 6390 W. Sahara Ave.

Single Central of Las Vegas
2235 E. Flamingo Rd., Ste. 109
641-8842
Hot Line: 866-6525
Non-profit dating and activity service

Singles Travel Club
Eva Lee, Pres.- 880-3663
Don Murschel, Treas. - 880-5828
Objective is to get group rates; singles travel together to eliminate cost of singles supplement. Meets 1st and 3rd Friday of the month at Skinny Dugan's Pub, W. Charleston Blvd.

SOLOS
First Presbyterian Church
1515 W. Charleston Blvd.
Las Vegas, NV 89102
384-4554
Rick Karns, Associate Minister
Discussion group meets Sunday 6 pm in Fireside Room. For singles only.

West Valley Assembly
876-8338
For singles of all ages; meets each Friday for fellowship, teaching and discussion.

SPORTS
(Also see individual sports in the Sports and Recreation Section.)

Las Vegas Fly Fishing Club
454-2191
Vern Baker, Pres.
Meets at O.C. Lee Building, 1250 S. Burnham Ave. every 3rd Tuesday at 6:30 pm.

Las Vegas Kart Club
438-3398
Don Daydon, Pres.
Meets 1st Wednesday at 7:30 pm; call for location. Go-cart racing. Race 2nd and 4th Saturday of the month at 6 pm in the summer and 2nd and 4th Sunday of the month at 9 am in the winter at Las Vegas Motor Speedway. Oldest racing club in Las Vegas.

Las Vegas Ski Club
458-0469
Meets at various times and locations; please call ahead.

Neon Divers
452-5723
Steve Castle, Pres.
Meets 1st Wednesday of the month at 7 pm at AA1 Neptune, Lake Mead Blvd.

Softball League for Women
251-9784
Pat Etheridge
Senior women's softball for ages 48 and older. Plays at Lorenzi Park most Sundays at 2 pm. Will have earlier hours in summer and evening games. All skill levels are welcome.

Southern Nevada Divers Assn.
644-7461
Michelle Adams, Pres.
Meets 2nd Tuesday of the month 7 pm at Denny's on Maryland Pkwy.

VOLUNTEER & ASSISTANCE

Adopt-A-Trail
363-1921
Kathy August
Highway cleanup, trail monitors, hike guides, and information desk volunteers.

Assistance League of Las Vegas
6126 W. Charleston Blvd.
Las Vegas, NV 89102
870-1158
Jeanette Davis, Pres.
Founded in 1976, Assistance League is a philanthropic organization of members who volunteer to support community-wide projects. Operates Just a Second thrift shop.

Children's Service Guild
735-6448
Peggy Welch, Pres.
Raises money for children who have been through the court system. Meets every Tuesday at Juvenile Court Bldg. at 9:30 am. Come and join us in our craftwork.

City of Hope
Sun City Summerlin Chapter #1499
meets 2nd Sunday of each month at 7 pm at Mountain Shadows Community Center, 9107 Del Webb Dr. For Seniors 50+, over 300 members. Fundraisers include fashion shows and luncheons, candy sales, show tickets, cruises, bowlaramas and much, much more.
Power of Life Chapter #1369 meets 3rd Sunday of each month at 1:30 pm at Best Western Mardi Gras, 3500 Paradise Rd. For Seniors 50+, 100 members.

Clark County Social Service Volunteer Program
1600 Pinto Ln.
Las Vegas, NV 89106
455-5719
Carolyn Forrester, Coordinator
The volunteer program gives support to social service clients.

Desert Springs Hospital Auxiliary
369-7782
Susan Jootberns, Volunteer Dir.
Money raised at bake sales, boutiques, and gift shops go to charities and scholarships. Patients, needs are attended to by volunteers.

Just a Second Boutique
570 S. Decatur Blvd.
Las Vegas, NV 89107
878-2558
Hours: Tue., Wed., Sat. 10 am - 4 pm

Las Vegas Civitan Club
791-6633   566-0625
Mark Singer
Volunteer community service organization focuses on mental and physical disabilities. Meets 2nd Wednesday of each month at Marie Callender's on Decatur Blvd. Call for additional information.

Nevada Donor Network Inc.
796-9600
Compassionate and talented volunteers are needed to donate time and skills.

PRN Home
896-5759
Dana Garner
Training program for office and patient care.

Retired Senior Volunteer Program
Catholic Charities of Southern Nevada
340 N. 11th St.
Las Vegas, NV 89101
382-0721
27 E. Texas Ave.
Henderson, NV 89015
565-6990
Juliette Parlow, Dir. - 382-0721
Finds volunteer jobs for seniors.

Score
(Special Corps of Retired Execs)
301 E. Stewart Ave.
Las Vegas, NV 89125
388-6104
Sherman Kerner, Chapter Chairman
"Wisdom and experience at work."
Small businesses seminars and professional assistance.

Salvation Army Women's Auxiliary
870-4430
Joanne Vaughn, Pres.
Replaces flooring and furnishings in transitional housing for low income.

St. Judes Women's Auxiliary
P.O. Box 42008
Las Vegas, NV 89116
386-0772
Eve Moss, Pres.
Raises money for St. Jude's Ranch, which provides for the welfare of abused, abandoned and neglected children.

St. Rose Dominican Hospital Volunteer Program
564-4543
Sharon Moxley, Manager

Provides service to patients and staff and runs the hospital thrift shop.

St. Vincent's Catholic Community Services
1501 Las Vegas Blvd. N.
Las Vegas, NV 89101
383-1163
Marlene Reichter - 383-0766
Multi-service social service agency providing assistance to seniors, youths, homeless, recent immigrants and families.

Sunrise Hospital Auxiliary
731-8188
Janet Delaney, Volunteer Coordinator
Proceeds from gift shop go toward charities and scholarships. Sees to comfort of patients.

United Way Services Inc.
1660 E. Flamingo Rd.
Las Vegas, NV 89119
734-2273
Garth Winckler, Pres. of Las Vegas organization
Hours: Mon.-Fri. 8 am - 5 pm
Positions are available working with the needy, elderly, handicapped and children; training is provided. See Sunday "Living Section" of the newspaper for a list of positions. Agency funds local charitable organizations. United Way is an umbrella organization for over 40 local agencies that provide a full range of human care services. United Way's Volunteer Bureau helps recruit volunteers for more than 130 local non-profit organizations. In 1996-97 the Las Vegas organization raised $7.8 million; 85.2 cents from every dollar goes to provide local services.

CIVIC & SERVICE ORGANIZATIONS

JAYCEES

Las Vegas Jaycees
457-8832
Cory Epps, Pres.
Meets Wednesday at 8 pm at Clubhouse at 1913 S. Eastern Avenue.

KIWANIS CLUBS

Henderson Kiwanis
558-7198
Olivia Purdie, Pres.

Green Valley Kiwanis
898-9386
Doug Hume, Pres.
Meets Monday 7:30 am at Greens Restaurant.

Kiwanis Club of Las Vegas
876-8080
Mark Zannis, Pres.
Meets noon on Wednesday at Chins Restaurant in the Fashion Show Mall.

Kiwanis Club of Southwest Las Vegas
795-0885
Rosa Herron, Pres.
Meets at noon on Wednesday at The Barking Frog on Spring Mountain Rd.

Las Vegas' Strip Kiwanis Club
254-2200

Rob Engleman, Pres.
Meets 7:30 am Friday at the Golden Eagle Restaurant on Paradise Rd.

North West Kiwanis Club
254-2200
Peter Jackson, Pres.
Meets 7 am Tuesdays at Magoos Restaurant on Cheyenne Ave.

Uptown Kiwanis Club
367-5412
Harris Lee, Pres.
Meets Thursday at noon at the Elks Club at 4100 W. Charleston Blvd.

OPTIMISTS CLUBS

"Friend of Youth" - Supports boys homes, scholarships, bicycle safety, and anti-drug program.

The Zone #2
368-3991
H. Jay Stone, Lt. Governor

Clark County Optimists Boys Home and Ranch
2521 Apricot Ln.
Las Vegas, NV 89108
594-1780
Tom Pitts, Pres.

Luncheon Optimist Club
732-1664
Paul Ruttan

Las Vegas Northwest Optimist Club
295-3521
Darwin Morgan, Pres.

Green Valley Optimist Club
435-3277
Barry Yost

LIONS CLUBS

Las Vegas Agila Lions Club
898-9527
John Eric Garde, Pres.

Las Vegas Breakfasters Lions Club
877-1483
Jerry Nebron, Pres.

Las Vegas Executives Lions Club
896-0443
Mark Soloman, Pres.

Las Vegas Golden Agila Lions Club
650-0793
Geny DelRosario, Pres.

Las Vegas Host Lions Club
796-9600
Raymond Christianson, Pres.

Los Prados Lions Club
655-0705   645-4647
Audrey Williams, Pres.

Las Vegas Paradise Valley Lions Club
382-6022
Robert Young, Pres.

Las Vegas Sundowners Lions Club
453-4958
Don Benshooe, Pres.

Las Vegas West Charleston Lions Club
877-5466
Bernie Lucido, Pres.

Lions Club Sight Conservation Committee
736-6506

Henderson/Green Valley Lions Club
897-6354
Paul Dreschler, Pres.

Boulder City Lions Club
293-3880
Stan Beans, Pres.

TOASTMASTERS

Toastmasters International
5775 W. Sahara Ave.
Las Vegas, NV 89102
367-1973
Organization that teaches communication and leadership skills.

EXCHANGE CLUB

**Las Vegas Breakfast
Exchange Club**
877-4343
Bob McArthur, Pres.
Meets at Las Vegas Club, Fremont and Main Sts. Thursday 7 am.

Exchange Clubs of Las Vegas
645-4844
National organization - supports Little League, soccer and the underprivileged. Meets noon Wednesday at the El Cortez Hotel.

SERTOMA CLUBS

Sertoma Club
Don Jay, Chairman - 385-4007
Walter Pinjuv - 384-2560
Assists speech and hearing impaired children; scholarship; contributes to UMC Hearing Dept. Meets 1 pm Tuesday at the Coachman's Inn, 3240 S. Eastern Avenue.

SOROPTIMISTS CLUBS

Contact number for all Soroptimist Clubs is 362-7666. Below is a list of the various clubs in Las Vegas and surrounding vicinities; please call for times and locations of meetings in your area.

**Soroptimists International of
Boulder City**

**Soroptimists International of
Creative Las Vegans**

**Soroptimists International of
Greater Las Vegas**

**Soroptimists International of
Henderson**

**Soroptimists International of
Las Vegas Valley**

**Soroptimists International of
Metropolitan Las Vegas**

ROTARY CLUBS

Boulder City
P.O. Box 60924
Boulder City, NV 89006
293-1067
Dick White, Pres.
Meets Wednesday noon at Two Gals.

Boulder City Sunrise
P.O. Box 60905
Boulder City, NV 89006
293-9256
Roger Hall, Pres.
Meets Thursday 7 am at Two Gals.

Green Valley
2887 Green Valley Pkwy., Ste. 335
Henderson, NV 89014
455-5995
Robert Gaston, Pres.
Meets Thursday 7 am at Renata's Restaurant.

Henderson
P.O. Box 90274
Henderson, NV 89009
565-9743
Steve Arrlington, Pres.
Meets Tuesday noon at Kiefer's Restaurant.

Las Vegas
P.O. Box 15152
Las Vegas, NV 89114
737-1122
Ralph Rohay, Pres.
Meets Thursday noon at Desert Inn on the Strip.

Las Vegas Fremont
P.O. Box 1148
Las Vegas, NV 89125
367-5244
Elise Sauer, Pres.
Meets Tuesday noon at the Las Vegas Club.

Las Vegas North
P.O. Box 4132
N. Las Vegas, NV 89030
731-8134   256-0782
B. J. Scott, Pres.
Meets Friday 7 am at Fiesta Hotel/Casino.

Las Vegas Northwest
P.O. Box 370995
Las Vegas, NV 89137
255-3465
Jim Veltman, Pres.
Meets Tuesday 7:15 am at TPC Club House.

Las Vegas Paradise
P.O. Box 72166
Las Vegas, NV 89170
382-0500
Loren Lomprey, Pres.
Meets Wednesday noon at Las Vegas Hilton Country Club.

Las Vegas Southwest
P.O. Box 26353
Las Vegas, NV 89126
897-4400
Jimmy Pettyjohn, Pres.
Meets Monday noon at the Elks Lodge on W. Charleston Blvd.

Las Vegas University
P.O. Box 71644
Las Vegas, NV 89170-1644
227-7044
Bill Pierce, Pres.
Meets Thursday 7:30 am at Las Vegas Country Club.

Las Vegas West
3675 S. Rainbow Blvd., Ste. 107-140
Las Vegas, NV 89103
877-2300
Scott Ruthe, Pres.
Meets Tuesday noon at Canyon Gate Country Club.

FRATERNAL ORGANIZATIONS

DEMOLAY

Demolay · Oasis Chapter #29014
383-9959
John Kielbaugh, Chapter Dad
Meets at 5:30 pm 1st and 3rd Sunday at Masonic Memorial Temple, 2200 W. Mesquite Ave. Open to young men 13-21 years old.

ELKS LODGES

Elks Lodge #1468
4100 W. Charleston Blvd.
Las Vegas, NV 89102
258-3557
Pat Bezenbower, Exalted Ruler

**Elks Lodge of
North Las Vegas #2353**
2939 Van Der Meer St.
N. Las Vegas, NV 89030
642-9431
Thomas Tucker

Elks Lodge #1682
1217 Nevada Hwy.
Boulder City, NV 89006
293-2457
Howard Tindall, Exalted Ruler

Elks Lodge #1759
***Improved Benevolent Protect.
of Order-Elks of the World***
1054 N. Rancho Dr.
Las Vegas, NV 89106
631-0331

Elks Paran Lodge #1508
1236 Blankenship Ave.
Las Vegas, NV 89106
648-8033

Fraternal Order of Eagles #1213, 1601 E. Washington Ave., Las Vegas, NV 89101

FRATERNAL ORDER OF EAGLES

Fraternal Order of Eagles #1213
1601 E. Washington Ave.
Las Vegas, NV 89101
642-1213
Meets 2nd and 3rd Tuesday of each month.

Fraternal Order of Eagles #2672
310 W. Pacific Ave.
Henderson, NV 89015
565-2672
Tom Rogers, Pres.
Meets 2nd and 4th Tuesday of each month.

INDEPENDENT ORDER OF FORESTERS

Independent Order of Foresters
1515 E. Tropicana Ave., Ste. 150
Las Vegas, NV 89119
739-8282
Fraternal organization over 100 years old, providing life insurance and investments for members. Over 10,000 members in Nevada.

KNIGHTS OF COLUMBUS

Las Vegas Council #2828
911 1/2 Ogden Ave.

Las Vegas, NV 89101
387-9312
Servando Cardenas, Grand Knight

KNIGHTS OF PYTHIAS

**Knights of Pythias
Las Vegas Lodge #11**
871-6256
Daniel Deanin, Chancellor Commodore
National organization that raises money for charities and United Cerebral Palsy and sponsors groups to help the homeless. Meets 2nd and 4th Thursday; call for location.

MASONIC LODGES

Vegas Lodge #32
632 E. Charleston Blvd.
Las Vegas, NV 89104
382-1174
Hours: 8 am - 2 pm Mon. - Fri.

Masonic Memorial Temple
2200 W. Mesquite Ave.
Las Vegas, NV 89106
382-6055
Hours: Mon. - Thu. mornings only.

Mount Moriah #39
480 Greenway Rd.
Henderson, NV 89015
564-2867

Acacia Lodge #49
2929 Van Der Meer St.
N. Las Vegas, NV 89030
399-0665

FRATERNAL ORGANIZATIONS

**Masonic Temple -
Boulder City #37**
901 Arizona St.
Boulder City, NV 89005
293-1809   293-0877

Daylight Lodge #44
2200 W. Mesquite Ave.
Las Vegas, NV 89106
384-7017

Oasis Lodge #41
2200 W. Mesquite Ave.
Las Vegas, NV 89106
383-9959 387-6016

Nellis Lodge #46
2200 W. Mesquite Ave.
Las Vegas, NV 89106
387-0046

Silver Cord Lodge #51
4401 Cory Pl.
Las Vegas, NV 89107
564-2867

YORK RITE - MASONS

Grand York Rite Committee
4409 St. Andrews Cir.
Las Vegas, NV 89107-2075
878-1074

Elks Lodge #1468, 4100 W. Charleston Blvd., Las Vegas, NV 89102

Bob Gilbert, Chairman
Royal Arch Masons Chapters
8 Chapters in the State of Nevada
8 Cryptic Masons Councils
9 Grand Sessions held every year at various locations. Contributes to research and medical fields.

MOOSE LODGES

Moose Lodge Las Vegas #1763
1600 Gragson Ave.
Las Vegas, NV 89101
399-9026

Moose Lodge Red Rock #252
4950 W. Charleston Blvd.
Las Vegas, NV 89102
878-9817

Moose Lodge Henderson #1924
22 W. Army St.
Henderson, NV 89015
565-6796

ORDER OF THE EASTERN STAR

**The Desert Rose Grand
Chapter of Nevada**
Meets 7:30 pm 2nd & 4th Mon., Tue. and Thu. at Price Hall Masonic Lodge, 2700 Colton Ave., N. Las Vegas.

Rosicrucian Order Amorc
645-6700
David Grower, Master
Meets 7:30 pm 2nd & 4th Monday at Commercial Square, Carriage Trade Center, 900 E. Karen Ave., Ste. 207.

SHRINERS

Zelzah Shrine Temple A.A.O.N.M.S.
2222 W. Mesquite Ave.
Las Vegas, NV 89106
382-5554
William Becker, Potentate

MILITARY and VETERANS CLUBS & ORGANIZATIONS

American Ex-Prisoners of War
293-2374
Jim Cronk, Commander
Organization for ex-prisoners of war. Does legislation for benefits through Veterans Administration. Donates money for Southern Nevada Veterans Memorial Cemetery in Boulder City and Nellis Federal Medical Center.

Air Force Association
453-5115
Mike Johnson, Pres.
Council meeting held 2nd Tuesday of each month at 6 pm at the Officers Club at Nellis Air Force Base.

Air Force Sergeants Assn.
453-5115
Mike Johnson, Pres.
Meets last Thursday of the month at 7:30 pm at Nellis Air Force Base.

The Key Foundation
594-5604
Terry Ryder, Pres.
Helps homeless veterans get jobs and housing; incorporated February 1991. The organization has placed 1,500 veterans and other homeless people in Las Vegas, provides food, clothing, transportation, housing and counseling.

AMERICAN LEGION

American Legion Post #8
733 Veterans Memorial Dr.
Las Vegas, NV 89101
382-8533
Mike Pipher, Commander
Meets 7 pm 1st and 3rd Tuesday.

American Legion Post #31
508 California Ave.
Boulder City, NV 89005
293-6374
David Mulligan, Commander
Meets 1st and 3rd Monday.

American Legion Post #40
P.O. Box 90081
Henderson, NV 90009
565-5433
Stan Ruvolo, Commander

American Legion Post #51
P.O. Box 2357
N. Las Vegas, NV 89030
385-2652
Doug Lawson, Commander

**American Legion J. Edgar
Hoover Police Post #55**
P.O. Box 603
Las Vegas, NV 89125
382-3312
Stan Kushel, Commander

**American Merchant
Marine Veterans**
293-7438
Meeting 11 am 3rd   Friday of each month at Police Protective Assn. on Burnham Ave. 1/2 block south of Charleston Blvd. All Merchant Marines are invited along with members of the Navy Armed Guard and Army Transport Services.

American War Mothers
642-2924
Joyce Hartley, Pres.
Meets 2nd Tuesday of each month. Call for location. Raises money with rummage and cake sales which is donated to the VA Clinic, 30th St., Senior Citizens Center and needy families.

**American Wheelchair
Veterans Association**
5355 Madre Mesa Dr.
Las Vegas, NV 89108
631-1900
James E. Smith, Pres.
Non-profit veterans organization; wheelchair sports - bowling, tennis, quad rugby, swimming, wheelchair marathons.

China-Burma-India Veterans
Silver State Basha #133
878-6903
Tim Schaefer
Meetings 4th Saturday of the month at noon. Call for information.

Civil Air Patrol
Nellis Senior Squadron
631-4575   652-8564
Major Arvid Schnackenberg, Squadron Commander
Meets every 2nd and 4th Wednesday at 1900 hours at the Officers Club at Nellis Air Force Base.

Henderson Squadron
US Air Force Aux. of Civil Air Patrol
433-1238   261-4800
Captain Fred Chatman
Meets 1st and 3rd Tuesday at 7 pm at Sky Harbor Airport. Search and rescue aerospace leadership organization for adults and teenagers.

Civilian Military Council
565-2085
Mayor Robert Groesbeck, Chairman
Joint-civilian military coordinating group that addresses matters that would interest the Las Vegas community.

**Council of Nevada Veteran's
Organizations**
1301 E. Webb St.
N. Las Vegas, NV 89030
399-2880
Mike Johnson, Pres.
Umbrella group for all veteran's organizations.

DISABLED AMERICAN VETERANS

D.A.V. Chapter #11
636-3070   486-6171
Steve Clark, Commander
Meets 7 pm 3rd Thursday of each month at Outpatient Clinic, Martin Luther King Blvd.

D.A.V. Auxiliary Unit #11
458-6514
Rose Thomas, Commander

D.A.V. #12 Boulder City
565-0521
Dan Johnson, Commander

D.A.V. Chapter #13
431-5251
Pete Petty, Commander

D.A.V. Woman's Auxiliary #13
649-9274
Dorothy Otts, Commander

D.A.V. Chapter #34
646-2160
Winston Bell, Commander

D.A.V. Women's Auxiliary #34
362-0296
Eva Garrett Johnson, Commander

**Disabled American Veterans
Department of Nevada**
William Brzezinski, State Commander
- 649-1496
Monika Diaz, D.A.V. Department Service Officer - 386-4051

**Governor's Commission For
Veterans Affairs**
Deputy Commissioner's Office
2915 W. Charleston Blvd., Ste. 5A
Las Vegas, NV 89102
636-3070

82nd Airborne Division Association, Inc.
253-6910
Eric Johnson, Chairman
Chuck Springer, Vice Chairman
Monthly meeting 2nd Thursday 7 pm at American Legion Post 8, 733 N. Veterans Memorial Dr. All paratroopers, glider troopers, and glider pilots are invited.

Fleet Reserve Association
P.O. Box 1824
Las Vegas, NV 89125
642-6000
Homer Williams, Pres.
Meets every 3rd Thursday at the Las Vegas Blind Center, 1001 N. Bruce St. Dinner at 6 pm, meeting at 7 pm.

Jewish War Veterans
Murray L. Rosen Post 64
2609 Springridge Dr.
Las Vegas, NV 89134
254-0150
Harry Hartstein, Commander
Meetings held 4th Sunday at 1:30 at the Rainbow Library.

Leatherneck Club
4360 W. Spring Mountain Rd.
Las Vegas, NV 89102
368-1775
Dick Byington, Commandant
Las Vegas headquarters and museum. Call for times and location of meetings.

Military Order of the Purple Heart
825 N. Lamb Blvd., #309
Las Vegas, NV 89110
459-0842
Harry Cohen, Commander
Support group of Purple Heart recipients.

RESERVE OFFICERS ASSOCIATION

Reserve Officers Assoc. of the U.S.
361-4983
Lieutenant Colonel Timothy Terrell, Pres.
An organization made up of reserve and warrant officers of all military services.

The Retired Officers Association
876-6530
Frank C. Fain, Pres.
Meets 2nd Thursday of each month at the California Hotel in the Ohana Room, cocktails at 6:30 pm, dinner at 7:30 pm.

Retired Officers Wives Club of Southern Nevada
897-8203
Donna Gavac, Pres.
Luncheons and bridge group.

Seabee Island X1
735-0126   255-6822
Normand Pratt
Meets 1st Thursday of the month at American Legion Post #8 at 7 pm.

Society of the Third Infantry Division O.P. 77
457-5722
Louis Conant, Secretary Treasurer
Third Infantry in existence since 1917. Anyone who served in war or peacetime or has been attached to the Third Infantry Division is welcome. Call for meeting times.

Veterans in Politics
2550 E. Desert Inn Rd., Ste. 320
Las Vegas, NV 89121
648-2167
Charles Stilson, Pres.
Political action committee. Meets 3rd Thursday of the month at the East Flamingo Library, 1 pm. Open to the public.

VETERANS OF FOREIGN WARS

VFW Post #1753
705 Las Vegas Blvd. N.
Las Vegas, NV 89101
384-4161
Lee Coke, Post Commander

VFW Ladies Auxiliary #1753
384-4161
Sheri Davidson, Pres.

VFW Post #10047
4337 Las Vegas Blvd. N.
Las Vegas, NV 89115
643-1177
Tim Parsons, Post Commander

VFW Ladies Auxiliary #10047
643-1177
Pearl Peterson, Pres.

VFW Post #10057
1905 N. H St.
Las Vegas, NV 89106
646-1052
Claude Brown, Post Commander

VFW Ladies Auxiliary #10057
646-1052
Patricia Feaster, Pres.

VFW Post #3848
401 Lake Mead Dr.
Henderson, NV 89015
564-5822
Gil Wagner, Post Commander

VFW Ladies Auxiliary #3848
564-5822
Alice Wagner, Pres.

U. S. Submarine Veterans of World War II - Silver State Chapter
731-0719
Ray Werbrich, Secretary/Treasurer
Meets 2nd Saturday of each month at Boulder Cascades, 1601 S. Sandhill Rd. at noon.

WAC #77
433-9000
Mildred Batalias, Pres.
Meets 3rd Tuesday of the month 1:30 pm at the Flamingo Library.

Women Marine Association - Sagebrush Chapter
2545 Reno Ave.
Las Vegas, NV 89120
736-2583
Mary Knapp, Pres.

Women Veterans of Nevada
867 N. Lamb Blvd., Space 75
Las Vegas, NV 89110
453-1701

Veterans Hotline: 399-2880

WOMEN'S ORGANIZATIONS

AMERICAN BUSINESS WOMEN'S ASSOCIATION

ABWA
Desert Dawn Chapter - #6101
564-1036
Earlene Gordon, Pres.
Meets 2nd Tuesday at various locations.

ABWA - Desert Winds - #6102
457-4445
Marie Gibbons, Pres.
Meets 4th Tuesday at various locations.

ABWA - Las Vegas Centennial Chapter - #6104
362-9548
Rama Shaw, Pres.
Meets 2nd Wednesday at Country Inn on Rainbow Blvd.

ABWA - Mojave Rose Chapter - (retired) #6105
616 Donner St.
Las Vegas, NV 89107
870-4347
Lynn Bonds
Meets 1st Wednesday at various locations.

ABWA - NLV Charter Chapter - #6174
649-3532
Minnie Walden, Pres.
Meets 4th Monday at Wendy's Human Resource Center on East Lake Mead Blvd.

ABWA - Drifting Dunes - #6103
869-3988
Kay Keckeisen, Pres.
Meets 3rd Monday at Holiday Inn on Flamingo and Paradise Rds.

ABWA - Las Vegas Gambeliers - #6315
657-0255
Jacqueline Cooper, Pres.
Meets 2nd Wednesday at Sizzler on Rainbow Blvd. and Spring Mountain Rd.

ABWA - Pinion Pine Chapter - #3660
431-7026
Sharon Rogers, Pres.
Meets 3rd Thursday at Magoos Hideaway on Sahara Ave. and Rainbow Blvd.

BUSINESS AND PROFESSIONAL WOMEN

Active Republican Women's Club
878-5534
Lia Roberts, Pres.
Meets 2nd Tuesday of the month at Marie Callendar's on West Flamingo Rd.

Altrusa Club of Las Vegas
878-6385
Janet Schlauder, Pres.
International Business and Professional Women's Club, organized in 1917, meets 2nd & 4th Tuesdays in members homes.

American Association of University Women Las Vegas
594-2929
Mary Stanley, Pres.
Meets the 4th Wednesday of each month at 6:30 pm at Emerald Springs Holiday Inn on Flamingo Rd. Promotes life-long education for women.

American League of Pen Women
9705 Sierra Mesa Ave.
Las Vegas, NV 89117
363-9920
Mary Shaw, Pres.
Founded in 1897. Composed of artists, writers and musicians. Luncheon meetings 2nd Saturday of the month at 1 pm at various locations. Call for information.

Aviva of Summerlin
233-8601
Shirley Ravich, Pres.
Meets 4th Monday of the month at the Summerlin Library.

B'nai B'rith Women
363-1068
Sydell Miller, National Membership Chairwoman
Business and professional women meeting on the last Sunday of each month at various locations.

Business and Professional Women
Meetings held the 4th Monday of each month at Denny's Restaurant, 3081 Maryland Pkwy. Dinner at 6 pm and business meeting.

Federally Employed Women
873-6023
Linda Robinson, Pres.
Meets 3rd Tuesday of each month. FEW was established 1968. Only national organization which focuses on eliminating sex discrimination, increasing career opportunities, advancing women in the federal sector.

Hadassah
656-1666
JoAnne Geller, Pres.
Health organization. Built and maintains hospital in Israel.

International Training in Communications
438-4464
Barbara Lyons, Pres.
Group's function is to develop communication skills and help express thoughts clearly.

The Jean Nidetch Women's Center
4505 S. Maryland Pkwy.
Las Vegas, NV 89154-2025
895-4475
Conee Spano, Dir.
Non-profit. Helps people get back into school. Information and referral service.

Junior League of Las Vegas
461 S. Decatur Blvd..
Las Vegas, NV 89109
732-3257
Luann Kutch, Pres.
Non-profit women's community service organization.

WOMEN'S ORGANIZATIONS

Las Vegas Christian Women's Club
254-6766
Meets every 3rd Wednesday of the month.

The Las Vegas Towne Club
648-9333
Yolanda Moreira, Pres.
Social club for women meets 4th Tuesday of each month.

Las Vegas Women in Communications
457-1694
Lynn Ann Martin, Pres.
Luncheons 2nd Thursday of every month at Palace Station.

League of Women Voters of Las Vegas
631-4998
Ruth Mills
Meets 3rd Saturday of the month at 8:30 am at the Mardi Gras on Paradise Rd.

Mesquite Club
702 E. St. Louis Ave.
Las Vegas, NV 89104

735-9048
Lois Mahood, Pres.
Women's social and civic club.

National Association of Female Executives
263-6728
Robyn Salisbury, Interim Pres.
Meets once a month on different days at Emerald Springs Holiday Inn on Flamingo Rd. Networking women's group.

National Assn. of Women Business Owners
732-4900
Nancy McRight, Pres.
Leadership and support group. Meets 4th Tuesday of each month at 5:30 pm at Southwest Gas Company.

National Federation of Press Women
1-702-827-9228
Shayne Del Cohen, Pres.
Professional journalists active in public relations, advertising and communications.

National Society of Daughters of the American Revolution
Valley of Fire Chapter
387-5520
Lee Cleven, Regent

Pomegranate Club
367-2057
Martha Shulman
Judaic needlework club. Meets 4th Monday of each month in the daytime and 2nd Tuesday of each month at night in different locations.

Professional Black Women's Alliance
631-0000
Faye Duncan-Daniel, Pres.
Meets 2nd Saturday at 10 am at West Las Vegas Library.

Republican Women of Las Vegas
877-0812
Meets 2nd Wednesday of the month at 11:30 am at Palace Station. Supports Republican candidates for office.

Shoshanim
459-2428
Meets 1st Monday of the month. Call for meeting times.

Southern Nevada NOW
P.O. Box 46693
Las Vegas, NV 89114-6693
387-7552
Patricia Ireland, National Pres.
National Organization for Women; Meets 3rd Saturday of the month at 10 am at various places. Political action organization for women's rights.

Vegas Valley Business and Professional Women's Club
361-8392
Rose Anna Cirac, Pres.
Meets 2nd Tuesday of each month at Carrows on West Sahara Ave.

Parks & Events Centers

Southern Nevada has over 151 parks (including rural) with over 60 parks in Clark County, 34 in Las Vegas, 23 in North Las Vegas, 21 in Henderson, and 13 in Boulder City. Clark County has 900 acres and Las Vegas has 540 acres developed for recreational use. Southern Nevada is also home to three state parks. Clark County has approximately 2.7 acres of park space for every 1,000 people, the city has 2.75 acres of park space for every 1,000 people. Most parks are open from about 7 am to 11 pm.

A variety of recreational facilities can be found, such as the Nellis Meadows BMX Track; Dog Fanciers and Horseman's Park for dog shows and equestrian events; Circus Circus Remote Control Aircraft Field and Park for model aircraft enthusiasts; remote control car track and an archery range at the Silver Bowl Sports Complex.

Sunset Park, the largest park in the county, has 324 acres of lighted ball fields and tennis courts, a swimming pool, 7 sandy volleyball courts, Frisbee golf course, horseshoe pits and a 13 acre pond with fishing. Lorenzi Park is the largest in the city with 60 acres.

Playgrounds at schools are for school use only from 8 am to 4 pm when schools are in session. The School Board and the County Commission endorsed the "Open Schools, Open Doors" program which will open schools for recreation programs after classes and when school is not in session at 77 area schools.

Alcohol is prohibited in parks and dogs must be on a leash in parks where they are permitted. Permits are required for groups of 25 people or more.

PARKS AND RECREATON DEPARTMENTS

Boulder City Parks & Recreation Dept.
900 Arizona St.
Boulder City, NV 89005
293-9256
Roger Hall, Dir.
Recreation classes and sports, municipal golf course, swimming pool and racquetball complex.

City of Las Vegas Parks & Leisure Activities
Administrative Offices
749 Veterans Memorial Dr.
Las Vegas, NV 89101
229-6297
David Kuiper, Dir.
Recreation: 229-6729
Municipal Sports Office: 229-2256

City of Las Vegas Parks & Leisure Activities
Parks Division
3100 E. Bonanza Rd.
Las Vegas, NV 89101
229-6571
David Lofgreen, Mgr.
Graffiti Hotline: 385-3473

Clark County Parks & Recreation Dept.
2601 E. Sunset Rd.
Las Vegas, NV 89120
455-8200
Glenn Trowbridge, Dir.

Henderson Parks & Recreation Dept.
240 Water St.
Henderson, NV 89015
565-4264
Steve Rongyocsik, Dir.
Leisure Line: 565-2134
For information on recreation and leisure activities
Sports Office: 434-4131
For information on youth and adult leagues and tournaments
Youth Center: 565-2124

North Las Vegas Recreation Dept.
1638 N. Bruce St.
N. Las Vegas, NV 89030
633-1171
Eric Dabney, Dir.

Camps Operated by Clark County:

Camp Lee Canyon
Mt. Charleston, NV 89124
This 17 acre campground has basketball courts, picnic areas, playground area, and restrooms.

Camp Potosi
Mountain Springs, NV
160 acres

COMMUNITY CENTERS & SCHOOLS

COMMUNITY CENTERS

Community centers offer a variety of recreation classes and activities, special interest workshops, cultural and educational offerings for children and adults of all ages, including senior citizens' programs. Children's after-school programs are also offered at the centers.

Boulder City Recreation Center
900 Arizona St.
Boulder City, NV 89005
293-9256
Roger Hall, Dir.
Hours: Mon. - Fri. 2:30 pm - 9 pm; Sat. - Sun. 1 pm - 5 pm

Boulder City Recreation Center
Swimming Pool & Racquetball Complex
861 Ave. B.
Boulder City, NV 89005
293-9286
Steve Corry, Aquatic Dir. & Recreation Superintendent
Hours: Adult Lap Mon. & Fri. 6:30 - 9 am & noon - 1 pm; Tue. & Thu. 5:30 am - 9 pm; Open Swim 4:30 pm - 7:30 pm; Sat. 1 pm - 5 pm; Sun. 1 pm - 3 pm
Racquetball Mon. - Fri. 7 am - 9 pm; Sat. 1 pm - 8 pm; Sun. 1 pm - 4 pm

Black Mountain Recreation and Aquatics Center
5999 Greenway Rd.
Hendeerson, NV 89015
565-2880
John Sefton, Center Coordinator
Hours: Mon. - Fri. 9 am - 8 pm; Sat. 9 am - 6 pm; Sun. 11 am - 6 pm. Workout room is open from 5:30 am - 9 pm
40,000 sq. ft. facility opened in Spring 1996. The center features a full-size gym, 6 meeting rooms, 3 racquetball courts, multi-use rooms, and an outdoor aquatics area with a zero-depth beach entry pool.

Charleston Heights Arts Center
800 S. Brush St.
Las Vegas, NV 89107
229-6383
Cassandra McGuire, Center Coordinator

Lorenzi Adaptive Center, 3333 W. Washington Ave., Las Vegas, NV 89107

Hours: Mon. & Thu. 1 pm - 9 pm; Tue. & Wed. 10 am - 9 pm; Fri. 10 am - 6 pm; Sat. 9 am - 5 pm; Sun. 1 pm - 5 pm

Chuck Minker Sports Complex
275 N. Mojave Rd.
Las Vegas, NV 89104
229-6563
Danny Higgons, Center Coordinator
Hours: Mon. - Fri. 7 am - 9:30 pm; Sat. 9 am - 5 pm; Sun. 10 am - 4 pm
Variety of classes, recreational activities and programs for all ages; weights, aerobics, 8 racquetball courts

City Sports
821 1/2 Las Vegas Blvd. N.
Las Vegas, NV 89101
229-2256
Dick Morgan, Supervisor
Hours: Mon. - Fri. 8 am - 5 pm

Doolittle Community Center
1901 N. J St.
Las Vegas, NV 89106
229-6374
Phil Thompson, Center Coordinator
Hours: Mon. - Fri. 9 am - 9 pm; Sat. 9 am - 4 pm
Supervised activities and field trips for children, outdoor pool, indoor

and outdoor basketball. Classes and programs for youths and adults. C.O.R.E. Program.

Dula Gym
441 E. Bonanza Rd.
Las Vegas, NV 89101
229-6307
Marilyn Louden, Center Coordinator
Hours: Mon. - Fri. 8 am - 5:30 pm
For seniors: fitness room, volleyball, paddle tennis, ping pong, badminton and basketball.

Guinn Community Center
6480 Fairbanks St.
Las Vegas, NV 89103
455-8393
Mary Ann Wainwright, Center Coordinator
Hours: Mon. - Fri. 5 pm - 9 pm; Sat. 1 pm - 5 pm
Dance, exercise room, martial arts, open basketball, volleyball and music and art classes.

Lorna J. Kesterson Valley View Rec. Center
500 Harris St.
Henderson, NV 89015
565-2121
Paul Widman, Center Coordinator

Hours: Mon. - Fri. 8 am - 9 pm; Sat. 9 am - 5 pm; Sun. 1 pm - 5 pm
Classes for dance, art, drama and exercise for adults and children. Summer camp program; full size gym, 3 racquetball courts, 6 meeting rooms, kitchen and multi-fitness room. Next to the facility are 4 lighted tennis courts, 2 sand volleyball courts and a basketball court.

Lorenzi Adaptive Center
3333 W. Washington Ave.
Las Vegas, NV 89107
229-6358
Cathy Watson, Center Coordinator
Hours: Mon. - Fri. 1 pm - 6 pm
Recreation for the developmentally disabled from 7 to 22 yrs.

Lowden Community Center
3333 Cambridge St.
Las Vegas, NV 89109
455-7169
John Hulme, Center Coordinator
Hours: Mon. - Fri. 8 am - 6 pm; Seniors: Mon. - Wed., Fri. 10:30 am - 2 pm; Tiny Tots (Ages 3 - 6): Tue. & Thu. 1 pm - 3 pm; After Schoolers (Ages 7 - 12): Mon. - Thu. 3 pm - 6 pm
Parks and recreation office; family, youth and social services providers; health district services; senior citizens programs; and children's library. Cooperative Extension Girl Scouts, Family Resource Center.

Mirabelli Community Center
6200 Elton Ave.
Las Vegas, NV 89107
229-6359
Sue Bartling, Center Coordinator
Hours: Mon. - Fri. 9 am - 7 pm; Sat. 11 am - 3 pm
Programs and classes for all ages; basketball and recreational activities.

North Las Vegas Neighborhood Recreation Center
1638 N. Bruce St.
N. Las Vegas, NV 89030
633-1600
Jody Davis, Center Coordinator
Hours: Tue. - Fri. 8 am - 9 pm; Sat. 9 am - 5 pm
Fitness center, racquetball court, game room for children, dance room and 3 lit tennis courts.

Northwest Community Center
6841 W. Lone Mountain Rd.
Las Vegas, NV 89108
Mike Ghorst, Center Coordinator
Recreation: 229-4794
Senior Activities: 229-4924
Lifetime Sports: 229-6772
Adaptive Recreation: 229-4796
Track Break & Martial Arts: 229-4794

Orr Community Center
1520 E. Katie Ave.
Las Vegas, NV 89119
455-7196
Sharon Lopez, Center Coordinator
Hours: Mon. - Fri. 10 am - 9 pm
Crafts, exercise, gymnastics and sports.

Paradise Community Center
4770 S. Harrison Dr.
Las Vegas, NV 89121
455-7513
Jacque Alter, Center Coordinator
Hours: Mon. - Fri. 7:30 am - 9 pm; Sat.
9 am - 4 pm; Track Break Program for
ages 6 - 12: Mon. - Fri. 7:30 am - 3 pm;
full day 7:30 am - 7:00 pm .
Fees: $7.00 and $30 per week.
Classes for youths and adults,
recreational programs; outdoor pool

Parkdale Community Center
3200 Ferndale St.
Las Vegas, NV 89121
455-7517
Marie Kirker, Center Coordinator

Hours: Mon. - Fri. 7:30 am - 7 pm; Sat.
10 am - 2 pm; after school program Mon.
- Fri. 3 pm - 7 pm; Track break Mon. -
Fri. 7:30 am - 3 pm
Recreational programs, physical fitness
classes, arts & crafts classes, outdoor
pool and basketball

Rafael Rivera
2900 E. Stewart Ave.
Las Vegas, NV 89101
229-4600
Lance Mecham, Center Coordinator
Hours: Mon. - Fri. 9 am - 8 pm; Sat. 9 am
- 5 pm. Year round track break, 2 tennis
courts, soccer, baseball field and
Mexican Fiesta.

Reed Whipple Cultural Center
821 Las Vegas Blvd. N.
Las Vegas, NV 89101
229-6211
Patricia Harris, Center Coordinator
Hours: Mon. & Thu. 1 pm - 9 pm; Tue. &
Wed. 10 am - 9 pm; Fri. 10 am - 6 pm;
Sat. 9 am - 5 pm
A wide variety of classes, programs,
performances and showings of performing
and visual arts

Silver Springs Recreation Center
1951 Silver Springs Pkwy.
Henderson, NV 89014
435-3814
Kurt Williams, Center Coordinator
Hours: Mon. - Fri. 8 am - 9 pm; Sat. 9 am
- 5 pm; Sun. 1 pm - 5 pm

Adult classes, community center,
weight room, gymnasium, outdoor
pool and diving pool and meeting
rooms for city-sponsored programs and
community use.
Supervised children's activities and
break out 7 am - 6 pm; Kid's Zone.

Stupak Community Center
300 W. Boston Ave.
Las Vegas, NV 89102
229-2488
Deb Massey, Coordinator
Hours: Mon. - Thu. 7:30 am - 8:30 pm;
Fri. 8:30 am - 8 pm; Sat. 9 am - 5 pm
Education services for at risk youths.
English as 2nd language for everyone.
Recreation for youths.

Sunrise Community Center
2240 Linn Ln.
Las Vegas, NV 89115
455-7600
Randy Reese, Center Coordinator
Hours: Mon. - Fri. 7:30 am - 9 pm; Sat.
10 am - 3 pm; Break program Mon. - Fri.
7:30 am - 3 pm
Classes and programs for all ages,
including Seniors on the Go. Outdoor
pool and basketball.

Von Tobel Recreation Center
3610 E. Carey Ave.
Las Vegas, NV 89115
455-7699
Michael Shumaker, Center Coordinator
Hours: Mon. - Fri. 7:30 am - 7 pm;

Sat. noon - 5 pm
Child development, workshops, martial
arts, youth and adult sports.

Walnut/Cecile Center
3880 Cecile Ave.
Las Vegas, NV 89109
455-8402
Quintin Dailey, Center Coordinator
Hours: Mon. - Fri. 8 am - 6 pm; Sat.
10 am - 5 pm
36 x 60 ft. modular building on 1/2 acre
site. Center for neighborhood recreation activities.

Whitney Community Center
5700 Missouri Ave.
East Las Vegas, NV 89122
455-7573
Robert Dwyer, Center Coordinator
Hours: Mon. - Fri. 8 am - 9 pm; Sat.
10 am - 3 pm; After School Drop-In
Program Mon. - Fri. 3 pm - 7 pm
Adult and youth classes and recreation-
al activities, basketball court available;
Senior center.

Winchester Community Center
3130 S. McLeod Dr.
Las Vegas, NV 89121
455-7340
Dan Skea, Center Coordinator
Hours: Mon. - Fri. 8 am - 9 pm; Sat.
9 am - 5 pm
Films, concerts, classes and programs
for all ages.

PARKS

COMMUNITY SCHOOLS

Facilities available to provide the youth
and adults of Southern Nevada with a
wide variety of classes, workshops and
programs in the arts, physical fitness,
self-help and recreational activities.
Costs vary with each activity.

Baker Park Community School
Fremont Jr. High
1020 E. St. Louis Ave.
Las Vegas, NV 89104
733-6599
Linda Ryan, Center Coordinator
Hours: Mon. - Thu. 3 pm - 9 pm; Fri.
noon - 6 pm
Leather creations, art, computers, ballet,
tap, folk dancing, jazz, country western,
drama, yoga, guitar, piano, voice,
basketball, soccer and cheerleading.
There are fall field trips, women's self
defense amd Greek folk dancing.

Becker Community School
9110 Hillpointe Rd.
Las Vegas, NV 89134
229-2482
Sue Ann Porter, School Coordinator
Hours: Mon. - Fri. 3:30 pm - 8 pm
Ballet, jazz, keyboard and voice lessons,
aerobics, gymnastics, computers,
modeling, math & reading, arts &
crafts, French and physical fitness.

Brinley Community School
6150 Smoke Ranch Rd.
Las Vegas, NV 89108
646-9046
Ken Brensinger, Center Coordinator
Hours: Mon. - Fri. 2 pm - 8 pm
Tole painting, tap, ballet, Spanish, judo,
keyboard, gymnastics, tennis, computers,

Lied Community School, 5350 W. Tropical Parkway, Las Vegas, NV 89130

cheerleading, modeling, cooking and
soccer, basketball and baseball pitching

**Charleston Heights Community
School**
Garside Jr. High
300 S. Torrey Pines Dr.
Las Vegas, NV 89107
878-8644
Mark Romeo, Center Coordinator
Hours: Mon. - Thu. 3 pm - 7 pm, Fri. 3
p.m - 6 pm
Tap, ballet, jazz, Spanish, private music
lessons, aquasize, judo, tennis, beginning
drawing, piano, voice, gymnastics
and basketball.

Clark Community School
4291 Pennwood Ave.
Las Vegas, NV 89102
365-9272
Brenda Boule, Center Coordinator
Hours: Mon - Thu. 2 pm - 10 pm
Judo, ballet, jazz, piano, soccer,
cheerleading, tennis and martial arts.

Johnson Community School
340 Villa Monterey Dr.
Las Vegas, NV 89128
229-6175
Ray Call, Center Coordinator
Hours: Mon. - Fri. 3 pm - 7 pm

Ballroom, modern dance, ballet, tap,
country western, jazz, Spanish, vocal
lessons, piano, aerobics, basketball,
cheerleading, tennis and martial arts.

Lied Community School
5350 W. Tropical Parkway
Las Vegas, NV 89130
768-2068
Stacy Nolan, Center Coordinator
Hours: Mon. - Fri. 8 am - 7 pm
Recreation classes, gymnastics, dance,
martial arts, computers, sign language,
Spanish, arts & crafts classes, soccer
and basketball.

Robison Community School
4794 Harris Ave.
Las Vegas, NV 89110
459-0201
Marc Walters, Center Coordinator
Hours: Mon. - Thu. 1 pm - 8 pm
Superhero drawing, creative dance,
keyboard, sign language, basketball, gymnastics, golf, senior classes and beginning computers.

CLARK COUNTY PARKS

**Clark County Parks &
Recreation Department**
Administrative Office
2601 E. Sunset Rd.
Las Vegas, NV 89120
455-8200
Sports & Activity Information: 455-8200
Glenn Trowbridge, Dir.
Publishes Clark County Parks &
Recreation guide biannually listing
classes, activities and programs for both
adults and children. The county main-
tains 45 parks and community centers.
The parks are open at 6 am in the sum-
mer and 7 am in the winter months and
close at 11 pm.

Alexander Villas Park
3620 Lincoln Rd.
Las Vegas, NV 89115
4.8-acre park with lighted ballfield, basketball courts, exercise course, jogging trails,
picnic facilities, playground, volleyball.

Beckley School Park
3223 S. Glenhurst Dr.
Las Vegas, NV 89121
4-acre park with ballfield, playground.

Blue Diamond Park
Blue Diamond, NV 89004
2.2-acre park with lighted ballfield, children's playground and picnic area.

Cannon School Park
5850 Euclid Ave.
Las Vegas, NV 89104
10-acre park with 2 lighted ballfields,
soccer field.

Cashman School Park
4622 W. Desert Inn Rd.
Las Vegas, NV 89102
9-acre park with 2 lighted ballfields,
soccer field, restrooms.

Davis Park
2796 Redwood St.
Las Vegas, NV 89102
8.26-acre park with exercise course,
jogging trails, picnic facilities, playground.

Dearing School Park
3046 S. Ferndale St.
Las Vegas, NV 89121
5-acre park with ballfield.

Desert Breeze
8425 Spring Mountain Rd.
Las Vegas, NV 89117
25 acres (245 acres when completed).
Three ballfields, 2 Rollerblade courts,
picnic tables, playground, 2 basketball courts, jogging and walking path.

Desert Inn Park
3570 Vista Del Monte Dr.
Las Vegas, NV 89121
5-acre park with ballfield, playground,
swimming pool, restrooms.

Dog Fanciers Park
5800 E. Flamingo Rd.
Las Vegas, NV 89103
455-7506
12-acre park, 4-acre lighted grassy show
area. *(See also Horseman's Park.)* Over
35 clubs, representing a variety of
breeds, hold regular events at the park.

Grapevine Springs Park
5280 Palm Ave.
Las Vegas, NV 89120
4-acre neighborhood park with natural
habitat, volleyball, jogging track, playground and picnic area.

Hidden Palms Park
8855 Hidden Palms Pkwy.
Las Vegas, NV 89123
7.09 acre park with basketball courts,
volleyball courts, tennis courts,
playground, jogging trail, picnic
area with covered shelter and with
adjacent barbecue area.

Horseman's Park
5800 E. Flamingo Rd.
Las Vegas, NV 89122
455-7509
Reservations: 455-8200
60-acre park *(including Dog Fanciers
Park)* with 320 permanent stalls, 2
arenas including a lighted rodeo and
show area, cutting area for day
use, picnic facilities, restrooms, shower
facility.

Joe Shoong Park
1503 Wesley St.
Las Vegas, NV 89104
5-acre park with exercise course, picnic
facilities, restrooms.

Robert E. Lake School Park
2904 Meteoro St.
Las Vegas, NV 89109
5-acre park with a ballfield, picnic facilities, playground.

Laurelwood Park
4300 Newcastle Rd.
Las Vegas, NV 89103
5-acre park with lighted ballfield, basketball court, jogging trails, playground, tennis courts, restrooms.

Lewis Family Park
1970 Tree Line Dr.
Las Vegas, NV 89122
11.2 acres, playground, horseshoes,
2 basketball courts, sand volleyball,
jogging and walking paths.

Maslow Park and Pool
4902 Lana Ave.
Las Vegas, NV 89109
4-acre park with lighted ballfield, picnic facilities, playground, soccer field,
swimming pool, restrooms.

Paul Meyer Park
4525 New Forest Dr.
Las Vegas, NV 89117
13-acre park with lighted ballfield, basketball court, exercise course, jogging
trails, picnic facilities, playground,
soccer field, volleyball court.

Mountain View School Park
5436 E. Kell Ln.
Las Vegas, NV 89115
6-acre park with 2 lighted ballfields.

Nellis Meadows
4949 E. Cheyenne Ave.
Las Vegas, NV 89115
18.5-acre park with picnic facilities, 2
ballfields, playground, BMX track,
restrooms. Clark County Parks and
Recreation, in conjunction with the
National Bicycle League, offers bicycle
motocross for all ages at the Nellis
Meadows BMX Track. Each rider is
required to join the league at a cost
of $30 per year. All minors must have
their parents' written permission to
participate in races. For further information
call 459-4665.

Overton Town Park
Overton, NV 89040
13-acre park with lighted ballfield, community center, horseshoe pit, picnic
facility, playground, tennis court,
restrooms.

Paradise Park
4770 S. Harrison Dr.
Las Vegas, NV 89121
21.5-acre park with lighted ballfield,
basketball court, community center,
exercise course, horseshoe pit, jogging
trail, picnic facilities, playground,
soccer field, swimming pool, lighted
tennis court, volleyball court, restrooms.
Park renovated in 1997.

Photo: Photostechnik International

Paradise School Park
851 E. Tropicana Ave.
Las Vegas, NV 89119
6-acre park with ballfield, playground,
picnic facility, tennis court.

Paradise Vista Park
5582 Stirrup St.
Las Vegas, NV 89119
5-acre park with picnic facilities and
playground.

Parkdale Park
3200 Ferndale St.
Las Vegas, NV 89121
4-acre park with basketball court,
community center, picnic facilities,
playground, swimming pool, volleyball
court, restrooms.

Potosi Park
2790 Potosi St.
Las Vegas, NV 89102
5-acre park with 2 lighted ballfields, volleyball court, restrooms.

Prosperity Park
7101 Parasol Ln.
Las Vegas, NV 89117
10-acre park with ballfield, basketball
court, exercise course, jogging trail,
picnic facilities, playground. Restrooms.

Shadow Rock Park
2650 Los Feliz St.
Las Vegas, NV 89115
Softball, jogging, picnic areas and
playgrounds.

Silver Bowl Sports Complex
6800 E. Russell Rd.
Las Vegas, NV 89122
36.9-acre park with 6 lighted ballfields,
archery, playground, soccer field and
restrooms.
  Circus Circus Radio Control Aircraft
Field located 1/4 mile north of stadium.
Remote Control Car Track for 1/4, 1/8
and 1/10 scale cars is located in the
south parking lot; archery range located
1/4 mile south of stadium. The Silver
Bowl Sports Complex covers 420 acres.

Spring Valley Park
4220 S. Ravenwood Dr.
Las Vegas, NV 89117
5-acre park with ballfield, basketball
court, picnic facilities, playground,
and restrooms.

Sunrise Park
2240 Linn Ln.
Las Vegas, NV 89115
7-acre park with 2 lighted ballfields,
basketball court, community center,
picnic facilities, playground, soccer
field, swimming pool, tennis court,
volleyball court and restrooms.

Sunset Park
2601 Sunset Rd.
Las Vegas, NV 89120
455-8200
324.5-acre park with 8 lighted ballfields, archery, basketball court, community center, exercise course, Frisbee
course, horseshoe pit, jogging trail, 13-
acre lake stocked with catfish in sum-

mer and rainbow trout in winter, model boat race area, over-the-line course, picnic facility, playground, soccer field, swimming pool, 8 lighted tennis courts, volleyball pits, playground designed for disabled children, restrooms. The Frisbee Golf Course is an 18-hole Championship Par 70 (5,491 ft.). Score cards are available at the park office during regular business hours. The course is open daily.

Tate School Park
2450 Lincoln Rd.
Las Vegas, NV 89115
33-acre park with playground.

Thomas School Park
1560 E. Cherokee Ln.
Las Vegas, NV 89109
6-acre park with ballfield & playground.

Ullom School Park
4869 Sun Valley Dr.
Las Vegas, NV 89121
5-acre park with soccer field, ballfield, playground.

Warm Springs Softball Complex
Eastern Ave./Warm Springs Rd.
Las Vegas, NV 89120
Lighted ballfields.

Whitney Park
5700 E. Missouri Ave.
Las Vegas, NV 89122
13-acre park with ballfield, community center, horseshoe pit, picnic facilities, playground, soccer field, volleyball court, pool, restrooms.

Winchester Park
3130 S. McLeod Dr.
Las Vegas, NV 89121
10-acre park with basketball court, bocce ball court, community center, horseshoe pit, jogging trail, picnic facility, playground, shuffleboard, tennis court, volleyball court, restrooms.

Winterwood Park
5310 Consul Ave.
Las Vegas, NV 89122
8-acre park with lighted ballfield, exercise course, picnic facilities, playground, soccer field, tennis court, restrooms.

CITY OF LAS VEGAS PARKS

City of Las Vegas Parks and Leisure Activities
749 Veterans Memorial Dr.
Las Vegas, NV 89101
229-6297
David Kuiper, Dir.
Cultural & Community Affairs: 229-6703
Recreation: 229-6454
Adaptive Recreation: 229-6358
Parks & Open Spaces: 229-6571
Park Reservations: 229-6718
Municipal Sports: 229-2256
Publishes "Beyond the Neon" listing of activities and Parks & Recreation facility locations. The city maintains 34 parks.

An San Sister City Park
Ducharme Ave./Villa Monterey Dr.
Las Vegas, NV 89128
15-acre park named in honor of Las Vegas' sister city in South Korea and featuring Korean design elements. First phase completed in early 1993. Playground, sand volleyball court, walking paths and shade trees.

Angel Park
Westcliff Dr./Durango Dr.
Las Vegas, NV 89134
10-acre park with children's play area, playground, tennis court, exercise course, fitness course, jogging path and restrooms.

Baker Park
1100 E. St. Louis Ave.
Las Vegas, NV 89104
7-acre park with baseball/softball field, children's play area, swimming/wading pool, tennis court, football/soccer field, exercise course, Frisbee golf course.

Bob Baskin Park
S. Rancho Dr./W. Oakey Blvd.
Las Vegas, NV 89102
5-acre park with children's play area, playground, picnic & barbecue facilities, swimming/wading pool, tennis court, exercise course, restrooms.

Bruce Trent Park
W. Vegas Dr./Rampart Blvd.
Las Vegas, NV 89128
10-acre park and softball complex with fitness court, jogging track, tennis courts, group picnic area with grills, volleyball, horseshoes, restrooms.

Charleston Heights Park
Maverick/Smoke Ranch Rd.
Las Vegas, NV 89108
6.45-acre park with children's play area, playground, picnic and barbecue

Angel Park, Westcliff Dr./Durango Dr., Las Vegas, NV 89134

facilities, swimming/wading pool, volleyball court, fitness court.

Chester Stupak Park
231 W. Boston Ave.
Las Vegas, NV 89102
1-acre park with children's play area, picnic facilities and basketball.

Children's Memorial Park
Gowan Rd./Torrey Pines Dr.
Las Vegas, NV 89108
8.2-acre park with 2 Little League fields, jogging track, physical fitness area, children's playground and restrooms.

Coleman Park
Daybreak Rd./Carmen Blvd.
Las Vegas, NV 89108
4.5-acre park with children's playground.

Cragin Park
900 Hinsen Ln.
Las Vegas, NV 89102
14-acre park with baseball/softball field, fitness court, tennis, playground and restrooms.

Dexter Park
Evergreen/Fulton Pl.
Las Vegas, NV 89107
3.80-acre park with baseball/softball field, children's play area, picnic and barbecue facilities, restrooms.

Doolittle Park
W. Lake Mead Blvd./J St.
Las Vegas, NV 89101
20.7-acre park with baseball/softball

field, children's play area, playground, picnic and barbecue facilities, swimming/wading pool, football/soccer field, basketball court, restrooms.

Ethel Pearson Park
Washington Ave./D St.
Las Vegas, NV 89106
2-acre park with children's play area, playground, barbecue facilities, tennis court, exercise course.

Ed Fountain Park
Vegas Drive/Decatur
Las Vegas, NV 89108
10.5-acre park with baseball/softball field, children's play area, playground, picnic and barbecue facilities, football/soccer field, horseshoe pit, volleyball court, restrooms.

Fitzgerald Tot Lot
H St./Monroe Ave.
Las Vegas, NV 89106
.5-acre park with children's play area, shuffleboard.

Freedom Park
Mojave/E. Washington Ave.
Las Vegas, NV 89101
29.5-acre park with a lake, fitness area, baseball/softball field, children's play area, beach volleyball, playground, picnic and barbecue facilities, football/soccer field, restrooms. Freedom Park is the home of the opening ceremonies of the annual Corporate Challenge held in the spring.

Hadland Park
2800 Stewart Ave.
Las Vegas, NV 89101
17.19-acre park with baseball/softball field, children's play area, playground, picnic and barbecue facilities, football/soccer field, pool, restrooms.

Heers Park
Smoke Ranch Rd./Zorro
Las Vegas, NV 89108
7-acre park with children's play area, playground, football/soccer field.

Hills Park
Hillpoint Dr./Rampart Blvd.
(Summerlin)
Las Vegas, NV 89134
6.7-acre park includes a village amphitheater, central pavilion, 7 picnic ramadas with grills, children's playground, baseball/softball fields, sand volleyball, 2 tennis courts, volleyball, basketball.

Huntridge Circle Park
Maryland Pkwy./Franklin Ave.
Las Vegas, NV 89104
3.6-acre park with playground and picnic facilities.

James A. Gay III Park
Morgan/B St.
Las Vegas, NV 89106
6-acre park with children's play area, tennis court, basketball court.

Jaycee Park
St. Louis/Eastern Ave.
Las Vegas, NV 89104
29-acre park with baseball/softball field, 1,088-yard tree-lined jogging track, children's play area, playground, picnic shelters with barbecue facilities, tennis, football/soccer field, volleyball court, horseshoe pits, bocce and shuffleboard courts, exercise course, basketball court, fitness court and restrooms.

Lorenzi Park
3333 W. Washington Ave.
Las Vegas, NV 89107
229-6297
Hours: daily 7 am - 11 pm
60-acre park with 4 lighted softball fields, soccer fields, outdoor basketball, children's playground, wheelchair fitness course, shuffleboard, tennis courts, jog track, restrooms and picnic and barbecue facilities. The park also contains a large lake; fishing is permitted with a valid license. The State of Nevada Historical Museum is

PARKS

CITY OF LAS VEGAS PARKS

located at the park; 486-5205. The Garden of the Pioneer Women is located within the park, as well as the Nevada Garden Club building; 878-4846. The Department of Parks & Leisure activities conducts activities at the Sammy Davis Jr. Festival Plaza, the Lorenzi Adaptive Center and the Derfelt Senior Center, all located within the park. To make tennis reservations, call 647-3434.

Lubertha Johnson Park
Balzar Ave./Concord St.
Las Vegas, NV 89106
1.67-acre park with children's play area.

Mary Dutton Park
Charleston Blvd./10th St.
Las Vegas, NV 89101
.3-acre children's playground.

Mirabelli Park
6200 Elton Ave.
Las Vegas, NV 89107
2-acre park with baseball/softball field, children's play area.

Mojave Ball Fields
Mojave Rd./Bonanza Rd.
Las Vegas, NV 89101
6-acre park with baseball/softball field, tennis court, restrooms.

Pueblo Park
W. Lake Mead Blvd./Pueblo Vista Dr.
(Summerlin)
Las Vegas, NV 89134
65-acre linear park
Two active play areas, jogging path, nature area, bike path, picnic area, basketball courts.

Rainbow Family Park
Oakey Blvd./O'Bannon Dr.
Las Vegas, NV 89117
10-acre park with baseball/softball fields, soccer field, fitness course, walking and jogging path, children's playground, covered group picnic area with grills and restrooms.

Rotary Park
W. Charleston Blvd./Hinson St.
Las Vegas, NV 89102

4.3-acre park with children's play area, playground, picnic and barbecue facilities, swimming/wading pool, horseshoe pit, volleyball pit, and restrooms. Ballfields at adjacent school.

South Meadows Park
Boston Ave. & Fairfield Ave.
Las Vegas, NV 89102
Basketball, football, soccer and playground.

Stewart Place Park
Marion Dr./Chantilly Ave.
Las Vegas, NV 89110
3.55-acre park with children's play area, playground, picnic and barbecue facilities.

Vegas Heights Tot Lot
Balzar Ave./Concord St.
Las Vegas, NV 89106
1-acre park with children's play area.

Wayne Bunker Family Park
Tenaya Way/Alexander Rd.
Las Vegas, NV 89129
12.5-acre park with playground areas, jogging track, volleyball, horseshoes,

restrooms, 3 picnic pavilions, barbecues and parking.

West Charleston Lion Park
Essex Dr./Fulton Pl.
Las Vegas, NV 89107
3.5-acre park with children's play area, playground, picnic facilities.

Wildwood Park
Shadow Mountain/Wildwood
Las Vegas, NV 89108
1.26-acre park with children's play area, picnic facilities, swimming/wading pool, exercise course.

Woofter Family Park
Vegas Dr./Rock Springs Dr.
Las Vegas, NV 89128
7.5-acre park with sand boxes, fitness course and jogging track, spray fountain and playground area.

BOULDER CITY PARKS

Bicentennial Park
Utah/Colorado
Boulder City, NV 89005
7-acre park with a gazebo and stage that is used for concerts. Park is host to Art in the Park, the Spring Jamboree and the Clark County Art Show. Children's play area on the Ave. G side.

Boulder City Parks & Recreation Dept.
900 Arizona St.
Boulder City, NV 89005
293-9256
Roger Hall, Dir.

Boulder City High School
5th St./Ave. G
Boulder City, NV 89005
4.7-acre park with an open play area, playground, tennis courts, baseball field, football/soccer field.

Boulder City Swimming Pool
861 Ave. B
Boulder City, NV 89005
293-9286

Central Park
5th St./Ave. B
Boulder City, NV 89005
5-acre park with an open play area, playground, tennis courts

Frank T. Crowe Memorial Park
Nevada Highway/Cherry St.
Boulder City, NV 89005
1-acre open green area, picnic tables and grills.

Del Prado Park
Utah St./Northridge
Boulder City, NV 89005
2.5-acres with playground, basketball courts, fitness center and open green area.

Elton M. Garrett Jr. High
Adams Blvd. & Ave. G.
Boulder City, NV 89005
2.7-acre park with an open play area,

playground, baseball field, football/soccer field.

Hemenway Park
Ville Dr.
Boulder City, NV 89005
4.6-acre park with an open play area, 2 gazebos, playground, basketball court, 2 lighted tennis courts, 2 ballfields, picnic facilities. Park offers a panoramic view of Lake Mead and bighorn sheep can be seen in the park from early summer until late fall.

Lakeview Park
Walker Way/Pyramid Ln.
Boulder City, NV 89005

Photo: Photohecbuk International

.75-acre neighborhood park with tot lot, basketball court, picnic tables with grills and grass play area.

North Escalante and South Escalante Plazas
Arizona/California
Boulder City, NV 89005
.5-acre facility which provides landscaped open space in the uptown area.

Oasis Park
Marita Dr./Sandra Dr.
Boulder City, NV 89005
5.5-acre park with an open play area, playground, baseball field, basketball courts, fitness course.

Reflections Center
Colorado St./Railroad St.
Boulder City, NV 89005
Beautifully landscaped area with 7 sculptures changing each year.

River Mountain Hiking Trail
55-year-old, 5.5-mile hiking trail originally built by the Civilian Conservation Corps between Red & Black Mountain. Look for sign between Lake View Subdivision and Highway 93.

Veterans Memorial Park
Buchanan Blvd./Airport Rd.
Boulder City, NV 89005

Whalen Baseball Field/Bravo Softball Field
Ave. B
Boulder City, NV 89005
7-acre lighted baseball, softball and youth soccer fields. Reservation and light tokens available by calling the Recreation Department.

Wilbur Square (Government Park)
Nevada Highway/Colorado St.
Boulder City, NV 89005
3.3-acre tree-shaded park on the highway through the city. Site of the annual Boulder City Hospital Auxiliary Art Show held in October.

NORTH LAS VEGAS PARKS

North Las Vegas Parks & Recreation Dept.
2200 Civic Center Dr.
N. Las Vegas, NV 89030
633-1171

Recreation Dept.
1638 N. Bruce St.
N. Las Vegas, NV 89030
633-1600
Eric Dabney, Dir.

Boris Terrace Park
2200 E. Cartier Ave.
N. Las Vegas, NV 89030
1.19-acre park with playground, picnic area, basketball courts.

Brooks Tot Lot
1421 Brooks Ave.
N. Las Vegas, NV 89030
.2-acre park with playground for tots.

City View Park
101 Cheyenne Ave.
N. Las Vegas, NV 89030
13.02-acre park with group picnic areas, large brick barbecue area, pond/waterfall area, 3 play equipment areas, horseshoe pits, open space for activities, scenic view overlook, fitness stations.

Cheyenne Ridge Park
3814 Scott Robinson Dr.
N. Las Vegas, NV 89031
5 acres with walking path, basketball court, sand volleyball, playground equipment & open space picnic tables.

Cheyenne Sports Complex
3500 E. Cheyenne Ave.
N. Las Vegas, NV 89030
Wayne Walder, Sports Coordinator
37.67-acre park with concession building, lighted soccer/football fields, 5 lighted tennis courts, 4 lighted softball fields, track & field and jogging course.

College Park
2613 Tonopah Ave.
N. Las Vegas, NV 89030
1.19-acre park with open play space and playground equipment.

Eldorado Park
5900 Camino Eldorado Blvd.
N. Las Vegas, NV 89031
9-acre park with shade structure, picnic area, playground for tots & walking path.

Nicholas E. Flores, Jr. Park
4133 Allen Ln.
N. Las Vegas, NV 89030
5-acres, playground, picnic area, horseshoe pits, shuffleboard, jogging track, exercise stations, and checkerboard tables.

Hartke Park/Pool Neighborhood Center
1638 N. Bruce St.
(adj. to J.D. Smith Jr. High)
N. Las Vegas, NV 89030
9.32-acre park with recreation offices, gymnasium, racquetball, 3 lighted tennis courts, 3 softball fields (2 lighted), a softball field, swimming pool, playground, picnic area.

Kiel Ranch
100 E. Carey Ave.
N. Las Vegas, NV 89030
Undeveloped area consisting of 3.73 acres. National Register of Historic Places. Native shrub and ranch features.

Hebert Memorial Park
2701 Basswood Ave.
(adj. to Lincoln School)
N. Las Vegas, NV 89030

3.48-acre park with baseball field, shade structure and playground.

Joe Kneip Park
2127 McCarran St.
N. Las Vegas, NV 89030
2.21-acre park with 2 lighted softball/baseball fields, soccer field, picnic area, parking.

Monte Vista Park
4910 Scott Robinson Dr.
N. Las Vegas, NV 89031
5 acres, picnic tables, jogging track and playground equipment.

Petitti Park/Pool
2505 N. Bruce St.
N. Las Vegas, NV 89030
9.23 acres, swimming pool, 3 softball/baseball fields, picnic area, parking lot, restrooms and playground.

Regional Park
4400 Horse Dr.
N. Las Vegas, NV 89031
120 acres. Miniature aircraft flying field, paved runway, parking facilities, portable toilets, shade shelter.

Richard Tam
Donna & Craig
N. Las Vegas, NV 89030
5 acres with active & passive play areas, 1 softball diamond and 60-foot unlighted picnic and barbecue area.

Rotary Tot Lot
2600 Magnet St.
N. Las Vegas, NV 89030
.12 acre park with playground for tots.

Tonopah Park
204 E. Tonopah Ave.
N. Las Vegas, NV 89030

.72-acre park with shade structure, basketball court, frontier village playground.

Valley View Park
2000 Bennett St.
N. Las Vegas, NV 89030
5.02-acre park with playground, open space, basketball courts.

Walker Park
2227 W. Evans Ave.
N. Las Vegas, NV 89030
3.08-acre park with picnic area, shaded structure, basketball courts, softball field.

Walker Pool/Park
1509 June Ave.
N. Las Vegas, NV 89030
10-acre park with swimming pool, playground area *(play booster, everglide)* picnic area with tables and grills, basketball courts.

Richard Walpole Rec. Area
1621 Yale St.
N. Las Vegas, NV 89030
1.32-acre park with basketball, playground, open space areas.

Richard Walpole Sr. Citizens Park
1620 Yale St.
N. Las Vegas, NV 89030
1.79-acre park with shade structure, horseshoes, picnic area, shuffleboard, open space and walking course.

Tom Williams
1844 Belmont St.
(adj. to Tom Williams Elementary School)
N. Las Vegas, NV 89030
3.22-acre school park with basketball, picnic area, playground, shade area.

PARKS

HENDERSON PARKS

Henderson Parks & Recreation Dept.
240 Water St.
Henderson, NV 89015
565-4264
Leisure Line: 565-2134
Steve Rongyocsik, Dir.
Maintains 21 parks.

Allegro Park
1023 Seven Hills Dr.
Henderson, NV 89015
5 acres, tot lot, open play turf, soccer/football field, parking, picnic area, barbecues and restrooms.

Arroyo Grande Sports Complex
298 Arroyo Grande Blvd.
Henderson, NV 89014
60-acre park with a four-field little league complex, a four-field softball/baseball complex, 2 baseball fields, several open play fields, basketball courts, play stations, tot lot, trail system and restrooms.

Burkholder Jr. High Baseball Field/Park
645 W. Victory Rd.
Henderson, NV 89015
8 acre park with lighted ballfields, practice soccer field and restrooms.

Civic Center Park
200 Water St.
(adj. to Henderson Convention Center)
Henderson, NV 89015
565-2121
5-acre park with tree shaded grass areas and restrooms.

Discovery Park
2011 Paseo Verde Pkwy.
Henderson, NV 89015
10-acre park in Green Valley Ranch allows users a wide range of activities. Lighted tennis courts, 2 lighted sand volleyball courts, lighted basketball court with 6 baskets, picnic, barbecue area, 3 horseshoe pits and ample parking.

Fox Ridge Park
(Green Valley)
420 Valle Verde Dr.
Henderson, NV 89014
5-acre park with playground, playing field, .25-mile walking path, picnic and barbecue facilities, shaded shelter, restrooms and amphitheater to accommodate theatrical productions and concerts.

Green Valley Park
370 N. Pecos Rd.
Henderson, NV 89014
5-acre park with a grass play area and

playground equipment, concrete basketball/volleyball court, horseshoe pits, picnic and barbecue facilities, and shade structure. Land donated by Pardee Construction Company.

Maintenance Yard & Nursery
405 Van Wagenen St.
Henderson, NV 89015
2 acres includes main shop, storage area for the division and a plant nursery for propagation.

McCaw Elementary School Park
57 Lynn Ln.
Henderson, NV 89015
7-acre park with grass and playground area used for various sports activities, 1 baseball/softball backstop and school physical education classes.

Morrell Park and Robert Taylor Elementary School Park
500 Harris St.
Henderson, NV 89015
18-acre park and 5-acre school park with 4 lighted tennis courts, lighted basketball court with 6 backboards, 2 lighted sand volleyball courts, 5 ball fields (4 lighted), 2 playground equipment areas, grass picnic area with grills, fitness and jogging course and

restrooms. Ballfields host Youth Baseball Leagues, Youth Softball Leagues, Women's Softball League and Co-Rec Adult Softball Leagues. Valley View Recreation Center contains a full gym, 3 racquetball courts, weight room and 6 meeting rooms.

Mountain View Park
1961 Wigwam Pkwy.
Henderson, NV 89014
7-acre park with lighted basketball court with 6 backboards, 2 tennis courts, softball/soccer field, children's play area, sand volleyball, picnic area and restrooms.

O'Callaghan Park and Fay Galloway Elementary School Park
601 Skyline Rd.
Henderson, NV 89015
16-acre and 6-acre school park with lighted baseball field, basketball court, handball courts, 4 lighted tennis courts, 2 horseshoe pits, 2 Frisbee golf target baskets, 2 playground equipment areas, shaded picnic areas, tot lot, .5-mile fitness and jogging course and restrooms. Site for Youth Baseball.

HENDERSON PARKS

Pecos Legacy Park
150 Pecos Rd.
Pittman Wash
Henderson, NV 89014
9-acre park with 2 lighted ballfields/soc-
cer fields, restrooms. Softball field, 2
lighted tennis courts, lighted basketball court with 6 backboards, open play
area, and children's play area.

River Mountain Park
1941 Appaloosa Rd.
Henderson, NV 89015
10 acres containing basketball and
roller hockey courts, restroom building,
ramada shelter, picnic tables, horseshoe pits, playground and parking area.

Sewell Elementary School Park
700 E. Lake Mead Dr.
Henderson, NV 89015
4-acre park with grass and playground
areas used for various sports activities
and school physical education classes.

Silver Springs Park
1950 Silver Springs Pkwy.
Henderson, NV 89014
12-acre park with grass recreational

areas; outdoor amphitheater to
accommodate theatrical productions
and concerts, ballfields, 2 tennis courts,
restrooms. Community center with pool.
The rim trail system that runs through
Silver Springs Park is a jogging and bicycling path that winds through Green
Valley and will eventually connect
with other segments of the City Trail
System.

Thurman White Middle School Park
1661 Galleria Dr.
Henderson, NV 89014
7-acre school park includes 2 lighted
baseball fields, an open grass area, basketball court, volleyball court and tennis courts

Titanium Field
Lake Mead Dr./Water St.
Henderson, NV 89015
7-acre park with grass area and softball field is used for various sports activities and special events such as carnival
grounds for Industrial Days and
Henderson Expo.

Wells Park
1608 Moser Dr.
(adj. to Edna Hinman Elementary School)
Henderson, NV 89015
10-acre park with basketball court,
playground equipment, shaded picnic
area, lighted adult softball field, 2 lighted tennis courts and restrooms.

Wetlands Park
This passive park, developed by Lake
Las Vegas, is a 7-mile-long network to
preserve indigenous plants and animals
along the Las Vegas Wash.

Youth Center Park
105 W. Basic Rd.
Henderson, NV 89015
565-2124
3-acre park with lighted basketball
court, shaded area, play area, small
grass field, swimming pool, children's
pool and diving tank.
Safekey: Program for working parents
Mon. - Fri. 7 am - 6 pm.

MAJOR EVENTS CENTERS

Artemus Ham Concert Hall
UNLV
4505 S. Maryland Pkwy
Las Vegas, NV 89154-5005
895-3801
Box Office: 895-3801
Larry Henley, Facility Mgr.
Capacity: 1,870
Use: Concerts, theater, dance

Cashman Field
850 Las Vegas Blvd. N.
Las Vegas, NV 89101
386-7100
Events: 593-4768
Don Ahl, Acting Mgr. of Operations
Capacity: Theater - 1,940-3,015 sq. ft.
permanent stage
Use: Fine arts events, concerts and
meetings
Stadium - 10,000
Use: Las Vegas Stars AAA baseball
Built in 1983 at a cost of $27 million,
Cashman has 122,000 sq. ft. of
exhibit space; 16 meeting rooms on two
levels comprising 17,500 sq. ft.
Parking for 2,608 vehicles; food and
beverage services available through
ARA Services.

Huntridge Performing Arts Theater
1208 E. Charleston Blvd.
Las Vegas, NV 89104
Hotline: 477-7703
Fun Hunt: 368-4868
Richard Lenz, Mgr./Chairman
Capacity: 647, Concerts 804
This 50-year old art deco style movie the-
ater is a registered historical landmark
and is being used for concerts, live the-
ater productions and specialty movies.

Judy Bayley Theatre
UNLV
4505 S. Maryland Pkwy
Las Vegas, NV 89154-5005
895-3801
Larry Henley, Facility Mgr.
Seating Capacity: 550
Use: Concerts, lectures, theater, dance

Las Vegas Convention Center
3150 Paradise Rd.
Las Vegas, NV 89109
892-0711
Rossi Ralenkotter, Marketing Dir.
Capacity: 100,000+ people; 1.3 million sq. ft.
Use: Conventions, meetings and trade
shows.

MGM Grand Garden
3805 Las Vegas Blvd. S.
Las Vegas, NV 89109
891-1111
Mark Prows, VP
15,222-seat sports arena and special
events center.
Total space: 275,000 sq. ft.
Exhibition space: Main floor - 60,000
sq. ft.; upper level 55,000 sq. ft. Hosts
major concerts of artists like Janet
Jackson, Phil Collins, Whitney Houston,
Bette Midler, Elton John and Rolling
Stones.

Sam Boyd Stadium
7000 E. Russell Rd.
Las Vegas, NV 89102
895-3761
Tickets: 895-3900

Pat Christenson, Dir.
Seating Capacity: 32,000 for football,
38,000 for concerts
Use: Concerts, "dirt & mud" events,
UNLV football and special events.

Sands Expo & Convention Center
201 E. Sands Ave.
Las Vegas, NV 89109
733-5556
Jeff Beckelman, VP of Mktg.
Total exhibit space: 935,000 sq. ft.
Meeting capacity: 40,000
Banquet capacity: 29,870
Parking: 1,000+ cars
Exhibit Hall A: 178,000 sq. ft.
Exhibit Hall B: 189,000 sq. ft.
Exhibit Hall C: 188,000 sq. ft.
Exhibit Hall G: 380,000 sq. ft.

Thomas & Mack Center
UNLV
4750 S. Swenson St.
Corner Tropicana Ave./Swenson St.
Las Vegas, NV 89154
895-3761
Pat Christenson, Dir.
Box office: 895-3900
Capacity: 18,651 for basketball, 19,383
for boxing and wrestling; 18,000 and
19,300 (round) for concerts.
Thomas & Mack Center charges $4 per
car and $6 for RV parking at all events.
Use: UNLV Runnin' Rebels basketball,
Las Vegas Thunder hockey, National
Finals Rodeo, concerts, boxing and
special events. Site of over 200 events
per year. Five meeting rooms and 1 specially designed restaurant/bar area provide 5,000 sq. ft. of additional meeting
space.

The Thomas & Mack Center opened
November 21, 1983 and was completed
at a cost of $30 million.

Thomas & Mack Center, UNLV, 4750 S. Swenson St.
Corner of Tropicana Ave./Swenson St., Las Vegas, NV 89154

PUBLIC BANQUET & MEETING ROOMS

Abacus & Quill
4161 S. Eastern Ave., Ste. E-8
Las Vegas, NV 89119
732-0889
Capacity: 16 theater style

Cafe Cappuccino
3420 S. Jones Blvd.
Las Vegas, NV 89102
362-2044
Caroline Guagliano, Gen. Mgr.
Capacity: 35-40 sit down

Calico Jack's Banquet Hall
8200 W. Charleston Blvd.
Las Vegas, NV 89117
233-5574
Jim Snow, Dir.
Hours: 7 days - 24 hours
Capacity: 25 - 125
Seminars, theme parties, wedding receptions, buffet and sit down dinners.

Camp Lee Canyon
Mt. Charleston, NV 89124
455-8200
John Hulme, Camp Mgr.
Located on 27 acres in Toiyabe National Forest 45 minutes from Las Vegas, the camp is available for groups and organizations that want a serene setting for retreats and daytime seminars. Facilities include basketball court, tennis court, picnic facilities and restrooms.

City of Las Vegas Parks and Leisure Activities
749 Veterans Memorial Dr.
Las Vegas, NV 89101
229-6718
Denise Robertson
Picnic and party services and park reservations for groups.

Clark County Parks and Recreation
Paradise Park: 455-7513
Sunset Park: 455-8200
Parks group areas available to groups for picnics.

Echo Bay Resort
Echo Bay
Overton, NV 89040
394-4000
Lorrie Young, Hotel Mgr.
Capacity: 120

Emerald Gardens
891 S. Rampart Blvd.
Las Vegas, NV 89128
242-5700
Par McGuire, Banquet Mgr.
Parties, weddings and banquets, seats 50 - 360.

Expedition Depot
1297 Nevada Hwy.
Boulder City, NV 89005
293-3776, ext. 204
Maggie Galloway, VP Mktg.
Capacity: 224
Weddings, parties and meetings.

Hartland Mansion
P.O. Box 85162
Las Vegas, NV 89185
387-0222 1-800-554-HART

Mansion address:
1044 S. 6th St.
Las Vegas, NV 89104
387-6700
Dr. Toni Hart
Capacity: 50 - 500
Everything available for the ultimate party or reception. Features 31,000 sq. ft. in mansion and a 3,000 sq. ft. cottage.

Henderson Convention Center
200 S. Water St.
Henderson, NV 89015
565-2171
Lisa Jolley, Convention Services Supvr.
Capacity: up to 800
Weddings, receptions, banquets, meetings, seminars and conventions. Catering kitchen, portable service bar available. Prices are for the use of the room(s) up to 12 hours, including decorating time. Rooms hold 120 each; double for two rooms, etc. Sizes and costs vary.
Deposit: $75 per room

Las Vegas Natural History Museum, 900 Las Vegas Blvd. N., Las Vegas, NV

Henderson Green Valley Elks Lodge #2802
631 E. Lake Mead Dr.
Henderson, NV 89015
565-9959
Shirley Gulick, Catering Dir.
Capacity: 250
Fee: $260 plus $100 refundable deposit
Bar, juke box, walk-in cooler. Newest Elks Lodge in the U.S., completely renovated.

Hippo & The Wild Bunch
4503 Paradise Rd.
Las Vegas, NV 89109
731-5446
Richard Martinez, Banquet Dir.
Capacity: Complete party planning, private facilities for 10 to 300 people. Indoor and outdoor catering. Your place or ours. Lush gardens and gazebo weddings.

Italian-American Club
2333 E. Sahara Ave.
Las Vegas, NV 89104
457-3866
Joe Tegano, Gen. Mgr.
Capacity: 300
Full food and beverage service available. Dance floor and stage.

Lake Mead Marina
322 Lakeshore Rd.
Boulder City, NV 89005
293-3484
Dave Fisher, Food and Beverage Mgr.
Capacity: 100

Las Vegas - Clark County Library District
District Headquarters
833 Las Vegas Blvd. N.
Las Vegas, NV 89101
382-3493
Tyrone Carpenter, Program Coordinator
Provides non-profit group/organization and commercial use of theaters, auditoriums, lecture halls and meeting rooms for workshops and seminars.

State registered non-profit organizations and their certified charters, open governmental meetings, and community specials. Interest groups have free use. Reservations can be made up to a year in advance depending on the facility.
Fees: Sliding scale for groups that are charged admission or holding closed or private meetings.

Las Vegas National Golf Club
1911 E. Desert Inn Rd.
Las Vegas, NV 89109
796-9018
Kristen Kasza, Banquet Mgr.
Capacity: Large room seats 150; smaller room seats 120

Las Vegas Natural History Museum
900 Las Vegas Blvd. N.
Las Vegas, NV 89101
384-3466
Marilyn Gillespie, Dir.
Capacity: 200 - 500

Las Vegas Racquet Club
3333 Raven Ave.
Las Vegas, NV 89139
361-4577
Christi McKee, Catering Coordinator
Capacity: up to 1,000
Garden weddings, receptions and celebrations. Private club on 10 acres with clubhouse and patio pavilions; pool and fountain. Hor d'oeuvres and formal buffet, open bar, champagne fountain, dance floor and music.
Fee: $45 per person

Las Vegas Villa - Liberace Mansion
4982 Shirley St.
Las Vegas, NV 89119
795-8119
Tom Fagan, Mgr.
Capacity: up to 1,300
Liberace's former home, this 20-room villa is available for receptions, luncheons and dinners.

Legacy Golf Club
130 Par Excellence Dr.
Henderson, NV 89014
897-2108
Linda Germano, Catering Mgr.
Clubhouse dining room can be used after sunset for private parties
Capacity: 250 - 300 buffet; 200 sit down.

Legends Ranch
8213 Rancho Destino Rd.
Las Vegas, NV 89123
253-1333 Ext.127
Tonya Kay, Coordinator
Capacity: up to 1,000
20-acre beautifully landscaped and uniquely designed Arabian estate. Owned by the producer of "Legends in Concert."

Lied Discovery Children's Museum
833 Las Vegas Blvd. N.
Las Vegas, NV 89101
382-3445
Capacity: up to 2,000
There are two rental options:
First floor capacity 800
Fee: $800 plus $4 per person
Gallery and courtyard capacity 250
Fee: $1,000 plus $4 per person.
Performance stage for entertainment, prep area for caterers, and dance floor.

Los Prados Country Club
5150 Los Prados Cir.
Las Vegas, NV 89130
645-4523
Mike Misowic, Banquet Mgr.
Capacity: Large banquet room 150. Small banquet room sit down 30. Patio room 70.

Mesquite Club
702 E. St. Louis Ave.
Las Vegas, NV 89104
734-6722 735-9048
Bette Butler
Capacity: 180
Fee: $500 room rental, available 7 am - midnight
Kitchen available; dance floor, stage, tables, chairs and portable bar.

Moonstruck Gallery
6322 W. Sahara Ave.
Las Vegas, NV 89102
364-0531
Denise Mrochek, Dir.
More than 3,500 sq. ft. of gallery space in Moonstruck's new 5,600 sq. ft. premises is available for special events and meetings. Moonstruck also presents free community events, seminars, craft demonstrations and workshops on an ongoing basis.

Nevada Institute for Contemporary Art
3455 E. Flamingo Rd.
Las Vegas, NV 89121
434-2666
Arlene Blut, Dir. of Development
Capacity: 200

Nevada State Garden Clubs, Inc.
3333 W. Washington Ave.
Las Vegas, NV 89107
878-4846
Lee Pearns, Pres.
Capacity: Up to 150
Fee: $250 refundable cleaning deposit secures the date; $500 room rental Kitchen and dry bar available. Stage, tables, chairs, no dance floor.

Nevada State Museum
700 Twin Lakes Dr.
Las Vegas, NV 89107
486-5205
Cleda Burney, Sec.
Capacity: up to 100
Available for private parties, group meetings and other functions.

North Las Vegas Host Lions Club
2934 Van Der Meer St.
N. Las Vegas, NV 89030
644-3872
W. J. Fields
Capacity: Up to 240
Fee: $550 room rental
Tables & chairs to seat 120; kitchen available, tended bar. Available 8 am - midnight.

Painted Desert Golf Club
5555 Painted Mirage Rd.
Las Vegas, NV 89129
645-2568
Tom Judson, Gen. Mgr.
After sunset, seats about 80.

Paradise Food Service
9457 Las Vegas Blvd. S.
Las Vegas, NV 89123
897-2287

Moonstruck Gallery, 6322 W. Sahara Ave., Las Vegas, NV 89102

Jack Stoerck
Capacity: Indoor up to 275; outdoor up to 1,200

Rainbow Gardens
4125 W. Charleston Blvd.
Las Vegas, NV 89102
878-4646
Kelly & Iwona Hulsey, Owners
Capacity: 50 - 400
Climate-controlled garden atmosphere. Full service banquet facilities. Formal dining 50 - 250; Garden Room 100 - 400; dance floor and music available in both rooms.

Richard Tam Alumni Center
UNLV
4505 S. Maryland Pkwy.
Las Vegas, NV 89154
895-3621
Jean Davis, Managing Asst.
Capacity: 250
Marietta Tiberti Grand hall, lounge and bar.

Sam Boyd Stadium
4505 S. Maryland Pkwy.
Las Vegas, NV 89154
895-3761 or 895-0992
Steve Sonnier, Dir. of Booking
Stadium Location: 6800 E. Russell Rd.
Capacity: 40,000

Silk Purse Ranch
8101 Racel St.
Las Vegas, NV 89131
645-1094
Maria Sileo, Coordinator
Capacity: 50 - 1000
Wedding and banquet garden with Victorian-style wedding gazebo. 5,400-sq. ft. pavilion and a 5-acre grove with stage and sound system.

Sunset Gardens
3931 E. Sunset Rd.
Las Vegas, NV 89120

456-9986
Tony Hulsey
Capacity: 300
2.5-acre garden setting. Can handle every detail, florist on premises. Available evenings only. $1,000 deposit. Approximately $40 per person includes buffet, full open bar (4 hours) and entertainment and photography.

Thomas and Mack Center
4505 S. Maryland Pkwy.
Las Vegas, NV 89154
895-3190
Michelle Payne, Catering Mgr.
Capacity: 250
Two rooms - full catering.

Tropical Gardens
3808 E. Tropicana Ave.
Las Vegas, NV 89121
434-4333 1-800-668-7080
Kristen James, Coordinating Dir.
Full service catered banquets for 20 - 500 people. Floral arrangements and event planning expertise.

VFW Post 1753
705 Las Vegas Blvd. N.
Las Vegas, NV 89101
384-4161
Larry Davidson
Capacity: 150
Hall rental, stage, catering available.

The Victorian Room
2800 W. Sahara Ave.
Las Vegas, NV 89102
252-8379
Monique Brae, Banquet Dir.
Capacity: 10 - 200.
Complete planning and catering for your party, seminars, banquets, weddings, high tea and luncheons. Disc jockey available and dance floor. Elegant Victorian theme.

Wet 'n' Wild · Las Vegas
2601 Las Vegas Blvd. S.
Mailing address: 2310 Paseo Del Prado, Ste. A220
Las Vegas, NV 89102
871-7811
Recorded Information: 734-0088
Offices/Group Information: 871-7811
Art Jimenez
Whether it's a birthday party for 20, a company party of 5,000 or an international convention gathering, Wet 'n' Wild can service the smallest to largest parties.
Capacity: The Picnic Plaza can be reserved for up to 2,000 guests, includes more than 100 picnic tables, two volleyball courts, horseshoe pits, the Trampoline Thing, and many more fun games. There are several other entertainment options including disc jockeys and live bands.
Fees: Discounted group rates for 25 to 100 people are $19.95 *(ages 10 and older)* and $16.95 *(ages 3 to 9.)* General admission tickets are $22.95 *(ages 10 and older)*, $16.95 *(ages 3 to 9)*, 1/2 price for senior citizens and children under 3 are free.
For more information on group or convention rates, children and spouse programs and coupons programs, please call 871-7811.

Wildhorse Country Club
1 Showboat Dr.
Henderson, NV 89014
434-9000
Kristen Kasza, Banquet Mgr.
Capacity: 50 - 250
Full service catering for business meetings, weddings, anniversaries, tournaments and outings after sunset.

Wooly Bully's
6020 W. Flamingo Rd.
Las Vegas, NV 89103
362-2116
Brian Weinstein, Operations Mgr.
Capacity: sit down dinner about 50, no charge for room, your choice of meals or finger foods.

(For catering and/or restaurant banquet facilities see the Restaurants Section. For hotel facilities see the Convention Section.)

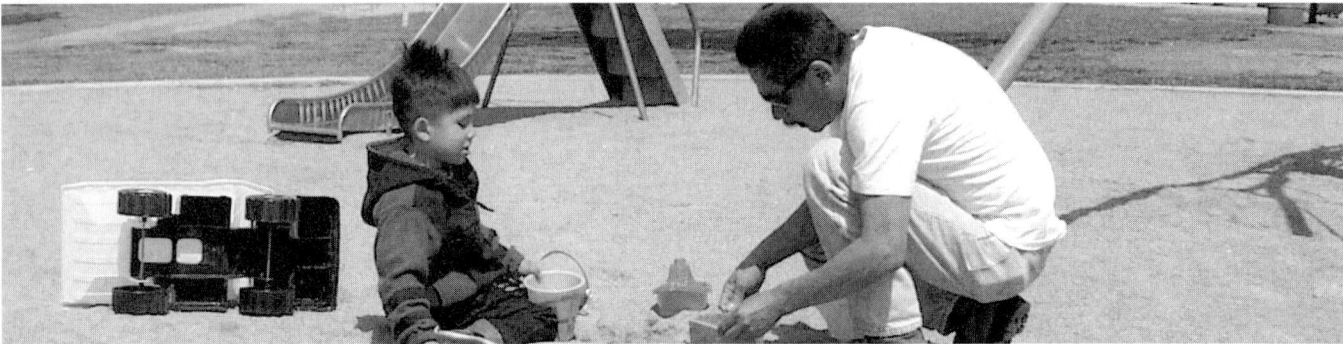

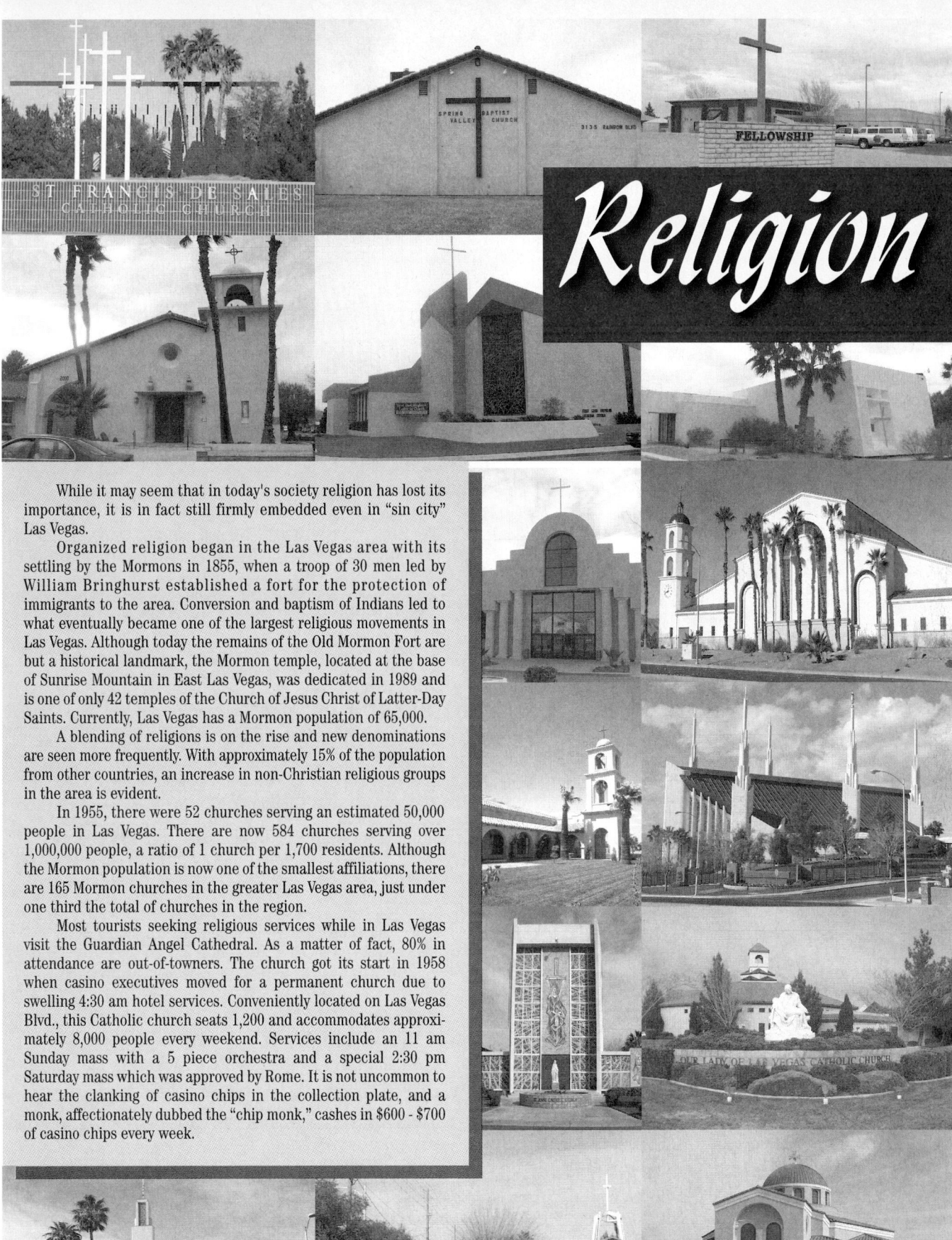

Religion

While it may seem that in today's society religion has lost its importance, it is in fact still firmly embedded even in "sin city" Las Vegas.

Organized religion began in the Las Vegas area with its settling by the Mormons in 1855, when a troop of 30 men led by William Bringhurst established a fort for the protection of immigrants to the area. Conversion and baptism of Indians led to what eventually became one of the largest religious movements in Las Vegas. Although today the remains of the Old Mormon Fort are but a historical landmark, the Mormon temple, located at the base of Sunrise Mountain in East Las Vegas, was dedicated in 1989 and is one of only 42 temples of the Church of Jesus Christ of Latter-Day Saints. Currently, Las Vegas has a Mormon population of 65,000.

A blending of religions is on the rise and new denominations are seen more frequently. With approximately 15% of the population from other countries, an increase in non-Christian religious groups in the area is evident.

In 1955, there were 52 churches serving an estimated 50,000 people in Las Vegas. There are now 584 churches serving over 1,000,000 people, a ratio of 1 church per 1,700 residents. Although the Mormon population is now one of the smallest affiliations, there are 165 Mormon churches in the greater Las Vegas area, just under one third the total of churches in the region.

Most tourists seeking religious services while in Las Vegas visit the Guardian Angel Cathedral. As a matter of fact, 80% in attendance are out-of-towners. The church got its start in 1958 when casino executives moved for a permanent church due to swelling 4:30 am hotel services. Conveniently located on Las Vegas Blvd., this Catholic church seats 1,200 and accommodates approximately 8,000 people every weekend. Services include an 11 am Sunday mass with a 5 piece orchestra and a special 2:30 pm Saturday mass which was approved by Rome. It is not uncommon to hear the clanking of casino chips in the collection plate, and a monk, affectionately dubbed the "chip monk," cashes in $600 - $700 of casino chips every week.

CHURCHES

AFRICAN METHODIST EPISCOPAL

First African Methodist Episcopal Church
2450 Revere St.
N. Las Vegas, NV 89030
649-1774
Sunday worship: 8 am, 11 am, 6 pm
Spencer Francis Barrett, Pastor

Holy Trinity AME Church
5243 W. Charleston Blvd.
Las Vegas, NV 89102
877-0790
Sunday worship: 8 am, 11 am
Emanuel Waffon III, Pastor

ANGLICAN

St Edward the Confessor
St Judes Chapel
Boulder City, NV 89005
221-0638
Sunday worship: Noon every other Sunday
Guest preachers

APOSTOLIC

Alpha & Omega Apostolic Church
2610 N. Martin Luther King Blvd.
Las Vegas, NV 89106
648-2111
Sunday worship: 11:30 am
Frank Gaston, Pastor

Apostolic Assembly
3100 E. Lake Mead Blvd.
N. Las Vegas, NV 89030
639-0037
Sunday worship: 10 am
Socorro Rios, Pastor
Spanish

Apostolic Church
1665 Lindell Rd.
Las Vegas, NV 89102
878-8000
Sunday worship: 10 am, 6:30 pm
Dallas Mefford, Pastor

Bible Way Fellowship Church
4900 Bevvie Dr.
Las Vegas, NV 89108
631-4990
Sunday worship: 11 am, 7:30 pm
Patricia Goss, Pastor

Calvary Apostolic Church
1401 N. Decatur Blvd., Ste. 4
Las Vegas, NV 89108
870-8501
Sunday worship: 11 am
John A. Brown, Pastor

Church of the Living God True Holiness
3665 N. Nellis Blvd.
Las Vegas, NV 89115
643-1197
Sunday worship: Noon, 7:30 pm
Leonard Johnson, Pastor

Church of the Lord Jesus
1260 W. Bartlett Ave.
Las Vegas, NV 89106
648-0332
Sunday worship: 11:30 am, 7:30 pm
C. Victoria, Pastor

Decatur Phesians Community Church
820 W. Bonanza Rd.
Las Vegas, NV 89106
647-4520
Sunday worship: 11:30 am, 7:30 pm
P. Washington, Pastor

Henderson Apostolic Mission
57 E. Basic Rd.
Henderson, NV 89015
565-0900
Sunday worship: 5 pm

Holy Ghost Temple
2624 Clayton St.
N. Las Vegas, NV 89030
646-0805
Sunday worship: 11:45
Louis Sansberry, Pastor

Mountaintop Faith Ministry
5435 W. Sahara Ave., Ste. D
Las Vegas, NV 89102
367-1636
Sunday worship: 10:30 am, 6 pm
Clinton House, Pastor

New Apostolic Church
3720 E. Haddock Ave.
Las Vegas, NV 89115
Sunday worship: 10 am, 5 pm
Hans Schneider, Pastor

New Life Christian Center
1229 Carson Ave
Las Vegas, NV 89101
387-5433
Sunday worship: 11 am, 6 pm
William R. Jones, Pastor

Newness of Life Apostolic Church
29 N. Mojave Rd.
Las Vegas, NV 89101
474-9744
Sunday worship: 11:30 am, 6 pm
C. E. Gamble, Pastor

Praise Tabernacle
1229 E. Carson Ave.
Las Vegas, NV 89101
435-6099
Sunday worship: 2:30 pm
R. P. Blizzard, Pastor

Spanish Apostolic Church
1401 Las Vegas Blvd. N.
Las Vegas, NV 89101
382-3347
Sunday worship: 10 am, 4:30 pm *(Bilingual)*; 5:30 pm *(English)*; 6:30 pm *(Spanish)*
Hector Flores, Pastor

Truth Christian Ministries
2070 Losee Rd.
N. Las Vegas, NV 89030
396-7066
Sunday worship: 10 am, 6 pm
Jerry Boyd, Pastor

ASSEMBLIES OF GOD

Assembly of God Celebration Worship Center
Call for time and location
631-4444
David Poole, Pastor

Assembly of God - Mountain View
3900 E. Bonanza Rd.
Las Vegas, NV 89101
452-8400
Sunday worship: 8 am, 10:40 am, 6 pm
Robert Goree, Pastor

Boulder City Assembly of God
Meets at Boulder City Women's Club
Boulder City, NV 89006
293-2400
Sunday worship: 10 a.m
Duane Jordan, Pastor

Calvary Community
2900 N. Torrey Pines Dr.
Las Vegas, NV 89108
658-3899
Sunday worship: 8:30 am, 11 am, 6 pm
Stan Steward, Pastor

Denomination	# of Churces
Apostolic	17
Assembly of God	16
Baptist	83
Catholic	23
Episcopal	10
Inter-Denominational	7
Jewish	13
Lutheran	18
Latter Day Saints	162
Methodist	15
Non-Denominational	57
Pentecostal	13
Other	150

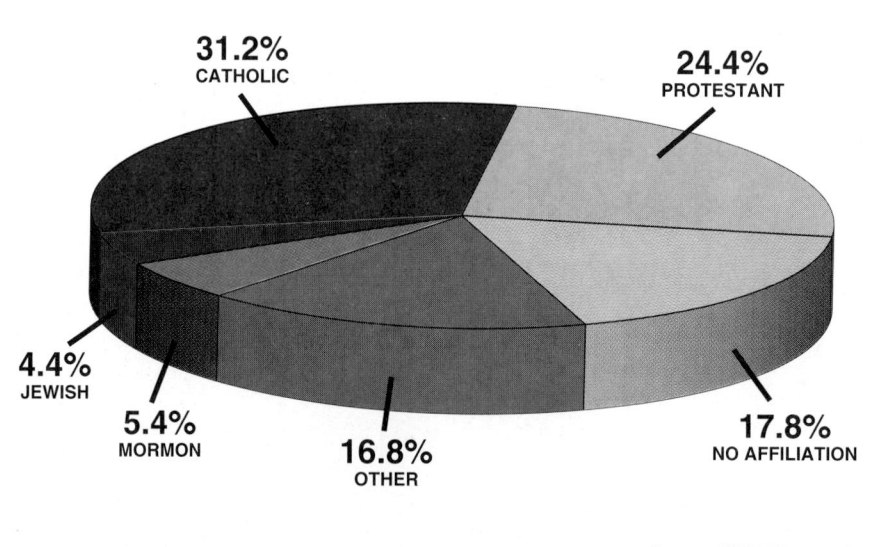

LAS VEGAS RELIGIOUS COMMUNITY
(APPROXIMATE BREAKDOWN)

31.2% CATHOLIC
24.4% PROTESTANT
4.4% JEWISH
5.4% MORMON
16.8% OTHER
17.8% NO AFFILIATION

Source: UNLV Research

Cristo Viene Asambleas De Dios
2333 E. Bonanza Rd.
Las Vegas, NV 89101
474-2909
Sunday worship: 10 am, 6 pm
Caesar Mendoza, Pastor

East Las Vegas Assembly of God
6060 Boulder Hwy., Ste. 5
Las Vegas, NV 89122
456-9820
Sunday worship: 10:45, 6:30 pm
James Martin, Pastor

Full Gospel Deliverance Church
910 S. First St.
Las Vegas, NV 89101
382-4711

Full Gospel Las Vegas Korean Church
1580 Bledsoe Ln.
Las Vegas, NV 89110
453-1223
Sunday worship: 8 am, 12:30 pm, 7:30 pm *(Korean)*; 10 am, 11 am, 6 pm *(English)*
Joel Kim, Korean Pastor
James Lee, English Pastor

Green Valley Assembly of God
711 Valle Verde Ct.
Henderson, NV 89015
454-2722
Sunday worship: 8:45 am, 11:15 am, 6 pm
Gary Morefield, Pastor

Harvest Church
3155 E. Patrick Ln., Ste. 4
Las Vegas, NV 89120
313-8000
Sunday worship: 10 am
Mike Teixeira, Pastor

Iglesia Evangelic Latina Amigos De Isreal
3939 Renate Dr.
Las Vegas, NV 89103
871-1900
Sunday worship: 6 pm
Oscar Benavita, Pastor

North Las Vegas Christian Center
3100 E. Lake Mead Blvd.
Las Vegas, NV 89115
452-3456
Sunday worship: 10 am
William Kowalski, Pastor

Spring Valley Assembly of God
7570 W. Peace Way
Las Vegas, NV 89117
873-1200
Sunday worship: 8:30 am, 10:45 am, 6 pm
David Childers, Pastor

Trinity Life Center
1000 E. St. Louis Ave.
Las Vegas, NV 89104
734-2223
Sunday worship: 9:30 am, 11 am, 6 pm
Randy Geer, Pastor

West Valley Assembly
8100 Westcliff Dr.
Las Vegas, NV 89128
242-2273
Sunday worship: 8:15 am, 9:45 am, 10:45 am, 11:30 am, 6 pm
Paul Goulet, Pastor

BAHA'I

Baha'i Faith of Boulder City
293-6663

Las Vegas
385-7650

Henderson
434-9234

North Las Vegas
648-6868

Paradise Valley
458-5152

Sunrise Manor
6444-8775

Clark County West
873-3318

BAPTIST

Bethany Baptist
210 Wyoming St.
Boulder City, NV 89005
293-1912
Sunday worship: 8 am, 10:30 am, 6 pm
George Huber, Pastor

Spring Valley Baptist Church, 3135 S. Rainbow Blvd., Las Vegas, NV 89102

Bethany Baptist
1229 W. Owens Ave.
Las Vegas, NV 89106
648-5665
Sunday worship: 11 am, 7:30 pm
Detonia Ackenson, Pastor

College Park Baptist
2101 E. Owens Ave.
N. Las Vegas, NV 89030
642-5921
Sunday worship: 9:45 am, 11 am, 7 pm

Community Baptist
245 E. Foster Ave.
Henderson, NV 89015
565-0071
Sunday worship: 11 am, 7 pm
S. Roberson, Pastor

Grace Immanuel Baptist
805 W. Barlett Ave.
Las Vegas, NV 89106
647-1907
Sunday Worship: 8 am, 11 am, 7 pm
Willie C. Wheaton, Pastor

Greater Calvary Baptist
317 Madison Ave.
Las Vegas, NV 89106
646-1559
Sunday worship: 11:30 am, 7 pm

Greater Carver Baptist
1221 N. J St.
Las Vegas, NV 89106
648-4111
Sunday worship: 11 am, 7 pm
Alphonse McCleod, Pastor

Greater Faith Baptist
2736 Chamberlain Ln.
N. Las Vegas, NV 89030
647-4110
Sunday worship: 11 am, 7 pm
Earl Henry, Pastor

Greater New Jerusalem Baptist
1100 N. D St.
Las Vegas, NV 89106
648-8438
Sunday worship: 8 am, 11 am, 6 pm
James M. Rogers, Pastor

Greater St. James Baptist
316 Madison Ave.
Las Vegas, NV 89106
646-4747
Sunday worship: 11 am, 7 pm
Donald Walker, Pastor

Highland Hills Baptist
615 College Dr.
Henderson, NV 89015
566-0200
Sunday worship: 8:30 am, 9:45 am, 11 am, 6 pm
John Mark Simmons, Pastor

Iglesia Bautista Monte Horeb
640 N. Eastern Ave.
Las Vegas, NV 89101
387-0881
Sunday worship: 11 am, 7 pm

Lone Mountain Missionary Baptist Church
6319 W. Lone Mountain Rd.
Las Vegas, NV 789108
645-7551
Sunday worship: 11 am, 6 pm

Macedonia Baptist Church
2600 Clayton St.
N. Las Vegas, NV 89030
646-9075
Sunday worship: 11:15 am
Johnnie Richardson, Pastor

Metropolitan Baptist Church
2200 E. Cheyenne Ave.
N. Las Vegas, NV 89030
657-0371
Sunday worship: 11 am, 7:30 pm
Tyrone Seals, Pastor

Mount Zion Missionary Baptist Church
3131 N. Rancho Rd.
Las Vegas, NV 89130
Sunday worship: 8 am, 10:45 am
Wayne Arnold, Pastor

Mt. Charleston Baptist
210 Kyle Canyon Rd.
Mount Charleston, NV 89124
872-7010
Sunday Worship: 11 am, 3 pm
Earl Greene, Pastor

New Bethel Baptist
400 W. Adams Ave.
Las Vegas, NV 89106
648-8663
Sunday worship: 11 am, 7 pm
Jesse L. Wesley, Sr., Pastor

New Hope Baptist
3739 Glen Ave.
Las Vegas, NV 89121
641-5131
Sunday worship: 12:30 p.m
Arvester Lee, Pastor

New Light Baptist
1165 Lawry Ave.
Las Vegas, NV 89106
648-6410
Sunday worship: 11 am
John Henry, Pastor

Oasis Baptist
4824 Desert Inn Rd.
Las Vegas, NV 89121
451-5694
Sunday worship: 11 am, 6 pm
Ron Dion, Pastor

Pleasant Grove
1189 Hassel Ave.
Las Vegas, NV 89106
648-1645
Sunday worship: 11 am
Terry B. Cox, Pastor

St. Johns Missionary
1439 Lawry Ave.
Las Vegas, NV 89106
648-2382
Sunday worship: 11 am, 5:30 pm
R. Perkins, Pastor

Second Baptist
500 Madison Ave.
Las Vegas, NV 89106
648-6155
Sunday worship: 11 am, 7 pm
Radio Broadcast: 8:15 am, KCEP 88.1 FM
Willie Davis, Pastor

Silverado Community Church
Meeting at Beatty Elementary
Las Vegas, NV 89123
269-1645
Sunday worship: 10 am
Chris Willeke, Pastor

Summerlin Community Baptist Church
2251 N. Rampart Blvd.
Las Vegas, NV 89128
387-7528
Sunday worship: 10:45 am
Dan R. Newburn, Pastor

Tried Stone Baptist Church
621 W. Carey Ave.
N. Las Vegas, NV 89030
642-4752
Sunday worship: 11:30 am
Pastor C. C. Smith

Trinity Missionary Baptist Church
953 E. Sahara Ave., Ste. 5
Las Vegas, NV 89107
735-3348
Sunday worship: 11 am, 3 pm
Robert A. Jackson, Pastor

True Love Missionary Baptist
1941 N. H St.
Las Vegas, NV 89106
648-3603
Sunday worship: 11 am, 7 pm

True Vine Missionary Baptist Church
500 Jackson Ave.
Las Vegas, NV 89106
648-6700
Sunday worship: 11 am
Bervin Oats, Pastor

CHURCHES

Victory Missionary Baptist
500 W. Monroe Ave.
Las Vegas, NV 89106
648-2286
Sunday worship: 11 am, 6 pm
Robert E. Fowler, Pastor

BAPTIST - AMERICAN

Fellowship Baptist Church
6210 W. Cheyenne Ave.
Las Vegas, NV 89108
645-2415
Sunday worship: 11 am
John O'Keefe, Pastor

First Baptist Church of Henderson
47 E. Atlantic Ave.
Henderson, NV 89015
565-8577
Sunday worship: 8 am, 11 am, 6 pm
Rick Wilder, Pastor

Unity Baptist Church
545 N. Marion Dr.
Las Vegas, NV 89104
459-2263
Sunday worship: 8 am, 10:45 am
Reginald Kamera, Pastor

Warm Springs Baptist Church
2075 E. Warm Springs Rd.
Las Vegas, NV 89119
361-7070
Sunday worship: 9:30 am, 11 am
Douglas Meye, Pastor

West Charleston Baptist Church
6701 W. Charleston Blvd.
Las Vegas, NV 89102
878-5798
Sunday worship: 8:15 am, 11 am, 6:30 pm
Richard Voth, Pastor

BAPTIST - BIBLE FELLOWSHIP

Bible Baptist Church
2238 Sandy Ln.
Las Vegas, NV 89115
452-2622
Sunday worship: 11 am, 6 pm
Pete McKenzie, Pastor

Gateway Baptist Church
1900 Gateway Rd.
Las Vegas, NV 89115
452-7111
Sunday worship: 10:50 am, 6 pm
Ron Patterson, Pastor

BAPTIST - CONSERVATIVE

Pilgrim Rest Missionary Baptist Church
1240 W. Adams Ave.
Las Vegas, NV 89106
648-5666
Sunday worship: 11 am
McKenley Hardmon, Jr., Pastor

The Good Samaritan Baptist
933 N. Pecos Rd.
Las Vegas, NV 89101
649-2670
Sunday worship: 11 am, 7 pm
Pal Lee Childress, Pastor

Valley Baptist Church
2844 Civic Center Dr.
N. Las Vegas, NV 89030
642-6357

Sunday worship: 10:45 am *(Spanish)*;
12:30 *(English)*
Robert Oliva, Spanish Pastor
Michael Jackson, English Pastor

BAPTIST - INDEPENDENT FUNDAMENTAL

Choice Hills Baptist Church
3700 E. Charleston Blvd.
Las Vegas, NV 89104
437-6994
Sunday worship: 11 am, 6 pm
Don Mathew, Pastor

Liberty Baptist Church, 6501 W. Lake Mead Blvd., Las Vegas, NV 89108

Liberty Baptist Church
6501 W. Lake Mead Blvd.
Las Vegas, NV 89108
647-4522
Sunday worship: 11 am, 6 pm
David Teis, Pastor

New Hope Baptist Church
5920 W. Flamingo Rd.
Las Vegas, NV 89103
253-6891
Sunday worship: 10 am, 11 am
Mark Patton, Pastor

Paradise Bible Baptist Church
2525 Emerson Ave.
Las Vegas, NV 89121
732-8555
Sunday worship: 10:45 am
Michael Matijevich, Pastor

BAPTIST - MISSIONARY

Greater Evergreen Missionary Baptist Church
1915 Lexington St.
Las Vegas, NV 89106
647-3071
Sunday worship: 11 am, 6 pm
Nathaniel Whitney, Pastor

Greater New Morning Star
2344 Webster St.
N. Las Vegas, NV 89030
642-0059
Sunday worship: 11 am
Charlie Banks, Jr., Pastor

Holy Cross Baptist Church
1328 West Lake Mead
Las Vegas, NV 89106
648-5959
Sunday worship: 11 am, 6:30 pm
George Turner, Pastor

Lamb Blvd. Missionary Baptist Church
500 N. Lamb Blvd.
Las Vegas, NV 89110
452-9146
Sunday worship: 11 am, 6 pm
Roy Wilson, Pastor

Mount Calvary Baptist Church
977 Hassel Ave.
Las Vegas, NV 89106
648-5929
Sunday worship: 11 am
Jack Douglas, Pastor

Mt. Sinai Missionary Baptist Church
1025 Balzar Ave.
Las Vegas, NV 89106
648-2300
Sunday worship: 8 am, 11 am, 6 pm
S. S. Rogers, Pastor

New Revelation Baptist Church
1311 W. Owens Ave.
Las Vegas, NV 89106
646-6572
Sunday worship: 11 am, 7 pm
Donall Horn, Pastor

Union Missionary Baptist Church
860 E. Twain Ave.
Las Vegas, NV 89109
733-7824
Sunday worship: 11 am
James Lucas, Pastor

BAPTIST - SOUTHERN

Southern Baptist Church Office
734-6470

Calvary Southern Baptist Church
1600 E. Cartier Ave.
N. Las Vegas, NV 89030
649-2644

Sunday worship: 8 am, 11:15 am
Jaffuf Haley, Jr., Pastor

Chinese Baptist Church
700 E. St. Louis Ave.
Las Vegas, NV 89104
696-1731
Sunday worship: 1:30 pm *(Cantonese)*
Joseph Cheung, Pastor

Desert Hills Baptist Church
4401 S. Nellis Blvd.
Las Vegas, NV 89121
451-2100
Sunday worship: 9:30 am, 6:30 pm
David Brown, Pastor

El Camino Baptist Church
4027 W. Washburn Rd.
N. Las Vegas, NV 89031
636-1000
Sunday worship: 11 am
Russ Daines, Pastor

Faith Christian Fellowship
421 S. Pacific Ave.
Henderson, NV 89015
565-7308
Sunday worship: 10 am, 6:30 pm
Bob Allen, Pastor

Fantastic First Southern Baptist Church
240 Cholla St.
Henderson, NV 89015
565-6072
Sunday worship: 8:30 am, 11 am, 6 pm
Rene Houle, Pastor

First Fil-Am Baptist Church
1426 E. Charleston Blvd.
Las Vegas, NV 89104
384-4209   385-7016
Sunday worship: 10:30 am, 7:15 pm
Edger Bello, Pastor

First Baptist Church
300 S. 9th St.
Las Vegas, NV 89101
382-6177
Sunday worship: 8 am, 10:45 am, 7 pm
Richard Johnson, Pastor

First Baptist Church
850 Ave. B.
Boulder City, NV 89005
293-1394
Sunday worship: 11 am, 7 pm
Dan Raley, Pastor

The First Korean Baptist Church
5700 Vegas Dr.
Las Vegas, NV 89108
646-4569
Sunday worship: 1 pm, 7:15 pm
Dennis Kim, Pastor

First Spanish Baptist Church
1490 E. University Ave.
Las Vegas, NV 89119
732-3385
Sunday worship: 11 am, 7 pm
Juan Sclafani, Pastor

First Southern Baptist Church
700 E. St. Louis Ave.
Las Vegas, NV 89104
732-3100
Sunday worship: 11 am, 6 pm
Dennis R. Tate, Pastor

Foothills Southern Baptist Church
6405 W. Cheyenne Ave.
Las Vegas, NV 89108
645-0479
Sunday worship: 11 am, 6 pm
Hoyt Savage, Pastor

Frontier Southern Baptist Church
3459 E. Cheyenne Ave.
N. Las Vegas, NV 89030
642-8776
Sunday worship: 11 am, 6 pm
Karel Sylvanus, Pastor

Grace Asia American Church
5904 Edrene Ave.
Las Vegas, NV 89108
735-1975
Sunday worship: 11 am, 6 pm
Marie Stapleton, Pastor

Green Valley Baptist Church
270 N. Valle Verde Dr.
Henderson, NV 89014
434-1906
Sunday worship: 9:45 am, 11 am, 6 pm
Mitch Martin, Pastor

Harbor Christian Fellowship
2675 S. Lamb Blvd.
Las Vegas, NV 89121
457-9300
Sunday worship: 11 am, 6 pm
Robert Walker, Pastor

Iglesia Bautista Israel
230 N. 10th St.
Las Vegas, NV 89101
382-1151
Sunday worship: 10:30 am, 11 am, 1:30 pm, 7 pm
Jose Aadam Gumedo, Pastor

Lake Baptist Chapel
8072 W. Sahara Ave., Ste. A
Meeting at R & R Plaza, Buffalo & Durango.
Las Vegas, NV 89117
254-3234
Sunday worship: 11 am, 6 pm
Charlie O. Jackson, Pastor

Mount Sinai Baptist Church
5424 Tamarus St.
Las Vegas, NV 89119
798-4060
Sunday worship: 11 am, 7 pm
Ozzie Barletta, Pastor

Nellis Baptist Church
4300 Las Vegas Blvd. N.
Las Vegas, NV 89101
644-1055
Sunday worship: 11 am, 7 pm
David Eaton, Pastor

Orchard Baptist Church
Meets at the Regency Village Mobile Home Clubhouse
432-3711
Sunday worship: 11 am, 7 pm
Tony Mayberry, Pastor

Palestine Baptist Church
5400 E. Carey Ave.
Las Vegas, NV 89115
438-3992
Sunday worship: 11 am
Bob Stringer, Pastor

Redrock Southern Baptist Church
5500 W. Alta Dr.
Las Vegas, NV 89107
870-9198
Sunday worship: 11 am, 6 pm
Steve Turrentine, Pastor

Spring Valley Baptist Church
3135 S. Rainbow Blvd.
Las Vegas, NV 89102
871-0150
Sunday worship: 9 am, 10:30 am, 6 pm
Johnny Nantz, Pastor

Sun City Community Church
8560 Del Webb Blvd.
Las Vegas, NV 89134
255-7729
Sunday worship: 11 am
Chip Bendel, Pastor

Sunrise Southern Baptist Church
1780 Betty Ln.
Las Vegas, NV 89110
452-8599
Sunday worship: 10:45 am
Bill Potts, Pastor

Tropicana Christian Fellowship
5000 Spencer Ave.
Las Vegas, NV 89119
798-0050
Sunday worship: 11 am, 5 pm
Tommy Starkes, Pastor

Twin Lakes Baptist
5700 Vegas Dr.
Las Vegas, NV 89108
648-5864
Sunday worship: 11 am, 7 pm
John Pretlove, Pastor

West Craig Road Baptist Church
7880 W. Craig Rd.
Las Vegas, NV 89129
656-7031
Sunday worship: 10:45 am, 6 pm
Roy Worthley, Pastor

Shadow Hills Baptist Church
4400 W. Oakey Blvd.
Las Vegas, NV 89102
878-6991
Sunday worship: 8 am, 9:10 am, 10:20 am, 11:30 am, 6 pm
Michael Rochelle, Pastor

BIBLE

Lake Mead Bible Church
Meets at 701 Skyline Rd.
Henderson, NV 89117
565-8301
Sunday worship: 9 am, 5:30 pm
Daniel Sabaka, Pastor

Las Vegas Bible Church
125 N. 14th St.
Las Vegas, NV 89101
385-3869
Sunday worship: 8 am, 10:15 am, 6 pm
John Mosqueda, Pastor

Our Lady of Las Vegas, 3050 Alta Dr., Las Vegas, NV 89107

Upland Bible Church
920 Upland Blvd.
Las Vegas, NV 89107
878-6291
Sunday worship: 9:30 am, 10:30 am
Richard Olsen, Pastor

BUDDHIST

Nan Hau Zen Buddhist Society
328 Xavier St.
Las Vegas, NV 89107
870-8240
Worship: Call for times
Reverend Chuan Yuan

Mojave Desert Zen Center
Meets at 919 E. Charleston Blvd.
Boulder City, NV 89014
293-4222
Sunday Worship: 9 am
Abbot Kwan Jok Poep Sa

Nevada Buddhist Association
4189 S. Jones Blvd.
Las Vegas, NV 89103
252-7339
Worship: On new moon & full moon days
Reverend Hui Kuang

Thai Buddhist Temple of Las Vegas
2959 W. Gowan Rd.
N. Las Vegas, NV 89030
648-9975
Worship: Daily 7 am, 4 pm
Abbott Naront Makobdee

CHARISMATIC

Golden Harvest Fellowship
2544 E. Charleston Blvd.
Las Vegas, NV 89104
383-8355
Sunday worship: 10:30 am
Pastor Dom Velasco

CATHOLIC - BYZANTINE

American Byzantine Catholic Shrine of Our Mother of Perpetual Help
1325 S. Eastern Ave.
Las Vegas, NV 89104
388-1169
Sunday Mass: 10 am
Father Alan Chegin

St. Gabriel the Archangel Byzantine Catholic Church
2250 E. Maule Ave.
Las Vegas, NV 89118
361-2431
Sunday Mass: 10 am
Father Stephen Washko

CATHOLIC - LATIN RITE

Our Lady of Victory Traditional Catholic Church
280 Hidden Well Rd.
Las Vegas, NV 89119
361-5605
Sunday Mass: 3:30 pm
Various visiting priests

St. Joseph Catholic Church
816 Ogden Ave.
Las Vegas, NV 89101
384-1223
Sunday Mass: 8 am, 9:30 am
Father Courtney Krier

CATHOLIC - ROMAN

Catholic Diocese of Reno - Las Vegas
336 Cathedral Way
Las Vegas, NV 89109
735-3500
Bishop Daniel Walsh

Christ the King
4925 S. Torrey Pines Dr.
Las Vegas, NV 89118
871-1904
Sunday Mass: 7:30 am, 9:30 am, 11:30 am, 6 pm
Father Bill Kenny

Guardian Angel Cathedral
302 Cathedral Way
Las Vegas, NV 89109
735-5241
Sunday Mass: 8 am, 9:30 am, 11 am, 12:30 pm, 5 pm
Saturday Vigil: 2:30 pm, 4 pm, 5:15 pm
Father James Crilly

Holy Family
4490 Mountain Vista St.
Las Vegas, NV 89121
458-2211
Sunday Mass: 7:30 am, 9:30 am, 11:30 am, noon, 7 pm
Father John McShane

Our Lady of Las Vegas
3050 Alta Dr.
Las Vegas, NV 89107
870-2767
Sunday Mass: 6:30 am, 8 am, 9:30 am, 11 am, 12:30 pm, 5 pm
Father Dave Casaleggio

RELIGION

CHURCHES

Prince of Peace
5485 E. Charleston Blvd.
Las Vegas, NV 89122
431-2233
Sunday Mass: 8 am, 10 am, noon, 5:15 pm
Father Francis Timoney

St. Andrew's
1399 San Felipe Dr.
Boulder City, NV 89005
293-7500
Sunday Mass: 8 am, 10:30 am
Father Joseph Annese

St. Anne's
1901 S. Maryland Pkwy.
Las Vegas, NV 89014
735-0510
Sunday Mass: 8 am, 9:30 am, 11 am, 12:30 pm, 5 pm
Spanish Mass: 6:15 pm
Father Robert Votta

St. Bridget's
220 N. 14th St.
Las Vegas, NV 89101
384-3382
Sunday Mass: 7:30 am, 9:30 am, 11:30 am
24 hour chapel for perpetual adoration.
Father James Swenson

St. Christopher's
1840 N. Bruce St.
N. Las Vegas, NV 89030
642-1154
Sunday Mass: 8 am, 9:30 am, 11 am
Spanish Mass: Sun. 1 pm, 5 pm, 7 pm
Father Greg Gordon

St. Elizabeth Ann Seton Catholic Church
1811 Pueblo Vista Dr.
Las Vegas, NV 89128
228-8311
Sunday Mass: 8 am, 10 am, noon, 5:30 pm
Father Kevin McAuliffe

St. Francis De Sales
1111 Michael Way
Las Vegas, NV 89108
647-3440
Sunday Mass: 7 am, 9 am, 11 am, 1 pm, 6 pm
Rev. James J. Bevan, Jr.

St. James the Apostle
820 N. H St.
Las Vegas, NV 89106
648-6606
Sunday Mass: 8 am, 10:30 am
Michael Blackburn, Pastor

St. Joan of Arc
315 S. Casino Center Blvd.
Las Vegas, NV 89101
382-9909
Sunday Mass: 8 am, 9:30 am, 11 am, 12:15 pm, 5 pm
Father Philip O'Donnell

St. Joseph - Husband of Mary
7260 W. Sahara Ave.
Las Vegas, NV 89117
363-1902
Sunday Mass: 8 am, 10 am, noon
Father Joseph Anthony

St. Paul Jung Ha Sang Korean
5225 Meikle Ln.
Las Vegas, NV 89115
453-0033
Sunday Mass: 1 pm
Father Michael Morrissey

St. Peter's Catholic Church
204 S. Boulder Hwy.
Henderson, NV 89015
565-8406
Sunday Mass: 8 am, 10 am, 11:30 am, 5 pm
Father Mark Roberts

St. Thomas More Catholic Community
130 N. Pecos Rd.
Henderson, NV 89014
361-3022
Sunday Mass: 8 am, 10 am, 11 am, noon
Father Daniel T. Nolan

St. Viator
2461 E. Flamingo Rd.
Las Vegas, NV 89121
733-8323
Sunday Mass: 8 am, 10 am, noon, 5 pm
Father Thomas Langenfeld

The Shrine of the Most Holy Redeemer
55 E. Reno Ave.
Las Vegas, NV 89119
891-8600
Mass Schedule: Mon. - Fri. 11:30 am; Sat. 4 pm, 5:30 pm; Sun. 8 am, 10 am
Holy Day Vigil: Same as Saturday
Holy Days: Same as Sunday
Father Patrick Leary
Dedicated in February, 1993, the largest church in Nevada (seating 2,200) was built to serve the expanding tourist population of Las Vegas.

CHRISTIAN

Canyon Ridge Christian
2620 Regatta Dr.
Meets at Cimarron Memorial High
Las Vegas, NV 89128
243-0000
Sunday worship: 9 am, 10:30 am
Kevin Odor, Pastor

Central Christian
3375 S. Mojave Rd.
Las Vegas, NV 89121
735-4004
Sunday worship: 8:30 am, 9:10 am, 11:30 am
Gene Appel, Sr. Pastor

First Church of Eternal Sovereignty
2657 Windmill Pkwy.
Las Vegas, NV 89014
260-1276
Call for information.
Christopher Hansen, Presiding Sovereign

Giving Life Ministries
416 Perlite Way
Henderson, NV 89015
565-4984
Sunday worship: 11 am, 7 pm
Dave Delaria, Pastor

Holy Ghost Ministries
900 Karen Ave.
Las Vegas, NV 89109
892-0987
Sunday worship: Noon
Elonzy Hauley, Pastor

Living Word Christian Church
3840 El Camino Rd.
Las Vegas, NV 89103
367-1773
Sunday worship: 10:30 am *(Cantonese)*
Mary Sheu, Pastor

The Potter's House
3400 S. Jones Blvd.
Las Vegas, NV 89102
248-6755
Sunday worship: 10:30 am, 7 pm
Duane Rens, Pastor

Rocka De Salvasion
3297 Las Vegas Blvd. N.
Las Vegas, NV 89115
644-3852
Sunday worship: 7 pm *(Spanish)*
Manuel Melendez, Pastor

Vegas Valley Christian
5515 Mountain Vista St.
Las Vegas, NV 89120
451-9211
Sunday worship: 10:30 am
Harold Dean, Pastor

CHRISTIAN DISCIPLES OF CHRIST

First Christian Church
101 S. Rancho Dr.
Las Vegas, NV 89106
384-1544
Sunday worship: 8:15 am, 10:45 am
Larry Hansmeier, Pastor

CHRISTIAN & MISSIONARY ALLIANCE

Christian Alliance Bible Church
4074 Schiff Dr.
Las Vegas, NV 89103
889-1290
Sunday worship: 10:30 am
Dan Young, Pastor

CHRISTIAN SCIENCE

First Church of Christ Scientist
300 S. Seventh St.
(7th & Bridger)
Las Vegas, NV 89101
384-3043
Sunday worship: 10 am
Reading room: 384-6185
Open daily

First Church of Christ Scientist
1419 5th St.
Boulder City, NV 89005
293-7740
Sunday worship: 11 am
Reading room: 534 Nevada Highway
Hours: Mon.-Sat. 10 am, 1 pm

CHURCH OF CHRIST

Boulder City Church of Christ
845 Cottonwood St.
Boulder City, NV 89005
293-4019
Guest speakers
Sunday worship: 10:30 am, 6 pm

Boulevard Church of Christ
4000 W. Oakey Blvd.
Las Vegas. NV 89102
877-9629
Sunday worship: 10 am, 6 pm
Randy Mabe, Preacher

St. Joseph - Husband of Mary
7260 W. Sahara Ave.
Las Vegas, NV 89117

Boulevard Iglesio De Cristo
4000 W. Oakey Blvd.
Las Vegas, NV 89102
877-3946
Sunday worship: 4:30 p.m
Manuel Arroyo, Preacher

Central Church of Christ
3984 Schiff Dr.
Las Vegas, NV 89103
871-1244
Sunday worship: 10 am, 6 pm
Dean Whaley, Preacher

The Church at Las Vegas
3388 S. Decatur Blvd.
Las Vegas, NV 89102
876-3499
Sunday worship: 10:30 am, 6 pm
Gospel broadcast: Sunday 7 am KORK AM-920
Darryl Reyman, Preacher

Church of Christ
131 E. King St.
Henderson, NV 89015
564-5959
Sunday worship: 10:30 am, 6:30 pm

Church of Christ
2626 N. Martin L. King Blvd.
Las Vegas, NV 89106
648-8283
Sunday worship: 11 am, 7 pm
Bob Hunter, Pastor

Church of Christ Las Vegas
3240 B Civic Center Dr.
N. Las Vegas, NV 89030
656-6138
Sunday worship: 10:30 am, 6 pm
Boyd Gilliland, Minister

Eastside Church of Christ
4690 E. Desert Inn Rd.
Las Vegas, NV 89121
435-1717
Sunday worship: 9:50 am
Guest speakers

Green Valley Church of Christ
28 Commerce Center Dr.
Henderson, NV 89014
456-2040
Sunday worship: 9:50 am, 5 pm
Barney Cargile, Pastor

North Las Vegas Church of Christ
2424 McCarran Ave.
N. Las Vegas, NV 89030
642-3141
Sunday worship: 9:50 am, 6 pm
Jack Freeman, Pastor

Vegas Drive Church of Christ
3816 Vegas Dr.
Las Vegas, NV 89108
648-4827
Sunday worship: 10 am, 6 pm
Keith Greer, Preacher

Valley Community
Meets at Masonic Temple
2200 W. Mesquite Ave.
Las Vegas, NV 89106
243-4331
Sunday worship: 10 am
Rick Smith, Pastor

Victory Road Church of Christ
104 W. Victory Rd.
Henderson, NV 89015
565-8186
Sunday worship: 10:30 am
Ron Edwards, Preacher

CHURCH OF CHRIST - HOLINESS

Pilgrim Church of Christ - Holiness USA
1515 N. D St.
Las Vegas, NV 89106
648-6504
Sunday worship: 11 am, 7 pm
David L. Harris, Pastor

CHURCH OF GOD

Church of God Family Worship Center
4000 W. Spring Rd.
Las Vegas, NV 89108
648-3418
Sunday worship: 8 am, 10:50 am, 6 pm
Douglas Galloway, Pastor

Friendship Church of God In Christ
2249 W. Washington Ave.
Las Vegas, NV 89106
646-1361
Sunday worship: 11 am, 8:30 pm
Billy Gilmore, Pastor

First Church of God
827 Balzar Ave.
Las Vegas, NV 89106
646-2824
Sunday worship: 11 am, 7:30 pm
Julia L. Daniels, Pastor

Gateway to Heaven
1425 Balzar Ave.
Las Vegas, NV 89106
646-1185
Sunday worship: Noon, 8 pm
Nathan Harris, Pastor

Iglesia De Dios
2540 Belmont St.
N. Las Vegas, NV 89030
642-4023
Sunday worship: 10 am, 6 pm
Samuel Diaz, Pastor

New Beginning Faith and Ministry
318 S. 11th St.
Las Vegas, NV 89101
382-4838
Sunday worship: 9:45 am, 11 am, 6 pm
Chuck Coleman, Pastor

North Las Vegas Church
2520 N. Belmont St.
N. Las Vegas, NV 89030
642-1945
Sunday worship: 11 am, 6 pm
Charlie Chancellor, Pastor

First Good Shepherd, 301 S. Maryland Pkwy., Las Vegas, NV 89101

Pentacostal Temple Church of God in Christ
1117 F St.
Las Vegas, NV 89106
648-6856
Sunday worship: 11:30 am, 7:45 pm
Leon Smith, Pastor

St. Paul Church of God in Christ
911 G St.
Las Vegas, NV 89106
648-4230
Sunday worship: 11 am, 8 pm
Bishop C. Hall, Pastor

CHURCH OF GOD IN CHRIST

Blood of the Lamb Cogic
630 N. Main St.
Las Vegas, NV 89101
382-8808
Sunday worship: 11:15 am, 7 pm
Mack O. Harris, Pastor

Ebenezer Church of God in Christ
1072 W. Bartlett Ave.
Las Vegas, NV 89106
646-1503
Sunday worship: 11:30 am, 8 pm
Bill McDonnell, Pastor

Friendship Church of God in Christ
2249 W. Washington Ave.
Las Vegas, NV 89106
646-1361
Sunday worship: 11 am, 8 pm
Billy Gilmore, Pastor

Grace Temple
721 W. McWilliams Ave.
Las Vegas, NV 89106
648-1900
Sunday worship: 11:45 am, 7:30 pm
Alonzo McGhee, Pastor

Greater Bethel Deliverance
2226 E. Cheyenne Ave.
N. Las Vegas, NV 89030
642-5131
Sunday worship: 11 am, 7:30 pm
Jerry Jimerson, Pastor

Greater Philadelphia
1200 N. D St.
Las Vegas, NV 89106
631-1321
Sunday worship: 11:15 am, 7:30 pm
Darrell Thomas, Pastor

House of Holiness
2301 N. H St.
Las Vegas, NV 89106
648-7937
Sunday worship: Noon, 8 pm
M. L. Sanders, Pastor

Israelite
1285 Miller Ave.
Las Vegas, NV 89106
648-9595
Sunday worship: Noon, 7 pm
Elder Gray, Pastor

Light House Church of God in Christ
2500 McLaurie Ave.
Las Vegas, NV 89121
457-4396
Sunday worship: 11:30 am, 6:30 pm
Charles Smith, Pastor

Lord of Hosts Ministries
1288 Miller Ave.
Las Vegas, NV 89129
638-2210
Sunday worship: 11 am, 7:30 pm
Robert Clemons, Pastor

Neway
320 W. Monroe Ave.
Las Vegas, NV 89106
647-4645
Sunday worship: 11:45 am, 7:30 pm
Harold Dorsey, Pastor

New Hope
839 Balzar Ave.
Las Vegas, NV 89106
648-0898
Sunday worship: 11:30 am, 6:30 pm
Chester L. Givens, Pastor

Powerhouse
1216 W. Adams Ave.
Las Vegas, NV 89106
646-2284
Sunday worship: 11:30 am, 7 pm
Willie Blanche, Pastor

Revival Temple
1603 N. Tonopah Dr.
Las Vegas, NV 89106
646-0738
Sunday worship: Noon, 8 pm
Eckstine McCurdy, Pastor

St. John
2301 Comstock Dr.
N. Las Vegas, NV 89030
646-9700
Sunday worship: 11:30 am, 6 pm
Robert Jefferson, Pastor

St Paul
911 N. G St.
Las Vegas, NV 89106
648-4230
Sunday worship: 11 am, 8 pm
Bishop C. Hall, Pastor

Tabernacle of Praise
2944 Civic Center Dr.
N. Las Vegas, NV 89030
633-5273
Sunday worship: 12:30 pm
Elder Michael Jackson, Pastor

Traveler's Rest
952 Balzar Ave.
Las Vegas, NV 89106
646-9077
Sunday worship: Noon, 7:30 pm
Elder Cleo Jamerson, Pastor

Tree of Life
4351 W. Charleston Blvd.
Las Vegas, NV 89102
259-9111
Sunday worship: 11 am, 5 pm
John Langford, Pastor

Trinity
1341 Blankenship Ave.
Las Vegas, NV 89106
648-6309
Sunday worship: Noon, 8 pm
Lawrence Daniels, Pastor

Vegas View
1906 Glider St.
N. Las Vegas, NV 89030
642-6211
Sunday worship: 8 am, 11:50 am, 7:45 pm
Claude H. Parson, Pastor

CHURCH OF GOD OF PROPHECY

Church of God of Prophecy
4780 Patterson Ave.
Las Vegas, NV 89104
431-2228
Sunday worship: 10:45 am, 6 pm
Archie Spangler, Pastor

RELIGION

CHURCHES

CHURCH OF JESUS CHRIST OF LATTER DAY SAINTS

Las Vegas Nevada Temple
827 N. Temple View Dr.
Las Vegas, NV 89110
452-5011
One of 50 temples, the $18 million Las Vegas Nevada Temple is situated at the base of Sunrise Mountain on a beautifully landscaped 12-acre site. A 13-foot gold leaf statue of an ancient prophet stands atop one of the six spires rising above the copper roof. Open to church members only, the temple serves 162 wards and is used for baptisms, marriages and an atmosphere of meditation. The Church has 18 stakes in the Las Vegas area where worship is held. Las Vegas has a Mormon population of 70,000, Nevada has 127,500 and the Church has a membership of 9.7 million worldwide.
Non-members may walk the grounds and enjoy the view of Las Vegas.
Grounds Hours: Tue.-Fri. 5:30 am - 8 pm; Sat. 7 am - 6 pm; closed 6 pm Sat. until 5:30 am Tue.

COMMUNITY

Bread of Life Deliverance Center
2721 Coran Ln.
Las Vegas, NV 89108
648-8844
Sunday worship: 11 am, 7 pm
Simmie Richard, Pastor

Faith Christian Church
1100 Buchanan Blvd.
Boulder City, NV 89005
293-2454
Sunday worship: 10 am
Robert E. Tedrow, Pastor

Grace Community
1150 Wyoming St.
Boulder City, NV 89005
293-2018
Sunday worship: 9 am, 10:30 am
Richard Smith, Pastor

Metropolitan Community
1140 Almond Tree Ln.
Las Vegas, NV 89104
369-4380
Sunday worship: 1 pm
Bill McDaniels, Pastor

New Hope Community
1641 E. Sunset Rd.
Las Vegas, NV 89119
361-4673
Sunday worship: 10:30 am
Harold McKellips, Pastor

ECKANKAR

Eckankar
3160 E. Desert Inn Rd., Ste. 14
Las Vegas, NV 89121
369-0101
Sunday worship: 10 am

EPISCOPAL

Episcopal Diocese of Nevada
737-9190

All Saints
4201 W. Washington Ave.
Las Vegas, NV 89107
878-2373
Sunday worship: 8 am, 10 am
Father John Yoder

Christ Church
2000 S. Maryland Pkwy.
Las Vegas, NV 89104
735-7655
Sunday worship: 8 am, 10:30 am, 6 pm
Father Massey Gentry

Church of Jesus Christ of Latter Day Saints
Las Vegas Nevada Temple, 827 N. Temple View Drive, Las Vegas, NV

Grace in the Desert
1910 Spring Gate Ln.
Meets at Summerlin Community Ctr.
Las Vegas, NV 89134
878-1919
Sunday worship: 8 am, 10:30 am
Father Sherman Frederick

St. Christopher's
812 Arizona St.
Boulder City, NV 89005
293-4275
Sunday worship: 10 am
Father Richard Lassiter & Katherine Rohde

St. Luke's
832 N. Eastern Ave.
Las Vegas, NV 89101
642-4459
Sunday worship: 10 am
Father Richard Henry

St. Matthew's
4709 S. Nellis Blvd.
Las Vegas, NV 89121
451-2483
Sunday worship: 9:45 am
Reverend Christie Leavitt

St. Thomas
5383 E. Owens Ave.
Las Vegas, NV 89110
452-1199
Sunday worship: 9 am
Father Billy Haycock

St. Timothy's
43 W. Pacific Ave.
Henderson, NV 89015
565-8033
Sunday worship: 10 am
Father Lloyd Rupp

EVANGELICAL

The Covenant Korean
2206 W. Bonanza Rd
Las Vegas, NV 89106
638-6207
Sunday worship: 7:30 pm
Chae K. Lee, Pastor

Grace Evangelical Free Church
920 S. Decatur Blvd.
Las Vegas, NV 89107
259-0515
Sunday worship: 10:30 am
Al Lewis, Pastor

Iglesia Evangelica Hispana Asambleas De Dios
3603 Las Vegas Blvd. N.
Las Vegas, NV 89115
644-3092

FOURSQUARE

Black Mountain Fellowship
317 S. Water St.
Henderson, NV 89015
564-2435
Sunday worship: 10 am, 5:30 pm
Roy Miller, Pastor

Calvary
2929 Cedar Ave.
Las Vegas, NV 89101
384-6960
Sunday worship: 8 am, 10:30 am, 5:30 pm
Rich Taylor, Pastor

Christian Center - Fourscore Gospel Church
571 Adams Blvd.
Boulder City, NV 89005
293-7773
Sunday worship: 10 am
Marjorie Kitchell, Pastor

Cornerstone Christian Fellowship
5825 W. Eldora Ave.
Las Vegas, NV 89102
871-5050
Sunday worship: 8:30 am, 10:45 am
Greg Massanari, Pastor

Grapevine Fellowship
2323 S. Nellis Blvd.
Las Vegas, NV 89104
451-8463
Sunday worship: 9 am, 11 am, 7 pm
Bud Higginbotham, Pastor
(This is also considered an Interdenominational Church.)

Isaac's Well
Meets at the Neighborhood Church Bldg. in Henderson
Las Vegas, NV 89015
399-1368
Saturday worship: 6 pm
Robert Lavala, Pastor

Meadows Christian Foursquare
Meets at Fellowship Community Church
6210 W. Cheyenne Ave.
Las Vegas, NV 89108
254-1725
Sunday worship: 4 pm
Ted Ramey, Pastor

Neighborhood Church
207 W. Basic Rd.
Henderson, NV 89015
565-9672
Sunday worship: 10 am, 6 pm
Don Frazier, Pastor

FULL GOSPEL

Antilepsis Full Gospel Ministries
5920 W. Flamingo Rd.
Las Vegas, NV 89103
227-6028
Sunday worship: 9 am
George Ward, Jr., Pastor

Full Gospel Mission Outreach Temple
1904 Stevens St.
Las Vegas, NV 89115
459-8933
Sunday worship: 11 am, 7 pm
Bertha Moores, Pastor

New Light Devine Temple Deliverance
1230 W. Owens Ave.
Las Vegas, NV 89106
638-1817
Sunday worship: 11 am, 6 pm
Milton Turner, Pastor

Praise Ministries
370 E. Windmill Ln.
Las Vegas, NV 89123
260-4777
Sunday worship: 11 am, 7 pm
Bill Toller, Pastor

Prayer Center
1316 Miller Ave.
Las Vegas, NV 89106
646-3415
Sunday worship: 11 am, 7 pm
Prince Davis, Pastor

Wellspring Church & Christian Center
1401 N. Decatur Blvd., Ste. 13
Las Vegas, NV 89108
631-5027
Sunday worship: 11 am, 7 pm
George and Sharon Stover, Pastors
(This is also considered an Interdenominational Church.)
Worship services translated to Spanish

GREEK ORTHODOX

St. John the Baptist Greek Orthodox Church
5300 S. El Camino Rd.
Las Vegas, NV 89118
221-8245
Sunday worship: 9 am, 10 am
Father Ilia Katre

JEHOVAH'S WITNESSES

Central Jehovah's Witnesses
1335 S. Mojave Rd.
Las Vegas, NV 89104
432-8603
Sunday worship: 6:30 pm

East Jehovah's Witnesses
3090 Mountain Vista St.
Las Vegas, NV 89121
454-3090
Sunday worship: 6:30 pm *(Spanish)*

Jehovah's Witnesses
601 Arrowhead Trail
Henderson, NV 89015
565-8220
Sunday worship: 9:30 am, 12:30 pm, 3:30 pm

Palomar Jehovah's Witnesses
1335 S. Mojave Rd.
Las Vegas, NV 89104
432-8603
Friday worship: 7:30 pm *(Spanish)*
Saturday worship: 1 pm *(English)*

Paradise Jehovah's Witnesses
2520 E. Patrick Ln.
Las Vegas, NV 89120
736-7450
Sunday worship: 9 am, 3 pm, 5 pm

Rancho Jehovah's Witnesses
5005 Donnie Ave.
Las Vegas, NV 89130
645-4590
Sunday worship: 9:30 am, 12:30 pm, 3:30 pm *(English);* 5 pm *(Spanish)*

Sunrise Congregation
1881 N. Walnut Rd.
Las Vegas, NV 89104
453-1277
Sunday worship: 9:30 am, 12:30 pm, 3:30 pm *(Spanish)*

Valle Verde Jehovah's Witnesses
2520 E. Patrick Ln.
Las Vegas, NV 89120
736-7450
Sunday worship: 9:30 am, 12:30 pm, 3:30 pm *(English);* 8 pm *(Korean)*

West Jehovah's Witnesses
5546 W. Oakey Blvd.
Las Vegas, NV 89102
877-1172
Sunday worship: 9 am, 12:30 pm, 3:30 pm

LUTHERAN

Calvary Lutheran
800 N. Bruce St.
Las Vegas, NV 89101
649-7788
Sunday worship: 9 am
Tom Morrison, Pastor

Christ Lutheran
111 N. Torrey Pines Dr.
Las Vegas, NV 89107
870-1421
Sunday worship: 7:30 am, 8:30 am
Praise worship: 10:30 am
Dr. Harry E. Olson, Jr., Pastor

Christ Lutheran
1401 5th St.
Boulder City, NV 89005
293-4332
Sunday worship: 8 am
Steven Cluver, Pastor

St. John the Baptist Greek Orthodox Church
5300 S. El Camino Rd., Las Vegas, NV 89118

Christ the Servant
2 S. Pecos Rd.
Henderson, NV 89014
263-0802
Sunday worship: 8 am, 10:30 am, 7 pm
Phil Hausknecht, Pastor

Community Lutheran Church
3720 E. Tropicana Ave.
Las Vegas, NV 89121
458-2241
Sunday worship: 8:30 am, 9:45 am, 11 am
Ray Christenson, Pastor

First Good Shepherd
301 S. Maryland Pkwy.
Las Vegas, NV 89101
384-6106
Sunday worship: 8:15 am, 11 am, 7 pm
David Hinck & Ed Zimbrick, Pastors

Good Samaritan
6500 W. Flamingo Rd.
Las Vegas, NV 89103
873-3589
Sunday worship: 8:30 am, 10 am
Tom Stutelberg, Pastor

Green Valley Evangelical
1799 Wigwam Pkwy.
Henderson, NV 89014
454-8979
Sunday worship: 9 am, 10:30 am
Don Pieper, Pastor

Holy Spirit Lutheran Church
6670 W. Cheyenne Ave.
Las Vegas, NV 89108
645-1777
Sunday worship: 8 am, 10:45 am
Paul E. Hansen, Pastor

Lamb of God Lutheran Church
6220 N. Jones Blvd.
Las Vegas, NV 89131
645-4998
Sunday worship: 8:15 am, 10:45 am
Wayne W. Koenig, Pastor

Mt. Olive Lutheran Church · WELS
3975 S. Sandhill Rd.
Las Vegas, NV 89121
451-1050
Sunday worship: 8 am, 10:30 am
James Panning, Pastor

Mountain View Lutheran Church · Missouri Synod
9550 W. Cheyenne Ave.
Las Vegas, NV 89129
360-8290
Sunday worship: 10:30 am
Terry Brandenburg, Pastor

Our Saviors Lutheran Church
59 Lynn Ln.
Henderson, NV 89015
565-9154
Sunday worship: 8 am, 10:45 am
Ed Brulming, Pastor

Redeemer Lutheran Church
1730 N. Pecos Rd.
Las Vegas, NV 89115
642-7744
Sunday worship: 8:30 am, 11 am
Ralph Buchhorn, Pastor

Reformation Lutheran Church
580 E. St. Louis Ave.
Las Vegas, NV 89104
732-2052
Sunday worship: 8:30 am, 10:45 am
Charles Bowker, Pastor

St. Andrew Lutheran Church
9107 Del Webb Blvd.
Las Vegas, NV 89134
255-1990
Sunday worship: 8:30 am, 10 am
Stephen Knudsen, Pastor

Summerlin Evangelical Lutheran Church
1911 Pueblo Vista Dr.
Las Vegas, NV 89134
254-8431
Sunday worship: 9 am
Jerome McWaters, Pastor

The Lakes Lutheran Church
8200 W. Sahara Ave.
Las Vegas, NV 89117
363-2515
Sunday worship: 8 am, 10:30 am
Thomas J. Unmacht, Pastor

METHODIST

Advent United Methodist Church
3460 N. Rancho Dr.
Las Vegas, NV 89130
645-0447
Sunday worship: 9 am, 11:15 am, 6 pm
Jeri Lee Harrell, Pastor

Celebration! United Methodist
2040 Desert Shadow Trail
Meets at Vanderburg Elementary in Green Valley Ranch
Henderson, NV 89012
361-4102
Sunday worship: 10:30 am
Jon Ierley, Pastor

Church of the Living Christ
Meets at Parson Elementary
649-2310
Sunday worship: 10:30 am
Michael Higgs, Pastor

Desert Springs United Methodist Church
Desert Vista Community Center
10360 Sun City Blvd.
Las Vegas, NV 89134
256-5933
Sunday worship: 8 am, 9:30 am
Ed Ramsey, Pastor

First Christian Methodist Episcopal
2727 Civic Center Dr.
N. Las Vegas, NV 89030
837-6846   395-2608
Sunday worship: 11:30 am
Salimu P. Autry, Pastor

First Henderson United Methodist Church
609 E. Horizon Dr.
Henderson, NV 89015
565-6049
Sunday worship: 8 am, 9:30 am
Marvin R. Gant, Pastor

First United Methodist Church
231 S. 3rd St.
Las Vegas, NV 89101
382-9939
Katherine Fuchs, Pastor
Sunday worship: 8:30 am, 10 am
Oldest church in Las Vegas

Green Valley United Methodist Church
2200 Robindale Rd.
Henderson, NV 89014
454-7989
Sunday worship: 8:15 am, 9:30 am, 11am
Dr. Robert Burns, Pastor

CHURCHES

Griffith United Methodist Church
1701 E. Oakey Blvd.
Las Vegas, NV 89104
384-5255
Sunday worship: 8:30 am, 10:45 am
Wayne Brown, Pastor

Korean United Methodist Church of Las Vegas
1701 E. Oakey Blvd.
Las Vegas, NV 89104
384-2203
Sunday worship: 12:30 pm
Eun Jin La, Pastor

Sunrise Mountain Church
2075 N. Lamb Blvd.
Las Vegas, NV 89110
437-8989
Sunday worship: 8:30 am, 10:45 am
Michael Downing, Pastor

Trinity United Methodist Church
6151 W. Charleston Blvd.
Las Vegas, NV 89102
870-4747
Sunday worship: 9 am, 10:30 am
Don Smith, Pastor

University United Methodist Church
4412 S. Maryland Pkwy.
Las Vegas, NV 89119
733-7155
Sunday worship: 8:45 am, 10 am, 11:15 am
Dr. John Blackwell, Pastor

Wesley United Methodist Church
2727 Civic Center Dr.
N. Las Vegas, NV 89030
642-0243
Sunday worship: 10 am
Billy Archibald, Pastor

Zion Methodist Church
2108 N. Revere St.
N. Las Vegas, NV 89030
648-7806
Sunday worship: 11 am, 6:30 pm
Marion Bennett, Pastor

MUSLIM

Masjid As-Sabur
711 W. Morgan Ave.
Las Vegas, NV 89106
647-2500
Sunday Taleem *(public)*: 1 pm
Imam Abdus-Salaam Haji, Pastor

ISLAMIC SOCIETY OF NEVADA

Jama Mosque
4730 E. Desert Inn Rd.
Las Vegas, NV 89121
458-1986
Friday service: 11 am
Guest speakers

NAZARENE

Charleston Heights Nazarene
6219 W. Washington Ave.
Las Vegas, NV 89107
870-9911
Sunday worship: 10:45 am, 6 pm
Bob Ogden, Pastor

Circle Church
4312 Rosebank Cir.
Las Vegas, NV 89108
636-8696
Sunday worship: 10 am
Ron Rogers, Pastor

First Church of the Nazarene
3825 Pecos McLeod
Las Vegas, NV 89121
451-6000
Sunday worship: 9:30 am, 10:50 am, 6 pm
Lane Zachary, Pastor

Grace Church of the Nazarene
Corner of Greenway Rd. & Horizon St.
Henderson, NV 89015
564-5922
Sunday worship: 10 am
David Smith, Pastor

The Lakes Lutheran Church, 8200 W. Sahara Ave., Las Vegas, NV 89117

Harvest Church of the Nazarene
Meets at Swainston Middle School
N. Las Vegas, NV 89030
656-1860
Sunday worship: 10 am
Bill Williams, Pastor

NONDENOMINATIONAL

Abundant Life Community Church
3210 N. Rancho Dr.
Las Vegas, NV 89130
877-4413
Sunday worship: 11 am, 6 pm
Mike Robinson, Pastor
(This is also considered an Interdenominational Church.)

Alcance Victoria
Meets at Von Tobel Junior High
N. Las Vegas, NV 89030
639-9472
Sunday worship: 5:30 pm
Gabriel Ortiz, Pastor (Spanish)

A Place for Miracles
2160 W. Charleston Blvd.
Las Vegas, NV 89102
388-9680
Sunday worship: 10:30 am
Mirkalice Gore, Pastor

Amistad Cristiana
901 Stewart Ave.
Las Vegas, NV 89101
386-9995
Sunday worship: 11 am, 6:30 pm

Calvary Chapel East
3430 E. Tropicana Ave.
Las Vegas, NV 89121
435-1777
Sunday worship: 8:30 am, 10:30 am, 6 pm
John Goad, Pastor

Calvary Chapel of Henderson
Meets at the Henderson Senior Center
600 W. Sunset Rd.
Henderson, NV 89015
456-3619
Sunday worship: 10 am, 6 pm
Chuck Trett, Pastor

Calvary Chapel Spring Valley
7175 W. Oquendo Rd.
Las Vegas, NV 89113
362-9000
Sunday worship: 8:30 am, 11 am, 6:30 pm
John Michaels, Pastor

Center Cross Chapel
2245 N. Decatur Blvd.
Las Vegas, NV 89108
384-1178
Sunday worship: 10 am
Peter Wells, Pastor

Chaplain of the Stars
3951 Kamden Way
Las Vegas, NV 89119
735-2933
Reverend Richard Gilster

Chinese Christian Church
3380 Arville St., Ste. G
Las Vegas, NV 89120
367-9882
Sunday worship: 10:30 am
Guest speakers *(Chinese)*

Christian Life Community
800 E. Karen Ave.
Las Vegas, NV 89109
731-6965
Sunday worship: 8 am, 10:45 am;
7 pm *(Spanish)*
Dennis Walker, Pastor
(This is also considered an Interdenominational Church.)

Church of God in Me
851 Hassell Ave.
Las Vegas, NV 89106
648-1259
Worship: Tue., Thu., Sat. 7 pm
Joseph Prange, Pastor
(For homeless men over 19 - meals & housing provided.)

Church of Scientology
Celebrity Center
1100 S. 10th St.
Las Vegas, NV 89104
366-0818
Sunday worship: 1 pm
Val Garcia, Pastor

City of the Palms Christian Fellowship
Call for location.
438-7700
Sunday worship: 10 am
Tom Griner, Pastor

Deliverance Thru Faith
1517 N. Las Vegas Blvd.
Las Vegas, NV 89101
388-9963
Sunday worship: 11 am, 6:30 pm
Carlton Mackie, Minister

Echoes of Faith River of Life
1401 E. Washington Ave.
Las Vegas, NV 89101
642-0011
Sunday worship: 8:30 am, 10:30 am, 6:30 p.m
Bertie McCoy, Pastor
(This is also considered an Interdenominational Church.)

Exodus Christian Fellowship
407 Spencer St.
Las Vegas, NV 89101
385-9200
Sunday worship: 10:30 am, 6:30 pm
Tony Giacopelli, Pastor

Faith Chapel Fellowship
2570 Duneville St.
Las Vegas, NV 89102
873-1445
Sunday worship: 11 am, 6 pm
Billy Cook, Pastor

Fellowship of Hope
1115 S. Casino Center Blvd.
Las Vegas, NV 89104
385-2606
Sunday worship: 9 am
R. Jones, Pastor

Genesis Christian Ministries
Meets at 5150 Duneville St.
Las Vegas, NV 89118
228-3890
Sunday worship: 10 am
Dennis McLaughlin, Pastor

Glad Tidings Christian Center
Meets at Garside Middle School
432-9201

God's Plan Christian Fellowship
205 N. 9th St.
Las Vegas, NV 89101
387-2093
Sunday worship: 11 am, 6 pm
Donald McCormick, Pastor

Greater Grace Ministries
5510 Meikle Ln.
Las Vegas, NV 89115
257-9440
Sunday worship: 10:30 am, 7 pm
Bill Reed, Pastor

Hallelujah Fellowship
800 N. Rancho Dr.
Las Vegas, NV 89106
646-7332
Sunday worship: 8:30 am, 11 am, 6 pm
Dennis Lee, Pastor

Higher Ground Christian Fellowship
Meets at Mendoza Elementary School
2000 S. Sloan Ln.
Las Vegas, NV 89122
440-6290
Sunday worship: 10:30 am
Ed Perkins, Pastor

Iglesia Ni Cristo
201 Taylor St.
Henderson, NV 89015
565-1908
Sunday worship: 8 am, 6 pm
June Macayan, Pastor

Institute of Divine Metaphysical Research
2645 S. Nellis Blvd.
Las Vegas, NV 89121
432-4424
Sunday worship: 11 am
Dean Covington Cormier, Pastor

Integrity Christian Fellowship
364-5421
Sunday worship: 11 am
Elder Ping Lee (Mandarin)

Jesus Is Lord Fellowship LV Chapter
3049 E. Charleston Blvd.
Las Vegas, NV 89104
385-1112
Sunday worship: 10 am, 6:30 pm
Robert Aquino, Pastor

Jesus Is the Answer
731 Fremont St.
Las Vegas, NV 89101
388-7777
Sunday worship: 10 am, 6 pm
Raymond MacIntosh, Pastor

Kingdom Harvest Worship Center Ministries
1911 N. H St.
Las Vegas, NV 89106
646-6399
Sunday worship: 11 am, 7 pm
Samuel Carroll, Pastor

Las Vegas Bible Church
125 N. 14th St.
Las Vegas, NV 89101
385-3869
Sunday worship: 8 am, 10:15 am, 6 pm
John Mosqueda, Pastor

Las Vegas Family Church
1740 Leonard Ln.
Las Vegas, NV 89108
648-3134
Sunday worship: 11:15 am
William Starr, Pastor

Meadows Christian Fellowship
1725 S. Rainbow Blvd.
Las Vegas, NV 89102
254-1725
Sunday worship: 9 am, 11 am, 7 pm
Ted Ramey, Pastor

Miracles Church for All People
1559 N. Decatur Blvd.
Las Vegas, NV 89108
648-8385
Sunday worship: 11 am, 7 pm
Buddy Eugene Yates, Pastor

The Moment of Truth Outreach Ministries
459-3908
Lunch at the park homeless feeding program; prison ministries
HIV Lifeline Radio Program: FM 88.1 - 10:45 am
Reverend Glories Powell, Pastor

Moments of Miracles
311 Madison Ave.
Las Vegas, NV 89106
647-5770
Sunday worship: 11 am, 7:30 pm
Amanda Irving, Pastor

My Father's House
1942 E. Sahara Ave.
Las Vegas, NV 89104
435-2700
Sunday worship: 10 am, 6:30 pm
Jose Boveda, Pastor

Namaste Life
Call for location and time of worship
880-9394
Dr. Fred McCoun, Pastor

New Light Divine Temple Deliverance
1230 W. Owens Ave.
Las Vegas, NV 89106
638-1817
Sunday worship: Noon, 6 pm
Milton Turner, Pastor

Northwest Christian Fellowship
Meets at Adcock Elementary School
100 Newcomer St.
Las Vegas, NV 89107
880-4243
Sunday worship: 10 am, 6 pm
Cary Smith, Pastor

Rainbow Christian Church
6005 W. Gowan Rd.
Las Vegas, NV 89108
396-6246

River of Life Word Ministries
5243 W. Charleston Blvd.
Las Vegas, NV 89102
258-9673
Sunday worship: 11 am, 6 pm
Sullivan Causey, Pastor

S M & A Outreach Ministries
553 E. Oakey Blvd.
Las Vegas, NV 89104
363-8030
Sunday worship: 10 am
Maria E. Mercadal, Pastor

Spiritual Life Ministries
Call for location and time of worship.
243-3887
Don Nelson, Pastor

Tabernacle Faith
2030 Yale St.
Las Vegas, NV 89107
657-2024
Sunday Worship: 11 am, 6 pm
Corine Claiborn, Pastor

Word of Life Christian Center, 3520 N. Buffalo Dr., Las Vegas, NV

Teaching of the Inner Christ
3160 S. Valley View Blvd., Ste. 105
Las Vegas, NV 89102
367-8911
Sunday worship: 11 am
Shirley Shaffer, Pastor

Times of Refreshing International Ministries
Meets at 1113 N. H St.
N. Las Vegas, NV 89030
263-9593
Sunday worship: 11 am
Jeffrey Reese, Pastor

United Faith Christian Deliverance Church
1114 N. H St.
Las Vegas, NV 89106
648-6377
Sunday worship: 11:30 am, 7:30 pm
Benjamin Johnson, Pastor

Upland Bible Church
920 Upland Blvd.
Las Vegas, NV 89107
878-6291
Sunday worship: 9:30 am, 10:30 am
Richard Olsen, Pastor

Victory Christian Center
6126 S. Sandhill Rd.
Las Vegas, NV 89120
456-4480
Sunday worship: 10 am, 6 pm
Bob & Martha Perry, Pastors
(This is also considered an Inter-denominational Church.)

Victory Outreach
810 E. Lake Mead Blvd.
N. Las Vegas, NV 89030
649-4423
Sunday worship: 10 am, 7 pm
Benny Jaques, Pastor

Vineyard Christian Fellowship of Las Vegas
3150 Builder Ave.
Las Vegas, NV 89101
438-7700
Sunday worship: 10 am
Dan Nezgoda, Pastor

Word of Grace Church
3825 Melody Ln.
Las Vegas, NV 89108
647-1617
Sunday worship: 10 am, 6 pm
Clint Glenny, Pastor

Word of Life Christian Center
3520 N. Buffalo Dr.
Las Vegas, NV 89129
645-1990
Sunday worship: 8 am, 10:30 am, 6:30 pm
TV Ministry: Channel 33 Sunday 8:30 am
David & Vicki Shearin, Pastors
(This is also considered an Inter-denominational Church.)

Zion Chapel Outreach Center
Meets at 950 Tonopah Dr.
Las Vegas, NV 89106
638-8191
Sunday worship: 11 am, 7 pm
A. J. Thompson, Pastor

INTERDENOMINATIONAL

Abundant Life Community Church
3210 N. Rancho Dr.
Las Vegas, NV 89130
877-4413
Sunday worship: 11 am, 6 pm

The Agape Love Center
1018 E. Sahara Ave.
Las Vegas, NV 89104
731-9429
Sunday worship: 11 am

Church of the Harvest
1000 Nevada Hwy.
Boulder City, NV 89005
293-5878
Sunday worship: 10:30 am
Bill Nordstrom, Minister

The Great Commission ID Church
3329 Coleman St.
N. Las Vegas, NV 89030
647-9522
Sunday worship: 11 am
Sylvester Hooks, Pastor

Hatcher Hallow Christian Ministries
1717 Ferrell St.
Las Vegas, NV 89106
631-0595
Daily prayer and counseling. No services. Travels throughout country and overseas to minister the word of God.
Evangelist Theresa Hatcher

CHURCHES

ORTHODOX

St Michael's Orthodox Church
5621 Judson Ave.
Las Vegas, NV 89115
452-1299
Sunday worship: 10 am
Father Paul Eyler

St. Paul
5400 Annie Oakley Dr.
Las Vegas, NV 89121
898-4800
Sunday worship: 9 am
Father Nicholas Soraich

St. Simeon's (Serbian)
3950 S. Jones Blvd.
Las Vegas, NV 89103
367-7783
Sunday worship: 10 am
Father Urosh Todorovich

PENTECOSTAL

Christ Holy Sanctified Church
30 W. Owens Ave.
N. Las Vegas, NV 89030
649-7169
Sunday worship: 11 am, 7:30 pm
Herman Ishmael, Pastor

Compassion Explosion
1116 Miller Ave.
Las Vegas, NV 89106
631-4454
Sunday worship: 11 am
Albert Williams, Pastor

El Shaddai Temple of Deliverance
1834 Roosevelt St.
N. Las Vegas, NV 89030
649-5505
Sunday worship: 11:30 am, 7:30 pm
Bishop Donald Fluker

Faith Temple COGICTH
907 W. Adams Ave.
Las Vegas, NV 89106
648-5905
Sunday worship: 11:30 am, 7:30 pm
Sylvester Tanner, Pastor

Full Gospel Temple of Jesus Christ
817 E. Carey Ave.
N. Las Vegas, NV 89030
649-8085
Sunday worship: 11 am, 6:30 pm
John Slack, Pastor

Goodwill Church of God in Christ
976 Hassell Ave.
Las Vegas, NV 89106
648-9682
Sunday worship: 11 am, 6:30 pm
Elder Williams, Pastor

Iglesia Pentecostes Elim Inc.
2215 Fairfield Ave.
Las Vegas, NV 89102
382-3555
Sunday worship: 6 pm
George Tobar, Pastor

Iglesia Pentecostal Unda Hispana
1545 N. Eastern Ave.
Las Vegas, NV 89101
649-4700
Sunday worship: 10 am, 7 pm
Firmen Gurrola, Pastor (Spanish)

Portals to Glory
2301 Comstock Dr.
N. Las Vegas, NV 89030
647-7393
Sunday worship: 11:45, 7 pm
Robert Jefferson, Pastor

Miracle Faith Temple
820 W. Bonanza Rd.
Las Vegas, NV 89106
646-7869
Sunday worship: 11:30 am

Starlight Church
812 W. Bonanza Rd.
Las Vegas, NV 89106
648-2175
Sunday worship: 11 am

Westminster Presbyterian, 4601 W. Lake Mead Blvd., Las Vegas, NV 89108

Trinity Life Center
1000 E. St Louis Ave.
Las Vegas, NV 89104
474-7534
Sunday worship: 7 pm
Alex Romano, Pastor

UPC - Gospel Lighthouse Church
Building church at Pecos Rd. and Patrick Ln.
Las Vegas, NV 89119
258-1258
Sunday worship: 10 am, 7 pm
David Sparks, Pastor

United Pentecostal Church of Jesus Christ
4775 Happy Valley Ave.
Las Vegas, NV 89121
565-8234
Sunday worship: 10 am, 7 pm
Pastor H. V. Covey

PRESBYTERIAN

Calvary Presbyterian
900 E. Karen Ave., Ste. A 218
Las Vegas, NV 89109
Sunday worship: 11 am, 7 pm
Daniel Uho, Pastor (Korean)

First Korean
3500 E. Harmon Ave.
Las Vegas, NV 89121
454-2525

First Presbyterian
1515 W. Charleston Blvd.
Las Vegas, NV 89102
384-4554
Sunday worship: 8 am, 11 am
Ames Broen, Pastor

Green Valley Presbyterian
1798 Wigwam Pkwy.
Henderson, NV 89014
454-8484
Sunday worship: 8:30 am, 11 am
Hilda Pecoraro, Pastor

Henderson Presbyterian
601 N. Major Ave.
Henderson, NV 89015
565-9684
Sunday worship: 8:30 am, 10:30 am
Ross Doyel, Pastor

Mountain View
8601 Del Webb Blvd.
Las Vegas, NV 89134
341-7800
Sunday worship: 8:30 am, 10:30 am
Thomas Tomlinson, Pastor

So-Mang Presbyterian Church CRC
3840 El Camino Rd.
Las Vegas, NV 89103
871-9588
Sunday worship: 1 pm
Pastor Chung Cho (Korean)

Spring Meadows Presbyterian
6001 W. Oakey Blvd.
Meets at Mountain View 7th Adventist Church at Jones & Oakey
Las Vegas, NV 89102
877-2776
Sunday worship: 10:30 am, 6 pm
Carl Robbins, Pastor
Radio broadcast: Sunday 8:30 am on KDWN 720 AM

Westminster Presbyterian
4601 W. Lake Mead Blvd.
Las Vegas, NV 89108
648-8437
Sunday worship: 8 am, 10:30 am
Ara Guekguezian, Pastor

Yung Kwang Korean Church
2200 S. Maryland Pkwy.
Las Vegas, NV 89104
650-3655
Sunday worship: 11 am, 1:30 pm
Mung Soo Lee, Pastor

QUAKERS

Religious Society of Friends
898-5785
Meets at 5 pm at First Christian Church, 101 S. Rancho Dr. at 4 pm on the first Sunday of every month for a public lecture and discussion.

RELIGIOUS SCIENCE

Christ Center for Positive Living
Meets at Clark County Library
1401 E. Flamingo Rd.
Las Vegas, NV 89119
454-8300
Sunday worship: 11 am
Raymond Cobb, Pastor

First Church of Religious Science
1420 E. Harmon Ave.
Las Vegas, NV 89119
739-8200
Sunday worship: 9 am, 10:30 am
Dr. Carlo Di Giovanna, Pastor

Desert Community Church
953 E. Sahara Ave.
Las Vegas, NV 89104
791-0202
Sunday worship: 11 am
Wes McPherson, Pastor

Religious Science Church of Las Vegas
4820 Alpine Pl., Ste. E101
Las Vegas, NV 89107
258-LOVE
Sunday worship: 9 am, 10:30 am
Rev. Sheila Weldon, Pastor

Sunrise Community Church
Henderson Convention Center
200 S. Water St.
Henderson, NV 89015
737-5219
Sunday worship: 5:30 pm
Jim Hamilton, Pastor

University of Metaphysics
925 E. Desert Inn Rd.
Las Vegas, NV 89109
369-9776
Sunday worship: 11 am
Dr. Paul Leon Masters & Dr. Sandra Masters

SALVATION ARMY

The Salvation Army
2828 E. Cheyenne Ave.
N. Las Vegas, NV 89030
651-9550
Sunday worship: 10:30 am
Lt. Bill Dickinson, Minister

The Salvation Army Church
2900 Palomino Ln.
Las Vegas, NV 89107
870-4430
Sunday worship: 9:30 am, 11 am, 6 pm
Lt. Colonel Jim Sullivan, Minister

The Salvation Army Community Center
830 E. Lake Mead Dr.
Henderson, NV 89015
565-9578
Sunday worship: 11 am, 6 p.m
Captain Delfino Garcia, Minister

SCIENTOLOGY

Church of Scientology
846 E. Sahara Ave.
Las Vegas, NV 89104
731-1500
Sunday worship: Noon
Reverends John Anderson, Mary Gay and Terri Bracken

SEVENTH-DAY ADVENTIST

Highland Square SDA
1720 N. J St.
Las Vegas, NV 89106
647-2627
Saturday worship: 11 am
Guest speakers *(African American)*

Las Vegas Spanish Church
100 E. Washburn Rd.
N. Las Vegas, NV 89031
Saturday worship: 8 am, 10:30 am
Orlando Magana, Pastor

Mountain View
6001 W. Oakey Blvd.
Las Vegas, NV 89102
871-0814
Saturday worship: 11 am
Dave Gemmell, Pastor

Paradise Seventh-Day Adventist Church
4575 S. Sandhill Rd.
Las Vegas, NV 89121
433-4703
Saturday worship: 11 am
Bob Hancock, Pastor

Seventh-Day Adventist
591 Adams Blvd.
Boulder City, NV 89005
293-2841
Saturday worship: 11 am
Bob Larson, Pastor

SYNAGOGUES

CONSERVATIVE UNITED SYNAGOGUE OF AMERICA

Midbar Kodesh Temple
33 Cactus Garden Dr.
Henderson, NV 89014
Service: Sat. 9 am
Isaac Soncino, Rabbi

Temple Beth Sholom
1600 E. Oakey Blvd.
Las Vegas, NV 89104
384-5070
Service: Sat. 9:30 am, Fri. 7:30 pm
Simon Bergman, Cantor

RECONSTRUCTIONIST

Beth Elohenu Messianic
Meets at 6210 W. Cheyenne Ave.
Las Vegas, NV 89108
248-1318
Service: 7:30 p.m 1st & 3rd Fri. of the month; every Sat. 10:30 am
Ira Weinstein, Rabbi

Lev Hashem
Meets at Redrock Baptist Church
55 W. Alta Dr.
Las Vegas, NV 89102
876-8983
Services: Fri. 7:30 pm
Bruce Lively, Spiritual Leader
For Christians and Jews

Valley Outreach
Meets at Lutheran Church
2 S. Pecos Rd.
Henderson, NV 89014
436-4900
Service: 8 pm 1st Fri. of each month
Richard Schachet, Rabbi

ORTHODOX

Congregation Shaarei Tefilla Forman-Glick
1331 S. Maryland Pkwy
Las Vegas, NV 89104
384-3565
Service: Fri. 1 hour before sundown; Sat. 8:30 am
Congregation participants

Or-Bamidbar Orthodox Synagogue
2959 Emerson Ave.
Las Vegas, NV 89121
369-1175
Service: Fri. 6:30 pm; Sat. 8:30 am
Nissim Elmalibch, Rabbi

Young Israel
1724 Winners Cup St.
Las Vegas, NV 89109
Service: Sat. 9 am
Yitchak Wyne, Rabbi

REFORM

Adat Ari El
3310 S. Jones Blvd.
Las Vegas, NV 89103
221-1230
Service: Fri. 7:30 pm
Gary Golbart, Rabbi & Cantor

Congregation Ner Tamid
2761 Emerson Ave.
Las Vegas, NV 89121
733-6292
Service: Fri. 7:30 pm
Sanford Akselrad, Rabbi

Temple Beth AM
9000 Hillpointe Rd.
Las Vegas, NV 89134
385-5366
Service: Fri. 7:30 pm
Mel Hecht, Rabbi

TRADITIONAL

Chabad of Southern Nevada
1254 Vista Dr.
Las Vegas, NV 89102
259-0770
Service: Fri. 8 pm; Sat. 10 am
Shea Harlig, Rabbi

Chabad at Summerlin
2620 Regatta Dr., Ste. 117
Las Vegas, NV 89128
Mikvah: 224-0015
Jewish Superphone: 259-1000
Pre-school: 259-0770
Services: Weekdays 7 am; Fri. 8 pm; Sat. 10 am; Sun. 8 am
Pre-school, Hebrew school, adult education
Yisroel Schanowitz, Rabbi

UNITARIAN UNIVERSALIST

Unitarian Universalist
6431 W. Sahara Ave., Ste. 250
Las Vegas, NV 89102
655-6068
Sunday worship: 11 am
Lay Led, Pastor

Unitarian Universalist
Meets at 2200 W. Mesquite Ave.
3616 E. Lake Mead Blvd.
Las Vegas, NV 89115
437-2404
Sunday worship: 10 am
Patricia Bowen, Pastor

UNITED CHURCH OF CHRIST

Community Church of Henderson - United Church of Christ
360 E. Horizon Dr.
Henderson, NV 89015
565-8563
Sunday worship: 10:30 am
Merrill W. Kanouse, Pastor

First Congregational Church
1200 N. Eastern Ave.
Las Vegas, NV 89101
642-2220
Sunday worship: 10:30 am
Jackie Brown, Interim Pastor

House of the Lord (UHCA)
1954 E. Charleston Blvd.
Las Vegas, NV 89104
598-0444
Sunday worship: 10:30 a.m, 7 pm
Rudy Gumallaoi, Pastor

UNITY

Unity Church of the Desert
1125 S. Maryland Pkwy.
Las Vegas, NV 89104
382-8688
Dial-a-Prayer: 384-9264
Sunday worship: 9:30 am, 11 am
Vivian Huber, Pastor

SCHOOLS - RELIGIOUS AFFILIATION

The following schools are listed by the denomination of their sponsorship, but are open to students of any denomination. All are licensed by the Nevada State Board of Education.

ASSEMBLY OF GOD

Mountain View Christian School
3900 E. Bonanza Rd.
Las Vegas, NV 89110
452-1300
Crystal Van Kempen McClannahan, Princ.
Grades: Pre-school *(2 yrs.)*, K-12
Abeka *(all Christian)* curriculum
School hours: 8:30 am-3 pm

Trinity Christian School
1000 E. St. Louis Ave.
Las Vegas, NV 89104
734-0562
Harry Hendrickson, Princ.
Grades: K-12

BAPTIST

Gateway Baptist Church School
1900 Gateway Rd.
Las Vegas, NV 89115
452-7111
Brent Fleshman, Princ.
Grades: K-8

Paradise Christian Academy
2525 Emerson Ave.
Las Vegas, NV 89121
732-8256
Michael Elliott, Princ.
Grades: Pre-school *(4 yrs.)*, K-10

Lake Mead Christian Academy
540 E. Lake Mead Dr.
Henderson, NV 89015
565-5831
Gayle Sue Blakeley, Adm.
Grades: K-12

West Charleston Baptist Center
6701 W. Charleston Blvd.
Las Vegas, NV 89102
870-2664
Linda Littlefield, Dir.
Grades: Pre-school *(2-5 yrs.)*

CATHOLIC

Bishop Gorman High School
1801 S. Maryland Pkwy
Las Vegas, NV 89104
732-1945
David W. Erbach, Princ.
Grades: 9-12

Our Lady of Las Vegas
2900 Alta Dr.
Las Vegas, NV 89107
878-6841
Gerald Streit, Princ.
Grades: Pre-school *(3 1/2 yrs.)* K-8

St. Anne's Elementary
1813 S. Maryland Pkwy
Las Vegas, NV 89104
735-2586
Phyllis Joyce, Princ.
Grades: Pre-school *(4 yrs.)* K-8

St. Christopher's Elementary School
1840 N. Bruce St.
N. Las Vegas, NV 89030
657-8008
Carol A. Haeberlin, Princ.
Grades: K-8

St. Francis De Sales
1111 Michael Way
Las Vegas, NV 89108
647-2828
Gloria Hagstrom, Princ.
Grades: K-8

RELIGIOUS ORGANIZATIONS

St. Joseph's Elementary
1300 Bridger Ave.
Las Vegas, NV 89101
384-6909
Linda Ballard, Princ.
Grades: 1-8

St. Viator's Elementary
4246 S. Eastern Ave.
Las Vegas, NV 89119
732-4477
William C. Langley, Princ.
Grades: K-8

CHRISTIAN & NON-DENOMINATIONAL

Christian Center Schools
571 Adams Blvd.
Boulder City, NV 89005
293-7773
Pastor Jim Kitchell, Dir.
Grades: K-8

First Christian Child Development Center
101 S. Rancho Dr.
Las Vegas, NV 89106
384-4839
Natalie Madden, Dir.
Grades: Kindergarten

Harbor Academy
2675 S. Lamb Blvd.
Las Vegas, NV 89121
457-9300
Robert Walker, Dir.
Grades: K-10
School uses the Abeka curriculum which emphasizes phonics in reading and mathematics basics.

Echoes Christian Academy
1608 Gragson Ave.
Las Vegas, NV 89101
649-8744
Cynthia Watson, Princ.
Grades: K-12

Maranatha Academy
2727 Civic Center Dr.
N. Las Vegas, NV 89030
399-4673
Roy Manibusan, Princ.
Grades: Pre-school and K-8

Shiloh Christian School
6701 W. Charleston Blvd.
Las Vegas, NV 89102
878-5798
Lois Cadwallader, Princ.
Grades: K-10

Vegas Valley Christian Pre-School
5515 Mountain Vista St.
Las Vegas, NV 89120
451-9665
Veronica Seibler, Dir.
Creative learning for ages 9 mos.-9 yrs.
Full or part-time Mon. thru Fri. 7 am - 6 pm

EPISCOPAL

All Saints Episcopal School
4201 W. Washington Ave.
Las Vegas, NV 89107
878-1205
Gloria Durling, Dir.
Grades: Kindergarten and Pre-school (3-4)

FOURSQUARE

Calvary Church Christian School
3005 Cedar Ave.
Las Vegas, NV 89101
382-5998
Deborah Lovell, Princ.
Grades: K-12

JEWISH

Jewish Community Day School of Las Vegas
2761 Emerson Ave.
Las Vegas, NV 89121
650-2800
Dr. Jerome Kutliroff, Dir.
Grades: K-6

Las Vegas Hebrew High
Congregation Ner Tamid
2761 Emerson Ave.
Las Vegas, NV 89121
733-6292
Jackie Fleekop, Dir.
Grades: K-9
Sponsored by Jewish Federation and local Synagogues community wide.
Meets Thursday evenings 6:30 pm - 8:30 pm
For information call Melanie Bash, 732-0556

Milton I. Schwartz Hebrew Academy
9700 W. Hillpointe Rd.
Las Vegas, NV 89134
255-4500
Roberta Sabbath, Dir.
Grades: Pre-school (3 yrs.) K-12

LUTHERAN

Faith Lutheran Jr/Sr High
1251 Robin St.
Las Vegas, NV 89106
648-7047
John Haynal, Princ.
Grades: 6-12

First Good Shepherd Lutheran
301 S. Maryland Pkwy.
Las Vegas, NV 89101
382-8610
James Kraft, Princ.
Grades: K-6

Redeemer Lutheran
1730 N. Pecos Rd.
Las Vegas, NV 89115
642-6144
Joyce Miskey, Dir.
Grades: K-6

METHODIST

Griffith United Methodist Day School
1701 E. Oakey Blvd.
Las Vegas, NV 89104
382-7836
Karen Bigelow-Varney, Dir.
Grades: Kindergarten and pre-school

Trinity United Methodist
6151 W. Charleston Blvd.
Las Vegas, NV 89102
870-4749
Pamela Troll, Adm.
Grades: Kindergarten and pre-school

PRESBYTERIAN

First Presbyterian Church Academy
1515 W. Charleston Blvd.
Las Vegas, NV 89102
382-3611
Jean Witmer, Dir.
Grades: K- 8

SEVENTH DAY ADVENTISTS

Las Vegas Jr. Academy
6059 W. Oakey Blvd.
Las Vegas, NV 89102
871-7208
Jim Hawkins, Prin.
Grades: K-8

BIBLE COLLEGE

Catholic Diocese of Las Vegas
336 Cathedral Way
Las Vegas, NV 89109
735-6044
Bishop Daniel Walsh
Master of religious education, master of pastoral studies degree and non-credit continuing education certificate in religious education or pastoral studies offered by Loyola University of New Orleans.

Logos Bible School
Hallelujah Fellowship
800 N. Rancho Dr.
Las Vegas, NV 89106
646-1899
Tim Bales, Dir.
The Las Vegas campus of the Florida-based Logos International Bible College and Graduate School offers degrees on the undergraduate and graduate level.

Wellspring Bible Institute
1401 N. Decatur Blvd., Ste. 18
Las Vegas, NV 89108
647-5479
Pastor Lou Grillo, Dean
Full gospel based institute of learning.

B'nai B'rith Women
254-5706
Micky Covner, Pres.
Contact Sydell Miller at 363-1088
International Jewish women's organization. Group offers women opportunities for networking, socializing, growth and development, as well as life-enhancement projects.

Catholic Daughters of the Americas
Nevada State Court
5454 Consul Ave.
Las Vegas, NV 89122
431-1503
Dee Schreiner, State Regent
A national charity organization open to practicing Catholic women 18 yrs. and over.

Ave Maria, Court, # 1420
1428 Norman Ave.
Las Vegas, NV 89104
382-6376
Pat Lenzendorf, Regent
Affiliated with St. Anne's Church -
Meets 2nd Thu. of the month.

Our Lady of Peace, Court #2307
4800 E. Vegas Valley Dr., Space 105
Las Vegas, NV 89121
457-8018
Stella Daszkowski, Regent
Affiliated with Prince of Peace Church - meets 2nd Thu. of the month.

Our Lady of the Rosary, Court #2226
358 Sunward Dr.
Henderson, NV 89014
436-3865
Ferrol Gillman, Regent
Affiliated with Holy Family Church - meets 2nd Mon. of the month.

Our Lady of the Valley, Court #2118
3320 S. Deuce St.
Las Vegas, NV 89121
732-9728
Charlotte Summers, Regent
Affiliated with St. Viator Church. Meets 3rd Thu. of the month.

St. Elizabeth Ann Seton, Court #2131
7409 Bagdad Ct.
Las Vegas, NV 89128
228-2108
Susan Dalton, Regent
Affiliated with St. Francis De Sales Church. Meets 2nd Wed. of the month.

Centrum of Las Vegas
387-5349
Christ-centered ministry of crisis-intervention and discipleship. Bible studies, Christian films and other services are available. Centrum operates a men's live-in facility at 9th and Carson.

Congregation Ner Tamid · Sisterhood
2761 Emerson Ave.
Las Vegas, NV 89121
733-6292
Janice Rounds, Pres.

Eckankar
Nevada Satsang Society Inc.
3160 E. Desert Inn Rd., Ste. 14
Las Vegas, NV 89121
369-0101

Gideon's International
4321 Mark Ave.
Las Vegas, NV 89108
648-9893

Greek Orthodox Youth
5300 S. El Camino Rd.
Las Vegas, NV 89118
221-8245
Father Ilia Katre, Ministry of the Church
Religious, cultural, educational, social and athletic programs and activities for middle school and high school.

Hadassah · Las Vegas Chapter
Jewish Women's Zionist Organization whose membership is open to anyone.
Meets the 3rd Mon. of each month.

Aviva of Summerlin
233-8601
Shirley Ravich, Pres.

Rishona
Renel Johnson, Pres.
288-3555

Shoshanim
256-4611
Jackie Fleekop, Pres.

Interfaith Student Center at UNLV
4765 Brussels Ave.
Las Vegas, NV 89119
736-0887
Joanna Pollard, Adm.
Serves the University, Jewish, Catholic and Protestant community.

Islamic Society of Nevada
4730 E. Desert Inn Rd.
Las Vegas, NV 89121
433-3431

Jewish Community Center of Southern Nevada
3909 S. Maryland Pkwy.
Las Vegas, NV 89119
794-0090
Laura Sussman, Exec. Dir.
Non-profit social, cultural and educational Jewish-oriented organization.

Jewish Family Service
3909 S. Maryland Pkwy., Ste. 205
Las Vegas, NV 89119
732-0304
Adrienne Rosenberg, Exec. Dir.
Family counseling, housing options for seniors.

Jewish Federation of Las Vegas
3909 S. Maryland Pkwy., Ste. 400
Las Vegas, NV 89119
732-0556
Ronni Epstein, Exec. Dir.
Serves as an umbrella organization developing community priorities. The Federation responds to local needs by allocating resources and coordinating specialized services.

Lighthouse Club
1515 W. Charleston Blvd.
Las Vegas, NV 89102
384-4554
Mature group meets for lunch and entertainment in social hall.

Lutheran Women's Missionary League
Mountain View Lutheran Church
9550 W. Cheyenne Ave.
Las Vegas, NV 89129
645-9222
Rachel Taylor, Pres.
Helen Pace, Publicity

National Conference of Christians & Jews (NCCJ)
913 E. Charleston Blvd., Ste. A
Las Vegas, NV 89104
387-6225
Jacque Matthews, Regional Dir.
Laura LeGrand, Asst. Dir.
Non-sectarian civic organization that promotes the eradication of prejudice and discrimination and the development or respect and tolerance among the diverse elements of America's population.

Nevada Buddhists Association
4189 S. Jones Blvd.
Las Vegas, NV 89103
252-7339

Salvation Army
2900 Palomino Ln.
Las Vegas, NV 89107
870-4430
Lt. Colonel Jim Sullivan, Clark County Coordinator

Sisterhood of Temple Beth Sholom
1600 E. Oakey Blvd.
Las Vegas, NV 89104

384-5070
Sandra Mallin, Pres.

Southern Nevada Baptist Assn.
1482 E. University Ave.
Las Vegas, NV 89119
732-4171
Harry Watson, Dir.

St. Jude's Women's Auxiliary, Inc.
P.O. Box 42008
Las Vegas, NV 89116
253-6896
Eve Moss, Pres.

St. Viator Winchestor Srs.
St. Viator Community Center
4320 Channel 10 Dr.
Las Vegas, NV 89121
733-7056
Jeff Yates, Dir.

RELIGIOUS STORES

Family Christian Bookstore
1230 S. Decatur Blvd.
Las Vegas, NV 89108
870-9550
Hours: Mon. - Sat. 9 am - 9 pm
Credit Cards: MC/Visa
Bibles, books, audio & video tapes, religious gift items and cards.

Beehive Book
4189 S. Sandhill Rd.
Las Vegas, NV 89121
732-9110
Hours: Mon. - Fri. 9 am - 6 pm; Sat. 9 am - 6 pm
Mormon items, books, CDs, audio & video tapes, sheet music and gift items.

Bell, Book & Candle
1725 E. Charleston Blvd.
Las Vegas, NV 89104
384-6807
Lucky Simone, Owner
Hours: 10 am - 9 pm
Wicca items, books, tapes, medallions, crucifixes, rosaries and unusual gift items.

Bertae Specialties
2401 W. Charleston Blvd.
Las Vegas, NV 89102
878-5113
Hours: Mon. - Sat. 10 am - 6 pm
Bibles, books, audio and video tapes, religious articles and gifts for all faiths.

The Chanukah Store & More
3050 E. Desert Inn Rd., Ste. 127
Las Vegas, NV 89121
732-2128
Hours: Mon. - Thu. 10 am - 5 pm; Fri. & Sun. 10 am - 3 pm *(Closed Saturdays)*
Chanukah and Judaic needs.

Christian Supply Center
1766 E. Charleston Blvd.
Las Vegas, NV 89104
382-7889
Hours: Mon. - Sat. 10 am - 8 pm

2550 S. Rainbow Blvd.
Las Vegas, NV 89102
876-2212
Hours: Mon. - Fri. 9:30 am - 5:30 pm; Sat. 9:30 am - 5 pm

643 Stephanie St.
Henderson, NV 89014
434-4020
Hours: Mon. - Sat. 10 am - 6 pm
Bibles, books, music, video tapes, cards and gifts as well as church and Sunday School supplies.

Dianetics Book Center
846 E. Sahara Ave.
Las Vegas, NV 89104
731-5525
Hours: 9:30 am - 9 pm
Scientology and Dianetics books. Life improvement courses and Dianetic therapy training.

Deseret Books
560 N. Nellis Blvd., Ste E 7
Las Vegas, NV 89110
453-5611
Kirk Tenney, Mgr.
Bibles, books, pictures and gift items.

336 S. Decatur Blvd.
Las Vegas, NV 89107
877-2066
Bibles, books, pictures and gift items.

1905 Green Valley Pkwy.
Henderson, NV 89014
896-6676
Hours: Mon. - Fri. 9 am - 9 pm; Sat. 9 am - 6 pm
Credit Cards: All major
LDS literature, genealogy supplies and other LDS related products, national trade titles and children's books.

Psychic Eye Book Shops, 3315 E. Russell Rd., Las Vegas, NV 89120

First Church of Religious Science · Las Vegas
1420 E. Harmon Ave.
Las Vegas, NV 89119
739-8200
Hours: Mon. - Fri. 9 am - 5 pm; Sun. 10 am - 11 am
Books, tapes and greeting cards.

Hallelujah Fellowship
800 N. Rancho Dr.
Las Vegas, NV 89106
646-7332
Hours: Mon. - Fri. 9 am - 5 pm; Sun. 10 am - 11 am, 12:30 pm - 1:15 pm
New and used books.

Latter Day Book & Craft
4660 W. Charleston Blvd.
Las Vegas, NV 89102
877-2880
LDS books, statues and crafts.

7450 W. Cheyenne Ave.
Las Vegas, NV 89129
645-7300
Hours: Mon. - Sat. 10 am - 6 pm

Mary's Grotto
1775 E. Tropicana Ave.
Las Vegas, NV 89119
739-0002
Hours: Mon. - Sat. 10 am-5 pm
Catholic book and gift store

Psychic Eye Book Shops
3315 E. Russell Rd.
Las Vegas, NV 89120
451-5777

953 E. Sahara Ave.
Las Vegas, NV 89104
369-6622
Hours: Mon. - Fri. 10 am - 9 pm; Sat. 10 am - 8:30 pm; Sun. Noon - 6 pm

4810 Spring Mountain Rd.
Las Vegas, NV 89102
368-7785
Hours: Mon. - Fri. 10 am - 9 pm; Sat. 10 am - 6 pm; Sun. 11 am - 6 pm
Specialists in New Age, self help, philosophy and occult.

Wellspring Bible & Book Store
1401 N. Decatur Blvd.
Las Vegas, NV 89108
631-5027
Hours: Tue. - Sat. 10 am - 6 pm
Religious books and thrift store.

RELIGION

RELIGIOUS MEDIA / BROADCASTING

MEDIA

The Beehive
1916 Maryland Pkwy.
Las Vegas, NV 89104
732-1812
Mormon newspaper.

Las Vegas Israelite
P. O. Box 14096
Las Vegas, NV 89114
876-1255
Biweekly Jewish community newspaper.

RELIGIOUS BROADCASTING

KILA · FM 90.5
731-5452
Non-commercial contemporary Christian music; SOS radio network.

KKVV · AM 1060
731-5588
Christian talk radio; broadcasts 6 am - 9 pm.

Cable Channel 46
Vision Interfaith Satellite Network
1-800-522-5131
Talk, music and worship.

Channel 57 · K57FA
Trinity Broadcasting Network
Christian programming.

SERVICES FOR TOURISTS

Guardian Angel Cathedral, 302 Cathedral Way , Las Vegas, NV 89109

Guardian Angel Cathedral, RC
302 Cathedral Way
Las Vegas, NV 89109
735-5241
Sunday Mass: 8 am, 9:30 am, 11 am, 12:30 pm, 5 pm
Saturday Vigil: 2:30 pm, 4 pm, 5:15 pm
Father James Crilly

Church at the Riviera
2901 Las Vegas Blvd. S.
Las Vegas, NV 89109
697-4142
Sunday Mass: 10 am
Chaplain Charles Bolin
The Riviera is the only hotel and casino anywhere in the world employing a full-

time chaplain. The sunday non-denominational service is held in the Mardi Gras Room. It is open to the general public, and a small group of local residents attend on a regular basis along with hotel employees and guests. Chaplain Bolin also offers counseling, hospital visits and other ministry relat-

ed services to the guests and employees of the Riviera. Two volunteer ministers, Wayne Harms, Pastor/Administrator and Phil Larimore, Pastor/Ministry coordinator assist.

Marriage

WEDDING CHAPELS

There are 31 wedding chapels in Las Vegas, all competing for the lucrative marriage business of the 109,378 couples who "tied the knot" in Las Vegas in 1997. The busiest days are New Year's Eve and Valentine's Day. The basic cost of the chapel wedding is $45 - $55 with a "suggested donation" to the minister of $25 - $30 in addition to the $35 for the license, which you must obtain at the courthouse. Most chapels will pick you up in their limousine and take you to the courthouse to get your license, then to the chapel and back to your hotel. The price can go up considerably if you want the extras, such as flowers, photographs, video of the ceremony and even wedding cake.

Many famous people have been married in Las Vegas, such as Elvis and Priscilla Presley, Frank Sinatra and Mia Farrow, Paul Newman and Joanne Woodward, Steve Lawrence and Eydie Gorme and Joan Collins and Peter Holm. The Little White Chapel advertises that "Joan Collins was married here" on their sign. The Little Church of the West advertises that "since 1942, more celebrities have been married here than any other one place in the world."

MARRIAGE INFORMATION & FACTS

MARRIAGE INFORMATION

Application:
Both parties must appear at:

County Clerk's Office
Courthouse
200 S. 3rd St.
Las Vegas, NV 89101
455-4416

Marriage Commissioner:
After 5 pm, holidays and weekends - 455-4415.

Proof of Identification:
Driver's license, certified copy of birth certificate,
Passport or military I.D. is required.

No waiting period or blood tests are required.

Consent:
All persons between the ages of 16 and 18 may marry if:
1. Consent is given by either parent in person at the time the license is applied for.
2. Notarized affidavit of consent of either parent when not present. Said notarized affidavit of consent must contain the birth date of the minor and state the relationship of the party giving consent. Proof of identity may be required of the person giving consent.

Hours:
8 am - midnight Monday - Thursday; 8 am Friday - midnight Sunday night. Twenty-four hours all Nevada holidays.

License Fees:
$35.00 paid in cash only.

Commissioner of Civil Marriages:
The office of the Commissioner of Civil Marriages is located at 309 S. Third Street (one block from the Marriage License Bureau).

Hours:
8 am until midnight Monday through Thursday and 8 am Friday until midnight Sunday. Twenty-four hours all Nevada legal holidays.

Ceremony Fees:
Monday - Friday 8 am - 5 pm - $35 cash.

Witnesses:
There shall be at least one witness present besides the person performing the ceremony.

Past Marriage Records:
To obtain information or certified copies of marriage certificates, address your request to:

Clark County Recorder
Courthouse
500 S. Grand Central Pkwy.
Las Vegas, NV 89106

Include the date of the marriage with your request. The cost is $7 per copy.

HOTELS WITH WEDDING CHAPELS

Bally's: Celebration
Circus Circus:
    Chapel of the Fountain
Excalibur: Canterbury
Flamingo: Garden Chapel
Imperial Palace:
    We've Only Just Begun
Monte Carlo: Chapel at Monte Carlo
NewYork NewYork: Wedding Chapel
Orleans: Chapel Orleans
Plaza: Love at the Plaza Chapel
Rio: Wedding Chapel
Riviera: Riviera Royale
Treasure Island:
    The Wedding Chapels
Tropicana: Island Wedding Chapel

RESIDENCE REQUIREMENT

The same day Governor Fred B. Balzar signed an act legalizing gambling in Nevada, he signed a bill lowering the residence requirements to six weeks for divorce. The bill took effect on May 1, 1931.

Clark County Courthouse
200 S. 3rd St.
Las Vegas, NV 89101
455-3156

The Clark County Clerk's Office issued 110,696 marriage licenses in 1997, most of which were issued to residents of other states. According to the 1990 census, there are 151,433 married households in Las Vegas, which is 56% of the metro area.

VALENTINE'S DAY
In 1998 the Clark County Court House issued 3,289 licenses on February 12, 13, 14, 15 and 16 for Valentine's Day.

FAMOUS WEDDINGS

Elizabeth Ruth Grable and Harry Haag James (1943)

Kirk Douglas and Ann Buydens (Sahara in 1954)

Joan Crawford and Alfred Steel (Flamingo in 1955)

Steve Lawrence and Eydie Gorme (1957)

Paul Newman and Joanne Woodward (El Rancho in 1958)

Sammy Davis Jr. and Loray White (1958)

Eddie Fisher and Elizabeth Taylor Todd (1959)

Mary Tyler Moore and Grant Tinker (1962)

Judy Garland and Mark Herron (1965)

Burt Bacharach and Angeline Dickinson (1965)

Jane Fonda and Roger Vadim (Dunes in 1965)

Charo and Xavier Cugat (Caesars Palace in 1966)

Frank Sinatra and Mia Farrow (1966)

Brigitte Bardot and Gunter Fritz Sachs (1966)

Ann-Margret Olsson and Roger Smith (1967)

Diana Ross and Robert E. Silberstein (1971)

Mickey Rooney (many times!)

Zsa Zsa Gabor and Michael John O'Hara (1976)

James Caan and Sheila Marie Ryan (1976)

Robert Goulet and Vera Novak (1982)

Richard Walter Burton and Sally Anne Hay (1983)

Telly Aristotle Savalas and Julie Ann Hovland (1984)

Bette Midler and Martin Rochus Sebastian von Haselberg (1984)

Joan Collins and Peter Holm (Little White Chapel in 1985)

Whoppi Goldberg and David E. Claessen (1986)

Dudley Stuart John Moore and Brogan G. Lane (1988)

Bon Jovi and Dorothea R. Hurley (1989)

Lorenzo Lamas and Kathleen Kinmont Smith (1989)

W. Axl Rose and Erin Invicta Everly (1990)

Red Foxx and Koho Cho (1991)

Melanie Griffith and Don Johnson (1991)

Richard Gere and Cindy Crawford (1992)

Bruce Willis and Demi Moore

Rich Little and Jennette Markey (1994)

Wayne Newton and Kathleen Ann McCrone (1994)

Ricki Lake and Robert Simon Sussman (1994)

Clint Eastwood and Dina Ruiz (1996)

WEDDING CHAPELS

A Chapel by the Courthouse
201 E. Bridger Ave.
Las Vegas, NV 89101
384-9099 1-800-545-8111
Joannie Richards, Mgr.
Hours: 8 am - midnight
Basic Cost: $40 - $199
Free limousine service; located behind the Golden Nugget Hotel. Checks and credit cards accepted.

A Special Memory Wedding Chapel
800 S. Fourth St.
Las Vegas, NV 89101
384-2211 1-800-962-7798
Joni Moss, Mgr.
Hours: Sun. - Thu. 8 am - 10 pm, Fri. 8 am - midnight, Sat. 8 am - 2 am
Basic Cost: $45 - $485
A gorgeous gazebo wedding in a garden setting. Some of the features on the premises to capture the enchantment of your storybook wedding day are a quaint New England chapel, a romantic curved staircase, unity and candlelight service, religious and civil ceremonies, free limousine service, photography and video-taping, flower shop, tux and gown shop, dressing rooms and professional wedding consultant. Also a drive-up window. Checks and credit card accepted.

Candlelight Wedding Chapel
2855 Las Vegas Blvd. S.
Las Vegas, NV 89109
735-4179
Doug Ferguson, Mgr.
Hours: 8 am - midnight
Basic Cost: Five packages ranging from $169 to $419
Free-standing western style chapel. Limousine service, church organist, flowers and photos available.

Canterbury Wedding Chapel
Excalibur Hotel
3850 Las Vegas Blvd. S.
Las Vegas, NV 89109
597-7777 1-800-811-4320
Renee Garduno, Chapel Mgr.
Basic Cost: Five basic wedding packages $275 - $795 including renewals.
Hours: Mon. - Fri. & Sun. 9 am - 7 pm; Sat. 9 am - midnight
Two wedding chapels. The Canterbury Wedding Chapel is decorated in beige and forest green with cathedral ceiling appearance. Medieval-theme costumes also available. Package can include a bridal bouquet, boutonniere, music, photos, videotape of ceremony, champagne and two ceremonial chalices. The large chapel seats 110. The smaller chapel seats 40.

Celebration Wedding Chapel
Bally's
3645 Las Vegas Blvd. S.
Las Vegas, NV 89109
739-4939 1-800-872-1211
Adriana Martinez, Chapel Dir.
Basic Cost: $80 - $1,280
Hours: 8 am - 10 pm
Two very elegant chapels with modern decor seat up to 50. Flowers, photographer and VHS videotape recordings available.

Chapel at Monte Carlo
Monte Carlo
3770 Las Vegas Blvd. S.
Las Vegas, NV 89109
730-7777 1-800-822-8651
Kathy Nelson, Mgr.
Basic Cost: $195 - $850
Hours: Sun. - Thu. 10 am - 8 pm; Fri. - Sat. 10 am - 9:30 pm
Adapts to the needs of the bride and groom. French Victorian decor accommodates 100 guests. Music, flowers, photos and wedding consultants.

Little Chapel of the Flowers, 1717 Las Vegas Blvd. S., Las Vegas, NV 89104

Chapel of Love
1431 Las Vegas Blvd. S.
Las Vegas, NV 89104
387-0155 1-800-922-5683
Donna Burleson, Chapel Dir.
Basic Cost: $14 - $379
Hours: Mon. - Thu. 9 am - 10 pm; Fri. - Sat. 8 am - 9 pm
Four chapels to choose from, each with a different atmosphere. Limo, flowers, photos, videos available. All major credit cards accepted.

Chapel of the Bells
2233 Las Vegas Blvd. S.
Las Vegas, NV 89104
735-6803 1-800-233-2391
Hours: Sun. - Thu. 9 am - 9 pm; Fri. -
Sat. 9 am - midnight
Basic Cost: Chapel fee $45 - $700
Elegant candlelight chapel garden weddings and renewal of vows. Organist, flowers, rings, videos, photos, limousine service and tuxedos and gowns available.

Chapel of the Fountain
Circus Circus
2880 Las Vegas Blvd. S.
Las Vegas, NV 89109
794-3777 1-800-643-6717
Glens Club, Mgr.
Hours: Sun. - Thu. 9 am - 6:30 pm; Fri. - Sat. 9 am - 10 pm
Basic Cost: $105 - $700
Chapel of the Fountain is richly decorated in blue, white and silver, accented by handcrafted stained glass windows. Behind the altar is the fountain for which the chapel is named. Its cascading waters are illuminated by colored lights. A professional photographer is available, along with VHS videotaping and a complete line of accessories, including fresh flowers, veils, garters, guestbooks, photo albums, and other gifts. Experienced wedding consultants assist with all arrangements.

Chapel Orleans
Orleans
4500 W. Tropicana Ave
Las Vegas, NV 89103
365-7555 1-888-365-7111 Ext 7555
Vickie Ruggeroli, Mgr.
Hours: Sun. - Thu. 10 am - 6 pm; Fri. 10 am - 7 pm; Sat. 10 am - 8 pm
Basic Cost: $100 - $695
Decorated in mauve and cream with marble columns. Reception facilities seat up to 500. Outdoor gazebo weddings are available.

Cupid's Wedding Chapel
827 Las Vegas Blvd. S.
Las Vegas, NV 89101
598-4444 1-800-543-2933
Judith Kerness, Chapel Dir.
Basic Cost: $75 - $549
Hours: Sun. - Thu. 9 am - 10 pm; Fri. - Sat. 9 am - 1 am
Limousine pick-up; flowers, rings, video, photos. Credit cards and checks accepted.

Garden Chapel
Flamingo Hilton
3555 Las Vegas Blvd. S.
Las Vegas, NV 89109
733-3232 1-800-933-7993
Windy Woolley, Chapel Mgr.
Hours: Sun. - Thu. 10 am - 6 pm; Sat. 10 am - 8 pm
Basic Cost: $375 - $995
Chapel can accommodate up to 65 guests. Tuxedo and gown rentals, candlelight ceremonies, full service floral packages, garden or indoor receptions overlook a quiet lagoon, 20 foot waterfalls and island with live flamingos, African penguins and swans.

Graceland Wedding Chapel
619 Las Vegas Blvd. S.
Las Vegas, NV 89101
474-6655 1-800-824-5732
Dale Johnson, Owner
Hours: Sun. - Thu. 9 am - 9 pm; Fri. - Sat. 9 am - midnight
Basic Cost: $50 -$200
Elvis impersonator - $120
Limousine, photos, video, flowers. Spanish spoken.

Hitching Post Wedding Chapel
1737 Las Vegas Blvd. S.
Las Vegas, NV 89104
369-8882 1-800-572-5530
Hours: 24 hours
Basic Cost: $50 - $75
Two 72-year-old chapels. Limousine, wedding rings, licenses, flowers, dressing room, music, witness and candlelight services. English and Spanish ceremonies performed.

Island Wedding Chapel
Tropicana Hotel
3801 Las Vegas Blvd. S.
Las Vegas, NV 89109
798-3778 1-800-325-5839
Cheryl Fretwell, Mgr.
Hours: Mon. - Sat. 9 am - 8 pm; Sun. 10 am - 6 pm
Basic Cost: $295 - $995
Enclosed chapel on grounds with waterfalls, fountains, greenery and flowers. Hawaiian ambience.

WEDDING CHAPELS

A Little White Chapel, 1301 Las Vegas Blvd. S., Las Vegas, NV 89104

Las Vegas Chapel
727 S. 9th St., Ste. C
Las Vegas, NV 89101
383-5909 1-800-452-6081
Barbara Montez, owner
Hours: By appointment 24 hours
"Elegant chapel." All wedding services
and accessories available.

Las Vegas Wedding Gardens
200 W. Sahara Ave.
Las Vegas, NV 89102
387-0123 1-800-843-2362
Donna Burleson, Chapel Dir.
Basic Cost: $149 - $399
Hours: Mon. - Thu. 8 am - 10 pm; Fri. -
Sat. 8 am - midnight; Sun. 8 am - 9 pm
Garden oasis setting. Reception facili-
ties on premises for up to 150 guests.
Limousine, photography and video and
flowers available.

Little Chapel of the Flowers
1717 Las Vegas Blvd. S.
Las Vegas, NV 89104
735-4331 1-800-843-2410
Brandon Reed Mgr.
Basic Cost: $169 - $345
Hours: 8 am -10 pm
A choice of two chapels, The Heritage
Chapel and the Victorian Chapel for a
traditional style wedding. Full service,
flower shop, limousine and professional
photographer.

The Little Church of the West
4617 Las Vegas Blvd. S.
Las Vegas, NV 89119
739-7971 1-800-821-2452
Greg Smith, Owner
Basic Cost: $65 - $499 (Minister paid sep-
arately)
Hours: 8 am - midnight
Opened in 1942 with the Last Frontier
Hotel. It has since been moved several
times. Building has been elected to the
National Register of Historic Places.

A Little White Chapel
1301 Las Vegas Blvd. S.
Las Vegas, NV 89104
382-5943 1-800-545-8111
Joannie Richards, Mgr.
Hours: 24 hours
Basic Cost: $45 - $499
Gazebo weddings, minister on duty at
all times and will perform the ceremony
any place. Free limousine service, live
organ music, witness, tuxedo and gown
rental.

Love at the Plaza Chapel
Plaza Hotel · Downtown
1 Main St.
Las Vegas, NV 89101
386-2110 1-800-241-5000
Jamie Ali, Mgr.
Hours: Sun. - Thu. 9 am - 6 pm; Fri. - Sat.
9 am - 9 pm
Basic Cost: $149 - $799

Civil or religious ceremonies. Overlooking
Fremont Street on the mezzanine level.
Free limousine service.

**New York New York
Wedding Chapel**
New York, New York
3790 Las Vegas Blvd. S.
Las Vegas, NV 89109
740-6625 1-888-652-NYNY
Marli Eyestone, Mgr.
Hours: Sun. - Thu. 10 am - 5:30 pm; Fri.
- Sat. 10 am - 7:30 pm
Basic Cost: $395 - $1,195
Thirties and Forties motif in ivory,
beige, burgundy and gold in front of
three windows overlooking "Central
Park."

Riviera Royale Wedding Chapel
Riviera Hotel
2901 Las Vegas Blvd. S.
Las Vegas, NV 89109
794-9494 1-800-242-7322
Jenita Rodgers, Mgr.
Hours: Mon. - Sat. 9 am - 9 pm; Sun. 9
am - 5 pm
Basic Cost: $179 - $975
Wedding ceremonies in both Spanish
and English. Receptions accommodating 40 guests, live piano music, complete florist, photographs and video.

**San Francisco Sally's
Victorian Chapel**
1304 Las Vegas Blvd. S.
Las Vegas, NV 89104
385-7777 1-800-658-8677
Joy Seaman, Mgr.
Hours: Mon. - Thu. 10 am - 6 pm; Fri. -
Sat. 10 am - 8 pm; Sun. 10 am - 4 pm
Basic Cost: $45 - Wear any clothes in
store for ceremony - $150.

Shalimar Wedding Chapel
1401 Las Vegas Blvd. S.
Las Vegas, NV 89104
382-7372 1-800-255-9633
Shawn Faeghi, Mgr.
Hours: 10 am - 10 pm
Basic Cost: $50 - $110
Located inside Howard Johnson's on the
Strip. Gazebo weddings, limousine ser-
vice, photos, witness, music and video.

Silver Bell Wedding Chapel
607 Las Vegas Blvd. S.
Las Vegas, NV 89101
382-3726 1-800-221-8492

Hours: Sun. - Thu. 8 am - midnight; Fri.
- Sat. 24 hours.
Basic Cost: $60
We pay for wedding license. Limousine
service, flowers, photos, witness, and
music. Checks and all major credit
cards accepted.

Wedding Chapel at the Rio
Rio
3700 W. Flamingo Rd.
Las Vegas, NV 89103
247-7986 1-888-746-5625
Mary Bray, Mgr.
Hours: Sun. - Thu. 9 am - 8 pm; Fri. - Sat.
9 am - 11 pm
Basic Cost: $400 - $1,395
Two chapels with seating up to 90
guests, theme honeymoon suites, flow-
ers and photographs.

**The Wedding Chapels at
Treasure Island**
Treasure Island
3300 Las Vegas Blvd. S.
Las Vegas, NV 89109
894-7700 1-800-866-4748
Cindy Carter, Mgr.
Hours: Sun. - Thu. 9 am - 8 pm; Fri. - Sat.
9 am - midnight
Basic Cost: Wedding packages starting
at $379
Two chapels created in an elegant
European style.

Victoria's Wedding Chapel
2800 W. Sahara Ave.
Las Vegas, NV 89102
252-4565 1-800-344-LOVE
Monique Bray, Pres.
Hours: Call for reservations
Full service wedding chapel. Decorated
with quiet elegance, nestled in a garden
setting.

**We've Only Just Begun
Wedding Chapel**
Imperial Palace
3535 Las Vegas Blvd. S.
Las Vegas, NV 89109
733-0011 1-800-346-3373
Joannie Richards, Mgr.
Hours: 9:30 am - 7:30 pm
Basic Cost: $55
Reception hall, banquets available,
music, flowers, photographs, videos, lim-
ousine service and wedding consultants.

CATERING ROOMS

CATERING / BANQUET ROOMS

The Grove at Silk Purse Ranch
645-1094
Five acres with flower gardens, lagoon
and waterscapes, majestic willow trees,
orchard, gazebo and picturesque mountain views.

Tropical Gardens
3800 E. Tropicana Ave.
Las Vegas, NV 89121
434-4333 • 1-800-668-7080
Tropical Gardens is fast becoming Las
Vegas' most popular site for weddings

and receptions, so don't wait to start
planning yours! Call now for more information or to schedule a personal tour.

**The Wedding Room
at the Cellar**
3601 W. Sahara Ave.
Las Vegas, NV 89102
362-6712 1-800-341-6046
Complete wedding package $124.95
includes meal for bride and groom, wedding cake, cake top, champagne toast
and glasses.

COORDINATORS

COORDINATORS

Andrea's Wedding Consultants
4012 S. Rainbow Blvd., Ste. K407
Las Vegas, NV 89103
367-7799 1-800-292-1177
Frank Harris, Mgr.
Chapel - candlelight ceremony in garden setting, minister, flowers, photos,
wedding cake and more arranged.

Catering to You
2770 Maryland Pkwy., Ste. 416
Las Vegas, NV 89109
737-6800

Carlyne Graves, Owner
We book 18 wedding chapels, churches,
Liberace and Hartland mansions. Call
for comparative prices.

UNUSUAL WEDDING IDEAS

A Aabells Beautiful Ceremony
437-1496
Choice of location. Minister on call. Rings, photography and accessories.

Absolutely Professional
898-2694
Chaplain Marlene Hetrick, "Chaplain at Large." Your choice of location

A. J. Hackett Bungy
810 Circus Circus Dr.
Las Vegas, NV 89109
385-4321
Jonathan Morrison-Deaker, Gen. Mgr.
Only in Las Vegas! Carry your bride over our 18 story threshold and take two plunges at once!

Alternative Lifestyle Commitments
1-888-638-4673
Weddings/Holy Unions. Gay, lesbian and regular weddings. Eternal Hope Ministry Chapel or location of your choice.

Chaplain of the Stars
735-2933
Rev. Richard Gilster
Will perform wedding ceremony at any location.

Graceland Wedding Chapel
619 Las Vegas Blvd. S.
Las Vegas, NV 89101
474-6655 1-800-824-5732
Dale Johnson, Owner
Basic Cost: $50; Elvis imitator $120
Hours: Sun. - Thu. 9 am - 9 pm; Fri. - Sat. 9 am - midnight

Lake Mead Cruises
480 Lake Shore Dr.
Boulder City, NV 89005
293-6180
Weddings on Lake Mead aboard a Mississippi paddlewheel boat. Charter or partial charters available

Las Vegas Helicopter, Inc.
3712 Las Vegas Blvd. S.
Las Vegas, NV 89109
736-0013 1-888-779-0800
Las Vegas night weddings and Grand Canyon day weddings.

A Little White Chapel
1301 Las Vegas Blvd. S.
Las Vegas, NV 89104
382-5943 1-800-545-8111
Joannie Richards, Mgr.
Hours: 24 hours
Basic Cost: $25 (plus donation to minister)
Drive-thru weddings.

A Little White Chapel in the Sky
1301 Las Vegas Blvd. S.
Las Vegas, NV 89104
382-5943 1-800-545-8111
Marriages made in heaven. A beautiful, romantic experience with your wedding service being performed in a hot air balloon. Two-day notice is required. The cost of $500 includes transportation from hotel to marriage bureau for license and return.

Mt. Charleston Restaurant and Lodge
Kyle Canyon Rd.
Mt. Charleston, NV 89124
872-5408
Plans are under way to build a chapel.

Old Nevada Chapel
Old Nevada, NV 89004
875-4191
Alan Levinson, Owner
Basic Cost: $150
Replica of a northern Nevada gold and silver era wedding chapel. Rent a stagecoach, ride horseback, rent shoot 'em up cowboys or rent entire town.

Pahrump Valley Vineyards
3810 Winery Rd.
Pahrump, NV 89048

1-702-727-6900 1-800-368-WINE
The state's only winery is located 65 miles west of Las Vegas. Rosebushes surround the garden gazebo. The bride and groom can request a private wine label that includes their wedding photo. Banquet and full restaurant facilities.

Scenic Weddings
P.O. Box 80601
Las Vegas, NV 89180
873-8316
Reverend Dyanne Maurer
"Be married in the great outdoors" anywhere. The Institute of Spiritual Awareness performs the ceremony. Interfaith / non-denominational services, Ceremony and party music available.

Wedding on Wheels
1301 Las Vegas Blvd. S.
Las Vegas, NV 89104
382-5943 1-800-545-8111
Joannie Richards, Mgr.
Hours: 24 hours
Basic Cost: $150
Get married in moving transportation while you drive down the Strip or while driving to Mt. Charleston or Red Rock Canyon.

WEDDING SERVICES & SUPPLIERS

WEDDING SERVICES

Several wedding events are held throughout the year at various centers, hotels and department stores. The Bridal Spectacular is held each year in February at the Cashman Field Center. A variety of exhibitors have display booths of interest to prospective brides and grooms.

The Perfect Wedding Guide
3871 S. Valley View Blvd., Ste. 11
Las Vegas, NV 89103
871-8083 1-800-841-8013
Haas Media Group, Inc.
Published six times a year with information on wedding and related services.

CAKES

Albertson Bakery
District Office - 368-4933
17 locations
2-tier wedding cakes $67.50 - $105.

Freed's Boulevard Bakery
4780 S. Eastern Ave.
Las Vegas, NV 89119
456-7762

Galleria Cakery
4300 Spring Mountain Rd.
Las Vegas, NV 89102
364-2253

Pastry Chef Bakery
608 S. Decatur Blvd.
Las Vegas, NV 89107
870-1418

ENTERTAINMENT
(Also see Conventions)

Musicians Union of Las Vegas
Local 369
3701 Vegas Dr.
Las Vegas, NV 89108
647-3690
Live music groups for all occasions.

FLORIST

A French Bouquet
2121 E. Tropicana Ave.
Las Vegas, NV 89119
739-8484
Hours: Mon. - Sat. 8 am - 6 pm; Sun. 10 am - 5 pm
Credit Cards: All major
FTD and Teleflorist wire service.

Awesome Blossoms
3140 S. Valley View Blvd.
Las Vegas, NV 89102
362-5002
Credit Cards: All major
Mainly a delivery service.

Bloom Saloon
3547 S. Maryland Pkwy.
Las Vegas, NV 89109
737-888
Hours: 7 am - 10 pm
Credit Cards: All major

GIFTS

D'Giovanna's Exclusive Favors & Gifts
6400 S. Eastern Ave., Ste. 15
Las Vegas, NV 89119
736-1186
Hours: Tue. - Sat. 10 am - 5 pm

INVITATIONS

Alligator Soup
4001 S. Decatur Blvd.
Las Vegas, NV 89103
367-0999
Hours: Mon. - Sat. 10 am - 6 pm; Sun. by appointment
Wedding invitations, announcements and accessories; calligraphy service.

Glee's Party Shop
4441 W. Charleston Blvd.
Las Vegas, NV 89102
870-8274
Hours: Mon. - Fri. 9 am - 9 pm; Sat. 9 am - 6 pm; Sun. 11 am - 5 pm

Hallmark Showcase
(Multiple locations listed below)
South Shore Center
8540 W. Lake Mead Rd.
Las Vegas, NV 89128
256-8274
Hours: Hours vary with each store
Credit Cards: MC, Visa, AMX
Gourmet and gift baskets, plants, invitations, cards and gifts

Meadows Mall
4300 Meadows Ln.
Las Vegas, NV 89107
878-1423

4616 W. Sahara Ave.
Las Vegas, NV 89102
259-7299

3462 Maryland Pkwy.
Las Vegas, NV 89109
734-6617

Madelyn R
4560 Spring Mountain Rd.
Las Vegas, NV 89104
222-9594
Hours: By appointment
Custom invitations for all occasions - weddings, Bar/Bat Mitzvahs, anniversaries, birthdays, business and personal stationary. Calligraphy.

Memorable Moments
9108 Crimson Clover Way
Las Vegas, NV 89134
228-0577
Penee Peltier
Invitations and baby announcements.

Papyrus
Fashion Show Mall
3200 Las Vegas Blvd. S.
733-0073
Hours: Mon. - Fri. 10 am - 9 pm; Sat. 10 am - 7 pm; Sun. noon - 6 pm
For a card that's a gift - fine greeting cards and papers, custom printed and engraved invitations, announcements and stationery.

Pretty Party Place
2718 Green Valley Pkwy.
Henderson, NV 89014
433-0676
Credit Cards: MC, Visa
Paper and plastic goods, invitations, cake tops, cake supplies. Complete line of wedding and party supplies.

LIMOUSINES
(See Transportation Section)

PARTY PLANNING
(See Convention Section)

WEDDING SERVICES & SUPPLIERS

PARTY SUPPLIES

Party Land
3129 N. Rainbow Blvd.
Las Vegas, NV 89108
645-9601
Hours: Mon. - Fri. 9 am - 9 pm; Sat. 9 am - 7 pm; Sun. 10 am - 5 pm
"Where fun parties begin."

PHOTOGRAPHERS / VIDEO

I Do Wedding Photography
3859 S. Valley View Blvd.
Las Vegas, NV 89103
221-7999

Multi-Media Video Productions
257-7477
Free pick up and delivery Nation's largest videotaping service.

West Coast Video
P.O. Box 50282
Henderson, NV 89016
876-8454

RENTAL

Ahern Party Rentals
4631 S. Industrial Rd.
Las Vegas, NV 89103
Roger Hanson
50,000 sq. ft. of gazebos, chafing dishes, silk trees and floral arrangements, linens, propane stoves and ovens, dance floors, china and silverware

RSVP Party Rentals & Decorating
5000 W. Charleston Blvd.
Las Vegas, NV 89102
878-0144
Complete wedding rentals.

TUXEDO & BRIDAL SHOPS

Celebrations Bridals
4517 W. Sahara Ave.
Las Vegas, NV 89102
222-0507
Hours: Mon. - Thu. 10 am - 8 pm; Fri. - Sat. 10 am - 6 pm; Sun. noon - 5 pm
Bridal gowns and bridal party gowns, formals, accessories & invitations.

David's Bridal
2600 W. Sahara Ave., Ste. 109
Las Vegas, NV 89102
367-4779 1-800-399-BRIDE
Hours: Mon. - Fri. 10 am - 9 pm; Sat. 10 am - 6 pm; Sun. 11 am - 5 pm
Bridal superstore.

Dandier Bridal Paradise
3335 E. Russell Rd.
Las Vegas, NV 89120
434-8011
Device Dandier
Hours: Mon. - Fri. 10 am - 7 pm; Sat. 10 am - 6 pm; Sun. noon - 5 pm
Bridal and bridal party gowns, formals, special occasions, shoes and accessories.

Designer Rentals for Her
4559 W. Flamingo Rd.
Las Vegas, NV 89103
364-Gown 1-800-249-5075
Joy Feller, Mgr.

Hours: Mon. - Fri. 10 am - 6 pm; Sat. 9 am - 5 pm; Sun. noon - 4 pm
Famous designer dresses for rent. Prom dresses, bridal, mother of the bride, evening gowns, dresses and suits. Over 400 fashions in stock in sizes 4 - 28.

Dolly's Bridal & Formal Wear
900 E. Karen Ave., Ste. D104
Las Vegas, NV 89109
737-0039 7737-0404 1-888-Dollys3
Hours: 9 am - 6 pm
Providing elegance in bridal and formal wear.

Emelia's Bridal & Formal Shoppe
5000 W. Charleston Blvd.
Las Vegas, NV 89102
878-7882
Hours: Mon. - Fri. 11 am - 6 pm; Sat. 10 am - 5 pm
Bridal gowns and accessories, veils and hairpieces, tuxedo rentals, bridesmaids, mother of the bride, invitations.

Formal Affair
3874 W. Sahara Ave.
Las Vegas, NV 89102
734-5683
Hours: Mon. - Fri. 10 am - 7 pm; Sat. 10 am - 6 pm; Sun. noon - 5 pm
Credit Cards: MC, Visa, Discover, AMX
Bridal and formal wear, tuxedo rental and sales. Complete line of bridal accessories, invitations, silk and fresh flowers and more.

Gary's Tux Shops
2797 S. Maryland Pkwy.
Las Vegas, NV 89109
732-7272 1-800-547-7757
Hours: Mon. - Fri. 10 am - 6 pm; Sat. 10 am - 4 pm; Sun. noon - 4 pm
Credit Cards: MC, Visa, Discover, AMX
Same day service - free hotel delivery.

Gingiss Formal Wear
Meadows Mall
4300 Meadows Ln.
Las Vegas, NV 89107
878-6885
Hours: Mon. - Fri. 10 am - 9 pm; Sat. & Sun. 10 am - 6 pm
Credit Cards: MC, Visa, AMX
Same day service.

Ilene's Bridal & Formal Wear
3049 Las Vegas Blvd. S.
Las Vegas, NV 89109
737-3858
Hours: Mon. - Sat. 9 am - 7 pm; Sun. 11 am - 7 pm
Bridal dresses and tuxedos. Free pick-up and delivery.

Mel-Aire Bridal & Formal Shop
953 E. Sahara Ave.
Las Vegas, NV 89104
369-4755
Airion Johnson
Hours: Mon. - Fri. 9:30 am - 6 pm; Sat. 9:30 am - 5 pm
Credit Cards: MC, Visa
Over 500 gowns from famous makers priced from $300 and up; sizes 3 to 20 and can special order to size 44; bridal hats, mantillas and veils. Tux department features After Six, Pierre Cardin and Raffanitta. Alteration and restoration services - no dry cleaning chemicals used.

Renta-Dress
2240 Paradise Rd.
Las Vegas, NV 89104
796-6444 1-800-375-2931
Hours: Mon. - Sat. 10 am - 7 pm; Sun. 11 am - 4 pm
Bridal, mother of the bride, bridesmaids, cocktail dresses, prom and formals, holiday and cruise. Pick-up to all Strip hotels and wedding chapels.

Tuxedo Junction
3540 W. Sahara Ave.
Las Vegas, NV 89102
873-8830
Hours: Mon. - Sat. 9 am - 6 pm; Sun. noon - 5 pm
Credit Cards: All major
Over 50 styles of tuxedos in over 75 colors, over 2,500 tuxedos in stock. Sizes to fit everyone, same day fitting.

GOWN AND FLOWER PRESERVATION

A Bridal Memory Gown & Floral Preservation
6115 W. Tropicana Ave., Ste. C4
Las Vegas, NV 89103
341-5635
Pam Deal
Freeze dried, heirloom keepsake cases.

WEDDING / RECEPTION ACCESSORIES

Pretty Party Place
2718 N. Green Valley Pkwy.
Henderson, NV 89014
433-0676
Hours: Mon. - Fri. 9:30 am - 9 pm; Sat. 9 am - 6:30 pm
Invitations, guestbooks, wedding favors.

DIVORCE FACTS

Nevada governor Fred Balzar signed a law in 1931 requiring a six-week residency for a divorce. The most famous divorce of that time was Clark Gable's in 1939. The local newspaper and the Chamber of Commerce publicized the divorce to promote the town as the divorce capital, a title which Reno held.

According to the Clark County Clerk's Office, there were 9,631 divorces granted in 1997. According to the 1990 census, there are 52,123 divorced households, which is 19 percent of the households in the county.

Attorney Referral:
State Bar of Nevada - 382-0502
Hours: Mon. - Fri. 8:30 am - 5 pm
Attorney Fees Breakdown:
$145 file complaint; $73 file answer
Court reporter can submit copies $1 per page; $3 to certify
Uncontested - Low $250, High $650

Brief summary of the divorce laws of the State of Nevada:

Six weeks residence of either party in the state is required before filing complaint (first paper) for divorce. Such residence must be actual, physical and corporeal. Constructive or technical residence will not be considered by the court. Contrary to general belief, there is no law in Nevada requiring newcomers to register with a county officer in order to establish residence.

Nevada is a community property state, which means you split your assets 50-50.

Recognized grounds for divorce are as follows:
1. Insanity existing for two years prior to the commencement of the action. Upon this cause of action the court, before granting a divorce, shall require corroborative evidence of the insanity of the defendant at that time, and a decree granted on this ground shall not relieve the successful party from contributing to the support and maintenance of the defendant, and the court may require the plaintiff in such action to give bond in an amount to be fixed by the court.
2. When the husband and wife have lived separate and apart for 1 year without cohabitation the court may, in its discretion, grant an absolute decree of divorce at the suit of either party.
3. Incompatibility. If defendant is willing to file a written appearance or waiver of time, the case may be tried in a few days after filing of the complaint. If the defendant will not file such appearance or waiver, a period of twenty days must elapse after service of summons on defendant before default of said defendant can be taken and the case tried.

When whereabouts of defendant is unknown, the summons must be published for a period of four weeks. Twenty days after such publication, default of the defendant may be taken if no appearance is made.

Facts constituting cause of action for divorce need not be stated in the complaint.

Upon application of either party and order of the court, certain papers in divorce actions may be sealed and shall not be open to public inspection.

Upon request of either party, the trial of a case may be heard in private, all persons except officer of the Court being excluded.

The divorce laws of this state apply to each and every county within the State of Nevada.

The District Court of Clark County is in session continuously.

Source of information:
Loretta Bowman,
County Clerk,
Clark County, Nevada.

Las Vegas is home to two daily newspapers, the *Las Vegas Sun* and the *Las Vegas Review-Journal*. In addition, from entertainment and dining guides to real estate and apartment rental magazines to news and business publications, Las Vegas offers unlimited information sources.

With the area's great cultural diversity, several ethnic publications are also available. The Las Vegas Convention and Visitors Authority Official Ethnic Destination and Visitors Guide is published semi-annually and has an annual circulation of 500,000. KINC Channel 15 is the local Spanish television network and KDOL AM 1230 is an area ethnic radio station.

"Experience Las Vegas" is the most complete guidebook and almanac about Las Vegas in the country, and is now produced semi-annually. Bigger and better than ever, it offers readers an extensive look at all that is Las Vegas.

Las Vegas has more than 30 AM and FM radio stations and 10 television stations; currently, it is the 61st largest television market in the U.S. With the addition of two new television newscasts in 1998, Las Vegas will have its first 10 pm news broadcasts. A 24-hour new channel, a joint project of the *Las Vegas Sun*, Prime Cable and KLAS-TV Channel 8, is scheduled to air April 1998 on cable channel 39, replacing the Travel Channel.

For the avid reader, there are many excellent book stores, including Borders, B. Dalton and Barnes & Nobel. You can also find many independent new and used book stores, where readers can locate new, inspirational and out-of-print works on all subjects.

MAGAZINES

Las Vegas Convention & Visitors Authority's Official Ethnic Destination/Visitors Guide
3838 Raymert Dr.
Las Vegas, NV 89121
456-3838
Fax: 456-4120
Diana Aird, Editor
Free 90-page color, glossy informational guide about Las Vegas' American Indian, African, Asian and European communities including information about restaurants, museums, shops and cultural festivals. Published twice a year. Call for copy at 892-7576.
Circulation: 500,000 annually

Las Vegas Magazine
3131 Meade Ave.
Las Vegas, NV 89102
257-2206
Debra Heiser and Virginia Thompson, Co-Publishers
Published quarterly. Features articles, fashion and food information and entertainment for both locals and tourists. Available at newsstands or through subscription.

Subscription: $15.95
Single copy: $3.95
Circulation: 91,000

Las Vegas Official Visitors Guide
Weaver Publications
5164 Paradise Rd.
Las Vegas, NV 89109
892-7575
Bruce Diebold, Pulisher.
Published semi-annually by Weaver Publications and The Las Vegas Convention & Visitors Authority. Las Vegas magazine geared toward the convention business.   Available free at select locations.

> Nevada's oldest continuously published magazine is Nevada Magazine, originally called Nevada Parks and Highways. Published by the State of Nevada since 1936.

Las Vegas Style
3201 W. Sahara Ave.
Las Vegas, NV 89102
871-6040
Larry Hall & Phil Hevener, Publishers

Published monthly. Las Vegas magazine available at newsstands around town, emphasis on hotel/casino business and entertainment.
Subscription: $28 yr
Single copy: $3.50
Circulation: 110,000 monthly

Nevada Business Journal
2127 Paradise Rd.
Las Vegas, NV 89104
735-7003
Lyle Brennan, Publisher
Monthly publication that provides coverage of business in Nevada, business news, business indicators, profiles of Nevada executives and companies.
Subscription: $44
Single copy: $3.95
Circulation: 16,000

Nevada Magazine
555 E. Washington Ave., Ste. 5600
Las Vegas, NV 89101
486-2433
State of Nevada, Owner
Richard Moreno, Publisher
Bimonthly, state-owned, non-profit magazine featuring articles and events about

all parts of Nevada.
Circulation: 100,000
Single copy: $3.95
Subscription: $16.95
Mail to: Nevada Magazine
P.O. Box 726
Mount Morris, IL 61054-7652

Nevada Woman
2685 S. Rainbow Blvd., Ste. 213
Las Vegas, NV 89102
258-4322
Paige Fleming, Publisher
Published bi-monthly. Glossy regional publication geared toward Nevada women 25 and older with diverse interests, incomes and careers.
Subscription: $15.95
Single copy: $3.95
Circulation: 25,000

Official Travel Planners Guide
Weaver Publications
5164 Paradise Rd.
Las Vegas, NV 89109
892-7575
Travel agents trade publication.

TELEVISION

Las Vegas is served by 10 local based television stations and approximately 50 cable stations. Las Vegas is rated the No. 61 television market in the country.

CHANNEL 3 KVBC · TV
NBC Affiliate
1500 Foremaster Ln.
Las Vegas, NV 89101
642-3333
Sunbelt Broadcasting, Owner
Rolla Cleaver, Gen. Mgr.

CHANNEL 4 UNLV · TV
4505 S. Maryland Pkwy.
Las Vegas, NV 89154
895-3876
Laurie Fruth, Gen. Mgr.
Broadcasts Las Vegas City Council and Clark County Commission meetings and student broadcasting.

CHANNEL 5 KVVU · TV
Fox Network Affiliate (Independent)
25 TV-5 Dr.
Henderson, NV 89014
435-5555
Meredith Corporation, Owner
Rusty Durante, Gen. Mgr.
On air since 1968.

CHANNEL 8 KLAS · TV
CBS Affiliate
3228 Channel 8 Dr.
Las Vegas, NV 89109
792-8888
Landmark Broadcasting
Dick Fraim, Gen. Mgr.
The first television station to go on the air in Nevada - July 22, 1953 - was once owned by Howard Hughes.

CHANNEL 10 KLVX · TV
PBS (Public Television)
4210 Channel 10 Dr.
Las Vegas, NV 89119
799-1010
Thomas Axtell, Gen. Mgr.
Clark County School District, Owner
Broadcasts 24 hours. National shows such as "Sesame Street." Broadcasts educational programs 7:30 am - 2:30 pm during the school year. Public Broadcasting Service programs begin at 3 pm.
Locally produced programs: "Nevada Week in Review" Friday 7:30 pm, features journalists discussing news events.

CHANNEL 13 KTNV·TV
ABC Affiliate
3355 S. Valley View Blvd.
Las Vegas, NV 89102
876-1313
Milwaukee Journal Broadcasting Inc.
Peter Bannister, Gen. Mgr.
Contact 13 - Consumer Line: 368-2255
Previously known as KSHO-TV, has been broadcasting since 1956.

Channel 15 KINC · Entravision, Inc.
500 Pilot Rd., Ste. D
Las Vegas, NV 89119
896-3095
Gabriel Quiroz, Gen. Mgr.
Spanish entertainment station affiliated with Univision.

CHANNEL 13 - KTNV-TV, 3355 S. Valley View Blvd., Las Vegas, NV 89102

CHANNEL 17 K17CT-TV
4674 S. Valley View Blvd.
Las Vegas, NV 89103
798-6646
Carol Mulanax, Mgr.
Alternative programming. Officials of America, one network, old TV shows, old movies and live football

> First commercial TV station. KLAS in Las Vegas broadcast on July 22, 1953.

CHANNEL 19 ESPN
Bristol, Connecticut
860-585-2000
All sports channel.

CHANNEL 21 KUPN · TV
920 S. Commerce St.
Las Vegas, NV 89106
382-2121
Mark Higgins, Gen. Mgr.
On air since 1984 - UHF. United Paramount Network (UPN). Broadcasts family entertainment, syndicated shows and sports including Runnin' Rebel Basketball.

CHANNEL 31 ESPN2
All sports network.

CHANNEL 33 KFBT · TV
(Cable channel 6) Independent
3840 S. Jones Blvd.
Las Vegas, NV 89103
873-0033
Daniel Koker, Owner
Jack Paris, Gen. Mgr.
Billed as "The Family Entertainer" featuring programs for all ages. Warner Bros. Network.

MEDIA 509

TELEVISION & CABLE TV

CHANNEL 39 KBLR - TV
Independent
5000 W. Oakey Blvd., Ste. B2
Las Vegas, NV 89102
258-0039
Summit Media Limited Partnership
Scott Gentry, Pres./Gen. Mgr.
Spanish-language television station.
Sports, news, movies, talk shows, game shows, music and newsmagazines.

CABLE TELEVISION

Prime Cable
121 S. Martin Luther King Blvd.
Las Vegas, NV 89106
383-4000
Harris Bass, Gen. Mgr.
Office Hours: Mon. - Fri. 8 am to 6 pm
Drive thru 7 am - 7 pm
To order: 383-4000

11 Water St.
Henderson, NV 89015
565-8855

508 Nevada Hwy., Ste. 5
Boulder City, NV 89005
294-0960
Prime Cable provides cable service to 280,390 subscribers in the Las Vegas area. The basic 49-channel service, which is a variety of shopping, sports, music and family programs, is $26.15 per month with a $25 deposit and installation fee. There is an additional fee of $10.95 per month for each of the premium channels, such as HBO 1, 2 and 3, the Movie Channel and Showtime (combined) and $4.95 for Cinemax. There are also additional charges for converter boxes and remote controls. Special request movies and events are available on a pay-per-view basis if you have a converter box; rates are $4.95 and up. Adultvision and Spice for a 6-hour block costs $6.95.

PROGRAMMING

A weekly programming guide can be found in the Sunday edition of the *Las Vegas Review-Journal*, as well as a daily listing in both the *Review-Journal* and the *Sun*.

CABLE STATIONS

Ch. 2   KUPN Independent *(Channel 2)*
Ch. 3   KVBC NBC
Ch. 4   Government Access/UNLV - TV
Ch. 5   KVVU Fox Independent
Ch. 6   KFBT Independent *(Channel 33)*
Ch. 7   WTBS Atlanta
Ch. 8   KLAS CBS
Ch. 9   KBLR Telemundo
Ch. 10 KLVX-PBS Public Broadcasting System
Ch. 11 WGN Chicago
Ch. 12 FX New Cable Network from Fox
Ch. 13 KTNV ABC
Ch. 14 The Weather Channel
Ch. 15 KINC (Spanish) Univision
Ch. 16 USA Network
Ch. 17 Fox Sports West
Ch. 18 TNT Turner Network TV
Ch. 19 ESPN Sports
Ch. 20 CNN Headline News
Ch. 21 Nickelodeon - Children
Ch. 22 CNN - Headline News
Ch. 23 American Movie Classics
Ch. 24 Comedy Central
Ch. 25 Discovery Channel
Ch. 26 Lifetime
Ch. 27 BET - Black Entertainment Television
Ch. 28 The Disney Channel
Ch. 29 CMT The Nashville Network - Country
Ch. 30 MTV Music Videos
Ch. 31 ESPN 2
Ch. 32 Arts & Entertainment
Ch. 33 VH-1 Music Videos
Ch. 34 On Screen Guide/Special Events
Ch. 35 CNBC - Entertainment
Ch. 36 E! Entertainment Television
Ch. 37 The Family Channel
Ch. 38 The Learning Channel
Ch. 39 The Travel Channel
Ch. 40 Turner Classics
Ch. 41 TV Land
Ch. 42 Kaleidoscope Movies
Ch. 43 The History Channel
Ch. 44 QVC (Shop by Phone)
Ch. 45 Sci Fi Channel
Ch. 46 Odyssey
Ch. 47 MSNBC
Ch. 48 Metro One
Ch. 49 C-Span News
Ch. 50 PPV Previews
Ch. 51 Showtime*
Ch. 52 The Movie Channel*
Ch. 53 Cinemax*
Ch. 54 HBO*
Ch. 55 HBO2*
Ch. 56 HBO3*
Ch. 57 PPV*
Ch. 58 PPV*
Ch. 59 PPV*
Ch. 60 PPV*
Ch. 61 Metro One
Ch. 83 Spice*
Ch. 84 Adultvision*
*Premium Services

FM RADIO STATIONS

Southern Nevada is served by 30 radio stations with a variety of formats. The *Las Vegas Sun* publishes a radio guide every Friday with shows for the coming week.

FM STATIONS

88.1 · KCEP
New Rhythm
330 W. Washington Ave.
Las Vegas, NV 89106
648-0104
Request line: 647-FM88
Economic Opportunity Board
Sherman Rutledge, Gen. Mgr.
Non-profit station; "pipeline to the African-American community."

89.5 · KNPR
Classical and news
5151 Boulder Hwy.
Las Vegas, NV 89122
456-6695
Request line: 451-8955
Fax: 458-2787
Nevada Public Radio Corp.
Lamar Marchese, Gen. Mgr.
Non-commercial public radio station. Presents the annual KNPR Artworks Market at Sunset Park each September.

90.5 · KILA
Christian adult contemporary
2201 S. 6th St.
Las Vegas, NV 89104
731-5452
SOS Radio Network
Jack French, Gen. Mgr.

91.5 · KUNV
Music and community affairs
4505 S. Maryland Pkwy
Las Vegas, NV 89154
895-3877
Request line: 895-3976
UNLV Board of Regents, Owner
Don Fuller, Gen. Mgr.
Jazz, underground rock, folk, bluegrass, blues.

> First radio station, KOH in Reno, broadcasted on November 11, 1928.

92.3 · KOMP
Album oriented rock
4660 S. Decatur Blvd.
Las Vegas, NV. 89103
876-1460
Request line: 876-3692
Concert Hot Line: 876-5667
Comment line: 873-2382
Lotus Broadcasting Corp.
Tony Bonnici, Gen. Mgr.

93.1 · KEYV
Oldies
1130 E. Desert Inn Rd.
Las Vegas, NV 89109
732-7753
Request line: 792-9336
Jacor Broadcasting
Mike Ginsburg, Gen. Mgr.
Big oldies.

94.1 · KMXB
Hot adult contemporary, rhythm
6655 W. Sahara Ave., Ste. 210
Las Vegas, NV 89102
889-5100
Request Line: 364-9400
American Radio Systems
Cindy Shloss, Gen. Mgr.
Rhythm requests.

95.5 · KWNR
New Country
1130 E. Desert Inn Rd.
Las Vegas, NV 89109
798-4004
Request line: 798-9500
Concert line: 739-9550
Jacor Broadcasting
Mike Ginsburg, Gen. Mgr.

96.3 · KKLZ
Classic Rock
4305 S. Industrial Rd., Ste. 120

Las Vegas, NV 89103
739-9600
Request line: 739-96FM
Concert Line: 739-8863
Apogee Communication
Eric Mastel, Gen. Mgr.

97.1 · KXPT
Adult Alternative
4660 S. Decatur Blvd.
Las Vegas, NV 89103
876-1460
Request line: 647-6468 (64POINT)
Lotus Broadcasting
Tony Bonnici, Gen. Mgr.
"The Point" quality music.

98.1 · 98.3 · 98.9 · 99.5
Refer to the call letters KHWY - all are broadcast simultaneously
Adult Contemporary
101 Convention Center Dr., Ste. P109
Las Vegas, NV 89109
737-9899
1-760-256-0326 (Barstow)
Tim Anderson, Gen. Mgr.
Transmitters cover I-15 from Las Vegas to Southern California, from Las Vegas to Arizona on Hwy. 95, Barstow to Laughlin on I-40; covers the whole Mojave Desert, broadcasts CALTRANS road reports.

FM & AM RADIO STATIONS

104.3 - KJUL, 1515 E. Tropicana Ave., Ste. 1000, Las Vegas, NV 89119

98.5 · KLUC
Contemporary hits
665 W Sahara Ave., Ste. D200
Las Vegas, NV 89102
253-9800
Request line: 364-9898
American Radio Systems Corp.
Rick Dames, Gen. Mgr.
"Top 40 Countdown" airs on Saturdays 8
am - noon with Rick Dees.

100.5 · KMZQ
Adult contemporary
6655 W. Sahara Ave.
Las Vegas, NV 89102
889-5100
Request line: 796-1100
American Radio Systems
Cindy Schloss, Gen. Mgr.
Klassy 100, sponsors concerts and
community events.

101.5 · KIXF
333 N. Rancho Dr., Ste. 134
Las Vegas, NV 89106
647-2222 1-800-278-4487
John Covington, Gen. Mgr.
Turquoise Broadcasting
Provides information and entertainment
for the highway traveler from Cajon
Pass in San Bernardino all the way to
Nevada state line.

101.9 · KFMS
Contemporary country
1130 E. Desert Inn Rd.
Las Vegas, NV 89109
732-7753
Request line: 732-1536
Jacor Broadcasting
Mike Ginsburg, Gen. Mgr.
Today's continuous country variety.

103.5 · KEDG
Modern rock
1455 E. Tropicana Ave.
Las Vegas, NV 89119
795-1035
Request Line: 798-1035
The Edge BBS: 795-0465 *(computer
bulletin board)*

Concerts/Events: 593-8400
Radiovision, Inc. (Suite 650)
Dax Tobin, Gen. Mgr.
"The Edge."

104.3 · KJUL
Nostalgic - hits from 40's, 50's and 60's
1515 E. Tropicana Ave., Ste. 1000
Las Vegas, NV 89119
248-9100
Contest line: 248-9105
Centennial Broadcasting
Harry Williams, Gen. Mgr.
"The Jewel."

105.1 · KVBC
News, sports and weather
1500 Foremaster Ln.
Las Vegas, NV 89104
Call-in line: 642-3230
Comment line: 657-3447
Patmor Broadcasting
Melinda Wirth, Gen. Mgr.
"Imus in the Morning" 5 am - 9 am.

105.5 · KQOL
Oldies
1515 E. Tropicana Ave.
Las Vegas, NV 89119
736-5105
Request line: 566-5105
Centennial Broadcasting
Harry Williams, Gen. Mgr.
American General Media Nevada
Oldies 50's through 70's.

106.5 · KSNE
Soft music
1130 E. Desert Inn Rd.
Las Vegas, NV 89109
796-4040
Studio line: 796-1065
Jacor Broadcasting
Mike Ginsburg, Gen. Mgr.
"The New Sunny 106.5."

107.3 · KIXW
333 N. Rancho Dr., Ste. 134
Las Vegas, NV 89106
647-2222 1-800-278-4487
John Covington, Gen. Mgr.

Turquoise Broadcasting
Provides information and entertainment
for the highway traveler from Cajon
Pass in San Bernardino all the way to
Nevada state line.

107.5 · KXTE
Alternative music
6655 W. Sahara Ave., Ste. C202
Las Vegas, NV 89102
367-9494
Request line: 791-1075
American Radio Systems
Alan Gray, Gen. Mgr.
Howard Stern - mornings 3 am - 11 am

AM STATIONS

530 · WNRM
McCarran Airport
Adam Mayberry, Public Info. Officer
Airport information & travelers advisory
information.

720 · KDWN
Talk/big band/news/sports
1 N. Main St.
Las Vegas, NV 89101
385-7212
Talk show line: 383-8255
Radio Nevada Corp.
Claire B. Reis, Gen. Mgr.
Michael Reagan - Mon. - Fri. 3 pm - 6 pm

840 · KXNT
Talk Radio
6655 W. Sahara Ave.
Las Vegas, NV 89102
262-6600
Call-in line: 733-5968
American Radio Systems
Tom Humm, Gen. Mgr.
Rush Limbaugh, Paul Harvey, Dr. Laura
Schlessinger, Art Bell and live local talk.
Also UNLV men's and women's basket-
ball. In the latest Arbitron ratings, KXNT
is rated the #1 AM station. 50,000 Watts
Programming Line.

920 · KBAD
Sports play-by-play
4660 S. Decatur Blvd.
Las Vegas, NV 89103
876-1460
Call-in line: 367-8402
Request line: 365-9200
Lotus Broadcasting
Tony Bonnici, Gen. Mgr.
Sports talk.

960 · KIXW
333 N. Rancho Dr., Ste. 134
Las Vegas, NV 89106
647-2222 1-800-278-4487
John Covington, Gen. Mgr.
Turquoise Broadcasting
Provides information and entertainment
for the highway traveler from Cajon
Pass in San Bernardino all the way to
Nevada state line.

970 · KNUU (KNEWS)
Total news, sports, information, talk
2001 E. Flamingo Rd., Ste. 101
Las Vegas, NV 89119
735-8644
Talk line: 735-8645
Bernstein & Rein.

Joe McMurray, Gen. Mgr.
Bruce Williams, Mon. - Fri. 7 pm - 10 pm;
Sat. & Sun. 10 p.m - 1 am; Oliver North,
Mon. - Fri. 1 pm - 3 pm
CBS News, Wall Street Journal, CBS
Sports, Dow Jones and AP news and
sports.

1060 · KKVV
Christian talk radio
3185 S. Highland Dr.
Las Vegas, NV 89109
731-5588
Las Vegas Broadcasters
Bill Ball, Gen. Mgr.

1140 · KXNO
All sports
6655 W. Sahara Ave., Ste. D208
Las Vegas, NV 89102
739-9383
American Radio Systems Corp.
Tom Humm, Gen. Mgr.

RADIO STATIONS BY FORMAT

ROCK:
FM 92.3, FM 96.3, FM 103.5,
AM 1140

TOP 40 ROCK:
FM 98.5

CONTEMPORARY:
FM 99.5, FM 100.5, FM 97.1

ADULT CONTEMPORARY:
FM 94.1, FM 100.5

COUNTRY:
FM 95.5, FM 101.9

OLDIES:
FM 93.1, FM 105.5

ALTERNATIVE:
FM 107.5

SOFT HITS:
FM 97.1, FM 106.5

NOSTALGIC:
FM 104.3, AM 920

CLASSICAL:
FM 89.5, FM 91.5 *(part-time)*

BIG BAND:
AM 720, AM 920

JAZZ *(all feature jazz part-time)*:
FM 91.5, FM 88.1, FM 89.5

AFRICAN AMERICAN:
FM 88.1

NEWS:
FM 89.5, FM 105.1, AM 720, AM 840,
AM 970, AM 1460

TALK:
AM 720, AM 840, AM 970, AM 1230

SPORTS:
AM 720, AM 920, AM 970, AM 1460,
AM 1340,

SPANISH:
AM 1280

RELIGIOUS:
FM 90.5, AM 1060

CHRISTIAN:
AM 1060

CHILDREN:
AM 1410

1230 · KLAV
Talk radio
1810 Weldon Pl.
Las Vegas, NV 89104
796-1230
Request line: 731-1230
Gore Overgaard Broadcasting
Lisa Lupo, Gen. Mgr.
Features over 20 on-air personalities.

1280 · KDOL
953 E. Sahara Ave., Ste. 253
Las Vegas, NV 89104
732-1664
Request line: 732-1003

S & R Broadcasting, Inc.
Paul Ruttan, Gen. Mgr.
Spanish language station. Music, games and news.

1340 · KRLV
Sports Radio Network
1515 E. Tropicana Ave., Ste. 240
Las Vegas, NV 89119
795-4700
Rod Stowell, Gen. Mgr.
Talk Radio. Vince Lupo, 5 am - 9 am; Lee Pete, 10 am - 11 am; Oliver North, noon

- 2 pm; Pat Choate, 2 pm - 4 pm; *(bought time),* 4 pm - 5 pm; Sport's Corner via live remote from the Imperial Palace, 5 pm - 6 pm; Larry King Live, 6 pm - 7 pm *(bought time),* 7 pm - midnight. High school sports on Fri. 7 pm - 10 pm. Weekends - NASCAR races official broadcaster live at race time. The Sports Corner is on Mon. - Fri. 5 pm - 6 pm and Sun. 5 pm - 8 pm. Wednesday is Hockey Time 4 pm - 7 pm and Thursday Motor Racing 4 pm - 7 pm.

1460 · KENO
CNN news and sports
4660 S. Decatur Blvd.
Las Vegas, NV 89103
876-1460
Request line: 367-UNLV
Lotus Broadcasting
Tony Bonnici - Gen. Mgr.
Las Vegas' first radio station, on air over 50 years.

NEWSPAPERS

NEWSPAPERS

Las Vegas has two major newspapers, the *Las Vegas Review-Journal* and the *Las Vegas Sun*. The *Review-Journal* was started in 1905 as the *Las Vegas Age* and after several owners sold to the current publisher, Don Reynolds, in 1949. The *Sun* was first published in 1950 by Hank Greenspun and is still published by the Greenspun family. In 1990 the *Review Journal* and the *Sun* entered into a joint operating agreement and now the *Review Journal* is published daily as a morning newspaper and the *Sun* is published Monday through Friday as an afternoon newspaper, with the weekend and holiday editions combined with the morning *Review-Journal*. Both newspapers maintain independent editorial departments while the advertising, circulation and production departments are combined.

The Clark County Library carries a large selection of local, state and out-of-state newspapers. *(See Cultural Arts Section for a list of libraries)*

NEWSPAPERS

Boulder City News
1227 Arizona St.
Boulder City, NV 89005
293-2302
Mike O'Callaghan, Publisher
Published weekly every Thursday morning.
Single copy: $.25
Subscription home delivery $20 per year
Circulation: 5,300

Henderson Home News
2 Commerce Center
Henderson, NV 89014
435-7700
Mike O'Callaghan, Publisher
Paul Szydelko, Editor
Tim O'Callaghan, General Manager
Bi-weekly *(Tue. & Thu. mornings)*
Single copy: $.50
Subscription home delivery $30 per year

Mail delivery: West of Mississippi - $50 - 12 mos., East of Mississippi - $60 - 12 mos.
Circulation: 15,500 daily
Green Valley Plus published by Henderson News is a free community newspaper published twice a month.
Circulation: 15,000

Las Vegas Review-Journal
1111 W. Bonanza Rd.
Las Vegas, NV 89125
383-0400
City Desk: 383-0264
Donrey Media Group
Sherman R. Frederick, Publisher

Las Vegas SUN, 800 S. Valley View Blvd., Las Vegas, NV 89107

Allan B. Fleming, Gen. Mgr.
Thomas Mitchell, Editor
Morning daily
Single copy: $.50 daily, $2.50 Sunday
Subscription home delivery - $14.00 per four weeks
Subscription: 383-0400
Delivery by mail: Sunday 4 weeks $30, daily 4 weeks $33, Sunday and daily 4 weeks out of state $36.
Circulation: 201,000 daily, 214,262 Sunday
Community newspapers published every

Wednesday. *View* newspapers packaged inside the *Review-Journal* and the *Sun*. Nonsubscribers receive *View* through the ad services department.
Kirk Kern, Editor
Henderson View
Circulation: 41,000 weekly
Northern View
Circulation: 39,000 weekly
Sunrise View
Circulation: 36,000 weekly
Northwest View
Circulation: 39,000 weekly
Southwest View
Circulation: 44,000 weekly

Summerlin View
Circulation: 38,000 weekly
Southeast View
Circulation: 48,000 weekly

Las Vegas Sun
Afternoon daily *(morning, weekends and holidays)*
800 S. Valley View Blvd.
Las Vegas, NV 89107
385-3111
Barbara Greenspun, Publisher
Brian Greenspun, Editor

Single copy: Monday - Friday $.50 daily, Saturday and Sunday combined with Review-Journal $2.50
Subscription home delivery: $14 for 4 weeks *(daily and Sunday)*
Subscription: 383-0400
Circulation: 37,709

USA Today
4625 S. Polaris Ave.
Las Vegas, NV 89103
798-7677
Chris Hansen, Cir. Mgr.
National newspaper published Mon. - Fri., $.50 per copy, various home delivery rates.

Latitude Newspapers
2949 E. Desert Inn Rd., Ste. 7
Las Vegas, NV 89121
650-9050
Fax: 650-9080
Bill Guthrie, Publisher
North by Northwest - first Wednesday of each month.
Circulation: 25,000
This Month in the Southwest - first Friday of each month.
Circulation: 19,000
This Week in Summerlin - every Wednesday.
Circulation: 15,500
This Week in Green Valley - every Friday.
Circulation: 18,500
Home delivered, free community newspaper.

OUT OF TOWN NEWSPAPERS

Las Vegas International Newsstand
3900 Paradise Rd.
Las Vegas, NV 89109
796-9901
Hours: Mon. - Fri. 9 am - 8 pm; Sat. - Sun. 9 am - 7 pm
Large selection of foreign and domestic newspapers and magazines. Special orders available.

SPECIALTY PUBLICATONS

Most of the following publications can be found at various locations free of charge, depending on the market the publication is targeting throughout Las Vegas.

Asian American Times
Asian American Media Corp.
2700 State St., Ste. 16
Las Vegas, NV 89109
796-5502
Tonie Sison, Publisher
Leading free Asian American newspaper; Nevada, California and Chicago circulation. Tabloid news.
Subscription: $20
Circulation: 8,000 - 10,000

Auto Trader
4205 W. Tompkins Ave., Ste. 7
Las Vegas, NV 89123
733-2886
Trader Publishing
Free classified weekly paper.

The Beehive
Beehive Press
1916 S. Maryland Pkwy.
Las Vegas, NV 89104
732-1812
Russell Taylor, Publisher
Monthly Latter Day Saints newspaper. Call for subscription.
Subscription: $6
Free throughout the Las Vegas area.
Circulation: 40,000

Bingo Bugle
3127 Industrial Rd.
Las Vegas, NV 89109
893-7774
Don Carrier, Publisher
Nevada Bingo, Inc., Owner
Monthly bingo players' news and guide. Available free at area bingo parlors.
Mail subscription: $20 year
Circulation: 35,000 in Nevada

Bioque Latino Americano
DePrensa/Latin American Press
P.O. Box 12599
Las Vegas, NV 89112
431-1904
Maggy Ruiz, Publisher/Editor
Distributed in Las Vegas and California casinos.
Subscription: $45
Circulation: 50,000

Bullseye
AWC/PAI
Nellis Air Force Base
NV 89191-5000
652-5814
Ed Scott, Editor
Weekly internal publication serving Nellis personnel with news and information and published by the *Las Vegas Review-Journal*.
Circulation: 10,000

The Card Player
3140 S. Polaris Ave., Unit 8
Las Vegas, NV 89102
871-1720
Fax: 871-2674
Linda Johnson, Publisher
Poker and gambling magazine published bi-weekly and available free at poker rooms throughout the United States.
Individual copies: $2.95 plus $1 postage per copy.
Circulation: 48,000

Cars & Trucks
900 S. Main St.
Las Vegas, NV 89101
224-5500
Lee Enterprise
Nifty Nickel Publications
Pete Bodnar, Publisher
Pictures and information on vehicles for sale. Available at convenience stores free of charge.
Circulation: 30,000

Casa Y Viviendas
709 N. Eastern Ave.
Las Vegas, NV 89109
383-0080
Eddie Escobedo, Sr. & Terry Tibbs, Publishers
Published quarterly. Free real estate and apartment guide. Distributed to Hispanic businesses.
Circulation: 45,000

Casino Games Magazine
Compass International
4933 W. Craig Rd., Ste. 248
Las Vegas, NV 89119
399-3998
Sam Micco, Publisher
Compass International
Quarterly guide to casino games. Main distribution through MLT Vacations.
Circulation: 166,000 copies per quarter

Casino Journal
5240 S. Eastern Ave.
Las Vegas, NV 89119
736-8886
Glenn Fine, Publisher
Monthly magazine with news and information about casinos and the casino business in Nevada and nationwide, with columns written by the most respected experts in the industry covering gaming finance, law, politics, marketing, tribal gaming, gaming development and human resources. The feature stories focus on leading gaming corporations, vendors and industry trends.
Subscription: $79 per year.
Circulation: 75,000

The Casino Player
5240 S. Eastern Ave.
Las Vegas, NV 89119
736-8886
Glenn Fine, Publisher
The nation's largest circulation consumer gaming publication with four regional editions targeting all the major gaming markets. Provides gamblers with expert opinions on gaming strategies, written by some of the most successful professional gamblers and recognized experts in the country.
Subscription: $24, $2.95 per issue
Circulation: 175,000

Checkered Flag
4429 Fern Brook Rd.
Las Vegas, NV 89103
454-9013
Ernest Figueroa, Publisher
Jeanne Riley, Editor
Monthly publication of the Las Vegas region of the Sports Car Club of America.
Subscription: $15 per year
Circulation: 400

CityLife
3335 Wynn Rd.
Las Vegas, NV 89102
795-0234   871-6780
Las Vegas Press
Bruce Spotleson, Publisher
Weekly newspaper with news and information on the arts, culture and entertainment. Available free at 7-11's and throughout Las Vegas.
Subscription: $50
Circulation: 40,000

Class!
6290 Harrison Dr., Ste. 10
Las Vegas, NV 89120
798-5757
David Phillips, Publisher
A free monthly publication by, for and about the high school students of Clark County.
Circulation: 20,000

Construction Notebook
3131 Meade Ave.
Las Vegas, NV 89102
876-8660
Sheila Dickinson, Publisher
Information source for contractors and the construction industry. Published weekly, the *Construction Notebook* categorizes permits, liens, new business licenses. The *Notebook* holds the plans and specifications for the jobs currently bidding and maintains a plan room for subscribers estimating work.
Subscription: $425 per year, $305 for 6 months
Circulation: 1,500

The Country Register
1736 E. Charleston Blvd., Ste. 350
Las Vegas, NV 89104
642-8775
Jeffrey Thomas, Editor
Published 6 times per year. Publication for country antique and collectible enthusiasts.
Subscription: $16 per year, $3 per issue
Circulation: 12,000

Deportimundo
845 N. Eastern Ave.
Las Vegas, NV 89101
657-0717
Eddie Escobedo, Jr., Publisher
Free Hispanic sports and entertainment newspaper.
Circulation: 7,000

El Mundo
845 N. Eastern Ave.
Las Vegas, NV 89101
649-8553
Eddie Escobedo, Sr., Publisher
Free weekly independent Spanish language newspaper.
Circulation: 23,000

End of the Line
P.O. Box 8
Searchlight, NV 89046
297-1218
Carl Weikel, Publisher
Monthly newsletter serving Las Vegas and extreme southern Nevada. Political, current events and entertainment.
Subscription: $16.05
Circulation: 800

Exito Deportivo
Latin American Press
P. O. Box 12599
Las Vegas, NV 89112
431-1904
Fax: 431-3339
Maggy Ruiz, Publisher/Editor
Only bilingual weekly sport and entertainment newspaper circulated in Nevada and California for over 18 years.
Subscription: $45 per year
Circulation: 50,000 *(Las Vegas)*

For Rent Magazine
7330 Smoke Ranch Rd., Ste. A
Las Vegas, NV 89128
255-3700
United Advertising Publications
Bi-weekly apartment guide available free at various locations including grocery stores and convenience stores.
Circulation: 40,000 monthly

Ray Koon's Gaming Gram
3271 S. Highland Dr., Ste. 705A
Las Vegas, NV 89109-1051
735-2550
Ray Koon, Publisher
Monthly newsletter provides professional overview of the gaming industry throughout the world.
Subscription: $150 quarterly, $600 yearly.
Circulation: 275

Gaming Today
P. O. Box 93116
Las Vegas, NV 89116
798-1151
Chuck Di Rocco, Publisher
Dirson Enterprises, Inc.
Weekly race and sports bettors news and information.
Subscription: $135 for six months, $180 per year; single issues $3.95

Greater Las Vegas Apartment Guide
4425 Spring Mountain Rd., Ste. 300
Las Vegas, NV 89102
736-3943
Haas Publishing Corp.
Monthly pocket-size apartment guide available at convenience stores and grocery stores.
Circulation: 30,000 monthly

Here Is Las Vegas
3750 S. Jones Blvd.
Las Vegas, NV 89103
221-8836
Decor Publications
Bruce Diebold, Publisher
Newcomers relocation guide published bi-annually. $5.95 per copy

Home Scene
900 S. Main St.
Las Vegas, NV 89101
224-5500
Lee Enterprise
Nifty Nickel Publications
Pete Bodnar, Publisher
Monthly news and guide to home and real estate. Published the fourth Friday of every month. Available free throughout Las Vegas.
Circulation: 23,000

MEDIA

SPECIALTY PUBLICATONS

Homebuyers Guide
1455 E. Tropicana Ave., Ste. 400
Las Vegas, NV 89119
891-8420
Walter Crowell, Publisher
Monthly guide to new home communities. Available free at grocery and convenience stores.
Circulation: 25,000

Home & Hearth Magazine
6120 W. Tropicana Ave.
Las Vegas, NV 89103
873-9802
Joyce Nolasco, Publisher
For people who love their home. Contains home projects, human interest stories, decorating, gardening and children's gardens
Subscription: $10
Circulation: 40,000

Homes and Living
2500 Chandler Ave., Ste. 1
Las Vegas, NV 89120
891-0095 1-800-247-6996
Terry Tebbs, Publisher
Home magazine published monthly.
Subscription: $15
Circulation: 30,000

Hospitality & Gaming Risk Management
3335 Wynn Rd.
Las Vegas, NV 89102
871-6780
Fax: 871-3740
Wick Communications
Alisa Fuller, Publisher
Subscription: $48 per year

Images of Las Vegas
2112 Santa Clara Dr.
Las Vegas, NV 89104
796-1778
Monica Ortiz, Publisher
Only bilingual variety monthly magazine.
Subscription: $20
Circulation: 10,000

In Light Times
P. O. Box 35798
Las Vegas, NV 89133
795-4801
Fax 259-6843
Michelene K. Bell, Publisher/Editor
Monthly newspaper dedicated to holistic health, spiritual growth and enlightenment. Distributed free at select locations.
Subscription: $24 per year

Indian Voices
618 E. Carson St., Ste. 305
Las Vegas, NV 89101
382-0808
Rose Davis, Publisher
Monthly Native American community news and enterprises.
Subscription: $24
Circulation: 15,000

The Jewish Reporter
3909 S. Maryland Pkwy., Ste. 400
Las Vegas, NV 89119-7528
732-0556
Rebecca Herren, Editor
Published twice a month and available at area synagogues and Federation Office.
Circulation: 8,500

Las Vegas Asian Journal
2770 S. Maryland Pkwy., Ste. 404
Las Vegas, NV 89109
792-6678
Asian Journal Publications
Corazon Oriel, Owner
Weekly ethnic newspaper targeting mainly Filipinos.
Circulation: 25,000

The Las Vegas Bugle
3131 Industrial Rd.
Las Vegas, NV 89109-1136
369-6260
Fax: 369-9325
Newspaper Services
Rob Schlegel, Publisher
Monthly lesbian and gay newspaper.
Subscription: $20, 1st Class Mail
Circulation: 15,000

Las Vegas Business Press
3335 Wynn Rd.
Las Vegas, NV 89102
871-6780
Las Vegas Press
Bruce Spotleson, Publisher
Business news and information. Published weekly.
Subscription: $68; single copies available at newsstands $1.25
Circulation: 8,500

Las Vegas Employment News
4040 Pioneer Ave., Ste. 201
Las Vegas, NV 89102
247-4151
Douglas T. Geinzer, Publisher
Bi-weekly employment newspaper available free throughout the Las Vegas area.
Subscription: $49.99 for 1 year, $29.99 for 6 months
Circulation: 40,000

Las Vegas Homes Illustrated
5825 W. Sahara Ave., Ste. G
Las Vegas, NV 89102
367-3439
T. C. Turpin, Publisher
Free bi-weekly homes magazine available at supermarkets and convenience stores.
Circulation: 15,000

Las Vegas Israelite
P.O. Box 14096
Las Vegas, NV 89114
876-1255
Michael Tell, Publisher/Editor
Bi-monthly newspaper serving the Jewish community. Available free at grocery and convenience stores throughout Las Vegas.
Subscription: $24 per year, $40 for 2 years
Circulation: 33,000 free plus 10,000 subscribers

Las Vegas Kidz
9208 Sienna Vista Dr.
Las Vegas, NV 89117
233-8388
Mya Lake-Collins, Publisher
Monthly Las Vegas parent's magazine with news and information.
Subscription: $20
Circulation: 40,000

Las Vegas Real Estate Showcase
3139 S. Eastern Ave.
Las Vegas, NV 89109
731-4000
Michael Abdoulah, Publisher
Harmon Publishing
Monthly magazine featuring pictures and information on homes from licensed real estate brokers. Available throughout Las Vegas free of charge.
Circulation: 30,000

Las Vegas Trader
4205 W. Tompkins, Ste. 7
Las Vegas, NV 89103
733-2886
Fax: 248-9764
Trader Publishing Co.
Classified photo ads for vehicles.

Look North
North Las Vegas Chamber of Commerce
2290 McDaniel St.
N. Las Vegas, NV 89030
642-9595
Ed Dodrill, Editor
Distributed to members, all businesses and residents of North Las Vegas.

Metropolitan Magazine
1201 Arville St.
Las Vegas, NV 89102
870-3435
Paul Brauner, Publisher
Free monthly - Nevada finest homes.
Circulation: 25,000

Mobile Home Finder
4685 Boulder Hwy.
Las Vegas, NV 89121
454-1050
Jim Blackwell, Publisher
Hi-Flyer Publications, Inc.
Monthly guide for manufactured homes for sale.
Circulation: 20,000

Mobile Home Living of Southern Nevada
3151 N. Rainbow Blvd., Ste. 183
Las Vegas, NV 89108
658-0587
Joe Carta, Publisher
Information on manufactured housing. Published monthly.
Subscription: $12

National Gaming Summary
5240 S. Eastern Ave.
Las Vegas, NV 89119
736-8886
Glenn Fine, Publisher
Published weekly about the national gaming industry.
Subscription: $398 per year, $7.65 per copy
Circulation: 2,100

Nevada Property Management Magazine
Nevada Apartment Association
2345 Red Rock St., Ste. 320
Las Vegas, NV 89102
368-3991
Marie Hamilton, Publisher
Bi-monthly trade publication for members of the Nevada Apartment Association.
Circulation: 760

DeCor Pub. of Here Is Las Vegas, 3750 S. Jones Blvd., Las Vegas, NV 89103

Nevada Business & Economics Indicators
Bureau of Business and Economic Research
University of Nevada, Reno - MS 032
Reno, NV 89557-0100
1-702-784-6877   735-7003
Connie Brennan, Editor
Annual publication of the Bureau of Business and Economic Research, College of Business Administration, University of Nevada, Reno. Focuses on the business and economic environment of Nevada and the western states.

Nevada Gaming News
325 Maryland Pkwy.
Las Vegas, NV 89101
678-6100
Jeff Burbank, Editor
Gaming fax newsletter.

Nevada Hospitality
5240 S. Eastern Ave.
Las Vegas, NV 89119
736-8886
Glenn Fine, Publisher
The official publication of the Nevada Hotel & Motel Association and the Nevada Restaurant Association. Published monthly.
Subscription: $45
Circulation: 12,000

Nevada Legal News
516 S. Fourth St.
Las Vegas, NV 89101
382-2747
Hoyt Sibley, Publisher
Legal and business newspaper containing public legal notices and public records. Available Monday through Friday. Also contains news articles of local and national interest.
Subscription: $60 for 3 months.
Circulation: 600

Nevada Senior World
2340 Paseo Del Prado, Ste. 304
Las Vegas, NV 89102
367-6709
Gilbert Moore, Publisher/Editor
Monthly senior newspaper available free throughout Las Vegas.
Subscription: $14.95
Circulation: 75,000

Nevada Times
P. O. Box 4142
N. Las Vegas, NV 89030
878-3504
Spur Enterprises, Inc.
Monthly mobile home, RV and senior half size newspaper. Available free at various locations throughout Las Vegas or by subscription. Oldest half size paper in the state. Oldest mobile home newspaper in the world. Started in 1952.
Subscription: $10

Nifty Nickel
900 S. Main St.
Las Vegas, NV 89101
224-5000   224-5500   224-5555
Lee Enterprises
Pete Bodnar, Publisher
Nickel classified ads. Distributed weekly on Thursday throughout Las Vegas at grocery and convenience stores and racks around Las Vegas. Also publishes *Cars & Trucks*, *Home Scene* and *Show Time*.
Circulation: 60,000 *(3 zones)*

Opus Magazine
2712 N. Green Valley Pkwy., Ste. 346
Henderson, NV 89014
434-4600
Matteson Media Grouping
Dale Matteson, Publisher
Published quarterly. Lifestyle for fine arts and fine living.
Subscription: $20 per year, single copy $5.95
Circulation: 16,000

A Perfect Wedding Guide
4001 S. Decatur Blvd., Ste. 37-482
Las Vegas, NV 89103
871-8083
Mark Shaffer, Publisher
Pocket-size guide published four times a year with wedding and honeymoon information and services. Available free.
Circulation: 60,000

The Ralston Report
2822 Ashby Ave.
Las Vegas, NV 89102
870-7997
John Ralston, Publisher
Statewide bi-weekly political newsletter by subscription only.
Subscription: $500

The Real Estate Book
4330 S. Valley View Blvd., Ste. 102
Las Vegas, NV 89123
367-7200
Freedom Enterprises Ltd.
Beverly Croft, Publisher
Pictures and information on homes, published monthly.
Subscription: $15
Circulation: 25,000

The Rebel Yell
4505 S. Maryland Pkwy., MSU 302
Las Vegas, NV 89154
895-3478
Univ. of NV Board of Regents
Darryl Richardson, Editor
UNLV student newspaper. Available free throughout the UNLV campus. Published twice weekly on Monday and Thursday from September through December and January through May.
Circulation: 6,000

Recycler Photo Classifieds
4440 S. Arville St., Ste. 1
Las Vegas, NV 89103
251-3730
Weekly classified ads. Offers free advertisement to private parties. Available at convenience stores and supermarkets
Price: $.50 per issue
Circulation: 35,000

Scope Magazine
820 S. Valley View Blvd.
Las Vegas, NV 89107
256-6388
Fax: 363-0461
Radiant City Publications
James P. Reza, Publisher
Bi-weekly alternative newspaper devoted to music, fashion and life-style and available free throughout Las Vegas.
Subscription: $20 for six monthly issues
Circulation: 40,000

Senior Press
3335 Wynn Rd.
Las Vegas, NV 89102
871-6780

Las Vegas Press
Bruce Spotleson, Publisher
Alternate for 40+ group events and happenings around town. Discount trips.
Subscription: $16
Circulation: 40,000 subscribers, 5,000 copies distributed free

Senior Spectrum
P. O. Box 40095
Reno, NV 89504
248-1240   1-800-253-3713
Chris & Connie McMullen, Publishers
Informing, serving and entertaining mature adults, published monthly.
Subscription: $10
Circulation: 40,000 in Las Vegas

Sentinel Voice
900 E. Charleston Blvd.
Las Vegas, NV 89104
380-8100
Griot Communications Group
Ramon Savoy, Publisher
Weekly newspaper, distributed Thursday, serving the African-American community of Las Vegas with local, state and national news concerning the black community.
Subscription: $25
Circulation: 7,000

Southern Nevada Realtor
Greater LV Assoc. of Realtors
1750 E. Sahara Ave.
Las Vegas, NV 89104
732-8177
Official publication of the Greater Las Vegas Association of Realtors. Monthly trade magazine sent free to realtors.
Subscription: Non-realtors $20
Circulation: 5,000

Southwest Lawn & Landscape
Plus Communications, Inc.
1455 E. Tropicana Ave., Ste. 175
Las Vegas, NV 89119
736-5958
Harry Sleight, Publisher
Monthly trade publication sent free to landscapers, nursery and property maintenance professionals.

A Taste of Vegas
236 S. Rainbow Blvd., Ste. 174
Las Vegas, NV 89128-5329
243-5922
John Bonds, Publisher
"Finally an honest Las Vegas dining guide you can trust." First monthly magazine focusing on restaurants and fashion. Official Comdex guide targeting all conventioneers.

Tiempo Libre
3320 Wynn Rd., Ste. D
Las Vegas, NV 89102
251-0726
Carlo Maffatt, Publisher
Weekly Spanish newspaper.
Circulation: 16,000

Today's Homes of Las Vegas
3139 S. Eastern Ave.
Las Vegas, NV 89109
731-4000
Harmon Publishing
Michael Abdoulah, Gen. Mgr.
Free monthly guide of homes for sale by realtors.
Circulation: 25,000

Trial Reporter
P.O. Box 8187
Phoenix, AZ. 85066-8187
385-7773
Andy Anderson, Publisher
Summarize civil jury trial. Published once a month.
Subscription: $275

Trip Sheet
2413 S. Eastern Ave., Suite 230
Las Vegas, NV 89104
641-3000
Craig Harris, Assoc. Editor
Monthly cabdrivers' newspaper.
Subscription: $24
Circulation: 5,000

Valley Explorer
1818 S. Industrial Rd., Ste. 105
Las Vegas, NV 89102
474-4187
Mark Steven Eisenberg, Publisher
Free newspaper for locals with entertainment suggestions in Las Vegas. Published the 1st and 3rd Thursday of every month, two-for-one coupons.
Circulation: 60,000

Valley Horse News
P. O. Box 34223
Las Vegas, NV 89133
658-0964
Fax: 658-0964
Available free at tack, feed and western stores.
Subscription: $24

Vegas People
P. O. Box 15477
Las Vegas, NV 89114
733-6072
Las Vegas International Press Club, Inc.
J. J. Cronan, Publisher/Editor
"Official publication for resort - casino industry employees"
Circulation: 10,000

MEDIA

ENTERTAINMENT GUIDES

After Dark in Vegas
3355 Spring Mountain Rd., Ste. 252
Las Vegas, NV 89102
367-1710
Angelo Contempo, Publisher
Weekly free adult entertainment guide.
Circulation: 25,000

Blues News
P. O. Box 27871
Las Vegas, NV 89126
251-9398   253-5252 (Blues Hotline)
Bill R. Cherry, Publisher/Editor
A non-profit organization dedicated to
"Keeping the Blues Alive."
Circulation: 3,000

Cityguide USA
535 E. St. Louis Ave.
Las Vegas, NV 89104
733-2880
Major Gateway Cities
Ken Tomono, Editor
Japanese language entertainment guide
for Las Vegas.
Subscription: $16 domestic or $41
international
Circulation: 30,000

Entertainment
6000 S. Eastern Ave., Ste. 4C
Las Vegas, NV 89119
795-0885   1-800-374-4464
Entertainment Publications
Published annually in October and
sold by charitable, educational and
community organizations.
Price: $30

Entertainment Today
2408 Chapman Dr.
Las Vegas, NV 89104
457-6808
Alisha Nelms, Publisher
Weekly entertainment guide distributed
on the Strip in hotels.
Subscription: $100 per year, $3 per issue
Circulation: 53,000

High Roller Magazine
3540 W. Sahara Ave., Ste. 164
Las Vegas, NV 89102
648-7709
Visitcom
Greg Wells, Publisher
Monthly free entertainment guide.
Circulation: 100,000+ per month

**The Insider Viewpoint of Las
Vegas**
9030 W. Sahara Ave., Ste. 423
Las Vegas, NV 89117
242-4482
Fax: 242-1028
Richard Reed, Publisher
Only complete free informational guide
in Las Vegas. Distributed at over 400
locations in Las Vegas.
Circulation: 100,000+ month *(worldwide)*
Subscription: $30 per year, single
issues $3

Las Vegas Advisor
3687 S. Procyon Ave.
Las Vegas, NV 89103
252-0655   1-800-244-2224
Fax: 252-0675
e-mail: lva@infi.net
Internet - http://www.infi.net/vegas/lva
Huntington Press
Anthony Curtis, Publisher
Monthly 12-page newsletter dedicated
to finding bargains offered by Las Vegas
hotel/casinos in lodging, dining, entertainment and gambling. Available by
subscription or single issues at the
Gambler's Book Club, 630 S. 11th St.
Subscription: $50 per year; single
copies $5.

**Las Vegas Lounge
Entertainment**
P. O. Box 80746
Las Vegas, NV 89180
256-3940
Fax: 228-1992
Las Vegas Lounge Entertainment
Daniel Gobel, Publisher
*"The ultimate bar and nightclub guide
in the entertainment capitol of the
world."* Available at Rebel and selected
Albertson's Stores.

Las Vegas Today
Desert Media Group
4440 S. Arville St., Ste. 12
Las Vegas, NV 89103
221-5000
Adam Slick, Editor
Hotel, casino, restaurant and entertainment
magazine published weekly. Available
free throughout Las Vegas at hotels and
motels, car rental agencies and other

tourist-oriented businesses.
Circulation: 50,000
Subscription: $75 per year, $2 per issue

Showbiz Magazine - Las Vegas Sun
800 S. Valley View Blvd.
Las Vegas, NV 89107
383-7185
Jim McGlasson, Mgr. Editor
Weekly TV and entertainment guide
available in hotels.

Show Time
900 S. Main St.
Las Vegas, NV 89101
224-5500
Capital Cities/ABC Inc.
Nifty Nickel Publications
Bill Davis, Publisher
Hotel entertainment and casino newspaper.
Published every Thursday and available
free throughout Las Vegas.
Subscription: $78

Spinzo Magazine
7056 Grasswood Dr.
Las Vegas, NV 89117
221-9295
Spinzo Inc.
Robert Spinzo, Editor
Published bi-monthly and focused on
Las Vegas with in-depth film and music
reviews. Also included is guide and
calendar of events.
Subscription: $12
Circulation: 30,000; 2,500 - 5,000 free
copies distributed

Today in Las Vegas
3626 Pecos/McLeod, Ste. 14
Las Vegas, NV 89121
385-2737
Lycoria Publishing Co.
Nicholas Naff, Publisher
Free weekly tourist entertainment and
dining magazine.
Circulation: 56,000

Tourguide Magazine
4440 S. Arville St., Ste. 12
Las Vegas, NV 89103
221-5000
Desert Media Group
Adam Slick, Editor
Weekly tourist magazine with informa-

tion on shows, dining, gaming and
events in Las Vegas. Copies are distributed each Friday to hotels and other
locations.
Subscription: $100
Circulation: 50,000

Vegas Times
900 E. Karen Ave., Ste. D111
Las Vegas, NV 89109
226-7731
Media Buying Services
Ron Macko, Publisher
Mail subscription: $24.95
Free community newspaper published
bi-weekly.

Vegas Visitor
P. O. Box 42249
Las Vegas, NV 89116
457-8689
Robert Supin, Publisher
Weekly hotel entertainment, gaming
and dining guide.
Subscription: $78 per year; mailed sin-
gle copies $3
Circulation: 25,000

Vegas Music & Film Magazine
2692 E. Florence St.
Las Vegas, NV 89120
736-3158
Adam Martinez, Publisher
Editorial coverage includes live music &
theater, monthly music reviews, new &
upcoming film releases, community
music.
Subscription: Free community newspaper
published monthly
Circulation: 80,000

What's On
4425 S. Industrial Rd.
Las Vegas, NV 89103
891-8811
What's On in Las Vegas Magazine
Murray Hertz, Publisher/Owner
Bi-weekly entertainment, restaurant,
features and television guide. Available
free at hotels and throughout Las Vegas.
Circulation: 150,000
Subscription: $34 per year, $4.95 per
issue by mail.

BOOKS OF LOCAL INTEREST

Amazing Las Vegas Trivia
Benjamin Blake & Hannah Erickson (1994)
Spiral-bound book of interesting Las Vegas trivia.
Price: $9.95

1996 American Casino Guide
Steve Paymar
Covers gambling facilities in 30 states, includes coupons. 176 pages
Price: $12.95

The Backyard Traveler Returns
Richard Moreno (1992)
62 outings in southern, eastern and historical Nevada. Paperback, 263 pages.
Price: $9.95

Bargain City
Anthony Curtis
Huntington Press (1995)
238-page guidebook and directory for "value-conscious casino consumers."
Price: $11.95

The Best of Nevada
Don and Betty Martin
Pine Cone Press (1992)
350-page book with information covering all of Nevada with more than 100 pages devoted to the Las Vegas area. This informative travel guide covers the major attractions such as hotels as well as beyond the casinos.
Price: $12.95

Bombs in the Backyard: Atomic Testing and American Politics
Costandina Titus
University of Nevada Press
Written by state senator and UNLV associate political science professor Dina Titus.
Price: $22.95

Casino
Nicholas Pileggi
Simon & Schuster
The story of the mob's downfall in Las Vegas.
Price: $24

The Cheapskate's Guide to Las Vegas
Connie Emerson
Carol Publishing Group (1995)
Presents sound advice on how to get maximum satisfaction in the "City Without Clocks" with minimum expenditure. From planning the trip to where to find penny slots. Paperback, 202 pages.
Price: $9.95

Comp City: A Guide to Free Las Vegas Vacations
Max Rubin
Huntington Press
A guide for anyone interested in earning casino freebies such as rooms, meals and shows. 300 pages.
Price: $39.95

The Complete Nevada Traveler
David W. Toll
Gold Hill Publishing Co. (1993)
A guide to Nevada and history of the different areas with hundreds of photos and maps with historical background and current travel information. Paperback, 256 pages.
Price: $15.95

Dining Out in Las Vegas
Elliot S. Krane
Elliot S. Krane and Associates, Inc. (1991)
Information and reviews on over 200 of Las Vegas' finest restaurants written by Elliot Krane, a long time Las Vegas restaurant critic.
Price: $8.95

Econoguide '96
Corey Sandler
Long Meadow Press (1995)
Chapters on shopping malls, buffets and food deals around Las Vegas, second half of book pertains to Reno-Tahoe area, 8 pages of discount coupons.
Price: $12.95

Experience Las Vegas
P.O. Box 35050
Las Vegas, NV 89133-5050
702-868-6310   800-881-7456
Fax: 838-4971
Internet Address:
www.experiencelasvegas.com
Bob Collins, Publisher
Todd Molinari, Vice Pres.
Phyllis Cohen, Editor
The largest and most complete full source reference directory on Las Vegas including accommodations, dining, entertainment and valuable relocation information covering southern Nevada. Published semi-annually. Available nationally in major book stores, locally wherever magazines and books are sold, at the Las Vegas Chamber of Commerce, or via mail order directly through Experience Las Vegas.
Price: $19.95

Family Fun "Las Vegas Style"
Services Unlimited (1995)
P. O. Box 28828
Las Vegas, NV 89126
Fun things for families to do in and around Las Vegas. Paperback, 160 pages.
Price: $10.95

Fear and Loathing in Las Vegas
Hunter S. Thompson
Fawcett Popular Library (1971)
The author's humorous story of his trip to Las Vegas to cover the Mint 400 Off-Road Race.
Price: $9.00

Fodor's Las Vegas
Fodor's Travel Publications
Random House, Inc. (1997)
Guidebook for tourists, includes Reno and Lake Tahoe.
Price: $13

Follow the Fun - Places to Go, Things to Do
Las Vegas Publishing House, Ltd.
P. O. Box 28887
Las Vegas, NV 89126
367-4939
100 page coloring book of things to do with kids in Las Vegas.
Price: $9.95

Frommer's Las Vegas
Mary Rakauskas
Simon & Schuster, Inc.
Guide for tourists containing descriptions of all major hotels in addition to sightseeing attractions. Paperback 230 pages.
Price: $13

Getting Established in Las Vegas
Ruth Catalano
Information and Assistance Network (1992)
3675 S. Rainbow Blvd.
Las Vegas, NV 89103
215-page book with information and personal advice for newcomers to Las Vegas.
Price: $7.95

The Hikers Guide to Nevada
Bruce Grubbs, Falcon Press (1994)
Statewide guide to Nevada's backcountry. Includes detailed descriptions, maps and photos of eighty hikes.
Price: $10.95

Hiking Las Vegas
Huntington Press
Anthony Curtis, Publisher
3687 S. Procyon Ave.
Las Vegas, NV 89103
252-0655
60 hikes within 60 minutes of the Strip, 200 pages.
Price: $17.95

Imperial Palace Auto Collection
Henry Rasmussen
Photos, overview and description of many of the more than 600 cars found in the Imperial Palace Auto Collection. Available only at the Imperial Palace Gift Shop, 96 pages.
Price: $4.95 paperback, $24.95 hardcover.

Las Vegas
Deke Castleman
Compass American Guide (1996)
History of Las Vegas and reviews of the hotels that made it what it is today. Points of interest and information, 292 pages.
Price: $16.95

Las Vegas Access
Access Press (1995)
Arranged by neighborhood so you can see at a glance where you are and what is around you. The text is color-coded according to the kind of place described. Paperback, 142 pages.
Price: $18

Las Vegas Agenda
Joyce Wisell
Fielding Travel Guides (1995)
The savvy guide to the capital of glitter and flash, where even breakfast is an extravaganza! This compact guide cuts through the chaos and takes you to the most exciting and offbeat places. Paperback, 178 pages.
Price: $14.95

Las Vegas & Reno Area Fun Guide
Derotha Sourwine
Gollehon Press Inc. (1990)
152-page pocket travel guide to the Las Vegas and Reno area.
Price: $3.95

Las Vegas: A Desert Paradise
Ralph J. Roske
Continental Heritage Press, Inc. (1986)
Large hardcover book tracing history of Las Vegas and business then and now written by a UNLV professor.
Price: $29.95

The Las Vegas Advisor Guide to Slot Clubs
Jeffery Compton
Huntington Press (1995)
1-800-244-2224
118-page book that takes you on a tour of southern Nevada slot clubs - separating the good from the bad and revealing strategies and insider tips that show you how to get more from the casinos than you ever imagined possible.
Price: $9.95

Las Vegas: As It Began - As It Grew
Stanley W. Paner
Nevada Publications
History of Las Vegas from the old Spanish Trail up through the building of Hoover Dam.
Price: $19.95 paperback, $29.95 hardcover

Las Vegas: Behind the Tables!
Barney Vinson
Gollehon (1986)
A behind the scenes look at casino management and stories.
Price: $4.95

Las Vegas: Behind the Tables! Part 2
Barney Vinson
Gollehon (1988)
Price: $5.95

Las Vegas Casino Employment Guide
Discover Las Vegas (1995)
4040 Pioneer Ave., Ste. 201
Las Vegas, NV 89102
247-4582
A complete and comprehensive book giving you inside tips on the Las Vegas casino job market. 96 pages.
Price: $12.95

Las Vegas: The Entertainment Capital
Don Knepp, Lane Publishing Co. (1987)
Menlo Park, Ca.
A sunset pictorial concentrating on the glamor of the entertainment industry in Las Vegas over the years, 288 pages.
Price: $14.95

Las Vegas Guide
Ed Kranmar/Avery Cardoza
Open Road Publishing (1995)
"We not only show you the unexplored Las Vegas - The world beyond the casinos - But the secrets within." 238 pages.
Price: $12.95

Las Vegas Ride Guide
Lamont J. Singley
Desert Quest Press (1995)
Maps and information for more than 30 trails and destinations that you can explore by mountain bike. Paperback, 79 pages.
Price: $8.95

Las Vegas With Kids
Barbara N. Land
Prima Publishing (1995)
Where to go, what to do in America's hottest family destination. This book contains a menu of child-appealing and family-oriented activities. Designed to help you plan your family adventures in Las Vegas. 251 pages.
Price: $12.95

BOOKS OF LOCAL INTEREST

Literary Las Vegas
Mike Tronnos (1995)
Twenty-four pieces about Las Vegas from various authors such as Tom Wolfe, Hunter S. Thompson, and Noel Coward. 358 pages.
Price: $12.95 paperback, $30 hardcover

The Nevada Adventure - A History
James W. Hulse
University of Nevada Press (1965)
Textbook once used by all schools and still used to teach the history of Nevada.
Price: $12.95

Nevada Ghost Towns & Mining Camps - Stan Paher's Illustrated Atlas
Stanley W. Paher
Nevada Publications
Illustrated atlas of the many old Nevada mining towns. Hardcover.
Price: $39.95

Nevada Ghost Towns & Mining Camps-Vol. 2 (Southern Nevada and Death Valley)
Stanley W. Paher (1993)
Illustrated atlas for the offbeat traveler with suggestions on where to explore in southern Nevada. Locations of ghost towns, old mines, caves, emigrant trails, gem fields and recreation areas. Contains 27 maps, 208 pages. Paperbound.
Price: $14.95

Nevada: Golden Challenge in the Silver State
Guy Shipler
Windsor Publications, Inc. (1990)
Big book concentrating mainly on the history of business in Nevada.
Price: $34.95

Nevada Handbook
Deke Castleman
Moon Publications, Inc. (1997)
Guide to Nevada off the beaten path. Comprehensive coverage of Nevada history, economy, politics, gambling, and prostitution. 400 pages.
Price: $16.95

Nevada - A History of Changes
David Thompson
Grace Dangberg Foundation (1986)
Nevada history. Contents cover the Indians, transportation, mining, ranching, government and gaming. 232 pages.
Price: $14.50

Nevada Place Names - A Geographical Directory
Helen S. Carlson
University of Nevada Press
Mixture of historical facts spiced with folklore on the origin of the names of numerous Nevada places.
Price: $16.95

Nevada Mountain Ranges
George Wuerthner (1992)
American & World Geographic Publishing
Whether you're planning a mountain trek or enjoying an armchair adventure, this is the best concise guide to Nevada's myriad mountain ranges. Paperback, 96 pages.
Price: $15.95

Nevada Towns & Tales, Volume I - North
Stanley W. Paher
Nevada Publications
Collection of stories and anecdotes by various authors on making Nevada what it is today.
Price: $14.95

Nevada Towns & Tales, Volume II - South
Stanley W. Paher
Nevada Publications
Collection of stories and anecdotes by various authors on making Nevada what it is today.
Price: $14.95

The Nevada Trivia Book
Richard Moreno
Gem Guides Book Company (1995)
Facts about interesting people, places and events that helped shape Nevada. Paperback, 206 pages.
Price: $9.95

Volume Two – Southern Nevada & Death Valley
Ghost Towns • Old Mines • Historic Places
Emigrant Trails • Placer Gold Sites • State Parks
Recreation Areas • Caves • Gem Fields • 4x4 Roads
★ 27 New Maps for Backroad Explorers ★

Nevada - True Tales From the Neon Wilderness
Jim Sloan
Eleven stories by a *Reno Gazette-Journal* reporter about Nevada's biggest events over the last few decades. 209 pages.
Price: $12.95

Nevada Wildlife Viewing Guide
Jeanne L. Clark
Falcon Press (1993)
This guidebook will lead you to fifty-five premier wildlife viewing areas and will better your chances of seeing wildlife once you get there. Included are detailed descriptions of each viewing site, maps and access information, helpful viewing tips, and more than forty color photographs. Paperback, 87 pages.
Price: $6.95

A Pictorial History of Las Vegas
Las Vegas Review-Journal
1111 W. Bonanza Rd.
Las Vegas, NV 89106
Hundred of photographs giving readers a glimpse of life in Las Vegas years ago - right up until today.
Price: $39.95

Planet Vegas
Collins Publishers (1995)
Coffee table book featuring over 200 color pictures taken by twenty top travel photographers. The photographers spent five days in May 1995 taking 6,000 shots; only the best 200 were printed in this book. 188 pages.
Price: $30.00

Resort City in the Sunbelt Las Vegas, 1930 - 1970
Eugene P. Moehring
University of Nevada Press (1989)
A scholarly study of the urbanization of Las Vegas written by a UNLV history professor.
Price: $29.95

Running Scared: The Life and Treacherous Times of Casino King Steve Wynn
John L. Smith
Unauthorized biography of Mirage Resorts Chairman Steve Wynn. 350 pages.
Price: $24

Senator Alan Bible & the Politics of the New West
Gary E. Elliott
University of Nevada Press
A 360 page, hardcover book with 18 photos which describes how Alan Bible worked to improve the National Park System.
Price: $34.95

Slot Machines: A Pictorial History of the First 100 Years
Marshall Fey
Liberty Belle Books

Pictures and history of coin operated gaming machines from the 1890s through today.
Price: $29.95 hardcover

Starting a Business in Las Vegas
Wendy Cole
Starting and choosing a business in Las Vegas; marketing, locations, franchises. 240 pages.
Price: $21.95

Touring Nevada: A Historic and Scenic Guide
Mary Ellen and Al Glass
University of Nevada Press (1983)
Well organized guide for people interested in the historical significance of the sights in Nevada. The book offers 34 one-day tours of Nevada, with the state divided into 7 geographic regions.
Price: $14.95

Ultimate Las Vegas and Beyond
David Stratton
Ulysses Press (1995)
Comprehensive coverage of the casino scene, including a chapter on gambling basics and strategies. The book also uncovers the little-known side of this community - the unique shopping districts, unusual restaurants, local arts and crafts shops - and takes the reader beyond the Strip to the surrounding areas. Paperback, 261-pages.
Price: $11.95

The Unofficial Guide to Las Vegas
Bob Sehlinger
Prentice Hall Travel (1996)
Tourist guide to Las Vegas. Uses a scale to rate hotels, casinos, entertainment and restaurants. Paperback 582 pages.
Price: $15.95

Vegas - Live and In Person
Jefferson Graham
Abbeville Press (1989)
Spotlights the people who live and work in Las Vegas and the history. Hardbound, 216 pages.
Price: $24.95

Viva Las Vegas - After-Hours Architecture
Alan Hess
Chronicle Books
History and review of Las Vegas architecture from the days of the first Strip hotel to the Mirage. Lots of photos.
Price: $18.95 paperback

The WPA Guide to 1930's Nevada
Russel R. Elliott
University of Nevada Press (1991)
First published in 1940, the text was compiled by workers of the Writers' Program of the Works Projects Administration (WPA) as a guide to Nevada.
Price: $15.95

Welcome to the Pleasuredome
David Spanmier (1992)
University of Nevada Press
A look at the excesses of Las Vegas, with profiles of the high rollers and the city's movers and shakers as well as those behind the scenes.
Price: $14.95

DIRECTORIES

Membership Guide
Las Vegas Chambers of Commerce
3720 Howard Hughes Pkwy.
Las Vegas, NV 89109
735-1616
Las Vegas Chamber of Commerce Member Directory, 210 pages.
Price: $24.95

The Community Services Directory (1997-1998)
HELP of Southern Nevada
953 E. Sahara Ave., Ste. 208
Las Vegas, NV 89104
369-4357
Community services directory covering areas of special assistance and help organizations. Listing includes agency address, personnel, agency function and eligibility requirements. Looseleaf binder.

Directions Official Street Guide
3105 Budding Blossom Ct.
Las Vegas, NV 89108
656-2161
Maureen R. Cooper, Publisher
Step by step directions to every street from Boulder City through North Las Vegas.
Price: $22.95

Distinguished Women in Southern Nevada
Carole Bellemyre, Publisher
Distinguished Publishing Co.
P. O. Box 12448
Las Vegas, NV 89112-0448
435-3838
Directory listing over 500 women in 75 professions. Published annually.

Distinguished Men in Southern Nevada
Carole Bellmyre, Publisher
Distinguished Publishing Co.
P. O. Box 12448
Las Vegas, NV 89112-0448
435-3838
Published annually. Pictorial, biographical directory lists more than 375 men in 73 professions.

Donnelley Directory
2030 W. Flamingo Rd., Ste. 220
Las Vegas, NV 89119
369-3700 / 1-800-533-5052
David Sobotko, Sr., Mktg. Mgr.
Donnelley Directory and Sprint Central Community action pages, white pages, yellow pages. Pages: 1,609+200-page white page business listings. Consists of

two volumes, one with white and yellow page business listings, and a second book with just residential listings. Semi-annual - Jan. & Jul.
Circulation: 850,000

Experience Las Vegas
P.O. Box 35050
Las Vegas, NV 89133-5050
702-868-6310   800-881-7456
Fax: 838-4971
Internet Address:
www.experiencelasvegas.com
Bob Collins, Publisher
Todd Molinari, Vice Pres.
Phyllis Cohen, Editor
The largest and most complete full source reference directory on Las Vegas including accommodations, dining, entertainment and valuable relocation information covering southern Nevada. Published semi-annually. Available nationally in major book stores, locally wherever magazines and books are sold, at the Las Vegas Chamber of Commerce, or via mail order directly through Experience Las Vegas.
Price: $19.95

The 1998 Front Boy Street Directory
Front Boy Service Co.
1149 S. Maryland Pkwy.
Las Vegas, NV 89104
384-7220
Detailed street maps book, available at some bookstores or at Front Boys. Published monthly.
Price: $21

Frontier Directory Co. of Nevada
6455 S. Industrial Rd., Ste. E
Las Vegas, NV 89118
451-4354
Brad Helland
Independent phone directory.

Hispanic Directories, Inc.
216 S. 7th St.
Las Vegas, NV 89101
384-5536
New official full-service Spanish telephone directory. Member of the Las Vegas Chamber of Commerce, Latin Chamber of Commerce and Better Business Bureau.

LAMBDA Business & Professional Association Directory 1998
QB Creative Services
792-6006
Directory of gay, lesbian and gay-friendly businesses in southern Nevada.
Circulation: 15,000

Las Vegas Living
5424 Aegean Way
Las Vegas, NV 89129
658-4102
Erin Cohen, Publisher
Homeowner's directory containing editorial articles.

1998 Las Vegas Perspective
Connie Brennan, Publisher
Connie & Associates
Sponsored by:
Las Vegas Review-Journal
Nevada Development Authority
Wells Fargo Bank
Published annually in May with key facts and figures about the Las Vegas metropolitan area. Available at any of the supporting companies listed.
Price: $25
Accompanying video also available:
Nevada Development Authority
3773 Howard Hughes Pkwy., Ste. 140 South,
Las Vegas, NV 89109
791-0000
Price: $25

Nevada International Trade Resource Directory
Commission on Economic Development
555 W. Washington Ave., Ste. 5400
Las Vegas, NV 89106
486-2700
Peter Cunningham
First point of reference for Nevada exporters who are looking for help in the field of international legal matters, language translation, international banking and other services.
Price: $35

Night Beat
3135 Industrial Rd.
Las Vegas, NV 89109
734-7223
Mike Peterson, Publisher
Gay classified monthly magazine.
Circulation: 150,000 annually

Recharger Magazine
4218 W. Charleston Blvd.
Las Vegas, NV 89102
870-0100
Recycling industry information for office products.
Circulation: 8,000+

Southern Nevada Business Directory
Center for Business & Econ. Research
4505 S. Maryland Pkwy.
Las Vegas, NV 89154
895-3191

Information on manufacturing and firms providing services in the southern Nevada area. Information about firm, company officials, SIC code, employees, addresses, phone numbers. 53,000 businesses.
Price: $75

Southern Nevada Hispanic Directory
709 N. Eastern Ave.
Las Vegas, NV 89101
383-0080
Eddie Escobedo, Jr., Publisher
Home delivery using R-J ad services. Free Spanish yellow pages.
Circulation: 60,000

UNLV
James Dickinson Library
Special Collections - Gaming Research Center
4505 S. Maryland Pkwy.
Las Vegas, NV 89154
895-3252
Information on Las Vegas and gaming in books, tapes, records, photographs, memorabilia, manuscripts and diaries.

VIP Directory 1998
Las Vegas Chamber of Commerce
3720 Howard Hughes Pkwy.
Las Vegas, NV 89109
735-1616
Lists chamber business and non-profit organizations and their contacts. Published annually in April.
Price: $24.95

Women's Yellow Pages
Carolyn Stephens, Publisher
3021 S. Valley View Blvd., Ste. 209
Las Vegas, NV 89102
362-6507
Directory of women-owned businesses and services.

Local Phone Book

Central Telephone - Nevada
Attn. Directory Department
330 S. Valley View Blvd.
Las Vegas, NV 89107
Phone 244-7400
Visa or MC orders: 1-800-877-7077
To order a local phone book from out of state, send $29.25 plus shipping and handling for yellow pages and $13.50 plus shipping and handling for white pages. There is no charge if you are a local resident.

BOOK STORES & NEWSSTANDS

Barnes & Noble
567 Stephanie St.
Henderson, NV 89014
434-1533
Pete Scott, Mgr.
Hours: Daily 9 am - 11 pm
27,000-square-foot store stocked with more than 150,000 titles and a music department with 50,000 CDs and tapes. Starbucks Cafe.

4505 S. Maryland Pkwy.
Las Vegas, NV 89154
Hours: Mon - Thu. 8 am - 11 pm; Sat. 11 am - 3 pm
College texts for UNLV, over 150,000

titles, newsstand and extensive children's department.

B Dalton Bookseller
3680 S. Maryland Pkwy.
Las Vegas, NV 89109
735-0008
Pat Morcinko
Hours: Mon. - Fri. 10 am - 9 pm; Sat. 11 am - 7 pm; Sun. 11 am - 6 pm

4300 Meadows Ln.
Las Vegas, NV 89107
878-4405
C. J. Rice
Hours: Mon. - Fri. 10 am - 9 pm; Sat. - Sun. 10 am - 6 pm

1300 W. Sunset Rd.
Henderson, NV 89014
434-1331
Travis Pugmire
Hours: Mon. - Sat. 10 am - 9 pm; Sun. 11 am - 6 pm
Credit Cards: MC, Visa, Discover, AMX

Bookstar
3910 S. Maryland Pkwy.
Las Vegas, NV 89119
732-7882.

4730 Faircenter Pkwy.
(Charleston and Decatur)
Las Vegas, NV 89102
877-1872

Hours: 9 am - 11 pm
Credit Cards: All major
Magazines, books and newspapers. Largest bookstores in Nevada with over 150,000 titles.

Book Warehouse
9155 Las Vegas Blvd. S.
Las Vegas, NV 89123
896-5344
Hours: Mon. - Sat. 10 am - 8 pm; Sun. 10 am - 6 pm
Credit Cards: MC, Visa
Factory outlet selling books at about one-fourth the regular price.

BOOK STORES & NEWSSTANDS

Borders Book Shop
2323 S. Decatur Blvd.
Las Vegas, NV 89102
258-0999

1445 W. Sunset Rd.
Henderson, NV 89014
433-6222
Hours: Mon. - Sat. 9 am - 11 pm: Sun.
9 am - 9 pm

2190 N. Rainbow Blvd.
Las Vegas, NV 89108
638-7866
Hours: Mon. - Sat. 9 am - 11 pm
Over 200,000 titles, newspapers and
magazines. Children's reading area and
a coffee bar. Weekly slate of performances,
readings and community meetings.

**Las Vegas International
Newsstand**
3900 Paradise Rd.
Las Vegas, NV 89109
796-9901
Evan Mader, Owner
Hours: Mon. - Fri. 9 am - 8 pm; Sat. -
Sun. 9 am - 7 pm

Largest selection of foreign and domestic newspapers and magazines in Las
Vegas. International candy and cigarettes, sports betting sheets and racing
forms.

Psychic Eye Book Shops
953 E. Sahara Ave.
Las Vegas, NV 89104
369-6622

4810 W. Spring Mtn. Rd.
Las Vegas, NV 89102
368-7785

3315 E. Russell Rd.
Las Vegas, NV 89120
451-5777
Robert Leysen, Owner
Hours: Mon. - Fri. 10 am - 9 pm; Sat. 10
am - 8:30 pm; Sun. noon - 6 pm
Credit Cards: Visa, MC
Psychic reading, astrology, new age self help.

**Readmore Magazine &
Book Stores**
2560 S. Maryland Pkwy.
Las Vegas, NV 89109
732-4453

6154 W. Flamingo Rd.
Las Vegas, NV 89103
362-3762.

4454 N. Rancho Dr.
Las Vegas, NV 89130
645-6644
Hours: Mon. - Sat. 9 am - 8 pm; Sun. 10
am - 5 pm
Credit Cards: MC, Visa
Large selection of magazines, paper-
backs and books.

UNLV Book Store
4505 S. Maryland Pkwy.
Las Vegas, NV 89154
895-3290
Doug Shaffer, Mgr.
Hours: Mon. - Thu. 7:30 am - 7 pm; Fri.
7:30 am - 4 pm; Sat. 11 am - 3 pm *(hours
vary during school year)*
Credit Cards: MC, Visa, AMX, Discover
New and used textbooks, books, UNLV
collectibles and clothing.

Waldenbooks
Meadows Mall
4300 Meadows Ln.
Las Vegas, NV 89107
870-4914

Hours: Mon. - Fri. 10 am - 9 pm; Sat. -
Sun. 10 am - 6 pm
Credit Cards: MC, Visa, AMX

Fashion Show Mall
3200 Las Vegas Blvd. S.
Las Vegas, NV 89109
733-1049
Greg Hertzog, Dist. Mgr.
Hours: Mon. - Fri. 10 am - 9 pm; Sat. 10
am - 7 pm; Sun. noon - 6 pm
Credit Cards: MC, Visa, AMX

USED BOOKSTORES

**Academy Fine Books &
Antiques**
2026 E. Charleston Blvd.
Las Vegas, NV 89104
Hours: Mon. - Sat. 10 am - 4 pm, Sun. 10
am - 2 pm
Vintage paperbacks, autographs, posters
and documents.

Albion Book Company
2466 E. Desert Inn Rd.
Las Vegas, NV 89121
792-9554
Mike Burdo
Hours: 10 am - 6 pm
Fine used, out-of-print and hard-to-find
books. Daily Grind Espresso Bar located
inside bookstore. Books bought and sold.

Book Magician
2202 W. Charleston Blvd.
Las Vegas, NV 89102
384-5938
Hours: Mon. - Sat. 9 am - 10 pm; Sun.
11 am - 7 pm
Military, science fiction and psychology.

Book Mart
512 Las Vegas Blvd. S.
Las Vegas, NV 89101
385-2841
Hours: Mon. - Sat. 9 am - 4 pm
Trade paperbacks.

Book Round-Up
858 S. Boulder Hwy.
Henderson, NV 89015
565-0665

Betty Wages
Hours: Mon. - Sat. 9:30 am - 5:30 pm
Over 30,000 new and used paperbacks.

The Book Shoppe
2232 S. Nellis Blvd., Ste. G1
Las Vegas, NV 89104
641-1155
Jeff Baker
Hours: Sun. - Thu. 10 am - 6 pm; Fri. -
Sat. 10 am - 8 pm
New and used books, special orders.

Bookends
3920 W. Charleston Blvd.
Las Vegas, NV 89102
878-9290
Hours: Mon. - Sat. 10 am - 6 pm; Sun.
noon - 6 pm
Fine used hardbacks and paperbacks,
bookbinding and restoration done
on premises.

Booklovers
3142 N. Rainbow Blvd.
Las Vegas, NV 89108
658-8583
Pat Gallotta
Hours: Mon. - Fri. 10 am - 7 pm; Sat. 10
am - 6 pm; Sun. noon - 5 pm
Very broad selection of hardbacks and
paperbacks. Buy, sell and trade.

Brats Book Exchange
4260 E. Charleston Blvd.
Las Vegas, NV 89104
459-0027

Hours: Mon. - Sat. 9:30 am - 5 pm
Sci-fi, fantasy, true crime non-fiction
and autobiographies.

Dead Poet Books
3858 W. Sahara Ave.
Las Vegas, NV 89105
227-4070
Rich & Linda Scalzi
Hours: Mon. - Sat. 10 am - 6 pm; Sun.
noon - 5 pm
Over 10,000 hardback and paperback books.

Ellens Books
312 E. Charleston Blvd.
Las Vegas, NV 89104
382-1646
Hours: Sun - Fri. 10 am - 6 pm
Children's books, cookbooks, karate,
horror and mysteries.

Gundy's Book World
1442 E. Charleston Blvd.
Las Vegas, NV 89104
385-6043
Sol Levco
Hours: Mon. - Fri. 10 am - 5:30 pm; Sat.
10 am - 3 pm
Hardcover and large selection of used
magazines.

Paperback Exchange
6700 W. Charleston Blvd., Ste. D
Las Vegas, NV 89102
870-5050
Jean Chatterton

Hours: Mon. - Sat. 10 am - 5 pm
Used paperbacks 1/2 off and hardcover
books, tapes, new CDs.

Parkland Books
3661 S. Maryland Pkwy.
Las Vegas, NV 89109
732-4474
Edwin Rothfuss
Hours: Mon. - Sat. 10 am - 6 pm
Out of print, old and rare books.

Plaza Books
7380 S. Eastern Ave.
Las Vegas, NV 89123
263-2692
John Hathaway
Hours: Mon. - Fri. 10 am - 7 pm; Sat. -
Sun. noon - 6 pm
Books on all subjects; rare and out-of-
print books. Large selection of fiction
and non-fiction. Trade and sell.

Rebelbooks
4440 S. Maryland Pkwy.
Las Vegas, NV 89119-7534
796-4141
Richard Field
Hours: Mon. - Thu. 8 am - 7 pm; Fri. 8
am - 4 pm; Sat. - Sun. 10 am - 4 pm
UNLV course required textbooks, medical technical and reference.

Pets & Animals

Nevada has abundant wildlife, with over 560 varieties of mammals, birds and reptiles. The state has some 23,000 wild horses and burros, more than half the population in the entire nation. Several sanctuaries in the Las Vegas area provide a glimpse of these area inhabitants. The Gilcrease Nature sanctuary provides numerous pathways and lush surroundings in which visitors may view many habitats for small animals and birds. Another favorite among is the Zoological Botanical Park, which is home to many varieties of wildlife, including the only Barbary apes available for viewing in the United States. Although the park has a large assortment of exotic animals, it also houses many of the area's own wildlife, including the threatened desert tortoise, and coyotes.

Aside from the many wild creatures, southern Nevada is home to a vast number of domesticated animals. To keep the population of these animals under control, there are limitations on the number of licensed animals allowed per household. Currently the state allows up to three dogs and three cats per family. Several care centers and organizations, including the Dewey Animal Care Center, provide low cost spaying and neutering for family pets. Other area organizations, such as the Animal Foundation of Nevada, offer inexpensive shot clinics throughout the year.

Area pet stores supply everything from the usual dogs, cats and birds to such exotic pets as Iguanas, prairie dogs and a vast variety of reptiles, spiders and amphibious creatures. Many local pet stores also provide in-house veterinarian care as well as grooming,making owning your pet an easy and enjoyable experience.

PET LAWS & ANIMAL CONTROL

PET LAWS

Licenses are required for all dogs and cats in Clark County. Residents are limited to three adult dogs and three adult cats per household. Special pet fancier's licenses are available allowing up to six dogs and six cats. All dogs must be restrained by leash; within the city, cats must be restrained by leash. Rabies shots are required every two years for both dogs and cats. Both dogs and cats must have rabies and license tags.

LICENSE FEES

Dogs: $20 for two year license for unaltered; $8 for altered.

Cats: $10 for one year license for unaltered; $4 for altered.

ANIMAL CONTROL

Dewey Animal Care Center
Clark County Animal Shelter
4800 W. Dewey Dr.
Las Vegas, NV 89118
873-3455
Dr. Joseph Freer, Dir.
Dewey Animal Care Center houses strays found in all of Clark County. Also provides adoption service, spay and neuter operations and shots. 300 animals average on hand at all times; handles 6,000 adoptions per year and reunites about 6,000 lost animals with their owners. In unincorporated Clark County in 1996-1997 fiscal year took in 15,200 dogs and cats of which 2,994 were adopted, 2,031 were reunited with their owners, 8,209 were euthanized and 1,733 were DOA. Animals are held six days before being destroyed. *Adopt a dog $36.00 regardless of sex and shots are included. Without shots $22.00 for dogs and $17.00 for cats. Adopt a cat $32 regardless of sex, shots included.*
Hours: Mon. 11 am - 3 pm; Tue. - Sat. 11 am - 5 pm

Boulder City Animal Control
1390 San Felipe Dr.
Boulder City, NV 89005
293-9283
Christina Jones, Supvr.
Animals for adoption. Animal control facility with full time officer. Mon. - Fri. call for hours.

City of Las Vegas
Animal Control
3150 Stewart Ave.
Las Vegas, NV 89101
229-6348
Sgt. Charlie Burger, Supvr.
Enforces animal control ordinances in the City of Las Vegas.

Clark County Animal Control
Field Service
4800 Dewey Dr.
Las Vegas, NV 89118
455-7710
Joe Boteilho, Mgr.

Henderson Animal Shelter & Animal Control
390 W. Athens Ave.
Henderson, NV 89015
565-2033
Vicki Cameron, Adm.
Hours: Mon. - Fri. 9 am - 4 pm; Sat. Noon - 4 pm
Animals for adoption.

> **UNWANTED ANIMALS**
> 20,000 unwanted dogs and cats were destroyed in Clark County in 1996. This figure does not include animals destroyed last year by private veterinarians.

ORGANIZATIONS and CLUBS

ORGANIZATIONS

The Animal Foundation of Nevada
700 N. Mojave Rd.
Las Vegas, NV 89101
384-3333
Mary Herro, Pres.
Hours: 11 am - 5 pm
This non-profit center provides low cost spay and neutering and shots. Fees range from $10.00 to neuter a male cat and $20.00 to spay a female cat; $20.00 - $25.00 to neuter a male dog and $25.00 - $40.00 to spay a female dog. Low cost shots: cats 4 in 1 - $8.00; dogs 7 in 1 - $18.00. Operates the Second Chance Adoption Center. Dogs $50.00 and Cats $35.00. Specials offered at various times.

Betty Honn's Animal Village
Animal Adoptions Ltd.
1442 Bermuda Rd.
Henderson, NV 89009
361-2484 361-5137
Dogs and cats are available for adoption by appointment. A cash donation is required to defray the costs.

Bonnie Springs
1 Bonnie Springs Ranch
Old Nevada, NV 89004
875-4191
Bonnie Levinson, Owner
Hours: 10 am - 6 pm
Admission: Free
Petting zoo with over 30 different species, exotic birds, porcupine, buffalo, deer, llamas, squirrels, foxes, bobcat, coatimundi, goat, pigs, sheep, wolf, lynx and big horn sheep.

Clark County Animal
Advisory Board
4800 W. Dewey Dr.
Las Vegas, NV 89118
455-7712
Business office for animal control; reviews laws pertaining to Clark County animal ordinances and makes recommendations on changes to the board of commissioners.

Dept. of Interior Bureau of Land Management
4765 W. Vegas Dr.
Las Vegas, NV 89108
647-5000
Gary McFadden
Debbie Palmira 452-5853
Call for information on adopting wild horses and burros in Nevada. It is estimated that there are 22,796 wild horses and 687 wild burros on public land in Nevada. (In the entire United States there are only 35,286 wild horses and 6,852 wild burros.)
Adoption Fee: Horse $125.00, burro $75.00

Gilcrease Nature Sanctuary
8103 Racel St.
Las Vegas, NV 89131
645-4224
Hours: Wed. - Sun. 11 am - 3 pm or by appointment for large groups
Admission: $3.00 adults, $1.00 children 6 and older, under 5 free.
Non-profit safe haven for exotic game birds and wildlife. Aviaries and small habitats for birds and animals, all in a beautiful setting filled with trees and flower-lined pathways. The sanctuary is home to the Wild Wing Project, Southern Nevada's only non-profit, federally licensed wildlife rehabilitation organization. School tours available.

Keepers of the Wild
4800 W. Dewey Dr.
Las Vegas, NV 89118
Jonathan Kraft, Owner
5.5-acre private exotic animal sanctuary

Las Vegas Valley Humane Society
2250 E. Tropicana Ave., Ste. 19
Las Vegas, NV 89119
434-2009
Judith Ruiz, Pres.
Non-profit organization devoting much of its efforts to pet overpopulation and animal welfare; adoption center. Adopts out of Petco at 2091 N. Rainbow Blvd. on Fri., Sat. and Sun. 11 am - 4 pm and Thu. 1 pm - 6 pm. Also works out of Sunset Eastern Animal Hospital.

Mirage Dolphin Habitat & Secret Garden
Mirage
3400 Las Vegas Blvd. S.
Las Vegas, NV 89109
791-7111
Julie Wignall, Dir. of Animal Care
Hours: Mon. - Fri. 11 am - 5:30 pm; Sat. - Sun. 10 am - 5:30 pm
Admission: $10.00, children under 10 free with adult; Wed. $5.00.
The $14 million, 2.5 million gallon salt water pool outdoor habitat houses seven Atlantic bottlenose dolphins. The Secret Garden contains 6 rare animal breeds including white lions and tigers.

National Wild Horse Association
P. O. Box 12207
Las Vegas, NV 89112
452-5853
Roberta Coleman, Pres.
Volunteer group devoted to the preservation of wild horses and burros.

The Nature Conservancy
1771 E. Flamingo Rd., Ste. 111B
Las Vegas, NV 89119
737-8744
Steve Hobbs, State Dir.
International organization devoted to preserving the environment.

Nevada Board of Veterinary Medical Examiner
1005 Terminal Way
Reno, NV 89502
322-9422

Nevada Society for the Prevention of Cruelty to Animals
4800 W. Dewey Dr.
Las Vegas, NV 89118
897-SPCA • 873-7722
Jennifer Palombi, Pres.
The only "no kill" animal sanctuary where a home-like atmosphere will be provided for the animals. The SPCA adopts out dogs for $50.00 and cats for $25.00. They are spayed and neutered and have received all necessary tests and shots.

PAVE
P.O. Box 27145
Las Vegas, NV 89126
367-6231
Veronica McPhelan, Pres.
All volunteer non-profit anti-vivisection organization. Incorporated 1984; quarterly newsletter, call for copy. Monthly public meetings at Border's Book Store on W. Sahara, 4th Thursday of each month at 5:30 pm; public invited.

Plant World Nursery
5301 W. Charleston Blvd.
Las Vegas, NV 89102
878-9485
Hours: Mon. - Sat. 8 am - 6 pm; Sun. 9 am - 5 pm
Besides being a nursery, Plant World has a bird aviary with hundreds of birds from parakeets to quail.

Red Rock Audubon Society
P. O. Box 96691
Las Vegas, NV 89193
363-6615
John Bialecki, Pres.
Conservation group active during fall and winter months. Monthly meetings and field trips; public invited.

Sierra Club
P. O. Box 19777
Las Vegas, NV 89132
363-3267 647-5459
Dave Brickey, Pres.
Group's function is to preserve and protect wild lands. Hiking, backpacking, skiing, pot-lucks and other activities.

Tortoise Group
739-7113
Betty Burge
739-8043
The desert tortoise is listed by the federal government as a "threatened species." The Tortoise Group offers homeless pet tortoises for adoption in hopes of stopping the poaching of wild ones.
Adoption information **739-7113**
Information about the Desert Tortoise **383-TORT**
Tortoise Rescue Service **593-9027**

Wild Wing Project, Inc.
6010 W. Cheyenne Ave., Ste. 15
Las Vegas, NV 89108
658-0166
Rescues and rehabilitates ill, injured and orphaned wild birds and wild animals. If

you have an injured wild bird, call to ask which vet that works with Wild Wing is closest to you. Holds open house once or twice a year at the Gilcrease Bird Sanctuary so the public can see the wild birds being rehabilitated.

Zoological Botanical Park
1775 N. Rancho Dr.
Las Vegas, NV 89106
648-5955
Pat Dingle
Hours: 9 am - 4:30 pm
Admission: Adults $5.00; children (2-12) and seniors (60+) $3.00
Exotic animals including rare barbary apes, golden eagles, a bengal tiger, jungle cats, an African lion, a large family of African green grivet monkeys and a collection of exotic birds and talking parrots. Western wildlife include coyotes, badgers, raccoons, lizards and desert tortoises; a children's petting zoo features goats, sheep, a llama, ducks and peacocks that can be fed. About 130 animals reside at the zoo.

PET CLUBS

Southern Nevada Dog Fancier's Park

5800 E. Flamingo Rd.
Las Vegas, NV 89122
564-3647
Terry Bounty 567-1227
15 acre park that serves as the site of various dog shows.

Black Mountain Kennel Club
Betty Heskett - 451-6954
Terri Bounty - 565-1277
Shows in April and October at Dog Fancier's Park.

Nevada Dog Fancier's Association
Clark Hazlett, Pres.
Jean Sharp - 458-4075
Meets 4th Monday of the month at 7:30 pm at Dog Fancier's Park.

Silver State Kennel Club
Peggy Falcone - 878-8683 or 258-SSKC
Shows held in April and October at the Silver Bowl

Vegas Valley Dog Obedience Club
368-0656
Sandy Burns, Pres.
Meets the first Tuesday of the month at Hines Ranch, 2614 Lindell Rd. at 8 am.

BOARDING & PET SITTING

Photo: Photoechnik International

BOARDING KENNELS

Animal Inn Kennels
3460 W. Oquendo Rd.
Las Vegas, NV 89118
736-0036
John A. Schoumaker
Hours: Mon. - Fri. 8 am - 6 pm; Sat. - Sun. 8 am - 5 pm
Rates: Cats $6.50, small $11.00, medium $13.00 and large dogs $15.00. Boarding, training, grooming.

Arkennels
1651 N. Rancho Dr.
Las Vegas, NV 89106
648-0414
Hours: Mon. - Fri. 7:30 am - 6 pm; Sat. 7:30 am - 1 pm
Rates: Cats $7.50, small dogs $8.50, large dogs $12.50, x-large $20.00.

Chaparral Animal Spa
2105 E. Alexander Rd.
N. Las Vegas, NV 89030
649-6383

Hours: 8 am - 5 pm; Fri. 8 am - 6 pm; Sun. 1 pm - 3 pm
Rates: Cats $6.50, small dogs $10.00, medium dogs $11.00, large dogs $12.00, x-large $13.00.

Paws 'N Claws Animal Lodge
640 Eastgate Rd.
Henderson, NV 89015
565-7297
Hours: Mon. - Fri. 8:30 am - 5:30 pm; Sat. 9 am - 4 pm
Rates: Cats $6.50, small dogs $9.50, medium dogs $10.00, large dogs $10.50, x-large $11.00 (weekly discounts).

Sue Zan Kennels
1788 N. Gateway Rd.
Las Vegas, NV 89115
452-7305
Susie Sadler
Hours: Mon. - Sat. 9:30 am - 6 pm; Sun. 10 am - noon
Rates: Cats $7.00 and dogs $8.00 - $12.00 (weekly rates available).
Will board anything that flies, swims, slithers or walks. Pick-up and delivery available. National and international certified master groomer and certified animal hygienist. Must have current proof of vaccination.

The Cat's Cradle
3310 E. Charleston Blvd.
Las Vegas, NV 89104
457-0370
Hours: Sat., Mon., Tue., Thu., Fri. 10 am - 5 pm
Exclusive cat hotel, home visits & specialty gifts

Tolgate Kennels
2670 Betty Ln.
Las Vegas, NV 89115
643-1015
Hours: Mon. - Sat. 8 am - 5 pm; Sun. and holidays 3 pm - 5 pm
Rates: Cats $7.50, dogs $10.00 - $12 .00 depending on breed.

PET SITTING SERVICE

Animal Crackers
564-PETS • 564-7387
Total in home pet care. Licensed, bonded and insured.

Cathy's Critters
632 Burton Ave.
Henderson, NV 89015
566-6947
Hours: 24 hours
Rates: Locally - 3 visits $15.00, other areas call for price and services. Licensed and bonded - care for all animals.

Critter Caravan
436-2823
Petsitting, daily pet care and pet transport

Home Sitting of Southern Nevada
243-9802
"Personalized Pet Care", plant care, mail pick-up, grocery shopping, elderly care and airport runs - 24 hours

In Charge Home Pet Sitting Service
7570 W. Flamingo Rd., Ste. 102
Las Vegas, NV 89117
870-0055
Jessie Reece, Pres.
Run by active seniors, 24 hour care or daily visits.

Pals for Pets
254-3485
Loving care for all types of pets.

Patti's Pampered Pet
873-7716
Professional and loving care in town or out of town.

Pet's Bed & Breakfast
395-0100
Bring your pet to our home. Elite and caring atmosphere.

PUBLICATIONS

Nevada Dog Fanciers Pet Guide
4305 Sawyer St.
Las Vegas, NV 89108
647-1983
Don Ploke. Editor/Pres.
Issued by the Nevada Dog Fanciers Association; lists all veterinarians, many breeders and all dog clubs in S. Nevada.

Nevada Dog Fanciers 1997 - 1998 Pet Owners Guide

BIRDWATCHING

If you like birdwatching, Sunset Park attracts mallards and geese that wait for people to feed them at the lake. Floyd Lamb State Park, which has a series of small lakes, is home to herons, egrets, cormorants, American coots and pied-billed grebes.

The Red Rock Audubon Society publishes a book, "Southern Nevada Birds" which sells for $4.00.

The Flamingo Hilton is home to 12 African penguins, a dozen Chilean flamingoes and sacred ibises and wood ducks in its 15 acre tropical wildlife habitat and pool area.

PETS & ANIMALS

SHOPPING FOR PETS

NEVADA ANIMALS

There are more than 370 species of birds, 129 species of mammals and 64 species of reptiles in Nevada.

Artistic Pets
6310 W. Flamingo Rd.
Las Vegas, NV 89103
362-4408
Cats, AKC puppies, ferrets, hamsters, guinea pigs, birds and exotics.

Aquarium World
2539 Wigwam Pkwy.
Henderson, NV 89014
435-FISH • 435-3474
Tropical and saltwater fish & reef maintenance service, equipment and supplies.

Aquatic Dreamscapes
2710 S. Maryland Pkwy.
Las Vegas, NV 89109
731-FISH • 731-3474
Newest & largest selection of marine and fresh water fish in Las Vegas. Live and frozen food.

Birds Nest
4970 S. Arville St.
Las Vegas, NV 89118
889-8303
Huge selection of exotic birds in stock; also boarding and grooming, cages, toys and hand-fed babies.

Exotic Pets
2105 N. Decatur Blvd.
Las Vegas, NV 89108
631-7387
Ken & Janice Foose, Owners
Hours: Mon. - Sat. 10 am - 7 pm;
Sun. noon - 5 pm
Anything from antelope to zebra can be ordered with 100% health guarantee. Specializing in reptiles and amphibians. Also birds, kangaroos, hedgehogs, possum, ferrets, sugar gliders, prairie dogs.

F.I.S.H.
300 Bruce St.
Las Vegas, NV 89109
388-0080
One of the largest selections in Nevada. Expanded pond, plants and aquariums.

Frisky Pet Center
Boulevard Mall
3548 S. Maryland Pkwy.
Las Vegas, NV 89109
737-5118
Pet supplies, live animals including puppies and kittens.

Jungleland Pets
667 N. Stephanie St.
Henderson, NV 89014
454-4677
Specializing in tropical fish, reptiles, birds and small animals. Full line of supplies.

Meadows Pet Center
4300 Meadows Ln., Ste. 2145
Las Vegas, NV 89107
870-0939
Fred Palmieri, Pres.
Largest pet store in Nevada.

Pet Kingdom
2431 E. Tropicana Ave.
Las Vegas, NV 89121
451-9123
Dogs, reptiles, monkeys, ferrets, hedgehogs, chinchillas, cats and many more. Complete line of pet supplies.

Petco (4 locations)
6125 W. Tropicana Ave.
Las Vegas, NV 89103
253-9828
Hours: Mon. - Sat. 9 am - 9 pm;
Sun. 10 am - 7 pm
Credit Cards: MC, Visa

Petsmart (4 locations)
2419 E. Tropicana Ave.
Las Vegas, NV 89121
451-9441
Hours: Mon. - Sat. 8 am - 9 pm,
Sun. 11 am - 6 pm
Credit Cards: MC, Visa, Discover

Puppies Plus
7380 S. Eastern Ave., Ste. 117
Las Vegas, NV 89123
269-1819
Puppies, kittens, reptiles, tame hand-fed birds and fish.

VETERINARIANS

All have 24 hour emergency service.

Animal Kindness Veterinary
4909 E. Bonanza Rd.
Las Vegas, NV 89110
453-2990
Jay Holt, DVM
Hours: Mon. - Fri. 7:30 am - 6 pm;
Sat. 7:30 am - 5 pm; Sun. 9 am - 11 am

Bonanza Cat Hospital
5000 E. Bonanza Rd.
Las Vegas, NV 89110
438-7000
Linda Steelman, DVM
Hours: Mon. - Fri. 7:30 am - 6 pm;
Sat. 9 am - 5 pm

Black Mountain Animal Hospital
1000 S. Boulder Hwy.
Henderson, NV 89015
565-6558
Randy Winn, DVM
Hours: Mon. - Fri. 7 am - 7 pm;
Sat. 7:30 am - 5 pm; Sun. 8 am - 4 pm

Gentle Doctor Animal Hospital
1550 S. Rainbow Blvd.
Las Vegas, NV 89102
259-9200
Dr. Gerald Pribyl, DVM
Hours: Mon. - Fri. 7:30 am - 6 pm;
Sat. 8 am - 4 pm; Sun. 8 am - 10 am

Green Valley Animal Hospital
6150 Mountain Vista Rd.
Henderson, NV 89014

456-4440
Bradley Gilman, DVM
Hours: Mon. - Fri. 7 am - 7 pm;
Sat. 7 am - 5 pm; Sun. 8 am - 5 pm

Lake View Animal Hospital
2939 Lake East Dr.
Las Vegas, NV 89117
254-8200
Mark S. Iodence, DVM
Hours: Mon. - Fri. 7:30 am - 6 pm;
Sat. 8 am - 4 pm; Sun. 8 am - 10 am

Sahara Pines Animal Hospital
6533 W. Sahara Ave.
Las Vegas, NV 89102
876-7580
Douglas Gensel, DVM
Hours: Mon. - Fri. 7 am - 6 pm;
Sat. 7 am - 5 pm

Summerlin Animal Hospital
8564 Del Webb Blvd.
Las Vegas, NV 89134-8567
255-8499
Frank Reynolds, Pres.
Hours: Mon. - Fri. 7:30 am - noon,
2 pm - 6 pm; Sat. 8 am - 2 pm

Warm Springs Animal Hospital
2500 W. Warm Springs Rd.
Las Vegas, NV 89119
361-2500
Hours: Mon. - Fri. 8 am - 6 pm
Equine and small animal medicine and surgery.

PET GROOMING

A Little Big Dog
2548 E. Desert Inn Rd.
Las Vegas, NV 89121
735-1769
"Your pet will be doggone happy" and cats, too.

Bark Avenue
5645 S. Eastern Ave.
Las Vegas, NV 89119
798-6694
If your dog isn't becoming to you, he should be coming to us. Fluff dry and hand scissoring.

Desert Breeze
3655 S. Durango Dr.
Las Vegas, NV 89117
256-6986
Over 20 years' experience. "Special care for your special pet."

Doggie Den
4347 Stewart Ave.
Las Vegas, NV 89110
452-9222
Since 1978, all-breed grooming.

Dorian's Cutting Edge
486 S. Pecos Rd.
Las Vegas, NV 89121
454-9777
Medicated bath, tick dipping and hand-stripping - no sedative.

Professional Grooming
2529 E. Desert Inn Rd.
Las Vegas, NV 89121
734-1033
No sedatives, medicated bath and tick dips. Bishon Frise experts.

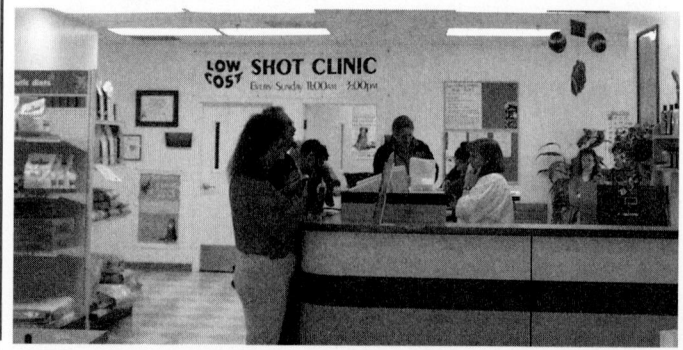

INDEX

INDEX

INDEX

INDEX

INDEX

INDEX

INDEX

INDEX

INDEX

INDEX

INDEX

INDEX

INDEX

INDEX of MAPS, CHARTS & GRAPHS

MAPS

INDEX OF ADVERTISERS

OVER 100,000 SQUARE FEET OF LAS VEGAS CASINO FUN & GAMES

America's Loosest Slots, Three Years in a Row - Casino Player magazine annual ranking

Fremont's Second Street Grill - Top 25 Las Vegas Restaurants - 1997 Zagat Survey

Award Winning Porters, Ales, and Lagers at Downtown Las Vegas' Only Microbrewery

With its Pacific Island flavor, the California Hotel & Casino caters to the Las Vegas visitor with a taste for tropical adventure. The Cal's first-class amenities include four distinctive restaurants and over 1,100 of some of the most liberal slots in America.

Glittering at the heart of the Fremont Street Experience, the Fremont Hotel & Casino has been a symbol of Las Vegas glamour for over 40 years. One of the secrets of the Fremont's longevity is their incredible restaurants, including the Second Street Grill –one of America's finest.

Set in the splendor of the Victorian era, the unique Main Street Casino, Hotel & Brewery is home to a fabulous collection of antiques, artifacts, and collectibles. Guests can enjoy downtown's only microbrewery, try a hancrafted beer, enoy live gaming action, or dine in elegance.

- **781 Deluxe Rooms & Suites**
- **21, Craps, Pai Gow & Live Keno**
- **1,100 Slots, Video Poker & Keno**
- **Sports Book**
- **Redwood Bar & Grill**
- **Pasta Pirate Restaurant**
- **24 Hour Restaurant & Snack Bar**
- **Swimming Pool**
- **Banquet/Meeting Facilities**

1-800-634-6255

- **447 Newly Remodeled Rooms**
- **1,100 Slots, Video Poker & Keno**
- **21, Craps, Pai Gow & Live Keno**
- **Race & Sports Book**
- **Second Street Grill**
- **Paradise Buffet**
- **Tony Roma's, Famous for Ribs**
- **Lanai Cafe, Chinese Specialties**
- **Banquet/Meeting Facilities**

1-800-634-6182

- **406 Deluxe Rooms & Suites**
- **21, Craps, Pai Gow & Live Keno**
- **900 Slots, Video Poker & Keno**
- **Garden Court Buffet**
- **Pullman Grille Steakhouse**
- **Triple-7 BrewPub**
- **Victorian Themed Casino**
- **Over $4 Million in Antiques**
- **Acres of Free Parking**

1-800-465-0711

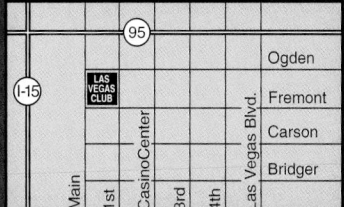

Hopes, dreams,
bricks and mortar.
What is it that
makes a home?

It's wedding photos. And school pennants.
And rooms designed for laughter.
What's your wish? Bank of America can
help make it possible. With our flexible
Home Equity Loans and Lines,
you can finance additions, renovations,
even your child's education.

Visit your local branch or
call 1-800-The-BofA.

put your life in motion

Las Vegas

Stock & Assignment

PHOTOTECHNIK
INTERNATIONAL

Experience LAS VEGAS

MAIL IN REGISTRATION CARD

Please register my name with *Experience Las Vegas* and send me the *"Valuable Coupon Package Worth Hundreds of Dollars"* in discounts for use when I visit Las Vegas. I would also like to be on your mailing list to receive discounts on future editions of *Experience Las Vegas* and exciting special offers from hotels and casinos. I understand this registration card does not obligate me in any way, I will only receive information by mail.

Name _____

Address _____

City_____ State _____ Zip _____

Telephone ( ) _____

$$$ RECEIVE VALUABLE COUPONS $$$

ORDER FORM

SEPARATE THIS ORDER FORM FROM THE ABOVE REPLY CARD
MAIL REGISTRATION CARD SEPARATELY

(INSERT THIS ORDER FORM IN AN ENVELOPE AND MAIL WITH YOUR CHECK, MONEY ORDER OR CREDIT CARD INFORMATION)

GIANT POSTER - $12.99

FABULOUS LAS VEGAS 1999 VIDEO $14.95

LAS VEGAS 1999 CALENDAR $4.99

GREATEST VEGAS VIDEOS

LAS VEGAS YESTERDAY &TODAY — RENO — BLASTED IN LAS VEGAS — LAUGHLIN

GAMING VIDEOS

CRAPS — WINNING SLOT SECRETS — BINGO! — WINNING LOTTO STRATEGY

BLACKJACK — VIDEO POKER STRATEGY — POKER HOW TO PLAY

QUAN.	PRODUCT	PRICE	TOTAL
	Giant Poster	$12.99	
	Las Vegas 1999 Calendar	$4.99	
	Fabulous Las Vegas Video 1999	$14.95	
	Las Vegas Yesterday & Today	$14.95	
	Blasted in Las Vegas	$14.95	
	Reno Video	$14.95	
	Laughlin Video	$14.95	
	Winning Lotto Strategy	$14.95	
	Video Poker Strategy	$14.95	
	Bingo!	$14.95	
	Poker How to Play	$14.95	
	Winning Slot Secrets	$14.95	
	Blackjack	$14.95	
	Craps, How to Play & Win	$14.95	
	Sub Total		
	Nevada Residents add 7% Sales Tax		
	Total Amount		

Payment by: ❏ Check or Money Order ❏ Visa ❏ MasterCard ❏ Amex ❏ Discover Card

Credit Card No._____

Exp. Date _____

Signature (req'd) _____

Name _____

Address _____

City _____ State _____ Zip _____

Day Phone (req'd) ( ) _____